THE HANDBOOK OF TEXAS

A Supplement

Volume III

An Official Project of the
American Revolution Bicentennial of Texas

THE
HANDBOOK OF
TEXAS

A Supplement

VOLUME III

ELDON STEPHEN BRANDA
Editor

Foreword by
JOE B. FRANTZ

AUSTIN

The Texas State Historical Association

JOE B. FRANTZ, *Director*
L. TUFFLY ELLIS, *Associate Director*

1976

Library of Congress Catalog Card Number: 76–55058
International Standard Book Number: 0–87611–027–8

PRINTED IN THE UNITED STATES OF AMERICA
THE UNIVERSITY OF TEXAS PRINTING DIVISION
AUSTIN, TEXAS

EDITORIAL STAFF

Editor

ELDON STEPHEN BRANDA

Editorial Associates

BARBARA F. CUMMINGS   JAMES C. MARTIN

CRYSTAL SASSE RAGSDALE

Editorial Assistants

ALWYN BARR

GRAHAM BLACKSTOCK

ROBERT G. BROWN

KAREN L. COLLINS

CHARLES A. DUVAL, JR.

WILLIAM T. FIELD

LISA B. FRANTZ

MARTHA DOTY FREEMAN

PHILLIP L. FRY

DAVID B. GRACY II

ELIZABETH LAND KADERLI

KAREN WILSON LENIART

FRANCES V. PARKER

MARY SHIELDS PEARSON

EDGAR P. SNEED

BARBARA J. STOCKLEY

LONN TAYLOR

ERNESTINE WHEELOCK

MELINDA ARCENEAUX WICKMAN

Staff Assistants

LARRY E. ABBOTT

JAMES E. ALVIS

ROY REID BARKLEY

MARTHA ANN CALVERT

WILLIAM RICHARD FOSSEY

ANITA LOUISE GLADE

MARLENE JOSEPH GLADE

CHARLES E. HANUS

STEPHEN F. JACKSON

JOHN WILLIAM JOHNSON

JEAN L. LEVERING

DAVID L. LINDSEY

PAUL S. LOFTON, JR.

DAVID L. MCWILLIAMS

DONNA WEST SHIPLEY

JOANNE SKILLING

RICHARD TAUSCH

ROBERT H. THONHOFF

PATRICIA WALSH

CARL R. ZIMMERMAN

FOREWORD

IN DECEMBER 1932 several members of his executive council wrote the director of the Texas State Historical Association that the Association's contribution to the Texas Centennial should be some sort of dictionary of Texas biography. Four years later Eugene C. Barker, reviewing Carlos E. Castañeda's first two volumes of *Our Catholic Heritage in Texas*, repeated the suggestion, though it was now too late for the centennial.

Then in the "Texas Collection" section of the July 1939 *Southwestern Historical Quarterly*, Walter Prescott Webb enlarged on these prior suggestions, named the project the Handbook of Texas, and began a study of ways and means. Webb, who had a penchant for promotion and an equal talent for starting projects and walking away from them, in time turned the Handbook program over to H. Bailey Carroll, under whose direction the first two volumes appeared in 1952.

In his 1939 prospectus Webb talked about the minimal interest in good Texas history and typically paraphrased the military adage, "If your position is weak, charge." The charge would be mounted, he said, with a Handbook of Texas History, modeled after Frederick W. Hodge's *Handbook of American Indians*, which had achieved the status of a Bible among American historians and anthropologists particularly.

"Such a work," wrote Webb, ". . . would be indispensable to every editor, reporter, library, scholar, and teacher in Texas. . . . It would set the standard for spelling . . . and furnish the starting point for every investigation of things pertaining to Texas history."

Indeed it would, and it has, and it does.

The Handbook of Texas quickly established a reputation that has made it a landmark in a profession not noted for innovation. When in the latter 1960's Yale University sponsored a symposium on state and local history, its theme revolved around the question of how other states might duplicate the Texas achievement. To date, no other state has launched a successful effort. *The Handbook of Texas* remains unique.

The first two volumes encompassed all the strengths and weaknesses of any pioneering effort. With more than a thousand contributors, many of them non-professional, errors and omissions naturally crept in. Before publication, Carroll directed his staff to begin a file for oversights, new topics, and corrections. Revision in a later edition became a goal.

But revision proved slow, tedious, and arduous. Under Carroll the principal supervisor was Barbara Cummings. For the past nine years the staff usually consisted of one person, Eldon Branda, assisted by other Texas State Historical Association employees as they could steal time from their assigned duties. Overall, Branda has been the chief person responsible for gathering, authenticating, correcting, collating, proofing—in short, editing.

The first two volumes required twelve years of work. This third volume, a supplement rather than a revision, has taken another dozen years, in large part because of Branda's passion for perfection. Like our predecessors, we have involuntarily accumulated a sizable file of new data and corrections for future volumes, even as we strove to bring this volume to press. Neither Branda, L. Tuffly Ellis, nor I intend to be around when a revised edition appears in some Buck Rogers future. Mortality expectations guarantee our absence.

Appropriately this new volume bears the seal of the American Revolution Bicentennial Commission of Texas, which augmented its good wishes with cash. Like the joke about the non-profit institution that never planned it that way, so we deserve no credit for completing this latest volume during the 200th Birthday year of the United States. We didn't plan it that way; it just took us till now!

Obviously we could not have completed such a long-running engagement without the benign neglect (to borrow a phrase from recent politicians) of The University of Texas at Austin, whose administration never asked us what we were doing with our time. Instead, it took for granted that we were performing some worthwhile task, if indeed it ever thought of us at all.

Meanwhile the University paid Branda's salary, and the Association paid for all other assistance from receipts from sales of the first two volumes, from income from its publication fund raised a quarter of a century ago by Leslie Waggener Jr. of Dallas, and with direct financial assistance from such friends as the W. St. John Garwoods, and The M. D. Anderson Foundation, The Brown Foundation, The H. Kempner Foundation, The Kathryn O'Connor Foundation, The Strake Foundation, The Texas Heritage Foundation, and The J. M. West Foundation.

Since its appearance nearly twenty-five years ago, the *Handbook* has enjoyed a steady sale—never less than $8,000 worth in any year, and of course much more in those seasons when the economy has peaked. As fast as schools, newspapers, and other such entities have worn out copies, they have ordered new ones, often three or four times. The *Handbook* rates as a staple, an item that belongs always on the shelves. And only the Lord knows how many wives have solved the problem of Christmas giving by presenting copies to husbands and children.

We here at the Association believe that the current volume will continue and even enhance this reputation. We have tried to produce a volume in the best Texas tradition, not of vainglorious boasting but of quiet, solid, continuing achievement.

Joe B. Frantz
November 1, 1976

INTRODUCTION

FOR YEARS many people have said that *The Handbook of Texas* was a misnomer. The name sounded like something you could roll up and stuff in your pocket, and I even had the audacity to suggest a change to a fancier name for Volume III. But that simple title has achieved a certain notoriety. Walter Muir Whitehill in the London *Times Literary Supplement* (November 13, 1970) wrote, "For preparing the best systematic work of reference on any of the fifty United States, the palm must go to the Texas State Historical Association for their two volume *Handbook of Texas*.... The *Handbook* is an invaluable tool for the scholar, the journalist, or anyone else; it is a shame that its successful completion has not yet inspired similar ventures in cooperative scholarship in other states." You just don't give up a name with that kind of integrity.

In preparing Volume III our objective was the same as that set forth by Walter Prescott Webb and H. Bailey Carroll, a work of significant information about the widest possible range of Texas topics, from prehistoric times to the present, arranged alphabetically for easy reference. From the moment that an announcement was made in 1963 that a supplement would be forthcoming, people expected it almost immediately. By 1969, one person (whom I know to be healthy) wrote, "I do not think that I shall live long enough to see the supplement in print!" At the same time we had visitors from other states who wanted to know how they could produce a similar work for their own states. We know of no such works in print as yet, although we would very much welcome forty-nine other state Handbooks, which collectively would be a valuable contribution to American history.

Work was underway on Volume III of *The Handbook of Texas* in 1964, under the direction of H. Bailey Carroll, director of the Texas State Historical Association. With the help of a small office staff, Barbara F. Cummings was responsible from 1965 to 1967 for soliciting articles and generally keeping things going by correspondence. Among the first articles written were those on towns and counties, but because of their statistical nature they were quickly out of date, which has been a problem we have faced all along. Joe B. Frantz and L. Tuffly Ellis became director and assistant director, respectively, of the Association in 1966, and they continued the project, appointing me editor in 1967. At that time it was estimated that, on the basis of articles then in our office, the supplement would be approximately three hundred pages, or almost one-sixth the size of Volumes I and II. Most articles still had to be edited, and somehow or another the supplement just grew, like a child who wanted to be as big as his parents.

Almost everything had to be revised over the next nine years, and we were always too optimistic about getting it out "next year." We were never happy with the population estimates of the 1960's anyway, and when the official United States census for 1970 appeared, all our town and county articles were again obsolete; generally, we could not add much to their earlier histories in Volumes I and II, except for corrections of errors. We did add articles on each of the Standard Metropolitan Statistical Areas in Texas, a new feature, and these should furnish a great deal more information about the more populous counties and the larger cities. Where we felt that a major city (such as Houston) was inadequately covered in Volume I or II, we tried to enlarge its coverage in Volume III. An early decision had been made to limit the addition of new material to towns of 1,000 or more population; however, we offer new articles on towns with less than 1,000 population if the town is a county seat, or wherever errors occurred in the previous work, or whenever the town reported some noteworthy historical event. Although the newer communities or towns with more than 1,000 population await their written histories, they are included here, for the most part just with census figures, so that their existence could be recorded (which points out the need for a continuing *Handbook* effort). In addition, any town that was not included in the previous volumes, regardless of its population and particularly if it no longer exists, is included in this volume. But alas! we missed Ding Dong, so appropriately located in Bell County.

When Volumes I and II were published in 1952, some critics complained about omissions. For instance, there was an article on Poetry, Texas, but none on poetry in Texas; there were articles on various ethnic groups, but none on Negroes. We paid attention. Not only is the Poetry Society of Texas represented here, but there is a long and comprehensive survey article on Literature in Texas, written by Mabel Major and Joe B. Frantz. In addition to Music in Texas we now have a history of Folk and Popular Music in Texas. In addition to Art in Texas we have Indian Rock Art in Texas. Although we added articles on the Negro, Mexican, Irish, English, Chinese, Japanese, and other ethnic groups in Texas, we failed to include them all. This volume contains no articles on Greeks or Italians in Texas, for those articles never arrived. Now I understand how the editors must have felt in 1952, that sinking feeling when something has been left out.

What we do have are articles of value to anyone interested in the history of Texas. The articles on the Office of Governor and the Office of Lieutenant Governor, with their ready-reference tables for who succeeded whom and why, should prove a valuable addition to the list of executive officers (1835–1845) found under the Republic of Texas article in Volume II. Perhaps one of the most important articles is that written by Governor Price Daniel on the Tidelands Controversy, a part of our history with far-reaching effects beyond Texas. Like that one, many of the articles have national importance. Two native Texans have been president and another has been vice-president of the United States in this century, and of course, since all are now deceased, their biographies are included. Texas has been the scene of tragedies that had to be recorded, so, sadly, we had to include accounts of the assassination of President John F. Kennedy, The University of Texas Tower Murders, and various scandals that the reader can find for himself without too much trouble. But there are happier recordings of history also, such as the fact that the Turkey Trot in Cuero was revived.

Even as late as 1975 a noteworthy Texas periodical complained, "Whither Ma?" because there was no article on Governor Miriam A. Ferguson in Volume I, implying discrimination against women. Since our policy has always been not to include living persons in the *Handbook* (Ma died in 1961), only now can we include her. There is a considerable increase in the number of biographies of women here, as well as a long survey article on Women in Texas by United States District Judge Sarah T. Hughes, and one on the Texas Women's Political Caucus. It may surprise many that the sophisticated East is represented in William F. Buckley, Sr., a native Texan, a graduate of The University of Texas law school, and son of a Duval County sheriff. There are articles on politics, politicians, government, sports, athletes, colleges and universities, academicians, scientists, state agencies, state parks, churches, museums, libraries, architecture, mineral resources, businesses, industries, labor, medicine, weather, radio, television, film, and artists in every medium (including two stars with the same last name who became symbols of completely different musical eras: one turn-of-the-century, male, and black, Scott Joplin; the other 1960's, female, and white, Janis Joplin). There is a look into the 1930's with an article on the Work Projects Administration in Texas (which we hope will end the confusion over its earlier name, the Works Progress Administration). We also hope that we have made clear the difference between the Permanent School Fund and the Permanent University Fund, the Available School Fund and the Available University Fund.

Recently a visitor from a foreign country was concerned that we did not make comment or render judgments in the *Handbook* articles. Suffice it to say that we have followed the good example of Volumes I and II in being more or less impersonal, with an occasional appraisal but never a eulogy. Biographies are still confined to those who are no longer living, and we have presented the facts by consulting the best sources available. Regretfully, because their deaths occurred too late for inclusion, we have not been able to include Harry Huntt Ransom, B. Iden Payne, Howard Hughes, Dillon Anderson, J. P. Bryan, J. Mason Brewer, and many others.

It must be understood that the work is not genealogical in nature, although genealogists have performed a tremendous service in their contributions through family records. But the purpose of the *Handbook* is not to trace family histories, for biographical entries are limited to those individuals whose lives made some impact on society, and very often that impact was felt outside the borders of the state. Some of the entries seemingly are not even of statewide importance, but who is to say that the last town crier of San Antonio did not merit inclusion? Or the Great Western, that fighting lady of the Mexican War? Or the Griffin Graffin? Such subjects might be the inspiration for some creative soul to say something important about humanity. In the right hands measured history becomes timeless literature, and perhaps the *Handbook* can be a useful tool, not only for the serious scholar but for the serious artist as well.

We retained the format of the earlier volumes, although some innovation was imperative, resulting in the creation of quite a bulky "*Handbook* Style Guide" for consistency. Names are important to us, and if a Texan of Mexican descent does not use the diacritical marks on his signature, then we leave them off also. The reader will note that we have done away with the hyphenated American, and so you will find Mexican Americans, Polish Americans, and Anglo Americans, but never (unless we slipped in proofing) any hyphenated ethnic group. Because Volume III contains articles which have not appeared before and at the same time adds new material to articles which appeared in Volumes I and II (both correcting errors and updating), there had to be a way of distinguishing between the two. The * preceding a subject title indicates that information on that subject may be found in either Volume I (A through K) or Volume II (L through Z). Because we repeated all titles from Volumes I and II, we were able to keep a strict alphabetical order, and Volume III at once became an index to all three volumes. Any errors in spelling of subject titles or alphabetical misplacement in the earlier work are noted in a bracketed statement following the correct title in its proper place. Errors in the text following repeated titles are pointed out in parentheses. Any encyclopedic work as large as the *Handbook* almost certainly will have errors, and we have been alerted to them by correspondents or stumbled on them ourselves for these many years. We know that we have not caught them all, but I do not know of a single correction sent to us that we have not, after careful research and verification, included in this volume. Since we do not repeat information given in Volumes I and II, those volumes remain essential to a complete examination of subjects treated here, although an article may have been updated or corrected in this volume. Some articles in the earlier work, such as those on Fletcher S. Stockdale and George W. Smith, contained serious errors, so we had to write entirely new articles for Volume III; but these are exceptions.

We made another change in style by placing all towns with the same name in boldface, followed by the town's county in parentheses. This ensures that towns of the same name will not be overlooked under one boldface title. One of the real difficulties in repeating all the titles from Volumes I and II was that so many official names of institutions, organizations, companies, etc., have changed in the last quarter century. Since old names are essential for reference, we have retained every title with a *see* reference to every new title. It seems that almost every college in Texas has become a university, for instance, often with many name changes in between. We have tried to record all name changes through the mid-1970's, and so we made a painstaking effort to utilize effectively the symbol ^{qv} (*quod vide*). The ^{qv}, which indicates that there are separate articles on the subjects so marked, is tied to all three volumes, not just to Volume III, so that any time it occurs here, one should look at that title first in Volume III; if an asterisk occurs there, one should go to Volumes I and II. The abundant use of this symbol throughout the articles will, we hope, keep you on an endless track through Texas history and not cause you the alarm that one reader felt when he wrote: "How dare you 'question' so many facts in a single article!"

The bibliographies speak for themselves, but I should like to give special thanks to Robert G. Brown of our staff who meticulously saw to their accuracy and consistency in form. If the serious researcher pursues those references and finds discrepancies in fact between what is found there and what is in the *Handbook* article, we suggest that the search for the truth continue by writing us, for our files will usually justify why we have used what we have used; and then, too, you may prove us wrong. Much of our information has come from the archives and library of the Barker Texas History Center at The University of Texas at Austin, the Texas State Library, and various state agencies in Austin, including the Bureau of Vital Statistics. Staff members of the Barker Texas History Center who have been helpful are too numerous to list without danger of missing someone, and the same is true for the Reference Department of The University of Texas at Austin Library. And of course we are forever indebted to the biennial *Texas Almanac* for the wealth of information it always provided.

Many of the articles were researched and written here in our office by staff members (listed on the editorial staff page) and most of these are unsigned. Those who typed the final manuscripts were Linda G. Sikes, Judith Ann Boyd (who produced most of the early work), Jolie Frantz, Susan Nasser Turner, Rebecca Jean McEvoy, Sharilyn Rae Howell, and finally, when we were always in a great hurry, Ruth Mathews. Other staff members of the Texas State Historical Association who helped in myriad ways are Colleen Kain, Janie Melton, Mary Standifer, Kenneth Ragsdale, Narcie Crosby, Lucretia Graham, Theresa Jamail Sewell, Barbara Going, Suann Waight, Candace O'Keefe, and Randall Paul. Unusually forbearing during this long process were Walter E. Neal, manager, and Norman T. Purcell, composing room supervisor, along with their typesetters and office personnel at The University of Texas Printing Division, who must have a special place in their hearts for Texas history. And of course we owe special thanks to the members of the Executive Council of the Texas State Historical Association, and especially to Joe B. Frantz and L. Tuffly Ellis for allowing this to go on all these years.

We especially thank all of those contributors who have waited so long to see their work in print. While it would be impossible to acknowledge here all of those experts in their respective fields who have made this book possible, we would like to cite a few who have contributed more than was reasonable to expect. Thomas Nolan Campbell, professor of anthropology at The University of Texas at Austin, could have published a book of his own with the number of scholarly articles he gave us on Indians in Texas; his answer to the query "Why so many Indians?" was the perfect one: since the *Handbook* carries all of the state's communities, even ghost towns, why not the Indian groups, which are equivalent to the earliest place names in Texas? Seth D. Breeding gave us, with few exceptions, all of the articles on lakes, dams, and reservoirs, with enough data to satisfy any water enthusiast. Southern Methodist University law professor Joseph W. McKnight made a special contribution in furnishing the many law articles, beginning with early Spanish Law in Texas. Altogether our list of contributors is a distinguished one. You will find signed articles by United States senators, federal judges, state governors, scientists, university and college professors (mainly historians), journalists, creative artists, and professionals from many fields. Not the least of our thanks go to the many dedicated local historians around the state who did original research and came up with some of the most interesting and informative articles. Knowing that payment was made for articles accepted in Volumes I and II, it seemed incredible that not one contributor to this volume ever asked how much we paid per word. We paid nothing, and yet we received more material than it was possible to use. That which we were not able to include has been placed in our files for possible future use. The nature of the *Handbook* demanded a certain conciseness and uniformity in style, so that some contributions may have been reduced in content, while others were lengthened to include pertinent new information.

One of the ever present dangers in editing the work was forgetting that the present is the past. An article which seemed perfectly fine in the present tense in 1968 became embarrassing in 1970 and outrageous in 1976. It must be remembered that in the earlier days of this compilation we had not yet landed a man on the moon. Now it is old hat. We have tried to update such facts, but where we have not we have at least tried to peg a certain accomplished fact to a very certain date. We cannot write the definitive book. Everything changes.

Eldon Stephen Branda
November 2, 1976

THE HANDBOOK OF TEXAS
A Supplement
Volume III

Note to the Reader

The * preceding a subject title indicates that information on that subject may be found in either Volume I (A through K) or Volume II (L through Z). Many subjects with this symbol will also have additional, updated, or corrective information in this volume. Since all titles from Volumes I and II are listed here, Volume III also serves as an index to all three volumes.

Biographies are limited to persons now deceased.

The symbols qv (*quod vide*, "which see") and qqv (the plural of qv) indicate that there are separate articles on the subjects so marked. As in Volumes I and II, the symbols are omitted after such obvious references as Stephen F. Austin, Sam Houston, the Alamo, the battle of San Jacinto, the Texas Revolution, the Mexican War, and the Civil War; nor are they included with the names of counties, towns, streams, elevations, railroads, natural regions, governmental positions, or fields of endeavor, since by the nature of this work the object has been to include all such topics of real significance. In Volume III the symbol is also omitted after the names of Indian groups and all colleges and universities for the same reason. In certain articles, particularly those which cover a broad subject, the symbol may occur with some of the topics mentioned above, but only when the editor has felt that the reader might wrongly assume that the more narrow subject is not included elsewhere.

THE HANDBOOK OF TEXAS
Volume III

A

Aba Indians. In 1683–1684 Juan Domínguez de Mendoza qv led an exploratory expedition from El Paso as far eastward as the junction of the Concho and Colorado rivers east of present San Angelo. In his itinerary he listed the names of thirty-seven Indian groups, including the Aba, from whom he expected to receive delegations on the Colorado River. Nothing further is known about the Aba, who seem to have been one of many Indian groups of north-central Texas that were swept away by the southward thrust of the Lipan-Apache and Comanche Indians in the eighteenth century. However, it is possible that the Aba were the same people as the Hape, a Coahuiltecan band of the same period that ranged from northeastern Coahuila across the Rio Grande into the southwestern part of the Edwards Plateau in Texas. This identification has yet to be demonstrated.

BIBLIOGRAPHY: H. E. Bolton (ed.), *Spanish Exploration in the Southwest, 1542-1706* (1916); C. W. Hackett (ed.), *Pichardo's Treatise on the Limits of Louisiana and Texas*, II (1934).

T. N. Campbell

Abau Indians. The similarity in the names Abau and Aba qv suggests that they may be variants of the same Indian group name, but this is contradicted by the fact that both Abau and Aba appear on the same list of Indian groups recorded by Juan Domínguez de Mendoza qv in 1683–1684, when he was in the western part of the Edwards Plateau. If Mendoza's Aba were the same as the Hape, then it is also likely that the Abau were the same as the Xiabu, who in other Spanish sources of the same time are identified with that section of the Rio Grande just downstream from modern Eagle Pass, Texas. In both cases it is possible to argue for Coahuiltecan affiliation and conclude that the ethnic identities were lost early in the eighteenth century.

BIBLIOGRAPHY: H. E. Bolton (ed.), *Spanish Exploration in the Southwest, 1542-1706* (1916); C. W. Hackett (ed.), *Pichardo's Treatise on the Limits of Louisiana and Texas*, II (1934).

T. N. Campbell

*Abbott, Jo.

*Abbott, Texas.

*Abercrombie, Leonard Anderson.

*Aberdeen, Texas.

*Aberfoyle, Texas.

Abernathy, Mollie D. Mollie D. Abernathy was born on April 27, 1866, in Hood County. She was the daughter of John N. M. and Elizabeth (Robertson) Wylie, both members of prominent ranch families. She grew up at Thorp Spring, where she became a member of the first class to enroll at Add-Ran College (forerunner of Texas Christian University). She spent the summers on her father's ranches in Erath and in Runnels counties, where she acquired the knowledge which was to make her one of Texas' leading cattlewomen.

On September 26, 1886, she married James William Jarrott, who served that year in the Texas legislature. The following year the couple moved to a ranch near Phoenix, Arizona, where their first child was born. In 1889 the family returned to Thorp Spring and in 1890 moved to Stephenville, where Jarrott became county attorney for Erath County. There three more children were born.

In 1900 Jarrott located a strip of vacant land lying between two railroad surveys and extending from the western boundary of Lubbock County to New Mexico. It was approximately one mile wide and one hundred miles long. Acting under the Four Section Act qv he filed on the vacancy for himself and twenty-four other families, and the Jarrotts moved to the Plains area in 1901. By 1902 Jarrott had settled the remaining families on the land, but incurred the animosity of the operators of the adjoining ranches. On August 28, 1902, he was shot to death by a then unknown assassin; thirty years later a convicted killer in Oklahoma, named John Miller, confessed to the Jarrott murder.

The young widow took over the operation of the ranch on the "Strip," expanding it from four to sixteen sections and developing under her "Swastika" brand a herd of registered cattle. Her affairs prospered, and she made additional profitable investments in the new city of Lubbock, where, among other properties, she built one of the large business buildings in the heart of town. In 1905 she married Monroe G. Abernathy, a real estate

[1]

operator for whom the South Plains towns of Monroe (later New Deal) and Abernathy were named. Mrs. Abernathy became a charter member of Lubbock's Business and Professional Women's Club and took an active interest in the League of Women Voters and the Woman's Christian Temperance Union. She was also a member of the Christian church. On June 4, 1960, she died in Lubbock, and was buried in the city cemetery.

BIBLIOGRAPHY: Seymour V. Connor (ed.), *Builders of the Southwest* (1959); Lubbock *Avalanche-Journal*, June 5, 1960.

Seymour V. Connor

*Abernathy, Texas. Abernathy, on the Hale-Lubbock county line, in 1965 was a farm market and shipping point with one hundred businesses, including a bank, a newspaper, a radio station, grain elevators, cotton gins, and other agriculturally related industries. In 1966 the town had thirteen churches, a public library, and a textile mill. The 1960 population was 2,491. Population for 1970 was 2,625.

*Abilene, Texas. Abilene, county seat of Taylor County, with an economy originally based on agriculture but shifting to oil and manufacturing since 1960, is the major distribution and retail center for the county and surrounding area. In 1964 over five hundred of the twenty-one hundred businesses in Abilene had a direct connection with the oil industry. In that year about ninety manufacturers produced clothing, cottonseed products, building materials, and machine shop products. Abilene had three hospitals, the West Texas Rehabilitation Center for crippled children, and the Abilene State School qv in 1966. The town had three colleges, Abilene Christian College (now University), McMurry College, and Hardin-Simmons University, thirty-three public schools, 132 churches, two libraries, a newspaper, five radio stations, and two television stations in 1966. Abilene's recreational facilities included four lakes, three golf courses, eleven parks, and a zoo. Dyess Air Force Base,qv a $100,000,000 Strategic Air Command installation, contributes to the Abilene economy. In 1962 the Atlas Intercontinental Ballistic Missile installations were completed and included twelve launching sites. Nike Hercules ground-to-air missile batteries were also in the Abilene area military complex. The 1960 population was 90,368; the 1970 population was 89,653. *See also* Abilene Standard Metropolitan Statistical Area.

*Abilene Christian University. Abilene Christian College (now University), Abilene, continued to be the largest Church of Christ qv institution of higher learning in the world. The college enrollment was national in character, representing fifty states and eighteen foreign countries. One-third of the students were nonresidents of Texas. While the student body increased from 1,493 to 3,346 between 1950 and 1972, the faculty-student ratio remained approximately one to twenty. Enrollment was 3,647 in 1974.

The college received accreditation by the South-ern Association of Colleges in 1951 and opened its graduate school in 1953. A jump in endowments from $873,000 to $5,200,000 financed construction of seven major projects during the period 1950 to 1965. Celebration of Don H. Morris' twenty-fifth anniversary as president in 1965 was the occasion for announcement of a $25,700,000 expansion program, which was to culminate in 1972. The program provides for ten new buildings, additional endowment, and academic enrichment. In 1974 John C. Stevens was president. In February, 1976, the name of the school was changed to Abilene Christian University.

BIBLIOGRAPHY: Abilene *Reporter-News*, May 22, 1965; *Texas Almanac* (1967, 1969).

Charles H. Marler

*Abilene Lake.

*Abilene and Northern Railway Company.

*Abilene *Reporter-News*.

*Abilene and Southern Railway Company.

Abilene Standard Metropolitan Statistical Area. The Abilene Standard Metropolitan Statistical Area, created in August, 1960, included the 1,863-square-mile area of Taylor and Jones counties. Abilene, the core city of the area, lies in the northeastern corner of Taylor County near the border of the two counties. A more realistic delineation of the Abilene metropolitan area would also include the counties of Callahan and Shackelford, lying some six miles east and northeast, respectively, of the Abilene city limits. Many hundreds of persons commute daily to work in the city from these counties. Clyde, in Callahan County, may be thought of as a suburb of Abilene. In 1960 the official metropolitan area had a population of 120,377, with 90,368 inhabitants in Abilene. The 1970 area population was 113,959, while Abilene had 89,653 residents. Stamford was the only other sizeable town in 1970, with 4,558 inhabitants. Other incorporated towns in the area are Merkel, Lawn, Tuscola, Buffalo Gap, Tye, Trent, Blair, and Impact in Taylor County; and Hamlin, Lueders, and Anson in Jones County.

The Abilene metropolitan area nearly doubled its population between 1940 and 1960. During the same period the city more than tripled its inhabitants. This large increase began with the opening in 1941 of Camp Barkeley,qv nine miles southwest of Abilene, and continued during the war boom. After the war Abilene shared in the oil development of some twenty counties which skirt the Permian Basin. In 1957 Taylor County had an aggregation of 423 producers, contractors, operators, and oil well service companies. Since then the petroleum industry has declined, and the static population of the area since 1960 reflects this loss. Still, the area remains a center of the oil industry. It is the headquarters for several oil firms, seven gasoline plants, and two oil refineries. Abilene, Anson, and Stamford furnish equipment to the surrounding oil fields. The Abilene metropolitan area also produces soft drinks, foods, clothing, concrete and clay products, structural steel, musical instruments, and watches.

Farming and ranching also contribute significantly to the income of the area. While most of the agricultural income of Taylor County comes from livestock (primarily cattle and sheep), Jones County relies on cotton, wheat, and other grains. The commercial towns of the area not only serve as gathering but also as processing centers. Cottonseed oil mills exist in Abilene, Hamlin, and Stamford; meat processing plants in Abilene; grain elevators in Anson and Stamford; and a flour mill in Stamford. The towns supply animal feeds and farm machinery to the outlying agricultural regions.

The Abilene area is a commercial center with fourteen printing and lithographing companies. Abilene, Anson, Hamlin, Merkel, and Stamford each publish a newspaper. Five radio and two television stations, all located in Abilene, serve the area. Abilene Christian University, Hardin-Simmons University, and McMurry College enroll over six thousand students annually. In addition to these educational facilities, Abilene has a public library. The Abilene State School qv has over one thousand patients. The West Texas Rehabilitation Center, Hendrick Memorial Hospital, and three other hospitals make the area a medical center of some importance. A good highway system, including Interstate 20, and a more than adequate water supply, augmented by the Hubbard Creek Reservoir, enhance the area. Dyess Air Force Base,qv located west of Abilene with over six thousand personnel, is a permanent Strategic Air Command U.S. Air Force Base.

The area offers the tourist a number of recreational and historical attractions. Culturally, Abilene added a fine arts museum and a community theater in 1966. All three colleges have active drama departments. The Abilene Philharmonic Association supports a symphonic orchestra. Twenty miles southwest of Abilene is Abilene State Park (see Parks, State), while Fort Phantom Hill Reservoir lies twelve miles northeast of the city. The Ernie Wilson Museum in Buffalo Gap preserves a collection of Indian artifacts, pioneer implements, and fossils. Fort Phantom Hill, the Butterfield Overland Mail Route,qqv and the Old Mackenzie Trail are other historical sites. Annual events in the area include the Cowboys' Christmas Ball qv in Anson, the Cowboy Reunion qv in Stamford, the Abilene Festival of the Arts, the Pecan Bowl qv in Abilene, and county fairs and livestock shows in both counties. Hardin-Simmons University hosts an intercollegiate rodeo each year. See also Standard Metropolitan Statistical Areas in Texas. [Callahan County was added to the Abilene Standard Metropolitan Statistical Area in April, 1973. Ed.]

Rupert N. Richardson

*Abilene State Hospital. See also Abilene State School.

Abilene State School. Abilene State School

(formerly Abilene State Hospital qv) was an epileptic colony until 1957, when it became an admission center for the mentally retarded from 115 West Texas counties. In 1964 some of the original buildings were still in use along with numerous replacements, and a new hospital was under construction; total value of the physical plant in 1969 was $7,406,609. The school was an independent school district, with classes conducted for the educable and trainable students. In 1964 the school's average daily census was 1,873; by 1970 the school census was 2,102. In 1970 L. W. Cain was superintendent.

BIBLIOGRAPHY: Board for Texas State Hospitals and Special Schools, *Report* (1964); *Texas Almanac* (1969); Texas Department of Mental Health and Mental Retardation, *Annual Report, 1970.*

*Abilene Trail. *See* Chisholm Trail and West Shawnee Trail.

*Ab initio Question.

*Ables, Texas.

*Abner, Texas.

*Abolition in Texas. *See also* Groce, Leonard Waller, for an account of the abolition laws of Brazil, which had an influence on Texas slave owners.

*Abra, Texas.

*Abram, Texas.

Abrams, Lucien. Lucien Abrams was born in Lawrence, Kansas, in 1871, the son of William Henry Abrams and Ella Murray (Harris) Abrams. In 1873 the Abrams family moved to Texas, and Lucien Abrams spent a major part of his life living and working in Dallas. He received his art education in New York, where he studied under Benjamin Constant at the Art Students League, and in Europe, where he worked under Lollin, Jean Paul Laurens, and James MacNeill Whistler. Abrams exhibited in England, throughout the United States, and in the Société National de Beaux Arts in Paris. At an exhibition of his work in 1925 at the Texas State Fair,qv the pictures shown were praised as examples of the "art nouveau."

Abrams was a member of the Lyme (Connecticut) Art Association, Société du Salon d'Automne, and the Society of Independent Artists. He is represented in many permanent collections, such as that of the Dallas Museum of Fine Arts.qv He died in Old Lyme, Connecticut, on April 14, 1941.

BIBLIOGRAPHY: Mantle Fielding, *Dictionary of American Painters, Sculptors, and Engravers* (1960); Frances Battaile Fisk, *A History of Texas Artists and Sculptors* (1928); McNay Gallery Files, San Antonio, Texas.

Caroline Remy

Abriache Indians. The Abriache (Abriade) Indians, who are generally considered to be Jumano, lived in the vicinity of present Presidio during the late sixteenth century. Their settlements seem to have been along the south bank of the Rio Grande, but they must have crossed to the north bank on occasion. The Abriache disappeared during the seventeenth century.

BIBLIOGRAPHY: J. C. Kelley, "The Historic Indian

Pueblos of La Junta de los Ríos," *New Mexico Historical Review*, XXVII–XXVIII (1952–1953); W. W. Newcomb, *The Indians of Texas* (1961); C. Sauer, *The Distribution of Aboriginal Tribes and Languages in Northwestern Mexico* (1934).

T. N. Campbell

*Absentee Voting. *See* Election Laws.

Academy of Freedom, Douglas MacArthur. *See* Howard Payne College.

*Academy of Science. *See* Texas Academy of Science.

*Acala, Texas.

*Acampo, Texas.

*Ace, Texas. Ace, in Polk County, was first named Geneva, with Mrs. W. H. Beazley as postmistress. The post office was discontinued, and the name Smithfield was given the community, which later became known as Ace.

Julia Beazley

*Acero Creek.

*Acheson, Alexander W.

Acheson, Sam Hanna. Sam Hanna Acheson, journalist and historian, was born in Dallas, Texas, on August 21, 1900, son of Alexander Mahon and Alice (Hanna) Acheson. He was educated in the public schools of Dallas, Austin College, and the University of Texas, from which he received an A.B. degree in 1921. After working for a Dallas business firm for two years, he joined the staff of the Dallas *Times Herald*,ᑫᵛ first as a reporter and then as assistant city editor. From 1925 he worked, first as a reporter and later as an editorial writer, for the Dallas *Morning News*,ᑫᵛ with which he remained until his retirement.

He was a member of the Enemy Alien Hearing Board of the Northern District of Texas from late 1941 until early 1943. He served in both world wars; in the latter he was commissioned as a captain, saw European service, received the Bronze Star Medal, and emerged as a major.

Acheson was a contributor to the *Bookman*, the *American Mercury*, and the *Dictionary of American History*. He wrote a historical play, *We Are Besieged*, and two books, *Joe Bailey, the Last Democrat* (1932) and *35,000 Days in Texas* (1938), the latter a history of the Dallas *Morning News* and its antecedents. He was one of the compilers of the biographical dictionary, *Texian Who's Who* (1937).

He was a fellow of the Texas State Historical Association ᑫᵛ and co-editor of a book the association published in 1963, *George Washington Diamond's Account of the Great Hanging at Gainesville, 1862*. He served long terms as secretary of the Dallas Historical Society and as corresponding secretary of the Philosophical Society of Texas;ᑫᵛ he was a member of the boards of directors of the Civil Federation of Dallas and the Dallas Community Chest Foundation. His memberships included the American Legion, the Military Order of the World Wars, and the Beta Theta Pi fraternity. An independent Democrat and Presby-

terian, he was known for his detailed knowledge of Dallas and Texas history and for his gentlemanly manners. He never married.

Following his retirement from the *News* on June 30, 1966, he served as consultant to the executive vice-president of the Southwestern Legal Foundation. He died at his Dallas home on March 7, 1972, and was buried in Denison.

BIBLIOGRAPHY: Dallas *Morning News*, March 8, 1972.

Wayne Gard

Achubale Indians. The Achubale Indians were one of twenty groups that joined Juan Domínguez de Mendoza ᑫᵛ on his journey from El Paso to the vicinity of present San Angelo in 1683–1684. Since Mendoza did not indicate at what point the Achubale joined his party, it is impossible to determine their range or affiliations. Indians between the Pecos River and the San Angelo area were being hard pressed by Apache Indians at that time, and it seems likely that the Achubale ranged between these two localities.

BIBLIOGRAPHY: H. E. Bolton (ed.), *Spanish Exploration in the Southwest, 1542–1706* (1916).

T. N. Campbell

*Ackerly, Texas.

*Acme, Texas.

*Acme Tap Railroad Company.

*Acol, Texas.

*Acton, Texas.

*Acuff, Texas.

*Acworth, Texas.

*Ad Hall, Texas.

*Ada, Texas. (Lampasas County.)

*Ada, Texas. (Nolan County.)

*Adaes, Settlement of.

*Adaes Indians.

Adair, Anthony Garland. Anthony Garland Adair, son of J. B. Adair, a Methodist minister, and Mattie (Palmer) Adair, was born in Queen City, Cass County, Texas, on March 28, 1889. He attended Wesley College, Terrell, Texas, and the University of Texas at Austin, where he was president of the Students' Assembly and Council, and a member of the Cofer Law Society.

After leaving the university and before World War I, Adair was editor of the Marshall *Messenger*. He entered the army in 1917, and on September 1, 1918, was commissioned a second lieutenant. On September 22, 1918, he married Gladys Marie Ingram, a school teacher, of Texarkana. They were the parents of two daughters and one son.

Following the war Adair was engaged in editing and publishing newspapers at Hico, Mexia, Breckenridge, and McCamey. He was twice named a delegate to national Democratic conventions, from Hico in 1920 and from Mexia in 1924. Becoming active in the American Legion, Adair was made commander of the 5th Division in 1930. In 1932 he moved his family to Austin to assume the duties of department historian for the legion. He became increasingly interested in historical projects, and in 1935 was named chairman of the Centennial Committee of the American Legion of Texas, which sponsored legislation to authorize the creation of a state museum. Adair conceived the idea of selling souvenir coins to raise money for the project, and fifty-cent silver coins commemorating Texas' one-hundredth year were minted by the federal government. Sales raised some $92,000. When the Texas Memorial Museum qv opened in 1939, Adair was named curator of patriotic exhibits, later curator of history, a position he held until his retirement in 1959.

He was co-author of several books, among them *Texas, Its History*, with Ellen B. Coats (1954), and *Austin and Commodore Perry*, with E. H. Perry, Sr. (1956). He edited a series of Texas history brochures including the *Texas Pictorial Handbook* and *Under Texas Skies*, and compiled a book of political cartoons of John Nance Garner qv (1958).

The Forty-seventh Texas Legislature named Adair commissioner for the 1945–1946 observance of the Texas Centennial of Statehood.qv He was an honorary life member of the Sons of the Republic of Texas, a life member of the Texas State Historical Association, a fellow in the Texas Academy of Science, a member of the Texas Press Association, the Knights of San Jacinto,qqv executive director of the Texas Heritage Foundation, a member of the Methodist church and of American Legion Post 76.

Adair died in Temple on December 14, 1966, and was buried in the State Cemetery qv at Austin.

Willena C. Adams

*Adair, Cornelia (Wadsworth) Ritchie.

*Adair, John George.

*Adair Normal School.

*Adams, Andy.

*Adams, Jed Cobb.

Adams, Nathan. Nathan Adams, Dallas banker and civic leader, was born in Pulaski, Tennessee, on November 26, 1869, the youngest of seven children of Nathan and Susan (Pankey) Adams. His father, an attorney and a Civil War hero, died when Nathan was five years old. After a term at Giles College, Nathan quit to become a cash boy in a store, then a messenger and clerk in a Pulaski bank, and later the manager of a bookstore. Borrowing seventy-five dollars to come to Dallas in December, 1887, he began work on January 1, 1888, as a clerk in the auditor's office of the Texas and Pacific Railroad. In April, 1889, he took a job as relief and general utility clerk at the National Exchange Bank, where he rose rapidly. On November 4, 1891, he married Elizabeth Kirby Ardinger. Mergers put him in the First National Bank in Dallas, of which he became president in 1929, board chairman in 1944, and honorary chairman in 1950. President of the Texas Bankers Association qv (1913–1914) and a member of the council of the American Bankers Association (1916–1929), he

did much to make Dallas the financial capital of the Southwest. He was a director of several corporations and engaged in many civic activities. During World War II he headed a Texas drive that sold $4,500,-000,000 in government securities. His favorite philanthropy was the Scottish Rite Hospital for Crippled Children, for which he raised more than a million dollars. A conservative in politics, he was outspoken in expressing his views. He played golf until he was seventy, rode horseback until he was about eighty, and was an ardent baseball fan. He was an Episcopalian. After four years of failing health, he died in Dallas on June 17, 1966.

BIBLIOGRAPHY: Dallas *Morning News*, February 9, 1933, August 14, 1949, June 18, 19, 1966; Dallas *Times Herald*, June 18, 19, 1966.

Wayne Gard

*Adams, Robert.

Adams, Walter R. Walter R. Adams, one of fourteen children of James and Emma Adams, was born in Purmela, Coryell County, Texas, on January 25, 1897. Adams attended Baylor University, served in the United States armed forces during World War I, and then taught school at Hay Valley, Purmela, and Ireland, Texas. He spent the rest of his life farming and writing, and he remained a bachelor. Three collections of his verse, *The Dead Lie Down* (1934), *Bachelor's Poppy* (1940), and *High to the Fruits* (1949), were published by the Kaleidograph Press of Dallas (*see Kaleidograph*). His poetry was published in many periodicals and anthologies, and he received numerous honors and literary awards. He was a charter member of the Texas Institute of Letters qv and the Fort Belknap qv Archives Association. At the time of his death at Gatesville on June 27, 1971, he was honorary vice-president of the Poetry Society of Texas.qv A collection of his works is on display at the restored Fort Belknap Museum near Graham.

BIBLIOGRAPHY: Vaida S. Montgomery, *A Century with Texas Poets and Poetry* (1934); Gatesville *Messenger*, July 1, 1971.

W. E. Bard

Adams, Wayman. Wayman Adams, son of Nelson Perry and Mary Elizabeth (Justice) Adams, was born in Muncie, Indiana, on September 23, 1883. His artistic ability was soon recognized. He studied painting under William Forsythe in Indiana, William Chase in Italy, and Robert Henri in Spain. In 1914 he won his first major award, the Thomas R. Proctor Prize of the National Academy in New York. Adams married Margaret Graham Burroughs on October 1, 1918; they had one son.

Adams was considered one of America's leading portrait painters long before he established permanent residence in Austin, Texas, in 1948. He maintained studios in New York City for most of the years of his career; his first sizeable commission was for a portrait of Booth Tarkington. He subsequently painted such notables as Presidents Harding, Coolidge, and Hoover, Vice-President Wallace, U.S. military generals Jonathan Mayhew Wainwright qv and Walter Krueger,qv industrialist B. F. Goodrich, Colonel E. M. House,qv Clara Driscoll

Sevier,qv golfer Bobby Jones, Texas Governors Beauford Jester qv and Allan Shivers, and J. Frank Dobie.qv His portrait of the great Russian cellist, Piatigorsky, is one of the most famous in American portraiture.

Adams taught at the Grand Central Art Galleries in New York and at the John Herron Art Institute in Indianapolis; in 1935 and 1936 he conducted an art school in Taxco, Mexico. He received an honorary Doctor of Arts degree at Syracuse University in 1943. He remained in Austin from 1948 to 1959, where he died, the victim of a heart attack, on April 7, 1959.

BIBLIOGRAPHY: *American Art Annual* (1929); *Who's Who in American Art* (1936); *Who's Who In America* (1950); Biographical File, Barker Texas History Center, University of Texas at Austin.

Joseph E. Blanton

*Adams, William.

*Adams, William Wirt.

*Adams Bayou.

*Adams Branch.

*Adams Creek.

*Adams-Oñis Treaty.

*Adams Store, Texas.

*Adamsville, Texas.

*Addicks, Texas.

*Addicks Lake. *See also* Addicks Reservoir.

Addicks Reservoir. Addicks Reservoir, formerly Addicks Lake, in the San Jacinto River Basin near Addicks in Harris County and on South Mayde and Langham creeks, tributaries to Buffalo Bayou, which is tributary to the San Jacinto River and the Houston Ship Channel.qv

Owned by the United States government, the project is operated by the United States Army Corps of Engineers, Galveston District, for flood protection of the Houston area. The reservoir is for floodwater retention only, with a capacity of 204,460 acre-feet and a surface area of 16,780 acres. The drainage area is 133 square miles above the outlet works.

BIBLIOGRAPHY: Texas Water Commission, *Bulletin 6408* (1964).

Seth D. Breeding

*Addielou, Texas.

*Addison, Oscar Murray.

*Addison, Texas.

*Addran, Texas.

*Add-Ran Christian University.

*Add-Ran College.

*Add-Ran Jarvis College.

*Adell, Texas.

*Adelsverein.

Ad Interim Government.

*Adjutant General.

*Adkins, Texas.

*Admiral, Texas.

*Adobe.

*Adobe Creek.

*Adobe Walls.

*Adobe Walls, Texas.

*Adobe Walls, First Battle of.

*Adobe Walls, Second Battle of. [This title was incorrectly listed in Volume I as Adobe Wall, Second Battle of.]

*Adobe Walls Mountain.

*Adoeette. *See* Big Tree.

*Adoue, Jean Baptiste.

Adoue, Jean Baptiste, Jr. Jean Baptiste Adoue, Jr., Dallas banker and mayor, was born into a pioneer family in Dallas on November 4, 1884. He was the son of Jean Baptiste Adoue qv and Mary (Simpson) Adoue. After receiving a law degree from the University of Texas in 1906, he practiced law in Dallas for a year, then joined his father in the National Bank of Commerce. On his father's death in 1924, he became president of the bank. He married Hester A. Allen on October 12, 1909, and, following her death, married Mary J. Wilson on May 12, 1937. An outstanding tennis player, he repeatedly won Texas, Southwestern, and Southern championships; in 1931 he went to Mexico City as nonplaying captain of the United States Davis Cup team. He engaged in civic activities, including two terms as head of the Community Chest and two years, 1939–1940, as president of the Dallas Chamber of Commerce. During several tempestuous terms as a city councilman, he frequently engaged in controversies with other members of the council; he served as mayor of Dallas for a two-year term, 1951–1953. He was a director of several financial, insurance, and business corporations. He died at his desk, of a heart attack, on November 17, 1956.

BIBLIOGRAPHY: Dallas *Morning News*, November 18, 1956.

Wayne Gard

*Adrian, Texas.

*Adriance, John.** John Adriance became a business partner of Morgan L. Smith qv (not Morgan R. Smith, as stated in Volume I).

BIBLIOGRAPHY: Adriance Papers (MS., Archives, University of Texas at Austin Library).

*Adsul, Texas.

*Advance, Texas.

*Adventist Churches in Texas.** [This title was incorrectly listed in Volume I as Adventists Churches in Texas.] Seventh-day Adventist church membership in Texas increased from 6,259 on January 1, 1950, to 9,495 on June 30, 1966. During the same period the number of churches increased from 79 to 118. Thirty-eight new church edifices were constructed between 1959 and 1966, serving key cities such as Dallas, Fort Worth, Houston, San Antonio, Austin, and Amarillo. In 1962 a camp-meeting pavilion with seating capacity for approximately five thousand persons was constructed in Keene.

As of June 30, 1966, the Texas Conference employed ninety-four pastoral and church workers. In addition, the conference operated thirty elementary schools, two secondary schools, and Southwestern Union Academy and College (see Adventist Schools in Texas). Twenty full-time literature evangelists were selling over $300,000 worth of books and periodicals yearly.

Also the conference operated five medical institutions—Hays Memorial Hospital, San Marcos (40 beds); Memorial Hospital, Beeville (74 beds); Menard Hospital and Retirement Home, Menard (70 beds); Santa Anna Medical Center, Santa Anna (30 beds for acute care and 78 for geriatrics); and Sunny Acres Manor, Rusk (48 beds). Seventy-two physicians and dentists operated self-supporting clinics as officials of Seventh-day Adventist Medical and Dental Association. Church headquarters for the Texas Conference of Seventh-day Adventists is in Fort Worth.

Don R. Christman

Adventist Schools in Texas. The early development of the Seventh-day Adventist educational system dates back to 1874. However, the first schools in Texas were established in 1890. In 1966 the Texas Conference of Seventh-day Adventists operated thirty elementary schools. Eighty teachers were employed for an annual enrollment of approximately 1,400 students. In addition the denomination maintained three secondary schools in Texas—Jefferson Academy at Jefferson, Valley Grande Academy at Weslaco, and Southwestern Union Academy at Keene. The schools accommodated both boarding and community students. The enrollment for the three academies was 350 students, with thirty teachers.

These schools, which are all coeducational, are operated on the philosophy that education should be threefold; equal development of mental, physical, and spiritual faculties is stressed. To accomplish this purpose, the schools adhere closely to educational standards established by the state, adding courses in Bible and allotting time for worship or inspirational studies. Health principles are taught and opportunity is given for students to work. Academy students assist with office work, janitorial services, laundry, cafeteria, grounds, broommaking, cabinetmaking, and other work. See also Southwestern Union College.

BIBLIOGRAPHY: E. M. Cadwallader, *Educational Principles in the Writings of Ellen G. White* (1950); *The Seventh-day Adventist Encyclopedia* (1966); Files of the Bureau of Public Relations, General Conference of Seventh-day Adventists, Washington, D.C.

I. V. Stonebrook

*Advocate of the People's Rights.

*Ady, Texas.

*Aeronautics Commission, Texas. The Texas Aeronautics Commission was reorganized in 1961. The number of commissioners was increased to six and the responsibilities of the commission were broadened. The commission was given authority to acquire land for aeronautical purposes and to cooperate in activities of federal and state agencies.

BIBLIOGRAPHY: University of Texas at Austin, *Guide To Texas State Agencies* (1964).

Aerospace Medical Division. See Brooks Air Force Base.

*Affleck, Isaac Dunbar.

*Affleck, Mary Hunt.

*Affleck, Thomas.

*Afton, Texas.

Aging, Governor's Committee on. See Governor's Committee on Aging.

*Agnes, Texas.

*Agrarian Movements in Texas.

*Agreda, María de Jesús de.

*Agricultural Adjustment Administration. See *also* Agricultural Stabilization and Conservation Service.

*Agricultural Education. See Education, Agricultural.

*Agricultural Experiment Station System. The Texas Agricultural Experiment Station, in the 1960's, concerned itself with problems confronting farmers and ranchers, rural and urban homemakers, and business firms depending on or serving agriculture which, together, make up 40 percent of the state's population.

Research was designed to point the way toward maintaining and improving productive resources; lowering production costs; improving quality of food, feed, and fiber products; expanding markets; devising new and better methods for growing, processing, and distributing and utilizing farm and ranch products.

At the Main Station, headquartered on the Texas A&M campus at College Station, are thirteen subject-matter departments, three regulatory services, three service departments, and the administrative staff. Field units were located in major agricultural areas of Texas to better serve the particular needs of those areas. Other stations operating cooperatively with the Texas Agricultural Experiment Station included those of the Texas Forest Service, Texas Parks and Wildlife Department, United States Department of Agriculture, the University of Texas, Texas Tech University, and Texas A&I University. Additionally, some experiments were conducted on farms and ranches, in rural homes, and in processing and distributing plants of industries serving agriculture.

The Texas Agricultural Experiment Station in 1965 was conducting more than four hundred active research projects, which included all phases of agriculture in the state. Among them were: the basic agricultural sciences, including biometrics, biochemistry, and biophysics; soil conservation and improvement; water conservation and use; grasses and legumes; grain crops; cotton and other fiber crops; vegetable crops; citrus and other subtropical fruits; fruits and nuts; oil seed crops; ornamental plants; brush and weeds; insects; plant diseases; beef cattle; dairy cattle, sheep, and goats; swine;

chickens and turkeys; animal diseases and parasites; fish and game; farm and ranch engineering; farm and ranch business; marketing agricultural products; home economics; and agricultural economics.

Hal R. Taylor

Agricultural Extension Service, Texas. [Earlier history appears under Texas Agricultural Extension Service, in Volume II.] The Texas Agricultural Extension Service is a joint undertaking between Texas A&M University and the United States Department of Agriculture and is carried out in cooperation with commissioners' courts and local people in each county.

In the 1960's the basic function of the service was to provide people with useful and practical information on subjects relating to agriculture and home economics and to encourage its use. Major areas of program emphasis were: efficiency in production; efficiency in marketing, distribution, and utilization of farm products; conservation, development, and wise use of natural resources; management on the farm and in the home; youth development; leadership development; family living; community improvement and resource development; and public affairs. The youth phase of the informal educational service was 4-H Club work.

The county extension staff was the organization's basic education unit. It had the responsibility of developing a county educational program based on the wants and needs of people as determined by the people themselves. Guidance in program development was provided by extension agents and appropriate subject matter specialists. Extension workers then brought to people the pertinent research information available, interpreted and demonstrated its application to the immediate situation involved, and encouraged the application of such research in solving practical problems.

The extension service endeavored to make the services of an agricultural and home demonstration agent, together with such assistants as might be needed, available in all counties of Texas. The headquarters staff of administrators and subject-matter specialists was located on the Texas A&M campus at College Station. For administrative purposes Texas was divided into twelve extension districts, each having a district agent for agriculture and one for home economics. Area subject-matter specialists were located at the various district headquarters.

Agricultural Extension Service programs were supported by the technical information and resources available from both Texas A&M University, including the Agricultural Experiment Station qv and the resident teaching staff, and the United States Department of Agriculture.

Hal R. Taylor

Agricultural and Mechanical College of Texas. See also Texas A&M University.

Agricultural Stabilization and Conservation Service. The Agricultural Stabilization and Conservation Service replaced the Agricultural Adjustment Administration.qv In 1949 substantial changes were made in the marketing quota provisions for cotton and rice, and the price support provisions were repealed with the enactment of the Agricultural Act of 1949. The Agricultural Act of 1954 repealed the authority for marketing quotas for corn, but authority for corn acreage allotments was retained. Acreage allotments and a commercial corn-producing area were not established for the 1959 and subsequent crops of corn since a majority of the corn producers voting in the referendum held on November 25, 1958, favored a price support program without acreage allotments.

In 1961 numerous changes were made in the wheat provisions of the act, and in 1962 further amendments were passed, effective with the 1964 and subsequent crops of wheat. A land use and a wheat marketing allocation program were also enacted by that law.

Hal R. Taylor

Agricultural Workers. *See* Labor, Migrant.

*Agriculture, State Department of.

*Agriculture in Texas. Since World War II the growth of urban areas and the mechanization of farming have produced great changes in Texas agriculture. By 1954 the number of Texas farms had declined 40 percent and the farm population had declined almost 50 percent in comparison with the 1937 census figures. The number of small farms continued to decline, while at the same time the size of the remaining farms doubled. This change was due primarily to increasing application of modern technology and technique. Mechanized equipment such as tractors, combines, trucks, and row strippers, as well as the increasing use of electricity and refrigeration became the rule rather than the exception on Texas farms in the 1950's.

Commercial fertilizers and insecticides also began to be employed widely, leading to increased crop yield. Texas farms increased usage of commercial fertilizers from 450,000 tons in 1948 to 600,000 tons in 1953. By 1960 the annual usage of fertilizer reached 708,036 tons; this trend continued during the 1960's, and the total amount of fertilizer used doubled between 1960 and 1966. By the latter date, land treated with fertilizer yielded an estimated $300,000,000 above costs.

Irrigation also became more widespread during the 1950's. Whereas less than 5 percent of Texas farms and only 3 percent of the total crop area were under irrigation in 1940, the area had increased to 10 percent by 1948. By summer, 1959, the irrigated area totaled 25 percent of the state's harvested cropland and was distributed throughout 239 Texas counties. Texas stood second only to California in irrigated cropland by 1960. More than 50 percent of the irrigation systems were located on the High Plains, and this area had the highest water consumption, partially due to the drouth in the 1950's. The increasing use of irrigation in the late 1950's and early 1960's led to rapid depletion of water resources, and in 1965 agricultural researchers intensified their programs to provide Texas with adequate water when the natural supply was exhausted. (*See* Irrigation.)

By the early 1960's certain trends in Texas agriculture could be observed. The increasing efficiency of machinery and the rising cost of living, as well as the high ratio of capital investment needed in modern agriculture, forced more than 50 percent of Texas farmers to supplement their income with off-farm employment.

The increasing application of technology led to larger farms. By 1963 the total number of Texas farms had decreased more than 31 percent, while the average acreage had increased from 438 acres in 1950 to over 600 acres. These farms paid more attention to calculated planning, accumulation of capital to meet higher production costs, and use of extensive credit. Use of machinery on farms increased from 10 percent in 1940 to 22 percent in 1959.

The rural farm population continued to decrease with the use of machinery. A shift from row crop to livestock farming on many Texas farms also contributed to the decline. By 1959 farm labor had decreased 27 percent since 1940. In 1963 only eighteen Texas counties registered an increase in farm population. Paralleling this trend was the rapid growth of rural non-farm areas or suburbia; by 1964 problems in rural areas approached those of urban areas as urbanization continued. Many farmers moved to the city and either continued their farming from an urban base or rented their land to tenants who remained in the rural area.

By the mid-1960's Texas farmers faced several problems. One of these was the restriction on the use of *bracero* labor, on which vegetable and fruit growers heavily depended. The organization of packinghouse and field labor by unions also increased the farmer's cost of production and led to increasing mechanization. Labor shortages in some cases forced old farmers to retire earlier than in the past. Widespread coverage by government social security and health plans, however, made such retirement easier than would have been the case in the 1930's.

By 1964 the principal Texas crops were valued at $1,343,000,000 and the state was engaged in developing a substantial international export trade. In 1963–1964 Texas was second only to Illinois in exporting agricultural products. Cotton continued to be the leading export, followed by grain sorghum, rice, and wheat. By 1967, 20 percent of Texas farm products were sold outside the United States, primarily to the European "Common Market" and to the European Free Trade Association. Texas exports yielded an estimated total of $484,000,000, with cotton bringing in $158,000,-000, followed by feed grains with $64,000,000, rice with $35,000,000, and wheat and flour with $23,-000,000.

Several non-traditional crops were expanded on Texas farms during the 1950's. Although castor beans were introduced in Texas during World War I, major interest in this crop was stimulated only after the Office of Defense Mobilization declared castor oil to be a strategic oil in 1950. Texas farms began developing different varieties of castor beans as a cash crop, and research with the original tall-growing castor bean variety led to the development of dwarf-internode castor beans, which made up almost all of Texas' production by the late 1950's. Starting with approximately three thousand unirrigated acres in 1957 centered around Plainview, Texas became the leading state in castor bean production by 1959 and had over ten thousand acres under cultivation in 1962. This crop was grown on a contract basis with processing firms. Development of a self-propelled combine with a two-row harvester, and construction of a crushing plant in Plainview in 1960 stimulated new interest in castor beans, which by this time had an annual value of $4,000,000.

Guar, a drouth-resistant annual summer legume which thrived on a wide variety of soils, was also introduced on Texas farms during the mid-1950's. Three main varieties were harvested between 1957 and 1959, two of which yielded over one thousand pounds per acre. With irrigation, crop yields as high as eighteen hundred pounds per acre were obtained. Guar was used mainly as livestock feed, as a soil conditioner, and as a source of mannogalactan gum, which was used in food, paper, and textile products.

Soybean cultivation was a third new crop to Texas farmers in the 1950's. With the development of non-shattering varieties suitable for irrigation, soybean acreage increased in Texas. Grown for seed, soybeans were planted on more than twenty-five thousand acres in 1956, mainly on the High Plains. By 1958 soybean acreage had increased to approximately sixty thousand acres. The seventy thousand acres under cultivation in the mid-1960's were valued at $4,322,000.

Grain sorghum became the second money value crop in the state, replacing corn as the principal feed grain crop. During the 1950's, 72 percent of all feed grain production in Texas was grain sorghum. Its ability to grow in a dry climate and its full adaptability to harvesting entirely by machines were two factors which stimulated the growth of grain sorghum. In 1955 Texas produced 141,570,-000 bushels, more than half of the nation's grain sorghum. The 22.5-bushel-per-acre yield that year was the highest since 1919, and the total harvest represented almost twice the average Texas production from 1944 to 1953. Although concentrated on the High Plains and East Texas coastal bend, grain sorghum was grown in 135 Texas counties and represented 37 percent of the total harvested acreage. Texas, with its 213,249,000 acres under cultivation in 1957, was the nation's most important grain sorghum-producing state. Total yield that year was 238,000,000 bushels. By 1964 Texas grain sorghum planted on more than five million acres was valued at $228,816,000. In 1966 Texas remained the nation's leading grain sorghum-producing state with 80 percent of the crop being used as a feed grain.

Oats accounted for 5 percent of Texas' harvested cropland in 1954. In the period from 1947 to 1956 the annual yield from 1,740,000 acres of oats under cultivation was 25,473,000 bushels. This total increased in the late 1950's mainly due to its cultivation for winter pasture and other forage uses. By 1964, 2,000,000 planted acres were valued at $17,827,000.

Barley production, after a peak year in 1944, had an average yield of 1,923,000 bushels annually from 1947 to 1956. In 1951 only 45,000 acres were planted, the smallest barley crop in recent times. In 1954 barley acreage amounted to only 1 percent of the total Texas harvested acreage. Acreage steadily increased from that time, however, and reached a total of more than 75,000 acres in 1958. Used as a commercial grain as well as for livestock, barley was grown chiefly in northwest Texas. In 1964 the acreage planted in barley was valued at $3,612,000.

The wholesale vegetable produce industry in Texas totaled $26,000,000 in 1940. In the 1950's tomatoes dropped from the most important crop, valued at $12,000,000 in 1952, to the third crop in the industry, valued at $5,000,000 in 1958, mainly because of drouth and acreage reduction in the East Texas coastal bend and Yoakum areas. Lowest planted acreage was 22,000 acres in 1957. During this time the tomato industry underwent several changes, including harvesting procedure, use of larger packaging crates, and a switch from rail to truck transportation. By 1960 thirteen major vegetable areas in Texas produced twenty major fresh-market vegetables valued at more than $69,000,000; processed vegetables alone were valued at $5,000,-000 annually, enabling Texas to rank fifteenth in the nation. Although there was a general lag in the development of the vegetable produce industry, partially due to the predominance of other enterprises such as cotton and cattle, greenhouse production of vegetables was expanded, and in 1961 the state had more than one hundred greenhouses producing vegetable crops. Major areas under vegetable cultivation included the Rio Grande Valley and parts of East Texas. Leading vegetables were onions and lettuce. *See also* Bee Industry, Cattle Industry, Citrus Fruit Production, Corn Culture, Cotton Culture, Dairying, Fruits Other than Citrus, Goat Ranching, Grape Culture, Grasses Native to Texas, Hay Production, Lumbering in Texas, Mule Raising, Onion Culture, Peanut Culture, Pecan Industry, Sheep Ranching, Spinach Culture, Sugar Production, Sweet Potato Culture, Swine Raising, Tobacco Culture, and Wheat Production.

BIBLIOGRAPHY: Texas Agricultural Experiment Station *Bulletins* (June, 1954–September, 1963); *Texas Agricultural Progress* (January–February, 1960, Winter, 1967); *Texas Almanac* (1955, 1957, 1963); *Texas Business Review* (October, 1951, June, 1955, February, May, 1958, July, August, September, 1959, April, August, 1960, March, 1961).

Charles Duval, Jr.

*Agua Azul Creek. Agua Azul Creek flows westward (not eastward, as stated in Volume I) into San Juanita Creek.

*Agua Caballo.

*Agua Dulce, Texas.

*Agua Dulce Creek.

*Agua Dulce Creek, Battle of.

*Agua Fria Mountain.

*Agua de Fuera Creek.

*Agua Negra Creek.

*Agua Nueva, Texas.

*Agua Piedra Creek.

*Agua Poquita Creek.

Agua Sucia Indians. The Agua Sucia ("dirty water") Indians are known from a single Spanish document of 1683 that does not clearly identify their area. They seem to have lived somewhere in west-central Texas. Their affiliations remain unknown.

BIBLIOGRAPHY: C. W. Hackett (ed.), *Pichardo's Treatise on the Limits of Louisiana and Texas*, I (1931).

T. N. Campbell

Aguajuani Indians. The Aguajuani Indians are known from a Spanish document of 1754, which placed them an unspecified distance north or northwest of Nacogdoches. They were evidently not the Yojuane, whose name (Jujuane) also appears in the same document. Aguajuani resembles Ahehouen, the name of an Indian group recorded in documents of the La Salle Expedition.qv These French documents indicate that in the late seventeenth century the Ahehouen lived inland somewhere north of Matagorda Bay, probably near the Colorado River. No relationship between the Aguajuani and the Ahehouen has thus far been established, and the linguistic and cultural affiliations of both groups remain unknown.

BIBLIOGRAPHY: I. J. Cox (ed.), *The Journeys of Réné Robert Cavelier, Sieur de La Salle*, II (1906); F. W. Hodge (ed.), *Handbook of American Indians*, I (1907); H. R. Stiles (ed.), *Joutel's Journal of La Salle's Last Voyage, 1684-7* (1906).

T. N. Campbell

Aguapalam Indians. This group of Indians is known only from one brief encounter by Spanish travelers near the close of the seventeenth century. At this time the Aguapalam and several other bands of Coahuiltecan Indians ranged over the Nueces-Frio area between San Antonio and Eagle Pass.

BIBLIOGRAPHY: F. W. Hodge (ed.), *Handbook of American Indians*, II (1910).

T. N. Campbell

*Aguastaya Indians. The Aguastaya (Aguastalla, Guasttaya) Indians were one of the small bands of Coahuiltecan Indians who, in the early eighteenth century, lived along the lower Medina River south of San Antonio. There they seem to have been living in close association with two other Coahuiltecan bands, the Payaya and the Mesquite.

The Aguastaya were listed as one of the Indian groups for whom San José y San Miguel de Aguayo Mission qv was established at San Antonio in 1720.

BIBLIOGRAPHY: F. W. Hodge (ed.), *Handbook of American Indians*, I (1907); M. K. Kress (trans.) and M. A. Hatcher (ed.), "Diary of a Visit of Inspection of the Texas Missions Made by Fray Gaspar José de Solis in the Year 1767–1768," *Southwestern Historical Quarterly*, XXXV (1931–1932); Pedro de Rivera y Villalón, *Diario y derrotero de la caminado . . . en las Provincias Internas de Nueva España* (1945).

T. N. Campbell

*Aguayo, Marquis de.

*Aguayo Expedition.

Aguida Indians. In 1683–1684 Juan Domínguez de Mendoza qv led an exploratory expedition from El Paso as far eastward as the junction of the Concho and Colorado rivers east of present San Angelo. In his itinerary he listed the names of thirty-seven Indian groups, including the Aguida, from whom he expected to receive delegations. Nothing further is known about the Aguida, who seem to have been one of many Indian groups of north-central Texas that were swept away by the southward thrust of the Lipan-Apache and Comanche Indians in the eighteenth century.

BIBLIOGRAPHY: H. E. Bolton (ed.), *Spanish Exploration in the Southwest, 1542–1706* (1916); C. W. Hackett (ed.), *Pichardo's Treatise on the Limits of Louisiana and Texas*, II (1934).

T. N. Campbell

*Aguilares, Texas.

*Aguja Canyon.

*Aguja Peak.

*Ahehouen Indians. The Ahehouen (Ahehoen, Ahekouen) Indians are known only from records of the La Salle Expedition.qv In 1687 Ahehouen lived somewhere north of Matagorda Bay, probably near the Colorado River. In 1754 Indians with a similar name, Aguajuani, lived an unspecified distance north or northwest of Nacogdoches. The Aguajuani are not to be confused with the Yojuane, whose name (Jujuane) also appears in the same document. No relationship between the Ahehouen and the Aguajuani has yet been established, and the linguistic and cultural affiliations of both groups remain unknown.

BIBLIOGRAPHY: I. J. Cox (ed.), *The Journeys of Réné Robert Cavelier, Sieur de La Salle*, II (1906); F. W. Hodge (ed.), *Handbook of American Indians*, I (1907); H. R. Stiles (ed.), *Joutel's Journal of La Salle's Last Voyage, 1684–7* (1906).

T. N. Campbell

Ahouerhopiheim Indians. In the latter part of the seventeenth century, according to records of the La Salle Expedition,qv the Ahouerhopiheim (Abonerhopiheim, Ahonerhopiheim) Indians occupied an inland area somewhere north of Matagorda Bay, probably near the Colorado River or between the Colorado and Brazos rivers. Although this name has passed into American Indian literature, there is some question about its accuracy. There is some evidence that on Henri Joutel's qv original manuscript two names appeared, Ahouergomahe and Kemahopiheim, and that a printer, through error, created a hybrid name, using the first and last parts of these names respectively. The linguistic and cultural affiliations of the Indians bearing these names remain unknown.

BIBLIOGRAPHY: I. J. Cox (ed.), *The Journey of Réné Robert Cavelier, Sieur de La Salle*, II (1906); F. W. Hodge (ed.), *Handbook of American Indians*, I (1907); H. R. Stiles (ed.), *Joutel's Journal of La Salle's Last Voyage, 1684-7* (1906).

T. N. Campbell

*Ahuache Spring.

Aieli Indians. In 1683–1684 Juan Domínguez de Mendoza qv led an exploratory expedition from El Paso as far eastward as the junction of the Concho and Colorado rivers east of present San Angelo. In his itinerary he listed the names of thirty-seven Indian groups, including the Aieli (Ayele), from whom he expected to receive delegations. Nothing further is known about the Aieli, who seem to have been one of many Indian groups of north-central Texas that were swept away by the southward thrust of the Lipan-Apache and Comanche Indians in the eighteenth century.

BIBLIOGRAPHY: H. E. Bolton (ed.), *Spanish Exploration in the Southwest, 1542–1706* (1916); C. W. Hackett (ed.), *Pichardo's Treatise on the Limits of Louisiana and Texas*, II (1934).

T. N. Campbell

Aijado Indians. The Aijado (Ahijao, Aijao, Ahijito, Aixao, Axtao, Ayjado, Ayjao) Indians have been the subject of much discussion, and their status is far from clear. Their earliest known area (seventeenth century) was either in north-central Texas or south-central Oklahoma, depending upon how one interprets the documentary evidence. An early attempt to identify the Aijado with the Eyeish (Caddo) of eastern Texas is no longer taken seriously. Some modern writers consider the Aijado as a Wichita group, possibly the same as that known in the eighteenth century as Taovaya.

BIBLIOGRAPHY: H. H. Bancroft, *History of the North Mexican States and Texas*, I (1884); H. E. Bolton, "The Jumano Indians in Texas, 1650–1771," *Quarterly of the Texas State Historical Association*, XV (1911–1912) and *Spanish Exploration in the Southwest, 1542–1706* (1916); G. E. Hyde, *Indians of the High Plains* (1959); A. H. Schroeder, "A Re-analysis of the Routes of Coronado and Oñate into the Plains in 1541 and 1601," *Plains Anthropologist*, VII (1962); S. L. Tyler and H. D. Taylor, "The Report of Fray Alonso de Posadas in Relation to Quivira and Teguayo," *New Mexico Historical Review*, XXXIII (1958).

T. N. Campbell

*Aiken, Herman.

Aiken, Texas. (Bell County.) Aiken was situated about ten miles north of Belton. In 1858 it was described as being "blessed with abundant spring water and a fine steam mill."

BIBLIOGRAPHY: *Texas Almanac* (1936).

*Aiken, Texas. (Floyd County.)

*Aiken, Texas. (Shelby County.)

*Aiken Creek.

*Air, Texas.

Air Conditioning in Texas. The earliest home air cooling in Texas was practiced by the Mexican and Spanish population. At an early date Spanish Americans constructed adobe houses with thick masonry walls with a door or a closable opening in each of the four walls. At night the opened doors and openings permitted an all-night flow of air through the rooms. This lowered the temperature of the entire adobe wall. At sunrise all openings were closed until sundown. The owner thus captured a mass of cool air in his home which lasted until "siesta" time after the midday meal. During the day, the semi-tropical sun would heat up the outer walls by direct radiation. For the night sleeping hours while the house was cooling for the next day, the adobe inhabitant and his family sometimes slept out-of-doors, where they could obtain the benefit of natural night cooling. The Spanish-speaking people acquired this practice from African and Asiatic Arabs who had learned to employ the existing forces of nature to keep cool. From Spain this practice entered Mexico and then Texas. The early white settlers in the state also built their homes so that they could be cooled by this system of cross ventilation.

Well water was also introduced as an air cooling medium at an early date. The water was pumped from the well to fan radiators installed in the space to be cooled. Unless the water was pumped for other uses subsequent to its application as a coolant, this was not an economical procedure in Texas since the well water was usually 62° to 72° F., and thus had little cooling potential.

In the dairy belts of Central Texas, the German farmers during the nineteenth century adopted evaporative cooling. This system, which was practiced extensively in Central and West Texas, originated for milk cooling. The evening milking was placed in metal cans and then fans blew air through wetted blankets covering the cans. This air took on "wet bulb" temperatures and cooled the milk to 70° to 75° F. This system was easily modified for home cooling, as is evident today in the wide range of evaporative coolers ranging from the desert variety to the sophisticated designs used in large homes, commercial structures, and government buildings. During this same period the more eastern North Texas low elevation cities experimented with every type of air-moving fan, with ice and dry ice, and with evaporative and sky-cooling devices to combat the summer heat waves.

Manufacturing of cooling devices began in Texas cities as early as 1870 and provided the beginning of a new type of industry. Air cooling with commercial ice dates back to approximately 1910, when ice could be purchased for as little as four dollars per ton. At first, the 300-pound blocks of ice were placed in a vault through which a fan blew ambient air into an outlet duct to the space to be cooled. By 1920 this procedure had been improved by placing the ice in an enclosed pool and circulating the ice water to fan radiators in order to cool rooms, auditoriums, and restaurants. The First Baptist churches of Dallas and Austin and the Highland Park Methodist Church were ice-water

cooled for many years. The first refrigerated air-cooled building in the Houston area was the Rice Hotel cafeteria, air-conditioned in 1922. In 1935 the Crystal Ballroom of the Rice Hotel became Houston's first air-conditioned ballroom.

By 1940 Texas had become a national manufacturing center for air cooling machines and inventions, which ranged from lowly desert coolers to the most sophisticated forms of evaporative coolers and reversed cycle refrigerators, as well as heaters for winter heating and summer refrigerated air cooling. The latter system was designed into one machine, usually called the "heat pump."

By 1963 there were 242 establishments in Texas manufacturing and selling air-conditioning equipment. Wholesale purchases had reached $168,044,-000 by that year. As of 1966 Texas ranked as the most air-conditioned area of the world, with Houston being the leading air-conditioned city. *See also* Refrigeration, History of, in Texas.

W. R. Woolrich

Air Control Board, Texas. The Texas Air Control Board, created in 1965, was composed of nine members, including the state commissioner of health, the executive director of the Texas Industrial Commission, and the executive director of the Texas Animal Health Commission as ex officio members; the remaining six members were appointed by the governor. The board was authorized to develop a plan for the control of air resources and to adopt necessary rules and regulations in preventing air pollution.

BIBLIOGRAPHY: University of Texas at Austin, *Guide To Texas State Agencies* (1966).

*Air Line Railroad Company.

*Aircraft Manufacture.** Aircraft manufacture and later its concomitant, electronics,qv have added significantly to the economy of the state. Though statistics concerning the industry are out of date almost before publication, aircraft manufacture had grown by the 1960's until it ranked sixth in the state in the number of employees, sixth in payroll accounts, and eighth in value added by manufacturing. These United States Census Bureau data did not include total figures of the National Aeronautics and Space Administration qv complex in Houston, a number of substantial governmental contracts in North Texas, and satellite plants.

The chief locale of the industry is the North Texas area and particularly the Grand Prairie-Richardson-Hurst-Euless-Arlington-Fort Worth salient, an area which ranks second only to the entire state of California in aircraft production. Other aircraft manufacturing enterprises or their subsidiaries are found in Bexar, Cameron, Harris, Harrison, Hunt, Kerr, McLennan, Medina, Stephens, and Young counties. The North American facility (later Ling-Temco-Vought) was followed in 1941 by the Fort Worth General Dynamics or "Convair" plant, noted for the production of bombers and the controversial TFX contract, a firm which in 1965 ranked first in the nation in the export of defense weapons. In 1950 Lawrence Bell established in a Hurst-Euless cow pasture the first plant in the world specifically designed to manufacture helicopters.

With the advent of electronics, other complexes, such as Texas Instruments and Collins Radio, have developed in Dallas County and branched elsewhere in Texas. The National Aeronautics and Space Administration in Harris County cooperates with other agencies in attempting to explore outer space. Thus, in Texas, aircraft are manufactured from the small one-man plane to vehicles capable of landing on the moon. See also Electronics Industry in Texas; Space Industry in Texas.

BIBLIOGRAPHY: Files of the Bureau of Business Research, University of Texas at Austin; Lloyd L. Turner, "The South's Biggest War Baby," Editor and Publisher (October 31, 1953); E. C. Barksdale, "The Genesis of the Aviation Industry in North Texas," No. 6, Texas Industry Series (1958).

E. C. Barksdale

*Airlines in Texas. See Aviation in Texas.

*Airville, Texas.

*Ais Indians.

*Akasquy Indians.

Akokisa Indians. The Akokisa (Arkokisa, Orcoquiza) Indians were Atakapan-speaking Indians who lived in extreme southeastern Texas between the Trinity and Sabine rivers. They were most commonly encountered around Galveston Bay. It seems likely that the Han and Coaque encountered by Cabeza de Vaca qv in the early sixteenth century were Akokisa, as well as the Caux, who held Simars de Bellisle qv captive in the early eighteenth century. Most of what is known about the Akokisa comes from mission records. In 1748–1749 some of the Akokisa entered San Ildefonso Mission qv on the San Gabriel River near present Rockdale, but they left this area when the mission was abandoned in 1755. Nuestra Señora de la Luz Mission qv was built near the mouth of the Trinity River for the Akokisa and the Didai in 1756 1757 and lasted until 1772. Thereafter little is reported about the Akokisa, although in 1805 they seem to have lived in two settlements, one on the lower Colorado River and the other near the coast between the Neches and Sabine rivers. It seems likely that the Akokisa survivors joined their relatives, the Atakapa, in southwestern Louisiana shortly before the Texas Revolution.

BIBLIOGRAPHY: H. E. Bolton, "The Founding of the Missions on San Gabriel River, 1745–1749," Southwestern Historical Quarterly, XVII (1913–1914), Athanase de Mézières and the Louisiana-Texas Frontier, 1768–1780 (1914), and Texas in the Middle Eighteenth Century (1915); M. C. Burch, "The Indigenous Indians of the Lower Trinity Area of Texas," Southwestern Historical Quarterly, LX (1956–1957); J. O. Dyer, The Lake Charles Atakapas (1916); A. S. Gatschet and J. R. Swanton, A Dictionary of the Atakapa Language (1932); W. W. Newcomb, Jr., The Indians of Texas (1961); J. R. Swanton, Indian Tribes of the Lower Mississippi Valley and Adjacent Coast of the Gulf of Mexico (1911), The Indians of the Southeastern United States (1946), and The Indian Tribes of North America (1952).

T. N. Campbell

*Akron, Texas.

Alabama, Texas. (Houston County.) Alabama was formerly a post office village and port of call for steamers on the Trinity River. Ten miles southwest of Crockett, the town was settled in the 1830's. In 1841 the Texas Congress chartered Trinity College to be situated at Alabama. In 1847 A. T. Monroe was postmaster, and during the Civil War, Thomas Jones was Confederate postmaster. Alabama appeared as a place name on maps as late as 1946.

BIBLIOGRAPHY: Viktor Bracht, Texas in 1848 (1931); Grover C. Ramsey, Confederate Postmasters in Texas (1963).

Cyrus Tilloson

Alabama, Texas. (Trinity County.) Alabama, named for the Alabama Indians, was established about 1865 on Alabama Creek approximately three miles west of the Neches River. At one time the community had a store, a cotton gin, a sawmill, and possibly a post office. A school was maintained there until the 1930's, when it was consolidated with the Centerville district. The population in 1967 was approximately twenty-five.

*Alabama-Coushatta Indian Reservation. Control of the Alabama-Coushatta Indian Reservation passed from the Board for Texas State Hospitals and Special Schools qv to the Commission for Indian Affairs qv in 1965.

*Alabama-Coushatta Indians. See also Alabama Indians; Koasati Indians.

*Alabama Creek.

*Alabama Grays. See Mobile Grays.

*Alabama Indians. The Alabama (Alibamo, Alibamu, Allibamon) Indians are Muskhogean-speaking Indians whose aboriginal home was in present Alabama and Mississippi. In the latter half of the eighteenth century the Alabama began to migrate in various directions, mainly eastward to Georgia and Florida and westward to Louisiana. Most of those who moved to Louisiana went farther westward and appeared in eastern Texas early in the nineteenth century. The Alabama who remained in the southeastern states were removed with the Creek Indians to Indian Territory in 1836, and today their descendants live in Hughes and Okfuskee counties, Oklahoma. A few Alabama still live in Louisiana (Calcasieu and St. Landry parishes), but most of the surviving Alabama live on the Alabama-Coushatta Indian Reservation,qv which was established in Polk County, Texas, in 1854. The main outlines of Alabama Indian history are well known, but a detailed Alabama ethnohistory has yet to be written. The early movements of the Alabama in Texas are poorly known because no one has taken the trouble to dig deeply into the local history resources of the area. See also Alabama-Coushatta Indian Reservation; Alabama-Coushatta Indians; Koasati Indians.

BIBLIOGRAPHY: G. T. Bludworth, "How the Alabamas Came South," Publications of the Texas Folklore Society, XIII (1937); C. E. Castañeda, Our Catholic Heritage in Texas, 1519–1936, V (1942); F. W. Hodge (ed.), Handbook of American Indians, I (1907), II (1910); A. Rothe, *Kalita's People: A History of the Alabama-Coushatta Indians of Texas* (1963); H. Smither, "The Alabama Indians of Texas," *Southwestern Historical Quarterly*, XXXVI (1932–1933); M. D. Wade, *The Alabama Indians of Texas* (1936); D. H. Winfrey and J. M. Day (eds.), *The Indian Papers of Texas and the Southwest, 1825–1916*, I–V (1966); M. H. Wright, *A Guide to the Indian Tribes of Oklahoma* (1951).

T. N. Campbell

*Alabama Red Rovers. *See* Red Rovers.

*Alabama Trace.

Alachome Indians. In the late seventeenth and early eighteenth centuries the Alachome Indians, apparently Coahuiltecans, ranged from northeastern Coahuila northward across the Rio Grande into the adjoining part of Texas south of the Edwards Plateau. The Alachome are not to be confused with the Chome; both names appear in the same document.
BIBLIOGRAPHY: M. A. Hatcher, "The Expedition of Don Domingo Terán de los Ríos into Texas," *Preliminary Studies of the Texas Catholic Historical Society*, II (1932); F. W. Hodge (ed.), *Handbook of American Indians*, II (1910).

T. N. Campbell

*Alamán, Lucas.

Alamita, Texas. Alamita, a small Mexican settlement situated at the crossing of the La Bahía Road qv and Alamita Creek in Karnes County, was the predecessor of old Helena, Texas, which was established in 1852. The name Alamita, meaning "little cottonwood," was also applied to nearby Alamita Crossing on the San Antonio River and to Alamita Lodge No. 200, A.F. and A.M., which was originally chartered in Helena in 1857 and later moved to Karnes City in 1925. *See* Helena, Texas.
BIBLIOGRAPHY: Thomas H. Puckett, *Alamita Lodge No. 200, A.F. & A.M.* (1957); Robert H. Thonhoff, *A History of Karnes County, Texas* (M.A. thesis, Southwest Texas State College, 1963).

*Alamito Creek.

*Alamo, Texas. Alamo, in Hidalgo County, had a population of 4,121 in 1960 and 4,291 in 1970, according to the United States census.

*Alamo, Battle of. *See* Alamo, Siege and Fall of.

*Alamo, Flag of the.

*Alamo, History of the. The Alamo was occupied by Mexican forces from 1821 to December, 1835 (not 1836, as stated in Volume I), when the fortress was surrendered to Texan forces.

*Alamo, Siege and Fall of.

*Alamo Alto, Texas.

*Alamo Cenotaph, The.

*Alamo Creek.

*Alamo de Cesario Creek.

*Alamo Express.

*Alamo Heights, Texas. Located in Alamo Heights are Texas Military Institute,qv a public swimming pool, a post office, and a shopping center, with the McNay Art Institute qv adjoining the municipality on the north. Adjacent to the Ar-

gyle Hotel qv is Cathedral House, headquarters of the Episcopal Diocese of West Texas, with conference center and chapel housed in the Spanish-style former Harry Halff residence and offices in a contemporary field-stone building. On Cathedral House grounds are the headwaters of the San Antonio River, described in diaries of Mary Adams Maverick qv in 1839 and a visiting Englishman, James Freemantle, in 1863. Newspapers which have been published in Alamo Heights include the Alamo Heights *Herald*, in the 1920's, and the Alamo Heights *News*, from 1939 to the early 1960's. Population in 1960 was 7,552; in 1970 it was 6,933, according to the United States census. *See also* Charles Anderson; Hiram W. McLane; and Argyle Hotel.

*Alamo Monument.

Alamo and San Jacinto Monthly. In the 1880's and 1890's two culturally oriented groups, the Alamo Society and the San Jacinto Society, combined to sponsor the *Alamo and San Jacinto Monthly*, devoted to the *belles lettres*. In 1893 it was edited by Jno. L. Brooks (of the San Jacinto Society) at Georgetown.
BIBLIOGRAPHY: T. E. Nelson Papers (MS., Archives, University of Texas at Austin Library).

*Alamo Star. *See* San Antonio *Herald*.

Alamo Village. Alamo Village is located six miles north of Brackettville on the Shahan Angus Ranch. This replica of a typical old West Texas town was first created as a set for a Western movie concerning the battle of the Alamo, but is still in use as a tourist attraction because of its historical accuracy and the thoroughness of its construction. From December, 1957, to September, 1959, when the filming of the motion picture *The Alamo* was begun, the Batjac Company pre-production crew supervised a building program that involved up to four hundred workmen at one time. Artisans for the adobe work were brought from Mexico, where bricks are still made the same way they were three centuries ago. More than one million individual adobes were used in this set, which covers a total area of more than four hundred acres. More than ten miles of underground wiring, both electrical and telephonic, were installed and are still in use. There are no "false front" streets; the village consists entirely of completed adobe and wood-constructed buildings which house a cantina and restaurant, a trading post, an Indian store, a church, a jail, a blacksmith shop, museums of artifacts and arrowheads, and a gallery of many modern-day celebrities who have performed on the dusty streets of this little village. There are horseback rides along some of the ranch trails and a short stagecoach ride down the hill from the Alamo Mission reconstruction, an authentic duplication of the mission as it was after the thirteen-day battle.

All of the buildings and facilities are controlled by the owner of the ranch and are open to the public.

D. Shaw

*Alamocito Creek.

*Alamosa Creek.

*Alanreed, Texas.

*Alarcón, Martín de.

*Alarm Creek.

*Alazan Bay.

*Alba, Texas.

*Albany, Texas. Albany, seat and principal commercial center of Shackelford County, was incorporated in 1927 with a council-mayor form of government. In 1966 Albany reported ninety-eight businesses, nine churches, a hospital, a bank, a library, and a newspaper. The most recent industrial developments include the manufacture of oil field equipment and pipe organs. Numerous visitors are attracted to the Fort Griffin Fandangle,qv a history-oriented theatrical production produced periodically by local residents. The 1960 population was 2,174; the 1970 population was 1,978.

*Albert, Texas.

*Albion, Texas.

Albuquerque, Texas. Albuquerque was located on the Clear Fork of Sandies Creek in Gonzales County, approximately two miles south of the junction of Gonzales, Wilson, and Guadalupe counties. The town was believed to be in Wilson County until a 1914 survey showed it inside the Gonzales County line. Probably the settlement was named by South Texans who had fought in New Mexico under Henry H. Sibley.qv

The town's official life spanned the fourteen years from 1870 through 1883. A United States post office, with William W. Davis as postmaster, operated from September 19, 1870, to February 20, 1877. Four months later, on June 11, 1877, the post office was reestablished with Mrs. Martha H. McCracken in charge. It was permanently discontinued on October 23, 1883.

Henry S. Hastings and Samuel McCracken—Mississippians and brothers-in-law—were the earliest settlers. At one time the town had a cotton gin, a blacksmith shop, a mercantile store, a saloon, a post office, a school, and several dwellings. On May 17, 1873, John Wesley Hardin killed Jack Helm qqv in Albuquerque, one of a series of violent acts of the Sutton-Taylor feud.qv Albuquerque quickly declined after business activities shifted to a new village, Union (sometimes referred to as Union Valley), located two miles south of the Albuquerque site.

BIBLIOGRAPHY: Roy Sylvan Dunn, "Life and Times in Albuquerque, Texas," *Southwestern Historical Quarterly*, LV (1951–1952).

Roy Sylvan Dunn

*Alcalde.

*Alcalde. Between the years 1952 and 1968 the *Alcalde* evolved from a news magazine format to a publication of longer, more comprehensive articles concerning topical matters at the University of Texas at Austin and studies of general interest in higher education. In 1968 *Alcalde* began using four-color covers. Membership in the Ex-Students' Association in 1968 was 22,000, and remained the only requirement for *Alcalde* subscriptions. The executive editor from 1952 to 1956 was John McCurdy, and from 1956 to 1973, Jack R. Maguire. Managing editors from 1952 to 1968 were Raymond West, Melvin R. Mason, Charles A. Seitz, Jack Maguire, Paul Tracy, Don Knoles, Roberta Love, and Pat Maguire.

Pat Maguire

Alcalerpaguet Indians. The Alcalerpaguet (Calexpaquet) Indians, who were probably Coahuiltecan in speech, lived on the south bank of the lower Rio Grande in northern Tamaulipas In the middle of the eighteenth century their settlements were reported to be a short distance downstream from present Reynosa. At times the Alcalerpaguet also foraged and camped on the Texas side of the Rio Grande.

BIBLIOGRAPHY: W. Jiménez Moreno, "Tribus e idiomas del Norte de México," *El Norte de México y el Sur de Estados Unidos* (1944); G. Saldivar, *Los Indios de Tamaulipas* (1943).

T. N. Campbell

*Alcantra, Battle of.

*Alcino, Texas.

Alcoa Lake. Alcoa Lake is in the Brazos River Basin in Milam County, seven miles southwest of Rockdale on Sandy Creek, a tributary of Yegua Creek, which is tributary to the Brazos River. The project is owned and operated by the Aluminum Company of America for industrial and recreational purposes. Construction was started February 17, 1952, and the dam and spillway were completed in October, 1952; the gates were not installed until January 31, 1953. Impoundment of water began with the inflow from runoff in early 1952. The 12.5-mile pipeline from the Little River pumping plant to the lake was placed in operation on January 13, 1953.

In 1966 the lake had a capacity of 10,500 acre-feet and a surface area of 703 acres at the top of the spillway gates. The lake was maintained at near-spillway level by pumping from Little River when necessary, and the water was used for condenser-cooling purposes for a steam-electric generating station. The drainage area was only six square miles, but this was an off-channel storage. Most of the water was pumped from Little River.

BIBLIOGRAPHY: Texas Water Commission, *Bulletin 6408* (1964).

Seth D. Breeding

*Alderbranch, Texas.

*Aldine, Texas.

*Aldredge, George N.

*Aldrete, José Miguel.

Aldrich, Roy Wilkinson. Roy Wilkinson Aldrich, whose term of service at the time of his retirement as a Texas Ranger qv was longer than that of any other Ranger, was born in Quincy, Illinois, on September 17, 1869. He spent his early childhood in Golden City, Missouri, and as a youth lived in

Arizona, Idaho, and Oklahoma Territory. When the Spanish-American War began he was commissioned as a second lieutenant in the Second Missouri Volunteer Regiment, and later saw service on the island of Mindanao during the Philippine Insurrection. He served with the British Army's remount service in South Africa during the Boer War. From 1903 to 1907 he was sheriff of Kiowa County, Oklahoma Territory, and from 1907 to 1915 he was in the real estate business in Corpus Christi and San Antonio.

In 1915 Aldrich enlisted in Company A, Texas Rangers. He was promoted to captain and quartermaster in 1918 and retired from that post in 1947. During his years as a Ranger, Aldrich became known in Texas academic circles for his interest in history and natural history. He aided Walter Prescott Webb qv while Webb was doing research in South Texas for his book, *The Texas Rangers* (1935); Aldrich's collections of flora and Indian artifacts were important sources of specimens for botanists and anthropologists at the University of Texas. The woods and pond of his home near Austin were the source of an important collection of fruit flies used by the university's Genetics Foundation. In 1958 Sul Ross State College (now Sul Ross State University) acquired his 10,000-volume library.

Aldrich never married. He died on January 29, 1955, and was buried in Oakwood Cemetery in Austin.

BIBLIOGRAPHY: W. F. Skyhawk, "Capt. Roy Aldrich," *The Pony Express*, XX (April, 1954); University of Texas, *The Genetics Foundation* (1955); Walter P. Webb, *The Texas Rangers* (1935); Austin *American*, August 15, 1952; Austin *American-Statesman*, January 30, 1955; Dallas *News*, January 16, 1927; Houston *Chronicle*, January 17, 1960.

Morris Cook

*Aldridge, Texas.

*Aledo, Texas.

*Aleman, Texas.

Alexander, Almerine M. Almerine M. Alexander was born in Kentucky about 1829. With his family he moved to Texas in the 1840's. In partnership with his father and brothers, he became one of the leading merchants in North Texas with stores in Dallas, Bonham, and Sherman. He raised the 34th Texas Cavalry for the Confederate Army in the winter of 1861–1862. As its first colonel, he led the regiment in action at Shirley's Ford and Newtonia, Missouri, and at Prairie Grove, Arkansas, in 1862. During early 1863, he was acting brigade commander of Joseph Warren Speight's qv Brigade (*see* Polignac's Brigade), before resigning because of chronic illness. He died suddenly in New Orleans in August, 1865.

BIBLIOGRAPHY: Alwyn Barr, *Polignac's Texas Brigade* (1964); Dallas *Herald*, August 19, 1865.

Alwyn Barr

Alexander, Birdie. Birdie Alexander was born in Lincoln County, Tennessee, on March 24, 1870, the daughter of George Washington and Mary Jane (Shores) Alexander. Her parents brought the family to Texas, where she was educated in Forney and Mary Nash College in Sherman. She then attended Ward Seminary in Nashville, Tennessee, where she majored in piano and voice, and graduated with honors in 1891. After her family moved to Dallas, where she lived for twelve years, she began teaching in the public schools, becoming supervisor of music in 1900. In Dallas she is credited with having laid the foundation for the system of music education in the public schools. She established the teaching of singing in all grades and was the first to form citywide choral groups for public performance. Under her direction the first operetta was performed at Turner Hall on May 24 and 25, 1901, to raise funds for the children's department of the Dallas Public Library. She produced and directed the Music Festival in May, 1912, at the Coliseum, and the first cantatas given by the schools. In 1910 she organized the Dallas High School orchestra, which continued to function with annual concerts. In the same year she inaugurated music appreciation lessons in the schools with the purchase of the first record player and recordings with funds subscribed by interested citizens. She instituted folk-dancing classes to teach rhythm in the lower grades.

Miss Alexander was a charter member of the first board of directors of the Music Supervisors' National Conference, and as chairman of the MSNC was responsible for the formation of the music department of the Texas State Teachers Association.qv In the summers of 1908, 1909, and 1910 she organized and taught courses in music education at the University of Texas. She also taught on the summer faculty at Northwestern University in Evanston, Illinois.

In 1912 she edited *Songs We Like to Sing*. Because of her health she moved to El Paso in 1913, and there until her death she taught piano and was a leader in musical activities. In 1941 the Texas Music Teachers' Association made her a life member "in recognition of her distinguished contribution to American music." She died in El Paso on August 2, 1960.

BIBLIOGRAPHY: Dallas *Morning News*, May 16, 1966.

Lelle Swann

*Alexander, Isaac.

*Alexander, James P.

*Alexander, Jerome B.

*Alexander, Robert.

*Alexander, William. [*See* first paragraph under this title in Volume I; second paragraph is applicable to another William Alexander, listed below.] William Alexander was born in 1819 in Woodford County, Kentucky, to a prominent family of farmers and stock raisers. He was a graduate of Centre College, Kentucky, and Yale University. He later studied law at Frankfort, Kentucky, and began his practice after moving to Galveston, Texas, in May, 1846. In 1857 he moved to Austin. He opposed secession and left Texas during the Civil War, traveling in Mexico and studying Spanish and Mexican law. After the war he served as attorney general of Texas under Provisional Governor A. J. Hamilton qv in 1865–1866. In September, 1867, he again was appointed attorney general of Texas by General Charles Griffin,qv commander of the Fifth Military District. He resigned in October, however, after a difference of opinion with Governor E. M. Pease qv over the validity of the Texas Constitution of 1866.qv Alexander was appointed attorney general of Texas for the third time in 1870 by Governor E. J. Davis qv and served until 1874. Thereafter he continued as an attorney in Austin, where he died on February 16, 1882.

BIBLIOGRAPHY: Austin *Daily Statesman*, February 19, 1882; Charles W. Ramsdell, *Reconstruction in Texas* (1910).

Alwyn Barr

*Alexander, William. [*See* second paragraph under this title in Volume I; first paragraph is applicable to another William Alexander, listed above.]

*Alexander, Texas. Alexander, in Erath County, was first named Harper's Mill when a post office was established there on August 21, 1876, with John D. St. Clair as postmaster. St. Clair was still postmaster when the name was changed to Alexander on May 17, 1881. [Homer Stephen's *The Frontier Postmasters* lists the earlier name incorrectly as Harpers Hill.]

BIBLIOGRAPHY: *Burke's Texas Almanac* (1881, 1882); Homer Stephen, *The Frontier Postmasters* (1952).

*Alexander Institute.

*Aley, Texas.

Alford, Needham Judge. Needham Judge Alford was born July 12, 1789, in North Carolina, the son of Jacob and Elizabeth (Bryant) Alford. An early Methodist preacher in Texas, Alford, along with Sumner Bacon,qv a Cumberland Presbyterian, held a two-day meeting in Sabine County near present Milam in the spring of 1832. The meeting was a test of their determination to preach in the area against the opposition of James Gaines qv and others. When a Mr. Johnson threatened to horsewhip the first preacher who entered the stand, Alford, a strongly built man, said, "I am as able to take a whipping as any man on this ground," and Johnson, taking notice of the muscular preacher, quietly retired. Before coming to Texas, Alford had been known in Louisiana as the bulldog preacher.

He was married to Martha Waddell (Waddle) in Franklin County, Mississippi, on February 18, 1815; they had nine children. Alford died September 19, 1869, in Limestone County near Horn Hill.

BIBLIOGRAPHY: George Louis Crocket, *Two Centuries in East Texas* (1932); Homer S. Thrall, *History of Methodism in Texas* (1872).

Helen Gomer Schluter

Alford's Bluff, Texas. Alford's Bluff, situated on the Trinity River in Trinity County, was described in 1867 as "just below Whiterock shoals on the site of the ancient Pueblo of Trinidad." It was noted for its chalybeate mineral springs.

BIBLIOGRAPHY: *Texas Almanac* (1936).

*Alfred, Texas. Alfred, in Jim Wells County, was founded in 1888 when the railroad arrived, and was originally named Driscoll, Texas (at that time Jim Wells County was uncreated and still a part of Nueces County). A post office was established in 1898 with Alfred Wright as postmaster. In 1904, when the St. Louis, Brownsville, and Mexico Railway built south from Robstown, establishing a railway station on the Robert Driscoll qv ranch, Mr. Driscoll wanted that station to be named after himself; N. T. Wright, the new postmaster of the old Driscoll, obliged, agreeing to change the name of his post office to Alfred, in honor of his father, Alfred Wright, who had been the first postmaster. In 1972 Alfred had a population of approximately twenty. *See* Driscoll, Texas (Nueces County).

Cyrus Tilloson

*Alfred, District of.

*Algereta, Texas.

*Algerita, Texas.

*Algoa, Texas. Algoa, in Galveston County, was not named for a British ship driven ashore by the 1900 hurricane (as stated in Volume I). The community had this name at least as early as 1891, for it is shown on a map of Galveston County compiled and drawn by Charles William Pressler,qv October 10, 1891, and traced in September, 1899. There was an ocean-going vessel aground about twelve miles from Algoa for more than a year after the Galveston Flood,qv but its name or registry had nothing to do with the naming of Algoa.

BIBLIOGRAPHY: Galveston County Map, 1891 (General Land Office, Austin, Texas, 1899).

J. A. McCaul

*Alguacil.

Alibates Flint Quarries. The Alibates Flint Quarries, near the Canadian River thirty-five miles north of Amarillo in Potter County, have been exploited by man for at least twelve thousand years for their distinctive and colorful variegated flint, which was fashioned into weapon points and implements by the earliest men on this continent. About 900 A.D., a pueblo-building people, known first as the Panhandle Puebloid culture and later as the Antelope Creek Focus, moved into the Canadian River valley and began extensive mining operations. The flint, banded in shades of blue-gray, red, white, or gray, was used locally for weapons and implements and was traded over an area of hundreds of miles radially.

The main exposure measures 50 to 300 feet wide, about 4,000 feet long, and 4 to 5 feet thick. The term Alibates was an unintentional corruption by Oklahoma geologist Charles N. Gould, in 1907, of the name of a nearby creek which had been named for Allen (Allie) Bates. Bates, a young cowboy who lived in a line camp at the quarry site in the late 1800's, was a son of W. H. Bates, one of the original owners of the L X Ranch.qv

Dr. H. P. Mera and Dr. Jesse Nusbaum of the laboratory of anthropology at Santa Fe, along with

Dr. Gould, visited the site in 1930, at which time the Alibates quarries were recognized as the source of the unique flint which earlier had been established as that used by the first men on the North American continent. In 1962 an appeal was made to the Department of the Interior to designate the Alibates quarries a national monument. A law was put into effect in 1965, establishing the Alibates Flint Quarries and Texas Panhandle Pueblo Culture National Monument (*see* Studer, Floyd V.). The monument was in a 600-acre tract which was expected to hold an interpretive center, a possible museum, and recreation facilities, such as a picnic area and trails for riding and hiking. A proposed visitor center and exhibits building would include displays depicting the living conditions of those peoples who lived at and used the quarries. *See* Pueblo Ruins of the Texas Panhandle; *see also* Archaeology.

BIBLIOGRAPHY: *American Antiquity*, XXIV (1958–1959); Panhandle Geological Society, *Alibates Flint Quarries* (1963).

Karen Collins

*Alice, Texas. Alice, seat of Jim Wells County, has an economy based on the oil and gas industry; livestock production; and the marketing of cotton, flax, grain, and vegetables. Industries manufacture oil well chemicals and supplies, fiberglass products, cottonseed oil products, and foods. In 1966 Alice reported 429 businesses, nineteen manufacturers, twenty churches, two libraries, two newspapers, three banks, a radio station, and a hospital. A city-county library was in the planning stage. The 1960 population was 20,861; the 1970 count was 20,121. It is questionable, because of lack of evidence, whether or not the original settlement was called Bandana, though it was called Kleberg before it was renamed Alice.

Alice Dam. *See* Alice Terminal Reservoir.

Alice Southwest, Texas. Alice Southwest, in Jim Wells County, had a population of 1,813 in 1960 and 1,908 in 1970, according to the U.S. census.

Alice Terminal Reservoir. Alice Dam and Alice Terminal Reservoir are in the Nueces-Rio Grande coastal basin in Jim Wells County, three miles north of Alice on Chiltipin Creek.

The reservoir was to be built in two stages. First stage construction started on September 27, 1963, and was completed in 1965. The project is owned by the Alice Water Authority, and is operated for a municipal water supply for the city of Alice. The water is obtained from Chiltipin Creek, supplemented by water from the Nueces River purchased by contract from the city of Corpus Christi.

The first stage reservoir has a capacity of 3,250 acre-feet and an area of 700 acres. The capacity eventually will be 7,050 acre-feet with an area of 880 acres. The desired level of the reservoir is maintained by water purchased from Lake Corpus Christi on the Nueces River. The lake is also used for recreational purposes. An intake structure and pumping plant were built at Lake Corpus Christi to deliver purchased water through 20.4 miles of pipeline. The drainage area to the reservoir is about 157 square miles.

BIBLIOGRAPHY: Texas Water Commission, *Bulletin 6408* (1964).

Seth D. Breeding

*Alief, Texas. Alief, in Harris County, reported two schools and three churches in 1966. At that time work was being done to extend the water and sewage system. In 1970 Alief was not reported in the U.S. census because it had less than 1,000 population, although estimates in 1972 indicate the population may have reached 1,000. *See also* Houston Standard Metropolitan Statistical Area.

*Alien Land Law.

*Alkali Creek.

*Allamoore, Texas.

*Allan, John T.

*Allcorn, Elijah.

*Allen, Augustus Chapman.

*Allen, Ebenezer.

Allen, George R. George R. Allen, born in Connecticut in 1830, came to Huntsville, Texas, probably before 1849, and advertised as a portrait painter. During his stay in Huntsville he painted portraits of Henderson K. Yoakum qv and members of the Sam Houston family, including Temple Lea Houston qv and his grandmother, Nancy Lea. Following his stay in Huntsville, Allen seemed to have made Galveston the center of his travels to various towns in the state. The date and place of his death are uncertain.

BIBLIOGRAPHY: Pauline A. Pinckney, *Painting in Texas: The Nineteenth Century* (1967).

Pauline A. Pinckney

*Allen, James L.

*Allen, John Kirby.

*Allen, John M.

*Allen, Martin.

*Allen, Richard.

Allen, Robert Thomas Pritchard. Robert Thomas Pritchard Allen was born in Maryland in 1813. He was graduated from the United States Military Academy in 1834, ranking fifth in a class of thirty-six. He resigned his commission in the United States Army in 1836 and entered the Methodist ministry. In 1847 he was appointed superintendent of the Kentucky Military Institute, a position he held intermittently until 1854. Some time thereafter he moved to Texas, and in 1857 was received by transfer into the Texas Conference, Methodist Episcopal church. In the same year he became superintendent of the Bastrop Military Institute.qv

In 1861 Allen served briefly as an instructor at Camp Clark.qv Next he proceeded to Richmond, Virginia, where he received a commission as colonel of the 4th Texas Infantry, then being organized at Richmond from separate companies arriving in Virginia. Some sort of report that Allen was a martinet, presumably spread by his former students, provoked so much objection that his appointment was revoked. Allen returned to Texas, where he organized and became first colonel of the 17th Texas Infantry, which was mustered into Confederate service in June, 1862. This regiment served as an element of Walker's Texas Division qv in the Trans-Mississippi Department.

In December, 1863, Allen was reassigned as commander at Camp Ford,qv a military prison near Tyler. Allen's considerable administrative ability and personal humanity made him so successful that after the war Camp Ford was never seriously cited by the Federal victors as the site of Confederate atrocities. In May, 1864, he was replaced at Camp Ford by Lieutenant Colonel John P. Border.qv Allen apparently returned to his regiment, though he may have resigned or been reassigned to other duties during the last year of the war. After the war Allen returned to Kentucky, where he resumed his old position as superintendent of the Kentucky Military Institute. He drowned while swimming off the coast of Florida on July 9, 1888.

BIBLIOGRAPHY: Harold B. Simpson (ed.), *Texas in the War, 1861–1865* (1965); F. Lee Lawrence and Robert W. Glover, *Camp Ford, C.S.A.* (1964).

Lester N. Fitzhugh

Allen, Samuel Ezekiel. Samuel Ezekiel Allen was born in Harris County on June 8, 1848, the son of Rebecca Jane (Thomas) and Samuel W. Allen.qv Allen was a rancher like his father, whose property he inherited and consolidated with some of his mother's land originally granted to her father, Ezekiel Thomas,qv and her great-uncle, Mosis A. Callihan.qv At the time of Allen's death in 1913 he was one of the largest taxpayers in Harris County, with ten to twenty thousand acres along Buffalo Bayou. At the time he also maintained a 10,000-acre "winter pasture" on the San Bernard River in Brazoria County and had additional grazing land in Galveston and Fort Bend counties. Earlier his holdings had gone as far as the Colorado River near Columbus.

For the headquarters of his ranch Allen chose a location near the mouth of Sims Bayou and used Buffalo Bayou for the transportation of cattle. Also he shipped cattle by rail, using his private station, El Buey. Besides his ranching activities Samuel Allen had varied business interests, including banking, shipping, and manufacturing. He founded and was one of the principal stockholders in the Oriental Textile Mills, at that time the largest manufacturer of press cloth for the cotton industry in the world, with offices in New York, London, and other major cities. He was also among the founders of a bank that has since merged into the Texas National Bank of Commerce, Houston.

In 1874 Allen married Rosa Christie Lum. They were the parents of six children, two of whom predeceased Allen. Samuel Ezekiel Allen died on June 23, 1913. After her husband's death, Mrs. Allen in 1917 began the dissolution of the Allen Ranch, which continued until her death in 1931. She was assisted by her grandson, Robert Cummins Stuart,

who helped her subdivide Allen Dale, Allen Farms, and Lum Terrace. Through those and other subdivisions many streets in Houston bear names connected with the Allen Ranch. Both Allen and his wife were buried in Glendale Cemetery, Harrisburg.

BIBLIOGRAPHY: Houston *Chronicle*, June 24, 1913; Houston *Post*, October 22, 1955; *Harris County Heritage Society Cookbook*, I (1964); Marguerite Johnston, *A Happy Worldly Abode, Christ Church Cathedral 1839–1964* (1964); Files (Baker, Botts, Shepherd, and Coates, Houston law firm).

Francita Stuart Koelsch

*Allen, Samuel T. Samuel Tabor Allen, son of Thomas and Eunice (Johnson) Allen, was born on July 19, 1809, in Connecticut (not New York, as stated in Volume I). He came to Texas by ship from New Orleans on July 21, 1830. In 1832 he was a prominent citizen of Anahuac and Liberty. He married a widow, Mrs. Matilda (not Hester) T. (Roberts) Connell, and they had two children. He was killed by Indians near Dawson in present Navarro County (not near Belton) in October, 1838 (not November, 1838).

BIBLIOGRAPHY: *Memorial and Biographical History of McLennan, Falls, and Coryell Counties* (1893); Harry McCorry Henderson, "The Surveyors Fight," *Southwestern Historical Quarterly*, LVI (1952–1953); Marc S. Simmons, "Samuel T. Allen and the Texas Revolution," *ibid.*, LXVIII (1964–1965).

Allen, Samuel W. Samuel W. Allen was born in Frankfort, Kentucky, on January 2, 1826. He was in Harris County on May 9, 1844, when he was married to Rebecca Jane Thomas, daughter of Ezekiel Thomas.qv Allen was not related to the Allen brothers who were the founders of the city of Houston.

Allen was a rancher and a partner in Allen and Poole, the largest shippers of cattle in southeast Texas. Allen later was a partner in a cattle enterprise with Shanghai Pierce.qv Allen bought Pierce's interest for $110,000, and Pierce left for Kansas City.

The Allen Ranch centered around present South Houston and extended from Clear Lake to the town of Harrisburg. When the Galveston, Houston, and Henderson Railroad opened in 1860, one stop was at Allen's private station, known as Dumont. The name has been preserved and is used at present for the railroad station in South Houston.

Allen died on August 8, 1888, and was buried in Glendale Cemetery, Harrisburg.

BIBLIOGRAPHY: Chris Emmett, *Shanghai Pierce, A Fair Likeness* (1953); Francis Richard Lubbock, *Six Decades in Texas* (1900); S. O. Young, *A Thumb-Nail History of the City of Houston, Texas* (1912); Jesse A. Ziegler, *Wave of the Gulf* (1938).

Francita Stuart Koelsch

Allen, Thomas. Thomas Allen was born in St. Louis, Missouri, in 1849, son of Thomas and Annie Allen. In his second year at Washington University in St. Louis, Allen accompanied a professor on a sketching expedition to the Rocky Mountains, and his notes and sketches were a spur to his interest in art. In 1871 he went to Paris, then to Düsseldorf, where he entered the Royal Academy in the spring of 1872. He visited many of the art centers of Europe while he studied.

He traveled to Texas in 1878–1879, where he made three notable paintings in San Antonio: "The Market Place, San Antonio" (exhibited at the Paris Salon in 1882); "Mexican Women Washing at San Pedro Spring"; and "The Portal of San José Mission." Two other works with settings probably in Texas are "The Covered Wagon" and "Toilers of the Plains." He painted the street scenes in San Antonio with great sensitivity, showing an appreciation of the simple and the commonplace.

The first American showing of Allen's work was at the National Academy of Design in New York. He was made a member of the American Society of Artists, and in 1884 he became an associate member of the National Academy. He was chairman of the Art Commission of Boston and prior to his death in 1924, he became president of the board of trustees of the Boston Museum of Fine Arts.

BIBLIOGRAPHY: Pauline A. Pinckney, *Painting in Texas: The Nineteenth Century* (1967).

Pauline A. Pinckney

*Allen, William Youel.

*Allen, Texas. Allen, in Collin County, had a 194.4 percent increase in population in a ten-year period, when the count rose from 659 in 1960 to 1,940 in 1970, according to the U.S. census.

*Allen Academy. Allen Academy, Bryan, a preparatory school and junior college for boys, was made a nonprofit educational trust in 1953 with plans for an extensive building program on its campus of more than 475 acres. Presidents of the academy have been J. H. Allen (1886–1919), R. O. Allen (1919–1926), N. B. Allen, Sr. (1926–1946), and N. B. Allen, Jr., since 1946. The 1970–1971 college enrollment was 300, with a faculty of 30. The academy held memberships in the Southern Association of Colleges and Schools, Secondary Division, and a number of other national and state associations.

H. Brownlee

*Allen Creek.

*Allendale, Texas.

*Allenfarm, Texas.

*Allen's Branch.

*Allen's Chapel, Texas.

*Allen's Creek.

*Alley, Abraham. Abraham (Abram) Alley was the son of Catherine (Baker) and Thomas Alley (not Cynthia and William A. Alley, Sr., as stated in Volume I). He was the only one of the five Alley brothers to marry. He died in 1862. [See bibliography under Alley, Thomas.]

Mrs. Walter G. Dick

*Alley, John.

*Alley, John C. John C. Alley was the son of Catherine (Baker) and Thomas Alley (not Cynthia and William A. Alley, Sr., as stated in Volume I). He was never married and did not live in Texas long enough to be entitled to land, as he was killed by Indians soon after his arrival in 1822. [See bibliography under Alley, Thomas.]

Mrs. Walter G. Dick

*Alley, Rawson. Rawson Alley was the son of Thomas Alley and his first wife (name unknown), and stepson of Thomas Alley's second wife Catherine (Baker) Alley (not the son of Cynthia and William A. Alley, Sr., as stated in Volume I); thus Rawson Alley was a half-brother to Abraham, John C., Thomas V., and William Alley.qqv [See bibliography under Alley, Thomas.]

Mrs. Walter G. Dick

Alley, Thomas. Thomas Alley, father of five sons, Abraham, John C., Rawson, Thomas V., and William,qqv and one daughter, Cynthia, was erroneously given the name William A. Alley, Sr., in Volume I. Thomas Alley lived in Pennsylvania and moved to Missouri in 1796. A resident of the District of Ste. Genevieve, Missouri, he had one son, Rawson, by his first marriage (wife's name unknown). A widower, he married Catherine Baker, a widow, on April 13, 1797; they were the parents of the remaining children listed above, and neither Thomas nor Catherine Alley ever came to Texas. Thomas Alley died in 1807 in Missouri, and his wife then married Alexander McCoy.

BIBLIOGRAPHY: "Register of non-Catholics Living in the District of Ste. Genevieve, Sept. 26, 1796–1812," Book D, Ste. Genevieve (Missouri) Church Records; Probate Records, St. Francois County, Missouri, File 31, Estate of Thomas Alley.

Mrs. Walter G. Dick

*Alley, Thomas V. Thomas V. Alley was the son of Catherine (Baker) and Thomas Alley (not Cynthia and William A. Alley, Sr., as stated in Volume I). [See bibliography under Alley, Thomas.]

Mrs. Walter G. Dick

*Alley, William. [This title was incorrectly listed in Volume I as Alley, William A., Jr.] William Alley was the son of Catherine (Baker) and Thomas Alley (not Cynthia and William A. Alley, Sr., as stated in Volume I). William Alley gave the townsite for Alleyton, Texas, in 1859, and he lived there until his death on August 15, 1869. [See bibliography under Alley, Thomas.]

Mrs. Walter G. Dick

*Alley, William A., Sr. [This article in Volume I should be discounted, as it was Thomas Alley, not someone named William A. Alley, Sr., who was the father of five sons, Abraham, John C., Rawson, Thomas V., and William Alley,qqv who came to Texas between 1822 and 1824. Neither of the parents of the five Alley brothers and their sister, Cynthia, ever came to Texas. See Alley, Thomas.]

Mrs. Walter G. Dick

*Alley Creek.

Alley Theatre. The Alley Theatre in Houston produced its first play in August, 1947, under the direction of Nina Eloise Whittington Vance. Mrs. Vance, a drama teacher at San Jacinto High School at the time, initiated the project by sending post-cards to approximately 150 persons whom she knew to be interested in the theater. As a result, one hundred people met to discuss the plausibility of forming a local theater group. Convinced the idea was sound, Mrs. Vance took on the triple role of business manager-producer-director. The group became professional in 1954 and existed without patronage until 1963, when it became possible to employ other personnel so that Mrs. Vance could concentrate on the role of director.

The first location for the group was in a former dance studio which had an opening on Main Street. A brick corridor led from Main to the back of the studio, hence the name "Alley Theatre." It seated eighty-seven persons. After a season and a half at this location, the group moved to a building at 709 Berry, which seated 215. Here the theater remained for eighteen and a half years before moving to the new $3,500,000 structure located in Houston's cultural complex, which included the Jesse H. Jones Hall for the Performing Arts qv and the Albert Thomas qv Convention Center.

Impetus for the new building came in 1962, when Houston Endowment Inc., a charitable organization established by the late Mr. and Mrs. Jesse H. Jones,qv donated a $400,000 downtown site at 615 Texas Avenue. The Ford Foundation pledged $1 million for construction, contingent on Houston residents raising $900,000. The local money was raised in 1963, and the Ford Foundation then boosted its pledge to $2 million, the largest grant ever given a resident professional theater. The foundation also pledged for operating expenses $100,000 a year for ten years.

Architect Ulrich Franzen designed the building to include two separate theaters, one seating 800 persons and another seating 300. The larger theater was designed with a modified thrust stage and allows for unusual exits and entrances. Built essentially for the classics, lighting takes the place of curtains. The smaller theater is a highly advanced replica of the playhouse's original small square arena under a hooded light grid.

The exterior of the structure is concrete, sand-blasted to give the look of aged stone. Nine towers are both decorative and utilitarian, housing elevators and air-conditioning equipment. A tunnel entrance gives credit to the original Alley entryway. Polished concrete, curved wood, and rich colors decorate the interior.

The new theater opened officially on November 26, 1968, with a special performance of Bertolt Brecht's *Galileo.* Tony Van Bridge, a Canadian, played the lead. By opening night more than 20,000 subscriptions had been paid. *See also* Theater in Texas.

*Alleyton, Texas.
*Alligator Bayou.
*Alligator Creek.
*Alligator Lake.
*Allison, Clay.

*Allison, John.
*Allison, John C.
*Allison, Texas. (Wheeler County.)
*Allison, Texas. (Wise County.)

Allred, James V. James V. Allred, Texas jurist, and governor from 1935 to 1939, was born in Bowie, Texas, on March 29, 1899, son of Mary (Hinson) and Renne Allred, Sr. Allred married Joe Betsy Miller of Wichita Falls on June 20, 1927. Three sons were born to the couple. After completing high school, Allred enrolled at Rice Institute but withdrew for financial reasons. He served with the United States Immigration Service until his enlistment in the United States Navy during World War I. After the war Allred began the study of law as a clerk in a Wichita Falls law office. In 1921 he received an LL.B. from Cumberland University, Lebanon, Tennessee, and began practice in Wichita Falls.

In 1923 Allred was named by Governor Pat M. Neff qv to the post of district attorney for the Thirtieth Texas District. In that office Allred earned a reputation as "the fighting district attorney" for his forthright opposition to the Ku Klux Klan.qv He was a candidate for the office of state attorney general in 1926 but was defeated by Claude Pollard qv by a close vote in the second primary. In 1930 Allred made a successful race for the same position by defeating the incumbent, Robert Lee Bobbitt. As attorney general, Allred won popular approval through a continuing campaign against monopolies and large businesses and against the efforts of corporations to influence state taxation and fiscal policies.

Allred's activities as attorney general, aided by the depression-born distrust of large corporations, made him a logical candidate for the governorship in 1934. He entered the campaign on a platform proposing the creation of a state commission for regulating public utility rates and practices, the imposition of a graduated chain store tax to neutralize the competitive power of chain enterprises, a system for regulating the activities of lobbyists, and opposition to a state sales tax as a revenue-increasing device because of the economic burden the tax would place on lower income groups. Other planks were his proposal to submit to the people the problem of state repeal of prohibition (in spite of his personal opposition to repeal), and his desire to see the basic pardoning power, used so freely by governors James Edward Ferguson and Miriam Amanda Ferguson,qqv transferred to a board of pardons and paroles. Allred's essentially middle-of-the-road outlook on fiscal matters was revealed in his assertion that sufficient state revenues for needed additional services could be raised by a more equitable system of property valuation and a more efficient use of existing revenues, rather than by increased general taxation.

Allred's principal Democratic opponents in 1934, both from Wichita Falls, were Tom F. Hunter, regarded basically as more liberal than the attorney general, and Charles C. McDonald, regarded as the candidate of the Ferguson faction. Allred gained a plurality in the first primary and won over Hunter by 40,000 votes in the run-off election. The governor devoted his ensuing administration to measures for cooperating with federal programs for combating the effects of the depression, accomplished in part through the activities of the Texas Planning Board,qv and to efforts to legislate his campaign proposals. Although several progressive measures were enacted in a regular session and three special sessions, the legislature refused to provide the revenues necessary for financing the programs. As a result, measures providing increased financial support to education, expanded highway construction, the creation of the state's Department of Public Safety,qv and the framework for old-age pensions and expanded state welfare services remained on insecure foundations.

Several significant factors worked to Governor Allred's credit in the election of 1936. He had been commended highly by President Franklin D. Roosevelt for Texas' cooperation and performance in the national recovery program, and that recognition had been a factor in causing the national Junior Chamber of Commerce to name Allred "Outstanding Young Man in America in 1935." Moreover, he had secured the enactment of a good portion of his 1934 pledges to the voters of the state. As a result, he polled a majority of 52 percent in the first primary in a field of five candidates and won by landslide proportions in the general election of 1936.

Allred's second administration brought a continuation of progressive legislation in the passage of the following measures: a teacher retirement system; broadened social security and welfare provisions; additional funds for education; expansion of the services of most existing state agencies; and increased compensation for state officials. Nevertheless, the legislature, in its regular session and one called meeting, again failed notably to provide the additional revenues for the services. The tendency of the legislature to appropriate freely from nonexistent funds forced Governor Allred to apply numerous vetoes in an effort to prevent financial chaos in the state.

Late in Allred's second term as governor, his nomination by President Roosevelt to a federal district judgeship was confirmed, and upon the completion of his gubernatorial term, he assumed his position on the bench. He resigned from the judgeship in 1942 to seek the Democratic nomination for the United States Senate, and after his defeat in that race by former Governor W. Lee O'Daniel qv he returned for a time to private law practice in Houston. In 1949 President Harry S. Truman returned Allred to the federal bench, where he remained until his death on September 24, 1959. He was buried in Riverside Cemetery in Wichita Falls.

BIBLIOGRAPHY: George N. Manning, Public Services of James V. Allred (M.A. thesis, Texas Technological College, 1950); Renne Allred, Jr., "My Brother, James V. Allred," Fort Belknap Genealogical Association, *Bulletin* (Fall, 1965); *Who's Who In America* (1948).

Floyd F. Ewing

*Allred, Texas.

*Alma, Texas.

*Alma Institute.

*Almazán, Fernando Pérez de.

*Almazán, Juan Antonio Pérez de.

*Almeda, Texas. The community formerly known as Almeda was by 1966 wholly within the city limits of Houston, Texas. *See also* Houston Standard Metropolitan Statistical Area.

*Almont, Texas.

*Almonte, Juan Nepomuceno.

*Almonte's Report on Texas.

*Aloe, Texas.

*Aloe Army Air Field.

*Alpha, Texas.

*Alpine, Texas. (Brewster County.) Alpine is a county seat, ranch marketing center, and tourist headquarters. Site of Big Bend Regional Library and Big Bend Historical Museum, Alpine reported thirteen churches in 1964 and 116 businesses in 1970. Manufactures include processing of fluorspar and production of candelilla wax. Population was 4,740 in 1960 and 5,971 in 1970.

*Alpine, Texas. (Brewster County.) Alpine is a the northeastern part of the county on the Judson Road out of Longview. The Alpine Presbyterian Church is the nucleus of the community.

*Alpine Creek.

*Alsa, Texas.

*Alsbury, Charles Grundison.

*Alsbury, Harvey.

*Alsbury, Horace (Horatio) A.

*Alsbury, Mrs. Horace (Horatio) A.

*Alsbury, Thomas P.

*Alsdorf, Texas.

*Alta Loma, Texas. Alta Loma, in Galveston County, had a population of 1,020 in 1960 and 1,536 in 1970, according to the U.S. census.

*Altair, Texas.

*Altavista, Texas.

*Althea, Texas.

*Alto, Texas. Alto, in Cherokee County, had a population of 869 in 1960 and 1,045 in 1970, according to the U.S. census.

*Altoga, Texas.

*Alton, Texas. (Denton County.)

*Alton, Texas. (Hidalgo County.)

*Altonia, Texas.

*Altsheler, Joseph Alexander.

*Alum, Texas.

*Alum Creek.

*Alvarado, Hernando de.

*Alvarado, Texas. Alvarado, a crossroads commercial center in eastern Johnson County, reported thirty-seven business establishments, a hospital, a newspaper, and a bank in 1966. The Alvarado Dam and Reservoir, completed in 1966, and the Old Settlers Reunion held each August encourage tourism. The 1960 census population of 1,907 increased to 2,129 by 1970. See also Fort Worth Standard Metropolitan Statistical Area.

Alvarado Dam and Reservoir. Alvarado Dam and Reservoir, two miles southwest of Alvarado, in Johnson County, is on Turkey Creek, a tributary of Chambers Creek and the Trinity River. Completed in 1966, its purpose is floodwater retention and municipal water storage. The drainage area is thirty-one square miles, and the capacity of the reservoir is 4,780 acre-feet. The dam is 3,200 feet long and has a crest width of fourteen feet; it has an elevation of 704.1 feet at the top of the dam, and the normal water level is 691.8 feet.

*Alvarez, Francisca (The Angel of Goliad).

*Alvin, Texas. Alvin, located in Brazoria County, reported 174 businesses, twenty-three churches, and a hospital in 1967. Educational institutions included four public schools located on one campus and Alvin Junior College, which moved to a new campus in 1963. Income was based on oil and gas and the production of rice, truck crops, and beef and dairy cattle. Industries manufactured chemicals, petroleum products, steel tanks, and processed rice. Population, which was 5,643 in 1960, almost doubled by 1970, when it was 10,671, according to the U.S. census.

Alvin Junior College. Alvin Junior College was created by an overwhelming popular vote of Alvin citizens in 1948 as a district with the same boundaries as the public school system. Classes began in the fall of 1949 with an enrollment of eighty-nine students. The school experienced a rapid growth between 1949 and 1974, when the enrollment was 2,133. Library holdings exceeded 18,000 volumes in 1969.

The junior college offered a basic liberal arts program of sufficient breadth to serve as a background for any professional career. In addition, several technical, specialized programs were provided for terminal training, including data processing, nursing, metal working, electronics, secretarial, and drafting.

In 1963 classes moved to a new million-dollar plant on a sixty-three-acre campus south of Alvin. Five initial components of the master plan—administration-classroom building, science laboratory-classroom building, student union, gymnasium, and maintenance shop—were completed to allow for expansion during several years of anticipated growth. An extension center in the Brazosport area opened in the fall of 1965 to supplement day and evening offerings on the Alvin campus.

A. B. Templeton served as head of the college from 1954 to 1964 and was succeeded by D. P. O'Quinn, who served as president of the college

and superintendent of the Alvin schools. Thomas V. Jenkins was president in 1974.

BIBLIOGRAPHY: Brazosport Facts, September 19, 1965.

*Alvord, Texas.

*Alzor y Virto de Vera, Joseph de. See Aguayo, Marquis de.

*Amanda, Texas.

*Amangual, Francisco.

Amargosa, Texas. Amargosa was originally a ranch settlement located on Amargosa Creek in present Jim Wells County and was owned by Manuel Barrera of Mier, Tamaulipas, Mexico, who received title to this part of La Tinaja de Lara Mexican land grant in 1836. By 1849 Amargosa was a prominent South Texas ranch, dealing in wool and hides, and was well stocked with sheep, goats, and horses. However, during the early 1850's, repeated Indian raids forced the occupants to leave, and in 1852 Hamilton P. Bee qv and associates took over the ranch. In 1854 Barrera's heirs and assigns had the ranch and the entire grant surveyed, and they won back the land in a suit.

By 1877 Amargosa had grown into a settlement of more than a hundred persons, and in that year a school was established, attended by about forty children. When the San Antonio-Aransas Pass Railroad bypassed Amargosa in 1898 the town lost its importance as a trade center. The school continued and became the Amargosa Common School District, but in 1926 the name was changed to El Carro. In 1935 another school was built four miles north of the original and was named Armagosa, thus changing not only the site but also the spelling. As of 1965 the only visible remains of the old Amargosa were two fort-type houses, one of which was in good condition, but the other was in ruins.

Agnes G. Grimm

*Amargosa Creek.

*Amarillo, Texas. Amarillo, seat of Potter County and commercial center for Potter and Randall counties and surrounding areas, encompassed in its city limits 60.28 square miles in 1966. In that year Amarillo reported 162 churches, forty-six public schools, a junior college, a business college, five hospitals, two newspapers, eight radio stations, and three television stations. City improvements effected during the late 1960's included a municipal building, a civic center, a branch library, and a corporation court building. Gas, oil, agriculture, and cattle represent the principal sources of income for the city. Amarillo ranked first in the nation in the growth of population for the decade 1950–1960 in the 130,000–150,000 bracket, showing an increase in population of over 85 percent, with 74,443 residents in 1950 and 137,969 in 1960; however, there was almost an 8 percent decline by 1970, when the population was 127,010, according to the U.S. census. Amarillo is the home of the largest feeder cattle auction in the world and the leading magazine concerned with horses, the *Quarter Horse Journal*. Nearby Lake Meredith, Alibates

Flint Quarries National Monument (*see* Alibates Flint Quarries), Palo Duro Canyon State Park (*see* Parks, State), and a tri-state fair are major tourist attractions. Amarillo is also a central medical center for the Panhandle area. Amarillo Air Force Base qv was deactivated on December 31, 1968. Among the 2,630 businesses reported in 1972 were industries concerned with petrochemicals, grain storage, processing, helium, meat packing, clothing, feed, leather goods, and cement. *See also* Amarillo Standard Metropolitan Statistical Area.

Amarillo Air Force Base. Following World War II, Amarillo Army Air Field qv was hurriedly closed down, and from 1946 to 1950, buildings were converted to peacetime uses or destroyed.

Reactivated as Amarillo Air Force Base in March, 1951, the base was assigned the task of training jet aircraft mechanics, becoming the first air force all-jet mechanic training base. In December, 1951, the first trainees from foreign countries arrived to participate in the training program.

By 1952 the training program reached a planned maximum of 3,500 students. Mechanic training continued throughout 1953 and 1954 and included a course on the B-47 jet bomber. In 1954 the base was declared a permanent installation. During 1955 four new courses were added and the number of students climbed to approximately five thousand. When the two-phase system of basic training began in 1956, Amarillo Air Force Base was selected as one of the bases to administer the technical second phase.

In the late 1950's the base continued to grow. In 1957 a guided missile training department was established, and facilities were expanded to accommodate an air wing of the Strategic Air Command. In July, 1958, a supply and administration school previously stationed in Wyoming relocated at the Amarillo base.

The base was redesignated Amarillo Technical Training Center in 1959, when the 4128th Strategic Air Command Wing concluded a joint-tenancy agreement with Air Training Command.

By May, 1960, the jet mechanic school had graduated one hundred thousand students. At that time Amarillo was the site of all Air Training Command resident training in administrative, procurement, and supply fields and continued to train thousands of jet aircraft mechanics, jet engine mechanics, and airframe repairmen.

The center entered a new era in February, 1966, with the formation of the 3330th Basic Military School. A personnel processing squadron was added the same month to support the school. In 1967 the center's facilities covered 5,273 acres, and its personnel numbered approximately 16,300.

By 1964 the Department of Defense had decided to reclose the base. The last class was graduated on December 11, 1968; the base was deactivated on December 31, 1968.

BIBLIOGRAPHY: *Jet Journal* (March 31, 1967); *Amarillo Air Force Unofficial Guide-Directory* (1966).

*Amarillo Army Air Field. *See* Amarillo Air Force Base.

Amarillo City Lake. *See* Bivins Lake.

Amarillo College. Amarillo College (not to be confused with an earlier Amarillo College qv which operated from 1897 to 1910) was approved by voters of the Amarillo Independent School District on July 16, 1929. During the following two months, the school board elected a college president, voters agreed to support the college, a seven-member faculty was hired, equipment was purchased, and students enrolled in regular classes.

Between 1929 and 1933 the junior college was accredited by the State Board of Education, qv the Association of Texas Colleges and Universities, qv the American Association of Junior Colleges, and the Southern Association of Colleges and Schools. The college was housed in the city auditorium until 1937, when it moved to an eighteen-acre campus. A physical plant of eleven buildings was in use by 1966, and plans called for additional construction to double floor space, as well as for acquisition of a vocational plant site which would double the campus area.

The college library contained approximately 27,000 books in the 1969 term. Associate degrees in arts, science, and applied science were offered, as were certificates of completion and technological certificates. The evening college provided academic, cultural, vocational, and high school completion courses. In addition to pre-professional programs, Amarillo College specialized in distributive education, trade and industrial education (including apprentice training), and vocational nursing to meet the needs of the immediate community.

Total enrollment increased from 125 students during the 1929–1930 school year, to 955 students in 1949–1950, and to 7,617 students in 1974–1975.

Six presidents served Amarillo College: B. E. Masters (1929–1935), J. F. Mead (1935–1946), A. M. Meyer (1946–1957), Joseph M. Ray (1957–1960), Albert B. Martin (1960–1974), and Charles D. Lutz, Jr. (1974–). Administration of the college passed from the board of trustees of Amarillo Public Schools to a board of regents in 1958.

*Amarillo College. Amarillo College, as shown in Volume I, was in operation from 1897 to 1910 and should be distinguished from Amarillo College listed above.

*Amarillo Creek.

Amarillo *Daily News*. The Amarillo *Daily News* in 1966 was published in the morning by the Globe-News Publishing Company, which also published the afternoon Amarillo *Globe-Times* qv and the Amarillo *Sunday News-Globe*. In 1955 the Globe-News Publishing Company was purchased by S. B. Whittenburg and associates.

Amarillo *Globe-Times*. The Amarillo *Globe-Times* became an afternoon newspaper in 1951 as a result of a merger between the Amarillo *News-Globe* qv and the Amarillo *Times*. In 1955 the owners of the former Amarillo *Times*, S. B. Whittenburg and associates, bought all stock in the Globe-News Publishing Company. In 1961 the Amarillo *Globe-Times* was awarded the Pulitzer Gold Award for Community Service, and in 1966 its circulation was 91,500. The owners of the newspaper also publish the Amarillo *Daily News* qv in the morning and the Amarillo *Sunday News-Globe.*

*Amarillo Lake.

Amarillo Medical Center. The Amarillo Medical Center, located on a 396-acre tract within the city limits of Amarillo, was planned to include health care, the training of doctors and nurses, and medical research programs. Projects completed or under construction by 1966 were the Veterans Administration Hospital (1939), the Potter-Randall County Medical Society headquarters building (1966), the Psychiatric Pavilion of Northwest Texas Hospital (1967), and the High Plains Baptist Hospital (1968). Construction started in 1966 on the Mary E. Bivins Nursing Home, the demonstration school of the Texas Department of Mental Health and Mental Retardation,qv the Killgore Children's Psychiatric Hospital, and the Amarillo Garden Center headquarters and therapeutic gardens. Plans were made for a vocational school for health occupations to be operated by Amarillo College, a cerebral palsy treatment center, a community blood center, and a fifty-two-acre park to be built by the city.
BIBLIOGRAPHY: City of Amarillo, *Official Notice of Bond Sale* (1966).

*Amarillo Mountain.

*Amarillo *News-Globe.* [Out of alphabetical order on page 39, Volume I.] The Amarillo *News-Globe* was merged with the Amarillo *Times* in 1951 and became the Amarillo *Globe-Times,*qv published in the afternoon.

Amarillo Standard Metropolitan Statistical Area. The Amarillo Standard Metropolitan Statistical Area, created in 1949 by the Bureau of the Budget, contains Potter and Randall counties. Amarillo, lying on the common border of the two counties, is the geographical center of the 1,812-square-mile area. In the United States census of 1950 the area had a population of 87,140, with 74,443 of those inhabitants living in Amarillo. By 1960 the metropolitan area population had increased to 149,-493, a 71.6 percent gain, while the city's population had increased to 137,969, an 85 percent gain. The tremendous growth of Amarillo during this period accounted for much of the population increase in Randall County, which went from 13,774 in 1950 to 33,913 in 1960; at the same time Potter County's population increased from 73,366 in 1950 to 115,-580 in 1960. By 1970, however, Amarillo's population had declined almost 8 percent, to 127,010 (a loss of 10,959 residents), and the entire two-county metropolitan statistical area population had similarly declined, by 5.3 percent, to 144,396 inhabitants. Amarillo's population included 86,477 in Potter County and 40,533 in Randall County; thus 95 percent of Potter County's 90,511 inhabitants (a decrease of 25,069 in the county since 1960)

lived in Amarillo in 1970, while 80 percent of Randall County's 53,885 inhabitants (an increase of 19,972 in the county since 1960) lived in the city in that year. It can be seen from the above figures that the dramatic thrust of Amarillo southward into Randall County accounted for the large increase in population in that county, while Potter County's population declined. The only other urban center in the metropolitan area is Canyon, in Randall County; its population increased from 2,622 in 1940, to 4,364 in 1950, to 5,864 in 1960, and to 8,333 in 1970. Smaller, unincorporated towns in the Amarillo Metropolitan Statistical Area are Umbarger in Randall County, and Cliffside, Bushland, St. Francis, and Ady in Potter County.

Farming and ranching have been the historic bases of the economy of the Amarillo area. Wheat, grain sorghums, and beef cattle are the major farm products, with the emphasis on beef cattle in Potter County and on grain sorghums and wheat in Randall County. Since 1930 the mechanization of agriculture and the size of the farms (including ranches) have increased in both counties. In 1959 the average-size farm was 3,650 acres in Potter County and 930 acres in Randall County. The amount of irrigated acreage increased significantly; nevertheless, the area is still essentially a dry-land farming region. Amarillo serves as the agricultural hub of the area. As a gathering, processing, and supplying center it has the largest cattle auction ring in the United States, grain elevators, meat processing plants, leather goods shops, animal feed companies, irrigation pump manufacturers, and farm machinery centers.

The agricultural economic base of the Amarillo metropolitan area has been increasingly supplemented by industry and commerce. Its transportation services are good, with three major railroads, three airports serving five major airlines, and an excellent highway system including Interstate 40. As a result of these connections, the Amarillo area is a major trade and banking center for the Texas Panhandle and the contiguous parts of New Mexico, Colorado, Kansas, and Oklahoma. Since 1940 both wholesale and retail sales have increased significantly. Comparatively, however, retail sales have lagged behind wholesale ones, both in rate of growth and in absolute value. Recently, petrochemical manufacturing based on natural gas has become important in the area. Mineral production is erratic but significant in value. Amarillo's unique helium production plants, which supply 60 percent of the world's helium, have become important because of their relationship to national security. Other manufactured goods include cement, signs, clothing, and oil field equipment.

Amarillo College (a municipal junior college) and West Texas State University, located at Canyon, serve the area's needs for higher education. In the 1972–1973 term 1,565 students attended these two institutions. In 1969 a branch of the Texas State Technical Institute qv was established at Amarillo. The school offers courses in vocational and technical education, and in the fall of 1972 it had an enrollment of 1,058 students. The Mary E. Bivins Memorial Library in Amarillo and the Randall County Library in Canyon help provide for the reading needs of the area. Nine radio stations, three newspapers, and three television stations keep the area informed. The new Amarillo Medical Center qv was planned to include the High Plains Baptist Hospital, an adult psychiatric hospital, and a children's psychiatric hospital. Six other hospitals and the only cerebral palsy clinic in the Texas Panhandle serve the Amarillo area. The only military installation in the area, Amarillo Air Force Base,qv was deactivated on December 31, 1968.

Located in Amarillo is the Musical Arts Conservatory of West Texas. Other cultural organizations of the city are the Amarillo Symphony Orchestra, the Amarillo Little Theater, the Amarillo Civic Ballet, and the Amarillo Guild of Organists. The Texas Panhandle Heritage Foundation sponsors the pageant "Texas" by Paul Green during the summer months in the Pioneer Amphitheater of Palo Duro Canyon State Park (see Parks, State). The music and drama departments of West Texas State University also furnish cultural entertainment.

The Amarillo metropolitan area features several recreational attractions. The scenic Palo Duro Canyon State Park, thirteen miles east of Canyon, is historically and geologically important. Buffalo Lake, a national wildlife refuge, lies twenty-five miles southwest of Amarillo. Fishing and boating are the major attractions of the refuge. Lake Meredith, an impoundment formed by the Sanford Dam on the Canadian River, stretches into northeastern Potter County. Although built primarily to furnish water to eleven cities, it has become a popular recreational center. In 1965 a national monument was dedicated on the southern shore of the lake for the Alibates Flint Quarries qv and the ruins of the Pueblo Indian culture (see Pueblo Ruins of the Texas Panhandle). In Amarillo the Fray Juan de Padilla qv Monument honors the first Christian martyr on present-day United States soil. Public consciousness of the region's historical and cultural heritage is reflected in the work of the Panhandle-Plains Historical Society,qv located on the campus of West Texas State University. The society publishes the annual *Panhandle-Plains Historical Review* and maintains the splendid Panhandle-Plains Historical Museum.qv A Texas League qv baseball team, the Amarillo Giants (called the Amarillo Sonics in the 1960's), offered sports entertainment. Some of the annual events in the area include the Amarillo Stock Show and Rodeo, the Tri-State Fair, and the Will Rogers Range Riders Rodeo. *See also* Standard Metropolitan Statistical Areas in Texas.

Frederick W. Rathjen

*Amateis, Louis.

*Ambia, Texas.

*Ambrose, Texas.

*Amediche Indians.

*Amelia, Texas.

*Amendments to Constitution. *See* Constitutional Amendments.

*American Association of University Women, Texas Division of. The Texas Division of the American Association of University Women held its twenty-first biennial convention in 1965. The division's eighty-four local city branches reported a total of more than seven thousand national members who hold academic degrees from one of the 884 American universities or colleges on the approved list of the A.A.U.W., which includes thirty-five Texas institutions.

Continuing the national association's program for practical educational work and the maintenance of high standards of education for women, the Texas Division has contributed to the establishment of the new national association's headquarters, the Educational Center, Washington, D.C. The A.A.U.W. Educational Foundation, created in 1958, has become a center for research in women's education, and a college faculty program for women has been added to other study and activity projects for the state division and its local branches.

The Helen Marr Kirby qv International Fellowship Fund, established in 1931 and completed in 1945, with an endowment increased to more than $61,000, provides an annual fellowship to a woman scholar from a foreign nation to pursue studies in an American university. These fellowship awards are made by the International Federation of University Women. Since 1948 the Margaret Lee Wiley Living National Fellowship Fund, unendowed, has provided annual fellowships to American women scholars for graduate study in the United States or abroad. These awards are made by the A.A.U.W. Educational Foundation. Texas contributes annually to other national fellowship funds, and local scholarships are granted by some city branches.

BIBLIOGRAPHY: Mrs. G. W. Dingus, *The Texas Division, American Association of University Women* (1941); Mrs. Hal P. Bybee, *Texas and A.A.U.W. Fellowships* (1941); Mrs. Earl Wyatt, *The Silver Anniversary of the Texas Division* (1951); Mrs. D. L. Pillow, *Texas Division A.A.U.W. Fellowships Program, 1953–1965* (1965); *Texas Division Bulletin, A.A.U.W.* (1950–1965).

Anna Irion Powell

*American Federation of Labor. *See* Labor Organizations in Texas.

American GI Forum of Texas. The American GI Forum of Texas was chartered as an independent veteran's organization on March 26, 1948. Its founder and first chairman was Hector P. Garcia of Corpus Christi, Texas, a veteran of World War II. Since then the Forum has established local GI forums, auxiliaries, and junior GI forums in most major towns and cities throughout the state. There are approximately two hundred such forums in the state, with a membership of approximately 10,000. Texas' state program has been so effective that similar organizations have been set up in other states, including Kansas, Ohio, New Mexico, Colorado,

Utah, Mississippi, Michigan, California, and Arizona.

Since its inception the GI Forum of Texas has taken part in many civil rights cases. It has worked toward developing leadership among American citizens of Mexican descent and has attempted to solve the many social, economic, and political problems affecting all citizens, but particularly those of the Mexican American.

All honorably discharged veterans may join the GI Forum regardless of race, color, or creed. All veterans' wives, mothers, sisters, nieces, cousins, and daughters may join the GI Forum Auxiliary. All persons, male or female, between the ages of fourteen and twenty-one years may join the Junior GI Forum. Because of the nature of the organization and because the Forum concentrates on the problems of those of Mexican descent, citizens of that group comprise approximately 98 percent of the organization.

The national GI Forum, known as the American GI Forum of the United States, is made up of the state organizations, the forums, auxiliaries, and juniors-at-large. The national board of directors, composed of the national officers and six representatives from each state and one representative from each forum-at-large, has supreme executive, administrative, legislative, and judicial powers.

Headquarters for the American GI Forum are usually located where the executive secretary resides. There is a yearly state convention. In 1968 the organization celebrated its twentieth anniversary in Del Rio, Texas, and its headquarters was in San Antonio. *See also* Mexican Americans in Texas.

*American Legion, Texas Department of.

*American Party in Texas. *See* Know-Nothing Party in Texas.

*Ames, Harriet (Moore).

*Ames, Texas. (Coryell County.)

*Ames, Texas. (Liberty County.)

*Amherst, Texas. Amherst, in Lamb County, became a station in 1913 for the ranch of William Electious Halsell qv (not W. N. Halsell, as stated in Volume I). In 1970 Amherst was incorporated and had a population of 825, according to the U.S. census.

*Amichel.

*Amigo, Texas.

Amistad Reservoir. Amistad Dam and Amistad Reservoir, authorized by Congress in 1960, are in the Rio Grande Basin, twelve miles northwest of Del Rio on the Rio Grande between the United States and Mexico. The dam and reservoir are in Val Verde County, Texas, and Coahuila, Mexico. The project, begun in August, 1963, and scheduled for completion in 1968, is owned by the United States and Mexico and operated by the International Boundary and Water Commission, United States and Mexico (formerly International Boundary Commission qv). The project was authorized by the commission for the purpose of flood control, water

conservation, irrigation, hydroelectric power, and recreation. Under terms of the treaty the United States will get 56.2 percent of the conservation storage and Mexico will get 43.8 percent.

The reservoir provides a conservation storage capacity of 3,550,000 acre-feet, has a surface area of 67,000 acres, and has a flood control storage capacity of 1,775,000 acre-feet. The total contributing drainage area above the dam is 126,423 square miles, with 82,690 square miles in the United States. There are two power plants of 66,000-kilowatt capacity each, one of which is on the United States side and the other on the Mexican side of the river. The dam was dedicated on September 8, 1969, by President Richard M. Nixon and Mexico's President Gustavo Díaz Ordaz. *See also* Rio Grande Flood Control.

BIBLIOGRAPHY: Texas Water Commission, *Bulletin 6408* (1964).

Seth D. Breeding

*Ammansville, Texas.

Amon Carter Museum of Western Art. The Amon Carter Museum of Western Art, in Fort Worth, was established under the will of the late Amon G. Carter,qv founder and publisher of the Fort Worth *Star-Telegram* qv and for many years prominent in the development of Fort Worth and West Texas. The museum houses the collection of American art assembled by Carter during his lifetime, including a large and distinguished collection of pictures and sculpture by Frederic Remington and Charles M. Russell. Additions to the basic collection broaden the scope of the museum to include contemporary as well as historic American works. The program of the museum is expressed in publications, exhibitions, and permanent collections related to the many aspects of American culture, both historic and contemporary, which find their identification as Western. All exhibitions are temporary, with frequent changes of the permanent collections and special exhibits prepared by the Carter Museum.

A reference library specializing in the museum's field of principal interest is housed in the same building and may be visited upon request during regular hours. Microfilm records of early newspapers of the American West are an important feature of the library collection.

Admission to the museum is free of charge at all times. The building, designed by the New York architect Philip Johnson, is of Austin shellstone trimmed with bronze and granite. Facing eastward, a superb view of downtown Fort Worth may be seen across the sunken plaza. A walk around the plaza brings the visitor to three large bronze sculptures by the English sculptor Henry Moore.

Mitchell A. Wilder

*Amory, Nathaniel C.

*Ampudia, Pedro.

*Amusements, Early.

*Amy, Texas.

*Anacacho, Texas.

*Anacacho Mountain.

Anachorema Indians. In the latter part of the seventeenth century the Anachorema Indians lived north of Matagorda Bay on or near one of the major streams in present Jackson County, apparently the Lavaca River. Their village, which was visited by La Salle in 1687, was one of many Indian settlements along this river. Of these various settlements, only the Anachorema and Quara villages are identified in the records of the La Salle Expedition.qv The Anachorema are not referred to by this name in later times, and their ethnic affiliation remains unknown. Since they lived in an area dominated by Karankawan groups, it is possible that they, too, were Karankawan. However, it is also possible that Anachorema is a French rendition of Aranama, the name of an Indian group which lived nearby at about the same time.

BIBLIOGRAPHY: C. W. Hackett (ed.), *Pichardo's Treatise on the Limits of Louisiana and Texas*, I (1931); J. G. Shea, *Discovery and Exploration of the Mississippi Valley* (1903).

T. N. Campbell

*Anachorema Village.

*Anacuas Creek.

*Anadarko Creek.

*Anadarko Indians. The Anadarko (Anadaca, Anduico, Nadaco, Nandacao) Indians, a tribe of the southwestern or Hasinai division of the Caddo Indians, lived near the boundary between present Nacogdoches and Rusk counties during the late seventeenth and early eighteenth centuries. Anadarko Creek in Rusk County received its name from these Indians. H. E. Bolton qv has suggested that Nabiri may have been an early name for the Anadarko, but this has yet to be demonstrated. In the late eighteenth century, after their numbers had been greatly reduced by disease and warfare, some of the Anadarko moved northward and lived along the Sabine River in present Panola County. After the Texas Revolution qv they migrated westward and, at various times, had settlements along the Brazos River and also between the Brazos and Trinity rivers north and northwest of present Waco. In 1854 they were placed on the Brazos Indian Reservation qv in modern Young County and in 1859 were removed to Indian Territory, now Oklahoma. Today their descendants live near the town of Anadarko (named for these Indians) in Caddo County, Oklahoma.

BIBLIOGRAPHY: H. E. Bolton, "The Native Tribes about the East Texas Missions," *Quarterly of the Texas State Historical Association*, XI (1907–1908); J. R. Swanton, *Source Material on the History and Ethnology of the Caddo Indians* (1942); D. H. Winfrey and J. M. Day (eds.), *The Indian Papers of Texas and the Southwest, 1825–1916* (1966).

T. N. Campbell

*Anagado Indians.

*Anahuac, Texas. Anahuac, seat of Chambers County, reported fifty-eight businesses in 1967. Connected with the Houston Ship Channel qv by a barge canal, the town serves a rice, cattle, and oil-producing area. Incorporated in 1949, Anahuac had

eleven churches, two public schools, a hospital, a library, and a newspaper by 1966. The 1960 population was 1,985; the 1970 population was 1,881.

*Anahuac Disturbances.

Anahuac Lake. Anahuac Lake is in the Trinity River Basin in Chambers County near Anahuac on Turtle Bay, a tributary to the Trinity River near its mouth. The project is owned and operated by the Chambers-Liberty Counties Navigation District. In 1966 the water was used mostly for irrigation with some used for industry and mining. Construction of the dam, levee, and spillway, which was an enlargement of an earlier project, began on March 17, 1953, and was completed in July, 1954. Impoundment of water had already started, and the water was in use from the smaller lake. The enlarged lake in 1966 had a capacity of 35,300 acre-feet and a surface area of 5,300 acres at elevation five feet above mean sea level. Water is pumped from the Trinity River into the lake at a point near its upper end. The drainage area to Anahuac Lake is 199 square miles, but the main source of the lake's water is the Trinity River.

BIBLIOGRAPHY: Texas Water Commission, *Bulletin 6408* (1964).

Seth D. Breeding

Anahuac National Wildlife Refuge. *See* Wildlife Areas in Texas.

*Anamis Village.

Anao Indians. In a Spanish missionary report of 1691, the Anao were listed among the enemies of the Hasinai Indians of eastern Texas. Twelve names occur on this list, and it is said that two or three of the groups named lived southeast of the Hasinai; the others lived to the west. The identity of the Anao remains undetermined. It is evident that the Anao were not the same as the Annaho, listed in documents of the La Salle Expedition qv (1687) as allies of the Kadohadacho on the Red River. The Annaho were Osage Indians whose base area at that time was western Missouri, and there is no record of their having lived as far south as eastern Texas or western Louisiana.

BIBLIOGRAPHY: P. Margry, *Découvertes et établissements des Français dans l'ouest et dans le sud de l'Amérique Septentrionale*, III, VI (1879); R. A. Smith, "Account of the Journey of Bénard de la Harpe: Discovery Made by Him of Several Nations Situated in the West," *Southwestern Historical Quarterly*, LXII (1958–1959); J. R. Swanton, *Source Material on the History and Ethnology of the Caddo Indians* (1942).

T. N. Campbell

*Anaqua, Texas.

*Anaquitas Creek.

*Anarene, Texas.

Anathagua Indians. The Anathagua (Anatagu) are known from a Spanish document of 1748 that lists twenty-five Indian groups of east-central and southeastern Texas who had asked for missions in that general area. About half the names on this list, including Anathagua, cannot be identified. It is possible but not demonstrable that the Anathagua were the same as the Quanataguo reported at San

Antonio de Valero Mission qv at San Antonio in the 1720's. J. R. Swanton included the Quanataguo in his list of Coahuiltecan groups, apparently because one Quanataguo woman was said to have married a Coahuiltecan. The list of twenty-five groups that includes Anathagua contains no names that can be identified as Coahuiltecan; the identifiable names indicate only Caddoans (including Wichita), Tonkawans, Atakapans, and Karankawans. Both Anathagua and Quanataguo bear some resemblance to Quiutcanuaha, the name of a group identified in 1691 as living an unspecified distance southwest of the Hasinai Indians of eastern Texas, but no identities can be established. The affiliations of all three groups remain undetermined.

BIBLIOGRAPHY: H. E. Bolton, *Texas in the Middle Eighteenth Century* (1915); C. W. Hackett (ed.), *Pichardo's Treatise on the Limits of Louisiana and Texas*, I (1931); F. W. Hodge (ed.), *Handbook of American Indians*, II (1910); J. R. Swanton, *Linguistic Material from the Tribes of Southern Texas and Northeastern Mexico* (1940) and *Source Material on the History and Ethnology of the Caddo Indians* (1942).

T. N. Campbell

Anchimo Indians. In 1683–1684 Juan Domínguez de Mendoza qv led an exploratory expedition from El Paso as far eastward as the junction of the Concho and Colorado rivers east of present San Angelo. In his itinerary he listed the names of thirty-seven Indian groups, including the Anchimo, from whom he expected to receive delegations. Nothing further is known about the Anchimo, who seem to have been one of the many Indian groups of north-central Texas that were swept into oblivion by the southward thrust of the Lipan-Apache and Comanche Indians in the eighteenth century.

BIBLIOGRAPHY: H. E. Bolton (ed.), *Spanish Exploration in the Southwest, 1542–1706* (1916); C. W. Hackett (ed.), *Pichardo's Treatise on the Limits of Louisiana and Texas*, II (1934).

T. N. Campbell

*Anchor, Texas.

*Anchorage, Texas.

Anchose Indians. The Anchose (Anchosa) Indians are known from a Spanish document of 1748 that lists the names of twenty-five Indian groups of east-central and southeastern Texas who had asked for missions in that general area. About half the names on this list, including Anchose, cannot be identified. The identifiable groups include Caddoans, Tonkawans, Atakapans, and Karankawans.

BIBLIOGRAPHY: H. E. Bolton, *Texas in the Middle Eighteenth Century* (1915); F. C. Chabot (ed.), *Excerpts from the Memorias for the History of Texas, by Father Morfi* (1932); C. W. Hackett (ed.), *Pichardo's Treatise on the Limits of Louisiana and Texas*, I (1931).

T. N. Campbell

*Andacamino Indians.** A few individuals are identified by this name (Spanish for "wanderer") in the records of San José y San Miguel de Aguayo Mission qv at San Antonio. It seems likely that this was a convenient term used by mission personnel to refer to displaced Indians of unidentifiable band or tribal origins. No such name appears in other eighteenth-century documents. J. R. Swanton listed Andacamino as a Coahuiltecan band, but he presented no evidence in support of this linguistic identification.

BIBLIOGRAPHY: F. W. Hodge (ed.), *Handbook of American Indians*, I (1907); J. R. Swanton, *The Indian Tribes of North America* (1952).

T. N. Campbell

*Ander, Texas.

*Anders Creek.

*Anderson, Bailey.

*Anderson, Bill.

*Anderson, Charles.

*Anderson, Charles Edwin.

*Anderson, James Monroe.

*Anderson, John.

*Anderson, John D.

*Anderson, Kenneth Lewis.

*Anderson, Monroe Dunaway.

Anderson, Ralph A. Ralph A. (Andy) Anderson, son of John and Anna Anderson, was born on May 14, 1890, in Pittsburgh, Pennsylvania. After two years at Carnegie Institute of Technology, he enlisted in the United States Army in 1917 at Fort Logan, Colorado, and served in the mounted engineers. After the armistice, he was sports editor of the Houston *Post* qv from 1919 to 1923. In 1920 he married Ruby Rose Ellison. They were the parents of one son.

While with the *Post*, Anderson was honored for his efforts in helping to establish sandlot baseball in Houston, and the Houston Amateur Baseball Federation. In 1923 he went into the business of constructing and operating golf courses in several small surrounding towns. In 1926 he became sports editor of the Houston *Press*, with which he was affiliated the rest of his life. An authority on hunting and fishing along the Texas Gulf Coast, he wrote a column on the subject and also conducted a radio program on outdoor sports for several years.

During World War II he actively promoted the sale of war bonds, and subsequently began rehabilitation work with returning disabled war veterans. This work included developing special social and recreational activities, with emphasis on the outdoors. He invented attachments for sports equipment to permit persons of various disabilities to participate. Under his direction annual wild game dinners were instituted in several veterans hospitals in South Texas; in addition to those hospitals, he visited 172 other veterans administration hospitals over the United States as volunteer-at-large, entertaining and instructing the veterans in recreational pursuits. Through his efforts, a park for handicapped veterans was established on the east shore of Lake Houston. Later the park was named for him.

His office at the Houston *Press* became a one-man bureau for helping the poor, the troubled, and also parolees. Through his column, he served as an intermediary between those in need and those in a position to help.

Anderson received national recognition for his

work. In 1953 he was chosen National Fisherman of the Year and was elected to the Fishing Hall of Fame of the Sportsman's Club of America. An elementary school in southwest Houston was named for him in 1961. He died on January 24, 1956, at his home in Houston.

BIBLIOGRAPHY: *Texas Press Messenger* (October, 1945); *Coronet* (June, 1952); *Field & Stream* (January, 1953); *Time* (July 5, 1954); *Editor & Publisher* (January, 1956); Houston *Press* (1926–1956).

Ruby E. Anderson

***Anderson, Simeon Asa.**

***Anderson, T. Scott.**

***Anderson, T. T. C.**

***Anderson, Washington.**

***Anderson, William Madison.**

***Anderson, Texas.** Anderson, seat of Grimes County, declined in population from a reported 400 in 1960 to an estimated 320 in 1971. A historic town, it has had an increasing tourist business.

***Anderson County.** Anderson County receives its principal income from gas, oil, beef and dairy cattle, and lumber, although manufacturers and the railway industry are the leading employers in the county. Between 1929 and 1973 over 205,000,000 barrels of oil were produced. In 1973 three-fourths of its agricultural income came from livestock and poultry. The county was 58 percent forested and had one saw mill in 1967. There are six salt domes with an estimated twenty-seven cubic miles of salt reserves. Lake Palestine was constructed without the use of federal funds in 1962 on the Neches River and provides water for municipal and industrial purposes, as well as serving as a recreation center. Major tourist attractions are the spring Dogwood Trail tours and the fall county fair. In 1965 a new prison farm was established in the county. The 1960 population was 28,162; the 1970 count was 27,789.

***Anderson Creek.**

***Anderson's Fort.** *See* Soldier's Mound.

***Anderson's Mill, Texas.**

***Andice, Texas.**

***Andrade, Juan José.**

***Andrew Female College.**

***Andrews, Frank.**

***Andrews, Henry Barclay.**

Andrews, Jesse. Jesse Andrews was born on April 9, 1874, in Waterproof, Louisiana, the son of Mark and Helen (McFerran) Andrews. He attended Jefferson College in Mississippi from 1887 to 1889 and then embarked on a career in the hardware industry. Andrews enrolled in the University of Texas in 1891. He was graduated in 1895 with a B.Litt. degree, obtained an LL.B. from the university in 1896, and passed the Bar examination. In 1899 Andrews entered the law firm with which he remained throughout his life. One of Andrews' major accomplishments was his stewardship of the Long-Bell Lumber Company, the world's largest lumber company in the 1920's. After leading the company through legal channels during the Depression, he became the real directing power of the company, serving as chairman of its board of directors.

Andrews was a trustee of the University of Kansas and maintained residences in both Houston and Kansas City. He was a member of the first zoning committee of the city of Houston and served as chairman of the Houston City Planning Commission for sixteen years. He also was a member of the Philosophical Society of Texas qv and served as both president and director of that organization.

At the time of his death on December 29, 1961, Andrews was an active Democrat, director and vice-chairman of the executive committee of Houston's Bank of the Southwest, director of the American General Life Insurance Company, and a trustee of the Robert A. Welch qv Foundation.

He was survived by his wife, the former Emilia Celeste Bujac, whom he married on November 8, 1900, and one son.

BIBLIOGRAPHY: Philosophical Society of Texas, *Proceedings* (1961); *Texian Who's Who* (1937).

***Andrews, Jessie.**

***Andrews, John.**

***Andrews, Matthew Thomas.**

***Andrews, Richard.**

***Andrews, Robert.**

***Andrews, Stephen Pearl.**

***Andrews, William.**

***Andrews, Texas.** (Andrews County.) Andrews, seat of Andrews County, had a 1960 population of 11,135 and a 1970 population of 8,625. In 1960 construction was completed on a new high school, a new city hall, and a hospital. Andrews is a marketing center for the production of oil and gas.

***Andrews, Texas.** (Harrison County.)

***Andrews County.** Andrews County, bounded on the west by the Texas-New Mexico line, ranked fifth in the state in total oil production in 1963 with 71,327,000 barrels of oil. The oil industry, with its production, processing, and supplying, is the major source of employment and income. Between 1930 and 1973 Andrews County wells produced over 1.5 billion barrels of oil. Although its population is over 80 percent urban, Andrews County has about eight thousand irrigated acres under cultivation and also has several large cattle ranches averaging eight thousand acres each. In 1960 the median annual income of the county was the fourth highest in the state. The population grew rapidly from 5,002 in 1950 to 13,450 in 1960. The population in 1970 had declined to 10,372.

***Andy, Texas.**

***Angel City, Texas.**

***Angelina.**

Angelina College. Angelina College was established on September 24, 1966, when an election was held in Angelina County creating the Angelina

County Junior College District, and providing $1,-500,000 in tax bonds. Seven persons were elected to the board of trustees for the junior college district, and they in turn elected Jack W. Hudgins, dean of Grayson County College, to be the first president of Angelina College.

The 140-acre campus is located within the city limits of Lufkin, Texas. Several buildings were completed by the fall of 1968, when students were enrolled for the first time. By 1974 the school had 1,403 students.

Jack W. Hudgins

*Angelina County. Angelina County, near the Louisiana state line in the heart of the East Texas Piney Woods belt, was 70 percent forested in 1970 with four active mills and many wood-using industries. The sawmills produced over sixty-nine million board-feet of lumber annually. The Sam Rayburn Reservoir, completed in 1964, provided water for industry, irrigation, municipal use, and recreation. A second major tourist attraction was the Angelina National Forest.qv The 1960 population was 39,814; the 1970 count was 49,349.

*Angelina National Forest. See National Forests in Texas.

*Angelina and Neches River Railroad Company.

*Angelina River.

*Angelita, Texas.

Angelo State University. Angelo State University (formerly Angelo State College), San Angelo, was established in 1928 as San Angelo College, a junior college program of the San Angelo Independent School District. A county junior college district created in 1945 operated the school until September 1, 1965. On that date the name was changed to Angelo State College, as the school became a four-year institution and joined the state system.

In 1965 the college maintained two campuses covering more than 160 acres—one campus on public school property separated from the other (occupied in 1947) by a narrow residential area. The campuses contained twenty-three buildings, including administration-classroom, auditorium, agriculture, home economics, gymnasium, vocational science, student center, dormitories, library annex, and auxiliary structures. Plans called for connection of the two campuses and construction of additional facilities, including a library, a science building, classrooms, dormitories, and a food service building. Library holdings numbered 100,000 volumes in 1969.

Enrollment, originally 112 students in 1928, climbed to 467 in 1946, to 979 in 1961, and to 4,312 in the fall of 1974.

An expanded curriculum provided for studies leading to B.A., B.S., and B.B.A. degrees in twenty major fields beginning in 1967. Degree plans included provisions for teacher certification at all levels.

In 1954 R. M. Cavness became the seventh president of the college and guided the institution through its transition from two-year to four-year status. Lloyd D. Vincent was president in 1974.

*Angier, Samuel T.

*Angleton, Texas. Angleton, seat of Brazoria County, was a business center for an oil and agriculture area in the 1960's; oil and chemical industries at nearby Chocolate Bayou added to the economy of Angleton. In 1966 the city reported a sixteen-bed hospital, a public library, two airports, two high schools, and one junior high school. In 1960 the population was 7,312; in 1970 it was 9,770.

Angleton South, Texas. Angleton South was an unincorporated town in Brazoria County with a population of 1,017 in 1970, according to the U.S. census.

*Anglo-Texan Convention of 1840.

*Angora Goat Industry. See Goat Ranching.

*Anguila Mesa.

*Angus, Texas.

*Anhalt, Texas.

*Animal Disease Investigations Laboratory. The Animal Disease Investigations Laboratory ceased operation on February 1, 1962.

Hal R. Taylor

*Anna, Texas. No reliable evidence can be found to support the exact origin of the name of Anna, Texas, although various sources claim the town was named for (1) Anna Greer (as stated in Volume I), (2) Anna Huntington, and (3) Anna Quinlan. The town, in Collin County, had a 1970 population of 736, according to the U.S. census.

J. Lee Stambaugh

*Anna Judson Female Institute.

*Annadale, Texas.

Annaho Indians. The Annaho Indians were mentioned in documents (1687) of the La Salle Expedition as enemies of the Kadohadacho Indians on the Red River. Annaho was an early name used by the French for the Osage, whose base area at that time was in western Missouri. The Annaho are not to be confused with the Anao, who were mentioned in a Spanish missionary report of 1691 as a group of Indians who lived near the Hasinai tribes of eastern Texas.

BIBLIOGRAPHY: P. Margry, *Découvertes et établissements des Français dans l'ouest et dans le sud de l'Amérique Septentrionale*, III, VI (1879); R. A. Smith, "Account of the Journey of Bénard de la Harpe: Discovery Made by Him of Several Nations Situated in the West," *Southwestern Historical Quarterly*, LXII (1958–1959); J. R. Swanton, *Source Material on the History and Ethnology of the Caddo Indians* (1942).

T. N. Campbell

*Annarose, Texas. [This title was incorrectly listed in Volume I as Annarosa, Texas.]

*Annas Indians. This name, recorded only in the early eighteenth century, refers to a small band of Indians who lived somewhere in the southern part of Texas. It seems likely that the Annas are the same as the Teaname, a Coahuiltecan group of northeastern Coahuila and adjoining parts of Texas, who in missions were also known as Peana and Teana.

BIBLIOGRAPHY: V. Alessio Robles, *Coahuila y Texas en la Epoca Colonial* (1938); F. W. Hodge (ed.), *Handbook of American Indians*, I (1907).

T. N. Campbell

***Annetta, Texas.**

***Annexation of Texas.** Although the date of Texas' legal entry into the Union was December 29, 1845, the formal transfer of authority from the Republic to the state was not made until a ceremony held on February 19, 1846 (not February 16, 1846, as stated in Volume I, which was the date the newly elected legislature met to prepare for the ceremony three days hence), when President Anson Jones qv declared, "The Republic of Texas is no more," and handed over the reins of state government to Governor James Pinckney Henderson.qv

***Annona, Texas.**

***Anranta Creek.**

***Anson, Texas.** Anson, seat of Jones County and commercial center for an agricultural and oil area, had in 1966 eighty-one business establishments, twelve churches, a forty-bed hospital, a library, and a city park. The 1960 population was 2,890; in 1970 it was 2,615. *See also* Abilene Standard Metropolitan Statistical Area.

***Antelope.**

***Antelope, Texas.**

***Antelope Creek.**

***Antelope Gap.**

***Antelope Gap, Texas.**

***Antelope Hill.**

***Antelope Hills.**

***Antelope Mesa.**

***Antelope Mountain.**

***Antelope Spring.**

***Anthony, D. W.**

***Anthony, Texas.** (Bexar County.)

Anthony, Texas. (El Paso County.) Anthony is located twenty miles north of El Paso on the Texas-New Mexico state line. Formerly called La Tuna qv for the Federal Correctional Institution qv located there, the community was incorporated in 1952 as Anthony, Texas. The post office was formerly in the New Mexico half of the city and was moved into Texas in 1942. A canning company was among the ninety-two businesses listed in 1960. Many residents are employed in nearby El Paso or at the White Sands Missile Range. The 1960 population was 1,082, and the 1970 count was 2,154.

***Anthony, Texas.** (Fannin County.)

***Anthony's Nose.**

***Antimony Smelter.**

Antioch, Texas. Antioch, in western Delta County, is a farming community which had a population of twenty-five in 1970. The blackland surrounding Antioch is a fine cotton-producing region, but the most important local product is honey. Since 1850, when Charles H. "Honey" Smith originated the industry, honey has been produced by the farmers of the vicinity, although the town itself was not established until 1890.

****Anti-Quaker.***

Antiquities Committee. *See* Padre Island Treasure.

***Anti-Saloon League, Texas Branch of.**

***Anti-Trust Regulation.** The anti-trust laws changed very little in the 1950's and 1960's. In 1951 the Texas legislature declared that an agreement between an employer and any labor organization whereby persons are denied the right to work because of membership or nonmembership in a labor organization, or whereby membership or nonmembership is made a condition of employment or continuance of employment, would be construed as a conspiracy in restraint of trade. In 1957 the legislature extended to any person or organization doing business in the state the right to have a judicial determination as to whether any of its existing procedures or methods of doing business "are or will be in violation of the anti-trust laws of the State of Texas" by instituting a suit for a declaratory judgment.

The responsibility of prosecution for violation of penal statutes is vested in the various district attorneys throughout the state, and there is no way, other than by a search of the court records in each of the 254 counties, to determine if anti-trust prosecutions have been filed under the penal provisions of Texas laws.

Civil enforcement of anti-trust laws is vested in the attorney general of Texas. In the years from 1950 through 1965, some twenty-five civil anti-trust actions were instituted, and judgments awarding civil penalties of approximately $1,200,000 were obtained. The case against Billy Sol Estes and Commercial Solvents Corporation regarding an alleged illegal attempt to eliminate competition in the liquid fertilizer business received the greatest amount of publicity of any of those anti-trust cases. Judgment was obtained against Estes for $547,500 and against Commercial Solvents Corporation, a nonresident corporation, in the amount of $150,000 in settlement of claims against them. Estes was prosecuted criminally on other alleged violations, rather than violation of penal provisions of the anti-trust law.

Hawthorne Phillips

***Anton, Texas.** Anton, in Hockley County, had a population of 1,068 in 1960 and 1,034 in 1970, according to the U.S. census.

***Antony, Edwin Leroy.**

***Apache Canyon.**

***Apache Indians.**

***Apache Mountains.**

*Apache Peak.

*Apache Spring Creek.

*Apacheria.

*Apalonia, Texas.

Apapax Indians. This name is known from a document of 1748 that lists twenty-five Indian groups of east-central and southeastern Texas which had asked for missions in that general area. About half of the names on this list, including Apapax, cannot be identified. The remainder consists of groups identifiable as Caddoans (including Wichita), Tonkawans, Atakapans, and Karankawans. The name Apapax bears some resemblance to Atakapa, but this may be fortuitous.

BIBLIOGRAPHY: H. E. Bolton, *Texas in the Middle Eighteenth Century* (1915); C. W. Hackett (ed.), *Pichardo's Treatise on the Limits of Louisiana and Texas*, I (1931).

T. N. Campbell

Apatin Indians. The Apatin Indians were one of five bands of Coahuiltecan Indians encountered near present Corpus Christi by a Spanish expedition in the middle eighteenth century. The Apatins are not mentioned in later documents.

BIBLIOGRAPHY: H. E. Bolton, *Texas in the Middle Eighteenth Century* (1915); G. Saldivar (ed.), *Archivo de la historia de Tamaulipas*, II (1946).

T. N. Campbell

Apaysi Indians. The Apaysi Indians were one of several bands of Coahuiltecan Indians whose range in the late seventeenth century was south of the Edwards Plateau. The Apaysi (Apayxam) are known from one brief encounter on the middle Frio River southwest of San Antonio. Since the name does not appear in eighteenth-century records, it seems likely that the Apaysi lost their identity among the various bands with which they were associated.

BIBLIOGRAPHY: F. W. Hodge (ed.), *Handbook of American Indians*, I (1907), II (1910).

T. N. Campbell

Apennapem Indians. The Apennapem Indians, apparently Coahuiltecans, lived along the lower Rio Grande. In the middle eighteenth century their principal settlements were on the south bank of the river about halfway between Camargo and Reynosa, Tamaulipas, Mexico. At times they foraged and camped on the Texas side of the Rio Grande.

BIBLIOGRAPHY: W. Jiménez Moreno, "Tribus e idiomas del Norte de México," *El Norte de México y el Sur de Estados Unidos* (1944); G. Saldivar, *Los Indios de Tamaulipas* (1943).

T. N. Campbell

*Apex, Texas.

Apion Indians. Apion Indians, known only from records of San Antonio de Valero Mission,qv in San Antonio, cannot be linked with any known group of Indians. The sounds suggest that the name may be a variant of Hape, but the Hape are believed to have become extinct by 1689. An early place name near Laredo, La Cañada de los Abiones, suggests residence in Coahuiltecan Indian territory. The records of Mission San Antonio de Valero also contain a reference to Capellone Indians, who may be the same, but nothing is known about the Capellone either.

BIBLIOGRAPHY: Bexar Archives Translations, Vol. 3 (typescript, Archives, University of Texas at Austin Library); H. E. Bolton, *Texas in the Middle Eighteenth Century* (1915).

T. N. Campbell

*Apostol Santiago Mission.

*Apple Springs, Texas.

*Appleby, Texas.

*Applegate, Texas.

*April 6, 1830, Law of. *See* Law of April 6, 1830.

Aquarena Springs. Aquarena Springs, a Texas tourist complex in San Marcos, had its beginning in 1849, when an earthen and rock dam impounding approximately thirty surface acres of water was constructed at the source of the San Marcos River. Noted for its clarity, the water originates from a multitude of natural springs.

In 1926, after a succession of owners, the dam and surrounding properties were acquired by Arthur Birch Rogers,qv a San Marcos citizen. In 1928 Rogers constructed the Spring Lake Hotel on the banks of the springs. The Depression of the 1930's, however, forced the resort to close, and later the hotel was leased to the Brown Schools as a home for exceptional children.

In 1946 Rogers' son, Paul J. Rogers, became interested in developing the area into a major tourist attraction, and he launched the first of an increasing fleet of glass-bottom boats. The popularity of the glass-bottom boat rides stimulated further development of the springs. During the latter part of 1950, the world's first submarine theater was constructed on the east bank.

During the first year after its formal opening to the public in March, 1951, approximately 20,000 people visited Aquarena Springs. Each year new facilities were added. In 1961 the Brown Schools relocated a short distance from the springs, and the old hotel was reopened after an extensive remodeling program.

In 1966 Aquarena Springs complex included a Swiss sky ride, glass-bottom boat rides, historical features in its hanging gardens, and an authentic Western town. Annual attendance soared to 400,000 visitors. During the winter period of 1966–1967, there was a major expansion of facilities to care for the increasing crowds.

Dorothy O. Worrell

*Aquilla, Texas.

*Aquilla Creek.

*Aragon, Texas.

*Arah, Texas.

*Aranama College. *See also* Presbyterian Education in Texas.

*Aranama Indians. The Aranama (Aname, Arrenamus, Auranean, Hazaname, Jaraname, Xaraname) Indians lived along the lower Guadalupe and San Antonio rivers near the coast. Although the evidence is scant, most writers today classify the Aranama as Coahuiltecan-speakers. Attempts to link the Aranama with groups named in the narrative of Cabeza de Vaca qv (Muruame) and in records of the La Salle Expedition qv (Anachorema, Erigoana, Quara) have not been very convincing and must be considered only as probabilities. Most of what is known about the Aranama comes from Spanish mission records. Espíritu Santo de Zuñiga Mission qv was moved in 1722 from Matagorda Bay to the lower Guadalupe River in order to serve the Aranama and Tamique. In 1749 this mission was moved to the vicinity of present Goliad, and many Aranama followed it to the new location. At various times in the late eighteenth century the Aranama deserted this mission and went north to live with other groups, particularly the Tawakoni. Each time the Spaniards induced them to return. A few Aranama were present at other missions—San Antonio de Valero qv at San Antonio, and Nuestra Señora del Refugio,qv near present Refugio. During the late eighteenth and early nineteenth centuries the Aranama slowly declined in numbers and finally disappeared about 1843. The last survivors were probably absorbed by Spanish-speaking people near the coastal missions. Some writers have implied that the Aranama were agricultural Indians in the pre-mission period, but acceptable evidence for this has never been presented.

BIBLIOGRAPHY: H. E. Bolton, *Athanase de Mézières and the Louisiana-Texas Frontier, 1768–1780,* II (1914) and *Texas in the Middle Eighteenth Century* (1915); C. E. Castañeda (ed.), *History of Texas, 1673–1779, by Fray Juan Agustín Morfi* (1935); F. W. Hodge (ed.), *Handbook of American Indians,* I (1907), II (1910); W. W. Newcomb, Jr., *The Indians of Texas* (1961); J. R. Swanton, "Linguistic Position of the Tribes of Southern Texas and Northeastern Mexico," *American Anthropologist,* XVII (1915), *Linguistic Material from the Tribes of Southern Texas and Northeastern Mexico* (1940), and *The Indian Tribes of North America* (1952).

T. N. Campbell

*Aransas, Texas.

*Aransas Bay.

*Aransas City, Texas. *See also* Lamar, Texas (Aransas County).

*Aransas County. Aransas County, a small Gulf Coast county divided into three parts by bays, has a varied economy. The total oil production between 1936 and 1973 was over sixty-four million barrels. Cattle ranching, shipping, and commercial and sport fishing are also important. Aransas Bay is bisected by the Gulf Intracoastal Waterway.qv A shipbuilding plant and a steel-form plant are found in the county seat, Rockport, and an aluminum plant is near Aransas Pass. The county benefited greatly from the settlement in 1953 of the Tidelands controversy,qv gaining 208 square miles of submerged land area. The tourist trade is a major source of the county's income. Attractions include Goose Island State Park (*see* Parks, State), a sand beach at Rockport, the Sea-O-Rama festival in June, and the Aransas National Wildlife Refuge.qv Population was 7,006 in 1960 and 8,902 in 1970.

*Aransas Harbor Terminal Company. The Aransas Harbor Terminal Company was incorporated under the laws of Texas on July 13, 1892, and its charter was amended in 1912. It was classified as a line haul carrier. In 1946 it operated a line from Aransas Pass to Port Aransas, a distance of 7.15 miles. It was controlled by the Baltimore Aransas Corporation, Baltimore, Maryland, until January, 1947, when the road was abandoned.

James M. Day

Aransas National Wildlife Refuge. Aransas National Wildlife Refuge, on a broad peninsula between San Antonio Bay and Saint Charles Bay overlooking Matagorda Island, was established on December 31, 1937. The United States Fish and Wildlife Service administers the refuge for the protection and management of the various species of wildlife inhabiting the area. In the 1960's it was the principal watering ground for the nearly extinct whooping cranes,qv less than forty of which were known to exist on the North American continent. The nesting ground of the whooping cranes is in the Woods Buffalo National Park in the Northwest Territory of Canada, some 2,500 miles from their Aransas wintering grounds.

Three hundred species of birds have been recorded in the region, including ibises, egrets, herons, Canada geese, most of the diving ducks, and snow and blue geese. There are, in addition, large numbers of white-tailed deer, javelinas, raccoons, and wild turkeys.

The Aransas National Wildlife Refuge contains 54,829 acres, most of which are upland. The remainder is composed of many ponds and marsh areas. The upland region has a cover of live oak, blackjack, sweet bay, brush, and open grasslands. Portions of the refuge are open to visitors throughout the year for purposes of observation.

BIBLIOGRAPHY: Claude F. Lard, *Aransas National Wildlife Refuge* (1964).

*Aransas Pass.

*Aransas Pass, Texas. Aransas Pass, located in Aransas, San Patricio, and Nueces counties, is a deepwater port on the Corpus Christi channel and the Gulf Intracoastal Waterway,qv as well as a center for commercial and sport fishing and seafood processing. The city's 162 businesses in 1970 included an aluminum plant and large petrochemical facilities. Population was 6,956 in 1960 and 5,813 in 1970.

*Aransas River.

*Arbadao Indians.

*Arbala, Texas.

*Arbuckle, Maclyn.

*Arcadia, Texas. (Galveston County.)

*Arcadia, Texas. (Shelby County.)

Arcahomo Indians. The Arcahomo (Axcahomo) Indians appear to have been related to the Tacame, a Coahuiltecan group that lived near the Gulf Coast between the San Antonio and Nueces rivers in the eighteenth century. Arcahomo may be a synonym for Tacame, or it may refer to a subdivision of the Tacame. It is also possible that the Arcahomo represent remnants of some former coastal group that became attached to the Tacame. The name Arcahomo appears only in records that pertain to San Francisco de la Espada Mission,qv in San Antonio, chiefly in connection with an episode of 1737, when all Indians deserted this mission.

BIBLIOGRAPHY: F. W. Hodge (ed.), *Handbook of American Indians*, II (1910).

T. N. Campbell

*Archaeology. *See also* Texas Archeological Society; *Bulletin of the Texas Archeological Society*; Archeologist, State.

Archeological Society, Texas. *See* Texas Archeological Society.

Archeologist, State. The office of State Archeologist was created by the Fifty-ninth Texas Legislature in 1965 and was at that time attached to the State Building Commission;qv the office was transferred to the Texas State Historical Survey Committee (now the Texas Historical Commission qv) on September 1, 1969. Responsibilities of the position include the systematic recording, investigation, preservation, and development of the state's archeological resources. Reconnaissance and excavations are carried out on state-owned land, at important historic sites, and where archeological sites are threatened by reservoirs, highways, and other types of construction. Archeological investigations are conducted for the Texas Parks and Wildlife Department, Texas Water Development Board,qqv and other state agencies.

Curtis Tunnell

*Archer. The brig *Archer* was first named *Galveston* (not *Galveston of Baltimore,* as stated in Volume I), renamed *Brazos,* and finally called *Archer* to honor Branch T. Archer.qv She was transferred to the United States Navy on May 11, 1846 (not June, 1846), and sold for $450 on November 30, 1846 (not 1847).

BIBLIOGRAPHY: Tom Henderson Wells, *Commodore Moore and the Texas Navy* (1960).

Tom Henderson Wells

*Archer, Branch Tanner.

*Archer City, Texas. Archer City, county seat of Archer County, had a 1960 population of 1,974, and a count of 1,722 in 1970. A farm market, retail, and oil trading center, Archer City had two hospitals and sixty businesses in 1970.

*Archer County. Archer County, on the north-central Texas rolling plains, is economically linked with the Wichita Falls Standard Metropolitan Statistical Area.qv Its shallow oil pool had produced over 402 million barrels from 1911 to 1973. Cattle ranching and cropping of small grains also rank among the principal industries, with dairy and hog production increasing. Tourist attractions include Lake Kickapoo, Lake Wichita, and several smaller lakes; Camp Cureton qv (site of a pioneer army camp); and a summer livestock show and rodeo are also offered. Population was 6,110 in 1960, and in 1970 it was 5,759.

*Architecture, Early Texas.

Architecture, Review of Texas. The architecture of Texas reflects the history of Texas in its emergence from a Spanish colony in the eighteenth century to a modern twentieth-century state. Five major architectural periods can be identified: Spanish Colonial, Pioneer Settlement, Greek Revival, Victorian, and Twentieth Century. The earliest remaining architecture is the eighteenth-century Spanish architecture of the missions (*see* Mission Architecture). These structures reveal the Baroque architecture of Spain as it was brought to these remote mission outposts by way of Mexico.

Following the Spanish architecture of the eighteenth century came the architecture of the Anglo American settlers who began to move into Texas in large numbers in the early 1820's. These pioneers brought with them the architecture of the American frontier—the log cabin and the frame house (*see* Architecture, Early Texas). Next came European immigrants who brought their native building traditions with them. Among these were French, Germans, Swedes, Alsatians, and Czechs. The most numerous were the Germans, whose fine timber and masonry buildings are still to be seen in Fredericksburg, New Braunfels, Mason, and La Grange. Particularly notable are their heavy timber frame houses, employing a medieval structural system which the Germans call *Fachwerk.*

From 1840 to 1870 the Greek Revival style dominated Texas architecture. Often erroneously called Southern Colonial, the style is neither Southern nor Colonial since it first appeared in the East in the early nineteenth century. It was, however, well suited to the climate and culture of the South, and it was primarily from the states of the Old South that it was introduced. Texas in the early nineteenth century was a frontier state, and the more sophisticated styles of the eastern states were slow in reaching the newly settled region west of the Mississippi. It was not until 1840 that the Greek Revival style appeared in Texas, Galveston and San Augustine being the first centers of the style.

The Greek Revival style takes its name from the fact that its principal feature was derived from the classic temple form of ancient Greece, the temple portico or porch which has a roof supported by a row of columns. These columns were of three types or orders: Doric, Ionic, and Corinthian. The Greek Revival style is formal in character, the building being arranged symmetrically about a central axis, the hall. This central hall is flanked by rooms on each side which are of the same width, in order to give the desired balance. The doorway is flanked by an equal number of windows on each side, and centered on the front of the house is a porch which features one of the classic orders.

The simple frame house of the Anglo American settlers continued to be the principal type of house built in Texas until the Civil War. These frame houses were often given a few classic details, such as a cornice, capped posts on the porches, and multipaned double-hung sash windows, all of which gave them a resemblance to the larger Greek Revival houses. As the farthest extension of the Old South, Texas possesses some of the most recently built Greek Revival homes, which can be seen in San Antonio, Austin, Waco, Jefferson, and Marshall. The Governor's Mansion qv in Austin, built by Abner Cook,qv is one of the most representative examples of the Greek Revival style in Texas. The most outstanding public building in the Greek Revival style is the Old Customs House in Galveston, built in 1858 by a United States Treasury Department architect.

Following the Civil War, from 1870 to 1900, Texas caught up with the main stream of American architectural fashion, which was the Victorian, so called for a lack of any better name to encompass the multitude of stylistic expressions of that complex period. The exuberance of the Victorian style reflects a period of rapid expansion and new fortunes. Turreted mansions sprang up in cities and towns all over the state. In contrast to the restrained classicism of the Greek Revival style, the Victorian style was rich in detail, exceedingly ornate, and strove for a romantic and picturesque effect. The buildings were seldom symmetrical, being characterized by the off-center tower and projecting bay to a central, balanced composition. Many materials were now available to the builder, and these were often combined to achieve greater richness. Sawmills had become widespread, and the frame houses were given elaborate gingerbread trim, made possible by the jigsaw. Architectural motifs from many historic styles were combined in an eclectic fashion, with the Medieval Romanesque and Gothic vying with the Renaissance for popularity. Civic and commercial architecture became important, and many handsome courthouses, banks, opera houses, and hotels were constructed.

The most significant building to be built during this period was the state capitol (see Capitol). Completed in 1888, this impressive red granite structure was designed by Elijah E. Myers,qv of Detroit, Michigan, in the Renaissance Revival style. Inspired by the national capitol in Washington, the building was originally intended to be of limestone. However, there was not a sufficient supply of the quality required to be found in Texas, so granite was used. The ruggedness of the granite gives the building a unique character, and the tall cast-iron dome adds a fine symbol to the state's most important building.

The county courthouses were second only to the state capitol in their architectural significance and reflected the pride of the people in their counties, at that time the most significant political, economic, and social units.

Many churches were built during the last two decades of the nineteenth century with the Medieval styles, Romanesque and Gothic, being favored. Richard Upjohn, the architect of Trinity Church in New York and the leading Gothic Revival architect in America, designed St. Mark's Episcopal Church in San Antonio, and his son, R. M. Upjohn, designed St. James' Episcopal Church in La Grange in 1885. Of all the cities in Texas, Galveston was undoubtedly the richest in its collection of Victorian architecture. One of the state's first professional architects, Nicholas Clayton,qv practiced there and added many fine buildings, including the Gresham house, now known as the Bishop's Palace.

The architecture of the first half of the twentieth century reflects the growing unity of architectural expression throughout the United States. Regional characteristics rapidly disappeared as a result of the spread of popular taste and the uniformity of architectural fashion. During the first thirty years of the twentieth century eclecticism was the accepted form of architectural expression. Among the styles revived by the architects were Colonial, Georgian, Spanish Renaissance, Italian Renaissance, and Tudor.

Soon after World War II, spurred by the schools of architecture and the high cost of eclectic ornamentation, the more practical contemporary forms of the leading modern architects were introduced. In addition to the Kalita Humphreys Theater, Dallas, by Frank Lloyd Wright, other examples are the Amon Carter Museum of Western Art,qv Fort Worth, by Philip Johnson; the Cullinan Wing of the Museum of Fine Arts, Houston,qv by Mies van der Rohe; and the Tennessee Gas Transmission Company Building, Houston, by Skidmore, Owings, and Merrill. Texas architects such as David Reichard Williams,qv who developed the indigenous ranch-style type of house; O'Neil Ford, who designed the Trinity University campus, San Antonio; Caudill, Rowlett, and Scott, who designed the Jesse H. Jones Hall for the Performing Arts,qv Houston; and Howard R. Meyer and Max Sandfield, who associated with W. W. Wurster of California to design the Temple Emanu-El, Dallas, are among those who have achieved national recognition.

BIBLIOGRAPHY: Drury Alexander and Todd Webb, *Texas Homes of the 19th Century* (1966); Dorothy Kendall Bracken and Maurine Whorton Redway, *Early Texas Homes* (1956); Clovis Heimsath, *Pioneer Texas Buildings* (1968); Frederick Law Olmsted, *A Journey Through Texas* (1857); Edward Muegge Schiwetz, *Buck Schiwetz' Texas* (1960); Samuel Edward Gideon (comp.), A Group of Themes on the Architecture and Culture of Early Texas (MSS., Architecture Library, University of Texas at Austin).

Drury B. Alexander

*Architecture as a Profession in Texas. In 1973 architecture was taught at Texas A&M University, the University of Texas at Austin, Texas Tech University, Rice University, and the University of Houston. All five schools of architecture are members of the Association of Collegiate Schools of Architecture and give the School Medal of the American Institute of Architects to qualified graduating seniors. The University of Texas at Arlington had a beginning program in architecture.

In 1973 there were seventeen local chapters of the American Institute of Architects in Texas. Together they form one of the national regions of the institute and are represented on the board of directors of the AIA by two regional directors. The Texas chapters are as follows: Abilene, Austin, Brazos, Corpus Christi, Dallas, El Paso, Fort Worth, Houston, Lubbock, Lower Rio Grande Valley, Northeast Texas, San Antonio, Southeast Texas, Texas Panhandle, West Texas, Waco, and Wichita Falls.

The Texas Society of Architects reached a membership of 2,250 in 1973. The TSA includes all AIA members in the state in its membership, with each chapter represented on its board of directors. The TSA represents the profession at the state level and maintains an office with a full-time executive director and staff in Austin, while the AIA represents the profession in regard to national affairs.

New responsibilities and challenges confronted the architect in this period of rapid urbanization of the population, accelerating technological changes, and social and economic readjustments. The architect has sought, through the years, to make communities cognizant of the basic need for a pleasant, as well as functional, urban environment, and the public has recently indicated a new sense of awareness and interest in accomplishing this objective. The architect, by his training and experience, is the natural leader of the team involving many specialists who coordinate all the elements of community planning into designs for more livable communities fundamentally related to their place and time.

George F. Harrell

*Archive War.

*Archives of Texas.

*Arciniega, Miguel.

*Arcola, Texas.

Arcos Buenos, Arcos Pordidos, and Arcos Tirados Indians. These three groups of Indians are known only from a Spanish document of 1693 which lists them among fifty "nations" that lived north of the Río Grande and "between Texas and New Mexico." This may be interpreted to mean the southern part of western Texas, since the document also mentions that the Apache were at war with the groups named. Nothing further is known about these Indians, whose names all refer to the condition of their bows ("good," "rotten," and "long," respectively).

BIBLIOGRAPHY: C. W. Hackett (ed.), *Historical Documents Relating to New Mexico, Nueva Vizcaya, and Approaches Thereto, to 1773*, II (1926).

T. N. Campbell

Arcos Tuertos Indians. The Arcos Tuertos Indians (Spanish for "twisted bows") were one of twenty Indian groups that joined Juan Domínguez de Mendoza qv on his journey from El Paso to the vicinity of present San Angelo in 1683–1684. The meeting occurred east of the Pecos River, possibly in the vicinity of present Reagan and Irion counties, and the Arcos Tuertos accompanied Mendoza to the Colorado River beyond San Angelo. They seem to have been one of the numerous bands of unknown

affiliation that ranged the transition zone between the southern High Plains and the Edwards Plateau prior to Apache dominance in the early eighteenth century.

BIBLIOGRAPHY: H. E. Bolton (ed.), *Spanish Exploration in the Southwest, 1542–1706* (1916).

T. N. Campbell

*Arden, Texas.

*Arenosa, Texas. *See* Ironosa, Texas.

*Arenosa Creek.

Aretpeguem Indians. The Aretpeguem Indians, presumably a Coahuiltecan band, lived on the south bank of the lower Rio Grande in northern Tamaulipas. In the middle of the eighteenth century their settlements were reported to be a few miles downstream from present Reynosa. At times the Aretpeguem foraged and camped on the Texas side of the Rio Grande.

BIBLIOGRAPHY: W. Jiménez Moreno, "Tribus e idiomas del Norte de México," *El Norte de México y el Sur de Estados Unidos* (1944); G. Saldivar, *Los Indios de Tamaulipas* (1943).

T. N. Campbell

*Argenta, Texas.

*Argo, Texas.

*Argyle, Texas.

Argyle Hotel. The building which became the Argyle Hotel was built in 1859 by Charles Anderson qv as a plantation house on a ranch in what is now the Alamo Heights area of San Antonio. When Anderson left the state during the Civil War the house stood unoccupied for several years, although there were plans for a Confederate arsenal to be built on the property. After the war Hiram W. McLane qv purchased the mansion; like Anderson, he raised horses and entertained in high style. In 1890 the ranch property was sold to a Denver investment company, which developed it into what is now Alamo Heights. The house was sold separately to two Scotsmen named Patterson, whose name was given the street which runs in front of the hotel. Calling the house Argyle, they operated it as a hotel for three years. A third story and a southwest wing were added after 1890; the second- and third-story front porches became modified colonial, and the lower front porch was made into a garden loggia.

Robert Emmit O'Grady and his sister Alice O'Grady, son and daughter of Katherine (Cahill) and John G. O'Grady,qv purchased the hotel and opened it on St. Patrick's Day, 1893. Victorian and European furnishings and decoration were added to the twenty-one guest rooms and various public rooms, and antique silver and fine china became part of the daily table service.

Miss Alice O'Grady, with George Bannister, the Argyle chef for thirty-five years, served a fine cuisine. Having collected and experimented with recipes from the time she helped her mother in the Kendall House (the O'Grady home and inn in Boerne), Alice brought to the Argyle a creative interest in cooking that made it outstanding for fine foods in the South. Her tiered wedding cakes, shipped in sheet-draped Pullman berths, were a must for brides of many South Texas families. Her brother Robert E. O'Grady, who was born in Boerne on November 14, 1870, assisted in the operation of the Argyle. He was elected mayor of the new township of Alamo Heights in 1922 and continued in that office until the early 1940's; he died on September 24, 1949. Through the years various O'Grady sisters, Kate, Lizzie, and Mary, assisted Alice and Robert in the hotel's management. Guests of national reputation came for meals, and several lived there for years. With Alice O'Grady's retirement in 1941, the hotel remained in private hands until it was bought in the 1950's by the Southwest Foundation for Research and Education qv of San Antonio and converted into an exclusive club whose members make an annual contribution in support of the medical research underway at the foundation; restoration and additions to the famous old Argyle Hotel have continued, and it was still in operation as a private club in the early 1970's.

BIBLIOGRAPHY: Lillie May Hagner, *Alluring San Antonio* (1940); Alice O'Grady (Sue Moore Gibson, comp.), *The Argyle Cookbook* (1940); Charles Ramsdell, *San Antonio* (1968); Ellis A. Davis and Edwin H. Grobe, *The New Encyclopedia of Texas*, I (1929?); Rudolph L. Biesele (book review of *The Argyle Cookbook*), *Southwestern Historical Quarterly*, XLIV (1940–1941); Ella K. Daggett, "Famous Contemporaries: The Argyle and the Menger," *Southern Home and Garden* (September, 1941); Files of the Texas Historical Commission, Austin.

*Arhau Indians.

*Ariel.

Arihuman Indians. The Arihuman Indians are known only from a Spanish document of 1683 which does not clearly identify their area, but it seems to have been east of the Pecos River in west-central Texas. Their affiliations remain unknown.

BIBLIOGRAPHY: C. W. Hackett (ed.), *Pichardo's Treatise on the Limits of Louisiana and Texas*, I (1931).

T. N. Campbell

*Ariola, Texas.

*Arispe, Texas.

*Arista, Mariano.

*Arkansas City, Texas.

*Arledge Field.

*Arlie, Texas.

*Arlington, Texas. Arlington, in Tarrant County, was an industrial center in 1973, producing machinery, auto parts, rubber products, and chemicals. Arlington was the site of a 5,800-acre industrial park, which was reported to be the largest of its kind in the nation. In 1957 a dam was completed, creating Lake Arlington in twenty-six days. In 1959 Arlington State College (now University of Texas at Arlington) was elevated to a four-year status and served the cultural needs of the community. The Six Flags Over Texas qv amusement park attracted thousands of tourists yearly. The population of Arlington had climbed from 7,692 in 1950, to 44,775 in 1960, and to 90,643 in 1970. *See also* Fort Worth Standard Metropolitan Statistical Area.

Arlington Baptist Junior College. *See* Bible Baptist Seminary.

*Arlington State College. *See also* University of Texas at Arlington.

Armadillo World Headquarters. *See* Music in Texas, Folk and Popular.

*Armagosa, Texas. *See* Amargosa, Texas, for the history of the earlier town, four miles distant, located on Amargosa (not Armagosa) Creek.

*Armagosa Creek. Although found on some maps with this spelling, Armagosa is a corruption of the word Amargosa; *see* Amargosa Creek.

*Armistead, William Thomas.

Armstrong, A. Joseph. A. Joseph Armstrong, the son of Andrew Jackson and Lotta (Foreman) Armstrong, was born in Louisville, Kentucky, on March 29, 1873. He received his B.A. degree from Wabash College in Indiana in 1902 and his M.A. degree in 1904. He taught at East Texas Baptist Institute in Rusk, Texas, one year and at Broadus College in West Virginia one year. From the fall of 1904 to 1907 he taught at Wesleyan University in Illinois. In 1908 he received a Ph.D. degree from the University of Pennsylvania.

In September, 1908, he was invited to relieve H. L. Hargrove, head of the Department of English at Baylor University in Waco, Texas, during Hargrove's one-year leave of absence. From 1909 to 1912 Armstrong taught English at Georgetown University in Kentucky, and in September, 1912, returned to Baylor University as head of the Department of English, a position he held for over forty years. On January 24, 1911, he married Mary Maxwell of Waco, whom he had met while both were teaching at East Texas Baptist Institute; they had one son.

During summers the Armstrongs, through their own travel bureau, conducted tours to Europe, and later Armstrong took groups to all parts of the world and conducted Browning pilgrimages for persons especially interested in the poet.

With his first editions and the portrait of Robert Browning by the poet's son, Robert Barrett Browning, given by the class of 1919, Armstrong began collecting items for a Browning Library at Baylor. He accumulated funds for the project by bringing poets, scholars, musicians, and lecturers to Baylor, including Robert Frost, Vachel Lindsay, Amy Lowell, and Carl Sandburg. The completed Armstrong Browning Library qv was opened in 1951 with Armstrong as director. He died on March 28, 1954.

Margaret Royalty Edwards

*Armstrong, Cavitt.

Armstrong, Frank B. Frank B. Armstrong, son of Richard Sands Armstrong, was born on May 10, 1863, at St. Johns, New Brunswick, Canada. After the death of his father, an amateur naturalist, the family moved to Medford, Massachusetts, and then to Boston. There Armstrong attended school, and following graduation he studied taxidermy for two years with Professor C. J. Maynard. At home in Boston, Armstrong wrote his first essays on ornithology, mammalogy, and oölogy.

In his early twenties Armstrong began a tour of the still sparsely settled Southwest and took an extensive tour of Mexico which lasted several years. During that time he made a fairly complete collection of Mexican birds and animals. Field work, with Laredo, Texas, as a center, took him through the border country, which then teemed with bird life and wild game.

In March, 1890, when Armstrong came to Brownsville, he was so pleased with wildlife in the area that he moved his collection and taxidermic studio there. He made exhaustive studies of subtropical bird life, and his later reputation was based chiefly on his work in tropical ornithology. The Armstrong collection of mounted birds, fishes, and animals attracted many visitors. He had assembled over eight hundred different specimens from that vicinity. He also contributed thousands of specimens to museums in Europe and the United States, including the Field Museum in Chicago and the Smithsonian Institution. At one time Southern Methodist University and Southwest Texas State University had specimens of Armstrong's work.

Armstrong married Marie Isabel Schodts of Brownsville on April 2, 1891. Their family consisted of three daughters and four sons. Armstrong died on August 20, 1915, and was buried in Brownsville's Old City Cemetery.

BIBLIOGRAPHY: Brownsville *Herald*, August 21, 1915; John Henry Brown, *Indian Wars and Pioneers of Texas* (189?); W. H. Chatfield, *Twin Cities of the Border* (1893).

Ruby Armstrong Wooldridge

*Armstrong, James.

*Armstrong, John Barclay.

Armstrong, Mollie Wright. Mollie (Wright) Armstrong was born on January 23, 1875, in Bell County, the daughter of Thomas C. and Elizabeth (Neal) Wright. She married Walter D. Armstrong of Brownwood. On September 1, 1899, when she began her practice, she became the first woman optometrist in Texas and the second in the United States. Dr. Armstrong was extremely active in the passage of the first optometry law in Texas, became a member of the Texas Board of Examiners in Optometry, and served as vice-president and president of the board, to which she belonged for twenty-four years. For the term 1923 to 1924 she was president of the Texas Optometric Association, and at another time served as the association's director of publicity. When the *Texas Optometrist* was first published, she was its editor. It was largely through her efforts that the first optometric professional liability policy was made available to optometrists nationwide, and she became a trustee of the American Optometric Association. In 1927 she was instrumental in the organizing of the Woman's Auxiliary to the Texas Optometric Association, in which she was honored with lifetime membership, and in

that year she was appointed national director by the president of the American Optometric Association Auxiliary. In Brownwood she was the organizer and first president of the American Legion Auxiliary, the Brownwood Business and Professional Women's Club, and the Brownwood Civic League. She served as director of the Brownwood Chamber of Commerce, and represented her district as a member of the State Democratic Executive Committee. She received every honor her state and national optometric associations could award.

In 1962 she retired from practice to write a complete history of Texas optometry. Dr. Armstrong died on May 23, 1964, at the age of ninety.

Gertrude Chambers

*Armstrong, Texas.

Armstrong Browning Library. The Browning Collection at Baylor University had its beginning in the personal collection of books assembled by Browning scholar A. Joseph Armstrong,qv chairman of Baylor's English department (1912–1952). Through the efforts of Dr. Armstrong the Browning Collection grew to rank unchallenged as the world's greatest assemblage of Browningiana. Of the approximately ten thousand volumes in the library in 1967, more than a thousand were rare books—all of the first editions of Robert Browning, all except one of the first editions of Elizabeth Barrett Browning, and 205 books from the Brownings' personal library. In addition, there were 3,097 original manuscripts and letters of the Brownings; 214 pamphlets, magazines, and newspapers from Robert Browning's personal collection; and 637 musical scores of the Brownings' poems. Special collections of Browning-related materials include the Shields Collection, the Meynell Collection, the Walter Savage Landor Correspondence and Manuscript Poems, the Slater Correspondence, the Edward Bulwer-Lytton Correspondence, the Isa Blagden Letters, the Edward Dowden Letters, the Frederick Leighton Letters, the Milsand-Browning Correspondence, and the Hagedorn Elizabeth Barrett Browning Collection.

The library has numerous holdings of Browning-associated materials, such as twenty-one original portraits of the Brownings, including an oil by the Brownings' son, Robert Wiedemann Barrett Browning; forty-eight original photographs; ten busts and statues; seven paintings and various furnishings owned by the Brownings, as well as many personal items. Recent acquisitions include one hundred Armstrong-Fannie Coddington Browning letters and hundreds of other Armstrong items.

Opened in 1951, the Browning Library is housed in the three-story, $1,500,000 Armstrong Browning Library building. Forty-two of the stained glass windows depict Browning themes, as do the heavy bronze entrance doors with panels illustrating Browning subjects. Terrazzo and marble floors and the marble and black-walnut-paneled walls maintain the Browning connection in design. There are work rooms for the library staff, graduate students, and visiting scholars, and classrooms for the Browning courses and the Department of English.

Lois Murray

*Armstrong County. Armstrong County is crossed by Palo Duro Canyon State Park (*see* Parks, State), its leading tourist attraction. The primarily agricultural economy of the county centers largely in cattle ranching. Large-scale farming of wheat and grain sorghums is also important, with over eighteen thousand acres depending on irrigation from underground water sources. Farm income for 1969 was $4,656,000. Population was 1,966 in 1960, and 1,895 in 1970.

*Armstrong Creek.

*Army of the Republic of Texas.

*Arneckeville, Texas.

*Arnett, Cullen Curlee.

*Arnett, William Washington.

*Arnett, Texas. (Coryell County.)

*Arnett, Texas. (Hockley County.)

*Arnim, Texas.

*Arno, Texas.

*Arnold, Hayden S.

*Arnold, Hendrick.

*Arnold, Ripley A.

*Arp, Texas.

Arpa, José. José Arpa, born in 1868 in Carmoria, Spain, was the son of Antonio Arpa and María de Garcia Perea Arpa. He studied in the School of Fine Arts in Seville, receiving special instruction from the historical painter Eduardo Cano de la Peña. While in the School of Fine Arts he received the Rome Prize three successive times, which allowed him six years of study in Rome. He was already well known in Europe when the Spanish government sent four of his paintings to the World's Fair at Chicago in 1893. Because of the recognition given his work in Spain and in the United States, the Mexican government sent a man-of-war to Spain to take the artist to Mexico, where he was to become the director of the Academy of Fine Arts in Mexico City. Although Arpa declined the position, he did stay in Mexico to paint.

Later, Arpa came to San Antonio, where his painting, "A Mexican Funeral," exhibited at the International Fair, brought him to the attention of Texans. Finding the atmosphere of San Antonio conducive to his creative work, Arpa remained in that city for many years painting and teaching.

His work was exhibited in the principal galleries of the United States. Arpa participated in the Texas Wildflower Oil Painting contests held by the San Antonio Art League, and in 1927 he won the state prize of $1,000 for "Verbena," which is now owned by the San Antonio Art League. In 1952 murals painted by Arpa were hung in the lobby of the Express Publishing Company of San Antonio. Arpa died in Seville, Spain, in October, 1952, at the age of ninety-four.

BIBLIOGRAPHY: Alamo Museum Files, San Antonio, Texas; Mantle Fielding, *Dictionary of American Painters, Sculptors, and Engravers* (1960); Frances Battaile Fisk, *A History of Texas Artists and Sculptors* (c. 1928); Esse Forrester-O'Brien, *Art and Artists of Texas* (c. 1935); Witte Museum Files, San Antonio, Texas.

Caroline Remy

*Arredondo, Joaquín de.

*Arrington, Alfred W.

*Arrington, George W.

*Arrington, William W.

*Arrowood, Charles Flinn.

*Arroya Reservoir.

*Arroyo, Texas.

*Arroyo Amaladeros.

*Arroyo Baluarte.

*Arroyo Colorado.

*Arroyo de los Angeles.

*Arroyo del Quenada.

*Arroyo del Tigre.

*Arroyo Dulce.

*Arroyo Hondo. *See* Neutral Ground.

*Arroyo Lagarto.

*Arroyo La Minita.

*Arroyo Leon.

*Arroyo Negro.

*Arroyo Nombre de Dios.

*Arroyo Palo Alto.

*Arroyo Primero.

*Arroyo Salado.

*Arroyo Santa Isabel.

*Arroyo Sauz.

*Arroyo Segundo.

*Arroyo Venado.

*Art, Texas.

Art, Indian Rock. *See* Rock Art, Indian.

Art in Texas. The history of art in Texas stretches back some eight thousand years, to the rock art qv by the early human inhabitants of West Texas in what is now the Pecos River and Devil's River country, scattered between Breckenridge and El Paso and north into the Panhandle.

Unfortunately the state no longer has its once large Indian population; remaining are the Alabama-Coushatta Indian Reservation qv in East Texas and the community of Tigua Indians qv at El Paso. The stylistic heirs of the early rock painters must be sought outside Texas' borders in the mural painters of such peoples as the Pueblos and Navahos, and in the hide painting of the Plains Indians.

The first artists and designers whose work may still be seen and felt as a part of living Texas culture were the Franciscan friars and their craftsmen, perhaps the best examples of whose art in Texas were in the missions of San Antonio. The builders of these missions, and particularly the stone carvers and artisans who ornamented the interior worship areas with icons and the exterior surfaces with exquisite stone sculpture and polychromed fresco designs, were the first artists of Western civilization to work and live in Texas.

Beginning in the 1820's one can look to on-the-spot paintings made in Texas for visual documentation of the early exploration and settlement period. George Catlin and William Ranney qqv contributed to this graphic record beginning in the 1830's with their paintings and drawings. From this time on, a steady supply of art work, both professional and amateur, by visitors and residents alike, was produced in Texas.

During the mid-nineteenth century a number of artists made their homes in and around San Antonio, painting the local scenery and events, and being commissioned to do portraits of members of early settler families. Perhaps the best known of these are the brothers-in-law Richard Petri and Hermann Lungkwitz.qqv Two lesser-known but no less exciting artists, both as to their historical and aesthetic values, were Carl G. von Iwonski and Theodore Gentilz.qqv

The end of the nineteenth century saw Edward L. Grenet and Thomas Allen qqv painting the Texas scene, particularly around San Antonio. Elisabet Ney qv came to Texas to continue her talented work as sculptor and her misunderstood life as rugged individualist. The turn of the century brought state support to art in the purchases and commissions of work by H. A. McArdle and W. H. Huddle,qqv among others. The Onderdonk family, particularly associated with the painting of Texas' hill country and San Antonio scenes, began its long period of activity in the 1890's with the work of R. J. Onderdonk.qv He was followed by his painter son, Julian Onderdonk.qv A successor to the Texas landscape painters, popular with the general public in the mid-twentieth century, was Porfirio Salinas, Jr.,qv of San Antonio.

Sculptors who worked in Texas during the early twentieth century, creating a number of monumental figures, were Pompeo Coppini qv (San Antonio and Austin), E. F. Cerrachio (Houston), and somewhat later, Alexander Phimister Proctor.qv Coppini is probably the best known of these three, having lived and worked for years in San Antonio, where he founded the Coppini Academy of Art. This academy is still in operation under the directorship of Coppini's pupil, Waldine Tauch. Work by New York sculptor Louis Amateis qv appeared in Galveston's statue commemorating Texas heroes. Other sculptors born in Texas, but working elsewhere during this period, were Bonnie MacCleary and Cleo Chandler.

Other artists had attained some prominence during the first three decades of this century. One was Seymour Thomas,qv who followed his painting career both here and abroad. Others, who worked and lived in Texas, were landscapist Charles H. Cox; Frank Reaugh,qv painter of Texas' longhorn cattle and ranch life; landscapist E. G. Eisenlohr;qv portraitist Mattie Simkins; Boyer Gonzales; and Charles Tidden. Peter Mansbendel became known

as a wood carver. Other artists were Emma Richardson Cherry, S. E. Gideon qqv and Raymond Everett.

The 1930's had a new generation of artists growing into professional maturity. They had reverence for the history and natural features of the state, but used these as subjects for the development of their own personal artistic expression. At the present time there are many prominent artists and sculptors working in the state. Among these, men and women who have continued to contribute immensely to their profession in Texas, are Otis Dozier, Everett Spruce, Jerry Bywaters, Ruth Pershing Uhler, William Lester, and Tom Lea. A number of artists have been associated both with Texas and neighboring states. Among them are Loren Mozley and the late Ward Lockwood, who have worked in both New Mexico and Texas. Frank Mechau, principally a Colorado artist, was a muralist in Texas during the 1930's and 1940's. Alexandre Hogue has worked in Texas, although he is primarily thought of as an Oklahoma artist. Xavier Gonzales lived and worked in San Antonio before going to Newcomb College in Louisiana.

A contemporary of these men, although his Texas career began somewhat later, is the sculptor Charles Umlauf, perhaps the most widely known sculptor ever to work and live in Texas. There is great difficulty in naming contemporary painters, due to the likelihood of omitting a deserving name. Outstanding among them, however, are Michael Frary, Kelly Fearing, and John Biggers.

Although the work of early Texas artists has been preserved over the years by their families and other private collectors, few museums have built collections of these vital and valuable works. The most notable exception at the present time is the Witte Memorial Museum,qv although valuable study in the field has been and is being done by the University of Texas at Austin and the Amon Carter Museum of Western Art.qv Even so, the greatest debt future generations will owe for preservation and knowledge of early Texas art will be to private collectors and researchers. Even research by these major institutions has depended largely on the willing help of non-paid or underpaid writers and researchers. The work of two new state agencies, the Institute of Texan Cultures and the Texas Fine Arts Commission,qqv in cooperation with other, older institutions, should prove invaluable in promoting appreciation of both past and contemporary art in the state.

The line of communication about art and artists, in Texas and the Southwest generally, has been limited. In the past a great talent could work for years without notice. A number of factors have combined to bring about a change. Probably the most important element in increasing knowledge and enjoyment of the visual arts in Texas has been the establishment and growth of such museums as the Marion Koogler McNay Art Institute and the Witte Memorial Museum qqv in San Antonio; the Dallas Museum of Fine Arts;qv the Fort Worth Art

Center, and the Amon Carter Museum in the same city; the Museum of Fine Arts, Houston;qv and the development of arts curricula and museums in the institutions of higher learning in Texas, particularly in the University of Texas at Austin, among the larger schools, and in recent years, the University of St. Thomas in Houston, among the smaller ones.

In the private sector of cultural development there are an increasing number of knowledgeable collectors in the state, along with the correlative growth of art galleries as successful business concerns; the only broad-based art magazine in the Southwest, *Southwestern Art*, was published in Texas in the 1960's. Continued development along the present worthwhile lines of art activity in Texas will be proportional to the accessibility of art and to the degree of increased communication and cooperation between art institutions, artists, laymen, and charitable foundations. *See also* Arts and Crafts in Texas.

BIBLIOGRAPHY: Pauline A. Pinckney, *Painting in Texas: The Nineteenth Century* (1967); Frances Battaile Fisk, *A History of Texas Artists and Sculptors* (c. 1928); Esse Forrester-O'Brien, *Art and Artists of Texas* (c. 1935); W. W. Newcomb, Jr., *The Rock Art of Texas Indians* (1967).

Mallory B. Randle

*Artesia Wells, Texas.

*Artesian Belt Railroad.

*Artesian Wells.

*Arthur City, Texas.

*Artillero Creek.

Arts and Crafts in Texas. A development in recent years which has proved increasingly important for art in Texas is the rebirth of the crafts tradition. A "craft," definitively, is work in any medium in which the finished product is predominantly handmade by one individual, with an emphasis on the satisfaction of utilitarian needs, but with an eye towards the satisfaction of aesthetic needs as well. Since contemporary thought includes the satisfaction of sensuous and contemplative needs within the concept of utility, the popular distinction between "the arts" and "the crafts" is probably obsolescent. Handmade products traditionally identified as "crafts," all of which are now being made in Texas, include pottery, weaving, jewelry, furniture, macrame, clothing and fabric design, leather work, glassware, wrought iron, and candles. A prolific and varied crafts tradition is a fertile matrix from and through which artistic expression of all kinds can obtain inspiration and realization. From the artist's viewpoint, training and experience in a crafts tradition, including the craftsman's intimate involvement with his medium and his concern for the total effect and purpose of his end product, often have a catalytic effect on the artist's realization of his own creative expression. From the layman's viewpoint, the availability of fine crafts enables him to surround himself with useful objects which are also aesthetically pleasing and generally only slightly more expensive than mass-produced items. In these ways a strong crafts tra-

dition is likely to strengthen the arts in Texas. *See also* Art in Texas; Pottery Industry in Texas.

Mallory B. Randle

Arts and Humanities, Texas Commission on the. *See* Texas Commission on the Arts and Humanities.

*Arvana, Texas.

*Asa, Texas.

Asbury, Samuel Erson. Samuel Erson Asbury, son of Felicia Swan (Woodward) and Sidney Monroe Asbury, was born September 26, 1872, at Charlotte, North Carolina, into a family that included four sons and four daughters.

In the fall of 1889 Asbury enrolled at the North Carolina State College of Agriculture and Engineering at Raleigh, working his way through school as a janitor in the chemistry building. He graduated in 1893 with a Bachelor of Science degree in chemistry and the next year was employed as an instructor in the Department of Chemistry; at the same time he began work toward a Master of Science degree in chemistry, which he completed in 1896.

Asbury began work as assistant state chemist in the North Carolina Experiment Station in 1895, and continued in this capacity until July, 1897. During the ensuing years Asbury took a succession of temporary assignments serving in the capacity of a chemist. He returned to his old job in the North Carolina Experiment Station in 1899 and worked at the station until November 1, 1904, when he accepted the position of assistant state chemist with the Texas Agricultural Experiment Station qv on the campus of the Agricultural and Mechanical College of Texas (now Texas A&M University). He held this position until he retired to modified service in 1940 and to complete retirement in 1945.

In the meantime, he helped put his brothers and sisters through college. He also took a year's leave of absence from his job at Texas A&M to do advanced study in physical chemistry at Harvard.

As assistant state chemist he tested seed, feed, and fertilizers, and became interested in experimenting with the growing of roses. By a judicious combination of aluminum sulphate and water, he succeeded in growing the roses to a height of forty to forty-five feet.

Soon after coming to Texas, Asbury became deeply interested in the early history of the state and became a collector of Texana, and of stories about early Texas leaders. After 1930 he became more and more absorbed in historical research, and the Texas Revolution qv became his chief concern. He planned the production of a musical drama to tell the story of that great event. In 1951 he published a pamphlet, entitled *Music As A Means of Historical Research*, in which he discussed music as a medium for the presentation of history. He proposed to produce an opera to interpret the Texas Revolution through a cycle of music-dramas, but it was never completed.

At the time of his death he held membership in

the Southern Historical Association and was a fellow of the Texas State Historical Association.qv He was the author of one article and the editor of another in the *Southwestern Historical Quarterly*.qv He was a member of the Bryan-College Station Poetry Society and was a critic of poetry. He attended the First Methodist Church in Bryan.

Asbury died in Bryan, Texas, on January 10, 1962, and was buried in the City Cemetery, College Station, Texas. His personal papers were deposited in the Texas State Archives and in the Texas A&M University Archives.

BIBLIOGRAPHY: Samuel Erson Asbury Papers, Texas A&M University Archives; Bryan *Daily Eagle*, May 26, 1953, December 29, 1957, January 11, 12, 1962; *Battalion*, September 20, 1945, October 1, 1952; Austin *American*, October 17, 1952; Dallas *Morning News*, December 18, 1937, February 22, 1959; Houston *Post*, April 4, 1954, January 12, 21, 1962; *Music Courier*, January 25, 1930; *Extension Service Farm News* (January, 1938).

Joseph Milton Nance

Asen Arcos Indians. This is one of twenty Indian groups that joined Juan Domínguez de Mendoza qv on his journey from El Paso to the vicinity of San Angelo in 1683–1684. Since Mendoza did not indicate at what point the Asen Arcos joined his party, it is not possible to determine their range or affiliations. However, since the Indians between the Pecos River and the Colorado River east of San Angelo were being hard-pressed by Apaches at this time, it seems likely that the Asen Arcos ranged somewhere between these two rivers. Asen Arcos is a shortening of Mendoza's phrase, "Los que asen Arcos," which is Spanish for "bow makers." This designation is of special interest because it suggests technological specialization by a single band.

BIBLIOGRAPHY: H. E. Bolton (ed.), *Spanish Exploration in the Southwest, 1542–1706* (1916).

T. N. Campbell

Ash, Texas. Ash, in southwest Houston County, was founded in 1870 and named for James B. Ash, a community leader. The town centered around a post office, a one-room school, a country store, and a cotton gin. After some thirty years of operation, the post office was closed, and a rural route from nearby Georgia Camp, commonly known as Creek, served the area. Since 1928 postal service has come from Austonio. In 1966 Ash was uninhabited.

*Ash Creek.

Ashburn, Isaac Seaborn. Isaac Seaborn Ashburn was born in Farmersville, Texas, on December 19, 1889, the son of a Methodist preacher. His parents were Isaac and Hannah (Strother) Ashburn. A legendary World War I figure, Ashburn was many times decorated for bravery. He received battlefield promotions, and his citations included the Distinguished Service Cross, Purple Heart, Legion of Honor, and Croix de Guerre with Palm. For twenty years he was colonel in command of the 360th Infantry Reserve, 90th Division. He retired from the army reserve as a major general.

In 1936 he founded and was the first publisher of *Texas Parade* qv magazine and was one of the organizers of the Texas Good Roads Association. Varied services to Texas included positions as commandant of Texas A&M College, vice-president and general manager of the Houston Chamber of Commerce, World War II director of civilian defense for Harris County, and executive secretary of Harris County Association of Industrial Peace.

Toastmaster, after-dinner speaker, and storyteller, "Colonel Ike" was one of the more widely known Texans of his day. Several Texas governors relied upon his advice and counsel. An imposing figure of six feet five inches, tipping the scales above three hundred pounds, he was the center of attraction in any group.

Most of his formal education was at old Polytechnic College at Fort Worth, which later was merged into Southern Methodist University. His journalistic career began when he was city editor of the Fort Worth *Record*.qv Ashburn died on February 2, 1961, at the Veterans Administration Hospital in Temple and was buried in Austin Memorial Park, Austin. He was survived by his widow, Bertha (Smith) Ashburn, and one son.

William B. Alderman

*Ashburn General Hospital. *See* Veterans Administration Hospital, McKinney, Texas.

*Ashby, Harrison Sterling Price.

*Ashe, Samuel Swann.

*Asherton, Texas. Asherton, in Dimmit County, had a population of 1,890 in 1960 and 1,645 in 1970.

*Asherton and Gulf Railway Company.

*Ashland, Texas.

*Ashtola, Texas.

*Ashwood, Texas.

*Asia, Texas.

*Askew, Texas.

*Aspermont, Texas. Aspermont, seat of Stonewall County, serves as a market for the ranching, farming, and oil-producing county. In 1970 the town had fifty business establishments. The 1960 population was 1,286, and in 1970 it was 1,198.

*Asphalt Belt Railway Company. The Asphalt Belt Railway Company was controlled until 1956 by the New Orleans, Texas and Mexico Railway through stock ownership; in that year it was merged into the Missouri-Pacific in the general consolidation of its subsidiaries. The line had extended from Asphalt Junction to Dabney.

James M. Day

*Asphalt Mountain.

*Assessor and Collector of Taxes. *See* Taxes, Assessment and Collection of. *See also* County and Precinct Officers, Terms of.

Association of College Teachers, Texas. *See* Texas Association of College Teachers.

Association for Graduate Education and Research (TAGER). *See* University of Texas at Dallas.

*Association of Texas Colleges and Universities. The Association of Texas Colleges and Universities, formerly Association of Texas Colleges, completely rewrote its constitution and bylaws in 1962. Under the new organization, the affairs of the association are handled by the following standing committees and commissions: Committee on Constitution and By-Laws, Committee on Audit, Committee on Resolutions, Committee on Nominations, Commission on Standards and Classification, Commission on School and College Relations, Commission on Cooperation in Higher Education, and Commission on Educational Policy.

The Commission on Standards and Classification has the responsibility of preparing the standards to be met by member institutions. The Commission on School and College Relations has, in addition to regular college officials, ex officio representatives from the Texas Education Agency qv and public school administrators. This commission has primary concern for the development of cooperative studies and programs between colleges and universities and secondary schools. The Commission on Cooperation in Higher Education is composed of representatives from the different types of colleges and universities, together with ex officio representatives from the Texas Education Agency and the Coordinating Board, Texas College and University System.qv This commission is primarily responsible for working on problems of inter-college relationships, on questions of subject matter fields, and on the total needs of higher education in Texas. The Commission on Educational Policy is concerned with the basic relationships of higher education to its various constituencies and to its support and service groups.

In 1966 the association's roster of members and affiliated institutions included fifty-four senior and forty-eight junior colleges. By 1973 most of the state's colleges and universities were members or affiliates of the organization.

W. B. McDaniel

*Astoria, Texas.

Astro-Bluebonnet Bowl. *See* Bluebonnet Bowl.

Astrodome. The Astrodome, the first fully air-conditioned enclosed, domed, multipurpose sports stadium in the world, officially is known as Harris County Domed Stadium. More than four million persons a year have visited the Astrodome each year since the stadium was opened in April, 1965. It has been used for major league baseball, major league soccer, collegiate football, championship boxing, Portuguese-style bullfighting, rodeos, horse polo, collegiate basketball, special concerts, conventions, and religious meetings.

First tangible efforts toward creation of the revolutionary stadium were made when the Harris County Park Commission was created by the Fifty-fifth Legislature of Texas. The bill enabled Harris County to submit a revenue bond issue to property owners to create a Houston sports center. Voters approved the issue by a vote of more than three to one on July 26, 1958. Later, the idea of having an all-purpose covered stadium was developed through the leadership of Judge Roy Hofheinz, and it was determined that a new bond issue should be held to authorize general obligation bonds.

On January 31, 1961, the voters of Harris County approved a general obligation bond issue of $18,-000,000 by a vote of 61,568 to 54,127. Ground was broken on January 3, 1962. After excavation work was completed it was found that more money was needed to complete the structure. On December 22, 1962, another bond issue of $9,600,000 was submitted to Harris County property owners, and it passed by a vote of 42,911 to 36,110. Although there were two lawsuits and other delays, construction on the stadium itself started on March 18, 1963, and was completed almost exactly two years later. The stadium structure itself cost $20,-000,000, but the overall cost has been well over $40,000,000, of which $31,600,000 came from two county bond issues, and $3,750,000 from the State Highway Department qv and the city of Houston for off-site improvements, including paved streets, bridges, and storm sewers. The Houston Sports Association, which leased the stadium from the county for forty years, added $7,000,000 for expensive apartments, restaurants, cushioned seats, and a $2,000,000 scoreboard.

The first event was held on April 9, 1965, when the Houston Astros qv played the New York Yankees in exhibition baseball. The Astros play all their home games in the Astrodome, as does the University of Houston football team. During 1968 professional football established itself in the Astrodome when the Houston Oilers qv began playing all of their home games in the Astrodome, beginning with a pre-season exhibition game with the Washington Redskins on August 1, 1968. Seating capacity of the Astrodome for baseball is 44,500, for football about 55,000, and for some events, 66,000. Temperature is a constant 73 degrees, with humidity at 50 percent. There are five restaurants. The stadium has a clear span of 642 feet, an inside height of 208 feet, a lighting maximum of 300 footcandles, an air filtering system of activated charcoal, and a man-made grass field called Astroturf.

Wayne Chandler

*Asylum Creek.

*Asylums. *See* Insane in Texas, Care of.

Atakapa Indians. The Atakapa (Attacapa, Attaquapa, Attencapa, Attuckapa, Hattakappa, Tuckapa, Zacapatac) Indians lived mainly in southwestern Louisiana, but their range extended westward into Texas a short distance west of the Sabine River. The name Atakapan is now used by linguists to refer to all groups who spoke a language similar to that of the Atakapa. These Atakapan groups include the Akokisa, Bidai, Deadose, and Patiri of Texas, the Opelousa of Louisiana, and the Atakapa of both Louisiana and Texas. The differences between these various groups seem to have been more geographic than cultural. All emphasized hunting, fishing, and food-gathering but occasionally practiced agriculture. Little is known about the Atakapa who lived in Texas. The Louisiana Atakapa lost their identity early in the present century. *See* Deadose Indians; *see also* Attacapa Indians.

BIBLIOGRAPHY: J. O. Dyer, *The Lake Charles Atakapas* (1917); A. S. Gatschet and J. R. Swanton, *A Dictionary of the Atakapa Language* (1932); F. W. Hodge (ed.), *Handbook of American Indians*, I (1907); II (1910); J. R. Swanton, *Indian Tribes of the Lower Mississippi Valley and Adjacent Coast of the Gulf of Mexico* (1911), *The Indians of the Southeastern United States* (1946), and *The Indian Tribes of North America* (1952).

T. N. *Campbell*

Atanaguaypacam Indians. The Atanaguaypacam Indians (Atanaguipacane), who were apparently Coahuiltecan in speech, lived on the Gulf Coast near the mouth of the Rio Grande. In the middle eighteenth century their settlements were reported to be along the shores of the numerous small bays and islands near the mouth of the Rio Grande.

BIBLIOGRAPHY: W. Jiménez Moreno, "Tribus e idiomas del Norte de México," *El Norte de México y el Sur de Estados Unidos* (1944); G. Saldivar, *Los Indios de Tamaulipas* (1943).

T. N. *Campbell*

Atasacneu Indians. The Atasacneu (Atasacnau) Indians are known from a Spanish document of 1748 which lists twenty-five Indian groups of east-central and southeastern Texas who had asked for missions in that general area. About half the names on the list, including Atasacneu, cannot be identified. The identifiable groups consist of Caddoans (including Wichita), Tonkawans, Atakapans, and Karankawans.

BIBLIOGRAPHY: H. E. Bolton, *Texas in the Middle Eighteenth Century* (1915); F. C. Chabot (ed.), *Excerpts from the Memorias for the History of Texas, by Father Morfi* (1932); C. W. Hackett (ed.), *Pichardo's Treatise on the Limits of Louisiana and Texas*, I (1931).

T. N. *Campbell*

*Atascosa, Texas.

*Atascosa County. Atascosa County, third largest strawberry grower among Texas counties in 1960, has a diversified agriculture, with cattle and other livestock accounting for two-thirds of the farm income, and watermelons, peanuts, and truck crops accounting for the rest. Between 1917 and 1973 over 102 million barrels of oil were produced. A strawberry festival is held each April. The population was 18,828 in 1960 and 18,696 in 1970.

*Atascosa River.

*Atascosito Road.

*Atascosito Spring.

*Atastagonie Indians.

Atayo Indians. The Atayo (Atoyo, Tayo) Indians were encountered by Cabeza de Vaca qv near or along the Texas coast, apparently about 1528. Their location cannot be determined, but it seems to have been in the central section of the coast. Attempts to identify the Atayo with groups known to Europeans over 150 years later are largely speculations based on phonetic similarities in names. The Atayo have been linked with the Adai, a Caddoan group of western Louisiana, but this is no longer taken seriously. They have also been linked with the Toho (or Tojo) and Tohaha, both of which did live inland near the coastal area possibly occupied by the Atayo.

BIBLIOGRAPHY: A. F. Bandelier (ed.), *The Journey of Alvar Nuñez Cabeza de Vaca* (1922); F. W. Hodge (ed.), *Handbook of American Indians*, II (1910); J. R. Swanton, *Source Material on the History and Ethnology of the Caddo Indians* (1942).

T. N. *Campbell*

*Atchison, Daniel D.

*Atchison, Topeka, and Santa Fe Railroad. [This title was incorrectly listed in Volume I as Atchinson, Topeka, and Santa Fe Railroad.] *See* Santa Fe Railroad System.

*Ater, Texas.

*Athapascan Indians.

*Athens, Texas. Athens, seat of Henderson County, had a 1960 population of 7,086 and a 1970 population of 9,582. Industries include the manufacture of high-fidelity record players, television sets, brick and pottery, furniture, women's clothing, and also the processing of food, oil, and gas. The town is also the site of Henderson County Junior College.

Atia and Atiasnogue Indians. These names occur in a Spanish document of 1748 which lists twenty-five Indian groups of east-central and southeastern Texas who had asked for missions in that general area. About half the names on this list, including Atia (Atai) and Atisnogue, cannot be identified. The others are identifiable as Caddoans (including Wichita), Tonkawans, Atakapans, and Karankawans.

BIBLIOGRAPHY: H. E. Bolton, *Texas in the Middle Eighteenth Century* (1915); F. C. Chabot (ed.), *Excerpts from the Memorias for the History of Texas, by Father Morfi* (1932); C. W. Hackett (ed.), *Pichardo's Treatise on the Limits of Louisiana and Texas*, I (1931).

T. N. *Campbell*

*Atkins Creek.

*Atlanta, Texas. Atlanta is the principal town in Cass County, serving a forestry, farming, and oil area. Among other plants there are a lumber mill, a feed mill, and a glove manufacturing plant. Twelve miles northwest of Atlanta is Atlanta State Recreation Park (*see* Parks, State), consisting of 1,475 acres along Lake Texarkana. The 1960 population figure was 4,076, and in 1970 it was 5,007.

*Atlantic and Pacific Railroad Company.

*Atlas, Texas.

*Atlee, Edwin A., Jr.

*Atlee, Edwin Augustus.

Atmospheric Research in Texas. *See* National Center for Atmospheric Research, Scientific Balloon Flight Station.

*Atravesada Hill.

*Atreco, Texas.

*Attacapa Indians. *See also* Atacapa Indians.

*Attorney General, Office of. *See also* State Executive Officers, Compensation of.

*Attoyac, Texas.

*Attoyac Bayou.

Attwater's National Wildlife Refuge. *See* Wildlife Areas in Texas.

*Atwell, James.

Atwell, William Hawley. William Hawley Atwell was born in Sparta, Wisconsin, on June 9, 1869. When he was two years old, his parents, Captain Benjamin D. and D. E. Emma (Greene) Atwell, moved to Texas, settling at Mesquite and then at Hutchins. Atwell attended Southwestern University, from which he was graduated in 1889. He then entered the law school of the University of Texas, where, two years later, he won the Debaters Medal and received his law degree. He began law practice in Dallas in 1891 and on December 7, 1892, married Susie Snyder. They became the parents of two sons.

Active in the Republican party ᵠᵛ in Texas, Atwell served as United States attorney for the northern district of Texas from 1898 to 1913. He was named the Republican candidate for governor in 1922. The following year President Warren G. Harding appointed him judge for the northern district of Texas. He was known for his close adherence to the United States Constitution, his vigor and long hours in trying cases, his dramatizing of naturalization proceedings, and his insistence on dignity in the courtroom, where he banned smoking, removal of coats, and any kind of lawyers' horseplay. Before retiring from the bench in 1958, he had heard more than eight thousand cases. Also a civic and fraternal leader, he helped to establish the Dallas Zoo and in 1925–1926 served as national Grand Exalted Ruler of the Benevolent and Protective Order of Elks. He died in Dallas on December 22, 1961.

BIBLIOGRAPHY: William Hawley Atwell, *Autobiography* (1935); Paul D. Casdorph, *A History of the Republican Party in Texas, 1865–1965* (1965); Dallas *Morning News,* December 23, 1961.

Wayne Gard

*Atwell, Texas.

Atz, John Jacob. John Jacob (Jake) Atz was born on July 1, 1879, in Washington, D.C. He is generally considered the greatest baseball manager in Texas League ᵠᵛ history. He began his major league playing career in 1902 with Washington of the American League and later played for the Chicago White Sox in 1907–1909. Here his major league career was ended when he was hit by a pitch thrown by Walter Johnson.

Atz signed as a playing manager of the Fort Worth Cats of the Texas League in 1914. Following an argument he quit in 1916, but returned in 1917. He led Fort Worth to seven consecutive championships during 1919–1925. He remained at Fort Worth until 1929, and continued his career thereafter with clubs in Dallas, Shreveport, New Orleans, Tulsa, and Galveston. He held the following records: twenty-two years as a player and manager; eighteen years as manager of one club (Fort Worth); longest continuous service at one club (fourteen seasons with Fort Worth); and seven successive first-place finishes.

Atz's real name was Zimmerman but, according to legend, he changed it because he had played on a succession of clubs which went bankrupt, and paying their players alphabetically, the clubs frequently would run out of money before reaching the end of the alphabet. The action was typical of his flamboyant personality, which has caused many people to call him "the grandest Texas League figure of all time." Atz died on May 22, 1945, in New Orleans, Louisiana.

Joe B. Frantz

*Aubrey, William.

*Aubrey, Texas.

*Auburn, Texas.

*Audelia, Texas.

Audie Murphy Veterans Administration Hospital. *See* Veterans Administration Hospital, San Antonio.

*Auds Creek.

*Audubon, John James.

*Augusta, Texas.

*Augustine, Henry W.

*Augustus, Texas.

*Aurelia Creek.

Aurora, Texas. (Jefferson County.) Aurora, a settlement on the northwest shore of Sabine Lake as early as 1840, was abandoned by 1890, and the site later became known as Port Arthur. *See* Port Arthur, Texas.

Aurora, Texas. (Wise County.) Aurora was founded in the southeastern part of the county in 1872. In the early 1880's Aurora was the largest town in Wise County and had a population of 2,500 at one time. The lack of a railroad and a yellow fever epidemic left Aurora practically uninhabited by 1890. The post office was probably closed before 1910. *See also* Newark, Texas.

*Aury, Louis-Michel.

*Austin. The sloop-of-war *Austin* was first named *Texas* (not *Austin of Baltimore,* as stated in Volume I); the name was changed to *Austin* on April 20, 1840, and the ship was turned over to the United States Navy on May 11, 1846. The *Austin* was later towed to Pensacola, Florida, where it was grounded and broken up for scrap.

BIBLIOGRAPHY: Tom Henderson Wells, *Commodore Moore and the Texas Navy* (1960).

Tom Henderson Wells

*Austin, Emily M. *See* Perry, Emily Austin Bryan.

Austin, Gene. Gene Austin (Eugene Lucas) was born in Gainesville, Texas, on June 21, 1900. He later took the name of his stepfather, Jim Austin, who had married his mother, Serena Belle (Harrell) Lucas. He grew up in small towns in Louisiana, joined the United States Army at the age of sixteen, and served in France during World

War I. He studied both dentistry and law in Baltimore, but he decided on a singing career.

Austin never learned to read music, although he composed more than one hundred songs. One of the original crooners, his tenor voice was well known in the early days of radio and on the hand-cranked phonographs of the 1920's and 1930's. His RCA-Victor recordings sold more than eighty-six million copies, one of which, "My Blue Heaven" (1927), sold more than twelve million records. Other hit songs Austin introduced were "My Melancholy Baby," "Girl Of My Dreams," "Ramona," "Carolina Moon," and "Sleepy Time Gal." His compositions included "When My Sugar Walks Down The Street," "How Come You Do Me Like You Do?" and "Lonesome Road." He made three movies, *Sadie McKee*, *Gift of Gab*, and *Melody Cruise*.

Austin was a nightclub entertainer in the 1930's, after which his career waned; in the late 1950's his life was dramatized in a television special, and he resumed nightclub appearances. He continued to write songs until about ten months before his death.

Austin ran unsuccessfully for the Democratic nomination for governor of Nevada in 1962. He was married five times, and on his death on January 24, 1972, in Palm Springs, California, Austin was survived by his wife and two daughters by a previous marriage.

BIBLIOGRAPHY: H. Allen Smith, "A Crooner Comes Back," *Saturday Evening Post*, August 31, 1957; *Newsweek*, May 6, 1957; Austin *American-Statesman*, January 25, 1972; Dallas *Morning News*, August 6, 1956; New York *Times*, January 24, 1972.

*Austin, Henry.

*Austin, James Elijah Brown.

*Austin, John. John Austin's wife, Elizabeth E. Austin, did not die in the cholera epidemic of 1833 (as stated in Volume I), although the epidemic did claim Austin's life. John Austin had obtained two leagues of land from the Mexican government in 1824, and after his death Elizabeth Austin turned over the upper league to Austin's father, John Punderson Austin.qv In 1834 she married T. F. L. Parrott, and on August 26, 1836, she and her husband sold for $5,000 the lower half of the John Austin league on Buffalo Bayou to Augustus C. Allen and John K. Allen qqv for the Allens' proposed town of Houston.

BIBLIOGRAPHY: David G. McComb, *Houston, the Bayou City* (1969); Sister M. Agatha Sheehan, *The History of Houston Heights, 1891–1918* (1956); Joe B. Frantz (ed.), "Moses Lapham: His Life and Some Selected Correspondence, II," *Southwestern Historical Quarterly*, LIV (1950–1951); H. Bailey Carroll, "Texas Collection," *ibid.*, LXVI (1962–1963).

Sister M. Agatha Sheehan

*Austin, John Punderson.

*Austin, Maria Brown.

*Austin, Moses.

*Austin, Stephen Fuller.

*Austin, Stephen F., Jr.

*Austin, William Tennant.

*Austin, Texas. Austin, county seat of Travis

County and capital of Texas, had as its first known settler Jacob M. Harrell,qv who in 1838 (not 1835, as stated in Volume I) lived on the north bank of the Colorado River near the present Congress Avenue bridge. Prior to 1838 Harrell had been living at the Reuben Hornsby qv settlement on the Colorado River south of Austin.

In 1970 Austin was the sixth largest and one of the fastest growing cities in the state. Research and science-oriented industries were increasing in number, and the city was a popular retirement area, noted (until the 1970's) for its low cost of living. Austin had a population of 132,459 in 1950, 186,-545 in 1960, and 251,808 in 1970. Between 1960 and 1970 the population increased 35 percent. *See also* Austin Standard Metropolitan Statistical Area.

*Austin *American*. The Austin *American*, a morning newspaper published in Austin, Texas, had a daily circulation of 68,666 in March, 1973. Combined with the evening Austin *Statesman* as the Austin *American-Statesman*, it had a circulation of 93,742 on Saturday and 104,422 on Sunday. *See also* Austin *Statesman*; Austin *American-Statesman*.

Austin *American-Statesman*. In November, 1973, the Austin *American*,qv a morning newspaper, and the Austin *Statesman*,qv an evening newspaper, were combined as an all-day newspaper, issuing four daily editions, with the name Austin *American-Statesman*.

*Austin Bayou.

Austin Caverns. Austin Caverns, Austin, Travis County, have been known since the mid-1800's. The cave was operated commercially for a short period in 1932 but was soon closed and the entrance blasted shut. Rainwater and quarrying have periodically reopened the cave, requiring further blasting and filling to keep it closed. A portion of the cave now serves as a storm sewer drain.

A. Richard Smith

*Austin *City Gazette*.

*Austin College. Austin College, Sherman, increased campus facilities with additions of a gymnasium and women's dormitory (1950), student union and health center (1951), men's and women's dormitories (1957), chapel (1958), 76,000-volume library and stadium (1960), music building (1962), Caruth Hall (1963), and science center and men's dormitory (1965). Adjacent to the campus, residences for the president and dean of the college were completed in 1957 and 1960.

The college received a $1,700,000 grant from the Ford Foundation in 1962, which it matched with over $3,700,000. Several private foundations and individuals also contributed generously to the school's expansion. Enrollment increased from 712 students in 1962 to 1,162 students in 1974. In 1953 John D. Moseley succeeded William Barnett Guerrant, Sr., as president of the Presbyterian college, and Moseley was still president in 1974. *See also* Presbyterian Education in Texas.

Austin Community College. Austin Community

College, a two-year institution of higher education, was established in Austin late in 1972 to serve the capital area of Texas. Students of all ages, ethnic groups, and educational backgrounds were enrolled; classes opened in September, 1973, in several locations in the city. Administrative offices were on the Ridgeview campus, the old Anderson High School building in East Austin.

The college holds membership in the Association of Texas Colleges and Universities,qv the American Association of Community and Junior Colleges, and the Texas Public Junior College Association. In 1974 it was a candidate for accreditation with the Southern Association of Colleges and Schools.

Thomas M. Hatfield was named president by the school board of the Austin Independent School District, the governing body of the college. The fall, 1974, enrollment was 7,061.

*Austin County. Austin County's economy is mainly agricultural, ranking high in livestock and poultry production, from which three-fourths of the county's farm income was derived in 1972. Rice and cotton are also cultivated in considerable quantity. Hardwood lumber and oil (over eighty-seven million barrels produced between 1915 and 1973) are other significant economic factors. Small industries, mostly growing out of lumbering and agriculture, are centered in Bellville, the county seat, and Sealy. The village of San Felipe and nearby Stephen F. Austin State Park (see Parks, State) are major tourist attractions. Austin County had a population of 13,777 in 1960 and 13,831 in 1970.

*Austin Dam and Suburban Railway Company.

*Austin Female Academy.

*Austin Female Collegiate Institute.

*Austin Lyceum.

*Austin and Northwestern Railroad Company. The Austin and Northwestern Railroad, although chartered by Iowa businessmen (as stated in Volume I), also had local businessmen on its board of directors. The charter granted by the secretary of state, dated April 29, 1881, shows that the promoters asked for a strictly commercial authorization, the line to run from Austin to Abilene, with a branch line or spur to run northwest from "at or near Burnet." Burnet was as far as the rails were laid, and the line was used to haul granite (not marble, as stated in Volume I) for the building of the Texas Capitol.qv The first train reached Burnet on April 30, 1882, but there was as yet no decision as to what stone was finally to be used in the building of the Capitol in Austin. The final decision to use granite was not reached until July 25, 1885, and the facts that the railroad existed for fifty-five of the seventy-one-mile distance from Austin to Granite Mountain qv and that the granite was offered free probably had something to do with the decision. A narrow-gauge railroad was built from Burnet to Granite Mountain.

Tad Moses

*Austin and Oatmanville Railway Company.

*Austin Presbyterian Theological Seminary. Austin Presbyterian Theological Seminary, Austin, had an average enrollment of 150 students between 1950 and 1965; enrollment for the 1972–1973 regular session was 144. New administration and classroom buildings were completed in 1963, as well as a home for the dean of students in 1965. The seminary library, remodeled in 1964, contained a collection of over 88,000 volumes in 1969, in addition to microfilms and microcards, minutes of Reformed churches, journals, and serials. A rare book collection included 5,000 volumes of materials written by reformers, such as Luther, Calvin, and Zwingli. The library mailing service provided books upon request to ministers and laymen. Additional building plans called for expansion of the chapel and for a new refectory and student union building.

In 1971 the faculty consisted of fifteen teaching members, including Rachel Henderlite, the first ordained woman minister in the Presbyterian church. Several assistantships are available. Sixty-seven percent of the Presbyterian churches in Texas were staffed by ministers who received at least one degree from the Austin seminary. *See also* Presbyterian Education in Texas.

*Austin School of Theology. *See also* Presbyterian Education in Texas.

Austin Standard Metropolitan Statistical Area. The Austin Standard Metropolitan Statistical Area consisted of Travis County and encompassed 1,015 square miles. Created in 1949 by the Bureau of the Budget, it had a population of 160,980 in 1950, while Austin, its central city, had 132,459. Ten years later Travis County contained 212,136 inhabitants and Austin, 186,545. The 1970 United States census showed a population of 295,516 in the metropolitan area and 251,808 in the city of Austin. Increasingly the county's population is being concentrated within the city limits of Austin. This trend is reflected in the 41 percent increase in the city's population and the 10 percent decrease in the non-Austin population of the county between 1950 and 1960. By the mid-1960's about 90 percent of the area's inhabitants lived in Austin. Other incorporated towns are Manor, West Lake Hills, Rollingwood, Pflugerville, and Sunset Valley. Smaller unincorporated communities include Jonestown, Creedmoor, Manchaca, Del Valle, Cedar Valley, Elroy, Bee Caves, Kimbro, McNeill, New Sweden, Garfield, and Littig.

Austin dominates the metropolitan area and is the home of its principal economic bases. The city serves as a headquarters for state and federal offices, educational institutions, insurance companies, associations and organizations, and conventions. Approximately eighty state and fifty federal agencies were the area's leading employers in 1966. They were closely followed by the educational institutions, trade and professional associations, insurance companies, Bergstrom Air Force Base,qv and the new United States Bureau of Internal Revenue

Regional Service Center. In 1960 over 50 percent of the area's population held white collar positions, while less than 8 percent were employed in manufacturing industries. Over two hundred manufacturers were located in Austin in 1966, but only twelve employed more than one hundred persons. The principal commodities produced and processed were foods and soft drinks, books and other printed materials, boats, concrete materials, furniture and fixtures, machinery and parts, bus bodies, nuclear devices, chemical products, lime and limestone, plastics, industrial instruments, electronic equipment, household cleaning utensils, and fabricated metal products. In the mid-1960's the Austin area was rapidly developing into a national center for public and private research in such fields as electronics, chemistry, and engineering. Conventions and tourism also have become major contributors to the income of the area. In 1966 Austin ranked third among Texas cities in the number of conventions hosted. The Southwest Conference qv football games of the University of Texas at Austin and the Texas League qv Austin Braves (now defunct) baseball team attracted a large number of sports fans. Agricultural activity in the metropolitan area is of relatively minor significance. Three-fifths of the farm income originates from the raising of dairy cattle, sheep, and poultry, while hay, grains, and cotton supply most of the remaining income.

The Robert Mueller Municipal Airport terminal, completed in 1961, serves three major airlines. Three railroads and a good highway system, which includes Interstate 35, also connect the area with the rest of Texas. A municipal auditorium and convention center, constructed in 1959, helped attract eighty-eight thousand delegates to the area in 1965. Nine radio stations, three television stations, and two daily newspapers distributed information throughout the Austin area. Five hospitals served the area. Bergstrom Air Force Base, located seven miles southeast of Austin, was a major air installation.

The University of Texas at Austin dominates the educational scene, enrolling a majority of the college students in the Austin area. Other schools are St. Edward's University, Huston-Tillotson College, Concordia Lutheran College, Austin Community College, the Austin Presbyterian Theological Seminary, and the Episcopal Theological Seminary of the Southwest. In addition to the huge library holdings of the University of Texas, Austin has its own public library and the Texas State Library and Archives. Austin is also a prominent cultural center of the Southwestern United States. The University of Texas annually presents an excellent fine arts program and its Cultural Entertainment Committee brings some of the world's finest artists to Austin. The city supports the Austin Symphony Orchestra, the Zachary Scott Theatre, and the Austin Civic Ballet. The Laguna Gloria Art Museum, the Elisabet Ney Museum,qqv and the University of Texas Art Museum house displays of the visual arts. Other museums, which concentrate on the his-

torical aspects of Texas, are the Texas Confederate Museum, the O. Henry Museum,qv the Daughters of the Republic of Texas qv Museum, the Daughters of the Confederacy qv Museum, the French Legation,qv and the Texas Memorial Museum.qv As the capital of Texas, Austin has many historical monuments, sites, and homes.

The area has extensive recreational facilities. In 1960 the completion of the Longhorn Crossing Dam created Town Lake. Together with the lake formed by Tom Miller Dam, Austin has twenty-eight miles of lake area within its city limits. Zilker Park, with its famed Barton Springs,qv is the city's biggest park. Since 1962 the annual Aqua Festival has developed into one of the nation's ten largest festivals. To the west of the Austin area lies the Highland Lakes country. After Lyndon B. Johnson qv became president of the United States in 1963, the Austin and Highland Lakes area received a substantial boost as a tourist mecca. *See also* Standard Metropolitan Statistical Areas in Texas. [Hays County was added to the Austin Standard Metropolitan Statistical Area in April, 1973. Ed.]

BIBLIOGRAPHY: Austin, Texas, Chamber of Commerce, *Austin Invites You to Share Texas' Scientific, Educational, and Recreational Center* (1966); Austin, Texas, Chamber of Commerce, *Directory of Associations Maintaining Headquarters in Austin, Texas* (1965); Austin, Texas, Department of Planning, *Basic Data About Austin and Travis County, 1965.*

Sam A. Suhler

*Austin State Hospital. The Austin State Hospital had an average daily population in 1968 of 3,313, and approximately 900 elderly patients were maintained on furlough in private facilities. The institution provided surgical services for residents and for persons from the Austin State School, Travis State School, and the Confederate Home for Men qqv (before it was closed in 1967). An adult out-patient clinic was operated by the hospital, with referrals to Travis County Mental Health and Mental Retardation Clinic, and to various home county community health centers around the state. Admissions of younger patients, alcoholic patients, and drug abusers increased in 1970, and the average daily census was 1,994. *See* Mentally Ill and Mentally Retarded, Care of, in Texas.

BIBLIOGRAPHY: Board for Texas State Hospitals and Special Schools, *Report* (1964); Texas Department of Mental Health and Mental Retardation, *Annual Report, 1970.*

*Austin State School. The Austin State School served as an admission center for 102 counties, with 2,291 students residing on the main and annex campuses in July, 1968. The annex, acquired in 1960, was one mile from the main school and was formerly occupied by the Texas Blind, Deaf, and Orphan School.qv Special education classes were conducted for the educable and trainable students. In 1970 the basic treatment programs were reorganized for greater emphasis on resident-centered services, and the census at the end of the year was 2,096. *See* Mentally Ill and Mentally Retarded, Care of, in Texas.

BIBLIOGRAPHY: Board for Texas State Hospitals and Special Schools, *Report* (1964); Texas Department of Mental Health and Mental Retardation, *Annual Report, 1970.*

***Austin State School Farm Colony.** *See also* Travis State School.

*Austin *Statesman.* The Austin *Statesman,* an evening newspaper published in Austin, Texas, had a daily circulation of 34,309 in March, 1973. Combined with the morning Austin *American* as the Austin *American-Statesman,* it had a circulation of 93,742 on Saturday and 104,422 on Sunday. *See also* Austin *American*; Austin *American-Statesman.*

***Austinia, Texas.**

***Austonio, Texas.**

***Austwell, Texas.**

***Authon, Texas.**

***Automatic Tax Board.** *See* Tax Board: To Calculate Ad Valorem Tax Rate.

***Autry, Micajah.**

***Available School Fund.** *See* School Fund, Available.

Available University Fund. *See* University Fund, Available.

***Avalon, Texas.**

***Avavare Indians.**

***Avery, Texas.**

***Avery Canyon.**

***Aves, Henry Damerel.**

***Aviation in Texas.** When World War II ended, all but twelve of the thirty-four army air force installations in Texas were deactivated. Most of the training sites reverted to the communities or counties from which they had been purchased or leased. The Flying Training Command was moved from Fort Worth to Washington, D.C. In 1947, when the United States Air Force became a separate military service, all of the active army air fields in the state became air force bases. At that time many of them were renamed for individuals lost during the war. San Antonio continued to serve as the focal point for Texas military aerial activity. Randolph, Kelly, and Brooks qqv served as pilot training bases. The old San Antonio Aviation Cadet Center was renamed Lackland Air Force Base,qv and it became the receiving and training center for all incoming enlisted personnel, as well as the location of the air force's Officer Candidate School. In 1950, with the onset of the Korean conflict, World War II installations at Del Rio, Harlingen, Victoria, Bryan, and Laredo were reactivated. New bases were built at Abilene and Austin. Following the Korean armistice, world conditions necessitated the continued operation of all of the Texas installations. In 1957, as an economy measure, Foster Air Force Base,qv near Victoria, was closed, and its air defense mission was transferred. Economy necessitated the closing of Harlingen in 1960. Its navigation mission was moved to James Connally Air Force Base,qv Waco. The Department of Defense announced in 1962, and again in 1965, that military installations in Texas and elsewhere would be deactivated for economic reasons. In 1967 James Connally Air Force Base was in the process of being closed.

In 1967 Randolph Air Force Base served as headquarters for the Air Training Command and also as the site of the United States Air Force Personnel Center. Limited flying training continued at Randolph, but was devoted solely to the training of instructor pilots for the training command's far-flung activities. Kelly Air Force Base was a major air materiel depot, responsible for the modification and maintenance of many types of aircraft, and also served as a supply point for parts and equipment which were shipped worldwide. The U.S. Air Force's Aerospace Medical Center was at Brooks. Personnel of that organization worked closely with those of the National Aeronautics and Space Administration's Manned Spacecraft Center,qv which, in 1967, directed the Gemini, Apollo, and other space programs. Located twenty-two miles southeast of Houston on a one-thousand-acre site which was selected in 1961, the center's facilities cost in excess of $150,000,000, and it was estimated that when the complex is completed the cost will exceed $250,000,000. This will make the Manned Spacecraft Center the most expensive aeronautical facility in Texas, if not in the nation. In 1964 the space center employed 2,900 people, and an additional 590 NASA employees worked at Ellington Air Force Base,qv Houston, which served as a support facility for the main center. (*See* Manned Spacecraft Center for more recent information.)

In 1967 the Air Training Command controlled the activities of seven of the thirteen active installations in Texas. Lackland continued to serve as a receiving center and officer training school. Sheppard Air Force Base,qv near Wichita Falls, and Amarillo Air Force Base qv trained aircraft and missile maintenance personnel. Laughlin Air Force Base, Del Rio; Reese Air Force Base, Lubbock; Laredo Air Force Base; and Webb Air Force Base,qqv Big Spring, were the pilot training installations within Texas. In the 1960's a student pilot received his flight training and his wings at the base where he entered the program. All pilot instruction was conducted in jet aircraft. Other major air commands were responsible for the remaining active installations in the state. The Tactical Air Command (TAC) controlled the operations of Perrin Air Force Base, near Sherman, and Bergstrom Air Force Base,qqv at Austin. In 1967 headquarters for TAC's 12th Air Force was located in downtown Waco, but plans had been made to transfer it to Bergstrom. Goodfellow Air Force Base,qv near San Angelo, was the home of the United States Air Force Security Service. Strategic Air Command (SAC) directed the activities of Carswell Air Force Base, Fort Worth, and Dyess Air Force Base, Abilene.qqv In addition, SAC shared the facilities at Amarillo and utilized the bombing range at Matagorda Island. Naval aviators continued to be trained at Corpus Christi and Dallas naval air stations,qqv and at Kingsville and Beeville naval auxiliary air stations.qqv The final phases of the navy's multi-engine training were carried out at Corpus Christi.

Kingsville and Beeville served as the bases providing the last stages of the naval aviator's all-jet training program. Upon completion of training at any of those installations the student was designated a naval aviator. Although the bulk of the army's aviation training was in Alabama in 1967, many Texas posts were equipped to handle light planes and helicopters. Jet aircraft, missiles, and space technology have resulted in new concepts and innovations in the field of aeronautics. As a result, major changes have taken place in the type of training provided aviation-oriented young men who entered the service.

As advances in aeronautical design and engineering have progressed, civil aviation interest has expanded. When the Texas State Aviation Association was organized in Dallas in 1948, there were 6,804 aircraft and 20,700 licensed pilots in the state. On January 1, 1965, the Federal Aviation Agency's records indicated that there were 11,093 airplanes registered in Texas, 7,381 of them in active use. Only 141 of these active planes were commercial aircraft, the remainder being classed as general aviation-type vehicles. In 1964 Texas had an average of 27.6 airplanes per one thousand square miles of territory, or 7.1 aircraft per ten thousand population. Pilot licenses had been issued to 31,-373 Texas residents in that year. On January 1, 1965, there were 812 active airports, compared with 669 on the same date in 1957, and 470 in 1948. Private facilities, 600 in all, comprised the bulk of the state's 812 airports. Itinerant aircraft traffic made Love Field,qv Dallas, the fifth busiest airport in the nation during 1964. Over 251,000 planes were recorded as having utilized its facilities.

While private aviation activity has shown a marked increase since 1948, a similar enthusiasm for commercial air travel has been noted. Dallas was rated tenth in the country as a commercial aviation center in 1964, recording 146,447 scheduled arrivals and departures. In 1966 eleven airlines served Texas, and thirty-one cities received regularly scheduled air service. The sixth largest air passenger carrier in the United States, Braniff International Airways, maintained its headquarters in Dallas. This company, which served most of the Central, Eastern, and Pacific Northwest portions of the nation, as well as Mexico, Panama, and South America, was almost entirely equipped with modern jet aircraft. Until 1955 three local service lines—Pioneer Airlines, Central Airlines, and Trans-Texas Airways—were located in the state. Pioneer, the oldest local service line in the state, was first established as Essair in 1939, but route disputes with Braniff curtailed its operations the same year. In 1945 it again offered local service, adopting the name Pioneer Airlines. Operating from Dallas, and utilizing DC-3 equipment, it served the greater portion of the state. In 1955 this firm merged with Continental Airlines of Los Angeles. In point of service Trans-Texas Airways ranked second, beginning its operations in 1947. Central Airlines, although organized earlier, did not inaugurate service

until 1949. Trans-Texas (later renamed Texas International) maintained its main offices in Houston and offered service to residents of Texas, Louisiana, Arkansas, Tennessee, and the Southwest. Central Airlines, serving North and Northwest Texas, Arkansas, Colorado, Kansas, Missouri, and Oklahoma, was based in Fort Worth.

The high-pitched whine of jet turbines has all but replaced the sound of reciprocating engines at most commercial and many private airports. It is doubtful that there is any part of Texas which has not heard the sound of some type of aircraft engine, and in some remote areas the airplane is a more common sight than the automobile. Aviation and its allied activities—aircraft sales, maintenance and repair, and airport operation and maintenance—have become big business in the state.

BIBLIOGRAPHY: Tom Compere (ed.), *The Air Force Blue Book*, I (1959); R. E. G. Davies, *A History of the World's Airlines* (1964).

Robert E. Hays, Jr.

*Avinger, Texas.

*Avoca, Texas.

*Avondale, Texas.

*Axson, Stockton.

*Axtell, Texas.

*Ayers, Lewis T.

Ayers, Texas. Ayers (Washington County), no longer in existence, was founded by David Ayers,qv who changed the spelling of his family name from Ayers. It was once a prosperous business town.
BIBLIOGRAPHY: *Texas Almanac* (1936).

*Ayish Bayou.

*Aynesworth, Kenneth Hazen.

*Ayr, Texas.

Ayres, Atlee Bernard. Atlee Bernard Ayres was born in Hillsboro, Ohio, on July 12, 1873, the son of Nathan Tandy and Mary Parsons (Atlee) Ayres. He came to Texas as a child with his family. They lived first in Houston and then moved in 1888 to San Antonio, where his father for many years managed the Alamo Flats, a luxury apartment hotel. In 1890 Ayres went to New York, where he studied at the Metropolitan School of Architecture, a subsidiary of Columbia University. There he won first prize in the school's annual design competition. He took drawing lessons at the Art Students League at night and studied painting under Frank Vincent Dumont on Sundays. Upon his graduation from the school of architecture in 1894 he returned to San Antonio, worked for various architects, then practiced in Mexico until 1900, when he began his own firm in San Antonio.

In Austin his firm designed the Blind Institute qv and, on the University of Texas campus, Carothers Dormitory and the Pharmacy Building. He drew plans for courthouses in Kingsville, Alice, Refugio, Del Rio, and Brownsville. In San Antonio he personally designed the exterior of the Municipal Auditorium (1923) and the Administration Building at Randolph Air Force Base,qv known as the "Taj

Mahal," with a tower which conceals a 500,000-gallon water tank. In 1924 his son, Robert M. Ayres, became part of the architectural firm of Atlee B. and Robert M. Ayres. In San Antonio the firm designed the thirty-five-story Smith-Young Tower, the Plaza and Menger hotels, and the Federal Reserve, Groos National, and Frost National banks. He designed the Spanish-style home of Marion Koogler McNay qv along with numerous other mansions in San Antonio. He was the author of the book *Mexican Architecture* (1926), a collection of photographs, drawings, and text on buildings of colonial Mexico.

Ayres was a charter member of the Texas Society of Architects. He was one of three architects instrumental in securing passage of state legislation in 1937 for the licensing of architects to practice, and he received license number 3. He married Olive Moss Cox in San Antonio in 1896, and the couple had two sons. After Mrs. Ayres' death in 1937 he married Katherine Cox, his second cousin, in 1940. Ayres died on November 6, 1969, in San Antonio, and he was buried in Mission Burial Park.

BIBLIOGRAPHY: E. A. Luck, *Greater San Antonio: The City of Destiny* (1919); M. J. Sullivan (ed.), *International Blue Book* (1912); Bonnie Sue Jacobs, "Trails and Tangents," San Antonio *Express*, March 15, 1972; Biographical File, Barker Texas History Center, University of Texas at Austin.

Ayres, Clarence Edwin. Clarence Edwin Ayres, longtime economics professor at the University of Texas at Austin and distinguished writer and theorist in the field of economics, was born in Lowell, Massachusetts, the son of William S. and Emma (Young) Ayres, on May 6, 1891. He received B.A. and M.A. degrees from Brown University in 1912 and 1914. He studied at Harvard in 1914 and received the Ph.D. degree in economics and philosophy from the University of Chicago in 1917. He was a member of Phi Beta Kappa. In 1918 Ayres wrote *The Nature of the Relationship Between Ethics and Economics*. After having taught at the University of Chicago, Amherst College, Reed College, the University of Wisconsin, and New York University, he came to the University of Texas in 1930, where he taught until 1969. He conducted graduate and senior seminars on institutionalism, formation of political economy, industrial economy, and the technological revolution in Western civilization.

From 1924 to 1925 he was an associate editor of the *New Republic* and also was a member of the editorial board of the *American Economic Review*. In 1936 he was director of the consumers division of the United States Department of Labor. It was during this time that he wrote *The Problem of Economic Order* (1938).

Ayres was brought into statewide and national news in the years following World War II, when he spoke out for academic freedom for university teachers. His article, "Academic Freedom in Texas" appeared in the *New Republic* in December, 1944. During this time he also wrote *The Theory of Economic Progress* (1944). In 1951 he was investigated by the state legislature at the behest of Marshall O. Bell, representative from San Antonio, who accused Ayres of advocating socialism and questioned the theories in Ayres' book, *The Divine Right of Capital* (1946). He was defended in the legislature by Representative John Barnhart. The board of regents took no action against Ayres. In 1952 his *The Industrial Economy: Its Technological Basis and Institutional Destiny* was a continuation of his probing into mid-twentieth-century economic practices and philosophies. He was a member of the Committee on the Southwest Economy for the President's [Harry S. Truman's] Council of Economic Advisors (1950–1953), and a director of the San Antonio branch of the Dallas Federal Reserve Bank (1954–1959).

In the 1960's Ayres was a governor of the Federal Reserve Board, received the University of Texas Students' Association award for teaching excellence, and was the first president of the Association for Evolutionary Economics (1966). He was a twenty-year national committeeman of the American Civil Liberties Union, and served as president of the Southwestern Social Science Association. In 1962 his *Toward a Reasonable Society: The Values of Industrial Civilization* was published.

Clarence Ayres was married to Ann Bryan in 1915; they had three children. His second marriage, in 1926, was to artist Gwendolen Jane. He had been visiting his summer home in New Mexico when he died in Alamagordo, New Mexico, on July 24, 1972.

BIBLIOGRAPHY: Biographical File, Barker Texas History Center, University of Texas at Austin.

*Ayres, David. David Ayres died on October 25, 1881 (not in 1878, as stated in Volume I).

BIBLIOGRAPHY: *Texas Christian Advocate*, November 5, 1881.

Walter N. Vernon

Ayres, Mother M. Angelique. Mother Mary Angelique Ayres, co-founder of Our Lady of the Lake College, was born Claudia Ayres, a daughter of Nannie (Lowry) and Eli Snow Ayres, at Kosciusko, Mississippi, on April 12, 1882. As the first American-born superior-general of the Sisters of Divine Providence qv and as dean of Our Lady of the Lake College, San Antonio, Texas, for more than forty years, Mother Angelique was directly responsible for instituting many of the modern administrative and educational concepts now prevailing in Texas institutions of higher learning. Mother Angelique took the A.M. degree at Catholic University of America and later matriculated in Columbia University for the Ph.D. degree. She was professor of English and mathematics at Our Lady of the Lake College, 1911–1912; professor of English, 1914–1943; registrar and dean, 1913–1924; dean until 1958; in 1943 she was elected superior general of the Organization of Sisters of Divine Providence. She was a member of the Southern Conference of College Deans and a co-founder and member-at-large of Delta Epsilon Sigma, national

Catholic honor fraternity. She was a frequent contributor to educational journals and collaborated with Sister M. Generosa Callahan on *The History of the Sisters of Divine Providence in Texas*. Ayres Hall, a girls residence hall at Our Lady of the Lake College, was named to honor the religious and educational distinction attained by Mother Angelique Ayres. She died on September 13, 1968, and was buried in Providence Cemetery in San Antonio.

BIBLIOGRAPHY: John Bennett Boddie, *Historical Southern Families*, X (1965); Sister Generosa Callahan, *History of the Sisters of Divine Providence in Texas* (1955); *Directory of American Scholars* (1942).

Mildred Alice Webb

*Ayuntamiento.

*Azle, Texas. Azle, in Tarrant and Parker counties, had a population of 2,969 in 1960 and 4,493 in 1970.

B

*B. O. Branch.

*Baber, Texas.

*Baby Head, Texas.

*Babyhead Creek.

*Babyhead Mountain.

Bache, Alexander Dallas. Alexander Dallas Bache was born in Philadelphia on July 19, 1806, eldest child of Sophia (Dallas) and Richard Bache.qv A great-grandson of Benjamin Franklin, in a family distinguished by its physicists and scientists, he served at Galveston as the first superintendent in Texas of the United States Coast Survey from 1846 to 1861. Although Commodore Edwin Moore,qv Captain George Simpton, and Captain Perry W. Humphrey of the Texas Navy qv had made surveys and maps of the Texas coast, and military engineers attached to General Zachary Taylor's qv army had surveyed the section of the coast between Corpus Christi and Paso Caballo in 1845–1846, Dr. Bache's charting of the Gulf Coast from Point Isabel (later Port Isabel) to Florida appears to have been the first scientific cartography of the coast of Texas. The numerous maps and charts made under his supervision during his fifteen-year tenure are in the National Archives. Being loyal to the Union and, perhaps, discouraged by the confiscation of his equipment by Confederate authorities, he returned to Washington after secession, and was adviser to the United States Navy Department during the Civil War. He wrote numerous reports of his surveys of the Texas coast, which appeared in the annual reports of his department, and he wrote articles which appeared in the early issues of the *Texas Almanac*.qv

Professor Bache made notable contributions to science during his national and international career. Among other distinctions, he was the first president of Girard College at Philadelphia. He died on February 17, 1867.

BIBLIOGRAPHY: *Dictionary of American Biography*, I (1957).

Hobart Huson

*Bache, Richard.

*Bachman, Texas.

*Bachman Branch.

*Back Peak.

*Backbone Creek.

*Backbone Ridge.

*Bacon, Sumner.

*Badger, Texas. (Burnet County.)

*Badger, Texas. (Ector County.)

*Badgett, Jesse B.

*Baffin Bay. During the latter half of the nineteenth century this body of water was recorded on maps as Salt Lagoon. Official designations today refer to it as Baffin Bay, although earlier in the twentieth century it was listed on maps as Baffins Bay (as shown in Volume I).

*Bagby, Arthur Pendleton.

*Bagby, Ballard C.

*Bagby, Thomas M.

*Bagby, Texas.

*Bagdad, Texas. (Taylor County.)

*Bagdad, Texas. (Williamson County.)

*Bagwell, Texas.

*Bahía Road. *See* La Bahía Road.

*Bailey, James Briton (Brit).

*Bailey, James Robinson.

*Bailey, Joseph Weldon.

*Bailey, Joseph Weldon, Jr.

*Bailey, Mollie.

*Bailey, Rufus William.

*Bailey, Texas.

*Bailey County. Bailey County, in the Panhandle on the New Mexico state line, ranked among the state's agricultural leaders in 1968. The county, with its 130,000 irrigated acres, excelled in crop value and in the production of grain sorghums and cotton (72,091 bales came from the county's twenty gins in 1968). In addition, alfalfa and truck crops were grown on a large scale. Farm income was $25,820,000 in the 1968 agricultural census. Population, which increased tenfold from 1920 to 1930 and doubled from 1930 to 1960, stood at 9,090 in 1960 and was 8,487 in 1970. Muleshoe National Wildlife Refuge,qv in southern Bailey County, is located on the western flyway.

*Bailey Creek.

*Baileyboro, Texas.

*Bailey's Prairie, Texas.

*Baileyville, Texas.

*Bainer, Texas. [Out of alphabetical order on page 106, Volume I.]

Baines, George Washington. George Washington Baines was born on December 29, 1809, near Raleigh, North Carolina, the son of Mary (McCoy) and Thomas Baines and the grandson of Baptist minister George Bains (English spelling), who emigrated from Ireland. The family moved to Georgia in 1817 and to a farm near Tuscaloosa, Alabama, the following year. With a sparse academic background and defrayment of expenses by cutting and rafting timber, the ambitious young man entered the University of Alabama. During his senior year in 1836, he was forced to withdraw because of ill health. He had been licensed to preach on July 20, 1834, and on August 7, 1836, he was ordained at Grant's Church, his father being one of the signers of both the license and certificate of ordination. In 1837 in the hope of recuperation he moved to Carroll County, Arkansas, where he founded three churches and baptized 150 converts. During three of his seven years in Arkansas, Baines held a commission from the Baptist Home Mission Board of New York. He was also a representative from Carroll County to the Fourth Legislature of Arkansas from November 7, 1842, to February 4, 1843.

On October 20, 1840, Baines married Melissa Ann Butler, daughter of Nealy Butler, and returned on horseback to the log cabin which he had built. One of the ten children born to the couple, Joseph Wilson Baines,qv was the father of Rebekah Baines Johnson,qv the mother of United States President Lyndon Baines Johnson.qv

In July, 1844, Baines moved to Mt. Lebanon, Louisiana, preaching there and at Minden, Saline, and other churches in the area. During his six-year Louisiana sojourn he served for a time as superintendent of schools in the Bienville Parish and assisted John Bryce in organizing the First Baptist Church of Marshall, Texas, in 1847. After a seventeen-day trek in 1850, Baines located his family at Huntsville, where he preached and also began a life-long friendship with Sam Houston. In 1851 he was pastor at Independence and in 1852 at Anderson, where he also assumed editorship of the first Baptist paper in Texas, *The Texas Baptist*, founded in 1855.

Baines was named president of Baylor University in 1861. Faced with almost insurmountable problems during the Civil War years, he maintained the fledgling school for two years at great sacrifice to his health. Baylor University conferred on him an honorary M.A. degree on July 27, 1861. Upon his resignation from the presidency, Baines moved to a farm near Fairfield and held churches in Freestone County. There his wife and youngest son died. On June 13, 1865, Baines married Mrs. Cynthia W. Williams. In the fall of 1866 he traveled as agent for the Baptist State Convention and the following year moved his family to Salado, where he was pastor. In 1877 he became an agent for the Education Commission of the Baptist State Convention, but in 1881 the Salado church insisted that he reenter the pastorate there. After the death of his wife, in January, 1882, he made his home with his daughter, Anna, in Belton until his death of malaria fever on December 28, 1882. He was buried at Salado.

BIBLIOGRAPHY: J. B. Link (ed.), *Texas Historical and Biographical Magazine*, I (1891).

Lois Smith Murray

*Baines, Joseph Wilson.

*Bainville, Texas.

*Baird, Charles.

*Baird, Raleigh William.

*Baird, Spruce McCoy.

*Baird, Texas. Baird, seat and commercial center of Callahan County, was a railroad division point in 1965. The town had twenty-three businesses in 1970, including an oil refinery and a feed mill. The county-owned hospital is in Baird. The 1960 population was 1,633; in 1970 the population was 1,538.

Bajunero Indians. In 1683–1684 Juan Domínguez de Mendoza qv led an exploratory expedition from El Paso as far eastward as the junction of the Concho and Colorado rivers east of present San Angelo. In his itinerary he listed the names of thirty-seven Indian groups, including the Bajunero (Baijunero), from whom he expected to receive delegations. Nothing further is known about the Bajunero, who seem to have been one of many Indian groups of north-central Texas that were swept away by the southward thrust of the Lipan-Apache and Comanche Indians in the eighteenth century.

BIBLIOGRAPHY: H. E. Bolton (ed.), *Spanish Exploration in the Southwest, 1542–1706* (1916); C. W. Hackett (ed.), *Pichardo's Treatise on the Limits of Louisiana and Texas*, II (1934).

T. N. Campbell

*Baker, Anderson Y.

*Baker, Andrew Jackson.

*Baker, Benjamin M.

Baker, Burke. Burke Baker was born in Waco, Texas, on August 9, 1887, the son of Nellie (Faulkner) and Robert Holmes Baker.qv He attended the University of Texas, receiving the B.A. degree in 1909. The following academic year, he studied at Harvard University. He married Bennie Brown of Cleburne on October 11, 1911, and they had two sons and two daughters. Following service in Houston with the Texas Trust Company and the Bankers Trust Company in 1915, Baker moved to Philadelphia, where he was named president of American Briquet Company. In 1919 he returned to Houston, where he was first an independent oil operator and then an insurance executive. In 1925 he founded Seaboard Life Insurance Company. He later became president and chairman of the board of American General Life Insurance Company and was also a director of the United Gas Corporation and the Manchester Terminal Corporation.

Baker was active in civic affairs, being general director of the city's first Community Chest campaign, chairman of the Civil Service Commission, and director of the Philosophical Society of Texas.qv

In December, 1961, he contributed $250,000 for the establishment of the Burke Baker Planetarium in the Houston Museum of Natural Science ᵠᵛ in the city's Hermann Park. Baker died on April 9, 1964, in Houston.

BIBLIOGRAPHY: Houston *Chronicle*, August 30, 1957, April 13, 1964; *Who's Who in the South and Southwest* (1961).

Clay Bailey

*Baker, Cullen Montgomery.

*Baker, D. Davis D.

*Baker, Daniel.

†Baker, DeWitt Clinton. DeWitt Clinton Baker was the son of Symonds William and Mary Ann (Watson) Baker (not Mary Bennington Baker, as stated in Volume I).

Ethel Mary Franklin Smith

*Baker, F. C.

*Baker, James Addison.

*Baker, James B.

*Baker, James H.

*Baker, John Holland.

*Baker, John Reagan.

*Baker, John W.

*Baker, Joseph. Joseph Baker was buried in Oakwood Cemetery in Austin (not Oakland Cemetery, as stated in Volume I).

Baker, Karle (Wilson). Karle (Wilson) Baker, known as the "poet of quiet things," was born in Little Rock, Arkansas, on October 13, 1878, the daughter of William Thomas and Kate Florence (Montgomery) Wilson. She received her early education in Little Rock Academy. After teaching for four years in Bristol, Virginia, and in Little Rock, in 1901 she came to Nacogdoches, Texas, where she married Thomas Ellis Baker on August 8, 1907; they had two children. Although not a college graduate, she attended the University of Chicago, where she came under the literary influence of William Vaughn Moody and Robert Herrick; the University of California; and Columbia University. In 1924 Mrs. Baker was awarded an honorary Litt.D. degree by Southern Methodist University. In 1925 she became acting professor of English at Stephen F. Austin State Teachers College (now Stephen F. Austin State University), and was assistant professor (1927–1934). She was a member of the Poetry Society of America and Phi Beta Kappa, a charter member of the Philosophical Society of Texas,ᵠᵛ and a fellow of the Texas Institute of Letters,ᵠᵛ which she served as president in 1938–1939. She was also a charter member and the first vice-president of the Poetry Society of Texas.ᵠᵛ

Mrs. Baker published her early work under the name of Charlotte Wilson. She contributed poems to a number of anthologies and to such magazines as *Scribner's*, *Harper's*, *Century*, *Atlantic Monthly*, and the *Yale Review Magazine*. Her first collection of poems was *Blue Smoke* (1919); selections from it were included in *Burning Bush* (1922); and various periodical pieces appeared in a third col-

lection, *Dreamers on Horseback* (1931). Her verses are primarily in the lyric tradition of British and American nature poets, and deal mainly with nature, Texas, the family, and home life. In 1925 she received the Southern Prize from the Poetry Society of South Carolina. Her prose works include a collection of children's stories, *The Garden of the Plynck* (1920); a volume of prose stories, *Old Coins* (1923); a collection of essays, *The Birds of Tanglewood* (1930); two novels, *Family Style* (1937) and *Star of the Wilderness* (1942); and *The Texas Flag Primer* (1925), which was adopted by the State Textbook Commission. She died in Nacogdoches on November 9, 1960.

BIBLIOGRAPHY: Houston *Post*, November 10, 1960; Nacogdoches *Daily Sentinel*, November 9, 1960; *Texian Who's Who* (1937); *Who's Who In America* (1950).

Sonja Fojtik

*Baker, Moseley (Mosely).

*Baker, Rhodes Semmes.

*Baker, Robert Homes.

*Baker, Waller Saunders.

*Baker, William Mumford.

*Baker, William R.

*Baker Creek.

*Baker Slough.

*Bakers Lake.

*Bakersfield, Texas.

*Balaxy Creek.

*Balch, Texas.

Balch Springs, Texas. Balch Springs, in east-central Dallas County, was settled in the 1850's. Named after an original family of settlers, the town developed around a trio of springs. In 1954 the community incorporated, choosing a mayor-council form of city government. In 1958 the city developed a modern fire department with three fire trucks. A post office branch station was opened in September, 1964. Local industry included the manufacture of steel joists and ornamental aluminum castings. Approximately 95 percent of the residents commuted to employment in nearby Dallas or Garland. Population in 1960 was 6,821; in 1970 it was 10,464.

*Balcon Creek.

*Balcones Creek.

*Balcones Escarpment.

Balcones Heights, Texas. Balcones Heights, in Bexar County, had a population of 950 in 1960 and 2,504 in 1970, according to the U.S. census.

*Bald Eagle Hill.

*Bald Eagle Peak.

*Bald Hill, Texas.

*Bald Knob.

*Bald Mountain.

*Bald Prairie, Texas.

*Bald Ridge, Texas.

*Baldridge Creek.

*Baldwin, Frank Dwight.

*Baldwin, Joseph.

*Baldwin, Texas.

*Baldy Mountains.

*Baldy Peak.

*Balis, Daniel E.

*Ball, George.

Ball, Thomas Henry. Thomas Henry Ball, born on October 29, 1819, in Northumberland County, Virginia, the son of Hannah (Gaskins) and David Thomas Ball, was an ordained Methodist minister. He married Susan Perrie and they had one son and two daughters. His wife died in 1853, and in the fall of 1855 he took his mother and three children to Huntsville, Texas, where he became president of Andrew Female College,qv a Methodist school.

In 1857 Ball married a widow, Mrs. M. O. (Spivey) Cleveland, and they had one son, Thomas Henry Ball.qv The senior Ball died of typhoid fever on November 30, 1858, and he was buried in Huntsville.

Mrs. Albert Ball

*Ball, Thomas Henry. Thomas Henry Ball did not run for governor in 1914 on the Prohibition ticket (as stated in Volume I); rather, he ran as a Democrat on a prohibition platform with the endorsement of many large newspapers. He was generally expected to win the election but was defeated in the Democratic primary by a comparative newcomer, James Edward Ferguson.qv The town of Tomball in Harris County was named for Thomas Henry Ball.

*Ball, W. B.

*Ballard Creek.

*Ballenger Bend.

Balli, Nicolás. Padre Nicolás Balli, about 1800, was granted the entire Isla de Corpus Christi, also known as Isla Blanca, for 400 pesos by King Charles IV, of Spain. It soon became known to most people as Padre Island. In 1810–1811 Padre Nicolás sided with the Royalists in the Mexican Revolution. Because of his royalist sympathies, the Mexican government refused to verify his title to the island and to other lands along the Rio Grande until after his death in 1839. *See also* Padre Island.

BIBLIOGRAPHY: Corpus Christi *Caller*, October 24, 1937; J. Frank Dobie, "Stories in Texas Place Names," in *Straight Texas* (1937); Florence Johnson Scott, *Historical Heritage of the Lower Rio Grande* (1937).

Cyrus Tilloson

Ballinger, Betty. Betty Ballinger was born on February 3, 1854, in Galveston, the daughter of Hally Jack and William Pitt Ballinger.qv She attended schools in New Orleans and Baltimore, returning to Texas in 1871.

In 1891 she, along with Hally Bryan Perry,qv formed the Daughters of the Republic of Texas,qv and Mrs. Anson Jones, the widow of the last president of the Republic, became the first state president.

She was also an organizer of the Wednesday Club, a literary club in Texas. She was active for years in the United Daughters of the Confederacy,qv Daughters of the American Revolution, and the National Society of Colonial Dames. She died on March 23, 1936, and was buried in Galveston.

Mildred E. Cherry

*Ballinger, William Pitt.

*Ballinger, Texas. Ballinger, seat of Runnels County, draws most of its income from agriculture, livestock, and petroleum. Of the twelve manufacturers which employed more than twenty-five workers each in 1965, three were concerned with petroleum and five with agriculture and livestock. Other manufacturers produced sheet metal, packaged meat, cottonseed oil, feed, and cheese. In 1966 the city reported 143 businesses, a hospital, ten churches, a city park and community center, a newspaper, a radio station, a library, and a small airport which was formerly an army training base. The Ballinger Museum was built in 1963. Rodeos held annually in June and Ballinger Lake provide recreation. The 1960 population was 5,043; in 1970 it was 4,203.

Balloon Flight Station. *See* National Center for Atmospheric Research, Scientific Balloon Flight Station.

*Balmorhea, Texas.

*Balsora, Texas.

*Baluarte Creek.

*Bammel, Texas.

*Banco Nacional de Tejas. *See* National Bank, First in Texas.

*Bancroft, Hubert Howe.

*Bancroft, Texas.

*Bandera, Texas. Bandera, seat of Bandera County, was a center for ranching supplies, marketing, and dude ranch activity in 1970. A mild year-round climate, scenic beauty, good water, and unlimited recreational facilities have made Bandera one of the most popular dude ranch centers in Texas. Bandera, with seventy-five businesses in 1970, had facilities for processing wool and mohair produced in that area. Some petroleum explorations have been conducted near Bandera with small results. In 1960 the population was 1,036; in 1970 it was 891.

*Bandera County. Bandera County, on the Edwards Plateau in southwest Texas, with its many spring-fed streams, is an important recreational area. Its dude ranches accommodate many tourists brought in by such attractions as the Marvin Hunter Historical Museum (formerly Frontier Times Museum), Bandera Pass, and the sites of Camp Montel qqv and Fort Forilla. Little farming or dairying is done, and aside from tourism, the economy centers on service industries and ranching, primarily sheep and goats. Some commercial use is also made of the county's cedar, pecan, cypress, and oak lumber. Population was 3,892 in 1960 and was 4,747 in 1970.

*Bandera Creek.

Bandera Falls, Texas. Bandera Falls is a small community in eastern Bandera County, approximately five miles south of Pipe Creek on Farm Road 1283. In 1966 it was a residential community of some ten houses.

*Bandera Mesa.

*Bandera Mountains.

*Bandera Pass.

Bane, John P. John P. Bane, at age twenty-six, formed the Guadalupe (County) Rangers in Seguin and became their first captain. They reported for duty on July 4, 1861, at Camp Clar, a training center on the San Marcos River. Mustered in on July 27, 1861, after a brief training period they gathered at Houston before going to Virginia, where they became Company D, 4th Texas Infantry (see Hood's Texas Brigade).

Bane was present at the battles of Eltham's Landing, Seven Pines, and Gaines' Mill. He received an arm wound in the last battle and was absent from the next five battles. Bane again saw action at Gettysburg, where he took command of the 4th Texas after Colonel John C. G. Key was severely wounded. Some weeks later, Key resumed command but apparently never became completely well. Bane again assumed command of the 4th Texas in the spring of 1864 prior to the opening of the Wilderness Campaign. Confederate records, however, indicate that Bane returned to Texas in the summer of 1864 for recruiting purposes and was there when the war ended. He signed a parole on honor in San Antonio on August 25, 1865, listing his home as Guadalupe County, Texas.

BIBLIOGRAPHY: Muster Rolls (Archives, Texas State Library); Service Record of John P. Bane, in War Department, Adjutant General's Office, Confederate Records (MS., National Archives, Washington, D.C.); Donald E. Everett (ed.), Chaplain Davis and Hood's Texas Brigade (1962).

· Donald E. Everett

*Bangs, Samuel.

*Bangs, Texas. Bangs, in Brown County, had a population of 967 in 1960 and 1,214 in 1970, according to the U.S. census.

*Bankers, Texas.

*Bankers Association. See Texas Bankers Association.

*Bankersmith, Texas.

*Banking Department of Texas.

*Banks, Nathaniel Prentiss.

Banks, Willette Rutherford. Willette Rutherford Banks, son of Jabe M. and Laura (McCurry) Banks, was born on August 8, 1881, in Hartwell, Georgia. Banks received a B.A. degree from Atlanta University (Georgia) in 1909, and an M.A. degree from Paul Quinn University (Waco, Texas) in 1922. He was married to Virginia Perry in 1911.

One of the leading Negro educators in America, Banks devoted his entire professional life to education for blacks, serving as teacher, principal, and college president. From 1909 to 1912 he was a teacher at Fort Valley Industrial School in Georgia; he was principal of Kowaliga Industrial School at Benson, Alabama, from 1912 to 1915; he then served as president of Texas College in Tyler until 1926, when he became principal at Prairie View State College (now Prairie View A&M University). During his tenure Banks insisted that the preparation of teachers was the first need of Negro education in the South, and that this could best be done in the state supported colleges. He worked for higher salaries, a larger physical plant, more books for the library (which was later named for him), and higher standards of professional efficiency. The result was that on December 6, 1934, the Southern Association of Colleges and Secondary Schools granted Prairie View a class "A" rating. Banks originated and continued a host of conferences and meetings with the aim of making the state college the focal point for all efforts at social and economic advancement. He sought to make the Prairie View program a model for the nation. Before Banks' retirement in 1946 (when he became president emeritus), the Texas legislature authorized the changing of the school's name from "College" to "University."

At a time when educational facilities were still segregated throughout Texas, Banks continued to work towards narrowing the gap that existed between quality education for blacks and for whites. In 1947 he was named vice-chairman of the board of regents of Texas State University for Negroes (now Texas Southern University). He also served on the boards of Morehouse College (Atlanta), Atlanta University, and Paine College in Augusta, Georgia. Banks lived most of his life in Prairie View, although he died in Corsicana on October 16, 1969; he was buried in Memorial Park, Prairie View.

BIBLIOGRAPHY: Who's Who in Colored America (1950); Biographical File, Barker Texas History Center, University of Texas at Austin.

George R. Woolfolk

*Banks and Banking in Texas.

*Bannister, Texas.

*Banquete, Texas.

*Banta, William.

*Baptist Church in Texas. The total number of Baptists of all sects in Texas in 1965 was approximately 1,850,000. There were 575,000 Negro Baptists in Texas in 1964. In 1965 there were 4,582 Sunday schools in the state with an enrollment of 1,690,855; there were over two thousand Baptist Training Unions with a membership of 433,573.

The colleges and universities affiliated with the Baptist General Convention of Texas had a total enrollment in 1965–1966 of 18,619, with an annual operating budget in excess of thirty-six million dollars. Southwestern Baptist Theological Seminary qv in Fort Worth enrolls over two thousand students annually and operates on a budget in excess of fifteen million dollars. In addition to these "Southern Baptist" educational institutions, the

Baptist Bible Fellowship and the World Baptist Fellowship maintain Bible Baptist Seminary qv in Grand Prairie and Arlington Baptist Junior College in Arlington.

Baptists continued to establish hospitals, including Baptist Memorial Hospital in San Antonio, 1948; Baptist Memorial Geriatric Hospital in San Angelo, 1950; and Baptist Hospital in Amarillo, 1967. The net worth of Texas Baptist hospitals in 1967 exceeded seventy million dollars.

BIBLIOGRAPHY: *Annual of the Baptist General Convention of Texas* (1965, 1966).

Jerry F. Dawson

*Baptist Standard. The *Baptist Standard* in 1966 had a weekly circulation of approximately 370,000, the largest of any publication in Texas and the largest circulation of any state Baptist paper in the United States.

John J. Hurt

*Baptiste Creek.

*Bar Association, Texas. *See* State Bar of Texas.

*Bar Gap.

*Baratt, William.

*Barbarosa, Texas.

*Barbed Wire.

*Barber Mountain.

*Barber's Hill Oil Field.

*Barbier, Sieur de.

Barclay, James. James Barclay, legislator and Indian agent, was one of the earliest settlers in present Tyler County. He was born in Tennessee on February 11, 1816, the son of Walter and Elizabeth (McQueen) Barclay. In 1826 he came to Texas with his father and brother, but they returned to Tennessee later in the same year. In February, 1836, the family settled permanently in Texas. Five years later James Barclay married Virginia Ann Foster and settled on the John Wheat survey a few miles southwest of the present city of Woodville. About 1841 the Alabama Indian tribe moved southward and established a village on the survey with Barclay's permission.

After the organization of Tyler County in 1846, Barclay played a prominent role in the government of the new county, serving in most of the county's elective positions. He was elected the first tax assessor-collector; in 1850 he was elected sheriff; and he was the county's chief justice during terms that began in 1856 and 1858. His activities as Indian commissioner and agent constituted another feature of his diversified public career. On February 3, 1854, James Barclay and Samuel Rowe were appointed commissioners to purchase a tract of land which is part of the Alabama-Coushatta Indian Reservation qv in Polk County. On May 12, 1858, Governor H. R. Runnels qv appointed Barclay agent for the Alabama, Coushatta, and Muscogie Indian tribes.

From November 7, 1859, to February 13, 1860, he served as the Tyler County representative in the Texas legislature. Returning to the legislature in December, 1863, Barclay represented Tyler and Hardin counties. He served on several legislative committees, including Indian affairs. During the administration of Governor Pendleton Murrah, qv Barclay served a second term as agent for the Polk County Indians from November 9, 1864, until he was replaced on August 29, 1865, by A. J. Harrison, an appointee of Provisional Governor A. J. Hamilton.qv After his removal as Indian agent, Barclay continued to operate his large plantation and to participate in civic affairs until his death at his Tyler County home on November 14, 1871. He was buried in the Hart Cemetery, about three miles south of Woodville.

BIBLIOGRAPHY: J. E. Wheat and Josiah Wheat, "The Early Days of Tyler County," *Tyler County Dogwood Festival Program* (1963); Dorman H. Winfrey and James M. Day (eds.), *The Indian Papers of Texas and the Southwest, 1825–1916* (1966).

Howard N. Martin

Barclay, William Anderson. William Anderson Barclay was born on December 23, 1849, in Woodville, Texas, the son of Jeremiah Todd and Elizabeth Anne (Rigsby) Barclay. After his father's death and his mother's remarriage, he was reared by his uncle, James Barclay.qv He left home at the age of sixteen and went to Cameron, Texas, where he worked as a store clerk. He married Martha King Ledbetter on February 14, 1871. Shortly after his marriage he was appointed a deputy sheriff of Milam County, continued to work in the store, while at night he delivered papers from one county seat to another, receiving the sum of fifty dollars per night because of the danger of Indians in the area. He also clerked in a Rockdale store before purchasing in 1873 a mercantile business at Yarrellton. In 1875 he sold his store and entered the cattle business with his wife's brother-in-law, William Sewell Goodhue Wilson of Belle Bayou. The Wilson-Barclay cattle were branded with the figures "28" and the Barclay cattle with the brand reversed, "82." Headquarters were established on Little Pond Creek in present Falls County. In 1876 he opened a store in Hico, and in 1878 he opened another store between Cameron and Waco near his homestead. His plantation, Crenshaw, eventually contained approximately six thousand acres.

A pioneer financier in Texas, Barclay established the first plow factory in Texas, the first cottonseed oil mill in Texas (having invented his own formula for extracting the oil), and helped to establish railroads, banks, lumber yards, furniture stores, and general mercantile stores. He was president of the Mexican-American Smelting and Refining Company, as well as owning private mines in Mexico. He invented a method of rewashing slag which proved to be extremely profitable. His Mexican mining ventures stopped abruptly when General Díaz was overthrown. He then turned to copper mines in Arizona and an apple orchard in Oregon. As he grew older he gradually converted his holdings into stocks and bonds.

Although he had little formal education, he was an inveterate reader, particularly of Texas history.

He died on October 24, 1927, and was buried in Temple.

Margaret Barclay Megarity

***Barclay, Texas.** Barclay, in Falls County, was founded by William Anderson Barclay qv (not S. F. Barclay, as stated in Volume I). Barclay owned a ranch on Little Pond Creek and later, in 1878, opened a mercantile store at a nearby crossroads; the settlement and post office established there were named in his honor. The estimated population for 1971 was seventy-two.

BIBLIOGRAPHY: Falls County Scrapbook (MS., Archives, University of Texas at Austin Library); Lillian Schiller St. Romain, *Western Falls County, Texas* (1951).

***Barcus, John M.**

Bard, John Pierre. John Pierre Bard was born in 1846 in France and was educated there. Shortly after the close of the Civil War he chaperoned a group of wealthy French boys on a tour of the Gulf of Mexico and the Caribbean; when the ship entered Corpus Christi Bay, Bard was impressed with its natural beauty and vowed to become a priest and return to Corpus Christi. In 1876 he went to Galveston, where he was ordained. A year later he returned to Corpus Christi and was sent to San Diego on April 14, 1877, to assist Farther Claude C. Jaillet qv with his visitation of about 200 ranches and missions in the area which extended from the Nueces River southward about 100 miles to Baluarte Creek and from Banquete westward to a point about forty miles beyond San Diego. Almost single-handedly, he built the only church to be built in Collins (Jim Wells County).

Called "Father Bard" or "Padre Pedro," he held services in Spanish, English, or German, though his native language was French. With San Diego as his headquarters, Father Bard served the immense area alone after 1883 until his death on March 4, 1920. He was buried in the St. Francis de Paula Church in San Diego.

BIBLIOGRAPHY: Sister Mary Xavier, *Father Jaillet: Saddlebag Priest of the Nueces* (1948); *idem*, Unpublished Notes (Archives, Incarnate Word Academy, Corpus Christi).

Agnes G. Grimm

***Bardwell, Texas.** Bardwell, in southeastern Ellis County, was established as early as 1892 (not 1906, as stated in Volume I). The town was named for John W. Bardwell (not J. Y. Bardwell), who was the owner of a gin, beside which Oris Wheatley built a store in 1892. Wheatley sold his store to a Mr. Willis (Ben or John) who became Bardwell's first postmaster in 1892. Bardwell had a population of 220 in 1960 and 277 in 1970, according to the United States census.

Bardwell Reservoir. Bardwell Reservoir is in the Trinity River Basin in Ellis County, three miles southeast of Bardwell on Waxahachie Creek, a tributary of Chambers Creek, which is a tributary of the Trinity River. The project is owned by the United States government, and was built by the United States Army Corps of Engineers, Fort Worth District. The Trinity River Authority qv will use the conservation storage and yield of the reservoir. Construction started on August 7, 1963, and impoundment of water began on November 20, 1965.

The reservoir has a total capacity of 140,000 acre-feet at the top of flood-control storage, including 53,550 acre-feet conservation storage, 1,320 acre-feet dead storage, and 85,130 acre-feet allocated to flood control. The top of conservation storage is at an elevation of 421 feet above mean sea level, where the surface area is 3,570 acres. The water yield from this reservoir will supply the cities of Waxahachie, Ennis, and possibly others. The drainage area above the dam is 176 square miles.

BIBLIOGRAPHY: Texas Water Commission, *Bulletin 6408* (1964).

Seth D. Breeding

***Bare Butte.**

***Barillos Creek.**

Barker, Eugene Campbell. Eugene Campbell Barker was born near Riverside (Walker County) on November 10, 1874, the son of Joseph [or Joe] and Fannie [or Fanny] (Holland) Barker. Shortly after his father's death in 1888, his mother moved the family to Palestine, where fourteen-year-old Eugene found employment in the Missouri-Pacific Railroad shops. In the months that followed, he became a fine blacksmith as he worked during the day and attended evening school in the home of Miss Shirley Green. He entered the University of Texas in September, 1895, an association that would continue until his death.

Despite financial handicaps (he served as night mail clerk on the Missouri-Pacific's Austin-to-Houston run), Barker received the B.A. degree in the spring of 1899 and the M.A. in 1900. He served the university as tutor in the Department of History (1899–1901); instructor (1901–1908); adjunct professor (1908–1911); associate professor (1911–1913); professor from 1913 until his retirement in 1951; and professor emeritus from 1951 until the end of his life in 1956—almost six decades altogether.

On August 6, 1903, Barker married Matilda LeGrand Weeden. In 1906 he took a leave of absence to complete his graduate work at the University of Pennsylvania, where he received the Ph.D. degree in 1908 (after a brief interval at Harvard). On the death of George P. Garrison qv in 1910, Eugene C. Barker became chairman of the Department of History, a position which he held until 1925. When the title of distinguished professor was created in 1937, Dr. Barker was among the first three chosen.

During the thirty-eight years of his full professorship, Barker did the bulk of his scholarly work. His first major project, inherited from Lester G. Bugbee qv and George P. Garrison, involved the life of Stephen F. Austin. Before finishing the classic biography of Austin, Barker collected, edited, and published *The Austin Papers*, a collection of correspondence that covered the years from 1789 to 1837 (published by the American Historical Association, 1924–1928, and the University of Texas Press,qv 1927). *The Life of Stephen F. Austin* was published in 1925, and republished several times. Barker's other major publications included *Mexico and Texas, 1821–1835* (1928); *Readings in Texas History* (1929); *The Father of Texas* (1935); in collaboration with Amelia W. Williams, *The Writings of Sam Houston* (1938–1943); and a series of public school textbooks for Row and Peterson done in collaboration with William E. Dodd, Henry S. Commager, and Walter Prescott Webb.qv

Meanwhile, Barker served as managing editor of the *Southwestern Historical Quarterly* qv and director of the Texas State Historical Association qv from 1910 until 1937. During that time he not only edited the *Quarterly* but contributed numerous articles to the publication, most of them dealing with some aspect of Texas or Mexican history. Through his articles Barker showed the general effect that Texas history had on the overall history of the American West. In this connection he explored some of the earlier myths that had gained widespread acceptance among American historians. The "conspiracy theory" of the conquest and annexation of Texas and the war with Mexico and the idea that the Texas Revolution and the Mexican War were all the fault of the Mexican people and government were among the misconceptions that he explored and explained.

In the midst of all of his research and publications, Barker found time for national professional associations. He was a lifetime member of the American Historical Association. Also, along with Clarence V. Alvord and others, he was instrumental in establishing the Mississippi Valley Historical Association (now the Organization of American Historians, publishers of the *Journal of American History*), and served this organization as its president, 1922–1923. During his later years he was interested in challenging Professor Charles A. Beard's economic interpretation of the Constitution of the United States.

Barker was instrumental in the origin of the Latin American Collection qv and the Littlefield collection of source materials on the history of the South, both integral parts of the University of Texas library. Barker's greatest contribution to the university, however, was in building the Department of History, which, during his career as a member, came to rank with the best in the state universities of the nation. After the Ferguson controversy of 1917–1918 (*see* Ferguson, James Edward), Barker exercised a remarkable influence as one of the leaders of the university faculty. As the years passed, Eugene C. Barker became a legend on the campus of the University of Texas; one of the great intangibles of his long and fruitful career concerned his influence on the thousands of young students who sat in his classes. When the University of Texas named the Eugene C. Barker Texas History Center qv for him (dedicated in 1950), it was the first time that such an honor had been accorded a living member of its faculty. Eugene C. Barker died on October 22, 1956. He was buried in Oakwood Cemetery in Austin.

BIBLIOGRAPHY: William C. Pool, *Eugene C. Barker: Historian* (1971).

William C. Pool

*Barker, William Louis.

*Barker, Texas.

*Barker Mountain.

*Barker Reservoir. Barker Reservoir is owned by the United States government and is operated by the United States Army Corps of Engineers, Galveston District, for flood protection to the Houston area. The dam was completed February 3, 1946, but was used for flood control in the spring of 1945. The reservoir is for floodwater retention only. In 1966 it had a capacity of 204,800 acre-feet and a surface area of 17,225 acres at the emergency spillway crest elevation of 107 feet above mean sea level. The drainage area was 134 square miles above the outlet works.

BIBLIOGRAPHY: Texas Water Commission, *Bulletin 6408* (1964).

Seth D. Breeding

Barker Texas History Center. *See* Eugene C. Barker Texas History Center.

*Barkley, Benjamin Franklin.

*Barksdale, Texas.

*Barnard, George.

*Barnard, Joseph Henry.

*Barnard Knob.

*Barnards Trading Post. *See* Barnard, George; Torrey Trading Houses.

Barnes, Charles Merritt. Charles Merritt Barnes was born on January 6, 1855, in Waterproof, Louisiana. Educated at Louisiana State University and the military college at Baton Rouge, he enlisted in the Louisiana State Militia before migrating with his family to Texas in 1872. Barnes settled in San Marcos and was soon admitted to the Bar.

After living a short time at Luling, he went to San Antonio in 1874 and practiced law several years. His interests soon turned to journalism, the military, and politics. He enlisted in the "Alamo Rifles" in 1875 and remained with that group until 1917, when he retired with the rank of major. During this period Barnes saw active duty along the Mexican border. He was color sergeant of Company G, 1st Texas Infantry (San Antonio Zouaves) in 1898, but he did not accompany his outfit to Cuba.

Barnes became a reporter for the San Antonio *Express* qv about 1880. He gained considerable prominence in this field until his retirement prior to World War I. The files of the *Express* are replete with stories written by Barnes featuring exploits of numerous frontier individuals. His articles appeared regularly in Sunday editions between 1902 and 1910. They were illustrated with line drawings by Leo Colton, the talented *Express* artist. In 1910 he published *Combats and Conquests of Immortal Heroes*, a collection of nineteenth-century San Antonio families, personalities, and events. He also published and wrote some verse. Barnes died on April 7, 1927, in San Antonio.

BIBLIOGRAPHY: San Antonio *Express*, April 11, 1886, May 4, 11, 18, 1902, April 8, 1927.

Hobart Huson

*Barnes, Texas.
*Barnes City, Texas.
*Barnesville, Texas.
*Barnett, George Washington.
*Barnett, S. Slade.
*Barnett, Thomas.
*Barnett Branch.
*Barnhardt Creek.
*Barnhart, Texas.
*Barnum, Texas.
*Barnum Draw.

Baromeo, Chase. Chase Baromeo, bass-baritone opera singer, was born Chase Baromeo Sikes, son of Clarence Stevens and Medora (Rhodes) Sikes, on August 19, 1892, in Augusta, Georgia. He held Bachelor of Arts (1917) and Master of Music (1929) degrees from the University of Michigan. Before coming to the University of Texas at Austin in 1938 to head the voice faculty in the music department of the new College of Fine Arts, Baromeo had an extremely successful operatic career. He made his debut in 1923 at the Teatro Carcano in Milan, Italy. From 1923 to 1926 he was a member of La Scala Opera Company in Milan, singing under Toscanini; because of the Italian difficulty in pronouncing his last name, Sikes became known professionally as Chase Baromeo, and he used that name for the rest of his life.

Baromeo also sang at the Teatro Colon in Buenos Aires, Argentina, in 1924, with the Chicago Civic Opera Company from 1926 to 1931, and with the San Francisco Opera Company in 1935. From 1935 to 1938 he was with the Metropolitan Opera Company in New York. At various times he performed with many of the leading symphony orchestras in the United States.

Baromeo was married to Delphie Lindstrom on May 12, 1931; they were the parents of three children, one of whom predeceased him. While with the University of Texas, he directed and performed in many university-staged operas. Chase Baromeo left the university in 1954 to join the University of Michigan faculty, from which he was retired at the time of his death in Birmingham, Michigan, on August 7, 1973.

Eldon S. Branda

*Barr, Amelia.
*Barr, Robert.
*Barr, Robert.
*Barr, William.
*Barr Creek.
*Barr and Davenport, House of.

Barreda, Celestino Pardo. Celestino Pardo Barreda, son of Don Eugenio Pardo and Doña Fermina de Barreda y Liaño, was born in La Penilla, Province of Santander, Spain, on January 1, 1858.

Barreda came to the United States in 1871 on the steamship *Germania*, arrived in New Orleans, and sailed to Port Isabel, Texas, shortly thereafter. After working a few months with his uncles, he was sent to schools in New Jersey and Massachusetts. In 1874 Barreda returned from the East to work for his uncles in Brownsville, but he soon went into the mercantile business for himself. By 1880 Barreda was a United States citizen and was accumulating ranch lands and city properties in Texas and Mexico. He acquired sugar plantations in Cuba and began shipping cattle throughout the southern United States and Cuba. As early as 1908 he was using the Rio Grande for irrigation purposes. By the 1920's Barreda had extensive land holdings in South Texas and was vice-president of the First National Bank in Brownsville, organizer of the Texas Bank & Trust Co., and active in many civic and social organizations.

On December 17, 1906, Barreda married Maria de Guinea in Matamoros, Mexico, and although they had no children of their own, they reared their orphaned niece and nephew. Barreda died on February 3, 1953, in Brownsville and was buried in Buena Vista Cemetery in that city.

BIBLIOGRAPHY: Barreda Bibliography and Papers (Stillman House Museum, Brownsville, Texas).

C. C. Stewart
Celia S. Santiso

*Barreda, Texas.
*Barrel Canyon.
*Barrel Springs Creek.
*Barrell Creek.

Barret, Lyne Taliaferro. Lyne Taliaferro Barret was born on November 1, 1832, in Appomattox, Virginia, youngest of nine children of Charles L. and Sarah (Taliaferro) Barret. The family moved to Texas in 1842 and, according to the census, he was a resident of Nacogdoches County in 1850. Barret is credited by petroleum historians as being the man who bored the first producing oil well in Texas. The well, completed between late summer and early fall (probably in early September), 1866, was located on a 279-acre lease, the Skillern Tract in Nacogdoches County; it was near Oil Springs, about twelve miles southeast of Nacogdoches. Barret used steam power and the rotary principle, with some crude tools made by a blacksmith, to bore 106 feet and hit oil. Production was rated at ten barrels a day. He had had the same Skillern Tract under lease to drill for oil in early 1859, but because of lack of machinery was unable to make it produce, a fact which perhaps prevented him from drilling the world's first producing oil well (the first having been drilled in Pennsylvania in August, 1859). In 1865 Barret formed the Melrose Petroleum Oil Company in partnership with four other men: Charles A. Hamilton, John T. Flint, John B. Earle, and Benjamin F. Hollingsworth.

In November and December, 1866, after his first success, Barret went to Pennsylvania to secure financing for drilling at least one more well, entered into an agreement with Brown Brothers of Titusville, Pennsylvania, and returned to Texas with John F. Carll (one of the early pioneers in Pennsylvania oil production) to attempt drilling. However, as the Texas oil venture was not immediately successful, the Pennsylvania firm lost interest and withdrew its support from drilling operations. Having failed to obtain solid backing, Barret never drilled another well. He ran a mercantile business in Melrose and managed his wife's land holdings. On March 23, 1913, he died and was buried in Melrose.

BIBLIOGRAPHY: Wayne Gard, *The First 100 Years of Texas Oil & Gas* (1966); Frank X. Tolbert, *The Story of Lyne Taliaferro [Tol] Barret* (1966).

Frank X. Tolbert

*Barrett, Don Carlos.

*Barrett, Montgomery (Monte).

*Barrett, Thomas.

Barrett, William Martin. William Martin Barrett was born in Dinwiddie, Virginia, in 1812, and came to Texas in 1841. With architecture as a profession, he was appointed in 1851 architect and contractor for the first permanent building of Austin College, in Huntsville. When Austin College was moved to Sherman in 1876, the building was used for public school purposes and in 1879 became the first building of the Sam Houston Normal Institute (now Sam Houston State University); it is still in use by the college and is the oldest building in Texas used continuously for educational purposes.

Barrett was a colonel in the Mexican War and also served as an officer in the Civil War. He was allegedly a cousin of William Barret Travis qv and a friend of Sam Houston (who was one of the trustees for Austin College). Barrett married his second wife, Mrs. Nancy Keenan Hamilton, in Huntsville on December 5, 1847. They were the parents of four children. Barrett died in Huntsville on September 18, 1867, of yellow fever.

BIBLIOGRAPHY: Frank W. Johnson, *A History of Texas and Texans* (1914); Minutes of the Meeting of the Board of Trustees of Austin College, June 24, 1851, and June 20, 1852; Huntsville *Item*, February 5, 1898.

Aline Law

Barrett, Texas. Barrett, in eastern Harris County, was a residential area composed predominately of Negroes. The population in 1960 was 2,364; in 1970 it was 2,750. *See also* Houston Standard Metropolitan Statistical Area.

*Barrilla Mountains.

*Barrio Junco y Espriella, Pedro del.

*Barrios y Jáuregui, Jacinto de.

*Barron, Samuel Benton.

*Barron Field.

*Barrons Creek.

*Barrow, Clyde Chesnut. Clyde Barrow was killed with Bonnie Parker qv near Gibsland, Louisiana (not in Arcadia, Louisiana, as stated in Volume I). His body was taken to Arcadia, Louisiana.

See also Hamer, Francis Augustus.

BIBLIOGRAPHY: H. G. Frost and J. H. Jenkins, *"I'm Frank Hamer"* (1968).

*Barry, James Buckner (Buck).

*Barry, Texas.

*Barsola, Texas.

*Barstow, George Eames.

*Barstow, Texas.

*Bart, Texas. *See* Artesia Wells, Texas.

*Bartholomew, Eugene Carlos.

*Bartlett, Churchill Jones.

*Bartlett, John Russell.

*Bartlett, Texas. Bartlett, in Williamson and Bell counties, had a population of 1,540 in 1960 and 1,622 in 1970.

*Bartlett and Western Railway.

*Bartlett-Condé Compromise.

*Barton, Donald Clinton.

*Barton, James M.

*Barton, Thomas Dickson.

*Barton, William.

*Barton Creek.

*Barton Springs.

*Barton Springs, Texas.

*Barton's Chapel, Texas.

*Bartonsite, Texas.

*Bartonville, Texas.

*Barwise, Joseph Hodson.

*Barwise, Texas.

*Barziza, D. U.

*Barzynski, Vincent.

*Baseball. *See* Texas League; Houston Astros (Baseball Club); Texas Rangers (Baseball Club).

*Basfords Bayou.

*Baskin, Texas.

*Bason Mill Creek.

*Bass, Sam.

Bass, Thomas Coke. Thomas Coke Bass was born in Mississippi or Tennessee. He was admitted to the Bar in January, 1858, at Aberdeen, Mississippi, but soon moved to Texas. In 1861 he was the first to raise a Confederate flag in Grayson County and commanded a military detachment which captured Fort Washita. Later he raised and became colonel of the 20th Texas Cavalry, which fought at Prairie Grove, Arkansas, in 1862. The regiment spent the rest of the Civil War defending the Indian Territory, serving at different times both as cavalry and as infantry. On July 10, 1867, Bass married Ada Dalton Hocker, and they had four children. With Silas Hare, he published the Sherman *Courier* in the late 1860's and was practicing law in that North Texas town as late as 1877.

BIBLIOGRAPHY: Graham Landrum, *Grayson County* (1960); Thomas Pilgrim and H. L. Bentley, *The Texas Legal Directory for 1876–77* (1877).

*Bass Creek.

*Bassets Creek.

*Bassett, Texas.

*Bassett Creek.

*Bastera, Prudencio. *See* Orobio y Basterra, Prudencio de.

*Bastrop, Baron Felipe Enrique Neri de. Felipe Enrique Neri, Baron de Bastrop, was born Philip Hendrik Nering Bögel in Paramaribo, Dutch Guiana, on November 23, 1759 (not in Holland about 1766, as stated in Volume I). He was the son of Maria Jacoba (Kraayvanger) and Conraed Laurens Nering Bögel (not Conrado Lorenzo Neri, Baron de Bastrop, and Susana Maria Bray Banguin, as stated in Volume I). He went to Holland with his parents in 1764, and in 1779 enlisted in the cavalry of Holland and Upper Issel. He married Georgine Wolffeline Françoise Lijcklama à Nycholt in Oldeboorn, Holland, on April 28, 1782. They settled in Leeuwarden where he was collector-general of taxes for the province of Friesland.

From his military service, marriage, and appointment as tax collector, it can probably be assumed that he was a staunch supporter of the aristocracy during the late eighteenth-century period of revolutionary upheaval. Although Bastrop always gave the French invasion of Holland as his reason for leaving the country, he actually left under entirely different circumstances. In 1793 he was accused of embezzlement of tax funds, a crime for which he did not stand trial, for he fled Holland. The Court of Justice of Leeuwarden on June 1, 1793, offered a reward of 1,000 gold Dutch ducats to anyone who brought him back. It was at this time that Philip Hendrik Nering Bögel changed the spelling of his name and adopted the title of Baron de Bastrop.

BIBLIOGRAPHY: Charles A. Bacarisse, "Baron de Bastrop," *Southwestern Historical Quarterly*, LVIII (1954–1955); Charles Albert Bacarisse, *The Baron de Bastrop: Life and Times of Philip Hendrick Nering Bögel, 1759–1827* (Ph.D. dissertation, University of Texas at Austin, 1955).

*Bastrop, Texas. Bastrop, seat of Bastrop County, was the home of eighty businesses in 1970, among which were plants specializing in wood products and oil-field equipment. There were two banks, a newspaper, and a Lower Colorado River Authority qv steam generating plant at the town. A second hospital and a housing development were completed in the late 1960's. Population was 3,001 in 1960 and 3,112 in 1970.

*Bastrop Academy.

*Bastrop Bay.

*Bastrop Bayou.

*Bastrop County. Bastrop County had a population of 16,925 in 1960, and by 1970 it had grown to 17,297. Lake Bastrop, completed in 1964, has added to the county's stature as a fishing resort area. Bastrop and Buescher state parks (*see* Parks, State), the Lost Pines,qv and a rodeo in August are other tourist attractions. Livestock raising and farming are the principal occupations of county residents. The average annual farm income in the early 1970's was $10 million, 90 percent of which was from livestock. In 1968 about twenty-five hundred bales of cotton were raised. Many of the small industries are associated with lumber, brick and tile, furniture, concrete, and tools.

*Bastrop Military Institute.

*Bastrop Park. *See* Parks, State.

*Bastrop and Taylor Railway Company. *See* Taylor, Bastrop, and Houston Railway Company.

Bata Indians. The Bata are known from a 1691 Spanish missionary report which identifies them as living about eighty leagues southwest of the Hasinai Indians of eastern Texas. Their affiliations remain unknown.

BIBLIOGRAPHY: J. R. Swanton, *Source Material on the History and Ethnology of the Caddo Indians* (1942).

                                          T. N. Campbell

Batayogligla Indians. Batayogligla (Batayolida) is the name of one band of Chizo Indians, who are considered by some writers to be a branch of the Concho. In the seventeenth and early eighteenth centuries the Chizo occupied the area now covered by northeastern Chihuahua, northwestern Coahuila, and the lower part of the Big Bend region of Trans-Pecos Texas.

BIBLIOGRAPHY: C. W. Hackett (ed.), *Historical Documents Relating to New Mexico, Nueva Vizcaya, and Approaches Thereto, to 1773*, II (1926); C. Sauer, *The Distribution of Aboriginal Tribes and Languages in Northwestern Mexico* (1934).

                                          T. N. Campbell

*Bateman, Texas.

*Baten, Anderson Edith.

Bates, Joseph. Joseph Bates was born in Mobile, Alabama, on January 19, 1805. A businessman rather than a lawyer, he became a prominent Whig politician and served as a representative in the Alabama legislature in 1829, 1836, 1837, and 1840. He was defeated for the state senate in 1838. Bates took part in the Seminole War of 1835 and became a major general of the Alabama militia.

He came to Galveston in 1843 and was elected mayor three years later. President Millard Fillmore appointed him United States marshal for the eastern district of Texas from 1850 to 1853. In 1854 he moved to a large plantation he had purchased on the west side of the San Bernard River in Brazoria County, where he engaged in farming and ranching until his death.

At the outbreak of the Civil War, Bates was appointed a colonel in the Confederate Army. He raised a regiment that later became, after several reorganizations, the 13th (Bates') Texas Infantry Regiment. Placed in command of the coast defenses between Galveston and Matagorda Island, he established headquarters at Velasco. From May to September, 1863, Bates and his regiment served in Louisiana under General Dick Taylor; for a time Bates was commander of the post at Brashear City.

Bates' moderation and firmness during Reconstruction qv went far in bringing about a peaceful adjustment of affairs in Brazoria County. A forceful and effective speaker, he was noted for his commanding physical appearance. He was a member of the Brazoria Lodge No. 327, A.F. and A.M. He was twice married. By his first wife, he had seven children. His second marriage was in 1851 to Mrs. Mary (Love) Morris of Galveston; they were the parents of five children. He died on February 18, 1888, and was buried in the Episcopal cemetery in Galveston.

BIBLIOGRAPHY: William Garrett, *Reminiscences of Public Men in Alabama* (1872); J. H. Brown, *Indian Wars and Pioneers of Texas* (189?); C. C. Nott, *Sketches in Prison Camps* (1965); *War of the Rebellion: Official Records of the Union and Confederate Armies* (1880–1901); Deed, Marriage, and Probate Records, Galveston and Brazoria Counties.

Cooper K. Ragan

*Bates, Texas.

*Bates Creek.

*Batesville, Texas. (Red River County.)

*Batesville, Texas. (Zavala County.) Batesville lost the county seat of Zavala County to Crystal City in 1928 (not 1927, as stated in Volume I).

*Batesville Hill.

*Bath, Texas.

*Batista Village.

*Batson, Texas.

*Batson Oil Field.

*Battle, Mills M.

*Battle, Nicholas W.

Battle, William James. William James Battle was born in Raleigh, North Carolina, on November 30, 1870. He later moved to Chapel Hill, where his father, Kemp P. Battle, served as president of the University of North Carolina. He received a B.A. degree from that institution in 1888 and a Ph.D. from Harvard University in 1893. In his first year at Harvard he held a Thayer scholarship, and the last two years a Morgan fellowship.

Battle was a tutor in Latin at the University of Chicago before coming to the University of Texas in 1893 as associate professor of Greek. He was promoted to professor in 1898 and was made dean of the College of Arts in 1908. Three years later Battle was made dean of the faculty, and in 1914 he was elected acting president of the university.

His two years as president were unhappy ones, because he was severely attacked by Governor James E. Ferguson,qv who charged that Battle had deceived the legislature and the governor about the university appropriation bill of 1915 and had used state money for purposes other than the items specified in the appropriation bill. His dismissal from the faculty was urged by Ferguson, but in October, 1916, the board of regents declared that the charges against Battle were unsubstantiated. In October, 1915, Battle had asked that he not be considered for a permanent appointment as president. When he stepped down as president in April, 1916, the board of regents elected Robert E. Vinson.qv

As a result of the political pressure Battle left the university in 1917 to teach at the University of Cincinnati. He remained there until 1920, when he returned to the University of Texas as professor of classical languages and chairman of the faculty building committee. He served in the latter position until 1948.

In addition to his academic work, Battle designed the seal of the university in 1901, edited the first student directory in 1900, and founded the first ex-student magazine. He furnished the money in 1898 to establish the University Co-Op and served as its first manager. The final announcement of courses was his idea, as was the English comprehension requirement.

In 1929 Southwestern University awarded Dr. Battle an honorary LL.D. degree, and he was honored with a second LL.D. degree by the University of North Carolina in 1940. He was a devout member of the Episcopal church and long served as senior warden of All Saints' Chapel near the University of Texas campus.

He retired from active duty in 1948 at the age of seventy-eight but continued to maintain an office on campus as professor emeritus. Books and papers published by Battle include *A Sketch of Grace Hall and All Saints' Chapel* (1940); *The Story of All Saints' Chapel, Austin, Texas, 1900–1950* (1951); and *Town and Gown Club, Memories of Past Days* (1952).

Battle returned to North Carolina in April, 1955, and died there on October 9, 1955. In his will he left his property in Austin and his 14,000-volume library to the University of Texas. He also provided means for setting up scholarships for the study of classical languages.

*Battle, Texas.

*Battle Creek.

*Battle Creek Fight. The Indians involved in the Battle Creek Fight (also known as the Surveyors Fight) on October 8, 1838, included not only Kickapoos (as stated in Volume I), but also Wacos, Tehuacanas, Ionies, and Caddoes. Authorities have disagreed on the number of surveyors who took part in this fight against approximately three hundred Indians. Their original mission was to survey land in what is now the southern part of Navarro County for ex-soldiers who had received bounty and headright certificates for their service in the Texas Revolution. It is known that two men in the original survey party were absent from the battle. The names of eighteen men have been listed as killed in the fight. Seven surveyors who survived and escaped were William Fenner Henderson,qv J. Baker, Walter Paye Lane,qv James Smith, and three others named McLaughlin, Violet, and Burton. Thus the original party would have consisted of twenty-seven men, with twenty-five participating in the Battle Creek Fight, in which eighteen were killed and seven escaped.

BIBLIOGRAPHY: Harry McCorry Henderson, "The Surveyors Fight," *Southwestern Historical Quarterly*, LVI (1952–1953).

Harry McCorry Henderson

*Battle of Flowers.

*Battleground Creek.

*Batts, Robert Lynn. Robert Lynn Batts had a son, as well as two daughters.

Baudin, Charles. Charles Baudin was born in Sedan (city on Meuse River in northeastern France) on July 21, 1784, the son of Pierre-Charles-Louis Baudin. At fifteen years of age he was accepted into service aboard the *Foudroyant* as a novice seaman. By 1808 he had risen to command successively the frigates *Piémontaise* and *Sémillante*. In a naval encounter with the British in the Indian Ocean he lost his right arm (1808). An ardent Bonapartist, he plotted the escape of Napoleon from France after Waterloo, but the emperor refused, preferring to throw himself upon the mercy of the British. With the second restoration of the Bourbons, Baudin's naval career was temporarily halted; he prospered as a merchant in Le Havre. In this capacity he befriended the penniless Pierre Soulé and provided for the latter's voyage to America (1825); Soulé was to become the well-known lawyer, senator, and diplomat of New Orleans.

After the revolution of July, 1830, Baudin rejoined the French navy and, on his return from a mission to Haiti, was on April 28, 1838, promoted to the grade of rear admiral. Soon after, he was charged with the command of the French expedition against Mexico in the so-called Pastry War. Promotion to vice admiral quickly followed this action.

Upon conferring with Barnard Bee qv in Veracruz harbor, Baudin determined to return homeward via Texas. Since Baudin lacked any instructions from his government concerning Texas, his visit was strictly personal, although he was accompanied by three vessels from his fleet and was welcomed by Texans as a harbinger of the official French recognition of the independence of Texas from Mexico. The visit occurred May 2–14, 1839, during which time Baudin's party traveled from Velasco to Houston to Galveston and was entertained by various leading citizens. His visit to President Lamar followed closely upon visits of Dubois de Saligny and Gaillardet.qqv The cumulative effect of these contacts, in conjunction with the diplomatic negotiations, was French recognition of Texas' independence, September 25, 1839.

After 1839 Baudin continued as a vice admiral until May 27, 1854, when he was finally promoted to admiral. He died only a few days later, on June 7.

BIBLIOGRAPHY: Eugène Maissin (James L. Shepherd, III, trans.), *The French in Mexico and Texas (1838–1839)* (1961); M. Prevost and Roman d'Amat (eds.), *Dictionnaire de biographie française*, V (1951); Frédéric Gaillardet (James L. Shepherd, III, trans.), *Sketches of Early Texas and Louisiana* (1966).

James L. Shepherd, III

Bauer, Paul. Paul Bauer, son of Matilda and Friederick Bauer, was born on October 30, 1855, at Yorktown, Texas, where his father, a German immigrant and master saddler, taught him the saddle and harness business. He went to Helena, San Diego, Pearsall, Oakville, and finally to Beeville in 1895. In 1878 he married Carrie Reagan, and of their six children, two sons continued in the saddle business. For nearly one hundred years the Bauers made saddles for cattlemen, Texas Rangers,qv sheriffs, and law enforcement officers throughout Texas, other states, Mexico, and South America. J. Frank Dobie qv was particularly fond of the Bauer saddle. In 1890 Bauer was justice of the peace in Live Oak County. Paul Bauer was in partnership with a son until his death. He died on October 28, 1934, and was buried in Beeville.

BIBLIOGRAPHY: Grace Bauer, History of Bee County, Texas (M.A. thesis, University of Texas, 1939); *Bee-Picayune* (Beeville), November 1, 1934; J. Frank Dobie, "On Silver Christmas Trees," San Antonio *Express*, December 22, 1960; Thelma Lindholm, *Live Oak County Centennial History, 1856–1956* (n.d.).

Grace Bauer

*Baugh, John J.

Baulard, Victor Joseph. Victor Joseph Baulard, son of Jean Antoine Baulard, was born in Besançon, France, in 1828. He came with his father to Texas in 1843 and settled at Galveston. Young Baulard apprenticed himself to Joseph W. Rice, a painter and merchant. In 1853 the two men established the firm of Rice & Baulard, dealers in paints, oils, glass, and allied goods. The firm became the largest of its kind in Galveston, with a trade extending throughout Texas and western Louisiana. Baulard was active in various civic, social, and benevolent organizations. In 1851 he married Clothilde L. Gillet; they had seven children. He died on October 3, 1889.

BIBLIOGRAPHY: Andrew Morrison (ed.), *The Industries of Galveston* (1887); Galveston *News*, October 4, 1889; Affidavit of Julie Baulard Borelly.

*Baum, Texas. See Sturgeon, Texas.

*Baumann Branch.

*Baxter, Texas.

*Baxter Springs Trail.

*Bay City, Texas. Bay City, seat of Matagorda County, is a commercial center for nearby petrochemical, petroleum, farming, and ranching interests. Among its 237 businesses listed in 1970 were several industries, the largest of which was a branch of Celanese Chemical Company. Other manufacturing and industrial concerns included rice mills, machine shops, sheet metal works, and the production of concrete, gases, feeds, and fertilizers. In 1965 the city completed construction of a new city hall and courthouse. The 1960 population was 11,656; in 1970 it was 11,733.

*Bay View College.

*Bayland Orphans' Home for Boys.

*Baylor, George Wythe.

*Baylor, Henry Weidner.

*Baylor, John Robert. John Robert Baylor married Emily Hammond in 1844 in Marshall, Texas; they were the parents of ten children.

*Baylor, Robert Emmett Bledsoe.

*Baylor County. Baylor County ranked in 1965 among the state's leading wheat-producing counties, but actually derived more income from cattle raising. The county's three thousand irrigated acres in 1964 (Lake Kemp and Diversion Reservoir on the Wichita River providing the water) also yielded several thousand bales of cotton as well as some grain sorghums. Total county farm income by 1970 exceeded eight million dollars annually. Oil production from 1924 to 1973 was 47,504,033 barrels. The county population was 5,893 in 1960 and 5,221 in 1970.

*Baylor Creek.

Baylor Creek Reservoir. Baylor Creek Reservoir is in the Red River Basin in Childress County, ten miles northwest of Childress on Baylor Creek, a tributary to Prairie Dog Town Fork of the Red River. The project is owned and operated by the city of Childress for municipal water supply and recreational purposes. Construction of the dam was started by the city on April 1, 1949, and completed in February, 1950. Deliberate impoundment of water was begun in 1949, and use of the water began in 1954. Adjacent to this reservoir is Lake Childress, which was built on a tributary to Baylor Creek in 1923. This lake had an original capacity of 4,600 acre-feet, and is still part of the city's water supply system. In 1966 Baylor Creek Reservoir had a capacity of 9,220 acre-feet and a surface area of 610 acres at the operating elevation of 2,010 feet above mean sea level. The drainage area above the dam is forty square miles.

BIBLIOGRAPHY: Texas Water Commission, *Bulletin 6408* (1964).

Seth D. Breeding

*Baylor Female College.

*Baylor Mountains.

*Baylor University. [The first president of Baylor University was Henry Lee (not Lea, as stated in Volume I) Graves,qv who received notice of his election on January 12, 1846, arrived in Independence in December, 1846, and entered upon his duties February 4, 1847. Ed.] Baylor University made unprecedented growth in both capital assets and academic standards during the thirteen-year administration of President William R. White. Between 1948 and 1959 the university departments affiliated with the highest accreditation agencies in their respective fields. Baylor's plant was increased in value some ten million dollars by addition of eleven new buildings, including Armstrong Browning Library,qv dormitories and apartments, music hall, School of Law, and Bible building.

Library holdings increased by 93,209 volumes between 1948 and 1965. The nucleus of the library collection was acquired in 1902 when the Erisophian, Philomathesian, Adelphian, Calleopean, and Burleson societies presented their libraries to the university. The F. L. Carroll Library, completed in 1903, was gutted by fire in 1922, but students were credited with saving most of the books. The rebuilt structure houses the main library. Special collections

in music, theology, law, Texana, and Robert Browning supplemented the general library, which in 1969 consisted of approximately 460,600 books and periodicals housed in fifteen units on the campus.

In June, 1959, Judge Abner V. McCall, former dean of the School of Law, was made executive vice-president with administrative responsibility, and White assumed public relations duties. In April, 1962, McCall was named president of the university. That same year White became Baylor's first chancellor, and in 1963 he was president emeritus.

McCall's administration was characterized by an emphasis on scholastic excellence with efforts to upgrade faculty, students, and facilities and to extend the graduate program. The university's College of Arts and Sciences provided special programs in American studies; B.S. degrees could be obtained in dental hygiene and pre-professional work in medical technology, physical therapy, dentistry, medicine, engineering, and forestry. A senior division of the United States Air Force Reserve Officers' Training Corps was located at Baylor. Doctoral programs were offered in English, chemistry, psychology, physics, and education. Graduate programs in many aspects of dentistry, medicine, and allied fields were sponsored in cooperation with the College of Medicine (Houston), College of Dentistry, and the Graduate Research Center (Dallas). The Master of Hospital Administration degree was offered for military personnel in cooperation with the Medical Field Service School at Brooke Army Medical Center, Fort Sam Houston.qqv

By 1965 Baylor's enrollment at Waco, including 268 students in the School of Law, reached 6,432—considered the maximum figure consistent with available facilities. The administration and teaching staff totaled 364 with 88 of these in part-time service. Approximately one-fourth of the faculty was involved in research, supported by various sources. Between 1845 and 1965, the institution graduated 36,121 students. In 1965, 74 percent of the students were Texans; the remainder represented every state in the Union and twenty-one foreign countries. Although Baptist in affiliation, Baylor had students from over thirty religious denominations.

Between 1960 and 1965 the Waco campus was extended by fifty-five acres; construction of a student health center, school of business, science building, and auxiliary buildings brought the investment in a total of thirty-two buildings to twenty-four million dollars. A second science building was constructed and a new library was ready for occupancy by 1968, when investments in Baylor's campuses at Waco, Dallas, and Houston totaled fifty-three million dollars, plus forty-two million dollars in endowments and other investments and assets. In 1970 enrollment was 6,632, and the faculty numbered 398. By 1974 the enrollment had increased to 8,130.

Lois Smith Murray

Baylor University College of Dentistry. Baylor University College of Dentistry held the distinction of being the oldest institution of higher learning in Dallas. The parent school, the State Dental College, received a license from the state of Texas in 1905 and opened its first class in 1906. A private institution, it met with little cordiality from the local profession, because many felt there were enough dentists with sufficient training working in the area. The difficult existence of the college eased somewhat in 1916, when the owners turned over management of the college to a group of local dentists who wanted to improve and enlarge its operation.

As this was a proprietary school with no university connection, mass induction of the 140-member student body for service in World War I appeared certain. The owners saved the situation by selling the college to Baylor University in the fall of 1918, when it became an integral part of the Baylor system.

In 1943, when Baylor University College of Medicine was moved to Houston, the College of Dentistry was left without faculty and facilities for basic science courses. Although extremely scarce during World War II, sufficient teachers and equipment were obtained to continue classwork without interruption. In 1948 a building program was begun, and the first new building, a large well-equipped clinic, was occupied in 1950.

Enrollment in 1950 numbered 242 students and 1 graduate student, compared to 428 students, 55 graduate students, and 74 dental hygiene students in 1965; total enrollment for the 1974–1975 regular term was 465. The Caruth School of Dental Hygiene was added in 1955 with a two-year curriculum which could be supplemented with work on the Waco campus for a bachelor's degree. Total faculty increased from 77 to 141 between 1950 and 1970. Keeping pace with the profession, the college met the rigid requirements for the Council on Accreditation of the American Dental Association. The graduate school offered an M.S. degree in dentistry and certificates in dental specialties, in addition to M.S. and Ph.D. degrees in the basic sciences. The building program included a basic science wing (1954) and a graduate research wing (1960), as well as expansion and improvements of classrooms, laboratories, and clinics. Library holdings grew from 6,843 books and journals in 1950 to approximately 17,000 volumes in 1965, including the Arthur Merritt and the Harold Judson Leonard collections. In 1974 Kenneth Randolph was dean.

Gladys Yates

*Baylor University College of Medicine. Baylor University College of Medicine, Houston, in 1966 was divided into nineteen departments, which collectively represented all traditional disciplines of the basic sciences and the clinical specialties of medicine.

In addition to the Roy and Lillie Cullen Building, occupied in 1947, the College of Medicine operated the following components of the Texas Medical Center:qv Jesse H. Jones Building for Clinical Research, M. D. Anderson Basic Science

Research Building, Jewish Institute for Medical Research, all completed in 1963, and Rayzor Student-Faculty Center.

Ben Taub General Hospital and Jefferson Davis Hospital, city-county facilities, and the Veterans Administration Hospital were staffed by the faculty of the College of Medicine. Other teaching hospitals were Methodist Hospital, St. Luke's Episcopal Hospital, Texas Children's Hospital, Houston State Psychiatric Institute (now Texas Research Institute of Mental Sciences), Texas Institute for Rehabilitation and Research, and to a limited extent, M. D. Anderson Hospital and Hermann Hospital.

In 1965 the College of Medicine shared the facilities of the Texas Medical Center Library, which contained 90,000 volumes and subscribed to 1,200 journals. Animals for research were provided by a vivarium affiliated with the College of Veterinary Medicine of Texas A&M University.

Faculty duties include a threefold combination of teaching, research, and public service. Perhaps the most noted research undertaken by the College of Medicine was Dr. Michael E. DeBakey's joint effort with the engineering faculty of Rice University to develop a mechanical heart. Hundreds of other significant medical research projects were undertaken in such areas as cancer biology, organ and tissue transplantation, computer analysis of health records, and virology.

The College of Medicine offered not only the M.D. degree but combined clinical and scientific degree programs for the M.D.-Ph.D. and M.D.-M.S. in specialty fields. During the 1964–1965 term 372 students enrolled and the faculty numbered 338 members. By 1965 the College of Medicine had graduated 3,290 physicians; enrollment for the 1974–1975 regular session was 710 students. In 1953 Dr. Stanley W. Olson succeeded Dr. Walter H. Moursund, Sr., as dean of the College of Medicine. In 1969 Baylor University College of Medicine became a private institution with Michael E. DeBakey as president.

BIBLIOGRAPHY: Walter H. Moursund, Sr., *A History of Baylor University College of Medicine, 1900–1953* (1956); J. R. Schofield (ed.), *Education of the Physician* (1965), *Education in the Basic Medical Sciences* (1966).

Russell Clem

Baylor University School of Nursing. Baylor University School of Nursing, Waco and Dallas, developed from a training school for nurses in the Texas Baptist Memorial Sanitarium, the forerunner of Baylor University Medical Center in Dallas. After a year's operation, the sanitarium closed to allow erection of a more suitable building. The training school was reactivated in October, 1909, when the new facility was ready for patients. Mildred Bridges served as director of the first training school and was succeeded by May Marr. During the early period, the school was considered necessary for hospital operation as pupils worked a seventy-eight-hour week doing housekeeping in addition to nursing chores. Mrs. Helen Holliday Lehman, director of the school for twenty-four years, gradually changed the twelve-hour day to an eight-hour one, and she relieved students of many housekeeping tasks.

Although the school had ties with Baylor University from its beginning, it was first called by its present name in 1924, when Elsa Maurer became the first director to have the title of dean. A total of 1,525 nurses were graduated under this program which was based on three years' work in the hospital rather than on academic achievement.

Since 1950 the school has been an integral part of Baylor University. During the administration of Zora McAnally Fiedler, the board of trustees changed control of the School of Nursing from Baylor Hospital directly to Baylor University, and the dean of the school became responsible to the president of the university. This move enabled the creation of a four-year degree program requiring sixty hours in nursing and seventy-five hours in general education. Between 1950 and 1965, 320 men and women were graduated under the new program. Enrollment for the 1974–1975 regular term was 209 at Waco and 192 at Dallas.

In 1954 Dean Frances McKenna succeeded in changing student hospital duty to an academic laboratory, and in 1964 Dean Anne Taylor obtained accreditation for the school by the National League for Nursing. Mrs. Geddes McLaughlin served as dean in 1974.

Sada F. Haynes

*Bayou, Texas.
*Bayou Alazan.
*Bayou Atascosa.
*Bayou Blue.
*Bayou Bonita.
*Bayou Carrizo.
*Bayou City.
*Bayou Din.
*Bayou La Nana.
*Bayou Lavaca.
*Bayou Loco.
*Bayou Morral.
*Bayou Pontizella.
*Bayou Vistador.
*Bayou Wander.
*Bays, Joseph.
*Bayside, Texas.

*Baytown, Texas. The towns of Pelly and Goose Creek, in 1947, did not consolidate with Baytown (as stated in Volume I). Pelly annexed unincorporated Baytown, and later, in 1947, Pelly and Goose Creek were consolidated, taking the name Baytown. Baytown, in Harris County, was incorporated in 1948, and it had a council-manager form of government. In 1966 there were seventeen public schools, a junior college, sixty-six churches, three banks, four hospitals, one daily newspaper, a radio station, and two public libraries. The city's economy has been greatly influenced by the surrounding petrochemical companies. By 1970

there were 414 businesses, a number of which were manufacturers. In 1951 buildings were completed for Lee Junior College, and in 1953 the Baytown-La Porte Tunnel, crossing the Houston Ship Channel,qv was opened. In 1965 construction was underway on a new high school, and the city began an extensive public improvement program. In 1960 Baytown had a population of 28,159; the 1970 population was 43,980. *See also* Houston Standard Metropolitan Statistical Area.

*Bayview, Texas.
*Bazette, Texas.
*Beach, Harrison Leroy.
*Beach Creek.
*Beach Mountains.
*Bead Mountain.
*Bead Mountain Creek.
*Beadle, Texas.
*Beal, John T.
*Beales, John Charles.
*Beales' Rio Grande Colony.
*Beall, Benjamin Lloyd.
*Beall, Jack. Jack Beall served in the United States House of Representatives from 1903 to 1915 (not in the United States Senate, as stated in Volume I).

*Beall, Thomas J.
*Beals Branch.
*Bean, Peter Ellis.
*Bean, Roy.
*Bean Hill, Texas.

Bean Indians. The Bean Indians (native name; does not refer to the common vegetable) are known from a single Spanish document of 1683 which does not clearly identify their area. Although it cannot be demonstrated, the Bean may have been the same people as the Teaname, also known as Teana and Peana, who at that time lived in northeastern Coahuila and the adjoining part of Texas (southwestern part of the Edwards Plateau).

BIBLIOGRAPHY: V. Alessio Robles, *Coahuila y Texas en la Epoca Colonial* (1938); F. W. Hodge (ed.), *Handbook of American Indians*, II (1910); C. W. Hackett (ed.), *Pichardo's Treatise on the Limits of Louisiana and Texas*, I (1931).

T. N. Campbell

*Beane Creek.
*Beans Creek.
*Bean's Place, Texas.
*Bean's Prairie, Texas.
*Bear Bayou.
*Bear Branch.
*Bear Creek.
*Bear Creek, Texas. (Comal County.)
*Bear Creek, Texas. (DeWitt County.)
*Bear Creek, Texas. (San Jacinto County.)
*Bear Grass, Texas.

*Bear Mountain.

*Bear Spring Branch.

*Beard, James.

*Bearhead Creek.

*Bear-pen Creek.

*Bears Foot Creek.

*Beasley, Texas.

*Beason Creek.

*Beattie, Texas.

*Beatty's Peak.

Beaty, John Owen. John Owen Beaty, educator and author, was born on December 22, 1890, in Crow, West Virginia, son of James Robert and Eula (Simms) Beaty. He received a B.A. and M.A. (1913) from the University of Virginia. He joined the army in 1917, remaining until 1919 on active duty, and until 1950 in the reserves, when he retired as a colonel. After graduate work at the University of Montpellier, France, he joined the faculty of Southern Methodist University, Dallas, as assistant professor of English in 1919. In 1921 Columbia University awarded him a Ph.D. degree. In 1926–1927 he was an American Kahn fellow working in Asia and Europe. From 1927 to 1957 Beaty served as head of the English department at Southern Methodist University, the last seventeen years in an honorary capacity. From 1926 to 1934 he was visiting professor during the summers at various universities, including the University of Texas.

In addition to teaching for thirty-eight years, Beaty wrote many books, including *An Introduction to Poetry* (1922), *An Introduction to Drama* (1927), *Texas Poems* (1936), *Swords in the Dawn* (1937), *Image of Life* (1940), and *Crossroads* (1956). His book *The Iron Curtain Over America* (1951), claiming that the Jewish people were responsible for the Communist expansion in Europe, was widely criticized. Beaty was also an editor with others of several compilations, and a prolific contributor to professional and popular magazines. He was a member of the Modern Language Association; Conference of College Teachers of English (president of the Texas group, 1937–1938); American Academy of Political Science; Order of the White Cross; and the Baptist church.

In 1920 Beaty married Josephine Mason Powell, and they had four children. Beaty died on September 9, 1961, in Barboursville, Virginia.

BIBLIOGRAPHY: *Who's Who In America* (1960); *Texian Who's Who* (1937); New York *Times*, September 13, 1961.

*Beau Monde.

*Beauchamp, Thomas D.

*Beauchamps Creek.

*Beaukiss, Texas.

Beaumier, Walter R. Walter R. (Beau) Beaumier, publisher of the Lufkin *News* and an East Texas civic leader for more than twenty years, was born at Hallettsville, Texas, on October 7, 1906, the son of Walter R. Beaumier, Sr. He attended schools at Bartlett, Schwertner, Salado, and Belton and after high school graduation took his first job in the sports department of the San Antonio *Express*,qv where he remained from 1924 to 1933. He was married to Mary Native of Paducah, Kentucky, on November 15, 1929, in Pearsall, Texas. They had one child, a daughter.

From 1935 to 1939 he served as editorial writer for the Beaumont *Journal*. He left there to become trade extension secretary of the Beaumont Chamber of Commerce. The following year he went to Lufkin as Lufkin Chamber of Commerce manager and was soon offered the management of the Lufkin *News*. He served as president of the Texas Press Association qv and was a member of the advisory councils of the University of Texas and Texas A&M. He became vice-president and general manager of the *News* in 1943 and continued in the capacity of publisher and vice-president until his death on September 1, 1965, in Houston, Texas. He was buried at Lufkin.

BIBLIOGRAPHY: Biographical File, Barker Texas History Center, University of Texas at Austin.

*Beaumont, Eugene Beauharnais.

*Beaumont, Jefferson.

*Beaumont, Texas. Beaumont, seat of Jefferson County, has access to the Gulf of Mexico through the Gulf Intracoastal Waterway.qv In 1970 there were 1,665 businesses in Beaumont, of which 122 were manufacturers. The city had over 160 churches, a four-year college, forty-four public schools, twelve hospitals, seven banks, two newspapers, five radio stations, two television stations, a public library, and recreational facilities. In 1960 Beaumont's population was 119,175; in 1970 it was 115,919. *See also* Beaumont-Port Arthur-Orange Standard Metropolitan Statistical Area.

*Beaumont and Great Northern Railway Company.

Beaumont-Port Arthur-Orange Standard Metropolitan Statistical Area. The Beaumont-Port Arthur-Orange Standard Metropolitan Statistical Area was originally created as the Beaumont-Port Arthur Standard Metropolitan Statistical Area by the Bureau of the Budget in 1949. The census report of 1950 listed Beaumont and Port Arthur separately with their metropolitan areas and also as a single metropolitan center. Beaumont had a population of 94,014 within its city limits and 112,216 in its metropolitan area; Port Arthur had 57,530 and 81,763, respectively. Together the Beaumont-Port Arthur area contained 193,979 inhabitants with 151,544 living in the two core cities. The combined metropolitan area included most but not all of Jefferson County, which had a population of 195,083 in 1950. In December, 1958, Orange County was added, enlarging the official metropolitan area from 945 to 1,301 square miles. In the 1960 census the area contained 306,016 residents; Beaumont had 119,175; Port Arthur had 66,676; and Orange, the largest city in Orange County, had

25,605. In 1970 the population of the area was 315,943, with 115,919 persons in Beaumont, 57,-371 in Port Arthur, and 24,457 in Orange. Other cities with more than one thousand inhabitants were Nederland, Port Neches, Pear Ridge, and Lakeview, in Jefferson County; and Bridge City, Vidor, Pinehurst, West Orange, and Cove City, in Orange County. Bevil Oaks, Sabine Pass, China, Pine Forest, Orangefield, and eleven smaller communities were also located within the area. In March, 1967, the Bureau of the Budget added Orange to the area's title, now officially designated as the Beaumont-Port Arthur-Orange Standard Metropolitan Statistical Area.

Beaumont, Port Arthur, and Orange were deep-water ports. The Sabine-Neches Waterway qv connects Beaumont, twenty-nine miles up the river, with the Gulf of Mexico. Because of this forty-foot-deep and four-hundred-foot-wide channel, Beaumont was Texas' second largest port. In 1963 it shipped over thirty million tons and ranked eighth in the nation in gross tonnage shipped. Port Arthur, located on Lake Sabine, nine miles from the Gulf of Mexico, shipped over twenty-eight million tons in 1963 and was the third largest port in Texas. The combined ports of Beaumont, Port Arthur, and Orange—the Sabine-Neches ports—ranked third in the United States behind New York and New Orleans. The principal foreign imports are petroleum products, while the main exports are lubricating and fuel oils, gasoline, wheat, rice, grain sorghums, dry sulphur, and coke. The chief coastal shipments include gasoline, crude oil, and sulphur.

The metropolitan area is a highly developed industrial center with manufacturing furnishing most of its income. Petroleum refining, petrochemicals, fabricated metals and machinery, and shipbuilding are the most important industries. In 1963 there were 265 manufacturing plants in the area, with 97 employing over twenty workers each. Popularly known as the "Golden Triangle," the Beaumont-Port Arthur-Orange oil refining and petrochemical complex has, along with the rest of the Texas Gulf Coast, about 20 percent of the petroleum refining capacity of the United States. Oil and gas fields, sulphur mines, and brine wells contributed most of the mineral wealth of the area. In 1963 Orange and Jefferson counties produced 12,-433,000 barrels of oil, 150,726,355,000 cubic feet of gas, and 2,436,000 barrels of hydrocarbon liquids. Jefferson County contributed about one-fourth of the sulphur produced in Texas. Brine, a 25 percent salt solution taken from the Spindletop Oil Field,qv is converted through electrolysis to chlorine and caustic soda for use in the petrochemical industry. Orange County is the lumber-producing center of the area with two active sawmills. Rice, the leading crop of the area, accounts for approximately 75 percent of the total farm income. Beaumont and Orange are large rice milling centers. Dairying and cattle ranching also contribute to the farm income. Port Arthur and Orange are commercial fishing centers.

Three railroads, three airlines and four airports, and a good highway system including Interstate 10 serve the area. Numerous radio and television stations, six newspapers, and public libraries in Beaumont, Nederland, Orange, Port Arthur, and Port Neches keep the area informed. Lamar University is located in Beaumont (with branches in Port Arthur and Orange). Culturally, Beaumont supports a symphony orchestra and an art museum, Port Arthur has an annual community concert series and a little theater, and Orange also has a community theatrical group. Annual events in the metropolitan area include the Neches River Festival, the South Texas State Fair, the Cav-Oil-Cade, and the YMBL Rodeo. Some historical sites include the Lucas Gusher Monument in the Spindletop Oil Field,qv the Temple to the Brave, the Richard W. (Dick) Dowling qv Monument, and the Clifton Walking Beam. The Gulf of Mexico, Sabine Lake, and the Neches and Sabine rivers offer opportunities for boating, fishing, and water sports. *See also* Standard Metropolitan Statistical Areas in Texas. [Hardin County was added to the Beaumont-Port Arthur-Orange Standard Metropolitan Statistical Area in April, 1973.   Ed.]

Preston B. Williams

*Beaumont and Saratoga Transportation Company.

*Beaumont, Sour Lake, and Western Railway.

*Beaumont Wharf and Terminal Company. The Beaumont Wharf and Terminal Company, operating a terminal and 3.85 miles of terminal track at Beaumont, was merged on May 3, 1957, with the Gulf, Colorado, and Santa Fe Railway Company.

James M. Day

*Beauxart Gardens, Texas.

*Beaver Creek.

*Beaver Dam, Texas.

*Beaver Hill, Texas.

*Beaver Lake.

*Beaverdam Creek.

*Bebe, Texas.

*Beccero Creek.

*Becerra Creek.

*Becker, Texas.

*Beckham, Robert H.

*Beckham, Texas.

*Beckman, Texas.

Beckmann, John Conrad. John (Johann) Conrad Beckmann, known for his artistic ironwork, was born on June 13, 1815, in Ruelle, Westphalia, near Osnabrück, Germany, the son of Johann Heinrich and Katarina Maria (Kohmoeller) Beckmann. He came to New York in 1839, traveling also to Baltimore and Cincinnati. He returned to Zurich, Switzerland, and brought his betrothed, Regina

Mueller, to New York, where they were married in 1841. His brothers Joe and Bernhart were already in New York.

Beckmann had been trained in Zurich as a locksmith, as a woodworking craftsman, and as a blacksmith. He came to San Antonio in 1841 and later worked for the United States government, setting up three forges in the Alamo for blacksmith work for the army and for the renovation of the Alamo. His first home, built in 1849 on Crockett Street, was behind the Alamo. His home on the southwest corner of Commerce and Casino streets, which he built later, was also the location of his blacksmith shop. With the urging of Dr. Ferdinand Herff,qv Beckmann fashioned hand-wrought iron bedsteads for his German friends.

He was active in the social, benevolent, athletic, musical, and educational affairs of San Antonio. He was a charter member of Alamo Masonic Lodge No. 44. A founder of the German-English School,qv he took part in the cornerstone laying in 1859, the hundredth anniversary of the birth of German poet Friedrich Schiller. He was a founder and charter member of early San Antonio German organizations: the Casino Club, the *Turnverein* (gymnastic club), *Krankenkassenverein* (hospitalization insurance association), *Arbeiter Verein* (workers association), the Beethoven *Maennerchor,* and the Teutonia Mixed Chorus.

Beckmann died on April 12, 1907, in San Antonio and was buried in the Alamo Masonic Cemetery. He was survived by one son. Although the Beckmanns had been the parents of seven children, several died in a cholera epidemic. Beckmann's portrait, painted by artist Edward Grenet qv in the early 1880's, is said to have encouraged the young artist in his career as a portrait painter.

BIBLIOGRAPHY: Frederick Charles Chabot, *With the Makers of San Antonio* (1937); *A Twentieth Century History of Southwest Texas* (1907); San Antonio *Express,* April 13, 1907.

S. W. Pease

*Becknell, William.

*Beckville, Texas.

*Becton, Edwin Pinckney.

*Becton, John May.

*Becton, Texas. The Becton, Lubbock County, post office was operated until August 30, 1942, when it was discontinued, the mail being sent to Lorenzo. As of January 1, 1970, population was approximately 100.

Cyrus Tilloson

Beddoe, Earl Percy. Earl Percy Beddoe was born on January 30, 1822, in eastern Tennessee, son of Philip Tolbert and Catherine (Parr) Beddoe. He married Martha Caroline Hembree on October 12, 1843, in Tennessee, and they were the parents of nine children.

After an education in civil engineering, Beddoe moved to Texas in 1845, lived in Marshall, where he built a tan yard, then in 1850 settled in Sabinetown, where he established a saddle and harness business. He served for a while there as school principal; he was named county surveyor of Sabine County and laid out the town of Hemphill as the new county seat in 1859.

Beddoe acted as a courier during the Civil War, and as a civil engineer he figured in the planning of fortifications at Sabine Pass in 1863. He helped plan and execute the embankments or breastworks fortifying Sabinetown in 1864.

In 1869 or early 1870 Beddoe and his family moved to Sabine Parish, Louisiana, but soon after 1871 they moved to Navarro County, Texas, where Beddoe died on November 27, 1876, in Chatfield.

Helen Gomer Schluter

*Bedford, Texas. Bedford, in eastern Tarrant County, had a post office from 1881 until about 1910. In 1950 the post office was reestablished. In 1952 the town was incorporated with a commission form of government, changing to an alderman form of government in 1965. The town reported seven churches, a hospital, and a library. The 1960 population was 2,706; the 1970 count was 10,049, according to the U. S. census. *See also* Fort Worth Standard Metropolitan Statistical Area.

Cyrus Tilloson

*Bedias, Texas.

*Bedias Creek.

*Bedias Road.

Bedichek, Roy. Roy Bedichek was born in Cass County, Illinois, on June 27, 1878, the son of James Madison and Lucretia Ellen (Craven) Bedichek. In 1884 he was brought by his parents to Falls County, Texas. He attended rural schools and Bedichek Academy, established at Eddy by his father. In February, 1898, he entered the University of Texas. Soon he began to work in the office of the registrar, John A. Lomax,qv who became his friend for life. In 1903 he received the B.S. degree and in 1925, the M.A.

He was a reporter for the Fort Worth *Record* qv (1903–1904) and taught in high schools in Houston (1904–1905) and in San Angelo (1905–1908). He served as secretary of the Deming, New Mexico, Chamber of Commerce (1908–1913) and edited the Deming *Headlight* (1910–1912). In 1910 he married Lillian Lee Greer, and they had three children.

In 1913 Bedichek returned to Austin and became secretary of the Young Men's Business League, which later merged with the chamber of commerce. In 1915–1916 he was executive secretary of Will C. Hogg's qv Organization for Promoting Interest in Higher Education in Texas. He served as city editor of the San Antonio *Express* qv for a year; then in the fall of 1917 he began work in Austin with the University Interscholastic League,qv a part of the Bureau of Extension. As director of the league he shaped its policies and made it a success. He ceased active direction in 1948 at the age of seventy.

In visiting schools over the state he formed the habit of camping out because suitable lodging was often unavailable. Camping stimulated his interest in wildlife, especially in birds. Urged by his close friends, J. Frank Dobie and Walter Prescott Webb,qqv he took leave of absence for a year beginning in February, 1946, and went into seclusion at Friday Mountain Ranch,qv Webb's retreat southwest of Austin, to write *Adventures with a Texas Naturalist* (1947). *Karánkaway Country* (1950) won the Carr P. Collins Award for the best Texas book of the year, as did *Educational Competition: The Story of the University Interscholastic League of Texas* (1956). A fourth book, *The Sense of Smell* (1960), appeared posthumously.

Bedichek liked to rise several hours before daybreak and study or write in a separate building beside his home. Every day he worked in his garden, swam, or walked. Without ever having been seriously ill, he died suddenly of heart failure on May 21, 1959. He was an excellent storyteller, a fine conversationalist, and a delightful correspondent. In 1967 a selection of his letters was being prepared for publication.

BIBLIOGRAPHY: *Texas Observer* (Austin), June 27, 1959; *Texian Who's Who* (1937); Stanley Walker, "The Lively Hermit of Friday Mountain," *Saturday Evening Post* (October 16, 1948).

Wilson M. Hudson

*Bee, Barnard E.

*Bee, Carlos.

*Bee, Hamilton Prioleau.

*Bee Branch.

Bee Caves, Texas. [This title was incorrectly listed in Volume I as Beecaves, Texas.] Bee Caves, sometimes referred to as Bee Cave, is located eighteen miles west of Austin in Travis County. It was founded about 1870 by Will Johnson, the name being derived from a large cave of wild bees discovered at the site. By 1873 Carl Beck had opened a store in an existing one-room rock house and had built a gin, a mill, and a cigar factory. A post office was opened soon after with Beck serving as postmaster, a position he held for the next forty-five years. By 1882 Bee Caves had a school operating in a ten-by-twelve-foot rock room. Johnson's son, Wiley, later established a trading post at the crossing of the two wagon roads. The store and trading post were operating in 1973, when the population was approximately fifty. *See also* Austin Standard Metropolitan Statistical Area.

*Bee Caves Creek.

*Bee County. Bee County is a ranching and farming area producing grain sorghums, cotton, flax, and broomcorn. Five thousand acres were irrigated in 1964. Small regional industries center in the county seat, Beeville; Pettus has petroleum industries. The county's oil production from 1930 to 1973 was 79,973,226 barrels. In 1954 the first United States Navy all-jet base opened at Beeville's

Naval Auxiliary Air Station,qv and in 1966 an airport began operation in Beeville. The county supports a library (completed in 1957), a hospital (1963), and Bee County College (1967). Population in 1960 was 23,755 and in 1970 was 22,737.

Bee County College. The Bee County Junior College District was created in November, 1965, and in December voters approved a tax to support the college and the issuance of bonds to erect buildings. The board of trustees and President Grady C. Hogue began the college program in September, 1967, with an enrollment of approximately six hundred students. The campus, donated by the A. C. Jones family, is about a mile north of Beeville. The library holdings totaled 13,500 volumes in 1969. The school provides the first two years of college degree programs; it offers technical courses in electronic data processing, drafting and design, electronics, and mid-management in business leading to associate's degrees; and it provides vocational courses in automotive mechanics, business and accounting, general business, data processing, secretarial, clerk-typist, and nursing, all leading to certificates. The college was approved by the Texas Education Agency and the Coordinating Board, Texas College and University System.qqv It is a member of the American Association of Junior Colleges, Texas Association of Public Junior Colleges, and Texas Association of Junior Colleges. In 1974 the college enrollment was 1,670.

*Bee Cove Creek.

*Bee Creek.

*Bee House Creek.

*Bee Industry. In 1954 honey production had decreased two million pounds from its 1953 total. The value of the 7,560,000 pounds produced by the 280,000 bee colonies was estimated at $1,100,000. Although by 1964 the number of colonies had declined to 252,000, production had risen to 12,096,000 pounds valued at $1,887,000. Texas ranked eighth in the United States in honey production in 1963. In 1966 the 12,189,000 pounds of honey produced by 239,000 colonies was valued at $1,914,000. In 1970 Texas continued to rank among the ten leading states in honey production.

BIBLIOGRAPHY: *Texas Almanac* (1955, 1965, 1967, 1971).

*Bee Mountain.

*Beecaves, Texas. *See* Bee Caves, Texas.

*Beech Creek.

*Beech Grove, Texas.

*Beecham Branch.

*Beef Canyon.

*Beef Creek.

*Beef Trail.

*Beehouse, Texas.

*Beeman, James J.

*Beeson, Benjamin.

*Beeson, Leander.

*Beeson, William E.

*Beeson's Ford.

*Beeville, Texas. Beeville, seat of Bee County, draws its economic life chiefly from agriculture, oil and gas, and nearby Beeville Naval Auxiliary Air Station.qv Beeville was the center of the major broomcorn growing area in the state. The city in 1970 had 258 businesses, including three banks, a newspaper, a radio station, and several small industries. Two hospitals, a library, a college, and twenty-five churches were also reported. The 1960 population was 13,811; the 1970 population was 13,506.

Beeville Naval Auxiliary Air Station. See Naval Auxiliary Air Station, Beeville, Texas.

*Behamon, Texas.

*Behrens, Texas.

*Behrenville, Texas.

*Behring Store, Texas.

Beitonijure Indians. The Beitonijure were one of twenty Indian groups that joined Juan Domínguez de Mendoza qv on his expedition from El Paso to the vicinity of present San Angelo in 1683–1684. Since Mendoza did not indicate at what point the Beitonijure joined his party, it is impossible to determine their range or affiliations. However, the Indians between the Pecos River and the San Angelo area were being hard-pressed by Apache at that time, and it seems likely that the Beitonijure ranged between these two localities.
BIBLIOGRAPHY: H. E. Bolton (ed.), Spanish Exploration in the Southwest, 1542–1706 (1916).

T. N. Campbell

*Bejar. See Bexar.

*Belcher, Edward.

*Belcher, Texas.

*Belcherville, Texas.

*Belco, Texas.

*Belfalls, Texas.

*Belfrage, Gustave W.

*Belgrade, Texas.

*Belk, Texas.

Belknap, Augustus. Augustus Belknap was born on March 19, 1841, in Newburg, New York, the son of Augustus Belknap. Educated in private military schools, he was in the hardware business from 1856 to 1861, when at the beginning of the Civil War he entered the 7th Regiment of the New York National Guard on April 19, 1861. After his term of duty expired he reenlisted with what later became the 67th Regulars, New York Volunteers. He was severely wounded at the battle of Fairoaks, and he saw action at Fredericksburg and Seven Pines. He was mustered out of service on February 9, 1863, with the rank of captain. He married (?) Pickard on December 9, 1863, and they had three daughters and one son. Belknap joined the Old Guard Metropolitan Regiment in New York City after the Civil War, and he became a junior partner in the hardware firm of William S. Dodge and Co.

In 1877 Belknap moved to San Antonio, where he became founder and president of the company which operated the city's only streetcar system. He was president and director of the Opera House Company and a director of the San Antonio Fair Association. He was elected alderman of the 2nd Ward in 1883 and 1885, and alderman-at-large in 1887, but he resigned later that year when he became the Republican candidate for Congress from the 10th District; he was defeated in that race.

Belknap was the founder and sponsor of the Belknap Rifles,qv which he organized in October, 1884. He died while visiting in Santa Barbara, California, on June 22, 1889, and his body was taken to the Belknap family vault in Greenwood Cemetery, Brooklyn, New York, where an honor guard of six members of the Belknap Rifles was in attendance.
BIBLIOGRAPHY: Frederick Charles Chabot, With the Makers of San Antonio (1937); A Twentieth Century History of Southwest Texas, I (1907); 100th Anniversary, Pioneer Flour Mills: San Antonio, Texas, 1851–1951 (1951?); San Antonio Express, June 24, 25, 1889.

S. W. Pease

*Belknap, Charles.

*Belknap, William Goldsmith.

*Belknap, Texas.

Belknap Coal Company. See Newcastle, Texas.

*Belknap Creek.

*Belknap Rifles.

*Bell, Charles Keith.

*Bell, James G.

*Bell, James Hall.

*Bell, John S.

*Bell, Josiah Hughes.

*Bell, Peter Hansborough.

*Bell, Thomas B.

*Bell, William.

*Bell Branch.

*Bell Branch, Texas.

*Bell County. Bell County, in east-central Texas, has an economy based on cotton and corn in the eastern and southern parts, and on livestock in the western part. Oats, poultry, and grain sorghums are the more important products, though cattle, sheep, goats, and hogs have increased in significance. Bell County ranked first in the state in turkey raising in 1970. Stillhouse Hollow Reservoir (sometimes called Lampasas Reservoir) was constructed for irrigation and flood control but is also a recreational area. Other tourist attractions are Belton Reservoir, Salado, a July rodeo, a fishing tournament, and Temple Pioneer Day in June. Bell County had a 1960 population of 94,097; in 1970 the population was 124,483. In 1972 Bell County was included in the Killeen-Temple Standard Metropolitan Statistical Area.qv

*Bell Hollow.

*Bell Mountain.

*Bellaire, Texas. Bellaire, in Harris County, has a council-manager form of government and is within the city limits of Houston. In 1966 the town reported four public schools, four banks, nine churches, and one library. At that time Bellaire had 202 businesses, including 10 manufacturers. The town's economy is directly influenced by a petroleum research laboratory and associated businesses and by Houston area concerns which employ many residents. In 1966 the city was involved in various paving and storm sewer-drainage projects. The 1960 population was 19,872, and the 1970 population was 19,009. *See also* Houston Standard Metropolitan Statistical Area.

Belle Branch, Texas. Belle Branch, situated in eastern Atascosa County about three miles south of Fashing, was a stage stop and a post office along the old San Patricio Trail qv in the 1870's. In 1963 only a few large building stones and a dirt-covered section of stone wall remained to mark the site.

*Belle Plain, Texas.

*Belle of Texas. See Scioto Belle.

*Bellevue, Texas.

*Bellisle, Simars de. See De Bellisle, François Simars.

*Bellmead, Texas. Bellmead, adjacent to northeastern Waco in McLennan County, recorded a population increase from approximately 800 in 1950 to 5,127 in 1960; the population was 7,698 in 1970, when eighty businesses were reported. *See also* Waco Standard Metropolitan Statistical Area.

Bellows, Warren Sylvanus. Warren Sylvanus Bellows was born in Kansas City, Missouri, on August 15, 1889. In 1911 he received his degree in civil engineering from the University of Kansas, and by 1921 had established a general contracting firm in Houston, the W. S. Bellows Construction Corporation. This firm was responsible for many of the major constructions in Houston in addition to several buildings in other Texas cities and on the campuses of the University of Texas, Texas A&M University, Southern Methodist University, and the University of Houston. These buildings include the Auditorium Hotel, one of the first of Bellows' constructions, completed in the 1920's, the Humble Headquarters Building, American General Insurance Company and Prudential Insurance Regional Headquarters buildings, the First City National Bank and the Bank of the Southwest buildings, all in Houston. One of the more recent Houston constructions was the Alley Theatre.qv Bellows' firm participated in the building of the Naval Air Station at Corpus Christi,qv built hotels in Galveston, Mobile, Alabama, and Fort Worth, and constructed the administration buildings on the campuses of the University of Texas and the University of Houston. Probably his most famous construction was the San Jacinto Monument,qv at 570 feet the tallest monument in the world when it was completed in 1939.

Bellows was a member of the American Society of Civil Engineers, 1946 president of the Associated General Contractors of America, chairman of the Houston Port Commission from 1950 to 1954, president of the Houston Chamber of Commerce in 1948–1949, member of the board of governors at the University of Houston, and member of the Texas Board of Corrections. He was also industrial member of the War Labor Board during World War II, director of the Gulf, Colorado and Santa Fe Railroad, director of YMCA, and trustee of the M. D. Anderson Foundation, Texas Medical Center, Southwest Research Institute,qqv Southwest Legal Foundation, and Board of Visitors of the University of Texas Cancer Foundation. Bellows was chairman of the Houston Symphony Society, belonged to the Philosophical Society of Texas,qv the Sons of the Republic of Texas,qv which in 1967 made him a knight of the Order of San Jacinto, and the Sons of the American Revolution, which awarded him the 1955 Good Citizens Award; he was a member of various other service and honorary organizations. His several awards included the Royal Order of Vasa from King Gustav VI of Sweden in 1956, the Service Award from the University of Kansas, and the first Annual Meritorious Award of the San Jacinto Chapter of Texas Professional Engineers.

On February 3, 1967, Bellows died in Houston, survived by his wife, Anna Williams Bellows, and four children.

BIBLIOGRAPHY: Houston *Chronicle*, February 5, 1967; *Houston Magazine* (March, 1951); Houston *Post*, February 5, 1967.

*Bells, Texas.

*Bell's Landing, Texas. *See* East Columbia, Texas.

*Bell's Slough.

*Bellville, Texas. Bellville, seat of Austin County, had a 1960 population of 2,218 and a 1970 population of 2,371. In 1970 Bellville had seventy-six businesses, including two furniture manufacturing companies.

*Bellwood, Texas.

*Bellwood Lake.

*Belmena, Texas.

*Belmont, Texas.

*Belo, Alfred Horatio.

*Belott, Texas.

*Belton, Texas. Belton was the marketing center in 1970 for the western part of Bell County, of which it is the county seat. The city's 105 businesses in 1970 produced insulating material, machinery, commercial gases, and other products. Belton sponsors a rodeo each July. The population of Belton in 1960 was 8,163; in 1970 it was 8,696.

*Belton Academy.

Belton Railroad Company. The Belton Railroad Company was chartered on April 14, 1960. It serves the Belton area, branching off the Katy lines to give access to the major railroad lines in Texas. It operates 8.26 miles of track.

James M. Day

*Belton Reservoir. Belton Reservoir is owned by the United States government and is operated by the United States Army Corps of Engineers, Fort Worth District. Construction began in July, 1949; the main structure was completed in April, 1954, and deliberate impoundment began March 8, 1954. In 1966 the reservoir had a capacity of 210,600 acre-feet and a surface area of 7,400 acres at the top of the conservation storage space at elevation of 569 feet above mean sea level. The reservoir provided 887,000 acre-feet of flood control storage capacity. The drainage area above the dam was 3,560 square miles.

The United States government leased for fifty years all facilities to Bell County Water Control and Improvement District in January, 1956. This district supplies Fort Hood, Killeen, and other areas with municipal water. An additional 113,700 acre-feet of conservation storage space was sold to the Brazos River Authority qv for $1,602,822 plus operational costs. The Brazos River Authority retained the right to purchase additional storage capacity from the federal government if the conservation storage capacity is enlarged.

BIBLIOGRAPHY: Texas Water Commission, *Bulletin 6408* (1964).

Seth D. Breeding

*Belzora, Texas.

*Ben Arnold, Texas.

*Ben Bolt, Texas.

*Ben Branch.

*Ben Ficklin, Texas.

*Ben Fort Creek.

*Ben Franklin, Texas.

*Ben Wheeler, Texas.

*Benavides, Alonso de.

*Benavides, Placido.

*Benavides, Santos.

*Benavides, Texas. Benavides, in Duval County, had a population of 2,112 in 1970.

*Benbrook, Texas. Benbrook, in western Tarrant County, in 1960 was an incorporated town with a population of 3,254; this figure represented a population increase of over 400 percent since 1950. In 1970 the population was 8,169. Benbrook had an independent branch of the Fort Worth post office. *See also* Fort Worth Standard Metropolitan Statistical Area.

*Benbrook Dam. *See also* Benbrook Reservoir.

Benbrook Reservoir. Benbrook Reservoir is in the Trinity River Basin in Tarrant County, ten miles southwest of Fort Worth on the Clear Fork of the Trinity River. The project is owned by the United States government, and is operated by the United States Army Corps of Engineers, Fort Worth District. Construction of the dam began on May 27, 1947, and was completed in December, 1950, with deliberate impoundment of water starting September 29, 1952. The reservoir storage capacity is used for flood control, flood regulation, and conservation, in addition to navigational and recreational purposes. The capacity is 88,250 acre-feet and the surface area is 3,770 acres at the top of the conservation storage space elevation of 694 feet above mean sea level. An uncontrolled concrete emergency spillway is located near the left end of the dam with a crest length of 500 feet. A 100-foot-long notch in the center of this section has a crest fourteen feet lower than the main spillway. The drainage area above the dam is 429 square miles.

BIBLIOGRAPHY: Texas Water Commission, *Bulletin 6408* (1964).

Seth D. Breeding

*Benchley, Texas.

*Bencini, Texas.

*Bend, Texas.

*Benedict, Harry Yandell.

Benedictine Sisters. *See* Sisters, Benedictine.

*Benford, Texas.

*Benhur, Texas.

*Benjamin, Texas. Benjamin, seat of Knox County, was incorporated in 1928 with a mayor-council form of government. In 1966 Benjamin reported a school, a library, four churches, and five businesses catering largely to the ranching industry. A public park was planned in 1966. The 1960 population was 338; in 1970 the population was 308.

*Benjamin Creek.

*Bennet, Valentine.

*Bennett, Joseph L.

*Bennett, Texas. (Parker County.)

*Bennett, Texas. (Yoakum County.)

*Bennett Creek.

*Bennetts Creek.

*Bennview, Texas. *See* La Salle, Texas. (Jackson County.)

*Benoit, Texas.

*Benonine, Texas.

*Bons Hole Creek.

*Benson, Ellis.

*Benton, Benjamin Franklin.

*Benton, Samuel L.

*Benton, Texas.

*Bentonville, Texas. (Fannin County.)

*Bentonville, Texas. (Jim Wells County.) Bentonville was established and had a post office as early as October 1, 1911 (not 1928, as stated in Volume I). Located on the route of the Texas-Mexican Railway, the town of Bentonville declined and the post office was discontinued in 1932. In 1971 Bentonville had an estimated population of twenty.

BIBLIOGRAPHY: *Texas Almanac* (1912).

*Bents Creek.

*Benvanue, Texas.

*Beramendi, Juan Martín de. *See* Veramendi, Juan Martín de.

*Béranger, Sieur.

*Berclair, Texas.

*Bergantin Creek.

*Bergheim, Texas.

*Berg's Mill, Texas.

*Bergstrom Air Force Base. Bergstrom Air Force Base was transferred to the Strategic Air Command at the beginning of 1949, and shortly thereafter the 27th Fighter Wing arrived. The 12th Fighter Wing moved to the base in December, 1950. With the arrival of the 42nd Air Division in 1951, Bergstrom became an important station of the Strategic Air Command. These two wings and the air division were active at Bergstrom through July, 1957.

In July, 1957, Bergstrom was transferred to the Tactical Air Command, and in January, 1958, the base was assigned to the Twelfth Air Force with headquarters in Waco.

With the deactivation of the 12th Fighter Wing in 1958, the 42nd Air Division came to a close. The 12th Wing had been in active service in the Austin area for over seven years, and the division had been active since March, 1951. In October, 1958, the base once again was transferred to the Strategic Air Command and became the home of the 4130th Strategic Wing. With this transfer, the base became a unit of the Second Air Force, operating the B-52 bomber and the KC-135 jet tanker. In September, 1963, the 4130th Strategic Wing was designated the 340th Heavy Bombardment Wing.

In July, 1966, Bergstrom Air Force Base again came under the jurisdiction of the Tactical Air Command. With the transfer, the base became a unit of the Twelfth Air Force and home of the newly reactivated 75th Tactical Reconnaissance Wing, which was equipped with the McDonnell Douglas RF-4C Phantom II jet, one of the newest aircraft in the air force's inventory.

By 1968 the Twelfth Air Force headquarters had been moved from Waco to Bergstrom Air Force Base. Under the 1967 military construction bill, more than six million dollars were earmarked for the base for operational, maintenance, supply, hospital, and administrative facilities. On July 15, 1971, the 75th Tactical Reconnaissance Wing was renamed the 67th Tactical Reconnaissance Wing; it was still a part of the Twelfth Air Force in 1973, when it was the only tactical reconnaissance wing west of the Mississippi River.

*Bering, Texas.

*Berkley Creek.

*Berkshire, Texas.

*Berlandier, Jean Louis.

*Berlin, Texas.

*Bermuda, Texas.

Bern Hill, Texas. Bern Hill, in the northwest corner of Shackelford County, was a rural school serving a farming community. It was never incorporated or known to have had a substantial population.

*Bernardo, Texas.

*Bernardo Plantation.

*Berry, Andrew Jackson.

*Berry, John.

*Berry, John Bate.

*Berry, John G.

*Berry, Joseph.

Berry, Kearie Lee. Kearie Lee Berry was born in Denton County, Texas, on July 6, 1893, the son of Thomas Eugene and Viola Eugenia (Riley) Berry. Berry was educated in the public schools of Denton and attended the University of Texas in Austin from 1912 to 1916, serving as vice-president of the Students' Association in 1915–1916; he left school in 1916 to enlist in the Texas National Guard qv and served for ten months on the Mexican border with the 2nd Texas Infantry. He returned to the university during 1924 and 1925 as a War Department student.

Berry was a prominent college athlete, earning four letters in football, three in track, and two in wrestling. He won the Southwest Conference qv heavyweight wrestling championship in 1915 and 1916, and continued his athletic involvement throughout his early military career. He was a member of the 2nd Texas Infantry football team in 1916, played on the Fort Benning, Georgia, team in 1925, and was head coach of the latter in 1926. In 1929, while assigned as assistant professor of military science and tactics at the University of Vermont, he served as freshman football coach and varsity basketball coach. Berry was elected to the Longhorn Hall of Fame in 1930.

Berry had a long and distinguished military career. He was commissioned a second lieutenant of infantry in the Officer Reserve Corps on August 15, 1917. Throughout World War I he served at various posts in the United States. In 1921 Berry was promoted to captain and became an infantry company commander at Fort Sam Houston.qv In 1935, following assignment in China, he was promoted to major. Berry was transferred to the Philippines in November, 1941, just before the outbreak of hostilities with the Japanese. At that time he was promoted to colonel (temporary). During the defense of the Bataan Peninsula, Berry and his command distinguished themselves in the battle of the "Pockets," which forced a temporary withdrawal of the Japanese forces. Following the surrender of Bataan on April 9, 1942, Colonel Berry survived the infamous "Death March" and forty months as a prisoner of war. He was promoted to brigadier general in 1946 and retired on May 2, 1947. Five days later he was appointed by Governor Beauford Jester qv as the adjutant general of Texas; he was promoted to major general in the Texas National Guard on June 5, 1947, and he continued as adjutant general for over fourteen years.

General Berry was awarded the following decorations: Distinguished Service Cross, Distinguished Service Medal, Silver Star, Bronze Star, Purple Heart, and the Legion of Honor from the Philippine Government. General Berry died at

Brooke Army Medical Center,qv San Antonio, Texas, on April 27, 1965.

BIBLIOGRAPHY: Files and Reports of the Adjutant General's Department of the State of Texas (Austin).

A. J. Matthews

*Berry, Manders.

*Berry Creek.

*Berryman, Helena Dill.

*Berrys Creek.

*Berry's Creek, Texas.

*Bertram, Texas.

*Berwick, Texas.

*Bess, Texas. (Dallas County.)

*Bess, Texas. (Duval County.)

*Besser, John S.

*Bessie, Texas.

*Bessmay, Texas.

*Best, Isaac.

*Best, Texas.

*Bethany, Texas. (Collin County.)

*Bethany, Texas. (Panola County.)

*Bethel, George Emmett.

*Bethel, Texas. (Anderson County.)

*Bethel, Texas. (Hopkins County.)

*Bethel, Texas. (Rusk County.)

*Bethel, Texas. (San Saba County.)

*Bethel, Texas. (Tarrant County.)

Bethel Church, Sabine County. Bethel Baptist Church (now called New Hope Baptist Church), organized in an area referred to as the "dark corner" of Sabine County, was located between the settlements of Milam and Sexton. It was constituted on February 7, 1841, in the home of Theophilus Harris as a Predestinarian Regular Baptist Church of Jesus Christ under the authority of Daniel Parker qv and his Pilgrim Church at Elkhart, Anderson County. The Bethel group had met earlier and asked to be aligned with the Union Association of the Pilgrim Church, but it appears that it never did in fact join the association.

Bethel Church was among the five East Texas Missionary Baptist churches which met at Union (Old North) Church four miles north of Nacogdoches on November 11, 1843, and organized the Sabine Baptist Association. They were the Union and Mount Zion, Nacogdoches County; Border and Bethel, Harrison County; and Bethel, Sabine County. The action of the Bethel Church in aligning itself with the Sabine Association naturally aroused the ire of Daniel Parker, his Predestinarian brethren in the Pilgrim Church, and the Union Association, who were opposed to missionary societies and boards, Bible societies, Sunday schools, and secret organizations, all of which were claimed to be purely devices of man with no scriptural authority for their existence. Parker's Pilgrim Church in regular conference on August 17, 1844, called upon the Bethel Church to surrender its authority as a church, since it had "departed from the faith and order." At a meeting held at Bethel Church between October 6 and 13, 1845, thirty-six persons were baptized into the Missionary Baptist belief.

The site of the old Bethel Baptist Church was deeded to the church on November 17, 1878, by Mrs. Julie R. Mason, widow of William Mason, who had obtained the land from the Republic of Texas in 1838. The white frame building and old cemetery are located in an opening of a heavily wooded forest; the oldest Baptist church in Sabine County, it has remained in continuous operation since it was founded, although the name was changed to New Hope Baptist Church.

BIBLIOGRAPHY: James Milton Carroll, *A History of Texas Baptists* (1923); Z. N. Morrill, *Fruits and Flowers of the Wilderness* (1872); William T. Parmer, *A Centennial History of Sexton and Jackson Masonic Lodges in Sabine County, Texas* (1960); *Monuments Erected by the State of Texas to Commemorate the Centenary of Texas Independence* (1938); "Records of an Early Texas Baptist Church," *Quarterly of the Texas State Historical Association*, XI (1907–1908).

Helen Gomer Schluter

*Bethlehem, Texas. (Milam County.)

Bethlehem, Texas. (Upshur County.) Bethlehem, in southeastern Upshur County, was founded in the early 1850's. The community serves a farming and ranching area but is composed almost entirely of retired persons. With one store, the town had a 1970 population of about twenty-five.

*Bettie, Texas.

*Bettina, Communistic Colony of. Ferdinand Herff qv came to Texas in 1847; therefore he could not have selected the site for the community in 1845 (as stated in Volume I); he did, however, live at Bettina when it was established near Llano in 1847. The community was named for Bettina von Arnim (not von Arnin).

*Betts, Jacob.

*Beulah, Texas.

*Beverly, Texas.

*Beverly Hills, Texas. Beverly Hills, in McLennan County, had a population of 1,728 in 1960 and 2,289 in 1970.

*Bevil, John. [This title was incorrectly listed in Volume I as Bevil, John R. John R. Bevil was one of the seven sons of John Bevil.]

Bevil Oaks, Texas. Bevil Oaks, in Jefferson County three miles northwest of Beaumont, was incorporated in 1963 with a population of 370. The name was taken from the names of two subdivisions, Bevil Acres and River Oaks. Since Bevil Oaks is a residential area, the incomes of its citizens, numbering 663 in 1970, are derived from businesses and industries outside the town's boundaries. *See also* Beaumont-Port Arthur-Orange Standard Metropolitan Statistical Area.

*Bevilport, Texas. Bevilport was named for John Bevil qv (not his son John R. Bevil, as stated in Volume I).

*Bevil's Settlement.

*Bewley, Anthony.

*Bexar.

*Bexar, Siege of.

*Bexar Archives. By 1971 all of the Bexar Archives in the Archives of the University of Texas at Austin had been reproduced on microfilm. The Bexar Archives, consisting of more than 250,000 pages of records pertaining to the military, civil, and political life of the Spanish province of Texas and the Mexican state of Coahuila and Texas, were produced during the period 1717 through 1836 (with referral to documents written as early as 1699). A useful reference to the work, *Guide To The Microfilm Edition Of The Bexar Archives, 1717–1803, 1804–1821, 1822–1836*, was published in three separate installments by the University of Texas Archives. The first, published in 1967, covers the period 1717–1803; the latter two, published in 1969 and 1971, cover the periods 1804–1821 and 1822–1836, respectively, and contain, in addition, indexes of all persons and places mentioned in the description of records of those periods.

By May, 1972, a total of 22,293 pages of typed translations of the original material had been completed at the University of Texas. Eighty-eight volumes (13,052 pages) cover the period between September 30, 1699, and September 29, 1779; thirty-eight volumes (8,486 pages) are dated between January 1, 1804, and September 30, 1808; and four volumes (755 pages) are translations of printed decrees dated June 14, 1803, to October 13, 1812. Each volume of translations contains an index of personal and place names. A master index is maintained of all proper names appearing in the volumes.

*Bexar County. Bexar County, with San Antonio as the county seat, is a major tourist and retirement area. In 1968 it had a farm income of $23,878,000, derived chiefly from beef, dairy cattle, grains, and vegetables. That same year 24,797 acres were irrigated. The county offers hunting of deer and turkey and fishing. Missions and historic sites are numerous in Bexar County, including the Alamo, Spanish Governors' Palace, and the Witte Memorial Museum.qqv The 1960 population of 687,151 had increased to 830,460 by 1970. Bexar County is also a major educational center with five senior colleges and several seminaries and smaller colleges. The economy of the area depends heavily on a large federal payroll from the various military bases and research facilities. San Antonio is the major distribution center for south-central Texas. *See also* San Antonio Standard Metropolitan Statistical Area.

*Bexar Presidio. See San Antonio de Bexar Presidio.

*Beyer, Texas.

*Beyersville, Texas.

*Biardstown, Texas.

Bibit Indians. The Bibit (Bibi, Mabibit) Indians were one of the many Coahuiltecan groups of the late seventeenth century that lived in north-eastern Coahuila and also ranged across the Rio Grande into the southwestern part of the Edwards Plateau. The Bosque-Larios Expedition qv of 1675 encountered the chief of a small group of Bibit who were hunting in the vicinity of present Kinney County. This leader reported that his band had recently declined in numbers because of a smallpox epidemic. The Bibit probably ranged even farther north into the Edwards Plateau, since in 1683–1684 Juan Domínguez de Mendoza qv listed the Bibi among the groups that he expected to see on the Colorado River east of present San Angelo.

BIBLIOGRAPHY: V. Alessio Robles, *Coahuila y Texas en la Epoca Colonial* (1938); H. E. Bolton (ed.), *Spanish Exploration in the Southwest, 1542–1706* (1916); C. W. Hackett (ed.), *Pichardo's Treatise on the Limits of Louisiana and Texas*, II (1934).

T. N. Campbell

Bible Baptist Seminary. Bible Baptist Seminary, Arlington, began as the Fundamental Baptist Bible Institute, chartered on March 15, 1939. In 1945 it was chartered as the Bible Baptist Seminary and was approved for veterans' training in 1952. In 1954 the Bible Baptist Institute, with a two-year curriculum leading to a Certificate of Theology, was opened. The coeducational seminary offered the Bachelor of Divinity, Bachelor of Religious Education, and Bachelor of Sacred Music degrees. Support for the school was provided by tuition and fees paid by students and from gifts and contributions from churches and individuals.

In 1956, after many years of occupying leased properties, the seminary purchased forty-six acres between Fort Worth and Dallas on U. S. Highway 80. Buildings included dormitories, a library, assembly and classroom building, a fine arts building, and a main building. In 1967 the library contained twenty-three thousand volumes.

In the first year of classes Louis Entzminger was the only full-time professor, teaching sixteen students. In 1962–1963 the student enrollment was 225; by the 1970–1971 regular term enrollment had increased to 469 students. In 1966 there were twelve full-time faculty members and four special instructors; in 1970 the faculty totaled twenty-three members. Entzminger, the first president, was succeeded by G. Beauchamp Vick (1948–1950), J. Frank Norris qv (1950–1951), Luther C. Peak (1951–1953), and Earl K. Oldham, who was elected president in 1953 and was still president in 1970. *See also* Baptist Church in Texas.

Bickett, John Hamilton, Jr. John Hamilton Bickett, Jr., judge, was born at Cameron, Texas, on July 29, 1892, son of John Hamilton and Minnie (Muse) Bickett. He attended the public schools at Cameron and later at Dallas and San Antonio, after which he entered the University of Texas. He was awarded B.A. and LL.B. degrees in 1914 and in the same year was admitted to the state Bar. From 1924 to 1934 he was a member of the state Board of Law Examiners, resigning to become chief justice of the court of civil appeals at San Antonio. In 1935 he again resigned to serve as general counsel of the Southwestern Bell Telephone Company.

He was appointed to the board of regents of the University of Texas in 1942, serving as chairman from 1943 to 1944, when he retired. Bickett, president of the State Bar of Texas,qv was a member of the Philosophical Society of Texas qv and the Presbyterian church.

In 1924 Bickett married Lula Wright Styles. He died on May 1, 1947, at Dallas.

BIBLIOGRAPHY: Philosophical Society of Texas, *Proceedings* (1947).

Bickler, Jacob. Jacob Bickler, son of Peter and Katherine (Schoeffling) Bickler, was born in Sobernheim, Germany, on November 20, 1849. At the age of fourteen, he came to Milwaukee, Wisconsin, to live with his father and stepmother. There he attended public school, Markham's Milwaukee Academy, and entered the University of Wisconsin in 1867. He received a B.A. degree in 1870 and an M.A. degree in 1871. During 1871 and 1872 he was principal of the La Crosse, Wisconsin, public school.

Bickler came to Austin in 1872 and was associated with his uncle, Phillip Bickler, as a teacher in Bickler German-English Academy until April 1, 1873, when he was appointed assistant draftsman and calculator in the General Land Office qv of Texas. There he met Martha Lungkwitz, eldest daughter of artist Hermann Lungkwitz.qv They were married on January 24, 1874, in Austin, and were the parents of nine children. In 1877 he founded the Texas German and English Academy in Austin for boys, which he successfully operated for ten years. He accepted the superintendency of Galveston public schools in 1887, returned to Austin in 1892, and founded Bickler Academy, a coeducational school, which flourished until his death. The curricula of his schools embraced many languages as well as music and liberal arts courses.

Bickler was fluent in six languages, his lectures were erudite and animated, and he was known as an outstanding teacher in preparing students for college work. Many graduates of his schools became leaders in public life, achieving success in the professions and business. Bickler Public School in Austin was named for him in recognition of his substantial contribution to the cause of education and character building. Bickler was an active member of the National Teachers Association and the Texas State Teachers Association,qv of which he was president in 1887. He wrote and presented a resolution at the 1891 association meeting calling upon the board of regents of the University of Texas in Austin to establish a Chair of Pedagogy (later School of Education) at the university, and this was accomplished within a few months. A member of the summer faculty at the University of Texas, he also conducted summer classes at Fredericksburg and Mason. He died in Austin on April 30, 1902, and was buried in Oakwood Cemetery.

Ralph A. Bickler

***Bidai Indians.** The Bidai (Beadeye, Bedias, Biday, Viday) Indians lived between the Brazos and Trinity rivers in southeastern Texas. Although at times they ranged a larger area, their main settlements were in the vicinity of present Grimes, Houston, Madison, Walker, and Trinity counties, and a number of place names record their former presence in this area. The Bidai were agricultural Indians. In 1748–1749 some of the Bidai were briefly at San Francisco Xavier de Horcasitas Mission qv before San Ildefonso Mission qv was built nearby for the Bidai, Deadose, and Akokisa. These missions, which were established on the San Gabriel River near present Rockdale, were abandoned by 1755. In 1756–1757 Nuestra Señora de la Luz Mission qv was established on the lower Trinity River for the Akokisa and Bidai, and some of the Bidai settled near this mission for a short time. In 1776–1777 the Bidai population was reduced by about 50 percent in a single epidemic and by 1820 only a few small groups of Bidai survived. Some of these joined the Akokisa; others joined the Koasati, who were living nearby; and still others were taken in 1854 to the Brazos Indian Reservation qv in present Young County. The last group eventually ended up in the Indian Territory, now Oklahoma, where their identity was soon lost. It was formerly thought that the Bidai spoke a Caddoan language, but it is now clear that their language was Atakapan.

BIBLIOGRAPHY: H. E. Bolton, "The Founding of the Missions on the San Gabriel River, 1745–1749," *Southwestern Historical Quarterly*, XVII (1913–1914), *Athanase de Mézières and the Louisiana-Texas Frontier, 1768–1780* (1914), and *Texas in the Middle Eighteenth Century* (1915); F. W. Hodge (ed.), *Handbook of American Indians*, I (1907), II (1910); A. F. Sjoberg, "The Bidai Indians of Southeastern Texas," *Southwestern Journal of Anthropology*, VII (1951); J. R. Swanton, *The Indians of the Southeastern United States* (1946), and *The Indian Tribes of North America* (1952); D. H. Winfrey and J. M. Day (eds.), *The Indian Papers of Texas and the Southwest, 1825–1916* (1966).

T. N. Campbell

***Biegel, Texas.**

***Biesele, Leopold.** Leopold Biesele settled on York Creek (not York's Creek, as stated in Volume I) in Guadalupe County.

Biesele, Rudolph Leopold. Rudolph Leopold Biesele, son of Julius and Hedwig (Bading) Biesele, was born on January 29, 1886, at a farming community on York Creek, near Zorn in Guadalupe County. He was educated at Blum School at York Creek, Seguin High School, the state normal school at San Marcos, and the University of Texas, where he received the B.A. degree in 1909, the M.A. in 1910, and the Ph.D. in 1928. After teaching in the New Braunfels, Corsicana, and Waco public schools, and at the University of Alabama and Louisiana Polytechnic Institute, he joined the permanent faculty of the University of Texas in 1931 and became professor of history in 1941. He served on the board of editors of the *Journal of Southern History*, 1945–1948, and of the *Southwestern Social Science Quarterly*,qv 1948–1957, and as book review editor and associate editor of the *Southwestern Historical Quarterly*,qv 1939–1957. Author of *The History of the German Settlements* *in Texas, 1831–1861* (1930), he also wrote workbooks and readings books for college American history courses, six articles on German colonization in Texas for the *Southwestern Historical Quarterly*, and numerous book reviews. Noted for his thoroughness, his kindness, and his devotion to his students, he supervised an unusual number of M.A. theses. He also served as an elder in the University Presbyterian Church and Westminster Presbyterian Church in Austin. Biesele was married in 1910 to Anna Emma Jahn of New Braunfels and had three sons and one daughter. He died in Austin on January 4, 1960, and was buried in the New Braunfels Cemetery.

David B. Trimble

*Big Aguja Mountain.

*Big Bear Creek.

*Big Bend Cave Dwellers. *See* Archaeology—Big Bend Area.

*Big Bend National Park.

*Big Blue Creek.

*Big Boggy Creek.

*Big Branch.

*Big Briary Creek.

*Big Brushy Creek.

*Big Caddo Creek.

*Big Canyon.

*Big Cedar Creek.

*Big Cow Creek.

*Big Creek.

*Big Creek, Texas.

*Big Cypress Creek.

*Big Eddy.

*Big Fivemile Creek.

*Big Foot, Texas. *See* Bigfoot, Texas.

*Big Head Mountain.

*Big Hill, Texas. (Gonzales County.)

*Big Hill, Texas. (Limestone County.)

*Big Hill Bayou.

*Big Island Slough.

*Big Jim.

*Big Lake.

*Big Lake, Texas. Big Lake, seat of Reagan County, serves an area devoted to petroleum production, farming, and ranching. Its fifty-five businesses in 1970 were concerned with oil well servicing, drilling, gasoline refining, ranching, machine work, motor rebuilding, dirt contracting, and trucking. The town reported an improved water system opened in 1959, a thirty-two-bed hospital completed in 1950, a high school completed in 1956, and, in the 1960's, a ten-acre park, as well as twelve churches, a newspaper, a radio station, a library, and one bank. The 1960 population was 2,668; the 1970 census count was 2,489.

*Big Lake and Central West Texas Oil Fields.

*Big Lucy Creek.

*Big Mineral Creek.

*Big Mountain.

*Big Mountain Creek.

*Big Mush.

*Big Onion Creek.

*Big Prairie Creek.

*Big Rocky Creek.

*Big Sandy, Texas. Big Sandy, in Upshur County, had a population of 848 in 1960 and 1,022 in 1970, according to the U.S. census.

*Big Sandy Creek.

*Big Satan Creek.

*Big Spring, Texas. Big Spring, seat of Howard County, depends largely on the petroleum industry, farming, cattle, and Webb Air Force Base qv for its livelihood. In 1966 the town reported fifteen schools, sixty churches, seven hospitals, three banks, a library, a newspaper, and a television station. By 1970 Big Spring had several hundred businesses, including manufacturers of petrochemicals, fertilizers, fiberglass pipe, and plastics. Public improvements completed since 1954 include a new police building and jail, a fire station, and water and sewer programs. Big Spring is the site of Howard County Junior College and is headquarters for the Colorado River Municipal Water District.qv The 1960 population was 31,230; in 1970 it was 28,735. The main tourist attraction is Big Spring State Park (*see* Parks, State).

*Big Spring Army Air Force Bombardier School. *See also* Webb Air Force Base.

*Big Spring Creek.

*Big Spring State Hospital. The Big Spring State Hospital in 1964 had under construction a fifty-two-bed medical-surgical building. Resident population averaged 945 patients in 1967, and an out-patient clinic provided follow-up care for eligible patients who were furloughed or discharged. In 1970 occupational and educational programs and special treatment grants were developed, and the average daily census was 978. *See* Mentally Ill and Mentally Retarded, Care of, in Texas.

BIBLIOGRAPHY: Board for Texas State Hospitals and Special Schools, *Report* (1964); *Texas Almanac* (1967); Texas Department of Mental Health and Mental Retardation, *Annual Report, 1970.*

*Big Stinking Creek.

*Big Sunday Creek.

*Big Thicket. Originally more than three million acres, the Big Thicket has been drastically reduced in size until by the early 1970's less than three hundred thousand acres remained. Some estimates show that fifty acres per day of the Big Thicket are destroyed by logging, hunting, construction, land speculation, land draining for farming, and, in some cases, intentional poisoning of vegetation and animal life.

The area retains, however, some aspects of its natural state. Four of the five carnivorous plants found in North America are still found in the Big Thicket. At least one thousand species of fungi which have never been classified grow within the forests, and twenty-one varieties of orchids still bloom. Although many of the animals native to the area are no longer there, the ivory-billed woodpecker, which was once thought lost, still remains, as does the bald eagle. Alligators can be found in the lowland areas, and more than three hundred species of birds inhabit the forests.

As early as 1927 attempts were made to set aside certain areas of the Big Thicket to preserve its original characteristics, and recommendations were made even then for a national park. The Little Thicket Nature Sanctuary, created by private acquisition of land from donations, was begun in the 1950's and has now grown to almost 1,500 acres. In the 1960's the Big Thicket Association was organized and was probably the largest and strongest private group involved in the preservation of the Big Thicket. In October, 1966, legislation was introduced by United States Senator Ralph Yarborough for the creation of a national park encompassing the East Texas Big Thicket area. The bill spent five years in committee and became a controversial issue; it was debated and reexamined through the early 1970's. On June 12, 1970, the Subcommittee of Parks and Recreation of the Committee of Interior and Insular Affairs held field hearings in Beaumont, Texas. The Big Thicket bill was finally passed in the United States Senate only to fail in the House. More bills were introduced, all unsuccessful, and by 1972 a Big Thicket national park had not been created. Plans varied from a 35,000-acre "string of pearls" park to a 191,000-acre park. On October 1, 1974, the United States Senate unanimously approved a proposal establishing an 84,550-acre Big Thicket National Preserve after accepting a compromise drafted in the House of Representatives. As approved by both houses the park would be a string of parks linked by corridors of parkland purchased over a six-year period. President Gerald R. Ford signed the bill into law, with an appropriation authorization for land acquisition and development, on October 12, 1974.

Proponents claimed that the economy of the area would expand with creation of a national park and that preservation of the area would be an aesthetic investment in the future and a guarantee that some spots in Texas would remain natural and beautiful, unspoiled by profiteering interests.

BIBLIOGRAPHY: William O. Douglas, *Farewell To Texas: A Vanishing Wilderness* (1967); Pete Gunter, *The Big Thicket: A Challenge for Conservation* (1971); Aline House, *Big Thicket: Its Heritage* (1967); Alexander Kress (comp.), *Ralph Yarborough: The Big Thicket's Advocate In Congress* (1970); Lois Williams Parker (comp.), *Big Thicket Bibliography* (1970); Subject File, Barker Texas History Center, University of Texas at Austin Library.

Melinda Arceneaux Wickman

*Big Timber Creek.

*Big Tree.

*Big Trestle Draw.

*Big Wells, Texas.

*Bigelow, Horatio.

*Bigfoot, Texas. [Out of alphabetical order on page 158, Volume I; Big Foot, Texas, should read Bigfoot, Texas.]

The body of W. A. A. (Bigfoot) Wallace qv was moved to the State Cemetery qv in Austin in 1899 (not 1936, as stated in Volume I).

BIBLIOGRAPHY: Stanley Vestal, *Bigfoot Wallace* (1942); Records (Cemetery Information Office, Board of Control, Austin).

Biggers, Don Hampton. Don Hampton Biggers, the eldest of four children of Samuel Washington Biggers, was born in Meridian, Texas, on September 27, 1868. About 1884 he left the small ranch in Stephens County to which the family had moved in 1876 to learn the printing trade in Colorado City.

His restless nature together with his varied career as a printer, editor, publisher, writer, and political publicist kept him almost incessantly on the move. At different times he resided in some two dozen Texas towns, as well as a few years in New Mexico, California, and Arizona.

He bought or established and sold within a year or two the following publications: Midland *Gazette* (1890), Ranger *Atlas* (1891), Clayton, New Mexico, *Democrat* (1897), *West Texas Stockman* (1898–1900), *Colorado Spokesman* (1900), Rotan *Advance* (1907–1909), *Oil Belt News* (1918), *Independent Oil News and Financial Reporter* (1921), *Biggers Monthly* (1922), and *Limelight* (1925).

A number of his books have become extremely rare, including his first one, *A Handbook of Reference . . . of Eastland County, Texas* (1889), and *History That Will Never Be Repeated* (1901, reprinted 1961). His best-known work is probably *From Cattle Range to Cotton Patch* (1905, reprinted 1944), first issued as a series of articles in the Dallas *Morning News* qv in 1904. Other books include a history of German settlement in Texas and a heavy satire about James E. Ferguson.qv He wrote hundreds of feature stories published in a dozen different newspapers and magazines, most of them either historical sketches of the open-range era in the cattle industry or vehement Progressive polemics.

Although his orientation was roughly that of a turn-of-the-century Progressive, the only consistent element in his political attitudes was a dislike for hypocrisy, injustice, and dishonesty. He served two terms in the Texas House of Representatives (1915 from Lubbock, and 1920–1921 from Eastland) and ran unsuccessfully for a third term in 1936. He conducted a bitter fight against the Ku Klux Klan qv of the twenties, was primarily responsible for the conviction of a famous ring of fraudulent oil field promoters, and with Louis Wiltz Kemp qv was instrumental in exposing the Ferguson highway scandals in 1925 (*see* Ferguson, James Edward; Ferguson, Miriam Amanda).

Biggers married Nettie Lee Cox on October 5,

1890, and died in Stephenville less than a month after she died, on December 11, 1957. The couple had six children.

BIBLIOGRAPHY: Seymour V. Connor, *A Biggers Chronicle* (1961).

Seymour V. Connor

*Biggers, Texas.

*Biggs Air Force Base. Biggs Air Force Base in 1964 continued as the home of a tow target squadron and heavy bomb wing and air refueling squadrons. On July 1, 1966, Biggs was transferred from the United States Air Force to the United States Army. *See* Biggs Army Airfield.

Maurer Maurer

Biggs Army Airfield. Formerly Biggs Air Force Base,qv this federal installation at El Paso was transferred from the United States Air Force to the United States Army on July 1, 1966. It operated as an adjunct to nearby Fort Bliss,qv serving in 1973 as a base for army helicopters and as the center for the aviation division and other tactical units of Fort Bliss. The 1970 United States census reported a population of 4,226 at Biggs.

*Bill Black Peak.

*Billam's Creek.

*Billingsley, Jesse.

*Billington, Texas.

*Bills Branch.

*Bills Creek.

*Billy the Kid. *See* Bonney, William.

*Biloxi, Texas.

*Biloxi Indians. The Biloxi (Balaxy, Baluxa, Beluxi, Bilocchi, Bolixe, Paluxy) Indians were Siouan-speaking Indians who originally lived near present Biloxi, Mississippi. After 1763 they crossed the Mississippi and settled near present Marksville, Louisiana. Early in the nineteenth century pressure from American settlers forced them farther westward, and some of the Biloxi entered Texas to settle on present Balaxy Creek in Angelina County. Other Biloxi from Louisiana moved up the Red River and joined Caddoan groups in northeastern Texas. Later in the nineteenth century the Biloxi of the Angelina County area moved westward to north-central Texas, particularly the vicinity of present Erath, Hood, and Somervell counties, which seems to explain the place-name Paluxy in that area. Most of the Biloxi survivors in Texas eventually entered Indian Territory, now Oklahoma, but a few Biloxi moved farther west and southwest and were associated with the Seminole in western Texas and northern Mexico.

BIBLIOGRAPHY: J. O. Dorsey, "The Biloxi Indians of Louisiana," *Proceedings of the American Association for the Advancement of Science*, XLII (1893); F. W. Hodge (ed.), *Handbook of American Indians*, I (1907), II (1910); K. W. Porter, "A Legend of the Biloxi," *Journal of American Folklore*, LIX (1946); J. R. Swanton, *Indian Tribes of the Lower Mississippi Valley and Adjacent Coast of the Gulf of Mexico* (1911) and *The Indians of the Southeastern United States* (1946); D. H. Winfrey and J. M. Day (eds.), *The Indian Papers of Texas and the Southwest, 1825–1916*, I–III (1966).

T. N. Campbell

Binford, Pauline (Larimer). Pauline (Larimer) Binford, daughter of Charles A. and Elizabeth (Wanamaker) Larimer, was born on June 17, 1893, near Library, Allegheny County, Pennsylvania, on a homestead owned by the family from the time of the American Revolution. Her father, a Presbyterian minister, died before her birth. She came to Texas with her mother in 1912, enrolling at Baylor College at Belton (later Mary Hardin-Baylor), from which she was graduated in 1916. She taught in Texas high schools for several years. On September 1, 1923, she married Benjamin Bryan Binford of Dallas, where she continued to reside until her death on August 28, 1966.

Mrs. Binford started her writing career early. Her first published poem appeared in the Pittsburgh *Sun* when she was thirteen years of age. Through the years she continued to write, contributing to a wide range of magazines, including religious periodicals, and was the recipient of numerous honors and prizes for her work. She is the author of two volumes of verse: *My Heart Knows a Song* (1948) and *Keep the Wonder* (1966), the latter being published only a few weeks before her death. Mrs. Binford was a life member of the Poetry Society of Texas.qv

W. E. Bard

*Bingham, Francis.

*Bingham Branch.

Binkley, William Campbell. William Campbell Binkley was born on April 30, 1889, at Newbern, Tennessee. He was educated at the University of California, receiving a B.A. degree in 1917, an M.A. degree in 1918, and a Ph.D. degree in history in 1920. Binkley began teaching history at Colorado College in 1921 and became a full professor in 1925. He was a student of the history of the West and the frontier, but his special interest was Texas history. From 1930 to 1953 Binkley was professor and chairman of the Department of History at Vanderbilt University. In 1953 he was named professor of history at Tulane University and editor of the *Mississippi Valley Historical Review*, positions he held until his retirement in 1963; he was given an honorary LL.D. degree by Tulane in 1964.

During his long teaching career Binkley spent many summers in Austin, teaching at the University of Texas and doing research; he was looked upon there as an ex officio member of the history department, working in harmony with those who were also interested in his special field, notably Eugene C. Barker and Walter Prescott Webb.qqv After his retirement from Tulane, where he was named professor emeritus, Binkley lived in Austin for a year, working on the official correspondence of the Republic of Texas. He returned to teaching at the University of Houston from 1965 to 1966, where he was distinguished professor of American history. He returned to New Orleans and taught history at University College, a part of the adult continuing education division of Tulane University, until February, 1970.

In addition to editing the *Mississippi Valley*

Historical Review, Binkley also edited the *Tennessee Historical Quarterly* and the *Journal of Southern History.* He was one of the founders of the Southern Historical Association and was active in that organization as well as in the Mississippi Valley Historical Association and the American Historical Association. He became a member of the Philosophical Society of Texas qv in 1940. Binkley wrote numerous articles for historical journals; his three major works were *The Expansionist Movement in Texas, 1836–1850* (1925), *Official Correspondence of the Texas Revolution, 1835–1836* (1936), and *The Texas Revolution* (1952).

William Campbell Binkley died August 19, 1970, and was survived by his wife, Vera (McGlothlin) Binkley, and two daughters. He was buried in Lake Lawn Park and Mausoleum, New Orleans.

BIBLIOGRAPHY: *Times-Picayune* (New Orleans), August 20, 1970; Files, Texas State Historical Association, Austin.

*Binner Branch.

*Birch, Texas.

*Birch Creek.

*Birch Hollow.

*Bircham Creek.

*Bird, John.

*Bird, Jonathan.

Bird, Stephen Moylan. Stephen Moylan Bird, direct descendent of Revolutionary War General Stephen Moylan, was born on October 12, 1897, in Galveston, Texas, the son of John Moylan and Alice Otis (Jones) Bird. He completed high school at the age of sixteen and wished to become a naturalist but, due to lack of funds, worked variously in railroading and as a clerk on the cotton exchange. In leisure moments he began to write brief lyrics, using streetcar transfers and the backs of envelopes for his manuscript paper.

In the winter of 1917–1918, Bird submitted some poems which were accepted for *Contemporary Verse* by the editor Charles Wharton Stork, who described the young poet as an "American Keats," although with a need for the full maturing of his poetic gift. In October, 1918, Bird became a cadet at West Point but felt the environment to be oppressive, and on January 1, 1919, he was found dead in his room, apparently a suicide. A posthumous collection of his verses, *In the Sky Garden,* was published in 1922 by the Yale University Press; it contained a number of imaginative lyrics on nature and one or two realistic poems.

BIBLIOGRAPHY: Stephen Moylan Bird, *In the Sky Garden* (1922).

Sonja Fojtik

*Bird Creek.

*Birds. *See also* Oberholser, Harry Church.

*Birds Creek.

*Bird's Creek Indian Fight. The Comanche chief Buffalo Hump qv was not killed in the Bird's Creek Indian Fight (as stated in Volume I). Although there may have been another chief by that name, the one referred to here was still living in 1861.

BIBLIOGRAPHY: Rupert N. Richardson, *The Comanche Barrier to South Plains Settlement* (1933).

*Bird's Fort.

*Birdsall, John. John Birdsall, son of Maurice (not Lewis, as stated in Volume I) Birdsall, was married (wife's name unknown) before he came to Texas; he had a son who lived in New York. Birdsall was not married to Mary Jane Allen (as stated in Volume I).

Dorothy Knox Houghton

*Birdville, Texas.

Birdwell, Alton William. Alton William Birdwell, oldest son of George Preston and Adelaide (Kilgore) Birdwell, was born near Elkhart, Texas, on September 18, 1870. In 1899 he enrolled at the University of Texas; he attended the University of Missouri in the summer of 1900 and the University of Chicago in the summers of 1910, 1912, and 1914; and he received his M.A. degree from George Peabody College for Teachers in August, 1915. In 1940 Southwestern University conferred on him an honorary LL.D. degree.

He began teaching in Smith County in 1892, and in 1899 he became principal of the North Side Elementary School in Tyler. In 1904 he became the first county school superintendent of Smith County, and in 1906 he became principal of Tyler High School. In 1910 he became professor of history at the Southwest Texas Normal School (later Southwest Texas State University); in 1911 he became head of the history department, and in 1915 he became dean of the college. When Stephen F. Austin State Teachers College (now Stephen F. Austin State University) was created in 1921, Birdwell became the first president and continued in that position until September 1, 1942. From 1925 through 1933 Birdwell spent a part of each summer teaching public school administration at George Peabody College for Teachers. He married Margaret Shipe in 1915.

His ambition throughout his life was to improve educational opportunities in Texas. He was president of the Texas State Teachers Association,qv a trustee of George Peabody College for Teachers, director of a bank, and a member of several professional associations. He was in great demand as a speaker and spoke in cities throughout the United States. Some two hundred of his speeches are in the Birdwell Collection in the Stephen F. Austin State University Library. He died on October 25, 1954, and was buried in Sunset Memorial Cemetery in Nacogdoches.

BIBLIOGRAPHY: Polly Anna Rawls Mallow, The Life and Work of Alton William Birdwell (M.A. thesis, Southern Methodist University, 1945); Patricia Ann Townsend, The Speeches of Doctor Alton W. Birdwell (M.A. thesis, Stephen F. Austin State University, 1956).

C. K. Chamberlain

Birkhead, Claude V. Claude V. Birkhead, Texas jurist and soldier, was born on May 27,

1880, at Phoenix, Oregon. His family moved to Texas during his youth, and he attended the public schools at Waco and the old Fort Worth University. Admitted to the State Bar of Texas qv in 1899, he moved to San Antonio. In 1910 he was appointed to the bench of the Seventy-third District Court; he resigned after his election to that post in 1912 to resume law practice. He was recognized as a leader of the Bar of Southwest Texas.

He enlisted in 1899 as a private in Company K, 1st Texas Infantry, and his long military record ended only with his death. Rapidly rising in the ranks he was colonel of field artillery of the Texas National Guard qv at the outbreak of World War I. As colonel of the 31st Field Artillery (Regiment), he entered federal service, and served in the American Expeditionary Force in France until the end of the war. Remaining in the Texas National Guard, he was the recipient of numerous promotions. In 1923 he was brigadier general of field artillery of the 36th Division.qv In 1936 he was promoted to major general and assigned as commanding general of the 36th Division, which was federalized on November 25, 1940. In September, 1941, he was placed in command of the internal security force of the Third Corps area, with headquarters at Baltimore. He was placed on the retired list, effective May 27, 1948. On December 6, 1947, he was appointed major general of the Texas State Guard qv Reserve Corps and assigned as its commanding general. On August 2, 1948, he was promoted to lieutenant general.

With an indefatigable interest in the welfare of veterans, he served as first department commander of Texas of the American Legion.qv He also served as president of the National Guard Association of the United States. He was on the board of directors of Peacock Military Academy qv for many years, and one of its dormitories was named in his honor. He died on November 19, 1950, in San Antonio.

Hobart Huson

*Birkmann, Gotthilf.

*Birome, Texas.

*Birthright, Texas.

*Biry, Texas.

Bishop, Curtis Kent. Curtis Kent Bishop, newspaperman and author of more than fifty books, was born in Tennessee on November 10, 1912, the son of D. E. and Annie (Cornelius) Bishop, and moved to Texas when he was a boy. He attended the University of Texas in the mid-1930's, during which time he was twice editor of *The Ranger*, the student magazine, and sports reporter for the student newspaper, the *Daily Texan*.qv He also worked as a reporter for the Austin *Tribune* and the Austin *American-Statesman* qv from the time he was sixteen, a job which he later took permanently. He wrote a column syndicated throughout Texas entitled "This Day in Texas." During World War II Bishop was with the Foreign Broadcast Intelligence Service in Latin America and the Pacific Theater of Operations.

On his return he became widely recognized for his books on sports and for his western novels, at least six of which were made into motion pictures. Other of his books were in the field of teen-age sports fiction, among them *Half-Time Hero* and *Dribble Up*. In the historical field he wrote *The First Texas Ranger: Jack Hays* and *Lots of Land*, the latter with Bascom Giles. He wrote hundreds of magazine articles and was given an award by *Look* magazine for a television play. His output was so prolific that he wrote under several pen names and for several different publishers.

As a result of the book written with Bascom Giles, the General Land Office qv of Texas employed him to examine its archives in order to help prepare the case for Texas in the famed tidelands controversy.qv At the time of his death he was administrative assistant in the public relations department of the General Land Office.

He married Grace Eyree and they had four children. He died of a heart attack on March 17, 1967, in Austin and was buried in Austin Memorial Park.

Joe B. Frantz

*Bishop, Texas. Bishop, in extreme southwestern (not southeastern, as stated in Volume I) Nueces County, is a site for petrochemical plants and petroleum processing. The major sources of farm income are cotton, grain sorghums, livestock, and poultry. Bishop reported eight churches, a state bank, and a weekly newspaper in 1966. The 1960 population was 3,722; the 1970 U.S. census count was 3,466. *See also* Corpus Christi Standard Metropolitan Statistical Area.

*Bishop Branch.

*Bishop College. Bishop College, Dallas, formerly in Marshall, elected its first Negro president, Joseph H. Rhoads,qv in 1929. That same year the college discontinued the high school department and received senior rank from the State Board of Education. In 1947 the Southern Association of Colleges and Secondary Schools granted accreditation, a junior college branch was opened in Dallas, and a graduate program leading to the M.Ed. degree was initiated. Rhoads also organized the Lacy Kirk Williams Ministers' Institute, which became nationally known as a training center for in-service ministers and lay church leaders.

M. K. Curry, Jr., assumed the presidency in 1952. Under his administration the graduate program in teacher education was terminated, a minimum endowment of $300,000 was raised, the faculty was strengthened, and the Marshall campus was renovated. Plans to move the college were formulated when, in 1957, the Hoblitzelle Foundation (*see* Hoblitzelle, Karl St. John) gave ninety-eight acres in south Dallas for a new campus. Four Baptist conventions joined in the purchase of an additional two-acre plot, and an anonymous gift increased the campus by 287 acres in 1964.

Initial construction in the multimillion-dollar expansion program on the Dallas campus provided an administration-classroom building, a gymnasium-auditorium, housing facilities, and a fine arts building, converted from the junior college branch. The move to the new campus was accomplished in 1961.

Additional construction included a student center (1962); men's dormitory and married-student apartments, classrooms, an infirmary, service buildings, and a stadium (1963); as well as approval of $2,500,000 for a library, a chapel, and a science building (1964). The college further acquired the Sabine Farms Community Center, twelve miles south of Marshall, and cooperated with various other community service agencies. Rechartered by the state in 1961, the college reduced the number of trustees but strengthened their power.

The church-related college was nonsectarian and interracial in selection of students and faculty. The college program, emphasizing liberal arts education, included summer sessions and an evening division of adult education. B.A. or B.S. degrees were available in about twenty major fields. By 1969 the library contained 75,000 volumes, in addition to collections of federal publications, clippings and pamphlets, and over 375 different periodicals and newspapers. During the 1974–1975 term Bishop College had an enrollment of 1,243 students and a faculty of approximately 100. M. K. Curry, Jr., was still president at that time.

Jack Herman

Biskatronge Indians. The Biskatronge (Biscatronge, Plañidores, Pleureurs, Weepers) Indians are known from a single document pertaining to the La Salle Expedition qv in the late seventeenth century. This document, the narrative of Anastasius Douay, indicates that the Biskatronge lived inland well to the north or northeast of Matagorda Bay, probably between the Colorado and Brazos rivers. Douay said that La Salle's party called these people "weepers" because they greeted the French by weeping for a quarter of an hour. Douay's Biskatronge cannot be identified with any Indian group named in Henri Joutel's qv journal of the same expedition. A. S. Gatschet equated the Biskatronge with the Coco, but his reasons for doing so were not made explicit. The affiliations of the Biskatronge remain undetermined.

BIBLIOGRAPHY: I. J. Cox (ed.), *The Journeys of Réné Robert Cavelier, Sieur de La Salle,* I (1905); A. S. Gatschet, *The Karankawa Indians, the Coast People of Texas* (1891); F. W. Hodge (ed.), *Handbook of American Indians,* I (1907), II (1910); J. G. Shea, *Discovery and Exploration of the Mississippi Valley* (1903).

T. N. Campbell

Bison. See Buffalo.

*Bissett Mountain.

*Bitter Creek.

*Bitter Creek, Texas.

*Bitter Lake Creek.

Bivins, Lee. Lee Bivins was born in Sherman on October 7, 1862, the son of O. C. Bivins. His career in cattle began at the age of sixteen, and his holdings came to include the L I T, L X,qqv Cross Bars, and Bonita ranches in the Panhandle; the Alibates Creek Ranch near Midland; the Coldwater Ranch

in Hansford and Sherman counties; and two ranches in New Mexico. By the time of his death, he was running around sixty thousand head of cattle on more than one million acres of land and was said to be the largest cattle operator in the United States.

Before Bivins moved to Claude in 1890, he was in the mercantile business in Sherman and Farmington. Later he owned stores in Claude and Amarillo. He had considerable oil and gas holdings, as well as some grain elevators. A dealer in real estate, he developed an addition to the city of Amarillo. He was instrumental in the organization of the Panhandle Livestock Association and served as president. Also, he was a long-time director of the Texas and Southwestern Cattle Raisers' Association,qv and an Armstrong County commissioner.

Bivins married Mary Elizabeth Gilbert; of four children born, only two boys lived to maturity. Bivins was a member of the Christian church, a civic worker, and a member of many organizations. He died in Wichita Falls on January 17, 1929, and was buried in Amarillo. His wife donated their home in Amarillo to house the city library. Bivins Lake is named for him.

BIBLIOGRAPHY: Seymour V. Connor (ed.), *Builders of the Southwest* (1959); J. W. Williams, *Big Ranch Country* (1954); Amarillo *News,* January 18, 19, 1929.

David B. Gracy II

*Bivins, Texas.

*Bivins Lake.** Bivins Lake, known also as Amarillo City Lake, is owned and operated by the city of Amarillo for municipal water supply to recharge the groundwater reservoir supplying the city's water-well field. The project was started in 1926 and was completed in 1927. Deliberate impoundment of water began in 1926. The lake has been full only a few times, and it has been empty on several occasions. The lake has a capacity of 5,120 acre-feet and a surface area of 379 acres at the spillway crest elevation of 3,634.7 feet above mean sea level. Water is not diverted directly from the lake, but the water in storage recharges, by infiltration, a series of ten wells that are pumped for the city supply. Runoff is insufficient to keep the lake full, and on several occasions there has been no storage. The drainage area above the dam is 982 square miles, of which 920 square miles is probably noncontributing. The lake was named for Lee Bivins.qv

BIBLIOGRAPHY: Texas Water Commission, *Bulletin 6408* (1964).

Seth D. Breeding

*Bizzell, William Bennett.

*Black, Harry Alfred.

*Black, John S.

*Black, Reading Wood.

*Black, William Leslie.

*Black, Texas.

*Black Bayou.

*Black Bean Episode.

*Black Creek.

*Black Cypress Bayou.

*Black Flattop Hill.

*Black Fork Creek.

*Black Hill.

*Black Hill, Texas.

*Black Hill Branch.

*Black Hills.

*Black Hills Creek.

*Black Hollow.

*Black Horse (Tu-ukumah).

*Black Jack, Texas.

*Black Jack Creek. *See also* Romberg, Johannes Christlieb Nathanael.

*Black Jack Grove, Texas. *See* Cumby, Texas.

*Black Jack Springs, Texas. *See also* Romberg, Johannes Christlieb Nathanael.

*Black Lake.

*Black Mesa.

*Black Mountain.

*Black Mountain Ridge.

*Black Mountains.

*Black Oak, Texas.

*Black Peak.

*Black Point, Texas.

*Black Prairie. *See* Texas Prairies.

*Black Spring Branch.

*Blackberry Creek.

*Blackburn, Ephraim.

Blackburn, James Knox Polk. James Knox Polk Blackburn was born in Maury County, Tennessee, in 1837 and moved with his family to Texas in 1856. He attended Alma Institute qv in Lavaca County for two years and then taught school until 1861. He then joined the force under Ben McCulloch qv which accepted the surrender of General David E. Twiggs qv in San Antonio.

Shortly afterward he enlisted in a company of cavalry drawn from Fayette, Lavaca, and Colorado counties, which became one of the elements of the 8th Texas Cavalry (*see* Terry's Texas Rangers). A few weeks after the battle of Shiloh he was elected first lieutenant of his company and shortly thereafter became captain. He served with his command in all major engagements until the battle of Farmington on October 7, 1863, when he was seriously wounded with a point-blank shot passing through both thighs. He refused to permit the surgeon to amputate and fell into the hands of the enemy, but he was paroled for hospitalization. After a severe illness and a long period of recovery, he was finally able to return to the Rangers in February, 1865, but could not assume command until he had been properly exchanged. His exchange was not validated until the surrender of Joseph E. Johnston's qv army.

His period of recuperation had been spent in Tennessee, and he decided to settle in Giles County, Tennessee, marrying Mary McMillan Laird. He became the owner of a plantation and for some time

also served the area in the Tennessee legislature. He died on July 6, 1923. Captain Blackburn wrote of his experiences in the Rangers, one of the few accounts by a participant.

BIBLIOGRAPHY: J. K. P. Blackburn, "Reminiscences of the Terry Rangers," *Southwestern Historical Quarterly,* XXII (1918–1919); L. B. Giles, *Terry's Texas Rangers* (1911).

Nowlin Randolph

*Blackfoot, Texas.

*Blackland, Texas.

*Blackland Army Air Field.

*Blacks Bayou.

*Black's Fort.

*Blackshear, Thomas Edward.

Blackstock, Leo Guy (Lee). Leo Guy Blackstock, known as Lee Blackstock, was born on November 1, 1899, at Whitt, in Parker County, the son of Rabun A. and Pearl (Mathis) Blackstock. He attended high school in Weatherford and then enrolled in the University of Texas (Austin), where he earned a B.A. degree in economics in 1923, an M.A. degree in business administration in 1925, and, while holding a full-time teaching position in the College of Business Administration, a J.D. degree (with highest honors) from the university's School of Law in 1933. He taught at Trinity University (1924–1925, when it was located at Waxahachie) and at Sam Houston State Teachers College (now Sam Houston State University) from 1925 to 1927. With brief interruptions he served on the faculty of the University of Texas at Austin from 1927 to 1971 in both the College of Business Administration and the School of Law.

On leave of absence from the university, Blackstock served from 1937 to 1939 as chief examiner of the gas utilities division of the Railroad Commission qv of Texas. Commissioned as a captain in the U. S. Army Reserve in 1936, Blackstock was on active duty in the army from November 1, 1940, to November 30, 1946. A graduate of the Command and General Staff School, Blackstock was assistant corps judge advocate of the Tenth Army Corps; he served in the Pacific Theater, participating in the New Guinea campaign of 1944, the initial invasion of the Philippines at Leyte in 1944, and the Mindanao campaign in 1945. He was assigned to the occupation forces in Japan from October, 1945, to November, 1946, where he was chief of the prosecution division, legal section, of the Supreme Command of the Allied Powers in Tokyo and was in charge of the prosecution of Japanese war criminals (classes B and C). He received numerous decorations and citations, including the Bronze Star. Released from active duty as a colonel, he remained in Japan as a civilian attached to the army from December 1, 1946, to August 8, 1948, continuing his work in the prosecution of war criminals. His work, however, did not prevent him from enjoying a close and warm relationship with many Japanese friends for the remainder of his life.

Following his work in Japan, Blackstock returned to the University of Texas, where he was professor of business law in the College of Business Administration and, from 1953 to 1966, visiting professor of military law in the School of Law. He retired from the university on May 31, 1971, when he became professor emeritus. His book, *Cases on Military Justice* (1954) was a significant contribution in that field. He was also the author of several other works and lectured extensively off campus on various aspects of law.

Lee Blackstock was married to Harriet L. Barrickman on June 30, 1923, at New Braunfels; they had two sons. On May 26, 1948, he was married to Hannah-Graham Delcher in two ceremonies (official and religious) at Yokohama and Tokyo, Japan. He died on September 4, 1972, and was buried in Fort Sam Houston Cemetery in San Antonio. Several years before his death he gave his fine collection of books on military law to the library of the University of Texas School of Law. In 1973 the Leo G. Blackstock Fund was established to provide an annual scholarship for a College of Business pre-law undergraduate student at the University of Texas at Austin, a fitting memorial to a sensitive and distinguished teacher, lawyer, and soldier.

BIBLIOGRAPHY: Biographical File, Barker Texas History Center, University of Texas at Austin.

Eldon S. Branda

*Blacktail Creek.

*Blackwell, Thomas H.

*Blackwell, Texas.

*Blackwell, Enid, and Texas Railway Company.

*Blair, William Cochran.

*Blair, Texas.

*Blairs Creek.

*Blair's Fort.

*Blake, Texas.

*Blakeney, Texas.

*Blalack, Texas.

Blalock, Bryan. Bryan Blalock, son of William Meredith and Willie (Boothe) Blalock, was born on November 16, 1895, on a farm four miles south of Marshall, in Harrison County. He finished high school in Marshall, then attended the University of Texas for two years. Before he was twenty-one he was elected and served for three years as Harrison County tax collector, then assisted in starting the Marshall *Morning News* (now the Marshall *News Messenger*). In 1921 he was elected manager of the Marshall Chamber of Commerce and served until 1930, when he joined in organizing the Texas Milk Products Company, serving as its president until 1943, when the firm was sold to the Borden Company. He expanded the operation from one plant to five and became vice-president and public relations director of Borden's southern division.

He served for seven terms as president of the Texas Dairy Institute and for many years served on national committees affecting the dairy industry. He organized the East Texas Dairy Finance Corporation, which loaned money to farmers to buy dairy cows.

During the last twenty years of his life Blalock became widely known for his unique style of platform speaking. Making more than 2,000 speeches in thirty-eight states and Canada, he was noted for his keen sense of humor and a fundamental philosophy embracing the free enterprise system.

Blalock was a Methodist and a Thirty-second Degree Mason. He married Irby Davis on September 18, 1918, and they had two daughters. He died on June 13, 1964, at Marshall, and was buried in Grange Hall Cemetery in Marshall.

BIBLIOGRAPHY: Longview *Daily News*, June 15, 1964.

Narcie Moore Crosby

*Blalock, Myron Geer.

*Blanchard, Texas.

*Blanco, Victor.

*Blanco, Texas. Blanco, in Blanco County, had a population of 789 in 1960 and 1,022 in 1970, a 29.5 percent increase during the ten-year period.

*Blanco Canyon.

*Blanco County. Blanco County had a growing tourist business after 1963 largely because President Lyndon B. Johnson's qv boyhood home was located at Johnson City, the county seat. The county also attracted hunting and fishing enthusiasts. Numerous spring-fed streams (notably the Blanco and Pedernales rivers), Blanco State Park, and Pedernales Falls State Scenic Park (see Parks, State) were major points of interest. Crop production in the hilly county was limited, the leading source of farm income being sheep ranching (one hundred thousand sheep and goats in 1965), though cattle were also numerous. Blanco County ranked high in the state in the production of turkeys as well, over one hundred thousand being fed in 1965. In 1970 the county still depended on sheep and goat ranching, and it ranked fourth among the turkey-producing counties in Texas. The 1960 population was 3,657; the 1970 count was 3,567.

*Blanco Creek.

*Blanco Masonic University.

*Blanco River.

*Blanconia, Texas.

*Blancpain, Joseph.

*Bland, Texas.

*Bland Creek.

*Blandlake, Texas.

*Blanket, Texas.

*Blanket Creek.

Blanton, Annie Webb. Annie Webb Blanton, daughter of Thomas Lindsay and Eugenia (Webb) Blanton, was born in Houston on August 19, 1870. She attended schools in Houston and La Grange and taught in Fayette County before moving to Austin about 1888. While attending the University of Texas, she taught in the Austin public schools.

Elected to Phi Beta Kappa, she received a B.Lit. degree in 1899. In 1901 she went to North Texas State Normal College (now North Texas State University) where she wrote a textbook, *Advanced English Grammar*, for use in her classes. In 1916 she was the first woman to be elected president of the Texas State Teachers Association.qv

Beginning in 1918 she served four years as state superintendent of public instruction, the first woman to serve in that elective state office. Through her leadership "The Better Schools Campaign" resulted in the passage of a constitutional amendment in 1920, which permitted "all districts to increase funds by local taxation." During that same period, Miss Blanton was an ardent supporter of woman suffrage, locally and nationally. In 1923 she received an M.A. degree from the University of Texas, and in 1927 she took a Ph.D. degree at Cornell University. At the University of Texas she was successively adjunct professor of school administration; professor of rural education; and chairman of the Department of Education. There are elementary schools named for her in Dallas and in Austin, as well as Blanton Dormitory for girls on the University of Texas campus. A member of numerous professional organizations, she served three terms as a vice-president of the National Education Association and six years as a member of the National Council of Education. In 1929 she "resolved to form an organization to help remove the barriers limiting the advancement of women educators," and on May 11, 1929, joined by eleven fellow teachers, she organized the Delta Kappa Gamma Society.qv From the twelve original members in the one state, the society had grown in forty years to some 108,000 members in fifty states, the District of Columbia, and six Canadian provinces. She died in Austin on October 2, 1945.

BIBLIOGRAPHY: Eunah Temple Holden, *Our Heritage in the Delta Kappa Gamma Society* (1960); *The Heroes and Heroines of Texas Education* (1954); *Who's Who of the Womanhood of Texas* (1923–1924).

Alice Duggan Gracy

Blanton, Thomas Lindsay. Thomas Lindsay Blanton was born in Houston on October 25, 1872, the son of Thomas Lindsay and Eugenia (Webb) Blanton (and brother of Annie Webb Blanton qv). He was educated in the public schools of Houston and La Grange and was graduated from the law school of the University of Texas in 1897. He married May Louise Matthews, daughter of J. A. and Sallie (Reynolds) Matthews,qqv in 1899, and five children were born to this union. He began the practice of law in Cleburne but soon moved to Albany, where he practiced until 1908, when he was elected district judge. He was reelected to that office in 1912.

In 1916 Blanton was elected to Congress as a Democrat; his first tenure ran from 1917 to 1929. In 1928 he did not seek reelection but was an unsuccessful candidate for the United States Senate. Upon the death of his successor, Robert Q. Lee,qv in 1930, he won election to Congress and served until 1937. He served on the House committees

on claims, education, irrigation and arid lands, railways and canals, woman suffrage, Indian affairs, and the District of Columbia. In 1932 he moved to the powerful Committee on Appropriations, where he remained until 1937.

Early in his career he incurred the wrath of Samuel Gompers and the labor leadership. In World War I he favored a "work or fight" amendment to the draft law. He opposed the railroad strike of 1921. He received many threats, and his car was once fired upon near Washington. In 1924 he proposed to stop all immigration for five years. In 1928 he introduced a bill to stop immigration for seven years, to require all aliens to register, and to deport those who did not become citizens. In 1935 he introduced a bill to outlaw Communists in the United States. In 1926 he forced the resignation of a District of Columbia commissioner for overcharging veterans in guardian fees. He caused an investigation at St. Elizabeth's Hospital; as a result, the court declared forty-five inmates sane and released them.

In his long career Blanton consistently opposed extravagance. On May 28, 1919, he introduced a resolution calling upon all government departments to furnish a list of employees earning money outside the government and the names of all relatives on the payroll. All Texans except Blanton voted against the resolution. His opposition to all congressional "junkets" and fringe benefits voted for themselves by Congressmen caused ill feeling toward him by his colleagues. After being defeated in 1936, he practiced law in Washington until 1938, when he returned to Albany to practice there.

The Dallas *Morning News* qv once observed that every delegation needed one Tom Blanton. In Congress he had a record of near perfect attendance and offered more objections to appropriations than any other member. Upon his retirement, the Washington *Post* said that he had saved the government millions of dollars and would be missed. He died in Albany on August 11, 1957, and was buried in the Albany Cemetery.

BIBLIOGRAPHY: F. C. Adams, *Texas Democracy*, II (1937); San Angelo *Standard-Times*, April 6, 1924; Abilene *Reporter-News*, August 12, 1957; *Biographical Directory of the American Congress, 1774–1961* (1961).

Thomas L. Miller

Blasig, Anne Justine. Anne Justine Blasig, author of *The Wends of Texas* (1954), was born on July 25, 1900, in Sealey, Texas, the daughter of Hermann and Caroline (Mennicke) Schmidt. In 1901 her parents moved to Galesburg, Illinois, then in 1908 to Dexter, Iowa. She worked her way through the University of Iowa, where she received a B.A. degree in history. In 1951 she received an M.A. degree in history from the University of Texas.

Anne Blasig taught in the public schools of New Braunfels, Brady, and Mercedes over a period of twelve years. In Brady she was instrumental in the establishment of the McCulloch County Library. She taught school in Harlingen for twenty-one years and was named outstanding teacher of the year before she retired in 1970. She was married to Carl A. Blasig on July 1, 1924, and the couple had one daughter.

Influenced by her Wendish heritage (her father served as the last Wendish-speaking Lutheran minister in Serbin, Texas, from 1922 to 1947), Anne Blasig first wrote her book, *The Wends of Texas*, as an M.A. thesis. She wrote numerous stories and articles and translated into English materials relating to the Texas Wends, including an old ship's register of Wendish immigrants. She contributed to the Wendish exhibit at the Institute of Texan Cultures qv during HemisFair qv in 1968 (*see also* Wends in Texas).

Anne Blasig died on August 30, 1971, in San Benito and was buried in Mt. Meta Cemetery there.

BIBLIOGRAPHY: Anne Blasig, *The Wends of Texas* (1954); Anne Blasig Papers (Archives, University of Texas at Austin Library); Files of the Institute of Texan Cultures, San Antonio; Austin *American*, September 2, 1971.

Mrs. Milton Walther

*Bleakwood, Texas.

*Bledsoe, A. A. Bledsoe died on October 8, 1882, at his home in Dallas County.

BIBLIOGRAPHY: Dallas *Weekly Herald*, October 12, 1882.

*Bledsoe, Jesse.

*Bledsoe, Joseph.

*Bledsoe, Jules.

*Bledsoe, Texas.

*Bleiblerville, Texas.

*Blessing, Texas.

*Blevins, Texas.

*Blewett, Texas.

*Blind Institute. *See* Texas School for the Blind.

Blinn College. Blinn College (formerly Blinn Memorial College qv), Brenham, received additional funds for buildings and improvements when voters in Washington County raised the tax levy and voted a bond issue in 1950. New construction included a library and fine arts building, agriculture building, athletic field facilities, and residence halls. In 1961 additional taxes provided for erection of an administration-science building and more dormitories. Since 1940, a museum project dedicated to T. P. Walker, who aided in collecting and organizing materials, has been established on the Blinn campus. Purpose of the project was to collect and preserve early Texana, particularly that relating to Austin's colony, the Declaration of Independence,qv natural history, Indians, and pioneers. Walker Museum also housed the H. Dornberger Coin Collection, containing more than five hundred pieces dating from 600 B.C. Accredited by numerous agencies, including the Southern Association of Colleges and Schools, the junior college provided both academic-transfer and vocational-terminal programs. Enrollment during the 1966–1967 regular term numbered 1,350 students under instruction of sixty faculty members. In 1967 the library con-

tained fourteen thousand volumes and other materials. By 1969 the library had increased its holdings to twenty-two thousand volumes. The enrollment for 1974–1975 was 1,642; James H. Atkinson was president at that time.

*Blinn Memorial College. *See also* Blinn College.

*Bliss, Don Alfonso.

*Bliss, Zenas Randall.

*Bliss Branch.

*Blix, Texas.

*Blocker, Abner Pickens (Ab).

Blocker, Dan. Dan Blocker, popular television star, was born on December 10, 1928, in DeKalb, Bowie County, northeast Texas, the son of Ora Shack and Mary (Davis) Blocker (his delayed birth certificate, filed by a doctor on March 22, 1929, recorded his name as Bobby Don Blocker). When he was six years old Dan Blocker moved with his parents to O'Donnell, in West Texas, where his father operated a general store. He attended local schools before entering, at the age of twelve, Texas Military Institute in San Antonio. He studied at Hardin-Simmons University and then entered Sul Ross State Teachers College (now Sul Ross State University) in Alpine in 1947. Always large in stature (reportedly, at fourteen pounds he was the largest baby born in Bowie County), Blocker stood over six feet and weighed 200 pounds as a youth of twelve; by the time he became a star football player at Sul Ross (the team he played on went through an undefeated season, won their conference championship, and played in Florida's Tangerine Bowl), he was six feet, four inches tall and weighed over 275 pounds.

While at college Blocker became interested in acting, and when he graduated from Sul Ross with a B.A. degree in speech and drama, he refused offers of professional careers in both football and boxing. He acted in summer stock in Boston and soon afterward was drafted for combat duty in Korea, where he served as an infantry sergeant with the army's 45th Division. In 1952 he returned to Sul Ross, where he took an M.A. degree; there he married his college sweetheart, Dolphia Lee Parker, on August 25, 1952; they had four children. Blocker taught school in Sonora, Texas, and Carlsbad, New Mexico, before moving to California in 1956 to work on a Ph.D. degree at the University of California at Los Angeles. He also worked as a substitute teacher at Glendale and began his career as a professional actor in Los Angeles. In 1959 he was cast in the role of "Hoss" Cartwright on the NBC network television production, "Bonanza," one of television's longest and most popular series. Enormously popular as an actor, he was also a successful businessman; he was co-owner of a nationwide chain of steak houses called Bonanza. Blocker received the Texan of the Year Award in 1963 from the Texas Press Association,qv and in 1966 he served as honorary chairman of the Texas Cancer Crusade. He played the role of "Hoss" Cartwright for thirteen seasons on national television, until his death on May 13, 1972, from complications following an operation. The television series was terminated soon after his death. Dan Blocker was buried in Woodmen Cemetery in DeKalb, Texas.

BIBLIOGRAPHY: Biographical File, Barker Texas History Center, University of Texas at Austin.

*Blocker, John Rufus.

*Blocker, Texas.

*Blocker Creek.

*Bloodgood, William.

*Bloomburg, Texas.

*Bloomfield, Texas.

*Bloomfield Branch.

*Blooming Grove, Texas.

*Bloomington, Texas. Bloomington, in Victoria County, had a population of 1,756 in 1960 and 1,676 in 1970, according to the U.S. census.

*Blossom, Texas.

*Blount, James H.

*Blount, James P.

*Blount, Stephen William.

*Blount, Thomas William.

*Blount Indians.

*Blow, George W.

*Blox, Texas.

*Bloys Camp Meeting.

*Blue, Texas.

*Blue Branch.

*Blue Creek.

Blue Gap, Texas. Blue Gap, sixteen miles east of Winters near the Runnels County line, was the second post office in the county, Walthall having been named the first. With James K. Paulk as postmaster, the Blue Gap post office was established in 1878 to accommodate ranchmen and a group of Texas Rangers qv stationed in the area. Named for a scenic pass through Table Mountain about a mile away, Blue Gap also served as a stagecoach stop for the Round Rock to Buffalo Gap line. In 1881 Content was established two miles north, and Blue Gap declined. In 1967 the restored post office building remained.

*Blue Mound.

Blue Mound, Texas. Blue Mound, north of Fort Worth, in Tarrant County, was an incorporated town with a population of 1,253 in 1960 and 1,283 in 1970, according to the U.S. census. See also Fort Worth Standard Metropolitan Statistical Area.

*Blue Mountain.

*Blue Mountains.

*Blue Ridge, Texas. (Collin County.)

*Blue Ridge, Texas. (Falls County.)

*Blue Ridge, Texas. (Fort Bend County.)

*Blue Sky Law.

Bluebonnet Bowl. The Bluebonnet Bowl, an annual post-season football classic, was initiated in Houston in 1959 as a result of the efforts of a civic group composed of Elvin Smith, Lou Hassell, and Eddie Dyer, which was appointed by the Houston Chamber of Commerce Athletics Committee in 1958. In the one year, between the inception of the idea for a Bluebonnet Bowl and its actual realization, the group managed to secure NCAA sanction, obtain Southwest Conference qv approval, and procure the use of Rice Stadium. The first game, on December 19, 1959, matched Clemson University against Texas Christian University's "Horned Frogs." In the first eight years of the Bluebonnet Bowl's existence, its success was evident as the television contract improved from the initial $16,-000 to the 1967 contract totaling $180,000. The proceeds from the Bowl games have been distributed to various Harris County charitable organizations. Beginning in 1968 the annual football game was played in the Astrodome,qv and the event was referred to as the Astro-Bluebonnet Bowl.

Lou Hassell

*Bluebonnets.

*Bluegrove, Texas.

*Bluetown, Texas.

*Bluff, Texas. (Bandera County.)

*Bluff, Texas. (Fayette County.)

*Bluff Creek.

*Bluff Dale, Texas.

*Bluff Springs, Texas.

*Bluffton, Texas.

*Blum, Leon.

*Blum, Texas. Blum, in Hill County, was incorporated in 1955 and in 1966 reported four churches, one school, and twelve business establishments. Farms nearby produced cotton, grains, and peanuts, and lime is processed northwest of the town. Tourism is of some importance since the town is located near Whitney Reservoir. Blum's population was 315 in 1960 and 382 in 1970, according to the U.S. census. The town installed water, gas, and sewer facilities between 1963 and 1966.

Blumenthal, Texas. (Colorado County.) Blumenthal, a German word meaning "valley of flowers," was established prior to 1840, for in that year Louis Cochand Ervendburg qv organized a congregation of seventy-two there. The settlement was located on Cummins Creek in the neighborhood of Frelsburg, Cat Spring, Bernardo, and New Ulm. It was not listed on any maps of the period, but was described in 1846 as a community having many German-owned farms.

BIBLIOGRAPHY: Rudolph Leopold Biesele, *The History of the German Settlements in Texas, 1831–1861* (1950).

*Blumenthal, Texas. (Gillespie County.)

*Blundell Creek.

*Bluntzer, Texas.

*Blythe Creek.

*Board Branch.

*Board of Control. The Board of Control was responsible for the administration of the state's eleemosynary institutions until 1949, when administration was transferred to the newly created Board for Texas State Hospitals and Special Schools.qv In 1951 the Budget Division of the Board of Control was transferred to the Governor's Office. In 1953 the old Board of Control was abolished and a new one composed of three part-time gubernatorial appointees was created. The board determines policy and appoints the director, who is the chief administrator. The agency's functions include serving as the chief purchasing office for state departments and institutions, auditing and certifying to the comptroller of public accounts qv all claims for goods sold to the state, and operating and maintaining the Capitol qv and other state office buildings, grounds, the State Cemetery,qv and other state property in Austin.

BIBLIOGRAPHY: Stuart A. MacCorkle and Dick Smith, *Texas Government* (1964); Texas Research League, *Purchasing, Warehousing, and Distribution* (1955), *Purchasing Functions of the Texas Board of Control* (1957); Wilbourn Eugene Benton, *Texas, Its Government and Politics* (1961).

Dick Smith

*Board House, Texas.

Board of Mansion Supervisors. The Board of Mansion Supervisors, created in 1931, was given the responsibility of planning for repairs on the Governor's Mansion.qv The board was abolished in 1965 and its powers and functions were given to the Texas Fine Arts Commission.qv

BIBLIOGRAPHY: University of Texas at Austin, *Guide To Texas State Agencies* (1966).

*Board for Texas State Hospitals and Special Schools. The Board for Texas State Hospitals and Special Schools was abolished in 1965, and its duties were transferred to other departments, primarily the Department of Mental Health and Mental Retardation.qv *See also* Indian Affairs, Commission for; Public Health, State Department of.

BIBLIOGRAPHY: University of Texas at Austin, *Guide To Texas State Agencies* (1966).

*Boards and Commissions. [*See* Volume I under this title for partial list. Many boards and commissions have had name changes since Volumes I and II were first published; both old and new titles may be found in the current work for updated accounts. A newly created board or commission will also be found under its own title; no attempt is made here to list them all under a single title. Ed.]

*Boardtree Creek.

Boatright, Mody Coggin. Mody C. Boatright, folklorist and English professor, was born on October 16, 1896, in Colorado City, Texas, the son of Eldon and Frances Ann (McAulay) Boatright. He served in the United States Army in 1918–1919. He received his B.A. degree from West Texas State Teachers College (now West Texas State University) in 1922 and his M.A. and Ph.D. degrees from

the University of Texas in 1923 and 1932. After serving as an instructor in the demonstration school at West Texas State, he taught English at Sul Ross State Teachers College (now Sul Ross State University) before being appointed an instructor at the University of Texas in 1926. His tenure at the University of Texas at Austin spanned forty-three years, during which he served as professor of English and chairman of that department. Boatright retired from the university in 1969 but retained an office on the campus as professor emeritus of English. Boatright married Elizabeth Reck in 1925, and they were the parents of a daughter. After his wife's death he married the artist Elizabeth E. Keefer in 1931, and they had a son.

Boatright was active in state and national folklore organizations, particularly the Texas Folklore Society,qv which he served as secretary-editor from 1943 to 1964. His interest in the folklore of cowboys and frontiersmen resulted in such books as *Tall Tales from Texas* (1934) and *Folk Laughter on the American Frontier* (1949). He found folklore in other areas also and published *Folklore of the Oil Industry* (1963). Along with Columbia professor William A. Owens, Boatright established an oral history project recording the folklore of the oil pioneers. The two men collaborated on a book entitled *Tales from the Derrick Floor* (1970). Boatright wrote and edited numerous articles for scholarly journals. He was named a Fellow of both the American Folklore Society and the Texas Folklore Society. He was also a member of the American Studies Association and the Modern Languages Association.

The students of the University Folklore Association dedicated the first number of their *Folklore Annual* to Boatright as a teacher who had inspired generations of students. At a dinner in his honor in 1965, emphasis was put on the kindness and fairness for which Boatright was widely known.

Boatright had a heart attack following an automobile accident which occurred while he and Mrs. Boatright were driving to Abilene on August 20, 1970, and was buried in Glenrest Cemetery in Kerrville.

BIBLIOGRAPHY: *Texian Who's Who* (1937); Austin *American-Statesman*, December 14, 1969, August 21, 1970; Dallas *News*, August 21, 1970; Biographical File, Barker Texas History Center, University of Texas at Austin.

Mary Shields Pearson

*Boatwright, Thomas.

Boaz, Hiram Abiff. Hiram Abiff Boaz was born in Murray, Kentucky, on December 18, 1866, the son of Peter Maddox and Louisa Ann (Ryan) Boaz. In 1873 his family moved to Tarrant County, Texas. After his graduation from Sam Houston Normal Institute (now Sam Houston State University), he taught in Fort Worth. He received B.S. (1893) and M.A. (1894) degrees from Southwestern University, the latter with highest honors. Ordained to the Methodist ministry, he served churches in Fort Worth, Abilene, and Dublin. In 1902 he became president of Polytechnic College (later Texas Woman's, now Texas Wesleyan) in Fort Worth, where he remained for nine years. Following a brief period as vice-president of Southern Methodist University, just being formed, he returned to Polytechnic College for five years.

After two years as secretary of the Methodist Board of Church Extension in Louisville, Kentucky, in 1920 he became the second president of Southern Methodist University, where he served until his election as bishop in the Methodist Episcopal Church, South, in 1922. Following four years as Methodist bishop in the Far East, he returned to the United States to serve as bishop in Arkansas, Oklahoma, Texas, and New Mexico, until his retirement in 1938. He then initiated and continued to help with the sustentation campaign for Southern Methodist University through which Dallas citizens contributed to the budget of the university. He was given honorary degrees from several institutions. He was a trustee of Southern Methodist and Southwestern universities. His publications include *Essentials of an Effective Ministry* and his autobiography, *Eighty-four Golden Years* (1951).

Boaz was married to Carrie Odalie Brown on October 4, 1894; they had three daughters. He died at the age of ninety-five in 1962 and was buried in Dallas.

BIBLIOGRAPHY: Hiram A. Boaz, *Eighty-four Golden Years* (1951); "Ninety-five Golden Years," *Mustang* (January–February, 1962); *Who's Who in the South and Southwest* (1950).

Howard Grimes

*Bob Creek.

*Bobcat Hills.

Bobida Indians. In 1683–1684 Juan Domínguez de Mendoza qv led an exploratory expedition from El Paso eastward as far as the junction of the Concho and Colorado rivers east of present San Angelo. In his itinerary he listed the names of thirty-seven Indian groups, including the Bobida, from whom he expected to receive delegations. This name does not appear in later documents. It is possible that Mendoza's Bobida were the same as the Bobole (Babele) who at the same time lived in northeastern Coahuila but ranged northward across the Rio Grande into the southwestern part of the Edwards Plateau, but this identity has yet to be demonstrated. If there is no relationship between the two, then it seems likely that the Bobida were one of many groups in north-central Texas that were swept away by the Lipan-Apache and Comanche invasions of the eighteenth century.

BIBLIOGRAPHY: V. Alessio Robles, *Coahuila y Texas en la Epoca Colonial* (1938); H. E. Bolton (ed.), *Spanish Exploration in the Southwest, 1542–1706* (1916); C. W. Hackett (ed.), *Pichardo's Treatise on the Limits of Louisiana and Texas*, II (1934).

T. N. Campbell

Bobole Indians. This was one of the more important groups of Indians of northeastern Coahuila during the latter half of the seventeenth century. At times the Bobole (Babele), who spoke a Coahuiltecan language, were in settlements on or near the Rio Grande in the present Eagle Pass area, and they also crossed into Texas to hunt bison in the southwestern part of the Edwards Plateau, particularly in the area of present Kinney and Edwards counties. Bobole males also accompanied various Spanish exploratory and military expeditions that crossed the Rio Grande into Texas.

In 1665 about three hundred Bobole warriors were with Fernando de Ascué when he penetrated southern Texas and decisively defeated the Cacaxtle. Later, in 1675, twenty-two Bobole were with the Bosque-Larios Expedition qv that crossed the Rio Grande near modern Eagle Pass. It is possible that the Bobole were the same people as the Bobida on the list of tribes made by Juan Domínguez de Mendoza.qv This list was made when Mendoza was at the junction of the Colorado and Concho rivers east of present San Angelo in 1684. If the two are identical, then the Bobole ranged much farther north in the western Edwards Plateau region than has been realized. Another Indian group with a similar name, Bobori, lived somewhere between Durango, Mexico, and Presidio, Texas, in 1693, but the relationship of these Bobori to the Bobole of northeastern Coahuila remains undetermined.

BIBLIOGRAPHY: V. Alessio Robles, *Coahuila y Texas en la Epoca Colonial* (1938); H. E. Bolton (ed.), *Spanish Exploration in the Southwest, 1542–1706* (1916); C. W. Hackett (ed.), *Historical Documents Relating to New Mexico, Nueva Vizcaya, and Approaches Thereto, to 1773*, II (1926).

T. N. Campbell

*Bobs Creek.

*Bobville, Texas.

*Bocherete Village.

*Bodano Bayou.

*Bodansky, Meyer.

*Boerne, Texas. Boerne, county seat of Kendall County, probably was named for Ludwig Börne, a German political journalist and satirist of radical views (not a poet and historian, nor was he a political refugee in West Texas, as stated in Volume I). Because of their association with the communistic colony of Bettina,qv it is likely that some of the founders of Boerne (spelled Börne in all of the town's early records) knew and admired Ludwig Börne's political views as set forth in his writings, and so they named the town for him. Ludwig Börne was born on May 6, 1786, at Frankfurt am Main, Germany, with the name Löb Baruch; a Jew, he changed his name in 1818 to Ludwig Börne and became a Lutheran, possibly to avoid prejudice against his writings. Börne never came to Texas; his collected works were published in 1829–1834, and he died in Paris, France, on February 12, 1837, about fourteen years before the townsite of Boerne was laid out.

Boerne was incorporated in 1909 with an alderman type of government. The town is a tourist center and a market for ranch products, while government installations near San Antonio add to its income. The town purchased grounds for a park in 1964 and planned a new library building. The building of Interstate Highway 10 initiated a residential building boom. In 1966 Boerne reported ten churches, a school, a bank, a library, a newspaper, and sixty-nine businesses, including four manufacturers. The 1960 population was 2,169; in 1970 it was 2,432.

BIBLIOGRAPHY: *Brockhaus Enzyklopädie* (1967); *Encyclopedia Americana* (1968); *Encyclopaedia Britannica* (1910); *The New Century Cyclopedia of Names* (1954).

Edith A. Gray
Eldon S. Branda

*Bofecillos Canyon.

*Bofecillos Mountains.

*Bog Creek.

*Bogart, Samuel A.

*Bogata, Texas. Bogata, in Red River County, served a farming and ranching area, with twenty-eight business establishments, six churches, a newspaper, a new sixty-bed nursing home, and a medical clinic reported in 1966. By 1965 the water and sewer systems had been improved, and a new school building was under construction. Bogata holds an annual rodeo in June. The 1960 population was 1,112, and the 1970 population was 1,287.

*Boggie Creek.

*Boggy Branch.

*Boggy Creek.

*Boggy Creek Lake.

*Bogus Springs, Texas.

*Bohemian.

*Boiling Mountain.

*Bois d'Arc Bayou.

*Bois d'Arc and Southern Railway Company.

*Boise, Texas.

*Bola, Texas.

*Bold Springs, Texas.

Boles, John. John Boles was born in Greenville, Texas, on October 27, 1895, the son of John Monroe and Mary Jane Boles. He attended the University of Texas, where he received a B.A. degree in 1917, then entered the army during World War I. On his release from the service he studied voice and made his first appearance on a stage in the lead role of a Broadway musical. He remained in the New York theater from 1923 to 1926. In 1927 Gloria Swanson brought him to Hollywood as the star of the silent film *Loves of Sunya*. He later won the top role in *The Desert Song*, at which time his baritone voice and good looks made him a matinee idol. During the 1930's he starred in pictures with Shirley Temple, Barbara Stanwyck, Rosalind Russell, and Irene Dunne. When his career began to wane he entered the oil business, later moving to San Angelo, Texas, where he lived for thirteen years prior to his death on February 27, 1969. He was married to Marcelite Dobbs on June 21, 1917, and they had two children.

BIBLIOGRAPHY: Austin *Statesman*, February 28, 1969; *Who's Who In America* (1946).

*Boles Orphan Home. In 1968 Boles Orphan Home campus consisted of more than one hundred acres adjacent to Lake Tawakoni near Quinlan, Texas. An elementary school and a high school, located on the campus, are staffed by state-supported teachers. A second unit of the Boles Home, the Sherwood and Myrtle Foster Home, is located at Stephenville, Texas. The total capacities of the Boles Home and the Foster Home remain at 250 and 64 children, respectively. The Boles Home is one of the largest children's homes in Texas and is the largest children's home supported and maintained by the Church of Christ.

*Boling, Texas.

*Bolivar, Texas.

*Bolivar Peninsula.

*Bolivar Point. *See also* Point Bolivar; Point Bolivar Lighthouse.

*Bolivar Roads.

*Boll, Jacob.

*Boll Weevil in Texas. The cotton boll weevil has destroyed billions of dollars worth of cotton in the United States since it crossed the Rio Grande into Texas in the early 1890's. This most costly of all cotton insects in the 1960's damaged cotton in excess of $200,000,000 annually.

In Texas, as elsewhere in the Southern cotton regions, the boll weevil has had an enormous impact on the economy. The rich blacklands, once the heart of the state's cotton belt, in the 1960's produced only a fraction of the output of former years. Cotton production, as a result, shifted westward, principally to the High Plains, and southward to the Rio Grande Valley. Those regions, through the use of irrigation, produced close to 20 percent of the nation's cotton.

The western portion of the state, because of its aridity, was long thought to be free of the danger of boll weevil infestation. However in 1960 the insects were found in the El Paso Valley, and in 1962 infestation of destructive proportions was noted on the High Plains. The boll weevil had successfully over-wintered (survived the winter) in the areas

The cotton industry of West Texas has cooperated with state and federal officials and the Mexican government in a program of research and eradication. Entomologists discovered that only those boll weevils completing diapause (physiological condition of an insect enabling it to survive periods of unfavorable environment without food) survive winter. Late season diapause control, through the use of undiluted Malathion, has been an important factor in the program. Only by such a program can the boll weevil be prevented from becoming permanent in the High Plains and the western cotton producing states, and the region saved from costly infestation and destruction. *See also* Agriculture in Texas; Bollworm, Pink.

BIBLIOGRAPHY: Joseph F. Spears, "Boll Weevil Counterattack: The Battle at the Cap Rock," *The Cotton Gin and Oil Mill Press*, LXVI (February 13, 1965); United States Department of Agriculture, Farmers' Bulletin No. 2147, *The Boll Weevil: How to Control It* (1962); The President's Science Advisory Committee, *Cotton Insects* (1965);

Texas Agricultural Extension Service, *Texas Guide for Controlling Insects* (1966).

L. Tuffly Ellis

*Bollaert, William. [*See* this title in Volume I for a more detailed account of William Bollaert's life; the following gives important data not included in that article. Ed.]

William Bollaert, of Dutch descent, was born in Lymington, Hampshire, England, on October 21, 1807. At the age of thirteen he entered the Royal Institution as a laboratory assistant in chemistry, where he stayed for five years and published in the *Journal of the Royal Institution* in 1823–1824. His journals written during a sojourn in Texas are invaluable to students of life and customs in the days of the Republic of Texas. From the time of his arrival at Galveston on February 20, 1842, until his departure from the same port on July 10, 1844, Bollaert traveled extensively in the Republic, recording impressions and data and sketching Texas scenes. He was married to Susannah McMorran on November 22, 1845, in Stamford, England; they had one son and four daughters. Bollaert died in London on November 15, 1876.

BIBLIOGRAPHY: Stanley Pargellis, "Introduction" (W. Eugene Hollon and Ruth Lapham Butler, eds.), *William Bollaert's Texas* (1956).

Joseph E. Blanton

*Bollworm, Pink. The pink bollworm, although not so destructive as the boll weevil, is a cotton pest of costly proportions. As late as 1952, cotton losses from this insect exceeded $28,000,000 in thirty-eight South Texas counties. In recent years, through the efforts of the Texas Department of Agriculture qv and cotton growers, losses have been reduced considerably.

The pink bollworm passes through four stages of development: egg, larva, pupa, and adult. The life cycle in midsummer is usually completed in twenty-five to thirty days, and as many as six generations of the insect may occur in a season.

To control effectively the pink bollworm in the state, the Texas Department of Agriculture has laid down rules and regulations, authorized by law, governing planting, cultivating, growing, and harvesting cotton. In order to prevent over-wintering (winter survival), shredding and plowing under of the cotton stalks by given dates is required. Federal quarantine regulates interstate movement of cotton from infested to noninfested areas. The use of insecticides, carbaryl, DDT, and Guthian plus DDT, have been especially effective in the control program. *See also* Agriculture in Texas; Boll Weevil in Texas.

BIBLIOGRAPHY: United States Department of Agriculture, Farmers' Bulletin No. 2207, *Controlling the Pink Bollworm on Cotton* (1965); Texas Agricultural Extension Service, Bulletin L-219, *Ways to Fight the Pink Bollworm* (1965); The President's Science Advisory Committee, *Cotton Insects* (1965); Texas Department of Agriculture, Proclamation No. 67, *Pink Bollworm Quarantine—Rules and Regulations* (1966).

L. Tuffly Ellis

*Bolt, Texas.

Bolton, Herbert Eugene. Herbert Eugene Bolton was born in Wilton, Wisconsin, on July 20, 1870, the son of Edwin Latham and Rosalie (Cady) Bolton. Bolton attended public schools in Wisconsin and the University of Wisconsin, where he was graduated with a B.L. in 1895. In 1895 he married Gertrude James, and they were the parents of six daughters and one son. He continued studies under Frederick Jackson Turner in 1896–1897. During 1897–1899 he was Harrison Fellow at the University of Pennsylvania, studying in American history under John Bach McMaster. He took his Ph.D. there in 1899. After teaching history and economics at the Milwaukee State Normal School in 1899–1901, Bolton went to the University of Texas as instructor in history in 1901, where he remained until 1909. Soon after his arrival at the University of Texas, he developed a lively interest in the history of Spanish expansion into North America, and from the summer of 1902 onward he made a series of pioneering forays into the archives in Mexico. At the invitation of the Carnegie Corporation, he prepared a report on materials in Mexican archives for a history of the United States, and this was published in 1913. Between 1906 and 1912 he studied the history of native Indians in Texas for the United States Bureau of Ethnology, and he wrote more than one hundred articles for the *Handbook of American Indians North of Mexico*. His interest in Texas history was reflected in over a dozen learned articles as well as in his published volumes on *Athanase de Mézières and the Louisiana-Texas Frontier, 1768–1780* (1914), and *Texas in the Middle Eighteenth Century: Studies in Spanish Colonial History and Administration* (1915). Although his later research and writing was more concerned with the Pacific Coast, Bolton retained a strong interest in Texas history and looked back with affection to his years at the University of Texas. His bibliography consists of ninety-four entries, including two dozen books written or edited. His concept of the Spanish Borderlands, the cresent-shaped area from Georgia to California, as a fruitful field for study and interpretation, was an important addition to historical thought.

From 1909 to 1911 Bolton was professor of American history at Stanford University, and from 1911 until his retirement in 1940 he was professor of history at the University of California, Berkeley. He served as chairman of the Department of History from 1919 to 1940, and from 1916 until 1940 he was director of the Bancroft Library. In 1920 he inaugurated at the University of California a course in the "History of the Americas," a study of the Western Hemisphere as a whole, which gave new insights into the dimensions of American history. He outlined this thesis in his presidential address to the American Historical Association at Toronto in 1952 under the title "The Epic of Greater America." Although he became professor emeritus in 1940, Bolton returned to teaching as lecturer in history from 1942 until 1944.

Bolton was tireless and enthusiastic in his research, in the exploration of old trails and historic sites, and in putting the results of his research and travel on paper. Not only a distinguished scholar and writer, he was also a great teacher. He gave time and energy unstintingly to this side of his profession. He lectured to large undergraduate classes, and his seminars became famous. Nearly three hundred M.A. theses and over one hundred doctoral dissertations were written under his supervision. He was noted for his ability to communicate his enthusiasm for scholarship and its presentation in readable form to his students. As scholar, writer, and teacher, he was an individual of remarkable power and influence.

On January 30, 1953, Herbert Eugene Bolton died at Berkeley, California, where he was buried.

John Haskell Kemble

*Bolton, John Thomas.

*Bomar, Texas.

*Bomarton, Texas.

*Bon Ami, Texas.

*Bon Wier, Texas.

*Bonanza, Texas.

*Bonaparte, Jerome Napoleon, Jr.

*Bonavía y Zapata, Bernardo.

*Boneo y Morales, Justo.

*Bonham, James Butler.

*Bonham, Texas. Bonham, seat and commercial center of Fannin County, in 1966 was a city of 217 businesses, principally connected with cotton, wood products, fertilizer, clothing, and metal products. In that year the city had three hospitals, two libraries (including the Sam Rayburn qv Memorial Library), a newspaper, and a radio and television station. Also situated in the town are a National Guard armory and a highway department office. Floods in the spring of 1966 did nearly twenty thousand dollars worth of damage to the streets of Bonham. A new high school was completed by 1969. The 1960 population of 7,357 increased to 7,698 by 1970.

*Bonilla, Antonio.

*Bonilla, Francisco Leyva de.

*Bonillo Creek.

*Bonita, Texas. (Comal County.)

*Bonita, Texas. (Montague County.)

*Bonito Creek.

*Bonnell, George W.

*Bonner, Mary.

*Bonner, Micajah Hubbard.

Bonner, Thomas Reuben. Thomas Reuben Bonner, son of William N. and Martha Ellen (Wade) Bonner, was born in Holmes County, Mississippi, on September 11, 1838. He moved with his parents to Rusk, Texas, in February, 1850. At twelve years of age he became an apprentice printer on the *Cherokee Sentinel*. Having only the rudiments of an education, he commenced at that time to educate himself by reading and self-directed study. In 1854 he left the *Sentinel* to take charge of his father's

farm and was a farmer at the outbreak of the Civil War. He entered Confederate service in April, 1862, as captain, Company C, 18th Texas Infantry. He was subsequently major, lieutenant colonel, and colonel of that regiment, which served in the Trans-Mississippi Department as an element of Walker's Texas Division.qv

After the war Bonner farmed until 1866, when he began reading law at Rusk in the office of his older brothers, F. W. and M. H. Bonner.qv Admitted to the Bar in 1867, he practiced law at Rusk until September, 1872, then moved to Tyler, where he entered the banking business with E. C. Williams. Bonner became a leading East Texas banker, railroad director, and financier. Bonner was apparently married twice during his lifetime, first to Cynthia A. Madden of Cherokee County and, in later years, to Mary Davenport. By his latter marriage he had two sons. Bonner served in the Texas legislature in 1866 from Rusk County. In 1876 he was elected to the legislature from Smith County and was speaker of the House during the ensuing session. A member of the Methodist church, he was an active Mason and was grand master in 1874. He died in 1891.

BIBLIOGRAPHY: John Henry Brown (ed.), *Encyclopedia of the New West* (1881); Sid S. Johnson, *Texans Who Wore the Gray* (1907).

Lester N. Fitzhugh

*Bonner Hollow.

*Bonney, William.

*Bonney, Texas.

*Bonnieview, Texas.

*Bono, Texas.

*Bonus, Texas.

Book Club of Texas. The Book Club of Texas was conceived in 1928 by H. Stanley Marcus and John Avery Lomax,qv both of Dallas. Formal organization occurred in 1929, with Marcus as president and Lomax as secretary. Its expressed purpose was the encouragement of graphic arts in Texas. The club's principal project was publication of limited editions of material about the Southwest. Such publications made major contributions to belles-lettres in Texas. Three books, *Code Duello* (1931), William Faulkner's *Miss Zilphia Gant* (1932), and Alexander Watkins Terrell's qv *From Texas to Mexico and the Court of Maximilian in 1865* (1933), were designated among the "Fifty Books of the Year" for 1932, 1933, and 1934 (national awards for book design and printing). Another club publication was *Tales of the Mustang* (1936) by J. Frank Dobie.qv By 1934 interest in the club had diminished; activities ceased in 1937. Club assets were transferred by Marcus to the Texas Folklore Society qv in 1941.

BIBLIOGRAPHY: Wilson M. Hudson, "Introduction," *The Story of Champ d'Asile* (1969); H. Stanley Marcus, "The Book Club of Texas," *News Notes*; *Bulletin of the Texas Library Association*, X (October, 1934).

*Booker, Shields.

*Booker, Texas.

*Boon Creek.

*Boon Slough.

*Boone, Hannibal Honestus.

*Boone Prairie, Texas.

*Boonsville, Texas.

*Boonville, Texas.

*Boot, The.

*Boot Canyon.

*Booth, Texas.

*Boothe Creek.

*Boquillas, Texas.

*Boquillas Canyon.

*Boquillas Hot Springs.

*Boraches Spring.

*Boracho Peak.

*Borden, Gail, Jr.

*Borden, John P.

*Borden, Paschal Pavolo.

*Borden, Thomas Henry.

*Borden, Texas.

*Borden County. Borden County was a sparsely settled ranching and farming area in the 1960's. The 1960 population of 1,076 decreased to 888 by 1970. Cattle and sheep were the chief livestock, while the crops included cotton, grain sorghums, and wheat (1,400 acres irrigated in 1964). A newer source of county income was oil; the yield from 1949 to 1973 was 190,990,228 barrels. The county's only areas of population concentration were Gail, the county seat, and Mesquite. The major recreational area was around Lake J. B. Thomas in the southeastern corner of the county.

*Bordentown, Texas.

*Border, John Pelham. John Pelham Border, son of William and Sarah Mell Border, was born on February 19, 1819 (not 1821, as stated in Volume I). He came to the United States with his parents in 1823 and settled in San Augustine, Texas, in 1835. He first served in the Texas Army qv from October to December, 1835, and participated in the successful Goliad Campaign of 1835.qv Border enlisted again on April 1, 1836, and joined Captain William Kimbro's qv Company at the Battle of San Jacinto. He was married to Catherine Elizabeth Harding on March 5, 1844 (not 1842). During the Civil War, in 1864, he was commandant at Camp Ford,qv the stockade for Federal prisoners. Border died on June 12, 1873, and in 1887 his widow married Oran Milo Roberts,qv governor of Texas from 1879 to 1883. Catherine Elizabeth Border Roberts died July 21, 1920, and was buried in the State Cemetery.qv

Kate Harding Bates Parker
Clara Elisabeth Bates Nisbet

*Border Patrol. In 1961 the Border Patrol Academy was moved from El Paso to the former U.S. naval base at Port Isabel. Fourteen-week sessions (usually three per year) were held for trainees, who daily attended classes for six hours and had two hours of physical training and firearms practice. There was no longer a maximum age limitation, and the minimum weight requirement was lowered to 140 pounds. All trainees had to learn to speak and write Spanish. Piper Super Cubs replaced helicopters as the standard air observation arm of the service, and horses were no longer used. In 1956 the service acquired transport aircraft for faster and more economical movement of illegal aliens. Three detention facilities, or staging points, were in operation in 1961; one each at El Centro, California; El Paso; and Port Isabel. Mexican aliens were concentrated at these points before being returned to Mexico. There were eleven Border Patrol sectors on the Mexican border, with strength fluctuating as needs dictated. Texas sectors were located at El Paso, Del Rio, Laredo, McAllen, and Brownsville. In each sector, substations were staffed with a small number of personnel used in maintaining roadblocks and backup stations. In 1952 Congress passed an act which gave border patrolmen the right to enter private lands, but not dwellings, to search and question persons as to alienage, and to arrest without warrant any alien who was likely to abscond. This act was effective within twenty-five miles of the United States boundary.

Ralph L. Nafus

*Borderville, Texas.

*Boregas Creek.

*Boren, Samuel Hampson.

*Borger, Texas. Borger, in southern Hutchinson County, was one of the largest centers for oil, carbon black, and petrochemical production and supplies in the state in the mid-1960's. In 1970 the town had a total of 354 businesses, including several manufacturers. In 1966 Borger reported eight schools, fifty churches, two banks, and two radio stations, as well as a newspaper, a library, a hospital, and a college. The 1960 population was 20,911, an increase of nearly three thousand since 1950; the 1970 population was 14,195, a decrease of 32 percent.

Borger City Junior College. *See* Frank Phillips College.

Borginnis, Sarah. Sarah Borginnis (best known as The Great Western), a legendary laundress of the Mexican War who stood six feet and two inches in height, was noted for outstanding feats of bravery performed in several battles of the war. She began her military career when she came to Corpus Christi in 1845 with her husband, a soldier in the United States 7th Infantry under General Zachary Taylor.qv Accompanying the army of occupation over Taylor's Trail qv as a laundress and cook, The Great Western first gained fame throughout the army for her actions at the crossing of the Arroyo Colorado in March, 1846, when she offered to wade the river and whip the enemy with a stout pair of tongs. She came to be known as the "Heroine of Fort Brown" for her bravery during the bombardment of the fort in May, 1846. At the battle of Buena Vista, she again demonstrated her fearlessness by loading cartridges, dressing wounds, and carrying wounded soldiers off the battlefield in the thick of the fight.

The Great Western seemed to have acquired several husbands during her lifetime, but little is known of them. After the Mexican War, she moved to El Paso and established a hotel where many Mexican War veterans stopped by to hail her on their way to California gold fields. John Salmon (Rip) Ford qv saw her in El Paso in 1849 and recorded that "she had the reputation of being something of the roughest fighter on the Rio Grande; and was approached in a polite if not humble manner." Later, Sarah Borginnis moved to Fort Yuma, Arizona, where she died and was buried in 1866 with full military honors.

BIBLIOGRAPHY: Brantz Mayer, History of the War between Mexico and the United States (1848); Memoirs of John Salmon Ford (MS., Archives, University of Texas at Austin Library); Buchanan A. Russell (ed.), "George Washington Trahern: Texan Cowboy from Mier to Buena Vista," Southwestern Historical Quarterly, LVIII (1954–1955); Samuel Emery Chamberlain, My Confession (1956); Edward S. Wallace, The Great Reconnaissance (1955); Lloyd Lewis, Captain Sam Grant (1950); J. Evetts Haley, Fort Concho and the Texas Frontier (1952).

Borglum, John Gutzon De La Mothe. Gutzon Borglum was born in Idaho, March 25, 1867, the son of Danish immigrants, James and Ida (Michelson) Borglum. Gutzon Borglum first studied art in California under William Keith and Virgil Williams. It was there that the large painting, "Stagecoach," now in the Menger Hotel,qv San Antonio, was completed. In 1890 he went abroad to study for two years in Paris at the Academie Julien and the École des Beaux Arts and also under individual masters. He exhibited in the Old Salon in 1891 and 1892 as a painter, and in the New Salon as a sculptor with "Death of the Chief."

After one year of work in Spain, Borglum returned to California and from there went to England in 1896. While in England he painted portraits and murals, illustrated some books, and produced sculpture, "Apache Pursued," executed at this time, is owned in replica by the Witte Memorial Museum,qv in San Antonio. Sculpture became his prime artistic medium; examples of his work include the head of Lincoln at the Capitol in Washington, D.C., a seated Lincoln in Newark, New Jersey, two equestrian statues of Philip Sheridan,qv and the "Wars of America" group. Most famous and monumental of his works are his Mt. Rushmore National Memorial mountain sculptures of Washington, Jefferson, Lincoln, and Theodore Roosevelt, in South Dakota, dedicated on August 10, 1927, and completed, after Gutzon Borglum's death, by his son Lincoln.

In 1925 the sculptor, with his family, moved to Texas to work on the monument to the trail drivers,qv commissioned by the Trail Drivers Association.qv The completed monument, one-fourth its originally planned size, stands in front of the Texas Pioneer and Trail Drivers Memorial Hall next to the Witte Museum in San Antonio. Borglum lived at the historic Menger Hotel, which in the 1920's was the residence of a number of artists.

His projected plan for the redevelopment of the Corpus Christi waterfront failed, although a model for a statue of Christ intended for it was later modified by his son and erected on a mountain top in South Dakota. While living and working in Texas, Borglum took vociferous interest not only in art but also in aspects of local politics. He preached the doctrine of change and modernity, although he was repeatedly berated by academicians. His work, however, remained true to his subjects and to life.

On November 6, 1941, Borglum died in Chicago, Illinois, survived by his wife Mary (Montgomery) Borglum and his two children. His first marriage to Mrs. Elizabeth "Lisa" Putnam in 1889 ended in divorce in 1908.

BIBLIOGRAPHY: Lincoln Borglum, My Father's Mountain: Mt. Rushmore National Memorial and How It Was Carved (1965); Robert Joseph Casey and Mary Borglum, Give the Man Room (1952); Frances Battaile Fisk, A History of Texas Artists and Sculptors (1928); Esse Forrester-O'Brien, Art and Artists of Texas (1935); National Geographic Society, America's Wonderlands (1959); San Antonio Light, June 20, 1937; Willadene Price, Gutzon Borglum, Artist and Patriot (1962).

Caroline Remy

Borobamo Indians. The Borobamo Indians are known from a single Spanish document of 1683 which does not clearly identify their area. They may have lived somewhere in west-central Texas. The affiliations of the Borobamo are unknown.

BIBLIOGRAPHY: C. W. Hackett (ed.), Pichardo's Treatise on the Limits of Louisiana and Texas, I (1931).

T. N. Campbell

*Borrado Indians. Borrado is a misspelled Spanish name that was used to refer to Indians who practiced body painting, usually in stripes. In Texas this name was applied to Indian groups in two separate areas, one in western Texas, the other in southern Texas and adjoining northeastern Mexico. In western Texas an early reference (1693) mentions "Borrados" and "other Borrados" who lived somewhere north of the Rio Grande and "between Texas and New Mexico." Today these Borrados still cannot be more precisely identified or located.

In the seventeenth and eighteenth centuries the second group of Borrado ranged over a large area that extended from Saltillo in southeastern Coahuila eastward across Nuevo León into Tamaulipas. In the eighteenth century they appeared in southern Texas, particularly along the coast and in the lower Rio Grande area. At various times during the second half of the eighteenth century groups of these Borrado entered three of the missions at San Antonio—Nuestra Señora de la Purísima Concepción de Acuña, San José y San Miguel de Aguayo, and San Juan Capistrano.qqv These Borrado spoke a Coahuiltecan language.

BIBLIOGRAPHY: H. E. Bolton, Texas in the Middle Eighteenth Century (1915); J. A. Dabbs, "The Texas Missions in 1785," Preliminary Studies of the Texas Catholic Historical Society, III (1940); C. W. Hackett (ed.), Historical Documents Relating to New Mexico, Nueva Vizcaya, and Approaches Thereto, to 1773, II (1926); F. W. Hodge (ed.), Handbook of American Indians, I (1907), II (1910); J. R. Swanton, Linguistic Material *from the Tribes of Southern Texas and Northeastern Mexico* (1940).

T. N. Campbell

*Borrego Creek.

Böse [Boese], Emil. Emil Böse was born in Hamburg, Germany, in 1868. He took his doctorate in Munich in 1893, under Karl von Zittel, after which he spent several years studying the Triassic rocks of the Italian Alps. Böse, one of several outstanding geologists who worked in northern Mexico and Texas in the early part of the twentieth century, is best known for outlining the basic stratigraphy of northern Mexico. Böse served as geologist for the Instituto de Geología de México from 1898 to 1915, and was responsible for the preparation of many of the guidebooks for the excursions and meetings of the International Geological Congress in Mexico City and environs in 1906. Although he published many articles and monographs during this period, his most important are probably the following: "Monografía Geológica y Paleontológica del Cerro de Muleros cerca de Ciudad Juárez, Estado Chihuahua, y descripción de la fauna Cretácea de la Encantada, Placer de Guadalupe, Estado de Chihuahua, México"; and "Faunas Jurásicas de Symon (Zacatecas) y faunas Cretácicas de Zupango del Río (Guerrero)."

In 1915 Böse joined the Bureau of Economic Geology of the University of Texas under the direction of Johan A. Udden.^{qv} He first worked with C. L. Baker and Wayne Bowman in Trans-Pecos Texas, but later studied the geology of North Texas and other parts of the state. He decided to return to Mexico during the latter part of World War I, but since he carried a commission as colonel (retired) in the German army, he was detained in San Antonio by United States authorities until the end of the war.

Until 1922 he was engaged as a consulting geologist in various parts of Texas, Oklahoma, New Mexico, and Mexico. In 1922 he joined O. A. Cavins, and others, in exploratory geology for the Richmond Petroleum Company of Mexico, S. A., a subsidiary of the Standard Oil Company of California. During this period he traveled much in Mexico, and his letters describing desert life in western and northern Coahuila during and following the Pancho Villa ^{qv} period are fascinating.

Böse's publications on the geology of Texas included several bulletins of the University of Texas, papers in the *American Journal of Science*, numerous bulletins and papers for the Instituto de Geología de México, and articles in the International Geological Congress journals and in various scientific bulletins. His last papers, published posthumously, were "Cretaceous Ammonites from Texas and Northern Mexico" and, with O. A. Cavins, "The Cretaceous and Tertiary of Southern Texas and Northern Mexico." He was the first to describe the Jurassic and Cretaceous peninsula in northern Mexico now known as the Coahuila Peninsula.

Emil Böse was killed in an automobile accident west of Sabinal, Texas, early in the fall of 1927.

He was survived by his wife and two children, who had returned to Munich in 1925.

BIBLIOGRAPHY: Emil Böse Papers (MS., Archives, University of Texas at Austin Library).

Keith Young

*Bosque County.** Bosque County, with 1,206 farms, was one of the leading oat-growing counties in Texas in 1963. Grains, cotton, and truck crops were also cultivated, but livestock and livestock products accounted for three-fourths of the farm income by 1973. Whitney Reservoir and Meridian State Park are tourist attractions. The 1960 population was 10,809; in 1970 the count was 10,966.

*Bosque Female Seminary and Male College.

*Bosque-Larios Expedition.

*Bosque River.

*Bosqueville, Texas.

*Bosqueville Male and Female College.

*Bostic, Caleb R.

*Bostick, Sion R.

*Boston, Texas.** Boston, seat of Bowie County, is within the city limits of New Boston. This older unincorporated city maintains its third-class post office independently of the second-class post office of the newer city. This situation creates the rare predicament of having two post offices about a mile apart under different names within a single corporate limit. Consolidation of the two post offices could come about by the adoption of a single name for the towns or by an act of Congress. Citizens of New Boston do not care to change their city's name and, since the older Boston is a county seat, an act of Congress is required to discontinue Boston's postal service, a necessary procedure in the consolidation of the post offices. The 1970 population was approximately two hundred. *See also* New Boston; Texarkana Standard Metropolitan Statistical Area.

BIBLIOGRAPHY: Dallas *News*, September 19, 1958.

Boswell, Margie Belle. Margie Belle Boswell was born in Pueblo, Colorado, on June 20, 1875, the daughter of A. G. and Mary Isabel (Whiteside) Huffmaster, who moved to Texas when she was an infant. From 1889 to 1892, she studied at Parker Institute,^{qv} Texas, then taught in the Fort Worth public schools until 1897, when she married W. E. Boswell. They had eleven children.

Mrs. Boswell conducted a poetry program over Station KFJZ in Fort Worth, taught verse technique, contributed poems to literary journals, and published eight books of poetry. Her last collection, *Selected Poems and Little Lines*, contained selections from earlier volumes. She wrote feature articles as well as verse and beginning in 1937 contributed a column to the Fort Worth *Press*. She died in Fort Worth on May 29, 1963.

BIBLIOGRAPHY: *Who's Who of American Women* (1938); Dallas *Morning News*, May 30, 1963.

Sonja Fojtik

*Botella Creek.

*Bougham Creek.

*Boulting House Mountain.

*Boundaries of Texas. When Texas won her independence in 1836 and was recognized by the United States in 1837, a new boundary agreement was necessary to determine the eastern boundary of Texas, and although no survey was made (as stated in Volume I) at that time, there was in 1840–1841 a survey made of that portion of the line between the Republic of Texas and the United States from the Gulf of Mexico to the Red River by a joint commission representing the two countries.

On July 5, 1848, the United States Congress passed an act giving its consent to the state of Texas to extend its eastern boundary from the west bank of the Sabine River (the term "Sabine River," used here, includes Sabine Pass and Sabine Lake) to the middle of that stream, and on November 24, 1849, the Texas legislature enacted such legislation, extending the state's boundary to the middle of the Sabine River. From that time the boundary was unchallenged until November 27, 1941, when Louisiana Governor Sam Jones wrote Texas Governor Coke Stevenson,^{qv} asserting that Louisiana's western border was the west bank of the Sabine River. Louisiana's claim rested on United States treaties of 1819 with Spain, 1828 with Mexico, and 1838 with the Republic of Texas, all of which designated the boundary of the United States as the western bank of the Sabine. However, the boundary of the United States to the west bank of the Sabine River was not identical to that of the Louisiana boundary, which extended only to the middle of the river. The state of Louisiana contended that the United States was negotiating on the state's behalf and consequently had no authority to grant Texas the western half of the river in the act of 1848.

It was more than twenty-seven years after Governor Jones' letter to Governor Stevenson in 1941 before Louisiana participated in any legal proceedings. United States District Judge Robert Van Pelt, special master for the United States Supreme Court, heard the claims and recommended to the Supreme Court, in a report filed on or about May 5, 1972, that the boundary between Texas and Louisiana should be the geographic middle of the Sabine River, Sabine Lake, and Sabine Pass. It was also recommended that Louisiana be awarded all islands which existed in the river on April 8, 1812 (the date Louisiana was admitted to the Union), subject, however, to any claims Texas might make to any such islands by reason of acquiescence and prescription; that all islands formed in the east half of Sabine River since 1812 be awarded to Louisiana; and that all islands formed in the west half of the river since 1812 be awarded to Texas.

Sixty-one square miles of the river and lake were involved in the dispute, but more than 35,000 acres of land, four producing oil wells, and $2.6 million in oil lease bonuses collected by Texas were directly involved in the case. Both states filed exceptions to the recommendations by the special master in July, 1972, and after answers to each state's exceptions, the United States Supreme Court was to rule on the master's report. The case was argued before the United States Supreme Court in December, 1972; the court's ruling came down early in March, 1973, saying, in effect, that the boundary was the geographic middle of the Sabine River; however, the case was sent back to the special master for further study in regard to the ownership of islands and also to determine the extension of the boundary into the Gulf of Mexico.

BIBLIOGRAPHY: Supreme Court of the United States, October Term, 1969, No. 36 Original, The State of Texas, Plaintiff, vs. The State of Louisiana, Defendant, *Report of Special Master* (1972); Austin *American-Statesman*, May 6, 1972; Files, Texas State Historical Association, Austin.

Eldon S. Branda

In the 1950's and 1960's two other important boundary disputes were settled. The controversy over state ownership of the 2,608,774 acres of Texas tidelands in the Gulf of Mexico between low tide and three leagues from shore was finally settled in 1960 after fourteen years of litigation involving three United States Supreme Court decisions, three acts of Congress, and two presidential vetoes. As a result of the last litigation, begun in 1957, Texas holds firm title to a three-league, as opposed to a three-mile, boundary in the Gulf. By August 31, 1966, the Texas Permanent School Fund (*see* School Fund, Permanent) had received $156,312,000 from leases of the oil-rich tidelands.

The other major boundary dispute in the 1950's involved the United States and Mexico and concerned acreage called "El Chamizal" along the Rio Grande at El Paso. In July, 1963, President John F. Kennedy and President Adolfo López Mateos announced an agreement by which the United States recognized the settlement proposed by the 1910–1911 arbitration commission. On September 25, 1964, President Lyndon B. Johnson ^{qv} and President López Mateos met on the boundary between El Paso and Ciudad Juárez to officially end the boundary dispute. *See also* Tidelands Controversy; Chamizal Dispute.

BIBLIOGRAPHY: Ernest R. Bartley, *The Tidelands Oil Controversy* (1953); Sheldon B. Liss, *A Century of Disagreement, the Chamizal Conflict, 1864–1964* (1965).

Bounds, Joseph Murphy. Joseph Murphy Bounds was born in 1822. He came to Collin County, Texas, before 1845 from Missouri and settled in McKinney, although he apparently was active as a traveling trader. In 1861 he raised a cavalry company in the county and by February, 1862, had been promoted to lieutenant colonel of the 11th Texas Cavalry. He led the regiment in the battle of Murfreesboro, Tennessee, but his promotion to colonel was never approved. He was assassinated on October 27, 1863.

BIBLIOGRAPHY: J. Lee Stambaugh and Lillian J. Stambaugh, *A History of Collin County, Texas* (1958); Seymour V. Connor, *The Peters Colony of Texas* (1959); Service Records of J. M. Bounds (Civil War Biographical File, Archives, University of Texas at Austin Library, originals in National Archives, Washington, D.C.).

*Bounty Certificates.

*Bourgeois d'Orvanne, Alexander.

*Bourland, James.

*Bourland, William H.

*Bourland Creek.

*Bovina, Texas. Bovina, in Parmer County, had a population of 1,029 in 1960 and 1,428 in 1970, according to the U. S. census.

*Bow Creek.

*Bowen, Reuben Dean.

*Bowen, William Abraham.

*Bower, John White.

*Bowers, Herbert Edmund.

*Bowers, John Henry.

*Bowers, Texas. (Milam County.)

*Bowers, Texas. (Polk County.)

*Bowie, James.

*Bowie, Rezin P.

*Bowie, Texas. Bowie, chief commercial center for Montague County, with fourteen manufacturing firms in 1963, was a center of diversified industry and a shipping point for cattle, cotton, truck crops, poultry, and eggs. It reported a gas plant, a dress factory, a slacks plant, and a few equipment manufacturers. Public improvement projects included a sewage treatment plant and an airport completed in 1965 and a new high school and a hospital in 1966. By 1967 the city had 258 businesses, eighteen churches, two banks, a library, a newspaper, and a radio station. The 1960 population was 4,566; the 1970 population was 5,185.

*Bowie County. The 1960 population of Bowie County was 59,971; the 1970 count was 67,813. The United States Army installations, Red River Army Depot and Lone Star Army Ammunition Plant,qqv employed large numbers of people. Texarkana was the largest incorporated area, with 30,497 inhabitants in 1970, and Boston was the county seat. Lake Texarkana was the largest tourist attraction. See Texarkana Standard Metropolitan Statistical Area.

*Bowie Knife.

*Bowie Mountain.

*Bowieville, Texas.

*Bowles, Chief (The Bowl).

*Bowles Creek.

*Bowman, John T.

*Bowman, John Tibaut.

Bowman, Joseph Wylie. Joseph Wylie Bowman, son of Joseph and Annie (Brakebill) Bowman, was born January 16, 1887, near Knoxville, Tennessee. The family moved to Texas in 1895 and Bowman attended country schools near Greenville and Rotan.

After three years as assistant cashier of the Cowboy State Bank in Rotan, Bowman operated a grocery store and an automobile agency in Greenville. In 1923 he began selling buses bought in Detroit and driven to Texas. In 1925 he bought rights to a bus line between Fort Worth and Dallas, and in 1929 he bought a bus company in Lubbock. From the latter eventually grew Texas, New Mexico, and Oklahoma Coaches, Incorporated, operating from western Oklahoma to Carlsbad, New Mexico. Bowman was a member and director of the Texas Motor Transportation Association and a member of the National Bus Owners' Association.

Bowman was active in religious and civic affairs. He helped build the Milam Home for Orphans in Lubbock and was active in other charities. An avid sportsman, he won many trophies and ribbons with his saddle horses and trotters at shows in West Texas and was recognized as one of the leading horse trainers in the Southwest.

Bowman married Bula Birdsong in 1909. The couple had no children. He died on December 19, 1943, and was buried at Greenville.

BIBLIOGRAPHY: Seymour V. Connor (ed.), *Builders of the Southwest* (1959); Lubbock *Evening Journal*, December 20, 1943.

Lawrence L. Graves

*Bowman, Thornton Hardie.

*Bowries Creek.

*Bowser, Oliver P.

*Bowser, Texas.

*Bowser Bend, Texas.

Box, John Andrew. John Andrew Box was born in Franklin County, Tennessee, on July 2, 1803, a son of Stephen F. and Keziah Box. He was married twice, first to a Miss Allbright, by whom he had four children, and then to Lucenda Yarbrough, by whom he had nine children. After coming to Texas in 1834, he was a member of the 2nd Regiment, Texas Volunteers, 1st Company, Infantry, and fought in the battle of San Jacinto as a member of that company under Captain Hayden Arnold.qv He was an early circuit rider for the Methodist church but discontinued his preaching after the battle of San Jacinto. On April 22, 1837, he, his father and brothers, plus 102 others from Mustang Prairie, petitioned the Texas Congress to create a constitutional county, and thus Houston County became the first county created by the Republic of Texas. Box died about 1874.

Edna Box Riley

*Box, John Calvin.

Box, Nelson A. Nelson A. Box was born in 1808 in Franklin County, Tennessee, a son of Stephen F. and Keziah Box. He emigrated from Tennessee to Blount County, Alabama, then to Texas in 1834. He married Elizabeth Garner and they had several children. After coming to Texas, Nelson Box enlisted in the Army of the Republic,qv and fought at the battle of San Jacinto in Captain Hayden Arnold's qv company.

In 1837 he and his father and brothers, along with other citizens of Mustang Prairie, were instrumental in the organization of Houston County, the first county of the Republic of Texas. Nelson Box died about 1849 and was buried in Box-Beeson Cemetery, three miles south of Crockett.

Edna Box Riley

Box, Thomas Griffin. Thomas Griffin Box, a son of Stephen F. and Keziah Box, was born in Franklin County, Tennessee, on January 12, 1817. He was married three times, first to Rachel Wilkerson, then to Amanda Georgia Alexander, and then to Sarah Crowson Massingale. He became a Methodist minister and immigrated to Texas in 1835. He enlisted in the Army of the Republic,qv and as a member of 2nd Regiment, Texas Volunteers, 1st Company, Infantry, in Captain Hayden Arnold's qv company, fought at the battle of San Jacinto. In 1837 he played a primary role, along with his father and brothers, in the petitioning of Congress to create Houston County, the first county created by the Republic of Texas. He died on February 18, 1859.

Edna Box Riley

*Box Church, Texas.

Box Colony. Michael James Box, at times a Texas Ranger,qv propagated a myth that a man could make twenty-five thousand dollars a day from the gold in "Red Mountain" near Durango, Mexico. Counterreports did not prevent him from collecting more than three hundred followers, including women, children, and his aged parents.

Departing from Laredo in March, 1861, the colonists experienced thirst, extreme fatigue, and the tyranny of Box's leadership during the next five months. As they neared their destination of the little mining town of Corneta, smallpox broke out, and Box had to obtain medical assistance through the governor of Durango.

None of the colonists could speak Spanish, a factor which contributed to their delusion. Box and ten men departed on a fruitless two-week search for Red Mountain. Upon the return of the party, the angry colonists threatened to kill Box, who immediately fell ill and pretended to be dying. Later the colonists attempted to have the governor of Durango prosecute Box, but the Mexican official refused. Thereafter the colonists broke into confused groups—one man was killed at a fandango, some were too poor to return to Texas, a dozen men went to work in the nearby mines, but most of the Texans returned home. Some of these were murdered en route. Box remained at Corneta as a miner, although other members of his family returned to Texas.

BIBLIOGRAPHY: James P. Newcomb, *Secession Times in Texas and Journal of Travel from Texas through Mexico to California, Including a History of the "Box Colony"* (1863).

Donald E. Everett

*Box Creek.

*Box Quarter, Texas.

*Boxelder, Texas.

*Boyce, Texas.

Boyd, Belle. Marie Isabel (Belle) Boyd, daughter of Benjamin Reed and Mary (Glenn) Boyd, was born in Martinsburg, Virginia (now West Virginia), on May 9, 1844. Known for her exploits as a Confederate spy during the Civil War, her memoirs of that period were published under the title *Belle Boyd in Camp and Prison* (1865). She married Samuel Wylde Hardinge, a Union naval ensign, on August 26, 1864, in England. They had one daughter. After her husband's death in 1866, she became an actress, using the name "Nina Benjamin," until she married an Englishman, John Swainston Hammond, on March 17, 1869, in New Orleans. They had four children, one of whom died as a youngster.

She was in Texas as early as 1869 when, in January of that year, she had a contract disagreement with Henry Greenwall qv in Houston. Belle and her family lived in many different places, including California, and Utica, New York (1874), Baltimore (1878), and Philadelphia (1881). They traveled farther south, finally settling in Dallas, Texas, sometime after 1881. They bought a fashionable home on Pocahontas Street, facing City Park, and lived there until the marriage ended in divorce on November 1, 1884. Belle Boyd returned to the stage, and on January 7, 1885, she married an actor, Nathaniel Rue High, who was eighteen years her junior. She sold the house in Dallas on July 29, 1887. Using her own name, Belle Boyd appeared as a lecturer on the Civil War in all parts of the country, always wearing a Confederate gray, double-breasted suit, with a cavalry-type hat, but emphasizing understanding and friendship between the North and South. Following a lecture in Kilbourn (now Wisconsin Dells), Wisconsin, she had a heart attack and died at the Hile House (later Brooks Hotel) on June 11, 1900. She was buried in Spring Hill Cemetery in that Wisconsin town. The house in which she lived in Dallas was razed in 1962.

BIBLIOGRAPHY: Louis A. Sigaud, *Belle Boyd, Confederate Spy* (1944); Dallas *Times Herald*, July 22, 1962, January 12, 1964; San Antonio *Daily Express*, December 30, 1884.

Mrs. Harry Joseph Morris

*Boyd, Frank Douglas.

*Boyd, John.

*Boyd, Richard Henry.

*Boyd, Texas.

*Boyds Chapel, Texas.

*Boydston, Texas.

*Boylan, James D.

*Boyle, Andrew Michael.

Boynton, Benjamin Lee. Benjamin (Ben) Lee Boynton was born on December 6, 1898, in Waco, Texas, the son of Charles Albert and Laura Bassett (Young) Boynton. The first Texan named to an All-American football team, quarterback Boynton began his football career at Waco High School where he was an all-round sports star (1913, 1914, 1915).

At a time when sports focus was on eastern collegiate football, Ben Lee Boynton attended Williams College, where during his sophomore year his kick-off returns placed him high among top contenders for national recognition. He played quarterback on an undefeated Williams team and was selected as one of the members of the All-Eastern eleven. At the close of the 1917 season International News Service placed him on their All-American team. He left school in 1918 and became a gunnery sergeant in the marine aviation corps during World War I. In 1919 he returned to Williams, where he became a legend in eastern collegiate football. Harvard, Yale, and Princeton were all defeated by Williams College in the years 1917, 1919, and 1920.

Boynton was named to Frank Menke's All-American teams for three seasons. He was one of the few players listed as three-time All-American by the Official Football Guide in 1919 and 1920. He was described as one of the best drop-kickers ever and a fine field general and open-field runner. He tied an all-time record for the longest scoring run by any method (110 yards) when he ran out a long punt return in the 1920 game against Hamilton College. He was also classed as one of the first great passers in football.

After graduation Boynton worked for Bethlehem Steel Company in Steeltown, Pennsylvania, and was on the professional football circuit for four years with five different teams, at one time playing on two teams at the same time—the Frankfort Yellow Jackets on Saturdays and the Buffalo All-Americans on Sundays. In pro football he was considered second only to Jim Thorpe in all-round football ability; he was described as a "brainy" fellow who could do anything.

In 1926 he organized the Southwest Football Officials Association and officiated at college and high school games until 1939, when he became a sportscaster for Southwest Conference qv games. Boynton served as a navy lieutenant commander during World War II. He was a long-time president of the Texas Golf Association and a Dallas insurance executive. He died in Dallas on January 23, 1963, and was survived by his wife, Katherine. Boynton was elected to the College Football Hall of Fame in 1962. He was also named to the Texas Sports Hall of Fame.qv

BIBLIOGRAPHY: Dallas *Morning News,* January 24, 1963; Dallas *Times Herald,* January 23, 24, 1963.

Boynton, Charles Albert. Charles Albert Boynton, the son of Alpheus S. and Jane Grannis (Cook) Boynton, was born on November 26, 1867, in East Hatley, Quebec, Canada. He received a B.S. degree from Glasgow (Kentucky) Normal University in 1888 and an LL.B. degree from the University of Michigan in 1891. That same year he was admitted to the Texas Bar and began practice in Waco. He married Laura Bassett Young on November 1, 1897; they had three sons.

Active throughout his life in Texas Republican politics, Boynton was a delegate to the Republican national convention of 1900 and in 1904 was chairman of the Texas delegation to the national convention in Chicago. He was appointed a United States district attorney by Theodore Roosevelt in June, 1906, to succeed Edwin H. Terrell,qv of San Antonio, and was reappointed by William H. Taft in 1910. Boynton had supported Taft at the 1908

Republican national convention. Boynton was the Texas Republican gubernatorial candidate against William P. Hobby qv in 1918. In 1924 President Calvin Coolidge appointed Boynton to the federal bench at El Paso, where he served until retiring in 1947. He lived in Dallas from 1947 until his death in 1956. Judge Boynton was an Episcopalian and had been active in Waco civic affairs until his elevation to the bench.

BIBLIOGRAPHY: *A History of Central and Western Texas* (1911); E. W. Winkler, *Platforms of Political Parties in Texas* (1916); *Texian Who's Who* (1937); Paul D. Casdorph, *A History of the Republican Party in Texas, 1865–1965* (1965).

Paul D. Casdorph

*Boynton, Charles Milton.

*Boynton, Edwin Curtis.

Boys Ranch. *See* Cal Farley's Boys Ranch.

*Boz, Texas.

*Bozar, Texas.

*Bozeman's Corner, Texas.

Brace, David Kingsley. David Kingsley Brace, a pioneer in the field of physical education testing, was born on September 4, 1891, in Lincoln, Nebraska, the son of David L. and Eleanor (Kingsley) Brace. He attended high school in Portland, Oregon, where he lettered in football and was captain of the track team. In 1915 he received his B.A. degree from Reed College (a member of that school's first graduating class) in Portland, where he again took part in football and track. At Teachers College, Columbia University, he received an M.A. degree in 1921 and a Ph.D. in 1927. After a year as general science and physical education teacher in a junior high school in Salem, Oregon (1915–1916), he spent four years in China, directing physical education at Chihli Provincial Higher Normal College, Paotingfu, and Tsing Hua College, Peking. From 1920 to 1926 he taught at Columbia University.

In 1926 he came to the University of Texas and established the Department of Physical and Health Education, serving as chairman from 1926 to 1958. He retired from active teaching in 1962, after thirty-six years on the faculty of the University of Texas (Austin).

His Brace Motor Ability Test was one of the first to use modern scientific methods to test physical skills. In 1915 his study, *The Family and Socialized Play,* won the Municipal League Prize in Portland, Oregon. In 1924 he published the first achievement tests for football and basketball. He was the author of, or contributor to, ten books from 1924 to 1958. In 1927 he wrote *Measuring Motor Ability.* His publications from 1922 to 1961 included pamphlets, booklets, and more than one hundred articles.

Brace's interests were in safety, motor learning studies, tests and measurements, and techniques and skills in sports. He was a member of the Austin Parks and Recreation Board from 1955 to 1968, and during his chairmanship of that board (1957–

1964), he, with other board members, pursued a policy of acquiring land for the city's future park needs. At various times he served as president of the American Academy of Physical Education, as principal specialist in physical education for the U.S. Office of Education, and as a member of the President's Council on Youth Fitness.

Brace was married to Dorothy Walton on December 25, 1915, in Portland, Oregon. After her death in 1935 he married Mary Elizabeth Bulbrook on July 12, 1936, in Fort Worth; they had two daughters. He died in Austin on December 27, 1971.

BIBLIOGRAPHY: Austin *Statesman*, December 28, 1971; Biographical File, Barker Texas History Center, University of Texas at Austin.

*Braches, Charles.

*Brachfield, Texas.

*Bracht, Viktor Friederich. Viktor Friederich Bracht held the position of deputy collector of customs at Carrizo (not Carrizo Springs, as stated in Volume I), in Zapata County, in the early 1870's.

BIBLIOGRAPHY: W. and D. Richardson, Richardson's New Map of the State of Texas Corrected for the *Texas Almanac* to 1867 (1866); J. David Williams, Map of Texas (1866?).

*Bracken, Texas.

*Brackenridge, George Washington.

*Brackenridge, John Thomas.

*Brackenridge, Mary Eleanor.

Brackenridge, Robert J. Robert J. Brackenridge, son of John Adams and Isabella (McCulloch) Brackenridge, was born in Boonville, Indiana, on December 28, 1839. The family moved to Texas in 1853. He was a cowboy and laborer on his father's farm as a boy and attended the common schools. In 1860 he entered Hanover College, Indiana. At the outbreak of the Civil War he returned to Texas and entered Confederate service under his brother, John Thomas Brackenridge.qv At Aransas Pass he was captured by General N. P. Banks'qv command, but was paroled through the influence of his brother, George W. Brackenridge, and Governor A. J. Hamilton,qqv both Texas Union men. During his parole he studied medicine in Mankato, Minnesota, and participated in a few skirmishes against the Sioux Indians. He matriculated at Rush Medical College, Chicago, graduating in 1867. He settled in Jackson County, Texas, but moved to Austin in 1874 and gave up the active practice of his profession. Appointed cashier of the First National Bank of Austin, he held this position until the sale of all the stock of the bank held by his family. In 1885 he married Mary T. Lyons; they had one child, Mary Eleanor. He was president of the Frontier Telephone and Telegraph Company for some years. He was active in the First Presbyterian Church, U.S.A., and in many religious endeavors. In 1886 he helped originate an organization known as the "Seven Churches," which had as its object the promotion of practical and everyday religion, and for many years he served as president of the Austin Bible Society. He was an active worker in the bond election

in 1914 to build a new city hospital, which about 1930 was renamed in his honor, Brackenridge Hospital. He died in Austin on June 26, 1918.

BIBLIOGRAPHY: La Prelle-Brackenridge Papers (MS., Austin Public Library); Austin *Statesman*, June 26, 1918; *Austin City Directory* (1930).

Elizabeth N. Kemp

Brackett, Oscar Bernadotte. Oscar Bernadotte Brackett was born on March 22, 1812, in Salina, Onondaga County, New York. He inherited a fortune in a salt works, then lost it in New York speculation. He married Emily Wood on May 16, 1832, then finished college in 1833.

Brackett came to Texas in 1841 from Syracuse with $20,000 in cash and some merchandising experience. His wife joined him two years later. With Peter Gallagher qv he purchased goods in New Orleans for a mercantile store which was established in downtown San Antonio, where the Frost National Bank is now located. The town of Brackettville was named for him after he set up a supply village on that site in 1852 for nearby Fort Clark.qv His business enterprises included ownership of land in the Fort Clark and Las Moras Creek area and the operation of a line of freight wagons which ran between San Antonio and Mexico. Despite the danger of Indians, Brackett and his wife often drove back and forth between San Antonio and Brackettville.

He served as an alderman in San Antonio (1847–1848) and was a Whig until the party's dissolution in 1855, after which time he was said to have "cooperated with Democracy." He died in San Antonio on December 2, 1857, and was buried in City Cemetery No. 1. He was survived by his wife and four daughters.

BIBLIOGRAPHY: John Henry Brown, *Indian Wars and Pioneers of Texas* (189?); Charles Frederick Chabot, *With the Makers of San Antonio* (1937); San Antonio *Ledger*, December 5, 12, 1857.

S. W. Pease

*Brackettville, Texas. Brackettville, seat of Kinney County, is a market and shipping point for the county. In 1970 Brackettville had forty businesses and one hospital. In addition to ranching, some income is derived from tourism, centered mainly on Fort Clark,qv which has been restored and opened as a guest ranch, and on Alamo Village,qv a replica of the Alamo used in several motion pictures. The 1960 population was 1,662; the 1970 count was 1,539.

*Brad, Texas.

*Bradburn, Juan Davis.

*Bradburn, William P.

*Braden Branch.

Bradford, Charles M. Charles M. Bradford was born in Pennsylvania in 1826. Moving to Louisiana on the eve of the Civil War, he joined the Louisiana military service for a four-month period in January, 1861. By early April he had become a major in Strawbridge's 1st Louisiana Infantry. Shortly afterward, when the unit was transferred to Pensacola, Florida, Bradford resigned his commission. Several months later, in September, 1861, he became a lieutenant colonel commanding the 3rd Battalion, Louisiana Infantry. In rapid order Bradford's eight-company battalion was shifted to Virginia, where it was active in the Norfolk-Portsmouth area throughout the fall of 1861. In mid-1862 Bradford became lieutenant colonel of the 15th Louisiana Infantry when his battalion was enlarged by two additional companies and converted into a regiment. Meanwhile, however, Bradford was court-martialed for conduct prejudicial to good order and military discipline and for disrespect toward his superior. Sentenced to loss of pay and suspension of rank for six months, he chose to resign his commission.

After moving to Owensville, Robertson County, Texas, in January, 1864, Bradford sought permission of Major General John Bankhead Magruder qv to raise a volunteer mounted regiment from state troops and from those subject to conscription. Appointed major, he served in quartermaster functions for several months until he finally gained command of what became known as Bradford's Battalion. The early summer of 1864 saw his companies chasing deserters and overawing disloyal elements in Bastrop, Austin, and Fredericksburg. Then, in July, 1864, he was named colonel, commanding Bradford's Regiment (a consolidation of his battalion, Mann's Battalion, Hoxey's Battalion, and Poole's Company of Texas cavalry). The new regiment was mustered into Confederate service in mid-1864 and took up defensive positions in the Galveston area for the duration of the war.

BIBLIOGRAPHY: *War of the Rebellion: A Compilation of the Official Records of the Union and Confederate Armies* (1880–1901); Service Record of Charles M. Bradford, in War Department, Adjutant General's Office, Confederate Records (MS., National Archives, Washington, D.C.).

Allan C. Ashcraft

*Bradford, Texas.

*Bradley, Edward R.

*Bradley, John.

*Bradley, John M.

Bradley, Palmer. Palmer Bradley was born in Tioga, Grayson County, Texas, on December 12, 1894, the son of Robert L. and Mary (Boxley) Bradley. About 1900 the family moved to Roswell, New Mexico, where Bradley attended public schools before entering the University of Texas in 1912; he received a B.A. degree from there in 1916. He served as a first lieutenant in the 42nd Field Artillery during World War I, then returned to the University of Texas and received a law degree in 1919. The following year Bradley moved to Houston to join the law firm now known as Andrews, Kurth, Campbell & Jones. Except for military service in World War II, when he served as commanding officer of the pilot school of the Pre-Flight Training School at Santa Ana, California, Bradley practiced law with this firm until his death. Bradley married Genevra Harris in Nacogdoches, Texas, on February 24, 1921; they had two children.

An authority on oil and gas law, Bradley helped organize in 1929 what is now the General Crude Oil Company in Houston and for many years served as one of its directors. He also helped organize the Southern National Bank of Houston in 1960 and was its board chairman for several years. He was a director of Trans-World Airlines, Inc., for a number of years after World War II.

Bradley won a number of tennis titles in Texas and New Mexico, and in 1931 he helped found the River Oaks Tennis Tournament, an annual event which has since grown to international significance. An avid collector of books, Bradley had a wide-ranging knowledge of Civil War history and had an excellent collection of books on this period. He was a member of the Texas State Historical Association qv and contributed numerous articles to the *Handbook of Texas*. He served for many years as chairman of the Houston chapter of the Civil War Round Table. Bradley died on June 13, 1968, and was buried in Glenwood Cemetery in Houston.

Robert L. Bradley

*Bradley, Thomas.

*Bradley, Texas.

*Bradley's Corner, Texas.

*Bradshaw, Texas.

*Brady, John Thomas.

*Brady, Texas. Brady, seat of McCulloch County, had a 1960 population of 5,338 and a 1970 population of 5,557. Industries include a wool-scouring plant and production of "sand-frac" sand used in the oil drilling industry. Surrounding ranches and farms produce cattle, sheep, goats, poultry, cotton, grain, and irrigated vegetables. In 1963 Brady Lake was completed. In 1970 Brady reported 146 businesses, twenty-two churches, two hospitals, a newspaper, a radio station, and a library. An annual three-day July Jubilee is held.

*Brady Bend.

*Brady Creek.

Brady Creek Reservoir. Brady Creek Reservoir is in the Colorado River Basin in McCulloch County, three miles west of Brady Creek, a tributary of the San Saba River. The project is owned and operated by the city of Brady as a municipal and industrial water supply. Construction began on December 27, 1961, and was completed on May 14, 1963, with impoundment beginning on May 22, 1963. The reservoir has a conservation storage capacity of 30,430 acre-feet and a surface area of 2,020 acres at the service spillway crest elevation of 1,743 feet above mean sea level. At the emergency spillway crest elevation of 1,762 feet above mean sea level the reservoir capacity is 90,480 acre-feet and the surface area is 4,464 acres. This provides 60,050 acre-feet of surcharge space for temporary retention of floodwaters between the crests of the service and emergency spillways. The drainage area of Brady Creek above the dam is 508 square miles.

BIBLIOGRAPHY: Texas Water Commission, *Bulletin 6408* (1964).

Seth D. Breeding

*Brady Mountains.

*Brady State School. *See also* Crockett State School for Girls.

*Bragg, Texas.

*Brahman Cattle.

*Bralley, Francis Marion.

*Bramlette, Edgar Elliott.

*Branch, Anthony Martin.

*Branch, Edward Thomas.

*Branch, Texas.

*Branchville, Texas.

*Brandon, Texas.

Braniff, Thomas Elmer. Thomas Elmer Braniff was born on December 6, 1883, in Salina, Kansas, the son of John A. and Mary Catherine (Baker) Braniff. He was a student in the public schools of Kansas City, Missouri, until 1901, when his family moved to Oklahoma City, where Braniff entered his father's insurance business. He opened his own insurance office at the age of seventeen, selling from a buckboard wagon to the first settlers of the new territory of western Oklahoma. He married Bess Thurman on October 26, 1912, and they had two children who predeceased them.

Braniff became one of the nation's leading insurance men, built Oklahoma City's first skyscraper, and became chairman of the board and president of Prudential Fire Insurance Company. In 1927, in partnership with several others, he purchased a second-hand airplane, bought out the interests of the others, and joined his brother, Paul, the following year in operating an airline between Oklahoma City and Tulsa. He became president of the T. E. Braniff Company, the first airline in the Southwest which became on November 3, 1930, Braniff Airways, Incorporated. In 1934 Braniff contracted to carry the United States mail from Chicago to Dallas by way of Kansas City, Wichita, and Oklahoma City.

Although Braniff had maintained an operations and maintenance base at Dallas' Love Field ᵠᵛ since 1934, it was on June 1, 1942, that all administration personnel were moved to Love Field; thus Dallas became the general headquarters of the entire company. On May 22, 1946, Braniff's application for 7,719 miles of international air routes to Central and South America was approved, and Houston was named as the international gateway for Braniff flights south. On August 16, 1952, Mid-Continent Airlines merged with Braniff, and Braniff became the sixth largest air carrier in the United States. In 1956 the company had so expanded its headquarters in Dallas that space was leased in the ten-story Braniff Airways Building. In 1968 Braniff International Airways served most of the Central, Eastern, and Pacific Northwest portions of the nation, as well as Mexico, Panama, and South America, and was the only major airline to retain the name of its founder.

Thomas Braniff made his home in Dallas but he received honors from all over the world. He was Catholic cochairman of the National Conference of Christians and Jews, and he and his wife set up the Braniff Foundation to support worthy religious, educational, and scientific undertakings. The University of Denver named him Aviation Man of the Year in 1952. He was one of the founders of the World Brotherhood movement. On January 10, 1954, Braniff died in the crash of a private plane in Louisiana.

BIBLIOGRAPHY: *Braniff Airways Story* (1963); *Who's Who In America* (1952).

*Brann, William Cowper.

*Branom, Texas.

*Bransford, Texas.

*Brashear, William C. William C. Brashear resigned from the United States Navy on December 20, 1839; he had command of the Texas steamer-of-war *Zavala* ᵠᵛ in 1841.

BIBLIOGRAPHY: Tom Henderson Wells, *Commodore Moore and the Texas Navy* (1960).

Tom Henderson Wells

*Brashear, Texas.

*Braswell, Radford O.

*Bray's Bayou.

Brazoria (schooner).

*Brazoria, Texas. Brazoria, in Brazoria County, had a population of 1,291 in 1960 and 1,681 in 1970.

*Brazoria Construction Company.

*Brazoria County. Brazoria County continued as one of the leading oil producing counties, having produced 30,441,922 barrels in 1972 and 923,660,366 barrels between 1902 and January 1, 1973. Brazoria remained one of the leading counties in cattle and rice production, and its average annual farm income in the early 1970's was over $22 million. The population of the county in 1960 was 76,204, and in 1970 it was 108,312. *See also* Houston Standard Metropolitan Statistical Area.

Brazoria National Wildlife Refuge. *See* Wildlife Areas in Texas.

Brazoria Reservoir. Brazoria Reservoir, an off-channel reservoir, is in the Brazos River Basin in Brazoria County, one mile northeast of Brazoria. The project is owned and operated by Dow Chemical Company for industrial water supply. Construction of the reservoir storage project began on March 1, 1953, and was completed on May 1, 1954. Diversion of water from the Brazos River by pumping into the reservoir began in April, 1954. The reservoir has a capacity of 21,970 acre-feet and a surface area of 1,865 acres at elevation 32.5 feet above mean sea level.

BIBLIOGRAPHY: Texas Water Commission, *Bulletin 6408* (1964).

Seth D. Breeding

*Brazos, Texas.

*Brazos County. Brazos County was one of the leading counties in dairying and poultry production in 1965. Diversified crops are raised in the cultivated areas, which include 18,000 irrigated acres.

The 1964 cotton crop, a principal product, was 29,-830 bales, the largest in more than fifty years. Industry and Texas A&M University are vital to county income. Light industries added since 1950 produce fertilizers, signs, fans, labels, aluminum products, batteries, trailers, concrete products, shoes, light machinery, and processed poultry. The population in 1960 was 44,895; in 1970 it was 57,978. *See also* Bryan-College Station Standard Metropolitan Statistical Area.

*Brazos Courier.

*Brazos Farmer.

*Brazos Flood of 1899.

*Brazos and Galveston Railroad Company.

*Brazos Indian Reservation. Zachariah Ellis Coombes qv (not Ellis Z. Coombes, as stated in Volume I) was educational instructor at the Brazos Indian Reservation.

*Brazos Institute.

Brazos Largos Indians. These Coahuiltecan Indians are known through a single missionary report (1794) from Nuestra Señora del Espíritu Santo de Zuñiga Mission qv near Goliad. In this report they are identified as a subdivision of the Aranama, and at that time only nine remained. The name, which is Spanish for "long arms" or perhaps "big arms," suggests that the Spaniards observed a physical difference between these and other Aranama groups. The original territory of the Brazos Largos was probably the same as that of the Aranama.

BIBLIOGRAPHY: E. L. Portillo, *Apuntes para la historia antigua de Coahuila y Texas* (1886).

T. N. Campbell

*Brazos Planter.

*Brazos Point, Texas. Brazos Point, in extreme northeastern Bosque County, was officially founded with the establishment of a post office there about 1873. About 1878 Tom Willingham built a store, a cotton gin, and a mill and placed Charles Walker Smith qv in charge of his interests. Brazos Point was a Brazos River crossing of the Chisholm Trail.qv

William C. Horton

*Brazos River.

Brazos River Authority. The Brazos River Authority is a public agency of the state established in 1929. It has statutory responsibility for developing and conserving the water resources of the entire Brazos River Basin and for putting these water resources to beneficial use in the best interest of the people of Texas. The Brazos River Basin covers approximately forty-two thousand square miles, about one-sixth of the area of the state. The 1929 act, a pioneering step in the history of water resources management, marked the first time anywhere in the United States that development and management of the water resources of an entire major river basin had been entrusted to a single public agency organized specifically for that purpose. The authority is governed by a board of twenty-one directors designated by the Texas Water Rights Commission qv subject to approval by the governor for six-year terms.

The authority in the early 1930's developed its first master plan for control, conservation, and development of the water resources of the Brazos Basin. The original master plan proposed the construction of thirteen major dams on the Brazos and its tributaries; this plan has been expanded to include a total of twenty-three reservoirs, six of which were completed and in operation and two of which were under construction in 1967. The first project built by the Brazos River Authority was Possum Kingdom Dam and Reservoir (see Possum Kingdom Reservoir), a water conservation and hydroelectric power project of 700,000 acre-feet capacity completed in 1941 on the main stem of the Brazos River northwest of Fort Worth. Financing of this project was obtained by a combination of state tax remissions and a federal WPA grant.

The authority had under construction a second project 150 river miles downstream from Possum Kingdom; this is the DeCordova Bend Dam and Reservoir, a water conservation and water supply project scheduled for completion in 1969. Its construction was being financed through a sixteen-million-dollar bond issue to be paid from revenues from water sales under contracts with two electric power companies. In the 1940's the authority began working closely with the United States Army Corps of Engineers after that agency was given responsibility by Congress for federal flood control activities throughout the nation. As a result of its cooperative program with the Corps of Engineers, the authority has arranged for inclusion of conservation storage space in Corps reservoirs throughout the Brazos Basin, and these reservoirs are thus integrated into the authority's basin-wide system of water supply reservoirs in accordance with its master plan for water resource development. In addition to the two projects owned and operated entirely by the authority, this agency has contracted with the federal government for conservation storage space in five Corps of Engineers reservoir projects in the Brazos Basin: Waco, Belton, Proctor, Stillhouse Hollow, and Somerville.qqv The authority has also agreed to contract for conservation storage space in the San Gabriel projects (Laneport and the North San Gabriel) and in projects proposed for construction on the Navasota (Millican and Navasota No. 2).

Additional needs in the Gulf Coast area south of Houston are met through two canal systems acquired in 1967 by the Brazos River Authority. These two systems, comprising the agency's newly established canal division, provide 130 miles of mainline canals which enable the authority to supply water from the Brazos Basin directly to water users throughout this growing industrial region as far east as Texas City and Galveston. Existing commitments for supply of industrial water through these canal systems include contracts with the Industrial Water Company (owned by American Oil Company and Union Carbide) at Texas City, with Sugarland Industries at Sugar Land, and with Monsanto Company and Houston Farms Development Company south of

Alvin. Water is also supplied through these systems for irrigation of more than thirty thousand acres of rice. In addition, the authority, at the request of the city of Galveston, has developed a plan for providing Galveston a treated surface water supply to replace its present well supply system; this proposed plan was under consideration by the city in 1967. Present water needs supplied through the canal systems are met primarily from natural flows of the Brazos River, supplemented as necessary by releases from the Brazos River Authority upstream reservoirs; future additional needs of the area can be met effectively by water released from the authority's upstream reservoir storage and delivered directly to water users through the facilities of its canal division.

Water quality is an increasingly important aspect of water resource management, and the authority is continually expanding its activities in this field. For many years the authority's primary concern has been the natural salt pollution occurring in the upper Brazos Basin. The authority spent considerable effort and money in the 1950's investigating this problem and defining the principal source of pollution. It has since obtained the participation of other agencies in efforts to solve this problem, and studies were under way in 1967 by the Corps of Engineers to develop a practical engineering solution. The authority is also concerned with problems of man-made pollution, and has recently developed plans for a centralized regional sewage system to serve the cities in the Waco metropolitan area and to prevent the development of potentially serious pollution problems in this growing urban complex. The authority expects to assume an increasingly active role, in close cooperation with the Texas Water Quality Board,qv in all aspects of water quality management throughout the Brazos Basin. Although a public agency of the state, the authority carries out all of its activities without the benefit of any tax money. It is entirely self-supporting, utilizing revenues from its operations to pay all its costs. See also Brazos River Conservation and Reclamation District in Volume I.

*Brazos River Conservation and Reclamation District.

*Brazos Santiago Pass.

*Brazosport, Texas. Brazosport, in southern Brazoria County, is a geographical division of several cities and communities largely within the confines of the Brazosport Independent School District, all represented by a single chamber of commerce. The economy is dependent on the huge Dow Chemical Company complex, along with a growing number of satellite and service industries. A shrimp fleet and a public port provide both commercial and recreational advantages, and the beaches are popular with both local and nearby Houston metropolitan area residents. Cities in the Brazosport division which were reported in the 1970 census are Clute, 6,023; Freeport, 11,997; Jones Creek, 1,268; Lake Barbara, 605; Lake Jackson, 13,376;

and Richwood, 1,452. Among the communities not reported in the census are Quintana, Grey Park, Oyster Creek, and Surfside. Velasco was absorbed by Freeport in 1957. Total population of the Brazosport area was 38,817 in 1970, according to the United States census. See also Houston Standard Metropolitan Statistical Area.

Brazosport College. Brazosport College, a two-year college at Lake Jackson, Brazoria County, was opened in September, 1968, in facilities provided by the Brazosport Independent School District at the Brazosport Education Extension Center in Freeport. The Brazosport Junior College District had been created by vote of the Brazosport Independent School District in November, 1948, but was not funded until 1967 when the school district authorized a tax for the college.

A board of regents was installed August 1, 1967. J. R. Jackson, named interim president, was elected full-time president on January 8, 1968, and he continued in that position in 1974.

A new facility for the college was completed on a 156-acre site at Lake Jackson in the spring of 1971. The school is accredited by the Southern Association of Colleges and Universities and the Association of Texas Colleges and Universities.qv

Total enrollment grew from 879 in 1968 to 2,925 in the fall of 1974. The staff, faculty, and other employees increased from 45 in 1968 to 109 in 1973. Graduates with associate of arts degrees increased from 25 in 1970 to 103 in 1973.

*Breckenridge, Texas. Breckenridge, seat of Stephens County, had a 1960 population of 6,273 and a 1970 population of 5,944. In 1970 its 212 businesses included industries concerned with sheet metal, oil field supplies, and clay products. The Breckenridge Boys Choir performed in the White House Youth Concert Series in 1962 and at the New York World's Fair in 1964. By 1966 a school building program had been completed. The town was named for John C. Breckinridge (not Breckenridge, as stated in Volume I), a United States senator from Kentucky, although the name of the town is spelled slightly different from that of the man it honors.

*Breckenridge Oil Field. See Ranger, Desdemona, and Breckenridge Oil Fields.

*Breece, Thomas H.

Breeding, David W. David W. Breeding was born about 1778 in Virginia and moved to Christian County, Kentucky, by 1810. He married Sarah Davis, and they had six sons (see below). In February, 1833, Breeding, with his family and two brothers (see below), moved to Colorado County, Texas. In 1838 the part of Colorado County where he settled became Fayette County, and Breeding was a member of the first board of land commissioners of the new county. He was also a juror at the first district court session held in Fayette County early in 1838. David Breeding died on December 28, 1843, and was buried at the Breeding family cemetery, five miles northeast of Fayetteville. Four of Breeding's six sons fought in various battles of the Texas Revolution. The sons were as follows:

1. Davis Breeding, the oldest son, died in Kentucky in 1828, unmarried.

2. John V. Breeding was born in 1807 in Virginia and came to Texas with his parents in February, 1833. He was in the Ranging Corps from November 24, 1835, to September 13, 1836. He served in the Texas Army qv from February 1 to May 10, 1836, and was in Captain William J. E. Heard's qv company under Sam Houston in the San Jacinto campaign, although he did not participate in the battle. John V. Breeding was the first sheriff of Fayette County after its organization in 1838, and also served under Colonel John Henry Moore qv on a campaign against the Comanche Indians from September to November, 1840. Breeding married Louisa Parks Ware on February 10, 1842, in Colorado County, and they had eight children. John V. Breeding died in 1869 in Fayette County, and was buried in the Breeding family cemetery near Fayetteville.

3. Richard Landy Breeding was born in 1810 in Kentucky and came to Texas with his parents in February, 1833. He was a juror at the first district court session held in Colorado County in April, 1837, and at the first district court session held in Fayette County early in 1838. Richard Breeding married Artemesia Ware on March 14, 1844, in Colorado County; they had twelve children. He died in 1880 in Hays County.

4. Napoleon Bonaparte Breeding was born in 1815 in Kentucky and came to Texas with his parents in February, 1833. He fought at the siege of Bexar in December, 1835. He served in the Texas Army from February 1 to May 10, 1836, and was in Captain William J. E. Heard's qv company in the San Jacinto campaign. Breeding was in Captain Stephen Townsend's company in 1836, and he participated in the Snively Expedition qv in 1843. The first marriage recorded in Fayette County was that of Napoleon Breeding to Charlotte T. O'Bar on January 19, 1838; they had six children. Breeding died about 1865 in Fayette County.

5. Fidelio Sharp Breeding was born about 1818 in Christian County, Kentucky, and came to Texas with his parents in February, 1833. He received a headright certificate for one-third league of land in Fayette County on January 19, 1838, and later he received 640 acres of land for participating in the battle of San Jacinto in Captain William J. E. Heard's qv company of "Citizen Soldiers." He seems to have been the only one of the brothers who actually participated in the battle. He joined the United States Army during the Mexican War and marched with the army from Veracruz, Mexico, to Mexico City during October and November, 1847. Breeding never married. He died in San Antonio in 1849, en route to the California gold mines with his brother, Benjamin W. Breeding.

6. Benjamin Wilkens Breeding was born in 1820 in Kentucky and came to Texas with his parents in February, 1833. Although only sixteen years old, Benjamin Breeding served in Moseley (Mosely) Baker's qv company which fought a detachment of Santa Anna's troops at the San Felipe Ferry in 1836. Later that year he and Thomas Chaudoin brought the "Twin Sisters" qv cannon, which had bogged down near Harrisburg, to Sam Houston's army at Bernardo Plantation.qv He then obtained leave to transport his parents beyond the Trinity River, and while he was gone, the battle of San Jacinto was fought. Breeding fought in a campaign against the Comanche Indians from September to November, 1840, and served in the Vasquez campaign in the spring of 1842. Breeding participated in the Woll campaign in 1842 and was a member of the Snively Expedition qv in 1843. During the Civil War he was a captain of a company in the Texas state troops. Breeding married Catherine Jane Mayhar in Colorado County on February 2, 1852; they had seven children. He died in 1902 in Hays County, Texas.

David W. Breeding had two brothers, Richard Landy and John Breeding, who also came to Texas with him in February, 1833. Richard Breeding never married, settled in Fayette County, and died in 1844. John Breeding married Elizabeth D. Russell in Christian County, Kentucky, on July 24, 1820, and they had at least four sons. His wife died in Kentucky, and he died on July 16, 1833, soon after settling in the jurisdiction of Brazoria; he left four young sons who were raised by his brother, David W. Breeding. They were as follows:

1. George William Breeding, oldest son of John Breeding, was born in 1821 in Kentucky. He served in the Confederate Army. On October 18, 1854, he married Isabelle Thomas Carlton in Colorado County; they had eight children. George Breeding died in 1902 in Tennessee.

2. Edward J. Breeding was born in 1823 in Kentucky, and he served under Edward Burleson qv in the Vasquez campaign in 1842. He also served in the Confederate Army. He married Henrietta Sutton in Fayette County on December 5, 1844; they had eight children. Edward Breeding died about 1875 in Gonzales County, Texas.

3. James Breeding was born in 1825 in Kentucky and served in the Vasquez campaign in 1842 and in the Woll campaign; he also served in the Confederate Army. He married Frances Adeline O'Bar in Fayette County on June 20, 1843; they had ten children. James Breeding died in 1869 in Fayette County, Texas.

4. Gustavus Breeding was born in 1827 in Kentucky, and he served in the Confederate Army. He married Jane Sutton in Fayette County on October 12, 1858; they had no children. Gustavus Breeding died in 1875 in Fayette County, Texas.

Seth Breeding
Betty Porter

*Breen, Charles.

*Bremond, Paul.

*Bremond, Texas.

*Brenan, William.

*Brenham, Richard Fox.

*Brenham, Texas. Brenham, seat of Washington County, had 252 businesses in 1970, including four new industries. The major businesses are concerned with agricultural produce, especially cotton. Brenham completed an airport and a new high school by 1966. In that year the city reported two hospitals, Blinn College, a library, a newspaper, and a radio station. The 1960 population was 7,740; in 1970 the count was 8,922.

Brennan, Thomas Francis. Thomas Francis Brennan was born on October 10, 1855, at Bally Cullen, Tipperary, Ireland, son of James and Margaret (Dunne) Brennan. He studied at St. Bonaventure's School, Allegheny, New York; Rouen University, France, 1873; and the University of Innsbruck, Austria, where he obtained a Doctor of Divinity degree in 1876. On July 4, 1880, he was ordained in Brixen, Austria, by Prince Bishop John de Leiss of Brixen and went to the Diocese of Erie, Pennsylvania, to work.

When Texas was divided into a third diocese in 1890, he was appointed the first bishop of Dallas. He was consecrated on April 5, 1891, by Bishop Tobias Mullen of Erie and installed in Dallas on March 8, 1891, in the Pro-Cathedral of the Sacred Heart. During his one-year tenure the Dallas diocese gained eleven priests, four religious communities, and twelve churches. Publication of *The Texas Catholic* by Bishop Brennan, one of his first works, continued for one year, then ceased until its revival in 1952.

Taking up his residence in Texas, Bishop Brennan, the youngest bishop in the United States at the time, found a diocese stretching over a territory of 110,000 square miles containing 108 counties in the northern and northwestern portion of Texas with El Paso and Culberson counties in the west added from the San Antonio diocese. It was poor in regard to churches, clergy, and number of institutions.

The young bishop immediately undertook the strengthening of the faith in his diocese. He toured his vast territory and talked to Catholics and non-Catholics alike. His dynamic personality, eloquent oratory, and linguistic talent (a master of seven or more languages) made him a well-known figure in the state and nation, and his letters and addresses appeared in the leading dailies of the nation.

After one year of vigorous zeal and work, Bishop Brennan resigned because of ill health and was transferred to Newfoundland; later he was called to Rome, where he labored until his death on March 21, 1916. He was buried in Frescati, Italy.

Sister M. Claude Lane, O.P.

*Breslau, Texas.

Brewster, Few. Few Brewster was born in Williamson County on May 10, 1889. After graduation from Killeen High School, he attended Baylor University and Howard Payne (where he was later awarded an LL.D. degree). Brewster transferred to the University of Texas, where he became a quiz-master and belonged to the Order of Chancellors while in the law department. Following his B.A. at Texas in 1913, Brewster completed work for the LL.M. in 1916, writing a thesis entitled "Trespass to Try Title in Texas." Later he was initiated into Phi Delta Phi fraternity. He practiced law in Temple from 1916 to 1929 except while serving as a second lieutenant in the infantry in World War I. He remained active in the American Legion. In 1918 Brewster married Myra Kilpatrick of Temple, and they had three children.

He served as county attorney of Bell County from October 7, 1919, to January 1, 1923. Then he served as district attorney to January 1, 1929, when he became district judge of the Twenty-seventh District. After several terms, he resigned to accept appointment in November, 1941, to the Supreme Court Commission of Appeals. When the Supreme Court was enlarged to nine members in 1945, he became an associate justice, being elected in 1948 and reelected in 1954.

While president of the Bell County Bar Association he became head of the Judicial Section of the Texas Bar Association for 1937–1938; served as secretary during 1938–1939; and became vice-president for 1939–1940. In April, 1940, he became the vice-president of the new State Bar of Texas qv and then president from July 6, 1940, to July 5, 1941. Besides being a frequent speaker, he published several articles, including "Benefit of Clergy" and "Prime Obligation" in the *Texas Bar Journal*; in the latter article he urged acceptance of an integrated Bar. His success as an administrator and judge was enhanced by his "tension-breaking humor," and he was a legal scholar whose work was carefully planned and executed. One outstanding example was his 400-page manuscript to serve as "a ready reference to the more important phases of the law relating to prohibited liquor and searches and seizures as declared in the Texas statutes and decisions." This study included digests of cases, forms, and an overall index for ready reference. The work was revised and ready for publication in 1930, but after some delay and condensation it was published under the title *Search and Seizure*.

Brewster served as an associate justice of the Supreme Court of Texas for twelve years, from September, 1945, to September 30, 1957, when he resigned because of ill health. He died at home of a heart attack on October 12 of that year and was buried at the State Cemetery qv in Austin.

BIBLIOGRAPHY: *Who's Who In America* (1952); Fort Worth *Star-Telegram*, March 22, 1954; Biographical File (Library, State Bar of Texas, Austin).

Robert C. Cotner

*Brewster, Henry Percy. Henry Percy Brewster died in Austin, Texas, on December 28, 1884 (not November 27, 1884, as stated in Volume I); his body was taken to Galveston and then buried in the Gulf of Mexico.

BIBLIOGRAPHY: Galveston *Daily News*, December 29, 1884; Houston *Chronicle*, December 31, 1884; San Antonio *Daily Express*, December 30, 1884; C. L. Greenwood Collection [Death Index] (Archives, University of Texas at Austin Library).

*Brewster County. Brewster County is Texas' largest county, with an area of 6,208 square miles. In 1970 the chief sources of income were cattle, sheep, and tourism. There was also a small irrigated farming area along the Rio Grande and some significant mineral deposits. Mercury was mined during 1966 in the Lone Star Mine, while the mine at Study Butte began operation in the fall of that year. The Big Bend Historical Museum is on the campus of Sul Ross State University in Alpine. The population was 6,434 in 1960, and in 1970 it was 7,780.

*Brewster Creek.

*Briar, Texas.

*Briar Branch.

*Briar Creek.

*Briary, Texas.

*Brice, Texas.

*Brick House Gully.

*Bridge City, Texas. Bridge City, an unincorporated community in Orange County between Port Arthur and Orange, quadrupled its population during the 1950's from 1,100 to 4,677 by 1960. Its location gives it ready access to the Southern Pacific Railroad and to the port facilities on the Neches River and the Sabine Lake. Further industrial incentive was stimulated by the completion of a nearby private electric power utility in 1962 which nearly doubled the electric capacity of the immediate area. Sixty-two businesses were reported in the community in 1970, when the community had a population of 8,164. See also Beaumont-Port Arthur-Orange Standard Metropolitan Statistical Area.

*Bridge Creek.

*Bridge Valley, Texas.

*Bridgeport, Texas. Bridgeport, in Wise County, had a population of 3,218 in 1960 and 3,614 in 1970.

Bridgeport Reservoir. Bridgeport Reservoir (mostly in Wise County, but extending into Jack County), which was completed in December, 1931, is operated in conjunction with Eagle Mountain Reservoir and Lake Worth for flood control and as a municipal and industrial water supply for Fort Worth and surrounding areas. According to annual water service reports filed with the Texas Water Commission, no water has been used for irrigation. On the basis of a survey made in 1956, the capacity of the reservoir is 270,900 acre-feet, and the surface area is 10,400 acres at the crest of the service spillway at elevation of 826.2 feet above mean sea level. A floodwater retardation capacity of 395,000 acre-feet is provided between the crest of the service spillway and the crest of the emergency spillway at 853 feet above mean sea level. The drainage area of the West Fork of the Trinity River at Bridgeport Dam is 1,111 square miles.

BIBLIOGRAPHY: Texas Water Commission, Bulletin 6408 (1964).

Seth D. Breeding

*Bridges, William B.

*Bridgetown, Texas.

*Brier Creek.

*Brigade Districts.

*Briggs, Clay Stone.

*Briggs, Elisha Andrews.

Briggs, George Waverley. George Waverley Briggs, journalist and banker, was born at Burford's Landing, near Camden, Alabama, on February 27, 1883, son of Alice (Burford) and Ritchie Jones Briggs, a Methodist, and later Congregationalist, minister. He attended public and private schools and the academy of Joseph Bickler qv in Austin. After studying at the University of Texas, Briggs became a reporter on the Austin Tribune (1905–1906). At later times he held the positions of staff correspondent of the San Antonio Express (1906–1910) and Dallas Morning News qqv (1911–1913), and managing editor of the Austin Statesman (1910–1911) and the Galveston News qqv (1913–1918). For the San Antonio Express he wrote a series of articles that became, in book form, The Texas Penitentiary (1909). As a result he was appointed a penitentiary commissioner of Texas. His work on the Dallas Morning News included a study of city and state housing, resulting in The Housing Problem in Texas (1911). Governor W. P. Hobby qv appointed Briggs commissioner of insurance and banking, 1918–1920. Briggs later became vice-president and trust officer of the City National Bank and its successor, the First National Bank, Dallas. He wrote the Digest of Texas Insurance and Banking Laws. Briggs was responsible for three major legislative acts: the Texas trust act, the common trust fund act, and the Texas probate code.

Briggs held office in many organizations: the American Red Cross, national and Dallas chambers of commerce, National Committee on Prisons and Prison Labor, Texas Tax League, Southwestern Legal Foundation, Texas Centennial qv Exposition, Dallas Historical Society,qv and the Philosophical Society of Texas.qv He was awarded, by George VI, the King's Medal for civilian service to the Allies in World War II. At the time of his death he was director of the Dallas Morning News.

In 1912 Briggs married Lorena May Foster, for many years a member of the board of regents of Texas State College for Women, Denton (now Texas Woman's University). Briggs died in Dallas on July 16, 1957, and was buried in Oakwood Cemetery, Austin.

BIBLIOGRAPHY: Philosophical Society of Texas, Proceedings (1957); Texian Who's Who (1937).

*Briggs, Texas.

*Brigham, Asa.

*Bright, David.

*Bright Star, Texas.

*Bright Star Educational Society.

*Brightman, John Claver.

Brindley, Paul. Paul Brindley was born in Maypearl, Texas, on December 27, 1896, the youngest son of George Goldthwaite and Mattie (Hanes) Brindley. The family resided at Maypearl and Temple. As a child he was crippled by osteomyelitis. He attended the University of Texas from 1918 to 1920 and received a B.S. degree from the medical branch in 1923 and an M.D. degree in 1925. He was then appointed instructor in pathology and served on the faculty of the medical branch continuously for thirty years. He was promoted to a professorship in 1929 and soon thereafter was made chairman of the Department of Pathology, a position he held until his death. He was the pathologist for all university medical branch hospitals and consultant in pathology at St. Mary's Hospital and the United States Public Health Hospital, both in Galveston, and to Lackland Air Force Base,qv in San Antonio. He did graduate work in pathology at the Mallory Laboratory of Boston City Hospital and at Mayo Clinic. In 1934 he became a fellow of the American College of Physicians and in 1947 a fellow of the American College of Pathologists. He was a member of numerous other state, local, national, and international scientific societies. He was considered the authority on the tropical disease, Madura foot. He published thirty papers in his field, established the Galveston chapter of the American Cancer Society, and posthumously received the Caldwell Memorial Award of the Texas Society of Pathologists in January, 1955. He twice served as president of the society.

On July 2, 1929, he was married to Anne Ammons. Brindley died on December 28, 1954, and a hall at the medical branch of the University of Texas was later named for him.

BIBLIOGRAPHY: Galveston News, September 5, 1965; Who's Who In America (1952); Texas State Journal of Medicine (February, 1955); MediTexan (January, 1955).

*Bringhurst, Nettie Power Houston. Nettie (Antoinette) Power Houston was married to W. L. Bringhurst on February 28, 1877 (not 1876, as stated in Volume I). She was given in marriage by Governor Richard Bennett Hubbard.qv

BIBLIOGRAPHY: William C. Crane, Life and Select Literary Remains of Sam Houston of Texas (1884); Austin Weekly Democratic Statesman, March 8, 1877; Dallas Herald, March 10, 1877; C. L. Greenwood Collection [Marriage Index] (Archives, University of Texas at Austin Library).

Brinker, Maureen Connolly. Maureen "Little Mo" Connolly Brinker was born in San Diego, California, on September 17, 1934, the daughter of Martin J. and Kathryn (Payne) Connolly. Her father was killed in an automobile accident when she was two years old, and she was reared by her mother and a great-aunt. As a child she was an accomplished horseback rider, winning prizes in San Diego horse shows. When she was ten her family moved near the Balboa (California) municipal tennis courts, where she became interested in tennis, and she soon began to devote her entire time to the game. Eleanor "Teach" Tennant, the famed California coach, considered her the perfect pupil.

Before she was twenty the five-foot-four-inch Maureen Connolly, called "Little Mo" by the press,

had on three occasions won both the Wimbledon (British) and United States tennis titles. In 1953 she won an unprecedented grand slam, taking the United States, Wimbledon, French, and Australian championships. For three years she was recipient of the U. S. Woman Athlete of the Year award. She was ranked with the great tennis players of all time when, at age nineteen, her career was cut short as a result of a horseback riding accident in the summer of 1954 in San Diego. The horse, frightened by an approaching truck, slammed against the vehicle, and Little Mo's right leg was smashed. She never played competitive tennis again.

In 1955 she was married to businessman Norman Brinker; they had two daughters. With her family she moved to Dallas in 1963, where she devoted herself to helping Texas youngsters discover tennis. Active in the Maureen Connolly Brinker Foundation for the advancement of tennis achievement among Texas junior tennis players, she gave numerous clinics and was cited as Dallas Woman of the Year for her work with youth. She was also active in the national Junior Wightman Cup program.

Maureen Connolly Brinker died, after a three-year bout with cancer, on June 21, 1969, in Dallas; she was buried in Hillcrest Cemetery there. The first annual Maureen Connolly Brinker Award to an outstanding junior girl tennis player was presented during the U. S. Lawn Tennis Association national championships at Philadelphia in early August, two months after the death of Little Mo.

BIBLIOGRAPHY: Austin American-Statesman, June 22, 1969; Austin Statesman, June 23, 1969.

*Brinker, Texas.

Brinkley, John Romulus. John Romulus Brinkley was born on July 8, 1885, probably in Jackson County, North Carolina. He attended elementary schools in the county, and in January, 1908, he married Sally Wike. They had three daughters and a son. In 1913 he divorced his wife and married Minnie Telitha Jones, of Memphis, Tennessee. He worked at odd jobs (a traveling medicine man at one time) in various parts of the country before entering Bennett Medical College in 1908. Although he was forced to drop out before his senior year and apparently never was graduated from a legitimate medical school, he adopted the title of doctor. During World War I, Brinkley was granted a reserve commission in the army medical corps. After a brief stay he settled at Milford, Kansas, where he built a hospital and first performed his famous operation involving a transplant of goat organs to humans for the purpose of sexual revitalization. Later he abandoned this technique in favor of others.

He became involved in a series of law suits beginning in 1930, when the Kansas State Medical Board revoked his license to practice. He then launched a short-lived but serious political career, running for governor of Kansas in 1930, 1932, and 1934. Meanwhile Brinkley had already begun to establish medical headquarters at Del Rio, Texas, and built a 75,000-watt radio station at Villa Acuña,

Coahuila, Mexico, three miles from Del Rio. It was the second most powerful radio station in the world. In 1933 he established a hospital at Del Rio, where he continued his unorthodox medical practice. Although Brinkley was widely criticized, especially by the American Medical Association, he was highly successful financially. In 1938 he moved his Del Rio hospital to Little Rock, Arkansas, where law suits totaling one million dollars were filed against him. He was eventually forced into bankruptcy. He died on May 26, 1942, in San Antonio and was buried in Memphis, Tennessee.

BIBLIOGRAPHY: Gerald Carson, *The Roguish World of Doctor Brinkley* (1960); San Antonio *Express*, May 27, 1942.

Brinkmann, Alexander. Alexander Brinkmann was born in a log cabin at Comfort, Texas, on March 26, 1868, the eldest child of Otto and Marie (Ochse) Brinkmann. He attended the six-grade Comfort school, then took a business course in San Antonio. In 1890 he married Emmie Bodemann; they had four sons and two daughters. With his father, Brinkmann engaged in the lumber business in Comfort and later was in partnership with Ed Steves & Sons of San Antonio, continuing this partnership until the early 1940's when he sold his interest. In 1928 he acquired the Carl Assmann library of Austin, which added to his already growing Texana collection. Besides an extensive collection of pictures of early settlers of the Texas hill country, Brinkmann also collected letters, documents, muster rolls, membership lists, and minutes of various groups and organizations, many of which are displayed in the Comfort Historical Museum, which he assisted in founding in 1933. His library of Texana and western Americana consisted of more than four thousand volumes at the time of his death in Comfort on August 29, 1947.

BIBLIOGRAPHY: Guido E. Ransleben, *A Hundred Years of Comfort in Texas* (1954).

Guido E. Ransleben

*Brinson, Enoch.

*Briscoe, Andrew.

*Briscoe, Mrs. Mary Jane Harris.

*Briscoe, Texas.

*Briscoe County. Briscoe County, with forty thousand irrigated acres in 1970, was heavily reliant on farming as a major source of revenue, the average annual farm income being over $10 million by 1970. The cotton crop and grain sorghum and wheat harvests are of prime importance, while lesser acreage is devoted to castor beans and sugar beets. Ranching in the county is almost entirely limited to cattle. The 1960 population was 3,577; the 1970 count was 2,794.

*Bristol, Texas.

*Brite, Lucas Charles, II.

*Brite, Texas.

*Brite College of the Bible.

*Britton, Forbes.

*Britton, Frank L.

*Britton, Texas.

Broadcasters, Texas Association of. *See* Texas Association of Broadcasters.

*Broaddus, Texas.

*Broadview, Texas.

*Broadway, Texas.

*Brock, Texas.

*Brodbeck, Jacob.

*Brogado, Texas.

*Bronco, Texas.

*Bronson, Texas.

*Bronte, Texas. Bronte, in Coke County, had a population of 999 in 1960 and 925 in 1970.

*Broocks, John Henry.

Broocks, Lycurgus Watters. Lycurgus Watters Broocks was born in San Augustine, Texas, in 1840, the son of Elizabeth Ann (Morris) and Travis Gustavus Broocks.qv He was associated in the mercantile business with his father and brothers. He enlisted in the Confederate Army when he was twenty-one and served as a private in Captain D. M. Short's Company, South Kansas-Texas Regiment, Mounted Volunteers. On May 2, 1863, he was appointed 2nd lieutenant and ordnance officer in Jackson's Cavalry Division, Department of Mississippi and Louisiana.

Broocks was a planter and had extensive land holdings. He was also an editor of the *South East Texan*, published in San Augustine. In 1866 he was married to Emma Alston Border, and the couple were the parents of two daughters. Broocks died in 1873 and was buried in the Broocks family cemetery five miles east of San Augustine.

BIBLIOGRAPHY: *War of the Rebellion: A Compilation of the Official Records of the Union and Confederate Armies* (1880–1901); Muster Roll, San Augustine County.

Kate Harding Bates Parker
C. Elisabeth Bates Nisbet

*Broocks, Moses Lycurgus.

*Broocks, Travis Gustavus.

*Brooke, George Mercer.

*Brooke, Roger.

*Brooke Army Medical Center.

*Brookeland, Texas. Brookeland, in Sabine County, was a post office as early as July 26, 1866 (not 1899, as stated in Volume I), when John C. Brooke, for whom the town was named, was appointed first postmaster. A November, 1867, listing by the U.S. Post Office in Washington, D.C., shows Brooke as postmaster in that year. In 1971 Brookeland had an estimated population of 213.

BIBLIOGRAPHY: John B. Sanders, *The Postoffices and Post Masters of Sabine County, Texas, 1845–1930* (1964); *Texas Almanac* (1868).

*Brookesmith, Texas.

*Brookhaven, Texas.

*Brooks, Bluford.

*Brooks, James Abijah.

*Brooks, John Sowers.

*Brooks, Micajah Madison.

*Brooks, Samuel Palmer.

*Brooks, Victor Lee. Victor Lee Brooks was instructor in the law department of the University of Texas from 1895 to 1896 (not from 1892 to 1893, as stated in Volume I). He was district judge of the Twenty-sixth District from February 1, 1904, to November 5, 1907, when he resigned (not from 1915 to 1917).

BIBLIOGRAPHY: Travis County Bar Association, *One Hundredth Anniversary of the District Courts of Travis County, Texas, 1840–1940* (1940).

James W. McClendon

*Brooks Air Force Base. Brooks Air Force Base had by 1960 transferred all flying activities to other air force bases. In 1959 the United States Air Force Aerospace Medical Center, assigned to Air Training Command, was organized at Brooks. That was the initial step toward placing management of aerospace medical research, education, and certain clinical practices under one command. In November, 1961, the Aerospace Medical Center was transferred to the Air Force Systems Command and became the Aerospace Medical Division, comprised of seven units: School of Aerospace Medicine, located at Brooks Air Force Base; the Wilford Hall Hospital, Epidemiological Laboratory, and the Personnel Research Laboratory, all located at Lackland Air Force Base,^{qv} Texas; the Aeromedical Research Laboratory at Holloman Air Force Base, New Mexico; the Aerospace Medical Research Laboratories at Wright-Patterson Air Force Base, Ohio; and the Arctic Aeromedical Laboratory at Fort Wainwright, Alaska.

Under the 1967 military construction bill, the base was scheduled to receive approximately $4,-185,000 for research and development, testing and medical facilities, and troop housing.

Dorman H. Winfrey

*Brooks County. Brooks County pioneered in scientific dairying in Texas, and milk and butter production remained important. Although ranching dominated the agriculture economy, the county had five thousand irrigated acres in 1965 and produced truck crops and grain sorghums. Oil production totaled 130,006,731 barrels between 1936 and January 1, 1973. Trade and small industries center in the county seat, Falfurrias, and Encino is the site of a refinery. The population was 8,609 in 1960 and 8,005 in 1970.

*Brooks Creek.

*Brookshire, Nathen.

*Brookshire, Texas. Brookshire, in Waller County, had a population of 1,339 in 1960 and 1,683 in 1970.

Brookside, Texas. Brookside, in northern Brazoria County, had a population of 560 in 1960 and 1,507 in 1970.

*Brookston, Texas.

*Broome, Texas.

*Brotherton, Robert.

*Brougham Creek.

*Brower, John.

*Brown, Aaron B.

*Brown, Edwy Rolfe.

*Brown, Frank.

*Brown, George.

*Brown, George William.

*Brown, Harry Wyse.

*Brown, Henry Stevenson.

Brown, Herman. Herman Brown, business executive and founder of Brown & Root, Incorporated, was born in Belton, Texas, on November 10, 1892, the son of Riney Louis and Lucy Wilson (King) Brown. After studying at the University of Texas in 1911–1912, Brown was employed by a contractor in Belton. In 1914 he accepted eighteen mules for back wages and went into the construction business. In 1919 he and his brother-in-law, Dan Root, became partners. In 1923 a third partner, Herman's brother George Rufus Brown, joined the firm. After Root's death in 1929, the brothers purchased the firm, retaining the name, and Herman became president. The company was widely known for constructing United States air and naval bases (in Spain, France, and Guam) and roads, dams, bridges, ships, and intricate plants, such as those for the manufacture of petrochemicals. During World War II the firm purchased the Big and Little Inch pipelines from the government and constructed more than 350 vessels for the navy. In 1961 the company received a planning contract for the two-hundred-million-dollar Manned Spacecraft Center ^{qv} in Houston.

In 1917 Brown married Margaret Root, sister of his partner, and they had two children. Brown died of a heart attack on November 15, 1962, in Houston, and was buried in Glenwood Cemetery. In December, 1962, the Halliburton Company of Dallas purchased Brown & Root, Incorporated.

Brown was a member of the board of directors of City National Bank, Houston; Eastern Transmission Corporation; Armco Steel Corporation; Brown Securities Corporation; Texas Railway Equipment Company; and was vice-president of Highland Oil Company.

BIBLIOGRAPHY: *Who's Who In America* (1960); Houston *Post*, November 17, 1962; Dallas *Morning News*, December 12, 1962.

*Brown, Jacob.

*Brown, James M.

*Brown, Jeremiah.

*Brown, John.

*Brown, John (Red).

*Brown, John (Waco).

*Brown, John Duff.

*Brown, John Henry.

*Brown, Reuben R.

*Brown, Richard.

*Brown, Thomas Jefferson. Thomas Jefferson Brown was the son of Ervin and Matilda (Burdett)

Brown. He obtained his law license in 1857, graduated from Baylor University law department in 1858, and was married to Louisa T. Estes on August 7, 1859 (not 1858, as stated in Volume I). Brown served in the 21st Texas Legislature during the regular session, January 8 to April 6, 1889; and in the 22nd Legislature during the regular session, January 3 to April 13, 1891, and in the called session, March 14 to April 12, 1892 (not from 1888 to 1890, as stated in Volume I).

BIBLIOGRAPHY: L. E. Daniell, *Personnel of the Texas State Government* (1892); *Biographical Encyclopedia of Texas* (1880); *Members of the Legislature of the State of Texas from 1846 to 1939* (1939); *Who Was Who In America* (1943).

***Brown, William M.**

***Brown, William S.**

***Brown, William S.**

***Brown County.** Brown County, with a balanced rural-urban economy, receives the larger portion of its farm income from sheep and cattle ranching and a minor portion from feed grains. In 1964 six thousand acres were under irrigation. Significant manufacturing, especially of brick and tile products, is carried on in Brownwood, the county seat. Between 1917 and 1973 over forty-two million barrels of oil were produced. Population was 24,728 in 1960; in 1970 it was 25,877.

***Brown Creek.**

***Brown Lake.**

***Browndell, Texas.**

***Brownfield, Texas.** Brownfield, seat of Terry County, was incorporated in 1920 with a council-manager form of government. The town's businesses in the 1960's were largely concerned with the agriculture and oil industries. In 1966 Brownfield reported thirty-eight churches, a hospital, two banks, a library, a newspaper, and a radio station. A post office building was completed in 1966. The 1960 population was 10,286; the 1970 count was 9,647.

Browning, David Greig, Jr. David Greig (Skippy) Browning, described as the greatest springboard diver the United States ever had, was born in Boston, Massachusetts, on June 5, 1931, the son of Martha (Hollingsworth) and David G. Browning, Sr. He came to Texas with his parents when he was three and began diving when he was four, under the direction of his father. The family lived for a time in Corpus Christi before moving to Dallas, where Browning in 1941 entered his first competition in swimming and diving contests.

After a brilliant high school diving career at Dallas Highland Park, where he was three times state diving champion, he enrolled at Wayne State University in Detroit, but after one semester he came to the University of Texas at Austin. He had learned a great deal from coach Clarence Pinkston at the Detroit Athletic Club and came within .2 point of making the 1948 Olympic team before he was seventeen. In April, 1949, he made his first national Amateur Athletic Union (AAU) bid at Daytona Beach, Florida, but was edged out by .06 point by the 1948 Olympic champion, Bruce Harlan of Ohio State. At their next competition four months later, in Los Angeles, Browning beat Harlan, winning his first national title. At the University of Texas Browning was named All-American diver in 1950, 1951, and 1952. In all three years he won the Southwest Conference qv diving championship in both the one- and three-meter boards. He dominated Southwest Conference diving for three years and was undefeated in dual meets during his entire collegiate career. He received a long list of diving awards, among which were eight AAU national diving titles and four National Collegiate Athletic Association (NCAA) titles. In the spring of 1952 at the intercollegiate competition at Yale he was given a perfect score of ten on a cutaway one and one-half pike, rated one of the most difficult of dives. He made up his own special dives and the AAU rules committee officially adopted some of them. The University of Texas yearbook, *Cactus*, listed Browning as a Goodfellow in 1951 and 1952.

At the 1952 summer Olympics in Helsinki, Finland, Browning, in his senior university year, was acknowledged as the world's diving champion when he was awarded the Olympic gold medal. The following August he won the championship of the National AAU outdoor meet at Newark, New Jersey. In 1952 he accomplished what no other diver ever had by winning the Amateur Athletic Union, National Collegiate Athletic Association, and the Olympic diving championships in all springboard events, both one meter and three meter. In 1954 he won his last AAU championship; he was sixty-five points ahead of his nearest competitor, something unheard of in that caliber diving competition.

He was married to Corinne (Cody) L. Couch on September 7, 1950, and was graduated from the University of Texas with a degree in business administration in January, 1953. He received his wings as a naval pilot at Pensacola, Florida, in June, 1955. Browning was in training for the 1956 Olympics, and favored to win another gold medal, when he was killed in the crash of his AFJS Fury, a jet carrier fighter, on March 13, 1956, on a training flight near Rantoul, Kansas. In 1957 Browning was named to the Helms Athletic Foundation Hall of Fame, in 1960 was selected for the University of Texas Longhorn Hall of Honor, and in 1962 was named to the Texas Sports Hall of Fame.qv

BIBLIOGRAPHY: Biographical File, Barker Texas History Center, University of Texas at Austin.

***Browning, George Washington.**

***Browning, James Nathan.**

***Browning, Texas.**

Browning Collection. *See* Armstrong Browning Library.

***Browns Creek.**

***Brown's Creek, Texas.**

Brown's Gin, Texas. *See* Pleasant Grove, Texas.

***Brown's Mountain.**

***Brownsboro, Texas.** (Caldwell County.)

*Brownsboro, Texas. (Henderson County.)

***Brownsville, Texas.** In 1960 the population of Brownsville was 48,040; in 1970 it was 52,522. It was the largest city in the Lower Rio Grande Valley area and the seat of Cameron County. *See also* Brownsville-Harlingen-San Benito Standard Metropolitan Statistical Area.

Brownsville-Harlingen-San Benito Standard Metropolitan Statistical Area. The Brownsville-Harlingen-San Benito Standard Metropolitan Statistical Area, which is identical to Cameron County, was designated a metropolitan area in 1960 as one of two such areas in the Lower Rio Grande Valley. The Valley covers 2,424 squares miles, 883 of which are in Cameron County, with its 1960 population of 151,098. The 1970 population was 140,-368. Cameron County gained 311 square miles of submerged land by the tidelands decision of the 1950's (*see* Tidelands Controversy).

The Valley is in the semitropical southern tip of Texas bordered by Mexico on the south, the Gulf of Mexico, South Padre Island, and Laguna Madre Bay on the east, and the King Ranch and the International Falcon Reservoir qqv on the north and northwest, respectively. Its climate and location make the Lower Rio Grande Valley a popular tourist area, tourism ranking as the second largest industry in the Valley. The leading industry is agriculture, due to the warm climate, fertile soil, and extensive irrigation. One of the most productive areas in the state, the Valley is the location of the majority of the citrus fruit crop. Other sources of income are related to the fishing and shipping facilities, oil and gas production, and diversified manufacturing.

Cameron County, which had in 1970 an effective buying income of $267,778,000 and employed 51,-100 people, is composed of two major cities: Brownsville, the county seat, with a 1970 population of 52,522, and Harlingen, with a 1970 population of 33,503. Harlingen, reporting 672 businesses in 1970, depends upon expanding agricultural, tourist, and industrial interests for its economy. Located in the geographic center of the metropolitan area, it is the wholesale and distribution center of the Valley. Harlingen also serves as a transportation center for surrounding farm and manufacturing interests as well as the financial center of the Valley for the cotton industries. During the first eight years of operation, barge tonnage shipped through the port of Harlingen multiplied eightfold. Local light industry includes the processing of cottonseed oil and foods, the manufacturing of agricultural chemicals, metal and concrete products, and printing, refrigeration, and aircraft concerns. Harlingen is a significant medical center, having the Harlingen State Chest Hospital, Harlingen State Mental Health Clinic qqv (now Rio Grande State Center for Mental Health and Mental Retardation qv), and the Valley Baptist Hospital, which has a cobalt radiation treatment center.

Brownsville reported 688 businesses in 1970, many of which were concerned with the processing and marketing of cotton, cereals, and vegetables. Other economic interests are centered in aviation, fishing, natural gas, retailing, and port transportation. As the terminus of the Gulf Intracoastal Waterway,qv Port of Brownsville serves as a major shipping center. Brownsville itself is an important tourist town and port of entry for Mexico. Large quantities of goods going into and from Mexico go through the city of Brownsville.

San Benito is the third largest town in the metropolitan area with a 1970 population of 15,176. Its economic importance rests upon fruit and vegetable marketing facilities. Other industries are expanding, however, particularly clothing manufacturing and vegetable packing, along with tourism.

Port Isabel, with a 1970 population of 3,067, competes with Port of Brownsville for the title of the leading shrimping center. Together the two ports with their four hundred trawlers caught almost fifteen million pounds of shrimp annually in the mid-1960's. Port Isabel also handles both deep-water and barge shipping. This town, along with the smaller communities of La Feria, Rio Hondo, and Los Fresnos, contributes to the area's trading, tourist, and agricultural marketing capacities.

The Laguna Atascosa National Wildlife Refuge,qv bordering the Laguna Madre, is a forty-five-thousand-acre refuge for wintering waterfowl and is a natural tourist attraction of the area. There are also many parks, lakes, and resacas. South Padre Island (developed since the opening of the Queen Isabella Causeway in 1954) and the eighty-mile Padre Island National Seashore qv area both provide recreational opportunities. The international Charro Days qv festival at Brownsville, Shrimp Festival at Port Isabel, "Life Begins at Forty" Golf Tournament, and Fiesta Turista at Harlingen, as well as many fishing tournaments, are additional tourist attractions in the area. The Confederate Air Force,qv based at Harlingen, holds an annual air show and maintains an aircraft museum.

Important historical sites include Fort Brown,qv the oldest permanent fort in Texas; Palmito Ranch,qv site of the last Civil War battle, and the Palo Alto and Resaca de la Palma battlefields qqv of the Mexican War.qv The area's only institution of higher education is the Texas Southmost College at Brownsville, a junior college with regional accreditation. *See also* McAllen-Edinburg-Pharr Standard Metropolitan Statistical Area; Standard Metropolitan Statistical Areas in Texas.

BIBLIOGRAPHY: Robert B. Williamson, *The Lower Rio Grande Valley of Texas: Economic Resources* (1966).

Verna J. McKenna

Brownsville Junior College. *See* Texas Southmost College.

***Brownsville and Matamoros Bridge Company.**

***Brownsville Wharf Case.**

***Brownwood, Texas.** Brownwood, seat of Brown County, has a diversified economy. To enhance Brownwood's importance as an industrial center, a portion of former Camp Bowie qv was purchased in 1963 for use as an industrial park. Plants in Brownwood manufacture industrial and transportation equipment, furniture, clothing, woolen goods, crushed stone, livestock drenches, feeds, and also food, glass, plastic, and leather products. Telephone and railway companies employ over seven hundred persons. In 1953 Daniel Baker College qv was merged with Howard Payne College,qv and a modern science building was added to the campus. When built in 1963, the Brownwood coliseum had the second largest lift slab dome in the nation. The city reported a total of sixty-one churches, six city parks, and new elementary and high schools in 1964. In 1970 there were 430 business establishments. The population in 1960 was 16,974; in 1970 it was 17,368.

*Brownwood North and South Railway Company.

Brownwood Reservoir. Brownwood Reservoir is in the Colorado River Basin in Brown County, eight miles north of Brownwood on Pecan Bayou, a tributary of the Colorado River. The project is owned and operated by the Brown County Water Improvement District No. 1 as a water supply for municipal, industrial, and irrigation uses.

The project was started in 1930, and was completed in 1933. The reservoir was filled during a large flood in 1932, but the water was released to enable completion of the dam. Deliberate impoundment began in July, 1933. During the drouth of 1934, water was released from Brownwood Reservoir for irrigation use near Bay City, about 500 miles downstream. On the basis of a survey made in 1959, the reservoir had a capacity of 143,400 acre-feet and a surface area of 7,300 acres at the spillway crest elevation of 1,424.6 feet above mean sea level. The drainage area above the dam is 1,535 square miles.

BIBLIOGRAPHY: Texas Water Commission, *Bulletin 6408* (1964).

Seth D. Breeding

*Bruce, William Herschel.

*Bruce, Texas.

*Bruce Field.

*Bruceville, Texas.

*Bruckisch, Wilhelm.

*Bruff, Samuel.

Brulay, George Paul. George Paul Brulay, son of Ambroise and Eliza (Vernon) Brulay, was born on December 6, 1839, in Paris, France. He was educated at home and at local schools until he was fourteen, when he boarded a merchant vessel and was shipwrecked off Colombia; stranded in Cartagena, he worked his way through the interior of the country for three years, then returned to Paris where he worked for a commission merchant. At eighteen he shipped out to Tampa, Florida, and from there to the Rio Grande Valley.

With his brother, Arthur, Brulay opened a business handling merchandise between Matamoros and Monterrey by mule caravans. They also used sailboats to deliver goods to coastal towns, and on one

of these trips his brother was lost at sea. In Brownsville Brulay operated a mercantile business under the firm name of Colon, Brulay & Company, until about 1876. On March 11, 1876, Brulay married Marie E. Boesch, and they had five children. In the early 1870's Brulay bought approximately four hundred acres of land east of Brownsville, naming it the Rio Grande Plantation. He first planted cotton and experimented with other produce, including sugar cane. He became a successful sugar cane producer; a mill, commissary, residences, a school house, and other buildings were constructed as the sugar cane industry grew. Small rail cars ran from the fields to the mills, and hundreds of laborers were employed. Brulay began irrigating his fields and held one of the first irrigation permits on the Rio Grande. The Brulay plantation home became a social gathering place not only for local people, but for state and foreign travelers as well. In 1891 the Brulay family also maintained a home in Brownsville. The sugar cane plantation was operated for several years after George Brulay's death on March 29, 1905. Brulay was buried in Buena Vista Park in Brownsville.

BIBLIOGRAPHY: L. E. Daniell, *Texas, The Country and Its Men* (n.d.); W. H. Chatfield (comp.), *Twin Cities of the Border* (1893); Eugenie Brulay Wortman, Life on the Brulay Plantation (MS., Archives, Texas Southmost College Library, Brownsville).

Grace Edman

*Brumley, Texas.

*Brundage, Texas.

*Bruni, Texas.

*Brunswick, Texas.

*Brush, Elkanah.

*Brush Creek.

Brushy, Texas. *See* Round Rock, Texas.

*Brushy Creek.

*Brushy Creek, Texas.

*Brushy Creek, Battle of.

Brushy Creek Reservoir. Brushy Creek Reservoir is in the Red River Basin in Fannin County, three miles north of Savoy on Brushy Creek, a tributary to the Red River. The reservoir extends into Grayson County. The project is owned and operated by the Texas Power & Light Company for the purpose of condenser cooling and other power plant uses for its Valley Creek steam-electric generating station. The project was started on April 18, 1960, and completed on September 5, 1961. The reservoir has a capacity of 16,800 acre-feet and a surface area of 1,180 acres at the service spillway crest elevation of 610 feet above mean sea level. The drainage area is eight square miles, but it is unimportant because the water level in the reservoir is maintained by the diversion of water from the Red River by two pumps installed in the plant at the mouth of Sand Creek.

BIBLIOGRAPHY: Texas Water Commission, *Bulletin 6408* (1964).

Seth D. Breeding

*Brushy Elm Creek.

*Brushy Knob.

*Brushy Lake.

*Brushy Mountain.

*Bruton Creek.

*Brutons Creek.

*Brutus.

*Bryan, Beauregard.

*Bryan, Francis Theodore.

*Bryan, Guy Morrison.

*Bryan, John Neely.

*Bryan, Lewis Randolph.

Bryan, Lewis Randolph, Jr. Lewis Randolph Bryan, Jr., was born in Quintana, Texas, on August 17, 1892, the son of Martha Jane (Shepard) and Lewis Randolph Bryan.qv Following the tropical storm of 1900, his family moved from Velasco to Houston, where he was graduated from the public schools. Thereafter, he attended Virginia Military Institute and received a law degree from the University of Texas in 1913. He practiced law in Houston until the United States entered World War I, at which time he was commissioned a captain in the army and assigned to the 36th Division.qv While serving in France, he gained promotion to major. In the postwar years, Bryan was a lieutenant colonel in the Texas National Guard qv and was made brevet colonel upon retirement in 1939.

In 1919 Randolph Bryan returned to Houston and joined the Lumberman's National Bank (renamed the Second National Bank in 1923) as assistant cashier. He rose to the presidency of the bank in 1944. He became vice-chairman of the board in January, 1956, at the same time the bank took the name Bank of the Southwest. At the time of his death on January 30, 1959, Bryan was also a director of the Fort Worth and Denver Railway Company and the Federal Reserve Bank of Dallas, Houston Branch.

Bryan was an Episcopalian and active in the religious and cultural affairs of Houston. As a great-grandson of Emily Austin Bryan Perry,qv sister of Stephen F. Austin, he inherited and nurtured an interest in Texas history. He was president of the San Jacinto Museum qv of History Association and the Philosophical Society of Texas qv in 1958. He was also a trustee of the Texas Gulf Coast Historical Association,qv which, beginning in 1961, has offered an annual prize in his honor for historical writing. He was a member of the Sons of the Republic of Texas qv and was made a Knight of San Jacinto in 1956.

Bryan was married in San Antonio on November 1, 1924, to Katharine McGown, and they had two sons.

James A. Tinsley

*Bryan, Moses Austin.

*Bryan, William.

*Bryan, William Joel.

*Bryan, Texas. Bryan, seat of Brazos County, had a 1960 population of 27,542 and a 1970 population of 33,719. A new county courthouse and two shopping centers were added, and the downtown business area was renovated. In 1970 Bryan had 505 businesses, fourteen churches, and a library. Industries included the manufacture of aluminum windows, furniture, rubber shoes, electronic components, and insecticides, and the processing of poultry. The city has several hospitals and clinics and a community center for senior citizens. *See also* Bryan-College Station Standard Metropolitan Statistical Area.

Bryan Air Force Base. Bryan Air Force Base, formerly Bryan Army Air Field,qv was placed on "inactive caretaker" status in May, 1960. On April 30, 1962, 1,991.39 acres of land, with roads, airfield pavements, utilities, and 180 buildings, were deeded to Texas A&M University. Private individuals purchased and removed 198 other buildings from the base.

Maurer Maurer

*Bryan Army Air Field. *See also* Bryan Air Force Base.

*Bryan Baptist Academy.

*Bryan and Central Texas Interurban.

*Bryan and College Interurban Railway Company.

Bryan-College Station Standard Metropolitan Statistical Area. One of the newer official Texas metropolitan areas, the Bryan-College Station Standard Metropolitan Statistical Area was so designated following the 1970 U. S. census. With the Texas A&M University System qv as the hub, the area includes all of Brazos County, consisting of 583 square miles. The population of the area increased 29.1 percent during a ten-year period, from 44,895 in 1960 to 57,978 in 1970. The adjoining towns of Bryan (the county seat) and College Station had population increases of 22.4 percent and 55.1 percent, respectively, with Bryan having a population of 27,542 in 1960 and 33,719 in 1970, while College Station's population increased from 11,396 in 1960 to 17,676 in 1970. All of the other towns are small, and the area as a whole comprises a rich farming district that had an annual agricultural income of over $14 million, 70 percent of which was derived from livestock and poultry, in the early 1970's. Cotton and grains are the chief crops.

The Texas A&M University System, with its $77 million yearly budget and over 150 research laboratories, provides the largest stimulant to the area's economy. While mineral production in the area is insignificant, there is an increasing number of agriculturally oriented industrial plants. Total employment in the area reached a figure of 22,890 by April, 1970.

Fishing and hunting are popular in the area for recreation. Bryan and College Station offer numerous cultural attractions, with the new Bryan Civic Auditorium and Texas A&M University sponsoring many events. In addition to the many athletic activities at Texas A&M, which attract visitors from within and outside the area, the new Texas International Speedway Road Course has gained national recognition. *See also* Bryan, Texas; College Station, Texas; Brazos County; Standard Metropolitan Statistical Areas in Texas.

*Bryan's Mill, Texas.

*Bryant, Benjamin Franklin. Benjamin Franklin Bryant settled on Palo Gaucho Creek in Sabine County (not in Shelby County, as stated in Volume I).

Helen Gomer Schluter

*Bryant, David E.

*Bryant Station, Texas.

*Bryarly, Texas.

Bryson, James Gordon. James Gordon Bryson was born on October 6, 1884. Forced to drop out of high school by his father's death, Bryson later worked his way through the University of Texas and received an M.D. degree in 1910. In Bastrop Dr. Bryson became one of central Texas' best known general practitioners during his thirty-seven-year career.

Bryson retired from practice in 1947 and spent most of his time working his Bastrop County farm. He also served as Bastrop's mayor and school board president. Bryson returned to the University of Texas at the age of seventy-two to study history. He was the author of two books: *One Hundred Dollars & a Horse* (1965) and *Shin Oak Ridge* (1964). Bryson married Lily Shuddemagen, and they had six children. He died on August 2, 1968.

BIBLIOGRAPHY: Austin *American*, August 3, 1968.

*Bryson, Texas.

*Bucareli.

*Buchanan, James Paul.

*Buchanan, William.

*Buchanan, Texas. (Johnson County.)

Buchanan, Texas. (Morris County.) *See* Cason, Texas.

*Buchanan County. *See also* Stephens County.

*Buchanan Dam, Texas.

*Buchanan Dam and Lake. *See also* Buchanan Reservoir.

Buchanan Reservoir. Buchanan Dam and Buchanan Reservoir were the first of a series of six projects owned and operated on the Colorado River by the Lower Colorado River Authority.qv The reservoir is in Burnet and Llano counties; its upper end extends into San Saba County. Begun in 1931, the dam was completed in 1938. Water released from Buchanan Reservoir is subsequently used at Inks, Lyndon B. Johnson, Marble Falls, Marshall Ford (Mansfield), and Austin plants for generation of power and for municipal and irrigation purposes. The reservoir has a capacity of 992,000 acre-feet and a surface area of 23,200 acres at the spillway crest elevation of 1,020.5 feet above mean sea level. Water released is used for the generation of power, irrigation, mining, municipal, and recreational pur-

poses. Normal water releases are controlled by the operation of the turbines in the powerhouse. Flood-water releases are from one or more sections of the gated spillways.

There are three generating units and allied equipment with a rated capacity of 11,250 kilowatts each. In addition to the three generating units, there is a pump-back unit which has a capacity of 840 cubic feet per second for returning water from the Buchanan tailrace (Inks Lake) into Buchanan Reservoir. The pump is driven by a 14,500-horse-power motor. This unit operates at off-peak times for power requirements when electric energy can be purchased at a lower rate than its cost during the time of greatest demand. The generating units and the pump are all located in the powerhouse structure. The drainage area is 31,250 square miles, of which 11,900 square miles are probably non-contributing.

BIBLIOGRAPHY: Texas Water Commission, *Bulletin 6408* (1964).

Seth D. Breeding

*Buchel, Augustus. Augustus Buchel (sometimes written as August C. Buchel, as shown in Volume I) was born at Guntersblum, Oppenheim, Germany, in 1815 (not 1811, as stated in Volume I), and was educated at Mainz and the École Militaire in Paris. Mahmoud II appointed him military instructor in the Turkish army upon his graduation. Buchel's advancement in Turkey was stymied because he was a Christian; therefore, when the Carlist War broke out in Spain, he joined the forces of Queen Maria Christina de Bourbon, who decorated him for meritorious service. In 1845 he went to Indianola, Texas. When the Mexican War erupted, Buchel raised and commanded Company H of the 1st Regiment of Texas Foot Riflemen (Volunteers). Although the company, composed of Buchel's fellow German immigrants, enlisted for six months, Buchel served only four, from May 1 until August 25, 1846.

Buchel became a United States citizen in 1852. During the mid-1850's he was deputy collector and inspector at the La Salle Custom House, District of Saluria, Texas. He fought in the border skirmishes against Juan N. Cortina qv shortly before the Civil War. In September, 1861, the Confederate government commissioned Buchel a lieutenant colonel and promoted him to colonel on May 2, 1863. [Buchel did not "enlist" as a colonel (as stated in Volume I), nor was he ever promoted to the rank of brigadier general (as stated in Volume I), although his tombstone in the State Cemetery in Austin reads "Brigadier General Confederate Army."] He served in Texas and Louisiana and was shot at the battle of Pleasant Hill, Louisiana, on April 9, 1864. After his death [April 11 and 12 have been cited, although his tombstone reads April 15, 1864] Brigadier General Hamilton P. Bee qv described Buchel as "a brilliant soldier of Prussia and an irreparable loss to our cause and his adopted country." He was buried in the State Cemetery qv in Austin.

The Texas legislature in 1887 created a county

named Buchel, presumably in his honor, but in 1897 the area was incorporated into present Brewster County.

BIBLIOGRAPHY: Service Records of Augustus Buchel (National Archives, Washington, D.C.); *War of the Rebellion: A Compilation of the Official Records of the Union and Confederate Armies* (1880–1901); *United States Senate Executive Documents*, 30th Cong., 1st Sess., Vol. I, No. 1; H. P. N. Gammel (comp.), *Laws of Texas, 1822–1897*, IX, X (1898); John Henry Brown, *History of Texas from 1685–1892* (c. 1892–1893).

Walter Rundell, Jr.

*Buchel, Texas.

*Buchel County (Defunct).

*Buck, Beaumont Bonaparte.

*Buck, Frank.

*Buck, Texas.

*Buck Branch.

*Buck Creek.

*Buck Hill.

*Buck Mountain.

*Bucker Creek.

*Buckeye, Texas.

*Buckeye Creek.

*Buckeye Rangers.

*Buckham Creek.

*Buckholts, Texas.

*Buckhorn, Texas.

*Buckley, Constantine W.

*Buckley, Samuel Botsford.

Buckley, William Frank. William Frank Buckley was born in Washington-on-the-Brazos, Washington County, on July 11, 1881, the fourth of eight children of John and Mary Ann (Langford) Buckley, of Irish ancestry. In the fall of 1882 the family moved to San Diego, Duval County, where John Buckley engaged in merchandising, politics, and sheep raising; he also served several elective terms as Duval County sheriff.

Growing up in a Spanish-speaking community, William F. Buckley became proficient in the language and a close friend of Spanish-speaking peoples, a quality he retained all of his life. One of his early influences was the widely educated parish priest, Father John Pierre Bard,qv of the Church of San Francisco de Paula in San Diego. After finishing school in San Diego, Buckley taught at a country school near Benavides, where all but a few of the students used the Spanish language. According to records at the University of Texas at Austin, he enrolled there in 1899 and was a student at the university until 1905, when his picture appeared with the law class of 1905. Because of his command of the language he received advanced credit in Spanish in his first years there and was an assistant in the Romance Languages department. During this time he was also, along with his sister, Priscilla, a Spanish translator in the General Land Office.qv With others he initiated the founding of the Austin chapter of Delta Tau Delta national college fraternity and later became one of its most liberal

financial supporters. A devout Catholic, his interest, along with that of others, led to the purchasing of property near the university for the Catholic Newman Club. When his father died in 1904 he was the oldest surviving son, and he undertook the care of his mother, whom he moved to Austin, along with his two brothers and two sisters, to a small house on the corner of Lavaca and 19th streets; Buckley later built a large house there (now the site of Cambridge Tower), where his mother lived until her death in 1930. He received a B.S. degree in 1904, an LL.B. degree in 1905, was a quizmaster in the School of Law, and was a member of the John C. Townes qv Law Society. In 1905 he was elected editor of the University of Texas yearbook, *The Cactus* (1906). Buckley received his license to practice law in Texas on June 8, 1906, and he was elected a member of the Texas Bar Association qv in 1909.

He went to Mexico City in 1908, passed law examinations there, and he and his brother Claude, also a lawyer, acted as counsel for many of the most important American and European oil companies doing business in Mexico. In 1911 they established their own law office with another brother, Edmund, in Tampico, Mexico. By 1914 William F. Buckley had given up his law practice, turning it over to his brothers so that he might engage in real estate and the leasing of oil lands. He acquired, improved, and sold land around the city of Tampico, and he founded the Pantepec Oil Company of Mexico. The Mexican Revolution was at its height in 1912, 1913, and 1914, and after the invasion and takeover of Vera Cruz by the United States Marines in April, 1914, President Woodrow Wilson offered the post of civil governor to Buckley, who indignantly refused the appointment because he was not in sympathy with Wilson's Mexico policy. Later that year Buckley served as counsel for the Mexican government at the ABC Conference at Niagara Falls when Argentina, Brazil, and Chile acted as mediators between the United States and Mexico. In December, 1919, he testified before the United States Senate Subcommittee on Foreign Relations as an expert witness on the conditions in Mexico. Knowing the language, the people, and the nature of revolutionary activities there, it was Buckley's belief that internal Mexican policies such as those approved of by American "specialists" would destroy American investments in Mexico. Because of his opposition to the government of General Álvaro Obregón, Buckley was expelled from Mexico in 1921. In January, 1922, he gave a full report of his expulsion to the secretary of state of the United States and urged that this country not recognize the Obregón government until certain agreements had been reached between the two countries.

Invited back to Mexico by President Plutarco Calles in 1924, Buckley returned for a visit, but in that year he transferred his Pantepec Oil Company to Venezuela. There, in a largely undeveloped oil region, Buckley fully committed himself to oil exploration. One of the first to use the "farm-out" system, Buckley made agreements with some of the largest oil companies, whereby the companies would take over the cost of exploring, drilling, and developing, and would in turn share the profits from oil and gas produced on his concessions. He made his first major deal, with Standard Oil, in the 1930's when a large oil field was found on Pantepec's Venezuelan concessions. Other major producers followed. During his entire career Buckley was primarily interested in unexplored territory, and in 1946 he began a diversification of his oil holdings with the forming of separate companies. Operations assumed an international scale with the leasing of land in Canada, Florida, Ecuador, Australia, the Philippines, Israel, and Guatemala.

In 1922 Buckley gave to the University of Texas his extensive files covering the tumultuous years of Mexican history from the time of his stay in that country. Included in the gift were thirty-five scrapbooks of newspaper clippings and three hundred folders containing copies of Buckley's confidential reports, annotated letters, statements, interviews, and other papers. In 1925, over the opposition of the university's librarian, Ernest W. Winkler,qv the entire collection was sent to Washington, D.C., for use by the State Department's Mixed Claims Commission (United States and Mexico). They were finally returned at the request of the University of Texas in 1929. The papers are housed in the Latin American Collection qv of rare books and manuscripts.

William F. Buckley was married to Aloise Steiner of New Orleans in 1917; a widely read man and always concerned with learning, he closely supervised the trilingual education of their ten children during the years the family lived in Paris, London, and the United States. In the 1920's he purchased the family estate, Great Elm, in Sharon, Connecticut, and later, for a winter home, the estate Kamschatka in Camden, South Carolina. Several of William and Aloise Buckley's children became national figures in their own right, with James Buckley elected to the United States Senate, and William F. Buckley, Jr., a nationally known writer, editor, and speaker for the conservative view in politics. Fergus Reid Buckley, another son, is a journalist and novelist. Members of the family also continued in active operation of the Buckley oil business.

Following a stroke on board the S.S. *United States*, between Paris and New York in late September, 1958, William F. Buckley was given the last rites of the Catholic church; he died in Lenox Hill Hospital in New York on October 5, 1958. He was buried in the Quaker Cemetery near his winter home in Camden, South Carolina.

BIBLIOGRAPHY: Priscilla L. Buckley and William F. Buckley, Jr. (eds.), *W. F. B.—An Appreciation* (1959); *Life* (December 18, 1970); *Time* (March 4, 1957); William F. Buckley Papers (MS., Latin American Collection, University of Texas at Austin); Biographical File, Barker Texas History Center, University of Texas at Austin.

Eldon S. Branda

*Buckleys Creek.

*Buckner, Aylett C.
*Buckner, Robert Cooke.

Buckner, Thomas Addison. Thomas Addison Buckner, born in Bandera County, Texas, on December 24, 1873, was the second son of Thomas L. and Martha (Buckelew) Buckner. Buckner married one of his school pupils, Harriet Caroline Mayfield, in 1892. During the early years of their marriage he taught school, was justice of the peace in Bandera, and was deputy district and county clerk of Bandera County, where both his grandfather and his father had served as county officials. Buckner began his newspaper career in the office of the Bandera *Enterprise* about 1896, later owning the newspaper. Subsequently he owned or managed newspapers at Comfort, Center Point, Ozona, Kerrville, and San Marcos, where he spent the years between 1921 and his death on January 23, 1950, actively engaged in operating the San Marcos *Record*. His two sons purchased interests in the paper in 1922 and 1932. He was also the father of two daughters.

Buckner was a member of the Baptist church, the Texas Press Association,qv on which he served as director on several occasions, and the Texas Editorial Association. One of the early presidents of the local Kiwanis Club, he was active in many civic organizations. During the time the San Marcos *Record* was under his management, Buckner was the recipient of many awards for excellence.

Babe Zimmerman

Buckner, Texas. (Collin County.) Buckner was established by Collin McKinney qv near the present site of McKinney, Texas, in 1840. In 1845 Buckner was selected as the headquarters for the agents of the Peters' Colony qv and for the Texas Emigration and Land Company.qv With the creation of Collin County in 1846 Buckner was chosen as the first county seat. In 1953 it was listed as a ghost town.

BIBLIOGRAPHY: Richard King, *Ghost Towns of Texas* (1953).

*Buckner, Texas. (Parker County.)

Buckner Baptist Benevolences. The Buckner Baptist Benevolences is a wide-scale operation that consists of various child- and adult-care units in several Texas cities. Originally known singly as the Buckner Orphans Home,qv this institution was founded by Robert Cooke Buckner qv in 1879 and acquired its present title in 1961.

A second child-care unit, Buckner Baptist Boys Ranch, was opened at Burnet in 1951. In Dallas a new vocational education building was opened at the children's home. The Mary E. Trew Home for the aged was founded in 1954, and a second home for the aged, Baptist Haven, was opened in Houston in 1955. Both had a capacity of twenty-four. A girls ranch began operation at Breckenridge in 1955 and was later moved to Lubbock and renamed Milam Girls Home.

A Department of Social Service was established in 1957. An extensive building program was carried out in 1958 and 1959, including a new cottage at the girls home in Lubbock; a bedroom wing and new cottages added to Baptist Haven in Houston; new residences for supervisors at the children's home in Dallas, boys ranch in Burnet, and Trew Home in Dallas; a bedroom and infirmary wing at Trew Home; and the Buckner Baptist Benevolences administration building at Dallas. In 1961 the charter of Buckner Orphans Home was changed to Buckner Baptist Benevolences, and where necessary each of the units received the name Buckner Baptist in their titles. In 1964 trustees approved a recommendation for two new units, one of which offered care to the aged with chronic health problems, and a maternity home, both to be built in Dallas. At their annual meeting in 1965 trustees voted to change the name of Buckner Baptist Girls Home in Lubbock to Buckner Baptist Children's Home, authorizing it as a residence for boys and girls.

Jack Edward Bird

*Buckner Orphans Home. *See also* Buckner Baptist Benevolences.

*Buckners Creek.

*Bud Matthews, Texas.

*Buda, Texas.

*Budconnor, Texas.

*Buena Creek.

*Buena Vista, Texas. (Ellis County.)

*Buena Vista, Texas. (Pecos County.)

*Buesing, Texas.

*Buffalo.

*Buffalo, Texas. (Henderson County.)

*Buffalo, Texas. (Leon County.) Buffalo is an agricultural center. In 1964 Buffalo's livestock auction sales amounted to $5,500,000. In that year fifty thousand hogs and sixty thousand cattle were shipped to buyers. Buffalo is the site of an Associated Heavy Equipment trade school, only three of which exist in the United States. In 1965 construction was underway on an $86,000 post office and federal building, as well as a new thirty-two-bed hospital. In 1967 Buffalo had sixty-one businesses, several of which were woodworking plants. The population was 1,108 in 1960; the 1970 population was 1,242.

*Buffalo Bayou.

*Buffalo Bayou, Brazos, and Colorado Railway Company.

*Buffalo Creek.

*Buffalo Draw.

*Buffalo Gap.

*Buffalo Gap, Texas.

*Buffalo Gap College. Buffalo Gap College was opened with a twenty year charter as Buffalo Gap High School, with William H. White as principal. The cornerstone of the building was laid in 1883. In 1885 the board of directors requested the school be designated Buffalo Gap College; the name was adopted by the fall of 1885, and degrees were offered. The former principal, William H.

White, became the college's first president (not J. N. Ellis, as stated in Volume I). By December of that year, 106 students were enrolled. The school had at least eight different presidents and reached an enrollment exceeding 200 students in 1891. The school was plagued with financial troubles, although at times it operated on a secure basis through the efforts of school officials. Enrollment for the school year 1900–1901 was 103 students (the school did not close in 1896, as stated in Volume I). During the school year 1901–1902, William H. White was returned to the presidency, but by December, 1902, the presbytery instructed the trustees to sell the property, as the school's charter was near expiration. By July, 1906, the transaction of sale of the college was completed.

BIBLIOGRAPHY: Tommie Clack, "Buffalo Gap College," *West Texas Historical Association Year Book,* XXXV (October, 1959).

*Buffalo Hump (Pochanaquarhip). Buffalo Hump was not killed in 1839 (as stated in Volume I). In 1858 he was a leader among the northern Comanches and was present when Major Earl Van Dorn qv attacked Wichita Village in Indian Territory. He was still living in 1861.

BIBLIOGRAPHY: Rupert N. Richardson, *The Comanche Barrier to South Plains Settlement* (1933).

*Buffalo Hunting.

*Buffalo Lake. Umbarger Dam and Buffalo Lake, in Randall County, are owned by the Fish and Wildlife Service, United States Department of the Interior. The dam was built by the Federal Farm Securities Administration to store water for recreational purposes. Construction of the dam was started in February, 1938, and was completed June 15, 1938. Impoundment began on June 9, 1938. The project was operated by the Soil Conservation Service, United States Department of Agriculture, until 1953, when the operation was assumed by the Forest Service, United States Department of Agriculture. In 1958 operation of the project was transferred to the Fish and Wildlife Service, United States Department of the Interior. Capacity of the lake is 18,130 acre-feet at the spillway crest elevation of 3,642.6 feet above mean sea level. Surface area at this elevation is 1,900 acres. The drainage area is 2,075 square miles, of which 1,500 square miles is probably non-contributing.

BIBLIOGRAPHY: Texas Water Commission, *Bulletin 6408* (1964).

Seth D. Breeding

*Buffalo Peak.

*Buffalo Point.

*Buffalo Springs, Texas. (Clay County.)

*Buffalo Springs, Texas. (Comal County.)

*Buffalo Wallow Fight.

*Buffington, Anderson.

*Bufford Creek.

*Buford, Texas.

*Buford Branch.

*Buford Creek.

*Bug Tussle, Texas.

Bugbee, Harold Dow. Harold Dow Bugbee, the artist-illustrator of the Texas Panhandle, was born on August 15, 1900, in Lexington, Massachusetts. When he was twelve, his parents, Charles H. and Grace L. (Dow) Bugbee, brought him to Texas, where they settled near Clarendon. Bugbee's formal education was at Clarendon College and at Texas Agricultural and Mechanical College (now Texas A&M University); he studied art at the Charles Cummings Art School in Des Moines, Iowa, and later in New York and in Taos, New Mexico.

In 1921 Bugbee sold his first painting and held his first exhibition. The owner of the Amarillo Hotel, Colonel Ernest O. Thompson,qv commissioned fourteen oils by the artist for the "Longhorn Room." Thompson later had Bugbee paint murals for the "Tascosa Room" of his Herring Hotel. Bugbee sold many of his paintings to ranchmen and collectors of western art, and he drew Christmas card designs that were used internationally. For eighteen years beginning in 1933, Bugbee illustrated books, pulp magazines (particularly Ranch Romances), historical editions of local and regional newspapers, trade publications such as The Shamrock, and thirty-four issues of the Panhandle-Plains Historical Review.qv During this period he was also exhibiting his works in New York, in galleries in the West, and frequently in Clarendon. In 1951 Bugbee became part-time curator of art (and later, until his death, curator) for the Panhandle-Plains Historical Society;qv he also contributed to the society's museum at Canyon many of his works, along with carefully documented murals, important for both their historic and artistic merit. A picture painted on wood panels hangs in the Hall of State qv in Dallas. Having spent much of his life on the family ranch, much of Bugbee's work provided an authentic insight into daily ranch life routine. One of the most familiar of his paintings is that of "Old Blue," the lead steer for the J A Ranch.qv

Bugbee's first marriage, to Katherine Patrick in 1935, ended in divorce. He later married Olive E. Vandruff, who survived him at his death in Clarendon on March 27, 1963.

BIBLIOGRAPHY: Price Daniel, Jr., Bugbee Bibliography (1964); Frances Battaile Fisk, A History of Texas Artists and Sculptors (c. 1928); Esse Forrester-O'Brien, Art and Artists of Texas (c. 1935); Mary Whatley Clarke, "Harold Dow Bugbee—Cowboy Artist," Cattleman, 37 (May, 1937); Jean Ehly, "Harold Dow Bugbee and the Texas Panhandle," Frontier Times, 41 (April–May, 1967); John L. McCarty, "Authentic Western Artist—Harold D. Bugbee," Quarter Horse Journal, 21 (December, 1968); John L. McCarty, "Some Memories of H. D. Bugbee," Southwestern Art, I (No. 3, n.d.); Biographical File, Barker Texas History Center, University of Texas at Austin.

Caroline Remy

*Bugbee, Lester Gladstone.

*Bugbee, Thomas Sherman.

Bugg, Willis Lemuel, II. Willis Lemuel Bugg was born in Georgia about 1802, the son of Willis Lemuel Bugg. He married Caroline Eidom in Georgia, then came to East Texas as a Cherokee County settler in the early 1840's with his wife and three children. Bugg became a landholder in Cherokee County and cultivated a cotton plantation. He, along with several of his wife's brothers, was instrumental in establishing the townsite of Knoxville, in Cherokee County, where he constructed the first cotton gin for commercial use in that area and where he operated the first mercantile store under the firm name of Bugg & Eidom. He and his son, John Randolph Bugg, led a group of Knoxville citizens in organizing the first Masonic lodge in Cherokee and Smith counties. He helped promote the first railroads through East Texas and supported the establishment of post offices in Troup, Tyler, and Omen.

BIBLIOGRAPHY: Hattie Joplin Roach, A History of Cherokee County, Texas (1934).

Mildred Alice Webb

*Build Butte.

Building Commission, State. See State Building Commission.

Building Materials and Systems Testing Laboratory, State. See Community Affairs, Department of.

*Buke Creek.

*Bula, Texas.

*Bulah, Texas.

*Bulcher, Texas.

*Buler, Texas.

*Bulger Creek.

*Bull Creek.

*Bull Hide Creek.

*Bull Hollow.

*Bull Lake.

*Bull Run Creek.

*Bull Wagon Creek.

*Bullard, Texas.

*Bullard Creek.

Bulletin of the Texas Archeological and Paleontological Society. See Bulletin of the Texas Archeological Society.

Bulletin of the Texas Archeological Society. The Bulletin of the Texas Archeological Society, published annually since 1929 (except in 1944), is the principal publication of the Texas Archeological Society.qv Entitled Bulletin of the Texas Archeological and Paleontological Society from 1929 to 1952, the bulletin was published at Abilene under the editorship of Cyrus N. Ray from 1929 to 1946 (Volumes 1–17) and at Lubbock under W. C. Holden from 1947 to 1952 (Volumes 18–23). From 1952 to 1965, the bulletin was published at Austin under successive editors Alex D. Krieger, E. Mott Davis, T. N. Campbell, and Dee Ann Suhm. Two special topic volumes have been published: An Introductory Handbook of Texas Archeology, authored by Dee Ann Suhm, Alex D. Krieger, and Edward B. Jelks; and The Gilbert Site, by Edward B. Jelks.

With the exception of these special topic volumes (Volumes 25 and 37), the bulletin contains papers on Texas archeology and related subjects, book reviews, and obituaries; earlier volumes also carried society news and notes which now appear in *Texas Archeology*, the society newsletter. Volumes average 200 to 300 pages and usually contain at least five papers; most articles are illustrated with photographs or line drawings. An index to Volumes 1–22 was published in 1953. The first two volumes (1929, 1930) used the spelling "Archaeological" rather than "Archeological."

Michael B. Collins

*Bullhead Creek.

*Bullhead Mountains.

Bullington, Orville. Orville Bullington, outstanding lawyer and civic leader of Wichita Falls and leading Republican in Texas for a number of years, was born in Indian Springs, Missouri, on February 10, 1882. His father, W. I. Bullington, was a druggist, teacher, and ordained Presbyterian minister, who moved from Tennessee in 1884 to Parker County, Texas, where he taught school. Orville Bullington received his secondary education in a Tennessee academy, then worked his way through Sam Houston Normal Institute (later Sam Houston State Teachers College and now Sam Houston State University), graduating in 1901. He taught school for two years before entering the University of Texas law school in 1903, finishing the three-year law course in two years.

In February, 1906, he opened a law office in Munday, serving as county attorney for a term. In June, 1909, he moved to Wichita Falls, where he practiced law for the remainder of his life. He was a member of local, state, and national Bar associations. At the beginning of World War I, he enlisted as a private and was discharged as a lieutenant colonel in the 8th Texas Infantry.

On June 28, 1911, he married Sadie Kell, daughter of Frank Kell,qv of Wichita Falls. Their only son, William Orville Bullington, died in 1951.

Bullington served as president of the chamber of commerce in 1929 and was active in other movements to advance Wichita Falls. His business investments included the American National Bank, Kemp Hotel Corporation, Wichita Falls and Southern Railroad (president, chairman of the board when the road was sold in 1953), and oil interests in the Wichita Falls area and the Texas Panhandle. He also had farm and ranch investments.

His association with the University of Texas was strong. He was active in the old B-Hall Association; was a member of the board of the Ex-Students' Association for twenty years and its president (1921–1923); member of the board of regents (1941–1947), during which time plans for the Barker Texas History Center qv were formulated. It was also during his tenure that Mrs. Frank Kell presented the Frank Kell Collection of Texana and Western Books. With Mrs. Kell, Bullington contributed to the endowment and added some of his own books to the collection. He was a patron of the Texas State Historical Association.qv He also served as president of the Sam Houston State College Ex-Students' Association (1928–1932).

After 1918, when he resigned from the Democratic party, Bullington was active in the Republican party and was the Republican nominee for governor in 1932, waging a vigorous campaign. Though unsuccessful, he polled the largest number of Republican votes to that time—198,000 to Miriam A. Ferguson's qv 328,000. He was a delegate to eight national conventions and a member of the state executive committee (1947–1951), serving as chairman (1951–1952). He died on November 23, 1956, in Wichita Falls.

BIBLIOGRAPHY: *Alcalde* (June, 1941); Dallas *Morning News*, October 16, 1932; *Southwestern Historical Quarterly*, LIV (1950–1951); Wichita Falls *Daily Times*, August 9, 1932, January 14, 1941; Wichita Falls *Times*, November 24, 1956, May 25, 1960.

Louise Kelly

*Bullis, John Lapham.

*Bullis, Texas.

*Bullis Gap Ridge.

Bullock, Henry Allen. Henry Allen Bullock, first black professor appointed to the faculty of Arts and Sciences at the University of Texas at Austin, was born on May 2, 1906, in Tarboro, Edgecombe County, North Carolina, the son of Jessie and Aurelia Bullock. He attended local schools and was graduated from Virginia Union University in Richmond, Virginia, in 1928, with a B.A. degree in social sciences and Latin classics; he received from the University of Michigan an M.A. degree in sociology and comparative psychology in 1929 and a Ph.D. degree in sociology in 1942. He was an Earhardt Foundation Fellow at the University of Michigan and was twice a General Education Fellow.

Bullock taught sociology at North Carolina Agricultural and Technical College in 1929–1930; he was head of the Department of Sociology at Prairie View A&M College, where he taught from 1930 to 1949. In 1949–1950 he was head of the Department of Sociology and chairman of the Division of Social Sciences at Dillard University, New Orleans. From 1950 to 1969 he was director of graduate research, head of the Sociology Department, and chairman of the Division of Social Sciences at Texas Southern University in Houston. In 1961 he was named a Minnie Stevens Piper Fellow as an outstanding Texas educator.

In the spring of 1969 Bullock became a visiting professor in the University of Texas at Austin History Department to teach a new course, "The Negro in America." He was then appointed a regular faculty member for the following fall semester and thus became the university's first Negro permanent faculty member. From 1969 to 1971 he was professor of history and sociology, and chairman and designer of the university's first ethnic studies program. Upon his retirement in 1971 he returned to his home in Houston.

Bullock's interest in the Negro in American society began during his student years. In the early 1930's he organized conferences in the South to train black teachers and administrators in more effective teaching techniques. His search for facts on education and employment culminated in the publication of "A Comparison of the Academic Achievements of White and Negro College Graduates," in the *Journal of Educational Research* in 1950, and "Racial Attitudes and the Employment of Negroes," in the *American Journal of Sociology* in 1951. The transition of the American black from a rural-oriented society to an urbanized society in this century led him to a study of crime rates among juveniles in the cities and the publication of "Urban Homicide in Theory and Fact," in the *Journal of Criminal Law, Criminology, and Police Science* (January–February, 1955), and "Significance of the Racial Factor in the Length of Prison Sentences," in the same journal in 1961. In "The Houston Murder Problem: Its Nature, Apparent Causes, and Probable Cures," he presented a special study for the office of the mayor of Houston in 1961. Various economic and ecological studies resulted in the publication of "Consumer Motivations in Black and White," in *Harvard Business Review* (May–June; July–August, 1961), and "Spatial Aspects of the Differential Birthrate," in the *American Journal of Sociology* (September, 1943). He was the author of numerous other publications.

Bullock also worked in the field of communications media. In 1957 he helped produce a series of twelve thirty-minute films, "People are Taught To Be Different," along with fellow faculty members of Texas Southern, for National Educational Television and Radio Center, Ann Arbor, Michigan. The film received second place in the world competition, presented by the Institute for Education by Radio-Television, at the Twenty-third American Exhibition of Educational Radio-Television Programs. He completed a study of the attitudes of young children toward the television series, "Discovery '63" on a grant from the American Broadcasting Company. Bullock believed that the black college should continue to exist to develop the leadership needed for blacks and for the nation, a view unpopular with many educators. He served on the Houston Community Council, the Texas Advisory Committee of the U. S. Civil Rights Commission, and the Advisory Group for Equal Employment for President Lyndon B. Johnson.ᑫᵛ For a number of years he wrote a weekly column for the black newspaper, the Houston *Informer*. His book, *A History of Negro Education in the South* (1967) won the Bancroft Prize in 1968, one of the highest honors obtainable in the historical profession.

Henry Allen Bullock died in Houston on February 8, 1973, and was buried in Paradise Cemetery there. He was survived by his wife, Merle (Anderson) Bullock and three children.
BIBLIOGRAPHY: Biographical File, Barker Texas History Center, University of Texas at Austin.

Naomi W. Ledé

*Bullock, James Whitis.

*Bullock, Texas.

*Bullock Bend.

*Bullock House.

*Bulls Eye, Texas.

*Bulverde, Texas.

*Buna, Texas.

Bunavista, Texas. Bunavista, an unincorporated center in southern Hutchinson County, was established during World War II to house employees of a government synthetic rubber plant. The plant was sold to a petroleum company, and much of the housing had been sold and removed from the premises by 1966. Population in 1960 was 2,067; in 1970 it was 1,402.

*Bunger, Texas.

*Bunker Hill, Texas.

Bunker Hill Village, Texas. Bunker Hill Village, in southwestern Harris County, was incorporated in December, 1954, and had a mayor-council form of city government. The city is completely restricted as a residential community and in 1966 had two public schools and two churches. In 1960 the population was 2,216; population in 1970 was 3,977. *See also* Houston Standard Metropolitan Statistical Area.

**Bunker's Monthly.*

Bunn's Bluff, Texas. Bunn's Bluff, in Orange County, was founded in 1867 near the present city of Orange.
BIBLIOGRAPHY: *Texas Almanac* (1936).

*Bunting, Robert Franklin.

*Bunton, John Wheeler.

Burch, Valentine Ignatius. Valentine Ignatius Burch was born near Bardstown, Kentucky, on February 14, 1813, the son of Samuel Lewis and Dorothea (Brown) Burch, both of Maryland Catholic stock. Burch was educated at nearby St. Mary's College. In 1826 the family migrated to Texas, settling first near Nacogdoches, later near San Augustine. Burch and his younger brother James enlisted in Captain William Kimbro's ᑫᵛ company on March 15, 1836, and participated in the battle of San Jacinto, where they assisted in the capture of Colonel Juan Almonte.ᑫᵛ The brothers reenlisted on June 4, 1836, in Captain Henry Reed's ᑫᵛ company and served until September 4 of that year.

After the revolution Burch settled at Colita in Polk County. In 1843 he married Helen Elmira Cauble, daughter of Peter Cauble,ᑫᵛ and settled at Peach Tree Village in Tyler County, where he managed the plantation of his father-in-law as well as his own property in several counties. There he was one of the charter subscribers for a private academy in 1870. The Burch home was a social center for years, as well as a haven for Catholic missionaries to East Texas. Burch died on November 26, 1892, and was buried in the family cemetery at Peach Tree Village. He was a member of the Texas Veterans Association.ᑫᵛ

BIBLIOGRAPHY: S. H. Dixon and L. W. Kemp, *Heroes of San Jacinto* (1932); Bounty and Headright Certificates and Muster Roll of the Texas Revolution (MS., General Land Office, Austin); *Historical Polk County, Texas* (1900); Emma R. Haynes, *History of Polk County* (1937); Aline Rothe, History of Education in Polk County, Texas (M.Ed. thesis, University of Texas, 1934).

John P. Landers

*Burdette Wells, Texas.

Burdine, John Alton. John Alton Burdine was born February 9, 1905, in Smithville, Mississippi, the son of W. B. and Margie (Knight) Burdine. He came to Texas as a youth with his parents. He graduated from the Paris, Texas, high school in 1921 and received a B.A. and an M.A. degree from the University of Texas in 1926. Except for graduate study at Harvard University, from which he received an M.A. degree in 1933 and a Ph.D. degree in 1939, and one year in Washington, D.C., he was a continuous resident of Texas. At the time of his death on September 15, 1967, he had been a member of the University of Texas community for more than forty years. He married Marian Griffith in 1931, and they had one child.

Burdine was vice-president of the university from 1941 to 1945, when he resigned because of his concern with the dismissal of Homer Price Rainey as president of the University of Texas. He resumed his career in the Department of Government only to return again to administrative functions when he became associate dean of the Graduate School and acting dean of the College of Arts and Sciences in 1957. He became dean of the College of Arts and Sciences in 1958 while continuing to play a significant role in the university's graduate program.

Burdine served on a large number of committees concerned with various aspects of governmental change in the state of Texas. For a time he was a consultant to the administrator of the Federal Security Agency and served in consulting capacities to the United States Civil Service Commission and the United States Employment Service. He held various committee assignments in the National Municipal League and the National Civil Service League. He assisted with the faculty fellowship program of the Fund for the Advancement of Education and was a member of the board of trustees of the College Entrance Examining Board.

His activities within his own academic discipline were equally broad. He served as a vice-president of the American Political Science Association, as an officer in several of its regional groups, and on committees of the Social Science Research Council. His many publications dealt with problems of administration at all levels of government.

In his broadly based social science career in Texas, in the South, and on the national scene, Alton Burdine played an influential role not only in developments that set the direction of both undergraduate and graduate education, but in developments in government and in the whole spectrum of social science generally.

W. Gordon Whaley

*Bureau, Allyre.

*Burford, Nathaniel Macon.

*Burges, Richard Fenner.

*Burgess, George Farmer.

*Burgess, Texas.

*Burgess Creek.

*Burk Station, Texas.

*Burkburnett, Texas. Burkburnett, in northeastern Wichita County, has a commission-manager form of government. In 1970 its 100 businesses served an oil, cattle, and farming area. The city completed a library in 1966 and was constructing an outdoor oil museum. The community reported fourteen churches, two banks, and a newspaper. The 1960 population was 7,621; in 1970 it was 9,230. *See also* Wichita Falls Standard Metropolitan Statistical Area.

*Burkburnett Oil Field.

*Burke, David N.

*Burke, James.

*Burke, John.

*Burke, Robert E.

*Burke, Texas.

*Burke Creek.

Burkett, George W. George W. Burkett was born in County Derry, Ireland, on November 12, 1847. He came to the United States during the Civil War and went to work for a contracting firm grading the roadbed of the Union Pacific Railway. After rising to gang foreman, he resigned to become a grading subcontractor for the Union Pacific in Utah until 1869, and for the Missouri, Kansas, and Texas Railway in Kansas until 1872. He then moved to Texas, where he was a grading subcontractor for the Texas and Pacific and for the Galveston, Harrisburg, and San Antonio railways, before becoming a general contractor for the International and Great Northern Railway. In that capacity he also built sections of line for the Trinity and Sabine, for the Santa Fe, for the Taylor, Bastrop, and Houston, and for the Missouri, Kansas, and Texas railways—often as a partner in Burkett, Murphy, and Burns.

In the late 1880's Burkett became one of the organizers and a vice-president of the First National Bank of Palestine, a director of the Taylor National Bank, and a stockholder in the First National Bank of Stephenville and the First National Bank of Orange. He was also president of the Taylor Water Works and Ice Company, a stockholder in the Palestine Cotton Seed Oil Company, a dealer in land and railroad ties, and president of the Palestine and Dallas Railway in the 1890's.

Burkett made his entry into state politics as a delegate to the Republican national conventions of 1884 and 1888. In 1892 he was a member of the state executive committee of the "Lily White" Republican organization (*see* Lily-White Movement), and in 1898 was on the executive committee of the regular Republican Party in Texas.[qv] He was the gubernatorial nominee of the E. H. R. Green [qv] faction but was withdrawn when the national executive committee recognized the opposing faction as representing Texas Republicans. In 1902 Burkett was the party candidate for governor in a harmony move between factions, being defeated by S. W. T. Lanham.qv In 1904 he was again a leader of one of the factions within the party, but he later served the regular party on its executive committee and as a presidential elector in 1908. He then joined the Progressive party as a follower of Theodore Roosevelt, acting as a presidential elector in 1912, as a member of the state executive committee from 1912 to 1916, and as a delegate to the national convention of 1916.

Burkett married Mary Hartley of Houston in 1880, and they had a son and a daughter.

BIBLIOGRAPHY: John Henry Brown, *Indian Wars and Pioneers of Texas* (189?); E. W. Winkler, *Platforms of Political Parties in Texas* (1916).

*Burkett, Texas.

*Burkeville, Texas. Henry Stephenson qv (not Stevenson, as stated in Volume I) was buried near Burkeville, in Newton County, in 1841.

*Burkland, Texas.

Burks, John C. John C. Burks was born in Georgia about 1835. He moved to Red River County, Texas, where he was practicing law and living with his wife and one daughter by 1860. In 1861 he joined the 11th Texas Cavalry and rose to colonel in 1862. He was killed while leading the regiment in a dismounted charge at the battle of Murfreesboro, Tennessee, in the winter of 1862-1863.

BIBLIOGRAPHY: S. S. Johnson, *Texans Who Wore the Gray* (1907); U.S. Census, 1860, Red River County, Texas (microfilm, University of Texas at Austin Library).

Burleigh, Texas. Burleigh, approximately eight miles east of Bellville in Austin County, was on the proposed route of a new Austin-to-Houston highway in 1966. A post office was established in a store around the turn of the century and christened Burleigh; some years later the post office was discontinued. The name remained, although the community dwindled to one home. In 1966 a store was in operation about three-fourths of a mile north of the original store. By 1971 the estimated population was sixty-nine.

*Burleson, Aaron B. Aaron B. Burleson was the son of Elizabeth (Shipman) [not Nancy (Christian), as stated in Volume I] and James Burleson.qv

Luther H. Hill

*Burleson, Albert Sidney.

*Burleson, David Crockett.

*Burleson, Edward. Edward Burleson was born in 1798 (not 1793, as stated in Volume I) and was the son of Elizabeth (Shipman) [not Nancy (Christian)] and James Burleson.qv Edward Burleson was married in 1816 (not 1813) at the age of seventeen, according to a letter he wrote to Mirabeau B. Lamar.qv

Luther H. Hill

*Burleson, Edward, Jr.

*Burleson, James. James Burleson, son of Aaron Burleson (born in 1749) was born on May 4, 1775 (not 1758, as stated in Volume I; the inscription on the centennial marker near Bastrop is incorrect, for if James Burleson were born in 1758, his father would only have been nine years old at the time). He was married to Elizabeth Shipman, and they had twelve children. He was married a second time, to Mary Christian, and they had one child, a daughter.

Luther H. Hill

*Burleson, Richard Byrd.

*Burleson, Rufus C.

*Burleson, Texas. Burleson, in Johnson County, was named for Rufus C. Burleson qv (not Edward Burleson,qv as stated in Volume I). Henry Renfro, owner of the land where the town was established and where he was a Baptist minister, named it for Rufus C. Burleson, his former teacher at Baylor University.

BIBLIOGRAPHY: Viola Block, *History of Johnson County and Surrounding Areas* (1970).

William C. Griggs

Burleson grew rapidly during the 1950's, extending its boundaries out from Johnson County into the metropolitan area of Tarrant County. Its population grew from 791 in 1950, to 2,345 in 1960, and to 7,713 in 1970. By 1970 Burleson reported a new bank, four schools, eleven churches, and a newspaper. *See also* Fort Worth Standard Metropolitan Statistical Area.

*Burleson College.

*Burleson County. Burleson County had a stable population of around eighteen thousand from 1900 to 1940 but has experienced a population decline since that time. The population was 13,000 in 1950, 11,177 in 1960, and 9,999 in 1970. The decline is paralleled in the dairy and poultry industries. Beef and swine production, on the other hand, is rising, and diversified crops are raised, partly on the county's nine thousand irrigated acres. About twelve thousand bales of cotton were grown in 1968. Some manufacturing is located in Caldwell. A new rodeo arena, country club, and inn have been constructed. Somerville Reservoir serves both Burleson and Washington counties as a municipal, industrial, and irrigation water supply.

*Burleson County (Judicial).

*Burleson Creek.

*Burleson Female Institute.

*Burlington, Texas. (Milam County.)

*Burlington, Texas. (Montague County.)

*Burlington Railroad System. The Burlington Railroad System in Texas, consisting of the Fort Worth and Denver Railway and its subsidiaries, included by merger in 1952 the following: the Wichita Valley Railroad Company, the Abilene and Northern, the Fort Worth and Denver South Plains Railway Company, the Fort Worth and Denver Northern, and the Fort Worth and Denver Terminal Railway Company. In December, 1954, the

Wichita Falls and Oklahoma Railway Company was dissolved. Roads included in the Burlington System in Texas were the Fort Worth and Denver and the Colorado and Southern. The Galveston Terminal, the Houston Belt and Terminal, and the Union Terminal were all owned in part by the system. Until 1964 the Burlington-Rock Island was included, but in that year the Chicago, Rock Island, and Pacific Railroad Company and the Colorado and Southern each purchased half of the company, and it lost all its operations in Texas. Together the roads in the Burlington system operated 1,115 miles of main line track in Texas in the mid-1960's.

James M. Day

*Burlington-Rock Island Railroad Company. In 1964 the Burlington-Rock Island Railroad Company sold out to the Colorado and Southern and the Chicago, Rock Island and Pacific, each purchasing one half of the railroad's property. *See also* Colorado and Southern Railroad; Chicago, Rock Island, and Pacific Railroad Company.

James M. Day

*Burnam, Jesse.

*Burnam, Texas.

*Burnam's Ferry.

*Burnell Switch, Texas.

*Burnet, David Gouverneur. David G. Burnet, first president *ad interim* of the Republic of Texas, was born on April 4, 1788 (not April 14, as stated in Volume I). He was buried in the Episcopal cemetery in Galveston; his body was removed to Magnolia Cemetery in that city in 1871, then finally reinterred in Lake View Cemetery in Galveston in 1894, beneath an imposing monument honoring both Burnet and General Sidney Sherman qv (Burnet's body was not moved to the State Cemetery qv in Austin, as stated in Volume I).

Inaugurated as vice-president on December 10, 1838 (he also served as secretary of state and Indian commissioner during his term as vice-president), Burnet took over as acting president of the Republic on December 12, 1840. President Lamar had requested a leave of absence because of illness and was granted one in December, 1840, by a joint resolution of Congress (Lamar did not resign, as reported in Volume I). Lamar returned to the capital on March 5, 1841, to reassume duties as president. Burnet was not made president again on December 13, 1841 (as stated in Volume I); Sam Houston became president on that date, after defeating Burnet in the 1841 election.

BIBLIOGRAPHY: Mary W. Clarke, *David G. Burnet* (1969); Joseph Milton Nance, *After San Jacinto* (1963); Stanley Siegal, *A Political History of the Texas Republic, 1836–1845* (1956); A. K. Christian, "Mirabeau Buonaparte Lamar," *Southwestern Historical Quarterly*, XXIII (1919–1920), XXIV (1920–1921); L. W. Kemp, Fort Worth *Star-Telegram*, May 13, 1928.

*Burnet, Pumphrey.

*Burnet, Texas. Burnet, seat of Burnet County, had a 1960 population of 2,214 and a 1970 population of 2,864. Burnet had three schools, a public library, and two hospitals. Businesses included feed

manufacturers, stone crushing facilities, and graphite processors. The economy is based on tourism, the quarrying of stone, farming, and ranching. Although a railroad was built from Austin to Burnet in 1882, it was not until 1885 (not 1882, as stated in Volume I) that the narrow-gauge line was completed from Burnet to Granite Mountain, where stone was quarried for building the state Capitol.qv

*Burnet County. Burnet County, with its series of man-made lakes on the Colorado River, is an especially scenic part of Central Texas. Lakes Buchanan, Travis, Marble Falls, Inks, and Lyndon B. Johnson (formerly Granite Shoals) draw tourists into the county, as do also the county's two state parks, its hunting facilities, and its historic sites. Mineral deposits are profitable; about $2,500,000 is gained annually from stone and graphite production. Ranching is diversified, with special emphasis on sheep production; poultry raising is also important. The population was 9,265 in 1960 and 11,420 in 1970.

*Burnet County (Judicial).

Burnett, John H. John H. Burnett was born in Greene County, Tennessee, on July 8, 1830, the son of Silas E. and Malinda (Howell) Burnett, both of whom were natives of Virginia. Burnett was reared in Summerville, Chattooga County, Georgia. During the Mexican War,qv he enlisted in Lieutenant Colonel James S. Calhoun's battalion of the Georgia mounted volunteers, a part of General Winfield Scott's army. He was in several engagements, including the storming of the castle of Chapultepec, was twice slightly wounded, and before the end of the campaign was promoted to lieutenant. After the war Burnett was made a colonel in the Georgia militia. He also was elected sheriff of Chattooga County, Georgia, at the early age of twenty-one and served for two years. Moving to Crockett, Houston County, Texas, in 1854, he engaged in farming and merchandising. Burnett took an active interest in public affairs and was elected to the Texas House of Representatives in 1857. In August, 1861, he was elected a member of the Texas Senate, representing the counties of Houston, Anderson, and Trinity, and served until February, 1862, when he resigned to command the 13th Texas Cavalry Regiment. His senatorial colleague, Anderson F. Crawford of Jasper County, became the lieutenant colonel of the regiment, which was soon dismounted and attached to the first brigade of Brigadier General Henry E. McCulloch's qv division of Texas infantry. Following service in Arkansas and Louisiana, upon surgeon's certificate, Burnett was transferred to post duty in early November, 1863, and never thereafter commanded his regiment in the field. He resigned his commission in April, 1864, because of continuing illness and disability.

Colonel Burnett returned to Crockett after the war, but in 1866 moved to Galveston and became a partner with W. B. Wall in the commission business. By 1875 his firm, J. H. Burnett and Company, was doing general contracting and building as well as engaging in a cotton brokerage business. The firm was one of the contractors for the third and last Tremont Hotel, completed about 1880. It engaged in railway construction and built seventy miles of the Gulf, Colorado, and Santa Fe Railway, the Gulf City Street Railway, and was the contractor for some $350,000 of Galveston streets and sidewalks. For a number of years Burnett was president and director of the Galveston National Bank and a large stockholder in several railroads. In 1899 he moved to Houston, where he had acquired extensive real estate holdings, and became president of the Planters and Merchants Bank. He was thought to be one of the largest taxpayers in South Texas at the time of his death, and his estate was appraised at more than a million dollars.

In 1851 Burnett married Catherine Beavers, daughter of General John F. Beavers of Summerville, Georgia. They were the parents of three children. He died on June 24, 1901, and was buried in Glenwood Cemetery, Houston.

BIBLIOGRAPHY: Joseph P. Blessington, *The Campaigns of Walker's Texas Division* (1875); *War of the Rebellion: A Compilation of the Official Records of the Union and Confederate Armies* (1880–1901); Service Records of John H. Burnett (National Archives, Washington, D.C.); John Henry Brown, *Indian Wars and Pioneers of Texas* (189?); Probate Records, Galveston and Harris Counties.

Anne A. Brindley

*Burnett, Samuel Burk.

*Burnetta College.

*Burney, George E.

*Burney, Hanse McCain.

*Burney, Robert Hanse.

*Burnham, Jesse. *See* Burnam, Jesse.

*Burnley, Albert Triplett.

Burns, Hugh. Hugh Burns, identified with much of the railroad construction in Texas, was born in 1846 in County Roscommon, Ireland. He came to the United States about 1850 with his parents, settling first at Nashville, Tennessee, then later at Madison, Illinois. Burns, along with his four brothers, was educated at the Christian Brothers College in St. Louis, but, seeking adventure, he left school when he was sixteen to drive a freight wagon of sugar from Ft. Smith, Kansas, to Denver, Colorado. He spent some time mining, but he lost his stake.

His first railroad construction work was in Missouri on the Ft. Scott and Gulf Railroad. Coming to Texas in the early 1870's, Burns went into partnership with a railroad builder, a Mr. Peters, who was working on the Southern Pacific in West Texas. Later he went into the railroad construction business for himself and accepted a contract with the Houston and Texas Central in East Texas. During the early 1880's, Burns formed a partnership with George W. Burkett qv and P. Murphy, and they contracted to build the International and Great Northern from Laredo to Palestine. While construction was progressing in Williamson County, Burns

bought a 3,000-acre ranch on the San Gabriel River seven miles from Taylor and eventually made his home there. Several other contracts followed; his last contract was for construction of a railway for the Jay Gould qv interests through the cotton lowlands of the Brazos River valley. Burns married Mary Clifford in 1881 in San Antonio. They lived in Taylor after Burns retired, but moved to San Antonio, where he died on March 11, 1911.

Mary Burns Mendel

*Burns, Rollie C.

*Burns, Waller T.

*Burns City, Texas.

*Burnside, Texas.

*Burnt House Creek.

*Burnt Oak Creek.

*Burr, Aaron (and Texas).

*Burr, Texas.

*Burrett Creek.

*Burro Creek.

*Burro Mountain.

*Burros Canyon.

*Burroughs, George H.

*Burroughs, James M.

*Burrow, Texas.

Burr's Ferry. Burr's Ferry was an old Sabine River crossing located ten miles northeast of Burkeville in Newton County. Both the ferry, discontinued in 1936 when a bridge was opened, and the town, which is in Louisiana, were named for Dr. Timothy Burr, a relative of Aaron Burr.qv Timothy Burr arrived from Mt. Vernon, Ohio, probably in about 1809 and chose a homesite near the mouth of Pearl Creek. However, the earliest record of Burr's land ownership was dated February 1, 1841, and on the boundary map the name of the ferry crossing was, in 1840, Hickman's Ferry. By 1849 the land at the ferry approach on the Texas side was owned by Dr. Burr's son, Bryant Burr, and was known as the Burr Plantation.

During the Civil War when the invasion of Texas by the Union forces in the spring of 1863 was threatened, breastworks were thrown up on the Louisiana side. Timber was cut on the Texas bank near the ferry so that Confederate artillery placed on the hills commanding the river would have an unimpeded view of the river crossing and an open field of fire. These breastworks are well preserved on the Louisiana side of the crossing.

Madeleine Martin

*Burr's Ferry, Browndell, and Chester Railroad.

*Burton, Isaac Watts.

*Burton, Texas.

*Burton Knob.

*Busby Branch.

*Bush Knob Creek.

*Bush Mountain.

*Bushdale, Texas.

*Bushland, Texas.

*Bushy Creek.

*Bustamante, Anastasio [or Anastacio].

*Bustamante, Texas.

*Buster, Texas.

*Bustillo y Zevallos, Juan Antonio (Bustillo y Cevallos).

*Butcherknife Hill.

*Butler, Anthony.

*Butler, George.

Butler, William G. William G. Butler, one of the earliest and most active trail drivers of South Texas, was born on June 14, 1831, in Scott County, Mississippi. In 1852 he moved to Karnes County, Texas, with his parents, Burnell and Sarah Ann (Ricks) Butler, and twelve brothers and sisters. In 1858 he married Adeline Burris, who bore him eight children.

During the Civil War, Butler volunteered for Confederate service and was mustered into the Escondido Rifles, a company of mounted riflemen raised in Karnes County in July, 1861. Later, as a member of Wilke's Cavalry, he was transferred to the Trans-Mississippi Department for service in Louisiana, Texas, and Arkansas.

After the war, like many other South Texans, Butler started ranching and trail driving "to connect the four-dollar cow with the forty-dollar market." He soon became one of the giants of the cattle industry in South Texas. His first string of cattle was driven to Abilene in the spring of 1868. For many years he and Major Seth Mabry of Austin were partners, and together they sent up the trail an estimated 100,000 head of cattle. In Karnes County, Butler owned nearly 75,000 acres of land, leased another 25,000, and stocked 10,000 head of cattle. Butler died in Karnes County on June 20, 1912, and was buried in the family cemetery at his home near Kenedy

BIBLIOGRAPHY: J. Marvin Hunter (ed.), *The Trail Drivers of Texas* (1925); J. Frank Dobie, *A Vaquero of the Brush Country* (1946).

Robert H. Thonhoff

*Butler, Texas. (Bastrop County.)

*Butler, Texas. (Freestone County.)

*Butler College. Butler College, Tyler, was still operating as a coeducational Negro junior college in 1948, when R. W. Puryear was president. With a new charter in 1951 and Claude Meals as president, the school made plans to become a four-year college with curricula leading to bachelor degrees; an emphasis of the educational program was on teacher preparation. Declining enrollment hindered the school's plans. A succession of new presidents included John H. Williams, Leon Fernandez Hardee, and Millard J. Smith. The physical plant in the 1960's consisted of fourteen buildings, three of which were faculty dwellings. Student enrollment declined from 203 in 1954 to 58 in 1969.

The college was closed prior to the fall term of 1972, never having attained an accredited four-year college status.

*Butler Creek.

*Butlerburg, Texas.

*Butte, George Charles. The family of George Charles Butte did not move directly from San Francisco to Dublin, Texas (as stated in Volume I); they came to Hunt County from California when Butte was nine years old. He was reared on a farm near Commerce, attended the public schools there before taking a degree at Austin College, and later moved to Dublin, Texas.

BIBLIOGRAPHY: Dallas *Morning News*, October 22, 1924.

W. Walworth Harrison

*Butterfield Overland Mail Route. The Butterfield or Southern Overland Mail began operating on September 15, 1858 (not 1808, as stated in Volume I) [some later printings of Volume I contain this correction], from San Francisco eastward and on September 16, 1858, from St. Louis westward. Stage service on the southern route terminated when an agreement was made in March, 1861, to modify the contract and move the route northward out of Texas.

BIBLIOGRAPHY: Waterman Ormsby, *The Butterfield Overland Mail* (1954).

*Butternut Creek.

*Button Prairie, Texas.

*Buzzard Mountain.

*Buzzard Peak.

*Buzzardwing Creek.

*Byars, Noah Turner.

*Byars' Institute.

*Byers, Texas.

*Byers Lake.

*Bynum, Texas.

*Byrd, Micajah.

*Byrd, William.

*Byrd, Texas.

*Byrds, Texas.

Byrne, Christopher Edward. Christopher Edward Byrne was born on April 21, 1867, in Byrnesville, Missouri, the son of Patrick and Rose Byrne. After attending the village school where his father taught, he earned an A.B. degree at the age of nineteen in 1885 from St. Mary's College, Kansas. After completing his studies at St. Mary's Seminary, Baltimore, on September 23, 1891, he was ordained into the Catholic priesthood in St. John's Church in St. Louis. He spent about twenty-eight years in parish work in St. Louis, Columbia, and Edina, Missouri, building churches and schools in each place. For many years he also did editorial work on the leading church publication in Missouri, *Church Progress*.

On November 27, 1918, he succeeded Bishop Nicholas A. Gallagher qv as fourth bishop of Galveston. During his tenure he ordained about 130 priests and received several hundred women into religious communities. In 1922 he sponsored a successful celebration of the Diamond Jubilee of the Galveston Cathedral and Diocese. Through his encouragement the church took a lead in planning the 1936 Texas Centennial qv program, beginning with the Field Mass at San Jacinto Battleground. He also endorsed and supported the collecting and preserving of the church's history by the Knights of Columbus, which resulted in the publication of the seven-volume history, *Our Catholic Heritage in Texas, 1519–1936,* by Carlos E. Castañeda,qv and the establishment of the Catholic Archives of Texas. During his administration the Catholic population of the Galveston diocese grew from about 70,000 to approximately 200,000. The number of schools increased from fifty-one in 1918 to more than one hundred in 1950.

Bishop Byrne was known to be an avid reader and an eloquent orator and was often the speaker at religious and civic ceremonies. He died on April 1, 1950.

Sister M. Claude Lane, O.P.

*Byrne, J. J. J. J. Byrne was killed by the forces of Apache chief Victorio qv (not Geronimo). [Some later printings of Volume I contain this correction.]

BIBLIOGRAPHY: Frank M. Temple, "Colonel E. B. Grierson's Victorio Campaign," *West Texas Historical Association Year Book,* XXXV (October, 1959).

*Byrne, James W.

*Byrom, John Smith Davenport.

*Byspot, Texas.

C

Caai Indians. The Caai Indians are known from a single 1691 Spanish missionary report. The name occurs on a short list of tribes that lived an unspecified distance southwest of the Hasinai. The Caai may be the same as the Caisquetebana, reported in 1690 as living north of Matagorda Bay and between the Guadalupe and Colorado rivers, and also the Caiasban, named in documents (1687) of the La Salle Expedition qv as enemies of the Kadohadacho on the Red River. These identifications cannot be demonstrated. If the names all refer to the same group of Indians, a considerable north-south range is indicated. The affiliations of these groups remain unknown.

BIBLIOGRAPHY: H. E. Bolton (ed.), *Spanish Exploration in the Southwest, 1542–1706* (1916); P. Margry, *Découvertes et établissements des Français dans l'ouest et dans le sud de l'Amérique Septentrionale,* III (1879); J. R. Swanton, *Source Material on the History and Ethnology of the Caddo Indians* (1942).

T. N. Campbell

*Caballo Muerto Mountains.

Cabell, Charles Pearre. Charles Pearre Cabell, son of Ben E. and Sadie E. (Pearre) Cabell, and grandson of William Lewis Cabell,qv was born on October 11, 1903, in Dallas. He attended Oak Cliff High School there. A graduate of the United States Military Academy at West Point in 1925 and the Air Corps Flying School in San Antonio in 1931, he spent thirty-eight years in the U.S. Army and Air Force before his retirement as a four-star general in 1963. Cabell was married to Jacklyn Dehymel in 1934; they had two sons and a daughter.

During World War II he was a member of the advisory council for the U.S. Army Air Force headquarters in Washington, D.C., before being assigned as commander of the 45th Combat Wing of the Eighth Air Force in the European Theater of Operations. He was director of plans for the U.S. Strategic Air Forces from May until July, 1944, when he became director of operations and intelligence for the Mediterranean Allied Air Forces until May, 1945. Cabell attended the Yalta Conference in 1945 and the London Conference of the United Nations in January–February, 1946. He had been promoted to colonel in 1942 and to brigadier general in 1944. Following the war he was the U.S. air representative on the military staff committee of the United Nations in New York. In 1951 he was appointed director of the staff for the Joint Chiefs of Staff, working closely with the highest military officers, including chairman of the Joint Chiefs of Staff, General Omar Bradley. From 1953 until his retirement in 1963, General Cabell was deputy director of the Central Intelligence Agency. In 1965 he was appointed as a consultant to the National Aeronautics and Space Administration.qv While he devoted most of his life to the military service, he maintained close ties with his home state and Dallas; he was a member of the Philosophical Society of Texas.qv Charles Pearre Cabell died in Arlington, Virginia, on May 25, 1971; he was buried in Arlington National Cemetery.

BIBLIOGRAPHY: *Who's Who In America* (1960); The Philosophical Society of Texas, *Proceedings* (1970); Biographical File, Barker Texas History Center, University of Texas at Austin.

*Cabell, William Lewis. William Lewis Cabell was graduated from the United States Military Academy at West Point in 1850 (not 1820, as stated in Volume I).

*Cabell, Texas.

*Cabello, Domingo.

Cabellos Blancos Indians. The Cabellos Blancos Indians (Spanish for "white hairs") are known only from a Spanish document of 1693 which lists the Cabellos Blancos as one of fifty "nations" that lived north of the Rio Grande and "between Texas and New Mexico." This may be interpreted to mean the southern part of western Texas, since the document also mentions that the Apaches were at war with the groups named. Nothing further is known about the Cabellos Blancos.

BIBLIOGRAPHY: C. W. Hackett (ed.), *Historical Docu-*

ments Relating to New Mexico, Nueva Vizcaya, and Approaches Thereto, to 1773, II (1926).

T. N. Campbell

*Cabellos Colorados.

Cabet, Étienne. Étienne Cabet, a French utopian, was born January 1, 1788, in Dijon, France. He first studied medicine and then law, and in 1812 he received a doctorate in law from the university at Dijon. Turning to politics, he served for a time as attorney general in Corsica, then became a member of the French Chamber of Deputies. In 1833 he launched the reform and anti-government journal, *Le Populaire*. In 1834 his revolutionary writings forced him into exile to avoid a jail sentence, and he went to London, where he came under the influence of the Welsh socialist, Robert Owen. During his five-year stay in London, Cabet was married to Delphine Lesage, a native of Dijon; they had one daughter. He returned to Paris in 1839, where he published a four-volume work, *Historie Populaire de la Révolution Française de 1789 à 1830* . . . He also published a novel, *Voyage et Aventures de Lord William Carisdall en Icarie* (1839), a work which depicted a perfect communist society. The book was a tremendous success (400,000 copies circulated by 1847), and Cabet gained a large following of socialist adherents. When the French government refused his request to try the communist experiment in France, Cabet obtained a grant of several thousand acres of land in Texas from the Peters Real Estate Company of Cincinnati (*see* Peters Colony).

His followers elected Cabet "dictator" of the proposed Icarian colony for a period of ten years, and although Cabet remained at the outset in France, sixty-nine or seventy men left Le Havre for Texas on February 3, 1848 (a day afterwards celebrated annually by the Icarians). They landed in New Orleans in late March and by May were in Texas. They settled in southwest Denton County, near present Justin (*see* Icarian Colony in Volume I). The Peters Company had not provided contiguous tracts of land for the colonists, and a company-imposed deadline of July 1, 1848, which required the settlers to make improvements on their land by that time, prevented them from exercising options for the additional hoped-for million acres. Ill with malaria, nine members died; most of the survivors returned to New Orleans via Shreveport, where they were joined by an additional group of twenty-eight Icarian men. In New Orleans they were joined by ninety newly arrived men, women, and children. They wrote Cabet for advice; against the counsel of his friends, Cabet left France on December 13, 1848, accompanied by a group of women and children.

Having heard of a Mormon group's abandonment of the town of Nauvoo, in western Illinois, a delegation left New Orleans in late December, 1848, to investigate the property. They returned in mid-February, 1849, and their favorable reports convinced the newly arrived Cabet that Nauvoo was the place for the colony to be reestablished. Two hundred and eighty-one Icarians traveled up the Mississippi River and arrived at the vacated town on March 15, 1849.

The colony elected Cabet to serve for one year as president. All money and property were communally owned, although an emphasis was placed on marriage and the family. From the beginning the colony was torn by strife and factionalism. Cabet returned to France in May, 1851, to answer charges of swindling, in the name of his Icarian venture, brought against him by the French Second Republic. Vindicated, he returned to Nauvoo in 1852. In 1854 he became an American citizen. A lack of money, increasing immigration into the colony, the drain of supplying a newly established Icarian colony in Adams County, Iowa, and, finally, violent internal conflicts among the members lead to a breakup within the colony in the fall of 1856. Cabet, in the defeated minority group, left Nauvoo in late October along with 180 of his followers; they went to St. Louis, Missouri, where within a week, on November 8, 1856, Cabet died. He was buried in Riddle Cemetery (now Holy Ghost Cemetery). His followers, feeling that Cabet had been buried without proper ceremony, exhumed his body in January, 1857, held a proper funeral service, and buried him again in the same cemetery plot.

BIBLIOGRAPHY: Jean Pierre Beluze, *Aux Icariens* (1849); Sylvester A. Piotrowski, *Étienne Cabet and the Voyage en Icarie* (1935); Albert Shaw, *Icaria* (1884); Alice Felt Tyler, *Freedom's Ferment* (1944); Emile Vallet (H. Roger Grant, ed.), *An Icarian Communist in Nauvoo* (1971); *Dictionary of American Biography*, II (1958); Étienne Cabet (Thomas Teakle, trans.), "History and Constitution of the Icarian Community," *Iowa Journal of History and Politics*, 15 (1917); Henry King, "M. Etienne Cabet and the Icarians," *Lakeside Monthly*, 6 (1871); New York Tribune, July 9, 1852; *Sunday Morning Republican* (St. Louis), November 9, 1856.

*Cabeza, Texas.

*Cabeza Creek.

*Cabeza de Vaca, Alvar Núñez.

Cabeza Indians. Cabeza (Cavesa, Caveza) is a name (Spanish for "head") that seems to have been applied to several Indian groups in North America. In 1693 a group of Cabeza was reported north of the Rio Grande, presumably in Trans-Pecos Texas. It is not known if these were the same as the Cabeza who lived in southern Coahuila during the same period and who were frequently recorded as being closely associated with the Toboso.

BIBLIOGRAPHY: H. E. Bolton, "The Jumano Indians in Texas, 1650–1771," *Quarterly of the Texas State Historical Association*, XV (1911–1912); H. E. Bolton (ed.), *Spanish Exploration of the Southwest, 1542–1706* (1916); C. W. Hackett (ed.), *Historical Documents Relating to New Mexico, Nueva Vizcaya, and Approaches Thereto, to 1773*, II (1926); W. Jiménez Moreno, "Tribus e idiomas del Norte de México," *El Norte de México y el Sur de Estados Unidos* (1944).

T. N. Campbell

Cabia Indians. The Cabia Indians, reported but not located in a document of 1690, have been identified with the Kabaye of the La Salle Expedition qv records, but this has never been demonstrated. J. R.

Swanton listed the Cabia among his Coahuiltecan bands. Since only the name is known, the status of the Cabia remains in doubt. It is possible that Cabia is merely a variant of the name Cava.

BIBLIOGRAPHY: F. W. Hodge (ed.), *Handbook of American Indians*, II (1910); J. R. Swanton, *Linguistic Material from the Tribes of Southern Texas and Northeastern Mexico* (1940).

T. N. Campbell

*Cabildo.

Cabra Indians. A settlement known as Cabras was reported near Nuestra Señora del Espíritu Santo de Zuñiga Mission ᵠᵛ (vicinity of present Goliad) in 1785. It has been assumed that Cabra Indians lived there, and the Cabra have been linked with the Kiabaha of the La Salle Expedition ᵠᵛ about one hundred years earlier. No demonstration of identity has ever been presented.

BIBLIOGRAPHY: H. H. Bancroft, *History of the North Mexican States and Texas*, I (1886); F. W. Hodge (ed.), *Handbook of American Indians*, I (1907), II (1910).

T. N. Campbell

Cacalote Indians. Cacalote ("crow" or "raven") is a name that was applied by the Spanish to several Indian groups in North America. Two Cacalote groups of northern Mexico can be connected with the Texas area. One of these lived south of the Rio Grande in Nuevo León and Tamaulipas in the seventeenth and eighteenth centuries and may at times have crossed into Texas. This was probably a Coahuiltecan group. The other Cacalote group lived south of the Rio Grande near present Presidio, Texas, in the early eighteenth century but is said to have ranged north of the Rio Grande in the late seventeenth century. These western Cacalote have been identified as Concho Indians, but this identification is debatable. Both Cacalote groups disappeared in the late eighteenth century.

BIBLIOGRAPHY: C. W. Hackett (ed.), *Historical Documents Relating to New Mexico, Nueva Vizcaya, and Approaches Thereto, to 1773*, II (1926); W. Jiménez Moreno, "Tribus e idiomas del Norte de México," *El Norte de México y el Sur de Estados Unidos* (1944); J. C. Kelley, "Factors Involved in the Abandonment of Certain Peripheral Southwestern Settlements," *American Anthropologist*, LIV (1952) and "The Historic Indian Pueblos of La Junta de los Ríos," *New Mexico Historical Review*, XXVII–XXVIII (1952–1953); C. Sauer, *The Distribution of Aboriginal Tribes and Languages in Northwestern Mexico* (1934).

T. N. Campbell

*Cacaxtle Indians. This was one of the more important early Coahuiltecan bands of southern Texas. Between 1653 and 1663 the Cacaxtle (Casastle, Cataxtle) and their allies repeatedly attacked the Spanish frontier settlements of Coahuila and Nuevo León, and two Spanish military expeditions in 1663 and 1665 finally crossed the Rio Grande to administer punishment. In two decisive battles a total of two hundred Cacaxtle were killed and about the same number captured. The captives were sold into slavery for work in the mines of Chihuahua and Zacatecas, a common procedure in northern Mexico during the seventeenth century. The location of the Cacaxtle in southern Texas cannot be precisely determined, but the data available suggest that it was

somewhere on the southward bend of the Nueces River in present La Salle and McMullen counties. However, on a map prepared by W. Jiménez Moreno the Cacaxtle are shown as living along the lower Pecos River. It seems likely that the Cacaxtle originally ranged from the Nueces southward across the Rio Grande into what is now northwestern Tamaulipas and northern Nuevo León. This hypothetical range is in accord with reports of repeated raids on Spanish frontier settlements prior to 1663. If Spanish records are accurate, the two battles mentioned above destroyed Cacaxtle power, for little is heard of them afterward. The name of this group appears to be derived from a Coahuiltecan word, "kakaxtle," which refers to a special netted frame used for carrying loads on the back.

BIBLIOGRAPHY: V. Alessio Robles, *Coahuila y Texas en la Epoca Colonial* (1938); H. E. Bolton (ed.), *Spanish Exploration in the Southwest, 1542–1706* (1916); C. E. Castañeda, *Our Catholic Heritage in Texas, 1519–1936* (1936–1958); D. A. Cossio, *Historia de Nueva León* (1925); W. Jiménez Moreno, "Tribus e idiomas del Norte de México," *El Norte de México y el Sur de Estados Unidos* (1944); F. Ruecking, Jr., "The Economic System of the Coahuiltecan Indians of Southern Texas and Northeastern Mexico," *Texas Journal of Science*, V (1953); J. R. Swanton, *Linguistic Material from the Tribes of Southern Texas and Northeastern Mexico* (1940).

T. N. Campbell

Cachaé Indians. This was a Caddoan tribe of the southwestern or Hasinai division in eastern Texas that is known from a single Spanish document written near the close of the seventeenth century. H. E. Bolton thought that Cachaé and Cataye were variants of the same name and that they were early names for the people later known as Hainai. It is true that Cachaé and Hainai seem to have occupied the same area. J. R. Swanton followed Bolton's interpretations and also identified the Caxo with the Cachaé. This is all a matter of modern inference and opinion. Cachaé, Caxo, and Cataye are all listed as separate tribes in the same document without any indication that they are names for the same people, and no early Spanish authority ever said that these names were synonyms for Hainai.

BIBLIOGRAPHY: H. E. Bolton, "Native Tribes about the East Texas Missions," *Quarterly of the Texas State Historical Association*, XI (1907–1908); J. R. Swanton, *Source Material on the History and Ethnology of the Caddo Indians* (1942).

T. N. Campbell

*Cachopostale Indians. The Cachopostale (Cachapostate) Indians, who spoke a Coahuiltecan language, were mentioned in a few documents of the early eighteenth century. These indicate close association with the Pampopa on the Nueces and Frio rivers between present San Antonio and Eagle Pass. The Cachopostale may be the same as the Postito, who entered San José y San Miguel de Aguayo Mission,ᵠᵛ in San Antonio, and were associated with Pampopa there until at least 1785.

BIBLIOGRAPHY: J. A. Dabbs, "The Texas Missions in 1785," *Preliminary Studies of the Texas Catholic Historical Society*, III (1940); F. W. Hodge (ed.), *Handbook of American Indians*, I (1907); J. R. Swanton, *Linguistic*

Material from the Tribes of Southern Texas and Northeastern Mexico (1940).

T. N. Campbell

*Cacti.

*Cactus, Texas.

*Cactus Branch.

Caddell, Andrew. Andrew Caddell was born October 21, 1795, in Person County, North Carolina, the son of John Calvin and Mary (Jay) Caddell. He married Rhoda Doty in 1818 in Tuscaloosa County, Alabama, and they were the parents of eleven children. He and his family came to the Sabine District, Texas, in April, 1834. He received a title grant of one league and one labor of land from the San Augustine board of land commissioners in 1834. Part of the grant was located in San Augustine County and part of it in what is now Young County.

Andrew Caddell was a member of Captain William Kimbro's qv company at the battle of San Jacinto. He received a commission as captain and later commanded a company of volunteers from San Augustine County. He served in the army from March 15 to June 15, 1836. Shortly after the Texas Revolution he moved to Nacogdoches County, where he was tax assessor and collector from 1846 to 1854. He moved to Bell County near Belton in 1867 and settled on a farm. He died in Bell County on October 15, 1869, and was buried there. One of his sons, John C. Caddell, was the first county clerk of Bell County. Another son, William Jay Caddell, also fought in the Texas Army.

Helen Gomer Schluter

*Caddo, Texas. (Milam County.)

*Caddo, Texas. (Stephens County.)

*Caddo Creek.

*Caddo Fork of the Sabine River.

*Caddo Grove, Texas.

*Caddo Indians.

*Caddo Lake. Caddo Lake, extending into Harrison and Marion counties in Texas, is in the Cypress Creek Basin in Caddo Parish, Louisiana, twenty-nine miles northeast of Marshall, on Cypress Creek. The Caddo Lake project is owned by the United States government and operated by the United States Army Corps of Engineers, New Orleans District. Federal authorization was an act of June 25, 1910, giving four-foot navigation depth above the dam to Jefferson, Texas. The project was started in 1913 and completed in 1914. Caddo Lake has a capacity of 175,000 acre-feet and a surface area of 32,700 acres at elevation 168.5 feet above mean sea level. Of this total, 58,000 acre-feet of the capacity and 11,000 acres of the surface area are in Texas. The lake has been used for navigation from Mooringsport, Louisiana, to Jefferson, Texas. The drainage area in Texas to Caddo Lake is 2,639 square miles.

BIBLIOGRAPHY: Texas Water Commission, *Bulletin 6408* (1964).

Seth D. Breeding

*Caddo Mills, Texas.

*Caddo Peak.

*Caddo Peak, Texas.

*Cadena Creek.

*Cadiz, Texas.

*Caesar, Texas.

Cagaya Indians. This name occurs in a single Spanish missionary report of 1691, which lists eight tribes that lived some eighty leagues southwest of the Hasinai Indians of eastern Texas. The Jumano (Chuman) are named on this list. The Cagaya may be the same as the Caynaaya, named in another document of the same year, along with Jumano and Cibola, as having been seen hunting bison near the Guadalupe River east of San Antonio. If Cagaya and Caynaaya were the same, then the Cagaya can be identified as Indians of Trans-Pecos Texas, the designated home of the Caynaaya, Cibola, and Jumano.

BIBLIOGRAPHY: H. E. Bolton, "The Jumano Indians in Texas, 1650–1771," *Quarterly of the Texas State Historical Association*, XV (1911–1912); J. R. Swanton, *Source Material on the History and Ethnology of the Caddo Indians* (1942).

T. N. Campbell

Caguate Indians. The Caguate (Caguase, Caguaze) Indians lived along the Rio Grande Valley below El Paso in the late sixteenth century. Some writers regard the Caguate as a Jumano band; others suggest that Caguate was probably an early name for the Suma, who occupied that area in the seventeenth and eighteenth centuries. The status of the Caguate remains in doubt.

BIBLIOGRAPHY: G. P. Hammond and A. Rey, *Expedition into New Mexico Made by Antonio de Espejo, 1582–1583, as Revealed in the Journal of Diego Pérez de Luxán, a Member of the Party* (1929); J. C. Kelley, "Factors Involved in the Abandonment of Certain Peripheral Southwestern Settlements," *American Anthropologist*, LIV (1952); C. Sauer, *The Distribution of Aboriginal Tribes and Languages in Northwestern Mexico* (1934).

T. N. Campbell

Caiasban Indians. The Caiasban Indians are known only from the 1687 records of the La Salle Expedition,qv which merely list these Indians as enemies of the Kadohadacho on the Red River. They may be the same as the Caai, named in a 1691 Spanish missionary report as one of the tribes that lived southwest of the Hasinai, and also the Caisquetebana, who in 1690 lived north of Matagorda Bay between the Guadalupe and Colorado rivers. These identifications cannot be demonstrated. If the names all refer to the same group of Indians, then a considerable north-south range is indicated. The affiliations of the three groups remain unknown.

BIBLIOGRAPHY: H. E. Bolton (ed.), *Spanish Exploration in the Southwest, 1542–1706* (1916); P. Margry, *Découvertes et établissements des Français dans l'ouest et dans le sud de l'Amérique Septentrionale*, III (1879); J. R. Swanton, *Source Material on the History and Ethnology of the Caddo Indians* (1942).

T. N. Campbell

*Caicache Indians. A few eighteenth-century maps show the Caicache (Kaikache) Indians on the

Texas coast between the Nueces River and the Rio Grande. The primary sources used by the cartographers have not been identified. Caicache may be a variant of either Aguichacha or Cacaxtle. In the seventeenth century the Aguichacha lived between Monterrey and Cerralvo (Nuevo León) and the Cacaxtle lived farther inland in southern Texas.

BIBLIOGRAPHY: W. Bollaert, "Observations on the Indian Tribes in Texas," *Journal of the Ethnological Society of London*, II (1850); F. W. Hodge (ed.), *Handbook of American Indians*, I (1907).

T. N. Campbell

*Caiman Creek.

Caimane Indians. The Caimane Indians are known from a Spanish document of 1683 which does not clearly identify their area, although it seems to have been east of the Pecos River. This name bears some similarity to Camama, the name of a band, presumably Coahuiltecan, known only from eighteenth-century records pertaining to San José y San Miguel de Aguayo Mission qv at San Antonio. As yet the two groups cannot otherwise be linked.

BIBLIOGRAPHY: C. W. Hackett (ed.), *Pichardo's Treatise on the Limits of Louisiana and Texas*, I (1931).

T. N. Campbell

*Cain City, Texas.

*Cairo Springs, Texas.

Caisquetebana Indians. The Caisquetebana Indians are known only from records of Alonso de León's qv various expeditions to the Texas coast in search of La Salle's Fort St. Louis.qv In 1690 De León visited a small settlement of these Indians north of Matagorda Bay and between the Guadalupe and Colorado rivers. The name suggests the possibility of linkage with the Caai, reported in 1691 as living southwest of the Hasinai, and also the Caiasban, named in the 1687 documents of the La Salle Expedition qv as enemies of the Kadohadacho on the Red River. These identifications cannot be demonstrated. If the names all refer to the same group of Indians, then a considerable north-south range is indicated. The affiliations of these groups remain unknown.

BIBLIOGRAPHY: H. E. Bolton (ed.), *Spanish Exploration in the Southwest, 1542–1706* (1916); P. Margry, *Découvertes et établissements des Français dans l'ouest et dans le sud de l'Amérique Septentrionale*, III (1879); J. R. Swanton, *Source Material on the History and Ethnology of the Caddo Indians* (1942).

T. N. Campbell

Cal Farley's Boys Ranch. Cal Farley's Boys Ranch was founded in 1939 by Cal Farley,qv a former Amarillo businessman and noted athlete, on the site of Old Tascosa.qv The original 120 acres were given by Julian Bivins, prominent Panhandle rancher. The ranch opened with headquarters in the Old Tascosa courthouse, built in 1872. The courthouse was also used as a home until 1963.

By 1966 over fourteen hundred acres had been added to the ranch, which cared for 346 formerly homeless boys between the ages of four and eighteen. Coming from thirty-seven states, the boys lived in eleven dormitories, nine of which housed thirty-six boys and two staff families, and two with ten boys from four to eight years old. In addition to

living facilities, there were sixteen other buildings for educational, sports, and vocational training. In addition to other sports, since 1944 the boys have participated in the annual Boys Ranch Rodeo.

By 1973 twenty-five hundred boys from every state and several foreign countries had been educated, trained, and cared for without cost to any governmental, church, or civic agency. The ranch is supported solely by contributions from persons interested in helping boys too young to help themselves.

Louie Hendricks

*Calabras, Isla de.

*Calahan, Texas.

*Calahorra y Saenz, Joseph Francisco.

*Calallen, Texas. Calallen, in Nueces County, had been annexed by Corpus Christi by 1970.

*Calamity Creek.

*Calaveras, Texas.

*Calaveras Creek.

*Calder, Robert James.

Caldwell, Colbert. [This title was incorrectly listed in Volume I as Coldwell, Colbert.] Colbert Caldwell was born in Bedford County, Tennessee, on May 16, 1822. After engaging in the Santa Fe trade between 1840 and 1845, he returned to Tennessee, studied law, and was admitted to the Bar at Shelbyville in 1846. He established his practice in Madison, Arkansas, and represented that district in the state legislature before he moved to Navasota, Texas, in August, 1858. On October 18, 1867, he was made associate justice in the Texas Supreme Court and held that position until he was removed by the commander of the military district of Texas on February 21, 1870. He also served as a member of the Constitutional Convention of 1868–1869,qv in which he was a leader of the Moderate Republicans and a nominee for president of the body. In 1876 Caldwell was judge of the Seventh Judicial District. He later served as United States collector of customs at El Paso.

Caldwell and his wife, the former Martha Julia Michie, were the parents of eight children. Caldwell died in Fresno, California, on April 18, 1892.

BIBLIOGRAPHY: H. L. Bentley and Thomas Pilgrim, *Texas Legal Directory for 1876–1877* (1877); J. H. Davenport, *History of the Supreme Court of Texas* (1917); Dallas *Herald*, March 28, June 12, July 11, 1868.

*Caldwell, John.

*Caldwell, Mathew.

*Caldwell, Pinckney Coatsworth. [This title was incorrectly listed in Volume I as Caldwell, Pinkney.] According to family records his full name was Pinckney Coatsworth Caldwell, and he was born on August 21, 1802 (not 1795, as stated in Volume I). [Some later printings of Volume I show the correct year, 1802, but continue to misspell the name.]

*Caldwell, Texas. Caldwell, the seat of Burleson County, had eighty-six businesses in 1970. The city's location at the intersection of State Highways 21 and 36 and at a railway division point enhance its importance. Several manufacturing plants are located in Caldwell; most of the products are related to agriculture, the area's chief source of income. In addition, a large aluminum ladder plant and a wood-preserving plant have been built in the town, and a municipal airport was completed by 1967. The population was 2,204 in 1960 and 2,308 in 1970.

*Caldwell County. Caldwell County has a dual-based economy. Between 1922 and 1973 over 227,-000,000 barrels of oil were produced, and recently the expanding industry has renewed drilling activity around Luling. Diversified agriculture includes certified planting seed, watermelons, livestock, poultry, and cotton. By 1964 two thousand acres had been irrigated. The 1960 population of 17,222 increased to 21,178 by 1970.

*Caledonia, Texas.

*Calf Creek.

*Calf Creek, Texas.

*Calgary, Texas.

*Calhoun, James Henry.

*Calhoun, John William.

*Calhoun, Texas. (Calhoun County.)

*Calhoun, Texas. (Colorado County.)

*Calhoun College.

*Calhoun County. Calhoun County, which gained 364 square miles of submerged lands from the decision in the 1953 Tidelands controversy,qv derives much of its income from the sea. The tourist industry makes use of the world's longest fishing pier and five hundred miles of coastline for fishing, duck hunting, and swimming. Commercial fishing and processing of seafoods are equally important. The Matagorda Ship Channel, with a turning basin completed in 1965, added to the facilities already offered by the Victoria Barge Canal and the Gulf Intracoastal Waterway.qv The production of oil (over seventy million barrels between 1935 and 1973), chemicals, and metal items is important in the overall economy. Agriculture is diversified, including cattle, cotton, rice, grain sorghums, and truck crops. About six thousand acres were irrigated in 1964. The 1960 population of 16,592 increased to 17,831 by 1970.

*California Column.

*California Creek.

*California Mountain.

*Calina, Texas.

*Call, Texas.

*Call Field.

*Call Junction, Texas.

*Callaghan Ranch. The Callaghan Ranch was operated in the 1960's by the Finley family. Joe B. Finley was general manager from 1923 through 1947. On June 12 of the following year, the Callaghan Ranch was partially liquidated, and original stockholders retired from the company. Acreage at

that time was reduced to 131,000 acres owned and 46,000 acres leased.

Hal R. Taylor

*Callahan, James Hughes.

*Callahan, Texas. (DeWitt County.)

*Callahan, Texas. (Webb County.)

Callahan City, Texas. Callahan City, Callahan County, was organized in 1877 at the same time as the county, but lost the county seat to Belle Plain the same year and ceased to exist soon thereafter.

Weldon Hart

*Callahan County. Callahan County has little industry, deriving its income largely from agriculture and oil. Ranching, predominantly beef cattle, sheep, and goats, provides the bulk of the farm income, but many acres are planted in various crops, including wheat, grain sorghums, cotton, peanuts, and oats. The oil yield from 1923 to 1973 was 60,648,860 barrels. The towns of Baird and Clyde reported new lakes built in their areas by 1966 and 1968, respectively. Tourist attractions are Camp Pecanqv (a Texas Ranger qv station abandoned in 1864), a livestock show, and a spring rodeo. The county population was 7,929 in 1960 and 8,205 in 1970.

*Callahan Divide.

*Callahan Expedition.

Callaway, Francis Oscar. Francis Oscar Callaway was born in Harmony Hill, Rusk County, Texas, on October 2, 1872. Four years later he moved with his parents, Christopher Columbus (Bud) and Louise Caroline (Atwood) Callaway, to Mercers Gap in Comanche County. There he entered Comanche High School, from which he was graduated in 1894. After teaching school for three years, he entered the University of Texas law school, received a degree in 1900, and began the practice of law. He was prosecuting attorney of Comanche County in 1900–1902. Serving three terms, he was elected to the United States Congress from the Twelfth District of Texas in 1910, 1912, and 1914.

Throughout his legislative career Callaway sharply questioned every federal expenditure. In 1912–1913 he served on the Committee on Expenditures in the Treasury Department and, in 1914–1915, on the Committee on Expenditures in the Department of the Interior. Until late 1915, when he was moved up to the important Naval Affairs Committee, he had not attracted a great deal of attention except for his vigorous opposition to huge rivers and harbors appropriations. It was hard for him to see merit in making the Texas Trinity and Brazos rivers navigable. Of these two rivers he once remarked that he had often waded across them, sometimes had spat across them, but never had to swim them.

He gained national attention in 1916 by his vigorous opposition to the naval appropriation bill. He thought the huge preparedness campaign unnecessary and felt that it favored the munition makers and others who would derive excessive profit from it. He also believed that an army of civilians could repel any invasion. So strong were his words against some congressmen that parts of his speech were expunged from the *Congressional Record*. He believed that submarines had made battleships obsolete and that international law would have to be rewritten to cover the situation.

He was defeated for renomination in 1916 by United States attorney James C. Wilson, largely on the issue of preparedness. His hometown newspaper, the Comanche *Chief*, at the time of his defeat said of Oscar Callaway, "One thing marks this man above his fellows and that is his absolute lack of fear of criticism. He has his convictions and lives up to them." In 1917 Callaway returned to Comanche, where he practiced law and engaged in farming and stock-raising until his death on January 31, 1947. He was buried in Oakwood Cemetery in Comanche. He was survived by his widow, the former Stella Couch, whom he had married on December 29, 1904. They had no children.

BIBLIOGRAPHY: *Biographical Directory of the American Congress, 1774–1961* (1961); Comanche *Chief*, March 24, July 28, 1916; Comanche *Vanguard*, February 18, July 28, 1915; Fort Worth *Star-Telegram*, November 30, 1915, February 8, May 19, July 16, September 11, 1916; *Who's Who In America* (1930).

Thomas L. Miller

*Callaway, Morgan, Jr.

Callender, William Larrabee. William Larrabee Callender, with his father and mother, Nathaniel and Olive Callender, moved from Shippensburg, Pennsylvania, where he was born in 1815, to several locations in New York and to the Ohio frontier. Callender learned the shoemaker's trade from his father and as a youth of thirteen read for college preparation while employed as a printer. He was graduated from Allegheny College in 1839 and after studying law in Frankfort, Kentucky, under James Harlan, was admitted to the Bar in 1848. Callender edited the Frankfort *Commonwealth* from 1850 to 1856, when he relocated in Victoria, Texas. He married Ann Matilda Kellogg in 1842, Lucy W. Roper in 1850, Alice F. Kibbe in 1862, and Sallie R. Sangster in 1869, having children with each marriage.

Though his views were decidedly Unionist, Callender was a much respected citizen of Victoria, where he conducted the Victoria Male Academy.qv He served as justice of the peace, district clerk, and attorney, while pursuing his avocation of reflecting on current and historical events through poetry and prose, much of which remains among the Callender manuscripts.

The firm of Glass and Callender conducted the bulk of legal business in Victoria County for two decades following the Civil War. For thirty years Callender led the Methodist movement in the area. At the time of his death in 1895, he was given generous recognition by the Texas Supreme Court. The Callender House of Victoria, cited by the United States Department of the Interior and the state of Texas, bears his name. Callender was buried in Evergreen Cemetery, Victoria.

BIBLIOGRAPHY: Callender Papers (MS., Callender House, Victoria); *Texas Bar Journal* (January, 1963); Victor M. Rose, *Some Historical Facts in Regard to the Settlement of Victoria, Texas* (1883).

Robert W. Shook

*Callett Creek.

*Callihan, Mosis A.

*Callihan, Texas.

*Callis, Texas.

*Callisburg, Texas.

*Calohan, W. Lod.

*Calvert, Texas. Calvert, in Robertson County, had a population of 2,073 in 1960 and 2,072 in 1970.

*Calvert, Waco, and Brazos Valley Railroad Company.

*Calvin, Texas. (Bastrop County.)

*Calvin, Texas. (Red River County.)

*Calvit, Alexander.

*Calzones Colorados.

Camai Indians. This name appears only in records of San Antonio de Valero Mission qv at San Antonio. It may refer to remnants of the Camaiguara, a Coahuiltecan band that lived near Cadereyta, Nuevo León, at the close of the seventeenth century, but documentary proof of this has not been found. J. R. Swanton listed the Camai as a Coahuiltecan band without presenting any evidence in support of this identification.

BIBLIOGRAPHY: G. García (ed.), *Documentos inéditos ó muy raros para la historia de México*, XXV (1909); F. W. Hodge (ed.), *Handbook of American Indians*, II (1910); J. R. Swanton, *Linguistic Material from the Tribes of Southern Texas and Northeastern Mexico* (1940).

T. N. Campbell

Camama Indians. The Camama Indians are known only from documents pertaining to San José y San Miguel de Aguayo Mission qv of San Antonio. They seem to have been among the Coahuiltecan bands for whom the mission was founded in 1720. Their aboriginal range was never recorded, but it was probably somewhere to the west or southwest of San Antonio.

BIBLIOGRAPHY: C. W. Hackett (ed.), *Pichardo's Treatise on the Limits of Louisiana and Texas*, I (1931); M. K. Kress (trans.), "Diary of a Visit of Inspection of the Texas Missions Made by Fray Gaspar José de Solís in the Year 1767–68," *Southwestern Historical Quarterly*, XXXV (1931–1932).

T. N. Campbell

*Camargo, Diego de (Antonio).

Camargo, Mexico. Camargo, Mexico, was founded on the south side of the San Juan River on March 5, 1749, by José de Escandón,qv governor of the colony of Nuevo Santander. At this time, Blas María de la Garza Falcón, a prominent rancher, and forty families from Nuevo León already occupied the general area of the San Juan Valley. Camargo was one of five such towns founded by Escandón and local cattle owners from 1749 to 1753 in the Trans-Nueces area.

Settlers who came to Camargo in 1749 brought 13,000 sheep to begin ranching; the following year they had increased their stock to 30,000 and their population to 700, thus becoming the largest of Escandón's settlements. In addition to the Spaniards, the town included 241 Indians from the six tribes of Tareguanos, Pajaritos, Paysanos, Venados, Cueroquemados, and Guajolotes living inside the walls of the Mission San Agustín de Laredo south of the town. Prominent ranchers, including Manuel and Joseph Hinojosa, Don Nicolás de los Santos Coy, and Captain Blas María de la Garza Falcón, braved two years of drouth, as well as floods and malaria, to continue ranching.

In 1751 Camargo remained the largest of the Rio Grande colonies, with ninety-six families numbering 637 persons. Although agriculture afforded the settlers a moderate income, their main subsistence came from cattle and sheep at Camargo. In 1753 Escandón used nineteen families to help found the *lugar* of Mier along the Rio Grande.

Camargo remained the largest goat and sheep ranching site of the Rio Grande settlements and in 1757 seventeen ranches contained 8,000 horses and mules, 2,600 cattle, and 72,000 sheep and goats. By this year constant migration into Camargo began to create the problem of inadequate land for new settlers and in 1767 a royal commission was appointed to survey the total land contained in the colony of Nuevo Santander. Camargo received 118 *porciones* as a result of this survey, the largest number granted to any of the settlements surveyed.

By 1800 Nuevo Santander had a population of 15,000, a large part of which resided in Camargo. After *de facto* Texas independence, Camargo joined the effort in 1839–1840 of the northern provinces supported by Anglo Americans to separate from Mexico and establish a Republic of the Rio Grande.qv

During the late 1800's, disputes arose over the *porciones* granted to Camargo, but in a series of rulings from 1889 to 1908 the Supreme Court validated all of the original *porciones* of the jurisdiction of Camargo. The present Texas town of Rio Grande City, however, is located on *porciones* eighty and eighty-one of the original jurisdiction of Camargo.

In 1967, along with other Mexican border towns, Camargo was badly damaged by the floodwaters of Hurricane Beulah.

BIBLIOGRAPHY: F. J. Scott, *Historical Heritage of the Lower Rio Grande* (1966); L. F. Hill, *José de Escandón and the Founding of Nuevo Santander* (1926); H. E. Bolton, *Texas in the Middle Eighteenth Century* (1915); *Texas Almanac* (1949); *Time* (October 6, 1967).

*Camberon Creek.

Cambridge, Texas. Cambridge was one of the principal towns in Clay County in 1878, but when Henrietta was later chosen as the county seat, Cambridge declined.

BIBLIOGRAPHY: *Texas Almanac* (1936).

*Camden, Texas.

*Camels Hump.

*Camels in Texas.

*Cameron, Ewen.

*Cameron, John.

*Cameron, William.

*Cameron, William Waldo.

*Cameron, Texas. (DeWitt County.)

*Cameron, Texas. (Milam County.) Cameron, the county seat, is a commercial center for an agricultural area. Among the five major industries is a door manufacturing plant, which has bolstered the town's economy since the plant's establishment in 1955. Cameron also has facilities for ginning, compressing, and warehousing cotton. In 1967 the town reported 139 businesses, two hospitals, seventeen churches, two banks, a newspaper, and a radio station. A new $85,000 library building and a new airfield runway were completed by 1966. The 1960 population was 5,640; the population in 1970 was 5,546.

*Cameron County. Cameron County, the southernmost Texas county, is one of the state's most productive agricultural areas. Under irrigation it produces citrus fruits, vegetables, and cotton. Many populous towns had developed by 1964, and tourism expanded because of the area's proximity to the Mexican border and the Gulf of Mexico. Other attractions include Padre Island,qv where recreational facilities have increased considerably, and the Laguna-Atascosa National Wildlife Refuge.qv The Loma Alta Reservoir was completed in 1962. The county gained 311 square miles of submerged land by the decision in the Tidelands controversy.qv Brownsville remains the county seat, and the 1960 census reported the county population as 151,098. The population in 1970 was 140,368. Charles Stillman,qv (not Charles Stillwell, as noted in Volume I) was an early promoter of the city of Brownsville. *See also* Brownsville-Harlingen-San Benito Standard Metropolitan Statistical Area.

*Camey Spur.

*Camilla, Texas.

*Camino Real. *See* Old San Antonio Road.

*Camole Indians.

*Camp, John Lafayette.

*Camp, John Lafayette, Jr.

*Camp Allison, Texas.

*Camp Austin.

*Camp Barkeley.

*Camp Belknap.

*Camp Ben McCulloch.

*Camp Blake.

*Camp Bowie. Troops stationed at Camp Bowie, by October, 1942, included men from the Third Army under General Walter Krueger qv (not Krueger, as shown in Volume I).

*Camp Branch.

*Camp Breckenridge.

*Camp Bullis.

*Camp Cabell.

*Camp Casa Blanca. *See* Camp Merrill.

*Camp Cazneau. Camp Cazneau, in Williamson County, was possibly named for William Leslie Cazneau qv by George W. Bonnell qv when he led the Travis Guards and Rifles qv on brief expeditions from Austin in search of Comanches during May and June, 1840. Cazneau was commissary general of the Republic of Texas when the Santa Fe Expedition qv camped at Camp Cazneau on what is generally considered to be the setting out point of the expedition. See also Kenney's Fort.

BIBLIOGRAPHY: H. Bailey Carroll, *The Texan Santa Fe Trail* (1951); Gerald S. Pierce, *Texas Under Arms* (1969).

Camp Charlotte. Camp Charlotte, Irion County, was on the Middle Concho River below the mouth of Kiowa Creek. The site, forty-five miles west of San Angelo and ten miles from the mail station called Head of the Concho, was at the junction of the Butterfield Overland qv and El Paso mail roads. The camp was a stockade with outside dimensions of 190 feet by 115 feet. The company stable, measuring 75 feet by 150 feet, was inside the stockade, while officers' quarters and the guard house were outside the east main gate. A stage station was built, and a civilian settlement arose around the camp. Later the camp was moved one mile east.

Parties of Indians were seen driving off livestock in 1874, but the troops were powerless to intervene as they were only infantry. A post office existed at Camp Charlotte from 1885 to 1899. The foundation and crumbling walls of the stage station are located near the headquarters of the former Sawyer Cattle Company Ranch (later the Rocker b Ranch), which was given to the Scottish Rite Hospital in Dallas by the owner, former United States Senator William A. Blakley in the early 1960's. A marker on the adjoining Cal Sugg Ranch designates the site of Camp Charlotte.

Grover C. Ramsey

Camp Clark. Camp Clark, situated in Guadalupe County on the south side of the San Marcos River, about seven miles from San Marcos, was one of the instruction camps founded by Governor Edward Clark qv in 1861. The 4th Texas Infantry Regiment was mobilized there. Several companies were organized at Camp Clark, where the men were trained for several months before going to active duty in the Civil War. The 4th Texas became part of Hood's Texas Brigade.qv

In 1862 Camp Clark served as a training camp for Colonel Peter C. Woods' qv 36th Texas Cavalry Regiment, which was composed mostly of Hays County men. Its officers were Woods, Major W. O. Hutchinson, and Captains James G. Storey, J. L. Holes, R. Blair, L. C. Schrum, J. K. Stevens, John Crook, and Eugene Millet. The regiment, called the 32nd Texas Cavalry by its members, served in the Red River campaign qv of 1864.

In 1966 a large cotton farm was on the site, and no signs of a camp remained.

BIBLIOGRAPHY: Dudley R. Dobie, A Brief History of Hays County and San Marcos, Texas (M.A. thesis, University of Texas, 1932).

Tula Townsend Wyatt

*Camp Collier.

*Camp Colorado.

*Camp Cooper.

*Camp Corpus Christi.

*Camp County. Camp County had a 1960 population of 7,849, which increased to a count of 8,005 by 1970. Lake O' the Pines (completed in 1959), the numerous small lakes within the county, an annual golf tournament, rodeos, and a peach festival provide recreation. Besides peaches, Camp County produces sweet potatoes, nursery products, and some commercial timber. Poultry and dairy and beef cattle contribute substantially to the farm income.

*Camp Creek.

Camp Creek Lake. Camp Creek Lake is in the Brazos River Basin in Robertson County, thirteen miles east of Franklin on Camp Creek, a tributary of the Navasota River, which is tributary to the Brazos River. The project is owned by the Camp Creek Water Company with offices in Bryan and operated for recreational uses. The project was started in August, 1948, and was completed on January 3, 1949, with deliberate impoundment beginning in November, 1948. The lake has a capacity of 8,550 acre-feet and a surface area of 750 acres at elevation 310 feet above mean sea level. The drainage area above the dam is forty square miles.

BIBLIOGRAPHY: Texas Water Commission, *Bulletin 6408* (1964).

Seth D. Breeding

*Camp Cureton.

*Camp Davis.

*Camp Dix.

*Camp Drum.

*Camp Eagle Pass.

*Camp Elizabeth.

*Camp Fannin.

*Camp Ford.

Camp Grierson. Camp Grierson, Reagan County, was eight miles south-southwest of Best. Because the camp was built near a spring of water at the head of a prong of Live Oak Creek, the road from Fort Concho to Fort Stockton qqv was routed through it. The camp guarded the Chidester Stage Line, and army details were posted there from 1878 to 1880. A large stone building, a corral, stables, and a guard house were built by the army. In 1963 remains of the camp included water pipes near the spring, walls two or three feet high, and marks of wagon wheels on the arroyo walls.

Grover C. Ramsey

*Camp Groce.

*Camp Harney.

*Camp Hatch. See Fort Concho.

Camp Holland. Camp Holland, located in Viejo Pass, twelve miles west of Valentine, Texas, was built in 1918 to protect the population from Mexican bandits. The camp was seldom occupied by troops. Instead it was used as a base for pack trains which supplied troops along the Rio Grande. Declared surplus in 1921, Camp Holland was sold at auction to C. O. Finley, the former owner.

BIBLIOGRAPHY: Kim Thornsburg, "Camp Holland," *Junior Historian*, XXVIII (December, 1967).

Kim Thornsburg

*Camp Hood. *See* Fort Hood.

*Camp Houston. *See* Fort Houston.

*Camp Howze.

*Camp Hudson.

*Camp Hulen.

*Camp Independence.

*Camp Ives.

*Camp Joseph E. Johnston.

*Camp Kenny.

*Camp Lake Slough.

*Camp Liendo.

*Camp Llano.

*Camp Logan.

*Camp Mabry. Camp Mabry, in northwestern Austin, was headquarters for the Texas National Guard qv (Army) and the Texas Air National Guard qv in 1970. The office of the adjutant general of Texas and his staff was located there, as were the Texas National Guard State Officer Candidate School, the Texas National Guard Armory Board, the United States property and fiscal officer, the senior army advisor, and the Texas State Guard, qv which takes over the responsibilities of the National Guard whenever it is mobilized for federal duty. Headquarters of the 36th (Texas) Division qv and the 36th Division Museum were at Camp Mabry, along with units of the 36th Infantry Brigade (Separate) and the 49th Armored Division. Also, one of the state's combined support maintenance shops was there.

Officer candidates and members of the twenty-seven Austin National Guard units participate in training demonstrations and testing of military equipment on the maneuver area of the post. The Officer Candidate School presents a training program paralleling exactly that administered by the Infantry School at Fort Benning, Georgia. The school, officially accredited on May 24, 1957, has graduated an annual average of 110 young men.

Parts of the original Camp Mabry grounds became the United States Army Reserve Armory and Camp Hubbard, a division of the Texas Highway Department.qv Modern equipment similar to that currently in use by the Army and the Air National Guard is displayed on the grounds near the entrance to Camp Mabry.

BIBLIOGRAPHY: Files of the Office of Adjutant General of Texas.

Albert E. Binotti

*Camp MacArthur.

*Camp McMillan.

*Camp Marfa. *See* Fort D. A. Russell.

*Camp Maxey.

Camp Melbourne. *See* Camp Melvin, Texas.

Camp Melvin, Texas. Camp Melvin, in Crockett County, was on the left bank of the Pecos River two miles west of the present Iraan-Rankin Road. Juan Domínguez de Mendoza,qv a Spanish explorer who camped at the site on May 22, 1684, called it San Pantaleón. Henry Connelley crossed there returning to Chihuahua from a trading trip through Texas in 1840. In 1868 the Fort Stockton qv commander was ordered to find a shorter route to the Concho River than the one by Horsehead Crossing.qv He used the route of Mendoza and Connelley.

Camp Melvin post office was opened on December 11, 1868, and was discontinued on September 28, 1870. Stage coaches often used the Camp Melvin crossing. The site lost its identity through a multiplicity of names, totaling twenty-four from 1684 to 1926. Those names were San Pantaleón, Connelley's Crossing, Camp Melbourne, Fennelly's Crossing, Pecos Crossing, Camp Melvin, Camp Milvin, Pecos River Station, Mail Station, Mail Station Bridge, Pecos Mail Station, Melvin Station, Melvin Mail Station, Ficklin, Crossing of the Pecos Station, Crossing of the Pecos, Pecos Crossing Bridge, Pecos Bridge, Pecos Stage Station, Pecos Station, Pontoon Bridge Crossing, Pontoon Crossing, Mail Station at Pecos, and Pontoon Bridge. Pontoon Bridge, the latest name used for the site, was last found on maps in 1926. Ruins are extensive.

Grover C. Ramsey

*Camp Merrill.

*Camp Montel.

*Camp Mystic.

*Camp Normoyle.

*Camp Nowlin.

*Camp Nueces.

*Camp Pecan.

*Camp Rabb.

*Camp Radziminski.

*Camp Rice. *See* Fort Hancock.

*Camp Ruby, Texas.

*Camp Sabinal.

*Camp Salmon.

*Camp San Elizario.

Camp San Felipe. Camp San Felipe was established in 1857 on San Felipe Creek at present Del Rio. The camp was considered an outpost of Fort Clark qv until 1876, when it was made a permanent post with Company E, 10th United States Cavalry stationed there. Lieutenant J. M. Kelley was the commanding officer. The installation remained in active use until 1896, when the government ordered it dismantled. All movable and usable parts were sold at auction; the medical and hospital supplies were sent to Fort Clark; and the reservation was returned to the original grantee, the Agricultural, Manufacturing, and Irrigation Company of Del Rio.

Axcie Seale

*Camp San Saba.

*Camp San Saba, Texas.

*Camp Seale, Texas.

*Camp Springs, Texas.

*Camp Stanley.

Camp Sweeney. *See* Southwestern Diabetic Foundation.

*Camp Swift.

*Camp Travis.

*Camp Van Camp.

*Camp Verde (1).

*Camp Verde (2).

*Camp Verde, Texas.

*Camp Wallace.

*Camp Waul.

*Camp Wichita.

*Camp Wolters. *See also* Fort Wolters.

*Camp Wood.

*Camp Wood, Texas.

*Camp Wood Creek.

*Camp Worth. *See* Fort Worth.

*Camp Worth, Texas.

Campbell, Charles A. R. Charles A. R. Campbell was born in 1865 in San Antonio. He acquired his early education there, received a medical degree from Tulane University, and returned to San Antonio, where he practiced many years. He was president of the San Antonio Academy of Medicine at one time.

Campbell early became interested in the extermination of fever-carrying mosquitoes. Discovering that the bat was a foe of the mosquito, he constructed large roosts in which bats could feed, sleep, and deposit guano, the latter of which attracted mosquitoes. In this manner Campbell provided for the eradication of large numbers of the insect and its concomitant disease, as well as benefiting himself financially from the sale of guano.

Campbell published his findings in *Bats, Mosquitoes, and Dollars* (1925), which was lauded by such notable naturalists as Theodore Roosevelt, Lord Rothschild, and Ernest Thompson Seton. Campbell was married to Ida Hoyer, and they had one son. He died on February 22, 1931.

BIBLIOGRAPHY: Biographical File, Barker Texas History Center, University of Texas at Austin.

S. W. Pease

*Campbell, Donald.

*Campbell, Henry Harrison.

*Campbell, Isaac.

*Campbell, Killis.

*Campbell, Michael.

*Campbell, Thomas Mitchell.

*Campbell, Texas.

*Campbell Branch.

*Campbell Creek.

*Campbell Draw.

*Campbells Creek.

*Campbell's Lake.

*Campbellton, Texas.

*Campground Creek.

*Camps, Texas.

*Campti, Texas.

*Camptown, Texas.

Cana Indians. The Cana (Cano) Indians are known only from records pertaining to San José y San Miguel de Aguayo Mission qv at San Antonio. It is said that they were among the Indians for whom this mission was founded in 1720. This rather clearly indicates that they were Coahuiltecans. It has been assumed by some writers that the Cana were the same as the Sana, but the Sana were not Coahuiltecans and did not appear at San Antonio missions until after 1740. In 1691 a group known as Canu was reported as living eighty leagues southwest of the Hasinai Indians of eastern Texas, but it cannot be proved that Canu and Cana were names for the same people. It seems likely that the Cana originally lived in the vicinity of San Antonio, perhaps to the west or southwest.

BIBLIOGRAPHY: C. W. Hackett (ed.), *Pichardo's Treatise on the Limits of Louisiana and Texas*, I (1931); F. W. Hodge (ed.), *Handbook of American Indians*, II (1910); M. K. Kress (trans.), "Diary of a Visit of Inspection of the Texas Missions Made by Fray Gaspar José de Solís in the Year 1767–68," *Southwestern Historical Quarterly*, XXXV (1931–1932); J. R. Swanton, *Source Material on the History and Ethnology of the Caddo Indians* (1942).

T. N. Campbell

Canabatinu Indians. This name is known from a single Spanish missionary report in 1691, which indicates that the Canabatinu were enemies of the Hasinai tribes of eastern Texas and lived an unspecified distance to the west of the Hasinai. J. R. Swanton suggested that the Canabatinu may have been a Wichita group, but he cited no evidence in support of this identification.

BIBLIOGRAPHY: J. R. Swanton, *Source Material on the History and Ethnology of the Caddo Indians* (1942).

T. N. Campbell

*Canadian, Texas. Canadian, seat of Hemphill County, had a population of 2,239 in 1960 and 2,292 in 1970, which was two-thirds of the county's total population.

*Canadian Academy.

*Canadian River.

Canadian River Compact. Shortly after 1900 interest began to develop in large-scale irrigation projects, requiring conservation storage of water. In 1918 Eagle Nest Reservoir was constructed on Cimarron Creek, a Canadian River tributary in New Mexico, to impound water for downstream irrigation. In 1925 an organization known as the Canadian River Development Association was formed to foster interstate flood control and irrigation projects, and in furtherance of such projects a compact apportioning the river's flows among the three riparian states was negotiated in 1926. The Oklahoma legislature ratified the agreement, as did the New Mexico legislature, with modification. The Texas legislature took no action in the matter, and the compact did not become effective.

Interest in the river's development continued, however, and in 1938 the United States Army Corps of Engineers was authorized to construct Conchas Reservoir on the river's main stem in New Mexico, to provide flood protection for all three states, and to supply water for a 34,000-acre irrigation project in the headwater state, New Mexico.

During the late 1940's, faced with the problems of declining water levels and rising water requirements, a number of pump-dependent Texas Panhandle communities pooled efforts to promote construction of a surface-water reservoir on the river's main stem near Sanford. This was to provide additional flood protection and store water for municipal, industrial, and recreational uses. To expedite the plan, the communities urged negotiation of a second compact to clearly define the rights of each state to use of Canadian River waters. On December 6, 1950, a second compact was signed in Santa Fe, New Mexico. The legislatures of the three states ratified the agreement in 1951. Acceptance by Congress followed, and the instrument was signed into law by the president on May 19, 1952.

With their equities in the river defined, New Mexico and Texas have been able to proceed with development projects—New Mexico at the Clayton and Ute sites and Texas at the Sanford site. Projects in Oklahoma were planned.

Sanford Dam, recently completed by the United States Bureau of Reclamation, will yield about 103,000 acre-feet of water annually for use in eleven Texas communities: Amarillo, Borger, Pampa, Plainview, Lubbock, Slaton, O'Donnell, Tahoka, Levelland, Lamesa, and Brownfield. The aqueduct system was to include more than three hundred miles of pipeline, pumping stations, and regulating reservoirs, as well as chlorinating facilities. Construction costs were expected to total about $103,-230,000. *See also* Canadian River Municipal Water Authority.

Hudson Davis

Canadian River Municipal Water Authority. The Canadian River project received federal authorization in December, 1950, and in 1953 the legislature authorized the Authority to organize as a legal entity and independent political subdivision of Texas. Eleven cities formed the Authority: Amarillo, Borger, Pampa, Plainview, Lubbock, Slaton, Brownfield, Levelland, Lamesa, Tahoka, and O'Donnell.

Under a tri-state compact (Texas, Oklahoma, and New Mexico), Texas was entitled to 100,000 acre-feet of water per year for use by the member cities and 51,000 acre-feet for use by industries. In 1960 a repayment contract between the United States government and the Canadian River Municipal Water Authority was executed for construction of the project. The repayment schedule for the Au-

thority provided for the repayment, with interest, over a fifty-year period. Each city negotiated a contract with the Canadian River Municipal Water Authority for that city's estimate of water needs and the city's assumption of a percentage of the construction debt. Sale of water to cities outside of the Authority is possible only by a city's willingness to release a portion of its water. The dam, crossing the Canadian River nine miles west of Borger, is 228 feet high and 6,380 feet long. The aqueduct system, with 322 miles of pipeline, ten pumping plants, and three regulating reservoirs, furnishes municipal and industrial water to the cities of the Authority. *See also* Canadian River Compact.

Doris Alexander

*Canales, Antonio. Antonio Canales was born about 1800 in Monterrey, Mexico. As a young lawyer and supporter of the Mexican Constitution of 1824 he joined with other leaders of the northern Mexican states in armed resistance to Santa Anna's *coup d'état* of 1834. He commanded the principal force in Tamaulipas. Proposing to join forces with the Texan revolutionary leaders, he sent observers to San Felipe. When he received the report that the true purpose of the Texans was to secede from Mexico, he declined an alliance but remained neutral throughout the war. In 1838 he became one of the principal leaders in the revived *federalista* revolution and became colonel of a regiment. Promoted to commander-in-chief, he participated in numerous battles with varying success. In 1839 he sponsored, along with Zapata and others, the Republic of the Rio Grande,^{qv} to be composed of the northern Mexican states and the trans-Nueces portion of Texas; Canales was appointed commander-in-chief of that incipient republic. Successful at first, he was later defeated and compelled to retreat to the Nueces for reorganization. In his second campaign of 1840, in which Samuel W. Jordan ^{qv} was commander of the Texian auxiliaries, he failed principally because of his vacillation. He made his peace with the *centralistas* and betrayed his Texian auxiliaries. As part of his treaty of submission, he received a commission as brigadier general in the Mexican Army, and in that capacity he led an expedition against the Texian outposts at Corpus Christi and Lipantitlan, but was eventually defeated and driven back to Mexico.

In 1846–1848 Canales served Mexico as a brigadier general, commanding guerilla troops and harassing General Zachary Taylor's ^{qv} advance into Mexico. He issued numerous manifestoes calling upon civilians to harass the invaders by every means.

Canales early identified himself with the state of Tamaulipas, where he served as governor in 1851. As surveyor-general he made numerous surveys in the area west of the Nueces which, prior to 1845, was regarded as part of the state of Tamaulipas. His surveys included the Rincon de Oso grant on which the city of Corpus Christi is sited. Canales seems to have died in 1852, while the governor of Tamaulipas.

BIBLIOGRAPHY: Vito Alessio Robles, *Coahuila y Texas Desde La Consumacion De La Independencia* . . . (1945); *Diccionario Porrua* (1964); Hobart Huson, *Iron Men* (1940); J. M. Nance, *After San Jacinto, The Texas-Mexican Frontier, 1836–1841* (1963).

Hobart Huson

Canaq Indians. These Indians are known only from a Spanish document of 1693 which lists them as one of fifty "nations" that lived north of the Rio Grande and "between Texas and New Mexico." This may be interpreted to mean the southern part of western Texas, since the document also mentions that the Apache were at war with the groups named. Nothing further is known about the Canaq. The name is similar to that of the Cana, who apparently lived in southern Texas, but no connection between the two can be established.

BIBLIOGRAPHY: C. W. Hackett (ed.), *Historical Documents Relating to New Mexico, Nueva Vizcaya, and Approaches Thereto, to 1773*, II (1926).

T. N. Campbell

*Canary, Texas.

*Canary Islanders.

*Canby, Edward R. S.

Cancepne Indians. The Cancepne (Cancepu, Concepue) Indians are known from a Spanish document of 1748 which lists the names of twenty-five Indian groups of east-central and southeastern Texas who had asked for missions in that general area. About half the names on this list, including Cancepne, cannot be identified. The others consist of groups identifiable as Caddoans (including Wichita), Tonkawans, Atakapans, and Karankawans.

BIBLIOGRAPHY: H. E. Bolton, *Texas in the Middle Eighteenth Century* (1915); F. C. Chabot (ed.), *Excerpts from the Memorias for the History of Texas, by Father Morfi* (1932); C. W. Hackett (ed.), *Pichardo's Treatise on the Limits of Louisiana and Texas*, I (1931).

T. N. Campbell

*Candelaria, Señora Andrea Castanon. [This title was incorrectly listed in Volume I as Candalaria, Señora Andrea Castanon.]

*Candelaria, Texas.

*Candelaria Mission. *See* Nuestra Señora de la Candelaria Mission.

*Candler Branch.

*Candlish, Texas.

*Cane Belt Railroad Company.

*Cane Bend.

*Cane Creek.

*Caney, Texas. (Hopkins County.)

*Caney, Texas. (Matagorda County.)

*Caney Bayou.

*Caney Creek.

*Canfield, Alanson Wyllys.

Cann, Texas. *See* Dreyfoos, Texas.

Cannaha and Cannahio Indians. These Indians are known only from the 1687 documents of the La Salle Expedition,[qv] which list them separately as enemies of the Kadohadacho on the Red River. In spite of this separate listing, it has been assumed that the two names refer to the same people, and the Cannaha-Cannahio have been equated with the Kannehouan, who in the same documents were placed far to the south of the Red River near the Gulf Coast. These identifications, which are based on phonetic similarities in names, ignore separate listing in the documents as well as differences in geographic location. Until better evidence is presented, the Cannaha and Cannahio must be considered as different peoples and unrelated to the Kannehouan.

BIBLIOGRAPHY: F. W. Hodge (ed.), *Handbook of American Indians*, I (1907), II (1910); P. Margry, *Découvertes et établissements des Français dans l'ouest et dans le sud de l'Amérique Septentrionale*, III (1879).

T. N. Campbell

*Cannai Creek.

*Cannan, William Jarvis. [This title was incorrectly listed in Volume I as Cannon, William Jarvis. Some later printings of Volume I contain this correction.]

*Cannon, Texas.

*Cannon Gully.

*Cannonsnap Creek.

*Cannonville, Texas.

*Canoe Bayou.

*Canon Creek.

Canonidiba Indians. The Canonidiba Indians are known from a single 1691 Spanish missionary report which lists them as a group that lived to the southeast of the Hasinai of eastern Texas. As no distance was specified, it is impossible to tell whether the Canonidiba area was in eastern Texas or western Louisiana. Their affiliations are unknown.

BIBLIOGRAPHY: J. R. Swanton, *Source Material on the History and Ethnology of the Caddo Indians* (1942).

T. N. Campbell

Canonizochitoui Indians. The Canonizochitoui Indians are known from a single 1691 Spanish missionary report, which lists them among the groups that lived southeast of the Hasinai. Since no distance was specified, it is impossible to tell whether these Indians lived in eastern Texas or western Louisiana. The latter part of the name, "-zochitoui," resembles Souchitiony, an early form of Doustioni, the name of a Caddoan tribe that lived near present Natchitoches, Louisiana, in the eighteenth century. No further evidence in support of this identification has been found.

BIBLIOGRAPHY: J. R. Swanton, *Source Material on the History and Ethnology of the Caddo Indians* (1942).

T. N. Campbell

*Cantau Creek.

Cantey Indians. This name appears in records of the La Salle Expedition,[qv] which indicate that in 1687 these Indians were enemies of the Kadohadacho. The Cantey have been identified as Lipan-Apache, but this identification is debatable. A better case can be made for identification of the

Cantey with the Chaquantie, who in 1700 lived on the Red River some sixty to seventy-five miles west of the Kadohadacho. This would place them in the area of present Lamar and Red River counties. Apparent variants of the name Chaquantie appear on several eighteenth-century maps, some of which show the name on the north side of the Red River, others on the south. Although it has been speculated that the Chaquantie were Caddoans, their affiliations have yet to be documented.

BIBLIOGRAPHY: F. W. Hodge (ed.), *Handbook of American Indians*, I (1907), II (1910); P. Margry, *Découvertes et établissements des Français dans l'ouest et dans le sud de l'Amérique Septentrionale*, III (1879).

T. N. Campbell

***Canton, Texas.** Canton, seat of Van Zandt County, had eighty-six businesses in 1970. The town has a municipal lake with recreational facilities. Canton reported seven churches, a school, a bank, a library, and a newspaper. The 1960 population was 1,114; the 1970 population was 2,283, an increase of over 100 percent.

***Cantona Indians.** Although they were reported as numerous and were widely distributed in east-central Texas, the Cantona Indians have generally been ignored in studies of Texas Indians. In the late seventeenth and early eighteenth centuries the Cantona were known to the Spanish by a variety of names, including Cantanual, Cantujuana, Cantauhaona, Cantuna, Mandone, and Simaomo (Simomo). During this period they ranged the prairies between the Guadalupe and Trinity rivers, particularly east of the present cities of San Antonio, Austin, and Waco. They were most frequently reported along the Colorado and Brazos rivers, where their skill and success in bison hunting were often mentioned. The Cantona were rarely encountered alone; instead they shared settlements with other Indian groups, and they seem to have been welcome nearly everywhere. At times they encamped with the Jumano and their associated tribes or with Coahuiltecans (Mescale, Payaya, Xarame) near San Antonio; farther east they sometimes shared villages with the Cava, Emet, Sana, and Tohoho, all considered to be Tonkawans; northeast of Austin they were closely associated with the Yojuane, also Tonkawan; in eastern Texas they were frequent visitors at the Hasinai Caddo villages; and later in the eighteenth century (1771) they were associated with Wichita groups (Tawakoni, Yscani) east of present Waco. A few Cantona also entered San Antonio de Valero Mission qv at San Antonio in the first half of the eighteenth century.

The linguistic and cultural affiliations of the Cantona are difficult to assess. J. R. Swanton listed the Cantona as a Coahuiltecan band, presumably because of their association with Coahuiltecan groups near San Antonio. Others have stressed association with Tonkawan peoples and have argued that the Cantona language must have been Tonkawan. It is clear that linguistic identification on the basis of association leads nowhere in the case of the Cantona. At one time or another the Cantona were associated with nearly every group in or near their area. The same judgment also applies to Cantona cultural affiliations. The Cantona disappeared in the second half of the eighteenth century. When last mentioned they were living with Wichita groups in the northern part of their range, and it seems likely that most of the Cantona survivors lost their ethnic identity among the southern Wichita groups, particularly the Tawakoni and Yscani.

One question deserves serious consideration: were the Cantona the same people as the Kanohatino named in documents of the La Salle Expedition?qv Both groups occupied the same general area at the same time, and their cultures as known seem to have been similar. This question can be answered only by further archival research.

The name Simaomo, clearly stated in one Spanish document to be an alternative name for the Cantona, is puzzling. Since another document mentions both Cantona and Simaomo as being represented in a large congregation of tribes or bands, it is impossible that Simaomo was the name of a Cantona subdivision that was sometimes used as a synonym for Cantona.

BIBLIOGRAPHY: H. E. Bolton, "The Jumano Indians in Texas, 1650–1771," *Quarterly of the Texas State Historical Association*, XV (1911–1912), *Athanase de Mézières and the Louisiana-Texas Frontier, 1768–1780*, I (1914), *Spanish Exploration in the Southwest, 1542–1706* (1916); C. W. Hackett (ed.), *Pichardo's Treatise on the Limits of Louisiana and Texas*, II (1934); F. W. Hodge (ed.), *Handbook of American Indians*, II (1910); J. R. Swanton, *Linguistic Material from the Tribes of Southern Texas and Northeastern Mexico* (1940), and *Source Material on the History and Ethnology of the Caddo Indians* (1942).

T. N. Campbell

***Cantwell, James William.**

Canu Indians. In a Spanish missionary report of 1691 the Canu Indians were mentioned as living about eighty leagues southwest of the Hasinai of eastern Texas. Although there is no proof, the Canu may have been the same as the Cana, one of the Coahuiltecan groups for which San José y San Miguel de Aguayo Mission qv was founded at San Antonio in 1720. Some writers have assumed that the Cana were the same as the Sana, but there is little evidence to support this identification.

BIBLIOGRAPHY: C. W. Hackett (ed.), *Pichardo's Treatise on the Limits of Louisiana and Texas*, I (1931); M. K. Kress (trans.), "Diary of a Visit of Inspection of the Texas Missions Made by Fray Gaspar José de Solís in the Year 1767–68," *Southwestern Historical Quarterly*, XXXV (1931–1932); J. R. Swanton, *Source Material on the History and Ethnology of the Caddo Indians* (1942).

T. N. Campbell

***Canutillo, Texas.** Canutillo, in El Paso County, had a population of 1,377 in 1960 and 1,588 in 1970.

***Canyon, Texas.** Canyon, county seat of Randall County, had 163 business establishments, three schools, a hospital, a newspaper, and a radio station in 1967. The economy was based on the production of wheat, grain sorghums, dairy products, and livestock. Canyon is the site of the Panhandle-Plains Historical Museum,qv located on the campus of West Texas State University. City projects completed by 1966 included water and sewer improvements and street extensions. The 1960 population was 5,864; the 1970 count was 8,333. *See also* Amarillo Standard Metropolitan Statistical Area.

*Canyon Creek.

Canyon Reservoir. Canyon Dam and Canyon Reservoir are in the Guadalupe River Basin in Comal County, twelve miles northwest of New Braunfels on the Guadalupe River. The project is owned by the United States government and operated by the United States Army Corps of Engineers, Fort Worth District. The Guadalupe-Blanco River Authority qv is the local cooperative agency. Guadalupe-Blanco River Authority, by paying part of the cost, will have rights to the conservation storage space and control over the use and release of conservation water. Construction was started on April 8, 1958, and impoundment of water began June 16, 1964.

The reservoir is for flood control, conservation storage, and recreation. The conservation storage capacity is 386,200 acre-feet with a surface area of 8,240 acres and a shoreline of sixty miles at elevation 909 feet above mean sea level. Conservation storage is for municipal, industrial, and irrigation uses and for the development of hydroelectric power downstream. The flood control capacity is 354,700 acre-feet between elevations 909 and 943 feet. The drainage area above the dam is 1,418 square miles.

BIBLIOGRAPHY: Texas Water Commission, *Bulletin 6408* (1964).

Seth D. Breeding

*Canyons of the Rio Grande. *See* Boquillas Canyon; Mariscal Canyon; and Santa Elena Canyon.

*Cap Mountain.

*Cap Rock.

Capellone Indians. This name, which is known only from the records of San Antonio de Valero Mission qv of San Antonio, cannot be related to any known group of Indians. It may be a variant of Apion, another unidentifiable group at the same mission. If the two are the same, a former place name near Laredo, La Cañada de los Abiones, suggests residence in Coahuiltecan Indian territory.

BIBLIOGRAPHY: H. E. Bolton, *Texas in the Middle Eighteenth Century* (1915).

T. N. Campbell

*Capers, William Theodotus.

*Capitals of Texas.

*Capitol. Elijah E. Myers qv (not Elijah Meyers, as stated in Volume I) was the architect of the capitol building in Austin. The 16th Texas Legislature convened in 1879 (not 1882), appropriated public land to be used to finance the building of a new state capitol, and created the Capitol Board. Debate had begun as early as 1875 over the appropriation, and one architectural plan for the building had been selected by the time the old capitol burned, November 9, 1881, making construction of the new capitol urgent.

*Capitol Boycott.

*Capitol Freehold Land and Investment Company, Limited.

*Capitol Syndicate. The 16th Texas Legislature appropriated land to finance a new capitol in 1879 (not 1881, as stated in Volume I) and also created the Capitol Board. The destruction of the old capitol building by fire on November 9, 1881, made construction of the new building urgent.

*Capitola, Texas.

*Caplen, Texas.

*Capote Creek.

*Capote Draw.

*Capote Peak.

Capps Corner, Texas. Capps Corner, in northeastern Montague County, was founded about 1925 in an area devoted to agriculture and oil. Named for E. G. (Cap) Adams, the town had a grocery store and a community center serving the rural area in 1966.

*Caps, Texas.

*Caput, Texas.

Caquixadaquix Indians. The Caquixadaquix Indians are known from a single 1691 Spanish missionary report which lists them among the groups which lived southeast of the Hasinai of eastern Texas. Since no distance was specified, it is impossible to tell whether they lived in eastern Texas or western Louisiana. The first part of the name, "Caquixa-," suggests Catqueza, the name of a tribe that lived southwest of the Hasinai. Since the same report also lists "Caquiza" as living to the southwest of the Hasinai, there seems to be no basis for giving serious consideration to linkage of Caquixadaquix with Catqueza. The affiliations of the Caquixadaquix remain unknown.

BIBLIOGRAPHY: J. R. Swanton, *Source Material on the History and Ethnology of the Caddo Indians* (1942).

T. N. Campbell

*Car-Stable Convention.

*Caracol Creek.

*Caradan, Texas.

*Carancahua, Texas.

*Carancahua Bay.

*Carancahua Creek.

*Carazones Peaks.

*Carbajal, José María Jesús.

*Carbon, Texas.

*Carbon Black Industry. During the 1950's Texas retained its position as the nation's leading carbon black producer, when approximately eighty-eight billion cubic feet of gas were burned annually to produce carbon black. In 1954 thirty Texas plants with a total daily capacity of approximately three million pounds were located in eighteen Texas counties and produced 65 percent of the nation's total carbon black. Most of the total production was utilized by rubber companies, although some was used to manufacture ink and paint.

Production continued to be concentrated in the Panhandle area, although some carbon black plants were located on the coast. The major locations included Borger, five plants (four furnace-type and one channel-type); Big Spring, two furnace-type plants; and Seagraves, two plants (one furnace-type and one channel-type). Other plants were located in Skellytown, Baytown, and Aransas Pass. Of the two methods of production, channel and furnace, the latter was becoming more popular by the 1960's.

In 1964 the industry recovered 1,166,000,000 pounds of carbon black valued at $86,500,000. Thirty-nine plants employed 1,954 persons and had a value added by manufacturing of $29,957,000. Also by 1964 the total daily capacity of Texas carbon black plants had increased to 3,945,000 pounds. In 1969 carbon black production was valued at $110,816,000.

BIBLIOGRAPHY: U.S. Bureau of Mines, *Mineral Facts and Problems* (1965); U.S. Bureau of Mines, *Minerals Yearbook*, I, III (1965).

*Carbondale, Texas.

Cardelle, Cara. *See* Kimball, Emmaretta Cara.

*Carden, Texas.

*Cárdenas, Alonso de.

*Cárdenas y Magaña, Manuel José de.

*Cardis, Louis.

*Cardwell, John.

*Carey, Texas.

*Carey Crane College. *See* William Carey Crane College.

*Carhart, Edward Elmer.

*Carhart, John Wesley.

*Carhart, Lewis Henry.

*Carizzo Creek.

*Carl, Texas.

*Carleton, William.

*Carlisle, James M.

*Carlisle, Texas. (Lubbock County)

*Carlisle, Texas. (Rusk County.)

*Carlisle, Texas. (Trinity County.)

*Carlisle Creek.

*Carlisle Military Academy.

*Carlos, Texas.

*Carlos Rancho, Texas.

*Carlow Creek.

*Carlsbad, Texas. In 1907 the Concho Land Company was organized by T. L. Clegg, E. D. Perry, and others who purchased the 60,000-acre Hughes Ranch in Tom Green County. They subdivided it into 160-acre farm tracts, placed them on the market, and laid out a 120-acre townsite called Hughes. In 1908 the company applied for a post office to be named Hughes, which was refused because of its resemblance to Hughes Spring. A well drilled in the center of the townsite proved of medicinal value, and a new petition for a post office

named Carlsbad was approved by the post office department. In 1910 the town was prospering when a three-year drouth hit the area; the town declined and never recovered. In 1970 there were three business houses and a population of approximately 100.

Cyrus Tilloson

*Carlson, Texas.

*Carlton, Charles.

*Carlton, Texas. Carlton, in Hamilton County, was not first named Charlton (as stated in Volume I). It was named for pioneer residents Francis Marion Carlton (not F. M. Charlton) and Samuel Latimore Carlton (not Samuel F. Charlton). The post office was established by March 17, 1879 (not 1900).

Kathryne Baker Witty

*Carlton College.

*Carmichael Bend.

*Carmine, Texas.

*Carmona, Texas.

*Carnes, Texas.

*Carney, Frank.

*Caro, Texas.

*Caro Northern Railway Company.

*Carolina Creek.

*Carpenter, David.

*Carpenter, Eugene R.

Carpenter, John William. John William Carpenter, business and civic leader, was born on a farm near Corsicana, Texas, on August 31, 1881, son of Thomas Wirt and Ellen Isaphene (Dickson) Carpenter. One of ten children, he was educated at a country school and, briefly, at North Texas State Normal College (now North Texas State University) and Draughon's Business College at Fort Worth. After helping on his father's farm as a youth, he worked for a short time for an implement supply firm in Corsicana. In 1900 he began work for the Corsicana Gas and Electric Company, first as a laborer digging post holes, then as lineman, plant engineer, bookkeeper, collector, superintendent of distribution, and general superintendent.

In 1905 he began work in the testing department of the General Electric Company at Schenectady, New York, where he also took an apprentice course in electrical engineering. From there he worked for General Electric in Ohio and Indiana for two years until, in 1909, he was called back to Corsicana to become president and general manager of the Corsicana Gas and Electric Company. On June 18, 1913, he married Flossie Belle Gardner; to this union three children were born.

In 1918 he became vice-president and general manager of the Dallas Power and Light Company. A year later he took the same position with the Texas Power and Light Company, serving as president from 1927 to 1949, and continuing as chairman of the board until 1953. In time he organized or managed nearly twenty-five major companies in the Southwest, including eleven utility companies, the Texas Refrigerator and Ice Company, the Lone Star Steel Company, and the Southland Life Insurance Company, which, under his management, became the fifteenth largest publicly owned life insurance company in the country. He also served on the boards of many corporations, including the St. Louis and Southwestern Railway Company (Cotton Belt).

His many civic activities included two years as president of the Dallas Chamber of Commerce, vice-presidency of the State Fair of Texas,qv and board or advisory posts with more than a score of organizations, including the National Safety Council, the National Conference of Christians and Jews, the Texas Research Foundation,qv the Texas Forestry Association, and the Southwestern Legal Foundation. He was a vigorous advocate of canalizing the Trinity River and was president of the Trinity Improvement Association from its formation in 1930 until his death. The John Carpenter Freeway, in Dallas, was named for him. He was a Presbyterian and a Democrat.

A man of large frame and driving energy, he kept up his habits of hard work until almost the end. He died in Dallas of a heart attack on June 16, 1959.

BIBLIOGRAPHY: Dallas Morning News, September 17, 1950, April 12, June 17, 1959.

Wayne Gard

*Carpenter, Texas.

*Carpenters Bayou.

*Carpenter's Bluff, Texas.

*Carper, William M.

*Carpers Creek.

*Carpetbaggers.

*Carr-Burdette College.

*Carrease Creek.

*Carricitos, Texas.

*Carrick, Manton Marble.

*Carrizitos Creek.

*Carrizo Arroyo.

*Carrizo Creek.

*Carrizo Indians. In both the eighteenth and nineteenth centuries Spaniards and Mexicans applied this name to a number of Coahuiltecan bands in northeastern Mexico and southern Texas, including those otherwise known as Casas Chiquitas, Comecrudo, Cotoname, Garza, Juncal, Pakawa, Pajaseque, Pinto, Tanpacuaze, Tejón, Tusane, Yemé, and Yué. Of these, the Comecrudo seem to have been most frequently called Carrizo. It seems to have become common practice to refer to most Indians along the Rio Grande below Laredo as Carrizo, which is Spanish for "reed" or "cane." Some sources say that the Carrizo were so called because canes were used to cover their house frames. Carrizo (Carcese) Indians from Mexico crossed the Rio Grande and raided ranches in the Brownsville area as late as 1855. The name Carrizo was still in use in 1886 when some thirty-five individuals were reported as living near present Charco Escondido,

about twenty miles south of Reynosa, Tamaulipas. These were descendants of groups formerly known as Casas Chiquitas, Comecrudo, Cotoname, Pakawa, and Tejón. A few Carrizo (Cotoname) lived on a ranch in southern Hidalgo County at the same time.

BIBLIOGRAPHY: H. E. Bolton, Texas in the Middle Eighteenth Century (1915); F. W. Hodge (ed.), Handbook of American Indians, I (1907), II (1910); M. K. Kress (trans.), "Diary of a Visit of Inspection of the Texas Missions Made by Fray Gaspar José de Solís in the Year 1767–68," Southwestern Historical Quarterly, XXXV (1931–1932); G. Saldivar (ed.), Archivo de la historia de Tamaulipas, III (1946); R. C. Troike, "Notes on Coahuiltecan Ethnography," Bulletin of the Texas Archeological Society, 32 (1962); D. H. Winfrey and J. M. Day (eds.), The Indian Papers of Texas and the Southwest, 1825–1916, III (1966).

T. N. Campbell

*Carrizo Mountain.

*Carrizo Springs, Texas. Carrizo Springs, seat of Dimmit County, was one of the state's leading shipping points for truck crops in 1970. In 1967 the town had a modern twenty-seven-bed hospital, nine churches, and 123 businesses, including packing sheds and an oil refinery. The 1960 population was 5,699; in 1970 the count was 5,374.

*Carrol Creek.

*Carroll, Benajah Harvey.

*Carroll, Benajah Harvey, Jr.

Carroll, Horace Bailey. H. Bailey Carroll, son of J. Speed and Lena (Russell) Carroll, was born in Gatesville, Texas, on April 29, 1903. He attended, successively, Southern Methodist University, McMurry College, Texas Technological College (now Texas Tech University) (B.A., M.A., 1928), and the University of Texas (Ph.D., 1935). He began teaching history at Texas Technological College in 1928 and subsequently taught at Texas Wesleyan, Lamar State, Hillsboro, West Texas State, Eastern New Mexico, and Arlington State colleges before returning to the University of Texas in 1942 as a member of the history department, director of research in Texas history, and associate director of the Texas State Historical Association.qv In 1946 he became professor of history, director of the association, and editor of its Southwestern Historical Quarterly and Junior Historian.qqv

Under his direction and co-editorship the two-volume Handbook of Texas was published in 1952. His first published work was Gúadal P'a (1941); the next year he edited Three New Mexico Chronicles. He compiled a bibliography of Texas County Histories (1943) and wrote Texan Santa Fe Trail (1951), followed by his indispensable check list of Texas History Theses (1955). These and twenty-six volumes of the Quarterly stand as a monument to his editorial skill and scholarly standards. Fourteen articles by him were published in learned journals, and he served six journals in various advisory capacities. He held honorary memberships in a number of regional societies, including the Sons of the Republic of Texas,qv and was a member of the Mississippi Valley Historical Association (now Organization of American Historians), American Association for State and Local History (vice-president), Texas Folklore Society,qv Bibliographical Society of the United States and Canada, and the Philosophical Society of Texas.qv He was a fellow of the Royal Geographic Society of London and of the Society of American Historians.

His monument is in his published works; his influence will be felt through the years through the work of his students, who caught some of his zeal for history and respect for the canons of historical evidence. He received a Rockefeller research grant and wide recognition for his pioneer leadership in the Junior Historian Movement,qv which originated in Texas and spread throughout the country.

He was over six feet tall, loose-jointed, and deliberate in movement and speech. If he had worn a mustache he would have resembled John Knott's qv drawings of Old Man Texas. He worked hard and effectively at teaching, editing, writing, and upbuilding the Texas State Historical Association. His devotion to his task was infectious; he had the knack of making business and professional men see that history was their business, too. Largely because of his efforts, interested citizens created a fund amounting in 1966 to nearly $140,000 for the benefit of the association. He initiated in 1948 a book publication program which has made possible the issuance of twenty books under the association's colophon by 1966.

He had great capacity for personal friendships with all sorts and conditions of men and was a charming raconteur. His memory was prodigious and remarkably accurate.

He was married on June 3, 1935, to Mary Joe Durning, and they had one son. A cerebral stroke in 1961 impaired his health permanently, although he continued his work almost to the day of his death, May 12, 1966.

Herbert Gambrell

*Carroll, James Milton.

*Carroll, Texas.

*Carroll Creek.

*Carrollton, Texas. Carrollton, in Dallas-Denton counties, had an increase in population from 1,610 in 1950, to 4,242 in 1960, to 13,855 in 1970. It was one of the fastest growing communities in the state. See also Dallas Standard Metropolitan Statistical Area.

*Carson, Samuel Price.

*Carson, William C.

*Carson, Texas.

*Carson County. Carson County is important in mineral and agricultural production. Natural gas from the giant field underlying the county contributes to a large carbon black industry and is piped to several out-of-state population centers. Oil, too, is produced in abundance; 149,196,744 barrels were obtained from 1921 to 1973, while the 1963 yield alone was 4,323,000 barrels. Carson County,

with moderately high farm income, had, in 1965, 127,000 acres of wheat in cultivation. Extensive acreage is also devoted to grain sorghums, cotton, and cattle grazing. Agricultural research is carried on at Pan-Tech Farms, under the auspices of Texas Tech University. An atomic energy plant is located at Pantex in the southwestern corner of the county. Population was 7,781 in 1960 and 6,358 in 1970.

*Carswell Air Force Base. Carswell Air Force Base, near Fort Worth, continued as a heavy bomber base during the 1950's. By the mid-1960's it had become the home of the 7th Heavy Bombardment Wing of the Strategic Air Command. The wing had three tactical squadrons, two bomb squadrons equipped with the Boeing B-52 bomber, and the 7th Air Refueling Squadron equipped with the Boeing KC-135 tanker.

The 7th Heavy Bombardment Wing, which has the distinction of serving in two world wars, entered the war in Vietnam in June, 1965, when its B-52's were transferred to Guam. In December, 1965, the wing returned to Carswell after four months of service and more than 1,300 bombing missions over South Vietnam.

BIBLIOGRAPHY: *Carswell Air Force Base Guide and Directory* (1967).

*Cart War.

*Carta Valley, Texas.

Carter, Amon Giles. Amon Giles Carter was born on December 11, 1879, in Crafton, Texas, the son of William Henry and Josephine (Ream) Carter. When eleven years old he quit school to help his family, did odd jobs in Bowie, and later worked in Oklahoma and California.

Carter came to Fort Worth in 1905 and became advertising manager of the Fort Worth *Star* the next year. Three years later, with the backing of Colonel Paul Waples, he bought the newspaper, renaming it the Fort Worth *Star-Telegram*,qv with Louis J. Wortham qv as editor. In 1923 Carter succeeded Wortham as publisher and president, and in 1925 he bought the rival Hearst paper, the *Record*.

Carter's energies were directed in diverse ways: in 1922 he established WBAP, the city's first radio station; in 1923 he was appointed to the first board of directors of Texas Technological College (now Texas Tech University), serving until 1927; through the *Star-Telegram* and his position as the youngest president of the Fort Worth Chamber of Commerce, Carter was able to promote and publicize the city. When oil was discovered in North Texas in the 1920's he helped persuade oilmen to move to Fort Worth, encouraging the building of skyscrapers such as the Sinclair, W. T. Waggoner,qv and Life of America buildings; he later served as director of the American Petroleum Institute.

Carter's influences on Fort Worth are inestimable. One of his special interests was transportation. In 1911 he headed a committee which brought the first airplane to the area; by 1928 he was a director and part owner of American Airways, which six years later reorganized as American Airlines, Inc. Prior to World War II he was the principal figure in bringing to Fort Worth a huge Convair complex, later to become General Dynamics. In 1952 he persuaded Bell Aircraft Corporation to locate a helicopter plant in nearby Hurst. Amon G. Carter Field, named for him in 1950, was involved in the Fort Worth-Dallas airport controversy (see Greater Southwest International Airport).

Carter was noted for his large-scale philanthropy. His wealth came mainly from the oil business; his first successful well was drilled in New Mexico in 1935. In 1945 the Amon G. Carter Foundation was established for cultural and educational purposes. Because of his outstanding service to Fort Worth and to Texas, Carter received innumerable honors. He was named "Range Boss of West Texas" in 1939 and "Ambassador of Good Will" in 1941 by the Texas legislature. He received the Exceptional Service Medal from the U.S. Air Force and the Frank M. Hawks Memorial Award from American Legion Post 501 of New York City.

Carter was married three times: to Zetta Thomas, by whom he had a daughter, to Nenetta Burton, who bore him a son and a daughter, and to Minnie Meacham Smith. He died on June 23, 1955, in Fort Worth. Under the terms of his will, the Amon Carter Museum of Western Art qv was established in Fort Worth. See also Texas Frontier Centennial.

BIBLIOGRAPHY: Seymour V. Connor (ed.), *Builders of the Southwest* (1959); Fort Worth *Star-Telegram,* June 24, 25, 1955.

Ben H. Procter

Carter, George Washington. George Washington Carter, a Methodist minister who entered Texas in 1860, addressed the Secession Convention qv in January, 1861. He was elected colonel of the 21st Texas Cavalry on March 8, 1862. The regiment marched to Arkansas in the summer of 1862, where it joined William H. Parsons' Brigade.qv Carter and his regiment saw action in Arkansas and Louisiana throughout the war, including the Red River campaign qv in the spring of 1864. After the war Carter became a speaker and writer for the Republican party qv in Texas, Louisiana, Ohio, and Washington, D.C.

BIBLIOGRAPHY: Service Records of G. W. Carter (Civil War Biographical File, Archives, University of Texas at Austin Library, originals in National Archives, Washington, D.C.); H. S. Thrall, *History of Methodism in Texas* (1872); E. W. Winkler (ed.), *Journal of the Secession Convention of Texas, 1861* (1912); Frank Brown, Annals of Travis County and the City of Austin (MS., Archives, University of Texas at Austin Library); E. W. Winkler (ed.), "The Bryan-Hayes Correspondence," *Southwestern Historical Quarterly,* XXVI (1922–1923).

*Carter, Robert Goldthwaite.

*Carter, Samuel C.

*Carter, Samuel Fain.

*Carter, William Samuel.

*Carter, Texas. (Parker County.)

*Carter, Texas. (Stephens County.)

*Carter Bend.

Carter Field. *See* Greater Southwest International Airport.

*Carter Lake.

*Carters Creek.

*Carterville, Texas.

*Carthage, Texas. Carthage, seat of Panola County, has been the site of much construction since 1950. In addition to a new county library building, other construction included a new city hall and a fire station in 1963, a chamber of commerce building and an airport in 1964, and a fifty-bed nursing home and a new federal building with a post office in 1965. Panola Junior College was founded there in 1947. There were 156 businesses in 1970. Petroleum, cattle, lumber, and meat processing were important industries. The 1960 population was 5,262; the 1970 total was 5,392. Jonathan Anderson (not Jonathan Allison, as stated in Volume I) donated the original one hundred acres for the townsite in 1848.

*Cartwright, Jesse H.

*Cartwright, John.

*Cartwright, Matthew.

*Cartwright, Thomas.

*Carvajal, José María Jesús. *See* Carbajal, José María Jesús.

Carvajal Crossing. Carvajal Crossing, a natural rock-bottomed ford across Cibolo Creek in Karnes County, was the best known ford along the old cart road that went from the Texas coast to San Antonio. Situated halfway between Goliad and San Antonio, the crossing was in close proximity to the old Fuerte del Santa Cruz qv and the ranch headquarters of Andrés Hernández,qv who may have had the first ranch in Texas. Old maps and journals designated the crossing at various times in history as Tawakoni Crossing, the Crossing of the Tehuacanas, or Cibolo Crossing. About 1830 José Luis Carvajal, scion of a Canary Islander qv family of San Antonio, acquired the ranch property adjoining the crossing, and since that time the ford has been called the Carvajal Crossing.

BIBLIOGRAPHY: Robert H. Thonhoff, "The First Ranch in Texas," *West Texas Historical Association Year Book,* XL (1964).

*Casa Blanca, Texas.

*Casa Blanca Creek.

Casa Blanca Lake. Country Club Dam and Casa Blanca Lake are in the Rio Grande Basin in Webb County, three miles northeast of Laredo on Chacon Creek, a tributary to the Rio Grande. Country Club Dam and Casa Blanca Lake are owned and operated by Webb County for recreational purposes. The first dam, built in 1946, with top elevation at 455 feet above mean sea level, was damaged by the first floodwaters impounded by piping underneath the earth embankment. Construction of the second dam began in 1947, and was completed in 1951. The lake has a capacity of 20,000 acre-feet and a surface area of 1,656 acres at elevation 446.5 feet above mean sea level. Among its recreational uses, the lake supplies water to a golf course owned by the county. The drainage area above the dam is about 117 square miles.

BIBLIOGRAPHY: Texas Water Commission, *Bulletin 6408* (1964).

Seth D. Breeding

Casa-Calvo, Marqués de. Sebastián Nicolás de Bari Calvo de la Puerta, Marqués de Casa-Calvo, was born in Havana on August 11, 1751, the son of Pedro Calvo de la Puerta, and Catalina de O'Farril. He joined the Company of Nobles as a cadet on April 1, 1763. On July 3, 1769, he was named interim-captain of cavalry volunteers, and on September 14 given full captain's rank. He transferred to the regular army with the rank of captain in 1776, advancing to the rank of colonel by 1802. Casa-Calvo participated in the reconquest of Louisiana by Spain in 1769. He fought in the campaign at Mobile during 1780, but a hurricane prevented him from fighting at Pensacola. When Manuel Gayoso de Lemos ᑫᵛ died in 1799, Casa-Calvo was sent by the captain-general of Cuba to take military command of Louisiana, which he did on September 18. The following June he was succeeded by Juan Manuel de Salcedo. Together with Salcedo, Casa-Calvo delivered Louisiana to the French on April 10, 1803, but remained in New Orleans after the American flag was raised. In 1805 and 1806 he led an expedition with Nicolás deFiniels ᑫᵛ into western Louisiana and Texas. His analysis of mission and presidial records at Nacogdoches and survey of the jurisdiction of Los Adaes persuaded him of the just claims of Spain to territory as far east as Arroyo Hondo, which formed the boundary between Louisiana and Texas. Upon his return to New Orleans in 1806, he was expelled from Louisiana by Governor W. C. C. Claiborne. He was almost shipwrecked off Pass Christian, but he survived the storm to arrive at Pensacola in March, 1806, where he asked permission to lead a military expedition against Louisiana. He regarded this as the only hope of saving Spanish North America from the rapacious conquest by Anglo Americans. He was a Knight of the Order of Santiago.

BIBLIOGRAPHY: Charles Gayarré, *History of Louisiana, the Spanish Domination* (1854); Micheline Walsh, *Spanish Knights of Irish Origin,* I (1960); Jack D. L. Holmes (ed.), *Documentos inéditos para la historia de la Luisiana, 1792–1810* (1963); Jack D. L. Holmes, "The Marqués de Casa-Calvo, Nicolás deFiniels, and the 1805 Spanish Expedition Through East Texas and Louisiana," *Southwestern Historical Quarterly,* LXIX (1965–1966); Archivo General Militar de Segovia, MS., Service Sheet; Archivo General de Indias, Papeles de Cuba, legajo 179-a (Seville, Spain).

Jack D. L. Holmes

*Casa Grande.

*Casa Mañana. *See* Texas Frontier Centennial.

*Casa Piedra, Texas.

*Casañas de Jesús María, Francisco.

*Casas, Juan Bautista de las.

*Casas Amarillas.

Casas Blancas, Texas. Casas Blancas, begun in 1776 as an outgrowth of the colonizing activities of Don José de Escandón,ᑫᵛ was located seven miles west of Roma in Starr County. Legend states that the property was owned by the García family and that through marriage the Gonzales family came to control a large interest. The two families began a bitter feud, in which a man was killed. After a ghostly form reportedly appeared, the inhabitants fled the town.

BIBLIOGRAPHY: Randall McMillon, "Vanished Towns of the Rio Grande Valley," *Junior Historian,* XV (1954–1955).

*Casas Blancas Creek.

*Casas Chiquitas Indians. These Indians, whose name is Spanish for "small houses," lived somewhere along the Rio Grande below Laredo during the second half of the eighteenth century. They are among the various small Coahuiltecan bands of that area which the Spaniards referred to as Carrizo.

BIBLIOGRAPHY: F. W. Hodge (ed.), *Handbook of American Indians,* I (1907).

T. N. Campbell

Casas Moradas Indians. The Casas Moradas (Spanish for "purple" or "mulberry-colored houses") are known only from a Spanish document of 1693 which lists them as one of fifty "nations" that lived north of the Rio Grande and "between Texas and New Mexico." This may be interpreted to mean the southern part of western Texas, since the document also mentions that the Apache were at war with the groups named. The document further states that the Casas Moradas consisted of "four nations of the same name." Nothing further is known about them.

BIBLIOGRAPHY: C. W. Hackett (ed.), *Historical Documents Relating to New Mexico, Nueva Vizcaya, and Approaches Thereto, to 1773,* II (1926).

T. N. Campbell

*Casas Revolution.

*Cascade Caverns. Cascade Caverns, five miles south of Boerne in Kendall County, was first commercially operated from 1933 to about 1941; it was reopened about 1950. Originally known as Hester's Cave, the cave became famous as a result of publication of Frank Nicholson's exaggerated account of explorations. A commercial tour passes through about a half-mile of flowstone-decorated passages and rooms. *See also* Caves and Cave Studies in Texas.

BIBLIOGRAPHY: Victor S. Craun, "Commercial Caves of Texas," National Speleological Society, *Bulletin Ten* (1948); Frank E. Nicholson, "Nature Discloses More Queer Life," Philadelphia *Public Ledger,* October 30, 1932.

A. Richard Smith

*Casconade Creek.

*Case, Joel Titus.

*Case Creek.

*Case School at Victoria.

*Caseyville, Texas.

*Cash, Texas.

*Cash's Creek.

Casiba Indians. This name is known from a single 1691 Spanish missionary report, which indicates that the Casiba Indians were neighbors of the Hasinai tribes of eastern Texas. It is said that they lived an unspecified distance southeast of the Hasinai. This location suggests that the Casiba were probably not the same as the Cassia, reported in 1687 documents of the La Salle Expedition qv as allies of the Kadohadacho on the Red River. The affiliations of both groups remain unknown.

BIBLIOGRAPHY: P. Margry, *Découvertes et établissements des Français dans l'ouest et dans le sud de l'Amérique Septentrionale*, III (1879); J. R. Swanton, *Source Material on the History and Ethnology of the Caddo Indians* (1942).

T. N. Campbell

*Casino Club.

*Casket Mountain.

Caso Indians. The Caso Indians are known from a Spanish document of 1748 which lists the names of twenty-five Indian groups of east-central and southeastern Texas who had asked for missions in that general area. Although it cannot be demonstrated, it seems likely that the Caso were the same as the Caxo, who were reported in a Spanish missionary report from eastern Texas in 1691. The Caxo are generally considered to have been Caddoans of the southwestern or Hasinai division.

BIBLIOGRAPHY: H. E. Bolton, *Texas in the Middle Eighteenth Century* (1915); F. C. Chabot (ed.), *Excerpts from the Memorias for the History of Texas, by Father Morfi* (1932); C. W. Hackett (ed.), *Pichardo's Treatise on the Limits of Louisiana and Texas*, I (1931); J. R. Swanton, *Source Material on the History and Ethnology of the Caddo Indians* (1942).

T. N. Campbell

Cason, Texas. Cason is in Morris County, ten miles east of Pittsburg. In 1856 J. W. Cason settled on the site. On May 5, 1857, a post office named Buchanan was established with John Henderson as postmaster. Then, on October 21, the post office was changed to Snow Hill. On January 14, 1878, Postmaster William M. Cason obtained a change of name to Cason in honor of his father. In 1971 Cason had a post office, a population of approximately 160, and five businesses.

BIBLIOGRAPHY: Fred I. Massengil, *Texas Towns* (1936).

Cyrus Tilloson

*Cass, Texas.

*Cass County. The county seat of Cass County was relocated at Linden in 1852 (not 1860, when Marion County was separated and organized, as stated in Volume I). Cass County, 71 percent forested, in 1964 reported twelve active sawmills capable of producing 73,000 board-feet of pine and hardwood lumber daily, as well as 235 railroad ties. A new paper mill in the 1970's was expected to increase the income from forestry. The county also produces gas, oil, iron ore, and lignite. Livestock and poultry are responsible for two-thirds of the agricultural income, and diversified field crops, truck farming, and fruit make up the remaining one-third. The 1960 population was 23,496; in 1970 the population was 24,133.

Cassia Indians. In the 1687 documents of the La Salle Expedition,qv the Cassia Indians were reported as allies of the Kadohadacho on Red River. Apparently the Cassia were not the same as the Casiba, reported in a Spanish document of 1691 as living southeast of the Hasinai tribes. The affiliations of both groups remain unknown.

BIBLIOGRAPHY: P. Margry, *Découvertes et établissements des Français dans l'ouest et dans le sud de l'Amérique Septentrionale*, III (1879); J. R. Swanton, *Source Material on the History and Ethnology of the Caddo Indians* (1942).

T. N. Campbell

*Cassin, Texas.

*Cassin Lake.

*Castolon, Texas. [This title was incorrectly listed in Volume I as Castalon, Texas.]

*Castolon Peak. [This title was incorrectly listed in Volume I as Castalon Peak.] Although sometimes called Castolon Peak because of its proximity to Castolon, Texas, the peak's actual name is Cerro Castellan.qv

Castañeda, Carlos Eduardo. Carlos Eduardo Castañeda was born on November 11, 1896, in Camargo, Tamaulipas, Mexico, the son of Timoteo and Elise (Leroux) Castañeda. He came to the United States in 1908, was graduated from Brownsville High School in 1916, and then embarked on a long and distinguished academic career. He received his A.B. in 1921, his M.A. in 1923, and Ph.D. in 1932, all from the University of Texas in Austin. During this period he also taught school in Beaumont and San Antonio, and at William and Mary College. In 1927 Castañeda became librarian of the García Collection, the nucleus of the Latin American Collection qv at the University of Texas. He was also an associate professor of history from 1939 until 1946, when he became professor of Latin American history, a position he held until his death.

Castañeda's interests centered in the history of the Catholic church.qv His principal work was the seven-volume *Our Catholic Heritage in Texas, 1519–1936*, with *Supplement* to 1950 (1936–1958). He translated Juan A. Morfi's qv *History of Texas, 1673–1779* (1935) and prepared (with Jack A. Dabbs) the *Guide to the Latin American Manuscripts in the University of Texas Library* (1939).

Castañeda was the recipient of many honors, among them the presidency of the American Catholic Historical Association (1939), Knight of the Order of the Holy Sepulchre (1941), and Knight Commander of the Order of Isabel the Catholic of Spain. He received the Serra Award of the American Academy of Franciscan History in 1951 and an LL.D. from Catholic University of America. In 1921 Castañeda married Elisa Ríos, and they had three daughters, one of whom predeceased him. He died on April 3, 1958.

BIBLIOGRAPHY: *Texian Who's Who* (1937).

Lota M. Spell

*Castañeda (Castonado), Francisco.

Castañeda, Pedro de. Pedro de Castañeda, a member and chronicler of the Coronado Expedition,qv was a native of Najera, a town in the state of Vizcaya in northern Spain. At the time of the organization of the Coronado Expedition, Castañeda was at a Spanish outpost at Culiacán, in northwestern Mexico. He was married and had at least eight children. Castañeda's original account has been lost, but a copy made in 1596 is in the Lenox Library in New York City. The original publication was entitled *Relación de la jornada de Cibola compuesta por Pedro de Castañeda de Nacera donde se trata de todas aquellos poblados y ritos, y costumbres, la cual fué el año de 1540*. The narrative appears most recently in both Spanish and English in George Parker Winship, *The Coronado Expedition, 1540–1542* (1964).

BIBLIOGRAPHY: George Parker Winship (trans. and ed.), *The Journey of Coronado, 1540–1542* (1904).

*Castaño de Sosa, Gaspar.

*Castell, Texas.

*Castillito Creek.

*Castillo, Diego del.

*Castillo Maldonado, Alonso de.

*Castle Canyon.

Castle Hills, Texas. Castle Hills, in Bexar County, had a population of 2,622 in 1960 and 5,311 in 1970.

*Castle Mountain.

*Castle Peak.

*Castleberry, Texas.

*Castleman, Sylvanus.

*Castleman Creek.

*Castrillón, Manuel Fernández.

*Castro.

*Castro, Henri.

*Castro County. Castro County, unlike many of the Panhandle counties, finds its underground treasure not in oil but in an abundant supply of water. In the mid-1960's it ranked among the state's leaders in acres irrigated with over four hundred thousand, and in agricultural production with a 1970 farm income of $56,000,000. Important crops are grain sorghums, wheat, cotton, sugar beets, soybeans, and castor beans. Cattle are also significant. The county's industries, centering in the county seat, Dimmitt, are largely connected with agriculture and irrigation. A county fair, with a Miss Grain Sorghum contest, in September and a fat stock show in March are tourist attractions. The population was 8,923 in 1960 and 10,394 in 1970.

*Castro Creek.

*Castro's Colony.

*Castroville, Texas. Castroville, in Medina County, was originally surveyed by John James (not Henry James, as stated in Volume I). The town had a population of 1,508 in 1960 and 1,893 in 1970.

Ruth C. Lawler

*Cat Creek.

*Cat Spring, Texas.

*Catarina, Texas.

*Catarina Creek.

Cataye Indians. The Cataye Indians, a Caddoan tribe of the southwestern or Hasinai division in eastern Texas, are known from a single Spanish document that was written near the end of the seventeenth century. H. E. Bolton assumed that Cataye was a variant of the name Cachaé, but these similar names both occur in the same document without any indication that they are variants of the same name. Bolton also argued that Cachaé was an early name for the Hainai (they seem to have occupied the same territory). J. R. Swanton accepted Bolton's interpretations and also linked Caxo with Cachaé. This is all largely a matter of modern inference and opinion. As no early Spanish authority ever stated that Cataye, Cachaé, Caxo, and Hainai were names that referred to the same people, the case is still open.

BIBLIOGRAPHY: H. E. Bolton, "The Native Tribes about the East Texas Missions," *Quarterly of the Texas State Historical Association*, XI (1907–1908); J. R. Swanton, *Source Material on the History and Ethnology of the Caddo Indians* (1942).

T. N. Campbell

*Catfish Bayou.

*Catfish Creek.

*Cathedral Mountain.

*Catholic Church in Texas. *See* Roman Catholic Church in Texas.

Catholic Education in Texas. *See* Roman Catholic Education in Texas.

*Catlin, George. It is possible that George Catlin came to the Panhandle area of Texas as early as 1834 with a Colonel Dodge (but not with Jefferson Davis in that year, as stated in Volume I).

*Cator, James Hamilton.

*Cator, Texas.

*Catqueza Indians. The Catqueza (Caquiza, Casqueza, Catcueza) Indians are known only from a brief period near the close of the seventeenth century. At this time they ranged an area east and northeast of San Antonio, principally in the Guadalupe Valley between present San Marcos and Gonzales. Certain Spanish documents indicate that the Catqueza were not Coahuiltecans. Some writers have suggested that they spoke Tonkawan, apparently because they lived in an area where other Tonkawans also lived. It is possible that the Catqueza were seventeenth-century migrants from western Texas or northern Mexico. They were sometimes associated with the Jumano and Cibola, and a Spanish document of 1691 mentions a Catqueza chief who was "reared in Parras, Saltillo, and Parral. Later he went to New Mexico and returned again to his people. . . ."

BIBLIOGRAPHY: H. E. Bolton, "The Jumano Indians in Texas, 1650–1771," *Quarterly of the Texas State Historical Association*, XV (1911–1912); C. W. Hackett (ed.), *Pichardo's Treatise on the Limits of Louisiana and Texas*, II (1934); F. W. Hodge (ed.), *Handbook of American Indians*, I (1907), II (1910); J. R. Swanton, *Source Ma-*

terial on the History and Ethnology of the Caddo Indians (1942).

T. N. Campbell

*Catsclaw Bend.

*Cattail Creek.

*Cattle Brands.

*Cattle Drives.

*Cattle Industry. Texas has long been the top ranking state in cattle numbers. On January 1, 1968, Texas reached an all-time high of 10,972,000 head. By 1973 there were 15,350,000 cattle and calves in Texas, with an inventory value of $3.5 billion. Beef cattle raising is the most widely distributed livestock enterprise in Texas. Dairy cow numbers have declined in recent years (*see* Dairying).

Cattle feeding was rapidly developing in many areas of the state. The April 1, 1968, report from the United States Department of Agriculture indicated there were 761,000 cattle and calves on feed in Texas. This figure represented a 250 percent increase over the 1958 figures. The principal reason for the change was the gain in commercial feedlots in the state. On April 1, 1968, there were 275 feedlots operating in Texas with a minimum capacity of 1,000 head each. Such feedlots accounted for 95 percent of all the cattle being fattened for the slaughter market in Texas. Marketings from Texas feedlots during 1968 approached 1.8 million head, an increase of 508 percent over the 1958 level, which moved Texas into third position in cattle feeding in the United States. The main feeding area is the northern end of the Panhandle area, which accounts for over half of all the cattle on feed in Texas. Paralleling the dramatic increase in the number of cattle being fed on the Texas plains has been the expansion of beef slaughter facilities. In the years from 1966 to 1968 slaughter capacity of plants in the plains area increased more than 100 percent. *See also* Livestock; Texas and Southwestern Cattle Raisers' Association.

Joe B. Frantz

*Cattle Raisers' Associations. *See also* Texas and Southwestern Cattle Raisers' Association.

*Cattle Rustling.

*Cattle Tick.

*Cattle Trails. Martín de León qv could not have driven cattle to Louisiana in 1763 (as stated in Volume I). He was born in 1765.

Cattleman, The. The *Cattleman* magazine was established by the Texas and Southwestern Cattle Raisers' Association qv in 1914 and is recognized as an authoritative voice of the cattle industry. Published monthly in Fort Worth, its issues go to every state in the union and to more than thirty foreign countries. Its pages are filled with articles by the world's leading authorities in the field of animal and plant sciences. The journal includes reference articles on animal breeding, health, nutrition, management, pastures, finance, taxation, and other related subjects.

News of the association and historical articles dealing primarily with the early days of the cattle industry also are featured each month. All articles have been indexed, making *The Cattleman* one of the most widely used livestock industry reference sources in the nation. Since the cattle industry was so closely intertwined with the early development of the frontier and continues to be a moving force in the economy, the magazine is in many respects a chronicle of the development of the great Southwest.

Dick Wilson

Catujano Indians. In the late seventeenth century the Catujano (Catajane, Catuxane) Indians, apparently a Coahuiltecan-speaking people, ranged from northeastern Coahuila across the Rio Grande into the southwestern part of the Edwards Plateau in Texas. They do not seem to have survived into the eighteenth century.

BIBLIOGRAPHY: H. E. Bolton (ed.), *Spanish Exploration in the Southwest, 1542–1706* (1916); F. W. Hodge (ed.), *Handbook of American Indians,* I (1907); W. Jiménez Moreno, "Tribus e idiomas del Norte de México," *El Norte de México y el Sur de Estados Unidos* (1944).

T. N. Campbell

Cauble, Peter. Peter Cauble was born in Guilford County, North Carolina, in 1786, the descendant of emigrants from the German Palatinate of the Rhine. About 1812 Cauble migrated to Alabama, where he farmed for a time and married Mary Ann Rotan.

Cauble came to Texas about 1829, and settled first in Nacogdoches County. He was living in the area of present Tyler County by 1831, being one of the first white settlers in Southeast Texas. He was a soldier in the volunteer "Army of the People of Texas" in 1835 and received a headright grant of 640 acres from the Republic of Texas in 1839. Thereafter he became a prosperous planter and stockraiser in Tyler County, owning about five thousand acres and eleven slaves in 1860. He built and maintained one of the first cotton gins in the county.

Having been a teacher in early life, Cauble was often referred to as "Professor Cauble." For years he served as road commissioner and justice of the peace. A large hewn-log house which he built at Peach Tree Village in 1835 was considered such a landmark in early times that it is mentioned in the legislative act establishing Polk County in 1846. Cauble died at Peach Tree Village on March 8, 1870.

BIBLIOGRAPHY: B. B. Paddock, *History of Central and Western Texas,* II (1911); Minutes of the Commissioners Court, Deed and Probate Records, Tyler County; Headright Grants of the Republic of Texas (General Land Office, Austin); J. E. Wheat (ed.), *Dogwood Festival Bulletins.*

John P. Landers

Caudle, John H. John H. Caudle was born in Alabama about 1835. He came to Texas, settled in Red River County as a merchant in the 1850's, and was married by 1860. In 1861 he was a member of the local Red River County Rangers, and in 1862 raised a company which joined the 34th Texas

Cavalry. The regiment served in the Indian Territory and, as part of what became Polignac's Brigade,qv fought at Shirley's Ford and Newtonia, Missouri, and Prairie Grove, Arkansas, in 1862. Then in the spring of 1863, the unit was reorganized and Caudle was placed in command, first as lieutenant colonel and later as colonel. He led the regiment in action at Vidalia and Harrisonburg and in the Red River campaign qv in Louisiana during 1864, continuing as its commander until it was disbanded in Texas in the spring of 1865. After the war he returned to Red River County, which he represented in Democratic congressional district conventions of 1871 and 1872.

BIBLIOGRAPHY: Alwyn Barr, *Polignac's Texas Brigade* (1964); U.S. Census, 1860, Red River County, Texas (microfilm, University of Texas at Austin Library); *Dallas Herald*, July 8, 1871, August 24, 1872.

Alwyn Barr

Caula Indians. The Caula were one of twenty Indian groups that joined Juan Domínguez de Mendoza qv on his journey from El Paso to the vicinity of present San Angelo in 1683–1684. Since Mendoza did not indicate at what point the Caula joined his party, it is impossible to determine their range or affiliations. However, the Indians between the Pecos River and the Colorado River east of San Angelo were being hard pressed by Apache at this time, and it seems likely that the Caula ranged between these two localities.

BIBLIOGRAPHY: H. E. Bolton (ed.), *Spanish Exploration in the Southwest, 1542–1706* (1916).

T. N. Campbell

*Causey Brothers, George and John.

*Causey Hill.

Caux Indians. These are the Indians who held François Simars de Bellisle qv captive for several months in 1719–1720. Their location has now been established as the vicinity of Galveston Bay in southeastern Texas. They have been tentatively identified as Coco, but their location and De Bellisle's description of their culture strongly indicate that they were the Akokisa, well known to the Spanish through missionary activity in this area later in the eighteenth century. The Akokisa were Atakapan-speaking Indians who dominated the coastal strip that lies between present Houston and Beaumont.

BIBLIOGRAPHY: H. Folmer, "De Bellisle on the Texas Coast," *Southwestern Historical Quarterly*, XLIV (1940–1941); P. Margry, *Découvertes et établissements des Français dans l'ouest et dans le sud de l'Amérique Septentrionale*, VI (1879); M. de Villiers and P. Rivet, "Les Indiens du Texas et les expéditions françaises de 1720 et 1721 à la Baie-Saint Bernard," *Journal de la Société des Américanistes de Paris*, XI (1919).

T. N. Campbell

*Cava Indians. In the late seventeenth century and during the first half of the eighteenth century the Cava (Caba, Cagua, Caouache, Lava) Indians lived on the coastal plain north of Matagorda Bay and between the Guadalupe and Colorado rivers. When encountered by Europeans they were usually occupying settlements jointly with other groups, especially Cantona, Emet, Sana, Toho, and Tohaha.

Between 1740 and 1750 some of the Cava entered San Antonio de Valero Mission,qv at San Antonio. The linguistic and cultural affiliations of the Cava are still debatable. Most writers have said that the Cava were probably Tonkawan; however, others have suggested either a Karankawan or a Coahuiltecan affiliation. Attempts to link the Cava with various groups encountered by the La Salle party, such as Kabaye and Kouyam, are not very convincing.

BIBLIOGRAPHY: H. E. Bolton (ed.), *Spanish Exploration in the Southwest, 1542–1706* (1916); F. W. Hodge (ed.), *Handbook of American Indians*, I (1907), II (1910); W. W. Newcomb, Jr., *The Indians of Texas* (1961); A. F. Sjoberg, "The Culture of the Tonkawa, A Texas Indian Tribe," *Texas Journal of Science*, V (1953); J. R. Swanton, *The Indian Tribes of North America* (1952).

T. N. Campbell

*Cavasso Creek.

*Cavazos, Texas.

*Cave, Eber Worthington.

*Cave Creek.

*Cave Dwellers in the Big Bend. *See* Archaeology, Big Bend Area.

Cave-Without-A-Name. *See* Kendall County; *see also* Caves and Cave Studies in Texas.

*Cavelier, René Robert. *See* La Salle, René Robert Cavelier, Sieur de.

*Caven, John William.

Caves and Cave Studies in Texas. Archeologists have shown that Texas Indians used natural shelters and cave entrances for living quarters and burial places during the last few thousand years, as indicated by artifacts, burials, petroglyphs, and pictographs. Frontiersmen later used caves for temporary shelters and easily defended forts. Occasional hermits made caves their permanent homes. None of these activities led to any concentrated efforts to explore and record the speleologic features of the state. During the Civil War, however, searches were made for bat caves that could furnish guano-derived saltpeter for use in munitions manufacture.

Early scientific work in Texas caves began about the turn of the twentieth century with the study of blind salamanders and crustacea from the San Marcos area, but cave exploration was still considered unimportant except as it affected investigations of economic mineral deposits in caves. Early references to caves are brief and include little detail and, rarely, cave maps.

With the rise of the National Speleological Society in the 1940's came a marked increase in local interest in speleology and spelunking. Out of this interest grew a number of local caving groups, including the University of Texas Speleological Society, Corpus Christi Speleological Society, Alamo Grotto, and Balcones Grotto. By 1948 enough work had been done in the state to prepare a book on Texas caves, which was published as *Bulletin Ten* of the National Speleological Society.

Following publication of *Bulletin Ten* there was a decline in exploration and scientific study until the mid-1950's. In 1957 Texas spelunkers recognized the need for a comprehensive collection of available material on Texas caves and began the *Texas Cave Survey*, edited by Donald Widener. The main purpose of this publication was to disseminate county-by-county cave information to members of the Texas Region of the National Speleological Society. Since 1961 this function has been fulfilled by the Texas Speleological Survey. A news magazine, the *Texas Caver*, containing accounts of trips as well as scientific articles, was begun in 1955; it remains the official publication of the Texas Speleological Association.

The revival of interest in the 1950's also resulted in annual conventions and projects, the latter intended for the detailed study of a cave or a small area. The noncommercial part of Longhorn Cavern qv was the object of the first and second region projects. Seven miles of passage were mapped in Powell's Cave in central Texas, and a large number of caves were located in San Saba County during other project meetings.

After the initial studies in the early 1900's, biospeleology (the study of the fauna and flora of caves) languished until the discovery of new biota and their description by out-of-state biologists. James R. Reddell of the Texas Speleological Survey began a thorough examination of the biology of Texas caves. He found many new species of fauna, and his work has been summarized in a published list. Geological, paleontological, and hydrological studies have only begun; several theses are just completed or in progress.

In the mid-1960's several active caving groups, all affiliated with the Texas Speleological Association (successor to the Texas Region), were conducting speleological studies in Texas and surrounding areas. Groups were located in Austin, San Antonio, Boerne, Dallas-Fort Worth, Georgetown, and Abilene.

Most caves in Texas occur in limestone and dolomite, but many also occur in gypsum. A few are known from volcanic rocks, sandstone, terrace gravels, and caliche. The Balcones Fault zone of central Texas is well known for its high concentration of caves; less known but equally important are the great number of caves in the rocks of the Ellenburger Group in the Llano region, in Permian gypsum beds in northwest Texas and Culberson County, and in Cretaceous limestone in the southwestern part of the Edwards Plateau. Several important caves are known in the Glass Mountains, the Big Bend, and other local areas of limestone.

The deepest known cave in Texas is Langtry Lead Cave (Val Verde County) at 367 feet below the entrance; longest is Powell's Cave (Menard County) with about thirty-eight thousand feet of mapped passage. Natural Bridge Caverns qv (Comal County) and Fern Cave (Val Verde County) are probably largest in terms of volume.

In 1967 eight caves were open for tourists; all are interesting, well lighted, and well maintained. They are: Cascade Caverns (Boerne), Caverns of Sonora (Sonora), Cave-Without-A-Name (Boerne), Cobb Caverns (Florence), Inner Space Cavern (Georgetown), Longhorn Cavern (Burnet), Natural Bridge Caverns (New Braunfels), and Wonder Cave (San Marcos).qqv

BIBLIOGRAPHY: National Speleological Society, *Bulletin Ten* (1948); James R. Reddell, "A Checklist of the Cave Fauna of Texas," *Texas Journal of Science*, XVII, XVIII, XIX (1965–1967); *Texas Caver*, I–XI (1955–1966).

A. Richard Smith

*Caviness, Texas.

*Cawthon, Texas.

Caxo Indians. The Caxo Indians, a tribe of the southwestern or Hasinai division of Caddo Indians, are known from a single 1691 Spanish missionary report. J. R. Swanton identified the Caxo with the Cachaé and followed H. E. Bolton in equating the Cachaé with the Hainai. This is strictly a matter of modern inference and opinion. Caxo and Cachaé both occur as names of tribes in the same document without any indication that they refer to the same people. Bolton argued that Cachaé was an early name for the Hainai (both names are associated with the same area) and that Cataye was a synonym for Cachaé. No early Spanish authority ever stated that Caxo, Cachaé, Cataye, and Hainai were different names for the same people.

BIBLIOGRAPHY: H. E. Bolton, "The Native Tribes about the East Texas Missions," *Quarterly of the Texas State Historical Association*, XI (1907–1908); J. R. Swanton, *Source Material on the History and Ethnology of the Caddo Indians* (1942).

T. N. Campbell

Caylor, Harvey Wallace. Harvey Wallace Caylor, a painter of Western scenes, was born near Noblesville, Indiana, on February 20, 1867, the son of Henry I. and Nancy Ann (Rambo) Caylor. At an early age Harvey Caylor showed talent and enthusiasm for drawing and took lessons from Frank Finch, a Noblesville artist. At the age of fourteen Caylor left home, working wherever he could and sketching as he went. Saving a small amount of money, he went to Indianapolis, where he studied art under Jacob Cox. Later, Caylor worked under Frederic Remington, who advised him to use nature as his teacher. This Caylor did as he began to explore the great West, learning about its people, its animals, and its physical appearance. It was not until 1886, after his marriage to Florence Nephler in Parsons, Kansas, that Caylor began serious work in putting what he had learned on canvas.

In 1890 Caylor and his wife settled on a ranch at Big Spring, Texas, although they still traveled widely through the West, stopping at ranches and camping out; they experienced the West Texas scene intimately and came to know many of the early cattlemen. Visual impressions of these experiences are shown in his paintings, such as "Going Up the Old Trail," which hangs in the Hoof and Horn Club in Kansas City, and other pictures in the collections of the Kansas City Stock Market, Howard County Junior College, banks of Big Spring, as well as in private collections. On December 24, 1932, Caylor died at Big Spring.

BIBLIOGRAPHY: Frances Battaile Fisk, *A History of Texas Artists and Sculptors* (c. 1928); Elsie Montgomery Wilbanks, *Art on the Texas Plains* (1959); Marilee Carr, "H. W. Caylor—Frontier Artist," *Junior Historian*, XXVI (1965–1966); Witte Memorial Museum Files, San Antonio, Texas.

Caroline Remy

Caynaaya Indians. The Caynaaya (Caynaagua) Indians are known mainly from a document of 1691 which reported these Indians encamped with Cibola and Jumano on the Guadalupe River east of San Antonio, where they were hunting bison. In this document it is stated that these three groups lived far to the west on the Rio Grande and that their country was adjacent to that of the Salineros, who lived along the lower stretches of the Pecos River. This seems to place the Caynaaya in Trans-Pecos Texas. As their name does not occur on contemporary lists of Indians living in western Texas, it is possible that the Caynaaya were also known by some alternate name. The Caynaaya were probably the same as the Cagaya, who are named in a Spanish missionary report of 1691 from eastern Texas. This report placed them about eighty leagues southwest of the Hasinai and lists them along with the Jumano (Chuman).

BIBLIOGRAPHY: H. E. Bolton, "The Jumano Indians in Texas, 1650–1771," *Quarterly of the Texas State Historical Association*, XV (1911–1912); J. R. Swanton, *Source Material on the History and Ethnology of the Caddo Indians* (1942).

T. N. Campbell

***Cayote, Texas.**

***Cayote Creek.**

******Cayuga***.** The steamer *Cayuga* was built at Pittsburgh, Pennsylvania (not Harrisburg, Texas, as stated in Volume I), in 1832 (not 1834 or 1835); it was purchased by Captain William P. Harris and Robert Wilson ^qqv^ from J. F. Ailes of New Orleans in the fall of 1834. The *Cayuga* was one of the earliest successful steamboat enterprises in Texas history.

BIBLIOGRAPHY: *Ship Registers and Enrollments of New Orleans*, III (1831–1840); Robert Wilson to Samuel May Williams, October 23, 1834 (Williams Papers, Rosenberg Library, Galveston).

William J. Doree

***Cayuga, Texas.**

***Cazneau, Jane Storms.** *See* McManus, Jane.

***Cazneau, William Leslie.**

***Cedar, Texas.**

***Cedar Arroyo.**

***Cedar Bayou.**

***Cedar Bayou, Texas.**

***Cedar Branch.**

***Cedar Creek.**

***Cedar Creek, Texas.**

Cedar Creek Reservoir. Cedar Creek Reservoir is in the Trinity River Basin in Henderson County, three miles northeast of Trinidad on Cedar Creek, a tributary to the Trinity River. The project is owned and operated by the Tarrant County Water Control and Improvement District No. 1 for municipal water supply. Construction started in April, 1961, and was completed in 1965. The reservoir has a capacity of 679,200 acre-feet and a surface area of 34,000 acres at operating elevation of 322 feet above mean sea level. The drainage area above the dam is 1,007 square miles.

BIBLIOGRAPHY: Texas Water Commission, *Bulletin 6408* (1964).

Seth D. Breeding

Cedar Grove, Texas. Cedar Grove, four miles northeast of Elmo in Kaufman County, was at the crossroads of the Austin-Clarksville and the Jordans Saline-Black Hill-Dallas roads. A post office was opened in 1850 and closed in 1874. Balances in its Confederate post office showed it to be the second most active in the county in the closing months of the Civil War. The community had Cedar Grove Lodge No. 308, A.F. and A.M., from 1868 to 1913. When the Texas and Pacific Railroad came to Wills Point in 1873, many Cedar Grove inhabitants moved there. Cedar Grove remained a trading center until the 1930's, when it still had two or three stores. A half-dozen residences and the Cedar Grove Cemetery were still there in the 1960's.

Grover C. Ramsey

***Cedar Hill, Texas.** Cedar Hill, in Dallas County, had a population of 1,848 in 1960 and 2,610 in 1970.

***Cedar Hollow.**

***Cedar Lake.**

***Cedar Lake, Texas.**

***Cedar Lake Creek.**

***Cedar Lake Slough.**

***Cedar Lane, Texas.**

***Cedar Mills, Texas.**

***Cedar Mountain.**

***Cedar Mountains.**

***Cedar Park, Texas.**

Cedar Springs, Texas. (Dallas County.) Cedar Springs, the pioneer settlement in northwest-central Dallas County, was settled by Dr. John Cole and family in May, 1843. By the end of that year it numbered fifteen inhabitants. Never incorporated, the community grew up around a small but constantly flowing spring in a clump of cedars in what is today the Oak Lawn neighborhood of the city of Dallas. Several stores, including a blacksmith shop, a harness maker's shop, and a whisky distillery (the first in the Three Forks of the Trinity area) were opened in what quickly became a favored rest camp spot for travelers across north-central Texas. The peak of the town's importance was perhaps reached by 1850, when it received 101 votes in a losing attempt to become the permanent site of the Dallas courthouse in a three-way contest with Dallas (191 votes) and Hord's Ridge (178 votes). However, Cedar Springs had largely disappeared by the time its area was annexed a number of decades later to the city of Dallas. The present-day city thoroughfare of Cedar Springs Road is the outgrowth of the pioneer trail connecting Cedar Springs with John Neely Bryan's qv settlement of Dallas four miles to the southeast. In 1936 the state of Texas erected at the site of Cedar Springs a granite marker which is located in Craddock City Park.

BIBLIOGRAPHY: John H. Cochran, *Dallas County: A Record of Its Pioneers and Progress* (1928).

Sam Acheson

*Cedar Springs, Texas. (Falls County.)

Cedar Springs, Texas. (Upshur County.) Cedar Springs, in northeastern Upshur County, was founded before the Civil War near a fine spring surrounded by large cedar trees. Most of the one hundred inhabitants in 1966 were employed at the Lone Star Steel Company three miles away. Population in that year was increasing because of the steel plant.

*Cedar Top.

*Cedar Valley, Texas.

*Cedar Valley Lands and Cattle Company.

*Cedarville, Texas.

Cedric, Texas. Cedric, one mile west of Ralls in Crosby County, was laid out in 1911 by Julian Bassett in an effort to kill the infant town of Ralls. Bassett had opened the town of Crosbyton in 1908, and in a successful attempt to secure the county seat for his town, built in 1911 the Crosbyton-South Plains Railroad from Lubbock to Crosbyton. The rail line crossed John R. Ralls' qv ranch, and Ralls decided in 1911 to open a town, named for him, along the railroad. Bassett, wishing to be rid of the competition posed by Ralls' townsite, on which he had not calculated, refused Ralls a depot and laid out Cedric. In Cedric, Bassett built four brick business buildings, which were never occupied, and a depot. Settlers in Ralls freighted supplies from the railroad stop in Cedric to their community. By 1915, when the Santa Fe Railroad bought the Crosbyton-South Plains Railroad and made Ralls a regular stop, Bassett had conceded that he could not destroy the rival settlement and sold Cedric to John Ralls, who moved Cedric's depot and sidewalks to Ralls.

BIBLIOGRAPHY: Lubbock *Avalanche*, June 10, 1951; Nellie Spikes and Temple Ellis, *Through the Years, A History of Crosby County, Texas* (1952).

David B. Gracy II

*Cedron Creek.

*Cee Vee, Texas.

*Cego, Texas.

*Cele, Texas.

*Celery Creek.

*Celeste, Texas.

*Celina, Texas. Celina, in Collin County, had a population of 1,204 in 1960 and 1,272 in 1970.

*Cement, Texas.

*Cement Production. By 1954 Portland cement production totaled 21,350,000 barrels valued at $53,500,000. Portland cement ranked next to petroleum minerals in 1964, when production increased to 29,600,000 barrels valued at $94,128,000. In the same year masonry cement production totaled 950,000 barrels valued at $2,917,000.

Figures for 1966 indicated that cement production for that year was 2 percent higher than the preceding year. Portland cement production exceeded 31,000,000 barrels valued at $100,166,000, while masonry cement production decreased to a total of 922,000 barrels valued at $3,013,000. In 1970 Portland cement production was over 35,000,000 barrels, valued at $107,370,000. Masonry cement production was 955,000 barrels, valued at $3,331,-000. Texas had nineteen cement producers located in Bexar, Dallas, Ector, Ellis, El Paso, Harris, Johnson, McLennan, Nolan, Orange, Potter, and Tarrant counties.

BIBLIOGRAPHY: *Texas Almanac* (1955, 1963–1971); Files of the Bureau of Business Research, University of Texas at Austin.

*Cementville, Texas.

*Cemetery, State. *See* State Cemetery.

Cenizo Indians. The Cenizo (Cenis, Ceniz, Seniso, Zenizo) Indians were well-known Coahuiltecan Indians of northeastern Mexico during the late seventeenth and early eighteenth centuries. Some entered Mission San Antonio Galindo Moctezuma (north of Monclova) in 1698, and shortly thereafter others entered San Francisco Solano Mission qv near present Eagle Pass. In 1718, when San Francisco Solano was transferred to San Antonio and became known as San Antonio de Valero,qv some of these Cenizo moved with it. The baptismal records at Valero include such names as Censoc, Censoo, Seniczo, Senixzo, Sinicu, and Sinnizo, all of which seem to be variants of Cenizo. However, H. E. Bolton has identified two groups: Cenizo (with Siniczo as a synonym) and Sinicu (with Censoc, Censoo, Seniczo, and Senixzo as synonyms). J. R. Swanton followed Bolton by listing Cenizo (Seniso) as separate Coahuiltecan bands. Reanalysis of the primary documents is needed in order to clarify this matter.

BIBLIOGRAPHY: F. W. Hodge (ed.), *Handbook of American Indians*, I (1907); M. D. McLean and E. del Hoyo (eds.), *Description of Nuevo León, Mexico, 1735–1740, by Don Josseph Antonio Fernández de Jáuregui Urrutia* (1964); E. L. Portillo, *Apuntes para la historia antigua de Coahuila y Texas* (1886); J. R. Swanton, *Linguistic Material from the Tribes of Southern Texas and Northeastern Mexico* (1940).

T. N. Campbell

*Census and Census Records. In 1850 the first United States census was taken, and Texas population was given as 154,034 whites (not 212,592 whites, as stated in Volume I), 397 free Negroes, and 58,161 slaves. In 1955 Texas had an estimated population of 8,657,000, ranking sixth in the nation. The official 1960 census recorded 9,579,677 persons living in Texas. By 1962 the population had passed the 10,000,000 mark with 75 percent of all residents classified as urban residents. The official 1970 population was 11,196,730.

*Centennial. *See* Texas Centennial.

*Centennial, Texas.

*Centennial Masonic Institute.

*Center, Texas. (DeWitt County.)

*Center, Texas. (Limestone County.)

*Center, Texas. (Shelby County.) Center, the county seat, reported 212 businesses in 1971. A hospital was located there. Manufacturers dealt largely with timber and poultry products. The population was 4,510 in 1960 and 4,989 in 1970.

*Center City, Texas.

*Center Creek.

Center Grove, Texas. Center Grove, in southern Houston County, was founded in 1925 as a combination of two earlier communities, Pine Grove and Center Hill. In 1966 the population of three hundred was engaged in farming and ranching. The community had a school.

*Center Mills, Texas.

*Center Point, Texas. (Kerr County.) Center Point was originally called Zanzenburg (not Zenzenburg, as stated in Volume I; for corrections of other errors, *see* Zanzenburg, Texas). Center Point's population was 506 in 1970.

*Center Point, Texas. (Upshur County.)

*Centerline, Texas.

*Centerpoint, Texas.

*Centerville, Texas. (Dallas County.)

*Centerville, Texas. (Leon County.) Centerville, the county seat, was a farm market and lumber-manufacturing center with forty businesses in 1970. The town had one newspaper. The population was 836 in 1960 and 831 in 1970.

Centerville, Texas. (Trinity County.) Centerville was founded in 1935 near the Centerville school district in the center of the county. Most of the four hundred inhabitants in 1966 were connected with farming, ranching, or forestry.

*Central, Texas.

*Central College.

*Central Colorado River Authority. *See* Colorado River Authorities.

*Central Denuded Region.

*Central Male and Female Institute.

*Central Mineral Region. *See* Geology of Texas.

*Central and Montgomery Railway Company.

*Central National Road of the Republic of Texas.

*Central Nazarene College.

*Central Plains Academy.

*Central Plains College and Conservatory of Music.

Central Texas College. Central Texas College, Killeen, was approved in a 1965 Bell County bond election, and opened on September 1, 1967. Situated five miles west of Killeen on the south side of U.S. Highway 190, the campus was formerly part of Fort Hood.qv Plans called for construction of administration, science, academic, technical-vocational, and physical education buildings, as well as a library, student center, dormitories, maintenance shop, and homes for the president and custodian.

The two-year curriculum included arts and sciences, business administration, vocational-technical education, and adult education. Luis M. Morton, Jr., was president in 1974, when student enrollment was 3,499.

*Central Texas and Northwestern Railroad.

*Centralia, Texas.

*Centralia Draw.

*Centro, Texas.

*Ceramic Industry.

*Cerro Alto Lake.

*Cerro Alto Mountain.

*Cerro Boludo.

Cerro Castellan. Cerro Castellan (sometimes called Castolon Peak), just north of the village of Castolon in southwestern Brewster County, has an elevation of 3,283 feet. The word *Castellan* means governor or warden of a castle.

*Cerro Diablo Mountain.

*Cestohawa, Texas.

Chabot, Frederick Charles. Frederick Charles Chabot was born on May 11, 1891, in San Antonio, the son of Charles Jasper and Pauline Minter (Waelder) Chabot. He was graduated from San Antonio High School in 1909, then studied music and languages at the Sorbonne and the University of Berlin. Returning to Texas, he embarked upon a career as a concert pianist and organist. He decided to enter the diplomatic service, utilizing his mastery of French, Spanish, German, Italian, Greek, and Dutch in preparatory studies at Emerson University and Washington University. Chabot served in United States embassies and consulates in such diverse places as Paris, Athens, Sofia, Rio de Janeiro, San Salvador, and Caracas.

After his retirement from the diplomatic service, Chabot returned to San Antonio and became engaged in the research and writing of history, concentrating primarily on the Spanish, Mexican, and early Texas Republic periods. His most notable works are *With the Makers of San Antonio* (1937); *Excerpts from the Memorias for the History of Texas, by Father J. A. Morfi* (1932), a translation of those parts of Juan A. Morfi's qv work which dealt with Indians in Texas; and *Texas in 1811*, a translation done in 1941. All three were publications of the Yanaguana Society,qv which Chabot founded in 1933.

Other significant contributions made by Chabot include his locating thirteen original paintings by Theodore Gentilz,qv which were later placed in the Alamo; helping in the restoration of La Villita qv in San Antonio and also the nearby San José Mission;qv and in 1935 compiling an album entitled *Pictorial Sketch of Mission San José*, which illustrated the grandeur, charm, and artistic beauty of this mission.

Chabot projected a definitive history of Bexar County from aboriginal times to statehood. Unfortunately he did not complete it; he died while on a research tour at San Luis Potosí, Mexico, on January 18, 1943, and was buried there.

BIBLIOGRAPHY: San Antonio *Light*, January 22, 1943.

Hobart Huson

*Chacon Creek.

*Chacon Lake.

*Chadwick, Joseph M.

*Chadwick, Texas.

Chaguane Indians. Near the end of the seventeenth century the Chaguane (Chaguame, Ohaguame) Indians were reported as living between present Eagle Pass and the Nueces River. Later the Ohaguame (presumably a copying error for Chaguame) were listed among the tribes resident at the nearby mission of San Juan Bautista,qv and still later the name Chaguane was recorded at San Antonio de Valero Mission,qv in San Antonio. It seems likely that these names refer to the same band of Coahuiltecan Indians. Chaguantapam, a similar name, also occurs in the records of San Antonio de Valero and may be a variant of Chaguane, but further study of the original documents is needed for demonstration of identity.

BIBLIOGRAPHY: Bexar Archives, Translations, Vol. 3 (typescript, Archives, University of Texas at Austin); F. W. Hodge (ed.), *Handbook of American Indians*, II (1910).

T. N. Campbell

Chaguantapam Indians. This name is known only from baptismal records at San Antonio de Valero Mission qv in San Antonio. J. R. Swanton listed the Chaguantapam as Coahuiltecan without presenting evidence in support of this identification. It is possible that Chaguantapam is a variant of Chaguane, a name which also appears in the same baptismal records, but proof of this depends on further study of the primary documents.

BIBLIOGRAPHY: H. E. Bolton, *Texas in the Middle Eighteenth Century* (1915); F. W. Hodge (ed.), *Handbook of American Indians*, II (1910); J. R. Swanton, *Linguistic Material from the Tribes of Southern Texas and Northeastern Mexico* (1940).

T. N. Campbell

*Chalk, Whitfield.

*Chalk, Texas.

*Chalk Creek.

*Chalk Hill, Texas.

*Chalk Mountain.

*Chalk Mountain, Texas.

*Chalmers, John G. John G. Chalmers married Mary Wade Henderson in 1827 (not 1807, as stated in Volume I).

*Chalmers, Texas.

Chamberlain, Hiram. Hiram Chamberlain was born on April 2, 1797, in Monktown, Vermont.

Ordained a Presbyterian minister in 1825, he embarked on a career of mission work that took him to Missouri and Tennessee before he arrived in Brownsville, Texas, where he organized the Presbyterian Church on February 23, 1850, said to be the first Protestant church on the lower Rio Grande. In 1854 he helped found the Rio Grande Female Institute.qv

Chamberlain, twice widowed, was married three times, first to Maria Morse, by whom he had one daughter (*see* King, Henrietta). He had no children by his second wife, whose name is not known. In 1842 he married Anna Adelia Griswold, and they had seven children. He enlisted in the Confederate Army in 1862, served as chaplain of the 3rd Regiment, Texas Infantry, C.S.A., and was discharged in 1865. Chamberlain died on November 1, 1866, in Brownsville, Texas.

BIBLIOGRAPHY: Florence Bell, *A History of the First Presbyterian Church of Brownsville, Texas* (n.d.); Tom Lea, *The King Ranch*, I (1957).

Margaret Puckett Tipton

*Chamberlain, Texas.

*Chamberlin, Chester Harvey.

Chambers, Barzillai J. Barzillai J. Chambers was born in Montgomery County, Kentucky, on December 5, 1817, the son of Walker Chambers and Talitha Cumi (Mothershead) Chambers. He was commissioned a captain of the Kentucky volunteers by his uncle, Thomas Jefferson Chambers,qv and arrived in Texas during May, 1837, as an aide-de-camp. After his discharge in 1838 B. J. Chambers became a surveyor, first in South Texas, and in 1839 in Robertson County. In 1847 he was elected district surveyor of Robertson Land District. He settled in Navarro County as a farmer and land dealer in 1855 and became an attorney in 1860. He was an ardent secessionist in 1860 and served in the Texas State Troops in 1864. In 1867 with W. F. Henderson he donated the land for the establishment of Cleburne as the county seat of Johnson County. In 1871 he and J. W. Brown opened a private bank, from which Chambers retired in 1875. He was an alderman, and in the late 1870's he was an incorporator of a proposed narrow-gauge railroad from Dallas to Cleburne.

Politically, Chambers first gained notice with a newspaper article in 1868 opposing the creation of an interest-bearing national debt. He opposed ratification of the state Constitution of 1876 qv because of its homestead exemption, and was defeated for the legislature in 1876. He became a member of the Greenback party qv after the Democratic national convention of 1876 refused to adopt as strong a greenback money plank as he wanted, and he began to publish a Greenback paper in Cleburne. In 1878 he was again defeated for the legislature as a Greenback party nominee in Johnson County. He was an active party organizer and writer and in March, 1879, attended the Greenback national convention at Chicago, where he was elected the Texas member of the national executive committee. In 1880 he was nominated for vice-president by the Union Greenback Labor party and later by the National Greenback party to promote harmony between the two factions. He was forced to end his campaign, however, after breaking two ribs in a fall from a train in July. He continued to be active in the Greenback party through 1884.

Chambers married Susan Wood in Limestone County in 1852, but she died in 1853. In 1854 he married Emma Montgomery, who died after having one child. The child died in infancy. Chambers then married Harriet A. Killough in Johnson County in 1861, and they had one son and two daughters. He was a Mason and a member of the Christian church. Chambers died on September 16, 1895.

BIBLIOGRAPHY: Thomas Pilgrim and H. L. Bentley, *Texas Legal Directory For 1876–77* (1877); A. J. Byrd, *History and Description of Johnson County* (1879); *A Memorial and Biographical History of Johnson and Hill Counties* (1892); Galveston *Weekly News*, March 18, July 15, 1880.

Alwyn Barr

*Chambers, Thomas Jefferson.

*Chambers, William Morton. William Morton Chambers was born in Culpeper County, Virginia, in 1822. He came to Texas in the early 1840's and settled in Liberty County. In the 1850's he moved to Chambers County, where he served as a judge and as a delegate to the Secession Convention qv of Texas in 1861. After service in the Confederate Army, he again served as probate judge of Chambers County and was later appointed judge of the First Judicial District. Cleared of charges of malfeasance in office in 1874, he was reappointed a judge. After his defeat as the Republican candidate for governor of Texas in 1876, his political career was unsuccessful. In 1882 he was defeated for representative from the First Congressional District by Charles Stewart.qv He was again defeated as a candidate for attorney general on the Nonpartisan ticket in 1888.

BIBLIOGRAPHY: *Report of the Secretary of State of the State of Texas for the Year 1882* (1882); Galveston *Weekly News*, January 17, 1876; U.S. Seventh Census, 1850, Liberty County, Texas, and U.S. Eighth Census, 1860, Chambers County, Texas (microfilm, University of Texas at Austin Library); E. W. Winkler, *Platforms of Political Parties in Texas* (1916).

Alwyn Barr

*Chambers of Commerce. The first two chambers of commerce in Texas were chartered by the Republic of Texas. Houston founded its chamber of commerce on January 28, 1840, seventy-two years after the organization of the first chamber of commerce in the United States. The Galveston Chamber of Commerce was chartered on February 3, 1845. The United States census of 1850 listed thirty towns in Texas. Only ten towns had over one thousand population, and Galveston, the largest, had only 4,177 persons.

More than a decade after the Civil War, when Texas had seventy-five urban communities, several other cities organized commercial associations— Austin in 1877; Fort Worth, 1882; Gainesville, 1888; Hillsboro, 1890; Dallas, 1893; San Antonio,

1894; Marlin, 1898; Waco, 1899; and Port Arthur, 1899.

The commercial organization movement gained full momentum during the first decade of the twentieth century, which opened with 124 Texas cities; forty-five additional towns appeared in the 1910 census. The growing urban populations and steadily increasing number of cities awakened a competitive spirit among the businessmen of the various communities in quest of their full share of prosperity. Realizing the advantages of organized effort, businessmen in every city in Texas organized chambers of commerce before the decade ended.

While vigorously building their own communities, Texas business interests moved rapidly into a program of statewide cooperation. Chamber of commerce executives organized their statewide association in 1906. Two years later the Texas Business Men's Association was founded. It functioned successfully as the first statewide chamber of commerce until 1914, when its career was abruptly ended by a temporary court injunction secured by the state attorney general on grounds that the association engaged in politics. The charge was never proved, and the lawsuit was dismissed five years later. Local chambers of commerce had not been included in the injunction.

Upon recommendation of the post-World War I Readjustment Conference, the Texas Chamber of Commerce was formed in April, 1919, but was dissolved four years later because Texas businessmen preferred regional organizations. The powerful West Texas Chamber of Commerce qv was founded in February, 1919. Although rudimentary commercial associations existed in other sections, additional regional chambers of commerce were not founded until 1926, when the present East Texas Chamber of Commerce qv was organized on March 24, and the South Texas Chamber of Commerce qv on November 16. The Lower Rio Grande Valley Chamber of Commerce came into existence in 1944.

During the last four decades chambers of commerce have been the propelling force in promoting highways, transportation, industry, business, agriculture, tourism, new community facilities and services, and applying new techniques to keep abreast of the rapidly and constantly changing economic and political conditions.

BIBLIOGRAPHY: Carl A. Blasig, *Building Texas* (1963).

Carl A. Blasig

*Chambers County. Chambers County, one of the state's pioneer oil-producing counties, yielded over 676,776,000 barrels from 1916 through 1972. Natural gas and sulphur are other important mineral resources. The state's fifth-ranked county in rice production, Chambers County reported a 1970 farm income of $14,000,000, with substantial amounts brought in by the sale of beef cattle and white clover seeds for pastures. Excellent hunting and fishing facilities and many historic sites support the tourist industry. The 1960 population of 10,379 increased to 12,187 by 1970.

*Chambers Creek.

*Chambers Peak.

*Chambers Terraqueous Transportation Company.

*Chambersville, Texas.

*Chambliss, Texas.

*Chamizal Dispute. The Chamizal dispute was formally settled on January 14, 1963, when the United States and Mexico exchanged ratifications of a treaty which generally followed the 1911 arbitration recommendations. The treaty awarded to Mexico 366 acres of the Chamizal area and seventy-one acres east of Cordova Island. Although no payments were made between the two governments, the United States received compensation from a private Mexican bank for 382 structures included in the transfer. The United States also received 193 acres on Cordova Island from Mexico, and the two nations agreed to share equally in the cost of relocating the river channel. In 1964 President Adolfo López Mateos and President Lyndon B. Johnson qv met on the border to officially end the dispute. In October, 1967, Johnson met with Mexican President Gustavo Díaz Ordaz on the border to formally proclaim the settlement.

An aura of suspicion had hovered over Mexico-United States relations until President John F. Kennedy agreed to settle the Chamizal dispute on the basis of the 1911 arbitration award. Now that the conflict has terminated, an irritating source of Communist propaganda, directed against United States "imperialism," has been silenced. In placating the Mexicans, the United States demonstrated its firm belief in the Good Neighbor Policy, and Latin American fears of United States hemispheric expansion have been allayed. As a result of the settlement, the United States is seen as pursuing a more conciliatory line toward Latin America for the sake of gaining good will. With the advent of the settlement, access was granted to diplomatic archival materials heretofore "classified" for security purposes. Analysis of these documentary sources revealed new and profound effects which the Chamizal conflict had had upon United States-Mexico relations. This settlement might well lead to the solution of other outstanding diplomatic problems, such as the one between the United States and Mexico regarding salinity in the Colorado River.

BIBLIOGRAPHY: Sheldon B. Liss, *A Century of Disagreement: The Chamizal Conflict 1864–1964* (1965); Austin *American-Statesman*, October 29, 1967.

Sheldon B. Liss

*Champ d'Asile.

Champion, Albert. Albert Champion, son of George and Marie (Bronzin) Champion, was born on May 9, 1816, in Revigno, Austria. In the early 1840's he settled in Mobile, Alabama, after several years at sea. He later moved to New Orleans, where he was joined by his younger brothers, Peter and Nicholas. When the village of Point Isabel, Texas (later Port Isabel), was founded, the Champions were among the first settlers. The brothers early secured sail lighters and became engaged in transporting goods and passengers from shipside off the bar to the wharves at Point Isabel. Champion later established the United States Mail Stage Line, which he operated from about 1858 to 1873, when Point Isabel and Brownsville were connected by rail. During the 1850's Champion established two ranches, La Florida, the oldest in Cameron County, and La Gloria. In 1850 he married Estéfana Solís of Point Isabel. He held the appointive office of road commissioner for many years and in 1873 Governor E. J. Davis qv appointed him pilot commissioner for the Brazos Santiago port. After suffering property damage from the occupation by Federal troops during the Civil War, Champion became a citizen of Brownsville, where he engaged in merchandizing and managed his ranches. He died there on September 20, 1890, and was buried in Brownsville's Old City Cemetery.

BIBLIOGRAPHY: Joseph Kleiber Letters (MS., Archives, Texas Southmost College); G. D. Kingsbury, "The Lower Rio Grande Valley," Kingsbury Papers (Archives, University of Texas at Austin); Brownsville *Herald*, January 17, 1937; *Daily Ranchero* (Brownsville), 1868–1870.

A. A. Champion

*Champion, Texas. Champion, in western Nolan County, was established in 1902, when the Carlisle Ranch sold several small sections on Champion (formerly Champlin) Creek. That same year a school was built and soon afterward a store. In 1917 a brick school building was completed. In 1947 a tornado struck the community, killing three persons. The population in 1971 was about sixteen.

Champion Creek Reservoir. Champion Creek Reservoir is in the Colorado River Basin in Mitchell County, seven miles south of Colorado City on Champion Creek, a tributary of the Colorado River. The project is owned and operated by the Texas Electric Service Company. The function of this reservoir is to supply water by pumping to Lake Colorado City to maintain the contents of the latter reservoir at a satisfactory level. The water is used from Lake Colorado City for municipal and industrial purposes. Construction began on May 5, 1958, and the closure was made and impoundment of water started in February, 1959. It was completed on April 30, 1959. The reservoir has a capacity of 42,500 acre-feet and a surface area of 1,560 acres at the service spillway crest elevation of 2,083 feet above mean sea level. The drainage area above the dam is 203 square miles. *See* Champlin Creek.

BIBLIOGRAPHY: Texas Water Commission, *Bulletin 6408* (1964).

Seth D. Breeding

*Champlin Creek.

*Chamuscado, Francisco Sánchez.

*Chance, Joseph Bell.

*Chance, Samuel.

*Chance, Texas. *See* Ariola, Texas.

*Chandler, Eli.

Chandler, Jesse Van Buren. Jesse Van Buren Chandler was born November 9, 1892, at Belton, Texas, the son of W. E. and Sarah (Dickey) Chandler. He married Helen Marie Airhart on July 24, 1915, and they had two sons.

Chandler, a dentist, graduated from the University of Texas Dental School, and practiced in Kingsville, Texas. Active in the business, educational, and cultural life of his community, he was also known as a writer of articles, short stories, and poems, serving as a member of the executive staff of the Southwest Writers Conference. He was appointed to the honorary position of Poet Laureate of Texas qv for the term 1959–1961. He died on January 9, 1968.

Margaret Royalty Edwards

*Chandler, Samuel Ezekiel.

*Chandler, Texas.

Chandor, Douglas Granville. Douglas Granville Chandor was born in Surrey, England, on August 20, 1897, the son of J. A. and Lucy Chandor. He enlisted in the First Life Guards at the age of seventeen when World War I began, later becoming an officer in the famous Scottish Lovat Scouts, the commandos of that time. During lulls in action at the front, Chandor first tried his hand at portraiture. At the end of the war he was discharged from the service because of typhoid and a permanently injured knee.

He studied art at the Slade School in London and six months later embarked on a career of portrait painting. Swiftly advancing in his profession, Chandor soon became known for his portraits and drew his clientele from high English society, including such persons as Prime Minister Stanley Baldwin, the Lord Mayor of London, Lady Mary Curzon, and Edward, Duke of Windsor.

Chandor arrived in New York City in 1926. Within a short time he had painted portraits of several prominent American figures, including Mary Anne Scripps, Mrs. Duke Biddle, and President Herbert Hoover and his entire cabinet. In his hotel studio Chandor later painted the only portrait of Eleanor Roosevelt, as well as portraits of President Franklin D. Roosevelt, Bernard Baruch, and Samuel T. Rayburn.qv He was called back to England twice during his career, once to paint Winston Churchill and once to paint Queen Elizabeth II. During his lifetime, Chandor painted approximately three hundred portraits, including many of Texans.

Chandor settled in Weatherford, Texas, in 1934 and married Ina K. Hill, a Texan, on April 17 of that year. At his home he planted an elaborate garden with a great variety of plants and trees, including pear, peach, and apricot groves; Chinese fountains and pagodas decorated the area. Chandor had almost completed work on his garden when he died suddenly on January 13, 1953. He was buried in Greenwood Cemetery in Weatherford.

BIBLIOGRAPHY: Malcolm Vaughan, *Of Douglas Chandor, His Art and His Weatherford, Texas, Garden* (n.d.).

*Chanes, Rio de. *See* Llano River.

*Chanesa, Texas.

*Chaney, Texas.

*Channelview, Texas. [This title was incorrectly listed in Volume I as Channel View, Texas.] Channelview, bordering on the northern edge of the Houston Ship Channel qv in eastern Harris County, began to increase in population beginning in 1940. The major population explosion occurred in the early 1960's, with an increase from 1,150 in 1960 to 7,860 in 1970. Local light industry included the production of petrochemical products, hydraulic equipment, boats, and boating equipment. The town reported 110 businesses in 1970. Channelview, in conjunction with four nearby communities, has supported the municipal San Jacinto College qv since its founding in 1961. *See also* Houston Standard Metropolitan Statistical Area.

*Channing, Texas. Channing, seat of Hartley County, was incorporated in 1960. It reported one public school and three churches in 1966. Cal Farley's Boys Ranch qv is twelve miles south of the city, and two sand and gravel plants are within a fifteen-mile radius. A volunteer fire department, organized in 1963, built in 1966 a new station which was paid for entirely by donations. Members pay annual dues to belong and receive no compensation for fire calls. In 1970 Channing reported ten businesses. The population for 1960 was 351; the population in 1970 was 336.

*Chaparrosa Creek.

*Chapel Hill, Texas. *See* Chappell Hill, Texas.

*Chapel Hill College. *See also* Presbyterian Education in Texas.

Chapin, Texas. *See* Edinburg, Texas; *see also* Closner, John.

*Chapman, R. M.

*Chapman, Texas.

*Chapman City, Texas.

*Chapman Ranch, Texas.

*Chappel, Texas.

Chappell Hill, Texas. Chappell Hill, in Washington County, was named for Robert Chappell, who settled there in 1841. The original spelling in the 1800's was Chappell Hill, although later many of the local people began using the spelling Chapel Hill (*see* Chapel Hill, Texas, in Volume I for the town's early history). In the 1970's the official name for the post office and town was Chappell Hill (its original spelling), and the community had a population of approximately three hundred and fifteen.

BIBLIOGRAPHY: Betty Plummer, *Historic Homes of Washington County, 1821–1860* (1971).

*Chappell Hill Male and Female Institute.

Chappell Hill Stitchery. The Chappell Hill, Texas (Washington County), stitchery project began as a sound baffle for the Old Rock Store on Main Street, an 1869 building which was restored in 1971 by men of the Chappell Hill Historical

Society as a meeting place for the society. Because of the reverberation of sound when the group met in the building, members temporarily suspended quilts and blankets on the two long side walls. The group decided to create two permanent wall panels of stitchery which would depict the history of the Chappell Hill area and at the same time solve the problem of acoustics.

Twenty-three members of the society worked for nine months on the first panel, thirty feet long and six feet wide, showing ten homes and buildings of the area which have historical markers. The panel's background material is a soft shade of green duck. Depictions of the area, in addition to the historic buildings, are representative animals, birds, trees, and flowers; they were created out of textured fabrics and threads (chosen according to color, texture, and pattern which best suited the subjects) and were then appliquéd to the panel. A second panel on the same historical theme, to be placed on the opposite wall, was in the process of completion in 1972.

BIBLIOGRAPHY: Betty Plummer, *Historic Homes of Washington County, 1821–1860* (1971); Brenham *Banner Press*, February 24, 1972.

Dorothy Zeiss

*Chaquantie Indians. In 1700 the Chaquantie (Chacacante, Chaquanhe, Chicacanti) Indians lived on the Red River some sixty to seventy-five miles west of the Kadohadacho. This would place them in the area covered by present Lamar and Red River counties. Apparent variants of this name appear on several eighteenth-century maps, some showing the name north of the river, others south. The Chaquantie may have been the same people as the Cantey, who were listed as enemies of the Kadohadacho in records (1687) of the La Salle Expedition.qv The Cantey have been identified as Lipan-Apache, but this identification is debatable. The geographic and historical facts lend more support to identification of the Cantey with the Chaquantie. Although it has been speculated that the Chaquantie were Caddoan, this has yet to be demonstrated.

BIBLIOGRAPHY: F. W. Hodge (ed.), *Handbook of American Indians*, I (1907), II (1910); P. Margry, *Découvertes et établissements des Français dans l'ouest et dans le sud de l'Amérique Septentrionale*, III (1879).

T. N. Campbell

*Charco, Texas.

*Charles, Isaac N. See Nidever, Charles Isaac.

*Charleston, Texas.

*Charlie, Texas.

*Charlotte, Texas. Charlotte, in Atascosa County, had a population of 1,465 in 1960 and 1,329 in 1970.

*Charlotte Lake.

*Charnwood Institute.

*Charro Days. Charro Days, Incorporated, a nonprofit corporation, sponsors the annual Brownsville pre-Lenten celebration in which local people wear colorful Latin American costumes. Great study and care are given to each regional costume and its accessories. Texas Southmost College Library has a collection of dolls in copies of authentic costumes. Music and dances appropriate to each region are taught in the schools and to the general public.

The fiesta features dances, parades, window exhibits, and other entertainment attractions. The streets are filled with strolling musicians, commonly called *mariachi* bands. Throughout the annual fiestas, which date back to 1938, the celebration has been phenomenally successful and continues to grow in favor with Mexican nationals, northern visitors, and local citizens. Crowds are often twice the city's population.

BIBLIOGRAPHY: Charro Days, Incorporated, Minutes and Records; "Rio Grande Cornucopia Under a Winter Sun," *National Geographic* (January, 1939); *México: Leyendas y Costumbres, Trajes y Danzas* (1945).

John H. Hunter

Charro Indians. Charro is the Spanish name for an otherwise unidentified group of Indians represented at San Antonio de Valero Mission qv in San Antonio.

BIBLIOGRAPHY: H. E. Bolton, *Texas in the Middle Eighteenth Century* (1915).

T. N. Campbell

*Charters, Municipal. See City Government.

Chase Field. See Naval Auxiliary Air Station, Beeville, Texas.

*Chatfield, Texas.

*Chautauqua, Texas.

*Chayopine Indians. [See Tiopine Indians for statement of special problems connected with proper identification of the Chayopine.] San Antonio mission records indicate that after 1750 the Tiopine came to be known as Chayopine. It is said that the Chayopine (Chapopine, Saiopine, Sayopine, Zaiopine) originally lived east of the Nueces River near the coast, which suggests occupation of the area in the vicinity of present Bee County. The Chayopine-Tiopine were associated with three San Antonio missions—Nuestra Señora de la Purísima Concepcíon de Acuña, San José y San Miguel de Aguayo, and San Juan Capistrano.qqv The mission records show that they deserted the missions rather frequently, sometimes in large numbers, and had to be persuaded or forced to return. A few Chayopine served as teachers and interpreters at the short-lived San Xavier qv mission near present Rockdale. In 1768 some of the Chayopine were reported as living on the Frio River, presumably south of San Antonio. It seems clear that the Chayopine spoke a Coahuiltecan language.

BIBLIOGRAPHY: H. E. Bolton, *Texas in the Middle Eighteenth Century* (1915); F. W. Hodge (ed.), *Handbook of American Indians*, I (1907), II (1910); J. R. Swanton, *Linguistic Material from the Tribes of Southern Texas and Northeastern Mexico* (1940).

T. N. Campbell

*Cheapside, Texas.

*Cheek, Texas.

*Cheisa, Texas.

Chelsa, Texas. See Simpsonville, Texas. (Upshur County.)

*Chemical Industries. Texas' chemical industry had its large-scale beginnings before World War II with the construction of plants for making bulk inorganic chemicals, and during World War II with development of petrochemical units to produce synthetic rubber and other strategic materials. Since 1950 the enormous proliferation of the industry has placed it first among all Texas manufactures in value added. Capital investment for new chemical manufacturing plants and equipment totaled about $457,000,000 in 1965, over 40 percent of all new manufacturing investment in the state.

Most of the new chemical plants fell into one of three broad product categories: petrochemicals, based on oil and gas, industrial inorganics; and finished products, such as detergents, paints, and medicinal preparations. The greatest growth has come in the first of these three.

In 1968 the Texas chemical industry employed more than sixty thousand workers, mostly in the coastal area. The Houston vicinity, including Freeport, Bay City, and Texas City, contained the heaviest concentration of plants. Second in size was the chemical industry of Beaumont-Port Arthur-Orange. Other major centers near the coast were Brownsville, Corpus Christi, Victoria, and Seadrift. Total chemical plant investment in 1968 within a 150-mile radius of Houston was estimated at seven billion dollars. Inland centers of chemical production included Big Spring, Borger, Denver City, Longview, Odessa, and Pampa.

Petrochemicals. The largest-volume petrochemical product was ethylene, produced in more than a dozen Texas plants, most of them along the coast. Ethylene is an intermediate product, used in the making of dozens of chemical outputs. Some of these are polyethylene, made in larger amounts than any other plastic, vinyl plastics, styrene plastics and rubber, and cellulose acetate, as well as solvents, cleaning agents, antifreeze compounds, and many other products. The preparation of most of these petrochemicals was carried on in several phases, often in different plants, which were frequently connected by pipelines. Hence the term "spaghetti bowl" has come into use to describe the elaborately interconnected production complexes that have grown up along the Houston Ship Channel and the Sabine-Neches Waterway.qqv

Synthetic rubber, pioneer product of the Texas petrochemical industry, was made in larger volume in 1968 and in a wider range of types than ever before. Ten Texas plants, along the coast from Houston to Beaumont-Port Arthur, and also in Borger and Odessa, turned out various polymers and copolymers for use as rubber. Texas in 1970 produced 80 percent of the nation's synthetic rubber.

Some of the basic building blocks of the petrochemical industry were compounds that could be separated or derived from either natural gas or petroleum: ethane and ethylene, butane and butylene, propane and propylene. Others, such as benzene, toluene, and xylene are produced only from oil.

In spite of the occurrence of oil and gas in almost all parts of Texas, most petroleum refining was carried on along the coast, where low-cost water transportation could be used. The petrochemical industry, closely tied technologically and economically to refining, developed principally in already established refining centers.

Most of Texas' major petrochemical products were organic chemicals, but a few were not. Synthetic ammonia, made from the hydrogen contained in natural gas, was in rapidly increasing demand for use in agricultural fertilizers. It was made not only in the Houston area but also in East Texas and on the High Plains, where demand was strong for agricultural chemicals. Texas was the leading state in production of fixed-nitrogen fertilizers, chiefly ammonia-based.

Carbon black, used largely in tire rubber, was an important product of the Texas chemical industry. In the past most of the carbon black plants based their production on natural gas and were located in the gas fields of the Texas Panhandle. However, the grades of black in demand for use in synthetic rubber in 1968 were more readily made from oil, and the industry has migrated to the Gulf Coast, where petroleum-based feedstocks can be purchased from the large coastal refineries.

Sulphur was also a Texas petrochemical to the extent that large amounts were recovered from hydrogen sulfide-bearing natural gas, mainly in the Permian Basin and Panhandle gas fields. Similarly, helium was extracted from natural gas at Amarillo, Dumas, Gruver, and Masterson, which were close to gas deposits that contained enough helium to justify its extraction. *See also* Petrochemical Industry.

Industrial inorganic chemicals. Aside from petrochemicals, Texas' largest-volume chemical outputs were generally those derived from salt, sulphur, sea water, oyster shell, and other raw materials drawn mainly from reserves along the Gulf Coast. These inorganics included chlorine, soda ash, caustic soda, and sulfuric acid, all of which figured very importantly in a wide variety of chemical process operations. In 1963 Texas plants shipped more chlorine (valued at $23,000,000) and more caustic soda (valued at $36,000,000) than plants in any other state. Most of this came from production centers in or near Corpus Christi, Houston, and Port Neches.

Finished chemical products. The end products turned out by the chemical industry in Texas fell mostly into three categories: detergents and soaps, paints and varnishes, and pharmaceutical chemicals. Output of these products tended to be more heavily concentrated in Dallas than in any other Texas city. In fact, one Dallas plant accounted for most of the state's total employment in soap manufacture.

The making of paint and related products was a significant manufacture in Dallas and particularly in Houston. Texas' seventy-eight paint plants shipped products valued at $118,000,000 in 1963.

Texas' drug industry was small and rather highly specialized. Substantial quantities of veterinary medicines were produced and also some synthetic organic chemicals for medical use. However, there were no major production centers in 1968. *See also* Carbon Black Industry; Helium Gas Production; Rubber, Manufacture of Synthetic; Sulphur Industry.

Robert H. Ryan

*Chenango, Texas.

*Cheneyboro, Texas.

Chennault, Claire Lee. Claire Lee Chennault, son of John Stonewall Jackson and Jessie (Lee) Chennault, was born September 6, 1890, in Commerce, Texas. A descendant of eighteenth-century Huguenot immigrants, he was related to Sam Houston paternally and to Robert E. Lee maternally. At an early age he moved with his family to the Tensas River region in northern Louisiana. His mother died when he was five years of age. He attended Louisiana State University but graduated from Louisiana State Normal College. On Christmas Day, 1911, he married Nell Thompson, and they were the parents of eight children. The marriage ended in divorce in 1946. He then married Anna Chan on December 2, 1947, and they had two children.

He taught in various Southern towns, including Athens, Louisiana; Biloxi, Mississippi; and Louisville, Kentucky. With the American entry into World War I, he was commissioned a first lieutenant and became a flight instructor. From 1919 to 1923 he was with the Mexican Border Patrol; from 1923 to 1926, with the Hawaiian Pursuit Squadron; and from 1930 to 1936 he was a member of the United States Pursuit Development Board and leader of the Air Corps Exhibition Group ("Three Men on a Flying Trapeze"). Deafness forced his retirement in 1937. In the same year he became advisor to Chiang Kai-shek and the Chinese Air Force. In 1941 he organized the American Volunteer Group (Flying Tigers) in China. This organization became the 14th Air Force in July, 1943, and Chennault was promoted to major general. His tour was marked by conflicts with the theater commander, Lieutenant General Joseph Stilwell. He retired again in July, 1945. He then organized and was chairman of the board of Civil Air Transport, and he maintained homes in Taipei, Taiwan, and near Monroe, Louisiana.

He was the author of an autobiography and several works on fighter tactics. Among his many decorations were the Distinguished Service Medal with cluster; Distinguished Flying Cross with cluster; Army and Navy Air Medal with cluster; Chinese Army, Navy, and Air Force Medal; Commander British Empire; Legion of Honor; Croix de Guerre with Palm; and Chevalier Polonia Restituta. He died of cancer on July 27, 1958, at the Ochsner Foundation Hospital in New Orleans. He was buried in Arlington National Cemetery. Monuments were erected to him in Taipei and at Chennault Air Force Base, Lake Charles, Louisiana.

BIBLIOGRAPHY: Keith Ayling, *Old Leatherface* (1946); Frank Cameron, *Hungry Tiger* (1964); Anna Chennault, *Chennault and the Flying Tigers* (1963), *A Thousand Springs* (1963); C. L. Chennault, *Way of a Fighter: Memoirs* (1949); W. F. Craven and J. L. Cate, *The Army Air Forces in World War II* (1948); *U.S. Air Force Biographical Dictionary* (1965); *Who's Who In America* (1957); *Time* (August 4, 1958); New York *Times*, July 28, 1958.

James W. Pohl

*Chenoweth, James Q.

*Chenoweth, John.

Chenti Indians. The Chenti (Chení) Indians are known only from the 1730's, when they were closely associated with the Lipan and other Apache groups in west-central Texas, particularly along the San Saba River. They were probably one of several bands that later came to be spoken of collectively as the Lipan-Apache.

BIBLIOGRAPHY: H. E. Bolton, "The Jumano Indians in Texas, 1650–1771," *Quarterly of the Texas State Historical Association*, XV (1911–1912); F. C. Chabot (ed.), *Excerpts from the Memorias for the History of Texas, by Father Morfi* (1932); W. E. Dunn, "Apache Relations in Texas, 1718–1750," *Quarterly of the Texas State Historical Association*, XIV (1910–1911).

T. N. Campbell

*Cheocas.

*Cheremusca Creek.

*Cherokee, Texas.

*Cherokee Academy (1).

*Cherokee Academy (2).

*Cherokee Bayou.

*Cherokee County. Cherokee County, 85 percent forested and with eight active lumber mills in 1964, produces fruits, poultry/dairy products, and vegetables. The county ranked seventh in egg production and had sixty Grade A dairies in 1959. Some cotton is grown, though not as much as formerly, partly because more land is being used for improved pastures. Cherokee is one of three major rose-producing and one of the top two plum-raising counties in Texas. In addition, petroleum, iron ore, and natural gas are important to the economy. Lake Jacksonville and Striker Creek Reservoir are major recreational centers. The 1960 population of 33,120 decreased to 32,008 by 1970.

*Cherokee Creek.

*Cherokee Indians.

*Cherokee War.

Cherry, Emma Richardson. Emma Richardson Cherry, born in Aurora, Illinois, in 1859, the daughter of Perkins and Frances Richardson, married Dillin Brook Cherry of Houston, Texas. Mrs. Cherry began her art career by studying at the Art Students League in New York City. Persuance of the study of art took her to Chicago, Venice, Rome, and Paris, where she studied at the Académie Julien. The works of Emma Cherry were soon winning awards in various American and European exhibitions. She won the gold medal from the Western Art Association in Omaha, Nebraska, a landscape prize from the Southern States Art League, and a still life prize in Nashville, Tennessee.

In Texas her paintings merited awards in the 1929 Texas Artists Exhibit and portrait prizes in Austin, Houston, and Dallas. Her works were exhibited in the Paris Salon and the French-Irish Exhibit in London. In the United States, paintings by Emma Cherry were displayed in the National Academy of Design, the Art Institute of Chicago, the Museum of Fine Arts qv in Houston, the Witte Memorial Museum qv in San Antonio, the Delgado Museum in New Orleans, and other museums. Some of her works are in the permanent collections of the Society of Civil Engineers in New York, the Elisabet Ney Museum qv in Austin, the San Antonio Art League, the Denver Art Association, the Museum of Fine Arts in Houston, and in public libraries.

Emma Cherry was a member of many of the leading art associations of the United States and contributed particularly to art in Texas by aiding in the founding of the Museum of Fine Arts in Houston and the Houston Art League. Interest in the preservation of some of the historic architecture of Texas led to her purchase of the William Marsh Rice qv house in Houston which, after her death, was given to the Harris County Heritage and Conservation Society. Mrs. Cherry died in Houston on October 29, 1954, at the age of ninety-five.

BIBLIOGRAPHY: Files of the Alamo Museum, San Antonio; Dorothy Kendall Bracken and Maurine Whorton Redway, *Early Texas Homes* (1956); Houston *Chronicle*, October 30, 1954; Esse Forrester-O'Brien, *Art and Artists of Texas* (c. 1935).

Caroline Remy

Cherry, Johnson Blair. Johnson Blair Cherry, famed high school and collegiate football coach and successful oil businessman, was born at Kerens, Navarro County, on August 7, 1901. Cherry began his coaching career at Ranger following graduation from Texas Christian University in 1924. After three years at Ranger, he moved to Northside High School in Fort Worth. In 1930 he was named head coach at Amarillo High School, embarking on a remarkable career that saw his fabled "Sandies" win eighty-six of ninety-one games and four state championships in seven years. In 1936 he married Florence Snodgrass of Amarillo; they had two children.

Cherry was hired at the University of Texas in 1937 by D. X. Bible, and served as first assistant on the Longhorn staff for ten years. When Bible retired following the 1946 season, Cherry was named head coach. Cherry accepted the challenge of following Bible and gambled on a new formation, the "T." Executed by quarterback Bobby Layne, the formation was an immediate success. In Cherry's four years at Texas, he had one Southwest Conference qv championship, three postseason bowl games, and an overall record of 32–10–1.

He resigned after the 1950 season (in which his Longhorns ranked No. 2 nationally and became the school's first team to win all of its Southwest Conference games) to enter the oil business in Lubbock. Cherry was voted into the Texas Sports Hall of Fame qv shortly before his death in Lubbock on September 10, 1966. He was buried in Llano Cemetery in Amarillo.

Jones Ramsey

*Cherry, Wilbur.

*Cherry Branch.

*Cherry Canyon.

*Cherry Creek.

*Cherry Mound, Texas.

*Cherry Spring, Texas.

*Cherry Springs Creek.

*Chester, Texas.

*Chesterville, Texas.

*Cheyenne, Texas.

*Cheyenne Indians.

*Chiamon Bayou.

Chicago, Texas. Chicago, two miles north of Lamesa in Dawson County, was created in 1903 when the post office in the county was moved from the Barton Ranch headquarters to a sparsely populated settlement in the area, which already had a few stores. That same year Lamesa was founded, and in 1905, when Lamesa won the county seat, the entire population of Chicago moved there.

BIBLIOGRAPHY: Royston E. Willis, Ghost Towns of the South Plains (M.A. thesis, Texas Tech University, 1941).

*Chicago, Rock Island, and Gulf Railway Company.

*Chicago, Rock Island, and Mexico Railway Company.

*Chicago, Rock Island, and Pacific Railroad. The Chicago, Rock Island, and Pacific Railroad was chartered on December 16, 1947, in Delaware as successor to the reorganization of the Chicago, Rock Island, and Pacific Railway Company, from which it took over property and operations. In Texas the Chicago, Rock Island, and Pacific operated 773.7 miles of track. In 1955 it acquired 38.7 miles of the Wichita Falls and Southern Railway Company. Prior to 1964 it leased the track of the Burlington-Rock Island Railroad, of which it controlled one-half the stock. In 1964 it purchased half ownership of the Burlington-Rock Island Railroad Company, the other half going to the Colorado and Southern. In addition, the Chicago, Rock Island, and Pacific owned one-half interest in the Galveston Terminal Railway Company and one-eighth interest in the Houston Belt and Terminal Railway Company and the Union Terminal. *See also* Rock Island System; Burlington-Rock Island Railroad Company.

James M. Day

*Chicago, Rock Island, and Pacific Railway Company. *See also* Chicago, Rock Island, and Pacific Railroad.

Chicago, Rock Island, and Texas Railway Company. *See* Chicago, Rock Island, and Pacific Railway Company; Rock Island System.

*Chicago, Texas, and Mexican Central Railway Company.

Chicano. The word "Chicano," while not a new word, came into more general usage in Texas during the civil rights movement in the 1960's, especially among young Americans of Mexican descent, who used the word to refer to themselves with pride in their cultural inheritance. Although the origin of the word is disputed, it is often cited as having originated in northern Mexico. It is possible that the word was derived from "Mexicano," with the "x" having had, from the early sixteenth-century Spanish, the phonetic equivalent of a sound between the English "sh" and "ch"; thus, Chicano would simply have been a shortened form of Mexicano. The word was used in the United States as early as the 1930's, and in Mexico long before that. In the past it was sometimes applied to lower class Mexicans by the upper class, but it no longer has that identity. Most Texans and Southwesterners of Mexican descent use the word with pride, although some continue to think the word degrading.

Generally, Texans use the word to denote those who are committed to working for a radical improvement in the social and economic status of United States citizens of Mexican descent. The activity of this group has been described as the Chicano Movement; in addition to actively seeking political and economic rights, the movement asserts that their language and heritage are important and that they have made a significant contribution to life in the United States. The Chicano Movement seeks to educate Chicano people concerning their history and customs, to increase their pride and effectiveness as individuals, and to promote institutionalized education within the Chicano communities. One of the efforts of the movement was the organization of Chicano theater groups in Texas and the Southwest; these dramatic groups performed skits portraying the realities of being a Mexican American at rallies, churches, universities, housing projects, and community centers. Perhaps the best known Texas group, active in the early 1970's, was the Teatro Chicano de Austin, which was inspired, as were the others, by El Teatro Campesino (The Farm Workers Theater) in Delano, California. *See also* Mexican Americans in Texas (and other allied subjects, including political and social organizations, listed at the end of that article).

BIBLIOGRAPHY: Ernie Barrios (ed.), *Bibliografía de Aztlán: An Annotated Chicano Bibliography* (1971); Ed. Ludwig and James Santibáñez (eds.), *The Chicanos: Mexican-American Voices* (1971); Wayne Moquin and Charles Van Doren (eds.), *A Documentary History of the Mexican Americans* (1971); Richard A. Garcia, Political Ideology: A Comparative Study of Three Chicano Youth Organizations (M.A. thesis, University of Texas at El Paso, 1970); Ysidro Ramon Macias, "The Chicano Movement," *Wilson*

Library Bulletin (March, 1970); Austin *American*, May 18, 1972; Austin *Statesman*, July 10, 1971; Dallas *Morning News*, February 26, 1973.

Eldon S. Branda

Chichitame Indians. This is the name of one band of Chizo Indians, who are considered by some writers to be a branch of the Concho. In the seventeenth and early eighteenth centuries the Chizo occupied the area now covered by northeastern Chihuahua, northwestern Coahuila, and the lower part of the Big Bend region of Trans-Pecos Texas.

BIBLIOGRAPHY: C. W. Hackett (ed.), *Historical Documents Relating to New Mexico, Nueva Vizcaya, and Approaches Thereto, to 1773*, II (1926); C. Sauer, *The Distribution of Aboriginal Tribes and Languages in Northwestern Mexico* (1934).

T. N. Campbell

*Chickasaw Indians.

*Chicken Bayou.

*Chicken Salad Case.

*Chico, Texas.

*Chicolete, Texas.

*Chicolete Creek.

*Chicony.

*Chicota, Texas.

Chief Justice of County. *See* County Judge.

*Chigger Creek.

*Chihuahua, Texas.

*Chihuahua Expedition. *See* Chihuahua Trail.

*Chihuahua Trail.

*Chilano Village.

*Child Labor Legislation in Texas.

Childhood Development, Early. *See* Community Affairs, Department of.

Children of God. In 1969 a communal group of approximately two hundred young primitive or fundamentalist Christians, part of a national group called the Children of God (which was started in Los Angeles, California, in the late 1960's with thirty-five members), established a 425-acre colony a few miles from the ghost town of Thurber, in Erath County. Members used only Biblical first names, gave to the commune their personal possessions, and divided themselves into twelve tribes (inspired by the twelve tribes of Israel), with each tribe responsible for certain work several hours each day, including camp maintenance, food preparation, procurement of food from neighboring towns, and care of livestock. Their main interest was in Bible study and discussions which were often characteristic of nineteenth-century revivals. There was a Montessori school there for the colony's children. Rock music with religious lyrics was a favorite communal experience. Most members of the group had a history of drug use and claimed that they had conquered the drug habit through a communion with God.

One of several such communal Christian groups formed in the United States in the late 1960's (such as the Jesus People, the God Squad, Teen Challenge, and others), the Children of God was the largest national organization; by 1971 it claimed a membership of 4,000 in every state in the union, mostly teen-agers and people in their early twenties. Many parents were outraged, claiming that their children were brainwashed or hypnotized by leaders of the group and were thus forceably alienated from their families.

On Moratorium Day, October 31, 1970, members of the Thurber group of the Children of God parked their bus next to the campus of the University of Texas at Austin, and made a dramatic appearance wearing sackcloth and carrying Bibles, to "witness Christ" among university students.

In November, 1971, the Thurber colony of the Children of God was evicted by the American Soul Clinic group, a non-denominational missionary organization which owned the property. Many members sought to join Children of God communes in other states and in foreign countries, particularly England, where in 1972 many such groups had been formed.

BIBLIOGRAPHY: Larry Moffitt, "Children of God on Parade," *Texas Ranger* (supplement to *Daily Texan*), November, 1971; San Antonio *Express*, February 22, 1972, August 19, 1972.

Children and Youth, Commission on Services to. Created by the 62nd Texas Legislature in 1971, the Commission on Services to Children and Youth is composed of twenty-eight members, eighteen of whom are appointed by the governor with the concurrence of the senate for overlapping terms of six years (the remaining are permanent ex officio members who are heads of various Texas state commissions and departments). The eighteen appointed members must be widely representative of the racial, ethnic, and economic makeup of the state's population, and six of them must be younger than twenty-one years of age at the time of appointment.

The commission reports periodically to the legislature its findings in a continuous study of matters relevant to the protection, growth, and development of children and youth, recommending changes in existing state programs or proposing new programs. It encourages public and private organizations in the state to participate in children and youth development programs, and it performs duties assigned to it by the governor or legislature which deal with the national White House conferences on children and youth.

BIBLIOGRAPHY: University of Texas at Austin, *Guide To Texas State Agencies* (1972).

Children's Home and Aid Society, Texas. *See* Gladney Home.

*****Childress, George Campbell.**

*****Childress, Texas.** Childress, seat of Childress County, had a 1960 population of 6,399 and a 1970 population of 5,408. In 1970 the town had 146 businesses, including railroad shops and a hobby-horse manufacturer, six schools, a library, and two grain elevators. The first commercially producing oil well in the area was drilled in 1961.

*****Childress Army Air Field.**

*****Childress County.** Childress County is a predominantly agricultural region. Wheat is produced at the rate of four million bushels annually, supplemented by cotton and grain sorghums. Beef cattle are the chief livestock, followed by sheep and swine. In 1964 the county had twenty thousand acres under irrigation, with water authority headquarters at Childress. There were 8,421 inhabitants in 1960 and 6,605 in 1970.

*****Childress Creek.**

*****Chilicotal Mountain.**

*****Chilili Indians.**

*****Chilipin Creek.**

*****Chillicothe, Texas.** Chillicothe, in Hardeman County, was incorporated in 1911. A farm market, the town had three grain elevators, a new guar processor, cotton gins, seven churches, a hospital, a bank, a library, and a newspaper in 1966. A new high school was completed in 1964. The 1960 population was 1,161, and in 1970 it was 1,116.

*****Chiltipin Creek.**

*****Chilton, George W.**

*****Chilton, Horace.**

*****Chilton, Robert Henry.**

*****Chilton, Texas.**

*****Chimney Creek.**

*****China, Texas.**

*****China Creek.**

*****China Grove, Texas.**

*****China Spring, Texas.** [This title was incorrectly listed in Volume I as China Springs, Texas.]

*****Chinati, Texas.**

*****Chinati Mountains.**

*****Chinati Peak.**

Chinese in Texas. The first sizable Chinese migration into Texas was in 1870 when a group of approximately three hundred laborers were brought to Calvert in the Brazos valley to help build a railroad to Dallas. When the road was finished many of them returned and settled in towns which had appealed to them along the route they had worked.

A decade later, when the building of the Southern Pacific line reached El Paso, another large group of Chinese laborers entered Texas. They worked east from El Paso on the now abandoned rail line that followed closely the Rio Grande between Langtry and Comstock. When their work was completed many of them, like their predecessors, settled in towns along the route, a large number concentrating in El Paso.

The next major influx came in 1917 when several hundred Chinese, who had become friendly with American troops during their invasion of Mexico in pursuit of Francisco (Pancho) Villa, settled at San Antonio under the sponsorship of General John (Black Jack) Pershing. With the Communist takeover of China in the late 1940's, a final wave of immigration occurred when many students and professional people fled their homeland.

The older Chinese Texans were primarily natives of Canton Province who came to Texas as laborers, stayed to establish small stores, and clung to old ways in small tight-knit enclaves in the cities. Their children were largely well educated and entered many professions; they, along with the more recent professional immigrants, make up a large group of teachers, college professors, doctors, architects, chemists, and engineers. In 1970 it was estimated that there were ten thousand Americans of Chinese ancestry living in Texas, the largest groups living in Houston, El Paso, and San Antonio.

BIBLIOGRAPHY: Edward E. Briscoe, Pershing's Chinese Refugees: An Odyssey of the Southwest (M.A. thesis, St. Mary's University, 1947); Myrtle R. Dove, The History of Toyah, Texas (M.A. thesis, Sul Ross State University, 1947); Files of the Institute of Texan Cultures at San Antonio.

William Field

*Chinquapin, Texas.

*Chinquapin Creek.

*Chiquihuitilla Creek.

*Chiquita Creek.

*Chireno, Texas.

*Chisholm, Jesse.

*Chisholm, Texas.

*Chisholm Creek.

*Chisholm Trail.

*Chisos Mountains.

*Chispa, Texas.

*Chispa Creek.

*Chispa Mountain.

*Chisum, John Simpson.

*Chisum Trails.

*Chita, Texas. (Jefferson County.)

*Chita, Texas. (Trinity County.)

*Chittenden, William Lawrence (Larry).

Chizo Indians. The Chizo (Chiso) Indians were nomadic desert people who lived in the area now covered by northeastern Chihuahua, northwestern Coahuila, and the lower Big Bend region of Trans-Pecos Texas. They were also known under the alternate name of Taquitatome. The names of several Chisos bands are known: Chizo proper, Batayogligla, Chichitame, Guazapayogligla, Osatayogligla, Satapayogligla, and Sunigogligla. Some writers consider the Chizo as an eastern subdivision of the Concho Indians. The Chisos Mountains of the Big Bend National Park qv are believed to have been named for the Chizo Indians, whose range included the present park area.

BIBLIOGRAPHY: J. D. Forbes, "Unknown Athapaskans: The Identification of the Jano, Jocome, Jumano, Manso, Suma, and Other Indian Tribes of the Southwest," *Ethnohistory*, 6 (1959); C. W. Hackett (ed.), *Historical Documents Relating to New Mexico, Nueva Vizcaya, and Approaches Thereto, to 1773*, II (1926); C. Sauer, *The Distribution of Aboriginal Tribes and Languages in Northwestern Mexico* (1934).

T. N. Campbell

*Choate, Texas.

*Chocolate Bayou.

*Chocolate Bayou, Texas.

*Choctaw, Texas.

*Choctaw Creek.

*Choctaw Indians.

*Choctaw, Oklahoma, and Texas Railroad Company. [This title was incorrectly listed in Volume I as Choctow, Oklahoma, and Texas Railroad Company.]

*Choice, Texas.

Chome Indians. In the late seventeenth and early eighteenth centuries the Chome, apparently Coahuiltecans, ranged from northeastern Coahuila northward across the Rio Grande into the adjoining part of Texas south of the Edwards Plateau. The Chome are not to be confused with the Alachome; both names appear in the same document.

BIBLIOGRAPHY: M. A. Hatcher, "The Expedition of Don Domingo Terán de los Ríos into Texas," *Preliminary Studies of the Texas Catholic Historical Society*, II (1932); F. W. Hodge (ed.), *Handbook of American Indians*, II (1910).

T. N. Campbell

*Chorruco Indians.

*Chriesman, Horatio.

*Chriesman, Texas.

*Chrisman, John H.

*Christen, Texas.

Christian, Charles. Charles Christian was born in Dallas, Texas, in 1919. Much of his youth was spent in Oklahoma City, where he stayed with his father and played bass and guitar in various small orchestras in that area. His first experiments with an amplified guitar were in 1937. When John Hammond, the music critic, heard him two years later, he persuaded the orchestra leader Benny Goodman to employ Christian in September, 1939. Although barely twenty years old, young Christian immediately became known among professional jazz men for his new sounds and new ideas in modern jazz. Only one other electric guitar had been recorded on jazz records when the first Christian-Goodman records were issued. Since then, all musicians have insisted on his large creative contribution to modern jazz. Christian featured a down-stroke technique almost exclusively. To musicians, his single-string solos, featuring altered chords, new melodic lines, rows of even beats, and contrasting dramatic aspects have become the base from which they have created an entirely new approach to modern jazz. Christian won *Down Beat* polls from 1939 through 1941 and in the *Encyclopedia Year Book* poll of 1956 was chosen "Greatest Ever." Always in delicate health, he died of tuberculosis in a Staten Island sanitarium in New York on March 2, 1942, leaving behind a stature, a memory, and a contribution that belie the slightly more than two years that he was on the national scene.

Joe B. Frantz

*Christian, Edward.

*Christian Church (Disciples of Christ) in Texas. The Disciples of Christ (Christian Church) in Texas resolved at their annual assembly held in Des Moines from September to October, 1956, to change their official name to Christian Church (Disciples of Christ) and the official name of their annual convention to the International Convention of Christian Churches.

In 1966 the Christian Church (Disciples of Christ) in Texas had a membership of 133,157. Headquarters for cooperative activity was the Texas Association of Christian Churches in Fort Worth, Texas. Most of the churches cooperated with the International Convention of Christian Churches, and many of them contributed directly to the ecumenical movement. *See also* Christian Church Schools in Texas.

BIBLIOGRAPHY: C. D. Hall, *Texas Disciples* (c. 1953).
Noel L. Keith

Christian Church Schools in Texas. There were four Christian Church (Disciples of Christ) schools in Texas in 1967. They were Texas Christian University, Jarvis Christian College, the Texas Bible Chair Foundation, and the Inman Christian Center. (*See* Texas Christian University; Jarvis Christian College.)

The basic presupposition of the work done by the Texas Bible Chair, adjacent to the campus of the University of Texas at Austin, was that the examination of faith and life in the Judeo-Christian tradition was essential to all higher education.

The chair was founded in 1905, largely through the efforts of Mrs. M. M. Blanks of Lockhart, who gave thirty thousand dollars to purchase the buildings. The first teacher to hold that chair was F. L. Jewett, who assumed that position in 1905 and retired in 1946. The United Christian Missionary Society, in cooperation with the Christian Churches (Disciples of Christ) in Texas supported the Bible chair. The United Society, however, withdrew financial and administrative support from 1932 to 1942 because of the depression. In 1946, P. G. Wassenich was called to serve the Texas Bible Chair.

The Inman Christian Center, formerly the Mexican Christian Institute, was a settlement house founded to meet the spiritual and social needs of Mexican Americans in the San Antonio area. Founders of the settlement house were on the Christian Women's Board of Missions of the Christian Churches (Disciples of Christ). The permanent location of the settlement was established November 23, 1913, in San Antonio.

The actual work of establishing the school was done by S. G. Inman,[qv] director of Mexican missionary work for the Disciples of Christ, and by Hugh McLellan, minister of San Antonio's Central Christian Church.

In 1961 the name of the institute was changed to the Inman Christian Center. The program of the center by 1967 consisted of kindergarten, clinics, library, girls' clubs, boys' clubs, naturalization classes, mothers' club, parents' forums, arts and crafts, woodcarving, leathercraft, Mexican folk dancing, and community organization.

The center has been a member of the National Federation of Settlements in New York since 1948. *See also* Christian Church (Disciples of Christ) in Texas.

Noel L. Keith

Christian College of the Southwest. Christian College of the Southwest, Mesquite, belonged to Christian Schools, Incorporated, of Dallas, a private nonprofit organization for kindergarten-through-college Christian education in Dallas County. In 1961 Garland industrialist Austin N. Stanton announced a gift of 16.6 acres adjacent to Garland Christian School for a college campus. Chartered by the state in March, 1962, the college operated on a limited basis beginning in September, 1962, in temporary quarters with 115 students enrolled in evening classes.

Originally known as Garland Christian College, the name was changed to Christian College of the Southwest in February, 1963, to indicate the institution's regional influence and service. Day and evening classes started in the fall of 1963 with 137 students, and enrollment climbed to 161 students by spring. The 224 students enrolled in the fall of 1965 were taught by eleven full-time and six part-time faculty members. In the 1966–1967 regular term, student enrollment had increased to 264, while the faculty numbered twenty-nine.

In February, 1964, the college acquired for its permanent campus a 181-acre site, situated within the Mesquite city limits and a few hundred yards from the boundaries of Dallas and Garland. Officials projected the development of a full university. A two-year curriculum was offered leading to an associate in arts or an associate in science degree. By 1965 the college had established seven departments: Bible and Biblical languages, business administration, English, history and government, mathematics, music, and speech and drama. A member of the Texas Association of Collegiate Registrars and Admissions Officers and the American Association of Junior Colleges, the school was not yet fully accredited in 1965. Library holdings numbered 3,300 volumes. James L. Jackson, dean of instruction, served as chief administrator of the college until July, 1965, when Willis E. Kirk became president.

In 1971 the college became a branch of Abilene Christian College. In 1974 Douglas Warner was executive director and the school was known as ACC Metrocenter. *See also* Church of Christ.

*Christian Courier. The *Christian Courier*, published by the Texas Association of Christian Churches, in 1964 introduced an area edition plan, a unique innovation in Disciples of Christ religious journalism. In 1966 five separate editions were circulated to some thirty-two thousand families, making the *Courier* the most widely distributed newspaper among thirty-nine state and area Christian Church organizations in the United States and

Canada. *See* Christian Church (Disciples of Christ) in Texas.

Hartwell Ramsey

*Christian Messenger.

*Christian Preacher.

*Christian Science Movement in Texas. In 1966 Texas had 108 Christian Science churches and societies, and organizations at twenty colleges and universities. Dallas had six churches and one society; Houston, seven churches and two societies; and San Antonio, four churches. The first Christian Science Sanatorium in the Southwest, called "The Leaves," was established in Richardson in 1966 for the exclusive use of those depending upon Christian Science for care and treatment of illness.

The churches in Texas supported a radio series called "The Bible Speaks To You," heard over thirty-four stations in Texas. Three of these stations broadcast the programs in the Spanish language. In 1966 Texas churches took part in the observance of the one hundredth anniversary of the Christian Science movement.

Lee Mitchell

*Christine, Texas.

*Christmas Creek.

*Christmas Mountains.

Christopher College of Corpus Christi. Christopher College of Corpus Christi in Corpus Christi, Texas, was first organized in 1957 as Mary Immaculate Teacher Training Institute, an affiliate of the Catholic University of America. Governed by the Sisters of the Incarnate Word and Blessed Sacrament,qv the school's primary purpose was to furnish education for aspirants of the Order. In January, 1958, the institute was chartered by the state of Texas, and classes began at Incarnate Word Academy. Shortly afterwards the institute began admitting non-members of the Order to its classes, and in 1961 its name was shortened to Mary Immaculate College. A growing, more heterogeneous student body and a shortage of space led to a complete reassessment of the college in 1964. The following year the institution was reorganized as a junior college, and in August, 1965, renamed Christopher College of Corpus Christi. In 1967 the coeducational college offered an associate of arts degree, and was a member of the Southern Association of Junior Colleges, the American Association of Junior Colleges, and the Association of Texas Colleges and Universities.qv Because of inadequate financial support the college was closed August 31, 1968. *See also* Roman Catholic Education in Texas.

*Christoval, Texas.

*Christy, William H.

*Chrystal Creek.

*Chubb, Thomas.

*Chucareto Creek.

*Chupaderas Creek.

*Church of Christ. The Church of Christ had grown to approximately 3,165 congregations served by approximately 2,500 ministers by 1966. Lubbock Christian College was established in 1957, Fort Worth Christian College in 1960, and Christian College of the Southwest in Dallas in 1964. Bible chairs have been established at all principal state-supported colleges and universities and at most of the regional schools. Homes for orphans are maintained at Quinlan, San Benito, Fort Worth, Lubbock, Medina, and Cherokee. Homes for the aged are located at Gunter and Houston. An international program called "Herald of Truth" is produced in Abilene and is broadcast on more than five hundred radio and television stations. Missionaries are supported in eighty nations. Southwestern Christian College is at Terrell. The church sponsors more than twenty youth camps. A newspaper dedicated to church news, the *Christian Chronicle*, is published in Abilene. The *Firm Foundation* continued to be published in Austin; in 1955 Reuel Lemmons replaced G. H. P. Showalter as editor.

BIBLIOGRAPHY: Stephen Daniel Eckstein, Jr., *History of the Churches of Christ in Texas, 1824–1950* (1963).

Reuel Lemmons

*Church Hill, Texas.

*Church Hill Academy.

*Church Mountain.

*Church of the Nazarene. The Church of the Nazarene is a Protestant, evangelical, perfectionist body which originated in the early twentieth century as a result of successive mergers of small perfectionist, or holiness, groups. Its official beginning as a national church occurred in 1908 in Pilot Point, Texas, when the Pentecostal Church of the Nazarene, formed the previous year from a union of the Church of the Nazarene on the West Coast and the Association of Pentecostal Churches in New York and New England, merged with the Holiness Church of Christ, a Tennessee-Arkansas-Texas group. Despite the name, the latter had no doctrinal connection with the religious body known as the Church of Christ.

The Holiness Church of Christ was itself the result of the merging of two groups: the New Testament Church of Christ, organized in Milan, Tennessee, in 1894 and then expanded to rural areas of West Texas; and the Independent Holiness Church, with congregations in East Texas. These joined forces in 1904 at Rising Star, Texas, and contributed about one hundred small churches to the Pilot Point merger of 1908.

Doctrinally, the Church of the Nazarene is of Methodist lineage, subscribing to the view expounded by John Wesley: that the moral depravity of the soul can be cleansed away by operation of the spirit of God in a religious experience subsequent to conversion. According to Nazarene belief, the experience, termed "entire sanctification" or "Christian perfection," is characterized by purifying of inner motives, although it does not perfect human judgment or preclude mistakes and temptations. Other doctrines of the Church of the Nazarene include those common to conservative Protestantism. Belief in the free agency of man and in universal atonement places this denomination among Protestant churches espousing Arminianism.

In Texas the Church of the Nazarene is divided into four districts. Each district, led by a district superintendent, holds an annual assembly and is accountable to a General Assembly, convening quadrennially, and to a Board of General Superintendents. By 1966 Nazarene congregations in Texas numbered 280, with a membership of around 18,000. Total giving for all purposes exceeded $2,800,000, and church property in this state was valued at $13,000,000.

Internationally, the denomination, with headquarters in Kansas City, Missouri, numbered 350,-000 members.

BIBLIOGRAPHY: Ernest W. Moore, Jr., History of the Church of the Nazarene in Texas (M.A. thesis, University of Texas at Austin, 1963); Maury E. Redford, Rise of the Church of the Nazarene (1961); Timothy L. Smith, Called Unto Holiness (1962).

Ernest W. Moore, Jr.

*Churchill Bridge, Texas.

*Cibola, Seven Cities of.

*Cibola Indians. This name, which means "bison," was used by the Spanish to refer to various Indian groups that specialized in bison hunting. In the Texas area one group of Cibola (Cibolo, Cibula, Sibolo, Sibula, Zivolo) lived in western Texas in close association with the nomadic branch of the Jumano. In the late seventeenth century both groups were bison hunters and traders who traveled widely in Texas and northern Mexico. In the warm season they ranged the area between El Paso and the Hasinai country of eastern Texas but spent the winter in the Indian towns near present Presidio. Such evidence as is available suggests that the Cibola were originally occupants of the southern plains between the Pecos and Colorado rivers. They appear to have been displaced by the southward movement of Apache groups and to have moved into the Trans-Pecos region. Continued Apache pressure in the eighteenth century led to their disappearance as an ethnic group. Some Cibola were evidently absorbed by the Apache and others by the Spanish-speaking population of northern Chihuahua. The linguistic affiliation of the Cibola remains unknown.

BIBLIOGRAPHY: H. E. Bolton, "The Jumano Indians in Texas, 1650–1771," Quarterly of the Texas State Historical Association, XV (1911–1912); J. D. Forbes, "Unknown Athapaskans: The Identification of the Jano, Jocome, Jumano, Manso, Suma, and Other Indian Tribes of the Southwest," Ethnohistory, 6 (1959); C. W. Hackett (ed.), Historical Documents Relating to New Mexico, Nueva Vizcaya, and Approaches Thereto, to 1773, II (1926); J. C. Kelley, "Factors Involved in the Abandonment of Certain Peripheral Southwestern Settlements," American Anthropologist, LIV (1952), "The Historic Indian Pueblos of La Junta de los Ríos," New Mexico Historical Review, XXVII–XXVIII (1952–1953), and "Juan Sabeata and Diffusion in Aboriginal Texas," American Anthropologist, LVII (1955); C. Sauer, The Distribution of Aboriginal Tribes and Languages in Northwestern Mexico (1934).

T. N. Campbell

*Cibolo, Texas.

*Cibolo Creek.

Cibolo Crossing. See Carvajal Crossing.

*Cibolo Settlement, Texas.

*Cidwell Branch.

*Cienega Creek.

*Cienega Mountain.

Cigar Manufacture. See Tobacco Culture.

*Cigar Mountain.

*Cigar Spring.

*Cincinnati, Texas.

Cinnabar. See Mercury Mining in Texas; Mineral Resources and Mining.

*Cipres, Texas.

*Circle, Texas.

*Circle Back, Texas.

*Circle Dot Ranch.

*Circle Ranch.

*Circleville, Texas.

*Cisco, Texas. Cisco, in Eastland County, has varied recreational facilities because of its nearness to Lake Cisco and its opportunities for fishing, hunting, golfing, skiing, picnicking, and swimming in the "world's largest concrete swimming pool." Manufactured products include pottery, gloves, roofing, steel tanks, mops and brooms, and aluminum windows. In 1967 Cisco reported two hospitals, a bank, 125 businesses, and a junior college. Conrad Hilton's first hotel was built in Cisco. In 1960 the population was 4,499, and in 1970 it was 4,160.

Cisco Junior College. Cisco Junior College, Cisco, founded in 1940, offered fundamental preparatory work for admission to senior colleges, including pre-pharmacy, pre-medical, pre-business administration, pre-law, journalism, and work leading to associate degrees in arts and sciences. Technical and vocational courses, such as electronic data processing and vocational nursing, were also offered to assist students in qualifying for employment in the shortest possible time.

The physical plant included an administration building housing the commercial department, a library which contained twelve thousand volumes by 1967, gymnasium, auditorium, administrative offices, and classrooms; a music hall; a student union; a fine arts building; and several dormitories. The college was accredited by the Texas Education Agency, the Association of Texas Colleges and Universities,qqv and the Southern Association of Colleges and Secondary Schools.

Presidents of Cisco Junior College were R. N. Cluck (1940–1946), O. L. Stamey (1947–1954), Carlos J. Turner (1954–1957), Grady C. Hogue (1957–1966), and W. Leland Willis (1966–1973). Enrollment for the 1974–1975 term was 1,442; at that time Norman E. Wallace, Jr., was president.

*Cisco and Northeastern Railway Company.

*Cistern, Texas.

*Citizen, The.

*Citrus Fiesta.

*Citrus Fruit Production. Citrus fruits in the Rio Grande Valley, after their peak harvests of 1947 and 1948, experienced disastrous freezes in 1949 and 1951 which killed 7,000,000 of the Valley's 9,000,000 producing grapefruit and orange trees. In 1952 the citrus fruit industry began rehabilitation of its groves, while the canning industry in South Texas temporarily turned to vegetable canning. By 1959 the United States Department of Agriculture census reported that the industry had been rebuilt to the extent of 3,165,932 grapefruit trees on 2,299 farms and 2,428,543 orange trees on 2,129 farms. Approximately 39,201 lemon trees, which continued to have limited significance because of their lack of cold resistance, were reported on 298 farms; lesser production of limes, tangerines, kumquats, and other citrus fruits was also reported in that year.

In 1964 the Texas citrus fruit industry produced 2,400,000 boxes of grapefruit valued at $8,016,000 and 1,000,000 boxes of oranges valued at $3,810,000. Tangerines, tangelos, and tangors, as well as limes, kumquats, and various ornamental hybrids such as calamondin and citrangequats, continued to have only small acreage in Texas.

Texas produced 5,600,000 boxes of grapefruit valued at $10,152,000 and 2,800,000 boxes of oranges valued at $5,808,000 in 1966, placing it second and third, respectively, in the nation in citrus fruit production. The 1967–1968 crop harvested by December, 1968, however, totaled only 2,800,000 boxes of grapefruit and 1,800,000 boxes of oranges. Light November showers necessitated irrigation of the Valley's citrus groves and cool weather in that month was beneficial in maturing and coloring the smaller-sized fruit of that year. Texas citrus fruit production for the 1968–1969 season was estimated to be 6,500,000 boxes of grapefruit and 4,100,000 boxes of oranges, a 126 percent increase over the 1966 crop and a 230 percent increase over the 1967 crop. Production for the 1970–1971 season was estimated to be 10,000,000 boxes of grapefruit and 5,900,000 boxes of oranges of all varieties.

BIBLIOGRAPHY: *Texas Agricultural Progress* (January–February, 1960); *Texas Almanac* (1963–1971); *Texas Business Review* (July, December, 1952; October, 1959; September, 1960); Texas Department of Agriculture, *Texas Citrus*, April 12, December 12, 1968.

*Citrus Grove, Texas.

*City Government. By 1965 over 60 percent of the 921 municipalities in the state were mayor-council cities. Although there has been a substantial growth in the number of incorporated communities in Texas over the last thirty years, the number with commission forms of government has steadily decreased and council-manager cities have increased.

BIBLIOGRAPHY: University of Texas at Austin, *Bibliography on Texas Government* (1964); Texas Municipal League, *Texas Home Rule Cities* (1964).

Stuart A. MacCorkle

*City Lake.

*City Planning. See Planning and Zoning.

Civil Air Patrol Commission. The Civil Air Patrol Commission was created by the 62nd Texas Legislature in 1971 for the purpose of improving and promoting the Texas Civil Air Patrol, a voluntary civilian organization. The commission also promotes financing of the Texas Civil Air Patrol and is active in aerospace education and training programs. Almost all of the state's air-oriented search and rescue operations are supplied by the Civil Air Patrol, and the commission helps in the deployment of the patrol's resources, manpower, and equipment for such emergencies. Working with the Department of Public Safety,qv the commission is also involved in improving civil defense capabilities. The commission is composed of nine members appointed by the governor with concurrence of the senate for six-year overlapping terms. Reports to the governor and the legislature are made by the commission.

BIBLIOGRAPHY: University of Texas at Austin, *Guide To Texas State Agencies* (1972).

*Civil Engineering in Texas. Since 1950 civil engineering in Texas has become even more vital to the state as industrial development has accelerated. Water as a resource has become a major Texas concern, and development of a statewide water plan has received strong sponsorship. Dams have been built or planned on all major streams, including the large Amistad Dam (*see* Amistad Reservoir) on the Rio Grande in cooperation with Mexico and the sixty-million-dollar Toledo Bend Dam (*see* Toledo Bend Reservoir) on the Sabine River in cooperation with Louisiana. Plans for transporting water long distances were developing. Control of industrial wastes and water pollution generally has become a major activity, and similar attempts to control air pollution were beginning.

Limited access highways have been constructed across the state, both north-south and east-west. In cities, highway interchanges have developed striking structural patterns. High bridges have been built at Corpus Christi and Port Arthur to allow passage of ocean-going vessels, and in West Texas notable bridges for highway and for railway use have been constructed high above the Pecos River. Tall buildings have become commonplace in the larger cities, but in Houston a unique structure, the Astrodome qv (officially named the Harris County Domed Stadium), an enclosed air-conditioned field and stadium for professional baseball and football games, gained worldwide attention and opened new possibilities for major sport exhibitions.

Phil M. Ferguson

Civil Law. See English Law in Texas; Spanish Law in Texas.

*Civil Service in Texas. Between 1950 and 1965 there was virtually no political sentiment for the passage of a general civil service law applicable to state employees. During that period, the state had only three governors, and none of them asked the legislature for such a law.

A Civil Service Act of 1947, which was applicable only to firemen and policemen in cities of 10,000 or more inhabitants, has been amended many times through population-bracket legislation in an attempt to tailor the general act to one or more specific cities within the bracket. A general merit system law applicable to employees of cities of 10,000 inhabitants or more was introduced in the 1963 and 1965 legislatures, but the bills were never reported out of committee. The Texas Public Employees Association, composed of 25,000 state and county employees, includes "A Well-Balanced Merit System" in its aims, but nowhere does it define what constitutes such a system. The Council of State Governments estimates that 6,400 state employees in Texas are covered by merit systems required under federal grants-in-aid.

The only significant personnel step taken in Texas between 1950 and 1965 was the passage of the Position Classification Act by the legislature in 1961, after the Texas Employment Commission,qv pursuant to legislation request, had made a job survey of more than 26,000 positions and had developed therefrom 1,200 individual class specifications. The Legislative Budget Board,qv composed of representatives from both houses of the legislature, was responsible for developing a salary plan to fit the class specifications.

The Position Classification Act provides for its administration through a classification officer in the office of the state auditor. That official was appointed by the auditor with the advice and approval of the joint Legislative Audit Committee. In 1965 there were some 69,000 state employees. Of that number, and exempted from the act, were approximately 23,000 staff and employees in higher education and 8,000 hourly wage employees of the Texas State Highway Department.qv Other miscellaneous exemptions included department heads and other executive personnel. The classification office estimated that slightly over 36,000 positions were subject to the act.

In 1966 the adoption of a general merit system law with provision for open, competitive examinations seemed unlikely in the foreseeable future. Neither the state nor its local governments have developed on any wide-scale positive personnel programs, despite the great extent and technical nature of state and local governmental functions in modern society.

BIBLIOGRAPHY: University of Texas at Austin, *Bibliography on Texas Government* (1964); University of Texas at Austin, *Guide To Texas State Agencies* (1964).

J. Alton Burdine

*Civil War.

*Civil War Industry.

Civilian (Galveston).

Civilian (Houston).

*CJ Mountain.

*Clairemont, Texas. Clairemont, a ranch center in central Kent County, was the county seat until 1954, when, after a two-year court dispute, Jayton was designated the county seat. The population in 1970 was approximately thirty-five.

*Clairette, Texas.

*Clam Lake.

Clancluiguyguen Indians. In the eighteenth century this presumably Coahuiltecan band, also known as Clancluiguygu and Tlanchuguin, lived on the north bank of the lower Rio Grande between present Zapata and Rio Grande City.

BIBLIOGRAPHY: J. Jiménez Moreno, "Tribus e idiomas del Norte de México," *El Norte de México y el Sur de Estados Unidos* (1944); G. Saldivar, *Los Indios de Tamaulipas* (1943).

T. N. Campbell

*Clapp, Elisha.

*Clara, Texas. (Bee County.)

*Clara, Texas. (Wichita County.)

*Clara Lake.

*Clardy, Texas.

*Clare Creek.

*Clarendon, Texas. Clarendon, marketing center and seat of Donley County, had several gins and hatcheries to accommodate the produce of the county in 1971, when 81 businesses were operating in the area. Since 1950 the manufacture of cotton bags and covers has been added to the local light industry. The 1960 population was 2,172; the 1970 population was 1,974. The Clarendon Press, longtime publisher of Western Americana, is located in Clarendon. *See also* Bugbee, Harold Dow.

*Clarendon College.

*Clarendon Junior College. Clarendon Junior College, Clarendon, continued to grow and prosper after an uphill effort to maintain an institution of higher learning in that city (*see* Clarendon College in Volume I). An enrollment of 228 students during the 1966–1967 regular term was the largest in the municipal junior college's history up to that time. Dormitory facilities were filled to capacity, and the number of faculty members increased to seventeen. Library holdings in 1969 were 10,000 volumes. Kenneth D. Vaughan served as president in 1974, when the enrollment had increased to 395.

*Clarendon Lake.

*Clareville, Texas.

*Clark, Addison.

*Clark, Charles A.

*Clark, Edward. Edward Clark, eighth governor of Texas, was the son of Elijah Clark, Jr (not John Clark, who was governor of Georgia from 1819 to 1823, as stated in Volume I). His father and John Clark were brothers.

Robert Stephen Wilson

*Clark, George. George Clark was defeated in the gubernatorial campaign of 1892 (not 1893, as stated in Volume I).

*Clark, Horace.

*Clark, James.

*Clark, James Benjamin.

*Clark, John C.

*Clark, Joseph Addison.

Clark, Joseph Lynn. Joseph Lynn Clark was born in Thorp Spring, Hood County, on July 27, 1881, the son of Ella Blanche (Lee) and Randolph Clark,qv and nephew of Addison Clark.qv During his undergraduate days at Texas Christian University, he played baseball and assisted in the organization of the Texas Intercollegiate Athletic Association, Texas' first intercollegiate sports organization. He was graduated from TCU in 1906. From 1906 to 1909 he was an instructor in history and English at Add-Ran College and from 1909 to 1910 an instructor at John Tarleton College. He attended summer sessions at the University of Virginia in 1907 and at the University of California in 1915; he also did graduate work at Columbia University in 1917 and at the University of Texas in 1927–1928 and 1932–1933. He was married to Sallie Frances Chism on August 28, 1913.

In 1910 he was named secretary to Harry F. Estill,qv president of Sam Houston Normal Institute (now Sam Houston State University), and was soon given the additional duties of registrar, purchasing agent, bookkeeper, and librarian. He taught history at Sam Houston and was named head of that department in 1916.

Clark was the author of two school textbooks, A New History of Texas (1928) and The Story of Texas (1932); he also wrote, with Elton M. Scott, The Texas Gulf Coast (1955). His book Thank God We Made It! (1969) was an account of the Clark family's role in higher education in Texas. He was one of the organizers and second president of the Texas College Classroom Teachers Association (later renamed the Texas Association of College Teachers qv). He was a long-time member, vice-president, and fellow of the Texas State Historical Association.qv Interested in race relations, he was a co-founder and member of the Texas Commission on Interracial Cooperation, and it is possible that his was the first college course offered in Texas on race relations. Clark died in Houston on September 13, 1969, and was buried in Huntsville.

BIBLIOGRAPHY: Sam Houston Alumnus (August, 1951); Texian Who's Who (1937); Biographical Files, Barker Texas History Center, University of Texas at Austin.

*Clark, Randolph.

*Clark, Randolph Lee.

Clark, Robert Carlton. Robert Carlton Clark, son of Sallie (McQuigg) and Addison Clark,qv was born at Thorp Spring, Texas, on March 4, 1877. He was graduated from Add-Ran College (now Texas Christian University) in 1893, at the age of sixteen. His early teaching was in the public schools of Mineral Wells and at Bay View College in Portland, Texas. While a graduate student at the University of Texas, he prepared transcripts of official documents in the national archives of Mexico. He was one of the early historians of Spanish-French relations on the Texas-Louisiana border. His earliest authoritative contribution, under the general title "The Beginnings of Texas,"

appeared in the Quarterly of the Texas State Historical Association qv (January and July, 1902).

In 1901–1902 he held a graduate scholarship at the University of Wisconsin; in 1903 he was appointed fellow in American history at the same university, where he was awarded the doctorate. He taught at Pennsylvania State College, then at the University of Oregon, where he became head of the Department of History. He was married first to Ann W. Wallace, by whom he had three children; he then married Marguerite Straugham, and they had two children. On December 4, 1939, he died in the classroom of a heart attack. He was buried in Eugene, Oregon.

                                        J. L. Clark

*Clark, Thomas Marshall.

*Clark, William, Jr. William Clark, Jr., was a delegate to the Secession Convention qv in 1861 and served in the Eighth Texas Legislature from 1859 to 1861. He died on January 3, 1871 (not January 7, 1859, as stated in Volume I).

                                        Palmer Bradley

*Clark, William H.

*Clark, William Thomas. William Thomas Clark was born in Norwalk, Connecticut (not Norfolk, Connecticut, as stated in Volume I).

*Clark, Texas.

*Clark Lake.

*Clark Seminary.

*Clarke, Anthony R.

*Clarks Creek.

*Clarkson, Texas.

Clarksville, Texas. (Cameron County.) Clarksville, a place of importance during the Civil War, was near the mouth of the Rio Grande, opposite the Mexican city of Bagdad. During the war with Mexico, a temporary army camp stood there, with William H. Clark,qv a civilian, in charge. Clark set up a country store and served as agent for the steamship lines using the port. The town quickly developed; houses were built upon stilts to be above high water. During the early part of the Civil War, Clarksville thrived on the trade of the Confederate blockade-runners, but in 1863 it was captured by the Federals, who held it most of the time until the end of the war. The last battle of the war was fought four miles away at Palmito Ranch.qv In 1867 Clarksville was almost destroyed by a hurricane, but survived during the days of the river steamer. In 1872 it received another blow when the railway was built from Brownsville to Point Isabel, and severe storms in 1874 and 1886 finished it. In 1953 the river had changed its course and flowed over the site of Clarksville.

BIBLIOGRAPHY: Houston Chronicle, April 19, 1926; Dick King, Ghost Towns of Texas (1953); Florence J. Scott, Old Rough and Ready on the Rio Grande (1935); Joseph C. Sides, Fort Brown Historical (1942).

                                        Cyrus Tilloson

*Clarksville, Texas. (Gregg County.) See Clarksville City, Texas.

*Clarksville, Texas. (Red River County.) Clarksville, seat of Red River County, is a farm-market supply center with small industries including clothing, boats, fences, brushes, and mobile home accessories included among the 164 businesses reported in 1967. In that year Clarksville had a county hospital, two banks, a library, twelve churches, a newspaper, and a radio station. Improvements had been completed on streets and the water and sewer systems by 1966. In 1970 there were 127 businesses. A 165-acre lake and an October fair provided tourist attractions. The 1960 population was 3,851; 1970 population was 3,346.

*Clarksville Academy.

Clarksville City, Texas. [This title was incorrectly listed as Clarksville, Texas, in Volume I.] Clarksville City, an incorporated town in Gregg County, had a population of 359 in 1960 and 398 in 1970.

*Clarksville Female Academy (Mrs. Weathered's School).

*Clarksville Female Institute.

*Clarksville Male and Female Academy.

*Clarkwood, Texas. By 1970 Clarkwood, in Nueces County, had been annexed by Corpus Christi.

Clato, Texas. See Ecleto, Texas.

*Claude, Texas. Claude, seat of Armstrong County, had a 1960 population of 895 and a 1970 population of 992. A commercial center for ranching and farming, Claude had thirty-one businesses in 1970.

*Clauene, Texas.

*Clawson, Texas.

*Clay, Nestor.

*Clay, Texas.

*"Clay Castle." The plantation house "Clay Castle" was located one and one-half miles west of Independence in Washington County.

*Clay County. Clay County continued in the 1960's the population decline that had begun several decades earlier; the county's 8,351 inhabitants in 1960 were reduced to 8,079 by 1970. Oil production has remained at an annual yield of over 3,700,000 barrels since 1946; from 1902 to 1973 a total of over 148,000,000 barrels were produced. Livestock accounts for three-fifths of the farm income; wheat, cotton, small grains, fruit, and dairying produce the remaining two-fifths.

Although many historical accounts of Clay County state that the county was named for Henry Clay, of Kentucky, some sources claim it was named for the clay soil found in the region. No conclusive evidence has been found for either opinion.

*Clay Creek.

*Clay Lake.

*Clays Creek.

*Clayton, Joseph Alvey.

Clayton, Nicholas J. Nicholas J. Clayton, fellow of the American Institute of Architects, was born on November 1, 1849, in Cork, Ireland. Following the death of his father, he was brought to America by his mother when he was two years old. In 1864, at the age of fifteen, he enlisted as a yeoman in the United States Navy.

After the Civil War Clayton studied sculpture, architecture, and structural engineering with W. H. Baldwin in Memphis. He went to Galveston on December 8, 1872, and soon established himself as an architect. His advertisement in the Galveston *City Directory* stated that he was the "earliest established professional architect in the state." Clayton received many important commissions during the 1880's and 1890's, designing residences, churches, schools, and commercial buildings in Galveston and throughout Texas. Among the most notable of his works are the Gresham residence (now the Bishop's Palace), the W. L. Moody Building, the Galveston *News* qv Building, all in Galveston, and St. Edward's University Main Building and St. Mary's Cathedral in Austin. As the first professional architect in Texas, Clayton had considerable influence in the establishment of architecture on a professional level in the state. Clayton married Mary Ducie, and they had five children. He died on December 9, 1916, in Galveston.

BIBLIOGRAPHY: Howard Barnstone, *The Galveston That Was* (1966).

Drury B. Alexander

Clayton, William Lockhart. William Lockhart Clayton, one of the nation's leading cotton merchants for over half a century, was born on a farm near Tupelo, Mississippi, on February 7, 1880. His parents were James Munroe and Martha Fletcher (Burdine) Clayton. He was educated through the seventh grade in the public schools of Tupelo and Jackson, Tennessee, where the family moved when he was six years old. Proficient in shorthand, young Clayton went to St. Louis in 1895 as personal secretary to an official of the American Cotton Company. From 1896 to 1904 he worked in the New York office of the American Cotton Company, rising to the position of sales department manager.

In 1904 Clayton formed a partnership to buy and sell cotton with two members of a Jackson, Tennessee, family prominent in banking, Frank E. and Monroe D. Anderson,qv the former Clayton's brother-in-law. A younger brother, Benjamin Clayton, joined the firm in 1905. Anderson, Clayton, and Company first opened its offices in Oklahoma City and experienced immediate success. In 1916 the firm moved its headquarters to Houston, where Clayton, as the partner most expert in foreign sales, led other cotton exporters in providing warehouse facilities, insurance, credit, and other services which European firms had formerly rendered. Later in the 1920's Clayton led the fight which forced the New York Cotton Exchange to accept Southern delivery on futures contracts, thus removing an impediment to the natural operation of the futures market.

When high tariffs and federal farm price supports tended to drive American-grown cotton out of the world market in the late 1920's and early 1930's, Clayton's firm responded by establishing cotton-buying offices in Latin America and Africa in order to supply its foreign sales agencies with cotton at competitive rates. Meanwhile, Anderson, Clayton, and Company increased investments in cotton gins, vegetable oil mills, commercial animal feeds, experimental seed farms, and other activities related to processing cotton and similar commodities which from the beginning had made the firm unique among cotton-merchandising organizations. Although Clayton retired from the partnership in 1940, he retained a major interest in the newly formed Anderson, Clayton, and Company, Incorporated, to which the principal assets of the partnership had been assigned. In post-World War II years he took a seat on the company's board of directors.

Clayton distinguished himself in public service as well as business. During World War I he served on the Committee of Cotton Distribution of the War Industries Board. In 1940 he was called to Washington to serve as deputy to the coordinator of inter-American affairs. For the next four years he held a variety of high-level positions with the Export-Import Bank, the Department of Commerce, and wartime agencies. From December, 1943, until October, 1947, he was assistant and then undersecretary of state for economic affairs, in which capacity he became a principal architect of the European Recovery Program, known commonly as the Marshall Plan. Returning to Houston late in 1947, he remained an occasional participant and frequent contributor to international conferences concerning world trade, the European Common Market, and related matters.

Clayton contributed personally and through the Clayton Fund to a variety of religious, charitable, and educational institutions, most notably to Johns Hopkins University (of which he was a trustee from 1949 to 1966), Tufts University, the University of Texas, Susan V. Clayton Homes (a low-cost housing project in Houston), and the Methodist church.

Clayton married the former Susan Vaughan of Clinton, Kentucky, on August 14, 1902. One son died in infancy, but four daughters survived their parents. Clayton died following a brief illness, on February 8, 1966. He was buried in Glenwood Cemetery, Houston.

BIBLIOGRAPHY: Ellen Clayton Garwood, *Will Clayton: A Short Biography* (1958).

James A. Tinsley

*Clayton, Texas.

*Claytonville, Texas.

*Clear Creek.

*Clear Creek, Texas. (DeWitt County.)

*Clear Creek, Texas. (Hemphill County.)

*Clear Fork of the Brazos River.

*Clear Fork Indian Agency. *See* Comanche Indian Reservation.

*Clear Fork of the Trinity River.

*Clear Lake, Texas.

*Clear Spring, Texas.

Clearwater, Theresa Clark. Theresa Clark Clearwater, daughter of William Henry Clark, was born December 19, 1853, at Clarksville in Cameron County. In 1872 she received a state teaching certificate and, at a salary of fifty-five dollars a month, became the teacher of the first school in Cameron County and one of the first certified teachers in the border area. In 1875 Theresa Clark married Joseph H. Clearwater; they had two children. After her husband's death in 1879 in Tampico, Mexico, she returned to Point Isabel, then moved to Brownsville where she taught school from 1882 to 1936. She died on September 28, 1938; a Brownsville elementary school was named in her honor.

BIBLIOGRAPHY: W. H. Chatfield, *Twin Cities of the Border* (1893); San Antonio *Express*, January 10, 1937.

Verna J. McKenna

*Clearwater, Texas.

*Cleason Creek.

*Clebarro College.

*Cleburne, Texas. Cleburne, county seat of Johnson County, had a 1960 population of 15,381 and a 1970 population of 16,015. In 1966 Cleburne reported forty-eight churches, a library, nine schools, two newspapers, a radio station, and three parks. In 1967 the town had 359 businesses, including twenty-nine manufacturers connected with pipe making, metal working, the manufacture of machine parts, textiles, air conditioners, and clothing. In the 1960's the town increased both in income and in population. Cleburne Reservoir was completed in 1965, supplying the city's water needs. Trends in land use are toward livestock raising rather than crop production. A new municipal building was completed in 1966. *See also* Fort Worth Standard Metropolitan Statistical Area.

*Cleburne Male and Female Institute.

Cleburne Reservoir. *See* Lake Pat Cleburne.

Clegg, George Austin. George Austin Clegg, one of the nation's most successful breeders of fine quarter horses, was born on April 22, 1872, at Thomaston, Texas, a village near Cuero. He attended the public school at Thomaston, St. Joseph's College in Victoria, and Baylor University. On July 12, 1897, he married Letitia Nichols of Cuero, and in 1904, they moved to Alice.

"Old Sorrel," foundation stallion of the King Ranch qv herd, was from Clegg's stock. Some other famous Clegg horses were Jodie Clegg and Cotton Eye Joe (sires); Jiggs and Medina Sport (roping horses); and racers, Rondo, Little Joe, and Hickory Bill.

Clegg started in 1905 with an especially good group of mares sired by Little Joe. In 1911 he was racing some of their offspring, and by 1916 Clegg was an established quarter horse breeder. In 1929 Clegg was involved in an automobile accident in which he was injured and his wife was killed. The stock market crash and continued depression wiped out Clegg's extensive ranch holdings and herd of racing horses. He lost a sheriff's race in 1934 in Alice. Because of his knowledge and integrity, he became a nationally recognized and much sought-after judge at horse shows. During June, 1952, Clegg took a boatload of cattle to Cuba for the King Ranch.

He died on January 10, 1959, at the home of his daughter in Alice. In appreciation of his accomplishments in the quarter horse field, the King Ranch donated the George Clegg Memorial Trophy to be presented to the grand champion of the Quarter Horse Show at the Jim Wells County Fair.

BIBLIOGRAPHY: Scrapbook of clippings (Christine Clegg Phillips, Alice, Texas); Alice *Daily Echo*, October 25, 1965; Alice *News*, November 4, 1965.

Agnes G. Grimm

*Clegg, Texas. In 1914 the post office at Clegg was established on Harry Hyman's ranch in southwestern Live Oak County. Hyman had cut his ranch into one-hundred-acre tracts for sale to farmers. S. A. Story was the first postmaster. In 1927 the post office was moved three miles northeast to Gay's store. On January 1, 1941, the post office was discontinued and mail was delivered by a rural route from George West. In 1963 there was a store and garage on U.S. Highway 59, known as the Clegg store, several miles from the original site.

Cyrus Tilloson

*Clem, John Lincoln.

*Clemens, Texas.

*Clemens Creek.

*Clements, Joseph D.

*Clemons, Lewis Chapman.

*Clemville, Texas.

*Cleo, Texas.

Cleto, Texas. *See* Ecleto, Texas.

*Cleveland, Texas. Cleveland is a marketing and processing center for lumber, oil, and agricultural products for Liberty County. In 1967 the town had 164 businesses, with eight manufacturers supplying lumber products and sand and gravel, and producing electronic components, hydraulic machinery, and oil field supplies. A forty-eight-bed hospital, five schools, a city park, and Stancil Memorial Park served the town. The 1960 population was 5,838; the 1970 population was 5,627. *See also* Houston Standard Metropolitan Statistical Area.

*Clevenger, Texas. *See* Tubbes, Texas.

*Click, Texas.

*Click Branch.

*Click Creek.

*Click Gap.

*Cliff, Texas.

*Cliffside, Texas.

*Clifton, John M.

*Clifton, Texas. (Bosque County.) Clifton reported a hospital, clinic, grain elevator and mill,

and 116 businesses in 1970. In 1960 the population was 2,335; in 1970 it was 2,578.

*Clifton, Texas. (Van Zandt County.)

*Clifton Academy.

*Clifton Junior College. Because of a decline in enrollment and income, it was decided in 1953 that Clifton Junior College, a successor to the old Clifton Academy qv in Clifton, Bosque County, would be merged with Texas Lutheran College qv in Seguin. A dormitory at Texas Lutheran College was named Clifton Hall as a reminder of the early educational interest of Norwegian settlers in Clifton. *See also* Lutheran Church in Texas; Clifton Lutheran Sunset Home.

W. A. Flachmeier

Clifton Lutheran Sunset Home. After Clifton Junior College qv was merged with Texas Lutheran College qv in Seguin the Clifton campus was converted in 1954 into a home for elderly people. Supported by the Evangelical Lutheran church, the home was soon filled to capacity. An infirmary was added, and extensive remodelling was undertaken with the help of Hill-Burton funds. Odie C. Pederson was the first superintendent; he was succeeded by Elmer Luckenbach.

W. A. Flachmeier

*Clifton-by-the-Sea, Texas.

*Clifty Creek.

Climate of Texas. *See* Weather in Texas.

*Climax, Texas. (Collin County.)

*Climax, Texas. (Nacogdoches County.)

*Cline, Henry B.

*Cline, Texas.

*Cline Mountains.

*Clint, Texas.

*Clinton, Texas. (DeWitt County.)

*Clinton, Texas. (Hunt County.)

*Clinton-Oklahoma Western Railway Company of Texas. The Clinton-Oklahoma Western Railway Company of Texas, leased from 1943 to 1948 to the Panhandle and Santa Fe Railway, was acquired by the Panhandle and Santa Fe Railway in December, 1948. At this time it operated 64.7 miles of track.

James M. Day

*Clisbee, Texas.

*Clodine, Texas.

*Cloice Branch.

Clopper, Nicholas. Nicholas Clopper was born in New Brunswick, New Jersey, on November 3, 1766. After unsuccessful business ventures in Pennsylvania and Maryland, he moved to Ohio about 1820. Two years later he came to Texas to Stephen F. Austin's colony, hoping to recoup his fortunes by trade and land speculation. From that date until his death on December 2, 1841, he divided his time between Ohio and Texas.

One of the first to see the potential of Buffalo Bayou as a trade route between the Brazos area and the sea, Clopper organized the Texas Trading Association in 1827 to conduct trade over the route. In 1826 he purchased the peninsula between Galveston and San Jacinto bays, now known as Morgan's Point. The sand bar blocking the entrance to San Jacinto Bay still bears his name. In 1835 Clopper presided over a meeting in Cincinnati, Ohio, which opened a subscription to purchase two cannon, the famous Twin Sisters,qv for the Texas revolutionaries.

Clopper, who married Rebecca Chambers in 1790, was the father of eleven children. One of his sons, Andrew M., was a courier for President David G. Burnet qv during the Texas Revolution. Another was lost at sea in 1822 or possibly killed by Karankawa Indians on the Texas coast. Two other sons, Joseph C. and Edward N., came to Texas with Clopper at various times. The printed letters and journals of the family tell much about life and events in Texas at the time.

BIBLIOGRAPHY: E. N. Clopper, *An American Family* (1950); *Quarterly of the Texas State Historical Association*, XIII (1909–1910).

Marilyn M. Sibley

*Clopton, Albert Gallatin.

*Close City, Texas. Close City is in western Garza County (not Graza County, as stated in Volume I).

Closner, John. John Closner, founder and main developer of Edinburg, Texas, also known as the "Father of Hidalgo County," was born in 1853 in Glaris, Wisconsin. He came to Texas in 1870, settling first in Bosque County. He arrived in Rio Grande City in 1883 with a capital of fifteen dollars, starting as a stage driver to Peña Station,qv and later obtaining the mail contract between Brownsville and Rio Grande City. In 1884 he moved to Hidalgo, then the county seat of Hidalgo County, where less than a dozen Anglo Americans lived. At a time when border banditry and cattle rustling were of prime concern, Closner was appointed deputy sheriff in 1884 and served until 1889, when he was elected sheriff and tax collector, positions he held until his retirement from public office in 1912.

As one of the Rio Grande Valley's largest landowners, his greatest contribution was in promoting irrigation and diversified farming. He bought land at twenty-five cents to one dollar an acre, until his holdings reached forty-five thousand acres. Constructing a canal system for carrying water from the Rio Grande to his crops, he experimented successfully with the growing of a wide variety of fruits and vegetables. His sugar cane won a gold medal at the St. Louis Exposition in 1904.

Through his influence and gift of two thousand acres, Closner, with the help of Lon C. Hill,qv Tom Hicks, and others, obtained the extension of the St. Louis, Brownsville, and Mexico Railway through Hidalgo County to Samfordyce. At San Juan (named for John Closner), a branch line was extended seven miles north to the 300,000-acre ranch of William Sprague. Closner and Sprague were the principal owners of this railroad project.

A townsite, laid out as Chapin and later renamed Edinburg, contained 1,400 acres donated by Closner and Sprague, who with D. B. Chapin were instrumental in having a special election called to move the county seat. The election was held October 8, 1908, and the vote was favorable for the move from Hidalgo to Edinburg. To prevent blocking of the move by those who objected, tents were set up to receive the county records, and men with wagons and mule teams made the move overnight.

Closner gave the city its first public school and was for years president of the Edinburg State Bank and director in several other Valley banks. He was the moving spirit behind Edinburg's irrigation system. He started a small private telephone system in 1902 which later developed into the Hidalgo Telephone Company, with Closner as president.

In 1888 he married Mary Elizabeth Doughtry of Brownsville, who died in 1903. They had three children. In 1904 he married Alice Doughtry, sister of his first wife. In 1923 the family moved to Brownsville, where Closner lived in retirement until his death in 1932. *See also* San Juan Plantation.

BIBLIOGRAPHY: J. L. Allhands, *Gringo Builders* (1931); Edinburg *Daily Review*, March 21, 1965; *Encyclopedia of American Biography* (1937); San Antonio *Express*, September 7, 1911.

Verna J. McKenna

*Clothing Manufacture. The manufacture of apparel and related items was, in number of employees and size of payroll, the fourth largest manufacturing industry in Texas in 1963. With 40,150 employees and a $124,809,000 payroll, the industry was outdistanced only by manufacturing of machinery, transportation equipment, and chemicals and allied products. More than a third of apparel manufacturing in Texas was concentrated in Dallas County, which had 12,355 employees and a payroll of $43,704,000.

A growing awareness of the power of the press and its relation to fashion apparel success caused the apparel manufacturers' organization to sponsor its first annual national press week in March, 1951. This successful endeavor has, through the years, brought Texas fashions into strong focus nationally, as wire services, syndicates, newspaper fashion editors, and magazines have related the Texas fashion story in headlines and pictures. The resulting value of lineage space given to Texas fashions has reached millions of dollars.

As women's and children's apparel manufacturers began springing up in all sections of Texas, the Dallas group enlarged its scope to include members from all over the state. Subsequently in 1961 the organization became the Texas Fashion Creators Association.

A stimulus to the Texas fashion industry was the erection of the fifteen-million-dollar Apparel Mart as part of a vast Dallas Market Center complex of five buildings. This center, already enlarged, draws buyers from nearly every state, as 3,000 lines of women's apparel and accessories, 550 of children's wear, 700 of men's apparel and accessories, plus 250 textile assortments are displayed. Mart officials report approximately seventy thousand buyers attend the market sessions in the Apparel Mart, with a 15 to 25 percent attendance growth at each market annually. Another factor catalyzing the fashion business in Texas was the relocation of the Army and Air Force Exchange Services from New York to Dallas on January 1, 1967.

In 1958 Texas Fashion Creators purchased *Dallas Fashion & Sportswear* magazine, later renaming it *Texas Fashions.* This magazine reached more than twelve thousand retailers in every state of the union, showing photographs and sketches of newly designed apparel and accessories, and offering constructive ideas for improving the state of the retail business. This medium is used as a sales promotion and public relations tool for the industry as a whole.

Other elements spotlighting Texas as a state of fashion must be attributed to fashion-minded retailers who wished to create unique concepts of fashion and quality in their stores. The influence of Neiman-Marcus,qv established in Dallas in 1907 by Herbert Marcus,qv has helped create the favorable fashion climate which exists in Texas.

As retailers and manufacturers of Texas advertised nationally and generated worldwide fashion promotions, the Texas fashion concept continued to flourish.

Velma McKee

*Cloud, John Wurts.

*Clouds Bayou.

Cluetau Indians. This name occurs in the records of San Antonio de Valero Mission qv at San Antonio. As no further record of this Indian group has been found, its affiliation remains unknown. J. R. Swanton listed the Cluetau as a Coahuiltecan band, but he presented no evidence in support of this linguistic identification.

BIBLIOGRAPHY: F. W. Hodge (ed.), *Handbook of American Indians,* II (1910); J. R. Swanton, *The Indian Tribes of North America* (1952).

T. N. Campbell

*Clute, Texas. Clute, in Brazoria County, continued to increase in population, reaching 4,501 in 1960 and 6,023 in 1970. *See also* Houston Standard Metropolitan Statistical Area.

*Clyde, Texas. Clyde, in Callahan County, had a population of 1,116 in 1960 and 1,635 in 1970.

Coaches Association. *See* High School Coaches Association.

*Coahoma, Texas. Coahoma, in Howard County, had a population of 1,239 in 1960 and 1,158 in 1970.

*Coahoma Draw.

*Coahuila and Texas. *See also* Nueva Estremadura; New Philippines.

*Coahuiltecan Indians.

*Coal Creek.

*Coal Kiln Draw.

*Coal and Lignite Deposits in Texas. *See also* Coal and Lignite Mining in Texas.

Coal and Lignite Mining in Texas. Undoubtedly early settlers mined both coal and lignite from numerous outcroppings across the state for use in their homes, stores, and blacksmith shops. Commercial mining, however, did not commence until the 1880's. The first year that coal production was listed for Texas was 1884, when 125,000 tons were mined. Production declined from 1885 to 1888. From 1889 to 1901, production climbed tremendously, reaching 1,107,953 tons in 1901. There was a slight recession in the industry in 1902–1903, but production had surpassed the 1901 total again by 1904, and began a steady climb until the all-time peak was reached in 1913 at 2,429,920 tons. The totals declined slightly in 1914–1916. In 1917, however, with the United States' involvement in World War I, production soared to near the 1913 peak. The industry underwent a sharp recession in the 1920's, and the Texas decline was not unique. Competition from petroleum and electricity had hurt the whole bituminous-lignite industry. There was a brief rise in production in 1927, then a steady decline until 1935, when a thirty-year low of 757,529 tons was reached. In the post-World War II period, mining practically ceased, total production being only 18,169 tons in 1950. The industry received a tremendous boost in the 1950's, when the Aluminum Company of America began using char produced from lignite at a plant near Rockdale. Production figures have not been released since 1953, but the ALCOA operation should consume approximately 300,000 tons of lignite per year.

Several methods have been used for extracting coal and lignite, including the pillar and stall, longwall, and strip mining. The tools used were few and rather primitive. Mining was usually by hand, although a few gasoline locomotives were used. The mines were generally small, yielding between 10,000 and 50,000 tons per year. The bulk of Texas' coal production was used within the state. Though railroads were early purchasers, they found the quality poor and used it only sparingly. Lignite was burned in homes; converted to briquettes which were used in boilers for producing steam for generating power; and reduced to activated carbon, a substance used as a clarifying agent in the sugar-refining industry. By-products of coal and lignite, including gas, coal tar, and char, were also important.

BIBLIOGRAPHY: United States Department of the Interior, Bureau of Mines, *Minerals Yearbook* (1932–1955); *Texas Almanac* (1910, 1925, 1926, 1931, 1949).

Dwight F. Henderson

*Coapite Indians. The Coapite (Coapiste, Guapica, Guapite) Indians were Karankawans who, when first reported by this name in the eighteenth century, lived on the Texas coast near Matagorda Bay, where they were closely associated with the Cujane and Karankawa proper. In 1722 Espíritu Santo de Zuñiga Mission qv was established for these Indians near Matagorda Bay, but hostilities between Spaniards and Indians soon led to its removal. In 1754 the Spanish again attempted to missionize the Coapite and their Karankawan associates by establishing Nuestra Señora del Rosario Mission qv near present Goliad. The Coapite were periodically in and out of this mission until as late as 1831. During this period a few Coapite entered Nuestra Señora de la Purísima Concepción de Acuña Mission qv at San Antonio. Some of the Coapite also entered Nuestra Señora del Refugio Mission qv when it was founded in 1793 and were reported as being there until 1828. After this, remnants of the Coapite seem to have merged with the group known to the Anglo American settlers as Karankawa, who disappeared in the middle of the nineteenth century.

BIBLIOGRAPHY: H. E. Bolton, "The Founding of Mission Rosario," *Quarterly of the Texas State Historical Association*, X (1906–1907) and "Records of the Mission Nuestra Señora del Refugio," *ibid.*, XIV (1910–1911); H. E. Bolton, *Texas in the Middle Eighteenth Century* (1915); W. E. Dunn, "The Founding of Nuestra Señora del Refugio, the Last Spanish Mission in Texas," *Southwestern Historical Quarterly*, XXV (1921–1922); F. W. Hodge (ed.), *Handbook of American Indians*, I (1907), II (1910); W. H. Oberste, *History of Refugio Mission* (1942).

T. N. Campbell

Coaque Indians. The Coaque (Caoque, Cadoque, Cahoque, Capoque, Cayoque, Coaqui) Indians were encountered by Cabeza de Vaca qv in 1528 on the Texas coast. They occupied one end of an island that is usually identified as Galveston Island. The Coaque have been consistently identified with the Coco, who were first known over 150 years later, at which time they lived on both sides of the Colorado River near the coast. It cannot be proved conclusively that these two names refer to the same people. A better case can be made for identification of the Coaque with the Akokisa, who in the eighteenth century lived in the vicinity of Galveston Bay. Both occupied the same area, and there are phonetic similarities in the names.

BIBLIOGRAPHY: A. F. Bandelier (ed.), *The Journey of Alvar Nuñez Cabeza de Vaca* (1922); F. W. Hodge (ed.), *Handbook of American Indians*, I (1907), II (1910).

T. N. Campbell

*Coastal Plains.

*Coat of Arms.

*Coats, Merit M.

*Coayo Indians.

*Cob Jones Creek.

Cobb Caverns. Cobb Caverns, in Williamson County, is located on the Cobb Ranch halfway between Florence and Georgetown. Although the cave had been known for several decades, it was not opened to the public until June, 1962. A commercial trail follows a high-ceilinged, linear passage for one thousand feet, past flowstone-coated walls, "totem poles," and boxwork. An additional one thousand feet of passage is not open to tourists. Indian artifacts are found in abundance in old campgrounds at nearby Cobbs Springs. *See also* Caves and Cave Studies in Texas.

BIBLIOGRAPHY: J. R. Reddell and R. Finch, "The Caves of Williamson County," *Texas Speleological Survey*, II (1963).

A. Richard Smith

*Cobb Creek.

*Cobb Gulley.

Cobolini, Louis. Louis Cobolini, known as "father of the port at Brownsville," was born on December 13, 1845, in Trieste, Italy, then a part of the Austrian Empire. As a young man he fought under Giuseppe Garibaldi for Italian independence and unification, and as a result he could not return to his home, which remained under Austrian control. Cobolini migrated to Galveston, Texas, in the mid-1860's. Beginning as a fish and fruit peddler, he soon acquired a small fishing schooner and became a commercial fisherman.

Active in Texas labor unions, he joined the Screwmen's Benevolent Association qv in December, 1882, supported its strike in 1885, and at one time served as its vice-president. He held both local and state offices in the Knights of Labor and in the Texas State Federation of Labor (*see* Labor Organizations in Texas). In 1894 Governor James Stephen Hogg qv appointed him state delegate to the National Farmers' Congress.

Interested in the development of Texas seaports, in the 1870's and 1880's Cobolini helped secure a federal project for a deepwater channel and port at Galveston. As he transferred his growing fishing business westward along the Texas coast, he helped to develop ports at Port Lavaca, Rockport, Aransas Pass, and Corpus Christi. In 1907 Cobolini moved his fishing operations to Port Isabel and settled in Brownsville. He was active in Brownsville politics, serving as city alderman from 1910 to 1912 and as city commissioner from 1921 to 1922. He was a strong advocate of municipally-owned utilities and a nationally known lecturer on the cause of labor and on the importance of seaport development. He was married to Elizabeth Grupe; they had two sons.

By 1910, as secretary of the Brownsville Chamber of Commerce, he championed the more ambitious plan of a deepwater port for Brownsville itself. He insisted upon a major port and channel facility capable of handling ships drawing thirty feet of water. In 1911, along with others, he helped organize the Brownsville Waterways Association; the association employed him for both technical and political promotion of the Brownsville port project, and federal funds were sought through U.S. Congressman John Nance Garner.qv In 1927 the Cameron County Commissioners Court also employed Cobolini to promote the project. While conducting army engineers on a field trip over the proposed channel site in mid-February, 1928, he became ill with pneumonia and died on February 27, 1928. A few months later Congress approved the Brownsville deepwater port project, and on May 14–16, 1936, Cobolini's granddaughter served as "Miss Port of Brownsville," for the port opening.

BIBLIOGRAPHY: Frank C. Pierce, *Brief History of the Lower Rio Grande Valley* (1917); *New Encyclopedia of Texas* (1929?); Brownsville *Herald*, May 10, 1936; Jim

Wells Papers (MS., Archives, University of Texas at Austin Library).

Edgar P. Sneed

*Coching Bayou.

*Cochran, Archelaus M.

*Cochran, James.

*Cochran, John Hughes.

*Cochran, Robert.

*Cochran, Samuel Poyntz.

*Cochran, Texas.

*Cochran County. Cochran County, on the New Mexico border, has enjoyed increasing agricultural production in the decades following 1950. By 1970 some 115,000 acres were under irrigation, and the annual farm income had reached fifteen million dollars. The county's twelve gins processed a 1970–1971 cotton yield of 38,765 bales. Livestock, too, was important. A fat stock show, one of the major tourists attractions of the county, is held each February. Oil production from 1936 to 1973 was over 239,000,000 barrels, providing another major source of income and employment. County population, 6,417 in 1960, decreased to 5,326 by 1970.

*Cocke, James Decatur.

*Cockrell, Alexander.

*Cockrell, Jeremiah Vardaman.

*Cockrell Hill, Texas. Cockrell Hill, in Dallas County, had a population of 3,104 in 1960 and 3,515 in 1970.

*Coco Indians. The Coco (Caaucozi, Caocasi, Cascossi, Coke, Quaqui, Quoaque) Indians were Karankawans who lived near the Gulf Coast between the Lavaca and Brazos rivers. They were most frequently linked with the lower Colorado River in the area now covered by Colorado, Wharton, and Matagorda counties. Most writers have identified the Coaque (Caoque) of Cabeza de Vaca qv with the Coco of the late seventeenth and eighteenth centuries, but this cannot be established beyond question. A. S. Gatschet equated the Diskatronge with the Coco without giving any apparent reason for doing so.

The Coco first became known through documents of the La Salle Expedition,qv which recorded them under the name Quoaque. Coco was the most commonly used Spanish designation for these people; the Anglo Americans referred to the Coco as Coke. In the latter half of the eighteenth century the Coco were represented at various Spanish missions—San Antonio de Valero at San Antonio, San Ildefonso and Nuestra Señora de Candelaria on the San Gabriel River near present Rockdale, Nuestra Señora del Rosario near modern Goliad, and Nuestra Señora del Refugio qqv near present Refugio. Some of the Coco remained in their ancestral area along the lower Colorado River, where they were encountered by Anglo American colonists in the early nineteenth century. Later these Coco merged with remnants of other Karankawan groups

and became known as Karankawa. The Karankawa became extinct by 1858.

BIBLIOGRAPHY: H. E. Bolton, "The Founding of the Missions on the San Gabriel River," *Southwestern Historical Quarterly*, XVII (1913–1914); H. E. Bolton, *Texas in the Middle Eighteenth Century* (1915); H. E. Bolton (ed.), *Spanish Exploration in the Southwest, 1542–1706* (1916); A. S. Gatschet, *The Karankawa Indians, the Coast People of Texas* (1891); C. W. Hackett (ed.), *Pichardo's Treatise on the Limits of Louisiana and Texas*, I (1931); F. W. Hodge (ed.), *Handbook of American Indians*, I (1907), II (1910); J. G. Shea, *Discovery and Exploration of the Mississippi Valley* (1903).

T. N. Campbell

Cocoma Indians. The Cocoma (Cocuma) Indians have been identified with the Macocoma, but this has yet to be fully demonstrated. When first encountered by the Spanish in 1675, the Cocoma lived in northeastern Coahuila and sometimes ranged northward across the Rio Grande into the southwestern part of the Edwards Plateau in Texas. However, in 1693 Cocoma were also reported as a tribe that lived between Durango, Mexico, and present Presidio, Texas. It is not certain that these two groups of Cocoma were the same people. The Cocoma of Coahuila and Texas were probably the same as the Macocoma of San Francisco Solano Mission qv (near present Eagle Pass) and its successor, San Antonio de Valero,qv at San Antonio. J. R. Swanton evidently considered them to be the same, since he listed the Macocoma as a Coahuiltecan band but omitted the Cocoma from his list.

BIBLIOGRAPHY: H. E. Bolton, *Texas in the Middle Eighteenth Century* (1915); H. E. Bolton (ed.), *Spanish Exploration in the Southwest, 1542–1706* (1916); F. W. Hodge (ed.), *Handbook of American Indians*, II (1910); J. R. Swanton, *Linguistic Material from the Tribes of Southern Texas and Northeastern Mexico* (1940).

T. N. Campbell

Cocomeioje Indians. This name appears only in the records of San Antonio de Valero Mission qv in San Antonio, and its status remains in doubt. The Cocomeioje may be the same as the Cocomegua, a Coahuiltecan band that lived near Cadereyta in north-central Nuevo León during the second half of the seventeenth century, but documentary proof of this has not been found.

BIBLIOGRAPHY: H. E. Bolton, *Texas in the Middle Eighteenth Century* (1915); J. R. Swanton, *The Indian Tribes of North America* (1952).

T. N. Campbell

*Codman, Texas.

*Coe, Philip Haddox.

*Coesfield, Texas.

*Coffee, Holland. Holland Coffee was born August 15, 1807, the son of Ambrose and Mildred (Moore) Coffee. By the time he was eleven years old he had lost both parents, and he apparently grew up in the home of his eldest brother, Jesse, in McMinnville, Tennessee.

Coffee was not killed by an Indian (as stated in Volume I). In 1846 a conflict over a point of honor between Coffee and Charles A. Galloway, husband of Coffee's niece, resulted in a duel between the two men, with Coffee being stabbed to death. Testimony by witnesses cleared

Galloway of blame, and no charges were filed against him. Coffee was buried in a red brick mausoleum on the Glen Eden Plantation,qv but during the construction of Lake Texoma his remains were moved to a nearby site.

BIBLIOGRAPHY: Audy J. and Glenna Middlebrooks, "Holland Coffee of Red River," *Southwestern Historical Quarterly*, LXIX (1965–1966).

Glenna P. Middlebrooks

*Coffee Creek.

*Coffee Mill Creek.

Coffee Mill Creek Lake. Coffee Mill Creek Lake is in the Red River Basin in Fannin County, twelve miles northwest of Honey Grove on Coffee Mill Creek, a tributary of Bois d'Arc Creek, which is tributary to the Red River. The project, built in 1938, is owned and operated by the United States Forest Service for recreational purposes. The reservoir has a capacity of 8,000 acre-feet and a surface area of 704 acres at the service spillway crest elevation of 496 feet above mean sea level. The drainage area above the dam is thirty-nine square miles.

BIBLIOGRAPHY: Texas Water Commission, *Bulletin 6408* (1964).

Seth D. Breeding

*Coffee's Station.

*Coffeeville, Texas.

Cohen, Henry. Henry Cohen, son of David and Josephine C. Cohen, was born on April 7, 1863, in London, England. He studied there at Jews' Hospital and at Jews' College. After being ordained a rabbi in 1884, Cohen assumed his first assignment, in Kingston, Jamaica. In 1885 he came to the United States and served a congregation in Woodville, Mississippi, until 1888, when he transferred to Galveston, Texas, to head the Temple B'nai Israel. The next year he married Mollie Levy of Galveston. The couple had two children.

After the storm of 1900 Cohen was a leader in keeping law and order in Galveston, often with the help of a shotgun. He served as a member of the storm relief commission and became widely known for his hospital and rehabilitation work and for his ministering to people of all religions.

One of Cohen's earliest interests was in immigration. He was instrumental in finding homes in less populated areas for immigrants who arrived at the port of Galveston. He also helped families in the New York slums to move to various regions of the South and Midwest. During World War I Cohen was responsible for getting Congress to provide Jewish naval chaplains; President Woodrow Wilson later referred to Cohen as the "first citizen of Texas." Following the revival of the Ku Klux Klan,qv the rabbi, along with James Martin Kirwin,qv became noted for his open attacks upon that organization.

In 1927 Cohen was appointed by Governor Dan Moody qv to the Texas Prison Board.qv Cohen won statewide fame as a prison reformer by advocating segregation of hardened criminals from first offenders, better medical facilities, and vocational training; all of Cohen's recommendations were later adopted.

In recognition of forty years of service as a rabbi, Hebrew Union College awarded Cohen the degree of doctor of Hebrew law in 1924. Texas Christian University also conferred on Cohen an honorary doctorate in 1948. A recognized authority on the Talmud, he published a number of essays, including *Settlement of the Jews in Texas* (1894), *Henry Castro, Pioneer and Colonist* (1896), and *The Galveston Immigration Movement, 1907–1910*; he was also coauthor of *One Hundred Years of Jewry in Texas* (1936?). Cohen was active in many organizations and committees, including the advisory board of Hebrew Union College and the Jewish Publication Society. He retired in September, 1949, after having served as a rabbi for sixty-five years. He died on June 12, 1952, in Houston and was buried in Galveston.

BIBLIOGRAPHY: Anne Nathan and Harry I. Cohen, *The Man Who Stayed in Texas* (1941); Houston *Post*, June 13, 1952.

James C. Martin, Jr.

*Coit, Daniel P.

*Coit, Texas.

*Coke, Richard. Richard Coke resigned as governor of Texas in December, 1876 (not 1877), and served in the United States Senate from 1877 to 1895 (not 1885, as stated in Volume I).

*Coke, Texas.

*Coke County. Coke County ranked among the state's leading counties in sheep production in 1965. Sheep, cattle, and goats are the chief source of agricultural revenue, although some grain sorghums and cotton are grown. Oil, however, is more important to the economy than agriculture; by 1973, 167,000,000 barrels had been produced since the county's first well was drilled in 1942. Historical sites, Oak Creek Reservoir, Mountain Creek Lake, and a county stock show are tourist attractions. Construction of the E. V. Spence Reservoir on the Colorado River near Robert Lee was completed by 1970. Population was 3,589 in 1960 and 3,087 in 1970.

*Coke-Davis Controversy.

*Coker Creek.

Colabrote Indians. In 1683–1684 Juan Domínguez de Mendoza qv led an exploratory expedition from El Paso as far eastward as the junction of the Concho and Colorado rivers east of present San Angelo. In his itinerary he listed the names of thirty-seven Indian groups, including the Colabrote, from which he expected to receive delegations. Nothing further is known about the Colabrote, who seem to have been one of many Indian groups of north-central Texas that were swept away by the southward thrust of the Lipan-Apache and Comanche Indians in the eighteenth century.

BIBLIOGRAPHY: H. E. Bolton (ed.), *Spanish Exploration in the Southwest, 1542–1706* (1916); C. W. Hackett, *Pichardo's Treatise on the Limits of Louisiana and Texas*, II (1934).

T. N. Campbell

Colas Largas Indians. The Colas Largas ("long tails") Indians are known only from a Spanish document of 1693 which lists them as one of fifty "nations" that lived north of the Rio Grande and "between Texas and New Mexico." This may be interpreted to mean the southern part of western Texas, since the document also mentions that the Apache were at war with the groups named. Nothing further is known about the Colas Largas.

BIBLIOGRAPHY: C. W. Hackett (ed.), *Historical Documents Relating to New Mexico, Nueva Vizcaya, and Approaches Thereto, to 1773*, II (1926).

T. N. Campbell

*Colbert's Ferry.

*Cold Creek.

*Cold Spring, Texas.

*Cold Spring Creek.

Cold Springs, Texas. Cold Springs, the name given as of 1965 to a church at the intersection of Farm Road 184 and State Highway 36 in southeastern Coryell County, was originally a community located some distance away, on land that was taken over by the Fort Hood ᵠᵛ military reservation during World War II. The settlement, established in the early 1880's and named for natural springs, was originally a farming and ranching community.

*Cold Springs Female College.

*Coldspring, Texas. Coldspring, seat of San Jacinto County, is the commercial center for the major products of the county: crops, livestock, and lumber. It reported eighteen businesses in 1970. The 1960 population was 655, with no major change estimated in 1970.

*Coldwater, Texas. (Dallam County.)

*Coldwater, Texas. (Sherman County.)

*Coldwater Creek.

*Coldwell, Colbert. [Incorrect spelling in Volume I of Caldwell, Colbert. *See* Caldwell, Colbert.]

*Cole, Aaron Shannon.

*Cole Creek.

*Coleman, Robert M.

*Coleman, Thomas M.

*Coleman, Walter Moore.

*Coleman, Texas. Coleman, seat of Coleman County, had a 1960 population of 6,371 and a 1970 count of 5,608. In 1964 Coleman reported thirty-two churches, six schools, two banks, and an enlarged hospital. Among the 138 businesses in 1970 were companies manufacturing brick and tile, boots, and air-diffusing equipment. Annual events include a rodeo in July and a livestock show in January.

*Coleman County. Coleman County had a population of 12,458 in 1960 and 10,288 in 1970. Over 80 percent of the county's farm income, which totaled nine million dollars annually by 1970, is derived from livestock, while diversified farming provides the remainder. Coleman County ranked ninth in Texas in turkey production in 1959 and fifth in sheep in 1960. The county, with substantial

mineral resources, produced 72,285,019 barrels of oil between 1902 and 1973. The fine silica sand found on Santa Anna Mountain and elsewhere contributes to ceramic tile and brick industries in the county seat, Coleman. A stock show and rodeo are tourist attractions, as are Hord's Creek Reservoir, Lake Scarborough, and Lake Coleman.

*Coleman Field.

*Coleman-Fulton Pasture Company.

Coleman Reservoir. Coleman Reservoir is in the Colorado River Basin in Coleman County, fourteen miles north of Coleman on Jim Ned Creek. This reservoir is owned and operated by the city of Coleman for municipal water supply. Construction was started in August, 1965, and completed on May 10, 1966, with deliberate impoundment beginning in April, 1966. The reservoir has a capacity of 40,000 acre-feet with a surface area of 2,000 acres at the service spillway elevation of 1,717.5 feet above mean sea level, and has a capacity of 59,000 acre-feet with a surface area of 2,530 acres at emergency spillway crest elevation of 1,726 feet above mean sea level. The drainage area above the dam is 292 square miles.

Seth D. Breeding

*Coles, John P.

*Coles Creek.

*Colete Village.

*Coleto, Battle of.

*Coleto Creek.

*Coletoville, Texas.

*Coley Creek, Texas.

*Coleysville, Texas.

*Colfax, Texas.

*Colita, Texas.

*Colita Academy.

*Collard, Elijah Simmons.

*Collard, William E.

*Collards Creek.

Collectors' Institute. Co-sponsored by the Texas State Historical Association ᵠᵛ and the Humanities Research Center of the University of Texas at Austin, the Collectors' Institute was a private association for collectors of library materials such as books, manuscripts, documents, maps, etc. Organized on November 23, 1968, with more than one hundred and fifty members, the institute elected officers and an eight-member board of directors. Two annual meetings are held, one in the fall, which focuses on the general subject of collecting, and another in the spring, a workshop exploring specific problems which confront collectors. The institute provides a research and communications framework within which solutions are sought for problems such as the preservation and restoration of collectors' holdings. Although many of the members collect Texana, the organization is not limited to those who collect Texas materials, but rather encourages all areas of bibliographic interest. Transcripts of the meetings are published and distributed to the membership. Jenkins Garrett was the first president of the Collectors' Institute, and Kenneth Ragsdale was acting secretary and coordinator of membership activities. Membership was approximately two hundred in September, 1975, when the Humanities Research Center became the sole sponsor of the institute.

*College Hill, Texas.

*College Hill Institute.

College of the Mainland. College of the Mainland, a two-year public community college in Texas City, serves the mainland portion of Galveston County. In 1965 the Galveston County Union Junior College District was created. In 1966 the Galveston Junior College District and the Union District were separated, the Union District becoming College of the Mainland, Union Junior College District. The college operated in temporary quarters in Texas City beginning in September, 1967, until a 120-acre campus on Farm Road 1764 could be completed in 1969.

Both college courses leading to an associate of arts degree and technical courses leading to an associate in applied science degree are offered. The first president of the school was Herbert F. Stallworth. Student enrollment in the fall of 1974 was 5,291; Fred Taylor was president in that year.

*College of Marshall. *See* East Texas Baptist College.

*College of Mines and Metallurgy. *See* Texas Western College; *see also* University of Texas at El Paso.

*College Station, Texas. College Station adjoins Bryan to form the urban heart of Brazos County. As its name implies, the city has always received its sustenance largely from Texas A&M University (formerly the Agricultural and Mechanical College of Texas) and activities related to the school. In 1970 some small local industries were among the city's seventy-seven businesses. During 1967 an unsuccessful campaign was underway to rename the city. College Station's population was 11,396 in 1960 and 17,676 in 1970. *See also* Bryan-College Station Standard Metropolitan Statistical Area.

College Teachers, Texas Association of. *See* Texas Association of College Teachers.

*Collegeport, Texas.

*Colleges, Association of Texas. *See* Association of Texas Colleges and Universities.

*Colley Creek.

Colleyville, Texas. Colleyville, in northeastern Tarrant County, was incorporated in 1957. In 1966 the city had four churches. The 1960 population was 1,491; the 1970 count was 3,368. *See also* Fort Worth Standard Metropolitan Statistical Area.

*Collier Creek.

*Collin County. Collin County in the 1960's was closely linked with the nearby Dallas metropolitan area. The rapidly growing cities produced a rise in the county population from 41,247 in 1960 to 66,920 in 1970. Many of the inhabitants commuted to jobs outside the county. Manufacturing and trade were the chief occupations, and agriculture remained important. The county ranked among the state's leaders in hog raising and dairying, there being seventy-one dairy herds and sixty Grade A dairies in the county in 1959. The beef cattle industry,qv more important economically, contributed a three-million-dollar income in 1966. Collin is also one of the major commercial oat-growing counties, while producing about thirty-five thousand bales of cotton annually. The Lavon Reservoir furnishes water for the growing industries and municipal needs. *See also* Dallas Standard Metropolitan Statistical Area.

*Collingsworth County. Collingsworth County, with about twelve thousand acres irrigated by 1964, obtained two-thirds of its fairly high farm income from cotton, wheat, and grain sorghums; cattle raising and guar cultivation contributed a lesser amount in the mid-1960's. In the early 1970's the county's average annual farm income was $10,000,-000, half of which came from livestock, the other half from cotton and grains. A September county fair and a horse show are held annually. The county population has decreased steadily since 1940, to 6,276 persons in 1960 and 4,755 in 1970.

Collins, Harry Warren. Harry Warren (Rip) Collins was born February 26, 1896, in Weatherford, Texas, the son of H. W. Collins. He is considered one of the greatest athletes in Texas history. Collins' punting and running ability, incubated at Bickler School, Austin Academy, and then Austin High School, led the Austin, Texas, high school to state football championships in 1913 and 1914. He enrolled at the Agricultural and Mechanical College of Texas (now Texas A&M University) and achieved national recognition in 1915 in a game against the University of Texas when he punted twenty-three times for a fifty-five yard average, leading the Aggies to a 13–0 victory. In 1916 Collins was a member of the famed Second Texas Infantry team. He returned to A&M in 1917 and led the team to an unbeaten, unscored-on season. He was described by coaches as very strong physically, standing six feet, one inch, and weighing approximately 190 pounds.

Collins signed a professional baseball contract with Dallas of the Texas League,qv where he pitched during the 1919 season. In 1920 he went up to the New York Yankees, thus launching an eleven-year career in the American League during which he compiled a 108–82 won-lost record. He closed out his professional career with Fort Worth of the Texas League in 1933.

Collins then began a law enforcement career. He served in the Texas Rangers,qv was elected sheriff of Travis County in 1940, and remained in this position until 1948. He became Bryan police chief in 1950, serving there until his retirement in 1959. Collins died on May 27, 1968, in Bryan, Texas.

BIBLIOGRAPHY: Austin *Statesman*, May 29, June 27, 1968.

George Breazeale

*Collins, Jasper.

*Collins, Richard M.

Collins, Vinson A. Vinson A. Collins, the son of Warren Collins, was born on March 1, 1867, near Honey Island, Texas. After receiving a teacher's certificate in 1887 in Polk County, he taught school until he entered Sam Houston Normal Institute (now Sam Houston State University) at Huntsville. In 1893 he graduated with honors from the institute and continued to teach until he passed the Bar examination and began law practice at Beaumont in 1901. He returned to Polk County and represented his district in the state Senate for two terms. In the legislature he was sponsor of a bill to have enacted into law the first workmen's compensation act; he also introduced the first bill providing for the eight-hour day for laborers. In Livingston he continued to practice law, was appointed for two terms to the board of regents of the state teachers colleges,qv and for a time served as its chairman. On July 5, 1966, Vinson A. Collins died and was buried at Livingston.

Sam Long

*Collins, Texas. (Jasper County.)

*Collins, Texas. (Jim Wells County.) Collins, Texas, was founded in June, 1878, when N. G. Collins bought almost half of a Mexican land grant along the San Fernando and San Diego creeks when it was subdivided to settle the estate of Marcelino López, original grantee from the state of Tamaulipas, Mexico. On this land a short distance below the juncture of the two creeks, and across from the Mexican settlement of Preseños, Collins laid off a townsite and named it Collins. He gave half of this townsite to the Texas-Mexican Railway to persuade the owners to build the railroad through Collins. The railroad reached Collins in March, 1879, when the town consisted of a lumberyard, three or four stores, a small Roman Catholic church built by Father John Pierre Bard,qv a dozen or so houses, and a two-story hotel. The stage from Brownsville came through Collins and stopped at the hotel.

The post office and most of the inhabitants, with their houses, moved to and started present Alice in 1888, when the San Antonio and Aransas Pass Railway bypassed Collins and intersected the Texas-Mexican Railway about five miles to the west.
BIBLIOGRAPHY: Jim Wells County Map, General Land Office, July, 1913; Nueces County Deed Records, Book N.

Agnes G. Grimm

*Collins Creek.

*Collinson, Frank.

*Collinsville, Texas.

*Collinsworth, George Morse.

*Collinsworth, James. The monument erected at the grave of James Collinsworth was dedicated on August 15, 1931 (not 1831, as stated in Volume I).

*Collom Spring Branch.

*Colmesneil, Texas.

*Cologne, Texas.

*Colonial Dames of America (Texas Branch).

*Colonization Contracts and Laws. *See* Mexican Colonization Laws, 1821–1830.

*Colony, Texas.

*Colony Creek.

*Colony Settlement, Texas.

Colorado. See Wharton.

*Colorado City, Texas. (Fayette County.)

*Colorado City, Texas. (Mitchell County.) Colorado City, county seat, was incorporated twice, in 1881 and again in 1907. By 1970 the city had 126 businesses, twenty-five churches, a hospital, a bank, a newspaper, and a radio station. Industries include an oil refining and asphalt plant, cottonseed oil mill, cotton compress, regional power plant, brick and tile factory, and a dairy. Lake Colorado City and Champion Creek Reservoir, both completed by 1959, provide facilities for water sports. The 1960 population was 6,457; the 1970 count was 5,227.

*Colorado College.

*Colorado County. Colorado County attracts hunters and history-minded sightseers. Eagle Lake boasts that it is the "goose-hunting capital of the world." Colorado ranks among the state's leading counties in rice production; truck crops, some cotton, numerous cattle, and a large poultry industry also contribute to a sizable farm income, which reached $20 million in 1970. Much natural gas, some oil, and sand and gravel are also produced. The population of the county has remained relatively stable since 1890. The 1960 population of 18,463 decreased to 17,638 by 1970.

*Colorado Female Academy.

Colorado Gazette and Advertiser.

Colorado Indians. The Spanish name Colorado ("red" or in some cases "painted") was given to many Indian groups in the New World. Only one of these can be related to the Texas area, the Colorado of northern Mexico, who seem to have ranged over the northern portions of Coahuila and Chihuahua at the close of the seventeenth century. In 1688 these Colorado participated in a revolt against the Spanish and tried to involve some of their Texas neighbors in the uprising, principally the Terocodame and Jumano.
BIBLIOGRAPHY: H. E. Bolton, "The Jumano Indians in Texas, 1650–1771," *Quarterly of the Texas State Historical Association*, XV (1911–1912); C. W. Hackett (ed.), *Historical Documents Relating to New Mexico, Nueva Vizcaya, and Approaches Thereto, to 1773*, II (1926).

T. N. Campbell

*Colorado River.

*Colorado River Authorities.

Lower Colorado River Authority: With a twelve-member board of directors appointed by the governor, the LCRA in 1966 operated six dams and reservoirs and two steam-generating plants.

Lake Buchanan and Buchanan Dam are 413 river miles from the mouth of the Colorado River. Down the river from this reservoir are Inks Lake and Inks Dam, Lake Lyndon B. Johnson and Alvin J. Wirtz Dam, Lake Marble Falls and Max Starcke Dam, Lake Travis and Mansfield Dam, and Lake Austin and Tom Miller Dam, the latter 297 river miles from the Gulf. These six dams have hydroelectric generating plants which, combined with the leased Comal Steam Plant at New Braunfels, have a generating capacity of 290,000 kilowatts. Added to this is the new LCRA Sim Gideon Steam Plant on Lake Bastrop, which was planned to have a 250,-000-kilowatt capacity when completed. This latter plant can be expanded to 565,000 kilowatts, according to state legislative authorization given during the 1961–1965 sessions to enable the agency to meet the expanding requirements for electric power and energy from the eleven electric cooperatives and thirty-three cities in the thirty-three-county, 31,000-square-mile area served by the LCRA.

The dams and reservoirs successfully controlled the record flood waters of over 3,000,000 acre-feet during a two-month period in the spring of 1957. In contrast, during the "dry" year of 1963, only 715,000 acre-feet of water entered the river above Austin, during which time the reservoirs were invaluable in providing water for municipal, industrial, and agricultural uses.

Central Colorado River Authority: The four community reservoirs at Santa Anna, Talpa, Novice, and Goldlusk were still in operation in 1967. The latter had silted so that its water condition was considered poor. The agency continues to construct small farm and ranch reservoirs and other conservation projects such as terraces and diversion channels. This agency operates within Coleman County.

Upper Colorado River Authority: This water conservation and development agency operates within Coke and Tom Green counties. San Angelo Dam and Reservoir, on the North Concho River just above San Angelo, was constructed by the United States Army Corps of Engineers. The UCRA has purchased the conservation storage of this reservoir.

Comer Clay

Colorado River Municipal Water District. The Colorado River Municipal Water District, created in 1949, was authorized to impound the storm and flood waters and the unappropriated flow of the Colorado River and its tributaries, and also to distribute such water to cities and other agencies for municipal, domestic, and industrial purposes. The district was originally brought into being and organized to furnish water to the cities of Odessa, Big Spring, and Snyder. The twelve-man board of directors governs the district and is composed of four men from each member city, appointed by the governing body of each city. The administration has a general manager, assisted by an administrative assistant and a staff of forty-two employees. Although the cities own the district, it operates independently, subject only to terms covered by a trust indenture. The principal office of the district is located in Big Spring, Texas.

By September, 1952, the new district had developed a water well field to provide water for the cities of Odessa and Big Spring. This well field has been enlarged and is now being artificially recharged during winter months with water from Lake J. Thomas. Surface water is injected into the de-watered aquifer and recovered in summer months to furnish water for peaking purposes. Upon completion of the dam and reservoir, known as Lake J. B. Thomas, having a capacity of 204,000 acre-feet, the city of Snyder received its first water on July 1, 1953, from this source. The district later contracted to furnish waterflood projects for oil companies; recovery of oil has been doubled or tripled by this means. These contracts are subject to cancellation if water is needed for municipal use.

Initially the district installed 115 miles of pipeline, varying from twenty-one to thirty-three inches in diameter. A series of pump stations capable of delivering a total of 44,000,000 gallons per day was developed. The district in 1966 operated eight pump stations and pumped water through some 200 miles of pipeline.

Originally the district issued $11,750,000 in revenue bonds, adding $4,600,000 more in 1958 for pipeline and terminal storage construction and $2,750,000 in 1963 for additional pipeline. Bond funds, without assistance from the state or federal government, have purchased land and financed the cost of a dam and channel for a lake, 200 miles of pipeline and rights-of-way, a pair of eighty-million-gallon storage reservoirs, a pair of fifteen-million-gallon reservoirs, eight pump stations and microwave equipment for automatic operation of the system, basic equipment and supplies, and several houses for key employees at pump station locations. It has also invested several hundred thousand dollars in dam improvement, recreation facilities, and extensive studies for a new lake and other improvements. Since the district's inception in 1951, an aggregate of over 117 billion gallons of water has been supplied to cities and oil field consumers; the district grossed over $23,000,000 in revenue. Recreation has been provided for thousands, and the district was on the threshold of providing another huge lake on the Colorado River.

A permit was granted on September 1, 1965, by the Texas Water Rights Commission qv authorizing the district to build a reservoir near Robert Lee in Coke County, which was scheduled to impound a maximum of 488,760 acre-feet of water on the Colorado River, and to divert 40,000 acre-feet per annum from this source. This permit, along with existing rights for Lake J. B. Thomas, authorizes the district to divert a total of 73,000 acre-feet annually from the Colorado River. Plans and specifications were being completed in 1966 for the dam and its related facilities. Construction of the dam began in 1966 and was completed by 1970. The new reservoir at Robert Lee, along with its related pipelines and other facilities, was financed through the sale of $30,000,000 in revenue bonds. Named the E. V. Spence Reservoir, it supplied approximately 70 percent of the city of Midland's water requirements in accordance with a sixty-year water sales agreement.

*Colorado and Southern Railroad. The Colorado and Southern Railroad was incorporated in 1898 in the state of Colorado. In Texas it operated 112.6 miles of first main track acquired when it purchased half ownership of the Burlington-Rock Island Railroad in 1964. It also owns 99.9 percent interest in the Fort Worth and Denver Railway, which leases, but does not operate, its track in Texas. In June, 1952, seven companies operated under lease and owned by the Colorado and Southern were acquired by the Fort Worth and Denver and thereafter dissolved. They were the Fort Worth and Denver South Plains Railway, the Fort Worth and Denver Northern Railway, the Fort Worth and Denver Terminal Railway Company, the Wichita Valley Railway, the Wichita Valley Railroad Company, the Abilene and Northern Railway, and the Stamford and Northwestern Railway Company. *See also* Burlington Railroad System; Burlington-Rock Island Railroad Company.

James M. Day

*Colorado Valley Railroad Company. *See* Kansas City, Mexico, and Orient Railway Company of Texas.

*Colored Orphans' Home, Gilmer. *See* State Colored Orphans' Home.

*Colquhoun, Ludovic.

*Colquitt, Oscar Branch.

*Colquitt, Texas.

*Colston Draw.

*Colt Revolver.

*Coltexo, Texas.

*Coltharp, Texas.

*Colton, Texas.

*Columbia, Texas. *See* West Columbia, Texas.

*Columbia College.

*Columbia Tap Railroad Company. *See* Houston Tap and Brazoria Railroad Company.

*Columbus, Texas. Columbus, seat of Colorado County, in 1970 had 94 businesses, including companies producing liquid petroleum gas, feeds, concrete, meat products, and sand and gravel. The 1960 population of 3,656 decreased to 3,342 by 1970.

*Columbus Tap Railway.

*Colville, Silas.

Comal, Texas. Comal, in the southern part of Comal County, is not to be confused with Comal Town qv or Comal Creek Settlement.qv Comal, eight miles southwest of New Braunfels, was established as a settlement on the Old San Antonio Road qv in 1846 and became a railroad section station on the Missouri, Kansas, and Texas Railroad about 1900. In 1967 its forty inhabitants were employed in farming, ranching, and working at a nearby quarry.

*Comal County. Comal County, located in the hilly terrain of south-central Texas, has an area of 567 square miles. In every census since 1850 Comal County has shown a gain in population; between 1960 and 1970 the population increased almost 22 percent, from 19,844 to 24,165 residents. Much of the county's income is derived from oil, gas, sand, and gravel. In 1966 the mineral value reached $3,948,214 and the income received from the sale of sand and gravel exceeded $3,000,000. A total farm income of approximately $3,000,000 in 1970 was derived primarily from the raising of sheep and goats; cattle, poultry, and row crops were also important. New Braunfels, county seat and largest city, is the site of several small manufacturing industries, including the Mission Valley textile mills, as well as many points of scenic and historic interest. County tourist attractions include Natural Bridge Caverns and Canyon Reservoir qqv on the Guadalupe River. Annual events for the county include the September county fair and the New Braunfels Wurstfest, held in November.

*Comal Creek.

*Comal Creek Settlement, Texas.

*Comal River.

*Comal Springs.

*Comal Town, Texas.

*Comal Union School.

*Comanche, Texas. Comanche, seat of Comanche County, had a 1960 population of 3,415 and a 1970 population of 3,933. Located in an area of diversified farming and ranching, Comanche had 108 business establishments in 1970, mainly concerned with the marketing and processing of peanuts, fruits, and livestock. Industries produce camping trailers, air conditioners, feeds, peanut products, and leather goods. The city operates a swimming pool, completed in 1953, and a park area at Lake Eanes, as well as a library, established in 1960, and a county airport. Comanche has two hospitals, several nursing homes, and a home for handicapped children. Also located in the city is Burks Museum, which attracts many visitors.

*Comanche County. Comanche County, the leading county in peanut production, realized five million dollars from its 1964 crop, which spread over 58,406 acres. Livestock, poultry, truck crops, fruit, pecans, and dairying are also important contributors to the farm income, which reached $22,000,000 annually by 1970. The county partially supports an airport and maintains five parks around Proctor Reservoir.qv These parks, along with Hodges Park, a January livestock show, a July rodeo, and an August peach and melon festival, furnish activities for county residents and tourists. The 1960 population was 11,865; the 1970 count was 11,898.

*Comanche Creek.

*Comanche Indian Reservation.

*Comanche Indians.

*Comanche Peak.

*Comanche Reserve. *See* Comanche Indian Reservation.

*Comanche Springs.

*Comanche Trail.

*Comancheros.

*Comb Creek.

*Combes, Texas.

*Combine, Texas.

Combs, David St. Clair. David St. Clair Combs was born in Johnson County, Missouri, in 1839, and accompanied his family to Texas in 1854, settling near San Marcos.

In August, 1861, at La Grange, he enlisted in Company D of the 8th Texas Cavalry, later known as Terry's Texas Rangers.qv Combs fought in all major engagements in which the Rangers participated through Chickamauga. While he was on furlough in Texas, he was transferred to the Trans-Mississippi Department, where he served to the end of the war. He fought in the battle of Palmito Ranch,qv on May 13, 1865, the last engagement of the Civil War.

After the war Combs was one of the first trail drivers, and from 1866 to 1879 he drove cattle and horses to Louisiana, Kansas, Iowa, Nebraska, and the Dakotas. In 1880 he and his partners ranched near San Angelo, but in 1882 they moved ranching operations to Brewster County. In 1900 he established Combs Ranch, one of the largest ranches of Brewster County, near Marathon. The ranch is still owned and operated by his descendants.

As one of the last surviving members of Terry's Texas Rangers, he was instrumental in getting L. B. Giles to write a history of the regiment; Combs' letter is the book's preface. In 1873 he married Eleanora Allen Browning. They lived in San Antonio during the time he operated the ranch in Brewster County. He died in 1926.

BIBLIOGRAPHY: L. B. Giles, *Terry's Texas Rangers* (c. 1911).

Nowlin Randolph

Combs, Jesse Martin. Jesse M. Combs, Texas jurist and United States representative from the Second Congressional District from 1945 to 1953, was born in Center, Texas, on July 7, 1889, son of Frank and May (Beck) Combs. After attending public school, he was graduated from Southwest Texas State Teachers College (now Southwest Texas University) in 1912. He was admitted to the Bar in 1918 and began practice in Kountze, Texas. He was county judge of Hardin County in 1919 and 1920, and served as district judge of the Seventy-fifth District from 1923 to 1925. He served as an associate justice of the Ninth Court of Civil Appeals from 1933 to 1943. He was president of the board of trustees of South Park Schools, Beaumont, Texas, from 1926 to 1940 and president of the board of trustees of Lamar College (now Lamar University) from 1940 to 1944. Combs was elected to Congress in 1944 and re-elected each term until 1952, when he did not seek reelection.

In Congress he was a leader in the dispute to retain the tidelands for Texas (*see* Tidelands Controversy). He helped to develop the Sabine River Authority,qv and in 1951 in the Ways and Means Committee he opposed a large reduction in the capital gains tax. He was instrumental in reshaping the House Committee on Un-American Activities. He was co-author of the act to provide federal aid to schools in defense areas. He was considered a liberal and generally supported President Truman except on the tidelands issue. He returned to Beaumont in 1953, where he died on August 21 of that year and was buried in Magnolia Cemetery.

BIBLIOGRAPHY: *Biographical Directory of the American Congress, 1774–1961* (1961); Dallas *Morning News*, August 23, 1953; *Who's Who In America* (1953).

Thomas L. Miller

Come Cibolas Indians. These Indians are known only from a Spanish document of 1693 which lists the Come Cibolas ("bison eaters") as one of fifty "nations" that lived north of the Rio Grande and "between Texas and New Mexico." This may be interpreted to mean the southern part of western Texas, since the document also mentions that the Apache were at war with the groups named. Nothing further is known about the Come Cibolas. They were evidently not the same as the Cibola, whose name occurs on the same list.

BIBLIOGRAPHY: C. W. Hackett (ed.), *Historical Documents Relating to New Mexico, Nueva Vizcaya, and Approaches Thereto, to 1773*, II (1926).

T. N. Campbell

Come Indians. The Come are known from a single Spanish document of 1683 in which they are identified only as "the people who eat." Since no native name is given, they cannot be related to other known groups. Their area seems to have been somewhere east of the Pecos in west-central Texas.

BIBLIOGRAPHY: C. W. Hackett (ed.), *Pichardo's Treatise on the Limits of Louisiana and Texas*, I (1931).

T. N. Campbell

Comecrudo Indians. The Comecrudo (Spanish for "raw meat eaters") Indians were a Coahuiltecan people who in the late seventeenth and eighteenth centuries lived in northern Tamaulipas. In the second half of the eighteenth century part of the Comecrudo lived along the south bank of the Rio Grande near Reynosa, and it may be inferred that they hunted and gathered wild plant foods on both sides of the river. At times the Comecrudo were also referred to as Carrizo, a Spanish name applied to many Coahuiltecan groups along the Rio Grande below Laredo. In 1886 the ethnologist A. S. Gatschet found a few elderly Comecrudo near Reynosa who could still speak their native language. Gatschet's Comecrudo vocabulary and texts helped to establish the linguistic affiliations of many Indian groups of southern Texas and northeastern Mexico.

BIBLIOGRAPHY: F. W. Hodge (ed.), *Handbook of American Indians*, I (1907); G. Saldivar, *Los Indios de Tamaulipas* (1943); J. R. Swanton, *Linguistic Material from the Tribes of Southern Texas and Northeastern Mexico* (1940).

T. N. Campbell

*Cometa, Texas.

*Comfort, Texas. The site for Comfort, in Kendall County, was first selected by Ernst Hermann Altgelt in July, 1854 (not August 27, 1854, as stated in Volume I). Altgelt, acting as agent for New Orleans cotton broker John F. C. Vles (who owned a league of land in what was then Bexar County), returned to San Antonio to notify Vles that the fifteen-hundred-acre site he had selected had a favorable potential for settlement; there were German settlers already in the area as early as 1852. He also wrote his father in Düsseldorf, Germany, for money to buy from Heinrich Schladoer a thousand acres of land adjoining the Vles tract. With Vles' power of attorney and his own land to develop, Altgelt returned to the site accompanied by a small party, including surveyor Friedrich Grothaus. They immediately began laying out town lots (in July and August, 1854) at the confluence of Cypress Creek and the Guadalupe River, near the site of an Indian village.

The site was officially ready for settlement when three hundred lots were offered for sale, of which thirty lots were purchased, and eight houses were built by late August, 1854, marking the real establishment of the town. The origin of the name of the town remains a matter for debate; for instance, some writers have suggested that the name Comfort was given because of the pleasant landscape, or perhaps as an inspiration to the early German settlers during the difficult first years of settlement. At no time was it given the name Camp Comfort (as suggested in Volume I).

It was thought that Comfort would be the county seat of Kerr County, which was organized in 1856, but Kerrville was chosen instead; however, for two years, from 1860 to 1862, Comfort was the county seat when Chief Justice Jonathan Scott had it moved there. The Kerr County seat was returned to Kerrville when Comfort was included within the boundary of Kendall County, which was organized in 1862.

In 1972 the town sponsored a museum with a collection of articles from early German families of the area. The population of Comfort, an unincorporated town, was not listed in the official U.S. census for 1970, which indicates that there were less than one thousand residents in the town in that year. A 1971 estimate given by the town claimed more than one thousand population.

BIBLIOGRAPHY: Rudolph L. Biesele, *The History of the German Settlements in Texas, 1831–1861* (1930); F. H. Lohmann, *Comfort* (1904); Guido E. Ransleben, *A Hundred Years of Comfort in Texas* (1954); Albert Schuetze, *Diamond Jubilee Souvenir Book of Comfort* (1929); Henry B. Dielmann, "Emma Altgelt's Sketches of Life in Texas," *Southwestern Historical Quarterly*, LXIII (1959–1960).

*Comisario.

*Commerce, Texas. Commerce, in northeastern Hunt County, is a growing industrial site specializing in dairy products, clothing, concrete products, confectioneries, wood products, chemicals, mobile homes, and printing. In 1970 the town had a newspaper, a new hospital, and 120 businesses, including at least seven manufacturers. Its population was 5,890 in 1950, 5,789 in 1960, and 9,534 in 1970, the latter figure representing a 64.7 percent increase in ten years.

*Commercial Chronicle.

*Commercial Intelligencer.

*Commission of Claims. See Court of Claims.

*Commission Form of City Government. See also City Government.

*Commissioner of Education. See Education, Commissioner of.

Commissioner of the General Land Office. See State Executive Officers, Compensation of.

*Commissioners Creek.

*Commissioners of Deeds.

*Commissions of Appeals.

*Commissions and Boards. [See Volume I under this title for partial list. Many commissions and boards have had name changes since Volumes I and II were first published; both old and new titles may be found in the current work for updated accounts. A newly created commission or board will also be found under its own title; no attempt is made here to list them all under a single title. For example, Commission for Indian Affairs will be found under Indian Affairs, Commission for.]

*Committee of Industrial Organizations. See Labor Organizations in Texas.

*Committees of Public Safety (Civil War).

*Committees of Safety and Correspondence.

Community Affairs, Department of. The Department of Community Affairs was created by the 62nd Texas Legislature in 1971 when the Division of State-Local Relations of the governor's office, created in 1969, was elevated to agency status. At the state level, it assists local governments by providing human, financial, and technical resources, and by coordinating federal and state programs which affect local governments. The department is composed of six divisions and several offices, all responsible to an executive director who is appointed by the governor with the concurrence of the senate.

Community Services Division. This division encompasses the activities and services of the Model Cities Program and the Community Development Program. The Model Cities Program, part of a national demonstration program in 147 U.S. cities, receives federal funds for social, economic, and physical projects designed to improve the quality of life in inner-city neighborhoods. The state program provides eight Texas cities (Austin, Eagle Pass, Edinburg, Houston, Laredo, San Antonio, Texarkana, and Waco) with technical and financial assistance; in so doing it provides a way of testing and developing programs of technical and financial assistance that will be applicable to all units of local government in Texas. The Community Development Program assists local governments in maximizing the available human, natural, and financial resources to achieve orderly growth and development. The program provides technical assistance and information on available state and federal programs to assist local governments. It also assists in the revitalization of small communities in Texas through the Texas Communities Tomorrow program.

Comprehensive Planning Assistance Division. This division administers funds provided by the U. S. Department of Housing and Urban Development to counties, Indian reservations, disaster areas, federally impacted areas, municipalities of less than 50,000 population, and municipalities of any size which are in redevelopment areas or economic development districts. To qualify, eligible recipients must present detailed programs concerning their needs.

Special Programs Division. This division includes the Office of Early Childhood Development, which develops and implements programs for children under six, encourages cooperation of all such community agencies in developing programs, compiles research, and conducts seminars on early childhood development; the Public Employment Program, created in response to the Emergency Employment Act of 1971 and funded by the U.S. Department of Labor, which provides transitional employment for the unemployed and underemployed in public service areas, primarily in local units of government; the Public Service Careers Program, also funded by the U.S. Department of Labor, which is a manpower program designed to provide training and supportive services to employ disadvantaged persons in state government; and the State Program on Drug Abuse, which provides direct assistance through community organization, fund raising, preparation of grant proposals, development of programs, and research in drug abuse prevention, treatment, rehabilitation, and law enforcement.

Housing Division. This division develops housing programs for the state and provides technical assistance and information concerning availability of federal and state housing programs to local governments and regional councils; it also assists in operating the State Building Materials and Systems Testing Laboratory, a laboratory created by the 62nd Texas Legislature in 1971 to assist local governments, the residential construction industry, and consumers by encouraging and facilitating the use of new methods and materials in residential construction and by testing and evaluating building materials, products, and systems.

Texas Office of Economic Opportunity. The primary concern of this division is the alleviation of poverty and poverty conditions in the state. It serves as the governor's representative in the operation of the Economic Opportunity Act in Texas, provides technical assistance for the development and administration of community action agencies, and assists any private or governmental groups engaged in anti-poverty programs in the state. The Governor's Youth Opportunity Program serves as a liaison between youth and government, concentrating on the training, education, and job placement of young people in Texas.

Office of Traffic Safety. This division helps local governments develop traffic safety plans and programs, provides limited traffic engineering services to small jurisdictions without such capabilities, and conducts and develops training programs for the public on highway safety.

BIBLIOGRAPHY: University of Texas at Austin, *Guide To Texas State Agencies* (1972).

Community Colleges in Texas. *See* Junior College Movement in Texas.

Community Development Program. *See* Community Affairs, Department of.

*****Community Property Law of Texas.** In Texas the community property system controls property rights of husband and wife. It is derived from the law of Spain (Castile) and is ultimately of Visigothic origin. The basic rule is that all property acquired during marriage is owned in common by the spouses except that acquired either by gift or inheritance, which acquisitions, along with the property brought into the marriage, are termed separate property. All the profits of separate property acquired during marriage are community property. As between the spouses, the community property may become separate property by an agreement entered into before marriage or by a gift, sale, or partition during marriage. Separate property may be converted into community property by sale. Otherwise, as long as its identity can be traced, it retains its separate character, but if separate property is so commingled with community property that it cannot be traced, the whole commingled mass is deemed common.

Prior to 1913, and in large measure up to 1968, management of community property was vested in the husband. Since 1967, management of community property is clearly divided between the spouses according to its source. Each spouse has control of his or her earnings, the profits of his or her separate property, and recoveries from personal injury to him or her amounting to community property. But if that common property over which one spouse has sole management power is mixed or combined with that which is subject to the sole control of the other spouse, the resulting mixture is subject to joint control of the spouses thereafter.

All jointly managed community property is subject to the liabilities of either spouse, and all community property, however managed, is liable for tortious wrongs committed by either spouse during marriage. But though that common property subject to the sole management of a spouse is subject to all liabilities of that spouse incurred before or during marriage, the common property subject to the sole control of one spouse is not subject to any nontortious liabilities incurred by the other and only to tortious liabilities incurred during marriage.

Each spouse has testamentary disposition of one-half of the community property, however managed during the joint lives of the spouses, and that share of the common property passes to his or her heirs on intestacy. In the absence of descendants, the share of a deceased spouse passes on intestacy to the other.

BIBLIOGRAPHY: William O. Huie, *The Community Property Law of Texas* (1951); Ocie Speer, *A Treatise on the Law of Marital Rights in Texas* (1929); Joseph W. McKnight, "Recodification and Reform of Matrimonial Property Law," *Texas Bar Journal*, XXIX (1966); Joseph W. McKnight (reviewer of book by William O. Huie), "Texas Cases and Materials on the Law of Marital Property Rights," *Texas Law Review*, XLVI (1967).

Joseph W. McKnight

*Como, Texas.

*Como Indians.

Comocara Indians. The Comocara are known from a single Spanish document of 1683 which does not clearly identify their area. They seem to have lived somewhere in west-central Texas. Their affiliations remain unknown.

BIBLIOGRAPHY: C. W. Hackett (ed.), *Pichardo's Treatise on the Limits of Louisiana and Texas*, I (1931).

T. N. Campbell

*Compromise of 1850.

*Comptroller of Public Accounts. *See also* State Executive Officers, Compensation of.

*Comstock, Texas.

*Comyn, Texas.

*Cona Indians.

*Concan, Texas.

*Concepcion, Texas.

*Concepción, Battle of.

*Concepción de Agreda, Pueblo of.

*Concepcion Creek.

*Concepción Mission. *See* Nuestra Señora de la Purísima Concepción de Acuña Mission.

Conchamucha Indians. In 1683–1684 Juan Domínguez de Mendoza qv led an exploratory expedition from El Paso as far eastward as the junction of the Concho and Colorado rivers east of present San Angelo. In his itinerary he listed the names of thirty-seven Indian groups, including the Conchamucha, from whom he expected to receive delegations. Nothing further is known about the Conchamucha, whose name is Spanish for "much shell" and suggests that they lived near the Concho River, so named because of its abundant freshwater mussel shells. The Conchamucha seem to have been one of many Indian groups of north-central Texas that were swept into oblivion by the southward thrust of the Lipan-Apache and Comanche Indians in the eighteenth century.

BIBLIOGRAPHY: H. E. Bolton (ed.), *Spanish Exploration in the Southwest, 1542–1706* (1916); C. W. Hackett (ed.), *Pichardo's Treatise on the Limits of Louisiana and Texas*, II (1934).

T. N. Campbell

*Conchaté Indians.

*Concho, Texas.

*Concho County. Concho County ranked fourth among Texas sheep counties in 1969 with over 140,000 head. Sheep, goats, and cattle account for two-thirds of the county's farm income, with chickens, turkeys, cotton, and small grains contributing the remainder of the $8.5 million annual income. Paint Rock and Eden are marketing centers for wool and mohair. In 1968 one thousand acres were under irrigation. Tourists are attracted to the fifteen hundred Indian pictographs on the bluff (*see* Rock Art, Indian) that gave Paint Rock its name, and to the annual Labor Day carnival. Population was 3,672 in 1960 and 2,937 in 1970.

BIBLIOGRAPHY: Forrest Kirkland and W. W. Newcomb, *The Rock Art of Texas Indians* (c. 1967).

*Concho River.

*Concho, San Saba, and Llano Valley Railroad Company.

*Concord, Texas. (Cherokee County.)

*Concord, Texas. (Hardin County.)

*Concord, Texas. (Hunt County.)

*Concord, Texas. (Leon County.)

*Concord, Texas. (McLennan County.)

*Concord, Texas. (Rusk County.)

*Concord, Texas. (Upshur County.)

*Concordia Lutheran College. *See* Lutheran Concordia College.

*Concordia Ranch.

*Concrete, Texas.

*Concrete College.

Concuguyapem Indians. The Concuguyapem (Couguyapem) Indians, apparently Coahuiltecan in speech, lived on the north bank of the Rio Grande between present Zapata and Rio Grande City. They are known only from the middle eighteenth century.

BIBLIOGRAPHY: W. Jiménez Moreno, "Tribus e idiomas del Norte de México," *El Norte de México y el Sur de Estados Unidos* (1944); G. Saldívar, *Los Indios de Tamaulipas* (1943).

T. N. Campbell

*Cone, Texas.

Conejero Indians. The Conejero (Conexero) Indians lived along the Canadian River in northwestern Texas during the seventeenth century. The name is Spanish for "rabbit people." The Conejero appear to have been an early band of Lipan-Apache.

BIBLIOGRAPHY: J. M. Espinosa, *Crusaders of the Rio Grande* (1942); F. W. Hodge (ed.), *Handbook of American Indians*, I (1907); A. H. Schroeder, *A Study of the Apache Indians: The Mescalero Apaches*, Part III (1960); A. B. Thomas, *After Coronado* (1935).

T. N. Campbell

*Conejo, Texas.

Conejo Indians. The Conejo (Spanish for "rabbit") Indians are considered to be a subdivision of the Concho, a Uto-Aztecan group of northern Chihuahua. In a Spanish document of 1693 the Conejo were identified as living north of the Rio Grande, presumably in what is now Trans-Pecos Texas, but in the first half of the eighteenth century the Conejo were known only from the lower Conchos River in Chihuahua.

BIBLIOGRAPHY: C. W. Hackett (ed.), *Historical Documents Relating to New Mexico, Nueva Vizcaya, and Approaches Thereto, to 1773*, II (1926); C. Sauer, *The Distribution of Aboriginal Tribes and Languages in Northwestern Mexico* (1934).

T. N. Campbell

*Conejos Creek.

*Confederacy, Texas in. *See* Civil War in Texas.

*Confederacy, United Daughters of the. *See* United Daughters of the Confederacy, Texas Division of.

Confederate Air Force. The Confederate Air Force was organized in 1957 by a group of Lower Rio Grande Valley ex-military pilots interested in buying and flying surplus World War II fighter aircraft. The group's purpose soon developed into an effort to preserve for posterity the remaining aircraft of the Second World War. On September 6, 1961, the organization was officially chartered as the Confederate Air Force.

Led by the mythical Jethro E. Culpepper, the CAF's membership is open to all who desire to preserve remaining World War II aircraft. Membership is on the basis of partnerships, whereby as many as four men pool their money to purchase a particular aircraft and then lease it to the CAF. All members are commissioned "colonel," the only rank in the CAF.

Established in their headquarters at the "Octagon," flying from "Rebel Field," near Mercedes, and having the unofficial motto of "Semper Mint Julep," the group realized a goal when they established a flying museum covering twenty-nine thousand square feet. The museum was dedicated in January, 1966, and contained aircraft representing the United States Army Air Force, Navy and Marine Corps Air Arms, the British Royal Air Force, and the German *Luftwaffe*. All fighter aircraft in the museum were fully operational and have been exhibited at various air shows from Texas to Canada.

With the growth of the CAF, a new bomb wing was established at Brownwood. In 1967 this section of the Confederate Air Force was attempting to purchase a Boeing B-29 "Superfortress."

During the Vietnam War, the CAF adopted "Purvis' Raiders," an armed helicopter group on duty in Southeast Asia. CAF air wings were furnished to the group and the airmen were designated honorary colonels.

The Confederate Air Force by 1967 had signed two movie contracts for films depicting air battles of World War II. In a British film entitled *The Battle of Britain*, the CAF was commissioned to do the flying in return for two British "Spitfires" and three German ME-109's to go into their flying museum. Another film commitment was *Tora, Tora, Tora*, a story depicting the Japanese preparations for and the bombing of Pearl Harbor. In 1968 the Confederate Air Force moved its headquarters from Mercedes to the Harlingen municipal airport. In addition to its World War II aircraft, the CAF was also collecting more modern aircraft.

BIBLIOGRAPHY: John Covington, "The Confederate Air Force," *Junior Historian*, XXVIII (1967–1968); Wynn Parks, " 'Flying Museum' from the Texas Valley," *Texas Star*, II (March 4, 1973).

*Confederate Courts in Texas.

*Confederate Home for Men. The Confederate Home for Men was used for the hospitalization of 828 elderly men in 1955. In 1963 its resident capacity was reduced from 800 to 500 by transferring patients to the Legion Annex of the Kerrville State Hospital qv and closing unsafe buildings. In 1965 the home was made a part of the Austin State Hospital,qv was renamed the Austin State Hospital Annex, and was under the management of the Texas Department of Mental Health and Mental Retardation.qv Early in 1967 the annex was closed.

BIBLIOGRAPHY: Board for Texas State Hospitals and Special Schools, *Report* (1964); *Texas Almanac* (1955, 1965); University of Texas at Austin, *Guide To Texas State Agencies* (1966).

*Confederate Woman's Home. Because there were only three occupants, the Confederate Woman's Home (also called the Confederate Home for Women) was closed in September, 1966, and these ladies were provided residence in a nursing home with the state paying all expenses. The home was originally dedicated by the United Daughters of the Confederacy on June 3, 1908. *See also* United Daughters of the Confederacy.

*Conglomerate Creek.

*Congregational Church in Texas. *See also* United Church of Christ.

*Congress of Mothers and Parent-Teacher Associations. *See* Texas Congress of Parents and Teachers.

*Congress of the Republic of Texas.

*Conkline Creek.

*Conlen, Texas.

*Conn, Texas.

Connally, Thomas Terry. Thomas Terry (Tom) Connally, the only surviving son of Jones and Mary Ellen Connally, was born on a farm in McLennan County on August 19, 1877. He moved to Falls County in 1882. After attending public school in Eddy, he received a B.A. degree from Baylor University in 1896 and a law degree from the University of Texas in 1898. Although turned down by the Rough Riders,qv he rose to the rank of sergeant major during the Spanish-American War.

Practicing law while not in office, Connally was elected in 1900 and 1902 to the Texas legislature, where he was known as a "young progressive." He was elected county attorney of Falls County in 1906 and 1908 and United States congressman from the Eleventh District in 1916. As a member of the House Foreign Affairs Committee, his first vote was in favor of declaring war against Germany in 1917. He resigned to become a captain in the army. Reelected to Congress in 1918, he continued to serve until 1929.

In 1928 Connally unseated U.S. Senator Earle B. Mayfield,qv becoming the only freshman Democratic senator in 1929. Best known for his Senate career, Connally was an able debater and an effectively picturesque figure who dressed in the style of William Jennings Bryan. His major assignments were to the Senate Finance Committee and the Senate Foreign Relations Committee, of which he was chairman, 1941–1946 and 1949–1953.

While in the Senate, Connally presented a plan to lessen the gold content of the dollar, which became a part of the Agricultural Adjustment Act of 1933. In spite of his usual loyalty to the Franklin D. Roosevelt administration, he voted against the National Industrial Recovery Act, which he considered unconstitutional, and openly fought Roosevelt's court reorganization plan. He was largely responsible for three national laws which particularly affected Texas—the Connally Hot Oil Act, the Jones-Connally Act, and a part of the Agricultural Adjustment Act of 1935, which subsidized the exportation of raw cotton.

Concerned with postwar peace settlements, he wrote the Connally Resolution calling for United States participation in the United Nations and served as a delegate to the 1945 meeting of the United Nations in San Francisco. Together with Arthur H. Vandenburg, he helped to determine bipartisan foreign policy during the Harry S. Truman administration.

Connally did not seek renomination in 1952. Reasons were his age, his close association with the then-unpopular Truman administration, and his opponent, Price Daniel, head of the popular move to regain the Texas tidelands (see Tidelands Controversy). By retiring, Connally preserved his unblemished record at the polls.

Connally married Louise Clarkson in 1904, and they had one son, Ben Clarkson Connally. Mrs. Connally died in 1935. The senator then married Lucile (Sanderson) Sheppard, widow of Senator Morris Sheppard,qv in 1942. He was a member of the Methodist church, the Masonic Order, and the Texas Knights of Pythias,qqv of which he was grand chancellor, 1913–1914. He died of pneumonia in Washington, D.C., on October 28, 1963, and was buried in Marlin, Texas.

BIBLIOGRAPHY: Tom Connally, My Name Is Tom Connally (1954); Biographical Directory of the American Congress, 1774–1961 (1961).

Frank H. Smyrl

*Connally Air Force Base. See also James Connally Air Force Base.

Connally Technical Institute. See Texas State Technical Institute.

*Connell, John.

*Connell, Wilson Edward.

*Connell, Texas.

*Connellee, Charles Ulrich.

Connelley's Crossing. See Camp Melvin, Texas.

*Conner, John Coggswell.

*Conner Creek.

Connolly, Maureen (Little Mo). See Brinker, Maureen Connolly.

*Connor, William Orr.

*Connor, Texas.

*Conoley, Texas.

*Conrad, Edward.

*Conrad, Frank Eben.

*Conroe, Texas. Conroe, seat of Montgomery County, serves an area devoted to petroleum and forestry, with forty related industries in the town, including creosoting, carbon black, and other chemical plants. Conroe's proximity to Houston has bolstered the economy and increased the population 30 percent between 1960 and 1970. The town reported many new improvements from 1957 to 1967, including four new school buildings, a modern city hall, a large library, a post office, an FM radio station, and remodeling and enlarging of the airport, hospital, and courthouse. In 1970 the town had 344 businesses, twenty-three churches, two radio stations, and a newspaper. The town also had a large Boy Scout facility at Camp Strake. Conroe's population was 9,192 in 1960 and 11,969 in 1970. See also Houston Standard Metropolitan Statistical Area.

*Conroe Oil Field.

*Consavvy Lake.

*Conscription under the Confederacy in Texas.

*Conservation of Natural Resources.

*Considérant, Victor Prosper.

*Constable. See also County and Precinct Officers, Terms of.

*Constitution of Coahuila and Texas.

*Constitution of 1824.

*Constitution of 1827. See Constitution of Coahuila and Texas.

*Constitution of 1836. See Constitution of the Republic.

*Constitution of 1845.

*Constitution of 1861.

*Constitution of 1866.

*Constitution of 1869.

*Constitution of 1876.

*Constitution Proposed in 1833.

Constitution Proposed in 1974. See Constitutional Convention of 1974.

*Constitution of the Republic.

*Constitutional Advocate and Brazoria Advertiser.

*Constitutional Amendments. By the time of the Constitutional Convention of 1974,qv the legislature had submitted 343 amendments to the voters since 1876. Of this number, 219 amendments had been approved by the voters.

Perhaps the most important amendment in recent times was that passed on November 7, 1972, when voters approved the adoption of an amendment which called for the establishment of a Constitutional Revision Commission and for the convening of the 63rd Texas Legislature as a Constitutional Convention at noon on the second Tuesday in January, 1974, for the purpose of writing a new constitution to be submitted to the voters of Texas for their approval or rejection. See Constitutional Convention of 1974.

*Constitutional Convention of 1836. *See* Convention of 1836.

*Constitutional Convention of 1845. *See* Convention of 1845.

*Constitutional Convention of 1861. *See* Secession Convention.

*Constitutional Convention of 1866.

*Constitutional Convention of 1868–1869.

*Constitutional Convention of 1875.

Constitutional Convention of 1974. Recognizing the need for a new state constitution, the 62nd Texas Legislature passed House Joint Resolution Number 61 in May, 1971, which called for the establishment of a Constitutional Revision Commission and for the convening of the 63rd Legislature as a Constitutional Convention at noon on the second Tuesday in January, 1974. House Joint Resolution Number 61 was presented to the voters of Texas as Constitutional Amendment Number 4 on November 7, 1972, and by a vote of 1,549,982 to 985,282 the voters approved the adoption of the amendment, which became Article XVII, Section 2 of the Constitution of 1876.qv

Following the mandate of the amendment, the 63rd Legislature passed Senate Concurrent Resolution Number 1 in February, 1973, establishing a Constitutional Revision Commission. The purpose of the commission was to ". . . study the need for constitutional change and . . . report its recommendations to the members of the legislature not later than November 1, 1973."

The thirty-seven members of the commission were appointed by a committee composed of Governor Dolph Briscoe, Lieutenant Governor William P. Hobby, Attorney General John Hill, Speaker of the House of Representatives Price Daniel, Jr., Chief Justice of the Supreme Court Joe R. Greenhill, and Presiding Judge of the Court of Criminal Appeals John F. Onion, Jr.; the appointments were ratified and confirmed by the legislature. Robert W. Calvert, former Speaker of the Texas House of Representatives and former chief justice of the Texas Supreme Court, was named chairman of the commission, and Mrs. Malcolm Milburn, former vice-chairman of the Texas Republican party,qv was named vice-chairman. The other members of the commission were as follows: Loys D. Barbour, Roy R. Barrera, Bill Bass, George Beto, Tony Bonilla, Mrs. Mary Beth Brient, Mrs. David F. (Ann) Chappell, Barbara Culver, William Donnell, Beeman Fisher, Peter T. Flawn, M. F. "Mike" Frost, Clotilde Garcia, Mrs. C. F. (Sibyl) Hamilton, Bill Hartman, Zan Holmes, Mrs. Faye Holub, Leon Jaworski, Leroy Jeffers, Andrew Jefferson, Jr., Page Keeton, W. James Kronzer, Jr., Earl Lewis, Honore Ligarde, Wales Madden, Jr., Mark Martin, Janice May, Mark McLaughlin, L. G. Moore, Raymond Nasher, E. L. Oakes, Jr., Don Rives, Preston Shirley, Jim W. Weatherby, and Ralph W. Yarborough.

The commission held its first meeting in March, 1973. After holding nineteen public hearings across

the state, the commission presented its recommendations for a new constitution to the legislature on November 1, 1973. The proposed constitution submitted by the commission represented the first thorough attempt to draft a new constitution for Texas since the Constitutional Convention of 1875.qv

On January 8, 1974, the 63rd Legislature convened as a Constitutional Convention in the chamber of the House of Representatives, with Lieutenant Governor William P. Hobby presiding as temporary chairman. Speaker of the House of Representatives Price Daniel, Jr., of Liberty County, was elected president of the convention, and State Senator A. M. Aikin, Jr., of Lamar County, was elected vice-president. Also during the first week of proceedings, the permanent rules of the convention were adopted, and the delegates were appointed to the eight substantive and five procedural committees.

Daniel, with approval of the convention, named the following delegates to head the convention committees: Neil Caldwell, of Brazoria County, chairman of the committee on finance, and H. Tati Santiesteban, of El Paso County, vice-chairman; Craig A. Washington, of Harris County, chairman of the committee on local government, and Charles Evans, of Tarrant County, vice-chairman; Dan Kubiak, of Milam County, chairman of the committee on education, and Bill Braecklein, of Dallas County, vice-chairman; Robert Maloney, of Dallas County, chairman of the committee on the legislature, and Ron Clower, of Dallas County, vice-chairman; L. DeWitt Hale, of Nueces County, chairman of the committee on the judiciary, and Oscar H. Mauzy, of Dallas County, vice-chairman; Bob Gammage, of Harris County, chairman of the committee on general provisions, and Hilary B. Doran, Jr., of Val Verde County, vice-chairman; Bill Meier, of Tarrant County, chairman of the committee on the executive, and Jim Vecchio, of Dallas County, vice-chairman; A. R. Schwartz, of Galveston County, chairman of the committee on rights and suffrage, and James R. Nowlin, of Bexar County, vice-chairman; Matt Garcia, of Bexar County, chairman of the committee on rules, and Richard S. Geiger, of Dallas County, vice-chairman; Jack Hightower, of Wilbarger County, chairman of the committee on administration, and Joe Allen, of Harris County, vice-chairman; Nelson W. Wolff, of Bexar County, chairman of the committee on submission and transition, and Gene Jones, of Harris County, vice-chairman; Max Sherman, of Potter County, chairman of the committee on style and drafting, and Tim Von Dohlen, of Goliad County, vice-chairman; Pike Powers, of Jefferson County, chairman of the committee on public information, and Eddie Bernice Johnson, of Dallas County, vice-chairman.

James F. Ray, who served as executive director of the Constitutional Revision Commission, was appointed executive director of the convention. Upon the completion of its work the convention was to submit a proposed new constitution to the voters of Texas for their approval or rejection.

After seven months and approximately five million dollars spent, the Constitutional Convention closed on July 30, 1974, having failed by three votes (118 for, 62 against, and 1 not voting) to produce a document to submit to the voters.

Mary Lucia Barras
Houston Daniel

*Constitutions of Texas. The Constitution of 1876,qv with 219 constitutional amendments,qv continued to be the fundamental law of Texas in 1974; however, the 63rd Texas Legislature convened as a Constitutional Convention on the second Tuesday in January, 1974, for the purpose of writing a new constitution to be submitted to the voters of Texas for approval or rejection in that year. *See* Constitutional Convention of 1974.

*Consular Service of the Republic of Texas.

*Consultation.

*Content, Texas. (Colorado County.)

*Content, Texas. (Runnels County.)

*Contraband Trace.

*Contrabando Mountain.

*Contrabando Water Hole.

*Convention of 1832.

*Convention of 1833.

*Convention of 1836.

*Convention of 1845.

*Conventions, State Party. *See* Political Parties; Election Laws.

*Converse, Texas. Converse, in Bexar County, showed the influence of the San Antonio area's continued growth, with a population of 900 in 1960 and 1,383 in 1970.

*Conway, Texas.

Cook, Abner Hugh. Abner Hugh Cook was born in Rowan County, North Carolina, on March 20, 1814. In 1835 he moved to Macon, Georgia, and two years later to Nashville, Tennessee. In 1839 he came to Austin, Texas, where he remained for the rest of his life. He married Mrs. Eliza Taylor Logan in 1842, and they had four sons.

Although nothing is known of his early life and training, Cook must have learned the building trade during his youth, for he brought with him a skill in designing and construction which soon established him as a master builder in the newly founded capital city of Austin. With apprentice training and the builder's handbooks which were the source of structural and architectural details, Cook produced some of the finest Greek Revival houses in Texas. Among these were the Governor's Mansion, Woodlawn Mansion,qqv and the Neill-Cochran House in Austin. In addition to designing and building fine residences, Cook was the contractor for several important public buildings during the forty-odd years that he practiced his trade in Austin. One of these was the Old Main Building of the University of Texas.

Abner Cook died on February 21, 1884, and was buried in Oakwood Cemetery in Austin.

BIBLIOGRAPHY: Samuel E. Gideon, *Historic and Picturesque Austin* (1936); August Watkins Harris, *Minor & Major Mansions in Early Austin* (c. 1955), *Buildings of the Seat of Government, 1840–1861* (1959); Roxanne Kuter Williamson, Victorian Architecture in Austin (M.A. thesis, University of Texas at Austin, 1967); Austin *Daily Statesman*, February 22, 26, 1884; Dallas *Morning News*, June 5, 1953.

Drury B. Alexander

*Cook, James.

*Cook, James R.

*Cook, Jim.

*Cook, John R.

*Cook Mountain.

*Cooke, Gustave.

*Cooke, John.

*Cooke, Louis P.

*Cooke, Wilds K.

*Cooke, William G.

*Cooke County. Cooke County has numerous attractions, including the Frank Buck Zoo, Fort Fitzhugh,qv Lake Texoma, and an August fair. Over nine million barrels of oil were produced in 1972, bringing the total production from 1926 through 1972 to 274,166,611 barrels. The farm income reached an estimated thirteen million dollars in 1970, 80 percent of which came from livestock and poultry. The county ranked eleventh in dairying in the state in 1959. It was also among the state's leaders in the production of oats, while other grains, cotton, fruit, nuts, and vegetables were grown in marketable quantities. Manufacturing is centered in Gainesville. The 1960 population of 22,560 increased to 23,471 by 1970.

Cooke County Junior College. Cooke County Junior College, Gainesville, celebrated its fortieth anniversary in 1965. The college, originally known as Gainesville Junior College, began as a movement initiated by Lee Clark, superintendent of the public schools, in November, 1923. As the first president, Clark organized and officially opened the doors of the three-room college in Newsome Doughtery Memorial High School on September 8, 1924. Gainesville Junior College was one of the first public junior colleges in Texas. H. O. McCain served as superintendent of schools and president of the college from 1929 to 1944. Roy P. Wilson, the third superintendent of schools to serve as college president, saw the college through the late World War II and postwar years, from 1945 to 1958. James K. Kearns succeeded Wilson. Under Kearns' administration the move was initiated to separate the junior college from the high school district, build new facilities, and make a county-wide junior college.

In May, 1960, Gainesville Junior College separated from the Gainesville Independent School District, and Cooke County Junior College District was organized. The same year, John H. Parker became the fifth president of the college and the first to serve the junior college district. Between 1952 and 1967 the enrollment grew from 55 to 1,104 students. Facilities expanded from the "little white house" on Lindsay Street to a million-dollar, sixty-acre campus on Black's Hill west of the city of Gainesville. The plant was composed of four structures—classroom-student union building, vocational-technical shop building, library-administration building, and science-mathematics building. In 1962 the college was fully accredited by the Southern Association of Colleges and Schools. Faculty numbered fifty-five members in 1970, and the library collection contained over 24,000 volumes. Eight major departments and the vocational-technical division offered a total of 141 courses, and there were thirty-five areas from which professional and pre-professional courses might be chosen. The college offered two summer sessions in addition to regular terms. Enrollment for the 1974 fall term was 2,126; Alton Laird was president in that year, and the school was renamed Cooke County College.

*Cookes Point, Texas.

*Cooks Creek.

*Cook's Fort.

*Cooks Slough.

*Cookville, Texas.

*Coolidge, Dane.

*Coolidge, Texas.

Coombes, Zachariah Ellis. Zachariah Ellis Coombes was born in Nelson County, Kentucky, on March 30, 1833, the son of William and Ivy (Green) Coombes. In 1843 he came with his family in an ox-drawn wagon to Dallas County, where they were early members of the Peters' Colony.qv At the age of twenty Coombes returned to Kentucky for additional education. Although preparing for the practice of law, he contracted with the Brazos Agency to conduct an Indian school at the Brazos Indian Reservation,qv located approximately fifteen miles from Fort Belknap qv in Young County. He married Rebecca Finch Bedford on December 28, 1856, and they had seven children.

Coombes enlisted in the Confederate Army on May 14, 1862, was promoted to lieutenant on April 24, 1863, and to captain of Company G, 31st Regiment, Texas Cavalry, in June, 1863. He served Dallas County as a judge from 1866 to 1868, as an alderman in 1871, and as a member of the House of Representatives of the Nineteenth Texas Legislature in 1885. Coombes died November 25, 1895, in Dallas, and was buried in the west Dallas cemetery.

Charles E. Coombes, Jr.

*Coon Creek.

*Coon Mountain.

*Coon's Rancho.

*Cooper, Dillard.

Cooper, Madison Alexander, Jr. Madison Alexander Cooper, Jr., son of Madison Alexander and Martha Dillon (Roane) Cooper, was born in Waco, Texas, on June 3, 1894. He entered the University of Texas in September, 1911; following his graduation with a B.A. degree in 1915, he returned to Waco to work in the family business, the Cooper Company, which at that time was one of the largest wholesale grocery firms in Texas. In May, 1917, he entered the U.S. Army officer training school at Leon Springs, Texas, was commissioned a second lieutenant, and then served in France during the war; he was promoted to captain before his discharge and return to Waco in May, 1919.

He worked for the Cooper Company for ten years and then tried other business ventures on his own. He had a strong interest in literature, particularly the short story, but he was mostly unsuccessful in this form of writing. When his parents died he lived alone in the three-story Victorian house his father had built, and in 1943, as a memorial to his parents, he set up the Cooper Foundation. Known locally as a wealthy, eccentric, bachelor businessman, Cooper did not reveal his ambition as a writer, so that when his novel, *Sironia, Texas* (which he worked on for eleven years), was published in New York in 1952, it came as a surprise to most people. The novel was reputed to be the longest work of fiction published up to that time, running 1,731 pages in two volumes. He received the Houghton Mifflin Fellowship Award for the novel; in 1953 the Texas Institute of Letters qv awarded him the McMurray Bookshop prize for the work. Cooper drew national attention with his first novel, and the work quickly became a best seller. The publicity subsided, and his second novel, *The Haunted Hacienda* (1955), which was the first of a planned trilogy, went largely unnoticed. In 1956 he was a regular contributor to the Dallas *Morning News* qv book page. He encouraged young writers, often with material aid, and anonymously sponsored many civic programs in Waco. After a long series of lawsuits over control of the family firm, Cooper sold his interests, and the business became known as the J. R. Milam Company in 1954.

Madison Cooper died on September 28, 1956, and was buried in Oakwood Cemetery in Waco. He left his entire estate of $2,844,544 to the Cooper Foundation, the income of which was to be used for the betterment of Waco. By 1971 the total assets of the foundation were several million dollars, and 163 grants amounting to more than $1.2 million had been donated to various Waco projects.

BIBLIOGRAPHY: Marion Travis, *Madison Cooper* (1971); Biographical File, Barker Texas History Center, University of Texas at Austin.

*Cooper, Oscar Henry.

*Cooper, Samuel Bronson.

*Cooper, William.

*Cooper, William.

*Cooper, Texas. Cooper, seat and commercial center of Delta County, had approximately sixty businesses in 1970, including seed-cleaning plants and no less than thirty-eight dairies. The city's population was 2,213 in 1960 and 2,258 in 1970. Cooper was the site of two hospitals which served the area.

Cooper was named the seat of Delta County when that county was organized in 1870; therefore the town's existence must date at least to 1870 (not 1874, as stated in Volume I). Post office records show that Thompson P. Pickins was named postmaster of Cooper on August 7, 1871.

*Cooper Canyon.

*Cooper Creek.

*Cooper Creek, Texas.

*Cooper Mountain.

*Cooperatives in Texas. In 1966 there were over seven hundred cooperative associations in Texas, about half of which were cotton gins. The remainder included grain elevators; fruit and vegetable, poultry, peanut, dairy, and livestock marketing associations; rural electrification cooperatives; rural telephone cooperatives; production credit associations; credit unions; and farm supply stores. Also included were regional associations, such as cottonseed oil mills, cottonseed breeding associations, cotton compresses, cotton and grain marketing associations, wholesale farm supply associations, and the Houston Bank for Cooperatives.

Texas cooperatives were represented by the Texas Federation of Cooperatives, the Texas Cooperative Ginners Association, the Texas Rural Electric Cooperatives Association, and the Texas Rural Credit Union Association. These organizations were assisted in research, service, and educational activities by the Farmer Cooperative Service of the United States Department of Agriculture, Texas Agricultural Experiment Station qv and Texas Agricultural Extension Service qv of Texas A&M University, and the Farm Credit Banks of Houston.

Bruno E. Schroeder

*Coopers Creek.

*Coopwood, Bethel.

Coordinating Board, Texas College and University System. The Coordinating Board, Texas College and University System, was created by the Fifty-ninth Legislature under the Higher Education Coordinating Act of 1965 to provide a strong central agency to coordinate all state-supported junior and senior colleges and universities in the state. The board is composed of eighteen lay individuals, appointed by the governor and approved by the Senate, who serve without pay for six-year overlapping terms. The members provide representation from all areas of the state and cannot be employed professionally for remuneration in the field of education during the term of office.

A commissioner of higher education is the chief executive officer and is appointed by the board.

The Coordinating Board was established to provide leadership and coordination for the institutions and governing boards of higher education so that the state of Texas could achieve excellence for the college education of its youth through the efficient and effective utilization and concentration of all available resources. The board has general and specific authority in areas of academic program, finance, and facilities and has been designated the administrator at the state level for certain federal educational programs. The Coordinating Board is charged with a vast array of responsibilities, including the elimination of costly duplication of programs and facilities, and the initiation of programs required by the exigencies of higher education.

Coordination of higher education in Texas is an outgrowth of a study made by the Texas Legislative Council qv in 1950. The report of the council led to the establishment of a temporary Texas Commission on Higher Education in 1953 to study the needs of higher education in the state and to submit recommendations. The temporary commission urged the creation of a permanent central agency for coordinating higher education, and the legislature enacted the required legislation for the permanent Texas Commission on Higher Education in 1955. The permanent commission, with limited statutory authority, was charged with providing leadership in coordinating services to the state senior colleges and universities, with developing formulas for funding the expenses in each institution, and for exercising control over their growth.

In 1963 a special Governor's Committee on Education Beyond the High School was appointed to make an extensive study of Texas' needs in higher education for the next decade. The committee issued its report on August 31, 1964, in which it recommended a comprehensive reconstitution of the coordinating authority in higher education. As a result of the report of the governor's committee, the legislature created the Coordinating Board, Texas College and University System.

BIBLIOGRAPHY: University of Texas at Austin, *Guide To Texas State Agencies* (1972).

Forrest E. Ward

Coospacam Indians. The Coospacam (Cospacam, Coospascan) Indians, presumably Coahuiltecan in speech, lived along the lower Rio Grande. In the middle eighteenth century they were reported on the south bank of the river about halfway between present Camargo and Reynosa, Tamaulipas.

BIBLIOGRAPHY: W. Jiménez Moreno, "Tribus e idiomas del Norte de México," *El Norte de México y el Sur de Estados Unidos* (1944); G. Saldivar, *Los Indios de Tamaulipas* (1943).

T. N. Campbell

Cootajanam Indians. The Cootajanam (Cootajan) Indians, apparently Coahuiltecan in speech, lived along the lower Rio Grande. In the middle eighteenth century they were reported to have had settlements on the north bank of the river in present Cameron and Hidalgo counties.

BIBLIOGRAPHY: W. Jiménez Moreno, "Tribus e idiomas del Norte de México," *El Norte de México y el Sur de Estados Unidos* (1944); G. Saldivar, *Los Indios de Tamaulipas* (1943).

T. N. Campbell

*Copane Indians. The Copane (Cobane, Coopane, Kopano) Indians were Karankawans who, in the eighteenth century, lived in the middle section of the Texas coast, mainly on and between Copano and San Antonio bays. Little is known about the Copane other than that they were represented at the coastal missions of Nuestra Señora del Rosario and Nuestra Señora del Refugio qqv between 1751 and 1828. It seems likely that the Copane who survived the mission period joined remnants of other Karankawan groups that became known as the Karankawa. All Karankawan groups became extinct by 1858.

BIBLIOGRAPHY: H. E. Bolton, "The Founding of Mission Rosario," *Quarterly of the Texas State Historical Association,* X (1906–1907), "Records of the Mission of Nuestra Señora del Refugio," *Quarterly of the Texas State Historical Association,* XIV (1910–1911), and *Texas in the Middle Eighteenth Century* (1915); W. E. Dunn, "The Founding of Nuestra Señora del Refugio, the Last Spanish Mission in Texas," *Southwestern Historical Quarterly,* XXV (1921–1922); F. W. Hodge (ed.), *Handbook of American Indians,* I (1907), II (1910); W. H. Oberste, *History of Refugio Mission* (1942).

T. N. Campbell

*Copano, Texas.

*Copano Bay.

*Copano Creek.

*Cope, Edward Drinker.

Cope, Millard Lewis. Millard Lewis Cope, son of James A. and Hattie B. (Parkinson) Cope, was born at Sonora, Texas, on December 21, 1905. He began his career in newspaper work while he was in public school, working as an odd-job boy for Sonora's *Devil's River News.* He went to Howard Payne College from 1923 to 1926, working summers for the San Angelo *Standard-Times.* He then went to the University of Missouri on a scholarship and received a degree in journalism in 1927. A year after graduation, Cope became co-editor of the San Angelo *Standard-Times* of the Harte-Hanks chain, an organization for which he worked until the end of his life. On January 1, 1930, he became publisher of the Sweetwater *Reporter,* then returned to the San Angelo newspapers, and in 1940 became publisher of the *Herald.* In 1945 he became editor and publisher of the Marshall *News Messenger* and served in this position for eighteen years.

During Cope's years at Marshall he rose to national prominence in his profession. In 1954 he was a member of the board of directors of the Southern Newspaper Publishers Association. He was elected president of the regional organization at its 1957 meeting. In addition to other newspaper duties, he and his son collaborated on a weekly syndicated release called "News Tips," distributed by the General Features Corporation of New York to approximately 125 newspapers in the United States and Canada. Cope wrote many articles as well as a number of booklets on Texas history.

On December 12, 1931, Cope married Margaret Kilgore of San Angelo. They had a son and a daughter. Cope received many local and national journalism awards, including, in 1959, the Missouri Honor Award Medal of Distinguished Service in Journalism from the University of Missouri. Howard Payne College named him "Man of the Year" in 1958, and four years later President John F. Kennedy named him to the National Advisory Council for the Peace Corps. Cope was a member of the American Society of Newspaper Editors. He was a member of the Texas Commission on Higher Education qv and was serving his second

three-year term as a director of the Associated Press when he died on January 4, 1964.

BIBLIOGRAPHY: Rebecca M. Cameron, "Millard Lewis Cope," *Harrison County Historical Herald,* I (November, 1964); San Angelo *Standard-Times,* April 11, 1945, January 19, 1965; "Christmas in Texas," Marshall *News Messenger,* December 24, 1953.

John N. Cravens

*Copeland Creek.

*Copenhagen, Texas.

*Copeville, Texas.

*Coplen, Texas.

*Coppell, Texas. Coppell, in northwestern Dallas County, increased its population 159.5 percent in ten years, from 666 in 1960 to 1,728 in 1970. *See also* Dallas Standard Metropolitan Statistical Area.

*Copper Production. The last reported copper production was eighteen tons in 1952 valued at $8,712. Most of the ore came from the Old Hazel Mine in Culberson County in the Trans-Pecos region. During the mid-1950's, however, most of the Texas copper mines were inoperative. Large deposits of ore are known to exist in the North Texas region but have not been developed because of their low copper content. In 1966 there existed a copper refinery and a copper smelter in El Paso County which were dependent upon ore from New Mexico, Mexico, and Arizona to produce refined copper, copper anode, and copper sulfate.

BIBLIOGRAPHY: *Texas Almanac* (1955, 1965); *Directory of Texas Manufacturers* (1966).

*Copperas Cove, Texas. Copperas Cove, formerly a farming and ranching center in Coryell County, is a retirement and military community at the edge of Fort Hood.qv Its population has grown rapidly from 1,052 in 1950, to 4,567 in 1960, and to 10,818 in 1970. Among its sixty-eight businesses in 1970 were manufacturers of mattresses, automotive chemicals, concrete, cabinets, and molding.

*Copperas Creek.

Coppini, Pompeo. Pompeo Coppini, sculptor, was born in Moglia, Italy, on May 19, 1870, son of Giovanni and Leandra (Raffa) Coppini. He grew up in Florence, Italy, where he was a student at the Accademia di Belle Arte and there studied under Augusto Rivalta, graduating with highest honors in 1889. On March 5, 1896, Coppini came to the United States without money and with no knowledge of English. On February 27, 1898, he married Elizabeth Di Barbieri of New Haven, Connecticut; he became an American citizen in 1902.

Coppini, hearing of Frank Teich's qv search for a sculptor, came to Texas in November, 1901; he was commissioned to model the statue of Jefferson Davis (and other figures) for the Confederate monument, subsequently erected on the Capitol qv grounds in Austin. Other Texas commissions followed, one of the best known being the Littlefield Fountain Memorial at the University of Texas at Austin which stands at the principal entrance to the university grounds. He also did the seven bronze statues along the south mall of the university. Other Texas works include a statue of the Reverend

Rufus C. Burleson [qv] at Baylor University in Waco, the monument to Sam Houston at Huntsville, a monument at Gonzales in commemoration of the first shot fired for Texas independence, a statue of a Confederate soldier at Victoria, busts of Jefferson Davis, Albert Sidney Johnston, Robert E. Lee,[qqv] and Stonewall Jackson for the Confederate monument at Paris, Texas, and a group statue called "The Victims of the Galveston Flood," which was given to the University of Texas at Austin. He also modeled a cowboy equestrian group at Ballinger and executed the bronze doors of the Scottish Rite Cathedral in San Antonio. The familiar cenotaph to the heroes of the Alamo on Alamo Plaza in San Antonio, a piece which aroused some controversy, is also a work by Coppini. One of his best known works is a statue of George Washington in Mexico City.

The appreciation of Texans for Coppini's artistic ability was further shown in the commission given him to design the commemorative half-dollar for the Texas Independence Centennial.[qv] Recognition and appreciation of his work extended to Italy, for in 1931 he was decorated "Commendatore" of the Crown of Italy for his contribution to art in America.

Coppini is represented in the United States by thirty-eight public monuments, sixteen portrait statues, and about seventy-five portrait busts. When expressing his own attitudes toward art and sculpture, Coppini was often critical of modernism, which he attributed to a general lack of screening of pupils in art schools. Coppini felt art training should be a regular branch of learning in a university, with strict standards that would assure adherence to classic and academic artistic traditions. For a short period of time Coppini was head of the art department of Trinity University in San Antonio. He died in San Antonio on September 26, 1957, and was buried in Sunset Memorial Park in a crypt of his own design. He was survived by his wife and foster daughter, sculptress Waldine Tauch.

BIBLIOGRAPHY: Lillian G. Burson, *Life and Works of Pompeo Coppini, Sculptor* (n.d.); *Pompeo Coppini, From Dawn to Sunset* (1949); Mantle Fielding, *Dictionary of American Painters, Sculptors, and Engravers* (1960); *Newsweek* (April 29, 1940); Esse Forrester-O'Brien, *Art and Artists in Texas* (c. 1935); *Who's Who In America* (1952); San Antonio *Express*, August 15, 1916; Biographical File, Barker Texas History Center, University of Texas at Austin.

*Copyrights in the Republic of Texas.

*Cora, Texas. Cora, first known as Troy, was renamed when the town became the first seat of Comanche County in 1856. It was a thriving frontier settlement, but its population declined and its businesses were abandoned after the change of the county seat to Comanche in 1859. In 1936 the log cabin containing two rooms with a dogtrot, which had been the first courthouse, was moved to Lake Eanes Park four miles south of Comanche. In the 1960's this building was moved again onto land adjoining the museum in Comanche, where it stands today with a historical marker. A high metal bridge over a branch of the South Leon River marked the site of Cora in 1967.

Margaret Tate Waring

*Corazones Draw.

*Corazones Peaks.

*Corbet, Texas.

*Cord Wood Creek.

*Cordaro, Texas.

*Cordele, Texas.

*Cordéro y Bustamante, Manuel Antonio. Antonio Cordéro y Bustamante was born in Cádiz, Spain, in 1753. He became a cadet in the Spanish army on December 7, 1767, and he held the same rank in America on September 6, 1771. He rose in rank, and by February 15, 1798, he had become governor of Coahuila.

He served in the Zamora Infantry, the Dragoons of Spain and Mexico, and the Presidial Companies of San Buenaventura. From 1777 until 1790 he fought in twenty-five campaigns in the Provincias Internas,[qv] four of them as subordinate and the rest as commander. He captured or killed 472 enemies and rescued six prisoners. He signed a peace treaty with the Mimbreños and Gileños in 1787. For ten months during 1790 and 1791 he had military command of Nueva Vizcaya, where he chased marauders and punished rebelling Indians who threatened the ranches. In a four-month campaign during 1794 he subjugated again the Gileña and Mimbreña Apaches who rose against the Presidio of Janos. In 1795 he directed an expedition against the Mescaleros at Presidio del Norte. On December 27, 1796, he became commander of troops operating on the Coahuila frontier. During the years 1795–1800 he built up the defenses of Coahuila and founded numerous towns and settlements. In September, 1805, he arrived at San Antonio with orders to reinforce the posts of Orcoquisas, Nacogdoches, and Adaes; until 1810 he remained in Texas, establishing settlements on the Trinity, Brazos, Colorado, San Marcos, and Guadalupe rivers. He attempted to bar North American colonists and ordered all Negro slaves entering Texas from Louisiana to be freed. Zebulon Pike [qv] described him as "five feet ten inches in height . . . fair complexion, and blue eyes . . . wears his hair turned back, and in every part of his deportment was legibly written 'The Soldier.' . . . Well-read and introspective, with a bachelor's fearlessness for his personal safety, he was one of the ablest Spanish military commanders on the frontier."

Cordéro became commandant general of the Western Interior Provinces in 1822 and was promoted to field marshal general, a position he held until his death in Durango in the spring of 1823.

BIBLIOGRAPHY: Zebulon M. Pike, *An Account of Expeditions to the Sources of the Mississippi* (1810); C. F. Castañeda, *Our Catholic Heritage, 1519–1936*, V (1942); Vito Alessio Robles, *Coahuila y Texas en la Época Colonial* (1938); Jack D. L. Holmes, "Showdown on the Sabine: General James Wilkinson *vs.* Lieutenant-Colonel Simón de Herrera," *Louisiana Studies*, III (1964); Nettie Lee Benson, "Texas Failure to Send a Deputy to the Spanish

Cortes, 1810–1812," *Southwestern Historical Quarterly,* LXIV (1960–1961).

Jack D. L. Holmes

*Cordova, Jacob de. *See* De Cordova, Jacob.

*Cordova, Phineas de. *See* De Cordova, Phineas.

*Cordova, Vicente.

*Cordova Island.

*Cordova Peak.

*Cordova Rebellion.

*Corinth, Texas. (Denton County.)

*Corinth, Texas. (Jones County.)

*Corinth, Texas. (Milam County.)

*Corley, Texas.

*Corn Creek.

*Corn Culture. Corn declined as the principal feed grain crop during the 1950's because of the displacement of animal power on Texas farms by machines and the development of a sturdier, less expensive grain sorghum. In 1954 Texas produced 33,184,000 bushels of corn valued at $48,117,000. At that time over two million acres were under cultivation and over 80 percent of the 1954 production consisted of hybrid varieties; in 1955 Texas ranked twelfth in the nation in corn acreage. Plantings decreased, however, and the corn acreage in 1957 was the smallest planted since 1875. The average yield at the same time increased, and in 1959 a record of twenty-eight bushels per acre was registered.

Acreage continued to decline during the 1960's, falling below one million acres in 1963 for the first time since 1869. The following year, the 23,-488,000 bushels harvested were valued at $29,595,-000. In 1966 Texas corn was attacked for the first time by maize dwarf mosaic virus. In that year Texas farmers lost over one million dollars because of the virus, and agricultural researchers turned to the development of a more resistant variety to prevent future losses. In 1970, 32,391,000 bushels of corn, valued at $45,995,000, were harvested from 531,000 acres.

Major corn-growing counties included Williamson, Lavaca, Bell, Collin, Falls, Fayette, and Hill. *See also* Agriculture in Texas.

BIBLIOGRAPHY: *Texas Almanac* (1955, 1963, 1965, 1972); Texas Agricultural Experiment Station, *Bulletin,* No. 878 (August, 1957); *Texas Agricultural Progress* (November–December, 1960, Fall, 1966); *Texas Business Review* (July, 1958).

*Corn Gap.

*Corn Hill, Texas.

*Corn Mountain.

*Cornelius Creek.

*Cornell, Texas.

*Cornersville, Texas.

*Cornet, Texas.

*Cornudas Mountains.

*Coronado, Francisco Vázquez de.

*Coronado Expedition.

*Coronal Institute.

*Corporations, Regulation of. *See* Anti-Trust Regulation.

*Corpus Christi, Texas. The population of Corpus Christi was 167,690 in 1960 and 204,525 in 1970. The city was an industrial-commercial center for the surrounding large agricultural-petrochemical area and the largest city in the Corpus Christi Standard Metropolitan Statistical Area. A United States naval air station was located there, and the port handled 29,854,615 tons of freight in 1969, making it the second port city in Texas in amount of total tonnage. The city's proximity to Padre Island insured a good tourist trade. *See also* Corpus Christi Standard Metropolitan Statistical Area.

*Corpus Christi Bay.

*Corpus Christi College-Academy. John Dunn, Jr. (not his cousin, John B. Dunn,qv as stated in Volume I), donated the land for Corpus Christi College-Academy. Part of the John B. Dunn museum collection was donated to Corpus Christi College-Academy.

Grace Dunn Vetters

*Corpus Christi *Gazette.*

*Corpus Christi de la Isleta.

Corpus Christi Junior College. *See* Del Mar College.

Corpus Christi Museum. The Corpus Christi Museum, established in 1957 with the aid of the local Association for Childhood Education, is supported by city, school, and private memberships. The collections of the museum are of a general nature, including natural history, marine science, geology, and exhibits on man. The programs of the museum are geared to education and information for all age levels. The Corpus Christi Museum, in its present location since 1967, is the only general museum in a 150-mile radius, and it draws visiting school groups from a thirteen-county area.

Aalbert Heine

Corpus Christi Naval Air Station. *See* Naval Air Station, Corpus Christi, Texas.

*Corpus Christi Pass.

*Corpus Christi, San Diego, and Rio Grande Narrow Gauge Railroad. *See* Texas-Mexican Railway Company.

Corpus Christi Standard Metropolitan Statistical Area. The Corpus Christi Standard Metropolitan Statistical Area, created in 1949 by the United States Bureau of the Budget, encompassed at that time the 838-square-mile area of Nueces County. In 1950 it had 165,471 inhabitants with 108,287 living in Corpus Christi. In 1960 the population was 221,573 and 167,690, respectively. In 1965 the Bureau of the Budget added San Patricio County to the official metropolitan area, increasing its size to 1,518 square miles. The 1970 population for the new area was 284,832. Corpus Christi in 1970 had a population of 204,525. Other towns with more than one thousand residents are

Robstown, Bishop, Sinton, Aransas Pass, Mathis, Taft, Ingleside, Portland, Gregory, Odem, Taft Southwest, North San Pedro, South San Pedro, and Port Aransas. Smaller communities include Driscoll, Banquete, Agua Dulce, Edroy, Saint Paul, Violet, and Chapman Ranch.

The port of Corpus Christi ranked ninth in the United States and second in Texas in 1969, handling more than twenty-nine million tons of cargo. A new system of channels forty feet deep and four hundred feet wide was completed in 1965, assuring entry of the latest supertankers into the port. Corpus Christi exports cotton, grain sorghums, and wheat. Its coastal shipments include fuel oils, gasoline, crude petroleum, and natural gas. Other major contributors to the income of the Corpus Christi area are petroleum and natural gas, manufacturing, agriculture, fishing, the Corpus Christi Naval Air Station,qv and tourism. The region has become the center of a large petroleum and petrochemical industry. Six oil refineries are located in close proximity to fifteen hundred oil wells. Short-distance pipelines connect Corpus Christi to one of the nation's largest supplies of natural gas. Oil and gas production was valued at sixty million dollars per year in 1965 and 1966. Twenty-two docks in the Corpus Christi port handle exclusively petrochemicals and petroleum products. Other manufactured goods of importance are metals, stone products, glass, chemicals, and gypsum products. Both Nueces and San Patricio are important agricultural counties. Cotton, grain sorghums, livestock, flax, and vegetables provide most of the farm income. Most of the towns in the area serve primarily as commercial centers for the surrounding farms. Corpus Christi, in addition to its port facilities for agricultural products, also has some food processing, meat packing, and cottonseed oil manufacturing. Aransas Pass and Corpus Christi, the commercial fishing headquarters of the area, are seafood processing centers. The Corpus Christi Naval Air Station adds twenty-one million dollars annually to the economy of the area.

The Corpus Christi metropolitan area offers numerous recreational facilities. Opportunities for boating, swimming, fishing, camping, and bird-watching are provided in the Padre Island National Seashore, the Aransas National Wildlife Refuge, the Rob and Bessie Welder Foundation and Refuge,qqv Goose Island State Park, and Lake Corpus Christi State Park (see Parks, State). Historically, the area includes Fort Lipantitlán, Fort Marcy,qqv the San Patricio cemetery, and a number of historical homes. Annual events include the Shrimporee in Aransas Pass, Buccaneer Days, the All-Texas Jazz Festival, the Navy Relief Festival, the New Year's Day Swim, and the Cinco de Mayo celebration in Corpus Christi. The major cultural attractions, all in Corpus Christi, are the Corpus Christi Museum,qv the Art Museum of South Texas, a symphony orchestra, and a little theater. Public libraries are located in Corpus Christi, Robstown, Aransas Pass, Sinton, Portland, Taft, and Odem. One junior college, Del Mar, and Texas

A&I University at Corpus Christi provide educational facilities for the area. Del Mar Technical Institute, a branch of Del Mar College, and the University of Texas Marine Science Institute at Port Aransas offer specialized training. See also Standard Metropolitan Statistical Areas in Texas.

Corpus Christi State School. Corpus Christi State School was opened June 1, 1970, as a residential school facility of the Texas Department of Mental Health and Mental Retardation.qv Damaged August 3, 1970, by Hurricane Celia, the school resumed partial operations by 1971. Programs included medical, recreational, speech stimulation and development, and outreach services. See Mentally Ill and Mentally Retarded, Care of, in Texas.

BIBLIOGRAPHY: Texas Department of Mental Health and Mental Retardation, *Annual Report, 1970.*

*Corral Creek.

Corrections, Texas Board of. In 1957 the legislature made several changes in nomenclature with regard to the Texas Prison System.qv The Texas Prison Board qv became the Texas Board of Corrections; the Texas Prison System became the Texas Department of Corrections; and the general manager of the Prison System became the director of corrections. The functions of each remained the same. See also Corrections, Texas Department of.

Dick Smith

Corrections, Texas Department of. In 1957 the Texas Prison System qv became known as the Texas Department of Corrections, administered by the Texas Board of Corrections,qv a nine-member policy-making group appointed by the governor for six-year overlapping terms. By December 31, 1964, prison population had increased to 12,278 from a 1947 figure of 5,762, creating more crowded conditions than at any other time in recent years. The average number of prisoners during 1966 was 12,-765. Prison population decreased from 12,854 at the end of 1965 to 12,392 on December 31, 1966.

Department assets, including land, buildings, and equipment, were $41,629,663 on August 31, 1964; on August 31, 1966, assets were $50,593,-667. In 1964 the department's income from agriculture and industries was $8,435,509 and operating expenses were $17,705,561. In 1966 agricultural and industrial income was $8,685,656 and operating expenses stood at $19,678,242. In 1960 daily cost per inmate was $1.42, compared to a national average of $3.51; cost in 1964 was $2.10; in 1966 daily cost was $2.36 compared to a national average of $5.50. Prison canteens yield approximately $156,000 annually, and the Texas Prison Rodeo,qv held each Sunday in October, yields approximately $167,000. Both sums are applied to educational and recreational programs not financed by legislative appropriation.

The Huntsville Unit, the Diagnostic Unit, and the administrative headquarters for the fourteen-unit system are in Huntsville. Headquarters includes general administration, finance department, personnel and machine records, bureau of classification and records, and a hospital. Construction of the Diagnostic Unit was completed in 1964. Used for orientation, testing, and classification of prisoners, the unit contains modern medical facilities for five hundred persons.

Other units and types of inmates are Central Unit, Sugar Land (first offenders over twenty-two years of age); Goree Unit, Huntsville (women); Jester Unit (formerly Harlem), Richmond (prerelease center); Ramsey Unit, Rosharon (recidivists over twenty-five); Wynne Unit, Huntsville (physically incapacitated and mentally defective prisoners of all ages); Clemens Unit, Brazoria (first offenders over twenty-two and recidivists between the ages of seventeen and twenty-one); Darrington Unit, Sandy Point (recidivists between the ages of twenty-two and twenty-five); Eastham Unit, Weldon (recidivists); Ferguson Unit, Midway (intermediate reformatory with emphasis placed on education and vocational training for first offenders between the ages of seventeen and twenty-one); Retrieve Unit, Angleton (second offenders and habitual offenders over twenty-five years of age); Ellis Unit, Huntsville (a maximum-security institution completed in 1963 for habitual offenders, agitators, malcontents, and high security risks); and Coffield Unit, Anderson County (constructed in 1965 as a medium security unit for 2,000 inmates). In November, 1971, the units housed a total of 15,689 prisoners. In that year the director was George J. Beto. *See also* Prison System in Volume II.

BIBLIOGRAPHY: *Texas Almanac* (1963, 1965, 1971); University of Texas at Austin, *Guide To Texas State Agencies* (1972).

*Corrigan, Texas. Corrigan, in Polk County, had a population of 986 in 1960 and 1,304 in 1970.

*Corrigan Settlement, Texas.

*Corsicana, Texas. Corsicana, seat of Navarro County, is a supply center for farm and oil products and a processing center for cotton. In 1967 the town had a new one-hundred-bed hospital, a municipal airport, churches of almost every denomination, and 542 businesses, including numerous manufacturers. Corsicana is the site of Navarro Junior College, the International Order of Odd Fellows state headquarters, and the Corsicana State Home.qv The 1960 population was 20,344; the 1970 population was 19,972.

*Corsicana Female Literary Institute.

*Corsicana Oil Field.

Corsicana State Home. Corsicana State Home, formerly the State Orphans' Home,qv is operated under the administration of the Texas Youth Council qv as a home for dependent and neglected children. A recent feature of the institution is the practice of sending school-age children to the Corsicana public schools on an annual contract basis. The cost of such an arrangement has proved to be considerably less than the school system formerly operated by the home.

On August 31, 1965, the Corsicana State Home was providing group care for 295 children under a system enabling each child to receive specialized attention according to individual need; by 1967 this total had increased to 350. In addition, a multiservice program was in operation assuring further care for eighty-five children, nine of whom were in paid foster homes.

BIBLIOGRAPHY: Texas Youth Council, *Annual Report* (1965); *Texas Almanac* (1967).

William T. Field

*Cortina, Juan Nepomuceno.

*Corwins Creek.

*Coryell, James.

*Coryell, Texas.

*Coryell County. Coryell County experienced a population boom following a post-World War II decline; the estimated 1955 population of 17,587 increased to an official 23,961 in 1960, and then to 35,311 in 1970. Much of the increase can be attributed to activity at Fort Hood,qv which covered much of the southern part of the county, and to an influx of retired persons, many of whom were military personnel. Belton Reservoir, Fort Gates,qv a March stock show, a June rodeo, and other attractions support an increasing tourist industry. Livestock (cattle, sheep, and goats) accounts for much of the county's farm income; fruits, truck crops, small grains, and cotton are of lesser importance. Cedar, limestone, sand, and gravel are commercially exploited. Industry was centered in Gatesville, the location also of two state penal institutions, the Gatesville State School for Boys and the Mountain View School for Boys.qqv In 1972 Coryell County was included in the Killeen-Temple Standard Metropolitan Statistical Area.qv

*Coryell Creek.

*Corzine, Shelby.

*Cós, Martín Perfecto de. Martín Perfecto de Cós, son of an attorney of the same name, was born in the port of Veracruz, Mexico, in 1800; he was not a leader under José Morelos in the Mexican Revolution of 1811 (as stated in Volume I, Cós having possibly been confused with José María Cos y Peréz, a contemporary of Morelos who supported the Mexican Revolution). Martín Perfecto de Cós was only ten or eleven years old in 1811; he became a cadet in the army in 1820, a lieutenant in 1821, and a brigadier general in 1833. Cós died in Minatitlán, Veracruz, on October 1, 1854, while serving as commandant general and political chief of the Tehuantepec Territory.

BIBLIOGRAPHY: Service Records, Historical Archives of the Defense Ministry, Mexico City.

*Cost, Texas.

*Costley, Michael.

*Cothran's Store, Texas.

*Cotland, Texas.

*Cotonam Indians. *See also* Cotoname Indians.

Cotoname Indians. In the second half of the eighteenth century the Cotoname (Catanamepaque, Cotomane, Cotonan) Indians lived on both sides of the Rio Grande below Camargo and Rio Grande

City, where they were sometimes called Carrizo, a Spanish name applied to many Coahuiltecan groups along the Rio Grande below Laredo. In 1886 a few Cotoname were still living at La Noria Ranch in southern Hidalgo County and at Las Prietas in northern Tamaulipas. At that time the ethnologist A. S. Gatschet was able to obtain a short Cotoname vocabulary which demonstrated that this group spoke a Coahuiltecan language.

BIBLIOGRAPHY: F. W. Hodge (ed.), *Handbook of American Indians*, I (1907); G. Saldivar, *Los Indios de Tamaulipas* (1943); J. R. Swanton, *Linguistic Material from the Tribes of Southern Texas and Northeastern Mexico* (1940); C. Thomas and J. R. Swanton, *Indian Languages of Mexico and Central America and Their Geographical Distribution* (1911).

T. N. Campbell

Cotten, Fred Rider. Fred Rider Cotten was born in Weatherford, Texas, on June 21, 1894, the son of J. T. and Sarah Ida (Rider) Cotten. Following graduation from the University of Texas law school, he worked with the Department of Justice in Washington, D.C., and was one of the agents assigned to the investigation of the German torpedoing of the ship *Lusitania*. When his father died, he returned to Weatherford to take over the family furniture and undertaking businesses, which he ran for fifty-two years.

An outspoken man, he was active in Parker County politics and for many years was Democratic chairman of precinct four. He was a city commissioner of Weatherford during the Depression years and was instrumental in the establishment of the local Public Works Authority which paved and curbed many of the Weatherford streets. The present city hall and Fort Worth Street overpass were built while he was commissioner.

Active in statewide organizations, he served as president of the Texas Funeral Directors' Association, the Texas Retail Furniture Dealers' Association, the Texas Swine Breeders' Association, the West Texas Historical Association,[qv] and the Texas State Historical Association.[qv] He was one of the organizers of the Hood-Parker Soil Conservation District.

As the local authority on Parker County history, he shows up regularly in books about that area. John Graves' remarkable work, *Goodbye to a River*, quotes Cotten rather frequently. He had also taken trips to Mexico, retracing the steps of Stephen F. Austin's prison journey from Texas to Mexico City, and had visited London to see what traces of the Republic of Texas he could find there.

Cotten died in Fort Worth on September 7, 1974. Interment was in Oakland Cemetery in Weatherford. Surviving were his wife, Mary Akard Cotten (with whom he had celebrated their fiftieth wedding anniversary in 1969), a son, and a daughter.

BIBLIOGRAPHY: Joe B. Frantz, "In Memoriam: Fred R. Cotten," *Southwestern Historical Quarterly*, LXXVIII (1974–1975).

Joe B. Frantz

*Cotten, Godwin Brown.

*Cottingham, Irvin Alexander.

*Cottle, George Washington.

*Cottle County. Cottle County is a predominantly agricultural area. The population continued a decline begun in the 1930's, with 4,207 persons in 1960 and 3,204 in 1970. Over half the residents reside in Paducah. Several large ranches are located at least partly within the county, but the major source of income is farming, for which ten thousand acres were irrigated in 1964. Cotton and small grains are the principal crops, and the cultivation of guar has been recently introduced. A livestock show and rodeo are sponsored in partnership with King County each April, and a Cottle County calf and pig show is held in January.

*Cotton, Texas.

*Cotton Belt System. *See* St. Louis Southwestern Railway of Texas.

*Cotton Bowl. The Cotton Bowl is both a stadium and the name for an annual New Year's Day football game. Home field for Southern Methodist University since 1947, the stadium was for several years also home field for the Dallas Cowboys,[qv] a professional football team. Once termed the "House that Doak Walker Built," the Cotton Bowl has had its capacity taxed most consistently by the New Year's Day game and by the Texas-Oklahoma game, both of which have attracted sell-out crowds continuously since 1946.

The Cotton Bowl classic is the only fully college-sponsored post-season game. The Southwest Conference [qv] football champion annually meets one of the nation's top rated teams, and on several occasions the winner has emerged as national champion.

Wilbur Evans

*Cotton Center, Texas. (Fannin County.)

*Cotton Center, Texas. (Hale County.) Cotton Center, in southwestern Hale County, was an unincorporated community of some 475 people and eleven businesses when, on June 2, 1965, it was struck by a tornado that killed one person, critically injured three, and virtually wiped out the town.

BIBLIOGRAPHY: *Fort Worth Star-Telegram*, June 3, 1965.

Cotton Compress Industry in Texas. The Texas cotton compress industry developed in antebellum days as a result of the need to lower the cost of transporting cotton on sailing vessels. Over $500,000 was invested in the industry at Galveston by 1860. After the Civil War, as cotton culture spread into the Texas hinterland, compresses were built in many Texas towns. The development of communications and the extension of railroads into cotton-producing regions of the state revolutionized the Texas cotton trade. The compress industry was a major factor in this change because it made the long-distance transportation of cotton by rail economically feasible. Interior cotton markets developed, and the old factorage system was disrupted.

When the Texas Railroad Commission [qv] came into existence in 1891, it soon provided rules and regulations governing the movement of cotton by rail; thus the cotton compress industry was one of the first to feel the effects of this regulatory agency. Measures adopted by the commission encouraged overdevelopment of the industry in the interior and intensified a struggle for control of cotton between port and hinterland interests.

Processes were developed in the 1890's to compress cotton to a high density at gins and thus eliminate the need for cotton compresses. Owners of these processes attempted to have the Texas Railroad Commission and the Interstate Commerce Commission set carload rates for cotton so compressed. The commissions refused to do so because of a belief that such a rate system would revolutionize the cotton trade and result in great loss to small operators in the cotton industry.

Since the 1920's the geographical trend of the cotton compress industry in Texas has been westward and southward as cotton culture has shifted to the High Plains and the Rio Grande Valley. Policies of the Commodity Credit Corporation have also been a factor in the movement.

Cotton compression has been a major industry in Texas both in terms of capital invested and labor employed. The declining fortunes of cotton in recent years, however, have taken a heavy toll in the trade. The prospects indicate a continued deterioration of a once flourishing industry. *See also* Cotton Culture; Textile Industry.

BIBLIOGRAPHY: Louis Tuffly Ellis, The Texas Cotton Compress Industry: A History (Ph.D. dissertation, University of Texas at Austin, 1964).

L. Tuffly Ellis

*Cotton Creek.

*Cotton Culture. Since the beginning of successful Anglo American settlement in Texas, cotton has been the area's principal cash crop. It remains so today, although its relative importance to the state's economy is now secondary to such products as oil, gas, and cattle. About 3 percent of the state's total area is devoted to cotton culture. Over 20 percent, or 121,726, of the nation's 600,000 cotton farms are in Texas, accounting for 30 to 34 percent of the total American cotton production. Texas is by far the top producer.

The most notable change in the production of cotton is the geographical trend from East and Central Texas to the High Plains and the Rio Grande Valley. High production in these latter two areas is obtained by extensive use of fertilizers and irrigation. Lubbock County now exceeds all other counties in Texas both in acreage and production.

Another notable feature of cotton culture is the decreasing number of farms and the total acreage devoted to production, although the average size of cotton farms is increasing. The highest number of acres planted, 18,443,000 in 1925, yielded an average of 115 pounds per acre, or a total of 4,163,000 bales. The high point of total production and value was reached in 1949, when 6,040,000 bales valued at $847,632,000 were produced. In 1967 the yield on 3,960,000 acres was 376 pounds

per acre, or a total of 2,767,000 bales valued at over one-half billion dollars. Improved seed, use of fertilizers, and better farming practices have contributed to the increased yield.

The industrialization of the state, the competition of synthetics, the depletion of formerly rich lands, the high cost of production, and the uncertain and continually changing policies of the federal government have all been major factors in the declining position of cotton culture in Texas, a trend certain to continue. Nevertheless, cotton remains the foundation for agriculture in Texas. *See also* Cotton Compress Industry in Texas; Textile Industry; Boll Weevil; Bollworm, Pink.

BIBLIOGRAPHY: William F. Harris, "Cotton's Place in the Economy of Texas," *Texas Business Review*, XLI (September, 1967); United States Department of Agriculture, *Texas Cotton, 1928–1937* (1939); United States Department of Agriculture, *Texas Cotton Statistics* (1951); Texas Agricultural Experiment Station, *Cash Receipts from the Sale of Texas Farm Commodities* (1967).

L. Tuffly Ellis

*Cotton Gin, Texas.

*Cotton Lake.

*Cotton Mills. *See* Textile Industry.

*Cotton Palace, The.

*Cotton Patch Bayou.

Cotton Research Committee. *See* Natural Fibers and Food Protein Committee.

*Cottondale, Texas. (Wharton County.)

*Cottondale, Texas. (Wise County.)

*Cottonseed Industry. After reaching a maximum of 233 cottonseed oil mills during the 1914–1915 season, the Texas total declined to forty-four mills in 1966–1967. The state produced more than 1,320,000 tons of cottonseed in 1966–1967. Most of this cottonseed was valued at $67.40 per ton, for a total of $88,968,000. The mills employed 2,361 people in 1966 and had a total payroll of more than eleven million dollars.

Although over 91 percent of the 1,177,000 tons of cottonseed produced in Texas during the 1967–1968 season was delivered to the cottonseed oil mills located throughout the state, the industry continued to decline. The amount of seed available for crushing decreased that season for the second year in a row. Thus the oil mills in the state employed fewer workers and had fewer products derived from cottonseed to sell. This in turn reduced the income derived from cottonseed which, in the case of many of the mills, was their only source of income. The price per ton received by the farmers for their cottonseed in the 1967–1968 season was down about thirteen dollars per ton from the previous season's average figure. Fort Worth cake and meal prices were down about three dollars from the $90.13 average price per ton for the previous season. The price of hulls during the same period increased about $5.50 per ton, the opposite of the cake and meal prices on the Fort Worth market.

During 1967 nine crude vegetable oil refineries processed the crude cottonseed oil for use by the twelve shortening, table oil, and margarine manufacturers located in the state. Cottonseed by-products are, at times, used in the manufacture of many additional items. Some of the potential users of cottonseed by-products located in Texas include paper mills and manufacturers of plastics, explosives, and pharmaceuticals.

BIBLIOGRAPHY: Publications of the Cotton Research Committee of Texas, University of Texas at Austin.

*Cottonwood, Texas. (Callahan County.)

*Cottonwood, Texas. (Madison County.)

*Cottonwood Arroyo.

*Cottonwood Creek.

*Cottonwood Draw.

*Cottonwood Mott Creek.

*Cotulla, Texas. Cotulla, seat of La Salle County, reported fifty-four businesses, including a newspaper, in 1970. In 1965 Cotulla completed installation of a natural gas system and an extension of the sewer system. The 1960 population was 3,960; the 1970 population was 3,415.

Couch, Texas. Couch, in Karnes County on the north bank of Hondo Creek seven miles southeast of Kenedy, was the center of a rich farming area populated largely by a group of Oklahomans who had come in the early 1890's. For that reason, the general vicinity of Couch was referred to as the Oklahoma Settlement. Old county records designated it as "Oaklahoma."

In the early 1890's Andrew J. Harryman bought sixty acres of land from J. M. and T. Y. Pettus. Eighteen acres of the tract were surveyed and plotted as the townsite of Couch, named after D. F. Couch, who was instrumental in bringing in the settlers from Oklahoma. The town of Couch had a post office established in 1896, a general store, a hotel, a Methodist church, and a public school. After the main road from Kenedy to Goliad was moved south of Couch, the post office of Couch was discontinued in 1909, and the town declined.

*Coughran, Texas.

*Council Branch.

*Council Creek.

*Council of Defense. See Texas State Council of Defense.

*Council, General. See General Council.

*Council House Fight, The.

*Council-Manager City Government. In 1964 the council-manager form of city government was used by 160 cities in Texas, of which 126 had charter provisions for the plan, 14 were general law cities adopting the plan by election, and the others adopted the plan by ordinance.

BIBLIOGRAPHY: Texas Municipal League, Directory of Texas City Managers (1964); International City Managers' Association, Yearbook (1964).

Joe A. Michie

*Council of Provisional Government, 1835. See General Council.

Counties, Texas Association of. See Texas Association of Counties.

*Country Campus, Texas.

*Counts Creek.

*County Attorney. See also County and Precinct Officers, Terms of.

*County Auditor.

*County Commissioners Court. See also County and Precinct Officers, Terms of.

*County Court, Clerk of. See also County and Precinct Officers, Terms of.

*County Health Officer.

*County Judge. See also County and Precinct Officers, Terms of.

*County Line, Texas.

*County Organization.

County and Precinct Officers, Terms of. Terms of all elective, constitutional county and precinct officers were changed from two to four years by a series of constitutional amendments adopted in 1954. Officers affected by the change were county commissioner, county judge, county attorney, sheriff, clerk of the county court, assessor and collector of taxes, county treasurer, justice of the peace, constable, and county surveyor. The district attorney and the clerk of the district court were also elected for four years. No change was made in the terms of the statutory county offices of county superintendent of schools, who already had a four-year term, and county school trustees, who were still elected for two years.

BIBLIOGRAPHY: Stuart A. MacCorkle and Dick Smith, Texas Government (1964); Clifton McCleskey, Government and Politics of Texas (1963); Wilbourn Eugene Benton, Texas, Its Government and Politics (1961).

Dick Smith

*County School Trustees. See also County and Precinct Officers, Terms of.

*County Superintendent of Schools. See also County and Precinct Officers, Terms of.

*County Surveyor. See also County and Precinct Officers, Terms of.

*County Treasurer. See also County and Precinct Officers, Terms of.

*Coupland, Texas.

*Coups de Flèches.

*Court of Claims, Texas.

*Courthouse Mountain.

*Courtney, Texas. (Grimes County.)

*Courtney, Texas. (Martin County.)

*Courtney Male and Female School.

*Courts. See Judicial System.

*Coushatta Indians. See Alabama-Coushatta Indians; Koasati Indians.

*Coushatta Trace.

*Cousins, Robert Bartow.

Cousins, Walter Henry. Walter Henry Cousins, the son of Henry Clay and Frances Cousins, was born on August 18, 1879, near Whitson, Coryell County, Texas. Cousins attended Whitson, Walker, and Haunted Hill schools. In 1898 his family moved west to Haskell County, where Walter worked as a bronc buster on the M N Ranch in Haskell, Throckmorton, and Knox counties. He was also camp cook for trail drives across Oklahoma during this period.

In 1902, after apprenticeship, Cousins became a licensed druggist. In that year he also married Sue Reeves McClendon. Cousins was appointed a member of the State Board of Pharmacy qv in 1913, becoming secretary of this board in 1920. He held this office until December 1, 1941, when ill health forced his retirement.

On April 15, 1915, Cousins bought and became editor of the *Southern Pharmaceutical Journal* in Dallas. That year he was elected secretary-treasurer of the Texas Pharmaceutical Association, and in 1918 he became president of the National Association of Retail Druggists. He owned drugstores in Munday and Wichita Falls.

Cousins helped to establish the Texas Cowboy Reunion qv at Stamford in 1930 and served as historian, vice-president, and president of the Reunion Association. He was author of the book *Cuz* (1922) and "Range Poems" in Lona Shawver's *Chuck Wagon Windies* (1934). He also wrote numerous poems, ballads, and articles which appeared in pharmaceutical journals and Texas Cowboy Reunion publications. He died in Dallas on February 6, 1942.

Laura Simmons

*Cousins Creek.

*Cove, Texas.

Cove City, Texas. Cove City, in Orange County, had a population of 1,749 in 1960 and 1,578 in 1970.

*Cove Spring, Texas.

*Covey, John Van Epps.

*Covington, Texas.

*Cow Bayou.

*Cow Branch.

*Cow Creek.

*Cow Gap.

*Cowan, William Jones.

*Cowan Creek.

*Cowboy, Texas.

Cowboy Reunion. *See* Texas Cowboy Reunion.

*Cowboy Strike.

Cowboys' Christmas Ball. *See* Anson, Texas (in Volume I).

*Cowden Ranch.

*Cowgill, Texas.

*Cowhouse Creek.

*Cowhouse Mountain.

*Cowhouse Mountains.

*Cowl Spur, Texas.

*Cowleech Fork of the Sabine River.

*Cox, Paris.

*Cox, Thomas B.

Cox, Texas. Cox, in northern Upshur County,

was founded in 1890. The community is located in a farming and ranching area, although many of the inhabitants are employees of the Lone Star Steel Plant several miles away. In 1966 the population was estimated at three hundred.

*Cox Creek.

*Coxey's Army in Texas.

*Coy City, Texas.

*Coyabegux Indians.

*Coyanosa Draw.

*Coyote Creek.

*Coyote Lake.

*Coyote Peak.

*Crabapple Creek.

*Crabb, Texas.

*Crabb's Prairie, Texas.

*Craft, Texas.

*Crafton, Texas.

Crafts in Texas. *See* Arts and Crafts in Texas.

*Crain, William H. William Henry Crain was born November 25, 1848 (not November 28, 1848, as stated in Volume I), and was elected to the United States House of Representatives in 1884 (not 1878), serving from March 4, 1885, until his death on February 10, 1896.

*Cramayel, Jules Edouard de. Jules Edouard Fontaine, Viscount de Cramayel, was the fourth of seven children born to Jean François Fontaine, Marquis de Cramayel, and Marie Josephine de Folard. Born in 1798 in France, Jules entered on a diplomatic career in 1818 and held successively the posts of secretary of the legations at Stockholm, Madrid, Vienna, Hanover, Lisbon, and Naples. As chargé d'affaires *ad interim* to Texas from January, 1843, to January, 1844, he reported frequently on what he believed to be the fraudulent practices of Henri Castro qv in bringing French immigrants to Texas, and he urged the French foreign minister to take steps to prevent further recruitment of colonists in France. Plagued by ill health, appalled at frontier conditions, and concerned over the revival of the question of annexation, he nonetheless fulfilled his duties and compiled massive and detailed memoranda on the civil administration and military and naval organization of the Republic of Texas. Although commended by the foreign minister when he left Texas, he remained without further assignment until 1848, when he went as minister plenipotentiary to Copenhagen. In 1849 he became an officer in the Legion of Honor. Unmarried, he died in Paris in 1871.

BIBLIOGRAPHY: Nancy N. Barker, "The Republic of Texas: A French View," *Southwestern Historical Quarterly*, LXXI (1967-1968).

Nancy N. Barker

*Crandall, Texas.

*Crane, John.

*Crane, Martin McNulty.

Crane, Royston Campbell. Royston Campbell Crane, son of Catharine (Shepherd) and William

Carey Crane,[qv] was born on February 16, 1864, in Independence, Texas, where his father was president of Baylor University. He was graduated from Baylor in 1884 and from the law school of the University of Texas in 1886. In 1950 Baylor University bestowed upon him the LL.D. degree.

Settling in Roby, Fisher County, Texas, in 1886, Crane practiced law, served as county attorney, and for a period published the *Fisher County Call*. In 1902 he moved to Sweetwater, where he was active in community affairs until his death on January 20, 1956. He was mayor of Sweetwater from 1902 to 1906 and postmaster from 1914 to 1921.

Crane was an avid collector of historical material bearing on the Southwest, and parts of his collections were obtained by Texas Technological College (now Texas Tech University) and Hardin-Simmons University. He initiated the movement for a West Texas Historical Association [qv] and led in calling the organizational meeting of that body in Abilene on April 19, 1924. He was president of the group until 1949, when he was made president emeritus. Crane published numerous historical articles in several different newspapers and contributed to the *Southwestern Historical Quarterly*.[qv] To the *West Texas Historical Association Year Book* he contributed at least twenty-seven articles and items and inspired a number of articles that were written by others.

Crane married Mamie Douthit on January 7, 1892. Their son, Royston Campbell Crane, Jr., became a nationally syndicated cartoonist.

BIBLIOGRAPHY: Marvin E. Burgess, Royston Campbell Crane (M.A. thesis, Hardin-Simmons University, 1948).

Rupert N. Richardson

*Crane, William Carey.

*Crane, Texas. Crane, seat of Crane County and a commercial center for local oil and ranching industries, had among its eighty-three businesses in 1970 several oil well supply plants and firms connected with natural gas and sour-gas sulphur. In 1962 the hospital was enlarged and modernized. The city also boasts a new library and courthouse. The population in 1960 was 3,796; in 1970 it was 3,427.

*Crane College. See William Carey Crane College.

*Crane County. Crane County, ranking fifth in the state in the value of its minerals in 1960, had 5,485 oil wells by 1964. Its total oil production from 1926 to 1973 was over one billion barrels. By 1964 oil revenue had exceeded $100,000,000 annually. An additional $500,000 was contributed annually by ranching. The 1960 population was 4,699; the 1970 count was 4,172.

*Crane Creek.

*Cranell, Texas.

*Cranes Mill, Texas.

*Cranfill, James Britton.

*Cranfills Gap, Texas.

*Cranford, John W.

*Cranz, Texas.

Crash at Crush. *See* Train Wreck Stunt.

*Cravens, Robert M.

*Crawfish Creek.

Crawford, Emmaretta Cara Kimball. *See* Kimball, Emmaretta Cara.

*Crawford, Robert.

*Crawford, Walter Joshua.

*Crawford, William Carrol.

*Crawford, William Lester.

*Crawford, Texas.

*Crawford Mountain.

*Crazy Cat Mountain.

Creager, Rentfro Banton (Rene B.). Rene B. Creager was born at Waco, Texas, on March 11, 1877, son of Katherine (Rentfro) and Francis Asbury Warwick Creager. In 1898 he received a B.S. degree from Southwestern University, which gave him an LL.D. in 1930. After graduation from the law school of the University of Texas in Austin in 1900, he began practice in Brownsville. Prior to 1916, when he became the gubernatorial candidate of the Republican party [qv] in Texas, Creager served as a collector of customs at Brownsville under both Presidents Theodore Roosevelt and William H. Taft. Upon the death of Henry F. MacGregor [qv] of Houston in 1923, Creager was elected the Texas member of the Republican National Committee, a position he held until his death. He retained a firm leadership over the state Republican party and played a prominent role in national Republican politics for many years. At the Republican national convention of 1920 he delivered the only speech seconding the nomination of Warren G. Harding. Following Harding's election, the President-elect and Mrs. Harding visited Creager at his home in Brownsville. The presidential party also did extensive fishing at nearby Port Isabel. Creager was offered the ambassadorship to Mexico by both Presidents Harding and Calvin Coolidge, but declined. He was the first national committeeman to come out in support of Herbert Hoover for the 1928 presidential nomination. Likewise, he was in the forefront of the movement to secure the 1936 nomination for Kansas Governor Alfred Landon. Creager was a close friend of and floor leader for Senator Robert A. Taft at the Republican national convention of 1948. In addition to his political activities, he was president of an oil company. He died on October 28, 1950, in Brownsville. He was survived by four children and his widow, the former Alice Terrell, whom he had married on February 3, 1904.

BIBLIOGRAPHY: *Who's Who In America* (1950); Austin *American*, October 20, 1950; Paul D. Casdorph, *A History of the Republican Party in Texas, 1865–1965* (1965).

Paul D. Casdorph

*Creamer, Texas.

Creath, Joseph Warner Dossey. Joseph Warner Dossey Creath, son of William Creath, was born in Mecklenburg County, Virginia, on February 3, 1809. J. W. D. Creath and four of his brothers became preachers. After graduation from

Virginia Baptist Seminary in 1837, he began an active ministry which was to last forty-four years. He and his wife were commissioned as missionaries to Texas in 1846, the first two Home Missions appointees by the newly created Southern Baptist Convention. From the time he began his work at Huntsville in 1846 until his death in 1881, Creath worked to strengthen virtually every facet of Baptist work in Texas. He served churches in Huntsville, Anderson, Cold Springs, and San Antonio, acted as president of the Southern Baptist Convention in 1876, and presided over the Texas Baptist Convention. From 1863 to 1865 he was sent by the Texas Baptist Convention to minister to Confederate soldiers. He played a leading role in raising funds to support Baylor University and for over two decades was connected with the school as a trustee; at one time he was president of the trustees. Creath was married twice and was the father of two children. He died near Cameron, Milam County, Texas, on July 28, 1881.

BIBLIOGRAPHY: Robert G. Torbit, *A History of the Baptists* (1950); J. M. Carroll, *A History of Texas Baptists* (1923).

Jerry F. Dawson

*Crecy, Texas.

*Creechville, Texas.

*Creedmoor, Texas.

*Creek, Texas.

*Creek Indians.

*Cresson, Texas.

*Crest, Texas.

*Crestonio, Texas.

*Crete, Texas.

Creuzbaur, Robert. Robert Creuzbaur was employed by the General Land Office qv of Texas as a map maker during the mid-1800's. Two of his maps are of particular importance. On July 10, 1848, he was commissioned to compile topographic information for a map of Texas for Jacob de Cordova,qv who was a land promoter; he also made a map from notes compiled by John S. (Rip) Ford qv on his exploring expedition in 1849 showing the route from Austin to Paso del Norte. This map was published for emigrants, and it gave the distances from one water hole to another as well as pertinent landmarks and detailed descriptions of the nature of the soil and terrain. This map is included in "Creuzbaur's Guide to California and the Pacific Ocean." Copies of Creuzbaur's maps are in the University of Texas Archives and at the General Land Office in Austin, Texas.

BIBLIOGRAPHY: Kenneth F. Neighbours, "The Expedition of Major Robert S. Neighbors to El Paso in 1849," *Southwestern Historical Quarterly*, LVIII (1954–1955).

Crews, Texas. (Gregg County.) Crews is also known as Swamp City, probably because of its location on the swamps of the Sabine River. It was named for Dr. C. C. Crews, a dentist in Longview and donor of the land on which the Crews Baptist Church was built. The town was founded in 1931 with an original population of three hundred; population had decreased to fifty by 1966. Oil pro-

vides the main industry and occupation of the inhabitants.

*Crews, Texas. (Runnels County.)

*Crier, John.

*Crier Creek.

Criminal Law. By an act of the Consultation qv of 1835 the English system of criminal law was adopted in Texas and criminal trials have since been conducted according to that system. (*See* English Law in Texas; Judicial System.) The process of criminal law was codified by the enactment of a Penal Code and a Code of Criminal Procedure in 1856, effective February 1, 1857. Allowing an accused person to testify under oath on his own behalf was a very significant reform adopted in 1889. A new Code of Criminal Procedure was enacted in 1965 after long study, and it has since been somewhat revised. Preparation of a new Penal Code has been under intensive study since 1965.

Serious crimes are termed felonies and are presented only by indictment of a grand jury,qv and are subject to jury trial qv by a jury composed of twelve persons. Felonies, including treason to the state, are punishable by death or confinement in the state's penitentiary. Less serious offenses are called misdemeanors, subject to fines or imprisonment in local jails for terms up to three years or both. Misdemeanors are usually instituted by information rather than grand jury indictment and are subject to trial by a jury of six. By ordinance municipalities define local offenses not inconsistent with state offences; local offences are tried in municipal courts. (*See* Jury Trial.)

BIBLIOGRAPHY: Charles S. Potts, "Early Criminal Law in Texas: From Civil Law to Common Law, to Code," *Texas Law Review*, XXI (1943); Charles T. McCormick and Roy R. Ray, *Texas Law of Evidence*, I (1956).

Joseph W. McKnight

Crimmins, Martin Lalor. Martin Lalor Crimmins, army officer, traveler, herpetologist, and military historian, was born on April 4, 1876, in New York City, the son of John D. and Lily (Lalor) Crimmins. From September, 1891, to October, 1895, he attended Georgetown College, Washington, D.C., after which he studied at the University of Virginia Medical School from November, 1895, to May, 1898. Shortly before graduation he joined the Rough Riders qv in San Antonio, owing his enlistment to the influence of Theodore Roosevelt, a family friend. He was commissioned second lieutenant, 69th Volunteer Infantry on August 29, 1898. The following month he was commissioned second lieutenant, United States Army, and assigned to the 18th Infantry Regiment at Cavite, Luzon, Philippine Islands. Thereafter, promotions continued until he reached his final rank of colonel on April 23, 1921. In 1926 he was retired for physical disability in line of duty. During his military service he traveled extensively in Europe, Asia, and Alaska.

As a herpetologist he did pioneer work in the field of snake-bite treatment, assisting medical experts in many experiments and lecturing throughout the United States. He inoculated himself with serum until he became immune and then gave blood transfusions to snake-bite victims. In April, 1953, he received the Walter Reed Award "in recognition of courageous service to mankind."

His later years were devoted to writing, mostly on historical subjects. More than two hundred of his articles appeared in publications including *West Texas Historical Association Year Book*, *Southwestern Historical Quarterly*, *Frontier Times*,qqv *New Mexico Historical Review*, *Journal of the American Military Institute*, *U.S. Infantry Journal*, *Military Surgeon*, *Army & Navy Courier*, *Military Engineer*, *Southern Medical Journal*, and *Texas State Journal of Medicine*. He was active in various scientific and historical associations in Texas.

On January 16, 1901, he married Margaret Custis Cole; his second marriage was to Josephine Yost on May 19, 1918. He died in San Antonio, his home since 1926, on February 5, 1955.

BIBLIOGRAPHY: Chris Emmett, *In the Path of Events with Colonel Martin Lalor Crimmins, Soldier, Naturalist, Historian* (1959).

Paul Adams

*Crim's Chapel, Texas.

*Crisp, Downing H. Downing H. Crisp died of yellow fever on June 3, 1844, in Galveston while in command of the Texas Navy qv ship, *Austin*.qv

BIBLIOGRAPHY: Tom Henderson Wells, *Commodore Moore and the Texas Navy* (1960).

Tom Henderson Wells

*Crisp, William M.

*Crisp, Texas.

Critz, Richard. Richard Critz was born in Starkville, Mississippi, on October 16, 1877, the son of George Edward and Ella (Richards) Critz. When Critz was fourteen, his family moved to Williamson County, Texas, where he went to school. He attended Southwestern University for a limited time, then studied law in a Georgetown law office while teaching in the local public schools. Admitted to the Bar in 1902, he practiced until 1910 at Granger, where he also served for some years as city attorney; he returned in 1910 to Georgetown to become county judge until 1918, after which he continued to practice there until 1927. Around 1920 Critz assisted the young Georgetown district attorney, Dan Moody,qv in his prosecution of sundry local members of the then resurgent Ku Klux Klan.qv When Moody became governor in 1927, he appointed Critz to the Commission of Appeals to the state Supreme Court,qqv on which Critz remained until elevated in 1935 to associate justice of the Supreme Court by appointment of Governor James V. Allred.qv Critz' judicial opinions are noteworthy for unusual conciseness and clarity, as well as for their logic and numerical abundance. He was defeated for renomination in the Democratic primary of 1944 and left the bench at the end of that year to practice law as a member of an Austin firm until his death on April 1, 1959.

On January 18, 1906, Critz married Nora Lamb of Granger, and they had two sons and two daughters. Justice Critz was a Democrat and a Methodist. He was buried at Austin in Capital Memorial Gardens Cemetery.

BIBLIOGRAPHY: *Texas Bar Journal*, III (1940), XXII (1959); *Texian Who's Who* (1937).

W. St. John Garwood

*Croaker.

*Crockery Creek.

*Crocket, George Louis.

*Crockett, David.

*Crockett, John McClannahan.

*Crockett, Texas. Crockett, seat of Houston County and commercial center for its farming, livestock-raising, and forestry industries, had a 1960 population of 5,356 and a 1970 population of 6,616. In 1970 Crockett reported 166 businesses, including at least ten manufacturers.

*Crockett County. Crockett County is the eighth-ranking Texas county in geographical area, yet its population always has been sparse and concentrated almost entirely in Ozona. The 1960 population was 4,209; by 1970 the count was only 3,885. The ruins of Fort Lancaster qv and the Crockett County Museum attract some tourist income. Crockett County, ranking second in the state in sheep raising in 1960, supports goats and cattle in smaller numbers. The chief wealth of the county, however, is in natural gas and oil. Between 1925 and 1973 over 221 million barrels were produced.

Crockett State School for Girls. The Crockett State School for Girls, formerly Brady State School,qv has been placed under the administration of the Texas Youth Council.qv The school provides a comprehensive program of treatment and training for delinquent girls. The average population during the 1964–1965 period was 171; in 1970 the school had 209 girls.

Separate dormitory facilities provide for housing younger girls apart from older, more serious offenders. The conversion of surplus federal government buildings has aided in the enlargement of academic and vocational training programs. A new chapel has been built on the premises, and a new gymnasium has enabled the staff to increase physical education and athletic activities at the school.

BIBLIOGRAPHY: Texas Youth Council, *Annual Report* (1965); *Texas Almanac* (1967, 1972).

William T. Field

*Croix, Teodoro de.

Croneis, Carey Gardiner. Carey Gardiner Croneis was born on March 14, 1901, in Bucyrus, Ohio, the son of Frederick William and Nell (Garner) Croneis. He received a B.S. degree from Denison University, Granville, Ohio, in 1922, an M.S. degree from the University of Kansas in 1923, and a Ph.D. from Harvard in 1928. His early career in education and geology was as an instructor in geology at the University of Kansas (1922–1923), the University of Arkansas (1923–1925), and Harvard, Radcliffe, and Wellesley (1925–1928). He worked on geological surveys in Arkansas, Kansas, and Illinois. In 1928 Croneis went to the University of Chicago where he was assistant professor of geology, associate professor (1931–1941), and professor (1941–1944). He created the geology section of the Chicago Museum of Science and Industry and was curator of paleontology at the Walker Museum at the University of Chicago (1928–1944). At the Century of Progress World's Fair he was in charge of the geology section (1933) and chief of basic sciences (1934). He produced films on geology for the University of Chicago and the National Parks Service.

During World War II Croneis was a consultant for the National Defense Research Committee and in this capacity helped plan the coastal defenses for the Brownsville, Texas, area. He also helped select the proving grounds for the United States Chemical Warfare Service in the Republic of Panama. In 1944 he was named president of Beloit College in Wisconsin. He designed a plan for the creation of the geology department at Rice University in 1953, and in January, 1954, he became the provost there and the first Harry C. Wiess professor of geology. Croneis was named acting president of Rice in 1960; in 1961 he became the university's first chancellor. He maintained a teaching load along with administrative responsibilities while he was also involved in Houston civic affairs. He was chairman of the Houston City Charter Committee, and he is credited with being influential in the decision to establish the Manned Spacecraft Center qv near Houston. Croneis was the founding president of the Houston Council on World Affairs, a charter member of the Texas Academy of Science,qv and a member of the Centennial Committee of the American Museum of Natural History in New York City. He was editor of Harper & Row's Geoscience Series (from 1941), associate editor of *Journal of Geology* (1930–1945), and author of *Geology of the Arkansas Paleozoic Area* (1930), and numerous scientific articles.

Croneis, a Phi Beta Kappa, was awarded nine honorary doctorates during his career; in 1967 he received the highest honor in professional geology, the Sidney Powers Memorial Medal, from the American Association of Petroleum Geologists, and the same year he was presented a gold medal by the Association of Rice Alumni for distinguished service to the university. He was elected a fellow of the World Academy of Art and Science. In 1970 the American Federation of Mineralogical Societies established in his honor five two-year scholarships for graduate study in earth sciences. Croneis was president of the Philosophical Society of Texas qv in 1971, and retired as chancellor emeritus of Rice University on August 31, 1971.

Carey Croneis was married to Grace Williams on September 15, 1923, and they had two daughters. He died in Houston on January 22, 1972, and was cremated. Memorial services were held for Croneis at Rice Memorial Chapel.

BIBLIOGRAPHY: Houston *Post*, January 23, 1972.

*Cronican, Michael.

*Crooked Branch.

*Crooked Creek.

*Crooked Lake.

*Crosby, Josiah Frazier.

*Crosby, Stephen. Stephen Crosby, for whom Crosby County was named, was land commissioner of Texas from August 4, 1851, to March 1, 1858.

*Crosby, Texas. Crosby, in Harris County, had a population of 1,118 in 1970.

*Crosby County. Crosby County, partly on and partly off the Cap Rock, ranked in the middle 1960's among the state's leading counties in irrigation with two hundred thousand irrigated acres. Cotton is produced in large quantity, the 1964 crop totaling 130,020 bales; other major crops include wheat, grain sorghums, and soybeans. Cattle raising contributed to a high farm income that averaged almost $26 million annually by 1970. Tourist attractions include White River Reservoir, Silver Falls Park, Blanco Canyon, and the site of an abandoned Quaker Colony qv at Estacado. The census reported a population of 10,347 in 1960 and 9,085 in 1970.

*Crosbyton, Texas. Crosbyton, seat of Crosby County, with sixty business establishments in 1970, is a commercial center for the area's farming and livestock activities. A bank and a clinic-hospital are located in the town, which had a population of 2,088 in 1960 and 2,251 in 1970.

*Crosbyton-South Plains and Santa Fe Railroad Company.

*Cross, Texas. (Grimes County.)

*Cross, Texas. (McMullen County.)

*Cross Creek.

*Cross Cut, Texas.

Cross Mountain. Cross Mountain or *Kreutzberg*, a rounded hill which stands apart from a line of hills north of Fredericksburg, became a landmark for the first colonists of Fredericksburg in 1846. John Christian Durst, the first person to hold title to the land, found on it the fallen remnants of a wooden cross, perhaps erected by Catholic missionaries going to the San Sabá de la Santa Cruz Mission.qv Durst set the cross in place. Although a sketch of the hill by Seth Eastman,qv dated February 24, 1849, shows no cross there, a large new wooden cross was erected before the end of that year by Father George Mensel, a priest at St. Mary's Catholic Church in Fredericksburg. The wooden crosses have been replaced often. Since June, 1940, the cross has been lighted at night. The present cross is made of sheet metal set in a concrete base, and an automatic time switch controls the lighting. To preserve Cross Mountain, the Gillespie County Historical Society in 1952 purchased the twelve acres it covers.

BIBLIOGRAPHY: Rudolph L. Biesele, *The History of the German Settlements in Texas, 1831–1861* (1930); *A Seth Eastman Sketchbook 1848–1849* (c. 1961); "Durst Family History," Fredericksburg *Radio Post* (n.d.); H. Gerlach,

Fest-Schrift zum 75-jährigen Jubiläum der St. Marien-Gemeinde zu Friederichsburg, Texas (1921).

Esther L. Mueller

*Cross Plains, Texas. Cross Plains, in Callahan County, had a population of 1,168 in 1960 and 1,192 in 1970.

*Cross Roads, Texas. (Delta County.)

*Cross Roads, Texas. (Denton County.)

*Cross Roads, Texas. (Henderson County.)

*Cross Roads, Texas. (Milam County.)

Cross Roads, Texas. *See also* Crossroads, Texas.

*Cross Timber Creek.

*Cross Timbers.

*Cross Timbers, Texas.

*Crossenville, Texas.

*Crossett, Texas.

Crossing of the Pecos Station. *See* Camp Melvin, Texas.

Crossing of the Tehuacanas. *See* Carvajal Crossing.

Crossroads, Texas. Crossroads, named for its location at a five-way intersection in southeastern Harrison County, was in 1965 a small rural community centered around two general stores facing each other across Farm Road 31. (*See also* Cross Roads, Texas, for other towns with this name.)

*Crosstimber Creek.

*Crossville Peak.

*Croton, Texas.

*Croton Breaks.

*Croton Creek.

*Croton Peak.

Crouch, Carrie Johnson. Carrie Johnson Crouch was born in Graham, Texas, on September 10, 1887, the daughter of Clark Wesley Johnson, a Graham lawyer who was the 1912 Republican nominee for Texas governor. She wrote *A History of Young County, Texas*, first published in 1937, and later, with extensive revision, published by the Texas State Historical Association qv in 1956. She was a member of the Fort Belknap qv Historical Society and the Fort Belknap Genealogical Association. On May 23, 1967, she died in Graham and was survived by one daughter.

Barbara Neal Ledbetter

*Crow, Texas.

*Crow Creek.

Crowell, Caroline. Caroline Crowell, daughter of William James and Frances (Eakins) Crowell, was born May 17, 1893, in Avondale, Pennsylvania. She received a B.A. degree in 1916 from Bryn Mawr and a B.S. degree in industrial chemistry in 1918 from Pennsylvania State College. During World War I she worked as a chemist in a munitions factory; following the war she was an industrial chemist with the Corning Glass Works in New York before attending the University of Pennsylvania

Medical School, where she received the M.D. degree in 1925.

After serving her internship at Woman's Hospital, Philadelphia, she came to Austin, where she was a staff physician at the University of Texas student health center from 1926 until her retirement in 1965. At the time she came to Texas she was one of only two doctors on the university campus and the only woman physician in Austin. From 1929 to 1932 she volunteered her services as night resident physician at Brackenridge Hospital. The niece of the noted nineteenth-century artist Thomas Eakins, Dr. Crowell donated to the university's art museum two of her uncle's works, "At the Piano" and "A Portrait of a Lady." She died on August 28, 1972, in Austin and was buried in Austin Memorial Park.

*Crowell, Texas. Crowell, seat of Foard County, is a market and shipping point for the surrounding cattle, cotton, and wheat areas. Crowell reported thirty-two business establishments in 1970. The population was 1,703 in 1960 and 1,399 in 1970.

*Crowley, Miles.

*Crowley, Texas. Crowley, in Tarrant County, had a population of 583 in 1960 and 2,662 in 1970.

*Crown, Texas.

*Crown Mountain.

*Crownest Creek.

*Crownover, John.

*Crowther, Texas.

Crozier, Harry Benge. Harry Benge Crozier, son of Henry and Sallie (Benge) Crozier, and grandson of William Cocke Young,qv was born on July 27, 1891, in Paint Rock, Concho County. He attended Southwestern University, but left school in 1912 to work for the San Antonio *Express*,qv beginning a writing career which spanned almost sixty years. First with the *Express*, and later with the Galveston *News*, the Fort Worth *Record* (*see* Fort Worth *Star-Telegram*), and the Dallas *Morning News*,qqv Crozier covered capitol news events and legislative sessions from 1913 to 1931.

Although never far from newspaper work, Crozier continued his writing career in allied fields; he was editor of the Texas and Southwestern Cattle Raisers' Association qv publication, the *Cattleman*,qv which he and Tad Moses took over and modernized with a new format that lasted thirty years; he was also public relations director for the American Petroleum Institute in New York, public relations director for the Texas Centennial qv in 1936, and director of information for the Texas State Department of Health.qv Crozier worked in the political campaigns of Senator Thomas Terry Connally qv and presidential candidates Al Smith and Wendell Willkie. Governor Coke Stevenson qv appointed him to the Texas Employment Commission qv and later appointed him chairman of that agency.

Crozier returned to public relations work in the 1950's, but he finally returned to journalism in

1961. His first marriage, to Grace Younger, with whom he had one son, ended in divorce; he later married Ruth Hey. Harry Crozier died on July 14, 1970, in Austin, and he was buried in the State Cemetery.qv

BIBLIOGRAPHY: Austin *Statesman*, July 14, 1970; San Antonio *Express*, July 15, 1970; Biographical File, Barker Texas History Center, University of Texas at Austin.

*Crozier, Robert Hoskins.

*Cruger, Jacob W.

*Cruger, James F.

*Cruger, William R.

Cruiamo Indians. These Indians are known only from a Spanish document of 1693 which lists the Cruiamo as one of fifty "nations" that lived north of the Rio Grande and "between Texas and New Mexico." This may be interpreted to mean the southern part of western Texas, since the document also mentions that the Apache were at war with the groups named. Nothing further is known about the Cruiamo.

BIBLIOGRAPHY: C. W. Hackett (ed.), *Historical Documents Relating to New Mexico, Nueva Vizcaya, and Approaches Thereto, to 1773*, II (1926).

T. N. Campbell

Crump, William Dorsey. William Dorsey Crump, son of Robert Henry and Sara (Dorsey) Crump, was born in Louisville, Kentucky, on August 21, 1844. Prior to his service in the Confederate Army, he attended the University of Kentucky. In 1874 he moved to Texas, settling near present Oak Cliff, and three years later he married Mary King of Dallas. In June, 1890, Crump moved his family to the South Plains region, where he helped organize and build the town of Lubbock. A Mason and a member of the Christian church, he was elected county judge in 1898 and served two terms. With others, he set up the Ripley Townsite Company, which created the town of Shallowater. He died on January 18, 1940.

BIBLIOGRAPHY: Seymour V. Connor (ed.), *Builders of the Southwest* (1959).

Roy Sylvan Dunn

Crush, Crash at. *See* Train Wreck Stunt.

*Crutcher Creek.

*Cryer Creek, Texas.

*Cryers Branch.

*Crystal City, Texas. Crystal City, seat of Zavala County and the world's largest shipping point for spinach, is a processing and shipping center for a cattle and vegetable area. The main industry in the town in the 1960's was a vegetable-packing plant which employed about six hundred persons. There were also a cattle chute factory and a cotton gin. Improvements on the airport and construction of a new city hall were completed by 1966, when the town reported 115 businesses, twelve churches, two hospitals, a bank, a library built in 1965, and a newspaper.

Between 1950 and 1960 the population of Crystal City increased from 7,198 to 9,101. During the 1960's the city was the scene of much political activity which gained national attention. Although almost 85 percent of the town's citizens were of Mexican ancestry, the mayor (who had served for over three decades) and all but one of the city council members were of non-Mexican descent. With the help of the Political Association of Spanish-Speaking Organizations qv (PASO), citizens participated in voter registration drives, and in a city election on April 7, 1963, a new mayor and city council were elected, all of whom were of Mexican descent. Many changes were made after the election, including the appointment of Mexican Americans as city manager and city attorney, positions usually held by Anglo Americans.

Political gains were not sustained, however, because of dissension within the new political structure. Anglo American businessmen formed the Citizens' Association Serving All Americans by 1965, and in the next election they were returned to power. By 1969 the conflict had spread to the local school system, and in the fall of that year Mexican American students in the high school went on strike, demanding a fuller representation in student affairs, bilingual education, Mexican American advisors, a Mexican independence day holiday, and Chicano qv cultural courses (by this time the word "Chicano" was used by many Mexican Americans, with pride, in referring to themselves). Soon thereafter a new school board consisting of Chicanos was elected. A new political party, Raza Unida,qv was active in the 1970 elections, and many offices in Crystal City were again held by Americans of Mexican descent. The end of the decade saw a decline in population in Crystal City, however, when the official U. S. census showed a count of 8,104 in 1970, a decrease of 11 percent since 1960.

BIBLIOGRAPHY: *La Raza Unida Party in Texas* (1970); *New Yorker* (April 17, 1971); Austin *American*, August 26, 1971; San Antonio *Express*, July 11, 25, 1971, September 2, 1971, March 15, June 16, 1972; San Antonio *Light*, October 10, 1971.

*Crystal City and Uvalde Railway Company. *See* San Antonio, Uvalde, and Gulf Railroad.

*Crystal Creek.

*Crystal Falls, Texas.

*Crystal Lake.

*Crystal Lake, Texas.

*Cuchendado Indians.

*Cuellar, Jesús (Comanche).

*Cuero, Texas. Cuero, seat of DeWitt County, is a center for the county's turkey and other farm products. Its 166 businesses in 1970 included a cotton mill, a creamery, a sausage plant, and a poultry-packing plant. The 1960 population of 7,338 declined to 6,956 by 1970.

*Cuero Creek.

*Cuero Field.

Cuero Quemado Indians. This name, which is Spanish for "burnt skin," was applied to a Coahuiltecan-speaking band that ranged both sides of the lower Rio Grande during the second half of the eighteenth century. Cuero Quemado may have been a local Spanish name for a downstream group of Tepemaca, who occupied the Rio Grande Valley between Laredo and Rio Grande City. The Cuero Quemado were sometimes known as Quemado.

BIBLIOGRAPHY: F. W. Hodge (ed.), *Handbook of American Indians*, II (1910); G. Saldivar, *Los Indios de Tamaulipas* (1943); R. C. Troike, "Notes on Coahuiltecan Ethnography," *Bulletin of the Texas Archeological Society*, 32 (1962).

T. N. Campbell

*Cuesta.

*Cuesta Blanca.

*Cuesta del Burro.

*Cuevas Creek.

*Cuevitas, Texas.

*Cuitao Indians. The Cuitao (Cuitoa, Cuitoat) Indians were known only in the seventeenth century. Their location hinges upon identification of a river referred to by the Spanish as Río Nueces. This was not the present Nueces River of southern Texas but a river much farther north. Two schools of thought have emerged concerning the identity of this river. One school identifies it as the Colorado River in west-central Texas, and the other identifies it as either the Red River or Canadian River of Texas and Oklahoma. Since each identification leaves certain important details unexplained, the status of the Río Nueces remains undetermined. However, it is important to note that, regardless of river identification, the Cuitao area was either in north-central Texas or that portion of Oklahoma north of it. A. H. Schroeder's suggestion that the Cuitao were probably a Wichita group therefore appears reasonable. The phonetic resemblance of Cuitao to Quitaca may be significant, especially since the Quitaca seem also to have been a Wichita group.

BIBLIOGRAPHY: H. H. Bancroft, *History of the North Mexican States and Texas*, I (1884); H. E. Bolton, "The Jumano Indians in Texas, 1650–1771," *Quarterly of the Texas State Historical Association*, XV (1911–1912), and (ed.), *Spanish Exploration in the Southwest, 1542–1706* (1916); G. E. Hyde, *Indians of the High Plains* (1959); A. H. Schroeder, "A Re-analysis of the Routes of Coronado and Oñate into the Plains in 1541 and 1601," *Plains Anthropologist*, VII (1962); S. L. Tyler and H. D. Taylor, "The Report of Fray Alonso de Posadas in Relation to Quivira and Teguayo," *New Mexico Historical Review*, XXXIII (1958).

T. N. Campbell

Cujaco and Cujalo Indians. The Cujaco and Cujalo, apparently names for two separate groups, are listed among twenty Indian groups that joined Juan Domínguez de Mendoza [qv] on his journey from El Paso to the vicinity of present San Angelo in 1683–1684. Since Mendoza did not indicate at what point the two groups joined his party, it is not possible to determine their range or affiliations. However, the Indians between the Pecos River and the San Angelo area were being hard pressed by Apache at this time, and it seems likely that the two groups ranged between these two localities.

BIBLIOGRAPHY: H. E. Bolton (ed.), *Spanish Exploration in the Southwest, 1542–1706* (1916).

T. N. Campbell

Cujalo Indians. *See* Cujaco and Cujalo Indians.

*Cujane Indians. The Cujane (Cohanni, Coxane, Cujano, Guyane, Kohani, Qujane, Quxane) Indians were Karankawans who, when first mentioned by this name in the early eighteenth century, lived on the Texas coast near Matagorda Bay, where they were closely associated with the Coapite and the Karankawa proper. At this time they seem to have ranged between the Colorado and Guadalupe rivers, but later this range was extended westward along the coast at least as far as Aransas Bay. In 1722 Espíritu Santo de Zuñiga Mission [qv] was established near Matagorda Bay for the Cujane and their Karankawan associates, but it was soon abandoned because of frequent hostilities between Spaniards and Indians. In the 1730's a few Cujane were persuaded to enter Nuestra Señora de la Purísima Concepción de Acuña Mission [qv] at San Antonio. In 1745, when Mission Espíritu Santo de Zuñiga was moved to the vicinity of present Goliad, some of the Cujane came but soon deserted the mission. Then in 1754 Nuestra Señora del Rosario Mission [qv] was established in the Goliad area for the Cujane, whose name at this time became a general name for all Karankawan groups except Copane. The Cujane were in and out of this mission until it was secularized in 1831. When Nuestra Señora del Refugio Mission [qv] was founded in 1793, some of the Cujane took up residence there, remaining until it was abandoned in 1828. The Cujane who did not enter missions continued to live along the nearby coast. Soon after Anglo American colonization of the coastal region the Cujane began to lose their ethnic identity among the coastal Indians generally referred to as Karankawa, who disappeared about 1858.

Attempts have been made to identify the Cujane with several groups named in records of the La Salle Expedition,[qv] particularly Ebahamo, Kouan, Kouyam, and Quinet. Since all of these groups evidently lived in or not far from the original Cujane area, sound correspondences in names provide the only basis for identification. Quinet and Kouan seem to be phonetically most similar to Cujane, but this needs the support of reliable documentary evidence. Identification of the Quevene of Cabeza de Vaca [qv] with the Cujane is dubious because 175 years or more separate the initial records of these groups.

BIBLIOGRAPHY: H. E. Bolton, "The Founding of Mission Rosario," *Quarterly of the Texas State Historical Association*, X (1906–1907), "Records of the Mission of Nuestra Señora del Refugio," *Quarterly of the Texas State Historical Association*, XIV (1910–1911), *Texas in the Middle Eighteenth Century* (1915); W. E. Dunn, "The Founding of Nuestra Señora del Refugio, the Last Spanish Mission in Texas," *Southwestern Historical Quarterly*, XXV (1921–1922); F. W. Hodge (ed.), *Handbook of American Indians*, I (1907), II (1910); W. H. Oberste, *History of Refugio Mission* (1942).

T. N. Campbell

*Culberson, Charles Allen.

*Culberson, David Browning.

Culberson, Olin Wellborn Nichols. Olin Wellborn Nichols Culberson, son of William Albert and Martha Artemesia (Richardson) Culberson, was born at Turnersville, Coryell County, Texas, on October 26, 1886. He was formally educated by his parents at the Culberson Select School, a family enterprise, and afterward labored as a railroad worker in Hillsboro until 1911. That year he was appointed deputy clerk of Hill County. The following year Culberson married Mary Lou Rochelle of Hubbard.

In 1918 Culberson resigned his office to serve in World War I. Upon returning to Hillsboro, he was twice elected county clerk of Hill County. As county clerk, he discovered and exposed a $263,000 road-bond fraud. In 1925 Culberson became county judge. During his two terms as judge, the recovered bond-fraud money was used to construct needed roads and bridges for Hill County. Refusing to run for a third term, Culberson moved to Edna, Texas, and purchased an interest in a dry-goods store. He moved to Austin in 1932. Asked to conduct a rate investigation of the Lone Star Gas Company, he accepted a position with the Texas Railroad Commission,qv serving first as chief examiner and later as chief of the gas utilities division. The sixteen major rate investigations he conducted for the commission antagonized certain gas interests. Pressure groups sought his removal. In 1939 he was discharged.

The following year, Culberson, a reform candidate, bested twenty opponents and was elected railroad commissioner. He was reelected three consecutive times. In addition to proposing a weekly meeting of the railroad commissioners and insisting on ten days' notice for all public hearings, Culberson was responsible for other important rulings. Political appointees were replaced by graduate petroleum engineers. The flaring of casinghead gas was stopped, and its return to the well became mandatory. A malodorant was added to natural gas. Annual inspections of liquefied petroleum gas installations in schools and public buildings were established. He implemented a new system of oil accounting and fought freight-rate discrimination against southwest Texas.

He served the Texas Firemen's and Fire Marshal's Association as their secretary for over forty years, and he was active in many charitable organizations. Culberson died on June 22, 1961, and was buried in the State Cemetery qv in Austin. In 1963 the Olin Culberson Memorial Research Center at Scott and White Hospital,qv a center for the study of cardiovascular diseases, was dedicated.

BIBLIOGRAPHY: Houston *Press*, June 24, 1961; Texas Railroad Commission, *A Resolution Memorializing the Services of the late Olin Culberson* (June 22, 1961).

Robert Stephen Peel

*Culberson County. Culberson County, with the highest mountains in Texas, has had decreasing numbers of cattle, sheep, and goats in recent years. With over 12,000 acres irrigated in 1960, cotton and truck crops were produced in increasing quantities. However, in 1970 cattle ranching was still the largest source of agricultural income. Petroleum, natural gas, and barite were valued at nearly $4,000,000 in 1963. Nine talc mines, a barite mine, and a marble mine exploit the mineral resources. The 1960 population of 2,794 increased to 3,429 by 1970.

*Culebra Creek.

*Cullen, Ezekiel Wimberly.

Cullen, Hugh Roy. Hugh Roy Cullen, son of Cicero and Louise (Beck) Cullen and grandson of Ezekiel W. Cullen,qv was born on July 3, 1881, in Denton County. His formal education was limited to a few years in the public schools in San Antonio. He married Lillie Cranz on December 29, 1903; they had four daughters and one son, Roy Gustave Cullen, who died in 1936.

At the age of sixteen Cullen worked for a cotton broker; he later went into that business for himself and also dealt in real estate. In 1911 Cullen moved to Houston and entered the oil business in 1918. His policy of drilling deep wells was so successful that he became known as the king of the wildcatters. He made major discoveries in the Houston area, notably at Pierce Junction, Blue Ridge, Rabb's Ridge, Humble, and the O'Connor field. He owned half of the South Texas Petroleum Company and later formed the Quintana Petroleum Company.

Cullen took an active interest in politics throughout his life. Firmly dedicated to states' rights, much of his energy was spent in opposition to the New Deal. He promoted W. Lee O'Daniel qv for governor in 1938 and 1940 and for senator in 1941. Although Cullen aided the Dixiecrat movement in 1948, he normally supported Republican candidates, particularly Dwight D. Eisenhower qv in 1952.

Cullen was a well-known philanthropist, giving over $11,000,000 each to his favorite projects, the University of Houston and Houston hospitals. In 1947 he established the $160,000,000 Cullen Foundation to provide for continual aid to education and medicine. By 1955 Cullen had given away an estimated 90 percent of his fortune.

He served in many capacities during his career, including chairman of the board of regents of the University of Houston, vice-president of the Texas World Fair Commission in 1939, and director of Boy Scouts of America. He received honorary degrees from the University of Pittsburgh in 1936, Baylor University in 1945, and the University of Houston in 1947. He was an honorary member of the American Hospital Association and a member of the Sons of the Republic of Texas.qv Cullen died in Houston on July 4, 1957.

BIBLIOGRAPHY: Ed Kilman and Theon Wright, *Hugh Roy Cullen* (1954); Houston *Post*, July 5, 1957; *Who's Who In America* (1956).

Rita Crabbe

*Culleoka, Texas.

*Cullinan, Joseph Stephen.

Cullum, Landon Haynes. Landon H. (Shino) Cullum, son of J. D. Cullum, Sr., was born in Dallas on February 25, 1889. He studied engineering and participated in athletics at the University of Texas until 1910, then joined the Gulf Pipe Line Company as an engineer, first at Beaumont and later in the Wichita Falls area.

Becoming an independent operator, he joined J. J. Perkins, Frank Kell,qqv and R. O. Harvey in forming the Harvey Lease Account, one of the strongest and most profitable independent oil firms in the state. They opened the South Electra field and operated in North Texas, Ranger, Desdemona, and other fields. In 1922 the firm was sold to Magnolia Petroleum Company qv for a seven-figure sum. Cullum and Perkins formed the Perkins-Cullum Production Company, which successfully operated in many fields in Texas and Oklahoma. Cullum was one of the organizers of the Texas Division of the Mid-Continent Oil and Gas Association, president of the North Texas Oil and Gas Association in 1935–1936, and active in other independent oil groups. His other business interests included buildings in Wichita Falls, farms, and ranches.

Cullum was a member of the first board of trustees of Hardin Junior College. He served from 1941 to 1957, during which time Hardin became a four-year college, expanded its campus, added a graduate department, and changed its name to Midwestern University. Cullum was active in University of Texas projects, including the Athletic Council, the Committee of 75 Development Board, and the Ex-Students' Association, of which he was a president. On May 28, 1921, he was married to Leila Beall Anderson of Wichita Falls, and they had three children. Cullum died on August 15, 1961.

BIBLIOGRAPHY: Wichita Falls *Record News*, August 16, 1961.

Louise Kelly

*Culver, Texas.

*Culvers Creek.

Cumby, Robert H. Robert H. Cumby was born in Charlotte County, Virginia, on August 24, 1825. In 1836 he moved to Lafayette County, Mississippi, with his family. He married and lived in Mississippi until 1849, when he moved to Rusk County, Texas, as a farmer. He was elected to the Eighth Texas Legislature. In 1861 he raised Company B, 3rd Texas Cavalry, and during 1862 rose to colonel of the regiment. In 1864 he was appointed a brigadier general of Texas State Troops. After the war he moved to Dallas, where he served as a constable in 1884.

BIBLIOGRAPHY: Dorman H. Winfrey, *A History of Rusk County, Texas* (1961); U.S. Census, 1860, Rusk County, Texas (microfilm, University of Texas at Austin Library); Dallas *Herald*, November 13, 1884.

*Cumby, Texas.

Cummings, Franklin. Franklin Cummings was born in Portland, Maine, on September 18, 1823, the son of Cyrus Cummings, a Methodist minister. He married Ann Mildred Jones in April, 1850, and brought his bride to Brownsville. He was attracted to the area because of its great potential as a deep-sea port. A graduate of Wesleyan University, with an LL.B. degree, he was an early partner of Stephen Powers,qv who established the first law office in Brownsville. In 1851 he was appointed postmaster, succeeding Stephen Powers, and he held this office for seven years. He was also a judge and one of the early mayors of the city. He was one of

the group of men who financed the building of the First Episcopal Church in Brownsville in 1851.

He served as county commissioner of Cameron County, as an officer in the Texas Volunteers at Fort Brown qv during the Civil War, and as a member of the Committee of Public Safety qv after the Cortina Raid. He was one of the men to whom a charter was issued for the building of the Rio Grande Railroad linking Brownsville with the seaport of Point Isabel, now Port Isabel, Texas. He died in Brownsville in 1874, survived by six children, including Joseph Franklin Cummings.qv

Eleanor Russell Rentfro

+Cummings, James.

*Cummings, John.

Cummings, Joseph Franklin. Joseph Franklin Cummings, son of Ann Mildred (Jones) and Franklin Cummings,qv was born in Brownsville, Texas, July 16, 1851. He attended Wesleyan University in Middletown, Connecticut, where his uncle, Joseph Cummings, was president of the university. On leaving Wesleyan, he entered West Point, where he was graduated in 1876 and then assigned to the 3rd U.S. Cavalry. He served in the Indian wars of 1876 and 1877 and was promoted to the rank of first lieutenant. Retiring from the army, Cummings was employed in Galveston, Texas, in 1888, as a teacher. He returned to Brownsville in July, 1888, to organize the local public school system. Within two years a new school building was finished, located on part of Washington Park. Because the school was well organized and thoroughly disciplined Cummings became known as the father of the Brownsville school system. Later the Cummings Junior High School was named for him. Cummings also organized the first company of the Brownsville Rifles and was made its captain.

In 1896 he married Katherine Garriga of Point Isabel, the sister of Marino Simon Garriga,qv Bishop of the Diocese of Corpus Christi. They had one son. Cummings died in Washington, D.C., in 1912 and was buried in Maryland in his mother's family burial plot.

BIBLIOGRAPHY: W. H. Chatfield, *Twin Cities of the Border* (1893).

Pierre Joseph Vivier, Jr.

*Cummings, Rebecca.

*Cummings, William.

*Cummings Creek.

*Cummins, James.

*Cummins, Moses.

Cummins, Robert James. Robert James Cummins was born in Moutmellick, Ireland, on March 1, 1881. He received his engineering degree in 1900 from Queen's College of the Royal University of Ireland, Galway. He came to the United States shortly afterward and worked for ten years as a civil engineer in Detroit, Michigan, both for the city and as a private consultant. In 1910 Cummins moved to Houston, where development of port facilities occupied much of his time for the next fifty years. For twenty-five years he was a member of the Houston Port Commission and for fifteen of those years served as vice-chairman. He laid out the harbors and designed the original facilities for the ports of Brownsville and Corpus Christi. Other major port facilities designed by him are in Freeport, Port Arthur, Beaumont, and Orange. At the time of his death, wharves he had designed were under construction at a cost of $2,-500,000 along the Houston Ship Channel.qv

In addition to carrying on his consulting practice, from 1918 to 1921 Cummins taught a senior class in engineering at Rice Institute. During the 1930's he served as engineering adviser to the Reconstruction Finance Corporation. He acted as adviser during construction of the San Francisco-Oakland Bay Bridge and on several construction programs of the Metropolitan Water District of Southern California. He received the United States Navy Certificate of Achievement in 1945 for his part in the design of the navy hospital in Houston.

A pioneer in welded, multi-storied construction, Cummins was largely responsible for its popularity along the Gulf Coast. He was structural engineer on numerous major buildings, notably the San Jacinto Monument qv and Houston's thirty-story First City National Bank Building. A member of American Society of Civil Engineers since 1920, he was president of the Texas section in 1940. Also, he was technical adviser to the International Boundary Commission,qv United States and Mexico; chairman of the board of directors, Travelers Aid Society; and director of the Houston Chamber of Commerce. On April 4, 1926, he married Sascha Morrison in Houston. He died there on June 11, 1960, survived by his widow, a son, and two daughters.

Uel Stephens

*Cummins, William Fletcher.

*Cummins Creek.

*Cundiff, Texas.

*Cundiff Creek.

*Cuney, Norris Wright.

*Cuney, Phillip M.

*Cuney, Texas.

*Cunningham, Abel Seymour.

*Cunningham, Leander Calvin.

Cunningham, Minnie (Fisher). Minnie (Fisher) Cunningham was born in New Waverly, Texas, on March 19, 1882, the seventh child of Captain Horatio White and Sally Comer (Abercrombie) Fisher. Taught by her mother at home, she learned about politics from her father. In 1898 she received a teaching certificate and taught for a year at Gourd Creek. In 1902 she became the first woman in Texas to receive a degree in pharmacy from the University of Texas medical school. In the same year she married B. J. Cunningham, a Galveston lawyer.

Soon after her marriage she became interested in both state and national women's suffrage movements. Elected president of the Texas Equal Suf-frage Association in 1911, she led the fight that won the vote for women in Texas in 1918. Her name is among the eighty-seven American women honored by a plaque in Washington commemorating the adoption of the Nineteenth Amendment. She was Texas chairman of the Liberty Loan Campaign during World War I. From 1932 to 1942 she served as information editor, Texas Agricultural Extension Service,qv Texas A&M College (now Texas A&M University). In Washington in 1942–1943 she worked with the United States Department of Agriculture, the Agricultural Adjustment Administration, and the Urban Rural Women's Conference. A tireless campaigner on state and national levels, she was a founder and executive secretary of the National League of Women Voters, and, with others, organized the Women's National Democratic Club in Washington, D.C., in 1923. She was an unsuccessful Liberal Democratic candidate for United States senator from Texas in 1928 and for governor in 1944. She died on December 9, 1964, in Conroe and was buried at New Waverly.

Lillian Collier

*Cunningham, Texas.

Cunquebaco Indians. The Cunquebaco Indians were one of twenty Indian groups that joined Juan Domínguez de Mendoza qv on his journey from El Paso to the vicinity of present San Angelo in 1683–1684. Since Mendoza did not indicate at what point the Cunquebaco joined his party, it is not possible to determine their range or affiliations. However, the Indians between the Pecos River and the San Angelo area were being hard pressed by Apache at this time, and it seems likely that the Cunquebaco ranged somewhere between these two localities.

BIBLIOGRAPHY: H. E. Bolton (ed.), *Spanish Exploration in the Southwest, 1542–1706* (1916).

T. N. Campbell

*Cupola Mountain.

*Cupples, George. George Cupples was elected second (not first, as stated in Volume I) president of the Texas Medical Association qv in November, 1853.

BIBLIOGRAPHY: Pat Ireland Nixon, *A History of the Texas Medical Association, 1853–1953* (1953).

*Cureton, Calvin Maples. Calvin Maples Cureton's wife's maiden name was Nora Morris (not Nora Norris, as stated in Volume I).

*Cureton, J. J. (Jack).

*Currency of the Republic. *See* Money of the Republic of Texas.

*Currie, L. W.

*Currie, Thomas White.

*Currie, Texas.

*Curry, Texas. (Milam County.)

*Curry, Texas. (Stephens County.)

*Curry Comb Branch.

*Curry-Comb Ranch.

*Curry's Creek.

*Curtis, Hinton.

*Curtis, James.

*Curtis, James, Jr.

*Curtis, Texas.

*Curtis Field.

*Cushing, Edward Benjamin.

*Cushing, Edward Hopkins.

Cushing, Thomas Humphrey. Thomas Humphrey Cushing was born in Massachusetts and enlisted there as a sergeant in the 6th Continental Infantry in January, 1776. A career army man, he succeeded Isaac Guion in 1799 as commander of United States troops on the Mississippi and Tombigbee rivers with headquarters near Natchez. He supervised the construction of American frontier forts in the Mississippi Territory, particularly Fort Stoddart. Commissioned a colonel on September 7, 1805, he was named commander of the posts west of the Mississippi the following May, and was ordered by General James Wilkinson qv to leave for Natchitoches with several cannon and howitzers. He was to prevent Spanish violations of American territory east of the Sabine River during the Neutral Ground qv dispute. He negotiated with Simón de Herrera qv during 1805, but failed to reach any agreement. Hostilities were avoided when Wilkinson arrived and signed the Neutral Ground Agreement on November 6, 1806. Cushing was commissioned brigadier general on July 2, 1812. Honorably discharged on June 15, 1815, he died on October 19, 1822.

BIBLIOGRAPHY: Francis B. Heitman (comp.), *Historical Register and Dictionary of the United States Army*, I (1903); Jack D. L. Holmes, "Showdown on the Sabine: General James Wilkinson *vs.* Lieutenant-Colonel Simón de Herrera," *Louisiana Studies*, III (1964); Jack D. L. Holmes (ed.), "Fort Stoddart in 1799: Seven Letters of Captain Bartholomew Schaumburgh," *Alabama Historical Quarterly*, XXVII (1965).

Jack D. L. Holmes

*Cushing, Texas.

*Cusseta, Texas.

*Custer, George Armstrong.

Custer City, Texas. Custer City was founded by Jim Jones when he established a cotton gin and flour mill one mile east of Rock School in Cooke County. Since the town's post office was established in 1876, it was originally called Centennial City. It was later renamed for Indian fighter George Armstrong Custer.qv With a population of 300 in 1882, the settlement had a sawmill, school, church, store, blacksmith shop, cotton gin, and flour mill; it became a ghost town by the 1930's.

BIBLIOGRAPHY: A. Morton Smith, *The First 100 Years in Cooke County* (1955); *Texas Almanac* (1936).

*Customs Service of the Republic of Texas.

*Cut, Texas.

*Cut Off Mountain.

*Cut 'n Shoot, Texas.

*Cutalchich Indians.

*Cuthand, Texas.

*Cuthand Creek.

*Cuthbert, Texas.

*Cuyler, Texas.

*Cyclone, Texas.

*Cyclone Branch.

*Cypress, Texas. (Franklin County.)

*Cypress, Texas. (Harris County.)

*Cypress Creek.

Cypress Creek, Texas. Cypress Creek, in eastern Kerr County, is a farming community. Its economic activities are centered in the town of Comfort, located in Kendall County.

*Cypress Mill, Texas. [This title was incorrectly listed in Volume I as Cypress Mills, Texas.]

*Cyril, Texas. *See* Joinerville, Texas.

*Czechs in Texas. By 1900 there were about fifteen thousand foreign-born Czechs living in Texas. The exodus of Czechs from rural communities began during World War I and continued at an increased pace during and after World War II. As it became more difficult for individuals to farm successfully, many Czech families left traditional agricultural pursuits and moved to Texas cities. Despite the change in life styles, large numbers of urban Czechs maintained active memberships in Czech social, fraternal, and religious organizations. Interest among the younger generation in the Czech language and culture continued to be strong. Fraternal theatrical groups put on plays in the Czech language, and Czech folk dancers in authentic costume were in demand for various celebrations. The Czech language was taught in several high schools and colleges. An extensive collection of Czech materials and the production of the slide show "The Czech Texan" by the Institute of Texan Cultures qv at San Antonio, helped bring into focus the life of the Texas Czechs.

Until the 1960's a Czech language press flourished in Texas, but as the younger generation became fluent in English, the use of Czech newspapers declined steadily. In the 1970's there were only a handful of survivors. The *Brethren Journal*, *Nasinec*, and *Vestnik* contain some articles in Czech. Only one paper, *Hospodar*, published in West, Texas, is printed entirely in Czech; many copies of *Hospodar* are sent to Czechoslovakia. *See also* Snook, Texas.

BIBLIOGRAPHY: Henry R. Maresh and Estelle Hudson, *Czech Pioneers of the Southwest* (1934); O. J. Pazdral, Czech Folklore in Texas (M.A. thesis, University of Texas at Austin, 1942); John M. Skrivanek, The Education of the Czechs in Texas (M.A. thesis, University of Texas at Austin, 1946); Robert L. Skrabanek, Social Organization and Change in a Czech-American Rural Community (Ph.D. dissertation, Louisiana State University, 1949).

D

*Dabney, Robert Lewis.

*Dabney, Texas.

*Daccus, Texas.

*Dacosta, Texas.

*Dad's Corner, Texas.

*Daffan, Katie.

*Daffan, Texas.

*Daggett, Ephraim M.

Daileyville, Texas. Daileyville was situated near Escondido Creek eight miles south of Helena in Karnes County and was founded in 1869 by brothers, Christopher P. and David Dailey. A post office was established at Daileyville from July 5, 1870, to May 27, 1884. The Dailey brothers operated a store there until they moved to Kenedy Junction in 1887.
BIBLIOGRAPHY: Robert H. Thonhoff, A History of Karnes County, Texas (M.A. thesis, Southwest Texas State College, 1963).

*Daily Advertiser (Galveston).

*Daily Bulletin (Austin).

*Daily Courier (Galveston).

*Daily Galvestonian. See Galvestonian.

*Daily Globe (Galveston).

*Daily News. See Galveston News.

Daily Texan. The Daily Texan, student newspaper at the University of Texas at Austin, began as a weekly in 1900 when two privately owned campus newspapers, the Calendar and the Ranger, were joined to form the Texan, with Fritz Garland Lanham qv as the first editor. In 1904 the student assembly took charge of operating the paper, and by 1907 the Texan had expanded to a semi-weekly. A student referendum in 1913 made the Texan a daily newspaper, and its first issue as such was on September 24, 1913; on that date the Daily Texan became, according to its editors, the first college daily in the South. A student-faculty conference was held in 1921 to establish the paper on a sound business basis, and the result was the formation of Texas Student Publications, Inc. (TSP), chartered by the secretary of state on July 6, 1921, as a non-profit corporation, and directed to issue, publish, and distribute the Daily Texan along with the Longhorn Magazine, the Cactus (yearbook), and such other publications that might in the future be authorized. By 1925 the newspaper was eight pages and had a circulation of 7,000. During the 1930's the charter for Texas Student Publications, Inc., was revised several times, in effect giving the board of regents of the university the authority to approve changes in the charter and subjecting all actions taken by the TSP board of directors to the approval of the regents.

On July 6, 1971, the fifty-year-old charter of the TSP expired, and although attempts were made to have it extended, the corporation was dissolved. By agreement with the board of regents and the board of directors of Texas Student Publications, Inc., all the assets of TSP became the property of the university, and the student publications continued to be published as an auxiliary enterprise of the university. Daily Texan and other TSP employees became university (or state) employees. The board of operating trustees of TSP in 1974 consisted of six students, three faculty members, and two professional newsmen.

From its early days, the Daily Texan fostered both the university song, "The Eyes of Texas," and the name "Longhorns" for the university football team. Over the years the newspaper, with the aid of national news gathering sources, provided the university community with coverage of local, state, national, and international news. Often controversial, it has taken editorial stands which were unpopular in many areas of the state. Although the editor has traditionally been elected for a one-year term by the university student body, there have been times when the editor was appointed; in the 1970's the editor continued to serve by student election. The Daily Texan was a consistent standout among college newspapers, and in 1965, 1969, and 1971 it was awarded the coveted Pacemaker Award (one of the top two) as a member of the Associated Collegiate Press (comprised of 1,200 university newspapers across the nation), from which it has nearly always held an All-American rating (the top ten to twelve newspapers). The long list of editors and staff members includes a large number who went on to become outstanding newspaper and press professionals. In the fall of 1973 the operations of the Daily Texan were moved from the Journalism Building to the new Texas Student Publications Building in the Communication Complex on the campus of the University of Texas at Austin.

*Daily Texian (Austin).

*Daily Times (Houston).

*Daingerfield, William Henry.

*Daingerfield, Texas. Daingerfield, seat and commercial center of Morris County, lists a roofing plant, a regional power plant, and nearby Lone Star Steel plant among its major business concerns. In 1967 the town had 100 businesses, thirteen churches, a bank, a library, and two newspapers. The Daingerfield State Park (see Parks, State) aids the tourist business. The 1960 population was 3,133; the 1970 population was 2,630.

Dairy Advisory Board. The Dairy Advisory Board, created by the 62nd Texas Legislature in 1971, is a three-member board appointed for two-year terms by the governor with the concurrence of the senate. One member must represent the dairy processing industries, one the dairy production industries, and one the consumers. The board acts as an advisory body to the commissioner of agriculture to determine proper apparatus for testing butterfat content and component parts of milk. In 1972 the Babcock test was the official dairy test used in Texas. The legislature provided for the approval of other testing equipment as it became available, contingent upon certain standards.

BIBLIOGRAPHY: University of Texas at Austin, *Guide To Texas State Agencies* (1972).

Dairy and Hog Farm, State. *See* State Dairy and Hog Farm; State Hog Farm; Texas Leander Rehabilitation Center.

*Dairying. Dairying in Texas has moved progressively away from small herds maintained on many farms, supplying milk, cream, or butter to be used at home or retailed. The bulk of production in 1963 was concentrated on fewer farms, operating large herds which were fed, managed, and milked scientifically. The farms wholesaled only whole milk. The trend of large concentrated dairy units coupled with greater production per cow influenced the decline in the number of Texas milk cows from 1,594,000, a peak reached in 1945, to 523,000 in 1965. In 1970 there were 355,000 milk cows. Gross income to farmers from dairying reached a peak of $213,500,000 in 1953, declined to $155,200,000 in 1960, and increased to $199,626,000 in 1970.

Dairying remained well distributed over Texas, with the greatest concentration around urban centers. Leading Texas counties by 1972 were Hopkins, Wise, Johnson, Harris, Erath, Fayette, Parker Tarrant, Nacogdoches, McLennan, Grimes, El Paso, and Bexar.

BIBLIOGRAPHY: *Texas Almanac* (1955, 1963, 1967, 1971, 1973).

*Daisetta, Texas. Daisetta, in Liberty County, had a 1970 population of 1,084.

*Dakin, Texas.

*Dalberg, Texas.

*Dalby, Texas.

*Dalby Creek.

*Dalby Springs, Texas. Dalby Springs, in southwestern Bowie County, was founded during the 1870's when people began to travel there to bathe in the medicinal red mineral water. Two hotels and several buildings were constructed. When the town's best known physician, Louis A. Seager, died in 1897, the town declined. Although some of the Dalby family still live in the area, the settlement is almost a ghost town with only a general store remaining. The original Black Spring was located northwest of the townsite.

BIBLIOGRAPHY: Margaret McWilliams, "Ghost Town of Red Gold," *Junior Historian*, XVIII (November, 1957); Frank Tolbert, "The Black Spring Wouldn't Freeze," *Dallas Morning News*, August 29, 1961.

*Dale, Texas.

*Dalhart, Texas. Dalhart, seat of Dallam County, had a 1960 population of 5,160 and a 1970 population of 5,705. In 1963 the town had eighteen churches, six schools, two banks, a library a hospital remodeled in 1959, and a million-dollar

senior citizens' home completed in 1960. In 1970 Dalhart had 166 businesses, mainly connected with irrigated grain growing and the cattle industry.

*Dalhart Army Air Field.

*Dallam, James Wilmer.

*Dallam County. Dallam County, bordering on both New Mexico and Oklahoma, ranked fifth among the state's leading counties in beef cattle in 1960. In addition, the county was a major grower of grain sorghums and wheat, having 58,000 acres under irrigation in 1964. Annual farm income was about $16,000,000 in the 1960's. The leading recreational area, Rita Blanca Lake, although located near Dalhart, the county seat, is actually in adjoining Hartley County, as is part of Dalhart itself. The county had 6,302 inhabitants in 1960 and 6,012 in 1970.

Dallardsville, Texas. Dallardsville, in southeastern Polk County, was founded about 1880. Its first post office was called Elbert. Named for one of the first settlers in the area, Dallardsville had at one time a cotton gin, a syrup mill, and a grist mill. In 1967 there were about three hundred fifty persons living in the town, which had one store, a consolidated high school, and a post office.

*Dallas, Texas. *See also* Dallas Standard Metropolitan Statistical Area.

Dallas Baptist College. Dallas Baptist College, Dallas, became the successor of Decatur Baptist College qv in September, 1965. The Decatur school moved to a 200-acre campus overlooking Mountain Creek Lake in the southwest Oak Cliff section of Dallas to form the nucleus of a new school. Opening with four contemporary buildings—administration and classroom, science, and two dormitories—the enrollment was about four hundred students in freshman and sophomore classes. Construction of a chapel and physical education building in addition to a temporary student center were the next projects planned. By 1973 the school had become a four-year senior college with 1,339 students enrolled. Charles P. Pitts served as president.

Sponsored by the Dallas Baptist Association, the college was operated by trustees elected by the Baptist General Convention of Texas.

Dallas Christian College. Dallas Christian College was opened in 1950 as a private coeducational college of the Texas Christian churches. The beginning enrollment was thirty-four students. Designed for the training of religious workers, the curriculum in 1974–1975 offered courses of instruction leading to the bachelor of arts, bachelor of science, bachelor of theology, and bachelor of religious education degrees; it also offered associate of arts degrees.

The school, originally situated on McKinney Avenue in Dallas, moved to a site at Carroll and San Jacinto streets and then to a new twenty-two-acre campus in suburban Farmers Branch in the fall of 1967. An anonymous gift provided the first thirteen acres, valued at $96,000, and an additional nine acres were purchased to assure adequate room for expansion. The campus consisted of four buildings in 1975.

The college library contained fifteen thousand volumes. Both the Veterans Administration and the United States Immigration Service recognized the college as fully acceptable to receive veterans and foreign transfer students.

By fall, 1974, the student body numbered 175 and the faculty consisted of twelve members. Presidents of the college have been Vernon Newland, J. T. Seagroves, William Nash, P. C. McCord, Harold D. Platt, Vernon Newland (a second term), E. Dean Barr, and Melvin M. Newland (son of the first president), who was president in 1975.

*Dallas and Cleburne Railroad Company. See Chicago, Texas, and Mexican Central Railway Company.

*Dallas, Cleburne, and Rio Grande Railway Company. See Chicago, Texas, and Mexican Central Railway Company.

*Dallas, Cleburne, and Southwestern Railway Company.

*Dallas College.

*Dallas County. In the 1950's and 1960's Dallas County was among the nation's leading agribusiness centers. Two-thirds of the farm income came from livestock, poultry, and dairying; grains, cotton, hay, and horticultural and truck farm products were the main crops. Manufacturers included those producing farm implements and cotton gin machinery. Other businesses included agribusiness publications, chemicals, warehousing, and the financing of agribusiness projects. Dallas was the largest city in the county, which contained 859 square miles in 1970; Dallas was also the county seat. The 1960 county population was 951,527; the 1970 population was 1,327,321. See also Dallas Standard Metropolitan Statistical Area.

Dallas County Community College District. The Dallas County Junior College District was created in May, 1965, and changed its name in 1972 to Dallas County Community College District. The district was created to establish and operate a system of public junior colleges in Dallas County. In the fall of 1966 El Centro College, the first of seven, opened in a remodeled eight-story department store building in downtown Dallas. The school, which enrolled about four thousand freshman students in 1966, had an enrollment of 6,099 in the fall of 1974.

The district opened Eastfield College and Mountain View College in 1970; their enrollments were 6,895 and 5,340, respectively, in 1974. Richland College, opened in 1972, had an enrollment of 8,257 in 1974. Three more colleges, Cedar Valley, North Lake, and Brookhaven, were planned for the future. All colleges were planned so that they would be capable of expansion to a capacity of 10,000 each. The schools offer courses equivalent to the first two years of standard university work, leading to associate degrees in arts and sciences. In addition, there are courses leading to associate degrees in applied arts and applied sciences in technical and occupational fields, including nursing, data processing, programming, drafting, electronics, culinary arts, mid-management, pattern drafting and draping, chemical technology, dental assisting, secretarial work, and library assisting.

Dallas Cowboys. The Dallas Cowboys, a professional football team, came to Dallas on January 28, 1960, when the National Football League awarded to Clint Murchison, Jr., and Bedford Wynne its thirteenth franchise. (Earlier, in 1952, the NFL had placed a franchise in Dallas, but it was later moved to Baltimore.) The Cowboys suffered through early lean years at the gate and on the field, but steadily gained in popularity and stature, climaxing the gradual upswing by winning the Eastern Conference championship in 1966 and losing only by a score of 34–27 to the Green Bay Packers in the NFL championship game. The Cowboys returned in 1967, again losing to Green Bay in the championship game. The Cowboys were National Conference champions in 1970 and 1971, winning the NFL title championship in the Super Bowl in 1971.

The original team was formed by a thirty-six-player pool, three selected from each of the other twelve teams in the league. Throughout its existence, the team has been coached by Tom Landry and played all of its home games in the Cotton Bowl qv until 1971, when Texas Stadium in Irving became the home field of the Cowboys.

Curt Mosher

*Dallas Fair. See State Fair of Texas.

Dallas-Fort Worth Airport. The Dallas-Fort Worth Airport, located north of the two cities, was officially opened on January 13, 1974. Covering approximately seventeen thousand acres, it was the largest airport in the world. See also Greater Southwest International Airport; Love Field.

*Dallas, Fort Worth, and Gulf Railway Company. See Dallas Terminal Railway and Union Depot Company.

Dallas-Fort Worth Standard Metropolitan Statistical Area. In April, 1973, the six-county Dallas metropolitan area and the two-county Fort Worth metropolitan area were combined, statistically, and Wise, Parker, and Hood counties were added, statistically, to create an eleven-county Dallas-Fort Worth Standard Metropolitan Statistical Area. See Dallas Standard Metropolitan Statistical Area; Fort Worth Standard Metropolitan Statistical Area.

*Dallas and Greenville Railway Company.

Dallas Health and Science Museum. The Dallas Health and Science Museum, one of the exhibition buildings at Fair Park, managed year-round programs to study the mind and body of man and the means by which science explores the universe. Founded in 1946, the museum was known as the Health Museum; in 1958 the officers and trustees added "Science" to its name. Supported by municipal and voluntary funds, it provided free admission and services for its visitors. The director in 1967 was H. D. Carmichael.

Besides the threescore permanent major scientific exhibits, the museum conducted a pre-schooler's program to explain the wonders of the universe and the structure, functions, and health of the human body. These themes were expanded and specialized in adult and youth classes studying topics such as hygiene, public health, advanced subjects in science technology, bomb shelters, and precious gem studies. Facilities of the museum included anatomical and astronomical models and puppets, equipment and vehicles for astronauts and aquanauts, a planetarium, the Civil Defense Emergency Operating Center for Dallas County, and a library dealing with topics on science and health.

*Dallas *Herald*.

*Dallas Historical Society. Additional holdings of the Dallas Historical Society include the papers of Hatton William Sumners, Thomas Bell Love, George Bannerman Dealey, and Sam Hanna Acheson;qqv the society also has portions of the libraries of William Lewis Cabell, Oscar Branch Colquitt,qqv and J. T. Trezevant.

Presidents of the society from 1950 to 1975 have been Edward H. Cary, Homer R. Mitchell, D. K. Woodward, Jr., Ben H. Mitchell, Lester T. Potter, Henry C. Coke, Jr., and W. W. Lynch. Sam Hanna Acheson, beginning in 1934, was a long-time secretary of the society. Herbert Gambrell became curator of the museum in 1934; he was subsequently named director and then historical director, a post he continued to hold in 1975. Virginia Leddy Gambrell became archivist in 1934 and director of the museum in 1948; she continued in that capacity in 1975.

Herbert Gambrell

Dallas *Journal*. The Dallas *Journal*, a six-day afternoon newspaper, was established on April 1, 1914, by A. H. Belo and Company, publishers of the Dallas *Morning News*,qv with Tom Finty, Jr., as editor, Harry Clay Withers as city editor, and Hilton R. Greer qqv as chief editorial writer. Its strong editorial page was later edited by Lynn W. Landrum.qv Both in news coverage and editorial positions, this spritely journalistic enterprise was concerned mainly with local and state affairs, although it was an early advocate of a league of nations to promote world peace. It was sold on July 1, 1938, to Karl Hoblitzelle qv and Alfred O. Andersson of Dallas, who consolidated it with the Dallas *Dispatch* under the name of the *Dispatch-Journal*. The name reverted to the Dallas *Dispatch* when it was sold on December 1, 1939, to J. M. West of Houston, whose heirs after his death discontinued its publication in 1942.

Sam Acheson

*Dallas Little Theater. *See* Theater in Texas.

*Dallas Male and Female College.

*Dallas *Morning News*. The Dallas *Morning News*, which had initially supported Franklin D. Roosevelt and his New Deal, found itself disagreeing with Roosevelt's domestic policies as the president's tenure in office stretched out to include a fourth term. It backed, however, Roosevelt's foreign policies, including unreserved support of America's participation in World War II after Pearl Harbor.

In the postwar period the paper reverted sharply to the conservative point of view that had dominated its editorial position throughout most of its earlier history. In 1952 and 1956 it supported Republican Dwight D. Eisenhower qv for president over Adlai Stevenson. In 1960 it supported Republican Richard M. Nixon over John F. Kennedy, although it took a neutral stance in 1964 in the contest between Lyndon B. Johnson qv and Barry Goldwater. In 1968 and 1972 it supported Richard Nixon.

In 1968 the *Texas Almanac*,qv Radio Station WFAA, and Television Station WFAA-TV were affiliates of the Dallas organization. In 1968 the paper had 1,342 persons employed with its newspaper and its radio and television stations; it had a Sunday circulation of 276,000 and a daily circulation of 236,273.

Sam Acheson

Dallas Museum of Fine Arts. The Dallas Museum of Fine Arts, located in Dallas' Fair Park Civic Center, is a public art museum operated by the city of Dallas and the Dallas Art Association. The director in 1968 was Merrill C. Rueppel. The Dallas Art Association, founded in 1903 with eighty members, antedates the museum, which opened in 1909 and was then known as the Dallas Free Public Art Gallery. It occupied a building in Fair Park which was later destroyed by a storm. In 1932 the name was changed to Dallas Museum of Fine Arts, and the same year the museum moved into the Dallas Power and Light Company building. In 1936 a museum building, financed by a $500,000 city bond issue, was erected in Fair Park. By this time the membership of the Dallas Art Association had reached 519, and an exhibition presented in conjunction with the Texas Centennial qv attracted 154,000 visitors.

In 1964 the museum added a two-story wing, virtually doubling its exhibition area, and completely renovated its older galleries. Since that time both the exhibitions and acquisitions programs have been intensified. In 1968 the museum housed a permanent collection of American and European painting and sculpture. The collection also included some fine examples of the art of ancient civilizations. A life-size Greek marble figure (fourth century B. C.) acquired by the museum in 1967 was described by authorities as one of the greatest examples of ancient Greek sculpture to be brought to the Western Hemisphere. Major exhibitions have included a Picasso retrospective, a Van Gogh watercolor and drawing show, a twentieth-century sculpture exhibition, and a Mark Tobey retrospective. The museum complements its major exhibitions with lectures, gallery talks, film and slide showings, and guided tours. A rapidly growing museum library provides a vital research resource for the museum staff, teachers, and art students. The membership of the Dallas Art Association as of April, 1968, was 1,765. Rueppel's predecessors as director of the Dallas Museum of Fine Arts were John S. Ankeney (1929–1933), Lloyd Rollins (1933–1936), Richard Foster Howard (1936–1941), and Jerry Bywaters (1941–1964).

Dallas Naval Air Station. *See* Naval Air Station, Dallas, Texas.

*****Dallas, Palestine, and Southeast Railroad.**

Dallas Standard Metropolitan Statistical Area. The Dallas Standard Metropolitan Statistical Area in 1970 included Collin, Dallas, Denton, Ellis, Kaufman, and Rockwall counties in north-central Texas, about three hundred miles inland from the Gulf of Mexico. When first organized by the United States Bureau of the Budget in 1949, the area contained only Dallas County, consisting of 859 square miles. In 1950 the population of the area was 614,-799, while the city of Dallas had 434,462 persons. In May, 1959, Collin, Denton, and Ellis counties were added to the area, increasing its size to 3,653 square miles. By 1960 the enlarged area had 1,083,-601 inhabitants, with 679,684 residing in Dallas. The Dallas metropolitan area expanded again in March, 1967, with the addition of Kaufman County and in April, 1967, when the inclusion of Rockwall County increased the area's size to 4,614 square miles. The 1970 census showed 844,401 persons in Dallas, and an area population of 1,555,950.

In addition to Dallas, the eighth largest city in the United States, the area had eighteen cities of more than ten thousand persons. Those in Dallas County were Balch Springs, Carrollton, Duncanville, Farmers Branch, Garland, Grand Prairie, Highland Park, Irving, Lancaster, Mesquite, Richardson, and University Park. Cities of more than ten thousand in other counties of the area were McKinney and Plano in Collin County, Denton in Denton County, Ennis and Waxahachie in Ellis County, and Terrell in Kaufman County. The metropolitan area also had an additional twenty-six towns with population between one thousand and ten thousand persons.

The Dallas area has been one of the fastest growing sections in America. Its rate of expansion in population, business activity, and buying income exceeded that of most areas in the United States. During the decade of the 1950's its metropolitan area increased in population by over 45 percent, while Dallas County gained almost 55 percent. Among the largest twenty metropolitan areas, Dallas ranked first in the rate of population growth during the first seven years of the 1960's, with a 26.7 percent increase.

After World War II the Dallas metropolitan area developed many science-oriented industries, which in the late 1960's accounted for about one-third of its total manufacturing employment. In 1940 the electronics (electrical equipment and scientific instruments) industry employed 624 persons, but by 1959 it employed approximately 11,400. During the same period, aircraft and aerospace industrial employment leaped from five thousand to over twenty

thousand. Industries concerned with printing and publishing, primary and fabricated metal products, non-electrical machinery, and food processing also made significant gains. Other important industries in the area were those involved with air-conditioning, building materials, oil field supplies and equipment, farm and cotton gin machinery, and automobiles. In July, 1967, the civilian labor force totaled 626,120, of which 610,670 were employed—602,-270 in non-agricultural work and 8,400 engaged in agricultural work.

Dallas, long the largest wholesale center in the Gulf Southwest, ranked twelfth in the nation in 1967 wholesale sales. The annual sales of over four thousand wholesale firms in the city totaled more than $5,600,000,000. Dallas was the country's third largest market city in apparel, gifts, and furniture. In 1959 about one-fifth of the furniture and fixture employees of Texas worked in the Dallas area. The opening of merchandise-mart facilities of more than three million square feet made Dallas one of the country's leading market centers for consumer goods.

By 1967 Dallas served as the headquarters of numerous industries, agencies, and businesses. Its property owners and railroad companies had developed more than twelve thousand acres into fifty planned industrial districts, providing sites for new manufacturing and distribution activities. The area was the insurance center of the Gulf Southwest. In 1967 the 178 home offices and numerous branch offices in Dallas had assets totaling $2,300,000,000. Although the area's oil production was negligible, the city was headquarters for many oil companies and issued ten petroleum journals. Dallas was also the nation's fifth largest center for distributing motion pictures to commercial theaters.

Twenty state and 115 federal agencies had offices in Dallas. In addition to serving as the regional center for several federal administrative offices, the city also was the headquarters of the Eleventh District Federal Reserve Bank, the fifth largest of the twelve in total reserves. Its Dallas member banks accounted for more than 20 percent of its deposits, resources, capital accounts, and outstanding loans. Dallas had the two largest banks in the South in terms of capital and surplus. Between June, 1960, and December, 1965, banks in the metropolitan area, which then did not include Kaufman and Rockwall counties, almost doubled their deposits, from $2,385,000,000 to $4,286,000,000.

Dallas was the leading agribusiness center of the Southwest. Its numerous plants distributed farm equipment, feeds and fertilizers, cotton gin machinery, and other farm and ranch supplies. Agriculture in the area was diversified after 1950 to meet the needs of the growing metropolitan population. Cotton production, the traditional agricultural base of the area, declined, while grains, feed crops, dairying, and beef cattle made significant gains. Still, Dallas was one of the larger international cotton markets. In addition, Collin, Dallas, and Denton counties were among the five leading oats-producing counties in Texas, and Collin County had sixty Grade A dairies.

Dallas has been a transportation center since the 1840's. Although the metropolitan area's motor vehicle registration increased over 38 percent between 1960 and 1965, the highway system, including interstates 20, 30, 35, and 45, adequately handled the additional traffic. Dallas served as a regional headquarters for many nationwide trucking lines and for both nationwide and worldwide airlines. With the improvement of Love Field qv in the 1950's, Dallas became the leading air traffic center in Texas. In 1965 the number of the area's enplaned air passengers rose to more than 2,789,-000, an increase of nearly 1,500,000 in five years, and represented 49 percent of the state's total air passengers. Both the total figure and the increase between 1960 and 1965 were more than double those for any other metropolitan area in the Gulf Southwest. Air travel originating in Dallas was 75 percent business, compared with a national average of 50 percent. By 1974 a new airport handled air traffic (see Dallas-Fort Worth Airport). The Dallas Naval Air Station qv trained marine and naval pilots and the air national guard. Several railroads also provided transportation for passengers and freight.

Dallas became the leading convention city of the South and ranked in the top five nationally by 1971 in the number of conventions hosted. The Dallas Memorial Auditorium, which seats almost twelve thousand, and air-conditioned hotels and motels easily handle the national and international conventions. The State Fair of Texas, qv the largest annual exposition in the world, in the 1960's attracted more than 2,500,000 visitors during its sixteen-day run each October; by 1971 that figure had increased to over 3,000,000.

Sports events attracted numerous visitors to the metropolitan area. The Cotton Bowl, qv a football stadium located at Fair Park, has been the home of the Southern Methodist University Mustangs and the site of the annual University of Texas University of Oklahoma football game, as well as the Cotton Bowl Classic on New Year's Day. It was also the home of the Dallas Cowboys qv of the National Football League until their new location, Texas Stadium in Irving, was completed in 1971. By the early 1970's other professional sports clubs were the Tornado, a soccer team; the Texas Rangers, qv an American League baseball franchise (formerly the Washington Senators), located in Arlington; the Chaparrals of the American Basketball Association; and the Dallas-Fort Worth Spurs baseball team of the Texas League. qv The World Championship of Tennis had its headquarters in Dallas. Other special events for sportsmen included the Southwestern Open Badminton Championship, the triennially-held National Skeet Shooting Championship Tournament, the Southwest Boat Show, and the Byron Nelson Golf Classic. Other annual events in the area are a rodeo at Mesquite, an industrial show and Jaycee Jubilee in Garland, a July Fourth celebration at Farmers Branch, a stock show at De Soto, and a community fair in Richardson. Within the metropolitan area are seven lakes which, in addition to providing an adequate water supply, offer opportunities for fishing and various types of water sports.

As an educational center in the early 1970's, the Dallas metropolitan area had more than fifty thousand students enrolled in colleges and universities, including Southern Methodist University, North Texas State University at Denton, Bishop College, Texas Woman's University, the University of Dallas, the University of Plano, and the Dallas County Community College District.qqv In addition to the college libraries, including the state's second largest at Southern Methodist University, the metropolitan area had seventeen city and county libraries. In 1961 Dallas acquired the Graduate Research Center of the Southwest, a private nonprofit corporation devoted to graduate education (now the University of Texas at Dallas). Other research agencies include the Science Information Center on the campus of Southern Methodist University and the Texas Research Foundation, qv a privately supported, nonprofit institution devoted to rebuilding Texas soil.

Medical research is carried on by the University of Texas Southwestern Medical School at Dallas. Baylor University has both a college of dentistry and a school of nursing located in the city. Wadley Research Institute and Blood Center is world-renowned in blood research and operates the largest blood bank in the region.

Cultural institutions in the city include the internationally famous Dallas Civic Opera, the nationally known Dallas Symphony Orchestra, the Dallas Theater Center, other musical and dramatic groups, and many lecture and concert series. Dallas also has twelve weeks of summer musical shows and an annual spring visit by the Metropolitan Opera Company of New York (see Music in Texas). Within the city are two museums for the fine arts; museums of history, health and science, and natural history (see Dallas Museum of Fine Arts; Dallas Health and Science Museum); an aquarium; an outstanding zoo; and a planetarium. Among the cultural attractions in other cities are Denton's concert and lecture series and Richardson's symphony orchestra. The hospitality shown by the Dallas Council on World Affairs and other agencies has made Dallas one of the most popular cities among foreign visitors. In 1973 the Fort Worth Standard Metropolitan Statistical Area qv and the Dallas Standard Metropolitan Statistical Area were combined, and three counties were added, to create an eleven-county Dallas-Fort Worth Standard Metropolitan Statistical Area.qv The new area includes Dallas, Tarrant, Denton, Collin, Rockwall, Kaufman, Ellis, Johnson, Hood, Parker, and Wise counties. See also Standard Metropolitan Statistical Areas in Texas.

BIBLIOGRAPHY: "The New Metro Dallas," Dallas (May, 1967).

Wayne Gard

Dallas State Hospital.

Dallas State Mental Health Clinic. The Dallas

State (Adult) Mental Health Clinic was established in 1958. It provided an out-patient psychiatric service for adults earning less than three thousand dollars per year. Patients furloughed or discharged from a psychiatric hospital are assisted by the clinic at home and on the job. The staff of the clinic also diagnoses, evaluates, and treats patients referred to the clinic from the community. Fees are based upon the individual's income and the number of dependents being supported by the patient.

By the 1970's "Adult" was dropped from the name, and the clinic was called the Dallas State Mental Health Clinic. Vocational rehabilitation programs, a halfway house, a graduate training program, and telephone consultations were provided by the clinic. In 1970 the 16,665 patient visits to the center showed a 20 percent increase over the previous year. *See* Mentally Ill and Mentally Retarded, Care of, in Texas.

BIBLIOGRAPHY: Board for Texas State Hospitals and Special Schools, *Report* (1964); Texas Department of Mental Health and Mental Retardation, *Annual Report,* 1970.

*Dallas Terminal Railway and Union Depot Company. The Dallas Terminal Railway and Union Depot Company owned 19.1 miles of terminal track at Dallas, and was owned and operated by the St. Louis Southwestern Railway Company through ownership of its entire capital stock. In 1953 the Interstate Commerce Commission authorized the St. Louis Southwestern to lease and operate the properties of the company which it had been operating up to that time under contract.

James M. Day

Dallas Texans. In the late 1950's Lamar Hunt of Dallas sought to obtain a professional football franchise for that city. Hunt was told by the National Football League (NFL) that there would be no expansion in the foreseeable future, so he set out to form a new league. He found other men to join him in this venture, and in 1959 Hunt formed the American Football League (AFL). Hunt named his team the Dallas Texans and hired Hank Stram, an assistant coach at the University of Miami, Florida, as his head coach.

The American Football League made its professional debut in 1960. Hunt's Texans finished their first season with an eight-win and six-loss record, placing second in the AFL's Western Division. The 1960 Texans were an exciting team with the league's most exciting player, Abner Haynes. The rookie from North Texas State won the league rushing title, was chosen the AFL's first "Player of the Year," and became the symbol of the dynamic new professional league.

In 1961 the team slipped to a six-win and eight-loss record. Stram rewarded Hunt with his first championship in 1962, when the Texans, bolstered by the addition of quarterback Len Dawson and rookie fullback Curtis McClinton, swept to the Western Division title with a spectacular eleven-win and three-loss season. Stram was named

"Coach of the Year," Dawson, "Player of the Year," and McClinton, "Rookie of the Year."

The Texans' foe in the 1962 championship game was the Houston Oilers,qv who were bidding for a pro football record of three straight championships. Behind by seventeen points, Houston tied the score by the end of the regulation sixty minutes, and the stage was set for one of the most exciting endings in sports history. The Texans and Oilers struggled through a fifth fifteen-minute period and were two minutes and fifty-four seconds into a record-breaking "sixth quarter" when rookie Tommy Brooker kicked a twenty-five-yard field goal to give the Texans a 20 to 17 victory in the longest football game ever played.

The Texans were champions, but all was not peace and tranquility in Dallas. The rival National Football League had placed a team, the Dallas Cowboys,qv there in 1960 to compete with the Texans. The fans were torn between two camps—the Texans and the Cowboys. In 1963 Lamar Hunt moved his team to Kansas City, Missouri.

Jim Schaaf

Dallas Theological Seminary. Dallas Theological Seminary, Dallas, opened in the fall of 1924 with twelve students who proposed to study with Bible teacher Lewis Sperry Chafer. The school was incorporated by the state on February 16, 1925, under the name Evangelical Theological College. Denominationally unaffiliated, the seminary served those of like faith in evangelical Protestantism and welcomed qualified men in sympathy with their doctrine.

In 1926 friends purchased the first portion of the present campus on Swiss Avenue. The following year, memorial gifts provided for the erection of Lidie C. Davidson Hall and D. M. Stearns Memorial Hall. In 1929 George T. Besel of Philadelphia purchased an apartment house, adding to the Swiss Avenue frontage to complete the five-acre campus.

The seminary pioneered in offering a four-year course for graduation leading to the master of theology degree. Incorporating essential theology courses offered in three-year programs, the new curriculum gave additional emphasis to systematic theology, Greek and New Testament exegesis, and English Bible exposition. Since 1935 courses in practical theology, missions, church history, and Christian education have been made available. In addition to the four-year Th.M. program for college graduates, the seminary program included a year of study leading to a Th.M. for those having graduated from a three-year seminary course, as well as a three-year Th.D. for those having completed a Th.M.

The name of the school was changed from Evangelical Theological College to Dallas Theological Seminary and Graduate School of Theology in July, 1936. The next major building, Lewis Sperry Chafer Chapel, was erected during 1952–1953. Mosher Library, suitable for a student body of five hundred and a collection of 125,000 volumes, was added in 1960. The campus plan called for future construction of classroom buildings, a student center, apartments, and dormitories.

In the regular 1972–1973 term, the faculty numbered twenty-eight. Enrollment averaged three hundred students between 1950 and 1965, and included 543 men during the 1972–1973 term. Chafer served as president of the seminary from 1924 to 1952, and was succeeded by John F. Walvoord in 1952.

*Dallas *Times Herald*. The Dallas *Times Herald* had a new president in 1941 when Tim Gooch succeeded Edwin John Kiest upon the latter's death in that year. The *Times Herald* obtained new presses and began constructing a five-story building in 1956. In 1965 work began on a new KRLD building, which was completed by 1967. Effective July 1, 1970, the *Times Herald* was acquired by the Times Mirror Company, publisher of the Los Angeles *Times*. In 1974 Tom Johnson was executive editor of the Dallas *Times Herald*.

Mary A. Aldridge

*Dallas and Waco Railway Company.

*Dallas and Wichita Railway Company.

*Dalrymple, William Cornelius.

*Dalton, Texas.

*Dalton Gang.

*Dalton Mountain.

*Dalworth Park, Texas.

Dam B Reservoir. Dam B Reservoir is in the Neches River Basin in Tyler and Jasper counties, one mile north of Town Bluff on the Neches River. The project is owned by the United States government and is operated by the United States Army Corps of Engineers, Fort Worth District. The Lower Neches Valley Authority, the cooperating state agency, has purchased the right for use of 77,600 acre-feet of conservation storage for municipal, industrial, and irrigation uses. Construction started in March, 1947. The dam and outlet works were completed on April 16, 1951. The capacity at the normal operating level at elevation eighty-three feet above mean sea level is 94,200 acre-feet, and the surface area is 13,700 acres. The capacity at the top of the gates and at uncontrolled spillway crest is 124,700 acre-feet. The drainage area above the dam is 7,573 square miles.

BIBLIOGRAPHY: Texas Water Commission, *Bulletin 6408* (1964).

Seth D. Breeding

*Dameron City, Texas.

*Damon, Texas.

*Damon's Mound.

*Damsite, Texas.

*Dan, Texas.

*Danbury, Texas.

*Danciger, Texas.

*Dancy, John Winfield Scott. John Winfield Scott Dancy was married a second time, on October 25, 1849, to Lucy Ann Nowlin.

Lucie C. Price

Danes in Texas. A few Danish settlers, mostly unknown, came to Texas in the first part of the nineteenth century, including Charles Zanco (or Lanco), who was a lieutenant at the Alamo. The Trube family came to Galveston in 1850, and Hans Peter Nielson Gammel,[qv] noted publisher and editor of Texana, came to Austin about 1878. In 1894, for the first time as a group, members of the Danish Folk Society (*Dansk Folkesamfund*) came to Texas from the north-central part of the United States, establishing Danevang in Wharton County. By 1910 other Danes had arrived either from other parts of the United States or directly from Denmark, some settling in Danevang and others in various parts of the state, especially Williamson, Swisher, and Lee counties. Farming was their principal occupation in Texas, and although many difficulties were encountered, the Danes' general goal of a prosperous agricultural community life was usually realized. *See also* Danevang, Texas.

BIBLIOGRAPHY: Anders Saustrup (trans.), *Danevang Community Anniversary, Danevang, Texas, 1894–1944* (MS., University of Texas Institute of Texan Cultures at San Antonio); Grace Cove Grantham, The Danes in Wharton County (M.A. thesis, Texas A&I University, 1947); Flora Thompson, "The Danes of North Lee County," *Lee County News*, July 28, 1966.

John L. Davis

*Danevang, Texas. Danevang, in Wharton County, was founded in 1894 (not 1904, as stated in Volume I), when the first settlers arrived after a contract between the *Dansk Folkesamfund* of America and the Texas Land and Cattle Company set aside land for the settlement. Members of the group had come from Slesvig (Schleswig), in the southern part of Jutland, and the eastern Danish islands of Fyn and Sjaelland by way of the Scandinavian colonies in the north-central part of the United States. About twenty persons, including families and single men, came with the first group. They used the Danish language (along with dialects); their children, learning English, were also taught the Danish language and culture in Saturday and vacation parochial classes.

In 1895 fifteen to twenty more families arrived, and L. Henningsen became the first pastor of the Grundtvigian Church (Danish Lutheran). Other settlers came in 1896 and 1897, and by 1908 there were sixty-four families in Danevang. In 1897 settlers formed their first cooperative, the Danish Mutual Insurance Company; in 1903 or 1904, after successfully growing cotton, they organized a farm cooperative. A community store, two gins (in Danevang and Midfield), a telephone system (1913), a blacksmith and welding shop, a community house, and a circulating library all were cooperative enterprises. In 1898 Herman P. Hermansen was chosen as the first postmaster and weather observer, positions he held until his death in 1928. In 1934 there were more than one hundred families in the Danevang settlement; in 1971 there were approximately sixty persons there. *See also* Danes in Texas.

BIBLIOGRAPHY: Annie Lee Williams, *A History of Wharton County, 1846–1961* (1964); Thomas P. Christensen, "Danevang, Texas," *Southwestern Historical Quarterly,*

XXXII (1928–1929); El Campo *News*, March 2, 1934; Houston *Press*, April 8, 1938; Waco *News-Tribune*, May 13, 1938.

Dangers, Gottlieb Burchard. Gottlieb Burchard Dangers was born on October 11, 1811, in Langenhagen, Hanover. He emigrated to America with his bride, Mathilde Max, arriving at Galveston in December, 1846. By February, 1847, Dangers founded at Indianola a religious congregation of seven hundred. He reached New Braunfels in the summer of 1847. Discovering that there was no salary for a minister, he bought land on the Guadalupe River and took up farming, an occupation he retained on the side throughout his ministry.

In 1849 Dangers became pastor at the unfinished *Vereinskirche* in Fredericksburg. His request that the octagonal church building be given to the congregation was granted by the German emigration officials. In November, 1849, Dangers began recording statistics of the Evangelical Protestant congregation in Fredericksburg. Diphtheria swept the county in 1861 and took many lives, among them Dangers' only son and three of his daughters. The neatly written record book he kept for twenty years shows that his ministry at Fredericksburg included 1,061 baptisms, 525 confirmations, 187 marriages, and 256 funerals. Dangers died in Fredericksburg on November 12, 1869.

BIBLIOGRAPHY: Rudolph Leopold Biesele, *The History of the German Settlements in Texas, 1831–1861* (1930); Robert Penniger (ed.), *Fest-Ausgabe zum 50-jährigen Jubiläum der Gründung der Stadt Friedrichsburg* (1896); Robert Penniger (ed.), Charles L. Wisseman (trans.), *Fredericksburg, Texas . . . The First Fifty Years* (1971); Gillespie County Historical Society, *Pioneers in God's Hills* (1960); Ella Gold, The History of Education in Gillespie County, Texas (M.A. thesis, University of Texas at Austin, 1945).

Esther L. Mueller

*Daniel, Ferdinand Eugene.

*Daniel, Texas.

*Daniel Baker College. *See also* Howard Payne College.

Daniels, Bebe Virginia. Bebe Virginia Daniels was born in Dallas on January 14, 1901, the daughter of Melville and Phyllis (Griffin) Daniels, both of whom were actors. Miss Daniels was introduced to the public at the age of two months when her mother carried her across the stage in a 1901 comedy entitled *Jane*. At four, she was cast in her father's touring troupe as the Duke of York in Shakespeare's *King Richard III*. By the time she was fourteen she had made a movie with Harold Lloyd, and she and the comedian went on to collaborate for over four years, averaging a movie a week. Her success with Lloyd led to starring roles in *Male and Female* and *Everywoman*, directed by Cecil B. de Mille, and she later appeared opposite such stars as Wallace Reid, Rudolph Valentino, and Edward G. Robinson. Her first talkie, *Rio Rita*, revealed that she could sing as well as act, and it may be her most remembered picture.

In 1930 Miss Daniels married Benjamin Bethel Lyon, an actor professionally known as Ben Lyon, who had achieved success in *Hell's Angels*. They were the parents of a daughter and an adopted son. In the 1930's the family moved to England, where they lived permanently except for a three-year stay in California after World War II. Miss Daniels was known during the war for her broadcasts back home of interviews with U.S. servicemen; she was thought to be the first woman civilian into Normandy after D-Day, interviewing soldiers in the field. The Lyons resumed a radio show they had begun before the war, "Hi Gang," and later starred in a weekly comedy serial for BBC-TV, "Life with the Lyons," which began in 1953. "The Lyons in Paris," another TV comedy, began in 1955. Bebe Daniels died March 16, 1971, in London.

BIBLIOGRAPHY: Edward Wagenknecht, *Movies in the Age of Innocence* (1962); Clarence Winchester (ed.), *World Film Encyclopedia* (1933); *Who's Who In America* (1934); Austin *Statesman*, March 16, 1971.

*Daniels, Joseph.

*Daniels, Williamson.

*Daniels, Texas.

*Daniels Creek.

*Dante, Texas.

*Danville, Texas. (Comal County.)

*Danville, Texas. (Gregg County.)

*Danville, Texas. (Montgomery and Walker counties.)

*Daphne, Texas.

*Daquinatino Indians.

*Daquio Indians.

*Darby, Texas.

*Darco, Texas.

*Darden, Stephen Heard.

*Darden, Texas. (Bowie County.)

Darden, Texas. (Polk County.) Darden, in northeast Polk County, was named for one of the early settlers in the area. The population of approximately seventy-five in 1966 was engaged in farming, ranching, and lumbering.

*Darden Canyon Creek.

*Dark Valley Creek.

*Darling, Texas.

*Darlington, John Washington.

Darnell, Linda. Linda Darnell, actress, was born in Dallas on October 16, 1923, and was christened Monetta Eloyse Darnell by her parents, Calvin Roy and Margaret Pearl Darnell. She appeared in many local theatrical affairs until 1938, when her mother took her to Hollywood for screen tests. An impressed director wrote in a part for her in *Hotel for Women*. Her second film, *Daytime Wife*, with Tyrone Power as the leading man, carried her to cinema stardom, although she returned to Dallas temporarily to receive her high school diploma. After several more films Miss Darnell sought more mature roles, and in 1946 she played the lead in *Forever Amber*. After thirty films in eleven years, as a leading Hollywood actress, Twentieth-Century Fox Studios terminated her contract; however, she continued in the film industry, acting in twenty more films and earning several million dollars. When her parts dwindled in number and importance, she made nightclub appearances and had occasional television roles. Other major films in which she starred were *Brigham Young*, *Mark of Zorro*, *Blood and Sand* (all opposite Tyrone Power), *A Letter to Three Wives*, and *Song of Bernadette*.

Linda Darnell married three times. Her first marriage, to Peverell Marley in 1943, ended in divorce in 1952. The couple had adopted a daughter in 1948. In 1954 she married Philip Liebmann, a New York brewery heir; they were divorced in 1955. Airline pilot Merle Roy Robertson became her third husband in 1957, but the marriage was ended in 1963. She was beginning a road-show engagement when she died in a fire at the home of a friend in a Chicago suburb, Glenview, Illinois, on April 10, 1965.

BIBLIOGRAPHY: Dallas *Morning News*, April 11, 1965; Kirtley Baskette, "The Needless Tragedy of Linda Darnell," *Good Housekeeping* (September, 1965).

Karen Collins

*Darnell, Nicholas Henry.

*Darrouzett, Texas.

*Darrs Creek.

*Darst Creek.

*Darwin, Texas.

Das Wochenblatt. See Trenckmann, William Andreas.

*Dashiell, Jeremiah Yellott.

*Dashiell, L. Travis.

Datana Indians. The Datana Indians are known from a 1691 Spanish missionary report which identifies them as a tribe living some eighty leagues southwest of the Hasinai Indians of eastern Texas. The affiliations of the Datana remain unknown.

BIBLIOGRAPHY: J. R. Swanton, *Source Material on the History and Ethnology of the Caddo Indians* (1942).

T. N. Campbell

*Datcho Indians.

*Datura, Texas.

*Daugherty, Jacamiah Seaman.

*Daugherty, James M.

*Daugherty, Texas.

Daughters of the American Colonists, Texas Society of. The Texas Society, Daughters of the American Colonists, was organized in Washington, D.C., in 1931. Membership in June, 1966, totaled 425 in ten chapters located in various Texas cities. The National Society, Daughters of the American Colonists, was organized in Washington, D.C., in April, 1921, and in 1966 had over ten thousand members in fifty states and the District of Columbia. According to its bylaws, "The object of this society shall be patriotic, historical and educational; to make research as to the history and deeds of the American colonists and to record and publish the same; to commemorate deeds of colonial interest; to inculcate and foster love of America and its institutions by all its residents; to obey its laws and venerate its flag—the emblem of its power and civic righteousness."

Josephine C. Kirby

*Daughters of the American Revolution, Texas Society of.

*Daughters of the Confederacy. See United Daughters of the Confederacy, Texas Division of.

*Daughters of the Republic of Texas. The Daughters of the Republic of Texas had 2,365 members in fifty-one chapters in May, 1966, an increase of 100 percent since 1947. A change in organization occurred when the state was divided into nine geographical districts composed of four to seven chapters each. Representatives, one from each district, elected by the entire membership replaced the former nine members-at-large on the board of management.

Custodianship of the Alamo continued to be the most important activity. Constant work was required to maintain the Alamo complex. Restoration of the convent walls, also called the Long Barracks, made possible by a donation from the Moody Foundation, was completed in the 1960's. A museum and conference room are located there. The DRT Library, a stone building added to Alamo Hall on the west side, was completed in 1950 by means of a gift from Mrs. John King Beretta in memory of her late husband. This small but important repository of books and documents pertaining to Texas, particularly of colonial and pre-colonial days and of the era of the Republic, is used by researchers in the field of history and genealogy. Containing many Spanish documents and manuscripts, it is especially noted for the William E. Howard Collection and a fine group of paintings by Theodore Gentilz.[qv]

On November 2, 1949, the state of Texas, by legislative act, gave to the Daughters the custodianship of the house in Austin which had been built and occupied by Alphonse de Saligny,[qv] chargé d'affaires of the Kingdom of France to the Republic of Texas. The property, known as the French Legation,[qv] has been carefully restored and furnished, and since April, 1956, has been open to the public. Excavation and research revealed the location and proportions of the old outdoor kitchen, which was rebuilt and furnished by Mr. and Mrs. Jack Beretta of San Antonio.

The Ezekiel W. Cullen [qv] chapter of San Augustine was given Cullen House, the former home of the man for whom the chapter was named, by his grandson, the late Hugh Roy Cullen [qv] of Houston. The chapter furnished the house with period furniture and maintains it as a meeting place and social center for the town. The S. Seymour Thomas [qv] Memorial Room contains a collection of paintings and memorabilia of the late artist, a native of San Augustine. The house is open to visitors from June through August.

In 1962 the Daughters published *Founders and Patriots of the Republic of Texas*, which contains the lineage of all members and is considered a significant addition to genealogical material of Texas.

The society owns the copyrights of several books and sells *Dr. James Harper Starr, Financier of the Republic of Texas*, by John N. Cravens, for the benefit of its historical publication fund.

Through the influence of the Daughters, in 1954 Governor Allan Shivers designated the first week in September as Texian Navy Week and September 2 as Texian Navy Day, which has become one of Texas' honor days, celebrated each year with appropriate ceremonies at Freeport and Old Velasco.

Much of the work of the DRT was performed in cooperation with the Texas State Historical Survey Committee (now the Texas Historical Commission qv) with many Daughters serving on the committees of their local counties. Through this agency they promote the recording of Texas history, the marking of significant sites, and the preservation and restoration of historic remnants, all of which have been the objectives of the DRT since its founding in 1891.

Rosa Tod Hamner

Davenport, Harbert. Harbert Davenport was born in Eastland, Texas, on October 19, 1882, the son of O. H. and Elizabeth (Merril) Davenport. In 1904 he married Elizabeth Pettit, and they had two sons. After living in Rusk for two years, they resided in Austin from 1906 to 1908, when Davenport received an LL.B. from the University of Texas. He practiced law in Anahuac until 1912, when he established permanent residence in Brownsville, becoming a law associate of Judge James B. Wells, Jr.qv During World War I he became a second lieutenant in the air corps.

Davenport was recognized as an authority on southwestern land and water law, and Spanish and Mexican law as it applied to Texas. Concerned with procuring needed water legislation for the Valley area, Davenport wrote "The Texas Law on Flowing Waters as Applied to Irrigation from the Lower Rio Grande." One of his important legal cases involved the disputed title to Padre Island. In 1944 the Supreme Court of Texas decided the case in favor of the descendants of Padre Nicolás Balli,qv who had received the original land grant from the Spanish government in 1800. Davenport was also recognized as a historian. Particularly interested in early Spanish expeditions, personnel of the Goliad campaign,qv and the history of the lower Rio Grande area, Davenport contributed several articles to the *Southwestern Historical Quarterly*.qv From 1922 to 1955 he was a member of the executive council of the Texas State Historical Association,qv and from 1939 to 1942 he was president of the association. He also served as a member of the Brownsville school board from 1924 to 1932, and contributed actively to the American Legion and other civic organizations. He died on February 23, 1957, and was buried in Buena Vista Cemetery in Brownsville.

BIBLIOGRAPHY: Brownsville *Herald*, February 24, 25, 1957.

Wortham Davenport
Harbert Davenport, Jr.

*Davenport, John G.

*Davenport, Peter Samuel.

*Davenport, Texas. (Anderson County.)

*Davenport, Texas. (Red River County.)

*Davenport Branch.

*Davenport Hill.

*Davidson, Asbury Bascom.** Asbury Bascom Davidson, son of William and Cathrina (McBank) Davidson, was born on November 13, 1855, in Lincoln County, Tennessee; he came to Texas with his parents sometime prior to 1870, settling in Williamson County. Davidson was educated during the 1870's at Southwestern University in Georgetown, later moving to Gonzales to study in a law office there. After being admitted to the Bar, he practiced for a time in Gonzales before moving to Cuero in the early 1880's, where he established his home and a law firm. There in the late 1880's, Davidson was elected district attorney for the Twenty-fourth Judicial District; he held that office for eight years, until he was elected state senator, serving for three terms in that capacity.

Davidson was elected lieutenant governor of Texas for three consecutive terms, serving from 1906 to 1912, one of the few men to serve in that office for that many successive terms. He also served as a member of the board of directors of the Agricultural and Mechanical College of Texas (now Texas A&M University). He was interested in the development of Texas inland waterways and was active in the Interstate Inland Waterway League of Louisiana and Texas after it was organized in 1905, serving on its Texas executive committee. Davidson was married to Minnie McClanahan in March, 1890. He died on February 4, 1920, and was buried in Hillside Cemetery in Cuero.

BIBLIOGRAPHY: *Proceedings of the Texas Bar Association* (1921); Biographical File, Barker Texas History Center, University of Texas at Austin.

*Davidson, Charles E.

*Davidson, James.

*Davidson, Robert Vance.

*Davidson, Samuel.

Davidson, Thomas Whitfield. Thomas Whitfield Davidson was born in Harrison County on September 23, 1876, the son of John Ransom and Sarah Josephine (Daniels) Davidson. After attending East Texas Normal College (now East Texas State University qv) in Commerce, teaching school in Harrison County, and attending summer sessions at Columbia University and the University of Chicago, Davidson was admitted to the Texas Bar in 1903 and began his practice in Marshall, where he was city attorney from 1907 to 1913. He was a delegate to the Democratic national convention which nominated Woodrow Wilson for president in 1912, when the delegates from Texas became known as the "Immortal 40." Elected to the Texas Senate in 1920, Davidson ran successfully for lieutenant governor in 1922, but was defeated in the race for governor in 1924, when Miriam A. Ferguson qv won the Democratic primary. .

Davidson returned to Dallas in 1927 to practice law, and he was president of the Texas Bar Association in that year. A leader of the "Roosevelt for President" movement in Texas in 1931, he helped bring about the nomination of Franklin D. Roosevelt in 1932. In 1936 Roosevelt appointed Davidson U.S. district judge for the Northern District of Texas. On April 12, 1936, he married Mrs. Constance Key Wandel; after her death in 1948 he married Bula Rose Davidson, who died in 1967. When Davidson retired from the bench in 1965 at the age of eighty-nine he was the oldest federal judge in the nation. One of his most famous cases was tried in New York in 1941: the notorious Trans Ocean News Agency trial, involving German propaganda activities in the United States.

T. Whitfield Davidson was a dedicated Episcopalian. He published a collection of lessons he used in his Sunday school classes; he also wrote *Wisdom of George Washington* (1964) and *Stealing Stick: The Folklore of Pioneer East Texas*, edited by Hobart Key, Jr. (1969). He died in Dallas on January 26, 1974, and was buried in a chapel he had built in memory of his mother at Diana, Upshur County.

BIBLIOGRAPHY: Biographical File, Barker Texas History Center, University of Texas at Austin.

*Davidson, William Francis H.

*Davidson, William Lewis. Davidson was appointed a member of the Court of Appeals (not the Court of Civil Appeals, as stated in Volume I) in early 1891. By amendment to the constitution adopted in August, 1891, and proclaimed in September, 1891, the Court of Appeals was abolished and the Court of Criminal Appeals was created. Davidson continued as a judge of the Court of Criminal Appeals until his death.

*Davidson Canyon Creek.

*Davidson Creek.

✝Davic, W. R.

*Davilla, Texas.

*Davilla Institute.

*Davis, Andrew.

Davis, Clare Ogden. Clare Ogden Davis, newspaperwoman and author, was born on November 26, 1892, in Kimball's Bend, Texas, the daughter of Charles Vance and Mary (Lawrence) Ogden. She entered Baylor College at Belton (now Mary Hardin-Baylor College) in 1913 and graduated from there, afterwards teaching history in Bonham and Cleburne high schools. Her first newspaper job was as a reporter in the Fort Worth office of the Dallas *Morning News*.qv There she was possibly the first Texas woman to cover police assignments. In Dallas in 1920 she married John Burton Davis,qv with whom she later collaborated on seven novels under the pen name of Lawrence Saunders. They had no children. During the early 1920's Mrs. Davis became manager of the Houston bureau of several Texas newspapers. From 1923 to 1925 she was in Europe, reporting on various international events; while there she met Joseph Conrad and obtained the last interview granted by the author before his death. Returning to Texas, she became Governor Miriam A. Ferguson's qv press secretary for one year, before moving in 1926 to New York City, where she wrote a column on child psychology and reported on such important events as the Lindbergh baby kidnapping. She was also a public relations counselor and was press agent for a national seed company for twenty-five years. It was probably during this time that she collaborated with her husband on the novels and took graduate studies in horticulture and landscape architecture at Columbia University.

Mrs. Davis returned to Texas in 1951 and worked as garden editor for the Austin *American-Statesman*,qv contributing a column, "In My Texas Garden." She was instrumental in starting the Garden Center in Zilker Park in Austin, and part of the park was named for her. She retired in 1965 when she suffered a stroke which left her paralyzed, and she died on May 17, 1970.

BIBLIOGRAPHY: Biographical File, Barker Texas History Center, University of Texas at Austin.

*Davis, Daniel.

Davis, Edgar B. Edgar B. Davis, philanthropist and oilman, was born February 2, 1873, in Brockton, Massachusetts. With only a high school education, Davis began making his first million dollars in the shoe business in Massachusetts about 1905, and later he made another fortune, about $3 million, as an early investor in foreign rubber plantations. After thirteen years he sold his holdings and gave much of the proceeds away to friends and associates. Davis came to Luling, Texas, about 1921 to investigate oil leases which he had bought from his brother. A deeply religious man, Davis believed that he was directed by God to come to Texas and to deliver Luling and Caldwell County from the oppressive one-crop economy which dominated the area. To do this he believed he would find oil, although geologists claimed there was none. On March 18, 1921, Davis formed the United North and South Oil Company. The first six wells were dry and Davis' company was heavily in debt, but the seventh, Rafael Rios No. 1, gushed in on August 9, 1922. This well opened up a field twelve miles long and two miles wide, located near Stairtown. By 1924 the field was producing 57,000 barrels of oil daily (*see* Luling Oil Field). On June 11, 1926, Davis sold the field for what may have been the biggest oil deal to that time, $12 million (one-half in cash), and to celebrate gave a free barbecue for friends, associates, and employees, to whom he gave from 50 to 100 percent of their total salaries to that date as bonuses. In addition, he gave the citizens of Luling a golf course, a Negro athletic clubhouse, other facilities, and endowments for each. He also established the Luling Foundation qv for the teaching of improved agricultural methods. In all, Davis donated at least $5 million to charity, as well as keeping *The Ladder*, a play written by his friend, James Francis Davis,qv running on Broadway for two years.

Davis discovered two more fields in the area, Buckeye and Darst Creek, and again gave most of the cash away when they were sold. With the depression of the 1930's Davis ran into financial problems again; by 1935 the development company was declared insolvent. He worked for twelve years paying off most of his indebtedness, always insisting that more oil could be found. Davis died in Galveston on October 14, 1951, and was buried in Luling at the site of one of his former homes. He never married. Though deeply religious, he belonged to no church, having attended each church in Luling regularly. He is credited with bringing to Luling and Caldwell County a diversified economy and with having a significant impact on farming in the area through the Luling Foundation farm.

BIBLIOGRAPHY: Biographical File, Barker Texas History Center, University of Texas at Austin.

*Davis, Edmund Jackson.

*Davis, George Washington.

*Davis, James. James Davis was born near Richmond, Virginia, on July 17, 1790 (not 1792, as stated in Volume I). He possibly attended West Point, but his name does not appear on any class list of graduates; he served in the War of 1812 and participated in the battle of New Orleans under Andrew Jackson. In 1834 (not 1842, as stated in Volume I) he came to Texas and settled at Grand Cane, Liberty County, where he developed a large plantation. Later he moved to Coldspring in present San Jacinto County, then a part of Liberty County. During the Texas Revolution, he and his squadron attempted to join Houston's army at San Jacinto, found Vince's Bridge qv destroyed, and captured the escaping Mexicans. He attended the Convention of 1845 qv (but not the Constitutional Convention of 1866,qv as stated in Volume I). He died on February 10, 1859 (not 1877, as stated in Volume I); he was buried in the Baptist cemetery at Coldspring. He was married to Anne Eliza Hill of Virginia. [All information furnished in Volume I which postdates 1859 must be attributed to another James Davis, a newspaperman of whom little is known. Ed.]

Mrs. T. A. Armstrong

Davis, James Francis. James Francis (J. Frank) Davis, author and playwright, was born on December 20, 1870, in New Bedford, Massachusetts, the son of James and Ann E. (Francis) Davis. He was educated at the public schools of New Bedford and Brockton, Massachusetts. Davis was married to Clara Franklin Draper on October 7, 1896. From 1886 to 1904 he worked as a newspaperman, salesman, and publicity man. In 1904 Davis began working for the Boston *American* as dramatic editor and special writer. In 1907 he became managing editor of the Boston *Tribune*; by 1908 he was a special political writer for the Boston *Herald*, then city editor of the Boston *Traveler* from 1908 to 1909, and associate editor of that paper in 1910, when, because of an injury, he retired to San Antonio,

Texas. From 1911 to 1914 Davis did advertising and publicity work in San Antonio, and he began writing fiction about 1915. Davis published several books and plays; *Gold in the Hills* (1930) was one of his better known plays. He wrote short stories and serials for many of the popular magazines of the day, such as *Collier's*, *Saturday Evening Post*, *Liberty*, *Scribner's*, *American*, and others. The setting for many of his stories was Texas and San Antonio, and he was made an honorary Texas Ranger qv for his vivid stories of early western life. In 1935 Davis became the state supervisor of the Texas Writers' Project of the Works Progress Administration (later called the Work Projects Administration qv), which published *Texas: A Guide to the Lone Star State* (1940) and guidebooks of San Antonio, Corpus Christi, Beaumont, Port Arthur, and Houston, all under Davis' direction. He died on April 6, 1942, in San Antonio and was buried in Mission Burial Park in that city.

BIBLIOGRAPHY: *Texian Who's Who* (1937); *Who Was Who In America* (1943); San Antonio *Express*, April 7, 1942.

*Davis, James Harvey.

*Davis, Jefferson.

Davis, John Burton. John Burton Davis, a newspaperman, war correspondent, and writer, was born in Perryville, Missouri, on October 14, 1893, the son of John Brooks and Laurette (Saunders) Davis. He attended high school in Brownsville, Texas, and Western Military Academy near St. Louis. In 1913 he entered the school of journalism at the University of Missouri, but withdrew in 1914 to live near the Texas-Mexican border. In 1915 he took his first newspaper job, with the Brownsville *Daily Herald*, covering such events as the Mexican Revolution and the activities of Francisco (Pancho) Villa;qv he acted as interpreter for General John J. (Black Jack) Pershing's punitive forces in their efforts to capture Villa. From 1919 to 1925 Davis worked on newspapers in Houston, San Antonio, Fort Worth, and Dallas. He was drama editor for the New York *Morning Telegraph* in 1925–1926; he also served as general press agent for Gene Buck in 1927 and associate agent for Florenz Ziegfeld in 1928–1929.

In World War I Davis served with the American forces in France and Germany. In World War II he was assigned by the Treasury Department to create publicity for war bonds, and he remained with the department for twenty years, retiring in 1962 to return to Austin.

Under the pen name of Lawrence Saunders, he collaborated with his wife, Clare Ogden Davis qv (whom he married in 1920), to write seven novels, most of which were serialized in popular magazines such as *Liberty*, *Collier's*, *Ladies' Home Journal*, and *Saturday Evening Post* and later published as books. Two of these, *Snowed Under* and *Lady Godiva*, were filmed, and one was produced as a drama. Davis died in Austin on April 15, 1970.

BIBLIOGRAPHY: Biographical File, Barker Texas History Center, University of Texas at Austin.

*Davis, Mollie Evelyn Moore.

Davis, Nathaniel Hart. Nathaniel Hart Davis, third son of Nathaniel Bowe and Martha D. Davis, was born in Fayette County, Kentucky, on November 6, 1815. In 1817 his family moved to Alabama, where he received his early education. He attended Transylvania University and later taught at Marion Military Academy. He received a license to practice law in Alabama in 1837. In 1840 he moved to Texas, arriving in Montgomery, Montgomery County, in April of that year. He served as county attorney, commissioner, and chief justice of Montgomery County, and as judge of the Thirteenth Judicial District from 1867 to 1870. Davis was a member of the Somervell Expedition,qv serving under Colonel Joseph L. Bennett,qv in whose home he had lived during his first years in Texas.

In 1851 Davis married Sarah Elizabeth White, a native of South Carolina, and they had seven children. He died on October 8, 1893, and was buried in Montgomery. Still standing in Montgomery in 1968 were the Davis law office and the early Davis home, built in 1845 and 1851, respectively. Both were recorded Texas historic landmarks.

BIBLIOGRAPHY: N. H. Davis Papers (MS., Archives, University of Texas at Austin Library); Houston *Post*, October 10, 1893.

Margaret Davis Cameron

Davis, Nicholas A. Nicholas A. Davis was born on August 8, 1824, near Huntsville, Alabama. Son of Rhoda and Nathaniel Davis, he came from a reputable and public-minded farm family of moderate means. Ordained a Cumberland Presbyterian minister, Davis married Nancy Isabella Worthington. Two daughters were born of this marriage before they migrated to Texas in November, 1857. Mrs. Davis died before he departed for Virginia in 1861 to serve as chaplain of the 4th Texas Infantry Regiment of Hood's Texas Brigade.qv Personable and aggressive, Davis received the acclaim of these soldiers, for whom he sought proper clothing and hospital care. His *Campaign from Texas to Maryland* (Richmond and Houston, 1863), written because he believed that the Texans had received insufficient praise, brought him wider recognition.

Returning to Texas on February 7, 1865, he married Mrs. Eliza E. Coley Radford, by whom he had three children. Plantations in East Texas acquired through this marriage, in addition to his own ranch near Bastrop, demanded much of Davis' time. Even so, the family moved about as he continued to preach in Milam, Jacksonville, Larissa, Rusk, and nearby communities. He established the first commercial fruit orchard at Jacksonville, founded several churches, served on the board of trustees of Trinity University, sought unity among Texas Cumberland Presbyterians who had been divided among three synods, became for a time secretary of the Southeast Texas Agriculture Society and president of the Rusk Transportation Company, and gave counsel to younger ministers and businessmen. Described by contemporaries as courageous and progressive, the versatile Davis died in San Antonio on November 19, 1894, while on a visit to his daughter.

BIBLIOGRAPHY: Donald E. Everett (ed.), *Chaplain Davis and Hood's Texas Brigade* (1962).

Donald E. Everett

Davis, Samuel Boyer. Samuel Boyer Davis was born in 1827 in Louisiana; he attended the United States Military Academy for about six months. He served on the Texas border during the early part of the Mexican War and later saw service as an officer of the 14th Infantry, Colonel P. O. Hébert,qv commanding. He was brevetted first lieutenant at Churubusco, suffered a wound at Molino del Rey, and was in action at Chapultepec and Mexico City. After the war, Davis resided in Texas until the Civil War. In mid-1861 Davis organized seven companies from Harris, Caldwell, Galveston, Leon, Montgomery, Washington, Liberty, and Fort Bend counties, formed them into Davis' Mounted Battalion, and became major of that unit. Davis also was assistant adjutant general at General P. O. Hébert's headquarters for the District of Texas. On December 7, 1861, Major Xavier B. de Bray qv assumed command of the mounted battalion when Davis assumed full-time administrative functions under Hébert. In February, 1862, three more companies from Montgomery, Grimes, and Harris counties were added to de Bray's command, resulting in its reorganization as the 26th Texas Cavalry. When Hébert appointed Davis colonel of the new unit, members of the regiment protested and claimed the right to elect their own officers. Davis then resigned from the unit and de Bray was elected regimental commander.

Davis returned to his adjutant's position at district headquarters, where he served for the duration of the conflict. As assistant adjutant general, his rank varied from captain to colonel. His final act in the Civil War was the signing of his parole on June 23, 1865, as Captain, Acting Assistant Adjutant General, Provisional Army Confederate States, Staff, Brigadier General P. O. Hébert.

Davis was first married to Mary Minerva Monk Clark, by whom he had two sons; his wife and children died in 1854 and 1855 during a yellow fever epidemic. On March 28, 1867, he married Rhoda Catherine Milby in Galveston; they had five daughters and three sons. Following this marriage he lived in Houston and Galveston; he died in 1885 while visiting in New Orleans.

BIBLIOGRAPHY: Service Record of Samuel Boyer Davis, War Department, Adjutant General's Office, Confederate Records (MS., National Archives, Washington, D. C.).

Allan C. Ashcraft

*Davis, Samuel S.

*Davis, Thomas.

*Davis, William Kinchen.

*Davis, Texas.

*Davis County.

*Davis Creek.

*Davis Guards.

*Davis Mountains.

*Davisville, Texas.

*Davy, Texas.

*Davy Crockett National Forest. *See* National Forests in Texas.

*Dawn, Texas.

Dawson, Joseph Martin. Joseph Martin Dawson, an influential and noted Baptist leader in Texas, was born in Maypearl, Ellis County, on June 21, 1879. He was the son of Martin Judy and Laura (Underwood) Dawson. Educated at Baylor University, from which he took both the A.B. (1904) and D.D. (1916) degrees, Dawson was a founder and editor of both the Baylor *Lariat* and *The Round Up*. He had been a licensed minister of the Baptist church since 1899, and from 1907 to 1908 was editor of the *Baptist Standard*. After serving pastorates in Lampasas, Hillsboro, and Temple, Dawson went to the First Baptist Church in Waco, where he remained for over thirty-one years. He married Willie Evelyn Turner on June 3, 1908; they were the parents of five children.

A firm believer in religious liberty, Dawson represented U.S. Baptists at the founding of the United Nations in San Francisco, where in 1945 he carried petitions calling for a declaration of religious liberty to be incorporated in the U.N. Charter. He was also an opponent of censorship; he shocked many observers when he testified before a state House committee hearing (concerning the adoption of textbooks and loyalty oaths in 1962) that "while I have spent most of my life trying to persuade people to be Christians, I would not raise a featherweight to compel them to be Christians." He was the first executive director of the Baptist Joint Committee on Public Affairs and one of the founders of Americans United for Separation of Church and State.

Joseph Dawson was the author of thousands of articles and news stories during his long career, along with many books, among them *The Spiritual Conquest of the Southwest* (1927), *A Century with Texas Baptists* (1947), *America's Way in Church, State and Society* (1954), his autobiography, *A Thousand Months To Remember* (1964), and *Jose Antonio Navarro* (1969). He died July 6, 1973, in Corsicana, and was buried in Oakwood Cemetery in Waco.

BIBLIOGRAPHY: Biographical File, Barker Texas History Center, University of Texas at Austin.

*Dawson, Nicholas Mosby.

*Dawson, Texas.

*Dawson County. Dawson County, at the eastern edge of the Cap Rock, is a productive agricultural and mineral county. Over 150 million barrels of oil were produced from 1937 through 1972. Natural gas liquids, gas, and stone are also commercially exploited. Sales from crops raised in the county amounted to thirty-five million dollars annually in the early 1970's. The county's farms, with extensive irrigation, yielded cotton in the amount of 117,363 running bales ginned in the 1971–1972 season and 213,496 running bales ginned in the 1972–1973 season. The county had twenty-six active gins in 1973. In addition, dairy-ing, grain sorghums, poultry, and beef cattle are important. An Old Settlers' Reunion in May and a fair in September are tourist attractions. The county population, 19,185 in 1960, was 16,604 in 1970.

*Dawson County (Defunct).

*Dawson Creek.

*Dawson Massacre.

*Dawson-Watson, Dawson.

*Day, James Monroe.

*Day, William H.

*Day, Texas. (Bowie County.)

*Day, Texas. (Washington County.)

*Day Land and Cattle Company.

*Daycao River.

*Dayton, Texas. Dayton, in Liberty County, almost doubled its population in the ten years following the 1950 census, with a reported figure of 3,367 in 1960. In 1970 the population was 3,804, and seventy-one businesses were reported.

*Dayton-Goose Creek Railroad Company.

*Dayton's Road.

*Dead Horse Creek.

*Dead Man's Canyon.

*Dead Man's Creek.

*Dead Man's Mountain.

*Dead Nigger Creek.

*Deadhorse Creek.

*Deadman Creek.

*Deadose Indians. The Deadose (Agdoza, Doxsa, Igodosa, Jacdoas, Judosa, Yacdossa) Indians are known to have existed only during the eighteenth century. It is now clear that they were closely related to the Bidai and spoke an Atakapan language. In the early eighteenth century they lived between the junction of the Angelina and Neches rivers and the upper end of Galveston Bay. Some time after 1720 the Deadose moved westward to an area lying between the Brazos and Trinity rivers in the vicinity of present Leon, Madison, and Robertson counties. Between 1749 and 1751 the Deadose, along with other Atakapan-speaking groups (Akokisa, Bidai, and Patiri), were represented at the short-lived San Ildefonso Mission qv near present Rockdale in Milam County. A few Deadose (Yacdossa) entered San Antonio de Valero Mission qv shortly afterward. In the second half of the eighteenth century the Deadose were at times closely associated with certain Tonkawan groups (Ervipiame, Mayeye, and Yojuane), and it was once thought that their language might have been Tonkawan. This view was abandoned because other evidence clearly indicated an Atakapan linguistic affiliation. The Deadose suffered heavily from European-introduced diseases, especially measles and smallpox, and they eventually lost their ethnic identity in the latter part of the eighteenth century. Remnants of the Deadose probably joined the Bidai, who survived into the nineteenth century, although some may have been absorbed by the Tonkawa.

J. R. Swanton erred in identifying the Yacdossa of Mission San Antonio de Valero as Coahuiltecans.

BIBLIOGRAPHY: H. E. Bolton (ed.), *Athanase de Mézières and the Louisiana-Texas Frontier* (1914) and *Texas in the Middle Eighteenth Century* (1915); P. P. Forrestal, "The Solis Diary of 1767," *Preliminary Studies of the Texas Catholic Historical Society*, I (1930); A. F. Sjoberg, "The Bidai Indians of Southeastern Texas," *Southwestern Journal of Anthropology*, 7 (1951); J. R. Swanton, *Linguistic Material from the Tribes of Southern Texas and Northeastern Mexico* (1940) and *The Indians of the Southeastern United States* (1946).

T. N. Campbell

*Deadwood, Texas.

*Deaf, Dumb, and Blind Institute for Colored Youth. *See* Texas Blind, Deaf, and Orphans School.

Deaf, State Commission for the. *See* State Commission for the Deaf.

*Deaf and Dumb Institute. *See* Texas School for the Deaf.

*Deaf Smith County. Deaf Smith County, one of Texas' leading agricultural counties, ranked fourth in the state in number of acres in wheat, tenth in farm income, and first in Irish potato production in 1960. In addition, grain sorghums, cotton, sugar beets, vegetables, and barley were cultivated in marketable quantities on the county's 377,-000 irrigated acres in 1964. Beef and dairy cattle and swine contributed to the county's $36,802,285 farm income in 1964. By 1970 the average annual farm income was over $86,000,000. Many of the businesses in the county seat of Hereford are devoted to supplying the farms or processing their products. The population was 13,187 in 1960 and 18,999 in 1970.

*Deaguane Indians. *See also* Doguene Indians.

*Deal, Texas.

Dealey, Edward Musgrove. Edward Musgrove (Ted) Dealey, a noted and often controversial publisher, was born on October 5, 1892, in Dallas, Texas, the son of Olivia (Allen) and George Bannerman Dealey.qv Dealey attended the Dallas public schools and Terrill School for Boys. He was graduated with a B.A. degree from the University of Texas in 1913 and received an M.A. degree from Harvard University in 1914. He continued at Harvard in the school of business until 1915, when he returned to Dallas as secretary to Cesar Maurice Lombardi,qv president of the A. H. Belo Corporation (publisher of the Dallas *Morning News*, Galveston *Daily News*, and the *Texas Almanac* qqv). That same year he began work as a reporter on the Dallas *Morning News*; from 1920 to 1924 he served as staff correspondent and from 1924 to 1928 edited a Sunday magazine supplement which was soon a popular feature, earning special recognition for its authentic material on Texas history and introducing the early work of such well-known Texans as J. Frank Dobie and Walter Prescott Webb.qqv

Dealey became a member of the board of directors of the A. H. Belo Corporation in 1926; in 1928 he joined the executive staff as assistant to the publisher. Dealey was named vice-president in

1932 and president in 1940. He was chairman of the board in 1960, a position from which he resigned in 1968 to become publisher emeritus. Dealey served on various other boards, such as the Texas Research Foundation,qv the Texas Newspaper Publishers Association, the Southern Newspaper Publishers Association, and the American Newspaper Publishers Association. He was also on the board of directors of Southland Paper Mills, Inc. Prominent in civil affairs, Dealey was a charter member of the Dallas Citizen's Council; he was also a member of the Dallas Historical Society qv and the Dallas Zoological Society. Among Dealey's publications were *Diaper Days of Dallas* (1966), *Sunset in the East* (1945), and several short stories. Dealey led fights against the Ku Klux Klan qv in the 1920's and against corruption at the Dallas courthouse in the 1940's. He received national attention for his verbal attack on the administration of President John F. Kennedy at a White House luncheon in 1961.

A Presbyterian, Dealey married Clara Mac-Donald on March 1, 1916; they had three children. On June 29, 1951, he was married a second time, to Mrs. Trudie Kelley. Dealey died at his home in Dallas on November 26, 1969, and was buried in the Dealey family plot in Grove Hill Memorial Park.

BIBLIOGRAPHY: *Who's Who In America* (1960); *Texas Almanac* (1969); Biographical File, Barker Texas History Center, University of Texas at Austin; Dallas *Morning News*, November 27, 1969, January 28, 1970; Austin *American-Statesman*, November 27, 1969.

*Dealey, George Bannerman.

*Dealey, James Quayle.

*Dean, John M.

*Dean, John M.

Dean, Texas. (Clay County.) Dean, in northwestern Clay County, first called Dean Dale, was named for C. C. Dean, a prominent rancher and early settler in the area. In 1904, with the coming of the railroad and mail delivery, the name was changed to Dean. At that time the town had a gin, a grain elevator, a section house, a store, a doctor's office, and a church. The town site was selected because of its facilities for shipping cattle, wheat, and cotton, the major sources of income. In 1963 Dean organized a rural fire district and purchased a fire truck; in 1966 it completed facilities for supplying the community with ample water. Still a ranching area, Dean receives some income from dairying.

*Dean, Texas. (Leon County.)

*Dean Dale, Texas. *See also* Dean, Texas. (Clay County.)

*Dean Law. *See* Prohibition Movement.

*Deanville, Texas.

*Dearborn, Texas.

*Deaver, Texas.

*De Bellisle, François Simars.

*DeBerry, A. W.

*DeBerry, Texas.

*De Bray, Xavier Blanchard.

*Debt of the Republic of Texas.

*Decatur, Texas. Decatur, seat of Wise County, completed a new water system and a city park in 1966. The city reported 115 businesses, fourteen churches, a hospital, a bank, and a newspaper in 1967. In 1965 the Decatur Baptist College moved to the Oak Cliff section of Dallas to form the nucleus of Dallas Baptist College. The types of business concerns most directly influencing the local economy were connected with agriculture, petroleum, meat processing, clothing, and glassware manufacture. The 1960 population was 3,563; the 1970 population was 3,240.

*Decatur Baptist College. See also Dallas Baptist College.

*Decker, Texas. (Nolan County.)

*Decker, Texas. (Travis County.)

*Decker Creek.

*Declaration of Independence.

*Declaration of November 7, 1835.

*De Cordova, Jacob.

*De Cordova, Phineas.

*De Cordova Bend.

*Decrow, Daniel.

*Decubadao Indians.

*Dee Mountain.

*Deep Creek.

*Deep Creek, Texas.

*Deep Draw.

*Deep Hole Creek.

*Deep Lake, Texas.

*Deer Creek.

*Deer Creek, Texas.

*Deer Park, Texas. Deer Park, an industrial section of eastern Harris County, was incorporated in 1948. Governed by the city manager-council system, the community endorsed a plan to expand educational opportunities in 1961 and municipal recreational facilities in 1964. Deer Park, in conjunction with surrounding communities, has supported San Jacinto Junior College since its opening in 1961. Industries include the manufacture of plastics, paper products, carbon, concrete products, lubricants, chemicals, petroleum products, and alkali materials. In 1970 the town reported eighty-six businesses. The city's population during the 1950's increased sixfold, from 736 in 1950 to 4,865 in 1960; the 1970 population was 12,773, a 162.5 percent increase. See also Houston Standard Metropolitan Statistical Area.

*Deerton, Texas.

*De Farnese, Count Charles.

*Defense Guard. See Texas State Guard.

DeFiniels, Nicolás. Nicolás deFiniels was born in France about 1767. He came to America with the French expeditionary force and served as a captain of engineers during the American Revolution. In 1797, armed with a passport from the Spanish minister to the United States, he went from Philadelphia to St. Louis to help with fortifications of upper Louisiana during the period when Spain feared a British attack from Canada. Despite jurisdictional disputes with the Flemish engineer, Luis de Vandembenden, and Colonel Carlos Howard, deFiniels drew several plans of the Missouri River and environs. Ordered to leave Louisiana and the Spanish service in 1798 by the minister of war in Spain, deFiniels went to New Orleans, where his patron, Governor-general Manuel Gayoso de Lemos,qv continued to employ him as an engineer and draftsman in drawing plans of Baton Rouge and New Orleans. A royal order of June 19, 1799, reinstated deFiniels in the service. He was a valuable member of the staff of Governor-general the Marqués de Casa-Calvo.qv In addition to his skill in cartography, deFiniels was an inventor of surveying instruments. Casa-Calvo chose him as chief surveyor of the 1805 expedition to western Louisiana and Texas. Leaving New Orleans in October, the party ascended by canoe up the Bayou de la Fourche de Chetimachas and descended the Atchafalaya River toward Texas. They charted the Gulf Coast and in particular the Mermentau, Calcasieu, Sabine, and Trinity rivers. The expedition employed the galiot Vigilante to explore San Bernardo Bay, from which point a land expedition trekked overland to Atascosito near the Trinity River, and thence to San Antonio and Nacogdoches. After three weeks of examining the mission records to determine the location of the mission and presidio of San Miguel de los Adaes,qv the expedition examined the region toward Arroyo Hondo, some two and one-half leagues west of Natchitoches and the boundary between Louisiana and Texas. Upon the return of the expedition to New Orleans in 1806, deFiniels and other Spanish officers were expelled from Louisiana by Governor William C. C. Claiborne. Lieutenant Colonel deFiniels was attached to the Pensacola garrison, where he soon became engineer-in-chief of West Florida, serving until 1819. He supervised fortifications at Pensacola, San Carlos de Barrancas, and Mobile, and in 1818, as a member of the Security and Vigilance Committee, was wounded when Andrew Jackson captured Pensacola. He was twice married. His second wife, Mariana Rivier, a native of Pensacola, bore him four sons, all of whom served in the Spanish Army.

BIBLIOGRAPHY: Jack D. L. Holmes (ed.), Documentos inéditos para la historia de la Luisiana, 1792–1810 (1963); Jack D. L. Holmes, "Some French Engineers in Spanish Louisiana," in John Francis McDermott (ed.), The French in the Mississippi Valley (1965); Jack D. L. Holmes, "The Marqués de Casa-Calvo, Nicolás deFiniels, and the 1805 Spanish Expedition Through East Texas and Louisiana," Southwestern Historical Quarterly, LXIX (1965–1966).

Jack D. L. Holmes

*Defunct Counties.

*Degener, Edward.

DeGolyer, Everett Lee. Everett Lee DeGolyer was born on October 10, 1886, at Greensburg, Kansas, the son of John W. and Narcissa Kagy (Huddle) DeGolyer. In 1889 the DeGolyer family moved to Joplin, Missouri, to try zinc mining, then to Oklahoma to examine the "land runs." His father, an amateur prospector, took part in the Cherokee Strip run in 1889 and for the next fifteen years moved his family around Oklahoma and southern Missouri, operating restaurants to make a living. Young DeGolyer, irregularly schooled, clerked in stores and learned to wait tables and to cook. The family settled in Norman, Oklahoma, in 1904, and DeGolyer entered the University of Oklahoma in 1906. At the university he had two notable teachers who spurred his interest in geology; he was appointed the first student assistant in that department. During the summers from 1906 to 1909, he was camp cook with the United States Geological Survey camps. As such, he met Dr. C. Willard Hayes, head of the geological surveys, who was concerned with salvaging Sir Weetman Pearson's vast investment in Mexican oil near Tampico. DeGolyer was taken along on Dr. Hayes' geological team, and where Pearson had failed with oil enterprises, DeGolyer succeeded. On December 27, 1910, the DeGolyer-located well, the famous Potrero del Llano #4, came in to become one of the greatest producing wells in history, and soon he was making other strikes in Mexico's Golden Lane. In 1910 he returned to Norman to marry Nell Goodrich, and the couple went back to Tampico. In 1911 Sir Weetman Pearson (later Lord Cowdray) sent DeGolyer back to the University of Oklahoma for his B.A. degree. With the Mexican Revolution and World War I, Mexican oil exploration was interrupted. Lord Cowdray's British firm established DeGolyer in New York, where, from 1916 until 1932, he served as head of an exploration company in the United States and Canada, the Amerada Corporation. With its subsidiary founded for technological innovation, Geophysical Research, Inc., Amerada became one of the historic American oil companies, primarily for its subsidy of applied geophysics in the search for oil. DeGolyer was largely responsible for the triumph of research methods which now govern oil production, and he was able to attract gifted scientists and utilize their knowledge. In 1932 he resigned from Amerada to work for himself. With H. C. Karcher, Eugene B. McDermott,qv and others he founded in 1932 the Geophysical Research Corporation, a general consulting service for all companies. From then on the Southwest became the center of his work, and in 1936 he and his family moved to Dallas.

During World War II, DeGolyer went to Washington, D.C., to serve from 1941 to 1943 as assistant deputy petroleum coordinator. He made confidential missions for the government to Mexico in 1942, and to Saudi Arabia in 1943–1944, to map potential oil supplies for the war and postwar needs. He played an important role in the development of Arabian oil.

DeGolyer was also interested in literature as well as scientific advancement. He gave a large collection of first editions of landmark books in science to the University of Oklahoma, a geological col-

lection to Southern Methodist University, and a collection of first editions of Whitman, Dickens, Kipling, Melville, and other nineteenth- and twentieth-century writers to the University of Texas at Austin, where he served as guest professor for one semester in 1940. In 1941 he financially aided the *Saturday Review of Literature*, later served as its board chairman, and saw it prosper. His library of Latin American and Western history and of American business history are part of the DeGolyer Foundation.qv

Sick the last seven years of his life, a victim of persistent anemia, DeGolyer committed suicide at his office in Dallas on December 9, 1956, and he was buried in that city.

Lon Tinkle

DeGolyer Foundation. The DeGolyer Foundation Library was established in 1957 as the result of a gift by the late Everett Lee DeGolyer qv and Mrs. Nell V. DeGolyer, and by a bequest under the will of Everett DeGolyer. The library is largely located at Fondren Library, Southern Methodist University, Dallas. It consists of approximately eighty thousand volumes bearing on the history of the Western United States and Mexico and on business and economic history. The collections are particularly strong in the history of exploration and of transportation technology. The Western history portion of the collection is said to be one of the three finest in the world, especially in the areas of Texas and California history.

In addition to the printed materials, the foundation has acquired by gift and by purchase several important groups of manuscripts. Chief among these are the papers of DeGolyer; the business papers of John Insley Blair, capitalist; the papers of Samuel M. Vauclain, longtime president of the Baldwin Locomotive Works; the specification records of the Baldwin Locomotive Works; the papers of the Muskogee Company, a railroad holding company; and the motive power files of the Burlington Railroad and the Fort Worth & Denver Railway. The foundation also owns a photographic collection of about 250,000 items on the West, Mexico, and railroads. The geology collection of the foundation is on loan to the Science Information Center of Southern Methodist University.

A subject guide for users of the library is published occasionally to communicate to interested persons what they may find in the library. Five of these publications were published between September, 1962, and June, 1966.

Everett L. DeGolyer, Jr.

*DeGraffenreid, Reese Calhoun.

*DeGress, Jacob C.

*Degüello, The.

*DeKalb, Texas. DeKalb, in Bowie County, had a population of 2,042 in 1960 and 2,197 in 1970.

*DeKalb and Red River Railroad Company.

Delaney, James Joseph. James Joseph Delaney, son of Henry H. and Sarah (King) Delaney, was born on April 6, 1879, in Bristol, Virginia. He was educated at King College (B.A., 1900; M.A., 1918; honorary Litt.D., 1923), University of Virginia, and Columbia University. Before coming to Texas, he served as superintendent of schools at Marion, Virginia, and as president of Euharlee Institute, Georgia. He came to Texas in 1904 as headmaster of Carlisle Military Academy (now the University of Texas at Arlington). He taught at Austin College in Sherman from 1908 until 1920, when he became headmaster of the University Training School in Dallas. In 1922 Delaney was chosen as the first president of Schreiner Institute, a position he held until retirement on July 14, 1950. His efforts resulted in Schreiner Institute's becoming a fully accredited junior college.

Delaney was the first junior college representative to be chosen president of the Association of Texas Colleges.qv He was president of the Southern Association of Junior Colleges (1945–1946) and a member of the Executive Committee for Secondary Schools of the Southern Association of Colleges (1939–1947). He served as a member of accrediting committees of both the Southern Association and the Texas Education Agency.qv He represented the Southern Association of Colleges and Secondary Schools in evaluating the work of Mexican colleges seeking accreditation. He attempted to promote better relations with Mexico, Central America, and South America by helping young men from those areas to obtain an education in Texas.

Delaney contributed much to the civic life of Texas. He served as president of the Kerrville Chamber of Commerce (1926–1927), as a director of the West Texas Chamber of Commerce qv (1937–1938), as a member of the board of directors, Texas Centennial of Statehood qv Commission (1946–1947), and as a director of the Federal Building and Loan Association. He was a member of the Texas Academy of Science, Texas State Historical Association,qqv Phi Gamma Mu, the International Rotary Club, the Democratic party, and the Presbyterian church. Delaney and Stella (Vineyard) Delaney, whom he married on June 6, 1906, were the parents of two children. Delaney died in Kerrville on June 28, 1959.

BIBLIOGRAPHY: *Presidents and Professors in American Colleges and Universities* (1935); *Texian Who's Who* (1937); *Who's Who in the South and Southwest* (1950); Bob Bennett, *Kerr County, Texas 1856–1956* (c. 1956).

Joe R. Baulch

*Delaney, William Shelby.

*Delaware Bend, Texas.

*Delaware Creek.

*Delaware Indians.

*Delaware Mountains.

*Delaware Spring.

*Delba, Texas.

*Del Carmen Range. *See* Sierra del Carmen.

*De León, Alonso.

*De León, Juan María Ponce.

*De León, Martín.

*DeLeon, Texas. DeLeon, in Comanche County, is a commercial center for a diversified agricultural area. In 1970 the town had sixty-eight businesses, including several industries producing brick, feeds, peanut products, and burlap bags. The town also had three new school buildings and a modern hospital; a peach and melon festival is held annually in August. The 1960 population was 2,022; the 1970 population was 2,170.

*De Leon's Colony.

*Delfina, Texas.

*Delgado, Antonio.

*Delhi, Texas. (Caldwell County.)

*Delhi, Texas. (Harris County.)

*Delia, Texas.

Dell City, Texas. Dell City, in northeastern Hudspeth County, was established in 1948 and by 1949 had a post office. With the use of irrigation water obtained from an underground lake, the semidesert area produces cotton, vegetables, fruit, nuts, alfalfa, watermelons, sheep, cattle, and poultry. In 1962 the town was incorporated and by 1966 reported a modern school system, seven churches, a medical center, and six cotton gins. Recreation facilities are chiefly connected with game hunting in the Guadalupe Mountains. In 1970 the town had twenty-five business establishments and a population of 383.

Cyrus Tilloson

*Della Plain, Texas.

*Della Plain Male and Female Institute.

Delma, Texas. *See* Snell's, Texas.

*Del Mar, Texas.

Del Mar College. Del Mar College, Corpus Christi, was established in 1935 under control of the board of trustees for the Corpus Christi Independent School District. A separate tax levy provided financial support. The junior college began as an evening school, with initial enrollment of 150 students. For some years the college met in the local high school, then moved to the educational building of a local church. In 1941 construction began on the present main campus. Enrollment grew slowly until 1946, when a vocational program was created. In 1947 a school of music was established.

The college separated from the school district in 1950 and since then has had its own board of regents elected by the college district. By 1950 academic enrollment increased to 1,250 and by the 1974–1975 term increased to 10,704 students. Participation in vocational and adult education programs accelerated at a similar pace. During the late 1950's, a technical institute was founded on a separate campus. Full-time faculty membership grew with enrollment, numbering about 200 instructors in 1974. Approximately sixteen new buildings were constructed between 1950 and 1965. The campus master plan called for additional facilities, with a new library building scheduled. Jean Richardson served as president in 1975.

*Delmita, Texas.

*Del Norte Gap.

*Del Norte Mountains.

*Del Rio, Texas. Del Rio, seat of Val Verde County, with 434 businesses in 1970, has increased its number of manufacturing companies. A fifty-acre industrial park was established to encourage manufacturers to move to Del Rio, the first new industry being a wool-scouring plant. Although the city gained several new industries, the pattern of economic activity continued to be dominated by Laughlin Air Force Base qv and by sheep and goat ranching; more of its basic income is received from Laughlin Air Force Base than from any other source. A new municipal building was completed in 1960, a county hospital in 1961, and a civic center, designed for use by conventions as well as for local entertainment and meetings, in 1964. The airport was modernized and enlarged and construction was begun on a new library building in 1964.

In 1966 the city reported thirty-one churches, two hospitals, two banks, two newspapers, and a radio station. The 1960 population of 18,612 increased to 21,330 by 1970. Historic sites include the Whitehead Memorial Museum, the site of the largest trading center between San Antonio and El Paso, and the Val Verde winery, the only commercial winery in Texas. The Amistad Dam, six miles north, formed reservoirs on the Rio Grande, Devil's, Pecos, and Concho rivers. Thousands of visitors pass annually into Mexico through Del Rio's port of entry over the international bridge. *See also* Amistad Reservoir.

*Delrose, Texas.

*Delta County. Delta County, a diversified agricultural area, gains most of its farm income from cotton, vetch, and small grains. Both beef and dairy cattle are raised, with a local dairy industry centering in the county seat, Cooper. The sale of honey brings the county some fifty thousand dollars annually. Water projects include Cooper Dam on Cooper Creek, a tributary to the South Sulphur River, and rectification of the channels of both the South and North Sulphur rivers. The 1960 population was 5,860; the 1970 population was 4,927.

Delta Kappa Gamma Society. The Delta Kappa Gamma Society was founded on May 11, 1929, at the Faculty Women's Club in Austin, Texas. It was originally chartered and incorporated in Texas in 1929, the amended charter permitting establishment of chapters anywhere in the world. Annie Webb Blanton,qv along with eleven other Texas women representing a cross section of educational work, began the society.

Delta Kappa Gamma is the largest organized group of women educators in the world. In 1975 more than one hundred thirty-three thousand members were in about twenty-five hundred chapters organized in every state of the United States, the District of Columbia, six provinces of Canada, Finland, Sweden, Norway, Mexico, and Guatemala. Members all over the world study and do research, teach in the schools of other nations, and occupy governmental or university positions.

The society supports eighteen annual international scholarships of $2,500 each for members for graduate study. Many state chapters give financial assistance for advanced study to members. At the 1964 convention the society set up the Delta Kappa Gamma Educational Foundation and authorized the transfer to this fund of $100,000. Its purpose was to provide graduate scholarships, fellowships, and grants. The Educator's Award of $1,500 was originally given to the woman author whose educational book was voted as the best published during the biennium. By 1975 that award, in the amount of $1,000, was given annually. The society's international offices are located in Austin.

*Del Valle, Texas. [This title was incorrectly listed in Volume I as Delvalle, Texas.]

*Delwin, Texas.

DeMazenod Scholasticate. *See* Oblate College of the Southwest.

*De Mézières, Athanase.

*Demijohn Bend, Texas.

*Democratic National Convention of 1928.

*Democratic Party in Texas. The Democratic party in Texas is as old as the state itself, having been brought along as part of the institutional baggage of the early arrivals. The dominant party from the beginning, it successfully overcame the pre-Civil War challenge of the American party (*see* Know-Nothing Party), the Reconstruction qv era victories of the Republican party,qv and the turn-of-the-century threat from the People's (Populist) party.qv Since Reconstruction the Democratic party in Texas has won every gubernatorial election, all but four of the presidential elections (through 1972), and the vast bulk of local elections, the principal exceptions occurring in the isolated areas of traditional Republican strength where local candidates avoid the Democratic label.

Despite that impressive record, the position of the Democratic party deteriorated considerably in the period following World War II. There was a tendency in 1952 and 1956 to dismiss Dwight D. Eisenhower's qv victories for the Republican party in Texas as the same kind of accident as had occurred in 1928 when Herbert Hoover carried the state. But even with native son Lyndon Baines Johnson qv as the vice-presidential candidate, the Democratic ticket headed by John F. Kennedy barely carried Texas in 1960. Although it carried the state for President Lyndon B. Johnson by a comfortable margin (63 percent) in 1964, the Texas Democratic party in 1968 was barely able to eke out a plurality for presidential nominee Hubert H. Humphrey (41.1 percent, compared to 39.9 percent for Republican Richard M. Nixon). In the 1972 presidential election Texas voted overwhelmingly for the Republican candidate, Nixon (2,298,896 votes), in preference to his Democratic opponent, George S. McGovern

(1,154,289 votes). Republican John Tower won Johnson's vacated Senate seat in a special election in 1961 and easily won again in 1966 and 1972. These elections, coupled with a strong Republican showing in the 1962, 1968, 1970, and 1972 gubernatorial elections and in certain congressional and legislative districts over a longer period of time, make clear that, while Texas is not yet a two-party state, it can no longer be taken for granted by the Democratic party.

In part, this evolution toward a two-party system derives from the distaste of some Texas voters for the liberalism of the national Democratic party and from their growing attachment to the Republican party. The electoral woes of the Democrats in Texas, however, are also due to persistent, wracking factionalism. Personality differences are no doubt a factor, but the factionalism that has been a recurring problem both in the party primaries and in the party organization seems basically to involve conflict along lines of ideology and group interests.

The liberal faction identifies with the modern national Democratic party and with the leadership and programs of Franklin Roosevelt, Harry Truman, John Kennedy, and Lyndon B. Johnson. Its orientation is to such groups as organized labor, Negroes and Latin Americans, those of lower socioeconomic status, and liberal intellectuals and professionals. Its concerns are with improved and expanded public services (including welfare), better protection of civil rights, and progressive taxation.

The conservative faction has long been identified with the Southern wing of the Democratic party, but in recent years its militant states' rights stand on such issues as civil rights, federal spending, and welfare programs has been considerably moderated. Even so, it is still seen as opposed to many if not most programs of the national Democratic party. The conservative faction draws some support from all classes of voters, but its most enduring strength is with the middle and upper classes. Its leadership and programs are generally attuned to business and industrial interests of the state.

Open conflict between these two factions can be traced as far back as 1946. The 1950's were especially turbulent as a result of Governor Allan Shivers' and the conservative Democrats' support of Eisenhower in 1952 and 1956. Ralph Yarborough emerged as the outstanding liberal figure, winning a seat in the United States Senate in a 1957 special election after narrowly failing to win the governorship. Shivers' successor in the governor's office, Price Daniel, took a more moderate stand on public issues and hence eased somewhat the electoral conflict, but the struggle for control of the party organization continued unabated. Liberals in the late 1950's put together their own statewide organization, called Democrats of Texas (DOT), but it collapsed in 1960. Liberal efforts in the 1960's to rebuild an effective state organization were uniformly unsuccessful.

The conservative Democrats by the early 1960's were in disarray as a result of lack of effective leadership and inroads made by the Republican party's capitalizing on hostility to the Kennedy administration. Some conservatives backed John Connally in the 1962 gubernatorial struggle, despite his somewhat more moderate stance. He won only after narrowly defeating the liberal choice in the Democratic primary (Don Yarborough) and after a surprisingly strong Republican bid by Jack Cox in the general election. Connally's efforts to rebuild the conservative faction received tremendous impetus near the end of his first term when he was wounded in the assassination of President Kennedy (see Kennedy, John Fitzgerald, Assassination of). Thereafter unassailable politically, Connally soon restored the conservative faction to its dominant position, but in so doing further alienated many liberals. His successor as governor, Preston Smith, showed some interest in muting the factional conflict, but its deep and pervasive roots made success difficult. As long as this factionalism continues, the Republican party will have a splendid opportunity to exploit the dissatisfactions of the losing faction.

The formal organization of the Democratic party in Texas, dictated by state laws which provide both temporary and permanent organs, remained unchanged throughout the 1950's and 1960's. The temporary party organs consist of a series of regularly scheduled (biennial) conventions beginning at the precinct level and limited to persons who voted in the party primary. The precinct convention's chief function is to choose delegates to the county convention held one week later. The delegates who gather at the county convention are likewise chiefly concerned with choosing delegates to the state convention held biennially in September for the purpose of formally choosing the state executive committee, adopting a party platform, and officially certifying the party's candidates to be listed on the general election ballot. In presidential election years there is also a state convention held in June to choose delegates to the national presidential nominating convention.

The permanent organs of the party are largely independent of the temporary ones just sketched. Voters in the Democratic primary in each precinct elect for a two-year term of office a chairman or committeeman who is formally the party's agent and spokesman in that precinct. A few of these precinct chairmen work diligently for the party and its nominees; some do very little. Normally the precinct chairman will be in charge of the conduct of the primary in his precinct, and, perhaps less assuredly, will serve as chairman of the precinct convention and of the delegation to the county convention.

The party's county executive committee is composed of the precinct chairmen plus a county chairman who is elected in the primary by the Democratic voters in the county as a whole. The county committee determines policy in such matters as the conduct and financing of the primary, and officially canvasses its results. It could serve as a focal point for party organizing and campaigning efforts, but rarely, if ever, is this the case.

The state executive committee is composed of one man and one woman from each of the thirty-one state senatorial districts, plus a chairman and vice-chairman, formally chosen by the state convention but informally chosen by a caucus of the delegates from each senatorial district. Occasionally a governor and his advisers will decide that a caucus nominee is simply unacceptable and then will substitute their own choices. By law the state committee is responsible for overseeing the party primary and for canvassing the returns. It also undertakes to do a limited amount of fund-raising and campaign work for the party, but such efforts are apt to be spasmodic and uninspired. The committee's role is to serve as an adjunct of the governor's office, designed to help him as best it can with political and policy problems.

It would seem that the governor is the dominant figure in the Democratic party. He controls the state convention, can veto choices for the state executive committee, and often intervenes to influence the selection of party officials at the local level. However, it also follows that there will be opposition to him from factional leaders, some of whom hold party and public office. The fact is that even the most influential governor cannot dislodge or defeat those opponents who have built up their own grass-roots support. There are in reality limits to the governor's ability to control the party apparatus; his powers are those of persuasion, not of dictation.

The position of the Democratic party in Texas has long been supreme, but the nationalization of American politics has unleashed forces which pose a serious threat, particularly in view of the party's divided condition. Party organization is decentralized, and its leadership is weak. There is as yet relatively little effort at systematic, organized politics. *See also* Political Parties; Election Laws; Governor, Office of.

Clifton McCleskey

*DeMontel, Charles S.

*DeMorse, Charles.

*De Moss, Charles.

*De Moss, Peter. In addition to two sons (as shown in Volume I), three daughters were born to Peter and Susanna De Moss after their arrival in Texas. Charles De Moss ᵠᵛ was his brother.

Emma Peper Nickelson

*Denhawken, Texas.

*Denison, Franklin L.

*Denison, James.

*Denison, James.

*Denison, Texas. Denison, in northeastern Grayson County, has become increasingly industrial, manufacturing such products as furniture, cotton textiles, boats, food products, and transit pipe. A second city hospital was constructed in 1963; Grayson County College was completed in 1965. The Thompson House, the earliest residence in existence in Grayson County, was moved to Denison and restored. The 1960 population was

22,748; the 1970 population was 24,923. *See also* Sherman-Denison Standard Metropolitan Statistical Area.

*Denison, Bonham, and New Orleans Railroad Company.

*Denison and Pacific Railway Company.

*Denison and Pacific Suburban Railway Company. The entire stock of the Denison and Pacific Suburban Railway Company was owned by the Texas and Pacific, though its tracks were also used by the Kansas, Oklahoma, and Gulf Railway of Texas. The road operated freight service only. In 1964 it operated over 4.4 miles in Texas, but the business was not profitable and the following year the Texas and Pacific abandoned the property.

James M. Day

*Denison and Southeastern Railway Company.

*Denison and Washita Valley Railway Company.

*Denman, Leroy Gilbert.

*Denning, Texas.

*Dennis, Isaac N.

*Dennis, Thomas Mason.

*Dennis, Texas.

*Denton, John B.

*Denton, Texas. Denton, seat of Denton County, in 1970 ranked as one of Texas' leading educational centers, with many public schools, North Texas State University, Texas Woman's University, Selwyn Preparatory School, and Denton State School ᵠᵛ for the mentally retarded. There were also orphanages and a children's camp. Two hospitals, three libraries, four banks, a newspaper, and a radio station served the rapidly growing city. A community center, a new federal building, and a municipal building were completed by 1968.

Local industrial activity included the production of bricks, plastics, clothing, boats, and trailers. Other industries were connected with the county's agriculture. The 1960 population was 26,-844; the 1970 population was 39,874. *See also* Dallas Standard Metropolitan Statistical Area.

*Denton Community, Texas.

*Denton County. In 1965 Denton County was strongly linked economically with Fort Worth and Dallas. Aside from the commuters who earned their living from the metropolitan areas, many Denton County inhabitants were employed in agriculture. The blackland county produced sizable quantities of cotton, oats, wheat, grain sorghums, peanuts, beef and dairy cattle, and sheep. The county seat, Denton, was the site of several large educational institutions, and recreational facilities were provided by Grapevine and Garza-Little Elm reservoirs. The population grew rapidly, from 47,432 in 1960 to 75,633 in 1970. *See also* Dallas Standard Metropolitan Statistical Area.

*Denton Creek.

*Denton Field.

Denton State School. Denton State School for the mentally retarded was authorized in 1957, and construction was completed in 1960. At the close of the 1963 school year, 367 students were enrolled in the academic and training program. About half of the total enrollment of 985 students had physical disabilities that made them completely bedfast or semi-ambulatory. In 1967 the school had a capacity of 1,750 students and was an admission center for thirty-seven counties. In 1970 the programs of vocational rehabilitation, education, recreation, and medical service were expanded and improvements were made. The census at the end of that year was 1,680. *See* Mentally Ill and Mentally Retarded, Care of, in Texas.

BIBLIOGRAPHY: Board for Texas State Hospitals and Special Schools, *Report* (1964); Texas Department of Mental Health and Mental Retardation, *Annual Report*, 1970.

*Denver City, Texas. Denver City, in Yoakum County, has a balanced economy based on agriculture, oil, and gas. Industries include gas plants, six cotton gins, chemical manufacturing plants, oil refineries, and cattle feedlots. Denver City reported 188 businesses, sixteen churches, a bank, a library, a semi-weekly newspaper, a radio station, and an improved hospital in 1967. The 1960 population was 4,302; the 1970 population was 4,133.

*Denworth, Texas.

De Pagès, Pierre Marie François. *See* Pagès, Pierre Marie François de.

*Dependent and Neglected Children, Home for. *See* Waco State Home.

*Deport, Texas.

*Derby, Texas.

*Dermadera Creek.

*Dermott, Texas. Dermott, in Scurry County, was named for P. S. McDermott (not P. S. Dermott, as stated in Volume I). [Although the historical marker for the town shows that a man by the name of "S. P. McDermott" was "an early postmaster," this is not reflected in the official records of the United States Post Office, General Services Administration, Washington, D.C. The official records show that the first post office at Dermott was established in 1902 and that William H. Smith was the first postmaster; the records also show that the second postmaster was Luther Edmondson, in 1910. There is no listing of a McDermott as ever having been postmaster of this town, although it is possible that the post office was located in a store owned by McDermott. Whether this man's initials were "P. S." or "S. P." is inconclusive, although the Scurry County tax rolls for 1902 and 1903 carry his name as "P. S. McDermott," as used in this article. Ed.]

BIBLIOGRAPHY: Scurry County Tax Rolls, 1902, 1903 (MS., Archives, Texas State Library); United States Post Office Records (Civil Archives Division of the National Archives, General Services Administration, Washington, D.C.).

*Dernal, Texas.

*DeRyee, William.

*Desdemona, Texas.

*Desdemona Oil Field. *See* Ranger, Desdemona, and Breckenridge Oil Fields.

*Desert, Texas.

*Desert Creek.

*DeShields, James Thomas.

Deshler, James. James Deshler was born at Tuscumbia, Alabama, on February 18, 1833, and was graduated from West Point in the class of 1854, ranking seventh in a class of forty-six. After serving in various western posts in Indian operations, Deshler joined the Confederacy as captain of artillery in the regular army at the outbreak of the Civil War. He was seriously wounded in the 1861 campaign in western Virginia. Upon recovery he was promoted to colonel and acted as chief of artillery in Lieutenant General T. H. Holmes' corps during the Seven Days battles. Thereafter he accompanied Holmes to the Trans-Mississippi and was captured in January, 1863, at Arkansas Post, where he commanded a brigade composed of the 10th Texas Infantry and the 15th, 17th, and 18th Texas Dismounted Cavalry.

After his exchange, Deshler was appointed brigadier general on July 28, 1863, and was assigned a brigade in Major General Pat Cleburne's division of the Army of Tennessee. At the battle of Chickamauga, Deshler commanded a brigade composed of the 6th, 10th, and 15th Texas Infantry (consolidated); the 17th, 18th, 24th, and 25th Texas Dismounted Cavalry (consolidated); and the 19th and 20th Arkansas Infantry. He was killed in action in that battle on September 20, 1863, and was buried in Oakwood Cemetery at Tuscumbia.

BIBLIOGRAPHY: U. S. War Department, *The War of the Rebellion: A Compilation of the Official Records of the Union and Confederate Armies* (1880–1901); *List of Field Officers, Regiments and Battalions in the Confederate Army* (n.d.); *Memorandum Relative to the General Officers Appointed by the President in the Armies of the Confederate States* (1905); Ezra J. Warner, *Generals in Gray* (1959); C. A. Evans, *Confederate Military History* (1899); George W. Cullum, *Biographical Register of the Officers and Graduates of the U.S. Military Academy* (1891).

Palmer Bradley

*De Solís, Gaspar José.

*De Sosa, Castaño. *See* Castaño de Sosa, Gaspar.

*De Soto, Luís.

*De Soto, Hernando, and De Soto Expedition. *See* Moscoso Expedition.

*De Soto, Texas. De Soto, in Dallas County, had a 1960 population of 1,969 and a 1970 population of 6,617. In 1970 De Soto had seventy-one businesses, new shopping centers, and several new schools.

Desprez, Frank. Frank Desprez, the eldest of the eleven children of Charles Desprez, jeweler and silversmith, was born in Bristol, England, on February 9, 1853. The Desprez family was of French descent. After concluding his education at Cosham School, Wiltshire, Desprez was apprenticed to a Bristol copper-engraving firm. Because of trouble with his right eye, he gave up engraving and came to Texas while still in his teens with his cousin

Willie Pinder. For about three years Desprez worked on a Texas ranch, though its location is unknown.

Shortly after his return to England, he became involved with the theater, a connection that lasted the remainder of his life. He was consecutively or concurrently theatrical secretary, playwright, drama critic, and editor of a theatrical newspaper. He wrote more than twenty dramatic productions, sometimes using a pseudonym. Many of these were short pieces presented as curtain raisers or after-pieces for the Gilbert and Sullivan operas produced by Richard D'Oyly Carte. Two of Desprez's supporting pieces contain references to his life in Texas.

Desprez was also an essayist and poet. Dozens of his pieces on travel, art, music, and famous personalities were published in English periodicals, most of them between 1905 and 1914. His best-known work, however, is a poem, "Lasca," about a Mexican girl and her cowboy sweetheart caught in a cattle stampede "in Texas down by the Rio Grande." The ballad-like poem, first published in a London magazine in 1882, has often been reprinted, usually with deletions and changes, and recited in many parts of the English-speaking world. Three times the poem has been the basis for a movie, with a fourth one in prospect. Between 1873 and 1882 at least four other of Desprez's poems were published, two of which are about Texas.

In 1883 Desprez married Jessie McQueen, the daughter of an officer in Her Majesty's dragoons; they had a son and two daughters. Desprez died in London on November 25 (or 22), 1916.

BIBLIOGRAPHY: Mabel Major, "The Man Who Wrote 'Lasca,'" *Southwest Review*, XXXVI (1951).

Mabel Major

*Dessau, Texas.

*Detmold, Texas.

Detobiti Indians. In 1683–1684 Juan Domínguez de Mendoza qv led an exploratory expedition from El Paso as far eastward as the junction of the Concho and Colorado rivers east of present San Angelo. In his itinerary he listed the names of thirty-seven Indian groups, including the Detobiti (Tobite), from which he expected to receive delegations. Nothing further is known about the Detobiti, who seem to have been one of many Indian groups of north-central Texas that were swept away by the southward thrust of the Lipan-Apache and Comanche Indians in the eighteenth century.

BIBLIOGRAPHY: H. E. Bolton (ed.), *Spanish Exploration in the Southwest, 1542–1706* (1916); C. W. Hackett (ed.), *Pichardo's Treatise on the Limits of Louisiana and Texas*, II (1934).

T. N. Campbell

*Detroit, Texas.

*Devereux, Julien Sidney. Julien Sidney Devereux was the son of John William Devereux (not John Ward Devereux, as stated in Volume I).

*Devers, Texas.

*Devil Hollow.

*Devil Ridge.

*DeVilbiss, John Wesley.

*Devil's Backbone.

*Devil's Courthouse Peak.

*Devils Fork Creek.

*Devil's Hill.

*Devils Lake. The Devils Lake project was owned and operated by Central Power and Light Company for generation of hydroelectric power. Construction of the dam was begun in 1927 and was completed in December, 1928. Devils Lake was inundated by Amistad Reservoir.qv It originally had a capacity of 9,200 acre-feet and a surface area of 406 acres at elevation 1,042.3 feet above mean sea level. The project was a one-unit plant with a capacity of 1,800 kilowatts. The drainage area above the dam was 4,053 square miles. *See* Water Power.

BIBLIOGRAPHY: Texas Water Commission, *Bulletin 6408* (1964).

Seth D. Breeding

*Devils River.

*Devils River, Texas.

*Devil's Sinkhole. Devil's Sinkhole, in Edwards County, was first named by Ammon Billings in 1876, when he discovered the entrance while pursuing Indians. The sixty-foot-diameter entrance bells out into a large room partly filled with fallen rock. The cave is blocked 310 feet below the surface by standing water. The impressive size and rumors of lost bat rooms have drawn cave explorers from all over the United States. The cave is no longer open to spelunkers, however, as a result of the death of a youth there in 1960. Guano has been mined sporadically from the cave for use as fertilizer. *See also* Caves and Cave Studies in Texas.

BIBLIOGRAPHY: Tom Meador, "A Brief History of the Devil's Sinkhole," *Texas Caver*, X (1965); J. R. Reddell and A. R. Smith, "The Caves of Edwards County," *Texas Speleological Survey*, II (1965).

A. Richard Smith

*Devine, Thomas Jefferson.

*Devine, Texas. Devine, in Medina County, showed an increase in population from 2,522 in 1960 to 3,311 in 1970, according to the United States census.

Devore, Cornelius. Cornelius Devore, son of Jesse Devore,qv was born in New Orleans on September 11, 1819. The family moved to Liberty Municipality in 1828. He volunteered for army service at the outbreak of the Texas Revolution. As a member of Captain William M. Logan's qv 3rd Infantry Company, he fought at the battle of San Jacinto. For his service from March 6 to June 6, 1836, he was awarded 320 acres of land. He was a member of the Texas Veterans Association.qv Devore, who never married, died on July 29, 1883.

BIBLIOGRAPHY: William M. Jones, *Texas History Carved in Stone* (1958); A. J. Sowell, *Early Settlers and Indian Fighters of Southwest Texas* (1900); S. H. Dixon and L. W. Kemp, *Heroes of San Jacinto* (1932).

Marshall Jackson

Devore, Jesse. Jesse Devore, descendant of a French Huguenot family, was born in Pennsylvania on January 16, 1789. He was living with his family in Catahoula Parish, Louisiana, when he became a soldier in the War of 1812, serving in General Andrew Jackson's army as a member of the 14th Regiment of Louisiana Militia stationed at Villeri Canal.

While living in Louisiana, Devore sold land to James and Rezin P. Bowie.qqv He later moved to Texas and in 1827 petitioned Anastacio Bustamante qv for land. On June 20, 1835, Devore received a league of land in Joseph Vehlein's qv colony, Liberty Municipality. At the outbreak of the Texas Revolution, Hugh B. Johnston, Benjamin Watson Hardin,qqv and Devore were named commissioners to organize militia for service in the war.

Devore was married twice; he had two daughters and a son, Cornelius Devore,qv by his first wife. In 1833 Devore was married to Rachel Falk, who also bore him several children. Devore died on January 24, 1849, in Liberty County.

BIBLIOGRAPHY: Arlene Pickett, *Historic Liberty County* (1936); Service Records of Jesse Devore (National Archives, Washington, D.C.); A. J. Sowell, *Early Settlers and Indian Fighters of Southwest Texas* (1900); S. H. Dixon, *Romance and Tragedies of Texas History* (1924).

Marshall Jackson

*Dew, Texas.

*Dewalt, Texas.

*Dewees, John Oatman.

*DeWees, William B. William B. DeWees was not the author of the letters compiled under the title *Letters from an Early Settler of Texas to a Friend* (as stated in Volume I). This book was written in 1852 by Emmaretta Cara Kimball,qv who collaborated with DeWees and put his reminiscences into the form of letters to one "Cara Cardelle" (not Clara Cardello). The authorship agreement between DeWees and Miss Kimball was affirmed in a contract filed at the Colorado County courthouse on December 17, 1852.

BIBLIOGRAPHY: Andrew Forest Muir, *Texas in 1837* (1958); Earl Vandale Collection, Archives, University of Texas at Austin.

*Dewees, Texas. (Waller County.)

*Dewees, Texas. (Wilson County.)

Deweesville, Texas. Deweesville, a small community about ten miles southwest of Falls City in Karnes County, was named after John O. Dewees, a prominent rancher in the vicinity during trail-driving days. In 1936 Deweesville had a school, a cotton gin, and a store. After the discovery of uranium in Karnes County in 1954, the first uranium ore processing mill in Texas was built by the Susquehanna-Western Corporation at Deweesville in 1961.

*Dewey, Texas.

*Dewey Lake.

*Deweyville, Texas.

*DeWitt, Green C.

*DeWitt County. DeWitt County, widely known for its turkey production and its Turkey Trot qv parade held at various times in Cuero, ranked tenth in the state in number of beef cattle and eighteenth in dairy cattle in 1959. In 1964

there were 1,680 farms with a total income of over eight and one-half million dollars; farm income had reached fifteen million dollars by 1970. Three-fourths of the farm income is derived from livestock and poultry, while grains, cotton, pecans, flax, and peanuts contribute a smaller amount. Textiles and leather goods are manufactured by local industries, and oil is produced in small quantities. The population was 20,683 in 1960 and 18,660 in 1970.

*DeWitt County (Judicial).

*DeWitt's Colony.

*Dewville, Texas.

*Dexter, Peter B.

*Dexter, Texas.

De Young, Harry Anthony. Harry Anthony De Young was born in Chicago, Illinois, on August 5, 1893. He studied art at the Art Institute of Chicago, where he was an honor student, and at the University of Illinois. For a time he taught at the Academy of Art in Chicago and was the director of the Midwest Summer School of Art at Paw Paw Lake, Michigan. He also taught at Bailey's Harbor (Wisconsin) School of Art and was director of the Glen Wood School of Landscape Painting in Illinois. In Texas the artist founded and directed the De Young Painting Camp in the Davis Mountains.

Recognition of De Young's work in 1925 won him the Fine Arts Building Purchase Prize of five hundred dollars at the Art Institute of Chicago and honorable mention in landscape painting at the American Artists Exhibition of Chicago. In 1927 he received honorable mention at the Chicago Galleries Association. In the Edgar B. Davis qv Competitive Exhibition in San Antonio in 1928 he won the member prize of two hundred dollars.

A mural representing the "Basket Maker Indians of West Texas," painted as a Public Works Administration project, is owned by the Witte Memorial Museum,qv San Antonio. "Cinchin' Up" is part of the San Antonio Art League Collection. Among other pictures of Texas subjects are his portraits of David Crockett and James Bonham,qqv which hang in the Alamo. Some of his other works are in the Chicago and Gary, Indiana, public schools, in Fort Davis, Texas, and in Brackenridge High School in San Antonio.

In 1942, at the height of his career, De Young suffered paralysis of his right side. He died in Waco, Texas, on January 9, 1956, survived by his wife and daughter.

BIBLIOGRAPHY: Mantle Fielding, *Dictionary of American Painters, Sculptors, and Engravers* (1960); Esse Forrester-O'Brien, *Art and Artists of Texas* (c. 1935); Witte Museum Files, San Antonio, Texas; *Who's Who in American Art* (1956).

Caroline Remy

De Zavala, Adina Emilia. Adina Emilia De Zavala, eldest of six children of Augustine and Julia (Tyrrell) De Zavala (originally "de" Zavala) and granddaughter of Lorenzo de Zavala,qv was born on November 28, 1861, in Harris County. The family lived at Galveston before moving to a ranch near San Antonio about 1873. The young Adina attended Ursuline Academy qv at Galveston from 1871 to 1873, was enrolled at Sam Houston Normal Institute (now Sam Houston State University) at Huntsville in 1879, from which she was graduated in 1881, and later attended a school of music in Missouri. She taught school at Terrell from 1884 to 1886 and later in San Antonio.

About 1889 she and other San Antonio women met to discuss Texas and its heroes; this group became one of the first societies composed of women organized for patriotic purposes in the state. In 1893 members of this De Zavala society became affiliated with the Daughters of the Republic of Texas (DRT).qv One of Miss De Zavala's greatest contributions to Texas was the preservation of a portion of the old San Antonio de Valero Mission,qv better known as the Alamo, preventing it from being razed in the early twentieth century. The state had purchased the chapel of the Alamo from the Catholic church in 1883, but in 1886 Hugo and Schmeltzer Company, a wholesale grocery firm, bought the Alamo mission convent, also known as the monastery, long barracks, or fortress, which was the scene of the major resistance by Alamo defenders against the Mexican forces headed by Antonio López de Santa Anna qv in 1836. As early as 1892, before her historical group affiliated with the DRT, Miss De Zavala extracted a verbal promise from the grocery firm to give her chapter first chance at buying the property.

Clara Driscoll qv joined the De Zavala chapter and the DRT in 1903, and the next year she purchased the Hugo and Schmeltzer Company property to prevent an "eastern syndicate" from acquiring it. The Texas legislature authorized state purchase of the property from Miss Driscoll in January, 1905, and gave custody of the Alamo to the DRT, but soon the women began to disagree upon procedures for preservation of the Alamo and upon exactly what constituted the Alamo at the time of its siege and fall in 1836. The women split into two factions, one led by Adina De Zavala and the other by Clara Driscoll, and fought for control of the state organization of the DRT and the Alamo. Certain legal aspects of the battle were settled by the state courts, which in a series of decisions ruled in favor of the Driscoll group as the de jure DRT in 1909.

While Miss Driscoll and others in the DRT expressed desires to destroy the dilapidated Hugo and Schmeltzer building in the mistaken belief that it was erected after the 1836 battle, Miss De Zavala led the opposition in a resolute and voluble stand against any such move and was instrumental in the preservation of portions of the original wall of the convent. Miss De Zavala and the DRT renewed the feud over historical questions revolving around the Alamo at intervals, and time has proved that Miss De Zavala was correct in most of her historical contentions concerning the mission.

In 1912 Miss De Zavala organized the Texas Historical and Landmarks Association,qv which placed thirty-eight markers at historic sites in Texas. She probably did more than any other one person in stirring interest in the preservation of San Antonio's Spanish Governors' Palace,qv which was finally purchased in 1928 by the city and restored. In the 1930's she helped establish the location near Crockett of sites of the first two missions established in Texas by the Spanish. Governor Pat Neff qv in 1923 appointed her to the Texas Historical Board,qv and she was one of the original members of the Committee of One Hundred appointed to plan for a state centennial. She also served on the advisory board of the Texas Centennial qv Committee. A charter member of the Texas State Historical Association,qv she was a member of the executive council of that body beginning in 1919. In 1945 she was elected an honorary life fellow of the association. A dedicated Catholic, Miss De Zavala was a member of the United Daughters of the Confederacy, Texas Folklore Society, the Philosophical Society of Texas,qqv the Texas Woman's Press Association, and many other organizations. She was author of a book, History and Legends of the Alamo and Other Missions in and Around San Antonio (1917); pamphlets, including The Story of the Siege and Fall of the Alamo, A Résumé (1911); and a contributor to the Handbook of Texas. Adina De Zavala died on March 1, 1955, and was buried at St. Mary's Cemetery in San Antonio.

BIBLIOGRAPHY: Adina De Zavala Papers (Archives, University of Texas at Austin Library); Adina De Zavala, History and Legends of the Alamo and Other Missions in and Around San Antonio (1917); L. Robert Ables, "The Second Battle for the Alamo," Southwestern Historical Quarterly, LXX (1966–1967).

L. Robert Ables

*De Zavala, Lorenzo.

*D'Hanis, Texas.

*Diablo Plateau. See Sierra Diablo.

*Dial, John.

*Dial, Texas. (Fannin County.)

*Dial, Texas. (Hutchinson County.)

*Dialects, Texan.

*Dialville, Texas.

Diamond, George Washington. George Washington Diamond, one of six brothers who immigrated to Texas before the Civil War, was born on December 26, 1835, in De Kalb County, Georgia, son of James and Nancy Diamond. He moved to Texas shortly after receiving a law degree in 1857 from Albany (now New York) University. He settled first in Rusk County, where he became co-publisher of the Henderson Times. When the Civil War began Diamond sold his interest in the newspaper and enlisted as a private on May 7, 1861, in Company B, 3rd Texas Cavalry Regiment.

Near the end of 1862 Diamond took leave from his unit to visit his brother James J. Diamond qv at Gainesville. This was only a few weeks after the "Great Hanging" at Gainesville qv in which James J. Diamond and other Confederate loyalists smashed an alleged "Peace Party Conspiracy"qv in north-central Texas by convening a "citizens court" that tried, condemned, and hanged thirty-nine prisoners charged with conspiracy and insurrection against the Confederate State of Texas. George Washington Diamond was asked to use the records of the court in preparing an official account of its work, a manuscript which he apparently completed before the end of 1876. It was not published during his lifetime, but was brought to light many years later by his granddaughter, Mrs. Harry Harlan of Dallas, and was published in 1963 by the Texas State Historical Association.qv

At Gainesville Diamond transferred to the 11th Texas Cavalry, CSA, in which his brother James J. Diamond was a colonel. He later raised a company of cavalry on the lower Brazos River and fought as a captain in the battles of Mansfield and Pleasant Hill, Louisiana, in 1864.

At the end of the Civil War, Diamond returned to Henderson, where he was elected state representative to the 11th Texas Legislature. The Reconstruction qv of Texas prevented this legislature from convening until 1870. Meanwhile, Diamond had moved with his family to Whitesboro, where he spent the remainder of his life. Although he practiced law during Reconstruction in the Grayson County seat of Sherman and held several county offices at various times, he was chiefly interested in newspaper work, serving for many years on the staff of the Whitesboro *News*. He died at Whitesboro on June 24, 1911, and was buried there.

BIBLIOGRAPHY: Sam Acheson and J. A. O'Connell (eds.), *George Washington Diamond's Account of the Great Hanging at Gainesville, 1862* (1963).

Sam Acheson

Diamond, James J. James J. Diamond, eldest of six sons born to James and Nancy Diamond in De Kalb County, Georgia, immigrated to Texas before the Civil War. As a Red River Valley cotton planter and slave owner who settled in Grayson County near Whitesboro, he became a leading spokesman for Southern rights and views immediately preceding the Civil War. He was a delegate from Texas to the 1860 Democratic national convention held in Charleston, South Carolina, and, following the nomination of Douglas for president, bolted the convention.

Upon the election of Lincoln in November, 1860, Diamond helped call a public meeting at Whitesboro on November 23, composed of citizens from Cooke and Grayson counties, and was named chairman of the committee that offered resolutions calling upon Governor Sam Houston "to ascertain the will of the people . . . by convention, or otherwise" on the question of Texas' remaining in the Union. Sent to Austin as one of the two delegates from Cooke County, he voted with the majority at the Secession Convention qv to sever the political ties of Texas with the Union. He was appointed a member of the convention's Committee of Public Safety,qv which served, in effect, as the interim government of Texas until March 2, 1861, when the referendum on the Ordinance of Secession was officially endorsed.

Diamond joined the 11th Texas Cavalry, organized in July, 1861, as a captain of a company, was quickly promoted to lieutenant colonel, and later held the rank of colonel. He was one of the organizers and managers of the "citizens court" formed in Gainesville in October, 1862, which brought to trial and hanged thirty-nine persons accused of a part in the "Peace Party Conspiracy."qv He died in Houston during the yellow fever epidemic of 1867. *See also* Gainesville, Great Hanging at.

BIBLIOGRAPHY: M. D. Lucas and M. H. Hall, *A History of Grayson County, Texas* (1936); Sam Acheson and J. A. O'Connell (eds.), *George Washington Diamond's Account of the Great Hanging at Gainesville, 1862* (1963); Graham Landrum, *Grayson County: An Illustrated History* (1960); A. M. Smith, *The First 100 Years in Cooke County* (1955); E. W. Winkler (ed.), *Journal of the Secession Convention of Texas, 1861* (1912).

Sam Acheson

Diamond, Texas. Diamond, in western Scurry County, is the location of a gas refinery around which are a few company-owned houses, but no stores or post office. The refinery, originally owned by the Lyon Oil Company, is in the Diamond M oil field, named for the local Diamond M Ranch.

Diana, Texas. *See* New Diana, Texas.

*Diboll, Texas. Diboll, in southwestern Angelina County, was established in 1894 by Thomas Lewis Latané Temple qv (not T. L. K. Temple, as stated in Volume I). The town reported fifty-eight businesses, three schools, and a bank in 1967. Industries included a large lumber mill and several companies manufacturing wood products. A new plywood mill had been built. The 1960 population was 2,506; in 1970 the population was 3,557.

*Dibrell, Joseph Burton.

*Dicey, Texas.

*Dickens, Texas. Dickens, seat of Dickens County, is the main market for the surrounding ranching area. The town had twelve businesses in 1970. The population was 302 in 1960 and 295 in 1970.

*Dickens County. Dickens County is divided, for the most part, into several large cattle ranches. There is, however, some irrigated farming, mainly cotton. Oil is present in small quantities. The marketing center is the county seat, Dickens, but the largest city is Spur. County population was 4,963 in 1960 and 3,737 in 1970.

*Dickenson, Almaron. The spelling of Almaron Dickenson's name has always been controversial. The marriage certificate and the application for headright land gave the name as Almeron Dickinson; an affidavit made by Mrs. Dickenson's last husband used the spelling Almaron Dickerson. *See also* Dickenson, Mrs. Almaron.

BIBLIOGRAPHY: Walter Lord, *A Time to Stand* (1961); Amelia Williams, "A Critical Study of the Siege of the Alamo and of the Personnel of its Defenders," *Southwestern Historical Quarterly*, XXXVII (1933–1934).

*Dickenson, Mrs. Almaron. Mrs. Almaron Dickenson (for variant spellings of the name, *see* Dickenson, Almaron) married John W. Hannag [or Hannig] (not Hanning, as stated in Volume I) in 1857.

BIBLIOGRAPHY: Curtis Bishop, "Forgotten Heroine," *Texas Parade*, XXIV (1964); Amelia Williams, "A Critical Study of the Siege of the Alamo and of the Personnel of its Defenders," *Southwestern Historical Quarterly,* XXXVII (1933–1934).

*Dickey Creek.

*Dickie's Spout, Texas.

*Dickinson, John.

*Dickinson, Texas. Dickinson, in north-central Galveston County, recorded a 74 percent increase in population during the 1950's and a 128.5 percent increase during the 1960's, with census figures showing 2,704 in 1950, 4,715 in 1960, and 10,776 in 1970. It was the largest unincorporated city in Texas in 1970. Although it was once called the "Strawberry Capital of the World," the area is shifting from an agricultural to a residential community. One hundred businesses were reported in 1970, including a printing firm and a refinery for mineral oil. *See also* Galveston-Texas City Standard Metropolitan Statistical Area.

*Dickinson Bayou.

*Dickson, Cambell.

*Dickson, David Catchings.

*Dickson Colored Orphanage.

*Dickson Gun Plant.

*Dickworsham, Texas.

Dico Indians. The Dico are known from a single 1691 Spanish missionary report which lists them among the groups that lived southeast of the Hasinai. Since the distance was not given, it is impossible to tell whether the Dico area was in eastern Texas or western Louisiana. Their affiliations are unknown.

BIBLIOGRAPHY: J. R. Swanton, *Source Material on the History and Ethnology of the Caddo Indians* (1942).

T. N. Campbell

Didrikson, Mildred Ella (Babe). *See* Zaharias, Mildred Ella (Babe) Didrikson.

*Dienst, Alex.

Dientes Alazanes Indians. The Dientes Alazanes (Spanish for "sorrel-colored teeth") are known only from a Spanish document of 1693 which lists them as one of fifty "nations" that lived north of the Rio Grande and "between Texas and New Mexico." This may be interpreted to mean the southern part of western Texas, since the document also mentions that the Apache were at war with the groups named. Nothing further is known about the Dientes Alazanes. The name reference to stained teeth suggests that these Indians may have lived in the southern high plains of western Texas, since tooth-staining by minerals in the water of that area occurs there.

BIBLIOGRAPHY: C. W. Hackett (ed.), *Historical Documents Relating to New Mexico, Nueva Vizcaya, and Approaches Thereto, to 1773,* II (1926).

T. N. Campbell

*Dies, Martin.

Dies, Martin. Martin Dies was born November 5, 1901, in Colorado City, Mitchell County, the son of Olive M. (Cline) and Martin Dies.qv He studied at Wesley College in Greenville and the University of Texas after graduating from Beaumont High

School, but he had to give up his law courses because of eye problems. Dies then moved to Washington to continue his studies and earned a law degree from National University in 1920. On June 3, 1920, he married Myrtle M. Adams; they were the parents of three sons. After practicing for a time in Marshall, Dies entered his father's law firm in Orange in 1922, and in 1931 he was elected to Congress as its youngest member. With a seat on the House Rules Committee, and then as the first chairman of the Un-American Activities Committee (created in May, 1938, and known popularly as the Dies Committee), Dies frequently made headlines with his probes of Nazi, Fascist, Communist, and other organizations termed "un-American" or subversive in the United States.

In January of 1945 the Dies Committee was given permanent status by a House vote (207–186), and that same year the committee recommended dismissal of some 3,800 government employees thought to be connected or in sympathy with subversive activities. After a Department of Justice investigation, only thirty-six were found to warrant dismissal. Also in 1945 Dies resigned his seat because of ill health; he won election as congressman-at-large in 1952, but lost in a bid for the Senate in 1957, serving the remainder of his term in the House. Dies served over two decades in Congress, voting steadfastly against foreign aid. He was the author of *The Trojan Horse in America* (1940) and *Martin Dies' Story* (1963); the files and papers collected by his committee were given to Texas A&M's Cushing Library. Martin Dies died in Lufkin November 14, 1972, and was buried in the Garden of Memories Chapel.

BIBLIOGRAPHY: *Who's Who In America* (1948); Biographical Files, Barker Texas History Center, University of Texas at Austin.

*Dies, Texas.

Dieterich, Francis. Francis Dieterich was born on February 2, 1815, in Cassel, Germany. He came to Texas in 1834 and settled in Refugio, where he petitioned for several leagues of land, which were granted; he also bought a lot there when the town was officially surveyed. In February, 1836, he joined a company of militia which became part of a regiment commanded by Lieutenant Colonel William Ward qv under Colonel James W. Fannin, Jr.qv He participated in the defense of the mission at Refugio, where he was taken prisoner on March 14, 1836, and his life was spared. He was again taken prisoner at Goliad but escaped the Goliad Massacre qv of March 27. After the war he applied for land and received two grants—640 acres of donation land in San Patricio County, and 320 acres of bounty land in Comal County.

In 1839 he moved to Austin and, in that community's first year of real settlement, went into business as a meat dealer. Records of sales from November 29, 1839, to September 14, 1841, show that Dieterich sold approximately 25,900 pounds of beef preceding and during preparation by the government for the Texan Santa Fe Expedition.qv He added to his land holdings by the purchase of three city lots in 1841. When the government of the Republic moved to Washington-on-the-Brazos in 1842, Dieterich moved there also to supply the government with goods. On returning to Austin in 1845, he opened a store at the corner of Congress Avenue and Pecan Street (now Sixth Street), and joined in business with George Hancock,qv who bought the site from Alexander Russell. Later he purchased lots on the east side of Congress Avenue, where he increased his trade by sales from his own storehouse. In 1846 he served as alderman of the city.

Dieterich was married three times: to Bessie Reed in 1834 or 1835, by whom he had twin children, one of whom survived; to Martha Ann Brown on March 12, 1845, Bessie having died sometime prior to 1845; and to Sarah Elizabeth Browning on June 17, 1847, Martha Ann having died in 1846. Francis and Sarah Dieterich were the parents of four children. He died in Austin on May 31, 1860, and was buried in Oakwood Cemetery.

BIBLIOGRAPHY: Dora Dieterich Bonham, *Merchant to the Republic* (1958); Frank Brown, Annals of Travis County, and of the City of Austin (MS., Archives, University of Texas at Austin Library); William H. Oberste, *Texas Irish Empresarios and Their Colonies* (1953); Austin-Travis County Collection, Austin Public Library, Austin; Dora Dieterich Bonham Collection (Archives, University of Texas at Austin Library).

Dora Dieterich Bonham

*Dietz, Texas.

*Dignowity, Anthony Michael.

Diju Indians. In 1683–1684 Juan Domínguez de Mendoza qv led an exploratory expedition from El Paso as far eastward as the junction of the Concho and Colorado rivers east of present San Angelo. In his itinerary he listed the names of thirty-seven Indian groups, including the Diju, from which he expected to receive delegations on the Colorado River. Nothing further is known about the Diju, who seem to have been one of many Indian groups of north-central Texas that were swept away by the southward thrust of the Lipan-Apache and Comanche Indians in the eighteenth century.

BIBLIOGRAPHY: H. E. Bolton (ed.), *Spanish Exploration in the Southwest, 1542–1706* (1916); C. W. Hackett (ed.), *Pichardo's Treatise on the Limits of Louisiana and Texas*, II (1934).

T. N. Campbell

*Dike, Texas.

*Dikes Creek.

*Dill, James.

*Dill Creek.

*Dillard, Frank Clifford.

*Dillard, Nicholas.

*Dillard Creek.

*Dilley, Texas. Dilley, in Frio County, had a population of 2,118 in 1960 and 2,362 in 1970.

*Dillon, Texas.

*Dilworth, Texas.

*Dime Box, Texas.

*Dimitt, Philip.

Dimitt's Landing. Dimitt's Landing in Calhoun County was founded in 1832 by Philip Dimitt qv and was the second settlement in that county. Located on the east bank of the mouth of the Lavaca River, Dimitt's Landing existed primarily around a pier and a warehouse for handling imports. However, shortly after the death of Dimitt in 1841, the town was abandoned. A centennial marker was placed on the site of the town, but this was destroyed by Hurricane Carla in 1961.

C. D. George

*Dimmit County. Dimmit County, a leading vegetable producer of the Winter Garden region qv of Texas, has an agricultural economy consisting primarily of cattle and truck crops. About fifteen thousand acres were irrigated in 1964. In the early 1970's oil production had become important. The 1960 population was 10,095; by 1970 it had decreased to 9,039.

Dimmit's Landing. *See* Dimitt's Landing.

*Dimmitt, Texas. Dimmitt, seat and trading center of Castro County, depends upon agriculture for most of its income. Local crops are stored in its grain elevators, while its new fertilizer plant produces for a wider market. A federal youth corps project was located within the city. The population increased from 2,935 in 1960 to 4,327 in 1970.

*Dimple, Texas.

*Dinero, Texas.

*Dinkins, Texas.

*Dinner Creek.

*Dinsmore, Silas.

*Diplomatic Relations of the Republic of Texas.

*Direct, Texas.

*Direct Navigation Company. *See* Houston Direct Navigation Company.

Directory of Texas Manufacturers. The *Directory of Texas Manufacturers* for 1976 was the twenty-seventh edition published by the Bureau of Business Research of the University of Texas at Austin. First published biennially, it has been revised annually since 1960. Each issue contains about nine hundred pages. For each manufacturing firm listed, information covers products manufactured (classified by the Standard Industrial Classification Code), address, chief executive officer, date of establishment of the firm, type of business organization, area of distribution, and employment. The publication is divided into three sections: an alphabetical listing, a geographical listing, and a products listing. A monthly supplement to the *Directory*, entitled *Texas Industrial Expansion*, is also published. In addition to listing new industries, this publication includes announcements of expansions, of changes of ownership, of mergers, and of changes of address for manufacturing concerns. The supplement also includes information on public utilities in Texas. The *Directory* had grown to such size by 1971 that a two-volume format was required.

Stanley A. Arbingast

*Dirt Farmers' Congress.

Disabled American Veterans, Department of Texas. The Disabled American Veterans, World War, was organized in Cincinnati, Ohio, in 1920 by Robert S. Marks, who became its first national commander. In June, 1921, the first Texas chapter, Harwood Davis Chapter Number One, was formed in Fort Worth. By July, 1921, there were more than twenty-five chapters throughout Texas. In May, 1923, the Department of Texas, Disabled American Veterans, World War, was organized at Kerrville, Texas. William Ellis Register was elected first department commander, a position which he held for two terms. Congress granted the organization a federal charter in 1932. This charter was amended in 1942 by the deletion of the words "World War." The purpose of the organization is to advance the interests of all wounded, gassed, injured, and disabled veterans of all wars.

Laurence R. Melton of Dallas was the first state commander to be elected to the office of national commander, for the term 1941–1943. During this term he was instrumental in securing an executive order from President Franklin D. Roosevelt for government agencies to cooperate in the hiring of the physically handicapped. This program has become national in scope and is now known as the President's Committee for the Hiring of the Handicapped. The DAV local and state organizations also grant scholarships to the winners of essay contests which are held each year. In 1966 there were more than one hundred chapters of the DAV, with more than eight thousand active members located in five regions throughout the state.

P. D. Jackson

Disch, William John. William John (Billy) Disch was born on October 20, 1874, in Benton County, Missouri. In 1886 the Disch family moved to Milwaukee, Wisconsin, where Disch first attended public schools. His greatest interest was baseball, and in 1898 he began his coaching career at Sacred Heart College in Watertown, Wisconsin. On December 25, 1909, he married Anna Marie Kuck.

He played professionally at Sioux Falls, South Dakota, from 1900 to 1902; at Fort Worth from 1903 to 1904; and at Galveston from 1905 to 1907. He simultaneously coached at St. Edward's University in Austin from 1900 to 1910, and in 1911 he joined the staff of the University of Texas, where he compiled one of the nation's best coaching records. From 1911 until his retirement in 1940, Disch's teams won twenty-one out of a possible twenty-six baseball championships.

Disch played an important role in persuading the Southwest Conference qv to adopt baseball in 1915, and in 1947, "Uncle Billy" was honored with the opening of Austin's Disch Field, named for him. He died on February 3, 1953.

BIBLIOGRAPHY: Austin *American,* February 4, 1953.

*Disciples of Christ (Christian Church) in Texas. See also Christian Church (Disciples of Christ) in Texas.

*District Court, Clerk of. *See also* County and Precinct Officers, Terms of.

*Dittlinger, Texas.

*Ditto, Texas.

*Diversion Lake.

*Divide, Texas. (Hopkins County.)

*Divide, Texas. (Nolan County.) *See also* Nolan, Texas.

Divine Providence, Sisters of. *See* Sisters of Divine Providence.

Division of Planning Coordination, Governor's Office. *See* Planning Coordination, Division of, Governor's Office.

*Division of Texas, Proposals for.

*Divot, Texas.

*Dixie, Texas. (Grayson County.)

*Dixie, Texas. (Young County.)

*Dixon, William (Billy).

*Dixon, Texas.

*Dixon Creek.

*Dixon Lake.

*Doan's Crossing and Store.

*Dobbin, Texas.

Dobie, Bertha McKee. Bertha McKee Dobie, daughter of Richard Alexander and Ray (Park) McKee, was born on July 8, 1890, on a farm in Susquehanna County (near Nicholson), Pennsylvania; at that time her parents had already established residence in Texas, but her mother had returned to Pennsylvania to have her first child. The family lived for short periods in the small Texas towns of Italy, Forreston, Coldspring, Waelder, and Aransas Pass before settling in Velasco when Bertha was seven years old. After graduation from high school she received a B.A. degree from Southwestern University in Georgetown (where she met her future husband) in 1910; she later took a masters degree in English from the University of Texas in 1918. She taught English and mathematics in Dalhart, Galveston, and Alexander Collegiate Institute (originally called Alexander Institute, now Lon Morris College) in Jacksonville.

Bertha McKee was married to James Frank Dobie qv on September 20, 1916, and in later years she was credited by her renowned husband as being his best literary critic and editor. Bertha Dobie became a writer in her own right, contributing a series of articles on gardening for Texas newspapers; she also wrote for numerous periodicals, including *Nature Magazine, New York Herald Tribune Magazine, Garden Digest, Holland's Magazine,*qv *Publications of the Texas Folklore Society,* and *Southwest Review.*qv She was assistant editor of the Texas Folklore Society's qv *Publications* from 1923 to 1935. Occasionally she conducted classes at the University of Texas for her faculty-member husband while he was away collecting materials for his books. She was well known for the flower garden at her home in Austin and was a guest lecturer on gardening at meetings throughout the state. Especially attuned to nature, Bertha Dobie was a member of the Audubon Society and was an interested participant in the formulation of plans for Paisano Ranch,qv a hill country (central Texas) retreat for Texas writers and artists. Upon the death of J. Frank Dobie, she edited his posthumous publications. She was named a distinguished alumna of Southwestern University on January 26, 1973.

Bertha McKee Dobie died on December 18, 1974, and was buried alongside her husband in the State Cemetery qv in Austin.

Eldon Branda

Dobie, James Frank. J. Frank Dobie, son of Richard Jonathan and Ella (Byler) Dobie, was born September 26, 1888, on his parents' ranch in Live Oak County, Texas. He was the oldest of six children. His early education was in ranch schools built by his father and neighbors. He attended high school in Alice, Texas, where he was graduated as salutatorian. In 1906 he entered Southwestern University, Georgetown, Texas, where he intended taking courses leading to a law degree so that he could "make speeches to the jury," but he became interested in English poetry and took a B.A. degree there in 1910 with the aim of teaching English.

Between college graduation and his first teaching job, he worked as a summer reporter on the San Antonio *Express*.qv He liked being a newspaperman and said if he had not contracted to teach school he would have remained in journalism. In the fall of 1910 he became principal of the high school in Alpine, Texas, also teaching English, history, Spanish, and geology. For a short time thereafter he returned to Southwestern to work as a fund-raiser and secretary to the president, as well as to teach in the preparatory school.

In 1913 he entered Columbia University, where he received his master's degree in 1914; he worked again as a reporter during the summer of 1914 on the Galveston *Tribune*, then returned to the University of Texas in Austin that fall. He never took a Ph.D. degree and was said to be the first native Texan without such a degree to rise above the rank of instructor in the University of Texas English department, where he became a full professor in 1933. He taught in that department from 1914 until 1947, but with several interruptions. During World War I he served as a first lieutenant in the United States Army. He managed a ranch owned by his uncle in 1920–1921, and while there he began to think about writing, particularly about the land he had grown up on.

In 1921 he again became a member of the faculty at the University of Texas, where he remained until 1923, when he left to serve as chairman of the English department at Oklahoma A&M College at Stillwater. He returned to the University of Texas in 1925 as adjunct professor. In that same year he sold an article on cowboy songs to *Country Gentleman*, a magazine with wide national circulation. Previously his published writings had been limited to articles for the publication of the Texas Folklore Society,qv which he, along with Professor Leonidas

Payne,qv had reorganized in 1922, and for which he served as editor and secretary from 1922 until 1942. His aim as a writer had become, as it was to remain, to "open the eyes of the people to the richness of their own tradition." With the publication of two books, *A Vaquero of the Brush Country* (1929) and *Coronado's Children* (1931), Dobie became a national literary figure. Many books followed, including *The Longhorns* (1941), *The Voice of the Coyote* (1949), and *Cow People* (1964). He also wrote a weekly Sunday column for Texas newspapers from 1939 until his death.

He lectured in American history at Emmanuel College, Cambridge University, England, in 1943–1944, and was awarded an honorary master of arts degree in June, 1944, from that university. He returned to England in 1945, and during 1945 and 1946 he gave lectures to American servicemen in Shrivenham, England, and in Germany and Austria.

Dobie, as a liberal Democrat, was often at odds with the University of Texas and state officials. He espoused academic freedom and decried the firing in 1944 of the university's president, Homer Price Rainey. After differences over his application for an extension of leave of absence, he was dropped from the University of Texas faculty budget in 1947. Though he never rejoined the university faculty, he continued to lecture on the campus, read manuscripts for the University of Texas Press,qv and often counseled with university administrators and faculty members.

He was appointed a member of the United States National Commission, UNESCO, in 1945–1946 and a consultant to the Library of Congress on American cultural history in 1964.

He died in his home in Austin on September 18, 1964. Four days before his death, his wife Bertha McKee Dobie qv (whom he married on September 20, 1916) received on Dobie's behalf the Presidential Medal of Freedom from President Lyndon B. Johnson qv in a ceremony in Washington, D.C. Services were held for Dobie in Hogg Auditorium on the campus of the University of Texas, and he was buried in the State Cemetery qv in Austin. Dobie's outstanding working library, manuscripts, letters, and collections are housed in the Dobie Room in the Academic Center at the University of Texas at Austin. *See also* Paisano Ranch.

Winston Bode

*Dobie, James M.

Dobie-Paisano Project. *See* Paisano Ranch.

*Dobrowolski, Texas.

*Dockum Creek.

*Doctors Creek.

Dodd, Texas. Dodd was the name given to a small community on Farm Road 303 in extreme southwestern Castro County. Before the road became a throughway, between 1955 and 1965, the settlement apparently marked the terminus of a local road. In 1966 Dodd consisted of little more than a gas station.

*Dodd Branch.

*Dodd City, Texas. (Fannin County.)

*Dodd City, Texas. (Travis County.)

*Doddville, Texas.

*Dodge, Texas. (McCulloch County.)

*Dodge, Texas. (Walker County.)

*Dodge City Trail. *See* Western Trail.

*Dodson, Archelaus Bynum. Archelaus Bynum Dodson, son of Obadiah and Sarah (Garrison) Dodson, was born December 31, 1807, in North Carolina. He came to Texas in 1826, settled in Harrisburg, and there married Sarah Randolf Bradley on May 17, 1835; they were the parents of six children.

In September, 1835, the tricolor flag made by his wife (presented to Robinson's Company, in which Dodson was a first lieutenant) was the first to fly over San Antonio when that city was captured following the siege of Bexar qv in December, 1835. Dodson was among those detailed to insure the safety of women and children in the Runaway Scrape qv early in 1836.

Following his participation in the battle of San Jacinto, Dodson lived in Fort Bend County. He and his family moved to Grimes County in 1844, where he gave ten acres of land to the Bethel Community for a church, a school, and a cemetery. After the death of his wife in 1848, Dodson married Louisa McWhorter in 1850. He brought his family to Live Oak County in 1860. Dodson spent the final years of his life in Alice, where he died March 10, 1898; he was buried in the Old Collins Cemetery about two miles east of the present city limits of Alice.

Agnes G. Grimm

*Dodson, Sarah (Bradley).

Dodson, Viola Ruth. Viola Ruth Dodson was born on the Perdido Ranch in Nueces County on September 3, 1876, the daughter of Milton and Susan Dodson. Her early schooling took place on the ranch and, for one year, in the public schools of Corpus Christi. She also attended Lagarto College.qv In 1935, at the insistence of J. Frank Dobie,qv to whose work she contributed material and information, she wrote a volume, entirely in Spanish, of southwest Texas folklore entitled *Don Pedrito Jaramillo*. Jaramillo qv was a faith healer and doctor, and the book contains many of his healing remedies. The library of the College of Physicians in Philadelphia acquired it as a reference book in the history of medicine, and it has become a classic in the field of folklore. Other writings included pieces for the Texas Folklore Society (of which she was a counselor), the *Southwest Review*, and *Frontier Times*.qqv Her aim was to present a true picture of the area between the Nueces and Rio Grande; having grown up speaking Spanish, as well as English, she often wrote in Spanish, as in the case of *Don Pedrito*. Miss Dodson died in Corpus Christi on July 19, 1963, and was buried in the Old Mathis Cemetery, Mathis, Texas, in San Patricio County.

BIBLIOGRAPHY: Biographical File, Barker Texas History Center, University of Texas at Austin.

Agnes G. Grimm

*Dodson, Texas.

*Doe Creek.

*Doe Run Creek.

*Dog Creek.

*Dogie Mountains.

*Dog-run Houses.

*Doguene Indians. The Doguene (Aguene, Deaguane, Deguene, Draguane) were Indians of the Texas coast among whom Cabeza de Vaca qv lived for a time, presumably about 1528. Their precise location cannot be determined, but geographic details in the Cabeza de Vaca narrative seem to indicate the vicinity of Matagorda Bay. About 160 years later, when Europeans again visited this section of the coast, it was occupied by Karankawan groups. In Volume I, Doguene and Deaguane were presented separately; they are variants of the same name. The Doguene lived in the vicinity of San Antonio Bay (not San Antonio, as stated in Volume I).

BIBLIOGRAPHY: A. F. Bandelier (ed.), *The Journey of Alvar Nuñez Cabeza de Vaca* (1922); F. W. Hodge (ed.), *Handbook of American Indians*, I (1907), II (1910).

T. N. Campbell

*Dogwood Bayou.

*Dogwood Creek.

*Dohoney, Eben LaFayette.

*Doke, Texas.

*Dokegood Creek.

*Dolchburg, Texas.

*Dollardsville, Texas.

*Dolores, Presidio of. *See* Nuestra Señora de los Dolores de los Tejas Presidio.

*Dolores, Texas. (Webb County.)

Dolores, Texas. (Zapata County.) *See* Nuestra Señora de Dolores.

*Dolores Creek.

*Dolores Mission. *See* Nuestra Señora de los Dolores de los Ais Mission.

*Dolores y Viana, Mariano Francisco de los.

*Dome Mountain.

*Dome Peak.

*Domenech, Emanuel Henri Dieudonné.

*Domínguez, Cristóbal.

Domínguez y Valdez, Juan. Juan Domínguez y Valdez was born in Havana, Cuba, in 1784. He began military training as a cadet in 1795 and joined the Mexican Army on October 9, 1813, when he landed at Vera Cruz. He was a lieutenant colonel in the Army of the Three Guarantees, supporting the Plan of Iguala which proclaimed Mexican independence in March, 1821. Domínguez retired in 1828 as a full colonel. He married Ignacia Quintanar, the niece of a general, in 1821, and by 1828 they had four daughters.

Domínguez was granted a colonization contract by the Texas government on July 6, 1829. By terms of this contract he was to bring 200 American and European settlers to Texas within a period of six years, to be located in an area bounded as follows: beginning on the Arkansas River where the river is intersected by the 23rd degree of longitude west of Washington, the boundary line between Mexico and the United States; thence south with said boundary line the distance of forty leagues; thence west twenty leagues; thence north on a line parallel with the 23rd meridian to the Arkansas River; thence with the right bank of the Arkansas River to its intersection with said 23rd meridian, the place of beginning.

Domínguez, who resided in Mexico, appointed Victor Blanco, lieutenant governor of Texas, to sign his contract. Domínguez brought no colonists to Texas, and his contract expired in 1835.

BIBLIOGRAPHY: Translations of Impresario Contracts, 1825–1835 (MS., Spanish Archives, General Land Office, Austin).

Virginia H. Taylor

Dominican College. Dominican College (formerly Sacred Heart Dominican College qv), located in Houston, grew out of the Convent of the Sacred Heart, a teacher-training school for the Sisters of Saint Dominic (*see* Sisters, Dominican), which was established in 1882 by Mother Mary Agnes Magevney at the request of Bishop Nicholas Aloysius Gallagher.qv The convent remained on Market Street in Galveston until 1926, at which time a forty-acre tract in south Houston was obtained and a four-story brick building was erected there.

In 1945 the college was formally organized as a women's junior college and affiliated with the Catholic University of America. Approved as a junior college by the State Department of Education in June, 1946, the school was chartered to operate as a senior college in September, 1946, and received state approval in 1948. The first degrees were conferred in 1949.

In June, 1947, St. Joseph's School of Nursing, conducted by the Sisters of Charity of the Incarnate Word,qv transferred its program of affiliation from the University of Houston. A four-year college course in nursing leading to the bachelor of science degree became operative in September, 1948. The college also awarded bachelor of arts degrees in seventeen major fields, and the music department offered programs leading to either a B.A. or a bachelor of music degree in liturgical music.

By 1965 the campus contained a main building, chapel, administration building, science building, music hall, student center, three dormitories, business center, art center, and a library subscribing to 250 periodicals and containing over 49,166 volumes. A few male students were enrolled in the early 1970's, but the college was primarily attended by female students. In the fall of 1974 the total enrollment was 265 students, the faculty numbered approximately fifty members, and Sister Antoinette Boykin was president. *See also* Roman Catholic Education in Texas.

Dominican Sisters. *See* Sisters, Dominican.

*Domino, Texas.

"Don Pedrito" Jaramillo. *See* Jaramillo, Pedro.

*Donaho Creek.

*Donahoe, Texas.

*Donahoe Creek.

*Donalson Creek.

*Donation Warrants.

*Donelson, Andrew Jackson.

*Donelton, Texas.

*Donie, Texas.

*Donley, Stockton P.

*Donley County.** Donley County bases its economy on ranching and farming. A great part of the farm income is derived from cattle and other livestock; crops include cotton, grain sorghums, and wheat, with 14,500 acres under irrigation. Interstate Highway 40 bounds the county to the north. Several fairs and festivals are held annually. The population was 4,449 in 1960 and 3,641 in 1970.

*Donna, Texas.** Donna, in Hidalgo County, received its income primarily from fruits and vegetables and the tourist trade in recent years. In 1967 Donna reported 110 businesses (including eight manufacturers), ten churches, a bank, a library, and a newspaper. The world's first American Legion hall, located in Donna, was designated a historical landmark in 1964. The 1960 census reported the population as 7,522; the 1970 census reported 7,365.

*Donnellan, Thurston John.

Donoghue, David Patrick. David Patrick Donoghue was born on January 19, 1891, in San Antonio, the son of Patrick and Statia Madeline (Fitzgerald) Donoghue. He was graduated in 1909 from St. Mary's University with a B.S. degree, and from 1909 to 1912 he studied mining engineering and geology at the University of Texas. He began his professional career associated with the United States Geological Survey (1911 to 1913). He worked as a scout, leaseman, and geologist for the J. M. Guffey Petroleum Company from 1914 to 1918, and from 1919 to 1921 he was a geologist for Gulf Production Company. On June 30, 1914, Donoghue married Agnes M. Kennedy. He acted as a consulting geologist in Fort Worth and Houston from 1921 to 1924, when he became assistant to the vice-president of Marland Oil Company. In 1925 he was made director of Texas Pacific Coal and Oil Company, and in 1929 he again became a consulting geologist. Donoghue became president of the Federal Royalties Company in 1933, a position which he held until 1951. From 1952 to 1958 he served as president of Lasca, Inc. In addition to his regular duties, Donoghue acted as consultant for the Consejo Nacional de Petroleos in Colombia from 1948 to 1949, and in 1948 he served as petroleum adviser for the United States mission in Libya.

Donoghue was active in numerous professional, religious, and civic organizations, including memberships in several southwestern historical societies. He served as vice-president of the American Association of Petroleum Geologists from 1927 to 1929, and he was director and vice-president of the Texas Independent Producers and Royalty Owners Association. He served as mayor of Westover Hills in Tarrant County from 1946 to 1948 and was commissioner from 1948 to 1949. Donoghue published many papers on petroleum appraisals, geology, engineering, and Texas history. He died on October 15, 1958, in Mexico City, and was buried in Greenwood Cemetery in Fort Worth.

*Donoho, William.

*Donovan, Texas.

*Doole, Texas.

*Doom, Randolph C.

*Dor, John M.

*Dora, Texas.

*Dorantes de Carranza, Andrés.

*Dorchester, Texas.

*Dorn, Andrew J.

*Dorr Creek.

*Dorras, Texas.

*Doss, Texas. (Cass County.)

*Doss, Texas. (Gillespie County.)

*Dot, Texas.

*Dotchetonne Indians. The Dotchetonne Indians are known only from records of the La Salle Expedition,qv which identify them as late seventeenth-century allies of the Kadohadacho. Although some writers state that the Dotchetonne lived in northeastern Texas, this has never been demonstrated. J. R. Swanton identified the Dotchetonne as a Caddoan group that lived on Bayou Dauchite in present northwestern Louisiana, but he presented no argument for this identification.
BIBLIOGRAPHY: F. W. Hodge (ed.), *Handbook of American Indians*, I (1907); P. Margry, *Découvertes et établissements des Français dans l'ouest et dans le sud de l'Amérique Septentrionale*, III (1879); J. R. Swanton, *Source Material on the History and Ethnology of the Caddo Indians* (1942).

T. N. Campbell

*Dothan, Texas.

*Dotson, Texas.

*Doty, Texas.

*Double Bayou.

*Double Bayou, Texas.

*Double Creek.

Double Horn, Texas. Double Horn, at the headspring of Double Horn Creek in Burnet County, was settled in 1855 by Jesse Burnam qv (or Burnham), Levi Fowler, and others. The creek had been named earlier when a pioneer found the horns of two bucks whose antlers were interlocked, presumably the result of a fight in which the deer could not separate themselves, thus dying of starvation. In 1855 William H. Holland qv taught in a school there, with thirty-five pupils, including the children of Noah Smithwick.qv From 1861 to 1865

the post office was operated by the Confederate States with P. M. Yett as postmaster. The post office was discontinued about 1910, when the village had a population of sixty-three.
BIBLIOGRAPHY: *Frontier Times*, December, 1949; Grover C. Ramsey, *Confederate Postmasters in Texas* (1963); Noah Smithwick, *Evolution of a State* (1900).

Cyrus Tilloson

*Double Horn Creek. [This title was incorrectly listed in Volume I as Doublehorn Creek.]

*Double Knobbs, Texas.

*Double Lakes.

*Double Mountain

*Double Mountain Canyon.

*Double Mountain Fork of the Brazos River.

*Doublehorn Creek. *See* Double Horn Creek.

*Doucette, Texas.

*Doud, Texas.

Dougherty, James Robert. James Robert Dougherty, son of Robert and Rachael (Sullivan) Dougherty, was born in San Patricio, Texas, on August 27, 1871. Dougherty became a teacher at Los Apaches, in Webb County, after certification by examination at the age of sixteen. Two years later he enrolled at St. Louis University, after which he attended the University of Texas in Austin. He studied law in the offices of Lon C. Hill and Judge Jim Wells,qqv and he was admitted to the Bar on March 4, 1895. He went to Beeville to practice law, and later his brother, J. Chrys Dougherty, joined him to form the law firm of Dougherty and Dougherty, an outstanding firm in South Texas for more than half a century. J. Chrys died in 1932, but the firm name remained unchanged. Dougherty helped to establish the legal precedent of private ownership of minerals in river beds of nonnavigable rivers.

He was a ranchman before he became a lawyer and dealt in livestock all his life. He developed a silver mine in Durango, Mexico, in 1916. He was instrumental in discovering a number of South Texas oil fields, including the Tom O'Conner, Greta, Pettus, Flour Bluff, Refugio, the Dougherty Field in Duval County, and several others. He became associated with Dr. W. E. Hewit in the formation of the oil company of Hewit and Dougherty, which operated over a wide area of South and West Texas. He spoke Spanish fluently and was a student of Latin, Greek, and French. He furnished capital to a publishing company in New York for the printing of translations from rare Latin and Greek manuscripts.

Dougherty married Genevieve Tarlton on April 24, 1911, and they had four children. He was a member of the board of regents of Texas A&I College (now Texas A&I University) at Kingsville for ten years, and was a member of the boards of regents of Incarnate Word and Our Lady of the Lake colleges in San Antonio. A decade before his death, he and his wife established the Dougherty Foundation as an aid to youths for obtaining an education. He died on July 8, 1950, in Corpus Christi and was buried at Beeville.

BIBLIOGRAPHY: Grace Bauer, *Bee County Centennial, 1858–1958* (1958); J. Frank Dobie, "Intelligent and Delightful Talk Finest Thing Society Offers," Fort Worth *Star-Telegram*, November 29, 1964.

Grace Bauer

*Dougherty, Texas.

*Doughty, Walter Francis.

*Douglas, James P.

Douglas MacArthur Academy of Freedom. *See* Howard Payne College.

*Douglas Mountains.

*Douglass, Kelsey Harris.

*Douglass, Samuel C.

*Douglass, Texas.

*Douglassville, Texas.

*Douro, Texas.

*Dove, Texas.

*Dove Creek.

*Dove Creek, Battle of.

*Dove Mountain.

*Dowell, Greensville S.

*Dowling, Richard W. (Dick).

*Downer, James Walker.

*Downie Creek.

*Downing, Texas.

*Downsville, Texas.

*Doyle, Texas.

*Doyle Creek.

*Dozier, Texas.

*Dozier Creek.

*Drainage Districts. *See also* Water Agencies and Programs, Local (and all *see* references following that article).

*Drama. *See* Theater in Texas.

*Drane, Texas.

*Drascoe, Texas.

*Draw, Texas.

*Dreamland, Texas.

*Dreben, Sam.

*Dreka, Texas.

*Drennan Creek.

*Dresden, Texas.

Dresel, Gustav. Gustav Dresel, born in 1818 in Germany, came to the United States in 1837 and in 1838 settled in Houston, where he obtained a position as bookkeeper and salesman in a general merchandise firm. Between 1838 and 1841 he traveled in parts of Texas (particularly the area around Houston), Louisiana, and Mississippi. He kept extensive accounts of his experiences and impressions in a diary called "Texanisches Tagebuch," which was published in the yearbook for 1920–1921 of the German-American Historical Society of Illinois. Later it was published in translation by the University of Texas Press ᵠᵛ in 1954 under the title *Gustav Dresel's Houston Journal*.

Dresel was the first German consul in Texas, serving in that capacity for Duke Adolph of Nassau, from whose country many of the German immigrants came. At the same time he was business manager in Texas for the German Society for the Protection of German Immigrants to Texas, located in Galveston. He died on September 14, 1848.

Max Freund

*Dressy, Texas.

*Drew's Landing, Texas. *See* Marianna, Texas.

Dreyfoos, Texas. Dreyfoos, also known as Patton and Cann, was established in Hemphill County in 1928, when the Cities Service Gas Company built a compressor station on land purchased from Dick Cann, a pioneer rancher. For a short time there was a post office there. In 1929 a two-year high school was built on land purchased from Ben Dreyfoos, and the community was called Dreyfoos, even though the official name was Patton. When founded, the town had an approximate population of forty; in 1966 the population was thirteen. Inhabitants were ranchers, farmers, or employees of Cities Service Gas Company. The school was still in use in 1966, employing one teacher.

*Dreyfuss, Sol. [Out of alphabetical order on page 518, Volume I.]

*Driftwood, Texas.

*Dripping Springs, Texas.

*Dripping Springs Academy.

*Driscoll, Clara.

*Driscoll, Robert.

*Driscoll, Texas. (Denton County.)

Driscoll, Texas. (Nueces County.) Driscoll was established in 1904, when the St. Louis, Brownsville, and Mexico Railway built south from Robstown, locating a station on Robert Driscoll's ᵠᵛ ranch. Driscoll named the site after himself, although there was already a town in the county bearing that name; the older town's name (later in Jim Wells County, created from Nueces County) was changed to Alfred (*see* Alfred, Texas). By 1920 the new Driscoll had a population of 500; the population was 669 in 1960 and 626 in 1970. The town was incorporated in the early 1950's and had six business establishments in 1970. *See also* Corpus Christi Standard Metropolitan Statistical Area.

Cyrus Tilloson

*Driskill, Jesse Lincoln.

*Drop, Texas.

*Drossaerts, Arthur Jerome.

Drouths in Texas. Drouths have been recorded as a problem in Texas since Spaniards explored the area. Alvar Núñez Cabeza de Vaca ᵠᵛ found a population of soil tillers near present-day Presidio, where it had not rained for two years. Regarding the white man as a god, they begged him to tell the sky to rain. In 1720 a summer dry spell in Coahuila killed 3,500 of the 4,000 horses which the Marquis de Aguayo,qv governor of Texas, was prepared to bring to Texas. A drouth in Central Texas dried up the San Gabriel River in 1756, forcing the abandonment of a settlement of missionaries and Indians.

Stephen F. Austin's first colonists also were hurt by drouth. In 1822 their initial food crop of corn died from lack of moisture. Each decade since has been marked by at least one period of severe drouth. Associated with dry times are grasshopper plagues, brush and grass fires, sand and dust storms, crop failures and depression, livestock deaths, disease resulting from insufficient and impure drinking water, and migrations of citizens from parched territory.

Information concerning pioneer-day drouths is sketchy because of the absence of official statistics; but data on some drouths, especially those during the nineteenth century, can be compiled from individual complaints recorded in newspapers, diaries, and memoirs. In later years, official detailed record-keeping makes possible a better understanding of the geographical distribution of drouths. Based upon the 1931–1960 average precipitation figures, drouth occurred when an area received, in a given year, less than 75 percent of its average rainfall. The number of drouth years in each of ten geographical areas of Texas in the seventy-two years between 1892 and 1964 was as follows: Trans-Pecos, sixteen years; Lower Rio Grande Valley, fifteen; Edwards Plateau, fourteen; South Central, fourteen; Southern, thirteen; North Central, twelve; Upper Coast, twelve; East Texas, ten; High Plains, nine; and Low Rolling Plains, seven. The incidence of widespread drouth thus computed shows: 1893, drouth in seven areas; 1901, six; 1910, nine (all but the Lower Rio Grande Valley); 1917, all ten; 1954, eight; and 1956, all ten. The greatest deficiency of statewide precipitation occurred during 1916–1917.

On occasion, attempts to make rain artificially have been instituted by both private individuals and public organizations, but these have met with little success. Constant improvement in moisture conservation and utilization, however, has aided Texans in their struggle with drouth. See also Weather in Texas; Rain Making; Rainfall in Texas; Agriculture in Texas.

BIBLIOGRAPHY: Roy Sylvan Dunn, "Weather Changes as Factors in Social Change," Proceedings of the Southwestern Sociological Society (1961); Roy Sylvan Dunn, "Drouth in West Texas, 1890–1894," West Texas Historical Association Year Book (1961); Ivan Ray Tannehill, Drought, Its Causes and Effects (1947); William Curry Holden, "West Texas Drouths," Southwestern Historical Quarterly, XXXII (1928–1929); J. W. Williams, "A Statistical Study of the Drouth of 1886," West Texas Historical Association Year Book (1945); Vance Johnson, Heaven's Tableland, The Dust Bowl Story (1947); Texas Almanac (1857–1965).

Roy Sylvan Dunn

Drug Abuse, State Program on. See Community Affairs, Department of.

Drummond, Thomas. Thomas Drummond was born in Scotland, probably in the county of Perth, around 1790. Little is known of Drummond's formal study of botany; he was perhaps encouraged in his scientific interests by an older brother who at one time was director of the Botanical Gardens at Cork, Ireland.

In 1825, upon the recommendation of the eminent botanist, Sir William Jackson Hooker, Drummond accompanied Sir John Franklin's second overland expedition to Arctic America. As assistant naturalist, his assignment was to make botanical explorations of the mountains of western Canada, where for two years he collected bird and plant specimens.

In 1830 Drummond made a second trip to America, this time to collect specimens from the western and southern United States. While in Missouri he learned of the work Jean Louis Berlandier qv was doing in Texas, and in March, 1833, he arrived at Velasco to begin his collecting work in that area.

Despite experiencing the great floods of the spring and summer of 1833 and contracting both cholera and diarrhea, Drummond spent twenty-one months working the area between Galveston Island and the Edwards Plateau, especially along the Brazos, Colorado, and Guadalupe rivers. His collections were the first made in Texas that were extensively distributed among the museums and scientific institutions of the world. He collected some seven hundred fifty species of plants and about one hundred fifty specimens of birds, a feat which was to stimulate the later studies of such botanical collectors as Ferdinand Jacob Lindheimer and Charles Wright.qqv Drummond had hoped to make a complete botanical survey of Texas, but he died in Havana, Cuba, in March, 1835, while making a short collecting tour of that island. See also Ottine Swamp.

BIBLIOGRAPHY: Samuel Wood Geiser, Naturalists of the Frontier (1948).

*Drumright, Texas.

*Dry Blanket Creek.

*Dry Branch.

*Dry California Creek.

*Dry Comal Creek.

*Dry Creek.

*Dry Cypress Creek.

*Dry Devils River.

*Dry Draw.

*Dry Elm Creek.

*Dry Frio River.

*Dry Hollow Creek.

*Dry Land Farming. See Agriculture in Texas.

*Dry Lipan Creek.

*Dry Run.

*Dry Valley Canyon.

*Dryburg, Texas.

*Dryden, William G.

*Dryden, Texas.

*Dryer, Texas.

*Dubbs, Emanuel.

*Dubbs Lake.

*Dubina, Texas.

*Dublin, Texas. Dublin, in southern Erath County, is a market center for an agricultural area, with several industries among its approximately eighty businesses in 1970, including two garment factories, a peanut processing plant, and several feed mills. A thirty-two-bed hospital, fifteen churches, two city parks, and a public library serve the city. The population in 1960 was 2,443; the 1970 population was 2,810.

*Dubois de Saligny. [This title was incorrectly listed in Volume II as Saligny, Alphonse de.] Jean Pierre Isidore Alphonse Dubois, son of Jean Baptiste Isidore Dubois (a tax inspector) and Marie Louise Rose Bertrand, was born on April 8, 1809, in the French town of Caen (Calvados) in Normandy. He entered on a diplomatic career in 1831 and became, successively, secretary of the French legations in Hanover, Greece, and the United States. While at this last post he was instructed by the French government to go to Texas to investigate the conditions and prospects of the new Republic.

During this mission in the spring of 1839 he visited Galveston, Houston, and the coastal area as far west as Matagorda. His reports to the French foreign minister influenced the French government to recognize Texas in a treaty of friendship, navigation, and commerce.

Appointed to head the new legation with the rank of chargé d'affaires, Dubois, or "A. de Saligny," as he now signed himself (he was not in fact a member of the French nobility), returned to Texas in January, 1840. He established his residence in Austin, then the capital of the Republic, and lived successively in the inn of Richard Bullock (see Bullock House) and in a nearby house on West Pecan Street where he entertained members of the Texas government. He bought approximately twenty-one acres of land on the east side of town and began construction there of the house known today as the French Legation.qv A strong supporter of Roman Catholicism, he worked effectively in this period with the Very Reverend Father John Timon and the Reverend John Mary Odin,qv later a bishop, for the restoration of church property. In acknowledgment of his efforts Pope Gregory XVI later awarded him the Order of Saint Gregory the Great. Drawn into Texas politics, he backed the controversial Franco-Texian Bill,qv became identified as a Houston man, and was a bitter enemy of the Lamar faction. His personal and political troubles culminated in the so-called "Pig War"qv with his landlord Richard Bullock and in his withdrawal in April, 1841, without instructions from the French foreign minister, to Louisiana. Dubois had earlier sold his still unfinished house and property to Odin, and he never again returned to the capital city of Austin.

Although the French foreign minister criticized Dubois for leaving his post without permission, he stood behind the agent in his quarrel with the Texas government and insisted on receiving an appropriate apology and promises to bring Bullock to trial. Somewhat tardily, Anson Jones, secretary of state in the second Houston administration, fulfilled these requirements and paved the way for Dubois' return to Galveston in April, 1842. He resumed cordial relations with the Houston administration, but, his health failing him, he departed for France in July. During his absence Viscount Jules de Cramayel qv served as chargé d'affaires ad interim.

Disappointed in his hopes for promotion to a more prestigious post, Dubois returned in January, 1844, to serve as the French representative until the annexation of Texas to the United States. During this last period of his mission he evinced a marked preference for Louisiana over Texas as a place of residence and came only infrequently and reluctantly to Galveston to fulfill his duties. With his British colleague, Captain Charles Elliot,qv he tried to stave off annexation, but, constrained by his instructions to a position of reserve, he could offer only the good offices and moral support of France in seeking to obtain Mexican recognition of the Texas Republic. Dubois withdrew to Louisiana in April, 1845, where he remained until 1846.

In 1849–1850 he served as French minister plenipotentiary to The Hague and in 1856 represented France on a commission to verify the Russo-Turkish border in Asia. Emperor Napoleon III appointed him minister plenipotentiary to Mexico in 1860. His dispatches from that post urging French intervention helped the emperor decide to undertake the military expedition that placed the ill-fated Maximilian and Charlotte on their Mexican thrones. In 1862 Dubois was promoted to the rank of Grand Officer in the Legion of Honor. While in Mexico he married María de la Luz-Josefa-Brigide del Corazón de Jesús de Ortiz de la Borbolla, by whom he had one son. Accused of dishonest financial operations and too close an association with the clerical party in Mexico, he was recalled in 1863 and returned to France in disgrace in 1864. Despite repeated attempts to vindicate himself, he was unable to obtain another assignment from the foreign ministry. He died in 1888 in his residence, known as "Le Prieuré," in St. Martin du Vieux Bellême, a village in Normandy.

BIBLIOGRAPHY: Nancy N. Barker, "The Republic of Texas: A French View," Southwestern Historical Quarterly, LXXI (1967–1968); Nancy Nichols Barker, The French Legation in Texas, I (1971), II (1973).

Nancy N. Barker

*Dubose, Texas.

*Dubuis, Claude-Marie.

*Duck Creek.

*Duck Creek, Texas.

*Ducos, Armand.

Dudley, Ray Lofton. Ray Lofton Dudley, son of Nicholas Lee and Cordelia (Stover) Dudley, was born on August 8, 1891, at Stoverville, Denton County, Texas. He attended Lewisville Academy, Denton High School, and North Texas State Teachers College (now North Texas State University), then taught in a rural school for three years. He entered Baylor University (class of 1915), but he did not stay to receive a degree. As a young man he held various newspaper positions in Dallas, Marshall, El Paso, Fort Worth, and Houston. His first connection with the oil industry was as oil editor of the Houston *Post*,qv a position he held briefly before becoming editor in 1918 of the *Gulf Coast Oil News* (later called *The Oil Weekly* and, still later, *World Oil*).

In 1918 he purchased *The Oil Weekly* and became president of Gulf Publishing Company, publisher of the magazine. In 1923 he became general manager for the Houston *Post Dispatch,* while retaining presidency of Gulf Publishing. Sixteen months later he retired from daily newspaper work and thereafter devoted full time to his oil publications.

Under his leadership Gulf Publishing Company became the world's largest specialized publisher on oil subjects. *World Oil, Pipe Line Industry,* and *Hydrocarbon Processing* were its major publications. The company also published composite catalogs serving major branches of the oil industry. These publications became known as "oil industry bibles."

Dudley became chairman of Gulf Printing Company, one of the largest printing firms in the South and Southwest, director of the American Petroleum Institute and Texas Mid-Continent Oil and Gas Association, and one of the founders of NOMADS, an organization made up of oil men with international business experience. His civic activities included serving as trustee of Baylor University, board member of both Hermann Hospital and the Texas Medical Center,qv president of the Houston Museum of Fine Arts,qv and board member of the Houston Symphony. He was one of the founders of the Houston Livestock Show and for a number of years owned a large ranch at Rio Frio in the Uvalde area. He and his wife, Frederica Gross, had four children. He died October 29, 1957, in Houston.

Silas B. Ragsdale

*Dudley, Texas.

*Dudley Creek

Duff, James. James Duff, born in Scotland about 1828, had become a San Antonio merchant by 1860. He served as commander of an irregular Texas Confederate military unit, Duff's Partisan Rangers. Unionism in the hill country qv brought about his assignment to that area in May, 1862. Leaving his duty station at San Antonio, Duff camped on the Pedernales a few miles west of the town of Fredericksburg and declared martial law in several precincts of Kerr and Gillespie counties. He dismissed the Unionist enrolling officer, Jacob Kuechler,qv and began what many hill country people regarded as a reign of unjustified terror. Captain Duff learned of Fritz Tegener's Battalion and its planned departure for Mexico and sent part of his troops in a pursuit which culminated in the battle of the Nueces qv on August 10, 1862. One participant in the encounter testified to Duff's presence at the "massacre" and his refusal to provide medical assistance to the defeated Germans. Another story had Duff arriving there after the battle. Harassment of Unionists continued in the Fredericksburg area until Duff's return to San Antonio. Duff's command was later expanded into the 33rd Texas Cavalry; he served on the Texas coast throughout the remainder of the war.

BIBLIOGRAPHY: U. S. War Department, *The War of the Rebellion: A Compilation of the Official Records of the Union and Confederate Armies,* 1–70 (1880–1901); Thomas C. Smith, *Here's Yer Mule* (1958); R. H. Williams, *With the Border Ruffians: Memoirs of the Far West* (1907); Guido E. Ransleben, *A Hundred Years of Comfort in Texas* (1954); Don H. Biggers, *German Pioneers in Texas* (1925); United States Eighth Census, 1860, Bexar County, Texas (microfilm, University of Texas at Austin Library).

Robert W. Shook

*Duffau, Francis T.

*Duffau, Texas.

*Duffau Creek.

Duggan, Arthur Pope. Arthur Pope Duggan was born on September 21, 1876, to Alston and Eliza Permelia (Malone) Duggan in Stringtown, Hays County. He grew up in San Saba, graduated from the Agricultural and Mechanical College of Texas (now Texas A&M University) in 1895, and from the University of Texas law school in 1899. On June 18, 1902, he married Sarah Elizabeth Harral in the home of her uncle, George W. Littlefield,qv in Austin. They had two children. When in 1912 Littlefield placed 79,000 acres of the 312,000-acre Yellow House Ranch qv on the market, Duggan was made sales manager. After Littlefield's death, Duggan became a trustee of the Yellow House Land Company and continued selling acreage for farms. He was state senator from the 30th Senatorial District in the Forty-third and Forty-fourth legislatures, 1933–1935. He was an authority on state education and taxes, and in 1916 he was instrumental in initiating free transportation for rural children in the Littlefield School District. He made a special study of the equalization of taxes which led to the legislature's providing for a Tax Survey Committee, which he served on as secretary, under the appointment of Governor Dan Moody.qv Duggan died on September 6, 1935, and was buried in the State Cemetery qv in Austin.

BIBLIOGRAPHY: Seymour V. Connor (ed.), *Builders of the Southwest* (1959); Duggan Collection (Southwest Collection, Texas Tech University); Lamb County *Leader* (Littlefield), June 27, 1963.

Alice Duggan Gracy

*Duggan, Edmund.

*Duggan, Thomas Hinds.

*Duggey's Lake.

Dugout, Texas. Dugout, McCulloch County, although no longer in existence, was described in 1877 as a thriving town with good churches and schools.

BIBLIOGRAPHY: *Texas Almanac* (1936).

*Dugout Creek.

*Dugout Draw.

*Dugout Mountain.

Duke, Cordia Sloan. Cordia (Cordelia Jane) Sloan Duke was born near Belton, Missouri, on January 10, 1877, the daughter of A. R. C. and Belle (Wingert) Sloan. She attended school in Overbrook, Kansas, where her family moved shortly after her birth. She passed the teacher's examination at the age of sixteen and taught school for several years in the Cherokee Nation, Oklahoma Territory, before coming to Sherman County, Texas, in 1906. There she taught in a four-pupil school located on a Texas strip between Oklahoma and the XIT Ranch.qv She homesteaded there and met Bob Duke, foreman of the Buffalo Springs division of the XIT and later manager of the ranch. They were married on January 9, 1907, and were the parents of three daughters.

During her years as a ranch wife, Mrs. Duke kept a diary, excerpts of which were used as the basis for a book entitled *6,000 Miles of Fence*, which she co-authored with Joe B. Frantz. She also wrote articles for *The Cattleman*. She was appointed Texas' first woman game warden in the late 1920's, a post she held for a number of years. After her husband's death in 1933, she moved to Dalhart, where she died on July 23, 1966, and where she was buried.

BIBLIOGRAPHY: Cordia Sloan Duke and Joe B. Frantz, *6,000 Miles of Fence* (1961); *Texas Parade*, XVII (May, 1962).

*Duke, Thomas Marshall.

*Dulaney Creek.

*Dulin, Texas.

*Dumas, Texas. Dumas, seat of Moore County, had a 1960 population of 8,477 and a 1970 population of 9,771. In 1970 Dumas reported 212 businesses and the addition of a school, library, and park. The town had a total of twenty-two churches, six public schools, two banks, a hospital, a library, a newspaper, a radio station, and a television station. Industrial growth included the addition of several chemical plants.

*Dumble, Edwin Theodore.

Dumont, Texas. (Harris County.) *See* South Houston, Texas.

*Dumont, Texas. (King County.)

*Dunagan, Texas.

*Dunbar, William.

*Dunbar, Texas.

Duncalf, Frederick. Frederick Duncalf was born in Lancaster, Wisconsin, on March 23, 1882. He attended Beloit College, where he received his B.A. in 1904, and the University of Wisconsin, where, as a student under Dana C. Munro, historian of the Crusades, he received his Ph.D. in 1914. He came to the University of Texas as a tutor in 1909; after two short intervals of teaching, at Bowdoin in 1910–1911 and at the University of Illinois in 1913–1914, he returned to the University of Texas as professor of medieval history, a post he held until his retirement in 1950.

During his tenure at the university he was responsible for the training of a group of medievalists who subsequently had distinguished careers in the same field at leading American universities. He also was instrumental in the inauguration of the university's Plan II program in 1936, the earliest honors program at any major state university. He was married to Alma Rather in 1914.

After his retirement in 1950 he continued his active intellectual life, teaching courses in church history at the Episcopal Seminary of the Southwest. He was made a Councillor of the Medieval Academy and a Fellow of the Royal Historical Society. His publications included *Parallel Source Problems in Medieval History* (1912), with August C. Krey; *A Brief History of the War* (1918); *Europe and Our Nation* (1932), with Eugene C. Barker;qv and *The Story of Civilization* (1938), with Carl Becker. His most important contribution to scholarship was the planning, with Krey, of a cooperative American *History of the Crusades*, the first volume of which appeared in 1955 and to which he contributed an important chapter. He died on March 29, 1963.

Archibald R. Lewis

*Duncan, John Martin.

*Duncan, William.

*Duncan, Texas. (Milam County.)

*Duncan, Texas. (Wharton County.)

*Duncan Creek.

*Duncan Field.

*Duncan Wood, Texas.

*Duncanville, Texas. Duncanville, located in Dallas County, had a 1950 population of 841, a 1960 population of 3,774, and a 1970 population of 14,105. Duncanville had a council-manager form of city government; its city hall was completed in 1961. In 1970 the city had 108 businesses. Dallas Baptist College, a four-year institution, is located near there. *See also* Dallas Standard Metropolitan Statistical Area.

*Dundee, Texas.

*Dunlap, Richard G.

*Dunlap, Texas. (Cottle County.)

*Dunlap, Texas. (Travis County.)

*Dunlay, Texas.

*Dunn, John.

*Dunn, John B.

Dunn, William Edward. William Edward Dunn was born in Sulphur Springs, Texas, on March 2, 1888, the son of James McMurry and Lucie (Ballinger) Dunn. He attended high school in Sulphur Springs and Austin. He was awarded a B.A. degree at the University of Texas in 1909, an M.A. at Stanford University in 1910, and a Ph.D. from Columbia University in 1917. He was a student of Herbert Eugene Bolton qv while at the University of Texas and went with Bolton to Mexico City to assist in research work on the early history of the Spanish Southwest. He returned to Austin in the fall of 1913 and became an instructor in history;

later he became an associate professor of Latin American history.

During World War I he left the university faculty to serve in the naval intelligence service, in which he saw duty in various Latin American countries. After the war he returned to the university, where he taught for a short while before resigning to become Latin American editor for the New York *Sun-Herald*. He was the author of *Commercial and Industrial Handbook on Peru* (1925) and of numerous historical monographs in the Latin American field.

His official United States government posts began in 1921 with his appointment as trade commissioner and acting commercial attaché at the United States Embassy in Lima, Peru, and continued through the years in various Latin American countries. He also held advisory posts in many of the Latin American countries and was active in investment and banking in New York City.

He married Linda Tays and they were the parents of two children. The family lived in Washington, D.C., and Dallas. Dunn died in Dallas on November 18, 1966, and was buried at Sulphur Springs.

Richard T. Fleming

*Dunn, Texas. Dunn, in south-central Scurry County, was named for Alonzo T. Dunn (not J. A. Dunn, as stated in Volume I); he was postmaster when the post office was established at his home on September 19, 1890. According to some accounts it was Dunn's wife who actually tended the mail while he farmed. The second postmaster, appointed June 21, 1898, was Isaac N. Anderson.

BIBLIOGRAPHY: Kathryn Cotten, *Saga of Scurry County* (1957); Scurry County Historical Survey Committee, *Historical Markers in Scurry County* (c.1969); United States Post Office Records (Civil Archives of the National Archives, General Services Administration, Washington, D.C.).

*Dunn Creek.

*Dunne, Edward Joseph.

*Duplex, Texas.

Dupre, Marcy Mathias   Marcy Mathias Dupre was born on September 4, 1866, near Winton in Gallia County, Ohio, to John and Nancy Sophia (Huntley) Dupre. He was graduated from Ohio State University in 1886 and married Sallie Bell Naasson in 1887; to them were born ten children. Upon his wife's death in 1908, Dupre married Zenobia Smith. He moved to Texas in 1888, pursuing a career of teaching and school administration in Shelbyville, Henderson, Troup, and Center; he became superintendent of schools in Lubbock in 1914. Dupre was an early advocate of the University Interscholastic League qv and was one of the active proponents of the movement to place high school football on a state championship basis, a development that came officially in 1921. He served on the committee of the West Texas Chamber of Commerce qv that successfully worked for the establishment of Texas Technological College (now Texas Tech University). He died on February 24, 1925, in Lubbock.

BIBLIOGRAPHY: Seymour V. Connor (ed.), *Builders of the Southwest* (1959).

David M. Vigness

*Durango, Texas.

*Durant, Texas.

*Durazno Bayou.

*Durham, George J. George John Durham, born May 12, 1820, was the third of seven children of William and Ester (Bloomfield) Durham and a younger brother of William Davis Durham.qv He was in Austin when surveyors laid out the site for the new capital in 1839 and purchased twenty-eight of the original lots. On December 23, 1852, he married Cassandra Lincecum, the daughter of Gideon Lincecum,qv and they were the parents of five children. He was elected the third mayor of Austin in 1852. In 1854, while in that office, he shot and killed a man who had attacked him with a cane; he was acquitted.

In 1861 Durham was a delegate to the Secession Convention qv and affixed his name to the declaration. Serving for a short time as an orderly sergeant in the Confederate Army, he was recalled to the capital to act as state war tax collector for Texas under the Confederacy. In 1865, upon the break-up of the Confederacy, he successfully resisted armed men who tried to remove funds from the comptroller's office. He ran for state treasurer on the ticket with James Webb Throckmorton qv in 1866, but was defeated. Durham was an ornithologist, an authority on Texas grapes, an excellent marksman, and a writer. Under the pen name "De Los Llanos" he contributed a series of hunting articles entitled "Shooting in Western Texas" to the *London Field* magazine. He was a correspondent of the Smithsonian Institution; he wrote two articles on grape culture and several articles on game in Texas for the *Texas Almanac* qv of 1868 and 1869. In 1867 he was elected a corresponding member of the Academy of Natural Science in Philadelphia. Durham died of typhoid in Austin on April 10, 1869, and was buried in the family plot at Oakwood Cemetery.

BIBLIOGRAPHY: Amelia E. Barr, *All the Days of My Life* (1913); Frank Brown, Annals of Travis County, and of the City of Austin (MS., Archives, University of Texas at Austin Library); Lois Wood Burkhalter, *Gideon Lincecum* (1965); Amelia W. Williams and Eugene C. Barker (eds.), *Writings of Sam Houston*, VIII (1943); Brownsville *Sentinel*, April, 1869; Dallas *Herald*, April 24, 1869.

Charles Durham Gouldie

Durham, William Davis. William Davis Durham was born at Bardswell, Norfolk, England, on July 4, 1815, the eldest of seven children of William and Ester (Bloomfield) Durham; he was a brother of George J. Durham.qv The family immigrated to the United States in 1833 (or 1835) and settled in New York. On October 22, 1835, William enlisted in the New Orleans Greys and landed at Velasco, Texas, three days later. As a member of that unit he participated in the siege of Bexar.qv When the Texas Army split, Durham marched to the east and fought at the battle of San Jacinto; his name is engraved (incorrectly, as William Daniel Durham) on the face of the San Jacinto monument.qv A victim of a yellow fever epidemic, he died in Houston on August 27, 1838, and was buried in the Old Founders Memorial Park. In 1936 the state erected a monument over his grave.

BIBLIOGRAPHY: S. H. Dixon and L. W. Kemp, *Heroes of San Jacinto* (1932); L. W. Kemp Papers (MS., Archives, University of Texas at Austin Library).

Charles Durham Gouldie

*Durnett, Samuel J.

*Durst, John.

*Durst, Joseph.

*Dust Bowl. *See also* Weather in Texas.

*Duster, Texas.

*Dutch Branch.

*Dutch Mountain.

*Dutchman Branch.

*Dutchman Creek.

*Dutchmans Creek.

*Duty, George.

*Duty, Joseph.

*Dutys Creek.

*Duval, Burr H.

Duval, Ella Moss. Ella Moss Duval was born in Pass Christian, Louisiana, in August, 1843, the daughter of Samuel and Isabel (Harris) Moss. When she was still in her teens, her mother took her to Dresden to escape the perils of the approaching Civil War and to give her the advantage of an uninterrupted education in Europe. After her Dresden stay she was sent to the fashionable Düsseldorf School for art instruction, studying under August Wilhelm Sohn. In her last year at Düsseldorf, Ella was awarded a prize of a year's study in Rome, but took money in lieu of the trip, and returned with her mother to New York. There, in 1877, she established herself as a successful artist, with a studio in New York's Domestic Building, where she received several commissions for portraits, including one of the second wife of Commodore Vanderbilt. In 1879 she married Burr G. Duval, and the couple went to Texas. In Austin she built a studio in their home and was soon teaching art classes.

The Duvals in the early 1880's moved to San Antonio, where the artist taught first in the French Building and later in her home in Maverick Grove. Portraits done at this time included those of Mrs. J. T. Woodhull, Dr. Ferdinand Herff,qv Miss Phillipa G. Stevenson, and that of Duval West,qv which now hangs in the courtroom of the United States District Court in Austin. While pursuing her art career Mrs. Duval constantly advocated the establishment of an academy of art in San Antonio. Until her death in 1911, in St. Louis, she made every effort to encourage San Antonio in its various art activities.

BIBLIOGRAPHY: Pauline A. Pinckney, *Painting in Texas: The Nineteenth Century* (1967).

Pauline A. Pinckney

*Duval, John Crittenden. John Crittenden Duval died on January 15, 1897 (not 1891, as stated in Volume I).

*Duval, Thomas Howard. Thomas Howard Duval moved to Texas in December, 1845, arriving in Austin late that month, or in January, 1846.

*Duval, William Pope. William Pope Duval's son, Thomas H. Duval,qv moved to Austin, Texas, in December, 1845, or in early January, 1846 (not 1839, as stated in Volume I).

*Duval, Texas.

*Duval County. Duval County, a South Texas county renowned for its politics and oil, ranked high among Texas oil-producing counties. From 1905 through 1972 the accumulated total oil production exceeded four hundred eighty million barrels. Beef cattle account for 80 percent of the farm income, with feed grains, vegetables, dairy cattle, and sheep contributing the remainder. The 1960 population was 13,398; by 1970 the population had decreased to 11,722.

*Dwight, Texas.

*Dwire, Texas.

*Dwyer, Edward.

*Dwyer, Thomas. Thomas Dwyer was born on August 17, 1819, in Cashel, County Tipperary, Ireland. He came to Texas February 8, 1845 (not 1849, as stated in Volume I), located at Quintana on September 1, 1845, where he went into the mercantile business, and later opened another store in Brazoria. He went to Brenham in 1858 and continued in the mercantile business there. Thomas Dwyer died on January 29, 1896 (not June 19, 1876), in Brenham.

Mrs. A. G. McNeese

*Dye, Texas.

*Dye Creek.

*Dyer, Clement C.

Dyer, Edwin Hawley. Edwin Hawley Dyer, son of Joseph Dyer, was born in Morgan City, Louisiana, on October 11, 1900. Following attendance at public schools there, he enrolled in Rice Institute, where he played football and baseball. He was a member of the class of 1924, but he did not graduate until 1936, following periods as a player with various minor league baseball teams.

He managed the Houston club of the Texas League qv for a time, winning league championships in 1939, 1940, and 1941, and in 1942 he was named minor league manager of the year for his direction of the Columbus, Ohio, team. Thereafter, he joined the St. Louis Cardinals and was manager of that club when it won the World Series championship in 1946, beating the Boston Red Sox four games to three.

After twenty-three years as a player, manager, and coach, Dyer came to Houston in 1948 and opened an insurance office, relinquishing managership of the Cardinals in 1950. On January 2, 1962, he suffered a stroke and on April 20, 1964, died of a heart attack. Survivors were his wife, the former

Geraldine Jennings of Timpson, a son, and a daughter. He was buried at the Garden of Gethsemane in Houston.

Dyer was described in the *Official Encyclopedia of Baseball* as a "slow-speaking and quick-thinking Texan." Considered one of the best teachers and developers of young baseball talent, he discovered such men as Stan Musial, Howard Pollet, and Jeffre Cross. Pollet and Cross were associated with him in his Houston business.

BIBLIOGRAPHY: *Newsweek* (May 4, 1964); *New York Times*, April 21, 1964; *Time* (May 1, 1964); *Houston Post*, April 21, 22, 23, 1964; *Official Encyclopedia of Baseball* (1956).

Clay Bailey

*Dyer, Isadore.

*Dyer, Leigh R.

*Dyer, Texas.

*Dyersdale, Texas.

Dyess, William Edwin. William Edwin Dyess was born on August 9, 1916, the son of Richard T. and Hallie (Graham) Dyess, in Albany, Texas. After completing his secondary education, Dyess enrolled at John Tarleton Agricultural College (now Tarleton State University) in Stephenville and was graduated from there in 1936. He subsequently entered the air force as a pilot trainee and was commissioned a second lieutenant in 1937.

In 1940, after serving at air bases in Louisiana and California, Dyess was promoted to first lieutenant and given command of the 21st Pursuit Squadron. Before being transferred overseas in 1941, Dyess married Marajen Stevick.

At the time of the Japanese attack on Pearl Harbor, Dyess and his squadron were stationed at Nichols Field near Manila in the Philippine Islands. Soon promoted to captain, Dyess fought in the "Battle of Bataan," was taken prisoner by the Japanese in April, 1942, and was forced to participate in the Bataan "Death March" to a Japanese prison camp.

Three hundred sixty-one days after his imprisonment, Dyess escaped. He then fought with Filipino guerrillas against the Japanese, was taken from the island by a United States submarine, participated in amphibious attacks against the Japanese from that vessel, and was finally returned on leave to the United States, where he confided to the War Department a wealth of information on Japanese warfare.

After a period of recuperation in an army general hospital and a promotion to lieutenant colonel, Dyess returned to active duty in late 1943. Soon after that, on December 22, 1943, he was killed at Burbank, California, when his plane crashed and burned. At the time of his death at age twenty-seven, he held the Distinguished Service Cross, the Legion of Merit, and the Silver Star. He was posthumously awarded the Soldier's Medal.

In January, 1944, the army and navy released a report on Japanese atrocities based primarily on the information of Dyess and two other officers who had escaped from Japanese prison camps. In the same month more than one hundred newspapers began serial publication of the story of Dyess' experience in the prison camps, which he dictated before his death. In December, 1956, Abilene Air Force Base was renamed Dyess Air Force Base qv in his memory.

BIBLIOGRAPHY: *Dallas News*, December 23, 1943, March 7, 1944; Austin *American*, January 28, 1944; William E. Dyess (Charles Leavelle, ed.), *The Dyess Story* (1944).

Dyess Air Force Base. In 1947 Abilene Army Air Base was closed and the 1,500-acre physical plant was deeded to the city. Following the outbreak of the Korean War, however, the base was modernized and reactivated as a Strategic Air Command installation. Abilene Air Force Base, as it was then known, was dedicated in April, 1956, and in December of that year the name of the base was changed to Dyess Air Force Base in memory of William Edwin Dyess,qv who was killed during World War II.

With the opening of the base came the activation of the 819th Aerospace Division Headquarters and the 819th Base Group. The first wing arriving at the base was the 341st Bombardment Wing, equipped with B-47 jet bombers and supported by the 11th Air Refueling Squadron's KC-97 tanker aircraft. Late in 1957 the 96th Bombardment Wing was transferred from Oklahoma to Dyess, where it became the base's principal unit.

In 1960 the 5th Army Missile Battalion, equipped with Nike Hercules missiles, was activated at the base. The following year the 578th Strategic Missile Squadron, using Atlas F missiles, was established at Dyess. The Atlas F was the last in the Atlas series of operational ICBM's and was an underground, silo-type weapon. Both missile units remained operational until the mid-1960's, when both were deactivated.

In July, 1965, Dyess Air Force Base was transferred to the Second Air Force, and a year later the 819th Strategic Aerospace Division was deactivated, leaving only the medical group of the division at the base. The three principal units assigned to Dyess in 1967 were the 96th Strategic Aerospace Wing, the 96th Combat Support Group, and the 516th Tactical Airlift Wing, the last of which was the principal tenant unit at the base. The mission of the 96th Aerospace Wing, with its B-52 jet bombers, was to provide a deterrent force in the event of an international crisis. Refueling support was provided by the 917th Air Refueling Squadron, using KC-135 tanker aircraft. The mission of the 516th Airlift Wing, equipped with C-130 aircraft, was to provide worldwide tactical support in the form of men and equipment.

By 1967 Dyess had become one of the most modern air force bases in the United States and had a military population of more than six thousand. It was still active in the 1970's.

E

Eagle, Joe Henry. Joe Henry Eagle was born in Tompkinsville, Kentucky, on January 23, 1870. After graduation from Burritt College at Spencer, Tennessee, in 1887, he moved to Texas, where he taught school at Vernon from 1887 to 1893, acting as superintendent of schools, 1889–1891. After studying law at night and in his spare time, he was admitted to the Bar in 1893 and was elected city attorney of Wichita Falls for 1894–1895. Eagle moved to Houston in 1895 and ran unsuccessfully for Congress as a Populist in 1896. Later he served six terms in Congress as a Democrat, under Woodrow Wilson from 1913 to 1921 and under Franklin D. Roosevelt from 1933 to 1937. While in the House, he was a strong advocate of credit for farmers and of the resulting Federal Farm Loan Act of 1916. He also secured the establishment of Ellington Air Force Base qv in 1917 and an appropriation of $4,000,000 to deepen and widen the Houston Ship Channel qv in 1919. In the 1930's, as earlier, he advocated social security benefits and promoted the construction of several PWA and WPA buildings in his district. In 1936 he ran unsuccessfully for the Democratic nomination for United States senator, then retired from Congress for a second time to practice law in Houston until 1957.

He married Mary Hamman, daughter of William H. Hamman,qv and they had a son and a daughter. Eagle died on January 10, 1963.

BIBLIOGRAPHY: Galveston *Daily News*, August 9, 1896; Houston *Post*, January 11, 1963; *Biographical Directory of the American Congress, 1774–1961* (1961); *Who's Who In America* (1934).

Alwyn Barr

*Eagle, Texas.

*Eagle Cove, Texas.

*Eagle Creek.

*Eagle Flat, Texas.

*Eagle Ford, Texas.

*Eagle Hollow.

*Eagle Island Plantation.

*Eagle Lake. The Eagle Lake project is owned by the Lakeside Irrigation Company. It was first owned by Wilham Dunovant, then by Rineyard-Walker and Company, and later by Eagle Lake Rice Irrigation Company, which became Lakeside Irrigation Company. The project was begun in 1899, and was completed in 1900 with impoundment beginning in that year. Water was diverted for the irrigation season of 1900. Eagle Lake has a capacity of 9,600 acre-feet and a surface area of 1,200 acres at elevation 170 feet above mean sea level. The lake provides means of storing water diverted from the Colorado River when excess flood flows occur. The early pumping installation consisted of pumps which were rope-driven by Corlis steam engines. Modern pumps driven by electric motors lift water from the Colorado River to a canal system that supplies water to the lake, or directly to the land to be irrigated, through a relift pumping station. The drainage area to the lake is about twenty square miles, but the area is relatively unimportant as a source of water supply. Water is pumped from the Colorado River when excess flow is available.

BIBLIOGRAPHY: Texas Water Commission, *Bulletin 6408* (1964).

Seth D. Breeding

*Eagle Lake, Texas. Eagle Lake, Colorado County, was founded by Austin's colonists on the site of an old Indian village. The family of Frank J. Cooke settled near Eagle Lake in 1835 and with other inhabitants joined the Runaway Scrape qv in 1836. It was a station in 1859 on the Buffalo Bayou, Brazos, and Colorado Railway. Carli Stucke and Matthew Barrett were Confederate postmasters during the Civil War. In 1960 Eagle Lake was an incorporated town of 3,565 inhabitants, showing an increase of 35 percent during the previous decade; the 1970 population count was 3,587. A center for rice drying and shipping, the town had manufacturing plants that produced concrete, truck beds, and farm trailers. Eagle Lake advertised itself as the "goose hunting capital of the world."

BIBLIOGRAPHY: *Frontier Times* (February, 1951); *Texas: a Guide to the Lone Star State* (1940).

Cyrus Tilloson

*Eagle Mills, Texas.

*Eagle Mountain.

*Eagle Mountain Lake. *See also* Eagle Mountain Reservoir.

Eagle Mountain Reservoir. Eagle Mountain Reservoir, formerly Eagle Mountain Lake,qv is owned and operated by the Tarrant County Water Control and Improvement District No. 1 to supply water to Fort Worth for municipal and industrial uses and for irrigation and recreation. Construction of the dam began on January 23, 1930, and was completed on October 24, 1932. Impoundment of water began on February 28, 1934. On the basis of a survey made in October, 1952, the capacity of the reservoir at the crest of the service spillway at elevation 649.1 feet above mean sea level was 182,700 acre-feet with a surface area of 8,500 acres. A floodwater retardation capacity of 365,200 acre-feet was provided between the crest of the service spillway and the crest of the emergency spillway at elevation 676 feet above mean sea level. The drainage area of the West Fork of the Trinity River at Eagle Mountain Dam was 1,970 square miles.

BIBLIOGRAPHY: Texas Water Commission, *Bulletin 6408* (1964).

Seth D. Breeding

*Eagle Nest Canyon.

*Eagle Pass, Texas. During the Mexican War a company of Texas Mounted Volunteers under the command of Captain J. A. Veatch qv established an observation post on the Rio Grande opposite the mouth of the Mexican Rio Escondido and by an old smuggler's trail which crossed the river at this point. The crossing, known as El Paso del Aguila, was so named because of frequent flights of Mexican eagles from the grove along the Escondido. Though abandoned by the military at the conclusion of hostilities, the site remained a terminus and crossing point for trappers, frontiersmen, and traders. Fort Duncan qv was established in 1849 (not 1850, as stated in Volume I) two miles upstream, and its proximity caused a rudimentary settlement to spring up at the crossing below the post. In 1850 General William Leslie Cazneau qv and his bride, Jane McManus qv (Cora Montgomery), were among the early settlers. The village, named after the crossing on the Rio Grande, changed from El Paso del Aguila to Eagle Pass as the Anglo presence grew. Concurrent with the growth of Eagle Pass below the fort, emigrants bound for the California gold fields (via Mazatlán) established a staging area above the post known as California Camp. The resulting trade and traffic brought a shift in the settlement of Eagle Pass from the old crossing downstream to its present location above the fort. John Twohig qv (not John Twong, as stated in Volume I), owner of the land, surveyed and laid out a townsite, naming it Eagle Pass (not El Paso del Aguila). The settlement and adjoining fort were frequently attacked by the Lipan and Comanche Indians. Piedras Negras, across from Eagle Pass, became a haven for fugitive Negro slaves, and both banks of the river were infested with outlaws. In 1855 J. H. Callahan qv crossed into Mexico at Eagle Pass with three companies of volunteer rangers in pursuit of Lipan-Apache and Kickapoo Indians. After a fight with Mexican forces on the Escondido, Callahan fell back on Piedras Negras and set the village afire as he crossed back into Eagle Pass. During the Civil War, a party of renegades crossed from Piedras Negras and attacked and drove off the Confederate troops garrisoned at Fort Duncan. The townsmen, fighting from behind a barricade of cotton bales, successfully drove off their assailants. Following Federal occupation of Brownsville in 1863, Eagle Pass became the only port in the Confederacy not under Federal blockade and thus was the terminus of the Cotton Road. A growth in stock raising and outlawry followed the war years. Bands of cattle thieves and fugitives led by King Fisher qv dominated Eagle Pass during the 1870's, notwithstanding the multiple intervention of the Texas Rangers.qv Not until the coming of the railroad in 1884 was law and order restored.

Seat of Maverick County, Eagle Pass had a 1960 population of 12,094 and a 1970 population of 15,364. It had a hospital, a library, a newspaper, a radio station, and twelve churches. A new city charter was adopted in 1964. The city serves as the center for a ranching, truck farming, and oil area. Industries include the manufacture of clothing; the processing of fluorspar, barite, and celestite; the production of oil and gas; and the processing of foods and feeds. Eagle Pass is the site of a United States radar base and immigration and customs station. In 1954 a flood inundated the city and destroyed approximately one-third of the international bridge connecting Eagle Pass and Piedras Negras, Coahuila, Mexico.

BIBLIOGRAPHY: Mrs. William L. Cazneau (Cora Montgomery), *Eagle Pass; or Life On The Border* (1852); Report of the Secretary of War (1850); R. W. Johnson, *A Soldier's Reminiscences in Peace and War* (1886).

Ben E. Pingenot

*Eagle Pass Army Air Field.

*Eagle Spring.

*Eagle Springs, Texas.

Eagleton, Clyde. Clyde Eagleton was born in Sherman, Texas, on May 13, 1891, son of Addie Christian (Parker) and Davis Foute Eagleton.qv He attended the Sherman public schools and Austin College, receiving a B.A. degree (1910) and an M.A. (1911). A Rhodes Scholar, Eagleton earned a second B.A. (1917) from Oxford University and a second M.A. (1928) from Princeton. He received a Ph.D. (1928) from Columbia University and an honorary doctorate (1941) from Austin College.

Eagleton served on the faculty of New York University from 1923 to 1956, and at various times he taught at the University of Louisville, Southern Methodist University, Daniel Baker College, University of Texas (Austin), University of Chicago, Stanford, Yale, University of Washington, and Académie de Droit International (The Hague, Netherlands). A legal expert with the Department of State (1943–1945), Eagleton served as assistant secretary of the Dumbarton Oaks Conference in 1944. In 1945 he was technical expert with the United States delegation to the Washington meeting of the Committee of Jurists, and adviser to the United States delegation at the San Francisco Conference for the founding of the United Nations. Eagleton was director of the Institute for the Study of International Law at New York University, and at the time of his death he was studying legal aspects of the use of international rivers. He wrote many articles for professional journals and periodicals and several books, including *The Responsibilities of States in International Law* (1928), *International Government* (1932, 1948, 1957), and *The Forces That Shape Our Future* (1945). In addition, he was co-editor of seven volumes of *Annual Review of United Nations Affairs* (1949–1956), published by New York University Press. He was a member of numerous national and international associations, the Presbyterian church, and the Texas State Historical Association;qv president of the American Branch of International Law Association; and at times a consultant to United Nations bodies.

He was married to Sara Virginia McKinney on September 15, 1917, and they had one son. Eagleton died January 30, 1958.

BIBLIOGRAPHY: *American Journal of International Law*, LII (1958); Austin College *Bulletin* (1958); New York

Times, January 31, 1958; *Who's Who In America* (1952).

N. Ethie Eagleton

Eagleton, Davis Foute. Davis Foute Eagleton was born on March 16, 1861, in Boon's Hill, Tennessee, son of Mary Ethlinda (Foute) and George Ewing Eagleton. He was educated by his father, a Presbyterian minister and educator, until 1879, when he attended Davidson College, North Carolina, for a short time. Following his father as principal of Ouachita Seminary, Mount Holly, Arkansas, in 1879, and Magnolia Academy, Arkansas, in 1880, he returned to Davidson College and received a B.A. degree (1884), an M.A. (1894), and an honorary doctorate (1914). He was principal of Fannin College at Bonham, Texas (1884–1886), principal of Ladonia Academy (1886–1888), and professor of English at Austin College (1888–1897). After resigning his position at Austin College, Eagleton opened Sherman Academy, which was later moved to Bonham as Bonham Academy. In 1898 he went to Calvert and conducted the public schools there until his return to Austin College in 1900.

Eagleton was the compiler and editor of *Writers and Writings of Texas* (1913) and *Texas Literature Reader* (1916, 1922); he was the author of several short works. In Sherman he was an elder of the College Park Presbyterian Church, which he had helped organize. He married Addie Christian Parker on June 19, 1890, at Mount Holly, Arkansas, and they had seven children. Eagleton died on June 9, 1916, and was buried in Sherman.

BIBLIOGRAPHY: *Alumni Monthly of Austin College* (July, 1916); Davis Foute Eagleton, *A Memorial Sketch of Rev. George Ewing Eagleton* (n.d.); Sherman *Daily Democrat*, June 9, 1916.

N. Ethie Eagleton

*Earle, Thomas.

*Earle, Texas.

Early, Texas. Early, in Brown County just outside of Brownwood, had a population of 819 in 1960 and 1,097 in 1970.

*Earth, Texas.** Earth, in Lamb County, was incorporated in 1947 and had an aldermanic-general form of government. In 1970 most of the business establishments were mainly concerned with farming; there was a rural school, a bank, four churches, and a newspaper. The 1960 population was 1,104; the 1970 population was 1,152.

*Earthquakes in Texas.** [The bibliography should read *Texas Almanac* (1926), not (1936), as shown in Volume I. Some later printings of Volume I contain this correction.]

*East, James H. (Jim).

*East Bay.

*East Bay Bayou.

*East Bernard, Texas.** East Bernard, in Wharton County, had a population of 1,159 in 1970, according to the U.S. census.

*East Black Hills.

*East Bosque River.

*East Branch.

*East Buffalo Creek.

*East Caddo, Texas.

*East Caddo Peak.

*East Columbia, Texas.

*East Creek.

*East Fork of the Angelina River.

*East Fork of the Trinity River.

*East Hamilton, Texas.

*East Line and Red River Railroad Company.

*East Mayfield, Texas.

*East Mesa.

*East Mountain, Texas.

*East Navidad River.

*East Nueces River.

*East Point, Texas.

*East San Jacinto River.

*East Sandy Creek.

*East Sweden, Texas.

East Tawakoni. East Tawakoni, a newly created town in Rains County, is a center for tourist activities around Lake Tawakoni. Population was 278 in 1970, according to the U.S. census.

*East Tempe, Texas.

*East Texas.

*East Texas Baptist College.** East Texas Baptist College, Marshall, was accredited by the Southern Association of Colleges and Secondary Schools; it offered a program of teacher education as well as a four-year liberal arts curriculum. Assets of the institution stood at $5,388,664 in 1965, which included $1,113,541 in endowment and annuity funds in addition to a plant of eleven permanent buildings on a 100-acre campus. The operating budget was in excess of $900,000 for 1965. Its library contained more than 65,000 volumes in 1969. Student enrollment was 771 during the regular session of 1974–1975.

*East Texas Baptist Institute.

*East Texas Chamber of Commerce.** The East Texas Chamber of Commerce continued to promote agricultural, forestry, industrial, and local community development in its area. In recent years agricultural research has been one of the chamber's paramount interests. The chamber has worked alone and with other groups in fostering agricultural tours, inaugurating programs, and promoting the location of the East Texas Research-Extension Center at Overton.

Timber growing for pulpwood has been encouraged to ensure additional income for farmers and an adequate supply of raw material for the large paper mills in the region. For many years the East Texas chamber has also been one of the sponsoring agents in holding annual forestry schools for young people.

During all sessions of both state and national legislatures, the taxation and legislation department keeps the membership informed of developments on a weekly basis. A county government institute has been a successful annual program, and a series of citizenship and career conferences on college campuses has been an annual activity of the public affairs department for many years. Industrial activities have been broadened to include semiannual tours to other areas of the nation in the interest of locating industry in East Texas. Through its library and research facilities, the chamber has also been instrumental in helping many communities to establish industrial foundations.

In recent years, the chamber has also worked actively in the fields of tourism, foreign trade, and water resource development. Trade tours to Latin American and European countries are conducted annually. The tourist department issues annual travel guides and maps, and it works with local communities in developing their tourist attractions.

The chamber maintains a research department, housed in a library which is the largest of its kind outside of the national chamber of commerce library. This department maintains a lending service to local chambers and business people throughout its region and publishes a quarterly directory of chambers of commerce in Texas. In addition, the chamber continued to publish its magazine, *East Texas*.

Camilla Koford

East Texas Chest Hospital. East Texas Chest Hospital, near Tyler, was formerly called East Texas Tuberculosis Sanatorium qv (1949–1950) and East Texas State Tuberculosis Hospital (1950–1971). In 1957 the hospital opened a six-floor air conditioned building, and by 1965 all patient areas were consolidated around the new building. The hospital began operating under the State Department of Public Health qv in 1965, when the Board for Texas State Hospitals and Special Schools qv was abolished. At that time the hospital capacity was 521, and patients were admitted from fifty-three Texas counties. In 1967 the hospital housed 400 patients.

When the legislature changed the name of the institution in 1971 it also established it functionally, for the first time, as a state facility treating a wide range of respiratory diseases and disorders, including tuberculosis. There was a decline in hospitalized TB patients and an increased reliance on out-patient clinics for less severe TB cases. An increase in the treatment of patients with chronic obstructive lung, cardiovascular, and pulmonary diseases was necessary because these disorders had become the most significant causes of total and permanent disability in Texas.

The hospital was enlarged to include an out-patient clinic and additional laboratories. Occupational, inhalation, and physical therapy departments were instituted, along with departments concerned with health education, alcoholism, drug education, pulmonary rehabilitation, and vocational rehabilitation. Research activities were expanded. The East Texas Chest Hospital had 3,476 visits to the out-patient clinic in 1970 and 4,554 visits in 1971. The average daily census for the hospital was 270 in 1970 and 234 in 1971; George A. Hurst was superintendent.

BIBLIOGRAPHY: Board for Texas State Hospitals and Special Schools, *Report* (1964); East Texas Chest Hospital, *Annual Report* (1971).

*East Texas and Gulf Railway Company.

East Texas Historical Association. In the summer of 1926, on the initiative of Professor W. F. Garner, chairman of the Department of History at Stephen F. Austin State College (now Stephen F. Austin State University), a group formed a tentative historical association. The Nacogdoches group, which included a number of Stephen F. Austin professors, invited the faculties of Sam Houston State Teachers College (later Sam Houston State College and now Sam Houston State University) and East Texas State Teachers College (now East Texas State University) to join the Stephen F. Austin faculty in creating the East Texas Historical Association. The first meeting of the association was held on the Stephen F. Austin campus on April 29–30, 1927. At the first meeting papers were read by Professor Eugene C. Barker qv of the University of Texas, President A. W. Birdwell qv of Stephen F. Austin, Professor J. T. Clark of Sam Houston, Professor J. G. Smith of East Texas State, Miss Martha Emmons of Nacogdoches High School, and the Reverend George L. Crocket qv of Nacogdoches.

The 1927 constitution provided for three types of membership: twenty-five dollars for life membership; three dollars for active members; and two dollars for corresponding members or members who lived outside of East Texas. Officers were elected, and the Reverend George L. Crocket became the first president. Forty-two members were declared charter members, and Professor Eugene C. Barker became a life member.

From 1928 to 1932 the association met annually: in 1928 and 1931 on the Sam Houston campus, in 1929 and 1932 on the East Texas State campus, and in 1930 on the Stephen F. Austin campus. After the 1932 meeting the East Texas Historical Association did not meet again until 1962.

On September 29, 1962, at the invitation of C. K. Chamberlain, chairman of the Department of History at Stephen F. Austin, a group of East Texans met and reorganized the association. A new constitution was adopted which provided for four types of memberships: patrons, sustaining members, regular members, and student members. The constitution also provided for two meetings of the association each year: a spring meeting on the invitation of a community or college and the annual fall meeting on the Stephen F. Austin campus.

Lee Lawrence, of Tyler, became the first president, and C. K. Chamberlain became editor-in-chief of *The East Texas Historical Journal*, published in March and October of each year by the association on the Stephen F. Austin campus. In the reorganization there were 425 charter members.

C. K. Chamberlain

*East Texas Normal College.

*East Texas Oil Field. One of the largest oil fields in the world (the largest until later discoveries in the Middle East), the East Texas Oil Field was discovered when C. M. (Dad) Joiner qv brought in a successful test on the No. 3 Daisy Bradford on the Juan Ximenes survey about seven miles from Henderson on the evening of Friday, September 5, 1930 (not October 6, 1930, as stated in Volume I). Several erroneous dates have been given to mark this occasion, including the September 3, 1930, date on the slab erected on the site by the Texas Centennial qv Commission. Many accounts give varying dates in early October, 1930; these discrepancies occurred because the well was not considered a sure producer by some oilmen until it was completed in October, though the head driller, E. C. Laster, entered the September 5 date in his logbook as the time when the drill stem test proved beyond reasonable doubt that high grade oil was present in the area. On that evening oil was struck in the Woodbine sand at approximately 3,580 feet and was allowed to run for a few moments, clearing the top of the derrick before being cut off and mudded in to prevent a blowout. An estimated crowd of two thousand people looked on, and by midnight Henderson citizens still thronged the streets while brisk trading went on with leases and royalties changing hands. Bottles of crude oil were brought into Henderson to convince the skeptical. Early estimates varied, some enthusiasts predicting a 10,000- to 20,000-barrel producer. In early September the Daisy Bradford No. 3 had changed the mood of the whole area from an agriculture-oriented community to that of a bustling oil town, with crowds anxiously awaiting the completion of the well. When the drill stem test was made on September 5, there was no pipe on the ground and storage tanks had yet to be completed.

Nearly all of the holdings near the well were owned by individuals. Most of the large oil companies had been skeptical of this area, but with Joiner's successful test they became eager buyers, seeking whole blocks near the Joiner well. Farmers were undecided whether or not to sell when thousands of dollars were suddenly offered, or to hold on for possibly much more money if the Daisy Bradford No. 3 proved beyond all doubt the existence of a new field. After almost a month's delay in running pipe and completing storage tanks, the well, having been bailed for two days previously, finally came in as a producer at approximately 8:30 P.M. on Friday, October 3, 1930, blowing oil over the derrick and running wild for a short time before it was brought under control and the oil turned into storage tanks.

The well was the center of attention in East Texas, and it was finally recognized by the oil fraternity as a good producer with oil of high gravity. By October 4, fifteen thousand people were crowded into Henderson. Major oil companies continued taking leases over a wide area, thus establishing the field, and cash in huge amounts was being paid to farmers who had suddenly become oilmen.

BIBLIOGRAPHY: Houston *Post-Dispatch*, September 7, 14, 21, 28, October 4, 5, 12, 1930.

Eldon S. Branda

*East Texas Railroad Company.

*East Texas State Teachers College. *See also* East Texas State University.

East Texas State University. East Texas State University, Commerce, has had its name changed twice since 1923, the year the legislature renamed all Texas normal colleges "teachers colleges." The educational scope of East Texas State Teachers College qv became much broader than teacher education, and consequently "Teachers" was dropped from the name in 1957. University status was recognized by the legislature in 1965, and the name was changed to East Texas State University. It was reorganized into three schools: graduate, education, and liberal arts.

Buildings on the 150-acre main campus numbered eighty-seven in 1965, while twenty-five were located on the 1,052-acre college farm. Value of the physical plant grew steadily from $175,000 in 1917, to $2,328,000 in 1947, and to $19,000,000 in 1965. The university operated on a six-million-dollar budget in 1965. Sixty-nine undergraduate majors in twenty-five academic departments were offered in 1965 in addition to thirty master's degree fields. Student enrollment in the regular 1974–1975 term was 9,241; F. Henderson McDowell was president at that time. In 1971 East Texas State University Center at Texarkana was opened with an enrollment of 323 students. By fall, 1974, enrollment had increased to 615; John F. Moss was president of the center at Texarkana.

*East Texas Tuberculosis Sanatorium. *See also* East Texas Chest Hospital.

*East Yegua Creek.

*Easter, Texas.

Easter Fires. *See* Fredericksburg Easter Fires.

*Easterly, Texas.

*Eastern (or Lower) Cross Timbers. It is not true that the Comanches or other Indians avoided the Cross Timbers (as stated in Volume I). Comanches raided east of them in the early years, and the Wichitas and others used the wood in the Cross Timbers, perhaps settling near them for this reason. Indians used the Cross Timbers as a north-south avenue which afforded secrecy from enemies.

W. W. Newcomb

*Eastern Interior Provinces. *See* Provincias Internas.

*Eastern Texas Female College.

*Eastern Texas Railroad.

*Easterwood, William Edward, Jr.

*Eastgate, Texas.

*Eastland, William Mosby.

*Eastland, Texas. Eastland, seat of Eastland County, had a population of 3,292 in 1960 and 3,178 in 1970. In the late 1960's Eastland had nineteen churches, four schools, a library, and a hospital. Industries included the manufacture of clothing, clay products, and petroleum products. Annual events include the Peanut Bowl and a fishing rodeo.

*Eastland County. Eastland County had a population of 19,526 in 1960 and a population of 18,092 in 1970. In the early 1970's the county's annual income from minerals (oil, gas, stone, and clays) was approximately $3 million. From 1917 to 1973 over 123 million barrels of oil were produced. Eastland ranks among the state's leading counties in production of peanuts. Its other crops include small grains, fruits, vegetables, and pecans. Most of the farm income (approximately $13 million annually) is derived from livestock, chiefly beef and dairy cattle, goats, sheep, hogs, and turkeys. Lake Cisco and Leon Reservoir are tourist attractions.

*Eastland, Wichita Falls, and Gulf Railroad Company.

*Eastman, Seth.

*Eastman, Texas.

*Eastman College.

*Easton, Texas. Easton revived in the late 1940's with the development of oil fields in the area. In March, 1949, a post office was again established, after which the town was soon incorporated. The incorporated area lay in Gregg and Rusk counties, with a population of 220 in 1960 and 297 in 1970.
Cyrus Tilloson

*Eaton, Texas.

*Ebahamo Indians. Most writers who have studied the documents of the La Salle Expedition qv consider Bahamo, Bracamo, and Ebahamo (Hebahamo) as variants of the same name for a single Indian group. This is clearly supported by sound correspondences. However, close analysis of these documents leads to some doubt about this presumed synonymy. The journal of Henri Joutel qv contains no names for the Indians who lived in the immediate vicinity of Fort St. Louis qv (Matagorda Bay) and who gave the French colonists so much trouble. He does refer to the Ebahamo, but only in connection with La Salle's last trip to the Hasinai country. The geographic features described by Joutel indicate that the Ebahamo were an inland group who lived in northern Jackson County or somewhere in that general vicinity. He does not identify the Ebahamo with the Indians who harassed Fort St. Louis. That they were not the same seems to be indicated by the fact that La Salle was curious about the Ebahamo language and is said to have recorded a few words. The Indians near the fort were called Bracamos by La Salle. Douay merely says that the neighboring Indian groups included the Quoaque (Coco), Bahamo, and Quinet. A few years later, after the Spanish found Fort St. Louis abandoned, Alonso de León qv reported that the Indians of the general vicinity were Bahamo and Quelanhubeche (Karankawa?). Thus the only Indians specifically linked with Fort St. Louis are the Bracamo. It seems safe to assume that Bracamo and Bahamo are variants of the same name and refer to the same people, but doubt remains as to whether Bahamo and Ebahamo are the same. Unless new documents become available, this situation may never be clarified. After 1690 the Spanish used other names for the Indian groups in this section of the Texas coast. These groups (Coapite, Cujane, and Karankawa) are all identifiable as Karankawan. Although they may not be strictly synonymous, it seems reasonable to conclude that Bracamo, Bahamo, and Ebahamo were French-derived names for two or more bands or tribes of Karankawan affiliation. This is supported by one bit of linguistic evidence: the word for "father" in Karankawan is *béhema*.

BIBLIOGRAPHY: A. S. Gatschet, *The Karankawa Indians, the Coast People of Texas* (1891); C. W. Hackett (ed.), *Pichardo's Treatise on the Limits of Louisiana and Texas*, I (1931); J. G. Shea, *Early Voyages up and down the Mississippi* (1861); J. G. Shea, *Discovery and Exploration of the Mississippi Valley* (1903); H. R. Stiles (ed.), *Joutel's Journal of La Salle's Last Voyage, 1684–7* (1906).
T. N. Campbell

*Eberle, Edward Walter.

*Eberly, Mrs. Angelina Belle.

*Ebony, Texas.

*Eca y Músquiz, José Joaquín de.

Echancote Indians. In 1683–1684 Juan Domínguez de Mendoza qv led an exploratory expedition from El Paso as far eastward as the junction of the Concho and Colorado rivers east of present San Angelo. In his itinerary he listed the names of thirty-seven Indian groups, including the Echancote (Enchacote), from which he expected to receive delegations on the Colorado River. Nothing further is known about the Echancote, who seem to have been one of many Indian groups of north-central Texas that were swept away by the southward thrust of the Lipan-Apache and Comanche Indians in the eighteenth century. The name Echancote is not to be confused with Echuntica, which referred to the Kotsoteka band of Comanche in later times.

BIBLIOGRAPHY: H. E. Bolton (ed.), *Spanish Exploration in the Southwest, 1542–1706* (1916); C. W. Hackett (ed.), *Pichardo's Treatise on the Limits of Louisiana and Texas*, II (1934).
T. N. Campbell

*Echo, Texas. (Coleman County.)

*Echo, Texas. (Orange County.)

*Eckert, Texas.

*Ecleto, Texas. Ecleto, originally an Indian word, was a popular name for a number of different places in Karnes County. The journal of John Charles Beales qv mentioned in 1834 the remains of an Indian encampment where the road from Goliad to San Antonio crossed El Cleto Creek. In the 1840's N. Doran Maillard qv listed the placename of Clato as being situated thirty-six miles south of San Antonio on the road to Goliad. In 1852 the post office of Cleto was established at the crossing of the San Antonio-Victoria road and Ecleto Creek, about seventeen miles north of the first Clato. By the time Karnes County was created in 1854, the post office name of Cleto was changed to

Ecleto. In the 1850's Kelly's Stage Stand,qv operated by Riley A. Kelly at Ecleto, was a way station for stages running between San Antonio and Victoria. During the Civil War, Ecleto was a Confederate post office and also the place for mustering a company of Confederate soldiers under Captain Thomas Rabb.qv In 1871 the post office at Ecleto was changed in name and moved to Riddleville, established about three miles southeast of Ecleto. In 1905 the post office name of Riddleville was changed officially to Gillett. Another post office named Ecleto, situated about six miles south of Gillett on the Dry Ecleto Creek, was established in 1921.

BIBLIOGRAPHY: Robert H. Thonhoff, A History of Karnes County, Texas (M.A. thesis, Southwest Texas State College, 1963).

Robert H. Thonhoff

*Ecleto Creek.

Economic Opportunity, Texas Office of. *See* Community Affairs, Department of.

*Ector, Mathew Duncan.

*Ector, Texas.

*Ector County. Ector County had a population of 90,995 in 1960 and 91,805 in 1970. Ector usually ranked first or second among Texas oil-producing counties; it is the site of one of the state's largest oil fields, which produced 1,794,939,269 barrels of oil from 1926 to January 1, 1973. The industries in the county seat of Odessa centered around petroleum. In the mid-1960's the largest petrochemical complex in the United States was constructed near the city. Cattle ranching and farming produced some income, but were far less important than oil. Tourist attractions are the famous Meteor Crater at Odessa,qv one of the largest in the United States; a replica of London's Globe Theater; and the Odessa College Museum. *See also* Odessa Standard Metropolitan Statistical Area.

*Ector County Oil Field.

Ector's Brigade. Ector's Brigade of the Confederate Army perfected its organization in October, 1862, when Mathew Duncan Ector,qv who had been promoted to brigadier general in August, assumed command in the reorganization of the troops of Lieutenant General E. Kirby Smith qv of the Department of East Tennessee. As originally organized, the brigade consisted of the 10th, 11th, 14th, and 15th Texas Dismounted Cavalry, and it fought as infantry throughout the war.

Later in 1862 the brigade joined the Army of Tennessee and participated in the battle of Murfreesboro as a part of Major General John P. McCown's division.

In May, 1863, the brigade was detached from the Army of Tennessee and attached to General J. E. Johnston's qv army in Mississippi. In September, 1863, the brigade, consisting at that time of the 9th, 10th, 14th, and 32nd Texas and the 29th North Carolina regiments, returned to the Army of Tennessee and participated in the battle of Chickamauga in Major General W. H. T. Walker's division. Brigadier General Nathan B. Forrest, in his

official report of the battle, stated that "the fighting and gallant charges" of the brigade "excited his admiration."

The brigade fought through the Atlanta campaign as a part of Major General Samuel G. French's division of Polk's (later Stewart's) corps of the Army of Tennessee. General Ector was badly wounded in July, 1864, and Brigadier General William H. Young qv succeeded him in command. The latter was in turn seriously wounded in September and the command devolved to Colonel David Coleman of the 39th North Carolina Regiment, which had previously joined the brigade. It participated in General John B. Hood's qv disastrous invasion of Tennessee in November and December, 1864, and surrendered at Mobile in the spring of 1865.

Ector's Brigade, the name by which it was usually known, had a record of consistent, steady valor throughout the Civil War.

BIBLIOGRAPHY: U.S. War Department, *The War of the Rebellion: A Compilation of the Official Records of the Union and Confederate Armies* (1880–1901); *List of Field Officers, Regiments and Battalions in the Confederate States Army* (n.d.); Ezra J. Warner, *Generals in Gray* (1959); C. A. Evans, *Confederate Military History* (1899).

Palmer Bradley

*Edcouch, Texas. Edcouch, in Hidalgo County, had a population of 2,814 in 1960 and 2,656 in 1970.

*Edd Creek.

*Eddleman, Texas.

*Eddy, Texas.

*Eden, Texas. (Concho County.) The population of Eden, in Concho County, was 1,486 in 1960. and 1,291 in 1970.

*Eden, Texas. (Nacogdoches County.)

*Edgar, Texas.

*Edge, Texas.

Edgecliff, Texas. Edgecliff, in Tarrant County, had a population of 339 in 1960 and 1,143 in 1970.

*Edgewood, Texas. Edgewood, in Van Zandt County, became the shipping point for Canton in 1878 (not 1888, as stated in Volume I), so the Texas and Pacific Railroad was there at least that early. In 1960 the population was 887; in 1970 it was 1,176.

BIBLIOGRAPHY: W. S. Mills, *History of Van Zandt County* (1950).

*Edgeworth, Texas.

*Edhube, Texas.

*Edinburg, Texas. Edinburg, seat of Hidalgo County, had a 1960 population of 18,706 and a 1970 population of 17,163. The economy was based on fruit and vegetable packing and processing, and oil and gas. Edinburg Junior College was renamed Pan American College in 1952, when it became a regional four-year institution; the name was changed again, in 1971, to Pan American University. (*See* Closner, John, for account of Edinburg's becoming a county seat. *See also* McAllen-Edinburg-Pharr Standard Metropolitan Statistical Area.)

Edinburg Junior College. *See* Pan American University.

*Edith, Texas.

*Edmonson, Texas.

*Edna, Texas. Edna, seat of Jackson County, is a marketing, supply, and processing center for rice, cotton, and livestock; it is also an oil industry center. The town was served by a new barge canal by the mid-1960's. The 1960 population was 5,038; the 1970 population was 5,332.

Edna Gladney Home. *See* Gladney Home.

*Ednas Creek.

*Edom, Texas.

*Edroy, Texas.

*Edruvera, Texas.

*Edson, Texas.

*Education. The Gilmer-Aikin Law,qv established in 1949, marked a major milestone in Texas public school education. By 1965 approximately 98 percent of Texas public school teachers had college degrees and about 40 percent had graduate degrees. The Texas Permanent School Fund (*see* School Fund, Permanent) totaled more than one-half billion dollars, with annual earnings used to defray current expenses of public schools (*see also* School Fund, Available). Earning power of the fund increased through legislative authorization permitting investment in corporate securities in addition to investments previously authorized in federal, state, and municipal bonds.

County-wide day schools for the deaf and special classes for non-English-speaking preschool children, emotionally disturbed children, minimally brain-injured children, and the educable mentally retarded were initiated. By 1965 ten pilot schools, using a longer school day and a shorter school term, were in operation in an attempt to educate the children of migratory workers. In the middle 1960's the Texas school-age population, ages six through seventeen, was increasing at the rate of about eighty thousand pupils per year; the 1963–1964 scholastic population represented an increase of approximately one million pupils over the comparable number in 1949–1950.

As the scholastic population and the cost of education increased, the number of school districts decreased, from 2,748 in 1949–1950 to 1,187 in 1970–1971. Small school districts in thickly populated areas were consolidated into larger units in order to effect a lower cost per pupil and to increase educational opportunities through providing better school facilities. Two factors then slowed the rate of consolidation. First, in many sparsely settled areas of Texas, further consolidation was difficult because of the time and distance involved in transporting young children from 100 to 125 miles each school day. Second, more than one hundred small Texas schools joined forces to improve their educational programs through sharing resources and working together in a statewide small schools project.

The capital investment in public school plants exceeded three billion dollars during the period from 1949 to 1968. A few schools built all or large parts of their plants underground to avoid noise, to reduce costs of construction and maintenance, and to provide less expensive, year-round climate control. School taxes were the subject of considerable controversy as school population increases necessitated more buildings, more supplies, more teachers, and more textbooks.

Academic requirements for teachers were strengthened during the period in an attempt to improve teacher preparation. All who began teaching after September 1, 1962, were required to have a minimum of twenty-four semester hours of college preparation in each subject area taught.

A uniform system for school finance accounting was made mandatory by direction of the legislature. Computers were used in some of the larger systems for both financial and pupil accounting. The rapid shift of the state economy from rural to urban brought a 30 to 40 percent reduction in the population of some counties. Those in industrial areas found it difficult to build enough classrooms to keep pace with the increases in scholastic enrollment. By the 1970's much experimental work was underway in classrooms. More audio-visual aids were in use, and new approaches to learning enabled pupils to progress at their own rate of speed. Closed-circuit television, team teaching, nongraded schools, accelerated classes, and electronic laboratories were some of the innovations. *See also* Education, Agricultural; Education, Negro; Education, Vocational; Texas Education Agency.

Lee Wilborn

*Education, Agricultural. In 1965 there were vocational agriculture departments in 1,022 high schools, representing a substantial increase over the 631 extant in 1947. Some 48,895 high school students received daily instruction in 1965, as compared to the 1947 figure of 25,000. Adult agricultural education more than tripled from 1947, with 67,653 persons enrolled in 1965. In addition to regular courses in classrooms, laboratories, and research centers, vocational agriculture teachers provided individual instruction to 41,895 young and adult farmers in 1965.

An agricultural education specialist program was established in 1958, which provided part-time instruction for 6,750 adults in all phases of agriculture. The Vocational Education Act of 1963 provided for the expansion of vocational agricultural education to include production agriculture training and off-farm occupation training for persons of all ages.

In 1970 vocational agricultural teachers were trained at Texas A&M University, Texas Tech University, Southwest Texas State University, East Texas State University, Sam Houston State University, Stephen F. Austin State University, Texas A&I University, and Prairie View A&M University.

John C. White

*Education, Commissioner of.

*Education, Negro. The period between 1950

and 1975 was one of tremendous change in the education of Negroes in Texas. The early 1950's marked a peak in Texas Negro education from the public school level to collegiate and professional training. Improvement in school buildings and facilities was the most obvious change. Equalization of teachers' salaries and the addition of funds for classroom instruction and libraries had their beginnings during this period. In higher education the state's oldest Negro college, Prairie View A&M,qv moved in the direction of improved technical training while developing better programs of teacher education to meet the needs of the growing public schools of the state.

There were also beginnings in other areas of professional education when Texas Southern University qv (established in 1947 in Houston) developed programs in law, pharmacy, and other disciplines unavailable to Negroes in the state. Special state funds were available through offices at Texas Southern for Negro students interested in enrolling in out-of-state institutions for studies in medicine, veterinary medicine, and several other fields.

The 1954 United States Supreme Court decision outlawing segregated education had tremendous influence on programs of education for Negroes. Texas has been one of the leaders in desegregation throughout the South. In Friona, in West Texas, two Negro students had been admitted before the 1954 decision. In 1964 Texas accounted for about 60 percent of the desegregated school districts in the South and for more than half of the Negroes attending biracial schools.

Negro education was in a period of transition throughout the post-World War II years, with the years of the 1960's marking the most revolutionary changes. Enrollment of Negro students in all levels of education has kept pace with the national trend. Even with desegregation, nearly all Negro institutions continued to grow, and efforts were increased to encourage other racial groups to attend such schools.

The transition in higher education was best illustrated by the development of various professional fields of study offered at Prairie View A&M University and Texas Southern University. For three-quarters of a century in Texas, Prairie View A&M was the focal point for training Negroes in agriculture. By 1950 provisions for pre-service and in-service training of professional workers reached a peak.

The Texas Association of New Farmers of America had chartered chapters in 178 high schools, with a membership of more than nine thousand high school boys studying vocational agriculture. The operating headquarters for the New Farmers of America program in Texas was Prairie View A&M University. Its state adviser was also stationed at Prairie View; the staff of the School of Agriculture, in cooperation with the state staff in agricultural education, sponsored and planned jointly such activities as the annual state NFA convention and state livestock and poultry judging contests. They also participated in various fairs, shows, contests, and conventions at local, district, state, and national levels. Similar responsibilities revolved around the Cooperative Extension Staff, consisting of three district supervisors and a state leader stationed at Prairie View. The program of training in agriculture, which from the beginning had been a single-track program in general agriculture, was reorganized into multiple curricular offerings, including agricultural education, engineering, economics, animal science, and plant science.

The progress of civil rights legislation and the process of racial school desegregation effected changes in the focal responsibility of Prairie View A&M University for Negroes in agricultural education in Texas. In 1965 the New Farmers of America was merged with the Future Farmers of America. The annual state conference of Negro teachers of vocational agriculture was discontinued. A similar change was made in 4-H Club work of the Extension Service and for conferences of extension agents. Sponsorship of segregated participation in various fairs, shows, and contests was discontinued.

In the process of initial adjustment to the transition, the number of Negroes teaching vocational agriculture had declined 20 percent and the number in agricultural extension had declined 8 percent by 1967. This change was more than matched by the increased employment of Negroes in professional positions which were formerly occupied almost exclusively by whites.

Since 1950 the Texas Education Agency qv has brought a considerable degree of uniformity into the programs of teacher education in colleges of the state. Efforts of the predominantly Negro institutions to achieve recognition by regional and national accrediting agencies have also brought about marked improvement in teacher education.

In 1945 Prairie View began offering four-year programs in architectural engineering, civil engineering, electrical engineering, and mechanical engineering. The enrollment in engineering in the academic year of 1945–1946 was twenty-eight; the first graduating class consisted of one person in mechanical engineering in 1948. In 1950 enrollment in engineering had grown to 40; in 1960, to 224; and in 1966, to 319. The total number of students receiving degrees from 1950 to 1967 was 250.

Significant developments in home economics education for Negroes have occurred, such as the integration of the Future Homemakers of America, the State In-Service Education Conference for Homemaking Teachers, and the Vocational Homemaking Teachers Association of Texas.

Several important changes in industrial education occurred in the 1960's. Two factors appear to have been closely associated with these changes: (1) the changing manpower requirements in Texas, and (2) passage of state and federal legislation designed to provide persons with the opportunity for gaining the skills and knowledge necessary to meet these requirements. Negroes in the state have been affected by these changes, as indicated by the increase in the number of persons engaged in training for individual pursuits.

There has been a noticeable increase in the number of students enrolled in vocational trade and industrial education programs in the high schools of the state. In addition, the number of schools offering these programs has increased significantly in recent years.

The Manpower Development and Training Act of 1962 has provided job-oriented industrial training for a large number of Negroes at several institutions in the state. The Gary Job Corps Center (*see* Job Corps Program in Texas) at San Marcos and the James Connally Technical Institute qv at Waco have also provided training in many different occupations ranging over a wide spectrum of industrial job fields.

Interest and enrollment in non-baccalaureate programs in vocational-industrial education and technology have increased, but in 1967 there was not a sufficient number of qualified teachers in this field.

In 1950 nearly half of the nursing graduates of Prairie View A&M University were located out of the state, mostly in California. In 1964 seventeen out of ninety nursing graduates were employed in Houston, the largest number in any Texas city. A program of public health nursing was established at Prairie View in 1954. That same year Negro students were admitted for the first time to other schools of nursing in Texas. A school of law was organized at Texas Southern University at the time of its establishment in 1947 as the second state institution for Negroes in Texas. As a result of desegregation in Texas universities, efforts in 1967 were made to phase out the law school at Texas Southern, but these plans were abandoned and the law school was still in operation in 1975.

Other specialized programs at Texas Southern were in question due to the close proximity of the state-supported University of Houston.qv Prairie View's Interscholastic League, which enrolled all Negro schools in the state until 1966, was merged with the University Interscholastic League qv by 1968.

In summary, Negro education since 1950 has been concerned with integration and meeting newer standards of accrediting agencies. Texas led the South in integration of students and teachers in public schools. Prairie View A&M University, like Texas Southern University, was gradually integrating. Prairie View moved toward a greater thrust in the technical fields, while Texas Southern was faced with a possible merger with the University of Houston. While Negro education as such was a dying term, the education of Negroes continued in the late 1960's to be of special concern because of the inadequacies faced by students still trapped by the forces of the social structure. *See also* Integration in Texas; Negroes in Texas; Texas Southern University; Prairie View A&M University; Huston-Tillotson College; Bishop College; Paul Quinn College; Jarvis Christian College; Texas College; Butler College; Mary Allen Junior College; Wiley College.

Curtis A. Wood
George R. Woolfolk

*Education, State Board of. The law passed in 1949 was the Gilmer-Aikin (not Gilmer-Aiken, as stated in Volume I) Law.qv *See also* Texas Education Agency.

Education, Texas Commission on Higher. *See* Coordinating Board, Texas College and University System.

*Education, Vocational. Since 1948 the vocational programs established and funded under the George-Barden and Smith-Hughes acts continued to grow and student enrollment increased. In 1959, under an amendment to the George-Barden Act, technical education was introduced in high schools and junior colleges. Nursing education was initiated under this act, whereby programs were conducted on a cooperative basis between hospitals and schools and junior colleges. Congressional acts increased the scope of vocational education. Programs of veterans' education and of civil defense adult education were introduced in Texas with funds provided in 1950 and in 1952, respectively. Under the 1961 Area Redevelopment Act, occupational training was established for unemployed persons in areas of the state where substantial unemployment existed. Also in 1961, programs to train unemployed youth and adults and to retrain adults in present employment were initiated under the Manpower Development and Training Act.

The most significant changes in vocational-technical education resulted from passage of the 1963 Vocational Education Act, which authorized grants to states to assist them in maintaining, extending, and improving existing programs of vocational-technical education and in developing new programs of high quality. These programs were directed toward immediate gainful employment and suited to the needs, interests, and abilities of persons to be trained or retrained. To insure that the programs were directed toward occupations for which there was a demand for personnel, surveys of actual occupational needs were made.

Vocational office education, occupation training for potential school dropouts, and work-study programs were initiated by the 1963 act. Funds were provided also for construction of area schools so that a comprehensive vocational program would be available in a specific geographical area to schools unable to conduct effective vocational education programs for high school or college students and adults. Amendments to the 1963 act provided for enlarging the scope of programs established under the George-Barden and Smith-Hughes acts and for orienting them toward gainful employment, namely, vocational agriculture, home economics, and industrial education. The program of health occupations, originally limited to nurse training, in 1967 included training for medical laboratory assistants and dental assistants and for other critical health areas.

J. W. Edgar

Education Agency, Texas. *See* Texas Education Agency.

Education Beyond the High School, Governor's Committee on. *See* Coordinating Board, Texas College and University System.

*Edward, David Barnett.

*Edwards, Benjamin W.

*Edwards, Gustavus E.

*Edwards, Haden.

*Edwards, Haden Harrison.

*Edwards, Lilburn U.

*Edwards, Monroe.

*Edwards, Peyton Forbes.

*Edwards Colony.

*Edwards County. The leading Angora goat-producing county in the United States, Edwards County also raises large numbers of sheep, cattle, and quarter horses. Crops are limited to small grains, hay, and pecans. Game preserves and hunting leases support a tourist industry. Devil's Sinkhole,qv a huge natural sink, can be viewed from above, but its entrance is closed to the public. It and Seven Hundred Springs, in the northeastern tip of the county, are popular sites for residents and visitors. A Texas Agricultural Experiment Station is located in the northwestern corner of the county. The population was 2,317 in 1960 and 2,107 in 1970, according to the United States census.

*Edwards Creek.

*Edwards Plateau.

Edwards Underground Water District. The Edwards Underground Water District was created by the legislature in 1959 for the purpose of conserving, protecting, and recharging the underground water in the district, and for the prevention of waste and pollution of underground water. The district was organized under a special law rather than under the general law which provides certain powers for underground water districts. It was given responsibility without authority, and its activities were thus limited to fact-finding and education.

The area of the district is generally the same as the boundaries of the Edwards Underground Reservoir designated by the State Board of Water Engineers, later known as the Texas Water Development Board.qv All of Uvalde County, most of Medina County, all but a small part of Bexar County, and a narrow strip across Comal and Hays counties comprise the district. Operations of the district have consisted chiefly of making a co-operative study with the United States Army Corps of Engineers to determine the recharge potential to the underground formation in the upper portions of the Nueces, San Antonio, and Guadalupe river basins which are hydrologically connected by the underground reservoir. The average recharge is 500,000 acre-feet of water a year. In 1966 usage was 256,000 acre-feet.

The state had prepared a comprehensive statewide water plan for use as a guide in water resource development and proposed to develop an arrangement for an integrated system of surface and ground water use for the Edwards (Balcones

Fault Zone) aquifer area by the Texas Water Development Board, the Edwards Underground Water District, the City Water Board of San Antonio, the San Antonio River Authority,qv the Guadalupe-Blanco River Authority,qv and the Lower Colorado River Authority.qv

*Egan, Texas.

*Egerton, Henry.

*Egg-Nog Branch.

*Egypt, Texas.

*Ehrenberg, Herman.

*Eight Mile Creek.

*Eight-Section Act.

*Eighteen Mile Coleto Creek.

*Eightmile Creek.

*Eighth Texas Cavalry. *See* Terry's Texas Rangers.

Eisenhower, Dwight David. Dwight David (Ike) Eisenhower, thirty-fourth president of the United States, was born in Denison, Texas, on October 14, 1890, to David J. and Ida Elizabeth (Stover) Eisenhower, the third of seven sons. The family moved to Abilene, Kansas, soon afterward and settled in a rural area where he earned spending money by doing odd jobs on neighboring farms. During his school years he was interested in history and mathematics and excelled at football, baseball, and boxing. He was graduated from high school in 1909 and worked at various jobs in the community the following year until he took the examination for entrance to West Point. He received his appointment on October 11, 1910, and left for the academy in June, 1911. While there he played halfback for the football team until a knee injury sidelined him. He was graduated June 12, 1915, at the top of the middle third of his class, which numbered 163. He was commissioned a second lieutenant and was assigned to the 19th Infantry at Fort Sam Houston qv in San Antonio on September 13, 1915. He received promotion to first lieutenant on July 1, 1916, the same day on which he was married to Mamie Geneva Doud. They had two sons.

He was promoted to captain on May 15, 1917, and to major on July 2, 1920. His abilities as a training officer quickly emerged and, during World War I, he was put in charge of Camp Colt, Gettysburg, Pennsylvania, where he was instrumental in developing tank corps personnel to operate the new machines of war. He received the Distinguished Service Medal at the end of the war for marked administrative ability.

In 1922 he went to the Canal Zone for a two-year period, after which he returned to the United States. He served under General John J. Pershing in Washington in 1927, during which time he was detailed to the American Battle Monuments Commission. He later served in Paris with the same commission.

He was assigned to the War Department in November, 1929, and served there until 1933, during which period he acted as special assistant to General Douglas MacArthur. Impressed with Eisenhower's abilities, MacArthur appointed Eisenhower his aide. In 1935 Eisenhower joined MacArthur in the Philippines as a member of the American Military Mission and served on MacArthur's staff. Eisenhower's assignment was the development of the Philippine Air Force and the development of the islands' defenses. In December, 1939, he returned to the United States.

He became chief of staff of the 3rd Division (1940), of the Ninth Corps (1941), and then of the Third Army (1941), becoming a brigadier general later in 1941. His impressive conduct of the war maneuvers in Louisiana in the fall of 1941 called attention to his military genius, and, five days after Pearl Harbor, he was summoned from Texas to Washington, where he was made chief of the War Plans Division, War Department, General Staff. He was promoted to major general in March and to lieutenant general in July, 1942. An official proclamation announced his appointment as commanding general of the European theater of operations, U.S.A., in June, 1942, with headquarters in London.

He was made commander of Allied forces landing in North Africa, November 8, 1942, and directed the invasions of Sicily and Italy. He was made full general in February, 1943, and left the Mediterranean theater of operations in December, 1943, to return to Britain to assume command of the troops preparing for the Second Front in Europe. With the official announcement of his appointment as supreme commander of the Allied Expeditionary Force in late December, 1943, Eisenhower was invested with the greatest military authority in history. He directed the Allied landing at Normandy on the French coast on June 6, 1944, which led to the fall of Germany. He was given the temporary rank of general of the army in December, 1944, a rank made permanent in 1946. On May 7, 1945, he received the surrender of the Germans at Rheims. He was in command of the United States Occupation Force in Germany in 1945, and he returned to the United States to serve as chief of staff from 1945 to 1948.

Interested in assuming useful civilian employment, he accepted the presidency of Columbia University in June, 1948. He held the office until December, 1950, at which time he took a leave of absence to become supreme Allied commander in Europe and was in charge of organizing the North Atlantic Treaty Organization (NATO) forces.

Apolitical all his life, he became sought after as a candidate for president of the United States by both parties. He disavowed all political ambitions, but the "I Like Ike" movement grew, and he resigned from the United States Army in July, 1952. He accepted the Republican nomination for president on July 11, 1952, and defeated Adlai Stevenson in the general election; he was inaugurated on January 20, 1953.

Reelected in 1956, he considered himself a moderate and aided in modernizing the outlook of the Republican party, as well as improving United States–Soviet relationships through such means as the Geneva Summit meeting, the Atoms-for-Peace program, and the Open-Skies proposal.

Shortly before he died, President Eisenhower set down a list of achievements during his administration of which he was most proud. Among them were:

Statehood of Alaska and Hawaii.

End of Korean War.

Largest reduction of taxes to that time.

First civil rights law in eighty years.

Prevention of Communistic efforts to dominate Iran, Guatemala, Lebanon, Taiwan, South Vietnam.

Initiation and great progress in most ambitious road program by any nation in all history.

Initiating a strong ballistic missile program.

Conceiving and building the Polaris program, with ships operating at sea, within a single administration.

Using federal power to enforce orders of a federal court in Arkansas, with no loss of life (Little Rock school crisis).

Upon completion of his eight years in office, he retired with his wife to his farm in Gettysburg, Pennsylvania, where he spent his time writing and indulging in his favorite sport, golf. He became increasingly conservative in his political views. He suffered from a chronic heart ailment and, after several remarkable recoveries from serious heart attacks, he died at Walter Reed Army Hospital on March 28, 1969. He was buried in a small chapel in the Eisenhower Center near the Eisenhower Library in Abilene, Kansas. See also Eisenhower Birthplace State Historic Site; Eisenhower State Recreation Park (both under Parks, State).

BIBLIOGRAPHY: Kenneth S. Davis, Soldier of Democracy (1945); Alden Hatch, General Ike (1944); Luman H. Long (ed.), The 1970 World Almanac and Book of Facts (1969); Francis T. Miller, Eisenhower, Man and Soldier (1944); Richard Rovere, Affairs of State: The Eisenhower Years (1956).

John G. Tower

Eisenlohr, Edward G. Edward G Eisenlohr was born in Cincinnati, Ohio, on November 9, 1872, and came with his family to Dallas, Texas, in 1874. He accompanied his parents to Europe at the age of fourteen, where he attended schools in Zurich and Karlsruhe. Eisenlohr returned to Dallas to work in a bank for nineteen years. His avid hopes for a career as an artist impelled him to paint and study during this period under Robert Onderdonk and Frank Reaugh.qqv While on a leave of absence from the bank he learned that one of his paintings had been accepted for the Spring Exhibition at the Cincinnati Museum, and, thus encouraged, he studied at Woodstock, New York, a summer school of the Art Students League He then traveled in Europe, studying in Zurich in the school of Gustave Schoeleher and in the Granducal Academy of Fine Arts. After two years Eisenlohr returned to Dallas to work and paint.

Exhibits of his work appeared at the National Academy in New York, the San Francisco World's Fair, the Corcoran Gallery in Washington, D.C., the Texas Centennial qv Exhibition at the Dallas Museum of Fine Arts qv in 1936, and in numerous one-man shows. He regularly exhibited with the Fort Worth Art Association. Eisenlohr won prizes in the Edgar B. Davis qv Competitions of the San Antonio Art League, in the 1930 Southern States Art League, and in the 1931 exhibit of the Dallas Art Association. He was a member of the Salmagundi Club, the Southern States Art League, the American Federation of Arts, and the Texas Fine Arts Association.qv Examples of Eisenlohr's work are in the permanent collections of the Dallas Museum of Fine Arts, the Elisabet Ney Museum qqv in Austin, the Isaac Delgado Museum in New Orleans, and the Witte Memorial Museum qv in San Antonio. He was a charter member of the First Unitarian Church of Dallas, formed in 1899, and often spoke at its services. He died in Dallas on June 6, 1961.

BIBLIOGRAPHY: Frances Battaile Fisk, *A History of Texas Artists and Sculptors* (1928); Esse Forrester-O'Brien, *Art and Artists of Texas* (c.1935); Witte Memorial Museum Files, San Antonio, Texas; *Who's Who in American Art* (1959).

Caroline Remy

***Elam, John.**

***Elam, Texas.**

***Elba Creek.**

***El Barroso Creek.**

Elbert, Texas. (Polk County.) *See* Dallardsville, Texas.

***Elbert, Texas.** (Throckmorton County.)

***Elberta, Texas.**

***Elbow Lake.**

***El Burro Creek.**

El Campanario. *See* Texas Old Missions and Forts Restoration Association.

***El Campo, Texas.** El Campo, in Wharton County, is a market and supply center for agricultural produce and oil, with industries producing metal products, garments, fertilizer, and meat and rice products. In 1970 the city reported 237 businesses, numerous churches, and one hospital. In 1960 the population was 7,700; the 1970 population was 8,563, an increase of 11.2 percent, according to the United States census.

El Campo South, Texas. El Campo South, an unincorporated town in Wharton County, had a population of 1,884 in 1960 and 1,880 in 1970, according to the United States census.

***El Cañon Mission.** *See* San Lorenzo de la Santa Cruz Mission.

***El Capitan.**

***El Chamizal.** *See* Chamizal Dispute.

***El Colorado, Texas.**

***El Copano.**

***Elder, Robert.**

***Elderville, Texas.**

***Eldorado, Texas.** Eldorado, seat and only town of Schleicher County, was incorporated in 1926. Of the forty-three businesses reported in 1970, most were concerned with wool and petroleum. In 1966 two high school buildings were completed. There was also a bank, a library, eleven churches, and a newspaper. In the 1960's there was a movement to change the name of the town to the correct Spanish, El Dorado. The 1960 population was 1,815; the 1970 population was 1,446, according to the United States census.

***Eldorado Center, Texas.**

***Eldridge, Joseph C.**

***Eldridge, Texas.**

***Election Laws.** A new election code was enacted in 1951 which made few important changes in the law. It did, however, provide for cross-filing of the candidates of one party by another in general elections. The election of 1952 saw its first and only use. In that year the Republican party qv cross-filed all but one of the Democratic party's qv candidates for statewide office to make it easier for Democrats to vote for General Dwight D. Eisenhower,qv the Republican candidate for president. This action no doubt aided him in carrying the state and produced a Democratic demand for its repeal and a refusal of the Democrats in 1954 to allow their candidates to be cross-filed. The device was repealed in 1955. In that year a new provision for reports of campaign expenditures reduced the number required to one before and one after an election.

In 1957 run-offs were provided for in special elections for United States senator and congressmen-at-large between the two highest in the initial election if no candidate received a majority. Run-offs were later provided for in special elections for district congressmen. Also in 1957 the scratch-out method of marking ballots was restored. For some years the voters had been allowed to use the cross mark in a square as the alternate method.

The prospective candidacy of Senator Lyndon B. Johnson qv for the presidency in 1960 produced important changes in the election law, which was enacted for his benefit in 1959. One law moved the dates of the primary elections from July and August (for run-off if necessary), where they had been long established, to the first Saturdays in May and June. This law also dispensed with the second series of precinct and county conventions previously held in the summers of even-numbered years to choose delegates to the September state convention. Beginning in 1960 one set of precinct and county conventions elected delegates who served in both the presidential and gubernatorial state conventions, the precinct conventions to be held earlier on the moved-up day of the first primary. The earlier dates for the primaries allowed Senator Johnson to be nominated for reelection to the United States Senate and simultaneously to have his name on the ballot as a presidential candidate. Opponents of Johnson resented these permanent changes in the primary arrangements. The changes had the bad effect of creating a much longer interval between the primary and the general election. A good effect, however, was that having one set of delegates to serve in both state conventions eliminated a possible shift in party control, which had sometimes happened in presidential election years in the former summer precinct and county conventions.

There were two other significant changes in the election law in 1959. First, it was required that when the voter first voted in a party primary or attended a party convention, his poll tax or exemption certificate (now registration certificate) be stamped with the name of the party in whose activity he was participating. During that year, he could not participate in the primary or convention of any other party. The other requirement was that the county executive committee, after canvassing the votes of a primary election, had to file the results with the county clerk. Previously, no official returns of primaries were required to be made except to party authorities.

In 1961 the voting strength in party conventions was shifted from the presidential to the gubernatorial vote in the last general election. In 1963 many minor changes and clarifications were made in election procedures. A voter registration system was set up to go into effect if the voters repealed the poll tax requirement in the Constitution of Texas. A temporary registration system for voting for national officials was also established, to be applied in case the poll tax was repealed for federal elections by a pending amendment to the Constitution of the United States.

The election of 1964 was the first one in which no poll tax was required to vote in federal elections, but the tax still survived for state and local elections. The Twenty-fourth Amendment to the United States Constitution went into effect, abolishing the poll tax as a voting requirement for president, vice-president, presidential electors, United States senators, and representatives in the United States Congress. Thus, in 1964 in Texas, ballots had to be provided for voters qualified for all elections and for those voting only in federal elections.

Early in 1966 the poll tax was judicially invalidated for all elections. Senate Bill 1 of the first called session of 1966 of the Texas legislature required voters to register, in person or by mail, with the county tax assessor once each year between October 1 and the following January 31. Persons eligible to register and vote had to be twenty-one years of age, residents of the state for one year, and residents of the district or county for six months. Persons over sixty who did not live in a city of 10,000 or more, or who moved, could vote without registering, except in counties of 500,000 or more, where the county commissioners could require all voters to register.

A state constitutional amendment submitted on November 8, 1966, was approved, removing the poll tax voting provision from the Constitution of Texas and embodying a requirement for annual registration. Another proposed amendment was approved, removing the year's residence requirement for persons who qualified to vote in another state for presidential electors and who lived in Texas at least thirty days, and allowing the legislature to provide for the reenfranchisement, under certain circumstances, of former Texas voters who had been away from the state for less than one year.

[In 1971 the legislature eliminated the annual voter registration requirement and provided, instead, a continuing registration system, whereby voters were automatically registered after participating in primaries or elections. Passage of a statute effective August 27, 1973, by the 63rd Texas Legislature, granted persons eighteen years of age all the privileges hitherto granted those twenty-one years of age; thus, men and women eighteen years of age were allowed, for the first time in Texas, the right to vote.—Ed.]

BIBLIOGRAPHY: J. M. Patterson, Jr. (comp.), *Texas Election Laws* (1966); Institute of Public Affairs, "Elections," *Reviews* of the 53rd–59th Legislatures (1953–1966).

O. Douglas Weeks

*Electra, Texas. Electra, in western Wichita County, is an oil and agricultural commercial center. Electra counts among its industries oil field equipment plants, petroleum processing, grain storage and processing, and the making of farm implements. By 1970 Electra had 116 businesses; a one-hundred-acre industrial park had been created in an effort to attract new industries. Other community assets were a twenty-five-bed hospital and a sixty-bed nursing home. The 1960 population was 4,759; the 1970 population was 3,895, according to the United States census. *See also* Wichita Falls Standard Metropolitan Statistical Area.

*Electra Oil Field.

*Electric City, Texas.

*Electric Fence.

*Electrical Power. By 1954 the total generating capacity of Texas electric power plants was 5,521,180 kilowatts, four times as much as in 1944. Of the 192 electric power plants, seventy-two were powered by steam and produced 4,971,400 kilowatts; 101 were powered by internal combustion engines and produced 196,990 kilowatts; nineteen were hydroelectric and produced 352,790 kilowatts. In 1963 the 176 electrical power plants in Texas increased their total generating capability to 11,990,392 kilowatts, more than twice the 1954 figure.

Although by 1970 the number of electric power plants had decreased to 171, their generating capability had risen to 25,117,928 kilowatts, almost five times the 1954 capacity. Of the total number of plants, eighty-two were steam-powered with a capability of 23,955,741 kilowatts, sixty-eight were internal combustion engines or gas turbine-powered with a capacity of 644,727 kilowatts, and twenty-one were hydroelectric with a capability of 517,460 kilowatts. Seventy-seven distribution cooperatives of the Rural Electrification Administration served 97 percent of the total Texas farms in 1970. *See also* Agriculture in Texas.

BIBLIOGRAPHY: *Texas Almanac* (1955, 1963–1971).

Electronics Industry. The electronics industry expanded rapidly in Texas during the 1950's. Advantages of locating plants in Texas included proximity to markets, cheap labor, good living conditions, freedom from labor strikes, and a favorable tax structure.

In the mid-1950's Houston became the home base for most electronics firms, most of which concentrated on geophysical instruments and automation systems. Total sales in that area in 1955 topped $10 million.

The second major concentration of the electronics industry in the state at that time was in the Dallas and in the Fort Worth standard metropolitan statistical areas.qv Texas Instruments, the world's only source of high temperature silicone transistors, reached $28 million in sales in 1955 and planned a new 250-acre plant north of Dallas. In that year, Texas Instruments supplied 85 percent of the transistors used in the newly developed transistor radios. Collins Radio maintained a $2 million plant near Richardson and was involved in the development of the microwave system of televising. Total 1955 sales for the Iowa-based company were $108 million. Texas Electronics became the only manufacturer of television picture tubes in the state and one of six such plants west of the Mississippi River.

Texas Instruments rapidly became the leader in the Texas electronics industry in the late 1950's. Compared to $44 million in 1956, the company's sales jumped to $67 million in 1957, a 45 percent increase. As military spending on electronic equipment reached 7 percent of all defense spending in 1958, Texas Instruments took on the manufacture of United States Air Force photographic mapping radar systems. The firm carried out eight mergers in the late 1950's, which boosted its sales by 1959 to $193 million. In the previous year Collins Radio, also of the Dallas area, was awarded a $3.3 million contract for the development of microwave link installations.

Texas firms in the 1950's ranged from small groups of research scientists in Austin to large corporations employing thousands of people in Dallas, Fort Worth, and Houston. Products ranged from high fidelity phonographs and television sets to defense microwave equipment and computers.

The electronics industry expanded greatly in the early 1950's with the aid of government contracts. By 1963 Texas had 291 establishments producing electronic parts and equipment. In 1964 a $2 million plant to manufacture inertial guidance systems was planned for Lubbock. In the same year Texas Instruments boosted its total annual sales to $233 million.

In February, 1966, Texas manufacture of electronic navigation and guidance systems, radar, and communication equipment was expanding at an ever-increasing rate. More than thirty-five thousand people were employed in large or small electronics plants in the Dallas metropolitan area alone. The war in Vietnam greatly stimulated the manufacture of military equipment at various Texas electronics firms. By 1966 Tracor, originally a small group of Austin scientists in the mid-1950's, had expanded its sales to $17 million and had branches in eight states; sales the following year reached $38 million. Developments included chaff dispensing systems for the United States Navy, chaff units for the United States Air Force, and the development of a sophisticated missile penetration system. Analytical and medical instruments, as well as anti-submarine warfare devices, were manufactured by this company. *See also* Aircraft Manufacture.

BIBLIOGRAPHY: *Texas Business Review* (August, 1956–February, 1966); *Texas Almanac* (1967).

Charles Duval, Jr.

*Eleemosynary Institutions.

*Elephant Mountain.

*Elevation, Texas.

*Elfco, Texas.

*El Fortín. *See* Presidio del Norte.

*El Gato, Texas.

*Elgin, John Edward.

*Elgin, Texas. Besides the earlier names of Glasscock and Hogeye, it is possible that Elgin, in Bastrop County near the Travis County line, began with the name of Lickskillet; a place close by, at least, was cited by that name by William M. Walton qv in 1915 in a remembrance of his trip to Texas in 1852. Walton recalled that he had spent the night on the prairie about where Manor now is, and that "in that great expanse of territory there was not a house, and only one at Elgin, which place was called 'Lickskillet' in memory of some instance where the participator had a short meal and had to lick the skillet to eke out his supper." The long (sixty-three years) period of Walton's recall of this story is not sufficient evidence for establishing Lickskillet as the earliest name for Elgin, and it is offered here only as a possibility.

In the early 1970's Elgin had over eighty business establishments. The most important were brick and tile industries and a cottonseed oil mill. Several firms throughout the region produced the sausage associated with Elgin's name. The 1960 population was 3,511. The 1970 population was 3,832.

BIBLIOGRAPHY: "Major Buck Walton's Stirring History," *Frontier Times*, 27 (October, 1949).

*Elguezábal, Juan Bautista.

*Elguezábal, Juan José.

*Eliasville, Texas.

*Eliga, Texas.

*El Indio, Texas.

Elisabet Ney Museum. The Elisabet Ney Museum building, originally the Austin studio of the sculptor Elisabet Ney qv (who called it Formosa), was built in 1892 and enlarged in 1902. The stone building alongside Waller Creek was set amid numerous trees and plants on property originally encompassing seven acres; the museum property has since been reduced to approximately one city block.

After the sculptor's death in 1907, the property was purchased by Ella (Dancy) Dibrell, wife of Joseph Burton Dibrell,qv by a deed dated March 28, 1909, for the purpose of preserving it as an art shrine and memorial to the artist. Ella Dibrell appointed a board of managers in that year, with Jospeh Draper Sayers,qv former governor of Texas, as chairman. The Ney sculptures were presented by the artist's husband, Edmund Duncan Montgomery,qv to the University of Texas, Austin, with the understanding that the collection remain in his deceased wife's studio-home.

One of the oldest art museums in Texas, the building was opened to the public in 1909, at first only for special exhibitions. In 1911 members of the newly organized Texas Fine Arts Association qv acted as hostesses for the museum, and by the 1920's the museum was open for exhibition once a week. Following Ella Dibrell's death in 1920, Formosa remained in the hands of the Dibrell family until 1932, when it was sold to the Texas Fine Arts Association. In 1941 the association deeded the site to the city of Austin's parks and recreation department, which in 1974 continued to maintain and operate the museum. Mrs. James W. (Willie) Rutland was curator of the museum from sometime prior to 1930 until 1967; from that time until the present (1974), Mrs. May Diane Harris has been director. Until 1973 the Elisabet Ney Museum emphasized the exhibition of contemporary art. In the spring of that year, however, it became a national historic site, and the new emphasis in 1974 was the operation of the museum as an edutional institution, showing a typical nineteenth century studio containing nineteenth century sculpture, consisting principally of pieces executed by Elisabet Ney during her career in Europe and in Texas.

*Elite, Texas.

*Eliza Russell and Little Penn Claims.

*Elizabeth, Texas.

*Elizabeth Creek.

*Elizondo, Ignacio.

*Elk, Texas.

*Elkhart, Texas.

*Elkhart Creek.

*Elkins, Texas.

*Elks, Benevolent and Protective Order of. The Benevolent and Protective Order of Elks continued many youth programs in the 1960's, including scholarships, scouting for boys and girls, aid to the needy, and many civic and community endeavors. The Elks operated a hospital for crippled children at Ottine, Texas, coupled with an accredited school for regular classroom work. With no foreign affiliation, the Elks national organization had about 2,300 lodges in 1964, with a combined membership of over 1,350,000. The Texas lodges numbered sixty-five, with a membership of 25,000. Fort Worth had the largest lodge in the state. The president of the Texas State Elks Association in 1972 was T. O. Wilkins of Lubbock.

John A. Fuhrhop

*Elkton, Texas.

*Ella, Texas.

*Ellen, Texas.

*Ellersly Plantation.

*Ellinger, Texas.

*Ellington Air Force Base. Ellington Air Force Base was designated as a permanent United States Air Force base in 1954. The base changed hands in April, 1958, when jurisdiction was transferred from Air Training Command to Continental Air Command under the immediate command of Headquarters, 4th Air Force Reserve Region, Randolph Air Force Base,qv Texas. In February, 1963, the 2578th Air Base Squadron was reactivated and assumed the duties as host unit. In 1964 missions included base logistics support, training of Air Force Reservists and Air National Guardsmen, air rescue, communications, and support of the National Aeronautics and Space Administration's Manned Spacecraft Center.qv The base was transferred to the Air National Guard on July 1, 1967.

*Elliot, Charles.

Elliott, Claude. Claude Elliott, the son of Robert Mitchell and Martha (Smith) Elliott, was born at Cross Plains, Texas, on September 21, 1896. After attending Abilene Christian College, Simmons College (now Hardin-Simmons University), and West Texas State College (now West Texas State University), Elliott began his teaching career at Sardis and at Donna. He received his B.A. degree from Southwest Texas State Teachers College (now Southwest Texas State University) in 1923 and served as superintendent of the La Feria schools, 1923–1928. In the meantime Elliott pursued his graduate studies at the University of Texas, where he was awarded the M.A. degree in 1928 and the Ph.D. degree in 1934. He married Emma Edwin Moore at San Marcos on September 6, 1927, and joined the faculty of Southwest Texas State Teachers College in September, 1929.

While a student at the University of Texas, Elliott studied history under Eugene C. Barker, Charles W. Ramsdell, Walter P. Webb,qqv and others. As a faculty member at Southwest Texas State, Elliott was a great influence in the growth and development of the school. Although classroom teaching was his primary interest, Elliott found time to serve as registrar and, later, as graduate dean. He also wrote widely in the general field of Southern and Texas history. He wrote *Leathercoat: The Life History of a Texas Patriot* (1938) and compiled and edited a check list of theses and dissertations, *Theses on Texas History* (1955). He served on the advisory council of the *Handbook of Texas* and contributed articles to the *Southwestern Historical Quarterly*,qv the *Georgia Historical Review*, the *Southwestern Social Science Quarterly*,qv and the *Journal of Southern History*. A fellow of the Texas State Historical Association,qv Elliott served the organization as vice-president, 1947–1952, and as president, 1953–1955. He died at Houston on October 1, 1958; he was buried at San Marcos.

BIBLIOGRAPHY: *Who's Who In America* (1952).

William C. Pool

Elliott, George Washington. George Washington Elliott, one of the first to introduce a herd of full-blood Durham cattle to Texas, was born in Boone County, Missouri, in 1830, one of eight children of Reuben and Elizabeth (Wilhite) Elliott. He married Harriett E. McQuity in 1869, and they had three children. Although a physician by profession, in 1878 Elliott moved to Bexar County, Texas, where he established a 1,700-acre ranch a few miles northwest of San Antonio. Interested in testing the endurance of Durham cattle in the Texas open range country, he built the first pasture fence and the first artificial watering tanks in Bexar County for forty-five purebred Durhams which he bred to stocker cattle. Elliott also cultivated hay to supply provender for the army post at San Antonio. In 1884 Elliott sold his ranch and stock, and two years later he established the 20,000-acre "T" Ranch in Upton County, on which he stocked one thousand head of cattle. For his headquarters he built a two-room rock house across from the old Butterfield Overland Mail Route ᵠᵛ station.

In 1890 Elliott sold the "T" Ranch to R. S. Benson and moved to Midland, where he was elected chairman of the board for the organization of the First National Bank. In Midland he devoted full time to the practice of medicine and was credited with designing and patenting the Elliott saddlebag, known and appreciated by country physicians. The saddlebag was made and sold by A. D. Mollier and Son of St. Louis, Missouri. At the turn of the century, Elliott moved to Fort Worth, where he died on May 12, 1910. He was buried in Oakwood Cemetery in Fort Worth.

BIBLIOGRAPHY: James Cox, *Historical and Biographical Records of the Cattle Industry and the Cattlemen of Texas and the Adjacent Territory*, II (1895); John Howard Grifin, *The Land of the High Sky* (1959); Midland *Reporter-Telegram*, October 18, 1953.

N. Ethie Eagleton

*Elliott, Robert Woodward Barnwell.

*Elliott, William.

*Elliott, Texas. (Robertson County.)

*Elliott, Texas. (Wilbarger County.)

*Elliott Canyon Creek.

*Elliott Creek.

*Ellis, A. (Alexander) Caswell.

*Ellis, Joseph L.

*Ellis, Richard.

*Ellis County. Ellis County in 1970 was part of the Dallas Standard Metropolitan Statistical Area. Interstate Highway 35 connected the county seat, Waxahachie, with Dallas, and while many Ellis County residents were employed in that large city, there was a thriving economic life within the county itself. Agriculture was important and diversified; the county had an average annual farm income of $24 million in the early 1970's. In 1972–1973, 68,060 bales of cotton were ginned, and livestock was marketed in a large quantity. In addition to several feedlots, the county had twenty-five cotton gins and fifteen grain elevators by 1970. Local industry had become a major source of revenue; building materials (especially brick), clothing, business forms, and other commodities were produced within the county. Local fairs and historical sites attracted

tourists. The Ellis County population was 43,395 in 1960 and had increased to 46,638 by 1970. *See also* Dallas Standard Metropolitan Statistical Area.

*Ellis Draw.

*Ellison Branch.

*Ellison Creek.

*Ellison Creek Reservoir. Ellison Creek Reservoir, in Morris County, was owned and operated in 1975 by the Lone Star Steel Company. Construction of the dam began in 1942 and was completed in April, 1943. The reservoir capacity is 24,700 acre-feet, and the surface area is 1,516 acres at the service spillway crest at elevation 268.1 feet above mean sea level. When the flow into the reservoir is inadequate, water is pumped into the reservoir from Cypress Creek. The drainage area of the Ellison Creek watershed at Ellison Creek Dam is thirty-seven square miles.

BIBLIOGRAPHY: Texas Water Commission, *Bulletin 6408* (1964).

Seth D. Breeding

*Ellison Ridge, Texas.

*Ellison Springs Indian Fight.

*Ellsworth, Texas.

Ellwood, Isaac L. Isaac L. Ellwood was born in Springfield Hollow, New York, on August 12, 1833. As a boy he exhibited the initiative and enterprise which were to make him one of America's great businessmen by selling sauerkraut to barge hands on the Erie Canal. In 1851 he followed the gold rush to California, returning in 1855 with a capital of nearly three thousand dollars with which he opened a hardware and implement store in DeKalb, Illinois. There he married Harriet Augusta Miller on January 27, 1859. The couple had six children.

Ellwood acquired several farm properties around DeKalb and after the Civil War began importing and breeding Percheron draft horses. His interest in farming directed his attention to the need for a fencing material which would contain livestock. He patented a type of barbed wire, but he concluded that the wire patented by Joseph F. Glidden was more practical. He formed a partnership with Glidden as the I. L. Ellwood Manufacturing Company in 1873 and began producing a two-strand, twisted barbed wire in a back room of his hardware store. Success was almost immediate, for the Glidden-Ellwood wire fulfilled a practical need, especially for ranchers on the western plains. In 1881 the company expanded and reorganized as the Superior Barbed Wire Company, and in 1898 it merged into the American Steel and Wire Company, a predecessor of United States Steel.

In the meantime Ellwood became interested in ranching, making a trip to Texas in 1889 and purchasing the well-known Renderbrook Ranch of some 130,000 acres in Mitchell County from John W. and Dudley H. Snyder,ᵠᵛ for which Ellwood adopted the Spade brand. In 1891 Ellwood acquired an additional 128,000 acres northwest of Lubbock from the Snyder brothers. He added 45,000 acres in 1902 and additional acreage in 1906 to bring the total size of this ranch, which was known as the Spade Ranch,qv to 265,000 acres, thereby increasing Ellwood's total Texas holdings to 395,000 acres.

After the merger with American Steel and Wire, Ellwood's chief interest focused on his Texas ranches, although his home remained in DeKalb, where he had other investments. Ellwood died in DeKalb, Illinois, on September 11, 1910.

BIBLIOGRAPHY: Seymour V. Connor (ed.), *Builders of the Southwest* (1959).

Seymour V. Connor

*Elm Bayou.
*Elm Branch.
*Elm Creek.
*Elm Flat, Texas.
*Elm Fork of Red River.
*Elm Fork of the Trinity River.
*Elm Grove, Texas. (Dallas County.)
*Elm Grove, Texas. (Hays County.)
*Elm Grove Creek.
*Elm Mott, Texas.
*Elm Mott Branch.
*Elm Mountain.
*Elm Ridge, Texas.
*Elmaton, Texas.
*Elmdale, Texas.
*El Mejicano.
*Elmendorf, Texas.
*Elmir Branch.
*Elmo, Texas.
*El Mocho. See Mocho.
*Elmont, Texas.
*Elmore, Texas.
*El Moro Creek.
*Elmton, Texas.
*El Muerto Peak.
*Elmwood, Texas.
*Elmwood Institute.
*Eloise, Texas.
*El Olso, Texas.
*El Orcoquisac.
*El Parr, Texas.

*El Paso, Texas. El Paso is a wholesale, retail, and manufacturing center with 3,404 businesses reported in 1970. Manufactures include cotton seed products, foods, clothing, petrochemicals, and minerals. In 1960 the population was 276,687, increasing to 322,261 by 1970. On the border opposite Ciudad Juárez, Mexico, El Paso enjoys a great tourist industry. The two cities are the largest border cities of both the United States and Mexico, with a combined population of approximately 840,000 within a twenty-mile radius. *See also* El Paso Standard Metropolitan Statistical Area.

El Paso Community College. Founded in 1969 as a public coeducational institution, El Paso Community College enrolled students for the first time in the fall of 1971. In 1972 there were 150 faculty members and 3,501 students. Alfredo de los Santos was president in 1974, when enrollment reached 7,443.

*El Paso County. El Paso County ranked second among the counties in livestock income in the late 1960's. With 55,000 acres of irrigated land, the production of cotton, alfalfa, vegetables, and fruits added to the economy. There were seventeen cotton gins, and manufacturing generally increased. The 1960 population of the county was 314,070, and this figure increased to 359,291 by 1970. *See also* El Paso Standard Metropolitan Statistical Area.

El Paso County Historical Society. The El Paso County Historical Society was organized on March 18, 1954, as a project of the Civic Improvement Committee, Women's Division, El Paso Chamber of Commerce, in order to "promote and engage in research into the history, archeology, and natural history of West Texas, Southern New Mexico, Eastern Arizona, and Northern Mexico; to publish the important findings; and to preserve the valuable relics and monuments."

The society quarterly, *Password*, edited since its beginning by Eugene O. Porter of the University of Texas at El Paso, is widely distributed among libraries, historical societies, and more than six hundred members of the society. In 1957 the society was given the Award of Merit of the American Association for State and Local History.

The El Paso County Historical Society organized community celebrations for the seventy-fifth anniversary of the coming of railroads to El Paso and the hundredth anniversary of the Butterfield Overland Route.qv It has cooperated with the Texas State Historical Survey Committee qv and local organizations in marking numerous historical sites and has preserved important historical records and memorabilia. Annual contests are held to stimulate significant historical research. At the annual El Paso Hall of Honor banquet at least two persons, living or dead, are enrolled in the El Paso Hall of Honor. Presidents of the society have been Paul Heisig, Frank Feuille III, Jack C. Vowell, Jr., John B. Neff, Joseph Leach, Richard C. White, Conrey Bryson, H. Gordon Frost, H. Crampton Jones, and Fred J. Morton.

Conrey Bryson

*El Paso and Northeastern Railroad Company.
*El Paso Polychrome Pottery.
*El Paso Southern Railway Company. Up to 1955 the El Paso Southern Railway Company owned its own line and leased it to the Southern Pacific. In that year the Southern Pacific took it over, and on November 1, 1961, merged it with the Texas and New Orleans Railroad and the El Paso and Southwestern Railroad of Texas.

James M. Day

*El Paso and Southwestern Railroad Company of Texas. Up to 1955 the El Paso and Southwestern Railroad Company of Texas owned its own line, but it was operated under lease by the Southern Pacific, into which it was merged in that year. In November, 1961, it was merged with the Texas and New Orleans Railroad and the El Paso Southern Railway Company.

James M. Day

El Paso Standard Metropolitan Statistical Area. The El Paso Standard Metropolitan Statistical Area, as designated by the Bureau of the Budget in 1949, included all of El Paso County, with an area of 1,054 square miles. In 1950 the area had 194,968 inhabitants, while its core city, El Paso, had 130,-485. In 1960 the population was 314,070 and 276,-687, respectively. The 1970 population showed 359,291 in the county and 322,261 in the city. Other towns with more than one thousand residents were Fabens, Anthony, Canutillo, and San Elizario. Smaller communities in the area were Socorro, Clint, Tornillo, Mesa, Vinton, and Alamo Alto.

A more realistic designation of the area would be a "standard international metropolitan area," including Ciudad Juárez, Mexico, across the Rio Grande from El Paso. Combined with the 522,032 residents of Juárez, the metropolitan area had a population of approximately 840,000 within a twenty-mile radius. The two cities are bound by historical, economic, and cultural ties. Products and persons pass daily over the international bridge. About thirty million persons and seven million motor vehicles annually cross from Juárez to El Paso. The reverse flow of human traffic is equivalent in volume.

The unity of the international metropolitan area is reflected by the trade between the twin cities. One-fifth of the retail sales in El Paso is purchased by citizens of Mexico. Downtown El Paso, near the international points of entry, had 30 percent of its retail sales volume furnished by purchasers from across the Rio Grande. As a result this Mexican patronage has offset the loss of downtown retail sales to the El Paso suburban competition. North American spending in Juárez, while less than Mexican spending in El Paso, is increasing. About one-third of the retail trade of Juárez is with customers from the United States. Mexican craft products promoted by PRONAF (Programa Nacional Fronteriza), amusements, and newly built supermarkets are increasingly patronized by North American buyers. Services like automobile repair work attract many. Bars, restaurants, and cabarets offer recreation for visitors. Curio shops catering more to the tourist than to the El Paso citizen continue to thrive. Retail liquor sales, however, have declined with the curtailment of wet goods that may be brought back monthly from Mexico.

In addition to Juárez and northern Chihuahua, El Paso serves as a trade center for Trans-Pecos Texas and southern New Mexico. The city's wholesale trade, which exceeds its retail sales, reflects this trade. While El Paso owed its early pros-perity to commerce and transportation, it has developed rapidly as a manufacturing center. Most important of its many manufacturers are those engaged in ore smelting, oil and copper refining, and the production and transportation of natural gas and electricity. Recently the clothing industry, especially Western apparel, has grown rapidly and now employs several thousand workers. El Paso has the largest custom smelter in the world—a copper plant which, using the electrolytic process, refines one-fourth of all copper processed in the United States (see Copper Production). Outside of El Paso, only Vinton, with a steel mill, has any manufacturing of significance. Agribusiness includes food processing (especially Mexican foods), meat packing, cottonseed oil manufacturing, and animal feed production.

Although El Paso dominates the economy of the area, El Paso County ranks second in the state in livestock income. The metropolitan area has two distinctive parts, the irrigated Rio Grande valley and the mountainous uplands. The valley is the center of the farming industry, with cotton, alfalfa, grains, and truck crops predominating. About fifty-five thousand acres are irrigated. Around half of the forty-nine thousand cotton bales ginned in the area are of the Supima variety, which is a highly valued, long-staple cotton. The pecan industry has expanded rapidly in the area. In the uplands cattle and sheep ranching are of major significance.

Basic to the El Paso economy are the surrounding military installations. (See Fort Bliss; Biggs Army Airfield.) Military spending in the area for goods and services increased from $15.7 million to $25.6 million and the personnel increased from seventeen thousand to forty thousand between 1965 and 1966. The military payroll for 1966 totaled more than $200 million, much of which was spent locally. Allied to the military impact upon the economy is the presence of a large number of civilian workers employed by the federal government and private companies at the White Sands Missile Range. The aggregate of non-military employees increased from about six thousand in 1965 to eleven thousand in 1966. A majority of them resided in El Paso. By 1970 the government payroll amounted to $325 million annually.

The El Paso area is a popular tourist center. With almost perfect weather the entire year, the city offers a number of attractions. Historical sites in the area include the old town of Ysleta, Old Fort Bliss, and Hueco Tanks.qqv Annual events include the Southwestern Livestock Show and the Southwestern Sun Carnival. Sports-minded persons could watch Texas League qv baseball, football in the Sun Bowl,qv as well as horse racing and bull-fighting in Juárez. Located within the area are the International Museum, the Fort Bliss Replica Museum, the El Paso Centennial Museum, and the El Paso Museum of Art, which houses the famous Kress Collection of Italian Renaissance art. The El Paso Symphony Orchestra, Playhouse El Paso, and the drama department of the University of Texas at El Paso provide cultural entertainment. The El

Paso Public Library, two English and one Spanish daily newspapers, three television and nine radio stations, three airlines, and a good highway system, including Interstate 10, served the metropolitan area. *See also* Standard Metropolitan Statistical Areas in Texas.

BIBLIOGRAPHY: *Community Economic Analysis, Chamizal Planning Program, El Paso, Texas* (1966); John M. Richards, *Economic Growth in El Paso, Texas, 1950–1962* (Special Report No. 1, Bureau of Business and Economic Research, August, 1964); *Texas Almanac* (1971).

Rex W. Strickland

*El Paso Terminal Railroad Company.

El Rincón. *See* Fuerte del Santa Cruz; Carvajal Crossing.

*Elroy, Texas.

*Elsa, Texas. Elsa, Hidalgo County, showed an increase in population from 3,847 in 1960 to 4,400 in 1970, according to the U.S. census.

*El Sal del Rey.

*El Sauz, Texas. (Starr County.)

*El Sauz, Texas. (Willacy County.) El Sauz, eight miles inland from the bay, in Willacy County, was considerably south of Alice and therefore not located between Alice and San Antonio (as stated in Volume I).

*El Señor San José.

*Elser, Maximilian.

*Elstone, Texas.

*Elton, Texas.

*El Turco (The Turk).

*Elwood, Texas. (Fannin County.)

*Elwood, Texas. (Madison County.)

*Ely, Texas.

*Elysian Fields, Texas.

*Emberson, John.

*Emberson, Texas.

*Emberson Lake.

*Emblem, Texas.

*Embryfield, Texas.

Emerald, Texas. Emerald, Crockett County, was established in 1889 about seven miles east of Ozona by the Gulf, Colorado, and Santa Fe Railway Company, which envisioned the extension of the railroad from its terminus at San Angelo to the site. T. W. Wilkerson of Fort Worth was the immigration agent. A church, saloon, and schoolhouse were provided by the railroad, and several families moved to the town. Mrs. John Noyes taught the first school in the county in 1889 at Emerald in a tent before the building was erected. Charles Hatch, the first postmaster, was followed by Edwin C. Moore, who served until the post office was discontinued in December, 1891. Emerald, then the only town in the county, lost the 1891 county seat election to the settlers around the E. M. Powell well, the present site of Ozona. The inhabitants of Emerald moved to Ozona and became its charter citizens.

BIBLIOGRAPHY: Ira Carson (comp.), *Ozona* (1966).

*Emerson College.

*Emet Indians. In the late seventeenth century and during the first half of the eighteenth century the Emet (Emat, Emiti, Ymette) Indians lived on the coastal plain north of Matagorda Bay and between the Guadalupe and Colorado rivers. When encountered by Europeans they were usually occupying settlements jointly with other groups, particularly Cantona, Cava, Sana, Toho, and Tohaha. Between 1740 and 1750 some of the Emet entered San Antonio de Valero Mission,qv at San Antonio. The linguistic and cultural affiliations of the Emet are still debatable. Most writers have stated that the Emet were probably Tonkawan, but some have suggested a Karankawan affiliation.

BIBLIOGRAPHY: H. E. Bolton (ed.), *Spanish Exploration in the Southwest, 1542–1706* (1916); F. W. Hodge (ed.), *Handbook of American Indians*, I (1907), II (1910); W. W. Newcomb, Jr., *The Indians of Texas* (1961); A. F. Sjoberg, "The Culture of the Tonkawa, A Texas Indian Tribe," *Texas Journal of Science*, V (1953); J. R. Swanton, *The Indian Tribes of North America* (1952).

T. N. Campbell

*Emhouse, Texas.

*Emigrants' Guides to Texas.

*Emilee, Texas.

*Emma, Texas.

*Emmaus, Texas.

Emmett, Chris. Chris Emmett was born near Energy, Texas, on June 30, 1886, the son of Thomas Addis and Laura Frances (Pickett) Emmett. He grew up in Hamilton and attended the University of Texas undergraduate and law schools, receiving the LL.B. degree in 1910. He practiced law in Hamilton for two years until 1912, when he took a position with the legal department of the Southern Pacific Railway Lines, the company with which he was associated for over thirty years in San Antonio and Houston. On August 26, 1922, he married Margaret Craig.

The study and writing of history was his spare-time activity. He was a collector of rare maps and drawings and presented numerous papers to several regional historical societies. His contributions to the Texas State Historical Association,qv of which he was a member, were placed in the Barker Texas History Center,qv University of Texas at Austin. He was president of the San Antonio Historical Association qv and helped organize the Harris County Historical Society. His book *Shanghai Pierce: A Fair Likeness* (1953), a biography of a cattle baron, won the 1953 Summerfield G. Roberts award of the Texas Institute of Letters qv for the best book on the Texas Republic. An earlier work, *Texas Camel Tales* (1932), was also widely acclaimed. Some of his other works were *Texas As It Was Then* (1935), *Give Way to the Right* (1934), *The General and the Poet* (1937), *In the Path of Events* (1959), and *Fort Union and the Winning of the Southwest* (1965).

After his retirement from the Southern Pacific, he lived for a time in Santa Fe, devoting his attention to New Mexican history. Chris Emmett died in Dallas on October 20, 1971, and was buried in Hamilton, Hamilton County.

BIBLIOGRAPHY: *Texian Who's Who* (1937); Dallas *Morning News*, October 21, 1971.

*Emmett, Texas.

*Emory, William Hemsley.

*Emory, Texas. Emory, seat of Rains County, is also the geographical and commercial center of the county. In 1970 Emory reported twenty-seven businesses, a public school, a bank, four churches, and a newspaper. The 1960 population was 559; the 1970 population was 693.

*Emory Peak.

Employment Program, Public. *See* Community Affairs, Department of.

*Empresarios.

*Enchanted Rock.

*Enchanted Rock, Legends of.

*Encinal, Texas.

*Encinal County.

*Encino, Texas.

*Endora Lake.

Enepiahe Indians. The Enepiahe (Exepiahohe) Indians are known only from records of the La Salle Expedition,qv which indicate that in the late seventeenth century these Indians inhabited an area north or northeast of Matagorda Bay, probably between the Colorado and Brazos rivers. Their linguistic and cultural affiliations remain unknown. Attempts to identify the Enepiahe with the Ervipiame are not convincing. The Enepiahe are known only from the late seventeenth century, at which time the Ervipiame were still living in the area around present Eagle Pass.

BIBLIOGRAPHY: I. J. Cox (ed.), *The Journeys of Réné Robert Cavelier, Sieur de La Salle*, II (1906); F. W. Hodge (ed.), *Handbook of American Indians*, I (1907); P. Margry, *Découvertes et établissements des Français dans l'ouest et dans le sud de l'Amérique Septentrionale*, III (1879).

T. N. Campbell

*Energy, Texas.

Engerrand, George Charles Marius. George Charles Engerrand, professor of anthropology at the University of Texas, was born on August 11, 1877, near Bordeaux, France, of French-Basque ancestry. Engerrand received his early education from private tutors, and at the age of eighteen he enrolled at the University of Bordeaux, where he received a licentiate in geology (1897) and a licentiate in botany (1898). At Bordeaux he was a student of the famed pioneer sociologist, Émile Durkheim. In 1898 he went to Brussels, Belgium, where he had been invited to teach by the great geographer, Élisée Reclus. Between 1898 and 1907 Engerrand held numerous research and teaching positions, some of them concurrently, at several Belgian institutions.

From 1907 until the political revolution in 1917 made it impossible to continue, Engerrand lived in Mexico and was, for most of this period, professor of archeology in the Museo Nacional de Arqueolo-

gía, Historia, y Etnología. He moved to Mississippi, where he taught geology until 1920, then to Austin, Texas, where he became adjunct professor of anthropology at the University of Texas. For the next forty-one years, until his retirement in 1961, Engerrand was a member of the Department of Anthropology of the University of Texas, from which he received a Ph.D. degree in 1935.

Engerrand received many academic honors in his lifetime, including La Croix de Chevalier de l'Ordre des Palmes, a French decoration given for distinguished teaching and scholarly publication. Known for the breadth of his intellectual interests, he was the author of seventy-five articles and several books. In 1898 Engerrand married Alice Delsaute, from whom he separated in 1902; two sons were born of this marriage. In 1904 he married Jeanne Richard, and they had one son and two daughters. Engerrand died in Mexico City on September 2, 1961. He was buried in Austin, Texas.

BIBLIOGRAPHY: Texas Archeological Society, *Bulletin*, XXXII (1961); *Daily Texan* (Austin), September 12, 1961.

Robert L. Wagner

*Engineering Experiment Station. *See* Texas Engineering Experiment Station.

Engineering Extension Service. *See* Texas Engineering Extension Service.

*Engle, Texas.

*Englehart, Texas.

*English, James N.

*English, John.

*English, William. William English (who spelled his name "Inglish," although all of his children used the spelling "English"), a resident of Teneha Municipality, was born about 1786 and died about 1836; thus he did not move to Louisiana in 1845 (as stated in Volume I). William English (Inglish) and his nine brothers and one sister moved from Tennessee to Texas in the 1820's. [Only the first two sentences of this subject entry in Volume I are correct. The remainder of that article pertains to an entirely different person, William K. English, who was a merchant from Nacogdoches in the early 1840's, moved to Louisiana in 1845, and died about 1850.]

Richard D. English

*English, Texas.

English Law in Texas. Oriented as they were to Anglo-American law, the leaders of the Texas Revolution qv of 1835 provided that all trials should be by jury and that the common law of England would be controlling in criminal matters. The Constitution of 1836 qv directed (Article IV, Section 13) that as soon thereafter as practicable the rest of the English system should be adopted "with such modifications as our circumstances . . . may require." Various elements of law patterned on the Anglo-American model were enacted during the late 1830's, but there was no general reception of English law until the Fourth Congress so provided in the act of January 20, 1840, with certain specific exceptions that perpetuated principles of

Spanish law in Texas;qv however, as was the case with reception of English law in many American states, there was no rigid adherence to all English precedents; the act was construed as adopting the common law of England as that system was understood in the United States during the colonial and national periods. Reception questions regarding statutes were generally plagued by problems associated with changing conceptions of American representative bodies as the source of new law. Distinctions arose between old statutes having become a part of the common law, and later statutes being but pronouncements of an assembly in which American colonies or states had no representation; hence, the most ancient of English statutes were accepted as part of the system, and the more recent were not by virtue of the statute alone. Out of an abundance of caution such archaic institutions as essoins, trial by battle, and wager of law were abolished by statute in 1846. Following the lead of other common law jurisdictions, Texas made all interested parties competent to testify in civil cases in 1871; however, an accused was not to become a competent witness in a criminal case until 1889. Since the rules of English law in Texas are pervasive rather than supplementary (as in the case of Spanish legal influences), only a few of the substantive and adjective aspects of the system can be noted here. An adversary system of contest is employed in the courts in which the judge acts as referee more than active participant. Generally speaking, any pursuant of remedies has the burden of proving allegations on which he relies; the standard of proof is on preponderance of the evidence in civil cases and beyond a reasonable doubt in matters criminal. An accused person is deemed to be not guilty as charged until the contrary is proved. Evidence of events is generally limited to that of the actual knowledge of witnesses.

Adulthood is obtained for all purposes at age 21, but mainly, except for jury duty and the general power to contract, substantial rights are acquired on marriage or on reaching 18. [By passage of a statute effective August 27, 1973, the 63rd Texas Legislature granted persons eighteen years of age all the privileges hitherto granted those twenty-one years of age, and indicated that the statute be construed liberally.—Ed.] Very liberal grounds exist for dissolution of marriage, but periodic payments in the way of support of a spouse after divorce is proscribed, except by agreement. Enforcible agreements are based on bargain, though in some instances writing is also required. Willful and careless conduct gives rise to liability for harm, though as a general rule any amount of fault on the part of the injured person is a complete defense to negligent injury. Though all ultimate titles to land emanate from the sovereign, title may be acquired by adverse possession by one citizen against another, but not against the sovereign. Broad protections are offered to debtors in protection of their homes, their wages in the

hands of their employers, and implements necessary for the exercise of their skills.

The system has been somewhat codified and reformed in the twentieth century, but it retains the principal hallmarks of the English tradition: a law officially unsystematized and generally not reduced to codification, and one that adheres strictly to judicial precedent and an almost superstitious reverence for jury trial.qv

BIBLIOGRAPHY: Charles T. McCormick and Roy R. Ray, *Texas Law of Evidence*, I (1956); Baker & Botts, "Texas Law Digest," *Martindale-Hubbell Law Directory*, V (1972); Ford W. Hall, "An Account of the Adoption of the Common Law in Texas," *Texas Law Review*, XXVIII (1950); Edward L. Markham, Jr., "The Reception of the Common Law of England in Texas and the Judicial Attitude toward that Reception, 1840–1859," *ibid.*, XXIX (1951); Charles S. Potts, "Early Criminal Law in Texas from Civil Law to Common Law, to Code," *ibid.*, XXI (1943).

Joseph W. McKnight

English in Texas. The first English in Texas, according to an early written account, were not settlers, but three seamen set ashore near Tampico, Mexico, by John Hawkins after a battle with the Spanish at Vera Cruz on Hawkins' third expedition to the Indies in the sixteenth century. The three seamen, David Ingram, Richard Twide, and Richard Browne, allegedly walked across lower Texas on their way north in 1568, and Ingram's brief account was included by the younger Richard Hakluyt in his publication in 1589 of *The Principall Navigations, Voiages and Discoveries of the English Nation* (though Hakluyt's doubts about the authenticity of the story caused its omission from subsequent editions). Scattered English farmers and businessmen may have settled in Texas prior to 1800. At least six Englishmen were awarded empresario qv contracts in the 1820's, though none were successful in bringing in families; in the 1830's attempts at colonization began on a much larger scale, though again with limited success. Beales' Rio Grande Colony qv included a few English families, and the contract granted by the Republic of Texas to the Peters Colony qv in 1841 eventually resulted in the scattered settlement of large areas in North Texas, covering parts of twenty-six present counties. William Kennedy qv failed in a contract to bring six hundred families to Texas, but he did attract a good deal of attention with his book, *Texas: The Rise, Progress, and Prospects of the Republic of Texas* (1841); William Bollaert,qv who published some of his own accounts of traveling in Texas in English magazines, was attracted to the new republic by Kennedy's book. A later colonization attempt was made in Bosque County in 1850 (*see* Kent, Colony of).

Ranching and land investment interests in the Panhandle undoubtedly reflected the greatest intercourse between England and Texas, especially in the boom years of 1880–1887. The English had invested about twenty-five million dollars in western ranches and directly controlled over twenty million acres of Panhandle land by the end of 1886, with the largest investor, Capitol Freehold Land and Investment Company, Limited,qv showing nominal capital of £1,532,226 in 1885. Concerned that Texas lands were becoming monopolized by foreign control, many Texans sought protection from the large corporations; in 1891 Governor James S. Hogg qv approved the Alien Land Law,qv prohibiting aliens from holding lands unless they became United States citizens. Even though the law was later changed and did not prohibit land ownership by alien corporations, British investments declined in the following decades. The benefits that British investors and managers conferred upon the land and economy of Texas are not easily measured. They helped to introduce barbed-wire fences, steel windmills, deep wells, and better breeds of cattle into the northwest part of the state, and they also made attempts to attract more settlers.

The English had considerable influence upon the diplomacy and laws of Texas during its years as a republic, resulting in several treaties and mediations (*see also* Anglo-Texan Convention of 1840; Diplomatic Relations of the Republic of Texas; English Law in Texas). The English culture in Texas through the nineteenth century, mostly through the settlement of Anglo Americans from other states, became so pervasive that it is difficult to isolate various contributions.

BIBLIOGRAPHY: Lady Clodagh Anson, *Victorian Days* (1957); Seymour V. Connor, *The Peters Colony of Texas* (1959); E. DeGolyer, *Across Aboriginal America; the Journey of Three Englishmen across Texas in 1568* (1947); W. Eugene Hollon and Ruth Lapham Butler (eds.), *William Bollaert's Texas* (1956); Lester Fields Sheffy, *The Francklyn Land and Cattle Company* (1963); Ephraim Douglass Adams (ed.), "Correspondence from the British Archives Concerning Texas, 1837–1846," *Quarterly of the Texas State Historical Association*, XV–XXI (1912–1917); J. Fred Rippy, "British Investments in Texas Lands and Livestock," *Southwestern Historical Quarterly*, LVIII (1954–1955); Files of the University of Texas Institute of Texan Cultures at San Antonio.

John L. Davis
Phillip L. Fry

*Enloe, Texas.

*Ennis, Cornelius.

*Ennis, Texas. Ennis, on Interstate Highway 45 in eastern Ellis County, had a population of 9,347 in 1960 and 11,046 in 1970. Ennis had a hospital, library, newspaper, two banks, and 190 businesses, including railroad shops, a cotton oil mill, and companies manufacturing business forms, roofing material, clothing, and doors. Nearby Lake Bardwell, completed in 1966, is a tourist attraction.

*Ennis Creek.

Enoch, Texas. Enoch, in central Upshur County, was founded around 1900. It is a Mormon community of farmers and ranchers, reporting one store and a service station in 1966. The population was estimated at 125 in 1966.

*Enochs, Texas.

*Ensign, Texas.

*Ensworth, Augustus S.

Environmental Science Park. *See* University of Texas Environmental Science Park.

*Eola, Texas.

*Eolian, Texas.

*Ephriam, Texas.

*Epidemics. *See* Medical History of Texas.

*Episcopal Church. *See* Protestant Episcopal Church.

Episcopal Theological Seminary of the Southwest. The Episcopal Theological Seminary of the Southwest, Austin, was founded in 1951 through the efforts of Clinton S. Quin qv and John E. Hines, Episcopal bishops, Diocese of Texas. During the first year of operation the school was officially connected with the Austin Presbyterian Theological Seminary qv and had an enrollment of seven students and a faculty of three part-time instructors. In 1952 the seminary was recognized by the Diocese of Texas, a board of trustees was appointed, and the school was chartered by the state.

A permanent site for the seminary, a five-acre tract of wooded ground five blocks north of the University of Texas at Austin, was given in 1953. Classes opened on the new site in September, 1954. In 1955 the seminary received endowments for a chair in theology and for operation of the school. That same year, the Church Historical Society was authorized to house its library and archives at the seminary, providing materials for the study of American church history.

Full accreditation was granted in 1956, the year a program in Latin American missions was initiated. In 1957 the seminary became a charter member of the Council of Southwestern Theological Schools and conducted its first series of summer institutes under the council's sponsorship. Reed House, a conference center in west Austin, was transferred to the seminary from the diocese in 1960, and a summer school for clergy of the Episcopal church in Mexico began. A program of short courses for clergymen was inaugurated in 1961, and in 1962 a program of visiting Fellows was commenced.

The seminary offered a curriculum leading to the following degrees: bachelor in divinity and diploma in sacred theology, bachelor of theology, and master of sacred theology. The main library contained over 36,000 volumes and was increasing by 3,000 volumes annually; by 1967 the library housed 45,000 volumes. Two special collections, 3,000 volumes from the former De Lancey Divinity School and the Black Library of English Literature and History, augmented library holdings.

During the 1970–1971 regular terms the seminary had forty students enrolled and a faculty of ten. T. H. Harvey served as dean of the seminary. *See also* Protestant Episcopal Church.

*Epperson, Benjamin Holland. Benjamin Holland Epperson died on September 6 (not September 16, as stated in Volume I), 1878.

BIBLIOGRAPHY: Galveston *Weekly News*, September 9, 1878.

*Epperson's Ferry.

*Epps Creek.

*Epworth, Texas.

*Equestria, Texas.

*Era, Texas.

*Erath, George Bernard.

*Erath, Texas.

*Erath County. Erath County is an agricultural area producing primarily poultry, dairy and beef cattle, peanuts, grain sorghums, and cotton. In 1960 Erath County ranked fifth in the state in dairies with 167, fourth in egg production, and sixth in turkey raising. The 1964 farm income reached $16,588,000; in 1970 it was $20,000,000. The 1960 population was 16,236; in 1970 it was 18,141.

*Erigoanna Indians. This group is known only from brief mention in French documents that pertain to the La Salle Expedition.qv In 1687 the Erigoanna Indians were enemies of the Ebahamo, a Karankawan group which lived in the vicinity of La Salle's Fort St. Louis qv near Matagorda Bay. A group of Ebahamo warriors told La Salle that their enemies lived farther inland to the northwest. Sound correspondences suggest that Erigoanna may be a French rendition of Aranama, the name of an early eighteenth-century Coahuiltecan group which lived within striking distance of the Ebahamo to the west and northwest, but this equivalence has yet to be demonstrated.

BIBLIOGRAPHY: A. S. Gatschet, *The Karankawa Indians, the Coast People of Texas* (1891); J. G. Shea, *Discovery and Exploration of the Mississippi Valley* (1903).

T. N. Campbell

*Erin, Texas.

*Erna, Texas.

*Ero, Texas.

*Erosion Control. *See* Conservation of Natural Resources.

*Erskine, Andrew Nelson.

*Erskine, Michael.

*Ervendberg, Louis Cachand. [This title was incorrectly listed in Volume I as Ervendberg, Louis Cochand.] According to the church book of the First Protestant Church at New Braunfels, Louis Cachand Ervendberg was born on May 3, 1809, at the village of Rhoden in the former principality of Waldeck in west-central Germany; however, it is possible that the name Ervendberg was assumed, for there is no record of a family by that name in his supposed birthplace. Ervendberg himself wrote his name in different ways, but for the most part he used the spelling as shown here, Louis Cachand Ervendberg.

BIBLIOGRAPHY: Samuel Wood Geiser, *Naturalists of the Frontier* (1948); Johannes Mgebroff, *Geschichte der Ersten Deutschen Evangelisch-Lutherischen Synode in Texas* (1902).

*Ervipiame Indians. The Ervipiame (Chivipane, Cibipane, Hierbipiane, Huvipane, Hyerbipiame, Yerbipiame, Yrbipia) Indians were first known in 1673, at which time they lived in northeastern Coahuila and were in close association with bands that have been identified as Coahuiltecan in speech. In 1675 they were encountered by the Bosque-Larios Expedition qv north of the Rio

Grande in the southwestern part of the Edwards Plateau, again with bands of Coahuiltecan affiliation. In 1698 some of the Ervipiame were in the missions of northeastern Coahuila. It was not until 1707 that the Ervipiame appeared in central Texas and became the dominant group in the Ranchería Grande qv de los Ervipiames, a series of settlements made up principally of Coahuiltecan refugees from northeastern Coahuila and the adjoining part of Texas, but later augmented by refugees from various Spanish missions in Texas and Coahuila. In 1722 the San Francisco Xavier de Nájera (Náxera) Mission qv was founded at San Antonio for the Ervipiame of Ranchería Grande, and their village near the mission was known as the Ervipiame suburb. Nearly all of the groups associated with the Ervipiame in this village were Coahuiltecans. Most of the evidence indicates that the Ervipiame were originally Coahuiltecans. After this the Ervipiame who remained at Ranchería Grande, or who retired to it from San Antonio after their mission was merged with San Antonio de Valero,qv were associated mainly with groups identified as Tonkawans—Tonkawa, Yojuane, and Mayeye. They were with these Tonkawans at San Francisco Xavier de Horcasitas Mission,qv founded about 1748 on the San Gabriel River near present Rockdale. In the latter part of the eighteenth century the name Ervipiame was rarely mentioned. It seems clear that they lost their identity among the various bands which in the nineteenth century came to be called Tonkawa.

Although most modern writers have concluded that the Ervipiame were Tonkawans, the historical evidence suggests that the Ervipiame were originally Coahuiltecans who later became so closely associated with Tonkawans that they were regarded as Tonkawan. Attempts to equate the Ervipiame with the Enepiahe of the La Salle Expedition qv documents are not convincing. The Enepiahe were known only in the late seventeenth century, at which time the Ervipiame were still in the vicinity of northeastern Coahuila.

BIBLIOGRAPHY: H. E. Bolton (ed.), *Athanase de Mézières and the Louisiana-Texas Frontier, 1768–1780* (1914) and *Spanish Exploration in the Southwest, 1542–1706* (1916); F. W. Hodge (ed.), *Handbook of American Indians*, I (1907), II (1910); W. W. Newcomb, Jr., *The Indians of Texas* (1961); A. F. Sjoberg, "The Culture of the Tonkawa, A Texas Indian Tribe," *Texas Journal of Science*, V (1953).

T. N. Campbell

*Erwin, Texas.

*Esbon, Texas.

*Escandón, José de.

*Escanjaque Indians. The Escanjaque (Ercansaque, Escansaque, Escanxaque, Esquansaque, Excanjaque) Indians are known only from the seventeenth century, and their area remains in doubt. Some writers have interpreted the evidence as indicating that the Escanjaque lived in north-central Texas; others have placed them in western Oklahoma. Early attempts to identify the Escanjaque with the Kansa were not successful because it was found that the Kansa lived elsewhere in the seventeenth century. It has been suggested that the Es-

canjaque were Apache, but today most writers are inclined to identify them as a Wichita group, possibly the same as the Yscani of the eighteenth century.

BIBLIOGRAPHY: H. H. Bancroft, *History of the North Mexican States and Texas*, I (1884); H. E. Bolton, "The Jumano Indians in Texas, 1650–1771," *Quarterly of the Texas State Historical Association*, XV (1911–1912); G. P. Hammond and A. Rey, *Don Juan de Oñate, Colonizer of New Mexico, 1595–1628* (1953); G. E. Hyde, *The Pawnee* (1951); A. H. Schroeder, "A Re-analysis of the Routes of Coronado and Oñate into the Plains in 1541 and 1601," *Plains Anthropologist*, VII (1962); S. L. Tyler and H. D. Taylor, "The Report of Fray Alonso de Posadas in Relation to Quivira and Teguayo," *New Mexico Historical Review*, XXXIII (1958).

T. N. Campbell

*Escobares, Texas.

*Escobas, Texas.

*Escondido Creek.

*Eskota, Texas.

*Espada Creek.

*Espada Mission. *See* San Francisco de la Espada Mission.

*Espantosa Lake.

Esparza, Gregorio. Gregorio Esparza was born in San Antonio de Bexar in 1803, the son of José Ignacio and Nicolasa (Ramírez) Esparza. He married Anna Salazar, and to this union a daughter and three sons were born.

During the siege of Bexar qv in December, 1835, Esparza served in the Texan forces under Captain Juan N. Seguin,qv while his brother, Francisco Esparza, also a native of San Antonio, served in the Mexican defense under General Martín Perfecto de Cós.qv Under the terms of capitulation granted to General Cós, those of his men who were natives of Texas were allowed to remain in Texas. In late February, 1836, when Mexican forces under General Antonio López de Santa Anna qv entered San Antonio, Gregorio Esparza and his family entered the Alamo to fight for Texas. Santa Anna ordered that the paroled men of General Cós hold themselves in readiness to join the attacking forces, but in a sworn statement on file in the General Land Office,qv Francisco Esparza declared he was never called to service.

On March 6, 1836, upon the fall of the Alamo, Francisco Esparza sought and obtained permission from General Cós to search for and bury the body of his brother. He found Gregorio in one of the small rooms of the Alamo. Francisco buried his brother in Campo Santo, on the west side of San Pedro Creek where Milam Square is now located. Thus Gregorio's body was not burned with those of the other Alamo defenders.

The heirs of Gregorio Esparza were granted a bounty warrant of 1,920 acres of land and a donation of 640 acres. At one time the court of claims rejected these warrants, but they were later approved.

BIBLIOGRAPHY: Frederick C. Chabot, *With the Makers of San Antonio* (1937); San Antonio *Express*, May 12, 19, 1907; Files of the General Land Office, Austin.

Thomas L. Miller

*Espejo, Antonio de.

*Esperanza, Texas. (Hudspeth County.)

*Esperanza, Texas. (Montgomery County.)

*Esperanza Creek.

*Esperson, Texas.

*Espinosa, Isidro Felix de.

*Espio Creek.

*Espiritu Santo Bay.

*Espíritu Santo de Zuñiga Mission. *See* Nuestra Señora del Espíritu Santo de Zuñiga Mission.

*Espopolame Indians. The Espopolame (Isopopolame) Indians, who presumably spoke a Coahuiltecan language, lived in northeastern Coahuila during the latter part of the seventeenth century. Apparently they were never seen in Texas. However, documents of Coahuila indicate that the Espopolame were closely associated with the Pinanaca, who in 1675 were encountered by the Bosque-Larios Expedition qv north of the Rio Grande near present Eagle Pass.

BIBLIOGRAPHY: V. Alessio Robles, *Coahuila y Texas en la Epoca Colonial* (1938); H. E. Bolton (ed.), *Spanish Exploration in the Southwest, 1542–1706* (1916); F. W. Hodge (ed.), *Handbook of American Indians*, I (1907).

T. N. Campbell

*Espuela Land and Cattle Company. *See* Spur Ranch.

*Esquien Indians.

*Esseville, Texas.

*Estacado, Texas.

*Estacado and Gulf Railroad Company.

Esteban. *See* Estevanico.

*Estelle, Texas.

*Estelline, Texas.

*Estepisa Indians.

Estes, Carl Lewis. Carl Lewis Estes, newspaper publisher and industrial leader, was born in New Market, Tennessee, on November 10, 1896, the son of Joseph Guinn and Della Marshall (Loy) Estes. He was educated in the public schools of Commerce and Denison and at East Texas State Teachers College (now East Texas State University).

As editor of his college newspaper, he became interested in journalism as a career, and he subsequently worked for the Commerce *Journal*, the Denison *Herald*, and the Tyler *Courier-Times*. He became a foreign correspondent for International News Service, spending 1927 in Paris and Stockholm. He founded the Tyler *Telegraph* in 1930 and four years later bought the Longview *Daily News* and the Longview *Morning Journal*. At Longview he also owned and published two weekly newspapers, the Longview *Lens* and the *Greggtonian*. He was married to Margaret McLeod. During the 1930's Estes was publisher of the Van *Free Press*, the Carthage *Panola Watchman*, the *East Texas Oil Magazine* (later the *Texas Oil Journal*), the *East Texas Dairyman*, the *Wood County Record*, and the Mineola *Monitor*.

Estes served in the cavalry in World War I and was a lieutenant commander in the navy during World War II. He was a delegate to the national Democratic convention in Houston in 1928 and a delegate-at-large to the national Democratic convention in Chicago in 1932. He later served as confidential adviser to Arthur H. James, Republican governor of Pennsylvania.

Estes was an originator of the Texas Rose Festival at Tyler, originator and first president of the East Texas Land and Royalty Owners Association, vice-president and secretary of Van Oil Royalty Association, and an originator of the East Texas Dairy and Milk Products Association.

Upon returning to Longview after World War II, he was effective in helping persuade a number of major industries to locate plants in the Longview area. As chairman of the Sabine Watershed Association, he was active in the development of the water resources of East Texas for industrial, recreational, and transportation uses. He died at his vacation home in La Jolla, California, on May 29, 1967, and was buried in Memory Park, Longview, Texas.

BIBLIOGRAPHY: Dallas *Morning News*, May 31, June 1, 1967; *Editor and Publisher Magazine*, July 1, 1967; *The Texas Press Messenger*, June, 1967; *Texian Who's Who* (1937).

C. Richard King

*Estes, William Lee.

*Estevanico.

Estill, Amanda Julia. Amanda Julia Estill, daughter of James Thomas and Ellen Elizabeth (Wiley) Estill, was born in Fredericksburg, Texas, on October 27, 1882. She attended the University of Texas and received the B.S. and M.S. degrees in 1904 and 1905. A versatile educator and writer, Miss Estill taught in the Fredericksburg schools from 1899 to 1900 and from 1905 to 1941, also serving for eleven years as high school principal. She was also a teacher and elementary school principal in La Feria from 1947 until 1951 before returning to Fredericksburg.

A member of the Texas Folklore Society,qv she served as its president in 1923–1924, and contributed numerous articles to that society's *Publications*. She was one of the first to write about the hill country's Sunday houses, Easter fires, Indian rock art,qqv and other landmarks in Gillespie County. She also contributed to the *American German Review*, wrote many historical pieces for the Fredericksburg chamber of commerce, and for twenty years was correspondent for the San Antonio *Express*.qv She served on the first board of directors of the Gillespie County Historical Society, and from 1943 to 1947 she was librarian at the Gillespie County Pioneer Museum and Library. She died on July 1, 1965, in Fredericksburg.

BIBLIOGRAPHY: Florence E. Barns, *Texas Writers of Today* (1935); Gillespie County Historical Society, *Pioneers in God's Hills* (1960); Ella Gold, The History of Education in Gillespie County, Texas (M.A. thesis, University of Texas, 1945); Fredericksburg *Standard*, July 7, 1965.

Esther L. Mueller

*Estill, Harry Fishburne.

*Ethel, Texas.

*Etholen, Texas.

*Etoile, Texas.

*Ettas Creek.

*Etter, Texas.

*Eugene C. Barker Texas History Center. The Eugene C. Barker Texas History Center at the University of Texas at Austin was moved in 1971 from the Old Library Building to Sid W. Richardson qv Hall, immediately east of the Lyndon Baines Johnson Library.qv In 1973 the center housed the Texas Collection,qv which consisted of a library with holdings of 104,000 titles, archives containing approximately seventeen million documents (including the Bexar Archives qv), a newspaper collection of Texas newspapers dating from 1829 to 1959, and the Frank Reaugh qv collection of paintings. The offices of the Texas State Historical Association qv were also located in the center.

In addition to the Eugene C. Barker Texas History Center, the Sid W. Richardson building also housed the Latin American Collection qv and the Lyndon B. Johnson qv School of Public Affairs. Formal dedication of the building took place on January 21, 1971, with an address delivered by the United States secretary of the treasury, John B. Connally (former governor of Texas).

*Eula, Texas.

*Eulalie, Texas.

*Euless, Texas. Euless, in eastern Tarrant County, revived in the late 1940's and early 1950's with the spread of the metropolitan areas of Dallas and Fort Worth and the building of Greater Southwest International Airport qv (formerly Amon G. Carter Field). In 1949 a post office was reestablished after having been discontinued for many years. In the early 1950's the town was incorporated; in 1960 it had a population of 4,263 and approximately fifty businesses. The city completed a fire station in 1965 and several buildings for police and city offices in 1966. By 1967 the city had 180 businesses, fifteen churches, one hospital, two banks, a library, and a newspaper. According to the United States 1970 census, Euless had a combined urban and rural population of 19,316 in 1970. *See also* Fort Worth Standard Metropolitan Statistical Area.

*Eulogy, Texas. Eulogy, in northern Bosque County, was founded on July 11, 1884, by Charles Walker Smith,qv who opened a dry goods store on the site on that date. The community was named by his sister, Julia Smith Mickey. When a post office was established in 1885, Smith became the first postmaster. The 1970 estimated population was fifty.

BIBLIOGRAPHY: William C. Pool, *Bosque Territory: A History of an Agrarian Community* (1964).

William C. Horton

*Eunice, Texas. (Leon County.)

*Eunice, Texas. (Swisher County.)

*Eureka, Texas.

*Eustace, Texas.

*Evadale, Texas.

*Evangelical Lutheran College. *See also* Lutheran Church in Texas.

*Evans, Augusta Jane.

Evans, Cecil Eugene. Cecil Eugene Evans was born on January 21, 1871, at Bowdon, Georgia, the son of Hiram Martin and Georgia (Striplin) Evans. He was educated at Oxford College, Alabama, where he took a B.A. degree in 1888. He received an M.A. degree from the University of Texas in 1906, and in recognition of his work as an educator, Southwestern University conferred on him an honorary LL.D. in 1923.

Evans taught in Alabama schools from 1889 to 1893, then moved to Texas in 1894 to teach at Mexia. He was superintendent of the public school at Anson from 1895 to 1902, at Merkel from 1902 to 1905, and at Abilene from 1906 to 1908. For three years beginning in 1908, he served as general agent for the Conference on Education in Texas, successfully conducting campaigns to secure three school amendments to the Texas Constitution. In addition, he was largely responsible for legislation designed to improve the public schools and teacher training. From 1917 to 1927 Evans served as a member of the Texas Textbook Board. His book *The Story of Texas Schools* (1955) is a volume on historical development of the public and private educational system of the state.

Evans came to Southwest Texas Normal School (now Southwest Texas State University) at San Marcos in 1911 as its second president. During his thirty-one years as president, Southwest Texas added two years of college work to the curriculum, then a full college course accredited by the American Association of Colleges, and finally a graduate program awarding master's degrees. During that time, the college plant expanded from an original eleven acres to more than double that size, and from a three-building institution to fifteen classroom and administration buildings, eight dormitories and cooperative houses, a forty-acre farm, a swimming pool, and a recreation park. Enrollment expanded from 600 to 1,600 students. Evans retired in 1942, at which time Lyndon Baines Johnson qv (at one time secretary to Evans) came from Washington to speak at the ceremony. Evans was a Democrat, Methodist, member of the National Education Association, and a trustee of Southwestern University. He was married to Allie Maxwell in Anson on May 18, 1899; they were the parents of one daughter. Evans died on August 23, 1958, and was buried at San Marcos.

BIBLIOGRAPHY: San Marcos *Record*, April 21, 1936; *Who's Who In America* (1934).

Tula Wyatt

Evans, Herschel. Herschel Evans was born in Denton, Texas, in 1909. As a youth he moved to Kansas City, where his cousin, Eddie Durham, already regionally famous as a trombonist and guitarist, persuaded him to switch from alto saxophone to tenor, the instrument on which he became internationally acclaimed by jazz critics.

In 1936 Evans joined the Count Basie band in Kansas City and almost immediately found himself in intraband competition with Lester Young, perhaps the best known of all tenor players. Accounts of the duels between the two musicians, some of which are recorded, are classics in jazz folklore; Young played a cool, controlled style, whereas Evans tended to be emotional and melting.

Evans played with Basie until his death by heart failure in New York City, February 9, 1939. His influence and warm tone have been continued through later tenormen like Illinois Jacquet and Buddy Tate. Evans scored his biggest success with Basie's record of "Blue and Sentimental," considered a jazz classic. He was also instrumental in working out the lead arrangement for Basie's theme, "One O'Clock Jump," another jazz standard, which began as a warm-up riff, or series of short musical phrases, without any idea of developing into a full-fledged lasting musical composition.

Joe B. Frantz

*Evans, Ira Hobart. Ira Hobart Evans' home was the site for a discussion of a historical society in the late 1880's, but it was not there (as stated in Volume I) that the nucleus of the Texas State Historical Association qv was formed. The association, as such, was first planned at an organizational meeting in one of the rooms at the University of Texas on February 13, 1897.

BIBLIOGRAPHY: "The Organization and Objects of the Texas State Historical Association," *Quarterly of the Texas State Historical Association*, I (1897–1898).

*Evans, John S.

Evans, Joseph Wood. Joseph Wood Evans was born in Augusta, Kentucky, on October 17, 1877, son of Joseph Madison and Alice (Humphreys) Wood. After graduation from Hanover College, Madison, Indiana, and military service in the Spanish-American War, he came to Houston in 1901. He was married to Emily Scott on October 31, 1906; they had two daughters. He entered the cotton brokerage business and in 1908 organized a major cotton exporting firm, Evans and Company. He was elected president of the Houston Cotton Exchange and Board of Trade in 1918.

In his determination to bring Texas cotton producers improved transportation facilities, he took a key role in the development of Houston as a deepwater port. He served as chairman of the Harris County Houston Ship Channel qv Navigation Commission from 1930 to 1945; during his tenure, shipping tonnage doubled and the port of Houston rose to third place in total tonnage and first place in cotton tonnage among the nation's deepwater ports.

He was chairman of the Houston War Work campaign and an official of the state Red Cross during World War I. Later he helped organize the Houston Community Chest and served on the state executive committee of the National Foundation for Infantile Paralysis. He was president of the Houston Chamber of Commerce in 1928. Elected a director of the United States Chamber of Commerce in 1933, he was named a vice-president of that organization in 1935.

Evans was a trustee of Hanover College; in 1938 he was a member of the original building fund campaign committee for the University of Houston. It was in recognition of his keen interest in higher education that, after his death at Houston on November 13, 1962, his widow, Emily Scott Evans, and daughter, Alice Evans Pratt, donated a substantial sum in his memory for the establishment of the extensive Joseph W. Evans Collection of bibliographical references at the M. D. Anderson qv Library, University of Houston.

BIBLIOGRAPHY. Houston *Post*, November 14, 1962; Max H. Jacobs and H. Dick Golding, *Houston and Cotton* (1949); *Who's Who In America* (1952).

John O. King

*Evans, Lemuel Dale.

*Evans, Moses.

*Evans Creek.

*Evans Point, Texas.

*Evansville, Texas.

*Evansville Peak.

*Evant, Texas.

*Eve, Joseph.

*Evea.

Evening Herald (Dallas).

*Everett Creek.

Everettsville, Texas. Everettsville was established in 1847 by one of General Zachary Taylor's qv officers, Colonel Jack Everett. Situated near Roma, in Starr County, the community was founded as a health spa around a sulphur spring. Distance, bad roads, and lack of transportation facilities crippled the town, leading to its decline.

BIBLIOGRAPHY: Randall McMillon, "Vanished Towns of the Rio Grande Valley," *Junior Historian*, XV (1954–1955).

*Evergreen, Texas. (San Jacinto County.)

*Evergreen, Texas. (Washington County.)

*Evergreen Plantation.

*Everitt, Stephen Hendrickson.

*Everitt, Texas.

*Everman, Texas. Everman, in Tarrant County, was incorporated in 1945 under a city council and mayor. By 1966 the city had seven churches, a bank, a newspaper, a city park, and a firehouse. The 1960 population was 1,076; the 1970 population was 4,570, showing a remarkable increase from the 451 reported in the 1950 census. *See also* Fort Worth Standard Metropolitan Statistical Area.

*Everts, Gustavus A.

Evia, José de. José Antonio de Evia was born in La Graña, Spain, in July, 1740, the son of master mariner Simón de Evia and Felipa de Gantes y Pravio. After studying at the Royal Naval School of El Ferrol, beginning January 1, 1753, he served on numerous naval vessels as a pilot. After serving in the coast guard of Cartagena de Indias in 1760, he sailed around Spain's *Mare Nostrum*, the Gulf of

Mexico. He made the round trip from Havana to New Orleans, Vera Cruz, and Mobile several times. In 1779 he commanded a launch at New Orleans and captured the English ship which tried to bring reinforcements and supplies to Manchak. Shipwrecked in the *Volante* off Mobile in February, 1780, he nevertheless captured the English ship and crew he was chasing. He also commanded the port of Mobile during its siege and capture by Gálvez. After convoying troop ships back to Havana, he served as courier between Bernardo de Gálvez,qv Gabriel de Aristizabal, and Juan Bautista Bonet. He served in the Royal Arsenal of Havana from March, 1782, until May, 1783, when he was assigned to the warship *San Cristóbal*. Promoted to frigate ensign in 1783, he was commissioned by Gálvez to draw up detailed plans of the entire Gulf Coast from West Florida to Tampico.

After an unsuccessful 1783 attempt, he embarked once again in 1785 and explored by lugger and canoe the rivers and inlets of Florida, Alabama, Mississippi, Louisiana, Texas, and Mexico, completing his arduous task at Tampico in September, 1786. He explored San Bernardo Bay and named Galveston Bay for his patron after taking detailed soundings of it. Supported by Gálvez, he was rewarded on July 2, 1787, with the post of captain of the port and commander of the coast guard of New Orleans at an annual salary of two thousand dollars. He left Havana with his wife, Francisca Ruiz Delgado, and his two sons for New Orleans, where he changed the spelling of his name to Hevia. In 1792 he was commissioned by Governor-general Carondelet to capture William Augustus Bowles, who had used Seminole Indians to attack and take the post of San Marcos de Apalachee. Upon the successful completion of the assignment, he returned to New Orleans, where he exercised the functions of port master throughout the Spanish occupation of Louisiana. His accurate and detailed charts, diaries, and descriptions of the Gulf area were the best by any navigator of the eighteenth century. They served as the basis of subsequent charts drawn by the Hydrographic Service of Spain, as well as key documents in the Spanish case against American claims to the Neutral Ground qv between Louisiana and Texas.

BIBLIOGRAPHY: Charles W. Hackett (ed. and trans.), *Pichardo's Treatise on the Limits of Louisiana and Texas*, I (1931); Jack D. L. Holmes, "Gallegos notables en la Luisiana," *Cuadernos de Estudios Gallegos*, LVII (1964), *José de Evia y sus Reconocimientos del Golfo de México, 1783–1796* (1967), and "Two Spanish Expeditions to Southwest Florida, 1783–1793," *Tequesta*, XXV (1965); Lawrence Kinnaird, "The Significance of William Augustus Bowles' Seizure of Panton's Apalachee Store in 1792," *Florida Historical Society Quarterly*, IX (1931).

Jack D. L. Holmes

*Ewell, Texas.

*Ewing, Alexander Wray.

*Ewing, Presley Kittrege.

Ewing, William Maurice. William Maurice Ewing, geophysicist and oceanographer, was born on May 12, 1906, in Lockney, Texas, the son of Floyd Ford and Hope (Hamilton) Ewing. He received three degrees from Rice Institute (now Rice University), a B.A. in 1926, an M.A. in 1927, and a Ph.D. in 1931. He taught physics at the University of Pittsburgh (1929–1930); physics, geology, and geophysics at Lehigh University (1930–1944); and geology at Columbia University (1944–1972). While on leave from the latter two universities, from 1940 to 1946, he was a research associate on national defense projects at Woods Hole (Massachusetts) Oceanographic Institute. Back at Columbia University in 1947, he became professor of geology, and in 1959 he was named Higgins Professor of Geology there. He was the first director of Columbia University's Lamont Geological Observatory (later Lamont-Doherty Geological Observatory), serving from 1949 to 1972.

As a pioneer oceanographer, Ewing led more than fifty expeditions to explore ocean bases. He made many contributions in the development of oceanographic instruments now in use for exploration of the oceans, including the development and use of the deep-sea camera and the piston cover. During the war he discovered the existence of the SOFAR Channel, a continuous layer in the deep ocean where sound energy is trapped by focusing, thus providing a mechanism for a long-range communications system. Over the years the vast collection of data that Ewing and his associates collected contributed enormously to the present concept of oceans as youthful features. His work in earthquake seismology confirmed the layered structure of oceans which had been first demonstrated by his refraction studies. Maurice Ewing, perhaps more than any other single person, laid the foundations for the revolutionary concept known as plate tectonics.

In 1954 he discovered the Sigsbee knolls in the deep basin of the Gulf of Mexico, and he suggested that they might be salt domes. Fourteen years later he was the chief scientist aboard the oceanographic research ship *Glomar Challenger* when oil deposits were discovered beneath those salt domes.

Known worldwide for his contributions in geophysics and oceanography, Ewing was named head of the Division of Earth and Planetary Sciences in the Marine Biomedical Institute of the University of Texas Medical Branch at Galveston in June, 1972; he was also named professor of geological sciences at the university. He published over three hundred papers in scientific journals and was on the editorial boards of several publications. He was elected to the National Academy of Sciences and to national academies of several other countries. He was also elected to foreign membership in the Royal Society of London. He served as president of the American Geophysical Union and of the Seismological Society of America. His contributions to geophysics were recognized by the conferring of eleven honorary degrees by universities around the world. In addition to numerous medals and prizes awarded him during his lifetime, President Richard M. Nixon presented him the national Medal of Science. He was a member of the Philosophical Society of Texas ᵠᵛ for more than twenty-five years.

Ewing was married to Avarilla Hildenbrand on October 31, 1928; they had one son. He was married to Margaret Sloan Kidder on February 19, 1944; they had two sons and two daughters. Both marriages ended in divorce. He was married a third time, on May 6, 1965, to Harriett Greene Bassett, who survived him when he died on May 4, 1974, at John Sealy Hospital in Galveston. He was buried at Palisades, New York. Ewing was awarded posthumously, in the fall of 1974, the Penrose Medal, highest honor of the Geological Society of America.

BIBLIOGRAPHY: *Who's Who In America* (1968); Biographical File, Barker Texas History Center, University of Texas at Austin.

*Ewing, Texas.

*Ewing College. *See also* Presbyterian Education in Texas.

*Ewing Lakes.

*Exall, Henry.

*Exall, Mrs. May Dickson.

*Examining Boards. In 1972 the state of Texas had thirty-four examining boards. The boards, with dates of establishment, were as follows:

Texas Board of Architectural Examiners, 1937

Texas State Board of Landscape Architects, 1969

Texas Board of Athletic Trainers, 1971

State Board of Barber Examiners, 1929

State Board of Examiners in the Basic Sciences, 1949

State Board of Chiropractic Examiners, 1949; an earlier board created in 1943 was declared unconstitutional in 1944

Texas Cosmetology Commission, 1971; replaced Board of Hairdressers and Cosmetologists, 1935

Texas State Board of Dental Examiners, 1897; replaced **District Dental Examining Boards, 1889**

Texas Board of Examiners in the Fitting and Dispensing of Hearing Aids, 1969

Board of Examiners of Land Surveyors, 1919

Board of Law Examiners, 1909

State Board of Library Examiners, 1919

Texas State Board of Medical Examiners, 1907

State Board of Morticians, 1953; replaced State Board of Embalming, 1903

Board of Nurse Examiners, 1909

Texas Board of Licensure for Nursing Home Administrators, 1969

State Board of Tuberculosis Nurse Examiners, 1950

Board of Vocational Nurse Examiners, 1951

Texas Optometry Board, 1969; replaced Board of Examiners of Optometry, 1922

State Board of Pharmacy, 1907

Texas Board of Physical Therapy Examiners, 1971

Texas State Board of Plumbing Examiners, 1947

Texas State Board of Podiatry Examiners, 1923; formerly known as the State Board of Chiropody Examiners

Texas Board of Polygraph Examiners, 1969

Texas Board of Private Investigators and Private Security Agencies, 1969

State Board of Registration for Professional Engineers, 1937

Texas State Board of Examiners of Psychologists, 1969

Texas State Board of Public Accountancy, 1945

State Board of Registration for Public Surveyors, 1955

Texas Real Estate Commission, 1949

Texas Structural Pest Control Board, 1971

State Board of Examiners for Teacher Education, 1905

State Board of Veterinary Medical Examiners, 1911

Texas Water Well Drillers Board, 1965

BIBLIOGRAPHY: University of Texas at Austin, *Guide To Texas State Agencies* (1972).

*Excelsior, Texas.

*Exchequer Currency of the Republic. *See* Money of the Republic.

*Exile, Texas.

*Extension Service, Agriculture. *See* Texas Agriculture Extension Service.

*Exter, Richard.

Exxon Company, U.S.A. *See* Humble Oil and Refining Company. [The name of Humble Oil and Refining Company was officially changed to Exxon Company, U.S.A. on January 1, 1973.]

*Eyeish Indians. *See* Ais Indians.

*"Eyes of Texas." The official song of the University of Texas at Austin was first performed at a varsity minstrel show on May 12, 1903 (not in 1906, as stated in Volume I). Originally created as a prank on William Lambdin Prather's qv statement, "The eyes of Texas are upon you," the song took on a note of seriousness and meaning upon Prather's death on July 24, 1905, when students asked permission to sing it at his funeral.

BIBLIOGRAPHY: Subject File, Barker Texas History Center, University of Texas at Austin.

*Eylau, Texas.

Eyth, Louis. Louis Eyth, born in 1838, migrated to Galveston, Texas, with some of his family at the age of fourteen. His only known art training came in the years he spent with the well-known daguerreotypists and artists, Blessing and Company. Eyth later applied for and received the commission of copying the early portrait of Stephen F. Austin, and that copy is now in the secretary of state's office in the Capitol.qv Eyth went to San Antonio, where he was commissioned, along with other Texas artists, by historian James DeShields,qv who needed illustrations for his books. Some of Eyth's paintings for DeShields remain only in photographic reproduction, works such as "Surrender of Geronimo" (1885), "Death of Bowie: A Command from the Mexicans that He Be Killed," and the "Battle of Plum Creek." Eyth had an ability to represent the historic scene with spirit and accuracy. The artist died about 1889.

BIBLIOGRAPHY: Pauline A. Pinckney, *Painting in Texas: The Nineteenth Century* (1967).

Pauline A. Pinckney

*Ezzell, Texas.

F

*Fabens, Texas. Fabens, in El Paso County, had a population of 3,134 in 1960; the town's population in 1970 was 3,241.

*Fails, Texas.

*Fair Oaks, Texas.

*Fair Play, Texas.

*Fairbanks, Texas.

*Fairchild Creek.

*Fairchilds, Texas. (Angelina County.)

*Fairchilds, Texas. (Fort Bend County.)

*Fairdale, Texas.

*Fairfield, Texas. Fairfield, seat of Freestone County, is an agricultural marketing center with shipping facilities, a rock quarry, and a sawmill. The 1960 population was 1,781; in 1970 it was 2,074. That year the community reported sixty-two business establishments.

*Fairfield Female Academy.

*Fairland, Texas.

*Fairlie, Texas.

*Fairmount, Texas.

Fairview, Texas. (Collin County.) Fairview, in south-central Collin County, had a population of 175 in 1960 and 463 in 1970.

*Fairview, Texas. (Hays County.)

*Fairview, Texas. (Howard County.)

*Fairview, Texas. (Milam County.)

*Fairview, Texas. (Wilson County.)

*Fairy, Texas.

*Falba, Texas.

*Falcon, Texas. Falcon, in southwestern Zapata County along the Rio Grande, and originally known as Ramireño, took its name officially in 1915 with the establishment of a post office. When construction on the International Falcon Reservoir qv began in 1950, Falcon was moved a few miles inland from its original location and split into three villages, each with the forename of Falcon. Old Falcon was inundated in 1953 when the waters of the reservoir covered the area.

Maria Grace Ramirez

Falcon Dam. *See* International Falcon Reservoir.

Falcon Heights, Texas. Falcon Heights, in

western Starr County, was founded in 1954 at the entrance to the crossing of International Falcon Reservoir qv dam. Most of the inhabitants were either migrant laborers or storekeepers supplying tourists with fishing and picnicking items. In 1970 the town had seven businesses and an estimated population of 341.

Falcon Reservoir. *See* International Falcon Reservoir.

Falcon Village, Texas. Falcon Village, in western Starr County, was founded in 1949 and named for International Falcon Reservoir.qv The federal government built the community for employees working on the dam and on associated projects. In 1966 there were about 140 inhabitants, all federal employees.

*Falconer, Thomas.

*Falfurrias, Texas. Falfurrias, seat of Brooks County and site of the Brooks County Hospital, was a commercial center with 106 businesses in 1970. Its income was derived from dairying, farming, ranching, small-scale manufacturing, and the oil industry. The population was 6,515 in 1960 and 6,355 in 1970.

*Fall Branch.

*Fall Creek.

*Fallon, Texas.

*Falls City, Texas.

*Falls County. Falls County by the 1960's had shifted from crop-oriented agriculture to a livestock and poultry-oriented agriculture. Cotton, corn, grain sorghums, vegetables, and fruits, however, retained economic importance. In 1972 the county had seven active gins available to process the 8,823-bale cotton crop. Bricks are made from the county's clay deposits. The 1960 population was 21,263; the 1970 count was 17,300, a decrease of 18.6 percent.

*Falls Creek.

*Fancher, Texas.

Fandangle. *See* Fort Griffin Fandangle.

*Fandango Creek.

*Fannett, Texas.

*Fannin, James Walker, Jr.

*Fannin, Texas.

*Fannin County. Fannin County, on the Red River, has many aquatic facilities, including Fannin Lake, Davy Crockett Lake, Coffee Mill Creek Lake, Brushy Creek Reservoir, and Bonham Lake. Added tourist attractions are Bonham State Park (*see* Parks, State) and the Sam Rayburn qv Memorial Library. Agriculture is diversified, with cotton, wheat, corn, and peanuts the most important crops. An increasing beef cattle industry partially offsets a decreasing dairy industry. The 1960 population was 23,880; in 1970 it was 22,705.

*Fannin Creek.

Fannin State Battleground Commission. The Fannin State Battleground Commission, created in 1947, was composed of three members appointed by the governor; its responsibility was to advise the state Board of Control qv in caring for the Fannin State Battleground. The commission was reorganized in 1965 as the Fannin State Park Advisory Commission, and control of the battleground was given to the Parks and Wildlife Commission.qv *See also* Parks, State.

BIBLIOGRAPHY: University of Texas at Austin, *Guide To Texas State Agencies* (1964, 1966).

*Fannin State Park. *See* Goliad State Park; Parks, State.

*Fant, Dillard Rucker.

*Fanthorp, Henry.

*Fanthorp Inn.

*Far West.

*Fargo, Texas.

*Farías, Valentín Gómez. *See* Gómez Farías, Valentín.

*Faris, Willis A.

Farish, William Stamps. William Stamps Farish, pioneer in East Texas oil field development, was born in Mayersville, Mississippi, on February 23, 1881, grandnephew of Jefferson Davis qv and son of Katherine (Power) and William Stamps Farish. He attended school at St. Thomas Hall, an Episcopal preparatory school at Holly Springs, Mississippi. After receiving a law degree from the University of Mississippi in 1900, Farish practiced law for three months at Clarksdale, Mississippi, before moving to Beaumont, Texas, when oil was discovered at Spindletop.qv He became supervisor of wells for the Texas Oil Fields, Limited, an English syndicate. The next year he organized the Brown-Farish Oil Company, which did contract drilling and traded in oil. The firm became bankrupt at Brown's death, but Farish succeeded in borrowing money to pay creditors. By 1904 Farish and Robert Lee Blaffer formed a partnership and engaged in contract drilling and lease trading. The next year Blaffer and Farish moved to Houston to be nearer the Humble field.

In 1915 Farish became president of the Gulf Coast Producers Association and subsequently was named president of the Texas-Louisiana Oil and Gas Association. In March, 1917, he and others organized the Humble Oil and Refining Company.qv Farish served as vice-president for five years and in 1922 became president. In 1933 he became chairman of the board of the Standard Oil Company of New Jersey, which held substantial stock interest in Humble, and in 1937 he became its president. One of the founders of the American Petroleum Institute, Farish served as its president in 1926. At the beginning of World War II, Farish was a member of the National Petroleum Industry War Council.

He was married to Libbie Randon Rice in Houston on June 1, 1911; they had a son and a daughter. Farish died on November 29, 1942, in Millbrook, New York, while visiting friends, and he was buried in Houston.

BIBLIOGRAPHY: Dallas *Morning News*, November 30, 1942; Henrietta M. Larson and Kenneth Wiggins Porter, *History of Humble Oil & Refining Company* (1959); *Who's Who In America* (1934).

Karen S. Collins

Farley, Cal. Cal Farley was born December 25, 1895, at Saxton, Iowa. He was among the six children of Frank and Jennie Farley, who later moved to a small farm near Elmore, Minnesota. Cal Farley settled in Amarillo in 1923, following a distinguished career as a soldier and champion athlete. In 1917 he was sent to Europe for combat in World War I, serving with Company C, 6th Engineers Regiment, Third Army Division. During the postwar occupation, the American Expeditionary Forces (AEF) and Inter-Allied Games athletic programs were held in Paris, France, where Farley was a member of the American team. A welterweight wrestler, he defeated Walter O'Conner for the AEF championship and George Bridges of Australia for the Inter-Allied Games title. Farley continued in professional wrestling after World War I, and he was also a minor league baseball player. He acquired a defunct tire shop and built it into a three-quarter-million-dollar-a-year business. He pioneered department store merchandising in Amarillo and for fifteen years broadcast a daily radio program. In 1924 Cal Farley married Mabel Fincher, and they had one child.

In January, 1934, Farley, along with others, started the Maverick Club, an organized program of athletics designed to keep boys off the streets. In 1966 Kids Incorporated (an outgrowth of the Maverick Club) was helping over ten thousand boys aged six to sixteen years become involved in athletics, and the boys were supervised by over 1,500 adult volunteers. There were some boys, however, who could not be helped by the Maverick Club because of their lack of supervision and encouragement at home. For these boys, termed "the lower 10 percent of our nation's youth," Cal Farley started his boys' ranch (*see* Cal Farley's Boys Ranch). The ranch was started in 1939, and as its work became more widely known and more requests were received to take boys from all over the country, Farley sold his business in 1947 so that he and his wife could devote their lives to helping homeless and delinquent boys.

For his career as an athlete, businessman, and humanitarian, Farley was honored many times. He was a district governor for Rotary International and a member of the Panhandle Sports Hall of Fame. For his work with boys, his awards included "Texas's Outstanding Citizen," the Veterans of Foreign Wars' Silver Citizenship Medal, Boys Clubs of America's Bronze Keystone Award, Doctor of Humanities degree from Texas Technological College (now Texas Tech University), and the Democracy in Action Award from students at Long Beach, California. On February 19, 1967, he died suddenly while attending non-sectarian chapel services with the boys at the ranch. Mrs. Farley died on March 19, 1967, at Hermann Hospital in Houston, Texas. Interment for the Boys Ranch founder and his wife was at the Llano Cemetery in Amarillo.

Louie Hendricks

*Farm Bureau Federation. *See* Texas Farm Bureau Federation.

*Farm Implements. In the 1950's Texas continued its mechanization revolution. In 1954 the number of horses and mules used on Texas farms decreased to 300,499, while the number of farms having one or more tractors increased to 174,040 out of a total of 292,946 farms; by 1959 the number of horses and mules had declined to the point that the agricultural census no longer reported them. Thirty-three Texas plants manufacturing agricultural implements attempted to satisfy the increasing demand for mechanization. By the early 1960's the number of firms manufacturing farm machinery and equipment had increased to seventy-nine, with a value added by manufacture of $12,929,000.

In the early 1960's Texas farms employed a total of 278,040 tractors, 197,792 trucks, and 40,723 grain combines on 210,000 farms. By 1964, 284,535 tractors, 211,041 trucks, 31,355 combines, and 15,737 balers were at work on Texas farms. The number of farm machinery and equipment manufacturers that year totaled eighty, with a value added by manufacture of $12,932,000. Four out of five bales of cotton produced in 1960 were machine-harvested, whereas in 1940 four out of five bales were harvested by hand.

The increased availability of electricity on Texas farms stimulated the development of irrigated farms and irrigation equipment. In 1960, 30,102 farms, or 12 percent of the total Texas farms, used some type of irrigation equipment. The result was that in 1960 there were approximately 5,338,890 acres under irrigated cultivation compared to 2,969,799 acres in 1950; by 1969 irrigated acreage had increased to 8,206,249 acres, representing less than 40 percent of the total cropland. *See also* Agriculture in Texas.

BIBLIOGRAPHY: *Texas Almanac* (1955, 1963, 1965, 1967, 1971).

*Farm Relief. *See* Agricultural Adjustment Administration.

*Farmer, Alexander.

*Farmer, Edward Disney.

*Farmer, Texas. (Crosby County.)

*Farmer, Texas. (Young County.)

*Farmers' Alliance. In 1887 the Farmers' Alliance, organized in Texas by such men as Charles William Macune,[qv] merged with the Farmers' Union of Louisiana (not the Farmers' Union founded in Texas in 1902, as stated in Volume I).

*Farmer's Branch.

*Farmers Branch, Texas. Farmers Branch, claimed to be the oldest community in Dallas County, recorded a fourteenfold population increase from 915 in 1950 to 13,441 in 1960. The 1970 population was 27,492. Originally known as Mustang Branch, the town was renamed Farmers Branch in the days of the Republic of Texas. *See also* Dallas Standard Metropolitan Statistical Area.

*Farmers Creek.

Farmers Creek Reservoir. Farmers Creek Reservoir, also known as Lake Nocona, is in the Red River Basin in Montague County, eight miles northeast of Nocona on Farmers Creek, a tributary of the Red River. The project is owned and operated by the North Montague County Water Supply District for municipal, industrial, and mining purposes. Construction of the dam began in September, 1959, and was completed in October, 1960. The lake has a capacity of 25,400 acre-feet and a surface area of 1,470 acres at elevation 827 feet above mean sea level. The capacity is 40,000 acre-feet with a surface area of 1,920 acres at the second-level spillway. Drainage area above the dam is ninety-four square miles.

BIBLIOGRAPHY: Texas Water Commission, *Bulletin 6408* (1964).

Seth D. Breeding

Farmers Hall, Texas. Farmers Hall, formerly Anhalt, is located in western Comal County. In 1966 it was a farming and ranching community of ten people, hosting festivals annually in May and October. *See* Anhalt, Texas, for general history of the area.

Farmers' Home Improvement Society. The Farmers' Home Improvement Society was founded in 1890 by Robert Lloyd Smith qv at Oakland, Colorado County, as a farmers' association for Negroes. The purpose of the society was to abolish the sharecropping and credit system which ensnared the Negro; to encourage self-sufficiency; to promote home and farm ownership; to promote crop diversification and use of improved farming methods; to foster cooperative buying and selling; to provide sickness and health benefits; and to encourage the social and moral elevation of its members. By 1898 the society claimed 1,800 members; by 1900 it had grown to eighty-six branches and 2,340 members; and by 1909 it boasted 21,000 members spread over Texas, Oklahoma, and Arkansas. In 1909 its cooperative business was estimated at fifty thousand dollars per year. In 1912 the membership owned 75,000 acres of land valued at considerably over one million dollars.

The society sponsored agricultural fairs which demonstrated the effectiveness of its program. In addition to the cooperative business, the society established the Farmers' Improvement Agricultural College at Wolfe City in 1906 and then the Farmers' Bank at Waco in 1911 to implement the overall program. For more than twenty years the society contributed more than any other organization to elevating the status of Negroes in Texas.

Lawrence Rice

*Farmers' Union.

*Farmers Valley, Texas.

*Farmersville, Texas. Farmersville, in Collin County, showed a population of 2,311 in 1970, up from the 2,021 population count in 1960.

*Farming. *See* Agriculture in Texas.

*Farmington, Texas.

*Farnsworth, Joseph Eastman.

*Farnsworth, Texas.

*Farrar, Lochlin Johnson.

*Farrar, Roy Montgomery.

*Farrar, Texas.

*Farrers Creek.

*Farris Chapel, Texas.

*Farris Creek.

*Farrsville, Texas.

Farwell, John Villiers. John V. Farwell was born in Steuben County, New York, on July 29, 1825, to Henry and Nancy (Jackson) Farwell. When John was thirteen his family moved to Ogle County, Illinois. In 1845 he was graduated from Morris Mount Seminary in Chicago. After working for a time for the city of Chicago, he became bookkeeper for a business firm.

In 1850 he was made general manager of Cooley, Wadsworth and Company. In 1867 Farwell took over the business. The John V. Farwell Company was the leading dry goods store in Chicago for many years.

Farwell rarely participated in politics, but in 1864 he was an elector for Abraham Lincoln. In 1869 he was appointed a commissioner for Indian Affairs by President Ulysses S. Grant. A devout Christian, Farwell headed the Chicago branch of the United States Christian Commission during the Civil War. He was a zealous supporter of the Young Men's Christian Association and built Farwell Hall to house it.

As a member of Taylor, Babcock and Company (*see* Capitol Syndicate), he helped finance the building of the Texas capitol qv in 1882. He was a director of the Capitol Freehold Land and Investment Company, Limited,qv organized in London in 1885. In addition, he was for a time managing director of the XIT Ranch.qv

Farwell was married twice—to Abigail T. Yates and to Emeret Cooley—and had a son and a daughter. He died on August 20, 1908. Farwell, Texas, was named for him and for his brother Charles.

BIBLIOGRAPHY: John V. Farwell, Jr. (comp.), *Some Recollections of John V. Farwell* (1911); (Mrs.) Abby (Farwell) Ferry, *Reminiscences of John V. Farwell* (1928); J. Evetts Haley, *The XIT Ranch of Texas* (1953); *Dictionary of American Biography*, VI (1943).

David B. Gracy

*Farwell, Texas. Farwell, seat of Parmer County, was incorporated in 1950. The town is the leading grain-shipping and supply center for the county and has a fertilizer plant, an irrigation pipe plant, and grain elevators. In 1967 it reported five churches, a school, a bank, a newspaper, and over ninety businesses. The 1960 population was 1,009; the 1970 population was 1,185.

*Fashing, Texas.

Fashions of Texas. *See* Clothing Manufacture.

Fasken, Texas. Fasken, in east-central Andrews County, on the line of the Midland and Northwestern Railroad, was opened in the summer of 1917 by the Midland Farms Company. The town was created primarily in the hope of providing revenue for the Midland and Northwestern. Though many lots were sold, few buyers moved onto the land, and the settlement, once boasting a general store and a post office, died with the railroad in the 1920's.

*Fastrill, Texas.

*Fate, Texas.

*Faught, Texas.

*Faulkey Gulley.

*Faulkner, Texas.

*Faunt Le Roy, Frederick Wiles.

*Faver, Milton. [This title was incorrectly listed in Volume I as Favor, Milton. Faver was generally known as Don Meliton (not Don Milton, as stated in Volume I).]
   BIBLIOGRAPHY: Leavitt Corning, Jr., *Baronial Forts of the Big Bend* (1967).

*Fawil, Texas.

*Fay, Edwin Whitfield.

*Fayette County. Fayette County led the state in number of farms in 1964, with 2,873 farms. It also ranked high among the counties in the raising of beef and dairy cattle. Both the hog and poultry industries were economically important. Major crops include peanuts, corn, grain sorghums, and cotton; fifteen thousand acres are in Coastal Bermuda grass. The county's average annual farm income in the early 1970's was $18.5 million. The population was 20,384 in 1960 and 17,650 in 1970.

*Fayetteville, Texas. (Fayette County.)

*Fayetteville, Texas. (Fort Bend County.)

*Fayetteville Academy.

*Fayetteville Male and Female Academy.

*Faysville, Texas.

*Fazenda, Texas.

*Federal Correctional Institution. *See also* La Tuna, Texas; Anthony, Texas.

*Federal Judicial Districts in Texas.

*Fedor, Texas.

*Feeble-Minded, Schools for. *See also* Mental Health and Mental Retardation, Department of.

*Feely, Texas.

*Fence-Cutting.

*Fenn, John Rutherford.

Fennelly's Crossing. *See* Camp Melvin, Texas.

*Fenton, David.

*Fentress, Texas.

*Ferguson, Alanson.

Ferguson, Daniel. Daniel Ferguson was born at Chireno, Texas, on December 8, 1891, son of Richard Oliver and Minnie Jane (Pate) Ferguson. He was educated in the Nacogdoches public schools

and was graduated from the University of Texas with an LL.B. degree in 1916.

His Dallas law practice was interrupted during World War I by service as a second lieutenant in the army air force. For forty years Ferguson was an attorney with the Magnolia Petroleum Company.qv During that time he built a remarkable private library on Texas and the Southwest; he used this collection to study the relationships of early churches and education in Texas, about which he published several articles. In 1956 Ferguson presented his library of approximately 5,500 volumes to the Bridwell Library of Southern Methodist University. A catalogue of the collection was published in 1960.

Ferguson was a trustee and member of the board of Oak Lawn Methodist Church, Dallas, and a member of the Texas State Historical Association.qv His first marriage was to Lucile Harding on June 27, 1923, and there were three children born of this marriage. Following the death of his wife in 1932, he married Miss Ten Tower on June 2, 1935. Ferguson died on December 17, 1963, and was buried at Grove Hill Cemetery, Dallas.
                                     Decherd Turner

*Ferguson, James Edward.

Ferguson, Miriam Amanda (Wallace). Miriam Amanda (Wallace) Ferguson, daughter of Joseph L. and Eliza (Garrison) Wallace, was born in Bell County on June 13, 1875. She attended Salado College and Baylor Female College at Belton. She married James E. Ferguson,qv also of Bell County, on December 31, 1899. Mrs. Ferguson served from 1915 to 1917 as the First Lady of Texas during the governorship of her husband, who was impeached early in his second term. When her husband failed to get his name placed on the ballot in the 1924 gubernatorial election, Mrs. Ferguson entered the race. Prior to that time she had taken little part in politics, but had devoted her time to rearing their two daughters.

Mrs. Ferguson promised the voters that, if elected, she would follow the advice of her husband. She campaigned with the slogan "two governors for the price of one" and her supporters quickly combined her first and middle initials to call her "Ma." Her campaign centered around her call for a vindication of the Ferguson name, her vehement attacks on the Ku Klux Klan,qv and her promise to reduce state expenditures by $15,000,000 a year. With prohibition a leading issue of the day, Mrs. Ferguson was associated with the so-called "wets" since she opposed any new liquor legislation. In the Democratic primary she trailed the Klan-supported prohibitionist candidate, Judge Felix D. Robertson of Dallas, but defeated him handily in the run-off election to become the Democratic nominee. In the general election she easily defeated George C. Butte,qv who had resigned as dean of the law school of the University of Texas to run as the Republican candidate. Mrs. Ferguson thus became the second woman governor in the United States and the first woman to be elected to that office.

The first administration of Mrs. Ferguson was characterized by disunity and strife, with few measures of importance being passed. She was able to fulfill her campaign promise to secure an act prohibiting the wearing of a mask in public, which was aimed at the Ku Klux Klan. State expenditures, however, were slightly increased, and she was unable to make the prison system self-sustaining. Pursuant to a campaign pledge, her administration became noted for its wide use of the governor's pardon power. She pardoned an average of one hundred convicts per month, which often brought the charge that Mrs. Ferguson was accepting bribes. There were also charges of graft in the letting of highway contracts and irregularities in the soliciting of advertising for the *Ferguson Forum*,ᑫᵛ the political mouthpiece of the Fergusons.

Mrs. Ferguson had said from the outset of her political career that she would not seek a second term in office, but in 1926 she opposed Attorney General Daniel James Moody ᑫᵛ and others for the Democratic nomination. The chief issue in the 1926 campaign was Mrs. Ferguson's administration, and Moody had little difficulty in winning the nomination and the governorship.

In 1928 Mrs. Ferguson did not run for office, but she sought election in 1930 after the Texas Supreme Court refused to order the Democratic State Executive Committee to put Jim Ferguson's name on the ballot. Mrs. Ferguson led in the first primary, but she was defeated in the runoff by Ross Sterling,ᑫᵛ who was elected governor in the general election.

The financial distress brought on by the Depression made 1932 an open year for politicians, and the Fergusons were not known to overlook political advantages. Mrs. Ferguson announced for governor in February with a promise to lower taxes. The campaign issue centered around the Sterling administration, especially the highway commission, and other financial problems. The election results showed that Mrs. Ferguson led Sterling by over 100,000 votes, but a second primary was necessary to determine the winner. A majority of Texas newspapers were against Mrs. Ferguson, and many of the state's prominent citizens spoke in Sterling's behalf, but by a close vote the Democrats again decided to nominate "Ma" Ferguson, thus depriving Sterling of a traditional second term. The Republicans nominated Orville Bullington,ᑫᵛ a Wichita Falls lawyer and business executive, to oppose Mrs. Ferguson. He waged an aggressive campaign and was able to get some Democrats to split the ticket. Mrs. Ferguson, however, had the political repercussions of the Depression in her favor and easily won by over 200,000 votes.

Mrs. Ferguson's second administration did not bring as much criticism as the first. It was conservative in financial matters, and the pardoning of prisoners continued. She proposed an income tax on the gross earnings of corporations, but the legislature did not follow her advice. Governor Ferguson chose not to succeed herself in 1934. Again in 1936 and 1938 the Fergusons preferred not to seek elec-

tion but did lend support to their choices for the governorship.

In 1940 the Fergusons could not resist a popular "draft," and Mrs. Ferguson at the age of sixty-five announced for a third term, again seeking to unseat an incumbent governor. Notwithstanding some bitter attacks on Governor W. Lee O'Daniel,ᑫᵛ her campaign lacked the traditional Ferguson vitality. Mrs. Ferguson's platform called for pensions for qualified citizens over the age of sixty-five, elimination of waste in government spending, meeting reasonable demands of labor, state and federal aid to tenant farmers, generous appropriations for education, and a third term for President Franklin D. Roosevelt. The popularity of Governor O'Daniel proved too great, however, even though the Ferguson name was still able to attract over 100,000 votes.

After the death of her husband in 1944 Mrs. Ferguson retired to private life in Austin. She continued an interest in politics but confined herself to less demanding activities. In 1955 past political differences were forgotten and more than three hundred state officials and friends honored Mrs. Ferguson at a banquet celebrating her eightieth birthday. On June 25, 1961, Mrs. Ferguson suffered a heart attack and died. She was buried alongside her husband in the State Cemetery.ᑫᵛ

BIBLIOGRAPHY: Ouida Ferguson Nalle, *The Fergusons of Texas* (1946); Seth McKay, *Texas Politics, 1906–1944* (1952).

James C. Martin, Jr.

Ferguson, Texas. (Hale County.)

Ferguson, Texas. (Jasper County.)

Ferguson Forum.

Fernández, Bernardo.

Fernando, Texas.

Fernando Creek.

Ferndale Club Lake.

Ferries.

Ferris, Charles Drake.

Ferris, Justus Wesley.

Ferris, Royal Andrew.

Ferris, Warren Angus.

Ferris, Texas. Ferris, in northern Ellis County (and partly in Dallas County), had a population of 1,807 in 1960; in 1970 it had 2,180.

Ferris Institute. *See* Speer Institute.

Ferry Lake.

Fetzer, Texas.

Feuds in Texas.

Ficklin. *See* Camp Melvin.

Ficklin, Benjamin Franklin.

Field, Joseph E.

Field, Scott.

Field Creek.

Field Creek, Texas.

Fielders Creek.

Fields, John F.

*Fields, Richard.

*Fields, Smallwood S. B.

*Fields, William.

*Fieldton, Texas.

*Fiesta de San Jacinto. *See also* Fiesta San Antonio.

Fiesta San Antonio. In 1961 the official name of the Fiesta de San Jacinto,qv held annually in April, was changed to Fiesta San Antonio, with all business of the celebration handled by the Fiesta San Antonio Commission, Inc., a coordinating body made up of representatives of the many participating groups. Instead of solely celebrating the victory of the Texans at the battle of San Jacinto, the purpose of the present-day fiesta is to encourage and help perpetuate the study of the history of Texas, to honor the heroes of the Alamo, and to enhance the importance of San Antonio as the meeting place, or confluence, of the great Anglo and Latin American cultures.

Among the more recent features of the week-long festivities are two illuminated night parades. The first, held at the beginning of fiesta week, is the "King's River Parade," which marks the entry into the city of King Antonio, the monarch who heads the procession of gaily decorated river floats. The other, at the close of the week, is a marching parade known as "Fiesta Flambeau." One of the most popular and highly successful additions to the gala week is the "Night in Old San Antonio," which is held on four succeeding nights. It is an authentically costumed re-creation of San Antonio's early life under six flags, held in La Villita,qv an internationally recognized historic restoration of the little village that existed at its present site before the time of the Alamo. *Terrell Webb*

*Fife, Texas.

*Fifteen-Mile Coleto Creek.

*Fifth Creek.

*Fifth Ferrying Group.

*Fifty Cent Act.

*Files, Texas.

*Filisola, Vicente.

Film Commission. *See* Texas Film Commission.

Film Industry in Texas. *See* Texas Film Industry.

*Fincastle, Texas.

*Fine Arts Association. *See* Texas Fine Arts Association.

Fine Arts Commission, Texas. The Texas Fine Arts Commission, created in 1965, consisted of eight members appointed by the governor for six-year terms. The commission coordinated efforts of state agencies in developing appreciation for the fine arts in Texas and acted in an advisory capacity regarding the construction and remodeling of state buildings and works of art. The duties of the Board of Mansion Supervisors,qv abolished in 1965, were transferred to the commission. The commission was made permanent in 1967, and its name was changed by the Sixty-second Texas Legislature in 1971, when the commission had an increased number of members. *See* Texas Commission on the Arts and Humanities.

BIBLIOGRAPHY: University of Texas at Austin, *Guide To Texas State Agencies* (1966, 1972).

*Finger, George W.

*Finhioven, Chief.

Finis, Texas. Finis, a Jack County frontier town located near the common meeting point of Young, Jack, and Palo Pinto counties, was founded in 1879 at a natural crossing on Rock Creek. Its name was derived from an early-day cattleman and merchant, Finis Marshall. Finis had a school, church, blacksmith shop, gin, and stage stand alongside the old Fort Belknap-Weatherford road. The town disappeared in the 1920's, except for a few foundations and the Finis cemetery.

Barbara A. Neal Ledbetter

*Fink, Texas. (Bell County.)

*Fink, Texas. (Grayson County.)

*Finlay, George P.

*Finlay, Texas.

*Finlay Mountains.

*Finley, Newton Webster. Newton Webster Finley did not serve as comptroller of Texas from 1894 to 1896 (as stated in Volume I). He was an associate justice of the Court of Civil Appeals for the Fifth Supreme Judicial District from 1893 to 1897, and he was chief justice of that court from 1897 to 1900.

BIBLIOGRAPHY: Ocie Speer, *Texas Jurists* (1936).

James W. McLendon

*Finley, Richard Watson.

*Finney, Texas. (Hale County.)

*Finney, Texas. (King County.)

*Finty, Tom, Jr.

Fire Protection Personnel Standards and Education, Commission on. The Commission on Fire Protection Personnel Standards and Education, created in 1969, was composed of eleven members, including the commissioner of the Texas Education Agency,qv the commissioner of higher education (Coordinating Board, Texas College and University System qv), and nine citizens appointed by the governor with concurrence of the Senate for six-year overlapping terms. An executive director, appointed by the commission, is the chief administrative officer.

Beginning operations in March, 1970, the commission certifies fire protection training and education programs as having attained minimum standards, certifies qualified instructors, directs research in the field of protection, and recommends curricula for advanced courses and seminars in fire science training in colleges and institutions of higher education. *See also* Firemen's Training School Advisory Board.

BIBLIOGRAPHY: University of Texas at Austin, *Guide To Texas State Agencies* (1972).

Firemen's Training School Advisory Board. First created in 1931, the Firemen's Training School

Advisory Board is composed of three members of the teaching staff of Texas A&M University and four representatives of the State Firemen's and Fire Marshals' Association of Texas. An adjunct of the Firemen's Training School, the board's duties are advisory only; they are concerned with the type and quality of training in the annual firemen's training courses and in the year-round training services offered at Texas A&M University. *See also* Fire Protection Personnel Standards and Education, Commission on.

BIBLIOGRAPHY: University of Texas at Austin, *Guide To Texas State Agencies* (1972).

*Fires, Amos J.

*First Creek.

*First Elm Creek.

*First United States Cavalry Volunteers. *See* Rough Riders.

*First Yegua Creek.

*Fiscal History of the Republic of Texas. *See* Money of the Republic.

*Fischer Store, Texas.

*Fish Creek.

Fish and Fishing Industry. *See* Marine Resources.

*Fish Lake.

*Fish Pond Creek.

*Fish Spring Branch.

*Fisher, George.

*Fisher, Henry Francis.

*Fisher, James.

*Fisher, John.

*Fisher, King. King Fisher was born in Texas (not Kentucky, as stated in Volume I) to Joby (Jobe) and Lucinda (Warren) Fisher in 1854. His father did not die of wounds received in a fight with Federal troops (as stated in Volume I), but died of natural causes.

BIBLIOGRAPHY: Ovie Clark Fisher, *King Fisher* (1966).

*Fisher, Orceneth.

*Fisher, Rebecca Jane (Gilleland).

*Fisher, Samuel Rhoads. Samuel Rhoads Fisher had four children (not three children, as stated in Volume I).

Tad Moses

*Fisher, William S.

*Fisher, Texas. (Dallas County.)

*Fisher, Texas. (Hunt County.)

*Fisher County. Fisher County had a population of 7,865 in 1960 and 6,344 inhabitants in 1970. The economy is diverse except for a lack of significant manufacturing. Petroleum production from 1928 through 1972 was 141,686,848 barrels. Crops, particularly cotton and small grains, were the greatest source of farm income, which was $7,-714,234 by the 1964 agricultural census. Cattle, sheep, and poultry also were raised commercially. Irrigated farming was practiced on 4,140 acres in 1964. By the early 1970's the county's average annual farm income was $12,000,000, evenly divided between livestock and crops; mineral production amounted to over $25,000,000 annually. A stock show and a fair in October are tourist attractions.

*Fisher Creek.

*Fisher-Miller Land Grant.

*Fisk, Greenleaf.

*Fisk, Texas.

*Fiskville, Texas.

*Fitzgerald, David.

*Fitzgerald, Edward.

*Fitzgerald, Hugh Nugent.

*Fitzgerald Creek.

*Fitzhugh, John P. T.

Fitzhugh, William F. William F. Fitzhugh, son of John and Sarah (Shelton) Fitzhugh, was born in Kentucky in 1818; as a child he moved with his parents to Missouri, and at the age of seventeen he volunteered for service in the Seminole War in Florida. Returning to Missouri, he participated in the campaign to expel the Mormons from that state. In 1845 he came to Texas with his parents, settling just south of the present town of Melissa. He married Mary Rattan and received a 640-acre headright. During the Mexican War he served in the 1st Regiment, Texas Mounted Volunteers, commanded by Colonel John Coffee (Jack) Hays.qv

Fitzhugh returned to Collin County after the war and divided his time between farming and serving with the Texas Rangers qv on the Indian frontier. In March, 1862, he entered Confederate service as first colonel of the 16th Texas Cavalry, a regiment which served in the Trans-Mississippi Department.

After the war Fitzhugh resumed farming at Melissa. He served as doorkeeper for the Constitutional Convention of 1875 qv and as Senate doorkeeper for the Fifteenth through the Eighteenth legislatures. On October 23, 1883, he was killed when he was thrown from a wagon. He was first buried in Forest Grove Cemetery near McKinney, but was subsequently reinterred in Fairview Cemetery in Denison. He was survived by seven children.

BIBLIOGRAPHY: *Weekly Democrat-Gazette* (McKinney), February 26, 1925; J. Lee Stambaugh and Lillian J. Stambaugh, *A History of Collin County, Texas* (1958).

Lester N. Fitzhugh

*Fitzhugh, Texas.

FitzSimon, Laurence Julius. Laurence Julius FitzSimon was born in San Antonio, Texas, on January 31, 1895. His parents, John Thomas and Theodora (Okelmann) FitzSimon, moved the following year to Castroville, where his father practiced medicine until his death in 1924. At the age of twelve, FitzSimon was sent to St. Anthony's College of the Oblate of Mary Immaculate Fathers in San Antonio. In 1911 he was sent by the Diocese of San Antonio to Rome to complete his studies for the priesthood. Ill health forced him to return to Texas in 1916. After recuperating for a few months, he joined the United States Navy, and was assigned to the minesweeper *Heron* during World War I.

Resuming his theological studies in 1919 at St. Meinrad's Seminary, Indiana, he was ordained on May 17, 1921. After teaching for four years at St. John's Seminary, San Antonio, and then serving as pastor at Runge, Karnes City, and Kenedy for seven years, he was transferred to Seguin in 1932. While there he directed the activities celebrating the founding of Seguin and wrote a history of Seguin and a pageant on the city's founding.

In 1941, when Bishop Robert E. Lucey of Amarillo was made archbishop of San Antonio, he appointed Father FitzSimon as chancellor of the archdiocese. It was a short assignment, however, for on August 5, 1941, the chancellor was named bishop of Amarillo. He was consecrated on October 22 and was installed on November 4. During his administration the number of churches, priests, schools, and institutions more than doubled.

FitzSimon was a scholar and historian. His Texana collection ranked among the best private historical libraries. During his custodianship of the Catholic Archives of Texas, he made frequent trips to France and Rome to gather materials on bishops and priests who had labored in Texas during the colonization period. For his research on these pioneer French priests of Texas, he was awarded in 1951 by the Cardinal Bishop of Lyons the title of *Chanoine d'Honneur de la Primatiale*, the first American to be so honored.

Suffering a stroke in May, 1954, FitzSimon never fully recovered, but he continued the work of his diocese and historical collecting. He died on July 2, 1958, at St. Anthony's Hospital in Amarillo.

BIBLIOGRAPHY: Catholic Archives, Chancery Office, Austin; *Who's Who In America* (1950).

Sister M. Claude Lane, O.P.

*Five Mile, Texas.

*Five Mile Mountain.

*Five-Mile Coleto Creek.

*Fivemile Creek.

*Flacco.

*Flag Branch.

†Flag Creek.

*Flag Mountain.

*Flagg, Texas.

*Flags of Texas.

*Flags of the Texas Revolution.

*Flake, Ferdinand.

*Flanagan, James Wainwright.

*Flanagan, James Winwright. James Winwright Flanagan was not a delegate to the Republican national conventions in 1872, 1876, and 1880 (as stated in Volume I), but his son, Webster Flanagan,qv was a delegate to each convention from 1872 until 1896.

BIBLIOGRAPHY: Paul D. Casdorph, Texas Delegations to Republican National Conventions, 1860–1896 (M.A. thesis, University of Texas at Austin, 1961).

*Flanagan, Webster. In addition to being a member of the Constitutional Convention of 1875,qv Webster Flanagan was also a member of the 1868–

1869 convention. He was a delegate to Republican national conventions from 1872 until 1896, and during a debate over a resolution on civil service in 1880 he made his famous "What are we here for?" speech, an honest appraisal of the spoils system which provoked comment throughout the country.

BIBLIOGRAPHY: Paul D. Casdorph, Texas Delegations to Republican National Conventions, 1860–1896 (M.A. thesis, University of Texas at Austin, 1961); C. W. Ramsdell, *Reconstruction in Texas* (1910).

*Flanagan, Texas.

*Flanakin, Isaiah.

*Flash.

*Flat, Texas.

*Flat Creek.

Flat Creek Reservoir. Flat Creek Reservoir is in the Neches River Basin in Henderson County, eight miles east of Athens on Flat Creek, a tributary of the Neches River. The project is owned and operated by the Athens Municipal Water Authority for municipal water supply, flood regulation, and recreation. Construction began on September 25, 1961, and the dam closure was made and deliberate impoundment of water started November 1, 1962. The project was completed at the end of May, 1963. The reservoir has a capacity of 32,840 acrefeet and a surface area of 1,520 acres at the service spillway crest elevation of 440 feet above mean sea level. The capacity at the top of the emergency spillway at elevation 446 feet above mean sea level is 43,000 acre-feet. The conservation storage has been reduced to 26,990 acre-feet because of allocation of 5,850 acre-feet to dead storage space. The drainage area of Flat Creek above the dam is twenty-one square miles.

BIBLIOGRAPHY: Texas Water Commission, *Bulletin 6408* (1964).

Seth D. Breeding

*Flat Fork, Texas.

*Flat Fork Creek.

*Flat Rock Branch.

*Flat Rock Creek.

*Flat Top Hill.

*Flat Top Knob.

*Flat Top Mountain.

*Flat Top Peak.

*Flatonia, Texas. Flatonia, in Fayette County, had a population of 1,009 in 1960 and 1,108 in 1970.

Flechas Chiquitas Indians. In 1683–1684 Juan Domínguez de Mendoza qv led an exploratory expedition from El Paso as far eastward as the junction of the Concho and Colorado rivers east of present San Angelo. In his itinerary he listed the names of thirty-seven Indian groups, including the Flechas Chiquitas, from whom he expected to receive delegations. Nothing further is known about the Flechas Chiquitas (Spanish for "little arrows"), who seem to have been one of many Indian groups of north-central Texas that were swept into oblivion by the southward thrust of the Lipan-Apache and Comanche Indians in the eighteenth century.

BIBLIOGRAPHY: H. E. Bolton (ed.), *Spanish Exploration in the Southwest, 1542–1706* (1916); C. W. Hackett (ed.), *Pichardo's Treatise on the Limits of Louisiana and Texas,* II (1934).

T. N. Campbell

Flechas Feas Indians. The Flechas Feas ("ugly arrows") are known from a Spanish document of 1683 that does not clearly identify their area. They seem to have lived east of the Pecos in west-central Texas. Their affiliations are unknown.

BIBLIOGRAPHY: C. W. Hackett (ed.), *Pichardo's Treatise on the Limits of Louisiana and Texas,* I (1931).

T. N. Campbell

*Flechazos Village.

*Fleeson, Isaac Neville.

*Fleming, James Richard.

Fleming, Lamar, Jr. Lamar Fleming, Jr., was born in Augusta, Georgia, on August 13, 1892, the son of L. L. Fleming, a prominent cotton merchant of that city and later of New York City. Lamar Fleming was educated in the public schools; he attended Harvard University until his junior year in 1911, when, for family financial reasons, he left school to join Anderson, Clayton, and Company in Oklahoma City, Oklahoma. He became the firm's representative in Holland and Germany in 1914, and from 1915 to 1922 he directed their operations in Italy under the name Lamar Fleming and Company. In recognition of his continuing interest in Italy, the Italian government awarded him the Italian Solidarity Star in 1962, the highest honor it can bestow upon the citizen of another country. From 1922 to 1924 Fleming lived in Liverpool, England, where his firm acted in partnership with D. F. Pennefather and Company.

Fleming became a resident of Texas in 1924. He retired from Anderson, Clayton, and Company in 1960, having served as president from 1939 to 1953 and chairman of the board from 1953 to 1960. Fleming helped his firm evolve from a co-partnership trading only in American-grown cotton into a publicly owned corporation dealing also in foreign cotton and coffee, grain, and vegetable oils. During the last decade of his business career, Fleming directed the firm into the food products field.

Fleming served on the governing boards of the University of Houston and Rice University, as well as Kinkaid School. He was a board member of Texas Children's Hospital and Baylor University Medical Foundation. He was vice-chairman of President Dwight D. Eisenhower's qv Commission on Foreign Economic Policy and was an adviser to the ninth session of the General Agreement on Tariffs and Trade Conference in Geneva. He served on the board of directors of the Federal Reserve Bank of Dallas. Although never a candidate for public office, he exercised a strong influence in local and state politics.

On February 7, 1920, Fleming married Clare Evelyn Knowles of England. They were the parents of four children. Fleming died in Houston on July 5, 1964.

BIBLIOGRAPHY: Lamar Fleming, Jr. (James A. Tinsley, ed.), *Growth of the Business of Anderson, Clayton & Co.* (1966); *Who's Who In America* (1960).

James A. Tinsley

Fleming, Richard Tudor. Richard Tudor Fleming, business executive and collector, was born in Temple, Texas, on April 12, 1890, the son of Richard Tudor and Edna (Griffin) Fleming. After graduation from Temple High School Fleming attended the University of Texas, where he lettered as a pole vaulter for the track team, was editor of the university yearbook, *Cactus,* and was one of three originators of the infamous *Blunderbuss,* an underground newspaper first published on April Fool's Day, 1913 (and published for sixteen years). He received a B.A. degree in 1912 and an LL.B. degree in 1915.

Fleming began his legal career in Houston, where he practiced from 1915 to 1928, with the exception of the years 1917 to 1919, when he served in the United States Army, rising to the rank of major. Back in Houston after World War I, he became president of the Houston Bar Association, executive secretary of the State Democratic Executive Committee, and one of the leaders in the fight against the Ku Klux Klan.qv He was married to Harriet H. Jameson on March 10, 1928; they had one son. In 1928 Fleming moved to New York as an attorney for Texas Gulf Sulphur Company. He advanced in the company through the years as assistant secretary, secretary and general counsel, and finally vice-president and general counsel from 1951 until his retirement a decade later.

His retirement from business opened a new career. A collector since his student days, he had particularly gathered all sorts of writings, paintings, photographs, and even sheet music and phonograph records by former University of Texas students and faculty. He offered his collection to the university, which installed the Richard T. Fleming Library of Texas Writers, with Fleming as volunteer founder, collector, and curator. For eleven years, until his death, he worked as a non-paid employee of the University of Texas at Austin, continuing to gather one of the most nearly complete collections of its kind in any major university.

Wherever he went, Fleming was outspoken and always gathered controversy. Short of stature, but with tremendous vitality, he made both a powerful advocate and adversary until the morning of his death on March 12, 1973. Following cremation, a memorial service was held for Fleming in Austin.

Joe B. Frantz

*Fleming Creek.

*Fletcher, Texas.

*Flewellen, Robert Turner.

*Flewellen, Texas.

*Flint, Texas.

*Flint Creek.

Flintoff, Thomas. Thomas Flintoff, born in Newcastle-upon-Tyne, England, in 1809, came to Texas around 1850; there he wandered from town to town seeking commissions for his portrait paintings. Though little is known of his early life, the fact that he had received some training is evident in his work, for his paintings show that he had at least been exposed to the elements of English romantic style. While he was in Galveston, Flintoff painted several portraits, including those of Pryor M. Bryan and his wife, Mary Angelica Bryan, Thomas Jefferson Chambers qv and his wife, Abbie Chambers, and a group portrait of William J. Jones'qv children. In late 1851 Flintoff went to Austin, where he was commissioned by the legislature to restore its portrait of Stephen F. Austin. One of his portraits of Austin was donated to Austin College at Sherman, Texas, in 1855. Other commissions followed, and Flintoff completed portraits of General Edward Burleson, Guy Morrison Bryan (now the property of the University of Texas at Austin), and George Washington Smyth qqv (now in the State Archives qv at Austin).

Thomas Flintoff disappeared from the scene in 1852 just as mysteriously as he had appeared a few years earlier. He eventually went to Australia, where he died in 1891.

BIBLIOGRAPHY: Pauline A. Pinckney, *Painting in Texas: The Nineteenth Century* (1967).

Pauline A. Pinckney

Flipper, Henry Ossian. Henry Ossian Flipper, the first black graduate of the United States Military Academy at West Point, received nationwide attention when he was dismissed from the army in a much publicized trial at Fort Davis,qv Texas, in 1881. Flipper was born of slave parents in 1856 at Thomasville, Georgia, and grew up in Atlanta. His own account of experiences at the academy was published as *The Colored Cadet at West Point* (1878). He was graduated fiftieth in a class of seventy-six on June 15, 1877, commissioned a second lieutenant, and assigned to Company A of the 10th United States Cavalry; he first reached Texas on his way to Fort Sill, Indian Territory. Company A entered Fort Davis in 1880, and by that time Flipper had already distinguished himself in the field, drawing praise from his commander for his performance in the campaign against the Apache chieftain Victorio.qv He was made acting assistant quartermaster, post quartermaster, and acting commissary of subsistence at Fort Davis, but by 1881, when Colonel William R. Shafter qv became commander, Flipper became aware of what he later termed a systematic plan of persecution. He was court-martialed and dismissed from the army on December 8, 1881, on charges of "conduct unbecoming an officer and gentleman," though the charge of embezzlement from commissary funds was unproved; accounts of the proceedings may be found in the San Antonio *Express*,qv November 2–December 14, 1881. A final confirmation of the verdict was rendered by President Chester A. Arthur on June 24, 1882. Flipper was unsuccessful in his later attempts at reinstatement, maintaining until his death that the charges were false.

After the trial Henry Flipper spent thirty-seven years as a civil and mining engineer on the mining frontiers of the Southwest and Mexico, usually maintaining residence in El Paso. Fluent in Spanish, he published articles on Spanish-American history and folklore. He was an executive for Colonel William C. Greene's mining promotions, and, in 1908, he acted as a consultant for Albert B. Fall, a position which continued through the chaotic political activities in the decade after Fall was elected senator from New Mexico in 1912. Flipper again drew national attention when he was reported to be allied with the forces of Pancho Villa,qv a rumor that he denied in a letter dated May 4, 1916, to the Washington *Eagle*. In 1919 Albert Fall summoned Flipper to Washington to act as interpreter and translator for his Senate subcommittee hearings, and in 1921, when he was secretary of the interior, he appointed Flipper to the post of assistant to the secretary of the interior. Flipper served in that capacity until March, 1923, after which he worked for various petroleum companies in Latin America until returning to Atlanta in 1931. His appointment was one of the highest federal positions held by a black in the early twentieth century, and his accounts of the American Southwest and the mining regions of Mexico are remarkable narratives of his struggle against discrimination on the frontier. Flipper died in Atlanta in 1940.

BIBLIOGRAPHY: J. Frank Dobie, *Apache Gold and Yaqui Silver* (1950); Theodore D. Harris (ed.), *Negro Frontiersman, The Western Memoirs of Henry O. Flipper* (1963); Bruce J. Dinges, "The Court-Martial of Lieutenant Henry O. Flipper," *The American West*, IX (January, 1962).

Phillip L. Fry

*Flo, Texas.

*Flomot, Texas.

Floods in Texas. *See* Weather in Texas.

*Flora, Texas. (Fort Bend County.)

*Flora, Texas. (Hopkins County.)

Florence, Fred Farrel. Fred F. Florence, Dallas banker and civic leader, was born in New York City on November 5, 1891, the son of Mose and Celia (Freedman) Florence. Brought to Texas by his parents in 1892, he was educated in the public schools of Rusk. In 1907 he began working for the First National Bank in Rusk and rose to the post of assistant cashier. In 1911 he went to Dallas and worked for the American Exchange National Bank. The next year he left to become cashier of the First State Bank at Ratcliff. Later he was vice-president, then president, of the Alto State Bank. In 1917 he enlisted in the aviation division of the United States Army, in which he became a second lieutenant. In 1919 he returned to the presidency of the Alto State Bank and was elected mayor of Alto. In 1920 he returned to Dallas as first vice-president of the Guaranty Bank and Trust Company, which in 1922 became the Republic National Bank and Trust Company, and in 1937 the Republic National Bank of Dallas.

On February 21, 1928, he married Helen Lefkowitz, and they had two children. In 1929 he became president of the Republic National Bank, which under his leadership became the largest bank in Texas. In 1957 he relinquished the presidency to become chairman of the executive committee, but retained the duties of chief executive officer.

In 1936 he served as president of the Texas Centennial qv Exposition and in 1937 was president of the Greater Texas and Pan American Exposition. In 1955–1956 he served as president of the American Bankers Association, and in 1956 he became chairman of the banking committee of President Dwight David Eisenhower's qv People to People Program. He was chairman of the board of the Lone Star Steel Company and a director of several corporations. Prominent in civic activities, he was vice-president of the Boy Scouts of America, a member of the executive committee of the board of Southern Methodist University, national chairman of the combined campaign of American Reformed Judaism, and for years head of the Dallas County March of Dimes. He received the Linz Award in 1944 for outstanding community participation and contributions, was named Press Club Headliner of the Year, 1955, and was awarded the Roman Catholic Benemerenti Award for work as general chairman of the St. Paul's Hospital Building Campaign. A building erected on the Southern Methodist University campus was named Florence Hall in his honor. He died in Dallas on December 25, 1960.

BIBLIOGRAPHY: Dallas *Morning News*, December 26, 1960; *Who's Who In America* (1960).

Wayne Gard

*Florence, Texas. Florence is in northwestern (not northeastern, as stated in Volume I) Williamson County. The town had a population of 610 in 1960 and 672 in 1970.

*Florence Hill, Texas.

*Flores, Manuel. Before the Texas Revolution, Manuel Flores lived in Natchitoches Parish, Louisiana, where he illicitly traded with the Caddo Indians who lived in the vicinity. In 1835 he failed in an attempt to keep the Caddo from making a treaty with the United States that called for the removal of the Indians from Louisiana. The next year, during the Texas Revolution, he unsuccessfully tried to recruit these Indians to the side of Mexico. He eluded U.S. military units and presumably fled to Mexico; by 1838 he was associated with the Mexican authorities at Matamoros as an emissary with the task of convincing the Texas Indians that they should overthrow the Texas Republic.

In the spring of 1839, under orders from Valentín Canalizo, he led an expedition from Matamoros that carried war supplies to those Indians in Texas whom the Mexicans were trying to organize. After killing four members of a party of surveyors between Seguin and San Antonio on May 14, the Flores group was trailed by a Texas Ranger qv company for two days, and a portion of the Ranger company, led by Lieutenant James O. Rice,qv confronted the Mexican group on the North San Gabriel River (not between Seguin and Bexar, as stated in Volume I) on May 17, 1839 (not May 14, 1837, as stated in Volume I). Flores' band was routed and Flores was reported among the dead. In the baggage removed after the skirmish, the Texans found several documents that seemed to link the Cherokee Indians with a Mexican plot to conquer Texas. These documents prompted President Mirabeau B. Lamar qv to demand that the Cherokees leave Texas, and this precipitated the Cherokee War.qv In 1936 a marker was erected near the site of the Rice-Flores engagement. *See also* San Gabriels, Battle on the. [This Manuel Flores has often been confused with the Manuel Flores whose biography follows.]

BIBLIOGRAPHY: William L. Mann, "James O. Rice, Hero of the Battle on the San Gabriels," *Southwestern Historical Quarterly*, LV (1951–1952); Joseph Milton Nance, *After San Jacinto* (1963); J. W. Wilbarger, *Indian Depredations in Texas* (1889); *House Committee Reports*, 27th Congress, 2nd Session (Serial No. 411), Report No. 1035; *House Executive Documents*, 25th Congress, 2nd Session (Serial No. 332), Document No. 351; *Senate Executive Documents*, 32nd Congress, 2nd Session (Serial No. 660), Document No. 14.

Roderick B. Patten

Flores, Manuel. Manuel Flores was born in San Antonio in 1801 (possibly as early as 1799), the son of José Antonio Flores de Abrego and María Antonia Rodríguez. He was a widower for the second time before he married María Josefa Courbiere in 1835.

In the fall of 1835 he became a member of the volunteer company organized by his brother-in-law, Juan N. Seguin.qv This company was composed of San Antonio area Mexicans who were sympathetic to the Texas colonists' stand against Antonio López de Santa Anna,qv president of Mexico. He participated in the expulsion of General Martín Perfecto de Cós qv at the siege of Bexar qv in December, 1835. The company disbanded, but was reorganized in Gonzales during the first week of March, 1836, and Flores became Captain Seguin's first sergeant. He fought in this capacity at the battle of San Jacinto.

In 1838 he and his wife established a ranch on the south side of the Guadalupe River across from Seguin, Texas. In the spring of 1842 Flores again took up arms in defense of Texas; he was a member of the party that pursued the army of Rafael Vásquez qv after the brief invasion of San Antonio by the Mexicans.

In 1853 he sold his ranch and established a new one in Atascosa County. His wife died the next year, and about 1858 he married Margarita Garza. He was a Mason in Alamo Lodge No. 44. Flores died on December 3, 1868. He has often been confused with the Mexican emissary, Manuel Flores,qv who was killed at the battle on the San Gabriels,qv May 17, 1839.

BIBLIOGRAPHY: Bexar County Probate Court Records (San Antonio); Bounty Certificate No. 414, General Land Office, Austin; John N. Seguin, *Personal Memoirs of John N. Seguin* (1858); Antonio Menchaca, *Memoirs* (1937).

Roderick B. Patten

*Flores, Vital.

*Flores Bayou.

*Flores y Valdez, Nicolás.

*Floresville, Texas. Floresville, seat of Wilson County, reported one hundred businesses, a hospital (completed in 1960), a bank, a library, and one newspaper in the early 1970's. Water and sewer systems improvements were completed by 1964, and a new city hall was built. Between 1955 and 1975 several new school buildings were constructed. The 1960 population was 2,126; the 1970 count was 3,707.

*Florey, Texas.

*Florida Treaty. See Adams-Oñis Treaty.

*Flour Milling in Texas. See Milling.

*Flournoy, George M.

*Flowella, Texas.

*Flower, State. See Bluebonnets.

*Flower Mound, Texas. Flower Mound, in south-central Denton County, reported a population of 275 in 1965. The United States census reported 1,685 in 1970.

*Flowers, Allen Gilbert.

*Flowers, Elisha.

Flowers, John Garland. John Garland Flowers was born at San Antonio, Texas, on October 17, 1895, the son of Richard Morton and Mary Frances (Butts) Flowers. He attended Southwest Texas State College (now Southwest Texas State University) from 1911 to 1913, received a B.A. degree from East Texas State College (now East Texas State University) in 1924, and earned an M.A. in 1925 and a Ph.D. in 1932 at Columbia University. He married Lora Hogan in 1916, and they had two children.

After teaching in the public schools of Texas from 1912 to 1917, Flowers was principal of the demonstration school and later director of teacher education at East Texas State College (1921–1928), professor of education at New Jersey State Teachers College (1928–1937), and president of Pennsylvania State College at Lock Haven (1937–1942).

In September, 1942, Flowers became the third president of Southwest Texas State College, a position he held for twenty-two years. He assumed a role of educational leadership at both the state and national levels. He served as a member and later as chairman of the standards committee of the American Association of Colleges for Teacher Education and was president of the association in 1950–1951. He was a member of the interim committee which founded the National Council for Accreditation of Teacher Education. In 1949 he was a special consultant to the educational branch of the American military government of occupied Germany, where he assisted in establishing a teacher-training program for Germany. In 1959 he was chairman of a committee appointed by the council of presidents of state-supported institutions of higher learning to study library needs in Texas colleges and universities.

Flowers was a director of the Texas Society for Crippled Children for three years, vice-president for a term, and president from 1949 to 1951. He was also governor of Rotary District 584 in 1957–1958.

Flowers retired on August 31, 1964, and died on February 23, 1965, in Harlingen.

L. E. Derrick

*Floy, Texas.

*Floyd, Dolphin Ward.

*Floyd, Texas. (Denton County.)

*Floyd, Texas. (Hunt County.)

*Floyd County. Floyd County ranked eighth in the state in crop production and seventh in total value of its farm products in 1960. With more than three hundred thousand acres irrigated in 1964, the county's main crops were cotton, wheat, grain sorghums, and vegetables. By 1970, two-thirds of the thirty-five million dollar average annual income came from crops. A harvest of 77,748 bales of cotton was turned out of the twenty-one gins in the county in 1970–1971. The population in 1960 was 12,369; in 1970 it was 11,044.

*Floydada, Texas. Floydada, seat of Floyd County, had 118 businesses in 1970, related primarily to agriculture. The school system had been expanded, and a forty-six-bed hospital was in operation. The town had twenty-two churches, a library, and three city parks. The U. S. census reported a population of 3,769 in 1960 and 4,109 in 1970.

*Fluvanna, Texas. Fluvanna, in northwestern Scurry County, was named by a Mr. Telford, surveyor for the realty company that developed the town in 1908 (not by W. S. Jones, as stated in Volume I); Telford's suggested name for the town came from his home county of Fluvanna in Virginia.

BIBLIOGRAPHY: Scurry County Historical Survey Committee, *Historical Markers in Scurry County* (1969).

Mrs. Wayne Boren

*Fly, Ashley Wilson.

*Fly, William Seat.

*Flynn, Texas.

*Foard, Robert J.

*Foard City, Texas.

*Foard County. Foard County in the 1960's obtained half of its farm income from beef cattle and the remainder from other livestock, poultry, wheat, cotton, grain sorghums, and a limited quantity of vegetables. Four gins in the county operated in 1966, handling some four thousand bales of cotton. Foard County produced nearly fifteen million barrels of oil between 1929 and 1973. In 1960 the population was 3,125; by 1970 it was 2,211.

*Fodice, Texas.

*Foik, Paul Joseph.

*Foley County.

*Folklore. See Texas Folklore Society; Folklore and Folk Music of Texas.

Folklore and Folk Music of Texas. For the most part, the study of Texas folklore and the work of the Texas Folklore Society qv have been synonymous. The society has brought together those most interested and informed on the subject from throughout the state and has stimulated a great amount of important collecting and writing, much of which was printed in the annual publications of the society. A list of contributors includes many of the most illustrious names in Texas letters: L. W. Payne, Jr., J. Frank Dobie, Walter Prescott Webb, John A. Lomax, Dorothy Scarborough, Mody Boatright,qqv and many others.

The work of the Texas folklorists has been in tune with the traditional orientation of the Texan. Whereas folklore activities in parts of the United States have tended to be academic, library-oriented, and antiquarian in approach, work in Texas has emphasized the living character of the lore and the human interest of traditional expressions and folkways. Consequently, the Texas folklorist has tended to underline the vitality of his materials, the men who performed, and the context in which the lore arose and persisted. Reportorial detail is often eschewed in favor of overall effect, often to the exasperation of folklorists outside the state.

Most Texas folklorists have been intimately involved in the life of a folk community at some important time in their lives, and it is from this experience that they tend to draw their materials. Consequently, the full range of Texas folk expression has not been explored with consistent thoroughness. The cowboy and the oilman have been widely studied, as have some other Anglo American folk communities. To a lesser extent Negro and Texas Mexican lore have been investigated, but only occasionally from the same inside vantage point. Almost completely neglected has been the lore of the resident immigrant groups.

Though the Texas Folklore Society continues to act as the focus for these activities, a number of investigators from other disciplines have recently made important studies in Texas traditions, especially in the field of folk music. Most notable are the many who have looked into the importance of Texas musicians in the early years of the recording industry. They have been able to show that not only have important performers with a traditional background come from Texas, but that some important folk styles were developed in whole or in part in the state. See Music in Texas, Folk and Popular.

These and other recent studies have emphasized the interplay between the many important folk cultures in the state. They point the direction of future work in folklore, in which sociological tools of investigation will be brought into greater use, especially in regard to the relation between the dominant Anglo American culture and those of Negro, Mexican, and European enclaves.

Roger D. Abrahams

*Follett, William W.

*Follett, Texas.

*Folsom Chapel, Texas.

*Foncine, Texas.

*Fontaine, Edward.

Fontaine, Jules Edouard, Viscount de Cramayel. See Cramayel, Jules Edouard de.

*Fontaine, William Winston.

*Food Processing, General. General food processing and associated industries as a whole in 1953 employed the greatest number of Texas workers, ranking above the chemical and transportation equipment industries. Employing 59,209 people, this industry had a value added by manufacture of $498,226,000. Throughout the 1950's the industry remained the least mechanized and the largest industrial employer in the state.

Expansion of Texas food processing plants and associated industries ranged from new breweries to rice packaging plants. Expansion in the beverage industry was particularly great, and by the mid-1960's Texas ranked among the leading states in the production of beer and canned soft drinks. Four nationwide companies operated breweries in Texas in 1965, while a fifth such brewery was scheduled to be constructed. Much of the new construction of food processing plants was concentrated in Houston, which ranked as the leading national coffee processing center.

By the early 1960's meat packing plants tended to decentralize and build new small plants far from their traditional centers and close to their raw materials. High wage rates and obsolescence in old centers, as well as abundant labor in small rural communities, influenced this relocation. In 1964 eight new plants were scheduled to be built in Texas and existing plants were modernized to include some automatic machinery.

A twenty-million-dollar sugar processing plant with a capacity of six hundred tons of beets per day was constructed in Hereford. In 1964 beet sugar was made in Texas for the first time.

In 1964 the food processing and associated industries employed over eighty thousand workers or approximately 13.2 percent of the state's total work force. Value added by manufacture totaled $923,362,000, and capital investment in the industry as a whole amounted to over five hundred million dollars. A 1965 survey indicated that the industry had expanded 15 percent over the previous year because of the population increase, larger family incomes, and greater agricultural production.

Many nonindustrial towns benefited from this expansion. The Paris soup cannery, the Corsicana potato chip plant, and the Plainview castor bean processing facility were all examples of the expansion and decentralization of the food processing and associated industries. By 1973, 85,000 Texans were employed in food processing, more than in any other manufacturing industry. Nearly five billion dollars worth of food products was being shipped annually.

BIBLIOGRAPHY: *Texas Business Review* (March, 1960, February, 1966); *Texas Almanac* (1955, 1965, 1973).

Foods in Texas. To name a particular food as typical Texas fare is difficult since the population of the state represents many nationalities and cultures, and "typical" depends on the area within the state. A crock of sauerkraut and boiled potatoes with pork and venison sausage is typical of the German-Texas communities in the counties of Mason and Gillespie, as chicken and dumplings, fried chicken, and cream peas are typical of counties in East Texas. Kolaches and strudels are delicacies found in the Czech areas, while smorgasbords of Swedish meatballs, baked fish, and *osta kaka* (sweet custard) are found in areas inhabited by large populations of Swedish Texans.

Barbecue, the food of the plainsmen, and chili, which is Latin American in origin, represent typical Texas dishes, though not as everyday fare. The method of preparation of barbecue is a matter of individual taste and convenience, but, traditionally, cooking takes place over reflected heat provided by a fire of hickory, oak, or mesquite wood which is built at one end of a long pit. The meat is then placed on a rack at the opposite end and sheets of corrugated steel are placed in positions to reflect the heat of the fire, thus allowing the meat to cook slowly. Brisket is considered the best cut of beef to use for this purpose because it has a covering of fat and good marbling. The meat is basted while cooking with a sauce or its own drippings, and turned often. The menu for a barbecue often includes pinto beans cooked with salt pork, potato salad, sliced onions, camp bread (cooked in a Dutch oven or heavy iron skillet), and boiled coffee. Cabrito (young goat), sausage, pork, and venison are also used for barbecuing.

Mexican food found in Texas is rarely found in Mexico. Much of it, such as tortillas and tamales made from masa flour, which is prepared from dry corn kernels, originated with the Indians. Chili, tamales, enchiladas, refried beans, and Mexican rice are served in every part of Texas, but the closer one gets to the United States-Mexico border, the more highly seasoned with green and red chili peppers the food becomes, since they are true Mexican condiments.

Many other cultures—Greek, Lebanese, Chinese, Italian, French, and Jewish—contribute to Texas menus and, in many cases, a Texas adaptation of the original recipe has become popular. For example, chestnut stuffing for roasting fowl evolved into sage stuffing primarily because the chestnut tree was not native to the land.

Many of the foodstuffs used in the preparation of Texas foods are produced in the state. Texas has long been identified with fine beef, but other kinds of meat are also produced in abundance— chickens, turkeys, sheep and goats, as well as swine. The Texas sportsman also provides game for his table and lists it as a favorite dish. Deer were plentiful in the 1970's, and the Texas housewife has learned how to prepare venison in many different ways. Other game birds such as duck, quail, dove, and pheasant are hunted in many areas of the state; the Gulf Coast provides redfish, red snapper, pompano, trout, flounder, crab, oysters, and shrimp.

Vegetables and fruits produced in the Rio Grande Valley rank with the finest in the world. This is especially true of the citrus crop. In the Stonewall area peaches are famous for their flavor, as are watermelons from the Luling area, strawberries from Poteet, and cantaloupes from the Pecos Valley. Producers of these various foods have conducted research and engaged home economists to test the uses of each. Under commercial supervision, recipes have been perfected for both domestic and institutional uses.

As Texans traveled more they became increasingly interested in continental cuisines; however, in the 1970's Texas menus, both in the home and in restaurants, continued to include frontier foods, Southern cooking, and individual ethnic favorites.

Mary Faulk Koock

*Foot, Texas.

*Foote, Henry Stuart.

*Forbes, John.

*Forbes, Robert M.

*Forbes, Texas.

*Ford, Henry.

*Ford, John Salmon (Rip).

*Ford, Texas.

*Ford and Neighbors Trail.

*Ford's Bluff, Texas.

*Fordtran, Charles. Charles Fordtran was married to Almeida (not Almeda, as stated in Volume I) Brookfield.

Pauline Brenstedt

*Fordtran, Texas.

*Forest, John Anthony.

*Forest, Texas.

*Forest Chapel, Texas.

*Forest Glade, Texas.

*Forest Grove, Texas. (Collin County.)

*Forest Grove, Texas. (Milam County.)

*Forest Hill, Texas. Forest Hill, in central Tarrant County, was incorporated in 1946 under general law. This city of seven churches and two public schools in 1966 also had a developing industrial area. The 1960 population was 3,221; the 1970 population was 8,236. *See also* Fort Worth Standard Metropolitan Statistical Area.

*Forest Hills Plantation.

*Forest Resources. *See* National Forests in Texas; Trees of Texas; Tree Farming.

*Forest Service, Texas. *See* Texas Forest Service.

*Forestburg, Texas.

Forests in Texas, National. *See* National Forests in Texas.

*Forky Deer Creek.

Fornell, Earl Wesley. Earl Wesley Fornell, son of Oscar and Theresa Fornell, was born on November 12, 1908, in Laketown, Wisconsin. He received his B.A. degree from the New School for Social Research in 1948 and his M.A. degree from the same school in 1949. From 1948 to 1950 he was documents specialist at Columbia University, where he received an additional M.A. degree in 1950. He was head of the government department at Amarillo College from 1950 to 1952 and an instructor in government at Rice University from 1952 to 1956. He received the Ph.D. degree in political history from Rice University in 1956. He joined the government faculty at Lamar State College of Technology (now Lamar University) in 1957 as an assistant professor and advanced to the rank of full professor in 1962.

Professor Fornell was a prolific researcher and author, writing over twenty articles for professional journals and two major books, *The Galveston Era* (1962) and *The Unhappy Medium* (1964). He was a contributor to the *Encyclopaedia Britannica* and the *Handbook of Texas*, and shortly before his death completed a manuscript on the Moodys of Galveston. In 1967 he was chosen a Fellow of the Texas State Historical Association.qv

Fornell was married to Martha Steinmetz in 1947. They resided in New York City before their move to Texas in 1950. Although living in Beaumont after 1957, he maintained a close interest in Galveston and Houston through research and writing. He served in the United States Army Air Force in World War II, attaining the rank of warrant officer. He was awarded the Silver Star for bravery in action. Fornell died on March 2, 1969, in Beaumont and was buried at Magnolia Cemetery in that city.

Ralph A. Wooster

*Forney, Texas. Forney, in northwestern Kaufman County, has an economy almost 50 percent dependent upon agriculture, with principal products being cotton, corn, wheat, hay, maize, and beef and dairy cattle. In 1967 Forney reported a new medical clinic, a bank, ten churches, and thirty-nine businesses. The 1960 population was 1,544; the 1970 population was 1,745.

Forrest, S. Lamar. S. Lamar Forrest was born on November 23, 1892, in Madison County, Texas, the son of Sidney Samuel and Ora Celia (Robinson) Forrest. He attended Clarendon College from 1908 to 1910, and was graduated from Seth Ward College in Plainview in 1912. He married Myrtle Robertson on October 13, 1916, and they had three children. Lamar developed a prosperous network of building supply stores in West Texas, gaining national recognition for his merchandising skill. In 1934 he became a director in the Lumbermen's Association of Texas and during 1937–1938 served as its president. In the following year he was made a director in the National Retail Lumber Dealer's Association and became its president in 1944. During World War II he was a member of the War Production Board and held the position of industrial advisor to the Office of Price Administration. He died of a heart attack on February 28, 1948.

BIBLIOGRAPHY: Seymour V. Connor (ed.), *Builders of the Southwest* (1959).

Roy Sylvan Dunn

*Forreston, Texas.

*Forsan, Texas.

*Forshey, Caleb G.

*Fort Anahuac.

*Fort Belknap.

*Fort Bend.

*Fort Bend County. Fort Bend County has ranked among the leading cotton-producing counties of East Texas although the annual average has decreased in recent years. Rice, grain sorghums, and cattle helped boost the farm income, which averaged twenty-four million dollars annually by 1972. A center for the sugar and rice industries, the county also processed petroleum in significant quantities, producing nearly 475,000,000 barrels between 1919 and January 1, 1973. The overall economy was linked with that of populous Harris County to the northeast. Three state prison farms—Harlem State, Central State, and Blue Ridge—are located in eastern Fort Bend County. Population was 40,527 in 1960, but had risen to 52,314 by 1970. *See also* Houston Standard Metropolitan Statistical Area.

*Fort Bliss. In 1944 the United States Army established an Air Defense Center for guided missiles at Fort Bliss. After its establishment the center grew rapidly.

Commemorating the hundredth anniversary of Fort Bliss in 1948, the citizens of El Paso presented Fort Bliss with a replica of the original post, standing near the southeast corner of the fort. Housing historic relics of the period, the replica is open to the public. In 1967 it was ranked as the fourth most popular tourist attraction in Texas.

In September, 1965, the army designated Fort Bliss as a basic combat training site. A year later the German Air Force Air Defense School was moved from Aachen, Germany, to Fort Bliss and established as an air defense facility for German trainees. In July, 1966, Fort Bliss also took over the facilities of Biggs Air Force Base qv and redesignated it as Fort Bliss Biggs Field.

By 1967 Fort Bliss had become the only air defense center of its type in the world. The physical plant included 1,130,000 acres, approximately 4,550 buildings, and a total value in land, buildings, and equipment of more than $650,000,000. More than thirty thousand soldiers as well as approximately five thousand federal civilian employees worked on the base, implementing the instruction of basic trainees and missilemen for worldwide air defense units. In 1970 personnel had decreased in number to about sixteen thousand military and thirty-six hundred civilian employees.

Individuals at the center received training ranging from basic marksmanship, map reading, and basic mathematics, to instruction on the most complex missile and electronic systems. Despite its modern programs and facilities, the Air Defense School was the army's oldest service school, tracing its origin directly to the Artillery Corps for Instruction founded in 1824 at Fort Monroe, Virginia. The Sergeant Major Academy was the top level academic institution for noncommissioned officers, and a separate instructional school was the Defense Language Institute Southwest, with the mission of teaching the Vietnamese language to military personnel.

Twenty-six miles to the north of Fort Bliss is McGregor Range. Part of the Air Defense Center, it was the western world's largest air defense guided missile range. The range covered an area of approximately 1,200 square miles and was the area in which missilemen from around the world held their annual service practice. Firing Nike-Ajax, Nike-Hercules, and Hawk missiles, various missile units were evaluated and scored in every phase of testing, which included live missile firings.

*Fort Boggy.

*Fort Bolivar Point. *See* Fort Travis.

*Fort Brazos Santiago. *See* Fort Polk.

*Fort Brown.

*Fort Burleson.

*Fort Chadbourne.

*Fort Chadbourne, Texas. Fort Chadbourne, Texas, is in northeastern Coke County (not northwestern Coke County, as stated in Volume I).

*Fort Chambers.

*Fort Cienaga.

*Fort Clark. Since it was inactivated by the army in 1946 and became the Fort Clark Guest Ranch, the old fort has attracted hundreds of distinguished visitors to explore problems far removed from Indian fights and Mexican border raids. In 1961, 1962, and 1964, business, civic, and intellectual leaders met there for the Rice University-sponsored Southwestern Assembly. A number of corporations and other organizations, including the American Philosophical Society, have had their regional meetings and executive conferences at the guest ranch.

Mrs. Walter C. Conway

*Fort Colorado.

*Fort Concho.

*Fort Crockett. Fort Crockett was built in 1897 (not in 1879, as stated in Volume I). [Some later printings of Volume I contain this correction.]

Fort Crockett was declared surplus by the army and transferred to the General Services Administration in September, 1953. In 1957 the land was put up for auction. A portion was purchased by the city of Galveston for a recreation area. Some of the property was retained by the government for the United States Air Force Reserve, Galveston district engineers, the United States Fish and Wildlife Service, and the Navy and Marine Reserve Training Center.

Dorman H. Winfrey

*Fort Croghan. During the late 1950's and early 1960's the Burnet County Historical Society began the reconstruction of Fort Croghan. Since all original buildings had been destroyed, old buildings in the area which had been built at the time of the fort were moved from their original locations to the fort's site. They included typical frontier log houses and one stone building which was one of the original homes of Hamilton Valley. Descendants of the first settlers in this area contributed authentic nineteenth-century articles to furnish the relocated buildings. By 1967 three buildings had been completely restored and were open to the public from April to November. The society in that year was also in the process of restoring a store building.

*Fort D. A. Russell.

*Fort Davis. During the 1930's the citizens of Fort Davis, Texas, began to consider preserving the old fort as a symbol of frontier civilization. Their campaign culminated in September, 1961, when Congress designated the fort as a national historic site and appropriated more than a million dollars to buy the 447-acre area and to repair the stone and adobe buildings which were largely ruins. Work progressed steadily, and thirteen buildings of the Officers Line were completely reroofed and reporched. Reconstruction plans included one of the best museums, from a military standpoint, under the jurisdiction of the National Park Service. The federal government took over administration in January, 1963. By the mid-1960's Fort Davis had been restored to its 1880 appearance. In 1966 approximately 135,000 visitors toured the fort.

BIBLIOGRAPHY: Barry Scobee, *Fort Davis Texas* (1963).

Barry Scobee

*Fort Davis, Texas. Fort Davis, seat of Jeff Davis County, reported fifteen business establishments in 1970. It is a commercial center for a large ranching area. Scenically located, it maintains a thriving tourist business. In 1960 the population was 850; in 1970 it was 896.

*Fort Defiance.

*Fort Duncan.

*Fort Elliott.

*Fort Esperanza.

*Fort Ewell.

*Fort Fisher. Fort Fisher, near Baylor University in Waco, was designated a museum site for the Texas Rangers.qv Completed in 1968, the reconstructed post on the banks of the Brazos River houses the Colonel Homer Garrison qv Museum and the headquarters for a company of Rangers. The museum exhibits works of contemporary Western artists and maintains an excellent collection of weapons connected with the history of the Rangers. Visitors are allowed to camp on the site of the old fort. The Texas Ranger Hall of Fame,qv located nearby, was officially dedicated on February 7, 1976.

Fort Fitzhugh. Fort Fitzhugh, the first settlement in Cooke County, was built about 1847 on a hill approximately three miles southeast of Gainesville. There are conflicting reports as to whether the troops who built and garrisoned the post were Texas Rangers qv or United States militia, but it is certain that they were commanded by William Fitzhugh,qv who rose to the rank of colonel in the

Confederate Army. The records do not reveal how long the fort was in operation.

Fort Fitzhugh was chosen the first seat of Cooke County and tentatively named Liberty until it was learned there was another Liberty in Texas. In 1850 a new townsite on Elm Creek was chosen and named Gainesville, and thereafter the fort was no longer used. In 1965 only a well, thirty feet northwest of the old fort on a branch of Elm Creek, and a caved-in ammunition dump, which once may have extended back into the stockade, remained. A plaque erected by the Boy Scouts during the county centennial in 1948 marks the site of Fort Fitzhugh.

BIBLIOGRAPHY: Gainesville *Daily Register*, August 19, 1950.

Maxine Fitzhugh Gentry

*Fort François. See Fort St. Louis.

*Fort Gates.

*Fort Graham.

*Fort Green. See Fort Travis.

*Fort Griffin. (Bell County.)

*Fort Griffin. (Jefferson County.)

*Fort Griffin. (Shackelford County.)

*Fort Griffin, Texas.

Fort Griffin Fandangle. The Fort Griffin Fandangle is an annual summer production held on two successive weekends in June in Albany, Texas. Originally conceived by Robert Edward Nail qv and directed by him until his death in November, 1968, the Fandangle was first performed in 1938 under the title "Dr. Shackelford's Paradise." The community effort has been in continuous performance with the exception of the war years and the years between 1957 and 1964.

Approximately two hundred Albany residents volunteer each year to act as performers for the panoramic production which presents the history of the area based on old family records. Original music is used as well as familiar ballads and folk songs. Costumes are made by local women. An annual parade precedes one of the performances and a barbecue dinner is served each evening on the courthouse square.

The production is held in a natural outdoor bowl on the ranch of Watt Matthews. Seating capacity is about 2,500. The purpose of the nonprofit production is the promotion of the educational and cultural values inherent in the community.

*Fort Griffin Trail. See Western Trail.

*Fort Hancock.

*Fort Hancock, Texas.

*Fort Hood. Fort Hood in 1976 had the largest concentration of armored power in the nation. The complex contained 217,000 acres and was the home of Headquarters, III Corps; two armored divisions, which were the 1st Cavalry Division and the 2nd Armored Division; the 13th Corps Support Command (COSCOM); and the 6th Air Cavalry (Air Combat), a helicopter brigade. In 1969 the Defense Atomic Support Agency turned over its base to Fort Hood, and it, together with an adjoining strategic air base (Robert Gray Army Airfield) became West Fort Hood. In 1976 Fort Hood had the largest population of any post in the free world, with approximately 47,600 military personnel, 4,700 civilian employees, and 60,000 dependents.

BIBLIOGRAPHY: *Texas Almanac* (1963, 1965, 1973).

*Fort Houston.

*Fort Hudson.

*Fort Inge.

*Fort Inglish.

*Fort Ives. See Camp Ives.

*Fort Jacksboro. See Fort Richardson.

*Fort Johnson.

*Fort Kenney. See Kenney's Fort.

*Fort Lacy. See Lacy's Fort.

*Fort Lancaster. In 1967 the ruins of Fort Lancaster, consisting of foundations of several dozen stone buildings, a burial area, lime kiln, and stone quarry, were being developed by Crockett County as a park. An archeological exploration of the site was undertaken during the summer of 1966 by the State Building Commission qv and Southern Methodist University. Various architectural features and thousands of artifacts which reflect life at a frontier fort—military insignia, buttons, buckles, gun parts, knives, liquor and medicine bottles, dishes, silverware, coins, and horse trappings—were recovered.

Curtis Tunnell

*Fort Leaton. In 1967 the ruins of Fort Leaton were acquired by the state, and the five-acre tract became Fort Leaton State Historic Site. See Parks, State.

Fort Le Dout. Fort Le Dout, in present Wood County, was established by the French as a trading post on the upper tributaries of the Sabine River. The founder and date of founding are unknown, and few traces of the post remain.

BIBLIOGRAPHY: *Texas Almanac* (1936, 1955).

*Fort Lincoln.

*Fort Lipantitlán.

*Fort McIntosh. Fort McIntosh became the campus of Laredo Junior College qv following deactivation by the army in 1946. The college also acquired the Fort McIntosh library and chapel through the Chief of Chaplains Association in Washington, D.C., on March 17, 1948. The college agreed to maintain the name "Fort McIntosh Memorial Library and Chapel" and to dedicate the chapel building as a memorial to veterans of Webb County killed during World War II.

Manuel B. Blanco

*Fort McKavett.

*Fort McKavett, Texas.

*Fort Marcy.

*Fort Martin Scott.

*Fort Mason.

*Fort Merrill.

*Fort Milam.

*Fort Moritas.

*Fort Parker.

*Fort Peña Colorado.

*Fort Phantom Hill. Fort Phantom Hill was restored in recent times as a tourist attraction in Jones County.

Fort Phantom Hill Reservoir. Fort Phantom Hill Reservoir, formerly known as Lake Fort Phantom Hill,qv is a tributary of the Clear Fork of the Brazos River. The project is owned and operated by the city of Abilene for municipal water supply and recreation. Construction started June 26, 1937, and was completed in October, 1938. The reservoir has a capacity of 74,310 acre-feet and a surface area of 4,246 acres at the spillway crest elevation of 1,635.9 feet above mean sea level. In May, 1952, the city began pumping water from the Clear Fork of the Brazos River into the reservoir to supplement runoff from Elm Creek. Diversion of water from Deadman Creek into Fort Phantom Hill Reservoir was started in May, 1955, to further supplement the water supply for the city of Abilene. The drainage area above Fort Phantom Hill Dam is 478 square miles.

BIBLIOGRAPHY: Texas Water Commission, Bulletin 6408 (1964).

Seth D. Breeding

*Fort Picketville.

*Fort Polk.

*Fort Prairie, Texas.

*Fort Quitman.

*Fort Quitman, Texas.

*Fort Ramirez.

*Fort Richardson.

*Fort Ringgold.

*Fort Sabine.

*Fort St. Louis.

*Fort Sam Houston. The United States Army Medical Training Center was transferred to Fort Sam Houston from Virginia in 1954 and placed under the jurisdiction of the Brooke Army Medical Center.qv Later, it was transferred to the jurisdiction of the post of Fort Sam Houston in the reorganization of the army in 1962. The Medical Training Center is the only center in the army which provides basic medical training.

In 1967 this three-thousand-acre post with its two thousand buildings held three major commands: Headquarters Fort Sam Houston, Headquarters Fourth United States Army, and Headquarters Brooke Army Medical Center. Fort Sam Houston is also the home of the United States Modern Pentathlon Training Center, where athletes train for Olympic team competition in horsemanship, swimming, épée fencing, shooting, and running. Other principal tenants included the Fort Sam Houston National Cemetery, the Army Engineers Map Plant, and a service center for the Army and Air Force Exchange System. Since 1967, Headquarters Fifth U. S. Army and the newly organized U. S. Health Service Command have been added to Fort Sam Houston.

*Fort San Jacinto.

Fort of Santa Cruz. See Fuerte del Santa Cruz.

Fort Sherman. Fort Sherman, established by Captain W. B. Stout in present Titus County in December, 1838, was located on the Cherokee Trail about one mile north of the Cherokee Crossing on Cypress Creek. After trouble between settlers and Indians, Stout established the fort to protect families living in that area. The fort was used until the Cherokee Indians were moved out of East Texas. In 1967 only a large abandoned cemetery remained at the site, which was about thirteen miles southwest of Mt Pleasant.

BIBLIOGRAPHY: Charles Adams Gulick (ed.), The Papers of Mirabeau Buonaparte Lamar, I–VI (1921–1928); Traylor Russell, History of Titus County, Texas (1965).

Traylor Russell

*Fort Smith.

*Fort Spunky, Texas.

*Fort Stockton.

*Fort Stockton, Texas. Fort Stockton, seat of Pecos County, has an economy based on ranching, irrigated farming, petroleum production and refining, and tourism. In 1970 its 232 businesses included those pertaining to gas and oil products, concrete pipe, seed delinters, paper products, and packaged meat. In 1967 Fort Stockton reported two banks, seventeen churches, a hospital, and a library. The 1960 population was 6,373; the 1970 population was 8,283.

*Fort Stockton Field.

*Fort Sullivan.

*Fort Taylor. See Fort Brown.

*Fort Tenoxtitlán.

*Fort Terán.

*Fort Terrett.

*Fort Travis.

Fort Wolters. Camp Wolters qv was deactivated in January, 1946. Local businessmen purchased the site, near Mineral Wells, and converted many of the buildings to private use. During the early months of 1951, however, it was announced that Camp Wolters would be reactivated by the air force and would be the home base for aviation engineers.

The camp was reactivated in February, 1951, and redesignated Wolters Air Force Base. It housed the newly formed Aviation Engineer Force. Special Category Army with Air Force (SCARWAF) personnel were trained at the base until July, 1956, when the army took over the base as a site for primary helicopter training.

The Primary Helicopter School became an official United States Army school in September, 1956, at which time there were 125 helicopters in its fleet. The school graduated its first class of thirty-five warrant officers in April, 1957, and during the first full year of operation trained approximately 250 students.

On June 1, 1963, Wolters Air Force Base was renamed Fort Wolters, a permanent installation, and in March, 1966, was designated as the United States Army Primary Helicopter Center.

Training increased at a rapid pace after 1965. More than fourteen thousand students had been trained by 1967, and the 1968 program called for the training of 575 students per month. The helicopter fleet increased from the original 125 to over 1,200 aircraft. The main heliport was enlarged to accommodate 550 aircraft, and in 1966 the Downing Army Heliport with a capacity of 350 aircraft was opened. A third facility was scheduled for completion in 1968.

In 1967 there were seventeen Primary I stage fields and eight Primary II stage fields located within thirty-one miles of the main heliport. In the same year, Southern Airways, the private company conducting the training under contract, employed over four hundred personnel. In addition the school housed 395 military flight instructors, most of them Vietnam veterans.

The training schedule for warrant officer candidates included a four-week pre-flight program. After its completion, the candidates advanced to the sixteen-week flight training course. The Primary I phase at Fort Wolters was conducted by instructor pilots of Southern Airways, while the Primary II, or advanced, phase was conducted by the military instructors.

Training facilities included three heliports housing over 1,200 helicopters and seven permanent stage fields. The ten tactical stage fields and eight refueling areas at the base each bore a Vietnamese name. The school utilized the Hiller OH-23D, Hughes TH-55A, and Bell TH-13 training helicopters. In 1968 additional TH-55A aircraft were to be added to the base's complement.

Fort Wolters was being phased out as of 1973.

BIBLIOGRAPHY: *A Salute to Fort Wolters, U.S. Army Primary Helicopter Center: 1967 Unofficial Directory & Guide* (1967); *Texas Almanac* (1973).

*Fort Worth.

*Fort Worth, Texas. *See also* Fort Worth Standard Metropolitan Statistical Area.

*Fort Worth Army Air Field. *See* Carswell Air Force Base.

*Fort Worth Belt Railway Company.

Fort Worth Children's Museum. *See* Fort Worth Museum of Science and History.

Fort Worth Christian College. Fort Worth Christian College, Fort Worth, was a private, coeducational junior college of the Church of Christ,qv offering standard liberal arts courses and a strong Bible department.

In 1956 the college obtained a forty-eight-acre campus. During 1957 a board of trustees was established, a state charter was granted, and Roy Deaver, first president of the college, began a campaign which produced $245,000 for construction of administration and classroom buildings.

College classes were offered for the first time in the fall of 1959 and expanded annually. Thomas B. Warren was appointed president the same year, and during his administration a cafeteria-audi-torium and a library-classroom building were added. Charles A. Guild succeeded Warren in 1961. Between 1961 and 1964, two dormitories, a president's home, and a gymnasium-auditorium were completed.

By 1965 twelve departments offered work leading to the associate in arts or associate in science degree. All work offered conformed to standards of accreditation agencies. In 1969 the faculty numbered eighteen, and the library holdings reached 13,500 volumes. Enrollment during the 1968–1969 regular term was 220 students. Curtis E. Ramey served as president of the college in 1965.

In 1971 the college became a branch of Abilene Christian College,qv and Thomas A. Shaver was executive dean. Enrollment was 104 during 1970–1971, and the faculty numbered fourteen. *See also* Church of Christ.

*Fort Worth and Denver City Railway Company. *See also* Fort Worth and Denver Railway Company.

*Fort Worth and Denver Northern Railway Company. *See also* Fort Worth and Denver Railway Company.

Fort Worth and Denver Railway Company. In August, 1951, the charter of the Fort Worth and Denver City Railway qv was amended to change the name to the Fort Worth and Denver Railway and to allow it to operate beyond the boundaries of Texas. By 1953 the entire line was dieselized for passenger service and most of it was dieselized for freight. The following year the company purchased the property of the Wichita Falls and Southern Railroad. In 1952 it acquired ownership of the Fort Worth and Denver Northern Railway, the Fort Worth and Denver South Plains Railway, the Fort Worth and Denver Terminal Railway, the Stamford and Northwestern, the Abilene and Northern Railway, the Wichita Valley Railway, and the Wichita Valley Railroad. The Fort Worth and Denver Railway is part of the Burlington System and in 1964 had 1,003 miles of track in Texas. *See also* Burlington Railroad System.

James M. Day

*Fort Worth and Denver South Plains Railway Company. *See also* Fort Worth and Denver Railway Company.

*Fort Worth and Denver Terminal Railway Company. *See also* Fort Worth and Denver Railway Company.

*Fort Worth Frontier Centennial Celebration. *See* Texas Frontier Centennial.

Fort Worth Museum of Science and History. The Fort Worth Museum of Science and History was originally called the Fort Worth Children's Museum when it was established in a classroom of the De Zavala Elementary School in 1939 by a group of school teachers, the Administrative Women in Education. In 1948, due to its growth, the museum was moved to the old Harding home on Summit Street, where it remained until 1953, when a new building was started through public funds. In 1961 and 1964 major wings were added by the Amon G. Carter qv Foundation, making it the world's largest children's museum. The name was changed to its present one in 1969. The museum is owned by the city of Fort Worth, controlled by a private board of twenty-six members, and receives financial support from the city, the county, and the museum's classes, gift shop, planetarium, and observatory.

As a museum of science and history, it was designed around family participation through a varied program of exhibits and specialized education. Within the museum are exhibit halls on man, Texas history, medical science, natural science, live animals, astronomy, and numerous other exhibit areas. The museum also houses the Noble Planetarium, a museum school handling over 4,500 students enrolled each year, a natural science research department, and a library. The museum's main collections cover the fields of anthropology, conchology, entomology, geology, herpetology, mammalogy, paleontology, and Texas Americana.

Helmuth J. Naumer

*Fort Worth and New Orleans Railway Company.

*Fort Worth Quartermaster Depot.

*Fort Worth *Record. See* Fort Worth *Star-Telegram.*

*Fort Worth and Rio Grande Railway Company.

Fort Worth Standard Metropolitan Statistical Area. The Fort Worth Standard Metropolitan Statistical Area, as designated by the Bureau of the Budget in 1949, was identical to Tarrant County and had a population of 361,253 in 1950. Fort Worth, the central city, had 278,778 residents. In December, 1958, the Bureau of the Budget added Johnson County to the official metropolitan area, increasing its size from 860 to 1,600 square miles. In 1960 the area had 573,215 inhabitants; Fort Worth had 356,268. The 1970 population for the area was 762,086 residents while Fort Worth numbered 393,476. Eight other cities had more than ten thousand residents by 1970—Arlington, Haltom City, Hurst, Euless, White Settlement, North Richland Hills, Bedford, and Cleburne. Twenty-five more towns had more than one thousand inhabitants.

During the 1950's and 1960's aircraft manufacturing became the major contributor of income in the area (*see* Aircraft Manufacture). General Dynamics, established in 1941, was Fort Worth's largest aircraft plant, employing more than eighteen thousand persons. Other aerospace firms manufacture helicopters, aircraft equipment, and guided missile parts (*see also* Electronics Industry). Arlington has a large automobile assembly plant. Other important manufactured goods are air-conditioning units, oilfield equipment, steel products, clothing, candies, plastics, and wood products. Fort Worth is the headquarters of numerous insurance firms, savings and loan associations, and petroleum companies.

The cattle industry, which gave Fort Worth its first boom, declined in relative importance during the 1950's and 1960's. The city still remains a major livestock center in the United States, due to the large investments of the Swift and Armour companies. Fort Worth also ranked fourth in the nation in grain storage capacity. It had eleven major grain brokers and elevator companies and was headquarters for the Texas Grain and Feed Association. Major agricultural products in the area are beef cattle, poultry, dairy goods, cotton, hay, and peanuts. Other businesses include flour milling, animal feeds, vegetable and cotton oils, peanut products, fertilizers, and farm equipment.

In 1963 a new city council together with prominent businessmen generated new life into the city government. Within two years multimillion-dollar bond issues created funds for a lavish convention center encompassing fourteen blocks (completed in 1967), new schools, flood control and water conservation, a new sports arena, an airport near Grapevine, and numerous city improvements and salary advancements.

Intellectual advancements, both educational and cultural, reflect Fort Worth's evolution, from "Cowtown, U.S.A." to a cosmopolitan center. The Fort Worth Public Library, which has seven branches, and six other public libraries serve the area. Over twenty-two thousand students attended seven institutions of higher learning—the University of Texas at Arlington, Texas Christian University, Texas Wesleyan College, Southwestern Baptist Theological Seminary, Southwestern Union College in Keene, Fort Worth Christian College, and the Bible Baptist Seminary. A new Tarrant County Junior College opened in September, 1967.

In 1963 the Arts Council of Greater Fort Worth was created by its citizens to raise funds for six cultural organizations. In 1967 the city had a symphony orchestra, civic opera association, community theater, and civic ballet organization. In July, 1958, the Casa Mañana, a well known theater-in-the-round, was opened, where outstanding musicals are presented. The Texas Boys Choir of Fort Worth is also well known. In 1962 and 1966 the Van Cliburn International Quadrennial Piano Competition was held in Fort Worth. Museums include the Amon Carter Museum of Western Art, the Fort Worth Museum of Science and History qqv (which was formerly called the Fort Worth Children's Museum, and includes the Noble Planetarium), the Fort Worth Art Center Museum, the Kimbell Art Museum,qv and the Texas Christian University Natural History Museum.

One of the biggest tourist attractions in the metropolitan area is Six Flags Over Texas,qv a twelve-million-dollar amusement park stressing the historic past of Texas. Annual area events include the Arlington Community Fair, the Southwestern Exposition and Fat Stock Show, and the Miss Texas Pageant. Opportunities for boating, fishing, and swimming are offered at Lake Arlington, Benbrook

Reservoir, Grapevine Reservoir, Lake Worth, Cleburne State Park, Eagle Mountain Reservoir, and Marine Creek Reservoir. Within Fort Worth, the Forest Park Zoo, the James R. Record Aquarium, and the Botanic Garden offer biological exhibits. Sports entertainment was provided by the Texas Rangers,qv an American League baseball franchise at Arlington; football at Texas Christian University and the University of Texas at Arlington; a national invitational golf tournament at Fort Worth's Colonial Country Club; and annual rodeos at Arlington and Fort Worth.

Three daily and over a dozen other newspapers were published in the area. Railroads, airlines, and an interstate highway system connected the area with the rest of Texas. The Greater Southwest International Airport and Meacham Field qqv are located near Fort Worth. By 1974 the new Dallas-Fort Worth Airport qv was opened. Also located in the area is Carswell Air Force Base.qv In 1973 the Dallas Standard Metropolitan Statistical Area qv and the Fort Worth Standard Metropolitan Statistical Area were combined, and three counties were added to create an eleven-county Dallas-Fort Worth Standard Metropolitan Statistical Area.qv The new area includes Dallas, Tarrant, Denton, Collin, Rockwall, Kaufman, Ellis, Johnson, Hood, Parker, and Wise counties. *See also* Standard Metropolitan Statistical Areas in Texas.

*Fort Worth *Star-Telegram*. In 1950 the Fort Worth *Star-Telegram* acquired the services of the New York *Times* News Service, the Chicago *Tribune* Service, and the Chicago *Daily News* and North American Newspaper Alliance. The circulation in 1974 was over 235,000 daily and 224,000 on Sundays. The *Star-Telegram* was owned by Carter Publications, Inc.

Fort Worth State Mental Health Clinic. The Fort Worth State Mental Health Clinic was established and opened with community cooperation in 1962. The staff evaluates, treats, and continues psychiatric support for adult patients returning to the community from a state hospital and those patients referred from within the community. Fees are based upon individual income and the number of dependents being supported by the patient. Approximately fifty persons received treatment in 1970.

BIBLIOGRAPHY: Board for Texas State Hospitals and Special Schools, *Report* (1964); Texas Department of Mental Health and Mental Retardation, *Annual Report* (1970).

*Fort Worth University.

Fortier, Honoré. François Honoré (Honorato) Fortier was born in New Orleans in 1764, the son of Michel and Perrine (Langlois) Fortier. He was engaged in the mercantile business with his brother, Jacques, and made several voyages from Louisiana to Europe in ships carrying tobacco and other colonial products. In 1801 he went to Mexico and asked permission of the viceroy to carry a portion of Louisiana's subsidy overland through the Provincias Internas qv to New Orleans because of the insecurity of maritime travel. The travelers journeyed from Vera Cruz to Mexico City by way of Puebla on April 15, 1801, and on June 10 they left Mexico City for the frontier. By June 19 they were in San Luis Potosí, where they rested until August 4. They reached Reynosa on September 8, and ascended the Rio Grande toward Camargo because of the swollen river. They swam their 700 mules and 215 horses over the river. A stampede on September 26 delayed the travelers until October 1. On October 7 they were forced to ford the Nueces River, and they continued toward the settlement at La Bahía qv and then toward San Antonio and Natchitoches. They described crossing the Guadalupe, Colorado, Trinity, and Sabine rivers, and by November 28 they had reached the Red River in Louisiana. They descended that river through the Spanish posts of Avoyelles and Pointe Coupée and arrived at New Orleans on the evening of December 5, having traveled 922 leagues in 77 days of actual travel. Fortier fought with the 4th Regiment of the 1st Division of Louisiana militia as a corporal during the War of 1812. He was married to Marie Asunción Brulé, a native of New Orleans, and they had two children. Fortier died in 1826.

BIBLIOGRAPHY: Estelle M. Fortier Cochran, *The Fortier Family and Allied Families* (1963); Archivo del Ministerio de Asuntos Exteriores (Madrid), Doc. LXIX; Stanley Faye, "Privateersmen of the Gulf and their Prizes," *Louisiana Historical Quarterly*, XXII (1939); Jack D. L. Holmes, "De México a Nueva Orléans en 1801: el Diario Inédito de Fortier y St. Maxent," *Historia Mexicana* (1966).

Jack D. L. Holmes

*Forward, Texas.

*Fossil Creek.

*Fossil Knob.

*Foster, Isaac.

*Foster, John.

*Foster, Lafayette Lumpkin.

*Foster, Randolph.

*Foster, Texas. (Fort Bend County.)

Foster, Texas. (Terry County.) Foster was founded in 1928. In 1966 the population was four, and the community was composed of a general store and a gin serving a farming area.

*Foster Army Air Field.

*Foster Branch.

Fosters Store, Texas. Fosters Store, near the Brazos River in eastern Burleson County, was in 1966 an unincorporated community of some ten people. The community, less than ten years old at that time, was devoted entirely to farming.

*Fostoria, Texas.

*Foundation School Program Fund. The Foundation School Program Fund was created by the Gilmer-Aikin (not Gilmer-Aiken, as stated in Volume I) Law.

The Foundation School Fund draws its revenue by transfer from the Omnibus Tax Clearance Fund. Since 1951 the tax sources from which the Omnibus Tax Clearance Fund draws its revenue have been altered by legislation. Receipts as of September 1, 1965, were made up from taxes on local oil production, natural and casinghead gas, sulphur, oil and gas regulation, cement, utilities, telephone companies, oil and gas well servicing, express companies, carline companies, Pullman companies, admission, cigarette, liquor, wine, ale, beer, telegraph, motor vehicle, stock share transfer, insurance companies occupation, coin device machine, miscellaneous occupation, cigarette and tobacco tax permit fees, liquor permit fees, and wine and beer permit fees. During the school year of 1965–1966, a total of $129,074,067 was drawn from the fund in support of public education.

J. W. Edgar

*Fountain, Albert J.

*Four Corners, Texas.

*Four Mile Creek.

Four Mile Prairie, Texas. Four Mile Prairie, in western Van Zandt County, was founded in 1847, one of the three Norwegian settlements established by Johan Reinert Reiersen.qv The community used the post office at neighboring Prairieville, one of the other Norwegian settlements, three miles west in Kaufman County. Still standing in the 1970's at Four Mile Prairie was a small white board-and-batten frame Lutheran church, built in 1875. *See also* Wærenskjold, Elise Amalie; Prairieville, Texas.

BIBLIOGRAPHY: C. A. Clausen (ed.), *The Lady with the Pen: Elise Waerenskjold in Texas* (1961).

*Four-Section Act.

*Four Sixes Ranch.

*Fourmile Draw.

*Fourth Creek.

*Fourth United States Cavalry.

*Fowler, Andrew Jackson.

*Fowler, John Hopkins.

*Fowler, Littleton. Littleton Fowler was born in Smith County, Tennessee, on September 12, 1803, and died on January 29, 1846. He was buried beneath the pulpit of the original log church which was McMahan's Chapel,qv in western Sabine County (not McMahon's Chapel in San Augustine County, as stated in Volume I).

BIBLIOGRAPHY: J. B. Sanders, *Index to the Cemeteries of Sabine County, Texas, 1836–1964* (c.1964); L. Fowler Woolworth, *Littleton Fowler—A Saint of the Saddlebags* (1936); "Texas Collection," *Southwestern Historical Quarterly*, XLV (1941–1942).

Helen Gomer Schluter

*Fowler Institute.

*Fowlerton, Texas.

*Fowlkes Station, Texas.

Fox, Oscar Julius. Oscar J. Fox, composer of Western songs, was born on a ranch in Burnet County, Texas, on October 11, 1879, son of Emma (Kellersberger) and Bennie Fuchs and grandson of Adolph Fuchs.qv After the death of Fox's mother, five months after his birth, he was reared in the home of an uncle, Hermann T. Fuchs. He attended school in Marble Falls until 1893, when he went to San Antonio and began the study of music. In

1896 he was sent to Zurich, Switzerland, by his grandfather, Getuli Kellersberger, to study piano, violin, and choral direction for three years. He then studied in New York City for two years before going to Galveston in 1902 as choirmaster of the First Presbyterian Church and later of St. Mary's Cathedral. He resigned in 1904 to accept a similar position at the First Presbyterian Church in San Antonio, where he served for ten years. He was conductor of the San Antonio Choir Club (1913–1915) and director of the men's and girls' glee clubs and the University Choral Society at the University of Texas (1925–1928). Fox was a member of the Texas Music Teachers Association; Sinfonia Fraternity of America; American Society of Composers, Authors, and Publishers; Composers-Authors Guild; and the Sons of the Republic of Texas.qv

Fox published the first of his more than fifty songs in 1923. He first achieved fame through his setting to music the cowboy songs collected by John A. Lomax.qv He never wrote lyrics, preferring to use outstanding poetry on which to base his original musical compositions. He drew strongly on his Texas background, and some of his better-known compositions were "The Hills of Home," "Old Paint," "The Old Chisholm Trail," "Whoopee Ti Yi Yo, Git Along, Little Dogies," "Will You Come to the Bower?" and "The Cowboy's Lament."

Fox married Nellie Tuttle in 1905, and they had three daughters. The last fifteen years of his life he taught voice and was organist and choir director at Christ Episcopal Church, San Antonio. He died on July 29, 1961, while visiting in Charlottesville, Virginia, and was buried in Mission Burial Park in San Antonio. On May 27, 1962, the state honored Oscar J. Fox by placing a red granite marker one mile south of Marble Falls on Highway 181. Inscribed on the marker beneath his name is the first bar of "The Hills of Home," a song which was his own favorite and one that has continued to be popular around the world.

BIBLIOGRAPHY: Carl Weaver, "Oscar J. Fox and His Heritage," *Junior Historian*, XXIV (1963–1964); Lota M. Spell, *Music in Texas* (1936); Dallas *Morning News*, July 30, 1961; *Daily Texan* (Austin), October 18, 1925; Biographical File, San Antonio Public Library; Biographical File, Barker Texas History Center, University of Texas at Austin.

S. W. Pease

*Fox City, Texas.

*Fox Mountain.

Fox Nation, Texas. Fox Nation was a place name along the San Patricio Trail qv in Live Oak County near the Comanche Crossing of the Nueces River in the 1850's. Named after the Fox family who settled in the vicinity in the early 1850's, Fox Nation was the predecessor of the stage stop and post office at Gussettville.

Robert H. Thonhoff

*Foy, Frederick.

*Foyle Creek.

*Fraimville, Texas.

*Frame Switch, Texas.

*Francis, Mark.

*Franciscan Missionaries in Texas. *See* Nuestra Señora de Guadalupe de Zacatecas; San Fernando de Mexico; Santa Cruz de Querétaro.

*Francisco Creek.

*Francitas, Texas.

*Franco, Texas.

Franco-Texan Land Company. The Franco-Texan Land Company, chartered under the laws of Texas on August 4, 1876, owned approximately 600,000 acres of land in Parker, Palo Pinto, Stephens, Callahan, Shackelford, Mitchell, Taylor, Nolan, Jones, and Fisher counties. The company had its origin in a land grant made by the Texas legislature to the Memphis, El Paso, and Pacific Railroad. The railway charter, granted in 1856, authorized the building of a railroad from a point on the eastern boundary of the state between Sulphur Fork and the Red River to a point on the Rio Grande opposite or near the city of El Paso, donating sixteen sections of 640 acres each for every mile of road constructed and placed in running order, on the completion of a minimum of ten miles, and eight sections per mile for the grading of a minimum of twenty-five miles of roadbed. By 1861 the Memphis, El Paso, and Pacific directors, originally a group of sincere and earnest Texans, had surveyed the center line of the road as far as the Brazos River and graded fifty-five miles on which they were ready to lay the track. When the outbreak of the Civil War suddenly halted all operations, the company could do no more than retain its corporate form for the duration of the war. In 1866 the legislature passed a relief act which extended the limitations on its contract for ten years. Interest revived and the Texas directors, in search of capital, brought John Charles Fremont into the company. Fremont, envisioning a transcontinental road on the 32nd parallel, beginning at San Diego and connecting with the East at Memphis, took control and promptly executed three mortgages secured by the road itself and the land grants yet to be received from the state of Texas. Fremont sold his securities in France and collected some five million dollars after he had succeeded, by highly questionable methods, in getting his "puffed-up" bonds quoted on the Paris Bourse.

Because the "French Bond Scandal" was widely publicized at home and abroad, and because little of the money was spent on the railroad, Congress refused to grant Fremont a transcontinental charter. He therefore compromised with the rival Texas and Pacific Company which, since it had to have the Memphis, El Paso, and Pacific to get across Texas, agreed to buy the embryo railroad and take over its liens. Ultimately Fremont was frozen out of the successor company, but the French bondholders did become the owners of the Texas land which secured their bonds, subject however to rules and regulations imposed by John A. C. Gray, the agent who put the Memphis, El Paso, and Pa-

cific into receivership and sold it to the Texas and Pacific.

The French bondholders received thirteen acres of land for each $100 bond, and this land constituted the capital stock of the Franco-Texan Land Company. The incorporators were H. E. Alexander and S. Pinkney Tuck of New York, and Claiborne S. West and H. C. Withers of Austin, Texas. Tuck, the company's secretary, came to Weatherford, Texas, and began the sale of land in 1878. Henry P. du Bellet, vice-secretary residing in Paris, staged a *coup d'état* in which the New York officers were ousted and Sam H. Milliken of Weatherford was elected president. Du Bellet then came to Texas and had a hand in the company's affairs until he too was ousted. Successive presidents were V. G. Frost of Palo Pinto, A. Chaptive of Paris, France, R. W. Duke and A. J. Hood of Weatherford, and George P. Levy of Paris, France. With the gradual increase in the value of Texas land, the Franco-Texan Land Company developed into something of a bonanza for the French and American directors who bought stock certificates for a few cents on the dollar and conspired to riddle the company's coffers. The losers were the French peasants who had invested their life savings in the Memphis, El Paso, and Pacific bonds.

In 1896, after years of local rivalry and dissension, the charter of the Franco-Texan Land Company expired by limitation. On request, the legislature allowed the company three additional years to liquidate its assets and conclude its business.

BIBLIOGRAPHY: Virginia H. Taylor, *The Franco-Texan Land Company* (1969).

Virginia H. Taylor

*Franco-Texian Bill. [This title was incorrectly listed in Volume I as Franco-Texienne Bill.] Although referred to by the press as the "Franco-Texienne Bill," the bill that was proposed to the Texas Congress appeared in printed form as follows: *A Bill To Be Entitled "An Act To Incorporate The Franco Texian Commercial And Colonization Company."* The two Frenchmen whose names appear in the bill as sponsors were Jean Pierre Hippolyte Basterrèche and Pierre François de Lassaulx (not Pierre Hassauex, as stated in Volume I). In the bill itself, the name "de Lassaulx" is misspelled as "de Hassaulx" on page one, and as "De Lassaulx" on subsequent pages. Various works have spelled the name still differently, "de Lassauix" and "de Hassauex," both of which are incorrect. The correct spelling, "de Lassaulx" may be found in the original handwriting of Dubois de Saligny,qv friend and confidant of Basterrèche and de Lassaulx, who made strenuous efforts to have this bill passed by the legislature of the Republic of Texas. The initial misspellings are quite likely the result of difficulty in reading the handwriting of Dubois de Saligny, according to Nancy N. Barker, who translated and edited the French commercial and diplomatic correspondence concerning Texas in a two-volume work entitled *The French Legation in Texas* (1971, 1973), published by the Texas State Historical Association.qv

*Frank, Texas. (Colorado County.)

*Frank, Texas. (Fannin County.)

Frank Phillips College. Frank Phillips College, Borger, was established as Borger City Junior College in 1948, and C. A. Cryer served as president of the college and superintendent of schools. The board requested and received permission from Frank Phillips, founder of Phillips Petroleum Company, which had extensive holdings in the Borger area, to change the name of the college.

J. W. Dillard served as dean in the planning stage and took over the presidency of the college in 1955. The college and Borger High School shared a physical plant that was completed in time for occupancy in the fall of 1948. During that year 250 students enrolled and the faculty numbered ten. In 1955 the college bought thirty acres in the southwest part of the city for a new campus, and facilities were ready for classes by the fall semester of 1956. Enrollment that year was 450 students, and the faculty had grown to twenty-nine members.

A fine arts building containing an auditorium, cafeteria, classrooms, offices, student lounge, and bookstore was completed in 1960. A $450,000 library opened in 1966, and it contained 21,000 volumes in 1969. With the addition of twenty acres to the campus the college physical plant was valued at three million dollars. Enrollment was 758 in the 1974 fall term, and the faculty consisted of over fifty instructors; W. E. Raab was president in that year.

*Frankell, Texas.

*Franklin, Benjamin Cromwell.

*Franklin, Texas. (El Paso County.) See Coon's Rancho.

*Franklin, Texas. (Lamar County.)

*Franklin, Texas. (Robertson County.) Franklin, the county seat, changed to an alderman form of government in 1951. City projects completed between 1951 and 1965 included a water system, paving, a sewage treatment plant, a city hall, and a fire station. In 1967 the city reported thirty-one business establishments, six churches, two public schools, a bank, a library, and a newspaper. Franklin serves as the commercial center for the eastern part of the county, while Hearne serves the south and west areas. The 1960 population was 1,065; the 1970 population was 1,063.

*Franklin College.

*Franklin County. Franklin County, producer of oil, livestock, and lumber, yielded over 134,063,-144 barrels of oil from 1936 to 1973. Oil and gas production and processing is the leading industry of the county, though livestock raising, the chief farm enterprise, is increasing in importance. Cotton, grain sorghums, fruit, and vegetables are also raised. The 1960 population of 5,101 increased to 5,291 by 1970.

*Franklin Mountain.

*Franklin Mountains.

*Franks, L. B.

*Frankston, Texas. Frankston, in Anderson County, had a population of 953 in 1960 and 1,056 in 1970.

*Franquis de Lugo, Carlos.

Frantz, Dalies Erhardt. Dalies Erhardt Frantz, eminent pianist and teacher at the University of Texas at Austin, was born on January 9, 1908, in Lafayette, Colorado, the son of William Henry and Amalia (Lueck) Frantz. He grew up in Denver, where he studied piano at an early age and became known as a child prodigy. Later he learned to play the organ and helped support himself by serving as organist and choirmaster in churches. His education was at the Huntington Preparatory School in Boston and under Guy Maier at the University of Michigan from 1926 to 1930. He received the Bachelor of Music degree with highest honors from that university; subsequently, he studied in Europe with Artur Schnabel and Vladimir Horowitz.

Following his debut with the Philadelphia Orchestra under Leopold Stokowski in 1934, he was signed by Columbia Concerts Corporation and began a long and brilliant career that took him from coast to coast in recitals and in appearances with most of the major orchestras in the United States. During this period he also taught two summer sessions at the University of Washington in Seattle and returned for further study at the University of Michigan. In 1934 he married Martha King of Detroit. They were separated five years later.

His eminence as a pianist attracted Hollywood's attention, and he appeared in several motion pictures. During World War II he served for a time as an intelligence officer in a West Coast fighter squadron, but was given a medical discharge before the end of the war.

In 1943 he joined the faculty of the University of Texas music department. In spite of physical misfortunes which continued to plague him, he pursued his teaching until the time of his death and was recognized as one of the outstanding music teachers in the country. He inspired a large number of student pianists, some of whom won national and international acclaim, and well-known professional pianists came to Austin to work with him. Some of his experiences and convictions about piano teaching were passed on to music teachers all over the United States through a series of articles in a publication of the National Piano Guild.

He died in Austin on December 1, 1965, and was buried at Capital Memorial Gardens in Round Rock, Texas.

Kent Kennan

Frantz, Ezra Allen. Ezra Allen Frantz was born in the Pleasant Hill community, Macoupin County, Illinois, on August 6, 1875, the son of Michael and Barbara (Brubaker) Frantz. In 1896 he married Mary Lavanna Buckley of Parker County, Texas; they were the parents of two sons and three daughters. A manufacturer of heavy machinery and chain stay fences in Sterling, Illinois, along with his brother Peter, he dissolved the partnership in

1900 in order to move to Texas. Except for three years in the 1920's in the real estate business in Miami, Florida, again as a partner with his brother, Frantz remained in Texas until his death.

In 1902 Frantz invented the first wire buckle for tying compressed cotton bales. This buckle made possible high density compressing and soon dominated the cotton buckle market, a position it held until the close of World War II. Frantz also held about a dozen other patents, including one for an improved piston ring and another for the first successful scratcher for oil drilling rigs. At one time he was president of seven different companies. Most of his career was spent in Weatherford, Texas, although he maintained his chief manufacturing plant in Memphis, Tennessee. He lived in Fort Worth from 1923 to 1932, where he reorganized distressed business firms and designed oil field machinery, particularly an improved pump jack. He served as general superintendent for the American Manufacturing Company during World War II when it received huge contracts for manufacturing naval shells. He was also quite active in various philanthropic religious organizations of several denominations. He died in San Angelo on August 31, 1964, and was buried in Weatherford, Texas.

*Fratt, Texas.

*Frazer, Hugh McDonald.

*Frazier, James.

*Frazier Canyon.

*Frazier Creek.

*Fred, Texas.

*Fredericksburg, Texas. Fredericksburg, seat of Gillespie County, had a 1960 population of 4,629 and a 1970 population of 5,326. The 225 businesses reported in 1970 included companies producing machine and aircraft parts, tents, baked goods, feeds, ice cream, peanut oil, furniture, clay products, processed poultry, and mineral and stone products. By 1967 Fredericksburg had a new National Guard armory, a new high school, and served as headquarters for the eleven-county Central Texas Electric Cooperative. The Gillespie County fair, the oldest in the state, held its diamond jubilee in 1963.

*Fredericksburg College.

Fredericksburg Easter Fires. The custom of lighting fires on hills the night before Easter is undoubtedly of North German origin. The German emigrants who founded Fredericksburg in 1846 came largely from the Hesse, Hanover, Westphalia, and Brunswick areas, where many villages built Easter fires on nearby hills, often with ceremony, dance, and song. Little is known of Easter fires in Fredericksburg before the Civil War; night fires burning in the hills at that time were usually attributed to Indians. After the war, however, the lighting of Easter fires became customary, especially on the hills around Fredericksburg and at Grapetown, Doss, and other communities. Through several generations, families tended Easter fires on hills

in their pastures. Later, Boy Scout troops prepared the fires. Seeing the bonfires in the hills, small children believed that the Easter rabbit was dyeing eggs that would appear in their Easter nests on Sunday morning.

Since 1948 an Easter Fire pageant written by William Petmecky has been presented annually at the fair grounds in Fredericksburg. In its theme, fantasy and folklore mingle with the historical background of the town. Fires on top of the surrounding hills furnish a backdrop for the pageant. The Easter Fire Association was merged with the Gillespie County Historical Society in 1950.

BIBLIOGRAPHY: Julia Estill, "Customs Among the German Descendants of Gillespie County," *Texas Folk-Lore Publications*, II (1923); James George Frazer, *The Golden Bough: A Study in Magic and Religion*, I (1958); Fredericksburg *Standard*, March 24, 31, 1948.

Esther L. Mueller

*Fredericksburg and Northern Railway Company.

Fredonia, Texas. (Gregg County.) Fredonia was platted in 1843. In the same year Haden Edwards qv established a ferry on the Sabine River at Fredonia where the present bridge is located. By 1872 Fredonia was virtually abandoned. At one time the town had three cotton warehouses, forty to fifty buildings, and a brick-making business.

*Fredonia, Texas. (Mason County.)

*Fredonian Rebellion.

*Free State of Van Zandt.

*Freedmen's Bureau.

*Freeland, Texas.

*Freeman, George R.

*Freeman, Texas.

*Freeman's Red River Expedition.

*Freemasonry in Texas. In 1965 (in addition to the Grand Lodge of Texas, having 971 subordinate lodges with a total membership of 244,476) organized Freemasonry in Texas was represented by a Grand Chapter of Royal Arch Masons consisting of 228 subordinate chapters with 45,825 members; a Grand Council of Royal and Select Masters consisting of 223 subordinate councils with 44,134 members; a Grand Commandery of Knights Templar consisting of 91 subordinate commanderies with 30,222 members; and the Scottish Rite of Freemasonry with bodies located in Galveston, Austin, El Paso, Houston, San Antonio, Dallas, and Waco, with a combined membership of 61,750 in their Lodges of Perfection.

Additional programs of public service in operation in 1965 by Texas Masonic organizations included: Knight Templar Educational Foundation, a loan fund for college education; Knight Templar Eye Foundation, for the prevention of blindness; Texas Public Schools Week, an observance in support of free public education; Texas Scottish Rite Foundation, a charitable and educational foundation contributing to worthy charities, providing aid at public disasters, and supporting a scholarship program for persons seeking graduate degrees in preparation for a career in government service; the Texas Grand Lodge Library, a general library containing outstanding collections of Texas history materials and Masonic publications; and in connection with Baylor University, the J. M. Dawson Studies in Church and State, dedicated to objective research and instruction in church-state relations.

BIBLIOGRAPHY: James D. Carter (ed.), *The First Century of Scottish Rite Masonry in Texas, 1867–1967* (1967).

James D. Carter

*Freemound, Texas.

*Freeport, Texas. (Brazoria County.) Freeport was the center of a highly industrial complex which included petrochemical and other plants in 1970. There was a deepwater port, with related industries such as marine repairs and shrimp processing. Historic Velasco qv was within the city limits. Freeport is part of Brazosport and in the Houston Standard Metropolitan Statistical Area.qv The 1960 population of 11,619 was almost double the 1950 population; by 1970 the population was 11,997.

*Freeport, Texas. (Hale County.)

*Freer, Texas. Freer, in Duval County, had a population of 2,724 in 1960 and 2,804 in 1970, according to the United States census.

*Freestone, Texas.

*Freestone County. Freestone County obtains most of its farm income from beef cattle, poultry, and swine. In the early 1970's its average annual farm income was about $9 million. Additional revenue is obtained from petroleum, over thirty-three million barrels having been produced from 1916 to January 1, 1973. The 1960 population was 12,525; the 1970 count was 11,116.

*Freestone Creek.

*Freie Presse für Texas.

*Freiheit, Texas.

*Frelsburg, Texas.

*French, George H.

*French, Henry R.

*French, James Henry.

French, John C. John C. French was born in New Jersey or Pennsylvania in the 1820's. He and his brother Samuel came to San Antonio in the 1840's. French entered the employ of Lewis and Groesbeck, dealers in groceries and banking. In 1854 the firm became Groesbeck and French, and later was run by French alone. In 1856 the French Building was completed; in 1868 it became the Bexar County courthouse and in 1878 housed the city government. San Antonio's first regular bank was organized by French and Erasmus Andre Florian, and it operated until the Civil War forced French to withdraw from active business, though he still retained large interests in San Antonio. He helped promote the Gulf, Western Texas, and Pacific Railway Company (*see* San Antonio and Mexican Gulf Railway).

French married Sally Roberts. He died in Cuero on May 16, 1889, and was buried beside his daughter in Philadelphia, Pennsylvania.

BIBLIOGRAPHY: Frederick C. Chabot, *With the Makers of San Antonio* (1937); Edward W. Heusinger, *A Chronology of Events in San Antonio* (1951).

S. W. Pease

*French Creek.

*French Embassy. [Often used as a popular name for the French Legation, this title is incorrect.] *See* French Legation.

*French John Creek.

French Legation. [This title was incorrectly listed in Volume I as French Embassy.] The French Legation in Austin was acquired by the state of Texas in 1949 and placed under the custodianship of the Daughters of the Republic of Texas.qv In the 1950's the legation was restored by the DRT and opened to the public as a museum in 1956. Draperies, upholstery, and furniture included in the building are typical of nineteenth-century France. The wine cellar had been rebuilt to its original size and contained several hundred-year-old wine casks.

The legation's kitchen was rebuilt later on its original foundation and represents the only known restoration of an early French kitchen in the United States. Duplications of every original item in the kitchen were used in the kitchen's reconstruction. It was dedicated and opened to the public in May, 1967. For earlier history of the legation *see* French Embassy, in Volume I.

BIBLIOGRAPHY: Daughters of the Republic of Texas, *Légation de France . . .* (1963).

*French in Texas.

*Frenchman Hills.

Frenstat, Texas. Frenstat, a farming community in southern Burleson County, had twelve inhabitants in 1966. The settlement was unincorporated and less than ten years old at that time.

*Fresenius, Texas.

*Fresno, Texas.

*Fresno Creek.

*Fresno Peak.

*Freyburg, Texas.

*Friar, Daniel Boone.

*Friar, Texas.

*Friar Branch.

*Friday, Texas.

*Friday Mountain.

Friday Mountain Ranch. Purchased by the noted historian Walter Prescott Webb qv in 1942, and strongly identified with him since that time, Friday Mountain Ranch was originally the site of Johnson Institute,qv a school which began operation in 1852. Located in Hays County, seventeen miles southwest of Austin, the ranch encompasses 630 acres of land along Bear Creek. The dominant landmark is Friday Mountain,qv an elevation of slightly more than one thousand feet, which stands only a few hundred yards away from the main stone building across Bear Creek.

The Institute, founded by Thomas Jefferson Johnson,qv was first quartered in log cabins; with the aid of associates and students, Johnson built an L-shaped building out of limestone quarried on the grounds, using long-lasting timbers of cedar and cypress. Two stories high, fronting south, the thick-walled structure had more the appearance of a fortress than of a school or residence. Construction probably began about 1853. Originally intended as a boys' school, the institute soon took in girls. Boys were housed in log cabins with puncheon floors, while the girls lived on the second floor of the main stone structure. The school was closed in 1872, but the main building, consisting of ten large rooms, two small ones, and seven fireplaces, remained in good repair.

Ownership of the land changed hands several times, once at public auction for taxes, before it was bought by Louis Kemp in 1908, who in turn sold it to his son, Thomas Jefferson Kemp, in 1921. Purchased from Kemp in 1942 by Walter Prescott Webb, it was Webb's desire "to preserve the building and to restore it as nearly as possible to its original state." He became engrossed with the ranch and was determined to restore its depleted grassland and water. During the drouth years of the late 1940's and early 1950's, he continued to apply commercial fertilizer to land no longer tillable, and planted seed, slowly restoring the soil and growing a turf of grass. He built barns, bought and sold cattle and hogs, cut cedar so the grass and oaks could grow. Game was plentiful, but no hunting was allowed.

In November, 1946, Webb met with his friend, Rodney J. Kidd, and they decided to open a boys' summer camp at the ranch the following summer. Friday Mountain Camp for boys has continued in operation every summer since its opening in 1947. Leaving the operation of the camp to Kidd, Webb maintained his interest in the soil, the water, and the grasses.

From 1949 to 1956 the Austin public schools engaged in a program, the first of its kind in Texas, to take sixth grade boys and girls, staggered throughout the school term, for a week's stay (Monday through Friday) at the ranch. Boys occupied cabins, and girls stayed on the second floor of the main house. The program stressed nature study, self-reliance, and appreciation of the pioneer spirit.

Throughout the years of Webb's ownership the great limestone building at Friday Mountain was the scene of retreats for Webb and his friends, with serious discussions mixed with good humor. Roy Bedichek,qv urged by Webb and J. Frank Dobie,qv went into seclusion at the ranch to write his classic *Adventures with a Texas Naturalist* (1947).

When Webb died on March 8, 1963, he had made arrangements for Rodney Kidd to purchase the ranch, knowing that his friend would continue to maintain the turf and operate the summer camp. Webb's friends continued to meet at the ranch occasionally to honor his memory, and on March 8, 1969, the great stone house was again filled with friends and admirers who came from all parts of Texas to create a perpetual memorial: The Walter Prescott Webb Great Frontier Foundation. Friday Mountain Ranch had brought together Webb's ideals of historical preservation and the conservation of natural and human resources. It remains a continuing memorial.

BIBLIOGRAPHY: T. U. Taylor, "Johnson Institute," *Frontier Times*, XVIII (February, 1941); Walter Prescott Webb, "Texas Collection," *Southwestern Historical Quarterly*, XLVI (1942–1943); Roy Bedichek, *Adventures with a Texas Naturalist* (1947); Dudley R. Dobie, *A Brief History of Hays County and San Marcos, Texas* (1948); Ronnie Dugger (ed.), *Three Men In Texas* (1967); C. B. Smith, Sr. (ed.), *Walter Prescott Webb: From the Great Frontier to the Threshold of Space* (1969).

Eldon S. Branda

*Friedland, Texas.

*Friend, William R.

*Friendship, Texas. (Denton County.)

*Friendship, Texas. (Milam County.)

*Friendship, Texas. (Williamson County.)

*Friendsted, Texas.

*Friendswood, Texas. Friendswood, in Galveston County, reported only 75 inhabitants in 1965, but by 1970, according to the United States census, the population was 5,675.

*Frijole, Texas.

*Frijole Peak.

*Frio County. Frio County had 10,112 inhabitants in 1960 and 11,159 in 1970. Frio County State Park (*see* Parks, State), the Big Foot Wallace Museum, and plentiful and diverse game support a small tourist industry. The Medina Electric Cooperative power plant, completed in 1962, is located in Frio County. A city-county library is maintained at the county seat, Pearsall. Minerals providing much of the county's wealth are silica, brick clay, gravel, gas, and oil. Over forty-one million barrels of oil were produced between 1934 and January 1, 1973. Over fifteen thousand irrigated acres yield carrots, watermelons, peanuts, broomcorn, and various grains, while cattle ranching is promoted in other areas of the county.

*Frio Creek.

*Frio Hill.

*Frio River.

*Frio Town, Texas.

*Friona, Texas. Friona, site of the only hospital in Parmer County, reported twelve churches, a school, a bank, a library, a radio station, and a newspaper in 1966. In 1967 the town was the farming-trading center of the county, with over 140 businesses principally concerned with wheat, vegetable and sugar beet processing, and cattle. In 1965 the town completed a high school. Incorporated in 1929 with a council-manager form of government, Friona almost doubled its population between 1950 and 1960, reporting 1,202 for 1950 and 2,048 for 1960. The 1970 population was 3,111.

*Frisco, Texas. Frisco, in Collin County, had a population count of 1,184 in 1960 and 1,845 in 1970, an increase of 55.8 percent.

*Frisco Creek.

*Frisco System in Texas.

*Fritch, Texas. Fritch, in southwestern Hutchinson County and partly in Moore County, was incorporated in 1959. Its industry centers around oil and gas, with some ranching and farming in the vicinity. In 1966 Fritch reported two schools, six churches, and one bank. In 1970 it had thirty businesses. Fritch offers water sports on nearby Lake Meredith and easy access to the Alibates Flint Quarries National Monument.qv The 1960 population was 1,617; the 1970 count was 1,778.

*Frog Creek.

*Frog Pond Creek.

*Frontera, Texas.

*Frontier Battalion.

*Frontier Echo.

*Frontier Regiment.

*Frontier Times. Frontier Times was purchased in 1957 by Joe Austell Small and issued as a quarterly until January, 1963, when it became a bimonthly. Texas material continues to be featured, but true stories of any state in the pioneer West are also included. Frontier Times was incorporated into Western Publications in December, 1962. The magazine is edited and published in Austin, Texas, and in 1974 had a circulation of over 150,000; Pat Wagner was editor. Beginning in 1973 Western Publications began printing in facsimile the original Frontier Times published by John Marvin Hunter,qv with the first issue dated October 1, 1923; by the summer of 1974 nine monthly issues had been printed in facsimile.

                                        Joe Small

*Frontier Times Museum.

Fronton, Texas. Fronton, in southwestern Starr County, was founded about 1770. The name is said to have been derived from a solid rock bank on the Rio Grande, downstream and across from the community. The bank was called El Acha but later became known as Fronton. In 1939 inhabitants of the community organized a cooperative irrigation system, the first in the area. The 1970 population was approximately one hundred.

*Froon, Texas.

*Frost, Samuel R.

*Frost, Texas.

*Frost Town, Texas.

*Fruitdale, Texas.

*Fruitland, Texas.

*Fruits Other Than Citrus. Following World War II, approximately 50 percent of the Texas fruit crop was sold fresh from market bins. With the advent of frozen foods, however, the demand for fully ripened fruits increased. By 1962 more than 60 percent of the Texas fruit crop went through some kind of processing, either drying, canning, or freezing. The location of Texas fruit industries near population centers was an advantage for the future growth of that industry. Problems encountered by fruit growers in the mid-1960's included rising production costs, bracero labor, lack of mechanization, and lack of water.

Peach production in 1954 totaled 180,000 bushels valued at $675,000. The following year, however, only thirty thousand bushels were produced because of a severe spring freeze. Despite this, Texas ranked sixth in United States production of peaches during the period from 1953 to 1957. The 1958 crop increased to approximately one million bushels, the largest harvest in nine years. In the 1959 agricultural census, Texas had 7,634 farms reporting 806,309 peach trees; the following year the number of trees had increased to approximately 1,500,000. Commercial output increased in the 1960's with production concentrated in ten Texas counties in west-central and East Texas totaling approximately 60 percent of the state's peaches. The frozen food industry's demand for larger tree-ripened peaches, as well as the market for fresh peaches in the summer, continued to increase in the early 1960's, and by 1964 production totaled 550,000 bushels valued at $1,760,000. In studies devoted to the development of an improved system of marketing, it was found that Texas peaches accounted for 65 percent of the total sales of stone fruit in the state. Production of peaches on more than seven thousand farms continued its expansion during the mid-1960's with the 1965 crop totaling 560,000 bushels valued at $2,016,000; the following year the harvest jumped to 700,000 bushels valued at $2,205,000. Texas peach trees at this time numbered over 600,000. The yield for 1970 was 688,000 bushels of peaches, worth $2,326,000.

In the 1950's pear production in Texas remained widely scattered, the chief concentration being in the Panhandle Plains, North Texas, and the upper Rio Grande Valley. Nearly all of the pears were sold locally or consumed at home. In 1960 Texas had 90,949 pear trees on 5,936 farms; four years later the number of pear trees had declined to 57,351.

In the late 1950's plums accounted for 30 percent of the total stone fruit sales in Texas. Commercial production was centered in East Texas. In 1960 the agricultural census reported 257,153 plum trees on 4,703 farms. The total number of plum trees decreased during the mid-1960's, numbering 117,878 in 1964. Production was estimated at 50,000 bushels in 1969.

Experiments were conducted in producing hybrid Texas grapes. By 1960 over one hundred experimental varieties, called French-American hybrids, illustrated the development of hybrids from old world grapes and American species. Several wild Texas grapes were used in this blending process. Grape production centered in Montague, Denton, Wise, Grayson, Wichita, San Patricio, El Paso, Reeves, and Wheeler counties on 2,847 farms. Although wineries at Del Rio, Newcastle, and Fredericksburg used a small portion of the harvest, most grapes were sold locally or consumed at home.

Texas was not a leading state in strawberry production, growing less than 1 percent of the nation's strawberries in 1958. The following year, however, the 600 harvested acres yielded 2,200 pounds per acre. In 1960 the Department of Agriculture indicated that annual Texas strawberry production had increased 13.7 percent over its 1949–1958 average of 1,478,000 pounds. Four years later the average annual total had climbed to 2,600,000 pounds. Texas was also one of the three states which grew early spring strawberries. Principal commercial strawberry shipments were made from Hidalgo, Atascosa, and Wood counties.

Blackberries, dewberries, and related berries were sold locally in many eastern and northeastern Texas counties. Smith County remained the nation's principal market and shipping point for blackberries during the 1950's and 1960's. The four main Texas varieties were cultivated on six thousand acres, with 90 percent of the average annual harvest of four million pounds being either canned or frozen; only 10 percent of the crop was sold fresh in markets in 1962.

Figs were grown in most parts of the state. Considerable commercial production was noted in the Gulf Coast area, with emphasis on preserving. Total 1964 production from the 57,466 fig trees located on 2,805 farms was over a million pounds. Cherry, apricot, avocado, mango, papaya, and persimmon trees scattered in areas across the state allowed limited production. *See also* Agriculture in Texas; Grape Culture.

BIBLIOGRAPHY: *Texas Business Review* (November, 1958, June, 1960, December, 1966); *Texas Almanac* (1955, 1963, 1965, 1967, 1971); *Texas Agricultural Progress* (January-February, 1960, July-August, 1962, January-February, 1963, Spring, 1964); Texas Agricultural Experiment Station, *Bulletin*, No. 986 (1961), No. 990 (1962).

*Fruitvale, Texas.

*Fry, Benjamin Franklin.

*Fry, Texas.

*Frydek, Texas.

*Frying Pan Ranch.

*Fuchs, Adolph.

*Fuchs, Texas.

*Fueldale, Texas.

Fuerte del Santa Cruz. Fuerte del Santa Cruz, situated on the west bank of Cibolo Creek near Carvajal Crossing qv in present Karnes County, was used as a Spanish garrison on two different occasions in the eighteenth century. The Spaniards referred to the wedge of land between the San Antonio River and Arroyo del Cíbolo as El Rincón, meaning "the corner." Because of Indian depredations in and around San Antonio, Governor Manuel de Sandoval qv in 1734 decided to protect the presidial horse ranch by moving it to this site on Cibolo Creek, sixteen leagues distant from San Antonio, where a garrison with a small detachment of soldiers was established. The site became known by various names: Fuerte del Santa Cruz; Fuerte del Santa Cruz de Cíbolo; Santa Cruz del Cíbolo; Fuerte del Cíbolo; and El Cíbolo. This first attempt to establish the fort was short-lived, however, for after two Indian raids in 1737 both the garison and the

horses were moved back to San Antonio.

In 1770 citizens of San Antonio remonstrated that the increasing hostility of Indians had caused the abandonment of numerous ranches to the south, and the governor was requested to reestablish the garrison. Accordingly, Governor Juan María Vicencio de Ripperdá qv ordered the fort to be built. By June, 1771, official recognition was again given the fort, and twenty soldiers were to be stationed there permanently. Plans to settle the frontier region of El Rincón, however, did not meet with success, for by the year 1782 Comanche depredations had become so severe that most of the ranches again were abandoned.

BIBLIOGRAPHY: Helmuth H. Schuenemann, "The Karnes County Story," *Karnes County Centennial* (1954); Herbert E. Bolton, *Texas in the Middle Eighteenth Century* (1915); Juan Agustín Morfi (C. E. Castañeda, trans.), *History of Texas, 1673–1779* (1935); Robert H. Thonhoff, A History of Karnes County, Texas (M.A. thesis, Southwest Texas State College, 1963).

Robert H. Thonhoff

*Fulbright, Texas.

*Fulcher Creek.

Fulgham, Robert Cummins. Robert Cummins Fulgham was born in Twiggs County, Georgia, on February 6, 1817, the son of Micajah and Rachel (Taylor) Fulgham, both of Virginia origin. The family left Georgia and settled in 1820 in Lawrence County, Mississippi, where in 1838 Fulgham married Eleanor Madoriah Kirkwood. In the following year the couple moved to Tyler County, Texas, and established a plantation near present Colmesneil. In 1839 Fulgham, together with his two brothers, Ezekiel and Jesse, and his father-in-law, George Kirkwood, received headright grants of 640 acres each from the Republic of Texas.

Fulgham was first clerk and later moderator of the Louisiana-Texas Predestinarian Baptist Association from 1850 to about 1870. In 1861 he became chief justice of Tyler County and served in that capacity during the entire Civil War period until removed by the Reconstruction qv government in 1867. Justice of the peace for many years, Fulgham was elected county tax assessor-collector in 1890 and served until his death on July 14, 1893.

BIBLIOGRAPHY: J. B. Boddie, *Historical Southern Families*, III (1959); Minutes of the County Court of Tyler County, Texas, 1861–1867 (County Clerk's Office, Woodville); H. P. N. Gammel (comp.), *Laws of Texas, 1822–1897* (1898).

John P. Landers

Fuller, Franklin Oliver. Franklin Oliver Fuller was born on November 2, 1872, in Melrose, Texas, the son of Benjamin Franklin and Josephine (Green) Fuller, who came to Texas from Alabama in 1838. Fuller married Lizzie Holt on April 28, 1895, in San Augustine. They lived in Huntsville, where he attended Sam Houston State College, later moving to Oakhurst, San Jacinto County, to teach school. They made their home in 1900 in Coldspring, where he was admitted to the Bar in 1901 and served as county attorney from 1904 to 1906.

Fuller served as state representative from the Nineteenth District, and was speaker of the House for the Thirty-fifth Legislature when impeachment proceedings were filed against Governor James E. Ferguson.qv He served in the Texas National Guard,qv and was commissioned captain in the United States Army Judge Advocate Department. He moved to Houston in 1920, where he died on August 7, 1934, survived by his wife and five children.

Billie Trapp

*Fullerton, Texas.

*Fullerville, Texas.

*Fullinwider, Peter Hunter.

*Fulmore, Zachary Taylor. Zachary Taylor Fulmore was appointed a member of the commission to select a site for and to organize the State School for the Colored Blind and Deaf (later Texas Blind, Deaf, and Orphan School qv) in 1887 (not 1875, as stated in Volume I).

*Fulshear, Churchill.

*Fulshear, Churchill, Jr.

*Fulshear, Texas.

*Fulton, George W.

*Fulton, George W., Jr.

*Fulton, James C.

*Fulton, Roger Lawson. Roger Lawson Fulton was defeated in his first campaign for mayor of Galveston in 1873 (not 1875, as stated in Volume I). He was first elected mayor in 1875 (not 1877); he was again elected mayor in 1883, and was re-elected for four two-year terms until he was defeated in 1893; thus, he served as mayor of Galveston for twelve years, ten of which were consecutive.

BIBLIOGRAPHY: *Charter and Revised Ordinances of the City of Galveston* (1875); *History of Texas together with a Biographical History of the Cities of Houston and Galveston* (1895).

Bob Dalehite

*Fulton, Samuel Moore.

*Fulton, Texas. Fulton, an unincorporated town

in Aransas County, had a population of 1,101 in 1970, according to the United States census.

*Funston, Texas. (Jefferson County.)

*Funston, Texas. (Jones County.)

*Fuqua, Benjamin.

*Fuqua, Texas.

*Furnash, Charles.

Furr, Crone Webster. Crone Webster Furr, food merchant, was born to John Allan and Martha Ann Furr on May 8, 1878, in Stanly County, North Carolina. He attended a country school near his birthplace.

In 1894 the family moved to Collin County, Texas, and young Furr became a farmer near McKinney; he began operating a small crossroads grocery store in addition to his farm. In 1896 he married Annie Furr (no relation), and they had three children. In 1904 he moved to Kirkland and established the Kirkland Mercantile Company. Four years later he organized the First State Bank of Kirkland. In 1924 Furr bought the M System franchise for grocery stores in the Amarillo area; in 1928 he acquired the franchise for Piggly Wiggly stores in Amarillo. By 1946 his family-run enterprises included forty-three supermarkets in an area from Denver, Colorado, to El Paso and Odessa in West Texas, and into eastern New Mexico and western Oklahoma, as well as a wholesale grocery firm in El Paso, a creamery, bakery, packing plant, and warehouse in Lubbock, and a packing plant in Amarillo. He was a deacon of the Polk Street Methodist Church in Amarillo. Furr died on October 30, 1946, in Amarillo and was buried there.

BIBLIOGRAPHY: Seymour V. Connor (ed.), *Builders of the Southwest* (1959); Amarillo *Sunday News-Globe*, August 14, 1938; *Furr's Magazine* (October, 1946); Amarillo *Daily News*, October 31, 1946; Lubbock *Morning Avalanche*, December 5, 1958.

Lawrence L. Graves

*Furrh, Texas.

*Fuzzy Creek.

G

GI Forum. *See* American GI Forum of Texas.

*G. T. T.

Gabriel Mills, Texas. Gabriel Mills, Williamson County, received its name about 1850, when a gristmill was built on the North Fork of the San Gabriel River by Samuel Mather. Later a post office was established. During the Civil War, Edmund Crim and H. T. Norton served as postmasters. Gabriel Mills continued as a post office until about 1910.

Cyrus Tilloson

*Gabriel Mountain.

*Gaceta de Tejas.

*Gaffords Chapel, Texas.

*Gage, David.

*Gage, Texas.

*Gageby, Texas. Gageby, formerly in Hemphill County and currently in northwestern Wheeler County, was founded in 1907 and named for nearby Gageby Creek. From 1910 to 1920 the town had a post office, a barber shop, a general store, a service station, a blacksmith shop, and an average population of ten. Gageby was a cream station from 1910 to 1925. During the 1930's and 1940's the population fluctuated between twenty and fifty. In 1945 the store was moved two miles southwest to U.S. Highway 83. The population in 1964 was two. By 1967 the count was five, but in 1970 no persons were reported living there.

*Gageby Creek.

*Gages Creek.

*Gail, Texas.

*Gail Peak.

Gaillardet, Frédéric. Théodore-Frédéric Gaillardet, early traveler and writer in Texas, was born April 7, 1808, in Tonnerre, France, the son of Jean-Baptiste and Geneviève-Henry Gaillardet. He took a law degree in Paris and returned to Tonnerre to practice, but soon became successful enough as a dramatist to have three plays produced in Paris in 1832 and 1833. As a dramatist Gaillardet is chiefly remembered for his first success, *La Tour de Nesle,* which was rewritten by Alexandre Dumas *père,* frequently revived during the nineteenth century, and twice translated into English. Dumas attempted to take all credit for the play, and Gaillardet retaliated with a duel and legal action. Before coming to America, he also published a well-received novel which became the source of several popular dramas and vaudevilles.

In 1837 Gaillardet arrived in New Orleans hoping to contribute articles to Parisian newspapers and also to start a wine importing business, but after bank failures and an epidemic of yellow fever in New Orleans, he conceived the plan of studying the political and social organization of the United States. After visits to Cuba, to Texas, and up the Mississippi River to Indian Territory, Gaillardet settled in New York, where he remained for more than eight years. There he wrote of French affairs for New York newspapers and of American affairs for French newspapers. He owned and edited in New York the leading French language newspaper in the Western Hemisphere, the *Courrier des États-Unis.*

Gaillardet's visit to Texas, from April to July, 1839, coincided with that of Alphonse Dubois de Saligny,qv who accompanied him in his calls upon General Sam Houston and Mirabeau B. Lamar. Gaillardet communicated to Europe a favorable impression of Texas, and his accounts and analyses of events in Texas no doubt helped in bringing about French recognition of Texas' independence from Mexico. Among his important dispatches from Texas are those urging French recognition, a description of the invasions of Anglo Americans into Texas, his accounts of the Texas Revolution, an analysis of the Republic, and a projection of the future for the French in Texas.

After his marriage Gaillardet established his residence in France, where he served as mayor of Le Plessis-Bouchard, and was working on the memoirs of his life in America, which was to have been a companion piece and corrective to Alexis de Tocqueville's *De la Démocratie en Amérique,* when he died in 1882. Parts of these memoirs appeared posthumously in 1883 under the title, *L'Aristocratie en Amérique.*

BIBLIOGRAPHY: Frédéric Gaillardet (James L. Shepherd, III, trans.), *Sketches of Early Texas and Louisiana* (1966).

James L. Shepherd, III

*Gaines, Edmund Pendleton.

*Gaines, James. Although James Gaines indicated that his home was in Natchitoches, Louisiana, on March 31, 1818, when selling a tract of land in Texas (as stated in Volume I), he apparently maintained operations on both sides of the Sabine River from 1812 to 1819; his often repeated claim that he came to Texas in 1812 to make it his home is probably accurate, although for safety's sake his wife and young children resided with her parents on the Louisiana side of the river during the years 1814 to 1819. Gaines apparently was not one of the Americans who resigned in disgust (as stated in Volume I) following the Mexican execution of prominent Spanish soldiers after the battle of Rosalis,qv for he later told Mirabeau B. Lamar qv that he had been commissioned by the Mexican Army to reconcile the other Americans to acceptance of the executions; he also recounted to Lamar an account of the battle of the Medina River,qv which indicates that he was still with the Mexicans in that battle, which followed the battle of Rosalis.

BIBLIOGRAPHY: Charles Adams Gulick, Jr. (ed.), *The Papers of Mirabeau Buonaparte Lamar,* I–VI (1921–1928); L. W. Kemp, General Biographical Notebook (MS., Archives, University of Texas at Austin Library).

Deolece Parmelee

*Gaines, Matthew.

*Gaines, Reuben R.

*Gaines County. Gaines County, through the use of underground water, had 275,000 acres irrigated by 1968. Cotton, grain sorghums, and truck crops accounted for most of the farm income, which amounted to $15,565,000 in 1968 and was averaging over $29,000,000 by 1970. The petroleum industry yielded over 748,000,000 barrels of oil from 1936 to 1973. Cattle and sheep were decreasing in numbers, while peaches and pecans were increasing in importance. The 1960 population was 12,267; in 1970 it was 11,593.

*Gaines Ferry. In 1837 the town of Pendleton, near Gaines Ferry, was surveyed by Thomas S. McFarland qv (not William McFarland,qv as stated in Volume I). *See* Pendleton, Texas (Sabine County).

Deolece Parmelee

Gaines House. The first house encountered by early settlers as they came to Texas via Louisiana and El Camino Real (Old San Antonio Road,qv present-day State Highway 21) was the Gaines house, located on the west bank of the Sabine River and built by James Gaines qv about 1812. Frederick Law Olmsted,qv in his *A Journey Through Texas* (1857), relates that it was the first house he encountered upon entering Texas, that it was a two-story log house with glass windows, and that it ranked high for comfort on the road.

Creation of the Toledo Bend Reservoir qv necessitated the inundation of land upon which the Gaines house was located; therefore, in 1968 the house was dismantled log by log and moved west to an acre of land opposite the road to Lows Chapel, just off Highway 21. The house was not reconstructed as late as 1974. *See also* Oliphint House.

Helen Gomer Schluter

*Gainesmore, Texas.

*Gainesville, Texas. Gainesville, incorporated in 1872, is the seat of Cooke County. Fifty-eight churches, eight schools, two banks, a hospital, and a public library were reported in 1966. Institutions in the county include Cooke County Junior College, which moved to a new campus in 1958; Camp Sweeney, operated for diabetic children by the Southwestern Diabetic Foundation; and Gainesville State School for Girls.qqv Among the city's 313 businesses in 1970 were industries which produced artificial lures, millwork, oil field equipment, clothing, paints, leather goods, iron castings, flour, gasoline, fertilizer, fiberglass items, geophysical instruments, mattresses, boat trailers, and concrete. By 1966 Moss Lake had been completed for use by the city. The population in 1960 was 13,083; the 1970 population was 13,830.

Gainesville, Great Hanging at. The Great Hanging at Gainesville in October, 1862, grew out of the discovery of an alleged "Peace Party Conspiracy"qv and prompt and vigorous moves by Confederate authorities to suppress it. In December, 1861, the Texas legislature had created thirty-three brigade districts designed to insure the internal security of the Confederate state of Texas. District Number 1, with headquarters at Gainesville, the seat of Cooke County, comprised eighteen north and northwest Texas counties, eight of which had cast majorities against the Ordinance of Secession by which Texas withdrew from the Union. Pro-Unionist counties included Cooke, Grayson, Montague, Wise, Jack, Collin, Fannin, and Lamar. (See Secession Convention; Secession in Texas.)

About September 1, 1862, Brigadier General William Hudson, commander at Gainesville, acting on reports reaching him of a Unionist underground movement, conferred with Colonel James Bourland qv (his provost marshal), Lieutenant Colonel James J. Diamond qv of the 11th Texas Cavalry, and others to design a plan by which they might obtain the secret schemes and operations of the conspirators. Through the Gainesville to Denton mail carrier and Colonel J. N. Chance, a resident of Wise County stationed at Gainesville, the military authorities penetrated a secret organization said to number several hundred men. Early on the morning of October 1, 1862, armed forces carried out raids in Cooke County and took sixty to seventy men into custody, bringing them to Gainesville and placing them under guard.

On the same day, Colonel William C. Young,qv commander of the 11th Texas Cavalry, presided over a mass meeting. He named a committee of five, which recommended the names of twelve citizens, military or civilian, who were to constitute a "citizens court." This court was instructed to examine all crimes and offenses committed, determine the innocence or guilt of the accused, and pronounce appropriate punishment. The jury elected Daniel Montague,qv long-time county surveyor and official for whom the adjoining county

had been named in 1858, as president of the court. Bourland was named constable of the court, and all other members were sworn into office by R. G. Piper, chief justice of Cooke County.

In the succeeding weeks the "citizens court" tried and found guilty thirty-nine of those charged with "conspiracy and insurrection," "disloyalty and treason," or a combination of such charges. The court sentenced them to be hanged, and the sentences were carried out in Gainesville. Three other prisoners who were members of Confederate military units were permitted trial by court martial, as they requested, and were subsequently hanged by its order.

The first published account of the organization and operation of the "citizens court" was that of Thomas Barrett,qv a member of the "citizens court." It appeared in Gainesville in 1885 entitled *The Great Hanging at Gainesville, Cooke County, Texas.*

Soon after the events occurred in the fall of 1862, George Washington Diamond,qv a former newspaper publisher of Henderson who had joined the 3rd Texas Cavalry, visited his brother James in Gainesville. G. W. Diamond was asked by his brother and other members of the "citizens court" to write a complete account of the "Peace Party Conspiracy" and the trial of those charged with participating in it. The original court records were turned over to him to be used as the basis of his account. Evidence indicates that he completed his account sometime between 1874 and 1876, but it remained unpublished in the hands of his descendants until January, 1963, when it was published by the Texas State Historical Association in the *Southwestern Historical Quarterly.*qqv It was later issued as a book entitled *George Washington Diamond's Account of the Great Hanging at Gainesville, 1862* (1963).

Sam Acheson

*Gainesville College.

*Gainesville Community Circus. At one time the third largest circus in the world, the Gainesville Community Circus had equipment valued between $60,000 and $100,000 in its circus barn, which was destroyed by an early-morning fire in 1954.

A nonprofit, community-wide hobby, the circus was manned completely by performers who served without pay. All performers were amateurs who had conventional ways of making a living; professional circus people were sometimes invited to go to Gainesville as instructors in circus skills.

The group performed in the Cotton Bowl qv in 1936 during the Texas Centennial.qv During 1947, one of its peak years, it played twelve engagements, which included twenty-nine performances to more than 120,000 circus fans. General Jonathan Wainwright,qv Elliott Roosevelt, and Frank Buck qv (a Gainesville native) have served as honorary ringmasters.

The United States Department of State in 1950 made a Voice of America movie about the Gainesville circus and distributed the film abroad, citing it as an example of cooperation and team spirit in American community life.

Seven tents, including the Big Top, parade wagons, calliopes, ring curbs, trapeze riggings, acrobatic props, and a twenty-four-year accumulation of costumes were lost in the 1954 fire, but three elephants were rescued. In the 1960's Gainesville Circus, Incorporated, continued as a nonprofit corporation.

Anita Brewer

*Gainesville, Henrietta, and Western Railway Company.

Gainesville Junior College. *See* Cooke County Junior College.

*Gainesville State School for Girls. The Gainesville State School for Girls was placed under the administration of the Texas Youth Council qv by the Fifty-fifth Legislature. From 1966 to 1967 the average population was 364; there were 390 girls there in 1973.

Intensified renovation of existing facilities, construction of additional dormitories, and the establishment of a security-treatment cottage have made the school one of the finest training institutions for delinquent females in America. A new hospital-reception building provides modern equipment for proper orientation and classification.

BIBLIOGRAPHY: Texas Youth Council, *Annual Report* (1965); *Texas Almanac* (1973).

William T. Field

*Galena Park, Texas. Galena Park, located near the highly industrialized Houston Ship Channel qv in Harris County, was incorporated in 1935, and has a home-rule type of municipal government. In 1966 there were four public schools within the city limits, a hospital, a bank, two libraries, and thirteen churches. In 1970 there were 100 businesses in Galena Park. The city's most important economic sources were the nearby steel mills, chemical plants, refineries, and other heavy industrial plants. Galena Park's population increased dramatically in three decades, from 1,562 in 1940, to 7,186 in 1950, to 10,852 in 1960, and then fell slightly, to 10,479 in 1970. *See also* Houston Standard Metropolitan Statistical Area.

　*Galgo, Texas.

　*Galilee, Texas.

　*Gallagher, Nicholas Aloysius.

　*Gallagher, Peter.

　*Gallagher's Ranch.

　*Gallatin, Albert. Albert Gallatin, a participant in the battle of San Jacinto, was in William Ware's qv (not William Ward's,qv as stated in Volume I) 2nd Company, 2nd Regiment of Texas Volunteers. Gallatin died on February 16, 1898 (not February 17, 1896), in Brazos County.

Albert R. Gallatin

　*Gallatin, Texas.

　*Galle, Texas.

　*Gallinas Creek.

　*Galloway, Texas.

　*Galvan Creek.

　*Galveston, Texas. Galveston, in Galveston County, changed its form of government in 1961 to the city manager-council plan. A new causeway had been added by 1964, giving greater access to the mainland at the west end of the city, and a modern toll-free ferry system was the link between the city and Bolivar Peninsula on the east. Bonds were voted in 1963 to build a bridge across San Luis Pass at the west end of the island to tie Brazoria County into the coastal highway from New Orleans to Brownsville. By 1966 the San Luis-Vacek Bridge had been completed.

In 1964 Galveston's principal exports were cotton, grain, flour, and cattle. Raw sugar was the major import. The city was the nation's major cotton port, shipping approximately one-third of the U.S. cotton exports. Customs receipts for the district in 1963 were $36,095,400. District headquarters for the United States Bureau of Customs and the United States Army Corps of Engineers were located in that city.

In addition to its import and export activities, Galveston was the home service port of the N. S. *Savannah*, the world's first nuclear-powered merchant vessel. Galveston's industries included grain elevators, cotton compresses, dry docks, boat and marine shops, off-shore drilling services, a large brewery, a nail factory, a metal container manufacturer, a tea blending plant, and commercial fishing.

Pelican Island, which adjoins Galveston, was in an advanced stage of development for industrial purposes in 1964. The Moody Center was given to the city of Galveston by the Moody Foundation in 1964 to increase Galveston's convention facilities. Institutions in Galveston included the United States Marine Hospital, the Moody State School for Cerebral Palsied Children,qv the biological laboratories of the Parks and Wildlife Department,qv the Texas Maritime Academy,qv St. Mary's Infirmary, and the Shrine Burn Hospital, one of three national Shrine hospitals for the study and treatment of children's burns. The 1960 population of the city was 67,175, and in 1970 it was 61,809. *See also* Galveston-Texas City Standard Metropolitan Statistical Area.

　*Galveston, Battle of.

　*Galveston Bay.

　*Galveston Bay and Texas Land Company.

　*Galveston *Beacon*.

　*Galveston, Brazos, and Colorado Railroad.

　*Galveston and Brazos Navigation Company.

　Galveston City Company. *See* Galveston, Texas; Borden, Gail, Jr.

　Galveston College. Galveston College, Galveston, was created in 1966, and David G. Hunt was named the first president in 1967. The college opened in September, 1967, with an enrollment of 672. The school offered the first two years of standard college work leading to an associate in arts or sciences degree, as well as technical and vocational courses leading to an associate in applied arts or sciences degree. During 1967–1968 the college held classes in college-owned and public school facilities. Its library contained 9,500 volumes in 1969. The school is a member of the American Association of Junior Colleges, the Texas Association of Junior Colleges, and the Texas Association of Public Junior Colleges. Melvin M. Plexco was president in the fall term of 1974, when enrollment was 1,888.

*Galveston County. Galveston County, on the Gulf Coast, produced oil, sulphur, field crops, poultry, and truck crops in 1970. From 1922 to 1973, oil production totaled over 336 million barrels. The county's economy centered around Galveston and Texas City, where industries and shipping were concentrated. As a result of the tidelands decision (*see* Tidelands Controversy), Galveston County received 609 square miles of submerged land. In 1960 the county had 140,364 inhabitants; in 1970 it had 169,812. *See also* Galveston-Texas City Standard Metropolitan Statistical Area.

*Galveston Female Collegiate Institute. *See* Galveston Seminary.

*Galveston Flood. *See also* Hurricanes in Texas.

*Galveston, Harrisburg, and San Antonio Railway. *See also* Peirce, Thomas Wentworth.

Galveston Historical Foundation. The Galveston Historical Society,^{qv} continuing to emphasize research, published and sold five thousand copies of *Historic Galveston Homes* in 1951. Ruth G. Nichols and S. W. Lifflander compiled a calendar of the Samuel May Williams ^{qv} papers; it was published by Galveston's Rosenberg Library ^{qv} in 1956 as *Samuel May Williams, 1795–1858.*

Aroused by the destruction of old homes in Galveston, but not organized to buy and own real property, the society formed the Galveston Historical Foundation on November 23, 1954, with Mrs. Paul Brindley as president. Its purpose was to preserve historic homes; in May, 1955, it acquired the Samuel May Williams-Philip Crosby Tucker ^{qv} home, built in 1839–1840. The house was opened to the public on April 15, 1959, after extensive preservation work and repairs. Projects in the mid-1970's included the restoration of Ashton Villa and a five-block area known as The Strand, of which two buildings had been sold by the foundation's revolving fund by 1974. Membership in the Galveston Historical Foundation was 1,200 in 1974; at that time the executive director was Peter Brink and the president was M. L. Ross. *See* Galveston Historical Society in Volume I.

Anne A. Brindley

*Galveston Historical Society. *See also* Galveston Historical Foundation.

*Galveston, Houston, and Henderson Railroad Company. The Galveston, Houston, and Henderson Railroad Company constructed the first railroad bridge crossing from Galveston to the mainland in 1858, a two-mile connection which opened the port to railroad service from Houston and beyond.

In the mid-1960's the road was owned jointly by the Missouri, Kansas, and Texas Railway Company and the Missouri-Pacific, each of which controlled 50 percent of the stock. It operated a little over twenty-five miles of first main-line track in Texas.

James M. Day

*Galveston, Houston, and Northern Railway Company.

*Galveston Island.

Galveston Island Junior College. *See* Galveston College.

*Galveston, La Porte, and Houston Railway Company. *See* Galveston, Houston, and Northern Railway Company.

*Galveston Medical College. *See* Texas Medical College.

**Galveston Medical Journal.*

*Galveston News. The A. H. Belo ^{qv} Corporation in 1923 sold the Galveston *News* to William L. Moody, Jr.,^{qv} and Louis C. Elbert succeeded John F. Lubben (not John F. Lubber, as stated in Volume I). In 1926 (not 1923) the Moody company bought the Galveston *Tribune*, and both papers, with Silas B. Ragsdale as managing editor, were published in the *News* plant.

The Moody Foundation in 1963 engineered the sale of the Galveston *News* and *Tribune* (plus the Texas City *Sun*, which it also owned) to the W. P. Hobby ^{qv} interests of Houston. In 1965 the *Tribune* was merged with the *News*, which became an afternoon paper Monday through Friday, with a Sunday morning edition. The old *News* building, designed by architect Nicolas Clayton,^{qv} and called a model for newspaper publishing when it was erected in 1883–1884, was abandoned in favor of a modern structure not far from the Galveston causeway, where the *News*, the Texas City *Sun*, and a mainland paper, *Today—News-Sun*, were published by Hobby's Galveston County Publishing Company. In June, 1967, the Galveston County Publishing Company was sold to a corporation headed by newspaper executives from Montgomery, Alabama, and Bristol, Tennessee. The *News* again became a morning paper, published by Galveston Newspapers, Inc. Les Daughtry served as publisher in Galveston.

Silas B. Ragsdale

*Galveston Plan of City Government. *See* Commission Form of City Government.

*Galveston and Red River Railroad Company. *See* Houston and Texas Central Railroad.

*Galveston, Sabine, and St. Louis Railway.

Galveston Screwmen's Benevolent Association. *See* Screwmen's Benevolent Association.

**Galveston Seminary.*

*Galveston State Psychopathic Hospital. *See also* University of Texas Medical Branch at Galveston.

*Galveston Terminal Railway Company. The Galveston Terminal Railway Company's 4.4 miles of track were operated under lease from June, 1931, by the Burlington-Rock Island, until that railroad was sold in 1964. The Galveston Terminal in the 1960's was controlled through stock ownership by the Chicago, Rock Island and Pacific, and the Colorado and Southern.

James M. Day

Galveston-Texas City Standard Metropolitan Statistical Area. The Galveston Standard Metropolitan Statistical Area was created by the United States Bureau of the Budget in 1949. In 1950 the population of the area, which consisted of 429 square miles of Galveston County, was 113,066, while Galveston, the core city, had 66,568 residents. In August, 1960, the Bureau of the Budget added Texas City to the area's title, now officially designated as the Galveston-Texas City Standard Metropolitan Statistical Area. The population figures for that year were 140,364 inhabitants in the area, 67,-175 in Galveston, and 32,065 in Texas City. The 1970 population of the area was 169,812 persons. The residents of Galveston and Texas City numbered 61,809 and 38,908, respectively. Other towns with more than one thousand persons are La Marque, Alta Loma, Port Bolivar, Bacliff, Dickinson, Hitchcock, and League City. Smaller communities include Kemah, Gilchrist, Friendswood, Arcadia, High Island, Algoa, San Leon, Clear Lake Shores, and Clifton-by-the-Sea.

Galveston and Texas City are deepwater ports. Texas City ranked fifth among the ports of Texas in 1971 with over seventeen million tons. The port of Galveston, located only ten miles from the open waters of the Gulf of Mexico, was ninth in total tonnage in Texas with 3,952,969 tons. Both cities have a forty-foot-deep ship channel and are protected by high seawalls and dikes. The major foreign imports are sugar and bananas, while wheat, dry sulphur, grain sorghums, and cotton are the main products shipped to foreign countries. Galveston is the chief cotton port in the United States. While Galveston handles most of the foreign trade, Texas City dominates the coastal shipping, which includes gasoline, fuel oils, kerosene, alcohols, petroleum asphalt, industrial chemicals, and coal tar products.

The leading industries of Galveston County are petroleum refining and petrochemicals (*see* Petrochemical Industry). Seven major petroleum and chemical plants, all located in Texas City, provide employment for more than nine thousand persons with an annual payroll of seventy-five million dollars. The metropolitan area has ten oil fields and over 450 producing wells. More fields are being developed offshore in the 609-square-mile tidelands of the county. The Wah Chang Corporation, located in Texas City since 1941, operates the world's largest tin smelter. It produces about one-third of the primary tin used by the United States and is the only tin smelter in the western hemisphere (*see* Tin Smelting in Texas). Galveston is less industrialized than Texas City; its major industries include seafood processing, shipbuilding, meat packing, brew-

ing, tea processing, flour milling, and metal production.

Despite the rapid industrialization of the area, agriculture and fishing remain an important part of the economy. Rice, grain, vegetables, hay, poultry, livestock, and dairy products contributed over five million dollars to the income of the county in 1966. About twelve thousand acres are irrigated in the county. In 1966 commercial fishermen caught over thirteen million pounds of shrimp, oysters, crabs, and fish in the Galveston waters. In 1970 the catch was 8,331,600 pounds, valued at $7,579,638. The island city is headquarters for a shrimp fleet.

The field of education employs over five thousand persons, with about three-fifths of these working at the University of Texas Medical Branch qv at Galveston. In 1966 the new Shrine Burn Hospital for children was added to the medical branch complex. The oldest educational institution in the area is Ursuline Academy qv in Galveston. The Texas A&M University research laboratory and the Texas Maritime Academy qv were located at Fort Crockett.qv Two new junior colleges, College of the Mainland and Galveston College,qqv began operation in September, 1967, at Texas City and Galveston, respectively. Rosenberg Library qv in Galveston and public libraries in Texas City, La Marque, and Friendswood serve the area. Cultural attractions include performances by the Galveston County Civic Music Association.

Galveston Island has always been a tourist mecca, but in recent years tourism has become important to the whole area. The thirty-three miles of sloping beaches on Galveston Island offer year-round fishing, swimming, boating, and surfing. The Sea-Arama, a Gulf marine aquarium opened in 1965, attracts thousands of visitors. Galveston, Texas City, and Kemah have piers and docking facilities for pleasure craft. Splash Day, which officially opens the summer tourist season, is the big annual event in the area. Galveston has one of the finest collections of Victorian buildings extant in the United States today. About forty-five buildings and sites, including the Bishop's Palace, The Oaks, and the Williams-Tucker Home, have historical markers. Three radio stations, two daily newspapers, two railroads, one airline, and a good highway system, including Interstate 45, serve the county. *See also* Standard Metropolitan Statistical Areas in Texas.

Anne A. Brindley
Agnes Lowry
Emmett Lowry
Meriworth Mabry
Pat Updegrove

*Galveston University. *See also* Presbyterian Education in Texas.

*Galveston *Weekly News*. *See* Galveston *News*.

*Galveston and Western Railroad.

Galveston Wharves. Prior to 1854 the wharves at Galveston were owned and operated by numerous individuals and companies, but on February 4, 1854, a charter was issued by the Texas legislature authorizing Michael B. Menard qv and associates to incorporate under the name of the Galveston Wharf and Cotton Press Company and to assume "complete control over all waterfront facilities then existing in Galveston." In 1860 the charter of the company was amended to give it the title of the Galveston Wharf Company. Nine years later the city obtained one-third of the company's stock. In 1940 the citizens of Galveston voted to purchase the facilities of the company. In 1967 the "Galveston Wharves" was really the Port of Galveston Authority, which operated the docks, warehouses, and railroad facilities for the port. It is the only major port terminal in the United States not supported by public funds. Its railroad operation consists of switching and loading, for which it operates five diesel switch engines and three locomotive cranes, as well as 45.8 miles of terminal track.

James M. Day

*Galvestonian.

*Gálvez, Bernardo de.

*Gambrell, James Bruton.

*Gambrell, Joel Halbert.

*Game, Fish, and Oyster Commission. *See also* Parks and Wildlife Department, Texas.

*Gammel, Hans Peter Nielson.

*Ganado, Texas. Ganado, Jackson County, had a population of 1,626 in 1960 and 1,640 in 1970.

*Gander Slu, Texas.

*Gano, Richard Montgomery. Richard Montgomery Gano was a colonel (not a brigadier general, as stated in Volume I) while serving with General John H. Morgan. He was made brigadier general in March, 1865, one of the last to be appointed. Gano was not the last living officer of equal or higher rank at the time of his death (as stated in Volume I). Many others survived him, the last being Brigadier General Felix Robertson,qv who died in 1928.

Gano's Texas Cavalry Battalion. Gano's Texas Cavalry Battalion, also called Gano Guards and Gano's Squadron, was composed of two companies of Texas cavalry which were the nucleus of the 7th Kentucky Cavalry Regiment, of which Lieutenant Colonel Richard M. Gano qv was the original commander. The battalion of five hundred men was merged into the Kentucky unit in September of 1862. *See* Gano, Richard Montgomery.
BIBLIOGRAPHY: Lester N. Fitzhugh, *Texas Batteries, Battalions, Regiments, Commanders and Field Officers, Confederate States Army, 1861–1865* (1959); Harry McCorry Henderson, *Texas in the Confederacy* (1955).

*Gant, William W.

*Gantt, William Henry.

*Gaona, Antonio.

*Gap Creek.

*Gapher Creek.

*Garay, Francisco.

*Garceno, Texas.

*García, Francisco. *See* Larios, Francisco García.

*García, Luciano.

*Garcia, Texas.

*Garcia Creek.

*Garcia Lake.

*García Library. *See* Latin American Collection.

*Garciasville, Texas.

*Garcitas Creek.

*Garden City, Texas. Garden City is the county seat of Glasscock County (not Glascock County, as stated in Volume I). The city had a population of 286 in 1970, most of whom ranched, farmed, or worked in oil fields.

Garden Ridge, Texas. Garden Ridge, in Comal County, was incorporated on April 4, 1972, and became the first new city in the county in 127 years. Located south of New Braunfels near the county lines of Comal, Bexar, and Guadalupe counties, Garden Ridge had a population of approximately 230 in 1972.

*Garden Valley, Texas.

*Gardendale, Texas.

Gardner, J. Alvin. J. Alvin Gardner was born in Colmesneil, Texas, on April 8, 1890. He moved to Beaumont six years later with his parents and was educated in the public schools there. He received his first taste of baseball when he served as bat boy for the Beaumont club of the South Texas League (*see* Texas League) in 1903–1904. He went to work in 1907 for Gulf Production Company and remained with that company for seventeen years, including service in Tampico, Mexico, where he organized a city baseball league.

Gardner lived in Shreveport from 1914 to 1918 and opened Gulf's Fort Worth office in 1918. The following year he was transferred to Wichita Falls in charge of its North Texas division. He resigned in 1924 to go into business as a drilling contractor and producer with his brother, Craig T. Gardner. One of the first stockholders in the Wichita Falls Texas League club in 1920, Gardner became a director in 1925. That same year he purchased majority control of the team and owned and operated it until 1929, when he sold his interest. At the October meeting of the Texas League in 1929 he was elected acting vice-president to conduct league affairs during president Doak Roberts' illness. When Roberts died, Gardner was elected to the presidency for a five-year term ending in 1934. He moved the league office to Dallas in November, 1931. Gardner died in Dallas on June 3, 1968, survived by his wife and one daughter; he was buried in Dallas.
BIBLIOGRAPHY: William B. Ruggles, *History of the Texas League of Professional Baseball Clubs* (1932).
Joe B. Frantz

*Gardner, J. W.

*Gardner, Texas.

*Garfield, Texas. (DeWitt County.)

*Garfield, Texas. (Travis County.)

*Garland, Texas. Garland, located in Dallas County, had a 1950 population of 10,571, a 1960 population of 38,501, and a 1970 population of 81,437. In 1970 Garland reported 1,042 businesses. Industries included aerospace, automotive, paint and varnish, electronics, and container manufacturers. *See also* Dallas Standard Metropolitan Statistical Area.

Garland Christian College. *See* Christian College of the Southwest.

*Garner, David.

Garner, John Nance. The thirty-second vice-president of the United States, John Nance Garner, was born on November 22, 1868, in a log cabin in Red River County, Texas, thirty miles from Indian Territory. He was the first of thirteen children born to John Nance and Sarah (Guest) Garner. He went to school at Antioch, to a boarding school at Bogata, and later to high school at Blossom Prairie, where he earned spending money by playing shortstop for the Coon Soup Hollow-Blossom Prairie baseball team. Love for the game stayed with him the remainder of his life, and he was a familiar figure at baseball games in Washington, often taking with him one Democrat and two Republicans in order to keep the party balance.

At the age of eighteen he spent one semester at Vanderbilt, developed a lung condition, and returned to Texas to read law in a Clarksville law firm. When he was twenty-one years old, he was admitted to the Bar. His first venture in politics was an unsuccessful bid for the office of city attorney. Shortly thereafter he sought a drier climate and moved to Uvalde. He joined the law firm of Clark and Fuller and was appointed to fill a vacancy as county judge. When the time came for election to the position, one of his opponents was Miss Mariette Rheiner; Garner won the election, and a few months later, on November 25, 1895, he and Miss Rheiner were married. On September 24, 1896, their only child, a son, Tully, was born.

Garner was elected to the state legislature in 1898. During his first term, he was a member of the judiciary committee, which newspapers christened the "Blue-beard Committee" because of its work on money-spending legislation. He won a second term in the state legislature, presented a redistricting plan which was approved, then ran for and won the new congressional seat.

Garner was thirty-five years old when he went to Washington as Democratic representative from the new Fifteenth Texas Congressional District. He entered the chambers for the first time on November 9, 1903, when Theodore Roosevelt was president and the Republican party was overwhelmingly in power. He fought for an income tax based on the theory of paying according to ability, favored a tariff to protect domestic producers, and was one of the first to conceive the idea of insuring bank deposits, a forerunner of what was to become the Federal Deposit Insurance Act. Never one for frills, Garner made few speeches in his years in public office, seldom taking the floor except when vital

issues were at stake. In 1909 he became party whip. By World War I, he was recognized as the leading House Democrat. Although an isolationist, he voted to declare war on Germany, and, because of his influence in the House, he acted as liaison between President Woodrow Wilson and the legislators during the years of the war.

In 1931, in his twenty-eighth year of service, Garner was elected Speaker of the House of Representatives. By that time he was being mentioned as a possible candidate for the presidency. He did not actively seek the nomination, but at the Democratic convention of 1932, he and Al Smith, along with Franklin Delano Roosevelt, became the principal contenders. Roosevelt won the nomination, and Garner, with Roosevelt's approval, was chosen by acclamation as the vice-presidential nominee. Roosevelt and Garner were elected on the Democratic ticket, assuming office on March 4, 1933. Much later Garner referred to the post as that of a "waiting boy." Publicly he observed silence on national issues; however, on assuming office a second time with Roosevelt (January 20, 1937), there appeared to be a marked separation in their thinking. As Roosevelt became more liberal, Garner, once considered a radical by his fellow legislators in Texas, became more conservative.

Though he disagreed with Roosevelt's attempts to reorganize the Supreme Court and opposed the recognition of Russia, the first open argument between them came over the sit-down strikes of 1937. When Roosevelt announced his intention to run for a third term, the split became more evident. In 1939 a "Garner for President" movement sprang up. When Roosevelt won the nomination a third time and was elected president with a new running mate, Garner stayed in Washington only long enough to attend the inaugural ceremonies. He believed that Roosevelt should not have run for a third term but should have left it wide open for any Democratic nominee, and Garner thought that as vice-president he had a good chance. However, despite his differences with Roosevelt, Garner remained a staunch, loyal, straight-ticket Democrat for the rest of his life.

He was seventy-one years old when he returned to Uvalde. In his thirty-eight years in Washington he had set a record for the longest period of continuous service in the chairs of the highest parliamentary bodies in the United States. John Nance Garner was the first Texan ever elected national Speaker and the first Texan ever elected vice-president. He paved the way for other Texans to hold high national office. He was one of only two men in our nation's history who served both as Speaker and as vice-president.

Garner remained intellectually bright and continued to be greatly interested in political activities. His famed "Quail Breakfast" for President Harry S. Truman at Uvalde on Truman's lonesome campaign train trail of 1948 gave Truman a boost that ballooned into enormous crowds throughout Texas, helping elect Truman president. He supported Adlai Stevenson at a similar breakfast in Uvalde in 1952. He endorsed John F. Kennedy in 1960 and Lyndon Baines Johnson qv in 1964. He endorsed Ralph Yarborough in campaigns for the Texas governorship and the U.S. Senate.

One of the most widely noted of many happy reunions at his Uvalde home was his 90th birthday in 1958, when former President Harry S. Truman, Majority Leader Lyndon B. Johnson, and Speaker Sam Rayburn qv came to help him celebrate. He died quietly of a coronary occlusion on November 7, 1967, fifteen days short of his ninety-ninth birthday. Services were conducted in St. Philips Episcopal Church, and he was buried in the Uvalde cemetery.

BIBLIOGRAPHY· George Rothwell Brown, *The Speaker of the House* (1932); Marquis James, *Mr. Garner of Texas* (1939); Bascom N. Timmons, *Garner of Texas* (1948); *Who's Who In America* (1934); Biographical File, Barker Texas History Center, University of Texas at Austin.

Ralph W. Yarborough

*Garner, Texas.

*Garner Army Air Field. Garner Army Air Field was closed in late 1944. Two years later Southwest Texas Junior College qv was established on the site after the land had been purchased from the city of Uvalde.

*Garrett, Alexander Charles.

*Garrett, Charles.

*Garrett, Christopher C.

*Garrett, Daniel Edward.

*Garrett, Jacob.

*Garrett, Patrick Floyd (Pat).

*Garrett, Texas.

*Garrett Creek.

*Garrett's Bluff, Texas.

*Garretts Creek.

Garriga, Mariano Simon. Mariano Simon Garriga, son of Frank and Elizabeth (Baker) Garriga, was born in Point (now Port) Isabel, Texas, on May 30, 1886. His schooling began in Port Isabel and continued in Brownsville and at St. John's Orphanage in San Antonio, Texas. He studied also at St. Mary's College, Kansas City; St. Francis Seminary, Milwaukee, Wisconsin; and in 1936 at St. Edward's University in Austin, Texas. He was ordained a Roman Catholic priest in San Antonio on July 2, 1911. From 1912 to 1915 Father Garriga was a missionary on horseback in West Texas and New Mexico. In 1915 he was recalled to San Antonio to be vice-rector of the newly established diocesan seminary. That same year, Father Garriga, who was to become the first native-born Roman Catholic bishop and third bishop of the Diocese of Corpus Christi, assisted in San Antonio at the first mass said by the first bishop of Corpus Christi.

A National Guard chaplain, he went into service in World War I, trained with the 144th Infantry, 36th Division,qv and served in all its engagements in France. (During World War II he was appointed vicar delegate of Texas and Louisiana in the military ordinariate of the United States.)

Between 1919, when he resigned from the army, and 1936, when he was consecrated titular bishop of Siene and coadjutor of Corpus Christi, with right of succession, he was pastor of St. Cecilia's Church, San Antonio. For a brief period following the war, he had served as president of Incarnate Word College in San Antonio. On November 18, 1926, Father Garriga was appointed historian of the Archdiocese of San Antonio in connection with the preparation of a history of the Catholic church in Texas.qv The restoration work of the San José y San Miguel de Aguayo Mission qv at San Antonio was also under his personal supervision. On November 26, 1935, he was invested as a domestic prelate, and was consecrated a bishop on September 21, 1936.

On March 15, 1949, Bishop Emmanuel B. Ledvina of the Corpus Christi diocese retired, and Bishop Garriga took over his administration. In 1959, in recognition of his work for both the church and Texas, he was named "Mr. South Texas" at Laredo's George Washington Day celebration.

Garriga was a member of the Veterans of Foreign Wars, Texas Historical Commission, Order of the Alhambra (which he served as Supreme Chaplain), and Order of the Holy Sepulchre of Jerusalem.

He died on February 21, 1965, in Corpus Christi, and was interred in the crypt of Corpus Christi Cathedral.

BIBLIOGRAPHY: Carlos E. Castañeda, *Our Catholic Heritage in Texas, 1519–1936*, VII (1958); *Texas Catholic Herald* (Diocese of Galveston-Houston), February 25, 1965.

Rita Crabbe

*Garrison, Caleb Jackson.

*Garrison, George Pierce.

Garrison, Homer, Jr. Homer Garrison, Jr., son of Homer and Mattie (Milam) Garrison, was born in the settlement of Kickapoo in Anderson County on July 21, 1901, the eldest of nine children. After graduation from Lufkin High School, he went to work in the office of his father, who was district clerk in Angelina County. Garrison received his first experience as a law officer at nineteen when he received an appointment as a deputy sheriff for Angelina County. In 1929 he became a state license and weight inspector for the Texas State Highway Department,qv and he joined the Texas Highway Patrol when it was organized in 1930.

When the Department of Public Safety qv (DPS) was created in August, 1935, Garrison became the first assistant director. Among his initial duties was the task of developing a training program for DPS officers. At the request of the governor of New Mexico, he was sent to that state to help organize the New Mexico State Police. During World War II he was offered an appointment by General Douglas MacArthur to reorganize and supervise the Japanese national police system for the War Department, but he declined in deference to his duties as director of the DPS and chief of the Texas Rangers.qv

Among the many honors bestowed upon him during the nearly thirty years he served as the head of the state law enforcement agency was the presentation of the sixth Paul Gray Hoffman Award, conferred annually by the Automotive Safety Foundation for distinguished service in highway safety. In 1963 Governor John Connally appointed Colonel Garrison director of Civil Defense and Disaster Relief for the state of Texas, and chairman of the State Defense Council. That same year the governor also named him director of the Governor's Highway Safety Commission. In May, 1966, he was elected chairman of the resolutions committee and a member of the steering committee of the Southern Region Highway Policy Committee of the Council of State Governments; in January, 1967, he was named a member of the National Motor Vehicle Safety Advisory Council.

Colonel Garrison became director of the Department of Public Safety and chief of the Texas Rangers in 1938. Under his leadership numerous major programs were developed, and the organization grew to a total of some 3,400 employees. The programs included crime control, police traffic supervision, driver licensing, vehicle inspection, safety responsibility, accident records, safety education, defense and disaster service, and police training.

Garrison married Mary Nell Kilgo on June 1, 1939, and they had one son. Garrison died on May 7, 1968; he was buried in the State Cemetery.qv A Texas Ranger museum was named for him at Fort Fisher.qv

Bill Carter

*Garrison, Texas. Garrison, in Nacogdoches County, was named for James Henry Garrison (not his son, George Franklin [Frank] Garrison, as stated in Volume I). A conveyance dated August 29, 1885, in the Nacogdoches County records shows that James Henry Garrison and William Craig conveyed land to the Houston, East and West Texas Railway, reserving eleven acres "at what will hereinafter be known as Garrison." Garrison had a population of 951 in 1960 and 1,082 in 1970.

Quillian Garrison

Garwood, Calvin Baxter. Calvin Baxter Garwood, son of Hettie (Page) and Hiram Morgan Garwood,qv was born at Bastrop, Texas, on March 26, 1894. His parents moved to Houston about 1900, and he received his early education there at Sacred Heart School and St. Thomas College, before graduating from Georgetown Preparatory School, Washington, D.C., in 1911. He took an A.B. degree from Georgetown University in 1915 and, after military service, an LL.B. from the University of Texas in 1920. Admitted to the Texas Bar in 1920, he resided in Houston throughout his life, practicing law. In 1931 he served as a substitute special judge of the 55th District Court, and in 1935 he was president of the Houston Bar Association.

In 1916 Garwood enlisted in the 2nd Infantry Regiment of the Texas National Guard,qv which was called into active federal service on the Mexican border. Commissioned 2nd lieutenant after about a year of this duty, he remained a National Guard officer almost continuously until his retirement as brevet brigadier general at the end of 1946; his assignments during these thirty years included active service in the two world wars and state service in the martial law episodes at Galveston and in the East Texas Oil Field.qv His part in the Meuse-Argonne (Champagne) offensive (1918) earned him the French Croix de Guerre with Gilt Star. His World War II decorations included Officer of the Order of the British Empire and U. S. Army Commendation Medal for his part in the military government training program.

Garwood was a director of the Second National Bank in Houston and a post commander of the American Legion. In 1921 he married Christie Moore, and they had two children. Following the death of his first wife in 1957, Garwood married Mrs. Daisy (Reisner) Long. He died on May 14, 1960, and was buried in Forest Park Cemetery, Houston.

W. St. John Garwood

*Garwood, Hiram Morgan. Hiram Morgan Garwood was married to Hettie (not Hattie, as stated in Volume I) Page.

W. St. John Garwood

*Garwood, Texas. Garwood, Texas, was named for Hiram Morgan Garwood qv (not W. T. Garwood, as stated in Volume I). [Some later printings of Volume I contain this correction.]

W. St. John Garwood

Gary, Hampson. Hampson Gary was born in Tyler, Texas, on April 23, 1873, the son of Franklin Newman and Martha Isabella (Boren) Gary. After graduation from the University of Virginia (Phi Beta Kappa) in 1894, he practiced law in Tyler. During the Spanish-American War, he was captain of Company K, 4th Texas Volunteer Infantry Regiment. After the war he served in the Texas National Guard qv as colonel of the 3rd Texas Infantry Regiment.

A member of the Texas House of Representatives, 1901–1902, and board of regents of the University of Texas, 1909–1911, Gary also served as a referee in bankruptcy for four years. In 1914 he was appointed special counsel to the State Department to assist in matters arising out of the war situation in Europe. In 1917 Gary was appointed by President Woodrow Wilson as diplomatic agent and consul general to Egypt in charge of American interests in Palestine, Syria, and Arabia, where he formed a close friendship with Field Marshal Viscount Allenby, who commanded British forces in the Near East. In 1919 Gary was called to Paris to assist the American Commission to Negotiate Peace and in 1920 he was appointed minister to Switzerland by President Wilson. He resigned from the diplomatic service to practice law in New York and Washington, D. C., from 1921 to 1934. A staunch

Democrat and friend of President Franklin Roosevelt, he was appointed a member of the first Federal Communications Commission in 1934 and later served as its general counsel, 1935–1938. He was appointed solicitor of the United States Export-Import Bank in Washington, D. C., 1938–1946. In 1901 he married Bessie Royall of Palestine. Gary maintained a lifelong interest in Texas history and was a contributor to the *Southwestern Historical Quarterly* qv and the *Handbook of Texas*. He died in Palm Beach, Florida, on April 18, 1952, and was buried in Arlington Cemetery, survived by a son and a daughter.

BIBLIOGRAPHY: Hampson Gary Papers (Tyler Junior College, Tyler, Texas); *Who's Who In America* (1950); Albert Woldert, *A History of Tyler and Smith County, Texas* (1947).

F. Lee Lawrence

*Gary, Texas.

Gary Air Force Base. Gary Air Force Base, formerly San Marcos Air Force Base,qv served as an army helicopter training school until it was deactivated in 1959. The base remained closed until December, 1964, when the Office of Economic Opportunity, through contract with the Texas Educational Foundation, Inc., established the Gary Job Corps Training Center on the 2,200-acre site. *See also* Job Corps Program in Texas.

*Gary Creek.

Gary Job Corps Training Center. *See* Job Corps Program in Texas; Gary Air Force Base.

Garza, Catarino Erasmo. Catarino Erasmo Garza, Texas journalist and Mexican revolutionary, was born in Matamoros, Mexico, on November 25, 1859, son of Maria (Rodriguez) and Encarnación Garza; he moved with his family to Brownsville, Texas, at an early age. He was educated at San Juan College in Matamoros and, as a young man, worked as a clerk in a store in Brownsville and as a traveling agent for the Singer Sewing Machine Company. For a brief period in the early 1880's he was an officer of the Mexican Consulate in St. Louis, Missouri. In 1884 he returned to Texas and joined the staff of a newspaper which vehemently attacked Mexico's dictator-president, Porfirio Díaz, published in San Antonio by Adolfo Duclós Salinas, a young Mexican exile. In 1885 Garza was publishing his own paper, *El Comercio Mexicano*, in Eagle Pass, where he became known for his intemperate attacks on local citizens as well as on the governments of Porfirio Díaz and General Bernardo Reyes, the governor of Nuevo León. On May 24, 1890, he married Concepción Gonzalez, the daughter of a Duval County rancher, and moved to his father-in-law's ranch at Palito Blanco, where he published a newspaper called *El Libre Pensador*.

In the summer of 1891 Garza began plotting with liberal elements in northern Mexico to overthrow the Díaz regime. On September 16, 1891, he led an army of two hundred followers, recruited in Texas, across the Rio Grande at La Grulla, in Starr County, and proclaimed himself in revolt against the Mexican government. He and his men penetrated some sixty miles south of Camargo before it became evident that they had no support in Mexico. They made their way back to Texas, but during the next few months Garza made at least two more raids into Mexico, using his Palito Blanco ranch as headquarters. On December 22, 1891, United States troops caught a group of Garza's men crossing the river into Texas near La Grulla, returning from a raid on the La Tortilla ranch in Mexico. A skirmish ensued in which a soldier was killed, but most of the revolutionists escaped. On January 5, 1892, Garza and his men were decisively defeated at La Joya, in Hidalgo County, by troops from Fort Ringgold.qv Garza escaped, however, and is believed to have fled the country and to have been killed in Nicaragua in the early 1900's.

BIBLIOGRAPHY: Frank Bushick, *Glamorous Days* (1934); Agnes Grimm, *Llanos Mesteñas* (1968); Gabriel Saldívar, *Documentos de la rebelión de Catarino E. Garza en la frontera de Tamaulipas y sur de Texas 1891–1892* (Mexico City, 1945); *El Correo de Laredo*, September 19, 26, 1891, January 12, 1892; *San Antonio Express*, December 23, 1891; *La Prensa* (San Antonio), February 13, 1938.

Lonn Taylor

*Garza County. Garza County, in West Texas at the eastern edge of the Cap Rock, derives its income chiefly from ranching, farming, and oil production. The range land, which exceeds fourfold the area used as farm land, is grazed predominantly by beef cattle. Major crops are cotton and grain sorghums, some of which are grown on irrigated lands. Between 1949 and 1968, cultivated land under irrigation increased from 2,000 acres to 14,891 acres. Similarly, annual cotton production increased from 10,800 bales in 1958 to 21,717 in 1968. Over 124 million barrels of oil were produced from 1926 to 1973. Construction included a county hospital, a park, a library, and an airport. Several historic sites, a rodeo in August, and a fair in October stimulate the tourist trade. The 1960 population was 6,611; in 1970 it was 5,289. Post is the county seat.

Garza Indians. The Garza Indians, a Coahuiltecan band of northeastern Mexico, were one of several groups commonly referred to as Carrizo, and sometimes ranged north of the Rio Grande. In the middle eighteenth century the Garza lived on the south bank of the Rio Grande near Mier and Revilla, and as late as 1828 some of these Indians were still living near Mier.

BIBLIOGRAPHY: F. W. Hodge (ed.), *Handbook of American Indians*, II (1910); R. C. Troike, "Notes on Coahuiltecan Ethnography," *Bulletin of the Texas Archeological Society*, 32 (1962).

T. N. Campbell

Garza-Little Elm Reservoir. Lewisville Dam and Garza-Little Elm Reservoir are in the Trinity River Basin in Denton County, two miles northeast of Lewisville on the Elm Fork of the Trinity River. The project is owned by the United States government and is operated by the United States Army Corps of Engineers, Fort Worth District, for flood control and conservation purposes. The reservoir inundated and incorporated Lake Dallas when the old Garza Dam was breached on October 28, 1957.

The city of Dallas purchased 310,000 acre-feet of conservation storage for $3,400,000 plus annual operational costs, and in addition reserved 105,000 acre-feet of storage in exchange for existing rights in the old Lake Dallas. The city of Denton purchased 21,000 acre-feet of conservation storage for $235,000 and certain annual operational costs. Construction began on November 28, 1948, and the main dam was completed in August, 1955. Deliberate impoundment of water began on November 1, 1954. The reservoir has a capacity of 464,500 acre-feet and surface area of 22,970 acres at the conservation storage space elevation of 515 feet above mean sea level. The reservoir provides 525,-200 acre-feet of flood control storage capacity. The drainage area above the dam is 1,660 square miles.

BIBLIOGRAPHY: Texas Water Commission, *Bulletin 6408* (1964).

Seth D. Breeding

*Gasconades Creek.

*Gasoline, Texas.

*Gaspar Flores Creek.

*Gaston, Texas. (Fort Bend County.)

*Gaston, Texas. (Rusk County.)

*Gastonia, Texas.

*Gates, Amos.

Gates, Isaac Edgar. Isaac Edgar Gates was born on June 26, 1874, in Mart, Texas, the son of William Collier and Nancy Caroline (Fowler) Gates. He received his early education in the public schools of McLennan County. The Missionary Baptist Church of Battle, Texas, ordained him to the ministry in 1894, and he began preaching, serving as pastor of small churches at Mart, Battle, China Springs, and Patrick, while at the same time pursuing studies at Baylor University. He received his B. A. degree in 1903. His first full-time pastorate was the First Baptist Church at Caldwell. After doing missionary work in Texas and Arkansas, he served as financial secretary for the raising of funds to build the Southwestern Baptist Theological Seminary.qv He was the first president of Wayland Baptist College at Plainview, Texas, from 1910 to 1915, and then became pastor of churches at Plainview, Amarillo, and San Antonio.

Known as a gifted speaker and humorist, he was the author of *Vital Themes for Thinking People* (1914) and an autobiography, *Watching the World Go By* (1930). Baylor University awarded him the honorary Doctor of Divinity degree in 1921. Gates was married to Stella Wood on February 26, 1893, and they had five children. Because of a heart condition he resigned as an active pastor in 1932. Gates died on July 17, 1933, and was buried in the family cemetery at Mart, Texas.

BIBLIOGRAPHY: Isaac Edgar Gates, *Watching the World Go By* (1930); *Who Was Who In America* (1943).

James O. Wallace

*Gates, John Warne.

*Gates, Samuel.

*Gates, William. William Gates' son, Charles, died in 1836 (not 1822, as stated in Volume I).

Mrs. Robert R. Truitt

*Gatesville, Texas. Gatesville, seat of Coryell County, had a 1960 population of 4,626 and a 1970 population of 4,683. The city contains Mountain View School for Boys,qv administered by the Texas Youth Council.qv In 1963 the Graves Memorial Library was completed. Industries among the 106 businesses in 1970 included the processing of meat and the manufacture of deck boats, toys and games, livestock feed supplements, plastic items, mattresses, and concrete.

*Gatesville State School for Boys. The Gatesville State School for Boys was placed under the administration of the Texas Youth Council qv by the Fifty-fifth Legislature. An extensive program was initiated by the council to transform the old school into six separate training units or schools, including a security-treatment institution and five open-type schools. The proposed program became a reality in April, 1963, with the completion of the Hackberry School.

The general superintendent directed the five open-type schools, which provided benefits from specialized programs of classification, care, treatment, and discipline. Each school was in turn directed by an assistant superintendent, aided by a principal and teachers of the academic and vocational school and by a professional counseling staff.

The Valley School was a training unit for 160 young males. It was situated three-quarters of a mile south of the old Main Campus. The school had its own dormitories, recreational facilities, kitchen and dining facilities, academic school, vocational workshops, and playgrounds. It enabled younger, lesser offenders to be separated completely from older offenders.

The Hackberry School, a training unit for 240 younger males, was situated three-quarters of a mile southeast of the old Main Campus. The school possessed all necessary facilities, including living, academic, recreational, and vocational accommodations. Its emphasis centered on the classification and treatment of younger males.

The Terrace School, one-half mile east of the old Main Campus, provided for the separation and classification of 240 youngsters of intermediate age and background.

The Riverside School was composed of two training units. One had complete facilities for living and recreation and for the academic and vocational training of 160 younger Negro offenders. The other was created by renovating and remodeling existing housing and training facilities. The latter unit accommodated 160 older Negro males.

The Hilltop School, formerly the Main Campus, provided facilities for classification and treatment of 250 young male offenders less sophisticated in delinquent activities than those housed in Mountain View School.qv The overall daily population average for all five units of the Gatesville school in 1969 was 1,830.

BIBLIOGRAPHY: Texas Youth Council, *Annual Report* (1965); *Texas Almanac* (1969).

William T. Field

*Gathings, James J.

*Gathright, Thomas S.

*Gatlin, Texas.

*Gato Creek.

*Gause, Texas.

*Gaut, Texas.

Gavilán Indians. Baptismal records at the San Antonio de Valero Mission qv of San Antonio indicate the presence there of a few Gavilán (Gabilán) Indians, presumably remnants of the Gavilán (Spanish for "sparrow hawk") who in the late seventeenth century lived in the Bolsón de Mapimí of Coahuila and Chihuahua but sometimes ranged northward to the Rio Grande. J. R. Swanton listed Gavilán as a Coahuiltecan band, but J. D. Forbes has recently presented evidence which suggests that the Gavilán spoke a Uto-Aztecan language.

BIBLIOGRAPHY: J. D. Forbes, "Unknown Athapaskans: The Identification of the Jano, Jocome, Jumano, Manso, Suma, and Other Indian Tribes of the Southwest," *Ethnohistory*, 6 (1959); F. W. Hodge (ed.), *Handbook of American Indians*, II (1910); J. R. Swanton, *The Indian Tribes of North America* (1952).

T. N. Campbell

*Gay Hill, Texas. (Fayette County.)

*Gay Hill, Texas. (Milam County.)

*Gay Hill, Texas. (Washington County.)

*Gayle, Alexander T.

*Gayle Creek.

*Gaylord, Texas.

*Gaylors Creek.

Gayoso de Lemos, Manuel. Manuel Gayoso de Lemos Amorín y Magallanes was born in Oporto, Portugal, on May 30, 1747, the son of Spanish consul Manuel Luis Gayoso de Lemos y Sarmiento and Theresa Angélica de Amorín y Magallanes. Educated in England, he joined the Spanish Lisbon Regiment as a cadet on July 7, 1771. He was commissioned sub-lieutenant on July 20, 1772, and was promoted through the years, reaching the rank of brigadier on September 4, 1795.

On November 3, 1787, he was named governor of the fort and district of Natchez. He served at that post from 1789 until August, 1797, during which time he encouraged American settlers, established posts as far north as Missouri, and organized militia, naval units, and defenses of the frontier to guard against possible attacks from Indians, American frontiersmen, or Jacobins. His valuable services in persuading the southern Indians to sign treaties in 1792, 1793, and 1795 secured a buffer zone between the American settlements and Spanish Louisiana. His close contacts with General James Wilkinson qv during the so-called "Spanish Conspiracy" introduced him to Philip Nolan,qv with whom he was tempted to form a business partnership in 1797 involving the importation of Texas horses into Louisiana and the trading of goods with Texas and Mexico.

Appointed governor-general of Louisiana and West Florida on October 28, 1796, he took office on August 5, 1797, and died in New Orleans of yellow fever on July 18, 1799, as Americans moved into the Natchez District. He was married three times: to Theresa Margarita Hopman y Pereira, of Lisbon, to whom two children were born; to Elizabeth Watts of Philadelphia; and to Margaret Cyrilla Watts, of Louisiana, to whom one son was born. Gayoso's correspondence with governors of Texas and the viceroy of New Spain during 1797–1799 concerned the activities of Philip Nolan, whom Gayoso considered a dangerous enemy of Spain, and the preservation of Louisiana as a barrier to American expansion into Texas and New Spain.

BIBLIOGRAPHY: Jack D. L. Holmes, *Gallant Emissary: the Political Career of Manuel Gayoso de Lemos in the Mississippi Valley, 1789–1799* (Ph.D. dissertation, University of Texas at Austin, 1959), *Gayoso, the Life of a Spanish Governor in the Mississippi Valley, 1789–1799* (1965), "La última barrera: la Luisiana y la Nueva España," *Historia Mexicana*, X (1961), "Gallegos notables en la Luisiana," *Cuadernos de Estudios Gallegos*, LVII (1964); *Dictionary of American Biography*, VII (1931); Irving A. Leonard, "A Frontier Library, 1799," *Hispanic American Historical Review*, XXIII (1943).

Jack D. L. Holmes

*Gazelle, Texas.

Gazette (Richmond).

*Gazley, Thomas Jefferson.

*Gazley Creek.

*Geies Indians. The name Geies (Geie, Geier) is mentioned in basic documents only once, by Damian Massanet,qv who said that these people were among the Indians who lived between Monclova and eastern Texas. Although it cannot be proved, it seems likely that Geies (or Geie) is merely a shortened form of Gueiquesale, the name of a Coahuiltecan group that ranged from northeastern Coahuila across the Rio Grande into the southwestern part of the Edwards Plateau during the seventeenth and early eighteenth centuries.

BIBLIOGRAPHY: F. W. Hodge (ed.), *Handbook of American Indians*, I (1907); J. R. Swanton, *Linguistic Material from the Tribes of Southern Texas and Northeastern Mexico* (1940).

T. N. Campbell

*Gem, Texas.

*Gemelo Mesa.

Genealogical Societies of Texas. Genealogical societies were organized in some thirty Texas communities between 1950 and 1965, mainly through the work of librarians and patrons of Texas history collections in public libraries.

The Texas State Genealogical Society, organized on November 28, 1960, at Hotel Texas, Fort Worth, by Edna Perry Deckler, then president of the Fort Worth Genealogical Society, was the largest in membership of the societies. In June, 1965, there were 690 individuals and libraries receiving the genealogical quarterly, *Stirpes*.qv

Some purposes of the societies are to stimulate interest in the local history and genealogy departments of public and private libraries and in the Texas State Library and the Archives of Texas;[qq] to enrich the wealth of genealogical and historical research material in Texas and to make it more readily available to all who seek family and local history; to sponsor schools and institutes for the scientific study of genealogical and historical research; and to publish magazines, bulletins, and books of genealogical records.

Edith Perry Deckler

*General Consultation. *See* Consultation.

*General Council.

*General Land Office. In December, 1960, the state resumed mineral development of the Gulf area after Texas ownership was confirmed by the United States Supreme Court on December 12, 1960 (*see* Tidelands Controversy). The mineral revenues were consigned to the Permanent School Fund.[qv] Although the financial potential of Texas public land has been generally limited to surface properties, mineral resources have become financially important in recent years. New departments and equipment have become necessary to manage the increased volume of business resulting from these modern trends. Land office operations are carried on by the following divisions: legal, sales and leasing, exploration and development, engineering, accounting and auditing, Spanish archives, records, veterans land program, and coastal areas management.

The state's entire submerged area of 4,145,674 acres includes 1,536,900 acres of beaches, islands, lands beneath bays and inlets, and other inland waters. Texas is the only public land state with complete control over the public lands within its boundaries and the proceeds resulting from the administration and sale of lands. *See also* Veterans' Land Board; Veterans' Land Board Scandal.

Virginia H. Taylor

General Land Office Commissioner. *See* State Executive Officers, Compensation of.

*"General Sherman."

*Geneva, Texas.

*Geneview, Texas.

*Genoa, Texas.

*Gentilz, Theodore. Jean Louis Theodore Gentilz was born in France in 1819 (not 1820, as stated in Volume I) and was a member of the second contingent of settlers brought to Texas by Henri Castro.[qv] Gentilz helped Castro in his colonization efforts by writing reports for him, by assisting in surveying the towns of Castroville and nearby Quihi, and in 1847 by helping to establish the town of D'Hanis. Gentilz returned to France at least twice; the second time, in 1849, he married Marie Fargeix (not Marie Fargeux, as stated in Volume I). Well educated and trained as an artist, Gentilz left in his numerous paintings a rich pictorial account of the people of San Antonio de Béxar and its environs that revealed perception and understanding as well as talent. His art train-

ing in Paris had included the disciplined draftsmanship of the French academic tradition. He had attended the National School of Mathematics and Drawing, and, while still a student, he compiled a manuscript on a method of perspective for artists, now in the Daughters of the Republic of Texas [qv] Library at the Alamo.

Among his many paintings are those depicting the life of the Mexican people in San Antonio, such as "The Tamale Seller" and "The Rooster Race" (1848). He painted the Spanish missions of San Antonio, and his historical paintings include "The Fall of the Alamo" and "Shooting of the Seventeen Decimated Texians." In 1882, when the artist was surveying and mapping northern Mexico, he painted scenes of Mexican people, such as "Selling of Cardinals on the Plaza." Gentilz also took interest in the Indians of Texas, sketching them on his survey trips, later expanding the sketches into oil paintings. "Comanche Chief" and "Fishing with Bow and Arrow" are among several of his paintings now at the Witte Memorial Museum [qv] in San Antonio. In the late 1960's Carmen Perry and Dorothy Steinbomer of San Antonio made a study and check list of Gentilz' works.

BIBLIOGRAPHY: Pauline A. Pinckney, *Painting in Texas: The Nineteenth Century* (1967).

Pauline A. Pinckney

*Gentry, Abram Morris.

Gentry, Brady. Brady Gentry was born on a farm near Colfax in Van Zandt County on March 25, 1895. He attended Cumberland University and Tyler Commercial College. He was admitted to the Bar at the age of twenty-one. During World War I he served as an infantryman in France, emerging from the service with the rank of captain.

He entered public service as a clerk in the office of the Van Zandt County tax collector. After moving to Tyler he served as assistant city tax collector. He was elected county attorney, and in 1930 he became county judge of Smith County, holding the office for four successive terms. During this period he was instrumental in developing the county's road system. In 1939 he was appointed chairman of the Texas Highway Commission by Governor W. Lee O'Daniel.[qv] He was the first man to serve as chairman of the commission for a full six-year term. (*See* Highway Department, Texas State.)

During his tenure on the highway commission, first steps were taken in the development of Texas' extensive farm-to-market road program. His work attracted national attention. In 1943 he was elected president of the American Association of State Highway Officials. He also served as a director of the Texas Good Roads Association. When his highway commission term ended in 1945, Gentry turned his full-time efforts to his Tyler law practice.

In 1952 he was elected to Congress from the Third District, serving two terms. As a member of the House committee on highways and roads, he was instrumental in shaping the legislation which launched the development of the national system of interstate and defense highways. In 1957, after his retirement from Congress, Gentry was tendered another appointment as chairman of the Texas Highway Commission. He declined the appointment, however, because of business and personal commitments.

Throughout his life Gentry was a staunch supporter of Southern Methodist University; he also was a benefactor of Tyler Junior College. Shortly after World War II, he helped form the Tyler Junior College District, and the old college gymnasium was named "Gentry Gym" in his honor. Gentry, a bachelor, died in Houston on November 9, 1966, after a lengthy illness.

D. C. Greer

*Gentry, Frederick Browder.

*Gentry, Texas.

*Gentry Creek.

*Gentry's Mill, Texas.

Geobari Indians. The Geobari Indians are known from a single Spanish document of 1683 which does not clearly identify their area. They seem to have lived somewhere in west-central Texas. Their affiliations are unknown.

BIBLIOGRAPHY: C. W. Hackett (ed.), *Pichardo's Treatise on the Limits of Louisiana and Texas*, I (1931).

T. N. Campbell

*Geographical Society. *See* Texas Geographic Society.

*Geological Surveys of Texas. The University Mineral Survey was created in 1901 to evaluate the mineral potential of state lands. It functioned until 1905, issuing eight publications and maps on mineral districts, mineral commodities, and mining law problems.

The Bureau of Economic Geology, established in 1909 as an organized research bureau of the University of Texas, has continued to function as a state geological survey for Texas. In 1966 the bureau was engaged in a four-point program of research and public service in earth science and Texas mineral resources as follows: basic geological research; geology applied to resource and engineering problems; systematic geologic mapping; and public-service mineral information, identification and testing, and compilation of mineral statistics. The bureau participates in other university research efforts in the fields of resources and earth sciences, such as the Center for Research in Water Resources. As part of its effort, the bureau publishes major reports in the University of Texas publication series; it also has its own series of reports of investigations, geologic quadrangle maps, guidebooks, geological circulars, and mineral resource circulars. The guidebooks include nontechnical publications of general interest.

The basic geologic data developed by the Bureau of Economic Geology in the form of scientific reports and geologic maps are used by many state and federal organizations in carrying out investigations in the public service. These include the Texas Water Development Board, Railroad Commission of Texas, Parks and Wildlife Department, Texas Highway Department, Texas Industrial Commission,[qqv] and numerous other state boards, conservation organizations, water districts, and chambers of commerce. The bureau also cooperates formally and informally with federal agencies, such as the Geological Survey, Bureau of Mines, Bureau of Reclamation, Corps of Engineers, and National Park Service. The mineral and geological information service offered by the Bureau of Economic Geology is used by public and private groups, corporations, and citizens. *See also* Geological Surveys in Texas, United States.

BIBLIOGRAPHY: Peter T. Flawn, "Geology in the State Government of Texas," Bureau of Economic Geology, *Geological Circular 65–5* (1965).

Peter T. Flawn

Geological Surveys in Texas, United States. The Geological Survey of the United States Department of the Interior has for many years conducted various geologic and geophysical studies, topographic mapping, water-resource investigations, and supervision of oil and gas leases on federally owned land in Texas. The survey's work is organized under four divisions: geologic, topographic, water resources, and conservation.

Geologic Division. In cooperation with the Bureau of Economic Geology of the University of Texas at Austin, the geologic division was making important contributions to the knowledge of the mineral composition, rock structure, mineral resources, and geologic history of the state. Regional investigations supplemented by chemical, physical, and paleontological research, in the laboratory and in the field, enable scientists to determine the nature of the rocks and minerals that make up the earth and how they were formed.

Regional geologic studies made by the United States Geological Survey in Texas included professional papers on the Sierra Blanca region, the Sierra Diablo, and the Guadalupe Mountains of the Trans-Pecos; on the Pennsylvanian and Permian rocks of north-central Texas; and on the rocks of the Del Rio-Indian Wells area. Professional papers, bulletins, and maps also have concerned economic mineral deposits such as the quicksilver deposits of the Terlingua district in the Big Bend region, the oil geology of the Horseshoe Atoll (a buried reef in west-central Texas that is the largest limestone reservoir in the United States), the uranium deposits of southern Texas, the oil-bearing Jurassic rocks of northeastern Texas, and the uranium-bearing black shales. Monographs have been written on fossils of the Woodbine Formation in northeastern Texas, the conodonts of the Llano uplift, the fusulines of north-central Texas, and the ostracods of the Glass Mountains in western Texas; an important aero-radioactivity map has been published on southern Texas.

Topographic Division. Since the 1880's the survey has been making topographic maps of Texas. The early maps show roads, towns and settlements, and political boundaries, but the physical features are only generalized. Some of these maps are valuable for historical studies, for they show roads and trails, water holes, river crossings, and other important landmarks used by the early travelers and the cattle drives. In recent years the topographic division of the Geological Survey has cooperated with several agencies of the state and is using the most modern mapping techniques for delineating in great detail the physical and cultural features of the state. More than 60 percent of Texas is now covered by detailed maps scaled either at 1 inch equivalent to 2,000 feet (1:24,000) or 1 inch equivalent to approximately 1 mile (1:62,500). The entire state is covered by maps scaled at 1 inch equaling about 4 miles (1:250,000).

Water Resources Division. The principal activities of the survey in Texas concern water resources. The survey works in cooperation with the Texas Water Development Board,qv the Texas Highway Commission (*see* Highway Department, Texas State), with local agencies, and with other federal agencies whose activities relate to water. Surface and ground water supplies are studied to solve many water problems, including quantity, quality, distribution, variability, and flooding.

Water resource investigations in Texas are concerned with both basic data collection and analytical and interpretive research. Data for stream-flow studies are collected at 651 stream sites; for storage studies at 58 reservoir sites; for chemical quality research at 221 stream sites and in 213 wells; for water-level studies in 880 wells; and for land-surface subsidence research at two sites.

Hydrologic studies are made of small watersheds, both rural and urban, for use in the design of watershed projects, drainage systems, flood control projects, water supply facilities, and highway culverts and small bridges. Continuing progress is made on a long-term project concerned with the accurate measurement of river basin drainage areas as the necessary topographic maps become available.

The chemical quality of waters in streams, wells, and reservoirs is investigated as an aid in the planning of water developments and in the management of the water resources of the state, and problem areas and probable sources of water salinity and pollution are identified so that water of the best possible quality can be provided to water users.

Reconnaissance studies of river basins have been made to aid in statewide water planning. The occurrence of ground water is studied and mapped by geologic formation (aquifer) and by geographic location. Ground water appraisal studies made for local agencies, counties, cities, and districts include appraisal of the ground water resources as to availability, dependability, quality and quantity, and the effect of water withdrawal on water levels and water quality. Detailed studies have been continued in several districts for many years: San Antonio and vicinity (along the Balcones Fault), Houston, Galveston County, and El Paso. Much of the water data has been set up for computer analysis, and

electrical analog models of several areas have been built. These enable the hydrologists to predict the changes in water level that will result in an area from any pattern of water use.

Conservation Division. In addition to administration of the Connolly Act of Compliance in oil and gas production in the state, the conservation division of the survey supervises mineral recovery operations in both mining and oil and gas production on federal lands. Currently, reimbursements to the government for oil and gas leases on federal lands in Texas amount to about $1.8 million annually. The division also has classified federal lands as to their mineral and water resources and their suitability for construction of dams, reservoirs, and power plants. *See also* Geological Surveys of Texas.

D. H. Eargle

*Geology of Texas.

*George, Freeman.

*George, Texas.

*George Creek.

*George West, Texas. George West, seat of Live Oak County, reported forty-five businesses, including a refinery and newspaper, in 1970. It is a market and shipping point for cotton and cattle. The 1960 population was 1,878, and in 1970 it was 2,022.

*George's Creek, Texas.

*Georgetown, Texas. (Grayson County.)

*Georgetown, Texas. (Williamson County.) Georgetown, the county seat, is a farming and ranching center. With 156 businesses in 1970, it had several industries producing crushed stone, furniture, grain and cotton products, and concrete. In 1966 Georgetown reported a new airport, a large park, and a new retirement hotel, as well as sixteen churches, a hospital, a library, a college, a newspaper, and a radio station. A major tourist attraction, opened in 1966, was Inner Space Cavern.qv Public improvements included four buildings at Southwestern University completed in 1966 and a proposed dam on the North Fork of the San Gabriel River. The population in 1960 was 5,218, and by 1970 it was 6,395.

*Georgetown and Granger Railroad Company.

*Georgetown Railroad Company. In 1958 the Georgetown Railroad Company was acquired from the Missouri-Pacific Railroad Company by businessmen in Georgetown who planned to use it to haul from a quarry at Georgetown to Round Rock. The Missouri-Pacific was planning to abandon the line at that time, but sold it instead. It operated 12.2 miles of line from Georgetown in the mid-1960's.

James M. Day

*Georgia Army.

*Georgia Battalion.

Geote Indians. The Geote (Geota, Teote) Indians are known from a Spanish document of 1748 which lists the names of twenty-five Indian groups of east-central and southeastern Texas who had asked for missions in that general area. About half the names on this list, including Geote, cannot be identified. The others consist of groups identifiable as Caddoans (including Wichita), Tonkawans, Atakapans, and Karankawans.

BIBLIOGRAPHY: H. E. Bolton, *Texas in the Middle Eighteenth Century* (1915); F. C. Chabot (ed.), *Excerpts from the Memorias for the History of Texas, by Father Morfi* (1932); C. W. Hackett (ed.), *Pichardo's Treatise on the Limits of Louisiana and Texas,* I (1931).

T. N. Campbell

*Geraghty, John.

Gerken, Rudolph Aloysius. Rudolph Aloysius Gerken, one of thirteen children of William and Elizabeth (Sudmeier) Gerken, was born in Dyersville, Iowa, on March 7, 1887. He was graduated from St. Joseph College, Rensselaer, Indiana.

He came to Texas and taught for two years, 1910–1912, in the public school at Scotland. Through the encouragement of Bishop Joseph Patrick Lynch qv of Dallas, he began studies for the priesthood at the old University of Dallas and at Kenrick Seminary, St. Louis, Missouri. On June 10, 1917, he was ordained in Sacred Heart Cathedral, Dallas, by Bishop Lynch. From 1917 to 1926, he served as pastor in various sections of West Texas and the Panhandle, building churches, schools, missions, and rectories.

On April 26, 1927, he was consecrated the first bishop of the newly created Diocese of Amarillo. During his six-year administration of the diocese, he built twenty churches, thirteen rectories, six schools, three hospitals, one college, one convent, and four homes for teachers. Bishop Gerken was named archbishop of Santa Fe in 1933, a position he held for ten years, before his death on March 2, 1943.

BIBLIOGRAPHY: *Who's Who In America* (1934).

Sister M. Claude Lane, O.P.

*Gerlach, George.

*Gerlach, John J.

*German, James L.

*German Attitude—Civil War.

German Emigration Company. *See* Adelsverein.

*German-English School.

*German Free School Association of Austin.

German Singing Societies. *See* Texas State Singing Society.

*Germania, Texas. *See* Paul, Texas.

*Germans in Texas. The background and culture of Germans in Texas has increasingly interested historians during the mid-twentieth century, and as a result materials have become more accessible to the general public through numerous books, paintings, restorations, and museums. Research into the background and activities of the Germans in Texas has produced valuable reference materials concerning their history and settlement. Two early landmark books in English, *The Germans in Texas* (1910), by Gilbert Giddings Benjamin, and *The History of the German Settlements in Texas, 1831–1861* (1930), by Rudolph L. Biesele,qv have

become guide posts for subsequent study. Not until the mid-twentieth century, however, was there a significant amount of published material in English. Translations were made by Arthur L. Finck of Ferdinand Charles von Herff's qv *The Regulated Emigration of the German Proletariat with Special Reference to Texas* (1949); by Chester W. Geue of Friedrich W. von Wrede's qv *Sketches of Life in the United States of North America and Texas* (1970); and by Charles L. Wisseman of Robert G. Penniger's qv *Fredericksburg, Texas . . . The First Fifty Years* (1971). Oscar Haas was the most consistent and prolific translator, his weekly articles appearing for a number of years in the New Braunfels *Herald*. His *History of New Braunfels and Comal County, Texas, 1844–1946* (1968) and an earlier work, *A Chronological History of the Singers of German Songs in Texas* (1948) are also important contributions, as was Lota M. Spell's qv chapter on German music in *Music in Texas* (1936).

In their letters and memoirs well-educated German women wrote vividly and thoughtfully of the family life of German pioneer settlers in mid-nineteenth-century Texas. Among those whose writings have survived are Emma Murck Altgelt, *Beobachtungen und Erinnerungen* (1930); Ottilie Fuchs Goeth, *Was Grossmutter erzaehlt* (1915), translated in 1969 by Irma Goeth Guenther as *Memoirs of a Texas Pioneer Grandmother*; Louise Romberg Fuchs, *Erinnerungen* (1928); and the letters of Elise K. Willrich and Amanda von Rosenberg. Clara Mattaei Palacios Reyes, granddaughter of Friedrich Schlecht, a Texas-German writer, lived near Bellville, and under the name Walther Grey wrote a dozen novels and short stories with backgrounds in Austin County. They were published in the Austin *Wochenblatt*. Her poems were written under the pseudonym "Gertrud Hoff." Selma (Metzenthin) Raunick qv compiled the authoritative listing of Texas-German prose and poetry, *Deutsche Schriften in Texas* (c. 1935–1936).

Biographies and check lists of Texas-German naturalists appeared in *Naturalists of the Frontier* (1937), by Samuel Wood Geiser, and in issues of *Field and Laboratory*, which Geiser edited for three decades. Irene Marschall King published a full-length biography of John O. Meusebach qv in 1967. Additional publications included Guido Ransleben's *A Hundred Years of Comfort in Texas* (1954); Gillespie County Historical Society's *Pioneers in God's Hills* (1960); Chester W. and Ethel H. Geue (eds.), *A New Land Beckoned* (1966); and Ethel H. Geue's *New Homes in a New Land* (1970). The last two books used early newspapers and ships lists to study German immigration from 1844 to 1861. A study of the German immigrant farmer and his farming in Texas was made by Terry G. Jordan in *German Seed in Texas Soil* (1966).

Texas-German periodicals, the majority of which remain to be translated, are rich in personal experiences. Yearbooks and calendars were published by the *Neu Braunfelser Zeitung*,qv the Bellville *Wochenblatt*, and the *Seguiner Zeitung*. The first

German language newspaper, the Galveston *Zeitung*, was established in 1846. It was possibly in 1853 that Adolf Douai, a former member of the Sisterdale Latin Colony (*see* "Latin Settlements" in Texas), first published the San Antonio *Zeitung*.qv

Studies have been made of the dialect in two of the most heavily populated Texas-German areas; Fred Eikel, Jr., in *New Braunfels German* (1966), and G. G. Gilbert, in *The Dialect Spoken in Kendall and Gillespie Counties* (1963), analyzed changes in the original German dialects brought to Texas.

Food is another important Texas-German heritage. The widely publicized Wurstfest held each year in New Braunfels, celebrations in Fredericksburg, the State Fair of Texas,qv fairs in Comal, Gillespie, and Kendall counties, and the long-observed annual Fourth of July celebration in Round Top all featured typical Texas-German food. Two cookbooks of interest are *Cooking in Comfort* (1961) and the *Fredericksburg Home Kitchen Cookbook*, first printed in 1916 and still in print in the 1970's.

The files and exhibits of the Institute of Texan Cultures qv at HemisFair qv in 1968 provided a comprehensive study of German culture in Texas; a growing awareness of fine German craftsmanship, especially in furniture, led to numerous private collections. Holdings and exhibitions were increased in the Witte Memorial Museum qv in San Antonio, Kammlah Museum in Fredericksburg, and at Winedale, a University of Texas project near Round Top (*see* Winedale Museum). The uniqueness of Texas-German architecture was recognized by Samuel Edward Gideon,qv who photographed numerous structures and published a booklet, *Fredericksburg, A Little Town in the Lone Star State* (193?). German houses, barns, and store buildings, often in ruin, were recorded in the paintings and drawings of Edward M. "Buck" Schiwetz in *Buck Schiwetz' Texas* (1960); photographs and drawings in Clovis Haimsath's *Pioneer Texas Buildings* (1968); and line drawings by Roy L. White in his book with Joe B. Frantz, *Limestone and Log* (1968). Private restoration of early structures of *Fachwerk* (timber framework with stone, brick, or adobe) aided in preserving the European architectural style which flourished in the Texas-German areas of the hill country of Central Texas.

Works of numerous Texas-German artists, the most prominent and prolific of whom were Frederick Richard Petri, Hermann Lungkwitz, and Carl G. von Iwonski,qqv are found in the permanent collections of the Witte Memorial Museum, Kammlah Museum, Texas Memorial Museum qv in Austin, and the Sophienburg Museum qv in New Braunfels. Pauline A. Pinckney, in *Painting in Texas: The Nineteenth Century* (1967), presented for the first time biographies and reproductions of the works of numerous Texas-German painters.

Crystal Sasse Ragsdale

Germany, Eugene Benjamin. Eugene Benjamin Germany, an organizer and president of Lone Star Steel Company, was born in Sweetwater, Nolan County, on September 18, 1892, the son of John Wesley and Arona (Lea) Germany. He attended public schools in Murchison and Grand Saline and from 1910 to 1912 was a student at Southwestern University at Georgetown. Germany taught school in Grand Saline for six years, worked in various oil fields for another six years, and then in Dallas formed the firm of E. B. Germany & Sons (originally Cranfill & Germany Company).

E. B. Germany was active in many fields, writing extensively for business and professional publications and publishing a regular column, "The Way I See It," in East Texas newspapers. Active in politics, he served as mayor of Highland Park from 1934 to 1942, and in 1940 he managed the campaign of John Nance Garner qv for the Democratic nomination for president. He twice served as state Democratic chairman, under governors W. Lee O'Daniel qv and Coke Stevenson,qv and in 1958 he was appointed chairman of the Texas Industrial Commission by Governor Price Daniel.

In 1947 Germany became president of Lone Star Steel Company, which, under his direction, was originally a government project. After his private acquisition in January, 1948, the company was expanded into a fully integrated steel mill, serving industrial markets throughout the United States. Among the many civic and professional organizations which Germany served either as a member or officer were the Dallas Methodist Hospital, the Scottish Rite Crippled Children's Hospital, and the Philosophical Society of Texas.qv He married Maggie Lee Wilson on June 8, 1915; they were the parents of two sons and a daughter. Germany died in Dallas on July 12, 1971, and was buried in Grand Saline. *See also* Iron and Steel Industry.

BIBLIOGRAPHY: *Who's Who In America* (1968); Philosophical Society of Texas, *Proceedings* (1970); Biographical File, Barker Texas History Center, University of Texas at Austin.

*Geronimo, Texas.

*Geronimo Creek.

Gertrude, Texas. Gertrude, in Jack County, was situated in the "Lost Valley" and during the 1870's was a post office for the cattlemen of that region.

BIBLIOGRAPHY: *Texas Almanac* (1936).

*Géry, Jean. *See* Henri, Jean.

*Gettysburg Peak.

*Gewhitt, Texas.

*Gholson, Albert G.

*Gholson, Benjamin Franklin.

*Gholson, Texas. (Lampasas County.)

*Gholson, Texas. (McLennan County.)

*Gibbons Branch.

*Gibbs, Barnett. Barnett Gibbs died on October 4, 1904 (not October 5, 1904, as stated in Volume I).

BIBLIOGRAPHY: Dallas *Morning News*, October 5, 1904.

*Gibbs, Texas.

Gibbs Brothers & Company. Gibbs Brothers & Company, Huntsville, a family partnership concerned primarily with land-owning and investments, is reputedly the oldest continuous business in Texas still on its original site and under the same ownership. It began when Thomas Gibbs moved to Texas in 1841 and opened a general mercantile store and was in 1847 joined by his brother, Sandford St. John Gibbs, to form the original partnership. The firm built the first brick building in Walker County, which is now commemorated by a Texas historical marker. Thomas Gibbs was the first-named executor in the will of Sam Houston, who was a regular customer of the firm. Gibbs Brothers & Company's private bank became the Gibbs National Bank in 1890 and the First National Bank in 1922. Also in 1922 the mercantile business was discontinued, and the firm thereafter concentrated on acquiring land and making other forms of investments.

J. Philip Gibbs, Jr.

*Gibbs Field.

*Gibson, Charles Reese.

*Gibson, Fenton M.

*Gibson, George Miles.

*Gibson Creek.

*Gibtown, Texas.

*Giddings, DeWitt Clinton.

*Giddings, George H.

*Giddings, Jabez Deming.

*Giddings, Texas. Giddings, seat of Lee County, had two banks, a hospital, thirteen churches, two weekly newspapers, and recreational facilities for swimming, fishing, and hunting in 1970. Its ninety businesses in 1970 were chiefly concerned with poultry and livestock processing and the manufacturing of boats and boat trailers. The 1960 population was 2,821; the 1970 total was 2,783.

*Giddings-Clark Election Contest.

*Gideon, Samuel Edward.

Gidley, William Francis. William Francis Gidley was born on November 5, 1882, in Holly, Michigan, the son of Benjamin Franklin and Anna (Bailey) Gidley. He received a B.S. in pharmacy and a degree in pharmaceutical chemistry from the University of Michigan in 1908. He married Mamie Winifred Belford on September 7, 1910, and they had four children.

He began work as a drugstore clerk in 1900. During the 1908–1909 academic year he was a tutor at the University of Michigan. In 1909 he was appointed dean of Mercer University College of Pharmacy, Macon, Georgia, serving for three years in that capacity. Thereafter he was bacteriologist and chemist of the city of Macon, Georgia, for two years. He was made professor of *materia medica* at Purdue University and served in that position for five years. In 1918 he was professor of pharmacy at Purdue and remained in that position until 1924.

During that time he was also chief of the medical staff of E. R. Squibb in New York for one year.

He came to the University of Texas as dean of the College of Pharmacy in 1924 and served in that capacity until 1947, when he resigned in favor of teaching duties in that department. He was the author of *Prefixes and Suffixes of Scientific Nomenclature* (1940). In 1957 he retired from the faculty.

He was a member of the American Pharmaceutical Association, which awarded him its Schlotterbeck Award, the American Association for the Advancement of Science, Texas Academy of Science, and the American Chemical Society. Gidley, a member of the Methodist church, died in Austin on May 18, 1965.

Fred C. Morse

Giesecke, Frederick Ernest. Frederick Ernest Giesecke was born on January 28, 1869, in Latium, Washington County, Texas, the son of Julius and Wilhelmina (Groos) Giesecke, both of whom had come to America from Hanover, Germany. In 1873 Giesecke moved with his parents to New Braunfels.

He was graduated from the New Braunfels public school in 1882 and the German-English School in San Marcos in 1883. In September, 1883, he entered Texas A&M College (now Texas A&M University) and graduated in June, 1886, at the head of his class. At the close of his senior year, at the age of seventeen, he was named an instructor in mechanical engineering. In addition to teaching, he also worked toward his master's degree, which he received in 1890.

In 1888 a Department of Drawing was created and Giesecke was made instructor and head of the new department. After becoming associate professor of drawing and acting head of the department, he married Hulda C. Gruene of New Braunfels. They had four children. Giesecke spent the summer of 1893 at Cornell University, studying architectural drawing; fifteen months abroad, during which he studied in Berlin; a year at Massachusetts Institute of Technology, where he earned his S.B. in architecture; and a year at the University of Illinois, where he earned his Ph.D.

He served as professor of architectural engineering and drawing at Texas A&M from 1906 to 1912 and as professor of architecture and architectural engineering at the University of Texas from 1912 to 1927. He then returned to Texas A&M, where he taught until his retirement in 1945. During the years of teaching, he wrote a textbook on descriptive geometry, as well as three textbooks, later combined (and revised in collaboration with two other professors) into one entitled *Technical Drawing*. This text became internationally used. In addition, he wrote some eighty articles.

Giesecke was elected national president of the American Society of Heating and Ventilating Engineers; in 1941 he received the F. Paul Anderson gold medal "in recognition of his notable contributions to the advancement of heating based on his research work." He died in New Braunfels on June

27, 1953. In honor of his contributions as a teacher, architect, engineer, and scholar, the F. E. Giesecke Memorial Fund was established on May 25, 1954, in Houston.

Uel Stephens

*Giladon Creek.

*Gilbert, Mabel.

*Gilbert, Preston.

*Gilbert, Sarah.

*Gilbert Creek.

*Gilburg, Texas.

Gilchrist, Gibb. Gibb Gilchrist was born on December 23, 1887, at Wills Point, Van Zandt County. He was the son of Angus Jackson and Katherine (Douglass) Gilchrist, who named him Gibb, even though his name appears on some official documents as Gilbert Houston Gilchrist (a name he chose to satisfy the registrar at the University of Texas). He attended Southwestern University at Georgetown for one year before entering the University of Texas in the fall of 1906. Awarded a degree in civil engineering in 1909, he became a civil engineer for the Santa Fe Railroad System in 1910, working on their expanding lines in West Texas and on the Gulf Coast until joining the United States Army in 1917.

At the end of World War I Gilchrist was discharged as a captain of engineers and took the position of division engineer in southwestern Texas for the newly created Texas State Highway Department;qv in 1924, he was named the state highway engineer for Texas. Because of political differences with the administration of Governor Miriam A. Ferguson,qv Gilchrist resigned as state engineer; from 1925 to 1927 he was a consulting engineer in Dallas, but by January, 1928, he was again in Austin as state engineer, holding that position until 1937. During this period many innovations in highway building were made in Texas. While Gilchrist seldom took personal credit for the changes, many lasting contributions came under his administration: beautification of roadways, including the planting of native shrubs and flowers; use of the first landscape architect in highway construction; development of the first roadside parks (an idea credited to a foreman in Fayette County); and the preservation of trees along proposed roadways. The mileage of paved roads in Texas more than doubled during Gilchrist's administration.

In 1937 Gibb Gilchrist was named dean of engineering at Texas A&M College (now Texas A&M University), and in 1944 he became president of the college, which included at that time presidency of the branch colleges and experiment stations as well. He served as chairman of the Engineering Committee of 75 of the President's Highway Safety Conference from 1946 to 1950 (appointed by President Harry S. Truman). One of the planners and organizers of the Texas A&M College System,qv Gilchrist became its first chancellor in September, 1948, becoming chancellor emeritus upon his retirement in 1953.

On March 29, 1920, Gilchrist married Vesta Weaver; they had one son. He belonged to numerous organizations, including the Philosophical Society of Texas and the Texas State Historical Association.qqv The city of Gilchrist, a resort area in Galveston County, was named for Gibb Gilchrist. He died on May 12, 1972, in Bryan.

BIBLIOGRAPHY: *Who's Who In America* (1952); R. Henderson Shuffler, "Aggies are Different," *Alcalde,* LX (November, 1971); Dallas *News,* May 13, 1972; Fort Worth *Star-Telegram,* May 13, 1972; Biographical File, Barker Texas History Center, University of Texas at Austin.

Gilchrist, Texas. Gilchrist, a resort area in Galveston County, was named for Gibb Gilchrist,qv a civil engineer for the Santa Fe Railroad System, who relocated and reconstructed the railroad from Port Bolivar to High Island following the 1915 Galveston storm. When this project was finished in 1916, the chief engineer, Frank Merritt, named the town in honor of Gilchrist. In 1970 the population was 750.

Giles, Alfred. Alfred Giles was born in London, England, on May 23, 1853, the son of Thomas and Sophia (Brown) Giles. He attended school in England, studied for the ministry, then turned to architecture, and was graduated from King's College, London. Giles came to the United States in 1872, and in 1875 he established the firm of Alfred Giles, Architect, in San Antonio, Texas.

He designed many buildings in Texas and northern Mexico, many of which still stood in 1970. In 1908 Giles was president of the San Antonio Architect's Society, which in that year activated the movement to revive the Texas State Association of Architects. Giles owned, with his father-in-law, John James,qv thirteen thousand acres of land near Comfort, where he raised horses, mules, registered Aberdeen Angus cattle, and Angora goats. He was active in the Texas Cattle Raisers' Association,qv was secretary of the Texas Sheep and Goat Raisers' Association, and was active in the American Aberdeen Angus Association. His ranch, Hillingdon, was cited as a model in Richard Harding Davis' book, *The West From A Car Window* (1892).

On December 15, 1881, Giles married Annie Laura James; they were the parents of eight children. Giles died on August 13, 1920, at his Hillingdon Ranch in Comfort.

BIBLIOGRAPHY: Richard Harding Davis, *The West From A Car Window* (1892); Vinton Lee James, *Frontier and Pioneer Recollections of Early Days in San Antonio and West Texas* (1938); Charles G. Norton (ed.), *Men of Affairs of San Antonio* (n.d.); Guido Ransleben, *A Hundred Years of Comfort in Texas* (1954); *Reference Work of Prominent Men of Southwest Texas* (n.d.); San Antonio *Light,* April 12, 1953.

Edith J. Scrimgeour Giles

*Giles, Texas.

*Gilhula Creek.

*Gill, Bennett Lloyd.

*Gill, John Porter.

*Gill, Texas.

*Gillaspie, James.

*Gilleland, Daniel.

*Gilleland, Johnson (or Johnstone).

*Gilleland Creek.

*Gillespie, Julian Edgeworth.

*Gillespie, Oscar William.

*Gillespie, Robert Addison. [This title was incorrectly listed in Volume I as Gillespie, Richard Addison.]

BIBLIOGRAPHY: F. B. Heitman, *Historical Register and Dictionary of the United States Army*, II (1903).

*Gillespie County. Gillespie County was named for Robert (not Richard, as stated in Volume I) Addison Gillespie. County tourist attractions include the Lyndon Baines Johnson Birthplace...and Ranch,qv the Lyndon B. Johnson State Historic Park (*see* Parks, State), and the Admiral Nimitz Center (*see* Nimitz Hotel) in Fredericksburg. Nine-tenths of Gillespie's agricultural income was from livestock in 1970, and it was among the leading counties in sheep and goat raising. Harvested crops included grains, peaches, other fruits, and truck crops. The 1960 population was 10,048; in 1970 it was 10,553.

Gillett, Harper Baylor. *See* Lee, Harper Baylor.

*Gillett, James Buchanan. James Buchanan Gillett married Helen Baylor, daughter of George Wythe Baylor.qv They had two sons. One died in childhood; the other, James Harper Gillett,qv later gained fame as a bullfighter in Mexico under the name of Harper B. Lee (*see* Lee, Harper Baylor). Gillett was divorced from his first wife in 1889; he later married Lou Chastain, and they had four children. Gillett wrote *Six Years with the Texas Rangers* (1921). [Bibliographical item in Volume I should read J. Marvin Hunter, "Captain James B. Gillett," *Frontier Times* (September, 1933), not (July, 1933).]

BIBLIOGRAPHY: Marshall Hail, *Knight in the Sun* (1962).

Gillett, James Harper. *See* Lee, Harper Baylor

*Gillett, James S.

*Gillett, Texas.

*Gillette, Charles.

*Gillette, Henry Flavel.

*Gilliland, Texas.

*Gills Creek.

*Gilmer, Alexander.

*Gilmer, Texas. Gilmer, seat of Upshur County, was incorporated in 1903 with a council-manager form of government. The town reported eleven churches, a hospital, two nursing homes, two banks, a library, and one newspaper in 1966. In 1970 Gilmer had 154 businesses, including industries concerned with pottery making and the manufacturing of dresses, flooring, electrical fittings, and feed products; lumber milling and meat processing were also important. The 1960 population was 4,312; the 1970 population was 4,196.

*Gilmer-Aikin Law. The law passed in 1949 was the Gilmer-Aikin (not Gilmer-Aiken, as stated in Volume I) Law.

*Gilmer Female College.

*Gilmer Male Academy.

*Gilmore, Clarence Edgar.

*Gilmore Creek.

*Gilpin, Texas.

Gincape Indians. This name appears only in the 1784–1785 baptismal records at San José y San Miguel de Aguayo Mission qv in San Antonio. Gincape is evidently a variant of Inocoplo, the name of a presumably Coahuiltecan people who lived in central Tamaulipas during the middle eighteenth century. This identification is supported by the fact that the Gincape entered the mission at the same time as Mulato, Salapaque, and Tenicapeme, all from Tamaulipas. Furthermore, G. Saldivar indicates that the Mulato of Tamaulipas constituted a subdivision of the Inocoplo.

BIBLIOGRAPHY: F. W. Hodge (ed.), *Handbook of American Indians*, I (1907); W. Jiménez Moreno, "Tribus e idiomas del Norte de México," *El Norte de México y el Sur de Estados Unidos* (1944); G. Saldivar, *Los Indios de Tamaulipas* (1943).

T. N. Campbell

*Gindale, Texas.

*Ginger, Texas.

*Ginhouse Lake.

*Ginsite, Texas.

*Gipaw, Texas.

Gipson, Frederick Benjamin. Frederick (Fred) Benjamin Gipson, noted Texas author, was born on a farm near Mason, Mason County, on February 7, 1908, the son of Beck and Emma Deishler Gipson. He was graduated from Mason High School in 1926; after working at a variety of farming and ranching jobs he entered the University of Texas in 1933, where he wrote for the *Daily Texan* qv and the *Ranger*, but he left school before graduating to become a reporter for the Corpus Christi *Caller-Times* in 1937. A year later he worked for the San Angelo *Standard-Times*, worked briefly for the Denver *Post*, and soon after began to sell stories and articles to pulp western magazines and to slick magazines such as *Liberty* and *Look*. By 1944 Gipson had published a story in the more prestigious *Southwest Review*;qv many of his short stories appearing in that journal in the 1940's were prototypes for the longer works of fiction that followed.

Gipson's first full-length book, *The Fabulous Empire: Colonel Zack Miller's Story* (1946), was moderately successful (25,000 copies sold), but it was his *Hound-Dog Man* (1949) that established Gipson's reputation when it became a Book-of-the-Month Club selection and sold over 250,000 copies in the first year of publication. Many critics and readers maintain that *Hound-Dog Man* was Gipson's best work, and it remains popular with a large audience. The rapid succession of books that followed brought increasing attention to the hill country writer: *The Home Place* (1950), later filmed as *Return of the Texan*; *Big Bend: A Homesteader's Story* (1952), with J. O. Langford; *Cowhand: The Story of a Working Cowboy* (1953); *The Trail-Driving Rooster* (1955); *Recollection Creek* (1955); *Old Yeller* (1956); and *Savage Sam* (1962).

Old Yeller was the novel that Gipson considered his best work; it probably sold more copies—nearly three million by 1973—than any other novel ever written by a Texan. Set in Gipson's familiar hill country of the 1860's, the novel is the story of several months in the life of a fourteen-year-old boy left in charge of the household while his father is away. "Old Yeller," a stray dog adopted by the boy, helps in the formidable task of protecting the family in the frontier wilderness. The dog is given considerable status in the novel, but because Gipson always allows the human element to predominate in his work he can be judged as more than a writer of animal stories. One of four Gipson works made into films, *Old Yeller* had its world premiere in San Angelo in 1957; its sequel, *Savage Sam*, dealing with the same family a few years later, had its first showing in Mason in 1963. The movie versions were produced by Walt Disney Studios and continue to be popular attractions around the world. Gipson was the recipient of the William Allen White Award, the first Sequoyah Award, the Television-Radio Annual Writers Award, and the Northwest Pacific Award. He was president of the Texas Institute of Letters qv in 1965. His first marriage, which ended in divorce, was to Tommie Wynn; they had two sons. In 1967 he was married to Angelina Torres. Gipson died at his ranch near Mason on August 14, 1973, and by a special proclamation of the governor was buried in the State Cemetery qv in Austin. Gipson's place in literature, according to one critic, was that of one who has "made the term Southwest literature legitimate and meaningful" and who "accomplished the rare but admirable feat of turning the bits and pieces of folklore into myth."

BIBLIOGRAPHY: Sam H. Henderson, "Fred Gipson," *Southwest Writers Series*, 10 (1967); Author and Biographical Files, Barker Texas History Center, University of Texas at Austin.

*Girard, Texas.

*Girvin, Texas.

*Girvin Butte.

*Gist, Texas.

Givens, Newton Curd. Newton Curd Givens was born in Kentucky in 1823, son of William and Elizabeth (Prather) Givens. He was appointed to the United States Military Academy from Madison, Indiana, was graduated, and was promoted to brevet second lieutenant, 1st Dragoons, on July 1, 1845.

In the Mexican War qv he was engaged in the battle of Buena Vista and was cited for gallant and meritorious conduct. From 1850 to 1859 he served at various posts in Texas: Fort Croghan, Fort Belknap, Fort Phantom Hill, and Camp Cooper.qqv He was acquitted in one court martial and was suspended for nine months (of which five and one-half months were remitted) in another court martial. He achieved the rank of captain on February 28, 1857.

Captain Givens, well known as a hunter of animals, kept a pack of trained dogs that were often used by other officers for special hunts. His place on a tract of land in Throckmorton and Shackelford counties in the 1850's, known as the Old Stone Ranch, was the most western ranch on the northwestern frontier at the time, beyond that of Indian agent Jesse Stem.qv The remains of two rock houses and two large rock-walled corrals, built in 1856, still stand near Albany, Texas.

Givens married Mary Louisa Power; they had one daughter, who died in infancy. He died in San Antonio on March 9, 1859, from tuberculosis, at age thirty-five.

BIBLIOGRAPHY: Don H. Biggers, *Shackelford County Sketches* (1908); Mildred P. Mayhall, *Indian Wars of Texas* (1965); W. B. Parker, *Notes Taken During the Expedition Commanded by Captain R. B. Marcy, U.S.A., through Unexplored Texas in the Summer and Fall of 1854* (1856); Rupert N. Richardson, *The Frontier of Northwest Texas, 1846–1876* (1963); Givens' letters and records (Archives, University of Texas at Austin Library, originals in National Archives, Washington, D.C.).

Mildred P. Mayhall

*Givens, Texas.

*Glade, Texas.

*Glade Creek.

*Gladewater, Texas.** Gladewater, in Gregg and Upshur counties, had a 1960 population of 5,742 and a 1970 population of 5,574. In the 1960's Gladewater had five schools, twenty-one churches, four parks, and five hospitals and clinics. Center of an oil and farming area, Gladewater had 161 business establishments in 1970, and its industries produced furniture, machines, tools, clothing, and lumber.

Gladney Home. The Edna Gladney Home, in Fort Worth, was Texas' first chartered child-placing charity. Founded in 1892 as Texas Children's Home and Aid Society by the Reverend I. Z. T. Morris, the society was chartered by the state on January 25, 1904, for the purpose of "procuring homes in Texas for homeless children." Edna Gladney joined the board in 1910.

Superintendent Morris died in 1914, leaving the society's work to his wife, Isabella, who carried on in his position until 1924. Because of her outstanding social work in Sherman in the years 1909–1918, Mrs. Gladney was asked to become the home's superintendent in 1925. Until retirement in 1959 she was the guiding spirit of the home's statewide operations. Her career inspired the motion picture, *Blossoms in the Dust* (1941), as well as magazine and newspaper stories.

Renamed the Edna Gladney Home in 1950, it was in the 1960's a maternity home and child-placing agency accredited by the Child Welfare League of America. Financed by fees, endowments, and contributions, complete medical care for unmarried mothers was provided, including professional counseling. Educational facilities such as accredited grade and high school courses, business courses, university-level extension courses, and a library were available for unmarried mothers. In 1968 the capacity of the home was ninety residents. Application was made by referring agencies or by the individual.

BIBLIOGRAPHY: Texas Department of Public Welfare, *The Unmarried Parent Needs Your Help* (1967).

Ruby Lee Piester

*Gladstell, Texas.

*Gladstone, Texas.

*Gladwin, John.

*Gladys City, Texas.

*Glanton, John Joel.

*Glasco, Jesse Martin.

*Glass, Anthony.

Glass, Herman A. Herman A. Glass was born on March 23, 1890, in Granite, Oklahoma, the son of John Thomas and Fannie (Bunkley) Glass. His youth was spent in Donley County. He attended school at McLean and at West Texas State College (now West Texas State University), where he received his B.A. degree. He received his M.A. degree from the University of Chicago and taught in the public schools at McLean and Clarendon, West Texas State College, East Texas State College, and North Texas State College (all now universities).

Glass pioneered the junior high school system in Wichita Falls, and after a twelve-year tenure there, became superintendent of schools at Bonham until 1938, when he was appointed director of textbooks for the state. He served in this capacity until his retirement in 1960. In recognition of his many services to education in Texas, the degree of Doctor of Humanities was conferred on him by Midwestern University at Wichita Falls in August, 1956. He was a charter member of the National Association of Textbook Directors and served as president and secretary of that organization.

Glass married Abbie Clibourne in 1922; they had one daughter. He died on February 19, 1963, and was buried in Memorial Park Cemetery, Austin.

Peggy M. Baker

*Glass, Texas. (Robertson County.)

*Glass, Texas. (Somervell County.)

*Glass Mountains.

Glasscock, Charles Gus. Charles Gus Glasscock was born on December 16, 1895, in Leon County, Texas, the son of J. B. and Elizabeth (Armstrong) Glasscock. He attended the public schools at Longview and Blanco, and Southwest Texas State College (now Southwest Texas State University) at San Marcos. Prior to World War I Glasscock and his three brothers performed as acrobats with Ringling Brothers; later they opened a vaudeville act at Madison Square Garden and performed on the big vaudeville circuits. In 1917 he married Lucille Freeman; they had two children. Rejected for military service in 1917, he worked briefly in the construction and taxicab businesses, then in the Texas oil fields. In December, 1919, Glasscock and his three brothers formed an oil syndicate. It was not until 1927 that their well near

Big Spring came in and Glasscock's career began a meteoric rise. In 1939 he moved to Corpus Christi and organized his own drilling company. His first venture into tidewater drilling was a rig in Corpus Christi Bay in 1948. Dissatisfied with the cumbersome method and expense of this new facet of the oil industry, Glasscock contracted with Bethlehem Steel for a barge-rig that could be towed to a drilling site for stationary mooring. The barge was 155 feet long and 52 feet wide, with draft of 5½ feet. The jackknife derrick was 132 feet high. The lower section of the barge could be dropped to the floor of the bay and the upper half could be elevated on caissons above wave interference. The unit cost $700,000. Auxiliary barges carried equipment and supplies. The innovation was a success, resulting in the construction of fleets of similar rigs. Use of the barge-rigs revolutionized tidewater drilling, made Glasscock the biggest offshore driller in the state, and gave him national prominence.

When the United States returned the tidelands of Texas to state ownership in 1953 (*see* Tidelands Controversy), new problems soon developed with deepwater drilling. Another Glasscock innovation resulted in "Mr. Gus," a modified barge-rig equipped to drill a fifteen-thousand-foot well. Its cost exceeded one million dollars. It was also a success and was soon emulated by competitors all over the world.

Glasscock also had extensive holdings in oil properties and real estate, with ranches in Texas, Montana, and Wyoming. He served on the staffs of Governors Robert Kennan and Jimmie Davis of Louisiana and Governor Price Daniel of Texas. He was a strong supporter of the University of Corpus Christi from that institution's founding. Glasscock died on January 25, 1965, in Corpus Christi

BIBLIOGRAPHY: Lucille Glasscock, *A Texas Wildcatter* (1952); *Time* (June 21, July 2, 1954); Corpus Christi *Caller*, May 8, 1962, January 26, February 2, April 5, 1965; Corpus Christi *Caller-Times*, October 15, 1951, January 13, 1957, January 23, 1966; Corpus Christi *Times*, September 12, 1962, January 25, 26, 1965.

J. E. Conner

*Glasscock, George Washington. George Washington Glasscock died on February 28, 1868 (not February 28, 1879, as stated in Volume I).

*Glasscock, George Washington, Jr.

*Glasscock, James A. James Abner Glasscock was born in Kentucky in 1816, the son of Thomas and Jane (Milligan) Glasscock and brother of George Washington Glasscock.qv He came to Texas before November 11, 1842, when he joined Captain Ewen Cameron's qv company for the Mier Expedition.qv He was imprisoned in Mexico from December, 1842, until September 16, 1844, when he was released by the Mexican government. He soon sailed from Vera Cruz for New Orleans.

Glasscock, Michael Cronican, and Frank Brown qqv went to San Antonio in 1848 and established the *Western Texian*, one of the first newspapers to be published in that town. Glasscock became sole proprietor on April 27, 1849. He returned to Austin in 1849 and worked for the *Texas State Gazette.*qv Sometime after October, 1850, he left for El Paso with Major R. S. Neighbors.qv He later went to California where, in 1859, he was living in Siskiyou County. He died in 1876.

BIBLIOGRAPHY: Frank Brown, Annals of Travis County and the City of Austin (MS., Archives, University of Texas at Austin Library); Jacobina B. Harding, A History of the Early Newspapers of San Antonio, 1823–1874 (Master's thesis, University of Texas at Austin, 1951); James M. Day (ed.), "Diary of James A. Glasscock, Mier Man," *Texana,* I (1963); Public Debt Papers of the Republic of Texas (Archives, Texas State Library).

Seth D. Breeding

Glasscock County. Glasscock County, a ranching, farming, and oil producing county in West Texas, had a 1960 population of 1,118 and a 1970 count of 1,155. Cattle and sheep, the chief livestock, contribute about one-half of the farm income; the remainder comes from grain sorghums, silage, and hay. During 1961–1962, about twenty-five sections of rangeland were subdivided and put under cultivation. More than twenty thousand acres were reported irrigated in 1968. The county produced 106,967,695 barrels of oil and a small amount of natural gas from 1925 to 1973.

*Glaze City, Texas.

*Glazier, Texas.

*Glecklar, Texas.

*Glen Cove, Texas.

*Glen Eden Plantation.

*Glen Rose, Texas. Glen Rose, seat of Somervell County, is primarily a resort and local market. Recreational facilities include camps and cottages for hunting, fishing, and swimming. Glen Rose reported thirty-three businesses in 1969. Dinosaur tracks found in the riverbed of the nearby Paluxy continue to be of interest. In 1966 the town had six churches, a hospital, a bank, and a newspaper. The 1960 population was 1,422; the 1970 population was 1,554.

*Glen Rose Collegiate Institute.

*Glen Spring, Texas.

*Glen Spring Draw.

*Glenblythe Plantation.

*Glendale, Texas.

*Glenfawn, Texas.

*Glenflora, Texas.

*Glenham, Texas.

*Glenn Creek.

*Glenrio, Texas.

*Glenwood, Texas. Although the Glenwood area, in Upshur County, was settled earlier, it was not until after the Civil War that the village flourished; in 1865 a post office was established, and Wiley Florence was the first postmaster. The post office was discontinued in 1932.

BIBLIOGRAPHY: G. H. Baird, A Brief History of Upshur County (1946).

*Glenwood Creek.

*Glidden, Texas.

*Globe, Texas.

*Glory, Texas.

*Goacher, James. James Goacher's name has been variously spelled in early Texas writings as Gotier, Gocher, Goucher, and Gotcher.

BIBLIOGRAPHY: John H. Jenkins (ed.), *Recollections of Early Texas* (1958).

*Goacher's Trace.

*Goat Creek.

*Goat Mountain.

*Goat Ranching. Texas was the nation's leading producer of mohair from Angora goats in the 1950's, 1960's, and 1970's, although there was a marked decline in both demand and prices for mohair by the early 1970's. In 1964, 3,978,000 goats produced 28,872,000 pounds of mohair valued at $27,428,000. By 1966 three-fourths of all Angora goats in the United States were located on less than eight thousand ranches near San Angelo, Rocksprings ("Goat Capital of the World"), and Uvalde. Mohair production that year totaled 28,770,000 pounds valued at $15,536,000. Production continued to be centered around the Edwards Plateau and nearby central and north-central Texas counties. In 1972, with 10,190,000 pounds of mohair valued at $8,458,000 from 1,521,000 animals shorn, Texas produced 97 percent of the nation's and nearly 50 percent of the world's mohair clip.

BIBLIOGRAPHY: *Texas Almanac* (1955, 1963, 1965, 1967, 1969, 1973).

*Gober, Texas.

*Gobler Creek.

Goddin, M. H. [Although there is a lack of biographical information available on M. H. Goddin, he is included here because of his prominence in the affairs of Texas, especially Huntsville, during the Reconstruction qv period. Ed.]

M. H. Goddin, a Republican, was a member of the Constitutional Convention of 1868–1869 qv from Polk County; he was later elected to the Constitutional Convention of 1875 qv from Walker County. Less than a week after the latter convention met, he resigned his position and was replaced by Andrew Todd McKinney,qv a Democrat from Huntsville. Goddin has been identified by several authorities, including S. S. McKay and J. E. Ericson, as one of six black members of the Constitutional Convention of 1875, but while editor of the Huntsville *Union Republican*, Goddin listed himself as a white member of a grand jury; he was also identified as white by the black folklorist, J. Mason Brewer. During Reconstruction he achieved a position of substantial importance in Huntsville. Moving there from Polk County, he held the position of district clerk by early 1870, and within a period of eighteen months he had become mayor of the city, editor of the Huntsville *Union Republican*, chief justice of the peace of Walker County, and a captain in the state guard. At the time of his resignation from the Constitutional Convention of 1875, some members of that body charged that he was *non compos mentis*. Whatever caused him to leave the convention may have led him to leave public life, for within two months of his resignation from the convention he had also resigned as justice of the peace.

BIBLIOGRAPHY: S. S. McKay (ed.), *Debates in the Texas Constitutional Convention of 1875* (1942); J. Mason Brewer, *Negro Legislators of Texas and Their Descendants* (1935); Fred Cockrell, "The Making of the Constitution of 1875," *West Texas Historical Association Year Book*, V (June, 1929); J. E. Ericson, "The Delegates to the Convention of 1875: A Reappraisal," *Southwestern Historical Quarterly*, LXVII (1963–1964); Huntsville *Union Republican*, February 15, 1871, April 5, 1871; Bonds and Oaths of Office (Archives, Texas State Library, Austin).

John Mauer

*Godley, Texas.

*Godley Creek.

*Goff Bayou.

*Goforth, Texas.

Goggin, James Monroe. James Monroe Goggin, son of Pleasant Moorman Goggin and Mary Otey (Leftwich) Goggin, was born on October 23, 1820, in Bedford County, Virginia. He attended the United States Military Academy at West Point in the class of 1842, although he did not graduate. Immigrating to the Republic of Texas, he served in the Texas Army as a lieutenant in the 1st Infantry and during that time, as well as later, acquired large land holdings, principally in Waller County. Goggin lived in Missouri, California, and Tennessee from 1844 until 1861, when he entered the Confederate Army as major of the 32nd Virginia Infantry. Commended for gallantry, Goggin was appointed brigadier general to rank from December 4, 1864, but probably because there was no vacant brigade at the time, the appointment was subsequently cancelled and he returned to staff duty at his former rank of major.

Following the war, Goggin returned to Texas and was a planter in Waller County until his removal about 1883 to Austin, where he died on October 10, 1889. Goggin married Elizabeth Nelson Page on February 13, 1860, and they had several children. Both Goggin and his wife were buried in Oakwood Cemetery at Austin.

BIBLIOGRAPHY: Service Records of J. M. Goggin, in War Department, Adjutant General's Office, Confederate Records (National Archives, Washington, D.C.); Ezra J. Warner, *Generals in Gray* (1959); U. S. War Department, *The War of the Rebellion: A Compilation of the Official Records of the Union and Confederate Armies* (1880–1901); Austin *Statesman*, October 11, 1889.

Palmer Bradley

*Gohlke, Texas.

Golconda, Texas. Golconda, created by an act of the legislature on August 27, 1856, as the first seat of Palo Pinto County, was the site of commissioners court meetings in 1857. Later the name Golconda was changed to Palo Pinto; the reason for this change is not recorded. The Postal Guide of the United States Post Office Department for the year 1858 lists as post offices both Golconda and Palo Pinto.

BIBLIOGRAPHY: Mary Whatley Clarke, *The Palo Pinto Story* (1956); *Texas Almanac* (1936).

*Gold, Texas.

*Gold Creek.

*Gold Mining in Texas.

*Golden, Texas.

*Goldenrod Creek.

*Goldfinch, Texas.

*Goldmine Creek.

*Goldsboro, Texas. Goldsboro is in northwestern Coleman County (not in the northeastern part of the county, as stated in Volume I). It had a population of approximately thirty in 1970.

*Goldsmith, Texas.

*Goldthwaite, George.

*Goldthwaite, Texas. Goldthwaite, seat of Mills County, had the world's largest sheep and goat auction business, as well as facilities for feeding and marketing turkeys and lambs and processing wool and mohair. In 1963 the city completed a water plant, and in 1965 improvements on the hospital were finished. In 1966 the town had six churches, a bank, library, newspaper, and radio station. Goldthwaite reported sixty-four businesses in 1970. The 1960 population was 1,383; the 1970 population was 1,693.

*Goliad, Texas. The Nuestra Señora del Espíritu (not Espírito, as shown in Volume I) Santo de Zuñiga Mission qv was located in Goliad in 1749. In the 1960's Goliad continued to attract tourists to its historic sites, such as the restored presidio La Bahía, qv and the "hanging tree." The city is a commercial center for the petroleum, ranching, and farming interests of Goliad County. In 1966 the city reported a bank, weekly newspaper, county library, county hospital, new fire station, and nursing home. In 1970 it reported sixty business establishments. The city government was administered by a mayor and two commissioners. The population was 1,782 in 1960 and 1,709 in 1970.

*Goliad Campaign of 1835. The man referred to in Captain George M. Collingsworth's qv report as being wounded in the shoulder during the taking of Goliad was a free Negro named Samuel McCulloch qv (not Greenberry Logan,qv as stated in Volume I). McCulloch's name is sometimes spelled McCullock or McCullough.

BIBLIOGRAPHY: Harold Schoen, "The Free Negro in the Republic of Texas," *Southwestern Historical Quarterly*, XL (1936–1937).

*Goliad Campaign of 1836.

*Goliad College.

*Goliad County. Goliad County is well known for its many points of interest, including the Goliad State Historic Park, Fannin Battleground State Historic Site, General (Ignacio) Zaragoza qv State Historic Site (*see* Parks, State), the recently restored La Bahía qv presidio, Trail of Six Flags, and the grave of Texans murdered in the Goliad Massacre qv in 1836, in whose honor an annual memorial service is held. In 1964 the courthouse was enlarged and modernized. By 1965 the annual production of oil had dropped one-half million barrels from the two million barrels produced in 1950. Total production reached 55,847,755 barrels in 1973 since its discovery in 1930. Ranching continued to be important, and Arabian, Appaloosa, and Quarter Horses were raised and sold in the county. A thirty-thousand-acre conservation program cleared brushlands for improved pasturage and provided for increases in cattle production. By 1965 the cultivated lands under irrigation had increased to three thousand acres. Crops included cotton, corn, grain sorghums, flax, and broomcorn. Population was 5,429 in 1960 and 4,869 in 1970.

*Goliad Declaration of Independence.

*Goliad Massacre.

*Goliad State Park. Nuestra Señora del Espíritu Santo de Zuñiga Mission qv (not the chapel of Nuestra Señora de Loreto Presidio,qv as stated in Volume I) is popularly known as La Bahía qv mission, and is part of the Goliad State Historic Park. See also Parks, State; La Bahía.

*Golightly, Thomas Jefferson.

*Golindo, Texas.

*Golly, Texas.

*Golondrina Creek.

*Gómez Farías, Valentín.

*Gomez, Texas.

*Gomez Peak.

*Gonzales, Rafael.

*Gonzales, Texas. Gonzales, seat of Gonzales County, is the center of a large poultry producing and farming area in which pecans, peanuts, corn, grain sorghums, cotton, and melons are the principal crops. Recent industrial developments include a poultry processing plant, a commercial pizza industry, numerous hatcheries, veterinary medicine manufacture, feed production, egg processing plants, a cottonseed oil mill, a cotton gin, a clay products factory, a spark plug reconditioning plant, and the manufacture of cotton bagging and twine. Gonzales reported twenty-two churches, two hospitals, and a convalescent home in 1966. In 1970 the town reported 190 business establishments. The population in 1960 was 5,829, and in 1970 the count was 5,854.

*Gonzales, Battle of.

*Gonzales Branch Railroad Company.

*Gonzales College.

*Gonzales County. Gonzales County derived one-half its farm income in the mid-1960's from poultry, particularly eggs, broilers, and turkeys. Hogs, pecans, peanuts, cotton, and a wide variety of vegetables were also important. In 1960 and 1968 Gonzales County ranked eighth in cattle raising in Texas. Commercial clays, sand, and gravel are produced and processed. Numerous historic sites, such as a museum commemorating the role played by Gonzales in the Texas Revolution qv and a statue by Pompeo Coppini,qv serve as tourist attractions.

The small town of Ottine is the site of both Palmetto State Park and the Texas Warm Springs Foundation.qqv County population was 17,845 in 1960 and 16,375 in 1970.

*Gonzales Creek.

*Good, John Jay.

*Good Creek.

*Good Hope, Texas.

Good Neighbor Commission. The Good Neighbor Commission, created in 1945, was composed of nine members appointed by the governor. The function of the commission was to promote favorable inter-American relations and to maintain an intrastate program of eliminating friction between English- and Spanish-speaking groups. In 1965 the Texas Council on Migrant Labor qv was abolished and its duties were transferred to the Good Neighbor Commission.

BIBLIOGRAPHY: University of Texas at Austin, Guide To Texas State Agencies (1972).

*Good Springs, Texas.

*Goodbread, Joseph G.

*Goodfellow Air Force Base. Goodfellow Air Force Base carried on primary pilot training from 1950 until June, 1954. From that time until September, 1958, the base conducted pilot training in the two-engined B-25 light bomber.

In October, 1958, the Air Training Command transferred Goodfellow Air Force Base to the United States Air Force Security Service, with headquarters in San Antonio. During the 1960's the base trained officers and airmen in technical skills used by the security service.

*Goodland, Texas. (Bailey County.)

*Goodland, Texas. (Robertson County.)

*Goodlett, Texas.

*Goodloe, Robert Kemp. Robert Kemp Goodloe was married to Nerisa Agnes Roberts on January 11, 1838, in San Augustine; they were the parents of ten children. Several years after his wife's death on July 10, 1868, Goodloe was married a second time, to Henrietta Martin, from whom he was probably separated by the time of his death on October 20, 1879. Robert Kemp and Nerisa Agnes (Roberts) Goodloe were both buried in the old Sabinetown Cemetery, sometimes called the Goodloe Cemetery or Beddoe Springs Cemetery, located in Sabinetown.

Helen Gomer Schluter

*Goodnight, Charles.

*Goodnight, Texas.

*Goodnight Academy.

*Goodnight-Loving Trail. Goodnight and Loving first drove a herd along the trail in 1866 (not 1886, as stated in Volume I). [Some later printings of Volume I contain this correction.]

*Goodnight Ranch.

*Goodnight Trail.

*Goodrich, Benjamin Briggs.

*Goodrich, John Calvin.

*Goodrich, Texas.

*Goodwyn Creek.

*Goose Branch.

*Goose Creek.

*Goose Creek, Texas. In 1947 Goose Creek, Pelly, and Baytown were not consolidated under the name Baytown (as stated in Volume I). Pelly first annexed unincorporated Baytown, then Pelly and Goose Creek were consolidated in 1947, taking the name Baytown. *See* Baytown, Texas.

*Goose Creek Oil Field.

*Gorbet, Chester S.

*Gordon, John Fletcher.

*Gordon, William Knox.

*Gordon, Texas.

*Gordonville, Texas.

Goree, Thomas Jewett. Thomas Jewett Goree was born in Perry County, Alabama, on November 14, 1835, son of Langston and Sarah Goree. The family moved to Texas in the 1850's, settling in Walker County in 1855. After attending Howard College in Marion, Alabama, Goree took an A.B. degree from Baylor University (then located at Independence). He read law for two years, then was admitted to the Walker County Bar in 1858, practicing law until 1861, when he enlisted as a scout in the Confederate Army. By the end of the war he was a major. He returned to the practice of law in Houston in 1865 and was also in the merchandising business in Walker County around 1873.

Goree was appointed superintendent of the Texas Prison System qv in 1877, at a time when that system was embroiled in controversy. He remained for fourteen years, leaving the state's employ in June, 1891. In that same year he was named general manager of the New Birmingham Company, an enterprise interested in the development of iron ore found in the Cherokee County area. The organization collapsed with the panic of 1893 (*see* New Birmingham, Texas). He then became associated with the Texas Sand Company in Galveston, and by 1900 he had left private business to work for the city of Galveston.

He was married to Elizabeth Thomas Nolley, and they had five children. A grandson, John William Thomason, Jr.,qv was a well-known writer-illustrator. Goree died in Galveston on March 5, 1905, and was buried in Huntsville. The Goree Unit of the Texas Prison System, which houses the state's women prisoners, was named in honor of Thomas J. Goree.

BIBLIOGRAPHY: Herman L. Crow, A Political History of the Texas Penal System, 1829–1951 (Ph.D. dissertation, University of Texas at Austin, 1964).

Herman Crow

*Goree, Texas.

*Gorey, Texas.

*Gorgas, William Crawford.

*Gorman, Texas. Gorman, in Eastland County, had a population of 1,142 in 1960 and 1,236 in 1970.

*Gorman Branch.

*Goshen, Texas. (Parker County.)

*Goshen, Texas. (Walker County.)

*Gossett, Texas.

*Gossett Creek.

*Gouge, William M.

*Gough, Lysius.

*Gough, Texas.

*Gould, Jay.

*Gould, Robert Simonton.

*Gould City, Texas.

*Gouldbusk, Texas.

*Gouldrich, Michael.

*Governor, Office of. The office of chief executive in Texas, if the earlier history of the area is considered, is older than the union of the American states and earlier by almost a century than the presidency of the United States. Although most historians settle for the year 1691 and the appointment of Domingo Terán de los Ríos qv as the beginning of Texas as a political entity, several support the year 1523, when the royal governor from Spain was Francisco de Garay.qv The long list of *gobernadores*, presidents, and governors provides a colorful index to the history of the state, and even though the basic duties of the chief executive have changed little since the Constitution of 1876,qv the personalities and politics of these officials have left their imprint on both the form and the function of state government. The following list of governors since the state was annexed to the United States, with dates of tenure in office, shows that most served more than the two-year term set by the Constitution of 1876 (extended by approval of the voters in 1972 to a four-year term, beginning in 1975).

Of these governors since statehood, only one, Edmund J. Davis, has been a Republican. W. Lee O'Daniel was the only governor who was not a voter at the time of his election, having refused to pay the required poll tax. James E. Ferguson was the only governor to be impeached, although Sam Houston was removed when he refused to take the oath of allegiance to the Confederacy and James W. Throckmorton was removed by the military. The youngest has been Dan Moody, who was thirty-three years old when elected. Two were born north of the Mason-Dixon line: Lawrence S. Ross (Iowa) and O'Daniel (Ohio). A large number of early governors were soldier-statesmen from the South. Miriam A. Ferguson was the state's only female chief executive, and she was the only governor elected to non-consecutive terms (Elisha Pease was appointed provisional governor almost ten years after serving two elective terms).

While the state's highest executive office often

GOVERNORS OF THE STATE OF TEXAS
SINCE ANNEXATION, 1845 TO 1975

NAME	TENURE OF OFFICE	COMMENTS
James Pinckney Henderson qv	Feb. 19, 1846–Dec. 21, 1847	
Albert Clinton Horton qv	May 19, 1846–Nov. ??, 1846	Acted as governor while Henderson was at war in Mexico.
George T. Wood qv	Dec. 21, 1847–Dec. 21, 1849	
Peter Hansborough Bell qv	Dec. 21, 1849–Nov. 23, 1853	Resigned to enter U.S. Congress.
James Wilson Henderson qv	Nov. 23, 1853–Dec. 21, 1853	Became governor when Bell resigned to take congressional seat.
Elisha Marshall Pease qv	Dec. 21, 1853–Dec. 21, 1857	
Hardin Richard Runnels qv	Dec. 21, 1857–Dec. 21, 1859	
Sam Houston qv	Dec. 21, 1859–March 16, 1861	Deposed when he refused oath of allegiance to Confederacy.
Edward Clark qv	March 16, 1861–Nov. 7, 1861	
Francis Richard Lubbock qv	Nov. 7, 1861–Nov. 5, 1863	Retired voluntarily to serve as advisor for Confederate Army.
Pendleton Murrah qv	Nov. 5, 1863–June 17, 1865	Administration ended with fall of Confederacy.
Fletcher S. Stockdale qv	June 17, 1865–July 21, 1865	Served as acting governor when Murrah fled to Mexico. Removed by U.S. authorities.
Andrew Jackson Hamilton qv	July 21, 1865–Aug. 9, 1866	Provisional governor.
James Webb Throckmorton qv	Aug. 9, 1866–Aug. 8, 1867	Removed by U.S. Military.
Elisha Marshall Pease qv	Aug. 8, 1867–Sept. 30, 1869	Provisional governor (appointed); resigned, leaving state without governor until Jan. 8, 1870.
Edmund Jackson Davis qv	Jan. 8, 1870–Jan. 15, 1874	Elected, then appointed provisional governor. At first refused to give up seat to Coke (*see* Coke-Davis Controversy).
Richard Coke qv	Jan. 15, 1874–Dec. 1, 1876	Resigned to enter U.S. Senate.
Richard Bennett Hubbard qv	Dec. 1, 1876–Jan. 21, 1879	
Oran Milo Roberts qv	Jan. 21, 1879–Jan. 16, 1883	
John Ireland qv	Jan. 16, 1883–Jan. 18, 1887	
Lawrence Sullivan Ross qv	Jan. 18, 1887–Jan. 20, 1891	
James Stephen Hogg qv	Jan. 20, 1891–Jan. 15, 1895	First native-born governor.
Charles Allen Culberson qv	Jan. 15, 1895–Jan. 17, 1899	
Joseph Draper Sayers qv	Jan. 17, 1899–Jan. 20, 1903	
Samuel Willis Tucker Lanham qv	Jan. 20, 1903–Jan. 15, 1907	Last Confederate veteran to be governor.
Thomas Mitchell Campbell qv	Jan. 15, 1907–Jan. 19, 1911	
Oscar Branch Colquitt qv	Jan. 19, 1911–Jan. 19, 1915	
James Edward Ferguson qv	Jan. 19, 1915–Aug. 25, 1917	Impeached.
William Pettus Hobby qv	Aug. 25, 1917–Jan. 18, 1921	
Pat Morris Neff qv	Jan. 18, 1921–Jan. 20, 1925	
Miriam Amanda Ferguson qv	Jan. 20, 1925–Jan. 17, 1927	First woman elected governor in the United States.
Daniel James Moody, Jr. qv	Jan. 17, 1927–Jan. 20, 1931	
Ross S. Sterling qv	Jan. 20, 1931–Jan. 17, 1933	

NAME	TENURE OF OFFICE	COMMENTS
Miriam Amanda Ferguson qv	Jan. 17, 1933–Jan. 15, 1935	Only governor elected to two non-consecutive terms.
James V. Allred qv	Jan. 15, 1935–Jan. 17, 1939	
Wilbert Lee O'Daniel qv	Jan. 17, 1939–Aug. 4, 1941	Resigned to enter U.S. Senate.
Coke Robert Stevenson qv	Aug. 4, 1941–Jan. 21, 1947	Became governor when O'Daniel resigned; elected to two additional terms.
Beauford Halbert Jester qv	Jan. 21, 1947–July 11, 1949	First to die while in office.
Allan Shivers	July 11, 1949–Jan. 15, 1957	First governor to be elected to three consecutive terms, after having served unexpired term of previous governor, for a total of seven and one-half years, longest of any governor.
Price Daniel	Jan. 15, 1957–Jan. 15, 1963	Three terms.
John Connally	Jan. 15, 1963–Jan. 21, 1969	Three terms.
Preston Smith	Jan. 21, 1969–Jan. 16, 1973	
Dolph Briscoe	Jan. 16, 1973–Jan. 21, 1975 Jan. 21, 1975–	By constitutional amendment, approved by Texas voters in 1972, the term of office for governor was increased to four years, effective in 1975. Briscoe, reelected in 1974, was the first governor to assume the four-year term, which began January 21, 1975.

[*See also* Republic of Texas (in Volume II), for list of executive officers, 1835–1845; Lieutenant Governor, Office of (in this volume), for list of lieutenant governors, 1845–1975.]

has been regarded as a stepping-stone to high national offices, few former governors have actually been successful in gaining them. Since 1876 only three, Coke, Culberson, and O'Daniel, have served in the United States Senate after their governorships; Ireland, Campbell, Moody, Allred, and Stevenson failed in bids for the U.S. Senate, while James Ferguson was defeated for the U.S. Senate as well as for nomination as president on the Know-Nothing party qv ticket. On the other hand, Price Daniel resigned his seat in the U.S. Senate to become governor. John Connally was appointed secretary of the treasury of the United States after his term of office, having served as secretary of the navy before his election, thus becoming the only Texas governor to hold high national office both before and after his term. For the most part, Texas governors returned to their previous occupations after stepping down, content to accept posts at the state level when they stayed in public life; several retired into obscurity.

. No definite pattern is discernible in the political experience, educational background, or occupation of those attaining the office of governor. In political experience, the area of law enforcement produced the largest number of successful candidates, with several having previously served as state attorney general or as a county attorney or district attorney. Former legislators and others who served in some capacity in state or local law enforcement or regulatory agencies were also successful. Most governors of Texas received at least some higher education from Texas institutions, while several held degrees from such schools as Harvard University, College of William and Mary, Virginia Military Institute, and the University of Virginia. In occupation or profession, the largest number have been lawyers, most of whom received legal training in Texas. No college professor or small-town merchant has ever been elected, but the occupations of those outside the legal profession have ranged from newspaper editor to flour manufacturer to housewife.

The religious background of candidates has played an important part in the elections for governor. All governors of Texas since annexation have been Protestants, mostly Baptists and Methodists, and only a very few have not been Masons. Although the proportions of church members in the state's total population have changed very little in this century, with Roman Catholics annually reporting almost as many members as the Baptists (who lead all denominations), no Roman Catholic has been elected chief executive since annexation.

Both the place of birth and the residence at the time of election have also been important in determining who was elected. More governors have come from East and Central Texas than any other geographic area, although in the 1960's and 1970's Preston Smith (Northwest), John Connally (South), and Dolph Briscoe (Southwest) were the first governors to come from their respective areas. Near the turn of the century the city of Tyler was the state's political stronghold. For many years the official residences (at the time of gaining office) for governors and other state officials were in East Texas, but by mid-century the central portion of the state claimed a higher percentage. Since 1876 McLennan and Smith counties have each sent three persons to the governor's chair, while Jefferson, Tarrant, and Bell counties have each sent two.

By tradition and general acceptance the governor has been the party leader in the state. The convention of rank and file delegates in each party, often called the "Governor's Convention" and held in September, gives the party's nominee an opportunity to put his own campaign promises into the state platform, as well as to secure control of the party machinery. Exceptions to the governor's control of the party have been few, and mostly since 1920, when Pat M. Neff gave the convention a free hand in writing a platform and selecting the state executive committee for the Democrats. Ross Sterling suffered loss of control to the opposing Ferguson-dominated convention in 1932, which put Mrs. Ferguson back in office. Another example of weak party leadership was O'Daniel, who seemed indifferent to party matters. By 1944 a large split had separated the Democrats, with former governors Moody and Allred each heading opposing forces which clashed over national and state Democratic policies. Moody, leader of the "Texas Regulars," and Allred, a "New Dealer" supporting President Franklin D. Roosevelt, clashed first at the national convention, with Governor Coke Stevenson trying to restore some unity by appeasing both factions. Allred and his forces won control at the state convention, severing the governor's hold almost completely.

Stevenson's separation from party control was a clear warning for future governors, however. Beauford Jester was able to steer his administration through a middle-of-the-road era which in effect gave leadership in the party back to the chief executive, a leadership all governors have enjoyed since. Allan Shivers demonstrated his control by leading a successful bolt from the Democratic ticket which supported Adlai Stevenson in the general election of 1952. He was supported in this remarkable move by his attorney general, Price Daniel, who ruled that Texans could write in the names of Dwight D. Eisenhower qv and Richard M. Nixon "without losing status as Democrats." Not coincidentally, Daniel was later to pursue the Tidelands Controversy qv to its conclusions during the administration of Eisenhower, who had been noncommittal about the tidelands before the election, while Adlai Stevenson was known to be unfavorable to Texas' position. Price Daniel was aided at his convention by the appearance of Sam Rayburn and Lyndon B. Johnson,qqv whose pleas for party harmony brought a largely divided Democratic party back under Daniel's control.

Recent governors have enjoyed long tenure and fairly strong party control. The Sharpstown Stock Fraud Scandal qv possibly kept Preston Smith from the third term which his three predecessors had enjoyed, however, and the rise of the Raza Unida party qv as a political force large enough to draw votes away from the Democratic contender in 1972 almost threw the election to the Republican candidate.

The office of governor is probably not as strong in Texas as in some other states. Legally, at least, the governor has little power over certain administrative functions and has no removal power over important elected officials. His privilege of legislative veto may be his strongest executive weapon. Politically, however, the governor has been an influence on the decisions of state government at almost all levels.

See also Democratic Party in Texas; Election Laws; Political Parties; Republican Party in Texas; State Executive Officers, Compensation of.

BIBLIOGRAPHY: Fred Gantt, Jr., The Chief Executive in Texas (1964); Stuart A. MacCorkle and Dick Smith, Texas Government (1968); Rupert N. Richardson, Texas, The Lone Star State (1943); Texas Almanac (1973); Biographical and Subject Files, Barker Texas History Center, University of Texas at Austin.

Phillip L. Fry

Governor's Commission on Physical Fitness. See Physical Fitness, Governor's Commission on.

Governor's Committee on Aging. The Governor's Committee on Aging was created in 1965 to coordinate services to the aged by government and private agencies and to aid in the establishment of new programs on the local level. The governor appointed ten members with six-year terms, including a chairman who supervised the work of an executive director. The committee was advised by the Governor's Citizens Advisory Council, which was composed of two members from each senatorial district. The Governor's Committee on Aging was the first permanent body created to work with this problem.

BIBLIOGRAPHY: University of Texas at Austin, Guide To Texas State Agencies (1966, 1972).

*Governor's Mansion. Construction of the mansion was supervised by Abner Hugh Cook qv (not Abner Coals, as stated in Volume I). See Board of Mansion Supervisors.

Governor's Office, Division of Planning Coordination. See Planning Coordination, Division of, Governor's Office.

*Governors' Palace. See Spanish Governors' Palace.

Governor's Youth Opportunity Program. See Community Affairs, Department of.

*Gox, Texas.

*Goyens, William.

*Graball, Texas.

*Graces Creek.

*Graceton, Texas.

Graduate Research Center of the Southwest. See University of Texas at Dallas.

*Graford, Texas.

*Gragg Creek.

*Graham, Beriah.

*Graham, Edwin S.

Graham, George. George Graham, son of Richard and Jane (Brent) Graham, was born in Dumfries, Prince William County, Virginia, about 1772. A lawyer, soldier, banker, and public servant, Graham was graduated from Columbia College (now Columbia University) in 1790 and practiced law in his native town. He represented his county in the Virginia general assembly and raised and commanded the Fairfax Light Horse during the War of 1812.

James Monroe appointed Graham chief clerk of the War Department in 1814, and he served as secretary of war ad interim from October 16, 1816, to December 9, 1817. Graham became known as a troubleshooter in the War Department. In 1815 he was appointed a member of a commission to treat with the British regarding the settlement of the War of 1812. Later he became a specialist in Indian problems.

In 1818 he was commissioned a special agent and sent on a confidential mission to Texas to determine the status of the Napoleonic exiles who had attempted to establish the colony of Champ d'Asile qv on the Trinity River. Graham arrived at Galveston in a smuggling boat in the late summer of that year. The French colony had already disintegrated upon his arrival, but he took occasion to consult with Jean Laffite qv and to inspect the Texas coast on behalf of the United States. The United States claimed Texas at that time on the basis of the Louisiana Purchase, but little was known about it. Graham was impressed by what he saw and recommended that his government occupy Texas immediately. The following year, however, the United States and Spain signed the Adams-Oñis Treaty qv setting the international boundary at the Sabine River. Graham's account of his mission stands as the first Anglo American account of a sea voyage to Texas (from Calcasieu Lake, Louisiana, to Galveston Island, after an overland trip by horseback) and gives an interesting view of Laffite and Galveston Island in 1818.

Graham was first married to a widow, Elizabeth Mary Anne Barnes (Hooe) Mason; they had two children. His second marriage was to a Miss Watson, and they also had two children. Graham was president of the Washington branch of the Bank of the United States from 1817 to 1823. From 1823 until his death in August, 1830, he served as commissioner of the general land office of the United States.

BIBLIOGRAPHY: James Grant Wilson and John Fiske (eds.), *Appletons' Cyclopaedia of American Biography*, II (1894–1900); Walter Prichard (ed.), "George Graham's Mission to Galveston in 1818: Two Important Documents Bearing upon Louisiana History," *Louisiana Historical Quarterly*, XX (1937); *Virginia Magazine of History and Biography*, XII (January, 1905); "The Brent Family," *ibid.*, XIX (January, 1911).

Marilyn M. Sibley

*Graham, Malcolm D.

*Graham, Malcolm K.

Graham, Samuel Stanley. Samuel Stanley Graham was one of the most decorated officers of the 36th Infantry Division (Texas National Guard) during World War II. He was born at Selma, Iowa, on November 16, 1895, the son of James Sherman and Lydia (Snode) Graham. Prior to World War II, he served for many years as professor of agriculture at Sam Houston State College (now Sam Houston State University), Huntsville, Texas.

Colonel Graham commanded the 2nd Battalion, 143rd Infantry Regiment, 36th Division (*see* Thirtysixth Division), and led it ashore at Salerno, Italy, on September 9, 1943. These were among the first Allied troops to land in Europe. Graham's decorations included the Distinguished Service Cross, Silver Star, Bronze Star, Legion of Merit, Purple Heart, and the Order of Suvorov (Russian). Graham died July 17, 1965, at San Antonio, Texas, and was buried in Huntsville.

Robert L. Wagner

Graham, Shadrack Edmond. Shadrack Edmond (Shad) Graham, filmmaker, was born in New York City on April 24, 1896, the son of Charles Edmond and Edith (Craske) Graham. His father and uncle (Robert E. Graham) were professional actors and his mother was a well-known ballerina. Shad Graham began his association with the film industry as a child actor in *The Great Train Robbery* (1903), but his main interest through the years was in the technical phase of the new art form. He spent fifty years with major motion picture companies in New York and Hollywood and later with his own company, Shad E. Graham Productions. His *Our Home Town* series, documentaries of small towns in many parts of the United States, especially in Texas, is of historical significance for the period following World War II.

Graham moved to Houston after the war, where he continued making documentary films while serving as Texas representative for Twentieth Century Fox Movietone News. His *Texas City Disaster 1947* won awards for that studio and focused international attention on disaster needs. Graham was a charter member of the Film Editors of New York City and Hollywood and a gold card member of the Motion Picture Pioneers Foundation. He was first married to Helen May in New York City on January 11, 1920; they had two children, and they were divorced in 1927. His second marriage was to Ruth Esther McLain, of Houston, on July 17, 1947, in New York City; they lived in Missouri City, Texas. Graham died on January 28, 1969, in Houston, and he was buried there. His documentary films were donated to the University of Texas at Austin, where a Shad E. Graham Memorial Student Film Fund and Memorial Film Library were established in 1969.

BIBLIOGRAPHY: Ilanon Moon (with Shad E. Graham), *Mama Was A Ballerina* (1971); *National Cyclopedia of American Biography*, 54 (1973).

Eldon S. Branda

*Graham, Texas. Graham, seat of Young County, in 1966 reported seventeen churches, a hospital, two libraries, two newspapers, and a radio station. In 1960 Lake Graham was completed, and in 1966 water plant extensions were put into operation. The city gains most of its income from the oil industry, tourism, and the manufacture of livestock feeds, garments, and leather goods. In 1970, 252 business and manufacturing establishments were located in Graham, including a manufacturing firm dealing with fiberglass and aluminum aerospace equipment. The 1960 population was 8,505 and the 1970 count was 7,477.

*Graham Lake. *See also* Lake Graham.

*Graham Mountain.

*Grains and Grain Production in Texas. *See* Agriculture in Texas and related articles.

*Grammont, John J. H.

*Granbury, Hiram Bronson. [This title was incorrectly listed in Volume I as Granberry, Hiram Bronson.] Hiram Bronson Granbury was born in Copiah County, Mississippi, on March 1, 1831, and was educated at Oakland College. Moving to Texas in the 1850's, he lived in Waco, where he was admitted to the Bar and served as chief justice of McLennan County from 1856 to 1858. On March 31, 1858, Granbury married Fannie Sims of Waco; they had no children. At the outbreak of the Civil War he recruited the Waco Guards, which became a unit in the 7th Texas Infantry in Brigadier General John Gregg's qv Brigade of the Confederate Army. He was captured at Fort Donelson and after being exchanged was promoted to colonel of the 7th Texas. In April, 1863, Granbury was at Port Hudson, Louisiana. In May he participated in the battle of Raymond, Mississippi (but was never stationed in northern Mississippi, as stated in Volume I), and shortly thereafter joined General J. E. Johnston's qv army, assembled for the relief of Vicksburg.

Granbury commanded the 7th Texas in Brigadier General Bushrod R. Johnson's Brigade of General John B. Hood's qv Corps at Chickamauga, where he was wounded. He participated in the battle of Missionary Ridge, where his commanding officer was James A. Smith (not James E. Smith) and shortly thereafter succeeded to brigade command. During the retreat from that battle he was particularly distinguished for his conduct at Ringold Gap, where he commanded his own brigade (not Hood's Texas Brigade qv). Granbury was commissioned brigadier general on February 29, 1864.

During the ensuing Atlanta campaign, Granbury served in Cleburne's Division of General J. E. Johnston's Army of Tennessee and was again particularly distinguished at the battle of New Hope Church. After the fall of Atlanta, Granbury led his brigade in Hood's disastrous invasion of Tennessee, and at the battle of Franklin on November 30, 1864, he was killed in action.

Granbury was first buried near Franklin, Tennessee. His body was later reinterred at the Ashwood Church Cemetery south of Columbia. On November 30, 1893, his remains were removed to Granbury, Texas, seat of Hood County, the town being named in his honor. His name on the statue in that town is mistakenly spelled "Granberry." *See also* Granbury's Texas Brigade.

BIBLIOGRAPHY: Ezra J. Warner, *Generals in Gray* (1959); U. S. War Department, *The War of the Rebellion: A Compilation of the Official Records of the Union and Confederate Armies* (1880–1901); *Confederate Veteran* (1893–1933); *List of Field Officers, Regiments, and Battalions in the Confederate Army* (n.d.); *Memorandum Relative to the General Officers Appointed by the President in the Armies of the Confederate States* (1905); Dudley G. Wooten, *A Comprehensive History of Texas* (1898); Stanley F. Horn, *The Army of Tennessee* (1941); Irving A. Buck, *Cleburne and His Command* (1908); Thomas R. Hay, *Hood's Tennessee Campaign* (1929); Joseph E. Johnston, *Narrative of Military Operations* (1874); *Granbury News*, November 30, 1893; W. M. Sleeper, *Waco Bar and Incidents of Waco History* (1941); C. A. Evans, *Confederate Military History* (1899).

Palmer Bradley

*Granbury, Texas. Granbury, seat of Hood County, was named in honor of Hiram Bronson Granbury qv (not Granberry, as shown in Volume I). This misspelling of Granbury's name probably stems from the fact that the name of the statue in this town is misspelled "Granberry." The town of Granbury had a 1960 population of 2,227 and a 1970 population of 2,473. In 1963 Granbury had seven churches, a bank, and a hospital. Sixty-five businesses were reported in 1970. Industries were concerned with the manufacture of toys and clothing and the processing of feeds, peanuts, and pecans.

*Granbury College.

Granbury's Texas Brigade. Granbury's Texas Brigade was formed in November, 1863, just prior to the battle of Missionary Ridge and was composed of the 7th Texas Infantry, the 6th, 10th, and 15th Texas Infantry (consolidated), and the 17th, 18th, 24th, and 25th Texas Dismounted Cavalry (consolidated) as a part of Major General Pat Cleburne's Division with Brigadier General James Argyle Smith as its commanding officer. At Missionary Ridge the brigade quickly established a record for consistent valor. General Smith was wounded there and was succeeded in command by Colonel Hiram Bronson Granbury qv of the 7th Texas. The brigade took its name from Granbury, who was subsequently promoted to brigadier general.

In the ensuing retreat of the Army of Tennessee from Missionary Ridge, Cleburne's Division, including Granbury's Brigade, probably saved the army by its rear guard stand at Ringold Gap for which it received the thanks of the Confederate Congress. The brigade fought in General Joseph E. Johnston's qv army throughout the entire Atlanta campaign, participating, in addition to countless skirmishes, in the battles of Resaca, New Hope Church, Kenesaw Mountain, Peachtree Creek, Atlanta, and Jonesboro. In General Cleburne's official report of New Hope Church he said: "The piles of dead on this front was but a silent eulogy upon Granbury and his noble Texans."

After the close of the Atlanta campaign the brigade participated in General John B. Hood's qv disastrous invasion of Tennessee, where the brigade was decimated in November, 1864, at the battle of Franklin, during which both Granbury and Cleburne were killed in action. At the succeeding battle of Nashville, the brigade was commanded by a colonel. What was left of it joined the remnants of the Army of Tennessee in North Carolina in the spring of 1865 and surrendered at Greensboro in April, being there commanded by Brigadier General D. C. Govan.

Granbury's Texas Brigade, although only organized as late as November, 1863, established a reputation for stark fighting ability unsurpassed by any brigade in the Confederate Army of Tennessee.

BIBLIOGRAPHY: U. S. War Department, *The War of the Rebellion: A Compilation of the Official Records of the Union and Confederate Armies* (1880–1901); *Confederate Veteran* (1893–1933); *List of Field Officers, Regiments, and Battalions in the Confederate Army* (n.d.); Dudley G. Wooten, *A Comprehensive History of Texas* (1898); Stanley F. Horn, *The Army of Tennessee* (1941); Irving A. Buck, *Cleburne and His Command* (1908); Thomas R. Hay, *Hood's Tennessee Campaign* (1929); Joseph E. Johnston, *Narrative of Military Operations* (1874).

Palmer Bradley

Grand Jury in Texas. The function of the grand jury (which seems to have been instituted in England about the middle of the twelfth century) is to determine cause for criminal prosecution. Instituted as a means of making the local community responsible for bringing its malefactors to justice, it has come to be regarded over the centuries as a safeguard against unwarranted prosecution, and as such it was incorporated in the Fifth Amendment to the United States Constitution, a provision which has not been made applicable to the states by the doctrine of selective incorporation; however, there is a correlative provision in the Texas Constitution of 1876 qv (Article I, Section 10) which requires grand jury indictment for prosecution for a felony (*see* Criminal Law; English Law in Texas). The indictment is termed a "true bill" against a prisoner; a decision not to indict is termed a "no bill."

The district judge (or in a county in which there are several district courts, the district judge designated for this purpose) appoints three to five jury commissioners, normally, during the term preceding that during which the grand jury for the county will serve. These commissioners make up a list of twenty persons to be summoned at the beginning of the next term of court. Anyone can challenge the qualifications of a prospective grand juror. The judge designates twelve of those whom he deems qualified as the grand jury, and he appoints one of them as foreman. The term of the grand jury is the same as that of the district court that organizes it, with some provision for extension at the judge's discretion.

The grand jury's investigation of any matter may be initiated by the court, the district attorney, its own members, or any credible person. The grand jury may summon witnesses by subpoena and examine them under oath. On completion of an investigation the grand jury determines by vote whether or not an indictment should be presented to the court, with nine votes necessary for a decision to indict; nine members also constitute a quorum. The grand jury may also make reports to the district court on conditions in the county or the misconduct of an individual.

Joseph W. McKnight

*Grand Lake, Texas.

*Grand Prairie, Texas.** Grand Prairie, in Dallas and Tarrant counties, had a 1960 population of 30,386, and an expanded 1970 population of 50,904. Headquarters of the Texas Junior Chamber of Commerce, the growing city was officially designated the "Gateway to Six Flags Over Texas,"qv a ten-million-dollar educational and entertainment center which opened in 1961. The Ling-Temco-Vought merger that same year presented Grand Prairie with its single greatest industry. In 1964 Grand Prairie had 115 industries among its several hundred businesses; it had sixty-two churches, four hospitals, and one public library. By 1970 businesses numbered 602. An eight-acre site in Grand Prairie was designated as the location for a planned Texas Sports Hall of Fame qv museum-library, but no construction had started by 1975; a fund-raising campaign was active at that time.

*Grand Prairies and the Lampasas Cut Plain.

*Grand Saline, Texas.** Grand Saline, in Van Zandt County, had seventy businesses in 1970, with several major industries engaged in mining and refining salt, manufacturing clothing, processing sulphur, and meat packing. The town also reported eleven churches, a public park and swimming pool, and a fifty-bed hospital. The population was 2,006 in 1960; it was 2,257 in 1970. *See also* Jordan's Saline, Texas.

*Grand Saline Creek.

*Grandfalls, Texas.

*Grandview, Texas.** Grandview, in southeastern Johnson County between Cleburne and Fort Worth, reported a post office, bank, and newspaper in 1966. In 1970 thirty business establishments were reported. The population in 1960 was 961, and in 1970 it was 935.

*Grange.

*Granger, Gordon.

*Granger, Texas.** Granger, in Williamson County, reported thirty-five businesses in 1970. The population was 1,339 in 1960 and 1,256 in 1970.

*Granger, Georgetown, Austin, and San Antonio Railway Company.

*Granite Knob.

*Granite Mountain.** Although the railroad line from Austin to Burnet was built in 1882, the special narrow-gauge railroad line which was laid to Granite Mountain to haul stone for the Texas Capitol qv was completed in 1885 (not 1882, as stated in Volume I). By that year the decision had been made to use the red Texas granite instead of limestone. *See also* Austin and Northwestern Railroad Company; Burnet, Texas.

*Granite Mountain and Marble Falls City Railroad Company.

Granite Shoals, Texas. Located near Lake Lyndon B. Johnson qv in Burnet County, Granite Shoals was an incorporated town of 342 residents in 1970.

Granite Shoals Lake. *See* Lake Lyndon B. Johnson.

*Granny Creek.

*Grannys Branch.

Grant, George W. George W. Grant was an early advocate of education in Walker County. In 1871 he initiated the holding of classes within the state penitentiary at Huntsville; he is credited with originating the idea of establishing Sam Houston Normal Institute (now Sam Houston State University) in that town in 1879 and was a member of the first board of directors of the institute. He and his brother operated a stage stop thirteen miles from Huntsville, and he served as county judge of Walker County from 1876 to 1878. He established Grant's Colony qv (which was named in his honor) several miles northeast of Huntsville to induce members of the Society of Friends (Quakers) to come to Walker County; he built farm homes and a meeting house for school and religious use.

He was married, but had no children. He died in 1889. His date of birth is uncertain, although the census of 1850 shows a George W. Grant, age 36, living in Walker County at that time.

BIBLIOGRAPHY: Huntsville *Item*, March 6, 1941; A History of the First Christian Church (Disciples of Christ), Huntsville, Texas, 1854–1936 (MS., Estill Library, Sam Houston State University).

Mary S. Estill

*Grant, James.

*Grant, Texas.

*Grant's Colony, Texas. *See also* Grant, George W.

*Grape Creek.

*Grape Culture. The growing of native grapes was continued in many Texas counties in the 1950's and 1960's. Commercial production remained limited and was largest in Montague, Denton, Wise, Grayson, Wichita, San Patricio, El Paso, Reeves, and Wheeler counties. In 1959 there were 2,847 Texas farms with 105,127 grapevines; production that year totaled 267,403 pounds. Five years later, however, the agricultural census reported a decline to 2,466 farms, 76,501 grapevines, and a total annual production of 161,922 pounds.

BIBLIOGRAPHY: *Texas Almanac* (1965, 1967).

*Grapefruit Culture. *See* Citrus Fruit Production.

*Grapeland, Texas. Grapeland, Houston County, had a population of 1,113 in 1960 and 1,211 in 1970.

Grapetown, Texas. Grapetown, in Gillespie County approximately ten miles southeast of Fredericksburg, was first settled shortly after the founding of Fredericksburg in 1846; the first landowner of record was John Hemphill, who received a deed to land there on May 13, 1848. Most of the early settlers were German immigrants, and several of these were freight drivers, carrying produce from the Fredericksburg area through San Antonio to Indianola on the coast. Ranching and later farming were the chief occupations. In 1860 Friedrich Doebbler opened the first business establishment, Doebbler's Inn, in his home; it served as a grocery and dry goods store, a post office, and a stopping place for travelers; it remained in operation until 1915. Children attended school in Fredericksburg until about 1870, when a school was opened in Grapetown. The last school there closed in 1944, when it was consolidated with the Rocky Hill School. In 1887 residents organized a singing club and a shooting club (which was still in existence in the 1960's).

Trade diminished in Grapetown about 1932, when the state highway was rerouted through Comfort. The population was approximately one hundred forty-five in 1900 and seventy in 1965. Most of the area residents were engaged in farming, and Grapetown's social gatherings consisted of occasional family reunions, parties, and regular target practices of the Grapetown Shooting Club.

*Grapevine, Texas. Grapevine, in northeastern Tarrant County, increased its water supply as well as its commercial and recreational facilities by the creation of Grapevine Lake. The city counts among its major industries the manufacture of metal products, rubber gaskets, house trailers, mattresses, and feeds. In 1966 the town reported eighteen churches, a hospital, a bank, two libraries, and two newspapers. The town had 136 business establishments in 1970. The population in 1960 was 2,821; the 1970 count was 7,023. *See also* Fort Worth Standard Metropolitan Statistical Area.

*Grapevine Creek.

*Grapevine Hills.

Grapevine Reservoir. Grapevine Reservoir is in the Trinity River Basin in Tarrant County, two miles northeast of Grapevine on Denton Creek, a tributary to the Elm Fork of the Trinity River. The reservoir extends into Denton County. The project is owned by the United States government and is operated by the United States Army Corps of Engineers, Fort Worth District, for flood control and the conservation of water. Conservation storage space has been purchased by the cities of Dallas and Grapevine, and Dallas County Park Cities Water Control and Improvement District No. 2. The water is used for municipal, industrial, manufacturing, and recreational purposes.

Construction began in January, 1948, and was completed in June, 1952. Deliberate impoundment of water began on July 3, 1952. The reservoir has a conservation storage capacity of 188,500 acre-feet and a surface area of 7,389 acres at elevation 535 feet above mean sea level. The shoreline is sixty miles long at this storage level. The flood control storage capacity is 247,000 acre-feet. The drainage area above the dam is 695 square miles.

BIBLIOGRAPHY: Texas Water Commission, *Bulletin 6408* (1964).

Seth D. Breeding

*Graphite, Texas.

*Grass Creek.

*Grass Fight.

*Grass Lake.

*Grassbur, Texas.

*Grasses Native to Texas.

*Grasshopper Creek.

*Grassland, Texas.

*Grassy Branch.

*Grassy Creek.

*Grassyville, Texas.

*Gratis, Texas.

*Gravelly Creek.

Graves, Harry N. Harry N. Graves was born at La Vernia, Texas, on April 4, 1877, the son of H. N. and Susan Graves. In 1884 the family moved to Georgetown, where he worked for the Georgetown *Democrat* for two years and then entered Southwestern University. Needing additional financial assistance, he went to work for the *Williamson County Sun* as assistant editor. He read law at night and served as a law-office stenographer. Graves was admitted to the Bar in 1896, when he was nineteen years old.

He practiced law for a short time in Sherman, then returned to Georgetown, where he was elected city attorney in 1898. For the next thirty-five years he was associated in law practice with his brother-in-law, D. W. Wilcox. He served three terms as city attorney in Georgetown and three terms as county attorney of Williamson County. While serving as county attorney, he assisted district attorney Dan Moody qv in the nationally famous prosecution of the Ku Klux Klan qv in Williamson County.

Graves served in the Texas House of Representatives from 1929 to 1937. While in the House, he wrote the bill that established the Texas Highway Patrol in 1930. He resigned from the legislature in October, 1937, to accept appointment to the Court of Criminal Appeals the same month. He served on the court from 1937 until his retirement on January 1, 1955. He was elected presiding judge of the court for the last four years of his service on the bench.

In 1908 Graves married Dorthula Wilcox of Georgetown. He was a member of the Methodist church. Graves died on December 3, 1957, and was buried in the State Cemetery qv in Austin.

BIBLIOGRAPHY: *Texas Bar Journal*, XXI (February 22, 1958).

Forrest E. Ward

*Graves, Henry Lee. [This title was incorrectly listed in Volume I as Graves, Henry Lea.] Henry Lee Graves died in Brenham on November 4 (not December 4, as stated in Volume I), 1881. [Later printings of Volume I contain these corrections.]

Graves, first president of Baylor University, at Independence, was graduated from the University of North Carolina in 1835, was tutor in mathematics at Wake Forest College from 1835 to 1837, and taught at Cave Springs, Georgia, in 1838. After attending the Hamilton Theological Seminary in New York, 1841–1843, he taught at Covington, Georgia, before receiving notice of his election to the presidency of Baylor University in 1846. He wrote many circular letters and articles on Baptist doctrine and Christian education and was a frequent contributor to *The Texas Baptist. See also* Baylor University.

Lily M. Russell

Graves, Marvin Lee. Marvin Lee Graves was born on March 26, 1867, at Bosqueville, McLennan County, Texas, the son of George W. and Mary Priscilla (Fowler) Graves. He was graduated from Southwestern University in 1885 and taught school in Williamson County for one year before becoming principal of Belton High School. During that same time he began premedical training under Dr. H. C. Ghent of Belton. In 1891 he received his M.D. degree from the medical school of Bellevue Hospital, New York. He began the practice of medicine in Waco, where he remained seven years before being appointed superintendent of Southwestern Hospital for the Insane (now San Antonio State Hospital qv) in San Antonio. In 1905 he was made professor of medicine and mental and nervous diseases at the University of Texas medical branch at Galveston.

He resigned in 1925 to continue his private practice and moved to Houston, where he was a member of the executive board of the Methodist Hospital. After his retirement in 1949 Graves became medical adviser to the American General Insurance Company. He served as president of the Texas Medical Association qv from 1913 to 1914, was a member of its board of trustees for ten years, and was elected to emeritus membership in 1937; he was also a Fellow of the American College of Physicians. Graves held honorary degrees from Southern Methodist University, Baylor University College of Medicine, and Southwestern University. He was a member of the boards of stewards of Methodist churches in Galveston and Houston for a total of forty-nine years. Graves married Laura Ghent in 1893. He died in Houston on November 19, 1953, survived by his wife, a son, and two daughters.

BIBLIOGRAPHY: *Texas State Journal of Medicine* (January, 1954).

*Graves, William Sidney.

*Gravis, Texas.

*Gray, Alfred Gilliat.

*Gray, Allen Charles.

*Gray, Andrew Belcher.

*Gray, Edwin Fairfax.

*Gray, Franklin C.

*Gray, George H.

Gray, James. James Gray was born in Edinburgh, Scotland, on November 9, 1815. He fought in William Warner Hill's qv company at San Jacinto. In 1850 he was living in San Antonio, where he was a tinsmith, and in 1860 he was a merchant in San Antonio. He married Simona Seguin, the daughter of Emeregildo Seguin, and developed the town of Graytown qv on property which she inherited. Gray died at Floresville on September 12, 1884, and was buried in the city cemetery there.

BIBLIOGRAPHY: Frederick Chabot, *With the Makers of San Antonio* (1937).

S. W. Pease

*Gray, Mabry B. (Mustang).

*Gray, Peter W.

*Gray, Thomas.

*Gray, William Fairfax.

*Gray County. Gray County's abundant crude oil and gas contributed to the county's petrochemical, carbon black, and heavy machinery industries, which were centered at Pampa. The 1972 production of 6,423,237 barrels of oil brought the accumulated total to 565,960,114 barrels since its discovery in 1925. The rangelands and cultivated areas provided a steady agricultural income, most of which came from cattle. Wheat and grain sorghums were among the crops grown in the mid-1960's on approximately 25,000 irrigated acres. Lake McClellan provided recreation opportunities. The 1960 population was 31,535; the 1970 count was 26,949.

*Grayback, Texas.

*Grayburg, Texas.

*Graydon, Texas.

*Grays Creek.

*Grays Prairie, Texas.

*Grayson, Ben S.

*Grayson, Peter William.

*Grayson, Thomas Wigg.

*Grayson College.

*Grayson County. Grayson County, with Sherman as the county seat, opened Eisenhower State Recreation Park (*see* Parks, State) two miles west of Denison Dam on land acquired from an army lease in 1954. Facilities included a large marina. In 1958 a three-acre site was acquired from the Eisenhower Birthplace Foundation and the city of Denison for the Eisenhower Birthplace State Historic Site (*see* Parks, State). The Hagerman National Wildlife Refuge,qv on the upper end of the Big Mineral Arm of Lake Texoma, was created to provide rest and feed for migratory waterfowl. The county has a diversified economy based on agriculture, industrial employment, and minerals. The 1960 population was 73,043, and the 1970 population was 83,225. *See also* Sherman-Denison

Standard Metropolitan Statistical Area.

Grayson County College. Grayson County College in Denison was organized as a junior college in 1963 by the Grayson County Development Council. In 1964 college bonds were sold, Cruce Stark became the college's first president, and construction of an eight-building campus began. Classes began in September, 1965, with an initial enrollment of 1,500 students. By 1969 the library contained 24,000 volumes.

The college offered courses leading to associate degrees in arts, engineering, science, and business administration. One- and two-year terminal courses were given by the technical-vocational division, and the evening division provided an adult education program. In 1972 the faculty numbered 112; student enrollment in the regular term of 1974 was 3,854. Truman Wester was president in that year.

*Grayton, Texas.

*Graytop.

*Graytown, Texas. *See also* Gray, James.

*Great Britain, Relations of Texas with. *See* Diplomatic Relations of the Republic of Texas.

Great Hanging at Gainesville. *See* Gainesville, Great Hanging at.

Great Southwest Railroad, Inc. The Great Southwest Railroad, Inc., was chartered on May 7, 1957, and began operation in May, 1959. In 1966 it was classed as a switching and terminal company and operated 9.3 miles of track in the Dallas-Fort Worth industrial district.

James M. Day

*Great Southwest Strike. *See* Southwest Strike.

"Great Western." *See* Borginnis, Sarah.

Greater Fort Worth International Airport. *See* Greater Southwest International Airport.

Greater Southwest International Airport. Greater Southwest International Airport originated in the 1940's when a regional airport for the Dallas-Fort Worth area was being considered. The Civil Aeronautics Administration (CAA) approached Arlington in regard to sponsoring an airport located midway between Dallas and Fort Worth to serve the North Texas area. Both Dallas and Fort Worth were interested in this project since expensive expansion of Love and Meacham fields qqv was necessary to accommodate four-engine planes.

Arlington agreed to be the official sponsor of such an airport, to which Braniff and American Airlines would deed one thousand acres of land on which the CAA would build the landing area; a seven-man board would control overall operation of the field. Clearing of the site began in May, 1942, while negotiations between the CAA and the cities of Dallas, Fort Worth, and Arlington were still in progress.

After the failure of agreement on plans for a joint regional airport (over the issue of which way the terminal building would face, along with other issues), Midway Airport was turned over to Arlington in July, 1943. During the remainder of World War II it was used as a training field and for test flights.

In 1946 Fort Worth hired a firm to prepare an airport plan for the city. One year later Fort Worth decided to develop Midway Airport as its major airport and redesignated the field Greater Fort Worth International Airport. Total development cost was an estimated eleven and one-half million dollars.

The 1948 CAA National Airport Plan recommended that Greater Fort Worth International Airport be expanded into the major regional airport. Despite Dallas opposition, Fort Worth development of the field continued, and in June, 1948, the city annexed the site. American Airlines spent approximately three million dollars expanding its facilities at the airport, a four-lane highway was constructed, and runways were paved. In 1950 the Fort Worth City Council voted to rename the airport Amon G. Carter qv Field.

In June, 1951, a $29,000,000 Fort Worth bond issue, which included $1,750,000 in aviation bonds, passed by a margin of thirty-six votes. This issue was part of the Love Field-Carter Field competition during the 1950's. Development of Carter Field continued with the backing of American Airlines, and in April, 1953, the airport was officially opened.

Two attempts were made during the 1950's to convert Carter Field into a joint area airport. Fort Worth unsuccessfully offered participation in Carter Field to Dallas on a full partnership basis in 1951. Again in 1954, Fort Worth unsuccessfully offered to sell Dallas one-half interest in the airport, to change the airport's name to the Dallas-Fort Worth International Airport, and to establish a joint airport authority. Dallas found certain terms unfavorable.

In September, 1955, Fort Worth petitioned the Civil Aeronautics Board (CAB) to investigate the adequacy of air service to Carter Field. The CAB ruled that air service was sufficient for the field at that time, but five years later it ordered American Airlines to provide two additional daily flights to Carter Field.

In an effort to compete more successfully with Love Field, Carter Field—renamed Greater Southwest International Airport—was sold to the city of Fort Worth in May, 1960, and a municipal board was created to supervise that city's airports. The north-south runway of the airport was extended over State Highway 183 in March, 1961, thereby breaking out of the hemmed-in boundaries of the field and making it easier to extend runways in the future.

During the period from 1959 to 1965, air traffic declined substantially at this field and by 1964 represented less than 1 percent of the state's total. Enplaned passengers declined from 174,240 in 1959 to only 29,131 in 1966. Such losses led to the virtual abandonment of the comparatively new airport by the mid-1960's. The number of total operations at the field increased from 148,596 in 1965 to only 185,790 in 1966.

After the CAB refused to designate either Greater Southwest International Airport or Love Field as a regional airport in 1964, both cities jointly financed a survey to select a regional airport site. In 1965 the survey recommended a location in the Grapevine area. Greater Southwest International Airport was included in the southern part of the new site, with future use undetermined. In 1967, as Dallas and Fort Worth were moving toward creation of a joint airport authority to supervise an area airport, Greater Southwest International Airport continued in operation. *See also* Love Field; Dallas-Fort Worth Airport.

BIBLIOGRAPHY: Fritz-Alan Korth, A Tale of Two Cities (Senior thesis, Princeton University, 1961); *Texas Business Review* (April, July, 1967).

Charles Duval, Jr.

Green, Ben King. Ben K. (Doc) Green, son of David Hugh and Bird (King) Green, was born March 5, 1912, in Cumby, Hopkins County, Texas. He moved with his family to Weatherford and attended high school there. A maverick then (and always), Green ran for a seat in the Texas legislature when he was about twenty-three years old, led the ticket in the primary, but lost in the runoff. As a boy Green fell in love with horses and the love affair never ended. He bred horses and lived the life of a cowboy for most of his life, although he traveled widely outside Texas and the United States. At one time or another he both claimed or denied that he attended Texas A&M, Cornell University, and the Royal College of Veterinary Medicine in England, but most of his expert knowledge about animals came from experience. He began writing rather late in life, and it was a memorable moment when he met Alfred A. Knopf, the New York publisher, telling the international sophisticate more than he wanted to know about horses and cows and people. The result was that Knopf published *Horse Tradin'* (1967), *Wild Cow Tales* (1969), *The Village Horse Doctor* (1971), and *Some More Horse Tradin'* (1972), each a strong seller. The books were immediately hailed by the critics, and *Horse Tradin'* has been cited as a classic of Western Americana. In 1973 Green received the Writers Award for contributions to Western literature from the Cowboy Hall of Fame in Oklahoma City. He also received a career award from the Texas Institute of Letters qv for his unique contribution to Texas literature.

Green wrote all of his books the way he operated best. He talked them, telling stories to a tape recorder and to his secretary. He wrote from his own experiences as a rancher, horse and steer trader, wild horse hunter, and horse doctor. He owned the only registered herd of Devon cattle in Texas and supported it on his farm in Cumby, where he also raised Percheron and quarter horses. He was tremendously in demand on the lecture circuit. Green placed his personal papers in the Jenkins Garrett

Collection of the University of Texas at Arlington Library.

Altogether, Green published eleven books between 1967 and 1974. His last book, *The Color of Horses* (1974), was the product of his arduous research through the years on the hide and hair of horses to determine what made color. Although the book is controversial in content, Green considered it his most worthwhile contribution, and he saw it come off the presses shortly before he died while sitting in his car on a roadside in northwest Kansas on October 5, 1974.

Ben K. Green was buried in a 100-foot-square knoll in the cemetery at Cumby, making good his oft repeated, "I never let myself be crowded in life, and by God, ain't nobody gonna close in on me when I'm dead!"

Joe B. Frantz

*Green, Duff.

*Green, Edward Howland Robinson.

*Green, George.

*Green, John Alexander.

Green, Rena Maverick. Rena Maverick Green, daughter of native Texans George Madison and Mary (Vance) Maverick, was born on February 10, 1874, in Sedalia, Missouri. She was educated at Mary Institute in St. Louis and Miss Stuart's School in Staunton, Virginia. She came to San Antonio with her family in 1896, and in 1897 she married Robert B. Green.qv They had four children.

Mrs. Green was a member of the San Antonio school board and the board of trustees of the San Antonio public library. She was one of the charter members of the San Antonio Conservation Society and of the Yanaguana Society and a member of the San Antonio Historical Association.qqv She was especially active in a series of controversies over the preservation of San Antonio's public parks as open spaces. In 1926 she served as Texas state chairman of the National Woman's party. She made two valuable contributions to Texas historiography through her editorship of manuscript material relating to her grandparents, Samuel Augustus and Mary (Adams) Maverick:qqv *Memoirs of Mary A. Maverick* (1921) and *Samuel Maverick, Texan* (1952). Rena Maverick Green died on November 29, 1962, in San Antonio.

BIBLIOGRAPHY: San Antonio *Express*, September 27, 1959; National Woman's Party, *How Texas Laws Discriminate Against Women* (1926).

Donald E. Everett

Green, Robert B. Robert B. Green, son of Martha (Fulton) and Nathaniel Otho Green, was born in San Antonio on May 16, 1865. He was educated at the San Antonio German-English School qv and Texas A&M College (now Texas A&M University). In 1899 he received a law degree from Cumberland University in Lebanon, Tennessee. Prior to that, in 1886, he served as secretary to Richard Coke,qv United States senator from Texas. He was appointed judge of the Thirty-seventh Judicial District of Texas in 1895, a position he held

until 1900, when he resigned to run for county judge of Bexar County. He was elected, and served until 1906, when he was elected to the state senate from the Twenty-fourth Senatorial District. He served in the Thirtieth Legislature, and was chairman of the senate investigating committee appointed to investigate the conduct of Senator Joseph Weldon Bailey.qv

Green was one of the organizers of the Belknap Rifles qv and was captain of that organization until it was disbanded in 1897. He was a leader in the movement for all-weather rural roads in Texas. In 1897 he married Rena Maverick (*see* Green, Rena Maverick). He died while on a hunting trip on December 1, 1907, and was buried in the Confederate Cemetery in San Antonio. Robert B. Green Memorial Hospital in San Antonio is named in his honor.

BIBLIOGRAPHY: San Antonio *Express*, December 8, 1907, May 1, 1949; San Antonio *Light*, December 2, 1907; William A. Cocke, *The Bailey Controversy in Texas*, I (1908); *Texas Legislative Manual for 1907* (1907).

Hobart Huson

*Green, Thomas. On January 31, 1847, Thomas Green was married to Mary Wallace Chalmers (not Mary Watson Chalmers, as stated in Volume I). He was buried in Oakwood Cemetery, Austin (not the Texas State Cemetery).

BIBLIOGRAPHY: Alexander Eanes Cemetery Record Book (MS., Austin-Travis County Collection, Austin Public Library); A. W. Williams and E. C. Barker (eds.), *The Writings of Sam Houston*, III (1938).

Lucy Price
Palmer Bradley

*Green, Thomas Jefferson.

*Green, Texas. Green, in Karnes County, began in the 1880's as a railroad switch named Nichols, halfway between Kenedy Junction and Pettus on the San Antonio and Aransas Pass Railway. One mile south of Green the town of Pullin was established in the early 1900's and at one time boasted a gin, two general merchandise stores, a cafe, confectionery, and post office. Because of poor railroad facilities, the businesses and post office were relocated at Green in 1907. Founded by William Green, a partner in the land promotional firm of Green and Welhausen of Yoakum, the town became the center of a cotton farming community and had a store, gin, Baptist church, and school. The post office of Green was discontinued in 1944. The 1970 population was thirty-five.

*Green Branch.

*Green Creek.

*Green DeWitt School, Texas.

*Green Lake.

*Green Lake, Texas.

*Green Mountain.

*Green Valley, Texas.

*Greenback Party in Texas.

Greenbelt Reservoir. Greenbelt Reservoir is in the Red River Basin in Donley County, five miles north of Clarendon on the Salt Fork of the Red River. The reservoir is owned and operated by the Greenbelt Municipal and Industrial Water Authority to supply water for municipal and industrial uses. Construction of the Greenbelt Dam began on April 12, 1966. Closure of the dam and deliberate impoundment of water began December 5, 1966.

The reservoir has a capacity of 59,800 acre-feet with a surface area of 1,990 acres at the service spillway elevation of 2,664 feet above mean sea level, and a capacity of 78,500 acre-feet with a surface area of 2,270 acres at emergency spillway crest elevation of 2,674 feet above mean sea level. The drainage area above the dam is 288 square miles.

Seth D. Breeding

*Greenbriar, Texas.

*Greenbriar Creek.

*Greenpond, Texas.

*Greens Bayou.

*Greens Creek.

*Greens Lake.

*Greenview, Texas.

*Greenville, Texas. Greenville, seat of Hunt County, experienced a 29 percent growth in population from 1950 to 1960, when the population was 19,087. By 1970 the population was 22,043, an increase of 15.5 percent for the ten-year period. Although the nearby United States Cottonseed Breeding Station was abandoned, the town gained sixteen new small industries which began producing ready-mix concrete, garments, tools, leather goods, and pesticides. The largest industry, Ling-Temco-Vought Aerosystems, Incorporated, employed 3,-758 in 1966. Civic improvements included expansion of the municipal airport and the city-owned electric plant. The electric plant's net revenues paid half the cost of operating the other functions and services of Greenville's government, which became a city manager-council system in 1953.

*Greenville and Northwestern Railway Company.

*Greenvine, Texas.

Greenwall, Henry. Henry Greenwall, a native of Germany, was brought to New Orleans by his parents in 1837, when he was five years old. He worked in a brokerage house until the end of the Civil War, when he and his brother Morris moved to Galveston to organize their own brokerage firm. In 1867 Augusta L. Dargon, an actress of note, became stranded in Galveston and indebted to the Greenwalls; the brothers took over the management of the actress' career. By November, 1867, they had remodeled the Galveston Theatre.

The following year they booked Sophie Miles in the Perkins' Theatre, Houston, which was lighted by gas lights for the first time. Accused of mistreating the troupe, the brothers countered with charges that the Houston contract had been violated. Henry Greenwall became known for keeping the opera house respectable. On January 7, 1869, he became involved in a disagreement with Maude St. Leon and Belle Boyd,qv who were performing in the play *Rosedale*, and the production was cancelled.

While Augusta Dargon toured Australia under the direction of Morris Greenwall, Henry persuaded Willard Richardson,qv founder and owner of the Galveston *News*,qv to erect the Tremont Opera House. In 1871 the Tremont was leased to Morris and Henry Greenwall, and the Sweeney and Combs Opera House in Houston was remodeled by the Greenwall Theatrical Circuit and renamed the Houston Theater. Greenwall added the Fort Worth Opera House to his chain in 1890, and in 1892 he brought the Waco Opera House under his supervision.

In an early civil rights case in June, 1873, Henry Greenwall was named defendant, charged with depriving a Negro of full enjoyment of the accommodations of Galveston's Tremont Opera House. Greenwall leased houses in Atlanta, Memphis, Nashville, and Savannah and established the American Theatrical Exchange in New York in opposition to the Theatrical Syndicate, which he refused to join. He then went to California, where he became ill. In 1909 he sold his interests in Galveston and Houston to Albert Weiss, but he kept his property in Dallas, Fort Worth, and Waco, under the management of Phil Greenwall.

Henry Greenwall died on November 27, 1913, in his apartment over the Greenwall Theatre in New Orleans. At the time of his death he was said to be the oldest active theatrical manager in the United States.

BIBLIOGRAPHY: C. Richard King, A History of the Theater in Texas, 1722–1900 (Ph.D. dissertation, Baylor University, 1962); J. S. Gallegly, *Footlights on the Border* (1962); John S. Kendall, *The Golden Age of the New Orleans Theatre* (1952); *The Bohemian Magazine* (December, 1901–January, 1902); Dallas *Weekly Herald*, March 6, 1875; Galveston *Weekly News*, June 7, 1875; Fort Worth *Record*, November 28, 1913; Galveston *Daily News*, November 29, 1913.

C. Richard King

Greenwood, Thomas Benton. Thomas Benton Greenwood, the son of Thomas Benton and Lucy H. (Gee) Greenwood, of Palestine, Texas, was born on July 2, 1872, in Louisburg, North Carolina. After graduation from the Palestine public schools he attended the University of Texas from approximately 1888 to 1890. Thereafter he read law in his father's office, was licensed in 1893, and practiced with his father until the senior partner's death in 1900. After 1900 he practiced alone, although he was often associated with his younger brother, A. G. Greenwood.

From 1907 to 1911 he served as regent of the University of Texas. His statewide prominence began with a single celebrated law case, *Anderson County v. I. & G. N. Railway Company* (1912–1918) in which he helped block removal of the railway company's shops and general offices from Palestine to Houston. Appointed on April 1, 1918, as associate justice of the Supreme Court of Texas, Justice Greenwood was thereafter elected and continuously reelected without opposition until relinquishing his office on December 31, 1934. He returned to law practice, this time at Austin in association with former governor Dan Moody qv and J. B. Robertson. That association continued until Greenwood's death.

Greenwood's judicial opinions in the relatively new and developing field of oil and gas law constitute much of today's decisional law in the same area. A member of the Texas Bar Association, its successor, the State Bar of Texas,qv and the American Bar Association, his committee work for these organizations contributed notably to modernizing the administration of justice. He held an honorary LL.D. degree from Austin College at Sherman.

In 1908 he married Mary Ezell of Palestine; they had no children. Greenwood was a member of the Southern Presbyterian church. He died in Austin on March 26, 1946, and was buried in the State Cemetery.qv

BIBLIOGRAPHY: *Texas Bar Journal,* 9 (1946), 24 (1961); Minutes of the Supreme Court of Texas, March 17, 1946.

W. St. John Garwood
Virginia Parton

*Greenwood, Texas. (Hopkins County.)

*Greenwood, Texas. (Parker County.)

*Greenwood, Texas. (Wise County.)

*Greer, Elkanah.

*Greer, Hilton Ross.

*Greer, John Alexander. John Alexander Greer was elected lieutenant governor of the state of Texas in 1847 (not 1845, as stated in Volume I), and he held that post until 1851 (not 1853).

*Greer, Nathaniel H.

*Greer, Thomas N. B.

*Greer County.

*Greer Mountains.

*Gregg, Alexander.

*Gregg, Alexander White.

Gregg, Edward Pearsall. Edward Pearsall Gregg, son of Nathan and Sarah Pearsall (Camp) Gregg, was born at Courtland, Alabama, on November 27, 1833. He received a general education at LaGrange College, Alabama, and came to Houston County, Texas, with his parents in 1852. He read law in the office of his brother, John Gregg,qv and was admitted to the Bar in 1854. In that year he moved with John Gregg to Fairfield, Texas, where he commenced practicing his profession. In 1858 he moved to McKinney, where he was living at the outbreak of the Civil War.

He entered Confederate service in March, 1862, as lieutenant colonel of the 16th Texas Cavalry. This regiment served in the Trans-Mississippi Department as an element of Walker's Texas Division.qv Gregg suffered two wounds during his service and was colonel and commander of the 16th Texas Cavalry at the end of the war. After the war Gregg located at Marshall, Texas. In 1867 he married Lucie Goree of Alabama, then in 1871 moved

to Sherman, Texas, where he was a leading member of the Grayson County Bar until his death on March 13, 1894.

BIBLIOGRAPHY: *Biographical Encyclopedia of Texas* (1880).

Lester N. Fitzhugh

*Gregg, John.

*Gregg, Josiah.

*Gregg, Texas.

*Gregg, County. Gregg County, with the lucrative East Texas Oil Field,qv was the leading oil-producing county in the state in 1961. From 1931 through 1972, the county's wells produced over two billion barrels of oil, over fifty-three million in 1972 alone; in that year the county ranked fourth in oil production. Agriculture, important before the oil discovery, had dwindled considerably, but there was still some production of beef cattle, truck crops, and nursery plants, particularly roses. The lumber industry, once of major importance, was reduced by 1966 to a daily output capacity of nine thousand board-feet from the one active mill. The county supports an airport and lends assistance to libraries of the principal cities. LeTourneau and Kilgore colleges are located in the county, and a stock show in the fall, a golf tournament in the spring, and nearby lakes attract tourists. Floods in the spring of 1966 did considerable damage and led to extensive road rebuilding. County population was 69,436 in 1960 and 75,929 in 1970.

*Greggton, Texas.

*Gregory, Edgar M.

*Gregory, Thomas Watt. Thomas Watt Gregory was offered the position of associate justice of the Supreme Court of the United States in 1916 to replace Associate Justice Charles Evans Hughes (not Chief Justice Hughes, as stated in Volume I); Gregory declined the offer of President Woodrow Wilson. [Charles Evans Hughes had resigned as an associate justice in 1916, and he was not appointed to the position of chief justice of the Supreme Court of the United States until 1930.]

BIBLIOGRAPHY: *Who's Who In America* (1934); *Who Was Who In America* (1943); Letter from Woodrow Wilson to T. W. Gregory, University Writings Collection, University of Texas at Austin.

Danny Farek

*Gregory, Texas. Gregory, in San Patricio County, had a 1960 population of 1,970 and a 1970 population of 2,246.

*Grenet, Edward. One of the better known of Edward Grenet's portrait paintings was that of his father's friend and neighbor, John (Johann) Conrad Beckmann qv (not Johann Conrad Backmann, as stated in Volume I).

BIBLIOGRAPHY: *A Twentieth Century History of Southwest Texas,* I (1907); San Antonio *Express,* April 13, 1907.

*Gresham, Walter. Walter Gresham served in the Texas House of Representatives from 1887 to 1892 (not 1866 to 1891, as stated in Volume I).

*Gresham, Texas.

*Greta, Texas.

Grevembert, Agustín de. Agustín de Grevembert, captain in the Attakapas Militia and the son of Louisiana explorer Juan Bautista Grevembert and Ana María Chenal, was sent from Louisiana to San Antonio, Texas, in 1775 with a sergeant, three militiamen, and a cargo of merchandise along the Camino Real qv to trade for Texas mules and horses. The goods were temporarily confiscated, but the Spanish governor of Texas, Juan María Vicencio de Ripperdá,qv later returned the goods with a warning not to attempt to trade with Texas again. Trade between the two Spanish provinces was illegal, although contraband continued to flow in both directions.

BIBLIOGRAPHY: Charles W. Hackett (ed. and trans.), *Pichardo's Treatise on the Limits of Louisiana and Texas*, III (1941); Jack D. L. Holmes, *Honor and Fidelity, The Louisiana Infantry Regiment and the Louisiana Militia Companies, 1766–1821* (1965).

Jack D. L. Holmes

*Grey Beard.

*Grice, Frank.

*Grice, Texas.

*Grierson, Benjamin Henry.

*Griffenhagen Report.

*Griffin, Charles.

*Griffin, J. L.

Griffin, Meade F. Meade F. Griffin, who served on both the Texas Supreme Court and the Court of Criminal Appeals, was born in Cottonwood, Callahan County, on March 17, 1897, the son of W. F. and Frances Lodi (Patterson) Griffin. Griffin received the A.B. degree in 1915 and the LL.B. in 1917 from the University of Texas, and in August, 1917, he was in the first graduating class of the Officers' Training Camp at Leon Springs. In World War I he rose to the rank of major of infantry; in World War II he was promoted to colonel, helping to establish the trial section of the U.S. Army's war crimes department at Wiesbaden, Germany, at the end of the war.

Meade Griffin was admitted to the Bar in 1917 and practiced in Tulia, where he was county attorney from 1917 to 1919 and mayor in 1919; he served as county judge in Hale County from 1923 to 1926 and as district attorney for the 64th Judicial District from 1927 to 1934. In 1949 Governor Beauford H. Jester qv appointed Griffin to the Texas Supreme Court, where he served as associate justice until his retirement in 1968. A year later he was appointed a special judge to the Texas Court of Criminal Appeals, becoming one of few men who have served on both of the highest courts in Texas. He also served as an assistant attorney general under Crawford Martin.qv

On June 2, 1917, Griffin married Eleanor Sykes, whom he divorced in 1950; they had two children. He married Dorothy Porter on November 8, 1950. He received the Rosewood Gavel Award from St. Mary's University in 1965 and was a member of the American Legion and the State Bar of Texas,qqv

for which he was chairman of numerous committees. Griffin died in Austin on June 3, 1974, and was buried in the State Cemetery.qv

BIBLIOGRAPHY: *Who's Who In America* (1968); Austin *American-Statesman*, June 4, 5, 1974.

*Griffin, Texas.

*Griffin Creek.

*Griffin Graffin Land Corner.** [The records division of the General Land Office qv in Austin has no record of an original landmark registered as "Griffin Graffin Land Corner" in Val Verde County (as stated in Volume I); however, the account still makes a good man-eating varmint (not varment) story. Ed.]

*Griffin Trail. *See* Western Trail.

*Griffing Park, Texas.** Griffing Park, in Jefferson County, had a population of 2,267 in 1960 and 2,075 in 1970.

Griffin's Point, Texas. *See* Point Peñascal.

*Griffith, John Summerfield.

*Griffith, Lycurgus E.

Griffith, Reginald Harvey. Reginald Harvey Griffith, son of Richard Henry and Mary Ann (Coleman) Griffith, was born in Charlotte, North Carolina, on February 3, 1873. He went to Greenville Military Institute, then to Furman University, where he received an M.A. degree in 1892. He also attended Johns Hopkins University. He taught English at Furman University in 1898–1899. In 1902 he became an instructor in English at the University of Texas, where he stayed the remainder of his academic life, taking the Ph.D. degree, meanwhile, from the University of Chicago in 1905. Furman University honored him with a Litt.D. degree in 1925. At the University of Texas he became curator of the Wrenn Library in 1918, full professor in 1919, and professor emeritus in 1952. It was under his direction that the first University of Texas dissertation in the Department of English was written.

Both author and co-editor of several literary studies, Griffith was particularly known for his two-volume work *Alexander Pope: A Bibliography* (1922, 1927) and was subsequently regarded as one of the world's foremost authorities on this eighteenth-century writer. He also wrote *Sir Percival of Galles: A Study of the Sources of the Legend* (1911), and he co-edited, with Howard Mumford Jones, *A Descriptive Catalogue of an Exhibition of Manuscripts and First Editions of Lord Byron* (1924). Known as the "godfather" of the rare books collections, Griffith was instrumental in the university's buying the Wrenn and Aitken collections; with the addition of the Miriam Lutcher Stark qv Library in 1926, the University of Texas was established as a major center for research in eighteenth-century literature.

He initiated and directed the Shakespeare Tercentenary Festival at the university; in 1933 he instituted the Texas Conference of College Teachers of English and became its first president. He was appointed chairman of a committee to investigate the creation of a university press; in 1950, when the University of Texas Press qv was established, the committee which he headed chose the first director; he was also the first chairman of the Faculty Advisory Board for the university press.

Griffith married Alice Mary Matlock on August 3, 1906; they had three children. He died on December 10, 1957, and was buried in Oakwood Cemetery in Austin.

BIBLIOGRAPHY: Mary Tom Osborne (ed.), *The Great Torch Race* (1961); *Texas Studies in English*, XXXVII (1958); *Who's Who In America* (1952); Biographical File, Barker Texas History Center, University of Texas at Austin.

Sarah L. C. Clapp
Fannie E. Ratchford

Griffith, Texas. (Cochran County.) Griffith was an unincorporated hamlet of some twenty-five persons in 1965. The town, established in 1934 by Henry Chipley, was first called Oasis. In 1950 it was renamed for Karl Griffith, local landowner and banker, who built a grain elevator there in that year. Other businesses in Griffith were a cotton gin, grocery store, and service station.

*Griffith, Texas. (Ellis County.)

*Grigsby, Joseph.

*Grigsby, Texas.

*Grigsby's Bluff, Texas.

*Grimes, Jesse.

*Grimes County. Grimes County was among the leading Texas counties in dairying in 1969. Along with beef cattle production, dairying accounted for the bulk of its farm income. Agricultural interests shifted from cotton production, which in 1967 averaged less than half of the 1950 output, to cattle raising and milk production. Other field crops, truck farming, and honey bees contributed to the agricultural income. Both lumber and oil production remained small. Since its discovery in 1952, only 308,072 barrels of oil had been produced by 1972. Tourist interest was drawn to antebellum and Civil War sites, as well as to the county's facilities for hunting and fishing. Population decreased from 12,709 in 1960 to 11,855 in 1970.

*Grimshaw, Texas.

*Grindstone Creek.

Grinstead, Jesse Edward. *See Grinstead's Graphic.*

Grinstead's Graphic. Grinstead's Graphic was published in Kerrville by Jesse Edward Grinstead from January, 1921, through May, 1925. The monthly pictorial magazine carried human interest stories, editorials, and various articles of hill country interest. The magazine's circulation was approximately three thousand. Grinstead also established and published the Kerrville *Mountain Sun* until 1917. As a free-lance writer he had over thirty novels and hundreds of short stories published, all predominantly Western in nature. In addition to his own name, Grinstead used William Crump Rush, Tex Janis, and George Bowles as pen names. Grinstead, born in Owensboro, Kentucky, on October 16, 1866, died in Kerrville on March 8, 1948.

Pat Wagner

*Griswald, Texas.

*Grit, Texas.

*Gritten, Edward.

*Groce, Jared E.

*Groce, Leonard Waller. Leonard Waller Groce's decision not to move to Brazil but to remain in Texas after the Civil War was probably influenced by events in Brazil which anticipated the abolition of slavery in that country, not by the actual abolition (as stated in Volume I), since abolition by law in Brazil did not occur until May, 1888, fifteen years after Groce's death. It is probable, though, that Groce anticipated abolition in Brazil much earlier, for the importation of slaves was negligible after 1850, the numerical strength of the free colored population was as great as that of the slave population, and the first statute aimed at eventual abolition was enacted by the Brazilian Parliament as early as 1868. Brazilian manifestos of May and November, 1869, announced a program of reform including eventual abolition of slavery, and in September, 1871, the "Law of Free Birth" was passed, providing that all children of slaves born thereafter were free, but apprenticed to their mothers' owners until the age of twenty-one. Groce, like many other slave owners in the South, certainly must have been aware of the agitation for abolition in Brazil in those years immediately following the American Civil War.

BIBLIOGRAPHY: Gilberto Freyre, *The Masters and the Slaves* (1956); C. H. Haring, *Empire in Brazil* (1958); Roy Nash, *The Conquest of Brazil* (1926).

Eldon S. Branda

*Groce's Ferry.

*Groce's Retreat.

Groesbeck, John D. *See* Groesbeck, John D.

*Groesbeck, Texas. Groesbeck, seat of Limestone County, serves as a marketing and shipping point for farm and ranch products and also manufactures bricks and mattresses. In 1969 the town had sixty businesses, including three manufacturers. One newspaper served the area. The 1960 population was 2,498; in 1970 the total was 2,396.

*Groesbeck Creek.

Groesbeck, John D. John D. Groesbeck (Groesbeck), son of Jacob D. and Catherine (Shever) Groesbeeck, was born on April 13, 1816, in Albany, New York. He came to Galveston in 1837, where he worked first as a surveyor and later entered the wholesale drug business. He moved his business to Houston in 1841, and in 1846 he entered the banking and mercantile business in San Antonio with Nathaniel Lewis.qv Their firm, located on the south side of Main Plaza, supplied the United States military posts in south-western Texas for several years. Groesbeeck and Lewis also published a newspaper, *The Western Texan*, which was edited by Henry Lewis. Groesbeeck served as an alderman of San Antonio in 1849 and again in 1855. He married Phoebe Henrietta Tuttle on April 18, 1848; they had four children. John Groesbeeck died on October 11, 1855, and was buried in San Antonio City Cemetery Number One.

BIBLIOGRAPHY: Frederick Chabot, *With the Makers of San Antonio* (1937); F. B. Baillio, *A History of the Texas Press Association* (1916); Austin *American*, September 23, 1955.

S. W. Pease

*Grogan, Texas.

*Grollet, Jacques.

*Groom, B. B.

*Groom, Texas.

Groos, Friedrich Wilhelm. Friedrich Wilhelm Groos, son of Karl Wilhelm Apollo and Sophie (Martin) Groos, was born on September 18, 1827, in Strass-Ebersbach, in the German Duchy of Nassau. He was educated as an architectural and civil engineer, and he came to Texas in 1848 with his father, three brothers, and four sisters. He lived first on a farm in Fayette County, but in 1850 he moved to San Antonio and took a position with the mercantile firm of Gilbeau and Callaghan. He represented that firm in Eagle Pass until 1854, when he formed his own merchandising and freighting company, F. Groos & Company, in partnership with his brothers, Carl and Gustav. The firm's main offices were in Eagle Pass, with branches in San Antonio, New Braunfels, and Matamoros. During the Civil War, Groos was engaged in shipping cotton to Mexico, and he resided in Monterrey. In 1866 he moved the firm's headquarters to San Antonio and made his home there for the rest of his life. F. Groos & Company's mercantile operations were displaced by its banking functions after the Civil War, and the firm operated as a private bank until 1912, when it was chartered as the Groos National Bank.

Groos was president of the San Antonio Casino Association and served for two terms on the San Antonio school board. For twenty years he was president of the San Antonio German-English School.qv He first married Gertrude Rodriguez, by whom he had seven children before her death in 1873. He then married Anna Siemering, by whom he had eight children. He died on January 27, 1912, and was buried in San Antonio City Cemetery Number One.

BIBLIOGRAPHY: Frederick Chabot, *With the Makers of San Antonio* (1937); Groos National Bank, *From Ox Carts to Jet Planes* (1954); August Santleben, *A Texas Pioneer* (1910).

S. W. Pease

*Groos, Johann Jacob. Johann Jacob Groos was nominated for commissioner of the General Land Office qv in 1873 (not 1872, as stated in Volume I).

*Grossville, Texas.

*Grosvenor, Texas.

*Grounds, Texas.

*Grove Creek.

*Grover, George W.

Grover, Walter E. Walter E. Grover was born on April 17, 1869, in Galveston, the son of Eliza (Crane) and George W. Grover.qv On November 14, 1905, he married Kate Duble; they had no children. Grover was an accountant and bookkeeper specializing in abstract and title work; he became an authority in the field of land titles. Following his retirement in 1950, Grover served two terms as president of the Galveston Historical Society qv and devoted full time to historical research, collections, and writing. He placed his own and his father's manuscripts in the Eugene C. Barker Texas History Center, the Rosenberg Library, and the San Jacinto Monument and Museum.qqv

A skilled sailor and ardent hunter and fisherman as a youth, Grover made a collection and description of bird eggs from the Galveston area for the Smithsonian Institution. He was acclaimed by the United States Coast Guard for his manuscript on the coast guard stations of Galveston, and a copy of that work was placed in the coast guard headquarters in New Orleans. He died on February 6, 1960, and was buried in the Old Episcopal Cemetery in Galveston.

BIBLIOGRAPHY: "Texas Collection," *Southwestern Historical Quarterly*, LXIV (1960–1961).

Anne A. Brindley

*Grover, Texas.

*Groves, Texas. Groves, adjacent to Port Arthur in Jefferson County, adopted a home rule charter in 1953 and a manager-council form of city government in 1959. Located on State Highway 87, and with the Kansas City Southern Railroad line and nearby Gulf Intracoastal Canal,qv Groves has ample transportation facilities for its development. Nearby oil, chemical, and shipbuilding industries provide employment for its rapidly expanding population. During the 1950's its population increased thirteenfold, from approximately 1,300 in 1950 to 17,304 in 1960. In 1970 the population was 18,067. Groves reported one hundred business establishments in 1973. *See also* Beaumont-Port Arthur-Orange Standard Metropolitan Statistical Area.

*Groveton, Texas. Groveton, seat of Trinity County, had a 1960 population of 1,148 and a 1970 count of 1,219. In 1972 Groveton had thirty-five business establishments.

*Groveton, Lufkin, and Northern Railway Company.

*Grow, Texas.

*Grubbs, Texas.

*Grubbs Self Help and Industrial School. *See* Arlington State College.

*Gruenau, Texas.

*Gruene, Texas.

*Grulla, Texas. Grulla, also called La Grulla, in Starr County, had a population of 1,194 in 1970, according to the United States census.

*Grumbles, John J.

*Gruver, Texas. Gruver, Hansford County, had a 1960 population of 1,030; in 1970 the United States census reported 1,265.

Guacali Indians. These Indians are known only from a Spanish document of 1693 which lists the Guacali ("fruit hamper") as one of fifty "nations" that lived north of the Rio Grande and "between Texas and New Mexico." This may be interpreted to mean the southern part of western Texas, since the document also mentions that the Apache were at war with the groups named. Nothing further is known about the Guacali.

BIBLIOGRAPHY: C. W. Hackett (ed.), *Historical Documents Relating to New Mexico, Nueva Vizcaya, and Approaches Thereto, to 1773*, II (1926).

T. N. Campbell

*Guadalajara, Diego de.

*Guadalupe, Texas.

*Guadalupe Bayou.

*Guadalupe-Blanco River Authority. The Upper Guadalupe River Authority did not emerge from the Guadalupe River Authority (as stated in Volume I). The Guadalupe River Authority merged with the newly created Guadalupe-Blanco River Authority in 1935. The Upper Guadalupe River Authority was created separately by the Forty-sixth Legislature and has responsibility only in Kerr County at the headwaters of the Guadalupe River (*see* Upper Guadalupe River Authority).

The Guadalupe-Blanco River Authority operates as a public corporation, does not have the power of taxation, and does not receive appropriations from the state. A thirty-year lease, with purchase option, was negotiated with the San Antonio City Public Service Board in 1942 for the Comal Steam Generation Plant. The plant was in turn subleased to the Lower Colorado River Authority.qv Income from the Comal plant lease provided the Guadalupe-Blanco River Authority with a small amount of capital with which to begin the development of the Guadalupe and Blanco rivers for the benefit of residents of the Guadalupe Valley.

A soil conservation program was initiated by the Authority in 1948, aimed at helping farmers and ranchers within the Guadalupe River Watershed to improve handling of rainfall and provide adequate drainage for low areas. The program consisted primarily of providing heavy equipment, such as motorgraders, draglines, etc., at cost to construct terraces, waterways, and drainage ditches.

Canyon Reservoir,qv constructed by the United States Army Corps of Engineers on the Guadalupe River in Comal County, was financed jointly by the United States government and the Guadalupe-Blanco River Authority. The reservoir, serving the joint purposes of flood control and water conservation, impounds 366,400 acre-feet of water at conservation pool level and has a planned surface

of 8,240 acres. The Authority also operates six small hydroelectric plants, which were purchased from private corporations in 1963. The small plants have an aggregate capacity of 16,080 kilowatts and function primarily from the flow of the Guadalupe River. The six small lakes formed by the hydroelectric dams are heavily used by recreationists from nearby communities.

Under lease-purchase option, the Authority's Calhoun Canal Division operates a system of canals in Calhoun County. The system distributes water from the Guadalupe River to Union Carbide Corporation and National Starch Corporation for industrial use and provides water to irrigate 7,500 acres of rice and 3,500 acres of other crops. The canal system is protected by the Lower Guadalupe Diversion Dam and Salt Water Barrier on the Guadalupe River constructed by the Authority in 1965. The unique "fabri-dam" automatically maintains a river surface at four feet above mean sea level, preventing intrusion of salt water into the canal system.

A master plan of development was prepared by the Authority to guide the future development of the Guadalupe River and its tributaries. The plan called for the construction of Cloptin Crossing Reservoir, on the Blanco River above Wimberley in Hays County; Lockhart Reservoir, on Plum Creek near Lockhart, in Caldwell County; and Cuero Reservoir above Cuero, in DeWitt and Gonzales counties.

John H. Specht

*Guadalupe Canyon.

*Guadalupe College. (Gonzales, Texas.)

*Guadalupe College. (Guadalupe City, Texas.)

*Guadalupe Colored College.

*Guadalupe County. Guadalupe County, adjoining Bexar County on the east and forming part of the San Antonio metropolitan area, continued in 1974 to attract tourists to its historic sites and festivals. The county ranked among the state's leaders in hog production; other livestock included dairy cattle, poultry, and sheep. Crops were diversified, emphasizing cotton, pecans, and vegetables. Oil was a major source of income; the 1972 production alone was 2,712,936 barrels, and by 1972 over 157,500,000 barrels had been produced since its discovery in 1922. Manufacturing was centered in the county seat, Seguin, the site of the city-county public library and the Guadalupe Valley Hospital, both completed in 1965. Work was projected for the late 1960's for the improvement of the county's roads and construction of an airport. The 1960 population was 29,017; in 1970 it was 33,554. *See also* San Antonio Standard Metropolitan Statistical Area.

*Guadalupe County (Judicial).

*Guadalupe Hidalgo, Treaty of.

*Guadalupe High School Association.

*Guadalupe Male and Female Academy.

*Guadalupe Mountains.

Guadalupe Mountains National Park. The first national park in the United States acquired mainly by purchase of private lands, Guadalupe Mountains National Park had its inception in 1961 when the federal government received 5,632 acres in the north McKittrick Canyon area from Wallace Pratt. The plan at that time apparently was to join this small amount of donated land to Carlsbad Caverns National Park, but in 1963 Senator Ralph W. Yarborough introduced a bill in the United States Congress to establish the park in Texas. In the next few years Senator Yarborough, Congressman Richard White, and Congressman Joe Pool persisted in efforts to publicize the mountains and to find support in Congress; on October 15, 1966, President Lyndon B. Johnson qv signed into law the bill creating the national park. Seventy thousand acres were purchased from J. C. Hunter, Jr., of Abilene, bringing the total land area to 77,518 acres in Hudspeth and Culberson counties.

Guadalupe Mountains National Park is sixty-five miles east of El Paso and thirty-five miles southwest of Carlsbad Caverns, New Mexico. The park area displays an extraordinary range of geologic features, from the world's best known fossil organic reefs (the Capitan is said to be the most extensive in the world) to the highest point in Texas, Guadalupe Peak.qv A region of diverse climate, wildlife, and vegetation, with characteristics of desert, forest, and mountain alike, the Guadalupe Mountains area is virtually unspoiled by man, and its geological importance and geographical location make it one of the most unusual wilderness areas in the United States.

BIBLIOGRAPHY: Freeman Tilden, *The National Parks* (1968); Ralph W. Yarborough, *The Guadalupe Mountains: A Congressional Record Bibliography* (1971).

*Guadalupe Peak.

*Guadalupe River. *See also* Guadalupe-Blanco River Authority; Upper Guadalupe River Authority.

*Guagejohe Indians.

*Guajillo, Texas.

*Guasa Indians. The status of the Guasa (Guaser, Guaza, Guesa, Huasa) Indians in Texas is far from clear. In a Spanish missionary report of 1691 a group identified as Guaza was reported as living about eighty leagues southwest of the Hasinai Caddo. This name did not appear again in documents until the second half of the eighteenth century, when the Guasa were identified as enemies of the Comanche and also as trading with various Indian groups in northeastern Texas. These Guasa seem to have been the Osage, who at that time were ranging from western Missouri into eastern Kansas and Oklahoma. At present it is not possible to link the Guaza of 1691 with the Guasa of the late eighteenth century.

BIBLIOGRAPHY: C. E. Castañeda, *Our Catholic Heritage in Texas, 1519–1936*, V (1942); F. W. Hodge (ed.), *Handbook of American Indians*, I (1907), II (1910); J. R. Swanton, *Source Material on the History and Ethnology of the Caddo Indians* (1942); R. C. Troike, "A Pawnee Visit to San Antonio in 1795," *Ethnohistory*, 11 (1964).

T. N. *Campbell*

*Guaycone Indians.

*Guayule Creek.

Guazapayogligla Indians. This is the name of one band of Chizo Indians, who are considered by some writers to be a branch of the Concho. In the seventeenth and early eighteenth centuries the Chizo occupied the area now covered by northeastern Chihuahua, northwestern Coahuila, and the lower part of the Big Bend region of Trans-Pecos Texas.

BIBLIOGRAPHY: C. W. Hackett (ed.), *Historical Documents Relating to New Mexico, Nueva Vizcaya, and Approaches Thereto, to 1773*, II (1926); C. Sauer, *The Distribution of Aboriginal Tribes and Languages in Northwestern Mexico* (1934).

T. N. *Campbell*

*Guda, Texas.

Gueiquesale Indians. The Gueiquesale (Guyquechale, Cotzale, Guisole, Heyquetzale, Huisocale, Quesal, Quisole) Indians were one of the dominant bands of Coahuila during the last half of the seventeenth century. At times they crossed the Rio Grande to hunt and forage for wild plant foods in the southwestern part of the Edwards Plateau. In 1675 the Bosque-Larios Expedition qv that penetrated Texas north of present Eagle Pass was accompanied by Gueiquesale warriors and also encountered other Gueiquesales beyond the Rio Grande. The Gueiquesales entered several missions in Coahuila but not in Texas. Although it has been commonly assumed that the Gueiquesales spoke a Coahuiltecan language, J. D. Forbes has recently objected to this linguistic identification. He prefers to leave their language unidentified. Geie (or Geies), the name of an early eighteenth-century group of the same area, may be a shortened form of Gueiquesale.

BIBLIOGRAPHY: V. Alessio Robles, *Coahuila y Texas en la Epoca Colonial* (1938); H. E. Bolton (ed.), *Spanish Exploration in the Southwest, 1542–1706* (1916); J. D. Forbes, "Unknown Athapaskans: The Identification of the Jano, Jocome, Jumano, Manso, Suma, and Other Indian Tribes of the Southwest," *Ethnohistory*, 6 (1959); F. B. Steck, "Forerunners of Captain de Leon's Expedition to Texas, 1670–1675," *Southwestern Historical Quarterly*, XXXVI (1932–1933); J. R. Swanton, *Linguistic Material from the Tribes of Southern Texas and Northeastern Mexico* (1940).

T. N. *Campbell*

*Guenther, Carl Hilmer.

*Guenther, Heinrich.

*Guerra, Texas.

*Guerrero, Vicente Ramón.

Guerrero, Coahuila, Mexico. *See* San Juan Bautista.

*Guerrero Decree.

*Guest Creek.

*Guffey, Texas.

*Guhlkainde Indians.

Guiguipacam Indians. The Guiguipacam (Iguiguipacam) Indians, apparently a Coahuiltecan band, lived along the lower Rio Grande. In the middle eighteenth century their principal settlements were on the south bank of the river just upstream from present Reynosa, Tamaulipas.

BIBLIOGRAPHY: W. Jiménez Moreno, "Tribus e idiomas del Norte de México," *El Norte de México y el Sur de Estados Unidos* (1944); G. Saldivar, *Los Indios de Tamaulipas* (1943).

T. N. Campbell

*Guilford, Texas.

*Guion, Texas.

*Guisole Indians.

*Guleke, James O.

*Gulf, Texas. (Matagorda County.)

*Gulf, Texas. (Upshur County.)

*Gulf, Beaumont, and Great Northern Railway Company.

*Gulf, Beaumont, and Kansas City Railway Company.

*Gulf, Colorado, and Santa Fe Railway Company. In 1964 the Gulf, Colorado, and Santa Fe Railway operated 1,665.5 miles of track in Texas. In addition it leased the Gulf and Interstate of Texas and owned one-fourth interest in the Houston Belt and Terminal and one-eighth in the Union Terminal. The following year it was taken over by the parent company, the Atchison, Topeka, and Santa Fe.

James M. Day

*Gulf and Interstate Railway Company. In 1925 the Gulf and Interstate Railway Company acquired the property of the Santa Fe Dock and Channel Company.

In the mid-1960's all but nine directors' qualifying shares were owned by the Atchison, Topeka, and Santa Fe. The road has 43.3 miles of first main track between High Island and Beaumont, which are operated under lease by the Gulf, Colorado, and Santa Fe Railway Company.

James M. Day

*Gulf Intracoastal Waterway. The Texas section of the Gulf Intracoastal Waterway was extended and improved during the 1950's and 1960's, with many tributary and feeder channels added. Petroleum and petroleum products continued to be the principal commodity transported over the waterway; other commodities included basic chemicals, building cement, iron and steel products, coal and lignite, plastics, and wheat and other agricultural products. Outbound and inbound commerce in 1967 amounted to approximately 55.5 million short tons, according to the United States Army Corps of Engineers, which operates the waterway. The canal was also used in the transportation of missiles and space vehicles moving to and from Texas. In 1971 the Texas section of the waterway broke previous records, handling over 67.6 million short tons of commerce.

*Gulf and Northern Railroad Company.

*Gulf Oil Corporation. The Gulf Oil Corporation began its second half century with completion in 1951 of the world's largest (at the time) catalytic cracking unit in Port Arthur, Texas, and in the same year began construction of plants in Port Arthur for the manufacture of ethylene and isooctyl alcohol, a major move in developing its petrochemicals capacity.

While the Fort Worth, Sweetwater, and Pittsburgh (Pennsylvania) refineries were dismantled in the 1950's after the facilities had become obsolete, the Port Arthur and Philadelphia refineries continued to expand and the Toledo and Cincinnati refineries were modernized. New refineries were built or acquired in the United States, with additions at Purvis, Mississippi, Santa Fe Springs, California, and Venice, Louisiana. Plans were made for a major refinery south of New Orleans.

Increasing its capital expenditures in the 1950's, Gulf joined with B. F. Goodrich Company to form a new company, Gulf-Goodrich Chemicals, Incorporated, through which Gulf maintained an important position in the manufacture of synthetic rubber from petroleum-derived feedstocks. It also acquired Warren Petroleum Corporation in 1956 and that same year increased its interest in British American Oil Company by trading Gulf's Canadian properties for 8,335,648 common shares of British American stock, bringing Gulf's interest in that company to 58 percent. Gulf also extended its exploration and production operations in the 1950's, including an extensive program for exploration of underwater leases in the Gulf of Mexico off Louisiana which has since become one of the company's leading domestic producing areas.

With the conclusion of World War II, Gulf, as a 55-percent participant in Kuwait Oil Company, resumed operations in Kuwait to put into production petroleum discovered there about the time of the war's outbreak. Production from these vast reserves climbed steadily and yielded for Gulf's interest an average of more than 1,300,000 barrels per day in 1967.

Gulf owned or had an interest in twenty-two refineries in addition to those in the United States. Adding to its European refining capacity, refineries at Milford Haven, Wales, and Huelva, Spain, went on stream in 1968 and a permit was obtained for construction of a refinery at Milan, Italy, to further strengthen Gulf's capacity to supply products for its growing European markets. Discoveries in Bolivia and Nigeria were developed in the 1960's and added significantly to Gulf's foreign oil production. Production from discoveries in Colombia and Cabinda was expected to begin before the end of 1968, and substantial discoveries were made in Ecuador. Gulf was producing oil and gas from eleven nations as its explorations continued in thirty countries.

A milestone in Gulf's marketing operations was reached in 1966. With the acquisition in 1960 of Wilshire Oil Company of California and in 1966 of mid-continental retail outlets and storage and distribution facilities of Cities Service Oil Company, Gulf for the first time had service station representation in all forty-eight adjoining states of the continental United States.

Gulf's transportation facilities moved more than a million barrels of crude oil daily from oil fields to refineries throughout the world by pipelines and tankers. In 1968 the world's largest ship, the 312,-000-deadweight-ton tanker, *Universe Ireland*, was placed in service for Gulf. It was the first of six such tankers planned for use by the company to deliver Middle Eastern and West African crudes to deepwater terminals at Bantry Bay, Ireland, and at Okinawa for transshipment to European and Far Eastern refineries by smaller vessels.

Refining capacity was increased along with Gulf's expansion in other petroleum operations. The company owned full or partial interest in thirty United States and foreign refineries. In 1967 the company processed an average of more than 1,295,000 barrels of crude oil daily. By the 1960's Gulf had become a major producer of petrochemicals, plastics, and agricultural chemicals. In 1967 Gulf entered the field of nuclear energy. In this program it began uranium exploration and acquired the General Atomic Division of General Dynamics Corporation, renaming the subsidiary Gulf General Atomic Incorporated. Research and development operations included both basic and applied research to cover every phase of its integrated interests.

At the end of 1967, with total assets of approximately $6,500,000,000 owned by more than 163,000 shareholders, Gulf Oil Corporation had some 58,000 employees working in more than fifty nations to provide the world with petroleum and other energy-producing products.

James A. Clark

*Gulf, Santa Fe, and Northwestern Railroad Company. *See* Pecos and Northern Texas Railway Company.

*Gulf, Texas, and Western Railroad Company.

*Gulf and West Texas Railroad Company.

*Gulf, Western Texas, and Pacific Railway Company. *See* San Antonio and Mexican Gulf Railway.

*Gum Creek.

*Gum Gully.

*Gum Spring Mill, Texas.

Gumpusa Indians. The Gumpusa (Campusa) Indians were Coahuiltecan Indians who are known through a single 1794 report from Nuestra Señora del Espíritu Santo de Zuñiga Mission qv near Goliad. In this report they are identified as a subdivision of the Arunama, and it is stated that at that time only twelve remained.

BIBLIOGRAPHY: E. L. Portillo, *Apuntes para la historia antigua de Coahuila y Texas* (1886).

T. N. Campbell

*Gun Canyon Creek.

*Gun Manufacturing in Texas During the Civil War.

*Gunsight, Texas.

*Gunsight Mountains.

*Gunter, Jot.

*Gunter, Texas.

*Gunter Bible College.

*Gurley, Davis R.

Gurley, Edward Jeremiah. Edward Jeremiah Gurley, brother of Davis R. Gurley,qv was born in Franklin County, Alabama, on June 7, 1827. He was graduated from LaGrange College, Alabama, in 1845, and received a master's degree in 1846. He read law in Tuscumbia, Alabama, and there married Annie Blocker, by whom he had two daughters. In 1852 they moved to Waco, Texas, where Gurley practiced law with his brother-in-law, Richard F. Blocker. When the Civil War began, Gurley raised the 30th Texas Cavalry in McLennan and surrounding counties and led the regiment as colonel in the Indian Territory and Arkansas. After the war Gurley returned to his law practice, which consisted largely of land litigation in McLennan, Falls, and Williamson counties; he also acquired extensive land holdings. He was a member of the Constitutional Convention of 1866 qv and was elected to the legislature in 1867. His first wife having died, he married Virginia (Jennie) Alexander in 1868, and they had one son. In his later years Gurley owned several plantations along the Brazos River; he was president of Lone Star Cotton Picking Machine Company and of the Collins Company, which owned land in the Mexican coffee region. He died on July 4, 1914.

BIBLIOGRAPHY: Virginia Gurley, Widow's Application for a Pension (Confederate Veterans Pension Index File, Archives, Texas State Library); John Sleeper and J. C. Hutchins (comps.), *Waco and McLennan County, Texas* (1876); *Biographical Encyclopedia of Texas* (1880); *Memorial and Biographical History of McLennan, Falls, Bell, and Coryell Counties, Texas* (1893); Thomas Pilgrim and H. L. Bentley, *The Texas Legal Directory for 1876–77* (1877); *Confederate Veteran,* XXIII (January, 1915).

*Gus, Texas.

*Gusher, Texas.

*Gussettville, Texas.

*Gustine, Lemuel.

*Gustine, Texas.

*Guthrie, Robert.

*Guthrie, Texas. Guthrie, seat of King County and commercial center for its ranches, reported seven businesses in 1970. The 1970 population was 125.

*Guthrie Lake.

*Gutiérrez de Lara, José Bernardo Maximiliano.

*Gutiérrez-Magee Expedition. Following the battle of Rosalis,qv Manuel María de Salcedo qv was one of the royalist officers executed; his uncle, Nemesio de Salcedo, was not present at this battle, nor was he executed (as stated in Volume I). Nemesio de Salcedo, who was commander-general of the internal provinces, returned to Spain in 1814 and died around 1819.

Gutsch, Milton Rietow. Milton Rietow Gutsch was born on March 7, 1885, in Sheboygan, Wisconsin, the son of Louis and Laura (Rietow) Gutsch. In 1904 he entered the University of Wisconsin, where he received a B.A. degree (1908), an M.A. degree (1909), and a Ph.D. degree (1916), specializing in medieval history. On August 29, 1918, he married Mary Mayfield. He began his career at the University of Texas in 1912 as an instructor in British history. He became adjunct professor in 1916, associate professor in 1922, and professor in 1927.

Early in his career at the university Gutsch became noted for his ability as a teacher and administrator. In 1927 he became chairman of the Department of History; in 1928 he was made secretary of the general faculty; and in 1944 he became secretary of the Faculty Council. He held these administrative positions until poor health forced his retirement in 1951. He wrote several articles and published in 1955, with H. Bailey Carroll,qv *Texas History Theses: A Check List of the Theses and Dissertations Relating to Texas History Accepted at the University of Texas, 1893–1951.* He also compiled Texas war records of World War I and served as managing editor of the *Texas History Teachers Bulletin* from 1912 to 1920. He died in Austin on January 1, 1967.

BIBLIOGRAPHY: Austin *American,* January 5, 1967; *Who's Who In America* (1960); Documents and Minutes of the General Faculty, University of Texas.

*Guy, Texas.

*Guyot, Jean Marie.

*Guy's Store, Texas.

*Gyp Hills.

*Gypsum Creek.

H

H-4 Reservoir. H-4 Reservoir is in the Guadalupe River Basin in Gonzales County, four miles southeast of Belmont on the Guadalupe River. The project is owned and operated by the Guadalupe-Blanco River Authority qv for the generation of hydroelectric power. The authority purchased this and five other projects located on the Guadalupe River by a contract which became effective May 1, 1963. Construction of the dam was begun in 1929 and completed in 1931, with impoundment of water and generation of power beginning at that time. The reservoir has a capacity of 6,700 acre-feet and a surface area of 800 acres at elevation 331 feet above mean sea level. The reservoir is maintained at practically constant level, except during floods, by regulating the power output to the water inflow. The hydroelectric power plant for this project is part of the dam structure. The power plant consists of one generating unit with all auxiliaries, with a generating capacity of 2,400 kilowatts. The river flow has been partly regulated since June, 1964, by releases from Canyon Reservoir.qv The drainage area above the dam is 2,038 square miles.

BIBLIOGRAPHY: Texas Water Commission, *Bulletin 6408* (1964).

Seth D. Breeding

*Haborth Hill.

*Hacanac Indian Province.

Hacanac Indians. The Hacanac were a Caddoan people encountered by the Moscoso Expedition qv in 1542 somewhere in northeastern Texas or in the adjoining parts of Arkansas and Louisiana. They may be the same as the Lacane, also mentioned in the records of the same expedition, whose name was regarded by J. R. Swanton as an early name for the people later known as Nacaniche. On the basis of sound correspondences in the names, Swanton has suggested that Hacanac, Lacane, Nacachau, Nacao, Nacaniche, Nacono, and Nakanawan were probably fragments of the same Caddoan tribe. This cannot be verified by such documentary evidence as is now available.

BIBLIOGRAPHY: J. R. Swanton, *Source Material on the History and Ethnology of the Caddo Indians* (1942).

T. N. Campbell

*Hacienda, Texas.

*Haciendita, Texas.

*Hackberry, Texas. (Cottle County.)

*Hackberry, Texas. (Edwards County.)

*Hackberry, Texas. (Lavaca County.)

*Hackberry Creek.

*Hackberry Draw.

*Hackett, Charles Wilson.

*Hackett Peak.

*Hackley Creek.

*Haddon, John.

*Hadley, Joshua.

*Hadra, Berthold Ernest.** Berthold Ernest Hadra was married first to Ida Weisselberg (not Eda Weiselberg, as stated in Volume I). *See* Hadra, Ida Weisselberg.

Hadra, Ida Weisselberg. Ida Weisselberg Hadra was born in Castroville, Texas, on January 4, 1861, the daughter of German immigrants Gustav Frederick and Anna (von Groos) Weisselberg. In 1872 Ida's father, a physician, took his family to Austin, where he had been appointed to a position in the State Lunatic Asylum (now Austin State

Hospital qv). This gave Ida the opportunity to study with the Austin portrait artist, Ella Moss Duval.qv In addition to a very successful portrait of her father, she also painted "A Neighbor" and "Portrait of a Child." When Mrs. Duval left Austin, Ida attended classes at the Texas Female Institute,qv where Hermann Lungkwitz qv was teaching landscape painting. Some of her landscapes include "View of the Military Academy from East Austin," "Seventh Street, Austin, Looking West," "The Old Ira Evans Home," and "The Old Duval Home."

In 1882 Ida married a physician, Berthold Ernest Hadra,qv and lived in San Antonio, where, until her death on November 3, 1885, she continued her studies with Mrs. Duval. Some San Antonio views include "Bridge over the San Antonio River," "San Antonio River Back of the Old Brewery," and two still-life paintings, "The Hunter's Quest" and "Products of the Garden."

BIBLIOGRAPHY: Pauline A. Pinckney, *Painting in Texas: The Nineteenth Century* (1967).

Pauline A. Pinckney

*Hady, Samuel C.

Haeser Indians. The Haeser (Saesse, Siaexer, Xaeser) Indians were Coahuiltecan-speaking Indians who, in the seventeenth century, ranged from northeastern Coahuila northward across the Rio Grande to the southwestern portion of the Edwards Plateau, particularly in the area of present Kinney County. Like other Indians of northeastern Coahuila at this time, the Haeser crossed the Rio Grande to hunt bison.

BIBLIOGRAPHY: V. Alessio Robles, *Coahuila y Texas en la Epoca Colonial* (1938); H. E. Bolton (ed.), *Spanish Exploration in the Southwest, 1542–1706* (1915); J. R. Swanton, *Linguistic Material from the Tribes of Southern Texas and Northeastern Mexico* (1940).

T. N. Campbell

*Hagansport, Texas. A post office was established at Hagansport in 1857 (not 1884, as stated in Volume I) and continued in operation until 1929 (not 1915).

Cyrus Tilloson

Hagar, Conger Neblett. Conger ("Connie") Neblett Hagar, known widely as "The Texas Bird Lady" for her many years of bird observation on the Texas coast, was the daughter of Robert S. and Mattie (Yeager) Neblett. She was born in Corsicana, Navarro County, on June 14, 1886. She studied voice and piano at Forest Park College in Saint Louis, taking post-graduate training at the University of Chicago and the American Conservatory. In 1935 she and her husband moved to Rockport, Texas, where she began to study birds seriously for the first time.

Connie Hagar spent the rest of her life as an amateur birdwatcher in Rockport, gaining the respect of professional ornithologists in Europe and the United States. She added over twenty new species to the avifauna list of the state and was the first to report numerous species of migratory birds, including several that were thought to be extinct.

In addition to the snowy plover, buff-breasted sandpiper, ash-throated flycatcher, and mountain plover (among others), she identified nine different species of hummingbirds, whose annual movement down the Texas coast had been unknown to science. The number of different birds in the Aransas Bay area reported by Connie Hagar was nearly five hundred.

Throughout her life Connie Hagar was a conservationist, teacher, and tireless bird watcher. She received a special citation in 1962 from the National Audubon Society, which convened in Corpus Christi that year largely to be near Rockport and the flyways. Connie Hagar married Jack Hagar in 1926. She died November 24, 1973, in Corpus Christi, and was buried in Rockport.

BIBLIOGRAPHY: Edwin Way Teale, *Wandering Through Winter* (1966); *Bulletin of the Texas Ornithological Society*, 21 (December, 1973); Derro Evans, "Notable South Texans," *Texas Parade*, 32 (December, 1971); Eleanor Anthony King, "Lady with Binoculars," *Audubon* (July, 1947).

*Hager, Texas.

*Hagerman, Texas.

Hagerman National Wildlife Refuge. Hagerman National Wildlife Refuge was established in February, 1946, on Lake Texoma near the town of Denison. The refuge consists of 11,320 acres, of which approximately 2,500 are open water. The area was created for the purpose of providing resting and feeding areas for migratory water fowl using the central flyway and for the protection of other mammals and birds occupying the upland sections. Almost 1,000 acres of farmland are cultivated by refuge personnel and cooperating farmers to supplement natural foods of ducks and geese.

Approximately 70 percent of the area is upland and consists of oak, elm, and pecan woodlands. Native bluestem grass is interspersed throughout the region. In February, 1951, oil was discovered on the refuge. One hundred and thirty-five wells were producing petroleum products in the 1960's.

The fall migration of ducks and geese is in excess of 100,000 birds. Among the seasonal visitors to the refuge are snow geese, white-fronted geese, Canada geese, mallards, pintails, American widgeons, and scaup duck.

BIBLIOGRAPHY: Fish and Wildlife Service, United States Department of the Interior, "Hagerman National Wildlife Refuge," *Refuge Leaflet 18.*

*Haggerty Creek.

*Hagler, Lindsay S.

*Hahn, Texas.

*Haidusek, Augustine.

*Hainai Indians. The Hainai (Aenay, Ainai, Ayenai, Aynai, Hini, Inay, Ioni, Ironeye, Ironi) Indians, one of the leading Caddoan tribes of the Hasinai confederation in eastern Texas during the seventeenth and eighteenth centuries, lived along the Angelina River, mainly in the vicinity of present Cherokee and Nacogdoches counties. After the Texas Revolution the Hainai, along with remnants of other Hasinai tribes absorbed by them, moved westward and at various times occupied settlements along the Brazos River, particularly between McLennan and Palo Pinto counties. Some Hainai joined the Taovaya (Wichita) Indians on the Red River. In 1854 the Hainai were placed on the Brazos Indian Reservation qv of present Young County. In 1859 they were taken to Indian Territory, now Oklahoma. Today their descendants are living with the Wichita in Caddo County, Oklahoma. Several place names in Texas mark former Hainai occupations—Ioni Creek in Anderson County and Ioni Falls, Ioni Creek, and the community of Ione, all in Palo Pinto County.

BIBLIOGRAPHY: H. E. Bolton, "The Native Tribes about the East Texas Missions," *Quarterly of the Texas State Historical Association*, XI (1907–1908); J. R. Swanton, *Source Material on the History and Ethnology of the Caddo Indians* (1942); D. H. Winfrey and J. M. Day (eds.), *The Indian Papers of Texas and the Southwest, 1825–1916*, I–III (1966).

T. N. Campbell

*Hainesville, Texas.

*Hairston Creek.

*Halbert, Nathan.

*Halbert, Texas.

*Haldeman, Horace.

Hale, Charles Haynes. Charles Haynes Hale, educator, was born on November 14, 1869, in Corinth, Arkansas, son of James Thomas and Elizabeth (Watson) Hale. He came with his family in 1885 to Flatwoods (now Huckabay), Texas. In 1889 he entered Add-Ran College (now Texas Christian University), and through the years he attended several universities, earning B.S., B.A., and M.A. degrees. Texas Christian University conferred an honorary Doctor of Laws degree on Hale in 1953. He taught at various schools and colleges, including Abilene Christian College and Tarleton State College (now Tarleton State University), from which he retired; he was founder, owner, and teacher of Huckabay Academy in the early 1900's. Hale married Dova Copeland in 1891; they had five children. He died on February 3, 1969, at the age of ninety-nine, and he was buried in Stephenville.

BIBLIOGRAPHY: Stephenville *Empire-Tribune*, February 7, 1969.

*Hale, John C.

*Hale, William G.

*Hale, Texas. (Dallas County.)

*Hale, Texas. (Fannin County.)

*Hale Center, Texas. Hale Center, in Hale County, in 1970 reported forty-three businesses, most of which were engaged in the processing and distribution of agricultural products. On the night of June 2, 1965, a tornado struck the city, leveling two hundred homes and destroying virtually all of the downtown business area, including twenty-nine business buildings, the city hall, and the fire station. Five people were killed and sixty were injured, while property damage was estimated at $8,000,000. All but one of the demolished businesses and most of the homes had been rebuilt by the end of 1965. The

All-American country fiddlers contest and homecoming celebration is one of the biggest annual events in the town. According to the United States 1970 census, Hale Center had a population of 1,964, a decrease from the 2,196 reported in the 1960 census.

*Hale City, Texas.

*Hale County. Hale County, an area of 979 square miles in the Panhandle, produced oil (57,-790,633 barrels between 1946 and 1973) and manufactured goods, but its economy was primarily devoted to farming. The county's farm income in the early 1970's was over $63,000,000 per year. Beef and dairy cattle, poultry, and eggs contributed to this figure, but the raising of crops was more important. With 404,283 irrigated acres, Hale was a leading county in crop revenue in 1968. Farms produced castor beans, cotton, grain sorghums, wheat, soybeans and other legumes, barley, sugar beets, and vegetables. Industries to process this output were located in Plainview, the county seat. Crops suffered from the tornadoes which hit the county in June, 1965, severely battering Hale Center and Cotton Center. According to the United States 1970 census, Hale County had a population of 34,137, a decrease from the 36,798 reported in the 1960 census.

*Hale Institute.

*Halesboro, Texas.

*Haley Branch.

Halff, Henry Mayer. Henry Mayer Halff, the son of Rachel (Hart) and Mayer Halff,qv was born in San Antonio on August 17, 1874. He was educated at Staunton Military Academy, Virginia, and Eastman Business College, Poughkeepsie, New York. He married Rosa Wechsler on January 1, 1905, and they became the parents of two sons and two daughters. Soon after their marriage they moved to Midland, where Halff actively engaged in the operation of ninety sections of rough semidesert land on which he ran cattle bearing the brands Circle Dot, Quien Sabe,qqv and J M. The range lay east of the Pecos River in Crane, Crockett, Midland, and Upton counties. Halff moved the headquarters for his cattle business to the old George W. Elliott qv rock house in Upton County. Halff advocated improvement in breeding cattle, and on the Quien Sabe Ranch alone he had three thousand top Herefords. Bulls from this herd were widely sought and sold throughout the Southwest.

Halff also imported Belgian stallions to improve his draft horses and bought thoroughbred stallions from racing stables to breed with local mares, producing wiry horses used as polo ponies. His polo teams competed at Fort Bliss;qv Aiken, South Carolina; Newport, Rhode Island; and Dedham, Massachusetts, where he won an international championship. The ponies were trained on the H. M. Halff Polo Farm in Midland and shipped from there to other parts of the United States, Canada, and England.

A pioneer in irrigation on the plains, Halff

drilled his first irrigation well on his Cloverdale Farm, five miles southeast of Midland. The wells drilled there became a source of Midland's water supply and yielded sufficient water to enable him to produce an excellent quality of grapes, melons, grain, and cotton. As early as 1908 water was hauled by ox team from there to use in drilling wells at East Upland, a part of his ranch in Upton County. Because of poor health, Halff moved to Mineral Wells in 1923. He died in Richardson on March 20, 1934, and was buried in Emanu-El Cemetery in Dallas.

BIBLIOGRAPHY: Grace Miller White, "The Activities of M. Halff and Brother," *Frontier Times*, 19 (January, 1942).

N. *Ethie Eagleton*

Halff, Mayer. Mayer Halff was born on February 7, 1836, in Lauterbourg, Alsace, France. At the age of fourteen he moved to Texas to help his brother Adolphe, who was peddling goods on horseback from Galveston to Liberty. Between 1850 and 1856 the brothers operated a store at Liberty, where they sold their goods to farmers and ranchers along the coast, accepting hides and cattle for merchandise. Mayer drove the cattle to market in New Orleans.

On August 25, 1856, Adolphe Halff was drowned when the *Nautilus*, a ship bound for Boston, sank. A younger brother, Solomon, came from Lauterbourg in 1857 to help Mayer with the store. In 1864 the brothers moved to San Antonio, where, with a cousin, they opened a wholesale store. Since there were few banks, the brothers entered the banking business and in 1891 were among the founders of the Alamo National Bank, of which Solomon was vice-president until his death on May 29, 1905. M. Halff also founded and was president of the City National Bank, chartered in 1898. At the peak of their careers, the brothers controlled more than a million acres of land in Bee, McMullen, Gaines, Presidio, Crockett, Midland, Upton, and Brewster counties and were part owners of the Laramie Cattle Company in Wyoming.

With the closing of the open range, the brothers bought 1,280 acres of land in Presidio County in 1882. Near a spring Halff built the headquarters for the Circle Dot Ranch,qv from which herds were driven northward up the Chisholm qv and other trails. In 1883 a small part of the land was leased to the United States Army for a post, with grazing and watering rights retained by the brothers. They began moving their herds to land near the Pecos River south of Fort Lancaster.qv In addition, they bought the J M Ranch in Crockett County and established headquarters at Camp Melvin.qv

In 1898 M. Halff and Brother began purchasing the desertland in Upton County. They drilled water wells and planned to concentrate the Circle Dot, Quien Sabe,qv and J M herds at that place. In 1900 Solomon Halff began selling his interests to Mayer and initiated the dissolution of the firm, which had opened up a great range in West Texas.

Mayer Halff was active in the Temple Beth-El, serving as its president for a time. He married Rachel Hart of Detroit, Michigan, and they were the parents of four children. Halff died on December 23, 1905, and was buried in the Beth-El Cemetery in San Antonio.

BIBLIOGRAPHY: J. Marvin Hunter (ed.), *The Trail Drivers of Texas* (1925); Grace Miller White, "The Activities of M. Halff and Brother," *Frontier Times*, 19 (January, 1942); Grover C. Ramsey, "Camp Melvin, Crockett County, Texas," *West Texas Historical Association Year Book*, XXXVII (1961).

N. *Ethie Eagleton*

*Halfway, Texas.

*Halifax Creek.

*Hall, David Graham.

*Hall, George B.

*Hall, Jesse Lee (Leigh).

*Hall, John W. (Captain Jack).

*Hall, Richard Moore.

*Hall, Robert. Robert Hall came to Texas aboard the side-wheeler *George Washington* (not the *Yellow Stone*, as stated in Volume I).

BIBLIOGRAPHY: Brazos [pseud.], *Life of Robert Hall, Indian Fighter and Veteran of Three Wars* (1898).

*Hall, Warren D. C.

*Hall, William J.

*Hall, William Sims.

*Hall, William Whitty.

*Hall, Texas.

*Hall County. Hall County had primarily an agricultural economy with particular emphasis on farming. Chief crops were cotton (60,000 bales in 1968), small grains, and alfalfa. There was some cattle raising, both beef and dairy, with a small amount of poultry production. Most of the industries of the county, including several new ones established in the 1960's, were linked to agriculture. The county hospital was in Memphis, and the headquarters of a watershed conservation district was located in Lakeview. Population for the county in 1960 was 7,322; the United States census report showed a 1970 population of 6,015.

*Hall Creek.

*Hall of State.

*Hallettsville, Texas. Hallettsville, seat of Lavaca County, was incorporated in 1870 with an alderman-mayor type of government. In 1966 Hallettsville had two banks, eleven churches, two newspapers, a hospital, and a library. An airport was completed and put into operation in August, 1966. The town reported eighty-two businesses in 1970, including fourteen manufacturers, primarily connected with metal works, meat packing, and cotton. In 1960 the population was 2,808; the United States census report showed a 1970 population of 2,712.

*Halls Bayou.

*Hall's Bluff, Texas.

*Hall's Branch.

*Hallsburg, Texas.

*Hallsville, Texas. According to the United States report of the 1970 census, Hallsville, in Harrison County, had a population of 1,038, an increase from the 684 reported in the 1960 census. The town had fifteen businesses in 1970.

*Hallville Masonic Institute.

*Halsell, J. Glenn.

*Halsell, John T.

Halsell, William Electious. William Electious Halsell was born in Wise County on June 7, 1851, the son of Electious and E. J. (Mays) Halsell. As a young man he became a trail driver, taking cattle to the northern markets. He bought a ranch which he sold in 1882 in order to buy a large spread in the Cherokee territory of Oklahoma. In 1901 he purchased 200,000 acres of land in Lamb and Castro counties from Capitol Freehold Land and Investment Company, Ltd.,qv when they dissolved their holdings. In 1924 the largest part of the ranch, which was named the Mashed O,qv was sold to farmers. Halsell established the towns of Amherst and Earth and built banks, hotels, and cotton gins. He kept the Spring Lake division of the ranch for himself, and he lived there most of the time. He died in California in 1934.

BIBLIOGRAPHY: Biographical File, Barker Texas History Center, University of Texas at Austin; C. D. Cates, *Pioneer History of Wise County* (1907).

*Halsell, Texas. (Clay County.)

*Halsell, Texas. (Lamb County.)

*Halstead, Texas.

*Haltom City, Texas. Haltom City, in Tarrant County, was incorporated in 1949. It is primarily a residential area adjoining Fort Worth. The population was 5,760 in 1950 and 23,133 in 1960. The United States report of the 1970 census showed another increase, to 28,127. *See also* Fort Worth Standard Metropolitan Statistical Area.

*Ham Creek.

*Hamberlin, Lafayette Rupert.

*Hamby, William Robert.

*Hamby, Texas.

Hamer, Francis Augustus. Francis A. Hamer, son of Frank and Lou Emma (Francis) Hamer, was born in Fairview, Texas, on March 17, 1884. Known commonly as Frank or Pancho, he grew up on the Welch Ranch in San Saba County. In 1894 the family moved to Oxford in Llano County, where Hamer worked at his father's blacksmith shop. In 1901 he and his brother hired out as wranglers on the Pecos County ranch of Barry Ketchum, brother of outlaw Tom "Black Jack" Ketchum.qqv In 1905 Hamer was a cowboy on the Carr Ranch, between Sheffield and Fort Stockton,qv where, after capturing a horse thief, he was recommended for a position with the Texas Rangers.qv

On April 21, 1906, Hamer enlisted as a Texas Ranger. Working primarily along the South Texas border, Hamer became known as an expert shot. In 1908 he resigned from the Rangers to become marshal of the lawless community of Navasota. Hamer brought order to the area, remaining as marshal until April 21, 1911, when he became a special officer in Harris County.

On March 29, 1915, Hamer rejoined the Rangers and began one of the most eventful periods of his peace officer career, patrolling the South Texas border from the Big Bend to Brownsville when arms smuggling, bootlegging, and banditry were rampant. From 1919 to 1920 Hamer served as a prohibition officer. Returning to the Rangers in 1920, he rose to the rank of senior captain and made Austin his permanent home.

During the following decade he was instrumental in restoring order in oil boom towns such as Mexia and Borger, and he participated in numerous fights with lawbreakers. In 1932 Hamer retired from active duty but retained his commission. Two years later he was called back to duty by Governor Miriam Ferguson qv to track down the nationally known outlaws Clyde Barrow and Bonnie Parker.qqv After a three-month search, he trapped them near Gibsland, Louisiana, on May 23, 1934, and with the aid of several local policemen shot and killed them. Congress awarded Hamer a special citation for catching the pair. During the late 1930's Hamer worked for various oil companies and shippers as a private agent preventing strikes and breaking up mobs. In 1948 he again was called to duty as a Ranger by Governor Coke Stevenson qv to help check the election returns in Duval County in the controversial United States Senate race. Afterwards he went into permanent retirement in Austin, where he died on July 10, 1955.

BIBLIOGRAPHY: H. G. Frost and J. H. Jenkins, *"I'm Frank Hamer"* (1968).

John H. Jenkins

*Hamilton, Andrew Jackson.

*Hamilton, David.

*Hamilton, James.

*Hamilton, Morgan Calvin.

*Hamilton, Robert.

Hamilton, Walton Hale. Walton Hale Hamilton, educator and lawyer, was born at Hiwassee College, Tennessee, on October 30, 1881, son of Hale Snow and Bettie Dixon (Hudgings) Hamilton. He attended Webb School, Bellbuckle, Tennessee, from 1898 to 1901 and Vanderbilt University from 1901 to 1903. He received a B.A. degree from the University of Texas in 1907. After teaching in the public schools of Belton and Temple until 1909, he became an instructor in medieval history at the University of Texas in 1909–1910. He received a Ph.D. degree in 1913 from the University of Michigan, and Yale University conferred on him an honorary M.A. degree in 1928. Hamilton was instructor of economics at the University of Michigan, 1910–1913; professor of political economy, 1913–1914; assistant professor of political economy at the University of Chicago, 1914–1915; and professor of economics at Amherst College, 1915–1923. From 1923 to 1928 he taught at

Robert Brookings Graduate School, and from 1928 to 1948 was professor of law at Yale, though he had never formally studied law. He became Southmayd Professor of Law, Emeritus, and won renown as a teacher and writer on legal and economic subjects and as a specialist in the law of social control of business.

Hamilton was with the law firm of Arnold, Fortas, and Porter in Washington, D.C.; a member of the National Recovery Administration Board, 1934–1935; a delegate of the United States government to the International Labor Conference at Geneva in 1935; special assistant to the attorney general of the United States, 1938–1945; and a member of the Georgia Bar. He also served on a presidential fact-finding board arbitrating a Pullman wage dispute. Hamilton was a prolific contributor to legal and economic periodicals and was the author of the following: *Current Economic Problems* (1915, 1925); *Price and Price Policies* (1938); *The Pattern of Competition* (1940); *Patents and Free Enterprise* (1941); and *The Politics of Industry* (1951); with others he also wrote *The Control of Wages* (1923); *The Case of Bituminous Coal* (1925); *A Way of Order for Bituminous Coal* (1928); *The Power to Govern* (1937); and *Antitrust in Action* (1940).

Hamilton married Lucile Elizabeth Rhodes in 1909; they had three children. After the death of Mrs. Hamilton, he married Irene Till on July 20, 1937; they had two children. He died in Washington, D.C., on October 27, 1958.

BIBLIOGRAPHY: *Who's Who In America* (1950).

Richard T. Fleming

*Hamilton, Texas. (Hamilton County.) According to the United States report of the 1970 census Hamilton had a population of 2,760 in 1970, a decrease from the 3,106 reported in the 1960 census. Hamilton had fourteen churches, two banks, and a school resulting from the consolidation of Hamilton and Fairy school districts by 1963. In 1970, 110 businesses were reported, including ten manufacturers. Garment, sheet metal, and ready-mix concrete industries were in operation in the early 1970's.

*Hamilton, Texas. (Harris County.)

*Hamilton Chapel, Texas.

*Hamilton County. Hamilton County, primarily an agricultural area, specialized in livestock and egg production. One gas field, a small amount of oil production, and the cutting of cedar posts produced a minor portion of the income. Trade and industry centered in Hamilton, the county seat, and in Hico. Tourist attractions included the Hico Old Settlers Reunion in August and a livestock show in March. The United States report of the 1970 census showed that the 1960 population of 8,488 had declined to 7,198 by 1970.

*Hamilton County (Judicial).

*Hamilton Creek.

*Hamilton Dam, Texas.

*Hamilton Field.

*Hamilton Pool, Texas.

*Hamiltonburg, Texas. *See* Three Rivers, Texas.

Hamlin, James Darlington. James Darlington Hamlin, son of James H. and Mary Jane (Gilman) Hamlin, was born on August 5, 1871, at St. Matthews, Kentucky. He attended Kentucky Wesleyan University and the University of Kentucky but left his native state in 1897 to seek his fortune in Alaska. He ended his journey at Amarillo, Texas, where he found relief from his chronic asthma. During the fall of 1897 he and Willis Day Twitchell qv established Amarillo College; Hamlin was named president of the college and professor of Latin and Greek, positions he held until 1909. He was admitted to the Bar about 1898 and practiced law until 1902, when he was elected county attorney for Potter County. About the same time he became Texas counsel for the Capitol Freehold Land and Investment Company, Ltd.,qv being named Texas representative of the firm in 1906. In 1905, as the agent for the Capitol Syndicate,qv he opened XIT Ranch qv lands to colonization and founded the town of Farwell, Texas; at the same time, and in partnership with John Hutson, Hamlin opened Texico, New Mexico, to settlement. From 1907 to 1919 he served as county judge of Parmer County. In 1916 he helped found the short-lived Panhandle-Plains Chamber of Commerce, which a few years later was amalgamated with the West Texas Chamber of Commerce.qv From 1934 to 1936 he served as president of the combined organization. In 1921 he, Thomas F. Turner,qv and several others organized the Panhandle-Plains Historical Society,qv and Hamlin, as a director, was later instrumental in the establishment of the Panhandle-Plains Historical Museum.qv In 1940 he retired from all business activities except the position of Texas representative of the John V. Farwell Company (Capitol Syndicate), a position he held until his death.

Hamlin was married in 1906 to Katherine Nichols. He died at Clovis, New Mexico, on January 10, 1950, and was interred at Farwell, Texas.

BIBLIOGRAPHY: James D. Hamlin Papers (MS., Southwest Collection, Texas Tech University); Amarillo *Daily News*, January 11, 1950.

Jimmy M. Skaggs

*Hamlin, Texas. Hamlin was the commercial center for the farming area in the northwest part of Jones County, located on the county line with Fisher County. In 1963 Hamlin reported a gypsum products plant, a cottonseed oil mill, a compress, and grain and feed plants, plus a hospital, post office, and bank. The town had eighty businesses in 1970, including eight manufacturers. The 1960 population was 3,791; the 1970 population decreased to 3,325. *See also* Abilene Standard Metropolitan Statistical Area.

*Hamlin Lake.

*Hamlin and Northwestern Railway Company.

*Hamman, William Harrison.

*Hammeken, George Louis.

*Hammett, Samuel Adams.

*Hammond, Texas. (Polk County.)

Hammond, Texas. (Robertson County.) Hammond was named for B. F. Hammond, who came to the area sometime before the Civil War and purchased two large plantations, one of which was located just west of the present village of Hammond. Founded in 1869 by the Houston and Texas Central Railroad, supposedly at the request of Hammond, the town probably had a post office by the next year. By 1900 the settlement had a railroad depot, a cotton gin, general store, jail, and school. The inhabitants were largely engaged in farming and cattle raising. In 1900 the population was 115; by 1930 it had decreased to 100. The population was forty in 1940, and the town had at least one business and a post office. By 1950, however, the post office was no longer in operation. The 1970 population was approximately forty.

*Hamon, Texas.

Hampton, John Howard. John Howard Hampton was born in Fort Worth, Texas, on January 16, 1898, the son of Ireland and Marian (Rieger) Hampton. After a year at Texas A&M and one year in the Marine Corps, he worked on ranches and raised some livestock of his own. In 1921 he worked on the Dallas *Morning News* qv and in 1926 he became editor of the *East Texas Magazine*. Hampton resumed ranching in 1931 near Clarksville, and in 1945 he purchased the A. B. Robertson Ranch. About 1950 he acquired part of the old Bell Ranch known as the Fort Bascom Ranch, near Logan, New Mexico. A resident of Lubbock, Hampton served as a director of the Panhandle-Plains Historical Society qv and as president of the West Texas Museum Association; he helped establish the Southwest Collection at Texas Technological College (now Texas Tech University). Hampton married Valvora Moore in 1929, and they had one child. Hampton died at his New Mexico ranch on June 1, 1967, and was interred in Lubbock.

BIBLIOGRAPHY: Lubbock *Avalanche-Journal*, June 2, 3, 1967; Howard Hampton Papers (MS., Southwest Collection, Texas Tech University).

Jimmy M. Skaggs

Hampton, Joseph Wade. Joseph Wade Hampton, one of the more able newspapermen of nineteenth-century Texas, was born on July 7, 1813, to Thomas F. and Elizabeth Hampton in Catawba County, North Carolina. In 1836 he married Sarah Stirewalt (who died in 1841 after bearing one daughter). Hampton learned the newspaper trade under Dr. Ashbel Smith, qv as he first apprenticed, then shared the editorial duties on the Salisbury, North Carolina, *Western Carolinian*. He assumed the editorship of the journal when Smith immigrated to Texas in 1837; he hoped to join Smith in establishing a newspaper in the new republic, but ill health forced him to remain in North Carolina.

Hampton probably hoped to regain his health when he left journalism and purchased a resort at Catawba Springs, North Carolina, in 1838. He could not stay out of journalism, however, and after he moved to Charlotte in 1841, he founded and edited the *Mecklenburg Jeffersonian*, a Democratic organ through which he continually squabbled with the Whigs in opposition newspapers. In 1844 he married Cynthia R. Wilson, first cousin of Samuel Polk (who was President James K. Polk's father). They had five children—three girls and two boys.

Hampton's health grew worse, and he reconsidered immigrating to Texas. Heavily in debt, he arrived in Montgomery, Texas, on December 28, 1848, but moved to Huntsville almost immediately. He taught English at the Huntsville Male Institute,qv studied law in the county clerk's office, and was named to the original board of trustees of Austin College.qv He moved again in 1850, to Austin, where he was offered a job on the *Texas State Gazette*;qv in October of the same year he was elected clerk of the legislature. In December Hampton purchased a one-third interest in the *Gazette*. He became publisher of the paper in 1853 and was elected public printer for the Fifth Texas Legislature. When ill health forced him to retire in 1854, he sold his interest in the paper to John Marshall.qv

Hampton died on June 13, 1855, after a short but active involvement in community and state affairs. He was a ruling elder and charter member of the First Presbyterian Church in Austin; he was a motivating force in the agricultural societies and Democratic parties of North Carolina and Texas; and he endeavored to bring the railroad into Charlotte and Austin. More important, he helped to improve the cultural and social life of Texans by advocating progressive causes, supporting various educational institutions, and editing widely read and influential newspapers. He was buried in Austin.

BIBLIOGRAPHY: Ronnie C. Tyler, *Joseph Wade Hampton, Editor and Individualist* (Southwestern Studies Monograph No. 23, 1969).

Ronnie C. Tyler

*Hampton, Texas. (Nacogdoches County.)

*Hampton, Texas. (Tyler County.)

*Ham's Hole.

*Hamshire, Texas.

*Han Indians. The Han Indians are known only from the narrative of Cabeza de Vaca,qv who encountered them in the vicinity of Galveston Bay in 1528. Since other Europeans did not visit this section of the Texas coast until some 150 years later, it is difficult to link the Han with later coastal Indian groups. Some writers have argued that the Han were Karankawans, but most consider them Atakapans, probably ancestors of the Akokisa who lived in this area during the seventeenth and eighteenth centuries. Linguistic evidence supports this identification. In both Akokisa and Atakapa *hañ* is the word for "house."

BIBLIOGRAPHY: A. F. Bandelier (ed.), *The Journey of Alvar Nuñez Cabeza de Vaca* (1922); A. S. Gatschet and J. R. Swanton, *A Dictionary of the Atakapa Language* (1932); F. W. Hodge (ed.), *Handbook of American In-*

dians, I (1907); W. W. Newcomb, Jr., *The Indians of Texas* (1961); J. R. Swanton, *The Indians of the Southeastern United States* (1946).

T. N. Campbell

Hanasine Indians. The Hanasine were one of twenty Indian groups that joined Juan Domínguez de Mendoza ᑫᵛ on his journey from El Paso to the vicinity of present San Angelo in 1683–1684. Since Mendoza did not indicate at what point the Hanasine joined his party, it is not possible to determine their range or affiliations. However, the Indians between the Pecos River and the San Angelo area were being hard pressed by Apache at this time, and it seems likely that the Hanasine ranged somewhere between these two localities.

BIBLIOGRAPHY: H. E. Bolton (ed.), *Spanish Exploration in the Southwest, 1542–1706* (1916).

T. N. Campbell

*Hancock, George Duncan.

*Hancock, John. John Hancock was married in November, 1855 (not 1885, as stated in Volume I). [Some later printings of Volume I contain this correction.]

Hancock, Joseph Curtis. Joseph Curtis Hancock was born on August 12, 1872, at Pine Hill, Rusk County, Texas, the son of Tyre and Caroline (Hillin) Hancock. He was graduated with a law degree from the University of Texas in 1897. In 1903 he entered the Texas legislature as the youngest member ever seated in the Dallas delegation up to that time. He served two terms, then practiced law in Dallas County. In 1917 Governor James E. Ferguson ᑫᵛ appointed Hancock the first chairman of the state highway commission (*see* Highway Department, Texas State), which was created in that year. He was reappointed to the same post by Governor William P. Hobby.ᑫᵛ He worked for the improvement of Texas highways throughout his life. Hancock married Ada Rike on February 10, 1898, and they had three children. He died in Dallas on January 8, 1957, and was buried in Laurel Land Cemetery near Dallas.

William B. Alderman

*Hancock, Winfield Scott.

*Hancock, Texas.

*Handley, Texas.

*Handy, Robert Eden.

*Hankamer, Texas.

*Hanks, Wyatt. Wyatt Hanks was born in Kentucky (not Arkansas Territory, as stated in Volume I) on November 27, 1795 (not 1794). He came to Texas in 1826; his brothers, James and Horatio, followed sometime later, probably in 1828. In 1840 Hanks was a trustee of the San Augustine Female Academy at San Augustine. He died in 1862 and was buried in Liberty County.

Mrs. William F. Hanks

*Hanna, Ebenezer. Ebenezer Hanna was the son of Jesse Pearce [Pierce] Hanna (not Jesse Pearch Hanna, as stated in Volume I).

Abigail Curlee Holbrook

Hanna, Erasmus Manley. Erasmus Manley Hanna, the son of Martha (Berryhill) and James Newton Hanna, was born in Henry County, Tennessee, in 1841. He studied medicine in Germany, then returned to Louisville, Kentucky, to take his medical degree before the Civil War. Hanna came to the East Texas area to practice medicine during the war; in the Reconstruction ᑫᵛ period he, along with other East Texas physicians, organized the first local medical society. Shortly after his marriage to Virginia Morris at Henderson, Texas, in 1870, Hanna again matriculated in the Louisville Medical School to pursue advanced studies. He returned to Texas a year later.

Hanna established permanent residence in Troup, Smith County, Texas, where he continued to practice medicine while entering into the economic and cultural life of the community. He established Hanna House, Troup's first hotel, in 1872; the first furniture store in 1873; and a theater and opera house in 1875. With his wife's uncle, William Wright Morris,ᑫᵛ he promoted the first railroads and clay industry in East Texas. He died at Troup in 1903. In 1967 a medallion and historical plaque were placed at the Hanna homesite, then occupied by a great-niece of Hanna.

BIBLIOGRAPHY: John Bennett Boddie, *Historical Southern Families,* VI (1962), X (1965); Mrs. Lucius Smith, *Some Important Personages in the East Texas Area* (1959).

Mildred Alice Webb

Hanna Valley, Texas. An earlier name for Regency, Texas, Hanna Valley was settled by Jesse P. Hanna and his five sons in 1856. It was then in Brown County, part of which is now Mills County. The settlement was attacked by Comanche Indians in 1863 (*see* Mills County in Volume II). The first post office was established in 1875 but was later discontinued. When it was reestablished, the name was changed to Regency.

BIBLIOGRAPHY: *Texas Almanac* (1936).

*Hanover, Hiram.

*Hanover, Texas.

*Hansford, John M.

*Hansford, Texas.

*Hansford County. Hansford County ranked among the leading counties in the state in wheat and grain sorghum production in 1969. More than half the farm income, $40,000,000 per year in the early 1970's, was derived from beef cattle. Irrigation (230,000 acres) and oil and gas development added to the growth of the county. The Cator Buffalo Camp, the Rolling Plains Mule Train Association, and a stock show draw tourists to the county. The population numbered 6,208 in 1960; the 1970 population was 6,351.

*Hanson, Texas.

*Hape Indians. In the second half of the seventeenth century the Hape (Ape, Jeapa, Xape) Indians, a Coahuiltecan-speaking band, ranged from northeastern Coahuila across the Rio Grande to the southwestern margin of the Edwards Plateau. The Bosque-Larios Expedition ᑫᵛ of 1675 encountered fifty-four Hape and Yorica adults a few miles north of the Rio Grande near present Eagle Pass. They were loaded with dried bison meat that was being taken back to their settlements south of the river. At this time it was learned that their local enemies included Ocana, Pataguo, and "Yurbipame," bands that ranged to the east along the Nueces and Frio rivers south of the Edwards Plateau. In 1688 the Hape numbered about 500, but shortly thereafter they were almost wiped out by a smallpox epidemic. By 1689 most of those who had survived the epidemic were slain by unspecified Indian enemies from the east.

BIBLIOGRAPHY: H. E. Bolton (ed.), *Spanish Exploration in the Southwest, 1542–1706* (1916); F. W. Hodge (ed.), *Handbook of American Indians*, I (1907).

T. N. Campbell

***Happy, Texas.**

***Happy Draw.**

***Haqui Indians.** The Haqui (Aqui, Hake, Hakesian) Indians are known only from records of the La Salle Expedition,qv which clearly indicate that at the close of the seventeenth century they lived in northeastern Texas between the Hasinai tribes and the Kadohadacho on the Red River (Texarkana area). The Haqui probably lived in the valley of either the Sabine or the Sulphur River. It has been suggested that the Haqui were the same as the Adai (Adaes), but this has not been demonstrated. At this time the Adai, a Caddoan people, were reported to be living on the Red River in northwestern Louisiana. However, it seems likely that the Haqui were Caddoan.

BIBLIOGRAPHY: I. J. Cox (ed.), *The Journeys of Réné Robert Cavelier, Sieur de La Salle*, II (1906); F. W. Hodge (ed.), *Handbook of American Indians*, I (1907); H. R. Stiles (ed.), *Joutel's Journal of La Salle's Last Voyage, 1684–7* (1906).

T. N. Campbell

***Harahey Province.**

***Harber Creek.**

***Harbin, Texas.**

***Harbor City, Texas.**

***Harcourt, Edward.**

***Hardeman, Bailey.**

***Hardeman, Thomas Jones.**

***Hardeman, William P.**

***Hardeman County.** Hardeman County gained several new industries between 1948 and 1966, including a gypsum plant, a power plant, and an oil refinery. Total crude oil production in 1972 was 823,320 barrels; production from its discovery in the county in 1944 to January 1, 1973, was 14,458,875 barrels. The main occupation was farming, with an average annual farm income of $7.7 million in the early 1970's coming from the production of wheat, cotton, and grain sorghums and the raising of cattle, horses, hogs, and poultry. Approximately 10,000 acres were irrigated, and commercial production of cucumbers was begun in the mid-1960's. The county supported a public library and a hospital; a new hospital building was completed in 1967. Construction of a new municipal building was planned. The 1960 population was 8,275; the 1970 census showed a population decrease to 6,795.

***Hardin, Augustine Blackburn.**

***Hardin, Benjamin Watson.**

***Hardin, Franklin.** Franklin Hardin, in making an application for a Mexican land grant, said that he came to Texas in 1826 (not 1825, as stated in Volume I).

BIBLIOGRAPHY: Mexican Titles, Spanish Documents, XXXIX (MS., General Land Office).

***Hardin, John Gresham.**

***Hardin, John Wesley.** John Wesley Hardin was captured in Florida on August 23, 1877 (not July 23, as stated in Volume I). The telegrams from John Barclay Armstrong,qv his captor, to the Texas Rangers qv telling of Hardin's arrest are all dated August. Hardin relates in his autobiography, which was written many years after the event, that his capture took place in July.

BIBLIOGRAPHY: Adjutant General's Papers (Archives, Texas State Library); Wayne Gard, *Frontier Justice* (1949); Walter Prescott Webb, *The Texas Rangers* (1935).

***Hardin, Milton Ashley.** Milton Ashley Hardin was born on November 4, 1813 (not in 1807, as stated in Volume I). He came to Texas in 1829 (not 1825) and on December 2, 1835, was appointed a second lieutenant in the Texas Army qv under Captain Henry Teal.qv In the summer of 1836 he transferred to Captain Amasa Turner's qv company on Galveston Island and on December 26, 1836, he resigned his commission.

BIBLIOGRAPHY: Pension Applications, Republic of Texas (MS., Archives, Texas State Library).

***Hardin, William.** William Hardin, in making an application for a Mexican land grant, said that he came to Texas at the beginning of 1827 (not in 1825, as stated in Volume I).

BIBLIOGRAPHY: Unfinished Mexican Titles, Spanish Documents, LXV (MS., General Land Office).

Hardin, William Barnett. William Barnett Hardin, a participant in the siege of Bexar,qv was born in Tennessee on April 20, 1806, the son of Benjamin and Martha (Barnett) Hardin. In 1826 he moved with his family to Texas, west of the present town of Moscow in Polk County, on the Coushatta Trace.qv On August 20, 1829, he married Ann Holshousen.

In November, 1835, Hardin began his military service as a sergeant in Captain Martin B. Lewis'qv company of East Texas volunteers. This company, recruited from the present counties of Jasper, Tyler, and Polk, marched from the Neches River to join the Texan army assembled outside San Antonio. Sergeant Hardin participated in the bitter house-to-house fighting that occurred in San Antonio during December, 1835. He received a leg wound on December 9, which left him slightly crippled for the remainder of his life. He continued his army service for several months after the capture of San Antonio, and by September, 1836, he was promoted to first lieutenant.

After Polk County was created out of the northern part of Liberty Municipality in 1846, Hardin served in several official positions. He surveyed land in the southern portion of the county and signed, as deputy surveyor, the field notes for numerous surveys in this area. He also served as an election judge in the western part of the county. He acted as an advisor on Indian affairs and helped prepare and circulate a petition to the legislature, asking that a reservation be established for the Alabama Indians. His signature appears first on this petition, which is dated October 29, 1853.

In 1855 Hardin moved his family to a new home on Long Tom Creek, about four miles northwest of Livingston. He was a trustee of the Methodist church in Livingston. Hardin died on July 28, 1885, and was buried in the Holshousen Cemetery on the Coushatta Trace west of Moscow.

BIBLIOGRAPHY: Thomas L. Miller, *Bounty and Donation Land Grants of Texas* (1967); Memorials and Petitions to the Texas Legislature (MS., Archives, Texas State Library); Muster Roll of Captain M. B. Lewis' Company (MS., Archives, Texas State Library); Public Debt Papers (MS., Archives, Texas State Library).

Howard N. Martin

*Hardin, Texas. (Hardin County.)

*Hardin, Texas. (Liberty County.)

*Hardin Branch.

*Hardin County. By January 1, 1973, Hardin County had produced 344,573,796 barrels of oil since the first discovery in 1893. The county was 90 percent forested, mostly in pine. Some farming also contributed to its income. Kountze, Silsbee, and Sour Lake were the centers for manufacturing and trade. The 1960 population was 24,629; the United States report of the 1970 census showed a population increase to 29,996.

Hardin Junior College. *See* Midwestern University.

*Hardin-Simmons University. Hardin-Simmons University, Abilene, added five dormitories, a student center, and a chapel-auditorium to its campus between 1950 and 1965. Construction of a million-dollar science center and a new library building was planned to meet expanding enrollment; by 1969 the library contained 180,000 volumes.

The university tightened admission and academic standards in the mid-1960's. After dropping the football program in 1963, the school placed a greater emphasis on intercollegiate basketball. By 1965 Hardin-Simmons University had granted 9,469 earned degrees since its founding in 1891. During 1965 and 1966 the school engaged in a $2,000,000 endowment campaign, and long-range plans anticipated $25,000,000 in endowment funds.

Evan Allard Reiff succeeded Rupert N. Richardson as president, and James H. Landes became chief administrator of the Baptist university in 1963. Enrollment for the 1974–1975 regular term was

1,630 students; faculty that year numbered over one hundred. Elwin L. Skiles served as president.

*Hardy, Dermott Henderson.

*Hardy, John Crumpton.

*Hardy, Rufus. Rufus Hardy immigrated to Texas with his family in 1861, settling on a farm in the Brazos River bottoms near Millican. Though he did return to Mississippi to attend Somerville Institute (as stated in Volume I), he received his early education in Texas. He graduated with a Bachelor of Law degree from the University of Georgia in 1875.

BIBLIOGRAPHY: Chandler A. Robinson, *Judge Rufus Hardy, Pioneer Texan* (1970), and (comp.), *The Collected Speeches of Judge Rufus Hardy* (1969).

Chandler A. Robinson

*Hardy, Texas.

*Hardy's Chapel, Texas.

*Hardys Creek.

*Hare, Silas.

*Hare, Texas.

*Hargill, Texas.

Harker Heights, Texas. Harker Heights, in western Bell County, is a suburb of Killeen and, like Killeen, is economically dependent on Fort Hood.qv The city was incorporated with a mayor and council government in 1960, at which time its population was less than one thousand. In 1966 Harker Heights had five churches and an elementary school which had been completed in 1964. A $300,000 paving program was completed in 1965. While the United States census did not indicate a population count for 1960, it did report a 1970 population of 4,216.

*Harkey Knobs.

*Harkeyville, Texas.

*Harlem, Texas.

*Harleton, Texas.

*Harley, James A.

*Harlingen, Texas. Harlingen, located in Cameron County, is an agricultural, industrial, and financial center in the Lower Rio Grande Valley. The largest industry was food processing and canning. Three cotton mills were operating in the mid-1960's, employing several hundred persons. Located on the former site of the navigation school of Harlingen Air Force Base (*see* Harlingen Army Air Field), the Marine Military Academy qv had students from twenty-seven states and some foreign countries. The new Harlingen International Airport terminal was completed in 1970. Adjacent to the airport is the Confederate Flying Museum at Rebel Field (*see* Confederate Air Force), which contains World War II combat aircraft. Harlingen is also the site of the Texas State Technical Institute,qv which began operating in November, 1967, and the Rio Grande State Center for Mental Health and Mental Retardation.qv The city has become a well-known retirement center. Businesses reported in 1970 totaled 672. The U.S. census report listed the 1970 population of Harlingen as 33,503, a decrease from the 41,207 reported in the 1960 census. *See also* Brownsville-Harlingen-San Benito Standard Metropolitan Statistical Area.

*Harlingen Army Air Field. Closed in February, 1946, Harlingen Army Air Field was reactivated as Harlingen Air Force Base in April, 1952. The reopening served as a major factor in the growth of the city of Harlingen. The base was again closed in 1962, and by 1963 the phase-out was completed.

Harlingen State Chest Hospital. The Harlingen State Chest Hospital was authorized in 1953 as the Harlingen State Tuberculosis Hospital, operating under the Board for Texas State Hospitals and Special Schools.qv The hospital opened in 1955, serving patients from twenty southeastern Texas counties. The hospital's patient capacity was 518. A full-time follow-up clinic was operated to serve indigent patients. The hospital began operating under the State Department of Public Health qv in 1965. In 1967 there were 234 patients.

In 1971 new programs were started at the hospital. The 62nd Texas Legislature changed the name of the hospital to Harlingen State Chest Hospital to designate a change in policy. Previously only tuberculosis patients were accepted; the new authorization provided for treatment of patients with all kinds of chest and respiratory diseases, particularly chronic obstructive lung disease. Efforts were made to merge the hospital programs with regional ones. Regional programs involved basic case finding and follow-up services, and some of the regional clinics were staffed with clinicians from the hospital. An interagency agreement was made in August, 1971, with the Rio Grande State Center for Mental Health and Mental Retardation qv for the use of buildings and other services.

In 1970 the out-patient clinic of Harlingen State Chest Hospital served 5,751 patients and in 1971 it served 7,523. The bed capacity of the hospital was reduced to 262 in 1971. Average daily patient census was 533 in 1970 and 457 in 1971. George H. Hobbs was the superintendent.

BIBLIOGRAPHY: Board for Texas State Hospitals and Special Schools, *Report* (1964); Harlingen State Chest Hospital, *Annual Report* (1971).

Harlingen State Mental Health Clinic. The Harlingen State Mental Health Clinic opened in October, 1962, at the former air base near the town. The clinic provided psychiatric treatment for adult indigent patients discharged or furloughed from San Antonio State Hospital,qv and referrals which might not require hospitalization. Fees were based on individual income and the number of dependents supported by the patient. In May, 1968, the name was changed to Rio Grande State Center for Mental Health and Mental Retardation.qv *See* Mentally Ill and Mentally Retarded, Care of, in Texas.

BIBLIOGRAPHY: Board for Texas State Hospitals and Special Schools, *Report* (1964).

Harlingen State Tuberculosis Hospital. *See* Harlingen State Chest Hospital.

*Harl's Creek.

*Harmon, Texas. (Chambers County.)

*Harmon, Texas. (Lamar County.)

*Harmon Creek.

Harmonson, Peter. Peter Harmonson, the son of Wallace and Polly (Curry) Harmonson, was born on December 18, 1797, in Bourbon County, Kentucky. He married Anna McGee on August 8, 1816; they had ten children.

Harmonson was one of the organizers of Denton County in 1846. He served as Denton's first sheriff and helped organize the first Methodist church there. In 1854 he moved to Fort Belknap and was appointed first chief justice of Young County in 1856. He was also one of the organizers of the first Methodist church in Young County. Harmonson died on January 9, 1865, of arrow wounds inflicted by Indians. He was buried at Johnson Station in Tarrant County.

BIBLIOGRAPHY: Denton County Commissioners Court Records; Young County Commissioners Court Records; Young County Probate Records.

Barbara Neal Ledbetter

Harmony, Texas. (Kent County.) Harmony, founded in 1900 about halfway between Jayton and Rotan, had at one time a store and a school. In 1966 there was nothing left of the community. The first name for the site was Tirkle Community. It is said that in the early days, after having trouble among themselves, the citizens settled their differences and renamed their town Harmony.

*Harmony, Texas. (Milam County.)

*Harmony, Texas. (San Augustine County.)

Harmony, Texas. (Tyler County.) Harmony was founded in 1890 eight miles southwest of Woodville. The community is in a farming and ranching area, with poultry raising as its main business. The 1966 estimated population was 250.

*Harmony Hill, Texas.

*Harney, William Selby.

*Harper, Alfred John.

Harper, George Franklin. George Franklin Harper, son of Henry and Jane (Cummings) Harper, was born on December 31, 1828, in Sangamon County, Illinois. He came to Victoria, Texas, in 1848 and on March 16, 1851, married his cousin, Keziah Harper. They had three children. During the Civil War Harper drove freight teams from Brownsville to San Antonio. His wife died soon after the war's end, and in 1869 he married her younger sister, Katherine Harper. They had one son.

Harper ranched and raised horses near Floresville until 1880, when he bought a section of land in Gillespie County and built a house on it near the Pedernales Springs. Mail was distributed weekly from this home, and when a post office was opened there in 1883, it was named Harper. Harper served as postmaster until 1890, as a county commissioner of Gillespie County from 1892 to 1898, and as a school trustee. He was also a director of the Harper Bank. In 1917 he moved to Bandera, and later to Florida, where he died on March 27, 1926. He was buried in Bartow, Florida.

BIBLIOGRAPHY: *Here's Harper: 1863–1963* (1963); Gillespie County Historical Society, *Pioneers in God's Hills* (1960).

Esther L. Mueller

*Harper, Henry Winston.

*Harper, Texas. Harper, in Gillespie County, was named for George Franklin Harper.qv

*Harpersville, Texas.

*Harrell, Jacob M.

*Harrell, Milvern.

*Harrell's Switch.

*Harriet, Texas.

*Harriet Lane. The *Harriet Lane* was named for the niece of President James Buchanan (not the niece of Andrew Johnson, as stated in Volume I).

*Harriet Mountain.

*Harris, Abner.

*Harris, David.

*Harris, DeWitt Clinton.

*Harris, Mrs. Dilue (Rose).

*Harris, Eli.

*Harris, Jane (Birdsall).

*Harris, John Birdsall.

*Harris, John Richardson.

*Harris, John Woods.

*Harris, Lewis Birdsall.

*Harris, Mose C.

*Harris, Samuel. Samuel Harris became private secretary to Governor Elisha Marshall Pease qv (not Governor James Wilson Henderson,qv as stated in Volume I) in December, 1853.

Katherine Hart

Harris, Thomas Green. Thomas Green Harris was born on May 27, 1854, at Sweetwater, Tennessee, the son of Ezekiel and Celina (Green) Harris. After attending Carson-Newman College at Jefferson City, Tennessee, where he received a B.A. degree in 1876 and an M.A. degree in 1880, he taught school in Ellijay, Georgia, before he came to Texas in 1879. He was superintendent of schools at Weatherford, Mansfield, and Plano, where he married Lou Oglesby on December 21, 1886. They moved to Dallas, where he became principal of the high school in 1887, remaining until 1891, when he became superintendent of the Dallas city schools. In 1893 he went to Houston as public school superintendent; in 1895 he took a similar position in Austin. In 1903 Harris moved to San Marcos and was named the first president of the Southwest Texas State Normal School (now Southwest Texas State University). He then went to the San Marcos Academy as its second president in 1911.

Harris retired from school work in 1915, but his love for schools later took him to Sul Ross College (now Sul Ross State University), where he taught mathematics for six years, after which he went to San Benito as superintendent of schools for three years. Harris and his wife were the parents of four daughters and two sons. He was a member of the Baptist church. He died on January 26, 1934, at San Marcos.

BIBLIOGRAPHY: Archives, Southwest Texas State University; San Marcos *Record,* January 30, 1934.

Tula Wyatt

Harris, Titus Holliday. Titus Holliday Harris, a pioneer in the field of psychiatry, was born on November 11, 1892, in Fulshear, Texas, to Robert Locke and Sally (Holliday) Harris. He attended Allen Academy (1908–1911) and Southwestern University (1911–1915), from which he received a B.A. degree. He received an M.D. degree from the University of Texas Medical Branch in 1919, interned at John Sealy Hospital in 1919–1920, and attended the New York Neurological Institute in 1923. In 1927 he worked at Manhattan State Hospital and Colorado State Psychopathic Hospital. Harris was married to Laura Randall Hutchings on December 17, 1927, and they had four children. He did further psychiatric study at the New York Psychiatric Institute in 1932–1933, and he was certified by the American Board of Neurology and Psychiatry in 1934.

He became the first chairman of the Department of Neurology and Psychiatry at the University of Texas Medical Branch in 1926. Under his guidance the department had become one of the largest and most highly acclaimed in the nation at the time of his retirement in December, 1962. In 1969 a higher percentage of medical students graduating from the University of Texas Medical Branch entered the field of psychiatry than from any other medical school in the nation; estimates place more than half of the psychiatrists practicing in Texas as graduates of Harris' residency training program.

He received numerous awards in recognition of his service in the field, including the Hogg Foundation qv Award in 1955 and the E. B. Bowis Award and Ashbel Smith qv Award in 1965. He was founder and editor of the monthly international journal *Diseases of the Nervous System* from 1940 to 1967 and the author and co-author of numerous papers in other professional journals. He was a member of some thirty associations and societies. Harris died in Galveston on April 22, 1969.

*Harris, William.

*Harris, William.

*Harris, William J.

*Harris, William Plunkett.

*Harris, Texas.

*Harris Bayou.

*Harris Chapel, Texas.

*Harris County. Harris County, home of the National Aeronautics and Space Administration

Manned Spacecraft Center,qv was among the leading oil, gas, and petrochemical areas in the 1950's and 1960's. The county is the center of one of the world's largest multicounty petrochemical developments and has a large production of cement, sand, lime, and clay. Since its discovery in 1905, 1,037,-007,984 barrels of oil were produced up to January 1, 1973. The county also had over 2,500 manufacturers in diversified fields. In the early 1970's the farm income averaged $26,000,000 per year, derived chiefly from rice, dairying, beef cattle, poultry, and vegetables; other leading crops included soybeans, grains, and cotton. The county supported approximately 60,000 irrigated acres. For recreation Harris County offers fishing and other saltwater activities and such attractions as Harris County Domed Stadium, completed in 1965 (see Astrodome), San Jacinto Monument, battleship *Texas*, and Jesse H. Jones Hall for the Performing Arts.qqv Houston, Texas' largest city, is the county seat. According to the United States report of the 1970 census, Harris County had a population of 1,741,912, a large increase from the 1,243,158 reported in the 1960 census. See also Houston Standard Metropolitan Statistical Area.

Harris County Domed Stadium. See Astrodome.

*Harris Creek.

*Harrisburg, Texas. (Harris County.)

*Harrisburg, Texas. (Jasper County.)

*Harrisburg and Brazos Railroad. See Harrisburg Railroad and Trading Company.

*Harrisburg County.

*Harrisburg Railroad and Trading Company.

*Harrison, Benjamin.

*Harrison, George.

*Harrison, Greenberry Horras.

*Harrison, James E.

*Harrison, Jonas.

*Harrison, Robert Henry.

*Harrison, Thomas.

*Harrison, Texas.

*Harrison Bayou.

*Harrison County. Harrison County, formerly a leading agricultural cotton-producing county, was, by the 1960's, drawing most of its wealth from manufacturing, lumbering, and commerce; beef cattle had replaced cotton as the chief agricultural money-maker. Located in northeast Texas on the Louisiana line, the county, 66 percent forested in 1965, had three lumber mills in operation. Oil (50,202,224 barrels produced between 1928 and January 1, 1973), gas, clay, and lignite were produced and processed, principally in Marshall and in Karnack, location of Longhorn Ordnance Works qv and Thiokol Chemical Corporation, a producer of solid fuel for rockets. As part of a campaign during the 1960's to end the prohibition that had been in force in the county since 1910, one new city, Uncertain, was created expressly for the purpose of legalizing the sale of alcoholic beverages in the Caddo Lake area. Caddo Lake and Lake O' the Pines in nearby Marion County were leading attractions for Harrison County residents and tourists, as were the many historic sites centering in Marshall. The 45,594 population in 1960 had decreased to 44,841 by 1970, according to the United States census.

*Harrison Times.

*Harrold, Texas.

*Harsleys Creek.

*Hart, John.

*Hart, Lawrence Joseph.

Hart, Meredith. Meredith Hart, son of Josiah Hart, was born in Kentucky in 1811. He came to Texas about 1833 by way of Arkansas, where he married Mary Riley; they had three sons and one daughter. He lived in Red River County (later Fannin County). Meredith was mustered into the Texas militia on July 20, 1835, serving in a cavalry company commanded by his brother, John Hart.qv He was discharged on August 29, 1841. Hart became a cattleman with operations in Hunt, Navarro, Erath, Comanche, and Johnson counties, selling stock at Fort Belknap qv and other army posts. His main route to market was overland to Shreveport and down-river to New Orleans. When Hunt County was organized in 1846 he was one of its commissioners. In 1855 he bought two sections of land in Johnson County and built a two-story frame house on Mustang Creek, a mile from present Rio Vista (landmarked by the Texas State Historical Survey Committee qv). After his wife's death, he married Cassandra Wilkins; they had two sons. Hart lost most of his holdings during the Civil War. He died in December, 1864, and was buried near his Johnson County homestead.

Weldon Hart

*Hart, Simeon.

*Hart, Texas.

*Hartburg, Texas.

Harte, Houston. Houston Harte, an active newspaperman in Texas for more than fifty years, was born on January 12, 1893, in Knobnoster, Missouri, the son of Edward Stettinius and Elizabeth (Houston) Harte. He attended the University of California for one year and was graduated from the University of Missouri School of Journalism in 1915. He was business manager in 1916 and then editor and publisher of the *Missouri Republican* in Boonville, Missouri, until 1920; Harte also served in the U.S. Army as a captain from 1918 to 1919.

In 1920 Houston Harte purchased the San Angelo, Texas, *Evening Standard*, and in partnership with Bernard Hanks in 1927 formed what became Harte-Hanks Newspapers, Inc. In 1972 the chain consisted of nineteen newspapers and one television station, including the Abilene *Reporter-News*, qv Corpus Christi *Caller-Times*, Paris *Evening News*, and San Antonio *Express* and *Evening News*. qqv

Total circulation of the chain, covering six states, was over 600,000 in 1972. Harte served on the board of the Associated Press from 1935 to 1946, and he received the medal of merit for journalism from the University of Missouri in 1931. He married Caroline Isabel McCutcheon on March 26, 1921; their two sons both became newspaper publishers.

Harte was instrumental in preserving Fort Concho qv in San Angelo, and he was on the committee that saved the Dwight D. Eisenhower qv Birthplace in Denison (*see* Parks, State). In 1949 Harte's edition of Old Testament stories entitled *In Our Image* was published by Oxford University Press. He was a member of the Texas Relief Commission in the first term of President Franklin Roosevelt. Houston Harte died in San Angelo on March 13, 1972, and was buried there in Fairmount Cemetery.

BIBLIOGRAPHY: Biographical File, Barker Texas History Center, University of Texas at Austin.

Edward H. Harte

*Hartley, Oliver Cromwell.

*Hartley, Texas.

*Hartley County. Hartley County, having an agricultural economy, ranked among the leading wheat-producing counties in the 1960's and early 1970's. The number of irrigated acres in wheat and grain sorghums was substantially increased during that period. Beef cattle contributed a major portion of the $15,000,000 average annual farm income in the early 1970's. Rita Blanca Lake, in the northern part of the county, is used for recreation. The 1960 population was 2,171; the 1970 population had increased to 2,782, according to the United States census.

*Hartman, Texas.

*Harts Camp, Texas.

*Harts Creek.

*Hartsbluff, Texas.

*Harvard, Texas.

Harvard Radio Astronomy Station. The Harvard Radio Astronomy Station on Mount Locke qv was constructed in 1956 and began operation in August of that year with one laboratory and a twenty-eight-foot dish antenna. Owned by Harvard University and the United States Air Force, the property initially cost $450,000. In 1962 a second laboratory and antenna were constructed near the first. The dish antenna spanned eighty-five feet and stood one hundred feet high. *See also* McDonald Observatory; University of Texas McDonald Observatory at Mount Locke.

Barry Scobee

*Harvey, William.

Harvey, Texas. (Andrews County.) Harvey was settled along the line of the Midland and Northwestern Railroad and was abandoned when the railroad ceased operations in the 1920's.

*Harvey, Texas. (Brazos County.)

*Harvey Creek.

*Harwood, Texas.

*Hashknife Ranch.

*Hasinai Indians.

*Haskell, Charles Ready.

*Haskell, Texas. Haskell, seat of Haskell County, had an airport, a bank, a hospital, eighteen churches, and a newspaper in 1967. In 1970, eighty-four businesses were reported. The most important industry was cotton ginning, the three gins handling an average of fifteen thousand bales per year. Lake Stamford, twelve miles southeast of Haskell, was built by the town in 1952 to provide water for municipal and industrial use, as well as for boating, fishing, and swimming. The 4,016 population in 1960 had decreased to 3,655 by 1970, according to the United States census.

*Haskell County. Haskell County in the 1960's and early 1970's was dependent upon farming and petroleum as chief sources of income. Between 1929 and January 1, 1973, nearly 77,000,000 barrels of oil were produced; a butane plant was established near O'Brien. In 1951 Lake Stamford in the southeast portion of the county adjoining Jones County was completed. Five types of soil in the area facilitated a broad spectrum of cultivated crops and pasturage. The leading crops in the county were wheat, cotton (80,185 bales in 1972), grain sorghums, and some Irish potatoes. Between 1960 and 1965 the number of cattle increased by 25 percent. The county supported a hospital at Haskell. The 1960 population was 11,174; the United States census report showed a decrease in population by 1970, when the count was 8,512.

*Haslam, Texas.

*Haslet, Texas.

*Hasse, Texas.

*Hasslers, Texas.

*Hastings, Frank S.

*Hastings, Thomas.

*Hastings, Texas.

*Hastings Oil Field.

*Hat Mountain.

Hatch, John Porter. John Porter Hatch was born at Oswego, New York, on January 9, 1822, the son of Moses Porter and Hannah (Reed) Hatch. He was graduated from the United States Military Academy in 1845. He served under General Zachary Taylor qv at Corpus Christi, Texas, fought in the battle of Resaca de la Palma, qv and then transferred into the service of General Winfield Scott. He participated in the capture of Mexico City, for which he was brevetted three times for gallantry.

Hatch was later assigned to frontier duty in Texas and New Mexico. He was serving as chief of commissariat in New Mexico when the Civil War began. Appointed brigadier general of volunteers, he took part in the first battle of Bull Run. In the second battle of Bull Run he suffered a head wound and was forced to retire from active duty for five months. In 1864 Hatch was assigned to the Army of the South and served with General William T. Sherman;qv again he was brevetted for gallantry.

After the war, as a major, Hatch took command of the 4th Cavalry at Fort Mason qv in Texas. Later he served at Camp Verde.qv He took command at Fort Concho qv (until 1868 named Camp Hatch in his honor) from June 9, 1870, to January 6, 1873, and later commanded Fort Clark qv from 1873 to 1875. He then served in the Indian Territory, Montana, and Washington Territory, where he retired as a colonel in 1886.

In 1851 Hatch married Adelaide Goldsmith Burckle of Oswego, New York; they had two children. Hatch died on April 12, 1901, and was buried in Arlington Cemetery, Washington, D.C.

BIBLIOGRAPHY: George W. Cullum, *Biographical Register of Officers and Graduates of the U. S. Military Academy*, II (1891); *Dictionary of American Biography*, VIII (1932); Files of the Oswego County (New York) Historical Association.

Susan Miles

*Hatchel, Texas.

Hatcher, John L. John L. Hatcher was born in Kentucky. He entered the St. Louis fur trade and became a noted hunter, trapper, and trader whose associates included William Bent and Lewis H. Garrard. He also acted as a guide for governmental exploring parties and military columns. In 1845 he accompanied Lieutenant Abert's party on an expedition from Bent's Fort through the country south of the Arkansas River. In 1850 he served as guide for Colonel Collier's party in New Mexico, and in 1851 he gave information to Lieutenant Parke, who was compiling a map of the little-known country south of the Arkansas River.

As one of the most valuable employees of Bent's Fort, Hatcher ranged from Old Mexico to the North Platte River. He traded with the Indians of West Texas and managed trade at Adobe Walls,qv a branch fort established by William Bent about 1843 and originally known as Bent's Post on the Canadian. The date of Hatcher's death is unknown.

BIBLIOGRAPHY: H. Bailey Carroll (ed.), *Guadal P'a, the Journal of Lieutenant J. W. Abert, from Bent's Fort to St. Louis in 1845* (1941); Lewis H. Garrard, *Wah-to-yah and the Taos Trail* (1927); George Bird Grinnell, "Bent's Old Fort and Its Builders," *Collections of the Kansas State Historical Society*, XV (1919), *Beyond the Old Frontier* (1913); David Lavender, *Bent's Fort* (1954); Mildred P. Mayhall, *The Kiowas* (1962).

Mildred P. Mayhall

*Hatchettville, Texas.

*Hatley Creek.

*Haulk, Texas.

*Havana, Texas.

*Havard, Valery.

*Haven, Texas.

*Haw Branch.

*Haw Creek, Texas.

*Hawk, Wilbur Clayton.

*Hawkins, Charles Edward.

Hawkins, Frank Lee. Frank Lee Hawkins was born on November 18, 1866, at Waxahachie, the son of Benjamin Franklin and Mary (Pinnell) Hawkins. He was educated at Marvin College in Waxahachie, Southwestern University, and the University of Texas, where he received the LL.B. degree with honors in 1889. He practiced law privately until 1894, then served as assistant county attorney, county attorney, and county judge in Ellis County. He was then district judge of the Fortieth Judicial District until appointed to the Court of Criminal Appeals by Governor Pat Morris Neff qv in 1921. Elected to the court in the next election, he was reelected until his voluntary retirement in 1950, having served continuously on the Court of Criminal Appeals longer than any other man, a period of thirty years, the last eleven of which he was presiding judge.

In 1889 Hawkins married Kate Briggs, and they had three children. He died in Austin on September 26, 1954, and was buried in the State Cemetery qv in Austin.

BIBLIOGRAPHY: *Who's Who In America* (1950); *Texas Bar Journal*, XIII (September, 1950), XVII (November, 1954).

W. St. John Garwood
Virginia Parton

*Hawkins, Joseph H.

*Hawkins, Walace E.

*Hawkins, William E.

*Hawkins, Texas.

*Hawkins' Lake.

*Hawkinsville, Texas.

*Hawley, John Blackstock.

*Hawley, Robert B.

*Hawley, Texas.

Hawpe, Trezevant C. Trezevant C. Hawpe was born on September 16, 1821, in Georgia. He lived in Kentucky and Tennessee before coming to Texas in 1846. He served as sheriff of Dallas County from 1850 to 1854 and as justice of the peace from 1854 to 1856; in 1860 he was elected county coroner. In the late 1850's he had a ranch at Pleasant Run, in Dallas County, where he raised thoroughbred horses and operated a steam-powered flour mill in partnership with D. Y. Ellis. Hawpe was the agent for several farm machinery companies and was an organizer and officer of the Dallas County Agricultural and Mechanical Association. In 1859 he advertised that he was interested in purchasing "tarantulas, centipedes, horned frogs, buffalo calves, mule-eared rabbits, and antelopes." In August, 1859, he was secretary of a public meeting held to expel Reverend Solomon McKinney, a suspected abolitionist from Dallas County, and in 1860 he was one of the organizers of a county convention to elect delegates to the state Secession Convention.qv

In early 1862 Hawpe recruited and became colonel of the 31st Texas Cavalry, which he commanded in the battles of Newtonia, Missouri, and

Prairie Grove, Arkansas. His regiment was dismounted in November, 1862, and Hawpe resigned his command and returned to Dallas, where he engaged in hauling supplies to the army in Arkansas and Indian Territory. In April, 1863, he was serving as a trustee of Dallas Male and Female College.qv In July, 1863, Hawpe's mill at Pleasant Run was destroyed by fire, and on August 14 he was killed in a personal disagreement in Dallas. At the time of his death, he was married and had seven children. He was buried in the Masonic Cemetery in Dallas.

BIBLIOGRAPHY: Alwyn Barr, *Polignac's Texas Brigade* (1964); John Henry Brown, *History of Dallas, Texas, from 1837 to 1887* (1887); Dallas *Herald*, July 3, 24, August 14, November 10, 1858, April 13, March 23, August 17, October 17, 31, December 12, 1860, March 13, 1861, November 22, December 20, 1862, April 8, July 22, August 19, 1863.

*Hawthorne, Texas.

*Hay, Samuel Ross.

*Hay, Stephen John.

*Hay Creek.

*Hay Hollow.

*Hay Production. Hay production in the 1950's was stimulated by declining cotton acreage, a greater attention to livestock, and increased planting of soil-building crops. Texas in 1954 harvested 1,389,000 tons valued at $36,114,000 from 1,376,000 acres. By 1963 this total had increased to 1,821,000 tons valued at $45,874,000 from 1,668,000 acres. Hay production in 1965 jumped to 2,217,000 tons valued at $49,000,000. In 1968 the production of hay, forage, and silage crops occupied more than three million acres and was valued at $100,000,000.

BIBLIOGRAPHY: *Texas Almanac* (1955, 1963, 1965, 1967).

*Hayden, Samuel Augustus.

*Hayes, William Robert.

*Hayes, Texas.

*Hayhurst, Texas.

*Haymond, Texas.

*Haymond Mountains.

*Haynes, John L. During the Civil War John Leal Haynes became an officer in the 1st Texas Cavalry (Union). He was promoted to colonel of the 2nd Texas Cavalry (Union) when it was organized in 1863 and commanded the consolidated regiment formed from both units in 1864. Following the war he served as internal revenue collector in Austin, 1865–1868. He ran unsuccessfully for the legislature in 1869 on the fusion ticket with A. J. Hamilton.qv Haynes then served as collector of customs at Galveston, 1869–1870, and at Brownsville, 1872–1884. He was active continuously in the Republican party qv after the Civil War, as a leader of the conservative faction in the late 1860's, as a member of the regular party in the 1870's, and as candidate for lieutenant governor on the "straight-out" Republican ticket in 1884.

Haynes was married and had four sons and one daughter. He was a member of the Grand Army of the Republic. He died in Laredo on April 2, 1888.

BIBLIOGRAPHY: Galveston *Daily News*, April 3, 1888; *Report of the Adjutant General of the State of Texas for the Year 1873* (1874); E. M. Winkler, *Platforms of Political Parties in Texas* (1916).

Alwyn Barr

*Haynes, Thomas N.

*Haynes, Thomas S.

Haynesville, Texas. Haynesville, in northwestern Wichita County, was founded in 1890 and was named for H. H. Haynes. With a population of seventy in 1970, the community served a farming area. *See also* Wichita Falls Standard Metropolitan Statistical Area.

*Haynie, John. John Haynie, pioneer Methodist minister, was the son of Spencer and Catherine (King) Haynie. He and his wife, Elizabeth (Brooks) Haynie, were the parents of nine children, one of whom was Dr. Samuel G. Haynie.qv He died at Rutersville (not La Grange, as stated in Volume I) and was buried in La Grange.

BIBLIOGRAPHY: Loyce Haynie Rossman, *Rev. John Haynie: Ancestry, Life & Descendants* (1963).

Loyce Haynie Rossman

*Haynie, Samuel G. Samuel G. Haynie was the son of John and Elizabeth (Brooks) Haynie.

*Haynie Chapel, Texas.

*Haynie Flat, Texas.

*Hayrick, Texas.

*Hayrick Canyon.

*Hayrick Mountain.

*Hays, John Coffee (Jack). John Coffee Hays came to Texas in late March or early April, 1836 (not 1837 or 1838, as stated in Volume I). He joined the Texas Army qv on May 1, 1836. He died on San Jacinto Day, April 21, 1883 (not April 25).

BIBLIOGRAPHY: James Kimmins Greer, *Colonel Jack Hays* (1952).

*Hays City, Texas.

*Hays County. Hays County capitalizes on its Balcones Escarpment qv location for agriculture. Although tourism is the main industry in the county, agriculture continued to provide approximately one-third of the total income. Livestock raising accounted for 90 percent of the farm income ($6,000,000 per year average in the early 1970's); the remainder came from grains, cotton, and cedar posts. After a slackening in the 1940's and 1950's the production of cotton increased during the 1960's. Tourists are attracted to Wonder Cave, Aquarena,qqv Pioneer Town, and guest ranches in the scenic hill country. The opening of Gary Job Corps Training Center qv in 1965, together with the growth of Southwest Texas State University, brought economic growth to the county. The 1960 population was 19,934; the United States report of the 1970 census showed that Hays County had an increase in population, with a count of 27,642.

*Haysland, Texas.

*Haystack, Texas.

*Haystack Mountain.

*Hazel Dell, Texas. [This title was incorrectly listed in Volume I as Hazle Dell, Texas.] Once reputed to be the capital of lawlessness in Comanche County (the town physician was said to be an expert on gunshot wounds), nothing remains at Hazel Dell except a few peaceful farm houses, an early cemetery with a boot-hill reputation, and a community center building. Early businesses included a sawmill, a variety of mercantile establishments, and a number of saloons, one of which included a bowling alley. Decline of this community began when it was bypassed by the railroad.

Margaret Tate Waring

*Hazen, William Babcock.

*Head, Henry Oswald.

*Head, James A.

*Head, Texas.

*Headrights.

*Headsville, Texas.

*Heald, Texas.

*Health, Public, in Texas. *See* Public Health, State Department of.

*Heard, Thomas Jefferson.

*Heard, William Jones Elliot.

*Hearne, Texas. Hearne, in southwestern Robertson County, was the site of 75 percent of the county's factories and accounted for 66 percent of the county's employment in 1961. In the 1960's Hearne businesses included a company manufacturing various metal products, a company making bathroom fixtures, and a company producing fertilizer, insecticides, and agricultural chemicals. The city acquired an airstrip in 1960. City improvements completed by 1966 included a water well and tower, an electric generator, road paving, and a ball park. The city reported ten churches, four public schools, two hospitals, two banks, a library, and a newspaper in 1967. In 1970 there were eighty-five business establishments. The 1960 population was 5,072; the United States census report showed a decrease in 1970, to 4,982.

*Hearne and Brazos Railway Company.

*Hearon, Richard Augustus.

Heart Transplants in Texas. Two Texas doctors have been particularly outstanding in the international field of human heart transplantation: Dr. Denton A. Cooley and Dr. Michael E. DeBakey. DeBakey made the earlier contributions with his perfection of the use of synthetic materials—particularly the knitted, crimped Dacron tube—for arterial grafts. Cooley, head of the cardiovascular surgical service at St. Luke's Hospital and professor of surgery at Baylor University, performed fourteen human heart transplants, one combined cardiopulmonary transplant, and a xenograft (with a sheep's heart). In addition, he performed the first heart-lung transplant, in a two-month-old infant girl with a total atrioventricular canal and severe pulmonary disease.

C. William Hall and Domingo Liotto spearheaded artificial heart research in collaboration with scientists and engineers at nearby Rice University. With Dr. E. Stanley Crawford these doctors were the first to install an implantable artificial ventricle in a patient, on July 19, 1963. Since then they have made so many technical advances that the development of a practical artificial heart seems imminent.

BIBLIOGRAPHY: Denton A. Cooley, "Cardiac Transplantation as Palliation of Advanced Heart Disease," *Archives of Surgery*, XCVIII (May, 1969); Michael E. DeBakey, "Human Cardiac Transplantation," *Journal of Thoracic and Cardiovascular Surgery*, LV (March, 1968); Adrian Kantrowitz, "Heart Transplantation," *Medical World News, Cardiovascular Review* (1970); Baylor College of Medicine, *Transplantation of Human Heart* (n.d.); *Medical Tribune*, February 3, 1969.

M. Doty

*Heartsill, William Williston.

*Heath, Ephraim Charles.

Heath, William Womack. William Womack Heath, United States ambassador to Sweden in 1967, was born in Normangee on December 7, 1903, the son of John Al and Runie (Hill) Heath. Graduating from high school at the age of fifteen, Heath taught school intermittently while attending Lon Morris Junior College, Texas Christian University, and the University of Texas at Austin. He was admitted to the State Bar qv in 1924, began his practice in Anderson, and was elected county attorney for Grimes County from 1925 to 1929 and county judge from 1931 to 1932. In 1933 Governor Miriam A. Ferguson qv appointed him secretary of state; upon completion of his term Heath moved to the post of assistant attorney general, where he remained until 1937.

Heath practiced law privately after 1937, representing many major insurance corporations; he was appointed to the board of regents of the University of Texas in 1959 and served as chairman from 1962 to 1966. His last official act as chairman was to disclose plans for the Lyndon B. Johnson Library qv and related buildings, but he stated that his proudest achievement was that peaceful integration was accomplished at the university during his tenure. On March 22, 1967, President Lyndon B. Johnson qv appointed him ambassador to Sweden; Heath took the oath of office on April 28 and had served only ten months before intense pressure from Swedish groups protesting U.S. involvement in Viet Nam forced his recall.

William Heath was married to Mavis Barnett on July 14, 1927. They were the parents of two daughters. Heath died on June 22, 1971, in Austin, and he was buried in the State Cemetery.qv

BIBLIOGRAPHY: Biographical File, Barker Texas History Center, University of Texas at Austin.

*Heath, Texas.

*Heath Creek.

Heaven, Texas. Heaven, in Cochran County, was established on a Santa Fe Railroad branch line about six miles south of the present site of Morton, a few years before the county was organized in 1924. Even though Morton was not on a railroad and Heaven was, when Morton obtained the county seat, Heaven was soon deserted.

BIBLIOGRAPHY: Roysten E. Willis, Ghost Towns of the South Plains (M.A. thesis, Texas Technological College, 1941).

*Hebbronville, Texas. Hebbronville, seat of Jim Hogg County, listed seventy-eight businesses in 1970. The 1960 population was 3,987; the 1970 population was 4,079.

*Hébert, Paul Octave.

*Hebron, Texas. (Denton County.)

*Hebron, Texas. (DeWitt County.)

*Hedgcoxe War.

*Hedley, Texas.

*Hedrio Creek.

Hedwig Village, Texas. Hedwig Village, primarily a residential area in southwestern Harris County, was incorporated in 1954. In 1966 there were two schools, a bank, a library, and two churches. According to the United States report of the 1970 census, Hedwig Village had a popuulation of 3,255, an increase from the 1,182 reported in the 1960 census. See also Houston Standard Metropolitan Statistical Area.

*Hedwig's Hill, Texas.

*Heel Top Creek.

*Hefner, Texas.

*Hegar, Texas.

*Heidenheimer, Texas. [This title was incorrectly listed in Volume I as Heindenheimer, Texas.]

*Heintzelman, Samuel Peter.

*Heinzeville, Texas.

*Helbig, Texas.

*Helena, Texas.

*Helium Gas Production. In 1964 an estimated 95 percent of the world's recoverable helium was within a 250-mile radius of Amarillo. Three new plants which began operating that year doubled the existing capacity. Production of refined helium was 304,909,000 cubic feet valued at $10,672,000, and crude production was 1,751,924,-000 cubic feet valued at $18,812,000 in 1964. In 1968 helium was extracted from natural gas of the Panhandle area at the U.S. Bureau of Mines plants at Amarillo in Potter County and Exell in Moore County, and at two privately owned plants in Moore and Hansford counties. Refined helium production in Texas in 1968 stood at 365,000,000 cubic feet valued at $9,560,000, and crude production totaled 1,043,700,000 cubic feet valued at $11,428,000. Crude unrefined helium was placed in underground storage at the government's Cliffside gas field near Amarillo. The helium industry celebrated its centennial at Amarillo in 1968.

BIBLIOGRAPHY: Texas Almanac (1963, 1965, 1967, 1970).

*Hell Creek.

*Hell's Half Acre.

*Helm, Jack.

*Helm, Mary Sherwood Wightman.

*Helmic, Texas.

*Helotes, Texas.

HemisFair. HemisFair, the first international exposition ever held in the southern half of the United States, opened in San Antonio, Texas, on April 6, 1968, and closed on October 6, 1968. It celebrated the 250th anniversary of the founding of San Antonio.

Built at a cost of $156,000,000, its theme was "The Confluence of Civilizations in the Americas." The Tower of the Americas, dramatically representing that theme, stood as the tallest observation tower in the Western Hemisphere, 622 feet. Built of slip-form concrete, its observation decks commanded a view of up to one hundred miles. A revolving restaurant occupied the 550-foot level and seated 312 people. It made one revolution per hour. Other decks were at the 570-foot level, and an open deck at the top stood at 605 feet. Glass-walled elevators on the outside went to the top of the structure in forty-three seconds. An engineering oddity, the wheel-shaped top house which included the restaurant and observation decks was built around the base of the tower and power-lifted to the top a few feet at a time. It began being lifted on January 3, 1968, and reached the top on January 24, 1968. It was built at a cost of $5,500,000.

The fair itself covered 92.6 acres in downtown San Antonio within easy walking distance of city hotels. The land, part of an urban renewal acquisition, was leased by the city to the fair organization. Part of the area was used as a parking lot which accommodated 5,000 vehicles. Some twenty-five foreign countries constructed buildings, and the federal government built the United States Pavilion at a cost of $6,750,000. Texas had the largest pavilion, a $10,000,000 structure housing the exhibits making up the Institute of Texan Cultures,qv the funds for which were provided by the Texas legislature. R. Henderson Shuffler was named director of the institute.

First envisioned in 1958 by a San Antonio merchant, Jerome K. Harris, HemisFair got underway in 1962. It was incorporated as a nonprofit organization under the direction of a group of business and professional residents of the city. Its incorporated name was San Antonio Fair. Chainstore owner and operator William R. Sinkin was elected president, Congressman Henry B. Gonzalez and Mayor Walter W. McAllister, Sr., were appointed honorary co-chairmen, and contractor H. B. Zachry was made chairman of the board. Gonzalez took the lead in promoting the fair in Washington. Erwin Dingwall, who directed the Seattle World's Fair in 1963, was named HemisFair director. He later left and represented the fair in Washington, and James M. Gaines replaced him.

The master plan for the fair was drawn by architect O'Neil Ford. The plan changed little during construction except that Ford wanted more of the old buildings left than finally remained. It was his idea to divert the San Antonio River, which flows through the city, into the HemisFair grounds. The Tower of the Americas was also his idea.

Marshall Steves succeeded Sinkin as fair president in 1965 and became responsible for raising the financial pledges necessary to build the fair; he succeeded in procuring $7,200,000. Governor John Connally was appointed commissioner general of the fair.

Aside from the cultural aspects of the fair as represented in the individual pavilions built by the countries, entertainment was provided in the form of the usual midway rides. A comprehensive view of the fair was available by means of the mini-monorail cars which toured the grounds at an elevated level over a one-and-a-half-mile route. Another view was available by means of the Swiss Skyride, cars on cables which traversed the area in a direct line from one side of the fair to the other. Many of the countries presented the crafts of their cultures in special shops where the products were available for purchase. Special free movies were presented in several pavilions, among them the three-dimensional color film in the Confluence Theater of the United States Pavilion entitled US. During the presentation of the film, screens expanded and interior walls disappeared, transforming a series of intimate studio theaters into one large arena with a vast panoramic screen.

In conjunction with the fair there were various presentations of theatrical performances with stage casts from New York as well as special performances of the Ballet Folklorico from Mexico, the Bolshoi Ballet from Russia, symphonies, and individual artist performances. These productions took place in the large new municipal auditorium on the fairgrounds.

Outdoor and indoor cafes and restaurants, featuring foods of the various nations, were scattered throughout the fair. Many free entertainment areas sponsored by various food and drink companies presented folk dances, singers, bands, and the like.

When the fair closed, it left to the city the convention center, exhibit areas, inter-American trade institute, stadium, military museum, and library. The final attendance figure was recorded at 6,384,482.

*Hemming, Texas.

*Hemphill, John.

*Hemphill, Texas. (Hays County.)

*Hemphill, Texas. (Sabine County.) Hemphill, the county seat, was incorporated in 1940 with a mayor-alderman form of government. Business establishments in the 1960's were largely concerned with the timber, broiler, and cattle industries. Major public projects were an electric system completed in 1950, a sewer system completed in 1961, and water system improvements completed by 1963. By 1966 the town had a school, a hospital, a bank, eight churches, and one newspaper. Hemphill reported fifty-six businesses in 1970. The 1960 population was 913 and the 1970 population was 1,005, according to the United States census.

*Hemphill County. Hemphill County was primarily a cattle ranching area, with wheat as a second source of income. Oil production increased but remained a minor industry. The Gene Howe Wildlife Management Area and the Washita watershed program have been established in the county since 1950. The county supported a hospital, to which additions were made in 1965; the courthouse was remodeled as well. Lake Marvin is in the east-central part of the county. The 1960 population was 3,185 and the 1970 population was 3,084, according to the United States census.

*Hempstead, Texas. Hempstead, seat of Waller County, was the market for the livestock and farm produce of the county. In 1970 the city had fifty-five businesses. According to the United States report of the 1970 census, Hempstead had a population of 1,891, an increase from the 1,505 reported in the 1960 census.

*Hen Egg Mountain.

*Henderson, James Pinckney. James Pinckney Henderson was not appointed a major general in the United States Army (as stated in Volume I). He served with the temporary rank of major general of Texas volunteers in United States service from July, 1846, to October, 1846.
BIBLIOGRAPHY: William Hugh Robarts, Mexican War Veterans: A Complete Roster (1887).

*Henderson, James Wilson. James Wilson Henderson was reelected to the legislature in 1857 (not 1855, as stated in Volume I).

*Henderson, John Nathaniel.

*Henderson, Thomas Stalworth.

Henderson, William Fenner. William Fenner Henderson, son of Thomas Henderson, was born in Raleigh, North Carolina, on July 28, 1817. He lived at Mount Pinson, Tennessee, until he came to Texas in 1836. He became a citizen of Coahuila and Texas at Nacogdoches on February 15, 1836. He served in the Texas Army, and after the revolution became a land surveyor and locator. In 1838 he participated in the Battle Creek Fight.qv Henderson was appointed district attorney of the Fifth Judicial District of the Republic of Texas by President Mirabeau Lamar. He practiced law in Corsicana until the Civil War, when he enlisted in a scout company formed by his brother in Mississippi. After the war he returned to Corsicana, but soon gave up the practice of law and moved to Bolivar Point, where he engaged in farming. After eight years he returned to Corsicana, where he died in 1890.

Henderson married Mary McCorry of Jackson, Tennessee, by whom he had a son and a daughter.

His second wife was Louisa Edwards of Christian County, Kentucky, by whom he had a son and a daughter.

BIBLIOGRAPHY: John Henry Brown, *History of Texas* (1893); James T. DeShields, *Border Wars of Texas* (1912); Annie Carpenter Love, *History of Navarro County* (c.1933); Walter P. Lane, *Adventures and Recollections of Walter P. Lane* (1887).

Harry McCorry Henderson

*Henderson, Texas. Henderson, seat of Rusk County, was an oil and agricultural center for the area. Among Henderson's businesses in the 1960's were companies making brick, clothing, lumber, furniture, picture frames, paint, oil tanks, ice-vending boxes, sawmills, plastic products, and church fixtures. In 1966 Henderson reported nineteen churches, two banks, two newspapers, two radio stations, a hospital, and a library. Businesses in 1970 totaled 328. The 1960 population was 9,666, and the United States census report showed a population increase in 1970 to 10,187.

*Henderson County. Henderson County continued to rely on light industry, minerals, and agriculture for its income. From 1934 to January 1, 1973, some 79,299,245 barrels of oil were produced, along with some natural gas. Similarly utilized were the deposits of sand, gravel, and clay, the last being used for brick and pottery manufacture. The river bottoms and the lakes, including Cedar Creek Reservoir completed in 1965, provided for hunting and fishing. These areas and various celebrations, including the Old Fiddlers Reunion, served as tourist attractions. Truck farming constituted a major portion of the row crops. The county was a center for the production of black-eyed peas. Recent county projects included an addition to the county hospital, road improvements, and courthouse beautification. From 1960 to 1970 the population in the county increased from 21,786 to 26,466, according to the United States census.

Henderson County Junior College. The creation of Henderson County Junior College, Athens, was approved in an election on May 3, 1946, which also authorized a tax for its support and elected a board of trustees. Students first registered in June, 1946, and classes were conducted in temporary quarters at Athens High School.

A gift from the city of twenty-three acres of land, formerly Athens Fair Park, and remodeling of the Cotton Palace, a large gymnasium on the site, enabled the college to move to a campus of its own for the fall semester of 1946. More bonds were voted in 1951 and other buildings were added. In 1962 fifteen acres adjoining the campus were purchased from the city, bringing total acreage to sixty-five. Plans were approved in 1963 to remodel the fire-damaged auditorium and to build a new administration building. By 1966 the physical plant included fifteen buildings.

Associate in arts or associate in science degrees were offered in two areas: preprofessional programs acceptable for transfer to four-year colleges; and technical, vocational, and semiprofessional fields. One- or two-year technical and vocational certificates were also offered in electronics technology, general office careers, and psychiatric and vocational nursing.

Athletic teams, known as the Cardinals, participated in intercollegiate competition as members of the Texas Junior College Football Federation and the Texas Eastern Athletic Conference. Five dormitories provided housing for students on campus, and free bus transportation was available to students residing within the county.

The college was accredited by the Texas Education Agency, the Association of Texas Colleges,qqv and the Southern Association of Colleges and Secondary Schools. By 1969 the library held 20,000 volumes of books, bound periodicals, and government documents. In the 1974–1975 regular term enrollment totaled 1,624 students and the faculty numbered over seventy. Orval Pirtle, the first president of the college, continued in that capacity until 1969. In 1970 T. M. Harvey became president.

*Henderson Female College.

*Henderson Male and Female College.

*Henderson Masonic Female Institute.

*Henderson and Overton Branch Railroad Company.

*Hendersons Chapel, Texas.

*Hendricks, Sterling Brown.

*Hendricks, Texas.

*Hendricks Oil Field.

*Heniocane Indians. This was one of the numerous Coahuiltecan bands of the latter part of the seventeenth century who lived in northeastern Coahuila and also ranged across the Rio Grande into the southwestern part of the Edwards Plateau. The Bosque-Larios Expedition qv of 1675 visited a Heniocane settlement of 178 persons in the vicinity of present Kinney County. This seems to have been the only recorded appearance of this band in the history of Spanish colonial Texas.

BIBLIOGRAPHY: H. E. Bolton (ed.), *Spanish Exploration in the Southwest, 1542–1706* (1916).

T. N. Campbell

*Henkhaus, Texas.

*Henly, Texas.

*Henning, Texas.

*Henning Creek.

*Henri, Jean.

*Henrietta, Texas. Henrietta, Texas, was not named for the wife of Henry Clay of Kentucky (as stated in Volume I), since Clay's wife's name was Lucretia.

Henrietta, with a mayor-council government, was the seat and commercial center of Clay County. Prominent among its sixty-five businesses in 1970 were firms producing cattle-branding equipment and leather goods. The United States report of the 1970 census indicated that like the population of Clay

County, that of the county seat was decreasing, from 3,062 in 1960 to 2,897 in 1970.

BIBLIOGRAPHY: *Dictionary of American Biography* (1943).

*Henry, John L.

*Henry, O. *See* Porter, William Sydney; *see also* O. Henry Museum.

*Henry, Robert Lee.

*Henry, Texas.

*Henry Chapel, Texas.

*Henry College.

*Henry's Chapel, Texas. Henry's Chapel (Cherokee County) is located about eight miles southeast of Troup, Texas (not on the Angelina River, as stated in Volume I).

Robert E. Hardwicke

*Henshaw Creek.

*Hensley, James.

*Hensley, William Richardson.

*Hensley, Texas.

*Hensley Field. *See also* Naval Air Station, Dallas, Texas.

*Henson Creek.

*Henson Mountain.

*Herbert, Claiborne C.

Herbert, Philemon Thomas. Philemon Thomas Herbert was born in Pine Apple, Alabama, on November 1, 1825, the son of John and Harriet (Waters) Herbert. He attended the common schools of the state and entered the University of Alabama in 1842. As a consequence of being indefinitely suspended from the university in June, 1844, for stabbing a fellow student, he left Alabama and came to Texas in 1845. In April, 1847, he enlisted at San Antonio as a private for six months' service in the 1st Texas Mounted Volunteers.

About 1850 Herbert moved to Mariposa, California, where he soon entered politics as a Democrat. He was elected to the California Assembly for the fourth (1853) and fifth (1854) sessions, and then as a representative to the Thirty-fourth Congress (1855–1857). On May 8, 1856, Herbert fatally shot an Irish waiter during a brawl at a Washington, D.C., hotel. Although acquitted of murder, Herbert found that the incident had ruined his political career. He therefore left California for the Gadsden Purchase area in the summer of 1859. After engaging briefly in mining, he settled in El Paso, Texas, to practice law.

Herbert, a fiery secessionist, was elected a delegate to the Secession Convention.qv That body subsequently appointed him a commissioner to encourage Arizona to join the Confederacy. With the outbreak of war, he entered the Confederate Army and saw action at the battle of Mesilla on July 25, 1861. Sometime after the arrival of Henry H. Sibley's qv Brigade, he went to Richmond, where he was commissioned a lieutenant colonel to recruit a regiment for the protection of Arizona. He suc-

ceeded in raising three companies which became known as Herbert's Battalion, Arizona Cavalry (also 1st Texas Arizona Battalion, Mounted Rifles), the last unit to leave Arizona and Trans-Pecos Texas when that area was abandoned in July, 1862.

After a brief respite in Texas, Herbert was ordered to Louisiana, where his battalion served as scouts. For a short time he was detached from his unit and placed on General Sibley's staff. As General Richard Taylor's forces retreated northward in April, 1863, Herbert helped protect the rear guard. The following May, he was promoted to the command of the 7th Texas Cavalry Regiment and saw action at the capture of Brashear City on June 23, the unsuccessful attack on Fort Butler on June 28, and the subsequent engagement at Cox's Plantation on July 13, 1863. For several months, beginning on September 30, 1863, Herbert was absent on sick leave. By February, 1864, he had rejoined his regiment for the Red River campaign.qv During the early phase of the battle of Mansfield,qv he was severely wounded. He was later removed to Kingston, Louisiana, where he succumbed on July 23, 1864, and was interred in Evergreen Cemetery there.

BIBLIOGRAPHY: *Biographical Directory of the American Congress, 1774–1961* (1961); James B. Sellers, *History of the University of Alabama* (1953); Rex W. Strickland, "P. T. Herbert: Ante-Bellum Resident of El Paso," *Password*, V (1960); U.S. War Department, *The War of the Rebellion: A Compilation of the Official Records of the Union and Confederate Armies* (1880–1901).

Martin Hardwick Hall

*Herbert Creek.

*Hereford, Texas. Hereford, seat of Deaf Smith County, had twenty-nine churches, eight schools, four parks, and a hospital in 1964. Located in an area of livestock production and diversified irrigated farming, Hereford had an economy based on the processing, storage, and shipping of cattle, grain sorghums, wheat, cotton, and a variety of irrigated vegetables. Production of sugar beets expanded in 1964 with the construction of a large processing plant. The city reported 358 businesses in 1970. According to the report of the 1970 United States census, Hereford had an increase in population from a reported 7,652 in 1960 to 13,414 in 1970.

*Hereford Cattle.

*Hereford College.

*Herff, Ferdinand.

*Herman Creek.

*Hermann, George Henry.

Hermann Sons. *See* Sons of Hermann, Order of.

*Hermann's University.

*Hermitage, Texas.

*Hermleigh, Texas. Hermleigh, in Scurry County, first surveyed in 1907, was developed on land that belonged to R. C. Herm (not Hern, as stated in Volume I) and Harry W. Harlin. The name "Hermlin," in honor of the two men, was rejected by the post office because of the similarity to "Hamlin," a nearby town. Instead, the town was named Hermleigh—"leigh" meaning meadow or field. (No evidence has been found to support the assertion that the town was named for W. J. Hermleigh, as stated in Volume I.) During World War I the name was changed to "Foch" in honor of the French general. In 1920, however, citizens circulated a petition to change the name, and post office records show that on January 1, 1921, the town was named Hermleigh again. The 1970 population was approximately seven hundred.

Mrs. Wayne Boren

*Hermosa, Texas.

Hernández, Andrés. A Spanish land grant (made by a compromise settlement over disputed land claims) to Andrés Hernández and Luís Antonio Menchaca qv on April 12, 1758, is the oldest land grant on record in the Spanish archives of the General Land Office qv in Austin (although there were grants prior to that date). The entire grant consisted of fifteen leagues and seven *labors* situated in the "Potrero del Rincón," the wedge of land between the forks of the San Antonio and Cibolo rivers in South Texas.

Andrés Hernández, son of Don Francisco Hernández and resident of the villa of San Fernando, was for many years a soldier of the San Antonio de Béxar Presidio.qv The grant made to him in 1758 consisted of four leagues and five *labors*, three-fifths of which lay in Karnes County and two-fifths in Wilson County.

Hernández had some ranch huts built near the bank of the Cibolo in order to raise horses, cattle, sheep, and goats. At the time of his official grant, he made sworn statements to the effect that he had been living on the ranch for more than five years by virtue of a grant of four *sitios* and eight *caballerías* of land called San Bartolomé, which had been made to his deceased father more than twenty-two years previously. It is possible that this was the site of the first ranch in Texas.

The ranch headquarters of Hernández was situated in the same locale as Fuerte del Santa Cruz.qv At first he owned everything on the west side of the Cibolo from Rincón to a distance of six leagues up the stream. Temporarily abandoned after a Comanche raid in 1783, the Hernández ranch was eventually divided among the heirs and sold to later purchasers.

BIBLIOGRAPHY: Bexar Archives (Translations, 1733–1759, Archives, University of Texas at Austin Library); Virginia H. Taylor, *The Spanish Archives of the General Land Office* (1955); Robert H. Thonhoff, "The First Ranch in Texas," *West Texas Historical Association Year Book* (1964).

Robert H. Thonhoff

*Herndon, John Hunter.

Herndon, Patrick Henry. Patrick Henry Herndon was born in Virginia in March, 1802, the son of John and Judith (Hampton) Herndon. Although it is known that he married Parmelee Smith, the date of his marriage and the date of his migration to Texas are not known. He settled in Navidad, Texas, and joined the defenders of the Alamo in 1836. As a private, Herndon served under David Crockett qv during the siege and was killed with the rest of the Alamo garrison on March 6, 1836.

BIBLIOGRAPHY: Amelia W. Williams, A Critical Study of the Siege of the Alamo and of the Personnel of its Defenders (Ph.D. dissertation, University of Texas, 1931); *Virginia Magazine*, IX (1902).

*Herndon, William Smith.

*Herndon, Texas.

*Herrera, Simón de. Simón de Herrera was born at Santa Cruz de Tenerife, in the Canary Islands, in 1754. He joined the Guimar Militia as sub-lieutenant on September 12, 1763, and was promoted to captain of militia on August 2, 1769. He transferred to the Zamora Infantry Regiment with the rank of sub-lieutenant on August 4, 1775. He was promoted through the ranks to lieutenant colonel in 1795. Among the posts at which he served was the government of Colotan, near Nayarit, Mexico, and the commandancy of the Militia of New Galicia. He created the Provincial Regiment of Guadalajara with battalions from Tepic, Bolaños, and several frontier companies from February 9, 1788, until June 21, 1794. He was then promoted to the government of the Province of Nuevo León, where he served as captain of the Lancer Company of Punta de Lampasas and commander of the provincial militia. Among his military actions was the expedition to South America in 1776 and the siege and capture of Portuguese colonies on the island of Santa Catalina, Puntagrosa, Santa Cruz, Ratones, and the fortified port of Feligrecia de San Antonio. He participated in the siege of Montevideo before returning to Spain to join in the blockade of Gibraltar until November 10, 1781. He returned to America with the Army of Operations and fought under the command of Bernardo de Gálvez at Guarico from February 10, 1782, until July 23, 1783. He then served as special courier to carry dispatches to Spain and France. Returning to Mexico, he formed a plan of the missions of Nayarit and Galicia, and by 1797 was ready to lead his provincial militia against 200 marauding Apaches and Comanches, an expedition which was singularly successful. He married an English lady at Cádiz and was well acquainted with George Washington and the intricate government of the United States. He was accused, along with his brother Pedro, who was left in command at Monterrey when Simón went to Texas, of extorting money from ranchers in lieu of their serving on the frontier. [For Herrera's activities in Texas, *see* account in Volume I.]

BIBLIOGRAPHY: Jack D. L. Holmes, "Showdown on the Sabine: General James Wilkinson *vs.* Lieutenant-Colonel Simón de Herrera," *Louisiana Studies*, III (1964).

Jack D. L. Holmes

*Herrera, Texas.

*Herring, Marcus de LaFayette.

*Herring, Texas.

*Herring Branch.

*Herron, Henry.

*Herron City, Texas.

Herty, Texas. Herty, a suburb of Lufkin in Angelina County, had a 1960 population of 1,400. Site of a color printing plant and the South's first newsprint mill, the town was named for a Dr. Herty who discovered a process for making newsprint from southern yellow pine. Population decreased to approximately 600 by 1970.

*Hester, Texas. (Hardin County.)

*Hester, Texas. (Navarro County.)

Hester's Cave. See Cascade Caverns; Caves and Cave Studies in Texas.

*Hettler, Texas.

*Hetty, Texas.

*Heugh, Texas.

*Hewetson, James.

*Hewitt, William M.

*Hewitt, Texas.

*Hext, Texas.

*Heyser, Texas.

*Heywood, Alba.

*Hiabu Indians. The Hiabu (Xiabu) Indians are known from a single Spanish encounter near Laredo at the close of the seventeenth century. It has been assumed that they ranged over both sides of the Rio Grande and that their language was Coahuiltecan. If this band survived into the eighteenth century, it must have been known by some other name. Juan Domínguez de Mendoza's qv list of 1684 (bands expected to arrive at the temporary San Clemente Mission qv east of present San Angelo) contains the names of several identifiable Coahuiltecan bands of northern Mexico. It is possible that Mendoza's Abau may be the group known as Hiabu along the Rio Grande about twelve years later.

BIBLIOGRAPHY: H. E. Bolton (ed.), *Spanish Exploration in the Southwest, 1542-1706* (1916); F. W. Hodge (ed.), *Handbook of American Indians*, I (1907); J. R. Swanton, *Linguistic Material from the Tribes of Southern Texas and Northeastern Mexico* (1940).

T. N. Campbell

*Hianagouy Indians.

*Hiantatsi Indians.

*Hickey, Texas.

Hickman, John Edward. John Edward Hickman, chief justice of the Supreme Court of Texas from 1948 to 1961, was born at Liberty Hill, Texas, on March 28, 1883, the son of Nathaniel Franklin and Mary J. (Porterfield) Hickman. By 1902 he had graduated from Liberty Hill Normal and Business College and taught briefly at a rural school at Hog Mountain in Bell County. Following summer study at Southwestern University, he attended the University of Texas from 1904 to 1906. After serving as principal and baseball coach at Lampasas High School, he entered the Law Department at the University of Texas. Hickman was graduated in 1910 and became quizmaster for the class of 1911. He practiced law briefly in Austin and then in Dublin, Texas. Hickman's wife, Ethel (Mark-

ward) Hickman, died in 1921, and in 1923 he married Lena Pettit.

While practicing law at Breckenridge, he was elected associate justice of the Eleventh Court of Civil Appeals at Eastland, taking office on January 4, 1927. Governor Dan Moody qv appointed Hickman chief justice of that court on February 4, 1928. In May, 1935, Hickman was appointed by the Supreme Court to Section A of the Supreme Court's Commission of Appeals. When the membership of the Supreme Court was increased to nine, Hickman and other commissioners took the oath as associate justices on September 21, 1945. Following the death of the chief justice, Governor Beauford Jester qv appointed Hickman to that high post, for which he qualified on January 7, 1948. In the general election of that year, Hickman was elected in his own right, and he was reelected in 1954.

In 1952-1953 Hickman became the first Texas jurist to serve as chairman of the National Conference of State Chief Justices. He was awarded the Hatton W. Sumners qv Award for "outstanding services" by the Southwestern Legal Foundation. He was honored by many organizations and received honorary degrees from Southwestern University and Southern Methodist University; he served the latter school as a trustee after 1921. A Methodist, Hickman taught a Sunday school class throughout his adult life. Justice Robert Calvert has recorded that Hickman inaugurated the practice of full court consideration of application for writ of error so that no litigant rights would be determined by only one "section" of the court. Hickman retired from the court in 1961 and died in Austin on April 26, 1962.

Hickman, Thomas R. Thomas R. Hickman, son of Walter B. and Mary Ann (McCormick) Hickman, was born in Cooke County, Texas, on February 21, 1886. Following graduation from Gainesville Business College in 1907, he joined the Miller Brothers 101 Ranch wild west show and was later appointed deputy sheriff of Cooke County. On June 16, 1919, Governor William Pettus Hobby qv appointed him a private in Company B of the Texas Rangers.qv By 1921 he had risen to captain, the rank he held until 1935 when he left the force following a dispute with Governor James V. Allred.qv

During the 1920's and 1930's, Hickman was assigned to maintain order in North Texas oil boom towns. These assignments, his work on the Oklahoma boundary dispute, and his many publicized encounters with bank robbers gave him an international reputation. His early interest in rodeo contests led to his appointment in 1924 as judge of the first American rodeo in England; in 1926 he judged the first rodeo held in New York's Madison Square Garden. In 1930 he toured Europe with the famed Cowboy Band of Hardin-Simmons University as the official representative of the state of Texas. In the 1950's he frequently served as sergeant at arms for Democratic party state conventions. On January 14, 1957, on Governor Allan Shivers' appointment, Hickman became a member of the Public Safety Commission, which governs the state's Department of Public Safety.qv On February 17, 1961, he became chairman of the commission, serving in that capacity until his death.

Hickman was married to Tina (Knight) Hickman; they had two sons. He died in Gainesville on January 29, 1962, and was buried in that city.

Kenneth Ragsdale

*Hickman Creek.

Hickmuntown, Texas. Hickmuntown, at the crossing of Highways 620 and 2222 in Travis County, was formerly known as Four Corners. In 1937, when the Lower Colorado River Authority qv began work on Mansfield Dam,qv the owner of the property, across which a railroad was to be built, requested that the name of the community be changed to Hickmuntown. It was probably named for the Hickman family who lived in the area, but a mistake was inadvertently made in the spelling. *See also* Austin Standard Metropolitan Statistical Area.

*Hickory Creek.

*Hickory Creek, Texas.

*Hickory Grove, Texas.

*Hicks, Archibald W. O.

*Hicks, Texas. (Lee County.)

*Hicks, Texas. (Tarrant County.)

*Hicks Creek.

*Hicks Field.

*Hicksbaugh, Texas.

*Hico, Texas. Hico, in Hamilton County, had a population of 1,020 in 1960 and 975 in 1970.

*Hidalgo, Francisco.

*Hidalgo, Texas. According to the United States report of the 1970 census, Hidalgo had a population of 1,289, an increase from the 1,078 reported in the 1960 census. The town reported forty-two businesses in 1970.

*Hidalgo y Costilla, Miguel.

*Hidalgo County. Hidalgo County, in the Lower Rio Grande Valley, was one of the leading farming counties. The income from agriculture in the early 1970's averaged over $85 million per year. The heavily populated southern portion of the county raised vegetables, fruits, and cotton, with the help of extensive irrigation. The northern portion was used primarily for ranching. The tourist industry had expanded, aided by the proximity to Mexico. Hidalgo County contained six centers of over ten thousand population, including Edinburg, the county seat. The county population in 1960 was 180,904; the 1970 census showed an increase in population to 181,535. *See also* McAllen-Edinburg-Pharr Standard Metropolitan Statistical Area.

*Hidden Valley, Texas.

*Hide and Tallow Factories.

Hidetown, Texas. *See* Mobeetie (Old), Texas.

Higgins, Michael Francis. Michael Francis (Pinky) Higgins was born on May 27, 1909, in Red Oak, Texas, to Michael Francis and Mattie (Orr) Higgins. He grew up in Red Oak, where he is said to have earned his nickname (Pinky) when, confined to bed because of illness, he showed up for a sandlot football game wearing his clothing over a pink nightgown.

He entered the University of Texas in the spring of 1927 and there played halfback on the football team of 1928. He played on the Texas baseball team during the 1928, 1929, and 1930 seasons, during which time he was all-conference third baseman. He was captain of the University of Texas team which won the Southwest Conference qv championship in 1930. He left the university in June of 1930 and signed with the Philadelphia Athletics for the then monumental bonus of $5,000. In 1938 Higgins established an American League and major league record by tallying twelve consecutive hits. In the 1940 World Series, he set three fielding records in addition to posting a .333 batting average. His lifetime average was .292.

He played for the Philadelphia Athletics, Boston Red Sox, and Detroit Tigers and set four batting and fielding records which still stood in 1969. He joined the Boston team as manager in 1955 and pulled them to fourth place in the league, thirty games above their 1954 showing, a feat which earned him manager-of-the-year honors. He managed the team for five years and later returned for two more years on the field before moving into the front office for Boston. He later joined the Houston Astros qv as a scout. He was elected to the Texas Sports Hall of Fame qv in 1965.

He died on March 21, 1969, in Dallas, having served thirty-nine years in major league baseball as a player, manager, and scout. He was survived by his wife Hazen, whom he married in 1935, and two children. He was buried at Hillcrest Memorial Park in Dallas.

BIBLIOGRAPHY: Biographical File, Barker Texas History Center, University of Texas at Austin.

Higgins, Pattillo. Pattillo Higgins, called the prophet of Spindletop (*see* Spindletop Oil Field), was born on December 5, 1863, in Beaumont, Texas, the son of Robert James and Sarah (Raye) Higgins. His education was limited to completion of the third grade. When he was quite young, he lost his left arm in a shooting accident. As a youth he worked in lumber camps along the Texas-Louisiana border. Higgins had the first practical idea that oil would be found beneath the small twelve-to-fifteen-foot rise in the coastal plain south of Beaumont that was to become famous in oil history as Spindletop.

Knowing that gas and crude oil were being used for fuel in the North and East and having studied government geological surveys, he formed the Gladys City Oil, Gas, and Manufacturing Company in 1892 with financial assistance from George W. Carroll and George W. O'Brien. The new company started three wells, each a mechanical failure due to the then unknown peculiarities of the salt dome geological formation. Released from the management of the company, Higgins persuaded Carroll and O'Brien to let him advertise for capital. His only response came from Anthony Francis Lucas.qv He drilled one failure in search of sulphur and found a showing of oil. Again in search of financial backing, Higgins was directed by William Battle Phillips qv of the University of Texas to the firm of Guffey and Galey in Pittsburgh, Pennsylvania. John Galey persuaded the Mellon brothers of Pittsburgh to provide funds for five tests of the Spindletop prospect. The first of these, known as the Lucas Gusher, came in, producing 100,000 barrels of oil per day and marking the beginning of the modern liquid fuel age. Left out of Lucas' second well, Higgins formed the Higgins Oil and Fuel Company, based on a fifteen-acre lease he controlled in the center of the field. He later sold his stock in this company and formed the Higgins Standard Oil Company. Higgins was considered one of the wealthiest oil men in the country, having made a fortune at Spindletop. In later years he operated as an independent and often pursued ideas which were practical but far ahead of the contemporary technological development. He explored most of the Texas Gulf Coast salt dome fields long before they were discovered as oilfields; he once stated that every acre of land between Brownsville and New Orleans was potential oil producing land. It has been said that Higgins was the advance man for an age of energy and mobility that radically changed the world.

In addition to being a self-taught geologist, Higgins was also a draftsman, cartographer, inventor, naturalist, mathematician, industrial designer, artist, and engineer. In 1908 he was married to Annie Jahn; they had three children. Higgins lived in Houston after Spindletop's discovery and later moved to San Antonio, where he died on June 5, 1955. He was buried in Mission Burial Park in San Antonio.

BIBLIOGRAPHY: Houston *Post*, June 6, 1955; James A. Clark and Michel T. Halbouty, *Spindletop* (1952).

James A. Clark

*Higgins, Texas.

*High, Texas.

*High Bridge, Texas.

*High Hill, Texas.

*High Island, Texas.

*High Plains.

*High Prairie, Texas.

High School Coaches Association. The Texas High School Football Coaches Association (later broadened to include other sports) was founded in 1929 by coaches Johnnie Pierce (Corsicana), Jesse Kellam (Lufkin), and Jimmie Kitts (Athens). Although participation was minimal during the first several years, the association began to flourish in 1933, when D. X. Bible, former Texas A&M University coach, consented to lecture at the as-

sociation's first annual coaching clinic. The purpose of the organization was to raise coaching standards and to put the game on a more wholesome basis. In appreciation of this goal, the state's high schools responded by making coaches a part of the teaching profession.

By 1941 the association had so grown in importance, scope, and accomplishments that the word "football" was dropped from its title and all major sports were then included. In 1967 the coaching clinic attained its all-time high enrollment when 4,814 coaches participated. The association uses its economic resources for insurance against injury in football, death benefits for players in all sports, and death benefits for the widows of coaches.

BIBLIOGRAPHY: Dallas *Morning News*, July 23, 1968.

Harold V. Ratliff

*Highbank, Texas.

*Highhill Creek.

*Highland, Texas. (Erath County.)

*Highland, Texas. (Nolan County.)

*Highland Bayou.

Highland Lakes. *See* Buchanan Dam and Lake; Buchanan Reservoir; Inks Lake; Lake Lyndon B. Johnson; Marble Falls Lake; Lake Travis; Lake Austin; Town Lake.

*Highland Park, Texas. The Highland Park townsite, a suburb of Dallas, was developed by John S. Armstrong (not John S. Anthony, as stated in Volume I). Both a street and a school were named for Armstrong. According to the United States report of the 1970 census, Highland Park had a population of 10,133, a decrease from the 10,411 reported in the 1960 census. *See also* Dallas Standard Metropolitan Statistical Area.

Pat H. Candler

*Highlands, Texas. The population of Highlands, in Harris County, grew to 4,336 in 1960 and declined to 3,462 in 1970. The town reported seventy businesses in 1970.

*Highsmith, Benjamin Franklin.

*Highsmith, Henry Albert.

*Highsmith, Malcijah Benjamin.

*Highsmith, Samuel.

*Hightower, Emmett.

*Hightower, Texas.

*Highway Department, Texas State. *See also* Highway Development in Texas.

*Highway Development in Texas. The 1950's and 1960's were the most dramatic years in the history of highway development in Texas. The age of the freeway dawned in the early 1950's. By the mid-1960's superhighways were a part of the everyday life of Texans in every corner of the state. Rapid growth of Texas' major cities was inseparably linked with highway development. The first large movements toward the suburbs occurred in the years immediately after World War II, when highway facilities were extended to serve them.

Many cities and towns around the great urban centers owed their existence to their proximity to good highway facilities.

The era also witnessed the decline of older modes of transportation and a growing dependence on highways. More than 1,800 Texas communities were served by no system of transportation other than the highway network in 1965. Impetus was given highway development throughout the nation in 1956 with the beginning of the National System of Interstate and Defense Highways. Popularly called the interstate highway system, this network is the world's greatest public works project. Scheduled for completion in the 1970's, the interstate system was conceived as a system of 41,000 miles, linking nearly every major population center in the nation. All routes on the network were to be constructed as controlled-access traffic arteries, with no stop lights or stop signs and no crossings at grade. The Texas portion of the interstate system is 3,027 miles, more than any other state's. The public road system of Texas included a total of 205,248 miles on January 1, 1966. Of this total, 79,834 were paved.

The overwhelming majority of the paved mileage, 63,040 miles, was maintained by the Texas Highway Department.qv City and county streets and highways composed the remainder of the public road system. Many miles of urban thoroughfares and principal routes in incorporated cities and towns are maintained by the state. Freeways and expressways make up much of the urban state-maintained mileage. A total of 4,890 miles of highways within incorporated cities and towns was under state maintenance on September 1, 1966.

State highways in Texas are built on a "pay-as-you-go" basis; when a highway facility is completed it is paid for. There are no tolls charged for the use of any state-maintained highway facility in Texas. Texas remains a leading state in the building of new highways, according to the United States Bureau of Public Roads. On June 30, 1966, Texas had 1,256 miles of highways underway. This included engineering and right-of-way planning as well as actual construction.

The 1950's and 1960's were characterized also by construction of multilane divided highway facilities. Expressway and freeway construction was accelerated, particularly in the major population centers of the state. On September 30, 1966, there were 4,063 miles of divided highways in service in Texas, of which 1,375 miles were in urban areas. In the same two decades, Texas also experienced tremendous growth in the farm-to-market system. In 1966 this system included more than 37,000 miles. Recognized as the most extensive network of secondary roads in the world, Texas farm- and ranch-to-market roads ultimately will total 50,000 miles.

Highway construction is one of the major activities and principal cost factors in the operations of the Texas Highway Department. The department budgeted approximately $380,000,000 for new construction and right-of-way purchase in the fiscal year ending August 31, 1966. This represents more than the total amount spent for construction during the first twenty years of the highway department's operation.

A key factor in the success of the highway program in Texas has been the development of the private contracting industry. Texas highways are designed and construction is supervised by the Texas Highway Department. Actual construction is performed by private contractors under a competitive bid system. More than three hundred contractors regularly bid on highway projects in Texas. Keen competition has caused development of better equipment and more efficiency among roadbuilders. These have made the extensive highway program in Texas possible within a sound financial framework.

Texas builds better highways more economically than most other states. For example, the national average cost of new interstate highway construction is about $1,200,000 per mile, compared to the average cost in Texas of $750,000 per mile. For the two-year period September 1, 1964, to August 31, 1966, the Texas Highway Department awarded contracts and started construction on 22,338 miles of highway at a cost of $741,448,209.17.

Twenty-year projections made in 1965 by the Texas Highway Department show that the state must build an average of $450,000,000 of new highway facilities each year. By 1985 annual construction will total $535,000,000 to keep pace with the growth of Texas and the demands this expansion will make on the highway network. In Texas 77.5 percent of all highway expenditures go for construction, compared to a national average of 63 percent. Maintenance of the highway system in Texas requires only 15 percent of total expenditures, compared to an average of 25 percent nationally. Administration costs have amounted to less than 1 percent.

Travel by automobile in Texas is expected to rise from more than fifty billion vehicle miles per year in the mid-1960's to seventy-nine billion vehicle miles in 1985. The number of motor vehicles in Texas will more than double. From some six million in Texas in 1966, vehicle registrations will climb to an estimated fourteen million in the mid-1980's. In the 1965–1985 period, estimates indicate Texas will require 17,000 construction miles of new expressway and freeway facilities. All systems—state, city, and county—will require $15,000,000,000 worth of new highway development in the twenty years preceding 1985.

Mileage of the various types of highway improvement in the state public road systems, as of the dates indicated, was as follows:

COUNTY AND CITY MAINTAINED PUBLIC ROADS
as of January 1, 1966

Primitive and Unimproved	13,159.49
Graded and Drained Earth	54,493.20

Soil Surface and Gravel or Stone	57,698.00
Low Type Bituminous	15,948.50
High Type Bituminous	464.47
Portland Cement, Brick, and Block	380.51
Total	142,144.17

STATE MAINTAINED HIGHWAYS AND FARM- OR RANCH-TO-MARKET ROADS
as of September 1, 1966

Bladed Earth	38.70
Graded and Drained Earth	27.23
Soil Surface and Gravel or Stone	12.96
Bituminous Surface less than 1" on All Bases	44,306.06
Bituminous Surface more than 1" on Flexible Base	9,575.16
Bituminous Surface more than 1" on Rigid Base	2,957.04
Concrete Pavement	1,525.47
Dual Surface	531.40
City Mileage maintained by State	4,744.39
Total	63,718.41

STATE MAINTAINED FARM- OR RANCH-TO-MARKET ROADS
as of September 1, 1966

Bituminous Surface less than 1" on All Bases	33,479.84
Bituminous Surface more than 1" on Flexible Base	989.28
Bituminous Surface more than 1" on Rigid Base	177.29
Concrete Pavement	154.71
Dual Surface	10.24
City Mileage maintained by State	1,158.34
Total	35,969.70

D. C. Greer

*Higo Indians.

*Hilburn, Texas.

*Hilda, Texas. (Guadalupe County.)

*Hilda, Texas. (Mason County.)

*Hildebrand, Ira Polk.

*Hilgartner, Henry Louis.

*Hill, Alexander Campbell.

Hill, Asa. Asa Hill, father of James Monroe Hill and John Christopher Columbus Hill,qqv has often been confused with Abram Wiley Hill of Bastrop who was born in 1815 and died in 1884. Asa Hill was born in North Carolina, moved to Georgia, and was married in 1811 to Elizabeth Barksdale (who after Hill's death married Alexander Thomson, Jr.qv). Asa Hill came to Texas in 1835 with members of his family, including his nephew Isaac Lafayette Hill.qv No original documents ever refer to Asa Hill as Abraham Webb (Asa) Hill (as shown in the articles on his sons in Volume I).

Luther Henry Hill

*Hill, Benjamin F.

Hill, Clyde Walton. Clyde Walton Hill was born in Austin, Texas, in 1883, son of Kate Easton (Raymond) and Robert Jerome Hill. He was educated in the Austin public schools, the University of Texas (B.A., 1906; LL.B., 1913), and Harvard University, where he did graduate work in drama and composition in 1908–1909. He returned to the University of Texas and was a member of the English faculty from 1909 to 1912. Moving to Dallas in 1915, he opened a law practice and later engaged in the real estate business, but eventually returned to teaching. Through the years he contributed verse and prose to leading magazines.

Hill was one of the founders of the Poetry Society of Texas,qv which he served as treasurer from 1921 to 1932. He wrote one volume of poems, *Shining Trails* (1926). He was best known for his poem "Little Towns of Texas," which captured the popular imagination. His poem "Wilson" found its way into the scrapbook of the World War I president. Hill married Louise Oram of Dallas. He died in Dallas on February 4, 1932.

BIBLIOGRAPHY: Hilton R. Greer, *Voices of the Southwest* (1922); Vaida Stewart Montgomery, *A Century with Texas Poets and Poetry* (1934).

W. E. Bard

*Hill, George Alfred, Jr.

*Hill, George Washington. George Washington Hill was not reappointed secretary of war and marine (navy) by President Anson Jones (as stated in Volume I). He was succeeded in that office on December 9, 1844, by Morgan Calvin Hamilton,qv whose appointment was not confirmed by the Senate but who served as acting secretary.

BIBLIOGRAPHY: E. W. Winkler (ed.), *Secret Journals of the Senate of the Republic of Texas, 1836–1845* (1911); Adjutant General, Navy Papers, 1839–1845 (Archives, Texas State Library, Austin).

*Hill, Isaac Lafayette. Isaac Lafayette Hill did not come to Texas with his immediate family (as implied in Volume I) but came with his uncle, Asa Hill qv and Asa's family in 1835.

Luther Henry Hill

*Hill, James Ewing.

*Hill, James Monroe. James Monroe Hill was the son of Asa Hill qv (not Abraham Webb [Asa] Hill, as stated in Volume I).

Luther Henry Hill

*Hill, John Christopher Columbus. John Christopher Columbus Hill was born on November 15, 1828 (not 1827, as stated in Volume I) and was the son of Asa Hill qv (not Abraham Webb [Asa] Hill). As a youth he gained the favor of General Pedro Ampudia qv and Antonio López de Santa Anna,qv but it is doubtful that he was ever legally adopted by either of them.

John C. C. Hill was married to Agustina Sagredo of Real del Monte (not Donna Augustina Lergreda of Real del Norte, as stated in Volume I). He visited Texas briefly in 1880, but subsequently returned to Mexico. In 1895, after the death of his wife (June 27, 1891), he returned to Austin and served as Spanish translator for the General Land Office qv until October, 1896; he then returned to Mexico. In 1899 he married a Mrs. Masterson. He died in Monterrey, Mexico, on February 16, 1904.

BIBLIOGRAPHY: Death Notice, *Quarterly of the Texas State Historical Association*, VII (1903–1904); *Diccionario Porrua* (1965); Austin *Statesman*, February 19, 1904.

Luther Henry Hill
Margaret Stanford

*Hill, Lon C.

*Hill, Robert Thomas.

*Hill, William G.

*Hill, William Pinckney. William Pinckney Hill, a native of Georgia, was the son of John and Sarah (Parham) Hill; his birthdate is not known, but he was somewhat older than his brother, U.S. Senator Benjamin H. Hill of Georgia, who was born in 1823. Before moving to Bastrop, Texas, in 1839, William Pinckney Hill received some college education and was active as a preacher. He subsequently practiced law in Marshall. In 1861 Jefferson Davis qv appointed him, under the Confederacy, district judge of the Eastern District of Texas, which held court on a circuit schedule in Galveston, Tyler, Austin, and Brownsville. Because Galveston was considered unsafe, Hill moved the court from Galveston to Houston in January, 1862. His court disposed of numerous cases under the Sequestration Act. As required by that act, he appointed at least five receivers to seize the property of alien enemies (United States citizens) and to garnish debts due them. He presided over eighteen admiralty cases by means of which the Confederacy confiscated enemy ships seized on the Texas coast.

In 1863 and again in 1865, Hill was widely mentioned as a candidate for governor, but declined to run. He was considered a principal contender for chief justice of the Supreme Court of the Confederacy, a court debated but never created by the Confederate Congress. In 1866 he was nominated for the Supreme Court of Texas, but refused to run. He practiced law in Galveston after the war; he died on April 30, 1870, while visiting his brother in Georgia.

BIBLIOGRAPHY: William M. Robinson, Jr., *Justice in Grey* (1941); Benjamin H. Hill, Jr., *Senator Benjamin H. Hill of Georgia* (1893); Nowlin Randolph, "Judge William Pinckney Hill Aids the Confederate War Effort," *Southwestern Historical Quarterly*, LXVIII (1964–1965).

Nowlin Randolph

*Hill, William Warner.

*Hill, Texas.

*Hill City, Texas.

Hill Country. The term "hill country" is loosely used to describe that area of the southern Edwards Plateau qv located on and just north of the Balcones Escarpment.qv Divided from the interior Coastal Plains qv to the southeast by the fault zone, the hill country rises as a series of low, wooded mounts on the uplifted side of this extended fracture in the limestone. Often defined by reference to the areas surrounding its small population centers, the hill country includes the communities of Llano, Marble Falls, Wimberley, San Marcos, Blanco, Johnson City, Stonewall, Bandera, Kerrville, Fredericksburg, and New Braunfels, with Austin at the eastern edge.

Because the topsoil is usually very thin with frequent outcroppings of limestone bedrock, the hill country is generally better suited to the grazing of cattle, sheep, and goats than to agriculture. Most rural residents of the area are ranchers, but some small farms do exist on the flood-plains where streams have deposited rich soil. Surface water is scarce; windmills dot the landscape and deep wells insure against the years when drouth causes the failure of normally active springs and flowing creeks.

Typical flora includes a cover of cedar, mesquite, post oak, live oak, prickly pear, laurel, sumac, and range grasses. Willow, cypress, cottonwood, and pecan trees thrive near reliable water courses. Peach orchards are common.

Fauna is characterized by an abundance of white-tailed deer, wild turkeys, raccoons, opossums, jackrabbits, and armadillos. Less frequently observed are the ring-tailed cat, gray fox, and bobcat. A wide variety of birds may be sighted in the hill country including everything from the paisano (roadrunner) to the Canada goose migrating along the great central flyway.

Many of the original hill country settlers purchased their land for a few dollars an acre from holders of Spanish or Mexican land grants or from wealthy land speculators. While some of these settlers moved to the Texas hill country from the East and Southeast, many came directly from Europe, especially from Germany. The customs, crafts traditions, and language of the "old country" were carefully preserved by these settlers and their descendants. In 1975 one could hear German spoken at the fairgrounds in Fredericksburg, where the radio station, on the afternoon German music program, might play any of nine different versions of the "Beer Barrel Polka." Many homes in the same locale are adorned with a distinctive Bavarian-like gingerbread woodwork that bespeaks a pride of hand craftsmanship.

Like some of the granite-hard post oak beams that for almost a century have supported many original settlers' homes, the residents of the hill country have proved durable. The land is often closely held, with the descendant of the original settler proud to consider the tradition of the land as part of his freehold. There is evidence everywhere of a determined effort by hill country folk to carve out of the landscape a permanent place for themselves and their families. Miles of laboriously hand-constructed stone fences trace the outlines of fields, pastures, and property boundaries. Two-story houses constructed of hand-quarried limestone blocks, eighteen to twenty-four inches thick, provided secure domicile with natural insulation against the extremes of 100-degree summer heat and the below twenty-degree weather of a Texas "blue norther." Many of these old stone houses have, with minimal care, remained in like-new condition; many of them are being lived in today.

In the 1970's the hill country atmosphere was best exemplified in the festivities that annually brought hill country residents and visitors together: the New Braunfels Wurstfest, the Blanco Old Fiddlers Contest, the Gillespie County Fair, and the Bandera Old Settlers Days. At these and similar expositions one could delight in hill country products from needlework to horseflesh and smoked sausage to bluegrass music. The local product, however, that was usually appreciated most by visitors to the area was the infectious spirit characteristic of these people who so strongly identify with their cultural heritage and the land around them.

Jim Alvis

*Hill County. Hill County, formerly among the top five cotton-producing counties, by 1965 had shifted to a varied economy including row crops, livestock, and light industry. Cotton production, after a slack period late in the 1950's, increased approximately 17 percent from 1960 to a 1964 total of 42,934 bales. During the 1968–1969 season, 46,980 running bales were ginned. An increase in light industry included printing and the manufacture of ready-mix concrete, furniture, pipe, and garments. Aquatic sports on Lake Whitney and the reconstruction of Fort Graham,qv built on the site of a Waco Indian village, and Towash, a former Indian community and trading post, supported a small industry. The 1960 population of 23,650 decreased to 22,596 by 1970, according to the United States report of the census.

*Hill Creek.

Hill Junior College. Hill Junior College, Hillsboro, was a reactivation of Hillsboro Junior College, which operated from 1923 to 1950 as a segment of the Hillsboro public school system. The old college was the first municipal junior college to be organized in the state. The reactivated district was enlarged through the voluntary annexation in June, 1961, of five independent school districts contiguous to the Hillsboro district: Abbott, Bynum, Covington, Itasca, and Whitney.

The new junior college district was a separate legal entity, having no connection with the independent school districts except geographically. Assessed valuation of the new district was approximately $20,000,000 in 1965. Enrollment for the 1962–1963 term, the first year of operation, was 154 full-time students. By the 1974–1975 regular term the student body had increased to 859 students.

The seventy-three-acre campus was situated on a tract east of Hillsboro. Five buildings, representing the first step in a long-range construction program, were completed by 1965—academic building, gymnasium and dressing rooms, fine arts building, men's dormitory, and student center and faculty offices. By 1969 the school's library contained 15,000 volumes. The faculty numbered nineteen full-time instructors and five part-time instructors in 1964–

1965; by the 1970–1971 regular term the faculty had increased to thirty-five.

The college sought to provide three types of training: academic and preprofessional courses; general and vocational education; and continued education for adults. The school was admitted to full membership in the Association of Texas Colleges qv in 1965. In 1964 a Confederate research center and college press were established. O. B. Bailey served as president in 1975.

Hillcrest, Texas. Hillcrest, on State Highway 71 in northwest Colorado County, was the site of a gas station, a store, a motel, and a few residences in 1970. County sources suggest that the town was probably named for the low hill in its vicinity.

*Hillebrand Bayou.

*Hillister, Texas.

*Hillje, Texas.

*Hills, Texas.

*Hills Prairie, Texas.

*Hill's Spur, Texas.

*Hillsboro, Texas. Hillsboro, seat of Hill County, in 1966 reported five schools, two hospitals, two newspapers, three banks, thirteen churches, a library, and a radio station. In 1962 Hill Junior College was reactivated. In 1970 Hillsboro had 192 businesses, including companies manufacturing asbestos-cement products, garments, furniture, paint, and cottonseed products. The 1960 population of 7,402 decreased to 7,224 by 1970, according to the United States report of the census.

Hillsboro Junior College. See Hill Junior College.

*Hillside, Texas.

*Hilltop, Texas.

*Hillyer, Hamilton Biscoe. [This title was incorrectly listed in Volume I as Hillyer, Hamilton Briscoe.] Hamilton Biscoe Hillyer came to Texas in 1847 (not 1845, as stated in Volume I). [Some later printings of Volume I contain this correction.] He quit school at thirteen because of poor health and worked along the San Antonio River as a ranch hand. He married Mary Emma Storey (not Story) on March 4, 1858. He died on December 10 (not December 25), 1903. [Some later printings of Volume I contain this correction.]

Lorena Hillyer Fox

*Hillyer Female College.

*Hinckley, Texas.

*Hindes, Texas.

*Hindman, Texas.

Hinehi Indians. The Hinehi were one of twenty Indian groups that joined Juan Domínguez de Mendoza qv on his journey from El Paso to the vicinity of present San Angelo in 1683–1684. Since Mendoza did not indicate at what point the Hinehi joined his party, it is not possible to determine their range or affiliations. However, the Indians between the Pecos River and the San Angelo area were being hard pressed by Apache at this time, and it seems likely that the Hinehi ranged between these two localities.

BIBLIOGRAPHY: H. E. Bolton (ed.), *Spanish Exploration in the Southwest, 1542–1706* (1916).

T. N. Campbell

Hines, Elbert. Elbert Hines was born on January 12, 1797, in Effingham County, Georgia. He married Mahana Melton in Pike County, Mississippi, on November 5, 1816, and they had eight children. In 1823 they came to Texas. Hines served as alcalde of the District of Sabine in 1826. He petitioned the Mexican government for a grant on three separate occasions between 1830 and 1835, but none of the petitions was completed. In 1838 he received a first class headright certificate for one league and one labor of land, which he located in Caldwell County. He died in Sabine County on July 6, 1862, and was buried in the Isaac Low qv Cemetery near old Sabinetown.

BIBLIOGRAPHY: Transcript of Nacogdoches Archives (MS., Archives, University of Texas at Austin Library); Character Certificate File, General Land Office, Austin; First Class Headright File, General Land Office, Austin.

Helen Gomer Schluter

*Hines Branch.

*Hinkle's Ferry, Texas.

Hinn, Albert. Albert Hinn was born in Fennimore, Wisconsin, on July 30, 1880, the son of Christopher and Annette (Hill) Hinn. While learning the milling business from his father, who operated a flour mill and mercantile business, Hinn received a B.A. degree in 1904 from the University of Wisconsin, where he directed the band for two years. In 1907 his father responded to advertisements of the Texas Land and Development Company qv of Plainview and the following year invested in area farm lands. Albert Hinn then moved to Plainview to enter the real estate business. On June 17, 1909, he married Lochie Ann Mayhugh; they had four children.

Envisioning the tremendous wheat-producing potential of the region, Albert Hinn purchased the Harvest Queen flour mill in 1910 and developed it into one of the major mills in Texas. Among its products were a special flour for commercial bakeries and a baking flour known as "Everlite" for household use. Hinn also built or acquired grain storage elevators at Plainview, Crosbyton, Ralls, Lorenzo, and Petersburg, and he introduced experimental varieties of wheat to the farms of the area.

His investments became quite extensive before the depression of the 1930's caused him considerable financial loss and forced him to devote his energies to saving the Harvest Queen mill (rebuilt in 1926 after a fire) from economic disaster. He died on July 19, 1940, in Temple and was interred in Plainview.

BIBLIOGRAPHY: Seymour V. Connor (ed.), *Builders of the Southwest* (1959).

Seymour V. Connor

Hinsa Indians. In 1683–1684 Juan Domínguez de Mendoza qv led an exploratory expedition from El Paso as far eastward as the junction of the Concho and Colorado rivers east of present San Angelo. In his itinerary he listed the names of thirty-seven Indian groups, including the Hinsa (Himsa), from which he expected to receive delegations on the Colorado River. Nothing further is known of the Hinsa, who seem to have been one of many Indian groups of north-central Texas that were swept away by the southward thrust of the Lipan-Apache and Comanche Indians in the eighteenth century.

BIBLIOGRAPHY: H. E. Bolton (ed.), *Spanish Exploration in the Southwest, 1542–1706* (1916); C. W. Hackett (ed.), *Pichardo's Treatise on the Limits of Louisiana and Texas*, II (1934).

T. N. Campbell

*Hinton, A. C.

*Hiram, Texas.

Hirsch, Maximilian Justice. Maximilian Justice (Max) Hirsch, who became a legend in his own time as a trainer of thoroughbred horses, was born on July 30 (sometimes given as July 12), 1880, in Fredericksburg to Jacob and Mary (Neffendorf) Hirsch. At the age of twelve he ran away from home to become an exercise boy. He became a jockey on the western circuit at fourteen and rode 123 winners in 1,117 races before he became too heavy. He became a trainer at age twenty, and between Gautaman, the first winner he saddled in 1902, and Heartland, who won at Aqueduct on April 2, 1969, the day before he died, Hirsch conditioned such famous horses as Grey Lag, Sarazen, Bold Venture, Dawn Play, Assault, Middleground, and High Gun. His winners included three Kentucky Derby victories—Bold Venture in 1936, Assault in 1946, and Middleground in 1950. Assault became a Triple Crown winner by taking the Preakness and Belmont Stakes as well as the Derby.

Hirsch trained horses for many years at the King Ranch qv stables, which produced Bold Venture, Assault, and Middleground. Assault, suffering from a serious foot injury, would never have been able to race again but for a special steel spring devised by Hirsch and inserted into the foot, thus enabling the animal to run without stumbling.

Hirsch was elected to the Hall of Fame in 1959, when a plaque commemorating him was placed in the Museum of Racing in Saratoga Springs, New York. He was married to Kathryn Claire; they had five children. During the latter years of his life he divided his time between his home at Queens Village, New York, and Columbia, South Carolina. He died April 3, 1969, in New Hyde Park, New York. A Catholic, Hirsch was buried in Holy Rood Cemetery in Westbury, New York. Following his death, he was elected, in 1970, to the Texas Sports Hall of Fame.qv

BIBLIOGRAPHY: Biographical File, Barker Texas History Center, University of Texas at Austin; Dallas *Morning News*, April 4, 1969; Houston *Post*, April 5, 1969; Fredericksburg *Standard*, April 9, 1969; San Antonio *Express*, April 5, 1969.

*Hisaw Creek.

*Histon Creek.

Historical Organizations in Texas. In 1968 the American Association for State and Local History listed sixty-seven associations in Texas made up of city, county, and regional societies, the purpose of which was to collect and preserve the history of an area. There were also specialized groups whose purpose was to gather and preserve the history of such subjects as churches, railroads, and aviation.

*Historical Records Survey. See Texas Historical Records Survey.

*Hitchcock, Andrew Jackson.

*Hitchcock, Lent Munson.

*Hitchcock, Texas. According to the United States census, Hitchcock, in Galveston County, showed a population increase from 5,216 in 1960 to 5,565 in 1970. The town reported twenty-five businesses in 1970.

*Hitchland, Texas.

*Hite, Rosalie Belle.

*Hitson Branch.

*Hitt, Texas.

*Hittson, John.

*Hixon, Texas.

*Hoard, Texas.

Hoban, Texas. Hoban, in Reeves County, named for a Catholic priest, was a switch built in 1910 on the Pecos Valley Southern Railway. Although it was never incorporated, a small community developed during the first few years of the operation of the switch. In 1948 a country store operated at the site. Hoban has since been abandoned.

*Hobart, Timothy Dwight.

*Hobart, Texas.

*Hobbs, Texas. (Bell County.)

*Hobbs, Texas. (Fisher County.)

*Hobby, Alfred Marmaduke.

*Hobby, Edwin E.

Hobby, William Pettus. William Pettus Hobby, editor, publisher, and governor of Texas from 1917 to 1921, was born in Moscow, Texas, on March 26, 1878, the son of Eudora Adeline (Pettus) and Edwin E. Hobby.qv One of six children, Hobby moved in 1893 with his family from Livingston to Houston, where he entered Houston High School. In 1895 he began working for the Houston Post qv as a circulation clerk. Hobby became a business writer for the Post in August, 1901. He began to take an active interest in politics, was a founder of the Young Men's Democratic Club of Houston, and in 1904 was secretary of the party's state executive committee. He became city editor, then managing editor of the Post, and participated in the covering of some of the most spectacular stories of the time. In 1907 he left the Post to become manager and part owner of the Beaumont Enterprise, which he soon acquired.

Hobby was elected lieutenant governor in 1914 and was reelected in 1916. He was married in 1915 to Willie Cooper, daughter of former United States Representative Samuel Bronson Cooper.qv She died in 1929. When Governor James Edward Ferguson qv was removed from office in 1917, Hobby became the twenty-sixth governor of Texas and the youngest man, at thirty-nine, to hold the office. Hobby served during an eventful period. During World War I he set up an effective military draft system for Texas, a state in which half of the country's military camps and most of its airfields were located.

In 1918 Hobby defeated Ferguson by the largest majority ever received in a Democratic primary. Hobby's administration saw the passage of measures for drouth relief, runoff requirements in party primaries, and state aid for schools and highways. He appointed the first Highway Commission in 1917. Laws included measures for oil conservation, the establishment of the oil and gas division of the Railroad Commission, the creation of the Board of Control,qqv and provision for free school textbooks.

After completing his term, he returned to the Beaumont Enterprise and purchased the Beaumont Journal. He retained control of both papers for more than a decade. In 1924 he became president of the Houston Post-Dispatch. When J. E. Josey acquired the newspaper in 1931 from Ross Sterling,qv Hobby continued in the presidency and maintained executive control. In 1939 he acquired the paper, again called the Post.

In February, 1931, Hobby married Oveta Culp of Killeen and Houston, a former parliamentarian of the Texas House, who became a Post staff member, served in World War II as commander of the Women's Army Corps, and served in the Dwight David Eisenhower qv administration as the first secretary of the Department of Health, Education, and Welfare. The Hobbys had a son and a daughter.

Under Hobby, the Post grew in circulation and prestige. The Houston Post Company also included the radio station, KPRC, and the television station, KPRC-TV. In August, 1955, Hobby became chairman of the board of the company, with Mrs. Hobby as president and editor.

Hobby died in Houston on June 7, 1964. A state historical marker at his birthplace was dedicated at Moscow in 1964. Hobby Field and Hobby Elementary School in Houston were named for him.

BIBLIOGRAPHY: James A. Clark (with Weldon Hart), The Tactful Texan: A Biography of Governor Will Hobby (1958); Library files of the Houston Post.

William P. Hobby, Jr.

*Hobby, Texas.

*Hobby's 8th Texas Infantry Regiment.

Hoblitzelle, Karl St. John. Karl Hoblitzelle, Dallas business and civic leader, was born in St. Louis, Missouri, on October 22, 1879, one of thirteen children of Clarence Linden and Ida (Knapp) Hoblitzelle. His father, a Confederate veteran, had settled in St. Louis after the Civil War and engaged in the saddlery and harness business. After graduation from high school, Karl worked briefly in a real estate business and in a soap factory, then started for himself in truck farming and poultry raising. When an attack of malaria caused him to give up this work, he began in 1904 as office boy, then secretary, for the director of works at the Louisiana Purchase Exposition. At the close of the fair, Hoblitzelle was made acting director of works in charge of demolition.

In 1905, with a brother and others, Hoblitzelle formed the Interstate Amusement Company, which later became the Interstate Circuit, of which he was president. The firm operated vaudeville houses in Dallas, Fort Worth, Waco, and San Antonio. With the advent of motion pictures, the company began showing films and by 1949 had expanded to more than 170 theaters in thirty-two cities and towns in Texas and New Mexico. In addition to his theater management, Hoblitzelle operated a farm and ranch in the Rio Grande Valley, engaged in oil production, and headed Hoblitzelle Properties. He became a director of the Republic National Bank in Dallas in 1928 and was chairman of its board, 1945–1955. He also served as a director of the Southwestern Life Insurance Company, the Republic Natural Gas Company, and the Texas Power and Light Company.

Hoblitzelle engaged in many civic activities. He was board chairman of the Southwestern Medical Foundation, the Texas Research Foundation, and the Hockaday School,qqv chairman of the commission for the Texas Centennial of Statehood,qv a trustee of Southern Methodist University, a director of the Dallas Citizens Council and several cultural organizations, president of the Civic Federation of Dallas, and a patron of the Texas State Historical Association.qv He established the Hoblitzelle Foundation, through which he distributed several million dollars to educational and charitable agencies and to which he left the bulk of his fortune. Although not a Catholic, he was honored by Pope Pius XII in 1954 for his philanthropic work. The Karl Hoblitzelle Clinical Science Center at Southwestern Medical School was named for him.

On April 7, 1920, Hoblitzelle married Esther Walker, a singer, recording artist, and star of musical comedies. She died in 1943. He died in Dallas on March 8, 1967.

BIBLIOGRAPHY: Don Hinga, *Forty Years of Community Service* (1946); Dallas *Morning News*, March 9, 1967.

Wayne Gard

*Hobson, Texas.

*Hochheim, Texas.

*Hochheim Prairie, Texas.

Hockaday, Ela. Ela Hockaday, founder of the Hockaday School qv in Dallas, was born at the family home in Ladonia, Fannin County, Texas, on March 12, 1875, the daughter of Thomas Hart Benton and Maria Elizabeth (Kerr) Hockaday. She received her early schooling in Bonham, Texas, where she lived with an elder sister following the death of her mother in 1881. Miss Hockaday received her B.A. degree from Denton Normal School (later North Texas State University) and studied in the graduate schools of Columbia University and the University of Chicago. In 1940 she was honored with an LL.D. from Austin College in recognition of her outstanding educational achievements.

Miss Hockaday began her teaching career as a classroom teacher in Sherman, Texas, and in 1901 was promoted to the position of principal of the Sherman schools. A few years later she was asked to head the Department of Biological Science at Oklahoma State Normal School in Durant. Following a successful tenure, she became a member of the faculty of the Oklahoma College for Women at Chickasha.

In September, 1913, Miss Hockaday was recommended to a group of Dallas residents by M. B. Terrill to organize and serve as headmistress of a preparatory school which would offer young ladies an education of quality equal to those offered by eastern schools. Miss Hockaday enlisted the help of Sarah B. Trent, with whom she had become acquainted while both were teaching at Oklahoma State Normal School, and in September, 1913, the Hockaday School for Girls (later Hockaday School) opened in a large house on Haskell Avenue.

Throughout her lifetime, Miss Hockaday planned and directed the activities and curriculum of the school. She was not content with a program confined solely to academic achievement. She believed that education should not end in the classroom and that its ultimate aim was the building of character.

Her home, The Cottage, was located on a corner of the Greenville Avenue campus and became a focal point for civic as well as school interest. She was often visited by outstanding persons in the fields of art, music, literature, and science and was instrumental in attracting notable people to Dallas as a part of her contribution to civic affairs. She was a recipient of the Zonta Club Award for outstanding service to the Dallas community. Miss Hockaday retired from her administrative duties at the school in 1946, at which time the school was incorporated as a nonprofit organization under the direction of a board of trustees. She served as president emeritus until her death on March 26, 1956. She was buried at the Hillcrest Memorial Cemetery.

Dorothy Bruton

Hockaday, James Addison. James A. Hockaday, a practicing physician in Port Isabel, Texas, for forty-seven years and a civic leader in the Lower Rio Grande Valley, was born on January 23, 1892, at Plattsburg, Missouri, the son of James Addison and Nana (Elliott) Hockaday. He attended schools at Holt, Missouri, and the University of Missouri at Kansas City, receiving his medical degree from the University Medical College of Kansas City in 1913. After serving in the medical corps during World War I, he moved his family to Port Isabel, Texas.

Hockaday married Clara Achterberg in Kansas City, Missouri, in 1913. She died in 1915; their only child, a son, died at age fifteen. In 1917 Hockaday married Ruby Dietz, and they had two sons. He was later married to Beulah Lee Rankin in 1935. She died in 1937, and on August 8, 1939, he married Jimmie Lee Jordan, who bore him two sons.

Hockaday was president of Cameron-Willacy County Medical Society, physician and surgeon for the Missouri-Pacific Lines for many years, and a member of the "Fifty Year Club of Physicians." He served as mayor of Port Isabel, 1946–1947, and from 1956 to April, 1966. A founder and lifetime director of the Texas International Fishing Tournament, he was recognized for his interest in oceanography, ornithology, taxidermy, and archeology— especially with respect to the life and history of the area in which he lived. He was a member of the Texas State Historical Association,qv Texas Historical Foundation, Cameron County Historical Survey Committee, and president and lifetime board member of the Lower Rio Grande Valley Historical Society. At the time of his death he had almost completed drafts for two books, one a history of Port Isabel and the other on Indians of the Lower Rio Grande Valley. His files of historical data were included in a memorial library in Port Isabel. He died on May 10, 1966, in Brownsville and was given a military burial at Port Isabel.

BIBLIOGRAPHY: *Texas Medicine* (July, 1966); Leonard King, *Port of Drifting Men* (1945); *Who's Who in the South and Southwest* (1956).

Verna J. McKenna

*Hockaday School. Hockaday School, founded by Ela Hockaday,qv moved in 1961 to air conditioned buildings on a 100-acre campus in North Dallas. The junior college division was closed in 1951, and in the 1960's the school consisted of grades one through twelve, including both resident and day students. The headmaster was Robert S. Lyle.

Robert S. Lyle

*Hockley, George Washington.

*Hockley, Texas.

*Hockley County. Hockley County in 1960 rated sixth among Texas counties in crop income, with $28,503,225, and third in cotton, with nearly 224,000 bales from its thirty-five gins. Cash receipts from crops in the early 1970's amounted to an average of $33,000,000 annually, ninety percent of which came from cotton. Other sources of farm income included grain sorghums, soybeans, castor beans, beef cattle, swine, and vegetables. Between 1937 and January 1, 1973, the county had a total crude oil production of 538,081,637 barrels. Hockley County, with Levelland, owned an airport. The 1960 population was 22,340; the report of the 1970 United States census showed a population of 20,396.

*Hodge, Alexander.

*Hodge, John C. M.

*Hodges, Galen.

*Hodges, James.

*Hodges, Texas.

*Hodgins, Texas.

*Hodgson, Texas.

*Hoen, Texas.

*Hoffman, David A.

Hoffmann, Gustav. Gustav Hoffmann was born in Stuhmbei, Prussia, on November 10, 1817. One of the original settlers of New Braunfels, he was elected the first mayor of that town in June, 1847, but resigned in March of the following year for an extended trip to Germany. On his return he resumed his occupation as a farmer.

Hoffmann had military experience in Prussia, and with the outbreak of the Civil War, he raised a company of cavalry from Comal County which joined Henry H. Silbey's qv Brigade in October, 1861, as Company B, 7th Regiment, Texas Cavalry. He participated in numerous battles and was seriously wounded during the assault on Fort Butler in June, 1863. He was promoted to lieutenant colonel on April 14, 1864, and became full-time commander of the 7th Texas Cavalry. At the war's end, he was paroled as a colonel at San Antonio on September 11, 1865.

Hoffmann returned to New Braunfels and in 1872 was elected a representative to the Thirteenth Legislature. He later moved to San Antonio, where he died on March 10, 1889. He was buried in New Braunfels.

BIBLIOGRAPHY: Rudolph L. Biesele, "Early Times in New Braunfels and Comal County," *Southwestern Historical Quarterly*, L (1946–1947); U. S. War Department, *The War of the Rebellion: A Compilation of the Official Records of the Union and Confederate Armies* (1880–1901).

Martin Hardwick Hall

*Hog Bayou.

*Hog Branch.

*Hog Creek.

Hog Farm, State. *See* State Dairy and Hog Farm; State Hog Farm; Texas Leander Rehabilitation Center.

*Hog Marsh.

*Hog Mountain.

Hog Raising. *See* Swine Raising.

Hogan, William Ransom. William Ransom Hogan was born in Toledo, Ohio, on November 23, 1908; he was the son of Lemuel Ransom and Irene (Logan) Hogan. Hogan was educated at Trinity University, where he received the B.A. degree in 1929, and the University of Texas, where he took the M.A. in 1932 and the Ph.D. in 1942. He began a teaching career at Ranger Junior College and High School (1929–1931), and from 1935 to 1938 he was a historian with the national park service. He was an archivist at Louisiana State University from 1938 to 1942; from 1942 to 1945 he was in military intelligence with the U.S. Army, attaining the rank of captain before returning to LSU to become head of the archives there in 1946. In that same year he became an associate professor of history at the University of Oklahoma.

In 1946 Hogan published his influential *The Texas Republic: A Social and Economic History*, an authoritative account of early Texas history and a standard source of information on the Republic. With Edwin A. Davis, Hogan edited *William Johnson's Natchez* (1951), and together they wrote *The Barber of Natchez* (1954). With his wife Jane, Hogan edited *Tales from the Manchaca Hills* (1960). He was a professor at Tulane University from 1947 until his death, serving for many years as chairman of the Department of History.

Widely admired by fellow historians and students, Hogan belonged to numerous professional organizations; he was a fellow of the Texas State Historical Association.qv He married Mrs. Jane Carpenter Ogg on June 20, 1949. He died in New Orleans on September 25, 1971. The Olympia Band provided the music at his funeral in New Orleans, and he was buried near Austin at Live Oak Cemetery.

BIBLIOGRAPHY: *Who's Who In America* (1968); Frank H. Wardlaw, "In Memoriam: William R. Hogan," *Southwestern Historical Quarterly*, LXXV (1971–1972); Author and Biographical File, Barker Texas History Center, University of Texas at Austin.

Hogeye, Texas. (Bastrop County.) Hogeye was two miles south of Elgin. It had three or four businesses and a stage station; it was a post-Civil War terminal of a freight line which used camels. Its post office was Youngs Settlement, which was open from 1855 to 1872. Only three cemeteries and some ruins of its stage station remained in 1968.

Grover C. Ramsey

Hogeye, Texas. (Hunt County.) Hogeye was two and one-half miles east of Celeste, which was its post office. Miller Lodge No. 224 was chartered there in 1858, and its lower floor was the Hogeye School. There was a grocery store and also a cemetery. Only the cemetery remains.

Grover C. Ramsey

Hogeye, Texas. (Jack County.) Hogeye was sixteen miles east of Jacksboro on the old Overland Mail Route.qv J. B. Earhart managed the stage station and a prosperous ranch there. A school and church were nearby.

Grover C. Ramsey

Hogg, Ima. Ima Hogg, only daughter of Sarah Ann [Sallie] (Stinson) and James Stephen Hogg qv (the first native-born governor of Texas), was born July 10, 1882, at Mineola. Named by her father for the heroine in a long epic poem by her uncle, Thomas Elisha Hogg,qv she was known affectionately during her lifetime as Miss Ima. At the age of nine she and her three brothers moved with their parents to the governor's mansion qv in Austin and remained in that city at the close of Governor Hogg's term in 1895. In the summer of that year Ima Hogg accompanied her mother to Pueblo, Colorado, where Sarah Ann Hogg died of tuberculosis on September 20, 1895.

Ima Hogg attended the University of Texas from 1899 to 1901. In the fall of 1901 she moved to New York City to continue her education in music. Her father had bought the Varner plantation near West Columbia in Brazoria County, was successfully practicing law in Houston, and was involved in the booming oil business in southeast Texas. Always close to her father, Ima Hogg was with him when he died in Houston on March 3, 1906. She continued her musical studies in piano both in the United States and Germany.

Ima Hogg moved to Houston in 1909 to teach piano. In 1913 she was one of the organizers of Houston's first symphony concert; she was the second president of the Houston Symphony Society (1917–1921) and was later returned to that office for ten one-year terms (1946–1956). Her life-long dedication to the Houston Symphony insured that orchestra's prestige, and she brought several world-famous conductors to lead it. She was also a longtime benefactor of the Houston Museum of Fine Arts,qv to which she donated important works of art, including paintings by Frederic Remington.

The Hogg family's wealth increased spectacularly in 1918, when the West Columbia Oil Field qv was developed. Called one of the great ladies of the twentieth century, Ima Hogg used the wealth that she inherited for the public good. In addition to founding the Houston Child Guidance Center as a pioneering institution in child psychiatry, she assisted in carrying out the will of her brother William Clifford Hogg,qv which resulted in the creation of the Hogg Foundation qv for Mental Health at the University of Texas at Austin, to which Ima Hogg continued her own support through the years. She served on the Houston School Board from 1943 to 1949, and she was active in the Texas Welfare Association, the League of Women Voters, the Daughters of the Republic of Texas,qv and the Texas State Historical Association.qv

Her interest in the history of the state was marked by enthusiasm, imagination, and strength of will, resulting in permanent gifts to the people of Texas. She restored her father's plantation home in Brazoria County, and the site became the Varner-Hogg Plantation State Historic Park (*see* Parks, State). In 1963 she purchased historic properties at Winedale in Fayette County, supervised extensive restoration there (she was an avid collector of early Texas furniture), and in 1965 she gave the property and buildings to the University of Texas at Austin as an outdoor museum and study center (*see* Winedale Museum). In 1966 she gave her fifteen-acre Houston River Oaks estate, Bayou Bend, along with $750,000 in stocks for maintenance of the mansion and its formal gardens, to the Houston Museum of Fine Arts.

Her influence extended past the borders of the state. In 1960 President Dwight D. Eisenhower qv appointed her to the advisory committee on the arts for the National Cultural Center in Washington, D.C., and the succeeding president's wife, Mrs.

John F. Kennedy, appointed her an advisor to the Fine Arts Committee for the White House in 1962. In 1966 the National Trust for Historic Preservation awarded her a citation for her accomplishments in historical preservation.

In 1948 she became the first woman president of the Philosophical Society of Texas;qv in 1963 she was the first woman recipient of the University of Texas' Distinguished Alumnus Award; in 1968 she was the first person to receive the Santa Rita Award, the highest honor bestowed by the University of Texas System,qv for her demonstrated concern for higher education.

In 1972 about three hundred friends honored Miss Ima with a dinner party at historic Winedale on the occasion of her ninetieth birthday. Three years later Ima Hogg was on vacation in London, where she died on August 19, 1975. Funeral services were held at Bayou Bend in Houston on August 22, and she was buried alongside her parents and three brothers in Oakwood Cemetery in Austin on August 23. The major beneficiary of her will was the Ima Hogg Foundation, a charitable nonprofit corporation organized in 1964.

Eldon S. Branda

*Hogg, James Stephen.

*Hogg, Joseph Lewis.

*Hogg, Thomas Elisha.

*Hogg, William Clifford. William Clifford Hogg was buried in Oakwood (not Greenwood, as stated in Volume I) Cemetery in Austin.

*Hogg Foundation. The Hogg Foundation for Mental Health continued to function as an integral part of the University of Texas System,qv responsible to its chancellor and to its board of regents, whose members were the trustees of the foundation. Begun in 1940 by a bequest from Will C. Hogg,qv it has expanded through grants by other family members, including brothers Thomas E. Hogg and Mike Hogg, their widows, and especially Miss Ima Hogg,qv who also served as advisor to Mike Hogg, executor of the will. Its annual income from endowment reached more than one-half million dollars by 1970. The largest grant from outside sources was made by the Ford Foundation in 1964 for the purpose of aiding the Hogg Foundation in mutual planning and programs with other foundations in the Southwest.

When the Hogg Foundation was originally organized within the university system, one of the main considerations of the donors was that the knowledge of human behavior and mental health which is to be found on a university campus be transmitted to the people of Texas. The foundation staff has been mindful of the Hogg family interest in reaching many colleges and communities.

A pluralistic concept of mental health was adopted by the Hogg Foundation from its beginning. All the forces acting upon man and his behavior—family, community, school, government, and others—were taken into account. Mental hygiene was defined broadly as the study and application of scientific principles of personality development toward the end of helping individuals "to utilize their capacities fully and to work with their fellows creatively."

Robert L. Sutherland served as director and president of the Hogg Foundation from 1940 until September 1, 1970, when Wayne H. Holtzman succeeded him in that office. Sutherland continued as Hogg Professor of Sociology.

The foundation staff was aided in its work by special consultants and by other advisors who assisted on certain projects. More than seventy members of the University of Texas faculty serve in some consulting capacity during the course of any year, and another fifteen consultants are drawn from state and community agency personnel or from the faculties of other colleges.

Long-term planning, as well as current policies of the foundation, is formulated through the help of its national advisory council, whose three members serve on a three-year, rotating basis. Meetings of two days' duration are held semiannually.

The foundation maintains three libraries. One is a collection of general mental health books and pamphlets; another is concerned with "the person in higher education." A third is the Regional Foundation Library, established through the cooperation of the Foundation Center of New York. This collection contains information on numerous foundations throughout the United States and particularly Texas and the Southwest.

The major thrust of the foundation has shifted from one emphasis to another through the years, depending upon the critical needs and opportunities of the time. In the early years attention was directed mainly to educating the people of Texas about mental health. The decade of the 1950's involved the foundation in programs for the education and training of professional mental health workers; the expansion of state and community services; the extension of mental health education by the large-scale distribution of pamphlets, books, radio, and television; the development of new research projects in the field of mental health; and the strengthening of cooperative efforts with other foundations in the Southwest. The decade of the 1960's brought increasing concern for the larger problems of society. Emphasis focused on campus mental health and intervention with special population groups ranging from disadvantaged ethnic minorities to the mentally ill and aged. Activities begun in the 1950's were continued in modified form.

More challenges and opportunities than ever were anticipated for the 1970's. The problems of environmental quality, the frustrations of awakening minorities, and the conflicts within everyone concerning the polarization of society were a few of the more salient issues.

Wayne H. Holtzman

Holcombe, Oscar Fitzallen. Oscar Fitzallen Holcombe was born in Mobile, Alabama, on December 31, 1888, the son of Robert Slough and

Sarah King (Harrell) Holcombe. When he was three years old his family moved from Alabama to San Antonio. His father died when Oscar was eleven, and the boy helped earn part of the family income by selling newspapers. When he was fifteen he quit school to work full time. In 1907 he went to Houston to work for an uncle who owned a lumber company. By the time he was twenty he was the assistant manager.

After a brief period as a salesman for a sash and door company, he went into the construction business, bidding successfully for contracts to build public schools in Texas. When he made his first race for mayor of Houston, in 1921, he estimated his yearly income at $30,000. In this first campaign he promised better business administration, reorganization of the city departments, paving, and new schools. Although opposed by the Ku Klux Klan,qv he won the election and began a twenty-two-year career as mayor, though not in consecutive terms. He acquired the nickname "old gray fox" because of premature grayness during this campaign.

During his early administrations Holcombe was instrumental in obtaining wider streets, better sewage systems, and the construction of a number of public buildings such as the municipal auditorium, farmers' market, and libraries. His main contribution, however, lay in the creation of the navigation district which included all of Harris County. He also created the new municipal offices of city manager, public service commissioner, and the city planning commission. The Houston Independent School District was also established under his guidance.

Holcombe served from 1921 to 1929, when he returned to the construction business. He ran again in 1933 and served until 1937. Other terms of service were from 1939 to 1944, 1947 to 1953, and 1956 to 1958, a total of eleven terms. He was part owner of the Southern Lumber Company and Southern Builders Corporation and was one of the early developers of several shopping centers and housing developments in the area.

He came out of semi-retirement in 1956 to run successfully against the incumbent mayor, Roy Hofheinz. Holcombe lost his last bid for reelection as mayor to Lewis Cutrer in 1958 over the issue of integrating public swimming pools. Holcombe refused integration, saying he wished to "prevent violence and bloodshed."

During his terms of office, Houston grew from an area of 34.4 square miles to 352 square miles; because the city was involved in a dramatic period of growth, Holcombe had the opportunity to demonstrate effectively his prime talent—that of builder. He married Mamie Gray Miller on May 3, 1912, and they had one daughter. He died of pneumonia on June 18, 1968, and was buried in Forest Park Lawndale Cemetery in Houston.

*Holder, Texas. (Brown County.)

*Holder, Texas. (Taylor County.)

*Holder, Texas. (Willacy County.)

*Holder Creek.

*Holding Institute.

*Holiday Creek.

*Holiness University. See Texas Holiness University.

*Holland, Bird.

*Holland, Francis.

*Holland, Frank P.

*Holland, James K.

Holland, John Henry. John Henry Holland was born in Hartford, Connecticut, about 1785. He moved to New Orleans sometime before 1803. He served as sheriff of Orleans Parish and subsequently practiced law in New Orleans. For many years he was associated with the Masonic Order in Louisiana. He was Grand Master of the Grand Lodge of Louisiana from 1825 to 1828 and again from 1830 to 1839. In 1825 he delivered the welcoming address, in French, to the Marquis de Lafayette at a special communication of the Grand Lodge of Louisiana. In 1827 he was credited with interceding with Manuel Mier y Terán qv to obtain the freedom of Adolphus Sterne,qv who was imprisoned at Nacogdoches for his part in the Fredonian Rebellion.qv During the 1830's Holland was a central figure in a controversy between French-speaking and English-speaking Masons over the control of Louisiana Masonry.

On January 27, 1836, Holland issued a charter for the first Masonic lodge in Texas, Holland Lodge No. 36 (now Holland Lodge No. 1), to a group of Masons in Brazoria. On September 22, 1837, he issued charters for Milam Lodge No. 40 at Nacogdoches and MacFarland Lodge No. 41 at San Augustine. On December 20, 1837, the Grand Lodge of Texas was organized, terminating Grand Master Holland's authority over Freemasonry in Texas.qv

Holland moved from New Orleans to Nacogdoches in April, 1839, and was joined there by his family in May, 1840. He was admitted to the practice of law in Texas in October, 1839. By March, 1846, he had returned to New Orleans. From 1856 to 1864 he was the Grand Master of the Grand Council of Royal and Select Masters of Louisiana. John Henry Holland died in New Orleans on March 29, 1864.

BIBLIOGRAPHY: James B. Scot, *Outline of the Rise and Progress of Freemasonry in Louisiana* (1873); *Biographical and Historical Memoirs of Louisiana*, II (1892); James Carter, *Masonry in Texas* (1955); L. W. Kemp Collection, (MS., Archives, University of Texas at Austin Library); New Orleans *Picayune*, March 30, 1864.

Chester V. Kielman

*Holland, Samuel Eley.

*Holland, Spearman.

*Holland, William.

*Holland, William H.

*Holland, Texas.

*Holland Creek.

*Holland Springs, Texas.

Hollander, Lee Milton. Lee Milton Hollander, son of Samuel and Amelia (Herstein) Hollander, was born on November 8, 1880, in Baltimore, Maryland. After the death of his father in 1886 he lived in Germany with his mother and returned to Baltimore in 1897. He attended Johns Hopkins University, where he received his B.A. degree in 1901 and his Ph.D. in 1905. He then went to Scandinavia and spent 1906–1907 studying North Germanic languages and literatures; this stay in northern Europe formally cultivated his interest in the field in which he held preeminence for more than sixty years. He taught German at the University of Michigan from 1907 to 1910, and German and Scandinavian languages at the University of Wisconsin from 1911 to 1918. Since the domestic reaction to World War I anathematized Germanic studies in the United States, Hollander spent 1918 to 1920 filing newspaper clippings in the University of Wisconsin library. In 1920 he moved to Austin, Texas, to teach in the Germanic languages department at the University of Texas. He was chairman of the department from 1929 to 1946; he retired in 1968, but continued to produce scholarly works.

Some of the most important of Hollander's numerous translations and studies are *The Poetic Edda* (1928), *Old Norse Poems* (1936), *The Skalds* (1945), *The Jomsvikinga Saga* (1955), *A Bibliography of Skaldic Studies* (1958), *Selections from the Writings of Kierkegaard* (1923, 1960), and the *Heimskringla* of Snorri Sturluson (1964). He pursued his work vigorously until the year of his death, when his translation of *Víga-Glúm's Saga* appeared (1972).

Hollander was noted for his meticulous learning, his sensitive translations, and his unflinching attention to the originals with which he worked. He insisted that even the most well known works in Old Norse had never been translated adequately because the translators did not know the language well enough and because they felt obliged to bowdlerize texts that they considered morally objectionable. For his work Hollander was named Knight of the Order of the Icelandic Falcon, member of the Norsk Videnskaps Akademi, president of the Society for the Advancement of Scandinavian Studies (twice, 1919–1921, 1960–1961), and honorary life member of the Viking Society for Northern Research, a distinction conferred on only twelve persons in the world.

Hollander married Jean Wright Fisher on June 27, 1912, and they had three children. He died in Austin on October 19, 1972, and was cremated. Memorial services were held at Woods Hole, Massachusetts.

BIBLIOGRAPHY: Edgar C. Polomé (ed.), *Old Norse Literature and Mythology: A Symposium* (1969); *Directory of American Scholars* (1969).

Roy R. Barkley

Holland's Magazine. *Holland's Magazine* was issued under the name *Street's Weekly* from 1876 through 1903, volumes 1 through 23. With volume 24, in 1905, the publication became a monthly magazine put out by Texas Farm and Ranch Publishing Company in Dallas, with Frank P. Holland,qv president and general manager, and Walter B. Whitman, editor. The contents usually included a number of fiction and nonfiction articles, often contributed by well-known writers; standard features, such as recipes and gardening notes; and vigorous editorials. By 1927 members of the Holland family occupied the top three positions: Frank P. Holland, Sr. (and later his wife), president; Frank P. Holland, Jr., vice-president and advertising director; and R. V. Holland, secretary-treasurer. In December, 1944, Mrs. Gussie Holland Lancaster became president. She was succeeded in May, 1945, by Brownlee O. Curry, who took the title of chairman of the board in August, 1946. By September, 1952, publishing of the periodical was taken over by Holland's Magazine Company. The last issue of the magazine (called *Holland's: The Magazine of the South* beginning with volume 48) was in December, 1953, with volume 72 ending a seventy-seven-year existence.

Karen Collins

*Holley, Mary Austin.

*Holliday, John J.

*Holliday, Texas. According to the United States 1970 census, Holliday, in Archer County, had a population of 1,048, a decrease from the 1960 population count of 1,139. The town had twenty-four businesses in 1970.

*Holliday Creek.

*Holliman, Kinchen.

*Hollingsworth, Orlando Newton.

*Hollis, Texas.

Holloway, Robert Fanning. Robert Fanning Holloway, son of John T. and Mary (Reid) Holloway, was born at Pritchett in Upshur County on February 24, 1867. He was graduated from Add-Ran Christian University (now Texas Christian University) in 1892. Shortly thereafter he became principal of Oak Cliff High School in Dallas. In 1896 he married Lou Ella Clark, daughter of Randolph Clark.qv They had two children.

He taught mathematics at Add-Ran Christian University, Add-Ran Jarvis College at Thorp Spring, and John Tarleton College at Stephenville. He was superintendent of schools at Comanche, 1911–1919; president of Randolph College at Cisco, 1922–1925; and superintendent of schools at Ranger, 1925–1934. From 1934 until his death in 1939, Holloway was manager and secretary-treasurer of National Educators Finance Corporation, an investment company owned and operated by and for teachers. He helped organize the University Interscholastic League and the Texas State Teachers Association,qqv serving the latter as director and as vice-president. He was active in the Christian church, serving several local congregations as a board member, Sunday school teacher and superintendent, and director of music. He died December 19, 1939, in Fort Worth and was buried in Stephenville.

R. R. *Holloway*

*Holly, Texas. (Houston County.)

*Holly, Texas. (Ward County.)

*Holly Creek.

*Holly Springs, Texas.

Hollywood Park, Texas. Hollywood Park, a Bexar County suburban town, was incorporated in 1955. According to the United States 1970 census, Hollywood Park had a population of 2,299, a substantial increase from the 783 reported in 1960. *See also* San Antonio Standard Metropolitan Statistical Area.

Holman, Eugene. Eugene Holman, geologist and chief executive officer of Standard Oil Company (New Jersey) from 1944 to 1960, was born in San Angelo on May 2, 1895, the son of James and Geneva (Moore) Holman. He lived in Monahans until 1912, when he entered Simmons College (now Hardin-Simmons University), Abilene. After earning a B.A. degree in 1916, he studied at the University of Texas, where he received an M.A. degree in geology in 1917. After a short employment with Producers Oil Company in Cuba, Holman joined the United States Army Air Service in 1918. In 1920 he began working for Humble Oil and Refining Company qv in Houston, and by 1925 he was chief geologist. In 1929 Standard Oil Company (New Jersey) employed Holman in New York in its foreign producing department. In 1939 Holman was selected to reorganize the company's marine department, and in 1940 he was elected to the Standard Oil Company (New Jersey) board of directors. In 1944 he became president and chief executive officer and from 1954 to 1960 was chairman of the board and chief executive officer. He retired in 1960.

Holman was a member of the American Association of Petroleum Geology, American Institute of Mechanical Engineers, the Mining and Metallurgical Society, and the Explorers Club. He wrote three articles for the *American Association of Petroleum Geologists Bulletin*. In November, 1923, he married Edith Carver Reid, and they had two children. Holman died on August 12, 1962, in New York City.

BIBLIOGRAPHY: Wallace E. Pratt, "Memorial," *American Association of Petroleum Geologists Bulletin*, XLVII (May, 1963).

Karen *Collins*

*Holman, James S.

*Holman, William W.

*Holman, Texas.

*Holmes, Edward L.

*Holmes, Thomas.

*Holmes, Willet.

*Holmes, Texas.

*Holmsley, James M. James Monroe Holmsley

was born on April 4, 1838, in Richland Township, Madison County, Arkansas, and died on April 28, 1881 (not 1898, as stated in Volume I), at Comanche, Texas. He was buried in Oakwood Cemetery in Comanche.

BIBLIOGRAPHY: Picture File, Barker Texas History Center, University of Texas at Austin.

*Holsinger, Juan José. Juan José Holsinger died on May 9, 1864, and was buried in Mexico City. His tombstone there carries a different spelling of his last name, reading "Juan J. Holzinger."

Andrew Forest *Muir*

*Holt, Benjamin.

*Holt, Texas.

*Holtke Hill.

*Holton, Gideon Nathaniel.

Holy Cross Sisters. *See* Sisters, Holy Cross.

Holy Ghost and Mary Immaculate, Sister-Servants of the. *See* Sister-Servants of the Holy Ghost and Mary Immaculate.

*Homan, William Kercheval.

*Home Creek.

*Homer, Texas.

*Homestead Grants.

*Homestead Law. By constitutional amendment adopted in 1970 the value of the urban homestead was raised from $5,000 to $10,000 without reference to improvements. In November, 1973, another constitutional amendment was adopted whereby a single adult was given the same homestead right as that given to the head of a family.

Joseph W. *McKnight*

*Homewood, Texas.

*Honabanou Indians.

*Hondo, Texas. Hondo, seat of Medina County, is on the Old San Antonio Road.qv The town had a new post office and a city-county hospital completed in the 1960's. Among its 100 businesses in 1970 were industries which produced porcelain bath fixtures, brick and tile, shelled pecans, and processed feeds. The 1960 population was 4,992; the United States census report showed that the population increased to 5,487 by 1970.

*Hondo Army Air Field.

*Hondo Creek.

*Hondo Pass.

*Honey, George W.

*Honey Creek.

*Honey Creek, Texas.

*Honey Grove, Texas. Honey Grove, in Fannin County, had in the 1960's a garment plant and various agribusinesses. According to the 1970 census the town had a population of 1,853, a decrease from the 2,071 reported in the 1960 census. In 1970 the city had forty-two businesses.

*Honey Grove Creek.

*Honey Island, Texas.

*Honey Springs, Texas.

*Hood, John Bell. John Bell Hood succeeded Joseph Eggleston Johnston qv (not Albert Sidney Johnston,qv as stated in Volume I) in command of the Confederate Army of Tennessee on July 18, 1864, and was later replaced in that command by the same Joseph Eggleston Johnston.

BIBLIOGRAPHY: Thomas Robson Hay, *Hood's Tennessee Campaign* (1929).

*Hood, Joseph L.

*Hood, Texas.

*Hood County. Hood County was chiefly a ranching and stock-farming area, with limited farming of peanuts, pecans, and grains. Acton State Park and the site of Fort Spunky qv are in the southeastern corner of the county. In 1960 the population was 5,443; the 1970 census showed a population increase to 6,368.

*Hoodoo War. *See* Mason County War.

*Hood's Texas Brigade.

*Hookersville, Texas.

*Hooks, Texas. Hooks post office, in Bowie County, was established on April 9, 1884, with James Smith serving as postmaster in that year (not in 1894, as stated in Volume I). The population of Hooks increased from 2,048 in 1960 to 2,545 in 1970. The city had forty businesses in 1970.

Cyrus Tilloson

*Hooks's Switch, Texas.

*Hooleyan, Texas.

*Hooper, Richard.

*Hooper Creek.

*Hoover, Texas. (Gray County.)

*Hoover, Texas. (Guadalupe County.)

*Hoover Knobs.

*Hoover's Valley, Texas.

*Hope, James.

*Hope, Texas.

*Hopes Creek.

*Hopewell, Texas.

*Hopewell Institute.

*Hopkins, David.

*Hopkins, Desmond Pulaski.

*Hopkins, Edwin Butcher.

*Hopkins, Matthew.

*Hopkins County. Hopkins County by 1968 had gained a new post office building, several schools, a water plant and system, a library, and a hospital. Hopkins was the leading dairy county in the state with 39,400 dairy cows in 1970; milk sales amounted to over 90 percent of the farm income. The production of grains, cotton, and hay contributed to the total farm income of over $28 million annually in the early 1970's. Total oil production from 1936 to January 1, 1973, was nearly 59,000,000 barrels. The livestock show in March and the dairy show in May are annual affairs. The 1960 population of 18,594 increased to 20,710 by 1970.

*Hopkinsville, Texas.

Hoppin, Agustus. Agustus Hoppin, born in Providence, Rhode Island, in 1828, the son of Thomas Cole and Harriet (Jones) Hoppin, was a participant in the Bartlett Survey of the western boundary of Texas as an illustrator. (*See* Bartlett, John Russell.) He had been educated at Brown University and Harvard Law School, but at the beginning of law practice he turned to illustrating books and magazines, among which were Oliver Wendell Holmes' *Autocrat of the Breakfast Table*, Washington Irving's *Sketch Book*, and Mark Twain's *Gilded Age*. On the Bartlett Survey, which he joined in 1850, Hoppin sketched in a humorous vein, choosing subjects that appealed to his mood. Happenings on Bartlett's route between Fredericksburg and Horsehead Crossing,qv on the Pecos in West Texas, are the essence of what might have appealed to the recorder of the local scene. Hoppin's work is simple, light, and effective, with little or no shading. Included in the report of the survey are Hoppin's drawings of "Prairie-Dog Town" and "Stampede of Wild Horses." The artist died in 1896.

BIBLIOGRAPHY: John Russell Bartlett, *Personal Narrative of Explorations and Incidents in Texas, New Mexico, California, Sonora, and Chihuahua*, I, II (1965); Pauline A. Pinckney, *Painting in Texas: The Nineteenth Century* (1967).

Pauline A. Pinckney

*Hord, William H.

*Hord Creek.

*Hords Creek.

*Hords Creek Reservoir. Hords Creek Reservoir is in the Colorado River Basin in Coleman County, five miles northwest of Valera on Hords Creek. The dam was started in February, 1947, and was completed in June, 1948, with deliberate impoundment of water beginning in April, 1948. In 1967 the reservoir had a conservation capacity of 8,640 acre-feet and a surface area of 510 acres at elevation 1,900 feet above mean sea level. Capacity at the crest of the emergency spillway was 25,310 acre-feet in 1967. The drainage area above the dam was forty-eight square miles.

BIBLIOGRAPHY: Texas Water Commission, *Bulletin 6408* (1964).

Seth D. Breeding

*Horger, Texas.

*Horn, Paul Whitfield.

*Horn Hill, Texas.

*Horne Branch.

*Hornica Creek.

*Hornsby, Reuben.

Hornsby, Rogers. Rogers Hornsby, son of Edward and Mary Dallas (Rogers) Hornsby, has been called the greatest right-hand hitter in the history of professional baseball. Born on April 27, 1896, on his father's Hereford cattle ranch near Winters, Texas, he played with Hugo, Oklahoma, and then Denison, Texas, in the lower minor leagues. When the St. Louis Cardinals purchased his contract for $500 in 1915, he went to the major leagues, beginning an illustrious career. At the time he weighed only 130 pounds, so he spent a winter at an uncle's farm near Lockhart, where he added thirty-five pounds. During his first full season in the major leagues he batted .313, a remarkably high figure for that era of dead ball.

Hornsby was one of the most controversial characters in baseball history. Although he did not drink, smoke, or otherwise dissipate, he was a compulsive horse player whose gambling activities frequently caused run-ins with baseball management. He read nothing but newspaper headlines, attended no movies, and did nothing to weaken his "batting" eyes or to interfere with his being in top physical condition at all times. One writer characterized him as "a liturgy of hatred." His only interest was in winning, so that he was as sarcastic and uncompromising with club owners as he was with careless players.

Hornsby managed five major league baseball clubs, being dismissed from each as the result of disagreement. He led the National League in batting seven times and batted over .400 in three years. In the successive years of 1921–1925 his batting averages were .397, .401, .384, .424 (a modern record), and .403, which Arthur Daley of the New York *Times* called "the most unbelievable period of batting greatness in baseball history." He always disclaimed any ability as a home run hitter, but twice led the National League in home runs with forty-two in 1922 and thirty-nine in 1925. His lifetime home run total was 301, part of it compiled during the dead ball era. He managed the St. Louis Cardinals to their first world championship in 1926. His lifetime batting average was .358, the highest in National League history and second only to the .367 of Ty Cobb. He was named most valuable player of the National League in 1925 and 1929. In 1942 he was elected to baseball's Hall of Fame. He was also named to the Texas Sports Hall of Fame.qv He earned approximately $750,000 in the days when income taxes were negligible.

Hornsby married three times and was the father of two sons. He died on January 6, 1963, in Chicago, of a heart attack following an operation for cataracts. A descendant of the pioneer Reuben Hornsby,qv Rogers Hornsby was buried at Hornsby Bend, Texas, a few miles east of Austin, in the old family cemetery. Commenting on his burial in central Texas, one eastern writer remarked on the irony of Hornsby's being interred "700 miles from the nearest big-time race track."

BIBLIOGRAPHY: Rogers Hornsby (J. Roy Stockton, ed.), *My Kind of Baseball* (1953); Rogers Hornsby and Bill Surface, *My War with Baseball* (1962).

Joe B. Frantz

*Hornsby Bend, Texas.

*Horrell-Higgins Feud.

*Horse Breeding. Because of the decline in the number of horses and mules on Texas farms, the census was no longer taken after the year 1950, when 387,393 horses and colts, and 128,558 mules and mule colts were reported. This compared with the 1,393,863 horses and 526,651 mules reported in the census of 1900.

However, this trend was reversed during the 1960's because of the recreational demand for horses. Texas A&M University authorities estimated that there were approximately 400,000 horses used for recreational, ranching, and breeding purposes. Mules were almost entirely replaced by tractors.

Western (or Quarter) Horses.

In the 1960's, despite the rising popularity of the Arabian and the Appaloosa, the Quarter Horse continued its reign in Texas. With 497,302 nationally registered Quarter Horses in the United States at the beginning of 1968, Texas had more than twice the number of any other state. The revival of Quarter Horse racing stimulated interest in the breed, and thoroughbred and Quarter Horse breeding received special attention at the King Ranch qv and several other places. Texas sprinters took part in many short races in other states, including the Labor Day All-American Futurity at Ruidoso Downs, New Mexico, where the purse was the largest offered in the country. In 1965 winnings totaled more than four hundred thousand dollars.

Interest in cutting horses culminated in the National Cutting Horse Association Futurity, established in 1962 and held each December since. Although the first two races were held in Sweetwater, the futurity was transferred to Dallas in 1964 to attract more entries. Limited to three-year-olds, this futurity offered a 1965 purse richer than the combined purses of the other top five cutting horse events in 1964. The 1968 competition, with a purse of $95,730, drew 230 horses from twenty-five states and Canada.

Prices for outstanding Quarter Horses continued to rise. In 1962 at Broken Arrow, Oklahoma, C. D. Johnson of Amarillo set a new auction price record by paying $86,000 for Clabber Bar, an eight-year-old sorrel stallion. A Texas stallion, Go Man Go, brought $125,000 at a private sale. (*See also* Clegg, George Austin.)

Work Horses.

With the increasing use of tractors on Texas farms, the number of work horses declined. In 1920 there were 991,362 horses used in agriculture; the figure had dropped to 387,393 by 1950. The number steadily declined, and by 1960 a combined total of only 218,000 horses and mules were used on Texas farms.

BIBLIOGRAPHY: *Quarter Horse Journal* (October, 1962, August, 1965, October, 1965, January, 1966); *Texas Almanac* (1948, 1955, 1965, 1969); *Texas Horseman* (May, 1960).

Wayne Gard

*Horse Creek.

*Horse Hollow.

*Horse Marines.

*Horse Mountain.

*Horse Pen Bayou.

*Horse Thief Canyon.

*Horse Thief Mountain.

*Horsehead Crossing. By 1975 there were two metal markers and one old granite monument commemorating Horsehead Crossing. One metal marker was located ten miles northwest of Girvin, in Pecos County, on the east side of Farm to Market Road 11 at an intersection with a gravel road, three miles from the crossing itself. On the riverbank, immediately north of the crossing, is the old granite marker, badly damaged, which was placed there in 1936, approximately ten to thirteen miles (not twenty miles, as stated in Volume I) northwest of Girvin, in Pecos County.

The second metal marker was located in the extreme southeast corner of Crane County, on U.S. Highway 67 about two miles east of the Pecos River, in a rest area that is twelve miles from the crossing itself. [The second monument mentioned in Volume I, "five miles east of Crane in Crane County," is not a proper identification, since five miles east of Crane would be in Upton County. There is no record of such a marker having been placed. Ed.]

Earl Ingerson

*Horsepen Creek.

*Horseshoe Mesa.

*Hortense, Texas. (Hidalgo County.)

*Hortense, Texas. (Polk County.)

*Horticulture. *See* Agriculture.

*Horton, Albert Clinton. Albert Clinton Horton was acting governor of Texas from May 19, 1846, to November, 1846, or perhaps as late as December, 1846 (but not July 1, 1847, as stated in Volume I).

BIBLIOGRAPHY: James T. DeShields, *They Sat In High Places* (1940); "Texas Collection," *Southwestern Historical Quarterly*, XLIX (1945–1946).

*Horton, Alexander.

*Horton, Texas. (Delta County.)

*Horton, Texas. (Jasper County.)

*Horton Gravel Railroad Company.

*Horton Town, Texas. *See* Neighborsville, Texas.

*Hoshall, Texas.

*Hoskins, Texas.

*Hospitals, State. *See* Austin State Hospital; Big Spring State Hospital; Dallas State Mental Health Clinic; East Texas Chest Hospital; Fort Worth State Mental Health Clinic; Harlingen State Chest Hospital; Harlingen State Mental Health Clinic; Kerrville State Hospital; Rio Grande State Center for Mental Health and Mental Retardation; Rusk State Hospital; San Antonio State Hospital; San Antonio State Chest Hospital; Terrell State Hospital; Texas Research Institute of Mental Sciences; Vernon Center; Wichita Falls State Hospital; *see also* Eleemosynary Institutions (in Volume I); Mentally Ill and Mentally Retarded, Care of, in Texas.

*Hostyn, Texas.

*Hot Oil.

*Hot Spring Creek.

*Hot Springs, Texas.

*Hot Sulphur Wells, Texas.

*Hot Wells, Texas.

*Hotchkiss, Archibald.

Houaneiha Indians. The Houaneiha Indians are known only from documents of the La Salle Expedition,qv in which they are identified as enemies of the Kadohadacho Caddo in the late seventeenth century. It is possible that they lived north of Red River and only entered present Texas to attack the Kadohadacho.

BIBLIOGRAPHY: F. W. Hodge (ed.), *Handbook of American Indians*, I (1907); P. Margry, *Découvertes et établissements des Français dans l'ouest et dans le sud de l'Amérique Septentrionale 1614–1698*, III (1879).

T. N. Campbell

House, Boyce. Boyce House was born in Piggott, Arkansas, on November 29, 1896, son of Noah E. and Margaret (O'Brien) House. House's family moved to Brownwood, Texas, when he was nine years old. At the age of nineteen he began his newspaper career, working on the staff of the Memphis *Commercial Appeal*. From 1919 to 1920 he operated his own paper, the Piggott (Arkansas) *Banner*. Returning to Texas, he worked as editor and reporter for the Eastland *Oil Belt News*, and later as a reporter in Ranger. House edited newspapers in the Texas oil field areas for more than ten years. Several of his books were about the oil rush in Texas, and much of his writing was based on material gathered in boom towns. He wrote of the human side of oil field life, concentrating on the people and their reactions to oil fever. House was technical adviser on the motion picture *Boom Town*.

He reached an estimated 300,000 people with his radio program in the early 1940's. While building interest in Texas history and legends, he also gave a wide audience to Texas poets by reading their poems on his programs. His column "I Give You Texas" was carried by approximately two hundred Texas newspapers. In addition, he contributed articles to the *Saturday Evening Post* and poetry to numerous anthologies. He was also well known for his compilations of Texas jokes.

He was a member of the Texas Folklore Society, the Poetry Society of Texas, the Texas Institute of Letters,qqv and the Texas Editorial Association. He died on December 30, 1961, in Fort Worth.

BIBLIOGRAPHY: *American Authors and Books* (1962); Don Morris, "Texas Booster," *Life* (March 17, 1947); *Publishers' Weekly* (January 29, 1962); *Who's Who In America* (1960).

Virginia Holliman Van Horn

*House, Edward Mandell.

*House, Robert Ernest.

*House, Thomas William.

*House, Texas.

*House of Barr and Davenport. *See* Barr and Davenport, House of.

*House Creek.

*House Mountain.

*House Mountain Branch.

*House Mountains.

*Housen Bayou.

*Houses. *See* articles under Architecture.

*Housetop Mountain.

*Housing Creek.

Housing Programs. *See* Community Affairs, Department of.

*Houston.

*Houston, Andrew Jackson. Andrew Jackson Houston was buried in the State Cemetery qv at Austin (not at the San Jacinto battlefield, as stated in Volume I).

*Houston, David Franklin.

Houston, Margaret Bell. Margaret Bell Houston, daughter of Lucy (Anderson) and Sam Houston, Jr.,qv and granddaughter of Sam Houston, was born at Cedar Bayou, Texas, in 1877. She was educated in the public schools and at St. Mary's College in Dallas, Texas. She wrote her first volume of poetry at age eleven. By the turn of the century she was widely known as a contributor of short stories and serials to reputable magazines.

Success in her writing ventures led her to New York, where she studied drama at the American Academy of Dramatic Arts and attended Columbia University. Later she moved to St. Petersburg, Florida. During her writing career she wrote some twenty novels and three collections of verse.

She was married twice, first to M. L. Kauffman and then to William H. Probert. She had one daughter, Katrina Kauffman, who predeceased her. Margaret Bell Houston died in St. Petersburg on June 22, 1966, and was buried at Restland Cemetery in Dallas.

BIBLIOGRAPHY: Vaida Stewart Montgomery, *A Century with Texas Poets and Poetry* (1934); St. Petersburg (Florida) *Times*, April 17, 1955, September 7, 1959; *Who's Who of American Women* (1958).

W. E. Bard

*Houston, Margaret Moffétte Lea.

*Houston, Sam.

*Houston, Sam, Jr.

*Houston, Temple Lea.

*Houston, Texas. (Anderson County.)

*Houston, Texas. (Harris County.) In 1970 Houston was the largest city in Texas and the South, the sixth largest city in the United States, and the third largest seaport (in terms of tonnage) in the nation. Located about fifty miles northwest of Galveston and the Gulf of Mexico in southeastern Texas, Houston, called the Bayou City, doubled its population in the twenty years between 1950 and 1970.

In 1950 the corporate city limits of Houston enclosed 160 square miles and 596,163 people (not 594,321, as stated in Volume I). At that time it was the fourteenth largest city in the United States. The United States census report for 1960 showed an increase in population to 938,219, making Houston the nation's seventh largest city. In 1970, according to the United States census, Houston's population had reached 1,232,802 (sixth largest in the United States), while the population in the Houston metropolitan area, 6,258 square miles which included Harris, Brazoria, Fort Bend, Liberty, and Montgomery counties, numbered 1,985,031 (*see* Houston Standard Metropolitan Statistical Area for the metropolitan area's growth between 1950 and 1970).

The seat of Harris County, Houston was the foremost manufacturing center in the state, a focal point for oil, gas, and petrochemical industries, and the world's leading producer of oilfield equipment. It was the most thoroughly air-conditioned city in the world—a response to high humidity, caused in part by a forty-six-inch annual rainfall, and high temperature, which ranges from an average forty-five degrees in January to ninety-three degrees in July. In Houston the timber and prairie regions of the county meet, with tall pines gracing the northwestern segment and the prairie predominating elsewhere. The flatness of the land has allowed an uninhibited urban spread in all directions.

Augustus Chapman Allen and John Kirby Allen,qqv two land speculators from New York, first introduced Texans to the new town of Houston through an advertisement on August 30, 1836, in the *Telegraph and Texas Register*,qv a bi-weekly newspaper published at Columbia. The two brothers, after purchasing the land, shrewdly named their town after a friend and hero of the moment, Sam Houston.qv (They did not intend the Houston site as a replacement for Harrisburg, as stated in Volume I, for they made an unsuccessful attempt to buy the burned village of Harrisburg, which had started to revive.) They employed Gail and Thomas Borden qqv to plat the site, and they promoted the place as a possible location for a new capital of the young Republic. Located on the banks of Buffalo Bayou, eight miles above Harrisburg, Houston could serve as a gateway between the cotton-rich Brazos Valley and Galveston, which in 1836 offered the best prospect for a deepwater port. Fortunately for the Allens the Texas legislature selected their town over fourteen others as the temporary seat of government. Thus overnight Houston became the most important town in Texas, even though at the time it was practically uninhabited. In January, 1837, the first steamboat, *Laura*,qv arrived, proving that the bayou was navigable, and during the spring, as several hundred people followed, a tent city arose to shelter the immigrants. The Allens erected an extended one-story wooden building called the Long Row, which was used by merchants, and they constructed a wooden capitol to quarter the government.

Local businessmen Thomas M. Bagby, Charles Shearn, William Marsh Rice, William J. Hutchins, Paul Bremond,qqv and A. S. Ruthven established trade connections with New York, Baltimore, Mobile, and New Orleans. Deep-draft vessels docking at Galveston transferred cargoes to smaller steamboats which plied the waters of Galveston Bay and Buffalo Bayou. Houston merchants thereby assembled for sale such items as coffee, flour, sugar, salt, nails, gun powder, soap, books, plows, cotton gins, ice, bricks, and medicine. In turn, from the interior (especially from the Brazos Valley), ox-drawn wagons brought cotton and hides for transshipment to the United States and elsewhere. The *Telegraph and Texas Register* began publication in Houston on May 2, 1837 (initial publication occurring on October 10, 1835, at San Felipe de Austin). The *Morning Star* qv began publication on April 8, 1839, thus qualifying as the second Houston newspaper (not the first, as stated in Volume I). Both papers reflected local interest in the cotton brokerage business, roads, railways, and projects to clear the bayou.

The legislature first met in Houston on May 1, 1837. It attempted soon after to improve Houston society by passing an anti-gambling law, and on June 5, 1837, it granted incorporation to Houston. Despite ordinances by the newly formed city council, the civilizing influence of the Masons, who first met in 1837 (*see* Freemasonry in Texas), and the strictures of the Presbyterians and the Episcopalians, who formed churches in 1839, Houston remained a rough frontier town in which drunkenness, dueling, brawling, speculation, counterfeiting, prostitution, and profanity prevailed. In 1838 John Herndon qv summarized conditions in Houston by calling it "the greatest sink of dissipation [*sic*] and vice that modern times have known."

Prompted apparently by the climate, the mud, the poor accommodations, the annual threat of yellow fever, and perhaps the desire for fresh land speculation, the legislators voted in 1839 to abandon Houston as the capital for the charms of Waterloo, a small western village shortly to be renamed Austin. Despite the removal of the government and a yellow fever epidemic which contributed to the 240 deaths in the latter half of 1839, Houston, which had an estimated population of two thousand, recovered as cold weather set in and the pattern of trade asserted itself. The Texas legislature permitted incorporation of a Houston chamber of commerce in January, 1840. Jacob de Cordova, Francis Lubbock, Henry Kesler,qqv E. S. Perkins, and John Carlos were early city leaders. The city council created a board of health in March, 1840, to help prevent future epidemics and on June 8, 1841, created the port of Houston. In spite of sporadic dredging which brought some improvement in the 1840's and 1850's, Buffalo Bayou remained almost impassable, with collisions, snagging, and grounding on sand bars occurring as common events.

Transportation facilities improved, however, when the Buffalo Bayou, Brazos, and Colorado Railway connected Harrisburg with Stafford's Point in 1853 and with the Brazos Valley in 1856. In 1856 Houston negated this threat to its future with the seven-mile long Houston Tap Railroad, which effectively "tapped" the Harrisburg line at Pierce Junction, thereby diverting traffic. Also in 1853, the Galveston and Red River Railroad (its name was changed in 1856 to the Houston and Texas Central), owned by Paul Bremond, began stretching to the northwest, reaching Hempstead in 1858. (Construction of this railway did not begin in 1858, as stated in Volume I.) In 1860 the Galveston, Houston, and Henderson Railroad spanned Galveston Bay, connecting Houston and Galveston. By 1861 Houston possessed rail connections southeast to Galveston, southwest to Columbia, west to Alleyton, northwest to Millican, and east to Beaumont.

The Civil War interrupted commercial growth, but the Confederacy placed an arsenal in the city, turned the courthouse into a cartridge factory, and used Houston as a distribution point. As the Union blockade became more effective and the strength of the South ebbed, inflation set in and commerce practically halted. With the collapse of the Confederacy, Houston was filled with refugees, restless soldiers, and freedmen. By the time the 34th Iowa Regiment and five companies of the 114th Ohio Regiment occupied the town, the treasury was empty, and Houston reflected the bitterness and confusion of the defeated South. Local leaders ignored sanitation, and in 1867 the city suffered one of its worst yellow fever epidemics.

In 1873 the Houston and Texas Central Railway reached Denison, giving the city rail connections with the North. In the 1870's major lines such as the Southern Pacific and the International and Great Northern connected with Houston, making the Bayou City a railroad center for the Southwest. The battle with the obstreperous bayou reopened during the Reconstruction qv era as leading citizens promoted a series of organizations—the Houston Direct Navigation Company,qv Houston Ship Channel Company (*see* Houston Ship Channel), and Buffalo Bayou Ship Channel Company—to dredge the channel to nine feet, eliminate snags, and remove sand bars. Hope soared in 1876, when Charles Morgan qv of the powerful Morgan Steamship Company (*see* Morgan Lines) completed a cut through Morgan's Point to permit his large steamboats to reach Houston's port. Morgan, however, placed a chain across the cut and exacted a toll. The Morgan Company, moreover, diverted freight to its railroads in 1880, and Galveston improved its harbor in 1896, thereby tarnishing the hopes of Houstonians for a prosperous ship channel.

By 1890 the population reached 27,557, which compared to 2,396 in 1850; 4,845 in 1860; 9,382 in 1870; and 16,513 in 1880. Houston then possessed 210 manufacturing companies, including four lumber firms, three ice factories, four foundries, four saddleries, and seven carriage and wagon establishments. The value added by manufacturing amounted to $3,195,000. Houston also boasted a mule-powered trolley system, several blocks of stone-paved streets, a public school system, a few telephone lines, and electric lighting for Main Street. However, George Clark Rankin,qv a Methodist minister who arrived in 1892, found Houston an insignificant town, possessing a malodorous bayou and intolerable mud.

In 1900 Houston's population reached 44,633, and by 1902 citizens had pushed back the mud with thirty-one miles of paved streets and an automatic street sweeper. Following the lead of Galveston, Houston adopted a commission form of government in 1905, but changed to a city-manager type in 1942 and to a mayor-council plan in 1947. Electric street cars replaced the mules in the 1890's, and in 1911 an electric interurban line connected Houston and Galveston. In 1912 Rice Institute opened its doors, enabling worthy Houston students the chance to attend college without paying tuition. South Texas Law School began in 1923; Houston Junior College, destined to become in 1934 the University of Houston, began in 1927; and Houston College for Negroes, which eventually became Texas Southern University, began in 1934 as part of the University of Houston. In 1914 George H. Hermann qv donated Hermann Park, which received a thirty-acre zoo in 1922. The city was ceded land for Memorial Park in 1924, the same year that River Oaks, which became Houston's most affluent residential section, was started. The public library, which was initiated in 1899, opened its doors in 1904 and moved to its present location in 1926. In 1913 the Symphony Society was formed, and in 1924 the Houston Museum of Fine Arts qv was opened. By 1930 Houston possessed three major newspapers—Houston *Post* (founded 1880), Houston *Chronicle* (1901), and Houston *Press* qqv (1911)—and four radio stations—KPRC (1925), KTRH (1930), KTLC (1930), and KXYZ (1930). The selection of Houston by the Democratic party as the national convention site for 1928 symbolized the growing importance of the city, which by 1930 had become the largest urban center in Texas. Its population had increased from 78,800 in 1910 to 138,276 in 1920, and then more than doubled by 1930 to 292,352.

The Bayou City's remarkable growth in the early twentieth century resulted primarily from the development of the ship channel and the oil industry. Agitation for a deepwater port led by Joseph Chappell Hutcheson, Thomas William House, Eber Worthington Cave, Thomas Henry Ball,qqv W. D. Cleveland, and others ultimately resulted in a channel eighteen feet deep, cut by the federal government in 1908. By November 10, 1914, the channel was deepened to twenty-five feet as a result of a joint federal and Harris County project. (Federal participation in channel development began in 1902, not after 1914, as stated in Volume I.) Although the two world wars temporarily curtailed growth, the Houston Ship Channel, periodically improved, experienced rapid expansion of business. By 1950 the port, second largest in the nation (although it fell to third in the 1960's), had become noted for grain, cotton, and oil exports. It contributed about 11 percent of Harris County income and served as the entrepôt for midcontinental United States.

Houston evolved as an oil center following the Spindletop Oil Field qv discovery in 1901 and the discoveries at Humble Oil Field in 1904, Pierce Junction in 1906, and Goose Creek Oil Field qqv in 1908. By 1929 there were forty oil companies with offices in Houston, the most important being the Texas Company (now Texaco Inc.), Humble Oil and Refining Company (now Exxon Company, U.S.A.), and Gulf Oil Corporation.qqv Sinclair Oil Company erected the first major refinery in Houston in 1918. Others followed and crude oil became the lifeblood of the Houston economy. The expanding oil activity of South Texas helped Houston endure the nationwide depression during the 1930's.

It is generally considered that Houston suffered less than many cities during the depression. The tonnage of the port dropped slightly in 1931 and 1932 but recovered strongly in 1933; bank clearings set a record of $2,000,000,000 in 1937; and no Houston bank failed. Nonetheless, from 1935 to 1936 the Works Progress Administration qv employed 12,000 people in Harris County and dispensed about $4,250,000 for a variety of road, water, school, and recreation projects, including development of Memorial Park and the San Jacinto Monument and Museum.qv In 1939 the agency still employed 4,900 persons in Harris County. By 1940 Houston's population was 384,514.

With the demands of World War II, the Houston economy surged ahead with $27,000,000 in defense contracts in December, 1940, and $83,000,000 the following February. The McEvoy Company, which made machine gun mounts, received the first prime contract, but Humble Oil obtained the first large contract—$19,000,000 for constructing a toluol plant at Baytown. Construction of concrete barges, steel merchant ships, and medium-sized war vessels became Houston's major activity. Houston Shipbuilding Corporation, a subsidiary of Todd Shipbuilding Corporation, leased Irish Bend Island in Buffalo Bayou in 1941, filled in the unused portion of the bayou to connect with the mainland, and began to produce steel merchant ships. Employment burgeoned from 6,000 in March, 1942, to almost 20,000 in July, 1942. The company reduced construction time for Liberty ships from 240 days to 45 days and launched its two-hundredth vessel in February, 1945. The other major Houston firm, Brown Shipbuilding Company, pioneered new techniques such as broadside launching at its Greens Bayou shipyard. In April, 1945, Brown, a subsidiary of Brown and Root, launched its three-hundredth warship.

Under the urgency of war the Armco-owned Sheffield steel plant, constructed in 1941, expanded to permit production from raw materials sent from

Mexico, Texas, and Oklahoma. It thus became the only fully integrated steel producer between the Mississippi River and the Rocky Mountains. The war also accelerated the growth of a Houston area chemical industry. Utilizing petroleum, sulphur, salt, gas, and sea water, such companies as Du Pont, Dow, Shell, Sinclair, Humble, Monsanto, and Goodyear produced plastics, magnesium, lubricants, materials for explosives, aviation gasoline, and fuel oil. The value of chemical products in the area skyrocketed from $30,000,000 in 1939 to $750,000,000 in 1949.

Closely related to this development was the rise of the natural gas industry, which in 1943 was relatively insignificant in Texas. Tennessee Gas Transmission Company placed 1,265 miles of pipeline into operation in October, 1944, to supply West Virginia and by 1950 had increased its capacity five times. After the war Texas Eastern Transmission Company, another Houston-based firm, bought the "Big Inch" and "Little Inch" pipelines to supply much of the eastern and midwestern portions of the nation.

Following World War II the business boom of the early 1940's continued, and the face of the city changed as new buildings went up, shopping centers blossomed, and new homes dotted the outskirts of the city. The chamber of commerce estimated a total of $427,000,000 for planned construction in April, 1946. Downtown merchants—Battlestein's, Sakowitz, Joske's, and Foley's—embarked on impressive building programs. Most impressive to the public was the value of real estate, when in 1946 downtown property for a new Woolworth store was sold at over $2,000 per front inch. Symbolic of the postwar building surge was the opening of the Shamrock Hotel in 1949. Built five miles from the downtown section by oil-wildcatter Glenn McCarthy, the $21,000,000 structure helped shift business activity southward along Main Street. Resplendent in sixty-three shades of green, the Shamrock, which opened in a blare of national publicity, represented great faith in the future. By 1970 that area of Houston had an impressive array of new buildings, and business interests were widespread throughout the city. For additional information on Houston and its metropolitan area from 1949 to 1970, see Houston Standard Metropolitan Statistical Area.

BIBLIOGRAPHY: Benajah Harvey Carroll (ed.), *Standard History of Houston, Texas* (1912); A. Pat Daniel, *Texas Avenue at Main Street* (1964); George Fuermann, *Houston: Land of the Big Rich* (1951), *Houston: the Feast Years* (1962), and *The Face of Houston* (1963); Ed Kilman and Theon Wright, *Hugh Roy Cullen: A Study of American Opportunity* (1954); Henrietta Larson and Kenneth W. Porter, *History of Humble Oil and Refining Company* (1959); David G. McComb, *Houston, the Bayou City* (1969); Marilyn McAdams Sibley, *The Port of Houston: A History* (1968); Bascom N. Timmons, *Jesse H. Jones: The Man and the Statesman* (1956); S. O. Young, *A Thumb-Nail History of the City of Houston, Texas* (1912) and *True Stories of Old Houston and Houstonians* (1913); Jesse A. Ziegler, *Wave of the Gulf* (1938); Writers' Program of the Work Projects Administration, *Houston: A History and Guide* (1942).

David G. McComb

*Houston Academy.

Houston Astros (Baseball Club). Houston was awarded a major league professional baseball franchise in the National League in October, 1960, when the league expanded from eight to ten teams. The Houston Sports Association received the franchise after operating the Houston Buff franchise in the American Association in 1961 and promising to build a new baseball park and an air-conditioned domed stadium. The club was first called the Houston Colt .45s, and held spring training in Apache Junction, Arizona, opening the first season on April 10, 1962, in Colt Stadium. In 1964 the club changed its spring training site to Cocoa, Florida. In 1965 the club changed its name to the Houston Astros and moved into the Astrodome.qv

Roy Hofheinz, a guiding force in the Houston Sports Association, purchased additional stock from his former partner, R. E. (Bob) Smith, in 1965, and became majority stockholder of the multimillion dollar venture. The ball club finished a surprising eighth in 1962 (64–96), ninth in 1963, 1964, and 1965, and eighth in 1966 (72–90). Official paid attendance the first year was 924,456. It dropped to slightly more than 700,000 in each of the next two years, increased to 2,151,470 the first year in the Astrodome, and dropped to 1,872,108 in 1966. In 1972 the Houston Astros had their best season up to that date, with a won-lost record of 84–69.

Wayne Chandler

*Houston and Austin Turnpike Company.

Houston Baptist University. Houston Baptist College (renamed Houston Baptist University in November, 1973), in Houston, was chartered in 1960 by the Baptist General Convention of Texas as a Christian four-year liberal arts college, the culmination of efforts of a college committee authorized in 1952. The college opened in September, 1963, with a freshman class of 191 students; a new class was added each year through 1966. For the term 1974–1975, enrollment had reached 1,216. Situated near the intersection of Southwest Freeway and Fondren Road in southwest Houston, facilities on the two-hundred-acre campus included two residence halls, theology building, physical education center, president's home, and academic quadrangle (containing administrative offices, classrooms, student center, cafeteria, library, and Denham Hall). Master plans called for addition of a fine arts complex, science building, library, chapel, and residence hall. The faculty increased each year, maintaining a ratio of one member to every seventeen students. Curriculum was maintained under six academic divisions: Christianity, education and psychology, languages, fine arts, science and mathematics, and social studies. Library holdings included about 50,000 volumes in 1969. Endowment funds from individuals and churches totaled more than $543,000 in 1964 and had grown to $3,500,000 by 1975. Physical worth of the university was estimated in excess of $22,000,000 in 1975. William H. Hinton served as first president of the institution and was still president in 1975.

*Houston Belt and Magnolia Park Railway. *See* Houston, Oaklawn, and Magnolia Park Railroad.

*Houston Belt and Terminal Railway Company. In the mid-1960's, all capital stock of the Houston Belt and Terminal Railway Company was owned by the Gulf, Colorado, and Santa Fe; the Missouri-Pacific; the Fort Worth and Denver; and the Chicago, Rock Island, and Pacific, which also leased the company. The Houston Belt and Terminal Railway Company owned the Union Passenger station in Houston and operated 13.1 miles of terminal track.

James M. Day

*Houston and Brazos Valley Railway.

*Houston *Chronicle.* Jesse H. Jones,qv owner of the Houston *Chronicle*, died in 1956, leaving the *Chronicle* and other Jones properties to Houston Endowment Inc., a philanthropic organization. Jones' nephew, John T. Jones, Jr., became president. In March, 1964, the Houston *Chronicle* purchased the physical assets of the Houston *Press*,qv which was liquidated by Scripps-Howard. Historical editions published by the *Chronicle* since 1950 included those on October 14, 1951; January 16, 1955; and February 4, 1962. The editor from 1961 to 1965 was William P. Steven.

On December 7, 1965, it was reported that John. W. Mecom, a Houston oil millionaire, had purchased the bulk of the Jesse H. Jones interests, including the Houston *Chronicle*; however, on June 7, 1966, the reported $84 million purchase fell through. Circulation of the *Chronicle* in 1968 was 280,000 on weekdays and 327,000 on Sundays. By October 12, 1975, circulation had increased to 298,991 on weekdays, 309,554 on Saturdays, and 369,288 on Sundays. At that time Houston Endowment, Inc., and J. Howard Creekmore were publishers, R. J. V. Johnson was corporate board president, and Everett D. Collier was vice-president and editor. Offices were located at 801 Texas Avenue.

*Houston College for Negroes. *See* Texas State University for Negroes; Texas Southern University.

Houston Community College. Houston Community College was founded in 1971. Enrollment in 1974 was 16,495, and the president was J. Don Boney.

*Houston County. Houston County, two-thirds forested with hardwoods and pine, is a small producer of natural gas and oil. Beef cattle, poultry, and dairying were the chief sources of farm income, which amounted to an annual average of $13 million in the early 1970's. The county was also one of the leading plum producers in Texas. The site of the first Spanish mission in East Texas, the Davy Crockett National Forest, Houston County Lake, and Lake Ratcliff made the county attractive to tourists. The 1960 population of 19,376 decreased to 17,855 by 1970.

Houston County Lake. Houston County Lake (formerly Little Elkhart Creek) is in the Trinity River Basin in Houston County, ten miles northwest of Crockett. The reservoir is owned by Houston County Water Control and Improvement District No. 1 for the purpose of supplying water to Crockett, Grapeland, and Latexo from the district's treating plants and water lines. Construction of the dam started on April 14, 1966, and was completed in December, 1966. The reservoir has a capacity of 19,500 acre-feet with a surface area of 1,282 acres at the service spillway elevation 260 feet above mean sea level and a capacity of 27,000 acre-feet with a surface area of 1,600 acres at emergency spillway crest elevation. The drainage area above the dam is forty-four square miles.

Seth D. Breeding

*Houston Direct Navigation Company.

*Houston, East and West Texas Railway.

Houston Endowment Inc. *See* Jesse H. Jones Hall for the Performing Arts; Jones, Jesse Holman.

Houston Foundation. *See* Welch, Robert Alonzo.

*Houston and Great Northern Railroad Company.

*Houston Heights, Texas.

Houston Intercontinental Airport. *See* Houston Standard Metropolitan Statistical Area.

*Houston *Morning Star. See Morning Star* (Houston).

Houston Museum of Fine Arts. *See* Museum of Fine Arts, Houston.

Houston Museum of Natural Science. The first Houston Museum and Scientific Society was formed in 1909. In 1914 the group persuaded city officials to buy part of the natural history collection assembled by H. P. Attwater, and in 1922 the remainder of the collection was bought by S. J. Westheimer and given to the city.

For more than thirty years after the purchases, the museum remained a city agency. In 1946 a nonprofit museum corporation was formed to maintain and operate the museum, and Robert A. Vines became director. He held the office until 1956.

T. E. Pulley became director in 1957; the first step toward the present museum was taken in 1959 after president Palmer Hutchison negotiated a ninety-nine year lease with the city for a four-and-a-half-acre site on the north edge of Hermann Park. At the same time, trustees received a $250,000 gift from the late Burke Baker,qv which assured construction of the Burke Baker Planetarium.

The museum and planetarium building was built in 1964 at a cost of $2.5 million. A $1.5 million addition to the building in 1969 more than doubled the size. The prime feature of the enlarged facility is a dinosaur display. Other displays include a space museum and geology, biology, and geography exhibits relating to the area. One of the important services performed by the museum is the teaching of science classes to children from the Houston public schools. Another important function is the identification and question-answering service it provides for the public at large.

*Houston North Shore Railway Company. In 1955 the Houston North Shore Railway Company had a complete line from Houston to Baytown, was controlled through stock ownership by the New Orleans, Texas, and Mexican Railway Company, and was operated under lease by the Beaumont, Sour Lake, and Western Railway Company. In 1956 it was consolidated with the Missouri-Pacific.

James M. Day

*Houston, Oaklawn, and Magnolia Park Railway Company.

Houston Oilers. The effort to obtain a professional football team for Houston began in 1958 when Houston tried to purchase the National Football League's Chicago Cardinals and move them to Houston. After two unsuccessful years Houston, through the influence of K. S. (Bud) Adams, Jr., became one of the charter members in the new American Football League founded in 1960, and the Oilers became part of the league's eastern division. The newly formed team played its first games in Jeppesen Stadium, a high school facility enlarged to over thirty-five thousand seats.

From 1960 to 1962 the Oilers dominated the new league. Under coaches Lou Rymkus and Wally Lemm, who both later received the coach of the year award, the Oilers won the first two AFL championships, first defeating Los Angeles 24–16 in 1960 and then San Diego 10–3 in 1961. In 1962 the Oilers took runner-up honors in the league, losing to Dallas 20–17 in professional football's longest contest, which lasted six quarters.

After 1962 the Oilers declined in prominence in the league, ending up in last place in the league in the 1964 season under coach Sammy Baugh. In 1965 the Houston club moved into the seventy-thousand-seat Rice Stadium, and although it remained in last place in the league, its attendance increased by over ninety thousand in that season. The following season the club was plagued with crippling injuries and ended up in a tie for last place in the league. In 1967 Houston again won the eastern division title before losing the league championship to Oakland 40–7. The Oilers thus became the first team in professional football history to come from last place to first place in one season.

The Oilers started a new era in 1968, when they moved into the Astrodome,qv the world's first air-conditioned, multipurpose sports complex, and the Oilers' third playing site since 1960. In 1968 Oilers officials estimated that more than one-half million fans attended their eleven home games.

With the merging in 1970 of the nation's two professional football leagues into a single organization (National Football League), the Houston Oilers became part of the American Conference of the National Football League. The American Football League was no longer in existence.

BIBLIOGRAPHY: Tex Maule, *The Game* (1967).

Jim McLemore

*Houston Port and Turning Basin. *See* Houston Ship Channel.

*Houston *Post*. The Houston *Post* continued to grow in prestige and circulation. As the Houston *Post-Dispatch*, the paper operated radio station KPRC in the 1920's. By the early 1950's the Houston Post Company had added the television station KPRC-TV to its holdings, and in January, 1955, a new $4,000,000 office building to house the *Post* was opened. In August, 1955, William Pettus Hobby qv became chairman of the board of directors; his wife, Oveta Culp Hobby, became president and editor. In 1963 the company purchased the News Publishing Company, a transaction which involved the sale of the Galveston *News*,qv the Galveston *Tribune*, and the Texas City *Sun*. In 1967 the Houston Post Company sold the Galveston area papers. With the death of Hobby in 1964, the *Post* remained under the management of Mrs. Hobby, assisted by their son, William P. Hobby, Jr., who served as executive editor and executive vice-president. In September, 1968, the *Post* had a paid circulation of 289,385 daily and 322,763 on Sundays. In 1969 William H. Gardner was named chief editorial writer and editor. By October 12, 1975, circulation had increased to 294,556 on weekdays, 330,032 on Saturdays, and 349,068 on Sundays. At that time Oveta Culp Hobby was editor and chairman of the board, William P. Hobby, Jr., was executive editor and president (although serving as lieutenant governor of Texas), and Edwin D. Hunter was vice-president and managing editor. Offices were located at 4747 Southwest Freeway, Houston.

Houston *Press*. The Houston *Press* was founded in September, 1911, and until its demise on March 20, 1964, it was the most colorful of the three Houston daily newspapers. The *Press* was a Scripps-Howard newspaper and had a general reputation for exposing the seamier side of life in Houston and for keeping Houston politicians on their toes. The *Press* style of journalism was established by its first editor, Paul C. Edwards, and that style flourished under later editors Marcellus E. Foster, 1926–1936 (who had founded and edited the Houston *Chronicle* qv), and George Carmack, 1946–1964. The *Press* began publication on the corner of Capital and Bagby streets; in 1927 it moved to Rusk and Chartres streets. In 1963 the *Press* averaged a daily circulation of nearly 90,000 and employed over 300 persons; however, it operated at a loss during the early 1960's. On March 20, 1964, president and publisher Ray L. Powers and editor Carmack announced to the assembled newspaper staff that it was preparing the last issue of the *Press*. The newspaper had been sold by Scripps-Howard to the Houston *Chronicle* for a price estimated in excess of four million dollars.

BIBLIOGRAPHY: Houston *Post*, March 21, 22, 1964; George Fuermann, *Houston: Land of the Big Rich* (1951); Writers' Program of the Work Projects Administration, *Houston: A History and Guide* (1942).

*Houston Railway Company.

*Houston Ship Channel. The Houston Ship Channel achieved its earliest significance as a link between interior Texas and the sea. As the waterway was the only one in Texas that was dependably navigable, planters over a large area adopted the practice of bringing cotton to Houston to be shipped by barge or riverboat to Galveston, thence by seagoing vessels to market. Goods destined for the interior came upstream, and visitors and immigrants made the route one of the most traveled in Texas in the prerailroad era. Although railroads tended to divert traffic from the channel, it remained an important transportation artery for bulky goods, especially cotton, throughout the nineteenth century.

After the discovery of oil in Texas early in the twentieth century, petroleum began to rival cotton as the most important cargo on the channel. Petroleum also led to the industrialization of the waterfront, for the long, protected channel with its nearby crude oil supplies proved an attractive location for oil refineries.

Although the channel was opened to deepwater vessels in 1914, shipping conditions created by World War I limited its use, and its deepwater development did not begin until after the war. In 1919 an ocean-going vessel, the *Merry Mount*, took the first shipment of cotton directly from Houston to a foreign market, thus inaugurating a trade that made Houston the leading cotton port in the United States within a decade. In the same period the growing popularity of the internal combustion engine boosted demands for petroleum products. By 1930 nine oil refineries were in operation along the channel and contributed to channel tonnage. Although the depression of the 1930's briefly interrupted the progress of the port, the Port of Houston ranked third in the nation in the amount of tonnage carried on the eve of World War II.

The war suspended normal shipping activities but gave impetus to the industrialization of the waterway. In addition to increasing the demand for customary petroleum products, the war inspired the development of synthetic rubber based on a byproduct of petroleum. Two synthetic rubber plants were located near the channel while the war was in progress, and after the war the channel became a center of the petrochemical industry. In the postwar years the port also became a major shipping point for midwestern grain. Growing foreign trade and new industry boosted the port to second in tonnage in the nation in 1948, and from then until 1964 it customarily ranked second or third. The combination of industry and transportation facilities influenced the National Aeronautics and Space Administration (*see* Manned Spacecraft Center) to select a site convenient to the channel as headquarters for the nation's space program in 1961.

Congress approved a project to widen the channel to 300 feet from Fidelity Island to the turning basin in 1945, and in 1957 army engineers recommended that the entire channel be deepened to forty feet. By 1964, the fiftieth anniversary of the deepwater channel, the federal government had expended $64,000,000 for channel improvement and maintenance, and the local government had invested $28,000,000 in port facilities. In return, all economic activities related to the channel were yielding $148,000,000 annually in taxes. The channelside industrial complex was valued at about $3,000,000,000; this complex and shipping activities gave employment to about 55,000 persons who received $314,000,000 in wages annually.

BIBLIOGRAPHY: Marilyn McAdams Sibley, *The Port of Houston: A History* (1968); Warren Rose, *Catalyst of an Economy: The Economic Impact of the Port of Houston, 1958–1963* (1965).

Marilyn McAdams Sibley

Houston Standard Metropolitan Statistical Area. The Houston Standard Metropolitan Statistical Area, created by the United States Bureau of the Budget in 1949, consisted at that time of the 1,711 square-mile area of Harris County. In 1950 this metropolitan area contained 806,701 inhabitants, while the city of Houston had 596,163 residents (*see also* Houston, Texas). For the decade 1950–1960 the metropolitan area ranked sixth in the rate of growth in the United States. On July 3, 1954, Houstonians celebrated "M Day" as the metropolitan population passed one million. In 1960, according to the United States census report, the number was 1,243,158 in the metropolitan area (Harris County) and 938,219 in Houston itself. In March, 1965, the Bureau of the Budget expanded the official metropolitan area to include not only Harris County, but also Brazoria, Fort Bend, Liberty, and Montgomery counties, an area of 6,258 square miles. It was estimated in that year that the city of Houston had a population of 1,091,800, while the new metropolitan area population increased to 1,673,000. Consequently, Houston became one of the largest and fastest growing metropolitan areas in the United States. The report of the 1970 United States census gave the city of Houston's population as 1,232,802 and that of the metropolitan area as 1,985,031.

Negroes, the largest minority group, made up 19.5 percent of the total population for the metropolitan area in 1960. In Houston itself the Negro population was 22.9 percent, as compared to 22 percent in 1930 and 39 percent in 1880. In the 1960's there was a decline in de facto segregation as Negroes moved out of the traditional housing areas and discrimination ended in public parks and buildings. Although much of the struggle for equal rights occurred without violence, a riot at Texas Southern University in May, 1967, resulted in 488 arrests and the death of a police officer. Difficulties with segregation in the public schools remained a problem, but it was clear by 1970 that the condition of racial separation had been irrevocably altered.

Between 1950 and 1970 Houston ranked as second or third largest seaport (slipping once in 1955 to fourth) in total tonnage in the United States, interchanging positions with New Orleans; the city was the third largest seaport in 1970. Its port is an inland waterway connected to the sea by a fifty-mile-long, four-hundred-foot-wide, and forty-foot-deep channel (*see* Houston Ship Channel). Between 1957 and 1965 the local Navigation District spent about $37,000,000 for improvements. While the port of Houston was first in Texas, Freeport, in Brazoria County, ranked seventh in the state in total tonnage in 1967. Chief foreign imports were fuel oils, iron ore and steel mill products, molasses, coffee, and gypsum. Houston and Freeport exported mainly rice, wheat, grain sorghums, cotton, caustic soda, and lubricating oils. Their coastal shippings included fuel and lubricating oils, gasoline and kerosene, crude petroleum and naphtha, jet fuel, caustic soda, and cement. In 1965 the Houston port handled over 3,800 vessels at its fifty-one public and fifty private berths.

Although the Houston area remained a retail and wholesale leader in Texas, the most spectacular accomplishments after 1950 came in manufacturing. Value added by manufacture in 1947 by 916 firms amounted to $385,549,000; in 1963 approximately 2,200 companies yielded $1,889,693,000; in 1969 manufacturing values had increased to $2,312,245,-000 from 2,500 manufacturing firms. Houston was, along with other metropolitan areas along the Gulf Coast, part of the leading petroleum refining complex in the United States. Many of the major oil companies had their headquarters in Houston. In 1966 sixty-five primary producers of metal, including Sheffield Steel in Houston and Dow Chemical, which extracts magnesium at Freeport, operated in the area. In 1965 Armco Steel Corporation expanded its production facilities and the United States Steel Corporation announced plans to build a steel mill in the Houston area. The most important manufacturing group, in terms of value produced, was the complex of approximately 180 chemical plants located along the Gulf Coast from Houston to the Louisiana border. This complex, although it extends far out of the Houston metropolitan area, was one of the largest in the United States and controlled about 85 percent of the nation's petrochemical capacity. The companies involved utilize the raw materials of the wider area and the production of neighboring chemical plants to create nylon, ammonia, glycerine, and plexiglass materials. Over 50 percent of the nation's synthetic rubber is produced in the Gulf Coast area.

Although the refineries and oil equipment manufacturers had long utilized electrical and automatic instruments, the National Aeronautics and Space Administration provided the main impulse for the new Houston electronics industry. Through the promotion and cooperation of Congressman Albert Thomas, Vice-President Lyndon B. Johnson, Humble Oil and Refining Company (now Exxon Company, U.S.A.), and Rice University,qqv in 1961 NASA selected a site thirty miles southeast of Houston at Clear Lake for the location of the Manned Spacecraft Center.qv The presence of the installation attracted over 125 space-related companies, placed Houston among the top ten metropolitan areas in the number of scientists, encour-

aged the growth of residential tracts such as Nassau Bay and Clear Lake City, and inspired the development of Bayport, the twenty-year industrial and residential product of Humble Oil and the Del E. Webb Corporation. In 1965 the $183,-000,000 center awarded about $34,000,000 in contracts to Houston-Gulf Coast industries. Rice University in 1963 established the first Department of Space Science in the United States, and in 1965 received a $3,700,000 contract to construct scientific satellites. The University of Houston and Texas A&M University also benefited from the presence of the Manned Spacecraft Center.

Houston had an ample water supply coming from Lake Houston (since 1954) on the San Jacinto River, Lake Livingston (1966) on the Trinity River, and artesian wells which tapped the nation's third largest aquifer. The area had a large supply of oil, gas, sulphur, lime, and timber. The value of the annual mineral production of the five counties was over $380,000,000. Nearly 60 percent of the total sulphur supply of the United States was produced within seventy-five miles of Houston. The forests to the north and east of the city supported lumber, plywood, building material, furniture, and paper milling industries.

Despite the heavy urbanization of the Houston area it remained in the 1960's an important agricultural region. More than half of the export tonnage of the port of Houston was agricultural commodities. Liberty, Harris, and Brazoria ranked among the top five counties in Texas in rice production. Harris and Brazoria counties were first and third respectively in the number of cattle. Harris was among the top five counties in Texas in egg production, and Brazoria County produced about one-fourth of the total fig crop in Texas. Swine, hay, grain sorghums, cotton, and truck crops were grown on a lesser scale. Agribusinesses included meat packing, food preparation, rice milling, animal feeds, cottonseed oil mills, and the only sugar cane refinery in Texas, at Sugar Land.

The appearance of Houston changed rapidly after 1950 with the construction of a series of modern office buildings. The Humble Building, at forty-four stories, was the tallest in the Southwest when it was completed. The planned fifty-story Shell Building was scheduled to be the tallest tower west of the Mississippi River and south of Chicago and New York. A number of high-rise apartments were added to the kaleidoscopic skyline, with 1963 the peak year for apartment construction. The largest subdivision in Houston's history, Sharpstown, began in 1954 on a 6,500-acre tract west of Bellaire. It included not only homes, but also schools, shopping malls, a high-rise apartment house, office buildings, and several country clubs. Harris County construction exceeded $500,000,000 per year after 1962 and totaled $604,900,000 in 1965.

The most spectacular construction in the area was the new Harris County Domed Stadium (*see* Astrodome). Completed in 1965, the enclosed, air-conditioned stadium, sometimes characterized as the

"Eighth Wonder of the World," covers nine and one-half acres and measures 218 feet high with a clear span of 642 feet. The stadium was the home of the National League Houston Astros qv baseball team and the University of Houston Cougars football team. Houston also had a professional football team, the Houston Oilers,qv formerly of the American Football League (now the American Conference of the National Football League); a professional basketball team, the Rockets of the National Basketball Association; and a professional hockey team, the Aeros of the World Hockey Association. Special sports events included the Houston Classic Invitational Golf Tournament, the River Oaks Tennis Tournament, the Houston Fat Stock Show and Rodeo, the Pin Oaks Stables Horse Show, the Houston International Golf Tournament, and the Bluebonnet Bowl qv football classic. Other annual events were the Houston International Flower and Garden Show, the Fishoree, the Bluebonnet Trail Trip, Sun Fest Days, the Fishin' Fiesta, and Sylvan Beach Day. Opportunities for swimming, fishing, water sports, and hunting were numerous.

Within the Houston metropolitan area is the historic site of Stephen F. Austin's Old Three Hundred qv settlement, including old Velasco, the site of the first capital of the Republic of Texas at West Columbia, Peach Point Plantation,qv and numerous other historic homes in the five-county area. Two state historic parks are located in the metropolitan area: the Varner-Hogg Plantation, the former home of James Stephen Hogg;qv and the San Jacinto battleground with a commemorative monument, a museum, and the battleship *Texas*.qv

As an educational center the Houston area had thousands of students enrolled in colleges and universities, including the University of Houston, Rice University, Texas Southern University, the University of St. Thomas, South Texas College of Law, Dominican College, Houston Baptist University, Houston Community College, North Harris County College, Brazosport College at Lake Jackson, San Jacinto College at Pasadena, Alvin Junior College, and Lee College in Baytown.qqv The Texas Medical Center,qv inspired by the M. D. Anderson Foundation,qv became operative in the 1950's and has made Houston world famous for the treatment of cancer and heart disease. In 1968 there were more heart transplant operations performed in Houston than anywhere else in the world (*see* Heart Transplants in Texas). The $125,000,000 investment was supported by sixteen institutions and fourteen medical organizations, including ten major hospitals, three medical schools, and three research institutes.

Since 1950 Houston has developed into a cultural center of considerable importance. In 1953 the University of Houston started KUHT-TV, the first educational television station in the United States. The Houston Symphony Orchestra, which celebrated its golden anniversary during the 1963–1964 season, was brought to greatness under Leopold Stokowski in the 1950's and Sir John Barbirolli in the 1960's. Other musical groups included the Houston Grand Opera Association, the J. S. Bach Society, the Houston Chorale, the Gilbert and Sullivan Society, the Music Guild, and the Houston All-City Symphony Orchestra. Ballet training was augmented in 1955 with the creation of the Houston Foundation for Ballet. Area members in the Southwest Regional Ballet Association were the Allegro Ballet, the Greater Houston Civic Ballet, and the Youth Ballet. Houston offered year-round drama in legitimate theaters and many little theater groups. The Alley Theatre,qv under the direction of Nina Vance, was considered one of the nation's foremost repertory theaters and represented the United States at the Brussels International Exposition in 1958; it received a third Ford Foundation grant, amounting to $2,100,000, in 1962 for development work and construction of new facilities. Additions were also made to the museums in the area. In 1958 Cullinan Hall, a $625,000 wing of the Museum of Fine Arts,qv opened. In 1964 the Burke Baker Planetarium in Hermann Park was completed as part of a projected expansion of the Houston Museum of Natural Science.qv The Contemporary Art Museum was dedicated exclusively to presenting all forms of avant-garde art. In October, 1966, the Jesse H. Jones Hall for the Performing Arts,qv one of the finest auditoriums for music and drama in the United States, opened in the Houston Civic Center.

Urban sprawl and an increasing number of automobiles emphasized the necessity for freeways and street improvements. The Gulf Freeway to Galveston opened in 1952 at an average cost of $573,-000 per mile. At that time it carried 75,000 vehicles daily, but by 1960 this figure increased to 100,000. Consequently Houston and state highway planners devised a 244-mile, $500,000,000 freeway system with inner and outer loops and expressways radiating from the heart of the city. Two of the highways, U.S. 75 (Interstate 45) and U.S. 90 (Interstate 10), and the loop Interstate 610 are portions of the United States Interstate and Defense Highway System. Houston's six major railroads handled over nineteen million tons of freight in 1965 and provided twelve passenger trains daily. Air transportation was improved with the completion of a new terminal in 1957. Within a short time, however, the ten major airlines operating in Houston completely utilized the facilities of the international airport. In 1962 construction began on the 7,300-acre Houston Intercontinental Airport in northern Harris County, with the terminal originally scheduled to open in late 1967. The Federal Aviation Administration began operating a control center in 1965. Although the massive airport was not completed after twelve years of planning, building, and controversy, a passenger plane made the first landing there on June 8, 1969. The airport was constructed under the linear expansion concept so that it could be enlarged with virtually no interrupted service. By 1969 approximately $110 million had been spent on the project, while the total investment was projected to reach $300 million by 1980. The airport was in full operation by 1970.

While Houston was by far the largest city in the Houston Metropolitan Statistical Area, there were other cities and towns which contributed to the region's overall prosperity. Pasadena, in Harris County, was the second largest city and a highly industrialized area. Baytown was also a center for industry along the ship channel, while Bellaire, largely residential, was research oriented and active in industry. The Clear Lake area was an association of cities (extending into the Galveston-Texas City Standard Metropolitan Statistical Area qv) that was closely allied with the activities of the Manned Spacecraft Center.

In Brazoria County, Brazosport was the group name for an area of many communities which had a joint school system and chamber of commerce; this group area contained one of the largest industrial complexes in the state. Angleton, seat of Brazoria County, was a center for petrochemical industries, rice, and cattle, while Freeport, in the same county, served as a deepwater port and petrochemical industrial site. Fort Bend County also contributed to the area's progress with petrochemical and agribusiness plants at Richmond (county seat) and adjoining Rosenberg. Sugar Land continued to maintain a large sugar refinery. This county area was still very much concerned with agriculture, providing a large income from cattle, rice, cotton, grains, vegetables, and poultry.

Liberty County showed an increase in industry with the introduction of petrochemicals and other manufactures along with a large oil production. The city of Liberty had a new port and barge canal, while Cleveland was the oil and lumbering center in the northwestern part of the county. Agriculture continued to be important, with a 1968 income of over $16 million. Rice, beef cattle, soybeans, and timber sales were especially important.

Montgomery County also had increasing industrialization along with urban development. It continued high in oil production, with over nine million barrels produced in 1968, and nearly 455 million barrels produced between 1931 and January 1, 1969. Conroe, the county seat, was the center of business activity. With three-fourths of the county forested, the timber industry continued to be economically important.

Many of the people in this five-county area worked in the city of Houston and commuted to their homes. Houston continued to grow as a cultural center for the whole metropolitan area. In 1973 Waller County was added to the Houston Standard Metropolitan Statistical Area. *See also* Houston, Texas; Standard Metropolitan Statistical Areas in Texas.

BIBLIOGRAPHY: A. Pat Daniel, *Texas Avenue at Main Street* (1964); George Fuermann, *Houston: Land of the Big Rich* (1951), *Houston: The Feast Years* (1962), and *The Face of Houston* (1963); Ed Kilman and Theon Wright, *Hugh Roy Cullen: A Story of American Opportunity* (1954); Henrietta Larson and Kenneth W. Porter, *History of Humble Oil and Refining Company* (1959); David G. McComb, *Houston, the Bayou City* (1969); Marilyn McAdams Sibley, *The Port of Houston: A History* (1968); Bascom N. Timmons, *Jesse H. Jones: The Man and the Statesman* (1956); *Texas Almanac* (1969).

David G. McComb

Houston State Psychiatric Institute for Research and Training. The Houston State Psychiatric Institute for Research and Training began operation in 1957 and moved into its new building in the Texas Medical Center qv in 1961. The institute conducted training in the treatment and prevention of mental illness and mental retardation. Out-patient clinics for adults and children functioned to train psychiatry residents. A special project provided follow-up care for area patients discharged or furloughed from the Austin State Hospital.qv Fees were based upon individual income and the number of dependents being supported by the patient. In 1967 the institution's name was changed to the Texas Research Institute of Mental Sciences.qv *See* Mentally Ill and Mentally Retarded, Care of, in Texas.

BIBLIOGRAPHY: Board for Texas State Hospitals and Special Schools, *Report* (1964).

*Houston Tap and Brazoria Railroad Company.

*Houston *Telegraph*. *See Telegraph and Texas Register*.

*Houston and Texas Central Railway Company.

*Houston, Trinity, and Tyler Railroad.

*Houstonian.

*Hovey, Texas.

*Howard, Ed.

*Howard, George Thomas.

*Howard, James W.

*Howard, Tilghman Ashurst.

*Howard, Volney Erskine.

*Howard, Texas. (Eastland County.)

*Howard, Texas. (Ellis County.)

*Howard Association.

Howard College at Big Spring. *See* Howard County Junior College.

*Howard County. New developments in the county after 1950 included a library, new buildings at Howard County Junior College, school expansions, and plans for a federal building. Major industries were connected with oil, chemicals, and carbon black, while Webb Air Force Base qv provided additional jobs. From 1925 to January 1, 1973, total oil production had reached 447,919,396 barrels. Three-fourths of the agricultural income was obtained chiefly from cotton and grain sorghums. Big Spring State Park, stock shows, a rodeo and old settlers reunion, and a rattlesnake roundup provided tourist and local interest. The 1960 population was 40,139; in 1970 the population decreased to 37,796.

Howard County Junior College. Howard County Junior College, in Big Spring, was created in 1945. E. C. Dodd was chosen first president of the college, to begin office in the spring of 1946. Negotiation with the federal government resulted in temporary quarters for the coeducational junior college in the hospital area of the former Big Spring Army Air Force Bombardier School, two and one-half miles west of town. The first session began in September, 1946, with an enrollment of 148.

In September, 1951, the college moved to new quarters on a one-hundred-acre site in southeast Big Spring. Enrollment increased from 337 to 879 between 1951 and 1964. The physical plant consisted of an administration-classroom-library building, practical arts building, greenhouse, music building, and dormitories, in addition to athletic facilities which included a stadium seating ten thousand persons.

The library collection contained over twenty thousand books in 1969, with from eight hundred to one thousand titles added annually. The library provided service primarily for students and faculty and secondarily for all citizens of the community. The college promoted lecture series, musical and stage productions, athletic events, and other activities.

Full accreditation was granted by the Southern Association of Colleges and Secondary Schools and by the Association of Texas Colleges.qv Courses of study designed for academic, pre-professional, and terminal technical or vocational fields were offered for regular, evening, and summer session students. By the 1974–1975 regular term, enrollment had increased to 1,373 students, and the faculty numbered over fifty. Charles D. Hays served as president. By 1974 the school's name had changed to Howard College at Big Spring.

*Howard Creek.

*Howard Hughes Airport Flying Training Detachment.

*Howard Payne College. Howard Payne College, Brownwood, was admitted to membership in the Southern Association of Colleges and Secondary Schools and the Southern Baptist Education Association in 1948 and in the American Council on Education in 1949. Graduate study was offered beginning in 1952.

Daniel Baker College,qv a few blocks away, merged with Howard Payne College in 1953. The main building of the former Daniel Baker College was remodeled for the Douglas MacArthur Academy of Freedom, a memorial to the late general, a museum depicting the concept of freedom throughout history, and a major program of study in the division of social sciences at Howard Payne College.

The following buildings were added to the twenty-five-acre Howard Payne campus: boys' dormitory (1947), library (1953), girls' dormitory (1955), U.S. Naval Reserve Electronics Facility (1957), Bible building (1958), science hall (1962), and student union and men's residence (1963). In addition, temporary buildings were

moved from Camp Bowie qv (1948), and the chapel, main building, religion center, and business building were renovated. The Department of Agriculture operated a 500-acre farm, with 155 irrigated acres, a herd of Angus and Hereford cattle, and a flock of Rambouillet sheep. A twenty-five-acre stadium site was also acquired on Brady Highway. The college joined the Lone Star Conference in 1956 for intercollegiate athletics.qv

By 1969 the library housed 79,000 volumes and regularly received 385 periodicals and newspapers. Microfilm and record collections were held by the central library, and a 3,000-volume education library was housed in the administration building.

The college offered bachelor's degrees in arts, science, music, and music education; it offered master's degrees in arts, education, and music. The curriculum was organized around five divisions: humanities, natural sciences and mathematics, professional studies, religion, and social sciences.

Guy D. Newman became president in 1955, upon the retirement of Thomas H. Taylor. The 1974–1975 regular term enrollment was 1,508 students, and in that year Roger L. Brooks served as president.

*Howard Wells, Texas.

*Howards Creek.

*Howard's Switch, Texas.

*Howe, Texas. According to the United States 1970 census, the population of Howe, in Grayson County, increased to 1,359 from a population count of 680 in 1960. The town had twenty businesses in 1970.

*Howellville, Texas.

*Howland, Texas.

*Howth, Texas.

*Howze, Robert Lee. Robert Lee Howze, son of James Augustus and Amanda (Brown) Howze, was commandant of cadets at the United States Military Academy, West Point (not superintendent of the academy, as stated in Volume I), from 1905 until 1909 (not after World War I). He was made a commander of the Puerto Rico Regiment of Infantry in 1909–1911 (not appointed governor general of Puerto Rico). He never left the service to later rejoin it (as implied in Volume I). He commanded the 38th (not 39th) Division in World War I. In 1921 he organized the 1st Cavalry Division at Fort Bliss,qv Texas, and served there until he went to Columbus, Ohio, in 1925 (not 1922). Camp Howze,qv near Gainesville, was named for him during World War II. The transport General Robert L. Howze was also named in his honor. Howze Field at West Point bears his name, as does Howze Stadium at Fort Bliss, Howze Street in El Paso, and Camp Howze in Korea. In addition to the Medal of Honor, he was awarded two Silver Star medals and the Distinguished Service Medal. A notable rescue occurred early in his career, in 1899, when Howze commanded a detachment which brought back twenty-nine Americans who had been

prisoners of insurgents in the Philippines for ten months or more.

Howze was married to Anne Chiffelle Hawkins on February 24, 1897; they had three children. He was buried at West Point.

BIBLIOGRAPHY: *Who Was Who In America* (1943).

Harriot Howze Jones

*Hoxey, Asa.

*Hoxie, Texas.

*Hoya, Texas.

*Hoyle, Stephen Z. (A.).

*Hoyt, Henry F.

*Hoyt, Samuel W.

*Hoyt, Texas.

*Hoyte, Texas.

*Huane Indians. The Huane (Juana, Juane, Xauana, Xaunzo, Xuana) Indians were first mentioned in 1683–1684 as one of the groups which Juan Domínguez de Mendoza qv expected to meet on the Colorado River east of present San Angelo. The Huane were one of the Coahuiltecan groups for whom the San José y San Miguel de Aguayo Mission qv was established at San Antonio in 1720. Their aboriginal range is not recorded, but it was probably the area just south of the Edwards Plateau.

BIBLIOGRAPHY: F. W. Hodge (ed.), *Handbook of American Indians*, I (1907), II (1910); M. K. Kress, "Diary of a Visit of Inspection of the Texas Missions Made by Fray Gaspar José de Solís in the Year 1767–68," *Southwestern Historical Quarterly*, XXXV (1931–1932); J. R. Swanton, *Linguistic Material from the Tribes of Southern Texas and Northeastern Mexico* (1940).

T. N. Campbell

Hubbard, James B. James B. Hubbard was born on June 10, 1874, in Rodney, Mississippi. He attended Jefferson College, the University of Texas, and the University of Chicago. After he was admitted to the Bar in 1895, he practiced law in Hempstead. In 1900 he became superintendent of schools in Belton, but in 1910 he returned to his law practice. That same year he married Belle Tyler, and they had two children.

Hubbard was president of the Texas State Teachers Association qv in 1905 and president of the Bell County Bar Association from 1918 to 1927. He was also co-author with C. P. Patterson qv of a civil government textbook, *A Civil Government of Texas* (1927), and collaborator with Henry Noble Sherwood on *Civics and Citizenship* (1934). Hubbard practiced law in Belton until his retirement in 1957. He died on October 17, 1959.

BIBLIOGRAPHY: *Texas Bar Journal* (November, 1958).

Dayton Kelley

Hubbard, Louis Herman. Louis Herman Hubbard, a prominent Texas educator and university president, was born February 10, 1882, in Mayaguez, Puerto Rico, where his father was U.S. consul. The son of Gorham Eustis and Louise (Monsanto) Hubbard, Louis Herman received a B.S. degree in 1903, an M.A. in 1918, and a Ph.D. in 1930, all from the University of Texas. He began his teaching and administrative career in the Sulphur Springs school system in 1902, but the next year he moved to the Belton system, where he remained until 1908.

Louis Hubbard returned to Belton as superintendent of schools in 1910 after serving as high school principal in San Angelo; he spent several summers as an instructor at Baylor University. From 1924 to 1926 he was a lecturer and dean of students at the University of Texas. He was named president of Texas State College for Women (now Texas Woman's University) in 1926, remaining in that position until his retirement in 1960. He married Bertha Altizer on July 31, 1912; they were the parents of a daughter and two sons. Hubbard was widely known in the educational field. His publications included *Handbook for English Teachers*, with H. W. Morelock (1914), two monographs entitled *The Improvement of College Teaching* (1927) and *The Private Endowment of Public Education* (1928), and his autobiography, *Recollections of a Texas Educator* (1964).

Hubbard died in Georgetown on August 13, 1973, and was buried in Oakwood Cemetery, Austin.

BIBLIOGRAPHY: Biographical File, Barker Texas History Center, University of Texas at Austin.

*Hubbard, Richard Bennett.

*Hubbard, Texas. According to the United States 1970 census, Hubbard, in Hill County, had a population decrease by 1970, to 1,572, from its 1960 population of 1,628. The town had forty-two businesses in 1970.

*Hubbard Creek.

Hubbard Creek Reservoir. Hubbard Creek Dam and Hubbard Creek Reservoir are in the Brazos River Basin in Stephens County, six miles northwest of Breckenridge on Hubbard Creek, a tributary of the Clear Fork of the Brazos River. The project is owned and operated by the West Central Texas Municipal Water District for supplying water to Abilene, Albany, Anson, and Breckenridge. Construction began on May 1, 1961, and the dam was completed on December 18, 1962. The reservoir has a capacity of 317,800 acre-feet and a surface area of 15,250 acres at an elevation of 1,183 feet above mean sea level, with a shoreline of 100 miles. Drainage area to the reservoir is 1,107 square miles.

BIBLIOGRAPHY: Texas Water Commission, *Bulletin 6408* (1964).

Seth D. Breeding

*Huckabay, Texas. Huckabay, in Erath County, was known as Flatwoods (not Falt Woods, as stated in Volume I) before the post office was established there with John Huckabay as postmaster. In 1970 the population was estimated to be 150.

*Huckins, James.

*Huckleberry Creek.

*Hud, Texas.

*Huddle, William Henry.

*Hudson, Charles S.

*Hudson, H. C.

*Hudson, William E.

*Hudsonville, Texas.

*Hudspeth, Claude Benton.

*Hudspeth County. In 1965 Hudspeth County had approximately forty thousand acres under cultivation in the vicinity of Dell City in addition to the farming area along the Rio Grande. The county produced about twenty thousand bales of cotton annually, as well as alfalfa, truck crops, cattle, and sheep. The average annual cash receipts from cattle and crops totaled $6,000,000 in the early 1970's. The ruins of Fort Hancock,qv scenic drives, and hunting areas support a small tourist trade. The 1960 population of 3,343 decreased to 2,392 by 1970.

*Hueco Mountains.

*Hueco Tanks.

Hueco Tanks State Park. See Parks, State; Tigua Indians.

*Huff, George.

*Huff, John.

*Huff, Robert E. Robert E. Huff was born on January 31, 1857 (not July 31, 1857, as stated in Volume I). He came to Texas alone (not with his family) in 1882 after graduating from Cumberland Law School at Lebanon, Tennessee. Robert and Elizabeth (Burroughs) Huff were the parents of four sons and three daughters.
BIBLIOGRAPHY: Jonnie R. Morgan, *The History of Wichita Falls* (1931); Frank W. Johnson, *A History of Texas and Texans*, IV (1914).

*Huff, Texas.

*Huffins, Texas.

*Huffman, Texas.

*Huffstuttle Creek.

*Hufsmith, Texas.

*Huger, Benjamin.

†Huggins, William O.

*Hughes, Edward Smallwood.

*Hughes, Howard Robard.

*Hughes, Isaac.

Hughes, John Reynolds. John Reynolds Hughes was born on February 11, 1855, in Henry County, near Cambridge, Illinois, to Thomas and Jennie (Bond) Hughes. In 1865 the family moved to Dixon, Illinois, where John attended country schools sporadically. Later the family moved to Mound City, Kansas; at age fourteen, Hughes left home to work on a neighboring cattle ranch but soon left there for Indian Territory. He lived among the Choctaws and Osage Indians for four years before moving to the Comanche Nation in 1874; there he traded in the Fort Sill area and became friends with Quanah Parker.qv After six years in Indian Territory, and after a brief stint as a trail driver on the Chisholm Trail,qv Hughes bought a

farm near Liberty Hill, in Travis County, and entered the horse business.

In May, 1886, Hughes set out to find a band of men who had stolen horses from his and neighboring ranches, and after trailing them for several months, he killed or captured the thieves in New Mexico and returned the horses to his neighbors; this exploit not only gained the attention of the Texas Rangers,qv but also apparently incurred the wrath of the Wild Bunch, a band of desperadoes led by Butch Cassidy. Persuaded to enlist in the Rangers at Georgetown, Hughes was sworn in on August 10, 1887, and joined Company D, Frontier Battalion,qv stationed at Camp Wood, Texas. He served mainly along the border between Texas and Mexico, and when the Frontier Battalion was abolished in 1900, he was made a captain in command of Company D in the new Ranger force. He was later appointed senior captain with headquarters in Austin, and on January 31, 1915, having served as a captain and Ranger longer than any other man, he retired from the force. Zane Grey's novel, *The Lone Star Ranger* (1914), is dedicated to Hughes and his Texas Rangers.

Hughes never married. He spent his later years prospecting and traveling by automobile. He became chairman of the board of directors and largest single stockholder of the Citizens Industrial Bank of Austin, but maintained his residence in El Paso. He was selected as the first recipient of the Certificate of Valor in 1940, an award set up to call attention to the bravery of peace officers of the nation. Hughes moved to Austin to live with a niece, and on June 3, 1947, at the age of ninety-two he took his own life; he was buried in the State Cemetery.qv
BIBLIOGRAPHY: Dane Coolidge, *Fighting Men of the West* (1932); Jack Martin, *Border Boss* (1942); *Austin American*, June 5, 1947; Fort Worth *Press*, February 3, 1934.

*Hughes, Reece.

*Hughes, Thomas Proctor.

*Hughes, William Edgar.

*Hughes, Texas. (Irion County.)

*Hughes, Texas. (Victoria County.)

*Hughes Creek.

*Hughes Springs, Texas. Hughes Springs, in western Cass County, had fifty-five businesses in 1970 serving a farming-lumbering area. Many inhabitants worked in the industries of surrounding towns, particularly Lone Star, Daingerfield, and Karnack. A new high school was built in 1963, and new water facilities were completed in 1965. Heavy floods in April and May, 1966, did extensive damage to streets, sewer plant, and water pipes. Population in 1960 was 1,813; the 1970 population was 1,701.

Hughey, Texas. Hughey, a small community north of Kilgore in Gregg County, experienced a brief boom in the early 1930's due to its proximity to the East Texas Oil Field.qv At one time Hughey had a school, a Baptist church, and several stores.

*Hugo, Texas.

*Hugo Mountain.

Huguenot Society of Texas. The Huguenot Society of Texas was organized on April 2, 1954, by Mrs. Earl Middleton of Austin as a unit of the National Huguenot Society. There were three chapters in Texas—Fleur de Lis (Austin area), St. Bartholomew (Houston area), and Navarre (Fort Worth area), which held meetings several times during the year and participated in the annual assembly of the state society. Each chapter had officers corresponding to those of the state and national societies.

Membership was by invitation, and lineal descent had to be established in the male or female line of (1) a Huguenot who emigrated from France to America or found refuge in some other country prior to the promulgation of the Edict of Toleration on November 28, 1787, or (2) a Huguenot who, in spite of religious persecution, remained in France.

Objectives of the society were to perpetuate the memory of the Huguenots, collect and preserve documents, and publish information on the Huguenots. Several resulting publications were contributed to libraries.

Edward N. McAllister

Huicasique Indians. In 1683–1684 Juan Domínguez de Mendoza qv led an exploratory expedition from El Paso as far eastward as the junction of the Concho and Colorado rivers east of present San Angelo. In his itinerary he listed the names of thirty-seven Indian groups, including the Huicasique, from which he expected to receive delegations. Nothing further is known about the Huicasique (Huicaxique), who seem to have been one of many Indian groups of north-central Texas that were swept away by the southward thrust of the Lipan-Apache and Comanche Indians in the eighteenth century.

BIBLIOGRAPHY: H. E. Bolton (ed.), *Spanish Exploration in the Southwest, 1542–1706* (1916); C. W. Hackett (ed.), *Pichardo's Treatise on the Limits of Louisiana and Texas,* II (1934).

T. N. Campbell

*Huizar, Pedro.

Hulen, John Augustus. John Augustus Hulen was born in Centralia, Boone County, Missouri, on September 9, 1871, the son of Harvey and Frances (Morter) Hulen. In 1873 he moved with his parents to Texas, where they took up residence in Gainesville. Hulen was educated in the public schools of Gainesville and at Staunton Military Academy in Virginia and Marmaduke Military Academy in Sweet Springs, Missouri. He graduated from Marmaduke in 1891 and married Frankie L. Race on February 14, 1893.

Hulen began his military record in 1889 as a private of the Gainesville Rifles. He was commissioned in 1891 and served as a lieutenant with Company G, 3rd Texas Volunteer Infantry, and in 1893 as captain, commanding Troop D, 1st Texas Volunteer Cavalry. Service in the Spanish-American War and participation in the campaign of the Philippine Insurrection followed. Mustered out of the service in 1901, he was then appointed adjutant general of Texas by Governor W. S. T. Lanham qv with the rank of brigadier general, serving in that capacity from June, 1903, until November, 1907.

In 1907 he was appointed passenger agent of the Frisco Railway lines in Houston. In 1910 he worked for the Trinity and Brazos Valley Railway Company and later took over as receiver and president of that company, which became the Burlington-Rock Island Railroad.

He was recalled to active service in May, 1916, to command elements of the Texas National Guard qv on the Mexican border. Following his release from active federal service in 1917, he participated in the mobilization of the Texas National Guard for service in World War I. Reentering active federal service, he commanded a brigade in France during that war. After the war he commanded the 36th Infantry Division qv with the rank of major general from 1923 until his retirement in 1935. He was promoted to the rank of brevet lieutenant general in recognition of his long and distinguished service at this time. Camp Hulen, the National Guard training field at Palacios, Texas, was named for him.

Awards received during his military career included the Silver Star for gallantry in action, the French Croix de Guerre, and the United States Distinguished Service Medal. He died at his home in Palacios, Texas, on September 14, 1957.

BIBLIOGRAPHY: Files and Reports of the Adjutant General's Department of the State of Texas (Austin).

A. J. Matthews

*Huling, Thomas B.

*Hull, Theodore Young.

*Hull, Texas. Hull, in Liberty County, had a 1970 population of 1,496.

*Hull Oil Field.

*Hulver, Texas.

*Humaña, Antonio Gutiérrez de.

*Humble, Texas. (Harris County.) The population of Humble in 1970 was 3,278, an increase from the 1960 population count of 1,711. The city reported ninety-six businesses in 1970.

*Humble, Texas. (Wilbarger County.)

Humble Camp, Texas. Humble Camp, in Kleberg County, just north of Kingsville, was established on the King Ranch qv by the Humble Oil and Refining Company qv in the early 1940's to provide housing for Humble employees. These company houses were torn down several years later, and no Humble oil camps were in existence by 1955.

*Humble Oil Camp, Texas. *See also* Humble Camp, Texas.

*Humble Oil Field.

*Humble Oil and Refining Company. The Humble Oil and Refining Company (now Exxon

Company, U.S.A.), with headquarters in Houston, maintained all of its operations in the United States. Early in 1963 the company moved into a new forty-four-story building, thus consolidating the work location of some 3,500 of its Houston employees. The building rises more than six hundred feet above the city and is considered a Houston landmark.

In the 1960's Humble had more than twenty-one thousand square miles of land under lease in the United States. The company operated approximately twenty-four thousand producing wells in twenty-one states with a daily production of about 600,000 barrels of crude oil. Humble-operated wells also produced approximately 2.6 billion cubic feet of natural gas daily. Six Humble refineries and plants processed about 800,000 barrels of crude oil daily and produced from that volume a great variety of products.

In the post-World War II period, the company built a products line from Baytown to the Dallas-Fort Worth area, and in June, 1950, the company completed an eighteen-inch direct line from West Texas to the Gulf Coast. In 1961 Humble Pipe Line Company and Interstate Oil Pipe Line Company merged to form a wholly-owned affiliate of Humble Oil and Refining Company with a combined network of more than twelve thousand miles of gathering and trunk lines. Humble Pipe Line system received and delivered daily more than one million barrels of crude oil and petroleum products. The company operated about 10 percent of the nation's petroleum transportation facilities. More than two million barrels of crude oil and oil products flowed daily through company lines or moved by tanker or barge. Aided by some chartered vessels, Humble's fleet of nineteen ocean-going tankers, ranging in capacity from 140,000 to 582,000 barrels, delivered approximately 400,000 barrels of crude oil and products to the eastern seaboard each day. Tows and barges of Humble's Inland Waterways system moved 300,000 barrels a day over the nation's rivers and other inland waterways.

Chief executive officers of Humble since 1948 have been Hines H. Baker, 1948–1957; Morgan J. Davis, 1957–1963; C. E. Reistle, Jr., 1963–1966; M. A. Wright, 1966–1976. The company continued to publish a quarterly, *The Humble Way*, in addition to *Humble News* (for employees) and three marketing, four plant, and two division publications.

On January 1, 1973, the name of the company was officially changed to Exxon Company, U.S.A. Operating only in the United States, Exxon Company, U.S.A., was a division of Exxon Corporation (which operated also in foreign countries). Names of the public affairs publications were changed to *Exxon USA* and *Profile*.

James A. Clark

*Hume Indians. In the latter part of the seventeenth century the Hume (Jume) Indians, a Coahuiltecan-speaking band, ranged over an area that extended from northeastern Coahuila across the Rio Grande into the southwestern part of the Edwards Plateau. In 1675 the leader of the Bosque-Larios Expedition qv interviewed a Hume chief some eighteen miles north of present Eagle Pass. This chief reported that his people had recently suffered from an epidemic of smallpox. In 1684, while he was at the San Clemente Mission qv east of present-day San Angelo, Juan Domínguez de Mendoza qv listed Humez among the bands he was expecting to arrive shortly. It seems likely that Mendoza's Humez are the same people as Bosque's Hume and that this band ranged northward well into the western part of the Edward's Plateau. So far as can be determined today, these Coahuiltecan Hume are not related to the Hume of Durango and Sinaloa in northwestern Mexico or to the Hume of Oaxaca in southern Mexico.

BIBLIOGRAPHY: H. E. Bolton (ed.), *Spanish Exploration in the Southwest, 1542–1706* (1916); J. R. Swanton, *The Indian Tribes of North America* (1952).

T. N. Campbell

*Humline, Texas.

*Humphrey, Texas.

*Humphreys, Ezekial.

*Humphreys, Milton Wylie.

*Hungerford, Texas.

Hunnicutt, Walter Scott. Walter Scott Hunnicutt was born on January 20, 1889, in Marlin, Texas. He entered the University of Texas, where he was student director of the band from 1910 to 1914 and composed "Texas Taps," also known as the University of Texas Fight Song. He was elected student president of the law department in his senior year and took his LL.B. degree in 1914. In 1914 he entered the law office of Tom Connally qv in Marlin; in 1915 he was elected city attorney of Marlin, serving until 1917, when he enlisted as a private in the infantry of the United States Army. In that same year he married Mary Lee Durham of Austin; they had two children. In 1919 he was appointed captain, Judge Advocate General's Department.

Separated from the army, Hunnicutt returned to Marlin in 1921, was county judge from 1922 to 1928, and city attorney of Marlin from 1929 to 1933, when he was appointed United States attorney for the western district of Texas. He moved to El Paso in 1933, was active in the El Paso Symphony until 1940, and composed the march "Texas Miner" for the Texas College of Mines and Metallurgy (now the University of Texas at El Paso).

Recalled to active duty as a lieutenant colonel in 1940, he served three years in Texas before going to the South Pacific for two and a half years as judge advocate general for Guadalcanal and other islands. He returned to the United States in 1945 and retired as a colonel in 1946. He died on November 27, 1963, and was interred in the national cemetery at Fort Bliss.qv

Charles Durham Gouldie

Hunt, James Winfred. James Winfred Hunt was born on July 9, 1875, at the Kaw Indian Agency, Indian Territory, the son of William and Elizabeth (Pruitt) Hunt. His father was a government physician at the time of his birth. When he was five the family moved to Estacado,qv a Quaker colony in Crosby County, Texas, and he grew up in that area working for neighboring ranchers.

He was graduated from Central Plains Academy, Estacado, in 1893. After graduation he edited the *Texan Press* at Plainview, and in 1903 he decided to enter the Methodist ministry. On January 16, 1906, he married Mary Anthony; they had five children. He held pastorates in Dumas, Snyder, and Abilene, and from 1916 to 1918 he was president of Stamford College. His principal achievement was his presentation of plans to the Northwest Texas Methodist Conference and the Abilene Chamber of Commerce which led to the founding of McMurry College. In 1923 he was named first president of that college and served in that capacity until his death on March 12, 1934. Hunt's published works include *The Saga of Grandma Rogers* (1926) and "Buffalo Days," a series in *Holland's Magazine* qv (1933).

Rupert N. Richardson

*Hunt, Memucan.

*Hunt, Texas. (Hunt County.)

*Hunt, Texas. (Kerr County.)

*Hunt County. Hunt County, although primarily a farming area, has had an increasing industrial economy. Cotton, grains, and other field crops accounted for two-thirds of the farm income, which was over $10 million in 1959 and approximately $13 million annually in the early 1970's. In 1964 the number of cotton bales produced in the county was 18,613, with fifteen gins to process them; in the 1968–1969 season 21,867 bales were ginned with twelve gins. The county produced 1,716,764 barrels of oil from 1942 to January 1, 1973. East Texas State University at Commerce and Lake Tawakoni in the southern part of the county have contributed to the growth of the county. The 1960 population was 39,399; by 1970 the population had increased to 47,948.

*Hunter, Eli.

*Hunter, John Dunn.

Hunter, John M. John M. Hunter, born on September 2, 1821, in Tennessee, was one of the pioneer merchants of Fredericksburg. In 1847 he joined German settlers in petitioning the Texas legislature for the creation of a new county. When Gillespie County was organized and elections held in 1848, he became the first county clerk. County and district court meetings were held in his store, located in the block east of Market Square. At closing time on the night of June 30, 1850, Hunter refused to sell whiskey to a soldier from Fort Martin Scott;qv a fight ensued and Hunter stabbed and killed the soldier. The next night, July 1, about fifty of the soldier's comrades returned, found that Hunter had left town, then proceeded to burn Hunter's store, destroying the county records housed in the building. The recording of county records was resumed after July 15, 1850.

Hunter, charged with manslaughter but never indicted, bought another lot on the same block, and by October 12, 1850, the district court was meeting in his new rock store. Hunter married Sophie Ahrens, who had come from Germany in 1845. He died on September 4, 1870.

BIBLIOGRAPHY: Rudolph L. Biesele, *The History of the German Settlements in Texas, 1831–1861* (1930); Robert Penniger, *Fest-Ausgabe zum 50-jährigen Jubiläum der Gründung der Stadt Friedrichsburg* (1896); Gillespie County Historical Society, *Pioneers in God's Hills* (1960).

Esther L. Mueller

Hunter, John Marvin. John Marvin Hunter, son of Mary Ann (Calhoun) and John Warren Hunter,qv was born in Loyal Valley, Texas, on March 18, 1880. His father, a school teacher, moved frequently, and Marvin spent his early boyhood in Voca, Camp San Saba, Mason, Menardville (renamed Menard), Fort McKavett, and Peter's Prairie. In 1891 his father became a newspaper publisher and editor, first in Menardville and, a year later, in Mason. Marvin learned to set type for his father's paper, and at seventeen he began work for the Llano *Times*. Late in 1897 he started the Comfort *Times*, but after a few months he discontinued the paper and worked as a printer for papers in Sonora, San Angelo, Brownwood, and El Paso. Throughout these early years Hunter became acquainted with many frontier characters, on both sides of the law, and his interest in recording history increased.

In 1900 he took a printer's job in Deming, New Mexico. A year later he married Hattie Westerman of Safford, Arizona, who died soon afterward. Returning to Texas, Hunter became editor and manager of a paper at Menardville. On December 23, 1903, he married Susie Rogers of Mason. They became the parents of two sons and two daughters. In 1904 Hunter launched the *Kimble County Crony.* In more than six decades of newspaper work he established, owned, or published sixteen newspapers; he settled in Bandera after buying a paper there in 1921. Two years later he began publishing the monthly *Frontier Times.*qv In 1927 he opened the Frontier Times Museum.qv He wrote an autobiography and several books and pamphlets on frontier history, some of which were: *Pioneer History of Bandera County* (c. 1922); *The Bloody Trail in Texas* (1931); *Old Camp Verde, the Home of the Camels* (1939); *Cooking Recipes of the Pioneers* (1948); and *Peregrinations of a Pioneer Printer* (1954). In addition, he edited *The Trail Drivers of Texas*, I (1920), II (1923) and was co-author of *Album of Gunfighters* (c. 1951). He was working on *The Story of Lottie Deno* when he died in Kerrville on June 29, 1957; this work was subsequently published by his children. His library and personal notes were placed in the Barker Texas History Center qv at the University of Texas at Austin.

BIBLIOGRAPHY: J. Marvin Hunter, *Peregrinations of a Pioneer Printer* (1954); Dallas *Morning News*, June 30, 1957.

Wayne Gard

*Hunter, John Warren.

*Hunter, Johnson Calhoun.

*Hunter, Robert Hancock.

*Hunter, William L.

*Hunter, Texas.

*Hunter Branch.

Hunter's Creek Village, Texas. Hunter's Creek Village in southwestern Harris County, was incorporated in 1954 and had a mayor–alderman form of city government. In 1966 the town had a school and a church. In 1960 the population was 2,478; by 1970 the population had increased to 3,959.

*Hunter's Retreat, Texas.

*Hunting Bayou.

*Huntington, Texas. According to the United States 1970 census, Huntington, in Angelina County, had a population of 1,192, an increase from 1,009 reported in 1960.

Huntley, Texas. Huntley was one of several names by which the settlement at Green's Bluff has been known. Located on the Sabine River in what is now Orange County, Huntley was one of the earlier names, for it is shown on the official boundary map drawn by A. B. Gray qv from the survey made in 1840 by the joint commission representing the United States and the Republic of Texas.qv Other names for the village that later became the present city of Orange were Green's Bluff and Madison.

Madeleine Martin

*Huntoon, Texas.

*Hunt's Store, Texas.

*Huntsville, Texas. Huntsville, seat of Walker County, was a center for the area's forestry industry, farming, livestock raising, and tourism. Among the first business enterprises was the Thomas and Sandford (not Sanford, as stated in Volume I) Gibbs general store, established in 1841 (not 1844). In 1970 Gibbs Brothers and Company qv was possibly the oldest continuous business in Texas still on its original site and under the same family ownership. In 1970 there were 182 businesses, including five industries employing twenty-five or more persons and producing pine lumber, bricks, and concrete blocks. The Texas Prison Rodeo qv was an annual event in October, and the Huntsville State Park (*see* Parks, State) offered major recreational and tourist facilities. In 1966 the city reported eighteen churches, two banks, two newspapers, a hospital, a library, and a radio station. A new library was opened in 1967. The doubling of both the student population and the faculty of Sam Houston State College (now Sam Houston State University) during the 1960's accounted for part of the city's growth and pro-

gress. Additional factors in this growth were the expansion and improvements at the Texas State Penitentiary, which provided new job opportunities for local labor. The 1960 population was 11,999; in 1970 the population was 17,610, an increase of 46.8 percent.

*Huntsville Academy.

*Huntsville Branch Railway Company.

*Huntsville Male Institute.

*Hurd, James Gardner.

*Hurd, Norman.

*Hurd, William A.

*Hurdleston, Charles H.

*Hurds Pasture Draw.

Hurley, Texas. Old Hurley, founded in 1907, was the first town established in Bailey County. Situated about three and one-half miles north of the present site of Muleshoe, it was opened by the Coldren Land Company. Old Hurley had a population of about twenty-five in 1908, when James Johnson bought the townsite. Later, when the Santa Fe Railroad determined its course from Lubbock to Texico, New Mexico, the Fairview Land and Cattle Company organized the Hurley Townsite Company, Incorporated, and bought land along the railroad. The company put New Hurley about three miles northwest of Muleshoe and on September 4, 1912, platted the town. Irrigation wells were drilled on surrounding forty-acre farms, and soon a broom factory was built in the new town. Because the company demanded more for the right-of-way through town than the railroad was willing to pay, the town of Muleshoe was organized and the depot put there. Hurley went to court but could not force the railroad to stop there. After the county courthouse was definitely established in Muleshoe in 1918, Hurley declined until the post office was discontinued in 1926.

BIBLIOGRAPHY: Roysten E. Willis, Ghost Towns of the South Plains (M.A. thesis, Texas Technological College 1941).

*Hurlwood, Texas.

*Hurnville, Texas.

*Huron, Texas.

*Hurricane Bayou.

*Hurricane Creek.

Hurricanes in Texas. The largest and most destructive storms which affect the Texas coast are the tropical cyclones which occur seasonally from late June through October. From 1818 to 1885 at least twenty-eight hurricanes struck Texas, and from 1885 through 1964 sixty-six tropical storms have been recorded, about two-thirds of which were of hurricane force (winds of more than seventy-four miles per hour). Two major hurricanes occurred in the five years from 1965 to 1970. Frequently these storms rushed inland, causing destruction and flooding in the interior, but the heaviest damage has always been to population centers along the coast.

A hurricane spoiled Jean Laffite's qv pirate encampment on Galveston Island in 1818, and "Racer's Storm" passed over the same area in 1837. Named for the Racer, a British sloop of war which encountered the storm in Yucatán Channel, the strong wind reached Brownsville about October 4, curved up the coastline over Galveston, and then moved eastward, reaching the Atlantic Ocean near Charleston, South Carolina. "Racer's Storm" wrecked nearly every vessel on the coast and blew away all the houses on Galveston Island. It sent flood waters inland fifteen to twenty miles over the coastal prairies.

Five years later, in September, 1842, Galveston was again prostrated. No lives were lost, but parts of the city were tossed about like "pieces of a toy town." Damage to ships and buildings amounted to $50,000. Another September storm in 1854 struck Texas between Galveston and Matagorda. Matagorda was leveled; Houston sustained a $30,000 loss; and heavy damage was reported at Lynchburg, San Jacinto, Velasco, Quintana, Brazoria, Columbia, and Sabine Pass.

The entire Texas coast felt the hurricane of 1867, which entered the state south of Galveston on October 3. Bagdad and Clarksville at the mouth of the Rio Grande were flattened, while Galveston was flooded and raked for a loss of $1,000,000.

On September 16, 1875, a hurricane washed away three-fourths of the buildings in the town of Indianola in Calhoun County and killed 176 citizens. Five years later, on October 12–13, 1880, many lives were lost and Brownsville was nearly destroyed by a tropical wind. A second hurricane in Indianola on August 19–20, 1886, struck the town, destroying or damaging every structure.

The "Great Galveston Storm" on September 8–9, 1900, is known as the worst natural disaster in United States history. Although the wind was estimated at 120 miles per hour, flooding caused most of the damage. The island was completely inundated. Property loss amounted to about $40,000,-000, and an estimated 6,000 to 8,000 persons perished. (See Galveston Flood in Volume I.) Again on August 16–19, 1915, Galveston received the brunt of a vicious hurricane. Damage amounted to $50,000,000, but only 275 lives were lost because of the protection afforded by a new sea wall.

At Corpus Christi a storm on August 18, 1916, inflicted over $1,500,000 damage and took twenty lives. Three years later, on September 14, 1919, the center of a hurricane moved inland just south of the city. Tides were sixteen feet above normal; the wind rose to 110 miles per hour; and damage was estimated at $20,272,000. Some 284 persons perished.

The center of a hurricane passed near Brownsville on September 4–5, 1933. The wind velocity was measured at 106 miles per hour before the anemometer blew away, and wind gusts were estimated at 125 miles per hour. Most of the citrus crop of the Lower Rio Grande Valley was ruined.

Forty persons were killed and five hundred were injured.

On June 27, 1957, Hurricane Audrey swept across the Gulf Coast near the Texas-Louisiana line. Nine lives were lost and 450 persons were injured. Property damage, particularly extensive in Jefferson and Orange counties, amounted to $8,000,000. The effect was more serious across Sabine Lake in Cameron Parish, Louisiana, where hundreds of persons lost their lives.

Hurricane Carla, one of the most widely known coastal storms of recent years, occurred on September 8–14, 1961. During the storm, a tornado ravaged Galveston Island; at Port Lavaca, Carla's wind gusts were estimated at 175 miles per hour. The total damage to property and crops amounted to over $300,000,000, with the heaviest losses sustained in the area between Corpus Christi and Port Arthur. Because 250,000 persons were evacuated from the coastal region, only thirty-four persons were killed and 465 were injured.

Hurricane Beulah, the third largest hurricane of the twentieth century, swept across South Texas on September 20–21, 1967. The storm, which had previously ravaged the Yucatán peninsula in Mexico, moved inland from the Gulf just south of Port Isabel early on the morning of the 20th. It struck Brownsville with winds estimated at 140 miles per hour, moved northwest across South Texas to the vicinity of Alice, then turned southwest, crossed the Rio Grande between Zapata and Laredo, and finally blew itself out in Mexico. Advance warnings permitted the evacuation of Port Isabel, Port Mansfield, and Port Aransas, but winds and rain caused considerable property damage there as well as in the resort areas of Padre Island. In Port Brownsville tides and high winds damaged a large portion of the shrimp fleet, and in the Lower Rio Grande Valley the citrus crop was ruined.

Beulah spawned 115 separate tornadoes, several of which occurred in populated areas. Tornadoes struck New Braunfels, Fulton, and Sweet Home, and were sighted as far north as Austin. Rains of up to thirty inches accompanied the storm, and these in turn caused floods which inundated a large part of South Texas for more than two weeks. Three Rivers, Sinton, Victoria, and Pleasanton were hit especially hard. In Harlingen rampaging water from the Arroyo Colorado threatened the entire city. Flood waters on the Rio Grande put large portions of Camargo and Reynosa, Tamaulipas, under water, and some 9,000 refugees crossed the border to Rio Grande City. On September 28 President Lyndon Baines Johnson qv declared twenty-four counties in South Texas disaster areas. Official estimates in these counties set the number of dead at eighteen, the injured or sick at 9,000, and the number of homes destroyed or heavily damaged at 3,000. Property damage was estimated at $100,-000,000, crop damage at $50,000,000. Some 300,-000 people were evacuated during the storm and subsequent flooding.

Reported to be the costliest in the state's history, Hurricane Celia ravaged Corpus Christi and its area on August 3, 1970. Previous to the storm the weather was deceptively calm with no heavy rains or gusty winds. Preliminary reports indicated the approach of a relatively mild storm. Formed as a tropical depression in the Gulf of Mexico, Celia first hit land at Port Aransas, Ingleside, and Aransas Pass. The eye of the storm moved in just north of Corpus Christi, then moved in several directions, sweeping that city, Portland, Taft, Bayside, Gregory, Fulton Beach, Rockport, and Key Allegro, and went on through Odem, Edroy, Sinton, Mathis, Agua Dulce, Robstown, Sandia, Orange Grove, and George West. Winds up to 161 miles per hour and gusts to 180 miles per hour were reported.

President Richard M. Nixon declared seven counties a major disaster area. An estimated thirteen persons died in the Corpus Christi area. Officials estimated damage to commercial buildings, automobiles, and homes in excess of $500,000,000. Crop losses and damage to farm equipment were estimated at more than $100,000,000. More than 3,500 persons left Corpus Christi, and entire cities were evacuated from the low-lying regions. Celia ended on August 5, in a series of thunderstorms near El Paso and the New Mexico border. Hurricane Celia did not produce torrential rains and flooding that so often accompany storms of this magnitude. The heaviest rainfall was 6.38 inches in Corpus Christi, and at Pearsall and Jourdanton, thirty to forty miles north of the hurricane center, there was no rain. Preliminary studies of the Bureau of Economic Geology at the University of Texas at Austin indicated that Celia differed significantly from previous storms that have struck the coast in that it was much narrower and correspondingly more intense in the affected area.

Other significant storms included those at Galveston Bay, 1776; Brazos Santiago, 1884; Sabine, 1886; Port Arthur, 1897; Velasco, 1909; near Freeport, 1932; near Seadrift, 1934; near Matagorda, 1941; Matagorda Bay, 1942; near Galveston, 1943; Aransas San Antonio Bay area, 1945; Freeport, 1949; and west of Port Arthur, 1963. While it is true that hurricane-inflicted damage to property has increased through the years, the death rate has not, because of the implementation of various precautionary measures. *See also* Tornadoes in Texas; Weather in Texas.

BIBLIOGRAPHY: W. Armstrong Price, *Hurricanes Affecting the Coast of Texas from Galveston to Rio Grande* (1956); John Edward Weems, *A Weekend in September* (1957); Joe Frantz, *Gail Borden* (1951); Ivan Ray Tannehill, *Hurricanes* (1945); Jim Wood and Grady Phelps (eds.), *Celia, the Saga of a Storm* (1970); *Texas Almanac* (1965, 1970); John T. Carr, Jr., "Hurricanes Affecting the Texas Gulf Coast," *Texas Water Development Board Report 49* (June, 1967); S. W. Geiser, "Racer's Storm (1837)," *Field and Laboratory*, XII (1944); New Orleans *Picayune*, October 24–27, 1837; San Antonio *Express*, September 18–30, 1967; *Time* (October 6, 1967); *Senator Ralph Yarborough's Newsletter*, October 12, 19, 1967; Austin *American-Statesman*, August 9, 1970; Corpus Christi *Caller-Times*, August 1–11, 1970.

Roy Sylvan Dunn

*Hurst, Texas. (Coryell County.)

*Hurst, Texas. (Tarrant County.) Hurst, in the Fort Worth suburban area, grew from an estimated one hundred persons in 1950 to an incorporated city of 10,165 in 1960. In 1966 the city reported sixteen churches, a bank, a library, and newspaper. In 1970 the number of businesses rose to 298. Northeast Campus of Tarrant County Junior College District qv began operations at Hurst in September, 1968. A Bell Helicopter factory has been established there also. Hurst experienced a substantial population growth, to 27,215 in 1970. *See also* Fort Worth Standard Metropolitan Statistical Area.

*Hurst Creek.

*Hurst Gap.

*Hurt, James Mann.

*Huston, Almanzon.

*Huston, Felix.

Huston-Tillotson College. Huston-Tillotson College, Austin, was a coeducational college of liberal arts and sciences, operated jointly under the auspices of the American Missionary Association of the United Church of Christ and the Board of Education of the Methodist Church. It was formed by merger of Samuel Huston College and Tillotson College,qqv which was effected in October, 1952. Huston-Tillotson remained primarily a Negro college after the merger, although there were no restrictions as to race.

The college was accredited or approved by the following bodies: Southern Association of Colleges and Schools, University Senate of the Methodist Church, American Association of Colleges for Teacher Education, Association of American Colleges, National Committee on Accrediting, Council for Higher Education of the United Church of Christ, Texas Education Agency,qv and Association of Texas Colleges.qv

Bachelor of arts and bachelor of science degrees were offered with major concentration in fifteen areas. In 1966 the twenty-three-acre campus contained an administration building, science building, two residence halls, student union-dining hall, gymnasium-auditorium, music hall, lounge, and two other halls. Its library housed 47,430 volumes by 1969. By the early 1970's new buildings included a classroom-administration building, a chapel, an addition of three wings to the women's dormitory, and an addition of two wings to the men's dormitory.

Mary E. Branch and William H. Jones, last presidents of Tillotson College, and Karl E. Downs, Robert F. Harrington, and Willis J. King, past presidents of Samuel Huston College, undertook cooperative sponsorship of several academic activities beginning in 1945. M. S. Davage served as interim president during the transition period. He retired in 1955 and was succeeded by J. J. Seabrook, the first permanent president of Huston-Tillotson. Upon Seabrook's retirement in 1965, John Q. Taylor King became president; King was still president in the 1974–1975 term, when the enrollment was 696 students.

*Hutcheson, Joseph Chappell.

Hutcheson, Joseph Chappell, Jr. Joseph Chappell Hutcheson, Jr., the son of Mildred (Carrington) and Joseph Chappell Hutcheson,qv was born in Houston on October 19, 1879. He entered into the practice of law with his father's firm of Hutcheson, Campbell and Hutcheson in Houston, where he practiced for seventeen years. In 1913 he was named chief legal advisor for Houston and in 1917 was elected mayor of that city. President Woodrow Wilson appointed him U.S. district judge for the Southern District of Texas in 1918, where he served until he was named federal appeals judge for the Fifth U.S. Circuit Court of Appeals by President Herbert Hoover in 1931. He served as chief judge of that court from 1948 to 1959. Known as an expressive idealist and pragmatist who championed individual rights, he never had a major ruling overturned upon appeal. During Prohibition qv he served as an advisor to the Wickersham Commission, and in 1945 he was named U.S. chairman to the British-American commission on the settlement of Jews in Palestine.

Joseph Hutcheson married Anne Elizabeth Weeden on December 21, 1905; they had two children. Hutcheson was educated at Bethel (Virginia) Military Academy, the University of Virginia, and the University of Texas, where he was graduated first in the class of 1900, the year he was also admitted to the State Bar.qv He was the author of *Law as Liberator* (1937) and *Judgment Intuitive* (1938). He died on January 18, 1973, in Houston.

BIBLIOGRAPHY: *Who's Who In America* (1968); Houston *Chronicle*, January 21, 1973; Houston *Post*, January 23, 1973; Biographical File, Barker Texas History Center, University of Texas at Austin.

*Hutcheson, Texas.

*Hutchings, Henry.

*Hutchings, John H.

*Hutchins, William J.

*Hutchins, Texas. The population of Hutchins, in Dallas County, in 1970 was 1,755, an increase from the 1,100 reported for the town in 1960. The town had thirty businesses in 1970.

*Hutchinson, Anderson.

*Hutchinson County. Hutchinson County relied chiefly on the petroleum and cattle industries in the 1960's. The county increased its production of wheat and grain sorghums by irrigation; sixty-five thousand acres were irrigated in 1968. New crops included sugar beets and soybeans. From 1923 to January, 1973, over 460,000,000 barrels of oil were produced. The county supported a library, a hospital, and an airport. The recreation area around Lake Meredith greatly increased the tourist trade. The population decreased from 34,419 in 1960 to 24,443 in 1970.

*Hutto, Texas.

*Huxley, Texas.

Huyuguan Indians. In the late seventeenth century a group referred to as Huhuguan (Huhuygam) Indians was reported as living in northeastern Coahuila. Later, in 1718, a group known as Huyuguan was encountered by the Spanish in Texas between present Austin and Houston, apparently in the vicinity of modern Austin County. These names evidently refer to the same people, and the chronology suggests migration from Coahuila to Texas. Many other Coahuiltecan groups also migrated to Texas during the same period.

BIBLIOGRAPHY: V. Alessio Robles, *Coahuila y Texas en la Epoca Colonial* (1938); F. L. Hoffmann (trans.), *Diary of the Alarcón Expedition into Texas, 1718–1719, by Fray Francisco Céliz* (1935).

T. N. *Campbell*

*Hyatt, Texas.

*Hydro, Texas.

*Hye, Texas.

*Hyer, Absalom.

*Hyer, Robert Stewart.

*Hylton, Texas.

*Hyman, Texas.

Hynds City, Texas. Hynds City, in northern Montague County, was founded in 1925, when oil production began in the area. The town, defunct by 1966, was named for Robert L. Hynds.

*Hynes Bay.

*Hynes Bay, Battle of.

*Hynesville, Texas.

*Hynson's Mountain.

I

*I O A Ranch.

*Iago, Texas.

*Iatan, Texas.

*Ibarvo, Antonio Gil. [This title was incorrectly listed in Volume I as Ibarvo, Gil Antonio.]

*Iberis, Texas.

*Ibex, Texas.

*Icarian Colony. *See also* Cabet, Étienne.

Ice Making, Mechanical. *See* Refrigeration, Early History of, in Texas.

*Iconoclast, The.

*Ida, Texas.

*Idalou, Texas. In 1960 Idalou, in Lubbock County, had a population of 1,274; in 1970 the population was 1,729, and thirty businesses were reported. *See also* Lubbock Standard Metropolitan Statistical Area.

Ideson, Julia Bedford. Julia Bedford Ideson, daughter of John Castree and Rosalie (Beasman) Ideson, was born at Hastings, Nebraska, on July 15, 1880. She received her early education in Visitation Convent in Hastings. After her parents moved to Houston, Texas, in 1891, she attended public schools. At the University of Texas (1899–1900; 1901–1903) she was a member of the first class in library science offered by the university.

In 1903 she was appointed librarian of the new Houston Lyceum and Carnegie Library in Houston. During the next ten years she developed an institution of high esteem in the city's cultural life. On leave from the library, she spent 1913–1914 in Paris, France, as secretary for the American Art Students' Club. During World War I, in Houston, Julia Ideson devoted her time and energy to furthering the United States war effort. As a member of the Harris County Women's Committee she worked for the Third Liberty Loan Drive. She organized the library for Camp Logan,[qv] an army camp near Houston, and later volunteered for library work overseas. In 1919 she was sent to Brest, France, with the American Library Association and was assigned to the Camp Pontenezeon library.

After her return to the United States, Julia Ideson, with the aid of the library board, the newspapers, and the staff and friends of the library, campaigned for an ordinance to set aside a percentage of the city's taxes for library purposes. In February, 1921, the ordinance received a favorable vote. Because the Carnegie building was too small for the growing city, Julia Ideson planned for a new building. Two city bond issues provided the funds, and the new building for the Houston Public Library was opened in October, 1926. Two new branch buildings were constructed from the proceeds of the sale of the old library site and building. In succeeding years Julia Ideson saw four other branches and a bookmobile added to the library system.

Julia Ideson was president of the Texas Library Association,[qv] 1910–1911; president of the Southwestern Library Association, 1932–1934; and first vice-president of the American Library Association, 1932–1933. She also served on numerous committees and policy-making boards for all three organizations. She was editor of two volumes of the *Handbook of Texas Libraries*, No. 2 and No. 4, published in 1908 and 1935, respectively.

Julia Ideson died in New Hope, Pennsylvania, on July 15, 1945, and was buried in Hollywood Cemetery in Houston, Texas. The central library building in Houston was named in her honor.

Louise Franklin

***Idlewilde, Texas.**

***Iiams, John.**

***Iiams, John, Jr.**

***Ijams, Basil G.**

***Ikard, William Sude.**

***Ike, Texas.** (Ellis County.)

***Ike, Texas.** (Live Oak County.)

***Ikin, Arthur.**

***Ilisee Indians.**

***Ilka, Texas.**

***Illinois Bend, Texas.**

***Illusion Lake.**

***Immermere, Texas.**

***Immigration Border Patrol.** *See* Border Patrol.

Impact, Texas. Impact, north of Abilene, voted incorporation in 1960 as the only wet town in dry Taylor County. When two liquor stores opened in Impact, Abilene lawyers went to court to oppose the incorporation of the town. In 1963 the Texas Supreme Court upheld the incorporation and also the selling of liquor in Impact. The town, covering forty-seven acres, was named for Impact, Inc., the advertising business of the town's mayor, Dallas Perkins. Impact's 1970 population was sixty-one.

***Imperial, Texas.** (Fort Bend County.)

***Imperial, Texas.** (Pecos County.)

***Imperial Colonization Law.** *See* Mexican Colonization Laws, 1821–1830.

***Imperial Valley Railroad.**

***Imperialist Creek.**

***Inadale, Texas.**

Incarnate Word, Sisters of Charity of the. *See* Sisters of Charity of the Incarnate Word.

Incarnate Word and Blessed Sacrament, Sisters of the. *See* Sisters of the Incarnate Word and Blessed Sacrament.

***Incarnate Word College.** Incarnate Word College, San Antonio, owned and operated by the Congregation of the Sisters of Charity of the Incarnate Word,[qv] continued as a Catholic women's college (although the nursing school has always admitted men as well) until the fall of 1971, when the college became fully coeducational. In 1965 the campus contained fourteen buildings, six of which were erected between 1955 and 1965, including a library, a gymnasium, a student center, a dormitory, a center for mentally retarded children and child evaluation and guidance clinic, and a fine arts center. By 1975 three more buildings were added: a nursing building, a dormitory, and a dining hall. In 1969 the library contained 78,962 volumes; by 1975 holdings had increased to 100,000 volumes.

The college was accredited by the Southern Association of Colleges and Schools as well as by various music, education, and nursing organizations. Master's degree programs were offered in the arts and sciences and in teacher education. In 1974–1975 the college had a total enrollment of 1,510 students and a faculty of 120. Sister Margaret Patrice Slattery served as president. *See also* Roman Catholic Education in Texas.

Independence.

*Independence, Texas. (Cherokee County.)

*Independence, Texas. (Hopkins County.)

*Independence, Texas. (Washington County.)

*Independence Academy.

*Independence Creek.

*Independence Day, Texas.

*Independence Female Academy. *See* Independence Academy.

*Independence Hill, Texas.

*Independent, Texas.

Independent Chronicle (Galveston).

*India, Texas.

Indian Affairs, Commission for. The Commission for Indian Affairs, composed of three members appointed by the governor, was created in 1965 to direct the improvement of the health, education, and economic resources of the Alabama-Coushatta Indian Reservation.qv The work of this commission was formerly done by the Board for Texas State Hospitals and Special Schools,qv which was abolished in 1965. In 1967 the Tigua Indian qv community in El Paso was placed under the jurisdiction of the commission.
BIBLIOGRAPHY: University of Texas at Austin, *Guide To Texas State Agencies* (1972).

*Indian Artifacts. *See* Archaeology.

*Indian Camp Creek.

*Indian Creek.

*Indian Creek, Texas.

*Indian Creek Academy.

*Indian Gap, Texas.

*Indian Head.

*Indian Hills.

*Indian Knob.

*Indian Mesa.

*Indian Mountain.

*Indian Peak.

*Indian Pottery. *See* Archaeology.

*Indian Relations: **Colonial Period.**

*Indian Relations: Republic of Texas.

*Indian Relations: Statehood.

*Indian Reservations.

*Indian Rock, Texas.

Indian Rock Art. *See* Rock Art, Indian.

*Indianola, Texas.

*Indianola Historical Society.

*Indianola Peak.

*Indianola Railroad.

*Indianola Storm.

*Indians of Texas. [The signature on this article in Volume I was left off; the author was W. E. S. Dickerson. Ed.]

*Indio, Texas. (Presidio County.)

*Indio, Texas. (Zavala County.)

*Indio Creek.

*Indios Bravos and Indios Reducidos.

*Industrial Accident Board.

Industrial Commission, Texas. The Texas Industrial Commission, created in 1920, was composed of nine members: two employers, two employees, and five persons from the general public. Appointed by the governor for six-year overlapping terms, the members represented different geographical areas of the state. The original function of the commission was to aid the governor in arbitrating labor-management disputes; this function was dropped and the commission was given, in 1959, the responsibility of promoting industrial development. The commission was not funded by the legislature until 1962, when a full-time executive director was hired. In 1965 a specialist in export development was added to promote foreign sales of Texas products.
BIBLIOGRAPHY: University of Texas at Austin, *Guide To Texas State Agencies* (1966, 1972).

*Industry. *See* Manufacturing in Texas.

*Industry, Texas.

*Inez, Texas.

*Inge, Texas.

*Inge Mountain.

*Ingleside, Texas. Ingleside, in San Patricio County, had a population of 3,022 in 1960 and 3,763 in 1970. The town had thirty-five businesses in 1970. *See also* Corpus Christi Standard Metropolitan Statistical Area.

*Inglish, Bailey.

*Ingram, Allen.

*Ingram, Ira.

*Ingram, John. John Ingram, who settled in Fayette County, participated in the siege of Bexar qv in the company of Captain R. Goheen (not Captain Mark B. Lewis,qv as stated in Volume I). John Ingram had also served at the battle of Gonzales qv in October, 1835, and he later fought at the battle of San Jacinto.qv [He should not be confused with another John Ingram, from Jasper County, who married Mary Conn and was a lieutenant in a company from Jasper County commanded by Captain Martin B. Lewis.qv Ed.]
BIBLIOGRAPHY: J. H. Kuykendall, "Reminiscences of Early Texans," *Quarterly of the Texas State Historical Association*, VI (1902–1903).

*Ingram, Seth.

*Ingram, Texas. Ingram, located in Kerr County, had a 1970 population of approximately 660. The site of the Kerr County Arts Foundation, Ingram had twenty-five business establishments in 1970.

*Ingrando Marsh.

Inhame Indians. In 1683–1684 Juan Domínguez de Mendoza qv led an exploratory expedition from El Paso as far eastward as the junction of the Concho and Colorado rivers east of present San

Angelo. In his itinerary he listed the names of thirty-seven Indian groups, including the Inhame, from which he expected to receive delegations on the Colorado River. Nothing further is known about the Inhame (Injame), who seem to have been one of many Indian groups of north-central Texas that were swept away by the southward thrust of the Lipan-Apache and Comanche Indians in the eighteenth century. It is possible that the Inhame were the same as the Sijame, a Coahuiltecan group of the same period, but proof of this is lacking.

BIBLIOGRAPHY: H. E. Bolton (ed.), *Spanish Exploration in the Southwest, 1542-1706* (1916); C. W. Hackett (ed.), *Pichardo's Treatise on the Limits of Louisiana and Texas,* II (1934).

T. N. Campbell

*Inks Dam and Lake. Inks Dam and Lake (or Inks Lake) is in the Colorado River Basin in Burnet and Llano counties, ten miles west of Burnet on the Colorado River, four miles below Buchanan Dam. The project is owned and operated by the Lower Colorado River Authority qv as one of a series of six dams and reservoirs on the Colorado River. Inks Lake has a capacity of 17,000 acre-feet and a surface area of 830 acres at spillway crest elevation of 880 feet above mean sea level. This lake is considered a constant-level one because the normal turbine discharge is coordinated with the inflow from Buchanan Reservoir so that the day-to-day fluctuation is small. However, during periods of floods the lake level will vary considerably. The power plant contains one 12,500-kilowatt generating unit with all auxiliary equipment. It is operated by remote control from Buchanan Plant, and the output is coordinated with the discharge from that plant. The drainage area is 31,290 square miles, of which 11,900 square miles is probably noncontributing.

BIBLIOGRAPHY: Texas Water Commission, *Bulletin 6408* (1964).

Seth D. Breeding

*Inks Lake State School. The Inks Lake State School was closed in 1950 when the land on which it was situated was returned to the Lower Colorado River Authority.qv The students were transferred to various other state institutions.

*Inland Waterways.

Inman, Samuel Guy. Samuel Guy Inman, who helped to formulate the United States' "Good Neighbor" policy toward Latin America and devoted his life to Christian missions and world peace, was born in Trinity County, Texas, on June 24, 1877, the son of Joel B. and Caroline (Rodgers) Inman. His parents died when he was young, and he spent his adolescence in Houston, the ward of Ed and Martha Kneeland. He was an enthusiastic worker in the Christian Endeavor Society of the Christian church. In 1897 he enrolled in Add-Ran Christian University (now Texas Christian University), and after two years he transferred to Kentucky University (later Transylvania College) and then to Columbia University. He accepted his first church office in 1901 as assistant pastor of the First Church of the Disciples of Christ (later Park Avenue Christian Church) in New York City. On May 31, 1904, Inman received his B.A. degree from Columbia University; on the same day he married Bessie Winona Cox. Immediately afterward he became pastor of Tabernacle Church in Fort Worth.

Inman began missionary work in Latin America in 1905; out of this work he became an expert in Latin American culture and politics, frequently serving the United States and Latin American governments in advisory capacities. In 1908 he founded El Instituto Del Pueblo in Piedras Negras, Coahuila, Mexico, and in 1913 he founded the Mexican Christian Institute (later the Inman Christian Center; see Christian Church Schools in Texas). He helped organize the first Congress on Christian Work in Latin America in 1916; this meeting sought to coordinate and encourage Protestant missionary endeavors in Latin America. Inman founded many schools in Latin America, the most ambitious project being the Colegio Internacional at Asunción, Paraguay.

In 1915 Inman began speaking out on hemispheric affairs. That year he helped to found and became secretary (until 1939) of the Committee on Cooperation with Latin America; in 1920 the committee appointed him editor of its monthly journal, *La Nueva Democracia*. With his publication in 1919 of *Intervention in Mexico*, Inman began a notable career writing on inter-American affairs in both Spanish and English. He was a delegate to the Fifth Pan American Conference at Santiago, Chile, in 1923; thereafter he participated in every Pan American Conference.

In 1923 Inman earned an M.A. degree from Columbia University while holding a position at Columbia as a lecturer. Both Transylvania College (in 1923) and Texas Christian University (in 1925) honored him with LL.D. degrees.

Inman's views on inter-American friendship influenced the Latin American policies of the Franklin D. Roosevelt and Harry S. Truman administrations. He assisted in the formulation of Roosevelt's "Good Neighbor" pronouncement in December, 1933. In 1935 he was the first American cultural attaché for Latin America and served on the League of Nations Commission to Latin American Republics. In 1936 he was a presidential adviser at the Buenos Aires Conference when Roosevelt reaffirmed the Monroe Doctrine. From 1937 to 1942 Inman was a professor at the University of Pennsylvania. Throughout his career he was a popular college lecturer on Latin American affairs. He teamed with Carlos Eduardo Castañeda qv to write *A History of Latin America for Schools* (1945).

In 1945 Inman was an adviser to the Inter-American Conference on War and Peace at Chapultepec, Mexico, and was a consultant to the State Department during the United Nations Conference on International Organization at San Francisco. In the immediate postwar years Inman was generally critical of United States neglect of Latin America and objected to its support of "reactionary" elements in Latin America. In May, 1948, the Colombian government appointed Inman as its delegate to the Bogatá Inter-American Conference. On March 3, 1950, Inman was decorated by the Mexican government for his devotion to inter-American cooperation and for his efforts in behalf of Mexico's revolutionary democracy.

During the 1950's and 1960's Inman continued to work for world peace, although he supported wars against "communist aggression"; he was a member of the Church Peace Union. He was also an outspoken critic of McCarthyism in the early 1950's. He published his best-known books during the 1950's: *The World Resolution* (1955), *The Voice of America—What Shall It Say?* (1955), and *The Rise and Fall of the Good Neighbor Policy* (1957).

Inman died on February 19, 1965, while attending the International Convocation on Peace in New York City; this conference was in response to Pope John XXIII's 1963 encyclical, *Pacem in Terris*. Inman was survived by his wife and all five of their children.

BIBLIOGRAPHY: William J. Castleman, *On This Foundation* (1966); *Who's Who In America* (1960); New York *Times*, February 21, 1965.

Edgar P. Sneed

Inman Christian Center. *See* Christian Church Schools in Texas; *see also* Inman, Samuel Guy.

Inner Space Cavern. Inner Space Cavern, a large commercial cave near Georgetown, Williamson County, was discovered by the Texas Highway Department qv while drilling to test underpass foundations in May, 1963. Early exploration by Texas spelunkers was permitted by way of a large-diameter hole drilled into the roof of one of the cave's rooms. The present entrance is an artificial tunnel equipped with a cable car. Most of this highly decorated and complex cave lies less than sixty feet below the surface. In two now-filled entrances to the cave a large variety of vertebrate fossils of late Pleistocene age was recovered.

A. Richard Smith

Inocoplo Indians. The Inocoplo Indians, who lived in central Tamaulipas, were also known by other names, among them Barroso, Mesquite, Mulato, Serrano, and Sincoalne. When their area was brought under Spanish control during the second half of the eighteenth century, the Inocoplo moved northward. Some of them entered the San Antonio de Valero Mission qv of San Antonio in 1784–1785 under the names Gincape (Inocoplo) and Mulato.

BIBLIOGRAPHY: F. W. Hodge (ed.), *Handbook of American Indians*, I (1907); W. Jiménez Moreno, "Tribus e idiomas del Norte de México," *El Norte de México y el Sur de Estados Unidos* (1944); G. Saldivar, *Los Indios de Tamaulipas* (1943).

T. N. Campbell

Insane in Texas, Care of. See also Mentally Ill and Mentally Retarded, Care of, in Texas; Mental Health and Mental Retardation, Texas Department of.

*Inspector of Hides and Animals.**

Institute of Marine Science. *See* University of Texas Marine Science Institute at Port Aransas.

Institute of Texan Cultures. The Institute of Texan Cultures was created by the Fifty-ninth Legislature on May 27, 1965. The agency was directed to develop and implement an appropriate plan for the state's participation in HemisFair qv in 1968; to plan exhibits related to the history of Texas, its development, resources, and contributions; and to design and erect a building suited to housing these exhibits, giving due consideration to its utility for state purposes after the fair. The importance of this project was indicated by the allocation of additional revenues by the Sixtieth Legislature, bringing the total investment to $10,000,000.

The institute, a permanent state agency located on HemisFair grounds in San Antonio, was designed to study the twenty-six ethnic groups which settled in Texas. While not a museum, the institute displayed relics, artifacts, and personal memorabilia, but only those which had a direct connection with telling the story of the people in each ethnic group. The exhibits made use of sound, color, movement, and atmospheric design. R. Henderson Shuffler guided the research projects and formed the original staff.

The institute's continued function is to bring together, on loan, fragments of Texas history collections from museums and archives throughout the state, to produce film strips and slide shows on segments of Texas history, and to publish historical pamphlets and books. The Institute of Texan Cultures was put under the University of Texas System qv effective June 5, 1969, and its official title became the University of Texas Institute of Texan Cultures at San Antonio. In February, 1973, the institute became, more specifically, a part of the University of Texas at San Antonio. Upon the death of Shuffler in 1975, Jack R. Maguire was named director.

David C. Tiller

Institute of Underwater Research. *See* Padre Island Treasure.

Instruction, Public. See Education; Education, Agricultural; Education, Commissioner of; Education, Negro; Education, State Board of; Education, Vocational; Texas Education Agency; Coordinating Board, Texas College and University System.

Insurance, State Board of. The old state Board of Insurance Commissioners qv was abolished in 1957 with the creation of the State Board of Insurance, composed of three gubernatorial appointees serving six-year terms. The board determines policy, makes rules, determines rates, and hears appeals. Administrative functions are left to the commissioner of insurance, who is appointed by the board. The agency's primary functions include chartering insurance companies, examining them periodically to see if they still meet the requirements of Texas laws, licensing out-of-state insurance companies to do business in Texas, and licensing insurance agents. The agency must approve policy forms. It also determines rates for all fire and casualty insurance.

BIBLIOGRAPHY: Stuart A. MacCorkle and Dick Smith, *Texas Government* (1964); Clifton McCleskey, *Government and Politics of Texas* (1963); Wilbourn Eugene Benton, *Texas, Its Government and Politics* (1961).

Dick Smith

*Insurance and Banking, Department of. *See* Banking Department of Texas.

*Insurance Commissioners, Board of. *See also* Insurance, State Board of.

*Intangible Tax Board. *See* Tax Board, State or Intangible.

Integration in Texas. Most Texas Negroes were traditionally concentrated in East Texas, but in recent years many joined the nationwide migrations into the cities. Their integration into Texas life as equals became a topic of general public concern when Heman Marion Sweatt, a Negro, won a lawsuit in 1950 seeking admission to the University of Texas (*see Sweatt* v. *Painter*).

During the last years of the administration of Governor Allan Shivers and the first part of Governor Price Daniel's administration, many conservative candidates for public office in Texas campaigned against integration with the idea that public opinion was against it. More liberal candidates generally were equivocal or avoided the subject. In 1957 the Texas legislature considered the last group of segregationist bills and passed two of them. Signed into law by Governor Daniel, they were later declared unconstitutional.

During the next two sessions the legislature was considering not segregationist, but integrationist bills, and while these did not advance beyond committee hearings, they foretold the new drift of the times. With the onset of the Southern demonstrations in 1961, most Texas politicians fell silent on race. Political pressures and public opinion had shifted. The minorities had begun to vote in large blocs in the big cities, and it had become politically costly to be known as a segregationist.

Some changes began to occur in Texas racial customs, although these changes did not reach to housing and economic discrimination. Except for a peripheral role played by the Southern Christian Leadership Conference in demonstrations in Huntsville, the militant civil rights organizations by and large skipped Texas in the first half of the 1960's. Nevertheless, the state experienced many civil rights demonstrations on campuses, in the streets, and at places of public accommodation, and Texans could not ignore what was happening in other parts of the country. Integration did not become the legal standard in Texas public facilities, but non-segregation did.

By 1966 school integration was more widespread in Texas than in the more Southern states, but was still basically limited by residential segregation and was token, especially in East Texas. A Dallas *Morning News* qv survey of school integration found that in 1962–1963 only 7,000 Negro school children were attending formerly all-white schools.

Four years later 100,000, or one out of four, were attending them. With federal money playing a much larger role in Texas in the 1960's than before, open rejection of the gradually stiffening federal desegregation guidelines for schools and hospitals was unusual. By 1966 all the state's colleges and universities had some Negro students, and the junior colleges also were integrating. At the University of Texas all official activities and approved housing were integrated.

In the summer and early fall of 1966, some Texas Mexican farm workers, affected by the Negroes' example nationally and by their fellow Chicanos' qv example in the California grape strike, struck farms in Starr County on the Texas border and then walked more than 400 miles from Rio Grande City to Austin to petition the governor and the legislature for a minimum wage of $1.25 an hour. Official Austin responded with resistance and confusion. The senior U.S. senator from Texas, Ralph Yarborough, joined their march in Austin and led them to the steps of the state Capitol, qv where he spoke during their rally. The Starr County strike failed, but a counterpart effort was launched in the more populous Lower Rio Grande Valley later in the decade.

Mexican Americans had been winning local elections, especially in South Texas, for some time. In the first half of the 1960's a few Negroes were elected to city councils, school boards, and the state legislature. Barbara Jordan of Houston, elected state senator in 1966 and a member of the United States Congress in 1972, was a Boston-educated Negro with an impressive speaking style; Houston also sent its first Mexican American to the state legislature. The judicial abolition of the poll tax further challenged the Anglos' traditional dominance of the state's politics. State-operated special schools for the handicapped and for girls had been integrated, and the prisons were being desegregated in varying degrees, with attempts being made in the state prison system qv to integrate on the basis of ethnic population ratios. Local police forces were hiring some Negroes. In response to federal law, public accommodations were generally open without regard to race, and by 1970 even rural East Texas had changed substantially in this respect.

If segregation by law was being eliminated in Texas, there was still plenty of segregation in fact. Despite the policy positions of their governing bodies, church congregations and local unions often reflected segregated patterns. Social segregation was still the practice and mostly still the rule. The pattern of lowly jobs and low pay continued, so there was little relative change in the actual life situations of the Negro people.

New studies measuring residential segregation by percentages indicated that in Texas in the 1960's Negroes, and to a lesser extent Mexican Americans, still lived apart in residential sections intended specifically for them. These sections, often slums, had predominantly black schools in them. Some resistance to integration developed among Negroes concerned that their neighborhoods and communities would lose identity without their own schools and that the academic competition, compounded by personal tension, might be too difficult in formerly all-white schools that had long enforced more rigorous academic standards. A hint of the size of this problem could be found in the fact that of the state's approximately 1,300 school districts, about 700 were automatically approved for federal funds in 1966–1967 because they were basically all-white or all-Negro districts.

As summer riots became frequent in ghettos in American cities, tension also developed in Texas, particularly in Houston and Dallas, where there were large Negro sections. Bad feeling broke out in urban areas between blacks and the police, ensuing sometimes in shootings and deaths.

While integration in Texas was thus evolving, the political climate on the subject was swinging back. The disorders in Texas and elsewhere estranged a number of theretofore moderate or fence-straddling whites in Texas. The state's more moderate and conservative politicians in the middle and later 1960's frequently exhorted their followers to oppose the crime, riots, and civil disobedience which had shaped Southern demonstrations. Conservative Texans of both parties in the Texas delegation in Washington generally voted against the civil rights acts of the 1960's, while the more liberal Texas congressmen voted for them with a minimum of remark. Thus, as the Negro movement and its allies were seeking, by a controversial variety of methods, to commit the national conscience to economic justice for Negroes, Texas politics' response was analogous to its first reaction to integration.

By 1970, however, segregation was a dead letter in Texas politics. None of the candidates for major statewide office that year openly questioned integration. The Nixon administration was enforcing the re-drawing of school boundaries in some of the cities to reduce somewhat the effects of residential segregation. The separatist movement that made some headway in the late 1960's among U.S. blacks had little sway in Texas, but appeared in the Chicano movement in the form of Raza Unida,qv a militant Mexican American organization that tried, with little success, to run third party candidates in 1970 and again in 1972.

In two decades there had been much change, but much was the same. See also Negroes in Texas; Education, Negro; Mexican Americans in Texas.

Ronnie Dugger

Interagency Councils. By 1972 the interagency councils, established by the 60th Texas Legislature in 1967, were the Interagency Council on Natural Resources and the Environment, the Interagency Human Resources Council, and the Interagency Transportation Council. Each council was chaired by the governor, was composed of representatives from state agencies, and received aid from the Division of Planning Coordination. The councils functioned as coordination, research, and policy-determining groups. The councils also advised the governor and reported to the legislature. See also Planning Coordination, Division of, Governor's Office.

BIBLIOGRAPHY: University of Texas at Austin, *Guide To Texas State Agencies* (1972).

*Intercoastal Canal. [This title is a variant and no longer used spelling of Intracoastal Canal.] See Gulf Intracoastal Waterway.

*Intercollegiate Athletics. From the horse and buggy era to the space age, intercollegiate athletics in Texas have spanned the past three-quarters of a century. In the mid-1960's history was made when the University of Houston, one of the leading independent college powers (now a member of the Southwest Conference qv), played its home football and basketball games in the world-famous Astrodome.qv

Teams from Texas annually ranked among the nation's elite, and several national, world, and Olympic champions have come from Texas. Texas Western College (now University of Texas at El Paso) had the nation's best basketball team in 1966, the El Paso school upsetting Kentucky in the National Collegiate Athletic Association (N.C.A.A.) finals. The University of Texas at Austin won the national championship in baseball on three occasions: 1949, 1950, and 1975. The state produced some of the world's best golfers and trackmen. University of Texas golfer Ed White was N.C.A.A. champion in 1935, and, from the same school, Ben Crenshaw was N.C.A.A. golf champion in 1971, 1972, and 1973; his teammate Tom Kite tied for the title in 1972; the team on which they played won the team national title in 1971 and 1972. Texas A&M University's Randy Matson broke the world record for the shot put in 1965. He bettered his own record on April 22, 1967, with a put of 71'5½", a mark which still stood in 1970. David Greig (Skippy) Browning, Jr., qv diver from the University of Texas, won eight Amateur Athletic Union (A.A.U.) titles, four N.C.A.A. titles, and an Olympic gold medal in the early 1950's.

In the mid-1970's five intercollegiate athletic associations operated in the state. The Southwest Conference sponsored the Cotton Bowl qv football classic played in Dallas each New Year's Day and furnished the host team. This conference produced seven national grid titles—Southern Methodist University in 1935, Texas Christian University in 1938, Texas A&M University in 1939, University of Texas in 1963, 1969, and 1970, and University of Arkansas in 1964. Through the 1975 season the University of Texas at Austin had won or shared twenty Southwest Conference football titles; Texas A&M University, eleven; the University of Arkansas, ten; Texas Christian University and Southern Methodist University, eight each; Rice University, six; Baylor University, four; and Texas Tech University, none. (The University of Houston did not participate in conference football until 1976.) In basketball for the same period the University of Texas won sixteen titles; the University of Arkansas, fourteen; Southern Methodist University, eleven; Rice University, nine; Texas A&M University and Texas Christian University, eight each; Baylor University, five; and Texas Tech University, three. The track championship had been won by Texas thirty-five times; Texas A&M University, twelve; Rice University, eight; and Baylor University, three. Baseball championships were won or shared by the University of Texas, fifty times; Texas A&M University, ten times; Texas Christian University, five times; Baylor University, twice; and Southern Methodist University, once.

Other conferences operating in Texas in 1973 included the Lone Star, Southland, Big State, and Southwestern Athletic, while North Texas State University was the only Texas member of the Missouri Valley Conference. All of these groups sponsored all major sports except the Big State Conference, which did not play football. The Lone Star Conference was composed of East Texas State University, Southwest Texas State University, Sam Houston State University, Texas A&I University, Stephen F. Austin State University, Howard Payne College, Sul Ross State University, Tarleton State University, Angelo State University, and Abilene Christian College. The Southland Conference was comprised of the University of Texas at Arlington, Lamar University, Arkansas State University, Louisiana Tech, and McNeese State (Louisiana). Texas teams in the Southwestern Athletic Conference included Prairie View A&M University and Texas Southern University. Members of the Big State Conference were St. Edward's University, St. Mary's University of San Antonio, Texas Lutheran College, Southwestern University, East Texas Baptist College, Le Tourneau College, and Huston-Tillotson College. Among the many independents were West Texas State University and Austin College. The University of Texas at El Paso, an independent, joined the Western Athletic Conference in 1969.

There were three major bowl games in the state, all approved by the National Collegiate Athletic Association. These were the Cotton Bowl at Dallas, the Sun Bowl at El Paso, and the Astro-Bluebonnet Bowl qqv at Houston.

Jones W. Ramsey

*Interior Provinces. *See* Provincias Internas.

International Bible College. International Bible College, San Antonio, celebrated its twenty-fifth anniversary in 1967. The school was founded by the Reverend Leonard W. Coote when World War II temporarily halted his missionary efforts with the Japan Apostolic Mission. He had previously established a Bible training school for native workers in Ikoma, Japan, and wanted to build a similar Bible training center in the United States. Chartered as a nonprofit institution and dependent on private contributions for support, the school was situated on a ten-acre campus atop "Hallelujah Hill" overlooking San Antonio. In 1965 the campus was comprised of fourteen buildings;

the library contained 3,000 volumes. By 1967 the campus included nineteen buildings. Curricula offerings in 1967 were a two-and-one-half-year course leading to a Christian Worker's certificate, a three-year ministerial diploma course, and two four-year Bible college courses—one leading to the Bachelor of Theology degree and the other to the Bachelor of Religious Education degree. A nonsectarian school, the International Bible College was affiliated with the North American Association of Bible Colleges and Bible Institutes. Enrollment for the 1972–1973 regular term was 200 students; faculty numbered seventeen members. David B. Coote served as president in 1972.

*International Boundary Commission. The name of this commission was changed to International Boundary and Water Commission, United States and Mexico,qv after February 3, 1944. The commission was located in El Paso.

International Boundary and Water Commission, United States and Mexico. The name of this commission was changed from International Boundary Commission qv after February 3, 1944.

International Falcon Reservoir. International Falcon Reservoir is located in the Rio Grande Basin, three miles west of Falcon Heights on the Rio Grande in Starr and Zapata counties, Texas, and in Estado de Tamaulipas, Mexico. The project, owned by the United States and Mexico, was authorized and operated by the International Boundary and Water Commission, United States and Mexico.qv In 1944 the United States and Mexico signed one of a series of treaties affecting the land and water boundary between the two countries. Among the most important clauses of the Water Treaty of 1944 were those providing for equitable distribution of the waters of the two principal international streams, the Colorado River and the Rio Grande. The treaty provided for the construction of necessary works for the maximum conservation and utilization of the waters of the Rio Grande. It also authorized the necessary international storage dams to be jointly constructed on the Rio Grande by the two governments through the International Boundary and Water Commission.

Falcon Dam was constructed for conservation, irrigation, power, recreation, and flood control uses. Under the terms of the treaty, the United States received 58.6 percent of the conservation storage and Mexico received 41.4 percent. The United States' share of the cost was thirty-five million dollars. Plans for the dam and two power plants were approved in the fall of 1949, construction began in 1950, and the date of completion was April 18, 1954. Deliberate impoundment began on August 25, 1953, and the project was dedicated on October 19, 1953.

The reservoir has a summer storage capacity of 2,371,220 acre-feet and a surface area of 78,340 acres at the conservation storage level at an elevation of 296.4 feet above mean sea level. Above this elevation there is 909,480 acre-feet of flood-control storage capacity. An additional 400,000 acre-feet of conservation storage is allowed during the winter, which reduces the flood-control capacity accordingly. The drainage area above the dam is 164,482 square miles, of which 87,760 is in the United States and 76,722 is in Mexico. A power plant with auxiliary equipment is located on each side of the river, and each plant has three 10,500-kilowatt generating units, with provision for a fourth unit when justified. The first generation of electricity occurred on October 11, 1954. *See also* Rio Grande Flood Control.

BIBLIOGRAPHY: Texas Water Commission, *Bulletin 6408* (1964).

Seth D. Breeding

*International-Great Northern Railroad Company. In June, 1951, the Interstate Commerce Commission approved the joint operation by the International-Great Northern and the Texas-Mexican Railway Company of the latter's line over the International Bridge at Laredo, each company to provide half of the equipment and crews furnished. In 1956 the railroad was consolidated with the Missouri-Pacific.

James M. Day

*International Railroad Company.

*Interscholastic League. *See* University Interscholastic League.

*Interstate Co-operation, Texas Commission on.

*Interurban Lines in Texas.

Intracoastal Canal. [This title was incorrectly listed in Volume I as Intercoastal Canal.] *See* Gulf Intracoastal Waterway.

*Invasions of Texas in 1842. *See* Mexican Invasions of 1842.

*Invincible.

*Iola, Texas.

*Ione, Texas.

*Ioni Creek.

*Iowa Colony, Texas.

*Iowa Park, Texas. Iowa Park, in central Wichita County, had eighty-five businesses, including several manufacturing companies, in 1970. The 1960 population of 3,295 increased to 5,796 by 1970. *See also* Wichita Falls Standard Metropolitan Statistical Area.

*Ira, Texas.

*Iraan, Texas.

*Irby, Texas.

*Iredell, Texas.

*Ireland, John.

*Ireland, Texas.

*Irene, Texas.

*Iriarte, Antonio de.

*Irigoyen, Josef.

*Irion, Robert Anderson. Robert Anderson Irion, son of Maacah (White) [sometimes found as Maacha (White)] and John Poindexter Irion (not Philip Irion, as stated in Volume I), was born on July 7, 1804 (not 1806). [Philip Irion, born in 1733, was his grandfather.]

Robert Anderson Irion came to Texas in 1832 following the death of his first wife, Ann A. Vick, in Vicksburg, Mississippi, leaving a daughter, Ann Elizabeth, with his deceased wife's relatives. According to the records in the Nacogdoches County Courthouse, Irion's second marriage, to Anna W. Raguet,qv was either on March 29 or on March 30, 1840 (not March 20, 1840, as stated in Volume I); some sources claim the marriage date was April 9, 1840, but no legal instrument has been found to verify this date (*see* Raguet, Anna W.). Robert and Anna (Raguet) Irion were the parents of five children.

BIBLIOGRAPHY: Irion Family Papers (in possession of Mrs. Anna Kathryn Holbrook, San Augustine, Texas); Marriage Records, Republic of Texas, 1840 (Nacogdoches County Courthouse, Nacogdoches, Texas); Shannon Irion and Jenkins Garrett (comps.), *Ever Thine Truly: Love letters from Sam Houston to Anna Raguet* (1975); Helen Hoskins Rugeley, "Anna Raguet Irion (1819–1883)," in (Evelyn M. Carrington, ed.), *Women in Early Texas* (1975).

Anna Kathryn Holbrook

*Irion County. Irion County is a leading sheep-raising area with a small amount of income from other livestock, alfalfa and small grains, and oil. The county produced over 15,000,000 barrels of oil from 1928 to January 1, 1973. Major tourist attractions include Dove Creek Battlefield (*see* Dove Creek, Battle of) and stagecoach stops. The 1960 population of 1,183 decreased to a 1970 population of 1,070.

*Irish Creek.

*Irish Creek Settlement.

Irish in Texas. Natives of Ireland were among the first settlers in Spanish-ruled Texas, and the story of the Irish in Texas is in many ways coincident with the founding of the Republic and the development of the state. The heritage of the Irish seems in retrospect to have peculiarly suited their migration to a new land, for the English dominance of Ireland must have been to the new colonists in Texas a close parallel to the oppression they eventually found in the new country. It is not surprising that as many as twenty-five Irishmen probably signed the Goliad Declaration of Independence,qv that four signed the actual Declaration of Independence,qv and that one hundred were listed in the rolls of San Jacinto, comprising one-seventh of the total Texan force in that battle.

Probably the first Irishman in Texas was Hugo O'Conor (*see* Oconór, Hugo), who became governor *ad interim* of Texas in 1767. Though his national origins are uncertain, O'Conor was almost certainly Irish, as his name suggests. His success in reinforcing San Antonio against raiding Apaches was a notable contribution to the further settlement of that region. Philip Nolan,qv a native of Belfast, Ireland, was said to be the first Anglo American to map Texas. Whatever his real mission in Texas,

Nolan's activities so aroused Spanish authorities that he was killed by a force sent to arrest him in 1801.

James Hewetson and James Power, along with John McMullen and James McGloin,qqv were the first Irishmen to receive empresario qv contracts from Mexico, successfully settling the areas now comprising Refugio and San Patricio counties.qqv Hewetson accompanied Stephen F. Austin to Texas on his first trip in 1821, and many Irishmen were counted in Austin's Old Three Hundred.qv De Leon's Colony qv at Victoria also included several Irish families, and it should be noted that all of these contracts, except to McMullen and McGloin, called for the settlement of Mexican as well as Irish families, specifically Roman Catholics. Some writers have maintained that the southern grants were made only to the Irish to create a buffer zone of devout Catholics between Mexico and the northern Anglo settlements, but it now seems clear that the McMullen-McGloin Colony qv was adjacent to the Power and Hewetson Colony qv only by sheer coincidence. During the days of the Republic the two colonies were on the frontier that saw the worst possible hardships for settlers.

In the war for independence, such Irishmen as Francis Moore, Jr., John Joseph Linn, Thomas William Ward,qqv and the four empresarios named above all played important roles. James Power used his influence to seat Sam Houston at the Convention of 1836.qv Eleven Irishmen died at the Alamo and fourteen were among those with James W. Fannin, Jr.,qv at the Goliad Massacre.qv Appropriately, Refugio and San Patricio counties were among the first created in Texas after the revolution; the date was March 17, 1836, Saint Patrick's Day.

The Mexican War qv (1846–1848) also saw a number of Irish Texans called to arms, with an episode which later caused much resentment toward Irish Americans. A group of deserters led by John Riley (or O'Reilly) joined the Mexican Army and fought in several engagements against the invading U.S. forces. Known as the Saint Patrick Battalion (Batallón San Patricio), the group gained the dubious honor of being the only unit in American military history known to have formed a separate corps in the enemy's army and then to have fought with distinction against its former comrades. Whether most of these men were Irish is questionable, however, and whether the deserters were Irish Texans is extremely doubtful. Riley, the Irish leader, was said to have been a sergeant in a British regiment stationed in Canada (from which he also deserted). Of the 260-odd deserters, all escaped or were killed except 65, who were either hanged or lashed and branded; all of these 65 were from regular U.S. regiments and therefore not part of the Texas volunteers under the command of Governor James Pinckney Henderson;qv only 27 of the captured men can be definitely classed as Hibernian. It is possible that the majority of this "Irish" battalion were English and German, since their names

register those nationalities, but the choice of the battalion's name was unfortunate for those Irishmen from the San Patricio area of Texas. Resentment over the episode was directed toward the Irish for many years in the United States, while in Mexico the renegades were regarded as heroes who had merely foreseen an act of aggression by the United States and had joined the other side.

The 1850 census listed 1,403 Irish in Texas; ten years later the number was 3,480. Notable Irish-born Texans in the nineteenth century included William Kennedy,qv whose book The Rise, Progress and Prospects of Texas (1841) encouraged immigration to the new Republic; Richard W. Dowling,qv whose company of all-Irish Confederates repulsed the Union fleet at Sabine Pass; Peter Gallagher,qv a Texas Ranger qv and later an organizer of Pecos County; Samuel McKinney,qv an early president of Austin College; and John William Mallet,qv first chairman of the University of Texas faculty.

Irish colonists in Texas endured the same problems of education, farming, and economic hardship as did other settlers, though perhaps with better success considering their proximity to hostile forces. The descendants of generations who had long fought and died for their civic and religious liberties, the Irish were quicker than most to recognize incursions upon their rights and to defend against them. (See also Refugio, Battle of; San Patricio, Battle of; San Patricio Minute Men; San Patricio Trail.)

BIBLIOGRAPHY: Hobart Huson, A Comprehensive History of Refugio County from Aboriginal Times to 1953 (1953); William H. Oberste, Texas Irish Empresarios and Their Colonies (1953); John C. Linehan, "The Irish Pioneers of Texas," American-Irish Historical Society Journal (1899); Edward W. Wallace, "The Battalion of Saint Patrick in the Mexican War," Military Affairs, XIV (1950).

Phillip L. Fry

*Iron Creek.

*Iron Jacket.

*Iron Mountain.

⁜Iron Ore Creek.

*Iron Ore Deposits.

*Iron and Steel Industry. The Lone Star Steel Company, which since the fall of 1947 had been making pig iron in its plant near Daingerfield, began in 1953 to produce steel ingots and steel pipe. It expanded its steel-making capacity in 1954 and again in 1956. In 1961, after borrowing $40,000,-000 from an insurance company, the company repaid the last of the more than $87,000,000 it had borrowed from the government.

In 1966 the Lone Star Steel Company sold its assets to the Philadelphia & Reading Corp., a New York holding company that in 1965 had bought 73 percent of the Texas firm's stock. Lone Star was reorganized as a subsidiary of Philadelphia & Reading and continued in operation.

In the late 1960's expansion of the steel industry was underway near Houston. The Armco Steel Corp. was built and subsequently expanded. This plant augmented Texas' two major steel plants already in operation at Houston and near Daingerfield.

Wayne Gard

*Ironosa, Texas.

*Irons, John.

*Irons, Martin.

*Irons Bayou.

*Ironton, Texas.

*Irrigation. Irrigation of land in Texas increased to 3,131,534 acres by 1950, due largely to the rapid development of irrigation on the High Plains, which was supplied exclusively with high quality groundwater from underlying Ogallala Sands. High Plains irrigation has continued to grow spectacularly—more rapidly than any development elsewhere —to 5,894,686 acres by 1974. It was one of the largest contiguous irrigation areas in the United States and represented 68 percent of all Texas irrigation (8,618,054 acres in 1974) and 15 percent of the nation's irrigated acreage.

The Winter Garden Region qv and adjacent areas below the Balcones Escarpment,qv the Trans-Pecos qv areas ot Reeves, Pecos, and Ward counties and the Marfa, Van Horn, and Dell City vicinities, several north-central Texas localities (where, especially after 1964, there was an increased use of the sprinkler system for peanut growing), and parts of the Gulf Coast were other important groundwater-supplied irrigated areas. Groundwater pumped from 90,469 wells supplied about 80 percent of the 8,618,054 acres of Texas irrigation in 1974.

Major areas supplied with surface water were the Lower Rio Grande Valley, portions of the Gulf Coast rice area, the El Paso Valley area along the upper Rio Grande in Texas, and alluvial lands along the lower Brazos River and other Texas rivers and tributaries. Better than 12,500,000 acre-feet of irrigation water was used on Texas crops and pastures in 1964, a comparatively dry year, and 13,082,262 acre-feet of irrigation water was used in 1974, another relatively dry year in the High Plains area. An increasing acreage in small tracts was being irrigated from small upstream impoundments. Over 11,000 sprinkler systems, with nearly 7,500 concentrated on the High Plains, were used to irrigate over a million acres in 1964, over one-third more than the 1958 amount. By 1974, 1,853,893 acres were irrigated by the sprinkler system. Most irrigation, however, employed surface systems—borders, rows, and field levees (rice). Many irrigation systems employed efficient pipelines or lined ditches to prevent water loss. In 1974 pipelines served 4,088,768 acres, mostly on the High Plains.

In 1948 only about one-tenth of Texas cropland harvested was irrigated, and less than one-third of the farm value of crops produced was from irrigated land. In 1966 about one-fourth of cropland acreage was irrigated and substantially over half the farm value of crops produced stemmed from irrigated land. By 1973, 72 percent of the value

of crop production was from irrigated land (this percentage of value varies from year to year, with wet or dry seasons).

Acreages of irrigated crops in 1974 were as follows (in terms of percent of total irrigated acreage): grain sorghum, 28; cotton, 24; pasture, hay, and other feeds, 11; wheat, 14; rice, 6; vegetables, 3; corn, 8; all others, 6. Citrus fruits and most of the vegetables were produced in the Lower Rio Grande Valley and the Winter Garden vicinity, although an increasing acreage of vegetables and sugar beets was grown on the High Plains; there were also important acreages in the El Paso Valley and Trans-Pecos area. Cotton and grain sorghum were important crops in nearly all irrigated areas, with special long-staple varieties of cotton produced in the Trans-Pecos area and El Paso Valley. Wheat was an important High Plains and north-central Texas irrigated crop. Rice was the major irrigated crop of the upper Texas Gulf Coast.

Water availability is the probable limiting factor in determining how much of the 37,000,000 acres of irrigable land in Texas is irrigated in the future. Groundwater is being used much faster than aquifers are recharging in the major groundwater-supplied irrigated areas. A new, comprehensive Texas Water Plan was developed in the 1960's, looking fifty years or so ahead to a Texas with over thirty million people and a dynamic industrial and agricultural economy. A need for more than sixteen million acres of Texas irrigation is visualized if water is not limited, physically or financially. It is probable, however, that ground- and surface water will be economically available to serve only a portion of this acreage. *See also* Agriculture in Texas; Water Agencies and Programs, Local (and all *see* references following that article).

BIBLIOGRAPHY: "Inventories of Irrigation in Texas 1958, 1964, 1969, and 1974," *Texas Water Development Board Report 196* (October, 1975).

Paul T. Gillett

*Irrigation Districts.

*Irrupien Village.

Irvine, Josephus Somerville. Josephus Somerville Irvine, son of Josephus and Jane (Patton) Irvine, was born in Lawrence County, Tennessee, on August 25, 1819. He was one of four brothers who served in the Texas Army qv from 1835 to 1836, one of whom was Robert Boyd Irvine.qv The Irvine family moved from Tennessee to Texas in 1830, settling first near Milam and four years later on a farm four miles south of San Augustine.

In the fall of 1835 Irvine enlisted in Captain Henry W. Augustine's qv company, and participated in the siege of Bexar.qv Irvine again volunteered for the Texas Army in March, 1836, and served in a company from Sabine County under Captain Benjamin Franklin Bryant.qv Attached to Colonel Sidney Sherman's qv 2nd Regiment, he fought in the battle of San Jacinto; it is possible that he was the youngest Texas soldier-participant in that battle. Irvine was discharged about May 1, but enlisted a third time on July 4, 1836, and served for three months in Captain William Scurlock's qv company from San Augustine.

Irvine served as county tax assessor and collector in Newton County from 1856 to 1860. At the outbreak of the Civil War, he raised and was captain of a company which became Company C of James B. Likens' Battalion of Texas Volunteers. After a reorganization of the battalion, it was designated the 11th or Spaight's (see Spaight, Ashley W.) Battalion of Texas Volunteers and Irvine was elected major. He led his troops in the battle of Fordoche or Stirling's Plantation on September 29, 1863, where his son, James Patton Irvine, was killed. Ill with yellow fever, Irvine resigned his commission in December, 1864.

Irvine married Nancy McMahon in 1838; they had eleven children. A member of the Methodist Episcopal church, he died on May 17, 1876, and was buried at Wilson's Chapel, Newton County. A state marker was erected on his grave in 1963.

BIBLIOGRAPHY: Cooper K. Ragan, Josephus Somerville Irvine, 1819–1876, The Worthy Citizen (1963); Cooper K. Ragan (ed.), "The Diary of Captain George W. O'Brien, 1863," Southwestern Historical Quarterly, LXVII (1963–1964).

Cooper K. Ragan

*Irvine, Robert Boyd. [This title was incorrectly listed in Volume I as Irvine, Robert Bruce.] Robert Boyd Irvine was born in Lawrence County, Tennessee, on January 8, 1813. He was the son of Josephus and Jane (Patton) Irvine and the oldest of four brothers who served in the Texas Army,qv one of whom was Josephus Somerville Irvine.qv His father died on the family's journey to Texas in 1830, and the family settled near Milam, Sabine County; four years later they moved to Ayish Bayou, four miles south of San Augustine.

Irvine enlisted in a San Augustine company of volunteers in October, 1835, and was in the battle of Concepción qv on October 28. He did not participate in the battle of San Jacinto; presumably he was in East Texas recruiting and obtaining supplies for Houston's army. Irvine drew pay as a captain of infantry from December 18, 1835, to August 27, 1836, with extra pay as assistant quartermaster from March 14, 1836, to August 27, 1836. He was paid as captain of the 1st Infantry Regiment from August 27, 1836, to May 18, 1837. President Houston nominated and the Texas Senate confirmed Irvine as a major of infantry in Colonel Amasa Turner's qv regiment in the regular army on May 22, 1837, making Irvine the first major commissioned in the regular army of the Republic after the permanent government was formed. A bounty warrant for 1,280 acres was issued to his heirs in 1845 for his twelve months' service in the Texas Army.

Irvine died on July 24, 1838, in San Augustine; he had never married. He was considered by his associates to be one of the most promising young men of the Republic.

BIBLIOGRAPHY: Cooper K. Ragan, Josephus Somerville Irvine, 1819–1876, The Worthy Citizen (1963); H. P. N. Gammel (ed.), Laws of Texas, I (1898); Ernest W. Wink-

ler (ed.), Secret Journals of the Senate of the Republic of Texas, 1836–1845 (1911); "Lecture on San Augustine" (1893), Oran M. Roberts Papers (MS., Archives, University of Texas at Austin Library); Comptroller's Military Service Records (MS., Archives, Texas State Library, Austin).

Cooper K. Ragan

*Irving, Texas. Irving, in Dallas County, had a tremendous growth in population over a twenty-year period, with a count of 2,621 in 1950, 45,985 in 1960, and 97,260 in 1970. In 1963 Irving had 730 businesses, seventy churches, sixteen public schools, three banks, and two hospitals. Manufacturing plants produced paint, cement blocks, aluminum products, millwork, roofing, chemical supplies, petroleum, and electronic components. In 1964 the world's largest truck terminal was located in Irving. The number of business establishments had increased to 1,077 by 1970. The University of Dallas was located in Irving. See also Dallas Standard Metropolitan Statistical Area.

*Isaacks, Elijah.

*Isaacks, Samuel.

*Isbell, William.

*Iser, Texas.

*Isinglass Canyon.

*Isla, Texas.

*Isla de Cordoba.

*Island, Texas.

*Island Creek.

*Isle Du Bois Creek.

*Isleta del Sur. See Corpus Christi de la Isleta; Ysleta, Texas.

*Islitas, Texas.

*Ismiquilpa Indians.

*Isopete. See Ysopete.

*Israel, Texas.

Isucho Indians. The Isucho Indians were one of twenty Indian groups that joined Juan Domínguez de Mendoza qv on his expedition from El Paso to the vicinity of present San Angelo in 1683–1684. Since Mendoza did not indicate at what point the Isucho joined his party, it is not possible to determine their range or affiliations. However, the Indians between the Pecos and the San Angelo area were being hard pressed by Apache at this time, and it seems likely that the Isucho ranged between these two localities.

BIBLIOGRAPHY: H. E. Bolton (ed.), Spanish Exploration in the Southwest, 1542–1706 (1916).

T. N. Campbell

*Italy, Texas. The population of Italy, in Ellis County, was 1,183 in 1960 and 1,309 in 1970, when the city reported twenty-five businesses.

*Itasca, Texas. The population of Itasca, in Hill County, declined to 1,383 by 1960 and grew to 1,483 by 1970. In 1970 the city listed thirty-eight businesses.

*Iturbide, Agustín de.

*Ivan, Texas. Ivan, in Stephens County, was a

post office location as early as 1898, when Lillian Brockmann was postmaster (thus established before the 1915 date given in Volume I). The post office was discontinued on December 31, 1953. The population in 1970 was approximately fifteen.

BIBLIOGRAPHY: *Texas Almanac* (1904).

Cyrus Tilloson

*Ivanhoe, Texas.

*Ivanhoe Creek.

*Iverson, Texas.

*Ives, Caleb Smith. [This title was incorrectly listed in Volume I as Ives, Caleb Semper.] Caleb Smith Ives was born on September 25, 1798, at Tinmouth, Vermont, the son of Jared and Joanna (Smith) Ives. He received a degree from Trinity College, Hartford, in 1830 and entered General Theological Seminary in New York the same year, completing his studies there in 1833. Ives was appointed missionary to Alabama by the Protestant Episcopal church; on February 6, 1834, he married Katherine Duncan Morison; they had three children. While serving as chaplain and professor of ancient languages at Mobile Institute, Ives was invited to perform duties of priest and schoolmaster in Matagorda, Texas. He arrived late in 1838 in time to celebrate the Holy Eucharist on Christmas Day, to his knowledge the first time it had been celebrated in Texas according to the Episcopal rite. He soon founded Matagorda Academy, said to be one of the best academies in Texas. With the organization of the first Episcopal parish in Texas, the most southern and western parish in the whole American church, Ives became rector of Christ Church.

BIBLIOGRAPHY: A. F. Muir, "Caleb Smith Ives, Priest, and the Beginnings of Christ Church, Matagorda, Texas," *Historical Magazine of the Protestant Episcopal Church,* XXVIII (December, 1959).

*Ivy Mountain.

*Iwonski, Carl G. von. Carl G. von Iwonski's oil portrait and his pencil sketch of the Herman Lungkwitz qv children are part of the art collection of the Texas Memorial Museum qv at Austin.

*Iza Settlement.

*Izoro, Texas.

J

*J A Ranch. The partnership between Charles Goodnight and John G. Adair's widow, Cornelia (Wadsworth) Ritchie Adair,qqv was not dissolved by Goodnight's being bought out (as stated in Volume I). According to the contract of sale dated May, 1887, Adair sold the tract of land known as the Quitaque Ranch to Goodnight, and Goodnight sold his one-third of the Palo Duro Ranch to Adair, who then owned the entire Palo Duro Ranch.

Richard Walsh became manager of the J A Ranch and consolidated Mrs. Adair's holdings from the scattered tracts of land having water into an area of some 450,000 adjoining acres. M. W. H. Ritchie, a grandson of Mrs. Adair, took over the management of the ranch in 1935. Ritchie served as president of the J A Cattle Company, which was formed in 1949 at the conclusion of the administration of Mrs. Adair's will. The company continued operations in 1970.

*J. Hall Creek.

*Jaboncillos Creek.

Jacinto City, Texas. Jacinto City, a residential area located in central Harris County, was incorporated in 1947. In 1966 the city had two public schools, a hospital, a bank, a library, and seventeen churches. According to the United States report of the 1970 census the population remained almost unchanged in ten years, having been 9,547 in 1960 and 9,563 in 1970. *See also* Houston Standard Metropolitan Statistical Area.

*Jack, Patrick Churchill.

*Jack, Spencer H.

*Jack, Thomas McKinney.

*Jack, William Houston.

*Jack County. Jack County, decreasing in population since 1940, had 7,418 inhabitants in 1960 and 6,711 in 1970, according to the United States report of the census. The petroleum industry, with over 142,000,000 barrels of oil produced from 1923 to 1973, was the chief source of revenue. The greatest part of the farm income in the 1960's was from livestock and products, with other income from mohair and such crops as grains, hay, and cotton. Tourism also contributed to the county income, and deer hunting was a popular attraction. Recreational activities centered around Lake Bridgeport and Fort Richardson State Historic Site (*see* Parks, State).

*Jack Creek.

Jack's, Texas. *See* New Columbia, Texas.

*Jacks Branch.

*Jack's Creek.

*Jacksboro, Texas. Jacksboro, seat of Jack County, had a 1960 population of 3,816 and a 1970 population of 3,554, according to the United States report of the census. In 1970 Jacksboro had 100 businesses, two newspapers, two banks, and a hospital. A new high school was built in 1964 to replace the building which burned in 1962. In 1963 a company manufacturing women's sportswear began operation. Oil and livestock provided other sources of income. An annual Frontier Fair held each May and a museum maintained at historic Fort Richardson qv have been developed as tourist attractions.

*Jacksboro College. *See* North Texas Baptist College.

*Jackson, Alexander.

*Jackson, Andrew.

*Jackson, Charles W.

*Jackson, Humphrey.

*Jackson, Isaac.

*Jackson, Joseph Daniel.

*Jackson, Thomas R.

*Jackson, Texas. (Montgomery County.)

*Jackson, Texas. (Shelby County.)

*Jackson, Texas. (Van Zandt County.)

*Jackson Branch.

*Jackson County. Jackson County was a leading producer of rice and cattle, although cotton, once the principal crop, was still of major importance. Cash receipts in 1968 totaled $12,092,000 from crops, and $5,319,000 from livestock and products. A number of industries in the county were connected with oil, and 469,216,194 barrels of oil had been produced from 1934 to January 1, 1973. Tourist attractions include hunting, fishing, missions, and historic homes. The 1960 population of 14,040 decreased by 1970 to 12,975, according to the United States census.

*Jackson Creek.

*Jackson Knob.

*Jackson Lake.

*Jacksons Bayou.

*Jacksonville, Texas. (Cherokee County.) Jacksonville had a population of 9,590 in 1960 and 9,734 in 1970, according to the United States report of the census. In the 1960's Jacksonville reported almost 400 businesses, including companies manufacturing cap pistols, clothing, baskets, furniture, precision tools, milk products, golf clubs, and charcoal. Additions were made to the campuses of Lon Morris College, Jacksonville College, and North American Theological Seminary. In 1970 the town had two hospitals, a children's clinic, a library, a newspaper, and over forty churches. Agriculture in the area is based on poultry, dairying, livestock, fruit, and varied truck crops. Lake Jacksonville, constructed in 1959, and an annual rodeo provide recreation for county residents.

*Jacksonville, Texas. (Washington County.)

*Jacksonville Baptist College. *See also* Jacksonville College.

Jacksonville College. Jacksonville College at Jacksonville, formerly known as Jacksonville Baptist College,qv continued under the ownership and operation of the Baptist Missionary Association of Texas. The junior college offered a curriculum in liberal arts, fine arts, and theology, as well as special training programs in business and music. Course work was approved or accredited by the Texas Education Agency and the Association of Texas Colleges.qqv During the 1962–1963 term the college had an enrollment of 147 students and a fourteen-member faculty; by the 1968–1969 regular term, student enrollment was 140, with a faculty of thirteen. The campus, situated on a high point overlooking the city, included eight permanent buildings in 1965 amid native oak and pecan trees. Completed in 1952, the library building housed 15,795 volumes by 1969. Additional construction plans called for dormitories, a student union-cafeteria, and married student apartments. In 1974 the Reverend Curtis M. Carroll was president, and the enrollment was 231 students.

*Jacksonville Collegiate Institute.

*Jacksonville Institute.

*Jacobia, Texas.

*Jacobs, John Cloud.

*Jacobs Creek.

*Jacob's Well.

*Jagavans Indians.

*Jahuey Creek.

Jaillet, Claude C. Known as the "Saddlebag Priest of the Nueces," Claude C. Jaillet was the son of Claude François and Marguerite (Dubois) Jaillet of Lyons, France, and was born on September 8, 1843. In 1862 he studied philosophy in the Séminaire d'Alix, then studied theology in the Grand Séminaire de St. François in Lyons, was made a deacon in 1866, and became a priest soon afterward.

On September 25, 1866, Father Jaillet embarked from Le Havre for the foreign missions in the United States. He arrived in San Diego, Texas, after traveling overland by horseback from Corpus Christi. He was San Diego's first Catholic priest, serving for fourteen years as pastor of the parish and missions which extended from Concepción in southeastern Duval County to Goliad on the San Antonio River. He was known throughout the Spanish-speaking area as Padre Claudio. In 1884 he became pastor of Saint Patrick's parish in Corpus Christi, where he remained until his death on November 27, 1929.

BIBLIOGRAPHY: Sister Mary Xavier, *Father Jaillet: Saddlebag Priest of the Nueces* (1948).

Agnes C. Grimm

*Jakehamon, Texas.

*Jakes Creek.

*Jalot, Medar.

*Jamerson Peaks.

*James, John.

*James, John.

*James, John Garland.

*James, John Herndon.

*James, Texas. (Shelby County.)

*James, Texas. (Upshur County.)

James Connally Air Force Base. James Connally Air Force Base, formerly Connally Air Force Base,qv discontinued pilot training in June, 1951, and instituted training for navigators, radar observers, and bombardiers. Later the base revived training for single engine pilots but was relieved of this responsibility in 1954. Bombardier training also ended at the base after a few years.

In March, 1958, the United States Air Force Instrument Pilot Instructor School moved to the base. Students from all allied countries were trained in the school until its relocation in 1961. A six-month radar course for officers, the only one of its kind in the air force, was situated at James Connally until the program was discontinued in 1962.

In January, 1966, the base was placed under the jurisdiction of the Tactical Air Command with a primary mission of supporting the Twelfth Air Force headquarters in Waco. When that headquarters relocated at Bergstrom Air Force Base qv in the summer of 1968, James Connally Air Force Base was scheduled to be closed.

Civilian installations replaced military ones during the phase-out. The James Connally Technical Institute was established on the base in April, 1965. In 1969 the name of the institute was changed to Texas State Technical Institute.qv The McLennan Community College was situated on the base and held its first classes in September, 1966. General Dynamics, in cooperation with the air force and the technical institute, also established a modification center at the base for B-58 bombers. The first aircraft were to arrive in July, 1967, with the technical institute providing many of the technicians for this project. After completion of the work on the B-58's, General Dynamics planned to conduct similar work on the F-111 aircraft. See Connally Air Force Base for earlier history.

James Connally Technical Institute. See Texas State Technical Institute.

*James River.

*Jameson, Green B.

*Jameson, Texas.

*Jamestown, Texas. (Newton County.) [This title was incorrectly listed in Volume I as Jameston, Texas.]

*Jamestown, Texas. (Smith County.)

*Jamison, Monroe Franklin.

*Jamison, Thomas.

*Jamison, Texas.

Janaque Indians. The Janaque Indians are known from a single Spanish document of 1683 which does not clearly indicate their area, but it seems to have been somewhere in west-central Texas. Their affiliations are unknown.
BIBLIOGRAPHY: C. W. Hackett (ed.), *Pichardo's Treatise on the Limits of Louisiana and Texas*, I (1931).
T. N. Campbell

*Jane Creek.

Janes, Texas. Janes was established in 1912 along the Santa Fe Railroad in Bailey County on land donated by E. K. Warren. The town soon had a general store, a hotel, and a bank. After Muleshoe was built between Janes and Hurley and was awarded the county seat, Janes' population moved there.
BIBLIOGRAPHY: Roysten E. Willis, Ghost Towns of the South Plains (M.A. thesis, Texas Technological College, 1941).

*January, James B. P.

*Japan, Texas.

Japanese in Texas. The first Japanese in Texas recorded by the census was a farmer in Dallas County in 1885; in 1890 only three persons were listed and in 1900 thirteen were recorded. In the next decade a fairly large number of Japanese came to Texas, mostly from California and Colorado, settling mainly in the southeastern and southwestern areas of the state. Near Webster in Harris County, Seito Saibara, the first Christian member of the Japanese Diet, formed a colony in 1902 that eventually brought in seventy families. At Terry in Orange County, K. Kishi arrived in 1907 after serving in the Russo-Japanese War; his 3,500-acre rice farm, tenant-farmed by fifteen to twenty Japanese families, was one of the largest rice farms in Texas until 1920, when Kishi changed over to truck farming because of a weak rice market. By 1927 Kishi owned some 10,000 acres of land, and his colony consisted of ten families. In the Rio Grande Valley, Japanese farmers turned to citrus and vegetable crops instead of rice. Early settlers (such as Seichi Noguchi, who came in 1913 and organized a farm cooperative in 1919 with six other Japanese farmers in Brownsville) experienced many setbacks at first. Wherever the Japanese farmed in Texas, however, their careful cultivation of nurseries, truck farms, rice crops, and citrus groves, as well as their introduction of many plants (such as camphor laurel trees, Satsuma oranges, and seed rice from Japan), established them as respected members of the agricultural community.

Even though very little has been written on Japanese in other parts of the state, many Japanese businessmen have been associated with exporting and importing since the turn of the century, several with large firms in northern Texas connected with the cotton industry. Takaski K. Tsutsumi was the manager of the Dallas office of Marimura, Arai and Company in 1919, a well known Japanese-American cotton import-export company, and S. Shima was president of the Southern Products Company, established in Dallas in 1911, with branch offices throughout the United States and in many foreign cities.

An unfortunate aspect of Japanese settlement in Texas was the attitude toward Asiatics by Americans during several crucial periods in this century. U.S. immigration restrictions in the early 1900's, Texas alien exclusion laws in the 1920's, and anti-Japanese sentiment in World War II were all hindrances to the assimilation of Japanese into Texas. On the other hand, several Texans of Japanese descent served with distinction in the military in World War II. Acceptance of the Japanese, as a people who have cherished the customs of their homeland while remaining dedicated to an American way of life, was rapid in the years following the war. Their contributions to the culture and economy of Texas continue to be widely recognized.

BIBLIOGRAPHY: Ellis A. Davis (ed.), *Encyclopedia of Texas* (19??); S. C. Hoyle, "How Orange County Solved the Japanese Question," *Farm and Ranch*, 43 (May 17, 1924); W. Jett Lauck, "Japanese Farmers in Texas," *The Texas Magazine*, VI (September, 1912); Frank X. Tolbert, "Old Colony of Japanese Farmers Almost Gone," Dallas *Morning News*, June 12, 1966; Lillie Mae Tomlinson, "The Japanese Colony in Orange County," *Texas History Teachers' Bulletin*, XIV (December 8, 1927); Files, Institute of Texan Cultures, University of Texas at San Antonio; Subject File, Barker Texas History Center, University of Texas at Austin.

Phillip L. Fry
John L. Davis

*Jaques, William Budd.

Jaramillo, Pedro. Pedro ("Don Pedrito") Jaramillo, *curandero* or "faith healer," was born of Tarascan Indian parents near Guadalajara, Jalisco, Mexico, in the mid-nineteenth century. He came to South Texas as a young man in 1881 and settled on the Los Olmos Ranch in the northern part of present Brooks County.

Don Pedrito related that when he was still a poor laborer in Mexico he suffered an affliction of the nose. One night he was in such pain that he went out into the woods to a pool of water. He lay down and buried his face in the mud at the edge, and remained there, treating himself for three days. When he had cured himself he returned to his house and fell asleep. A voice awakened him and told him that he had received the gift of healing from God. He began his practice as a faith healer almost immediately, prescribing the first thing that he thought of, and making no charge for his services.

At that time the only doctor between Corpus Christi and Laredo lived in San Diego; therefore, Don Pedrito's powers were often sought. At first he treated only close neighbors but soon began visiting ranches throughout the region between the Nueces River and the Rio Grande. Dressed as a Mexican peasant, wearing heavy shoes, sombrero, and a cowboy vest, he either walked or rode a donkey on his healing missions. As his fame spread, an increasing number of patients came to his home. Most of his patients were poor Mexican Americans, and often Don Pedrito would provide the remedies he prescribed.

He constantly received money through the mail in the form of donations, usually in the amount of a fifty-cent piece or a dollar bill. He made generous donations to several area churches and to the constant stream of poor people visiting his ranch. He bought food in wagonload lots and kept his storeroom well stocked. More than $5,000 in 50-cent pieces was found at his home when he died.

Don Pedrito never married, but he adopted two boys. He died on July 3, 1907, and was buried in the old ranch cemetery near Falfurrias. His resting place has become a shrine and is visited by several hundred persons yearly. A biography of him, *Don Pedrito Jaramillo: Curandero*, was written in Spanish by Viola Ruth Dodson qv and published in 1934.

BIBLIOGRAPHY: Ruth Dodson, *Don Pedrito Jaramillo: Curandero* (1934); Wilson M. Hudson (ed.), *The Healer of Los Olmos and Other Mexican Lore* (1951).

Agnes C. Grimm

*Jarbo Bayou.

*Jardin, Texas.

*Jarrell, Texas.

*Jarvis, James Jones.

*Jarvis, Van Zandt.

*Jarvis, Texas.

*Jarvis Christian College. Jarvis Christian College, at Hawkins, was a church-related senior college affiliated with the Christian Church (Disciples of Christ qv) and, since 1965, with Texas Christian University. In 1958 an autonomous board of trustees replaced the Texas board of trustees (members of the Disciples of Christ) and the Department of Institutional Missions of the United Christian Missionary Society in guiding the maintenance and operation of the school. The former governing bodies retained representation on the board with additional members from the Board for Fundamental Education and the constituency of the college.

Physical improvement of the original 456-acre campus (not 465 acres, as stated in Volume I) included commercial electrification replacing the campus power plant, a central deep-well water system, a filtration plant and water tower, and a gas line tie-in replacing field gas. Oil discovery in 1941 provided revenue for endowment, capital reserves, and operating costs. Additional property acquisitions brought total acreage to approximately two thousand by 1958. The campus proper comprised a 242.5-acre plot on Highway 80, midway between Dallas and Shreveport. The plant included approximately forty-five buildings. Since 1954 an extensive building program has been underway, including a fellowship center, a health center, four dormitories, a 34,000-volume library, and a communications center. The building program during the 1960's was estimated at six million dollars. By 1969 the library contained 41,560 volumes.

Enrollment increased from 299 students in 1959 to 551 in the 1968–1969 regular term. Selective admissions aided in the quest for quality rather than quantity. Applicants were not restricted in racial background, although only Negroes had enrolled. The faculty numbered fifty-three in the 1968–1969 term. The president in 1969 was J. O. Perpener. The curriculum, accredited by the Southern Association of Colleges and Secondary Schools in 1950, consisted of a standard liberal arts program, teacher education program, and a two-year, terminal agro-industrial program. Junior college work and the high school department were discontinued in 1938. By the 1972–1973 regular term, the faculty numbered thirty-seven and there were 623 students. John P. Jones was president in 1974, when there were 509 students enrolled. *See also* Christian Church Schools in Texas.

*Jasper, Selden L. B.

*Jasper, Texas. Jasper, seat of Jasper County, was incorporated in 1927 and has a council-manager form of government. In 1966 the town had a business college, two libraries, two hospitals, two banks, twenty-two churches, two newspapers, and one radio station. Between 1962 and 1965 improvements and additions were made to the water and sewage systems, and a new fire and police building was completed in 1966. In 1970 there were 197 businesses, including sixteen manufacturers. The economy was supported by lumber concerns, a poultry-processing plant, oil, and tourism.

The town's economy was impaired by the loss of several companies. In 1959 the biggest industrial fire in Jasper's history forced the closure of a lumber mill and a loss of income to more than two hundred workers. Several companies moved their personnel, thus causing additional payroll losses. However, in the mid-1960's a 148-acre industrial park was established, and according to the United States report of the 1970 census, Jasper's population rose from 4,889 in 1960 to 6,251 in 1970.

*Jasper Collegiate Institute.

*Jasper County. Jasper County, 90 percent forested, had an economy based principally on lumbering and petroleum. The petroleum industry by 1965 was adding to the economy between two and three million dollars annually; in 1968 crude oil production was 542,810 barrels, and the total crude output from 1928 to 1973 was 9,284,974 barrels. Livestock production had superseded crop farming in importance by 1969, as cash receipts from livestock totaled $4,859,000, and from crops, $171,000. An increasing tourist trade was developed around Sam Rayburn Reservoir, Martin Dies State Park, and Dam B Reservoir (also called Town Bluff Reservoir). The 1960 population was 22,100; the 1970 population was 24,692, according to the United States census.

*Jasper Creek.

*Jasper and Eastern Railway Company.

*Jáuregui y Urrutia, Joseph Fernández de.

*Java, Texas.

*Javelina.

*Jaybird-Woodpecker War.

*Jayton, Texas. Jayton replaced Clairemont as seat of Kent County in 1954; although an election on March 29, 1952, resulted in this decision, court suits delayed the actual move to Jayton until July 29, 1954, according to the commissioners court minutes. In 1970 Jayton reported four churches, a school, a bank, a library, a newspaper, and twenty-two businesses. Jayton is a commercial center for surrounding farms and ranches and is the location of a county-supported rest home. The 1960 population was 649; the 1970 population was 703.

*Jean, Texas.

*Jeanetta, Texas.

*Jeddo, Texas.

*Jedionda Indians. The Jedionda (Jediondo,

Gediondo, Hediondo, Hediodondo) Indians, whose name is Spanish for "stinkers," were encountered early in January, 1684 (not in 1683, as stated in Volume I) by Juan Domínguez de Mendoza qv on his journey from El Paso to the vicinity of present San Angelo. They were in a settlement on the Pecos River, apparently that section which today divides Pecos and Crane counties. They built thatched houses, hunted bison, and had horses and guns. They also had a large wooden cross painted red and yellow, as well as a white taffeta banner bearing two blue crosses. They were living in constant terror of Apache raids and met Mendoza's armed party with obvious relief and enthusiasm. When Mendoza declined to remain and help them fight Apaches, the whole Jedionda settlement seems to have joined the expedition and followed it to the Colorado River beyond present San Angelo. The linguistic and cultural affiliations of these people remain undetermined.

BIBLIOGRAPHY: H. E. Bolton (ed.), *Spanish Exploration in the Southwest, 1542–1706* (1916).

T. N. Campbell

*Jeff Davis County. Jeff Davis County, with cash receipts from livestock totaling $2,414,000 in 1969, also relied heavily on tourist trade for its income. The Davis Mountains State Park, Fort Davis, McDonald Observatory, qqv and Limpia Canyon are among the most scenic spots in Texas. In 1966 the county had only four towns. The county supported a library and the Fort Davis Historical Society. The population in 1960 was 1,582; in 1970 it was 1,527.

Jefferson, Blind Lemon. Blind Lemon Jefferson, son of Alec and Classie Jefferson, was born near the small town of Wortham, Texas, in July, 1897 (an estimated date since no records are available). He was born blind and was known all his life as Blind Lemon Jefferson.

Jefferson received no formal education and instead traveled from town to town in the Wortham area, playing his guitar and singing songs, most of which were his own compositions. He later moved to the Dallas-Fort Worth area and became a well-known figure in the "Deep Elm" district of Dallas. There he met Huddie Ledbetter qv (better known as "Leadbelly"), and for a time they played together in some of the brothels of Texas' cities. Leadbelly's "Blind Lemon Blues" was in honor of his friend.

Jefferson was discovered by a talent scout for Paramount Records while in Dallas and was taken to Chicago. He made seventy-nine records for Paramount in the 1920's, each estimated to have sold one hundred thousand copies; he also made two recordings under the "Okeh" label. Recognized as one of the earliest representatives of the "classic blues" field, and considered to be one of the best folk blues singers of the 1920's, Jefferson is said to have influenced such artists as Louis Armstrong, Bessie Smith, and Bix Beiderbecker, and to have encouraged "Lightnin'" Hopkins when Hopkins was an eight-year-old boy in Buffalo, Texas.

It is not definitely known whether Jefferson was married, although one source says he married in

1922 or 1923 and had a son. He died in late December, 1929, in Chicago. While Jefferson may not have been poisoned by a jealous woman, as one source indicated, there is evidence that his death did occur under "mysterious circumstances." Blind Lemon was buried in the Wortham Negro Cemetery, and his grave was marked as an official Texas historical monument.

BIBLIOGRAPHY: Rudi Blesh, *Shining Trumpets* (1958); Samuel B. Charters, *The Country Blues* (1959); Dave Dexter, Jr., *Jazz Story from the 90's to the 60's* (1964); Nat Hentoff and Albert McCarthy (eds.), *Jazz* (1961); Alan Lomax, *Folk Songs of North America* (1960); John A. Lomax and Alan Lomax, *Negro Folk Songs as Sung by Lead Belly* (1936); Marshall Stearns, *The Story of Jazz* (1962); Houston *Post*, October 18, 1967.

Marilynn Wood Hill

*Jefferson, John R., Jr.

Jefferson, Texas. (Jefferson County.) Fragmentary evidence indicates that in the 1830's one or more communities along Cow Bayou in the municipality of Jefferson (later Jefferson and Orange counties as well as parts of Chambers, Hardin, and Jasper counties) were referred to as Jefferson, and one of these communities (no longer existent) served as a post office and temporary seat before Beaumont became the county seat in 1838. *See also* West, Claiborne.

BIBLIOGRAPHY: Dermot H. Hardy and Ingham S. Roberts, *Historical Review of South-East Texas* (1910).

Madeleine Martin

*Jefferson, Texas. (Marion County.) Jefferson, seat of Marion County, is located on Caddo Lake. (It was never the seat of Jefferson County, as stated in Volume I.) Jefferson was laid out as a townsite in 1843 and in 1846 (not 1843) became the seat of Cass County upon that county's separation from Bowie County. The Cass County seat was moved to Linden in 1852.

Jefferson is known for places of historic interest, including some forty homes, churches, and other structures listed as worthy of preservation because of historical and architectural significance. Approximately twelve homes have been listed on the National Register in Washington, D.C. Every year Jefferson sponsors a three-day spring pilgrimage to view these sites.

Jefferson reported eighty-six businesses in 1970. In 1960 the population was 3,082; in 1970 the census count was 2,866.

BIBLIOGRAPHY: Seymour V. Connor, "County Government in the Republic of Texas," *Southwestern Historical Quarterly*, LV (1951–1952); H. P. N. Gammel (ed.), *Laws of Texas* (1898); L. W. Kemp, *Signers of the Texas Declaration of Independence* (1944); T. C. Richardson, *East Texas: Its History and Its Makers* (1940).

Madeleine Martin

*Jefferson County. Jefferson County, originally the Cow Bayou settlement (not the Cypress Bayou settlement, as stated in Volume I) of the municipality of Jefferson, had as its first county seat in 1837 a small community called Jefferson (no longer existent, and not to be confused with Jefferson in present Marion County). The present county seat is Beaumont. [*See* Jefferson, Texas (Jefferson County), and Jefferson, Texas (Marion County), for correction of this error; *see also* West, Claiborne.]

The income from crude minerals in Jefferson County was $78,838,440 in 1967. From 1901 to 1973 more than 416 million barrels of oil were produced in the county. Rice was still the leading crop in the mid-1970's. In 1960 Jefferson was the sixth most populous county, with a population of 245,659; in 1970 the population was 244,773.

BIBLIOGRAPHY: Seymour V. Connor, "County Government in the Republic of Texas," *Southwestern Historical Quarterly*, LV (1951–1952).

Madeleine Martin

*Jefferson and Northwestern Railroad Company.

*Jeffry, Texas.

*Jenkins, Charles H.

*Jenkins, James R.

*Jenkins, John H.

*Jenkins, Texas.

*Jennings, Elzy Dee.

*Jennings, Thomas Jefferson.

*Jennings, Texas.

*Jennings Lake.

*Jensen, Texas.

*Jericho, Texas.

*Jermyn, Texas.

*Jernigan Creek. Jernigan Creek was named for Curtis Jernigan (not a member of the Curtis Jernigin family, as stated in Volume I).

BIBLIOGRAPHY: Ikie Gray Patteson, *Loose Leaves: A History of Delta County* (1935).

*Jernigan Thicket. [This title was incorrectly listed in Volume I as Jernigin Thicket.] Jernigan Thicket was named for Curtis Jernigan (not Jernigin, as stated in Volume I).

BIBLIOGRAPHY: Ikie Gray Patteson, *Loose Leaves: A History of Delta County* (1935); Delta County records (Delta County Courthouse, Cooper, Texas).

*Jerry's Branch.

*Jesse Arroyo.

Jesse H. Jones Hall for the Performing Arts. On June 1, 1962, John T. Jones, Jr., nephew of Jesse Holman Jones,qv announced that Houston Endowment Inc. had offered to underwrite the construction costs for a performing arts hall in Houston. The Houston Endowment Inc., a charitable foundation endowed by Jesse H. Jones and his wife, Mary Gibbs Jones, for the purpose of supporting any charitable, educational, or religious undertaking, made possible the establishment of a permanent home for the Houston Symphony Orchestra, the Houston Grand Opera Association, and the Houston Ballet Foundation.

The city council of Houston passed an ordinance accepting the offer made by John Jones on June 6, 1962, and, on December 4, 1962, the council passed an ordinance officially naming the prospective building the Jesse H. Jones Hall for the Performing Arts. On January 10, 1964, groundbreaking for the building took place. On October 20, 1965, the cornerstone was laid and, on October 2, 1966, the building became the property of the city of Houston.

The site for the building was provided by the city and the total construction cost was $7.4 million. It was the first new building to be completed in the planned $40 million Civic Center complex. It occupied a full city block and consisted of a grand lobby decorated with sculpture by Richard Lippold, a minor lobby, and the main hall, which seated 3,001. A counter-weighted ceiling contained panels which could be lowered to reduce seating capacity. The stage measured 55 feet by 120 feet, the largest in the city in 1968. Other facilities included a room for performing artists to entertain friends and press, a rehearsal room, and offices for the administrative staff. Total space measured one million cubic feet.

*Jester, Beauford Halbert.

*Jester, George Taylor.

*Jester, Texas.

*Jesús, María, y José Mission.

*Jewell, Texas.

*Jewett, Texas.

*Jewry in Texas. From the 1850's to the 1870's, European Jews immigrating to Texas came mostly from Germany; from the 1880's to the outbreak of World War I in 1914, they came mostly from countries farther east. The immigration of eastern European Jews into Texas was expedited between 1907 and 1914 by the so-called "Galveston Plan" or "Galveston Movement," which resulted in the entry through Galveston of about ten thousand Jews. The plan, executed largely through the philanthropy of New York Jewish financier Jacob H. Schiff and the efforts of Rabbi Henry Cohen qv of Galveston, was designed to steer European Jewish immigrants away from the comparatively congested Atlantic seaboard to the less populous southern and southwestern sections of the United States.

By 1930 the Jewish population in Texas stood at approximately fifty thousand. In 1958 it was around 58,200; in 1960 near 60,900; and in 1964 about 63,385. Despite the slight population increase, the proportion of Jews in the total population of the state declined between 1930 and 1964 from approximately .86 percent to .61 percent.

In 1964 thirty Texas cities and towns had 100 or more Jewish residents. Dallas, with an estimated 19,500 Jewish inhabitants, and Houston, with approximately 19,000, had the largest Jewish communities in the state and, between them, accounted for over half of the Jewish population in Texas. Other cities with relatively sizable Jewish communities in 1964 were San Antonio, with about 6,000; El Paso, with 4,400; Fort Worth, with 2,600; and Galveston, with about 2,000 Jews.

There were about fifty-four Jewish houses of worship in the state in 1966, seven of which were in Houston and its suburbs, five in Dallas, and three in San Antonio. Other Texas cities with temples or

synagogues include Abilene, Amarillo, Austin, Beaumont, Brownsville, Bryan, Corpus Christi, Corsicana, Denison, El Paso, Fort Worth, Galveston, Harlingen, Kilgore, Laredo, Longview, Lubbock, McAllen, Marshall, Port Arthur, San Angelo, Schulenburg, Texarkana, Tyler, Victoria, Waco, Wharton, and Wichita Falls.

In March, 1928, the "Kallah of the Texas Rabbinical Association" was established in Houston. The organization, devoted to discussion of religious and rabbinical questions, was, at the time of its establishment, unique in American Jewry. In the area of social welfare, the Pauline Sterne Wolfe Memorial Home for Orphans and Widows, largely used for indigent and ill children of all faiths, was built in Houston in 1930–1931. Various Jewish community councils, federations, and welfare funds served the social and cultural needs of the larger Texas Jewish communities, with eleven such agencies reported in existence in 1965. A Jewish home for the aged, Golden Manor, opened in San Antonio during the middle 1960's.

Three Jewish periodicals were published in the state in 1965, of which the oldest, the weekly *Jewish Herald-Voice* (Houston), had been founded in 1908. The others were the weekly *Texas Jewish Post* (Dallas-Fort Worth), founded in 1947, and the monthly *Jewish Digest* (Houston), founded in 1955.

BIBLIOGRAPHY: *American Jewish Year Book* (1961, 1965); Bernard Postal and Lionel Koppman, *A Jewish Tourist's Guide to the United States* (1954); *The Standard Jewish Encyclopedia* (1962); *Texas Almanac* (1960, 1967); *The Universal Jewish Encyclopedia*, IV, V, X (1948); Files, Institute of Texan Cultures, University of Texas at San Antonio.

Sam A. Suhler

*Jiba, Texas.

*Jim Hogg County. Jim Hogg County was largely devoted to ranching and petroleum. Oil production began in 1922, and by 1973 total crude production had reached 92,984,804 barrels. Truck crops and peanuts were the main contributors to the agricultural income, which amounted to $116,000 in 1968. Cash receipts from livestock and products in that same year were $2,774,000. The 1960 population was 5,022; in 1970 the population was 4,654, according to the United States census.

*Jim John Creek.

*Jim Little Creek.

*Jim Nail Branch.

*Jim Ned.

*Jim Ned Creek.

*Jim Wells County. Jim Wells County has increased its emphasis on the oil industry. From 1933 to 1973 almost 416,000,000 barrels of oil were produced. In 1968 the county had a farm income that was divided among beef cattle, dairy cattle, and crops, with grain sorghums leading in numbers of bushels produced. Although dairying had been decreasing, there were fifty-five Grade A dairies in the county in 1964. From 1968 to 1969, 6,989 bales of cotton were produced by four gins.

The county has an October fair and a June rodeo. The 1960 population of 34,548 had declined to 33,032 by 1970, according to the United States census.

*Jimkurn, Texas.

*Jimmys Creek.

*Jims Bayou.

*Jines, Texas.

*Joaquin, Texas.

Job Corps Program in Texas. Following the passage of the Federal Economic Opportunity Act into law on August 20, 1964, the United States Office of Economic Opportunity began awarding contracts to establish vocational training centers. By the mid-1960's Texas had established one of each of the three types of centers: urban center for men, urban center for women, and rural center for men.

On December 16, 1964, the Texas Educational Foundation, Inc., a private, nonprofit, Texas corporation, was awarded a contract to establish the Gary Job Corps Training Center at San Marcos. In June of 1966 this foundation was awarded a second contract to establish the McKinney Center for Women. In addition to these two urban centers, the New Waverly Conservation Center, funded by the Office of Economic Opportunity and operated by the Forest Service of the United States Department of Agriculture, was completed in August, 1965.

A three-man board of trustees of the Texas Educational Foundation was appointed by Governor John Connally and included J. R. Thornton of San Marcos, Cecil Ruby of Austin, and Arleigh Templeton, president of Sam Houston State College (now Sam Houston State University). At Governor Connally's request, Opportunities Incorporated, another nonprofit organization composed of a group of Texas-based business and industrial firms, provided technical advice and assistance in designing the curricula for both urban centers. This support group of approximately one hundred firms also assisted in the placement of the Gary center graduates and periodically audited the training program to insure that training courses were in line with industrial needs and techniques.

The Gary Job Corps Training Center was located four miles southeast of San Marcos on the former site of Gary Air Force Base.qv The first trainees arrived in March, 1965, and on April 10, 1965, President Lyndon B. Johnson qv dedicated the training center. From the date of its opening, the center offered thirty-eight vocational choices to young men between the ages of sixteen and twenty-one. Between 1965 and 1967 the Gary Job Corps Training Center became the largest such training center in the nation, having approximately 3,000 trainees in 1967.

The McKinney Center for Women, established in June, 1966, was located in the facilities formerly used by the Veterans Administration Hospital, McKinney.qv With space for 600 young women, the center offered vocational training in industrial fields. With the cut-back of funds from the Office of Economic Opportunity, the New Waverly Conservation Center, which had provided facilities for a maximum of 225 young men to receive rural vocational training, was closed in June, 1969.

In 1969 the responsibility for establishing vocational training centers was changed from the Office of Economic Opportunity to the United States Department of Labor. In 1970 the Department of Labor entered into a contract with the Texas Educational Foundation, Inc., for the establishment and operation of a training center at El Paso. The El Paso Residential Manpower Center was opened in September, 1970, with fifty students, at the old Hotel Cortez in downtown El Paso. In 1975 there were 250 trainees, with 200 resident and 50 nonresident students. In that same year there were 2,200 male trainees at the Gary Job Corps Training Center in San Marcos and 620 women trainees at McKinney Center for Women in McKinney. There were definite plans formulated in 1975 to make all three centers coeducational in 1976.

The number of trustees on the board of the Texas Educational Foundation, Inc., was increased from three to five in late 1970; in addition to original members Thornton and Templeton (Ruby had resigned), Herman S. Wigodsky, Alfred Henry, and Roy Barrera served on the board beginning in 1970. The first executive director of the foundation was O. J. Baker, who served until his death in May, 1970; at that time Wallace D. Dockall became executive director, and he remained in that position in 1975.

Trainees in all three centers received sufficient technical knowledge and supervised practice to permit them to obtain gainful employment in a defined occupation upon completion of training. General education courses were offered in basic and remedial reading, writing, mathematics, and communications skills. Trainees who so desired could take the General Educational Development (G.E.D.) test; each student who passed was awarded the equivalent of a high school diploma. Although the program provided a maximum of two years training, the average trainee spent approximately one year in the Job Corps.

The average Job Corps trainee in Texas was seventeen and one-half years old, was unemployed but looking for work at the time of his application to the program, had been out of school eleven months, had completed eight and one-half years of formal education, and had a fifth-grade achievement level. The average trainee came from a family of six, which lived in overcrowded, substandard housing, and his parents were either unemployed or held unskilled jobs.

*Jobe's Creek.

*Joe.

*Joe Beatty Creek.

*Joe Lee, Texas.

*Joel, Texas.

*John B. Denton College.

*John Ray Creek.

*John Tarleton Agricultural College. *See* Tarleton State College (in Volume II); *see also* Tarleton State University.

*Johns, Clement Reed.

*Johns, Edward.

*Johns, Stephen B.

*Johns Creek.

*Johnson, Achilles Edmond Challis.

*Johnson, Adam Rankin.

*Johnson, Britton (Brit). [Britton (Brit) Johnson was not born on the ranch of the Moses Johnson qv referred to in Volume I, but was a close friend of Samuel Parker Johnson qv whose grandfather was a Moses Johnson, a member of Peters' Colony qv and not to be confused with the Moses Johnson who was a physician.]
BIBLIOGRAPHY: Benjamin Capps, *The Warren Wagontrain Raid* (1974); Newcastle *Register*, January 13, 1966.

*Johnson, Cone.

Johnson, Elizabeth E. (Lizzie). Elizabeth E. (Lizzie) Johnson, early businesswoman and cattle dealer, was born in Missouri in 1843, the daughter of Catherine (Hyde) and Thomas Jefferson Johnson.qv At the age of sixteen she began teaching bookkeeping at Johnson Institute,qv and later taught in Manor, Lockhart, and Austin. Her proficiency in bookkeeping eventually led to her handling books for cattlemen in St. Louis.

On June 1, 1871, she registered her brand and went into the cattle business. She married Hezekiah G. Williams of Austin on June 8, 1879, a preacher and widower with several children; he also entered the cattle business in 1881. Lizzie insisted on operating her business independently from that of her husband, and she is believed to have been one of the few women to drive her own herd up the Chisholm Trail qv to Kansas. She also invested money in real estate and eventually owned land in Llano, Hays, and Trinity counties, small ranches in Culberson and Jeff Davis counties, and various lots and buildings in Austin. After her husband's death in 1914, Lizzie kept to herself and subsisted on the barest of necessities. She died in Austin on October 9, 1924, and was buried in Oakwood Cemetery in that city. At the time of her death the value of her real estate alone was $164,339. The total value of her holdings was approximately $200,000. *See also* Friday Mountain Ranch.
BIBLIOGRAPHY: Biographical File, Barker Texas History Center, University of Texas at Austin; Emily Jones Shelton, "Lizzie E. Johnson: A Cattle Queen of Texas," *Southwestern Historical Quarterly*, L (1946–1947); T. U. Taylor, "Johnson Institute," *Frontier Times*, XVIII (February, 1941).

M. Doty

*Johnson, Francis White.

*Johnson, Henry W.

*Johnson, Hugh Blair. [This title in Volume I was an incorrect spelling of the subject's name and was therefore out of its proper alphabetical place. See Johnston, Hugh Blair.]

*Johnson, Isaac W.

*Johnson, Jack. John Arthur Johnson, known as Jack Johnson, was world heavyweight boxing champion from December 26, 1908, to April 5, 1915. Born in Galveston on March 31, 1878, he learned the art of boxing there at an early age. From the time he was fourteen he was defeating larger and older opponents on the streets of Galveston, and as a young man he traveled around the United States, seeking matches and usually winning. When he defeated Tommy Burns in 1908 he became the first black man to hold the world's heavyweight title.

Though largely uneducated, Johnson had a quick wit and a flamboyant life style. During a time of great racial prejudice he managed to gain international recognition (along with a great deal of hatred) for his prowess in the boxing ring. He was married four times, first to Mary Austin, a Negro girl from Galveston, in 1898; they separated in 1901 and were subsequently divorced. His next three wives were white: Etta Duryea, whom he married in 1909 (she committed suicide in 1912); Lucille Cameron, whom he married in 1913 (they were divorced twelve years later); and Irene Pineau, whom he married in 1925.

Charged with violation of the Mann Act, Johnson fled the United States in 1913 and did not return until 1919. He returned voluntarily and served eight months of a one-year prison sentence in 1920. He wrote an autobiography in 1926, but it was not published until 1969. Jack Johnson died in an automobile accident in Raleigh, North Carolina, on the way to New York from a lecture tour in Texas, on June 10, 1946.

The Great White Hope, a Broadway play based on Johnson's life, opened in New York in 1968. Although successful on the stage, and later made into a film, the dramatic work takes great liberty with the facts of Johnson's life, although it does convey to a large extent the bigotry and controversy which surrounded Johnson's career as a heavyweight boxing champion.
BIBLIOGRAPHY: John Arthur Johnson, *Jack Johnson is a Dandy: An Autobiography* (1969).

Eldon S. Branda

Johnson, John Arthur. See Johnson, Jack.

*Johnson, John R.

Johnson, Joseph Burton. Joseph Burton Johnson was born in Georgia about 1811 and served as major of the Regiment of Cavalry of the 2nd Florida Brigade during the Mexican War. He came to Texas and by 1860 had acquired substantial slave and agricultural holdings near Fairfield.

With the coming of the Civil War, Johnson recruited ten companies of state troops in the Freestone County area and was elected their regimental commander. On November 2, 1861, he was commissioned colonel of the Freestone County Regiment Number One, a part of the 19th Brigade of

Texas State Troops. In March, 1862, Johnson became senior colonel, commanding the 19th Brigade of the Texas militia, and on August 1, 1863, he was commissioned brigadier general of the 19th Brigade. After the war Johnson returned to Fairfield, where he resumed his agricultural activities. In 1873 he was chosen Master of Grangers from Freestone County. He died on January 18, 1874, and was buried in the family plot near Fairfield.

BIBLIOGRAPHY: Service Record of Joseph Burton Johnson, Confederate Records (MS., National Archives, Washington, D.C.); J. B. Johnson Records (MS., Archives, Texas State Library); J. B. Johnson Records (MS., Freestone County Historical Survey Committee); U.S. War Department, *The War of the Rebellion: A Compilation of the Official Records of the Union and Confederate Armies* (1880–1901).

Allan C. Ashcraft

*Johnson, Joshua Foster.

Johnson, Lyndon Baines. Lyndon Baines Johnson, thirty-sixth president of the United States, was born near Stonewall, Texas, on August 27, 1908, the son of Rebekah (Baines) and Samuel Ealy Johnson, Jr.qqv

He attended school in Albert and Johnson City and was graduated in 1924 from Johnson City High School. After spending nearly a year working at various jobs in Texas and California, he entered Southwest Texas State Teachers College (now Southwest Texas State University), defraying his expenses first as school janitor and then as secretary in the college president's office. Here he became active in campus politics and formed lasting friendships with men who would later prove significant in his political life. He interrupted his college career in 1929 to teach at the Welhausen School for Mexican Americans in Cotulla, Texas. In 1930 he was graduated from Southwest Texas State Teachers College and began teaching debating and public speaking at Sam Houston High School in Houston.

In the fall of 1931 Johnson worked in the campaign of Richard Mifflin Kleberg,qv candidate from the 14th United States District of Texas for the House of Representatives. When Kleberg won, Johnson moved to Washington as his legislative secretary. He first made an impact on Washington when in 1933 he was elected speaker of the "Little Congress," an organization of congressional secretaries modeled after the senior House of Representatives. He is also credited with having persuaded his employer, Congressman Kleberg, to reverse his opposition to the Agricultural Adjustment Administration bill, which President Franklin D. Roosevelt sent to Congress. He enrolled in night law school at Georgetown University in 1934–1935.

On July 25, 1935, Johnson was named state administrator of the National Youth Administration for Texas, the youngest NYA state administrator in the nation. For almost two years he ran one of the most effective state organizations, drawing attention to himself again both in Texas and beyond.

When Congressman James Paul Buchanan qv of the 10th United States District of Texas died on the previous February 5, Johnson won the election on April 10, 1937, over eight opponents. Two months earlier President Roosevelt had called on Congress to enlarge the Supreme Court, a request that provoked a national storm of opposition. In his campaign for Congress, Johnson took a calculated risk by coming out wholeheartedly for Roosevelt's administration, including the so-called Supreme Court packing plan. The fact that Johnson won on a platform of straightforward advocacy of the New Deal brought him to Roosevelt's attention. Shortly after President Roosevelt docked at Galveston for a visit to the state, young Congressman-elect Johnson was asked to ride through Texas on the special presidential train. The result was that he almost immediately came to know the president and his advisers better than would the ordinary freshman legislator. Shortly after he was sworn in on May 14, 1937, he received an appointment to the House Committee on Naval Affairs through the direct intervention of the president.

As a congressman Johnson proved to be as active as in his earlier positions. He helped with the formation of the Lower Colorado River Authority qv and pushed through for Austin one of the nation's first slum clearance programs. In 1940 Johnson was named a delegate to the Democratic national convention and later in the year was placed in charge of the Democratic Congressional Campaign Committee, charged with raising and disbursing money for the 150 Democratic candidates for Congress.

When Senator Morris Sheppard qv died on April 9, 1941, Johnson announced his candidacy for Sheppard's unexpired term from the steps of the White House. However, he faced a particularly formidable opponent, Governor W. Lee O'Daniel,qv then at the height of his popularity. On June 28 Johnson lost the Senate race to Governor O'Daniel by 1,311 votes. When at the end of the year the Japanese bombed Pearl Harbor and the United States retaliated by declaring war, Johnson became the first member of the House of Representatives to enter the armed services. The following June 9, 1942, as a lieutenant commander in the navy, he received a Silver Star from General Douglas MacArthur for gallantry in action in New Guinea, but in July President Roosevelt ordered all members of Congress in the military forces back to their desks in Washington. Johnson was then made chairman of a special investigating subcommittee of the Naval Affairs Committee, in which position he brought to light abuses and laxities in naval practices. In that same year his wife bought a small, impoverished Austin radio station, KTBC, for $17,500. In 1943 Johnson was one of only two Texas congressmen to side with President Roosevelt in voting against the bill to raise the wartime price ceiling on petroleum. In 1945 Johnson was named a member of the newly created House Committee on Post-War Military Policy, and he saw his draft of a "work or fight" bill permitting the government to freeze essential workers in their jobs and to penalize those refusing war jobs enacted by Congress. In the postwar 80th Congress he voted for the Taft-Hartley Act, dubbed by organized labor as a "slave labor" act, a stance that was to cause him considerable political problems later, particularly in the senatorial race of 1948.

In 1948 Johnson ran for the United States Senate, with former Governor Coke R. Stevenson qv as his principal opponent. Stevenson, a highly successful wartime governor, also had the support of the state officials of the American Federation of Labor, a reaction against Johnson's stand on Taft-Hartley. In the runoff election, Johnson won by 87 votes out of almost one million cast, which earned him the nickname of "Landslide Lyndon." The closeness of the result led Stevenson to file a lawsuit that went all the way to the United States Supreme Court, where Justice Hugo Black issued an order that Johnson's name should be put back on the ballot for the November election against the Republican candidate, Jack Porter. Johnson then defeated Porter by a two-to-one margin.

In the Senate Johnson distinguished himself by his hard and purposeful work. He refused to be either doctrinaire or labeled, sometimes lining up with the so-called Southern Bloc and other times going in other directions. Although in 1948 he had called the Truman civil rights program "a farce and a sham—an effort to set up a police state in the guise of liberty," in the next year he delivered another speech on the Senate floor on civil rights in which he said, "Some may feel moved to deny this group or that the homes, the education, the employment which every American has the right to expect, but I am not one of those." He refused to attend the Southern Caucus that same year.

In July, 1950, Johnson introduced a resolution to establish the Preparedness and Investigating Subcommittee to the Senate Armed Services Committee, and he was designated as chairman when the Senate passed his resolution. In the next two years the subcommittee issued forty-four reports, ranging from manpower requirements to industrial might to waste.

At the beginning of 1951, when he was barely 43 years old, Johnson was named majority whip by the Democratic members of the Senate, the youngest member ever to hold a position of Senate leadership. Senator Richard Russell of Georgia, then probably the most powerful Democrat in the Senate, named Johnson as floor manager for the Universal Military Training bill. In the election of 1952, when Texas voted for Dwight D. Eisenhower, qv the Republican candidate, Johnson announced his full support for the Democratic nominee, Adlai E. Stevenson.

When the new Senate was organized at the beginning of 1953, Johnson was named minority leader, again the youngest man ever to be named its floor leader. As minority leader, Johnson automatically became chairman of the Democratic Steering Committee and the Democratic Policy Committee. He won particular attention for breaking traditional Senate procedures by ignoring strict seniority in assigning capable young senators, some of them freshmen, to important committees. For instance, he assigned Stuart Symington to Armed Services, Hubert H. Humphrey to Foreign Relations, Mike Mansfield and Herbert Lehman to Banking and Currency, and John F. Kennedy to Labor and Public Welfare. Johnson both talked and practiced "the politics of responsibility," saying that as a minority leader he felt that the politics of partisanship were not in the nation's service.

When in 1954 the United States Supreme Court handed down its historic decision in *Brown* v. *Board of Education of Topeka, Kansas*, declaring racial segregation in the public schools as unconstitutional, Johnson refused to sign the "Southern Manifesto" protesting the Supreme Court decision. He also helped arrange the bipartisan Senate committee to investigate Joseph McCarthy's actions in the Senate. This was the select committee that censured the controversial senator. In November, 1954, the Democrats won control of the Senate by one vote, so that when the new Congress was formed at the beginning of 1955, Johnson was named Senate majority leader, again at age 46 the youngest majority leader in history. His career was interrupted when on July 2, 1955, he suffered a heart attack that threatened his life and his political future. He remained in Bethesda Naval Hospital for five weeks, and many questioned whether he would ever be able to work effectively again. But by the end of the year he was back at his post, working as hard as ever, a pace he continued for the next thirteen years.

At the Democratic national convention in Chicago in August, 1956, Johnson was considered a dark horse for the presidency. Although his supporters did manage to round up eighty votes, the convention delegates voted overwhelmingly to renominate Stevenson. When Stevenson threw the vice-presidency open to the convention, Johnson supported John F. Kennedy against the Tennessee senator, Estes Kefauver, the ultimate winner. Back in the Senate in January, 1957, Johnson nominated Kennedy for the vacant seat on the Foreign Relations Committee. But the principal accomplishment of Johnson in 1957 was steering through the Senate the first significant civil rights bill in eighty-two years. To a great extent passage of this bill is looked upon as the work of Johnson, who was able to carry only four other Southern senators along with him, including Ralph Yarborough of Texas. But he did stave off uncompromising Southern opposition to the bill on the one hand and the almost equally uncompromising liberal opposition on the other, and he somehow steered the bill safely through the Senate. Basically the new law empowered the federal government to intervene on behalf of any person whose civil rights had either been denied or threatened.

When later in 1957 the Russians launched Sputnik, the first man-made earth satellite, Johnson organized and became the first chairman of the Senate Committee on Aeronautical and Space Sciences. This committee wrote the National Space Act establishing the National Aeronautics and Space Administration (NASA) qv and guaranteeing that control of the space program would remain in civilian hands. Altogether the Johnson years as Senate majority leader were marked by his and Speaker of the House Sam Rayburn's qv attempts to work with the Eisenhower administration wherever possible, and the consensus in Congress was that during his last six years in office President Eisenhower received more assistance from Rayburn and Johnson, both Texas Democrats, than he did from his own party leadership in the Congress.

When the presidential election year of 1960 rolled around, Johnson played an evasive role as a candidate. Finally on July 5 he announced his candidacy, but by then John F. Kennedy had too large a delegate lead for Johnson to overcome. Johnson ran second on the first ballot at the Democratic national convention, but Kennedy easily won the first ballot majority. Kennedy then surprised many citizens by offering the vice-presidential nomination to Johnson, and Johnson surprised just as many by accepting. When in November the Kennedy-Johnson ticket won over the Richard Nixon-Henry Cabot Lodge ticket by the closest vote margin in the 20th century, Johnson was given a large share of the credit because of his ability to persuade leadership in several Southern states to support Kennedy. As vice-president, Johnson became chairman of the President's Committee on Equal Employment Opportunity, and he represented the president at the first anniversary of the new Republic of Senegal and in Paris at the tenth anniversary of Supreme Headquarters Allied Powers, Europe (SHAPE). He spent considerable time abroad representing the president in such countries as Viet Nam, the Philippines, the Republic of China, Thailand, Pakistan, Germany, Sweden, Jamaica, Lebanon, Iran, Cyprus, Turkey, Greece, Norway, Finland, Denmark, and Iceland.

On his Pakistan trip in May, 1961, Johnson startled the world by inviting a camel driver, Bashir Ahmed, to visit him in Texas, and the world was even more startled when during the following autumn Bashir arrived in the United States as a guest of Johnson. Johnson received considerable attention when on May 30, 1963, in an address at Gettysburg, he spoke the following words: "One hundred years ago, the slaves were freed. One hundred years later, the Negro remains in bondage through the color of his skin. The Negro today asks justice. . . . Until justice is blind to color, until education is unaware of race, until opportunity is unconcerned with the color of men's skins, emancipation will be a proclamation but not a fact."

On November 22, 1963, President Kennedy was in Texas visiting several cities in quest of political support, with Johnson and other Texas dignitaries accompanying him. About 12:30 p.m. of that day Kennedy was assassinated in Dallas, and Johnson was sworn in as president by United States District Judge Sarah T. Hughes on Air Force One at Love Field in Dallas at 2:38 p.m. (*See* Kennedy, John Fitzgerald, Assassination of.) Through tragedy the first real Texan had become president. (Eisenhower, of course, was born in Denison, Texas, but lived in the state such a short time that he had no memory of the period.) Johnson was elected to a full four-year term as president on November 3, 1964.

As president, Johnson inaugurated the Great Society and over the next five and one-half years pushed through hundreds of acts that left the United States with certain Johnson imprints that won't likely disappear within the foreseeable future. He was particularly effective in civil rights activities, especially with the Civil Rights Acts of 1964, 1965, and 1968. He pushed through such programs as federal aid to education, Medicare, and the "war on poverty" (later largely dismantled by the succeeding Nixon administration). Under his administration the Department of Transportation, the Department of Housing and Urban Development, the Inter-American Development Bank, and the Asian Development Bank, and the American Revolution Bicentennial Commission were created. Other programs dealt with wilderness areas, clean air, clean rivers, scenic rivers and scenic trails, water pollution, water desalting, hazardous radiation protection, aircraft noise abatement, heart, cancer, and stroke research, drug controls, gun controls, model cities, urban mass transit, safe streets, aid to handicapped children, school breakfasts, child nutrition, guaranteed student loans, care for older Americans, Indian bill of rights, flammable fabrics, public broadcasting, freedom of information, presidential disability, small business aid, truth in securities, truth in lending, truth in packaging, food for peace, fair immigration, Virgin Islands elections, international monetary reform, outer space treaties, arts and humanities foundations, and libraries of all sorts. He also added more areas to the National Park Service than any other president in history, including in Texas the Guadalupe Mountains National Park.qv

Johnson's hyperactivity in trying to overcome omissions of the past and to point the way to a more equitable future for all American citizens sometimes led to more than the American public was able to digest. Also he raised expectations of many previously disadvantaged people to such heights that their patience could not always endure the sometimes slow upward evolution toward improvement of the quality of their lives. When these dissatisfactions were coupled with an escalating unpopular war in Southeast Asia, which Johnson had inherited from his two predecessors and which required nearly five more years for his successor to terminate, dissidence in the United States reached an unparalleled height. The result was that the Johnson accomplishments were marred with all sorts of demonstrations, especially by American youth and by minority groups. Although Johnson did succeed in bringing North Viet Nam to a peace negotiating table in Paris, and although on March 31, 1968, he removed himself as a political factor by renouncing any intention to accept candidacy for reelection, the peace he sought eluded him.

After his retirement, Johnson returned to his LBJ Ranch outside Stonewall, where he lived until his death from a coronary on January 22, 1973. In retirement he completed plans to deed a large portion of his property, including his birthplace and his residence in Stonewall and his boyhood home in Johnson City, to the federal government, which in turn designated the area as a national historic site. The site is unique in the whole national historic complex, for nowhere else do we have the entire career of a president encapsulated within a twenty-mile radius. Here is the site where Johnson was born, where he mailed his first letter, where he attended his first school, where he probably kissed his first girl, where he was graduated from high school, where he left to hitchhike to California as a young man, where he took off for college, where he made his first political speech, where he brought the leaders of the world to discuss national and international problems, and where he died and was buried.

Johnson's papers are housed in the huge Lyndon Baines Johnson Library,qv built by the University of Texas at Austin and deeded to the Archives of the United States. The Lyndon B. Johnson School of Public Affairs at the university also represents a step forward in training career public servants.

Johnson was married on November 17, 1934, to Claudia Alta (Lady Bird) Taylor in St. Mark's Episcopal Church in San Antonio. Mrs. Johnson herself became an international figure, particularly for her work in conservation and beautification. The Johnsons had two children—Lynda Bird, born March 19, 1944; and Luci Baines, born July 2, 1947. *See also* Lyndon Baines Johnson Birthplace, Boyhood Home, and Ranch; Lyndon Baines Johnson Library; and Lyndon B. Johnson State Historic Park (under Parks, State).

Joe B. Frantz

Johnson, Lyndon Baines, Library. *See* Lyndon Baines Johnson Library. *See also* Lyndon Baines Johnson Birthplace, Boyhood Home, and Ranch; Lyndon B. Johnson State Historic Park (under Parks, State).

*Johnson, Middleton Tate.

*Johnson, Moses.

Johnson, Rebekah (Baines). Rebekah (Baines) Johnson, one of three children of Ruth (Huffman) and Joseph Wilson Baines,qv was born on June 26, 1881, at McKinney, Texas. In 1883 she moved with her parents to Austin, where her father served for four years as secretary of state under Governor John Ireland.qv In 1887 the family moved to Blanco. She attended Baylor University in 1901; in 1902 she transferred to the University of Texas; in the 1904–1905 school year she was a student at Baylor Female College (now Mary Hardin-Baylor

College) in Belton. After her father's death in Fredericksburg on November 18, 1906, she moved into the family home in that town, where she taught and corresponded for daily newspapers.

On August 20, 1907, she married Samuel Ealy Johnson, Jr.,qv and they had five children, one of whom was Lyndon Baines Johnson,qv thirty-sixth president of the United States. After the death of her husband in 1937, she made her home in Austin. She died on September 12, 1958, and was buried in the family plot at Johnson City.

BIBLIOGRAPHY: Rebekah Baines Johnson (J. S. Moursund, ed.), *A Family Album* (1965); Waco *Tribune-Herald*, December 1, 1963; Austin *Statesman*, December 16, 1964; Dallas *Morning News*, March 4, 1965.

Dayton Kelley

*Johnson, Robert Dabney.

Johnson, Samuel Ealy, Jr. Samuel Ealy Johnson, Jr., son of Eliza (Bunton) and Samuel Ealy Johnson, Sr.,qv was born at Buda, Texas, on October 11, 1877. He moved with his parents to Gillespie County, where he attended school at Johnson City. Although forced to leave school at an early age, he passed the teacher's examination and was awarded a teaching certification.

Johnson taught school in 1896 at White Oak School in Sandy and later at the Rocky School near Hye. In 1904 he was elected to the state legislature from the Eighty-ninth District, succeeding his future father-in-law, Joseph Wilson Baines.qv He served in the twenty-ninth, thirtieth, thirty-fifth, thirty-sixth, thirty-seventh, and thirty-eighth legislatures. He was the author of the Alamo Purchase Bill (which appropriated $65,000 for the purchase of the Alamo property), a bill providing $3,000,000 to aid drouth-stricken farmers and ranchers of West Texas, the Blue Sky Law,qv and other important legislative measures.

On August 20, 1907, Johnson married Rebekah Baines (*see* Johnson, Rebekah Baines). The couple were parents of five children, including Lyndon Baines Johnson,qv thirty-sixth president of the United States. In 1906 Samuel E. Johnson, Jr., suffered severe financial losses, which wiped out his cotton holdings and left him deeply in debt.

For a number of years he was engaged in real estate transactions. In 1935 and 1937 he was stricken with heart attacks. He died on October 23, 1937, and was buried in the family cemetery at Johnson City.

BIBLIOGRAPHY: Rebekah Baines Johnson (J. S. Moursund, ed.), *A Family Album* (1965).

Dayton Kelley

Johnson, Samuel Ealy, Sr. Samuel Ealy Johnson, Sr., tenth child of Jesse and Lucy Webb (Barnett) Johnson, was born in Alabama on November 12, 1838. He moved first with his parents to Georgia and later to Lockhart, Texas, where the family settled in 1846. His parents died in the late 1850's, and Sam Johnson, along with his brother Jesse Thomas, built a portholed rock barn as a headquarters for their cattle business at what is now Johnson City.

Sam Johnson enlisted in Colonel Xavier Blanchard de Bray's qv regiment on September 18, 1861, and served until the end of the Civil War on the coast of Texas and in Louisiana. He was present at the battle of Galveston and at the battle of Pleasant Hill qqv in Louisiana. After the war he returned to Lockhart and Johnson City and resumed his cattle buying. He and his brother became trail drivers, taking cattle to Kansas and Montana in the years 1870 to 1873.

Johnson was married to Eliza Bunton on December 11, 1867, in Lockhart, and the couple set up housekeeping in the log cabin at Johnson City which the two brothers had used before the war. They moved to Caldwell County and later to Buda in Hays County, where all but the oldest of their nine children were born. The family returned to Blanco County about 1889 and settled on the Pedernales River about twelve miles from Johnson City.

Johnson died of pneumonia at Stonewall, Texas, on February 25, 1915. One of his grandsons, Lyndon Baines Johnson,qv became thirty-sixth president of the United States.

BIBLIOGRAPHY: J. Marvin Hunter (ed.), *The Trail Drivers of Texas* (1924); John W. Speer, *A History of Blanco County* (1885); John S. Moursund, *Blanco County Families for One Hundred Years* (1958); Rebekah Baines Johnson (J. S. Moursund, ed.), *A Family Album* (1965); William C. Pool, Emmie Craddock, David E. Conrad, *Lyndon Baines Johnson: The Formative Years* (1965).

Dayton Kelley

Johnson, Samuel Parker. Samuel Parker Johnson, son of J. Allen Johnson (one of the founding fathers of Young County) and grandson of Moses Johnson (a member of Peter's Colony qv), was born in Choctaw County, Mississippi, on October 20, 1829, the oldest of four boys and many half-sisters.

Johnson was well known as a frontiersman in North Texas, spending about thirty-five years "in the saddle" as a guide, scout, militiaman, ranger, and cavalryman, but he was best known as a buffalo hunter and Indian fighter during the Indian depredations. His brother Reuben was killed by Indians in 1867.

Johnson took an uncompromising stand against Indians throughout his life, and in his later years he refused to attend reunions of old acquaintances when he knew that Indians would be present.

He was married to Elizabeth Adrian Steadham, and they were the parents of three children. He died on February 27, 1910, and was buried in the Fort Belknap qv civilian cemetery.

Barbara Neal Ledbetter

*Johnson, Thomas.

Johnson, Thomas Jefferson. Thomas Jefferson Johnson was born in Norfolk County, Virginia, on October 8, 1805. He was educated under the tutelage of Martin Ruter qv at Augusta College in Kentucky, and as a young man he went to Jefferson City, Missouri, to teach school. He married Catherine Hyde in Franklin County, Missouri, on May 7, 1837; they had six children. Johnson and his family came to Texas in 1844 and settled at Hunts-

ville. He taught school there and at Lockhart and Webberville before opening his own school, Johnson Institute,qv in Hays County. The institute was a family enterprise, with Johnson, his wife, son, and three daughters, including Elizabeth E. (Lizzie) Johnson,qv all teaching there. Johnson was affectionately known as "Old Bristle Top" to his students. He died on September 2, 1868, and was buried in a cemetery on the institute grounds. *See also* Friday Mountain Ranch.

*Johnson, W. A.

*Johnson, William H.

*Johnson, William M.

*Johnson, Texas.

*Johnson City, Texas. Johnson City, seat of Blanco County, gained nationwide fame in the 1960's as the home of President Lyndon B. Johnson qv and experienced a rise in the tourist industry, long its major source of income. The city is a trading center for the ranches of the area, with fifty-two businesses in 1970, and it is the headquarters of the large Pedernales Electric Cooperative. A housing project for aged and low-income families was completed in the late 1960's, along with other public improvements. The 1960 population was 611; the 1970 census showed a count of 767.

*Johnson County. Johnson County is a leading dairy and livestock area with a balanced urban-rural economy. In 1960 the county ranked tenth in the state in total sales from livestock and associated products and fifth in number of dairy cows, with 170 Grade A dairies. Since 1962 there has been some production of oil in the county; 194,000 barrels of oil had been produced by 1973. Tourist attractions include Cleburne State Recreation Park (*see* Parks, State) and Pat Cleburne Reservoir. The 1960 population of 34,720 had increased by 1970 to 45,769.

*Johnson Creek.

Johnson Creek Reservoir. Johnson Creek Reservoir is in the Cypress Creek Basin in Marion County, thirteen miles northwest of Jefferson on Johnson Creek. The project is owned and operated by the Southwestern Electric Company and is used for cooling water for a steam-electric generating station. Construction of the dam was begun June 16, 1960, and was completed August 4, 1961; impoundment of water began on the day of completion. The reservoir has a storage capacity of 10,100 acre-feet with a surface area of 650 acres at an elevation of 280 feet above mean sea level. The drainage area of Johnson Creek above the dam is eleven square miles. Runoff from Johnson Creek will be supplemented by pumping from Lake O' the Pines.

BIBLIOGRAPHY: Texas Water Commission, *Bulletin 6408* (1964).

Seth D. Breeding

*Johnson Draw.

*Johnson Fork.

*Johnson Institute. *See also* Friday Mountain Ranch; Johnson, Thomas Jefferson.

Johnson Library. *See* Lyndon Baines Johnson Library.

*Johnson Mine, Texas.

*Johnson Peak.

*Johnsons Creek.

*Johnsons Lake.

*Johnsons Run.

*Johnston, Albert Sidney. On April 6, 1862, Albert Sidney Johnston did not win the battle of Shiloh (as stated in Volume I) but was killed while leading his forces to a short-lived victory on that date. The Confederates were vanquished on April 7, 1862, by General U. S. Grant's troops.

BIBLIOGRAPHY: Charles P. Roland, *Albert Sidney Johnston: Soldier of Three Republics* (1964).

D. C. Greer

*Johnston, Hugh Blair. [This title was incorrectly listed in Volume I, page 916, as Johnson, Hugh Blair. With the exception of the misspelling of his name, the facts found under that title in Volume I are correct.] Hugh Blair Johnston was married to Martha White, daughter of Matthew G. White.qv

*Johnston, James H.

*Johnston, James Steptoe.

*Johnston, Joseph Eggleston.

Johnston, Ralph A. Ralph A. Johnston, son of Reuben Jefferson and Elizabeth (Gilbreath) Johnston, was born December 31, 1899, at Albertsville, Alabama. He grew up and went to school in Okemah, Oklahoma, enlisted in the U.S. Army during World War I, and attended the University of Oklahoma from 1918 to 1922, where he majored in geology. From the time he finished school he was involved in the oil business, first in Oklahoma and then, for the remaining thirty-five years of his life, in Houston, Texas.

In 1931 he was operating as an independent oil producer with offices in Houston. He was chairman of the board of Texas National Petroleum Company (until it was bought by Union Oil Company of California), of South Coast Life Insurance Company, and of University Savings and Loan Association; he was also a director of the University State Bank of Houston and the Security State Bank at Pearsall. He had extensive ranch operations in Medina, Frio, and Madison counties, was a director of the Texas and Southwestern Cattle Raisers' Association,qv and was a trustee of the National Cowboy Hall of Fame and Western Heritage Center at Oklahoma City.

Amassing a fortune as an oilman, insurance executive, banker, and rancher, Johnston devoted much of his time to insuring the growth of the city of Houston. He was a moving spirit in the affairs of the Houston Livestock Show and Rodeo and served as its president from 1951 to 1954. He helped acquire the land for the Houston Intercontinental Airport and turned it over to the city at cost, knowing that increased air traffic was an important factor in Houston's growth. Johnston was married to Merle May on November 5, 1927, and they were divorced in 1961; they had two children. He was married again on February 9, 1962, to Dolores Franklin Jones, a widow with one son.

In 1962 Johnston endowed a laboratory at the Baylor College of Medicine, and before his death he established the Ralph A. Johnston Foundation for charitable purposes. He was a longtime friend of J. Frank Dobie qv (whose last book was dedicated to Johnston and Walker Stone, editor-in-chief of Scripps-Howard newspapers); following Dobie's death it was Johnston who bought Paisano Ranch qv from the Dobie estate in order to take it off the market. Dobie's friends wanted the ranch to be preserved forever as a cultural retreat for Texas writers and artists, and although Johnston offered to underwrite the whole project, funds were raised with an auction of paintings by leading artists of the Southwest at a gala dinner held in Houston on May 11, 1966. Johnston, in addition to donating at the auction, had already contributed 10 percent of the original purchase price of the ranch, plus all legal fees, interest, and interim costs. Altogether, his was the greatest single contribution to the preservation of the ranch, and the Ralph A. Johnston Foundation continues to provide annual fellowships for residents of Paisano. One of Johnston's last acts before his death on August 8, 1966, was to sign the deed transferring Paisano Ranch to the University of Texas at Austin, with strict provisions for its use as a retreat for writers and artists. Johnston was buried in Forest Park Cemetery in Houston. *See also* Paisano Ranch.

Eldon S. Branda

*Johnston, Rienzi Melville. [This title was incorrectly listed in Volume I as Johnston, Renzi Melville.]

*Johnston, Thomas J.

*Johnsville, Texas.

*Johntown, Texas.

*Joiner, Columbus Marvin. Columbus Marvin (Dad) Joiner brought in a successful test on the No. 3 Daisy Bradford oil well on the Juan Ximenes survey about seven miles from Henderson on the evening of Friday, September 5, 1930 (not September 8, 1930, as stated in Volume I), thus opening up the largest oil field in the world up to that time. The Daisy Bradford, after almost a month's delay in running pipe and completing storage tanks, finally came in as a producer on Friday, October 3, 1930. *See also* East Texas Oil Field.

BIBLIOGRAPHY: Houston *Post-Dispatch*, September 7, 14, 21, 28, October 4, 5, 12, 1930.

Eldon S. Branda

*Joiner, Texas.

*Joinerville, Texas.

*Joliet, Texas.

*Jolly, Texas.

*Jollyville, Texas.

*Jonah, Texas.

*Jonah Creek.

*Jones, Allen Carter.

*Jones, Anson.

*Jones, Augustus H.

*Jones, Charles Adam.

Jones, Clifford Bartlett. Clifford Bartlett Jones, son of Charles Adam and Virginia (Bartlett) Jones, was born in Rico, Colorado, on April 9, 1885, and was reared in Kansas City, Missouri. He attended Central High School there from 1899 to 1903; in 1904 he became purchasing agent for the Kansas City Bag Manufacturing Company, and in 1907 he became vice-president and treasurer of the Jacques Steel Company in Kansas City. After his father moved to Texas as resident manager of the S. M. Swenson qv and Sons' Spur Ranch,qv Jones came along as his assistant four years later, in 1911. When his father moved to Freeport in 1913, Clifford Jones became manager of the ranch, and he continued as manager until 1939, when he was elected as the third president of Texas Technological College (now Texas Tech University), a position he held until 1944. Jones had been active in early efforts to obtain a state college for West Texas, and he was a member of the first board of directors of Texas Tech after the school was created. He was chairman of the board until he resigned to accept the presidency.

Jones was elected a director of Lubbock National Bank in 1944 and was later named chairman of the board. He also served as a director of the Mercantile National Bank in Dallas and as board chairman of the Spur Security Bank, of which he was president from 1936 to 1962. He was also president of the Spur Chamber of Commerce and mayor of Spur. He held directorships in several railroad companies, Southwestern Public Service Company, Mercantile Security Life Insurance Company of Dallas, and Lubbock Dodge Motors. He held honorary degrees from Texas Technological College, Southwestern University, and McMurry College.

Jones was one of the organizers and the third president of the West Texas Chamber of Commerce.qv He helped organize and was president of the Fort Worth–Roswell Highway Association, and he served a term as vice-president of the Texas Highway Association. He was a member of the Philosophical Society of Texas.qv Jones was married on June 24, 1908, to Alice Louise Palmer; she died in 1919. He was married to Audrey Barber on September 27, 1922. He died on November 27, 1972, in Lubbock, and he was buried in that city.

BIBLIOGRAPHY: Who's Who In America (1952).

Jones, Dudley W. Dudley W. Jones, son of Henry W. and Nancy (Evans) Jones, was born in 1842, in Titus County, Texas. He studied law at Maury Institute, Tennessee, and then returned home to Mount Pleasant to enlist as a private in the 9th Texas Cavalry. After serving for a year in Missouri and the Indian Territory, the regiment was sent east of the Mississippi in 1862. When the regiment was reorganized at Corinth, Mississippi, Jones was elected colonel, despite his youth, and he led the unit through campaigns in Tennessee, Mississippi, Georgia, and the Carolinas.

After the war Jones returned to Texas and was admitted to the Bar. In 1866 he was elected to the Eleventh Texas Legislature; a short time later he went to Houston to begin newspaper work. He was connected with the Houston Journal and bought the Houston Democrat with Major R. H. Purdom in 1868. The men commenced publication of the paper, renamed the Houston Times, about June 15, 1868. At the time of his death on August 14, 1868, Jones was senior editor of the Ku Klux Vedette. He was buried in Houston.

BIBLIOGRAPHY: Sidney Smith Johnson, Texans Who Wore the Gray (1907); Victor M. Rose, Ross' Texas Brigade (1881); Traylor Russell, History of Titus County, Texas (1965); Members of the Legislature of the State of Texas from 1846 to 1939 (1939); Dallas Herald, December 15, 1866, February 2, 1867, March 2, 23, 1867, May 30, 1868, June 27, 1868, August 22, 1868; Houston Weekly Telegraph, August 20, 1868; Northern Standard (Clarksville), September 12, 1868.

Jones, Enoch. Enoch Jones, son of Thomas Griffith and Susan (Jones) Jones, was born in 1802 in Wooster, Ohio. While a young man, he contracted to construct locks for the western division of the Pennsylvania Canal; in 1832, as an engineer with the same company he constructed the dam at Johnstown, Pennsylvania. Moving to Detroit, he began a store and engaged in the manufacturing of lumber.

Jones immigrated to Texas sometime before 1837 and in partnership with John William Smith qv acquired a vast amount of land, which he sold at a profit when he returned to Detroit. He moved to St. Louis, where he started an extensive wholesale business while Smith continued to make large land purchases in Texas. Smith died in 1845 and Jones returned to Texas, landing at Galveston on February 11, 1846. He settled in San Antonio and opened a large mercantile store on Main Plaza, meanwhile engaging in a variety of occupations. He sold horses and property and was an incorporator and director of the San Antonio and Mexican Gulf Railway. After the Texas Revolution he had bought a large amount of script, which the United States redeemed in full when Texas became a state. Eventually he acquired almost 175,000 acres on the Medina River and built a large mansion, which Count Adolph von Ormy bought in 1885. (See Von Ormy, Texas.)

Jones married three times. His first wife was Sophronia Hoyt of Cleveland, Ohio, and they had a son. He married Mrs. Olive Ann (Selkirk) Webb, a widow with two children, and they had two more children. His last wife was Charlotte Thompkins of Stillwater, New York; they had four children. Jones died on August 7, 1863, and was buried in City Cemetery No. 1 in San Antonio.

BIBLIOGRAPHY: Biographical File, Barker Texas History Center, University of Texas at Austin; Frederick C. Chabot, With the Makers of San Antonio (1937); San Antonio Express, July 19, 1931; Telegraph and Texas Register,

February 24, 1838; *Texas State Gazette*, September 28, 1850, March 1, 1851, October 23, 1852.

S. W. Pease

*Jones, Evan. [This title was incorrectly listed in Volume I as Jones, Evans.] Jones was born in Kentucky (not Missouri) and moved to Missouri (not Kentucky, as stated in Volume I).

BIBLIOGRAPHY: Roscoe C. Martin, *The People's Party in Texas* (1934); Ralph Smith, "The Farmers' Alliance in Texas, 1875–1900," *Southwestern Historical Quarterly*, XLVIII (1944–1945).

*Jones, George Washington.

*Jones, Henry.

*Jones, James Henry.

*Jones, James W. Although James Wales Jones was buried in Prairie Lea, Texas (as stated in Volume I), in 1953 he and his wife were reburied in the Texas State Cemetery,qv Austin. Jones was born in Columbia County, Georgia, on January 13, 1797, the son of Thomas and Sarah Jones; he served in the Texas Army qv under Captain Wylie Martin qv from March 7 to June 7, 1836.

BIBLIOGRAPHY: Bexar Bounty File (General Land Office, Austin).

Ruth Scudder Castleman

Jones, Jesse Holman. Jesse Holman Jones, Texas lumberman, banker, and statesman, was born in Robertson County, Tennessee, on April 5, 1874, the son of William Hasque and Laura Anna (Holman) Jones. In 1883 W. H. Jones moved his family to Dallas, Texas, primarily to secure better educational opportunities for the children, and for the remainder of the decade he divided his attention between tobacco and farming interests in Tennessee and investments in Texas.

Jesse Jones began his business career in the early 1890's in the lumber firm of his uncle, M. T. Jones, and held positions as manager of the Dallas office and general manager of the company from 1895 to 1905. During this time he moved to Houston, the eventual center of his many enterprises, and established the South Texas Lumber Company. From lumber, Jones expanded into banking, real estate, commercial buildings, and to a position as owner and publisher of the Houston *Chronicle*.qv In December, 1920, Jones married Mary Gibbs of Mexia.

Jones' first appointment to a major federal government position came in 1932, when President Herbert Hoover named him to the board of the Reconstruction Finance Corporation (RFC). He remained in Washington under President Franklin D. Roosevelt as chairman of the board of RFC (1933–1939), member of the board of the Export-Import Bank (1936–1943), administrator of the Federal Loan Agency (1939–1945), and secretary of commerce (1940–1945). He was best known in Washington as the supervisor of the basic New Deal lending programs, and his role and activities in that capacity were recorded in his book, *Fifty Billion Dollars* (1951). Jones followed policies regarded by most New Deal colleagues as conservative to reactionary; nevertheless, particularly through his activities in RFC and in spite of his insistence on strict adherence to bankers' principles in matters of collateral and repayment terms, he assisted in saving hundreds of individual banks, railroads, and factories from disaster and the nation as a whole from a serious threat to its investment capital. Although a controversial figure within the administration, Jones' competence and stature as a banker and his ability to serve as an intermediary between the administration and the business community gave him a significant role in the Roosevelt official family. In addition to his financial duties, Jones helped to shape and administer the economic policies of the World War II military effort and related domestic programs.

Jones was disappointed by his failure to gain the Democratic vice-presidential nomination in 1940. This, plus his established disagreement with much of the New Deal and wartime domestic programs, led to his gradual identification with the anti-Roosevelt political factions and his open participation as a conservative in the heated debates on postwar domestic policy which accompanied the 1944 election. Jones' role in the controversy led Roosevelt to ask for his resignation in January, 1945, from the Department of Commerce and the Federal Loan Agency and to propose alternative assignments. Jones rejected the proposal and submitted resignations from all of his federal positions. He completed his break with the Roosevelt-Truman wing of the Democratic party by turning the editorial support of his Houston *Chronicle* against the party nominees in 1948 and 1952.

Jones' far-ranging public contributions extended from several positions with the International Red Cross to such activities as director-general of the Texas Centennial qv celebration from 1926 to 1934, chairman of the Texas committee for the New York World's Fair of 1939 and the San Francisco Golden Gate Exposition, to membership on many public and private boards and commissions. The Texas legislature, in recognition of his services to the state and the nation, commissioned an official portrait, which was unveiled in the state Capitol qv in 1935. Jones died in Houston on June 1, 1956. Jones and his wife had set up a charitable foundation, Houston Endowment Inc. *See also* Jesse H. Jones Hall for the Performing Arts.

BIBLIOGRAPHY: Jesse H. Jones, *Fifty Billion Dollars* (1951); Bascom W. Timmons, *Jesse H. Jones* (c.1956).

Floyd F. Ewing

*Jones, John B.

*Jones, John C.

*Jones, John Rice, Jr.

*Jones, John Rice, III.

*Jones, Levi.

Jones, Margaret Virginia (Margo). Margaret Virginia (Margo) Jones was born on December 13, 1913, in Livingston, Texas, the daughter of Pearl (Collins) and R. H. Jones. At age fourteen she entered the College of Industrial Arts (now Texas Woman's University) in Denton, taking a B.A. degree in drama in 1931 and an M.A. degree in psychology a year later. During the summer of 1933 she studied directing at the Pasadena Summer School of Theater, then for one year was director of the Ojai (California) Community Players. In 1935 she embarked on a world tour, studying theater in Japan, China, India, France, and England. Margo Jones served as assistant director of the Houston Little Theatre of the Federal Theatre Project from February to August, 1936, and as director of the Community Players in Houston for six years.

In October, 1942, she became an instructor in drama at the University of Texas at Austin, teaching, acting, directing, and producing plays there until June, 1944. While a member of the university faculty, she made trips to the Pasadena and Cleveland playhouses in the role of producer and director. Imbued with the idea of establishing a repertory company, she applied for and received a grant from the Rockefeller Foundation in 1944, which permitted her to spend a year traveling and studying various methods of theatrical production. She had held the fellowship for less than three months when an invitation came for her to co-direct the original production of Tennessee William's *The Glass Menagerie*. Shortly after the New York success of this play, in February, 1945, Miss Jones arrived in Dallas to present her idea for a repertory theater in the city and to secure financial support for the project.

In June, 1947, Margo Jones' Theatre-in-the-Round opened in the Gulf Oil Building of the Texas State Fair qv in Dallas, the first professional repertory theater in the United States to use arena staging as its sole method of production. Both classical and original plays were presented in the theater, and Miss Jones became the champion of a number of young playwrights, particularly Tennessee Williams and William Inge. The 1947 season opened with Inge's *Farther Off from Heaven* (later made into the motion picture *Dark at the Top of the Stairs*), and that same year Theatre-in-the-Round presented the premiere of Williams' *Summer and Smoke*. In 1955 *Inherit the Wind*, by Jerome Lawrence and Robert E. Lee, was given its initial production at the Margo Jones theater. During her management of the theater, Miss Jones produced eighty-five plays, fifty-seven of which were new scripts.

Meanwhile Broadway was becoming acquainted with Margo Jones' work through her staging of Maxwell Anderson's *Joan of Lorraine* (with Ingrid Bergman) and such productions as *Summer and Smoke* in 1948 and *Inherit the Wind* in 1955. She also authored a book entitled *Theatre-in-the-Round* (1951).

Margo Jones died in Dallas on July 24, 1955, as a result of an accidental inhalation of carbon tetrachloride fumes. She was buried at Livingston. The Margo Jones theater in Dallas was closed in 1959.

BIBLIOGRAPHY: Margo Jones Theatre Collection (Dallas Public Library); Don Burton Wilmeth, A History of the Margo Jones Theatre (Ph.D. dissertation, University of Illinois, 1964); William Shapard, Margo Jones and Her Theatre in Dallas (M.A. thesis, Southern Methodist University, 1960).

Ronald L. Davis

Jones, Morgan. Morgan Jones, son of Morgan and Anne Jones, was born in Montgomery County, Wales, in 1840, and migrated to America in 1866. In Washington, Jones became associated with John Charles Fremont and for a period did railroad construction work in the Southwest for Fremont. Thereafter, Jones engaged in railroad construction on the Texas and Pacific under the direction of General Grenville M. Dodge. He built more than a thousand miles of railroad in Texas and earned the reputation of completing projects on time against all handicaps and difficulties.

While building railroads in the Fort Worth-Dallas vicinity, Jones conceived the idea of promoting a railroad from Fort Worth to Denver, Colorado, a dream that was realized on the completion of the Fort Worth and Denver City Railway in 1888. In this undertaking, also, he was associated with Dodge. Jones was president of the Fort Worth and Denver City Railway from 1883 to 1899, but for a period he did not accept his salary as president because he was continuing in the railroad construction business.

In 1890 Jones and Dodge built the Wichita Valley Railway from Wichita Falls to Seymour; in the early 1900's Jones was instrumental in linking Seymour and Abilene, Abilene and Ballinger, and Anson and Hamlin with railroad service. During later undertakings he was assisted by his nephew, Percy Jones.qv

Although his fortune, which was valued at several million dollars at his death, was begun through railroad construction, Jones' business interests were broad and varied, including mining in Mexico and Colorado, lumbering in Louisiana, and cottonseed milling in West Texas. He was never married. He died at Abilene on April 11, 1926.

BIBLIOGRAPHY: Abilene *Reporter News*, April 12, 1926; Richard C. Overton, *Gulf to Rockies: The Heritage of the Fort Worth and Denver–Colorado and Southern Railways, 1861–1898* (1953).

Rupert N. Richardson

*Jones, Oliver.

Jones, Percy. Percy Jones, son of Tom and Jane Elizabeth (Goodwin) Jones was born in Fence Houses, Durham, England, on January 23, 1885, and was educated at Barnard Castle School. In 1903 he came to America and joined his uncle, Morgan Jones,qv in railroad building and operation. He was engineer in the construction of the Abilene and Northern and Abilene and Southern railroads, was president of the Abilene and Southern for a period beginning in 1926, and was later president of the Paris and Mt. Pleasant Railway Company. He was also president of the Western Compress and Storage Company.

Oil discoveries on land which Jones had bought in Kent and Howard counties brought him a substantial fortune, which he augmented by development through his own oil company. He was a philanthropist, making most of his benefaction anonymously.

Jones married Ruth Legett on December 25, 1915; the couple had a son and two daughters. He died in Abilene on February 11, 1951.

BIBLIOGRAPHY: Abilene *Reporter News*, February 12, 1951.

Rupert N. Richardson

*Jones, Randal.

*Jones, Simeon.

Jones, Tignal W. Tignal W. Jones, son of Willis H. and Mary H. (Taylor) Jones, was born near Lewisberg, North Carolina, on November 25, 1820. He was educated at Nashville University, Tennessee, then studied law and was admitted to the Alabama Bar in 1844. In 1846 he served as first lieutenant of Company E, 1st Alabama Regiment, and participated in the siege of Vera Cruz during the Mexican War.

After the war, in 1847, Jones returned to Talladega, Alabama, to practice law. In 1856 he moved to Tyler, Texas, and was elected a member of the Secession Convention.qv With the coming of the Civil War, Jones enlisted in the Confederate Army and eventually became colonel of the 1st Cavalry Regiment, Texas State Troops. Following the war, he returned to Tyler and resumed his law practice from 1872 to 1879.

Jones married twice. In 1854, in Talladega, he married Mary E. Barclay, who died six months later. He married Mrs. Martha Bell on December 18, 1856, in Tyler, and they had two children, one of whom died in infancy. The date of Jones' death is not known; he is believed to have been buried in Oakwood Cemetery, Austin.

BIBLIOGRAPHY: Sidney Smith Johnson, *Texans Who Wore the Gray* (1907); William S. Speer (ed.), *The Encyclopedia of the New West* (1881); Service Record of T. W. Jones, Confederate Records (MS., National Archives, Washington, D.C.).

Allan C. Ashcraft

*Jones, Travis Fleming.

*Jones, William E.

*Jones, William Jefferson.

Jones, Texas. Jones, in eastern Van Zandt County, was founded about 1850 and was probably named for early settlers at the site. In a farming and ranching area, the town still existed in 1970, but no population figure was available.

*Jones County. Approximately three-fourths of the farm income in Jones County in the late 1960's was from cotton and grains. Cash receipts from crops were $8,762,000 in 1968, while those from livestock and products amounted to $3,999,000. Petroleum production increased in importance, with nearly 171,000,000 barrels produced from 1926 to January 1, 1973. The 1960 census reported 19,299 residents in the county; the 1970 population was 16,106, according to the United States census. Tourist attractions include Fort Phantom Hill,qv the Cowboys' Christmas Ball in Anson, the Cowboy Reunion qv in Stamford, and Lake Fort Phan-

tom Hill. *See also* Abilene Standard Metropolitan Statistical Area.

*Jones Creek.

*Jones Creek, Texas. (Brazoria County.) Jones Creek, in the geographical division of Brazosport in Brazoria County, was an unincorporated community with a population of 1,268 in 1970.

*Jones Creek, Texas. (Wharton County.)

*Jones Creek, Battle of.

*Jones Field.

Jones Hall. *See* Jesse H. Jones Hall for the Performing Arts.

*Jones and Plummer Trail.

*Jones Prairie, Texas.

*Jonesboro, Texas.

*Jonesborough, Texas. Four spellings, all given by men who lived there or in the vicinity, are as follows: Jonesborough, Jonesboro, Jones Borough, and Jones Boro.

BIBLIOGRAPHY: "Texas Collection," *Southwestern Historical Quarterly*, XLVIII (1944–1945).

Jonestown, Texas. Jonestown, a small unincorporated community on Lake Travis in western Travis County, was founded about 1939 by Emmet A. Jones and his brother, Warren Jones. Jonestown had a service station, hardware store, sub-post office, grocery store, beauty and barber shops, and community house in the 1960's. About three hundred families were living in the town, many of whom commuted to work in Austin. *See also* Austin Standard Metropolitan Statistical Area.

*Jonesville, Texas. (Angelina County.)

*Jonesville, Texas. (Harrison County.) Jonesville, known as Border from January 18, 1847, to September 5, 1849, assumed its present name on November 13, 1849.

Lena F. Nunley

Joplin, Janis. Janis Lyn Joplin, generally regarded in the 1960's as the top female performer in blues and rock music, was the daughter of Seth Ward and Dorothy Bonita (East) Joplin. She was born on January 19, 1943, in Port Arthur, and attended schools there before entering Lamar State College of Technology (now Lamar University) in the summer of 1960 and the spring of 1962. She also attended the University of Texas at Austin from June, 1962, until January, 1963.

While she was in Austin Janis Joplin sang in a small tavern operated by the country and western singer Kenneth Threadgill. In and out of college, sometimes working as a keypunch operator, she performed in clubs both on the West Coast and in Austin until she reentered Lamar State College in 1965.

In 1966 she returned to San Francisco, where she became lead vocalist with a rock music group called Big Brother and the Holding Company. They opened at the Avalon ballroom in San Francisco in June, 1966, and became an immediate success, with word spreading quickly throughout the Haight-

Ashbury "hippie" community about the exciting new singer who belted out a shattering emotional sound. International acclaim followed her performance at the Monterey (California) International Pop Festival in June, 1967, where she stopped the show with her rendition of "Love is Like a Ball and Chain." The performance was recorded in the film *Monterey Pop* (1968).

With nationwide press coverage Janis Joplin began a national tour of major United States cities, before audiences of young people who often reacted in frenzied adoration, leaving their seats, dancing, surging to the singer's platform. One account described her performance as "cross-stepping from one side of the stage to the other, making an urgent sort of pleading gesture toward the audience with her outstretched hand," and voicing "a kind of stuttering, staggering outcry," bringing the audience to its feet. Her American tour was followed by appearances in London, Paris, and other European cities. Commanding as much as $50,000 a performance, she was named the most popular female singer in the Jazz and Pop Third Annual Readers Poll.

She performed with several different bands from 1966 to 1970. Described variously as the "Judy Garland of Rock," the "Hippie Queen of Show Business," and the "Lioness of Rock" (because of her long colorful mane of hair), Janis Joplin became a symbol of the cultural style of many young people during the late 1960's. A reviewer in the New York *Times* said, "As a performer, she was everything we had ever hoped for in our music. She was so great that even the traditionalism of her lyrics of love, sex, and loss was overwhelmed by the majesty of her style." Living and performing at a frantic pace, the singer explained, "I think you can destroy your now by worrying about tomorrow."

Janis Joplin died, presumably from an overdose of drugs, in Hollywood, on October 4, 1970, and she was cremated. Her last album was recorded just before her death. Entitled *Pearl* (the name by which some of her close friends knew her), the recording drew unanimous praise, including a *Time* magazine review which described it as "the best ever recorded by a white female blues singer," and the New York *Times*, which said that it insured Janis Joplin "a fast and firm place in musical history forever."

BIBLIOGRAPHY: *Who's Who In America* (1970); *Current Biography*, XXXI (March, 1970); *Newsweek* (October 19, 1970); *Time* (October 19, 1970, February 15, 1971); Austin *Statesman*, October 5, November 3, 8, 1970; New York *Times*, October 11, 1970, January 31, 1971; San Antonio *Express-News*, August 23, 1970; *The Evening Star* (Washington, D. C.), October 5, 1970; *Washington Post*, October 6, 1970.

Eldon S. Branda

Joplin, Scott. Scott Joplin, known as the "King of Ragtime," was born in Texarkana, Texas, on November 24, 1868, son of Giles and Florence (Givens) Joplin. Coming from a musical family, young Scott taught himself to improvise on the piano in such a remarkable manner that a German musician in Texarkana volunteered to give him free lessons in piano technique, sight reading, and harmony.

In his early teens, Joplin was an itinerant pianist, playing in red-light districts of towns in Texas, Louisiana, and in the Mississippi Valley. By 1885 he was playing in the "parlors"—the only places open to black musicians during this era—of St. Louis, where a primitive sort of music called "jig-piano" was in vogue. The bouncing bass line and the ornate, syncopated melodic line were later called "ragged time," then simply "ragtime."

In 1894 Joplin moved to Sedalia, Missouri, the town most closely associated with his musical work. He continued to play in saloons, but he began serious study of advanced harmony and composition. In 1899 he published his best known song, "Maple Leaf Rag," named after a local club. The song not only sold more than a million copies, but has become an enduring number in the popular category.

As a result of "Maple Leaf" royalties, Joplin no longer had to work in honky-tonks and he could devote himself to serious composition. In 1900 he moved to St. Louis. Along with his continued composition of new ragtime music he wrote a ragtime opera, *A Guest of Honor*, in 1903. After one performance the opera score disappeared and has never been found. Joplin's second opera, *Treemonisha*, is the first grand opera by a black American; it was completed in 1911. It deals with the theme that runs through all of Joplin's activities—that the salvation of his people lay in education. The orchestration for this opera was also lost, although the piano-vocal score was later published and a new orchestration made for several performances in 1972.

In recent years ragtime has been re-evaluated as a valid art form, and Joplin's piano pieces, largely neglected for a half century, are now being compared with the short works in dance form of Mozart, Chopin, Schubert, and Brahms. As early as 1911 *American Musician* (June 24) wrote that "he had created an entirely new phase of musical art. . . . It has sprung from our soil practically of its own accord." In 1971 Harold C. Schonberg wrote in the New York *Times* (January 24) that "Joplin was a real composer. . . . Scholars are going to have to get busy on Joplin." Another critic writing in *Stereo Review* (April, 1971) wrote that "Joplin's piano rags . . . are just about perfect music by any standard. His . . . rags can only be described as elegant, varied, often subtle, and as sharply incised as a cameo. They are the precise American equivalent, in terms of a native style of dance music, of minuets by Mozart, mazurkas by Chopin, or waltzes by Brahms. They can be both lovely and powerful, infectious and moving."

Joplin was married twice. His first marriage was to Belle Hayden in 1900; they had a daughter who died in infancy. They were separated in 1906, and shortly thereafter Belle Joplin died. After that he moved to New York, from where he toured as the "King of Ragtime" in vaudeville, cut piano rolls of his own works, and continued to compose. In 1909 he married Lottie Stokes, who subsequently ran a theatrical and musical boarding house in New York. Joplin died in New York City on April 1, 1917, and was buried in St. Michael's Cemetery there.

In 1971 the collected works of Scott Joplin were published in two volumes by the New York Public Library as its first publication in the *Americana Collection Music Series*. Volume I contains fifty-one works for piano, while Volume II contains his works for voice. Each volume has a biographical and evaluative essay. Also included are a rollography and a discography of 78 rpm recordings of Joplin's compositions. A revival of interest in Joplin was further stimulated by the release in 1973 of the motion picture, *The Sting*, which had a musical score consisting mostly of Joplin rags. The movie won an academy award in 1974 for its music, although the commercial rewriting of the composer's works was not a true representation of Scott Joplin's musical genius.

BIBLIOGRAPHY: Rudi Blesh and Harriet Janis, *They All Played Ragtime* (1958); New York Public Library, "Collected Works of Scott Joplin," *Americana Collection Music Series* (1971); Joshua Rifkin (liner notes, Nonesuch Record Album H-71248), *Piano Rags by Scott Joplin* (1970); "Rebirth of Ragtime," *Life* (July 21, 1972); "From Rags to Rags," *Time* (February 7, 1972); Austin *American*, May 16, 1972, January 5, 1973.

Joe B. Frantz

*Joplin, Texas.

*Joppa, Texas.

*Jordan, Louis John.

Jordan, Powhatan. Powhatan Jordan was born in Portsmouth, Norfolk County, Virginia, in 1827, the son of Meritt and Paulina (Voinard) Jordan. He was graduated with a B.A. degree from a Virginia military academy and received his doctor of medicine degree from Columbian College, District of Columbia, in 1850.

Jordan moved to Texas in 1856, taking employment as a civilian surgeon at Fort Inge.qv He settled in San Antonio in 1857 to practice medicine, and in 1858 he helped organize the San Antonio Board of Health, of which he was elected secretary. He was also connected briefly with several Texas Ranger qv outfits, serving first as surgeon to John Salmon (Rip) Ford's qv expedition against the Comanches in 1858.

With the outbreak of the Civil War, Jordan raised a company of volunteers in Bexar County, which was mustered into Confederate service on October 4, 1861, as Company A, 7th Regiment, Texas Cavalry of the Sibley Brigade (*see* Sibley, Henry Hopkins). He served throughout the New Mexico campaign and was promoted to major in 1862. At the battle of Glorieta Pass on March 28, 1862, he commanded the battalion of the 7th Regiment. On April 20 he was taken prisoner by the Federals and sent to Camp Douglas, Illinois. He was exchanged at Vicksburg, Mississippi, however,

and shortly after his return to San Antonio in November, 1862, he was promoted to lieutenant colonel. After the Teche campaign in Louisiana he resigned his field commission on July 2, 1863. From 1864 until the end of the war, he served as assistant surgeon in charge of the post hospital at Sabine Pass, Texas. After the war, Jordan returned to San Antonio and in 1876 was one of the incorporators of the Western Texas Medical Association. In 1883 he settled at Beaumont and resumed his medical practice. From 1884 to 1894 he was a member of the Texas Medical Association.qv

Jordan married Jessie Alberta Edwards in 1864; they had four children. He was married a second time, to Ada Hoskins in 1874. Jordan died in 1904.

BIBLIOGRAPHY: Frank W. Johnson, *A History of Texas and Texans* (1914); L. E. Daniell, *Types of Successful Men of Texas* (1890); Pat Ireland Nixon, *A Century of Medicine in San Antonio* (1936); U.S. War Department, *The War of the Rebellion: A Compilation of the Official Records of the Union and Confederate Armies* (1880–1901).

Martin Hardwick Hall

*Jordan, Samuel W.

*Jordan Creek.

*Jordan Gap.

Jordan's Saline, Texas. Jordan's Saline, in northeastern Van Zandt County, was located one and a half miles southeast of the Texas and Pacific Railway depot at Grand Saline. Since Indian times the area has been known for its salt. In 1845 a salt-producing plant was established and the community was named Jordan's Saline. In 1848 the town had the county's first courthouse, first post office, and first manufacturing plant, a hide tannery. When the county was divided in 1850, Jordan's Saline lost the county seat to Canton. As the only source of salt between Dallas, Shreveport, and Jefferson, the community's prosperity multiplied when the railroad was built through the county in 1872. Under the direction of Samuel Q. Richardson the salt plant was modernized. On the land deeded by Judge Richardson to the railroad in return for a depot, the town of Grand Saline developed and expanded to include what was Jordan's Saline. Soon afterwards the older town lost the post office. *See also* Grand Saline, Texas.

*José María.

*Joseph (José).

*Joseph, Texas.

*Josephine, Texas.

*Joshua, Texas.

*Joshua Creek.

*Joske, Julius.

*Josselet, Texas.

*Josserand, Texas.

*Jotars Indians.

*Jourdanton, Texas. Jourdanton, seat of Atascosa County, had a 1960 population of 1,504 and a 1970 population of 1,841, according to the United States report of the census. In 1969 Jourdanton reported fifty-five buisnesses, six

churches, a bank, a hospital, and a rest home. Industries included processing of gasoline and feeds, the cultivation of grains and vegetables, and the raising of livestock. Jourdanton was the third-place winner in a national clean town contest in 1962 and 1963.

*Journal and Advertiser (San Augustine).

Journal of Air Law and Commerce. The Journal of Air Law was founded in 1930 and was published under that name until 1939, when it became the Journal of Air Law and Commerce. It was published at Northwestern University until 1961, when its editing was undertaken by the School of Law at Southern Methodist University; volumes 28 through 36 and a cumulative index through volume 35 have since been published at SMU. During the academic year 1971–1972 the thirty-seventh volume was issued. Though supervised by the law faculty, the journal is contributed to and edited by a self-perpetuating board of student editors. It is financed by the law school and annual subscribers, which in 1971 numbered approximately 1,700. This is the only journal in the English language devoted principally to developments in the law of aviation and aerospace. Its circulation is, therefore, both national and international.

Joseph W. McKnight

*Journalism in Texas, Early.

*Joutel, Henri.

*Jowers, W. G. W.

Joy, Jimmy. See Maloney, James Monte.

*Joy, Texas. (Cass County.)

*Joy, Texas. (Clay County.)

*Joyce, Texas. (Bowie County.)

*Joyce, Texas. (Webb County.)

*Jozye, Texas.

Juamaca Indians. This otherwise unidentified Indian group was represented at San Antonio de Valero Mission qv in San Antonio. J. R. Swanton listed the Juamaca as Coahuiltecan, but no evidence has been found which supports this identification.

BIBLIOGRAPHY: H. E. Bolton, Texas in the Middle Eighteenth Century (1915); J. R. Swanton, Linguistic Material from the Tribes of Southern Texas and Northeastern Mexico (1940).

T. N. Campbell

*Juan Cordona Lake.

*Juanita Creek.

*Juanity Creek.

*Jud, Texas.

*Judicial Counties. See Defunct Counties.

*Judicial Districts, Administrative.

Judicial Qualifications Commission, State. See State Judicial Qualifications Commission.

*Judicial System. In 1970 Texas had fourteen courts of civil appeals (as opposed to eleven in 1948), and 211 district courts (as opposed to some 120 in 1948). Another district court, in McLennan County, was added on January 1, 1971, bringing the total to 212 district courts.

Whereas (as stated in Volume I) since 1876 all appellate court judges have held office for six years, district judges for four years, and other judges for two years, the tenure for the latter has now changed so that all trial court judges hold office for four-year terms.

While previously the association of judges met annually in Austin, since 1950 the Judicial Section of the State Bar has held annual conferences in many different cities over the state.

In 1965 the Constitution was amended to provide for involuntary retirement and removal of judges. The amendment provided for compulsory retirement of a district or appellate judge at the end of the term in which he reached age seventy-five, and further provided that the legislature might lower the maximum age if it wished. The amendment created a nine-member State Judicial Qualifications Commission, qv to be appointed by the chief justice of the Supreme Court, the governor, and the State Bar. qqv In a case of alleged disability or misconduct of a judge, the commission will investigate and, if necessary, hold hearings. The Supreme Court, upon recommendation of the commission, may remove a judge for misconduct or retire the judge in case of disability.

Tom Reavley

*Judkins, Texas.

Judosa Indians. Although formerly referred to as an unidentified group that lived near the mouth of the Trinity River, the Judosa are now known to be the same as the Deadose, an Atakapan (Attakapan)-speaking group of southeastern Texas. See Deadose Indians.

T. N. Campbell

*Judosa Village. See also Judosa Indians.

Judson, George H. George H. Judson was born in 1823 near Woodbury, Connecticut, son of a farmer. He was educated as a lawyer and came to East Texas in the 1840's, practicing that profession for a time before entering the mercantile business. He moved to New Braunfels, where he continued in business and married a Miss Campbell. George Wilkins Kendall, qv a prosperous sheep raiser, advised Judson to get into the sheep business, and in 1861 Judson moved to a place about ten miles from San Antonio, on the Austin Road. His neighbors, mostly German, often called upon Judson for legal advice. During the Civil War he officiated as purchasing agent for the Confederacy and handled thousands of bales of cotton in exchange for supplies for the army. Judson died August 3, 1902, and was buried in City Cemetery No. 4, San Antonio.

S. W. Pease

*Judson, Texas.

*Jug Creek.

*Julia Pens, Texas.

*Julian, Isaac Hoover.

*Juliette Fowler Homes for Orphans and Aged.

*Juliff, Texas.

*Julimes Mission. *See* San Francisco de los Julimes Mission.

*Jumano Indians.

*Jumbo, Texas.

Juncal Indians. Juncal (Juncataguo, Juncata, Junced, Zuncal) Indians were one of five bands of Coahuiltecan Indians encountered by an Escandón (*see* Escandón, José de) expedition in the middle eighteenth century near present Corpus Christi. At this time the Juncal were also referred to as Carrizo, a name commonly applied by the Spanish to Coahuiltecan bands along the Rio Grande below Laredo. During the same period Juncal families entered San Antonio de Valero Mission qv at San Antonio.

BIBLIOGRAPHY: H. E. Bolton, *Texas in the Middle Eighteenth Century* (1915); F. W. Hodge (ed.), *Handbook of American Indians*, II (1910); G. Saldivar (ed.), *Archivo de la historia de Tamaulipas*, II (1946); J. R. Swanton, *Linguistic Material from the Tribes of Southern Texas and Northeastern Mexico* (1940).

T. N. Campbell

*Junco y Espriella, Pedro del Barrio. *See* Barrio Junco y Espriella, Pedro del.

*Junction, Texas. Junction, seat of Kimble County, is a livestock market and tourist center for the county. The town reported seventy-eight businesses, including three manufacturers, and a newspaper, a county hospital, and an airport in 1969. The 1960 population was 2,441, a slight drop from the 1950 population. In 1970, however, the population rose to 2,654, according to the United States census.

*June, Texas.

*"Juneteenth."

*Junior, Texas.

*Junior College Movement in Texas. The first junior colleges in Texas were private, often church related, schools. Many of them over the years changed names, or became four year institutions, or went out of existence, or changed from private to public junior colleges. In 1974 there were eight private junior colleges that reported their activities to the Coordinating Board, Texas College and University System.qv They were the following: Concordia Lutheran College, Austin; Jacksonville College, Jacksonville; Lon Morris College, Jacksonville; Schreiner College, Kerrville; Southern Bible College, Houston; South Texas Junior College, Houston; Southwestern Junior College of the Assemblies of God, Waxahachie; and Southwestern Christian College, Terrell. [The history of each of these schools, in addition to the histories of those private schools which later became four-year institutions or those which ceased to exist, may be found under their own titles. Ed.]

Despite the fact that junior colleges, as independent or private institutions, have enjoyed a long history in Texas, the public junior or community college movement in the state came quite late. The first public junior college, created as such, was established in 1922 at Wichita Falls as Wichita Falls Junior College (later renamed Hardin Junior College, now Midwestern University,qv a four-year institution). In common with the earliest colleges of many other states, the junior college at Wichita Falls was based on an existing independent school district and was established as an extension of the high school in that district. Despite the absence of legal provisions for the establishment and maintenance of public junior colleges prior to 1929, seventeen such local institutions were established between 1922 and 1928 as auxiliary units of the public schools, under the sponsorship and initiative of the boards of trustees of the respective independent (or, in some cases, municipal) school districts. A 1929 law validated the existence of those public junior colleges already established and specified the legal process whereby additional such colleges might be created.

In 1929 the first Texas legislation pertaining to junior colleges gave local districts specific junior college taxing powers. Since junior college districts were coterminous with independent school districts at that time, this meant, in effect, a surcharge on the existing property tax rates. The first direct state support came under legislation approved in the legislative session of 1941. At that time, $50 per full-time fall-enrolled student was granted by the legislature. The same legislation brought junior colleges under the administrative supervision of the Texas Education Agency.qv

This situation lasted until 1965, when, as a result of the extensive study and recommendations of the Governor's Committee on Education Beyond the High School (1964), junior colleges were made part of higher education and placed under the general supervision of the Coordinating Board, Texas College and University System. The Coordinating Board authorizes the creation of public junior colleges and specifies the standards they must meet in order to receive state financial assistance. The effect of transferring supervision to the Coordinating Board greatly strengthened the response to the state's need for public two-year post-secondary education. As in a number of other states, Texas' community or junior colleges had suffered from an excessive sense of identification with the secondary school system.

Two important exceptions to the Coordinating Board's jurisdiction over local public junior colleges were made by the legislature. Excluded were programs approved by, or subject to the approval of, the State Board for Vocational Education (whose members are the same as the State Board of Education) and construction financed by local property taxes. The first exception apparently was made to assure eligibility for federal vocational aid, since Congress requires that a single state agency administer vocational funds for both public schools and institutions of higher education. Boards of trustees or regents actually govern the respective institutions and are responsible for all administrative functions, but they operate within the policies and guidelines set by the state level agencies. These local boards consist of from seven to twelve members who are elected by voters residing within the junior college districts.

The community college movement has been especially significant because it has been a process of adding on rather than subtracting from other institutions of higher education. Community college enrollments are to a large extent composed of students who would not otherwise attend a college or university. The accessible locations of these institutions, permitting students to live at home, and their relatively low costs have opened the doors of higher educational opportunity to many young people for whom they would have been closed but for the community college's existence. Because of their smaller size and community orientation, they are more likely able to provide the kind of setting where each student can be treated as an individual and where his or her problems will be dealt with personally by staff, faculty, and administration. Their open-door admissions policy, where persons of all ages, all levels of achievement, and all types of objectives can find satisfactory programs geared to their personal needs, has thrust upon the community colleges a great social responsibility in terms of the education of culturally and educationally disadvantaged students. Because the demand for skilled technicians has grown, the most hopeful prospect for satisfying that demand has been offered by the vocational-technical programs in the community junior colleges, and these are offered in close conjunction with programs of academic orientation. In so doing, the community colleges proclaim in a unique way that there is dignity in all man's pursuits. Community colleges also have had the advantage of more community interest and involvement than was usually the case with a senior institution, being creatures of the communities in which they were located. Local consent was necessary for their establishment. Local support was vital to their development and growth. Local people served on their boards of trustees and determined their policies. Local pride was evidenced in their physical plants and their programs.

In 1968 Texas had forty public community/ junior college districts with forty-two operationally separate colleges or campuses. These two-year postsecondary educational institutions enrolled 86,913 students in the fall of 1968. General revenue appropriations in the form of state aid to public junior colleges totaled $29,072,825 in 1968, with $23,571,825 designated for general academic courses and $5,501,000 earmarked for technical-vocational programs. Although sizeable in comparison to other states, the junior college movement in Texas in 1968 was characterized, as in most states, by its emphasis on the freshman and sophomore years of a baccalaureate degree. The traditional junior college was only on the verge of becoming the comprehensive community college.

Stimulated in part by the passage of the Federal Vocational Education Amendments of 1968 and the State Technical-Vocational Act of 1969, enrollment in Texas public community/junior colleges skyrocketed after 1968, with over 185,000 students enrolled in the fall of 1973. The phenomenal growth in enrollments in these public two-year colleges made them the fastest growing segment of postsecondary education in Texas.

The number of public community college districts also increased markedly—from forty in 1968 to forty-seven in 1974. These forty-seven districts operated fifty-three separate colleges or campuses in 1974: Alvin Junior College, Alvin; Amarillo College, Amarillo; Angelina College, Lufkin; Austin Community College, Austin; Bee County College, Beeville; Blinn College, Brenham; Brazosport College, Lake Jackson; Central Texas College, Killeen; Cisco Junior College, Cisco; Clarendon College, Clarendon; College of the Mainland, Texas City; Cooke County College, Gainesville; Dallas County Community College District, Dallas (which included Eastfield College at Mesquite, El Centro College at Dallas, Mountain View College at Dallas, and Richland College at Dallas); Del Mar College, Corpus Christi; El Paso Community College, El Paso; Frank Phillips College, Borger; Galveston College, Galveston; Grayson County College, Denison; Henderson County Junior College, Athens; Hill Junior College, Hillsboro; Houston Community College, Houston; Howard College at Big Spring, Big Spring; Kilgore College, Kilgore; Laredo Junior College, Laredo; Lee College, Baytown; McLennan Community College, Waco; Midland College, Midland; Navarro College, Corsicana; North Harris County College, Houston; Odessa College, Odessa; Panola Junior College, Carthage; Paris Junior College, Paris; Ranger Junior College, Ranger; San Antonio Junior College District, San Antonio (which included San Antonio College and St. Philip's College, both at San Antonio); San Jacinto College, Pasadena (which included North Campus at Houston and South Campus at Pasadena); South Plains College, Levelland; Southwest Texas Junior College, Uvalde; Tarrant County Junior College District, Fort Worth (which included Northeast Campus at Hurst and South Campus at Fort Worth); Temple Junior College, Temple; Texarkana Community College, Texarkana; Texas Southmost College, Brownsville; Tyler Junior College, Tyler; Vernon Regional Junior College, Vernon; Victoria College, Victoria; Weatherford College, Weatherford; Western Texas College, Snyder; Wharton County Junior College, Wharton. [The history of each of these schools in addition to the histories of those public junior colleges which later became four-year institutions or those which ceased to exist, may be found under their own titles. Ed.]

In 1974 state aid appropriations to public junior colleges rose to a total of $94,712,526. Of that amount, $37,160,645 (or almost 40 percent) was tagged for occupational curricula and represented a seven-fold increase in state aid for these career oriented programs since 1968. Not only did Texas public community colleges expand dramatically their technical-vocational programs (almost 700 different ones were in existence in 1974), but efforts to serve new and emerging student populations of all ages led to increased emphases on adult and continuing education and on compensatory (or developmental) education programs. The growth and success of the two-year college movement in Texas was one of the most significant developments in education the state has experienced. The community college, the only native American institution in our educational system, seemed destined to continue playing an important role in Texas education. Enrollment projections in 1974 forecast for the year 1980 a public community college student headcount of 262,000, or a growth of about 40 percent above the 1974 enrollment.

Raymond M. Hawkins

*Junior Historian Movement. Continuing to operate as a young persons branch of the Texas State Historical Association,qv 403 chapters of the Junior Historians had been chartered in the state by 1975. There were 126 active chapters during the 1974–1975 school year, when Kenneth B. Ragsdale was the association's director of educational services.

A major change occurred in September, 1970, when the organization's publication, the *Junior Historian* (published since January, 1940, under that title), was changed in format and title to the *Texas Historian*. The magazine continued to publish material concerning Texas history which was written by and for young people. In December, 1975, the magazine had a subscription list of 2,200.

*Juno, Texas.

Jury Trial in Texas. Trial by a petit (or petty) jury (the ultimate origins of which are obscure) in both civil and criminal cases is one of the principal hallmarks of English law in Texas.qv As a result of persistent agitation of Anglo American colonists for this mode of trial, the 1827 Constitution of Coahuila and Texas qv provided that jury trial should be established in Texas. This was implemented in 1830 by the institution of a seven-man jury for criminal cases and in 1834 by a provision enacted for a twelve-man jury (with eight votes necessary for a verdict) for civil and criminal trials in Texas. The latter law was drafted by Thomas Jefferson Chambers qv and is referred to as Chambers' Jury Law. Because of the conditions of the times, it never became operative. The lack of jury trials was one of the Texan grievances voiced in their Declaration of Independence.qv

The Consultation qv of 1835 adopted the English common law jury of twelve for criminal trials, with unanimity required for a verdict. A right of jury trial in civil cases came in 1840 with the adoption of English law in Texas. The right was extended in 1841 to matters of equity as well as law. Under the Constitution of 1876 qv (Article I, Section 15), however, the right extends only to those proceedings in which the right was then accorded. Under that provision jury trials are excluded in election contests, probate matters in county court, most habeas corpus proceedings, adoptions, the review of certain administrative decisions, certain contempt proceedings, and incidental and ancillary matters.

When trial by jury is appropriate, in a civil case it may be demanded by either party or it may be waived by both parties. In criminal cases a jury trial is automatically accorded to the accused, but in most cases it may be waived by the accused. A jury of twelve is impaneled in the district, domestic relations, and juvenile courts, while a jury of six is used in county and other inferior courts. Though Texas juries were once impaneled from a body of free male citizens over twenty-one years of age, with certain other restrictions with respect to literacy, character, interest in the dispute, and property holding, women have been included since 1955 and property qualifications were removed in 1969. [By passage of a statute effective August 27, 1973, the 63rd Texas Legislature granted persons eighteen years of age all the privileges hitherto granted those twenty-one years of age; thus, those persons eighteen years old or older may now serve on juries. Ed.]

In selecting a jury of twelve from the panel of the week, which is called by lot, each party in a civil trial is allowed six challenges without cause and an unlimited number of challenges for cause. In criminal trials the number of challenges without cause are generally more numerous and depend on the seriousness of the offence charged. The most common challenge is one for biased views with respect to the facts or the parties. In the course of the trial and in charging the jury, a Texas judge may not comment on the evidence. In civil cases the judge charges the jury to find the facts in dispute based on the evidence presented, and according to the facts found by the jury, the court renders judgment.

In criminal trials the jury is charged to find a general verdict of guilty or not guilty, and all verdicts of guilty must be unanimous. A jury that cannot achieve unanimity is termed a "hung jury," and a new trial may be had. Whereas in English law sentencing was always left to the judge, a Texas statute of 1846 allowed the jury to sentence except in capital cases or if the penalty was fixed by law. In 1857 the first of these restrictions was removed; the jury was also allowed to suspend sentence. With the revision of the Code of Criminal Procedure in 1965, a two stage procedure was instituted for criminal trials under which the question of guilt and punishment (in the event of a verdict of guilty) are presented to the jury at two separate hearings.

As an aid to understanding testimony, juries elsewhere are allowed to leave the courtroom to view a scene or some object that cannot be brought into the courtroom; this procedure of jury views is not allowed in Texas.

BIBLIOGRAPHY: Roy W. McDonald (Frank W. Elliott, ed.), *Texas Civil Practice in District and County Courts*, III (1970); Jack Pope, "The Jury," *Texas Law Review*, XXXIX (1961), "The Proper Function of Jurors," *Baylor Law Review*, XIV (1962), "The Judge-Jury Relationship," *Southwestern Law Journal*, XVIII (1964); Charles S. Potts, "Early Criminal Law in Texas: From Civil Law to Common Law, to Code," *Texas Law Review*, XXI (1943); Charles W. Webster, "Jury Sentencing—Grab-Bag Justice," *Southwestern Law Journal*, XIV (1960); H. D. Wendorf, "Some Views on Jury Views," *Baylor Law Review*, XV (1963).

Joseph W. McKnight

*Jusepe (José, Joseph).

*Justice of the Peace. *See also* County and Precinct Officers, Terms of.

*Justiceburg, Texas.

*Justin, H. J. (Joe).

*Justin, Texas.

K

*Kabaye Indians. The Kabaye (Cabaie) Indians are known only from records of the La Salle Expedition,[qv] which indicate that these Indians lived inland well to the north or northeast of Matagorda Bay, probably near the Brazos River. The Kabaye have been confused with the Kiabaha, which these records clearly identify as a separate and distinct group who lived in the same area. The Kabaye have not been successfully identified with any specific Indian group in the same area known to the Spanish. However, the similarity in names suggests that the Kabaye of the French may have been the Cava (Caba) of the Spanish.

BIBLIOGRAPHY: I. J. Cox (ed.), *The Journeys of Réné Robert Cavelier, Sieur de La Salle*, II (1906); F. W. Hodge (ed.), *Handbook of American Indians*, I (1907); H. R. Stiles (ed.), *Joutel's Journal of La Salle's Last Voyage, 1684–7* (1906).

T. N. Campbell

*Kadane Corner, Texas.

*Kadodacho Indians.

*Kaffir, Texas.

Kaleidograph. Kaleidograph, originally called *Kaleidoscope*, was a poetry magazine published in Texas from 1929 to 1959. For the history of this magazine, *see* biographical articles on its founders, Montgomery, Vaida Stewart, and Montgomery, Whitney Maxwell.

*Kalgary, Texas.

*Kamay, Texas.

*Kamey, Texas.

*Kanawha, Texas.

*Kannehouan Indians. The Kannehouan (Cannehovan, Kannehonan, Kannehonau, Ouanahinan) Indians are known only from documents of the La Salle Expedition,[qv] which indicate that in the late seventeenth century these Indians lived inland well to the north or northeast of Matagorda Bay, probably near the Brazos River. Their affiliations remain undetermined. The Kannehouan have been erroneously identified with the Tahiannihouq, who were mentioned in the same documents as enemies of the Kadohadacho on the Red River. It is doubtful if the Tahiannihouq lived within the limits of present Texas. The Kannehouan have also been identified with the Cannaha and Cannahio, two separately listed groups likewise identified in the La Salle Expedition documents as enemies of the Kadohadacho. These identifications are conjectures based on similarities in names and do not meet the test of locational geography.

BIBLIOGRAPHY: F. W. Hodge (ed.), *Handbook of American Indians*, I (1907), II (1910); P. Margry, *Découvertes et établissements des Français dans l'ouest et dans le sud de l'Amérique Septentrionale 1614–1698*, III (1879).

T. N. Campbell

*Kanohatino. *See also* Kanohatino Indians.

Kanohatino Indians. The Kanohatino (Ayano, Canatino, Coannotino, Kanoutinoa, Konatine, Quanoatinno) Indians are known from documents of the La Salle Expedition,[qv] which indicate that in the late seventeenth century these Indians lived inland well to the north or northeast of Matagorda Bay, apparently along the Brazos River. The Kanohatino were expert bison hunters and were said to have forty settlements along the river. At this time the Kanohatino were at war with the Hasinai. Some modern writers have suggested that the Kanohatino were probably an early group of Wichita Indians, but this cannot be demonstrated. It is possible that the Kanohatino of the French sources were the same people as the Cantona of the Spanish sources. Both groups occupied the same general area during the same period, and the brief descriptions of their cultures show notable similarities. Further archival research is needed to prove or disprove this possible identity.

BIBLIOGRAPHY: I. J. Cox (ed.), *The Journeys of Réné Robert Cavelier, Sieur de La Salle*, I (1905); C. W. Hackett (ed.), *Pichardo's Treatise on the Limits of Louisiana and Texas*, I (1931); F. W. Hodge (ed.), *Handbook of American Indians*, I (1907); P. Margry, *Découvertes et établissements des Français dans l'ouest et dans le sud de l'Amérique Septentrionale 1614–1698*, II (1879); W. W. Newcomb, Jr., *The Indians of Texas* (1961).

T. N. Campbell

*Kansas City, El Paso, and Mexican Railway Company of Texas. *See* El Paso and Northeastern Railroad Company.

*Kansas City, Mexico, and Orient Railway Company of Texas. In 1964 the Kansas City, Mexico, and Orient Railway had 601 miles of track in Texas, and on August 1, 1964, it was taken over by the Atchison, Topeka, and Santa Fe and merged with it.

James M. Day

*Kansas City Southern Lines in Texas. The

Kansas City Southern Lines was the trade name for two railroad lines operating in Texas in 1970 under the management of Kansas City Southern Industries, Inc. One line, the Kansas City Southern Railway Company,qv maintained ninety-nine miles of track in Texas as part of its line from Port Arthur, Texas, through Shreveport, Louisiana, and Texarkana, Texas, into Kansas. This line provided the shortest route to Gulf of Mexico ports for agricultural products of the middle Missouri Valley; it crossed the Kansas-Missouri and Missouri-Arkansas bituminous coal fields, and it served important oil fields and refineries. The other line, the Louisiana and Arkansas Railway Company,qv maintained 157 miles of track in Texas as part of a line from Farmersville, Texas, to Shreveport, Louisiana. Kansas City Southern Industries also owned and operated the Port Arthur Canal and Dock Company.

James M. Day

*Kansas City Southern Railway Company. *See also* Kansas City Southern Lines in Texas.

*Kansas and Gulf Short Line Railroad Company.

*Kansas, Oklahoma, and Gulf Railway Company of Texas. The Kansas, Oklahoma, and Gulf Railway Company of Texas consisted of an 8.8-mile line between the Oklahoma border and Denison, Texas; in 1928 it became a subsidiary of the Kansas, Oklahoma, and Gulf Railway Company. In December, 1964, the parent company was purchased by the Texas and Pacific Railway Company,qv and at the same time the Kansas, Oklahoma, and Gulf Railway Company of Texas was dissolved.

James M. Day

*Kapp, Ernst.

*Karankawa Bayou.

*Karankawa Indians. In the late seventeenth and early eighteenth centuries the name Karankawa (Carancagua, Carankahua, Caronkoway, Coronk, Korenkahe, Kronk, Quelanhubeche) referred to a relatively small tribe of coastal Indians who lived in an area that extended from Matagorda Bay eastward to the Brazos River. This name was later used in a broader sense to refer to other coastal groups who spoke the same language, particularly the Coapite, Coco, Copane, and Cujane. In the nineteenth century the name Karankawa was commonly used to refer to surviving remnants of all these groups as well as to stray individuals and families of other coastal but non-Karankawan groups who had banded together for mutual protection.

In popular literature it is often assumed that Karankawan Indians occupied all of the Texas coast, but this assumption is not supported by historical evidence. During the eighteenth century the Karankawans were most commonly seen along the coast between the Brazos River and Aransas Bay. At times they traveled eastward for trade or war with the Atakapan groups who lived between present Houston and Beaumont. The coastal section south of Aransas Bay was occupied by Coahuiltecan groups until the late eighteenth century, and the Karankawans made little use of this area until the nineteenth century, when pressure from Anglo American colonists forced them westward and southward.

Some writers have given the impression that most of the coastal Indians known to Cabeza de Vaca qv between 1528 and 1535 were Karankawans. In the light of band and tribal distributions over 150 years later, when the coastal Indians became better known, it appears that Cabeza de Vaca first lived among Atakapans near Galveston Bay, then moved westward to live among Karankawans in the middle section of the coast, and finally entered the Coahuiltecan area west of the San Antonio River. Some of the more inland groups encountered by Cabeza de Vaca may have been Tonkawans.

The Karankawa tribe was represented in various Texas missions in the eighteenth century. In 1722 the Nuestra Señora del Espíritu Santo de Zuñiga Mission qv was established in their territory near Matagorda Bay, but frequent hostilities between Spanish soldiers and the Indians led to its removal to the San Antonio River in 1726. After the same mission was moved to present Goliad in 1749, some Karankawa entered it and remained until about 1793. Karankawa were also present at nearby Nuestra Señora del Rosario Mission,qv established in 1754, as well as at Nuestra Señora del Refugio Mission qv farther south, established in 1791 (with construction in 1793). A few Karankawa also entered Nuestra Señora de la Candelaria Mission,qv a short-lived mission established on the San Gabriel River near present Rockdale. Many Karankawa never entered missions, or entered them only for short periods. These continued to range the coast, but their numbers were steadily reduced by disease and warfare with Anglo American settlers. As stated above, in the nineteenth century these survivors joined remnants of other coastal groups and were generally known to Anglo Americans as "Kronks." They slowly gave way to the settlers by moving westward and southward along the coast. The last survivors crossed into Mexico and lived in northern Tamaulipas, mainly near Reynosa, until 1858, when they recrossed the Rio Grande and were said to have been "exterminated" in a single battle with settlers who lived along the north bank of the river.

Several Indian groups named in documents of the La Salle Expedition qv have been tentatively identified with the Karankawa tribe. Korenkahe (Koienkahe) seems reasonable, but Keremen and Korimen do not because both of these names occur on the same list with Korenkahe. Internal evidence in these documents suggests that Keremen and Korimen represent a duplication.

BIBLIOGRAPHY: Anonymous, *Reports of the Committee of Investigation Sent in 1873 by the Mexican Government to the Frontier of Texas* (1875); H. E. Bolton, *Athanase de Mézières and the Louisiana-Texas Frontier, 1768–1780* (1914) and *Texas in the Middle Eighteenth Century* (1915); F. W. Hodge (ed.), *Handbook of American Indians,* I (1907), II (1910); Albert S. Gatschet, *The Karankawa Indians, The Coast People of Texas* (1891); W. W. Newcomb, Jr., *The Indians of Texas* (1961); R. P. Schaedel, "The Karankawa of the Texas Gulf Coast," *South-*

western *Journal of Anthropology,* V (1949); M. de Villiers du Terrage and P. Rivet, "Les Indiens du Texas et les expéditions Françaises," *Journal de la Société des Américanistes de Paris,* XI (1919).

T. N. Campbell

*Karen, Texas.

*Karnack, Texas.

*Karnes, Henry Wax.

*Karnes City, Texas. Karnes City was formally organized when the Cuero, Texas, firm of Buchel, Wagner and Company purchased a 1,000-acre tract of land on December 12, 1890, and platted the townsite on this tract in March, 1891. Because of a similarity between Karnes, the original name suggested for the new town, and Kerens, Texas, the post office department added "city" to Karnes. Within three years Karnes City had established such a position in Karnes County as to petition for an election to remove the county seat from Helena to Karnes City. The move was effected in January, 1894.

The economy of Karnes City was based on area ranching, farming, uranium mining, and oil and gas production. In the early 1960's agriculture decreased while livestock raising increased. A new high school was completed in 1961. Karnes City had eight churches, a bank, a library, a newspaper, a radio station, and a hospital by 1970. Eighty-two businesses were reported in 1970; industries included fiberglass and furniture factories and plants processing petroleum, sulphur, and flax fibers. The town had a 1960 population of 2,693; the United States census for 1970 listed a population of 2,926.

Robert H. Thonhoff

*Karnes County. Karnes County is a cattle ranching, farming, and petroleum area. In 1968 livestock furnished the chief source of livelihood, yielding $6.6 million; all other agricultural products earned $2.6 million. The leading crops were flax (Texas' leading county in the raising of flax in 1965), broomcorn, cotton, corn, small grains, and truck crops. Oil production in 1972 was 2,740,635 barrels. Total oil production from 1930 to January 1, 1973, was 79,688,843 barrels. The first commercial deposits of uranium in Texas were discovered in Karnes County in 1954, and uranium mining in Karnes and neighboring counties was sufficient in 1968 to keep a uranium-ore-processing mill near Falls City in operation. Texas' oldest Polish settlement, Panna Maria, is in this county (*see* Poles in Texas). Major tourist attractions are a youth fair, a horse club show, and a carnival. County population declined from 14,995 in 1960 to the 1970 United States census count of 13,462.

*Karon, Texas.

Karper, Robert Earl. Robert Earl Karper was born near Chambersburg, Pennsylvania, on October 9, 1888, the son of William Edward and Della Emma (Laughlin) Karper. He graduated from Kansas State College in 1914 with a B.S. degree in agronomy. In 1914–1915 he taught and conducted research in agronomy at Oklahoma A&M College.

On March 8, 1915, he married Sophia Grace Dickinson; they had two children.

Karper was appointed superintendent of Texas Agricultural and Mechanical College (now Texas A&M University) experiment station at Lubbock in 1915. Largely as a result of station research, improved grain sorghum varieties became an important money crop on the Texas South Plains. Karper was made assistant director of the Texas Agricultural Experiment Station System qv in 1925. In 1928 he received an M.S. degree from Texas A&M and was appointed the school's vice-director and agronomist in charge of sorghum investigations. At his own request he returned to the Lubbock experiment station in 1940 to devote full time to sorghum research.

Karper was selected Man of the Year in Texas Agriculture in 1944, and in 1947 he was elected Fellow of the American Society of Agronomy. He began work with the Rockefeller Foundation in developing sorghum farming in Mexico and Latin America in 1954 and helped establish the foundation's large experimental station in Bogotá, Colombia. He retired in 1958, but as Agronomist Emeritus at Texas A&M he continued his experiments in sorghums. He died in Scotsdale, Arizona, on February 7, 1965.

BIBLIOGRAPHY: Seymour V. Conner (ed.), *Builders of the Southwest* (1959); *Texian Who's Who* (1937); Houston *Post,* February 9, 1965.

*Kasoga, Texas.

*Kate Creek.

*Katemcy, Texas.

*Katemcy Creek.

*Katherine, Texas.

*Katy, Texas. Katy, extending into Fort Bend, Harris, and Waller counties, was a rural community of 1,569 people in 1960; it had a 1970 population of 2,923, according to the 1970 United States census. Its seventy businesses were largely concerned with the petroleum industry.

*Katy Railroad. *See* Missouri, Kansas, and Texas Railroad System.

*Kaufman, David Spangler. David Spangler Kaufman and his wife Jane Baxter (Richardson) Kaufman (daughter of Daniel Long Richardson qv) were the parents of four children (not three, as stated in Volume I). They were as follows:

Anna Maria Kaufman was born on December 6, 1843; she died in 1881.

Daniel Richardson Kaufman was born on March 29, 1845. In order to inherit one-twelfth of his grandfather's considerable estate, Daniel Richardson Kaufman's name was changed to Daniel Kaufman Richardson by the time of the 1850 Sabine County census. This condition for inheritance was imposed in the will of his grandfather, Daniel Long Richardson. In 1865, however, when his brother, David Spangler Kaufman, Jr., died, leaving him the only surviving son of his father, Daniel changed his name back to the one given him at birth. The change was made in 1866 in the district court, Washington County.

David Spangler Kaufman, Jr., was born on March 17, 1847; he died in 1865.

Sam Houston Kaufman was born on March 10, 1850; he died on August 14, 1851.

BIBLIOGRAPHY: Daniel Long Richardson will, Probate Court Records, Sabine County; Mary S. Estill, "The Education of Anna Kaufman," *Texana* (Fall, 1966).

Helen Gomer Schluter

*Kaufman, Texas. Kaufman, seat of Kaufman County, was a farm marketing center in 1960 with a population of 3,087. By 1970 Kaufman reported ninety-one businesses, including eight manufacturers. Its industries included meat packing, cotton compressing, metal working, and fertilizer and water pump manufacturing. By 1970 Kaufman had a population of 4,012, according to the United States census.

*Kaufman County. Kaufman County, a part of the Dallas Standard Metropolitan Statistical Area,qv had an agricultural economy that was augmented in the 1960's by an influx of industry. The county produced cotton, hay (in 1969 the second leading county in Texas), oats, vetch, beef cattle, poultry, and dairy products. In recent years some cotton and grain acreage was given over to livestock pastures. There was some oil production in the southeast part of the county. Many county residents commuted to Dallas to work. Local industries have increased considerably, largely accounting for the increase in population from 29,931 in 1960 to 32,392 in 1970, according to the United States census report. Tourist attractions in Kaufman County included Terrell Lake, Cedar Creek Reservoir (sometimes known as Joe B. Hogsett Reservoir), and the Porter Farm, a model farming enterprise (*see* Knapp, Seaman Asahel).

*Kaufman Masonic Institute.

*Keachi College.

Keane, John. John Keane, major league baseball manager, was born in St. Louis, Missouri, on November 3, 1911. He considered a vocation as a Catholic priest, but instead became a professional baseball player. He moved to Houston in 1935 to play for the Houston Buffs and appeared headed for the major leagues when he was struck by a pitched ball. He lay in a coma for six weeks. After his recovery he managed the Albany, Georgia; Rochester, Minnesota; Columbus, Ohio; and Omaha, Nebraska, teams. In 1946 he returned to Houston as manager. In 1959 he joined the St. Louis Cardinals as a coach, becoming manager in 1961. The Cardinals barely missed winning the pennant in 1963 after a streak of nineteen victories in twenty games. In 1964 they won the National League pennant and defeated the New York Yankees in a seven-game World Series. Hailed as Manager of the Year, Keane startled the baseball world by leaving the Cardinals for the Yankees, where his teams were plagued by injuries before his release

in 1966. He died in Houston on January 6, 1967.

Joe B. Frantz

*Kearby, Jerome Claiborne.

*Keechi, Texas.

*Keechi Creek.

*Keenan, Charles G.

*Keenan, Texas.

*Keene, Texas. Keene, in central Johnson County, reported twenty-four businesses in 1969. The population in 1960 was 1,532; the 1970 census showed a count of 2,440. Each summer the Seventh-day Adventists of the Southwest hold a reunion in Keene. *See* Adventist Churches in Texas.

*Keeney's, Texas.

*Keep, Imla.

Keeter, Texas. Keeter, in Wise County, was founded about 1880 and named for John Keeter, who gave the land for the settlement. Along with Friendship and Garvin, two similar settlements nearby, Keeter provided community life for farmers in southern Wise County around the turn of the century. After 1945 the *Texas Almanac* qv no longer reported a population for Keeter.

Keidel, Wilhelm Victor. Wilhelm Victor Keidel was born in Hildesheim, Germany, in March, 1825, son of Dr. Georg and Mrs. Keidel. He was educated at Georg Augusts University at Göttingen in the field of medicine and came to Texas in 1845. When the Mexican War broke out, he enlisted in the United States Army for six months. He went to Fredericksburg and in 1847 served as the doctor for the German Emigration Company (*see* Adelsverein). In 1848 he was elected the first county judge of Gillespie County.

To encourage settlers to move into the rich bottom lands of Gillespie County along the Pedernales River, Keidel offered his medical services without charge to the colonists who would join him in settling there. He treated both settlers and Indians, the latter paying him with fresh venison and wild turkey hung on his fence. He served as trustee for the Live Oak school and was active in the cultural-political club of the Live Oak-Pedernales community. In a statewide mass meeting of German societies at San Antonio in 1854, he was elected a vice-president of the general organization.

Keidel married Albertina Kramer, who died giving birth to their only son; in 1856 he married Caroline Kott, and they had one son; his second wife died of fever in 1865. Keidel died on January 9, 1870, and was buried in the cemetery on his farm.

BIBLIOGRAPHY: Solms-Braunfels Papers (MS., Archives, University of Texas at Austin Library); Rudolf Leopold Biesele, *The History of the German Settlements in Texas, 1831–1861* (1930); Gillespie County Historical Society, *Pioneers in God's Hills* (1960); Robert Penniger, *Fest-Ausgabe zum 50-jährigen Jubiläum der Gründung der Stadt Friedrichsburg* (1896).

Esther L. Mueller

*Keiller, William.

*Keith, Texas.

*Keithton, Texas.

*Kell, Frank.

*Kellarville, Texas.

*Keller, John.

*Keller, Texas. Keller, formerly a small rural community in north Tarrant County, has become a suburban community of Fort Worth. In 1960 it had a population of 827; by 1970 its population had increased to 1,474, according to the United States census report. In 1970 Keller listed twenty two businesses. *See also* Fort Worth Standard Metropolitan Statistical Area.

*Keller Creek.

*Kellerville, Texas.

*Kelley, Texas.

*Kelley Creek.

*Kelley Peak.

*Kellog Canyon.

*Kellogg, Albert Gallatin.

*Kellogg, Texas.

*Kelly, George Addison.

*Kelly, John.

Kelly, Lawrence Vincent. Lawrence Vincent Kelly, founder and general manager of the Dallas Civic Opera, was born in Chicago, Illinois, on May 30, 1928, the son of Patrick James and Thelma (Seabott) Kelly. He was a student at Chicago Music College (1942–1945) at the same time that he attended Loyola Academy, from which he was graduated. He went to Georgetown University in Washington, D.C., and returned to Chicago in 1950 to assist in the family real estate business; upon his father's death he became business manager and later secretary-treasurer and director. He attended DePaul University Law School at night (1950–1951), became a vice-president and director of Dearborn Supply Company (1951–1952), and established himself as an insurance broker in 1953.

In 1953 Kelly was a cofounder of the Lyric Theatre of Chicago, an opera company of which he was secretary-treasurer from 1953 to 1956 and managing director from 1954 to 1956. For two years, under Kelly's guidance, Chicago was the scene of "some of the most brilliant nights of opera seen in the United States," according to one writer. In June, 1956, however, the founders of the company had a disagreement, and Kelly moved to New York City for a year. Considering where he might start a new opera company, he chose Dallas as a likely place. Through the efforts of music critic John Rosenfield,qv Kelly was brought to Dallas, and by March, 1957, the Dallas Civic Opera was chartered, with Kelly as general manager. In November, 1957, the company presented in a gala concert the world-renowned Maria Callas, an opera star who had been presented by Kelly in her American debut three years earlier in Chicago. That first season only one opera was mounted; it had a brilliant cast headed

by Giulietta Simionato in a new production of Rossini's *L'Italiana in Algeri*, designed and staged by the famed Franco Zeffirelli in his American debut. This production set a quality standard for the future of the company, and Kelly's subsequent pattern of originality established the Dallas Civic Opera internationally. Over the next seventeen years Dallas opera lovers saw the American debut of such singers as Teresa Berganza, Jon Vickers, Joan Sutherland, and many others. Kelly also introduced a distinguished group of theatrical directors and designers, and the company had its own scenic department, which built productions for other companies as well. He was also a cofounder and director of the Performing Arts Foundation of Kansas City, Missouri.

Early in 1974 Kelly took on the responsibility of acting manager of the Dallas Symphony Orchestra, which was in serious financial trouble. Several months later he became seriously ill and had to resign that position. He went to Kansas City, Missouri, for treatment, and he died there on September 16, 1974. A Requiem Mass was held for Lawrence Vincent Kelly at Christ the King Catholic Church in Dallas on September 19, the day before he was buried in the family plot in Chicago.

BIBLIOGRAPHY: *Who's Who In America* (1968); Dallas *Morning News*, October 12, 1958, May 19, 1974, September 17, 18, 22, 1974; Biographical File, Barker Texas History Center, University of Texas at Austin.

Eldon S. Branda

*Kelly, Texas. (Bexar County.)

*Kelly, Texas. (Uvalde County.)

*Kelly Air Force Base. Between 1950 and 1967 the Kelly Air Force Base work force grew from 12,500 to 31,400, and the physical facilities were greatly expanded and modernized. This growth was due to the expanded logistics mission of the San Antonio Air Materiel Area, the largest organization on the base, and to the transfer of various activities from neighboring Brooks Air Force Base.qv Kelly Field's logistics mission was considerably enlarged in scope during the Korean conflict.

During the 1950's Kelly's skyline was altered by the removal of the last World War I hangars and the construction of a one-million-square-foot maintenance hangar—the largest structure in the world without center columns. New additions included a 11,550-foot runway, shops, modern warehouses, and hangars and taxiways for the Texas Air National Guard.qv In August, 1953, the headquarters of the United States Air Force Security Service moved to Kelly and occupied a new administration building and other facilities constructed for them. Kelly also acquired the 172-acre San Antonio Air Force Station near Fort Sam Houston qv in July, 1955.

In 1960 an aeromedical airlift squadron and a Texas Air National Guard fighter-interceptor squadron moved to the base when the airdrome at Brooks Air Force Base was closed permanently. Kelly also completed 592 additional housing units in May, 1960. Modern industrial facilities constructed during the 1960's included a mechanized central receiving operation, one of the fastest and most efficient underground aircraft fuel and de-fuel systems in the air force, an electronics repair facility, a precision-measuring equipment laboratory, a nickel-braze repair facility, and one of the Southwest's most modern automatic data-processing equipment complexes with related high-speed communications equipment. An automated air freight terminal, in addition to serving domestic flights, began to operate as an inland aerial port of embarkment for Southeast Asia in 1964. The following year Kelly received the assignments and personnel from other deactivated air force installations and at the same time stepped up its support for Southeast Asian operations.

In 1967 the San Antonio Air Materiel Area served as the worldwide logistic support manager for twenty aircraft systems, including the C-5, B-58, and F-106. It also managed all air force reentry systems, 60 percent of the air force's propulsion systems, and almost three hundred thousand stock items. In the base's shops, B-52 bombers, T-34 and T-56 turboprop engines, and other aerospace equipment were overhauled. This assignment entailed more than six hundred million dollars worth of materiel and services. Kelly Air Force Base, with its work force of over thirty thousand in 1967, had an annual payroll of $222,000,000.

Edna S. McGaffey

*Kelly Creek.

*Kelly Plow Company.

Kelly's Stage Stand. Kelly's Stage Stand, situated at the Ecleto Creek crossing of the San Antonio-Victoria road in northeastern Karnes County, was a way station for stages from the 1850's to about 1871. Operated by Riley A. Kelly, the stage stand was the nucleus of the settlement of Ecleto before the post office and livery stable were moved to Riddleville in 1871.

Robert H. Thonhoff

*Kellyville, Texas.

*Kelsay, Texas.

Kelsey, John Peter. John Peter Kelsey was born in Poughkeepsie, New York, on January 11, 1818, the son of James and Rachel (Du Boise) Kelsey. In 1839 he signed on as a master mechanic with a building firm bound for Galveston, Texas; he built the first two-story house in that city. From Galveston he traveled to southwest Texas, Camargo and Monterrey, Mexico, and to New Orleans, Louisiana, where he borrowed money from a brother to buy merchandise. With his goods he sailed to Corpus Christi Bay, where he set up a tent on the Aubrey and Kinney Ranch (*see* Kinney, Henry Lawrence) and began selling his goods; shortly thereafter he built a one-room store. In October, 1847, he married Amanda Brooks; they adopted two daughters, one of whom died of yellow fever at the age of seven.

Kelsey moved to Rio Grande City in 1848 and established a mercantile-commission business. Much of his merchandise was furnished by the Brownsville, Texas, wholesale house of José San Román.qv In 1852 he was elected (and later reelected) chief justice (later called county judge) of Starr County. He purchased thousands of acres of ranch land in Jim Hogg County and may have introduced barbed wire into this section of Texas. He also experimented with crossbreeding to improve his cattle and sheep stock. In 1861 Kelsey's Unionist sympathies forced his departure from Texas; he transferred his mercantile business and home to Camargo, Mexico. During the Civil War he did a thriving business in the contraband cotton trade. He returned to Rio Grande City in the late 1870's. In 1882, and again in 1886 and 1888, he was elected county judge of Starr County. Ranching became his chief interest, which he carried on in Starr and Jim Hogg counties until his death on May 9, 1898. He was buried in the old cemetery in Rio Grande City. The Kelsey Memorial Methodist Church in Corpus Christi was named in honor of John Peter Kelsey and his wife in 1948.

BIBLIOGRAPHY: Anna Marietta Kelsey, *Through the Years* (1952); John Henry Brown, *Indian Wars and Pioneers of Texas* (1896); José San Román Collection (MS., Archives, University of Texas at Austin Library); Corpus Christi *Caller*, May, 1898; Brownsville *Herald*, May, 1898.

Shirley Brooks Greene

*Kelsey, Texas.

*Kelsey Creek.

*Kelton, Texas.

*Keltys, Texas. Keltys, a suburb of Lufkin in Angelina County, had a 1960 population of 1,056. In 1969 it had four businesses, including a large lumber mill. At the time of the 1970 census, Keltys was unincorporated and had somewhat less than 1,000 population.

*Kemah, Texas. Kemah, a community on Galveston Bay in Galveston County, was incorporated during the 1960's and by 1970, according to the United States census, had a population of 1,144. In 1970 it listed thirty-one businesses.

*Kemp, Joseph Alexander. Joseph Alexander Kemp died in Austin, Texas (not in Wichita Falls, Texas, as stated in Volume I), and he was buried in Wichita Falls.

BIBLIOGRAPHY: Wichita Falls *Record News*, November 17, 1930.

Mrs. Ken Lively

Kemp, Louis Wiltz. Louis Wiltz Kemp, son of Dempsey and Martha (Taylor) Kemp, was born in Cameron, Texas, on September 4, 1881. He attended high school in Cameron and studied engineering at the University of Texas from 1901 to 1903. He married Violet Volz on October 7, 1925, and they had two sons.

Kemp began employment with the Texas Company (now Texaco Inc.qv) in 1908 and continued in that service until his retirement. His spare time was spent in the study of Texas history. The State Cemetery qv in Austin was little known in 1932, and Kemp brought this to the attention of the Texas State Highway Department,qv which paved the roads within the cemetery grounds and dedicated them to Louis Kemp. A red granite marker honoring Kemp for his role in the reburial of many Texas heroes and statesmen in the cemetery was placed on the grounds.

At the end of his career he was considered one of the best informed men on Texas history. He checked and verified numerous inscriptions on historical monuments and, along with others, located the massacre site and burial place of Fannin's men. He was the prime mover in the plan to construct the San Jacinto Monument and Museum qv and was instrumental in having drives built in the San Jacinto Battleground area so that spots which had been accessible only by foot or on horseback might easily be reached. He was a member of the board of the Texas State Library qv and chairman of the board of Texas historians for the Texas Centennial.qv He was one of the directors of compilation of the book *Monuments Erected by the State of Texas to Commemorate the Centenary of Texas Independence* (c. 1939), published as the report of the Commission of Control for Texas Centennial Celebrations. He was the author or coauthor of several works, including *The Signers of the Texas Declaration of Independence* (1944) and *The Heroes of San Jacinto* (1932). He served as president of the Texas State Historical Association qv from 1942 to 1946. His collection of Texana was bought by Houston Endowment Inc. and the University of Texas at Austin and was placed in the Eugene C. Barker Texas History Center qv at the university.

Kemp died on November 15, 1956, in Houston, where he was buried. He was later reburied in the State Cemetery on May 5, 1957, beside the granite marker placed there to honor him.

BIBLIOGRAPHY: Austin *American-Statesman*, July 19, 1936; Dallas *Morning News*, March 2, 1953; Houston *Post*, March 30, 1962.

Gibb Gilchrist

Kemp, Samuel Barnet. Samuel Barnet Kemp was born on December 26, 1871, in Merrilltown, Travis County, Texas, son of James Barnet and Eliza Sofronia (Woodward) Kemp. Kemp was educated at Texas A&M and the University of Texas, receiving an LL.B. degree from the latter in 1900. Kemp practiced law in Austin from 1900 to 1908, moved to Robert Lee, Texas, and was county judge of Coke County from 1914 to 1915. In 1916 Kemp was assistant United States attorney, District of Hawaii, and was circuit court judge of the First Circuit, Hawaii, from 1917 to 1918. Kemp was associate justice of the Supreme Court of the Territory of Hawaii from March 7, 1918, to April 17, 1922. He was attorney general of Hawaii from 1937 to 1938, and he was again appointed Supreme Court associate justice in 1938. Kemp became chief justice of the Supreme Court of Hawaii on June 20, 1941, and remained in that position until his retirement in 1960.

Kemp married Mae S. Hope on December 30, 1904, in Caldwell, Texas, and they had one daugh-

ter. He died on August 14, 1962, in Honolulu, Hawaii, and was buried there.

BIBLIOGRAPHY: *Who's Who In America* (1952); *Alcalde*, LI (January, 1963).

*Kemp, Texas. Kemp, in Kaufman County, had a population of 816 in 1960; the town had forty businesses and 999 inhabitants in 1970, according to the United States census.

*Kemp City, Texas.

*Kemper, Samuel.

*Kemper City, Texas.

*Kempner, Harris.

*Kempner, Texas.

*Kendalia, Texas.

*Kendall, George Wilkins.

*Kendall, Joel Sutton.

*Kendall County. Kendall County was primarily a producer of sheep, goats, and cattle. Feed crops, pecans, and cedar posts also contributed to the economy. The county derived important income from tourist and hunting businesses. The 1960 population was 5,889; the 1970 population rose to 6,964, according to the United States census.

Two caves in Kendall County attracted visitors. Although there were indications of previous entry, the Cave-Without-A-Name was officially brought to the public's attention in May, 1939. Located eleven miles northeast of Boerne, the cave was commercially developed for tourists, and the name was changed to Century Cave in the early 1960's; however, the name was changed back to Cave-Without-A-Name in 1975. The other attraction, located south of Boerne, was Cascade Caverns.qv

*Kendall Valley, Texas.

*Kendleton, Texas.

*Kendrick, Harvey W.

*Kendrick, John Benjamin.

*Kenedy, Mifflin.

*Kenedy, Texas. Kenedy, serving the diversified agricultural area of Karnes County, in 1970 had 140 businesses, ten churches, two newspapers, a radio station, a hospital, and a large livestock exchange. The population of Kenedy declined from 4,301 in 1960 to 4,156 in 1970, according to the United States census.

*Kenedy County. Kenedy County had an economy almost totally devoted to natural gas and petroleum production and to cattle ranching. In 1967 income from gas and oil amounted to $12,-794,368; in 1968 receipts from sale of livestock came to $3,282,000. There were two large ranches (*see* Armstrong, Texas, and King Ranch) occupying most of the area, and there were eighteen other farms and ranches there in 1969. The 1960 population was 884; by 1970 the population had declined to 678, according to the United States census.

*Kennard, Texas.

*Kennedale, Texas. Kennedale, Tarrant County, became an incorporated suburban community near

Fort Worth during the 1960's. Its population doubled during the decade, increasing from 1,521 in 1960 to 3,076 by 1970, according to the United States census. *See also* Fort Worth Standard Metropolitan Statistical Area.

Kennedy, John Fitzgerald, Assassination of. On November 21, 1963, President John Fitzgerald Kennedy left Washington for Texas to attend several official functions, to present his administration's views in personal speeches, and to help reunify the conservative and liberal wings of the Democratic party in Texas,qv He flew to San Antonio to join Vice-President Lyndon B. Johnson qv in dedicating the United States Air Force School of Aerospace Medicine, attended a testimonial dinner in Houston for United States Representative Albert Thomas,qv and flew to Fort Worth to spend the night. Kennedy addressed a breakfast there on November 22, flew to Dallas, and began a motorcade trip in an open car with his wife, Governor John Connally, and the governor's wife through town to the Trade Mart, where Kennedy was to speak at a luncheon. About 12:30 p.m., as the car started down the Elm Street hill leading beneath a railroad overpass in Dealey Plaza, several shots were fired, wounding Kennedy and Connally. They were rushed to Parkland Memorial Hospital, where the president was pronounced dead at 1:00 p.m. from wounds in the neck and head. Connally, hit in the back, wrist, and thigh, recovered. At 2:38 p.m. Johnson was sworn in as president by U. S. District Judge Sarah T. Hughes at Love Field qv on the plane that would return Kennedy's body to Washington that evening.

Between 1:45 and 2:00 p.m. of the same day, Lee Harvey Oswald qv was arrested in the Texas Theatre in the Oak Cliff section of Dallas and charged with the murder of policeman J. D. Tippit.qv On November 23 he was charged with murdering Kennedy with a rifle from the sixth floor of the Texas School Book Depository. On November 24 Oswald was shot and killed by Jack Ruby,qv a Dallas lounge operator, in the basement of the city jail while being transferred to the county jail. Ruby was indicted for murder on November 26, 1963, and was convicted on March 14, 1964. The conviction was appealed, and in November, 1966, a new trial with a change of venue was ordered. Ruby died before the second trial could begin.

On November 29, 1963, President Johnson established the President's Commission on the Assassination of President Kennedy, consisting of seven men representing the United States Supreme Court, Senate, House of Representatives, and the public. The commission met first on December 5, 1963, and submitted its multivolume report on September 24, 1964. Several books and articles also were published which were critical of the commission's report or offered alternate theories about the circumstances and events connected with the assassination.

BIBLIOGRAPHY: *Report of the Warren Commission on the Assassination of President Kennedy* (1964).

*Kennedy, Samuel.

*Kennedy, William.

*Kennedy, William.

*Kenney, John Wesley.

*Kenney, Martin McHenry.

*Kenney, Texas.

*Kenney's Fort.

*Kennon, Alfred.

*Keno Creek.

*Kenser, Texas.

Kensing, Texas. Kensing is the easternmost community in Delta County; it is located in the rich bottom lands that make up the delta formed by the North Sulphur and South Sulphur rivers. The community had a population of fifty in 1969. Kensing was established about 1900 by D. G. Fleniken and his father-in-law, a Mr. Sansing, who were partners in establishing a sawmill and in dividing the area into town lots. They derived the town's name by combining the last syllables of their own names. In the 1850's, before there was a town of Kensing, the area was reportedly a haven for horse thieves.

*Kent, Andrew.

*Kent, Texas.

*Kent, Colony of.

*Kent County. Kent County had a petroleum-ranching-farming economy, in 1965 ranking thirty-third in the state in the production of oil and gas. From 1946 through 1972, 215,550,007 barrels of oil were produced. Cattle ranches occupied most of the area, but cotton and grain cultivation also contributed to the county's economy. The county seat was moved from Clairemont to Jayton in 1954 after a two-year court fight between the two communities. The county's population declined from 1,727 in 1960 to 1,434 in 1970, according to the United States census.

*Kentucky Mustangs.

*Kentucky Town, Texas.

Keralum, Pierre Yves. Pierre Yves Keralum, whose family name was often abbreviated to Kalum (or Kalim), was known to many in the Lower Rio Grande Valley as *El Santo Padre Pedrito*. He was born in Quimper, Brittany, France, on March 2, 1817. Following his secondary education he became apprenticed to a cabinetmaker and then moved to Paris to study architecture. Following success as an architect in Paris, at age twenty-eight he entered the Quimper diocesan seminary; in 1851 he made his profession as an Oblate of Mary Immaculate and was ordained in 1852. To utilize Father Keralum's knowledge of architecture at a time when the Oblate Order was founding missions, the Order sent him to Texas. Departing Le Havre in March, 1852, on *La Belle Assise*, Father Keralum reached New Orleans in early May and continued immediately to Galveston, arriving there on May 14. In October, 1852, he departed for Brownsville, where he was a missionary, architect, and builder for the rest of his life. A circuit priest, he rode horseback from ranch to ranch, visiting some seventy ranches three times every year, many of them in difficult wilderness areas along the lower Rio Grande. He practiced holy poverty to such an extent that he was often rebuked by his superiors. He often utilized his skill in cabinetry by constructing coffins for parishioners who had died.

Father Keralum's first known construction work in Texas was at Roma, where he was architect, stonecutter, and mason. On September 18, 1854, a cornerstone was laid and the church was dedicated to the Virgin Mary under the title of the Refuge of Sinners. He then designed the Church of the Immaculate Conception for Brownsville, the foundation of which was laid in 1854 and the cornerstone placed in 1855. After several difficult years of building, the church was dedicated in June, 1859; it achieved cathedral status in 1874. Toward the end of his career, Father Keralum designed the Church of San Augustine for the plaza at Laredo (1872) and assisted the secular priests with its construction.

On November 9, 1872, almost blind, Father Keralum left Brownsville to make his circuit of distant mission stations; he reached a scheduled ranch stop north of present Mercedes on November 12, but when he did not reach the next ranch as scheduled, an alarm went out. His horse was located on November 15; Keralum was presumed dead when three months later a Requiem Mass was celebrated for him in Brownsville.

In 1882, almost ten years after the disappearance of Father Keralum, the remains of a saddle placed on the fork of a tree were found. Nearby were the skeletal remains of Keralum, identified by instruments of his calling, including his Oblate cross, chalice, paten, and rosary, in addition to a watch and eighteen dollars in silver. He was interred at the Church of the Immaculate Conception in Brownsville; some of the remains of Padre Pedrito were placed in a cemetery in Mercedes, but these were later removed to the Provincial Cemetery in San Antonio.

BIBLIOGRAPHY: Bernard Doyon, *The Cavalry of Christ on the Rio Grande, 1849–1883* (1956); P. F. Parisot, *The Reminiscences of a Texas Missionary* (1899).

Eugene George

*Keremen Indians.

*Kerens, Texas. Kerens, in eastern Navarro County, is the site of a $25,000,000 petrochemical complex manufacturing fertilizer and employing about two hundred men. In 1967 the town reported fifty-six businesses, ten churches, a hospital, a bank, a newspaper, and four schools. City improvements included a National Guard qv building and the paving of all streets. In 1970 business establishments numbered thirty. In 1960 the population was 1,123; the 1970 census count was 973.

*Kermit, Texas. Kermit, seat of Winkler County, had a 1960 population of 10,465 and a 1970 population of 7,884, according to the United States census. In 1967 there were twenty-five churches and a hospital in Kermit. The town provided services to the surrounding ranches; petroleum industries there processed natural gas, oil, liquefied petroleum products, carbon black, and sulphur. The number of businesses reported in 1970 was 156.

*Kerr, Alfred Benjamin Fontaine.

*Kerr, James.

*Kerr, John Steele.

*Kerr, Peter. Peter Kerr was born in Carlisle, Pennsylvania, on September 12, 1795. He pronounced his name "Carr," and some contemporary accounts spell his name "Carr." After his notable activities in the Austin colony and in the Texas Revolution, Kerr became one of Texas' earliest cattlemen. By 1840 he was raising cattle in Travis County and branding them with his registered KER brand. He was a resident of Burnet County by 1851 (not 1856, as stated in Volume I), where he purchased a league of land from John Hamilton. In addition to supplying beef to the army, he profited from real estate investments. Kerr wrote his famous, disputed will three days before his death on December 21, 1861. His heirs took the will to court, and in 1868 the Texas Supreme Court ruled in their favor, leaving the county with only two acres for a public school.

Tad Moses

*Kerr, William.

*Kerr County. Kerr County, on the Edwards Plateau in south-central Texas, derived most of its income from ranching and tourism. Sheep, Angora goats, and cattle were the principal livestock. The picturesque Guadalupe River, the hunting leases on wooded, rolling hills, and the many summer camps annually attracted thousands of tourists; in addition, numerous real estate developments provided country homes for families living in Texas' urban centers. Captain Eddie Rickenbacker's ranch, stocked with deer and antelope imported from Africa, India, and Japan, was open for hunting. The Texas Lions Camp for Crippled Children, established in 1952, expanded its facilities to care for eight hundred children. The many youth camps, including private, church, and Boy and Girl Scout camps, accommodated thousands of youngsters during each summer season. Kerr County listed an airplane factory and two furniture factories among its major industries. The population was 16,800 in 1960; it rose to 19,454 by 1970, according to the United States census.

*Kerr Creek.

Kerrdale, Texas. Kerrdale was located in Newton County about five miles southeast of Burkeville. It was named for J. J. Kerr, the first and only postmaster. Established in 1907 to serve the Spear's Chapel community, it was discontinued in 1909 when the Jack's post office was established at New Columbia only two or three miles away.

Madeleine Martin

*Kerrick, Texas.

*Kerrville, Texas. Kerrville, seat of Kerr County, had a 1960 population of 8,901 and a 1970 population of 12,672, according to the United States census. In 1966 Kerrville had fifteen churches, six schools, four hospitals, two newspapers, a junior college, a library, and a radio station. In 1970, 332 businesses were reported. Kerrville's economy was based on tourism, wool, mohair, and cattle, supplemented with aircraft manufacturing and three government hospitals.

Kerrville State Hospital. The Kerrville State Hospital was the Kerrville State Sanatorium,qv a tuberculosis hospital exclusively for Negroes until 1949, when all patients were transferred to the East Texas State Tuberculosis Hospital qv in Tyler. In 1951 the institution was designated as a branch of the San Antonio State Hospital qv to serve its aged psychotic patients. It became a separate institution in 1952 and acquired its present name in 1959. The Fifty-eighth Legislature appropriated funds to operate the Legion Annex as a part of the hospital and changed its function from a tuberculosis facility to a mental hospital. Average population in 1967 was 1,600. In 1970 the hospital received patients from ten surrounding counties and offered new services including expanded recreational activities. A new 28-bed general psychiatric ward was added also. The average daily census in 1970 was 1,276. See Mentally Ill and Mentally Retarded, Care of, in Texas.

BIBLIOGRAPHY: Board for Texas State Hospitals and Special Schools, *Report* (1964); Texas Department of Mental Health and Mental Retardation, *Annual Report,* 1970.

*Kerrville State Sanatorium. *See also* Kerrville State Hospital.

*Kertman, Texas.

*Kesler, Henry.

*Kessler, Texas.

*Ketchum Boys. Samuel W. Ketchum was born on January 4, 1854, in Caldwell County, and Thomas Edward "Black Jack" Ketchum was born in San Saba County on October 31, 1863 (not in Tom Green County, as suggested in Volume I); they were the sons of Green Berry and Temperance Katherine (Wydic) Ketchum and grew up in San Saba, Texas. Their father had been coroner of Christian County, Illinois, before coming to Texas to ranch (he may also have been a doctor, as suggested in Volume I). Samuel Ketchum married Louisa J. Greenlee in San Saba on February 4, 1875, according to family records; Thomas never married. It is possible that many of the crimes attributed to Black Jack Ketchum were committed by a Will "Black Jack" Christian and his brother, and that Tom Ketchum inherited the name and reputation after Christian was killed; however, the facts of Tom Ketchum's career (as stated in Volume I) indicate that his notoriety outdistanced that of Christian.

Berry Spradley

*Ketchum Mountain.

*Key, Joseph S.

Key, Valdimer Orlando, Jr. V. O. Key, Jr., was born on March 13, 1908, in Austin, Texas, the son of V. O. and Olive (Terry) Key, and spent his early life in Lamesa in West Texas. He attended Mc-Murry College for two years, then the University of Texas, where he received the B.A. and M.A. degrees in 1929 and 1930; in 1934 he was graduated from the University of Chicago with a Ph.D. degree in political science. While at Chicago, he met Luella Gettys, also a political scientist, and they were married on October 27, 1934. He was a member of Phi Beta Kappa.

Key's career was largely devoted to teaching and writing. He taught first at the University of California at Los Angeles (1934–1936); later he taught at Johns Hopkins (1938–1949), Yale (1949–1951), and Harvard (after 1951) and served terms at all three schools as departmental chairman. In 1958 he was elected president of the American Political Science Association.

Professor Key served in several governmental positions. Under President Franklin D. Roosevelt he served on the staffs of the National Resources Planning Board (1937–1938) and the Bureau of the Budget (1942–1945); under President John F. Kennedy he was a member of the Committee on Political Campaign Expenditures.

Key published numerous articles and books. His *Southern Politics in State and Nation* (1949) won the Woodrow Wilson Award of the American Political Science Association. He also wrote *Politics, Parties, and Pressure Groups* (1942); *A Primer of Statistics for Political Scientists* (1954); *American State Politics: An Introduction* (1956); and *Public Opinion and American Democracy* (1961). His *Southern Politics in State and Nation* (1949) includes a chapter on Texas politics.

Key was Jonathan Trumbull Professor of American History and Government at Harvard University when he died on October 4, 1963, in Brookline, Massachusetts.

BIBLIOGRAPHY: *American Political Science Review,* LVIII (1964); *Biographical Directory of the American Political Science Association* (1961); *Who's Who In America* (1960); New York *Times,* October 4, 1963.

O. Douglas Weeks

*Key, William Mercer.

*Key, Texas.

*Keys Creek.

*Keyser Creek.

Kiabaha Indians. The Kiabaha (Kiaboha, Kiahoba, Kioboba, Niabaha) Indians are known only from records pertaining to the La Salle Expedition,qv which indicate that in the late seventeenth century these Indians lived inland to the north or northeast of Matagorda Bay, probably near the Brazos River. The Kiabaha have been confused with the Kabaye, which the records clearly identify as a separate and distinct group of Indians who lived in the same area. Thus far no one has successfully demonstrated that the Kiabaha were related to any other known group of Indians.

BIBLIOGRAPHY: I. J. Cox (ed.), *The Journeys of Réné Robert Cavelier, Sieur de La Salle*, II (1906); F. W. Hodge (ed.), *Handbook of American Indians*, I (1907); H. R. Stiles (ed.), *Joutel's Journal of La Salle's Last Voyage, 1684–7* (1906).

T. N. Campbell

*Kiam, Texas.

*Kiamatia.

Kiber, F. (Faustino). F. (Faustino) Kiber, an early developer of the drainage system in Brazoria County, was born in Ludiano, Switzerland, on February 15, 1852. He was educated in his native land and became fluent in five languages. He lived for a time in Italy and in England, and in 1872 he immigrated to New York City, where he was an interpreter in the construction department of the New York Central Railroad.

In 1874, looking for better business opportunities, he traveled to Chicago, Memphis, and New Orleans before coming to Texas. Landing at Galveston, he stayed for short periods of time in Houston and Austin before locating at Brenham, where for many years he operated a confectionary business with a large wholesale trade. After selling this business, he returned to Houston, where he spent four years in the hotel business.

Kiber purchased a league of land in Brazoria County, but finding the property unproductive and uninhabitable unless properly drained, he turned his attention to an effective drainage system for the entire area. He sold a half interest in his purchase to Lewis Randolph Bryan,qv and their operations made them the pioneer promoters of drainage in that part of Texas. The league of land was divided into lots and blocks, becoming the Bryan and Kiber subdivision on which the city of Angleton is located.

Kiber was one of the first in the area to cultivate orange, grapefruit, and fig trees; his close friendship and frequent correspondence with Luther Burbank, the world renowned horticulturist, whetted his interest in the development of the grafting process in the cultivation and growth of fruit-bearing trees.

F. Kiber was active throughout his life in the real estate business, formed the Angleton State Bank (now the 1st National Bank), owned and operated the electric service company for the city, operated the Angleton Gin Company, and was active in the promotion of the Intercoastal Canal System (now the Gulf Intracoastal Waterway qv). He married Emma Catherine Dwyer in 1888; they had one daughter. Kiber died on January 3, 1927.

Catherine Elsbury McNeese

*Kichai Indians.

*Kickapoo, Texas.

*Kickapoo Creek.

*Kickapoo Indians. After Texas became a republic some Kickapoo moved to Oklahoma, while others, with Seminoles and runaway Negro slaves, negotiated with the Mexican government for the land near Santa Rosa, Coahuila, now Muzquiz, in return for protecting the Mexican colonizers against the harassing Comanches, Apaches, and Lipans. Today, after more than one hundred years in Mexico, isolated in a remote village in the foothills of Sierra Hermosa de Santa Rosa, they maintain their ancient culture to a remarkable extent. They have accepted a few aspects of the Mexican culture, including Spanish, but the language spoken among them is still Algonquian. They have never allowed either evangelization or schooling. They believe in the Great Spirit who with many assistants attends to their pleas. Their religion is the most cohesive element in their lives. From a former economy of agriculture, hunting, trapping, horse raising, and trading, they have become migrant workers in the United States from California to New York, utilizing automobiles to follow the harvests. This mobility has been facilitated by the fact that they enjoy dual Mexican-American citizenship. Each fall they return to their village in Mexico for the winter months to build their ancient-type houses, like those they constructed around the Great Lakes, and to observe their myriad ceremonies.

BIBLIOGRAPHY: Alfred Barnaby Thomas, *Teodoro de Croix and the Northern Frontier of New Mexico* (1941); United States Senate Document 215, 60th Congress, 1st Session (*Affairs of the Mexican Kickapoo Indians*); Dorman H. Winfrey (ed.), *Texas Indian Papers, 1825–1843* (1959); Secretaría de Gobierno, Estado de Coahuila, *Código de Colonización y Terrenos Baldíos* (1850); Felipe A. Latorre & Dolores L. Latorre, *The Mexican Kickapoo Indians* (1975).

Dolores L. and Felipe A. Latorre

*Kickapoo Spring.

*Kicking Bird.

*Kidd-Key, Mrs. Lucy.

*Kidd-Key College.

*Kiest, Edwin John.

*Kildare, Texas.

*Kildare and Linden Railway Company.

*Kildoogan Creek.

*Kilgore, Constantine Buckley.

*Kilgore, Texas. Kilgore, in Gregg and Rusk counties, had a 1960 population of 10,092 and a 1970 population of 9,495, according to the United States census reports. Although oil and gas were the town's primary industries, publishing houses and companies producing bathroom fixtures, wax products, clothing, livestock feeds, and air-conditioning units were also significant. The total number of businesses in 1970 was 394. Kilgore supported a municipal hospital and was the site of the East Texas Treatment Center for the handicapped.

Kilgore College. Kilgore College, Kilgore, was established in 1935 through the efforts of citizens of Kilgore Independent School District. From 1935 to 1946 Kilgore College operated under the direction of the school district's board of trustees; W. L. Dodson was superintendent. In January, 1946, invitations were issued to neighboring school districts to join in forming a union district for junior college purposes. Seven districts accepted: Sabine (1946), White Oak (1946), Leverett's Chapel (1946), London (1947), Overton (1947), Gaston (1948), and Gladewater County Line (1951). A board of nine trustees from the union district directed the affairs of the college after 1946, and Dr. B. E. Masters served as president.

Kilgore College offered senior college and university preparatory courses, terminal technical and vocational courses, and an adult education program in the evening division. Associate of arts, science, and business administration degrees were offered. The curriculum was grouped into business administration, engineering-science, fine arts, liberal arts, and technical-vocational divisions.

The Texas Education Agency, the Association of Texas Colleges,qqv and the Southern Association of Colleges and Secondary Schools approved or accredited Kilgore College as a two-year college. The library contained approximately forty thousand volumes in 1969. Twelve permanent buildings were in use by 1966. Additions of business, technical-vocational, fine arts, and library buildings were planned.

The college engaged in intercollegiate competition in football, basketball, golf, tennis, and track as a member of the Texas Junior College Football Federation and the Texas Eastern Conference. The Rangerettes, a nationally known precision drill corps of fifty-three co-eds, was organized in 1940.

By the 1974 fall term, 3,169 students were enrolled. The faculty numbered approximately 120. In 1954 Masters retired as president emeritus, and Cruce Stark succeeded him. Upon Stark's resignation in 1964, Randolph C. Watson became president, and he was still president in 1974–1975.

*Kilian, John.

*Killeen, Texas. Killeen, located in Bell County, had a 1950 population of 7,045, a 1960 population of 23,377, and a 1970 population of 35,507, according to the United States census reports. Its rapid growth was attributed to the military installations: Fort Hood,qv Killeen Base, and Robert Gray Army Airfield. In 1967 Killeen had thirty churches, twelve schools, and the newly opened Central Texas College. In 1970 the town reported 414 businesses. For statistical purposes, in 1972 Killeen was included in the Killeen-Temple Standard Metropolitan Statistical Area.qv

Killeen-Temple Standard Metropolitan Statistical Area. The Killeen-Temple Standard Metropolitan Statistical Area, newest of such designated statistical areas in Texas, was created in 1972. It was composed of Bell and Coryell counties, which included a geographical area of 2,090 square miles. The total population in 1970 was 159,794, with 124,483 in Bell County and 35,311 in Coryell County. The two principal cities, both in Bell County, were Temple, with a 1970 population of 33,431, and Killeen, with a 1970 population of

35,507. See also Standard Metropolitan Statistical Areas in Texas.

*Killough Creek.

Kimball, Emmaretta Cara [pseud. Cara Cardelle]. Emmaretta Cara Kimball, daughter of Isaac and Abigail (Stevens) Kimball, was born on April 13, 1829, at Wallingford, Connecticut. She and her two brothers were orphaned at an early age and were educated in the home of an aunt, Anna Stevens, in Massachusetts. She came to Texas in 1851 to join her brother, Justin Aquilla Kimball, a Baptist minister who had a school in Columbus. While living in Columbus, she became acquainted with William B. DeWees,qv and in 1852 she collaborated with him in writing his reminiscences, which were published as Letters from an Early Settler of Texas to a Friend, "compiled by Cara Cardelle."

Emmaretta Kimball married Marquis Lafayette Crawford on June 11, 1855, at Columbus. They later moved to Bell County, Texas, where Crawford died in 1903. They had one son and five daughters. Emmaretta Kimball Crawford died on April 13, 1906, and was buried at Brady, Texas.

BIBLIOGRAPHY: Biographical File, Barker Texas History Center, University of Texas at Austin; Conroe Courier, July 16, 1942.

Kimball, Justin Ford. Justin Ford Kimball, educator and lawyer, was born near Huntsville, Texas, on August 25, 1872, the son of Justin A. and Elizabeth (Ford) Kimball. He received his A.B. and A.M. degrees from Mount Lebanon (Louisiana) College in 1890 and began his teaching career in the rural schools of Louisiana. He later taught in Mexia, Texas.

Kimball continued in various capacities in the public school system of Texas before receiving his M.A. degree at Baylor University in 1899 and his LL.D. degree in 1920. Kimball was the originator of the Blue Cross Plan of Hospitalization, which he began while serving as vice-president of Baylor University and working there on a plan for the installation of the Baylor College of Medicine and Baylor Hospital in Dallas. In recognition of his having originated the American plan of group hospitalization, he was made an honorary life member of the American Hospital Association.

He went into law practice in Waco in 1902 but returned to the field of education in 1905, the year he married Annie Lou Boggess. During the years that followed he served in many professional leadership capacities having to do with the guidance and development of various teaching systems in the state. In 1914 he was superintendent of schools in Dallas. He died on October 7, 1956, in Dallas.

BIBLIOGRAPHY: Who's Who In America (1950).

*Kimball, Texas.

*Kimbell, George C.

Kimbell, Kay. Kay Kimbell was born in Oakwood, Leon County, on June 15, 1886; he was the son of B. B. and Mattie (Jones) Kimbell. He attended the public schools in Whitewright, Grayson

County, but quit school in the eighth grade to work as an office boy in a grain-milling company in Whitewright, where he later founded the Beatrice Milling Company. This firm grew into Kimbell Milling Company, the pilot organization of a diversity of interests that Kimbell later founded or directed. At one time he was reportedly the head of seventy corporations, including flour, feed, and oil mills, grocery chains, an insurance company, and a wholesale grocery firm.

Kay Kimbell was an art collector as well as an industrialist. He established the Kimbell Art Foundation in Fort Worth in 1936, and after his death the foundation was moved into the Kimbell Art Museum,qv which had been provided for in Kimbell's will. The collection of art that Kimbell and his wife amassed included pieces from the prehistoric period to the modern, with outstanding examples of art by English painters from the 18th century as well as European masterpieces from the Renaissance period. The Kimbell's home in Fort Worth was often visited by touring groups before the museum was completed, and the collection was internationally known and acclaimed for its number of definitive works.

Kay Kimbell married Velma Fuller on December 25, 1910. They had no children. He died on April 13, 1964, in Fort Worth and was buried in Whitewright, Texas.

BIBLIOGRAPHY: *Who's Who In America* (1960); Dallas *Herald*, April 14, 1964; Houston *Post*, April 14, 1964.

Kimbell Art Museum. The Kimbell Museum in Fort Worth is a legacy of Kay Kimbell,qv who before his death in 1964 directed that his foundation "build a museum of the first class within Fort Worth." Designed by Louis I. Kahn of Philadelphia, the building is located on a nine-and-one-half-acre site donated by the city of Fort Worth in Amon Carter Square Park, near the Amon Carter Museum of Western Art qv and the Fort Worth Art Center Museum. A series of cycloid vaults enclosing 120,000 square feet of space, the museum employs a unique method of natural lighting; it was built at a cost of $6.5 million and opened in October, 1972.

The Kimbell Art Foundation consisted of the estate of Kay Kimbell; after Kimbell's death his widow, Velma (Fuller) Kimbell, gave her entire share of the community property to the foundation, the sole purpose of which is support of the Kimbell Art Museum. The art collection, acquired over a period of thirty years by the Kimbells, contains works of artists from prehistoric times to the modern period. The foundation's goal has been to acquire definitive works in excellent condition. Examples of the later European Renaissance, nineteenth-century French and American, and British painting in the grand tradition are found in the museum. The Kimbell collection has an international reputation for the fine quality of its art objects.

BIBLIOGRAPHY: *Texas Star*, II (February 4, 1973); Fort Worth *Star-Telegram*, February 17, 1974.

*Kimble, Herbert Simms.

*Kimble County. Kimble County, located on the Edwards Plateau, had an economy centered on sheep and goat raising, hunting, and tourism. Hunters killed over 9,000 deer in the county in 1968. The county ranked fifth in the state in number of Angora goats in 1960. The county supported a library, a hospital built in Junction in 1958, and an airport. In 1965 a private dam was completed on the Llano River. The 1960 population was 3,943; the 1970 population was 3,904, according to the United States census report.

*Kimbro, William.

*Kimbro, Texas.

*Kincaid, Texas.

*Kincaid Creek.

*Kinchelo Creek.

*Kinchelo Peak.

*Kincheloe, William.

*Kinder, Texas.

*Kindred, Texas.

*King, Amon Butler.

King, Henrietta. Henrietta Maria Morse (Chamberlain) King, the only child of Maria (Morse) and Hiram Chamberlain,qv was born on July 21, 1832, in Boonville, Missouri. Her mother's death in 1835 and her father's missionary work in Missouri and Tennessee often made her childhood lonely; as a result she became strongly self-reliant and introspective, and she maintained close attachments with her family. She attended Female Institute of Holly Springs, Mississippi, for two years. She moved to Brownsville, Texas, probably in 1849, for she was residing there when her father organized the Presbyterian church in Brownsville on February 23, 1850. In 1854 she taught briefly at the Rio Grande Female Institute qv before her marriage to Richard King qv on December 10, 1854; they had five children.

In 1855 Henrietta and Richard King established their home on the Santa Gertrudis ranch (*see* King Ranch). Not only was Henrietta King wife and mother, but she also was supervisor of housing and education for the families of Mexican American ranch hands. Upon her husband's death in 1885 she assumed full ownership of his estate, consisting chiefly of 500,000 acres of ranchland between Corpus Christi and Brownsville and $500,000 in debts.

Under Henrietta King's skillful and personal supervision, and with the assistance of her son-in-law, Robert Justus Kleberg,qv the King Ranch was freed of debt and increased in size. By 1895 the 650,000-acre ranch was engaged in experiments in cattle and horse breeding, in range grasses, and in dry and irrigated farming. That year she gave Robert J. Kleberg her power of attorney and increased his ranch responsibilities. The ranch continued to grow, reaching a size of 1,173,000 acres by 1925.

Mrs. King was interested in the settlement of the region between Corpus Christi and Brownsville. About 1900 she offered 75,000 acres of right-of-way to Uriah Lott and Benjamin Franklin Yoakum,qqv who planned to construct the St. Louis, Brownsville, and Mexico Railway. In 1904 she furnished townsites for Kingsville and Raymondville, located along the railway. She founded the Kleberg Town and Improvement Company and the Kingsville Lumber Company to sell land and materials to settlers in Kingsville. As the town grew she invested in the Kingsville Ice and Milling Company, Kingsville Publishing Company, Kingsville Power Company, Gulf Coast Gin Company, and Kingsville Cotton Oil Mill Company. She constructed the First Presbyterian Church building there and also donated land for Baptist, Methodist, Episcopal, and Catholic churches; she constructed a high school and presented it to the town. Among Mrs. King's many charities were donations of land for the Mexican American Industrial Institute and for the Spohn Sanitarium (see Spohn, Arthur Edward). In her last years she provided land and encouragement for the establishment of South Texas State Teachers College (now Texas A&I University).

Henrietta King died on March 31, 1925, on the King Ranch and was buried in Kingsville.

BIBLIOGRAPHY: Tom Lea, *The King Ranch*, I, II (1957); C. R. Wharton, *Texas Under Many Flags* (1930); Corpus Christi *Caller-Times, King Ranch: 100 Years of Ranching* (1953); Biographical Files, Barker Texas History Center, University of Texas at Austin.

*King, Henry C.

*King, John Jefferson.

*King, Richard. According to an affidavit subscribed and sworn to by Richard King before F. J. Parker, United States commissioner, Eastern District of Texas, on April 11, 1870, the date of his birth was July 10, 1824 (not July 10, 1825, as stated in Volume I).

*King, Samuel Alexander.

*King, Valentine Overton.

*King, Wilburn Hill.

*King, William P.

*King, William P. One of the defenders of the Alamo, William Phillip King was born on October 8, 1820 (and was not twenty-four years old in 1836, as stated in Volume I). Family records show that William Phillip's father, John Gladden King, died in 1856, and that his brother, John Gladden King, Jr., was born on January 30, 1826, and was later in service with a Texas Ranger qv company under John Coffee Hays.qv It seems probable, then, that the John G. King from Gonzales who died with William P. King at the Alamo was no relation.

Mrs. Jack Shelton

*King, William P.

*King, Texas. (Coryell County.)

*King, Texas. (Hartley County.)

*King County. King County, in West Texas, had four small communities and four large cattle ranches which accounted for almost the entire area. Although ranching was its major industry, the county also derived income from oil production and from irrigated cotton farming. Nearly thirty-one million barrels of oil were produced from 1943 through 1972. The 1960 population of 640 declined to 464 by 1970, according to the United States census.

*King Creek.

*King Mountain.

*King Ranch. The King Ranch in recent decades has become a diversified enterprise. While continuing to develop its cattle activities, centered around Santa Gertrudis cattle, the ranch derived sizeable incomes from oil and gas production, horse breeding and racing, and timber.

During the 1920's and early 1930's the King Ranch was in serious financial difficulties resulting from poor beef-marketing conditions. Oil was the salvation of the ranch. Beginning in 1925 the ranch and Humble Oil and Refining Company qv negotiated for oil-drilling and mineral-recovery rights on the ranch. Agreement was not reached until 1933 because Humble's top management was uncertain as to the oil potential of this region in Texas. It was the company's geologist William E. Pratt who finally convinced Humble to gamble on the largest oil-lease contract negotiated in the United States. Its subsequent leases with neighboring ranches gave Humble nearly two million acres of mineral rights between Corpus Christi and the Rio Grande. Drilling on the King Ranch was minor until 1945, when the Borregas Field was discovered. After that several major oil and gas discoveries were made on the ranch (see Oil Fields, Major, to 1968). Humble constructed a large refinery in Kingsville to handle its South Texas production.

In the early 1940's the King Ranch began breeding and racing both American quarter horses and English thoroughbreds. After the ranch's Assault raced to win the Triple Crown in 1946 and became for a time racing's all-time money winner, the ranch expanded its horse-breeding operations. A 680-acre bluegrass farm in Kentucky was bought in 1947. Ranch horses have been regular winners since then. In 1954 and 1955, for example, High Gun won $478,500, and in 1955 Rejected entered forty races, won ten, placed second in ten, and won a total of $544,000.

The King Ranch entered the timber business in 1967 when it purchased 50,340 acres of timberland in Harris, Montgomery, Liberty, and San Jacinto counties in Texas for a reported price of $17.6 million.

Cattle operations of the King Ranch have become worldwide. In 1947 its ranch in Chester County, Pennsylvania, was expanded to about 17,000 acres. In 1952 the King Ranch bought ranges in Cuba and Australia. The Cuban ranch encompassed 38,400 acres but was lost during the Cuban revolution. The Australian ranch was expanded in 1958, in conjunction with Australian businessmen, into a three-million-acre range in the northwest region. By 1958 the King Ranch also had cattle ranges of 147,000 acres in Brazil (operated in conjunction with Swift & Co.) and of 22,000 acres in Argentina. All of these ranges, like those of the home ranch itself, were devoted to the development and promotion of Santa Gertrudis cattle.

The King Ranch has long held significant banking and mercantile interests in Kingsville, Texas, a town located in the heart of the ranch. The ranch has long supported the agricultural educational programs of Texas A&I University and Texas A&M University.

Edgar P. Sneed

*Kings Branch.

*Kings Creek.

*King's Fort. *See* Kaufman, Texas.

*King's Highway. *See* Old San Antonio Road.

*King's Memorial State Park.

*Kings Mill, Texas.

*King's Mountain.

Kingsboro, Texas. *See* Kaufman, Texas.

*Kingsbury, Gilbert D.

Kingsbury, W. G. W. G. Kingsbury was born at Booncillo, Oneida County, New York, on November 6, 1823. Educated at the district school and at a seminary at Cazanovia, he studied dentistry in Baltimore. In January, 1846, Kingsbury went to Texas to set up practice. One of his acquaintances there was the Texas Ranger qv Samuel Hamilton Walker,qv whom he accompanied to Mexico in the Mexican War; although he went along as a civilian dentist, he received several wounds during that conflict. After the war he practiced dentistry in various West Texas towns, finally settling in San Antonio, where he was to practice for the next twenty-five years.

Kingsbury's writings concerning Texas caused the governor to appoint him commissioner of immigration, and as long as the Bureau of Immigration existed, he was stationed in St. Louis. He represented several railroads in Europe; with headquarters in London from 1875 to 1884, he also used the title of Texas land and emigration agent. He is credited with having induced thousands of people to immigrate to Texas by his speeches, pamphlets, articles, and books, published in several languages, describing for immigrants all aspects of the state. In 1872 Governor Edmund Jackson Davis qv appointed Kingsbury one of three representatives of Texas at the World's Fair in Vienna in 1073. Kingsbury and his wife, Elizabeth, had three sons. He died on September 11, 1896, and was buried in the City Cemetery in Boerne.

BIBLIOGRAPHY: John Henry Brown, *Indian Wars and Pioneers of Texas* (1896); W. G. Kingsbury (comp.), *Western Texas* (1877).

S. W. Pease

*Kingsbury, Texas.

*Kingsland, Texas.

*Kingston, William.

*Kingston, Texas.

*Kingsville, Texas. Kingsville, seat of Kleberg County, had 288 business establishments in 1970, primarily related to nearby ranching, chemical, and petroleum industries. In addition to the King Ranch qv headquarters, a large Humble Oil qv refinery, a Celanese plastics-processing plant, a naval auxiliary air station, and Texas A&I University, Kingsville had a one-hundred-bed hospital, eleven schools, thirty-seven churches representing fifteen denominations, a newspaper, a radio station, and a seventeen thousand-volume library. Recent city projects included street and water improvements, the completion of a chamber of commerce building in 1956, a new high school in 1964, and new facilities for the police in 1967. The 1960 population of 25,297 increased by 1970 to 28,711, according to the United States census.

Kingsville Naval Auxiliary Air Station. *See* Naval Auxiliary Air Station, Kingsville, Texas.

*Kinkler, Texas.

*Kinney, Henry Lawrence.

*Kinney County. Kinney County, in southwest Texas, had an economy based primarily on sheep and goat ranching; in 1968 the county produced 955,000 pounds of wool. Intensive farming became possible in the 1960's with the irrigation of 10,000 acres; feed grains, wheat, and winter vegetables were grown. Alamo Village qv and guest ranches attracted tourists, and the county's large deer population attracted hunters. The 1960 population of 2,452 decreased by 1970 to 2,006, according to the United States census.

*Kinney and Uvalde Railway Company. *See* Asphalt Belt Railway Company.

*Kinsolving, George Herbert.

*Kiomatia, Texas.

*Kiowa-Apache Indians.

*Kiowa Creek.

*Kiowa Indians.

*Kiowa Peak.

*Kirby, Helen Marr (Swearingen). Helen Marr (Swearingen) Kirby died on October 29 (not November 29, as stated in Volume I), 1921.

*Kirby, John Henry. While John Henry Kirby was an extremely successful lumberman and an acknowledged philanthropist, it is not true (as stated in Volume I) that labor troubles were absent while he was head of his companies. Labor difficulties plagued the Kirby Lumber Company in East Texas in 1903 when payrolls were not met; conditions were somewhat relieved when the company went into receivership from 1904 to 1909 because of financial difficulties. After Kirby regained full control of his company in 1909, he actively opposed the formation of unions by his workers, instructing his managers to do everything necessary to discourage workers from attending meetings. He was largely successful in defeating a viable labor organization for lumber workers.

BIBLIOGRAPHY: George T. Morgan, Jr., "The Gospel of Wealth Goes South: John Henry Kirby and Labor's Struggle for Self-Determination, 1901–1916," *Southwestern Historical Quarterly,* LXXV (1971–1972).

*Kirby, Robert Harper.

*Kirby, Texas. Kirby, in Bexar County, had 680 residents in 1960 and 2,558 residents in 1970. *See also* San Antonio Standard Metropolitan Statistical Area.

*Kirby Lake. Construction of Kirby Lake was started in 1927, and the dam was completed in 1928. This project was built to supplement the water supply from Lake Abilene. In 1967 Lake Kirby had a capacity of 7,620 acre-feet and a surface area of 740 acres at elevation 1,785 feet above mean sea level. The drainage area above the dam was forty-four square miles.

BIBLIOGRAPHY: Texas Water Commission, *Bulletin 6408* (1964).

Seth D. Breeding

*Kirby-Smith, Edmund. *See* Smith, Edmund Kirby.

*Kirbyville, Texas. Kirbyville, in central Jasper County, reported seventy-one businesses in 1970. The 1960 population was 1,660, and the 1970 population was 1,869, according to the United States census.

*Kirk, Texas. (Bexar County.)

*Kirk, Texas. (Limestone County.)

*Kirkendell Creek.

Kirkland, Olea Forrest. Olea Forrest Kirkland was born near Mist, Arkansas, on November 24, 1892. He attended local secondary schools, then Hendrix College in Conway, Arkansas, for a year. After attending commercial art school in Battle Creek, Michigan, he was drafted into the military service during World War I. Discharged in 1919 after serving in France, he settled in Dallas, where he was employed by an engraving firm. In 1925 he established an advertising-art studio which specialized in drawings of industrial machinery for catalogue illustrations.

Kirkland had begun to paint with watercolors while in the army and continued to paint landscapes and scenes of Dallas slums whenever time permitted. In 1932 he became interested in paleontology and was soon an avid fossil collector. On collecting trips, Indian artifacts as well as fossils were often found, and archeology became his paramount interest.

In 1933 Kirkland was introduced to Indian rock paintings (*see* Rock Art, Indian) when he visited the Paint Rock site on the Concho River. He returned the following summer to make exact scale copies in color of these pictographs. Over the next eight years he copied rock art at more than eighty sites.

The 160 watercolor copies of rock art which Kirkland painted were reproduced in 1967 in *The Rock Art of Texas Indians* (with text by W. W. Newcomb, Jr.). The originals are in the collection of the Texas Memorial Museum qv at the University of Texas at Austin. Kirkland also wrote papers on rock art, including a number of articles for the *Bulletin of the Texas Archeological and Paleontological Society.*qv

He was president and a founder of the Dallas Archeological Society, a director of the West Texas Historical and Scientific Society,qv a regional vice-president of the Texas Archeological and Paleontological Society,qv and a Fellow of the Texas Academy of Science.qv

Kirkland died on April 2, 1942, following a heart attack. He was survived by his wife, Lula (Mardis) Kirkland, and a son and daughter by a previous marriage.

W. W. Newcomb, Jr.

*Kirkland, Texas.

*Kirkley, Bertha.

*Kirkpatrick, Elbert W.

*Kironona Indians. The Kironona (Kiranona, Kikanona, Kirona, Kironuona) Indians are known from one document (Douay narrative) of the La Salle Expedition,qv which indicates that in the late seventeenth century these Indians lived inland well to the north or northeast of Matagorda Bay, probably near the Brazos River. They were not mentioned by Henri Joutel qv (same expedition), as has sometimes been stated (and as stated in Volume I), and it is impossible to identify Douay's Kironona with any one of the Indian groups named by Joutel. A. S. Gatschet was firmly convinced that Kironona was another form of the name Karankawa. The Kironona area indicated by Douay, however, was rather far inland from the Karankawa. Furthermore, the Kironona were described as meeting La Salle's party with ears of corn in their hands, which seems to indicate that they were an agricultural people. This does not agree with what is known about the culture of the specific tribe later known as Karankawa. The affiliations of the Kironona have yet to be determined.

BIBLIOGRAPHY: I. J. Cox (ed.), *The Journeys of Réné Robert Cavelier, Sieur de La Salle,* I (1905); A. S. Gatschet, *The Karankawa Indians, the Coast People of Texas* (1891); F. W. Hodge (ed.), *Handbook of American Indians,* I (1907); J. G. Shea, *Discovery and Exploration of the Mississippi Valley* (1903).

T. N. Campbell

*Kirtly, Texas.

*Kirvin, Texas.

Kirwin, James Martin. James Martin Kirwin, son of Patrick and Mary (Ryan) Kirwin, was born on July 1, 1872, in Circleville, Ohio. He attended St. Joseph's College in Bardstown, Kentucky, and received a B.A. degree from St. Mary's College, Lebanon, Kentucky, in 1890. His theological training was received at Mount St. Mary's of the West, Cincinnati, Ohio, where he was ordained into the Catholic priesthood on June 15, 1895. In August, 1896, he was appointed rector of the cathedral parish in Galveston, Texas.

Kirwin quickly became active in civic affairs in

the Galveston area, an uncommon practice for priests at that time. He first attracted public attention and appreciation for his special efforts during the yellow fever epidemic of 1897. At the outbreak of the Spanish-American War in 1898 he helped to form a volunteer regiment and was elected its chaplain, serving during the war with the rank of captain. After the war he was chaplain of the Camp No. 7 group of the United Spanish War Veterans.

Much of Kirwin's prominence came after the Galveston Flood qv of 1900. He helped organize a committee of public safety to restore order, drafted the order putting the city under martial law, supervised the disposal of the dead, and served as a member of the central relief committee that aided surviving flood victims. He delivered the opening prayer at the cornerstone ceremonies for the seawall in 1902 and officiated at the completion of the seawall in 1905. In 1901 Kirwin was cited by the fire department for bravery in his efforts to rescue persons in a great fire that threatened the entire city; afterwards he conducted a study of fire protection needs for the city. He was active in the American Prison Relief Society during this period.

In 1907 the city of Galveston appealed to Kirwin to mediate the Southern Pacific dock strike after the company's importation of Negro laborers threatened major violence. Kirwin ended the strike by securing concessions on both sides.

In 1909 Kirwin organized the Home Protective League, which succeeded in removing saloons from residential areas of Galveston. The league lobbied in the state legislature for a law empowering cities to restrict saloons. The crusade and the law received national publicity in the temperance movement (see Prohibition Movement).

In 1911 Kirwin became vicar general for the Galveston diocese and became president and professor of St. Mary's Seminary at La Porte, Texas. When American troops landed in France in World War I, General John J. Pershing called on Kirwin to serve as chaplain of his troops, but his diocesan duties prevented his acceptance of the call. He vigorously supported the war effort as chairman of the "four-minute men" speakers in Galveston and as chairman of the home services activities of the Galveston chapter of the American Red Cross.

During the war and in the early 1920's Kirwin was outspoken against extremists who would violate the Constitution in the name of patriotism. He was especially critical of the Ku Klux Klan.qv (See also Cohen, Henry.) In 1922 Pope Pius XI gave him the title of monsignor, and in 1923 he received an honorary Doctor of Laws degree from Notre Dame University. Kirwin died suddenly on January 24, 1926. He was buried in Circleville, Ohio.

BIBLIOGRAPHY: George T. Elmendorf (comp.), *Memoirs of Monsignor J. M. Kirwin* (1928); Galveston *Daily News*, January 25, 1926.

James C. Martin, Jr.

*Kit, Texas.

*Kit Carson Creek.

*Kit Mountain.

*Kitalou, Texas.

*Kitchai Indians.

*Kitchens Creek.

*Kittle, Texas.

*Kittrell, Norman Goree.

Kittrell, Pleasant Williams. Pleasant Williams Kittrell was born in Granville County, North Carolina, on April 13, 1805. He attended the University of North Carolina and graduated from Jefferson Medical College in Philadelphia in 1826. He practiced medicine in North Carolina and in Greensboro, Alabama, where he had moved in 1838. He served in both the North Carolina and Alabama legislatures. In 1850 he moved to Texas and settled near Huntsville. He continued to practice medicine while engaging in planting. In 1855 and 1857 he was elected to the lower house of the Sixth and Seventh Texas legislatures, representing Grimes, Walker, and Madison counties.

In both legislatures Kittrell was chairman of the House committee on education when the legislature took up the matter of higher education in Texas. The Senate had considered creating a state college in 1855 and passed an enabling bill in 1857. But the House of Representatives was split between the "No University," the "One University," and the "Two University" advocates, and they argued the matter to death. Kittrell and his committee were "One University" men, but they fell barely short of a House majority when the "No's" and "Two's" joined to defeat the committee resolution which would have at least committed the legislature in principle to creation of a "Texas University."

Kittrell died on September 25, 1867, of yellow fever during the yellow fever epidemic that struck Huntsville that summer.

BIBLIOGRAPHY: H. Y. Benedict, *A Source Book Relating to the History of the University of Texas* (n.d.).

Kittrell, William Henderson (Bill). William Henderson Kittrell, Texas political personality, was born on April 29, 1894, in Alexander, Erath County, the son of William and Laura Jane (Henderson) Kittrell. He was reared in Cisco, Texas, and graduated from high school there. He later attended the University of Texas. His grandfather, Pleasant Williams Kittrell qv was an early-day physician and legislator.

Kittrell spent most of his life working for the Democratic party qv and Democratic politicians, but he found his niche as a friend of the political great rather than as an officeholder. It was said of him in the 1940's that he knew every political figure of consequence in the United States. He was a political crony of James A. Farley, the former Democratic national chairman and postmaster general. He was a personal friend of President Franklin D. Roosevent. As secretary of the Texas delegation to the Democratic convention of 1932, he was active in the negotiations which switched the Texas and California delegations to Roosevelt, giving him the nomination. Kittrell also knew Presidents Harry S.

Truman, Dwight D. Eisenhower,qv John F. Kennedy, and Lyndon B. Johnson.qv On a northbound Katy train early in World War II, Kittrell introduced Eisenhower, then a lieutenant colonel, to Sid Richardson,qv the Fort Worth oilman who was to become one of Eisenhower's principal backers for the presidency.

Kittrell operated a newspaper clipping service in Dallas, where he had moved as a young man, but he also worked as a lobbyist, often without pay. He shouldered much of the actual work of putting through the constitutional amendment and the state appropriation that made the Texas Centennial Exposition possible (see Texas Centennial). He helped to locate it in Dallas and later served as general manager. He also accepted occasional presidential assignments. During World War II he was a senior lend-lease mission officer for the State Department in Libya, Turkey, Egypt, Lebanon, and Israel. He was a transportation officer at the San Francisco meeting which set up the United Nations in 1945. In the early part of the Kennedy Administration, he was consultant to the Office of Civilian Defense Mobilization.

Always a worker behind the scenes at Texas Democratic conventions, Kittrell helped crush an anti-Roosevelt movement called the Texas Regulars at the Dallas convention in 1944. In that same year he was elected secretary to the Texas Democratic Executive Committee. After the split between conservative and liberal elements of the Texas party, Kittrell was identified with the liberal wing, though his friendships spanned the gap. He died in Dallas on April 24, 1966.

BIBLIOGRAPHY: Dallas *Morning News*, February 12, 1961, April 25, 1966.

Paul Crume

*Kittrell, Texas.

*Klaerner, Christian.

*Kleberg, Marcellus E.

Kleberg, Richard Mifflin. Richard Mifflin Kleberg, son of Alice Gertrudis (King) and Robert Justus Kleberg,qv was born on the King Ranch qv on November 18, 1887. He attended public schools in Corpus Christi. After graduation from the University of Texas in Austin in 1911, he studied law there and was admitted to the Bar. Kleberg was active in the management of the King Ranch from 1913 to 1924 as foreman and part owner. He was an expert marksman and horseman, and in his early life he was an active rodeo participant.

He was elected in November 1931 as a Democrat to the Seventy-second Congress to fill the vacancy created by the death of Republican Harry McLeary Wurzbach.qv Kleberg was reelected to the Seventy-third Congress and to five succeeding congresses before being defeated in 1944 by John Lyle. He was known as the "Cowboy Congressman." Kleberg selected Lyndon Baines Johnson qv as his first administrative assistant, providing Johnson with the opportunity to begin his own political career. Sam Houston Johnson succeeded his older brother as Kleberg's administrative assistant in 1935.

Kleberg served on the committee on agriculture during his entire tenure in Congress (November 24, 1931, to January 3, 1945). He sponsored the bill to establish the Farm Credit Administration and was also author of the Duck Stamp Law. He sponsored the Migratory Bird Conservation Act and worked for laws to combat the pink bollworm.qv In the early New Deal days Kleberg went along with the Democratic leadership, supporting the bank moratorium and establishment of the Reconstruction Finance Corporation, but he soon opposed most New Deal legislation. In 1943 he was against price controls on live beef and began to oppose President Franklin D. Roosevelt; in 1944 he endorsed Thomas E. Dewey for president. Along with his agricultural and ranching interests, Kleberg was well informed on military affairs.

After retirement from Congress, he served as chairman of the board of King Ranch and as a member of the State Game and Fish Commission (1951–1955). He died on a visit to Hot Springs, Arkansas, on May 8, 1955, and was buried in Chamberlain Burial Park in Kingsville, Texas.

BIBLIOGRAPHY: *Biographical Directory of the American Congress, 1774–1961* (1961); *Congressional Directory* (1931–1945); San Antonio *Express*, April 24, 1932; Sam Houston Johnson, *My Brother Lyndon* (1969); Alfred Steinberg, *Sam Johnson's Boy* (1968).

Thomas L. Miller

*Kleberg, Robert Justus.

*Kleberg, Robert Justus.

Kleberg, Robert Justus, Jr. Robert Justus Kleberg, Jr., son of Alice Gertrudis (King) and Robert Justus Kleberg,qv was born March 29, 1896, in Corpus Christi. He was the grandson of Henrietta (Chamberlain) and Richard King,qqv founder of the King Ranch qv in South Texas. He began his ranching career there in 1916 and managed the ranch after his father's death in 1932. He was named president of the operation when it became a family corporation in 1935.

In addition to the King Ranch, estimated to be between eight hundred thousand and nine hundred thousand acres in six South Texas counties, Kleberg also managed holdings in Florida, Kentucky, and Pennsylvania in the United States, and in Brazil, Argentina, Spain, Morocco, and Australia. He is credited with the development of the first United States breed of beef cattle, the Santa Gertrudis, perfected over thirty years of breeding. He became known in the field of agriculture with his development of grazing grasses. He received an honorary Doctor of Agricultural Science degree (1941) from Texas A&M College (now Texas A&M University) and a Doctor of Science degree (1967) from the University of Wisconsin, where he had done undergraduate work.

Under Kleberg's direction, the King Ranch also developed thoroughbred racetrack winners, averaging $825,000 a year in purse money. The best known winner was Assault, the Triple Crown winner in 1946, and Middleground and Bold Venture, both Kentucky Derby winners.

Kleberg had other business, banking, and railroad interests. He was married to Helen Campbell on March 2, 1926; they had one daughter. He died October 13, 1974, in a Houston hospital; he was buried at the King Ranch.

BIBLIOGRAPHY: *Who's Who In America* (1968); Austin *American-Statesman*, October 15, 1974; Biographical File, Barker Texas History Center, University of Texas at Austin.

*Kleberg, Rudolph.

*Kleberg, Texas. Kleberg, in Dallas County, grew steadily during the 1950's and 1960's, with a population of 3,572 reported in 1960 and 4,768 in 1970, according to the United States census. *See also* Dallas Standard Metropolitan Statistical Area.

*Kleberg County. Kleberg County, with a ranching, farming, and petrochemical economy, is located on the Gulf coastal bend; its 850 square miles of area includes 236 square miles of submerged lands involved in the Tidelands Controversy.qv Between 1926 and January 1, 1973, the county produced 254,442,852 barrels of oil. Tourist attractions included the King Ranch qv headquarters, Baffin Bay, and the Museum of Frontier America. Texas A&I University and the Presbyterian Pan American School are located in the county. The 1960 population was 30,052; it increased by 1970 to 33,166, according to the United States census.

*Klegg, Texas. [This title in Volume I should be eliminated. No post office with the name Klegg, Texas (in Jim Wells County, as stated in Volume I), ever existed in the state of Texas, according to the Civil Archives Division of the National Archives, General Services Administration, Washington, D.C. It is probable that this entry in Volume I was confused with Clegg, Texas qv (in Live Oak County), which was named for George Clegg, a rancher there. Ed.]

Kleiber, Joseph. Joseph Kleiber, son of John George and Teresa (Zola) Kleiber, was born at Strasbourg, Alsace-Lorraine, France, on May 28, 1833. He immigrated to the United States, lived in New Orleans for a time, and then moved to Point Isabel (now Port Isabel), Texas. In 1856 he married Emma Henrietta Butler; they had five children. Kleiber purchased a drugstore in Brownsville, Texas, in 1860; he continued to operate it while he served as Confederate postmaster in Brownsville. During the Federal occupation of Brownsville he moved his family to Matamoros, Mexico; there he sold merchandise to Confederate forces and engaged in the contraband cotton trade. After the Civil War Kleiber reestablished his mercantile business and his home in Brownsville; he soon became associated with Simon Celaya (*see* San Román, José), Humphrey Eugene Woodhouse, John Salmon (Rip) Ford,qqv and others in building the Rio Grande Railroad between Port Isabel and Brownsville (*see* Port Isabel and Rio Grande Valley Railway) and became the company's secretary and auditor. In August, 1874, Kleiber resigned his railroad posts and became a real estate dealer in central Texas. He died in Austin on August 13, 1877, and was buried in the Old City Cemetery in Brownsville. Writing in English, Spanish, and French, Kleiber left a collection of letters, dated October 11, 1860, to July 10, 1877, which give a picture of the life and times of South Texas during that period.

BIBLIOGRAPHY: Joseph Kleiber Collection (MS., Archives, University of Texas at Austin Library); J. L. Allhands, *Gringo Builders* (1931); Tom Lea, *The King Ranch*, I, II (1957); LeRoy P. Graf, Economic History of the Lower Rio Grande Valley, 1820–1875 (Ph.D. dissertation, Harvard University, 1942).

John H. Hunter

*Klein Branch.

*Kleis, Theobald G. [Out of alphabetical order on page 969, Volume I.]

Klepper, Frank Earl. Frank Earl Klepper, landscape painter, lithographer, and etcher, was born in Plano, Texas, on May 3, 1890, the son of J. B. and Mary Caroline (Cunningham) Klepper. After early training with private instructors, he studied at the Art Institute in Chicago and at the American Art Training Center in Bellevue, France; while in Paris he was also a student of the American artist Henry B. Lachman. For his work Klepper received various medals and awards, including the 1920 Texas Artists gold medal, the Woman's Forum Medal at the 1922 Texas Artists exhibit, and the purchase prize at the 1928 Texas Artists showing. Klepper won awards at the 1929 San Antonio Art League's Edgar B. Davis qv Competition and at the 1930 (Tinker Prize, landscape) and 1932 Southern States Art League's competitive exhibitions. One of his bookplate designs merited the 1932 Litche prize. Klepper is represented in the collections of the Woman's Forum in Dallas, in Plano and McKinney high schools, in the Chicago Vanderpoel Memorial Collection, in the permanent works at the Fine Arts Club of Arkansas in Little Rock, and in the Dallas Museum of Fine Arts.qv He died in 1954.

BIBLIOGRAPHY: Witte Memorial Museum Files, San Antonio, Texas; *Who's Who in American Art* (1953).

Caroline Remy

*Klimek, Texas.

Klingelhoefer, Johann Jost. Johann Jost Klingelhoefer was born on July 11, 1802, in Eibelshausen, Nassau, Germany, the son of Johann Jost Klingelhoefer. Educated as a surveyor, he studied at Schmalkalden and at Dresden. He and his first wife, Elisabet Weil, had four children; after her death he married Elisabet Heiland, by whom he had two children. The family sailed to the United States under the auspices of the German Emigration Company, the Adelsverein,qv and settled in Fredericksburg in 1847.

He soon began to participate in the political activities of Fredericksburg. He was forced to give up the elective office of chief justice and probate judge of Gillespie County in 1850, when Lyman Wight,qv his Mormon opponent, contested the election; however, he was elected to the office in 1851, later serving as justice of the peace from 1852 to 1853 and from 1856 to 1861. In 1853 he helped to organize and was a charter member of the *Reform Verein*, a local discussion club which strove to interest its members in political and agricultural matters through public debates and discussions and the reading of newspapers, magazines, and books. He was a staunch Unionist during the 1850's and 1860's. He died on May 1, 1886, and was buried in the old section of the City Cemetery in Fredericksburg.

BIBLIOGRAPHY: Rudolph Leopold Biesele, *The History of the German Settlements in Texas, 1831–1861* (1930); Robert Penniger (ed.), *Fest-Ausgabe zum 50-jährigen Jubiläum der Gründung der Stadt Friedrichsburg* (1896); Gillespie County Historical Society, *Pioneers in God's Hills* (1960); Gillespie County Probate Court Minutes, Vol. A; Solms-Braunfels Archives (Typescript, Archives, University of Texas at Austin Library).

Esther L. Mueller

*Klondike, Texas.

*Klump, Texas.

*Knapp, Bradford.

*Knapp, Seaman Asahel.

*Knapp, Texas. It is inconclusive that Knapp, in Scurry County, was named for a pioneer named Benjamin Knapp (as stated in Volume I), and although it has been suggested that the town was named for another man, George Knapp, no evidence has been presented for either of these claims. The original name for the townsite was "Bison," but this name was rejected by postal authorities when the post office was established in 1890, with Alf Sloan as the first postmaster of Knapp. Herman von Roeder became postmaster in 1912 (not 1900), when the post office was located in his general store. The post office was closed in 1959.

BIBLIOGRAPHY: Scurry County Historical Survey Committee, *Historical Markers in Scurry County* (1969).

Knickerbocker, Hubert Renfro. Hubert Renfro Knickerbocker, internationally known writer and Pulitzer Prize-winning journalist, was born in Yoakum, Texas, on January 31, 1898, the son of Rev. Hubert Delancey and Julia Catherine (Opdenweyer) Knickerbocker. After graduation from Southwestern University in 1917, he served briefly with the United States Army on the Mexican border and then delivered milk in Austin. In 1919 he went to Columbia University to study psychiatry.

Knickerbocker's career in journalism began in 1920, when he became a reporter for the Newark, New Jersey, *Morning Ledger*; in 1922 he reported for the New York *Evening Post* and the New York *Sun*, then returned to Texas as journalism department chairman at Southern Methodist University for the 1922–1923 term. He went to Munich, Germany, with the intention of studying psychiatry, but historic events and his reporter's instinct intervened. He was a witness to the Beer Hall Putsch of Adolph Hitler on November 8–9, 1923. Shortly afterward he became assistant Berlin correspondent for the New York *Evening Post* and the Philadelphia *Public Ledger*. In 1928 he became chief Berlin correspondent for these two newspapers and continued in that capacity until 1941. His friends tell the story that he secured his promotion by introducing his predecessor, Dorothy Thompson, to Sinclair Lewis and by promoting their subsequent romance and marriage. From 1925 to 1941 Knickerbocker

was also a European correspondent for International News Service.

From 1923 to 1933 Knickerbocker based his activities in Berlin. Only from 1925 to 1927 did he divide his time between Berlin and Moscow, where he reported for INS. In Germany he became an important public figure, publishing six books in German and writing columns in two major German newspapers, *Vossische Zeitung* and *Berliner Tageblatt*. He circulated in highest German political, social, and cultural circles. His critical views on Soviet economy and foreign affairs were generally well received in Germany, especially his *Der rote Handel lockt* (1931), which was published in English as *The Red Trade Menace* (1931). In 1931 Knickerbocker won the Pulitzer Prize for his articles describing and analyzing the Soviet Five-Year Plan. His strong opinions on Hitler and the Nazi movement, however, made his position difficult when Hitler became a major political figure in 1932. With the Nazi take-over in 1933, Knickerbocker was deported and forced to report on Germany from beyond the frontiers of Hitler's Third Reich.

In 1933 Knickerbocker made an extensive research tour of Europe; he interviewed hundreds of public figures and many heads of state, asking the question beginning to trouble most Europeans and some Americans: "Will war come to Europe?" In his book *Will War Come to Europe?* (1934) he forecast a general European war. The remainder of Knickerbocker's life was spent witnessing, reporting, and interpreting the events foreshadowing and encompassing World War II. He covered the Italo-Abyssinian War in 1935–1936, the Spanish Civil War in 1936–1937, the early phases of the Sino-Japanese War in 1937, the *Anschluss* and the Czech crisis in 1938, the defeat of France in 1940, and the Battle of Britain in 1940.

In March and April, 1940, Knickerbocker devoted himself to the American lecture circuit, strongly urging active American support of the war against the Axis Powers. Repeatedly in late 1940 and in 1941 he toured the United States declaring that "we should go into war today." On April 24, 1941, he spoke on the University of Texas campus, and on November 20, 1941, after a speech at Southern Methodist University, he exchanged heated remarks with students who opposed United States entry into the war. Knickerbocker summed up his views in the book *Is Tomorrow Hitler's?* (1941).

In 1941 Knickerbocker went to work for the Chicago *Sun* as its chief foreign correspondent in the Far East and South Pacific. In 1942 he followed Allied troops into North Africa, reporting for the *Sun* and acting as the official correspondent for the 1st Division of the U.S. Army. During the remainder of the war he reported the European theater of military operations.

After the war Knickerbocker turned to radio journalism, going to work for Station WOR, Newark, New Jersey. He was on assignment for WOR with a team of journalists touring Southeast Asia when they were all killed in a plane crash near Bombay, India, on July 12, 1949.

Knickerbocker was married first to Laura Patrick in 1918, and they had one son; his second marriage was to Agnes Schjoldager, and they had three daughters.

BIBLIOGRAPHY: New York *Times*, May 5, 1931, July 13, 1949; Dallas *Morning News*, July 13, 1949; *Who's Who In America* (1948); Biographical File, Barker Texas History Center, University of Texas at Austin.

Edgar P. Sneed

*Knickerbocker, Texas.

*Knight, James.

*Knight, Texas. (Dallas County.)

*Knight, Texas. (Polk County.)

*Knights of the Golden Circle.

Knights of Labor. *See* Labor Organizations in Texas.

*Knights of Pythias.

Knights of San Jacinto. *See* Order of San Jacinto.

*Knights of the White Camelia.

*Knippa, Texas.

*Knobb, Texas.

*Knobbs Creek.

*Knobview, Texas.

*Knost, Texas.

Knott, John Francis. John Francis Knott, political cartoonist, was born on December 7, 1878, in Austria, the son of Francis Joseph and Anna (Hajek) Knott. At the age of five he came with his parents to Sioux City, Iowa, where he was educated in the public schools. As a youth he became an apprentice draftsman in a Chicago architect's office. He also attended night classes, including one in life drawing at the Holme School of Illustration (subsequently the Chicago Academy of Art), which then included the cartoonist John T. McCutcheon and the type designer Fred Gowdy among its instructors.

Knott moved to Dallas, Texas, in 1901 to work for a commercial engraver, and four years later he began his connection with the Dallas *Morning News*,qv first as a commercial artist but mainly as its staff cartoonist. He was married on February 22, 1907, to Carrie Louise Bowen of Dallas, and they had four children. He took a leave in 1910 to study drawing and painting in the Royal Academy of Art in Munich, Germany. He returned to the newspaper in Dallas in 1912, where he stayed for the remainder of his life.

Knott's daily cartoons were widely reproduced in magazines and other publications in the United States and abroad. His most memorable creation is the character of "Old Man Texas," a typical figure of a bygone era that has attained semi-legendary stature. Originals of more than fifteen thousand of Knott's cartoons are extant, the largest collection being in the archives of the Dallas Historical Society in the Hall of State qqv at Dallas. He received a Pulitzer Prize Committee citation in 1936, the National Headliners Club award in 1939, and the National Safety Council citation in 1941. Baylor University conferred an honorary degree of Doctor of Literature upon him in 1920. He was a member of the Philosophical Society of Texas.qv

Knott was an accomplished painter in oils, notably portraits, but he left only a limited number of completed examples of such work. He was greatly interested in art education and assisted many younger artists in his years as an instructor in the Dallas Public Evening School at the N. R. Crozier Technical High School. He died on February 16, 1963, in Dallas, and he was buried in Restland Cemetery.

BIBLIOGRAPHY: *Who's Who In America* (1940); Dallas *Morning News*, October 1, 1935, February 17, 1963.

Sam Acheson

*Knott, Texas.

*Know-Nothing Party.

*Knox, John Armoy.

*Knox City, Texas. Knox City, in Knox County, listed 1,805 inhabitants in 1960; in 1970 there were 1,536 inhabitants and fifty-five businesses.

*Knox County. Knox County, in northwest Texas, was largely farming and ranching country. Some thirty-eight thousand acres produced cotton, wheat, grain sorghums, guar (a forage crop), and truck crops, which accounted for a large part of the $11 million farm income averaged between 1970 and 1975. In 1966 the county harvested 16,818 bales of cotton; in the 1968–1969 season the county's eight gins ginned a total of 21,919 bales of cotton. Over thirty-seven million barrels of oil were produced between 1946 and 1972 in the oil fields in southern Knox County. The United States census reported a 1970 population of 5,972; this was a decline from the 1960 figure of 7,857, continuing the population decline that began prior to 1940.

Koasati Indians. The Koasati (Conchata, Coosada, Cooshate, Coushatta) Indians are Muskhogean-speaking Indians who originally lived in Alabama. In the 1790's one group of Koasati crossed the Mississippi and settled on the lower Red River in Louisiana. Some of these later moved farther west to the vicinity of present Opelousas and then on to the Sabine River. In the early nineteenth century some of the western Louisiana Koasati entered Texas and settled on the lower reaches of the Neches and Trinity rivers. Batista and Colete, two of their villages, were frequently mentioned in documents of the first half of the nineteenth century. Diseases reduced their numbers, and eventually some of the Koasati united with the Alabama, who had also settled in southeastern Texas. The others returned to Louisiana and acquired lands in present Allen and Jefferson parishes, where their descendants still live.

The Koasati who joined the Alabama in Texas went to the Alabama-Coushatta Indian Reservation qv that was established in present Polk County in 1854. In 1836 the Koasati who had remained in Alabama were removed with the Creeks to Indian Territory, and their descendants now live in central

Oklahoma. Today the Koasati of Louisiana outnumber those in both Oklahoma and Texas. A detailed ethnohistory of the Texas Koasati has yet to be written. *See also* Alabama-Coushatta Indians.

BIBLIOGRAPHY: W. E. S. Folsom-Dickerson, *The White Path* (1965); F. W. Hodge (ed.), *Handbook of American Indians*, I (1907); D. Jacobson, "The Origin of the Koasati Community of Louisiana," *Ethnohistory*, 7 (1960); H. Smither, "The Alabama Indians of Texas," *Southwestern Historical Quarterly*, XXXVI (1932–1933); J. R. Swanton, *Early History of the Creek Indians and Their Neighbors* (1922), *Social Organization and Social Usages of the Indians of the Creek Confederacy* (1925), *Religious Beliefs and Medical Practices of the Creek Indians* (1925), and *The Indians of the Southwestern United States* (1946).

T. N. Campbell

*Koehl Mill, Texas.

Koenigheim, Marcus. Marcus Koenigheim was born in Westphalia, Germany, about 1828. He immigrated to Philadelphia and then moved to San Antonio. During the Civil War he returned to Philadelphia where he married Elizabeth Levyson; they had eight children. Koenigheim returned to San Antonio and engaged in a prosperous mercantile business.

In 1870 he loaned fifteen hundred dollars to Bart DeWitt, who purchased land in West Texas to lay out a town which he named St. Angela, but within five years he was unable to pay back the loan. Koenigheim took the land as payment and became one of the first town builders of St. Angela, which soon became known as San Angela, and finally as San Angelo. He was murdered by a burglar on October 9, 1893, at his home in San Antonio. *See also* San Angelo, Texas.

BIBLIOGRAPHY: San Angelo *Standard-Times*, February 20, 1968.

*Koerth, Texas.

*Kokernot, David L. David Levi Kokernot, son of Levi Moses and Elizabeth (Cohen van der Beugel) Kokernot, was born in Amsterdam, Holland, on December 28 (not December 12, as stated in Volume I), 1805. He was married only to Caroline Josephine Dittmar (not Maley, although she was the daughter of Mrs. Julia Ann Maley), who survived him by seven years; it was his son, L. M. Kokernot (not himself, as stated in Volume I), who married Sarah Littlefield in 1866. In 1835 he lived within the present limits of Baytown (not in Nacogdoches, where he visited only occasionally). He served in the battle of Concepción and the Grass Fight qqv as a private (not a second lieutenant), but he was commissioned an officer later, on November 29, 1835. From 1838 to 1849 he was a resident of Liberty County; he moved to Columbus in 1849 and to Gonzales County in 1853 (not 1855). During the Civil War he served briefly in Louisiana and later in a Lavaca County home guard unit (but not in Terry's Texas Rangers,qv in which his son served). David L. Kokernot died on December 10, 1892, and was buried in the Kokernot family cemetery in the Big Hill district of southeastern Gonzales County (not in the city of Gonzales, as stated in Volume I).

Kent Gardien

Kokernot, Herbert Lee. Herbert Lee Kokernot was born in Gonzales County on December 28, 1867, son of L. M. and Sarah (Littlefield) Kokernot, and grandson of David L. Kokernot.qv He graduated from Moulton (Texas) Academy and studied at Southwestern University and the University of Texas. From 1888 to 1897 Kokernot engaged in the mercantile business in Gonzales. On October 28, 1891, he married Elizabeth Vanham of Gonzales; they had three children.

Herbert Kokernot acquired the practical and business skills of cattle ranching on his father's ranch in Gonzales County. In 1883 Kokernot's father acquired ranch holdings in Brewster County in partnership with James Francis Miller qv and W. B. Sayers. In 1897 the younger Kokernot bought out the partners and operated Brewster and Lubbock county ranches in association with his uncle, John W. Kokernot, until 1915. A few years later his son, Herbert Lee Kokernot, Jr., took charge of the 06 Ranch in Brewster, Jeff Davis, and Pecos counties (*see* Kokernot Ranch).

In 1907 Kokernot settled in San Antonio. He was president of the Southwestern Cattle Raisers' Association (*see* Texas and Southwestern Cattle Raisers' Association), president of the Alpine-Marfa Highland Hereford Association, and president and co-founder of the Texas Livestock Marketing Association.

He served as a regent of the Agricultural and Mechanical College of Texas (now Texas A&M University), a trustee of Baylor University, and president of the board of San Marcos Baptist Academy. He was co-founder and chairman of the board of the Baptist Foundation of Texas and served as vice-president of the Baptist General Convention of Texas. He died in San Antonio on April 16, 1949, and was buried in Mission Burial Park in that city.

BIBLIOGRAPHY: *The New Encyclopedia of Texas*, I (n.d.); *Who's Who In America* (1948); San Antonio *Express*, April 18, 1949; Alpine *Avalanche*, April 22, 1949.

Elton Miles

*Kokernot, Texas.

*Kokernot Ranch.

*Kokernot Spring.

*Kokomo, Texas.

*Kone, Edward Reeves.

Konkone Indians. In the latter part of the seventeenth century, according to records of the La Salle Expedition,qv the Konkone (Komkome, Konkome, Korkone) Indians seem to have ranged an inland area somewhere north or northeast of Matagorda Bay, possibly near the Brazos River. It has long been assumed that this name is a variant of the name Tonkawa, but this identification rests solely on the similarity of sounds in certain variants of the names. It is true that groups considered to be Tonkawan in affiliation were in or near this area, but during the same period Spanish records indicate that the "Tanquaay" lived much farther north. The question of Konkone identity is still open.

BIBLIOGRAPHY: I. J. Cox (ed.), *The Journeys of Réné Robert Cavelier, Sieur de La Salle*, II (1906); F. W. Hodge (ed.), *Handbook of American Indians*, II (1910); H. R. Stiles (ed.), *Joutel's Journal of La Salle's Last Voyage*,

1684-7 (1906); J. R. Swanton, *Source Material on the History and Ethnology of the Caddo Indians* (1942).

T. N. Campbell

*Konohasset, Texas.

*Konz, Adam.

*Koocksville, Texas.

*Kopperl, Moritz.

*Kopperl, Texas.

*Korville, Texas.

*Kosarek, Texas.

*Kosciusko, Texas.

*Kosse, Texas.

Kouan Indians. The Kouan (Quouan) are known only from records of the La Salle Expedition,qv which indicate that in the late seventeenth century these people lived inland north or perhaps northeast of Matagorda Bay and not far from the Colorado River. The Kouan have been confused with the Kouyam, whose name also occurs on the same French list of Indian groups in this area. Both Kouan and Kouyam have been identified with the Cujane, a Karankawan tribe that, according to later Spanish sources, lived in the same general area. These identifications have not been demonstrated. On the basis of sound correspondences in the names, identification of Kouan with Cujane seems more plausible.

BIBLIOGRAPHY: I. J. Cox (ed.), *The Journeys of Réné Robert Cavelier, Sieur de La Salle*, II (1906); F. W. Hodge (ed.), *Handbook of American Indians*, I (1907); H. Joutel, *Journal historique du dernier voyage que M. de la Salle fit dans le golf de Mexique* (1713); H. R. Stiles (ed.), *Joutel's Journal of La Salle's Last Voyage, 1684-7* (1906).

T. N. Campbell

*Kountze, Texas. The population of Kountze, in Hardin County, was 1,768 in 1960 and 1,703 in 1970. In 1970 the city listed sixty businesses.

Kouyam Indians. The Kouyam (Kavagan, Kouyan, Kouayan, Kouayon) Indians are known only from records of the La Salle Expedition,qv which indicate that in the late seventeenth century these Indians lived inland north or perhaps northeast of Matagorda Bay not far from the Colorado River. The Kouyam have been confused with the Kouan, whose name also occurs on the same French list of tribes living in the area. Both Kouyam and Kouan have been identified with the Cujane, a Karankawan tribe that, according to later Spanish sources, lived in the same area. These identifications have not been demonstrated conclusively. On the basis of sound correspondences in the names, identification of Kouan with Cujane seems more plausible.

BIBLIOGRAPHY: I. J. Cox (ed.), *The Journeys of Réné Robert Cavelier, Sieur de La Salle*, II (1906); F. W. Hodge (ed.), *Handbook of American Indians*, I (1907); H. R. Stiles (ed.), *Joutel's Journal of La Salle's Last Voyage, 1684-7* (1906).

T. N. Campbell

Krauskopf, Engelbert. Engelbert Krauskopf was born at Bendorf on the Rhine near Coblenz, Germany, on August 21, 1820. As a youth in Germany he learned the trades of cabinetmaker and gunsmith. He sailed from Antwerp in November, 1845,

arriving in Texas early in January, 1846. One of his first jobs was as a hunter for John O. Meusebach qv in New Braunfels. As an early settler in Fredericksburg, he made furniture and repaired guns. He also ran a sawmill and a small cotton gin.

During the Civil War when ammunition was scarce, he and Adolph Lungkwitz, a local silversmith, perfected two machines which they used to make gun caps, and they soon had the only gun cap factory in this section of the country. Saltpeter for black powder came from bat caves in Gillespie County, and the quicksilver and copper were obtained in Galveston or from Mexico. Krauskopf was the captain of a home guard company of fifty-seven men in Fredericksburg during the Civil War. As an amateur botanist he was credited with identifying a red-flowered yucca, now listed in the catalogue *Flora of Texas* under the *Liliaceae* plant family. He married Rosa Herbst of Rothweil, Württemberg, Germany; they had six children. He died July 11, 1881, and was buried in the City Cemetery, Fredericksburg.

Bruce Kowert

*Kreigle, Texas.

*Kress, Texas.

*Kretson, Texas.

*Kreutzberg.

*Kristenstad, Texas.

Krueger, Walter. Walter Krueger, a distinguished military general and resident of San Antonio for many years, was born in Flatow, Germany, the son of Julius O. H. and Anne (Hasse) Krueger, on January 26, 1881. Krueger moved with his family to the United States when he was eight years old and settled in the Middle West. He attended Cincinnati Technical School from 1896 to 1898, and although Krueger did not continue his academic education as a civilian, he attended many military schools and colleges and served as instructor or professor at many of them. He was the author or translator of several books on military history and tactics.

Beginning his military career in 1898 as a private in the Spanish-American War, Krueger served during several wars and military engagements, progressed through the officer ranks, and was promoted to lieutenant general commanding the Third Army headquarters in San Antonio by 1941. At the request of General Douglas MacArthur, Krueger assumed command of the Sixth Army in Australia in 1943. In that year the Sixth Army began two years of fighting to capture the islands of the South Pacific, including New Britain, Leyte, Mindoro, and Luzon. Krueger was promoted to full general by 1945. The Sixth Army was deactivated in January, 1946, and Krueger retired, returning to San Antonio, where he had made his permanent residence.

Krueger married Grace Aileen Norvell on September 11, 1904, and they had three children. He died August 20, 1967, in Valley Forge, Pennsylvania, and was buried at Arlington National Cemetery.

BIBLIOGRAPHY: *Who's Who In America* (1952); *News-*

week (February 4, 1946); Dallas *Morning News,* November 22, 1944, January 14, 1965; New York *Times,* August 21, 1967; San Antonio *Express,* September 20, 1953.

*Krum, Texas.

*Krunk's Lake, Texas.

*Kruse, Texas.

*Ku Klux Klan.

*Ku Klux Klan (1920's).

*Kuasse Village.

*Kuechler, Jacob.

*Kurten, Texas.

Kurth, Ernest Lynn. Ernest Lynn Kurth, industrialist and philanthropist, was born on July 25, 1885, at Kurth Station, Polk County, Texas, the son of Hattie (Glenn) and Joseph Hubert Kurth.qv He attended local schools in Angelina County and then Southwestern University, where he received the B.A. degree in 1905. He was associated with his father in his numerous business enterprises and became general manager of the Angelina County Lumber Company.

Upon his father's death in 1930 he became vice-president and later president of the family lumber business, which he expanded and modernized, adding other lumber operations and lands. Perhaps Ernest Kurth's most significant venture was his decision in 1936 to organize a company to produce newsprint from southern yellow pine, based on the research of Charles Herty, a Georgia chemist. With the assistance of Herty and East Texas businessmen, Kurth built the Southland Paper Mills, which began production in 1940. This was the first newsprint made from southern pine pulp and opened a new era for uses of southern forest products.

He served as president, director, or board chairman of the Southland Paper Company, the Angelina County Lumber Company, the Lufkin National Bank, the Lufkin Foundry, East Texas Theatres, KTRE radio and television, Angelina and Neches River Railroad Company, and other business enterprises. In addition, he was president of the Southern Pine Association, Lufkin Chamber of Commerce, and the East Texas Chamber of Commerce.qv He was vice-president of the National Lumberman's Manufacturers Association. For many years he was chairman of the Lufkin school board and a trustee for Southwestern University, which awarded him an honorary LL.D. degree in 1938. He was president of the Philosophical Society of Texas qv in 1952.

Kurth contributed generously to Texas Methodist enterprises. He was president of the board of directors of Lufkin Memorial Hospital, which he was instrumental in founding. In 1910 he married Isla Kinsolving of Corsicana; they had two children. He died on October 26, 1960, and was buried in the Glendale Cemetery in Lufkin.

BIBLIOGRAPHY: Lufkin *Daily News,* October 30, 1955, October 27, 1960, March 15, 1966; Kurth Papers, Forest History Collections, Stephen F. Austin State University Library, Nacogdoches; *Who's Who In America* (1961).

Robert S. Maxwell

Kurth, Joseph Hubert. Joseph Hubert Kurth, industrialist and political leader, was born on July 3, 1857, in Bonn, Germany. Little is known of his parents except that his father was a businessman, able to send his son to the university. Following a student demonstration which ended in a riot, young Kurth left Bonn fearing arrest and later migrated to the United States. He landed at Galveston, Texas, in 1878, with no funds, no laboring skills, and speaking only broken English. He began as a laborer in a Galveston sawmill, and after working in a number of sawmills in southeast Texas, he purchased a small mill in Polk County at a point (later called Kurth Station) on the Houston, East and West Texas Railway. In 1882 he met and married Hattie Glenn of Hartley, Texas; they had six children.

In 1888 Kurth purchased a sawmill plant two miles west of Lufkin. Here at Keltys, in 1890, with S. W. Henderson, and Eli and Sam Wiener, Kurth formed the Angelina County Lumber Company, which grew into one of the giants of East Texas lumbering. Surviving depressions, accidents, and fires, Kurth steadily expanded the company until by 1912 it was a million-dollar operation. During the same years, he had helped to found and direct the Lufkin National Bank, the Lufkin Foundry, the Angelina and Neches River Railroad, and a number of other sawmill ventures. In addition the company owned more than 150,000 acres of choice pine lands.

Kurth was active and influential in the Republican party,qv holding a number of local and state party offices. In 1924 he was the Republican candidate for lieutenant governor of Texas. For many years he was a trustee for the local school district and provided the funds for the Kurth Memorial Library in Lufkin; he also contributed to religious causes. He died on June 16, 1930, and was buried in Glendale Cemetery in Lufkin.

BIBLIOGRAPHY: Lufkin *Daily News,* June 16, 17, 1930, March 15, 1966; Frank W. Johnson, *A History of Texas and Texans,* V (1914); Kurth Papers, Forest History Collections, Stephen F. Austin State University Library, Nacogdoches.

Robert S. Maxwell

*Kurth, Texas.

*Kuykendall, Abner. The Abner Kuykendall who came to Texas from Tennessee in 1831 was not the son of the Abner Kuykendall (as stated in Volume I) who came to Texas from Arkansas in 1821. Although he was uncertain of their relationship, the younger Kuykendall always referred to the famous Abner Kuykendall as "uncle."

The younger Abner Kuykendall was born in Tennessee on January 6, 1807, son of Matthew and Nancy (Johnson) Kuykendall. He joined the Austin colony in March, 1831, and in 1834 married Mariah Duff; they had eleven children. During the Texas Revolution he enlisted in the regiment commanded by Edward Burleson qv but was on detached duty when it fought in the battle of San Jacinto. He died in 1868 in Texas.

BIBLIOGRAPHY: Carr Pritchett Collins, *The History of the Woodall, Dollahite, Miles, Kuykendall Families in East Texas* (1961).

Mrs. A. M. Allison

*Kuykendall, Barzillai.
*Kuykendall, Gibson.
*Kuykendall, James Hampton.
*Kuykendall, Joseph.
*Kuykendall, Robert H.
*Kuykendalls Creek.
*Kwahari Indians.

*Kyle, Texas. Kyle, in Hays County, had a population of 1,023 in 1960 and 1,629 in 1970; there were twenty-five businesses operating in Kyle in 1970.

*Kyle Baptist Seminary.

*Kyle Mountain.

*Kyote, Texas.

L

*L I T Ranch. Charles S. McCarty (not Charlie C. McCarty, as stated in Volume II) was the manager of the L I T Ranch when it opened.

*L S Ranch.

*L X Ranch.

*La Baca County.

*Labadie, Nicholas Descomps.

*La Bahía. By the early 1800's the Nuestra Señora del Espíritu Santo de Zuñiga Mission, Nuestra Señora de Loreto Presidio,qqv and a civil settlement were all called La Bahía. At present the presidio is more generally referred to as Presidio La Bahía. Many notable battles, involving the Spaniards, Mexicans, Indians, and Anglo Americans, took place at La Bahía. The fort was captured and held for a while by the Gutiérrez-Magee-Kemper filibusters (see Gutiérrez-Magee Expedition); later the filibuster groups of James Long and Henry Perry qqv fought to capture it. In 1835 the Anglo Texans, under George Morse Collinsworth,qv captured La Bahía, and there in December, 1835, Captain Philip Dimitt's qv Texans signed the Goliad Declaration of Independence.qv In January, 1836, James Walker Fannin qv commanded the presidio. Upon General José Urrea's qv threat to the fort, Colonel Fannin withdrew his force and demolished the fortifications, buildings, and houses of the settlement. He was overtaken and defeated in the battle of Coleto,qv surrendered, and marched back to La Bahía. Imprisoned there a week, Fannin and his men were marched out and massacred on March 27, 1836, by the Mexican Army. After the defeat of the Mexicans at San Jacinto, the burned bodies of the Texans were buried outside the presidio at a spot now marked by a memorial.

In 1840 the Catholic church reestablished its ownership of La Bahía presidio with its chapel. This chapel existed only for the presidio soldiers, and it should not be confused with the nearby mission Nuestra Señora del Espíritu Santo de Zuñiga. Because of inadequate funds for its maintenance, the presidio fell into ruins, though church services have been continuously held in the chapel since 1840. The presidio was restored by 1967 through the efforts of the Kathryn O'Connor Foundation. On April 9, 1968, Mrs. Lyndon B. Johnson, wife of the president of the United States, unveiled and dedicated the National Historic Landmark plaque that is located at the presidio entrance.

The site of Nuestra Señora del Espíritu Santo de Zuñiga Mission, one-fourth mile north of the presidio, is now a part of the Goliad State Historic Park (see Parks, State).

BIBLIOGRAPHY: C. E. Castañeda, Our Catholic Heritage in Texas, 1519–1936 (1936–1958); Kathryn Stoner O'Connor, Presidio La Bahía del Espíritu Santo de Zuñiga, 1721–1846 (1966); Harbert Davenport, "The Men of Goliad," Southwestern Historical Quarterly, XLIII (1939–1940).

Kathryn Stoner O'Connor

*La Bahía Road.

*Labatt, Texas.

*LaBelle, Texas.

*La Blanca, Texas.

*Labor.

Labor, Migrant. As early as 1912 farmers in other states sought the services of Texas farm workers. In that year the Arizona Salt River Egyptian Cotton Growers Association launched the first active recruitment campaign on record to lure Texans to the fields of other states.

Since that time a growing number of Texans have joined the ranks of migrant farm workers, a group described by the Texas Legislative Council (see Legislative Council, Texas) in its report to the Fifty-fifth Texas Legislature as "workers whose principal source of income is earned from temporary farm employment and who in the course of a year's work move one or more times, often through several states." In 1966 Texas had by far a larger migrant worker population than any other state.

There is little evidence that Texas farm workers found it necessary to find employment away from home before the early twentieth century. Until the early 1900's Texas farms were chiefly family farms, with the owner performing his own farm work with little or no outside assistance. Three major developments changed the complexion of farm labor requirements and led to the development of a migratory work force: the development of new cotton producing areas in Texas, the partial mechanization of cotton production, and the introduction of fresh fruit and vegetable industries into South Texas. Although new areas of farm employment opened up, mechanization and the seasonal nature of the crops provoked a need for workers to move with the crops in order to remain employed for any appreciable length of time.

As automobiles and trucks came into widespread use between 1900 and 1930, migrants could travel farther, stay longer, and, consequently, make more money. They began to travel in crews headed by a labor contractor, or crew leader, who found employment for his crew. These early crews concentrated mainly on harvesting Texas crops during this period. However, the migrants soon learned that wages were higher and work opportunities better in other states. By the early 1920's numbers of Texans sought the more lucrative jobs in the Rocky Mountains and Midwestern sugar beet industries. In 1925 a number began to work in temporary Mississippi Delta jobs. The 1930's were bleak years for Texas migrants. The decline in demand for workers plus the swelling of the agricultural work force by other victims of the Depression made it more difficult than ever to find adequate employment.

The 1940's wartime manpower shortage should have alleviated the underemployment of the American farm worker. Instead it brought a form of labor competition, the foreign agricultural worker. In August, 1942, the United States signed with Mexico the first intergovernmental agreement for importation of Mexican nationals to work in American agriculture. These workers were known as "braceros." The international agreements were re-negotiated and refined year after year until, in 1951, the Eighty-second Congress seemed to recognize that the bracero was here to stay. In July, 1951, Congress, with Public Law 78, gave the secretary of labor authority to arrange for importation of temporary agricultural workers from Mexico to fill farm labor shortages. Designed as a temporary two-year emergency measure, Public Law 78 was periodically extended by Congress until, after thirteen years of operation, it was finally allowed to expire in December, 1964. In addition to the braceros an unknown number of illegal Mexican entrants (known colloquially as "wetbacks") swelled the farm worker force. The competition in the Texas fields from Mexican nationals who could afford to work for lower wages than the domestic worker added impetus to the movement out of Texas by the domestic worker.

The annual migratory exodus from Texas rose from 4,315 persons in 1939 to 70,607 in 1954. The United States Department of Labor estimated that the annual number of Texans leaving for temporary out-of-state farm work was about 66,500 by the mid-1960's. An additional thirty to forty thousand traveled the highways for temporary work on Texas farms. These figures included only those migrants who found jobs through public or licensed private employment services. Including the nonworking family members who traveled with the workers and those migrants who found employment without using the agencies, more than 150,000 Texans left their homes each year to follow the crops through Texas and other parts of the nation. Most of these made permanent homes in the South Texas area, from San Antonio to the Mexican border

and to the Gulf of Mexico, the heaviest concentration living in the Lower Rio Grande Valley.

Characteristically, the Texas migrant in the 1960's was a citizen of Mexican-American descent. His income was less than one thousand dollars per annum. He left his home between March and June for farm work and usually returned no earlier than October. He often took his family with him, and thus his children's education was haphazard; the Texas Education Agency qv estimated that there were over forty-eight thousand migrant children in Texas. Because of his poverty, his lack of education, the discrimination he might suffer because of his ancestry, and the fact that he might speak only Spanish, the Mexican American migrant was never assimilated fully into Texas or United States society.

Until recently agricultural workers were specifically exempt from major federal and state social and labor legislation. The 1962 Federal Migrant Health Act provided very limited health services for migrants. In 1964 Congress included a section for migrant farm workers in the Economic Opportunity Act, the war on poverty legislation. Under Title III-B of this act, the Office of Economic Opportunity made available over $8 million in grants for the operation of programs in Texas benefiting migrant farm workers. The Eighty-ninth Congress included coverage of some agricultural workers in its 1966 minimum wage legislation. As of February 1, 1967, a relatively small percentage of the migrants received one dollar per hour for their services.

Documented studies show that migrant workers suffer from a variety of characteristic problems unknown to most other American workers: unusually low wages, inadequate housing while on the job, frequent exploitation by crew leaders, inadequate educational opportunities, lack of coverage under child labor and wage payment and collection legislation, and exclusion from the collective bargaining protection of the National Labor Relations Act. Over thirty states have enacted legislation designed to meet one or more of these needs. Texas has enacted only one law specifically aimed at the migrant problem: a requirement that persons seeking migratory work have a health certificate showing results of a recent tuberculosis examination. *See also* Agriculture in Texas; Mexican Americans in Texas.

BIBLIOGRAPHY: George Otis Coalson, The Development of the Migratory Farm Labor System in Texas: 1900–1954 (Ph.D. dissertation, University of Oklahoma, 1960); Ruth Graves, A History of the Interrelationships Between Imported Mexican Labor, Domestic Migrants, and the Texas Agricultural Economy (M.A. thesis, University of Texas, 1960).

Ruth Graves

Labor, Texas Council on Migrant. The Texas Council on Migrant Labor, created in 1957, was an ex officio board consisting of the chairman of the Texas Employment Commission, commissioner of the State Department of Public Welfare, director of the Good Neighbor Commission, commissioner of the State Board of Education, director of the Texas Department of Public Safety, commissioner of the State Department of Public Health, and commissioner of the Bureau of Labor Statistics.qqv The council was responsible for coordinating efforts of state agencies in improving travel and living conditions of migrant laborers. The council was abolished in 1965, and its duties were given to the Good Neighbor Commission.

BIBLIOGRAPHY: University of Texas at Austin, *Guide To Texas State Agencies* (1966).

*Labor Legislation. *See* Union Regulation in Texas; Child Labor Legislation in Texas.

*Labor Organizations in Texas. The rapid industrialization in the years during and immediately following World War II increased the number of nonagricultural workers, and thereby the potential union membership in Texas. Organizational drives by several national unions proved quite successful in the immediate postwar period, and by 1946 about 350,000 Texans were union members. Of these, approximately 225,000 were in unions affiliated with the American Federation of Labor (AFL), and roughly 60,000 were in the Congress of Industrial Organizations (CIO) affiliated unions; the remainder were in unaffiliated unions, such as the Railroad Brotherhood and the Southwestern Telephone Workers (the two largest independent groups) or company unions, such as that for the Humble Oil and Refining Company's qv employees. During the decade following the war, Texas' union membership grew at a rate greater than that of the nation as a whole, yet the increase was primarily a result of rapid economic and population growth, for the percentage of nonagricultural workers unionized remained relatively stable at a little below 20 percent, compared to a national average of about 30 percent. Total union membership in Texas reached about 375,000 by the mid-1950's, or approximately 17 percent of the nonagricultural labor force. The vigor of CIO organizational efforts was demonstrated by an increase in membership in its affiliated unions to something over 100,000, while membership in the AFL unions had remained stable and the membership in unaffiliated unions had actually declined to about 40,000.

Much of the union growth was in the larger industrial establishments. Over 60 percent of those manufacturing plants employing more than 250 workers were organized in 1955, while less than 10 percent of those employing less than 250 workers had unions. In addition, most of labor's strength was in new industries—over 75 percent of the workers in transportation, communication, and the manufacture of transportation equipment were union members; two-thirds of employees of paper, primary metals, and chemical manufacturers were unionized; and over half of those working in the petroleum industry were organized. The older industries— lumber, textiles, food, and agricultural processing— remained less than 25 percent unionized. Union membership was, therefore, both numerically and

proportionately strongest in those geographic areas where new industry flourished. Almost half of the state's union members were found in the Houston-Beaumont area and about one-third in the Dallas-Fort Worth complex. Yet the character and size of the industrial establishment seemed more critical than the location. Wherever large heavy industry was found, so were unions. There were, for example, large locals of the steelworkers in Daingerfield, the auto workers in Greenville, the rubber workers in Bryan, and the oil workers in Tyler, Borger, and Dumas, towns where there were few other union members. By the same token, most small industries in Houston, Dallas, and especially San Antonio were organized.

In July, 1957, the twenty-one-year split between the AFL and the CIO in Texas was bridged when, after eighteen months of negotiations, the Texas Federation of Labor and the Texas State CIO Council merged into the Texas State AFL-CIO. The merger agreement was delayed primarily by differences over representation in and leadership of the new body; jurisdictional disputes between former AFL and CIO unions; and disagreement over the role, scope, and power of the state organization, which was more philosophical than a reflection of the craft-industrial union conflict. Disagreement over policy between the chief officers of the state AFL-CIO, one of which represented the old AFL group and the other the old CIO unions, flared into a floor fight between their supporters for control of the 1961 state convention. That dissension, which threatened to split Texas labor again, involved personalities as well as the craft-industrial union conflict. With the magnanimity of the winners and the grace of the losers a split was avoided. The ill will, however, between craft and industrial unions which has divided American labor throughout its history remained strong in Texas labor in the 1960's. This dissension helps to explain the continued decline of affiliation by local unions with the state organization. By 1966 only a little more than half the membership of AFL-CIO unions were affiliated with Texas State AFL-CIO, compared to about 60 percent affiliated at the time of merger. Equally, if not more, responsible for disaffiliation was the dissatisfaction over the growing assessments by the state AFL-CIO on local unions, monies necessary to continue its increasing social and political activities.

Only since the war years has organized labor emerged as a political and social entity in Texas. The CIO, through its Political Action Committee, contributed greatly to the 1944 presidential campaign in Texas and gave support to Homer Rainey in the 1946 Democratic gubernatorial primary. The state AFL did not openly enter politics until 1948, when it endorsed Coke Stevenson over Lyndon Baines Johnson qqv in the senatorial primary and supported Roger Evans for governor. Ralph Yarborough's several statewide races received extensive support in the 1950's, and his election as United

States senator marked labor's first important political victory.

Although in the 1950's there was reason to think that labor's support was more to be avoided than sought in Texas, a state with strong anti-union attitudes, by the time of the merger labor's endorsement was being sought by both local and statewide candidates. In 1958 the state AFL-CIO began to rate members of the legislature and to work actively in legislative races, with little success except in areas of great union strength, where a considerable number of labor-supported candidates were being elected by the mid-1960's. Organized labor also began to play a growing role in other areas. Representatives of organized labor were being regularly placed on local charity committees, social service committees, planning committees, and the like. In 1954 the Texas Federation of Labor began to grant several college scholarships, and organized labor provided extensive support for the Warm Springs Foundation ᑫᵛ at Gonzales for the operation of a rehabilitation hospital for the physically impaired. A youth conference was sponsored annually by Texas AFL-CIO, and the state organization entered several court cases relating to insurance rates, poll tax, and other issues with implications for all Texans, not just union members. Unions in Texas likewise were active in civil rights movements and helped organize several demonstrations. Although there was some internal dissatisfaction with this aspect of labor's social role, integration within most unions was accomplished smoothly.

Increased activity outside the sphere of wages, hours, and working conditions grew in an era when labor was losing strength in the nation and in Texas. Internal division, along with a variety of other factors, retarded union growth. The exposés of labor racketeers in the mid-1950's had a great impact on public opinion, already hostile in Texas, although none of the exposés directly involved Texas unions. Automation, with the accompanying loss of jobs, struck hard at several unions. Membership continued to grow slowly until about 1960, when it peaked at something over 400,000, with about 375,000 of these in AFL-CIO unions. By 1964 this had declined to 370,000 total members, 320,000 in AFL-CIO unions, 39,000 in national unions outside the AFL-CIO, and the remainder in local unaffiliated, mostly company, unions.

BIBLIOGRAPHY: United States Department of Labor, Bureau of Labor Statistics, *Bulletin No. 1320* (1962), *Bulletin No. 1493* (1966); Frederick Meyers, "The Growth of Collective Bargaining in Texas," *Proceedings of the Seventh Annual Meeting of the Industrial Research Association* (1955).

James V. Reese

*Labor Statistics, Bureau of. The Bureau of Labor Statistics in 1972 included seven divisions. In addition to the divisions which enforced state law regarding labor, boxing and wrestling, licensing of employment agencies, mobile homes, and steam boiler inspection, the bureau added a safety division which investigated and corrected dangerous practices in oil fields and refineries, compiled accident statistics, and investigated violations of various state laws. An accounting division was also added to maintain the financial and accounting records of the bureau.

BIBLIOGRAPHY: University of Texas at Austin, *Guide To Texas State Agencies* (1972).

*Laborcitas Creek.

*LaBranche, Alcée Louis.

Lacane Indians. The Lacane (Lacame) Indians were a Caddoan people encountered by the Moscoso Expedition ᑫᵛ in 1542 somewhere in northeastern Texas or in the adjoining parts of Arkansas and Louisiana. They may be the same as the Hacanac, also mentioned in the records of the same expedition. J. R. Swanton believed that Lacane was an early name of the people later known as the Nacaniche. On the basis of sound correspondences in the names, Swanton has suggested that Hacanac, Lacane, Nacachau, Nacao, Nacaniche, Nacono, and Nakanawan were probably fragments of the same Caddoan tribe. This cannot be verified by such documentary evidence as is now available.

BIBLIOGRAPHY: J. R. Swanton, *Source Material on the History and Ethnology of the Caddo Indians* (1942).

T. N. Campbell

*La Casa, Texas.

La Casita, Texas. La Casita, in southern Starr County about one mile west of Garciasville, consisted of several grocery stores and filling stations and had a population of about six hundred in 1966. The inhabitants were principally engaged in farming and ranching.

*Laceola, Texas.

*La Cerda, Texas.

*Lacey, Howard.

*Lacey, Martin.

*Lacey, William Demetris.

*Laceyville, Texas.

*Lackland Air Force Base. Lackland Air Force Base, San Antonio, expanded its training program after World War II. In 1948 the number of enlistees exceeded the capacity of the base, and the overflow was directed to Sheppard Air Force Base.ᑫᵛ In the same year a training program for women in the United States Air Force was introduced, and in January, 1949, the officer candidate school at the base became coeducational. The outbreak of the Korean war brought a large influx of new recruits to the base.

With the close of the Korean hostilities, Lackland continued to expand by activating the officer military school and the language school, as well as reestablishing the preflight school for aviation cadets. The officer military school, designed to provide basic training to personnel with direct commissions, was in operation throughout the 1960's. The language school offered intensive instruction in English to foreign personnel participating in the air force's technical and flying training programs.

All basic training returned to Lackland at the

end of 1955. Technical training also gained impetus the following year when a technical training school was established at the base. In the following two years, the air force's marksmanship school and sentry dog training program were established at Lackland. In 1958 Lackland was transferred from the Technical Training Command to Air Training Command. In July, 1959, the air force's officer training school opened; the following year aviation cadet training was discontinued, thus terminating the base's flying programs.

The base continued to expand with the growth of its training programs. In mid-1961 a plan to enlarge Lackland Annex (Medina Facility) was submitted, and a large building to house the Department of Cryptographic Training, a hospital, and modern barracks were constructed. In July, 1966, Lackland doubled its physical plant by acquiring 3,500 acres from the Atomic Energy Commission's Medina Base facility.

By 1966 officers and men from fifty-two allied nations had attended Lackland's language school. The following year, the final class of legal officers graduated from the officer military school, although course material was maintained in current status after termination of the school's activities. The officer training school, having grown into the largest single source for new air force officers, had commissioned more than twenty-seven thousand second lieutenants by June, 1967.

More than twenty-five million dollars were earmarked for the base under the 1967 military construction bill. The sum was spent for expanding training, maintenance, and supply facilities, as well as troop housing and community facilities.

LaCoste, Jean Batiste. Jean Batiste LaCoste was born in Gascony, France, in 1823; he came to the United States in 1848, landing first at New Orleans and then migrating to San Antonio, where he established several business enterprises. LaCoste was a warm adherent of Emperor Ferdinand Maximilian of Mexico and moved to Matamoros to serve the imperial cause. With the collapse of the French adventure LaCoste returned to San Antonio and began rebuilding his economic fortunes. He built and operated the first ice plant in San Antonio. He married Manuela Menchaca, the daughter of José Antonio Menchaca,qv in 1852. They had six children. LaCoste died on October 24, 1887, and was buried in the San Fernando Catholic Cemetery.

S. W. Pease

*LaCoste, Texas.

*Lacy, Texas. *See also* Lacy-Lakeview, Texas.

*Lacy Creek.

Lacy-Lakeview, Texas. Lacy-Lakeview, in McLennan County, was originally two separate communities which incorporated as one city in 1953. Known since the turn of the century for the spring-fed Day's Lakes, the area had two steel and machine plants, three oil terminals, and some retail businesses in 1967. Most of the inhabitants worked in Waco. In 1966 the city reported three churches and three public schools. The population of the area began increasing when James Connally Air Force Base qv was reopened. The 1960 population was 2,272, and the 1970 population was 2,558, according to the United States census.

*Lacy's Creek.

*Lacy's Fort.

*Ladd, Texas.

*Ladies' Battalions and Legions.

*Ladonia, Texas.

*Ladonia Male and Female Institute.

Ladrón de Guevara, Antonio. Antonio Ladrón de Guevara, a resident of Nuevo León, undertook an expedition through Nuevo León, Coahuila, and Texas in the early eighteenth century and wrote his account of the ranches, settlements, missions, and Spanish frontier policy in 1739. The guidebook served in planning defenses on the northern frontier and in changing local administration. Ladrón de Guevara also helped the expedition of José de Escandón qv for the pacification and settlement of Nuevo Santander, which, together with Nuevo León, Coahuila, and Texas, formed the Provincias Internas de Oriente (*see* Provincias Internas). Among the Texas sites he described were the presidios of San Juan Bautista qv and San Antonio de "Vejar." His analysis of the role of Texas in the frontier defensive cordon is of great interest.

BIBLIOGRAPHY: Antonio Ladrón de Guevara, *Noticias de los poblados de que se componen el Nuevo Reyno de León y las Provincias de Coahuila (Nueva Extremadura) y Texas (Nuevas Philipinas)* (J. Porrúa Turanzas edition, Madrid, 1962).

Jack D. L. Holmes

*LaFayette, Texas.

*La Feria, Texas. La Feria, in Cameron County, had an economy based on agriculture, commerce, and some industry. The town reported ninety industries in 1967, including fruit and vegetable canning companies; manufacturers of carnival equipment, cotton trailers, and liquid fertilizer; and three cotton gins. The tourist trade expanded considerably, and recreational tourist facilities were available at the community center park. The 1960 population of 3,047 decreased to 2,642 by 1970, according to the United States census.

*Laffite, Jean.

*Lagarto, Texas.

*Lagarto College.

*Lagarto Creek.

*La Grange, Texas. (Fayette County.) La Grange, the county seat, is an agricultural and commercial center. The town had 140 businesses in 1967, including factories producing metal and machine parts, truck bodies and trailers, sausage, milk products, concrete, granite, mattresses, feeds, and furniture. In 1970 the town reported 106 businesses. La Grange had a hospital and two rest homes. The Old Faison Home Museum had been restored by a garden club. The 1960 population was 3,623; the 1970 population decreased to 3,092, according to the United States census. In 1975 there was a considerable increase in economic activity in La Grange and its environs because of the beginning of construction of a huge power plant, which was to furnish future energy needs for the city of Austin.

*La Grange, Texas. (Red River County.) *See* Madras, Texas.

*La Grange Collegiate Institute.

*La Grange Female Institute.

*La Grange *Intelligencer.*

*La Grange Male and Female Seminary and Boarding School.

*La Grange *Paper.*

*La Grange Select School.

La Grulla, Texas. *See* Grulla, Texas.

*Laguna, Texas. (Falls County.)

*Laguna, Texas. (Uvalde County.)

*Laguna Atascosa.

Laguna Atascosa National Wildlife Refuge. The Laguna Atascosa National Wildlife Refuge was established in 1946 twenty-five miles northeast of San Benito, partially bordering the shallow waters of Laguna Madre. Its name was derived from its largest lake, Laguna Atascosa. The refuge included coastal prairies, salt flats, ridges supporting thorny shrubs, and brushlands with mesquite, huisache, ebony, retama, granjeno, and scattered cacti and yucca. Approximately one thousand acres were farmed to supply winter food for geese. A total of 314 bird species were observed on the refuge. Containing over forty-five thousand acres, it was administered by the Fish and Wildlife Service of the United States Department of the Interior. *See also* Wildlife Areas in Texas.

BIBLIOGRAPHY: Fish and Wildlife Service, United States Department of the Interior, "Laguna Atascosa National Wildlife Refuge," *Refuge Leaflet 28.*

*Laguna Creek.

Laguna Gloria Art Museum. The Laguna Gloria Art Museum is located on the land Stephen F. Austin once selected for his homesite in Austin, Texas, and was the former home of Clara Driscoll Sevier.qv The Mediterranean-style villa overlooking Lake Austin was built in 1916 on twenty-eight acres of land and served as the winter residence for Mr. and Mrs. Sevier until 1929. Clara Driscoll, who dropped her married name after her divorce, conveyed the property to the Texas Fine Arts Association qv Holding Corporation in 1943. In 1961 the management was assumed by Laguna Gloria Art Museum, Inc., whose members also serve as the Austin chapter of the TFAA. In 1965 the Austin chapter was given control of the property rights of Laguna Gloria.

The museum schedules art exhibitions and sponsors children's and adults' art classes. A two-day "Fiesta," sponsored by the Women's Art Guild and held each May, attracts more than twenty thousand patrons who purchase works of art from hundreds of artists' booths set up on the estate grounds. The museum has a permanent collection of American art and maintains a sales and rental gallery. The city of Austin contributes substantially to maintenance of the museum.

Carol Spencer

*Laguna Grande.

*Laguna Larga.

*Laguna Madre.

*Laguna Plata.

*Laguna Rica.

*Laguna Salada.

*Laguna Vista, Texas.

*La Harpe, Bénard de.

*Lahey, Texas.

*Lahey Creek.

*Laird Hill, Texas.

*Lajitas, Texas.

*Lajitas Mesa.

*La Joya, Texas. La Joya, in Hidalgo County, had a population of 1,217 in 1970.

*La Junta de los Ríos.

Lake, Mary Daggett. Mary Sabina (Daggett) Lake was born on November 11, 1880, in Fort Worth, Texas, the daughter of E. M. and Laura Alice (Palmer) Daggett.

She attended the public schools of Fort Worth and Cottey College in Missouri, where she majored in botany and music. For twelve years she was research assistant in a private herbarium, which prepared her as a botanical authority. She was educational director of the Garden Center of Fort Worth from 1935 until her death in 1955. In this capacity she inaugurated nature classes for children, began a gardener's library, conducted workshops and flower shows, and promoted soil conservation as well as highway beautification.

As a charter member of the Fort Worth Garden Club she helped organize the Texas Federation of Garden Clubs (renamed the Texas Garden Clubs, Inc.) and was the state president from 1939 to 1941. In 1943 she was made a life member of both the Texas Garden Clubs, Inc., and the National Federation of Garden Clubs. She was a popular speaker on botanical subjects, a flower show judge, and an organizer of garden clubs throughout the Southwest.

From 1926 to 1955 she served on the Fort Worth Park Board, becoming its president in 1946. Her article "Wildflowers of Texas," written with Miss Eula Whitehouse, still runs annually in the *Texas Almanac.*qv During the Texas Centennial qv she was historical research chairman, interviewing old-timers and writing a series that ran in the Fort Worth *Star-Telegram.*qv From 1937 to 1955 she was garden editor of this newspaper. In recognition of her accomplishments Texas Christian University awarded her an honorary LL.D. degree in 1946. She was married to Will F. Lake on March 23,

1899, and they had three children. She died on March 1, 1955.

BIBLIOGRAPHY: Mary Daggett Lake Collection, Fort Worth Public Library.

Abby Hardy Moran

*Lake, Texas.

*Lake Abbott.

*Lake Abilene. The Lake Abilene project was started in 1919. The earthwork was completed in May, 1921, and the entire project was completed by August 1, 1921. The lake had a capacity of 9,790 acre-feet and a surface area of 641 acres at the spillway elevation of 2,018.8 feet above mean sea level. The drainage area of Elm Creek above the dam is 102 square miles.

BIBLIOGRAPHY: Texas Water Commission, *Bulletin 6408* (1964).

Seth D. Breeding

Lake Amon G. Carter. Lake Amon G. Carter is in the Trinity River Basin in Montague County, six miles south of Bowie on Big Sandy Creek, a tributary of the West Fork of the Trinity River. The project is owned and operated by the city of Bowie to supply water for municipal and industrial uses. Construction began in July, 1955, and was completed in August, 1956. The lake has a capacity of 20,050 acre-feet and a surface area of 1,540 acres at the service spillway crest elevation of 920 feet above mean sea level. The capacity is 30,050 acre-feet at the crest of the emergency spillway. The drainage area above the dam is 100 square miles.

BIBLIOGRAPHY: Texas Water Commission, *Bulletin 6408* (1964).

Seth D. Breeding

Lake Arlington. Lake Arlington is in the Trinity River Basin in Tarrant County, seven miles west of Arlington on Village Creek, a tributary of the West Fork of the Trinity River. Construction of the dam began on May 15, 1956, and was completed on July 19, 1957. The project is owned and operated by the city of Arlington. The Texas Electric Service Company has a contract with the city to use the lake water for condenser cooling in the Handley Steam-Electric Generating Plant. The lake has a capacity of 45,710 acre-feet with a surface area of 2,275 acres at the spillway crest elevation of 550 feet above mean sea level. Water is diverted from the lake as a water supply for Arlington. The Texas Electric Service Company circulates water from the lake to a power plant for condenser-cooling purposes. The drainage area above the dam is 143 square miles.

BIBLIOGRAPHY: Texas Water Commission, *Bulletin 6408* (1964).

Seth D. Breeding

Lake Arrowhead. Lake Arrowhead is in the Red River Basin in Clay County, thirteen miles southeast of Wichita Falls on the Little Wichita River. Lake Arrowhead is owned and operated by the city of Wichita Falls as a municipal water supply. Construction began on May 17, 1965, and the dam was completed in December, 1966. Lake Arrowhead has a capacity of 228,000 acre-feet and a surface area of 13,500 acres at spillway crest elevation 926 feet

above mean sea level. The spillway is a 1,525-foot-long concrete broad-crested weir with an ogee discharge section. The drainage area above the dam is 832 square miles.

Seth D. Breeding

*Lake Austin.

(1) Lake Austin (Matagorda County).

(2) Lake Austin, in Travis County, is one of six Lower Colorado River Authority (*see* Colorado River Authorities) projects on the Colorado River, immediately downstream from Lake Travis, which supplies the water to Lake Austin for constant level reservoir operation. The reservoir has a capacity of 21,000 acre-feet with a surface area of 1,830 acres at an uncontrolled spillway crest elevation of 492.8 feet above mean sea level. Lake Austin is operated at a practically constant level since electrical generation is coordinated with the turbine discharge at the Marshall Ford power plant at Mansfield Dam, twenty-one miles upstream. There are two generators with all necessary auxiliaries in the powerhouse at Tom Miller Dam (formerly Austin Dam), having a capacity of 6,750 kilowatts each. The electrical power can be delivered directly to the city of Austin's distribution system or to the Lower Colorado River Authority's interconnected transmission system. The drainage area above the dam is approximately 38,240 square miles, of which 11,900 square miles is probably noncontributing. The runoff is largely controlled by reservoirs upstream.

BIBLIOGRAPHY: Texas Water Commission, *Bulletin 6408* (1964).

Seth D. Breeding

*Lake Balmorhea. Lake Balmorhea was created in 1917 by the construction of the main dam and Rentz Dike. A survey in 1948 determined the capacity of Lake Balmorhea as 6,350 acre-feet with a surface area of 573 acres at an elevation of 3,187 feet above mean sea level. A principal source of water for Lake Balmorhea is the flow from San Solomon Springs. This flow is supplemented by water delivered to the lake from Toyah Creek by the Madera Diversion Dam and canals. Surplus water from Phantom Lake Canal is also stored in the lake until needed for irrigation. The drainage area is twenty-two square miles, including Sandia Creek and the Madera Canal drainage area.

BIBLIOGRAPHY: Texas Water Commission, *Bulletin 6408* (1964).

Seth D. Breeding

Lake Barbara, Texas. Lake Barbara, part of the Brazosport geographical division in Brazoria County, had a population of 477 in 1960 and 605 in 1970, according to the United States census. *See* Brazosport, Texas.

Lake Bastrop. Bastrop Dam and Lake Bastrop are in the Colorado River Basin in Bastrop County, three miles northeast of Bastrop on Spicer Creek. The project is owned and operated by the Lower Colorado River Authority ᵠᵛ as a source of cooling water for the Sim Gideon Steam Power Plant. Construction of the dam began in May, 1963, and was completed in 1964. The lake has a capacity of

16,590 acre-feet and a surface area of 906 acres at the operating elevation of 450 feet above mean sea level. In addition to furnishing industrial water, the lake provides recreational facilities to the public. The drainage area above the dam is nine square miles, but runoff is supplemented by pumping from the Colorado River to maintain a full lake.

BIBLIOGRAPHY: Texas Water Commission, *Bulletin 6408* (1964).

Seth D. Breeding

*Lake Blue Wing.

*Lake Brelsford.

*Lake Bridgeport.

*Lake Brownwood.

Lake Buchanan. *See* Buchanan Dam and Lake; Buchanan Reservoir.

Lake Buffalo Springs. Lake Buffalo Springs is in the Brazos River Basin in Lubbock County, nine miles southeast of Lubbock on the northern branch of the Double Mountain Fork of the Brazos River. The project is owned and operated by the Lubbock County Water Improvement District No. 1, and water may be used for municipal, industrial, and recreational purposes. Construction began in early 1958, and was completed at the end of 1959. The drainage area above the dam covers a large area, 6,000 square miles, but only about 340 square miles contributes to runoff. The lake has a capacity of 5,360 acre-feet and a surface area of 225 acres at the spillway elevation of 3,015 feet above mean sea level.

BIBLIOGRAPHY: Texas Water Commission, *Bulletin 6408* (1964).

Seth D. Breeding

Lake Cherokee. Lake Cherokee is in the Sabine River Basin in Gregg and Rusk counties, twelve miles southeast of Longview on Cherokee Bayou. Lake Cherokee is owned and operated by the Cherokee Water Company to supply water for municipal, industrial, and recreational purposes. Construction began in February, 1948, and was completed on November 19, 1948. The lake has a capacity of 46,700 acre-feet and a surface area of 3,987 acres at the crest of the service spillway at an elevation of 280 feet above mean sea level. The capacity is 68,700 acre-feet at the crest of the emergency spillway. The city of Longview diverts water for municipal use. From the lake the Southwestern Power Company circulates water for condenser cooling of the steam-turbine generating units in the Knox Lee Power Plant. The drainage area above the dam is 158 square miles.

BIBLIOGRAPHY: Texas Water Commission, *Bulletin 6408* (1964).

Seth D. Breeding

*Lake Childress.

*Lake Cisco. The Lake Cisco project is owned and operated by the city of Cisco for municipal water supply. Construction of the dam was completed on September 7, 1923. In 1967 Lake Cisco had a capacity of 26,000 acre-feet and the surface area was 1,050 acres at the spillway crest elevation of 1,520 feet above mean sea level. However, by

court order, the operating level was established with a capacity of 8,800 acre-feet and a surface area of 445 acres. The flow of Sandy Creek impounded in Lake Cisco has been supplemented since May, 1956, by pumping from Battle Creek into Lake Cisco. The drainage area to Lake Cisco is twenty-six square miles.

BIBLIOGRAPHY: Texas Water Commission, *Bulletin 6408* (1964).

Seth D. Breeding

Lake Colorado City. Lake Colorado City is in the Colorado River Basin in Mitchell County, six miles southwest of Colorado City on Morgan Creek, a tributary of the Colorado River. The project is owned and operated by the Texas Electric Service Company to provide water for municipal and industrial uses and to produce steam-electric power. Deliberate impoundment of water began in April, 1949, and the dam was completed in September, 1949. Water use for condenser-cooling purposes began in June, 1950. The lake has a capacity of 31,000 acre-feet and a surface area of 1,655 acres at elevation 2,070.1 feet above mean sea level, the crest of the service spillway. Runoff from Morgan Creek impounded into Lake Colorado City is supplemented with water pumped from Champion Creek Reservoir to maintain Lake Colorado City at a satisfactory level. The drainage area above the dam is 322 square miles, of which thirty-two square miles is probably noncontributing.

BIBLIOGRAPHY: Texas Water Commission, *Bulletin 6408* (1964).

Seth D. Breeding

*Lake Corpus Christi. The Wesley E. Seale Dam and Lake Corpus Christi are owned by the Lower Nueces River Water Supply District. Construction began on November 19, 1955, and was completed on April 26, 1958, submerging the old Mathis Dam and the old Lake Corpus Christi. The capacity of the reservoir in 1967 was 302,100 acre-feet, and the surface area was 22,050 acres at the top of the spillway gates at elevation 94 feet above mean sea level. The water is used for municipal, industrial, and recreational purposes. The drainage area of the Nueces River at Wesley E. Seale Dam is 16,656 square miles.

BIBLIOGRAPHY: Texas Water Commission, *Bulletin 6408* (1964).

Seth D. Breeding

*Lake Creek.

*Lake Creek, Texas.

*Lake Creek Railway Company.

Lake Creek Reservoir. Lake Creek Reservoir is in the Brazos River Basin in McLennan County, four miles southwest of Riesel on Manos Creek. The project is owned and operated by the Texas Power & Light Company, and is used to provide condenser-cooling water for a steam-electric generating station. Runoff from Manos Creek is supplemented by pumping from Brazos River. Construction began on September 8, 1951, and the dam was completed in May, 1952. The reservoir has a capacity of 8,400 acre-feet and a surface area of 550 acres at the maximum conservation storage level at elevation 405 feet above mean sea level. The drainage area above the dam is seventeen square miles; runoff is conserved to supplement the amount pumped from the Brazos River.

BIBLIOGRAPHY: Texas Water Commission, *Bulletin 6408* (1964).

Seth D. Breeding

*Lake Crook. Lake Crook, constructed in 1923, had a capacity of 9,960 acre-feet and a surface area of 1,226 acres at the spillway crest elevation of 476 feet above mean sea level in 1967. The drainage area above the dam was fifty-two square miles.

Seth D. Breeding

*Lake Dallas. See also Garza-Little Elm Reservoir.

*Lake Dallas, Texas. In 1970 Lake Dallas, in Denton County, had a population of 1,431, according to the United States census. See also Dallas Standard Metropolitan Statistical Area.

Lake Daniel. Gonzales Creek Dam and Lake Daniel are in the Brazos River Basin in Stephens County, seven miles south of Breckenridge on Gonzales Creek. The project is owned by the city of Breckenridge for municipal and industrial water supply. Construction of the dam began on December 15, 1947, and was completed on September 1, 1948; the lake was filled by June, 1949. A small diversion dam and pumping equipment installed near the city were placed in operation in March, 1951. The lake has a capacity of 10,000 acre-feet and a surface area of 950 acres at the operating level elevation of 1,278 feet above mean sea level. The drainage area above the dam is 115 square miles.

BIBLIOGRAPHY: Texas Water Commission, *Bulletin 6408* (1964).

Seth D. Breeding

*Lake Dunlap. [This title was incorrectly listed in Volume II as Lake Dunlop.] Lake Dunlap is in the Guadalupe River Basin in Guadalupe County, nine miles northwest of Seguin on the Guadalupe River. The lake was completed in 1928, and in 1967 it had a capacity of 5,900 acre-feet and a surface area of 406 acres at elevation 575 feet above mean sea level. The water is diverted by a canal to the powerhouse about two miles downstream from the dam. The hydroelectric power plant for this project contains two generating units with all auxiliaries, and has a total capacity of 3,600 kilowatts. The river flow has been partly regulated since June, 1964, by releases from Canyon Reservoir. The drainage area above the dam is 1,653 square miles.

The project is owned and operated by the Guadalupe-Blanco River Authority qv for generation of hydroelectric power. The authority purchased this and five other projects located on the Guadalupe River by a contract which became effective May 1, 1963.

BIBLIOGRAPHY: Texas Water Commission, *Bulletin 6408* (1964).

Seth D. Breeding

*Lake Eanes.

*Lake Eddleman. See also Lake Graham.

*Lake Erie Canyon Creek.

*Lake Fork, Texas.

*Lake Fork of the Sabine River.

*Lake Fort Phantom Hill. See also Fort Phantom Hill Reservoir.

*Lake Gibbons.

Lake Gladewater. Lake Gladewater is in the Sabine River Basin in Upshur County in northwest Gladewater on Glade Creek. The project is owned and operated by the city of Gladewater for municipal water supply and recreation. Construction was started on October 15, 1951, and completed on August 29, 1952. The lake has a capacity of 6,950 acre-feet and a surface area of 800 acres at the service spillway elevation of 300 feet above mean sea level. The drainage area above the dam is thirty-five square miles.

BIBLIOGRAPHY: Texas Water Commission, *Bulletin 6408* (1964).

Seth D. Breeding

Lake Graham. Lake Graham is in the Brazos River Basin in Young County, two miles northwest of Graham on Salt Creek, a tributary of the Brazos River. The project is owned and operated by the city of Graham in connection with former Lake Eddleman for municipal water supply. Construction of Graham Dam began on September 17, 1956, and was completed on June 15, 1958. The date that the two lakes became one was sometime after June, 1959. The new Lake Graham is connected with the former Lake Eddleman by a canal, forming one lake called Lake Graham. The combined capacity is 53,680 acre-feet with an area of 2,550 acres at the spillway elevation of 1,076.3 feet above mean sea level. Water is used for municipal purposes and for condenser-cooling water for a steam-electric generating plant at the Texas Electric Service Company. The drainage area above the Graham Dam is 168 square miles; above Eddleman Dam it is 37 square miles; therefore, Lake Graham has a contributing drainage area of 205 square miles.

BIBLIOGRAPHY: Texas Water Commission, *Bulletin 6408* (1964).

Seth D. Breeding

*Lake Halbert. Lake Halbert, in the Trinity River Basin, is owned and operated by the city of Corsicana for municipal, industrial, and recreational purposes. Construction of the dam was started in 1920 and was completed in 1921. In 1950 the spillway was raised one foot, to the elevation of 368 feet above mean sea level. The capacity was estimated to be 7,420 acre-feet, with a surface of 650 acres. The drainage area above the dam is twelve square miles.

BIBLIOGRAPHY: Texas Water Commission, *Bulletin 6408* (1964).

Seth D. Breeding

*Lake Hamilton.

Lake Hawkins. Wood County Dam No. 3 and Lake Hawkins are in the Sabine River Basin in Wood County, three miles northwest of Hawkins on Little Sandy Creek. The project is owned and operated by Wood County for flood regulation and recreational purposes. Construction began on June 9, 1961, and the dam was completed on September 17, 1962. The lake has a capacity of 11,890 acre-feet and a surface area of 776 acres at the service spillway crest elevation of 343.75 feet above mean sea level. A flood retardation surcharge capacity of 8,210 acre-feet is provided between the crests of the service spillway and the emergency spillway. The drainage area of Little Sandy Creek above the dam is thirty square miles.

BIBLIOGRAPHY: Texas Water Commission, *Bulletin 6408* (1964).

Seth D. Breeding

Lake Holbrook. Wood County Dam No. 2 and Lake Holbrook are in the Sabine River Basin in Wood County, four miles northwest of Mineola on Keys Creek. The project is owned and operated by Wood County for flood regulation and recreational purposes. Contruction began on June 20, 1961, and the dam was completed on November 28, 1962. The lake has a capacity of 7,990 acre-feet and a surface area of 653 acres at the service spillway crest elevation of 372 feet above mean sea level. Flood retardation surcharge capacity of 6,390 acre-feet is provided between the crests of the service spillway and the emergency spillway. The drainage area of Keys Creek above the dam is fifteen square miles.

BIBLIOGRAPHY: Texas Water Commission, *Bulletin 6408* (1964).

Seth D. Breeding

Lake Houston. San Jacinto Dam and Lake Houston are in the San Jacinto River Basin in Harris County, four miles north of Sheldon and eighteen miles northeast of Houston on the San Jacinto River. The project is owned and operated by the city of Houston for municipal, industrial, recreational, mining, and irrigation purposes. Construction began in November, 1951, and the dam was completed in December, 1953. On the basis of a sedimentation survey made in 1965, the lake has a storage capacity of 146,700 acre-feet and a surface area of 12,240 acres at the spillway crest elevation of 43.8 feet above mean sea level. The drainage area above the dam is 2,828 square miles.

BIBLIOGRAPHY: Texas Water Commission, *Bulletin 6408* (1964).

Seth D. Breeding

Lake J. B. Thomas. Colorado River Dam and Lake J. B. Thomas are in the Colorado River Basin in Scurry County, seven miles northeast of Vincent and sixteen miles southwest of Snyder on the Colorado River. The lake extends into Borden County. The project is owned by the Colorado River Municipal Water District,qv which was created in July, 1949, and was built to furnish water to the cities of Big Spring, Odessa, and Snyder for municipal, industrial, and recreational purposes. The project includes a dam across nearby Bull Creek, together with a 13,000-foot-long canal to divert the flow of Bull Creek by gravity into Lake J. B. Thomas. The project was started on March 26, 1951, and was completed in September, 1952. Although deliberate

impoundment of water began in July, 1952, there was little storage until July, 1953. The diversion dam on Bull Creek was washed out by a flood in April, 1954, but it was repaired the following month. The lake has a capacity of 203,600 acre-feet and a surface area of 7,820 acres at the service spillway crest elevation of 2,258 feet above mean sea level. The drainage area above the dam is 3,524 square miles, of which 2,590 is probably noncontributing. The drainage area includes 426 square miles above Bull Creek diversion dam, of which thirty-two square miles is probably noncontributing.

BIBLIOGRAPHY: Texas Water Commission, *Bulletin 6408* (1964).

Seth D. Breeding

*Lake Jackson, Texas. Lake Jackson became the largest town in Brazoria County by 1970, when the United States census counted 13,376 people; the 1960 population was 9,651. The city reported ninety-two businesses in 1970. *See also* Houston Standard Metropolitan Statistical Area.

Lake Jacksonville. Gum Creek Dam and Lake Jacksonville are in the Neches River Basin in Cherokee County, five miles southwest of Jacksonville on Gum Creek. The project is owned and operated by the city of Jacksonville for municipal water supply and for recreation. Construction of the dam began early in 1956, and it was completed in June, 1957. The lake has a capacity of 30,500 acre-feet and a surface area of 1,320 acres at the service spillway crest elevation of 422 feet above mean sea level. The capacity is 46,500 acre-feet with a surface area of 1,760 acres at the emergency spillway level. The drainage area is forty-one square miles.

BIBLIOGRAPHY: Texas Water Commission, *Bulletin 6408* (1964).

Seth D. Breeding

*Lake Jane.

*Lake Kemp. Lake Kemp was never used as a source for generating electrical power (as stated in Volume II). Lake Kemp has a capacity of 461,800 acre-feet and a surface area of 20,620 acres at spillway crest elevation of 1,153 feet above mean sea level. The project is owned by the city of Wichita Falls and Wichita County Water Improvement District No. 2. Water released from Lake Kemp travels by river channel about twenty miles to a diversion dam where it is diverted for distribution by two canal systems for irrigation. Municipal and industrial waters are diverted by a pumping plant and by pipeline systems. The drainage area of the Wichita River to Lake Kemp is 2,086 square miles.

BIBLIOGRAPHY: Texas Water Commission, *Bulletin 6408* (1964).

Seth D. Breeding

*Lake Kickapoo.

Lake Kurth. Lake Kurth, in the Neches River Basin in Angelina County, eight miles north of Lufkin, is an off-channel storage project of the Angelina River. The project is owned and operated by the Southland Paper Mills, Inc., for industrial use in producing paper. A large part of the diverted water is returned to the Angelina River. Construction began on May 26, 1959, and was completed on July 21, 1961. The lake has a capacity of 16,200 acre-feet and a surface area of 800 acres at the spillway crest elevation of 197.5 feet above mean sea level. The lake is held at normal level by pumping from the Angelina River flow and from water purchased from Striker Creek Reservoir. This pumped storage makes the four-square-mile drainage area to the lake unimportant.

BIBLIOGRAPHY: Texas Water Commission, *Bulletin 6408* (1964).

Seth D. Breeding

*Lake Leon.

*Lake Lovenskiold.

Lake Lyndon B. Johnson. Wirtz Dam and Lake Lyndon B. Johnson, formerly Granite Shoals Lake, are in the Colorado River Basin in Burnet and Llano counties, four miles southwest of Marble Falls on the Colorado River. The project is owned and operated by the Lower Colorado River Authority qv primarily for generating hydroelectric power. It is one of a series of six projects on the Colorado River. The other five are Buchanan Dam and Buchanan Reservoir, Inks Dam and Inks Lake, Max Starcke Dam and Marble Falls Lake, Mansfield Dam and Lake Travis, and Tom Miller Dam and Lake Austin. It is the second project downstream from Buchanan Reservoir and uses the controlled discharge of water from the Buchanan electrical generating plant together with the added flow of the Llano River for power generation. Construction was begun in September, 1948, and was completed in November, 1951. The reservoir, at normal operating elevation of 825 feet above mean sea level, has a capacity of 138,500 acre-feet and a surface area of 6,200 acres. Under normal conditions the water level fluctuates over a small range because the power plant operation is coordinated with the inflow. Water from this reservoir is used for the generation of power, and water is released to Marble Falls Lake for use at the Max Starcke Dam electrical generating plant. Except during floods, the only water released is through the turbines for the generation of power. The drainage area is 36,290 square miles, of which 11,900 square miles is noncontributing. However, the river flow is determined by the controlled discharge of Buchanan Reservoir and Inks Lake plants upstream on the Colorado River, plus the entire unregulated flow from the Llano River. The power plant contains two 22,500-kilowatt generating units with auxiliary equipment for connecting to the transmission system.

BIBLIOGRAPHY: Texas Water Commission, *Bulletin 6408* (1964).

Seth D. Breeding

*Lake McDonald. *See* Lake Austin.

*Lake McQueeney. The Lake McQueeney and Abbott Dam project is owned and operated by the Guadalupe-Blanco River Authority qv for generation of hydroelectric power. Construction of the dam was begun in 1927 and was completed in 1928. The lake has a capacity of 5,000 acre-feet and a

surface area of 396 acres at an elevation of 528 feet above mean sea level. It is maintained at an almost constant level by regulating the power output to the water inflow. The hydroelectric power plant for this project is part of the dam structure containing two generating units with all auxiliaries. The total generating capacity is 2,800 kilowatts. The river flow has been partly regulated since June, 1964, by releases from Canyon Reservoir. The drainage area above this dam is 1,684 square miles.

BIBLIOGRAPHY: Texas Water Commission, *Bulletin 6408* (1964).

Seth D. Breeding

*Lake Marvin.

Lake Meredith. Lake Meredith is on the Canadian River in Hutchinson County, ten miles northwest of Borger. The lake extends into Moore and Potter counties. The project was built and financed by the federal government under the jurisdiction of the Bureau of Reclamation, and is owned and operated by the Canadian River Municipal Water Authority.qv Construction of the dam began on March 11, 1962, and was completed in 1965. Lake Meredith has a total storage capacity of 1,407,600 acre-feet and a surface area of 21,640 acres at an elevation of 2,965 feet above mean sea level. Water is diverted, filtered, treated, and pumped to cities and towns in the area for municipal supply. The pumping plants and pipelines make up a major item of investment of the project's total estimated cost of $103,230,000. The drainage area of the Canadian River above Lake Meredith is 20,220 square miles, but the contributing drainage area to the Canadian River below Ute Dam near Logan, New Mexico, and above Lake Meredith is only 6,018 square miles.

BIBLIOGRAPHY: Texas Water Commission, *Bulletin 6408* (1964).

Seth D. Breeding

Lake Mexia. Bistone Dam and Lake Mexia are in the Brazos River Basin in Limestone County, seven miles southwest of Mexia on the Navasota River. The project, owned and operated by the Bistone Municipal Water Supply District, furnishes water for Mexia and Mexia State School.qv Construction of the dam began on July 26, 1960; it was completed on June 5, 1961. The lake has a capacity of 10,000 acre-feet and a surface area of 1,200 acres at the spillway elevation of 448.3 feet above mean sea level. Drainage area above the dam is 198 square miles.

BIBLIOGRAPHY: Texas Water Commission, *Bulletin 6408* (1964).

Seth D. Breeding

*Lake Mineral Wells. The original dam for Lake Mineral Wells was begun in 1918 and was completed in September, 1920. In 1921 a contract was let for improving the spillway and installing pumps, pipeline, and filter-plant equipment. Storage capacity was increased in 1943 by raising the height of the spillway two feet. The lake has a capacity of 8,420 acre-feet and a surface area of 646 acres at the spillway crest at an elevation of 863 feet above mean sea level. The capacity before enlargement was 7,300 acre-feet. The drainage area above the dam is sixty-three square miles.

BIBLIOGRAPHY: Texas Water Commission, *Bulletin 6408* (1964).

Seth D. Breeding

Lake Murvaul. *See* Murvaul Lake.

*Lake Nasworthy. In 1967 Lake Nasworthy was owned by the city of San Angelo. The project was originally constructed by the West Texas Utilities Company in 1929–1930 to supply municipal and industrial water to the city of San Angelo, and water for irrigation. The project was sold to the city of San Angelo in May, 1950. On the basis of a survey made in 1953, the capacity of Nasworthy was 12,390 acre-feet and the surface area was 1,596 acres at the top of the collapsible floodgates at an elevation of 1,872.2 feet above mean sea level. The drainage area at Nasworthy Dam is 3,833 square miles, of which 1,178 square miles is probably noncontributing. Twin Buttes Reservoir, completed in February, 1963, regulates the flow into Lake Nasworthy.

BIBLIOGRAPHY: Texas Water Commission, *Bulletin 6408* (1964).

Seth D. Breeding

Lake Nocona. *See* Farmers Creek Reservoir.

*Lake Nolte.

Lake O' the Pines. Ferrells Bridge Dam and Lake O' the Pines are in the Cypress Creek Basin in Marion and Harrison counties, nine miles west of Jefferson on Cypress Creek. The lake extends into Morris, Camp, and Upshur counties. The project is owned by the United States government and is operated by the United States Army Corps of Engineers, New Orleans District. The lake is used for flood control, water and wildlife conservation, and recreational purposes. Construction was started in January, 1955, and completed on December 11, 1959. The lake has a capacity of 254,900 acre-feet and a surface area of 18,680 acres at an elevation of 228.5 feet above mean sea level, at the top of the conservation storage space. The flood control storage space is 587,200 acre-feet. The drainage area above the dam is 850 square miles.

BIBLIOGRAPHY: Texas Water Commission, *Bulletin 6408* (1964).

Seth D. Breeding

Lake Palestine. Blackburn Crossing Dam and Lake Palestine are in the Neches River Basin in Anderson and Cherokee counties, four miles east of Frankston on the Neches River. The lake extends into Henderson and Smith counties. The project is owned and operated by the Upper Neches River Authority for industrial, municipal, and recreational purposes. Construction of the dam began on May 30, 1960, and was completed on June 13, 1962. The lake has a capacity of 30,500 acre-feet and a surface area of 4,000 acres at an elevation of 317 feet above mean sea level at the operating level. At the emergency spillway crest elevation, the capacity is 57,550 acre-feet with a surface area of 6,800 acres. An enlargement is planned to increase the capacity to 410,000 acre-feet. The

drainage of the Neches River above the Blackburn Crossing Dam is 839 square miles.

BIBLIOGRAPHY: Texas Water Commission, *Bulletin 6408* (1964).

Seth D. Breeding

Lake Palo Pinto. Palo Pinto Creek Dam and Lake Palo Pinto are in the Brazos River Basin in Palo Pinto County, fifteen miles southwest of Mineral Wells on Palo Pinto Creek. The project is owned by the Palo Pinto County Municipal Water District No. 1. Construction of the dam was started on March 21, 1963; storage began on April 16, 1964, and the dam was completed on November 13, 1965. The reservoir has a conservation capacity of 42,200 acre-feet with dead storage capacity of 1,900 acre-feet and a surface area of 2,661 acres at the spillway crest elevation of 867 feet above mean sea level. The drainage area above the dam is 471 square miles.

BIBLIOGRAPHY: Texas Water Commission, *Bulletin 6408* (1964).

Seth D. Breeding

Lake Pat Cleburne. Lake Pat Cleburne, formerly Cleburne Reservoir, is in the Brazos River Basin in Johnson County, six miles south of Cleburne on Nolands River. The project is owned and operated by the city of Cleburne for a municipal water supply. Construction started on August 9, 1963, and was completed in 1964. The reservoir has a capacity of 25,600 acre-feet and a surface area of 1,545 acres at the service spillway crest elevation of 733.5 feet above mean sea level. All of this capacity is allocated to conservation storage. The drainage area above the dam is 100 square miles.

BIBLIOGRAPHY: Texas Water Commission, *Bulletin 6408* (1964).

Seth D. Breeding

*Lake Pauline.

*Lake Pauline, Texas.

Lake Quitman. Wood County Dam No. 1 and Lake Quitman are in the Sabine River Basin in Wood County, four miles north of Quitman on Dry Creek, a tributary of Lake Fork of the Sabine River. The project is owned and operated by Wood County for flood regulation and recreational purposes. Construction of the dam began on June 1, 1961, and was completed on June 1, 1962. The lake has a capacity of 7,440 acre-feet and a surface area of 814 acres at the service spillway crest elevation of 395 feet above mean sea level and is used for flood retardation and recreational purposes. The drainage area of Dry Creek above the dam is thirty-one square miles.

BIBLIOGRAPHY: Texas Water Commission, *Bulletin 6408* (1964).

Seth D. Breeding

Lake Randall. Lake Randall is in the Red River Basin in Grayson County, four miles northwest of Denison on Shawnee Creek. The project was started and completed in 1909. The lake has a capacity of 5,400 acre-feet and a surface area of 172 acres at an elevation of 640 feet above mean sea level. The drainage area above the dam is eleven square miles.

This small area does not produce the needed run-off, and a supplementary water supply has been pumped from Lake Texoma into Lake Randall since July, 1962.

BIBLIOGRAPHY: Texas Water Commission, *Bulletin 6408* (1964).

Seth D. Breeding

*Lake Rita Blanca.

*Lake Sabine.

*Lake Scarborough.

Lake Stamford. Lake Stamford is in the Brazos River Basin in Haskell County, ten miles south-east of Haskell on Paint Creek, a tributary of the Clear Fork of the Brazos River. The project is owned and operated by the city of Stamford as a water supply for itself and several other communi-ties. The water is also used for condenser cooling at a steam-electric generating plant. Construction of the project started on July 14, 1951, and was com-pleted in March, 1953. The lake has a capacity of 60,000 acre-feet and a surface area of 5,125 acres at the spillway crest elevation of 1,416.8 feet above mean sea level. The drainage area above the dam is 360 square miles.

BIBLIOGRAPHY: Texas Water Commission, *Bulletin 6408* (1964).

Seth D. Breeding

*Lake Sweetwater. Lake Sweetwater is owned and operated by the city of Sweetwater to provide water supply for municipal and industrial purposes. Construction of Sweetwater Dam was begun in 1928 and was completed in 1930. The lake has a capacity of 11,900 acre-feet and a surface area of 630 acres at elevation 2,116.5 feet above mean sea level. The drainage area above the dam is 104 square miles.

BIBLIOGRAPHY: Texas Water Commission, *Bulletin 6408* (1964).

Seth D. Breeding

*Lake Tahoka.

*Lake Tampaquas.

Lake Tawakoni. Iron Bridge Dam and Lake Tawakoni are in the Sabine River Basin in Rains and Van Zandt counties, nine miles northeast of Wills Point on the Sabine River. The lake extends into Hunt County. The project is owned and oper-ated by the Sabine River Authority.qv Construction of the dam was begun in January, 1958, and was completed in December, 1960. The lake has a ca-pacity of 936,200 acre-feet and a surface area of 36,700 acres at the spillway crest elevation of 437.5 feet above mean sea level. The shore line of 200 miles is in Rains, Hunt, and Van Zandt counties. The water is used for municipal, industrial, and irrigation supplies. The drainage area above the dam is 756 square miles.

BIBLIOGRAPHY: Texas Water Commission, *Bulletin 6408* (1964).

Seth D. Breeding

*Lake Texoma. Lake Texoma in 1967 had a storage capacity of 2,733,300 acre-feet and a surface area of 91,200 acres. When the content drops below 2,250,100 acre-feet, the lake is divided into two pools by levees around the Cumberland oil field. The drainage area is 39,719 square miles, of which 5,936 square miles is probably noncontributing.

BIBLIOGRAPHY: Texas Water Commission, *Bulletin 6408* (1964).

Seth D. Breeding

*Lake Trammell.

*Lake Travis. The capacity of Lake Travis is 1,172,000 acre-feet and the surface area is 18,930 acres. The capacity between elevations of 681.1 and 714.1 feet (crest of uncontrolled spillway) above mean sea level is 778,000 acre-feet and is reserved for flood control. The power installation consists of three generating units with a rated capacity of 22,500 kilowatts, each with all the allied equip-ment for connecting to the transmission system. The drainage area above the dam is 38,130 square miles, of which 11,900 is probably noncontributing. Run-off is partly regulated by Buchanan Reservoir and other reservoirs upstream.

BIBLIOGRAPHY: Texas Water Commission, *Bulletin 6408* (1964).

Seth D. Breeding

*Lake Trinidad.

Lake Tyler. Whitehouse Dam and Lake Tyler are in the Neches River Basin in Smith County, twelve miles southeast of Tyler on Prairie Creek. The project is owned and operated by the city of Tyler as a water supply for municipal, domestic, and industrial uses. Construction of Whitehouse Dam began on April 30, 1948, and the structure was completed on May 13, 1949. The lake has a capacity of 43,400 acre-feet and a surface area of 2,450 acres at the spillway crest level of 375.5 feet above mean sea level. The drainage area above the dam is forty-five square miles.

BIBLIOGRAPHY: Texas Water Commission, *Bulletin 6408* (1964).

Seth D. Breeding

*Lake Victor, Texas.

*Lake View, Texas.

*Lake Waco.

*Lake Walk. The Lake Walk project was started in December, 1928, and was completed in May, 1929. Lake Walk was inundated by Amistad Reser-voir qv in the late 1960's. The lake originally had a capacity of 5,400 acre-feet with an area of 380 acres at the spillway crest elevation of 1,001 feet above mean sea level. The hydroelectric power plant at Lake Walk had one generating unit with a capacity of 1,350 kilowatts, and the drainage area above the dam was 4,104 square miles. *See also* Water Power.

BIBLIOGRAPHY: Texas Water Commission, *Bulletin 6408* (1964).

Seth D. Breeding

Lake Waxahachie. Lake Waxahachie is in the Trinity River Basin in Ellis County, four miles southeast of Waxahachie on the South Prong of Waxahachie Creek. The project is owned and oper-ated by Ellis County Water Improvement District No. 1 as a water supply to the city of Waxahachie. Construction began on April 18, 1956, and the dam was completed in November, 1956. The lake has a capacity of 13,500 acre-feet and a surface area of 645 acres at the spillway crest elevation of 531.5 feet above mean sea level. The drainage area above the dam is thirty square miles.

BIBLIOGRAPHY: Texas Water Commission, *Bulletin 6408* (1964).

Seth D. Breeding

*Lake Wichita. The Lake Wichita project, begun in 1900, was completed the following year. Originally, Lake Wichita water was used for municipal purposes and for irrigation. In 1966 the city of Wichita Falls sold some water from the old canal system for cooling purposes and other needs at a steam-electric generating plant. The lake has a total capacity of 14,000 acre-feet and a surface area of 2,200 acres at an elevation of 980.5 feet above mean sea level. The drainage area above the dam is 143 square miles.

BIBLIOGRAPHY: Texas Water Commission, *Bulletin 6408* (1964).

Seth D. Breeding

Lake Winnsboro. Wood County Dam No. 4 and Lake Winnsboro are in the Sabine River Basin in Wood County, six miles southwest of Winnsboro on Big Sandy Creek. The project is owned and operated by Wood County for flood regulation and recreational purposes. Construction began on June 15, 1961, and the dam was completed on September 17, 1962. During 1966 the crest of the service spillway was raised two feet to an elevation of 419 feet. The lake has a capacity of 8,100 acre-feet and a surface area of 806 acres at the service spillway crest elevation of 419 feet above mean sea level. A flood retardation surcharge capacity of 8,170 acre-feet is provided between the crests of the service spillway at 419 feet and the emergency spillway at 427 feet above mean sea level. Drainage area of Big Sandy Creek above the dam is thirty-one square miles.

BIBLIOGRAPHY: Texas Water Commission, *Bulletin 6408* (1964).

Seth D. Breeding

*Lake Worth. The Lake Worth water supply has been increased by construction of Bridgeport Reservoir and Eagle Mountain Reservoir, and through purchase of water from Benbrook Reservoir. The lake has a capacity of 33,660 acre-feet and a surface area of 3,267 acres at the spillway crest elevation of 594.3 feet above mean sea level. The storage capacity is no longer a major factor because the normal maximum water elevation is maintained through releases from larger storage reservoirs upstream. The drainage area to Lake Worth is 2,064 square miles.

BIBLIOGRAPHY: Texas Water Commission, *Bulletin 6408* (1964).

Seth D. Breeding

Lake Worth Village, Texas. Lake Worth Village, an incorporated, suburban community in Tarrant County, is encompassed by the city of Fort Worth. The United States census reported a population for Lake Worth Village of 3,833 in 1960 and 4,958 in 1970. *See also* Dallas-Fort Worth Standard Metropolitan Statistical Area.

*Lakeland, Texas. (Liberty County.)

*Lakeland, Texas. (Nacogdoches County.)

*Lakenon, Texas.

Lakeside Heights, Texas. Lakeside Heights, a resort and retirement community in Llano County on Lake Lyndon B. Johnson, was founded in 1957. In the late 1960's the population was approximately one hundred fifty.

*Laketon, Texas.

*Lakeview, Texas. (Dallas County.)

*Lakeview, Texas. (Hale County.)

*Lakeview, Texas. (Hall County.)

*Lakeview, Texas. (Jefferson County.) The United States census reported a population for Lakeview of 3,849 in 1960 and 3,567 in 1970.

*Lakeview, Texas. (McLennan County.) *See also* Lacy-Lakeview, Texas.

*Lakeview, Texas. (Orange County.)

*Lakota, Texas. *See* Bennett, Texas.

*La Leona, Texas.

*Lallemand, Charles François Antoine.

*Lamar, Mirabeau Buonaparte.

*Lamar, Texas. (Aransas County.) The present site of Lamar in Aransas County was originally in Refugio County before that county was divided in 1871 to create Aransas County. Lamar, promoted by James W. Byrne, George Robert Hull, and George Armstrong, was founded in 1839 at Lookout Point, on the channel entrance to Copano Bay, as a rival town to Aransas City, which was located across the channel, at Live Oak Point. James Power,qv who lived at Live Oak Point, strongly opposed the building of the new town, which he could view from the gallery of his own home.

In 1839 Byrne and his associates made application to President Mirabeau B. Lamar to remove the customhouse from Aransas City to Lamar, claiming that they had twenty houses under construction and that the number of inhabitants at Lamar more than doubled that of Aransas City. Despite the protestations of Power and the citizens of Aransas City, the removal of the customhouse to Lamar was approved, and Aransas City subsequently went into decline.

From that time Lamar prospered as a port town, an industrial site for salt works, and a population center for Refugio County. During the Civil War, however, Lamar was bombarded and destroyed by Federal troops so that only the ruins of a few old homes and a Catholic chapel, Stella Maria (originally known as St. Joseph's Chapel), all built of shell and lime, remained.

Lamar (though now in Aransas County) is the only Refugio County coastal town of the period of the Republic which exists in 1976. Some of the ruins, including the chapel, are still there. In 1976 there were approximately one hundred fifty people living at or near the unincorporated townsite of Lamar, although the figure is unreliable because a number of populated resort areas nearby are often referred to as Lamar.

BIBLIOGRAPHY: Hobart Huson, *Refugio*, I (1953), II (1955); William H. Oberste, *Texas Irish Empresarios and Their Colonies* (1953).

*Lamar, Texas. (Falls County.)

Lamar, Texas. (Refugio County.) *See* Lamar, Texas. (Aransas County.)

*Lamar County. Lamar County, with an average annual farm income of $15 million in the early 1970's, was among the leading blackland agricultural counties, with livestock and poultry providing the chief source of income. Row crops were decreasing in importance. Most of the industries in the county were located in Paris, the county seat. The major tourist attractions were the Paris art fair in May, an August rodeo, and historic sites. The 1960 population was 34,234, and the 1970 population was 36,062, according to the United States census.

*Lamar Female Seminary. *See also* Presbyterian Education in Texas.

*Lamar State College of Technology. *See also* Lamar University.

Lamar University. Lamar State College of Technology,qv Beaumont, became Lamar University by legislative act on August 23, 1971. Before reaching university status, the college received permission from the legislature in 1953 to retain tuition collections and issue bonds for permanent construction and equipment to ease an enrollment boom. Two years later a constitutional amendment placed Lamar in the building program available to other state colleges. The campus, which began as fifty-nine acres and grew to over one hundred acres, accommodated twenty-nine permanent buildings in 1965 compared to five in 1950, when it was admitted to the state system from junior college status. Plant worth increased from $1,899,789 to $19,935,942 during this period. New additions included engineering, home economics, and physics buildings as well as a million-dollar expansion of the library, which contained 176,988 volumes by 1969.

Enrollment climbed steadily, from 1,538 in 1950 to 9,926 in the 1966–1967 regular term. Teaching load was carried in 1966–1967 by 325 faculty members, 40 percent of whom had doctorates, contrasted with seventy faculty members in 1950. Six thousand baccalaureate degrees were granted from 1953 to 1965; graduate programs were authorized in 1960. In addition to M.A. and M.S. degrees, the college offered master's degrees in engineering science, business administration, and education. By the 1974–1975 regular term a total of 11,080 students were instructed by over six hundred faculty members. John E. Gray served as president.

In 1971 enabling legislation authorized Lamar University to operate lower division colleges in Orange and Jefferson counties. The Orange Center branch was founded in 1971; now known as Lamar University at Orange, the center had 415 students during the 1974–1975 regular term, and Joe Ben

Welch was director. The Port Arthur branch was opened in September, 1975, as Lamar University at Port Arthur, with 562 students taking credit and non-credit courses; W. Sam Monroe was director. The Port Arthur branch was formerly a city-owned, non-profit school dating back to 1909; for its earlier history, *see* Port Arthur College.

Lamar University at Orange. *See* Lamar University.

Lamar University at Port Arthur. *See* Lamar University; *see also* Port Arthur College.

*La Marque, Texas. [This title was incorrectly listed in Volume II as Lamarque, Texas.] La Marque, in Galveston County, was incorporated in 1953. In 1967 the city reported seven schools, a bank, a library, a newspaper, and twenty churches. La Marque had 126 business establishments in 1970. The numerous industries in Texas City employed many of the inhabitants of La Marque. The 1960 population of 13,969 increased to a 1970 census count of 16,131. *See also* Galveston-Texas City Standard Metropolitan Statistical Area.

*Lamasco, Texas.

*Lamb, George A. Richard Bankhead, with whom George A. Lamb came to Texas in 1834, died on January 17, 1835 (not October 20, 1834, as stated in Volume II). Lamb married Mrs. Sarah Bankhead on June 27, 1835 (not September 8, 1835).

BIBLIOGRAPHY: L. W. Kemp, San Jacinto Notebook (MS., Archives, Texas State Library, Austin).
Margaret Craig

*Lamb County. Lamb County ranked high in the state as an agricultural county. In the early 1970's the county had an average annual farm income of $57 million. In the 1972–1973 season thirty-two gins processed 106,069 bales of cotton. The county was a leader in grain sorghums and had a large beef income. Approximately 400,000 acres were irrigated in 1972. From 1945 through 1972, 12,021,447 barrels of oil were produced. There was some industry, such as the manufacture of cottonseed oil, concrete pipe, and fertilizer. The predominantly rural population was 21,896 in 1960 and decreased to 17,770 by 1970, according to the United States census.

*Lamb Creek.

*Lambert, Walter.

*Lambert, Will.

*Lambert, Texas.

*Lambs Creek.

*Lambs Head Creek.

*La Merle, Texas.

*Lamesa, Texas. Lamesa, seat of Dawson County, was the banking and marketing center of the county. Among the city's businesses in 1970 were several small industries mostly connected with agriculture, especially with cotton growing. Some oil field supplies were also manufactured. By 1970, 312 businesses were reported. Nursing homes, a hospital, a library, and two newspapers served the community, which had a population of 12,438 in 1960 and 11,559 in 1970, according to the United States census.

*Lamesa Field.

*Lamkin, Texas.

*Lamont, Texas.

*La Mota Mountain.

*Lampasas, Texas. Lampasas, seat of Lampasas County, completed a new high school in 1956, a new library in 1962, and a nursing home (with fifty beds) and a grade school in 1963. In 1966 Lampasas reported twenty-one churches, two hospitals, two banks, a library, a newspaper, and a radio station. In mid-1966 the Lampasas county-city airport was opened. The city's 126 businesses, including eleven manufacturers, were largely concerned with poultry processing, feed manufacture, and plastic and styrofoam products in 1970. The 1960 population of Lampasas was 5,061; the 1970 population had increased to 5,922, according to the United States census.

*Lampasas County. Lampasas County, among the leading Texas sheep raising counties in 1970, also produced some cattle and goats. Limited cropping was practiced, with an emphasis on sorghums, small grains, and cotton. The major tourist attractions of the county were a June rodeo and recreational facilities on the Colorado River and Highland Lakes in neighboring Burnet County. The 1960 population of 9,418 decreased slightly to 9,323 by 1970, according to the United States census.

*Lampasas Cut Plain. See Grand Prairies and the Lampasas Cut Plain.

*Lampasas River.

*LaNana Bayou.

*Lanark, Texas.

*La Navidad en las Cruces.

*Lancaster, Joseph.

*Lancaster, Texas. Lancaster, in Dallas County, had twenty-six churches, five schools, and a library in 1963. The town reported ninety businesses in 1970. Lancaster had a 1960 population of 7,501, which increased to a 1970 census count of 10,522. See also Dallas Standard Metropolitan Statistical Area.

*Lancaster Tap Railroad.

*Land, Texas.

*Land Appropriations. As of August 31, 1965, the free public school fund had received a total of $599,534,721 from mineral lease bonuses, rentals, and royalties. This can be broken down as follows: bonuses, rentals, and royalties from minerals other than oil and gas, totaling $36,862,101; oil and gas lease bonuses from submerged lands, totaling $212,645,651, and on shore (including riverbeds), amounting to $46,019,750; oil and gas lease rentals from submerged lands, totaling $26,466,174, and

on shore (including riverbeds), equaling $17,-980,129; oil and gas lease royalties from submerged lands, totaling $122,211,488, and on shore, $137,-349,428. See also School Fund, Available; School Fund, Permanent; Tidelands Controversy.

As of the same date the University of Texas permanent fund had received a total of $449,177,887 from the sale of the original fifty leagues and mineral lease bonuses, royalties, and rentals derived from the 2,104,909 acres of West Texas lands which were granted by the Constitution of 1876 qv and the legislature in 1883. As of that date $4,-009,057 had been paid into the University available fund from surface easements and sale of sand, gravel, and caliche.

The permanent fund is invested in government bonds and corporate securities as prescribed by the state constitution. One-third of the income from such investment accrues to the Texas A&M University System qv available fund and two-thirds to the available fund of the University of Texas System,qv as prescribed by the legislature in 1931. See also University Fund, Available; University Fund, Permanent; Lands, Texas Public.

Berte R. Haigh

*Land Board, State.

Land Board Scandal. See Veterans' Land Board Scandal.

*Land Bounties. See Land Grants: Bounty and Donation. For general information, see Lands, Texas Public.

*Land Colonization. See Mexican Colonization Laws; Land Speculation. For general information, see Lands, Texas Public.

*Land Districts.

*Land Excess.

*Land Fraud Board.

*Land Grants.

*Land Grants for Internal Improvements.

*Land Office. See General Land Office; Old Land Office Building.

*Land Scrip.

*Land Speculation. See also Veterans' Land Board.

*Land Vacancy.

*Landa Park.

*Lander, Texas.

*Landergin, Texas.

*Landers Branch.

Landrum, Lynn Wiley. Lynn Wiley Landrum was born on August 24, 1891, at Whitewright, son of Sam Houston and Mary Cutlen (Dickey) Landrum. Educated in public and private schools in Texas and Tennessee, he attended Miami University, Oxford, Ohio, before entering the University of Texas, from which he received an LL.B. degree in 1917. He served in the army during World War I, and was discharged in 1919 with the rank of first lieutenant. Reentering the army in August, 1942, he served in the American military government in France and Germany; he was the chief military government officer at Würzburg, Germany, when released from the service as a lieutenant colonel in December, 1945.

Landrum began his newspaper career in 1919, serving as a printer and editor on several Texas and Oklahoma weekly newspapers before joining the Dallas *Morning News* qv as an editorial writer in 1921. He was married in 1922 to Anna Belle May of Dallas, and they had one son. In 1933 Landrum was named chief editorial writer for the Dallas (Evening) *Journal*, serving until that newspaper was sold in 1938. He was then named editorial columnist of the Dallas *Morning News* and held that post until his death. His talents as a forceful and incisive commentator on public affairs reached their most sustained expression in his "Thinking Out Loud" column. Dedicated to controversy, the column was undeviating in its adherence to the conservative point of view, and it became one of the most widely read newspaper features in Texas. Landrum enjoyed a large and devoted following among like-minded readers, but he had the opposition of other thousands who disagreed with his political and social philosophy.

Although he never practiced law, Landrum was a member of the Dallas Bar Association. He was a lay leader in the Methodist church and belonged to the First Methodist Church of Dallas. He was greatly in demand as a public speaker and was long a member of speaking teams of the National Conference of Christians and Jews. He died in Dallas on August 31, 1961, and was buried in Whitewright.

BIBLIOGRAPHY: Dallas *Morning News*, September 1, 1961.

Sam Acheson

Landrum, Miriam Gordon. Miriam Gordon Landrum was born on November 25, 1893, in Waco, Texas, the daughter of Sam Houston and Mary Cutlen (Dickey) Landrum. After graduation from the public schools in Altus, Oklahoma, she received a diploma from Kingfisher College in 1915 and attended the University of Texas from 1916 to 1917. She began her study of piano in Whitewright, Texas, and continued it throughout her college years. She taught piano at Radnor College, a finishing school in Nashville, Tennessee, from 1911 to 1912. She studied under Gertrude Concannon, Charles Haubiel, and Rudolph Ganz, and worked under Isadore Philipp and Robert Casadesus in France.

Returning to Austin, Miss Landrum became associated with piano instruction at the University of Texas from 1922 to 1925. In 1930 Miss Landrum and her associates established the Texas School of Fine Arts qv in Austin. Along with Anita Gaedcke she jointly directed the school until 1942, when Miss Landrum became sole owner and director. She held that position until her death. She was a charter member of the National Guild of Piano Teachers and served as a member of its board

of trustees. She also wrote numerous articles in professional magazines. Miss Landrum was active in many religious and cultural activities, including the founding of the Austin Symphony. She died in Austin on January 2, 1967, and was buried in Whitewright.

BIBLIOGRAPHY: *Who's Who of American Women* (1958); Austin *American-Statesman*, April 24, 1962; Austin *American*, January 3, 1967.

*Landrum, Willis H.

*Landrum, Texas. (Cameron County.)

*Landrum, Texas. (Cherokee County.)

*Lands, Texas Public.** The "reserved area" of Texas public lands is composed of the beds of navigable rivers and lakes and the submerged coastal areas. The involved lands are permanently reserved to the state, with the minerals therein appropriated to the free public school permanent fund. The United States Supreme Court in 1950 decreed federal ownership of that land in the Gulf of Mexico lying between the three-mile and three-league limits off the Texas coast. This area, comprising an estimated 1,878,394 acres, was "returned" to Texas by a congressional act on May 23, 1953, and the Supreme Court finally confirmed Texas' ownership of the area in a new court case on December 12, 1960.

The estimated "off-shore" portion of the reserved area, including beach areas, islands, land beneath bays and inlets, and submerged lands to the three-league limit, is 4,045,000 acres. The total appropriation from the public domain to the free public school fund, as of 1964, amounted to 42,-561,400 acres. *See also* Land Appropriations; School Fund, Available; School Fund, Permanent; University Fund, Available; University Fund, Permanent; Tidelands Controversy.

BIBLIOGRAPHY: Jerry Sadler, *History of Texas Lands* (1964).

Berte R. Haigh

*Lane, George.

Lane, Horatio Gates.** Horatio Gates Lane was born in Bedford County, Tennessee, on March 21, 1832, the son of Isham H. and Theodosia (Edwards) Lane. The family came to Texas in 1849 when Lane was seventeen. He taught in a private school, read law in Joseph Lewis Hogg's qv law office at Rusk, and was admitted to the Bar on May 4, 1857. He married Sarah Elizabeth Virginia Hall of Rusk, and they had twelve children.

Lane moved to Homer, Angelina County, where he practiced law and taught school a short time before the Civil War. He enlisted in the Confederate Army as a private in February, 1862, rising to the rank of captain by the war's end. He then returned to Homer to practice law, but during the radical Reconstruction qv period Lane refused to take the "ironclad oath" and was not permitted to vote or practice law. Lane served as a state district judge and as district attorney for the Third Judicial District of Texas. He moved from Homer to Fort Worth in 1892, where he died on March 3, 1911. He was buried in Jacksonville. Confederate veterans of Jacksonville named their camp H. G. Lane Camp Number 614 in his honor.

BIBLIOGRAPHY: Mamie Yeary, *Reminiscences of the Boys in Gray, 1861–1865* (1912); H. L. Bentley and Thomas Pilgrim, *The Texas Legal Directory for 1876–1877* (1877).

John N. Cravens

*Lane, J. S.

*Lane, Jim. *See* Cook, Jim.

*Lane, Jonathan.

*Lane, Walter Paye. Walter Paye Lane was one of four wounded (not five, as stated in Volume II) of the seven survivors of the Battle Creek Fight qv (also called Surveyors Fight) on October 8, 1838. He was with a group of twenty-five (not twenty-three) surveyors who were attacked by Indians, among whom were not only Kickapoos (as stated in Volume II), but also Wacos, Tehuacanas, Ionies, and Caddos. Two of the original survey party of twenty-seven men were absent from the battle; eighteen (not sixteen) of the twenty-five participants were killed; and seven escaped, including Lane.

BIBLIOGRAPHY: Harry McCorry Henderson, "The Surveyors Fight," *Southwestern Historical Quarterly*, LVI (1952–1953).

*Lane, Texas. (Hartley County.)

*Lane, Texas. (Hunt County.)

*Lane, Texas. (Webb County.)

*Lane City, Texas.

*Lanely, Texas.

*Laneport, Texas.

*Laneville, Texas.

*Lang, John J.

*Lang, L. Willis.

*Lang, William W.

*Lang Creek.

*Lang Mountain.

*Langenheim, William.

*Langham Creek.

*Langtry, Texas.

*Langum Creek.

Lanham, Fritz Garland. Fritz Garland Lanham was born in Weatherford, Texas, on January 3, 1880, the son of Sarah Beona (Meng) and Samuel Willis Tucker Lanham.qv He attended schools in Washington, D.C., and in 1897 was graduated from Weatherford Junior College. He received a B.A. degree from the University of Texas in 1900; he was the first editor of the *Texan*, a university weekly newspaper which was the predecessor of the *Daily Texan*.qv In 1909 he was admitted to the Texas Bar qv and opened a law office in Weatherford.

Lanham was elected representative from the Twelfth Texas Congressional District on April 19, 1919, and served until January 3, 1947. During the early years of World War II he handled the legislation for the construction of defense housing for industrial workers. The outstanding law bearing his name was the Lanham Act, which gave greater trademark protection to American businessmen. For a number of years after retirement from Congress, Lanham was a registered lobbyist in Washington for the National Patent Office, the American Fair Trade Council, and the Trinity Improvement Association of Texas.

His career was many-faceted. He taught Greek at Weatherford Junior College, toured for a year with a theatrical company, covered Texas League qv baseball one season as sportswriter for the Dallas *Morning News*,qv spoke frequently as a lay preacher in the Methodist church, and entertained on numerous occasions as an amateur magician.

Lanham married Beulah Rowe of Austin, Texas, in 1908. After her death in 1930, he married Mrs. Hazel Head in 1932. He moved from Washington to Austin in 1961, where he died of a heart attack on July 31, 1965. He was buried at Weatherford.

BIBLIOGRAPHY: Escal F. Duke, The Life and Political Career of Fritz G. Lanham (M.A. thesis, University of Texas, 1941); Fort Worth *Star-Telegram*, August 2, 1965; *Congressional Record*, Eighty-ninth Congress, First Session, III.

Escal F. Duke

*Lanham, Samuel Willis Tucker.

*Lanham, Texas.

Lanier, Sidney. Sidney Lanier, poet, critic, and musician, was born in Macon, Georgia, on February 3, 1842, the son of Robert S. and Mary Jane (Anderson) Lanier. Graduating from Oglethorpe College in 1860, Lanier joined the Macon Volunteers at the outbreak of the Civil War and participated in several battles; later he served as a scout and in the signal service. On November 2, 1864, he was captured and eventually imprisoned at Point Lookout, Maryland, where hardships and illness led to tuberculosis. After his release in February, 1865, he walked home, arriving in Macon on March 15, desperately ill. These experiences are reflected in his antiwar novel *Tiger-Lilies* (1867) and were to make the remainder of his life a battle against time, poverty, and ill health.

On December 19, 1867, Lanier married Mary Day. Four sons were born to the couple. He practiced law with his father to support his family, and his health grew worse. In 1872 he left his family in Macon and arrived in San Antonio on November 24, 1872, via New Orleans, Galveston, Houston, and Austin.

Lanier wrote more than one hundred letters from Texas, but apparently no poetry. He wrote three short essays: "The Texas Trail in the '70's," a portion of which was printed under the title "The Mesquit [*sic*] in Texas"; "An Indian Raid in Texas"; and "The Mexican Border Troubles." All were published in the New York *World*, under the pseudonym "Otfall," in 1872 and 1873. A long article, "San Antonio de Bexar," with descriptions of places, peoples, and "northers," and with historical accounts based on Henderson Yoakum's qv *History of Texas* (1856), appeared in the July-August, 1873, edition of *The Southern Magazine*.

Lanier left Texas in March, 1873. He became

first flutist in the Peabody Orchestra in Baltimore, and in 1876 he wrote a cantata for the Centennial Exposition in Philadelphia. He published a volume of poems in 1877. In 1879 he gave lectures at Johns Hopkins University (published later as *The Science of English Verse*, 1880). He died on September 7, 1881, in Lynn, North Carolina, and was buried in Greenmount Cemetery, Baltimore.

Most important of those works posthumously published are *Poems of Sidney Lanier* (1884), *The English Novel and the Principle of its Development* (1883), *Music and Poetry* (1898), *Retrospects and Prospects* (1899), and *Shakespeare and His Forerunners* (2 vols., 1902). Lanier's interests were equally divided between music and literature. He is noted for his disputed theory that laws of music and poetry are identical, both based on the physics of sound: duration, intensity, pitch, and tone color. His best poem, "The Marshes of Glynn," with its scene of the sea marshes near Brunswick, Georgia, reflects this theory.

BIBLIOGRAPHY: Charles R. Anderson (ed.), *The Centennial Edition of Sidney Lanier* (1945); Lincoln Lorenz, *The Life of Sidney Lanier* (1935); Edwin Mims, *Sidney Lanier* (1905); Aubrey S. Starke, *Sidney Lanier* (1933).

Ruth S. Angell

*Lanier, Texas.

*Lann, James W.

*Lannius, Texas.

*Lansing, Texas.

*Lantana, Texas.

*La Paloma, Texas.

*Lapara, Texas.

*La Parita Creek.

*Lapham, Moses.

La Plata, Texas. La Plata, formerly called Grenada, was created on October 3, 1890, when Deaf Smith County was organized. The town served as the first county seat. A small courthouse was built, and the town grew to include such buildings as a post office, a school, a jail, a Presbyterian church, and eighteen residences. The population declined during the dry years of 1893 and 1894. In 1898 a railroad was built through the southern part of Deaf Smith County and into New Mexico. In the general election of November 8, 1898, the citizens voted to move the county seat to the railroad. Nine houses and the courthouse and jail were loaded onto wagons and moved to the site of Hereford.

Vern Witherspoon
Grover C. Ramsey

*La Porte, Texas. La Porte, in Harris County, was incorporated in 1948 and had a mayor-commissioner form of government. In 1966 the city was involved in extensive water and sewer expansion. La Porte had seven public schools, a college, a library, a municipal airport, two banks, sixteen churches, two newspapers, and considerable industrial growth in the 1960's. In 1970 the town reported 136 business establishments. La Porte had a population of 4,512 in 1960 and a population of 7,149 in 1970, according to the United States census. See *also* Houston Standard Metropolitan Statistical Area.

*La Porte, Houston, and Northern Railroad.

*La Portilla, Felipe Roque de. See Portilla, Felipe Roque de la.

*La Portilla, José Nicolás de. See Portilla, José Nicholás de la.

*La Prensa. Ignacio E. Lozano, founder and publisher of *La Prensa*, died in 1953. The paper was continued by his widow, Alicia Lozano, until June 14, 1957, when she suspended its publication. She blamed falling circulation on a decline in the non-English-reading public. In June, 1959, *La Prensa* was purchased by Dudley Dougherty and Eduardo Grenas Gooding, who published it as a bilingual weekly paper. In early 1960 Dougherty became sole owner and publisher; in May, 1961, he transferred ownership to Robert T. Brinsmade, but he continued to provide financial backing. The last issue of *La Prensa* appeared on January 31, 1963, two weeks short of its fiftieth anniversary.

BIBLIOGRAPHY: San Antonio *Light*, June 14, 1957, March 2, 1963.

*La Pryor, Texas.

*La Purísima Concepción de Acuña Mission. See Nuestra Señora de la Purísima Concepción de Acuña Mission.

La Raza Unida Party. See Raza Unida Party.

*L'Archeveque, Jean.

*Laredo, Texas. Laredo, seat of Webb County, relies on cattle raising, farming, manufacturing, imports-exports, tourism, and oil production for its income. Located in the city is the only antimony smelter in the United States. Approximately 60 percent of the total import-export trade and more than half the tourist trade between Mexico and the United States pass through Laredo. The town had two newspapers, two radio stations, and a television station in 1966, as well as a hospital, two colleges, a library, and forty-three churches. The Laredo International Civic Center, with a capacity for two thousand, was completed in 1965. An expressway, a senior citizens home, and an addition to the hospital were in operation by 1966. Nearby Laredo Air Force Base qv brought an increase in population and has become an important economic asset to the city. Among the many businesses in 1967 were forty-five industrial plants, five of which employed over a hundred workers each. Business establishments numbered 854 in 1970. The citizens of Laredo, primarily of Mexican descent, numbered 60,678 in 1960 and 69,024 in 1970, according to the United States census. See *also* Laredo Standard Metropolitan Statistical Area.

Laredo Air Force Base. Laredo Air Force Base, formerly Laredo Army Air Field,qv was officially reactivated in April, 1952, after a contract between the United States and the city of Laredo had been signed. The base's new mission was to provide basic training for jet pilots; the first class of qualified pilots was graduated in September, 1952.

In 1961 the base became one of the undergraduate pilot training bases of the Air Training Command. The students received a fifty-three-week training course on the base, which included the three phases of pilot training and experience in the T-41, T-37, and T-38 aircraft. From the inception of the training program, the Laredo Air Force Base student roster included United States officers and foreign trainees from twenty-four allied countries. By 1967 Laredo Air Force Base had trained nearly eight thousand pilots. The base was still operating just outside Laredo in 1975.

*Laredo Archives. After the death in 1959 of Sebron (Seb) Sneed Wilcox,qv who was responsible for the preservation of the Laredo Archives, the original manuscript materials were placed in the library at St. Mary's University in San Antonio. Organization of the collection was under the direction of Brother Paul Novosal. The earliest document found in the archives is from 1749, but the main records begin with the year 1768, when Laredo was granted a charter by the Spanish Crown, and cover the period through the Mexican administration, to 1846; a collection of papers dealing with local and border interests, from 1846 to 1875, is also included.

Typescript copies were made from the original documents, and portions of these copies were placed in the Archives Division of the Texas State Library,qv the University of Texas at Austin Library, the National Archives in Washington, D.C., and in Laredo, Texas. A microfilm copy of the complete set of records was made for Texas Tech University, and that copy was placed in the Texas Tech Library.

BIBLIOGRAPHY: Walter Prescott Webb, "Texas Collection," *Southwestern Historical Quarterly*, XLIV (1940–1941); Seb S. Wilcox, "The Spanish Archives of Laredo," *ibid.*, XLIX (1945–1946); H. Bailey Carroll, "Texas Collection," *ibid.*, LXV (1961–1962).

*Laredo Army Air Field. *See also* Laredo Air Force Base.

Laredo Junior College. Laredo Junior College was created by voting citizens in the Independent School District of Laredo on September 28, 1946. Classes began in September, 1947, with an enrollment in excess of eight hundred students. Enrollment increased rapidly as World War II veterans entered, and it reached a peak of 1,745 students in 1950.

The main 146-acre campus was situated at the western edge of Laredo on the south portion of old Fort McIntosh,qv approximately three-quarters of a mile across the Rio Grande from Mexico. By 1965 the physical plant included thirty-two buildings. Library holdings grew from approximately 5,600 volumes in 1949 to 30,000 volumes in 1969. The college was fully accredited by major agencies.

During the first years of the school's operation the curriculum was grouped into four divisions: liberal arts, adult education, vocational education, and terminal education (an accelerated elementary and high school program). As veterans completed their studies, the vocational and terminal departments were assimilated into the adult education division, or evening school. The liberal arts division increased in enrollment, faculty, and course offerings. Overcrowding of library, science, and gymnasium facilities resulted. A master building plan for a new 1,500-student college to be constructed on the same site was completed in 1964.

By the 1974–1975 regular term, student enrollment totaled 3,925. W. J. Adkins served as the first president of the college and was succeeded by Ray A. Laird. Domingo Arechiga became president in June, 1974.

*Laredo Seminary. *See* Holding Institute.

Laredo Standard Metropolitan Statistical Area. The Laredo Standard Metropolitan Statistical Area was created by the United States Bureau of the Budget in 1949. In 1950 the area, which consists of the 3,293 square miles of Webb County, had a population of 56,141; Laredo had 51,910 inhabitants. In 1960 the totals were 64,791 and 60,678, respectively; by 1970 the population of Webb County rose to 72,859, and Laredo had an increase to 69,024, according to the report of the United States census for 1970. Smaller communities are Mirando City, Bruni, Oilton, Aguilares, and Mills Bennett. A more realistic designation of the area would include Nuevo Laredo and the northwestern part of the Mexican state of Tamaulipas across the Rio Grande from Laredo. Combined with the 125,-000 residents of Nuevo Laredo, the area had a population of approximately 200,000.

Laredo and Nuevo Laredo are bound by historical, economic, and cultural ties. About eight million persons and 2,500,000 motor vehicles annually cross the border, passing over the international bridge which joins the two cities. A great majority of the Laredo population is of Mexican descent. Export, import, and tourist trade funnels through Laredo from all parts of the United States and Mexico. The city is a principal port of entry on the United States-Mexico border, handling about 60 percent of the total export-import trade and over half the tourists of Mexico and Texas. Laredo is the retail shopping center for much of adjacent Mexico. Exports from Laredo (with motor vehicles and electrical equipment the major export items to Mexico) were valued at $486 million in 1962 and over $1 billion in 1972. Imports from Mexico were valued at almost $147 million in 1962 and approximately $549 million in 1972.

Wearing apparel manufacture is a major enterprise in Laredo, with three firms employing more than one hundred workers. The city has the only antimony smelter in the United States. Other commodities manufactured in the area are tires, tile and brick, saddles, insecticides, candles, Mexican food, dairy products, bakery goods, soft drinks, and ready-mix concrete. Some petroleum is produced in Webb County. More important are farming and ranching, with two-thirds of the farm income in the county coming from livestock and poultry. Along the Rio Grande both irrigated and dryland farming produce fruits, vegetables, feeds, and cotton. Laredo Air Force Base,qv reactivated in 1952, has become an important economic asset to the area.

Culturally, Laredo has a civic music association and a little theater. Museums include the old capitol building of the Republic of the Rio Grande qv and the Margaret Jones Cactus Garden, one of the oldest cactus nurseries in the United States. Other historical attractions are Fort McIntosh, the old Dolores Mission,qqv San Agustín Plaza and Sección Original, and the Erastus (Deaf) Smith qv historical marker. Laredo Junior College, on the grounds of Fort McIntosh, enrolled 3,925 students in the 1974 fall term. In 1963 the city completed a new high school with all its classrooms completely underground. Recreational facilities include hunting, fishing, swimming, and water sports at Casa Blanca Lake, International Falcon Reservoir, and various ranches in the county. Annual events include the Laredo International Fair and Exposition, George Washington's Birthday Celebration, and the Border Olympics. Across the border Nuevo Laredo offers weekend bullfights during the summer months, in addition to gift shops, restaurants, and nightclubs throughout the year.

Laredo is the southernmost terminal point of Interstate 35 and U.S. Highways 81 and 59. The international bridge, destroyed by flood in 1954, was rebuilt and expanded to four lanes by February, 1957. Two railroads connected Laredo with northern and eastern points, while air service was provided by Texas International Airlines (formerly Trans-Texas Airways) from Laredo Municipal Airport. Laredo had a public library, a daily and a weekly newspaper, and one television and two radio stations in the late 1960's. See also Standard Metropolitan Statistical Areas in Texas.

Rogelia O. Garcia

*Laredo *Times*.

*La Reforma, Texas.

*La Réunion.

*Largin, Texas.

*Lariat, Texas.

*Larios, Francisco García.

*Larissa, Texas.

*Larissa College.

*Lark, Texas.

LaRoche, Daniel Constant. Three men of the same family, each named Daniel Constant LaRoche, contributed to the economy and culture of the Lower Rio Grande Valley.

The elder Daniel Constant LaRoche was born in Honfleur, Normandy, France, in the 1820's and went to sea as a young man. He migrated to the United States in the 1850's; in New York he met and married Elizabeth Cunhalt, a German immigrant; they moved to New Orleans and later to Point Isabel (now Port Isabel), Texas. LaRoche served in the Confederate Navy and was captured during the battle of Mobile Bay; he escaped and made his way to Bagdad, a Mexican boom town on the mouth of the Rio Grande. There he helped to run cotton through the Federal blockade. After the Civil War, LaRoche resettled his family at Point Isabel and participated in the coastal trade. He died at Point Isabel in the mid-1880's.

The eldest son and namesake of Daniel Constant LaRoche was born at Point Isabel in 1859 and followed the family tradition by becoming a seaman and pilot in the vital coastal transportation that connected the Rio Grande Valley with the remainder of Texas. He died at Port Isabel in 1917.

The third Daniel Constant LaRoche was born at Point Isabel on January 11, 1877. He broke the family's seagoing tradition and devoted himself to local transportation, tourism, and politics. He and two brothers, William and Frank, established a ferry line between Port Isabel and Padre Island and promoted the southern tip of the island for recreation. LaRoche participated in exploratory plans for a ferry, causeway, and road complex along Padre Island, linking its Corpus Christi and Port Isabel ends. He was a county commissioner of Cameron County for four terms, serving on the county court that initiated highway construction. He died at Brownsville on November 11, 1949, and was buried in the old cemetery at Port Isabel, not far from his father and grandfather.

Clarence J. LaRoche

*Larrison Creek.

*Larry Creek.

*Larue, Texas.

*La Salle, René Robert Cavelier, Sieur de.

*La Salle, Texas. (Calhoun County.)

*La Salle, Texas. (Jackson County.)

*La Salle, Texas. (La Salle County.)

*La Salle, Texas. (Limestone County.)

*La Salle County. La Salle County, primarily a cattle ranching area, also raised small crops of peanuts, vegetables, and watermelons. From 1940 through 1972, nearly eight million barrels of oil had been produced in the county. La Salle County partially supported a public library and in 1965 was given a permit to construct a reservoir on the Nueces River for the purpose of flood control. The major tourist attraction is a July rodeo. The population in 1960 was 5,972, but by 1970 it had declined to 5,014, according to the United States census.

*La Salle Expedition. H. E. Bolton qv (not H. H. Bolton, as stated in Volume II) offered evidence as to the location of Fort St. Louis qv on Garcitas Creek. [Some later printings of Volume II contain this correction.]

*La Sal Vieja.

*Las Anchas Creek.

*Las Animas Creek.

*Lasara, Texas.

*Lasater, Edward Cunningham.

"Lasca." *See* Desprez, Frank.

***Lasca, Texas.**

***Las Escobas, Texas.**

***Las Hermanitas.**

***Las Islitas, Texas.**

***Lasker, Morris.**

***Las Moras, Texas.**

***Las Moras Creek.**

***Las Moras Mountain.**

***Las Raices Creek.**

***Lassater, Texas.**

***Las Tiendas, Texas.**

***Las Vegas, Texas.**

***Latch, Texas.**

***Latex, Texas.**

***Latexo, Texas.**

***Latham Creek.**

***Latimer, Albert Hamilton.**

***Latimer, Henry Russell.**

***Latimer, James L.**

***Latimer, James Wellington.**

***Latimer County.**

***Latin American Collection.** [The Latin American Collection was officially renamed the Nettie Lee Benson Latin American Collection in the fall of 1975. Formerly housed on the eighth floor of the main library building at the University of Texas at Austin, the collection was moved to the south section of the newly completed Sid Richardson Hall in early 1971. The original García library, purchased in 1921, was the nucleus of the collection, and it contained approximately 25,000 printed items and 400,000 (not 200,000, as stated in Volume II) pages of manuscripts; other corrections to the Volume II article include the acquisition of the W. B. Stephens collection in 1938 of 1,300 (not 12,000) printed items, and the addition in 1943 of the Sánchez Navarro family papers of some 75,000 (not 40,000) pages. Head librarians of this important collection have been Carlos Eduardo Castañeda qv (1921–1927), Lota May Spell qv (1927–1942), and Nettie Lee Benson (1942–1975), for whom the collection is now named. Upon Miss Benson's retirement at the end of August, 1975, Laura Gutiérrez-Witt was named head librarian. Ed.]

In 1961 additions were made to the already extensive holdings of the Latin American Collection at the University of Texas at Austin. The acquisitions included Pedro Martínez Reales' gaucho library of 1,500 books, pamphlets, and articles on the literature of the Argentine cowboy and over three hundred editions of the nineteenth-century epic gaucho poem *Martín Fierro* by José Hernández. In 1963 the Arturo Taracena Flores collection of 10,000 books, pamphlets, and broadsides, as well as numerous periodicals, newspaper clippings, and maps on nineteenth- and twentieth-century Guatemala and other Central American countries, were added. The Simón Lucuix library of 26,000 volumes on Uruguay and the Río de la Plata area was received the following year. In 1975 more than a million manuscript pages were added to the holdings of the collection when the business records (dating from 1830 to 1960) of the St. John d'el Rey Mining Company were given to the university. The firm, originally owned and operated by the British, but located since 1960 in Cleveland, Ohio, operated gold and iron ore mines in Brazil; the holdings include a complete collection of the company's annual reports from 1830, demographic records, photographs, mining and geological reports, correspondence, land deeds, and employee records.

By late 1975 the Latin American Collection had grown into a library of 2,000,000 pages of manuscripts, 5,000 broadsides, 2,500 maps, 10,000 photographs, 3,000 bound volumes of newspapers, 9,000 reels of microfilm, and 320,000 bound volumes of books, pamphlets, and serials. Its wealth of information has given the collection an international reputation. Scholars from all over the world come in ever-increasing numbers to make use of its resources, or they obtain access to the material through inter-library loan or photocopies.

Nettie Lee Benson

***"Latin Settlements" of Texas.**

***Latium, Texas.**

***Lattimore, John Compere.**

***Lattimore, Offa Shivers.** Offa Shivers Lattimore was born in Marion, Alabama (not Perry, Alabama, as stated in Volume II). He moved with his parents to Texas when he was twelve years old; the family settled in Falls County.

Lattimore was assistant county attorney for Tarrant County from 1890 to 1894 (not assistant county auditor in 1894). He was county attorney of Tarrant County from 1900 to 1904 (not from 1898 to 1904). He died on October 27, 1937 (not October 14, 1937), and was buried in the State Cemetery qv in Austin (not in Rose Hill Cemetery, Fort Worth).

H. S. Lattimore

***La Tuna, Texas.** Formerly called La Tuna for the Federal Correctional Institution qv located nearby, the community was incorporated in 1952 as Anthony, Texas. *See also* Anthony, Texas (El Paso County).

Laughlin Air Force Base. Laughlin Air Force Base, at Del Rio, formerly Laughlin Army Air Field,qv was closed in late 1945 and its facilities turned over to the U.S. Army Corps of Engineers. Until 1952 parts of the base were leased to local ranchers and used for goat grazing. In May, 1952, Laughlin was reactivated and the 3646th Pilot Training Wing was formed there. The original single-engine pilot training mission of the base was never implemented. Later that same year the base's mission was changed to F-84 jet fighter pilot training. Laughlin was also used during this period for advanced fighter aircraft gunnery training.

The base was transferred to the Strategic Air

Command in 1957 and the 4080th Strategic Reconnaissance Wing moved there from Georgia. The wing, using the RB-57 as its basic aircraft, began a program of high-altitude weather reconnaissance. The first U-2 aircraft arrived at the base in mid-1957, and the reconnaissance wing became responsible for training all pilots and maintenance crews for the U-2 aircraft. By 1959 the base had expanded its facilities by five hundred housing units and plans were made to provide undergraduate pilot training for one-half of the students stationed at Laredo Air Force Base.qv The U-2's stationed at the base were of great importance during the 1962 Cuban crisis. A Laughlin-based U-2 provided the first conclusive evidence of a Soviet missile buildup in Cuba; likewise the only casualty due to enemy action in the crisis was a U-2 pilot stationed at Laughlin Air Force Base.

In April, 1962, the base was transferred to the Air Training Command, and the reactivated 3646th Pilot Training Wing graduated its first class later that year. The reconnaissance wing continued its mission until it was transferred to an Arizona base in July, 1963.

Laughlin expanded its training programs during the 1960's to include "para-sail" training, automated trainee scheduling, and a continuous flow launch and recovery system.

Since its reactivation, Laughlin has trained foreign students regularly under the military assistance program in the fields of pilot training, maintenance, safety, and operations. In April, 1967, there were twelve foreign trainees at the base. By February, 1967, the 3646th Pilot Training Wing had graduated its one-thousandth trainee since the reactivation of the base. Under the 1967 military construction bill, Laughlin was to receive $736,000 for operational, training, and administrative facilities. Undergraduate pilot training continued at Laughlin in the 1970's.

*Laughlin Army Air Field. See also Laughlin Air Force Base.

*Laura.

*Laurel, Texas. (Newton County.)

*Laurel, Texas. (Webb County.)

*Laureles, Texas.

*Laureles Ranch.

*Laurelia, Texas.

*Lavaca Bay.

*Lavaca County. Lavaca County ranked third among Texas counties in 1964 in number of farms, with 2,685. It was one of the leading counties in hog, beef cattle, and poultry production, and cotton, rice, and grains were its main crops. From 1941 through 1972 the county yielded almost six million barrels of oil. In 1960 a Lavaca County office building was completed, and by 1967 the courthouse had been enlarged and renovated. The major tourist attractions were a June Tom-Tom celebration in Yoakum, the Shiner Mayfest, and a rodeo. The

1960 population was 20,174; the 1970 population decreased to 17,903, according to the United States census.

*Lavaca River.

*Lavender, Eugenie (Mrs. Charles).

*Lavender, Texas. (Limestone County.)

*Lavender, Texas. (Smith County.)

*La Vernia, Texas.

*La Villa, Texas. La Villa, in eastern Hidalgo County, reported seven businesses in 1970; the population of La Villa was 1,261 in 1960 and 1,255 in 1970, according to the United States census.

*La Villita.

*La Viuda Mountain.

*Lavon, Texas.

Lavon Reservoir. Lavon Reservoir is in the Trinity River Basin in Collin County, two miles west of Lavon and twenty-two miles northeast of Dallas on the East Fork of the Trinity River. The project is owned by the federal government and is operated by the United States Army Corps of Engineers for flood control and conservation of water supply. The North Texas Municipal Water District has purchased the 100,000 acre-feet of conservation space in the reservoir for municipal, industrial, and domestic water supply.

Construction of the dam began in January, 1948, and the main dam was completed in 1952. The reservoir has a capacity of 143,600 acre-feet and a surface area of 11,080 acres at the top of the conservation storage space, at an elevation of 472 feet above mean sea level. The flood-control storage capacity at the top of the taintor gates is 279,800 acre-feet. The drainage area above the dam is 770 square miles.

BIBLIOGRAPHY: Texas Water Commission, *Bulletin 6408* (1964).

Seth D. Breeding

Law, Francis Marion. Francis Marion Law, son of Francis Marion and Mary Jane (Howell) Law, was born on January 3, 1877, in Bryan. He was graduated with a B.S. degree from the Agricultural and Mechanical College of Texas (now Texas A&M University) in 1895 and was a law student at the University of Texas for one term, in 1896–1897. He did not complete his study of law at the university, but went to work as a bookkeeper (and later assistant cashier) at the First National Bank of Bryan from 1897 to 1908. He was employed as a cashier at the First National Bank in Beaumont from 1910 to 1915 and as an officer of the First National Bank (now First City National Bank) in Houston from 1915 until his retirement in 1955, serving that institution as vice-president (1915–1930), president (1930–1945), and chairman of the board (beginning in 1945).

Law was elected president of the Texas Bankers Association in 1924 and president of the American Bankers Association in 1933. Following the Bank Holiday of 1933 he spent much of his time in

Washington, D.C., helping in the revision of the National Banking Act and in drafting a charter for the Federal Deposit Insurance Corporation. During that time of slow economic recovery he sought a rapprochement between conservative bankers and the federal government, particularly with President Franklin D. Roosevelt, whom he presented to the American Bankers Association at their convention in Washington in 1934. Law served on the board of directors of Texas A&M College from 1919 to 1947 and was chairman of that board from 1922 to 1944. He was president of the Houston Symphony Society, a director of the Houston Baptist Hospital, a regent of the University of Houston, and was active in numerous Houston civic projects, including work in behalf of the Port of Houston. He was on the board of directors of several corporations, including the Burlington-Rock Island Railroad, the Maryland Casualty Company, the Pritchard Rice Milling Company, and the Mound Company. Law was a member of the Philosophical Society of Texas qv for thirty years. He was married to Frances Mann on April 20, 1898, and they had two children. He died at age ninety-three on June 2, 1970, in Houston and was buried in Glenwood Cemetery there.

BIBLIOGRAPHY: University of Texas at Austin, *Cactus*, IV (1897); *Who's Who In America* (1948); Philosophical Society of Texas, *Proceedings* (1970).

Law, Robert Adger. Robert Adger Law was born on March 8, 1879, in Spartanburg, South Carolina, the son of Anna Elizabeth (Adger) and Thomas Hart Law, a Presbyterian minister. Law was graduated in 1898 with a B.A. from Wofford College, in 1902 with an M.A. from Trinity College (now Duke University), and in 1905 with a Ph.D. from Harvard under tutelage of the noted Shakespearean authority, George Lyman Kittredge. In 1906 Law joined the Department of English at the University of Texas, where he taught for fifty-one years before retiring in 1957. On March 30, 1910, Law was married to Elizabeth Mortimer Manigault, and they had four children.

His numerous publications in the field of Elizabethan literature and his eminence in national and regional modern language societies have served to identify Texas with the best traditions of American scholarship. In 1949 his alma mater, Wofford, conferred upon him the Litt.D.; in 1940 Austin College at Sherman honored him with the LL.D. He served the University Presbyterian Church of Austin as deacon, elder, and teacher of a Bible class. Broader interests involved him in the work of the Synod of Texas, the General Assembly, and the Austin Presbyterian Theological Seminary. He was Professor Emeritus of English when he died on August 17, 1961, in Austin and was buried in Oakwood Cemetery in that city.

BIBLIOGRAPHY: *Harvard University Directory* (1913); *Directory of American Scholars* (1942); *Texian Who's Who* (1937).

Thomas P. Harrison

*Law, Texas.

*Law of April 6, 1830.

Law Enforcement Officer Standards and Education, Commission on. The Commission on Law Enforcement Officer Standards and Education, created in 1965, was composed in 1972 of thirteen members: the commissioner of higher education (Coordinating Board, Texas College and University System qv), the commissioner of the Texas Education Agency,qv the director of the Department of Public Safety,qv the attorney general, and nine citizens appointed by the governor with concurrence of the Senate for six-year overlapping terms. An executive director, appointed by the commission, was the chief administrative officer.

The commission was created to improve law enforcement officer training and education and to direct research in this field. The commission was authorized to certify training programs as having attained minimum standards, to certify instructors, and to certify law enforcement officers as having achieved certain standards of education, training, and experience. The program was voluntary under the original law, but 1969 amendments made such training and education mandatory for all peace officers. A 1971 amendment established minimum requirements and training standards for all reserve officers. The commission's program includes a system of regional training centers, junior college programs in police science, and introductory courses for high school seniors.

BIBLIOGRAPHY: University of Texas at Austin, *Guide To Texas State Agencies* (1972).

*Law Schools.** The seven law schools in existence in 1947 were still in operation in 1967; the number was increased to eight that year with the addition of one at Texas Technological College (now Texas Tech University) authorized by the Fifty-ninth Legislature in 1965. In the early 1970's the Coordinating Board, Texas College and University System,qv studied applications of three universities—North Texas State University, the University of Texas at Dallas, and Texas A&M University—to establish new law schools. The board appointed an advisory committee of eight Texas attorneys and a committee of representatives from the eight Texas law schools and the three applicant universities to study the condition of legal education in Texas. The committees' report to the board recommended that the applications for new law schools be denied, but that legal education be improved in existing college and university departments, and that legal curricula and government funding be revised to meet developing needs of law schools and the legal profession.

Enrollment in the law schools grew from 2,145 in 1947 to 5,617 in 1972, with by far the largest increases at the University of Texas at Austin and the University of Houston, both state supported. Enrollment at Houston, St. Mary's, and Southern Methodist is divided between day and evening classes. In 1975 the University of Texas

School of Law, with 1,701 day school students, ranked as second largest in the nation.

BIBLIOGRAPHY: American Bar Association, Section of Legal Education and Admissions to the Bar, *Review of Legal Education* (1947, 1965); Association of American Law Schools, *Proceedings* (1965); Coordinating Board, Texas College and University System, *Lawyers for Texas* (1973).

Marian Boner

*La Ward, Texas.

*Lawhon, David E. David Ervin Lawhon was born on June 15, 1811, in Tennessee and died on February 14, 1884 (not 1886, as stated in Volume II), in Williamson County.

BIBLIOGRAPHY: Lawhon Family Papers (Archives, University of Texas at Austin Library).

Henderson Shuffler

*Lawn, Texas.

Lawrence, Adam. Although Adam Lawrence's 1824 application for land in Austin's colony indicates that he was born in 1799, he stated in 1874 that he was born in Logan County, Kentucky, on October 24, 1802, and that he immigrated to Texas in 1820. During the 1820's and 1830's "Ad" Lawrence acquired a general reputation as a hunter and Indian fighter. In 1831 he received a grant of one-fourth league of land in Austin's colony, adjacent to Simon Miller's qv grant on New Year and Cedar creeks in Washington County. This grant was augmented in 1838 by a grant of three-quarters of a league, which he eventually located in Madison and Trinity counties. He married Sarah Lucinda Miller sometime between 1831 and 1836. In 1838 he settled in southeastern Williamson County, at a place later known as Lawrence Chapel,qv where he became a prosperous rancher and farmer. There he built a log church for use by circuit preachers and by the school teacher he hired for the community.

Lawrence served with William Barret Travis'qv scouting company as the Texas Army converged on San Antonio in the fall of 1835. He was a private in Henry Reed's qv company, Army of the Republic of Texas,qv from June 4 to September 4, 1836, and in 1848 he received a bounty grant of 320 acres of land in Calhoun County for these services. Disappointed at the failure of the Confederacy and disturbed by the increasing population, he moved to California in 1866 and ranched on the San Gabriel River there. However, he returned to Texas in 1873 and died on October 2, 1878, at Lawrence Chapel.

BIBLIOGRAPHY: John P. Landers, "Adam Lawrence of New Year Creek," *Southwestern Historical Quarterly*, LXVIII (1964–1965); J. H. Kuykendall, "Reminiscences of Early Texans, II," *Quarterly of the Texas State Historical Association*, VI (1902–1903); Applications for Republic Pensions (MS., Archives, Texas State Library); Audited Military Claims, Republic of Texas (MS., Archives, Texas State Library); Book of Applications for Land, Austin's Colony (MS., General Land Office); First Class Headright File (MS., General Land Office).

*Lawrence, John W. John W. Lawrence was married to Mrs. Louisa J. Tryon (not Tyron, as stated in Volume II), widow of William Milton Tryon.qv

*Lawrence, William.

*Lawrence, Texas.

Lawrence Chapel, Texas. Lawrence Chapel, a small farming community in southeastern Williamson County, was founded in 1838 by Adam Lawrence,qv Austin colonist, Indian fighter, and veteran of the Texas Revolution. Although the settlement once possessed a school, a Masonic lodge, and several stores, all that remained in 1965 was a church, a cemetery, and several houses.

BIBLIOGRAPHY: John P. Landers, "Adam Lawrence of New Year Creek," *Southwestern Historical Quarterly*, LXVIII (1964–1965).

John P. Landers

*Lawson, Texas.

*Lawsonville, Texas.

*Lazare, Texas.

*Lazbuddie, Texas.

*Lazelle, Henry Martyn.

*Lea, Albert Miller.

*Lea, Nancy Moffette.

*Lea, Pryor.

Leach, John Sayles. John Sayles Leach was born on September 30, 1891, on a farm near Allen, Texas. His parents died when he was young, and he was reared by his grandfather. He was graduated from Baylor University in 1915 with a B.A. degree. Shortly thereafter, in September, 1916, he joined the Texas Company qv (now Texaco Inc.qv) and became one of its salesmen a year later in Waco.

Following service in the army in World War I Leach was named Texaco agent at Wichita Falls. Three years later he was transferred to Dallas, where he became assistant sales superintendent of that district in 1924. He became assistant sales manager of Texaco's southern territory in 1927 and two years later sales manager of this eleven-state area. He was elected vice-president of the company in 1938, with offices at Houston; executive vice-president in 1950 when he was transferred to New York; and president in 1952. In 1953 he was named chairman of the board and chief executive officer, a post he held until he reached retirement age in 1956.

During World War II Leach served as chairman of the Marketing and Distribution Committee, District 3, of the Petroleum Industry Council, and in 1950 he was recipient of the Texas Mid-Continent Oil and Gas Association's Distinguished Service Award. In 1952 he received an honorary LL.D. from Baylor University. He served on the governing board of Rice University and as a trustee of Baylor. After his retirement Leach returned to Houston, where he lived until his death on March 16, 1964. He was buried in Glenwood Cemetery in Houston.

BIBLIOGRAPHY: Dallas *Morning News*, March 18, 1964; Houston *Post*, November 21, 1956, June 22, 1958, March 17, 1964; Houston *Press*, March 17, 1964.

Clay Bailey

*Lead Mountain.

*Lead and Zinc Production. Lead and zinc have not been mined in Texas since 1952. Between 1885

and 1952 the total lead production in the state amounted to 5,443 short tons and the total zinc production amounted to 837 short tons. Lead was formerly produced as a by-product of silver mining, mainly from the Presidio Mine in Presidio County and the Bird Mine in Brewster County. Zinc production had come chiefly from the Bonanza and Alice Ray mines in Hudspeth County, with small amounts also from the Chinati and Montezuma mines in Presidio County and the Buck Prospect in Culberson County. *See also* Mineral Resources and Mining in Texas (in Volume II).

Although no longer a producer of lead and zinc, in the 1960's and early 1970's Texas had two primary lead smelters, located at Dallas and El Paso, processing ore and concentrates from western states and Mexico. In addition, seven secondary smelters, which treated scrap material and supplied 60 percent of the total United States lead, were located in Texas: three each in Houston and Dallas and one in Fort Worth.

Zinc production in Texas likewise depended upon imported ore. In the mid-1950's zinc smelting was one of the state's leading primary metal industries, and the plant at Corpus Christi was one of five in the nation which used the electrolytic process. Plants at Amarillo and Dumas smelted zinc by the horizontal-retort method. Texas plants also produced by-products such as sulfuric acid, cadmium, and zinc sulfate crystals; the smelter at El Paso produced 40,000 tons of zinc oxide in 1955. By 1961 the Corpus Christi plant supplied 18 percent of the nation's cadmium.

In 1957 rapidly mounting domestic stocks curtailed zinc production. By 1961, however, Texas led the nation in slab zinc production, producing 191,053 tons out of the national total of 846,795 tons. In that year, Texas zinc smelting facilities had expanded to five electrolytic, seven horizontal-retort, and four continuous vertical-retort smelters. The Corpus Christi plant alone had an annual capacity of 100,000 tons in 1964.

BIBLIOGRAPHY: *Texas Almanac* (1955, 1965, 1973); U.S. Bureau of Mines, *Minerals Yearbook*, I, III (1965); *Mineral Facts and Problems* (1965); *Directory of Texas Manufacturers* (1966); *Texas Business Review* (December, 1956, May, 1958, August, September, 1964).

Charles Duval

*Leaday, Texas.

*League, Hosea H.

*League City, Texas. The United States census reported a population for League City (Galveston County) of 10,818 in 1970. *See also* Galveston-Texas City Standard Metropolitan Statistical Area.

*League of Texas Municipalities. *See also* Texas Municipal League.

*League of United Latin American Citizens (LULAC). The League of United Latin American Citizens was founded at a meeting in Corpus Christi on February 17, 1929 (not April 17, 1929, as stated in Volume II); Ben Garza was selected first permanent chairman, and M. C. Gonzales was elected secretary. The purpose of the league was to unite efforts of heretofore separate groups to better the lot of Americans of Mexican descent.

LULAC concentrated in the early 1970's on establishing a liaison between city officials and the Mexican American population through the appointment of community relations committees and police review boards.

The Supreme Council of Texas LULAC Councils, headed by Tony Bonilla as state director in 1971, worked on programs to stop discriminatory hiring practices, to combat tuberculosis, and to lower the illiteracy rate among Mexican Americans. The LULAC Economic Development Association (LEDA) was also established.

The major emphasis of LULAC programs has always been in the field of education. Other priorities include civil rights, better housing, job training, and job placement. LULAC councils are active in Texas, New Mexico, Arizona, Colorado, and California. *See also* Mexican Americans in Texas.

BIBLIOGRAPHY: Weslaco LULAC Council 291, *The LULAC Story* (n.d.); Austin *American-Statesman*, August 29, 1971.

Ernestine Wheelock

*Leagueville, Texas.

*Leakey, Joel.

*Leakey, Texas. Leakey, seat of Real County, is a commercial center for livestock ranches. The 1960 population was 587; by 1970 the population had decreased to 393, according to the United States census. In 1970 the town had twenty-two business establishments.

*Leal, Antonio.

*Leander, Texas.

*Leary, Texas.

*Leather Industry. In 1939 Texas had thirty-three leather industry establishments, eight of them in Dallas, six in Fort Worth, and the rest scattered throughout the state. Thirteen of these were engaged in the making of saddlery harnesses and related products, four made leather luggage, six made industrial leather belting and packing leather, and six made leather footwear. By 1947 the number of establishments had increased to fifty-one, but only four of these had more than one hundred employees.

By 1963 Texas had eighty-four leather and leather-products plants, only twenty-seven of them employing twenty or more persons. Most of the larger plants were engaged in the making of boots and shoes, a branch of the industry that employed 1,784 workers and turned out shipments with a total value for the year of $16,500,000. Texas' largest leather-products center was Yoakum, with seven leather industry plants in 1967, two of them among the largest in the state. These two produced casual footwear, saddlery goods, belts, gloves, and other personal accessories of leather. Another of the state's largest leather plants, at Gainesville, turned out women's shoes and moccasins. Other leading fabricating centers were at El Paso, San Antonio, Dallas, Nocona, San Angelo, and Fort Worth. All these cities had leather industry plants that employed 100 or more persons in 1963, and most of them had smaller leather plants as well.

In spite of the identification of hides and leather goods with Texas' historical past, the state ranked low in leather production in the 1960's. The leather industry has, in fact, failed to keep pace with the American economy in general, and, nationwide, employs no more workers now than in the early days of the twentieth century. With centralization and mechanization the number of leather and leather-products plants has declined nationally, and there has been a rapid shift toward the use of synthetics and other leather substitutes.

Robert H. Ryan

*Leatherwood, Texas.

*Leavell, William Hayne.

Lebanese-Syrians in Texas. Texas' Arabic-speaking Lebanese-Syrian minority, numbering approximately 10,000 in 1970, originally arrived via New York or Mexico from the Middle East. Heaviest immigration, from 1880 until World War I, was caused by political, economic, social, and religious discrimination against Christians.

Characterized as highly individualistic yet clannish, adaptable, hard working, cosmopolitan, and nationalistic, Texas' Lebanese-Syrian communities sprang up in all metropolitan centers. The first generation, led by young men, were peddlers and small businessmen. Second and third generations diversified and made real contributions in retailing, wholesaling, medicine, oil, literature, education, politics, jurisprudence, and manufacturing.

Ethnic heritage is preserved by national churches, and almost all Lebanese-Syrians in Texas are Christians. Over half belong to the Lebanon-based Maronite Rite Catholic church, although only one church, St. George's (1925), was established (in San Antonio). Syrian Orthodox churches are Beaumont's St. Michael's (1898), Austin's St. Elias (1932), Houston's St. George's (1937), and El Paso's St. George's (1954), and serve the minority of this national group. Few Moslems settled in Texas.

A multitude of community and family social clubs throughout Texas belong to the Southern Federation of Syrian Lebanese American Clubs, organized in Austin in 1931 to provide scholarships, promote Americanization, and maintain strong ethnic pride. Close ties and visits to families in Lebanon and Syria, speaking Arabic in the home, and social solidarity have preserved Lebanese-Syrian ethnic communities in all large Texas cities. Lively folk festivals such as those in Austin and San Antonio have popularized Arabic foods, dances, and music.

BIBLIOGRAPHY: M. J. Gilbert (ed.), *Archdiocese of San Antonio: Diamond Jubilee, 1874–1949* (1949); Philip K. Hitti, *The Syrians in America* (1924); *Magic Is the Night: The Lebanese Colony of San Antonio* (Festival program, 1964).

James P. McGuire

*Lebanon, Texas.

*Lebo Lake.

Leclerc, Frédéric. Frédéric Leclerc, born in the Loire Valley, France, around 1810, was educated as a physician and awarded the M.D. degree from the University of Paris. He then traveled to the United States (1837) and visited Texas for several months in 1838. His treatise on Texas appeared in two installments in the Parisian periodical, *La Revue des Deux-Mondes* (March 1 and April 15, 1840). The publication in book form, which followed the same year, was complemented by a handsome new map of the region, made by the geographer Charles Picquet and incorporating information furnished by Leclerc.

On January 15, 1839, Leclerc was appointed chief physician of the General Hospital of Tours, France, a post that he retained until 1872. In that year, following separation from his wife, he resigned his position and returned to the United States. His death occurred at Bloomfield, San Juan County, New Mexico, January 3, 1891. He was a member of several learned societies, including the Society of Natural History of France and the Entomological Society of France.

BIBLIOGRAPHY: Frédéric Leclerc (James L. Shepherd, III, trans.), *Texas and Its Revolution* (1950); Thomas W. Streeter, *Bibliography of Texas, 1795–1845*, Part III, Vol. II (1960).

James L. Shepherd, III

Ledbetter, Huddie. Huddie Ledbetter, known as Leadbelly, was born in 1885 near Mooringsport, Louisiana, the son of a Negro tenant farmer, Wess Ledbetter, and his half-Indian wife, Sallie. Ledbetter attended public schools in Louisiana, then in East Texas after his family purchased a small farm near Boulder when he was ten. Having learned to play the six-string guitar, he left home in 1901 to make his way as a minstrel, first on Fannin Street in Shreveport, and later in Dallas and Fort Worth. He spent summers working as a farmhand in the blackland counties east of Dallas and supplemented his income by singing and playing his guitar in saloons and dance halls during the winter. While working in Dallas, he met Blind Lemon Jefferson,qv and it was as his partner that Leadbelly first began to play the twelve-string guitar.

In 1918, under the name of Walter Boyd, Leadbelly was convicted of murder and sentenced to thirty years in the Texas penitentiary. Pardoned in 1925, he resumed his life of odd jobs until 1930, when he entered the state prison in Angola, Louisiana, on a charge of assault with intent to murder. It was there that his music attracted Texas folklorist John Avery Lomax qv and his son Alan. As a result of their intervention, Leadbelly was released from prison, and for several months he toured with the Lomaxes, giving concerts and assisting them in their continued efforts to record the work songs and spirituals of Negro convicts. Soon after their arrival in New York City, Leadbelly's singing and his unconventional background combined to bring him national prominence. In 1935 he married a Shreveport laundress, Martha Promise, at the Lomax home in Wilton, Connecticut. Recordings, particularly his rendition of "Goodnight, Irene," and concerts at several American universities, including Harvard, furthered his reputation. He continued to perform both in this country and in Europe until his death in New York City on December 6, 1949.

BIBLIOGRAPHY: Moses Asch and Alan Lomax (eds.), *The Leadbelly Songbook* (1962); John A. Lomax and Alan Lomax, *Negro Folk Songs as Sung by Lead Belly* (1936); Marshall W. Stearns, *The Story of Jazz* (1960).

Christine Hamm

*Ledbetter, William Hamilton.

*Ledbetter, Texas. Ledbetter is in northeastern Fayette County (not northwestern Fayette County, as stated in Volume II).

Ledvina, Emmanuel Boleslaus. Emmanuel Boleslaus Ledvina, son of George Emmanuel and Mary (Kiefer) Ledvina, was the second bishop of Corpus Christi (formerly the vicariate of Brownsville). He was born on October 28, 1868, in Evansville, Indiana, and attended parochial schools in Evansville and St. Louis. In 1883 he enrolled in St. Meinrad College, Indiana, and in 1888 entered St. Meinrad Seminary to complete his studies for the priesthood. He was ordained by the bishop of Indianapolis on March 18, 1893.

After assignments in Evansville, Indianapolis, and Princeton, he became secretary in 1907 of the Catholic Church Extension Society, an organization devoted to financing churches and missions within the United States. In 1908 he was named first vice-president as well as general secretary of the society, a post he held until his appointment as bishop of Corpus Christi in 1921. Through his work with the society, he gained a basic background on the condition of the Catholic church in Texas and especially the Lower Rio Grande Valley area, where missionary work was concentrated.

In 1918 Ledvina was raised to monsignor; in 1919 he was made an honorary canon of Our Lady of Guadalupe Basilica in Mexico. Upon the resignation of the Most Reverend Paul Joseph Nussbaum,qv first bishop of Corpus Christi, Ledvina was appointed to the See. He was consecrated in Indianapolis on June 14, 1921, and installed as bishop of Corpus Christi on July 12, 1921.

During the twenty-eight years of his administration, the number of priests increased from 32 to 160; more than fifty new churches, fifty-three mission chapels, and forty-seven rectories were built. Corpus Christi College-Academy, the new Spohn Hospital, and St. Joseph Home and St. Joseph's Academy, Laredo, were also constructed. Under his direction the Corpus Christi Cathedral was erected in 1940, and in 1947–1948 a combined rectory and chancery office was added.

Bishop Ledvina resigned in 1949 because of failing health; he was succeeded by his coadjutor bishop, Mariano Simon Garriga.qv Ledvina died on December 15, 1952, and was buried in a crypt under the main altar of Corpus Christi Cathedral.

Sister M. Claude Lane, O.P.

*Lee, Fitzhugh. Fitzhugh Lee was the son of Sydney Smith Lee and the grandson of Henry ("Light Horse Harry") Lee. [The nickname is mistakenly attributed to Sydney Smith Lee in Volume II.] He died in 1905 (not 1903, as stated in Volume II).

Ann Young

Lee, Harper Baylor. Harper B. Lee, son of Helen (Baylor) and James Buchanan Gillett,qv and grandson of James S. Gillett and George Wythe Baylor,qqv was born in Ysleta, Texas, on September 5, 1884. He was named James Harper Gillett, but in 1889 his parents were divorced and his mother changed his name to Harper Baylor Gillett. In 1895 his mother married Samuel M. Lee, and he was given his stepfather's surname. It was under this name, Harper Baylor Lee, that he became famous as a bullfighter.

Harper B. Lee was educated in Guadalajara, Mexico, where his stepfather was employed by Hampson & Smith, a railroad construction firm. After his graduation from the Colegio de Estudios Altos, he worked for Hampson & Smith as a timekeeper, gang boss, and engineering assistant, and he engaged in amateur bullfights. In 1908 he began his professional career as a *matador*, under the tutelage of Francisco Gómez, known as El Chiclanero. He made his debut in Mexico City's *plaza de toros* El Toreo on May 16, 1909. During his career he suffered two nearly fatal injuries from gorings. He retired in October of 1911, having appeared in 52 *corridas* and having killed 100 bulls. According to Barnaby Conrad, Lee was the greatest North American, and perhaps the finest non-Latin, professional bullfighter. He was especially noted for his work with the *banderillas*.

After his retirement from the bullring Lee worked as a construction superintendent at Camp Travis qv in San Antonio and also in the San Antonio military censorship office. After an estrangement of eighteen years, Lee and his real father met in San Antonio in 1914. The following year, on April 21, 1915, Lee married Roxa Dunbar in San Antonio. They had no children. He dropped his stepfather's surname in 1915, and under the name Harper B. Gillett, he worked on his father's ranch at Marfa from 1920 to 1923. When his father retired in 1923, leaving the ranch to another son by a second marriage, Harper and his wife moved to San Antonio, where they operated a five-acre chicken ranch until Harper's death from cancer on June 16, 1941. He was buried in Mission Cemetery Park in San Antonio. The headstone reads Harper B. Gillett, with no mention of Harper B. Lee, *matador*.

BIBLIOGRAPHY: Marshall Hail, *Knight in the Sun* (1962); Barnaby Conrad, *Gates of Fear* (1957).

*Lee, Joseph.

*Lee, L. W.

Lee, Nelson. Nelson Lee was born in Brownsville, Jefferson County, New York, in 1807, the son of Parmer Lee. His early life was spent as a raftsman on the St. Lawrence and Mississippi rivers. Beset with "an intense longing to rove out into the world," Lee fought in the Black Hawk

War, served as a seaman on the *Delaware* and *Ontario*, chasing pirates between Africa and Brazil, and moved to Texas in 1840. Joining the Texas Navy,qv he sailed to Yucatan with Commodore Edwin Ward Moore.qv He joined the Texas Rangers qv under John Coffee Hays qv in the early 1840's and fought in numerous Indian battles, including the engagement at Enchanted Rock.qv He participated in the Plum Creek Fight qv and the battle of the Salado (1842).qv On October 17, 1842, he joined the Somervell Expedition qv as a member of Captain Philip Haddox Coe's qv Company, 1st Regiment. He participated in the Mier Expedition,qv but he managed to escape capture when the Texans surrendered; he was the first to bring news of the expedition's defeat back to Texas. Between 1844 and 1846 Lee was a mustanger and cattle drover, gathering and buying herds in far western and southern Texas to be sold in Louisiana. Lee served as one of Samuel Hamilton Walker's qv scouts in the Mexican War,qv serving under John C. Hays on the Rio Grande, in the battle of Monterrey, and on Hays' march to Mexico City.

From 1848 to 1855 Lee continued his livestock-droving activities. In 1855 he and some other men began an overland journey to California with a herd of horses, leaving from Brownsville. On April 2, 1855, his party was attacked by Comanches, and all members except Lee were killed. Lee was held captive by the Comanches for three years, so that he was able to observe closely the way of life of that tribe. In 1858 he escaped and made his way to El Paso after suffering great hardships and near starvation. He sailed to New York, arriving on November 10, 1858, where he immediately dictated an account of his life and captivity to the editors of Baker Taylor Company. Early in 1859 this account was published as *Three Years Among the Camanches* [sic]: *The Narrative of Nelson Lee, the Texan Ranger, containing a Detailed Account of His Captivity. . . .* Of this classic work, Walter Prescott Webb qv stated that "there is no better description of the life of the Texas Rangers than that of Nelson Lee." The fresh and vivid account of his captivity and of the habits of the Comanches is also considered valuable. Nothing is known of Lee's activities after the publication of his book.

John H. Jenkins

*Lee, Robert Edward.

*Lee, Robert Quincy.

Lee, Umphrey. Umphrey Lee, fourth president and first chancellor of Southern Methodist University and an authority on the Wesleyan movement, was born in Indiana, on March 23, 1893, the son of Josephus Lee and his second wife, Esther (Davis) Lee. After the family moved to Texas, he attended Daniel Baker College at Brownwood and was graduated from Trinity University at Waxahachie in 1914. He enrolled in Southern Methodist University on its opening day and was first president of the student body. He received an M.A. degree in 1916 from the School of Theology, but his interest was in cultural history rather than formal theology. From 1916 to 1917 he studied at Columbia University and Union Theological Seminary in New York. He was ordained in 1918 and became a Methodist pastor in Cisco, Texas. He established the Wesley Bible Chair at the University of Texas in Austin in 1919 and then became pastor at Ennis.

In 1923 he was appointed to the Highland Park Methodist Church in Dallas, a small but growing congregation, and during the remainder of his life (except for three years as dean of the School of Religion at Vanderbilt), Dallas was his home. He was professor of homiletics at Southern Methodist University (1927–1932), president of the Civic Federation of Dallas, and a participant in many civic activities. While affiliated with Southern Methodist University he also completed his Ph.D. at Columbia. He became president of his alma mater, Southern Methodist University, in 1939 and influenced the rapid development of the institution. During his tenure assets increased from $7,000,000 to $27,500,000, enrollment increased from 2,152 to 4,960, a Phi Beta Kappa chapter was installed, and eighteen major buildings were constructed. After a heart attack he resigned in 1954 to become chancellor, with less strenuous duties.

Lee played an important role in uniting the three branches of Methodism. He lectured in many universities and was the author of numerous books on religion. He was the recipient of a dozen honorary degrees. He married Mary Margaret Williams of Gatesville in 1917; they had one son. Lee died in his office on the Southern Methodist University campus on June 22, 1958, as he was finishing proof sheets on his tenth book.

BIBLIOGRAPHY: *Who Was Who In America* (1960); Umphrey Lee, *Our Fathers And Us* (1958).

Herbert Gambrell

Lee College. Lee College, Baytown, was established as a junior college in September, 1934, with 165 students and a faculty of two full-time and eleven part-time instructors. Until 1951 college classes were held in the Lee High School building. In 1965 the college plant consisted of four complexes erected between 1951 and 1962: a main building, a gymnasium, a liberal arts building, and a library containing 51,940 volumes by 1969. Several off-campus sites were used for technical and vocational training. The junior college offered the first two years of most degree programs for accredited transfer to senior institutions. Two-year courses in business and drafting and a one-year course in vocational nursing were included in the curricula, as well as evening courses. College policy allowed any course of educational value if twelve or more people wanted to register for it. Data processing and computer programming classes necessitated installation of $200,000 worth of equipment. In 1963 new technical and vocational classes were added under the Manpower Development Training Act. In the 1968–1969 regular term, enrollment reached 2,068 students, with eighty-five faculty members. Richard D. Strahan served as president. Enrollment for the fall term of 1974 reached 5,009. Jim D. Sturgeon was president in 1974.

*Lee County. Lee County listed beef and dairy cattle, hogs, and poultry as leading sources of farm income, which averaged $10.5 million annually by 1972. Cotton, once the leading product, decreased in importance. Farmers also produced small amounts of peanuts and grains. The 1960 population of 8,949 (approximately the same figure as in 1880) declined to a 1970 census count of 8,048. Peak population of the county was 14,595 in 1900.

*Leedale, Texas.

*Lee's, Texas.

*Lee's Mill, Texas.

*Leesburg, Texas.

*Leesville, Texas.

*Leevan, Texas.

*Lefevre, Arthur.

*Lefors, Texas.

*Leftwich, Robert.

*Leftwich Colony. See Robertson Colony.

*Léger, Theodore.

*Leggett, Texas.

*Legion, Texas.

*Legion Creek.

Legislative Budget Board. The Legislative Budget Board, created by the Texas legislature in 1949, was composed of the lieutenant governor and the speaker of the House of Representatives, ex officio, four senators appointed by the lieutenant governor, and four representatives appointed by the speaker. Two of the members of the House were required to be the chairman of the revenue and taxation committee and the chairman of the appropriations committee. Two of the members from the Senate were required to be the chairman of the finance committee and the chairman of the state affairs committee. The board appointed the budget director, who was responsible for preparing the budgetary requests of all state spending agencies and the appropriation bills to effectuate them. The board then presented the budget and the drafts of the appropriation bills to each regular session of the legislature.

BIBLIOGRAPHY: Stuart A. MacCorkle and Dick Smith, *Texas Government* (1964); Clifton McCleskey, *The Government and Politics of Texas* (1963); Wilbourn Eugene Benton, *Texas, Its Government and Politics* (1961); University of Texas at Austin, *Guide To Texas State Agencies* (1956, 1964, 1972).

Dick Smith

Legislative Compensation. The Constitution of 1876 qv set the legislator's compensation at five dollars per day for the first sixty days of a regular session and two dollars thereafter. During the thirty days of a special session he would receive five dollars a day. A constitutional amendment adopted in 1930 changed the per diem to ten dollars for the first 120 days of a regular session and five dollars thereafter. The special session per diem was ten dollars. In 1954 another constitutional amendment raised the per diem to not more than twenty-five dollars for the first 120 days of a regular session and nothing thereafter. During special sessions the per diem was twenty-five dollars. Still another constitutional amendment, adopted in 1960, allowed the legislature to pay its members an annual salary not to exceed $4,800, in addition to a per diem of twelve dollars during the first 120 days of a regular session and during 30 days of each special session. This was amended once again, in April, 1975, so that members of the legislature (although still meeting only every other year) received an annual salary of $7,200, plus a per diem of thirty dollars during both the regular and special sessions. A limit of 140 days was placed on the regular session.

BIBLIOGRAPHY: Stuart A. MacCorkle and Dick Smith, *Texas Government* (1964); Clifton McCleskey, *The Government and Politics of Texas* (1963); Wilbourn Eugene Benton, *Texas, Its Government and Politics* (1961).

Dick Smith

Legislative Council, Texas. The Texas Legislative Council, established in 1949, was the legislature's research agency. The council was composed of the speaker of the Texas House and president of the Texas Senate, ex officio, ten representatives appointed by the speaker, and five senators appointed by the president of the Senate. The council selected an executive director who supervised a professional staff. After the staff completed a study, either on the initiative of the council or on the request of the legislature, their report was approved by the council and submitted to the legislature, along with such drafts of legislation as the council deemed proper.

BIBLIOGRAPHY: Stuart A. MacCorkle and Dick Smith, *Texas Government* (1964); Clifton McCleskey, *The Government and Politics of Texas* (1963); Wilbourn Eugene Benton, *Texas, Its Government and Politics* (1961); University of Texas at Austin, *Guide To Texas State Agencies* (1956, 1964, 1972).

Dick Smith

Legislative Reapportionment. See Legislature of Texas.

*Legislature of Texas. Two important adjuncts of the Texas legislature came into being as a result of enactments of the Fifty-first Legislature: the Legislative Council and the Legislative Budget Board.qqv The council was created to aid the legislature by making special investigations and gathering information for the legislature. The budget board, composed of the presiding officers and four members of each house of the legislature, has the responsibility of coordinating the financial program of the state.

A constitutional amendment adopted in 1960 provided annual salaries for members of the legislature (see Legislative Compensation). In response to the annual salary provision, the legislature adopted the Legislative Reorganization Act of 1961, a major purpose of which was the establishment of standing committees to function during interims, as well as during sessions. Special committees and general investigating committees were also authorized.

In 1964 the United States Supreme Court decreed that apportionment of representation in state legislatures must be based solely upon population. Pursuant to that order, the Texas legislature in 1965 enacted reapportionment statutes based upon the last preceding federal census. Proposed constitutional amendments which would have increased the membership of the Senate to thirty-nine, and the term of members of the House of Representatives to four years, were defeated by the voters. In 1976 the Senate was still limited to 31 members, elected for four-year terms, and the House of Representatives was composed of 150 members still elected for two-year terms.

Dorsey B. Hardeman

*LeGrand, Alexander.

*LeGrand, Edwin Oswald.

*Lehman, Texas.

Lehmann, Herman. Herman Lehmann, son of Moritz (Maurice) and Augusta Johanna (Adams) Lehmann, German immigrants, was born June 5, 1859, near Loyal Valley in southeastern Mason County. His parents were married in Texas in 1849; after his father died in 1864 his mother married Philipp Buchmeier (Buchmeyer) in 1866. In May, 1870, when he had never been to school and spoke only German, Herman, almost eleven, and a younger brother, Willie, were captured by raiding Apaches; two younger sisters who were with them were not taken.

Willie escaped and returned home in about nine days. Herman was adopted by his Apache captor, Carnoviste, and initiated into the rigors of primitive Indian life. He underwent harsh tribal training and initiation, became a warrior, and took part in expeditions against the Texas Rangers,qv Comanches, Mexicans, and white settlers, ranging with the tribe from the Guadalupe Mountains in New Mexico down into the Mason County-San Saba region and into Mexico. After Carnoviste was killed, and Lehmann himself had killed an Apache medicine man, he spent a year alone on the plains of West Texas before joining the Comanches. Known as Montechena (Montechina), he had also been called at various times En Da and Alaman. With the Comanches he fought the Tonkawas and United States Cavalry, and he again took part in Indian raids. He was with the last Kwahadi remnant which joined the reservation at Fort Sill. He was adopted by Quanah Parker qv but was ultimately recognized as a white captive and forced to return in May, 1878, to his Texas family, who had thought him dead for the eight years he lived with the Indians.

At home he refused to eat pork or sleep in a bed, and he embarrassed his family by sometimes appearing before his mother's hotel guests with his body painted, dressed only in leggings, breech clout, and feathers. He startled a revival meeting with an Indian dance, thinking the congregation was praying for rain. His brother Willie kept him from killing the neighbors' calves and hogs and from stealing horses from adjoining farms. He relearned German, learned English, engaged in numerous odd jobs, tried to go to school for a single day, and worked as a trail driver.

Although he never adjusted to white society fully, Herman did accept his role in the Loyal Valley community, and his easygoing nature and good humor seem to have made him many friends. After an unhappy earlier marriage ended in divorce, he married Miss Fannie Light in 1890, and the couple had two sons and three daughters. Later Herman, as a Comanche, was given Oklahoma lands by the United States government, and he spent much of his time with his red brothers.

He was a local celebrity throughout the Texas hill country, giving many public exhibitions of skill at riding, roping, and shooting with a bow and arrow. In later years he met many of the Texas Rangers and soldiers he had fought against as an Indian. He died February 2, 1932, and was buried in Loyal Valley.

BIBLIOGRAPHY: Henry Buchmeyer, *The Life and Hardships of My Mother, Augusta Johanna Buchmeyer* (n.d.); Chester William and Ethel Hander Geue, *A New Land Beckoned* (1966); A. C. Greene, *The Last Captive* (1971); J. Marvin Hunter, *Horrors of Indian Captivity* (1937); Jonathan H. Jones, *A Condensed History of the Apache and Comanche Tribes* (1899); Herman Lehmann (J. Marvin Hunter, ed.), *Nine Years Among the Indians, 1870–1879* (1927).

A. C. Greene

Leidigh, Arthur Henry. Arthur Henry Leidigh, the son of Theodore F. and Elizabeth (Reed) Leidigh, was born on August 14, 1880, at Hutchinson, Kansas. He received a B.S. in agriculture from Kansas State College in 1902, and from 1903 to 1908 he was employed as superintendent of the United States Department of Agriculture experiment stations at Channing and at Amarillo, Texas. In that position he experimented with and developed several strains of grain sorghums, including Dwarf Kafir and Sunrise Kafir, both of which are widely grown on the South Plains. In 1911 he became professor of agronomy at Kansas State College and two years later joined the faculty of the Agricultural & Mechanical College of Texas (now Texas A&M University) as agronomist of the Texas Agricultural Experiment Station.qv In 1923 he became assistant director of the experiment station and earned an M.S. degree from Texas A&M before he left in 1925 to become the first dean of agriculture at the newly established Texas Technological College (now Texas Tech University). He resigned from this post in 1945 but continued to teach in the agronomy department until 1950, when he retired as dean emeritus.

Leidigh was active in the First Presbyterian Church of Lubbock, which was the subject of his book, *The First Fifty Years* (1954). He was a member of the Governor's Cotton Committee of Texas, the Texas Committee on Electricity in Relation to Agriculture, the Texas State Planning Board, the American Society of Agronomy, and Phi Kappa Phi. In 1947 he was elected a fellow of the Texas Academy of Science.qv

Leidigh married Mary Josephine Edwards on June 28, 1911; they had three children. He died in Lubbock on April 30, 1955, and was interred in Tech Memorial Park in that city.

BIBLIOGRAPHY: Seymour V. Connor (ed.), *Builders of the Southwest* (1959).

Jimmy K. Skaggs

*Leigh, Texas.

*Lela, Texas. Although the town was earlier known as Story, its name was changed to Lela by 1903 or 1904 (not 1910, as stated in Volume II). Lela was listed as a post office by 1904, whereas no listing was given for Story in that year.

BIBLIOGRAPHY: *Texas Almanac* (1904).

*Leland, Texas.

*Lelia Lake, Texas.

*Lelia Lake Creek.

*Lellan, Texas.

*Leming, Texas.

*Lemonville, Texas.

*Lemsky, Frederick.

*Lena, Texas.

*Lencito Draw.

*Lenorah, Texas.

Lentz, Sallie McGee. Sallie McGee Lentz, daughter of Harry W. and Sallie (Starr) McGee, and granddaughter of James Harper Starr,qv was born on November 2, 1896. She married J. Fred Lentz on January 15, 1923, and they had two daughters. She and her husband built a private history library and also assembled a collection of Indian artifacts and early Texas bonds, stamps, and currency.

Sallie Lentz wrote and spoke for local, regional, and state organizations and published a number of articles, one of which was "Highlights of Early Harrison County" in the October, 1957, issue of the *Southwestern Historical Quarterly*.qv She was instrumental in the organization of the Harrison County Historical Society in 1959 and served as its first president. She was also a charter member of the East Texas Historical Association.qv She died on June 1, 1962, in Harrison County. In the fall of 1962 her Harrison County friends established the Sallie McGee Lentz Memorial Fund.

BIBLIOGRAPHY: Eugene Spruell, "Sallie McGee Lentz," *Harrison County Historical Herald*, I (November, 1964).

John N. Cravens

*Lentz Branch.

Lenz, Louis. Louis Lenz, son of Charles and Emma (Muller) Lenz, was born in Yorktown, De-Witt County, Texas, on December 18, 1885. He spent his boyhood in Cuero and attended public schools and Guadalupe Academy. In 1903 he enrolled at Texas Agricultural and Mechanical College (now Texas A&M University) and graduated in 1907 with a degree in civil engineering. He was an avid football fan, and from his freshman year through Thanksgiving, 1966, he attended every Texas A&M–University of Texas football game played.

Following graduation, Lenz worked for a time in the right-of-way section of the Southern Pacific Railroad and in 1912 worked at locating and constructing a railroad in Uruguay. In 1915 he married Neal Woodson. He worked as chief engineer for the Vacuum Oil Company until 1931, when that company merged with Magnolia Petroleum Company,qv and Lenz served as division engineer for Magnolia in Lake Charles, Louisiana, until retirement in 1951.

After his retirement, Lenz moved to Houston, where he began devoting his time to collecting Texana. In 1956 he designed the special medallion authorized by Congress to commemorate the 120th anniversary of the Texas Declaration of Independence.qv In 1963 his collection of over four thousand books and journals was acquired by the University of Texas. The collection contained many writings on early Texas (in English as well as Spanish) and Mexican documents dealing with Texas lands and land grants. The entire collection is housed in the Barker Texas History Center qv of the University of Texas at Austin.

Lenz died on May 17, 1967, in Houston and was buried in Forest Park Lawndale Cemetery in that city.

BIBLIOGRAPHY: Houston *Chronicle*, August 25, 1965, May 25, 1966, May 18, 1967.

Clay Bailey

*Lenz, Texas.

*Leo, Texas. (Cooke County.)

*Leo, Texas. (Lee County.)

*Leon County. Leon County, 42 percent forested, reported a farm income of $12 million in 1972, nine-tenths of which was derived from livestock and poultry. Over three thousand bales of cotton are produced annually; however, watermelon is the main crop. The county's oil and gas fields produced over thirteen million barrels of oil from 1936 through 1972. Tourists enjoyed fishing, hunting, and visiting the site of Fort Boggy.qv The 1960 population was 9,951 and the 1970 population was 8,738, according to the United States census. The decrease in population continued the downward trend begun in 1930, when the county's population reached a peak of nearly 20,000.

*Leon Creek.

*Leon Junction, Texas.

*Leon Mountain.

*Leon Powell, Texas.

Leon Reservoir. Leon Reservoir is in the Brazos River Basin in Eastland County, seven miles south of Ranger on the Leon River. The project is owned and operated by the Eastland County Water Supply District as a municipal and industrial water supply for Ranger, Olden, and Eastland. Construction began on January 13, 1953, and the dam was completed in June, 1954. The reservoir has a capacity of 27,290 acre-feet and a surface area of 1,590 acres at the service spillway elevation of 1,375 feet above mean sea level. The storage capacity at the crest of the emergency spillway is 40,210 acre-feet. The drainage area above the dam is 252 square miles.

BIBLIOGRAPHY: Texas Water Commission, *Bulletin 6408* (1964).

Seth D. Breeding

*Leon River.

*Leon River, Texas.

*Leon Springs, Texas.

*Leon Springs First Officers Training Camp.

*Leon Springs Reservoir.

Leon Valley, Texas. Leon Valley, in Bexar County, was a rapidly growing suburban community on the northwest fringe of San Antonio. The United States census reported a population for Leon Valley of 536 in 1960 and 1,960 in 1970.

*Leona, Texas.

*Leona Creek.

*Leona River.

*Leonard, Texas. The United States census reported a population for Leonard, in Fannin County, of 1,117 in 1960 and 1,423 in 1970. Leonard reported forty-two businesses in 1970.

*Leonard Mountain.

*Leoncita Creek.

*Leonidas, Texas.

*Leopard Creek.

*Leota, Texas.

*Leroy, Texas.

*Lesassier, Luke.

*Lesley, Texas.

Leslie, Andrew Jack. Andrew Jack Leslie was born in 1815 in Tennessee. On September 11, 1842, he was in San Antonio, for he was captured along with fifty-one others by Mexican General Adrian Woll qv in the invasion of that city. They were marched to Mexico and imprisoned in Perote, near Vera Cruz. Leslie was in the group of thirty that were released on May 24, 1844. Texas awarded him a tract of land near Helotes on which he lived until his death. Affectionately known by relatives and friends as "Uncle Jack" Leslie, he remained unmarried. On November 10, 1881, he recorded a will making his nephew, Sam G. Leslie, his sole beneficiary, and specifying ground under a spreading oak overlooking Helotes Creek as his final resting place. He died on February 6, 1885, and was buried there.

S. W. Pease

*Leslie, John Douglass.

*Lester, James Seaton.

*Letona, José María.

*Letot, Texas.

LeTourneau, Robert Gilmour. Robert Gilmour LeTourneau was born on November 30, 1888, in Richford, Vermont, the son of Caleb T. and Elizabeth (Lorimer) LeTourneau. He received a primary education and then on his own learned mechanics and engineering through correspondence courses. In 1929 he became a contractor and builder of land-leveling equipment. In 1946 he located his operations in Longview, Texas, constructing a steel mill to supply his assembly plants. In 1953 LeTourneau sold his earth-moving business to Westinghouse Air Brake Corporation; thereafter his plants constructed logging, construction, road, mining, and oil drilling equipment. Most notable was the construction of mobile platforms for offshore oil drilling.

LeTourneau devoted much of himself and his wealth to private education. He founded LeTourneau Technical Institute (later known as LeTourneau College qv); he was also a trustee of John Brown University, Siloam Springs, Arkansas, and a member of the board of reference of Wheaton College in Illinois. He was also active in the Christian Business Men's Committee International, serving a term as its president. LeTourneau died on June 1, 1969, in Longview, and he was survived by his wife, Mary Evelyn (Peterson) LeTourneau, and their five children.

LeTourneau College. LeTourneau College in Longview, Texas, was formerly known as LeTourneau Technical Institute.qv It was a four-year, multidenominational, and coeducational college, offering programs in arts and sciences, technology, and engineering. The expansion program included a new science building in 1965. The library contained 54,000 volumes in 1969. Student enrollment numbered 726 in the 1974–1975 regular term, and the faculty totaled over fifty. Harry T. Hardwick served as president.

*LeTourneau Technical Institute. *See also* LeTourneau College.

LeTulle, Victor Lawrence. Victor Lawrence LeTulle, son of Captain Victor D. and Helen Virginia (Willard) LeTulle, was born at Columbus, Texas, on July 5, 1864, and was educated in the public schools of Colorado County. He moved to Bay City in 1900, when the town was in its infancy. He was engaged in farming, ranching, banking, and various mercantile enterprises in Matagorda County. He bought a canal system from Ross S. Sterling qv and built it into the world's largest privately owned irrigation system. The system provided a capacity to irrigate more than one hundred thousand acres per year and gave impetus to the rice farming industry in Matagorda County. He owned some sixty thousand acres of plantation lands in Matagorda and Brazoria counties. A philanthropist, he gave a nine-thousand-acre farm, dormitory, and hospital to the Buckner Orphans Home qv in Dallas; a memorial church sanctuary, municipal park, and gas utility system to Bay City; and monetary gifts to a Houston hospital.

He married Sallie West Bell on January 29, 1890. After her death on May 24, 1933, he married Essie Bell, a sister of his first wife, on July 19, 1935. He died on May 1, 1944, and was buried in Cedarvale Cemetery, Bay City.

Frances V. Parker

*Levee Improvement Districts.

*Levelland, Texas. Levelland, in central Hockley County, is the principal commercial center of the county, dealing largely in cotton, cottonseed processing, and petroleum refining. South Plains College was opened in the city in 1958. In 1967 Levelland reported thirty-five churches, eleven public schools, two hospitals, two banks, a library, a newspaper, and a radio station. Levelland reported 252 business establishments in 1970. The 1960 population of 10,153 increased to a 1970 census count of 11,445.

*Leverett's Chapel, Texas.

*Levi, Texas.

*Levita, Texas.

*Lewis, Asa M.

*Lewis, Charles W.

*Lewis, Gideon K.

*Lewis, Ira Randolph.

*Lewis, John M.

*Lewis, Judd Mortimer.

Lewis, Kendall. Kendall Lewis was born in western Virginia prior to 1800; he grew up with his family in Choctaw Indian country in western Georgia. He married a Choctaw woman, and they had six children. When the Choctaws began moving west in the late 1820's, he moved his family to the Caddo Lake area of Texas; in the early 1830's he moved to present Titus County, Texas, settling on Swannano Creek. The Lewis family may have been the first permanent settlers of this region; Lewis owned the first tract of land surveyed in Titus County, surveyed on March 30, 1838; he also patented the league and labor of land to which he was entitled. After the Ripley family had been killed by Choctaw Indians in Titus County in 1841, white settlers became so hostile toward the Lewis family that they were forced to move to Oklahoma in 1842; Lewis lived in the Choctaw Nation until his death.

BIBLIOGRAPHY: Traylor Russell, *History of Titus County* (1965).

Traylor Russell

*Lewis, Mark B. Mark B. Lewis (often confused with Martin B. Lewis qv) came to Texas with John A. Quitman's qv volunteers on April 9, 1836; he joined William Strickland's company on April 12, 1836. He was with a group headed by Erastus (Deaf) Smith and John Coffee Hays qqv when they raided Laredo in March, 1837. In April and May, 1838, Lewis was chief clerk of the commission on public lands. From June, 1838, to January, 1839, and from January, 1840, to March, 1840, he served as chief clerk in the comptroller's bureau of the treasury department, and in November and December, 1839, he was clerk of the Senate. Lewis was a prominent speaker at a meeting held in Austin in April, 1842, to generate enthusiasm for a war against Mexico, and in November, 1842, he raised a company of volunteers in Travis County to join the pursuit of General Adrian Woll.qv

BIBLIOGRAPHY: James H. McLendon, "John A. Quitman and the Texas Revolution," *Southwestern Historical Quarterly*, LII (1948–1949); Joseph M. Nance, *After San Jacinto: The Texas-Mexican Frontier, 1836–1841* (1963), *Attack and Counterattack: The Texas-Mexican Frontier, 1842* (1964); Civil Service Claims, Republic of Texas (MS., Archives, Texas State Library); Audited Military Claims (MS., Archives, Texas State Library).

Lewis, Martin B. Martin B. Lewis (often confused with Mark B. Lewis qv), was born in Clark County, Indiana, on January 13, 1806, the son of Sally (Lemasters) and Samuel S. Lewis.qv He married Nancy Moore in Vermillion County, Indiana, on October 25, 1825; they had eleven children. He and his family came to Texas in January, 1830, settling first on Ayish Bayou in what is now San Augustine County and then on Indian Creek near Bevil's Settlement, in what is now Jasper County. In August, 1832, Lewis was a sergeant major in the battalion commanded by James Whitis Bullock,qv and he participated in the battle of Nacogdoches.qv In November and December, 1835, he was captain of a company of East Texas volunteers which took part in the siege of Bexar.qv In July, 1836, when a Mexican invasion of Texas by General José Urrea qv was feared, Lewis raised a company of Jasper volunteers and marched to join the Texas Army qv on the Coleto. He resigned this command in August, 1836.

Lewis served as county surveyor of Jasper County from its organization in 1836 until 1845. In 1844 he was also chief justice of Jasper County. In 1845 he patented title to 2,958 acres of land in Jasper County. He left Texas for California in 1849, and in 1863 he settled at Millertown, in Fresno County, California. He died sometime before 1885.

BIBLIOGRAPHY: Civil Service Claims, Republic of Texas (MS., Archives, Texas State Library); Pension Claims, Republic of Texas (MS., Archives, Texas State Library); Audited Military Claims, Republic of Texas (MS., Archives, Texas State Library); Character Certificate File (MS., General Land Office); Vol. K, Deed Records of Jasper County, Texas.

Madeleine Martin

*Lewis, Nathaniel C.

*Lewis, Samuel K.

*Lewis, Samuel S.

*Lewis, William.

*Lewis, Yancy.

*Lewis Ferry, Texas.

*Lewis Hill.

*Lewis Lake.

*Lewisville, Texas. Lewisville, in Denton County, had a 1960 population of 3,956 and a 1970 population of 9,264, according to the United States census. In 1967 Lewisville had fifteen churches, five schools, and two banks. The town reported 140 businesses in 1970. Industries included production of feeds, apparel, boats, and furniture. Lewisville Lake Park served as a recreational center for the Dallas-Fort Worth area. *See also* Dallas Standard Metropolitan Statistical Area.

*Lexington, Texas.

*Leyendecker, Texas.

*Liberty.

*Liberty, Texas. (Liberty County.) Liberty, the county seat of Liberty County, in the 1970's continued as a prosperous port on the barge canal which connected with the Houston Ship Channel.ᑫᵛ Industries included those connected with sulphur, chemicals, steel, and lumber. By 1975 several new public buildings had been built, including a library, a museum, and a theater. The United States census reported a population for Liberty of 6,127 in 1960 and 5,591 in 1970.

*Liberty, Texas. (Milam County.)

*Liberty City, Texas.

*Liberty County. Liberty County is a large producer of commercial lumber and petroleum. In the early 1970's the income from minerals averaged $39 million yearly, ranking Liberty County among the leading oil producing counties of the state. By January 1, 1973, the county had produced 421,-222,851 barrels of oil since its discovery in 1905. In 1973 the county's land was 62 percent forested. Rice, the leading crop, was cultivated on forty-six thousand irrigated acres and contributed most of the farm income, which averaged $15 million annually in the early 1970's. Soybeans were increasing in importance. The 1960 population was 31,595; the 1970 population increased slightly to 33,014, according to the United States census. See also Houston Standard Metropolitan Statistical Area.

Liberty Grove, Texas. Liberty Grove, on Cooper Creek in southern Delta County, was founded in 1848. The town was located in the area to be flooded by Cooper Reservoir at its completion in the late 1960's. The inhabitants, never more than fifty, numbered twenty-five in 1966, all of whom were farmers.

*Liberty Hill, Texas. (Hays County.)

*Liberty Hill, Texas. (Milam County.)

*Liberty Hill, Texas. (San Jacinto County.)

*Liberty Hill, Texas. (Williamson County.)

*Liberty Normal and Business College.

*Liberty Springs, Texas.

*Liberty Volunteers.

*Libraries in Texas.

*Library, State. See Texas State Library.

*Lick Creek.

*Liendo Plantation.

*Lieutenant Governor, Office of. Since World War II the office of lieutenant governor has become increasingly important. The lieutenant governor has become more than a neutral moderator as presiding officer of the Senate by taking an active part in the legislative process. From his position he exerts influence, not only on lawmaking, but also on administration and public policy generally. He is not a widely known officer and his position and influence are not generally understood by the public. His importance is known, however, within legislative circles and among those closely associated with governmental affairs. The degree of his power and influence depends substantially on the personality of the individual occupying the office and on his desire and ability to wield the power. It is also contingent upon his support by the Senate and to a certain extent upon his role among the various "power teams" of state government. The lieutenant governor's annual salary is the same as that paid to members of the legislature ($7,200 in 1975). By constitutional amendment, approved by Texas voters in 1972, the term of office for lieutenant governor was increased from two years to four years, effective with the election of 1974 (when William P. Hobby was reelected to the first four-year term, beginning January 21, 1975).

From the accompanying table, it might first be noted that it was not customary for lieutenant governors to succeed themselves even for a second term during the period prior to 1894. During that time only J. A. Greer, R. B. Hubbard, and T. B. Wheeler were elected to second terms of office. It is also noticeable that after serving one term, the incumbent frequently did not run again for lieutenant governor.

Beginning with the election of George T. Jester in 1894, the practice changed. It then became common for the lieutenant governor to be elected for two terms. The only lieutenant governors who have not been reelected for at least a second term since that date were Will H. Mays, W. A. Johnson, Lynch Davidson, and T. W. Davidson. Of that group Johnson is unique in that he was defeated for reelection. The other exceptions to the two-term tradition chose not to run for reelection to office.

The first lieutenant governor to serve more than two terms was A. B. Davidson. It was not until the 1920's that Barry Miller served that long. Since Miller's tenure Ben Ramsey and Preston Smith have been reelected for more than two terms. Ramsey holds the record, having been elected lieutenant governor for an unprecedented six terms.

The table also shows that the office of lieutenant governor has been vacant on several occasions. Seven times the lieutenant governor has succeeded to the governor's office. One lieutenant governor (Jones) was removed from office, and one (Flanagan) was elected to the United States Senate and never occupied the lieutenant governor's office. The fact that the office was vacant seems never to have raised problems. The Texas Constitution provides that the president pro tempore of the Senate performs the two constitutional duties of the office but without actually succeeding to the office. He presides over the Senate when it is in session and is available to succeed to the governorship if that position should become vacant. At no time in Texas history has succession officially gone beyond the lieutenant governor. On a number of occasions when the lieutenant governor is acting temporarily as governor while the latter is out of the state, the

LIEUTENANT GOVERNORS OF THE STATE OF TEXAS
SINCE ANNEXATION, 1845 TO 1975

[Note that election years rather than inauguration years are used in the table; thus, prior to the Constitution of 1876 qv the dates fall on odd-numbered years, whereas from 1876 to the present the dates fall on even-numbered years.]

NAME	TERMS SERVED	COMMENTS
Nicholas Henry Darnell qv	1845–March, 1846	Mistakenly declared elected and inaugurated. Resigned when votes recanvassed.
Albert Clinton Horton qv	1846–1847	Officially sworn in on March 26, 1846, after declared elected. Acted as governor several months while Governor James Pinckney Henderson qv was at war in Mexico.
John Alexander Greer qv	1847–1849; 1849–1851	First to serve two terms.
James Wilson Henderson qv	1851–1853	Succeeded to governorship November, 1853, when Governor Peter Hansborough Bell qv resigned to serve in U.S. Congress.
David Catchings Dickson qv	1853–1855	
Hardin Richard Runnels qv	1855–1857	First to be elected governor (1857).
Francis Richard Lubbock qv	1857–1859	Second to be elected governor (1861).
Edward Clark qv	1859–1861	Succeeded to governorship March, 1861, when Sam Houston vacated the office.
John McClannahan Crockett qv	1861–1863	Acted as governor a few weeks when Governor Francis Richard Lubbock qv entered Confederate Army.
Fletcher S. Stockdale qv	1863–1865	Technically succeeded to governorship when Governor Pendleton Murrah qv fled after the Civil War. Removed by U.S. authorities.
George Washington Jones qv	1866–1867	Removed from office by U.S. authorities in 1867.
James Winwright Flanagan qv	1869	Elected but never inaugurated. Selected to serve as U.S. Senator.
Richard Bennett Hubbard qv	1873–1876; 1876	Second to be elected for two terms, but succeeded to governorship in December, 1876, when Governor Richard Coke qv resigned to enter the U.S. Senate.
Joseph Draper Sayers qv	1878–1880	Later elected governor, 1898–1902, as third lieutenant governor to be elected governor.
Leonidas Jefferson Storey qv	1880–1882	
(Francis) Marion Martin qv	1882–1884	Ran unsuccessfully for governor and lieutenant governor at later dates.
Barnett Gibbs qv	1884–1886	
Thomas Benton Wheeler qv	1886–1888; 1888–1890	Third to be elected for two terms.
George Cassety Pendleton qv	1890–1892	
Martin McNulty Crane qv	1892–1894	
George Taylor Jester qv	1894–1896; 1896–1898	Two terms.

NAME	TERMS SERVED	COMMENTS
James Nathan Browning qv	1898–1900; 1900–1902	Two terms.
George D. Neal qv	1902–1904; 1904–1906	Two terms.
Asbury Bascom Davidson qv	1906–1908; 1908–1910; 1910–1912	First elected for three terms.
William Harding Mays qv	1912–1914	
Wiliam Pettus Hobby qv	1914–1916; 1916–1917	Succeeded to governorship after impeachment of Governor James Edward Ferguson qv (September, 1917).
W. A. Johnson qv	1918–1920	First to be defeated for immediate reelection.
Lynch Davidson	1920–1922	
Thomas Whitfield Davidson qv	1922–1924	
Barry Miller qv	1924–1926; 1926–1928; 1928–1930	Second to be elected for three terms.
Edgar E. Witt qv	1930–1932; 1932–1934	Two terms.
Walter Woodal	1934–1936; 1936–1938	Two terms.
Coke Robert Stevenson qv	1938–1940; 1940–1941	Succeeded to governorship when Governor Wilbert Lee O'Daniel qv resigned to enter U.S. Senate (August, 1941).
John Lee Smith	1942–1944; 1944–1946	Two terms.
Allan Shivers	1946–1948; 1948–1949	Succeeded to governorship on death of Governor Beauford Halbert Jester qv (July, 1949).
Ben Ramsey	1950–1952; 1952–1954; 1954–1956; 1956–1958; 1958–1960; 1960–1961	First to serve more than three terms. Resigned when appointed to Railroad Commission qv (September, 1961).
Preston Smith	1962–1964; 1964–1966; 1966–1968	Elected governor in 1968.
Ben Barnes	1968–1970; 1970–1972	Defeated in race for governor in 1972.
William P. Hobby	1972–1974; 1974–	By constitutional amendment approved by Texas voters in 1972, the term of office for lieutenant governor was increased to four years, effective in 1975. Hobby, reelected in 1974, was the first lieutenant governor to assume the four-year term, which began January 21, 1975.

[See also Republic of Texas (in Volume II), for list of executive officers, 1835–1845; Governor, Office of (in this volume), for list of governors, 1845–1975.]

lieutenant governor also leaves the state to permit the president pro tempore to act as "governor for a day."

Another conclusion to be drawn is that the nominee of the Democratic party qv almost invariably has been elected to the office of lieutenant governor. Only during the turbulent years surrounding the Secession, Civil War, and Reconstruction qqv periods have nominees of other parties been successful. During the first decade of Texas statehood, nominations were generally made by personal announcement or by caucus. Most of the candidates were from the Democratic party, and a person was never elected with a clear majority. The rising competition of the Know-Nothing party qv forced the Democratic party to nominate by convention beginning in 1885. In 1859 Houston and Clark, running as independents with Know-Nothing backing, defeated the Democratic incumbents Runnels and Lubbock. The Democrats recaptured the offices in 1861 but were ousted from office by the military rule after the Civil War. A Republican governor was then selected, but the lieutenant governor's position remained vacant. In 1873 the Democrats again captured both offices, retaining them to the present.

The only other serious challenge to Democratic supremacy came with the rise of the Populist party in Texas.qv In the 1890's that party represented a real threat. Since the turn of the century the domination of the Democratic party has been complete.

The advent of the direct primary in 1906 and the double primary in 1918 brought about a change in the nomination procedure. The real contest for state office now occurred in the primary, with the general election usually being a mere formality in the lieutenant governor's race. As a general rule if a candidate were running to succeed himself, he had little opposition, but when the office was open, there were several contenders for the office. Usually the candidate who led in the first primary would win the nomination and election, but there are several notable exceptions to this rule.

The first to show that leading in the first primary did not assure victory was T. W. Davidson in 1922. He came from behind to win by a substantial margin in the second primary and the general election. Others who overcame a first primary deficit were Edgar Witt in 1930, Coke Stevenson in 1938, Ben Ramsey in 1950, and Preston Smith in 1962. In their bids for reelection all (except Davidson, who chose not to run) won rather easy victories.

The lieutenant governors of Texas have generally been men who were active in state politics before election to that office. Ordinarily they have served in the legislature, particularly in the Senate. They have sometimes aspired to the office as a climax to a political career, although frequently they have hoped to use the lieutenant governorship as a stepping-stone to higher office.

Contrary to some opinion, the office of lieutenant governor has not proved to be a stepping-stone to other offices, particularly to that of governor. In the early days of statehood several lieutenant governors entered the governor's race, but few were elected. Of the first eight lieutenant governors, seven ran for governor, and two were elected under rather unusual circumstances. In 1857 H. R. Runnels defeated Sam Houston, who was running for governor as an independent, while F. R. Lubbock was elected lieutenant governor. Two years later Houston defeated Runnels in his bid for reelection, while Clark defeated Lubbock for the lieutenant governor's post. At the next election (1861), both Lubbock and Clark ran for governor, and Lubbock was elected by a margin of 124 votes.

Later ex-lieutenant governors Jones, Martin, and Gibbs ran unsuccessfully for governor. It was not until 1898 that another former lieutenant governor was elected governor. Joseph D. Sayers has the unique distinction of having served one term as lieutenant governor (1878) and then twenty years later being elected governor, occupying that post for two terms.

Long tenure in the lieutenant governor's office has not aided in a later campaign for governor.

Three of the four individuals who have been elected governor (without first having succeeded to the office by a vacancy) served only one term as lieutenant governor (the exception being Preston Smith, who served three terms as lieutenant governor). On the other hand, several who were elected to two or more terms as lieutenant governor failed miserably in a subsequent race for governor.

Seven lieutenant governors have inherited the governor's office without being elected to it. Three governors resigned to serve in the United States Congress (Bell, Coke, O'Daniel); one governor resigned at the time of Secession (Houston); one governor vacated his office and fled from the country (Murrah); one governor was impeached and removed from office (Ferguson); and one governor died in office (Jester). Of the seven lieutenant governors who succeeded to the governor's office, three later ran for the office and were elected to additional terms (Hobby, Stevenson, and Shivers); two ran and were defeated (Henderson and Clark); and two did not run again (Hubbard and Stockdale, who only served technically as governor before being removed by U.S. authorities).

Lieutenant governors have continued to be ambitious to be elected governor, but without notable success. Through the election of 1974, twenty former lieutenant governors have run for the office of governor. Of that twenty, seven have been elected governor, but only four of the seven were elected without first having succeeded to the office due to a vacancy. With only four out of twenty having attained the goal through election, it seems doubtful that the office of the lieutenant governor should be termed a stepping-stone to the governorship.

BIBLIOGRAPHY: J. William Davis, *There Shall Also Be A Lieutenant Governor* (1967).

J. William Davis

Light Crust Doughboys. One of the original groups of western swing, the Fort Worth Doughboys, later the Light Crust Doughboys, first performed in late 1931 advertising Light Crust Flour over a Fort Worth radio station. The flour mill executive who hired and promoted the group was Wilbert Lee "Pappy" O'Daniel.qv The trio, known in pre-radio days as the Aladdin Laddies, consisted of Bob Wills (*see* Wills, James Robert), Herman Arnspiger, and Milton Brown. By early 1932 Arnspiger had left the group and had been replaced by Sleepy Johnson. Johnson, Wills, and Brown, along with Brown's younger brother, Durwood, recorded two songs for RCA Victor Records in February, 1932. With headquarters in Fort Worth, the group toured the Southwest, and their immediate popularity gave the city a reputation as the "cradle of western swing." Membership in the group changed drastically during the years immediately following the group's founding, and by 1933 none of the original members were associated with the Doughboys. At one time the group included such notables as Leon Huff and Leon McAuliffe.

When O'Daniel formed his own flour company

in 1935, he organized another country-western group called the Hillbilly Boys. This group was prominent in O'Daniel's successful 1938 gubernatorial campaign.

BIBLIOGRAPHY: Bill C. Malone, *Country Music U.S.A.* (1968).

*Lightfoot, Henry W.

Lightfoot, Jewel Preston. Jewel Preston Lightfoot, attorney general of Texas, was born on January 21, 1873, in Columbia County, Arkansas, son of Elijah Ward and Lucy Adele (Reynolds) Lightfoot. After attending public schools, he entered Jeff Davis College, Pittsburg, Texas, from which he was graduated in 1890. While working as a night railroad telegrapher, Lightfoot studied law. In 1898, after admission to the state Bar, he was elected Camp County attorney. After three terms, he was called to Austin as state prosecutor of anti-trust cases in 1905. As assistant to the attorney general, Robert Vance Davidson,qv Lightfoot directed prosecution of the Waters-Pierce Oil Company (*see* Waters-Pierce Case), resulting in the largest fine ever imposed by the state. In 1910 Governor Thomas Mitchell Campbell qv appointed Lightfoot attorney general. After serving three terms, Lightfoot resigned in 1912 to enter private law practice in Austin. From 1918 to 1926 he was general counsel for Wilson and Company, packers of Chicago, and then moved to Fort Worth as a member of the Lightfoot, Robertson, Saunders and Gano law firm.

Lightfoot was a member of the Fort Worth Chamber of Commerce and the Dallas and Fort Worth, state, and national Bar associations. He wrote several books on Masonic law and statutes. He married Fredonia Baudouin on September 15, 1896, and they had five children. He died on July 14, 1950, in Fort Worth and was buried in the State Cemetery qv in Austin.

BIBLIOGRAPHY: Philosophical Society of Texas, *Proceedings* (1950); *Texian Who's Who* (1937).

*Lightner, Texas.

*Lignite, Texas. (Burleson County.)

*Lignite, Texas. (Wood County.)

*Lignite Deposits. *See* Coal and Lignite Deposits in Texas.

*Ligon Hill.

*Lihe Creek.

*Lilac, Texas.

*Lilbert, Texas.

*Lillard, Texas.

*Lillian, Texas.

*Lilly, Texas.

*Lilly Creek.

*Lily-White Movement.

*Lime City, Texas.

*Limestone County. Limestone County had changed from a cotton and truck crop area to a livestock raising area by 1966. By 1973 about 80 percent of the county's $10 million average annual farm income was derived from cattle and hogs. That same year there were textile mills in the county, but raw cotton production was limited. Over 111,000,000 barrels of oil were produced from 1920 through 1972. The 1960 population was 20,413; by 1970 the population had decreased to 18,100, according to the United States census. A county improvement project was to connect Lake Mexia, Confederate Reunion Grounds, and Fort Parker qv by a system of roads.

*Limestone Creek.

Limita Indians. The Limita ranged along the Canadian River in Texas and New Mexico during the late seventeenth century. They seem to have been an early Lipan-Apache band. The Limita were either closely associated with the Trementina or were the same people. In contemporary documents both names were sometimes equated with Cipayne, the name from which Lipan probably evolved.

BIBLIOGRAPHY: J. M. Espinosa, *Crusaders of the Rio Grande* (1942); Albert H. Schroeder, *A Study of the Apache Indians: The Mescalero Apaches*, Part III (1974); A. B. Thomas, *After Coronado* (1935).

                                    T. N. Campbell

Limited Sales and Use Tax. *See* Sales Tax, State.

*Limpia Creek.

*Lincecum, Gideon.

*Lincoln, Texas.

*Lindale, Texas. The United States census reported a population for Lindale, in Smith County, of 1,285 in 1960 and 1,631 in 1970. The town had forty-two businesses in 1970.

*Linden, Texas. Linden became the seat of Cass County in 1860 (not 1852, as stated in Volume II). It had an economy supported by cattle, poultry, timber, and truck crops in the 1950's and 1960's. A twenty-eight-bed hospital was completed in 1961, and plans were made for a $350,000 expansion. A medical clinic valued at one hundred thousand dollars began operations in 1963. By 1966 a new high school had been built and improvements had been made in the grade and junior high schools. In 1970 Linden had fifty-five businesses. Numerous residents worked in the arsenal, chemical plant, and iron and steel plants in nearby counties. The 1960 population of 1,832 increased to 2,264 by 1970, according to the United States census.

*Lindenau, Texas.

*Lindheimer, Ferdinand Jacob. The home in which Ferdinand Jacob Lindheimer published the *Neu-Braunfelser Zeitung* qv was restored to its original state in 1968 by the New Braunfels Conservation Society. The house is typical of the ancient *Fachwerk* (half-timber construction) which the German settlers adapted to Texas cedar and limestone; the house includes Lindheimer's office and print shop, a parlor, a bedroom, a wine cellar, and a kitchen. Some of the articles included in the house, such as the desk, a pewter bowl, and a china coffee pot, were originally Lindheimer's.

*Lindleys Creek.

Lindsay, Benjamin Franklin. Benjamin Franklin Lindsay (not Lindsey, and mistakenly included in the last paragraph of the entry on Benjamin Lindsey in Volume II) was the name of a father and son whose family settled near San Augustine, Texas, about 1824 (not 1832). The elder Lindsay came with his wife and nine children from Tennessee; his son bearing the same name took part in the battle of San Jacinto and was issued a headright certificate by the San Augustine County Board on June 22, 1838. He was living in Hunt County in September, 1881, when he sold his veterans donation certificate of 1,280 acres of land to R. Garcia.

BIBLIOGRAPHY: Jovita Courtney, *After the Alamo–San Jacinto* (1964); L. W. Kemp, San Jacinto Notebook (MS., Archives, Texas State Library, Austin).

Margaret Craig

*Lindsay, Livingston.

*Lindsay, Texas.

*Lindsay, Benjamin. [Delete last paragraph in this article in Volume II, and *see* Lindsay, Benjamin Franklin, in this volume. Ed.]

Lindsey, Matthew Clay. Matthew Clay Lindsey was born in Henderson County, Texas, on October 20, 1877, the son of John Jackson and Laura E. (Powers) Lindsey. The family moved to Eastland County in 1887 and later to Palo Pinto County. Lindsey went to public schools in Strawn and Palo Pinto and attended the University of Texas in Austin for two semesters in 1899–1900.

After serving briefly as principal of a two-teacher school at Strawn, he began working as a cashier in a Palo Pinto bank. On June 2, 1901, he married Eunice D. Cunningham, and the following year the couple moved to Big Spring. The next year the family moved to Dawson County, where Lindsey and his father organized the Lamesa Town Company, which laid out the town that was to become the county seat in 1905. At that time Lindsey was elected the first county judge of Dawson County. He was reelected for a second term, but thereafter turned his energies to an abstract business he founded in 1907.

In 1905, shortly after the death of a two-month-old son, Lindsey's wife died. On October 29, 1908, he married Tommie Smith, who bore him six children. After selling his business in 1918, he moved his family to Gaines County, where he had purchased a ranch which he stocked with registered Aberdeen Angus cattle. The agricultural recession following World War I forced him to sell his herd and ranch, and he returned to the Lamesa real estate business. There he became a specialist in mineral properties and oil royalties and soon recouped his personal fortune. An oil field near Lamesa and three buildings in the town bear his name. A community leader, he was a member of several civic organizations. He died on December 1, 1955, and was buried in Lamesa Memorial Park. A history of Dawson County which he compiled was published posthumously as *The Trail of Years in Dawson County* (1958).

BIBLIOGRAPHY: Seymour V. Connor (ed.), *Builders of the Southwest* (1959).

Seymour V. Connor

Lindsey, Therese Kayser. Therese Kayser Lindsey was born in Chappell Hill, Texas, in 1870, daughter of Albert and Mary (Lawrence) Kayser. She received her education in the Tyler public schools and at Southwest Texas Normal School (now Southwest Texas State University), with additional studies at the University of Chicago, Harvard University, and Columbia University. In 1892 she married Sam A. Lindsey. She traveled extensively in America and Europe, although she resided in Tyler for many years.

She wrote poems, stories, and plays and received a number of awards for her work. Two of her books, *Blue Norther* (1925) and *The Cardinal Flower* (1934), contained lyrics dealing mainly with Texas and nature. A third volume, *A Tale of the Galveston Storm* (1936), was a long narrative poem based on a true incident of the 1900 disaster. She also published *Collected Poems* (1947). A member of poetry societies in America and England, Mrs. Lindsey initiated the movement which resulted in the formation of the Poetry Society of Texas,[qv] and she served as its first corresponding secretary and then as vice-president. She was also donor of the "Old South Prize," one of the society's major annual awards. She died in Tyler on April 3, 1957, and was buried in Oakwood Cemetery in that city.

BIBLIOGRAPHY: *Texian Who's Who* (1937); Mabel Major and T. M. Pearce (eds.), *Signature of the Sun: Southwest Verse, 1900–1950* (1951).

Sonja Fojtik

*Lindsey Spring Branch.

*Lindsley, Henry Dickinson.

*Lindsley, Philip.

*Lingleville, Texas.

*Linguist Creek.

*Linn, John Joseph.

*Linn, Texas.

*Linn Creek.

*Linn Flat, Texas.

*Linney Creek, Texas.

*Linnville, Texas.

*Linnville Bayou.

*Linwood Crossing, Texas.

*Liotot. Liotot came to Texas with La Salle in 1685 (not 1865, as stated in Volume II).

*Lipan, Texas.

*Lipan-Apache Indians.

*Lipan Creek.

*Lipan Flat.

*Lipan Spring.

*Lipantitlán Expedition.

*Lipscomb, Abner Smith.

*Lipscomb, Texas. Lipscomb, seat of Lipscomb County, had two businesses in 1970. The population has remained approximately two hundred since 1910, with no substantial change in 1970.

*Lipscomb County. Lipscomb County, with a ranching economy, produced approximately twenty-three million barrels of oil between 1956 and January 1, 1973. Cattle raising is predominant. Lipscomb County ranked seventh in the state in wheat acreage in 1960, with 95,529 acres; in 1968 wheat acreage amounted to 100,400 acres. The 1960 population was 3,406; the 1970 census count was 3,486.

*Lipsitz, Louis.

*Liquor Control Board.

*Liquor Laws. See Prohibition Movement.

*Lisbon, Texas.

*Lisle, Texas.

*Lissie, Texas.

*Literary Intelligencer.

Literature of Texas. Texas literature may be divided into two parts: "Early, or before 1918," and "Contemporary." The literature, though primarily in English, begins with Spanish fact-narratives, folk plays, songs, and legends. Álvar Núñez Cabeza de Vaca's qv The Relation . . . (1542), Pedro de Castañeda de Nacera's Narrative of the Coronado Expedition (MS. before 1596), and Fray Alonso de Benavides'qv Memorials (1630–1634), even in translation, are good reading. Spanish folk dramas and songs, still largely unpublished, live orally today along the Rio Grande as they did when the first Anglos came into the Valley. Legends of saints and missions, of lost mines and buried treasures, are told. Some of this literature has been collected and translated by folklorists such as J. Frank Dobie, Adina De Zavala,qqv M. R. Cole, and Américo Paredes.

Early Nonfiction Prose: Anglo (as well as Spanish) literature in Texas began with narrative, descriptive, factual prose, with legends and tall tales at times added. Belles lettres rooted in the region developed later.

Mary Austin Holley,qv cousin of Stephen F. Austin and visitor to his colony, was the author of Texas (1833), the first book in English that can be called Texas literature, and seemingly the first Texas book in the English language. Consisting of twelve letters to the people back East, it was expanded in 1836 into History of Texas. After David Crockett's qv death in the Alamo, a book entitled Col. Crockett's Exploits and Adventures in Texas (1836) appeared. Although partially, if not wholly spurious, it is in the lively frontier style of his authenticated narratives.

John Crittenden Duval,qv whom J. Frank Dobie called the "Father of Texas Literature," was also active in the Texas Revolution.qv Duval escaped from the Goliad massacre qv and lived out his life in Texas. Early Times in Texas (serial form, 1868–1871; book, 1892) tells of his escape and living by

his wits in the canebrakes. Like Robinson Crusoe it is good reading for both adults and adolescents. Young Explorers, published in the same volume, is a juvenile. The Adventures of Big-Foot Wallace (1872), although lacking the unity of content and style of Early Times, contains something for all: tall tales, legends, true adventure, and straight history. The chapters on the Mier Expedition qv are the best published account of that ill-fated episode. Another unfortunate affair of the Texas Republic was reported by George W. Kendall qv of the New Orleans Picayune in Narrative of the Texan Santa Fé Expedition (1844).

Most travelers in early Texas wrote favorably of the inhabitants, but not Frederick Law Olmsted qv in A Journey Through Texas (1857). He found the prairie charming, but the people crude, the food bad, and the coffee "revolting." Later he made his reputation as a planner of parks, two of which are Central Park in New York City and Forest Park in St. Louis.

Among the many ex-Confederate soldiers who came to Texas following the Civil War was young Sidney Lanier.qv He wrote his impressions of Texas for Eastern newspapers, and one charming essay, "San Antonio de Bexar," was published in his Retrospects and Prospects (1899). Also in the wake of the war came Federal troops. With General George A. Custer qv was his young wife, Elizabeth. Texas at first seemed "the stepping off place," but she came to enjoy the life and wrote a lively account of her experiences in Tenting on the Plains (1887).

The first of the cowboy writers was Charlie Siringo,qv a native Texan, who rode the range for nearly twenty years. He turned author in 1886 with A Texas Cowboy; or Fifteen Years on the Hurricane Deck of a Spanish Pony, later revised as Riata and Spurs (1912). Will Rogers once said it was "the cowboy's Bible when I was growing up." Siringo's narrative began what is one of the chief contributions of Texas to American literature—books of the cattle kingdom.

Early Fiction: Of the works of fiction written before 1918 that are set in Texas, only a few are of interest to persons other than literary historians. The first Texas novel L'Héroïne du Texas, the amateurish author identified only as Mr G . . . n F . . . . . .n, is identified with Champ d'Asile qv (Camp Refuge), a short-lived French colony on the Trinity River. Published in Paris in French in 1819, it was not available in English until Donald Joseph's translation of 1937.

Timothy Flint's Francis Berrian (1826), although set only partially in Texas, is of more significance, as it introduces two motifs that often reappear in Texas fiction: Whites, preferably pretty girls, captured by and rescued from Indians; and the conflict between Protestant Anglos and Catholic Mexicans, the hero usually Anglo. Mexico versus Texas qv (1838), however, is a novel which culminates in the marriage of a Catholic and a Protestant, probably written by a Catholic priest, Anthony Ganilh, who used A. T. Myrthe as a pen name.

The Travels and Adventures of Monsieur Violet (1843) by Frederick Marryat, a retired British naval officer and prolific writer, is pure adventure that ranges over much of the American West, including Texas of Revolution times. Another prolific novelist, Karl Bostl, an Austrian whose pseudonym was Charles Sealsfield, used Texas as the setting for *The Cabin Book* (1844) in which the hero becomes a general in the Texas Army.qv Of Frenchman Oliver Gloux's more than twenty novels of the American West, only one, *The Freebooters, a Story of the Texas War* (c.1860), is of Texas. His pen name was Gustave Aimard.

Charles Wilkins Webber qv in *Old Hicks, the Guide* (1845) added the search for a lost Spanish mine to Texas adventure fiction; and Alfred W. Arrington,qv writing as Charles Summerfield in *The Rangers and Regulators of Tanaha . . . a Tale of the Texas Republic* (1856), contributed the bandit motif. Jeremiah Clemens in *Mustang Gray* (1858) fictionalized the life of Mabry Gray,qv soldier-bandit of early Texas.

Before the end of the nineteenth century each of three women who won national fame for romantic fiction wrote a novel of Texas. Augusta Jane Evans qv at fifteen wrote *Inez, a Tale of the Alamo* (1855). She became widely read with such novels as *St. Elmo* (1866) and *Vashti* (1869). Much superior to *Inez* is *Remember the Alamo* (1886) by Amelia Barr,qv an Englishwoman who lived fourteen years in Texas. Of her more than fifty novels, only this one is of Texas.

The first novel deeply rooted in Texas is *Under the Man Fig* (1895) by Mary (Mollie) E. Moore Davis.qv The story, rather improbable in itself, skillfully employs the legend of the man-fig trees, and the characters are convincing. *Under the Man Fig* combines Old South romanticism and the newer local-color realism.

As if to put right the romantic portrayal of the life of the cowboy that by the turn of the century was flourishing in the dime novels, Andy Adams,qv a real Texas cowhand, wrote *Log of a Cowboy* (1903). The narrative of the long drive from south of the Rio Grande to market in Montana is as devoid of artificial plot as any actual drive. No love-romance intrudes. J. Frank Dobie said, *"Log of a Cowboy* is the best book that has ever been written of cowboy life, and it is the best that ever can be written." Later novels by Adams fall short of this, his first.

In contrast to the artlessness of *Log of a Cowboy* is the art and artifice of O. Henry's short stories with Texas settings, most of which were published in *The Heart of the West* (1907). O. Henry's Texas stories are in the plotted Bret Harte local-color pattern with the characteristic O. Henry surprise ending added. (*See* Porter, William Sydney.)

Of the writers of fact narratives of Texas before 1918, only Duval and Siringo are often read today; and of the writers of fiction, only Adams and O.

Henry are read. Mary E. Moore Davis' *Under the Man Fig* is overdue a revival.

Early Poetry: Early Texas poetry followed two traditions: the lyric and the story-telling ballad. Most of the writers are remembered for only one or two poems each. Mirabeau B. Lamar,qv soldier-statesman, as a poet is known chiefly for two lovely-lady lyrics, "Carmelita" and "The Daughter of Mendoza." His only volume is *Verse Memorial* (1857). The poetic reputations of two of his associates in affairs-of-state rest on one poem of each: Reuben M. Potter qv for "Hymn to the Alamo"; and Lamar Fontaine, the son of Lamar's secretary, Edward Fontaine,qv for "All Quiet Along the Potomac," a poem that others also have claimed. Mary E. Moore Davis during her girlhood in Texas, writing as Mary Evelyn Moore, gained renown with Civil War poems published in newspapers. "Lee at the Wilderness" and "Minding the Gap" were widely circulated through the South.

After the Civil War, with the developing of the cattle industry, the ballad or ballad-like poem of the range became popular. These were usually sung or recited. The names of the composers of most of the cowboy ballads have been lost.

Even the skillful and rather long recitative piece "Lasca"qv (1882), the best known of all Texas poems, was passed around and handed down orally. By the time it got into print in the United States, lines had been lost and the author known by name only as Frank Desprez.qv Not until recent years has he been traced to England, where, after three years "occupied on a Texas ranch," he returned and became a professional writer. However, nothing else Desprez wrote during a long career is so widely known as "Lasca," still a favorite recitation.

Another famous cowboy recitation is "The Cowboys' Christmas Ball" by Larry Chittenden,qv an Eastern newspaper reporter who became a poet-ranchman in Texas. His poem so immortalized the Anson ball of 1885 that it is redanced each Christmas in costume with dancers coming from hundreds of miles. Chittenden's volume *Ranch Verses* (1893) has seen sixteen editions.

John P. Sjolander,qv a young Swede, came to the Texas Gulf Coast in 1871, liked it, stayed, built boats, farmed, and wrote poems for periodicals. Not until 1928 were his poems gathered into a volume, *Salt of the Earth and Sea*. Using skillfully both the lyric and the narrative forms, Sjolander wrote with honesty and feeling of nature and people. Before his death in 1939, he was called the "Dean of Texas Poets." With Sjolander as the bridge, Texas poetry moves from the Early into the Contemporary.

Contemporary Literature: In the years following World War I, Texas, along with other southwestern states, experienced a literary renaissance. It was marked by discussions of regionalism, orally and in print; meetings of writers, some of which resulted in organizations; the founding of presses; and the developing of magazines and book-review sections of newspapers. In Texas John H. McGinnis and Henry

Nash Smith, editors of the *Southwest Review*,^{qv} led the regionalism movement. For a time New Mexico and Oklahoma writers received the most national attention. Texas, however, since World War II, has stepped to the fore.

The publications of the Texas Folklore Society,^{qv} begun in 1916, are of value both as source material for writers and as literature. (*See also* Book Club of Texas.) The yearbooks of the Poetry Society of Texas,^{qv} issued annually since 1922, have contained some of the finest Texas poems, as have volumes of poetry sponsored by the society. The Texas Institute of Letters,^{qv} founded as part of the Centennial ^{qv} activities of 1936, encourages Texas writers with large cash awards and the resulting attention of publishers and readers. Each of these societies presents writers and editors in lectures. Since the middle 1950's other reviews and journals have appeared as outlets for writers in Texas, notably the *Texas Quarterly*.^{qv} The rise of the University of Texas Press ^{qv} since 1951 under the directorship of Frank H. Wardlaw has also brought international attention to Texas literature, particularly in the fields of criticism and Latin American studies. The University of Texas Press publishes some American poetry, but no novels. It is, however, building a distinguished list of translations of novels from Latin America hitherto unavailable in English.

Contemporary Poetry: The 1920's through the 1940's were the great decades of Texas poetry. Nearly a score of men and women were writing verses that pleased both the critics and the public; Texas poets, as in other parts of America, were in demand for platform readings. Nature lyrics dominated, often with philosophical or religious implications. The literary ballad frequently used the story as the medium for a general truth.

Karle Wilson Baker,^{qv} one of the seven founders of the Poetry Society of Texas in 1921, set high standards with her two earliest volumes published by the Yale University Press (1919, 1922). Writing not many, but exquisite, lyrics until within a few months of her death in 1961, Mrs. Baker is Texas' most distinguished poet. Her poems are in the Wordsworth-Emerson tradition of philosophical nature poetry. She also wrote essays and novels.

The most widely read of Texas poets is Grace Noll Crowell, with more than a dozen volumes, most of them published by Harper Brothers. Her themes are usually nature and home. However, it may be that her fine religious poems are her most lasting work.

Glen Ward Dresbach, who lived for a time in far West Texas, wrote of settlers from the woodlands adjusting to life on the plains. In his character narratives he has aptly been compared to Robert Frost.

Among the other Texas poets who contributed to the poetic excitement of these years, a number of whom were writing on into the 1960's, are Walter Adams, Carlos Ashley, Frances Alexander, Ruth Averitt, Stanley Babb, William E. Bard, George

Bond, Margie B. Boswell,^{qv} Hilton Ross Greer,^{qv} Hazel Harper Harris, Clyde Walton Hill,^{qv} Margaret Bell Houston,^{qv} Siddie Joe Johnson, Fania Kruger, Tom McNeal, Vaida Montgomery,^{qv} Whitney Montgomery,^{qv} Patrick Moreland, Berta Hart Nance,^{qv} Lexie Dean Robertson,^{qv} Grace Ross, Goldie Capers Smith, and Fay Yauger. A number of these poets are widely known for a special poem: Clyde Walton Hill for "Little Towns of Texas," Margaret Bell Houston for "Song from Traffic," Fania Kruger for "Passover," Whitney Montgomery for "Death Rode a Pinto Pony," Berta Hart Nance for "Cattle," and Fay Yauger for "Planter's Charm." Mrs. Yauger's poem has rightly been called the finest Texas poem. Hilton Ross Greer had a notable influence on Texas poetry through his long presidency of the Poetry Society, as did the Montgomerys through their editing and publishing *Kaleidograph*.^{qv}

Among the writers who matured poetically after World War II are William Barney, Robert Lee Brothers, Everett Gillis, David Russell, and Arthur Sampley—all of whom have been active in the Poetry Society. Each has won the Texas Institute of Letters Poetry Award. Among more recent winners of this award are William Burford, Vassar Miller, Thomas Whitbread, Roger Shattuck, and Frederic Will. William Barney and Arthur Sampley also have received major awards of the Poetry Society of America, as did Fania Kruger and Fay Yauger earlier.

In the fifties and sixties, Texas poetry had become less lyric and story-telling, more intellectual and symbolic, often experimental, and puzzling to the uninitiated. Such is true of American poetry as a whole, with a resultant decline in audience.

Contemporary Nonfiction Prose: An era in Texas prose that began in the 1920's ended with the deaths of Roy Bedichek (1959), Walter Prescott Webb (1963), and J. Frank Dobie ^{qqv} (1964), often called the triumvirate of Texas writers. Close association enriched their lives and augmented their works.

It has been said that J. Frank Dobie made the Texas Folklore Society, and that the Texas Folklore Society made Dobie. Many of his articles appeared in the *Publications* of the society, of which he was the editor for twenty years. His first book, *Coronado's Children* (1930), established him as a collector and raconteur of tales of lost mines and buried treasures. *Apache Gold* (1934) and *Tongues of the Monte* (1935) came from this same rich lode. The history and legends of animals—longhorns, mustangs, coyotes, rattlesnakes, and bears— were other rich sources. Dobie wrote, too, of Texas pioneers—rangers, vaqueros, and cow people. And best of all, in articles, books, lectures, and conversation, Dobie revealed himself as a genial, freedom-loving individual. "Mr. Texas" became his sobriquet. As a person and as a writer, J. Frank Dobie put his brand on the life and literature of Texas.

Walter Prescott Webb, a scholarly researcher and original interpreter of facts, wrote history that is also literature. Whether analyzing the American frontier itself, or as an influence on European history, Webb always gave attention to how he said a thing as well as to what he said. Recognized as Texas' most distinguished historian, Webb was also one of its finest writers.

Roy Bedichek, through the encouragement of Dobie and Webb, became a writer after he was seventy years old. In his last ten years he wrote four books, the research for which as a hobby had covered decades. Bedichek is the Thoreau of Texas literature; all of Texas is Walden Pond. His first book, *Adventures with a Texas Naturalist* (1947), and his *Educational Competition* (1956), have already been hailed as standards in their respective fields.

Closely associated with Dobie in the Texas Folklore Society was John Avery Lomax,qv co-founder with L. W. Payne.qv Beginning with the publication of a volume of cowboy ballads in 1910, Lomax went on to become a professional collector of folk songs for books and for the Library of Congress record collection. *Adventures of a Ballad Hunter* (1947) established him as a writer as well as a collector. His tales of the finding of the ballads are as interesting as the ballads themselves. J. Evetts Haley, for a time in Austin, was also an associate of Dobie and Webb. His *Charles Goodnight* (1936) is a fine book of a man and a ranch.

The present recorders of legends and fact, while owing much to these older men, show some differences, though it is too early to generalize with surety. Folklorists Mody Boatright,qv Américo Paredes, and Wilson Hudson are more inclined to analyze and catalogue than were Lomax and Dobie. The *Publications of the Texas Folklore Society* under the editorship of Boatright and Hudson include scholarly articles as well as folk tales and songs. Boatright's *Gib Morgan: Minstrel of the Oil Fields* (1945) and *Folk Laughter on the American Frontier* (1949), and Paredes' *With a Pistol in His Hand: A Border Ballad and Its Hero* [Gregorio Cortez] (1958) are the products of scholarship and good writing.

Some historians in Texas are taking small segments of place and time and expanding the episodes with sensory details, such as John Edward Weems' *A Weekend in September* (1957), Lon Tinkle's *Thirteen Days to Glory* (1958), and Frank X. Tolbert's *The Day of San Jacinto* (1959).

Other authors have utilized a grander canvas. Paul Horgan in *Great River: The Rio Grande in North American History* (1954) encompasses more than four centuries and eighteen hundred miles and writes more like a poet and musician than a straight historian. In fact he is all three. *Great River* won a Pulitzer Prize and is the basis for a symphony. William H. Goetzmann's *Exploration and Empire* (1966), also a Pulitzer Prize winner, brings a searching examination to the federal government's role in charting the American West and making it habitable. John Graves in *Goodbye to a River* (1960) employs the literary frame-plot to

pattern his historical tales. Willie Morris in *North Toward Home* (1967) chronicles his development from a bright young Mississippian of narrow vision through his intellectual growth in Texas to his position as the youngest editor in the history of historic *Harper's Magazine*.

Texas cities, too, have their historians. Judged as literature, Green Peyton's *San Antonio, City in the Sun* (1946) and John William Rogers' *The Lusty Texans of Dallas* (1951) are outstanding. David G. McComb's *Houston: City on the Bayou* (1969), Robert L. Martin's *The City Moves West* (1969), and Kenneth W. Wheeler's *To Wear a City's Crown* (1968) have all broken new ground as studies in urban development.

Of the many factual books on oil, Carl Coke Rister's qv *Oil: Titan of the Southwest* (1949) and John S. Spratt's *The Road to Spindletop* (1955) have received the Carr Collins Texas Institute of Letters Award for the best Texas book of the year. Boyce House's qv *Were You in Ranger?* (1935) was one of the earliest of the well-written oil books, albeit with a determinedly light touch.

The line between history and biography is always thin. In a biography of such an epoch-making figure as Sam Houston, it is scarcely discernible. Marquis James in *The Raven, a Story of Sam Houston* (1929) employs many of the devices of the novelist—the expansion of episodes, the telescoping of time, and suspense. A Pulitzer Prize winner, *The Raven* endures as one of the top American biographies. Llerena B. Friend's *Sam Houston, The Great Designer* (1954) adds significantly to the portrait of Texas' leading soldier-statesman. The result of a quarter of a century of research, Eugene C. Barker's qv *The Life of Stephen F. Austin* (1925) is usually regarded as the first fine biography in Texas literature.

Other able writers also have turned to the Texas Revolution and Republic for biographical studies. Constance Rourke mixes tall tales and facts in *David Crockett* (1934); Stanley Vestal attempts to separate tall tales from facts in *Big-Foot Wallace* (1942). Joe B. Frantz in writing the biography *Gail Borden, Dairyman to a Nation* (1951) traces the beginnings of an industry. Herbert Gambrell in *Mirabeau Buonaparte Lamar* (1934) and in *Anson Jones, the Last President of the Republic* (1948) likewise is the historian-biographer.

Civil War heroes have their Texas biographers. Carl Coke Rister in *Robert E. Lee in Texas* (1946) writes of a neglected period of Lee's career. Colonel John W. Thomason, Jr.,qv in *Jeb Stuart* (1930) writes as only a soldier-artist-novelist could write. Frank Vandiver in *Mighty Stonewall* (1957), always conscious of style, has written what is perhaps the definitive life of Thomas Jonathan Jackson.

Monumental in scope is the work on Mexico-Texas relations during the period of the Texas Republic by Joseph Milton Nance. The first volume, *After San Jacinto*, appeared in 1963; the second, *Attack and Counterattack*, was published in 1964.

Although many books on Texas outlaws are mere sensationalism, a number can be classed as literature. Among these are Lyle Saxon's *Lafitte the Pirate* (1931); Wayne Gard's *Sam Bass* (1936); Burton Rascoe's *Belle Starr* (1941); Lewis Nordyke's ^{qv} *John Wesley Hardin* (1957); and Ramon F. Adams' *A Fitting Death for Billy the Kid* (1960).

C. L. Sonnichsen in *Roy Bean, Law West of the Pecos* (1943) portrays a picaro rather than a villain. In *Ten Texas Feuds* (1957) Sonnichsen tells of good men committing bad deeds.

Philip Graham in *Life and Poems of Mirabeau B. Lamar* (1938), Dobie in *John C. Duval, First Texas Man of Letters* (1939), Fayette Copeland in *Kendall of the Picayune* (1943), E. Hudson Long in *O. Henry, The Man and His Works* (1949), Rebecca Smith Lee in *Mary Austin Holley* (1962), and Wilson Mathis Hudson in *Andy Adams* (1964) combine biography and literary criticism.

Two Texas women who have won national renown have gone far afield for their material: Edith Deen in *All of the Women of the Bible* (1955) and *Family Living in the Bible* (1963); and Francis Mossiker in *The Queen's Necklace* (1961) and *Napoleon and Josephine* (1964).

Three Texans, who had built writing reputations while living in the East, backtracked to Texas and wrote autobiographically of the state. They are Stanley Walker,^{qv} *Home to Texas* (1956); Mary Lasswell, *I'll Take Texas* (1958); and William A. Owens, *This Stubborn Soil* (1966).

Joseph Martin Dawson and Louis Herman Hubbard,^{qqv} after retiring from distinguished careers, wrote full-length autobiographies. The Reverend Dawson's book, *A Thousand Months To Remember* (1964), incorporates important aspects of the religious development of Texas. Dr. Hubbard's *Recollections of a Texas Educator* (1964) is as much a history of the schools he served as of himself. Both men have been president of the Texas Institute of Letters.

Contemporary Fiction: Texas historical and biographical novels often read so much like fact that the reader needs to be warned by subtitle or preface. Such is true of two novels of Jim Bowie: Monte Barrett's ^{qv} *The Tempered Blade* (1946) and Paul Wellman's *Iron Mistress* (1951). Colonel John W. Thomason explains in the preface of *Lone Star Preacher* (1941) that the character Praxiteles Swan of Civil War days is a composite of two men. Laura Krey's *And Tell of Time* (1938) is the fictionized story of her grandparents during the Reconstruction.^{qv} William Goyen's *The House of Breath* (1950) is seemingly of his own home and youth. In these novels either real or composite people are the major characters, and actual events make the main plot.

J. Y. Bryan's *Come to the Bower* (1963) and William Humphrey's *The Ordways* (1965) employ historical people and events as characters and background which are important to the plot. Bryan's novel, beginning in Louisiana, climaxes at the battle of San Jacinto; Humphrey's, beginning near Clarksville, Texas, loops back to Shiloh and then roams over much of Texas. Both novels received the Jesse H. Jones ^{qv} fiction award of the Texas Institute of Letters.

Tom Lea sets two of his novels in the past: *The Hands of Cantu* (1964) in sixteenth-century Mexico and Texas; and *Wonderful Country* (1952), also of the border, in the nineteenth century. Although the action of *The Brave Bulls* (1949) is set in modern Mexico, the significance of its encounters between man and bull is symbolically extended to imply man's conflict with the fear of death. Paul Horgan's *The Devil in the Desert* (1950), a novelette based on fact, likewise is a morality and a great book. The time is mid-nineteenth century, the place the Texas side of the Great River. The ultimate victory of good over evil is told in terms of an elderly priest and a rattlesnake.

Dorothy Scarborough,^{qv} the first of the contemporary Texas novelists to gain national recognition, sets her plots chiefly in her own time. Of her four novels of the East Texas cotton country, the first and best is *In the Land of Cotton* (1923). *The Wind* (1925), set in the recent past in West Texas, is one of the rare Texas novels in which the protagonist is defeated. The wind is the villain.

The great novel of the cotton country is George Sessions Perry's ^{qv} *Hold Autumn In Your Hand* (1941). Sam Tucker, a tenant farmer, is every farmer since time began who struggles through the seasons to make a crop. Perry flavors this and his other tales with humor.

Fred Gipson,^{qv} too, flavors with humor *Hound-Dog Man* (1949) and *Old Yeller* (1956), tales of men and boys and dogs. Dillon Anderson makes humor the main ingredient of his picaresque tales, *I and Claudie* (1951) and *Claudie's Kinfolks* (1954). His third book, *The Billingsley Papers* (1961), is sophisticated satire of wealthy city-Texans.

David Westheimer's *Summer on the Water* (1948), like *The Billingsley Papers*, is set in the Houston area, but it is a humorless story of the complex and often tragic relationship between wealthy whites and their Negro servants. Westheimer's later and better known book, *Von Ryan's Express* (1964), which was made into a movie, is a thrilling adventure story of American officers escaping from an Italian prison camp.

Beginning in the 1930's, the Texas oil fields have been the subject of high-grade novels. Among them are: Karle Wilson Baker's *Family Style* (1937), Edwin Lanham's *Thunder in the Earth* (1941), Mary King's *Quincie Bolliver* (1941), and William A. Owens' *Fever in the Earth* (1958).

Three of Owens' novels are of the Red River country, where he grew up: *Walking on Borrowed Land* (1954), *Look to the River* (1963), and *This Stubborn Soil* (1966). The first of these, set on the Oklahoma side of the river, is one of the few novels by Texans, white or black, in which Negroes are the major characters. Mason Brewer, a Negro well known in Texas folklore circles, has published a book of poems and two of folktales, but no fiction.

Although the Western, with stereotyped plot and characters, is the most-read Texas fiction, only a few novels of the range since *Log of a Cowboy* can be considered as literature. Among these few are Larry McMurtry's three nonhero novels, *Horseman, Pass By* (1961), made into a movie as *Hud*; *Leaving Cheyenne* (1962), filmed as *Lovin' Molly*; and *The Last Picture Show* (1966), also made into a film; and Benjamin Capps' *The Road to Ogalalla* (1964), *Sam Chance* (1965), and *Woman of the People* (1966).

Loula Grace Erdman, the outstanding novelist of the Texas Panhandle, in *The Edge of Time* (1950) and *Many a Voyage* (1960), writes of women adapting woodland culture to the treeless plains. Miss Erdman's Dodd Meade $10,000 prize-winning novel, *The Year of the Locusts* (1947), however, is of her native Missouri.

Town and city novels of Texas are in the minority; yet a number are significant in portraying the varied facets of urban life. Mary Stuart Chamberlain's *We Inheritors* (1937) is a study of the effect of oil money on the second generation. Anne Pence Davis' *The Customer Is Always Right* (1940) concerns the lives of personnel of a large department store during the changing seasons. Madison A. Cooper's qv *Sironia, Texas* (1953), one of the longest novels in the language, reveals the private, often in contrast to the public, lives of men and women in a growing town. Al Dewlin's *Twilight of Honor* (1961) deals with the world of attorneys and courts. Leonard Sanders' *The Wooden Horseshoe* (1964) is about the political life of a young city. With the rapid change in Texas from a rural to an urban economy, more city novels are due.

Katherine Anne Porter, a superb stylist and one of America's most distinguished writers, though born and bred in Texas, prefers to be considered a Southerner. Much of her writing is of the Old South and based on her grandmother's tales. The setting of a number of her stories is indefinite. However, "Old Mortality" (1939), one of the most perfect, is specifically Texas, as is the unforgettable short story, "Holiday" (1960). Her one novel, *Ship of Fools* (1962), is international in scope. Miss Porter, a master of the shorter forms of fiction, in 1965 received a Pulitzer Prize for *Collected Stories*.

Texas fiction in the mid-1960's was rapidly catching up with nonfiction in volume and quality. Though not yet alongside fact-writing, fiction was only a few steps behind.

Drama: The most neglected type of Texas writing is the drama. For a time, when the Little Theater Movement qv was at its peak, a number of one-act plays were written. Two memorable ones are indictments of injustices toward Negroes: John William Rogers' *Judge Lynch* (1925) and Kathleen Witherspoon's *Jute* (1931). Sam Acheson's qv *We Are Besieged* (1941) concerns the fight at the Alamo. This heroic tragedy, however, found a more suitable medium in Ramsey Yelvington's qv *A Cloud of Witnesses* (1959), a full-length poetic drama for outdoor performance. Robert Nail qv at Albany has raised the historical spectacle to a high artistic level in his *Fandangle*,qv produced annually. Texans seem to like best large productions given under the sky or in a domed coliseum.

The Juvenile: The juvenile, a specialized form of literature, is one of the most alive forms of writing in Texas. Some of the outstanding writers, most of whom have won the Juvenile Award of the Texas Institute of Letters, are Charlotte Baker, Camilla Campbell, Wanda Jay Campbell, Anne Pence Davis, Irmengarde Eberle, Loula Grace Erdman, Fred Gipson, Carol Hoff, Byrd Hooper, Siddie Joe Johnson, John Latham, Jeanette Sebring Lowrey, Jessie Brewer McGaw, Lee McGiffin, Esse Forrester O'Brien, Nancy Paschal, Leigh Peck, and Ramona Maher Weeks. A number of these will also be recognized as writers of adult books.

BIBLIOGRAPHY: E. Douglas Branch, *The Cowboy and His Interpreters* (1926, 1961); Walter S. Campbell (Stanley Vestal), *The Book Lover's Southwest* (1955); Glen Dawson, *Southwest Books* (1954); Sam H. Dixon, *The Poets and Poetry of Texas* (1885); J. Frank Dobie, *Guide to Life and Literature of the Southwest* (1943, 1952); David Fonte Eagleton, *Writers and Writings of Texas* (1913); Edwin W. Gaston, Jr., *The Early Novel of the Southwest* (1961); Mabel Major, Rebecca W. Smith, and T. M. Pearce, *Southwest Heritage, A Literary History* (1938, 1948); Mabel Major and T. M. Pearce, *Signature of the Sun: Southwest Verse, 1900–1950* (1950); L. W. Payne, Jr., *A Survey of Texas Literature* (1928); Lawrence Clark Powell, *Books: West Southwest* (1957); C. W. Raines, *A Bibliography of Texas* (1896, 1934); John William Rogers and J. Frank Dobie, *Finding Literature on the Texas Plains* (1931); Lyle Saunders, *Guide to the Literature of the Southwest* (1952); Goldie Capers Smith, *The Creative Arts in Texas* (1926); C. L. Sonnichsen, *The Southwest: The Record in Books* (1965); Thomas W. Streeter, *Bibliography of Texas, 1795–1845* (3 parts, 5 vols., 1955–1960); Mary Tucker, *Books of the Southwest: A General Bibliography* (1937); Ernest W. Winkler (ed.), *Check List of Texas Imprints, 1846–1860* (1949); Ernest W. Winkler and Llerena B. Friend (eds.), *Check List of Texas Imprints, 1861–1876* (1963).

Mabel Major
Joe B. Frantz

*Littig, Texas.

*Little, John.

*Little, William W.

*Little Aguja Canyon.

*Little Aguja Mountain.

*Little Arkansas Creek.

*Little Blanco River.

*Little Boggy Creek.

*Little Brazos River.

*Little Brushy Creek.

*Little Caddo Creek.

*Little Camp Creek.

*Little Caney Creek.

*Little Cedar Creek.

*Little Chicago, Texas.

*Little Cow Creek.

*Little Creek.

*Little Cypress Creek.

*Little Duck Creek.

*Little Elkhart Creek. *See also* Houston County Lake.

*Little Elm, Texas.

*Little Elm Creek.

*Little Hackberry Creek.

*Little Keechie Creek.

*Little Lake.

*Little Lake Creek.

*Little Llano River.

*Little Loco Bayou.

*Little Mineral Creek.

*Little Mountain Creek.

⁺Little Mustang Creek.

*Little Pecan Creek.

Little Penn Claim. *See Eliza Russell* and *Little Penn* Claims.

*Little Pine Creek.

*Little Pine Island Bayou.

*Little Piney Creek.

*Little Postoak Creek.

*Little Red Mud Creek.

*Little Red River.

*Little River.

*Little River, Texas.

*Little River Fort.

*Little Rocky Creek.

*Little St. Louis, Texas.

*Little Saline Creek.

*Little Sandy Creek.

*Little Stinking Creek.

*Little Sunday Creek.

*Little Theater Movement. With the end of World War II and with renewed interest in theater to supplement and substitute for the decrease in the touring professional theater, the community theater flourished in Texas on a broadened scale from Amarillo and Midland to Beaumont and Port Arthur. Every major city had at least one local theater; some, such as Houston and Dallas, had more than one within the city limits and one in almost every suburb. In many cities of twenty-five thousand or less it was the major cultural activity.

Much of the impetus came with the industrial expansion of Texas, which brought into the state many residents who had known the theater elsewhere and wanted it in their new communities; also the spectacular growth of educational theater sharply honed the urge for theater activity among its trained theater graduates and excited the interest of those from other disciplines.

By the late 1960's some of the larger community theaters were professional in all but name, with volunteer actors and technicians trained in the universities and on the professional stage. Some had full-time, salaried directors; a few had paid staffs in addition. Others had operating budgets of fifty thousand dollars or more, with paid memberships nearing two thousand. Some had their own buildings—not remodeled garages, but theaters designed for their function—costing one hundred thousand dollars or more. *See also* Theater in Texas.

Gynter Quill

*Little Twin Sisters Peaks.

Little Victorio Canyon. *See* Victorio Canyon.

*Little Walnut Creek.

*Little White Oak Creek.

*Little White Rock Creek.

*Little Wichita River.

*Little York, Texas.

*Littlefield, George Washington. George Washington Littlefield's mother's maiden name was Mildred Terrell Satterwhite, and she was the widow of John Henry White at her marriage to Fleming Littlefield (Volume II gives her last married name as Mildred M. Littlefield). Littlefield enlisted in a company of volunteers under Captain Isham G. Jones in May, 1861; this company, which became a part of Terry's Texas Rangers,qv was sworn into Confederate service on September 11, 1861 (not August, 1861, as stated in Volume II). Littlefield was in eastern Tennessee under General James Longstreet's command during November and December, 1863. Severely wounded at Mossy Creek on December 26, 1863, he was given a battlefield commission as major. He married Alice Payne Tillar (not Tiller). In 1901 he purchased the 312,-175-acre southern or Yellow House division of the XIT Ranch.qv He then created the Littlefield Lands Company qv in 1912 and sold land to farmers in and around the town of Littlefield.

BIBLIOGRAPHY: David B. Gracy II, *Littlefield Lands: Colonization on the Texas Plains, 1912–1920* (1968).

*Littlefield, Texas. Littlefield, seat of Lamb County, was begun and developed by George W. Littlefield qv through the Littlefield Lands Company,qv which began operations in August, 1912, with Arthur P. Duggan as the sales manager. A public library was created in 1914, but no building was constructed to house it. Neal A. Douglass (not Douglas, as stated in Volume II) published the Lamb County *News* in 1917 and 1918.

In the 1950's and 1960's Littlefield was the retail and commercial center for Lamb County and parts of Hockley and Bailey counties, a region devoted to irrigated farming of cotton, grain sorghums, and vegetables. Agricultural industries, such as fertilizer and irrigation equipment manufacturing and cotton compressing, were located in Littlefield. By the mid-1960's Littlefield had two hospitals, two banks, twenty-one churches, a library, a newspaper, and a radio station; the town had completed water and storm sewer improvements, a new high school, and a downtown beautification project. In 1970 Littlefield reported 197 business establishments. The 1960 population was 7,236; the 1970 census reported 6,738 people.

Littlefield Lands Company. The Littlefield Lands Company was organized in August, 1912, by Major George Washington Littlefield qv to sell 79,-040 acres of his Yellow House Ranch qv in southwestern Lamb County for farming purposes. As general manager of the company, Littlefield selected James Phelps White,qv his partner in the Yellow House Ranch, and as sales manager, Arthur Pope Duggan,qv a nephew by marriage.

The center of the operation was the town of Littlefield, which was platted on the Santa Fe Railroad's main line from Lubbock to Texico, New Mexico, then under construction. The town's official opening was held on July 4, 1913. From a population of thirty in December, 1912, the number of residents in Littlefield and on land purchased from the company grew to approximately one thousand by March, 1917. Largely because of an ensuing two-year drouth which drove settlers from the community, the population dwindled to about four hundred by 1920 and two hundred fifty by 1923.

Though the plains were experiencing a land boom in 1906–1914, prospective buyers required proof of the land's agricultural utility. Littlefield Lands consequently established a demonstration farm for both dryland and irrigated crops and put in five irrigation plants.

The land was sold primarily through independent land agents under contract to Littlefield. R. C. Rawlings, the principal agent, made more than one-fourth of the 464 recorded sales. By 1920 the company had sold 47,601 acres of farming and grazing land and 148 town lots.

Among the settlers at Littlefield was a colony of Mennonites. Though about eighty buyers came from East Texas and the northern states, about twice as many originated from the states of the Great Plains. At Littlefield there was no friction between entrenched rancher and incoming farmer. In fact, through economic assistance, the rancher's land company, as Littlefield Lands, fostered settlement.

The drouth of 1917–1919, combined with the tightened credit in the United States caused by World War I and by America's entry into the conflict, stopped the flow of prospective buyers to Littlefield, and the land was taken off the market in July, 1918. The subdivision was reopened for sale in September, 1920, but at Littlefield's death in November, the unsold town lots passed to Duggan's wife by inheritance. The company was run by Littlefield's estate until April, 1923, when the newly organized Yellow House Land Company bought the ranch for further subdivision and sale. See also Yellow House Ranch.

BIBLIOGRAPHY: David B. Gracy II, *Littlefield Lands: Colonization on the Texas Plains, 1912-1920* (1968).

David B. Gracy II

*Littlejohn, Elbridge Gerry.

*Littles Chapel, Texas.

*Littleton, John.

*Littleton, Martin Wiley.

*Live Oak, Texas. (Bee County.)

Live Oak, Texas. (Bexar County.) Live Oak is a recently developed suburban community northeast of San Antonio. Incorporated in the 1960's, the town first appeared on the United States census rolls in 1970, when a population of 2,779 was reported. See also San Antonio Standard Metropolitan Statistical Area.

*Live Oak, Texas. (Concho County.)

*Live Oak, Texas. (Hays County.)

*Live Oak, Texas. (Milam County.)

*Live Oak Branch.

*Live Oak County. Live Oak County derived the bulk of its average annual farm income, $9 million in the early 1970's, from cattle. A sizeable portion of county income also came from grain sorghums and cotton. From 1931 through 1972, over thirty-eight million barrels of oil had been produced. The county had several tourist attractions: Lake Corpus Christi, Fort Merrill, and Fort Ramirez.qqv The 1960 population was 7,846; the 1970 population decreased to 6,697, according to the United States census.

*Live Oak Creek. See Liveoak Creek.

*Live Oak Female Seminary. See also Presbyterian Education in Texas.

*Live Oak Hill, Texas.

*Lively. The schooner *Lively*, bringing supplies to Stephen F. Austin's colony of three hundred families, was wrecked on Galveston Island on its second voyage in 1822. It is not true that the passengers were lost (as stated in Volume II), though this belief has persisted in Texas to the present time. Confusion actually began with the first voyage, when the settlers landed on the Brazos, thinking it to be the Colorado River. When Austin failed to find them on the Colorado, he assumed they were lost at sea; actually, they attempted a settlement, but had little contact with other settlements, and all but two or three returned to the United States. By the time of the second voyage, rumors were apparently so widespread that those on the second voyage were never able to correct them, although such men as Thomas Marshall Duke qv were actually on board the second trip. According to Duke, the passengers were rescued and taken on board the *John Motley*, which then landed them near the Colorado River.

BIBLIOGRAPHY: Lester G. Bugbee, "What Became of the *Lively*?" *Quarterly of the Texas State Historical Association*, III (1899–1900); John A. Lomax, "Lester Gladstone Bugbee," *Southwestern Historical Quarterly*, XLIX (1945–1946).

William J. Doree

*Lively, Robert Maclin.

*Liveoak Creek.

*Liveoak Draw.

*Liverpool, Texas.

*Livestock. Texas has always been among the leading livestock states in the nation, usually ranking first in total number of cattle, beef cattle, sheep, and goats. Between 1936 and 1965 (with the exception of 1939, 1943, and 1951), Texas' annual cash receipts from livestock and livestock products were always exceeded by those from crops. Beginning in 1966, however, and in each succeeding year, cash receipts from livestock exceeded those from crops at an ever increasing rate, so that by 1972 they accounted for about two thirds of the state's total farm receipts. In that year cash receipts from livestock amounted to over $2.5 billion, 72 percent of which came from cattle production. Texas in the mid-1970's continued to lead all states in total cattle, beef cattle, sheep and wool, and goats and mohair. *See also* Cattle Industry; Dairying; Goat Ranching; Horse Breeding; Mule Raising; Poultry Production; Sheep Ranching; Swine Raising.

*Livestock Sanitary Commission.

*Livingston, Texas. Livingston, seat of Polk County, was incorporated in 1902 with a city manager-alderman form of government. In 1966 it reported a hospital, a library, a newspaper, a radio station, and fourteen churches. In that same year Livingston completed a sewage treatment plant and other public improvements. Among its businesses were industries concerned with lumber milling and oil field supplies, although the town served as a commercial center for farm and ranch products as well. Livingston reported 131 businesses in 1970. The 1960 population was 3,398, and the 1970 census counted 3,925 people.

*Livingston and Southeastern Railway Company.

*Llaneros Tribes.

*Llano, Texas. Llano, seat of Llano County, had an economy based on livestock, tourism, and processing of granite and talc. In 1966 Llano had fourteen churches, a hospital, a bank, a library, and a newspaper. In 1970, 106 business establishments were reported. The 1960 population was 2,656; the 1970 population was 2,608, according to the United States census. The population has remained relatively stable since 1940. Improvements in the town included a public swimming pool completed in 1955 and a community center building and rodeo arena completed in 1960.

*Llano County. Llano County, a livestock-raising area, received 90 percent of its farm income, an annual average of $7 million in the mid-1970's, from cattle, sheep, and goat ranching. The county was also among the leading swine-producing areas. The only crop of importance in the 1960's was peanuts. Some income was derived from the sale of fence posts, firewood, and deer leases. Llano was the number one deer-hunting county in the state. The Highland Lakes country, Enchanted Rock, Bettina Communistic Colony, and Packsaddle Mountain qqv attracted thousands of tourists annually. The 1960 population was 5,240; the 1970 census reported a population of 6,979.

*Llano Estacado.

*Llano Estacado Institute.

*Llano Estacado Railroad.

*Llano River.

*Llanoria and the Llanorian Mountains.

*Llanos-Cárdenas Expedition.

*Llanos del Cibolo. *See* Llano Estacado.

*Lloyd, Texas.

*Loafer Creek.

*Lobo, Texas.

*Local Option. *See* Prohibition Movement.

*Locker, Texas.

*Lockett, Texas.

*Lockettville, Texas.

*Lockhart, Byrd.

*Lockhart, Matilda.

*Lockhart, Texas. (Caldwell County.) Lockhart, seat of Caldwell County, was an agricultural center in the 1960's and 1970's; businesses included a garment factory, a feed mill, seed farms, and a producer of charcoal products. The town had a hospital, sixteen churches, a high school and junior high, a public library, and a large senior citizens home. Businesses totaled 112 in 1970. The 1960 population was 6,084; the 1970 population rose to 6,489, according to the United States census.

*Lockhart, Texas. (DeWitt County.)

*Lockhart Academy.

*Lockhart Mountain.

*Lockney, Texas. Lockney, in central Floyd County, had seventy-five businesses serving a productive farming area in 1970. A large modern elementary school was completed in 1964, and the town also had a new twenty-four-bed hospital, nineteen churches, and a new city hall and fire station. The 1960 population was 2,141; the 1970 census reported 2,094.

*Lockney Christian College.

*Loco, Texas.

*Locust, Texas.

*Lodge Creek.

*Lodi, Texas. (Marion County.)

*Lodi, Texas. (Wilson County.)

*Loeb, Texas.

*Loebau, Texas.

Loftin, James Otis. James Otis Loftin, son of Sam R. and Lila (McLellan) Loftin, was born at Thornton, Texas, on July 19, 1877. He attended North Texas State Normal College (now North Texas State University) from 1905 to 1907 and received his B.A. degree from Southwest Texas State Teachers College (now Southwest Texas State University) in 1925 and his M.A. degree from Colorado State College in 1927. After a series of teaching and administrative positions, principally in San Antonio, he served as president of Texas College of Arts and Industries (now Texas A&I University) in Kingsville from 1934 to 1941. He then became president of San Antonio Junior College (now San Antonio College) and was largely responsible for the development of the college's educational program and physical plant. Loftin served as president of the Texas State Teachers Association qv from 1933 to 1934. He was married four times and had two children. He was killed in an automobile accident on December 31, 1955. He was buried at the Sunset Memorial Park in San Antonio.

BIBLIOGRAPHY: *Who's Who In America* (1952); San Antonio *Express*, January 1, 1956.

James O. Wallace

*Logan, Greenberry. [This title was incorrectly listed in Volume II as Logan, Greenbury.] Signatures on documents indicate that Logan spelled his first name as shown here. Logan was born a slave in Kentucky in 1799 and was emancipated by his father, David Logan. He came to Texas from Missouri in 1831, received a grant of one-fourth league of land on Chocolate Bayou in what is now Brazoria County, and leased a blacksmith shop on Francis Bingham's qv plantation. In June, 1832, he took part in the battle of Velasco.qv In 1834 he purchased the freedom of Francis Bingham's slave, Caroline, and married her; they subsequently operated a boarding house at Columbia (now West Columbia).

Logan joined the Texas Army qv on October 7, 1835 (not October 10). In 1838 he received a donation of one league of land as compensation for being permanently disabled in the Texas Revolution. In 1841 he complained to Robert M. Forbes qv (not R. F. Forbes) that the Constitution of the Republic qv deprived him of "every privilege dear to a freeman . . . no vote or say in any way," and asked that his bounty land be declared tax exempt by Congress, but a bill to do so failed to pass. In 1853 he located additional bounty and donation grants in Brown and Callahan counties. He was still living in March, 1881, when he filed a survey for a headright augmentation grant in Zavala County.

BIBLIOGRAPHY: Thomas Lloyd Miller, *Bounty and Donation Land Grants of Texas, 1835–1888* (1967); W. P. Zuber, "Biographies of Texas Veterans" (MS., Archives, University of Texas at Austin Library); Memorials and Petitions, Papers of the Legislature (MS., Archives, Texas State Library); Congressional Papers, Sixth Congress (MS., Archives, Texas State Library); First Class Headright File (MS., General Land Office, Austin).

*Logan, William G.

*Logan, William M.

*Logan, Texas.

*Logtown, Texas.

*Lohn, Texas.

*Lois, Texas.

*Lolita, Texas.

*Loma, Texas.

Loma Alta Reservoir. Loma Alta Reservoir is in the Nueces-Rio Grande Coastal Basin in Cameron County, eight miles northeast of Brownsville. The reservoir is off-channel from the Rio Grande. The project is owned and operated by the Brownsville Navigation District. Construction was started on November 10, 1958, and was completed in March, 1963. This project impounds surplus Rio Grande water to supply municipal and industrial needs. The reservoir has a capacity of 26,500 acre-feet and a surface area of 2,490 acres at the spillway crest elevation of 17.5 feet above mean sea level. The level is maintained by pumping from the Rio Grande during off-season irrigation demands.

BIBLIOGRAPHY: Texas Water Commission, *Bulletin 6408* (1964).

Seth D. Breeding

*Loma Alto, Texas.

*Loma Vista, Texas.

*Lomax, John Avery.

*Lomax, Texas.

*Lombardi, Cesar Maurice.

*Lometa, Texas.

*Lomo, Texas.

*Lomo Alto.

*Lomo San Caja.

*Lon Morris College. Lon Morris College, Jacksonville, continued to operate under the Texas Conference of the Methodist Church, which covered the eastern one-fourth of Texas. The first junior college in the state to be admitted to the Southern Association of Colleges and Secondary Schools, Lon Morris College also chartered the first Texas chapter of Phi Theta Kappa, national junior college scholarship fraternity. Construction on the twenty-six-acre campus included eight major buildings and twelve minor buildings between 1954 and 1965. Value of the physical plant increased from $461,193 in 1952 to over $2,250,000 in 1965. During this period enrollment doubled from approximately two hundred to four hundred full-time students. Endowments exceeded $710,000 in 1965 and were increasing monthly. The building program provided for completion of a cafeteria and student center (1958); science hall, library and administration building (1961); physical education and gymnasium building (1964); and boys dormitory (1965). The library contained nineteen thousand volumes by 1969. Expansion of dormitory facilities to accommodate 600 full-time students was expected to conclude this phase of the school's physical growth. C. E. Peeples served as president during the expansion period. By the 1974 fall term, student enrollment was 312. John E. Fellers was president in 1974.

*London, Texas.

*Lone Camp, Texas.

*Lone Cedar, Texas.

*Lone Elm, Texas. (Ellis County.)

*Lone Elm, Texas. (Kaufman County.)

*Lone Grove, Texas.

*Lone Gum Tree Creek.

*Lone Jack Mountain.

*Lone Man Mountain.

*Lone Mountain.

*Lone Oak, Texas.

*Lone Oak Mountain.

*Lone Star, Texas. (Cherokee County.)

*Lone Star, Texas. (Comal County.)

Lone Star, Texas. (Morris County.) The United States census reported a population for Lone Star of 1,513 in 1960 and 1,760 in 1970. The city reported fifty businesses in 1970.

*Lone Star, Texas. (Wise County.)

Lone Star Army Ammunition Plant. In 1964 the Lone Star Army Ammunition Plant, previously named Lone Star Ordnance Plant,qv continued as a government owned, contractor operated ammunition-loading plant, the lands of which are considered a part of the greater Red River Army Depot reservation. In the late 1960's approximately sixty-five hundred civil service employees and a limited number of military personnel worked in the Red River Army Depot, which included some eighty-five thousand supply items and seventy-seven hundred types of shells in its warehouse and underground ammunition dumps. See also Red River Army Depot.

BIBLIOGRAPHY: Texas Almanac (1963, 1969).

*Lone Star Boys' State.

*Lone Star Flag. See Flags of Texas.

*Lone Star Ordnance Plant. See also Lone Star Army Ammunition Plant.

*Lone Tree, Texas.

*Lone Tree Creek.

*Lone Wolf. It is possible that Lone Wolf was not one of the signers of the treaties of Medicine Lodge, Kansas, in 1867 (as stated in Volume II). His name does not appear as either Lone Wolf or Guipago (his Kiowa name) on the original manuscripts of the treaties, although it is possible he was there under some other name, as Indians sometimes went under various names in different periods. The official documents show ten Kiowa signers for one treaty and thirteen for the other (not nine, as stated in Volume II).

*Lone Wolf Mountain.

*Lone Woman Mountain.

*Lonely Lee Mountain.

*Long, James.

*Long, Jane Herbert Wilkinson.

*Long, John Benjamin.

†Long, Stephen Harriman.

Long, Walter Ewing. Walter Ewing Long, Austin businessman and civic leader, was born November 1, 1886, near Ladonia, Fannin County, the son of Andrew Davison and Alice Madora (McCown) Long. He graduated from high school in Ladonia in 1905 and from Austin College in Sherman with a B.A. degree in 1910 and an M.A. degree

in 1911. He received a law degree with honors from the University of Texas in 1914, but instead of practicing law he took a job with the San Antonio Chamber of Commerce. Long became secretary of the Austin Chamber of Commerce in 1915; he later was manager of that group for thirty-five years.

Walter Long was active in every concern that affected Austin. Considered the father of Austin's city planning, he also helped organize the Colorado River Improvement Association, which evolved into the Lower Colorado River Authority and built the dams forming what is now the Highland Lakes chain (see Colorado River Authorities). Long obtained options on land eventually used to increase the size of the University of Texas campus, and in 1922 he arranged a sale of bonds to construct the Stephen F. Austin Hotel, for many years a convention center in the city. In 1925 he founded the Texas Legislative Service and supervised its activities for forty years; he gave its collection of legislative history (1925–1965) to the Texas State Library.qv After his retirement in 1949, Long continued to work on various committees and to write on his favorite subjects, Austin and central Texas. Among his many publications were Flood to Faucet (1956), The Longhorn Crossing (1960), For All Time to Come (1964), and Stephen F. Austin's Legacies (1970). He was appointed to the Texas State Library and Historical Commission qv in 1954, and he served as president of the Texas Fine Arts Association.qv He was also a member of the executive council of the Texas State Historical Association.qv Walter Long was married to Janet Kaape on March 30, 1915, and they were the parents of two children. Long died in Austin on November 8, 1973, and was buried in Oakwood Cemetery.

BIBLIOGRAPHY: Joe B. Frantz, "In Memoriam: Walter E. Long," Southwestern Historical Quarterly, LXXVII (1973–1974); Austin American-Statesman, August 9, 1966, November 9, 1973; Biographical File, Barker Texas History Center, University of Texas at Austin.

†Long Branch.

*Long Branch, Texas.

*Long Creek.

*Long Draw.

*Long Expedition.

*Long Hollow.

*Long John Hollow.

*Long King Creek.

*Long Lake, Texas.

*Long Mott, Texas.

*Long Mountain.

*Long Mountain, Texas.

*Long Point, Texas. (Fort Bend County.)

*Long Point, Texas. (Washington County.)

*Long Siding, Texas.

*Long Slough.

*Long Station, Texas.

*Long Tom Creek.

*Longfellow, Texas.

*Longhorn Cattle.

*Longhorn Cavern. *See also* Parks, State.

*Longhorn Ordnance Works.

*Longley, William Preston.

*Longview, Texas. Longview, seat and principal commercial and industrial center of Gregg County, in the 1960's seemed to be leveling off in the population growth that had been so dramatic since the discovery of oil in the early 1930's. The population, 13,758 in 1940, had leaped to 24,502 by 1950; a further increase, to 40,050 in 1960, was less significant, in that it largely represented the annexation of nearby Greggton. In 1970 the United States census reported 45,547 people. The Longview metropolitan area had spread to the east by 1967, extending into Harrison County. Several new industries had joined the predominantly oil-connected older ones, notably a large brewery. The city had 1,168 business establishments in 1970. Two hospitals, several clinics, and LeTourneau College qv were located in Longview.

Longview Heights, Texas. Longview Heights, on United States Highway 80 in far western Harrison County, is the name of a suburb of Longview. The community is strictly residential.

*Longview and Sabine Valley Railway.

*Longworth, Texas.

*Lonnie, Texas.

*Lonsdale, Texas.

*Lookout, Texas.

*Lookout Mountain.

*Looney, James.

*Looney, Joseph K.

*Looney, Samuel.

*Looneyville, Texas.

*Loop, Texas.

*Looscan, Adele Lubbock Briscoe. Adele Lubbock Briscoe Looscan died on November 23, 1935 (not November 24, 1935, as stated in Volume II). She was buried in Glenwood Cemetery in Houston (not in the Harris family cemetery in Harrisburg). BIBLIOGRAPHY: Houston *Post*, November 24, 1935.

*Lopeno, Texas. [This title was incorrectly listed in Volume II as Lopena, Texas.] Lopeno, in southern Zapata County, was inundated by the waters of International Falcon Reservoir qv in 1953. A new town was built on higher ground, and in the early 1970's it had a population of approximately one hundred.

*López, Nicolás.

*Lopez Creek.

*Lopez Peaks.

*Loraine, Texas.

*Lord, George.

*Lorena, Texas.

*Lorenzo, Texas. Lorenzo, in western Crosby County twenty miles east of Lubbock, had thirty-four businesses in 1970, including a cotton compress and six gins, grain elevators, a chemical plant, and a large textile mill. A bank and weekly newspaper served the city. Its population has changed only slightly, from 939 in 1950, to 1,188 in 1960, to 1,206 in 1970, according to the United States census.

*Loreto, Presidio of. *See* Nuestra Señora de Loreto Presidio.

*Los Adaes.

*Los Adaes Mission. *See* San Miguel de Linares de los Adaes.

*Los Adaes Presidio. *See* Nuestra Señora del Pilar de los Adaes Presidio.

*Los Alamos Creek.

*Los Angeles, Texas.

*Los Apaches, Texas.

*Los Charco Creek.

*Los Ebanos, Texas.

*Los Fresnos, Texas. The United States census reported a population for Los Fresnos, in Cameron County, of 1,289 in 1960 and 1,297 in 1970. In 1970 Los Fresnos reported thirty businesses, including banking facilities.

*Los Horconsitos.

*Los Indios, Texas.

*Los Lingos Creek.

*Los Machos, Texas.

*Los Morteros Creek.

*Los Ojuelos, Texas.

*Los Olmos Creek.

*Losoya, Texas.

*Los Pastores.

Los Preseños, Texas. Los Preseños, in present Jim Wells County, was a Mexican ranch settlement started by Marcelino López of Camargo, Tamaulipas, Mexico, in 1831 after he applied for title to the land on August 2, 1831, in Camargo. The name of his grant was "Charco de los Preseños." It consisted of four sitios along San Fernando Creek and was part of the huge original San Fernando grant.

By June 23, 1832, López had improved his grant to the extent that he received title to the land. The first settlers were herders, who built their jacales near the southeast corner of the grant along San Fernando Creek, about two miles east of present Alice.

In 1849 the trade route from Corpus Christi to Laredo, and later to Eagle Pass, established by Henry Lawrence Kinney and William Leslie Cazneau,qqv passed through Los Preseños. Although no great houses were ever built there, Los Preseños was known to travelers as a place where food could be found. A trading post was established there, which was frequented by mustangers and sometimes raided by Indians. It continued to exist until Collins, Texas, was established in 1878. Father Claude C. Jaillet qv records a yellow fever epidemic there in 1867.

BIBLIOGRAPHY: Nueces County Deed Records, Book D; Sister Mary Xavier, *Father Jaillet: Saddlebag Priest of the Nueces* (1948); Felix von Blucher, Nueces District Map (compiled 1870); Corpus Christi *Star*, August 25, 1849.

Agnes G. Grimm

*Los Saenz, Texas. *See* Roma-Los Saenz, Texas.

Los Surdos Indians. The Los Surdos (possibly Los Sordos, "the quiet people") are known from a Spanish document of 1683. Since no native name is given, they cannot be related to other known Indian groups. They seem to have lived somewhere in west-central Texas.

BIBLIOGRAPHY: C. W. Hackett (ed.), *Pichardo's Treatise on the Limits of Louisiana and Texas*, I (1931).

T. N. Campbell

Lost Battalion. The 2nd Battalion, 131st Field Artillery Regiment, 36th Infantry Division (*see* Thirty-sixth Division)—better known as the Lost Battalion—was mobilized on November 25, 1940, from the Texas National Guard.qv The unit began training on January 14, 1941, at Camp Bowie,qv near Brownwood. After spending August and September on maneuvers in Louisiana swamps, the 2nd Battalion left for San Francisco by train on November 10, 1941. Their destination was known to them only by the code name PLUM.

Boarding the American ship *Republic* on November 21, the 2nd Battalion sailed from Angel Island, off the coast from San Francisco. The ship spent less than one day in Honolulu and was seven days out of Hawaii in a convoy with ten other ships when Pearl Harbor was bombed by the Japanese on December 7, 1941.

Because the Philippines were also attacked a few hours after Pearl Harbor, the convoy changed course. Supplies were picked up in Suva Harbor in the Fiji Islands, and the *Republic* docked in Brisbane, Australia, on December 21. Here the battalion spent Christmas and left on the Dutch ship *Bloemfontein* on December 28, 1941. After a three-day stop at the port of Darwin, the group proceeded to Surabaya (Soerabaya) Harbor on the island of Java in the (then) Dutch East Indies.

The battalion was immediately moved inland to the Malang airfield, where it assisted the United States Army Air Forces in keeping remnants of the Philippine-based 17th Bombardment Group active in an increasingly desperate campaign. Between February 28 and March 10 the battalion engaged the Japanese, who had invaded Java from east and west. By March 10 the entire battalion, along with some Dutch, Australian, and British forces, had surrendered and were taken as prisoners of war.

Because the United States War Department would not or could not disclose information about what happened to the unit, American newspapers named it the Lost Battalion. For the next forty-two months the men of this battalion were confined in prison and work camps from Singapore to Manchuria. Suffering from tropical diseases and malnutrition and with little or no medical help from the Japanese, many of these men worked as prison laborers on such projects as shipbuilding and road and railroad construction. Pierre Boulle's book, *The Bridge Over The River Kwai* (later a motion picture entitled *The Bridge On The River Kwai*), was based on the construction of the Burma-Thailand railroad, upon which many Lost Battalion men worked.

Liberation came in August, 1945, shortly after the explosion of the atomic bomb (the battalion officially celebrates August 14 as its liberation day). A yearly reunion was initiated on November 30–December 2, 1945, in Abilene. Beginning with its second reunion in Wichita Falls, the battalion decided to meet on the weekend nearest August 14 of each year.

BIBLIOGRAPHY: Hollis G. Allen, *The Lost Battalion* (1963); Abilene *Reporter-News*, November 10, 1971.

John William Johnson

*Lost Creek.

*Lost Draw.

*Lost Lake.

*Lost Mine Peak.

*Lost Mule Creek.

*Lost Nigger Expedition. *See* Nolan Expedition.

*Lost Pines of Texas.

*Lost Prairie, Texas.

*Lost Valley Creek.

*Lothrop, John T. K.

*Lott, Elisha Everett.

*Lott, Uriah.

*Lott, Texas.

*Lotta, Texas.

*Lou, Texas.

*Louetta, Texas.

*Loughery, Robert W.

*Louise, Texas.

*Louisiana and Arkansas Railway Company. *See also* Kansas City Southern Lines in Texas.

*Louisiana Railway and Navigation Company of Texas.

*Louisiana Western Extension Railroad.

Loupé, Armand Victor. Armand Victor Loupé (Loupy) was a Frenchman, reputedly from Louisiana, who was an original colonist of the Power and Hewetson Colony qv in Texas during the late 1820's and 1830's. He was one of the colony's official surveyors. He received a grant of one league as a colonist, dated November 26, 1834. Loupé was one of the party of Refugians who participated in George Morse Collingsworth's qv capture of Goliad on October 10, 1835, and was a member of Philip Dimitt's qv garrison. He also supplied James Walker Fannin's qv army at Goliad with beef, horses, and oxen during their occupation and later

received several land bounty warrants for this service to the Republic of Texas. His name is listed
among those who signed the Goliad Declaration of
Independence.qv Loupé served as interpreter for
Henry Wax Karnes and Henry Teal qqv on their
mission to Matamoros in 1837, and later he became
involved in the Federalist Wars of the northern
Mexican states. He was probably a part of Captain
Ewen Cameron's qv company of Texans who were
in Mexico at various times from 1838 to 1840. Victor Loupé attached himself particularly to Colonel
Antonio Zapata qv and was shot with that leader
at Monclova, Mexico, in March, 1840.

BIBLIOGRAPHY: D. W. C. Baker, *A Texas Scrap Book*
(1875); Carlos Maria Bustamante, *El Gabinete Mexicano*
(1842); Hobart Huson, *Refugio*, I (1953); Thomas Lloyd
Miller, *Bounty and Donation Land Grants of Texas, 1835–
1888* (1967); Virginia H. Taylor Houston, "Surveying in
Texas," *Southwestern Historical Quarterly*, LXV (1961–
1962); R. M. Potter, "Escape of Karnes and Teal From
Matamoros," *Quarterly of the Texas State Historical Association*, IV (1900–1901); Audited Military Claims, Republic (Archives, Texas State Library, Austin).

Hobart Huson

*Love, James. James Love practiced law at
Barbourville, Kentucky (not Barboursville, Kentucky, as stated in Volume II).

Jimmie Hicks

*Love, John G.

*Love, Robert Marshall.

Love, Thomas Bell. Thomas Bell Love, son of
Thomas Calvin and Sarah Jane (Rodgers) Love,
was born in Webster County, Missouri, on June 23,
1870. He was graduated with a B.S. degree from
Drury College in Springfield, Missouri, in 1891.
He was married to Mattie Roberta Goode on June
11, 1892, and they had three children. Before moving to Dallas in 1899, he was city attorney of
Springfield, Missouri (1892–1894), a member of
the board of managers of the Missouri State Hospital, and secretary of the Democratic State Central
Committee of Missouri (1896–1898). Love was a
prominent figure in Texas political life for the first
three decades of the twentieth century. He was elected to the Texas House of Representatives from
Dallas County in 1902, 1904, and 1906, the last
term serving as speaker of the House of Representatives. Love was an expert on taxes, insurance, and
banking and had an important role in the passage
of the reform legislation of 1905 and 1907 related
to these issues. At the conclusion of the 1907 legislative session, Governor Thomas Mitchell Campbell qv appointed him commissioner of the newly
formed Department of Insurance and Banking (*see*
Banking Department of Texas). He resigned from
the office in 1910 to resume law practice in Dallas
and to become associated with the Southwestern Life
Insurance Company and the Western Indemnity
Company.

Love did not retire from politics, however, for
he was a leading spokesman for the prohibitionist
forces in the 1911 submission campaign and he
was an early supporter of Woodrow Wilson for
the Democratic nomination in 1912. In 1917 President Wilson appointed him assistant secretary of

the Treasury Department and placed him in charge
of the Bureau of War Risk Insurance. Returning
to Texas in 1919, Love was elected national Democratic committeeman from Texas in 1920, and he
served in that capacity until 1924. He was a leader
of the anti-Ferguson forces (*see* Ferguson, James
Edward, and Ferguson, Miriam Amanda) in the
gubernatorial campaign of that year. In 1928 he
opposed the nomination of Alfred E. Smith and
bolted the party during the election to help organize the Hoover-Democrat Clubs that went into
the Republican column that year. The last elected
office he held was that of state senator (1927–
1931). Love died in Dallas on September 17, 1948.

James A. Tinsley

*Love Field. After the Air Transport Command
selected Love Field as its operational base in 1944,
Dallas purchased additional land to permit the extension of the field's runways by the U.S. Army. The
U.S. Army Air Force spent over five and one-half
million dollars rebuilding and extending the runways. This modernization prompted Dallas to develop Love Field as a super-airport after World
War II.

When Fort Worth began development of Midway Airport in 1947, Dallas responded with an
expansion program for Love Field. Two runways,
additional land, and a new terminal building were
included in a program which totaled fourteen million dollars. In 1950 the Dallas City Council voted
to expend $1,302,299 on Love Field to prevent the
loss of air traffic. This trend continued during the
1950's with Dallas citizens approving two bond
elections in 1952, one of which included twenty
million dollars for Love Field's improvement. Construction on the new air terminal began in April,
1954, and by 1957 the $7,750,000 building was
completed. In 1964 it was the largest air terminal
in the Southwest; continued modernization increased the building's value to over twelve and
one-half million dollars.

By 1961 a small group of thirty-six Dallas residents opposed further expansion of the field because of the safety factors involved, but were unsuccessful in securing an injunction against further
development. Expansion continued and Dallas became the leading air traffic center in Texas between
1959 and 1965. Passenger air traffic to Love Field
doubled during this time, 1965 being a peak year
with 2,800,000 passengers, representing 49 percent
of the state's total air traffic. The following year
enplaned passengers increased to 3,169,225 and the
total number of operations at Love Field jumped to
319,575. In January, 1974, the new Dallas-Fort
Worth Airport qv replaced Love Field. *See also*
Greater Southwest International Airport; Dallas
Standard Metropolitan Statistical Area.

BIBLIOGRAPHY: Fritz-Alan Korth, A Tale of Two Cities
(unpublished senior thesis, Princeton University, 1961);
Texas Business Review (April, 1967, July, 1967).

Charles Duval, Jr.

*Lovelace, Edward.

*Lovelace, Texas.

*Lovelady, Texas.

*Lovell, Benjamin Drake.

*Lovells Lake.

*Lovenskiold, Charles Grimus Thorkelin de.

Lovett, Edgar Odell. Edgar Odell Lovett was born in Shreve, Ohio, on April 14, 1871, the son of Zephania and Maria Elizabeth (Spreng) Lovett. Following graduation from Shreve High School, he entered Bethany College, Bethany, West Virginia, graduating from this institution in 1890 at the age of nineteen. From 1890 until 1892 he was professor of mathematics at West Kentucky College; In 1892 he became an instructor at the University of Virginia, where he continued his studies and received the degrees of M.A. and Ph.D. in 1895. The following year he studied in Europe at the universities of Christiana and Leipzig, receiving the degrees of M.A. and Ph.D. from the latter university in 1896.

In 1897 he lectured at Johns Hopkins University and the universities of Virginia and Chicago, relinquishing these connections in September, 1897, to become instructor in mathematics at Princeton University. He was promoted to assistant professor of mathematics at the school in 1898, and from 1900 to 1905 he held the rank of professor of mathematics. During the period 1905 through 1908 he was both professor and head of the Department of Mathematics and Astronomy at Princeton.

In 1907 Lovett was asked to head Rice Institute (now Rice University), then being planned at Houston; he was recommended for the post by Woodrow Wilson, then president of Princeton. He accepted in 1908, moved to Houston, and was formally inaugurated as the first president of the institute on October 12, 1912, continuing in this capacity until his retirement on March 1, 1946. Thereafter, he was associated with Rice as president emeritus, director, and consultant.

Lovett was a member of many learned societies, including Phi Beta Kappa, the London Mathematical Society, the American Association for the Advancement of Science, Circolo Matematico di Palermo, Société Mathématique de France, and the Royal Astronomical Society. The degree of LL.D. was conferred on him by Drake University, Tulane University, Baylor University, and Bethany; that of Sc.D. was conferred upon him by Colorado College.

In 1898 Lovett married Mary Allen Hale of Mayfield, Kentucky, and they had two daughters and two sons. He died on August 13, 1957, and was buried in Glenwood Cemetery, Houston.

BIBLIOGRAPHY: American Philosophical Society, Yearbook (1957); New York Times, August 14, 1957; Houston Post, August 14, 1957; Houston Chronicle, August 14, 1957; Houston Press, August 14, 1957; Texian Who's Who (1937).

Clay Bailey

*Lovett, Robert Scott.

*Loving, James C.

*Loving, Jesse P.

*Loving, Oliver.

*Loving, Texas.

*Loving County. By 1963 Loving County was receiving over ten million dollars annually from petroleum. From 1925 through 1972, over sixty-four million barrels of oil were produced. The introduction of automation into the oil fields of the county decreased the number of jobs available and was partially responsible for the decline in population. The county had the state's smallest agricultural income, amounting to $146,491 in 1959, most of which came from cattle sales. In 1968 the agricultural income was $136,000. Red Bluff Reservoir on the Pecos River provided irrigation and fishing. In 1966 there were about a dozen large cattle ranches, more than four hundred oil wells, eleven farms mostly irrigated, and an elementary school. The 1960 population was 226 and the 1970 population was 164, according to the United States census.

Low, Isaac. Isaac Low was born July 7, 1781, probably near Knoxville, in Tennessee. He married Elizabeth Parsons on September 25, 1804, in Tennessee; they had twelve children. Isaac Low and his family came to Sabine County, Texas, in August, 1828. In 1835 Low received about a league and a labor of land from the Mexican government, and he operated a ferry on this land grant near the mouth of Lows Creek and the Sabine River. Here during the Runaway Scrape,qv it is alleged that he and his oldest sons worked day and night for several days ferrying the panic-stricken settlers back to the United States. This site is now under the waters of Toledo Bend Reservoir. In 1840 Low served as a commissioner of Sabine County, investigating fraudulent land certificates; he may have held other civil jobs in the county. He died August 27, 1853, at his home near Sabinetown, Texas, and was buried in the old Isaac Low Cemetery, now near the shore of Toledo Bend Reservoir.

Helen Gomer Schluter

*Lowake, Texas.

*Lowber, James William.

*Lower Colorado River Authority. *See* Colorado River Authorities.

Lower Concho River Water and Soil Conservation Authority. The Lower Concho River Water and Soil Conservation Authority was created in 1939 by the Forty-sixth Legislature and covers only Concho County. The district is not authorized to levy or collect taxes or assessments payable out of taxes or assessments or in any other way to pledge the credit of the state. The act authorized the governor to appoint a nine-man board of directors, two members of which were to reside within each of the four commissioners' precincts in Concho County and one director at large. Three directors were to be appointed every two years, each serving a six-year term.

This authority has been diligent in its endeavor to cooperate with any adjacent authorities to promote the conservation of soil and water, but it has not seen fit to attempt to construct a major dam itself due to the fact that the cost would be too great for the needs of the smaller towns in the county. However, this authority has cooperated with the Upper Colorado River Authority qv in efforts to build a major dam just a few miles below the mouth of the Concho River on the Colorado River.

This authority has the power to develop and generate water power and electric energy within the boundaries of the district and to distribute and sell water power and electric energy within and outside the district, but such use must be subordinate and inferior to all requirements for domestic, municipal, and irrigation purposes. It also has the power to provide by adequate organization and administration for the preservation of the equitable rights of the people of the different sections of the watershed area in the beneficial use of storm, flood, and unappropriated flow waters of the Concho and Colorado rivers.

Scott L. Hartgrove

*Lower Indian Reserve. *See* Indian Reservations.

*Lower Keechi Creek.

*Lower Neches Valley Authority.

*Lower Pine Creek.

Lowman, Harmon Luther. Harmon Luther Lowman, the son of Quincy Joseph and Mellie (Scott) Lowman, was born on November 30, 1894, at Staples, Texas. He was a student at Coronal Institute in San Marcos from 1909 until 1911. He was enrolled in a pre-law course at Washington and Lee University from 1915 until April, 1917, when he volunteered for military service. Lowman served with the 345th Field Artillery, 90th Division, in the American Expeditionary Forces and attained the rank of first lieutenant. After the war he accepted a position as replacement teacher in his home town of Staples and decided to devote his life to teaching.

Lowman received an A.B. degree from Southwest Texas State Teachers College (now Southwest Texas State University) in 1924, an M.A. degree from the University of Texas in 1925, and a Ph.D. degree from the University of Chicago in 1930. He was director of the Demonstration School and professor at Stephen F. Austin State Teachers College (now Stephen F. Austin State University) from 1925 until 1936, superintendent of the Livingston, Texas, schools in 1936–1937, and superintendent of the Goose Creek district (Baytown) schools and president of the district's Lee Junior College from 1937 to 1940. In 1941, after serving for one year as executive secretary of Southern Methodist University, he became president of Sam Houston State Teachers College (now Sam Houston State University).

During the twenty-three years that Lowman was president of Sam Houston State Teachers College, enrollment increased from 1,200 to 5,200, the annual budget went from $488,000 to $6 million, and the value of college buildings increased from $1,180,000 to $21 million. In addition to promoting the school's growth, Lowman was concerned with the welfare of students, especially those in financial need. He often helped poor students with his own money and at times took students into his home so that they could remain in school. In recognition of his generosity, the board of regents in 1963 named the new student union building the Lowman Student Center.

Lowman married Marguerite Hightower on April 6, 1918. They had two sons. Lowman was a member of the National Education Association and the Texas State Teachers Association.qv He was author of *History of Teacher Training in the Gulf States* (1930). He died on January 26, 1964, and was buried in the Oakwood Cemetery in Huntsville.

John Payne

*Lowrey-Phillips School.

*Loyal Union League.

*Loyal Valley, Texas.

Loyola Beach, Texas. Loyola Beach, in southern Kleberg County, is situated on Caroline Beach. About 1909 two men by the names of Morgan and Miller brought in two artesian wells. A few people settled around one of the wells and the settlement became known as Loyola Beach. The origin of the name is unknown. In 1966 Loyola Beach consisted of a small seafood restaurant, a picnic supply store, beer establishments, and summer cottages. Within a radius of a half-mile, about thirty-five or forty people lived at Loyola Beach in 1966.

*Lozano, Texas.

*Lozier Creek.

*Luanna, Texas.

*Lubbock, Francis Richard.

*Lubbock, Thomas S. Thomas S. Lubbock died on January 9, 1862 (not January 23, 1862, as stated in Volume II), at Nashville, Tennessee, of typhoid fever.

BIBLIOGRAPHY: Robert Franklin Bunting Papers (Archives, University of Texas at Austin Library).

*Lubbock, Texas. Lubbock, seat of Lubbock County, was the center for the state's largest and richest irrigated agricultural area. Business concerns other than agricultural, with a direct influence on the local economy, were Reese Air Force Base,qv government offices, the manufacture of equipment, trucking, and wholesale distribution. In the late 1960's the town had 204 manufacturing concerns, over two hundred churches, fifty-three public schools, eight hospitals, two colleges, six banks, two libraries, and three newspapers. Lubbock reported 2,954 businesses in 1970. Significant city improvements since 1952 included a water treatment plant, remodeling of the airport, two high schools, a federal building, a post office, and numerous elementary and junior high school buildings. The 1960 population was 128,691, almost twice the 1950 population; the 1970 census reported 149,101 people. *See also* Lubbock Standard Metropolitan Statistical Area.

*Lubbock Army Air Field. *See* Reese Air Force Base.

Lubbock Christian College. Lubbock Christian College, Lubbock, opened in September, 1957, as a private liberal arts junior college of the Church of Christ.qv Enrollment increased from an original 102 students to 753 in the 1969 regular term. Eleven semi-permanent buildings were moved from Clovis Air Force Base, New Mexico, and from Reese Air Force Base,qv and were remodeled to serve as classrooms, apartments, dormitories, student recreational areas, and dining facilities. The first permanent buildings that were constructed consisted of administration-library (1958) and women's and men's dormitories (1960). In 1969 the library's holdings totaled 28,016 volumes. In fall, 1970, the college began accepting upper-level students, and on December 13, 1972, the school was fully accredited as a senior college. There were 1,055 students registered in the fall, 1974, term, when W. Joe Hacker, Jr., was president.

*Lubbock County. In 1959 Lubbock County was Texas' leading county in three areas: it registered the largest farm income, $62,193,584; it ginned the largest number of bales of cotton, 211,-079; and it reported the largest income from the sale of livestock and related products, $22,033,295. The county ranked second in income from the sale of field crops. By 1964 the county ranked second in both total farm products sales and all crops sales. Throughout the 1960's and early 1970's Lubbock County continued to rank high in all of these categories, and it was usually first or second in the number of bales of cotton ginned. Between 1941 and January 1, 1973, the county produced approximately ten million barrels of oil. Tourist attractions included Mackenzie State Park, part of Yellow House Creek canyon, and the Museum of Texas Tech University.qv The 1960 population for the county was 156,271; the 1970 population rose to 179,295, according to the United States census. *See also* Lubbock Standard Metropolitan Statistical Area.

Lubbock Standard Metropolitan Statistical Area. The Lubbock Standard Metropolitan Statistical Area consists of Lubbock County, an area of 893 square miles. The city of Lubbock is the single large metropolitan center, and there are twenty-three small communities, of which five—Abernathy, Idalou, Slaton, Shallowater, and Wolfforth—are incorporated. Lubbock County was organized in 1891, making the area one of the more recently settled metropolitan areas in Texas. The population figure for the statistical area was 156,271 in 1960, with 128,691 living in Lubbock. By 1970 the report of the United States census listed the figures as 179,295 and 149,101, respectively.

Lubbock County is located in the southern portion of the High Plains, a fairly level area with low humidity, nearly constant winds, and an average annual rainfall of 18.08 to 18.89 inches. The area has a 208-day growing season and is a major cotton and grain sorghums growing and marketing center. By 1960 Lubbock was the third largest inland cotton market in the world and consistently led the state during the 1960's in cotton production. In 1962, 292,595 bales of cotton were produced; in 1964, 205,000 acres of the 330,000 acres irrigated were planted with cotton. In 1968–1969 Lubbock County led the state in bales of cotton ginned with 180,765 bales, while in 1972–1973 it was second, with 226,837 bales. The area was one of the leaders in grain sorghums production also, with 7,-898,000 bushels produced in 1968 on 137,600 acres. During the 1960's and 1970's the area ranked among the highest in total farm income in the state, with $62,193,584 in 1960, $55,140,983 in 1964, and an annual average of $70 million in the early 1970's. In 1959 the area had the largest income from the sale of livestock and products with $22,033,295, but by 1968 cash receipts from livestock and products dropped to $16,651,000, which was still seventh highest in the state.

In 1966 the Lubbock area ranked seventh in Texas in per capita buying income with a total of $381,315,000. It also ranked seventh in total retail sales and first in retail sales per capita. Agribusiness, retail trade, and oil production were the major contributors to this prosperity. Total crude oil production from 1941 to 1973 was 10,477,099 barrels. Retail and wholesale trade also augmented the area's economy significantly, with the city of Lubbock dominating a trade sales area encompassing a wide section of the High Plains area of West Texas and New Mexico. By 1963 there were at least 350 wholesale firms and approximately 1,387 retail outlets. These income sources, in addition to the more than two hundred manufacturing concerns, thirty-two of which employed over fifty workers, made Lubbock a growing commercial, financial, marketing, and banking center of the Southwest.

The city of Lubbock provided three newspapers and was served by six banks, eight hospitals, two libraries, and fifty-three public schools. Culturally and recreationally the city supports a symphony orchestra, a community theater, Spitz Planetarium, and events at Fair Park Auditorium. In the city are thirty-two parks and Mackenzie State Park (*see* Parks, State) with its preserved and protected prairie dog town. Nearby, the people of the county have access to Buffalo Springs Lake. There are other opportunities for public entertainment and enlightenment at Texas Tech University, the second largest state-owned college in Texas. Lubbock Christian College also serves the city. Reese Air Force Base,qv a jet training center, plus naval, air force, and army reserve training centers give additional impetus to the growth and economy of the area. *See also* Standard Metropolitan Statistical Areas in Texas.

BIBLIOGRAPHY: L. L. Graves (ed.), *A History of Lubbock* (1962).

Seymour V. Connor

Lubbock State School. Lubbock State School, which opened in 1969, serves the mentally retarded from a fifty-two-county area in the Panhandle and South Plains of Texas. Located in Lubbock, the school has special treatment programs for all ambulatory residents, an extensive recreational program, speech therapy and language development classes for more than sixty students, and a work program on campus for approximately seventy-five students. By the early 1970's the school was able to accommodate over six hundred students.

From the beginning an outreach program was designed and operated to delay or prevent institutionalization of persons evaluated by the Diagnostic and Evaluation Center. Out of the 234 persons evaluated in 1970, about 50 percent were delayed or prevented institutionalization by the program. Six local communities aid the school with the outreach programs in their communities.

Census in the early 1970's was 660, and the superintendent was John W. Gladden. *See* Mentally Ill and Mentally Retarded, Care of, in Texas.

BIBLIOGRAPHY: Texas Department of Mental Health and Mental Retardation, *Annual Report, 1970.*

*Luby, James O.

*Lucas, Anthony Francis.

*Lucas, Texas. (Collin County.)

*Lucas, Texas. (Jefferson County.)

*Lucas Creek.

*Lucas Gusher. *See* Spindletop Oil Field.

*Luce Bayou.

*Luckenbach, Texas.

Luckett, Philip Noland. Philip Noland Luckett was born in 1823 (?) in Virginia. He was living in Ohio when he supposedly received an appointment to enter the United States Military Academy at West Point in 1841, although he is not listed in G. W. Cullum's *Biographical Register of the Officers and Graduates of the U.S. Military Academy at West Point.* By 1847 Luckett had established his residence in Corpus Christi, Texas, as a physician, and in 1850 he was listed on the rolls as a surgeon in John S. Ford's qv company of Texas Rangers.qv Luckett was a delegate to the Secession Convention qv in 1861, representing Nueces and Webb counties. In September, 1861, he formed the 3rd Texas Confederate Infantry in Brownsville, under the overall command of Ford, but by the end of the year Luckett was in San Antonio on detached duty, serving on a court of inquiry.

On July 12, 1863, Luckett's 3rd Infantry reached Galveston from Brownsville. Soon promoted from colonel to brevet brigadier general, Luckett was ordered on August 8, 1863, to take command of the eastern sub-district of Texas, but by January, 1864, he was on detached duty at Shreveport, Louisiana. In April of that year his unit was attached to William Read Scurry's qv 3rd Brigade, under John G. Walker, and Luckett took command after Scurry was killed at the battle of Jenkins'

Ferry. Relinquishing his command on December 21, 1864, Luckett was again on detached duty on a court of inquiry, and illness kept him in Shreveport for several months early in 1865. Alexander Watkins Terrell qv reported having met Luckett, Thomas Jefferson Devine,qv and Thomas C. Hindman (of Arkansas) in Monterrey, Mexico, in July, 1865. The men were undoubtedly fleeing the Federal takeover of Texas. Devine and Luckett were arrested upon their return to Texas and imprisoned in Fort Jackson, Louisiana, in November, 1865. Petitions entrusted to General Philip Henry Sheridan qv for Luckett's pardon were delayed for several months, and by the time his release from prison came, Luckett was in failing health.

Unable to engage in business, Luckett remained in New Orleans. He joined relatives in Cincinnati, Ohio, just before he died on May 21, 1869. Widely admired in Texas and Louisiana as an officer devoted to the cause of the South, Luckett was also well known for his fair treatment of soldiers and his courage and independence as a commander.

BIBLIOGRAPHY: A. W. Terrell, *From Texas to Mexico* (1933); Cincinnati *Daily Enquirer*, May 24, 1869; New Orleans *Daily Picayune*, May 23, 1869.

S. W. Pease

*Luckett, Samuel Magoffin.

*Luckie, Samuel H.

*Ludecus, Eduard.

*Lueders, Texas. Lueders, in Jones County, was not permanently settled until 1899, when the Webb and Hill Land and Cattle Company agreed to colonize the community. Lueders was named for Frederick Lueders (not Leuders, as stated in Volume II, although records show Luders and Leuders, as well as Lueders). W. J. Herrington settled in the vicinity of the future townsite in 1889 (not in the community in 1888), although the first farming may have been done as early as 1877 by M. McDaniel. August Lieb had cleared a farm in 1879. The Texas Central Railroad Company qv first came through Lueders in February of 1900. The town had a population of 654 in 1960 and 511 in 1970.

BIBLIOGRAPHY: Anson *Western-Enterprise*, August 24, 1933.

Tad Moses
Jimmy M. Skaggs

*Luella, Texas.

*Lufkin, Texas. Lufkin, seat of Angelina County, had a population of 17,641 in 1960 and 23,049 persons in 1970, according to the United States census. In 1966 Lufkin reported forty-nine churches, twelve schools, two banks, two hospitals, and a city library. In 1970 it had 485 businesses. The largest manufacturing plants included those producing lumber, newsprint, furniture, iron and steel castings, and oil field and sawmill machinery. Lufkin State School qv for the mentally retarded, the Texas division headquarters of the United States Forest Service, and the Texas Forest Products Laboratory were located in Lufkin.

*Lufkin, Hemphill, and Gulf Railway Company.

Lufkin State School. In 1961 the Lufkin Radar Base of the United States Air Force was acquired from the federal government and converted to serve as a school for mentally retarded. The 292 students were transferred from other state schools. All were ambulatory, and some were enrolled in the education program. By 1970 the maximum capacity of the school was increased to approximately 1,000 students with the completion of a building project which included five buildings and two dormitories. The physical therapy program was enlarged, and a reevaluation of 400 students was completed. In the same year the school cooperated with Angelina College to offer a two-year associate degree program for mental retardation technicians. The census at the end of 1970 was 928 students, and William W. Beaver was the superintendent. *See* Mentally Ill and Mentally Retarded, Care of, in Texas.

BIBLIOGRAPHY: Board for Texas State Hospitals and Special Schools, *Report* (1964); Texas Department of Mental Health and Mental Retardation, *Annual Report,* 1970.

Lugplapiagulam Indians. In the middle eighteenth century the Lugplapiagulam (Hueplapiagulam), whose name is said to mean "ground chili pepper," lived along the lower Rio Grande between present Rio Grande City and the mouth of the river. The maps of Jiménez Moreno and G. Saldivar place this group in present Zapata County, but the available records do not specify any particular locality.

BIBLIOGRAPHY: W. Jiménez Moreno, "Tribus e idiomas del Norte de México," *El Norte de México y el Sur de Estados Unidos* (1944); G. Saldivar, *Los Indios de Tamaulipas* (1943).

T. N. Campbell

*LULAC. *See* League of United Latin American Citizens.

*Luling, Texas. Luling, in southern Caldwell County, was a center for petroleum and for farm produce, particularly watermelons. In 1967 the town had a hospital, a new city hall, an airport, a municipal swimming pool, and twenty-two churches, and it was the headquarters of the Luling Foundation.^{qv} A watermelon thump was held annually in June. Luling reported 160 businesses in 1970, including meat processing and oil field servicing operations. The 1960 population of 4,412 increased to 4,719 by 1970, according to the United States census.

*Luling Foundation. In the 1960's the Luling Foundation, establshed by Edgar B. Davis,^{qv} had several demonstration projects in improved grasses and their response to different rates of applications of commercial fertilizer, as well as the control of weeds by use of herbicides. The Texas random sample turkey meat production tests were run for several years, which gave information on vitality, feed conversion, early finish, and uniform development. The foundation was one of the first Texas testing stations for grain evaluation tests for beef cattle. Soil and water conservation practices have always been strongly advocated, and a diversified agricultural program included developing and improving native pecan groves.

*Luling Oil Field.

*Lull, Texas.

*Lumber and Lumbering. In 1954, 86 percent of Texas' 644 sawmills were located in East Texas. More than one billion board feet valued at $61,460,000 were removed from Texas forests. Production of pulpwood was approximately 1,014,000 cords valued at $13,200,000. In 1960 there were about 250 sawmills operating in Texas and over 1,000 wood-using manufacturers in the state.

Lumber production during the late 1950's and early 1960's declined, reaching a low of 703,600,000 board feet for 1961. By 1964, however, approximately two hundred sawmills removed 995,200,000 board feet of lumber valued at $101,500,000. The value of the 1,443,000 cords of pulpwood produced increased to $18,500,000. By 1967 Texas lumber production had again decreased, to 792,800,000 board feet, cut mainly by a few large sawmills removing more than ten thousand board feet per day, and valued at $75,000,000. Texas pulpwood production that year increased to 1,993,000 cords valued at $39,862,000. In 1967 the value of all lumbering operations in Texas amounted to $153,062,000. By 1971 the number of sawmills in East Texas was reduced to 122, and lumber production amounted to 955,000,000 board feet. There were seven pulp mills in that year, and they produced 2,674,000 cords of pulpwood. *See also* Paper, Manufacture of.

*Lumberton, Texas.

*Lumm, Texas.

*Lumpkin, Pleides O.

*Lund, Texas.

Lundy, Benjamin. Benjamin Lundy was born in Sussex County, New Jersey, of Quaker parentage on January 4, 1789. Lundy became active in the antislavery movement in the 1820's. He organized abolitionist societies, lectured extensively, and contributed to many abolitionist publications. Believing that the slavery problem could be solved by settling free Negroes in thinly populated regions, he visited Haiti and Canada and, between the years 1830 and 1835, paid three visits to Texas in hopes of obtaining land for such a colony. While in Texas he talked to free Negroes, planters, and Mexican officials and visited Nacogdoches, San Antonio, and the Brazos and Rio Grande areas. He concluded that Texas was an ideal place for his colonization experiment; the Mexican government was friendly to his proposal. The Texas Revolution intervened before Lundy could carry out his plans, and the Republic of Texas legalized slavery. Lundy charged that the revolution was a slaveholders' plot to take Texas from Mexico and to add slave territory to the United States. He began publishing the *National Enquirer and Constitu-*

tional Advocate of Universal Liberty in Philadelphia in August, 1836, to set forth his thesis. In the same year he published *The War in Texas*, a pamphlet arguing against the annexation of Texas to the United States. Lundy won many influential adherents, among them John Quincy Adams, who represented Lundy's views in the United States Congress. Adams, Lundy, and their followers were instrumental in delaying the annexation of Texas for nine years. (*See also* Bangs, Samuel.)

Lundy died on August 22, 1839. After his death his children collected some of his writings, including his accounts of his Texas journeys, and printed them as *The Life, Travels and Opinions of Benjamin Lundy* (1847).

BIBLIOGRAPHY: *Dictionary of American Biography* (1933).

Marilyn M. Sibley

***Lungkwitz, Herman.** Herman Lungkwitz's paintings, drawings, and sketches were being catalogued and registered by the Texas Memorial Museum qv in Austin in 1972. Two portraits of the Lungkwitz children by the German artist Carl G. von Iwonski qv have been located in the museum collections.

***Lusk, Samuel.**

***Lusk, Texas.** (Throckmorton County.)

***Lusk, Texas.** (Washington County.)

***Lutcher, Henry Jacob.**

***Luther, Texas.**

***Luther Rice Baptist Female College.**

***Lutheran Church in Texas.** The Lutheran church had a landmark year in 1960, when there was a three-way merger, on the national level, of the American Lutheran Church, the Evangelical Lutheran Church, and the American Evangelical Lutheran Church. In Texas it meant the union of the Texas Circuit and the Texas District of the American Lutheran Church.

The Texas District (ALC) had observed its centennial in 1951, including in their celebration a pilgrimage to the first Lutheran church built on Texas soil at Neighborsville, now at the edge of New Braunfels. The district continued supporting Texas Lutheran College,qv Lutheran General Hospital, and Lutheran Welfare Society, as well as missions in India and New Guinea. It consisted of 98,514 baptized (68,996 confirmed) members in 218 congregations served by 186 pastors; it also included thirteen pastors serving as teachers and administrators, plus twenty-five retired pastors.

Only a year after the merger of 1960 another merger was effected on the national level, bringing together the Augustana Lutheran Church (formerly a member of the American Lutheran Conference), the United Lutheran Church, and the American Evangelical Lutheran Church, all of which had components in Texas, including the Texas Conference of the Augustana Lutheran Church, the Texas Synod of the United Lutheran Church, and Danevang qv Lutheran Church.

On January 1, 1961, the Texas Conference surrendered its identity to a new and larger church by uniting with the Texas Synod of the United Lutheran Church, at one time called Texas Synod II. This body, like the Texas Conference, had long joined in support and management of Texas Lutheran College, participated in the work of the Lutheran Welfare Society, and had become a partner in Lutheran student service (now called campus ministry). It also had a periodical called the *Texas Lutheran*.qv By the date of the merger it consisted of sixty pastors, fifty-six congregations, and 19,258 baptized members. The third group involved in the merger was the congregation at Danevang, which had until then been a member of the American Evangelical Lutheran Church. Like the parent body it had dropped the "Danish" from its name and called itself simply the American Evangelical Lutheran Church.

There is another body of Lutherans in Texas besides the two that grew out of mergers—the Texas District of the Lutheran Church, Missouri Synod. It has been in existence ever since a colony of 558 Wends qv settled in the part of Bastrop County which is now Lee County. In Germany they had lived partly in Prussia and partly in Saxony, in an area called Lusatia. When they reached Texas in 1855 they soon made contact with another contingent of Lutherans from Saxony which had come to America in 1839 and settled in Perry County, Missouri, most of them in St. Louis. They had organized the conservative Missouri Synod, which soon became the leader of a federation known as Synodical Conference. The Wends were received as a section of the Western District of that body and then as partners in the new Southern District of the Lutheran Church, Missouri Synod. In 1903 they were recognized as the Texas District. The relationship assured them of pastors for the new congregations surrounding the original settlement and for the immigrants from northern states which provided nuclei for new churches. As a result they soon had congregations in various parts of Texas, especially in the larger cities. To assist in securing an adequate number of pastors for the growing district, they established Lutheran Concordia College qv in 1926. Like the Lutheran Church, Missouri Synod, generally, the Texas District emphasized a parochial school in every parish. At the close of 1970 there were 102,322 baptized members in 285 congregations, served by 225 pastors and 375 teachers (125 men and 250 women).

Arrangements were completed in 1970 whereby the Texas District of the Lutheran Church, Missouri Synod, became a full partner in Lutheran Social Service of Texas. Texas Lutherans generally were also involved in Lutheran Council U.S.A., which superceded the National Lutheran Council, a less inclusive agency.

Increasing cooperation of people with diverse national backgrounds was greatly facilitated by the common use of the English language. In the 1970's worship services in languages other than English had become a rarity except in Spanish-speaking areas of the Rio Grande Valley.

W. A. Flachmeier

*Lutheran Concordia College. Lutheran Concordia College, Austin, added a junior college department in 1951 and made the college department coeducational in 1955. Training for women was limited to preparation for teaching in Lutheran elementary schools. In 1959 the Synodical Convention passed a resolution allowing qualified deaconess students to take their first two years of training at synodical schools, including Concordia. In 1965 the school's name was changed from Lutheran Concordia College to Concordia Lutheran College. In 1966 the curriculum was expanded to provide for students aiming for vocations other than church work. In 1967 the high school department was discontinued. In 1966 the college had nine major buildings on its twenty-acre campus, including a library completed in 1949; library holdings in 1969 were 8,500 volumes. The junior college was a member of the Association of Texas Colleges and Universities,qv the Texas Junior College Association, the American Association of Junior Colleges, and the Southern Association of Junior Colleges. The college student enrollment for the 1968–1969 regular term was 195, with a faculty numbering twenty-two. In 1974 the president of the college was Ray Martens. Enrollment rose to 384 in the regular fall term of 1974. See also Lutheran Church in Texas.

*Lutie, Texas.

*Luxello, Texas.

*Luzon, Texas.

*Lyday's Fort.

*Lydia, Texas.

*Lyford, Texas. It is not conclusive that Lyford, in Willacy County, was named for William H. Lyford, an attorney for the Rock Island Railroad (as stated in Volume II). It is possible that this is the same man whose Christian name was Will (not William) Hartwell Lyford, a railroad attorney who resided in Chicago. More evidence is needed to determine the reason for the naming of the town.

The population of Lyford was 1,554 in 1960 and decreased to 1,425 by 1970, according to the U.S. census report. The city had twenty-four businesses in 1970.

*Lykes, James McKay.

*Lynch, Francis J.

*Lynch, James.

Lynch, Joseph Patrick. Joseph Patrick Lynch was born in St. Joseph, Michigan, on November 16, 1872, the son of John V. and Veronica (Botham) Lynch. He was graduated from St. Charles College, Ellicott City, Maryland, and began theological studies at St. Mary's Seminary, Baltimore, where he changed his course to law.

While practicing law near Chicago, Lynch met Bishop Edward Joseph Dunne qv of Dallas, who was looking for volunteer workers in his Texas dio-

cese. Influenced by Bishop Dunne, he gave up his law practice, entered Kenrick Seminary, St. Louis, completed his studies for the priesthood, and was ordained on June 9, 1900.

For two years he worked as an assistant at the cathedral in Dallas and was then appointed pastor at Weatherford, where he built the present church. In 1905 he built a church in Handley, Texas. For the next eight years he served St. Edward's parish, Dallas, where he built a church, a rectory, and a school. During this time he also held several responsible diocesan offices, including vicar-general.

When Bishop Dunne died suddenly in 1910, Lynch was made apostolic administrator of the vacant See, in effect becoming the youngest bishop in the United States at the age of thirty-eight; the following year he was appointed bishop. During his forty-three years of service in the Dallas (now Dallas-Fort Worth) diocese, its territory was divided three times to make the El Paso, Amarillo, and Austin dioceses. The Catholic population grew from 20,000 in 1911 to about 125,000 in 1954. Bishop Lynch supervised the building of 150 churches and scores of other buildings, including St. Joseph's Hospital in Paris, St. Paul's Nurse's Home, St. Rita's Home for Working Girls, Dunne Memorial Home for Boys, and Mt. St. Michael's Home and School for Girls. In 1915 the first mission church for Mexicans was built in Dallas; the first church for Negroes was built in 1929 at Fort Worth.

Lynch was a widely respected speaker; he was an orator at the bicentennial of San Antonio in 1931 and also at the centennial commemorating the fall of the Alamo. He died on August 19, 1954, in Dallas and was buried in Calvary Hill Cemetery in that city.

BIBLIOGRAPHY: Catholic Archives, Chancery Office, Austin.

Sister M. Claude Lane, O.P.

*Lynch, Nathaniel.

*Lynch, Nicholas.

*Lynch Creek.

*Lynchburg, Texas.

Lynching in Texas. Prior to the Civil War, legal justice on the frontier in Texas was perhaps better evidenced by its absence than by its effective application. Many communities numbered more drifters than settled families, and those who considered themselves permanent members of society (usually those who had property interests) frequently adopted the frontier practice of executing their own justice, very often through the method of lynching. Lynchings by vigilance committees were often welcomed by communities that had little or no other method of law enforcement, although it was not uncommon for such committees to become as lawless as those they professed to punish. The first major outbreak of lynchings in Texas occurred in the late 1850's and continued throughout the Civil War and Reconstruction.qqv The greatest number of lynchings during this period stemmed from deeply ingrained racial animosities, aggravated by intense factional loyalties of the secession movement, rabid patriotism that developed in the Confederacy, and fear of the white for his social and economic supremacy in the face of Negro emancipation.

In the last years before the Civil War, abolitionists and Negroes were the targets of sporadic outbursts of violence which at times resulted in lynchings. A typical lynching incident occurred in 1860 in Tarrant County when suspected incendiary fires touched off a riot; two men from the North, already suspected of inciting Negroes to revolt, were seized by the mob, and in the general atmosphere of suspicion and violence their presence in the vicinity of the fires sufficed to condemn them. The two were summarily hanged.

Proslavery vigilante groups began to form and were active during the first two war years; they were responsible for hanging or burning an estimated ten whites and sixty-five Negroes. Throughout the Civil War, and notably in Cooke, Denton, and Wise counties where Union sympathizers were suspected of organizing opposition to the Confederacy, groups of men seized and hanged numbers of people. The most notorious occurrence of lynching during this time in Texas history was the so-called Great Hanging at Gainesville,qv in which forty prisoners were hanged at the insistence of a mob. The incident originated in the arrest of suspected members of a group organized to resist Confederate conscription. Although the affair was given a semblance of legality by the use of militia and a token trial, the mob so intimidated the jury, which it had appointed, that all pretense of impartial justice disappeared.

Most lynchings during the Civil War were more or less spontaneous outbreaks of mob hysteria. During Reconstruction, however, organized terror, particularly at the hands of the Ku Klux Klan,qv became more common and assumed the proportions of a race war. In the first three postwar years at least 500 whites and 500 blacks were murdered, but while whites killed about 450 freedmen only five whites were reported murdered by Negroes. Local units of the Ku Klux Klan, their membership often consisting of leading citizens, employed a variety of tactics from intimidation to murder in order to suppress Negroes. Whites who advocated racial equality or who sought to aid freedmen were harassed and sometimes hanged by Ku Klux Klan and kindred groups. The stationing of Negro troops at Federal posts in Texas was regarded by many white Texans as a provocation and probably added to the sufferings of freedmen. (See Knights of the Golden Circle; Knights of the White Camelia.)

Not all hangings in the post-Civil War era stemmed from racial hatred. The Ku Klux Klan and a variety of extralegal vigilante groups often adopted the role of superintendent of community order and morals, assaulting and sometimes lynching whites who violated their peculiar moral codes. Along the western Texas frontier, as well as in other locations, lawless men displaced by the Civil War congregated and spread fear. Often residents took the law into their own hands and dispensed vigilante justice. At Fort Griffin, where one of the most active of these vigilance committees operated, seven men were lynched within three months; attached to their bodies were warning notes to others whom the committee found offensive. This, while extreme, was not an exceptional procedure for these committees.

The trend from the 1880's into the twentieth century was for lynchings to be the product of spontaneous mob violence against persons held by legal authorities. Most often the victims were Negroes accused of crimes against whites. In other cases mobs were incited by a popular tendency to inflict sterner justice than that meted out by the courts. In 1872 three men were taken from the Comanche jail and lynched, and similar incidents occurred during every year from 1880 through the first decade of the twentieth century. In the 1890's the Texas Volunteer Guard qv was called out numerous times to prevent lynchings of prisoners, but in spite of this, a mob at Wichita Falls took two bank robbers from jail in 1896 and lynched them; other lynching of prisoners occurred in spite of the presence of state troops. In 1901–1902 Navarro, Grayson, and other counties saw similar lynchings in which local authorities could not prevent mobs from seizing prisoners.

Lynchings diminished greatly after the first decade of the twentieth century because of the increased efficiency of local law enforcement and the increased popular respect for law. In 1927 a bank robber was lynched in Eastland after having murdered an officer in the jail, and in 1931 there was one lynching. See also Negroes in Texas; Riots in Texas.

BIBLIOGRAPHY: Thomas Barrett, *The Great Hanging at Gainesville, Cooke County, Texas* (1885); Wayne Gard, *Frontier Justice* (1949); *Reports of the Adjutant General of Texas* (1870–1938); Edgar P. Sneed, "A Historiography of Reconstruction in Texas: Some Myths and Problems," *Southwestern Historical Quarterly*, LXXII (1968–1969).

Marilyn von Kohl

*Lynch's Ferry.

Lyndon B. Johnson School of Public Affairs. *See* Lyndon Baines Johnson Library.

Lyndon B. Johnson Space Center. *See* Manned Spacecraft Center.

Lyndon Baines Johnson Birthplace, Boyhood Home, and Ranch. The birthplace home of President Lyndon Baines Johnson qv is located adjacent to the LBJ Ranch, near Ranch Road 1, near Stonewall, Texas. The home was constructed in the 1880's by Sam Ealy Johnson,qv the president's grandfather, and it was here that the president's father, Sam Ealy Johnson, Jr.,qv brought his bride, Rebekah (Baines) Johnson,qv in 1907. Lyndon Baines was born in the home on August 27, 1908; the Johnsons lived there until 1913, when they moved to Johnson City. The family sold the house in 1923, and though it was demolished after much deterioration, some of the original materials were used in the construction of a smaller house on the same site in 1935. The Johnson City Foundation acquired the building in 1964 and reconstructed it to its 1907 size and appearance. The home is now open to the public, having been refurnished with authentic pieces and family mementos.

The boyhood home of President Johnson in Johnson City was built in 1886 and, though modest, reflects the Victorian style of the period. After the family moved there in 1913, the home remained the official residence of Lyndon Johnson until he married Claudia Alta Taylor in 1934; Johnson's first political speech in his race for Congress in 1937 was made on the east porch of the house. The home was dedicated as a museum by Judge Homer Thornberry on May 13, 1965, and like the birthplace contains authentic period items and family furnishings. It is also open to the public.

The LBJ Ranch is in the heart of the Texas hill country, on the banks of the Pedernales River, and is the present home of President Johnson's widow. The history of the ranch goes back to the time of the Republic of Texas when a young widow from Georgia, Rachael Means, was granted a tract which included the present property. In 1872 the land was sold by the Means family, and the property changed hands several times until about 1894, when a one-room stone house was constructed by a German family named Meyer; the small house became the nucleus of the present home.

In 1909 the property was purchased by Clarence Martin, a relative of the Johnsons, and in 1951 Senator (later President) and Mrs. Lyndon B. Johnson acquired the property, which consisted of 438 acres. *See also* Lyndon B. Johnson State Historic Park (under Parks, State).

Lyndon Baines Johnson Library. The Lyndon Baines Johnson qv Library, constructed on the campus of the University of Texas at Austin, was completed in 1971 and dedicated on May 22, 1971. The nation's sixth presidential library, it was the first to be located on a university campus. There it serves as a center for scholarly research and as a historical museum.

Scholarly interest in the Johnson Library centered on its unusually rich archives of manuscripts and audio-visual records. Photographic negatives, motion picture films, and sound recordings added to the dimensions of the archives. An extensive collection of political cartoons captured highlights of American government and politics since the 1930's.

More than 30,000,000 pages of manuscripts, mostly papers of President Johnson, formed the core of the research collection. As the most comprehensive single collection of materials on a president of the United States, it spanned Lyndon Johnson's entire political career. Added to the Johnson papers were those of Mrs. Lyndon B. Johnson and many of Johnson's contemporaries and associates. The library continues to gather these materials from historically minded individuals to preserve them for the nation's heritage.

Operated by the National Archives and Records Service, the Johnson Library is one of a system of presidential libraries devoted to objective research through preservation of materials related to the men who have held the awesome job of president of the United States. Chester A. Newland was named first director of the Johnson Library in October, 1968. He was succeeded by Harry Middleton in 1970.

Related to the establishment of the Lyndon Baines Johnson Library, but under the administration of the University of Texas at Austin, the Lyndon B. Johnson School of Public Affairs was opened in September, 1970, under the directorship of John A. Gronouski, former postmaster general and United States ambassador to Poland. The school is located in Sid W. Richardson qv Hall, adjacent to the Johnson Library, on the campus of the University of Texas at Austin.

*Lynn Bayou.

*Lynn County. Lynn County, a leader in the production of cotton and grain sorghums, with the help of extensive irrigation, ranked first among Texas counties in amount of cotton ginned in 1972. Nine-tenths of its 1972 farm income of $30,000,-000 was derived from crops, while the rest was from livestock. Nearly eight million barrels of oil have been produced by the county's young petroleum industry from 1950 through 1972. In the 1970's the county continued to have a large cotton and grain sorghum production, most harvested on the county's 92,000 irrigated acres. Tourists visited the county for its February livestock show. The 1960 population of 10,914 declined to 9,107 by 1970, according to the United States census.

*Lynn Creek.

*Lyon, Cecil Andren.

*Lyons, Texas.

*Lyonsville, Texas.

*Lyra, Texas.

*Lystra, Texas.

Lytle, John Thomas. John Thomas Lytle, son of Francis and Margaret (Collins) Lytle, was born on October 8, 1844, at McSherrystown, Adams County, Pennsylvania. Lytle migrated with his family in 1860 to San Antonio, Texas, where he worked in the Bexar County clerk's office until 1861, when poor health forced him to resign. He then moved to a ranch in Atascosa County, owned by an uncle, William Lytle, where outdoor work restored his health. From 1863 until 1865 he served in Company H, 32nd Texas Cavalry (Wood's Regiment), rising to the rank of sergeant. After his discharge he returned to the Atascosa County ranch, but in 1867 he established his own ranch near Castroville.

In 1871 Lytle formed a partnership with a cousin, Thomas M. McDaniel, in present Lytle, Texas, for the purpose of trailing the herds of area ranchers to northern railheads and ranges. During the next three years he personally conducted a number of drives to Kansas. In 1874 Charles Armand Schreiner qv of Kerrville and John W. Light of Kimble County joined the firm, thereby increasing its capital and prestige. Operating out of Lytle and Kerrville, the trailing firm became one of the most outstanding in Texas, ultimately handling in excess of one-half million cattle. The size of the operation forced Lytle to turn active management of trail herds over to employees, but he continued to supervise the organization of the drives in Texas and the sale of cattle at the railheads. In 1887 Schreiner bought full control of the firm, whereupon Lytle became general manager of the American Cattle Syndicate's Texas holdings, but in 1891 he resigned to devote full time to his own ranching enterprises.

With George W. Saunders qv and Jesse Presnall, he had in 1886 established the Union Stock Yards in San Antonio; three years later, with Thomas Jefferson Moore, W. H. Jennings, and John Rufus Blocker,qv he purchased the half-million-acre Piedra Blanca Ranch in Coahuila, Mexico; he was also one of the founders of the Southwestern Livestock Commission Company at Fort Worth. In 1901 he was elected vice-president and member of the executive committee of the Texas Cattle Raisers' Association.qv Three years later he was named secretary of the organization, a salaried position he held until his death.

Lytle married Elizabeth Noonan of Medina County in 1869; they had two children. Lytle died of influenza on January 10, 1907, in San Antonio.

BIBLIOGRAPHY: Gus L. Ford (ed.), *Texas Cattle Brands* (1936); J. Evetts Haley, *Charles Schreiner, General Merchandise* (1944); J. Marvin Hunter (comp. and ed.), *The Trail Drivers of Texas* (1925); Jimmy M. Skaggs, "John Thomas Lytle: Cattle Baron," *Southwestern Historical Quarterly*, LXXI (1967–1968).

Jimmy M. Skaggs

*Lytle, Texas. Lytle, in extreme northwestern (not northeastern, as stated in Volume II) Atascosa County, was named for John Thomas Lytle,qv who donated the land for the town (not William Lytle, as stated in Volume II, although perhaps a Lytle Station had been named earlier for William Lytle). The town was founded about 1880 with the coming of the railway. The United States census reported a population for Lytle of 798 in 1960 and 1,271 in 1970. The town had twenty-seven businesses in 1970.

BIBLIOGRAPHY: J. Marvin Hunter (comp. and ed.), *The Trail Drivers of Texas* (1925); C. L. Patterson, *Atascosa County, Texas* (1938); Jimmy M. Skaggs, "John Thomas Lytle: Cattle Baron," *Southwestern Historical Quarterly*, LXXI (1967–1968).

*Lytle Creek.

*Lytle Gap.

*Lytle Lake.

*Lytton Creek.

*Lytton Springs.

*Lytton Springs, Texas.

M

*M. D. Anderson Foundation. *See also* University of Texas M. D. Anderson Hospital and Tumor Institute at Houston.

*Mabank, Texas. Mabank had a 1960 population of 944 and a 1970 population of 1,239, according to the United States census.

*Mabelle, Texas.

*Mabry, Evans.

*Mabry, Hinche Parham.

*Mabry, William S.

*Mabry, Woodford Haywood.

Mabry, Texas. Mabry, near Clarksville in Red River County, was founded prior to 1860 by the Mabry family, the first settlers in the area. At the townsite, Mabry built a horse-powered cotton gin and a steam gristmill and gin. By 1900 the town had two churches and employed three teachers in its school. The 1967 population was estimated at seventy-five, continuing a decline begun earlier. The present inhabitants of Mabry engage in cattle raising or work in nearby towns.

*McAdams, Texas. McAdams, in Walker County, was named for John McAdams, Jr. (not his son Hiram McAdams, as stated in Volume II).

It had a post office as early as 1889 (not 1904) and as late as 1913. Mary Frances (Bankhead) McAdams, widow of John McAdams, Jr., was its first postmistress of record, 1889–1891.

Margaret Craig

*McAdams Mountain.

*Macado Creek.

*McAdoo, John D.

*McAdoo, Texas.

*McAllen, Texas. McAllen, in Hidalgo County, was an agricultural, oil, and tourist center in 1970. The city had a 200-bed hospital, and had recently built a new air-conditioned high school, the first school in the nation featuring on-site power generation with natural-gas-powered turbines and high-frequency lighting. The tourist industry expanded considerably. In 1967 the town listed 828 businesses, including forty-five manufacturers. There were sixteen schools, fifty-two churches, two banks, a hospital, a library, a newspaper, and a radio station. In 1970 McAllen reported 860 businesses. Since 1950 public improvements have included the building of a city hall, civic center, airport terminal, golf course, and three fire stations, and the purchase of the international bridge. The 1960 population was 32,728; the 1970 population was 37,-636, according to the United States census. *See also* McAllen-Edinburg-Pharr Standard Metropolitan Statistical Area.

McAllen-Edinburg-Pharr Standard Metropolitan Statistical Area. The McAllen-Edinburg-Pharr Standard Metropolitan Statistical Area, which is coextensive with Hidalgo County, was designated a metropolitan area in 1966 as one of two such areas in the Lower Rio Grande Valley. The Valley covers 2,424 square miles, 1,541 of which are in Hidalgo County. The county's 1960 population was 180,904. The 1970 population was 181,535, according to the United States census.

The Valley is in the semitropical southern tip of Texas bordered by Mexico on the south, the Gulf of Mexico, South Padre Island, and Laguna Madre Bay on the east, and the King Ranch ^{qv} and the International Falcon Reservoir ^{qv} on the north and northwest, respectively. Its climate and location make the Lower Rio Grande Valley a popular tourist area, tourism ranking as the second largest industry in the Valley. The leading industry is agriculture, due to the warm climate, fertile soil, and extensive irrigation. One of the most productive areas in the state, the Valley is the location of most of the state's citrus fruit crop. Other sources of income are related to the fishing and shipping facilities, oil and gas production, and diversified manufacturing.

Hidalgo County ranked fifth among counties in 1962 gas production. One of the leading farm counties in the state, it had an average annual agricultural income of over $85 million in the early 1970's. Among the principal towns of the area, McAllen, with its 1970 population of 37,636, was noted for its oil refineries, chemical plants, fruit, vegetable-packing and -processing plants, and expanding tourist industry. The county seat, Edinburg, with its 1970 population of 17,163, also had oil and gas operations among its 308 business establishments. Mission and Mercedes, with respective 1970 populations of 15,043 and 9,355, had important citrus fruit industries along with businesses related to cotton, vegetables, and livestock. Mission was a center for livestock pest (screwworm) eradication in 1966. Mercedes had industries for marketing and processing, meat packing, boot making, and farm chemical manufacturing. Weslaco, with a 1970 population of 15,313, was a citrus fruit center and was noted also for vegetable marketing and processing and cattle feeding. Pharr, with a 1970 population of 15,829, was also a citrus-vegetable center. Other towns in Hidalgo County contributing through agribusinesses included Donna, Alamo, San Juan, Elsa, Edcouch, Hidalgo, Penitas, and seventeen other communities.

The 1,981-acre Santa Ana National Wildlife Refuge ^{qv} for migratory birds is situated along the Rio Grande in Hidalgo County and augments the natural tourist attractions of the area. There are also many parks, lakes, and resacas. Other tourist at-tractions are the annual Citrus Fiesta ^{qv} in Mission and the South Texas Lamb and Sheep Exposition in Donna, both held in January; the Rio Grande Valley Livestock Show held in Mercedes during March; and numerous rodeos. The Confederate Air Force, ^{qv} organized in Mercedes, maintains its museum at Harlingen and holds its annual air show of World War II airplanes at Harlingen's municipal airport in October. Mission is the site of William Jennings Bryan's winter home, and Donna has the world's first American Legion hall, designated a historical landmark in 1964.

The area's only institution of higher education is Pan American University in Edinburg (formerly Pan American College, renamed from Edinburg Junior College in 1952 when it became a four-year institution). Weslaco is the site of experimental and laboratory operations of Texas A&M University, Texas A&I University, and the United States Department of Agriculture. *See also* Brownsville-Harlingen-San Benito Standard Metropolitan Statistical Area; Standard Metropolitan Statistical Areas in Texas.

BIBLIOGRAPHY: Robert B. Williamson, *The Lower Rio Grande Valley of Texas: Economic Resources* (1966); *Texas Almanac* (1968).

Verna J. McKenna

*****McAnelly, Cornelius.**

*****McArdle, Henry Arthur.** While in San Antonio, Henry (Harry) Arthur McArdle was commissioned by James Thomas DeShields ^{qv} (not Shields, as stated in Volume II). McArdle died on February 16, 1908 (not June 18, 1907).

BIBLIOGRAPHY: Frances Battaile Fisk, *A History of Texas Artists and Sculptors* (1928); Mrs. Esse Forrester-O'Brien, *Art and Artists in Texas* (1935); Pauline A. Pinckney, *Painting in Texas: The Nineteenth Century* (1967).

MacArthur, Douglas, Academy of Freedom. *See* Howard Payne College.

*****McBain, Texas.**

*****McBees Creek.**

*****McBride, Texas.**

McCaleb, Walter Flavius. Walter Flavius McCaleb, son of John Lafayette and Elizabeth (Sweeten) McCaleb, was born in Benton, Texas, on October 17, 1873. McCaleb married Idéalie Marie McCaleb of New Orleans on June 28, 1901. They had four children. He was married a second time, to Edna Lang of Baltimore on June 11, 1960.

He showed an interest in history at an early age while he was a student at San Antonio Academy. ^{qv} McCaleb became acquainted with the Bexar County courthouse papers concerning the Spanish regime in Texas history. While exploring the Bexar Archives ^{qv} he uncovered references to the Aaron Burr ^{qv} conspiracy and the history of the Spanish missions in Texas.

Entering the University of Texas, he communicated his interest and findings in the Bexar Archives to George P. Garrison ^{qv} of the Department of History, who collaborated with McCaleb in laying plans for the transfer of the Bexar Archives to the University of Texas. He was graduated from the university in 1896 with a Bachelor of Literature degree. He took his M.A. there in 1897 and proceeded to the University of Chicago with a fellowship in history from 1897 to 1900; he received his Ph.D. there in 1900. Under his traveling fellowship at Chicago he carried on further research on the Burr conspiracy in Mexico, England, Kentucky, Tennessee, and Louisiana, and in the Library of Congress in Washington, D.C.

His life's work on the Burr conspiracy coincided with business and journalistic endeavors. In 1903 the first edition of *The Aaron Burr Conspiracy* was published, with a second edition coming out in 1936. In 1963 McCaleb published *New Light on Aaron Burr*, and three years later the two books were consolidated into one volume.

The Aaron Burr conspiracy has been a controversial subject receiving wide notice. For more than 150 years many historians considered Burr both the originator and the protagonist of a plan to separate the western portion of the United States from the eastern, to "liberate" the Spanish colonies, East and West Florida, Texas, and Mexico, and to combine them all into a great empire. Many critics have endorsed McCaleb's conclusion as to Burr's nontreasonable purposes.

McCaleb was an editor on the staff of *The New International Encyclopedia* from 1901 to 1903; associate editor of the *Public Ledger* in Philadelphia in 1904; and reviewer for the New York *Times*, the *Nation*, and the *American Historical Review.* He was an officer of many banks and insurance companies, serving as president of the American Home Builders, principal field representative of the Federal Home Loan Bank, and, in 1937, special advisor to the secretary of the interior of the United States.

In the academic field he was a fellow of the Texas State Historical Association qv and one of its first-year members. McCaleb's writings were not confined to his favorite subject. He was also the author of fifteen other books, among them *Conquest of the West* (1947), *The Mier Expedition* (1950), *The Spanish Missions of Texas* (1954), and *The Santa Fe Expedition* (1964).

McCaleb's poems appear in three volumes: *Winnowings of the Wind* (1910), *Khorasan* (1962), and *No Port of Call* (c. 1964). His intellectual curiosity and writings continued until his death at the age of ninety-four on March 2, 1967, at Austin, Texas. He was buried there in Mount Calvary Cemetery.

Richard T. Fleming

***McCall, John Dodd.**

***McCallum, Arthur Newell.**

McCallum, Jane LeGette Yelvington. Jane McCallum was born in La Vernia, Texas, December 30, 1878, the daughter of Alvaro Leonard and Mary Fullerton (LeGette) Yelvington. She was educated in the schools of Wilson County, Texas; at Zealey's Female College in Mississippi; and at the University of Texas in Austin. She was married to Arthur Newell McCallum qv in 1896, when he was school superintendent of La Vernia, and later moved with him to Kenedy and Seguin. In 1903 her husband began his long career as superintendent of schools in Austin; the capital city became the permanent home for the McCallum family.

In connection with her efforts for woman suffrage, prison reform, prohibition, education, child labor laws, and other governmental concerns, Jane McCallum was a leader of numerous organizations. In January, 1927, she was appointed secretary of state and served in that office under two governors, until 1933. She was state chairman of publicity for the Texas Educational Amendment; state chairman of the Ratification Committee for the 19th Amendment; executive secretary of the Texas Joint Legislative Council during the Thirty-eighth and Thirty-ninth legislatures; presidential elector in 1940; state Democratic committeewoman for the Twentieth Senatorial District in 1942; and Travis County's first woman grand jury commissioner. During her service as secretary of state, Jane McCallum found and rescued from decay the original Texas Declaration of Independence,qv an accomplishment which she often looked upon as one of her more important contributions to Texas.

As a private citizen she was active in many groups, including the League of Women Voters, Colonial Dames of America, and Austin Woman's Club. Also, she was a public speaker and writer. Among her written works are *Women Pioneers* (c. 1929); the Texas chapter in *National History of Woman Suffrage* (Vol. VI) by Ida Harper; "Woman and Her Ways," written weekly for the Austin *Statesman*;qv and articles for *Texas Magazine*, *Texas Parade*, and *Holland's Magazine*.qqv On August 14, 1957, Jane McCallum died; she was buried in Oakwood Cemetery, Austin, Texas.

BIBLIOGRAPHY: Florence E. Barns, *Texas Writers of Today* (1935).

Henry D. McCallum

***McCamey, Texas.** McCamey, in Upton County, had a 1960 population of 3,375. Located in an oil and ranching area, McCamey completed two new parks, several school system buildings, a post office building, a new city hall, a hospital, and a museum between 1950 and 1966. In the latter year, the town had seventeen churches, three libraries, a bank, a newspaper, and a radio station. In 1970 McCamey reported sixty-eight businesses. The 1970 population was 2,647, according to the United States census.

***McCaulley, Texas.**

***McClain, A. W.**

***McClanahan, Texas.**

***McClellan, George Brinton.**

***McClellan, William B.** William Brownlow McClellan was born in 1810 in Tennessee (not a native of North Carolina, as stated in Volume II; another William B. McClellan was born in North Carolina and came to Texas from Tennessee, settling at Burton in Washington County as a merchant and farmer in 1841). William Brownlow McClellan learned the printing trade at Pensacola, Florida, and came to Austin, Texas, from Florida (not to Washington County from Tennessee in 1841). In Austin, McClellan's first wife, Caroline (Rawlins) McClellan, died in 1840. After editing the La Grange *Intelligencer* qv during the early part of 1844, McClellan moved back to Austin by 1845 and served on the executive committee of the Texas Bible Society. He returned to La Grange about 1850 and married Amanda Fitzallen Moore. From February 24 to September 29, 1855, he edited the La Grange *Paper*.qv McClellan died in Austin in 1871.

BIBLIOGRAPHY: Leonie R. Weyand and Houston Wade, *An Early History of Fayette County* (1936); *National Register* (Washington, Texas), July 31, 1845; *Northern Standard* (Clarksville), March 20, 1844; *Texas State Gazette*, August 14, 1852; United States Census, 1850, Fayette County, Texas (microfilm, University of Texas at Austin Library).

Thomas C. McClellan

*McClellan Creek.

*McClellan Creek Lake.

*McClelland, Brainard Taylor.

*McClelland, Samuel.

McClendon, James Wooten. James Wooten McClendon, a chief justice of the Court of Civil Appeals, was born November 1, 1873, in West Point, Georgia. His parents were James Wooten and Annie Eliza (Thompson) McClendon. After attending public schools in Georgia, McClendon moved to Texas and received his B.A. degree from the University of Texas in Austin in 1895. In 1897 he was a member of the first graduating class of the University of Texas law school, and he began law practice that year in Austin.

James McClendon was named associate justice on the Texas Supreme Court Commission of Appeals on October 7, 1918, and served there until December, 1923. He was appointed chief justice of the Court of Civil Appeals by Governor Pat Neff qv in 1923; he served in that position until 1949, when he retired. As chief justice in 1948, McClendon presided over the landmark case of Heman Marion Sweatt against the University of Texas, in which Sweatt, a black postal employee, charged that he could not enter law school because of his race (*see Sweatt* v. *Painter*). McClendon's decision, later overruled by the U.S. Supreme Court, favored the university and upheld the state's "separate but equal" provisions in running state schools.

McClendon married Anne Hale Watt on December 14, 1904; they were the parents of two children. A member of numerous judicial and honorary societies, McClendon also served as director and a member of the board of editors of the *Texas Law Review*.qv He died in Austin on January 9, 1972, and was buried in the State Cemetery.qv

BIBLIOGRAPHY: *Who's Who In America* (1960); Austin *American*, January 10, 1972.

McCloskey, Augustus. Augustus McCloskey was born in San Antonio on September 23, 1878. He attended Atascosa School, St. Joseph's Academy, and St. Mary's College in San Antonio, and studied law while working as a stenographer from 1903 to 1907. He was admitted to the Bar in San Antonio in 1907, and served as Bexar County judge from 1920 to 1928. In 1927 and 1928 he was president of the Highway Club of Texas and in 1928 was a delegate to the national Democratic convention in Houston. He apparently defeated Harry McLeary Wurzbach qv for Congress in 1928 and served from March 4, 1929, to February 10, 1930, when his opponent replaced McCloskey after successfully contesting the election. He then returned to law practice in San Antonio, serving also as judge of the corporation court from January, 1943, to July, 1947. McCloskey died on July 21, 1950, and was buried in San Fernando Cemetery in San Antonio.

BIBLIOGRAPHY: *Biographical Directory of the American Congress, 1774–1961* (1961).

McCloskey, John J. John J. McCloskey, instrumental in the founding of the Texas League,qv had a long, colorful career in baseball, contributing substantially to the development of professional baseball in the Southwest. McCloskey was born in Louisville, Kentucky, on April 4, 1862, and began playing professional baseball there in 1882. He usually played outfield or first base but during his career played every position. He not only played on teams in established leagues but also barnstormed with special teams and groups.

In 1884 he toured as battery mate for Phil (Red) Ehret, and one of their stops was in El Paso. In the fall of 1887 he organized a barnstorming Joplin, Missouri, team that toured the Southwest. The team played exhibitions in Fort Worth, Waco, and Austin. In Austin the Joplin team challenged and beat the touring New York Giants in both of the two games played; New York refused to play a third game. Austin businessmen and baseball fans were so impressed that they invited McCloskey to organize professional baseball in Texas. The result was the founding of the Texas League.

During the league's first year in 1888 McCloskey managed the Austin team, transferring it later in the season to San Antonio. He managed the 1889 Houston team that won the league pennant. In the 1890's the Texas League functioned intermittently, and McCloskey alternated as manager of teams in Texas and elsewhere. In 1895 and 1896 he managed the Louisville team in the National League. In 1899 he umpired in both the Southern Association and the Texas League. After managing a number of Pacific Coast teams, he managed the National League St. Louis Cardinals during the 1906, 1907, and 1908 seasons. During 1914–1917 he helped to organize and to direct the Rio Grande League, managing its El Paso team in 1915. During World War I he guided an independent circuit of United States Army teams.

In 1919 he again worked in the Texas League as manager of the Beaumont team. During the 1920's McCloskey managed, coached, and scouted for a number of major and minor league teams, and in 1931 he returned to Texas in an unsuccessful attempt to organize a Panhandle League. Thereafter, he retired to Louisville; he died there on November 17, 1940. For his great contribution to baseball in the state, John J. McCloskey was elected to the Texas Sports Hall of Fame.qv

William B. Ruggles

*McCloskey Veterans Administration Center. *See also* Veterans Administration Hospital, Temple.

*McClung Creek.

*McCollum, Texas.

*McComb, Joe S.

*McComb, John Evans.

*McConnell, Thomas.

*McConnico, Texas.

*McCook, Texas.

*McCord, Adelaide. *See* Menken, Adah Isaacs.

*McCord, J. E.

*McCormick, Andrew Phelps.

*McCormick, Arthur.

McCormick, Charles Tilford. Charles Tilford McCormick, son of Joseph Manson and Mary (McCoun) McCormick, was born on June 29, 1889, in Dallas, Texas. After attending the Dallas public schools he entered the University of Texas and received his B.A. degree in 1909. He received an LL.B. degree *cum laude* in 1912 from Harvard Law School. In 1920 he married Ireline DeWitt in Dallas. Practice in his father's Dallas law firm from 1912 to 1922 was interrupted by two years (1917–1919) in the United States Army, during which time McCormick rose to the rank of captain. From 1919 to 1920 he worked for Standard Oil of New Jersey.

In 1922 McCormick returned to the University of Texas as a professor of law to begin more than forty years as a distinguished teacher, scholar, and writer. In 1926 he went to the University of North Carolina School of Law, serving as dean from 1927 to 1931. He taught at Northwestern School of Law from 1931 to 1940. In 1940 he returned to the University of Texas as dean of the law school. He modernized the curriculum, established a legal aid clinic, recruited an outstanding young faculty, and initiated other needed improvements that enhanced the prestige of the law school. Upon his resignation as dean in 1949 he became Distinguished Professor of Law. In 1961 he was made Dean Emeritus.

McCormick published *Handbook on the Law of Damages* (1935), *Texas Law of Evidence*, with Roy Robert Ray (1937), *Handbook on the Law of Evidence* (1954), and *Cases and Materials on Federal Courts*, with James H. Chadbourn (1946). He coauthored later editions with the same and additional authors. He wrote more than fifty articles for scholarly publications.

Among his professional honors were his appointment by the United States Supreme Court to the First Judicial Conference Advisory Committee on Rules of Civil Procedure, and by President Dwight David Eisenhower qv to the National Oliver Wendell Holmes Devise Committee. He was a member of the American Law Institute; American, Texas, Illinois, and Chicago Bar associations; Philosophical Society of Texas;qv and Phi Delta Phi. He was president of the Order of the Coif and of the Association of American Law Schools. An honorary Doctor of Law degree was conferred on him by Southern Methodist University.

A member of All Saints Episcopal Church in Austin, he served on the vestry, was a senior warden, chancellor of the parish, and a trustee of Grace Hall. He died in Austin on December 22, 1963, and was buried in Austin Memorial Park.

BIBLIOGRAPHY: "Charles Tilford McCormick Memorial Resolution," University of Texas Documents and Minutes of the General Faculty (1964); Association of American Law Schools, *Proceedings*, Part I (1964); The Philosophical Society of Texas, *Proceedings* (1964); *Who's Who In America* (1962); "Charles T. McCormick, A Personal Appreciation," *Texas Law Review* (November, 1949); "Charles T. McCormick, Dedication," *Texas Law Review* (December, 1961); "Memorial," *Texas Bar Journal* (1964).

Helen Hargrave

*McCormick, David.

*McCormick, "Frenchy."

*McCormick, George.

*McCormick, George, Jr.

*McCormick, John.

*McCoy, John C.

*McCoy, Thomas.

*McCoy, Texas. (Atascosa County.)

*McCoy, Texas. (Kaufman County.)

*McCoy, Texas. (Red River County.)

*McCoy Creek.

*McCoy School, Texas.

*McCrabb Creek.

*McCrearey, James K.

*McCrocklin, Jesse Lindsay.

*McCroskey, John.

*McCulloch, Ben.

*McCulloch, Henry E. Henry E. McCulloch died at Rockport, Texas (not Seguin, as stated in Volume II), although he was buried at Seguin.

Palmer Bradley

McCulloch, Samuel. Samuel McCulloch (also spelled McCullock, McCullough), a free Negro, was the son of Samuel J. McCulloch. He was born in Abbeville District, South Carolina, on October 11, 1810. He was taken to Montgomery County, Alabama, in 1815, and came to Texas with his father and three sisters in May, 1835. They settled on the Lavaca River in what is now Jackson County, and his father, describing himself as a single man, obtained a headright certificate for one-third of a league of land. McCulloch joined George Morse Collinsworth's qv company of Texas troops on October 5, 1835, and participated in the October 9 attack on Goliad, where he was seriously wounded in the right shoulder during the attack on the *cuartel*. He was the only Texas soldier wounded in that engagement. In a petition to the Texas Congress, McCulloch described himself as "the first whose blood was shed in the War for Independence."

Samuel McCulloch married Mary Lorena Vess, daughter of Austin colonist Jonathan Vess, on August 11, 1837. They had at least four children before she died on November 8, 1847. In 1837 he petitioned Congress to grant him his headright land, his army bounty, and citizenship in the Republic. He received a bounty certificate for one league of land in 1838 as a permanently disabled veteran of the Texas Revolution, but his citizenship and headright land were denied to him under Section 10 of the Constitution of the Republic.qv In December, 1840, the Fifth Congress passed a law exempting McCulloch, his sisters, and their descendants from the Act of February 5, 1840, which required all free blacks to leave the Republic. In January, 1858, the Seventh Legislature passed an act granting McCulloch a headright certificate for one league and one labor of land.

In August, 1840, McCulloch participated in the Plum Creek Fight,qv and in 1842 Clark L. Owen qv sent him into San Antonio as a spy after its capture by General Adrian Woll.qv He moved to Wallace Prairie, in Grimes County, in 1842 but returned to Jackson County in 1845. In 1852 he, his father, and his children moved to Bexar County, where he located two-thirds of his bounty league on the south bank of the Medina River, near Von Ormy. In his later years he was an active member of the Texas Veterans Association.qv William Physick Zuber qv said of McCulloch that "he was generally recognized as an honorable white man, and treated as such." One of his sons, William R. McCulloch, served in the Confederate Army. Samuel McCulloch died on November 1, 1893, and was buried in the McCulloch Cemetery, near Macdona in Bexar County.

BIBLIOGRAPHY: H. P. N. Gammel, *The Laws of Texas, 1822–1897*, I, IV (1898); W. P. Zuber, "Biographies of Texas Veterans" (MS., Archives, University of Texas at Austin Library); Memorials and Petitions, Papers of the Legislature (MS., Archives, Texas State Library, Austin); Congressional Papers, Fifth Congress (MS., Archives, Texas State Library, Austin); First Class Headright File (MS., General Land Office, Austin).

Lonn Taylor

*McCulloch County. McCulloch County, primarily a ranching area with some small grain, cotton, and oil production, had a crop income of $1,-673,000 and a livestock and products income of $5,192,000 in 1968. The average annual farm income in the early 1970's was $8.5 million. Tourist attractions include Brady Lake, a January livestock show, and an April horse show. The 1960 population was 8,815; the 1970 population was 8,571, according to the United States census.

*McCullough, John.

*McCullough Female Seminary. *See* Galveston Seminary.

*McCullum Creek.

*McCurley, Texas.

*McDade, Texas.

*McDaniel, George White.

McDavitt, William Early. William Early McDavitt, son of Marcellus and Charlotte (Hoey) McDavitt, was born on March 6, 1876, in Auburn, Kentucky. Following his early education, McDavitt attended college in Quincy, Illinois. He came to Texas and set up business at Alvin, where he planted and raised fruits such as figs, peaches, and pears. It was at Alvin that he married Estella Lacy on April 6, 1900; they had four children. The couple moved to Corsicana, where McDavitt engaged in shipping. News reports about a "Valley of the Nile" located at the southern tip of Texas caused McDavitt to leave for Brownsville in 1904.

In touring the Rio Grande Valley he visualized the possibilities of growing vegetables and fruits to be shipped to big markets in the East, Midwest, and elsewhere. With his brother, Karl H. McDavitt, he soon developed an extensive packing and shipping business.

McDavitt was a pioneer in the shipping of vegetables by railway, steamship, and airplane. In fifty years of active business he sent over fifty thousand loaded cars from the Rio Grande Valley.

McDavitt was active in service and professional organizations. He was a member of the United Fruit and Vegetable Association. He helped to organize the Texas Citrus, Fruit and Vegetable Growers and Shippers, of which he became a director. Shortly before his retirement in 1954 he proposed the organization of the Associated Growers of Brownsville. He died on November 10, 1955, and was buried in Buena Vista Park, Brownsville.

BIBLIOGRAPHY: Marcellus McDavitt, "William Early McDavitt" (MS., Archives, Texas Southmost College); J. L. Allhands, *Gringo Builders* (1931).

Joe Lindaberry

McDermott, Eugene B. Eugene B. McDermott was born February 12, 1899, in Brooklyn, New York, the son of Owen and Emma (Cahill) McDermott. Destined to become a highly respected industrialist and patron of the arts and education, McDermott received an M.E. degree from Stevens Institute of Technology in 1919 and an M.A. from Columbia University in 1925. With another young scientist, J. C. Karcher, McDermott was recruited by Everett Lee DeGolyer qv to develop seismic exploration for the Geophysical Research Corporation. Karcher and McDermott perfected their instruments for use in oil detection before coming to Texas, and McDermott, personally directing his crews, located ten major salt domes in his first two years with the company. He was credited with more than ten inventions, among them the reflection seismograph, a system using underground explosions and the resulting shock waves to determine the structure of the earth.

Eugene McDermott was a cofounder in 1930 with J. C. Karcher of Geophysical Services, Inc., the company which in 1951 became Texas Instruments, Inc. A vice-president, president, and board chairman of GSI, McDermott was the first board chairman of TI, chairman of the executive committee from 1958 to 1964, and after 1964 a company director.

McDermott married Margaret Milam on December 1, 1954; they had one daughter. The McDermotts were well known in Texas for their philanthropy, and both were directors of SMU's Fine Arts Association, as well as contributors to educational funds in the Dallas area. They were largely responsible for the renovation of the former Gillespie County Courthouse in Fredericksburg. With his former associates Erik Jonsson and Cecil Green, McDermott was instrumental in establishing the University of Texas at Dallas. He was on the boards of numerous civic and business organizations and was a trustee of the Texas Research Foundation and Southwestern Medical Foundation;qqv he also established the Eugene McDermott Center for Study of Human Growth and Development at the University of Texas Southwestern Medical School at Dallas in 1972, and a permanent fellowship for Paisano Ranch.qv A contributor of numerous articles to technical journals, McDermott was the author (with William H. Sheldon) of *Varieties of Juvenile Delinquency* (1949). McDermott died in Dallas on August 24, 1973.

BIBLIOGRAPHY: *Who's Who In America* (1960); Austin *American-Statesman*, August 26, 1973; Dallas *Morning News*, August 26, 1973.

*McDiarmid, Errett Weir.

*Macdona, Texas.

*McDonald, Donald.

*McDonald, William Jesse.

*McDonald, William Johnson.

McDonald, William Madison. William Madison (Gooseneck) McDonald was born on June 22, 1866, at College Mound, Kaufman County, Texas. His father had been a slave, his mother a freewoman. He was educated at Wilburforce College in Nashville, Tennessee, with the aid of Jed Cobb Adams qv and other white friends.

McDonald became prominent in Texas Republician politics in 1892, when he was elected to the party's state executive committee. For more than thirty years he remained a notable figure of the party and attended many Republican national conventions. After the death of Norris Wright Cuney qv in 1897, McDonald became leader of the Texas Negro Republicans. In the late 1890's, McDonald formed what amounted to a political partnership with Edward Howland Robinson Green,qv who became active in Texas Republican politics as a member of the "Black and Tan" faction. The two men remained together for many years and sur-

vived many political battles until 1912, when the Bull Moose upheaval shattered the Republican hegemony.

McDonald moved to Fort Worth and founded the Fraternal Bank and Trust Company, which quickly became the chief depository of funds for the state's Negro Masonic lodges. Green and McDonald attempted a comeback in 1920 by supporting General Leonard Wood for the Republican presidential nomination. However, an opposing Texas Republican presidential faction, led by Rentfro Banton Creager qv of Brownsville, backed Warren G. Harding, who won the party's nomination. After the 1920 election, McDonald was no longer a major leader in the Texas Republican party.qv He supported Democrats Al Smith and Franklin D. Roosevelt, before returning to the Republican party to support Thomas E. Dewey for president. McDonald died in Fort Worth on July 5, 1950, and was survived by his fifth wife; an only child, a son, died some thirty years previously. He was buried in Trinity Cemetery, Fort Worth.

BIBLIOGRAPHY: Paul D. Casdorph, *A History of the Republican Party in Texas, 1865–1965* (1965); Arthur H. Lewis, *The Day They Shook the Plum Tree* (c. 1963); E. W. Winkler, *Platforms of Political Parties in Texas* (1916); Dallas *Morning News*, September 18, 1949, July 6, 10, 1950.

Paul D. Casdorph

*McDonald Creek.

*McDonald Observatory. *See also* University of Texas McDonald Observatory at Mount Locke; Harvard Radio Astronomy Station.

*McDonough, John Henry.

*McDow, Texas.

*McDowell Creek.

*Macedonia, Texas. (Liberty County.)

*Macedonia, Texas. (Panola County.)

*Macey, Texas.

*McFaddin, William M.

*McFaddin, William P. H.

*McFaddin, Texas.

*McFadin, David Hutchinson.

*McFarland, Achilles.

*McFarland, John.

McFarland, Mae Wynne. Mae Wynne McFarland was born September 23, 1884, in Huntsville, Texas, the daughter of Gustavus Adair and Samuella (Gibbs) Wynne. She attended the University of Texas; on April 14, 1914, she married Ike Barton McFarland. As lobbyist for women's patriotic societies she was active in urging the Texas legislature to enact into law a prohibition against the destruction of wild flowers along the public highways. She was also devoted to the project of having historical markers placed along the state's highways. A student of early Texas history, she specialized in the history of Huntsville and Walker counties and compiled a study of veterans of the War of 1812 who came to Texas. Mrs. McFarland died January 7, 1962, and was buried in the Oak Wood Cemetery in Huntsville.

Mary Lewis Ulmer

*McFarland, Thomas S.

*McFarland, William.

*McFarland Creek.

*McFarland Lake.

*MacFarlane, Dugald.

*McFarlin, John Green.

*McGary, Dan L.

*McGaughey, W. L.

*McGee, Joseph J.

*McGee, Joseph J.

*McGee, Texas. (Denton County.)

*McGee, Texas. (Montague County.)

*McGee Bend Project. The McGee Bend Project, to construct a dam and reservoir on the Angelina-San Augustine county line which touched the counties of Jasper, Sabine, and Nacogdoches, began in the late 1950's. Finally completed in 1965, the dam and reservoir were renamed for the late Samuel Taliaferro Rayburn,qv speaker of the United States House of Representatives. *See also* Sam Rayburn Dam and Reservoir.

BIBLIOGRAPHY: *Texas Almanac* (1955, 1965).

McGiffin, Philo Norton. Philo Norton McGiffin, son of the Reverend Nathaniel and Margaret (Leet) McGiffin, was born in Fairhaven, New York, on May 6, 1900. He received the B.A. degree from Hamilton College in 1923 and the LL.B. from the University of Southern California in 1926. In 1938 McGiffin became the chief editorial writer of the Buffalo (New York) *Evening News* and served in the same capacity for the St. Petersburg (Florida) *Times* from 1939 to 1940. He came to Texas in September, 1940, as professor of English and later taught history at Arlington State College (now the University of Texas at Arlington), where he served until his death.

During World War II McGiffin was radio news analyst and commentator for Texas Quality Network. He innovated the practice of comparing foreign military operations and geography with distances between Texas towns, thus in a sense bringing Guadalcanal and Normandy home to Cuero and Waxahachie and other Texas localities. For two years after the war he was political analyst and editorial writer for the Fort Worth *Press*. The author of three historical novels for youth, *The Domino Horse, Sam Henderson—Texas Ranger*, and *Red Lion*, McGiffin was a member of the Texas State Historical Association,qv Sigma Delta Chi, and Delta Theta Phi. The McGiffin Memorial Award to outstanding undergraduate history students at Arlington is named in his honor. He was married to Lee McGiffin, and they had one son. McGiffin died on April 12, 1964.

E. C. Barksdale

*McGirk, Texas.

*McGloin, James. [The *see also* reference in Volume II should read McMullen-McGloin Colony (not McMullin-McGloin Colony).]

*McGough Springs.

*McGowan, Alexander D.

*McGraw Creek.

*MacGregor, Henry Frederick.

McGregor, Stuart Malcolm. Stuart Malcolm McGregor was born on February 24, 1892, at Coleman, the son of Jesse and Gabriella Baldwin (Edwards) McGregor. After graduation from Coleman High School in 1910, he entered the University of Texas where he received a B.A. degree in 1914 and a Master of Journalism in 1915, the first degree granted by its School of Journalism. That same year he was editor of the *Daily Texan*,qv the student newspaper.

McGregor worked on the Austin *American* and Austin *Statesman* qqv before entering the aviation branch of the United States Navy during World War I, during which he held the rank of ensign. He moved to Dallas in 1919 to join the Texas Chamber of Commerce as its director of public relations and statistician. On January 1, 1923, he became a member of the staff of the Dallas *Morning News* qv and remained with it and its affiliated *Texas Almanac* qv until his retirement in 1961. He was married in 1923 to Louise Merritt Lawrence of Dallas, and they had one son.

From 1925 through the 1961–1962 edition, McGregor compiled and edited the *Texas Almanac*, co-edited the agriculture and business pages of the Dallas *Morning News*, and was associate editor of its editorial page. In 1960 he was chosen as the first living member of the Journalism Hall of Fame at the University of Texas. He was cited in 1961 by the Southwestern Journalism Forum at Southern Methodist University for his thirty-seven years of outstanding service to Texas as editor of the *Texas Almanac*. In 1962 he won the McMurray Award of the Texas Institute of Letters qv for outstanding service to Texas writers and researchers as editor of the same publication. He served as a vice-president of the Texas State Historical Association,qv which in 1944 elected him one of its Fellows. He was a member of the Texas Academy of Science, Philosophical Society of Texas,qqv Texas Institute of Letters, and Critic Club of Dallas. Besides his newspaper and yearbook work, his writings included articles for the *Southwestern Historical Quarterly*,qv *Encyclopædia Britannica, Economist* (London), and other publications. He died in Dallas on March 14, 1963, and was buried in Hillcrest Memorial Cemetery.

BIBLIOGRAPHY: *Who's Who In America* (1958); Dallas *Morning News*, March 15, 1963.

Sam Acheson

*McGregor, Texas. McGregor, in southwest McLennan County, was named for Gregor Carmichael McGregor (not J. C. McGregor, as stated in Volume II). [Some later printings of Volume II were corrected to read G. C. McGregor.] It is a commercial suburban center sixteen miles west of Waco. Major industrial products include upholstered furniture, prefabricated buildings, porcelain enamel, solid propellant fuel for rocket engines and power packages, and cabinets and store fixtures. An agricultural experiment station situated south of McGregor conducts research on cotton, grain, and cattle. In 1966 McGregor reported sixty-nine businesses, twelve churches, and one bank. In 1970 the town reported eighty businesses. The 1960 population was 4,642. According to the United States census, the 1970 population was 4,365. *See also* Waco Standard Metropolitan Statistical Area.

*McGrew Creek.

*McGuffin, Hugh.

*McHenry, John.

*McHenry, Lydia Ann.

*McIntosh, George S.

*McKay, Daniel.

*Mackay, Texas.

*McKee Creek.

*McKees, Texas.

*McKenzie, John Witherspoon Pettigrew.

*Mackenzie, Ranald Slidell.

McKenzie, Texas. McKenzie, in southeastern Mitchell County, was named for F. S. McKenzie, who gave land for a school in 1908. A small community developed, but declined when the school was abandoned in 1934. Located in a ranching area, the settlement no longer existed in 1966 although its cemetery was still in use.

*McKenzie College.

*McKenzie Creek.

*McKenzie Draw.

*Mackenzie Peak.

*McKibben, Texas.

*McKie, William Junius.

*McKim Creek.

*McKinney, Andrew Todd.

*McKinney, Buckner Abernathy.

*McKinney, Collin. Collin McKinney moved to Lincoln County, Kentucky, with his family in 1780 (not 1870, as stated in Volume II). [Some later printings of Volume II contain this correction.]

*McKinney, Samuel.

*McKinney, Thomas F.

*McKinney, Texas. McKinney, seat of Collin County, had a 1960 population of 13,763. In 1962 McKinney had thirty-nine churches, nine schools, two hospitals, and a library; by 1970 business establishments numbered 222. Diversified manufactures included textiles, garments, feeds, seat covers, dairy products, and bakery goods. In 1970 the population was 15,193, according to the United States census.

*McKinney Bayou.

McKinney Center for Women. *See* Job Corps Program in Texas.

*McKinney Lake.

*McKinney Mountains.

*McKinney Spring, Texas.

*McKinney, Williams and Company.

*McKinsey, Hugh.

*McKinstry, George B.

*McKnight, Alexander Hearne.

*McKnight, George.

McKnight, Joseph Banning. Joseph Banning McKnight, son of Joseph P. and Mary (Elkins) McKnight, was born in Dallas on November 7, 1869. With a very rudimentary preparatory education he enrolled in the Memphis Hospital and Medical College (now the University of Tennessee) to study medicine. After receiving his M. D. degree in 1893 he stayed on at the college for an internship and spent a year in residence at St. Joseph's Hospital, Memphis. In later years he did postgraduate study at Rush Medical School Polyclinic in Chicago, the Trudeau School of Tuberculosis at Saranac Lake, New York, and Charity Hospital in New Orleans.

Dr. McKnight commenced his medical practice in Menardville (now Menard) and served that community, Fort McKavett, and the surrounding countryside before moving to Brady in 1908. Late in 1913 he was appointed head of the newly founded state tuberculosis colony at Carlsbad, a small hospital with facilities for fifty-seven patients. McKnight accepted the appointment for one year, but stayed on to serve as superintendent and medical director until his retirement on April 1, 1950, when the legislature honored him by naming the facility McKnight State Sanatorium.qv Under his direction the hospital expanded into a treatment center with over 1,000 beds; more than 28,000 patients were treated during his tenure.

In 1915 McKnight founded the first training school in Texas for nurses of tuberculosis patients. During World War I he served as examiner of men found unfit for service by reason of diseases of the chest. In 1918 he was instrumental in establishing an extension service which supplied printed information with respect to the study and prevention of tuberculosis, especially directed to the pupils of Texas public schools. Throughout his career he actively supported reforms in public health. In 1922 he was a member of the building committee for the federal Veterans Administration Hospital, Kerrville,qv and in 1935 he helped to establish the Kerrville State Sanatorium qv for Negroes. He was active in the affairs of the American Medical Association and held various offices in the Texas Medical Association qv and in local medical groups. He became a Fellow of the American College of Chest Physicians in 1939, a member of the American Trudeau Society in 1941, and a member of the American Association of Railway Surgeons in 1948.

He was married to Geraldine Mabel Latham on June 19, 1894, and his wife worked with him toward the eradication of tuberculosis in Texas. McKnight died in San Angelo on January 27, 1961, a short time after the death of his wife; both were buried in San Angelo.

BIBLIOGRAPHY: Texarado McKnight Peak, *The McKnight Families and their Descendants* (1965).

Joseph W. McKnight

*McKnight, Samuel Ewell. [This title was incorrectly listed in Volume II as McKnight, Samuel Elkins.] Samuel Ewell McKnight, son of Joseph P. and Mary (Elkins) McKnight, was born on January 11, 1864, in Waxahachie, Ellis County (not in Dallas County, as stated in Volume II). He died on September 24 (not September 25), 1940.

*McKnight State Sanatorium. The name was changed to McKnight State Tuberculosis Hospital in the mid-1950's. Treatment was expanded to include patients of all ages; a sheltered workshop project involved chronic patients for whom discharge seemed unlikely. The capacity of the hospital was 454 patients in 1964, and the number of patients in 1967 was 265.

On September 1, 1969, the land and facilities of the hospital were deeded by the State Department of Public Health qv to the Texas Department of Mental Health and Mental Retardation.qv The name was changed to San Angelo Center,qv and its function changed from a tuberculosis hospital to a retardate residential facility. All but about twenty-five tuberculosis patients were transferred to other tuberculosis hospitals. The remaining tuberculosis patients were treated at the San Angelo Center by special contract between the Texas Department of Mental Health and Mental Retardation and the State Department of Public Health.

BIBLIOGRAPHY: Board for Texas State Hospitals and Special Schools, *Report* (1964).

*Macksville, Texas.

McLane, Hiram H. Hiram H. McLane was born January 26, 1820, in Orange County, Indiana, the son of William McLane, who had taken part in the Gutiérrez-Magee Expedition.qv He came to Texas in 1858 and bought a ranch near Helena (now Old Helena) in Karnes County. After the Civil War he came to San Antonio, where he married Emma E. Hurd of New York. They had one child who died in infancy. About this time he bought the 1,400-acre ranch that is now Alamo Heights, adjoining San Antonio, from Charles Anderson,qv who had raised sorrel stallions to sell to the army. McLane continued to raise and sell horses in addition to his mining and ranching interests in Mexico. On the ranch was an ante-bellum mansion where McLane lived for thirty years with his collection of rare books and violins. It was only after the property was sold for the Alamo Heights real estate development around 1890 that the house became known as the Argyle (a hotel) and later the famous eating establishment run by Robert O'Grady and his sister, Alice O'Grady. (*See* Argyle Hotel.)

McLane's interest in Texas history led him in 1886 to write (from his father's reminiscences) the novel, *Irene Viesca, A Tale of the Magee Expedition in the Gauchipin War in Texas, A.D. 1812–13. The Capture of the Alamo* (1886), a play, was written to raise money for a monument on the Alamo grounds. His small booklets on capital and labor, *Watchman! What of the Knights?* (1886) and *The Three Friends, and the Proposed Reform* (1887), were printed in San Antonio. He died February 13, 1907, in San Antonio and was buried in the Alamo Masonic Cemetery.

BIBLIOGRAPHY: Lillie May Hagner, *Alluring San Antonio* (1940); Alice O'Grady (Sue Moore Gibson, comp.), *The Argyle Cook Book* (1940); Rudolph L. Biesele, "The Argyle Cook Book," *Southwestern Historical Quarterly*, XLIV (1940–1941); San Antonio *Daily Express*, February 14, 1907.

S. W. Pease
Crystal S. Ragsdale

*McLaughlin, James Wharton.

*McLaughlin Creek.

*McLean, Ephraim W.

*McLean, John Howell.

*McLean, William Pinckney.

*McLean, Texas. In 1970 McLean, a commercial center on Interstate Highway 40 in southeastern Gray County, had a population of 1,183, according to the United States census. This figure represented a decline from the 1960 population of 1,330. The town had a hospital, a library, a newspaper, and a bank. By 1970 businesses totaled fifty. In addition to a garment factory, there were several industries connected with petroleum and its products.

*McLeary, James Harvey.

*McLemore, Atkins Jefferson.

*McLendon's, Texas.

*McLennan, Neil.

McLennan Community College. The McLennan Community College was the first public junior college in Texas to include the word "community" in its name. The McLennan County Junior College District was approved by the citizens of the county on November 2, 1965. Under president Wilbur A. Ball, the college began operations in September, 1966, in temporary quarters on the deactivated James Connally Air Force Base.qv A 160-acre site, a former home of W. W. Cameron,qv was purchased later for a permanent campus. The original faculty numbered fifty-one and the student enrollment was 886. The 1974 regular fall term enrollment was 3,438 and the faculty had increased to 170. The school offers courses in the first two years of bachelor's degree programs, and technical and vocational courses. The college is a member of the American Association of Junior Colleges and the Texas Public Junior College Association, as well as an affiliate member of the Association of Texas Colleges and Universities.qv Its 1969 library holdings numbered 19,800 volumes.

*McLennan County. McLennan County, with a large urban population around Waco, ranked sixth among Texas counties in number of farms in 1960. The county was the headquarters for several farm organizations, including the Texas Farm Bureau,qv the Texas Cotton Association, and the Texas Certified Seed Association. Average annual agricultural income reached $29,000,000 in the early 1970's, three-fourths of which was derived from livestock and poultry. McLennan County ranked tenth among Texas counties in value of its manufacturing in 1958. Between 1953 and 1966 the county completed a courthouse, annex building, the Heart o' Texas Coliseum, 180 miles of farm-to-market roads, and the widening of two major highways. Tourist attractions included Lake Waco, Cameron Park, the Heart o' Texas Fair, Mother Neff State Park, and Waco Springs. James Connally Air Force Base,qv which was closed in 1966, was the site of James Connally Technical Institute.qv In 1969 the Texas State Technical Institute qv was established by the state to replace the James Connally Technical Institute. The county supports McLennan Community College, established in 1965, which has grown in size and enrollment. United States governmental agencies in the county in 1970 included the regional office and hospital of the Veterans Administration and an air traffic control facility of the Federal Aviation Administration. The Twelfth Air Force headquarters remained until 1968, when it moved to Bergstrom Air Force Base.qv Watershed projects in the county from 1950 to 1966 included Cow Bayou, Castleman Creek, Hog Creek, and Elm Creek. The 1960 population was 150,091; the 1970 population, according to the United States census, was 147,553. *See also* Waco Standard Metropolitan Statistical Area; Waco, Texas.

*McLeod, Hugh. General Hugh McLeod was the son of Hugh and Isabella (Douglas) McLeod. Late in 1842 he married Rebecca Johnston Lamar, a first cousin of Mirabeau B. Lamar.qv They had a son, Cazeneau McLeod, in 1847, and a daughter, Isabella Douglas McLeod, who died in infancy about 1850.

Hugh McLeod, Jr.

*McLeod, Texas.

*McMahan, Texas.

*McMahan's Chapel.

*McManus, Jane.

*McManus, Robert O. W.

*McMillan Mountains.

McMillin, Alvin Nugent (Bo). Alvin Nugent (Bo) McMillin was born in Prairie Hill, Texas, on January 12, 1895, the son of Ruben Thomas and Matilda (Riley) McMillin. His long football career began at North Side High School in Fort Worth. His team won the state championship during his senior year in 1915. In 1916 McMillin and most of the Fort Worth team followed their coach, Robert L. Myers, to Centre College, Danville, Kentucky, but due to insufficient credits McMillin en-

tered a year later than his teammates. World War I interrupted enough of the 1918 season that players were given an additional year of eligibility. In 1919 McMillin was selected as Walter Camp's All-America quarterback. The 1921 season gave McMillin and Centre College national attention when the college defeated the previously unbeaten (for six years) Harvard University team, with McMillin scoring the winning touchdown.

In 1922, after receiving an A.B. from Centre College, Bo McMillin began his coaching career with Centenary College, Shreveport, Louisiana; in 1925 he was coaching at Geneva College in Pennsylvania. From there he went to Kansas State in 1928 and Indiana University in 1934, where he remained until 1948. He took the Indiana team to its first Big Ten championship in 1945. In 1948 he began coaching professional football with the Detroit Lions. He moved to the Philadelphia Eagles in 1951, but later that same year was forced to retire because of illness.

During his career he was assistant football coach of the Chicago *Tribune* All-Star Football Team in 1936 and head coach in 1938. He was president of the National Football Coaches Association in 1940; president of the American Football Coaches Association and member of their rules committee; voted "Football Man of the Year" for 1945 by the Football Writers Association of America; named "Coach of the Year" by fellow coaches polled by the New York *World Telegram*; and enshrined in the Texas Sports Hall of Fame qv and the College Football Hall of Fame. He was credited with inventing the "Crazy T" and the five-man backfield. McMillin was a Democrat and a Roman Catholic.

Bo McMillin married Maud Marie Miers on January 2, 1922; they had one daughter. After his first wife died in 1926, McMillin married Kathryn Gillihan on October 6, 1930, and they had three sons and one daughter. McMillin died March 31, 1952.

BIBLIOGRAPHY: Flem Hall, *Sports Champions of Fort Worth, Texas 1868–1968* (1968); *Who's Who In America* (1946); Fort Worth *Star-Telegram*, April 1, 1952.

*McMillin, Texas.

*McMullen, John.

*McMullen, John.

*McMullen College.

*McMullen County. McMullen County, primarily a ranching and petroleum area, produced more than thirty-four million barrels of oil between 1919 and January 1, 1973. Livestock accounted for 90 percent of the agricultural income. The county has an archival collection and museum, sponsored by the county historical survey committee, and an annual rodeo. The 1960 population was 1,116; the 1970 population was 1,095, according to the United States census.

*McMullen-McGloin Colony.

*McMurray, DeWitt.

*McMurry College. McMurry College, Abilene, added three dormitories, a student center, classroom building, band hall, library, administration building, and science building to its campus between 1946 and 1966, bringing the total value of the physical plant to more than $10,000,000. Endowment reached $2,500,000 during 1965.

Enrollment figures showed an increase from 610 students in 1946 to 1,361 students in the 1973–1974 regular term; in 1973 the faculty numbered ninety-three members. Its library holdings numbered 81,340 volumes in 1969.

During homecoming each year students erect an authentic reproduction of an American Plains Indian village, don costumes, and demonstrate the original American way of life before thousands of visitors. Thomas K. Kim was president in 1974, when 1,291 students were enrolled.

*McNair, James.

*McNair, Texas. McNair, in Harris County, was an unincorporated town with a population of 1,880 in 1960 and 2,039 in 1970.

*McNamara, Texas.

*McNary, Texas.

McNay, Marion Koogler. Jessie Marion Koogler McNay was born on February 7, 1883, in De-Graff, Ohio, the daughter of Marion A. and Clara (Lippincott) Koogler. At the age of one she moved with her parents to El Dorado, Kansas, where her father was a doctor and surgeon for the Santa Fe Railroad. She attended El Dorado public schools and began sketching and painting at an early age. Entering the University of Kansas in 1900, she studied drawing, and in 1902 she continued her art studies at the Art Institute of Chicago. At the institute she dropped the name Jessie, preferring the name Marion. She continued to study art after her graduation and worked for a brief period of time as a medical illustrator for a surgeon in Chicago.

She married Don Denton McNay on December 9, 1917, in Marion, Ohio, where her father had retired in 1912. Her husband was in the United States Army and was sent to Laredo, where she accompanied him. Transferred to Florida, McNay became ill and died soon after. In the years following his death Marion McNay was married and divorced four times. After the first divorce in 1925 she and her mother resided in San Antonio, where she returned to her art studies. She married Dr. Donald Taylor Atkinson of that city and began the construction of a large Spanish-style home in Sunset Hills on the outskirts of San Antonio. Her family had become wealthy when oil was discovered on their property near El Dorado. She was able to build and decorate the mansion as she chose.

Up to this time Mrs. McNay's art purchases had been few, and the paintings she owned were principally her own works; however, with the completion of her house, she began to collect the works of others. The first oil painting she bought was one by Diego Rivera, then generally unknown to the public, entitled "Delfina Flores." Following this purchase she attended an art exhibition in Chicago

and bought fourteen watercolors. She continued her own art work but spent much of her time accompanying her husband on trips abroad and to Mexico. She also began to take an interest in the art colony in Taos, New Mexico, where she often visited.

In 1936 she was divorced from Dr. Atkinson and again took the name McNay. Two brief marriages followed. She was converted to Catholicism in 1937 and thereafter supported its charities and various of its individual clergy.

The idea for a modern art museum and school of art came to her in 1942. As a result, the San Antonio Art Institute opened in the fall of 1942 in the former aviary in back of the McNay residence. Thereafter her energies were directed toward the furthering of the institute and the building of a collection to enhance the worth of the museum. Her aim was to put together a group of paintings which would exemplify the development of modern art.

Before her death from pneumonia on April 13, 1950, she had largely accomplished this goal. In her will she left her collection of art, her home, and a large perpetual endowment in trust for the museum. It was the largest single public gift in the city's history. On November 4, 1954, the Marion Koogler McNay Art Institute qv was opened to the public.

BIBLIOGRAPHY: Lois Wood Burkhalter, *Marion Koogler McNay: A Biography* (1968).

Elizabeth L. Kaderli

McNay Art Institute. *See* Marion Koogler Mc-Nay Art Institute.

*McNeel, Daniel.

*McNeel, George W.

*McNeel, John.

*McNeel, John Greenville.

*McNeel, Pleasant D.

*McNeel, Sterling.

*McNeil, Texas.

*McNeill, Angus.

*McNelly, Leander H.

*McNutt, Elizabeth.

*McNutt Creek.

Macocoma Indians. The Macocoma (Mecocoma, Ntacocoma) Indians are known only from early eighteenth-century records at San Francisco Solano Mission (near present Eagle Pass) and San Antonio de Valero Mission qqv (at San Antonio). It has been assumed but not fully demonstrated that the mission Macocoma were the same as the Cocoma who lived in northeastern Coahuila and the adjoining part of Texas in 1675. However, in 1693 Cocoma were also reported as living between Durango, Mexico, and present Presidio, Texas, a fact which complicates the status of the Cocoma. It is not certain that these two groups of Cocoma represented the same people. J. R. Swanton evidently considered the Macocoma and Cocoma (Coahuila-

Texas) as the same, since he identified only the Macocoma as a Coahuiltecan band.

BIBLIOGRAPHY: H. E. Bolton, *Texas in the Middle Eighteenth Century* (1915), (ed.), *Spanish Exploration in the Southwest, 1542–1706* (1916); C. W. Hackett (ed.), *Historical Documents Relating to New Mexico, Nueva Vizcaya, and Approaches Thereto, to 1773*, II (1926); F. W. Hodge (ed.), *Handbook of American Indians*, II (1910); J. R. Swanton, *Linguistic Material from the Tribes of Southern Texas and Northeastern Mexico* (1940).

T. N. Campbell

*Macomb, David B.

*Macon, Texas.

*McPherson, Chalmers.

*McQueeney, Texas.

*McRae, Thaddeus.

*Macrod, Texas.

*McShane, Texas.

*McSpaddens Lake.

*Macune, Charles William. [This title was listed as Macune, C. W. in Volume II.] Charles William Macune was born on May 20, 1851, in Kenosha, Wisconsin, son of William and Mary Almira (McAfee) Macune. He came to Texas as a young man and was living in Burnet by 1874. Macune married Sally Vickery on September 1, 1875; they had six children. His early career included the establishment of a newspaper, an unsuccessful hotel venture at Georgetown, and the study of both law and medicine. He practiced medicine at Fredericksburg and Junction.

Macune joined the original State Farmers Alliance (*see* Farmers' Alliance) and soon gained recognition as an advocate and organizer of farmer cooperatives. At a meeting at Cleburne in 1886, he participated in the creation of a new State Farmers Alliance and was appointed chairman of the executive committee and then president pro tem. He helped to form cooperative stores and urged the creation of cooperative compresses and mills and the buying of bagging. He opposed the idea of a third political party and urged support for James Stephen Hogg qv for attorney general and later for governor when Hogg pledged regulation of railroads by a commission in 1890. Macune presided at a convention in Waco in 1887 when the old and new farmers' alliances and the Farmers' Union of Louisiana became the National Farmers Alliance and Cooperative Union of America. Macune was elected the national alliance's first president that year (not in 1886, as stated in Volume II). Under Macune's direction the National Farmers Alliance was devoted to programs of economic self-help through cooperatives and by judicial and legislative action against business practices that hurt farmers. In January, 1889, president Macune and secretary E. B. Weaver established the national headquarters of the National Farmers Alliance at Washington, D.C.; as a leading stockholder and editor, Macune founded the *National Economist*, the official organ of the movement. At the national convention of 1889 at St. Louis, Macune stepped

down as president in favor of Leonidas L. Polk but was immediately elected chairman of both the national executive committee and of the national legislative committee. Macune was a delegate to the January, 1892, convention in St. Louis that founded the Populist party (*see* Populist Party in Texas), but he continued to fight efforts to engage the National Farmers Alliance in political activity. The Populists complained of the lukewarm support being given by the *National Economist*, and in November, 1892, H. L. Louck became president of the alliance, defeating Macune. Foreseeing that the *National Economist* was to become a Populist organ, he resigned as editor and as a member of the national executive committee and returned to Texas. In 1893 he dropped out of the alliance.

After his newspaper venture at Cameron foundered, Macune moved to Beaumont, where he practiced law. When his daughter developed tuberculosis, he took his family to the Davis Mountains. In 1900 Macune was appointed a supply preacher for the Central Methodist Conference, and he preached in small Texas towns and did missionary work among the miners at Thurber. He retired in 1918. Macune then joined his son, a preacher at Eagle Pass, and carried on volunteer medical work among the poor. He continued this work at Del Rio until 1921, when he moved to Fort Worth. He died November 3, 1940, and was buried in Mt. Olivet Cemetery, Fort Worth.

Macune wrote a brief history of the Texas alliance and the subtreasury plan which he proposed at the alliance meeting in St. Louis in December, 1889. The work is preserved in the Eugene C. Barker Texas History Center qv at the University of Texas at Austin.

BIBLIOGRAPHY: C. W. Macune, "The Farmers Alliance" (MS., Archives, University of Texas at Austin Library); Ralph A. Smith, "Macunism," *Journal of Southern History*, XIII (1947); *Dictionary of American Biography*, XI (1960); James C. Malin, "The Farmers' Alliance Subtreasury Plan and European Precedents," *Mississippi Valley Historical Review*, XXXI (1944–1945); John D. Hicks, *The Populist Revolt* (1931); Chester McArthur Destler, *American Radicalism, 1865–1901* (1946).

*Macune, Texas.

*McVeigh School.

*McWilliams, William.

*Madden, Texas.

*Madera Canyon.

*Madera Mountain.

*Madera Springs, Texas.

*Madero, Francisco.

*Madero, Texas.

*Madison County. Madison County, in the Post Oak Belt, has a small mineral production and is 18 percent forested. Farming in the early 1970's included truck crops, dairying, and poultry raising, with 90 percent of the agricultural income coming from beef cattle and other livestock. Tourist attractions include Spanish Bluff and Robbins' Ferry qqv on the Trinity River. A new courthouse was completed in 1970. The 1960 population was 6,749; the 1970 population, according to the United States census, was 7,693.

*Madison County (Judicial).

*Madisonville, Texas. Madisonville, seat of Madison County, is a farm and lumber area market. In 1968 the town had a sawmill, garment factory, bottling plant, and hospital. In 1970 Madisonville reported ninety-five business establishments. The Madisonville Sidewalk Cattlemen's Association holds a convention each June. According to the United States report of the 1970 census, Madisonville had a population of 2,881, an increase from the 2,324 reported in the 1960 census.

*Madras, Texas.

*Maetze, Ernst Gustav.

*Magee, Augustus William.

*Magee Bend.

*Magenta, Texas.

*Magic City, Texas.

*Magill Creek.

*Magnesium Industry in Texas. After 1952 no estimate of Texas magnesium production was reported by the United States Bureau of Mines. The two Dow Chemical Company electrolytic plants at Freeport continued to be a primary source of magnesium in the nation and one of the largest Texas industries. Ample deposits of dolomitic limestone and magnesite, the principal world source of refractory magnesium oxide, also existed in Burnet and other Texas counties.

The two Dow plants, recovering magnesium from sea water, had a combined capacity of 92,000 short tons annually. In addition to magnesium, they produced refractory magnesia, magnesium chloride, caustic-calcined magnesia, and magnesium hydroxide. A smaller Freeport plant produced periclase from magnesium hydroxide.

During the 1960's the recovery of magnesium and the manufacture of magnesium compounds increased in Texas. The Dow plants at Freeport increased their capacity to 100,000 short tons annually through improved processing. By 1964 the American Smelting and Refining Company in Houston was engaged in secondary magnesium production, and in Round Rock the production of dead-burned dolomite had begun. In the early 1970's Texas produced more than half the world's magnesium, most of which was used for weapons and industry.

BIBLIOGRAPHY: *Mineral Facts and Problems* (1965); *Minerals Yearbook* (1964); *Texas Almanac* (1973).

*Magnet, Texas.

*Magnolia, Texas. (Anderson County.)

*Magnolia, Texas. (Eastland County.)

*Magnolia, Texas. (Montague County.)

*Magnolia, Texas. (Montgomery County.)

*Magnolia Beach, Texas.

*Magnolia Hotel.

*Magnolia Park, Texas.

*Magnolia Petroleum Company. The Magnolia Petroleum Company merged with Socony Mobil Oil Company on September 30, 1959. Its operations became part of Mobil Oil Company, which had been formed in March, 1959, as an operating division of Socony Mobil, responsible for all operations, except marine transportation, in the United States and Canada. Magnolia Pipe Line Company was not absorbed into Mobil Oil Company but remained a common carrier affiliate of Socony Mobil.

James A. Clark

*Magnolia Springs, Texas.

*Magoffin, James Wiley. James Wiley Magoffin was appointed a special agent by President James K. Polk to aid S. W. Kearny (not S. W. Kearney, as stated in Volume II) in occupying New Mexico.

*Magoffin, Joseph.

*Magoffinsville, Texas.

*Magruder, John Bankhead.

Maguage Indians. *See* Olive Indians.

*Maha, Texas.

*Mahan, Patrick.

*Mahl, Texas.

*Mahomet, Texas.

*Mahon, Texas.

*Mahoney, Texas.

Mahuame Indians. The Mahuame (Mayhuam) Indians were first recorded in 1674 as living in northeastern Coahuila, but they were also seen near the Rio Grande and probably crossed the river at times to hunt on the Texas side. In 1699 some of the Mahuame entered San Juan Bautista qv Mission near present Eagle Pass. It is possible that the Mahuame were the same as the Merhuan, who were at San Antonio de Valero Mission qv in San Antonio, but there is no proof of this. H. E. Bolton qv once suggested that the Mahuame may have been the same as Cabeza de Vaca's qv Mariame of the Texas coast. This identification has not been accepted.

BIBLIOGRAPHY: C. E. Castañeda, *Our Catholic Heritage in Texas, 1519–1936*, I (1936); F. W. Hodge (ed.), *Handbook of American Indians*, I (1907), II (1910); F. B. Steck, "Forerunners of De Leon's Expedition to Texas," *Southwestern Historical Quarterly*, XXXVI (1932–1933).

T. N. Campbell

Mail Station Bridge. *See* Camp Melvin, Texas.

Mail Station at Pecos. *See* Camp Melvin, Texas.

*Maillard, Nicholas Doran P.

*Mails. *See* Postal System of the Republic of Texas.

*Mainzer Adelsverein. *See* Adelsverein.

Maissin, Eugène. Born in France in 1811, Louis-Eugène Maissin in early youth determined to spend his life at sea; he remained a naval officer throughout his adult life. He is chiefly remembered as the historian of the French expedition to Veracruz, Mexico, in 1838 and of Admiral Charles

Baudin's qv visit to Texas in May, 1839. During this period, Maissin was successively second aide-de-camp to the admiral, his chief of staff, and his first aide-de-camp, the last two offices being combined as one at the time of the visit to Texas. The book he wrote closely mirrors Baudin's interpretation of the events of this expedition. It is in the form of a diary that the writer kept from December 26, 1838, to October 20, 1839; it is especially valuable for some colorful word portraits of the Mexican leaders (including Santa Anna, Mariano Arista,qqv and Guadalupe Victoria) with whom Maissin came into contact. The original French publication was as an appendix to a large illustrated volume by Pharamond Blanchard and Adrien Dauzats, *San Juan de Ulua* (Paris, 1839). Maissin's death occurred in 1851.

BIBLIOGRAPHY: Eugène Maissin (James L. Shepherd, III, trans.), *The French in Mexico and Texas (1838–1839)* (1961).

James L. Shepherd, III

Major, James Patrick. James Patrick Major was born in Fayette, Howard County, Missouri, on May 4, 1836, the son of Samuel Collier Major. He was graduated from the United States Military Academy in the class of 1856, twenty-third in a class of forty-nine.

After some months at the Cavalry School at Carlisle Barracks, Pennsylvania, Major joined the 2nd United States Cavalry in Texas, with the rank of second lieutenant. He served in that command until the outbreak of the Civil War, participating in various forays against hostile Indians and being particularly distinguished in the action at Wichita Village, where he killed three Comanches with his own hands.

Major resigned from the United States Army on March 21, 1861, and was commissioned as a lieutenant in the Confederate Army. He was first aide-de-camp to both Major General David Emanuel Twiggs and Colonel Earl Van Dorn qqv at San Antonio and also acted as dispatch bearer between the Confederate capitals and Texas.

As a lieutenant colonel in the Missouri State Guard, Major participated in the battle of Oak Hills (Wilson's Creek) in August, 1861. In 1862 he was both acting engineer and acting chief of artillery to Major General Van Dorn at Vicksburg, with the rank of lieutenant colonel. He participated in the battle of Corinth in October and was recommended by Van Dorn for promotion to brigadier general.

Transferred to the Trans-Mississippi Department, Major commanded a brigade of Texas cavalry in Major General Richard Taylor's army in 1863 during the operations in lower Louisiana and on the Teche, where Taylor commended his conduct as "above all praise." He was promoted to brigadier general on July 23, 1863.

For a time Major was in command of the defenses at Galveston until the opening of the Red River campaign qv in the spring of 1864. At the battles of Mansfield and Pleasant Hill,qqv as well as in the ensuing pursuit of the Union Army, he commanded a division of cavalry with distinction. For the remainder of the war, Major was in command of a cavalry brigade in Louisiana.

At the conclusion of the war, Major returned to Austin, where he was a planter. On April 23, 1859, he married Eliza Chalmers of Austin, daughter of John G. Chalmers,qv onetime secretary of the treasury of the Republic of Texas, and a younger sister of Thomas Green's qv wife. Mrs. Major died in 1868, leaving one surviving child, a daughter.

Major remained in Austin for an indeterminate time before his marriage in 1871 to Mrs. Emily Schiff of New Orleans. Their only child died in infancy. On May 7, 1877, Major died suddenly while on a trip to Austin. He was buried in Donaldsonville, Louisiana.

BIBLIOGRAPHY: Ezra J. Warner, *Generals in Gray* (1959); U.S. War Department, *The War of the Rebellion: A Compilation of the Official Records of the Union and Confederate Armies* (1880–1901); C. A. Evans, *Confederate Military History* (1899); J. B. Blessington, *Campaigns of Walker's Texas Division* (1875); Richard Taylor, *Destruction and Reconstruction* (1879); Dabney Maury, *Recollections of a Virginian* (1894); *Northern Standard* (Clarksville), April 30, 1859; *Daily Picayune* (New Orleans), May 12, 1877; *Tri Weekly State Gazette* (Austin), September 21, 1868; *Democratic Statesman* (Austin), May 9, 1877; John D. Winter, *Civil War in Louisiana* (1963).

Palmer Bradley

Major, Mabel. Mabel Major, one of the state's leading authorities on Southwestern literature, was born in Ogden, Utah, on September 20, 1894. She was the daughter of David E. and Mollie (Ashcraft) Major. After receiving the B.A. degree from the University of Missouri in 1914 she taught English in Higginsville, Missouri, but she returned to the university for a B.S. in 1916 and an M.A. in 1917, later doing graduate work at the universities of Chicago and California. She first came to Texas to teach high school at Big Spring, but in 1919 she became a member of the English department at Texas Christian University, where she remained until her retirement in 1963.

An effective and stimulating teacher for several generations of students, Mabel Major wrote or edited numerous books on literature and folklore. Among her publications were *Browning and the Florentine Renaissance* (1924) and *British Ballads in Texas* (1932); with Rebecca W. Smith, she edited *The Southwest in Literature* (1929), John C. Duval's qv *Early Times in Texas* (1936) and *The Adventures of Big Foot Wallace* (1936), and William Sylvester Bartlett's *My Foot's in the Stirrup* (1937); with T. M. Pearce, she edited *Signature of the Sun: Southwest Verse, 1900–1950* (1950) and *Southwest Heritage: A Literary History* (1938, rev. 1972). She belonged to many social and literary groups, and upon her death she left $10,000 to a scholarship for students of Southwestern literature at TCU. Mabel Major died in Fort Worth on June 3, 1974, and was buried in Paris, Missouri.

BIBLIOGRAPHY: *Texian Who's Who* (1937); *Dallas Morning News*, June 5, 1974.

*Major Longs Creek.

*Major Peak.

*Majors, Texas.

*Majors Field.

*Makemson, William K.

*Makeup, Texas.

*Malaguita Indians. The Malaguita (under the less accurate title Malaguite Indians in Volume II; also called Malagueco, Maraquita, Marahuiayo, Marhita, and other variants) are known primarily from the eighteenth century. During this period they seem to have ranged widely on both sides of the lower Rio Grande in southern Texas and northern Tamaulipas. This range must have included at least the lower part of present-day Padre Island, since one of its Spanish names was La Isla de los Malaguitas. During the first half of the eighteenth century the Malaguita participated in Indian raids on Spanish settlements of northeastern Nuevo León. In the second half of the same century Malaguita families entered missions distributed over a large area in Texas and northeastern Mexico: Nuestra Señora de la Purísima Concepción de Acuña, San Francisco de la Espada, and San Juan Capistrano at San Antonio; Nuestra Señora del Refugio qqv at present Refugio, Texas; San Agustín de Laredo and San José de Camargo at Camargo, northern Tamaulipas; and San Bernardo and San Juan Bautista qv near modern Guerrero, northeastern Coahuila. It is evident that the Malaguita lost their identity through dispersion and absorption into local mission Indian populations in both Texas and Mexico.

Swanton listed the Malaguita as probable Coahuiltecan-speakers, but some doubt remains about their linguistic status. Attempts to equate the Malaguita with the Maliacone Indians recorded by Cabeza de Vaca qv in the 1530's are not very convincing, although it must be admitted that the two groups seem to have lived in the same general area. Occasionally it is stated that the Malaguita were Apache, but all the available evidence is to the contrary.

BIBLIOGRAPHY: H. E. Bolton, *Guide to Materials for the History of the United States in the Principal Archives of Mexico* (1913) and *Texas in the Middle Eighteenth Century* (1915); C. E. Castañeda, *Our Catholic Heritage in Texas, 1519–1936*, IV (1939); J. A. Dabbs, "The Texas Missions in 1785," *Preliminary Studies of the Texas Catholic Historical Society*, III (1940); J. A. Fernández de Jáuregui Urrutia, *Descripción de Nuevo Reino de León, 1735–1740* (1963); F. W. Hodge (ed.), *Handbook of American Indians*, II (1910); J. R. Swanton, *Linguistic Material from the Tribes of Southern Texas and Northeastern Mexico* (1940); R. S. Weddle, *San Juan Bautista: Gateway to Spanish Texas* (1968).

T. N. Campbell

*Malakoff, Texas. Malakoff, in west-central Henderson County, was incorporated in 1949 and in 1966 reported three schools, five churches, a hospital, a clinic, a bank, and a newspaper. In 1970 there were forty-five businesses, including six light industries. Nearby Cedar Creek Reservoir was completed in 1965 for conservation and recreational purposes. Between 1960 and 1970 the population

increased from 1,657 to 2,045, according to the United States census.

*Malden, Texas.

*Malden Lake.

*Maldonado, Rodrigo.

*Malhado Island.

*Maliacone Indians. The Maliacone (Malican, Malicona, Maticone) Indians were reported by Cabeza de Vaca qv as one of the tribes encountered during his sojourn in Texas (1528–1534). Their precise location cannot be determined, but the available data suggest an area near the lower Nueces River. Attempts have been made to link the Maliacone with various Indian groups reported in later French and Spanish sources, such as the Meracouma and Manico Indians, but these linkages are based on slight phonetic resemblances in the names and are not convincing. The affiliations of the Maliacone remain unknown.

BIBLIOGRAPHY: A. F. Bandelier (ed.), *The Journey of Alvar Nuñez Cabeza de Vaca* (1922); F. W. Hodge (ed.), *Handbook of American Indians*, I (1907), II (1910).

T. N. Campbell

*Mallard, Texas.

*Mallard Creek.

*Mallet, John William.

*Mallet Expedition.

*Mallopeme Indians. *See also* Mayapem Indians.

Malone, Clarence M., Sr. Clarence M. Malone, Sr., was born to William and Julia (McLeod) Malone on August 11, 1885, in San Angelo. He moved with his parents back to their home in Hays County in 1887. At the age of fifteen he was put in charge of a 750-acre farming, ranching, and gin operation. In 1902 Malone began work for the Trinity and Brazos Valley Railway Company as a stake driver. He later went into the operating department of the railroad and in 1905 was named auditor in Houston for the newly organized Houston Belt and Terminal Railway Company.

In 1910 Malone became secretary of the Bankers Trust Company. He remained in that position until 1917, when he and his associates organized the Guardian Trust Company in Houston, of which he later became president. When President Franklin Roosevelt declared a bank holiday, Malone took the lead in refusing to comply with this order, feeling that it was an encroachment on free enterprise.

From 1917 to 1945 Malone developed many of Houston's finest additions, as well as real estate properties in Brownsville and the Rio Grande Valley. He was active in many civic affairs and was a member of the American Bankers Association and the Texas Bankers Association.qv

In 1945 the Guardian Trust Company merged with the Second National Bank and Malone became vice-chairman, continuing in that capacity with the Bank of the Southwest. Impressed with the importance of soil conservation, Malone was well known in the field. In 1949 the Texas Scripps-Howard newspapers called him the "No. 1 Non-Farming Soil Conservation Supporter of Texas," honoring him at their fourth annual "Save the Soil and Save Texas" awards program. He was also the organizer of the Houston Dairy Fund Association in 1916 for which he raised $125,000 to help farmers develop high quality dairy herds and learn the system of testing milk for butterfat. In 1950 Malone organized the Texas Friends of Conservation; in 1958 he received the American Forestry Association's Conservation Award in Tucson, Arizona, for his work in preserving forest resources. In addition to his conservation work, Malone was associated with the United Business Committee of the National Association of Manufacturers.

Malone was first married to Mildred Ward, and they had two children. He later married Alice Bragg, and they also had two children. He died on November 11, 1960, and was buried in Houston.

Gertrude Chambers

Malone, Frederick J. Frederick J. Malone was born in Limestone County, Alabama, on June 12, 1826. He left school at Oxford College, Mississippi, to volunteer for service in the Mexican War. He was promoted to lieutenant and was wounded at Buena Vista. In 1849 he joined the gold rush to California but returned to Mississippi to marry Abbie Humphries in 1850. That same year he moved to Lavaca County, Texas, and to Goliad County as a cattleman in 1861. In 1862 he helped raise troops for the 31st Texas Cavalry and was elected major. He commanded the regiment from the fall of 1863 to the end of the war, leading it at the battle of Stirling's Plantation and during the Red River campaign qv of 1864 in Louisiana. After the war he moved to Rockport in 1869 and to Bee County in 1875, again as a cattleman. He had nine children and was a Methodist and a Democrat. Malone died in 1891 while serving on the county commissioners court.

BIBLIOGRAPHY: Alwyn Barr, *Polignac's Texas Brigade* (1964); Mrs. I. C. Madray, *A History of Bee County* (1939).

Alwyn Barr

*Malone, John.

*Malone, William T.

*Malone, Texas. (Hill County.)

*Malone, Texas. (Hudspeth County.)

*Malone Mountains.

Maloney, James Monte [pseud. Jimmy Joy]. James Monte Maloney was born on April 30, 1902, in Mount Vernon, Texas. He took the name "Joy" during his college days at the University of Texas, where the band he formed to help pay his expenses through school became known as "Jimmy's Joys." In the years that followed his college career, he became widely known as an orchestra leader whose theme song was "Shine on Harvest Moon."

His interest in music began when, as a boy, he listened to Negro rhythms in the small town in which he grew up. He entered the School of Engineering at the Agricultural and Mechanical College of Texas (now Texas A&M University) but soon transferred to the School of Business Administration at the University of Texas. He played in orchestras and bands at both schools and soon formed his own band after his transfer to the University of Texas. While at the university he was elected president of the Longhorn Band and also became its assistant director.

After graduation he turned to band direction in earnest. He subsequently played at state functions such as the Texas Gubernatorial Ball, and his was the official Kentucky Derby Orchestra for three successive seasons. His wife, Sally, and two daughters resided in Dallas, where Jimmy made his headquarters. He took pride in being an honorary Texas Ranger,qv a Kentucky Colonel, and the man who "discovered" the singer Patti Page. He died of cancer on March 7, 1962, in Dallas, Texas.

*Malta, Texas.

Maltby, William Jeff. Most of what is known about William Jeff Maltby is through his partly autobiographical book, *Captain Jeff* (1906), reprinted in 1965 and 1967. Although based on facts, the account cannot be fully verified.

William Jeff Maltby was born in Sangamon County, Illinois, on December 17, 1829. He was married, probably in June, 1858. He was an early settler in Burnet County, and for a time, between his Civil War service and his appointment to the Texas Rangers,qv he was engaged in the cattle business in Burnet, Lampasas, Llano, and San Saba counties. Maltby's military career (he also worked for the army for a time as a civilian) spanned the war with Mexico, the Civil War, and the era of Reconstruction. qv He had a long career as Indian fighter, builder of several forts in Texas, and Texas Ranger. After his retirement to his farm in Callahan County, Maltby also became widely known for his contributions to the improvement of horticultural and agricultural methods in the area. He died on his farm in 1908.

His book is filled with narratives of his experiences with the Indians and with the Texas frontier, and much of what he writes may be a composite of legends, stories, and experiences, his own and others', including his account of his hair-breadth encounters with a Kiowa chieftain named Big Foot.

*Malvado, Texas.

*Malvern, Texas.

*Mambrino, Texas.

*Mamie, Texas.

*Mammoth Creek.

Mamuya Indians. These Indians are known only from a Spanish document of 1693 which lists the Mamuya as one of fifty "nations" that lived north of the Rio Grande "between Texas and New Mexico." This may be interpreted to mean the southern part of western Texas, since the information was obtained at the junction of the Rio Conchos with the Rio Grande (near present Presidio, Texas) and the documentation mentions that the Apache Indians were at war with the groups named.

BIBLIOGRAPHY: W. B. Griffen, *Culture Change and Shifting Populations in Central Northern Mexico* (1969); C. W. Hackett (ed.), *Historical Documents Relating to New Mexico, Nueva Vizcaya, and Approaches Thereto, to 1773*, I (1926).

T. N. Campbell

*Man, William Whitaker.

Mana Indians. The Mana Indians, who are known from a single Spanish document of 1683 (early copyists altered the name to Mano and Chano), cannot be related to any other known group. Their area is not specified but seems to have been somewhere in west-central Texas.

BIBLIOGRAPHY: C. W. Hackett (ed.), *Pichardo's Treatise on the Limits of Louisiana and Texas*, I (1931), II (1934).

T. N. Campbell

*Manadas Creek.

*Manahuilla Creek.

*Manam Indians. The Manam (Manan) Indians are known from a single Spanish encounter in 1690, at which time they were living along the Guadalupe River east and northeast of San Antonio. Here they were closely associated with seven other groups—Apasxam, Cava, Emet, Panasiu, Sana, Tohaha, and Tohoho. Swanton's assessment of the Manam as probably Coahuiltecan in speech is questionable, since their associates do not appear to have been Coahuiltecan. It has also been suggested by Hodge that the Manam were the same people as the Mazame, which is not acceptable because the Mazame are known only from western Coahuila and eastern Chihuahua.

BIBLIOGRAPHY: L. Gómez Canedo, *Primeras exploraciones y poblamiento de Texas, 1686–1694* (1968); F. W. Hodge (ed.), *Handbook of American Indians*, I (1907); P. O. Maas (ed.), *Viajes de misioneros Franciscanos á la conquista del Nuevo México* (1915); J. R. Swanton, *Linguistic Material from the Tribes of Southern Texas and Northeastern Mexico* (1940).

T. N. Campbell

*Manchaca, Texas.

*Manchester, Texas. (Fort Bend County.)

*Manchester, Texas. (Harris County.)

*Manchester, Texas. (Red River County.) Following the appointment of Joseph E. Srygley as postmaster, the town's name was changed from Taylor (name of early settlers in the community) to Manchester on August 11, 1880. It was named for Manchester, Illinois (not New Hampshire, as stated in Volume II), the former home of the Srygleys.

Fannie Belle Srygley

*Manchola, Rafael.

*Manda, Texas. Manda, Travis County, was named for Amanda Gustafson, whose brother, Otto Bengtson (not Bengston, as stated in Volume II), operated the store which contained the post office.

S. P. Engelking

*Manere Mountain.

*Maney, Texas.

*Mangum, Texas.

*Manheim, Texas.

*Manico Indians. In 1690 the Manico (Manicu, Minicau) were reported as encamped with five other bands on the upper branches of the Frio River, probably in present Medina County, west of San Antonio. Baptismal records indicate that some of the Manico were at San Francisco Solano Mission qv in northeastern Coahuila in 1705, and in 1708 unmissionized Manico were living to the east of the missions of northeastern Coahuila, evidently across the Rio Grande in Texas. The available evidence suggests that the range of the Manico was in Texas between the Rio Grande and the southern edge of the Edwards Plateau, or west and southwest of present-day San Antonio. Attempts to link the Manico with other groups that lived farther east, such as the Maliacone of Cabeza de Vaca qv and the Meracoumen of the La Salle Expedition qv chroniclers, are not convincing. Hodge listed Minicau as a variant of Piniquu, which also is doubtful. Nigco, a group name recorded (1730) in the baptismal records of San Antonio de Valero Mission qv of San Antonio, may be a variant of Manico, but the only support for this is phonetic similarity of the names. Swanton thought that the Manico may have spoken a dialect of Coahuiltecan, which is supported by their territorial range and ethnic associates.

BIBLIOGRAPHY: L. Gómez Canedo, *Primeras exploraciones y poblamiento de Texas, 1686–1694* (1968); F. W. Hodge (ed.), *Handbook of American Indians*, I (1907), II (1910); P. O. Maas (ed.), *Viajes de misioneros Franciscanos á la conquista del Nuevo México* (1915); J. R. Swanton, *Linguistic Material from the Tribes of Southern Texas and Northeastern Mexico* (1940).

T. N. Campbell

*Mankins, Texas.

*Manley, John Haywood.

*Manlove, Bartholomew.

*Mann, Charles L.

*Mann, Pamela.

*Mann, Texas. (Reeves County.)

*Mann, Texas. (Tyler County.)

Manned Spacecraft Center. The origins of the Manned Spacecraft Center (MSC), the astronautical complex near Houston, are to be found in the national commitment to a broad program of space exploration, including manned space flight, which the United States made in response to the Soviet Union's successful space launches, begun in 1957.

On October 4, 1957, the U.S.S.R. orbited the first artificial earth satellite, *Sputnik I*. A month later, *Sputnik II*, weighing some 1,100 pounds and carrying a dog, went into orbit. These achievements, followed by the explosion at launch of this country's Vanguard rocket designed to orbit a tiny research satellite, shocked the American public. Nine months of debate over national purposes, capabilities, and shortcomings produced the National Aeronautics and Space Act, signed into law by President Dwight D. Eisenhower qv on July 29,

1958. The act created a new federal agency, the National Aeronautics and Space Administration (NASA). Absorbing the pioneer National Advisory Committee for Aeronautics (NACA), as well as space-allocated funds and several space projects from the Department of Defense, NASA was to be the focus of the nation's efforts in the space age.

The most publicized aspect of NASA's variegated program was the drive to put a manned satellite into orbit around earth. Established in November, 1958, and entitled Project Mercury, the manned satellite undertaking was managed by the Space Task Group, composed of former NACA scientists and engineers, with headquarters at NACA's Langley Aeronautical Laboratory, later renamed Langley Research Center, at Langley Air Force Base, Virginia. Project Mercury, proceeding under the assumption that the U.S.S.R. had man-in-space intentions, organized civilian, military, industrial, and academic resources to send a man into orbit and recover him.

From 1959 through 1961, Project Mercury, training seven military test pilots as "astronauts," continued under the Space Task Group. In May, 1961, after the Soviets launched Yuri Gagarin into a one-orbit flight around earth, and after a Mercury space capsule carried Alan B. Shepard on a suborbital flight downrange from Florida into the Atlantic, President John F. Kennedy set as a national goal the achievement of a manned landing on the moon by the end of the decade.

The extension of NASA's jurisdiction to the moon, and perhaps beyond, meant an enormous expansion of its research and development operations. NASA began to reorganize and increase its space establishments to carry to completion Project Mercury, to carry out Project Gemini (which was to perfect rendezvous and docking techniques essential to NASA's plans for lunar landing and return), and to carry out Project Apollo, the moonflight program itself. Central to the agency's new future was the creation of a manned space development aggregation, including the rocket launch facilities at Cape Canaveral (later Cape Kennedy), Florida; the Marshall Space Flight Center, Huntsville, Alabama; a planned rocket assembly and test plant in southeastern Mississippi on the Pearl River; and a new space management, crew-training, and flight control center at a site to be selected.

NASA formed a site survey team to investigate the qualifications of twenty prospective locations, from Florida to California. The NASA investigators measured each place by definite criteria: proximity of academic institutions with adequate research facilities; availability of water power and other utilities; temperate climate; adequate housing, land, and air and water transportation; and attractive cultural and recreational facilities. On September 19, 1961, Administrator James E. Webb of NASA formally announced that the new Manned Spacecraft Center would be built in southeastern Harris County, Texas, about twenty-five

miles from downtown Houston, at the edge of Clear Lake, an inlet of Galveston Bay. Rice University would transfer a tract of one thousand acres to the federal government for the construction of the center.

Civic leaders and congressmen from other states doubted that Houston and environs met all of NASA's official criteria or at least any more than their towns did. They inquired about the roles of Vice-President Lyndon B. Johnson,qv chairman of the high-level National Aeronautics and Space Council, and Representative Albert Thomas,qv also a Democrat and Texan and chairman of the Independent Offices Subcommittee of the House Appropriations Committee, in the choice of the Houston area. Webb and other NASA officials denied all charges and suggestions of political influence, pointed to Houston's obvious attractiveness in relation to NASA's criteria, and added that the planned expansion of the Cape Canaveral launch facilities, the establishment of the Michoud Plant on the Pearl River, and proximity to the Marshall Space Flight Center in northern Alabama made the choice appropriate. MSC, Michoud, Marshall, and Cape Canaveral would be integrated into a space engineering (development) as opposed to a science (research) enterprise.

The U.S. Army Corps of Engineers then began construction at Clear Lake. The Space Task Group, redesignated the Manned Spacecraft Center, remained in Virginia pending its move into temporary offices in southeastern Houston. Thus it was from the Langley Research Center that John H. Glenn's three-orbit flight in February, 1962, and M. Scott Carpenter's duplicate mission the following May were planned and effected. By the time Walter M. Schirra circumnavigated earth six times in October, 1962, the transfer of about eleven hundred persons and direction of the Mercury, Gemini, and Apollo projects to Houston was essentially complete.

Construction at Clear Lake continued on schedule as Project Mercury ended after L. Gordon Cooper's twenty-two-orbit mission in May, 1963. The following February, a month after the Saturn moon rocket proved itself by orbiting a payload of 37,000 pounds, and less than two months before the initial, unmanned, suborbital launch of a Gemini spacecraft, most MSC personnel moved into their new quarters at the center.

In October, 1966, the MSC had a work force of more than five thousand housed in some fifteen functional structures located on 1,620 acres. Dominating the landscape was the nine-story project management building, where the MSC hierarchy and many of the center's Gemini and Apollo engineering staffs had offices. Nearby were computer buildings, spacecraft environment chambers, and astronaut training facilities, including a large centrifuge. When flight missions are in progress, attention focuses on the Mission Control Center, where, once a spacecraft is launched, mission direction is assumed and maintained until the astronauts successfully enter earth's atmosphere from space.

In preparation for an Apollo spacecraft to carry three astronauts to the surface of the moon, the *Apollo 7* spacecraft was launched from Cape Kennedy, Florida, on October 12, 1968, and completed an eleven-day, three-man, 163-orbit mission. This was a successful test of the three-man spacecraft which was later modified after a fire had killed three astronauts, Roger B. Chaffee, Virgil I. Grissom, and Edward H. White, on the launching pad at Cape Kennedy in January, 1967. Soon after *Apollo 7*'s successful mission, *Apollo 8*, *Apollo 9*, and *Apollo 10* were launched in final preparation for the projected lunar landing. These flights were all successful.

Apollo 8 was launched in December, 1968, with astronauts Frank Borman, William Anders, and James Lovell aboard. This was the first time men saw the hidden side of the moon. The flight was significant in its successful moon orbit and return trip to earth, preparatory to the moon-landing flight. *Apollo 9* was the first mission to take the moon-landing module (LEM) into space. Launched March 3, 1969, the three-man crew, James A. McDivitt, David R. Scott, and Russell L. Schweickart, spent approximately ten days testing docking maneuvers with the LEM that would be used in the moon mission. On May 19, 1969, *Apollo 10*, carrying astronauts Thomas P. Stafford, John Young, and Eugene Cernan, was launched into what NASA officials called a dress rehearsal for the moon landing. Landing sites on the moon were examined, and most of the maneuvers and checks necessary in the moon landing were rehearsed.

The objective of landing a man on the moon within the decade of the 1960's was realized when *Apollo 11* was launched July 16, 1969, with Neil A. Armstrong, Edwin E. Aldrin, Jr., and Michael Collins aboard. On July 20, 1969, Neil Armstrong made his historic walk as the first man on the moon; Edwin E. Aldrin, Jr., was the second. The moon walk received worldwide television coverage; some claimed that one out of every four people on earth witnessed some part of the *Apollo 11* moon flight. The Apollo crew conducted various scientific experiments on the moon's surface and set up several instruments for continual relaying of information back to NASA installations on earth. The astronauts brought back samples of lunar material with them when they returned July 24, 1969. The next flight to the moon, *Apollo 12*, launched November 14, 1969, was similar to the previous mission, with increased experimentation and scientific apparatus taken and more moon rocks returned. Charles Conrad, Jr., Richard F. Gordon, Jr., and Alan L. Bean (a native Texan) were the second United States crew to go to the moon, with Conrad and Bean the third and fourth men to walk on its surface. On April 11, 1970, the *Apollo 13* mission was launched to follow *Apollo 11* and *Apollo 12* in format. However, before the crew, consisting of Fred W. Haise, Jr., James A. Lovell, Jr., and John L. Swigert, Jr., reached the moon's orbit, an overpressurized liquid oxygen tank exploded, blowing a hole in the service module. The explosion knocked out the command ship's life support systems and made the completion of the moon landing mission impossible. With a crippled and potentially dangerous spacecraft, the astronauts returned safely on April 17, 1970. Despite the *Apollo 13* failure, *Apollo 14* was launched on January 31, 1971, with astronauts Alan B. Shepard, Edgar D. Mitchell, the fifth and sixth men to walk on the moon, and Stuart A. Roosa, the third man on the team. This *Apollo 14* flight coincided with the 13th anniversary of America's entry into the space age. On January 31, 1958, a Jupiter C rocket had put the *Explorer I* satellite into orbit. The anniversary was perhaps significant due to the fact that during 1971 the future of the United States program was questioned and threatened by critics. Thousands of people employed by the NASA complex and hundreds of support industries connected with the space program sought reaffirmation of United States space goals.

The Manned Spacecraft Center, which was officially renamed the Lyndon B. Johnson Space Center on August 27, 1973, brought millions of dollars and thousands of people to the upper Texas coast. Housing developments, apartment projects, motels, and shopping centers are located on sites that were previously open prairies. Within twenty years, according to one projection, more than 200,000 people will live around MSC. Within fifty years, according to another estimate, one million people will inhabit the Clear Lake area, with some 7,800,000 people in greater Houston itself. The future of the space industry in Texas and of that prophesied metropolitan area depends on the future commitments of NASA. *See also* Space Industry in Texas.

BIBLIOGRAPHY: Stephen B. Oates, "NASA's Manned Spacecraft Center at Houston, Texas," *Southwestern Historical Quarterly,* LXVII (1963–1964); Loyd S. Swenson, Jr., James M. Grimwood, and Charles C. Alexander, *This New Ocean: A History of Project Mercury* (1966); James M. Grimwood, *Project Mercury: A Chronology* (1963); Loyd S. Swenson, Jr., "The Fertile Crescent: The South's Role in the National Space Program," *Southwestern Historical Quarterly,* LXXI (1967–1968); Houston *Post,* July 16, 1969, January 31, 1971; New York *Times,* October 11, 1968.

Charles C. Alexander

*Manning, Texas.

Mano Indians. The Mano ("hand") Indians are known from a single Spanish document of 1683. Since no native name is given, the Mano cannot be related to other known groups. Their area is not clearly identified but seems to have been somewhere in west-central Texas.

BIBLIOGRAPHY: C. W. Hackett (ed.), *Pichardo's Treatise on the Limits of Louisiana and Texas,* I (1931).

T. N. Campbell

*Manor, Texas.

Manos Coloradas Indians. The Manos Coloradas (Spanish for "red hands") Indians seem to have ranged northeastern Coahuila during the second half of the seventeenth century. The name appears on a list of eighteen groups whose representatives appeared in 1674 at the Spanish settlement of San Ildefonso de Paz on the Río Sabinas. Thereafter nothing more is heard of them until the name appears in the baptismal records of San Antonio de Valero Mission ^{qv} at San Antonio in the middle eighteenth century. Swanton listed them as of probable Coahuiltecan affiliation.

BIBLIOGRAPHY: V. Alessio Robles, *Coahuila y Texas en la Epoca Colonial* (1938); F. W. Hodge (ed.), *Handbook of American Indians*, II (1910); J. J. Figueroa Torres, Fr. *Juan Larios: Defensor de los Indios y fundador de Coahuila, 1673–1676* (1963); J. R. Swanton, *Linguistic Material from the Tribes of Southern Texas and Northeastern Mexico* (1940).

T. N. Campbell

*Manos de Perro Indians.** In the early eighteenth century these coastal Coahuiltecans, whose name is Spanish for "dog feet," ranged over the peninsulas and islands in the vicinity of Aransas Bay. The major islands within their range were St. Joseph's and Mustang, which they seem to have shared with the Piguique. Manos de Perro individuals and families entered the Nuestra Señora del Espíritu Santo de Zuñiga Mission ^{qv} near Goliad, and in 1756 they began to arrive at Nuestra Señora de la Purísima Concepción de Acuña Mission ^{qv} in San Antonio.

BIBLIOGRAPHY: H. E. Bolton, *Texas in the Middle Eighteenth Century* (1915); J. A. Dabbs, "The Texas Missions in 1785," *Preliminary Studies of the Texas Catholic Historical Society*, III (1940); M. A. Habig, *The Alamo Chain of Missions: A History of San Antonio's Five Old Missions* (1968); F. W. Hodge (ed.), *Handbook of American Indians*, I (1907), II (1910); J. R. Swanton, *Linguistic Material from the Tribes of Southern Texas and Northeastern Mexico* (1940).

T. N. Campbell

*Manos Prietas Indians.** In the late seventeenth century this name, Spanish for "dark hands," was applied to a Coahuiltecan group that lived in northeastern Coahuila but ranged across the Rio Grande into Texas south of the Edwards Plateau. In the 1670's some of the Manos Prietas entered Mission Nuestra Señora de la Victoria (Santa Rosa de Nadadores) in Coahuila, and after 1718 a few of these found their way to the San Antonio de Valero Mission ^{qv} at San Antonio.

BIBLIOGRAPHY: V. Alessio Robles, *Coahuila y Texas en la Epoca Colonial* (1938); C. E. Castañeda, *Our Catholic Heritage in Texas, 1519–1936*, I (1936); F. W. Hodge (ed.), *Handbook of American Indians*, I (1907), II (1910); F. B. Steck, "Forerunners of De Leon's Expedition to Texas," *Southwestern Historical Quarterly*, XXXVI (1932–1933); J. R. Swanton, *Linguistic Material from the Tribes of Southern Texas and Northeastern Mexico* (1940).

T. N. Campbell

Manos Sordos Indians. These Indians are known only from a Spanish document of 1693 which lists them as one of fifty "nations" that lived north of the Rio Grande and "between Texas and New Mexico." This may be interpreted to mean the southern part of western Texas, since the document also mentions that the Apache Indians were

at war with the groups named. Nothing further is known about the Manos Sordos ("still hands").

BIBLIOGRAPHY: C. W. Hackett (ed.), *Historical Documents Relating to New Mexico, Nueva Vizcaya, and Approaches Thereto, to 1773*, II (1926).

T. N. Campbell

Mansfield, Jayne. Jayne Mansfield was born Vera Jayne Palmer in Bryn Mawr, Pennsylvania, on April 19, 1933. Her parents were Vera (Jeffrey) and Herbert Palmer. After her father's death in 1938, her mother married Harry L. Peers and the family moved to Dallas. She attended public schools in Dallas and was graduated in 1950. During high school she married Paul Mansfield and they had one daughter. The couple attended Southern Methodist University, the University of Texas (Austin), and the University of California at Los Angeles. Her first film, *Female Jungle*, led to other parts and eventually to the starring role in *Will Success Spoil Rock Hunter?* In March, 1957, she and Mansfield were divorced. On January 13, 1958, she married Niklos (Mickey) Hargitay, a Mr. Universe titleholder (for outstanding physique), and they had two sons. After divorcing Hargitay she married Matt Cimber-Ottaviano in 1964, and they had one daughter. The buxom blonde actress died in an automobile accident on June 29, 1967, near New Orleans, Louisiana. She was director of Jayne Mansfield Productions and lived in New York City. Other films in which Jayne Mansfield appeared were *The Girl Can't Help It, Kiss Them for Me,* and *The Wayward Bus.*

BIBLIOGRAPHY: Dallas *Morning News*, June 30, 1967; New York *Times*, June 30, 1967; *Who's Who In America* (1966).

*Mansfield, Joseph Jefferson.**

*Mansfield, Texas.** Mansfield, in southeastern Tarrant County, reported five churches, a hospital, a bank, a library, and a newspaper in 1966. In 1970 it reported sixty businesses. In progress were improvements on the water and sewer systems. The 1960 population was 1,375; the 1970 United States census listed the population as 3,658. *See also* Fort Worth Standard Metropolitan Statistical Area.

*Mansfield, Battle of.**

*Mansfield Dam.** *See also* Lake Travis.

*Mansion House.**

*Mansker Lake, Texas.**

*Manso Indians.** The Manso (Maise, Mansa, Manse, Manxo) Indians, also known under the alternate name of Gorreta (Gorrite), were first reported in 1598, when they were living along the Rio Grande near present El Paso. It is commonly held that the Manso were the same as the Tanpachoa, reported in the same area in 1583–1584, but this has yet to be conclusively demonstrated. The greater part of the Manso area was in New Mexico north and northwest of El Paso. In 1659 Nuestra Señora de Guadalupe Mission was established for the Manso at present Juárez, Chihuahua. In the seventeenth century the Manso were closely associated with various Apache bands, par-

ticularly those that later became known as Mescalero Apache Indians, and in the eighteenth century
the Manso lost their ethnic identity among these
Apache. A few remnants of the Manso were reported as living in the vicinity of El Paso as late
as 1883. The linguistic affiliation of the Manso is
still being debated. Some writers consider that the
Manso spoke a Uto-Aztecan language; others, possibly swayed by common association of the Manso
with the Apache, think that the Manso spoke Atha-
paskan. It seems likely that both interpretations are
correct, and that the Manso eventually lost their
original language through absorption into southern
Apache bands.

BIBLIOGRAPHY: A. F. Bandelier, *Final Report of Investi-
gations among the Indians of the Southwestern United
States*, III (1890); J. D. Forbes, "Unknown Athapaskans:
The Identification of the Jano, Jocome, Jumano, Manso,
Suma, and Other Indian Tribes of the Southwest," *Ethno-
history*, 6 (1959); A. E. Hughes, *Beginnings of Spanish
Settlement in the El Paso District* (1914); C. Sauer, *The
Distribution of Aboriginal Tribes and Languages in North-
western Mexico* (1934).

T. N. Campbell

*Manson, Texas.

*Mansons Creek.

*Manton, Edward T.

*Manton, Texas.

*Mantua, Texas.

*Mantua Seminary.

Manucy, Dominic. Dominic Manucy was born
December 30, 1823, in St. Augustine, Florida,
son of Pedro and Maria (Lorenzo) Manucy. Hav-
ing completed his theological studies at Spring Hill
College, Mobile, Alabama, he was ordained on
August 15, 1850.

After twenty-four years service in the Mobile
Diocese, Manucy was appointed first vicar apostolic
of Brownsville, a newly created vicariate covering
the territory lying between the Nueces River and
the Rio Grande. Manucy and his cousin Anthony
Pellicer,qv who had been appointed first bishop of
San Antonio, were consecrated as bishops on December 8, 1874. Bishop Manucy was installed in
Brownsville in the Church of the Immaculate Conception by Bishop Claude-Marie Dubuis qv on February 11, 1875.

Respecting the priority of the Oblate Fathers, a
missionary society working in the area since 1852,
Bishop Manucy moved his offices to Corpus Christi,
where he built St. Patrick's Church. By 1884 nine
churches had been built and the construction of
three more was in progress, all debts were paid,
three convents for Sisters had been established, and
the plans for a boys' high school in Corpus Christi
were being completed.

On his transfer to the Diocese of Mobile in
1884 Manucy retained the jurisdiction over
Brownsville as its administrator. Because of illness,
the debt and worries of the Mobile Diocese, and
the distance from Brownsville, he sent in his
resignation and asked to return to Brownsville.
His request was granted in 1885, but before he

could make the move, he died on December 4,
1885. Manucy was buried in a crypt in the Mobile
cathedral.

BIBLIOGRAPHY: Francis Alfred Messing, Dominic
Manucy, Vicar Apostolic of Brownsville, Texas, and Third
Bishop of the Diocese of Mobile, Alabama, 1823–1885
(M.A. thesis, Notre Dame Seminary, New Orleans,
1964); Catholic Archives, Chancery Office, Austin.

Sister M. Claude Lane, O.P.

Manufacturers, Directory of Texas. See *Directory of Texas Manufacturers.*

***Manufacturing Industries in Texas, Growth
of.** The period since the end of World War II
has seen a continuation of the war-stimulated
growth in Texas manufacturing. The first postwar
census of manufactures gave data for 1947, which
showed an increase over 1939 of 93 percent in
production workers and 285 percent in value added
by manufacture. By 1947 the conversion to peacetime activities was generally complete, so the comparison between 1939 and 1947 census figures
reflects the permanent effect of the wartime expansion on Texas manufacturing.

The increase in the value added by manufacture
between 1939 and 1947 was due in part to the rise
in the level of prices. The wholesale price index of
the Bureau of Labor Statistics was 92 percent higher
in 1947 than in 1939, but even after making allow-
ance for this price increase the output of manufacturing plants doubled.

The difference between the percentage increase
in employment and in output represented the rise in
the productivity of labor. Much of the manufacturing capacity added during the war was highly
automated, resulting in increased output per worker.
Both measures of manufacturing activity are significant, since a factory not only turns out products,
but also creates jobs which add to the total income
in the state.

The composition of Texas manufacturing in
1947, as shown by the census of manufactures,
differed substantially from the prewar years. The
greatest relative increase in value added by manufacture was in instruments, primary metals, chemicals, transportation equipment, paper and allied
products, electrical machinery, and fabricated
metals. The largest industry in 1939, petroleum
refining, and the second largest, food processing,
showed substantial growth and retained their respective positions in 1947, although their rates of
growth were substantially below those registered
by the smaller, newer industry groups.

The postwar changes in Texas manufacturing in
general have been a continuation of the trends
established during the war. The most recent detailed
data available for value added by manufacture
covers the year 1967. The greatest rate of growth
between 1947 and 1967 was shown in electrical
machinery, which was forty-one times as large in
1967 as in 1947. This category includes the products that are commonly referred to as the electronics
industry, although no product group with this designation has been set up in the Standard Industrial

Classification. In spite of its spectacular rate of growth, this industry ranked only eighth in size in 1967, but its dynamic increase during the twenty-year period marks it as a strategic industry in the future development of Texas manufacturing. The value added by manufacture compiled by the Bureau of the Census is affected by changes in the level of prices, but during the period 1947 to 1967 the wholesale price index increased only 30.7 percent, so most of the rise in value added by manufacture reflected an increase in the physical volume of output.

The chemical industry, which was the fifth largest in the state in 1939 and third largest in 1947, had advanced to first place in 1967 with value added by manufacture almost nine times the 1947 level. Although the rate of increase in the chemical industry was lower than for electrical machinery, transportation equipment, and primary metals, its size makes the rate of growth it achieved spectacular. Twenty percent of the total increase in value added by manufacture for the entire state was concentrated in the chemical industry.

Food processing dropped from second place in value added by manufacture in 1947 to fourth place in 1967 but continued by a wide margin to employ the largest number of persons of any industry group in the state.

The disparity between the growth in the number of employees and value added by manufacture is the result of the difference in the productivity of labor, which is largely the result of variations in the amount of capital investment required by the industry. In 1967 the petroleum industry produced $75,970 of value added by manufacture per production worker, while the food-processing industry produced $22,941 per production worker. The apparel industry showed the lowest productivity per production worker at $7,198. It ranked third in employment in 1967 but tenth in value added by manufacture. Petroleum and coal products, which in Texas consist almost entirely of petroleum products, showed a value added by manufacture per production worker of $12,000 in 1947 and $75,970 in 1967. The number of production workers in the industry decreased 20 percent during the period while value added by manufacture increased 400 percent. The chemical industry showed almost as high a value added by manufacture per employee as petroleum, $66,348. These two industries in 1967 represented 66 percent of the value added by manufacture in Texas but employed only 11 percent of the production workers.

The major concentrations of manufacturing in Texas are in the northern portion of the state with a narrow strip across the blacklands to San Antonio and in the southeastern part of the state along the Gulf of Mexico. The Beaumont-Port Arthur-Orange, Houston, and Galveston-Texas City standard metropolitan statistical areas qqv reported 42 percent of the total value added by manufacture in the state in 1967. The Dallas and Fort Worth standard metropolitan statistical areas qqv accounted for 28 percent of the total, leaving only 30 percent of the total for the remainder of the state. The standard metropolitan statistical areas not in the two major concentrations accounted for 15 percent of the total, with 15 percent in smaller cities throughout the state.

Individual industries show a considerable degree of geographic concentration. Petrochemicals and refining activity are largely concentrated in the Beaumont-Port Arthur and Houston areas, with smaller concentrations along the Gulf Coast, in the Panhandle, the Permian Basin, El Paso, and East Texas. Apparel plants are concentrated in the Dallas area and to an increasing degree along the Rio Grande and in San Antonio, where a large pool of labor is available. Food-processing plants are scattered throughout the state and are the major representatives of manufacturing industry in the Lower Rio Grande Valley. Aircraft and automobile production is largely concentrated in the Dallas and Fort Worth areas. The aircraft industry came to North Texas during World War II, and the automobile industry is market-oriented. Marine-transportation manufacturing is found along the Gulf Coast, particularly in the Beaumont-Port Arthur-Orange, Galveston-Texas City, and Houston standard metropolitan statistical areas. The leading areas of concentration of the manufacture of electrical machinery and scientific instruments are Dallas, Houston, and Fort Worth. The electronics industry has been gaining a substantial foothold in Austin and promises to show considerable growth there.

The future growth of manufacturing in Texas appears to be dominated by the new industries founded on recent advances in science and engineering. This does not mean that all growth will be concentrated in these industries, for other classifications may be expected to continue to expand with the growth of population in the Southwest. The fastest growth rates, however, are likely to be achieved by these science-oriented industries.

The upward trend in the industries related to the exploration of space was given substantial support by the location of the Manned Spacecraft Center qv in Houston, and future historians may find that the location of this facility in Texas will rank as important to the industrial history of the state as the discovery of oil at Spindletop,qv which ushered in the oil industry at the beginning of the century. The first impact of the Manned Spacecraft Center was felt by industry in the Houston area, but cities all over the state have felt the effects of the attraction this facility has for supporting industries.

The increased support of the leaders in the state for improvements in education from the elementary schools through the graduate schools is an encouraging sign, for the newer industries are influenced in their location by the quality of research and graduate-level teaching in the universities. It is also significant that a strong nucleus of science-oriented manufacturing firms in the state has developed. The firms that have developed instruments, the science of oil exploration, and the manufacture of petrochemicals, aircraft, and electronic devices for civilian and military uses create a strong attraction for other science-oriented concerns. Industries of this type offer the greatest potential for expanding the manufacturing output of the state in the next decade. *See also* Chemical Industries; Food Processing, General; Aircraft Manufacture; Electronics Industry.

John R. Stockton

*Manvel, Texas.

*Manzanet, Damian. *See* Massanet, Damian.

*Maple, Texas.

Mapleton, Texas. Mapleton, in southwestern Houston County, was first known as Stumpville as a result of the number of stumps left after the clearing of the land in 1924 by T. J. Maples, his father, and brothers. In 1950 the Maples family erected a sign naming the community Mapleton. The chief occupations of the inhabitants are farming and ranching.

Mapoch Indians. This name is connected with the Texas area by a Spanish document of 1693 which lists the Mapoch as one of fifty "nations" that lived north of the Rio Grande "between Texas and New Mexico." This may be interpreted to mean the southern part of western Texas, since the name was collected near present Presidio, Texas, and the same document mentions that the Apache were at war with the groups named. Although it cannot be proved, there may be a connection between these Mapoch and the Mapoch recorded at Parras, Coahuila, in 1634–1635. Mapochi also appears as the name of an Indian leader (Galivan or Ocome) in western Coahuila during the second half of the seventeenth century.

BIBLIOGRAPHY: W. B. Griffen, *Culture Change and Shifting Populations in Central Northern Mexico* (1969); C. W. Hackett (ed.), *Historical Documents Relating to New Mexico, Nueva Vizcaya, and Approaches Thereto, to 1773*, II (1926).

T. N. Campbell

*Marak, Texas.

*Marathon, Texas.

*Maravillas Creek.

*Marble Falls, Texas. Marble Falls, in Burnet County, is a stone-processing and trading center. Despite a flood in 1957, recreational and retirement facilities in and around the town were enlarged as tourists and new residents came to the numerous lakes in the vicinity. The population in 1960 was 2,161 and increased only slightly to 2,209 by 1970, according to the United States census.

*Mable Falls Alliance University.

Marble Falls Lake. Max Starcke Dam and Marble Falls Lake are in Burnet and Llano counties near Marble Falls on the Colorado River at the upper reaches of Lake Travis. The project is owned and operated by the Lower Colorado River Authority qv primarily for the purpose of generating hydroelectric power and is one of six Lower Colo-

rado River Authority projects on the Colorado River. Construction of the dam was begun in November, 1949, and was completed in October, 1951; deliberate impoundment of water began in July, 1951. The lake is operated at a nearly constant level as the turbine discharge is correlated with the inflow from Granite Shoals plant. Except during floods, the only water released from Marble Falls Lake to Lake Travis immediately downstream is through the turbines for generation of power. Marble Falls Lake has a capacity of 8,760 acre-feet and a surface area of 780 acres at elevation 738 feet above mean sea level, which is the normal operating level at the top of the gates. The drainage area is 36,325 square miles, of which 11,900 square miles is noncontributing; however, the riverflow is regulated by upstream reservoirs and power plant operation. The power plant at the dam contains two 16,000-kilowatt generating units with auxiliary equipment for connecting to the transmission system.

BIBLIOGRAPHY: Texas Water Commission, *Bulletin 6408* (1964).

Seth D. Breeding

*Marcado Creek.

*Marcelinas Creek.

*Marco, Texas.

*Marcos, Fray. *See* Niza, Fray Marcos de.

*Marcus, Herbert. *See also* Neiman-Marcus Company.

*Marcy, Randolph Barnes.

*Marcy, Texas.

*Marcy Trail. *See* Marcy, Randolph Barnes.

*Marekville, Texas.

*Mares, José.

*Marfa, Texas. Marfa, seat of Presidio County, serves as the commercial and tourist center of the county and nearby areas. The town had several small local industries among its seventy-nine businesses reported in 1970. The 1960 population of 2,799 decreased to 2,647 by 1970, according to the United States census.

*Marfa Army Air Field.

*Margaret, Texas.

*Margaret Houston Female College.

*Margaret Peak.

*Margil de Jesús, Antonio.

Margo Jones Theatre-in-the-Round. *See* Jones, Margaret Virginia (Margo).

*María de Agreda, Madre. *See* Agreda, María de Jesús de.

*Mariame Indians. The Mariame (Marian, Mariane, Mariave) Indians were those with whom Cabeza de Vaca qv lived for a while between 1528 and 1534. Their precise location cannot be determined, but it is generally held that the Mariame lived near but not on the Texas coast, somewhere in the vicinity of Matagorda Bay. Certain features of Mariame culture were briefly described by Cabeza de Vaca. The Mariame have long been equated with the Muruam Indians, who lived at the San Antonio de Valero Mission qv during the eighteenth century but were first recorded in 1707 as living in the vicinity of present Eagle Pass. When one considers the fact that the Mariame were reported some 175 years before the Muruam became known and also that the two groups lived in widely separated areas, the identification of Mariame with Muruam becomes questionable. H. E. Bolton qv once suggested that the Mariame may have been the same as the Mahuame Indians, but the same criticism applies. The Mahuame, who were first recorded in 1674, lived in northeastern Coahuila. It is of interest to note that no one has suggested identification of the Mariame with the Mariguan of southern Tamaulipas. The Mariguan did not live much farther from the Mariame than the Muruam and Mahuame of northeastern Coahuila. The question of Mariame identity is still open.

BIBLIOGRAPHY: A. F. Bandelier (ed.), *The Journey of Alvar Nuñez Cabeza de Vaca* (1922); F. W. Hodge (ed.), *Handbook of American Indians*, I (1907), II (1910); W. Jiménez Moreno, "Tribus e idiomas del Norte de México," *El Norte de México y el Sur de Estados Unidos* (1944); J. R. Swanton, *Linguistic Material from the Tribes of Southern Texas and Northeastern Mexico* (1940).

T. N. Campbell

*Marianna, Texas.

*Mariano Creek.

*Marie, Texas.

*Mariensfield, Texas. *See* Stanton, Texas.

*Marienthal, Texas.

*Marietta, Texas.

*Marilee, Texas.

*Marine Creek.

Marine Military Academy. The Marine Military Academy is located at Harlingen, Texas, in the facilities of the air force navigation school at the deactivated Harlingen Air Force Base (*see* Harlingen Army Air Field). It is a nonprofit educational institution incorporated in April, 1963. The first classes began in September, 1965, at Harlingen.

A college preparatory course of grades nine through twelve was offered within an atmosphere traditional to the Marine Corps. The academy not only stressed a strong academic program, but also the development of character, leadership, patriotism, and *esprit de corps*. The academy, accredited by the Texas Education Agency, qv was the first military academy in the nation to be patterned on the ideals and traditions of the Marine Corps and commissioned as a Marine Corps Junior ROTC unit. Enrollment in the second year of operation was 138 cadets; in 1970 enrollment was 145 students, coming from twenty-seven states and some foreign countries. The faculty and staff consisted primarily of retired and reserve marines. By 1970 the academy offered instruction in grades seven through twelve. Brigadier General Hunter Hurst, USMC (Ret.), assumed the presidency of the school in 1968.

W. A. Gary

Marine-Related Affairs, Texas Council on. The Texas Council on Marine-Related Affairs was created in 1971 as an advisory body to assist in the comprehensive assessment, coordination, and planning of marine-related affairs at all levels. The council is composed of twelve members, and its affairs are administered by an executive director appointed by the council. Members of the council serve for overlapping terms of six years.

BIBLIOGRAPHY: University of Texas at Austin, *Guide To Texas State Agencies* (1972).

*Marine Resources of Texas.
Navigation.

Since completion of the Gulf Intracoastal Waterway qv along the Texas coast in 1948, new channels have been dredged to link the coastwise channel with several cities. Especially important connecting channels reach from Trinity Bay up the deepened Trinity River to Liberty; from Matagorda Bay to Port Lavaca and Red Bluff; from San Antonio Bay to Victoria; from the Gulf to Port Mansfield; and from Laguna Madre up the Arroyo Colorado to Harlingen. By far the most used of these has been the Matagorda Channel to Port Lavaca and Red Bluff. As a result of channel and port improvement and of industrial growth along the coast, traffic on the waterway increased from twenty-nine million tons of cargo in 1956 to fifty-one million tons in 1965.

Recreation and Resort Areas.

Development of coastal resort and recreational areas advanced during the 1950's and 1960's, particularly on Padre Island. In 1963 an eighty-mile length of the island was designated as Padre Island National Seashore qv and placed under jurisdiction of the National Park Service, which planned to preserve the seashore in its natural state, but to make it more accessible to visitors. It was officially dedicated as a national seashore on April 8, 1968. Commercial facilities for tourists have been expanded, especially in the vicinities of Corpus Christi and Port Isabel.

Oil and Natural Gas.

The disappointing record of offshore oil and gas production from areas along the Texas coast has not discouraged exploratory drilling, which, in fact, increased during the mid-1960's. In 1966 sixty-nine offshore wells were completed in Texas, though only one produced oil and one other gas. The fact that the same geological formations that produce oil and gas on the coastal plains continue far out under the waters of the Gulf has sustained the belief that major petroleum deposits remain to be found in the submerged continental shelf.

Oysters and Shell.

During the decade from 1956 to 1966, production of shell from Texas reefs averaged 11,700,000 cubic yards a year, and output was remarkably stable. State figures indicated a record year in 1960–1961 with 12,131,000 cubic yards of shell recovered. During the decade two major cement plants were built at Corpus Christi and near Houston to manufacture shell-based Portland cement.

Conflicts of interest between shell producers and commercial oyster producers and sports fishermen continued to cause controversy. However, surveys of coastal shell resources revealed that large producible reserves still existed, and oyster production increased dramatically. From a low of 69,000 pounds of shelled oysters in 1950, production rose to 5,112,000 pounds in 1966.

Commercial Fisheries.

Texas' coastal fisheries caught a wide variety of finfish and shellfish, but only a few types were significant in value or quantity. The dominant catch, shrimp, totaled sixty million to seventy-five million pounds in the period from 1950 to 1965. Of the thirty-five-million-dollar value of all commercial landings in 1965, shrimp accounted for thirty-one million dollars. The catch of menhaden, used for animal feeds and industrial purposes but not for human consumption, has been erratic in Texas waters. Though menhaden landings exceed shrimp in quantity during good years, the value of menhaden is far less. The sixty-one-million-pound catch of menhaden in 1965 was valued at $1,000,000.

Robert H. Ryan

Marine Science, Institute of. *See* University of Texas Marine Science Institute at Port Aransas.

*Mariner, Charles.

*Marion, Texas. (Angelina County.)

*Marion, Texas. (Brazoria County.)

*Marion, Texas. (Guadalupe County.)

*Marion County. Marion County is among the major recreational areas of the state. Major tourist attractions are the historic buildings in Jefferson, Caddo Lake, and Lake O' the Pines. By 1963 the oil and gas industry had become important, and by January 1, 1973, Marion County had produced 42,123,719 barrels of oil since 1910. The county was 80 percent forested and engaged in limited commercial timbering in the late 1960's. Farm income was derived from truck crops and dairying but primarily from beef cattle and other livestock. The 1960 population was 8,049; the 1970 population was 8,517, according to the United States census.

Marion Koogler McNay Art Institute. The residence of Marion Koogler McNay qv in San Antonio, Texas, was constructed in 1927 by architects Atlee B. Ayres qv and Robert M. Ayres of San Antonio. When Mrs. McNay died in 1950 she willed her home and art collection to become a museum of modern art for San Antonio and Texas. In November, 1954, the museum was opened to the public. It is privately administered by trustees and has no admission charge.

The collection includes major examples of most of the artists who charted the course of twentieth-century painting. Its greatest strength lies in the area of the first generation of the postimpressionists, including Gauguin, Cézanne, Picasso, Rouault, Van Gogh, and Braque. The original collection also includes works of Chagall, Degas, Matisse, Renoir,

and Seurat. In addition to modern French art, there are watercolors by Winslow Homer, John Marin, Childe Hassam, Mary Cassatt, and Maurice Prendergast. In 1955 the museum received the Frederick G. Oppenheimer Collection of medieval and Gothic art. Two galleries of the museum are devoted to the permanent collection of New Mexican arts and crafts. In 1969 additions to the collection included graphics, tapestries, and prints. The Emily Wells Brown Wing, which opened in 1970, added new gallery and auditorium space to the expanding museum.

It is not possible for the entire McNay collection to be exhibited simultaneously, although the major paintings are kept on permanent display. Each month a temporary exhibition allows portions of the collection to be seen, generally in context with outstanding related examples borrowed from public and private owners.

In addition to its program of changing exhibitions, the institute sponsors a series of formal lectures given by outstanding authorities. Informal guided tours are held regularly and special tours are arranged on request. Various art classes are offered on the grounds of the institute, and a large art library supplements the collections. Motion pictures and concerts are also presented. Museum attendance in 1969 was approximately 120,000.

*Mariscal, Texas.

*Mariscal Canyon.

*Mariscal Mountains.

Marjorie, Texas. Marjorie, in southern Milam County, is a switch on the Missouri-Pacific Railroad four miles west of Rockdale. During the 1930's a line of the Rockdale, Sandow, and Southern Railroad Company was built from Marjorie to Sandow, six miles to the south.

BIBLIOGRAPHY: Lelia M. Batte, *History of Milam County, Texas* (1956).

*Markham, Texas.

*Markley, Texas.

*Marley Peaks.

*Marlin, William N. P.

*Marlin, Texas. Marlin, seat of Falls County, had a population increase through the decades up to 1950, after which the population began to decline. Among the businesses listed in the 1960's were light industries which processed poultry, cottonseed, stock feeds, hand-rolled soap, and novelty candles. The town reported 140 business establishments in 1970. Marlin has long been known for its mineral waters and has maintained three large hospitals. The 1960 population was 6,918; the 1970 population, according to the United States census, was 6,351.

*Marlin City Lake.

*Marlow, Texas. (Fort Bend County.)

*Marlow, Texas. (Milam County.)

*Marnels, Texas.

*Marquart, Texas.

*Marquez, Texas.

*Marquis, Robert Lincoln.

*Marriner, Harry Lee.

*Marrs, Starlin Marion Newberry.

*Mars, Texas.

*Marsh, Frank Burr.

*Marsh, Shubael.

Marsh, William John. William John Marsh, son of James and Mary Cecilia (McCormick) Marsh, was born June 24, 1880, in Woolton, Liverpool, England. Marsh attended Ampleforth College in Yorkshire, England, and he studied harmony, composition, and organ. He came to Texas in 1904 and became a naturalized citizen in 1917. He was professor of organ, composition, and theory at Texas Christian University, and he was a choir director and organist.

During his career as composer, teacher, and performer, Marsh published over one hundred works, mainly classical and sacred music. He composed "O Night Divine," a Christmas song; "The Flower Fair at Peking," a one-act Chinese opera, reputedly the first opera to be composed and produced in the state of Texas; the official Mass for the Texas Centennial;qv and the state song, "Texas, Our Texas," which John Philip Sousa once described as the finest state song he had ever heard. Marsh also composed numerous pageants, masses, anthems, and cantatas.

In 1921 and 1922 Marsh won first prize in San Antonio for the best song by a Texas composer; he won double first prizes in Dallas in 1929 for vocal and piano and won the Texas Federation choral prize in that same year. He died February 1, 1971, in Fort Worth.
BIBLIOGRAPHY: Lota M. Spell, *Music In Texas* (1936); *Who's Who In America* (1946); *Daily Texan*, February 2, 1971.

*Marsh, Texas. (Dallas County.)

*Marsh, Texas. (Potter County.)

*Marshall, John F. According to an article announcing his marriage in the newspaper which he edited, *The Mississippian*, John Marshall's middle initial was F. (not shown in Volume II), and he was married to Ann (not Anne) P. Newman of Jefferson, Mississippi, on September 16, 1850, in Shelbyville, Mississippi.
BIBLIOGRAPHY: *The Mississippian* (Jackson, Mississippi), September 20, 1850.

Lucie C. Price

*Marshall, Texas. Marshall, seat of Harrison County, had a 1960 population of 23,846 and a 1970 population of 22,937, according to the United States report of the census. Marshall had thirty-eight churches, two hospitals, two banks, four city parks, and a public library in 1963. In 1970 the city reported 445 businesses, including approximately forty manufacturers that produced chemical, iron, steel, clay, wood, clothing, and dairy products. A large tile plant was constructed in 1964, and there was a manufacturer of solid propellant rocket engine fuel. Among the educational institutions were twelve public and parochial schools and three colleges. Marshall was the site of the central East Texas fair. On February 9, 1972, the Western Union telegraph office at Marshall, the first telegraph office in Texas (since February 14, 1854) was closed.

*Marshall Conferences.

*Marshall Creek.

*Marshall and East Texas Railway Company.

*Marshall Ford, Texas.

*Marshall *Review*.

*Marshall, Timpson, and Sabine Pass Railroad Company.

*Marshall University.

*Marston, Texas. (Palo Pinto County.)

*Marston, Texas. (Polk County.)

*Mart, Texas. Mart, in McLennan County, had a 1960 population of 2,197 and a 1970 population of 2,183, according to the United States report of the census. In 1966 the city reported eleven churches, two banks, and two city-owned lakes. In 1970 there were fifty-five businesses. Located in an area of diversified agriculture, Mart's economy is based on cotton, grains, cattle, and a company manufacturing clothing. *See also* Waco Standard Metropolitan Statistical Area.

*Martha, Texas.

*Martha's Chapel, Texas.

Martin, Albert. Albert Martin, a native of Tennessee, was a resident of Gonzales in 1835 and participated in the battle of Gonzales.qv Martin was also a participant during the siege of the Alamo, acting as an emissary and messenger for William B. Travis.qv On February 24, 1836, Travis sent Martin from the Alamo to Gonzales to recruit reinforcements with a message "To the People of Texas and All Americans in the World." Martin hastily assembled recruits there, while others carried the plea to the surrounding settlements. George C. Kimbell, John William Smith,qqv and Martin made their way through the Mexican lines in the early morning hours of March 1; the safe arrival of the thirty-two men from Gonzales was the cause for great celebration in the Alamo. Martin was about thirty years old when he died in the Alamo massacre on March 6, 1836.
BIBLIOGRAPHY: Walter Lord, *A Time to Stand* (1961); Amelia Williams, "A Critical Study of the Siege of the Alamo and of the Personnel of Its Defenders," *Southwestern Historical Quarterly*, XXXVII (1933–1934).

Martin, Clarence White. Clarence White Martin, son of William Washington and Mary Elizabeth (Routh) Martin, was born in San Marcos on November 26, 1868. He grew up in Blanco and surrounding counties, where his father was an attorney. After finishing high school, he worked for several years on his uncle's ranches near Midland and Colorado City. He returned home and in 1891 was appointed justice of the peace of Precinct No.

1 of Blanco County. In 1892 he married Frank Barnett Johnson, daughter of Samuel Ealy Johnson qv and aunt of President Lyndon B. Johnson.qv They had one son. After his marriage Martin studied law in his father's office.

In 1893 he was elected to the Twenty-third Legislature to represent the Ninety-eighth District. He resigned in 1894 and moved to Kerrville, where he and his father established a law office.

Martin moved to Fredericksburg in 1896 and in 1902 was elected judge of the Thirty-third Judicial District, which included Blanco County. He was reelected for three additional terms of four years. During his first term of office as district judge he participated in the statewide campaign to save the Alamo. He collected public contributions, then helped to persuade the state legislature to appropriate the remainder of the purchase price. Martin appealed for funds in the towns of his judicial district, at state meetings of various organizations, and over a wide area of the state. He was said to have been responsible for half of the total amount of $20,000 that was collected. Martin's letters to Adina De Zavala qv show that both of them drafted bills for the purchase of the Alamo. At the request of Miss De Zavala he went to Austin to guide the Alamo Purchase Bill through the Twenty-ninth Legislature. It was passed by an overwhelming majority.

Martin resigned from office in 1915 and resumed the private practice of law. For a time he lived in Austin and was a partner of C. C. McDonald, former attorney general. In 1917 he became the chief defense attorney for Governor James E. Ferguson qv in the latter's impeachment trial before the Texas Senate. During the last years of his life he owned and operated a farm and ranch in Gillespie County near Stonewall. This property was traded by his widow to Lyndon B. Johnson and is now the LBJ Ranch (see Lyndon Baines Johnson Birthplace, Boyhood Home, and Ranch). Martin died in Fredericksburg on August 31, 1936, and was buried in the Johnson family cemetery near Stonewall.

BIBLIOGRAPHY: Rebekah Baines Johnson (J. S. Moursund, ed.), *A Family Album* (1965); James T. DeShields, *The Fergusons* (1932); Letters of Judge Clarence Martin, Adina De Zavala Papers (MS., Incarnate Word College Library, San Antonio).

Sister Francis Xavier Brannen

Martin, Crawford Collins. Crawford Collins Martin, the son of William Marvin and Daisy (Beavers) Martin, was born in Hillsboro, Hill County, on March 13, 1916. He attended public schools and Hill Junior College before enrolling in the University of Texas School of Law, finishing his law degree at Cumberland University in Lebanon, Tennessee. Martin practiced law in Hillsboro after being admitted to the Bar in 1939; he served in the U.S. Coast Guard in World War II. He was elected mayor of Hillsboro in 1947, and in 1948 he was elected to the Texas Senate (a position his

father once held), successfully holding that seat for fourteen years.

Crawford Martin was appointed secretary of state by Governor John Connally in 1963. In 1966 he was elected to the first of three terms as attorney general; he became well known for his reorganization and modernization of that office. Divisions of antitrust, consumer protection, crime prevention, and water control were added to the official duties of the attorney general by Martin, who made drug abuse and organized crime his principal targets. He was the first attorney general of any state to file suit against drug companies for fixing prices of antibiotics, successfully recovering over four million dollars for Texas consumers. His office was involved in litigation to finally establish the Sabine River boundary between Texas and Louisiana (see Boundaries of Texas).

Crawford Martin was married to Margaret Ann Mash on May 14, 1941. They were the parents of a son and two daughters. Martin died in Austin on the last business day of his third term of office, December 29, 1972, and was buried in the State Cemetery.qv

BIBLIOGRAPHY: *Texas Parade*, XXVII (January, 1967), XXIX (January, 1969), XXXI (January, 1971); Biographical File, Barker Texas History Center, University of Texas at Austin.

*Martín, Hernán.

Martin, Louis. Louis (Ludwig) Martin, born November 25, 1820, in Erndtebrück, Prussia, was the son of Nicholas and Hedwig (Sinner) Martin. According to ship lists, he arrived in Port Lavaca on the *Johann Dethardt* in 1844 and was in New Braunfels in 1845. He married Elisabet Arhelger, daughter of Johann Jacob and Elisabet (Mueller) Arhelger of Rittershausen, Nassau, Germany, who had immigrated to Texas in 1845. They had eight children. He signed the petition of December 15, 1847, asking the Texas legislature for the creation of a new county and was elected sheriff in the first Gillespie County election, June, 1848. He became the county's first district clerk in 1850.

In 1853 Martin moved with his family to Willow Creek, a tributary of the Llano River, and named the settlement Hedwig's Hill for his mother and daughter. He was postmaster there in 1858 and often provided lodging to travelers passing through. He was one of the Mason Minute Men who organized in 1861 to protect the frontier against Indians. He was also on the 1864 muster roll of Mason's Company No. 1 for local defense.

As a trader and freighter, he transported and sold cotton on the Mexican border for English gold during the Civil War. Near the Nueces River in June, 1864, his wagon train was waylaid; he and his second-in-command, Eugene Frantzen, were hanged by Confederate sympathizers. His widow and her brother, William Arhelger, went by wagon from Mason County and brought the two bodies to Fredericksburg, where they were buried in a common grave.

BIBLIOGRAPHY: Rudolph Leopold Biesele, *The History of*

the German Settlements in Texas, 1831–1861 (1930); Chester William Geue and Ethel Hander Geue, *A New Land Beckoned* (1966); Stella Gipson Polk, *Mason and Mason County: A History* (1966); Robert Penniger, *Fest-Ausgabe zum 50-jährigen Jubiläum der Gründung der Stadt Friedrichsburg* (1896); Gillespie County Historical Society, *Pioneers in God's Hills* (1960); *Mason County News* (Centennial Issue, 1958).

Esther L. Mueller

*Martin, (Francis) Marion.

*Martin, William Harrison.

Martin, William Patrick. William Patrick Martin was born on July 9, 1891, in Fisher County, Texas, the son of J. P. and Josephine (Lynde) Martin. He received a B.S. degree in agronomy from Texas Agricultural and Mechanical College (now Texas A&M University) in 1915. On October 14, 1917, he married Iris Sikes, and they had two sons. Iris Martin died in 1922, and on April 17, 1928, Martin married Annie Blevins in Dallas. In 1936 he began developing the now famous Martin Combine Milo Maize, which was first offered to the public in the spring of 1941. Martin was selected as Top West Texan in 1943. He died on November 26, 1965, and was buried in Resthaven Mausoleum in Lubbock.

BIBLIOGRAPHY: Seymour V. Connor (ed.), *Builders of the Southwest* (1959).

Roy Sylvan Dunn

*Martin, Wylie.

*Martin County. Martin County has an economy based on cotton, grains, and livestock, primarily cattle and sheep. Between 1945 and January 1, 1973, nearly sixty million barrels of oil were produced. Truck farming was increasing with the development of irrigation. The county population was 5,068 in 1960; the 1970 population was 4,774, according to the United States census.

*Martin Creek.

*Martin Springs, Texas.

*Martindale, Texas.

*Martínez, Antonio María.

*Martínez, Francisco.

*Martinez, Texas.

*Martinez Creek.

*Martins Creek.

*Martin's Creek, Texas.

*Martins Mills, Texas.

*Martinsville, Texas.

*Martos y Navarrete, Angel de.

*Marvel Wells, Texas.

*Marvin, Enoch Mather.

*Marvin, Texas. (Lamar County.)

*Marvin, Texas. (Robertson County.)

*Marvin College.

Marvin Hunter Historical Museum. *See* Frontier Times Museum.

*Mary, Texas.

*Mary Allen Junior College. Mary Allen Junior College, Crockett, under the sponsorship of the Presbyterian church until 1943, was reestablished by the General Missionary Baptist Convention of Texas after 1944. G. L. Prince, the first president to serve under the administration of the Baptists, guided the institution through the period from 1941 through 1953, during which time the physical plant was expanded; in 1966 the plant included eleven buildings. The school offered Associate in Arts and Bachelor of Theology degrees. Courses were offered in elementary education, business administration, secretarial science, and religion. In 1969 the faculty numbered fourteen, and the enrollment for the fall, 1969, term was eighty-one students; Ira L. Clark was president. The school was officially closed in September, 1972.

*Mary Hardin-Baylor College. Mary Hardin-Baylor College had a predominately female enrollment of 711 and a faculty of sixty-two during the regular term of 1968–1969; the fall, 1974, enrollment was 902. From 1954 to 1966 four buildings were added, and in 1968 the Townsend Memorial Library holdings totaled 60,484 volumes. The college offered bachelor's degrees in science, arts, and musical education. William G. Tanner succeeded Leonard L. Holloway as president in 1968. In 1974 Bobby E. Parker was president.

Mary Immaculate College. *See* Christopher College of Corpus Christi.

*Mary Nash College.

*Maryetta, Texas.

*Maryneal, Texas.

*Marys Bayou.

*Marys Creek.

*Marystown, Texas.

*Marysville, Texas.

Masacuajulam Indians. In the middle eighteenth century the Masacuajulam (Imasacuajulam) Indians lived along the lower Rio Grande somewhere between present Zapata, Texas, and the mouth of the river. The maps of Jiménez Moreno and Saldivar show this group on the north bank of the Rio Grande in present Zapata County, but the known documents do not permit such a precise placement. The name is said to mean "those who travel alone."

BIBLIOGRAPHY: W. Jiménez Moreno, "Tribus e idiomas del Norte de México," *El Norte de México y el Sur de Estados Unidos* (1944); G. Saldivar, *Los Indios de Tamaulipas* (1943).

T. N. Campbell

*Mashed O Ranch.

*Mason, Charles.

*Mason, John Thomson.

*Mason, Texas. Mason, seat of Mason County, is a commercial center for the livestock-raising area and a headquarters for hunters. The town has wool and mohair warehouses and livestock auctions. In 1966 Mason reported nine churches, a hospital, a library, and a newspaper; in 1970 it reported eighty-eight business establishments. The site of Fort Mason qv is near the town. The 1960 population was 1,910; the 1970 population was 1,806, according to the United States census.

*Mason County. Major enterprises in Mason County include ranching, hunting, and tourism. Cattle, sheep, goats, and hogs provided 75 percent of the county's income in 1973; the crop income was largely from peanuts. Tourist attractions include Fort Mason Museum (*see* Fort Mason) and deer and turkey hunting. In 1960 Camp Gene Ashby was built for the purpose of giving the orphans of Texas a place to hunt; local ranchers furnished the land, transportation, and rifles for the orphans. The county celebrated its centennial in June, 1958. The 1960 county population of 3,780 decreased to 3,356 by 1970, according to the United States census.

***Mason County War.** Five men were hanged near Hick Springs (not Hicks Springs, as stated in Volume II).

Margaret Bierschwale

***Mason Creek.**

***Masonic Collegiate Institute.**

***Masonic Female Institute.**

***Masonic Institute of San Augustine.**

***Masonic Order in Texas.** *See* Freemasonry in Texas.

***Masons Creek.**

Mass Transportation Commission, Texas. The Texas Mass Transportation Commission, composed of six members appointed by the governor, was created in 1969 to assist in the development of public mass transportation, including mass transit systems and other modes of modern transportation. It recommends legislation and represents the state before federal and state agencies.

BIBLIOGRAPHY: University of Texas at Austin, *Guide To Texas State Agencies* (1972).

***Massanet, Damian.**

***Massey, Texas.**

***Massey Lake, Texas.**

***Masters, Texas.**

***Masterson, Thomas G.**

***Masterson, Texas.**

***Mastersville, Texas.**

***Matador, Texas.** Matador, seat of Motley County, is the commercial center for the Matador Ranch qv and for cattle, quarter horses, and farm produce. The town had two hospitals, seven churches, a bank, and a weekly newspaper in 1966, along with recreational facilities at Jameson Lake and Virginia Walton Park. In 1970 the town reported thirty businesses. The 1960 population was 1,217; the 1970 population was 1,091, according to the United States census.

***Matador Land and Cattle Company, Limited.** In 1951 Lazard Brothers and Company, acting on behalf of itself and a number of American corporations, purchased the stock of the Matador Company for $23.70 per share. The property acquired by the new stockholders included approximately 400,000 acres at the Matador Division, 395,000 acres at Alamositas, a herd of 1,400 horses, and 46,000 head of cattle. The land and livestock were divided among the various corporations. In the main the Alamositas Division was divided among relatively few persons and organizations whose interests centered on ranching. The original ranch, the Matador Division, was sold by its owning corporations to individuals or groups of individuals who in turn engaged in cattle-raising and farming activities.

BIBLIOGRAPHY: W. M. Pearce, *The Matador Land and Cattle Company* (1964).

W. M. Pearce

***Matador Ranch.** *See also* Matador Land and Cattle Company, Limited.

***Matagorda, Texas.**

***Matagorda Bay.**

***Matagorda *Bulletin*.**

***Matagorda County.** Matagorda County is a leading cattle- and rice-producing area; cotton, grain sorghums, and corn are other leading crops. In the early 1970's farm income averaged $21,000,000 annually, three-fourths from rice, cotton, and other crops. Between 1904 and January 1, 1973, total crude oil production had reached 205,586,629 barrels in the county. Gas, shell, clay, sand, and gravel were also important mineral resources. Major tourist attractions included fishing and water sports, an October rice festival, and a March fair. The 1960 population was 25,744; the 1970 population increased to 27,913, according to the United States census.

***Matagorda Island.**

***Matagorda Peninsula.**

***Matamoros Expeditions.**

***Matamoros Prisoners.**

***Matate Creek.**

***Mather, William Tyler.**

Mathews, Edward Jackson. Edward Jackson Mathews was born on October 21, 1878, at Clopton, Alabama, but at an early age came to Waller County, Texas, with his parents, I. P. and Martha (Wall) Mathews. His formal education began in a country school and continued through Hempstead High School, from which he graduated in 1896. He taught in the public schools for six years, acting as superintendent of Salado schools his last year. Following a period as an employee of a business concern at Waco, he entered the University of Texas in 1907; he received his B.A. degree in 1910 and his M.A. degree in 1918. During his first student year he became an assistant to the registrar; from 1909 to 1911 he was secretary to the president. Beginning in 1911 he served both as registrar and secretary of the board of regents. In 1914 he was made assistant dean of the College of Arts. He carried the three major responsibilities for about ten years, interrupted by military service during World War I. Mathews gave up his other positions and in 1935 assumed the position of registrar and dean of admissions. Having reached the age for retirement in 1949, he received the title Dean of Admissions, Emeritus, and continued in modified service until 1959, when he was fully retired.

Mathews' contribution to educational administration outside the university was noteworthy. In 1916 he aided the organization of the Association of Texas Colleges (later the Association of Texas Colleges and Universities qv), twice serving as president of the association. He was twice president of the Texas Association of Collegiate Registrars and Admission Officers, and in 1926 he served as president of the American Association of Collegiate Registrars and as president of the Southern Association of Colleges and Secondary Schools. He was a member of the Commission on Secondary Schools of the Southern Association for many years and in 1929 served as its chairman. For a number of years he was a special consultant of the Monterrey (Mexico) Institute of Technology. In 1934 Mathews received an honorary Doctor of Laws degree from Southwestern University. In 1948 at the celebration of its golden jubilee, Our Lady of the Lake College of San Antonio gave him a citation recognizing his service to education and his assistance to the college in its formative years. In 1956 the Monterrey Institute of Technology presented the University of Texas an oil portrait in recognition of his services.

Mathews married Ravenna Wakefield, and they had three children. He died on May 31, 1964, in Austin and was buried in Austin Memorial Park.

Herschel T. Manuel

*Mathews, J. F.

*Mathis, Texas. In contrast to its rapid rise in population during the 1950's, Mathis, in coastal San Patricio County, had a population decrease in the 1960's, from 6,075 in 1960 to 5,351 in 1970, according to the United States census. Calling itself the "Caliche Capital of Texas" because of its processing of road-building materials, Mathis also included the manufacture of oil field equipment, fertilizer, and ready-mix concrete among the 106 businesses reported in 1970. *See also* Corpus Christi Standard Metropolitan Statistical Area.

*Matinburg, Texas.

*Matlock, Avery L.

*Matthes, Benno.

Matthews, John Alexander. John Alexander Matthews was born in Spearsville, Union Parish, Louisiana, on March 2, 1853, the son of Joseph Beck and Caroline (Spears) Matthews. While he was still an infant, the family moved to Freestone County, Texas. Before the end of the Civil War they were living in Palo Pinto, then called Golconda, and soon thereafter the family settled permanently near Fort Griffin.qv He married Sallie

Ann Reynolds (*see* Matthews, Sallie Reynolds) on December 25, 1876. They had nine children.

He was engaged in cattle raising throughout his life. In 1872 he was in charge of driving a herd of cattle from southeastern Colorado to the Humboldt River in Nevada. In 1880 he entered a ranching partnership with George Thomas and William D. Reynolds,qqv which was dissolved by mutual consent in 1885. With his part of the division he then established the ranch which, with some additions, became known as the J. A. Matthews Ranch Company, with Lambshead Ranch as its headquarters. He joined the Northwest Texas Cattle Raisers Association in 1877, the year it was organized (now the Texas and Southwestern Cattle Raisers' Association qv). He was county judge of Shackelford County in 1895–1896. He was a member of the Presbyterian church and a founder of Reynolds Presbyterian Academy (*see* Reynolds Presbyterian College) in Albany, Texas. He died in Albany on April 25, 1941, and was buried in that town.

BIBLIOGRAPHY: Sallie Reynolds Matthews, *Interwoven: A Pioneer Chronicle* (1936).

Robert Nail

*Matthews, Mansell W.

Matthews, Sallie Reynolds. Sallie Ann Reynolds was born at the Cantrell Ranch in Buchanan County (now Stephens County), Texas, on May 23, 1861, the daughter of Barber Watkins and Anne Marie (Campbell) Reynolds. She married John Alexander Matthews qv on December 25, 1876; they had nine children. Mrs. Matthews wrote an autobiographical account of life on the Texas frontier entitled *Interwoven: A Pioneer Chronicle*, which was published in 1936. The book served as a reference on life and customs of the pioneer period of West Texas, and it was used as the basis of the original script for the Fort Griffin Fandangle.qv Mrs. Matthews died on September 14, 1938, in Albany, Texas, and was buried in that city.

Robert Nail

*Matthews, William.

*Matthews, Texas.

*Matthews Branch.

*Mattson, Texas.

Matucar Indians. This name is known only from baptismal records at the San Antonio de Valero Mission qv of San Antonio. J. R. Swanton listed the Matucar as Coahuiltecan, but he presented no evidence in support of this linguistic identification. Although there is as yet no proof, it is possible that Matucar is a variant of Matucapam, the name of a group of Indians who lived in central Tamaulipas during the eighteenth century.

BIBLIOGRAPHY: F. W. Hodge (ed.), *Handbook of American Indians*, II (1910); W. Jiménez Moreno, "Tribus e idiomas del Norte de México," *El Norte de México y el Sur de Estados Unidos* (1944); J. R. Swanton, *Linguistic Material from the Tribes of Southern Texas and Northeastern Mexico* (1940).

T. N. Campbell

*Maud, Texas. Maud, in Bowie County, had a 1960 population of 951 and a 1970 population of

1,107, according to the United States census. Maud reported eighteen businesses in 1970.

*Maudlowe, Texas.

*Mauriceville, Texas.

*Maurin, Texas.

*Maverick, Mary Adams.

Maverick, Maury. Fontaine Maury Maverick, son of Albert and Jane Lewis (Maury) Maverick and grandson of Samuel Augustus Maverick,qv was born in San Antonio, Texas, on October 23, 1895. He was educated in the public schools of San Antonio, Virginia Military Institute, the University of Texas in Austin, and the University of Texas School of Law. In World War I Maverick was a first lieutenant in the 28th Infantry, 1st Division; he received the Silver Star and other decorations in the Argonne offensive, an engagement in which he was twice critically wounded. He married Terrell Louise Dobbs (who after his death married Walter Prescott Webb qv) on May 22, 1920, and they had two children.

He served as tax collector of Bexar County (1930–1934), congressman from the Twentieth District (1935–1938), mayor of San Antonio (1939–1941), and member of the War Production Board and chairman of the Smaller War Plants Corporation (1941–1946). As a New Deal congressman he attracted national attention as the organizer of a group of "maverick" congressmen who tried to "out-New Deal" the New Deal. He was influential in the passage of the Patman Bonus Bill, neutrality legislation, a measure strengthening TVA, the Public Utilities Holding Company Act, legislation establishing the National Cancer Institute, and in the defeat of bills which threatened civil liberties. As mayor of San Antonio, Maverick was generally credited with bringing reform to the Alamo city with an honest and efficient administration. He was most proud of his leadership in the restoration of La Villita,qv a Spanish village in the heart of San Antonio.

In World War II Maverick gained a reputation as an able administrator and a champion of small business as chairman of the Smaller War Plants Corporation. As a lawyer, Maverick gained fame as a defender of civil liberties. He was the author of A Maverick American (1937), In Blood and Ink: The Life and Documents of American Democracy (1939), and numerous articles on public affairs. He died in San Antonio on June 7, 1954.

BIBLIOGRAPHY: Robert C. Brooks, "One of the Four Hundred and Thirty-Five: Maury Maverick, of Texas," in J. T. Salter (ed.), The American Politician (1938); Bruce Catton, The War Lords of Washington (1948); Richard B. Henderson, Maury Maverick: A Political Biography (1970); Maury Maverick, A Maverick American (1937); Anna Rothe (ed.), Current Biography (1944).

Richard B. Henderson

*Maverick, Samuel Augustus.

*Maverick, Texas.

*Maverick County. Maverick County is predominantly a ranching area with an increasing amount of irrigated farming. From 1929 to 1963 over 3,500,000 barrels of oil were produced, and by January 1, 1973, total crude production had reached 13,557,765 barrels. Major business concerns included two clothing manufacturers, two ore-grinding companies, and government projects, particularly the international bridge at Eagle Pass. Maverick County is also a popular tourist trade center, offering visitors access to markets at Piedras Negras, Mexico, and providing attractions such as Fort Duncan Park and an eighteen-acre recreation area completed in 1967; San Bernardo Mission ruins, and Presidio del Rio Grande (see San Juan Bautista) are nearby in Mexico. The county supports a hospital and contributes support to a library. The 1960 population was 14,508; the 1970 population was 18,093, according to the United States census.

*Maverick Creek.

*Maverick Mountain.

*Mavericks and Mavericking.

*Maxdale, Texas.

*Maxey, Samuel Bell.

*Maxey, Thomas Sheldon.

*Maxey, Texas.

*Maxon, Texas.

*Maxon Creek.

*Maxwell, Thomas Owen.

*Maxwell, Texas.

*Maxwelton, Texas.

*May, Texas.

Mayapem Indians. During the eighteenth century the Mayapem (Mallopeme) Indians ranged both sides of the Rio Grande in southern Texas and northern Tamaulipas. In the latter half of that century they entered missions on the south bank of the river—San Agustín de Laredo at Camargo and San Joaquín del Monte near Reynosa. A few Mayapem also moved northward to San Antonio, Texas, and entered San José y San Miguel de Aguayo Mission.qv These people probably spoke a Coahuiltecan language.

BIBLIOGRAPHY: H. E. Bolton, Guide to Materials for the History of the United States in the Principal Archives of Mexico (1913); F. W. Hodge (ed.), Handbook of American Indians, I (1907), II (1910); W. Jiménez Moreno, "Tribus e idiomas del Norte de México," El Norte de México y el Sur de Estados Unidos (1944); G. Saldivar, Los Indios de Tamaulipas (1943); J. R. Swanton, Linguistic Material from the Tribes of Southern Texas and Northeastern Mexico (1940).

T. N. Campbell

Mayborn, Ward Carlton. Ward Carlton Mayborn, publisher, was born on October 10, 1879, in Kinsman, Ohio, the son of Leroy and Lura (Burns) Mayborn. He was an advertising copywriter for a lumber company in Akron, Ohio, then joined the staff of that city's edition of the Cleveland Press in 1898, beginning an association with the E. W. Scripps (later Scripps-Howard) newspapers which lasted thirty years. By 1911 his work on various newspapers had established Mayborn as one of the leading businessmen in the Scripps-Howard national organization.

Mayborn's first job in Texas was in 1919, when he became business manager of the Dallas *Dispatch* and the Houston *Press*,qv both under Scripps ownership. In 1922 he founded the Fort Worth *Press* and the El Paso *Herald-Post*; until 1929 he was Southwest manager for the Scripps-Howard newspapers. During this period other Scripps-Howard newspapers in Albuquerque, Oklahoma City, and Omaha were assigned to his management. In 1925 he designed and built a building for the Fort Worth *Press* and in 1927 planned and built a new home for the Houston *Press*.

In 1929 he left the Scripps-Howard organization to become a publisher in his own right. With his sons, he purchased the Temple (Texas) *Daily Telegram*, a newspaper still being published in 1970 by one of his sons. From 1930 to 1937 Mayborn was publisher of the Baltimore (Maryland) *News American*.

Mayborn was often called upon to maneuver production economics to strengthen newspapers during the Depression; to do this he guided mechanical mergers in cities around the country. From 1941 to 1945 Mayborn served as assistant to publisher Marshall Field in founding the Chicago *Sun* and carrying the newspaper through its critical first years. When his son purchased the Sherman (Texas) *Democrat* in 1945, he returned to Texas to become publisher of that newspaper. He remained there until shortly before his death. While publishing the Sherman *Democrat*, Mayborn was a leader in the Texas Daily Newspaper Association and served as chairman of its education committee; he was instrumental in organizing a program of summer internships for college journalism students and semiannual press seminars at the University of Texas at Austin. He was a member of Sigma Delta Chi, professional association of newsmen.

On July 3, 1900, Mayborn married Nellie Childs Welton in Cleveland, Ohio, and they had three children. His wife died in 1928. He married Norma Brown on June 6, 1942. Mayborn died in Sherman, Texas, on March 1, 1958.

DeWitt C. Reddick

*Maydelle, Texas.

*Mayes, William Harding.

*Mayeye Indians. The Mayeye (Macheye, Maheye, Maiece, Maieye, Malleye, Maye, Muleye) Indians, a Tonkawa Indian tribe, are known principally from the eighteenth century. It is generally agreed that the Meghey (Maghay, Meghty) of the La Salle Expedition qv records were the same as the Mayeye of later times. The Meghey lived inland north or northeast of Matagorda Bay, probably between the Colorado and Brazos rivers. In the early eighteenth century the Spanish found the Mayeye in the same general area and also farther north in the valley of the Brazos River, particularly east

of present Temple. Later (about 1748) the Mayeye entered San Francisco Xavier de Horcasitas Mission qv on the San Gabriel River near modern Rockdale. A few years afterward, when the San Gabriel missions were abandoned, some of the Mayeye entered San Antonio de Valero Mission qv at San Antonio, where they were recorded as late as the 1760's. Sometime in the 1770's a group of non-missionized Mayeye moved southward to the coast and joined the Coco Indians, a Karankawa Indian tribe that lived along the lower Colorado River. In 1805 some Mayeye were reported farther west near the mouth of the Guadalupe River. Little is known of the Mayeye afterward, but it seems likely that the coastal Mayeye were absorbed by Karankawan groups. It also seems likely that some of the Mayeye may not have moved to the coast; if so, these Mayeye were probably absorbed by other Tonkawan groups of east-central Texas. A. F. Sjoberg has suggested that the Mayeye may have been the same as the Yakwal, a legendary Tonkawan people reported by late nineteenth-century Tonkawa as having once lived near the Texas coast.

BIBLIOGRAPHY: H. E. Bolton, *Athanase de Mézières and the Louisiana-Texas Frontier, 1768–1780* (1914) and *Texas in the Middle Eighteenth Century* (1915); F. W. Hodge (ed.), *Handbook of American Indians*, I (1907), II (1910); P. Margry, *Découvertes et établissements des Français dans l'ouest et dans le sud de l'Amérique Septentrionale*, III (1879); W. W. Newcomb, Jr., *The Indians of Texas* (1961); A. F. Sjoberg, "The Culture of the Tonkawa, A Texas Indian Tribe," *Texas Journal of Science*, V (1953).

T. N. Campbell

*Mayfield, Allison.

Mayfield, Earle Bradford. Earle Bradford Mayfield, son of John Blythe and Mary (D'Guerin) Mayfield, was born at Overton, Rusk County, Texas, on April 12, 1881. After completing high school at Timpson, he received a diploma from Tyler Business College and was graduated from Southwestern University at Georgetown in 1900. He attended the law school of the University of Texas, 1900–1901. In 1907 he began law practice in Meridian. He served in the Texas Senate from Bosque County (1907–1913) and was a member of the Texas Railroad Commission qv (1913–1923).

Mayfield was one of six candidates for the Democratic nomination for United States senator in 1922, challenging the elderly Senator Charles A. Culberson's qv bid for a sixth term. Supporting the Volstead Act and with the endorsement of Senator Morris Sheppard,qv he obtained the nomination in a bitter runoff campaign against former Governor James E. Ferguson,qv in which Ferguson was billed as the antiprohibitionist candidate and Mayfield as the Ku Klux Klan qv candidate. He avoided the Klan issue and spoke out against federal control of freight rates. In the general election Mayfield was opposed by an Independent Democratic-Republican fusion candidate, George E. B. Peddy,qv but defeated him by a vote of two to one.

Peddy demanded an investigation of the election by the United States Senate, complaining that his name was not printed on the ballot, that Mayfield missed the filing dates, spent too much money in his campaign, and was supported by the Ku Klux Klan. After two years, the Senate found in favor of Mayfield and permitted him to take his seat.

Seeking renomination in 1928, Mayfield led a field of six candidates in the first Democratic primary, but in the runoff he was defeated by Congressman Tom Connally.qv In the 1930 Democratic primary for governor, he ran seventh in a field of eleven.

Mayfield married Ora Lumpkin on June 10, 1902, and they had three sons. After leaving the Senate, Mayfield lived in Tyler, where he practiced law and was president of the Mayfield Wholesale Grocery Company until his retirement in 1952. He was granted an honorary Doctor of Humane Letters degree from John Brown University of Siloam Springs, Arkansas. He died on June 23, 1964, and was buried in the Oakwood Cemetery in Tyler.

BIBLIOGRAPHY: *Biographical Directory of the American Congress, 1774–1961* (1961); Seth Shepard McKay, *Texas Politics, 1906–1944* (1952).

Frank H. Smyrl

*Mayfield, James S. James S. Mayfield was secretary of state from February 8, 1841, to September 7, 1841 (not February 8 to April 30, 1841, as stated in Volume II), although Joseph Waples and Samuel A. Roberts qqv were acting secretaries of state, April 30 to May 25, and May 25 to September 7, 1841, respectively.

BIBLIOGRAPHY: George P. Garrison (ed.), *Diplomatic Correspondence of the Republic of Texas,* I (1907).

*Mayfield, Texas.

*Mayflower, Texas.

*Mayhard Creek.

*Mayhaw Bayou.

*Mayhew Creek.

Mayhill, Texas. Mayhill, a residential suburb on the southeast corner of Denton, in Denton County, had an estimated 1969 population of 150. *See also* Dallas Standard Metropolitan Statistical Area.

*Maynard, Texas.

*Maynard Creek.

MAYO. MAYO, the Mexican American Youth Organization, was founded in March, 1967, in San Antonio. The founders were Juan Patlan, Mario Compean, Willie Velasquez, Jose Angel Gutierrez, and Ignacio Perez. Consisting mainly of young high school and college-age Chicanos,qv the membership numbered about 1,000 in 1974. MAYO meets twice a year, once in May for election of officers and once in the fall for evaluation of projects. MAYO was an active political organization, with projects such as school walk-outs during the 1967–1969 period and the Winter Garden Project in 1969 and 1970 designed to draw attention to the political and educational policies of state and local government concerning Chicanos. MAYO was instrumental in organizing the larger Raza Unida

party qv in Texas in 1970 and 1971, and continued in the 1970's to support the growth of that party in other states.

Jose Angel Gutierrez was the first president of MAYO; in 1974 Alberto Luera held the office. *See* Mexican Americans in Texas.

*Mayo, William Leonidas.

*Mayor-Council Form of City Government. The mayor-council form of city government in Texas has assumed two types. Both the weak mayor-council and the strong mayor-council types are characterized by a mayor elected at large and a council elected either by wards, at large, or a combination of the two methods. In the weak mayor-council type, the mayor is not a chief executive in the true sense. His powers are limited with reference to appointments and removals, as well as veto, and there are a large number of elected officials and boards. Many legal powers of the council prevent him from effectively supervising city administration. In the strong mayor-council form, the mayor has the power to appoint and remove most department heads, and only a few officials are elected. In addition, he prepares the budget for the council's consideration, and he possesses an effective veto power. As of early 1964, 563 of the 891 Texas cities, towns, and villages used one of the two types of mayor-council government. In the 1960's this form of government continued to be the most popular in general-law cities and towns, but steadily declined in favor among home-rule cities. Of the 188 home-rule cities in 1969, only twenty-five had the mayor-council form of city government.

BIBLIOGRAPHY: Institute of Public Affairs, The University of Texas, *Forms of City Government* (1963); *Texas Almanac* (1969).

Stuart A. MacCorkle

*Maypearl, Texas.

*Maysfield, Texas.

*Mazape Indians.

*Mazatlan, Texas.

*Meacham Field.

*Meadow, Texas.

*Meadow Creek.

*Means, William.

Mears, Thomas Robert. Thomas Robert Mears was born on January 8, 1871, in Cornersville, Mississippi, the son of Erwin Jasper and Elizabeth (Moses) Mears. At the age of twenty he came to Texas, eventually settling in Pidcoke. He married Mrs. Rose Belcher Watkins, a widow with four children, in 1894.

In 1902 he purchased a farm at Mound, Texas. After being elected to the Texas state legislature in 1904, Mears sold his farm and moved into Gatesville, seat of Coryell County. From 1904 to 1909 he served in the Twenty-ninth and Thirtieth legislatures. He studied law on his own, and in the fall of 1909 he was admitted to the Bar. He served as county attorney of Coryell County for fifteen years and also served as mayor of Gatesville from 1910 to 1924. Mears often chaired local Democratic conventions and was a delegate to two national Democratic conventions. He continued to practice law until the spring of 1966. Mears died on February 22, 1967, and was survived by his widow from a second marriage, Mildred Watkins Mears, and two daughters. He was buried in the City Cemetery at Gatesville.

BIBLIOGRAPHY: Mildred Watkins Mears, *Coryell County Scrapbook* (1963); Resolution of the 52nd Judicial District Bar Association; Gatesville *Messenger*, May 20, 1966.

Merle Mears Duncan

*Meat Packing. During the 1950's and through the 1960's meat packing in Texas expanded from an industry characterized by a large number of small, low-volume firms to an industry comprising a small number of large slaughterhouses and wholesale distributors. By 1955 Texas had 218 large or medium sized plants with 10,464 employees and a total value added by manufacturing of $68,548,000. From 1954 to 1958 the total sales volume of Texas packing plants increased 12 percent as the industry spent $2,952,000 in new capital investments. By 1959 the 220 Texas packing plants had a volume of 1,490,477,000 pounds of meat and cured products.

Texas slaughterers received more than 84 percent of their cattle from Texas suppliers in the South Texas Plains. Cows, calfs, and range sheep constituted the major livestock from this area, while substantial numbers of stocker-feeder cattle and lambs were shipped outside the state for slaughter. In 1966 two hundred of the eight hundred slaughtering plants were classified as medium to large producers. Total red meat production for 1968 had increased to 1,763,000,000 pounds. In 1968 the Texas industry slaughtered 2,782,000 cattle, 345,200 calves, 1,978,000 hogs, and 1,404,000 sheep and lambs.

BIBLIOGRAPHY: *Texas Almanac* (1955, 1965, 1967, 1969); Files of the Bureau of Business Research, University of Texas at Austin.

*Mebane, Alexander Duff.

*Mecca, Texas.

*Medford, H. C.

*Mediavilla y Azcona, Melchor de.

*Medical Association of Texas. [The detailed account in Volume II under this title is essentially correct, although it does not give the original official name of the organization nor its present official name, the Texas Medical Association.] The first president was Joseph Taylor (not George Cupples,qv as stated in Volume II). The initial membership was thirty-five (not forty-eight) members. *See* Texas Medical Association.

BIBLIOGRAPHY: Pat Ireland Nixon, *A History of the Texas Medical Association, 1853–1953* (1953).

*Medical Branch of the University of Texas. *See* University of Texas, Medical Branch of.

*Medical Censors, Board of.

*Medical History of Texas. Two new medical schools have been established by the state legis-

lature, bringing the total number of schools in the state to five. The South Texas Medical School, a branch of the University of Texas in San Antonio, was established in 1958, and it is now the University of Texas Medical School at San Antonio.qv Classes began in 1966. In 1969 the University of Texas Medical School at Houston qv was established. The first classes began in 1970.

In the 1960's state medical facilities made significant progress in heart disease and cancer research. In 1967 there were 570 hospitals in Texas that were registered with the American Hospital Association. *See* Texas Medical Association; Heart Transplants in Texas; Mentally Ill and Mentally Retarded, Care of, in Texas.

*Medicine Mound, Texas.

*Medicine Mounds.

*Medill, Texas.

*Medina, Texas.

*Medina County. Medina County is primarily a farming and ranching area; farmers gained $15,-000,000 annually in cash receipts from crops, livestock, and products in the early 1970's. Grains, cotton, broomcorn, and truck crops constitute the major crops grown. Irrigation is made possible by Medina Lake. Crude oil production began in 1901 and through 1972 had reached a total of 4,875,631 barrels. Income from tourism and recreation is also important to the county; tourist attractions include dinosaur tracks in the Hondo Creek bed, historic buildings in Castroville, the site of Fort Lincoln,qv fishing and recreational facilities on Medina Lake, and deer and turkey hunting. Population was 18,904 in 1960 and had increased to 20,249 by 1970, according to the United States census.

*Medina Lake. Medina Lake is in the San Antonio River Basin in Medina and Bandera counties, eight miles northwest of Rio Medina on the Medina River, a tributary of the San Antonio River. The Medina Valley Irrigation Company built Medina Dam during 1912 and 1913. Impoundment of water began May 7, 1913. The Medina Valley Irrigation Company went into receivership in 1917 and emerged later as the Bexar-Medina-Atascosa Counties Water Improvement District No. 1, the present owner of the project.

According to a 1948 survey, the capacity of Medina Lake was 254,000 acre-feet and the surface area was 5,575 acres at the spillway crest at an elevation of 1,064.5 feet above mean sea level. Water released from Medina Lake is diverted for irrigation at the Medina Diversion Dam four miles downstream. The drainage area of the Medina River watershed to Medina Lake is 634 square miles.

BIBLIOGRAPHY: Texas Water Commission, *Bulletin 6408* (1964).

Seth D. Breeding

*Medina River.

*Medina River, Battle of the.

*Medio Creek.

*Medlin Branch.

*Meek, Edward Roscoe.

*Meeks, Texas.

*Megargel, Texas.

Meharg, Emma (Grigsby). Emma (Grigsby) Meharg, Texas' first woman secretary of state, was born on August 14, 1873, at Lynnville, Tennessee. She was the daughter of Jasper N. and Mary Amanda (Calvert) Grigsby. In 1883 the family moved to Italy, Texas, where she attended public school. She was graduated from Southwestern Normal College in 1895. She married Samuel W. Meharg, a native of Anniston, Alabama, on June 24, 1902, and went as a bride to Plainview, Texas, where her husband became principal of the public school. Mrs. Meharg also taught school both in Italy and Plainview. The couple had two children.

Appointed secretary of state by Governor Miriam A. Ferguson,qv Mrs. Meharg served during 1925 and 1926. In her official biennial report Mrs. Meharg made a number of recommendations for changes in laws relating to corporations, securities, administration of the secretary of state's office, and the institution of a civil service system for state employees. Subsequent legislatures enacted into law many of her proposals. She strongly recommended that the office of the secretary of state be made an elective office, rather than appointive, because the duties of the office were of a more public nature than at the time of the adoption of the Constitution of 1876.qv She also advocated adoption of a constitutional amendment to raise the salary of the secretary of state from the $2,000 per year set by the Constitution of 1876. During her administration as secretary of state many historical records were taken out of storage, restored, and processed for easy reference and exhibit.

Mrs. Meharg was a leader in civic, cultural, church, and political affairs. She served on the Plainview board of school trustees and on the board of regents for Texas Technological College (now Texas Tech University) from 1932 to 1937. Mrs. Meharg died at Plainview on September 4, 1937, and was buried there.

BIBLIOGRAPHY: Dallas Morning News, December 26, 1926.

Elora B. Alderman

*Meldavis, Texas.

*Meldrum, Texas.

Melenudo Indians. The Melenudo Indians, known only from the middle eighteenth century, appear to have been a band of Lipan-Apache Indians. They were reported as enemies of the Hasinai Caddo and also the Yojuane Indians, a Tonkawan tribe. One source indicates that the Melenudo were neighbors of the Yojuane. This suggests that the Melenudo were ranging an area west or southwest of present Waco.

BIBLIOGRAPHY: H. E. Bolton, Texas in the Middle Eighteenth Century (1915); W. E. Dunn, "Apache Relations in Texas, 1718–1750," Quarterly of the Texas State Historical Association, XIV (1910–1911).

T. N. Campbell

*Melish Map.

*Melissa, Texas. Various sources attribute the naming of Melissa, Texas, to Melissa Huntington (or Hunington, as stated in Volume II) or to Melissa Shirley, but there is no reliable evidence to support either of these claims; therefore, the origin of the name remains undetermined. In 1969 the population estimate was 375.

J. Lee Stambaugh

*Melon, Texas.

*Melon Creek.

*Melrose, Texas.

Melton, Amos W. Amos W. Melton was born December 31, 1906, in Bellevue, Clay County, Texas, the son of E. Frank and Jessie Jo Melton. The family moved to Fort Worth, where Amos received his education. In 1924 he graduated from North Side High School and in 1928 graduated from Texas Christian University, where he lettered in football, won the Bryson Poetry Prize, and edited the school newspaper. In 1928 he toured Japan, Korea, Manchuria, and China for six months. In 1929 he became a reporter for the Fort Worth Star-Telegram,qv later serving as an assistant financial editor and sportswriter, specializing in golf and football coverage. In 1951 he and L. R. "Dutch" Meyer coauthored Spread Formation Football.

Melton entered the U.S. Army Air Forces in June, 1942, as an intelligence officer; in 1944 he was assigned to the Office of Strategic Services, in which he served twenty months in China. For a time after the surrender of the Japanese in 1945 he was a major and commanding officer in Peking. For his services he received the Bronze Star, the Legion of Merit, the Asiatic-Pacific Theatre Ribbon with two campaign stars, and a special decoration from the Nationalist Chinese government.

Upon returning to Fort Worth, he worked first at the Star-Telegram, then in 1949 as sports editor of the Fort Worth Press. In June, 1950, he returned to TCU as business manager of athletics and director of sports publicity, and in March, 1952, he became director of information services; in November, 1959, he became an assistant to the chancellor, and in February, 1963, he was named assistant chancellor. The Ex-Students' Association of T.C.U. honored him in 1961 as their "Most Valuable Alumnus." He died on September 5, 1966, and was survived by his wife, the former Grace Bullock, and a daughter.

BIBLIOGRAPHY: This is T.C.U. (1966); Texas Christian University Public Relations Office biographical data; Fort Worth Star-Telegram, September 6, 1966.

Ben H. Procter

*Melvin, Texas.

Melvin Mail Station. See Camp Melvin, Texas.

*Memphis, Texas. Memphis, seat of Hall County, had a 1960 population of 3,332 and a 1970 population of 3,227, according to the United States census. Serving as market and banking center of the county, Memphis had grain and cotton storage and processing facilities, a synthetic material plant, and a hospital. In 1970 the town had 111 businesses.

*Memphis, El Paso, and Pacific Railroad.

*Menard, Michel B. [This title was listed in Volume II as Menard, Michel Branamour; however, since variant spellings of the middle name occur in all reference materials—Branamour, Brindamour, Branaman—only the middle initial can be certain, as Menard signed his name "Michel B. Menard," or "M. B. Menard." No full original spelling of the signature has been located or submitted.]

*Menard, Pierre J.

*Menard, Texas. Menard, seat of Menard County, in 1966 had thirteen churches, two banks, and a retirement home operated in conjunction with the hospital. In 1970 the town reported forty-two businesses. Menard is a market for cattle, wool, and mohair. Diversified farming, tourists, and oil production also add to local income. The 1960 population was 1,914; the 1970 United States census reported 1,740.

*Menard County. Menard County is primarily a sheep- and cattle-ranching area, with cash receipts from livestock and products totaling $4,500,000 annually in the early 1970's. There is also a small amount of oil, sand, gravel, and natural gas production. Five shallow oil fields have been developed since 1941, and by January 1, 1973, total crude oil production had reached 2,607,045 barrels. Major business concerns of the county are sheep shearing, livestock feeding, and furniture manufacturing. In addition, the county has a church-operated hospital. Tourism is attracted by hunting, fishing, the San Sabá Presidio,qv the county-built Camp Sol Mayers for Boy Scouts, and a state park on the Fort McKavett qv ruins. Population decreased from 2,964 in 1960 to 2,646 in 1970, according to the United States census.

*Menard County (Judicial).

*Menard Creek.

*Menard's Chapel, Texas.

*Menchaca, José. [This José Menchaca (in Volume II) should not be confused with either of the two men named José Antonio Menchaca, whose biographies follow.]

*Menchaca, José Antonio. José Antonio Menchaca, a Canary Islander qv descendant and the son of Juan Mariano and Maria Luz Guerra Menchaca (not Marcos and Josefa Cadena Menchaca, as stated in Volume II—these were his grandparents), was born in San Antonio in January, 1800. Before 1825 he married Teresa Ramón. They had four children.

Menchaca did not assist in the Texan siege of Bexar qv in December, 1835 (as stated in Volume II). He was a prominent citizen of Bexar and returned from a visit to Coahuila to find his house destroyed in the storming of San Antonio. He joined the Texas forces as second sergeant in Juan N. Seguin's qv company when Antonio López de Santa Anna qv and his troops marched into the city in February, 1836. The company left Gonzales as part of Sam Houston's army, and Menchaca fought for Texas in the battle of San Jacinto. He continued to serve in the Texas Army qv after the revolution and captained a company of cavalry that patrolled the San Antonio frontier to protect the settlements from Indian raids.

It is not true that Menchaca was sent in 1838 by President Mirabeau B. Lamar qv (who was not yet president) to confer with Vicente Cordova and Manuel Flores qqv on conditions in East Texas (as stated in Volume II); he was serving as mayor *pro tem* of San Antonio in 1838. [This José Antonio Menchaca should not be confused with the José Antonio Menchaca qv of Nacogdoches who was accused of treason during the Cordova Rebellion qv in 1838 and later pardoned by Mirabeau B. Lamar in 1839. *See* article below.]

In addition to his public service in San Antonio as alderman for several terms and as mayor *pro tem*, Menchaca was elected sergeant-at-arms of the House of Representatives in the Eighth Texas Legislature. He was an early member of the Holland Lodge, the oldest chapter of the Masonic Order in Texas.qv His last public service was made possible by Governor Oran Milo Roberts,qv who appointed him public weigher of San Antonio in August, 1879, a few months prior to his death on November 1, 1879.

There is no evidence to support the view that the village of Manchaca in Travis County was named for him (as stated in Volume II), although it is possible that Manchaca Springs in the area was earlier named for some member of this well-known family, and the village named after the springs.

BIBLIOGRAPHY: Antonio Menchaca, *Memoirs* (1937); San Antonio City Records, 1837–1849 (Archives, University of Texas at Austin Library); San Antonio *Daily Express*, August 15, November 2, 1879.

　　　　　　　　　　　　　　　　Roderick B. Patten

Menchaca, José Antonio. José Antonio Menchaca was born in Mexico in 1796, the son of José Maria and Maria Rivas Maldonado Menchaca. He settled in the Neutral Ground qv in western Louisiana and married Maria Feliciana Santa de los Sanches on August 1, 1825, in Natchitoches, Louisiana. In 1827 they moved to Nacogdoches, where he became a tailor and played a prominent role in local politics before the Texas Revolution.

He was a captain in the Texas militia when, on August 6, 1838, he was commanded by Major General Thomas J. Rusk qv to order members of his company who were participating in the Cordova Rebellion qv to return home and obey the laws. Although he visited the rebel camp and reported their strength to Rusk, he was later arrested and jailed, along with others, and charged with treason. On January 7, 1839, he went on trial at San Augustine, was found guilty, and sentenced to be hanged on February 22. He was pardoned on February 18 by President Mirabeau B. Lamar qv in response to a petition by several citizens of San Augustine and on Menchaca's promise to leave the Republic. He moved his family to the Mansfield, Louisiana, area and continued his trade as a tailor; by 1866, however, he was again living in the vicinity of Nacogdoches.

[This José Antonio Menchaca should not be confused with the José Antonio Menchaca qv who fought at the battle of San Jacinto and who was mayor *pro tem* of San Antonio during the Cordova Rebellion and subsequent trial. *See* article above.]

BIBLIOGRAPHY: R. B. Blake Research Collection (MS., Archives, University of Texas at Austin Library); United States Sixth Census, 1840, Natchitoches Parish, Louisiana; United States Seventh Census, 1850, De Soto Parish, Louisiana.

Roderick B. Patten

Menchaca, Luis Antonio. A grandson of Joseph (José) de Urrutia,qv Luis Antonio Menchaca was a resident of the villa of San Fernando in the middle 1700's and at one time was the captain of the royal San Antonio de Béxar Presidio.qv

Menchaca and Andrés Hernández qv were (by a compromise settlement over disputed land claims) recipients of a Spanish land grant dated April 12, 1758. This land grant, the oldest on record in the Spanish archives of the General Land Office qv (although there were grants prior to that date), consisted of fifteen leagues and seven labors situated between the forks of the San Antonio and Cibolo rivers in Karnes and Wilson counties.

The grant to Menchaca consisted of eleven leagues and two labors (the remaining four leagues and five labors went to his co-recipient, Andrés Hernández), one-fourth of which lay in Karnes County and three-fourths in Wilson County. The area was bounded on the south and west by the San Antonio River, and it became the ranch known as Pataguilla.

BIBLIOGRAPHY: Bexar Archives (Translations, 1758–1769, Archives, University of Texas at Austin Library); Virginia H. Taylor, *The Spanish Archives of the General Land Office* (1955); Robert H. Thonhoff, "The First Ranch in Texas," *West Texas Historical Association Year Book* (1964).

Robert H. Thonhoff

*Menchaca, Miguel.

*Mendica Indians.

*Mendon, Texas.

*Mendota, Texas.

*Mendoza, Juan Domínguez de.

*Mendoza, Texas.

*Menefee, George.

*Menefee, John Sutherland.

*Menefee, Thomas.

*Menefee, William.

*Menenquen Indians. This name and several variants of it (Menanque, Menaquen, Menanquen, Menequen) are said to appear in the baptismal records (1740–1750) of San Antonio de Valero Mission.qv Alice C. Fletcher and H. E. Bolton qv (in Hodge's *Handbook of American Indians*) have suggested that in the middle eighteenth century the Menenquen may have lived somewhere along the Guadalupe River east or southeast of San Antonio because mission records indicate intermarriage in the "gentile state" (unbaptized) with the Cava who ranged that area. Swanton listed the Menenquen as probably of Coahuiltecan affiliation, presumably because so many groups at the Valero mission were Coahuiltecans. Fletcher and Bolton also suggested that the Menenquen may have been the same people as the Meracouman and Merhuam, a judgment that seems to have been based on rather slight phonetic resemblances in the names. On phonetic grounds the Menenquen might also be linked with the Manico. It is evident that at present no one knows who the Menenquen were or where they originally lived.

BIBLIOGRAPHY: F. W. Hodge (ed.), *Handbook of American Indians*, I (1907), II (1910); R. G. Santos, "A Preliminary Survey of the San Fernando Archives," *Texas Libraries*, XXVIII (1966–1967); J. R. Swanton, *Linguistic Material from the Tribes of Southern Texas and Northeastern Mexico* (1940).

T. N. Campbell

*Menger Hotel.

*Menken, Adah Isaacs.

*Menlow, Texas.

Mennonites in Texas. Of Anabaptist origin in Switzerland in 1525, the Mennonites resorted to considerable migration to find freedom from compulsory military service and to escape religious persecution. Although Mennonites had been coming to the United States since 1683, the first church established in Texas was in 1905. The congregation founded in Tuleta that year was still active in 1957; another one in Richmond lasted only until 1908. A group numbering over one hundred persons settled temporarily in Dimmit County between 1911 and 1914; between 1915 and 1918 another 160 Mennonites established a colony near Littlefield. By 1920, of the 79,363 Mennonites in the United States, there were about 700 in Texas.

There was considerable colonization in North and West Texas through the 1930's. A small congregation was established at Texline, while the one at Coldwater once numbered 209 members. Except for the two churches at Perryton and Waka, which were later consolidated, Mennonite communities soon left North and West Texas. The earlier ones left because of unfavorable weather for farming and because of conscription during World War I, and the later ones left because of drouth and sand storms in that area in the 1930's.

In the 1930's and 1940's the Mennonites increased their activity in the South Texas area. Centers were started in Premont and Mission. Seven missions, claiming 271 members in 1957, were established between Laredo and Brownsville among the Mexican Americans. Other congregations were located at Mathis, Alice, and Corpus Christi.

In 1957 some 500 Texans, situated mostly in South Texas, claimed spiritual brotherhood with the 152,579 Mennonites in the United States.

BIBLIOGRAPHY: *The Mennonite Encyclopedia* (1957);

Census of Religious Bodies, 1926: Mennonite Bodies (1928); C. Henry Smith, The Story of the Mennonites (1950); Adolph Schock, In Quest of Free Land (1964); Paul S. Taylor, "Historical Notes on Dimmit County," Southwestern Historical Quarterly, XXXIV (1930–1931).

David B. Gracy II

Mental Health and Mental Retardation, Texas Department of. The Texas Department of Mental Health and Mental Retardation was created in 1965 from the Board for Texas State Hospitals and Special Schools qv by a legislative act. The function of the department is to provide for the conservation and restoration of mental health among the people, to provide for the effective administration and coordination of mental health services at state and local levels, and to provide, coordinate, develop, and improve services for the mentally ill or mentally retarded person. The act transferred the powers, duties, and functions relating to the commitment, care, treatment, maintenance, education, training, and rehabilitation of mentally ill or mentally retarded persons, or relating to the administration of these services, previously vested in the Board for Texas State Hospitals and Special Schools and in the Division of Mental Health and the Office of Mental Health Planning of the state department of Public Health,qv to the new department. The department is authorized to create additional state schools, hospitals, and research institutes within the limits of legislative appropriation.

The department consists of the Board of Mental Health and Mental Retardation, a commissioner of mental health and mental retardation, a deputy commissioner for mental health services, a deputy commissioner for mental retardation services, an executive director, and a staff under the direction of the commissioner and the deputy commissioners. The board is composed of nine members, appointed by the governor and confirmed by the Senate, who serve six-year terms. The board sets departmental policy, while the commissioners have administrative control of the department. In 1970 the chairman of the board was Ward Burke, and the commissioner was David Wade.

By 1970 state services included hospitals for the mentally ill, schools for the mentally retarded, mental health outpatient clinics, rehabilitation centers, local community mental health centers, and a research institute. In the last several years there has been an increasing emphasis placed on the goal of delivering mental health and mental retardation facilities at a local or community level. In addition, the department is beginning research in programs involving alcoholism, drug abuse, and child and adolescent services. See also Mentally Ill and Mentally Retarded, Care of, in Texas.

BIBLIOGRAPHY: The University of Texas at Austin, Guide To Texas State Agencies (1966); Texas Department of Mental Health and Mental Retardation, Annual Report, 1970.

Mentally Ill and Mentally Retarded, Care of, in Texas. [See Insane in Texas, Care of (Volume I) for an earlier account.] The Fifty-first Legislature created the Board for Texas State Hospitals and Special Schools qv in 1949 to replace the Board of Control qv in the supervision of the mental hospitals, tuberculosis hospitals, and schools for the mentally retarded.

A special session of the legislature in 1950 gave the board $5,000,000 per year for seven years to improve the physical plants. Under the resulting building program, the system of state hospitals and special schools was expanded to provide 7,609 beds for residents. Federal money under the Hill-Burton Act was utilized to make added hospital improvements. The conversion of abandoned military installations for use by patients and students, plus gifts of land and buildings, increased the inventory of physical properties.

Inadequate professional staffs were engulfed in a tidal wave of admissions. In 1951 first admissions reached 3,335, but discharges numbered 1,875. Treatment was primarily custodial care. While funds were spent on new physical plants at Austin, Big Spring, San Antonio, and Wichita Falls, funds for consultants were also increased. Only as the system began to provide higher salaries and employ more professional staffs did the hospital program move away from the custodial concept toward that of intensive treatment and rehabilitation and the early return of patients to their homes and communities.

As originally established, admission to a state mental hospital was generally by involuntary commitment following a trial by jury. The 1913 and 1925 acts by the legislature to eliminate or limit the right of a jury trial qv were held unconstitutional by state courts. In 1935 voters approved a constitutional amendment to the effect that a person may be admitted temporarily, without a jury trial, for observation or treatment for mental illness for a period not to exceed ninety days. The legislature in 1955 provided that all initial involuntary commitments should be of the temporary variety.

In 1956 the people again amended the Constitution, providing both that competent medical or psychiatric testimony must be the basis for any indefinite commitment to a mental institution and that trial by jury in such cases is not mandatory but may be waived. Adoption of this constitutional amendment provided the impetus for further legislative acts defining the procedures for admission to and release from state mental institutions.

The Texas Mental Health Code revisions substituted the term "mental illness" for previous legal usages of "insanity," "lunacy," and "unsound mind." A mentally ill person was defined as one whose mental health is substantially impaired. In amendments to the Code of Criminal Procedures, however, the term "insanity" continued to be used because it is an established concept in the criminal law dealing with the question of the accountability of a person for his conduct and his capacity to help in his own defense. The Texas Mental Health Code provided procedures for the admission of patients to the state mental hospitals, Veterans Administration hospitals, and private mental hospitals. It recognized four categories of patients by providing different procedures for their admission: voluntary patient; involuntary emergency patient; involuntary temporary patient, or ninety-day patient; and involuntary indefinite patient.

In 1959 an optional procedure for release from mental institutions by obtaining a judicial order stating that a patient is no longer mentally ill or incompetent was amended. The emergency admission procedures were tightened in 1961, requiring a warrant from a magistrate before a person could be taken into custody.

In 1957 the Houston State Psychiatric Institute for Research and Training qv was established, and later, in 1967, the name was changed to the Texas Research Institute of Mental Science.qv In conjunction with its extensive research program, the institute provided outpatient clinics and follow-up clinics for former patients of state hospitals. The institute also provided training programs for resident psychiatry trainees, clinical psychology interns, and social work and occupational therapy students.

Mental health clinics providing outpatient care were established in Dallas and San Antonio in 1958, and in Fort Worth and Harlingen in 1962. Efforts to extend the program of outpatient care resulted in the development of aftercare for patients released from the state hospitals and a contract program, utilizing local medical resources, including hospital beds. By 1970 the San Antonio Adult Mental Health Clinic qv was absorbed into the San Antonio State Hospital.qv The Harlingen clinic was renamed Rio Grande State Center for Mental Health and Mental Retardation qv in 1968.

In 1963 Texas received the first of two allotments from the federal government to support the development of comprehensive mental health planning. The Office of Mental Health Planning was established, and a citizens committee devised a general plan for state mental health services. The plan was completed late in 1964, and the Fifty-ninth Legislature in 1965 enacted a major portion of the committee's recommendations.

Effective September 1, 1965, the Texas Mental Health and Mental Retardation Act created the Texas Department of Mental Health and Mental Retardation.qv The department supervised the same mental health and mental retardation services, excluding the tuberculosis hospitals and Confederate homes, that the former board supervised. Its purpose was to provide for the conservation and restoration of mental health among the people. The department administered and coordinated mental health services at state and local levels to the end that mentally retarded persons would be afforded the opportunity to develop their mental capacities to the fullest practicable extent and that mentally ill persons would be provided treatment promising the best chances for recovery.

In 1967 Amarillo State Center for Human Development and Beaumont State Center for Human Development were established, as authorized by the legislature, offering services designed to help individuals remain in their communities as an alternative to placement in a residential state school.

By 1970 the state had eight mental hospitals, admitting more than 20,000 patients that year, an increase from 17,736 admitted in 1969. That hospitals served more people with greater efficiency than previously is evidenced by a shorter hospital stay (an average of forty-five days) per person. The discharges from the hospitals also increased with 22,164 patients discharged during 1970, compared with 18,575 in 1969. The daily hospital census average declined to 12,416. The Vernon Center qv was the newest facility, established in 1970.

New laws permitted a closer working relation between the mental health hospitals and centers and the mental retardation services. Transfers of special cases between hospitals and schools provided for care appropriate to the needs of individual patients. The "unit system" was implemented in the state hospitals during 1970. Patients from the same geographic area but with different forms of mental illness were placed in treatment programs with each other.

In the area of mental retardation the state maintained ten state schools in 1970, including the four newest: Richmond State School,qv opened in 1968; San Angelo Center,qv opened in 1969; Lubbock State School,qv opened in 1969; and Corpus Christi State School,qv opened in 1970. A new state school in Brenham was under construction. By the end of the fiscal year 1970, 12,088 individuals resided in these ten state schools, and an estimated 96 percent of the mentally retarded who were community residents were being served by new noninstitutional programs.

In community services the state has expanded to meet the increasing trend to treat mentally ill and mentally retarded persons at the community level. Ten mental health and mental retardation regions of Texas coordinate the community services of twenty-three centers. During 1970, $4.5 million was appropriated for grants-in-aid to community centers, and local matching funds totaled about $3 million. Outreach programs from the mental health and mental retardation facilities, mental health counseling services, alcoholism and drug abuse programs, and the community centers were only a part of the total picture of community services available.

The care of the mentally ill and mentally retarded in Texas was not limited to state facilities. Approximately twenty-three private residential facilities are licensed by the Public Welfare Department qv for children under sixteen years. These private institutions offer resources similar to those given individuals living in state schools. A few private hospitals also care for the same type of mentally ill person that the state hospitals serve, but the private facilities are limited in scope, and the state serves by far the majority of the mentally ill and mentally retarded in Texas. *See also* Abilene State School; Austin State Hospital; Austin State School; Big Spring State Hospital; Dallas State Mental Health Clinic; Denton State School; Fort Worth State Mental Health Clinic; Kerrville State Hospital; Lufkin State School; Mexia State School; Rusk State Hospital; Terrell State Hospital; Texas Leander Rehabilitation Center; Travis State School; Wichita Falls State Hospital.

BIBLIOGRAPHY: Texas Department of Mental Health and Mental Retardation, *Annual Report, 1970.*

*Mentone, Texas. Mentone, seat and only town of Loving County, had improved the county courthouse and landscaped the grounds by 1966. Mentone had only two businesses in 1967 and only one in 1969. An unincorporated town, Mentone had a population of 110 in 1960 and an estimated 1973 population of fifty.

*Mentz, Texas.

*Mepayaya Indians.

*Meracouman Indians. The Meracouman (Meraquaman, Muracuman) Indians are known only from records of the La Salle Expedition,qv which indicate that in the late seventeenth century these Indians lived north or northeast of Matagorda Bay, probably near the Colorado River. Although it has been argued that the Meracouman were Karankawans, the only basis for this is that they probably lived in or near the area later occupied by groups designated by Spanish sources as Karankawan. Attempts to link the Meracouman with tribes known both earlier (Maliacone) and later (Manico, Menenquen, and Merhuan) are not convincing. The linguistic and cultural affiliations of the Meracouman remain undetermined.

BIBLIOGRAPHY: F. W. Hodge (ed.), *Handbook of American Indians,* I (1907); P. Margry, *Découvertes et établissements des Français dans l'ouest et dans le sud de l'Amérique Septentrionale,* III (1879); H. R. Stiles (ed.), *Joutel's Journal of La Salle's Last Voyage, 1684–7* (1906).

T. N. Campbell

*Mercedes, Texas. Mercedes, in Hidalgo County, during the 1960's was a center for cotton, vegetable, and livestock marketing and processing. Other industries included meat packing, box and boot making, and farm chemicals. By 1970 the number of businesses reported was 140. The 1960 population was 10,943; the 1970 population had decreased to 9,355, according to the United States census.

*Mercer, Asa Shinn.

*Mercer, Charles Fenton.

*Mercer, Eli.

*Mercer, Elijah G.

*Mercer Colony.

*Mercer's Bluff.

*Mercers Creek.

*Mercer's Gap, Texas.

*Merchant, Clabe W.

*Merchants War.

*Mercury, Texas.

*Mercury Mining in Texas. In 1954 the federal government's price guarantee of $225 per flask and increased national consumption of mercury stimulated further recovery of mercury from cinnabar deposits around Terlingua in Brewster County. The following year two Texas mines were producing mercury for the open market.

From 1955 to 1957 private interests and a company under federal contract conducted drilling operations without much success. The establishment of thirty-ton rotary furnaces by Lone Star Mercury in their operations in 1956 made little difference in production. Texas-produced mercury continued to be insignificant, and in 1960 Texas and Arizona had a combined production of only 128 seventy-six-pound flasks out of the nation's total of 33,233.

Mercury consumption in the United States reached 78,000 flasks in 1963, the highest in history. The following year, mercury sold for $265 per flask, the highest price in many years. A 1963 Bureau of Mines survey of potential mercury resources, based on 1961 technology and production costs, indicated Texas mercury potential equaled 17,500 flasks.

Diamond Shamrock Chemical Company, formerly Diamond Alkali before its merger with Shamrock, leased mercury mineral rights on 28,000 acres near Terlingua and Study Butte in 1964. A price rise in mercury to $775 per flask led to considerable exploration and development by the company in 1965. In that year Texas produced a small quantity of mercury, the first in nearly five years.

Diamond Shamrock began expansion of its Study Butte facilities in 1967 with the addition of a mercury furnace and processing plant with a capacity of 100 tons of cinnabar ore per day. Most of the mercury recovered by Diamond Shamrock went into the production of chlorine and caustic soda at its Deer Park plant near Houston. By 1971, because of decreased demand for mercury, the mines in the Terlingua area were again shut down. *See also* Mineral Resources and Mining in Texas.

BIBLIOGRAPHY: *Texas Business Review* (August, 1964, September, 1964); U. S. Bureau of Mines, *Mineral Facts and Problems* (1965); U.S. Bureau of Mines, *Minerals Yearbook, 1965* (1967); Bureau of Business Research, *Texas Industrial Expansion 1968* (April, 1968); *Texas Almanac* (1973).

Mercy, Sisters of. *See* Sisters of Mercy.

*Mercy Academy.

*Mereta, Texas.

Merhuan Indians. The Merhuan (Merguan, Merhuam) Indians are known only from the baptismal records of the San Antonio de Valero Mission qv at San Antonio. Their aboriginal area and affiliations are unknown. They were apparently not the same as the Muruam, who were at the same mission, and attempts to equate the Merhuan with both Meracouman and Menenquen are not convincing.

BIBLIOGRAPHY: H. E. Bolton, *Texas in the Middle Eighteenth Century* (1915); F. W. Hodge (ed.), *Handbook of American Indians*, I (1907), II (1910).

T. N. Campbell

*Meridian, Texas. Meridian, seat of Bosque County, is the farm and ranch commercial center for the county. In 1967 the town reported a hospital, fifty businesses including several manufacturing industries, and a tourist industry based on nearby Meridian State Recreation Park (*see* Parks, State). By 1970 businesses numbered thirty-four and included a turkey processor and a clothing plant. The population was 993 in 1960 and increased to 1,162 by 1970, according to the United States census.

*Meridian Creek.

*Meridian Junior College.

*Meridian Knobs.

*Meridian Mountain.

*Merit, Texas.

*Merito, Texas.

*Merkel, Texas. Merkel, in northwestern Taylor County, changed from township to mayor-alderman city government rule. The headquarters of the Taylor Electric Cooperative and the REA Telephone Cooperative were located in Merkel. Civic improvements since 1965 included a modern sewer plant, a new fire station, and an expansion and remodeling of the city hall. The town reported fifty-five businesses in 1970. The 1960 population was 2,312; the 1970 population was 2,163, according to the United States census. *See also* Abilene Standard Metropolitan Statistical Area.

*Merle, Texas.

*Meroney, William Penn.

Merrill, Hamilton Wilcox. Hamilton Wilcox Merrill was born at Byron, New York, on February 14, 1814, the son of Asa and Penelope (Dalliba) Merrill. He was graduated from the United States Military Academy at West Point in July, 1838, was assigned to the 2nd Dragoons as second lieutenant, and, after serving in the wars against the Seminole Indians in Florida, was made first lieutenant and sent to Baton Rouge, Louisiana. In 1845 he was at the arsenal in Austin, Texas. On March 1, 1846, he became a captain. After participating in the battle of Molina del Rey on September 8, 1847, he was breveted major for gallant conduct. He also fought in the capture of Mexico City.

Merrill remained in Texas and in the summer of 1850 was sent to command Fort Martin Scott.qv While at this post, he assisted in negotiating a treaty with the Indians on Spring Creek near the San Saba River. On July 6, 1851, he was ordered to establish Fort Mason.qv He did much to get the fort buildings underway, then was transferred to Fort Worth qv in July of 1852, and later was sent to Fort Belknap.qv

In 1856 he married Louisa Kauffman; they had one son. He resigned his commission on February 28, 1857, to practice law in New York. He was of-fered a commission in the Union Army, but did not accept the offer. He died at his home in New York City on July 14, 1892, and was buried at Woodlawn in that city.

BIBLIOGRAPHY: George W. Cullum, *Biographical Register*, I (1868); Frederick J. H. Merrill, *The Ancestry of Hamilton Wilcox Merrill* (1899); M. L. Crimmins (ed.), "W. G. Freeman's Report on the Eighth Military Department," *Southwestern Historical Quarterly*, LIII (1949–1950); New York *Daily Tribune*, July 16, 1892.

Margaret Bierschwale

*Merrills Creek.

*Merrilltown, Texas. [This title was incorrectly listed in Volume II as Merrillton, Texas.] Merrilltown, in Travis County just north of Austin, was a town and a post office in 1858 (not founded in 1877, as stated in Volume II). It was named for Captain Nelson Merrill (not Merrillton), who settled there in 1837 and later operated a store and post office; the stage also stopped there.

BIBLIOGRAPHY: Mary S. Barkley, *History of Travis County and Austin, 1839–1899* (1963); *Texas Almanac* (1858).

Merriman, Eli T. Eli T. Merriman was the first regular medical doctor to locate in San Marcos, Texas. He was born in Bristol, Connecticut, in 1815, and graduated from Yale University in 1833. He received his medical degree at Pennsylvania and Vermont Academy of Medicine. He came to San Marcos in 1847, moved to Brownsville in the early 1850's, and then moved to Banquette. He served in the Confederate Army as a doctor. After the war he settled in Corpus Christi, working during the yellow fever epidemic which raged in that city. He fell a victim in 1867 and was buried in Bayview Cemetery, Corpus Christi.

Eli Merriman, William Lindsey, and Edward Burleson qv bought land where the town of San Marcos presently stands and laid out the townsite, selling the first lots in 1851. Burleson died on December 26, 1851, and Lindsey and Merriman completed the project. Merriman's log cabin, built in 1847, was restored, moved to Aquarena Springs,qv and awarded a medallion by the Texas State Historical Survey Committee qv in 1963.

BIBLIOGRAPHY: Tula Townsend Wyatt, *One Hundred Years of Medicine in Hays County* (1955); Dudley Dobie, *A Brief History of Hays County and San Marcos, Texas* (M.A. thesis, University of Texas at Austin, 1932); Hays County Court Records, 1848–1852 (County Clerk's Office, San Marcos).

Tula Townsend Wyatt

*Merriman, Texas.

*Merritt, Robert Clarence.

*Mertens, Texas.

*Mertzon, Texas. Mertzon did not become the county seat of Irion County until 1936 (not 1910, as stated in Volume II). An election was held on September 7, 1936, to remove the seat from Sherwood to Mertzon, but the results were questioned in court. The election was later decreed valid, and in January, 1937, the court met to receive bids on bonds for erecting a courthouse and jail in Mertzon.

In 1970 Mertzon had fifteen businesses and its population was 513, according to the United States census.

BIBLIOGRAPHY: Leta Crawford, *A History of Irion County* (1966).

*Mesa, Texas.

*Mesa de Anguila.

Mescal Indians. [Out of alphabetical order and incorrectly listed as Mescale Indians on page 179, Volume II.] In the late seventeenth century, when first mentioned in documents, the Mescal (Mescate, Mexcal, Mezcal, Miscal, Mixcal) Indians ranged from the Río Sabinas of northeastern Coahuila across the Rio Grande at least as far as the southern margin of the Edwards Plateau in Texas. North of the Rio Grande they were often encountered along the Nueces and Frio rivers. These Mescal were among the Indians for whom the mission San Juan Bautista qv was founded at its first location on the Río Sabinas in 1699. Some Mescal families also entered San Francisco Solano Mission,qv for a few were reported there in 1706 when it was located near present Zaragoza, Coahuila. Still other Mescal migrated northeastward to the area that became known as Ranchería Grande,qv near the junction of the Little and Brazos rivers in east-central Texas. Here, in 1716, Spaniards reported a number of refugee groups from northeastern Coahuila and vicinity—Ervipiame, Mescal, Mesquite, Pamaya, Payaya, Sijame, Ticmamar, and Xarame.

The few Mescal at San Francisco Solano Mission probably followed this mission when it was moved from Coahuila to San Antonio, Texas, in 1718 and became known as San Antonio de Valero.qv However, many of those reported in Valero records may have come from Ranchería Grande. The Mescal of San Juan Bautista seem to have remained with the mission when it was moved from the Río Sabinas to present Guerrero, Coahuila, near the Rio Grande. Some were reported there as late as 1738.

The Mescal slowly lost their ethnic identity through fragmentation during the eighteenth century. Some of those at Ranchería Grande must have been absorbed by the local groups that later became known as Tonkawa. The remainder faded into the mission Indian populations of Coahuila and Texas.

Without question the Mescal spoke a Coahuiltecan dialect. At times the Mescal have been confused with the Mescalero, an Apache group of southeastern New Mexico and southwestern Texas. Both names derived from the mescal plant (maguey or century plant) whose root crowns were used extensively for food.

BIBLIOGRAPHY: V. Alessio Robles, *Coahuila y Texas en la Epoca Colonial* (1938); H. E. Bolton (ed.), *Spanish Exploration in the Southwest, 1542–1706* (1916); J. J. Figueroa Torres, *Fr. Juan Larios: Defensor de los Indios y fundador de Coahuila, 1673–1676* (1963); L. Gómez Canedo, *Primeras exploraciónes y poblamiento de Texas, 1686–1694* (1968); W. B. Griffen, *Culture Change and Shifting Populations in Central Northern Mexico* (1969); M. A. Hatcher, "The Expedition of Don Domingo Terán de los Ríos into Texas," *Preliminary Studies of the Texas*

Catholic Historical Society, II (1932); F. W. Hodge (ed.), *Handbook of American Indians*, I (1907), II (1910); P. O. Maas (ed.), *Viajes de misioneros Franciscanos á la conquista del Nuevo México* (1915); R. G. Santos, "A Preliminary Survey of the San Fernando Archives," *Texas Libraries*, XXVIII (1966–1967); J. R. Swanton, *Linguistic Material from the Tribes of Southern Texas and Northeastern Mexico* (1940); R. S. Weddle, *San Juan Bautista: Gateway to Spanish Texas* (1968).

T. N. Campbell

*Mescalero Apache Indians.

*Meshaw, Texas.

*Mesmeriser Creek.

Mesquite, Texas. (Borden County.) Mesquite is a small unincorporated farm and ranch community in northwestern Borden County near the former town of Tredway. The community consisted in 1970 of only a few houses and a dilapidated unused school building.

*Mesquite, Texas. (Dallas County.) In the two decades from 1950 to 1970 Mesquite experienced exceptional growth. Located in the metropolitan area of Dallas, Mesquite businesses increased from 175 in 1957 to 432 in 1970. Developments included a large shopping center, an industrial park, and Christian College of the Southwest, established in 1962. From a 1950 population of 1,696, the population rose to 27,526 by 1960, and increased to 55,131 by 1970, according to the United States census. *See also* Dallas Standard Metropolitan Statistical Area.

*Mesquite Branch.

*Mesquite Creek.

*Mesquite Indians. The name Mesquite (Mesquita, Mesquitte, Mezquite) was applied by the Spanish to Indian groups in both southern and western Texas, but there is no indication that the Mesquite Indians of these areas were related to each other. Other Mesquite Indians lived in Tamaulipas, but these were not involved in the Texas area, at least not under that particular name.

The Mesquite of southern Texas ranged over a territory that extended from the Medina River near present San Antonio northeastward to the Brazos River in the vicinity of modern Milam County where, along with other Coahuiltecans, they lived for a time in the Tonkawa-dominated settlements known collectively as Ranchería Grande qv Along the Medina River the Mesquite were in close association with the Aguastaya and Payaya. The Mesquite were listed among the Coahuiltecan bands for which the San José y San Miguel de Aguayo Mission qv was founded in 1720 at San Antonio, and some were also at nearby San Antonio de Valero Mission.qv

In western Texas Mesquite Indians were reported as early as 1693 in a document which lists fifty "nations" that lived north of the Rio Grande and "between Texas and New Mexico." These were evidently the same as the Mesquite of the early eighteenth century who lived along the lower Conchos River of northern Chihuahua and which some writers identify as a division of the Concho Indians.

BIBLIOGRAPHY: H. E. Bolton, *Texas in the Middle Eighteenth Century* (1915); C. W. Hackett (ed.), *Historical Documents Relating to New Mexico, Nueva Vizcaya, and Approaches Thereto, to 1773*, II (1926); F. W. Hodge (ed.), *Handbook of American Indians*, I (1907); J. C. Kelley, "The Historic Indian Pueblos of La Junta de los Ríos," *New Mexico Historical Review*, XXVII (1952), XXVIII (1953); C. Sauer, *The Distribution of Aboriginal Tribes and Languages in Northwestern Mexico* (1934); J. R. Swanton, *The Indian Tribes of North America* (1952).

T. N. Campbell

*Mesquite Landing.

*Metcalf Gap.

*Metcalf Gap, Texas.

*Metcalfe, Charles B

*Meteor Crater at Odessa.

*Meteorites in Texas. The number of recognized meteorite localities in Texas increased to 104 by 1962, and additional reports up to 1966 raised the number to 128. Some authorities are studying meteorite localities which are in close proximity with the idea that they may be related, and the count of localities would thus be somewhat reduced.

Of the named meteorites, thirty-four are irons; one is a pallasite (part iron, part olivine); and ninety-three are of various stony types, mostly chondrites. The ones of stone always greatly outnumber all others.

At least seventeen of the localities are sites of multiple pieces, especially as the stones often fall in groups. The Plainview, Dimmitt, and Tulia showers in the Panhandle have yielded hundreds of specimens due to extensive collecting efforts in favorable, almost rock-free country, and a cooperating population. There have been two iron showers in the state; one of these resulted in the formation of the Meteor Crater at Odessa.qv

The Odessa crater has been further explored by Glen Evans. Ninety-three drill holes demonstrated the absence of meteoritic material beneath the crater and confirmed the theory that a sufficiently large impacting meteorite does not bury itself, but it is ejected from the crater created by explosion and falls in fragments on the surrounding area. However, it was shown at Odessa that there was a buried, adjoining, seventy-foot-diameter crater containing a concentrated cluster of badly oxidized meteoritic nickel-iron. This smaller crater was clearly of the impact type and did not explode; there are probably one or more similar smaller impact sites nearby.

The Odessa Meteoritical Society has erected a small museum on the northeast rim and is upgrading and safeguarding the crater area, which has received a Texas State Historical Survey Committee qv marker and was designated a Registered Natural Landmark in 1965 by the National Park Service.

The Sierra Madera structure, marked by an irregular set of hills just east of a highway twenty miles south of Fort Stockton, is considered by some authorities to be the site of a possible huge meteorite impact. That considerable geologic disturbances occurred is a well-established fact. Some authorities argue that the absence of derangement with depth and the presence of shatter cones in the dolomite of the central area denote an impact from above. According to this theory, all meteorite fragments and the accompanying crater itself were eroded away long ago, leaving only an anticlinical reaction exposed. Other authorities dispute this interpretation, and the structure is still under detailed investigation.

Texas has had only nine cases of "falls"—meteorites recovered from a witnessed fireball. All were of some stony type. By an unusual coincidence, two occurred in northeast Texas in 1961 within approximately one hundred miles of each other and within a period of only a little over one hundred days.

The Harleton, Texas, eighteen-pound chondrite fell in a man's back yard near Marshall, Texas, shortly before 10:30 p.m. on May 30, 1961, and was recovered within thirty minutes from a reported depth of about two feet in soft sand. It was distributed among scientists for a careful study of a freshly fallen meteorite, especially with respect to cosmic-ray-induced effects.

On September 9, 1961, at 10:08 p.m., a detonating fireball was witnessed passing northward just east of the Fort Worth-Dallas region. It terminated near Bells, Grayson County. Some ten ounces of a very rare carbonaceous chondrite was retrieved from the meteorite over a six-month period. Only about twenty ounces of this substance had been known previously to fall in the world. This type of meteorite is quite fragile. Only one piece was recovered in a fresh condition; all the others became wet from the torrential rains of Hurricane Carla of that year.

BIBLIOGRAPHY: Brian Mason, *Meteorites* (1962); Edna O'Connell, *A Catalog of Meteorite Craters and Related Features* (1965).

Oscar E. Monnig

*Metheglin Creek. Metheglin Creek rises in southeastern Coryell County (not northern Bell County, as stated in Volume II); the creek begins about two miles north of The Grove, a small community in Coryell County, and flows south into Bell County. The word "metheglin," originally Welsh, describes a beverage usually made of fermented honey and water. See Volume II for an account of how the creek got this name.

BIBLIOGRAPHY: U. S. Geological Survey Topographic Map, "The Gatesville Quadrangle" (1958).

*Methodist Church in Texas. In 1951 the All Texas United Evangelistic Mission was carried out in all Methodist churches in the state. A total of 23,272 new members were received into the church. More than 1,300 pastors and 17,000 lay workers participated in the campaign. In 1950 the enrollment in the Sunday schools of Texas Methodist churches was 374,123. By 1965 it had increased to

497,033, plus some 40,000 members in Negro Methodist churches. Church membership between 1890 and 1950 had a net gain of 327 percent. By 1959 the number of members had risen to 823,735, not including some of the smaller Methodist sects. The Methodist Student Movement had its beginning in 1900 at Urbana, Illinois; by the 1960's its work in Texas was carried on by every sizeable institution, representing an investment of many millions of dollars in buildings and operating expenses.

Missionary donations among the Sunday schools increased more than tenfold between 1900 and 1958. Vacation schools reported 62,574 children in 1948 and 97,459 in 1958. Since 1950 ten homes for the aged have been constructed and three new hospitals have been acquired. Per capita contributions among Texas Methodists in 1948 was $35.00, but by 1956 it had increased to $59.85, thus resulting in larger sums for church purposes.

The Woman's Society of Christian Service in 1957 reported 92,248 members. There were 1,013 Methodist mens' clubs in Texas in 1957. The church's builders clubs between 1955 and 1960 aided in constructing many new church buildings throughout the state.

The Methodist church and the Evangelical United Brethren church merged as the United Methodist church in April–May, 1968, in Dallas. Just preceding this union, the Methodist church had five conferences in Texas with 723,248 members, and two Negro conferences (which were in the process of being merged with the five white ones) with 35,772 members. There were 5,850 members of Mexican descent in the Rio Grande Conference, 27,675 Negro members in the Christian Methodist Episcopal church, 34,000 members in the African Methodist Episcopal church, and about 500 in the African Methodist Episcopal Zion church. The total Methodist membership represented by these major branches of Methodism in the state in 1967 was 827,037.

BIBLIOGRAPHY: Olin W. Nail (ed.), *History of Texas Methodism, 1900–1960* (1961); Walter N. Vernon, *William Stevenson, Riding Preacher* (1964).

Olin W. Nail

Methodist Education in Texas. Methodist schools in Texas began with the establishment of Rutersville College qv in 1840. Named for Martin Ruter qv and authorized by the Republic of Texas, it was the first Methodist and Protestant school in Texas. In 1875 it merged with three other schools to form the Methodist-church-supported Southwestern University qv in Georgetown. From 1840 the number of such schools increased rapidly. Two other early schools were Alexander Institute, later Lon Morris College, and Blinn Memorial College,qqv which became county supported in 1934. Westmoorland College, the original Methodist-owned San Antonio Female College in 1860, became the University of San Antonio in 1937; it later became a part of the Presbyterian-supported Trinity University.qqv

The number of Methodist colleges declined during the 1900's. Many schools were absorbed into larger institutions, some were merged, and a number were closed. Consolidation increased during the Depression and World War II, and by 1969 ten Methodist-supported educational institutions remained. Their total enrollment for the 1968–1969 term was 17,230 students.

Only three institutions have enrollments over 1,000 students. Texas Wesleyan College qv in Fort Worth was founded in 1891 as Polytechnic College,qv and in the 1973 fall term enrollment stood at 1,712 students. Southern Methodist University,qv established in 1911, was the result of attempts to found an educational institution of the Methodist church in a metropolitan area. The university is the largest Methodist educational institution in Texas, and the 1973 fall term enrollment was 10,402 students. As of 1969, McMurry College,qv founded in 1920 in Abilene, was the youngest of the senior colleges supported by the Methodist church in Texas.qv It now ranks as the third largest Methodist school with 1,361 students reported for the 1973 fall term enrollment.

In addition to colleges, the Methodist church established many small secondary schools in the past century to meet the need for education in the small communities in Texas. As public secondary education developed in Texas, many of these church schools changed into special purpose schools, such as college preparatory, or else they ceased to function.

BIBLIOGRAPHY: Olin W. Nail (ed.), *History of Texas Methodism, 1900–1960* (1961); *Texas Almanac* (1969).

Metropolitan Areas in Texas. *See* Standard Metropolitan Statistical Areas in Texas.

Metropolitan Technical Institute. Metropolitan Technical Institute, Dallas, grew out of three parent schools: Tyler Commercial College, Metropolitan College, and Rutherford School of Business.

Tyler Commercial College dated from 1898. In 1903 the citizens of Tyler financed construction of the commercial college building. The college added the School of Radio to its Department of Telegraphy in 1922, and Metropolitan Technical Institute traces its origin to that school. Metropolitan College was founded in Dallas in 1887 and was purchased in 1899 by the partnership of W. W. Darby, E. W. Gause, and Alfonso Ragland. Ragland bought the interests of his partners in 1902.

Mr. and Mrs. Tracy H. Rutherford established the Rutherford School of Business in 1928. They purchased Metropolitan College in 1947, forming by consolidation the Rutherford-Metropolitan Schools. In 1957 Rutherford, an alumnus and former faculty member of Tyler Commercial College, added that school to his holdings, which included schools of business in Dallas and in Fort Worth. Also in 1957, Tyler Engineering College was created from the former school of radio and television and occupied a facility across the street from the commercial college. Because Dallas was a world center of electronics, a decision was made in 1960 to move the engineering college from Tyler to Dallas. A new corporation was formed, and the name of the school changed to Metropolitan Technical Institute. Hampton Rutherford became president of the institute, expanded the faculty, and added equipment to the laboratories.

During the 1960's Metropolitan Technical Institute averaged an enrollment of 600 students per year. The school offered a twenty-four-month course in automation with majors in electronic engineering, data processing, and computer programming. The staff included forty instructors and five placement counselors.

*Metting, Texas.

*Meuly, Conrad.

*Meusebach, John O.

*Meusebach-Comanche Treaty. The original Meusebach-Comanche Treaty document was returned to Texas from Europe in 1970 by Mrs. Irene Marschall King, granddaughter of John O. Meusebach.qv The document was presented by Mrs. King and her sister, Mrs. Cornelia Marschall Smith, to the Texas State Library qv in 1972.

BIBLIOGRAPHY: Austin *American*, October 23, 1970, May 19, 1972; Irene Marschall King, *John O. Meusebach* (c. 1967).

*Mexía, José Antonio. [This title was incorrectly listed as Mexia, José Antonio in Volume II.]

*Mexia, Texas. Mexia, in Limestone County, was named for Enrique Antonio Guillermo Mexía (not a Mexican general, Jorge Hammerking Mexia, as stated in Volume II—a misspelling of Jorge Hammeken y Mexía). Enrique Antonio Guillermo Mexía was the son of General José Antonio Mexía qv and the uncle of Jorge Hammeken y Mexía.

Mexia is the site of the Mexia State School,qv established in 1946, and plants making military supplies and metal products. Businesses totaled 150 in 1970. The 1960 population of 6,121 decreased to 5,943 by 1970, according to the United States census.

BIBLIOGRAPHY: Ray A. Walter, *A History of Limestone County* (1959).

*Mexia Oil Field.

*Mexia State School. Mexia State School (formerly Mexia State School and Home) is now a school for the mentally retarded. In 1967 enrollment was 2,735. Students were received by transfer from three admitting schools. Twelve ward buildings and service facilities were completed in 1963 as a part of the program to replace the temporary wartime structures. Training included arts and crafts, recreation, vocational skills, music, and academic courses.

By 1969 the vocational skills program had expanded. Mexia State School was one of the first to be selected by the Texas Education Agency qv to establish a vocational education program for the mentally retarded. A work-opportunity program provided jobs for at least 250 people in assembly work, and the Cen-Tex Sheltered Workshop was established off campus for the employment of the state school residents in furniture repair and refinishing. Other trades included in the expanding vocational work program were horticulture, mechanical maintenance, and construction trades. A new campus gymnasium was built late in 1969 and recreational classes for the residents increased. A hospital improvement project was granted recently which provided better health care at the school. By the end of 1970 the census for the school was 2,502 people; Malcolm Lauderdale was the superintendent. *See* Mentally Ill and Mentally Retarded, Care of, in Texas.

BIBLIOGRAPHY: Texas Department of Mental Health and Mental Retardation, *Annual Report, 1970*; Board for Texas State Hospitals and Special Schools, *Report* (1964).

*Mexía's Expedition. [This title was incorrectly listed as Mexia's Expedition in Volume II.]

*Mexican Advocate.

Mexican American Joint Council. The first Mexican American Joint Council was held on January 7, 1967, in Austin, Texas, when a conference of Texas Mexican American leaders convened to form a new group. Members of the council belong to, but do not represent, other Mexican American organizations in the state. A political activist group headed by Dr. George I. Sánchez,qv the council's chief purpose was stated as being the involvement of Mexican Americans more thoroughly in politics in order to secure the benefits accruing from political power. By such means the organization hoped to make possible better wages, better schools, better communities, and a better society overall for the Mexican American.

Other conference resolutions adopted at the time were: to erase the required entrance exams for admittance to the University of Texas System; to dissolve the Texas Rangers;qqv to promote legitimate labor unions; to support farm labor strikers in the Valley area; to form voter registration drives; and to participate more vigorously in city and county elections. *See also* Mexican Americans in Texas.

Mexican Americans in Texas. Because of the state's intimate historical relationship with Mexico and its geographical boundary with that nation, approximately two million people of Mexican descent lived in Texas by 1970. This population was increasing faster than any other ethnic group. The group is highly heterogeneous because of the place of origin in Mexico, the time and place of settlement in this country, and the varied circumstances encountered in the particular development of the individual Mexican American as a Texan. This heterogeneity makes difficult any generalization about the group, which has been called variously "Latin American," "Spanish American," "Mexican," and "Texas Mexican." Under these names widely varying patterns of life evolved within the group; sub-groups that are noticeably different from each other can be found in all geographical areas of the state.

Texans of Mexican descent have some fundamental features in common, however. The majority have retained Spanish as the language used in the home, a bond which provides a sense of cultural homogeneity. A further bond has been formed from the feelings which have arisen as a result of the discriminatory treatment sometimes received by the Mexican American as a member of a socioeconomic minority group. Groups organized to secure better conditions for the Mexican American in the fields of education, job procurement, housing, health, and general welfare have been founded by leading Mexican Americans. See American GI Forum; League of United Latin American Citizens (LULAC); MAYO; Mexican American Joint Council; Political Association of Spanish-Speaking Organizations (PASO); Raza Unida Party; see also Chicano; Integration in Texas; Labor, Migrant; and Crystal City, Texas (for a note on Mexican American participation in local politics).

George I. Sánchez

Mexican Christian Institute. See Christian Church Schools in Texas.

*Mexican Citizen.

*Mexican Colonization Laws, 1821–1830.

*Mexican Creek.

*Mexican Government of Texas.

*Mexican Invasions of 1842.

*Mexican War.

*Mexico, Texas.

*Mexico versus Texas. [This title was incorrectly listed in Volume II as Mexico vs. Texas.] The novel Mexico versus Texas (1838) was republished as Ambrosio de Letinez, or The First Texian Novel in 1842, when the author's name was given as A. T. Myrthe (not A. F. Myrtle, as stated in Volume II), a pseudonym, probably, for Anthony Ganilh (not Anthony Gamilh), who copyrighted the work in 1842. A facsimile reproduction of the 1842 edition was printed in 1967 by the Steck Company of Austin.

*Meyerdale School, Texas.

*Meyer's Canyon.

*Meyersville, Texas.

*Mezes, Sidney Edward.

*Mgebroff, John.

*Miami, Texas. Miami, seat of Roberts County, was known as the last real cowtown in the Panhandle. Twenty-one businesses were reported in 1970, and the town was the center for a ranching area, oil businesses, and pipeline offices. The 1960 population was 656; the 1970 population was 611.

*Mica, Texas.

Michaelis, Aline (Triplett). Aline (Triplett) Michaelis was the daughter of Frank and Betty (Herndon) Triplett. Born in 1885 in St. Louis, Missouri, she received her early education there and in Kansas City. The Kansas City Star published some of her early poems. After her marriage to Frederick G. Michaelis on September 18, 1907, and their removal to Beaumont, Texas, she became society editor of the Beaumont Enterprise. She also wrote a daily poem and other features and became known as the "Rhyming Optimist." Later her poems were syndicated by King Features Service and appeared in more than forty newspapers in the United States, Canada, and Cuba, some of which were collected in her book, Courage and Other Poems (1931). She was poet laureate of Texas qv from 1934 to 1936. She died on August 10, 1958, in Beaumont and was buried in Austin.

BIBLIOGRAPHY: Margaret Royalty Edwards, Poets Laureate of Texas (1956).

Margaret Royalty Edwards

*Michigan Draw.

*Mickey, Texas.

*Mico, Texas.

*Middle Bayou.

*Middle Bernard Creek.

*Middle Bosque River.

*Middle Concho River.

*Middle Fork of the Wichita River.

*Middle Pease River.

*Middle Sulphur River.

*Middle Valley Prong of the San Saba River.

*Middle Water, Texas.

*Middle Yegua Creek.

*Middleton, Texas.

*Midfields, Texas.

*Mid-Kansas, Texas.

*Midkiff, Texas. (Midland County.)

Midkiff, Texas. (Upton County.) Midkiff, in Upton County, was created when the oil boom began in the Spraberry area in 1950–1951. Originally called Hadacol Corner, the post office department refused the original name application. Near the site of the original Midkiff, in Midland County, which is now a ghost town, Midkiff now consists of a post office, a community hall, four churches, and several small stores. The population in 1970 was seventy-five, although approximately five hundred people, mostly residing in oil field camps, lived nearby.

*Midland, Texas. Midland, seat of Midland County, is a banking, administrative, and distributing center for the oil, cattle, and agricultural industries. In 1966 Midland reported eighty-two churches, two hospitals, four banks, a library, two newspapers, five radio stations, and a television station. A new city hall building was completed in 1966. In 1970 Midland reported petrochemical plants among its 1,376 businesses. Midland saw a dramatic increase in its population, from 21,713 in 1950 to 62,625 in 1960; there was a decline by 1970, when the United States census reported a population of 59,463. See also Midland Standard Metropolitan Statistical Area.

*Midland Army Air Field.

*Midland Christian College.

Midland College. Midland College was created as a part of the Permian Junior College System qv when that system was established in 1969. The college, located in Midland, used facilities of the Midland public schools, and there were 780 students enrolled in the regular term of 1970–1971. A bond issue for construction of new buildings for Midland College was defeated in November, 1971, mainly by the voters of Odessa, in Ector County, and the resulting controversy between the two cities led to the disannexation of Midland College from the Permian Junior College System and to the creation of Midland's own junior college district (see Permian Junior College System for an account of the legal process). In the fall of 1974 Midland College had an enrollment of 2,135 students, and Al G. Langford was president.

*Midland County. Midland County is a farming, ranching, gas, and major petrochemical area. The agricultural income averaged $7.5 million annually in the early 1970's, mostly from livestock and livestock products. Cotton, grains, and some vegetables were also produced. By January 1, 1973, total crude oil production had reached 294,257,917 barrels since production began in 1945. The county supports a library, a museum, and two foster homes. In 1958 a new building for the library was completed; an annex to the courthouse was occupied in 1964, and an agricultural exhibits building was built in 1966. Within the county in 1969, a Permian Basin Oil Museum was being developed to record the history of oil discovery and production in that area. The 1960 population was 67,717; the 1970 population had declined to 65,433, according to the United States census. See also Midland Standard Metropolitan Statistical Area.

*Midland and Northwestern Railway Company.

Midland Standard Metropolitan Statistical Area. The Midland Standard Metropolitan Statistical Area encompasses the 938 square miles of Midland County, designated as a standard metropolitan statistical area in August, 1960. In 1960 the population of the county was 67,717, with 62,625 living in the city of Midland. By 1970 the populations were 65,433 and 59,463, respectively.

The economy of the area is based principally on the discovery, development, and marketing of the rich oil and mineral deposits in the underlying Permian strata. Administrative headquarters for the Permian Basin qv oil fields of West Texas and southeast New Mexico are in Midland, where more than 650 oil and affiliated firms were located by 1966.

Although situated in a semiarid section of the High Plains with problems of little moisture, incessant wind, and intense sunlight, the area has a productive agricultural economy. The raising of livestock on more than 523,000 acres of grazing land increased substantially between 1959 and

1973 due to the development of commercial feedlots. Eighty percent of the annual farm income, which averaged $7.5 million in the early 1970's, was from beef cattle, sheep, and poultry; the remainder was from crops, mainly cotton, sorghums, and other grains, produced on approximately ten thousand acres of irrigated farmland.

The location of Midland for air and highway traffic is advantageous for industrial and administrative growth. Manufacturing value average for the period 1973–1974 was $19,037,000, and effective buying income of the metropolitan area residents in 1972 was $281,972,000. Wages paid to residents of the area amounted to $163,734,224 in 1972, when there were 19,678 people employed.

Midland, seat and largest city of Midland County, supports a park system for recreation as well as a community theater, a symphony orchestra, a civic music association, and a museum. See also Midland, Texas; Midland County; Odessa Standard Metropolitan Statistical Area; Standard Metropolitan Statistical Areas in Texas.

BIBLIOGRAPHY: Texas Almanac (1969, 1973).

Richard L. Mahan

*Midline, Texas.

*Midlothian, Texas. Midlothian, in Ellis County, had a 1960 population of 1,521 and a 1970 population of 2,322, according to the United States census. Midlothian had fifty-six businesses in 1970.

*Midway, Texas. (Bell County.)

*Midway, Texas. (Dawson County.)

Midway, Texas. (Hamilton County.) Midway, in the central portion of the county, at one time had a service station and garage and a grocery store on the highway between Hamilton and Pottsville. Apparently the owners of the businesses and their families were the only inhabitants of the place. In 1966 the businesses were closed and Midway was abandoned.

*Midway, Texas. (Henderson County.)

*Midway, Texas. (Lavaca County.)

*Midway, Texas. (Madison County.)

*Midway, Texas. (Polk County.)

Midway, Texas. (Starr County.) Midway, halfway between Rio Grande City and Roma, was the site of the county's two dairies, with a total of over one thousand dairy cattle. Irrigated farms surrounded the town, which reported about three hundred inhabitants in 1966. In that year the town had a cafe, a service station, and a grocery store.

*Midway, Texas. (Upshur County.)

Midway Airport. See Greater Southwest International Airport.

*Midway Branch.

*Midwest, Texas.

*Midwestern University. Midwestern University, at Wichita Falls, became a fully state-supported university, effective September, 1961. By 1966 Midwestern had more than doubled its enroll-

ment, physical plant, and faculty, and had become a center of education for north-central Texas and southern Oklahoma. The hundred-acre campus contained twenty-eight buildings in 1965, including a new library, men's and women's dormitories, and a science building, as well as a remodeled and enlarged student center. Physical facilities of the university were then valued at $5,851,306. Undergraduate and graduate programs came under four academic divisions: business administration and economics; education; humanities and social sciences; and sciences and mathematics. In 1969, 168 full-time faculty members carried on the instructional program; enrollment for the 1974 regular fall term reached 4,154; library holdings numbered 126,000 in 1969. John Grove Barker served as president in 1974.

*Midyett, Texas.

*Miears, Texas.

Miembros Largos Indians. The Miembros Largos (Spanish for "long limbs") Indians were mentioned in two late seventeenth-century lists of Indians that lived in western Texas. In 1683 they were recorded as a tribe known to the Jumano; their area was not identified, but it was said to be large and the people numerous. In 1693 they were named as one of fifty "nations" that lived north of the Rio Grande and "between Texas and New Mexico." This may be interpreted to mean the southern part of western Texas, since it was said that the Apache were at war with them. The linguistic and cultural affiliations of the Miembros Largos remain unknown.
BIBLIOGRAPHY: C. W. Hackett (ed.), *Historical Documents Relating to New Mexico, Nueva Vizcaya, and Approaches Thereto, to 1773,* II (1926) and *Pichardo's Treatise on the Limits of Louisiana and Texas,* I (1931).

T. N. Campbell

*Mier Expedition.

*Mier y Terán, Manuel de.

Migrant Labor. *See* Labor, Migrant.

*Mikeska, Texas.

*Milam, Benjamin Rush.

*Milam, James.

*Milam, Jefferson.

*Milam, Texas.

*Milam, Municipality of.

*Milam County. Milam County, the site of several Spanish missions, derives its income mainly from livestock and crop farming. Beef and dairy cattle, chickens, and hogs are the main livestock, while major crops include cotton, grain sorghums, corn, and peanuts. A large lignite deposit provides fuel for an aluminum plant located in Rockdale. Total crude oil production from the year 1921 to January 1, 1973, was 6,467,177 barrels. Tourist attractions include a county fair in Cameron every August and a Frontier Days celebration in Rockdale every June. Indian battlegrounds, mission sites, and Fort Sullivan,qv along with hunting and fish-

ing, are other popular attractions. The population in 1960 was 22,263; in 1970 it was 20,028, according to the United States census.

*Milam Creek.

*Milam Guards.

*Milam Liberal Institute.

*Milam Male and Female Institute.

*Milano, Texas.

*Milburn, David H.

*Milburn, Texas.

*Milby, William Polk.

*Mildred, Texas.

*Miles, Albert Baldwin.

*Miles, Edward.

*Miles, Texas. Jonathan Miles, for whom the town of Miles, in Runnels County, was named, was a pioneer cattleman of San Angelo (but not a railroad contractor, as stated in Volume II).

Susan Miles

*Miley, Texas.

*Milford, Texas.

*Military Board. *See* Texas State Military Board.

Military History of Texas and the Southwest. *Military History of Texas and the Southwest,* a quarterly, began publication in 1971. Under the ownership of Jay A. Matthews, Jr., the journal published articles and documents on military strategy, tactics, organizations, units, personalities, incidents, and experiences involving Texas and the Southwest. The publication was the successor to the National Guard qv Association of Texas publication, *Texas Military History.*qv

*Military Institute. *See* Texas Military Institute (Galveston).

*Military Mountain.

*Military Road.

*Mill Branch.

*Mill Creek.

*Mill Creek, Texas.

*Mill Creek Hills.

*Mill Creek Lake.

*Millard, Henry.

*Miller, Barry.

*Miller, Burchard.

*Miller, Clarence Heath. Clarence Heath Miller, in addition to receiving an M.A. degree from the University of Edinburgh, Scotland, in 1880, also received an LL.B. degree from the University of Texas in 1886. He inaugurated the case study system while dean of the University of Texas law department.

James W. McClendon

Miller, Edmond Thornton. Edmond Thornton Miller, for many years professor of economics and leading authority on Texas finances, was born on

June 6, 1878, in Fort Worth, the son of Henry and Eliza (Hollis) Miller. Educated at Weatherford College (A.B., 1897), the University of Texas (A.B., 1900, and A.M., 1901), the University of Chicago, and Harvard University (A.M., 1903, and Ph.D., 1909), he became an instructor in economics at the University of Texas in 1904, adjunct professor in 1913, and full professor in 1917, a position he held until his death in 1952. In 1913 Miller married Emily Maverick of San Antonio, member of a pioneer Texas family. They had three children. His book *Financial History of Texas* (1916) was long the standard work in its field. He was appointed in 1927 to the Texas Tax Survey Committee and in 1947 to the Governor's Tax Study Committee of the Texas Economy Commission. He published many scholarly articles and reviews, and one of his last studies was a comprehensive review of the state tax system, published in the *Southwestern Historical Quarterly* qv for July, 1951. Miller was also a collector of and authority on United States currency. He died on May 6, 1952, and was buried in Austin Memorial Park.

Clarence E. Ayres

*Miller, James B.

*Miller, James Francis.

*Miller, James H. C.

*Miller, James Weston.

*Miller, Lewis B.

*Miller, Pierce.

Miller, Robert Thomas. Robert Thomas Miller, son of Thomas McCall and Annie Eloise (Gillum) Miller, was born on September 21, 1893, in Austin, Texas. Miller graduated from the public schools in Austin and attended the University of Texas for two years. He then entered the cotton and produce business, and later became active in banking.

In 1933 Miller was elected mayor of Austin, serving until 1949 when he voluntarily retired from office. His administration was marked by large land acquisitions, including those for City Park, airport expansion, and Bergstrom Air Force Base, qv and by the construction of a new Lake Austin Dam, later named Tom Miller Dam. In 1955 Miller was again elected mayor and served until 1961. Politically, Miller was a moderate Democrat and close friend and ally of Lyndon B. Johnson and Sam Rayburn.qqv During the 1930's Miller and Johnson were successful in securing for Austin the first federal housing project in the nation. In 1960 Miller was active in Johnson's efforts to become the Democratic presidential nominee.

He married Nellie May Miller of Austin, on April 30, 1918, and the couple had two children. He retired from office in 1961 and died on April 30, 1962. He was buried in Oakwood Cemetery in Austin.

*Miller, Samuel.

*Miller, Samuel R.

*Miller, Simon. Simon Miller was born in Bedford County, Virginia, in 1782, the son of Captain Simon and Elizabeth (Reade) Miller. He married Lucinda Rucker in Virginia in 1802. The couple settled first in Rutherford County, Tennessee; about 1809 they moved to Missouri (later Arkansas) Territory.

Simon Miller was one of the original Old Three Hundred qv colonists who came to Texas in December, 1821, and camped on New Year Creek in present Washington County. He received title to a sitio of land in Fort Bend County on August 7, 1824, his residence at the time. Miller returned to Washington County about 1826 and obtained a quarter of a league on Cedar and New Year creeks in 1831. It is still not certain whether it was he or his son of the same name who, in 1836 along with John Alcorn, volunteered to bear an order to Captain Henry Teal,qv and who, upon sighting two Mexicans whom they mistakenly took for spies of General Antonio Gaona,qv returned to inform the delegates of the Convention of 1836 qv of an imminent attack, thereby hastening the adoption of the Constitution, although the attack never occurred. Simon Miller died on August 31, 1836, in Washington County.

John P. Landers

*Miller, Stewart Alexander.

*Miller, Thomas R.

*Miller, Thomas Scott.

Miller, W. Henry. W. Henry Miller was born on April 13, 1882, at Boonsville, Wise County, Texas, the son of Charles G. and Sarah (Manley) Miller. He attended schools in Boonsville and in 1901 graduated from Peaster College. In 1902 Miller moved to the South Plains and attempted to secure lands under the Four-Section Act.qv In the years following he was involved in various business ventures, including the mercantile business in Indian Territory, the Littlefield development in Lamb County, promotion of the sale and use of silos all over North Texas, and an oil company during the Burkburnett oil boom in 1918 (see Burkburnett Oil Field). In Houston Miller published his own paper, *The Heights Weekly,* in which he wrote a column, "Jake Thompson's Talk on the Topic of the Day." In 1953 Miller's book, *Pioneering North Texas,* a comprehensive work covering North Texas, was published. Included in the book is the author's family history, accounts of pioneer life, Indian depredations, the Civil War and Reconstruction,qqv and the barbed wire qv wars and grazing lease scandals of the area.

Miller married Carrie T. Hawthorne in 1919. He died in Houston on May 24, 1953, and was buried at Boonsville, Texas.

Carrie Hawthorne Miller

*Miller, Washington D.

*Miller, William Parsons.

*Miller County, Arkansas.

*Milling. With favorable railroad rates on wheat transportation, Texas flour, meal, and animal feed millers have become market oriented, locating and relocating plants where there is ready access to consumer markets—in urban areas, on major rail lines, and near Gulf Coast shipping points. This reverses the past traditions of large mills located in grain-producing regions and of numerous small mills scattered over the state. Even so, the largest number of grain mills in Texas continued to be small operations producing animal feeds for local markets. In 1954 grain mills employed 5,966 persons in all capacities and had a value added by manufacture of $48,327,000. That year's production declined to a postwar low for the 166 Texas mills (excluding sixteen rice mills); for example, only 26 million bushels of wheat were ground as compared with over 50 million bushels in 1947, and Texas' thirty wheat flour and meal millers had a total flour production of over 11.2 million hundred-weight sacks.

Texas ranked sixth in the nation in wheat flour production in 1957 with a total production of fourteen million sacks milled from 32 million bushels of wheat. By 1958 almost all of Texas' wheat milling was in the hands of three major flour and meal producers (General Mills, Burrus Mills, and Pioneer Mills) and seven smaller producers (including Fant Milling of Sherman, Seguin Milling, Graham Mills, and Morrison Milling of Denton). In that year General Mills operated at Kenedy the only guar mill in Texas, and it established at Garland the state's first refrigerated and prepared bakery products plant. In 1960 General Mills introduced a new process which sharply cut the handling and processing steps in flour milling. Called the Bellera "air spun" process, it was hailed as the most important development in the milling industry in fifty years. In July, 1965, General Mills closed down two of its mills in Texas as a result of overcapacity in the milling industry and of rising material, transportation, and manufacturing costs.

By 1963 Texas had 211 mills of all types (excluding sixteen rice mills), twenty-five of them producing wheat flour; these mills employed 6,190 Texans and added $83,489,000 in value by manufacture.

Although by 1970 a total of twenty-six mills continued to produce wheat flour in Texas, the process of corporate consolidation in the previous decade had reduced both the number of the business organizations operating mills and the number of Texas-based enterprises. Burrus Mills had become a division of ELTRA Corporation of New York; Fant Mills was operated by Nebraska Consolidated Mills Company; and the H. Dittlinger Roller Mills Company of New Braunfels was a division of Flour Mills of America, Inc., of Kansas City. In addition to General Mills' continuing operations in Texas, two of its principal competitors, Quaker Oats Company and Peavey Company of Minneapolis, located large mills in Houston and Dallas, respectively. Major locally owned mills were Pioneer Flour Mills, Superior Foods of Fort Worth, and the mills of Kimball, Inc., located in Fort Worth, Gruver, Seguin (Seguin Milling Company), and Graham (Graham Mill and Elevator Company). Morrison Milling Company in Denton and Wendland Farm Products, Inc., of Temple were the only other Texas-based mills of consequence. Most wheat milling was concentrated in the Sherman, Dallas-Fort Worth, and San Antonio areas.

In 1954 Comet Rice owned and operated three of the sixteen rice mills located mainly along the Gulf Coast. In that year rice milling employed 1,304 personnel and had a value added by manufacturing of $8,554,000. As Texas rice farmers expanded cultivation, the rice-milling industry almost tripled the value added by manufacturing to $20,749,000 in 1958 and $24,432,000 in 1963. The number of rice mills and employees remained approximately the same during this time. In 1970 there were still nine rice mills operating, mainly in the Houston and Beaumont-Port Arthur-Orange standard metropolitan statistical areas.qqv The two Comet Rice mills in Houston and Beaumont dominated this industry, but Riviana Foods of Houston and General Foods Corporation of White Plains, New York, also operated large rice mills in Houston. See also Rice Culture; Wheat Production.

BIBLIOGRAPHY: Melvin R. Mason, "Flour Milling in Texas," Texas Business Review (September, 1958); U. S. Department of Commerce, 1958 Census of Manufactures (1958); U. S. Department of Commerce, 1963 Census of Manufactures (1963); University of Texas at Austin, Directory of Texas Manufacturers (1954, 1970); Dallas Times Herald, August 1, 1960; Texas Almanac (1957, 1967, 1969).

*Mills, Anson.

Mills, Charles Wright. C. Wright Mills was born in Waco on August 28, 1916, the son of Charles G. and Frances (Wright) Mills. He spent his childhood in Fort Worth, Dallas, and Sherman before attending the University of Texas, which awarded him B.A. and M.A. degrees in 1939. Mills received a Ph.D. from the University of Wisconsin in 1941. He then served as associate professor of sociology at the University of Maryland until 1945, when he received a Guggenheim Fellowship. From

1945 to 1948 Mills was director of the labor research division of the Bureau of Applied Social Research at Columbia University. He was made assistant professor of sociology at Columbia in 1946, associate professor in 1950, and full professor in 1956. Mills was visiting professor at the University of Chicago in 1949, at Brandeis University in 1953, and Fulbright professor at the University of Copenhagen during the 1956–1957 academic year.

Mills became widely known for his social criticisms of contemporary America. His major publications included: *The New Men of Power, America's Labor Leaders* (1948); *White Collar* (1951); with Hans Gerth, *Character and Social Structure* (1954); *The Power Elite* (1956); *The Causes of World War Three* (1958); *The Sociological Imagination* (1959); *Listen, Yankee; The Revolution in Cuba* (1960); and *The Marxists* (1962).

Mills married Yaroslava Surmach on June 11, 1959. He died on March 20, 1962, in New York.

*Mills, John T.

*Mills, Robert. Robert Mills and his brother David G. Mills were reputed to have built up before the Civil War a fortune worth between three and five million dollars (not three and five hundred million dollars, as stated in Volume II).

*Mills, Roger Quarles.

*Mills, William Wallace.

*Mills Branch.

*Mills County. Mills County was primarily a ranching area during the 1960's, with cattle, sheep, goats, and poultry bringing in 90 percent of the farm income in 1966. In the early 1970's receipts from total agricultural production averaged $8.5 million annually. In 1969 a limited amount of stone production was reported. A blouse factory and processing-storage facilities for wool and mohair are located in the county. Hunting and fishing along the Colorado River attract tourists. Population decreased from 4,467 in 1960 to 4,212 by 1970, according to the United States census.

*Mills Creek.

*Millsap, Texas.

*Millsaps, Isaac.

*Millseat, Texas.

*Millville, Texas.

*Millville Male and Female Academy.

*Millwood, Texas.

*Milner, Robert Teague.

*Milton, Texas. (Lamar County.)

*Milton, Texas. (Tyler County.)

*Milvid, Texas.

*Mimbres Apache Indians.

*Mims, Charles D.

*Mims, Joseph.

*Mims, Texas.

*Mina, Francisco Xavier. Francisco Xavier Mina was a student at the University of Zaragoza (not Zaragaza, as stated in Volume II). [Some later printings of Volume II contain this correction.]

*Mina, Municipality of.

*Mina Expedition. *See* Mina, Francisco Xavier.

*Minden, Texas.

*Mine Creek.

*Mineola, Texas. Mineola, in Wood County, had eighteen churches, two hospitals, a library, a newspaper, and a radio station in 1966. In 1970 the community reported 120 businesses. Located in a farming and oil-producing area, Mineola has railroad shops and manufacturers of clothing, oil field equipment, creosoted posts, and food products. Mineola is active in the Sabine River development program to make the river navigable. Mineola had a 1960 population of 3,810 and a 1970 population of 3,926, according to the United States census.

*Miner, Joel. On June 2, 1845, Joel Miner married Cynthia B. Tannehill.

Lucie C. Price

*Mineral, Texas.

*Mineral Creek.

*Mineral Resources and Mining in Texas. Minerals and mineral products of Texas, presented alphabetically below, include only those items in which a significant change has occurred since the more complete listing appeared in Volume II. Major mineral groups are treated separately, under their own headings, in this volume.

Asbestos. Further exploration in an area northwest of Allamoore in Hudspeth County was underway in the 1970's to determine the extent of a high quality amphibole-type asbestos associated with talc.

Asphalt. Numerous deposits of asphalt-bearing rocks occur in Texas. They include asphaltic Cretaceous limestones that crop out in Bexar, Burnet, Kinney, Uvalde, and other counties. Large amounts of the asphaltic limestone are quarried in Uvalde County for use chiefly as paving material. Asphaltic Cretaceous sandstones, which are not currently produced, occur in Cooke, Montague, Uvalde, and other counties.

Barite. Deposits of barite (barium sulfate) are widely distributed in Texas, but most are minor. They occur in Baylor, Brewster, Brown, Culberson, Gillespie, Hudspeth, Jeff Davis, Llano, Taylor, and other counties. During the 1960's barite was mined in the Seven Heart Gap area for use as a weighting agent in rotary-drilling muds.

Brines. Chemical plants using shallow brines are located in Gaines, Terry, and Ward counties. Magnesium chloride brines are obtained from wells in Borden County.

Burning Clay. Highly refractory clays used in making fire brick occur in the Eocene Wilcox strata of East Texas and are produced in Cherokee, Henderson, Hopkins, and Wood counties.

Carbon Black. See Carbon Black Industry.

Coal. Bituminous coal of the Pennsylvanian, Early Permian, and Cretaceous ages showed slight production in the 1960's. With increasing shortages of other fuel sources for generating electricity, however, further development of coal resources was expected in the 1970's. *See* Coal and Lignite Deposits in Texas.

Evaporites. Anhydrite is mined in Nolan County. No potash is produced in Texas.

Ferroalloy Metals (Chromium, Manganese, Molybdenum, Tungsten). A large deposit of a molybdenum mineral occurs north of Van Horn in Culberson County, but in the mid-1970's no molybdenum was being mined in Texas.

Fluorspar. Additional uses of fluorspar or fluorite have been in aerosols, refrigerants, plastics, and solvents. A fluorspar mine was operating in the Christmas Mountains of Brewster County in 1973.

Gem Stones. Collecting gem rocks and mineral specimens has attracted numerous fans ("rock hounds") and has proved quite profitable. Agate, jasper, cinnabar, fluorite, topaz, calcite, opal, petrified wood, and tektite were among stones collected by lapidarists. Quantities have not been recorded, but production value was estimated to exceed $150,000 annually during the late 1960's.

Glass Sands. Glass sands are produced from the Cretaceous in Somervell County and from the Eocene in Limestone County. Former production was in Atascosa and Coleman counties.

Granite. Granite, with other igneous rocks, occurs in the Franklin Mountains of El Paso County, the Chisos Mountains of Brewster County, the Chinati Mountains of Presidio County, and the Quitman Mountains of Hudspeth County.

Graphite. The only active mine still producing elemental graphite in the United States in 1973 was in Burnet County.

Helium. See Helium Gas Production.

Iron Ores. Deposits near Lone Star in Morris County are mined for use in producing pig iron and steel. Deposits in Cass, Cherokee, and Nacogdoches counties are exploited for use in the manufacture of Portland cement and as a mineral feed supplement.

Lead. Known deposits of lead and zinc are small and have not been mined in Texas since 1952.

Lime Materials. Cretaceous limestones are used in lime plants in Bexar, Bosque, Comal, Dallas, El Paso, Jasper, Johnson, Travis, and Williamson counties. Oyster shells are used in plants in Brazoria, Calhoun, Harris, and Nueces counties.

Magnesium. See Magnesium Industry in Texas.

Magnesium Chloride. Magnesium chloride brines are known to occur in Upper Permian strata in Borden County where they are obtained from wells for use in producing magnesium metal and chlorine at a plant southwest of Snyder.

Marble. In Culberson County, white brucite marble is quarried at Marble Canyon north of Van Horn for use as terrazzo chips and aggregate for exterior panels, and the same use is made of marble quarried in Burnet County.

Mercury. Mercury minerals occur in the Terlingua district of Brewster and Presidio counties, where mining has been carried on intermittently since 1896. Because of depletion of ore bodies and, in some cases, encroachment of groundwater, all of the operating properties in the area ceased to be commercially productive during the 1950's. Several old mines were reopened in the Terlingua area after 1965 when the price of mercury reached a high of $775 per flask (76 pounds), but concern for environmental pollution resulted in decreased demand; by 1971 the mines were again closed. Uses for mercury are in mercury-cell caustic-soda chlorine plants, in electrical apparatus, in dental preparations, in fungicides and bactericides, and in industrial instruments. *See* Mercury Mining in Texas.

Perlite. Perlite, a siliceous rock, occurs with other Tertiary igneous rocks in the Pinto Canyon area of Presidio County, about forty miles southwest of Marfa. During 1964–1967 the perlite was produced from an open pit and processed at a grinding plant nearby. Crude perlite mined outside of Texas is expanded at plants in Dallas, Fort Worth, Tomball, LaPorte, Midland, and Sweetwater for use as lightweight aggregate, filler, filter aid, insulation, and for other purposes.

Salt. See Salt Industry.

Silver. See Silver and Silver Mining.

Soapstone and Talc. Deposits of talc occur in pre-Cambrian rocks in the Allamoore-Van Horn area of Culberson and Hudspeth counties. The talc was discovered in Hudspeth County in 1932 by William Rossman. Commercial production of talc began in 1950 and considerable development occurred during 1961–1964. Six companies now mine talc, which is used in ceramic products, paint, roofing, insecticides, and for other purposes. A talc-processing mill operates at Allamoore. Soapstone deposits are mined near Willow City in northeastern Gillespie County and processed at a grinding mill in Llano for use in ceramic products and insecticides.

Sulphur. Sulphur areas include portions of Crockett, Culberson, Pecos, Reeves, and Tom Green counties. The sulphur is produced by the Frasch method in Culberson and Pecos counties. In addition, sulphur-bearing material has been produced in Culberson County for use as a fertilizer. *See* Sulphur Industry.

Tin. See Tin Smelting in Texas.

Titanium. A titanium mineral, ilmenite, occurs in sandstones in Burleson, Fayette, Lee, Starr, and other counties. Known occurrences of titanium minerals in Texas are not considered to be of commercial quantity.

Turquoise. Known deposits of turquoise in Texas have been depleted.

Uranium. Uranium ore was discovered in South Texas in the fall of 1954. A pilot, making an airborne scintillation survey to relate radioactivity to oil fields, noted a radioactive anomaly in the Tordilla Hill area of Karnes County. A short time later, an amateur rock collector discovered a deposit of uranium minerals at the foot of Tordilla Hill. A thorough search of the area followed. In South Texas, significant deposits of uranium minerals have been found in Tertiary strata within an area that extends along the Coastal Plains from northern Fayette County to southern Starr County. The uranium ore is mined from huge open pits in Karnes and Live Oak counties. Two mills for processing the ores are located in Karnes County; a third mill is in Live Oak County. An important deposit of uranium ore, not yet mined, occurs 300 feet below the surface in sand that overlies the Palangana salt dome in Duval County.

Uranium minerals also have been found in (1) the Trans-Pecos area of West Texas, including occurrences in Brewster, El Paso, Hudspeth, and Presidio counties; (2) the Red River area of North Texas; (3) the Llano Uplift area of Central Texas, including the Baringer Hill pegmatite that is now beneath the waters of Lake Buchanan; and (4) the Panhandle area of northwest Texas, where nearly 800 tons of uranium ore were obtained a number of years ago from prospects in Crosby and Garza counties.

According to the U. S. Atomic Energy Commission, Texas possessed—in January, 1971—an estimated 6.6 million tons of ore containing 10.4 thousand tons of U_3O_8.

BIBLIOGRAPHY: Bureau of Economic Geology Files, University of Texas at Austin; *Texas Business Review* (August, 1964, September, 1964); *Texas Almanac* (1973).

William L. Fisher
Berte R. Haigh

*Mineral Rights and Royalties in Texas. There has been a trend toward higher royalties with respect to oil and gas since the mid-1950's. Basic royalty on oil and gas was increased from 1/8 to 1/6 by the public school and other state land boards in 1955 and by the Board for Lease of University Lands in 1960 on gas and in 1961 on oil. The practice of overriding royalties being utilized as a portion of leasing and development promotion fees with respect to oil and gas, in amounts ranging from 1/32 to 1/4, has increasingly become a common practice. *See also* Natural Gas; Oil, Discovery and Production of.

Berte R. Haigh

Mineral Spring, Texas. *See* Sulphur Spring, Texas.

*Mineral Springs, Texas.

*Mineral Waters. *See* Mineral Resources and Mining in Texas.

*Mineral Wells, Texas. Mineral Wells, in eastern Palo Pinto County, reported thirty-seven churches, two banks, two newspapers, a business college, a radio station, and a hospital in 1966. Businesses totaled 365 in that year, including thirty-five manufacturers. A center for recreation, retired persons, health seekers, and conventioneers, Mineral Wells has industries which produce clay, plastic, and aluminum products, aircraft equipment,

clothing, boxes, and industrial filters. Fort Wolters,[qv] a helicopter training base, is located nearby. The 1960 population was 11,053 and the 1970 population, according to the United States census, had increased substantially to 18,411.

*Mineral Wells College.

*Minerva, Texas.

*Mingo, Texas.

*Mings Chapel, Texas.

*Mingus, Texas.

*Mingus Lake.

*Mining in Texas. *See* Mineral Resources and Mining in Texas.

*Minita Creek.

*Mink, Texas.

*Minna Creek.

*Minneosa Creek.

*Minter, Texas.

*Minutemen.

*Miracle, Julian Pedro.

*Miranda, Bernardo de.

*Mirando City, Texas.

*Mission, Texas. Mission, in southwestern Hidalgo County, reported eight schools, two banks, twenty-four churches, a newspaper, a radio station, a library, and a hospital in 1966. In 1970 the city had 212 businesses, including thirty-two industrial plants, and was a center for livestock pest (screwworm) eradication. Mission was also a center for tourism and agribusinesses. The 1960 population was 14,081; the 1970 population was 13,043, according to the United States census.

*Mission Architecture.

*Mission Bay.

*Mission Hill, Texas.

*Mission River.

*Mission Valley, Texas.

*Missions of Texas.

*Mississippi and Pacific Railroad.

*Missouri City, Texas. Missouri City, a suburb of Houston along the Harris-Fort Bend county line, had a 1960 population of 604 and a 1970 population of 4,136, according to the United States census. *See also* Houston Standard Metropolitan Statistical Area.

*Missouri Compromise and Texas.

*Missouri, Kansas, and Texas Extension Railway Company.

*Missouri, Kansas, and Texas Railroad System of Texas. On July 1, 1960, the Missouri, Kansas, and Texas Railroad system of Texas ("Katy"), a wholly-owned subsidiary, was taken over by the Missouri-Kansas-Texas. In 1964 the Katy system in Texas operated 1,135.3 miles of first main track. Subsidiaries were the San Antonio Belt and Terminal, the Texas Central, the Wichita Falls and Northwestern of Texas, and the Wichita Falls Railway. In 1964 it owned one-half interest in the Galveston, Houston, and Henderson Railroad, one-eighth interest in the Union Terminal, and one-third in the Texas City Terminal. In 1968 the Katy system owned 907 miles of mainline track.

James M. Day

*Missouri-Pacific System in Texas. In 1956 the Missouri-Pacific consolidated its holdings in Texas into one company. It still owns one-half interest in the Galveston, Houston, and Henderson and the Houston Belt and Terminal railroads, one-third of the Texas City Terminal, and two-fifths of the Fort Worth Belt Railway. In 1964 it operated 2,089.8 miles of first main track in Texas. By 1968 the Missouri-Pacific system owned 1,952 miles of mainline track in Texas.

James M. Day

*Mitchasson, Edward F.

*Mitchell, Asa.

*Mitchell, Eli.

*Mitchell, Joseph Daniel.

*Mitchell, Warren Jordan.

*Mitchell Branch.

*Mitchell County. Mitchell County, a farming and ranching area, gained three-fifths of its farm income in the early 1970's from livestock, mainly sheep, cattle, hogs, and poultry, and about two-fifths from crops, particularly small grains, cotton, hay, and forage. Between 1920 and January 1, 1973, total crude oil production had reached 72,342,064 barrels. Other mineral products included asphalt, concrete, sand, and gravel. A city-county airport was paved and a county library was completed by 1966. Major tourist attractions included Lake Colorado City, Champion Creek Reservoir, the Colorado City historical museum, a June Tumbleweek rodeo, and deer, turkey, quail, and dove hunting. The 1960 population was 11,255; the 1970 population was 9,073.

*Mitchell Creek.

*Mitchell Draw.

*Mitchell Mesa.

*Mitchell's Branch.

*Mitre Peak.

*Mixon, Texas.

*Mixons Creek.

*Mobeetie (New), Texas.

*Mobeetie (Old), Texas.

*Mobile, Texas.

*Mobile Grays.

*Moccasin, Texas.

*Mocho.

*Mock, William N.

*Mockingbird.

Model Cities Program. *See* Community Affairs, Department of.

*Moffat, Texas.

*Moffitt, John H.

*Moglia, Texas.

*Mohair Production. *See* Goat Ranching.

*Molina, Miguel.

*Moline, Texas.

Molyneaux, Peter. Peter Molyneaux, a journalist and lecturer who championed free trade and Southern conservatism, was born in New Orleans, Louisiana, on April 18, 1882. The son of James and Rosana (Lawlor) Molyneaux, he was of Irish ancestry and was the eldest of seven children. He attended parochial schools but quit at fifteen. After several minor jobs, he became a reporter for the New Orleans *Daily News* in 1902; later he wrote for the *Item* and the *Daily States* there. He married Etna Ester Ellzey on April 12, 1906. In 1908 he entered Meadville (Pennsylvania) Theological School; he studied economics, sociology, and philosophy for two years. After working briefly for the Philadelphia *Record*, he joined the staff of the Houston *Post* qv in 1911. In 1913–1914 he wrote for the San Antonio *Express*,qv which sent him to Mexico to report on the civil strife there. After another brief period on the Houston *Post*, 1914–1915, he became, late in 1915, chief editoral writer for the Fort Worth *Star-Telegram*,qv where he remained until 1924.

He was editor of the *Texas Monthly*, 1928–1930; editor and publisher of the *Texas Weekly*,qv 1930–1940; editor of the *Southwestern Banker*, 1935; editor of the *Texas Digest*, 1935 (and later); and editor of the *Southern Weekly*, 1943. In 1940 he began contributing a weekly column, "A Texan Looks at the World," to the Dallas *Morning News*.qv He wrote several pamphlets on economics and two books, *The Romantic Story of Texas* (1936) and *The South's Political Plight* (1947). He was a trustee of the Carnegie Endowment for International Peace, attending a conference which it sponsored in London in 1935, and a member of the Philosophical Society of Texas.qv Southern Methodist University gave him the honorary degree of Doctor of Laws. He died in Dallas on January 9, 1953.

BIBLIOGRAPHY: *Texian Who's Who* (1937); *Who's Who In America* (1950); Dallas *Journal*, April 22, 1936; Dallas *Morning News*, January 10, 1953.

Wayne Gard

*Monahans, Texas. Monahans, seat of Ward County, was incorporated in 1955. A commercial center for ranching, oil, and tourism, Monahans reported thirty-one churches, four parks, a hospital, a library, two newspapers, a radio station, and two banks in 1966. In that year Monahans was headquarters for ten oil field supply firms, for numerous oil well servicing companies, and for the district offices of twelve major oil companies. Industries included the manufacture of oil field equipment and tools and the processing of petroleum and chemical products. In 1970 the town had 222 businesses. The deepest natural gas wells in the world were drilled south of Monahans. Monahans Sandhills State

Scenic Park (*see* Parks, State) and its museum draw tourists to the city. Monahans had a 1960 population of 8,567 and a 1970 population of 8,333.

*Monaville, Texas.

*Monclova, Conde de.

*Monclova, Mexico.

*Moneto Creek.

*Money of the Republic of Texas.

*Monia Creek.

*Monington, Texas.

*Monks, John L.

*Monkstown, Texas.

*Monodale, Texas.

*Monroe, Texas. (Dallas County.)

*Monroe, Texas. (Lubbock County.)

*Monroe, Texas. (Rusk County.)

*Monroe City, Texas.

*Mont, Texas.

*Mont Belvieu, Texas. Mont Belvieu, in Chambers County and near Houston, had a 1970 population of 1,144, according to the United States census. The town had eleven businesses in 1970.

*Montague, Daniel.

Montague, Texas. (Coryell County.) Montague is an unincorporated village in the Copperas Cove division of Coryell County, an adjunct of Fort Hood.^{qv} It had a 1970 population of 1,265, according to the United States census.

*Montague, Texas. (Montague County.) Montague, the seat of Montague County, had five churches and a school in 1967. The town reported five businesses and an estimated population of 206 in 1970. The 1970 United States census showed a population of 1,170 in the combined Montague-Forestburg division of Montague County.

*Montague County. Montague County, an agricultural, oil, and manufacturing area, reported forty oil fields in 1955. Total crude production from 1924 to January 1, 1973, was 221,513,829 barrels. Since 1950 cattle have become increasingly more important to the county's economy. In the early 1970's livestock accounted for two-thirds of all farm income, while peanuts, grains, and vegetables accounted for the remaining portion. Montague was one of the few counties in which native grapes were grown commercially. In 1960 Farmers Creek Reservoir was completed, providing facilities for water sports. Other tourist attractions included Spanish Fort ^{qv} ruins, Lake Amon G. Carter, a monthly raccoon hunt, an October sidewalk art show, an August rodeo, and Jim Bowie Days. The 1960 population was 14,893; the 1970 population was 15,326, according to the United States census.

*Montague Creek.

*Montalba, Texas.

*Monte Alto, Texas.

Monte Alto Reservoir. Monte Alto Reservoir is in the Nueces-Rio Grande Coastal Basin in Hidalgo County, four miles north of Monte Alto. The reservoir, shown on early maps as Mestenas Reservoir, also is known as Willacy Reservoir. It is an off-channel storage reservoir to the Rio Grande. The project, constructed in 1939, is owned and operated by the Hidalgo-Willacy Counties Water Control and Improvement District No. 1. Monte Alto Reservoir has a capacity of 25,000 acre-feet and a surface area of 2,371 acres at elevation 56.5 feet above mean sea level. Water is diverted from the Rio Grande, in Cameron County, by a gravity canal system. From this main canal, water is diverted to another canal, known as Mestenas Canal, for distribution to land during the irrigation season or to a pumping plant that lifts surplus water to Monte Alto Reservoir for storage. When needed for irrigation, this water is released by gravity from the reservoir back to the Mestenas Canal for distribution.

BIBLIOGRAPHY: Texas Water Commission, *Bulletin 6408* (1964).

Seth D. Breeding

*Monte Christo, Texas.

*Monte Verdi.

*Montell, Texas.

*Montell Creek.

*Monteola, Texas.

*Monterey, Texas. (Angelina County.)

Monterey, Texas. (Lubbock County.) Monterey, the first town in Lubbock County, was established just north of a site which is now the campus of Texas Tech University in the spring of 1890 by W. E. Rayner, a professional promoter and real estate man. Shortly thereafter, Frank E. Wheelock and Rollie C. Burns ^{qqv} established a settlement nearby, which they named North Lubbock. To avoid a rivalry over which town was to be the county seat, Rayner, Wheelock, and Burns compromised and established another town one mile south of North Lubbock. The compromise site was named Lubbock but was laid out on the plan of Monterey. At that time Monterey had thirty-two buildings and a population of forty. Residents from both towns moved their buildings to the new site.

BIBLIOGRAPHY: Roysten E. Willis, Ghost Towns of the South Plains (M.A. thesis, Texas Technological College, 1941).

David Gracy II

*Montezuma Affair.

*Montford, Texas.

*Montgomery, Cora. *See* McManus, Jane.

*Montgomery, Edmund Duncan.

*Montgomery, James S.

Montgomery, Vaida Stewart. Vaida Stewart Montgomery was born in Childress, Texas, on August 28, 1888, daughter of William Riley and Butriss E. (Fowler) Stewart. After completing public school education in Ellis, Cottle, and Hardeman counties, she entered Metropolitan Business

College in Dallas in 1917. Her first marriage was to J. Arthur Boyd on March 5, 1905; they had two children. On June 9, 1927, she married Whitney Maxwell Montgomery.qv She was a member of the Texas Institute of Letters, the Poetry Society of Texas qqv (its recording secretary in 1944 and 1945), and the Poetry Society of America. She edited and contributed to several magazines and published handbooks on versification and writing, a reference volume entitled *A Century with Texas Poets and Poetry* (1934), and two books of lyrics, *Locoed and Other Poems* (1931) and *Hail for Rain* (1948), dealing mainly with Texas, the Southwest, and general philosophical themes. Vaida Montgomery received numerous prizes for her poetry. She won first prize in 1939 and 1944 in the Old South contest of the Poetry Society of Texas, and in December, 1942, and in February, 1944, she received the Critics award from that society. *Hail for Rain* received the Texas Institute of Letters annual award for poetry in 1948.

In May, 1929, the Montgomerys published the first issue of their poetry magazine, which was called *Kaleidoscope* during the first three years of its existence. The name was changed to *Kaleidograph* qv as a gesture of courtesy to a New York periodical which used no poetry but had adopted the name *Kaleidoscope* a month before the initial appearance of the Montgomerys' journal. *Kaleidograph* provided incentive for many aspiring Texas poets by furnishing them an outlet for their verse. At one time circulation reached approximately two thousand, the peak for most poetry magazines, and *Kaleidograph* had subscribers in every state, as well as in many countries. For the first twenty-five years *Kaleidograph* was a monthly, but during its last five years it appeared as a quarterly. It ceased publication upon Mrs. Montgomery's death in 1959.

In 1930 the Montgomerys' Kaleidoscope Publishers (subsequently changed to Kaleidograph Press) began activity by publishing three books. Output increased rapidly during the next few years, and almost all its publications were books of poetry, except for a few handbooks on versification and other volumes of prose. In addition to publishing the works of individual writers, the Montgomerys coedited several annual anthologies of poems selected from the pages of *Kaleidograph* magazines. Over the years Kaleidograph Press published books by poets from all regions of the United States, as well as from Canada, Newfoundland, and England. From 1931 to 1956, it sponsored an annual book publication contest, in which one or two titles were selected and published. During the twenty-six years in which contests were conducted, thirty-six winners were chosen.

Vaida Stewart Montgomery died in Dallas on July 24, 1959.

BIBLIOGRAPHY: *Who's Who In America* (1952); *Texian Who's Who* (1937); Vaida Montgomery, *A Century with Texas Poets and Poetry* (1934).

Sonja Fojtik

Montgomery, Whitney Maxwell. Whitney Maxwell Montgomery, son of Prosper K. and Margaret (Cook) Montgomery, was born on a farm near Eureka in Navarro County on September 14, 1877. Although his formal education ended with the eighth grade, he acquired a love of poetry from his father and was contributing verse to magazines at the age of nineteen. Although he remained on the farm as a farmer and stockman until he was fifty years old, he continued to write.

On June 9, 1927, he married a fellow poet, Vaida Stewart Boyd (*see* Vaida Stewart Montgomery), and established their home in Dallas. There, in May, 1929, he and his wife launched *Kaleidoscope* (later *Kaleidograph* qv), *A National Magazine of Verse*, and shortly afterward also entered the field of book publication. They issued the magazine monthly until 1954 and quarterly from 1954 to 1959; during the same period they published more than five hundred books of verse.

Both Whitney and his wife received numerous prizes. He won the ballad contest of the Poetry Society of Texas qv in 1941, 1942, 1943, and 1945, and received its Alamo prize in 1943. He received the poetry book award of the Texas Institute of Letters qv in 1946 for *Joseph's Coat* and also was given the Billy Chandler Memorial Award that year. His other books of verse are *Corn Silks and Cotton Blossoms* (1928), *Brown Fields and Bright Lights* (1930), and *Hounds in the Hills* (1934). He also edited *The Road to Texas* (1940) and with his wife jointly prepared five other anthologies.

He was a member of both the Poetry Society of Texas (an organizer and vice-president) and the Poetry Society of America. He served as president of the Texas Institute of Letters in 1940. For his accomplishments as poet, editor, and publisher, Southern Methodist University conferred on him the degree of Doctor of Literature in 1956.

On July 24, 1959, his wife died, and Montgomery decided to discontinue *Kaleidograph*. He died on December 7, 1966.

BIBLIOGRAPHY: *Who's Who In America* (1950); William E. Bard, "Whitney Montgomery—Notable Poet, Texan," Dallas *Times Herald*, June 3, 1956.

George Bond

*****Montgomery, William Reading.**

*****Montgomery, Texas.**

*****Montgomery County.** Montgomery County has an economy based on oil, forestry, and livestock. Total oil production between 1931 and 1973 was over 500 million barrels. In 1964 the county had twelve lumber mills, leading all Texas counties in the number of mills. Part of the Sam Houston National Forest qv is located in the northern part of the county, and the W. G. Jones State Forest is in the central part. The county has completed numerous improvements since 1957, among them a library, a county airport, a courthouse, and a hospital. Many inhabitants of the county commute to Houston. The 1960 population was 26,839; the 1970 population was 49,479, an increase of over 84 per cent, according to the United States census report. *See also* Houston Standard Metropolitan Statistical Area.

*Montgomery Institute.

*Montgomery *Patriot*.

*Monthalia, Texas.

*Monticello, Texas. (Fort Bend County.)

*Monticello, Texas. (Titus County.)

*Montopolis, Texas.

*Montrose, Marcus A.

*Monty, Texas.

*Monument, Texas.

*Monument Draw.

*Monument Hill.

*Monument Peak.

*Mooar, J. Wright. Josiah Wright Mooar's brother was John Wesley Mooar qv (not Webb Mooar, as stated in Volume II). The brothers operated in Colorado City, Texas (not Colorado Springs).

BIBLIOGRAPHY: Wayne Gard, *The Great Buffalo Hunt* (1959); Josiah Wright Mooar, "The First Buffalo Hunting in the Panhandle," *West Texas Historical Association Year Book*, VI (1930); J. Wright Mooar, "Buffalo Days," *Holland's*, 52 (January, 1933); Josiah Wright Mooar Papers (MS., Archives, University of Texas at Austin Library).

Mooar, John Wesley. John Wesley Mooar, son of John Allen and Esther K. (Wright) Mooar, and the brother of Josiah Wright Mooar,qv was born on June 12, 1846, at Pownal, Bennington County. Vermont. In 1861 he went to New York City where he worked for some ten years; after receiving a shipment of buffalo hides from his brother, John Wesley arranged to have them marketed through his business connections there. Soon a full partner in the enterprise, John Wesley joined his brother at Dodge City in November, 1872, and in 1873 their outfit crossed into Texas to hunt. In succeeding years, the two partners ranged from Kansas to Texas; as business manager, John Wesley was responsible mainly for marketing and shipping. After one of their more successful seasons of buffalo hunting, he delivered to Denison, Texas, four thousand hides which he freighted with eighteen teams of six yoke of oxen, three wagons being drawn by each team. After hunters had killed off the last buffalo herds in Texas, the brothers began a successful cattle business and settled in what is now Fisher County. John Wesley died in Colorado City, Texas, on May 24, 1918, and was buried there.

BIBLIOGRAPHY: Wayne Gard, "The Mooar Brothers, Buffalo Hunters," *Southwestern Historical Quarterly*, LXIII (1959–1960); Wayne Gard, *The Great Buffalo Hunt* (1959); B. B. Paddock, *A Twentieth Century History and Biographical Record of North and West Texas* (1906); John Wesley Mooar Papers (MS., Southwest Collection, Texas Tech University).

*Mood, Francis Asbury.

Moody, Daniel James, Jr. Dan Moody was born at Taylor, Williamson County, Texas, on June 1, 1893, the son of Daniel James and Nannie Elizabeth (Robertson) Moody. He graduated from Taylor High School and attended the University of Texas from 1910 to 1914, taking law courses during the last two years. He was admitted to the Bar in 1914 and began practice in Taylor with Harris Melasky. His early career was interrupted by service in World War I, during which he served as second lieutenant and captain in the Texas National Guard qv and second lieutenant in the United States Army. He returned to his practice after the war and in 1920 entered upon a period of public service. In successive public offices he had a record of being the youngest elected to such positions as: county attorney of Williamson County, 1920–1922; district attorney of the Twenty-sixth Judicial District, 1922–1925; attorney general of Texas, 1925–1927; and governor of Texas, elected for two terms, 1927–1931.

During his term as district attorney of the Twenty-sixth Judicial District, which included Williamson and Travis counties, and at the peak of Ku Klux Klan qv agitation, he prosecuted a group for criminal activities claimed to have been connected with the Klan and sent some of them to prison. He achieved statewide recognition for such prosecutions and, despite denunciations of the Klan, was elected attorney general, going into office at the start of the first administration of Governor Miriam A. Ferguson.qv State highway contract scandals developed within a few months, and Moody as attorney general prosecuted cases to set aside what he charged were "unconscionable" highway contracts. When these cases were won, he became the likely candidate to oppose Mrs. Ferguson when she sought a second term. The campaign has been characterized as one of the most spectacular in Texas history. After winning the first 1926 primary with 49.9 percent of the total vote, Moody defeated Mrs. Ferguson 495,723 to 270,595 in a runoff. He won renomination for the governorship in the first Democratic primary of 1928 with a clear majority. In the presidential campaign of 1928 the state Democratic party qv was rent with dissension on the prohibition and Catholic issues. Despite Governor Moody's appeals for support of the Democratic slate from top to bottom, Herbert Hoover won Texas.

As governor, Moody pursued a strong reform program. He halted a liberal convict pardon policy which had been initiated by the Fergusons and inaugurated a reorganization of prison management. He also instituted a complete reorganization of the state highway system, including a program for a connected network of roads; the cost of highways was cut by almost half that under the Ferguson administration. The office of state auditor and the auditing of state accounts were begun during his administration. Although his proposals were in accord with the thought of the progressive forces of his time, he was not successful in securing enactment of other reforms he advocated, such as important changes in the Constitution and laws. He supported a strong civil service law, the reorganization of the state government, the authorization of the governor to appoint executive officers elected under the Constitution of 1876,qv and constitutional change to permit the legislature to enact laws separating the subjects of taxation. He was no more successful than his predecessors in advocating such reforms.

In 1931 when he retired from the governorship he remained in Austin and again entered private law practice. At the request of President Franklin D. Roosevelt in 1935, he served as special assistant to the United States attorney general, in charge of prosecution of income tax evasion cases in Louisiana. He represented Texas in *State of Texas* v. *New Mexico*, a boundary dispute, and represented the governor of Texas in cases involving the right of the governor to declare martial law in the mid-1930's. He last entered active politics in the primary in 1942 as a candidate for the United States Senate against former governors W. Lee O'Daniel and James V. Allred.qqv Moody was third in the race. It was his only political defeat.

Moody remained active in party politics; he became a recognized leader of the conservative viewpoint that opposed the New Deal and the renomination of President Franklin D. Roosevelt in 1944. Although most of the conservative "Texas Regular" delegates in the convention walked out, Moody, an organizer of this anti-Roosevelt movement, did not. He stayed on and cast half of the Texas nominating votes for a conservative presidential aspirant; then he stayed within the Democratic party in the general election. Although a Democrat, he supported Republican Dwight D. Eisenhower qv for president in 1952 and 1956 and Republican Richard M. Nixon in 1960.

He served on numerous committees of the State Bar;qv one that he chaired was the special committee to study all phases of the lawyer-client relationship when the lawyer is a member of the legislature. The University of Texas School of Law honored him in 1959 by dedicating their Law Day activities to him. He served as a trustee of the University of Texas Law School Foundation.

He married Mildred Paxton of Abilene on April 20, 1926, and they had two children. He died on May 22, 1966, in Austin and was buried in the State Cemetery.qv

Richard T. Fleming

*Moody, Robert.

Moody, William Lewis. William Lewis Moody was born in Essex County, Virginia, on May 19, 1828. He received a law degree from the University of Virginia in 1851 and moved to Texas in 1852. Poor health forced him to end his law practice at Fairfield and move to Galveston as a merchant. In 1861 he raised Company G of the 7th Texas Infantry, which was captured at Fort Donelson in 1862. After spending time in camps at Douglas, Chase, and Johnson's Island, he was exchanged in the fall of 1862, sent with his regiment to Mississippi, and promoted to lieutenant colonel. He was

commended for bravery at Raymond and was incapacitated by a wound at Jackson, Mississippi, in 1863. Moody was then promoted to colonel and assigned to post duty at Austin until the end of the war.

In 1866 Moody again lived in Galveston, where he became one of the leading cotton factors and bankers of the city. He was also president of the Galveston Cotton Exchange several times during the 1870's, 1880's, and 1890's; president of the National Bank of Texas; owner of several cotton compresses in Galveston; and a director of the Gulf, Colorado, and Santa Fe Railway Company. In addition, he was a member of the Texas legislature in 1874 and a delegate to state and national Democratic conventions; he was active in efforts to make Galveston a deepwater port.

Moody married Pherabe Elizabeth Bradley on January 19, 1860; they had three sons and three daughters. He died on July 17, 1920, and was buried in Chesterfield County, Virginia, where he had lived as a child.

BIBLIOGRAPHY: S. C. Griffin, *History of Galveston, Texas* (1931); S. S. Johnson, *Texans Who Wore the Gray* (1907).

Moody, William Lewis, Jr. William Lewis Moody, Jr., son of Pherabe Elizabeth (Bradley) and William Lewis Moody,qv was born near Fairfield, Texas, in Freestone County, on January 25, 1865. He was educated in Virginia, completed studies at Virginia Military Institute, studied in Germany, and eventually returned to study law at the University of Texas. In 1886 Moody became a junior partner in his father's cotton-factoring firm, W. L. Moody & Co. His essential interest was that of expanding credit for the factorage business, but his experience along with his financial ability soon made him one of the outstanding capitalists in the United States.

In 1890 he married Libbie Rice Shearn of Houston, and for a time lived in New York City, where he was in charge of the New York branch of his father's firm. They had four children. Preferring Texas for their residence, however, the couple returned to Galveston. In 1907 he organized the City National Bank of Galveston, which was later renamed the Moody National Bank.

Other enterprises organized by Moody included the Moody Bank, Unincorporated, of Galveston; American National Insurance Company, one of the largest in the South; and National Hotel Company, a chain which expanded from the Atlantic seaboard to the Rocky Mountains. In 1920 he established the American Printing Company of Galveston; in 1923 he acquired the Galveston *News*,qv the oldest newspaper in Texas. He later purchased the Galveston *Tribune* and successfully consolidated the two newspapers; they remained Moody enterprises until they were sold in 1964. He supported the city of Galveston as a Gulf port and resort center, purchasing a two-and-one-half-million-dollar Galveston Wharves qv bond issue when there were no other bidders, and giving the city control of the properties. Along with banking, cotton, and insurance, one of Moody's prime business interests was ranching. During his lifetime he owned several hundred thousand acres of land in Texas, Oklahoma, West Virginia, and the Republic of Mexico.

Moody died on July 21, 1954, and was buried in Hitchcock, Texas. The bulk of the fortune of Moody and his wife was transferred to the Moody Foundation, one of the largest private foundations in the nation. The stated purposes of this foundation were to assist religious, charitable, scientific, and educational organizations within Texas. Another of many philanthropies left to Texas was the Moody State School for Cerebral Palsied Children qv in Galveston.

BIBLIOGRAPHY: Moody Papers and Moody Foundation Papers, Galveston, Texas; "Mr. W. L. Moody, Jr., 1865–1954," *The House of Moody*, XXI (c.1954).

Earl Wesley Fornell

*Moody, Texas. Moody, in McLennan County, had a 1960 population of 1,074 and a 1970 population of 1,286, according to the United States census. The town had thirty-two businesses in 1970.

Moody College of Marine Sciences and Maritime Resources. Founded as the Texas Maritime Academy,qv the Moody College of Marine Sciences and Maritime Resources took on the new name in the fall of 1973, although it remained a component in the Texas A&M University System;qv at that time there were 110 students enrolled, and William H. Clayton was provost. Enrollment had increased to 218 by 1974.

*Moody State School for Cerebral Palsied Children. The Moody State School for Cerebral Palsied Children was transferred in 1965 to the Medical Branch of the University of Texas at Galveston. *See also* Moody, William Lewis, Jr.; University of Texas Medical Branch at Galveston.

BIBLIOGRAPHY: University of Texas at Austin, *Guide To Texas State Agencies* (1966).

*Moodys Creek.

Moon, William Washington. William Washington Moon was born on March 25, 1814, in Madison County, Alabama, the son of Joseph and Martha (Moore) Moon. His father was killed in the battle of Horseshoe Bend on March 27, 1814, and his mother died at his birth. He grew up in Jackson County, Alabama, in the home of an uncle, and married Sophronia E. Sublett on May 12, 1834. He served in the Indian wars in Florida in 1836, and in 1838 the Moons, with a caravan of friends and relatives, came to Bastrop, Texas. He was granted land in Milam's District in 1839 (*see* Milam County; Robertson Colony). He served as a Texas Ranger,qv taking part in the Plum Creek Fight.qv He made his first trip to San Marcos Springs in 1843, and after two years moved there and started a settlement; other settlers soon arrived. His wife died in 1846, leaving him with four small daughters. He enlisted for service in the Mexican War on October 22, 1846, from San Marcos.

Moon was among the signers of a petition for the creation of Hays County. In the first county election on August 7, 1848, Moon was elected constable. He had a hotel in 1849, which became a stage stop in 1850. He was elected sheriff of Hays County on August 29, 1851. He joined the home guard and served as captain in 1860–1861, and during the Civil War he served in the 36th Texas Cavalry Regiment in the Confederate Army. After the war he operated a freight line for a time and is said to have had a blacksmith shop on the corner of what is now East Hutchinson and Union streets in San Marcos. He died on January 7, 1897.

BIBLIOGRAPHY: *Hays County Historical and Genealogical Quarterly*, I (November, 1967); Court Records, Hays County.

Tula Townsend Wyatt

*Moonshine Hill.

*Moore, Edwin Ward. Edwin Ward Moore was born July 15, 1810 (not June, 1810, as stated in Volume II), in Alexandria, Virginia. Moore returned to Galveston in 1860, where he built the Galveston Custom House (not post-office building). Moore died October 5, 1865, in New York City (not Virginia).

BIBLIOGRAPHY: Tom Henderson Wells, *Commodore Moore and the Texas Navy* (1960).

Tom Henderson Wells

*Moore, Francis.

*Moore, Francis, Jr.

*Moore, G. Bedell.

*Moore, George Fleming.

Moore, John Creed. John Creed Moore was born at Red Bridge, Hawkins County, Tennessee, on February 28, 1824, the son of Cleon and Margaret (Creed) Moore. After attending Emory and Henry College in Virginia, he was graduated from the United States Military Academy at West Point on July 1, 1849. After serving as an artillery officer in the Seminole Indian wars in Florida and at posts in Santa Fe and Fort Union, New Mexico, and in Baton Rouge, Louisiana, Moore worked as a civil engineer, and then as a teacher in Kentucky schools and colleges.

Moore entered the Confederate Army from Texas as a captain in the regular army. On September 2, 1861, Moore was commissioned colonel of the 2nd Texas Infantry Regiment at Houston and was promoted to brigadier general on May 26, 1862. His regiment, which he commanded, fought at Shiloh in April. As a brigade commander in Maury's Division, he particularly distinguished himself at Corinth in October, 1862. After the surrender at Vicksburg and his later exchange, he was assigned to duty with General Braxton Bragg's Army of Tennessee; he participated in the battles of Lookout Mountain and Missionary Ridge. Thereafter, at the request of Major General Dabney H. Maury, he was assigned to the latter's command at Mobile.

Moore resigned his commission as a general officer on February 3, 1864, apparently because he did not have a command, although Maury requested that his resignation be refused, assuring Moore that a brigade would be found for him. Thereafter, with the rank of colonel, he served in the ordnance department in charge of the arsenal at Selma, Alabama.

After the war Moore returned to Texas, where he taught school at several places, including Galveston, Kerrville, Mexia, and Dallas. At some indeterminate date after his graduation from West Point, Moore married Augusta E. Clark of New York; they had four children. Moore died on December 31, 1910, at the home of his daughter in Osage, Coryell County, Texas.

BIBLIOGRAPHY: Service Record of John C. Moore, Confederate Records (MS., National Archives, Washington, D.C.); U.S. War Department, *The War of the Rebellion: A Compilation of the Official Records of the Union and Confederate Armies* (1880–1901); Personal Statement (Records, United States Military Academy); C. A. Evans (ed.), *Confederate Military History* (1899); Ezra J. Warner, *Generals in Gray* (1959); Bob Bennett, *Kerr County, Texas* (1956); Dallas *Morning News*, January 1, 1911.

Palmer Bradley

*Moore, John Henry.

*Moore, John Matthew.

*Moore, John W.

*Moore, Littleton Wilde.

*Moore, Luke.

Moore, Robert Lee. Robert Lee Moore, son of Charles J. and Louisa Ann (Moore) Moore, was born on November 14, 1882, in Dallas, the fifth of six children. After attending school in Dallas, at the age of sixteen he was admitted to the University of Texas (at Austin), where he soon came under the influence of George Bruce Halsted, an internationally known mathematician. Under Halsted, Moore received the B.S. and M.A. degrees, both in 1901. After a year as a fellow in mathematics at the university and a year teaching mathematics in a high school in Marshall, Moore went on to graduate study at the University of Chicago. There he worked under Eliakim Hastings Moore (no relation) in one of the most active centers of mathematical research in the country.

After receiving his doctoral degree at Chicago in 1905 Moore taught at the University of Tennessee (1905–1906), Princeton University (1906–1908), Northwestern University (1908–1911), and the University of Pennsylvania (1911–1920). In 1920 Moore returned to the University of Texas as associate professor of mathematics and three years later was appointed professor. From 1907 to 1919 he published seventeen papers, thirteen of which appeared in the journals of the American Mathematical Society (AMS) and the National Academy of Sciences, and from 1914 to 1927 he was associate editor of the *Transactions* of the AMS. His field of mathematics—today called point-set topology—was a distinct and novel subject, and Moore eventually succeeded in developing his own unique approach within it. During the next twenty years at the University of Texas Moore published forty-one papers and received some of the highest honors in the American mathematical community. He was vice-president of the AMS, 1923; colloquium lecturer of the AMS in 1929, the lectures developing into

the publication *Foundations of Point Set Theory* (1932, rev. ed. 1962) as *Colloquium Publication* volume 13; elected a member of the National Academy of Sciences, 1931; fifth visiting lecturer of the AMS (and the first American to be so honored), 1931–1932; and president of the AMS, 1937–1938.

Moore had also developed a distinctive teaching method which involved the individual student in creating his own proofs and theorems within the framework set by Moore. Between 1920 and 1969, fifty doctoral students were trained in the "Moore method" of teaching (as it is known); Moore regularly taught a sequence of undergraduate courses as well. That three of his doctoral students were elected to the National Academy of Sciences was one measure of the quality of his teaching. He retired from teaching in 1969. Four years later the physics, mathematics, and astronomy building on the university campus was named the Robert Lee Moore Hall.

On August 19, 1910, Moore married Margaret MacLelland Key of Brenham, Texas; they had no children. He died on October 4, 1974, and was buried in Austin Memorial Park.

Albert C. Lewis

*Moore, Thomas.

*Moore, Thomas C.

Moore, Thomas Jefferson. Thomas Jefferson Moore, son of Jefferson and Susan (Jeffreys) Moore, was born on March 31, 1847, in Tuscaloosa County, Alabama. In 1855 Moore migrated with his family to a farm near Seguin, Texas. After serving as an enlisted man in the 32nd Texas Cavalry from 1863 to 1865, he and his father operated a freight company which served the Seguin area.

In 1870 Moore began buying Texas cattle and trailing them to northern railheads for sale. In the late 1870's he established a ranch near Llano, while continuing his trailing operations, and began experimenting with stock breeding. Besides extensive holdings in Llano and Webb counties, in 1889 he, along with John Thomas Lytle, John Rufus Blocker,qqv and W. H. Jennings, purchased the one-half-million-acre Piedra Blanca Ranch [sometimes incorrectly called "Piedra Blanco"] in Coahuila, Mexico, which Moore directed from Llano. In the late 1890's he became the president of the Llano County Bank (present Moore State Bank) of Llano.

Moore married Carrie Roberts in 1875, and they had one child. Moore died at Llano on May 31, 1911, and was buried in that city.

BIBLIOGRAPHY: J. Marvin Hunter (comp. and ed.), *The Trail Drivers of Texas*, II (1925); Jimmy M. Skaggs, "John Thomas Lytle: Cattle Baron," *Southwestern Historical Quarterly*, LXXI (1967–1968).

Jimmy M. Skaggs

*Moore, Texas.

Moore Air Force Base. After the close of the Weaver H. Baker Memorial Sanatorium qv in 1954, this installation, formerly Moore Field,qv was reactivated under the name of Moore Air Force Base.

Some four thousand air force pilots received their primary flight training and military and academic instruction at this base until December, 1960. From July, 1959, until deactivation of the base, the six-month training program featured jet plane flight instruction. In February, 1962, approximately one-half of the site was turned over to a private industry concerned with the eradication of the screwworm fly from the southwestern United States.

*Moore County. Moore County, a leading natural gas producer, is one of two areas in the state in which helium is found. There were twenty-one industrial plants with payrolls of over twelve million dollars in 1964. Between 1926 and 1973 over thirteen million barrels of oil were produced. Moore County ranked sixth among Texas counties in wheat acreage in 1960, and its 84,300 acres in 1968 placed it fourteenth in the state. The county had over 200,000 irrigated acres in 1972. By the early 1970's livestock (cattle, hogs, and poultry) brought in two-thirds of the average annual farm income of $40 million, replacing crops as the major source of farm income. Lake Meredith in the southeast corner of the county is a water supply and recreational center. The 1960 population was 14,773; the 1970 population was 14,060.

*Moore Creek.

*Moore Field. See also Moore Air Force Base.

*Moore's Fort.

Moores' Landing. Moores' Landing was located on the William Crutcher and James B. Floyd surveys in Bowie County on the banks of the Sulphur Fork of the Red River, about two miles west of the Texas-Arkansas state line. While Moores' Landing was still in existence, the Sulphur Fork carried twenty feet of water and was navigable for at least fifty miles upstream. Moores' Landing lost its importance when the Texas and Pacific Railway was completed between Jefferson and Texarkana in 1873. It was named for the Moores family, early settlers in Bowie and Cass counties.

Virginia H. Taylor

*Moores Peak.

*Moores Station, Texas.

*Mooresville, Texas.

*Mooring, Texas.

*Moorman, Charles Watson (Watt). Charles Watson Moorman married the sister of Ephraim M. Daggett qv (not Ephriam M. Daggett, as stated in Volume II).

*Mopechucope (Old Owl). See Buffalo Hump.

*Mora.

*Morales, Texas.

*Moran, Texas.

*Moras Mountain.

*Moravan, Texas.

*Moravia, Texas.

*Morbana Indians.

*More, Robert Lee.

*Morehouse, Edwin.

*Moreland, Isaac N.

Morelock, Horace Wilson. Horace Wilson Morelock was born on May 16, 1873, in Cleo, Tennessee. His parents were William M. and Sarah Lucretia (Weatherly) Morelock. Recipient of a Peabody Scholarship, he enrolled in the University of Nashville in 1895, and later received his B.A. degree, with honors, from the University of Tennessee in 1902. That fall he became professor of English at Tusculem College, Tennessee.

In 1904 he was named superintendent of city schools in Kerrville, Texas. He married Willa Royston Battaile of Houston on June 24, 1907, and they had three children.

In 1910 Morelock was named chairman of the Department of English at West Texas State Normal College (now West Texas State University). To further his professorial training he entered Harvard University in 1917, became an Austin Scholar, and received an M.A. degree. His return to West Texas State Normal College was followed by appointment to the presidency of Sul Ross State Teachers College (now Sul Ross State University) in 1923, where he served until 1945. In this capacity he helped save the institution from legislative extinction and worked toward making it a fully accredited college. Morelock was also a community leader in the Alpine area, assisting in the long campaign which resulted in the creation of Big Bend National Park.qv

His works include: *A Handbook for English Teachers* (1914), *Big Bend Panorama* (c. 1953), and *Mountains of the Mind* (c. 1956). He received an honorary LL.D. degree from Trinity University in San Antonio and was president emeritus of Sul Ross from 1945 until his death on August 4, 1966, at Austin, where he was buried in Memorial Park.

Willa B. Morelock

*Morfi, Juan Agustín.

*Morfit, Henry Mason.

*Morgan, Abel.

Morgan, Charles. Charles Morgan was born on April 21, 1795, in Killingworth (presently Clinton), Connecticut, the son of George and Betsey Morgan. He moved to New York City at the age of fourteen and soon began a ship chandlery and import business. That venture led to investments in merchant shipping and ironworks, and to management of several lines of sailing and steam packets trading with the South and the West Indies. In 1837 Morgan opened the first scheduled steamship line between New Orleans and Galveston (*see* Morgan Lines). From that axis he expanded his regular service to Matagorda Bay ports in 1848, Brazos Santiago in 1849, Vera Cruz in 1853, Key West in 1856, Rockport, Corpus Christi, and Havana in 1868, and New York in 1875. He was also both partner and rival of Cornelius Vanderbilt in attempts to establish an isthmian transit across Nicaragua in the 1850's.

During the Civil War, Morgan's vessels were seized or chartered for military and naval service by both sides, but he profited from wartime charters and machinery contracts and resumed his regular routes in 1866. As before the war, he dominated intra-Gulf trade through excellent service and his possession of exclusive United States mail contracts.

Much of Morgan's postwar career was devoted to integrating his water lines with rapidly developing rail carriers in Louisiana and Texas. He was also deeply involved in the interport rivalries of New Orleans, Mobile, Galveston, and Houston. Among railroads, he organized, reorganized, and/or managed the New Orleans, Mobile, and Texas; the New Orleans, Opelousas, and Great Western; the Louisiana Western in Louisiana; the Gulf, Western Texas, and Pacific; the Houston and Texas Central; the Texas and New Orleans; and associated lines in Texas. He also built at his own expense, in the 1870's, Houston's first deepwater ship channel to the Gulf.

In 1877 he created Morgan's Louisiana and Texas Railroad and Steamship Company as a holding company to control and operate his integrated water-rail services. The system was absorbed under lease by the Southern Pacific Company between 1883 and 1885.

On July 5, 1817, Morgan married Emily Reeves; they had five children. After her death in 1850, he married Mary Jane Sexton on June 24, 1851. He died on May 8, 1878, in New York City. *See also* Morgan Lines.

BIBLIOGRAPHY: James P. Baughman, *Charles Morgan and the Development of Southern Transportation* (1968); S. G. Reed, *A History of the Texas Railroads* (1941).

James P. Baughman

*Morgan, George Washington.

*Morgan, James.

*Morgan, John Day.

*Morgan, Texas. (Bosque County.)

*Morgan, Texas. (Lynn County.)

*Morgan Center, Texas.

*Morgan Creek.

*Morgan Lines. The Morgan Lines, originated by Charles Morgan,qv did not operate a steamer from New Orleans to Galveston in 1835, nor did Morgan Lines' ships ply Texas waters in 1836 (as stated in Volume II). The possibility of Morgan's extending service to the Gulf of Mexico may have been considered as early as 1835, but the first recorded voyage was that of the Morgan Lines' steamship *Columbia*, which arrived at New Orleans on November 18, 1837, and made its inaugural voyage to Galveston on November 25, 1837, thus making Charles Morgan's entrance into the economic life of the Gulf of Mexico. [The possibility of the earlier 1835 date appears to have originated with Lewis E. Stanton's *An Account of the Dedication of Morgan School Building, Clinton, Conn.* (1873), but no evidence in customs, shipping, or commer-cial lists of 1835–1836 can be found to support this contention.]

BIBLIOGRAPHY: James P. Baughman, *Charles Morgan and the Development of Southern Transportation* (1968).

*Morgan Mill, Texas.

*Morgans Peak.

*Morgan's Point, Texas.

*Moritas Creek.

*Morman Creek.

*Mormon Mill Colony.

*Mormons in Texas. From 1857 to the 1890's there were only a few Mormons scattered over the state. For example, Nathaniel Hunt Greer,qv a Texan who had joined the church and migrated to Utah in the 1850's, was called with his family to return to Texas on a mission. He remained for more than twenty years, providing a modest center of Mormon teaching during the years of the Civil War and Reconstruction.qqv There may have been a few other families with a similar history.

At the end of the nineteenth century a Mormon colony was established at Kelsey in Upshur County. John and Jim Edgar and their families, after migrating from Alabama to Arizona, returned eastward in 1897 and decided to settle at Kelsey. They encouraged other Mormons to join them; the colony was officially organized in 1901 and by 1918 had reached a population of about six hundred. After World War I hostility increased toward these Mormons; their meetings were harassed and neighbors refused to sell them land. When the railroad through Kelsey failed in the early 1920's, the community declined. Although stores were closed, and eventually children were taken by bus to schools in Gilmer, a Mormon congregation carried on and still existed in 1966 at Kelsey; relations with neighbors had become friendly.

Real progress of the Church of Jesus Christ of Latter-Day Saints in Texas did not result from converting individuals and then persuading them to migrate to Utah; nor could anachronistic religious colonies such as Kelsey hope to have much influence. Texas converts to Mormonism had to remain in their home communities to build up congregations. This was the task of the revived missionary proselytizing that started just before the turn of the century. With the formal abandonment of polygamy in 1890, Mormons hoped for a more favorable reception. Progress was not spectacular; for many years positions of leadership had to be filled by Utah missionaries, but the number of Texas Mormons steadily increased. In 1915 proselytizing was extended to Spanish-speaking people. By the beginning of World War II there were Mormon congregations in all major Texas cities. Proselytizing by Mormon missionaries continued in the 1960's under the direction of the present Texas Mission headquartered in Richardson and the Spanish American Mission headquartered in San Antonio.

After World War II membership had increased

sufficiently to allow the organization of Mormon "stakes" (corresponding roughly to dioceses) in El Paso (1952), Houston and Dallas (1953), San Antonio (1958), Beaumont (1961), and Corpus Christi (1964). In such areas the full church program was carried out, and leadership was assumed by local members. In other areas congregations were often smaller or more widely scattered. At the end of 1965 there were 30,818 members of the Church of Jesus Christ of Latter-Day Saints in Texas, with a total of 122 congregations.

Among Spanish-speaking congregations the use of English was encouraged. In 1964–1965 an experimental program of language instruction was conducted in San Antonio. About the same time several Spanish- and English-speaking units were merged, and worship, conferences, and auxiliary programs were integrated.

To provide religious instruction for Mormon young people of high school age, seminary classes were held daily for one hour. The first such class was organized at El Paso in 1955. By June, 1966, there were seventy such classes with a total enrollment of 1,150 students. For college students the church sponsored Deseret Clubs or Institutes of Religion at nine colleges and universities: Lamar University, Odessa College, San Antonio College, Texas Tech University, the University of Texas at El Paso, the University of Houston, Texas A&M University, East Texas State University, and the University of Texas at Austin.

The Reorganized Church of Jesus Christ of Latter-Day Saints has also been active in Texas. Several members of the old Lyman Wight qv colony joined this denomination, which has its headquarters in Independence, Missouri. It was proselytizing in Texas as early as the 1880's and has continued this activity. In 1966 it had thirty-three congregations and a total membership of 4,046 in the state.

BIBLIOGRAPHY: Norman B. Ferris (ed.), "The Diary of Morris J. Snedaker, 1855–1856," Southwestern Historical Quarterly, LXVI (1962–1963); Eliza M. Wakefield, Texas and the Greers (1953); Carl R. Hearne, The History of the Mormon Colony of Kelsey (M.A. thesis, East Texas State Teachers College, 1949); Journal History, History of the Church, History of the Texas Mission, and History of the Spanish-American Mission (MSS., Church Historian's Office, Salt Lake City, Utah).

Davis Bitton

Morning Herald (Galveston).

Morning Star (Houston).

*Moro Mountain.

*Moros Creek.

*Morphis, James M.

*Morrell, Z. N.

*Morrill, Amos.

*Morrill, Texas.

*Morris, Francis Asbury.

*Morris, George W.

Morris, Harold. Harold Morris, one of the first Texans to achieve prominence in the field of serious music, was born in San Antonio, Texas,

on March 17, 1890, the son of Harold and Nellie (Meyer) Morris. He earned his B.A. degree at the University of Texas. At the Cincinnati Conservatory he earned degrees of Master of Music in 1922 and Doctor of Music in 1939. From 1922 to 1939, Morris served as a faculty member at the Institute of Musical Art at Juilliard in New York City. In 1939 he joined the faculty of Teachers College at Columbia University.

In addition to teaching and composing, Morris toured, giving recitals and lectures. He held the guest music lectureship at Rice Institute (now Rice University) in 1933. In 1939 and 1940 he gave lectures and recitals at Duke University.

His compositions include three symphonies, piano and violin concertos and sonatas, chamber music, and solos. Several of these works have been awarded prizes such as the Juilliard Publication Award, the New York State and National Awards of the National Federation of Music Clubs, the Publication Award of the National Association of American Composers and Conductors (NAACC), the Philadelphia Music Guild Award, the Fellowship of American Composers Award, and the Award of Merit from the NAACC for service to American music. His original manuscripts are in the Texas Composers' Collection of the School of Fine Arts at the University of Texas at Austin.

Morris was active in professional organizations. He organized the American Music Guild. From 1936 to 1940 he served as United States director of the International Society for Contemporary Music. He was a life member of the NAACC and served as its vice-president.

On August 20, 1914, he married Cosby Dansby; they had one daughter. He died on May 6, 1964.

BIBLIOGRAPHY: Lota M. Spell, Music in Texas (1936); David Ewen (ed.), The Year in American Music (1948).

Alice C. Cochran

Morris, Jerry Walter. Jerry Walter Morris, who for fifty years, from 1902 to 1952, was identified with professional baseball in Texas, was born on January 30, 1880, at Rockwall, Texas. A student at the University of Texas, he left in 1902 to play with Corsicana of the Texas League, qv a league in which he spent the next twenty-six years as player, manager, club executive, and, for five years, league president. He was one of the earliest collegians to leap directly into organized baseball.

Headlines and records seemed to follow Morris. In his first season at Corsicana his club had baseball's highest winning percentage (.793), set a world record for consecutive victories (twenty-seven), never relieved a pitcher all season, and figured in the game's greatest slaughter—a 51–3 victory over Texarkana. All this was done with an eleven-man squad. While a student at the University of Texas, where he frequently played without shoes, Morris had been known as the "Barefoot Boy at Texas." He received a law degree from the University of Texas in 1906 and tried to combine law and baseball careers until 1910, when he decided that baseball was his life's work. In 1916 he became president of the Texas League and helped to arrange the Dixie Series, a thirty-seven-year match between the Texas League and the Southern Association champions. For several years he owned one-half interest in the Fort Worth Cats, and again, after 1922, he was part owner and secretary-business manager for six years for the Dallas baseball team. He also served as business manager for the Shreveport, Tyler, and Fort Worth teams.

Known throughout the sports world, he held the following personal records: club manager in his third year of organized baseball; organizer of more leagues (fourteen) and president of more (seven) than any other man on record; at one time president of three leagues concurrently—the East Texas, Evangeline, and Cotton States; builder of nine baseball parks; developer of numerous baseball players for the major leagues, including Rogers Hornsby;qv and once, in an emergency, Texas League president and umpire simultaneously. He died on August 2, 1961, of a heart attack following a surgical operation. In December, 1966, he was elected to the Texas Sports Hall of Fame.qv

Joe B. Frantz

*Morris, John D.

*Morris, Joseph Robert.

Morris, Ned Bradford. Ned Bradford Morris was born near Henderson, Texas, on September 4, 1860, the son of Mary (Bradford) and Stephen Decatur Morris.qv He married Minnie Louise Gould, one of the first female graduates of the University of Texas, on March 27, 1889. He was admitted to the Bar at Henderson, then was elected county attorney of Rusk County. Active in the Democratic party,qv in 1895 he was a leader in the party's "silver" wing and in 1896 and 1900 was a presidential elector for Texas. In 1899 he was appointed an assistant attorney general, but served less than two years. As a special investigator and prosecutor for Governor Joseph Draper Sayers,qv he helped to restore order to a portion of East Texas which had been subject to mob rule. In later life Morris practiced law in Houston and died there on November 29, 1929.

BIBLIOGRAPHY: John Bennett Boddie, *Historical Southern Families*, VI (1962); Walter Prescott Webb Files (Southern History Center, University of Texas at Austin Library); W. W. Morris Papers (MS., Archives, University of Texas at Austin Library).

Mildred Alice Webb

*Morris, Richard.

*Morris, Robert C.

Morris, Shadrach H. Shadrach H. Morris was born on December 12, 1790, in Kentucky or Tennessee. Morris served in the War of 1812 in a Louisiana regiment and lived in Sabine Parish, Louisiana, by 1827. A few years later Morris moved his family across the Sabine River into Sabine County, Texas, and received a Mexican land grant in 1835. His land was located on the western bank of the Sabine River at the mouth of the Palo Gaucho Bayou. He gave 200 acres of land here

to establish the town of Sabinetown. Here, Shadrach Morris operated a hotel and stagecoach stop. The two huge oak trees which stood at either corner of his hotel still stood on the bank by the waters of what is now Toledo Bend Reservoir in 1970. During the Runaway Scrape,qv Shadrach Morris took his family back to live in Sabine Parish, Louisiana, until 1857, when they returned to Sabine County, Texas. Morris married Mary Nelson of Mississippi about 1823; they had eleven children. He died January 18, 1864.

Helen Gomer Schluter

Morris, Stephen Decatur. Stephen Decatur Morris, son of Mary (Batchelor) and Aquilla Morris, was born in Halifax County, North Carolina, in 1819. After studying at the University of North Carolina he went to Coosa County, Alabama, where he studied law, was admitted to the Bar, and married Mary Elizabeth Bradford on January 5, 1842. Morris brought his family and slaves to Texas in 1848, settling near Henderson in Rusk County. He and his brother, William Wright Morris,qv were interested in promotion of railroads in East Texas and in development of Rusk County and Smith County resources. He moved to Troup, in Smith County, about 1871, where he collaborated with his son-in-law, Erasmus M. Hanna,qv in getting the International-Great Northern Railroad to pass through Troup. He died there on October 16, 1898.

BIBLIOGRAPHY: John Bennett Boddie, *Historical Southern Families*, X (1965); W. W. Morris Papers (MS., Archives, University of Texas at Austin Library).

Mildred Alice Webb

*Morris, William Wright.

*Morris, Texas. (DeWitt County.)

*Morris, Texas. (Falls County.)

*Morris County. Morris County, in northeast Texas, had approximately 80,000 acres in timber in 1969. The county also had extensive deposits of iron ore, furnishing raw material for a steel plant in Lone Star. Increasing numbers of beef cattle were the major source of farm income, with limited production of peanuts, grains, and vegetables. The many lakes and forested areas offer hunting, fishing, and sightseeing for tourists. The Daingerfield State Recreation Park (*see* Parks, State) is located southwest of Daingerfield. The 1960 population was 12,576; the 1970 population was 12,310.

*Morris Ferry, Texas.

*Morris Hill.

*Morris Ranch.

*Morris Ranch, Texas.

*Morris Sheppard Dam. *See also* Possum Kingdom Lake.

*Morrison, Moses.

*Morrison Creek.

Morrisstown, Texas. *See* Todville, Texas.

*Morse, Charles S.

*Morse, Texas.

*Morton, John V.

*Morton, William.

*Morton, Texas. Morton, seat of Cochran County, was a banking, distributing, and marketing center for farms and ranches in northwestern Texas and eastern New Mexico. The city's eighty-six businesses in 1970 included plants refining sulphur and gas. A hospital and numerous public improvements were added to the town in the 1950's and 1960's; the population was 2,731 in 1960 and 2,738 in 1970, according to the United States census.

*Morton Valley, Texas.

*Moscoso de Alvarado, Luis de.

*Moscoso Expedition.

*Moscow, Texas.

*Moscow, Camden, and San Augustine Railroad.

*Moser, Christopher Otto.

Moses, J. Williamson. J. Williamson Moses, son of Hannah (Lazarus) and Isaac Clifton Moses, was born on the family plantation near Old Hopewell, South Carolina, on September 1, 1825, and educated in Charleston and Philadelphia, Pennsylvania. After traveling in Florida, Georgia, and Alabama he arrived in Galveston from Mobile in 1845. He was at Wilbern (?) or Webber's Prairie, between Austin and Bastrop, in 1847. [There is some question regarding the name "Wilbern Prairie" in this area, while Webber's Prairie was well known in the 1840's. See Webberville, Texas.] In 1848 he joined the surveying party of Baron Weisberg, which surveyed land in Kendall, Gillespie, Mason, and Llano counties. He received land grants as part of his pay. From 1850 to 1860 he was with the Texas Rangers.qv He married Anna Cuellar on October 15, 1854, and generally made his home in or near Corpus Christi. He was elected justice of Precinct No. 3 (Rockport) in Refugio County in 1850.

During the time he lived in Banquete, Texas, and operated a mercantile business, he became involved with a group opposing the end of free range. Perhaps because of his opposition to the fence laws, a mob attempted to lynch him; he was saved when Captain John Rabb of the Texas Rangers arrived in time to cut him down. After that he moved with his family to Alto de Vivanco, near Saltillo, Mexico. During this time he wrote extensively of his impressions of northern Mexico. In 1871 he was chief justice of Aransas County, studied law, and was admitted to the Bar. He was postmaster in Rockport in 1871–1872. For a time he practiced law in San Diego, Texas.

Moses wrote his memoirs, "Early Times in Texas," but they were never published. Under the name "Sesom," his name reversed, he wrote for the San Antonio Express qv from 1887 to 1890 on his life in Mexico, Texas, and Florida. He died in Nueces County on August 17, 1929.

BIBLIOGRAPHY: H. L. Bentley, The Texas Legal Directory for 1876–77 (1877); Mrs. Frank de Garmo, Pathfinders of Texas: 1836–1846 (1951); Hobart Huson, Refugio, II (1955); Biographical File, Barker Texas History Center, University of Texas at Austin.

Hobart Huson

*Moses Bayou.

*Moses Lake.

*Mosheim, Texas. [This title was incorrectly listed in Volume II as Moshiem, Texas.]

*Moss Bluff, Texas.

*Moss Branch.

*Moss Creek.

*Moss Hill, Texas.

Moss Lake. Moss Lake is in the Red River Basin in Cooke County, eleven miles northwest of Gainesville on Fish Creek. Moss Lake is owned by the city of Gainesville as a water supply. Construction started on December 8, 1964, and was completed on September 24, 1966. Deliberate impoundment of a limited amount of water began in April, 1966.

The reservoir has a capacity of 23,210 acre-feet with a surface area of 1,125 acres at the service spillway elevation of 715 feet above mean sea level and a capacity of 36,400 acre-feet with a surface area of 1,500 acres at the emergency spillway crest elevation. The drainage area above the dam is sixty-nine square miles.

Seth D. Breeding

*Mossy Grove, Texas.

*Mossy Lake.

*Mostyn, Texas.

*Motley County. Motley County, formerly only a cattle-raising area, gained a part of its income from cotton and grains grown chiefly on irrigated land. In 1969, 4,000 acres were reported under irrigation. The county also had oil and gas resources. From 1957 to January 1, 1973, total crude oil production was 5,346,701 barrels. Tourists were drawn to the area for hunting, the April stock show in Matador, and the Roaring Springs Old Settlers Reunion. A new airport was completed about 1955 and a golf course about 1958. A large game preserve for antelope and deer has been established. The 1960 population was 2,870; the 1970 population was 2,178.

*Motley County Railroad.

*Motor Transportation and Regulation. See Railroad Commission.

Motor Vehicle Commission, Texas. The Texas Motor Vehicle Commission regulates manufacturers, distributors, and franchised dealers of new motor vehicles regarding manufacturers' warranties and fraud, unfair practices, discrimination, and other abuses. The commission was created in 1971 to carry out the duties and functions conferred upon it by the Texas Motor Vehicle Commission Code of 1971. Four of the six members must be licensed automobile dealers; the members serve for overlapping terms of six years. The commission also has the responsibility of establishing qualifications for licensing dealers, manufacturers, and distributors of new motor vehicles in Texas.

BIBLIOGRAPHY: University of Texas at Austin, *Guide To Texas State Agencies* (1972).

*Mott, Texas.

*Mott Creek.

*Mottley, Junius William.

*Motto, State. *See also* Texas, Origin of Name.

*Moulton, Texas.

*Mound, Texas.

*Mound Creek.

*Mound Lake.

Mound Prairie, Texas. Mound Prairie, which was located eight miles from Palestine in Anderson County on Mound Prairie Creek, was one of the county's oldest settlements. The name "Mound Prairie" came from an Indian mound located on a level stretch of treeless territory. Mound Prairie was in the heart of the plantation country and was a very prosperous community after its founding, probably in 1832. The town had among its businesses a gun factory, a blacksmith shop, a carriage repair shop, a ten pin alley, a Methodist church, a Baptist church, and the Mound Prairie Institute.qv During the Civil War the Confederate government operated a foundry there, where guns, skillets, ploughs, and iron singletrees were manufactured. In conjunction with the foundry, a mill manufactured woolen and cotton goods. The town declined after the Civil War, and few traces remained in the 1960's. Mound Prairie Cemetery perpetuates the name.

Carl L. Avera

*Mound Prairie Creek.

*Mound Prairie Institute.

*Mount Alamo.

Mount Alamo, Texas. Mount Alamo, a proposed mountain resort in the hills of Kendall County, was planned in 1912 under the direction and initiative of the (San Antonio) Fredericksburg and Northern Railway. A nearby nine-hundred-foot tunnel, the first railroad tunnel in the state, was designed to facilitate the transportation of people and building materials to both Mount Alamo and Fredericksburg. The settlement was to be on a ridge of hills between Fredericksburg and Comfort. According to promotional literature, the town was to be located close to the Guadalupe River; however, the nearest river was the Pedernales, some fifteen miles north. None of the lots were sold, and in spite of ample publicity and financial support, the mountain resort project failed to materialize because of lack of local support.

Carl Zimmerman

*Mount Barker.

*Mount Blanco, Texas.

*Mount Bonnell.

*Mount Calm, Texas.

*Mount Calvary Seminary.

*Mount Carmel, Texas.

*Mount Catherine.

*Mount Connor.

*Mount Emory.

*Mount Enterprise, Texas.

*Mount Enterprise Male and Female Academy.

*Mount Enterprise Male and Female College.

*Mount Franklin.

*Mount Holland, Texas.

*Mount Hope, Texas. (Cooke County.)

*Mount Hope, Texas. (Tyler County.)

*Mount Hudson.

*Mount Jake.

*Mount Joy, Texas.

*Mount Livermore.

*Mount Locke.

Mount Lucas, Texas. Mount Lucas, three miles south of Dinero in southeastern Live Oak County, was founded in 1914 at the point where a Missouri-Pacific Railroad depot was located. The community was named after Cyrus Lucas and for a long while was centered on a ranch owned by his daughter. In the late 1950's the depot, still bearing the name Mount Lucas, was relocated a mile north of Dinero and railroad track was relaid to the east of old Mount Lucas. Several years after its relocation, the depot was sold and removed.

Carl Zimmerman

*Mount Nebo.

*Mount Olive, Texas. (Lavaca County.)

*Mount Olive, Texas. (Mills County.)

*Mount Ord.

*Mount Pleasant, Texas. Mount Pleasant, seat of Titus County, had a 1960 population of 8,027 and a 1970 population of 8,877. The town supported industries largely concerned with poultry processing, meat packing, garment manufacturing, oil refining, lumber processing, and feed milling. Between 1956 and 1966 the town had completed Lake Tankersley, three school buildings, a post office building, and additions to the water and sewer systems. In 1966 Mount Pleasant reported thirty-one churches, three hospitals, two banks, a library, two newspapers, three nursing homes, and a radio station. In 1970 the town reported 258 business establishments.

*Mount Selman, Texas.

*Mount Sharp.

*Mount Sharp, Texas.

*Mount Sylvan, Texas.

*Mount Vernon, Texas. (Franklin County.) Mount Vernon, seat of Franklin County, is a commercial center for surrounding lumbering, oil, and livestock interests. In 1964 three industries concerned with plastics located in Mount Vernon. The town reported fifty-five businesses in 1970, including five industries employing 200 to 350 workers, and an industrial park area owned by Franklin County Industrial Foundation. A modern twenty-eight-bed hospital, a city lake and park, and thirty-five churches served the town. The 1960 population was 1,338; the 1970 census showed a population of 1,806.

*Mount Vernon, Texas. (Washington County.)

Mountain, Texas. Mountain, a suburb of Gatesville in central Coryell County, lies on U. S. Highway 84. While most of the 1965 estimated population of two hundred were employed in Gatesville or Fort Hood,qv others operated or worked on nearby farms and ranches. The original community, before it was absorbed into Gatesville, consisted of little more than a church, a school, and residences.

*Mountain City, Texas.

*Mountain Creek.

*Mountain Creek Lake. Mountain Creek Lake, in the Trinity River Basin four miles southeast of Grand Prairie on Mountain Creek, was constructed in the years 1929–1936. The capacity of the reservoir is 25,720 acre-feet, and the surface area is 2,940 acres at the top of the spillway gates at elevation 458 feet above mean sea level. The drainage area of the Mountain Creek watershed at the dam is 295 square miles.
BIBLIOGRAPHY: Texas Water Commission, *Bulletin 6408* (1964).

Seth D. Breeding

*Mountain Home, Texas. Mountain Home, in Kerr County, had a post office earlier than 1890 (the date given in Volume II). There was settlement in the area as early as 1853, evidenced by the fact that the first school was built in the community that year. The site of the post office changed many times and at one time there was no post office. Later the name of the community was changed to Eura for the postmaster Aubrey Taylor's wife. In 1923 postmistress Mrs. N. B. Estes changed the name back to Mountain Home.
BIBLIOGRAPHY: Matilda Real, A History of Kerr County, Texas (M.A. thesis, University of Texas at Austin, 1942).

*Mountain Peak, Texas.

*Mountain Springs, Texas.

*Mountain View, Texas.

Mountain View College. *See* Dallas County Community College District.

Mountain View School for Boys. The Mountain View School for Boys in Gatesville, Texas, was established on September 5, 1962, as a facility for chronic, serious offenders previously held at the Gatesville State School for Boys.qv Administration of the school was conducted by the Texas Youth Council qv and was both physically and administratively separate from other Gatesville facilities. The school was constructed to accommodate 480 male offenders, and during the period 1964–1965, the average population was 316.
BIBLIOGRAPHY: *Annual Report of the Texas Youth Council to the Governor* (1965).

William T. Field

*Mountains of Texas.

*Mouser, David.

*Mouzon, Edwin Dubose.

*Mowatt, Texas.

Mozelle, Texas. Mozelle, in south-central Coleman County, was the location of a rural school. By 1966 the community consisted of only a few nearby residences and the school.

*Mozo, Texas.

*Muchakooaga Peak.

*Mucorrera Creek.

*Mud, Texas.

*Mud Bayou.

*Mud Creek.

*Mud Lake.

*Muddy Creek.

*Muela Creek.

Muele Indians. The Muele Indians are known from a Spanish document of 1683, in which they are identified as "the nation that grinds." Their area is not clearly identified, but it seems to have been somewhere east of the Pecos River in west-central Texas. Their affiliations are unknown.
BIBLIOGRAPHY: C. W. Hackett (ed.), *Pichardo's Treatise on the Limits of Louisiana and Texas,* I (1931).

T. N. Campbell

*Muellersville, Texas.

*Muenster, Texas. Muenster, in west-central Cooke County, is the business center for an agricultural area important for dairy products, grain production, and championship breeding stock. Cheese and milk, feeds, ladies garments, and wood carvings were the major products of the city's seventy-five businesses in 1970. Muenster had a new million-dollar hospital, a bank, and several churches. The 1960 population was 1,190 and the 1970 population was 1,411.

*Muerto Creek.

Muir, Andrew Forest. Andrew Forest Muir was born in Houston, Texas, on January 8, 1916, the son of J. B. and Annie Jane (Ewing) Muir. He attended Houston public schools and graduated from Rice Institute (now Rice University) with a B.A. degree in 1938. He earned his master's degree there in 1942 and completed studies in United States history, modern European history, and American literature at the University of Texas in 1949 to earn his Ph.D. He taught at Iolani School, Honolulu; Schofield Junior College, Hawaii; Daniel Baker College, Brownwood; and Polytechnic Institute in Puerto Rico before receiving his doctorate, after which he became a professor of history at Rice, the post he held at the time of his death.

As associate editor of the *Journal of Southern History* he wrote on the political, economic, and social history of Texas from 1821 to 1874, on the Church of England in Hawaii to 1902, and on Queen Emma of Hawaii, 1836–1885. He was also a contributor to the *Handbook of Texas* and the *Southwestern Historical Quarterly,*qv and he edited

Texas in 1837 (1958) for the University of Texas Press.qv He was a contributor to the book page of the Houston *Post*.qv

He died on February 3, 1969, in Houston, where he was buried.

*Mujeres Creek.

*Mukewater Creek.

*Mula Creek.

*Mulato Creek.

*Mulato Indians. The Mulato, a subdivision of the Inocoplo, originally lived in central Tamaulipas. When their area was brought under Spanish control in the middle eighteenth century, the Mulato moved northward. Sometime prior to 1784 some of them came to San Antonio and entered San José y San Miguel de Aguayo Mission.qv Confusion may arise when *mulato* (Spanish for "mulatto") occurs in documents. The context must be carefully examined to determine if *mulato* refers to a caste or to a specific Indian group, as in this case. Swanton identified the Mulato as Coahuiltecans, but this needs confirmation.

BIBLIOGRAPHY: F. W. Hodge (ed.), *Handbook of American Indians,* I (1907); W. Jiménez Moreno, "Tribus e idiomas del Norte de México," *El Norte de México y el Sur de Estados Unidos* (1944); G. Saldivar, *Los Indios de Tamaulipas* (1943); J. R. Swanton, *Linguistic Material from the Tribes of Southern Texas and Northeastern Mexico* (1940).

T. N. *Campbell*

*Mulberry, Texas. (Fannin County.)

*Mulberry, Texas. (Red River County.)

*Mulberry Basin.

*Mulberry Creek.

*Muldoon, Michael.

*Muldoon, Texas.

*Mule Creek.

*Mule Ear Peaks.

*Mule Raising. Mule raising in Texas suffered under the impact of mechanization on Texas farms. The number of mules in Texas declined steadily: 400,000 mules in 1944, 160,000 in 1949, and 75,000 in 1954. After 1955 the United States Department of Agriculture no longer reported mules as a separate category in its agricultural statistics; instead it combined mules with horses. In that year the 68,000 mules in Texas were valued at $2,-584,000. By the late 1960's the mule had become a rarity on Texas farms.

BIBLIOGRAPHY: *Texas Almanac* (1955).

*Muleshoe, Texas. Muleshoe, seat of Bailey County, was a trading and shipping center for the agricultural products of the area. The 172 businesses in 1970 were largely connected with agriculture. In 1967 there were two hospitals, two banks, a newspaper, a radio station, a library, and a new statue of the city's namesake, the mule. By 1969 the town had a new municipal center. Population was 3,871 in 1960; 4,525 were reported in the 1970 census.

Muleshoe National Wildlife Refuge. The Muleshoe National Wildlife Refuge, situated twenty miles south of Muleshoe, Texas, was established in October, 1935, and is administered by the United States Fish and Wildlife Service in the Department of the Interior. The refuge area comprises 5,809 acres, broken by two caliche outcroppings in the form of rimrock near the northern and western boundaries, with frequent prominent draws leading to the lakes in the region. When all lakes were filled, five hundred surface acres of water became available for wintering waterfowl.

Over five thousand acres of short grass range lands were placed under a managed grazing program. Refuge personnel farmed on 160 acres of land providing a supply of grain sorghums and wheat for wildlife foods. Migrating waterfowl utilizing the area in the past were Canada geese, snow geese, pintails, blue-winged teal, American widgeon, mallards, brown cranes, and a wide variety of songbirds. Approximately 750,000 ducks mass in the area in the fall and winter.

Animals in the refuge include prairie dogs, coyotes, badgers, cottontails, and jackrabbits.

BIBLIOGRAPHY: United States Department of the Interior, "Muleshoe National Wildlife Refuge," *Refuge Leaflet 19.*

*Muleshoe Ranch.

*Mulkey, Abe.

*Mullin, Texas.

*Mullin Creek.

*Mumford, Texas.

*Muncy, Texas.

*Munday, Texas. Munday, in southeastern Knox County, served an important commercial vegetable growing area. Cotton was the principal crop, but irrigation in recent years has made profitable the cultivation of onions, sweet and Irish potatoes, cucumbers, melons, and cantaloupes. In 1967 Munday had four cotton gins, three grain elevators, vegetable-packing and -processing sheds, and a large plant for the manufacture of agricultural insecticides and various forms of fertilizers; that year the town supported a modern school system, eight churches, and seventy-five business establishments. The town reported sixty-five businesses in 1970. Munday was the home of a vegetable festival sponsored each year by the chamber of commerce. The petroleum industry around Munday has developed rapidly in recent years, and the town has become a petroleum center for two counties. The 1960 population was 1,978, and the 1970 population was 1,726, according to the United States census.

*Munger, Robert Sylvester.

*Munger, Texas.

*Mungerville, Texas.

*Municipal Government. *See* City Government.

Municipal Sales Tax. *See* Sales Tax, Municipal.

*Municipalities, League of Texas. *See* League of Texas Municipalities.

*Muñoz, Manuel.

*Muñoz, Pedro.

*Munson, Henry J.

*Munson, Thomas Volney.

*Munson, William Benjamin.

*Munson, Texas.

*Munz, Texas.

Murchison, Clinton Williams. Clinton Williams Murchison, oil operator and international financier, was one of the nation's richest men in the 1960's. The son of John Weldon and Clara (Williams) Murchison, he was born on April 11, 1895, in Tyler, Texas. He was brought up in Athens, Texas, where his father was a banker. He briefly attended Trinity University in San Antonio and served as a lieutenant in the army in World War I.

After the war, he and his boyhood friend Sid W. Richardson qv began buying oil leases in the Burkburnett Oil Field qv and went on in the early 1920's to establish their own drilling companies. In 1925 Murchison announced his intention to retire with a reported fortune of $5,000,000, but after the death of his wife in 1927 he returned to active drilling in the Pecos area. In 1929 he founded the Southern Union Gas Company, which utilized the natural gas from his wells as a fuel product, and he became a pioneer in the modern natural gas industry. During the 1930's and 1940's his American Liberty Oil Company owned a large number of producing wells in the East Texas Oil Field.qv

In 1947 Murchison became president of the Delhi Oil Company, which in 1955 became the Delhi-Taylor Oil Company, with reported assets of over $71,000,000. In 1953 Delhi's Canadian interests were transferred to Canadian Delhi Petroleum, Ltd. By 1955 he also controlled Life Companies, Inc. (with assets over $138,000,000), Transcontinental Bus Company, Union Chemical and Materials Company, Henry Holt and Company, and Martha Washington Candy Company.

In 1954 he and Sid Richardson helped Robert R. Young qv gain control of the New York Central Railroad by purchasing 800,000 voting shares of New York Central stock. Murchison is best remembered in financial circles for his struggle with Allan Kirby, Young's former partner, over control of the Alleghany Corporation. Following a bitter proxy contest, the 1961 stockholders' meeting voted to give Murchison control of the giant railroad and investment corporation, but in 1963 Murchison transferred his controlling shares to the Kirby interests.

The management of all of Murchison's businesses, with the exception of his oil companies, was vested in Investment Management Corporation, an organization founded in 1952 and managed by Clint Murchison, Jr., and John Murchison. Although he retired from his major interests in his last years, he continued to operate a country-style "trade" store in Athens.

Murchison married Anne Morris of Tyler in 1919; they had three children. Ann Morris Murchison died in 1927, and in 1942 Murchison married Virginia Long, of Commerce, Texas. He died on June 20, 1969, and was buried in Athens.

BIBLIOGRAPHY: Austin American-Statesman, June 20, 21, 1969; Dallas Morning News, June 21, 1969; Houston Post, October 6, 1962; New York Times, February 7, 1960.

Frank X. Tolbert

*Murchison, John.

*Murchison, Texas.

*Murchison Creek.

*Muriel, Texas.

*Murphree, David.

Murphy, Audie Leon. Audie Leon Murphy, the nation's most decorated soldier of World War II, was born on June 20, 1924, near Kingston, Hunt County, the son of Emmett and Josie (Killian) Murphy. A tenant farmer, the father moved the family several times in the area; when he later abandoned them it became part of Audie Murphy's job to provide food for the family by hunting squirrel and other game, a task he later said perfected his marksmanship. When the mother died, the younger children were placed in the Boles Orphan Home.qv Audie Murphy lived for a time in Celeste with the family of John Cawthon, and his education ended in the eighth grade after he attended schools in Greenville and Celeste.

Audie Murphy was working in Greenville in a radio shop when he joined the infantry of the U.S. Army on his eighteenth birthday. The Marines had rejected him when he tried to enlist after the Japanese bombed Pearl Harbor, and even at his induction Murphy stood only five feet seven inches and weighed 130 pounds, an unlikely candidate for combat duty. After final training at Fort Meade, Maryland, he reached North Africa as a replacement in an infantry company in 1943, just as the war was ending there. He took part in the campaigns for Sicily and Italy, and he was in the first wave of the invasion of southern France (Operation Dragoon) in August, 1944, earning the Distinguished Service Cross for his action against a German garrison, and later being wounded in the foot.

On January 26, 1945, near Holtzwihr, France, Murphy, by then a commissioned battlefield lieutenant and the only officer left in his company, performed the feat that earned him the Congressional Medal of Honor. After three days of fighting and with only thirty men left in his unit (Company B, 15th Infantry Regiment, 3rd Division), they were attacked by six tanks and at least a company of German infantrymen. Murphy ordered his men into the woods while he remained forward with a telephone to direct artillery fire almost upon himself. He used the machine gun on a burning tank destroyer to kill or wound fifty of the enemy, and was himself wounded in the leg. In addition to the Medal of Honor, Murphy received every combat decoration offered by the U.S. Army. Among the twenty-four awards were the Silver Star with Oak Leaf Cluster, Legion of Merit, Bronze Star, Croix de Guerre with Silver Star (one French and one Belgian), and Purple Heart with two Oak Leaf

Clusters. When he returned to Texas at the end of the war in Europe in 1945, greeted by parades in San Antonio, Dallas, and Farmersville, Audie Murphy had not yet reached twenty-one years of age.

Murphy first hoped to become a veterinarian after the war. Faced with a lack of formal education and with the prospect of supporting his younger brothers and sisters, he accepted an offer by several men in the movie industry—including the actor James Cagney—to come to Hollywood. The option on his first contract was dropped soon after his first picture, but Universal-International studios put him in *The Kid from Texas*, and Murphy's fortunes brightened. Western pictures became his standard vehicle, and he was later to say that he "made the same Western about thirty times—with different horses." More successful were several non-Western films such as *The Red Badge of Courage* and *The Quiet American*. The movie version of his autobiography, *To Hell and Back* (1949), recaptured in realistic detail his wartime exploits.

Murphy was first married to Wanda Hendrix, an actress. After their divorce he married Pamela Archer in 1951; they were the parents of two sons. Murphy died in the crash of a private plane while on a business trip near Roanoke, Virginia, on May 28, 1971. A funeral service was held at Forest Lawn Memorial Park in Los Angeles, with burial in Arlington National Cemetery. The Veterans Administration Hospital, San Antonio,qv is named in honor of Audie Murphy.

BIBLIOGRAPHY: *Newsweek* (June 14, 1971); *New Yorker* (June 21, 1952); Austin *American*, May 31, 1971, June 1, 1971; Dallas *Morning News*, June 1, 1971, January 25, 1974; San Antonio *Express-News*, August 29, 1971; Biographical File, Barker Texas History Center, University of Texas at Austin.

W. Walworth Harrison

*Murphy, William Sumter.

*Murphy, Texas.

*Murphy Creek.

*Murrah, Pendleton.

Murray, William Henry ("Alfalfa Bill"). William Henry ("Alfalfa Bill") Murray was born in the village of Toadsuck, near Collinsville, Texas, the son of Uriah Dow Thomas and Bertha Elizabeth (Jones) Murray, on November 21, 1869. He attended College Hill Institute in Springtown, Texas, and obtained a teaching certificate when he was nineteen years old. While still in his teens Murray joined the Farmers' Alliance qv and became a vigorous defender of farmers' interests both as a political orator and as a reporter for the *Farmer's World*. He was twice an unsuccessful candidate for the Texas Senate. After teaching school and editing a newspaper, he passed the Bar examination in 1897 and began practicing law in Fort Worth.

In 1898 Murray moved to Tishomingo, Indian Territory, then the capital of the Chickasaw Nation. There he became active in the politics of the territory, serving as legal advisor to the governor of the Chickasaw Nation and as a delegate to the Sequoyah Constitutional Convention, a movement which advocated separate statehood for eastern Oklahoma. On July 19, 1899, Murray married Mary Alice Hearrell, one-sixteenth Chickasaw, and became an intermarried Chickasaw citizen.

Soon after their marriage the couple moved to a farm at Twelve Mile Prairie, where Murray raised alfalfa. He earned the nickname "Alfalfa Bill" from delivering lectures to local farm organizations on the merits of cultivating that crop.

Murray presided over the Oklahoma Constitutional Convention, which met in 1906 and 1907. Many of the articles incorporated into the Constitution bear the imprint of his agrarian-Progressive philosophy. Among its provisions were a plan for agricultural education, severe restraints on corporations, prohibition of convict labor, and child-labor protection. Later he served as Speaker of the Oklahoma House of Representatives and United States congressman, and twice he ran unsuccessfully for governor. In 1919 he began plans for establishing an agricultural colony in Bolivia. In 1924 he led a group of eighty-six colonists to that country, but drouth, locusts, and an unfavorable political climate combined to prevent the colony's success. He returned to the United States in 1929.

The next year Murray ran for governor a third time, campaigning as a champion of the farmer. He hitchhiked to some of his speaking engagements to dramatize his affinity with the common people. Murray was elected to office on a platform which included lowering the state's property taxes and distributing free seed to destitute farmers.

Governor Murray attracted national attention because of his personal eccentricities and his dramatic use of executive power. In July, 1931, he defied a court order to open a free bridge across the Red River and then called out the National Guard to prevent the use of a parallel toll bridge (*see* Red River Bridge Controversy). During his term as governor, Murray launched a grass-roots presidential campaign, but he received little support outside his own state.

William Murray died on October 15, 1956, and was buried in Tishomingo, Oklahoma, beside his wife. He had one daughter and three sons, one of whom became governor of Oklahoma in 1950.

BIBLIOGRAPHY: Keith Bryant, Jr., *Alfalfa Bill Murray* (1968); Gordon Hines, *Alfalfa Bill: An Intimate Biography* (1932); William H. Murray, *Memoirs of Governor Murray and True History of Oklahoma*, I, II, III (1945).

Will Fossey

Murray, William Owen. William Owen Murray, son of William O. and Ella (Peacock) Murray, was born April 11, 1890, in Floresville. He began his legal and political career in Wilson County, where he was elected county judge in 1914, just before graduating from the University of Texas law school. He had previously attended West Texas Military Academy in San Antonio.

Murray was in public office for more than fifty years, with only a two-year interruption for World

War I service as a field artillery captain in the 36th Division,qv 1917 to 1919. He was elected district attorney of the 81st Judicial District in 1920 and district judge in 1926. In 1932 he was elected to the Fourth Court of Civil Appeals at San Antonio, where he served continuously for thirty-three years, part of the time as chief justice. During his long career as an appellate judge, he wrote 1,564 opinions, plus 56 dissenting and concurring opinions.

Murray was married to Louise Green; they had four sons. He was a Mason and a Presbyterian. He died February 18, 1974, in San Antonio, and he was buried in Sunset Memorial Park in that city.

BIBLIOGRAPHY: Biographical File, Barker Texas History Center, University of Texas at Austin.

*Murray, Texas.

*Muruam Indians. The Muruam (Moroame, Moruame) Indians were first recorded in 1707 at San Francisco Solano Mission qv near present Eagle Pass. Later, between 1721 and 1775, considerable numbers of Muruam were at San Antonio de Valero Mission qv of San Antonio. Their early presence in the Eagle Pass area suggests that they were Coahuiltecans. At San Antonio they frequently intermarried with both Coahuiltecan and Tonkawan groups, a fact which is probably the basis for J. R. Swanton's judgment that they may have been either Coahuiltecan or Tonkawan in language. The Muruam have long been equated with Cabeza de Vaca's qv Mariame, who lived near the Texas coast (vicinity of Matagorda Bay). This identification seems to be based entirely on similarity in names. The Mariame were known nearly 175 years before the Muruam entered written records. The presence of the Muruam in the Eagle Pass area when first known casts doubt on their identification with the Mariame, who lived a considerable distance farther east. Identifications based on phonetic similarities in names should meet the test of locational geography as well as chronology.

BIBLIOGRAPHY: F. W. Hodge (ed.), Handbook of American Indians, I (1907), II (1910); F. L. Hoffman (trans.), Diary of the Alarcón Expedition into Texas, 1718–1719, by Fray Francisco Céliz (1935); J. R. Swanton, Linguistic Material from the Tribes of Southern Texas and Northeastern Mexico (1940).

T. N. Campbell

*Murvaul Bayou.

Murvaul Lake. Murvaul Lake is in the Sabine River Basin in Panola County, ten miles southwest of Carthage on Murvaul Bayou. The project is owned and operated by the Panola County Fresh Water Supply District No. 1 with offices in Carthage. Construction began on September 26, 1956, and was completed on June 1, 1958. The lake has a capacity of 45,840 acre-feet and a surface area of 3,820 acres at the spillway crest elevation of 265.3 feet above mean sea level. Water is used for municipal, industrial, and recreational purposes. The drainage area above the dam is 115 square miles.

BIBLIOGRAPHY: Texas Water Commission, Bulletin 6408 (1964).

Seth D. Breeding

*Muscle Creek.

*Muse, Katie Cabell Currie.

*Muse, Kindred H.

Museum of Fine Arts, Houston. The Museum of Fine Arts in Houston, the first art museum in Texas, was opened in 1924. Since that time, as a result of private funds and donations, wings have been added, several galleries completed, and remodeling achieved. In 1926 two units were added; in 1953 the Robert Lee Blaffer Memorial Wing and the Frank Prior Sterling Galleries reached completion; and in 1958 the Junior Gallery and Cullinan Hall, designed by Mies van de Rohe, became part of the museum. In 1961 James J. Sweeney became museum director and expanded the collections with both classic and contemporary art pieces.

The permanent collections include a distinguished group of Renaissance paintings and small bronzes; the Robert Lee Blaffer Memorial Collection with works by Cézanne, Renoir, Vuillard, Vlaminck, and Toulouse-Lautrec; the Samuel H. Kress Collection of Spanish and Italian High Renaissance; the Bayou Bend Collection of Indian Art of the Southwest; the Bayou Bend Collection of prints, drawings, and watercolors; and the sixty-seven paintings and one bronze by Frederic Remington, considered one of the finest Remington collections in the United States. Bayou Bend, the former home of Miss Ima Hogg,qv was given to the museum in March, 1966. It houses a collection of American decorative arts spanning the late seventeenth, eighteenth, and early nineteenth centuries.

Museum activities center around an annual series of exhibitions with accompanying lectures, films, conducted tours, and musical programs. Each year thousands of Houston sixth-graders are conducted through the museum as a part of their studies. The museum also houses an art school, established in 1926, which has both junior and adult divisions and gives instruction in several areas of art. Adult students could earn their Bachelor of Fine Arts degrees by supplementing their art studies with sixty semester hours from an accredited college or university. See also Museums in Texas.

Emeline A. Smith

Museum of Texas Tech University. The Museum of Texas Tech University, formerly called the West Texas Museum, was created by the Plains Museum Society, which was formed on March 27, 1929, in Lubbock with sixty-nine charter members; the name of the society was changed to West Texas Museum Association on June 12, 1935. Plans for a three-story museum had been drawn, but funds for construction were not available until the Centennial qv Commission of Control made partial construction possible through its allocation of $25,000. Previously, in the summer of 1935, sixty-seven counties had agreed to pool their Centennial interests for a regional museum and for thirty-five historical markers, a goal which was only partially fulfilled through the allocation. The basement was completed and formally dedicated on March 5, 1937. In 1948 the Texas Technological College (now Texas Tech University) board of directors, at the request of the West Texas Museum Association, allocated $184,381 from the surplus of the veterans' program which, added to funds previously raised, made completion of the museum, at a cost of $226,000, a reality. The formal opening in 1950 coincided with Texas Tech's silver anniversary.

The South Plains mural in the rotunda, completed by artist Peter Hurd in 1954, featured individuals who were outstanding in the history of the area. The hall of earth and man, an archaeological and paleontological gallery, and other galleries devoted to the South Plains and its history, depicted the growth of the region. A large art gallery, an auditorium, and a planetarium offered facilities for year-round exhibits, classes, and lectures.

In 1969 the museum was officially renamed, and in the fall of 1970 the Museum of Texas Tech University moved into a new $2.5 million facility on a seventy-six acre tract. (The rotunda housing the Hurd mural was no longer a part of the museum, but remained on the campus as Holden Hall.) Adjacent to the museum is the Ranching Heritage Center,qv an outdoor exhibit depicting the development of ranching through more than twenty historical structures, relocated and authentically restored and landscaped on the site. The Moody Planetarium offers lecture-demonstrations on a regular basis. Collections in art, archaeology, biology, geology, history, and paleontology are housed in the museum and are used for research and exhibition. Permanent exhibits include a depiction of the heritage of the Llano Estacado, completed in 1973, and the hall of early Texas cultures, which opened in the fall of 1974. Special emphasis on man and his environment helped to interpret the university's role with its International Center for Arid and Semi-Arid Land Studies. In September, 1974, a Master of Arts degree in museum science was offered by Texas Tech University, utilizing the museum's collections and facilities in cooperation with related departments on the campus.

The West Texas Museum Association continued its support of the Museum of Texas Tech University, its publication, *Museum Journal* (begun in 1934) continued to publish articles on the history of the Panhandle area. *Museum Quarterly*, first published in 1972, is devoted to the activities of the museum.

The museum, through research conducted by staff members and students, issues two series of scholarly publications: *Occasional Papers of the Museum of Texas Tech University* and *Special Publications of the Museum of Texas Tech University.*

Lou Keay
Frances Stinson

Museums in Texas. The number and variety of Texas museums has increased rapidly since World War II. Most numerous are history museums, often devoted to the history of local regions, historic personages, or special subjects. In 1968 there were more than two hundred such museums scattered over the state, supported mostly by local historical societies or municipalities. Many were small, confined to a room or a hallway in a county courthouse, and staffed by volunteers. Many of the larger and more professional museums included history exhibits and collections of historic materials. Museums devoted to or including historic topics were the Panhandle-Plains Historical Museum,qv Canyon; the Hall of State,qv Dallas; the Sam Houston Memorial Museum, Huntsville; the Museum of Texas Tech University,qv Lubbock; the San Jacinto Monument and Museum of History;qv and the Texas Memorial Museum,qv University of Texas at Austin. There were also many historic houses and historic sites, some containing museums. Included among these were the French Legation qv in Austin, the Lyndon Baines Johnson qv homes (see Lyndon Baines Johnson Birthplace, Boyhood Home, and Ranch), the Dwight David Eisenhower qv birthplace in Denison, the Fort Davis National Historic Site (see Fort Davis), the Alamo qv and the missions in Texas (see Missions of Texas), the battleship *Texas* qv in the San Jacinto Battleground Park, the Varner-Hogg Plantation House at Varner-Hogg State Park (see Parks, State), the Winedale Museum,qv near Round Top, and others.

Texas could boast fifteen museums devoted solely to art, including the Dallas Museum of Fine Arts,qv the El Paso Museum of Art, the Amon Carter Museum of Western Art,qv the Fort Worth Art Center, the Kimbell Art Museum qv in Fort Worth, the Museum of Fine Arts qv in Houston, and the Marion Koogler McNay Art Institute qv in San Antonio. A number of art museums are associated with colleges and universities, including Hardin-Simmons University, Abilene; Texas Woman's University, Denton; the University Art Museum, University of Texas at Austin; the Owen Fine Arts Center, Southern Methodist University, Dallas; and the Art Gallery at Texas Christian University, Fort Worth.

By 1970 there were more than a dozen museums of natural history and science in Texas. Among these were the Dallas Museum of Natural History, the Houston Museum of Natural Science,qv and the Witte Memorial Museum qv in San Antonio, the latter a general museum which also included art and history. A number of natural history museums were associated with universities and colleges, such as the Texas Memorial Museum of the University of Texas at Austin, which also included Texas history; the Centennial Museum of the University of Texas at El Paso; the Strecker Museum of Baylor University, Waco; and the Museum of Texas Tech University, Lubbock, which was also an art and history museum. Specialized natural history museums included the Odessa Meteorite Museum and the A. V. Lane Museum of Archaeology at Southern Methodist University, Dallas.

Children's museums included the Fort Worth Children's Museum (renamed Fort Worth Museum of Science and History qv in 1969), the Corpus Christi Museum,qv and the Austin Natural Science

Center. Many other museums offer special children's programs and classes. Planetaria are found at the Houston Museum of Natural Science, the Dallas Health and Science Museum, the El Paso Centennial Museum, the Fort Worth Museum of Science and History, and the Museum of Texas Tech University.

In the larger museums and particularly those associated with universities, extensive teaching and research collections are maintained, and active research programs conducted. Most Texas museums also have active publication, lecture, film, loan, and other programs.

BIBLIOGRAPHY: *Museums Directory of the United States and Canada* (1965), *Texas Museum Directory* (n.d.); *Texas Museum Directory* (revised 1968).

W. W. Newcomb, Jr.

*Musgrove, Texas.

*Music in Texas. The history of music in Texas since 1950 is largely a reflection of the cultural boom that has swept the United States since World War II. Musical activities of every type have increased, resident opera companies have been founded, symphonies have been reorganized and expanded, choral and ballet groups have been formed, and all have played to larger audiences and received more financial support than ever before. At the same time each of these groups has suffered from rising costs and, in many cases, general public apathy. Foundation grants and generous support from civic-minded individuals and businesses have made possible much of the progress made by musical organizations in Texas.

In many respects music in Texas has come of age during the past twenty-five years. A number of the state's musical institutions have become truly professional, several of them internationally renowned. The Houston Symphony, for example, has enjoyed phenomenal growth. Conducted from 1948 to 1954 by Efrem Kurtz, the orchestra during the 1954–1955 season gave ten concerts under the direction of Thomas Beecham. That same year Leopold Stokowski was engaged as conductor and musical director; he remained in that capacity for six seasons. In 1961 John Barbirolli, formerly conductor of Halle Orchestra of Manchester, England, became the symphony's head. During the 1963–1964 season, Barbirolli took the group on a three-week tour of the East, whereupon the Houston Symphony became the first orchestra from the Southwest to play in New York and Washington, D.C. In 1969 Barbirolli was conductor emeritus. In 1973 Lawrence Foster was conductor. Through the years Miss Ima Hogg [qv] was a principal benefactress of the Houston Symphony.

The Dallas Symphony has also enjoyed considerable success, its former conductors including Antal Dorati, Walter Hendl, Paul Kletzki, and Georg Solti. In 1967 the orchestra was under the musical direction of Donald Johanos and performed in the renovated McFarlin Auditorium on the campus of Southern Methodist University. In the decade between 1950 and 1960 the symphony grew from seventy to ninety-two musicians, and the number of performances increased from thirty concerts a year to one hundred and fifty. In 1973 Max Rudolf was artistic adviser and Louis Lane was principal guest conductor.

When the founder and initial director of the San Antonio Symphony, Max Reiter,[qv] died in December, 1950, Victor Alessandro became that orchestra's head and at that time was the only native-born Texan to serve as musical director of a major symphony orchestra. Under Alessandro's leadership, the San Antonio Symphony's budget more than doubled; its artistic accomplishments both symphonic and operatic—revealed a similar growth. A grant from the Ford Foundation made possible the production of several American operas as a part of the regular symphony season, including Floyd's *Susannah,* Hanson's *Merry Mount,* and Bernstein's *Trouble in Tahiti.* In 1961 Alessandro initiated an annual Rio Grande Valley International Music Festival, which attracted music lovers from South Texas and Northern Mexico to the Valley for a week of concerts, opera, and student performances. In 1973 Alessandro remained as the conductor.

Community orchestras like the Amarillo Symphony have also achieved notable progress. Since 1948 the Amarillo podium has been occupied by native Southwesterners: A. Clyde Roller from 1948 to 1963, and Thomas Hohstadt from 1963 to 1969. In 1967 the Amarillo Symphony consisted of eighty-five members, all local talent. Comparable orchestras in Austin, Wichita Falls, El Paso, Beaumont, and Lubbock all played significant roles in bringing live concerts to their areas—often with high artistic results and despite sharp financial limitations. In 1964 Midland and Odessa strengthened their musical resources by combining their two symphonies into an interurban orchestra under the direction of Lara Hoggard; in 1969 Robert G. Mann was the conductor. In 1969 Ezra Rachlin conducted the Fort Worth Symphony, and Maurice Peress conducted the Corpus Christi Symphony; Peress also directed the Austin Symphony in 1970.

The San Antonio Symphony was the first professional resident opera producer in Texas. In 1945 conductor Max Reiter conceived a plan for extending the symphony season by adding a springtime opera festival and launched the venture with *La Bohème,* starring Grace Moore. Since 1945 the San Antonio Symphony has presented an annual season of opera—four different works given each year, one performance each, divided between two successive weekends. While stars from the Metropolitan and New York City operas are imported for leading roles, the chorus is drawn largely from three local colleges. Most of the sets were designed by Peter Wolf of Dallas. With the exception of two seasons the opera has closed its financial books in the black (unheard of in the operatic world). Seating capacity of San Antonio's Municipal Auditorium is nearly 6,000, and symphony officials look on a crowd of 4,500 as a poor showing.

Fort Worth followed San Antonio's resident company in 1946 when three housewives founded the Fort Worth Opera Association. One of the company's prime ambitions has been to provide opportunity for gifted local singers, with professionals used only for stellar roles. *La Traviata* launched the organization in November, 1946. From 1955 to 1969 conductor Rudolf Kruger, who formerly worked with the Columbia (South Carolina) Symphony and the Chicago Light Opera, served as Fort Worth's musical director and general manager. Under his supervision four operas were performed each season, spaced over fall, winter, and spring; two performances were given of each work, and most productions were in English.

Texas' third resident opera company, the Houston Grand Opera Association, began in January, 1956, with *Salomé*, starring Brenda Lewis. In 1969 the company's musical director was Walter Herbert, who had held similar posts earlier with the New Orleans and Fort Worth operas. His Houston company presented four or five works annually, usually in the original language. Only the leads were assigned to noted singers, and local talent was employed whenever artistically feasible. The Houston company proved dynamic in repertory, presenting such seldom-heard works as Rossini's *Cenerentola* (1957), Strauss' *Elektra* (with Inge Borkh, in 1958, a Texas premiere), and Wagner's *Die Walküre* (in 1959, the first time a *Ring* opera had been staged in Texas in twenty years).

The Dallas Civic Opera, formed in 1957 by Lawrence V. Kelly,qv formerly of the Chicago Lyric Theatre, received national and international acclaim. A concert by Maria Callas got the project off to a brilliant start on November 21, 1957, followed shortly by a production of Rossini's novelty *L'Italiana in Algeri*, with Giulietta Simionato. "For a cou· ple of nights running," *Newsweek* magazine wrote, "Dallas was the operatic capital of the United States."

Afterward, Dallas presented a number of remarkable productions and artists. In 1958 Callas returned for *La Traviata*, in a production produced by the renowned Italian designer, Franco Zefirelli, and highly praised performances of Cherubini's *Medea*, staged by Alexis Minotis of the Greek National Theater—a production later loaned to London's Covent Garden and Milan's La Scala. The 1960 Dallas season saw the United States debut of Joan Sutherland in Zefirelli's production of Handel's *Alcina*, an American premiere. Another American premiere, Monteverdi's seventeenth-century classic *L'Incoronazzine di Poppea*, was produced by the Dallas company in 1963 and later was leased by several major European houses. In 1965 the Dallas production team, headed by Kelly, joined to produce Handel's *Julius Caesar* for the newly formed Kansas City Performing Arts Foundation, and this premiere production was presented that fall for Dallas Civic Opera's season.

Since 1939 Dallas has sampled a season of the Metropolitan Opera's productions in the spring of each year. The Dallas company tried not to duplicate the New York company's repertoire and artists; instead the aim was to give Texas a look at European productions. While building a permanent repertory, each year manager Kelly borrowed at least one production from abroad—in 1960 *Alcina* from Venice's La Fenice, *Figlia del Regimento* from Palermo, and in 1961 *La Bohème* from Spoleto. In addition to Sutherland's United States debut, Dallas Civic Opera has enjoyed those of Teresa Berganza, Luigi Alva, Nicola Monti, Denise Duval, Montserrat Caballe, Gwyneth Jones, Jon Vickers, and Magda Olivero.

Musical comedy has also received considerable attention in Texas since World War II. The Starlight Operettas were begun in Dallas in 1941 in an outdoor arena-and-bandshell on the fair grounds, but were renamed the State Fair Musicals in 1951, when the shows were moved into the Music Hall. Outstanding Broadway and Hollywood talent was imported each summer for musicals of recent vintage, as well as the older "operetta" type of show. In 1952 the musicals opened with William Warfield and Leontyne Price in Gershwin's *Porgy and Bess*, the premiere of a production which the state department later sent to Moscow. Each year during the State Fair of Texas qv the national company of a current Broadway musical was brought to the Music Hall. Mary Martin began her tour in Irving Berlin's *Annie Get Your Gun* at the fair in October, 1947, and succeeding years saw productions of *South Pacific*, *Guys and Dolls*, *The King and I*, *My Fair Lady*, *The Sound of Music*, and *Funny Girl*.

Houston instituted the summer season of Broadway musicals, and Fort Worth's Casa Mañana was revived in 1958, introducing "musicals-in-the-round" to the Southwest. *See also* Music in Texas, Folk and Popular; Texas State Singing Society.

BIBLIOGRAPHY: Ronald L. Davis, *A History of Opera in the American West* (1965); "Stars over Texas," *Opera News* (November 14, 1964); Marshall Terry, "Culture in Dallas," (in) *Goals for Dallas* (1966); *Texas Almanac* (1969).

Ronald L. Davis

Music in Texas, Folk and Popular. As a transitional state between the South and the West, Texas has blended the country music of the South with the cowboy and other laments of the West. At the same time the state has contributed a number of performers and composers of national and even international stature.

The Old South, Anglo American tradition shows up in musical tastes in Texas as it does in speech patterns, architecture, food habits, voting attitudes, racial attitudes, and religion. In early Texas the country fiddler was the valued entertainer, as the people stomped or circled or squared at house parties and other country dances. Later the guitar was added, and now and then a banjo or mandolin. Fiddling contests were at least a century old when Texas became a Republic, and "old fiddlers' reunions" came to be a mark of country fairs, convocations of veterans of various wars, and the like. By World War I the one- and two-participant fiddler and guitar groups had developed into string bands which played regularly for entertainment. Meanwhile Texans played at home, for Sunday school and church, and for school commencements and similar activities. The folk songs created by Texans and imported from the South dealt primarily with the problems of rural and country people, and these two areas kept country music alive in the state. Usually the songs dealt with sadness, even catastrophe: "Letter Edged in Black," "Put My Little Shoes Away," "In the Baggage Coach Ahead," for instance. Equally popular were the religious and semireligious songs, such as "Whispering Hope," "Tell Mother I'll Be There" (inspired by President William McKinley's telegram to his dying mother), "When They Ring Those Golden Bells," "When the Roll Is Called Up Yonder," "Life Is Like a Mountain Railroad," and "The Old Rugged Cross."

A second strain fed into Texas, as it did throughout the remainder of the South, through the Afro-American tradition, especially in East Texas. Since both white and black groups dealt with the miseries of life and of work, they often interchanged their musical approaches until the researcher frequently finds it difficult to tell which songs are black inspired and which should be shared with the whites. "John Henry" is a good example. Although in early Texas black fiddlers were common, gradually the black gave up the fiddle for a guitar. The black particularly fastened "the blues" on Texas as a musical form. In turn blues evolved into the jazz form.

A similar evolution holds true for ragtime; its acknowledged father, Scott Joplin,qv grew up in Texarkana. From Joplin to W. C. Handy and his form of blues, with a combination of black and Latin American rhythms, into the popular music of the 1920's was a logical progression.

Both whites and blacks also shared Protestant religious traditions, and small rural churches with their thin paperback hymnals and all-day singing conventions frequently linked with graveyard working and dinner on the ground, both at revival times and in between, fueled development of this form. Traveling quartets became a feature of the Texas scene, particularly after 1920, when ownership of radio sets became widespread. The Stamps-Baxter Publishing House in Dallas, founded by V. O. Stamps of Gilmer, was one of the more important gospel publishing houses anywhere. The Stamps Quartet with its theme song, "Give the World a Smile," emanating out of Station KRLD in Dallas, became nationally known. The writer once heard a midnight concert by the Stamps Quartet from a radio station in Colombia while he was driving in the mountains near Huancayo, Peru.

In the latter nineteenth century Texas developed its historic range cattle and cowboy culture, which produced its own set of songs. In a sense these songs were as much work songs as were those dealing with miners, lumbermen, and union labor dissenters in other sections of the United States. The cowboy songs brought in still another cultural group, the Mexicans, who contributed so much both to the technique and folklore of the range cattle industry. Black cowboys, of whom there may have been as many as 5,000, added to the cultural and ethnic mixture.

The rise of a cowboy literature, both serious and at the "penny-dreadful" level, was well known. The cowboy, who came out of an Anglo American, black, and Mexican background, borrowed from this fused background to sing to the cattle and to while away his loneliness. When a later Texan, Gene Autry, sang for motion pictures, he introduced another element—the Singing Cowboy, who has continued in the movies to the present. Meanwhile Nathan Howard "Jack" Thorp published his Songs of the Cowboys in 1908 and John A. Lomax qv brought out his Cowboy Songs and Other Frontier Ballads in 1910. These two books helped perpetuate and popularize so-called cowboy music. Basically cowboy music was borrowed and did not contribute so much as it reflected. At least two of Texas' more "serious" composers utilized cowboy materials—Oscar J. Fox qv of San Antonio and David Guion of Brownwood and Dallas, whose "Home on the Range" is almost a regional anthem and was reputedly the favorite song of former President Franklin Delano Roosevelt. But many of the cowboy songs have been turned out by Tin Pan Alley in New York and by popular writers in airconditioned studios in Hollywood.

The term "cowboy songs" borders on being a generic term. One of the most popular and enduring is "New San Antonio Rose" by Bob Wills (James Robert Wills qv), who grew up in Turkey, Texas, on the fringe of the Texas Panhandle. Nowhere does the song hint at cowboys, but it is accepted in the cowboy tradition. Wills himself is remembered for having introduced "western swing" as a form of musical entertainment and for having pioneered the use of a string section in his western band. After he gained popularity, he and his band members donned broad-brimmed, high-crowned hats and the other accouterments of the show cowboy, but they had no real connection with cowboy culture. Composers of more modern cowboy songs were as diverse as Owen Wister, the Philadelphia-reared author of the novel The Virginian; Maurice Woodward Ritter,qv otherwise known as Tex Ritter, whose rendition of "High Noon" catapulted him into the Cowboy Music Hall of Fame; and Tex Fletcher, who hawked his song "Strawberry Roan" at rodeos and Wild West shows.

In central Texas the German Texans, Polish Texans, and Czech Texans have kept alive the central European musical influence through their German brass bands ("um-pah-pah" bands, as they are usually dubbed) and polka bands. Whether the music is played at a commercial dance hall or at a picnic of a benevolent society such as the Sons of Hermann,qv the music forms the background for what are essentially family affairs, with children, parents, and grandparents sharing their beer drinking and general *Gemütlichkeit* while an accordion, sometimes a brass horn or tuba, and any other instrument pound away.

The Mexican influence, following geography, is naturally strongest in the area from San Antonio to the Rio Grande. *Corrida* ballads, songs imported from the haciendas of Mexico, and protest songs are most frequently performed, usually in Spanish. Any aspiring folklore singer in Texas must perforce be bilingual, because the Mexican American songs are as dear to Anglo Americans as they are to their originators. The Mexican folk songs such as "La Cucaracha" and "El Rancho Grande" are as popular in the United States as they are in Mexico.

Another group are the so-called Cajun singers, who drifted from French Louisiana into Texas, particularly after the discovery of oil around Spindletop qv in 1901 and around Kilgore in the 1930's. Although they weren't the first Cajuns to enter Texas, the Cajuns' fiddle and accordion were not too much heard until World War II. Again, Cajun music has transcended its ethnic bounds, so that songs like "Joli Blon" and "Jambalaya" are as popular among Anglo Americans outside Texas as they are within the state, even though most Anglo singers have to mumble the words.

All of these strains combined served to give music in Texas considerable vigor and variety. As Bill Malone, the principal chronicler of country music, has written, "the folk music of Texas never existed in a vacuum. Just as it was never purely Anglo, neither was it totally rural and agricultural."

Meanwhile the larger cities were developing "sin streets," where a somewhat more commercial form of Negro blues was played, frequently associated with the town red-light district. In Dallas the area was known as "Deep Ellum." Here visitors could hear that newfangled musical form called jazz, syncopated and uninhibited. Although Texas never produced a separate brand of jazz such as New Orleans jazz, Kansas City jazz, or Chicago jazz, it produced any number of fine performers who again won international recognition. Scott Joplin has been mentioned. Jack Teagarden (Weldon Leo Teagarden qv) from Vernon and Peck Kelley from Houston won national followings, and Teagarden was sent abroad by the United States Department of State in its export of American culture. Ornette Coleman of Fort Worth has become one of the nation's most influential and controversial reed players on the contemporary scene. As an influence on jazz pianists Teddy Wilson of Austin ranks only behind the legendary Earl Hines. Wilson became famed in general history as the first black musician ever to play publicly in an integrated orchestra when he joined the Benny Goodman trio with Goodman and Gene Krupa in the middle 1930's, thereby opening new employment opportunities for black musicians.

On the other hand, no Texas jazz or popular orchestra ever became nationally known. Bob Wills, of course, and his bands were modeled loosely on the big band swing music of the 1930's and were nationally known, but were never really considered in the popular music category. In California, for instance, Wills frequently outdrew such national "name bands" as Benny Goodman and Glenn Miller, and with his mating of white hoedown music and black blues he is credited with having influenced the rock music that has dominated so much of the popular music scene since the latter 1950's.

During the 1920's hotels in the larger cities maintained "house bands" which broadcast "by remote control" over radio stations that blanketed the state. In Dallas, for instance, the Adolphus Hotel featured an orchestra led by Herman Waldman, while across the street the Baker Hotel's Peacock Terrace was presenting an orchestra under the direction of that inimitable pianist-raconteur, Ligon Smith. Between performances the hotels presented such nationally known touring dance bands as Herbie Kay, Hal Kemp, and Isham Jones. Dorothy Lamour, later a motion picture star, was a favorite entertainer around the Fort Worth-Dallas area during that period.

Texas has certainly produced its share of famous musicians. Besides those already mentioned, Blind Lemon Jefferson qv became a nationally known exponent of the "field holler-work shout" form of singing in the earlier part of the twentieth century. In later years Lightning Hopkins and Mance Lipscomb, from the same genre, have achieved similar reputations among the knowing. The first black country singer to achieve national fame, Charlie Pride, lives in Dallas. Huddie Ledbetter qv (Leadbelly), though born in Louisiana, spent much of his time in Texas and has become something of a legend, even to the point that Hollywood has made a movie of his frazzled life.

Trini Lopez of Dallas has become a popular Mexican American singer of international reputation, with a large number of hit records and appearances in movies to his credit. Johnny Rodriguez of San Antonio and Freddie Fender (Baldemar G. Huerta) of San Benito have also gathered a wide following of both Anglos and Chicanos, qv singing in both languages. Fender's route to popularity is illustrative of the seasoning that frequently accompanies a musician en route to stardom. He joined his family as a migrant worker when he was about ten, worked beets in Michigan and cucumbers in Ohio, baled hay and picked tomatoes in Indiana, and picked cotton in Arkansas. He became a high school dropout and then joined the marines. Out of the service, he returned to the Rio Grande Valley to play beer joints and Chicano dances and to sing Tex-Mex rockabilly music. Later he spent three years in Angola State Prison in Louisiana for possession of marijuana. Back again in the Valley, he worked as a mechanic for $1.60 an hour and made $28 a night on weekends picking a guitar, attended college for two years, and then struck popular fancy with his bilingual recording of "Before the Next Teardrop Falls."

Besides such Country Music Hall of Fame members as Ritter and Wills, Texas has contributed

Jimmy Rodgers (James Charles Rodgers [qv]), born in Mississippi but a Texan during his peak years, Ernest Tubb, and George Jones. Perhaps one reason for fastening a country music culture on Texas was the fact that radio reached its pinnacle about the same time that the Texas oil fields, both in the Permian Basin and in East Texas, were reaching their zeniths. Oil workers thronged to honky-tonks to listen to performers like Bob Wills, sang their songs at work, purchased their phonograph records, and listened to their songs over the radio. Station WBAP in Fort Worth was undoubtedly one of the pioneers in broadcasting radio barn dances, as well as live "hillbilly" groups, cowboy bands, and gospel singers. Possessed of unusually high wattage, Texas stations with their Texas music were listened to throughout the nation.

The first national hillbilly hit was "The Prisoner's Song," recorded by Vernon Dalhart (born Marion T. Slaughter) in Jefferson, Texas (his professional name derived from the Texas towns of Vernon and Dalhart), in 1924. At the time Dalhart's record was the biggest selling record in any field of music, even outselling such stellar performers as Enrico Caruso and Paul Whiteman. The first of the singing cowboys was Carl Sprague, born in Alvin, who commenced his career in 1923. Jules Verne Allen was another early Texas cowboy singer who was also a genuine cowboy.

During World War II, when rural and small town Texans were uprooted from their traditions, they assuaged their nostalgia in the shipyards of Houston and Brooklyn and the defense factories in California and Massachusetts by singing their country and western songs at work, purchasing records by their favorite performers wherever they could, and flocking out to hear itinerant country musicians whenever they appeared in the vicinity. Similarly, second-generation Italians from Mamaroneck, New York, and second-generation Norwegians from Hibbing, Minnesota, were deposited by the military in Texas, where they were likewise exposed to country and western music and its performers. When they left Texas during or after the war, they took along their own brand of nostalgia for the music they had heard. Such music was inescapable, for so many of the radio stations in the Southwest played little else. In Mineral Wells a Texas-based company, Crazy Water Crystals, became a national advertiser of hillbilly music during the 1930's and thereafter, even to the point of presenting future musical comedy star, Mary Martin of nearby Weatherford, as its lead singer. Although Miss Martin never became a country and western singer, she knew how to handle such a tune whenever the circumstances called for its rendition.

In the 1960's a phenomenon developed in Austin, where a type of music known as "red-neck rock" emerged. Another fusion of cultures, it drew from the huge University of Texas student body with its cosmopolitan and sophisticated qualities, from its proximity to San Antonio, from the Mexican American population to the south and the surrounding German communities, from Austin's sizable black population, and from the so-called "cowboy singers" who wandered through.

In a sense Austin country rock was also a product of the counterculture that evolved during the 1960's and 1970's, with a country bar called Threadgill's as its center. Kenneth Threadgill is an older person who prides himself on having obtained the first beer license in Travis County following the end of prohibition. When the students discovered his bar in the 1960's, after it had operated as a working-class bar for thirty years, they changed it into a student hangout. Threadgill himself knew all of the old Jimmy Rodgers songs and could render an authentic Rodgers "blue yodel." At Threadgill's in the 1960's a shy girl who hung around the bar but seldom spoke was encouraged one night to get up and sing. The reaction by the audience was instantaneous. From that time forward Janis Joplin [qv] developed into one of the symbols of the youth revolt. Although her short life ended in 1970, already several books have been written about her, and serious sessions at historical and sociological society meetings have been held to examine her meaning as a symbol for the alienated young.

Soon after, on the south side of Austin an abandoned armory was turned into a somewhat raffish nightclub known as Armadillo World Headquarters. Here its owner, Edward Wilson, promoted all sorts of red-neck rock concerts, featuring artists on tour but also attracting a number of local performers. The concerts were greeted as so fresh and uninhibited in their concepts that a number of nationally known rock, as well as country and western, musicians were persuaded to move to the environs of Austin to pursue a "new sound" in their music. The spiritual godfather of this group has been Willie Nelson, who has attracted other performers into the area. Recognized musicians such as Waylon Jennings, Doug Sahm, Jerry Jeff Walker, Ray Wiley Hubbard of Denton, Rusty Wier of Dripping Springs, and David Allen Coe were featured regularly. Meanwhile the performers have made a strong attempt to keep music in Austin somewhat free of form and to avoid the commercialism of other performing and recording singers. Other clubs in Austin have followed the lead of the Armadillo, until Austin has become a beehive of musical activity. None of this enlargement was planned—it just "growed." The story of the Armadillo World Headquarters has been written up in such national magazines as *Time* and in such famed newspapers as the London *Times* and the New York *Times*. Whether Austin can continue to grow as a music center and avoid the straitjacket of commercialism remains to be seen. But in musical circles around the world, musicians and dilettantes now speak of "the Austin Sound." *See also* Folklore and Folk Music of Texas; Music in Texas; Texas State Singing Society.

BIBLIOGRAPHY: William A. Owens, *Swing and Turn: Texas Play-Party Games* (1936); Alan Lomax, *The Folk Songs of North America* (1960); N. Howard Thorp,

Songs of the Cowboys (1908); John A. Lomax, Cowboy Songs and Other Frontier Ballads (1910); Bill C. Malone, Country Music, U.S.A. (1968); Charles Townsend, San Antonio Rose: The Life and Music of Bob Wills (1976); Norman L. McNeil, The British Ballad West of the Appalachian Mountains (Ph.D. dissertation, University of Texas, 1956).

Joe B. Frantz

Musical Arts Conservatory of West Texas. The Musical Arts Conservatory of West Texas, Amarillo, was organized in 1929 as a private, coeducational institution offering courses from kindergarten to fourth-year college level. In 1939 it was incorporated, and its present home was purchased in 1940. The president of the school in 1973 was Gladys M. Glenn.

From 1950 to 1967 (the last reporting date) the school faculty increased from twenty-one to twenty-two and the student enrollment from 551 to 600. The school was accredited by the Texas State Board of Education qv in 1939 and became a charter member of the Texas Association of Music Schools. In 1967 the school maintained a musical kindergarten, had elementary, junior, and senior high school courses culminating in recognized high school credit, and maintained a four-year college course leading to the Bachelor of Music degree and the Bachelor of Fine Arts degree in ballet. The library contained several hundred volumes of books, music, current music and art magazines, and hundreds of recordings. Twenty-eight studios and two recital halls were available for conservatory activities.

*Muskhogean Indian Family.

*Musquito.

*Músquiz, Ramón.

*Musquiz Canyon.

*Mussina, Simon.

*Mustang, Texas. (Denton County.)

*Mustang, Texas. (Falls County.)

*Mustang, Texas. (Limestone County.)

*Mustang, Texas. (Washington County.)

*Mustang Bayou.

*Mustang Branch.

Mustang Branch, Texas. *See* Farmer's Branch, Texas.

*Mustang Canyon.

*Mustang Creek.

*Mustang Hill, Texas.

*Mustang Island.

*Mustang Mott.

*Mustang Ridge.

*Mustangs.

"Mustangs" Sculpture. *See* Proctor, Alexander Phimister.

Myer, Albert James. Albert James Myer was born in Newburgh, New York, on September 20, 1828, the son of Henry Beekman and Eleanor Myer. He received the B.A. degree from Geneva (now Hobart) College in 1847, the M.A. from

Geneva in 1851, and the M.D. from the University of Buffalo in 1851.

After private practice in Florida, Myer became an assistant surgeon in the United States Army in 1854 and went with recruits to Fort Duncan,qv Texas, where orders soon transferred him to Fort Davis.qv He served at Fort Davis from January, 1855, until orders transferred him back to Fort Duncan in late 1855. There he remained as the post doctor until July, 1857, when he returned to the East.

From Fort Duncan, in October, 1856, Myer proposed a military signaling system, in which he had been interested since 1851. After it received the qualified approval of an army board in 1859, Myer tested and developed it, principally in the New York harbor area, and in June, 1860, became a major and the army's first signal officer. His system, first made operational in the Navajo Expedition, 1860–1861, used a flag for daytime and a kerosene torch for nighttime signaling, and this later became known as wigwag signaling.

Thus Myer founded the U.S. Army Signal Corps, which took form during the Civil War, and he became its chief signal officer. While introducing magneto-electric telegraphy into the signal corps, he collided with the rival United States Military Telegraph and was relieved as the chief signal officer in late 1863 and from active service in 1864. Myer won restoration to active service as a colonel in 1867 and remained chief signal officer until his death. He did not attain the regular rank of brigadier general until 1880. Meanwhile in 1870, he and the signal corps became responsible for the nation's weather service, which he organized and made world renowned. He must be numbered, therefore, among the principal founders of the United States Weather Bureau.

On August 24, 1857, Myer married Catherine Walden; they had six children. Hobart College awarded him the honorary LL.D. degree in 1872 and Union College the honorary Ph.D. in 1875. Myer died in Buffalo, New York, on August 24, 1880. He was buried in Buffalo's Forest Lawn Cemetery. Fort Myer, Virginia, bears his name.

BIBLIOGRAPHY: Paul J. Scheips, Albert James Myer, Founder of the Army Signal Corps: A Biographical Study (Ph.D. dissertation, American University, Washington, D.C., 1965).

Paul J. Scheips

*Myer Branch.

*Myers, Elijah E.

Myers, Julius. Julius Myers, called the last American town crier to ply his trade, was born in New York City in 1868 and attended schools there. He came to Texas seeking relief from respiratory trouble in 1882 and settled in Luling; in 1912 he moved to San Antonio. Mounted on his horse "Tootsy," Myers was seen daily on the streets of San Antonio announcing current or future attractions with his megaphone. With a decorative costume for each occasion, he advertised such events as sales and theater attractions, charity affairs, and sporting events. Because too many others were attempting to emulate him, a city ordinance in December, 1927, ordered an end to such advertising. Friends of Myers petitioned city hall for his exception from the ordinance, but to no avail. The following March, however, indulgent officials permitted him to inform the city of baseball games, but he was not allowed to use his horse. Despite repeated protests by his family, advancing age, and failing health, he continued as town crier until his death on September 18, 1929. Myers was survived by his wife and four children.

BIBLIOGRAPHY: San Antonio *Express*, September 19, 1929.

S. W. Pease

***Myers, Texas.**

***Myers Settlement, Texas.**

***Mykawa, Texas.**

***Myra, Texas.**

***Myrtle, Texas.**

***Myrtle Springs, Texas.**

N

Naaman Indians. The Naaman Indians, an unidentified group, are known only from records of Alonso de León's qv various expeditions to the Texas coast in search of La Salle's Fort St. Louis.qv In 1690 De León encountered the Naaman, whom he reported as a "large nation," north of Matagorda Bay between the Guadalupe and Colorado rivers. In later times the Naaman must have been known by another name, possibly as Aranama. The Aranama lived along the lower Guadalupe River during the eighteenth century.

BIBLIOGRAPHY: H. E. Bolton (ed.), *Spanish Exploration in the Southwest, 1542–1706* (1916).

T. N. Campbell

Naansi Indians. The Naansi Indians are known from only one document (Douay narrative) of the La Salle Expedition,qv which indicates that at the end of the seventeenth century these Indians were numerous and lived between the Hasinai and Kadohadacho tribes. This suggests that they may have occupied the valley of either the Sabine River or the Sulphur River. The Naansi cannot be identified with any other Indian group listed for this general area in French or Spanish documents. Since the Naansi lived between two areas dominated by Caddoan tribes, it seems likely that they too were Caddoan; but this cannot be demonstrated.

BIBLIOGRAPHY: I. J. Cox (ed.), *The Journeys of Réné Robert Cavelier, Sieur de La Salle*, I (1905); F. W. Hodge (ed.), *Handbook of American Indians*, II (1910).

T. N. Campbell

***Nabedache Indians.**

***Nabeyxa Indians.** The Nabeyxa (Nabeyeyxa) Indians are referred to in a single Spanish document written late in the seventeenth century. As the name occurs in a list of twenty-one tribes, nineteen of which are clearly Caddoan, it seems likely that the Nabeyxa were a small and perhaps peripheral tribe of the southwestern or Hasinai group of Caddo Indians in eastern Texas. J. R. Swanton has suggested that this name may be a synonym for Nabedache, but both names occur on the same list.

BIBLIOGRAPHY: J. R. Swanton, *Source Material on the History and Ethnology of the Caddo Indians* (1942).

T. N. Campbell

***Nabiri Indians.** Although it is generally held that the Nabiri (Nabiti, Nahiti, Nahiri, Naviti) Indians were a Caddoan tribe of the southwestern or Hasinai division in eastern Texas, their identity otherwise is far from clear. H. E. Bolton qv thought that the Nabiri might be the same as Henri Joutel's qv Noadiche (Nahordike), presumably a variant of Nabedache, and also suggested that the Nabiri might be the group later known as Anadarko. J. R. Swanton reviewed Bolton's argument and further suggested that the Nabiri might be the tribe later known as Namidish. The arguments presented by Bolton and Swanton are not convincing, and it seems unlikely that all of these interpretations are correct. The proper identification of the Nabiri must await better evidence. Bolton's study of Spanish documents convinced him that the Nabiri lived on the Angelina River near the spot where Cherokee, Nacogdoches, and Rusk counties meet. These documents clearly indicate that the Nabiri lived on the northern margin of the area occupied by Hasinai tribes.

BIBLIOGRAPHY: H. E. Bolton, "The Native Tribes about the East Texas Missions," *Quarterly of the Texas State Historical Association*, XI (1907–1908); J. R. Swanton, *Source Material on the History and Ethnology of the Caddo Indians* (1942).

T. N. Campbell

*Nabors Creek.

***Nacachau Indians.** The Nacachau (Nacachao, Nacaha, Nacachua) Indians, a tribe of the southwestern or Hasinai division of Caddo Indians, lived in eastern Texas during the late seventeenth and early eighteenth centuries. Their settlements were east of the Neches River in the area now occupied by Cherokee County. In 1716 the San Francisco de los Neches Mission qv was built for the Nacachau and other nearby Hasinai tribes. After this very little is heard of the Nacachau, and it is probable that they were absorbed by one or more neighboring Hasinai groups. On the basis of sound correspondences in the names, J. R. Swanton has suggested that the Hacanac, Lacane, Nacachau, Nacaniche, Nacau, Nacono, and Nakanawan were probably fragments of the same Caddoan tribe. This cannot be verified by such documentary evidence as is now available.

BIBLIOGRAPHY: H. E. Bolton, "The Native Tribes about the East Texas Missions," *Quarterly of the Texas State Historical Association*, XI (1907–1908); F. W. Hodge (ed.), *Handbook of American Indians*, II (1910); J. R. Swanton, *Source Material on the History and Ethnology of the Caddo Indians* (1942).

T. N. Campbell

*Nacaniche Indians. The Nacaniche (Nacan, Nacanish, Naconicho) Indians were a tribe of the southwestern or Hasinai group of Caddo Indians who lived in eastern Texas during the late seventeenth and early eighteenth centuries. The precise location of their settlements remains unknown, but Naconiche Bayou in Nacogdoches County probably indicates one of their favored localities. J. R. Swanton believed that their remnants were probably absorbed by the Hainai. He also thought that Nacaniche might be a later form of Lacane, the name of a group encountered by the Moscoso Expedition qv in 1542 somewhere in northeastern Texas or in the adjoining parts of Arkansas and Louisiana. In fact, on the basis of sound correspondences in the names, Swanton has suggested that Hacanac, Lacane, Nacachau, Nacaniche, Nacao, Nacono, and Nakanawan were probably fragments of the same Caddoan tribe. This cannot be verified by such documentary evidence as is now available.

BIBLIOGRAPHY: J. R. Swanton, *Source Material on the History and Ethnology of the Caddo Indians* (1942).

T. N. Campbell

*Nacau Indians. The Nacau (Nacao, Nacoho, Nocao) Indians, a Caddoan tribe of the southwestern or Hasinai division, lived in eastern Texas during the late seventeenth and early eighteenth centuries. H. E. Bolton's qv analysis of Spanish documents led him to place the Nacau in the northeastern part of present Nacogdoches County, but J. R. Swanton's map of Caddoan tribes places them farther to the northeast, apparently in the area where the present counties of Nacogdoches, Rusk, and Shelby join. In 1716 the Nuestra Señora de Guadalupe de los Nacogdoches Mission qv was established for the Nacogdoche and Nacau tribes. After this date little is heard of the Nacau, who were probably absorbed by the Nacogdoche. On the basis of sound correspondences in the names, J. R. Swanton has suggested that Hacanac, Lacane, Nacachau, Nacau, Nacaniche, Nacono, and Nakanawan were probably fragments of the same Caddoan tribe. This cannot be verified by such documentary evidence as is now available.

BIBLIOGRAPHY: H. E. Bolton, "The Native Tribes about the East Texas Missions," *Quarterly of the Texas State Historical Association*, XI (1907–1908); J. R. Swanton, *Source Material on the History and Ethnology of the Caddo Indians* (1942).

T. N. Campbell

*Nacisi Indians.

*Naclina, Texas.

*Nacogdoche Indians. The Nacogdoche (Nacadocheeto, Nacodissy, Nacodochito, Nagodoche, Nasahossoz, Naugdoche, Nocodosh) Indians, a Caddoan tribe of the Hasinai group in eastern Texas, lived in the vicinity of present Nacogdoches in the seventeenth and eighteenth centuries. In 1716 the Nuestra Señora de Guadalupe de los Nacogdoches Mission qv was established in the principal Nacogdoche settlement and was intermittently maintained until 1773. The tribe was greatly reduced by disease and warfare by 1800. Although many Nacogdoche seem to have been absorbed by the population of the Spanish settlement established at Nacogdoches in 1779, others lost their identity among other nearby Hasinai tribes, especially the Hainai and Anadarko, who moved westward to the Brazos River shortly after the Texas Revolution and were eventually taken to Indian Territory, now Oklahoma. Descendants of the Nacogdoche are probably included in these Hasinai survivors, who today live in Caddo County, Oklahoma.

BIBLIOGRAPHY: H. E. Bolton, "The Native Tribes about the East Texas Missions," *Quarterly of the Texas State Historical Association*, XI (1907–1908); F. W. Hodge (ed.), *Handbook of American Indians*, II (1910); J. R. Swanton, *Source Material on the History and Ethnology of the Caddo Indians* (1942).

T. N. Campbell

*Nacogdoches, Texas. Nacogdoches, seat of Nacogdoches County, was incorporated in 1939 with a commission-manager form of government. Nacogdoches tripled its land area in 1962 and by 1966 had developed a thirty-two-acre city park and increased water and sewer facilities. In 1969 Nacogdoches reported 360 businesses, including thirty-two manufacturers largely concerned with wood products, livestock and poultry, and dairy products. In the same year Nacogdoches had eighteen churches, three libraries, two radio stations, and a newspaper. The United States census reported a population for Nacogdoches of 12,674 in 1960 and 22,544 in 1970.

Two famous old trees were located in Nacogdoches. The Old North Church Oak, just north of the city limits, a few yards east of U.S. Highway 59, had provided shelter for Anglo American settlers in 1832 who began holding worship services beneath this post oak. In 1852 the present frame church replaced the original log church which stood beside the tree. The Indian Mound Oak, a southern red oak, was located across the street from Nacogdoches High School. It rose from a prehistoric Indian mound, the only remaining one of four original mounds. The oak and its companion six-foot-high mound were on the old campus of Nacogdoches University.

BIBLIOGRAPHY: John A. Haislet (ed.), *Famous Trees of Texas* (1970).

*Nacogdoches, Battle of.

*Nacogdoches Archives.

*Nacogdoches County. Nacogdoches County in 1968 was 67 percent forested and supported a small lumber industry with two mills. It was among the leading Texas counties in income from broilers, poultry, dairying, and total livestock. In 1968 Nacogdoches County ranked third in egg production with nearly 9.6 million dozen, fifth in sales from livestock and products with an income of $26,158,000, and fourteenth in number of dairy cows. In the early 1970's agricultural income averaged $30,500,000 annually. The Sam Rayburn Lake, completed in 1965, was fast becoming a major recreational center of the county. The 1960 population was 28,046; the 1970 population was 36,362, according to the United States census.

*Nacogdoches Rebellion, 1838. *See* Cordova Rebellion.

*Nacogdoches and Southeastern Railroad Company. In 1954 the Nacogdoches and Southeastern Railroad Company road was controlled through stock ownership by Olin Industries, Inc., and was in operation from Nacogdoches to Hayward, a distance of two miles. On July 17, 1954, operations of the company were discontinued.

James M. Day

*Nacogdoches University.

*Naconiche Bayou.

*Nacono Indians. The Nacono (Macono, Nacomone, Nocono) Indians, a tribe of the southwestern or Hasinai group of Caddo Indians in eastern Texas, lived along the Neches River during the late seventeenth and early eighteenth centuries, particularly in the vicinity of present Cherokee and Houston counties. For a short time the Nacono were served by the San Francisco de los Neches Mission,qv which was established in 1716. After 1727 little is heard of the Nacono, who appear to have been absorbed by one or more neighboring Hasinai tribes. On the basis of sound correspondences in the names, J. R. Swanton has suggested that the Hacanac, Lacane, Nacachau, Nacau, Nacaniche, Nacono, and Nakanawan were probably fragments of the same Caddoan tribe. This cannot be verified by such documentary evidence as is now available.

BIBLIOGRAPHY: H. E. Bolton, "The Native Tribes about the East Texas Missions," *Quarterly of the Texas State Historical Association*, XI (1907–1908); F. W. Hodge (ed.), *Handbook of American Indians*, II (1910); J. R. Swanton, *Source Material on the History and Ethnology of the Caddo Indians* (1942).

T. N. Campbell

*Nacoste Creek.

*Nada, Texas.

*Nadamin Indians. The Nadamin Indians are known only from the late seventeenth century, when they were identified in records of the La Salle Expedition qv as allies of the Kadohadacho Caddo. J. R. Swanton suggested that the Nadamin may have been the same people as the Sadammo, but this does not seem reasonable. In the expedition documents the Nadamin were listed as allies of the Kadohadacho, whereas the Sadammo (Caitsodammo) were listed as enemies. The identity of the Nadamin remains undetermined.

BIBLIOGRAPHY: F. W. Hodge (ed.), *Handbook of American Indians*, II (1910); P. Margry, *Découvertes et établissements des Français dans l'ouest et dans le sud de l'Amérique Septentrionale*, III (1879); J. R. Swanton, *Source Material on the History and Ethnology of the Caddo Indians* (1942).

T. N. Campbell

Nagel, Charles. Charles Nagel was born in Bernardo, Texas, on August 9, 1849, the son of Dr. Hermann and Friederike (Litzmann) Nagel, both natives of Prussia. His father was a graduate in medicine of the University of Berlin. Coming to America in 1847 his parents first settled in Colorado County, later moving to Millheim settlement in Austin County in 1855. Opposed to both slavery and secession, Dr. Nagel took the fourteen-year-old Charles to Mexico in 1863. They later traveled by ship to New York, thence to St. Louis in 1865 where his mother joined them. Charles attended country schools in Texas, completed high school in St. Louis in 1868, and was graduated from St. Louis Law School in 1872. This was followed by a year of study at the University of Berlin. He was awarded the honorary LL.D. degree by Brown University, Villanova University, and Washington University in 1911, and Doctor of Political Science degree by the University of Berlin in 1928.

He began a career as an attorney in St. Louis in 1873. Active in public affairs and politics, Nagel was elected a member of the Missouri House of Representatives (1881–1883), president of the St. Louis city council (1893–1897), and member of the Republican National Committee (1908–1912). In March, 1909, President Taft appointed him secretary of commerce and labor, the first native-born Texan to become a member of a president's cabinet. He was also a founder of the United States Chamber of Commerce. Following four years' service in Washington, Nagel returned to his law practice in St. Louis. In his later years Nagel wrote *A Boy's Civil War Story* (1934), an account of his boyhood in Texas.

On August 4, 1876, in Louisville, Kentucky, Nagel married Fannie Brandeis, sister of United States Supreme Court Justice Louis D. Brandeis. After her death in 1889 he married Anne Shepley in 1895. He was the father of six children. He died in St. Louis on January 5, 1940.

BIBLIOGRAPHY: F. C. Shoemaker (ed.), *Missouri and Missourians* (1943); "Historical Notes and Comments," *The Missouri Historical Review*, XXXIV (1940); *Encyclopedia of Biography* (1941); *Who Was Who In America* (1943).

Cooper K. Ragan

*Nagle, James C.

*Nail, James H.

Nail, Olin Webster. Olin Webster Nail, Methodist minister and church historian, was born June 12, 1890, in China Spring, Texas, the son of Daniel Marion and Martha Jane (Cox) Nail. Nail was educated at Baylor Academy and Southwestern Preparatory School and attended Southwestern University in 1913. He received an A.A. degree from Meridian College in 1915 and earned an A.B. degree in 1922 and a B.D. degree in 1924 from Southern Methodist University. Nail was a graduate student at the University of Chicago and Chicago Theological Seminary in 1930 and received the Doctor of Theology degree from Iliff School of Theology in Denver in 1937. He taught at the

Southern Methodist University Pastor's School in 1937 and later served on the board of managers of that school.

Nail was licensed to preach by the Methodist Episcopal church in 1907 and was ordained a deacon in 1913 and an elder in 1917. He was a member of the West Texas Conference beginning in 1924 and preached in many small Texas towns between 1925 and 1937. Nail also preached in San Antonio and Austin, serving Austin churches for over fifteen years. Nail was president of the West Texas Conference Historical Society for a number of years beginning in 1933 and was on the Methodist committee for the Centennial ꞯᵛ in 1936. Nail served as secretary of the Southwest Texas Conference for twelve years and was editor of the West Texas Conference annual journal. He edited *Texas Methodist Centennial Yearbook* (1934) and *History of Texas Methodism, 1900–1960* (1961), and he prepared *The First Hundred Years of the Southwest Texas Conference of the Methodist Church, 1858–1958*, for the Southwest Texas Conference.

Nail married Mary Alice Crowson on September 30, 1915; they had two children. Nail died May 22, 1971, in Garland and was buried in China Spring.

BIBLIOGRAPHY: *Texian Who's Who* (1937); Austin *American*, May 26, 1971.

Nail, Robert Edward. Robert Edward Nail, playwright and director, was born in Wolfe City, Texas, on September 13, 1908, the son of Etta (Reilly) and Robert Edward Nail, Sr. Nail graduated from Albany High School and later attended Lawrenceville School in Lawrenceville, New Jersey. As a Princeton University undergraduate, he studied drama, and his play, *The Time of Their Lives*, received an award for best undergraduate play. He graduated from Princeton in 1933. Nail became director of the Fort Worth Little Theater in 1933, and in 1936 he began directing the Dallas Little Theater (*see* Little Theater Movement). He taught in Albany High School in 1938.

Nail wrote several plays, but he was best known as creator and director of the Fort Griffin Fandangle,ꞯᵛ presented first in 1938 as a senior play written by Nail and based on events from *Interwoven: A Pioneer Chronicle* (1936) by Sallie Reynolds Matthews ꞯᵛ and *The Quirt and the Spur: Vanishing Shadows of the Texas Frontier* (1909) by Edgar Rye.ꞯᵛ The production became an annual community project; Nail wrote and directed a new script each year based on local county history. Nail held an honorary Doctor of Humanities degree from Hardin-Simmons University and was a member of the Texas Fine Arts Commission,ꞯᵛ appointed by Governor John Connally. Nail died on his ranch near Albany on November 11, 1968, and was buried in the Albany cemetery.

BIBLIOGRAPHY: Biographical File, Barker Texas History Center, University of Texas at Austin.

∗Nails Creek.

Nakanawan Indians. Nakanawan (Nakahanawan) is the name of a Caddoan group obtained by J. Mooney from a Caddo informant in the 1870's.

This informant later told J. R. Swanton that Nakanawan was another name for the Hainai, but Swanton believed that the name referred to some other Caddoan group that had been absorbed by the Hainai. This seems likely inasmuch as the Hainai absorbed remnants of several Caddo tribes. On the basis of sound correspondences in the names, Swanton has suggested that the Hacanac, Lacane, Nacachau, Nacau, Nacaniche, Nacono, and Nakanawan were probably fragments of the same Caddoan tribe. This cannot be verified by such documentary evidence as is now available.

BIBLIOGRAPHY: J. Mooney, *The Ghost Dance Religion and the Sioux Outbreak of 1890* (1896); J. R. Swanton, *Source Material on the History and Ethnology of the Caddo Indians* (1942).

T. N. Campbell

Nanatsoho Indians. The Nanatsoho (Nadsoo, Natsoho, Natsvto) Indians, a Caddoan tribe, lived on the Red River during the seventeenth and eighteenth centuries in what is now Bowie and Red River counties. They were one of the four tribes of the Kadohadacho group, which also included the Kadohadacho, Nasoni (upper), and Natchitoches (upper). Early in the nineteenth century the Nanatsoho lost their ethnic identity. It seems likely that remnants of the Nanatsoho were absorbed by the Kadohadacho and that their descendants were living with the Caddo who now reside in Caddo County, Oklahoma.

BIBLIOGRAPHY: J. R. Swanton, *Source Material on the History and Ethnology of the Caddo Indians* (1942).

T. N. Campbell

Nance, Berta Hart. Berta Hart Nance, daughter of a pioneer family, was born near Albany, Texas, on October 6, 1883. She was educated in the public schools and was graduated from Reynolds Presbyterian Academy in Albany. She began writing poetry at an early age and became a charter member of the Poetry Society of Texas ꞯᵛ at its organization in 1921. Her poems, widely published through the years, received critical acclaim. She studied music and was an accomplished violinist as well as a talented singer.

In 1934, suffering from tuberculosis, she took up residence in Tucson, Arizona, where she continued to live until the time of her death in 1958. She was the author of three books of verse: *The Round-up* (1926); *Flute in the Distance* (1935); and *Lines from Arizona* (1938). Her poem, "Cattle," with the lines "Other states were carved or born, Texas grew from hide and horn," has been widely praised.

BIBLIOGRAPHY: Hilton Ross Greer and Florence Elberta Barns (eds.), *New Voices of the Southwest* (1934); Vaida Stewart Montgomery, *A Century with Texas Poets and Poetry* (1934).

W. E. Bard

∗Nance's Mill, Texas.

∗Nancy, Texas.

∗Naples, Texas. Naples, in northeastern Morris County, made major improvements in water, sewer, and street systems during the 1960's. In 1960 the city reported six churches, a hospital, a bank, and a newspaper. In 1970 there were forty businesses. The 1960 population was 1,692; the 1970 United States census figure was 1,726.

*Napoleonic Exiles. *See* French in Texas.

Napuap Indians. The Napuap (Nacuap, Napuat) Indians were one of five Coahuiltecan groups reported to be living in the vicinity of present Corpus Christi during the middle eighteenth century. The name appears only in documents pertaining to expeditions sent out by José de Escandón qv from what is now Tamaulipas. In later times the Napuap were probably known by some other name.

BIBLIOGRAPHY: H. E. Bolton, *Texas in the Middle Eighteenth Century* (1915); G. Saldivar (ed.), *Archivo de la historia de Tamaulipas*, 11 (1946).

T. N. Campbell

*Narciseno Creek.

*Narcisso, Texas.

Narcotics and Dangerous Drugs, Research Advisory Panel. The Research Advisory Panel—Narcotics and Dangerous Drugs, was created in 1971 to approve or disapprove research projects in the fields of narcotics and dangerous drugs for which legal immunity was requested for the researcher and his subjects. Composed of seven members, including representatives from the State Department of Public Health, the Department of Mental Health and Mental Retardation, the State Board of Pharmacy, the office of attorney general, and the University of Texas System qqv (three members), the panel could approve projects which then would be furnished narcotics or dangerous drugs by the Department of Public Safety.qv As long as a person was acting within the authority of a panel-approved research project, he had immunity from prosecution for violation of drug laws.

BIBLIOGRAPHY: University of Texas at Austin, *Guide To Texas State Agencies* (1972).

Narrows, The. The Narrows was a part of the Sabine River which began about eight miles north of Orange where the stream divided into what was known as the East and West channels. Since these two channels were not as wide as the course of the river above and below, the men who piloted riverboats up and down the stream called them "The Narrows" (both channels being used for navigation). The East Channel at its upper end is no longer connected with the river.

BIBLIOGRAPHY: Map dated May 21, 1840 (General Land Office, Austin); Maps and records (State Land Office, Baton Rouge, Louisiana).

Madeleine Martin

*Naruna, Texas.

*Narváez Expedition. *See* Cabeza de Vaca, Alvar Núñez.

NASA. *See* Manned Spacecraft Center.

Nasayaha Indians. The Nasayaha (Nasayaya) Indians, a Caddoan tribe of the southwestern or Hasinai division, are known from a single Spanish document that was written near the end of the seventeenth century. H. E. Bolton's qv analysis of geographic data in this document led him to place the Nasayaha near the boundary between present

Nacogdoches and Rusk counties in eastern Texas. He also suggested that the Nasayaha were probably the same as the Nasoni (lower group) who lived in the same area and whose name appears frequently in later documents. J. R. Swanton somewhat reluctantly accepted Bolton's identification. The main difficulty with this interpretation is that both Nasayaha and Nasoni are listed as separate tribes in the same early document, a fact which Bolton and Swanton seem to have ignored. More convincing evidence is needed in order to show that Nasayaha and Nasoni are different names for the same people.

BIBLIOGRAPHY: H. E. Bolton, "The Native Tribes about the East Texas Missions," *Quarterly of the Texas State Historical Association*, XI (1907–1908); J. R. Swanton, *Source Material on the History and Ethnology of the Caddo Indians* (1942).

T. N. Campbell

*Nash, Texas. (Bowie County.) Nash, Texas, with a 1960 population of 1,124, showed an increase in the 1970 census, with a count of 1,961. The town reported twenty-two businesses in 1970.

*Nash, Texas. (Ellis County.)

*Nash Creek.

*Nashville-on-the-Brazos, Texas.

*Nashville Colony. *See* Robertson Colony.

*Nasoni Indians. The Nasoni (Assony, Nasoui, Nassonite, Nisohone, Nazone) Indians, a Caddoan tribe of northeastern Texas in the seventeenth and eighteenth centuries, was divided into two parts that may be designated as Upper Nasoni and Lower Nasoni. The Upper Nasoni were associated with the northern or Kadohadacho group of Caddoan tribes and lived along the Red River in what is now northern Bowie County. The Lower Nasoni were among the southwestern or Hasinai group of Caddoan tribes and lived in the vicinity of present Rusk County. The Upper Nasoni were under French influence from 1719 until 1762 (a French post was built in their main settlement), but the Lower Nasoni were under Spanish influence (San José de los Nazones Mission qv was founded among them in 1716). In the latter part of the eighteenth century both groups were greatly reduced in numbers by disease and warfare and by 1880 seem to have lost their identities among neighboring Caddo groups. It seems likely that the Upper Nasoni were absorbed by the Kadohadacho and the Lower Nasoni by the Anadarko. If so, unidentifiable descendants of both groups may be represented among the surviving Caddo who today live in Caddo County, Oklahoma.

BIBLIOGRAPHY: H. E. Bolton, "The Native Tribes about the East Texas Missions," *Quarterly of the Texas State Historical Association*, XI (1907–1908); F. W. Hodge (ed.), *Handbook of American Indians*, II (1910); J. R. Swanton, *Source Material on the History and Ethnology of the Caddo Indians* (1942).

T. N. Campbell

*Nassau Farm.

*Nat, Texas.

*Natalia, Texas. Natalia, in southeastern Medina County, had a population in 1970 of 1,296. The town reported eighteen businesses in that year.

*Natchitoch Indians. The name Natchitoch (Natchitoches, Nachitoch, Nachitos, Nacitos, Naketosh, Natsytos) is primarily linked with a group of Caddo Indians who lived on the Red River in northwestern Louisiana, but in the late seventeenth century one Natchitoch village was found among the Kadohadacho Caddo of extreme northeastern Texas. This village was on the south bank of the Red River in present Bowie County. In the nineteenth century some of the surviving Natchitoch Indians of Louisiana joined remnants of two Caddoan groups of Texas, the Kadohadacho and Hasinai, and eventually reached the Brazos Indian Reservation qv of present Young County. In 1858 these various Caddoan groups were moved to Indian Territory, now Oklahoma. Their descendants now live in the vicinity of Caddo County, Oklahoma.

BIBLIOGRAPHY: F. W. Hodge (ed.), *Handbook of American Indians*, II (1910); J. R. Swanton, *Source Material on the History and Ethnology of the Caddo Indians* (1942) and *The Indian Tribes of North America* (1952); D. H. Winfrey and J. M. Day (eds.), *The Indian Papers of Texas and the Southwest, 1825–1916* (1966).

T. N. Campbell

*Natchitoches, Louisiana.

Nation, Carry Amelia (Moore). Carry Nation, daughter of George and Mary (Campbell) Moore, was born on November 25, 1846, in Garrand County, Kentucky. The Moore family moved to Missouri in 1855, but with the outbreak of the Civil War, the slave-owning family moved to a farm in Grayson County, Texas. Her mother was mentally ill, and the family's financial situation became desperate after a drouth. In 1865 the Moores moved to Belton, Missouri, where on November 21, 1867, Carry married Dr. Charles Gloyd, an alcoholic. They had a daughter, but Carry soon left her husband because of his addiction. Gloyd died soon thereafter, and she taught school for the next four years. In 1877 she married David Nation, a Christian church minister, lawyer, and newspaper editor.

The Nations moved to a seventeen-hundred-acre plantation on the San Bernard River in Texas. After failing to make the plantation a success, the Nations operated a hotel in Columbia, Texas. After some success they purchased a hotel in Richmond. Through the husband's position as correspondent for the Houston *Post*,qv the Nations became involved in local outbreaks of racial violence. Because of activities of the anti-Negro faction, the Nations moved to Medicine Lodge, Kansas, in 1889.

During her stay in Texas, Mrs. Nation underwent numerous mystic experiences. She came to believe that she had been elected by God and that she spoke through divine inspiration. In Kansas she began a crusade which lasted the rest of her life against liquor and tobacco. She organized a local chapter of the Woman's Christian Temperance Union and became a national leader of the more extremist element of that organization. She wrecked saloons and berated persons who sold liquor. In 1900 she adopted the hatchet as her tool of destruction. The sale of souvenir hatchets and earnings from nationwide lecture tours allowed her to pay the fines which resulted from more than thirty arrests. She propagandized through several short-lived publishing efforts, including *The Hatchet*, *The Home Defender*, and *The Smasher's Mail*, and in 1904 she published her autobiography, *The Use and Need of the Life of Carry A. Nation*.

Devoting her life to what she felt was her predestined work, she never enjoyed a happy marriage; David Nation divorced her in 1901. She continued to tour American cities and universities, including the University of Texas in 1902 and 1904 (where in 1902 she was ordered off campus by President William Lambdin Prather qv for delivering a temperance speech to a group of young men); she lectured in the British Isles in 1908. Declining health forced her retirement to a farm in the Ozark Mountains. Shortly afterward, on June 2, 1911, she died in Leavenworth, Kansas, and was buried in Belton, Missouri. Her grave remained unmarked until 1924, when it was located and a marker erected with the words, "Carry A. Nation, 'Faithful to the Cause of Prohibition.' She hath done what she could."

BIBLIOGRAPHY: Carleton Beals, *Cyclone Carry* (1962); *Dictionary of American Biography*, VII (1934); Sam Woolford, "Carry Nation in Texas," *Southwestern Historical Quarterly*, LXIII (1959–1960).

James C. Martin

National Aeronautics and Space Administration (NASA) in Texas. *See* Manned Spacecraft Center.

*National Bank, First in Texas.

**National Banner.*

National Center for Atmospheric Research, Scientific Balloon Flight Station. The National Center for Atmospheric Research (NCAR) Scientific Balloon Flight Station occupies over four hundred acres, seven miles northwest of Palestine, Texas, just off U.S. Highway 287 and west of the municipal airport.

Established in 1963 by the National Center for Atmospheric Research of Boulder, Colorado, it was the first permanent facility devoted exclusively to scientific ballooning. Since its inception there has been a continuing effort to expand the facility and make the unique qualities of balloons for scientific research more readily available to scientists. In addition to scientific experiments, many flights designed to contribute improvements to balloon technology have been made.

The facility was open, within practical limits, to all scientists with balloon-borne experiments to fly. In many cases the NCAR provided scientists with a variety of technical assistance and field services, thus sparing them the burden of becoming experts in balloon technology.

The balloon flight station's services were provided by a complement of experienced private contractor personnel, under close NCAR supervision.

The principal financial support for NCAR comes from the National Science Foundation.

J. C. Warren

*National Colonization Law. *See* Mexican Colonization Laws, 1821–1830.

*National Farmers' Alliance and Industrial Union. *See* Farmers' Alliance.

*National Forests in Texas. By 1968 there were a total of 658,023 acres of national forests covering parts of eleven East Texas counties. This woodland was located on four national forest areas totaling 1,716,967 acres. Angelina National Forest had 154,389 acres of timbered land; Davy Crockett National Forest had 161,336 acres; Sabine National Forest had 183,843 acres; and Sam Houston National Forest had 158,235 acres. The forests were administered by a forest supervisor of the Forest Service, United States Department of Agriculture, with his administrative headquarters in Lufkin. Seven local offices supervised by district forest rangers were: Angelina district at Lufkin (Angelina National Forest); Neches district at Crockett (Davy Crockett National Forest); Trinity district at Groveton; Tenaha district at San Augustine (Sabine National Forest); Yellowpine district at Hemphill; Raven district at Huntsville (Sam Houston National Forest); and Big Thicket district at Cleveland.

The forests' estimated total net growth per year was over 175,000,000 board-feet and was valued at approximately seven million dollars. One-third of this growth was removed annually by cutting to improve the remaining stand. Over the years some 60,000 acres of national forest land were artificially reforested.

Various uses were made of Texas' national forests. State regulated hunting and fishing was permitted, federal grazing permits were issued to ranchers, and use by the public for recreation was encouraged. In 1968 more than two million people made use of recreational facilities established throughout the national forests. The recently developed Sam Rayburn and Toledo Bend reservoirs extend into national forest land and have been utilized by the Forest Service to improve recreational facilities. By 1973 all four of the national forests had slightly increased acreage, and with the addition of Caddo National Grasslands (17,729 acres in Fannin County) and Cross Timbers National Grasslands (20,272 acres in Wise County and 71 acres in Montgomery County) the U.S. Forest Service administered a net acreage of 697,265 and a gross area of 1,755,028 acres in Texas. *See also* Panhandle National Grasslands; Tree Farming; Big Thicket.

BIBLIOGRAPHY: *Texas Almanac* (1963, 1965, 1967, 1969, 1973).

*National Guard. *See* Texas National Guard.

National Guild of Piano Teachers. The National Guild of Piano Teachers (NGPT) had its beginning in Texas in 1929 when the first All-Southwestern Piano Playing Tournament was held.

It was first incorporated in California in 1933 by Irl Allison, former teacher of piano in various colleges in Texas, for the purpose of sponsoring the National Piano Playing Tournament. At first it was a voluntary membership organization and the purpose was then, as now, to encourage piano pupils of all ages and stages of advancement to continue their studies. In 1943 Allison returned to Texas and operated the organization out of Austin until it was rechartered and reincorporated in 1946.

In 1958 the National Guild of Piano Teachers, along with the Fort Worth Piano Teachers Forum, the Fort Worth Chamber of Commerce, and Texas Christian University, inaugurated the Van Cliburn International Piano Competition, held quadrennially in Fort Worth, with a grand prize of ten thousand dollars. In 1966 the Junior League of Fort Worth became a fifth sponsor. Irl Allison and Grace Ward Lankford were the cofounders of the competition.

Since its founding, the guild has sponsored the National Piano Playing Tournament in many music centers of the nation and in foreign countries. In 1967 more than seventy-five thousand piano students in more than 750 cities were auditioned and adjudicated by more than three hundred examiners made up of leading piano teachers of the United States and some foreign countries. Since its organization, the NGPT has awarded approximately eight hundred scholarships of $100 each to high school graduates.

Allison was president of the organization until 1955, when his son, Irl Allison, Jr., took office. Headquarters of the guild was in Austin. Membership was approximately seventy-six thousand students and teachers in 1968, the largest concentration being in Chicago. Dallas, New York City, and Honolulu ranked next in order out of the seven hundred chapters in the United States.

Irl Allison

National Intelligencer (Galveston).

National Intelligencer (Houston).

*National Road.

National Trail. The National Trail was proposed by Texas cattlemen in the 1880's in an attempt to thwart proposed northern quarantines against Texas cattle. Texas fever,qv caused by ticks indigenous to the Texas Southwest, had inflicted heavy losses upon the northern range cattle industry by the early 1880's, and these losses had resulted in northern cattlemen (roughly all those north of the 32nd parallel) lobbying for state and territorial quarantines against infected livestock. Since it was much less expensive for Texas cattlemen to trail their herds to northern railheads and ranges and then ship them by rail rather than ship directly from Texas, most Texans saw these proposed quarantines as a threat to their economic well-being. When the cattle industry convention met on November 17, 1884, at St. Louis, such prominent Texas cattlemen as Richard King, B. B. Groom, C. C. Slaughter, and John T. Lytle qqv pushed through a resolution calling upon Congress, "in the interest of cheaper food," to create and maintain a National Trail from Doan's Crossing qv on the Red River north through the Indian Territory, the present Oklahoma Panhandle, Colorado, Nebraska, Wyoming, South Dakota, and Montana to the Canadian border. Partially in retaliation, the following year, Colorado, Kansas, Nebraska, New Mexico, Wyoming, and Canada passed quarantine laws against Texas cattle, seriously restricting northern drives during the regular trailing season. Finally, on January 7, 1886, Texas Congressman James Francis Miller qv of Gonzales introduced the National Trail proposal in the United States House of Representatives. The measure was blocked in the House committee on commerce by northern cattle interests and by Texas railroads, which presumably wanted to replace the trail with rails. The failure of the National Trail, the northern quarantines, along with the western migration of the farmers and barbed wire,qv sounded the death knell of trailing.

BIBLIOGRAPHY: *Proceedings of the First National Convention of Cattle Growers' of the United States Held in St. Louis, Mo., November 17th to 22d, 1884* (1885); Joseph Nimmo, *Report of the Chief of the Bureau of Statistics on Range Cattle Traffic* (1885); Ernest Staples Osgood, *The Day of the Cattlemen* (1929).

Jimmy M. Skaggs

*National Vindicator.

Natural Bridge Caverns. Natural Bridge Caverns, the largest known caverns in Texas, were discovered on March 27, 1960, by four spelunkers who were students of St. Mary's University in San Antonio. The caverns are located in the hill country, midway between New Braunfels and San Antonio, off FM Road 1863. The name was derived from the sixty-foot natural limestone slab bridge which spanned the amphitheater setting of the caverns' entrance.

Development of the caverns began on March 25, 1962, and they were opened to the public on July 3, 1964. During excavation of the entrance trail, arrowheads and spearpoints dating from 5,000 B.C. were found as well as, just inside the entrance, jaw bones of a grizzly bear that became extinct over eight thousand years ago. The caverns are almost 100 percent active and still growing, and the temperature is seventy degrees year around. Because of constant drips and flowing water, the formations retain a luster that can be seen in few caverns. Under these growth conditions the formations appear to be made of wax, yet are as hard as limestone. The type of formations change from room to room; the largest, named the "Hall of the Mountain Kings," is 350 feet long, 100 feet wide, and 100 feet high. Among numerous formations found here the most distinct is a type described as "Fried Eggs" (because that is what they look like), a rare cave formation. The developed portion of the cave, with one-half mile of paved trails and illuminated by 35,000 watts of indirect lighting, extended to as much as 260 feet below ground level; portions of the cave are still under exploration.

Clara Heidemann

Natural Fibers and Food Protein Committee. The Cotton Research Committee, created in 1941, was renamed the Natural Fibers and Food Protein Committee by the 62nd Texas Legislature in 1971. The committee is composed of four ex officio members: the presidents of the University of Texas at Austin, Texas A&M University System, Texas Tech University, and Texas Woman's University. The term of office is indefinite. The committee appoints a director as its chief administrative officer.

The committee contracts with the above institutions for research in four principal areas: marketing and economic research, fiber and textile products research, and cottonseed and oilseed research. In 1969 responsibilities of the committee were expanded by the legislature to include study of increased use and outlet for farm products, especially cotton, wool, mohair, oilseed products, and other textile products. In 1970 the committee was assigned to research and test for flame retarding finishes and flammability standards for the state.

BIBLIOGRAPHY: University of Texas at Austin, *Guide To Texas State Agencies* (1972).

*Natural Gas. Texas is not only the largest producer of natural gas, but is also the largest consumer of this vital natural resource. Natural gas is second only to crude petroleum in value of Texas mineral products, and liquefied natural gasolines and petroleum gases are together the state's third most important natural resource.

By the end of 1967 a total of 262,800,000 million cubic feet of natural gas had been discovered in Texas, and production to that date had amounted to 130,380,000 million cubic feet of gas. Marketed production for the year of 1967 reached 7,188,900 million cubic feet. About one-half of the state's giant 1967 production was used by Texans; the remainder was sold to other states at a price of $488 million. Estimated proved recoverable reserves of natural gas of all types in Texas at the end of 1967 totaled 125,400,000 million cubic feet, or 42.8 percent of the natural gas reserves in the United States.

Of the total 1968 natural gas production of 8,-937,025 million cubic feet, an estimated 7,550,000 million cubic feet was marketed at a value of just over a billion dollars. Proved reserves of natural gas in Texas at the end of 1968 were calculated at 119,001,106 million cubic feet, a loss of 6,400,000 million cubic feet from the previous year. Losses in natural gas reserves in recent years have stemmed from declining discoveries of new reserves; in 1968 only 830 million cubic feet of new reserves were discovered.

By-products of the production and processing of natural gas in 1968 were 331.6 million barrels of natural gasoline, ethane, butane and propane, and other hydrocarbon liquids which were valued at $547 million dollars. Since the production of liquefied petroleum gas also exceeded new discoveries, the total proved reserves of liquefied petroleum gas fell by 97 million barrels to 4,005 million barrels.

The Railroad Commission,qv the state regulatory agency for the natural gas industry, reported a total natural gas production of 8,963,484 million cubic feet in 1969. Three-fourths of this production (6,838,026 million cubic feet) came from 23,689 producing gas wells, while the remaining natural gas was produced from crude petroleum wells. The 1969 marketed production of 7,314,839 million cubic feet represented the first decline in annual marketed natural gas production in Texas since 1932. While Texans consumed 3,879,427 million cubic feet of natural gas in 1969, the remaining 3,435,412 million cubic feet were exported from the state, principally by four large transmission enterprises (Natural Gas Pipeline Company of America, Northern Natural Gas Co., El Paso Natural Gas Co., and Tennessee Gas Pipeline Co.).

Approximately 2.4 million Texas consumers in 1969 were serviced by commercial distributors, the largest being Lone Star Gas Company, United Gas Distribution Company, Houston Natural Gas Corporation, Southern Union Gas Company, and Pioneer Natural Gas Company. In addition, consumers in seventy-two Texas communities were serviced by municipally owned natural gas plants; most of these communities were small, but they included San Antonio, Corpus Christi, Del Rio, and Bay City, and they accounted for about 30 percent of the natural gas distributed in Texas. While some 91 percent of Texas consumers were individuals and families using natural gas for domestic purposes, about 88 percent of the natural gas was consumed by commercial and industrial enterprises. In 1969 commercial distributors earned nearly one-half billion dollars from the sale of natural gas for commercial and industrial use in Texas; domestic users in Texas paid nearly two hundred million dollars. Gross income by these commercial distributors for all gas sales and operations in Texas in 1969 was just under one billion dollars. State gross receipts taxes collected for that year amounted to $1,446,000. (Domestic and industrial consumption figures in this paragraph do not include those for distribution plants wholly owned by municipalities, as they make no reports to the Railroad Commission.)

Perhaps the most important industrial use for natural gas in Texas was in the generation of electrical power. At the beginning of 1969, 98.3 percent of the electric capacity of the state depended upon fuel-driven generators, leaving only 1.7 percent to be derived from hydroelectric installations. Almost all fuel-driven generators, with a capacity of 24.5 million kilowatts, utilized natural gas.

Natural gas leases and royalties continued to be a major source of income for the Permanent School Fund and the Permanent University Fund qqv (see also Land Appropriations; Lands, Texas Public.

Among the state's largest producers of natural gas were: Atlantic Richfield Co., Cities Service, Gulf Oil Corp.,qv Humble Oil & Refining Co.,qv Mobil Oil Corp., Pan American Petroleum Corp., Phillips Petroleum Co., Shell Oil Co., Sun Oil Co., and Texaco Inc.qv

BIBLIOGRAPHY: Robert M. Lockwood, Statistical Report, Natural Gas in Texas (February 18, 1971), Files of the Bureau of Business Research, University of Texas at Austin; Railroad Commission of Texas, Annual Report of the Oil and Gas Division (1968); Railroad Commission of Texas, Seventy-Eighth Annual Report, Gas Utilities Division (1969); United States Bureau of the Census, Statistical Abstract of the United States: 1969 (1969); The Oil Producing Industry in Your State (1969); World Oil, February 15, 1971; Texas Almanac (1969).

James A. Clark
Robert M. Lockwood

*Natural Regions of Texas.

*Natural Resources. See Grasses Native to Texas; Lumber and Lumbering; Marine Resources; Mineral Resources and Mining in Texas (and related articles); Natural Gas; Oil, Discovery and Production of (and related articles); Soils of Texas; Water Resources (and related articles).

*Natural Resources, Conservation of. See Conservation of Natural Resources.

*Naval Air Station, Corpus Christi, Texas. The conclusion of World War II drastically altered the need for naval aviators trained at the Naval Air Station, Corpus Christi. Two postwar reorganizations reduced the station to a subordinate command by 1947; naval auxiliary air stations at Kingsville and Beeville qqv were shut down for several years.

In late 1948, however, Naval Air Advanced Training Command transferred its headquarters from Jacksonville, Florida, to Corpus Christi, and the naval air station became a permanent installation. The following year the navy's precision flight team, the "Blue Angels," changed to jets and relocated their headquarters at the Corpus Christi station. Although deactivated during the early part of the Korean War, the "Blue Angels" were reorganized in 1951 and remained at Corpus Christi until their 1955 transfer to Pensacola, Florida.

During the 1950's the station's assembly and repair department was renamed and given greater responsibility. This department employed a majority of the four thousand civilian workers at the station. In late 1959 the department was shut down and its facilities remained idle until converted into the Army Aeronautical Depot Maintenance Center in 1961.

During the 1960's the naval air station retained its original mission of providing fully trained aviators of multi-engine land and sea planes for the sea services. Training programs became longer because of the increasing complexity of aircraft and associated equipment. Cadets, commissioned officers, and flight students from many countries participated in the station's training program. The naval air station had graduated a total of 61,000 aviators by 1966. More than three million dollars were set aside for the base under a 1967 military construction bill to improve utilities and troop housing.

BIBLIOGRAPHY: Corpus Christi and the Navy: Unofficial Directory and Guide (1967).

*Naval Air Station, Dallas, Texas. In 1950 the naval reserve squadron stationed at Dallas Naval Air Station became the first naval air reserve squadron to be recalled to active duty as the result of the Korean conflict. During that war the runway at the station was lengthened to accommodate FH-1 "Phantom" jets which arrived in April, 1952. In 1954 the "Phantom" gave way to the swept-wing F-9F "Cougar" and later to the more advanced FJ "Fury" jets, requiring installation of a new type of arresting gear on the runway. This was the first such gear to be used at a reserve naval air station.

In the early 1960's the Dallas station continued to grow. Extensive repair work was undertaken on the main runway and the installation of a new mobile arresting gear on the alternative runway enabled the station to continue full operation despite the runway's 5,200-foot length. In 1963 Dallas became the first naval reserve station to be equipped with F-8 "Crusader" jets. By 1967 two jet fighter squadrons, three antisubmarine warfare patrol squadrons, and four tactical support squadrons made up the major contingents at the Dallas field. The navy maintained a complement of approximately 650 officers and men on active duty, and approximately 120 members of the Marine Air Reserve Detachment were located there. The Texas Air National Guard qv also had facilities at the station for KC-97 tankers. By 1967 the station was three times its original size and its real estate had a fifteen-million-dollar evaluation. New construction was underway in the late 1960's.

BIBLIOGRAPHY: *Golden Triangle Cities Salute Naval Air Station Dallas: Unofficial Directory and Guide* (1966).

Naval Auxiliary Air Station, Beeville, Texas. The Naval Auxiliary Air Station in Beeville was created in late 1942 by the conversion of a municipal airport under construction into a military field. It was named for Lieutenant Commander Nathan Chase, who was killed on a training flight at Pearl Harbor in 1925. During World War II, Chase Field conducted a flight training program from which many naval aviators graduated. After the war navy cutbacks forced the field to close in July, 1946, but it became operative again in June, 1953, with a new runway added. In November, 1953, the field was officially designated as a naval auxiliary air station.

Jet training began in August, 1954. Three training squadrons provided training in instrument flying, jet systems, formation flying, weapons delivery, air-to-air combat, and weapons systems; the Grumman "Cougar" jet and the "Tiger" were used to train marine and navy jet pilots.

Chase Field received almost thirteen million dollars under a 1967 military construction bill. In addition to expenditure on real estate, the sum was spent on operational, training, maintenance, and administrative facilities, troop housing, and utilities.

BIBLIOGRAPHY: *Your Navy in Beeville: Unofficial Directory and Guide for Chase Field, Beeville, Texas* (1967).

Naval Auxiliary Air Station, Kingsville, Texas. The Naval Auxiliary Air Station at Kingsville, one of the three advanced air training bases of the Naval Air Training Command, was commissioned in July, 1942. At that time its facilities were 85 percent complete; the field did not have a name, being officially designated as "P-4." During World War II, four squadrons taught fighter and bomber tactics as well as gunnery for combat aircrewmen. For a short time the field handled an overflow of basic training recruits from an Illinois naval training center. At the end of the war, pilot training at the base dropped sharply.

In September, 1946, the station was closed and turned over to the city of Kingsville, which leased the base to Texas College of Arts and Industries (now Texas A&I University) as an agricultural station. The base was reactivated in April, 1951, as an auxiliary air station under the command of the chief of naval air advanced training located at the Naval Air Station at Corpus Christi. Three training squadrons used the two-seated TF-9J and the single-seated AF-9J. In the 1960's student pilots reported to Kingsville from Pensacola, Florida, where they had received basic flight training. Training at Kingsville included three weeks of ground school in addition to high altitude, air-to-air combat, and formation flying, as well as landings aboard aircraft carriers in the Gulf of Mexico. The station trained almost three hundred men per year during the mid-1960's and received more than $3,800,000 under a 1967 military construction bill which was used to improve operation and maintenance facilities as well as troop housing.

BIBLIOGRAPHY: *Naval Air in Kingsville: 1966 Unofficial Guide* (1966).

*Naval Station, Orange, Texas. *See also* United States Naval Inactive Ship Maintenance Facility, Orange, Texas.

*Navarro, Angel, III.

*Navarro, José Antonio. *See also* Navarro House Museum.

*Navarro, Texas. (Leon County.)

*Navarro, Texas. (Navarro County.)

Navarro College. *See* Navarro Junior College.

*Navarro County. Navarro County has had the longest consistent oil production in Texas. From 1895 to January 1, 1973, 192,853,287 barrels had been produced. The county also had the first oil refinery west of the Mississippi River. Farm income averaged $16.5 million annually in the early 1970's, two-thirds coming from livestock, the remainder from crops (mainly cotton and sorghums). Navarro Mills Reservoir on Richland Creek was completed in 1963. The 1960 population was 34,423; the 1970 United States census reported 31,150 inhabitants.

Navarro House Museum. The José Antonio Navarro qv building complex of three buildings—house and kitchen (*circa* 1850) and two-story office (somewhat earlier)—at the corner of South Laredo Street and Nuevo Street in San Antonio, was scheduled for demolition in 1960; it was bought and restored by the San Antonio Conservation Society ᵠᵛ by 1965. The buildings were stuccoed Texas limestone; the house and separate small kitchen in Texas cottage style had deep front porches. The furniture in the buildings—Texas, Mexican, and Louisiana-French—was in use in San Antonio during Navarro's time. Documents and pictures concerning his life are on display. The Y-shaped complex, open to the public and operated as a house museum, was among those submitted to the National Register of Historic Places of the United States Department of the Interior.

Navarro Junior College. Navarro Junior College, Corsicana, was organized in 1946 by vote of Navarro County citizens. Classes opened the same year at the former Air Activities Field six miles south of Corsicana, with an enrollment of 238 students and a faculty of fifteen instructors.

Bond elections supporting the college passed in 1949, 1959, and 1965. Enrollment increased gradually until the campus was moved to a sixty-four-acre site on the western edge of the city limits in 1951. Enrollment on the new campus grew to 516 students in 1955 and doubled in the following decade to 1,184 students in 1965. By the fall of 1974, student enrollment was 1,274, and the faculty numbered about eighty.

In 1965 the campus contained an administration-library-auditorium building, hall of science, cafeteria, four dormitories, gymnasium, student union, technical building, and shop building. During 1966, two dormitories, a technical-vocational building, library, and women's physical education building were constructed at a cost of approximately two million dollars.

In 1969 the college library held 22,000 volumes, bound periodicals, and government documents. The R. S. Reading collection of Indian artifacts is on permanent display at the college.

Fully accredited by major agencies, the college offered work leading to an associate degree in most basic academic and technical fields, as well as offering secretarial certificates, certificates in business, and psychiatric technicians' certificates (in cooperation with Terrell State Hospital ᵠᵛ). An evening division provided an adult education program of college, technical, and special short courses.

Ray L. Waller served as first president of the college and was succeeded, upon his death in 1956, by Ben W. Jones. In 1974 Kenneth P. Walker was president, and by that year the school's name had been changed to Navarro College.

＊Navarro Mills, Texas.

Navarro Mills Reservoir. Navarro Mills Reservoir is in the Trinity River Basin in Navarro County, sixteen miles southwest of Corsicana on Richland Creek. The reservoir extends into Hill County. The project is owned by the United States government and is operated for flood control and recreational purposes by the United States Army Corps of Engineers, Fort Worth District. The Trin-

ity River Authority ᵠᵛ purchased the conservation storage space of 63,000 acre-feet and controlled diversion and conservation uses. Construction of the project began on December 23, 1959, and deliberate impoundment of water began on March 15, 1963. The reservoir has a total capacity of 63,300 acre-feet at the top of conservation storage at elevation 424.5 feet above mean sea level. It has a surface area of 5,070 acres, shoreline of thirty-eight miles, and flood control capacity of 148,900 acre-feet. The drainage area above the dam is 320 square miles.

BIBLIOGRAPHY: Texas Water Commission, *Bulletin 6408* (1964).

Seth D. Breeding

＊Navasota, Texas. Navasota, in southwestern Grimes County, is a banking and commercial center for parts of Grimes, Brazos, and Waller counties. Navasota industries produced foods, charcoal, lumber, feeds, boats, and oil field equipment. Navasota was served by a cotton gin and warehouse, two banks, a hospital, a library, a newspaper, and a radio station. The Texas State Highway Department ᵠᵛ maintained an office in Navasota. The town reported 110 businesses in 1970. In 1960 the population was 4,937; in 1970, according to the United States census, the population was 5,111.

＊Navasota River.

＊Navasota County.

Nave, Royston. Royston Nave was born in La Grange, Texas, on November 5, 1886, the son of Jack and Lou (Royston) Nave. Part of his boyhood was spent in San Antonio; by 1910 he was painting in Fort Worth. In New York he studied art under Walt Kuhn, Lawton Parker, Irving Wiles, and Robert Henri, and after that he painted landscapes and portraits in the western United States. After two years as an artillery officer in World War I he returned to New York to paint, and his works appeared in exhibitions with the Eclectics, a group of painters composed of Sidney Dickinson, Philip Hall, George Luks, Eugene Higgins, and others. His works were shown in the National Academy School of Fine Arts in New York and in the Pennsylvania Academy of Art, Philadelphia, where his portrait "Norma" received notice; other showings included the St. Louis Museum, the International Show in Pittsburgh, and the Milch Galleries in New York. He was a member of the Salamagundi Club, one of the oldest art clubs in the United States. Nave was described as a rapid painter. His works include landscapes, seascapes, Texas wild flowers, still lifes, and portraits in oil, mostly in contemporary styles. He modeled a bronze head for his mother's grave in La Grange and painted a portrait of Mrs. Rebecca Jane Fisher,ᵠᵛ now in the collection of paintings in the state Capitol ᵠᵛ in Austin.

Nave died on February 26, 1931, in Harlingen and was buried in Victoria. In 1932 his widow, Mrs. Emma McFaddin McCan Nave, built in Victoria a Greek temple-type building, designed by architects Atlee B. Ayers qv and Robert M. Ayres, to house Nave's paintings. An early catalogue listed sixty-nine paintings in the Royston Nave Memorial building in Victoria.

BIBLIOGRAPHY: Mantle Fielding, *Dictionary of American Painters, Sculptors, and Engravers* (1960); Frances Battaile Fisk, *A History of Texas Artists and Sculptors* (1928); Daniel Trowbridge Mallett, *Mallett's Index of Artists* (1948); Esse Forrester-O'Brien, *Art and Artists of Texas* (1935); San Antonio *Express*, March 1, 1931, December 25, 1932; Biographical File, Barker Texas History Center, University of Texas at Austin.

Crystal S. Ragsdale
Margaret Crain Lowery

*Navel Lake.

*Navidad, Texas.

*Navidad River.

*Navigation Districts. *See also* Water Agencies and Programs, Local.

*Navo, Texas.

*Navy, Texas. *See* Texas Navy.

Naylor, Joe Oliver. Joe Oliver Naylor was born in San Antonio, Texas, on March 28, 1893, son of John Decatur and Anna (Miller) Naylor. He attended public school and business college in San Antonio and in 1921 established the Naylor Printing Company, incorporated in 1935 as The Naylor Company, located in San Antonio. Under his direction it became a large regional book publishing house, operating its own printing and binding plant and devoting its entire facilities to book publishing. Naylor was well known for his encouragement of regional authors and for his interest in the preservation and publication of Texas folklore and history. He published a historical and literary quarterly, *Naylor's Epic-Century*, for twenty-two years.

He married Valerie Stone, and they had two children. After Mrs. Naylor died, Naylor married Rita Hall in 1943. He died in San Antonio on January 25, 1955.

BIBLIOGRAPHY: "Naylor of Texas, Regional Publisher for 15 Years," *Publisher's Weekly*, July 20, 1946; "Obituary Notes," *ibid.*, February 19, 1955; "Texas Collection," *Southwestern Historical Quarterly*, LIX (1955–1956).

Virginia Holliman Van Horn

Naylor's Epic Century. See Naylor, Joe Oliver.

*Nazarene Church. *See* Church of the Nazarene.

*Nazareth, Texas. Nazareth, first known as Wind, was begun as an Irish settlement when two brothers, A. V. and J. A. McCormick, were joined by another brother, T. P. McCormick, and his bride, from Hornell, New York, in 1892. At the invitation of T. P. McCormick thirty Irish families arrived from Austin and several East Texas towns, Arkansas, and New York that same year. Because of the dryness of the region and the difficulty in obtaining supplies and of selling the produce they raised, the Irish settlers all left within two years. In 1902, at the request of T. P. McCormick, Joseph Reisdorff qv became the first resident parish priest. A cemetery was established in 1906.

Fr. Reisdorff became interested in colonizing the town, and he changed its name to Nazareth.

Through his advertising in newspapers and writing to friends and acquaintances, German Catholic settlers were attracted, coming from Germany, Texas, Nebraska, and Indiana. Later, between 1913 and 1917, German families arrived from Nebraska, Ohio, and Oklahoma. Through the first drouth-plagued years, horse raising and then sheep raising were tried. A short-lived broom industry was begun, using the broomcorn raised on the farms. The blacksmith business became important in the town.

In 1970 Nazareth had approximately 275 inhabitants and twenty businesses.

BIBLIOGRAPHY: Charles P. Flanagin, Origins of Nazareth, Texas (M.A. thesis, West Texas State Teachers College, 1948).

*Nazro, Texas.

*Neal, George D.

Neal, Margie Elizabeth. Margie Elizabeth Neal, first woman member of the Texas Senate, was born near Clayton, in Panola County, on April 20, 1875, the second of four children of William Lafayette and Martha (Gholston) Neal; for most of her life, however, she was a resident of the county seat at Carthage. She attended, but did not graduate from, Sam Houston State Teachers College (now Sam Houston State University). After a short teaching career in Panola County and in Fort Worth she returned in 1903 to Carthage, where her father bought the *Texas Mule*, a weekly newspaper. With two men to do the mechanical work she became editor and publisher of the paper, which she immediately renamed the *East Texas Register*; she continued its publication until 1911, when she sold it.

Her first public services to the state included appointment as the first woman member of the board of regents of the State Teachers Colleges qv (1921–1927); district chairman in the fight for women's suffrage (which was won in 1920); first woman member of the State Democratic Executive Committee; and delegate to the national Democratic convention in San Francisco (1920). In 1926 she was elected from Panola County to the Texas Senate; she served four consecutive terms. She introduced the bill that created the State Board of Education,qv sponsored a bill that introduced public school physical education classes, and actively supported a bill that made the study of state and national constitutions mandatory. She was instrumental in the passage of legislation providing for the rehabilitation of handicapped persons and was on the board of the Texas Society for Crippled Children.

In 1935 she continued her career in public affairs in Washington, D.C., working with the National Recovery Administration and the federal Social Security Administration. She transferred to Texas and worked in San Antonio and Dallas, where she was with the federal Manpower Commission as a community facilities analyst. She resigned in 1945 and returned to her home in Carthage, where she continued to participate in community affairs for many years. She never married. On June 15, 1952, an appreciation party was held in Carthage for Margie Neal; among the speakers honoring her were United States Senator (later President) Lyndon Baines Johnson qv and Governor Allan Shivers. She died on December 19, 1971, in Carthage, and she was buried there.

BIBLIOGRAPHY: *Texian Who's Who* (1937); Dallas *Morning News*, June 9, 1952; *Panola Watchman* (Carthage), December 20, 1971; Tyler *Courier-Times-Telegram*, April 26, 1953; Biographical File, Barker Texas History Center, University of Texas at Austin.

*Neal, Texas.

Neale, William. William Neale, born on June 19, 1807, in Bexhill, Sussex, England, left home at thirteen and signed up as a cabin boy on an English ship which had been sold secretly to Mexico. Refitted as a Mexican man-of-war, the ship and its English crew took part in the shelling and surrender of the castle of San Juan de Ullóa and Vera Cruz in 1821. Neale then took a discharge from the Mexican Navy and worked for a British mining company in Mexico. He sailed back to England in 1826 and married Una Rutland on October 1, 1827. He and his wife came to the United States, settled first in Pottsfield, Pennsylvania, moved south in 1833, and arrived in Matamoros, Mexico, in 1834.

Seeing the need for overland transportation from the landing at Bagdad, Mexico, where ocean-going ships had to unload freight and passengers going to the river port of Matamoros, Neale began a stage route. He was involved in the Mexican War as a civilian, his stages or "hacks" being used by General Pedro Ampudia qv to remove the Mexican wounded after the battle of Palo Alto.qv He and his family were part of the frantic congestion of civilians and fleeing Mexican soldiers trying to cross the Rio Grande after the defeat of Mexican troops at the battle of Resaca de la Palma.qv From a windmill on the Mexican side of the river he witnessed General Ampudia's bombardment of Fort Brown.qv

During his years on the Mexican border he was an unofficial consul for Americans in diverse matters that included being asked to locate runaway slaves and having Mrs. Neale go to General Ampudia to secure the release of Henry Lawrence Kinney,qv who had been arrested by the Mexicans. In 1856 when steamboats began going directly to Matamoros, he discontinued his Bagdad stage line and established a mercantile business at a steamboat landing twenty-five miles up-river from Brownsville at Nealeville (also called Santa Maria). In 1859 Juan Nepomuceno Cortina qv and his men crossed at La Bolsa Bend of the Rio Grande and burned Neale's store, along with journals he had been keeping for years, and in Brownsville they killed Neale's son.

In the Civil War Neale served as captain of a company of home guards at Fort Brown, was a second lieutenant in the 3rd Texas Infantry Regiment, an inspector for cotton going into Mexico, and the enrolling and passport officer for General Hamilton Prioleau Bee.qv He witnessed naval actions of the Federal blockade at the mouth of the Rio Grande and the burning of Fort Brown. When the Federal troops occupied Brownsville in 1863, he returned to Matamoros to live.

He finally settled in Brownsville in 1865, where he had been mayor (1858–1859). He served as mayor again from 1866 to 1869. By the 1890's he was known as Brownsville's oldest inhabitant and recognized as an authority on the town's history. His address at the centennial celebration (Independence Day) in Brownsville, July 4, 1876, "The History of Brownsville, Texas, from 1848 to 1876," was published in the *Evening Ranchero* in Brownsville, July 5, 1876. He died in Brownsville on April 6, 1896, and was buried there. His home was given to the Brownsville Art League in 1950 and was moved to a location south of the United States Custom House.

BIBLIOGRAPHY: W. H. Chatfield, *The Twin Cities of the Border* (1893); Harbert Davenport, "The Life and Background of William Alfred Neale," *Southwestern Historical Quarterly*, XLVII (1943–1944); John C. Rayburn and Virginia Kemp Rayburn (eds.), *Century of Conflict, 1821–1913* (1966).

John C. Rayburn

*Neale, Texas.

*Neals, Texas.

*Neblett, Robert Caldwell.

*Nebletts Creek.

*Nebo, Texas.

*Nebo Mountain.

*Necessity, Texas.

*Nechanitz, Texas. The Matejowsky store, around which Nechanitz grew, was destroyed by fire in January, 1971.

Nechaui Indians. The Nechaui (Nechavi) Indians are known only from the late seventeenth and early eighteenth centuries, during which time they were listed as one of the Caddoan-speaking tribes of the southwestern or Hasinai division. Their principal village was on the Neches River, apparently in what is now southern Cherokee County. As their name is similar to the Hasinai name for the Neches River (Nachawi, "Osage orange"), it may be that the Nechaui were a more southerly group of Neche Indians. Sometime in the eighteenth century the Nechaui seem to have been absorbed by one or more neighboring Hasinai tribes.

BIBLIOGRAPHY: H. E. Bolton, "The Native Tribes about the East Texas Missions," *Quarterly of the Texas State Historical Association*, XI (1907–1908); F. W. Hodge (ed.), *Handbook of American Indians*, II (1910); J. R. Swanton, *Source Material on the History and Ethnology of the Caddo Indians* (1942).

T. N. Campbell

*Neche Indians. The Neche (Nacha, Naesha, Nascha, Nesta, Nouista) Indians, one of the Caddoan-speaking tribes of the Hasinai confederation, lived along the Neches River in present Cherokee and Houston counties during the seventeenth and eighteenth centuries. The Neches River received its name from this tribe. The San Francisco de los Neches Mission qv and its associated presidio were established near the Neche in 1716. The mission was abandoned in 1719, reestablished in

1721, and finally removed from the region in 1730. One of the major Hasinai fire temples was near the Neche, and there was also a lesser fire temple in the principal Neche settlement. In the nineteenth century the Neche lost their ethnic identity among the surviving remnants of Hasinai tribes, who in 1855 were placed on the Brazos Indian Reservation qv in present Young County. In 1859 all the Indians of this reservation were removed to Indian Territory, now Oklahoma. Although it has been suggested that the Nechaui were a more southerly group of Neche, this has yet to be proved.

BIBLIOGRAPHY: H. E. Bolton, "The Native Tribes about the East Texas Missions," *Quarterly of the Texas State Historical Association*, XI (1907–1908); W. J. Griffith, *The Hasinai Indians of East Texas as Seen by Europeans, 1687–1772* (1954); F. W. Hodge (ed.), *Handbook of American Indians*, II (1910); J. R. Swanton, *Source Material on the History and Ethnology of the Caddo Indians* (1942).

T. N. Campbell

*Neches, Texas.

*Neches, Battle of the.

*Neches County (Judicial).

*Neches River.

*Neches River Boundary Claim.

Necpacha Indians. The Necpacha (Nacpacha) Indians are known only from records at San Antonio de Valero Mission qv in San Antonio. J. R. Swanton listed them as Coahuiltecan, but this identification seems to have been based on similarity of the name to the names of other Coahuiltecan bands, such as Pachal and Pachalaque.

BIBLIOGRAPHY: F. W. Hodge (ed.), *Handbook of American Indians*, II (1910); J. R. Swanton, *Linguistic Material from the Tribes of Southern Texas and Northeastern Mexico* (1940).

T. N. Campbell

*Nederland, Texas. Nederland, in Jefferson County, changed to a home rule type of government with a mayor and four councilmen in 1955. Industries processed petroleum and chemical products. In 1966 Nederland reported fourteen churches, a hospital, a newspaper, a bank, and a library. In 1970 it had 136 business establishments. Population was 12,036 in 1960; the 1970 United States census report showed an increase to 16,810. *See also* Beaumont-Port Arthur-Orange Standard Metropolitan Statistical Area.

*Nedra, Texas.

*Needle Peak.

*Needmore, Texas. (Bailey County.)

*Needmore, Texas. (Delta County.)

*Needmore, Texas. (Nacogdoches County.)

Needmore, Texas. (Terry County.) Needmore was founded in 1907 as a school district. The school was later moved to Meadow, and only a general store and gin remained in 1966. The population at that time was four.

*Needmore Creek.

*Needville, Texas. The population of Needville, in Fort Bend County, was 861 in 1960 and 1,024 in 1970. The town had forty businesses in 1970.

Neff, Pat Morris. Pat Morris Neff was born near McGregor, Texas, on November 26, 1871, the son of Noah and Isabella (Shepherd) Neff, who came from Virginia in 1855. He attended school at Eagle Springs in Coryell County, McGregor High School, and Baylor University, where he took an A.B. degree in 1894. To earn money for a law degree, Neff taught school for two years at Magnolia, Arkansas, then entered the University of Texas law school, receiving his degree in 1897. In that same year he began law practice in Waco (1897–1921) and took an A.M. degree at Baylor. Later Howard Payne College (1921), Austin College (1921), Baylor University (1924), and Georgetown University of Kentucky conferred upon him the honorary LL.D. On May 31, 1899, he married Myrtle Mainer, a former Baylor classmate; they had two children.

Neff, a Democrat, began his political career as a member of the Texas legislature (1901–1905), serving as Speaker of the House for the last two years—the youngest ever to preside at that time. He was elected county attorney of McLennan County in 1906, serving until 1912. He spent the next eight years in private practice, during which time he led a successful prohibition campaign in McLennan County.

Neff defeated Senator Joseph Weldon Bailey qv to become the twenty-sixth governor of Texas in 1921 and was elected to a second term. During the Neff administration (1921–1925) two new colleges were established: Texas Technological College (now Texas Tech University) and South Texas State Teachers College (now Texas A&I University). Twice Governor Neff exercised the power of martial law: in a railroad labor dispute in Denison (Federated Shop Craft Union Strike) and during the time of oil field lawlessness in Limestone and Freestone counties, resulting from the discovery of a large oil pool near Mexia. President Calvin Coolidge named Neff to the National Board of Mediation (1927–1929), and Governor Dan Moody qv placed him on the Railroad Commission qv (1929–1931).

In 1932 Neff assumed the presidency of Baylor University (1932–1947), where he had been chairman of the board of trustees since 1903; campus facilities and enrollment were greatly increased following World War II. He was named president emeritus of Baylor after his resignation and spent much of his time building the Neff Collection of the Texas History Collection at Baylor.

The colorful orator, statesman, educator, and religious leader died of a heart attack at his home in Waco on January 20, 1952, and was buried in the Oakwood Cemetery in Waco.

BIBLIOGRAPHY: Emma Morrill Shirley, *The Administration of Pat M. Neff, Governor of Texas, 1921–1925* (1938); *Encyclopedia of Southern Baptists* (1958); *International Who's Who* (1949); Jacob F. Wolters, *Martial Law and Its Administration* (1930); *Texian Who's Who* (1937); *Who's Who in American Education* (1941).

Lois Smith Murray

*Neff, Texas.

*Negley, Texas.

*Negro Creek.

*Negro Education. *See* Education, Negro.

Negroes in Texas. From the first, the Negro has shared and shaped Texas history. Among the members of the Narváez expedition cast ashore in 1528 with Cabeza de Vaca qv was Estevanico qv (Steven, Stephen) "a Moorish slave." Negroes were also on several other early expeditions, including those under Coronado and Alarcón,qqv and a few lived in the early settlements, particularly San Antonio, both as freemen and as slaves. A census of 1785 listed 41 Negro slaves in the province, while a more detailed tally in 1792 counted 34 Negroes and 414 mulattoes, with no indication of whether they were slave or free, in a population of 3,992. The sizable influx of Negroes into Texas, however, began with immigration from the United States in 1821.

The legal position of slavery under the Mexican Republic was tenuous, but the colonists nevertheless brought their chattels. In 1826 there were 443 Negro slaves among the 1,800 persons in Austin's colony, and by the time of the Texas Revolution approximately 10 percent of the estimated total Texan population of fifty thousand were Negro. (*See* Mexican Colonization Laws, 1821–1830.)

Prior to the Texas Revolution and the subsequent legalization of the traditional customs of the American South toward the Negro, Texas held a special attraction for the black American. During the latter years of Spanish rule, numerous runaway slaves had sought refuge in the sparsely settled territory. If apprehended, they faced reenslavement by the Spanish but avoided the harsh punishment usually the lot of a runaway captured by his former owner in the United States. After the Mexican Revolution the appeal was even greater, for the threat of reenslavement was gone, and the runaway found freedom and legal equality.

The free black from the United States likewise found a better lot in Texas. Under Spanish law he was confronted with relatively few restraints on his activities. His equality was assured under the Mexican Constitution, and the Mexican government even considered several proposals to encourage free Negro immigration from the United States. Although no systematic plan for settlement was ever effected, a few Negroes came, received land, and shared in the trials and rewards of the frontier community, seemingly with little resentment from their white neighbors.

Ironically, several free Negroes served with distinction in the Texas Revolution, which resulted in the loss of their legal equality. As in the southern United States, the free Negro presented something of a dilemma for the Republic of Texas. While not given citizenship, he faced a better lot in Texas than in the American South. The obligations of the Republic to grant land to free Negroes who were residents before the Texas Declaration of Independence qv were honored, and harsh laws regulating the free Negroes, when enacted, were seldom enforced. Even after annexation, when anti-Negro feelings grew with the sectional crisis, the Negro could still find in Texas the isolation which was his only hope for peace and security.

The Negro population proportionally grew much more rapidly than the white from the Revolution to the Civil War, especially after annexation, when property became more secure. In 1848 there were 42,455 slaves in a population of 158,356. By 1860 just over 30 percent (182,921) of the total Texas population of 604,215 was black, but only 355 free Negroes were reported. The rest were held in bondage which differed little from that of the rest of the South. If, however, as has been generally conceded, slaves belonging to small slaveholders lived a less trying existence, then the institution of slavery was probably less harsh in Texas, for more than 50 percent of slave owners held five or fewer slaves and only 10 percent owned more than twenty slaves. Some scholars have also proposed that the proximity of Mexico and freedom made contented slaves desirable, and therefore better treatment characterized the Texas institution. The absence of major slave insurrections has likewise been cited as evidence of relatively good treatment of Texas slaves; however, the lack of adequate information on slave runaways and disturbances render such judgments subjective and tentative. All that is certain is that practices in Texas differed from those in the rest of the South so slightly as to be hardly discernible.

As the sectional crisis matured in the middle 1850's, efforts were made to increase controls and restraints over both slaves and free Negroes, particularly through a strengthened patrol system and stringent vagrancy laws. Secession and the war seemed to have had little impact on the Texas Negro. The primary result of the war was a sizable increase in the Negro population resulting from the influx of slaves who were sent from the Mississippi Valley out of the reach of Northern armies.

Freedom came to Negro Texans on June 19, 1865, when General Gordon Granger qv proclaimed the return of federal control. "Juneteenth" qv thereby became a major annual holiday for Negroes. In only a few cases did federal authorities have to force an owner to release his chattels, and the attempt of the Eleventh Legislature to establish a peonage system for the Negro was subverted by the Freedmen's Bureau.qv Freedom, if not equality, for blacks was reluctantly accepted by the whites.

During congressional Reconstruction (*see* Reconstruction in Texas) and the administration of Edmund J. Davis,qv Negroes participated actively in public affairs. In February, 1868, Negroes exercised the franchise for the first time, electing nine delegates to the Constitutional Convention of 1868–1869,qv but they played only a minor role in writing the new constitution. In 1869 two Negroes were elected to the Senate and nine to the House of the Twelfth Legislature; in the Thirteenth Legislature there were two Negro senators and five representatives. None had a major role in lawmaking. While no Negro ever held a statewide elective office, the power of the black man was great within the Republican party.qv Under the leadership of such men as G. T. Ruby and Matthew Gaines,qqv blacks greatly influenced party policy and provided most of the Republican votes in the state. Many Negroes held local office, especially in those areas of heavy Negro population, but only a few counties ever had a majority of Negro officials; even those counties with large Negro majorities always had some white officials.

While the political influence of the Negro began a rapid decline with the return of the Democrats to power in 1874, it did not disappear. Five Negroes attended the Constitutional Convention of 1875,qv and under the leadership of Norris Wright Cuney qv and later William Madison (Gooseneck) McDonald,qv Negroes actively participated in the Republican party until about the turn of the century. While the party won no statewide elections, even despite "fusion" politics with the Greenback and Populist parties,qqv its control of federal patronage gave it some power. In the "Black Belt" counties, Negroes continued to hold local offices until the 1890's, and Negroes served in every legislature except one until 1897.

When the "Lily-White" faction (see Lily-White Movement) captured control of the Republican party, the Negro voice in selection of candidates and drawing of policy ended. The passage of the Terrell election law paved the way for the poll tax and the white primary, and the Negroes' influence in public affairs came to a halt (see Election Laws). Not until the outlawing of the white primary by the federal courts in the Texas case of Smith v. Allwright in 1944 did Negroes again influence Texas politics.

While the Negro population of Texas steadily increased in number—253,471 in 1870, 620,722 in 1900, 854,964 in 1930, and 1,187,125 in 1960— the proportion of black to white Texans steadily declined. From a high of almost 31 percent in 1870, the ratio slipped to 20 percent in 1900, under 15 percent in 1930, and less than 11 percent in 1960. While the natural increase of the Negro population remained high, a steady black emigration from the state combined with high white immigration resulted in the decline in the relative position of the Negro population. From the beginning a great majority of Negroes lived in rural East Texas, but a major population shift by black Texans after 1920 brought many Negroes to the cities. In that year 70 percent of the Negro population lived in rural areas, but by 1960 only 25 percent lived there. Agricultural change was one of the major motivating factors in this move.

Freedom from slavery did not mean immediate freedom from the soil. The nature of the economy, the attitudes of the whites, and the training of Negroes all combined to assure that for more than half a century after emancipation a majority of working Negroes would be engaged in agricultural pursuits. Except for those performing domestic service, almost all Negroes in the early years of freedom worked on farms. A slow drift to other occupations began, but by 1910, when the first comprehensive data on Negro employment was gathered, 60 percent were still engaged in agriculture. The hired-hand system dominated the period immediately following emancipation and remained the lot of a large, if decreasing, portion of Negro agriculturalists well into the twentieth century. Although statistical data is not entirely satisfactory, it is clear that in 1910 approximately two-thirds of the Negroes in agriculture were still hired hands at least a portion of the time and that these accounted for more than a third of the 358,981 gainfully employed Negroes. By 1930 agricultural laborers amounted to about 40 percent of those engaged in agriculture, or about 20 percent of all working Negroes.

While the number of Negro farmers increased steadily from emancipation to the Great Depression, the number tilling their own land reached a plateau of roughly twenty thousand by 1900. An increasingly high portion of Negroes were tenants. In 1900, 69 percent of Negro farmers were tenants compared to less than 50 percent of white farmers, and in 1930, 76 percent of Negro farmers were sharecroppers compared with less than 60 percent of whites. In addition, the average size of both owned and rented farms was much smaller among blacks than whites.

Between 1930 and 1960 the occupational makeup of the Negro population changed spectacularly. In 1930 roughly 43 percent of gainfully employed Negroes were in agriculture, 29 percent in domestic service, 14 percent in manufacturing, 7 percent in transportation, 6 percent in professions, and the remainder scattered in various jobs. The depression and federal farm programs drove the tenants from the land. The economic boom and the relaxation of racial barriers during and following World War II opened numerous occupational opportunities. By 1960 only 8 percent of working Negro Texans were engaged in agriculture, 16 percent worked as laborers, 7 percent were in professions, and approximately 20 percent were in each of the following areas: domestic service, crafts and operations, and service industries.

Until these changes in occupational status, the black community made only slow social and economic progress. Segregated in public and private affairs—by custom until the late 1880's and thereafter by an ever-growing body of Jim Crow legislation—Negroes were thrown on their own meager resources in the struggle for social betterment. In spite of the efforts of Negro churches, fraternal organizations, and self-help groups like the Farmers' Home Improvement Society,qv the race as a whole lived a precarious existence on the edge of subsistence, remaining all but overwhelmed by the problems created by poverty and ignorance: high rates of birth, death, crime, illiteracy, malnutrition, broken homes, and contagious disease. Even with the changes following World War II, the average family income of Texas Negroes in 1960 was one-half that of white families, and their educational level was considerably lower. Only 50 percent of Negro dwelling units were sound, compared to 80 percent for whites, and 40 percent of Negro homes were overcrowded, compared to 20 percent for whites.

Perhaps the most tragic illustration of the position of Texas Negroes was lynching. While several Negroes were lynched before emancipation, such actions only became common as a part of white efforts to restore social and political control over the Negro after emancipation. Although the practice was clearly widespread from about 1870, the exact number of lynchings before 1882 is unknown. From that year to 1936, when apparently the last lynching occurred, 345 Negroes were lynched, thus ranking Texas third among the states in this gruesome category. At least three Negroes were lynched every year from 1889 to 1922, with the greatest number occurring around the peak years of 1895, when twenty Negroes were lynched, and 1897, when twenty-three Negroes were killed by mobs. The last year of considerable mob violence was 1922, when sixteen Negroes were lynched. Only rarely were members of lynch mobs punished in spite of the illegality of lynching.

Several race riots likewise marred the state's history. A clash between Negro troops and citizens of Brenham in 1866 ended with a portion of the city in flames. In 1887 violence erupted in Matagorda County and was controlled only by the arrival of the militia; five Negroes died and several were wounded. While not entirely white against black, there were deep racial overtones to political rivalries which ended in violence in Nacogdoches, Grimes, and Walker counties in the 1890's. Negro soldiers were again participants in racial violence in 1906 when a barroom brawl degenerated into a major race riot in Brownsville. One white was killed, and the riot led to a congressional investigation of great importance. In 1917 Houston suffered the worst race riot in the state's history as Negro soldiers and white citizens clashed, with seventeen whites killed and thirteen Negro soldiers later executed for murder. Two years later several persons of both races were shot and the Negro section of town burned in a riot in Longview. Marshall also experienced racial violence in 1919. Under pressures created by the advancement of Negro workers in defense plants, Beaumont's racial feelings exploded in June, 1943. By the time troops moved in to quiet the troubles, two persons had been killed and scores injured. The "Negro Revolution" beginning in the 1950's provoked no major racial violence in Texas in spite of the long tradition of racial conflict. While mobs gathered at the scene of several integration attempts and Negro houses were bombed when neighborhood integration was attempted, no lives were lost, few people were injured, and property damage was slight. In 1967 a riot occurred on the campus of Texas Southern University which resulted in the death of one policeman.

Some early attempts at school integration, such as the integration of Mansfield schools in 1956, were halted by mobs, but by 1966 only four of 1,170 school districts maintained mandatory separation of the races. In 1966 three Negroes—two representatives and one female senator—were elected to the state legislature for the first time in seventy years. While *de jure* segregation had all but disappeared in the state, *de facto* segregation remained. The Negro had made progress in almost all areas, but as the 1960's ended, great problems remained to be solved before Negro Texans could escape the stigma of their color. *See also* Integration in Texas; Lynching in Texas; Riots in Texas; Education, Negro.

BIBLIOGRAPHY: Mary Elizabeth Estes, An Historical Survey of Lynching in Oklahoma and Texas (M.A. thesis, University of Oklahoma, 1942); Charles E. Hall, *Progress of the Negro in Texas* (1936); Leonard Brewster Murphy, A History of Negro Segregation Practices in Texas, 1865–1958 (M.A. thesis, Southern Methodist University, 1958); Lawrence D. Rice, The Negro in Texas, 1874–1900 (Ph.D. dissertation, Texas Technological College, 1967); R. L. Skrabanek and J. S. Hollingsworth, "The Non-White Population of Texas," Texas Agricultural Experiment Station *Bulletin 1059* (1966).

James V. Reese

*Neibling, Frederic.

*Neighbors, Basley (Busby) G.

*Neighbors, Robert Simpson.

*Neighborsville, Texas. [This title was incorrectly listed in Volume II as Neighborville, Texas.] Both spellings, Neighborsville and Neighborville are found in writings concerning this early Comal County settlement, although on the plat of the town in the deed records the name was spelled with an "s."

BIBLIOGRAPHY: Deed Records, Vol. G, Comal County.

*Neil Creek.

*Neill, Andrew.

Neill, David Jasper. David Jasper Neill was born in Arkansas on March 25, 1857, the son of George and MaryAn (Munn) Neill. As a resident of Gorman, Eastland County, he became associated with the Texas Farmers' Union qv and was named lecturer in 1904. The following year he was elected state lecturer and was unanimously reelected in 1906. On August 5, 1907, he became the first West Texan elected president of the state union. He received the endorsement of Texas, Oklahoma, Illinois, Kansas, and Missouri to seek the presidency of the national union, but declined to make the race. For five years he served as editor of the *National Co-Operator*, then retired to his farm near Gorman; his last public service was to represent Eastland County in the Thirty-fifth and Thirty-sixth state legislatures.

Neill and his wife, America Cantley, were the parents of seven children. He died on June 28, 1937, in Gorman and was buried there.

BIBLIOGRAPHY: C. Richard King, "Dave J. Neill and the Farmers' Union," *West Texas Historical Association Year Book*, XL (1964).

C. Richard King

***Neill, James Clinton.**

Neiman-Marcus Company. The Neiman-Marcus Company of Dallas was founded in 1907 by Herbert Marcus qv and Alfred L. Neiman. Objectives of the store were to provide the very finest in specialty items and to introduce Dallas women to the latest fashions. It was one of the first stores in Dallas to offer ready-made garments and to sell designer items from New York and Paris. Not only Texas women became customers, but a worldwide clientele was attracted. Neiman-Marcus was unique in that, unlike the specialty stores in larger cities, it offered a wide variety of the world's finest items under one roof. In 1932 Neiman-Marcus created great attention with the idea, novel for a store outside of New York, of advertising nationally. An annual Fashion Exposition, distinguished service awards in the field of fashion, and the International Fortnights were Neiman-Marcus traditions that became trademarks in the fashion world and promoted Dallas as a fashion center in the Southwest.

The company began with a $35,000 investment, selling only women's garments and millinery in a two-story building on Elm and Murphy streets; it grew to a full-scale department store offering services in everything from a travel agency and portrait studio to restaurants. In addition to the two founders, Mrs. Carrie Marcus Neiman, wife of Alfred Neiman and sister of Herbert Marcus, was a store executive. In 1928 Alfred Neiman sold out his interest when he and Carrie Neiman were divorced. From then until 1969 Neiman-Marcus was family owned and operated, with the four sons of Herbert Marcus, Sr., joining the business. Stanley Marcus became vice-president in 1935 and president in 1950 after his father's death.

By 1976 Neiman-Marcus operated two stores in Dallas, one in Fort Worth (with another planned), one in Houston, one in Bal Harbour, Florida, one in Atlanta, Georgia, one in St. Louis, Missouri, and one in Chicago, Illinois; another was planned for Los Angeles, California. A number of boutiques were located in hotels in Texas. The original store in Dallas employed thirty-five people in 1907; the number of employees totaled 1,700 in 1956 and approximately 3,700 in 1971 in all the Neiman-Marcus stores. The first store had a net sales of $163,036 in 1907; in 1950 the company's net sales totaled $22,938,000; and by 1969 net sales amounted to $69,706,000. Some stock of Neiman-Marcus Company was sold publicly for the first time in July, 1959. In April, 1969, Neiman-Marcus merged with Broadway-Hale Stores, Inc., of California, now called Carter Hawley Hale Stores, Inc., of which Stanley Marcus was named executive vice-president in 1975. Stanley Marcus was also chairman of the executive committee of Neiman-Marcus Company, of which his son, Richard Marcus, was president in 1976.

BIBLIOGRAPHY: Zula McCauley, *The First Forty Years* (1947); Frank X. Tolbert, *Neiman-Marcus Texas* (1953).

***Neinda, Texas.**

***Nelleva, Texas.**

***Nelson, Albert Aldrich.**

***Nelson, Allison.** Allison Nelson was not a graduate nor did he ever attend the United States Military Academy (as stated in Volume II). He was promoted to brigadier general in September, 1862, but was never made major general.

BIBLIOGRAPHY: Marcus J. Wright (comp.) and Harold B. Simpson (ed.), *Texas in the War, 1861–1865* (1965); *List of Cadets Admitted into the United States Military Academy, West Point, N.Y., From its origin till September 1, 1886.*

Palmer Bradley

***Nelson, James.**

***Nelson, Orville Howell.**

***Nelson Creek.**

***Nelson Switch, Texas.**

***Nelsonville, Texas.**

***Nelta, Texas.**

***Nemo, Texas.**

***Neraz, John Claudius.**

***Neri, Felipe Enrique.** *See* Bastrop, Baron Felipe Enrique Neri de.

***Nesbitt, Texas.**

***Nesters.**

Nettie Lee Benson Latin American Collection. *See* Latin American Collection.

Neu, Charles Ternay. Charles Ternay Neu, son of Jacob and Magdalena (Weihing) Neu, was born in Brenham, Texas, on February 18, 1885. After graduation from Brenham High School, Neu taught at West, Texas, before entering the University of Texas, where he obtained a bachelor's degree in 1908 and a master's degree in 1909. At the university he assisted George P. Garrison qv in the editing of *Diplomatic Correspondence of the Republic of Texas* (1908, 1911). He became a Fellow of the Texas State Historical Association qv in 1910.

He taught history in the public schools of Greenville, Cisco, and Dallas; in 1917 he joined the faculty of East Texas State Teachers College (now East Texas State University) at Commerce, where he became head of the Department of History in 1925. Neu obtained his Ph.D. degree in history in 1928 at the University of California at Berkeley, studying under Herbert Eugene Bolton.qv He contributed numerous articles and book reviews to historical journals and was the author of "The Republic of Texas," in *The State of Texas Book* (1937), edited by Arthur W. Stikle, and "The Annexation of Texas," in *New Spain and the Anglo-American West: Historical Contributions Presented to Herbert Eugene Bolton* (1932).

On June 12, 1912, he married Johnie Marshall of Greenville, Texas, and they had one son. Neu died on May 8, 1950, in Commerce, Texas.

BIBLIOGRAPHY: Brenham *Daily Banner-Express*, August 9,

1919; Commerce *Daily Journal*, May 9, 1950; C. T. Neu, The Foreign Relations of the Republic of Texas 1836–1846 (Ph.D. dissertation, University of California, 1928).

Nannie M. Tilley

Neu Braunfelser Zeitung. The *Neu Braunfelser Zeitung*, the German newspaper in New Braunfels, began bilingual publication in 1950, at which time the title of the paper was changed to the New Braunfels *Zeitung-Chronicle*. When the paper was bought by the New Braunfels Herald Publishing Company in 1957, the German section was dropped. In 1964 the New Braunfels *Zeitung-Chronicle* was published weekly on Sunday, and its sister publication, the New Braunfels *Herald*, was published weekly on Thursday, each with a circulation of 5,000. In 1966 the New Braunfels *Zeitung-Chronicle* was merged with the New Braunfels *Herald* and publication of the New Braunfels *Herald and Zeitung* was begun weekly on Thursday. Paid circulation in October, 1970, was 7,705.

Marjorie Cook

*Neuse Store, Texas.

*Neut, Texas.

*Neuthard School.

*Neutral Ground.

*Neuville, Texas.

*Nevada, Texas.

*Nevantine Village.

*Neville, Texas.

*New Baden, Texas.

*New Berlin, Texas.

*New Bern, Texas.

*New Bielau, Texas.

*New Birmingham, Texas.

*New Birthright, Texas.

*New Blox, Texas.

*New Bluffton, Texas.

New Boston, Texas. New Boston, in the center of Bowie County, developed a mile north of the courthouse in Boston when the Texas and Pacific Railroad was built through the county in 1874. Most of the businesses of Boston relocated near the railroad stop, which was called New Boston. In 1970 the town listed seventy-seven businesses. The population doubled during the 1940's from 1,111 in 1940 to 2,688 in 1950. The 1960 population was 2,773; the 1970 United States census showed a population of 3,699. *See also* Texarkana Standard Metropolitan Statistical Area; Boston, Texas.

*New Braunfels, Texas. New Braunfels, seat of Comal County, in the 1960's had industries which included a cotton mill, a textile mill, a lime kiln, a flour mill, feed mills, a road material manufacturing plant, various meat and poultry plants, and a large work clothes rental service. In 1970 the city had 420 business establishments. The 1960 population of 15,631 increased to 17,859 by 1970, according to the United States census.

New Braunfels was not only an industrial center but also a popular year-round vacation spot. Landa Park and Canyon Reservoir (fifteen miles north of the city) provided fishing, boating, and other recreational facilities. A new tourist attraction, Natural Bridge Caverns,qv opened in 1964. The annual New Braunfels Wurstfest, celebrated during the first part of November, was patterned after the famed Munich *Oktoberfest*. The festival's food and entertainment have attracted thousands to New Braunfels each year. The restored home of famed botanist and newspaper publisher, Ferdinand Lindheimer,qv on the Comal River was open to the public. At the one hundred twenty-fifth anniversary celebration of the founding of New Braunfels in April, 1970, a *Fachwerk* memorial of two walls of cedar timbers and stone was erected bearing the names of over two hundred of the original German settlers. The *Fachwerk* (half-timber) structure so characteristic of early buildings in the New Braunfels area was influenced by an ancient German architectural style. *See also* Veramendi Estate—New Braunfels.

*New Braunfels Academy. The original long, one-story building of the New Braunfels Academy was razed in 1913 to be replaced by a two-story school building on the same location on East Mill and Academy streets. A fine photograph of the old building hangs in the Sophienburg Museum.qv

New Braunfels *Herald and Zeitung. See Neu Braunfelser Zeitung.

*New Camp, Texas.

New Camp Ruby, Texas. New Camp Ruby, Texas, in central Polk County, was founded in 1925 as a sawmill camp by W. T. Carter and Brothers of Camden. It once was connected with Camden by a railroad and consisted of a consolidated high school, a post office, a barber shop, and a large mercantile store. The village was named for Ruby Moore by the lumber camp boss, A. B. Clayton. In 1966 the only remaining business was the mercantile store under the management of M. W. Redd. The population in 1966 was about one hundred.

*New Caney, Texas.

New Clarkson, Texas. New Clarkson, in northeastern Milam County, was a small farming community in the 1960's, with a store owned by Jim Hauk. Some cabins, built on a lake, have made the community a resort area.

New Columbia, Texas. New Columbia was located in Newton County on the Sabine River eight miles east of Burkeville. It appears as a townsite on an 1839 map of Jasper County made by Martin B. Lewis,qv county surveyor, but records do not show who laid it out or when. Before and after the Civil War it was a boat landing with a store, warehouse, and five or six residences. In the latter part of the nineteenth century there was also a racetrack, and races were run regularly.

About 1908 two brothers, A. A. (Jack) and J. Polk McMahon, operated the McMahon Handle Company, manufacturers of handles and railroad ties. The ties were rafted downstream to Bon Wier, and the handles were hauled overland to Rosepine, Louisiana, and then shipped by rail to northern distributors. At that time the first post office was established. Because of other Texas towns named Columbia, the post office was named Jack's, for one of the handle factory partners. Operations ceased and the post office closed in 1914 because of declining business.

BIBLIOGRAPHY: County Maps (General Land Office, Austin).

Madeleine Martin

New Corn Hill, Texas. New Corn Hill, in Williamson County, is located east of Interstate Highway 35 between the settlements of Theon and Schwertner, near the Bell County line. *See also* Corn Hill, Texas.

*New County Line, Texas.

*New Diana, Texas.

New Era (Austin).

*New Fountain, Texas. The historic Weimers Oak, located near the New Fountain Methodist Church, was named for the John Weimers family, early German settlers. The tree often shaded open-air prayer meetings of the pioneers in the area.

BIBLIOGRAPHY: John A. Haislet (ed.), *Famous Trees of Texas* (1970).

*New Hagansport, Texas.

*New Harmony, Texas.

*New Harp, Texas.

*New Home, Texas. New Home, in northern Lynn County, incorporated in 1963, had an economy based on agriculture. By 1966 the town had completed a post office building, a city hall, and a fire station. New Home had three churches and a public school in use by 1966. The town reported nine businesses in 1970. The 1970 population was 252.

*New Hope, Texas. (Cherokee County.)

*New Hope, Texas. (Collin County.)

*New Hope, Texas. (Dallas County.)

*New Hope, Texas. (Denton County.)

*New Hope, Texas. (Franklin County.)

*New Hope, Texas. (Jones County.)

*New Hope, Texas. (San Jacinto County.)

New Hope, Texas. (Wilson County.) New Hope was a post office from June 9, 1873, to May 17, 1880.

*New Hope, Texas. (Wood County.)

*New Loco, Texas. *See* Loco, Texas.

*New London, Texas. New London, in Rusk County, had a population of 899 in 1970, according to the United States census.

*New Lynn, Texas. [This title was incorrectly listed as Newlynn, Texas, and thus out of alphabetical order on page 275, Volume II.] New Lynn, in Lynn County, had a population of eighteen in 1969.

*New Mexico v. Texas.

*New Moore, Texas.

New Mountain, Texas. New Mountain, in eastern Upshur County, had an estimated population of fifty in 1966. The community was located in a farming and ranching area.

*New Orleans Greys. The New Orleans Greys' experiences from October, 1835, and during the following months of revolution in Texas were well chronicled by the young German, Herman Ehrenberg,qv who was to survive the Goliad massacre qv on Palm Sunday. The first unit of the New Orleans Greys, of which Ehrenberg was a member, sailed on the steamboat, *Washita*, up the Mississippi River, thence up the Red River, where they temporarily stopped at Alexandria. Under the command of their newly elected captain, Thomas H. Breece,qv they sailed on to Natchitoches. From there they marched overland, crossed the Sabine River into Texas, and after two days reached San Augustine.

BIBLIOGRAPHY: Herman Ehrenberg, *With Milam and Fannin: Adventures of a German Boy in Texas' Revolution* (1968); Frank C. Lockwood, "Native German Early Leader in Southwest," Dallas *Morning News*, February 11, 1940; Clarence Wharton, "100 Years Ago Today," Houston *Chronicle*, October 13, 1935.

New Philippines. New Philippines (Nuevas Filipinas, Nuevas Filippinas, Nuevas Philipinas, Nuevo Reyno de Filipinas) was the name used for Texas about the time, 1716, when Don Martín de Alarcón qv was appointed governor of the Kingdom of the New Philippines. In 1719 the second Marquis de San Miguel de Aguayo qv was appointed governor and captain-general of the Province of Texas [New Philippines] and of Coahuila [New Kingdom of Estremadura] (*see* Nueva Estremadura). The Medina River was for more than a century to be designated as the official boundary between Texas (New Philippines) and Coahuila. The boundaries then ran from the coast of the Gulf of Mexico to the *lomeria* (hill country) of the Apaches, which formed its northern boundary, ending at the Red River, the boundary of Louisiana. Yoakum's *History of Texas* shows the map of "Spanish-Texas" with the New Philippines clearly marked, although the source of the map is not given. *See also* Coahuila and Texas.

BIBLIOGRAPHY: Eleanor Claire Buckley, "The Aguayo Expedition into Texas and Louisiana, 1719–1722," *Quarterly of the Texas State Historical Association*, XV (1911–1912); I. J. Cox, "The Southwest Boundary of Texas," *ibid.*, VI (1902–1903); Charles Wilson Hackett (ed.), *Pichardo's Treatise on the Limits of Louisiana and Texas*, I (1931); José Porrúa Turanzas (ed.), *Documentos para la historia eclesiástica y civil de la Provincia de Texas o Nuevas Philipinas, 1720–1799* (1961); H. Yoakum, *History of Texas* (1855).

*New Salem, Texas. (Milam County.)

*New Salem, Texas. (Rusk County.)

*New Summerfield, Texas.

*New Sweden, Texas.

*New Taiton, Texas.

*New Tira, Texas.

*New Ulm, Texas.

*New Washington, Texas.

*New Washington Association.

*New Waverly, Texas.

New Waverly Conservation Center. *See* Job Corps Program in Texas.

*New Wied, Texas. In 1971 portions of the original building in New Wied, Comal County, where the orphans and the family of Louis Cochand Ervendberg qv lived had been preserved and incorporated in a later Victorian house. Still owned by descendants of the original family, the house contained many of the old kitchen utensils, farm and carpenter's tools, and furniture. The area immediately around the house still retained the wilderness quality which characterized it more than a hundred years ago.
BIBLIOGRAPHY: Samuel Wood Geiser, *Naturalists of the Frontier* (1948); Frederick Law Olmsted, *A Journey through Texas* (1857).

*New Willard, Texas.

*New Year Creek.

*New York, Texas.

*New York Creek.

*New York, Texas, and Mexican Railway.

*Newark, Texas. Newark, in Wise County, has had five names, beginning with Odessa in 1855, when a post office with that name was established and Benjamin B. Haney was the first postmaster. Huff Valley, Sueville, and Ragtown were other names for the community until finally it was called Newark in 1893. When a neighboring settlement, Aurora, failed in 1893, several families moved their houses to Newark. Remnants of Caddo Indian culture have been located in graves and village sites in the area. The population in 1960 was 392 and in 1970 was 407, according to the United States census.
BIBLIOGRAPHY: Etta Bearden Pegues, *Newark, Its Heritage and Landmarks* (1969).

*Newburg, Texas. Newburg, in Comanche County, was originally named South Leon and was founded in 1854 by pioneer families located on the Mercer, Mountain, and South Leon creeks. By the end of 1855 the settlement consisted of thirty to forty families. Ranching continued to be the primary occupation in the 1960's. Although there were no businesses operating, an active church and community center were maintained in 1967. The population for 1970 was thirty-five.
Margaret Tate Waring

*Newby, Texas.

*Newcastle, Texas. Attempts at strip, pit, and slope mining were made in the Fort Belknap qv area, two miles south of Newcastle, in Young County, in the 1880's and early 1900's. In 1906 a few families in wagons came to nearby Whiskey Creek for the Merrill and Clark Strip Mining Company, living in a settlement of tents, dugouts, and box houses called "Tent Town" and "Rag Town." In May, 1907, the Wichita Falls and Southern Railway lines were laid from Olney to the Whis-

key Creek operation of the Belknap Coal Company. The first shaft was sunk in March, 1908, and the first car of coal reached Wichita Falls in mid-1908. After that a number of railroad workers went to work in the mines. Early in 1908 Samuel H. Hardy suggested as the town's name that of his birthplace, Newcastle upon Tyne, England. The post office was moved from old Fort Belknap on March 4, 1908. Called "City of Newcastle, the Birmingham of the Southwest," townsite lots were sold in mostly speculative buying. In October, 1908, the Newcastle *Register* began publication, and in the next three years a bank, churches, and a school were established. In 1909 there were fifty-six miners on the Belknap Coal Company payroll; by October of that year eight hundred people were living in the town.

In September, 1909, the miners struck, forming Local 2853 of the United Mine Workers of America. Another strike lasted twenty-two months (1914–1915), and strike-breaking miners were imported from Alabama. The coal from Newcastle was used by the railroad itself and by small industries in Wichita Falls and other towns in North Texas and Oklahoma. By 1942 all mining operations at Newcastle had ceased, although the influence of a mining culture remained with mining songs and ballads brought by miners from the South and East. In 1965 the town had a bank, a newspaper, five churches, and a school. Eleven businesses were reported in 1970. The population in 1960 was 617 and in 1970 was 624, according to the United States census.
BIBLIOGRAPHY: Barbara Neal Ledbetter, *Newcastle, Texas: A Coal Mining Town* (1964).

*Newcomb, James Pearson. The family of James Pearson Newcomb immigrated to Texas in October, 1839 (not 1840, as stated in Volume II), settling originally in Victoria. He moved to San Antonio with his father in 1847. In 1851 (not 1854) the orphaned Newcomb began his journalistic career at the age of thirteen in San Antonio as a printer's devil on the *Western Texan*. Together with F. M. Whitemond in 1854, Newcomb started publication of the *Alamo Star*,qv and in 1855 (not 1854) he established the San Antonio *Herald* qv with J. M. West. He published the first issue of the *Alamo Express*,qv a pro-Union paper, on August 18, 1860, as a weekly; it became a tri-weekly on February 4, 1861, with J. B. Maccus, Jr., as Newcomb's associate.

Newcomb joined with A. W. Gifford in 1879 in publishing the *Texas Sun* in San Antonio, a newspaper Gifford had started in Kansas City in 1877 and had published in Houston. In 1880 Newcomb published *The Surprise*, a forerunner of the *Evening Light*, which Gifford and Newcomb founded in January, 1881. His connection with the paper as its editor and publisher ended in 1883 with its reorganization and change of name to the San Antonio *Light* qv (not with his death in 1907).
BIBLIOGRAPHY: The Newcomb Papers (Archives, University of Texas at Austin Library); Newcomb Newspaper Collection and Letters (San Antonio Public Library); Ja-

cobina Burch Harding, A History of the Early Newspapers of San Antonio, 1823–1874 (M.A. thesis, University of Texas, 1951).

James Pearson Newcomb, Jr.

Newell, Chester. Chester Newell, Episcopal clergyman, was born in Massachusetts on July 8, 1803; he graduated from Yale in 1831 and from the Episcopal Theological Seminary in Virginia in 1834. After serving as a missionary in Tennessee, he came to Texas in 1837. For a year he operated a school at Velasco, and afterward spent some time at Houston gathering material for a history, after which he returned to New York.

In 1838 he published *The History of the Revolution in Texas, Particularly of the War of 1835 & 1836; Together with the Latest Geographical, Topographical and Statistical Account of the Country . . . .* In that year he applied for appointment as a missionary to Texas, but he was refused because of complaints from Texas that he had neglected exercising his ministerial office while there. He subsequently served as chaplain in the United States Navy, from which he retired in 1865. He died in Savannah, Georgia, on June 24, 1892, apparently never having revisited Texas.

BIBLIOGRAPHY: A. F. Muir, "William Fairfax Gray," *Historical Magazine of the Protestant Episcopal Church,* XXXVIII (1959); Minutes of the Foreign Committee, Domestic and Foreign Missionary Society, Episcopal Church (MS., Archives of General Convention, Episcopal Church Historical Society, Austin).

Lawrence L. Brown

*Newell, John D.

*Newgulf, Texas.

*Newlin, Texas.

*Newline, Texas.

*Newlynn, Texas. *See* New Lynn, Texas.

*Newman, Albert Henry.

*Newman, Joseph.

*Newman, Texas.

*Newman Creek.

*Newman Peak.

*Newport, Texas.

*Newsome, Texas.

*Newspapers of Texas. Trends developing prior to 1950 in the number of daily newspapers and circulation in Texas continued to 1965. Thirteen new dailies were started, eleven discontinued publication, and three merged with other dailies. Of the thirteen new dailies, seven were suburban, a reflection of population shifts in the state. The notable success of the Southwest edition of the *Wall Street Journal* at Dallas, which began publication in 1948, was indicative of the industrial, commercial, and financial growth in the state and region. Daily newspapers remained almost constant at 114, one less in 1965 than in 1950. In the number of dailies per state, Texas ranked third behind California and Pennsylvania.

Between 1950 and 1965 daily circulation increased by 26 percent, growing from 2,439,000 to 3,072,000, a figure slightly larger than the total number of households in the state. About 80 percent of Texas households received one or more daily newspapers in 1965.

The rise and fall of the total number of weekly newspapers provided an indication of the social and economic changes taking place in the state. After a seven-year decline which began in the middle of World War II, weeklies increased for several years until various influences, including the wage-and-hour law, Korean War, and continued urbanization, reversed the trend in 1951. After a five-year decline, total weeklies leveled off largely as a result of the economies afforded by offset printing and central printing plants. Of the 567 weeklies in the state in 1965, more than 200 were printed offset, which largely accounted for the increase of weeklies over a three-year span. Circulation in 1965 was approximately 1,050,000, of which about 48,000 was free. Paid circulation was about 12.5 percent larger than in 1950. In number of weeklies per state, Texas ranked third behind California and Illinois.

Newspapers in the standard metropolitan statistical areas,qv which had 83 percent of all daily circulation, increased in size per issue by more than one-third from 1950 to 1965. While the amount of space devoted to news increased, the proportion of news to advertising stayed about the same. The news comprised approximately 40 percent of total space for smaller papers and 32 percent for larger papers.

News content changed to meet the need for greater social responsibility, and there was an increase in the amount of space devoted to medicine, science and education, economic affairs, mental health, government, civil rights, and international news. Through temperateness and a relatively progressive outlook on racial integration, the Texas press played a significant role in the efforts that brought improvements in racial problems in the state without the violence that occurred in many other states.

Chain ownership increased in the state for both daily and weekly newspapers. In 1965 eleven Texas-based chains owned 59 of the 114 daily newspapers, and 3 Texas dailies were owned by out-of-state chains. The growth of multiple ownership can be attributed largely to efforts to cope with the economic problems of newspaper publishing and to the need for suburban dailies in the large metropolitan areas. The largest chain in the state was Harte-Hanks Newspapers, Inc., with ownership of thirteen daily newspapers in Abilene, Big Spring, Corpus Christi, Denison, Greenville, Marshall, Paris, San Angelo, and San Antonio.

In the ten years after 1965 the major trends noted for the previous fifteen years continued. Daily newspapers increased by 4, to 118, only 27 of those being morning papers. In number, Texas moved to second in the nation. Fifty-five dailies used offset printing by 1974, the two largest being the *Wall Street Journal* (Southwest edition) and the Beaumont *Enterprise-Journal.* There were 565 weekly newspapers in the state in 1975, 17 of which were Negro publications with circulations ranging from 40,000 to 2,000. Six were in Houston, four in Dallas, two each in San Antonio and Fort Worth, and one each in Austin, Lubbock and Waco.

The trend toward chain ownership continued slowly. Harte-Hanks Newspapers, Inc., became national in scope. By 1974 it controlled forty-seven daily and weekly newspapers, and its gross revenue for the previous year was $83,000,000. It was one of the ten largest newspaper chains in the country.

By 1976 seventeen Texas newspapers were 110 or more years old. They were the Galveston News,qv 1842; Dallas Morning News qv (by virtue of being a part of the newspaper institution which originated in the Galveston News, although established in Dallas only in 1885); Bay City Tribune, 1845; Seguin Gazette, 1846; Victoria Advocate,qv 1846; Rusk Cherokeean, 1847; Gladewater Mirror, 1849; Huntsville Item, 1850; New Braunfels Herald and Zeitung (originally Neu Braunfelser Zeitung qv), 1852; Bastrop Advertiser, 1853; Gonzales Inquirer, 1853; Goliad Advance-Guard, 1855; Colorado County Citizen, 1857; Cameron Herald, 1860; Jasper News-Boy, 1865; Jefferson Jimplecute, 1865; and San Antonio Express,qv 1865. See also Journalism in Texas, Early; Texas Press Association.

BIBLIOGRAPHY: Advertising Age, 45 (July 22, 1974); N. W. Ayer & Sons Directory of Newspapers and Periodicals (1951, 1966); Editor and Publisher Yearbook (1966); Media Records Blue Book (1950, 1965); Journalism Quarterly, 33 (Winter, 1956), 34 (Winter, 1957); Files of the Texas Press Association; Files of the Texas Daily Newspaper Association; Joe Belden, Texas-Louisiana Markets & Media (1956–1961).

Ernest A. Sharpe

*Newton, James Oscar.

Newton, Lewis William. Lewis William Newton was born in Smithfield, Texas, on May 2, 1881, the son of John Milton and Elizabeth (Autry) Newton. He attended Polytechnic College in Fort Worth from 1898 to 1901 and then the University of Texas, where he received the B.A. degree (1904) and M.A. degree (1907). He married Jodie Short on June 14, 1903; they had three children. Newton taught school in Bonham, San Antonio, and Fort Worth (where he was superintendent of schools) before joining the history department at North Texas State Normal College (now North Texas State University) at Denton in 1919. Newton served as director of the Department of History at North Texas from 1925 until his retirement in 1951. He was awarded a Ph.D. by the University of Chicago in 1929. He wrote A Social and Political History of Texas (1932), Texas, Yesterday and Today (1949), and numerous workbooks used in teaching history and geography in Texas public schools. Newton died on September 16, 1965, and was buried in Roselawn Cemetery in Denton.

BIBLIOGRAPHY: Texian Who's Who (1937); Dallas Morning News, September 18, 1965.

*Newton, Texas. Newton, seat, chief market, and commercial center of Newton County, had approximately fifty businesses in 1970. Newton's 1960 population was 1,233; the United States 1970 census showed a count of 1,529.

An area running north and south between Jasper and Newton contained probably the largest stand of Magnolia pyramidata (pyramid magnolia) to be found in the United States. The national champion pyramid magnolia was located nine miles west of Newton, behind the Newton Wildlife Kingdom office. The national champion Quercus incana (bluejack oak), of a tree family of shrubs or small trees, was also located in Newton. Towering sixty-five feet, it was growing alongside State Highway 87, about half a mile northeast of downtown Newton.

BIBLIOGRAPHY: John A. Haislet (ed.), Famous Trees of Texas (1970).

*Newton County. Newton County, 93 percent forested in 1968, had lumbering as its chief industry. The oil industry was second in importance; 28,187,262 barrels of oil were produced between 1937 and January 1, 1973. The raising of poultry and livestock were chief agricultural enterprises. Toledo Bend Reservoir, on the Sabine River at the Louisiana border, was a major tourist attraction. The national champion water tupelo tree, almost 100 feet tall, was located thirteen miles northeast of Bon Wier. The 1960 population of 10,372 increased to 11,657 by 1970, according to the United States census.

BIBLIOGRAPHY: John A. Haislet (ed.), Famous Trees of Texas (1970).

*Newton Creek.

*Newtown, Texas.

*Ney, Elisabet. Elisabet Ney's portrait was painted by Friedrich Kaulbach (not Karlbash, as stated in Volume II). In 1971 only two of Miss Ney's ideal pieces (non-portrait sculpture) were not located in Texas. "Sursum," a marble piece showing two figures representing strength and weakness, has been in a private collection in La Salle, Illinois, since the 1890's, and "Lady Macbeth" has been at the Smithsonian Institution since 1920. Schwabing, where Miss Ney's studio was located near Munich, Germany, is still a center for artists' studios and apartments in what is now metropolitan Munich. The Austrian housekeeper, Cencie Simath, who looked after the welfare of both Miss Ney and Dr. Edmund Duncan Montgomery,qv came with the couple to the United States in 1870. Miss Ney tried for years to have an art department created at the University of Texas and wanted to have a free academy of fine arts on the grounds of her studio, Formosa, in Austin; however, her efforts came to naught during her lifetime. See also Elisabet Ney Museum.

BIBLIOGRAPHY: Frances Battaile Fisk, A History of Texas Artists and Sculptors (1928).

Ney Museum. See Elisabet Ney Museum.

*Neyland, Texas.

*Neylandville, Texas.

Niblett's Bluff. Niblett's Bluff is located in Calcasieu Parish, Louisiana, on the old east channel of the Sabine River about ten miles northeast of

Orange. According to the 1840 official survey by a joint commission representing the United States and the Republic of Texas, the bluff was then known as Millspaw's (Millspaugh's), and the settlement was called Jericho. Except for the map and survey, no other record of either name has been located. By 1860 both the site and the settlement were called Niblett's Bluff. This site was one of the early crossings from Opelousas and the Atakapa country in southern Louisiana into Texas.

During the Civil War, especially in 1863 and 1864 when the Federals were probing for a point through which to invade Texas, Niblett's Bluff was a gathering place for recruits and supplies for the Confederacy's Trans-Mississippi Department. There was also a military hospital there. In 1958 the Louisiana and Texas divisions of the United Daughters of the Confederacy ᵠᵛ erected a gray granite marker at the cemetery site as a memorial to more than thirty men buried there.

In the riverboat and lumbering eras of post-Reconstruction ᵠᵛ time Niblett's Bluff enjoyed a period of growth and prosperity. A post office was established in 1873 but was discontinued in 1884. From 1877 to the 1930's the Lutcher-Moore Lumber Company of Orange used the bluff area as a log yard for its Orange sawmill and as a railroad terminal. Logs were delivered from forests in Louisiana and rafted downstream. On January 7, 1966, Lutcher-Moore Lumber Company conveyed a tract of thirty-one acres to Louisiana for future development as a historical state park. All that remains of Niblett's Bluff is a widely scattered rural community, a church and cemetery, and a few vacation homes.

BIBLIOGRAPHY: Cooper K. Ragan, "The Diary of Captain George W. O'Brien, 1863," *Southwestern Historical Quarterly*, LXVII (1963–1964); Frank E. Vandiver and Eugene C. Barker, "Letters from the Confederate Medical Service in Texas, 1863–1865," *Southwestern Historical Quarterly*, LV (1951–1952); "Niblett's Bluff Prepared For Battle That Never Came," Lake Charles *American Press*, August 15, 1965; "Map of the River Sabine from Its Mouth on the Gulf of Mexico in the Sea to Logan's Ferry" (A. G. Gray map, 1840, General Land Office, Austin, Texas).

Madeleine Martin

Nicaragua, Texas. Nicaragua, a ghost town of Karnes County, was situated at the intersection of the road leading east from Wofford Crossing and the San Antonio-Goliad Road, about two miles south of Helena. Its name may have been connected with the proslavery filibustering and short-lived dictatorship of William Walker in Nicaragua in 1855–1857. Nicaragua was a place name on the maps of Karnes County from 1859 to 1867.

Robert H. Thonhoff

*Nicholas, Texas.

*Nichols, Ebenezar B. The E. B. Nichols firm, in Galveston, represented the Peirce (not Pierce, as stated in Volume II) and Bacon Line. *See* Peirce, Thomas Wentworth.

Nichols, Texas. (Karnes County.) Nichols was a switch built in the 1880's halfway between Kenedy Junction and Pettus by the San Antonio and Aransas Pass Railway. The town of Green developed at the site of Nichols Switch in 1907. *See also* Green, Texas.

Robert H. Thonhoff

*Nichols, Texas. (Kendall County.)

*Nichols Creek.

*Nicholson, James.

*Nicholson Creek.

*Nickelville, Texas.

*Nickle, Texas.

*Nickleberry, Texas.

*Nidever, Charles Isaac.

*Niederwald, Texas.

Nigco Indians. This name apparently occurs only in the baptismal records (1730) of San Antonio de Valero Mission ᵠᵛ in San Antonio. Although J. R. Swanton listed Nigco as a separate Coahuiltecan band, it seems likely that Nigco is a variant of some other group name, possibly Manico, who lived west and southwest of San Antonio in the late seventeenth century.

BIBLIOGRAPHY: F. W. Hodge (ed.), *Handbook of American Indians*, II (1910); J. R. Swanton, *Linguistic Material from the Tribes of Southern Texas and Northeastern Mexico* (1940).

T. N. Campbell

*Nigger Branch.

*Nigger Creek.

*Nigger Head Hill.

*Nigton, Texas.

*Nile, Texas.

*Niles City, Texas.

*Nimitz, Charles H. Charles H. Nimitz was the son of Charles Henry (sometimes found as Karl Heinrich) Nimitz and Dorothea Magdelena (Dressel) Nimitz (not Meta Merriotte Nimitz, as stated in Volume II). [The confusion results from the fact that Charles H. Nimitz's father was married a second time, in November, 1847, to Meta Merriotte (or Meyerotto or Meierrotte, according to different accounts).]

Charles H. Nimitz was married to Sophie Dorothea Mueller. Nimitz was elected to the Twenty-second Legislature in 1890 (not in 1880).

BIBLIOGRAPHY: Sister Joan of Arc, *My Name Is Nimitz* (1948); Gillespie County Historical Society, *Pioneers in God's Hills* (1960); L. E. Daniell, *Personnel of the Texas State Government* (1892); Alwyn Barr, "Records of the Confederate Military Commission in San Antonio, July 2–October 10, 1862," *Southwestern Historical Quarterly*, LXXI (1967–1968).

Nimitz, Chester William. Chester William Nimitz was born on February 24, 1885, in Fredericksburg, Texas, the son of Chester Bernard (who died before his son was born) and Anna (Henke) Nimitz; his grandfather was Charles H. Nimitz.ᵠᵛ He and his mother lived in Fredericksburg until 1891, when his mother married his father's brother, William Nimitz, and they moved to Kerrville. He attended Tivy High School there before his appointment to the United States Naval Academy in

1901. Nimitz graduated seventh in his class of 114 in 1905, served in the Asiatic Fleet, and was commissioned ensign in 1907. His first ship command was the gunboat *Panay*. Although he received a court-martial early in his career for grounding the destroyer *Decatur* in Manila Bay, he steadily rose in the navy until he attained the rank of fleet admiral on December 19, 1944.

Beginning in 1908 he commanded a succession of submarines, and in 1913 he was assigned to study diesel engines in Germany and Belgium, after which he supervised construction of the first diesel engines for an American ship, the tanker *Maumee*. The European tour was also his honeymoon with his bride, Catherine Vance Freeman, whom he married on April 9, 1913. They had three daughters and one son.

During World War I, Nimitz served as aide and later as chief-of-staff to Admiral Samuel S. Robison, commander of the Submarine Force, United States Atlantic Fleet. In 1918 he was senior member of the Board of Submarine Design. He studied at the Naval War College in 1921–1922. In August, 1926, Nimitz installed one of the first Naval Reserve Officers' Training Corps programs, at the University of California. After various command assignments, including in 1933 his first major ship command, the heavy cruiser *Augusta*, he was promoted to rear admiral on June 23, 1938.

After the Japanese attack on Pearl Harbor in 1941, he was made admiral and became commander-in-chief of the Pacific Fleet and Pacific Ocean areas. Nimitz organized and directed the fleets that destroyed Japanese naval power in World War II. As fleet admiral he signed the instrument of Japanese surrender on the battleship *Missouri* in Tokyo Bay on September 1 (Washington, D.C., time), 1945. From 1945 to 1947 he served as chief of naval operations.

In 1947 Nimitz returned to Berkeley, California, where he was designated special assistant to the secretary of the navy for Pacific Ocean areas. His later years were devoted to various projects on behalf of his country and the United Nations. He received numerous honors from foreign governments and universities as well as from the United States, including the Distinguished Service Medal. He died at his residence on Yerba Buena Island in San Francisco Bay on February 20, 1966, and was buried in the Golden Gate National Cemetery in San Bruno, California.

BIBLIOGRAPHY: Naval Historical Foundation, *Fleet Admirals, U.S. Navy* (1966); E. B. Potter, "Chester William Nimitz, 1885–1966," *United States Naval Institute Proceedings*, XCII (1966); Sister Joan of Arc, *My Name Is Nimitz* (1948).

William R. Braisted

*Nimitz Hotel. The old Nimitz Hotel building in Fredericksburg was not razed (as stated in Volume II), although the ship-like superstructure was removed in the 1920's. The tall stone wall surrounding the back portion of the property is also still standing. Next to the hotel building were an arbor covered with Madeira grapevines, a bath-house, flower gardens, and a vegetable garden that always included parsley and leeks. Up the street from the hotel a historical marker on a Texas German stone house designates the birthplace of Fleet Admiral Chester William Nimitz.qv It was the home of his maternal grandfather, Heinrich Henke, Sr.

Much remodeled in 1926–1927, the Nimitz Hotel closed its doors as a business in the fall of 1963, and in September, 1964, the property bounded by East Main, Washington, and Austin streets was purchased by the Fleet Admiral Chester W. Nimitz Memorial Naval Museum Inc., a non-profit corporation. The museum opened in 1967 on the anniversary of Nimitz's birth, February 24, and by spring numerous exhibits had arrived from the United States Department of the Navy. In March, 1969, Governor Preston Smith signed a bill that officially made Fredericksburg the site of the Nimitz Memorial Museum.qv In 1971 plans were made to restore the hotel to its nineteenth-century appearance; included was the reinforcement of the old stone stables, bathhouse, and the stone walls enclosing the back yard and the old wagon yard behind the hotel. Among the original rooms remaining were the old Casino or ballroom, five drummers' or traveling salesmen's display rooms, and the flagstone-floored kitchen. The reconstruction of the three decks and a captain's bridge that had been part of the old hotel's East Main Street entrance was planned.

BIBLIOGRAPHY: Gillespie County Historical Society, *Pioneers in God's Hills* (1960); Fredericksburg *Standard*, April 28, 1971; *Radio Post* (Fredericksburg, Texas), May 6, 1971.

Nimitz Memorial Museum. Officially called the Admiral Nimitz Center, in honor of Chester William Nimitz,qv the museum was opened in 1967; it was at that time still under construction in the old Nimitz Hotel qv building in Fredericksburg. Open daily, the center features remnants of old Fredericksburg, exhibits which highlight the career of Admiral Nimitz, and relics of the Pacific Theater of Operations in World War II. [For a history of the building itself, *see* Nimitz Hotel.]

Douglass Hubbard

*Nimrod, Texas. (Eastland County.)

*Nimrod, Texas. (Liberty County.)

*Nine, Texas.

*Nine Mile Creek.

*Nine Point Draw.

*Nine Point Mesa.

*Ninemile Draw.

*Ninetieth Division. In 1947 the 90th Division was reactivated as an army reserve unit. Each summer, units of the division engaged in two-week training exercises at Fort Hood,qv Texas; Camp Polk, Louisiana; and Fort Chaffee, Arkansas. The division participated in two reorganizations of the army reserves: in 1959 under the "Pentomic" concept and in 1963 under the "ROAD" program. At the time of the division's deactivation in December, 1965, units were located in forty Texas cities. Thereafter, the reserve personnel and facilities of the old 90th Division became a part of the 90th U. S. Army Reserve Command (ARCOM), with headquarters located at San Antonio.

Dorman H. Winfrey

*Nineveh, Texas.

*Nipple Mountain.

*Nitre Peak. [Since there is no such peak with this name, this title was incorrectly listed in Volume II; see Mitre Peak.]

*Niven, William.

*Nix, Texas.

Nixon, George Antonio. George Antonio Nixon, land commissioner for the Galveston Bay and Texas Land Company,qv which sold land on the empresario grants of David Gouverneur Burnet, Joseph Vehlein, and Lorenzo de Zavala,qqv arrived in Nacogdoches in June, 1834, to issue titles to new settlers who had bought land in those grants. By the end of 1835 he had issued over one thousand titles. Little is known of him before or after that year. Captain Peyton S. Wyatt qv spoke of him as Major George A. Nixon, and he was chairman of the Committee of Vigilance and Safety in Nacogdoches in December, 1835 (see Committees of Safety and Correspondence). Nixon was still there in 1841, when Adolphus Sterne qv mentioned him in his diary.

Presumably he spent the last years of his life in Jasper County, for his will was probated there; however, no county records of his life or death survived the courthouse fire of October 28, 1849. There is a January, 1854, reference to an incomplete original probate which lists the bulk of his estate as having been eleven leagues of land on the Brazos River above Tenoxtitlán.qv

BIBLIOGRAPHY: Claude Elliott, "Alabama and the Texas Revolution," *Southwestern Historical Quarterly,* L (1946–1947); Ralph Smith, The Life of Alexander Horton (M.A. thesis, University of Texas, 1936).

Madeleine Martin

Nixon, Pat Ireland. Pat Ireland Nixon, son of Robert Thomas and Frances Amanda (Andrews) Nixon, was born at Old Nixon, Guadalupe County, Texas, on November 29, 1883. He attended Luling High School and Bingham School in Asheville, North Carolina, then enrolled in the University of Texas, from which he graduated with a B.S. degree in 1905. He entered Johns Hopkins University School of Medicine and received his M.D. degree in 1909.

Nixon opened his medical office in 1911 at San Antonio, where he served for more than fifty years as physician and surgeon. In 1912, with seven other doctors, he founded the organization that grew into the present Bexar County Medical Library. He held membership in the Texas State Historical Association,qv which he served as president from 1946 to 1949. He founded the San Antonio Historical Association qv and served as its president in 1941.

Trinity University in San Antonio awarded him an honorary D.Litt. degree in 1963.

In 1936 his first book, *A Century of Medicine in San Antonio,* was published. This was followed by *The Medical Story of Early Texas, 1528–1853* (1946); *Laurel Heights Methodist Church, 1909–1949* [with C. Stanley Banks] (1949); *A History of the Texas Medical Association, 1853–1953* (1953); *The Early Nixons of Texas* (1956), which received the Summerfield G. Roberts' award; *A Crowning Decade, 1949–1959* [with C. Stanley Banks] (1959); *The Texas Surgical Society* [as coauthor] (1965); and *In Memoriam, Olive Read Nixon* (1965). He contributed numerous articles to historical and professional magazines. For thirty-five years he was an ardent collector of books relating to the history of Texas, and his library of two thousand volumes was given to Trinity University in 1964.

He was married on July 3, 1912, to Olive Gray Read of Mineola, Texas. They had four sons. Nixon died on November 18, 1965, and was buried in Sunset Memorial Park at San Antonio.

George P. Isbell

*Nixon, Texas. The population of Nixon in 1960 was 1,751 and in 1970 was 1,925, according to the United States census. The city had fifty-four businesses in 1970.

*Niza, Marcos de.

*Noack, Texas. Noack, seven miles east of Taylor (not nine miles west, as stated in Volume II), in Williamson County, is widely known as a community center and gathering place for farm families and town dwellers in the area, particularly at the local cafe and bar. The sign above the bar reads, *"In Noack ist das Leben schön"* (In Noack life is wonderful). The famous old carved European bar which came to Noack by way of Fort Worth was destroyed by fire (along with the cafe and bar) in 1970. However, rebuilding of the establishment was begun immediately and was completed within the year. The gin had burned down in 1969. An estimated population of sixty was recorded in 1970.

BIBLIOGRAPHY: Austin *American-Statesman,* August 3, 1969.

*Nobility, Texas.

Noble, Texas. Noble, in the southwest corner of Lamar County, is approximately on the survey line of the Central National Road,qv which, in 1844, was run from central Dallas County, 130 miles to northwest Red River County, through Lamar County. In 1970 Noble had a population of forty.

BIBLIOGRAPHY: J. W. Williams, "The National Road of the Republic of Texas," *Southwestern Historical Quarterly,* XLVII (1943–1944).

*Nobles Creek.

*Nockernut, Texas.

*Nocona, Peta.

*Nocona, Texas. Nocona, in north-central Montague County, is a leather goods manufacturing

center. In 1963 one boot factory had 130 employees, and a subsidiary employed 80 persons in 1964. In 1970 the city had eighty-six business establishments. Construction after 1950 included two new bank buildings and a community center. In 1960 the population was 3,127; the 1970 population, according to the United States census, was 2,871.

*Noelete, Texas.

*Noelke, Texas.

*Nogalus, Texas.

*Nokoni Indians.

*Nolan, Philip. Philip Nolan was the son of Peter and Elizabeth (Cassidy) Nolan. He and his wife, Frances (Lintot) Nolan, had one son.

Nolan, Texas. Nolan, in eastern Nolan County, was established in 1928, a consolidation of two older towns: Old Nolan, founded in 1897 about five miles west of Nolan, and Dora, about five miles east. Each had churches, a school, a gin, stores, and a post office. About 1928 the schools of both were consolidated and the name Nolan given to the site. Many inhabitants of both towns moved to Nolan. A school building was completed in 1930. In 1966 the school served about four hundred students. The area, also known as Divide,qv produces cotton, feeds, sheep, cattle, and hogs. Irrigation was in the experimental stage. There was one business in the town in 1970 and the population was 131.

*Nolan County. Nolan County is a farming and ranching area with a large oil production. In 1953 Lake Sweetwater and Oak Creek Reservoir were completed to increase the water supply. In 1958 a coliseum was completed, and large additions to the county-supported hospital were made. A county-city library and a new high school were in use by 1966. Tourist attractions included Trammell Lake, a January cutting horse contest, a February rattlesnake roundup, a livestock show, and a girls' rodeo. Oil production was over sixty million barrels between 1939 and 1963. By January 1, 1973, total crude oil production had reached 114,956,087 barrels. Cotton, grain sorghums, and small grains are grown, and the county has over four thousand irrigated acres. Other business concerns directly influencing the economy of the county are gypsum processors, cement manufacturers, and meat-packing plants. The 1960 population of 18,963 decreased to 16,220 by 1970, according to the United States census.

Nolan Creek. [This title was incorrectly listed in Volume II as Nolans Creek.] Nolan Creek rises in north and south forks in western Bell County and flows east-southeast about sixteen miles into the Leon River just east of the town of Belton.

*Nolan Expedition.

*Noland's River, Texas.

*Nolans Creek. See Nolan Creek.

*Nolan's River.

*Nolanville, Texas. Influenced by the nearness of Fort Hood qv and Killeen, the population of Nolanville, in Bell County, had risen to 902 by 1970.

*Noleda, Texas.

*Nolte, Texas.

*Nolton Creek.

*Nome, Texas.

*Nona, Texas.

*Nonapho Indians.

*Nondacau Indians.

*Non-Partisan Taxpayers' Convention of 1871. See Taxpayers' Convention of 1871.

*Noodle, Texas.

*Noodle Creek.

*Noonan, George Henry. George Henry Noonan died on August 11, 1907 (not August 17, 1907, as stated in Volume II). [The bibliography under this article in Volume II should read A Twentieth Century History of Southwest Texas, I (1907), not History of Southwest Texas, I (1907).]

BIBLIOGRAPHY: San Antonio Daily Express, August 12, 1907.

Joseph Dixon Matlock

*Noonday, Texas. (Harrison County.)

*Noonday, Texas. (Smith County.)

*Nopal. See Cacti.

*Nopal, Texas. (DeWitt County.)

*Nopal, Texas. (Presidio County.)

*Nopal, Texas. (Willacy County.)

*Norasena Creek.

*Nordheim, Texas.

Nordyke, Lewis Thaddeus. Lewis Thaddeus Nordyke was born on December 25, 1905, in Cottonwood, Texas, Callahan County, the son of Charles T. and Nancy N. (Coffey) Nordyke. He grew up on a farm and later described his boyhood in his last book, Nubbin Ridge. He attended a country school at Turkey Creek, was graduated from John Tarleton College Academy High School in 1927 and attended John Tarleton Junior College. He taught at the college for two years after his graduation and before enrolling in the University of Missouri School of Journalism.

His first newspaper job was with the Stephenville Empire-Tribune in 1933. Nordyke worked for the Associated Press in Amarillo, Dallas, and Houston before returning to Amarillo in 1937 to join the Globe-News staff. Except for one year spent as associate editor of The Country Gentleman (Philadelphia), a national farm magazine, he remained with the Globe-News until 1951. In the late 1940's he was a daily columnist and political editor of the Amarillo newspaper. In 1935 he married Dorothy Beeman of Amarillo, and they had two daughters.

Nordyke was the author of Cattle Empire (1949), Great Roundup (1955), John Wesley

Hardin (1957), *The Truth About Texas* (1957), and *Nubbin Ridge* (1960). He served on the Texas Youth Development Council and the state Prison and Paroles Board. He died in Marfa on July 8, 1960, and was buried in the Llano Cemetery in Amarillo, Texas.

M. H. Loewenstern

*Norfleet, Texas.

*Norfolk, Texas.

*Noriacitas Creek.

*Norias, Texas.

*Normal Schools. *See* State Teachers Colleges.

*Norman, Texas.

*Norman Hill.

Normandy, Texas. (Henderson County.) Normandy was established in the fall of 1845 by Johan Reinert Reiersen,qv of the district of Christiansand, Norway, as the first of three Norwegian settlements in Texas that he founded. He brought his parents and his own family to Normandy, and other colonists followed. When in the summer of 1847 a number of the settlers who had moved onto the adjoining Neches River bottom lands died, many of the others moved to Four Mile Prairie (Van Zandt County) and Prairieville (Kaufman County), also established by Reiersen. After 1848 Normandy seems to have merged into the Brownsboro settlement, which had been established nearby. *See also* Brownsboro, Texas.

BIBLIOGRAPHY: C. A. Clausen (ed.), *The Lady with the Pen, Elise Waerenskjold in Texas* (1961).

*Normandy, Texas. (Maverick County.)

*Normangee, Texas.

*Normanna, Texas.

*Normanville, Texas.

*Normoyle, Texas.

*Norris, James M.

Norris, John Alexander. John Alexander Norris was born on October 14, 1877, at Alleyton, Colorado County, Texas, the son of Samuel Waller and Lucy Lavinia (Davidson) Norris. He attended Baylor University from 1894 to 1897 and returned there in 1920 to obtain a Bachelor of Arts degree. He also attended the College of Engineering at the University of Texas in Austin in 1905 and took additional engineering work at the university during later years.

As one of Texas' pioneer civil engineers Norris was influential in the beginning of water resources development in the state. He was appointed to the Texas State Board of Water Engineers (now the Texas Water Rights Commission qv) in 1918 and served with that agency until 1936. He was chairman of the board during the last sixteen years of his service. In 1929 Norris was one of those responsible for the creation of the Brazos River Conservation and Reclamation District qv (now the Brazos River Authority qv), which was the first such state agency created in the United States for the control and development of the waters of an en-

tire river basin. He was also instrumental in the creation of the Lower Colorado River Authority qv in 1934 and other similar water conservation and development agencies.

Norris became chief engineer and general manager of the Brazos River Conservation and Reclamation District in 1936 and was responsible for the construction of Morris Sheppard Dam and Possum Kingdom Lake,qqv the first dam and reservoir on the Brazos River. During later years he was in private engineering practice until his retirement.

He was a member of the American Society of Civil Engineers, serving as president of the Texas section from 1924 to 1925. He also belonged to the National Society of Professional Engineers. Norris worked for passage of the Texas Engineering Registration Act in 1937.

Norris married Jessica Bullock on October 31, 1907, in Wharton County, Texas; they had five children. He died on March 14, 1963, in Austin, Texas.

Seth D. Breeding

Norris, John Franklyn. John Franklyn (J. Frank) Norris, son of James Warner and Mary (Davis) Norris, was born on September 18, 1877, in Dadeville, Alabama. He came to Texas with his family in 1888 and settled in Hubbard. Norris married Lillian Gaddy on May 5, 1902; they had four children.

Norris was called to the Baptist ministry in 1899 by a Mount Calm, Texas, congregation which he served until he received an A.B. degree from Baylor University in 1903. After earning an A.M. degree from Southern Baptist Theological Seminary, Louisville, Kentucky, in 1905, he was pastor of McKinney Avenue Baptist Church in Dallas from 1905 to 1908. In 1907 he became business manager of the *Baptist Standard* qv and in 1908 also became its editor; he severed connection with the publication in 1909. As editor of the *Standard* Norris conducted his first crusade, attacking horse racing and gambling; he was instrumental in passage of the 1910 Texas racetrack law. He then directed his crusading zeal to the prohibition movement qv; he also pressed for laws regulating dancing and the length of ladies' skirts and laws against women smoking and wearing bobbed hair.

Norris became pastor of the First Baptist Church of Fort Worth in 1909 and almost immediately engaged in bitter controversy with the city's political leaders. His notoriety increased when his church was destroyed by fire under questionable circumstances. He was accused of arson and then of perjury but was acquitted in both trials.

In 1921 Norris became embroiled in controversy with state Baptist leaders, charging them with "modernist" theological tendencies and with permitting Baylor University to teach evolution. Leaders of the General Baptist Convention of Texas suspected Norris of a power play and objected to his disruptive tactics; the convention censored him in 1922 and expelled him and his Fort Worth church in 1924. Continuing to oppose the convention leadership, Norris held revivals at convention meetings and helped to organize in 1927 the rival Fundamental Baptist churches with headquarters in Chicago. Norris concentrated his campaign for strict fundamentalist orthodoxy in the World's Christian Fundamental Association, which he had helped to organize in 1919. When the association convened in Fort Worth in 1923, Norris staged a "trial" of several Texas colleges, particularly Southern Methodist University and Baylor University, charging them with teaching heretical doctrines, especially evolution. Norris claimed responsibility for the dismissal of several college professors. He fought most of his life against what he considered was an attack by science upon the inerrancy of the Bible.

In the mid-1920's Norris again attacked Fort Worth and Tarrant County politicians for being influenced by bootleggers and Catholics. In 1926 he was indicted for the murder of D. E. Chipps, a friend of Fort Worth mayor H. C. Meacham. Although Norris shot the unarmed Chipps three times during an argument in the minister's study, he won another acquittal with his plea of self-defense.

Norris's constant crusading won him wide support. By 1925 his Fort Worth church had become the largest Baptist church in the world, with a congregation of 8,000, Sunday school of 7,500, choir of 600, and forty-piece orchestra. He compounded his influence through his own radio station and newspaper, the *Searchlight* (begun in 1921 and changed to the *Fundamentalist* in 1927). The height of his popularity was reached perhaps during the 1928 presidential campaign; some political analysts are inclined to agree with Norris's claim that his assault on Al Smith helped to carry Texas for Herbert Hoover. Then in 1929 while he was in Austin, the First Baptist Church of Fort Worth was again destroyed by a fire of mysterious origin. Because of the depression during the 1930's, his church recovered slowly from the loss. While his congregation supported one of the nation's largest private relief efforts, he ardently supported the New Deal program. After 1935 Norris was simultaneously pastor of the Fort Worth church and the Temple Baptist Church in Detroit, Michigan, and he boasted a combined congregation of twenty-five thousand.

During his ministry Norris conducted revival meetings in forty-six states and made several crusading trips around the world. In 1947 he was granted an audience with Pope Pius XII, although he was an outspoken critic of Roman Catholicism. In the 1940's Norris crusaded against communists, who he believed had heavily infiltrated the churches, universities, and federal and state governments. The highlight of this campaign came when the Texas House of Representatives invited Norris to address it on April 20, 1949.

In May, 1951, Norris resigned his pastorship of the Detroit church and in November of that year resigned from the Fort Worth church because of poor health. He died on August 20, 1952, while attending the Fundamental Baptist Youth Camp at Keystone Heights, Florida.

BIBLIOGRAPHY: Kenneth K. Bailey, *Southern White Protestantism in the Twentieth Century* (1964); E. Ray Tatum, *Conquest or Failure? A Biography of J. Frank Norris* (1966); C. Allyn Russell, "J. Frank Norris: Violent Fundamentalist," *Southwestern Historical Quarterly,* LXXV (1971–1972); *Who's Who In America* (1950); Fort Worth *Press,* August 20, 1952; Fort Worth *Star-Telegram and Sunday Record,* July 18, 1926.

*Norris, Samuel.

*Norse, Texas. Norse, in southwestern Bosque County, at one time had a post office and several stores and was the focal point of Norwegian community life in the area. The village had disappeared by the 1970's except for Our Savior's Lutheran Church and adjoining cemetery. The church, located about a mile from the old Norse site, remains a community gathering place. Cleng Peerson,qv the father of Norwegian immigration to Texas, was buried there. A map in *The Norwegian Texans* (1970) locates Norse in relation to the other Norwegian settlements in Bosque County.

Phil Hewitt

North American Theological Seminary. The North American Theological Seminary, Jacksonville, Texas, was established in 1955 by the education committee of the North American Baptist Association as a national seminary. Ground was broken in 1956 on a seventeen-acre campus site given by J. M. Travis and William S. Gober.

An administrative wing, a reading room, and five classrooms were completed for the opening on September 8, 1957. A charter class of fifty-seven students enrolled, and the chapel was dedicated in January, 1958. Later additions to the campus included a bookstore, a student center, a music hall, a library, and student housing projects. The library contained 7,880 volumes in 1969.

The seminary provided specialized training for Baptist pastors, evangelists, missionaries, ministers of education, and ministers of music. Degrees offered in 1966 were bachelor, master, and doctor of theology; bachelor of divinity; and bachelor, master, and doctor of religious education. Admission to degree programs required some college work, although certification and diploma courses in Christian training and music were open to all, regardless of academic background.

During the 1972–1973 term the seminary had seven faculty members and twenty-seven students. John W. Duggar served as president.

*North Bosque River.

*North Canadian River.

*North Concho River.

*North Creek.

*North Croton Creek.

*North Elm, Texas.

*North Elm Creek.

North Fork Buffalo Creek Reservoir. North Fork Buffalo Creek Reservoir is in the Red River Basin in Wichita County, five miles northwest of

Iowa Park on North Buffalo Creek, a tributary to the Wichita River. This project, owned and operated by the Wichita County Water Control and Improvement District No. 3 as a municipal water supply for Iowa Park, was started on May 14, 1964, and completed on November 10, 1964. The reservoir has a capacity of 15,400 acre-feet with a surface area of 1,500 acres at the service spillway elevation 1,048 feet above mean sea level, and a capacity of 19,000 acre-feet with a surface area of 1,730 acres at emergency spillway crest elevation. The drainage area above the dam is thirty-three square miles.

BIBLIOGRAPHY: Texas Water Commission, *Bulletin 6408* (1964).

Seth D. Breeding

*North Fork of the Red River.

*North Fork of the Wichita River.

*North Franklin Peak.

*North Galveston, Houston, and Kansas City Railroad.

*North Grape Creek.

North Harris County College. The North Harris County Junior College District was created in 1972. W. W. Thorne was named president of North Harris County College in that year, and 1,548 students were admitted for the first time in the fall of 1973. There were 2,874 students enrolled in the fall term of 1974.

*North Hopkins, Texas.

*North Houston, Texas.

North Lake. North Lake is in the Trinity River Basin in Dallas County, two miles southeast of Coppell on the South Fork of Grapevine Creek. The project is owned and operated by the Dallas Power & Light Company for condenser-cooling water for the North Lake Steam-Electric Generating Station. Construction of the dam was begun by the Dallas Power & Light Company in 1956 and was completed in August, 1957. Deliberate impoundment of water began in March, 1957. Actual water use began in 1960 when the first generating unit was placed in operation. The lake has a capacity of 17,000 acre-feet and a surface area of 820 acres at the normal operating elevation of 510 feet above mean sea level. Make-up water to maintain the lake at operating level is pumped through a pipeline from the Elm Fork of the Trinity River. The drainage area above the dam is three square miles.

BIBLIOGRAPHY: Texas Water Commission, *Bulletin 6408* (1964).

Seth D. Breeding

*North Liberty, Texas.

*North Llano River.

*North Mesquite Creek.

*North Palo Pinto Creek.

*North Pease River.

*North Pleasanton, Texas.

*North Prairie Creek.

North Richland Hills, Texas. North Richland Hills, in northeast Tarrant County, is a suburban community located between Fort Worth and Grapevine. The population in 1960 was 8,662; in 1970 it was 16,514. *See also* Fort Worth Standard Metropolitan Statistical Area.

*North Rusk, Texas.

North San Pedro, Texas. North San Pedro, an unincorporated community in Nueces County, had a population of 2,229 in 1970.

*North Side Belt Railway.

*North Sulphur River.

*North Texas Agricultural College. *See* Arlington State College; University of Texas at Arlington.

*North Texas Baptist College.

*North Texas Regional Union List of Serials. The North Texas Regional Union List of Serials was discontinued during the academic year of 1953–1954. The last edition published was the revised edition of 1948.

David A. Webb

*North Texas and Santa Fe Railway Company.

*North Texas State College. *See also* North Texas State University.

North Texas State University. In May, 1961, North Texas State College qv became North Texas State University. The school awarded its first doctoral degrees in education in 1953, in music in 1955, and was authorized in 1964 by the Texas Commission on Higher Education qv to offer doctoral programs in biology, chemistry, physics, and business administration. Situated on a three-hundred-acre campus in southwest Denton, the university was the largest institution of higher learning serving the Dallas-Fort Worth metropolitan area. As such, the university was designated by the commission as the area school to develop doctoral programs in scientific fields (other than engineering and medicine), in the fine arts, humanities, social sciences, and mathematics.

Enrollment during the school's seventy-fifth anniversary in 1964–1965 reached nearly twelve thousand students, and the same year approximately 50 percent of the 450 faculty members held doctorates. In 1974 the regular term enrollment was 15,875, and the faculty numbered about eight hundred.

The library contained 711,224 volumes plus several thousand periodicals and audio-visual materials in 1969. Research projects in physical and biological sciences numbered fifty-seven in 1965 and were financed by $300,000 in grants. Between 1951 and 1965 sixteen buildings costing approximately fifteen million dollars were constructed. By 1971 there were more than fifty buildings on the university campus, valued at over forty million dollars. New structures completed by that time were a library building, a social science building, and a fine arts building. Several buildings were undergoing major renovation, including the chemistry, historical, and auditorium buildings, and a $5.5 million coliseum was under construction in 1971.

John J. Kamerick was president in 1969, and in 1971 John L. Carter, Jr., was acting president, before Calvin Cleave Nolen was named permanent president that same year.

*North Tule Draw.

*North Uvalde, Texas.

*North Valley Prong of the San Saba River.

*North Wichita River.

*North Zulch, Texas.

Northcrest, Texas. Northcrest, in McLennan County, grew from a population of 625 in 1960 to a population of 1,669 by 1970. *See also* Waco Standard Metropolitan Statistical Area.

*Northeast Texas Railroad Company.

**Northern Standard.*

*Northern Trail.

*Northfield, Texas.

*Northington, Texas.

*Northrup, Texas.

*Northrup Creek.

*Northwest Texas Baptist College. *See* Decatur Baptist College.

*Northwest Texas Stock Association. *See* Cattle Raisers' Associations; Texas and Southwestern Cattle Raisers' Association.

*Northwood, Texas.

*Norton, Anthony Banning. [This title was incorrectly listed in Volume II as Norton, Anthony Bannon.] Anthony Banning Norton was the son of Daniel S. and Sarah (Banning) Norton.

Norton, Homer Hill. Homer Hill Norton was born December 30, 1896, in Carrollton, Alabama, son of the Reverend and Mrs. John W. Norton. He grew up and was educated in Birmingham, where his father served as a Methodist minister. Norton excelled in athletics at Birmingham Southern College, lettering in four sports. After graduation in 1916 he entered professional baseball, playing with teams in Alabama, North Carolina, and Florida. On December 2, 1917, Norton married Mabel Telton, and they were the parents of four daughters. He ended his baseball career in 1920, when he took a football coaching position at Centenary College in Shreveport, Louisiana. There he served with Alvin Nugent (Bo) McMillin qv and Earl Davis before taking over as head coach in 1926 and compiling a record of sixty wins, nineteen losses, and nine ties.

In 1934 Norton moved to Texas A&M College (now Texas A&M University) and by 1939 had brought football glory to the Texas Aggies. Norton, with All-Americans Joe Boyd and John Kimbrough, led the Aggies in 1939 to an unbeaten season, a national championship, and victory over Tulane in the Sugar Bowl. Defeat by the University of Texas in 1940 prevented a second unbeaten season and invitation to the Rose Bowl. Trips to the Cotton Bowl qv in 1941 and 1942 and to the Orange Bowl

in 1944 highlighted Norton's later years at A&M. When his tenure ended in 1947, he had served longer than any other Aggieland coach at that time. His overall record there was eighty-two wins, fifty-two losses, nine ties, and three Southwest Conference qv championships.

His coaching career spanned three decades (1920–1947). He developed four All-Americans: guard Joe Eugene Routt,qv 1936 and 1937; tackle Joe Boyd, 1939; back "Jarrin'" John Kimbrough, 1939 and 1940; and guard Marshall Robnet, 1940. Norton was elected to the Helms Athletic Foundation's Hall of Fame, A&M's Athletic Hall of Fame, and the Texas Sports Hall of Fame.qv

After retiring Norton became sports columnist for the Houston *Post* qv and owned and operated several restaurants and a motel. In 1953, after his wife's death, he married Christine Sheppard, and they had one daughter. Norton died on May 26, 1965, and was buried in Forest Park Lawndale Cemetery in Houston.

BIBLIOGRAPHY: Houston *Post*, May 27, 29, 1965.

Billy M. Jones

*Norton, James.

*Norton, Milford Phillips.

Norton, Nimrod Lindsay. Nimrod Lindsay Norton was born near Carlisle, Nicholas County, Kentucky, on April 18, 1830, the son of Hiram and Nancy (Spencer) Norton. He was educated at Fredonia Military Academy in New York and Kentucky Military Institute. On October 27, 1853, he was married to Mary C. Hall in Nicholas County; they had eight children. They moved to Missouri, where he farmed; at the beginning of the Civil War, Norton organized one of the first companies north of the Missouri River for the defense against Federal troops. In May, 1864, he was chosen as one of the Missouri representatives in the Confederate States Congress.

After the war Norton returned to Missouri, but in 1867 he and his family moved to DeWitt County, Texas. They then moved to Salado, in Bell County, where in 1873 he was a charter member of the Grange,qv an agrarian order which powerfully influenced the Constitutional Convention of 1875.qv A section of the Constitution of 1876 qv provided for the designation, survey, and sale of three million, fifty thousand acres of public land in the High Plains qv to pay for the construction of a new state capitol.qv Governor Oran Milo Roberts qv selected Norton as commissioner to supervise the survey of those lands for the state in July, 1879. With surveyors and a ranger escort, Norton made the necessary land surveys that opened the Llano Estacado qv to settlement, making its possibilities known for the first time. In his diary (from August to December, 1879) and in his letters to Governor Roberts, Norton described the country, the daily camp life, and the flora and fauna that the survey party encountered.

In 1880 Norton was appointed a member of the three-man capitol building commission; they considered eleven designs submitted for the capitol, made a survey of various rock quarries in the Austin area, and studied qualities of various building materials. On February 1, 1882, Norton and another capitol building commissioner, Joseph Lee,qv shoveled the first spade of dirt for the beginning of construction. Norton, with his two business partners, W. H. Westfall and G. W. Lacy, ended the capitol limestone-granite controversy by donating all the red granite needed for construction from Granite Mountain qv in Burnet County.

Although Norton had purchased land in the Montopolis (now Austin) area in 1872 and journeyed to Austin to supervise the annual Travis County fairs, he continued to live in Salado. He and his family were living in Austin later, however, and in 1893 he built a large home north of the present Travis County courthouse. Norton died on September 28, 1903, in Austin, and he was buried in Oakwood Cemetery there.

BIBLIOGRAPHY: Anthony Garland Adair and E. H. Perry, Sr., *Austin and Commodore Perry* (1956); Clement A. Evans (ed.), *Confederate Military History*, XI (1899); Frederick W. Rathjen, "The Texas State House," *Southwestern Historical Quarterly*, LX (1956–1957).

Lucie C. Price

*Norton, Texas.

*Norton Creek.

*Norway, Texas.

*Norwegian Lutheran College of Clifton. *See* Clifton Junior College.

*Norwegians in Texas. Most Norwegians who came to Texas were from the rural areas of Norway and became farmers in their new homeland. The first known settler, Johannes Nordboe, was in his seventies when he came to Texas to live with his wife and three sons on a farm a short distance from Dallas in 1841. In 1845 Johan Reinert Reiersen qv had land for his colony surveyed several miles west of the Neches River in Henderson County. The 1850 United States census listed 105 Norwegian-born persons living in Texas. Cleng Peerson,qv who had corresponded with Johannes Nordboe, came to Texas with Ole Canuteson and Carl Engebretson Quæstad.qv The three scouted along the Bosque River, and in 1854, when Bosque County was created, they led the first Norwegian settlers into the area. Among the first settlers were Hendric Dahl and Jens Ringness.qv Ole Ringness,qv the son of Jens Ringness, invented the disc plow. Immigration to Texas, particularly to the settlement of Norse, continued until 1872, and old-world customs were maintained until the early years of the twentieth century.

By 1940, however, the language had all but disappeared, and descendants of the original pioneers had been integrated into the fabric of Texas rural life. Some of the architecture of the Bosque County area showed European influence, and names on mailboxes were still largely Norwegian. An old-world custom which remained in 1970 was the annual smorgasbord held at Our Savior's Lutheran Church, near old Norse in Bosque County.

BIBLIOGRAPHY: William C. Pool, *Bosque Territory* (1964); Institute of Texan Cultures, *The Norwegian Texans* (1970).

Phil Hewitt

*Notla, Texas.

*Nottawa, Texas.

*November 7, 1835, Declaration of. *See* Declaration of November 7, 1835.

*Novice, Texas.

*Novohrad, Texas.

Novrach Indians. In 1683–1684 Juan Domínguez de Mendoza qv led an exploratory expedition from El Paso eastward into the western part of the Edwards Plateau. When he was somewhere in the general vicinity of present Junction, Texas, he listed the names of thirty-seven Indian groups, including the Novrach (later copied as Nobrach and Nohorach), from whom he was expecting to receive delegations. Nothing further is known of the Novrach. Since the thirty-seven groups named in this document include peoples from across the Rio Grande in northern Mexico as well as from farther east in Texas, it is now impossible to identify their aboriginal range.

BIBLIOGRAPHY: Herbert Eugene Bolton (ed.), *Spanish Exploration in the Southwest, 1542–1706* (1916); C. E. Castañeda, *Our Catholic Heritage in Texas, 1519–1936*, II (1936); C. W. Hackett (ed.), *Pichardo's Treatise on the Limits of Louisiana and Texas*, II (1934).

T. N. Campbell

*Noxville, Texas.

*Nubbin Ridge.

*Nubia, Texas.

*Nuckols, Milton B.

*Nueces, Battle of the. *See also* Duff, James; Sansom, John William.

*Nueces Bay.

*Nueces County. Nueces County, a South Texas coastal county, has continued industrialization and agricultural development as well as expansion of port facilities and petroleum processing. Agricultural income in the early 1970's was approximately $22 million annually. The county was first in the state in acreage of grain sorghums harvested in 1969, although cotton production had dropped to twentieth in the state from a twelfth ranking in 1964. Total oil production in the county from 1930 to January 1, 1973, was almost 472 million barrels. Political changes in the county were noted when the first Republican state representative in recent history was elected in 1963. The 1960 population of 221,573 made Nueces County the fifth most populous county in the state; the 1970 census was 237,544, making it the eighth most populous county in the state. *See also* Corpus Christi Standard Metropolitan Statistical Area.

*Nueces River.

*Nueces Valley, Rio Grande, and Mexico Railway Company.

*Nuecestown, Texas. Nuecestown, a small early settlement in Nueces County, had been absorbed within the city limits of Corpus Christi by 1971. The famous Nuecestown raid occurred on the evening of May 13, 1875, at the large frame building containing the home and general store of T. J. Noakes, who also ran the United States post office there. Noakes, his wife, their three small children (one an infant), and one customer, John Smith, all inside the building, were surrounded by a large force of Mexican bandits. The bandits, on horseback with their hostages on foot, had just come from a raid on the outskirts of Corpus Christi. After a series of terrifying confrontations with the bandits, Noakes and his wife and children were able to escape before the raiders burned the building, the children escaping through underground tunnels. Smith was severely wounded. Later all of the twenty or more captives from Corpus Christi were released or escaped from the raiders. An American was killed in pursuit of the bandits.

BIBLIOGRAPHY: Leopold Morris, "The Mexican Raid of 1875 on Corpus Christi," *Quarterly of the Texas State Historical Association*, IV (1900–1901).

Nuestra Señora de la Bahía del Espíritu Santo de Zuñiga Mission. *See* Nuestra Señora del Espíritu Santo de Zuñiga Mission.

Nuestra Señora de la Candelaria Mission. Nuestra Señora de la Candelaria Mission had three locations. The second site (1755) is commemorated with a marker at Aquarena Park in San Marcos. A marker near Sabinal refers to the third site south of Barksdale. With its third and last location the mission is often referred to as Nuestra Señora de la Candelaria del Cañon.qv

BIBLIOGRAPHY: Texas Legislative Council, *Historic Forts and Missions in Texas—Restoration and Preservation*, Report 59–7 (1966).

Nuestra Señora de la Candelaria del Cañon Mission.

Nuestra Señora del Carmen. *See* Corpus Christi de la Isleta.

Nuestra Señora de la Concepción del Socorro.

Nuestra Señora de Dolores.

Nuestra Señora de los Dolores de los Ais Mission.

Nuestra Señora de los Dolores de Benevente, Pueblo of.

Nuestra Señora de los Dolores del Río de San Xavier Mission. *See* San Francisco Xavier de Horcasitas Mission.

Nuestra Señora de los Dolores de los Tejas Presidio.

Nuestra Señora del Espíritu Santo de Zuñiga Mission. A marker in Goliad State Historic Park (*see* Parks, State) near Goliad marks the reconstructed buildings of the mission. The mission should not be confused with the chapel of the nearby Nuestra Señora de Loreto Presidio;qv only the Nuestra Señora del Espíritu Santo de Zuñiga is a true mission. The confusion has resulted because both the mission and the presidio have been called La Bahía;qv in the 18th century this was the

common name for the locations and communities associated with the mission and presidio. The restored presidio is located one-fourth mile north of the mission.

BIBLIOGRAPHY: Kathryn Stoner O'Connor, *Presidio La Bahía del Espíritu Santo de Zuñiga, 1721–1846* (1966); Texas Legislative Council, *Historic Forts and Missions in Texas—Restoration and Preservation*, Report 59–7 (1966).

Nuestra Señora de Guadalupe.

Nuestra Señora de Guadalupe de Albuquerque, Pueblo of.

Nuestra Señora de Guadalupe Mission.

Nuestra Señora de Guadalupe de los Nacogdoches Mission.

Nuestra Señora de Guadalupe de Zacatecas, College of.

Nuestra Señora de Loreto Presidio. The Nuestra Señora de Loreto Presidio, with its accompanying Nuestra Señora del Espíritu Santo de Zuñiga Mission,qv has occupied three different locations. The first presidio site, on the west bank of Garcitas Creek about two miles above its mouth in Victoria County, was partially excavated by the Texas Memorial Museum qv in 1951. Many thousands of Spanish colonial artifacts from Presidio Loreto and some French colonial artifacts from La Salle's Fort St. Louis qv were recovered from the site.

The presidio and mission were moved to the second location in 1726 as a result of repeated harassment by the Indians and their killing of Captain Domingo Ramón.qv A place on the Guadalupe River ten leagues to the northwest was chosen, at what is now known as Mission Valley, Victoria County. Here the fort and mission were reestablished, suitable stone buildings erected, and the formal names of both retained. Successful farms and cattle ranches here enabled the presidio and mission to supply other Texas missions, besides providing for their own Aranama Indians, with ample food.

In the fall of 1749, however, the presidio and mission of La Bahía qv were again moved. Under the plan of José de Escondón qv for realigning the Texas forts further west along the route from Mexico to San Antonio, a site on the San Antonio River near present Goliad was chosen. The presidio was situated on the south bank of the San Antonio River at a location suitable for the defense of a fort. The mission was located a mile or two on the northeast side of the river in plain view of the presidio.

The presidio chapel on the third location has been incorrectly known as La Bahía mission, because it has been confused with Nuestra Señora del Espíritu Santo de Zuñiga Mission, traditionally known as La Bahía mission. The chapel existed only for the presidio soldiers and cannot be accurately called a mission. The mission ruins are now in Goliad State Historic Park (*see* Parks, State).

At the urging of Bishop Mariano Simon Garriga,qv the complete restoration of the presidio and chapel was undertaken in 1963. From 1963 to 1967 the Kathryn O'Connor Foundation, with permission of the Catholic bishop of Corpus Christi and under direction of architect-restorer Raiford Stripling and archaeologist R. E. Beard, restored the presidio to its original appearance. In the excavations to shore up the weakened and leaning walls, evidence was found of nine layers of previous occupation. Thousands of artifacts, such as shards, guns, and many other articles, were found. These are now on display in the museum, located in the restored officers' quarters. The site was returned to Bishop Thomas Drury on August 25, 1966.

On April 9, 1968, Mrs. Lyndon B. Johnson, wife of the president of the United States, unveiled and dedicated the National Historic Landmark plaque that is located at the presidio entrance. The presidio is located one-fourth mile south of the Goliad State Historic Park.

In 1971 plans were made for a Spanish Texas Microfilm Center to be established by the Sons of the Republic of Texas qv and to be housed in the jail portion of the presidio. The center would contain microfilm copies of documents relating to the exploration, settlement, and development of present-day Texas and records of the Roman Catholic church.

BIBLIOGRAPHY: C. E. Castañeda, *Our Catholic Heritage In Texas, 1519–1936* (1936–1958); Kathryn Stoner O'Connor, *Presidio La Bahía del Espíritu Santo de Zúñiga, 1721–1846* (1966); William H. Oberste, *History of Refugio Mission* (1942); Juan Antonio de la Peña (Peter P. Forrestal, trans.), *Peña's Diary of the Aguayo Expedition* (1935); Domingo Ramón (Paul J. Foik, trans.), *Captain Don Domingo Ramón's Diary of His Expedition into Texas in 1716* (1933); Harbert Davenport, "The Men of Goliad," *Southwestern Historical Quarterly,* XLIII (1939–1940).

Kathryn Stoner O'Connor
Curtis Tunnell

*Nuestra Señora de la Luz Mission.

*Nuestra Señora del Pilar de los Adaes Presidio.

*Nuestra Señora del Pilar de Bucareli. *See* Bucareli.

*Nuestra Señora del Pilar de Nacogdoches.

*Nuestra Señora de la Purísima Concepción de Acuña Mission.

*Nuestra Señora de la Purísima Concepción de los Hainai Mission.

*Nuestra Señora del Refugio Mission. The second site of the mission Nuestra Señora del Refugio, in the town of Refugio, is partially covered by a modern church, Our Lady of Refuge. Traces of rock foundations of this second site remain beneath this present church and lawn. There seems to be no information available concerning remains at the first site across the county line in Calhoun County.

BIBLIOGRAPHY: Texas Legislative Council, *Historic Forts and Missions in Texas—Restoration and Preservation*, Report 59–7 (1966).

*Nuestra Señora del Rosario Mission. The site of this mission is located four miles west of the town of Goliad on United States Highway 59, south of the San Antonio River, the land belonging to Goliad County (but not in Goliad State Park, as

stated in Volume II). The state of Texas archeologist considers the remains of this mission, with the foundations of the quadrangle still in evidence, among the best preserved in the state.

BIBLIOGRAPHY: Texas Legislative Council, *Historic Forts and Missions in Texas—Restoration and Preservation*, Report 59–7 (1966).

*Nuestro Padre San Francisco de los Tejas Mission.

Nueva Estremadura. Nueva Estremadura (or Extremadura), another name for Coahuila,qv was known as early as 1602, when three priests from Zacatecas were assigned to a Saltillo convent. They traveled twenty-five leagues inland, reaching a valley abundantly supplied with water. After seeing the pastures and realizing the possibility for the raising of sheep for wool, the priests gave it the name of Nueva Estremadura, for that western portion of Spain which borders Portugal.

The new province was north of the New Kingdom of León, east of Nueva Vizcaya (Chihuahua), west of the Río Bravo (Rio Grande), and south of the Apaches. Through the center of the province ran the Mexican Río de los Conchos. A map in Yoakum's *History of Texas* shows Coquila (Coahuila) or Nueva Estremadura lying below the Medina River and the New Philippines qv (Texas).

BIBLIOGRAPHY: I. J. Cox, "The Southwest Boundary of Texas," *Quarterly of the Texas State Historical Association*, VI (1902–1903); Charles Wilson Hackett (ed.), *Pichardo's Treatise on the Limits of Louisiana and Texas*, I (1931); Henderson Yoakum, *History of Texas* (1855).

Nuevas Filipinas. *See* New Philippines.

Nuevas Philipinas. *See* New Philippines.

*Nuevo Reyno de la Montaña de Santander y Santillana.

Nuez Indians. The Nuez Indians are known from a single Spanish document of 1683 which merely identifies them as "people of the nut." Since no native name is given, they cannot be related to other groups. Their area seems to have been somewhat east of the Pecos in west-central Texas.

BIBLIOGRAPHY: C. W. Hackett (ed.), *Pichardo's Treatise on the Limits of Louisiana and Texas*, I (1931).

T. N. Campbell

*Nugent, Thomas Lewis.

*Nugent, Texas.

*Nugent Mountain.

*Núñez, Alvar, Cabeza de Vaca. *See* Cabeza de Vaca, Alvar Núñez.

*Nunn, David A.

Nuns in Texas, Early Pioneer. The first religious order to come to Texas were the Ursulines, who came from New Orleans to establish the Ursuline Academy qv on January 16, 1847. Other orders followed, coming from all classes of society and trained in particular areas of teaching and nursing, to teach the Gospel, as Franciscan missionaries had done during the Spanish period. After long and arduous travels, they often found empty buildings awaiting them and had to gather furniture, equipment, and supplies for convent, school, or hospital. As with other pioneer women and men they had to endure yellow fever epidemics, hurricanes, Indian raids, and other hardships of the frontier.

Schools operated by orders of nuns added quality and variety to Texas culture. In 1847, for example, Ursuline Academy in Galveston offered courses of study in reading, grammar, composition, rhetoric, poetry, English literature, French literature, sacred and profane history, chronology, mythology, ancient and modern geography, the principles of natural philosophy, arithmetic, chemistry, astronomy, music, drawing, and plain and ornamental needlework. Other schools offered geometry, algebra, ethics, logic, and, somewhat later, various commercial subjects. They attempted to combine practical and cultural fields.

Those who came before 1900 and established headquarters in the state were the Ursuline Nuns (1847), Sisters of the Incarnate Word and Blessed Sacrament (1852), Sisters of Divine Providence (1866), Sisters of Charity of the Incarnate Word (1866), Sisters of St. Mary of Namur (1873), Holy Cross Sisters (1874), Sisters of Mercy (1875), Dominican Sisters (1882), and Sister-Servants of the Holy Ghost and Mary Immaculate (1893).qqv

BIBLIOGRAPHY: Files of the Catholic Archives of Texas (Austin).

Sister M. Claude Lane, O.P.

*Nursery, Texas. (Dallas County.)

*Nursery, Texas. (Victoria County.)

*Nussbaum, Paul Joseph.

*Nussbaumer, Texas.

*Nye, Texas.

O

*O Bar O Ranch.

*O. Henry. *See* Porter, William Sydney.

O. Henry Museum. The O. Henry Museum is the house occupied by William Sidney Porter qv [pseud. O. Henry] from 1893 to 1895. Built in Austin, Texas, in 1888 as a rent house, it was later purchased by Herman Becker who, as an admirer of O. Henry, gave it to the Rotary Club. The Rotarians moved it to a temporary location until a suitable permanent site could be found. On January 23, 1934, the Rotary Club gave the house to the Daughters of the American Revolution,qv the Daughters of 1812, and the Daughters of the Republic of Texas.qv These organizations then gave it to the city of Austin. In March, 1934, the house was moved to its original location in Brush Park and was formally opened to the public on June 2, 1934.

The museum contains a few pieces of furniture once owned by O. Henry and his wife; the remainder of the house was furnished with period pieces donated by interested persons. The desk which once belonged to O. Henry contained a complete set of his works as well as books written about him and scrapbooks containing a variety of newspaper clippings. The property was maintained and operated by the parks and recreation department of the city of Austin.

*O. P. Q. Letters.

*O2 Ranch.

*O X Ranch.

*Oak Branch.

*Oak Creek.

Oak Creek Reservoir. Oak Creek Reservoir is in the Colorado River Basin in Coke County, five miles southeast of Blackwell on Oak Creek. The project is owned and operated by the city of Sweetwater to supply municipal and industrial water to Sweetwater, Blackwell, Bronte, and Robert Lee. Construction began on July 10, 1950, and the project was completed in May, 1952. Deliberate impoundment of water began on May 12, 1953, when runoff was first available, and use of water began in September, 1953. The reservoir has a capacity of 39,360 acre-feet and a surface area of 2,375 acres at the service spillway crest elevation of 2,000 feet above mean sea level. The drainage area above the dam is 244 square miles.

BIBLIOGRAPHY: Texas Water Commission, *Bulletin 6408* (1964).

Seth D. Breeding

*Oak Forest, Texas.

*Oak Grove, Texas. (Bowie County.)

*Oak Grove, Texas. (Denton County.)

*Oak Grove, Texas. (Ellis County.)

*Oak Grove, Texas. (Grayson County.)

*Oak Grove, Texas. (Tarrant County.)

*Oak Grove, Texas. (Wood County.)

*Oak Hill, Texas. (Milam County.)

*Oak Hill, Texas. (Rusk County.)

*Oak Hill, Texas. (Travis County.)

*Oak Hills.

*Oak Island, Texas. (Bexar County.)

Oak Island, Texas. (Chambers County.) Oak Island, named for an island of oak trees near the mouth of Double Bayou, was founded in 1951 by real estate developers Charles Troy and R. L. Hall on the site of a fishing camp. In 1966 it had 147 residents and a seasonal population of five hundred to six hundred tourists. The inhabitants included workers on nearby offshore drilling rigs and persons engaged in fishing, oystering, and boat manufacturing. A municipal water system was installed in 1966. The village was still unincorporated in 1970.

*Oak Ridge, Texas.

Oak Shade, Texas. Oak Shade, in southeastern Polk County in the heart of the Big Thicket,qv was named for a group of shady oak trees. In 1966 the population of about seventy-five was engaged in ranching, oil field work, and lumbering.

*Oakalla, Texas.

*Oakflat, Texas.

*Oakhurst, Texas.

Oaklahoma, Texas. *See* Couch, Texas.

*Oakland, Texas. (Colorado County.)

Oakland, Texas. (Van Zandt County.) Oakland was founded about 1880 in an area of scrub oak trees. The population of the farming and ranching community has remained fairly constant during the life of the community and was approximately twenty-five in 1970.

*Oaks, Texas.

*Oakville, Texas. (Live Oak County.)

*Oakville, Texas. (Milam County.)

*Oakwood, Texas.

*Oasis, Texas. (Cochran County.) *See also* Griffith, Texas.

*Oasis, Texas. (Dallas County.)

*Oatman Creek.

*Oatmeal, Texas.

*Oatmeal Creek.

*Obar Creek.

*Obar Hill.

Oberholser, Harry Church. Harry Church Oberholser, son of Jacob and Lavera S. Oberholser, was born June 25, 1870, in Brooklyn, New York. He attended Columbia University in the late 1880's but did not take a degree from that institution; he returned to school in 1914 and received B.A. and M.S. degrees from George Washington University in that year; in 1916 he received a Ph.D. degree, also from George Washington University. He worked for the United States Bureau of Biological Survey (later the U.S. Fish and Wildlife Service) from 1895 to 1941, first as an ornithologist, later as a biologist, and finally as an editor. In 1941 he moved to Cleveland, Ohio, as curator of ornithology at the Cleveland Museum of Natural History.

Beginning in 1904, in addition to his regular work, Oberholser taught courses in zoology and ornithology at several colleges, delivered many series of lectures on conservation and birds, and made extensive ornithological explorations in the United States and Canada.

In 1900, when Oberholser was sent to the Big Bend area of Texas by the U.S. Bureau of Biological Survey to conduct field investigations on the distribution of birds and mammals, he began collecting material which resulted in the monumental two-volume work published by the University of Texas Press qv in 1974, eleven years after his death. Entitled *The Bird Life of Texas*, the work contains 1,108 pages, including thirty-six watercolors and thirty-six black-and-white drawings of Texas birds

by wildlife artist Louis Agassiz Fuertes, who accompanied Oberholser and Vernon Bailey, a mammalogist, to the Big Bend. The book also contains thirty-eight photographs and numerous distribution maps.

Oberholser died in 1963, leaving approximately 12,000 pages of manuscript encompassing nearly fifty years of findings on taxonomy of North American birds which in any way related to Texas. Edgar B. Kincaid, Jr., a student of Texas bird life, was chosen to edit the work. Kincaid had previously worked with Oberholser in condensing and updating his data; their objective was to reduce the work to publishable length, from three million to one million words. Kincaid retained detailed descriptions of plumages and taxonomic treatment, considered by Oberholser to be his most important scientific contribution; all other sections were condensed.

Publication of the two-volume work was made possible by a gift from Verna Hooks (Mrs. Marrs) McLean, who established a fund at the University of Texas at Austin in honor of her mother, Corrie Herring (Mrs. Joseph Lamar) Hooks. Mrs. Hooks, of Beaumont, had heard Oberholser lecture in her hometown, and she later furnished many of her records for use in his book.

Microfilm copies of Oberholser's original uncut manuscript are in the archives of the University of Texas at Austin and in the library of the Smithsonian Institution in Washington, D.C. Other publications by Oberholser include *Birds of Mt. Kilimanjaro* (1905), *Birds of the Anamba Islands* (1917), and *The Bird Life of Louisiana* (1938). He was a Fellow in the American Ornithologists' Union and in the Ohio and Indiana academies of science. He was a member of many ornithological and natural history societies all over the United States and in many foreign countries, including South Africa, India, Australia, Switzerland, Germany, and Denmark.

Oberholser was married to Mary Forrest Smith on June 30, 1914; he died in Cleveland, Ohio, on December 25, 1963. (*See* Birds, in Volume I, for Oberholser's article on birds in Texas.)

BIBLIOGRAPHY: Harry C. Oberholser [Edgar B. Kincaid, Jr. (ed.), Pat I. Nixon (Foreword), John W. Aldrich (Preface)], *The Bird Life of Texas* (1974); *Who's Who In America* (1948); Austin *American-Statesman*, September 29, 1974.

Oberholtzer, Edison Ellsworth. Edison Ellsworth Oberholtzer was born on May 6, 1880, in Patricksburg, Indiana, son of Augustus and Mary Anne (Collins) Oberholtzer. He was educated at Westfield College in Illinois and Indiana State Normal School. He received an M.A. degree from the University of Chicago in 1915 and a Ph.D. from Columbia University in 1934. Honorary LL.D. degrees were conferred on him by the University of Tulsa in 1921 and by the University of Houston in 1950.

Oberholtzer served an apprenticeship in teaching and administration in small schools in Indiana from 1898 through 1903. From 1906 through 1911 he was supervising principal in Terre Haute and superintendent of schools in both Evansville and Clinton, Indiana. In 1913 he was named superintendent in Tulsa, Oklahoma, a post he held until 1923.

Oberholtzer's contributions to Texas were made in the fields of public schools and university education. He served as superintendent of schools in Houston for over two decades, 1924–1945. During this period he was instrumental in establishing Houston Junior College (1927), and eliciting the support of Hugh Roy Cullen,qv Houston philanthropist, in transforming that junior college into the University of Houston. He served as part-time president of Houston Junior College and the University of Houston, 1927 1945; president of the University of Houston, 1945–1950; and president emeritus until his death in 1954.

Oberholtzer was a member of many state and national professional organizations as well as numerous civic groups. His publications included textbooks for public schools and articles in leading professional journals.

A member of the Methodist church, he married Myrtle May Barr on March 26, 1899; they had three children. Oberholtzer died in Houston on June 18, 1954, and was buried in Forest Park Mausoleum.

BIBLIOGRAPHY: *Who's Who In America* (1951).

James W. Reynolds

*Obi Hill.

*Oblate, Texas.

Oblate College of the Southwest. Oblate College of the Southwest, San Antonio, was founded by the congregation of the Missionary Oblates of Mary Immaculate to prepare students for the Catholic priesthood and was the first formally established permanent seminary in Texas. The school opened in 1903 as San Antonio Philosophical and Theological Seminary. In 1905 a high school department was added, known as St. Anthony's Apostolic School (*see* St. Anthony Seminary).

In 1920 the institutions separated. The apostolic school remained on the original site as a minor seminary or preparatory high school to the college. The major seminary moved to Castroville, where it was known as Sacred Heart Scholasticate. Both schools increased in enrollment.

A larger building was completed in San Antonio for the scholasticate in 1927. It was given the name De Mazenod Scholasticate in honor of Bishop Charles Eugene de Mazenod, founder of the order in 1816. After being returned to San Antonio, the seminary continued operations on a new campus, gradually expanding its facilities. A chapel was dedicated on the campus in 1960. In 1962 the institution's name was officially changed to Oblate College of the Southwest.

The seminary affiliated with the Catholic University of America, Washington, D.C., in 1947, to insure academic growth. In 1950 the state chartered the seminary to grant academic degrees, and a bachelor's degree in theology was offered. Admission was restricted to students preparing for ordination who had completed four years of college.

During the 1972–1973 regular term, the college had an enrollment of fifty-nine students and a faculty of sixteen members. In 1969 its library contained 25,000 volumes. Patrick Guidon was the director in 1972.

Oblate Fathers Trail. The Oblate Fathers Trail, designated by road markers in 1949 by the Brownsville Historical Association, was the route traveled in 1849 and through the 1850's by the Oblate Fathers of Mary Immaculate in their parish and missionary work. Bishop John Mary Odin qv of the Diocese of Galveston had called upon this priestly order to assist him in the organization of the Catholic church in the Rio Grande Valley. The trail began at Our Lady Star of the Sea Church at Port Isabel, proceeding to Brownsville at Immaculate Conception Cathedral and to Villa Maria Chapel, and on up the valley to San Pedro, Encantada, Las Rusias, San Benito, Santa Maria, Mercedes, Hidalgo, McAllen, La Lomita, Mission, Habana, Grulla, Rio Grande City, Roma, Zapata, San Ignacio, and Laredo. The octagonal bronze plaques were placed on the property of each early church.

BIBLIOGRAPHY: Brownsville Historical Association Minutes (1949); *Centenary Souvenir of the Arrival of the Missionary Oblates of Mary Immaculate in the Rio Grande Valley of Texas* (1949); J. T. Canales (Letter listing markers, Archives, Texas Southmost College Library, Brownsville).

Grace Edman

*Obodeus Indians.

*Obori Indians. [This title was incorrectly listed in Volume II as Obozi Indians.] The name of this group is usually rendered as Obozi, but Obozi is the result of an early copyist's error. The Obori are mentioned in a document of 1683 which lists numerous Indian groups known to the Jumano of western Texas. The Jumano claimed that all of these Indians were friends with whom they frequently traded in their extensive travels. It has been generally assumed that the Obori lived somewhere in Texas, but the document of 1683 does not specify where any of the Jumano's friends lived. The Obori cannot be equated with any other group known either before or after 1683. Although Swanton doubtfully listed the Obozi (Obori) as Coahuiltecan in speech, this should not be taken seriously.

BIBLIOGRAPHY: C. W. Hackett (ed.), *Pichardo's Treatise on the Limits of Louisiana and Texas*, I (1931), II (1934); F. W. Hodge (ed.), *Handbook of American Indians*, II (1910); J. R. Swanton, *Linguistic Material from the Tribes of Southern Texas and Northeastern Mexico* (1940).

T. N. Campbell

*Obregon, Texas.

*O'Brien, Texas. O'Brien, in Haskell County, experienced a major loss of life and property in and around the town from a tornado on March 13, 1953. In 1958 the town was incorporated. It reported a school, a library, and two churches in 1966.

Most of O'Brien's businesses in 1967 were connected with cotton ginning, seed and grain, and oil. Significant city improvements completed in the 1960's included a city hall, a fire station, a sewer system, and a school building. Four businesses were reported in 1970. The 1960 census reported a population of 287, a decrease from the estimated 800 in 1940. The 1970 population was 258, according to the United States census.

*Ocana Indians. In the latter part of the seventeenth century the Ocana (Acani, Ocane, Cane, Ocame, Ocano) Indians ranged over a fairly large area in northeastern Coahuila and the adjoining part of Texas south of the Edwards Plateau. In 1674 they were twice encountered with other Indian groups just north of the Rio Grande, and in 1684 Juan Domínguez de Mendoza qv heard of "Acani" when he was in the western part of the Edwards Plateau. Again in 1691 and 1694 the Ocana were encountered with other groups both north and south of the Rio Grande. Later some of the Ocana entered missions in northeastern Coahuila, particularly San Bernardo (see San Juan Bautista) in 1703 and San Francisco Solano qv in 1706. Evidently a few Ocana families at Solano followed this mission when it was moved to present San Antonio in 1718 and became known as San Antonio de Valero Mission.qv One Ocana was baptized at Valero as late as 1728. It seems apparent that the Ocana declined in numbers in the early eighteenth century and lost their identity among the mission Indian populations of Coahuila and Texas. Swanton listed the Ocana as probable Coahuiltecan-speakers.

BIBLIOGRAPHY: H. E. Bolton (ed.), Spanish Exploration in the Southwest, 1542–1706 (1916); L. Gómez Canedo, Primeras exploraciones y poblamiento de Texas, 1686–1694 (1968); C. W. Hackett (ed.), Pichardo's Treatise on the Limits of Louisiana and Texas, II (1934); E. L. Portillo, Apuntes para la historia antigua de Texas y Coahuila (1886); R. G. Santos, "A Preliminary Survey of the San Fernando Archives," Texas Libraries, XXVIII (1966–1967); J. R. Swanton, Linguistic Material from the Tribes of Southern Texas and Northeastern Mexico (1940); R. S. Weddle, San Juan Bautista: Gateway to Spanish Texas (1968).

T. N. Campbell

*Ocean.

*Ocean Shipping. The 370-mile Texas Gulf Coast had become a major seaboard by 1954 when a total of 138,360,878 tons were shipped through twenty-six Texas ports. By 1959 this amount increased to 160,535,334 tons. For the 1954–1963 decade averaged Texas $2,676,000,000 yearly in foreign trade—$2,113,000,000 in exports and $563,000,000 in imports—and led all states in the export of chemical and petroleum products, ranked second in argicultural products, fourth in food products, and eighth in manufactured items.

Port Mansfield, in Willacy County, became Texas' thirteenth deepwater port in 1962. The other deepwater ports were (in order of importance by shipping tonnage in 1971): Houston, Beaumont, Corpus Christi, Port Arthur, Texas City, Freeport, Port Aransas (Harbor Island), Brownsville, Galveston, Orange, Port Isabel, and Sabine

Pass. These thirteen major ports accounted for 183,-801,593 tons of the state's total shipping of 195,995,241 tons in 1971, with Houston alone handling over sixty-eight million tons of cargo. The port of Houston annually ranked second or third in the nation in tonnage among deepwater ports. Among Texas' major shallow-water ports were Port Lavaca, Sweeny, Dickinson Bayou, and Rio Hondo-Harlingen. Traffic along the Gulf Intracoastal Waterway,qv which linked most of Texas' major ports, continued a steady increase during the 1950's, 1960's, and early 1970's; short tons of commerce amounted to 24,700,000 tons in 1954, 34,000,000 in 1960, 55,500,000 in 1967, and an all-time high of 67,617,562 in 1971.

BIBLIOGRAPHY: Texas Almanac (1955–1973).

*Ocee, Texas.

*Ochiltree, Thomas Peck.

*Ochiltree, William Beck.

*Ochiltree, Texas.

*Ochiltree County. Ochiltree County was the leading Texas county in wheat acreage in 1968, with 186,800 acres, and was seventh in wheat production. It also had a large annual grain sorghum crop. About 60 percent ot the county's average annual farm income of $34 million in the early 1970's was from beef cattle and hogs. From 1951, when production began, to January 1, 1973, the county had produced 83,052,896 barrels of oil. A major tourist attraction was Wolf Creek Park. The 1960 population was 9,380; the 1970 United States census reported a population of 9,704.

*Ochoa, Texas.

Ochs, Heinrich. Heinrich Ochs was born on October 19, 1821, in Irmenach, Germany, and was educated in Coblenz. He taught school for ten years before immigrating to America with his grandfather and two brothers. He went first to New Braunfels, then to Fredericksburg, where on New Year's Day, 1852, he relieved Pastor Gottlieb Burchard Dangers qv as teacher, thus beginning a teaching career which was to last forty-five years. His first classes were held in the Vereinskirche in Fredericksburg, where he taught all subjects; later he specialized in Latin, German, and mathematics. He taught in the county courthouse in 1857 and in the school on Market Square in 1869 and 1873. Ochs became an American citizen in 1858 and was county clerk of Gillespie County from 1859 to 1869, with an office in his schoolroom. After the Civil War, in May, 1869, the military government appointed another county clerk. Ochs married Elizabeth Otto of Westphalia, Germany, in Fredericksburg on July 23, 1854, and the couple had six children.

Ochs was a writer, speechmaker, sage, and poet. "Emigration," his introduction to Robert G. Penniger's qv story of Fredericksburg, defended young Germans who came to America to escape poverty and to raise their families in honor and independence. His somewhat didactic poems (there were over three hundred) have several themes: national holidays and personages, German spirit and culture, and Texas German life. Of the latter, "The County Fair," "The Blue Texas Sky," "On the Pedernales," and "Upon Landing in Galveston, October 28, 1851," are of interest. He died on February 6, 1897, and was buried in the Fredericksburg cemetery.

BIBLIOGRAPHY: Don Hampton Biggers, *German Pioneers in Texas* (1925); Robert Penniger (ed.), Charles L. Wisseman, Sr. (trans.), *Fredericksburg, Texas: The First Fifty Years* (1971); Selma Metzenthin-Raunick, *Deutsche Schriften in Texas*, I (c. 1935–1936), *German Verse in Texas* (1932); Gillespie County Historical Society, *Pioneers in God's Hills* (1960); Ella Gold, The History of Education in Gillespie County, Texas (M.A. thesis, University of Texas, 1945).

Esther L. Mueller

*Ocker, Texas.

*O'Connor, Dennis Martin.

*O'Connor, Elizabeth Paschal.

*O'Connor, Thomas.

*Oconór, Hugo.

O'Daniel, Wilbert Lee. Wilbert Lee O'Daniel, Texas governor and United States senator, was better known in Texas as W. Lee (Pappy) O'Daniel. He was born in Malta, Ohio, on March 11, 1890, the son of William Barnes and Alice Ann (Thompson) O'Daniel. His father, a Union veteran, was killed in an accident soon after the birth of Wilbert; before the boy was five years old his mother remarried and went to live on a farm in Reno County, Kansas. O'Daniel was educated in the public schools of Arlington, Kansas, and spent a year in a business college in Hutchinson.

At eighteen O'Daniel became a stenographer and bookkeeper for a flour-milling company in Anthony, Kansas. Later he worked for a larger milling company in Kingman, rose to the post of sales manager, and eventually went into the milling business for himself. On June 30, 1917, in Hutchinson, he married Merle Estella Butcher; they had three children. In 1919 a merger took him to Kansas City, and in 1921 he moved to New Orleans.

In 1925 O'Daniel became sales manager for the Burrus Mill and Elevator Company of Fort Worth and moved to that city. In 1928 he was made general manager, and in 1933–1934 he was president of the Fort Worth Chamber of Commerce. He hired a group of jobless musicians and named them the Light Crust Doughboys;qv they became increasingly popular on radio programs which O'Daniel directed. He wrote the song "Beautiful Texas" and many other songs and poems.

In 1938 O'Daniel, unknown in politics and unable to vote because he had not paid his poll tax, entered the Democratic race for governor against twelve opponents, four of them seasoned politicians. Making full use of another musical group, the Hillbilly Boys, he campaigned on a platform of the Ten Commandments, mother love, abolition of the poll tax, and a promise of a state pension for every oldster. He also used as slogans the Golden Rule and "Less Johnson grass and politicians and more smokestacks and businessmen." In spite of a late start, he won without a runoff.

Although he failed in his efforts to end the poll tax or to increase old-age assistance, he won reelection in 1940. In 1941, in the middle of his second term as governor, he ran for a vacated seat in the United States Senate. Pitting his strength against twenty-five other candidates, including Representative Martin Dies and Representative Lyndon B. Johnson,qqv he won in a special election. In 1942 he was elected to a full six-year term after winning the Democratic nomination over two other former governors without a runoff.

O'Daniel was ineffective in the Senate, and it was reported that no proposal he ever made there received more than four votes. He did not seek another Senate term. After dealing in real estate in Washington for a short time, he moved to Dallas and formed an insurance company, which he headed. In 1956 and again in 1958 he sought the Democratic nomination for governor, but ran a poor third in each race. He died in Dallas on May 11, 1969, and was buried in Hillcrest Memorial Park.

BIBLIOGRAPHY: Seth Shepard McKay, *W. Lee O'Daniel and Texas Politics, 1938–1942* (1944); Dallas *Morning News*, May 12, 1969.

Wayne Gard

*Odds, Texas.

*Odds Creek.

*Odell, Willmot Mitchell.

*Odell, Texas.

*Odell Creek.

*Odem, Texas. Odem, in San Patricio County, had a population of 2,088 in 1960 and 2,130 in 1970, according to the United States census.

*Odessa, Texas. *See also* Odessa Standard Metropolitan Statistical Area.

Odessa College. Odessa College was opened in 1946 in Odessa as Odessa Junior College, a two-year school with an enrollment of 184 students. Classes met in the senior high school building for three years pending completion of a thirty-five-acre campus. In 1949 the college administration separated from the public school system, and the Odessa Junior College District, with a nine-member board of regents, governed in place of the Ector County board of education.

Located on the twenty-four-building campus is the Globe of the Great Southwest, an authentic replica of Shakespeare's theater, used for dramatic productions. A radio station, KOCV-FM, provides training for radio-speech students.

The 1965–1966 catalog listed 436 courses in forty-seven fields under the divisions of arts and sciences, fine arts, education and psychology, business administration, and engineering. Associate degrees in arts, science, and applied science were offered, as was a registered nursing program. The evening school presented terminal, adult, and vocational education courses in addition to academic curricula.

Enrollment increased from 1,565 students in 1949 to 3,708 students during the regular 1974–1975 term. By 1974 the faculty numbered 130 members. Library holdings grew from 600 volumes in 1949 to 35,773 volumes in 1969. The college was fully accredited by major agencies, including the Southern Association of Colleges and Secondary Schools. Murry H. Fly served as the first president of the college, and in 1974 Philip T. Speegle was president.

In 1969 Odessa College, along with the proposed Midland College,qv became a part of the Permian Junior College System,qv but that system was dissolved when citizens of Midland voted to disannex in December, 1972.

Odessa Standard Metropolitan Statistical Area. The Odessa Standard Metropolitan Statistical Area, covering the 907 square miles of Ector County, was designated a standard metropolitan statistical area in September, 1960. The population figure that year for Ector County was 90,995, of which 80,338 lived in the major city, Odessa. The 1970 census counted populations for the county and city of 91,805 and 78,380, respectively.

Area economy was based principally on the discovery, development, and marketing of the rich oil and mineral deposits in the underlying Permian strata. Odessa was an industrialized area built around one of the largest inland petrochemical complexes in the nation (see Petrochemical Industry). Other industries included eight natural gas, two carbon black, and rubber and nylon fiber plants. The city also served as headquarters for numerous oil industry manufacturing and service companies. Much of Odessa's labor force was employed in the oil fields, even though drilling activity in the area had declined.

Despite the semiarid nature of this section of the High Plains, the area's agriculture remained profitable with the aid of irrigation qv and the development of sturdier strains of cotton; livestock raising, an important factor in the economy, benefited after 1959 with the development of commercial feedlots. In the early 1970's the average annual farm income was over $1 million, mostly from beef cattle and poultry.

Effective 1965 buying income of Ector County residents was $209,682,000, with $197,032,000 of the total amount located within the city limits of Odessa. By 1972 the effective buying income for the area was $332,727,000. Wages paid to residents of the area amounted to $195,519,824 in 1972, when there were 26,245 persons employed.

Odessa, seat and largest city of Ector County, is served by Odessa College. The city contained a recreational park system and a museum constructed near the site of a large meteor crater (see Meteor Crater at Odessa). Other communities in the statistical area include Penwell, Notrees, Goldsmith, North Cowden, Judkins, and Scarborough. Eighty-nine percent of area residents were classified as urban in the 1970 census. See also Ector County; Permian Basin; Midland Standard Metropolitan Statistical Area; Standard Metropolitan Statistical Areas in Texas.

BIBLIOGRAPHY: Texas Almanac (1969, 1973).

Richard L. Mahan

*Odin, John Mary.

*Odlum, Benjamin Digby.

Odoesmade Indians. The Odoesmade Indians are known only from documents of 1691, at which time they were encountered by Spaniards just south of the Rio Grande in northeastern Coahuila. They must also have ranged north of the Rio Grande at least as far as the southern edge of the Edwards Plateau. Swanton considered them to be of Coahuiltecan affiliation.

BIBLIOGRAPHY: L. Gómez Canedo, Primeras exploraciones y poblamiento de Texas, 1686–1694 (1968); M. F. Hatcher, "The Expedition of Don Domingo Terán de los Ríos into Texas," Preliminary Studies of the Texas Catholic Historical Society, II (1932); J. R. Swanton, Linguistic Material from the Tribes of Southern Texas and Northeastern Mexico (1940).

T. N. Campbell

*O'Donnell, Texas. O'Donnell, located on the Lynn and Dawson county line, served as a commercial center for the surrounding agricultural region. The town was incorporated in 1960 with a population of 1,356. In 1966 O'Donnell reported five churches, a bank, and a newspaper. A water utilities system was completed in the late 1960's. Sixty-two businesses operated within the city in 1970, when the United States census count was 1,148.

*Oenaville, Texas.

*O'Farrall, Texas.

*Ogburn, Texas.

*Ogden, Duncan Campbell.

*Ogden, Frederick W.

*Ogden, James M.

*Ogden, Wesley.

*Ogden, Texas. (Comal County.)

*Ogden, Texas. (Cottle County.)

*Ogg, Texas.

*Ogles, Texas.

*Oglesby, Texas.

O'Grady, Alice. See Argyle Hotel.

O'Grady, John G. John G. O'Grady was born in Westport, Ireland, and came to Boston in 1848. He had prepared for the priesthood, but in America he studied medicine for a time, then traveled west. It is possible that he was in the United States infantry, for he was at Fort McKavett qv before he opened a mercantile business there; at Fort McKavett he married Katherine (Kate) Cahill of Tipperary, Ireland, in 1856, and they had eight children. When Fort McKavett closed (for the first time) in March, 1859, the couple moved to Boerne, a stage stop on the military road from San Antonio to Fort Concho qv and Ben Ficklin.qv He supplied feed to government teams hauling freight and opened an adobe-built inn for travelers which he called Kendall House, for Kendall County, which

O'Grady helped organize. The inn was located on the south bank of Cibolo Creek and on the east side of the road as it entered Boerne from San Antonio. Today the remaining portion of the inn is known as Stotts House. According to legend Robert E. Lee,qv on his last tour of duty for the United States in early 1860, stopped at Kendall House. Because of Indian raids on the settlements in the Boerne area, O'Grady often took part in the pursuit of marauding bands. During the Civil War he served as postmaster of Boerne and in January and February, 1872, contributed a meteorological register to the Smithsonian Institution. He died sometime in the 1870's, and two of his children, Robert Emmit O'Grady and Alice O'Grady,qqv continued the hospitality of Kendall House at the Argyle Hotel qv in San Antonio.

BIBLIOGRAPHY: Merrill Bishop and Joseph Roemer, *The Gentleman Commander* (1936); Ellis A. Davis and Edwin H. Grobe, *The New Encyclopedia of Texas*, I (1929?); S. W. Geiser, "Men of Science in Texas, 1820–1880," *Field and Laboratory* (October, 1959); "The O'Grady Family in Texas," *The Texas Pioneer* (January–February, 1930).

O'Grady, Robert Emmit. *See* Argyle Hotel.

*Ohio, Texas. (Cameron County.)

*Ohio, Texas. (Hamilton County.) Ohio, about six miles northeast of Evant in south-central Hamilton County, was settled in 1879 by William Thatcher Baker (not J. A. Baker, as stated in Volume II). He built a store and gin on his farm before 1882 (not in 1885) and encouraged settlement. On May 4, 1882 (not 1888) he was appointed postmaster, and he gave the station the name Ohio for the state in which he was born. The post office was moved away several years later.

Mrs. M. Brents Witty

*Oil, Discovery and Production of. Lyne Taliaferro Barret qv (not Lynis T. Barrett, as stated in Volume II) drilled the first producing oil well in Texas in 1866.

During the period from 1956 to 1966 there were no oil booms in Texas like those that characterized earlier decades; however, drilling in known fields and wildcatting continued. In the 1950's and 1960's about 3,000 wildcat wells were drilled annually, with one in five achieving production. A billion-barrel-a-year production level was reached in those decades. Price levels for gasoline and other petroleum products declined some in the 1960's from prices in the 1950's, but price levels were more stable.

Texas production has become relatively smaller in a world of oil that has grown larger: 9 percent in the mid-1960's compared to 22 percent in 1950. However, Texas oil was still a vital force in Texas life and on the national level as well. Oil production accounted for 62 percent (or $3.5 billion) of the total value of all mineral production (or $5.6 billion) in Texas in 1968.

Petroleum operations by 1967 created more than $4 billion a year in income, payrolls of $1.5 billion, and employment for 203,500 persons, approximately one out of every sixteen workers. In 1967, 199 of the 254 counties produced oil or gas in commercial quantities. Texas' reserves were approximately 46.5 percent of the nation's total in 1967. [*See* production table on page 670. Ed.]

James A. Clark

*Oil, Economic Importance of. Texas is the leading state in mineral production and value. The five most valuable minerals in 1966 were petroleum, natural gas, natural gas liquids, cement, and sulphur. Millions of dollars were invested in Texas in the production and refining of oil, and it was estimated that Texas petroleum industry taxes accounted for 21.8 percent of all state taxes, with the industry paying $262 million to the state government in 1967. In addition, oil production on public school and university lands resulted in major contributions to educational funding (*see* School Fund, Permanent; University Fund, Permanent). In 1967 the value of Texas crude oil, natural gas, and gas liquids was $4.9 billion, while the crude oil value alone was $3.4 billion. Over one billion barrels of oil were produced in Texas in 1967 and represented about one-third of all United States production. The approximately 18.6 billion barrels of oil reserves (including 14.5 billion in crude oil and 4.1 billion in natural gas liquids) in Texas were estimated at 46.5 percent of all United States oil reserves in 1967.

Refineries continued to be one of the state's leading manufacturing industries, employing 33,500 persons in 1967. The oil industry affords additional employment to thousands of Texans who operate the state's more than 15,000 service stations, work on drilling rigs, operate producing leases, serve in engineering and geological capacities, furnish legal advice, manufacture oil field equipment, and operate oil field trucking companies. An estimated 203,500 persons were employed by the state's petroleum industry by 1967.

Petroleum products continued to be the chief source of electrical power in Texas. Of the 164 electric power plants on January 1, 1967, 80 were powered by steam, using oil and gas for heat; 61 were powered by internal combustion engines or gas turbines. These 141 power plants, converting energy from oil or its by-products, produced 96.5 percent of the state's electric power.

Oil production was approximately 1 billion, 88 million barrels in 1968; 1 billion, 107 million barrels in 1969; and 1 billion, 208 million barrels in 1970. Meanwhile, proved crude oil reserves in Texas continued a decline that began in 1967; proved reserves of 13 billion, 810 million barrels in 1968 (44.7 percent of the United States reserves) declined to 13 billion, 63 million barrels in 1969. With a sharp decline in oil exploration in the late 1960's, discoveries of new oil reserves diminished; most Texas oil production, therefore, came from already established oil reserves.

James A. Clark

*Oil, Refining of. [The bibliography should read C. A. Warner (not Warren), *Texas Oil and*

TOTAL PRODUCTION OF OIL IN TEXAS*

(1946–1970)

(In thousands of barrels)

Year	East and E. Central	Gulf Coast	North	Panhandle	Southwest	West	West Central	Texas Total
1946	172,195	167,248	45,336	30,470	138,495	180,813	22,083	756,640
1947	173,063	175,555	48,077	31,347	153,932	206,515	28,131	816,620
1948	174,117	182,610	50,453	30,795	165,547	259,454	35,783	898,759
1949	139,547	139,312	48,583	33,034	126,806	210,872	38,472	736,626
1950	143,550	143,873	53,317	33,057	134,017	263,475	46,552	817,841
1951	160,358	171,690	57,283	30,978	163,624	341,845	66,205	991,983
1952	159,926	164,031	63,294	29,018	161,857	341,853	89,812	1,009,791
1953	152,624	161,205	66,983	27,260	161,646	327,500	102,359	999,577
1954	138,009	149,586	68,006	30,910	150,314	308,036	109,574	954,435
1955	140,931	155,212	73,498	33,015	158,021	344,605	117,199	1,022,481
1956	138,542	157,478	77,148	36,155	160,461	386,883	122,220	1,078,887
1957	129,177	151,020	75,522	38,218	148,092	401,779	114,191	1,057,999
1958	102,828	126,521	71,804	38,329	122,003	353,298	95,174	909,957
1959	103,987	126,340	72,683	39,170	123,083	384,140	95,007	944,410
1960	95,968	115,506	70,025	38,096	116,881	367,348	88,260	892,084
1961	99,083	113,854	69,602	37,819	118,883	371,188	84,337	894,766
1962	97,862	115,548	70,170	36,849	121,681	370,589	81,323	894,022
1963	95,557	122,648	70,132	36,504	129,537	380,369	80,673	915,420
1964	94,808	121,607	70,235	36,055	133,810	390,832	81,260	928,607
1965	92,341	118,103	68,384	35,254	135,363	400,308	83,057	932,808
1966	104,320	126,633	68,376	34,009	149,218	427,601	90,169	1,000,326
1967	115,623	140,396	66,910	32,957	166,259	459,458	92,244	1,073,847
1968	122,260	143,176	61,678	31,708	169,355	472,424	87,224	1,087,825
1969	133,068	145,242	56,897	28,637	169,217	491,719	82,365	1,107,146
1970	168,320	161,664	54,101	26,923	173,558	544,050	79,007	1,207,623
Total	3,248,064	3,596,058	1,598,497	836,567	3,651,660	8,986,954	2,012,681	

* Data compiled by staff of the Texas State Historical Association from annual reports of the Railroad Commission of Texas, Oil and Gas Division. The Railroad Commission reports are by districts as follows: East and East Central— Districts 5, 6, 6E; Gulf Coast—District 3; North—District 9; Panhandle—District 10; Southwest—Districts 1, 2, 4; West—Districts 8, 8A; West Central—Districts 7B, 7C.

BIBLIOGRAPHY: Railroad Commission of Texas, *Annual Report* (1946–1970).

Gas Since 1543 (1939) (not 1938). Some later printings of Volume II contain the first part of this correction.]

In 1967 there were forty-eight operating refiners in Texas. In that year they processed 961,000,000 barrels of oil, an amount equal to 86 percent of state crude production. Of Texas refining, 87 percent was done on the Gulf Coast, and more than one out of every four gallons of United States major oil products was made in Texas refineries. The state's refinery capacity was three million barrels of crude oil daily, which was 27.2 percent of the national total.

James A. Clark

*Oil City, Texas.

*Oil Field Machinery and Procedures. Ac-

cording to 1963 U. S. Bureau of the Census figures, there were 183 oil field machinery manufacturers in Texas. They employed 17,578 persons and had payrolls amounting to $110 million annually. Value added by manufacture in 1963 was $243 million and the value of shipments in that year amounted to $394 million.

In recent years the industry and the Railroad Commission qv have begun to protect Texas water supplies from disposal of the salt water that is frequently produced in large quantities with oil drilling. Approximately 90 percent of the salt water was being pumped back into underground formations where it would not harm fresh water and where it would repressure old oil fields to increase recovery. A $10 million pipeline project completed in 1964 hauled more than 500,000 barrels a day of brakish water to stimulate oil production in fields 160 miles from the source. Great emphasis was being placed on secondary recovery projects in which the operators put gas or water back into oil-producing formations to increase recovery. In 1965 it was estimated that 25 percent of Texas production was from fields undergoing such treatment.

James A. Clark

*Oil Fields, Major, to 1940.

Oil Fields, Major, 1940 to 1968. By 1968 there were 8,708 oil fields in Texas, ninety-five of which were classified by the *Oil & Gas Journal* as giant fields which had 100 million barrels or more reserves. In 1967 Texas oil fields produced 1,119,000,-000 barrels of oil, while the giant fields produced 776,000,000 barrels, or 69.3 percent of the state's total. Since 1940 the following giant fields were discovered and are listed in chronological order: Fullerton Fields, Andrews County; Quitman Fields, Wood County; Katy North Field, Harris County; New Hope Field, Franklin County; Russell and North Fields, Gaines County; TXL and North Field, Ector County; Tijerina-Canales-Blucher Field, Jim Wells-Kleberg counties; Midland Farms Fields, Andrews County; Block 31 Field, Crane County; Dollarhide Field, Andrews County; Levelland Field, Cochran County; Borregas Field, Kleberg County; Chocolate Bayou and South Field, Brazoria County; Jameson Field, Coke County; Spraberry Trend Field, Dawson-Glasscock-Midland counties; Shafter Lake Field, Andrews County; Diamond M Field, Scurry County; Kelly-Snyder Field, Scurry County; Cogdell Field, Kent-Scurry counties; Pegasus Field, Upton County; Salt Creek Field, Kent County; Prentice Field, Terry-Yoakum counties; Neches Field, Anderson County; Dora Roberts Field, Midland County; Alazan North Field, Kleberg County; and Fairway Field, Anderson-Henderson counties.

BIBLIOGRAPHY: *Oil & Gas Journal*, February 5, 1968.

James A. Clark

*Oil Industry, Regulation of. In the years from 1940 to 1967 the Texas Railroad Commission qv and the state legislature began to overhaul the regulatory structure of the state concerning the oil and gas industry. Rules were changed to encourage development of publicly owned Texas offshore acreage. The commission in 1963 changed its procedure for setting production allowables from a day basis to a percentage allowable. In 1964 the commission changed the yardstick by which it assigns allowables to new wells so as to reward the more widely spaced wells with higher production rates. A trend toward wider spacing of wells was set in motion so that fields could be developed with fewer wells and less cost. The legislature passed a pooling statute in 1965 which set up provisions that enabled various owners of a field to combine smaller tracts of land into a larger unit where a single well would be drilled; then, all would share in the proceeds.

Control of pollution in connection with oil and gas production became in the 1960's an important new Railroad Commission responsibility. In 1965 the legislature directed the commission to be "solely responsible for the control and disposition of waste and the abatement of pollution of water, both surface and subsurface, resulting from activities associated with the exploration, development, or production of oil or gas." The commission chairman, in order to provide adequate coordination between the Water Quality Board qv and the commission, was named a member of the former organization. *See also* Railroad Commission.

James A. Clark

*Oil Springs, Texas. Oil Springs, Nacogdoches County, was the site of the first producing oil well in Texas, a well drilled by Lyne Taliaferro Barret qv (not L. T. Barrett, as stated in Volume II).

*Oilla, Texas.

*Oilton, Texas.

*Ointemarhen Indians.

*Ojo de Agua.

*Okay, Texas.

*Oklahoma, Texas.

*Oklahoma City and Texas Railroad Company.

*Oklahoma Draw.

Oklahoma Settlement, Texas. *See* Couch, Texas.

*Oklaunion, Texas.

*Okra, Texas.

*Ola, Texas.

*Old Blue Mountain.

*Old Boston, Texas.

Old Carolina, Texas. Old Carolina was a noted watering place on the Trinity River in Walker County in 1867.

BIBLIOGRAPHY: *Texas Almanac* (1936).

*Old Cuero, Texas.

*Old Elizabethtown, Texas.

*Old Evergreen, Texas.

Old Fort Griffin Town, Texas. Old Fort Griffin Town was an army camp town established in the northeast corner of Shackelford County near Fort Griffin qv in 1852. Nothing remains today but a few rock foundations.

BIBLIOGRAPHY: *Texas Almanac* (1936).

*Old Franklin, Texas.

Old Gay Hill, Texas. Old Gay Hill was located about two miles west of the present town of Gay Hill in Washington County, possibly as early as the 1830's. In the 1960's no trace remained of the once flourishing town of churches and shops.

BIBLIOGRAPHY: *Texas Almanac* (1936).

*Old Glory, Texas.

*Old Land Office Building.

Old Military Road. The Old Military Road between Fort Brown qv at Brownsville and Fort Ringgold qv at Rio Grande City was built as a possible supply route for Zachary Taylor qv during the Mexican War. Taylor had set up a supply base at Camargo opposite Rio Grande City for his movement into the interior of Mexico. Although most historians agree that the bulk of supplies and troops were transported upriver by steamboat, the road was used when the river was low and when time was an important factor; the trip up the meandering river took almost two days. Writers disagree as to who actually laid out the road. Credit is given to both George Brinton McClellan qv and Gordon Meade, who were engineers with Taylor. The road went through most of the old towns of the Rio Grande Valley. In the 1960's, most of the old road was paved and was a portion of U.S. Highway 281.

BIBLIOGRAPHY: J. Lee Stambaugh and Lillian J. Stambaugh, *The Lower Rio Grande Valley of Texas* (1954); Virgil N. Lott, The Rio Grande Valley (MS., Archives, University of Texas at Austin).

Dixie L. Jones

*Old Mill.

*Old Ocean, Texas.

*Old Owl (Mopechucope). *See* Buffalo Hump.

Old Preston Road. The Old Preston Road was originally part of a major Indian trail which extended from near present St. Louis, Missouri, to southwestern Texas. Between 1840 and the coming of the railroad three decades later, the road was the principal immigrant route into northern Texas. It was completed in 1843 by soldiers under the command of Colonel William G. Cooke,qv who had been in charge of surveying a route for the Military Road qv for the Republic of Texas.

The road started near the community of Preston Bend in present Grayson County. Emigrants from the north crossed the Red River just below its confluence with the Washita River at a ford known as Rock Bluff Crossing. From there the route generally followed the divide between the East Fork and the Elm Fork of the Trinity River. The southern terminus was at the settlement of Cedar Springs, now a part of downtown Dallas.

Texas cattlemen knew the road as part of the Shawnee Trail.qv By 1870 the main cattle trails were farther west, but the Preston Road was still the most important route for immigrant and freighter traffic in north-central Texas. However, the Missouri, Kansas, and Texas Railroad bridge across the Red River was built in 1872 at Denison, some twelve miles downstream from Preston, and, with the major flow of traffic bypassing it both east and west, the road declined in importance. After little more than a year it had only the same status as other local rural roads.

Within the city limits of Dallas, Texas State Highway 289 is routed along a boulevard called Preston Road. Between Dallas and the intersection with U. S. Highway 82 west of Sherman, the state highway closely parallels a great section of the route of the original Old Preston Road.

BIBLIOGRAPHY: Charles W. Pressler, Map of the State of Texas, 1858, 1867 (Map Files, Archives, University of Texas at Austin Library); Mattie Davis Lucas and Mita Holsapple Hall, *A History of Grayson County, Texas* (1936); J. Lee Stambaugh and Lillian J. Stambaugh, *A History of Collin County, Texas* (1958).

Jean T. Hannaford

*Old River.

*Old Round Rock, Texas. *See also* Round Rock, Texas.

*Old Salem, Texas.

*Old San Antonio Road. The Old San Antonio Road crossed the Rio Grande at Paso de Francia qv (not Pado de Francia, as stated in Volume II). *See also* San Antonio Crossing.

*Old Somerset, Texas.

*Old Spanish Trail. The Old Spanish Trail was a national highway, completed in the 1920's, which ran from St. Augustine, Florida, across the southern United States to San Diego, California. The Texas portion of the road began at the southwestern Louisiana border at Orange, passed through Beaumont, Houston, and San Antonio, and ended at El Paso. The name Old Spanish Trail was chosen by an organization formed in December, 1915, in Mobile, Alabama, to promote the construction of a southern transcontinental highway. The group, which called itself the Old Spanish Trail Association, also publicized the route to tourists, and by August, 1926, had distributed 83,000 maps and travel service booklets. In 1919 the group established headquarters at the Gunter Hotel in San Antonio. By 1929 the highway was completed.

The present highway does not follow the route of the Old San Antonio Road qv (as implied in Volume II), which was sometimes referred to as the Old Spanish Trail and went from Bexar (now San Antonio) east to Nacogdoches and north of what is now known as the Old Spanish Trail. An 1829 map drawn by Stephen F. Austin shows that the Opelousas Road,qv an east-west trail running through southwestern Louisiana and southeastern Texas, had a branch trail going down to Harrisburg (now Houston). The same map shows that a trail existed from what is now Houston to what is now San Antonio, but it was unnamed on that map and did not correspond to what was sometimes called the Old Spanish Trail during the Spanish colonial period.

BIBLIOGRAPHY: *Year Book, The Old Spanish Trail* (1926); James Wadsworth Travers, *From Coast to Coast Via the Old Spanish Trail* (1929); *Old Spanish Trail Travelog* (September, 1927, March, 1928).

Will Fossey

Old Station. Old Station was the familiar name of the temporary settlement that Green DeWitt qv established in 1825 near the Lavaca River, about six miles above its mouth. It was to be a port for receiving immigrants bound for his colony, but it was abandoned in 1827 when all the colonists were ordered to remove to Gonzales.

BIBLIOGRAPHY: Eugene C. Barker (ed.), *Austin Papers,* II (1924); Ethel Zivley Rather, "De Witt's Colony," *Quarterly of the Texas State Historical Association,* VIII (1904–1905).

*Old Stone Fort.

Old Stone Ranch. *See* Givens, Newton Curd.

Old Tascosa, Texas. *See* Tascosa, Texas.

*Old Three Hundred.

*Old Town, Texas.

*Old Union, Texas.

*Old Warren, Texas.

Old West. Old West*, a quarterly, was established in 1964 as a sister publication to *True West* and *Frontier Times*.qqv Owned by Joe Austell Small, it was part of Western Publications, Inc.,qv and was edited and published in Austin, along with several other magazines. *Old West* was devoted to true accounts of the frontier West and specialized in the reprinting of rare works on Western Americana. In 1974 it had an international circulation of almost 130,000. Pat Wagner was editor.

Joe Small

*Olden, Texas.

*Olden Lake.

*Oldenburg, Texas.

*Oldham, Williamson Simpson.

*Oldham County. Oldham County, primarily a ranching area, also produced some wheat and grain sorghums. From the discovery of oil in 1957 to January 1, 1973, over 882,000 barrels of oil have been produced. A county pavilion was built in Vega, the county seat, and Cal Farley's Boys Ranch qv is located in the northeastern part of the county. The 1960 population of 1,928 increased to 2,258 by 1970, according to the United States census.

*Oletha, Texas.

*Oleys Creek.

*Olfin, Texas.

*Olga, Texas. (Bexar County.)

*Olga, Texas. (Nolan County.)

*Olin, Texas.

Oliphint, Alfred Davenport. Alfred Davenport Oliphint (sometimes spelled Oliphant) was born on March 10, 1799, in Kentucky and married Jemina Allen about 1823. They lived in Mississippi and were the parents of several children. After his wife's death in 1835 Oliphint married Martha Ann Causey in Mississippi on October 20, 1836, and they had four children. Oliphint came to Texas probably in 1839; he received a "third class" headright certificate on December 18, 1839, for land provided by the act of January 4, 1839, "to late emigrants," and obtained his headright on the Neches River in Cherokee County on April 1, 1844. It is not known if Oliphint ever lived, even briefly, on his headright. The family probably was living in the Oliphint House qv near Milam, Sabine County, in 1842.

Oliphint attended a mass meeting of over eighty men in Milam on March 31, 1845, to draft resolutions of views on annexation. He was a charter member of the Jackson Masonic Lodge No. 35 at Milam from 1847 until it was terminated in 1857 and was treasurer from 1849 to 1857. In 1860 he became affiliated with the newly organized Sexton Lodge No. 251. He was elected justice of the peace, Milam precinct, in December, 1845, and was chief justice of Sabine County, 1848–1852.

Although over the age of sixty he was involved in activities of the Confederacy during the Civil War. He was a slave owner, and it is said that slaves were auctioned from a cypress tree stump in front of his home. He died on September 26, 1880, in Sabine County and was buried in the Sneed-Scurlock cemetery in Sabine County. *See also* Oliphint House.

BIBLIOGRAPHY: Robert Austin Gomer (Helen Gomer Schluter, comp.), *Memories of Sabine County* (1966); John Barnette Sanders (ed.), *The 1850 Census, Sabine County, Texas* (1964), *The 1860 Census, Sabine County, Texas* (1965); San Augustine *Red-Lander*, June 13, 1845; Houston *Chronicle*, February 16, 1964; Election Registers, 1842–1846, 1846–1854 (Archives, Texas State Library, Austin); Files of the Texas Historical Commission, Austin; Sabine County Scrapbook (Archives, University of Texas at Austin Library).

Helen Gomer Schluter

Oliphint House. The Oliphint house in Sabine County, east of Milam near Texas State Highway 21 leading to the Sabine River bridge, is one of the few remaining Anglo American houses of the pre-Republic period and probably the oldest still standing. Apparently it was one of two houses built between 1812 and 1815 by James Gaines qv and spared through his influence when Ignacio Pérez qv burned homes and other improvements from Nacogdoches to the Sabine River in 1820. The two-story double-log structure was built on the Camino Real qv some fifty yards off the road. It was identical to the famous old house at Gaines Ferry qv which was occupied by Gaines and his family from 1815 to 1843. Since the site of the old Gaines house qv was inundated by waters of the Toledo Bend Reservoir, the "twin" Oliphint house survives as a replica of the Gaines house.

The Oliphint house is a fine example of early Texas architecture. There is a long gallery or porch across the front and two large square rooms flanking an open dog-trot on each floor. Originally there were four fireplaces. Logs in the walls were carefully hewn, with mortise and tenon joints. At one time slave quarters stood nearby. The property on which the house stands was sold about 1840 to Wilford Oliphint, but the deal seems to have fallen through, and the valid deed, dated February 17, 1843, conveyed the house and land from James Gaines to Martha A. Oliphint (wife of Alfred Davenport Oliphint qv). The Oliphints and their descendants occupied the house until the later years of the nineteenth century. Although there were plans for restoration of the house, no real progress was being made in 1971.

BIBLIOGRAPHY: Houston *Chronicle*, November 14, 1937, February 16, 1964; San Augustine *Red-Lander*, June 13, 1845; Files of the Texas Historical Commission, Austin; Sabine County Scrapbook (Archives, University of Texas at Austin Library); Deed Records, Sabine County, Texas.

Deolece Parmelee

*Olivares, Antonio de San Buenaventura.

*Olive, Texas.

Olive Indians. The Olive Indians, whose native name was Maguage, had somewhat uncertain links with Texas. During the colonial period the Olive lived in southern Tamaulipas, but they seem to have been brought there by a missionary in the sixteenth century. Published sources indicate that this missionary, Father Olmos, found the Olive Indians somewhere to the north in "Florida." Since at that time everything north and northeast of the Rio Grande was regarded by the Spaniards as Florida, it has been assumed that Father Olmos must have encountered the Olive or Maguage somewhere in southern Texas.

BIBLIOGRAPHY: H. E. Bolton, "The Spanish Occupation of Texas, 1519–1690," *Southwestern Historical Quarterly,* XVI (1912–1913); W. Jiménez Moreno, "Tribus e idiomas del Norte de México," *El Norte de México y el Sur de Estados Unidos* (1944); J. A. Mason, "The Native Languages of Middle America," in *The Maya and Their Neighbors* (1940); C. Reyes, *Apuntes para la historia de Tamaulipas en los siglos XVI y XVII* (1944).

T. N. Campbell

*Oliver Creek.

*Olivia, Texas.

*Ollie, Texas.

*Olmito, Texas.

*Olmos, Texas. (Bee County.)

*Olmos, Texas. (Maverick County.)

*Olmos, Texas. (Starr County.)

*Olmos Creek.

Olmos Dam and Reservoir. The Olmos Reservoir project is owned and operated by the city of San Antonio for flood protection of the city's business section. It was justified because of the great damage caused by the flood of September, 1921. Construction was started in 1925 and was completed in 1926. The reservoir has a capacity of 15,500 acre-feet and a surface area of 1,050 acres at the top of the dam at elevation 728 feet above mean sea level. The reservoir basin is maintained empty, and the area is used for parks and playgrounds except when needed for floodwater storage. The drainage area above Olmos Dam is thirty-two square miles.

BIBLIOGRAPHY: Texas Water Commission, *Bulletin 6408* (1964).

Seth D. Breeding

Olmos Park, Texas. Olmos Park, Bexar County, a suburban community encircled by the city of San Antonio, had a population of 2,457 in 1960 and 2,250 in 1970, according to the United States census.

*Olmsted, Frederick Law.

Olmus, Texas. Olmus, in southern Guadalupe County, was a farming and ranching community when a post office was established there on December 9, 1879, with Samuel S. Newton as first postmaster. As of May 1, 1904, money orders could still be obtained at the Olmus post office (located in a home), but the post office was discontinued on January 14, 1905. A one-room schoolhouse and a tavern were located there at one time.

BIBLIOGRAPHY: Post Office Records, Civil Archives Division of the National Archives (General Services Administration, Washington, D.C.).

Olney, Texas. Olney, in northern Young County, has maintained a stable population for the past several decades; the United States census reported 3,872 people in 1960 and 3,624 in 1970. The town continued as a commercial center for nearby farms, ranches, and oil operations; a hospital and a nursing home were located there. An aircraft plant and a boiler works were the principal industries of Olney. The city had 116 businesses in 1970.

Olton, Texas. Olton, in Lamb County, was incorporated in 1930 under general law. A low-cost housing project was completed in 1965. The town reported four schools, thirteen churches, a hospital, a bank, a library, and a newspaper the following year. The community was primarily dependent on agriculture, although it had seventy-eight businesses in 1970. The 1960 population was 1,917; the 1970 population count was 1,782, according to the United States census.

*Omaha, Texas.

*Omega, Texas.

*Omen, Texas.

*Omenaosse Indians.

Omohundro, John Burwell, Jr. John Burwell (Texas Jack) Omohundro, Jr., was born on July 26, 1846, to John B. and Catherine Baker Omohundro, at Palmyra, Virginia, the fourth of twelve children. He received some formal elementary education. In his early teens he left home, made his way alone to Texas, and became a skilled cowboy. Unable to join the Confederate Army in 1861 because of his age, he nevertheless entered Confederate service as a courier and scout. In 1864 he enlisted in General J. E. B. Stuart's command, serving as a runner, scout, and spy.

In 1866 Omohundro resumed his life as a Texas cowboy. He participated in several early cattle drives, including a drive across Arkansas to meat-short Tennessee. Grateful citizens of Tennessee nicknamed him "Texas Jack." He may also have served for a time as a Texas Ranger.qv In 1869 he moved northward and became a scout and buffalo hunter.

Omohundro traveled to Chicago in December, 1872, to co-star with "Buffalo Bill" Cody in *The Scouts of the Prairie,* one of the original Wild West shows. Critics described him as physically impressive and magnetic in personality. During the 1870's, Texas Jack divided his time between the Eastern stage circuit and the hunting ranges of the Great Plains. He guided hunting parties which included European nobility. The Texas Jack legend grew in many "Dime Novels," particularly those written by Colonel Prentiss Ingraham. In 1900 Joel Chandler Harris featured Texas Jack in a series of fictional accounts of the Confederacy for the *Saturday Evening Post.* Thereafter, the legend of Texas Jack faded.

On August 31, 1873, Omohundro married Guiseppina Morlacchi, a dancer-actress from Milan, Italy. Texas Jack died on June 28, 1880, of pneumonia, in Leadville, Colorado, and was buried in Evergreen Cemetery in that town.

BIBLIOGRAPHY: J. C. Dykes, "Dime Novel Texas; or,

the Sub-Literature of the Lone Star State," *Southwestern Historical Quarterly*, XLIX (1945–1946); "Texas Collection," *ibid.*, LXII (1958–1959); Prentiss Ingraham, *Texas Jack, the Mustang King* (1891); Joel Chandler Harris, *On the Wing of Occasions* (1903); Herschel C. Logan, *Buckskin and Satin: The Life of Texas Jack (J. B. Omohundro)* (1954); Windham Thomas Wyndham-Quin (Horace Kephart, ed.), *Hunting in the Yellowstone, by the Earl of Dunraven: On the Trail of the Wapiti with Texas Jack in the Land of Geysers* (1925).

Edgar P. Sneed

*Onalaska, Texas.

*Onapiem.

*Oñate, Juan de.

Onderdonk, Eleanor R. Eleanor R. Onderdonk was a distinguished painter and art curator. The daughter of Emily (Gould) and Robert Jenkins Onderdonk,qv she was born in San Antonio, Texas, on October 25, 1884. Her formal education in art began at the Art Students League in New York and continued under John F. Carlson at Woodstock, New York, and then under other artists such as Frank Du Mond. She was a painter of miniatures and landscapes, receiving in 1929 a prize in the Southern States Art League Exhibition for a miniature, "Portrait of a Lady." Other works were exhibited in the Southern States Art League annual exhibitions and the annual watercolor exhibitions at the Pennsylvania Academy of Fine Arts.

In 1927 Eleanor Onderdonk became curator of art at the Witte Memorial Museum qv in San Antonio, a position she held until her retirement in 1958. As curator she had little time to devote to her own work, but in her position she promoted art in Texas. Her efforts contributed to San Antonio's development as an art center. She died in San Antonio on November 11, 1964. A memorial gallery at the Witte Memorial Museum bears her name.

BIBLIOGRAPHY: Witte Memorial Museum Files, San Antonio, Texas.

Caroline Remy

*Onderdonk, Frank Scovill.

*Onderdonk, Gilbert.

*Onderdonk, Julian.

*Onderdonk, Robert Jenkins.

*One Eye Creek.

*Onion Creek.

*Onion Creek, Texas.

*Onion Culture. Onion production was one of the most important truck crops in Texas during the 1950's. Nineteen counties, concentrated on the Rio Grande plains of South Texas, led the state in onion production and made Texas a leading onion-producing state. The state's 45,000-acre average from 1949 to 1953 represented 36.8 percent of the nation's total onion acreage. Hidalgo County maintained a strong lead in onion production.

In 1958 the Texas onion production was centered in three main areas: South Texas, with 27,000 acres under cultivation; the High Plains, with 5,-600 acres; and north-central Texas, with 4,700 acres. Together these three areas produced a crop valued at $13,879,000 for 1958, a 20 percent increase over the 1949–1957 average.

By the early 1960's seven High Plains counties had been particularly successful in cultivating irrigated onions, and, while onion cultivation declined in north-central Texas, the Trans-Pecos counties of Reeves, Pecos, Presidio, El Paso, and Culberson were establishing significant acreages in onions. At the same time research which had begun in 1933 at Crystal City led to the development of onion hybrids, two of which were used extensively in South Texas. The 1964 agricultural census reported 643 farms with approximately 29,106 acres under onion cultivation. In 1966 onions ranked second in state vegetable values with a total value of $19,168,000 for early spring, late spring, and early summer varieties; by 1972 value of the state's onion crop rose to $24,750,000, placing onions ahead of carrots as the most important cash vegetable crop in Texas.

BIBLIOGRAPHY: *Texas Agricultural Progress* (January–February, 1960); *Texas Business Review* (February, 1958, July, 1959); *Texas Almanac* (1967, 1969).

*Onion Gap.

*Onion Top.

*Opdyke, Texas.

*Opelika, Texas.

*Opelousas Road. *See* La Bahía Road.

*Opera in Texas. *See* Music in Texas.

*Oplin, Texas.

Oposme Indians. The Oposme (Oposime, Oposine, Opoxme) Indians, apparently a Concho band, lived on both sides of the Rio Grande in the vicinity of present Presidio in the late seventeenth and eighteenth centuries. Their main settlement, known as San Francisco de la Junta, was on the south bank of the Rio Grande near the mouth of the Conchos River. In the late eighteenth century the Oposme lost their identity in the Spanish-speaking population of northern Chihuahua

BIBLIOGRAPHY: C. W. Hackett (ed.), *Historical Documents Relating to New Mexico, Nueva Vizcaya, and Approaches Thereto, to 1773*, II (1926); J. C. Kelley, "Factors Involved in the Abandonment of Certain Peripheral Southwestern Settlements," *American Anthropologist*, LIV (1952); J. C. Kelley, "The Historic Indian Pueblos of La Junta de los Ríos," *New Mexico Historical Review*, XXVII (1952), XXVIII (1953); C. Sauer, *The Distribution of Aboriginal Tribes and Languages in Northwestern Mexico* (1934).

T. N. Campbell

*Opossum Creek.

*Opossum Hollow.

Oppenheimer, Daniel. Daniel Oppenheimer, son of Joseph and Yetta Oppenheimer, was born in Burgkunstadt, Bavaria, on November 22, 1836. He came to Texas in 1854 and settled first in Palestine. He moved to Rusk, where he and his brother Anton, in 1858, opened the firm D. & A. Oppenheimer, a general store with a banking department. In 1861 Oppenheimer closed the business and joined the Confederate Army, serving as a first lieutenant in the 10th Texas Cavalry. He was wounded at the battle of Nashville and was hospitalized at Franklin, Tennessee, where he was captured by Federal troops. He returned to Texas after the war, and he and his brother reestablished D. & A. Oppenheimer in San Antonio. The company became one of San Antonio's major retail establishments, and its banking department was important in the development of South Texas in the 1870's and 1880's. The retail division of the firm eventually became the American Hat and Shoe Company, of which Oppenheimer was president. The banking department has continued to the present time under the name D. & A. Oppenheimer, Bankers, and is one of the few remaining private banks in the United States.

In the 1880's Oppenheimer and his brother, in partnership with William Cassin, acquired several thousand acres of land and eventually established a ranch near Carrizo Springs, where they engaged in stock raising.

Oppenheimer married Louisa Goldstein of New York on August 29, 1869; they had seven children. He died in San Antonio on December 7, 1915.

BIBLIOGRAPHY: Jesse D. Oppenheimer, *I Remember* (1965); San Antonio *Express*, May 14, 1913, December 8, 1915; San Antonio *Light*, February 10, 1958; *The Wall Street Journal*, February 5, 1968.

Opportunities Incorporated. *See* Job Corps Program in Texas.

*O'Quinn, Texas.

*Oran, Texas.

Orancho Indians. This name appears on a long list of Indian groups from which Juan Domínguez de Mendoza qv expected to receive delegations in 1684 when he was in the western part of the Edwards Plateau. Sound correspondences in names suggest linkage with Uracha, a band recorded (1764) in baptismal records of San Antonio de Valero Mission qv at present San Antonio. Nothing further is known about the identity of either group. J. R. Swanton listed the Uracha as probably Coahuiltecan in speech, but no evidence has been found that supports this assessment.

BIBLIOGRAPHY: H. E. Bolton (ed.), *Spanish Exploration in the Southwest, 1542–1706* (1916); C. E. Castañeda, *Our Catholic Heritage in Texas*, II (1936); C. W. Hackett (ed.), *Pichardo's Treatise on the Limits of Louisiana and Texas*, II (1934).

T. N. Campbell

*Orange, Texas.** Orange, seat of Orange County, was the location of the largest ethylene plant in the United States. This deepwater port city also had other petrochemical plants, steel works, shipbuilding facilities, rice mills, and seafood- and vegetable-processing plants. Two-thirds of the deepwater port's foreign export was rice. The city had 368 businesses in 1970, including thirty-six manufacturers. The 1960 population was 25,605; the 1970 census showed a population of 24,457. *See also* Huntley, Texas; Beaumont-Port Arthur-Orange Standard Metropolitan Statistical Area.

*Orange County.** Orange County, 64 percent forested, had five active lumber mills in 1968. The area was highly industrialized as a result of the expansion of the petrochemical industry. Over 105 million barrels of oil had been produced in the county from 1913 to January 1, 1973. Rice was the principal source of agricultural income; lumber and small crops were also important to the economy. The population had increased to 60,357 by 1960 and reached 71,170 by 1970, according to the United States census. *See also* Beaumont-Port Arthur-Orange Standard Metropolitan Statistical Area.

*Orange Grove, Texas.** Orange Grove, in Jim Wells County, declined in population from 1,109 in 1960 to 1,075 by 1970, when the town had twenty businesses.

*Orange Hill, Texas.

Orange Naval Station. *See* United States Naval Inactive Ship Maintenance Facility, Orange, Texas.

*Orange and Northwestern Railway Company.** In 1955 the Orange and Northwestern Railway Company operated from Orange to Newton on 61.5 miles of track. It was controlled by the New Orleans, Texas, and Mexican Railway Company, a subsidiary of the Missouri-Pacific which in 1956 was consolidated with the mother company.

James M. Day

*Orangedale, Texas.

*Orangefield, Texas.

*Orangeville, Texas.

Orcampion Indians. This name developed from a printing error in one edition of Henri Joutel's qv journal of the La Salle Expedition.qv No Indian group with the name Orcampion (Orcamipia, Orcampiou) seems to have existed. The names of two separate Indian groups, Orcan and Piou, were combined to give an erroneous hybrid name. *See* Orcan Indians; Piou Indians.

T. N. Campbell

*Orcan Indian Village. *See also* Orcan Indians.

Orcan Indians. The Orcan Indians are known only from documents of the La Salle Expedition,qv which indicate that in the late seventeenth century these people lived inland well to the north of Matagorda Bay, probably near the Brazos River or between the Brazos and Trinity rivers. In some editions of Henri Joutel's qv journal the names of two groups, Orcan and Piou, were erroneously combined to give a hybridized name, Orcampion or Orcampiou, which in later Spanish publications came out as Orcamipia. The linguistic and cultural affiliations of the Orcan and Piou remain undetermined. It has been suggested that the Orcan may have been the same as the Ebahamo, but no evidence can be found to support this interpretation.

BIBLIOGRAPHY: I. J. Cox (ed.), *The Journeys of Réné Robert Cavelier, Sieur de La Salle*, II (1906); F. W. Hodge (ed.), *Handbook of American Indians*, II (1910); H. R. Stiles (ed.), *Joutel's Journal of La Salle's Last Voyage, 1684–7* (1906).

T. N. Campbell

*Orchard, Texas.

*Orcoquisac.

*Orcoquisac Mission. *See* Nuestra Señora de la Luz Mission.

*Orcoquiza Indians.

*Ord, Edward Otho Cresap.

*Ord Range.

Order of San Jacinto. The Order of San Jacinto was probably created in 1842 but no later than January, 1843, by Sam Houston during his second administration as president of the Republic of Texas. The Republic conferred knighthood in the Order of San Jacinto on its diplomatic representatives and on those who distinguished themselves in service to Texas. In 1939 the Sons of the Republic of Texas qv revived the Order of San Jacinto so that the organization could honor distinguished Texans.

BIBLIOGRAPHY: Amelia W. Williams and Eugene C. Barker (eds.), *The Writings of Sam Houston, 1813–1863*, III (1940).

Hobart Huson

*Ore City, Texas.

Oregon City, Texas. *See* Seymour, Texas. (Baylor County.)

*Orejone Indians. In the early eighteenth century these Coahuiltecan Indians lived near the Texas coast between the San Antonio and Nueces rivers. What is now Bee County may have been the approximate center of their territorial range. The Orejone (Orejón, Orejana) was the principal band for which San Juan Capistrano Mission qv was established at San Antonio in 1731, and at this mission they frequently intermarried with the Pamaque, their former neighbors. Some Orejone were also at the nearby Nuestra Señora de la Purísima Concepción de Acuña Mission qv as early as 1733. A few Orejone individuals were taken from San Antonio to the short-lived Nuestra Señora de la Candelaria Mission qv on the San Gabriel River near present Rockdale in Milam County, where they served as interpreters. Since Orejone were reported near the coast as late as 1780, it is evident that not all of them entered the San Antonio missions. The Spanish name Orejón suggests that these people had something distinctive about their ears, perhaps mutilation and enlargement of the lobes for wearing earplugs.

BIBLIOGRAPHY: H. E. Bolton, *Texas in the Middle Eighteenth Century* (1915); F. W. Hodge (ed.), *Handbook of American Indians*, II (1910).

T. N. Campbell

*Organized Labor in Texas. *See* Labor Organizations in Texas.

*Oriana, Texas.

*Orient, Texas.

*Orient Railroad. *See* Kansas City, Mexico, and Orient Railroad.

*Orla, Texas.

*Orlena, Texas. *See* Delaware Bend, Texas.

*Oro Verde, Texas.

*Orobio y Basterra, Prudencio de.

Ororoso Indians. This name, which is Spanish for "horrible," is obviously not the name by which these Indians called themselves. The Ororoso were one of twenty Indian groups that joined Juan Domínguez de Mendoza qv on his expedition from El Paso to the vicinity of present San Angelo in 1683–1684. As Mendoza did not indicate at what point the Ororoso joined his party, it is impossible to determine their range or affiliations. However, the Indians between the Pecos River and the San Angelo area were being hard pressed by Apache at this time, and it seems likely that the Ororoso ranged between these two localities.

BIBLIOGRAPHY: H. E. Bolton (ed.), *Spanish Exploration in the Southwest, 1542–1706* (1916).

T. N. Campbell

*Orozimbo Plantation. Orozimbo, the two-story plantation home of James Aeneas E. Phelps, qv no longer exists, although Orozimbo Oak, a towering live oak tree which supposedly once shaded the house, still stands off County Road 26 in Brazoria County.

BIBLIOGRAPHY: John A. Haislet (ed.), *Famous Trees of Texas* (1970).

*Orrick, James.

*Orrs, Texas.

*Orsay, Henry.

*Ortaquilla Creek.

*Orth, Texas.

*Ortiz, Ramón.

*Orton, Richard David.

*Osage, Texas. (Colorado County.)

*Osage, Texas. (Coryell County.)

Osatayogligla Indians. Osatayogligla (Osatayolida) is the name of one band of Chizo Indians, who are considered by some writers to be a branch of the Concho. In the seventeenth and early eighteenth centuries the Chizo occupied the area now covered by northeastern Chihuahua, northwestern Coahuila, and the lower part of the Big Bend region of Trans-Pecos Texas.

BIBLIOGRAPHY: C. W. Hackett (ed.), *Historical Documents Relating to New Mexico, Nueva Vizcaya, and Approaches Thereto, to 1773*, II (1926); C. Sauer, *The Distribution of Aboriginal Tribes and Languages in Northwestern Mexico* (1934); J. R. Swanton, *The Indian Tribes of North America* (1952).

T. N. Campbell

Osborn, Benjamin. Benjamin Osborn was born in 1783 in South Carolina and married Leah Stark, also of South Carolina; they moved to Tennessee, where their sons, John Lyle (or Loyle) and Thomas Osborn qqv were born. Daughters Mariah, Louisa, and Adeline were also born in Tennessee. Sometime after 1821 the family moved to Marshall County, Mississippi, near Holly Springs and Mt. Pleasant, and thence to Texas. They crossed the Sabine River on Christmas Day, 1825, and settled near Matagorda, where their son, Claiborn Osborn qv was born.

Osborn was one of the forty-nine signers of the four resolutions drawn up by Thomas Marshall

Duke,qv alcalde of the District of Mina, after the Fredonian Rebellion.qv At Duke's behest the Stephen F. Austin colonists met at the Bay Prairie home of surveyor Bartlett Sims,qv January 4, 1827, and unanimously resolved to support the Mexican government. Osborn received a headright of 4,420 acres of land in Austin's Little Colony, in what is now Bastrop and Travis counties, on November 30, 1827.

He and his wife died of yellow fever in 1829. Their headright was divided among their children, and their daughter Louisa was reared by Colonel William G. Hill qv and his wife of Brazoria and Galveston.

BIBLIOGRAPHY: Eugene C. Barker (ed.), *The Austin Papers*, II (1919); Worth Stickley Ray, *Austin Colony Pioneers* (1970); Bastrop County Records.

Verna J. McKenna

Osborn, Claiborn. Claiborn Osborn was born April 6, 1826, near Matagorda, Texas, the son of Leah (Stark) and Benjamin Osborn.qv After his parents' deaths in 1829 his older brother, John Lyle Osborn,qv built a log house on Wilbarger Creek in Bastrop County for his orphaned brothers and sisters on the Osborn headright land. In 1840 the fourteen-year-old Claiborn accompanied his brother John Lyle and others on a buffalo hunt in what is now Williamson County. Near Rice's Crossing on Brushy Creek, Claiborn and a companion were attacked by Indians, and Claiborn was severely wounded, scalped, and left for dead. Rescued, he was taken to the W. F. Wells home, where Mrs. Wells and her mother took soot from the fireplace and mixed it with cobwebs to stop the flow of blood, then applied flax to his scalped head. He was taken to Noah Smithwick's qv home at Webber's Prairie and then to his sister's home at Hamilton Fort.

Osborn recovered and in 1854 married Almira Jane Leverett of Colorado Community; the couple had ten children. They tried living near Llano, but Indian depredations forced them back to the Osborn homestead in Bastrop County. Here he built a small Methodist church, Osborn's Chapel. He and his family were strong supporters of the annual camp-meeting at the old Colorado Chapel, a few miles south of Webberville, on the Colorado River. He died on March 8, 1899, and was buried in the old Manor cemetery in the hills above Webberville.

BIBLIOGRAPHY: John H. Jenkins III (ed.), *Recollections of Early Texas* (1958); Worth Stickley Ray, *Austin Colony Pioneers* (1970); J. W. Wilbarger, *Indian Depredations in Texas* (1889).

Verna J. McKenna

Osborn, John Lyle. John Lyle (or Loyle) Osborn, a veteran of the Texas Revolution, was born in Tennessee on January 31, 1808, the eldest son of Leah (Stark) and Benjamin Osborn.qv In 1832 he built a log house (still standing in 1970) for his orphaned brothers and sisters on the Osborn headright on Wilbarger Creek near Elgin. Located on a road crossing, the Osborn house became a stopping place for travelers on the road from Webberville to Elgin.

According to William Physick Zuber,qv Osborn first belonged to Colonel James Walker Fannin's qv command. He was in the advance guard under Captain Albert Clinton Horton qv when it was cut off from Fannin's ill-fated army, thus escaping the Goliad massacre.qv He joined Captain Moseley Baker's qv company and was detailed with others as a teamster on baggage guard during the battle of San Jacinto.qv He also served as a volunteer in Captain James Smith's qv company of cavalry. His discharge papers were signed at Matagorda by Joseph Washington Eliot Wallace.qv

Slightly crippled from birth, Osborn had married Hannah Hadden, who died within two months of their marriage. He never remarried; he made his home with his brother, Claiborn Osborn,qv and his brother's family in the log house on Wilbarger Creek. He died February 15, 1889, in Bastrop County.

BIBLIOGRAPHY: D. W. C. Baker, *A Texas Scrap-Book* (1935); Pension Papers (Archives, Texas State Library, Austin).

Verna J. McKenna

*****Osborn, Nathan.**

Osborn, Thomas. Thomas Osborn, veteran of the Texas Revolution, was born on October 12, 1812, in Giles County, Tennessee, the second son of Leah (Stark) and Benjamin Osborn.qv He came to Texas with his family in 1825. Osborn's participation in the battles of the Texas Revolution began on June 26, 1832, with the battle of Velasco,qv when he served in Captain Henry Stevenson Brown's qv company of eighty men. In October, 1835, he was one of the three hundred volunteers in the siege of Bexar,qv and on October 28, 1835, he was with a volunteer detachment of ninety men from Captain T. F. L. Parrott's company at the battle of Concepción,qv where he was badly wounded. In the Goliad campaign of 1836 qv Osborn, with his brother John Lyle Osborn,qv was a member of Captain Albert Clinton Horton's qv company in an advance group which was cut off from Colonel James W. Fannin's qv besieged army. He was not in the battle of San Jacinto,qv having been detailed to guard Texas families during the Runaway Scrape.qv He received both bounty and donation warrants for his service in these battles for Texas independence. In 1841 he married Mary Augustine McCulloch, and the couple had ten children. He died on May 16, 1883, in Red Rock, Bastrop County, and was buried there.

BIBLIOGRAPHY: D. W. C. Baker, *A Texas Scrap-Book* (1935); Charles Adams Gulick, Jr. (ed.), *The Papers of Mirabeau Buonaparte Lamar*, I (1921).

Verna J. McKenna

*****Oscar, Texas.**

*****Osceola, Texas.**

*****Oso, Texas.**

*****Oso Creek.**

Oswald, Lee Harvey. Lee Harvey Oswald, alleged assassin of President John F. Kennedy, was born in New Orleans, Louisiana, on October 18, 1939, the third son of Marguerite Claverie Oswald.

His father, Robert Lee Oswald, had died of a heart attack two months earlier. Young Oswald was placed in a Lutheran orphanage at the age of three, but he was removed when his mother left for Dallas in January, 1944, and remarried.

His schooling began in Benbrook, Texas, but he reentered the first grade in Covington, Louisiana, in 1946; he continued his education in Fort Worth in January, 1947, as a result of his mother's separation and divorce. After he and his mother moved to New York in August, 1952, he became a chronic truant and was placed under psychiatric care. They moved again to New Orleans in January, 1954; the next year Oswald left school and tried unsuccessfully to join the Marine Corps in 1955. He found a job and used his spare time to pursue his growing interest in communist literature. He returned to Fort Worth with his mother in July of the following year and in October, 1956, joined the Marine Corps. He served fifteen months overseas, mostly in Japan, and later in California. After an appeal based on the illness of his mother, he was released early from the service in September, 1959.

A month later Oswald left for the Soviet Union, entering through Finland. He tried to commit suicide when ordered out of Russia, but while attempting to renounce his United States citizenship he was permitted to remain and work in a Russian radio factory. On April 30, 1961, he married Marina Nikolaevna Prusakova. A daughter was born in February, 1962, and after prolonged efforts he was allowed to return with his family to the United States in June.

Oswald lived in Fort Worth until October, when he moved to Dallas. He worked there until April, 1963; it was during this month that he allegedly shot at Major General Edwin A. Walker, who had resigned from the army in 1961. In late April, upon his return to New Orleans, he organized a so-called Fair Play for Cuba Committee. He went to Mexico in September in an unsuccessful effort to get a visa to Cuba and the Soviet Union, and he returned in October to Dallas. A second daughter was born at that time.

Oswald was arrested on November 22, 1963, and later charged with the assassination of President John F. Kennedy and the murder of policeman J. D. Tippit.[qv] It was alleged that Oswald positioned himself in a sixth-story window of the Texas School Book Depository building and there fired on the motorcade of President John F. Kennedy and Governor John Connally. It was also claimed that Oswald killed policeman J. D. Tippit shortly after the assassination while resisting arrest. Oswald was finally arrested in a movie theater that same day in the Oak Cliff section of Dallas. Two days later, on November 24, Oswald was shot and killed by Jack Ruby[qv] in the basement of the city jail while being transferred to the county jail. He was buried in Fort Worth. See also Kennedy, John Fitzgerald, Assassination of.

BIBLIOGRAPHY: Report of the Warren Commission on the Assassination of President Kennedy (1964).

*Otey, Texas.

*Oteys Creek.

*Otis Chalk, Texas.

Otomoaco Indians. The Otomoaco (Amotomanco) Indians are known from the late sixteenth century, at which time they lived on the lower Conchos River of northern Chihuahua and also along the Rio Grande between present Presidio and El Paso. The Otomoaco have been convincingly identified as a sedentary branch of the Jumano Indians, for which the name Patarabueye is sometimes used today. One Spanish source seems to relate the Otomoaco with the Tecolote of the eighteenth century.

BIBLIOGRAPHY: H. E. Bolton (ed.), Spanish Exploration in the Southwest, 1542–1706 (1916); G. P. Hammond and A. Rey, Expedition into New Mexico Made by Antonio Espejo, 1582–1583, as Revealed in the Journal of Diego Pérez de Luxán, a Member of the Party (1929); J. C. Kelley, "Factors Involved in the Abandonment of Certain Peripheral Southwestern Settlements," American Anthropologist, LIV (1952); W. W. Newcomb, Jr., The Indians of Texas (1961); C. Sauer, The Distribution of Aboriginal Tribes and Languages in Northwestern Mexico (1934).

T. N. Campbell

*Otter Creek.

*Ottine, Texas.

Ottine Swamp. Ottine Swamp in Palmetto State Park has attracted wide attention because of its unusual ferns, grasses, and plants, as well as species of birds unusual to the area. Thomas Drummond,[qv] the Scottish botanist, collected rare plant specimens in the area between March, 1833, and December, 1834. In 1934 Ottine Swamp was cited by the legislature as an area which needed to be preserved and made available to the public. See Parks, State (Palmetto State Scenic Park).

BIBLIOGRAPHY: Samuel Wood Geiser, Naturalists of the Frontier (1937); Texas State Parks Board, Palmetto State Park, Ottine, Texas (1956); Austin American-Statesman, August 8, 1971.

*Otto, Texas. (Falls County.)

*Otto, Texas. (Hardin County.)

*Ottowa, Texas.

*Our Lady of the Lake College. Our Lady of the Lake College, San Antonio, increased its enrollment between 1950 and 1974 from 431 to 1,999 predominantly women students. Faculty increased from 56 to 140 members between 1950 and 1972. An annex to the Speech Center, two dormitories, a priest-professors' residence, Worden School of Social Service building, and an extensive refurnishing of the library were projects undertaken during this time. Library holdings grew from 51,000 in 1950 to approximately 83,000 bound volumes by 1969. Curriculum changes encompassed the addition of a speech pathology major, the opening of the Graduate School of Education (1950), the offering of graduate courses in history and English (1958), and the beginning of the Division of Graduate Studies, including majors in speech and English (1964). Preprofessional programs in medicine, dietetics, and law were offered as well as one- and two-year secretarial programs. Research development began in the fields of sociology, classical song translations of St. Basil, undergraduate science, and botanical study of cacti of the Southwest. College endowments totaled $677,461 in 1965. Principal support was given by the services of the Sisters of Divine Providence.qv In 1974 Gerald P. Burns served as president. *See also* Roman Catholic Education in Texas.

*Our Lady of Victory College. Our Lady of Victory College, Fort Worth, Texas, was closed in 1958 and was absorbed into the University of Dallas. *See also* Roman Catholic Education in Texas; University of Dallas.

*Oury, William Sanders.

*Ousley, Clarence.

*Ovalo, Texas.

*Overcup Pond.

*Overcup Slough.

*Overland Mail and Mail Routes. *See* Butterfield Overland Mail Route; San Antonio-San Diego Mail Route.

Overton, Marvin Cartmell. Marvin Cartmell Overton was born in Morganfield, Kentucky, on June 13, 1878, the son of George Buck and Sue Jane (Lawson) Overton. Leaving high school after two years, he worked at various jobs, entered the Louisville School of Medicine from which he was graduated in 1902, and then began the practice of medicine in Lubbock. He helped build Lubbock's first hospital in 1908. After 1925 he limited his practice to pediatrics. His book, *Your Baby and Child* (1936), went through four printings.

Overton owned a drugstore, opened two residential additions in Lubbock, cofounded the town of Abernathy with M. G. Abernathy (*see* Abernathy, Mollie D.), and was a bank president, an alderman, and a school board member. A school in Lubbock was named in his honor. Overton's philanthropy included significant contributions to the Methodist Student Center at Texas Technological College (now Texas Tech University) and several scholarship funds at that school as well as at McMurry College. He was married in 1902 to Georgia Robertson, and they had four children. After her death in 1916 he was married to Nannie Jennings in 1918, and they had two children. He died on September 1, 1955, and was buried in Lubbock.

BIBLIOGRAPHY: Seymour V. Connor (ed.), *Builders of the Southwest* (1959).

Ernest Wallace

*Overton, Texas. Overton, in Rusk and Smith counties, is a petroleum center. The town had twelve industries, employing a total of 268 workers, which included petroleum, construction, building supplies, lumbering, gas processing, and manufacturing. In 1970 Overton had sixty businesses and was the site of the East Texas Agricultural and Mechanical Research Center; it had a thirty-eight-bed hospital, eight churches, and a city park with recreational facilities. The 1960 population was 1,950; the 1970 United States census reported a population of 2,084.

*Ovilla, Texas.

*Owen, Clark L. Clark L. Owen was the son of Abraham Owen (not C. L. Owen, as stated in Volume II).

Earl Owen Cullum

*Owen Branch.

*Owens, Texas. (Brown County.)

*Owens, Texas. (Crosby County.)

*Owensville, Texas.

Owentown, Texas. Owentown, in central Smith County, was a switch on the Cotton Belt Railroad (*see* St. Louis Southwestern Railway of Texas) between Tyler and Texarkana. In 1942 many warehouses and other facilities were built at the site to serve Camp Fannin.qv Named for Cliff E. Owen of Tyler, the town gained many small industries which occupied the old warehouses in postwar years. In 1949 the East Texas Tuberculosis Sanatorium qv (now the East Texas Chest Hospital qv) was established nearby, in the hospital facilities of old Camp Fannin about one and one-half miles from present Owentown. The population in 1976 was about two hundred, and the area was mostly residential, with some small industries located there. *See also* Tyler Standard Metropolitan Statistical Area.

*Owl Creek.

*Owlet Green, Texas.

Owsley, Alvin Mansfield. Alvin Mansfield Owsley, lawyer and diplomat, was born in Denton, Texas, on June 11, 1888, son of Alvin Clark and Sallie (Blount) Owsley. He attended North Texas State Teachers College (now North Texas State University), Virginia Military Institute, from which he was graduated in 1909, and the University of Texas law school.

He was admitted to the Texas Bar in 1912; that same year he was elected to the Texas House of Representatives and served one term. He began the practice of law with his father in Denton and was elected county and district attorney in 1915. In May, 1917, he entered the United States Army and attained the rank of lieutenant colonel before his discharge two years later. He resumed his Denton law practice and late in 1919 was appointed assistant attorney general of Texas. Early in 1921 he accepted an appointment as head of the Americanization commission of the American Legion,qv and the following year he was elected national commander of the organization.

He began a new law practice in Dallas and in 1928 ran third in the Texas Democratic primary for United States senator. Owsley was named minister to Romania in 1933 and two years later became the first United States minister to the Irish Free State. In 1937 he was made minister to Denmark but resigned after two years to support Vice-President John Nance Garner qv for the 1940 presidential nomination. Later he served for several years as an executive of Ball Brothers Company, manufacturer of glass containers. In 1944 and 1948 he supported Thomas E. Dewey for president.

Owsley was a member of the American and Texas Bar associations and of the Dallas Historical Society.qv He was awarded the Legion of Honor, rank of commander (France) in 1923, and the Order of Polonia Restituta (Poland) in 1924.

On May 25, 1925, he married Lucy Ball; they had three children. Owsley died in Dallas on April 3, 1967, and was buried in Hillcrest Memorial Park in that city.

BIBLIOGRAPHY: Dallas *Morning News*, April 4, 1967.

Wayne Gard

*Ox Yoke Creek.

*Oxbow Creek.

*Oxford, Texas.

*Oyster Bayou.

*Oyster Creek.

*Oyster Creek, Texas.

*Oyster Culture. *See* Marine Resources of Texas.

*Ozona, Texas. Ozona, county seat and only town of Crockett County, began at a water well on Johnson Draw on the property of E. M. Powell. When Crockett County was organized in 1891, the county seat was located at the Powell well, despite the presence of an established town, Emerald, seven miles to the east. The inhabitants of Emerald moved to the Ozona site and became some of its charter citizens. Shortly after the county seat election a frame schoolhouse and a courthouse were built. A post office was established in 1891 with Frank M. Boykin as postmaster, and by 1893 two saloons and a large mercantile store were in business. In 1922 a flood killed fifteen people and destroyed forty-six businesses and 330 homes. The discovery of oil in Crockett County in 1925 produced a boom in Ozona, and oil soon replaced ranching as the major industry. The population steadily increased from 427 in 1900, to 1,200 in 1920, and to 2,885 in 1950. In 1960 the population rose again, to 3,361, but the 1970 United States census reported a population of 2,864, a decline. In 1970 the town reported seventy-two businesses, including plants processing petroleum and feeds, and a bank.

BIBLIOGRAPHY: Mrs. Ira Carson (comp.), *Ozona* (1966).

P

*P. D. Creek.

*Pa Creek.

*Paac Indians. As early as 1675 the Paac (Pahaque) Indians were listed as one of numerous Indian groups encountered by Spaniards in northeastern Coahuila. Some fifteen years later they were clearly linked with the adjoining part of Texas between the Nueces River and the Rio Grande. In 1690 they were reported at a temporary settlement on the Nueces River, probably in modern Dimmit or Zavala County, a settlement which they shared with eight other groups. The next year (1691) they were again reported in what is now southern Maverick County, some ten miles north of the Rio Grande, this time sharing a *ranchería* with five other groups. There is little reason to doubt that the Paac and their associates spoke a Coahuiltecan dialect, as Swanton has indicated. Paac may have been an early name for the Pakawa, who lived in the same general area during the first part of the eighteenth century.

BIBLIOGRAPHY: L. Gómez Canedo, *Primeras exploraciones y poblamiento de Texas, 1686–1694* (1968); M. A. Hatcher, "The Expedition of Don Domingo Terán de los Ríos into Texas," *Preliminary Studies of the Texas Catholic Historical Society*, II (1932); F. W. Hodge (ed.), *Handbook of American Indians*, II (1910); Esteban L. Portillo, *Apuntes para la historia antigua de Coahuila y Texas* (1886); J. R. Swanton, *Linguistic Material from the Tribes of Southern Texas and Northeastern Mexico* (1940).

T. N. Campbell

*Paachiqui Indians. The Paachiqui (Paachique, Pacchiqui, Parchiqui) Indians are known only from the late seventeenth century, at which time they seem to have been a minor Coahuiltecan band that ranged the area southwest of present San Antonio between the Rio Grande and the southern edge of the Edwards Plateau. In 1690 the Paachiqui were visited by Spaniards at a *ranchería* on the Nueces River, probably in Dimmit or Zavala County, where they were encamped with eight other Indian groups. The next year (1691) they were seen nearby on the Frio River, this time with twelve other groups. Thereafter nothing more is heard of them. It seems clear that the Paachiqui were not the same people as the Pachaque of Coahuila.

BIBLIOGRAPHY: L. Gómez Canedo, *Primeras exploraciones y poblamiento de Texas, 1686–1694* (1968); M. A. Hatcher, "The Expedition of Don Domingo Terán de los Ríos into Texas," *Preliminary Studies of the Texas Catholic Historical Society*, II (1932); F. W. Hodge (ed.), *Handbook of American Indians*, II (1910); J. R. Swanton, *Linguistic Material from the Tribes of Southern Texas and Northeastern Mexico* (1940).

T. N. Campbell

*Pacaruja Indians. The Pacaruja Indians were reported as having lived on the Texas coast between the Nueces River and the Rio Grande during the eighteenth century. This late report (1861) is based on hearsay and has not been verified by contemporary documents. Pacaruja may be a corruption of Pajarito, the name of a Coahuiltecan group known to have lived along the lower Rio Grande during the same period.

BIBLIOGRAPHY: F. W. Hodge (ed.), *Handbook of American Indians,* II (1910); W. Jiménez Moreno, "Tribus e idiomas del Norte de México," *El Norte de México y el Sur de Estados Unidos* (1944); J. R. Swanton, *Linguistic Material from the Tribes of Southern Texas and Northeastern Mexico* (1940).

T. N. Campbell

*Pace, Julian Harrison.

*Pachal Indians. The Pachal (Pacgal, Pachol, Paschal, Patehal) Indians, also known by the Spanish name Manos Blancas (white hands), originally ranged the area in Texas that lies between the southern margin of the Edwards Plateau and the Rio Grande. In 1690 they were reported sharing a temporary settlement with eight other Indian bands on the Nueces River, probably in present Dimmit or Zavala County. In the following year they were found on the Frio River, apparently in modern Frio County, where they shared an encampment with twelve other groups. Later the Pachal entered two missions in northeastern Coahuila, San Juan Bautista qv in 1699, at its first location on the Rio Sabinas, and San Bernardo Mission qv in 1703, near present-day Guerrero. Some Pachal were still at the latter mission in 1727. These Indians seem to have lost their identity by the middle eighteenth century among the mission Indian populations of northeastern Coahuila.

BIBLIOGRAPHY: V. Alessio Robles, *Coahuila y Texas en la Epoca Colonial* (1938); L. Gómez Canedo, *Primeras exploraciones y poblamiento de Texas, 1686–1694* (1968); M. A. Hatcher, "The Expedition of Don Domingo Terán de los Ríos into Texas," *Preliminary Studies of the Texas Catholic Historical Society,* II (1932); F. W. Hodge (ed.), *Handbook of American Indians,* II (1910); P. O. Maas, *Viajes de misioneros Franciscanos á la conquista del Nuevo México* (1915); J. A. de Morfi, "Descripción de territorio del Real Presidio de San Juan Bautista," *Boletín de la Sociedad Mexicana de Geografía y Estadística,* LXX (1950); M. Orozco y Berra, *Geografía de las lenguas y carta etnográfica de México* (1864); J. R. Swanton, *Linguistic Material from the Tribes of Southern Texas and Northeastern Mexico* (1940); R. S. Weddle, *San Juan Bautista: Gateway to Spanish Texas* (1968).

T. N. Campbell

*Pachalaque Indians. The Pachalaque (Pachalaca, Pachalate) Indians were associated with Nuestra Señora de la Purísima Concepción de Acuña Mission qv in San Antonio, which they began to enter as early as 1733. Their aboriginal range is unknown, but it is suspected that they came from the area south or southwest of San Antonio. Swanton listed them as probable Coahuiltecan-speakers. The Pachalaque are not to be confused with the Pajalat, who were also at Mission Concepción as well as at nearby San Francisco de la Espada Mission.qv The separateness of Pachalaque and Pajalat is supported by mission records, which list individuals of both groups on the same page and include one reference to the marriage of a Pachalaque to a Pajalat. However, the similarities in the names Pachalaque and Pachaloco raise questions of possible identity that cannot be answered at present.

BIBLIOGRAPHY: H. E. Bolton, "Spanish Mission Records at San Antonio," *Quarterly of the Texas State Historical Association,* X (1906–1907); H. E. Bolton, *Texas in the Middle Eighteenth Century* (1915); F. W. Hodge (ed.), *Handbook of American Indians,* II (1910); J. R. Swanton, *Linguistic Material from the Tribes of Southern Texas and Northeastern Mexico* (1940).

T. N. Campbell

Pachaloco Indians. The Pachaloco (Pacholoco, Panchaloco) Indians are known only as one of the Indian groups that entered mission San Juan Bautista qv near present-day Guerrero, northeastern Coahuila, in 1701 or shortly thereafter. Some of them were still at this mission as late as 1762. Swanton listed them as probable Coahuiltecan-speakers. The similarities in the names Pachaloco, Pachalaque, and Pastaloca raise questions of possible identity that cannot be answered at present.

BIBLIOGRAPHY: F. W. Hodge (ed.), *Handbook of American Indians,* II (1910); L. Naranjo, *Lampazos: sus hombres, su tiempo, sus obras* (1934); J. R. Swanton, *Linguistic Material from the Tribes of Southern Texas and Northeastern Mexico* (1940); R. S. Weddle, *San Juan Bautista: Gateway to Spanish Texas* (1968).

T. N. Campbell

Pachaque Indians. In 1675 the Pachaque (Pachaga, Pachajuen, Pachaquen, Pachoque, Parchaque, and other variants) Indians ranged northeastern Coahuila, especially that part between the Rio Sabinas and the Rio Grande, and in 1690–1691 they were also recorded as living in the same area. In the first half of the eighteenth century some of the Pachaque found their way to two missions of San Antonio—Nuestra Señora de la Purísima Concepción de Acuña and San Antonio de Valero.qqv Although the names are similar, the Pachaque do not seem to have been the same as the Paachiqui, who lived south of the Edwards Plateau in Texas and were associated with a different set of Coahuiltecan bands.

BIBLIOGRAPHY: V. Alessio Robles, *Coahuila y Texas en la Epoca Colonial* (1938); H. E. Bolton (ed.), *Spanish Exploration in the Southwest, 1542–1706* (1916); L. Gómez Canedo, *Primeras exploraciones y poblamiento de Texas, 1686–1694* (1968); M. A. Hatcher, "The Expedition of Don Domingo Terán de los Ríos into Texas," *Preliminary Studies of the Texas Catholic Historical Society,* II (1932); F. W. Hodge (ed.), *Handbook of American Indians,* II (1910); P. O. Maas, *Viajes de misioneros Franciscanos á la conquista del Nuevo México* (1915); R. G. Santos, "A Preliminary Survey of the San Fernando Archives," *Texas Libraries,* XXVIII (1966–1967); J. R. Swanton, *Linguistic Material from the Tribes of Southern Texas and Northeastern Mexico* (1940).

T. N. Campbell

*Pacheco, Rafael Martínez.

*Packing Plants. *See* Meat Packing.

*Packsaddle Mountain.

*Packsaddle Mountain Fight.

Pacpul Indians. In the late seventeenth century the Pacpul (Pachul, Pacpol, Papul, Paquil) Indians ranged a large area south of the Edwards Plateau in Texas as well as the adjoining part of northeastern Coahuila. In 1689 Pacpul were reported at Mission Caldera in Coahuila, and one of their leaders, Juan (or Juanillo), was sent by the Spaniards northward to find Jean Henri,qv who was thought to be a refugee from the La Salle Expedition qv and who had become a leader of several associated Indian bands in Texas. Juan found Henri in the Sierra de Sacatsol, a local name for the eroded southern margin of the Edwards Plateau, and escorted him to a point where contact could be made with a Spanish military unit.

In 1691 a Spanish missionary party encountered Pacpul at a *ranchería* in what is now southern Maverick County, some ten miles north of the Rio Grande. Five other Indian peoples shared this settlement with the Pacpul. A Pacpul man guided the same Spanish party to the site of present San Antonio and also served as an interpreter to the Payaya, who lived along the San Antonio River. After this no more is heard of the Pacpul, and it is assumed that they lost their identity early in the eighteenth century.

BIBLIOGRAPHY: V. Alessio Robles, *Coahuila y Texas en la Epoca Colonial* (1938); H. E. Bolton (ed.), *Spanish Exploration in the Southwest, 1542–1706* (1916); L. Gómez Canedo, *Primeras exploraciones y poblamiento de Texas, 1686–1694* (1968); C. W. Hackett (ed.), *Pichardo's Treatise on the Limits of Louisiana and Texas*, II (1934); F. W. Hodge (ed.), *Handbook of American Indians*, II (1910); J. R. Swanton, *Linguistic Material from the Tribes of Southern Texas and Northeastern Mexico* (1940); Elizabeth Howard West, "De León's Expedition of 1689," *Quarterly of the Texas State Historical Association*, VIII (1904–1905).

T. N. Campbell

Pacuache Indians. In the late seventeenth and early eighteenth centuries the Pacuache (Pacuachiam, Pacuaxin, Paguache, Pajauche, Paquasian, and other variants) Indians ranged the area that lies between the Rio Grande and the southern edge of the Edwards Plateau, sometimes crossing the Rio Grande into northeastern Coahuila. Juan Domínguez de Mendoza qv heard of them in the western part of the Edwards Plateau in 1684. In 1690 they were reported at an encampment on the southern margin of the Edwards Plateau, along with seven other groups, and in the same year they were also reported at a *ranchería* on one of the upper tributaries of the Frio River west or northwest of San Antonio. The following year (1691) they were visited by Spaniards at a settlement farther down the Frio River, apparently in present Frio County, a settlement which they shared with twelve other Indian bands. In 1693 they were again met by Spaniards between the Nueces River and the Rio Grande.

Some of the Pacuache entered San Bernardo Mission qv when it was established in 1702 near modern Guerrero in northeastern Coahuila, and they were still at this mission in 1708, although much reduced by epidemics. A few Pacuache survived at San Bernardo until at least 1738. Six miles northeast of Guerrero one of the commonly used fords for crossing the Rio Grande was known as "Paso Pacuache." However, many Pacuache seem to have remained in their traditional territory, for between 1709 and 1718 they were reported on both the Nueces and Frio rivers. By 1724–1725 Apache attacks on the Pacuache were recorded. In 1729 Pacuache were seen hunting bison in northeastern Coahuila, apparently somewhere south of present Del Rio, Texas.

Some Pacuache also entered San Antonio de Valero Mission qv shortly after it was established at San Antonio in 1718, and in 1747–1748 a few of these were taken to the short-lived San Xavier Missions qv near present Rockdale, Texas, to serve as teachers and interpreters. After 1750 the Pacuache seem to have been absorbed into the mission Indian population of Coahuila and Texas.

That the Pacuache spoke a dialect of Coahuiltecan is well established. However, there is much confusion concerning the Pacuache name variants. Hodge, Swanton, and others considered Pacuache and Pacuachiam as two separate Coahuiltecan groups, but nothing can be found to support this judgment. In primary sources the two names refer to groups in the same area at the same time, but no single source lists the two names together, either in the natural habitat or in missions. It now seems clear that these two names refer to the same people. Some writers have equated Pacuache with Paachiqui, Pachaque, Pachoche, and Pakawa, but these linkages are not supported by convincing evidence.

BIBLIOGRAPHY: V. Alessio Robles, *Coahuila y Texas en la Epoca Colonial* (1938); H. E. Bolton, *Texas in the Middle Eighteenth Century* (1915) and (ed.), *Spanish Exploration in the Southwest, 1542–1706* (1916); C. E. Castañeda, *Our Catholic Heritage in Texas, 1519–1936*, II (1936), V (1942); W. E. Dunn, "Apache Relations in Texas, 1718–1750," *Quarterly of the Texas State Historical Association*, XIV (1910–1911); L. Gómez Canedo, *Primeras exploraciones y poblamiento de Texas, 1686–1968* (1968); C. W. Hackett (ed.), *Pichardo's Treatise on the Limits of Louisiana and Texas*, II (1934); F. W. Hodge (ed.), *Handbook of American Indians*, II (1910); F. L. Hoffman (ed.), *Diary of the Alarcón Expedition into Texas, 1718–1719, by Fray Francisco Céliz* (1935); F. L. Hoffman (ed.), "The Mezquía Diary of the Alarcón Expedition into Texas, 1718," *Southwestern Historical Quarterly*, XLI (1937–1938); P. O. Maas, *Viajes de misioneros Franciscanos á la conquista del Nuevo México* (1915); J. R. Swanton, *Linguistic Material from the Tribes of Southern Texas and Northeastern Mexico* (1940); R. S. Weddle, *San Juan Bautista: Gateway to Spanish Texas* (1968).

T. N. Campbell

*Pacuachiam Indians. *See also* Pacuache Indians.

*Paddock, Buckley B.

Padgitt, Kate Ross. Kate Ross Padgitt, daughter of Catherine (Fulkerson) and Shapley Prince Ross,qv was born on January 6, 1851, in a log cabin near the Waco Springs,qv possibly the first white child born at Waco, Texas. She was graduated from Waco University, and on her birthday in 1870 she dedicated the important Waco Suspension Bridge across the Brazos River. A steamboat plying the Brazos was named for her, the *Katie Ross*. She organized the Possum Club, first social and hunt club in Waco.

She was married to Tom Padgitt qv on January 2, 1878, and they were the parents of six children. She was active in charitable works and at one time served as president of the Veterans' Association of the Republic of Texas. Kate Ross Padgitt died on

January 18, 1912, and was buried in Oakwood Cemetery in Waco.

BIBLIOGRAPHY: John Sleeper and J. C. Hutchins (comps.), *Waco and McLennan County, Texas* (1876); William Sleeper and Allan Sanford, *Waco Bar and Incidents of Waco History* (1941); Raymond L. Dillard, The Ross Family (M.A. thesis, Baylor University, 1931); Waco *Tribune-Herald*, January 6, 1929.

Merle Mears Duncan

Padgitt, Tom. Tom Padgitt was born on December 13, 1846, in Gallatin, Tennessee. In 1853 his family moved to Texas and settled at Goose Creek and then Houston. In 1858 Padgitt went to work for his uncle, a saddle and harness maker. During the Civil War he worked in a Confederate Army saddle shop in Houston; after the war he opened his own saddle and harness shop in Bryan and then extended his business into Kosse, Groesbeck, and Corsicana.

In 1872 Padgitt opened a saddle and harness shop in Waco. During World War I his company filled American and British contracts; later the company carried on extensive trade with Latin America and became one of the most widely known firms in the South.

Padgitt organized the first fire-fighting brigade in Waco, and also the "Red Stockings," Waco's first professional baseball club. He was a leader in the development of the Waco Cotton Palace qv and built a natatorium which housed Waco's first indoor swimming pool. He was married three times, first in 1870 to Amanda Hutchison; they had one daughter before Amanda died. His second wife was Kate Ross Padgitt,qv daughter of Shapley Prince Ross qv and sister of Lawrence Sullivan Ross;qv they were married in 1878 and had six children. Following the death of his second wife, Padgitt married Fannie S. Wall on October 6, 1914. Padgitt died October 19, 1926, and was buried in Oakwood Cemetery in Waco.

BIBLIOGRAPHY: Waco *Tribune-Herald*, October 20, 1926, June 28, 1936, April 3, 30, 1967.

Merle Mears Duncan

*Padgitt, Texas.

*Padilla, Juan de.

*Padilla, Juan Antonio.

*Padillo Creek.

*Padre Island. Padre Island is a long, narrow barrier island along the Texas Gulf Coast. Geologic studies indicate that during the Wisconsin glacial stage the ocean level was lowered considerably through removal of water to support extensive glaciation over the world. At that time the Texas shoreline was much farther to the east and south in what is now the Gulf of Mexico. As the glaciers of the world melted, the sea level rose and the Texas shoreline moved slowly back toward the present mainland. Padre Island began to form about 3,000 B.C., when the sea level had risen to within some twenty or thirty feet of its present level. A series of offshore islands developed by about 2,000 B.C., and these eventually joined to form the thin, elongated nucleus of present Padre Island.

Since then the island has grown in width. Longshore currents and wave action have continually added materials to the Gulf shore, and the prevailing easterly winds and hurricane-driven waters have carried these materials across the island into the Laguna Madre depression that separates Padre Island from the mainland. This dynamic situation continues today and provides an interesting environment for recreational use. *See also* Padre Island National Seashore.

Vegetation on the island is sparse and adapted to the unstable land surface. Land animals are few and small in size, but the beach and the interior ponds and lakes teem with shore birds and migratory waterfowl. Few people have been able to live there permanently. Like many such sparsely occupied areas, Padre Island has a rich folklore, which is based mainly on pirates, treasure-laden wrecked ships, and predatory Indians. *See also* Padre Island Treasure.

BIBLIOGRAPHY: Writers' Round Table, *Padre Island* (1950); P. S. Galtsoff (ed.), *Gulf of Mexico: Its Origin, Waters, and Marine Life* (1954); T. N. Campbell, "Archeology of the Central and Southern Sections of the Texas Coast," *Bulletin of the Texas Archeological Society*, 29 (1960).

T. N. Campbell

Padre Island National Seashore. In 1958 Senator Ralph Yarborough introduced the initial bill in the United States Congress calling for Padre Island National Seashore. After years of discussion, controversy, and hearings, the Yarborough bill was passed in 1962, creating a seventy-four-mile-long national seashore area administered by the National Park Service.

On April 8, 1968, before an estimated crowd of 7,500, the Padre Island National Seashore was dedicated by Mrs. Lyndon B. Johnson, who was accompanied by some eighty United States and foreign journalists and Washington officials, including Secretary of the Interior Stewart L. Udall. Although the National Park Service estimated in the early 1960's that the cost of buying the park site would be $4 million, the overall cost was given in 1968 as $21,889,917.

Padre Island National Seashore covers about two-thirds of Padre Island,qv a section some eighty miles in length that includes the eastern boundaries of three coastal counties—Kleberg, Kenedy, and Willacy. Shorter sections at each end of the island were not included; small county parks and commercial developments already existed when the Padre Island National Seashore bill was passed by Congress and the Texas legislature. Nueces County has a park at the northern end of the island and Cameron County maintains another at the southern end. Areas between the county parks and the national seashore remain under private or corporate ownership.

The chief attraction of Padre Island is its wide eastern beach of fine sand and shell fragments that slopes gently into the Gulf of Mexico, making it ideal for swimming, surf fishing, and strand-line play. This is the longest beach of its kind in the United States. Along the beach is a belt of sand dunes that rise to heights of twenty to thirty-five feet. In the interior of the island there are numerous deflated basins that become ponds and lakes in wet periods. In addition to these basins there are extensive dune fields of great scenic beauty, particularly early or late in the day. The National Park Service plans to alter the landscape as little as possible, so that visitors can experience the wind, sand, sea, and sky with minimal distraction.

Land animals are few and small in size, but the beach and the interior ponds and lakes teem with shore birds and migratory waterfowl. The Gulf shore is a beachcomber's paradise. In places the variety of seashells is phenomenal, and everywhere innumerable natural and man-made objects are cast ashore, especially after storms. The island has always been a lonely place because few people, including the Indians, have been able to live there permanently. Like many such sparsely occupied areas, Padre Island has a rich folklore, which is based mainly on pirates, treasure-laden wrecked ships, and predatory Indians. Its status as a national park will keep most of it free from further settlement and commercial development. See Padre Island in Volume II for detailed early history of its settlement; see also Padre Island Treasure.

BIBLIOGRAPHY: C. McCampbell, *Texas Seaport: The Story of the Growth of Corpus Christi and the Coastal Bend Country* (1952); V. Smylie, *Padre Island, Texas* (1960); Writers' Round Table, *Padre Island* (1950); Corpus Christi *Times*, April 9, 1968; Houston *Post*, July 3, 1968.

T. N. Campbell

Padre Island Treasure. When in 1967 a General Land Office [qv] field representative officially reported the discovery of a sunken Spanish ship off Padre Island near Port Mansfield, recovery attempts for Spanish artifacts from the ship were already in full operation by a private out-of-state salvaging firm. The salvaging company did not have a permit to operate within the state.

Acting in accordance with a 1960 United States Supreme Court ruling that title to all submerged coastal lands out to a distance of 10.35 miles belonged to the state of Texas, Land Commissioner Jerry Sadler requested the Texas attorney general's office to bring suit against the salvagers in December, 1967. Kenedy County 28th District Court granted a temporary injunction in January, 1968, to halt further recovery operations and removal of objects. After considerable controversy and confusion over rights of the state, rights of private firms, and the land commissioner's jurisdiction, the Indiana salvage firm began returning treasure to the state. The salvage firm then filed suit in a federal court against the state actions, and between 1968 and 1971 rulings were handed down verifying federal jurisdiction in the case, and an injunction was filed to halt state proceedings in the original suit. In 1971 the presiding federal judge urged a compromise settlement. Although the re-covered treasure was in the state's possession, the final judgment in the federal case would determine permanent ownership of the treasure.

The Padre Island artifacts recovered from the salvaging company were taken first to the General Land Office, then to the Texas Memorial Museum,[qv] and finally, in October, 1969, to the University of Texas Balcones Research Center in Austin. Reclamation and identification by the state continued in 1971, with cooperation between state and private facilities, although property rights of the collection were still in litigation in 1971.

The find was considered by most antiquarians and archeologists as a major discovery and has been cited as the earliest Spanish material ever recovered from American waters. Among the 400-year-old objects recovered from the wreck were a small solid gold crucifix, one gold bar, several silver discs, cannons, crossbows, and three astrolabes. The astrolabes, considered by some as the most valuable objects, were used in navigation and are extremely rare today.

It has been claimed that the wreck was part of a flota of twenty ships which set sail in 1553 for Spain from Vera Cruz, Mexico, laden with gold and silver from the Mexican and South American mines. Blown off course by storms, most of the ships were sunk or run aground off the Texas coast. Approximately three hundred people survived the wrecks and managed to reach Padre Island; for six weeks the survivors attempted to reach Mexico, but were killed off by Indians. Only two men, Fray Marcos de Mena and Francisco Vasquez, are known to have survived. Much of the silver from the flota was recovered by the Spanish government about one year after the wrecks, but the rest of the cargo remained until rediscovered in 1967.

As a result of the difficulties surrounding the salvaging attempts the 61st Texas Legislature passed the Antiquities Bill in September, 1969, to fix procedures in artifact recovery attempts. The bill provided for a committee with the authority for the designation and regulation of archeological landmarks and the protection and preservation of the archeological resources of Texas. Strict limitations were placed on all salvaging and excavation attempted by private individuals or companies.

On recommendation of the Antiquities Committee, the Institute of Underwater Research, a privately financed nonprofit organization, was formed in 1970 to locate other sunken ships in the same area as the 1967 find. In addition, the organization was to function in assisting artifact recovery attempts by any properly licensed salvaging company, although as of 1971 no permits had been issued for salvaging. The institute was composed of an eighteen-man team that surveyed an area about twenty-five miles long near Port Mansfield. Sixteen possible sites of sunken Spanish ships were located and mapped for future investigation. The legislature appropriated $125,000 for recovery of artifacts from shipwreck sites in 1971.

BIBLIOGRAPHY: General Land Office, *Treasure Tempest*

in Texas (1970); Marjie Mugno, "Padre's Spanish Treasure," *Texas Highways* (February, 1971).

Melinda Arceneaux Wickman

*Padrone Hill.

*Paducah, Texas. Paducah, county seat and principal marketing and shipping point of Cottle County, had a hospital under construction in 1966, a new post office, and a retirement home. Among its businesses in the 1960's were a farm equipment plant and a flying service. A state game preserve near the city attracts tourists. The city reported seventy businesses in 1970. The population, 2,392 in 1960, was 2,052 in 1970, according to the United States census.

*Paesta Creek.

Pagaiam Indians. The Pagaiam (Pagayam, Paguayam) Indians are known only from a list of Indian groups recorded in 1684 by Juan Domínguez de Mendoza qv when he was in the western part of the Edwards Plateau. It is said that delegations from these various groups were expected, but their territorial ranges are not indicated. Although it cannot be conclusively demonstrated, it seems likely that the Pagaiam are the same people as the Bagnam, a Coahuiltecan group encountered by Spaniards in 1675 near the southern margin of the Edwards Plateau in the vicinity of present Edwards, Kinney, Real, and Uvalde counties.

BIBLIOGRAPHY: H. E. Bolton (ed.), *Spanish Exploration in the Southwest, 1542–1706* (1916); C. E. Castañeda, *Our Catholic Heritage in Texas, 1519–1936*, II (1936); C. W. Hackett (ed.), *Pichardo's Treatise on the Limits of Louisiana and Texas*, II (1934).

T. N. Campbell

Page, Paul DeWitt. Paul DeWitt Page, son of Patrick D. and Ann (Mitchell) Page, was born on August 23, 1868, at Evergreen, Alabama. His family moved to Bryan, Texas, in 1872, and about fourteen years later Page moved to Bastrop, where he studied law in the office of Hiram Morgan Garwood qv and Captain B. D. Orgain.

After a year of law study at the University of Texas in Austin, Page returned to Bastrop, where he served as county attorney (1898–1904) and county judge (1904–1909). Elected in 1914 as Democratic state senator from the district including Bastrop County, he held that office continuously until 1922.

Page also was interested in local community development. He founded the present Citizens State Bank of Bastrop in 1909 and took a part in establishing Bastrop State Park and Camp Swift,qv an infantry training camp of World War II.

Page married Blanche Garwood in 1898, and they had two children. After the death of his wife, he was married to Mary Higgins. Page died on August 18, 1945, at Bastrop and was buried in Fairview Cemetery in that city.

W. St. John Garwood

Pagès, Pierre Marie François de. Pierre Marie François de Pagès, French naval officer, world traveler, and writer, was born of a noble family in Toulouse in 1748. Following the settlement of the Seven Years' War and the relaxed French-Spanish rivalry in North America, Pagès crossed Texas on the first lap of a journey around the world. Leaving his naval vessel at Santo Domingo on June 30, 1767, he sailed to New Orleans, traveled by the Mississippi and Red rivers to Natchitoches, then across Texas and into Mexico by way of the Old San Antonio Road.qv He returned to France by way of the Far East and then wrote an account of his adventure. The English translation of his book, *Travels Round the World in the Years 1767, 1768, 1769, 1770, 1771* (1791), is perhaps the oldest description of Texas in an English-language book. Pagès later became a captain in the French navy, received the Croix de St. Louis, and became a corresponding member of the Académie des Sciences. He accompanied an expedition toward the South Pole in 1773–1774 and one toward the North Pole in 1776. After fighting with the French navy in the American Revolution, he retired to a plantation in present Haiti, where he was killed in a slave uprising in 1793.

BIBLIOGRAPHY: *Biographie universelle: ancienne et moderne*, XXXI (n.d.); *Nouvelle biographie générale*, XXXIX (1862).

Marilyn M. Sibley

*Paguan Indians. The Paguan (Paguanan, Paguona, Pahuanan, Pguan, Poguan, Puyua) Indians were first mentioned in 1690, at which time they seem to have lived somewhere in Texas south of the Edwards Plateau. In 1707–1708 they were living east of the missions of northeastern Coahuila, which would place them in Texas, possibly in the vicinity of present Dimmit and La Salle counties. Later (1743–1751) a few Paguan entered San Antonio de Valero Mission qv of San Antonio. Hodge, Swanton, and others have listed the Paguan and Paguanan as separate Coahuiltecan groups, but no convincing evidence has been found that supports this judgment. The similarity of Paguan to Payuguan has led to some difficulty in separating variants of the two names. Bolton (in Hodge) suggested that these two names may actually refer to the same people, which now appears unlikely.

BIBLIOGRAPHY: F. W. Hodge (ed.), *Handbook of American Indians*, II (1910); A. de León and others, *Historia de Nuevo León, con noticias sobre Coahuila, Tejas y Nuevo México* (1909, 1961); P. O. Maas, *Viajes de misioneros Franciscanos á la conquista del Nuevo México* (1915); R. G. Santos, "A Preliminary Survey of the San Fernando Archives," *Texas Libraries*, XXVIII (1966–1967); J. R. Swanton, *Linguistic Material from the Tribes of Southern Texas and Northeastern Mexico* (1940); R. S. Weddle, *San Juan Bautista: Gateway to Spanish Texas* (1968).

T. N. Campbell

*Paguanan Indians. The name Paguanan now appears to be a variant of Paguan. *See* Paguan Indians.

T. N. Campbell

Paiabuna Indians. In 1683–1684 Juan Domínguez de Mendoza qv led an exploratory expedition from El Paso as far eastward as the junction of the Concho and Colorado rivers east of present San

Angelo. In his itinerary he listed the names of thirty-seven Indian groups, including the Paiabuna (Paganuma), from which he expected to receive delegations on the Colorado River. Nothing further is known about the Paiabuna, who seem to have been one of many Indian groups of north-central Texas that were swept away by the southward thrust of the Lipan-Apache and Comanche Indians in the eighteenth century.

BIBLIOGRAPHY: H. E. Bolton (ed.), *Spanish Exploration in the Southwest, 1542–1706* (1916); C. W. Hackett (ed.), *Pichardo's Treatise on the Limits of Louisiana and Texas*, II (1934).

T. N. Campbell

*Paige, Texas.

*Paine Female Institute.

*Paint Creek.

*Paint Gap.

*Paint Gap Hill.

*Paint Mountain.

*Paint Rock, Texas. Paint Rock, seat of Concho County, had seven business establishments in 1970. The town served as the market and shipping point for the large quantity of wool and mohair produced in the county. The 1970 population was 193, according to the United States census.

Painter, Theophilus Shickel. Theophilus S. Painter, the son of Franklin Verzelius Newton and Laura (Shickel) Painter, was born at Salem, Virginia, on August 22, 1889. He received the B.A. degree from Roanoke College in 1908 and the Ph.D. from Yale in 1913. He did post-doctoral work at the University of Würzburg from 1913 to 1914. From 1914 to 1916 he was instructor in zoology at Yale. In 1916 he was appointed adjunct professor of zoology at the University of Texas, where he remained for the next fifty years. In 1939 he was awarded the title of Distinguished Professor of Zoology. In 1944 Painter was appointed acting president of the University of Texas, and from 1946 to 1952 he served as president. He resigned in that year, but continued as professor of zoology until his retirement from active teaching in 1966.

Painter's contribution to zoology was primarily in the field of genetics. His earlier researches were in the cytology of spiders. He was widely known for his investigations of chromosomes in the salivary glands of fruit flies, and his later work in cytogenetics brought him the Daniel Giraud Elliot Medal from the National Academy of Sciences in 1938. One of America's foremost geneticists, in 1969 he became the first recipient of the Anderson Award for scientific creativity and teaching, given by the University of Texas M. D. Anderson Hospital and Tumor Institute qv in Houston.

Painter married Anna M. Thomas in 1917. They had four children. Painter was a member of the National Academy of Sciences, the American Philosophical Society, the American Society of Zoologists, the American Society of Naturalists, and the American Society of Anatomists. From 1917 to 1919 he served as a captain in the U.S. Army Aviation Service. Painter died on October 5, 1969, and was buried in Austin Memorial Park in Austin.

BIBLIOGRAPHY: *American Men of Science*, V (1967); *Texian Who's Who* (1937); University of Texas, *The Genetics Group, Department of Zoology* (1952); Austin *Statesman*, October 6, 7, 1969.

Paintings, Indian Rock. *See* Rock Art, Indian.

*Paisano. *See* Birds.

*Paisano Creek.

Paisano Fellowship. *See* Paisano Ranch.

*Paisaño Pass.

*Paisaño Peak.

Paisano Ranch. Paisano Ranch, fourteen miles southwest of Austin in the Texas hill country, was the 254-acre country place of J. Frank Dobie qv at the time of his death on September 18, 1964. Dobie had previously owned a larger place, Cherry Springs Ranch, near Marble Falls, but he sold it following a severe illness; in 1959 he bought the smaller place closer to Austin, which had been called Shady Creek Ranch by the previous owners, George and Pearl Turney.

The first owner of the land that is now Paisano was James S. Burton, who surveyed and received 160 acres of it about 1860. On August 14, 1863, Burton sold the property to Frederick and Lucy Kunze, who built a log cabin (now hidden in the walls of the present house); they sold the property on September 15, 1865, to John Daniel Wende and his wife Mary. The Wendes increased the size of the ranch to Paisano's present acreage, built additional rooms to the cabin, built the stone walls which still crosscut the property, and reared a son and a daughter there. John Wende died in 1897, and five years later his widow moved to Austin. For twenty-six years the ranch was uninhabited, until March, 1928, when it was sold by the surviving son, John Charles Wende, to Anton and Minnie Holm. The Holms sold it in 1943 to R. L. and Dicy Springfield, who in turn sold it the following year to George and Pearl Turney, the last owners before Dobie.

Dobie first thought of calling it Wild Gobbler Ranch but decided on Paisano, another name for the long-legged, cuckoo-like bird that runs more than it flies, better known in Texas as the roadrunner or chaparral. The paisano was Dobie's symbol, and he used it on his bookplates and on other printed works and objects. For a while he kept a few cattle and sheep at Paisano, but he sold them, preferring the deer and wild turkeys and other wildlife that abounded there. A refuge for him, Dobie described Paisano as "not an estate, not a ranch, not a farm, it is merely a place of some acres in the hills west of Austin, Barton Creek winding through it."

One-hundred-foot limestone cliffs, the delight of free-roaming goats, drop down to Barton Creek, which flows near the front of the Paisano ranch house. Plum and grape thickets grow near the creek along with pecan trees and sycamores; scrub oak, cedar, cedar elm, and redbud spread over the whole ranch, from a crumbling old log cabin which still stands secluded at one edge, up to and around the horse barn and meadows; umbrella-shaped China trees, elm and live oak, fig and pear trees surround Paisano's six-room main house, the back part of which has thick stone walls over one hundred years old. When cedar logs are lit in the massive stone fireplace in the living room, the ranch house can be kept warm in the coldest weather, a place for company or contemplation.

At a dinner meeting of the Philosophical Society of Texas qv in Austin on December 5, 1964, less than three months after Dobie's death, a casual conversation began between the writer's widow, Bertha McKee Dobie,qv and two men who had been close friends of Dobie. Frank H. Wardlaw, director of the University of Texas Press,qv and Lon Tinkle, Southern Methodist University professor and book critic for the Dallas *Morning News*,qv believed that the most fitting memorial to J. Frank Dobie would be Paisano preserved for all time. Even then they knew that preservation was not enough, that there must be use. Ideas flowed. It could be a continuation of Dobie's legendary generosity of time, advice, energy, and loan of material to other writers. After all, Dobie once said that all any man needed for a suitable habitat was grass, water, and trees. Thus began the Dobie-Paisano project.

A steering committee, mostly friends of Dobie, was appointed by Frank Wardlaw, who headed the project, and a campaign began which covered the state, the Southwest, and reached as far as Washington, D.C., where Walker Stone, editor-in-chief of Scripps-Howard Newspapers and a longtime friend and ex-student of Dobie at Oklahoma A&M, helped with the project.

Since the Dobie estate was being liquidated and a number of people were interested in buying the ranch, Ralph A. Johnston,qv a prominent Houstonian who was also a close friend of Dobie, decided to buy it (in a sixty-second decision after a call from Glen Evans of Midland) in order to take it off the market so that there would be time for Dobie's friends to raise funds for its purchase.

All along, the Texas Institute of Letters qv played an important role, and it was certain that it would in some way be partly responsible for the project to save Paisano for the use of writers and artists. The idea of deeding the property, once acquired, to the University of Texas at Austin was presented to the chancellor of the university, Harry Huntt Ransom. The university agreed to accept the property once the title was clear.

Various gifts were received, the largest of which was Ralph Johnston's, who not only had put up the original purchase price of $76,200 to hold it, but contributed 10 percent of that amount plus all legal fees, interest, and interim costs. The drive for funds was climaxed with a gala dinner and auction of paintings by leading artists of the Southwest in the Crystal Ballroom of the Rice Hotel in Houston on the night of May 11, 1966. Donors to the project were invited to the dinner-auction, a glittering social occasion which honored the memory of J. Frank Dobie, his widow Bertha McKee Dobie, and Ralph A. Johnston, the greatest single contributor to the project. Also honored were the artists who donated their paintings: John Biggers, Bill Bomar, Jerry Bywaters, Otis Dozier, Kelly Fearing, Michael Frary, John Guerin, Alexandre Hogue, Peter Hurd, Gillis King, Tom Lea, William Lester, A. Kelly Pruitt, Buck Schiwetz, Everett Spruce, Olin Travis, Bror Utter, Olaf Weighorst, Donald Weismann, and Ralph White. One of the two John Biggers paintings was donated by J. Mason Brewer, and the Olaf Weighorst work was a gift of Miss Madlin Stevenson.

The paintings, auctioned by famed cattle auctioneer Walter S. Britten, brought in a total of $35,950, with Johnston again making the largest contribution, $5,300 for Peter Hurd's "Border Country." Some of the paintings bought were donated back by the buyers and now hang in the ranch house at Paisano. The dinner, attended by some 500 persons, netted another $7,650. Cochairmen for the successful dinner-auction were Lloyd Gregory, of Houston, and Frank Wardlaw. The principal speaker at the dinner preceding the auction was Stanley Marcus, who praised Dobie for his contributions to freedom of thought and expression in Texas.

The $43,600 brought in by this affair, along with the substantial gifts made by various individuals and foundations since the beginning of the campaign, fell just short of the $76,200 purchase price of the ranch, but the full amount was raised shortly thereafter.

The deed giving Paisano to the University of Texas at Austin was signed by Ralph Johnston two days before his death on August 8, 1966. It was the oilman-rancher's last piece of business, a truly philanthropic one; few knew that throughout the campaign for saving Paisano Johnston had been suffering a terminal illness. Mr. Dobie's last book before his death, significantly, had been dedicated to Johnston and his friend Walker Stone.

It was now possible to make definite plans, and in accordance with the original idea, Paisano would not only be preserved, but used. It would be used by creative people, writers or artists who would receive fellowships to live and work at Paisano Ranch. An advisory board was appointed by Chancellor Harry Ransom and Herbert Gambrell (president of the Texas Institute of Letters) to assist in planning the procedure for selecting fellowship recipients and other details concerning the Paisano project. Frank Wardlaw was named board chairman and Wilson Hudson, U. T. professor, was appointed secretary.

Money was needed for providing the fellowships, and this was generously provided initially by the

Carr P. Collins Foundation (Dallas), Raymond Dickson Foundation (Hallettsville), George Waverly Briggs qv Foundation (Dallas), J. R. Parten Foundation (Houston), Eugene McDermott qv Foundation (Dallas), and other private donors. In the beginning, a part of the contributions was used for the maintenance of Paisano Ranch, but this operation was taken over by the university in October, 1968.

In its final plan the Dobie-Paisano project, jointly administered by the University of Texas and the Texas Institute of Letters, provided for the use of Paisano as a place for a writer or artist to live for six months, with a stipend of $3,000, so that the recipient might work unimpeded towards his artistic goal. The university could at its discretion use Paisano for such purposes as field trips for botanists, zoologists, geologists, etc., so long as such use did not interfere with the work of the writer or other creative person in residence. Some of the conditions attached were that Paisano would be kept in its more-or-less natural state with no attempt to landscape it, that it would be a nature sanctuary with hunting perpetually prohibited, that the ranch house would be kept in simple style much as it was when Dobie occupied it, and that furniture, pictures, and other of Dobie's things would be kept there for all time. The university could in the future build other modest structures on other parts of the ranch to make possible the use of Paisano by more than one writer or artist at the same time.

The two permanent fellowships, awarded semiannually were the Eugene McDermott Foundation-Texas Institute of Letters Fellowship (August 1–January 31) and the Ralph A. Johnston Memorial Fellowship (February 1–July 31). Applicants must be Texans or other persons whose lives or works have been somehow identified with the state, although there is no restriction on subject matter. To show serious intent, applicants must submit examples of work previously accomplished along with a detailed plan for work they expect to do at Paisano. Judges for the competition are selected by the president of the university and the president of the Texas Institute of Letters.

The first six-month fellowship was awarded in June, 1967, and the awards continued on a six-month basis until December, 1972, when the board extended the period to one year (with a stipend of $6,000), beginning with the then-current fellow.

Because of the difficulty of judging writers with artists, the board determined that, beginning with the August, 1971, term, every third fellowship would be awarded to an artist (or photographer), following two successive awards to writers.

There was a departure from both of these determinations in 1975, when two artists were selected for six-month fellowships (with stipends of $3,000). It was not known early in 1976 whether future fellowships would be for six-month or one-year terms.

Bill Porterfield, a writer, was the first Paisano Fellow in June, 1967; he was succeeded by the following (all writers unless otherwise noted): A. C. Greene, February, 1968; Eldon Branda, August, 1968; José Cisneros (artist), February, 1969; Jack Canson, August, 1969; Robert Grant Burns, February, 1970; Victor White, August, 1970; Ben Freestone (artist), February, 1971; Oattis E. (Wynn) Parks, Jr., August, 1971; Gary Cartright, February, 1972; Jim Bones (photographer), August, 1972; Claude Stanush, August, 1973; C. W. Smith, August, 1974; Ann Matlock (weaver), August, 1975; John Christian (photographer), February, 1976.

With the succession of Paisano fellows the ranch acquired some small memento from each, spontaneously given, so that Dobie's affection for the refuge is continually refurbished. Animals on the place have included "Chapter" and "Verse," two wild horses that couldn't stay; a big white country tomcat, "Blanco Posnet," who (in the words of Bernard Shaw) just "shewed up"; and "Mody Goatright," an inimitable, car-climbing goat who disdained the company of Paisano's wild herd to enjoy the eccentricities of writers and artists (and named in affection for Dobie's good friend, folklorist Mody Boatright qv).

What will be produced at Paisano will depend on what Mrs. Dobie described as the talent, temperament, and will of its occupants. "Not for everyone," she wrote, "is the serene beauty of cliffs, running streams and trees, or quietness. The Dobie-Paisano Project will stand or fall by the quality of work done there." Paisano remains not only a fitting permanent memorial for J. Frank Dobie, but the suitable habitat he envisioned for any man, and particularly the artist: a place of grass, water, and trees.

Eldon Branda

*Pajalat Indians. The Pajalat (Cajalate, Pajalac, Pajalache, Pajalatam, Pallalat, Paxolot, and numerous other variants) Indians are known only from the eighteenth century. Their aboriginal range seems to have been the area immediately south of San Antonio, between the Frio and the San Antonio rivers. Many Pajalat moved to present San Antonio and entered Nuestra Señora de la Purísima Concepción de Acuña and San Francisco de la Espada qv when those missions were established there in 1731. A Pajalat chief was the first governor of the Indian settlement associated with Mission Concepción. These Indians seem to have left at least a temporary mark on local geography at San Antonio. The *acequia* or main irrigation canal at Concepción was known as the Pajalache or Concepción ditch, and as late as 1820 an eminence in the vicinity of San Antonio was known as Los Pajalaches Hill.

The Pajalat are not to be confused with the Pachalaque, who were also at Concepción. The separateness of Pajalat and Pachalaque is supported by mission records, which list individuals of both groups on the same page and include one reference to the marriage of a Pajalat to a Pachalaque. A few Pajalat from San Antonio seem to have found their way to Nuestra Señora del Refugio Mission qv after it was moved to the site of present Refugio in 1791. The record clearly shows that the Pajalat spoke a Coahuiltecan dialect.

BIBLIOGRAPHY: C. E. Castañeda, *Our Catholic Heritage in Texas, 1519–1936*, II (1936), VI (1950); J. A. Dabbs, "The Texas Missions in 1785," *Preliminary Studies of the Texas Catholic Historical Society*, III (1940); E. del Hoyo, *El cuadernillo de la lengua de los Indios Pajalates* (1965); M. A. Habig, *The Alamo Chain of Missions: A History of San Antonio's Five Old Missions* (1968); F. W. Hodge (ed.), *Handbook of American Indians*, II (1910); R. G. Santos, "A Preliminary Survey of the San Fernando Archives," *Texas Libraries*, XXVIII (1966–1967); J. R. Swanton, *Linguistic Material from the Tribes of Southern Texas and Northeastern Mexico* (1940); V. H. Taylor, *The Letters of Antonio Martinez, Last Spanish Governor of Texas, 1817–1822* (1957); C. I. Wheat, *Mapping the Transmississippi West, 1540–1861*, I, Maps 115 and 149 (1957).

T. N. Campbell

Pajarito Indians. Pajarito, which is Spanish for "little bird," occurs as a group name in two different sections of Texas. It appears in an early list (1693) of tribes reported as living in western Texas (north of the Rio Grande and "between Texas and New Mexico"). Nothing further is known of these Pajarito. The second group of Pajarito were Coahuiltecans who lived in southern Texas and northeastern Mexico during the latter half of the eighteenth century. The earliest records place these Pajarito in northeastern Nuevo León. Later some of the Pajarito seem to have migrated northwestward to the north bank of the Rio Grande above present Laredo. Eventually most of the Pajarito ended up along the lower Rio Grande near the coast, principally in northern Tamaulipas. A small group of Pajarito entered the mission at Camargo. The Pacaruja of the South Texas coast may be the same as the Pajarito.

BIBLIOGRAPHY: C. W. Hackett (ed.), *Historical Documents Relating to New Mexico, Nueva Vizcaya, and Approaches Thereto, to 1773*, II (1926); F. W. Hodge (ed.), *Handbook of American Indians*, II (1910); W. Jiménez Moreno, "Tribus e idiomas del Norte de México," *El Norte de México y el Sur de Estados Unidos* (1944); J. R. Swanton, *Linguistic Material from the Tribes of Southern Texas and Northeastern Mexico* (1940).

T. N. Campbell

Pajaseque Indians. The Pajaseque (Pausaqui, Paxaseque) Indians were one of five Indian groups encountered by a Spanish exploring party near present Corpus Christi in 1746–1747. At this time the Pajaseque were also referred to as Carrizo, a general name commonly applied to Coahuiltecan bands near the Rio Grande below Laredo. Later some of these Pajaseque entered San Antonio de Valero Mission qv at San Antonio.

BIBLIOGRAPHY: H. E. Bolton, *Texas in the Middle Eighteenth Century* (1915); F. W. Hodge (ed.), *Handbook of American Indians*, II (1910); G. Saldivar (ed.), "Reconocimiento de la costa del Seno Mexicano, por José de Escandón," *Archivo de la Historia de Tamaulipas*, II (1946); J. R. Swanton, *Linguistic Material from the Tribes of Southern Texas and Northeastern Mexico* (1940).

T. N. Campbell

Pakan, Texas. Pakan, in southwestern Wheeler County, was founded in 1904 by thirteen Slovak families from Chicago led by Sam Pakan, Sr., for whom the town was named. A one-room school was built and operated until 1908, when state aid was procured and the school was enlarged. The chief occupations of the people were farming and stock raising. In 1966 the community was no longer in existence.

Pakana Indians. The Pakana (Kakan Tallahassee, Pacadia, Pacana, Pachina, Pakan Tallahassee, Puccunna) Indians, a subdivision of the Muskogee or Creek Indians, originally lived in Alabama. French records indicate that some of the Pakana moved westward to Louisiana in 1763 or 1764, but Spanish records mention Pakana (Pacadia, Pachina) as living between the Sabine and the Mississippi as early as 1746. In 1805 these Pakana were living on the upper Calcasieu River about forty miles from Natchitoches. Later in the nineteenth century remnants of these Pakana joined the Alabama Indians in Texas, among whom they lost their ethnic identity sometime before 1900. Today descendants of the Pakana who remained in Alabama live with the Creek Indians in Oklahoma.

BIBLIOGRAPHY: C. W. Hackett (ed.), *Pichardo's Treatise on the Limits of Louisiana and Texas*, IV (1946); J. R. Swanton, *Indian Tribes of the Lower Mississippi Valley and Adjacent Coast of the Gulf of Mexico* (1911), *The Indians of the Southeastern United States* (1952).

T. N. Campbell

*Pakawa Indians. In the early eighteenth century the Pakawa (Pacao, Poco, Pacoa, Pacque, Pacuq, Paikawa, and other variants) Indians lived along the Frio and Nueces rivers southwest of San Antonio. The name is said to mean "tattooed," and Spaniards in northeastern Mexico sometimes referred to the Pakawa as Pintos, a term commonly used to denote tattooing. After 1703 some Pakawa attached themselves to San Bernardo Mission qv near present-day Guerrero in northeastern Coahuila, and a few families also entered Mission Candela farther south in Coahuila in 1713. In 1731 several hundred Pakawa began to enter missions at present San Antonio. Some went to Nuestra Señora de la Purísima Concepción de Acuña and San Antonio de Valero missions,qqv but most entered San Francisco de la Espada qv and became its leading group until this mission was secularized in 1794. Other Pakawa refused to enter missions and moved down the Rio Grande to the delta region, where in 1886 A. S. Gatschet found two Pakawa survivors living near Reynosa, Tamaulipas. Samples of speech recorded by Gatschet clearly indicate that the Pakawa spoke a Coahuiltecan dialect. There is some evidence that the names Pacao and Pacoa refer to separate but closely related Coahuiltecan groups. It is possible that Pakawa may be a later name for the Paac, a group that lived in northeastern Coahuila and the adjacent part of Texas in the late seventeenth century.

BIBLIOGRAPHY: H. E. Bolton, *Guide to Materials for the History of the United States in the Principal Archives of Mexico* (1913); J. A. Dabbs, "The Texas Missions in 1785," *Preliminary Studies of the Texas Catholic Historical Society*, III (1940); M. A. Habig, *The Alamo Chain of Missions: A History of San Antonio's Five Old Missions*

(1968); F. W. Hodge (ed.), *Handbook of American Indians*, I (1907), II (1910); R. G. Santos, "A Preliminary Survey of the San Fernando Archives," *Texas Libraries*, XXVIII (1966–1967); J. R. Swanton, *Linguistic Material from the Tribes of Southern Texas and Northeastern Mexico* (1940); R. S. Weddle, *San Juan Bautista: Gateway to Spanish Texas* (1968).

T. N. Campbell

*Palacios, Texas. Palacios, in Matagorda County, had a population of 3,676 in 1960 and 3,642 in 1970, according to the United States census report. The city reported sixty-five businesses in 1970.

*Palafox, Villa of. The villa of Palafox (Palafos, Palafoz) was founded on April 27, 1810, on the sixty-seven-league Joaquin Galan land grant of 1786. Its founder, Manuel Antonio Cordéro y Bustamante,^{qv} located it midway between Laredo and Presidio del Rio Grande (*see* San Juan Bautista) and named it for the hero of the siege of Saragossa, Spain, Joseph Palafox, who held off the forces of Napoleon in 1809. Juan José Díaz administered the villa as an Indian outpost and distributed lands to settlers.

The villa of Palafox survived an Indian attack in 1813, and in 1815 it had grown so that settlers there were urged to help in establishing other settlements. By then it was said to have had a church, San José de Palafox. The villa was abandoned from 1818 to 1826, however, because of continuing Indian raids. In the 1818 Comanche raid buildings were burned and nearly all of the inhabitants were massacred. A century later, remains of the stone fort were said to still bear marks of the fire. An 1824 plat map of the villa on the Rio Grande, beside a creek, shows nine structures and three walled areas on three city blocks laid out around an empty square. With continued Indian hostilities the villa made little progress, and on Stephen F. Austin's 1828(?) map of Texas, Palafox is shown with the notation, "Destroyed by the Indians."

Attempts were made to restore it under the name of Houston in the 1840's, but by 1850 the name Palafox was again in use. The Palafox, Burkeville, Sabine, and Rio Grande Railroad, chartered in 1854, was never built. In the 1880's there were two large stores (the Cantu and Alexander stores); a post office operated from 1886 to 1887 and again from 1905 to 1922. An 1888 map drawn by William Sidney Porter ^{qv} shows Palafox with no roads leading to it and no adjoining settlements. The 1910 census listed forty inhabitants. Jack Walker, the settlement's last inhabitant, left in 1938. Ruins of twenty-three stone buildings remained in the 1960's. In 1966 the M. A. Hirsch estate owned the site.

BIBLIOGRAPHY: David G. Chandler, *The Campaigns of Napoleon* (1966); Early Martin, Jr., *Two Maps of William Sidney Porter (O. Henry)* (1929); Mattie Austin Hatcher, *Opening of Texas to Foreign Settlement, 1801–1821* (1927); Hobart Huson, Case 2500, District Court, Refugio (1940); *Texas Almanac* (1857); Stephen F. Austin, Villa of Palafox (1824) and Map of Texas (1828?) (MSS., Archives, University of Texas at Austin Library).

Grover Cleveland Ramsey

*Palangana, Texas.

*Palaquesson Indians. The Palaquesson (Alakea, Palaquessou, Palaquechaune, Paloguesson) Indians are known only from the records of the La Salle Expedition,^{qv} which indicate that in the latter part of the seventeenth century these Indians lived southwest of the Hasinai tribes, probably between the Brazos and Trinity rivers in the general vicinity of present Grimes County. At this time the Palaquesson made their living by hunting bison and growing corn, and they were reported as living in ten villages. La Salle thought that their language resembled that of the Hasinai, whom he had previously visited, and this suggests that the Palaquesson were Caddoans.

BIBLIOGRAPHY: C. W. Hackett (ed.), *Pichardo's Treatise on the Limits of Louisiana and Texas*, I (1931); F. W. Hodge (ed.), *Handbook of American Indians*, II (1910); H. H. Stiles (ed.), *Joutel's Journal of La Salle's Last Voyage, 1684–7* (1906).

T. N. Campbell

*Palava, Texas.

*Paleo-Indians.

*Palestine, Texas. Palestine, seat of Anderson County, is a commercial center which derives its income from manufacturing, agriculture, and railroading. In 1970 Palestine had two hospitals and 359 businesses, including companies producing glazed tile, hydraulic cement, clothing, containers, and food, chemical, and petroleum products. In 1961 the National Center for Atmospheric Research ^{qv} located its Scientific Balloon Flight Station in Palestine. The 1960 population was 13,974; the 1970 population was 14,525, according to the United States census.

*Palisada Spring.

*Palito Blanco, Texas.

*Palito Blanco Creek.

*Palm, Svante.

*Palm, Texas.

*Palm Valley, Texas.

*Palma Canyon.

*Palmer, Texas.

*Palmetto, Texas.

*Palmetto Creek.

*Palmetto State Scenic Park. *See* Parks, State.

*Palmito Ranch, Battle of.

*Palo Alto, Texas.

*Palo Alto, Battle of.

*Palo Alto Creek.

*Palo Blanco, Texas.

*Palo Blanco Creek.

*Palo Duro Canyon.

*Palo Duro Canyon State Scenic Park. *See* Parks, State.

*Palo Duro Creek.

*Palo Gaucho Bayou.

*Palo Pinto, Texas.

*Palo Pinto County. Palo Pinto County, predominantly a livestock raising area, has increased its production of cattle, sheep, and goats since 1945. Small acreage has been allotted to grain, cotton, peanuts, fruits, and vegetables. From 1902 to January 1, 1973, 11,236,999 barrels of oil had been produced in the county. The major tourist attraction is Possum Kingdom Lake qv and park. The 1960 population was 20,516; the 1970 population was 28,962, according to the United States census.

*Palo Pinto Creek.

*Palo Pinto Mountains.

*Paloduro, Texas.

*Paloduro Creek.

*Palomas Indian Village.

*Paluxy, Texas.

*Paluxy College.

*Paluxy Creek.

Pamaya Indians. In 1691 the Pamaya (Pamai, Pamau, Paniaya) Indians were encountered by Spaniards in northeastern Coahuila about twenty-five miles south of the Rio Grande, where they were encamped with five other Indian groups. Sometime before 1716 the Pamaya migrated to east-central Texas, for in that year they were reported at a large settlement known as Ranchería Grande,qv which was some six or seven miles west of the Brazos River above its junction with the Little River (northern Milam County). Here some two thousand Indians were congregated, most of them Coahuiltecan bands from northeastern Coahuila and the adjoining part of Texas. Presumably they had moved as a result of pressures from both Spaniards and Apaches.

In 1718–1719 a number of Pamaya entered San Antonio de Valero Mission qv at present San Antonio, and in 1722 some of the Pamaya came to San Xavier de Nájera Mission,qv which had been established (no structures were ever built) near the Valero mission for Indians from Ranchería Grande. It is supposed that these San Antonio Pamaya lost their identity in the general mission population of Valero. However, it seems likely that other Pamaya remained in east-central Texas and were absorbed by local Indian populations, particularly the Tonkawan groups that later ranged the area.

BIBLIOGRAPHY: H. Carter, Doomed Road of Empire: The Spanish Trail of Conquest (1963); L. Gómez Canedo, Primeras exploraciones y poblamiento de Texas, 1686–1694 (1968); C. W. Hackett (ed.), Pichardo's Treatise on the Limits of Louisiana and Texas, II (1934); M. A. Hatcher, "The Expedition of Don Domingo Terán de los Ríos into Texas," Preliminary Studies of the Texas Catholic Historical Society, II (1932); F. W. Hodge (ed.), Handbook of American Indians, II (1910); J. R. Swanton, Linguistic Material from the Tribes of Southern Texas and Northeastern Mexico (1940); G. Tous, "Ramon's Expedition: Espinosa's Diary of 1716," Preliminary Studies of the Texas Catholic Historical Society, I (1930).

T. N. Campbell

*Pamoque Indians. The Pamoque (Pamaque, Pamaca, Pamache, Panague) Indians were Coahuiltecan-speaking Indians who in the early eighteenth century ranged between the lower San Antonio and Nueces rivers. However, they are most firmly associated with the area around the mouth of the Nueces River on Nueces and Corpus Christi bays. They were closely related to the Pasnacane, Piguique, and Viayan; in fact, some Spanish writers considered these three groups as subdivisions of the Pamoque. The Pamoque were frequently mentioned with the Orejon, who appear to have lived farther inland north of the lower Nueces River. Some of the Pamoque entered San Antonio missions (Nuestra Señora de la Purísima Concepción de Acuña and San Juan Capistrano qqv); others went to Nuestra Señora del Refugio Mission qv near the coast, and some of these survived well into the nineteenth century, perhaps as late as 1828, before losing their ethnic identity. Identification of the Pamoque with the Panequo reported in documents (1687) of the La Salle Expedition qv has been suggested but not demonstrated.

BIBLIOGRAPHY: H. E. Bolton, Texas in the Middle Eighteenth Century (1915); F. W. Hodge (ed.), Handbook of American Indians, II (1910); J. R. Swanton, Linguistic Material from the Tribes of Southern Texas and Northeastern Mexico (1940).

T. N. Campbell

*Pamorano Indians. The Pamorano (Pamorane, Pamozane) Indians, who were presumably Coahuiltecan in speech, lived in northern Tamaulipas during the eighteenth century. Although it has been stated that a Pamorano group once lived north of Laredo, no satisfactory evidence of this has yet been presented.

BIBLIOGRAPHY: F. W. Hodge (ed.), Handbook of American Indians, II (1910); G. Saldivar, Los Indios de Tamaulipas (1943); R. C. Troike, "Notes on Coahuiltecan Ethnography," Bulletin of the Texas Archeological Society, 32 (1962).

T. N. Campbell

*Pampa, Texas. Pampa, seat of Gray County, served as a commercial center for the surrounding wheat growing, cattle raising, and oil producing territory. In 1967 Pampa had thirty-four industrial plants that produced petrochemical products, furniture, industrial machines, sheet metal products, and heavy machinery. A total of 460 businesses was reported in 1970. Modern schools, public buildings, hospitals, and convention facilities were noted aspects of the community. Pampa recorded a 50 percent increase in population during the 1950's; in 1960 the population was 24,664. By 1970 the population had decreased to 21,726, according to the United States census.

*Pampa Army Air Field.

*Pampopa Indians. The Pampopa (Apompia, Pampoca, Pamposa, Panpoa, and other variants) Indians are known mainly from the first half of the eighteenth century, during which time they were frequently reported in rancherías on the Medina, Frio, and Nueces rivers west, southwest, and south of present San Antonio. This would place their range in the area now covered by Bexar, Medina, Frio, Atascosa, La Salle, and McMullen counties.

In 1727 about five hundred Pampopa were said to be on the Nueces River, apparently on the great southward bend of that river in La Salle and McMullen counties. Some Pampopa entered the mission of San Juan Bautista,qv near present Guerrero, Coahuila, in 1701 and were reported still there as late as 1762. A few Pampopa individuals seem also to have been at nearby San Bernardo Mission qv in 1747. Relatively large numbers of Pampopa entered the San Antonio missions, a few going to San Antonio de Valero Mission,qv but most of them (at least two hundred) going to San José y San Miguel de Aguayo qv in the early 1720's. During the 1730's the Pampopa sometimes deserted Mission San José to return to their traditional range. Some Pampopa were still living at San José as late as 1793. It is evident that they eventually lost their identity in the mission Indian populations of northeastern Coahuila and southern Texas. The linguistic evidence clearly indicates that the Pampopa spoke a Coahuiltecan dialect.

BIBLIOGRAPHY: P. P. Forrestal, "The Solís Diary of 1767," Preliminary Studies of the Texas Catholic Historical Society, I (1931); F. W. Hodge (ed.), Handbook of American Indians, I (1907), II (1910); P. O. Maas, Viajes de misioneros Franciscanos á la conquista del Nuevo México (1915); J. R. Swanton, Linguistic Material from the Tribes of Southern Texas and Northeastern Mexico (1940); G. Tous, "The Espinosa-Olivares-Aguirre Expedition of 1709," Preliminary Studies of the Texas Catholic Historical Society, I (1930); R. S. Weddle, San Juan Bautista: Gateway to Spanish Texas (1968).

T. N. Campbell

*Pan American Camp, Texas.

*Pan-American Railway Company.

Pan American University. Pan American University (formerly Pan American College), Edinburg, opened in 1927 as Edinburg Junior College. Since 1952 the school has been a four-year institution. In 1961 a new campus was completed. In September, 1965, Pan American College became the twenty-second state-supported Texas college. Three types of degree programs were offered: bachelor of arts, bachelor of science, and bachelor of business administration. Student enrollment increased steadily from 2,355 in 1965, to 4,092 in 1968, to 6,694 in 1974. The steadily growing college library contained approximately 85,000 volumes in 1969. The school's name was changed to Pan American University in 1971. Ralph Schilling served as president in 1974.

Panasiu Indians. In 1690 the Panasiu (Sampanasiu, Sampansia) Indians were reported to be living along the Guadalupe River east or northeast of San Antonio, an area which they shared with Apasxam, Cava, Emet, Manam, Sana, Tohana, and Tohoho. The two variants of the name are early copyists' errors. Sana and Panasiu, names of separate groups, were combined to form a single name.

BIBLIOGRAPHY: L. Gómez Canedo, Primeras exploraciones y poblamiento de Texas, 1686–1694 (1968).

T. N. Campbell

*Pancake, Texas.

*Pancho Villa. See Villa, Francisco (Pancho).

*Pandale, Texas.

*Pandora, Texas.

Panequo Indians. The Panequo (Panego) Indians are known only from documents (1687) of the La Salle Expedition,qv which indicate that these Indians lived well inland to the north or northeast of Matagorda Bay, possibly near either the Colorado or the Brazos River. Identification of the Panequo with the Pamoque (Pamaque) has been suggested but not demonstrated, and it seems likely that the two groups were unrelated.

BIBLIOGRAPHY: F. W. Hodge (ed.), Handbook of American Indians, II (1910), P. Margry, Découvertes et établissements des Français dans l'ouest et dans le sud de l'Amérique Septentrionale 1614–1698, III (1879).

T. N. Campbell

*Panequo Village. See also Panequo Indians.

*Panhandle, Texas. Panhandle, seat of Carson County, is a regional marketing and shipping center' for wheat, cattle, and petroleum products. The town also had some manufacturing, including aluminum window and athletic equipment plants, among the fifty-five businesses reported in 1970. The population was 1,958 in 1960 and 2,141 in 1970, according to the United States census.

*Panhandle, The Texas.

*Panhandle Cattle Raisers' Association. See Cattle Raisers' Associations.

*Panhandle and Gulf Railway Company.

*Panhandle Herald.

Panhandle National Grasslands. In 1958 the United States Forest Service established the Panhandle National Grasslands, with headquarters at Amarillo. The unit contained some 300,000 acres, mostly in small tracts of land scattered over North Texas, western Oklahoma, and northeastern New Mexico. Tracts in Texas amounted to 117,268 acres in Dallam, Fannin, Gray, Hemphill, Montague, and Wise counties. Most of the grasslands came from the dust bowl lands purchased by the federal government in the 1930's and 1940's under the Bankhead-Jones Farm Tenant Act. The grasslands were administered under a policy of multiple uses: soil recovery and conservation, range, watershed protection, recreation, and wildlife.

A forest supervisor in Amarillo administered the unit, assisted by rangers in Clayton, New Mexico; Cheyenne, Oklahoma; and Texline, Alvord, and Bonham, Texas. The land provided seasonal forage for 15,000 cattle. Areas for picnicking, fishing, and boating were developed in association with some 1,600 acres of lakes. Deer, antelope, Barbary sheep, ducks, geese, turkey, quail, and other small game were available in limited numbers for hunting under state laws. On July 1, 1970, the forest supervisor's office in Amarillo was closed, and headquarters for grassland districts in the southwestern region of the United States were located at Albuquerque, New Mexico. See also National Forests in Texas.

BIBLIOGRAPHY: Texas Almanac (1963, 1973); United States Forest Service (Southwestern Region), Panhandle National Grasslands.

*Panhandle Oil Field.

Panhandle-Plains Historical Museum. The Panhandle-Plains Historical Museum, the first state museum in Texas, was financed by a combination of private donations and state funds appropriated by the Texas legislature. The museum is located on the campus of West Texas State University at Canyon and contains the headquarters for the Panhandle-Plains Historical Society.qv The society began a fund drive to build the museum in 1929, and on April 14, 1933, the first unit was opened to the public. Another unit was finished in 1952, and the newest unit was added in 1968; by 1972 there were tentative plans for further expansion. The museum includes major collections in anthropology, geology, paleontology, and natural history, along with other collections on the cattle industry and the fine arts. It houses relics of the Southwest, pieces of furniture, skeletal remains of prehistoric animals, and the Indian collection of Colonel Charles Goodnight.qv The core of the museum archives is a collection of records of the early days in Texas, which consists of personal interviews and written records of the larger ranches in the area. C. Boone McClure was succeeded by James A. Hanson as director of the museum in September, 1974.

BIBLIOGRAPHY: Subject Files, Barker Texas History Center, University of Texas at Austin.

Panhandle-Plains Historical Review. See Panhandle-Plains Historical Society.

Panhandle-Plains Historical Society. The Panhandle-Plains Historical Society continued to hold its annual meetings at its headquarters in the Panhandle-Plains Historical Museum qv on the West Texas State University campus at Canyon.

The *Panhandle-Plains Historical Review,* with volume forty-four in 1971, continued to be published annually by the society. In 1972, with over 1,000 members, the Panhandle-Plains Historical Society had more than doubled its membership since 1948. Virgil P. Patterson was serving his second year as president of the society in 1972, and C. Boone McClure was executive director.

*Panhandle Railway Company.

*Panhandle and Santa Fe Railway Company.

*Panhandle Water Conservation Authority.

*Panilla Creek.

*Panna Maria, Texas. *See also* Poles in Texas.

*Panola, Texas.

*Panola County. Panola County, on the Texas-Louisiana line, is the site of five large refineries. Gas and oil production value was in excess of ninety million dollars annually, and wells numbered 1,000 for gas and 550 for oil in 1964. By 1973 total crude production had reached 40,694,478 barrels since its discovery in 1917. The county, 63 percent forested, had three sawmills with a daily capacity of forty-three thousand board-feet of lumber in 1966. The number of beef cattle, chief source of the agricultural income, tripled during the decade from 1950 to 1960, while crop production declined. Panola County is also known for its Appaloosa and Quarter horses. Murvaul Lake, dedicated in 1959, proved to be a boon to industry as well as a recreational facility. The 1960 population was 16,870; the 1970 population was 15,894, according to the United States census.

*Panola County (Judicial).

Panola Junior College. Panola Junior College, in Carthage, was originally called Panola County Junior College when it opened in 1948; its name was changed to Panola College in 1953 and then to Panola Junior College by the 1971–1972 term. In an election on June 14, 1947, voters approved the establishment of a countywide, tax-supported coeducational junior college. On January 19, 1948, it formally opened in temporary buildings secured as surplus from the War Assets Administration. In June, 1948, voters approved a bond issue of $400,000, which was utilized to construct the first three units of a permanent plant on the thirty-five-acre campus. A student union building was opened in 1957, and in 1959 a boys' dormitory was occupied. New science, library, and fine arts buildings, plus renovation of the administration building, doubled the capacity of the plant in 1966. The new library contained approximately fifteen thousand volumes by 1969.

The college is accredited by the Southern Association of Colleges and Secondary Schools and is a member of the American Association of Junior Colleges, the Association of Texas Colleges and Universities,qv and the Texas Association of Junior Colleges. The college offered the Associate in Arts and Associate in Science degrees, as well as several special certificates. In 1964 the college had a faculty numbering twenty-three and a regular term student enrollment numbering 390. In 1968 the enrollment stood at 605 and the faculty numbered thirty-five. The 1974 regular term enrollment was 832, and Arthur M. Johnson served as president.

*Pansy, Texas.

Pantapare Indians. The Pantapare (Ippantapaje) Indians were one of five groups recorded as living in the vicinity of present Corpus Christi in the middle eighteenth century. They were probably the same as the Pantipora, who lived in Nuevo León during the preceding century.

BIBLIOGRAPHY: H. E. Bolton, *Texas in the Middle Eighteenth Century* (1915); A. de León and others, *Historia de Nuevo León, con noticias sobre Coahuila, Tamaulipas, Texas, y Nuevo México* (1909, 1961); G. Saldivar (ed.), *Archivo de la historia de Tamaulipas,* II (1946).

T. N. Campbell

Pantego, Texas. Pantego, in Tarrant County, had a population of 238 in 1960 and 1,168 in 1970, according to the United States census. *See also* Fort Worth Standard Metropolitan Statistical Area.

*Pantex, Texas.

*Pantex Ordnance Plant.

*Panther Canyon.

*Panther Creek.

*Panther Mesa.

*Panther Mountain.

*Panther Peak.

*Paouite Indians.

*Papalote, Texas.

*Papalote Creek.

Papanac Indians. The Papanac (Panac, Papan, Papanacua, Papanaque, Paponoca, and other variants) Indians were first reported in 1675 as living in northeastern Coahuila and adjoining parts of Nuevo León and Texas, and in 1684 Juan Domínguez de Mendoza qv heard of them when he was in the western part of the Edwards Plateau in west-central Texas.

A Papanac group was encountered by Spaniards in 1690 on the Nueces River, apparently in modern Dimmit or Zavala County, where they shared the same rancheria with eight other groups. The next year, 1691, Papanac were found farther east, on or near the Frio River, perhaps in present Frio County, this time associated with twelve other groups.

In 1700 some of the Papanac entered San Francisco Solano Mission qv when it was established in northeastern Coahuila. Shortly after 1703, Papanac families entered San Bernardo Mission qv near present-day Guerrero, Coahuila, but in 1708 it was recorded that unmissionized Papanac still lived north of the Rio Grande. After 1718 there were also Papanac families at San Antonio de Valero Mission.qv These probably followed Mission San Francisco Solano when it was transferred from Coahuila to San Antonio and renamed San Antonio de Valero. The Valero records identify Papanac individuals as late as the middle eighteenth century.

Statements by missionaries support Swanton's identification of the Papanac as Coahuiltecan-speakers. These people evidently lost their ethnic identity in the late eighteenth-century mission Indian population of Coahuila and Texas.

BIBLIOGRAPHY: L. Gómez Canedo, Primeras exploraciones y poblamiento de Texas, 1686–1694 (1968); M. A. Hatcher, "The Expedition of Don Domingo Terán de los Ríos into Texas," Preliminary Studies of the Texas Catholic Historical Society, II (1932); F. W. Hodge (ed.), Handbook of American Indians, II (1910); P. O. Maas, Viajes de misioneros Franciscanos á la conquista del Nuevo México (1915); Esteban L. Portillo, Apuntes para la historia antigua de Coahuila y Texas (1886); R. G. Santos, "A Preliminary Survey of the San Fernando Archives," Texas Libraries, XXVIII (1966–1967); J. R. Swanton, Linguistic Material from the Tribes of Southern Texas and Northeastern Mexico (1940); R. S. Weddle, San Juan Bautista: Gateway to Spanish Texas (1968).

T. N. Campbell

*Paper, Manufacture of. In response to increasing demand for paper and related products, Texas' pulp and paper industry has continued to grow since the early 1950's. Orange Pulp and Paper Company, the state's pioneer paper manufacturer, became a division of Equitable Bag Company and specialized in making lithographed kraft paper shopping bags for sale to department stores.

Champion Papers, Inc., expanded its Pasadena plant, built in 1937 (not 1939, as stated in Volume II) as a 150-ton mill employing 385 persons, to a 1967 capacity of 850 tons of pulp and 500 tons of paper a day, with more than 1,400 employees. Champion was still the largest mill in Texas in 1967, producing high-grade publication and writing papers from southern yellow pine.

Southland Paper Mills, Inc., which began operation in 1940 with a production capacity of 150 tons a day, was expanded to a 1967 capacity of one thousand tons. The plant made both newsprint and kraft paper, and it supplied paper to most Texas newspapers, many of which were stockholders in the firm. In 1967 Southland opened a new mill just outside Houston. (See Kurth, Ernest Lynn.)

Three other large paper mills have been established in Texas since World War II. The first was operated by Eastex, Inc., a subsidiary of Time, Inc. The plant at Evadale was opened in 1954 as a joint venture of Time, Inc., and the Houston Oil Company, which had large timberland holdings. Later the publishing company became sole owner. The Eastex plant had a capacity of more than 800 tons a day of bleached market pulp and paper in 1967, and expansion was under way to increase capacity to 1,150 tons.

A new paper mill was established at Orange in 1967, when Owens-Illinois, Inc., completed a $100,-000,000 plant for the manufacture of 325,000 tons a year of containerboard to be used as shipping boxes.

Completed in 1972 was the Texarkana Mill of International Paper Company, located near Atlanta, in Cass County. Costing approximately $72,000,-000, the mill was to produce 154,000 tons annually of coated bleached board for packaging and 60,000 tons of bleached hardwood pulp. The Texas paper industry was favored by market growth and by the availability of timberland, which gave promise of continued growth.

Robert H. Ryan

*Paphar Creek.

Paquache. See San Antonio Crossing.

*Paradise, Texas.

*Paradise Creek.

Parampamatuju Indians. In the middle eighteenth century the Parampamatuju (Parammatugu) Indians were listed as one of many groups that lived along the lower Rio Grande between its mouth and the vicinity of present Camargo, Tamaulipas. The maps of Jiménez Moreno and Saldivar place the Parampamatuju on the north bank of the Rio Grande in modern Hidalgo County, but this localization is only a matter of cartographic convenience. The name is said to mean "men who are painted bright red."

BIBLIOGRAPHY: W. Jiménez Moreno, "Tribus e idiomas del Norte de México," El Norte de México y el Sur de Estados Unidos (1944); G. Saldivar, Los Indios de Tamaulipas (1943).

T. N. Campbell

*Parantone Indians. These Coahuiltecan Indians are known through a single missionary report (1794) from Nuestra Señora del Espíritu Santo de Zuñiga,qv near Goliad. In this report they are identified as a subdivision of the Aranama, and at that time only twenty-one remained. The original territory of the Parantone was probably the same as that of the Aranama.

BIBLIOGRAPHY: Esteban L. Portillo, *Apuntes para la historia antigua de Coahuila y Texas* (1886).

T. N. Campbell

*Parathee Indians.

Parchaque Indians. The Parchaque (Pachague, Pachaque, Parchaca) Indians were Coahuiltecan Indians who are known only from the late seventeenth century. At this time they lived in northeastern Coahuila but sometimes crossed the Rio Grande to forage in Texas south of the Edwards Plateau. Apparently they were not the same people as the Paachique, whose name sometimes appeared on the same local list of bands. Identifications of Parchaque with Pachoche and Pakawa are not phonetically acceptable.

BIBLIOGRAPHY: H. E. Bolton (ed.), *Spanish Exploration in the Southwest, 1542–1706* (1916); F. W. Hodge (ed.), *Handbook of American Indians*, II (1910); J. R. Swanton, *Linguistic Material from the Tribes of Southern Texas and Northeastern Mexico* (1940).

T. N. Campbell

*Parchina Indians.

*Pardo, Manuel.

*Pardons and Paroles, Board of.

*Paredes, Alonzo de. *See* Posadas, Alonzo de.

*Parida Creek.

*Parilla Creek.

*Paris, Texas. Paris, seat of Lamar County, is an industrial center for an agricultural area. During the 1960's the city had three hospitals, a junior college, a commercial college, two libraries, two newspapers, two radio stations, forty churches, and a large soup plant. Lake Crook, Lake Gibbons, and Pat Mayse Reservoir provide recreational facilities as well as a municipal water supply. The city reported 480 businesses in 1970. The 1960 population was 20,977; the 1970 population was 23,441, according to the United States census.

*Paris, Choctaw, and Little Rock Railroad Company.

*Paris Female Institute.

*Paris Female Seminary.

*Paris and Great Northern Railroad Company.

Paris Junior College. Paris Junior College, Paris, was established on June 24, 1924, by the board of trustees of the city schools as a municipal junior college and part of the public school system. Classes first met in the high school building with an enrollment of ninety-one students. The college moved to the old post office building in September, 1925, and in 1931 the college became an independent unit of the public school system with its own administration and president. Accredited in 1934 by the Southern Association of Colleges and Secondary Schools, the college formed the Paris Junior College District in 1937, coterminous with the public school district. A new forty-acre campus, including main building, gymnasium, and stadium, was made possible in 1940 through a bond issue, the Work Projects Administration,qv and private gifts. The same year final separation from the public school district was made by election of a board of regents for the junior college.

During the 1963–1964 school year, the college added two dormitories housing seventy-two students each, a student center, and a library which contained 12,347 volumes by 1967. Regular term enrollment was 539 in 1967 and the faculty numbered thirty-two. Enrollment increased to 782 students by the regular term of 1969, and the library contained 16,704 volumes. Enrollment in the fall of 1974 was 1,793. Louis B. Williams was president in that year.

*Paris and Mt. Pleasant Railway Company.

*Parita, Texas.

*Parita Creek.

*Park, Milton.

*Park, Texas. (Bowie County.)

*Park, Texas. (Fayette County.)

*Park Springs, Texas.

*Parker, Benjamin F.

*Parker, Bonnie. Bonnie Parker was killed with Clyde Barrow qv eight miles from Gibsland, in Bienville Parish, Louisiana (not in Arcadia, Louisiana, as stated in Volume II), and was taken to Arcadia later that day. She was buried in West Dallas Fishtrap Cemetery. *See also* Hamer, Francis Augustus.

BIBLIOGRAPHY: H. G. Frost and J. H. Jenkins, "*I'm Frank Hamer*" (1968).

*Parker, Cynthia Ann.

*Parker, Daniel. Daniel Parker's church, which he organized in Lamotte, Crawford County, Illinois, was formally named the Pilgrim Predestinarian Regular Baptist Church of Jesus Christ. It is probably the first Primitive Baptist church in Texas, having been brought to Texas in 1834. *See also* Bethel Church, Sabine County.

Parker, Edwin B. Edwin B. Parker was born in Shelby County, Missouri, on September 7, 1868. He attended Central College in Fayette, Missouri, and was awarded the LL.B. degree by the University of Texas in 1889. He returned to Missouri and became secretary to the vice-president and general manager of the Missouri, Kansas, and Texas Railroad; he became assistant general passenger agent and continued in this position until 1893. He then practiced law at Houston, Texas, with the firm of Baker, Botts, Baker & Lovett (later Baker, Botts, Parker & Garwood), becoming a partner of this firm in 1897. From 1920 to 1922 he served as general counsel and board member of the Texas Company qv (now Texaco Inc.) in New York City. He retired from active law practice in 1925. While in Houston, he served as president of the City Park Board, president of the Houston Lighting and Power Company, and vice-president of the Guardian Trust Company and the South Texas Commercial Bank.

When the United States entered World War I, he went to Washington and volunteered as a dollar-a-year man. He helped organize the War Industries Board and Priorities Commission, to which he was appointed a member by President Woodrow Wilson. He also served as chairman of the United States Liquidation Commission, was umpire for the Mixed Claims Commission, United States and Germany in 1923, and was commissioner of the Tripartite Claims Commission involving the United States, Austria, and Hungary in 1926.

Parker was on the board of trustees of the Carnegie Endowment for International Peace and on the board of George Washington University; he was a member of the American Society of International Law, and the Council on Foreign Relations. He was awarded the United States Distinguished Service Medal and named officer of the Legion of Honor (France), Commandeur de l'Ordre de la Couronne (Belgium), and Order of Polonia Restituta, grade of Commander with the Star (Poland).

Parker married Katherine Putnam in 1894. He died in Washington, D.C., on October 30, 1929, and was buried in Greenwood Cemetery, Houston.

Richard T. Fleming

*Parker, Gustavus A.

*Parker, Isaac.

*Parker, James W.

*Parker, Jesse.

*Parker, John.

*Parker, Joshua.

Parker, Matthew. Matthew Parker, son of Jesse and Sarah (Wiley) Parker, was born in Franklin County, Georgia, on May 17, 1801. He came to Texas about 1822 and received a land grant located in present-day Sabine County. About 1826 he married Mary Isaacks, and they had twelve children. Mary died in 1845, and two years later Parker married Elizabeth Low. They had four children.

On December 20, 1836, Parker was appointed chief justice of Sabine County by Sam Houston. In 1840 he became commissioner on the land board in the same county. About 1855 Parker moved near Nordheim, in DeWitt County, where he died on March 19, 1862. He was buried in the Taylor Cemetery, approximately three miles south of Cuero.

Helen Gomer Schluter

*Parker, Quanah.

*Parker, Silas M.

*Parker, William.

*Parker, Texas. (Collin County.)

*Parker, Texas. (Johnson County.)

*Parker County. Parker County was a leading fruit, vegetable, and livestock producing area dur-

ing the 1960's. The income from livestock products was $12,692,018 in 1960, fourth highest in the state. The 1964 estimated income from fruit and vegetables was $1,300,000, with peanuts and pecans also contributing sizeable amounts. In 1964 livestock products totaled $8,319,645. With 165 Grade A dairies in 1965, the county was ninth in the state in number of dairy cows. Goat, sheep, and poultry raising were also important enterprises. By the early 1970's the average annual farm income was approximately $13 million. Oil production was negligible prior to 1966. Total crude production by 1973 was 822,713 barrels. Major tourist attractions include Weatherford Lake, Chandor Gardens, Texas Railroad Museum, the Double Log Cabin memorial, and Willow Park. The county partially supports Weatherford College and Weatherford Public Library.

The eastern part of the county during the 1960's was populated rapidly; small communities and housing developments sprang up as the suburban perimeter of Fort Worth extended into the county. The 1960 population was 22,880; the 1970 population was 33,888, according to the United States census.

Parker County Institute. *See* Parker Institute.

*Parker Creek.

Parker Institute. Parker Institute, at Whitt in northwestern Parker County, was established by a Professor Bales and his wife in 1881. In 1884 the Whitt Methodist Church assumed control of the school and chartered it under state law. Professor Amos Bennett, a graduate of DePauw University, became head of the institute. For the next nine years Bennett was a one-man faculty assisted by student instructors. The curriculum stressed Greek, Latin, higher mathematics, and physics, although the institute had no laboratory. In its twelve years of existence Parker Institute awarded only three, possibly four degrees. In June, 1891, Miss Beulah Sprueill (later Mrs. Sam B. Cook) became the school's first graduate. Jefferson Davis Sandefer,[qv] who later was president of Hardin-Simmons University for over thirty years, graduated the following June. Miles Lasater also is said to have graduated from Parker Institute although the date is not known. The last graduate, in June, 1893, was Charles Shirley Potts,[qv] later dean of the Southern Methodist University law school for twenty years. In 1893 Parker Institute surrendered its charter and became a public school.

BIBLIOGRAPHY: C. E. Bloss, "Old Parker Institute," *Texas Outlook* (March, 1938); Weatherford *Democrat*, August 11, 1939; Joe Harper, The History of Education in Parker County, Texas (M.A. thesis, Southwest Texas State College, 1951).

Charles E. Hanus

*Parker's Fort. *See* Fort Parker.

*Parks, William.

*Parks, Texas.

*Parks, State. In early 1972 Texas owned seventy-three parks of which thirty-eight were classified as recreation parks, eleven as scenic parks, nine as historic parks, and fourteen as historic sites; one, Hueco Tanks State Park, although unclassified in title, was both an historic and a recreation park. The classification of "recreation park" is applied to those areas designed primarily for the provision of outdoor recreational activities in an attractive natural setting. Generally such parks are water oriented and are located within an easy driving distance of large concentrations of people. The classification of "scenic park" is applied to those areas which preserve unique natural features of the state. Recreational facilities are usually provided at these parks, but are not allowed to impair the unique feature which the park was established to protect. The "historic park" and "historic site" classifications are applied to those areas set aside to perpetuate or memorialize a historic event, feature, or personage. Historic parks are normally large enough to incorporate recreational facilities.

The seventy-three parks in 1972 consisted of 75,-572 acres, of which 15,317 acres were water areas. The largest area of water in the state park system was Lake Corpus Christi, approximately 13,838 surface acres. Largest land acreage in a state park was in Palo Duro Canyon State Scenic Park, which consisted of 15,104 acres. The legislature authorized a $75,000,000 state park acquisition and development bond program in the form of a constitutional amendment which was approved by the voters of Texas on November 11, 1967. The legislature also enacted a bill which authorized the Texas Parks and Wildlife Commission qv to establish a state system of scientific areas for the purposes of education, scientific research, and the preservation of flora or fauna of scientific or educational value. During 1969 the legislature specifically directed that the first research area be established by transferring 717.3 acres of Buescher State Recreation Park to the University of Texas System,qv the area to be used by the University of Texas M. D. Anderson Hospital and Tumor Institute qv as a science park for medical and ecological research purposes. (See University of Texas Environmental Science Park.)

In 1972 the Texas Parks and Wildlife Department's qv policy continued to be to concentrate each year on the development of specified parks as part of a long-range program to improve the entire state park system.

A description of the individual state parks as they existed in 1972 follows (only those which have a number following the title were part of the parks system early in that year):

[Information on lakes, reservoirs, mountains, etc., which do not carry a qv below, may be found under their own titles. Ed.]

Abilene State Recreation Park (1.), located in Taylor County approximately twenty miles southwest of Abilene, and deeded to the state in 1933 by that city, consists of 490 acres. Nearby is the early frontier town of Buffalo Gap, through which passes the famous Butterfield Overland Mail Route.qv The park itself was a frequent campground for the Comanche Indians. Camping, swimming, hiking, and fishing are offered.

Acton State Historic Site (2.), located in Hood County approximately eight miles east of Granbury, is a .006-acre cemetery plot marking the 1860 burial site of Elizabeth Crockett, the second wife of David Crockett.qv A monument was erected by the state in 1911.

Alamo. The most famous of Texas historic sites, the Alamo is administered exclusively by the Daughters of the Republic of Texas.qv Located in downtown San Antonio, it has long been the foremost shrine of Texas history. *See* Alamo, History of the.

Atlanta State Recreation Park (3.), located in Cass County approximately twelve miles northwest of Atlanta on the southern bank of Lake Texarkana, was acquired in 1954 by a Department of the Army license. The 1,475-acre park offers camping, boating, fishing, swimming, and water skiing to its visitors.

Balmorhea State Recreation Park (4.), located in Reeves County four miles southwest of Balmorhea at the northern entrance to the Davis Mountains, was acquired in 1935 by deeds from private owners and the Reeves County Water Improvement District No. 1. In the 1940's a law suit resulted in the state's loss of most of the park, reducing it to the present park of forty-eight acres. The park provides camping and picnicking facilities as well as swimming in its two-acre springfed pool.

Bastrop State Scenic Park (5.), located in Bastrop County one mile east of Bastrop, is the site of the famous "Lost Pines," a timbered region isolated from the East Texas Piney Woods. The park consists of 2,033 acres, adjoining 900-surface-acre Lake Bastrop nearby, and was purchased by the state from the city of Bastrop and private owners in 1933–1935. The park offers nature study, fishing, camping, golfing, and swimming to visitors.

Battleship Texas. A former United States Navy battleship, the U.S.S. *Texas* is moored near the San Jacinto Monument qv in east Harris County and is administered by the Battleship *Texas* Commission. *See* San Jacinto Battleground State Historic Park, below; *see also Texas* in Volume II.

Bentsen-Rio Grande Valley State Scenic Park (6.), acquired by the state in 1944 and located along the Rio Grande in Hidalgo County six miles west of Mission, is a favorite spot for bird watchers. Many rare specimens are found in this 588-acre park, including Lichenstein's Oriole, Hooded Oriole, Gray Hawk, Pauraque, Groove-billed Ani, Longbilled Thrasher, Green Jay, Kiskadee Flycatcher, and Red-eyed Cowbird.

Big Spring State Recreation Park (7.), located in Howard County three miles south of Big Spring, consists of 332 acres transferred to the state in 1934 and 1935 by the city. The "big spring" nearby was the only watering place in a sixty-mile radius for herds of buffalo, antelope, and wild horses, and was used as a campsite by early Indians, explorers, and settlers. A drive to the top of a scenic mountain provides a panoramic view of the surrounding country. Hikers encounter varied geological formations.

Blanco State Recreation Park (8.) is located on the Blanco River one mile south of Blanco. This area was used as a campsite for early explorers and settlers. The 110-acre park has swimming, fishing, picnicking, and camping facilities. The land was acquired by the state in 1933 and 1934 by deeds from private owners.

Bonham State Recreation Park (9.), located in Fannin County four miles southwest of Bonham, offers scenic beauty as well as recreational activities centered on a sixty-five-acre lake. A wide variety of flowers, shrubs, and trees are found in this 300-acre park. Swimming, boating, fishing, and camping facilities are available. Bonham, which provided the park area to the state in 1933 and 1934, features the Sam Rayburn Library.qv

Brazos Island State Scenic Park (10.) is located in Cameron County approximately twenty-four miles east of Brownsville and is just north of the mouth of the Rio Grande. This undeveloped park consisting of 217 acres was created by legislative act in 1957 from lands held by the General Land Office qv and offers ocean fishing, surfing, and swimming as well as camping and nature study. Nearby are three battlegrounds: sites of the Mexican War battles of Palo Alto and Resaca de la Palma,qqv and the battle of Palmito Ranch,qv the last land engagement of the Civil War.

Buescher State Recreation Park (11.) [out of alphabetical order on page 339, Volume II], located in Bastrop County two miles northwest of Smithville, is part of one of the original Austin land grants. The park was acquired by the state between 1933 and 1936. The Old San Antonio Road,qv once connecting San Antonio de Bexar with the missions in East Texas, ran near the present-day park. This 1,013-acre park has picnicking, camping, and fishing facilities, and a scenic park road connects it to nearby Bastrop State Scenic Park. The park was reduced from 1,730 acres to 1,013 acres when part of the land was transferred to the University of Texas System to be used by the University of Texas M. D. Anderson Hospital and Tumor Institute qv as a science park for medical and ecological research purposes. (*See* University of Texas Environmental Science Park.)

Caddo Lake State Scenic Park (12.), located in Harrison County sixteen miles northeast of Marshall, consists of 478 acres, including an abandoned thirty-acre log pond. The park was acquired by the state in 1933–1937 and is accessible to nearby Caddo Lake.qv Picnicking, camping, boating, fishing, and nature study facilities are provided.

Cleburne State Recreation Park (13.), located in Johnson County approximately fifteen miles southwest of Cleburne, consists of 498 acres, including a 116-surface-acre lake. The state acquired this area from Johnson County, Cleburne, and private owners in 1935–1936. Fishing, boating, swimming, picnicking, and camping facilities are provided.

Copano Bay Causeway State Recreation Park (14.), located in Aransas County five miles north of Rockport, offers swimming, boat ramps, and pier fishing in Copano Bay. The park consists of six acres and was transferred from the jurisdiction of the Texas State Highway Department qv in 1967.

Copper Breaks State Recreation Park (15.), located in Hardeman County twelve miles south of Quanah, was acquired during 1970. It is a scenic area of 1,933 acres containing canyons that hold small lakes created by earthen dams. Recreational facilities were planned.

Daingerfield State Recreation Park (16.), acquired in 1935 and located in Morris County five miles southeast of Daingerfield, consists of 551 acres, including an eighty-surface-acre lake. The park provides picnicking, camping, boating, swimming, fishing, and nature study facilities.

Davis Mountains State Scenic Park (17.), located in Jeff Davis County approximately five miles northwest of Fort Davis, offers camping, picnicking, hiking, and a nature trail. The land was acquired by the state in 1933–1937. Indian Lodge, a resort hotel, is located in this 1,869-acre park. A scenic drive loops through the Davis Mountains. Nearby points of interest include Fort Davis National Historic Site (*see* Fort Davis), McDonald Observatory,qv the ghost town of Shafter, and scenic Limpia, Madera, Musquiz, and Keesey canyons.

Dinosaur Valley State Scenic Park (18.), located in Somervell County four miles west of Glen Rose, was acquired in 1969 through the State Park Acquisition and Development Bond Program. Initial park facilities were under construction in 1970. Within the park's 1,270 acres are found tracks representing three types of dinosaurs: the sauropods (*Brontosaurus* type), the theropods (*Tyrannosaurus rex* type), and the ornithopods (duckbilled dinosaur). It was at this location that the first sauropod tracks in the world were found.

Eisenhower Birthplace State Historic Site (19.) is located in the city of Denison in Grayson County. The three-acre site acquired in 1958 features the birthplace and early home of Dwight David Eisenhower,qv thirty-fourth president of the United States. A crank-type telephone with personal greetings from "Ike" is a main attraction.

Eisenhower State Recreation Park (20.), located in Grayson County approximately seven miles northwest of Denison, was named for Dwight David Eisenhower,qv thirty-fourth president of the United States. The 457-acre park site was transferred in 1954 by the Department of the Army to the state and is located on the shores of Lake Texoma, one of the largest man-made reservoirs in the United States. Facilities for picnicking, camping, fishing, boating, swimming, water skiing, and hiking are provided.

Falcon State Recreation Park (21.), located in Starr and Zapata counties thirty-two miles from Zapata, is located on Falcon Reservoir. The park was leased in 1954 from the International Boundary and Water Commission.qv Picnicking, camping, water skiing, swimming, and fishing facilities are provided in this 573-acre park. A 3,000-foot lighted airstrip is also available. Nearby points of interest are Mexico and Fort Ringgold qv in Rio Grande City.

Fannin Battleground State Historic Site (22.), located in Goliad County ten miles east of Goliad, is the site of the surrender of Colonel James Walker Fannin, Jr.,qv at the battle of Coleto qv on March 20, 1836, to Mexican General José Urrea.qv This thirteen-acre historic site was acquired by the Board of Control qv in 1914 and was transferred to the Parks and Wildlife Department in 1965. Nearby are Goliad State Historic Park (where Fannin and his men were massacred several days after their surrender) and General Zaragoza State Historic Site; also in the area are the restored Nuestra Señora de Loreto Presidio qv and the ruins of Nuestra Señora del Rosario Mission.qv

Fort Griffin State Historic Park (23.), deeded to the state by Shackelford County in 1935 and located fifteen miles north of Albany, offers picnicking, fishing from the Brazos River banks, and nature and historical studies. In the 503-acre park the ruins of old Fort Griffin qv are located on a bluff overlooking the townsite of Fort Griffin (the townsite is not in park boundaries). This park is the home of the official state Longhorn herd.

Fort Lancaster State Historic Site (24.), acquired in 1968 and located in Crockett County thirty-four miles west of Ozona, was named for old Fort Lancaster qv which was established at this site on August 20, 1855, by Captain Stephen D. Carpenter, 1st U.S. Infantry. The fort guarded the San Antonio-El Paso Road, protecting supplies and immigrants from hostile Indians. Historic ruins are found on this thirty-nine-acre site.

Fort Leaton State Historic Site (25.), acquired in 1967 and located about four miles east of Presidio, was named for a pioneer trading post established about 1846, at the site of Presidio del Norte,qv and taken over in 1848 by Ben Leaton, a former soldier of the Mexican War. The historic ruins of Fort Leaton qv are located on this five-acre site.

Fort McKavett State Historic Site (26.), acquired in 1967–1968 and located twenty-three miles west of Menard, in Menard County, is the site of the fort established on March 14, 1852, by Major Pitcairn Morrison of the 8th U.S. Infantry. Built by the U.S. War Department as protection for frontier settlers, it was originally called Camp San Saba (not to be confused with the Camp San Saba qv in southern McCulloch County) and was later renamed for Captain Henry McKavett, 8th U.S. Infantry, who was killed at the battle of Monterrey. Ruins of the fort, abandoned in 1883, are located on this one-acre site.

Fort Parker State Recreation Park (27.), acquired in 1935–1937 and located in Limestone County nine miles south of Mexia, was named for old Fort Parker,qv which was established in 1834 for protection from Indians. A replica of the fort is located on nearby Old Fort Parker State Historic Site. This 1,485-acre park contains a lake of 750 surface acres for water-oriented activities. Picnicking and camping facilities are provided.

Fort Richardson State Historic Site (28.), acquired in 1968 from the city of Jacksboro and located one-half mile south of the town, is the site of old Fort Jacksboro, founded in 1866 when six companies of the 6th U.S. Cavalry, under the command of H. H. McConnel, camped in Jacksboro. In 1867 the fort was renamed for Israel Richardson, who was fatally wounded at the battle of Antietam in 1862. Fort Richardson qv was part of the defensive system intended to protect the frontier, the cattle industry, and the Butterfield Overland Mail Route.qv The fort ruins, a museum, and picnic grounds are located on this forty-one-acre site.

Frio State Park. No longer administered by the Texas Parks and Wildlife Department, Frio State Park, fifty-one acres ten miles south of Pearsall, was transferred to Frio County.

Galveston Island State Recreation Park (29.), located in Galveston County approximately eight miles southwest of Galveston, is an undeveloped area of sand dunes and grasslands, including two miles of beach on the Gulf of Mexico. The 1,922-acre area was acquired during 1970.

Garner State Recreation Park (30.), acquired in 1934–1936 and located on the Frio River in Uvalde County fourteen miles north of Concan, was named for John Nance Garner,qv who served as vice-president of the United States from 1933 to 1941. Picnicking, camping, boating, fishing, swimming, and hiking facilities are provided in this 630-acre park. Nearby are the locations of Nuestra Señora de la Candelaria Mission,qv on the San Gabriel River just east of the town of San Gabriel; Camp Sabinal,qv five miles west of the town of Sabinal; and Fort Inge,qv on the Leona River south of Uvalde.

General Zaragoza State Historic Site (31.), a three-acre site acquired in 1961 from Goliad County and located two miles south of the town of Goliad, is the birthplace of General Ignacio Zaragoza,qv who assumed command of the Mexican army that met and defeated the French in 1862. The French proposed to march into Texas and establish liaison with Confederate forces and supply them with aid. Nearby are located Fannin Battleground State Historic Site and Goliad State Historic Park.

Goliad State Historic Park (32.), located on the San Antonio River one mile south of Goliad, contains reconstructed buildings of the Nuestra Señora del Espíritu Santo de Zuñiga Mission,qv originally established in 1722 and popularly referred to as La Bahía qv mission. This 209-acre park offers camping, fishing, hiking, and nature and historical studies. Other historic sites are nearby: the restored Nuestra Señora de Loreto Presidio (traditionally known as La Bahía presidio); the ruins of Nuestra Señora del Rosario Mission;qqv the General Zaragoza State Historic Site; and the Goliad Memorial Shaft, marking the common burial site of James Walker Fannin, Jr.,qv and several hundred other victims of the Goliad Massacre.qv *See also* Goliad State Park; La Bahía.

Goose Island State Recreation Park (33.), located in Aransas County approximately twelve miles northeast of Rockport, consists of 307 acres bounded by St. Charles and Aransas bays. Goose Island and the adjacent mainland were purchased by the state between 1931 and 1935. Boating, swimming, fishing, and camping are permitted. The "Big Tree," estimated to be 2,000 years old and certified as the largest Live Oak in Texas in 1969, is in the park. The Aransas National Wildlife Refuge,qv wintering grounds for the rare and endangered Whooping Cranes,qv is just across St. Charles Bay.

Governor Hogg Shrine State Historic Site (34.), located in the town of Quitman in Wood County, is a seventeen-acre memorial to James Stephen Hogg,qv governor of Texas from 1891 to 1895. The shrine was provided for by legislative act in 1941, and the site was acquired in 1946. It has a museum of furnishings which include some belonging to Governor Hogg while he was justice of the peace and editor of the weekly newspaper in Quitman.

Hueco Tanks State Park (35.), acquired from El Paso County in 1969 and located twenty-two miles northeast of El Paso, contains a unique attraction of natural "cisterns" formed by depressions in limestone which store water during the wet season. As this was the only water site for many miles, the Apaches, Kiowas, and Comanches camped here and left behind cave drawings telling of their adventures (*see* Rock Art, Indian). Evidence has been found that an early Pueblo tribe called the "basket makers" inhabited the area around 300 to 500 A.D. The site was included in the original Spanish land grant to the Tigua Indians, many of whom still live in nearby Ysleta (*see* Tigua Indians). Both historic and recreational, this 738-acre park provides picnicking, hiking, and archaeological study. *See also* Hueco Tanks.

Huntsville State Recreation Park (36.), acquired in 1937–1938 and located nine miles southeast of Huntsville, consists of 2,122 acres including 215-surface-acre Lake Raven (given the Indian name for Sam Houston). The park offers boating, fishing, swimming, camping, hiking, and nature studies and adjoins the Sam Houston National Forest.qv Sam Houston's homestead and grave are located in nearby Huntsville.

Independence State Park, acquired by legislative enactment in 1947, was leased to Baylor University until the year 2062. A seven-acre park, it was situated twelve miles north of Brenham in Washing-

ton County. It is no longer listed with the Texas Parks and Wildlife Department.

Indianola State Historic Park, acquired in 1958 by deed from Calhoun County, was transferred back to the county by 1971. The park contains three hundred acres along the shores of Lavaca Bay some thirteen miles southeast of Port Lavaca. The park features a swimming beach and facilities for fishing, boating, camping, and picnicking. The park area has a rich history of attempts by Spaniards, Frenchmen, Germans, and Americans to establish settlements. In 1856 the first camels for the "camel experiment" (*see* Camels in Texas) arrived at Indianola from North Africa. The park is not administered by the Texas Parks and Wildlife Department.

Inks Lake State Recreation Park (37.), located in Burnet County approximately thirteen miles west of Burnet, consists of 1,200 acres acquired in 1940 from the Lower Colorado River Authority qv and others. Adjacent to Inks Lake, the park provides picnicking, camping, boating, swimming, water skiing, fishing, golfing, and hiking facilities. Longhorn Cavern qv and a federal fish hatchery are located a few miles from the park; also nearby are quarries that furnished granite for the Capitol qv building.

Jeff Davis State Recreation Park (38.), located in Hill County approximately four miles southeast of Hillsboro, is a thirty-eight-acre wooded area with picnicking facilities. The area was acquired in 1924 and later leased to the American Legion qv for park purposes; although a part of the parks system, it is not operated by the Texas Parks and Wildlife Department.

Jim Hogg State Historic Park (39.), located in Cherokee County two miles northeast of Rusk, was dedicated as a memorial to James Stephen Hogg,qv first native-born governor of Texas. The 177-acre park, acquired in 1941 from Rusk, is located in the East Texas Piney Woods region.

Kerrville State Recreation Park (40.), located in Kerr County four miles southeast of Kerrville, offers boating, fishing, swimming, camping, picnicking, and hiking. This 497-acre park, acquired in 1934 from Kerrville, is adjacent to the Guadalupe River; old Camp Verde qv is nearby.

Lake Arrowhead State Recreation Park (41.), located in Clay County eight miles south of Wichita Falls, offers boating, swimming, and fishing. The 524-acre area was acquired in 1970 from the city of Wichita Falls.

Lake Brownwood State Recreation Park (42.), acquired in 1934 and located in Brown County twenty-two miles northwest of Brownwood, is situated near the geographical center of Texas. The park consists of 538 acres adjacent to Lake Brownwood and has facilities for camping, water skiing, fishing, swimming, and hiking. For a time the park was called Thirty-Sixth Division qv State Park.

Lake Colorado City State Recreation Park (43.), located in Mitchell County approximately eleven miles west of Colorado City, is an unusual scenic site for the West Texas area as it provides a variety of water-oriented activities. The 500-acre park was acquired in July, 1970, through a lease agreement with the Texas Electric Service Company and is adjacent to Lake Colorado City.

Lake Corpus Christi State Recreation Park (44.), located in San Patricio, Jim Wells, and Live Oak counties, approximately six miles southwest of Mathis, was leased in 1934 from the city of Corpus Christi. Water skiing, swimming, hiking, camping, and bird watching can be enjoyed. The park consists of 350 acres of land in San Patricio County and 13,838 surface acres of Lake Corpus Christi. Padre Island National Seashore qv is nearby.

Lake Fairfield State Recreation Park (45.), located in Freestone County, was in 1971 the newest addition to the park system.

Lake Somerville State Recreation Park (46.), located in Lee and Burleson counties, fifteen miles northwest of Brenham, consists of two areas (Nails Creek and Birch Creek) on Somerville Reservoir which are operated as a single park. The 940-acre park was leased from the Department of the Army in July, 1970; recreational facilities are being provided.

Lake Whitney State Recreation Park (47.), acquired by lease from the Department of the Army in 1954 and located in Hill County four miles west of Whitney, offers picnicking, camping, water skiing, boating, fishing, swimming, and geological study. Two hard-surface airstrips are also found in this 1,315-acre park. The park is adjacent to Lake Whitney.

Lipantitlán State Historic Site (48.), acquired in 1937 and located in Nueces County nine miles east of Orange Grove, is a five-acre area marking the site of a fort constructed in 1833 by the Mexican government in anticipation of trouble with Texas settlers. Fort Lipantitlán qv fell to Texas forces in 1835 (*see also* Lipantitlán Expedition). Lake Corpus Christi State Recreation Park is nearby.

Lockhart State Recreation Park (49.), acquired in 1934–1937 and located in Caldwell County four miles southwest of Lockhart, offers picnicking, camping, swimming, and fishing. This 257-acre park also housed a Confederate gunpowder factory. This Plum Creek Fight qv (1840) took place in the area.

Longhorn Cavern State Scenic Park (50.), located in Burnet County eleven miles south of Burnet, consists of 708 acres containing the famous and beautiful Longhorn Cavern.qv Scheduled tours conducted through the cavern, a nature trail, museum, and restaurant are operated in connection with the cavern. The cave was used by prehistoric man, Indians, robbers, and early white settlers; it also housed a Confederate gunpowder factory. This park, though part of the system, is not operated by the Parks and Wildlife Department. Inks Lake State Recreation Park is nearby.

Lyndon B. Johnson State Historic Park (51.), located in Gillespie County fourteen miles west of Johnson City, contains 269 acres obtained through private donations in 1967. The park was officially opened to the public in June, 1970, and features wildlife displays, nature trails, and picnic grounds. The ranch home of former President Lyndon Baines Johnson qv is located on the north bank of the Pedernales River across Ranch Road 1 from the park. A reconstruction of the Lyndon B. Johnson birthplace, located east of the ranch house at the end of Park Road 49, is open to the public. *See also* Lyndon Baines Johnson Birthplace, Boyhood Home, and Ranch.

Mackenzie State Recreation Park (52.), located in the city of Lubbock and named for General Ranald Slidell Mackenzie,qv is a 542-acre park offering a variety of recreational activities. The park is operated by Lubbock's parks and recreation department, and it features a cultivated prairie dog town.

Martin Dies, Jr., State Recreation Park (53.), located in Jasper and Tyler counties approximately ten miles southwest of Jasper, is adjacent to Town Bluff (also called Dam B) Reservoir. Picnicking, camping, water skiing, swimming, and fishing are offered. This 705-acre park, leased from the Department of the Army in 1964, is located at the edge of the Big Thicket qv and is eighteen miles from the Alabama-Coushatta Indian Reservation.qv

Meridian State Recreation Park (54.), acquired in 1933–1935 and located in Bosque County four miles southwest of Meridian, contains 461 acres on Bee Creek, which has bream, catfish, crappie, and bass fishing. Picnicking, camping, swimming, boating, and hiking are offered.

Mineral Wells State Park. No longer administered by the Texas Parks and Wildlife Department, Mineral Wells State Park, fifty-five acres in Palo Pinto County, was transferred to the city of Mineral Wells.

Mission San Francisco de los Tejas State Historic Park (55.), established in 1957 and located in Houston County approximately twenty-two miles northeast of Crockett, contains the replica of old San Francisco de los Tejas Mission,qv established in 1690. The 118-acre park is situated in the wooded area of David Crockett National Forest (*see* National Forests in Texas).

Monahans Sandhills State Scenic Park (56.), acquired in 1956–1957 and located in Ward and Winkler counties five miles northeast of Monahans, is a unique area of rolling sand dunes. Dune buggy rides are scheduled throughout the day. The 3,840-acre park has a museum which features the burial site of a prehistoric Indian.

Monument Hill State Historic Site (57.), located in Fayette County two miles southwest of La Grange, contains the tomb of and memorial to Texans who died in the Dawson Massacre qv and to those members of the Mier Expedition qv who were victims of the Black Bean Episode.qv The site is situated on a river bluff overlooking the Colorado River. The original .36-acre site of the tomb was acquired in 1949 by the Texas Parks and Wildlife Department; in 1956 the Catholic Archdiocese of San Antonio donated an additional 3.58 acres. *See also* Monument Hill.

Mother Neff State Recreation Park (58.), located in Coryell County eight miles west of Moody, was named for Isabella E. Neff, mother of Governor Pat Morris Neff,qv who in 1916 left a six-acre tract to the state for religious, educational, fraternal, and political purposes. The probation of Mrs. Neff's will in 1921 led to the creation by the legislature in 1923 of the state's Parks Board.qv Mother Neff State Park was the first official state park in Texas. In 1934 Pat Neff deeded 253 acres to the state for the balance of the park's total 259 acres. Adjacent to the Leon River, the park is now used primarily for camping, fishing, picnicking, bird watching, and nature study.

Normangee State Park. No longer administered by the Texas Parks and Wildlife Department, Normangee State Park, 500 acres in southwestern Leon County, was transferred to the town of Normangee.

Old Fort Parker State Historic Site (59.), located in Limestone County five miles north of Groesbeck, is the site of the old fort established in 1834. On this site the nine-year-old Cynthia Ann Parker qv was abducted by Comanche and Kiowa Indians. She was raised among the Indians, married Chief Peta Nocona qv and lived with the Indians for many years. Her son, Quanah Parker,qv was a well-known Comanche chief. A replica of the stockade fort can be inspected on a self-guided interpretive tour. This eleven-acre site was acquired in 1936; nearby is Fort Parker State Recreation Park.

Palmetto State Scenic Park (60.), located fifteen miles northwest of Gonzales, is a unique botanical area of sub-tropical vegetation, artesian wells, and natural springs. The 178-acre park offers picnicking, camping, fishing, and a nature study trail. The San Marcos River flows through this park, which was acquired in 1934–1937. Nearby Gonzales and Ottine played an important part in early Texas history. *See also* Ottine Swamp.

Palo Duro Canyon State Scenic Park (61.), located in Armstrong and Randall counties twelve miles east of Canyon, covers 15,104 acres of scenic geological formations that are millions of years old. Along with camping and picnicking facilities, there are riding stables, a sky ride, a miniature train ride, a prairie dog town, and an amphitheater. The musical drama *Texas*, produced by Paul Green, is presented each summer. The park, acquired in 1933, is particularly suited for nature and geological study.

Pedernales Falls State Scenic Park (62.), located in Blanco County approximately ten miles east of Johnson City, is an undeveloped scenic area including picturesque white water areas at the Pedernales Falls. Wildlife is abundant throughout the park. The 4,860-acre park was acquired from a private owner under the State Park Acquisition and De-

velopment Bond Program during 1970 and was officially opened to the public in June, 1970.

Port Isabel Lighthouse State Historic Site (63.), located in Cameron County in the city of Port Isabel (formerly Point Isabel), is a one-half acre tract acquired in 1950 upon which the historic Port Isabel Lighthouse qv was built in 1852.

Port Lavaca Causeway State Recreation Park (64.), located in Calhoun County on the west side of Lavaca Bay, consists of two acres and features a 3,200-foot-long lighted fishing pier extending into Lavaca Bay. The pier was formerly the old causeway until it was damaged by Hurricane Carla in 1961; the acreage and pier were then transferred from the Highway Department to the Texas Parks and Wildlife Department.

Possum Kingdom State Recreation Park (65.), located in Palo Pinto County thirty-two miles east of Breckenridge, is adjacent to Possum Kingdom Reservoir and was acquired in 1940 from the Brazos River Authority.qv The 1,615-acre park, situated in picturesque Palo Pinto Mountains, offers picnicking, camping, swimming, boating, water skiing, hiking, and a nature study trail. A portion of the official state herd of Texas Longhorns is maintained in the park. Originally much larger than its present 1,615 acres, much of the land was given back to the Brazos River Authority in 1965.

San Jacinto Battleground State Historic Park (66.), located in Harris County approximately ten miles east of Pasadena, is the site of the famous battle between the Texas and Mexican armies which, on April 21, 1836, won independence for Texas. The San Jacinto Monument and Museum qv commemorate those who participated in the battle. The 445-acre park is adjacent to the Houston Ship Channel,qv where the U.S.S. *Texas* (*see Texas*), a survivor of the battleship class, is moored. (For the origins of the park, *see* San Jacinto State Park in Volume II).

San José Mission State and National Historic Site (67.), located in Bexar County approximately six miles from downtown San Antonio, contains within its sixteen acres a restoration and replication of the mission established in 1720 by the Franciscan fathers. The park was established in 1941 by joint agreement of the federal government, the state of Texas, and the Catholic Archdiocese of San Antonio. San José Mission is known as "Queen of the Missions" because of its unique architecture and its artistically famous "Rose Window." The grounds also contain the Indian quarters, granary, mill, convents, and defense structures. (*See* San José y San Miguel de Aguayo Mission.)

Stephen F. Austin State Historic Park (68.), acquired in 1940 and located in Austin County approximately six miles east of Sealy, is the site of the township of San Felipe, seat of government of the Anglo American colonies in Texas. The Convention of 1832, the Convention of 1833, and the Consultation qqv (1835) were held here. A replica of Stephen F. Austin's home is found in this 664-

acre park, which offers picnicking, camping, swimming, and fishing facilities. There is also a nine-hole golf course.

**Thirty-Sixth Division State Park. See* Lake Brownwood State Recreation Park, above.

Tips State Recreation Park (69.), located in Live Oak County one mile west of the city of Three Rivers, consists of thirty-one acres adjacent to the Frio River. Picnicking, camping, and fishing are permitted. This park, acquired by the state in 1925, is leased to the city of Three Rivers, although it is included as a part of the state parks system.

**Tyler State Recreation Park* (70.), acquired in 1934–1935 and located ten miles north of Tyler, in Smith County, consists of 994 acres, including a 64-surface-acre lake. Picnicking, camping, boating, fishing, swimming, and hiking facilities are provided. Nearby Tyler, noted for its rose nurseries, sponsors a rose festival each fall.

Varner-Hogg Plantation State Historic Park (71.), located in Brazoria County two miles east of West Columbia, features the completely furnished old plantation home of Governor James Stephen Hogg.qv The park depicts traditional life in the early days of Texas from 1835 to 1850. There are scheduled guided tours of the home. This sixty-six-acre park, acquired in 1956, permits picnicking. The land originally belonged to Martin Varner,qv a member of Stephen F. Austin's Old Three Hundred qv colony.

Velasco State Recreation Park (72.) is an undeveloped area lying between mean low and high tide along the entire coastline of Brazoria County. Karankawa Indians were early inhabitants of the nearby area.

Washington-On-The-Brazos State Historic Park (73.), located in Washington County approximately eighteen miles northeast of Brenham, is the site of the first settlement of Stephen F. Austin's land grant (1821). This seventy-one-acre park is the site where the Convention of 1836 qv met, where it drew up the Declaration of Independence and the Constitution of the Republic,qqv and where it organized an *ad interim* government.qv Also located on this park site was the first capitol of the Republic of Texas (1836), the first county seat of Washington County (1837), and the home of the last president of the Republic of Texas, Anson Jones.qv The park features a number of historic structures; an auditorium and a museum were under construction in 1970. *See also* Washington State Park in Volume II.

Zaragoza State Historic Site. See General Zaragoza State Historic Site, above.

Vernen Liles
Marjorie Seidel

***Parks Board, State.** *See also* Parks and Wildlife Department, Texas.

***Parks Creek.**

***Parks Mountain.**

Parks and Wildlife Commission, Texas. *See* Parks and Wildlife Department, Texas.

Parks and Wildlife Department, Texas. The Texas Parks and Wildlife Department was created by the Fifty-eighth Legislature, replacing the Texas Game and Fish Commission (*see* Game, Fish, and Oyster Commission) and the State Parks Board.qv The merger became effective on August 23, 1963. Governed by the Texas Parks and Wildlife Commission, which is appointed by the governor, the department was headed by an executive director named by the commissioners. The first executive director of the new department was J. Weldon Watson. The first three members of the Texas Parks and Wildlife Commission were chairman Will E. Odom, A. W. Moursund, and James M. Dellinger.

Vernen Liles

***Parlin, Hanson Tufts.**

***Parmer, Allen.**

***Parmer, Martin.**

***Parmer County.** Parmer County, a leading agricultural area, in 1964 was fifth in total value of farm products sales ($38,482,906), sixth in total sales from crops ($29,905,283), and twentieth in sales from livestock (approximately $8,577,600). Wheat production in 1968 was 3,724,000 bushels, second largest in the state. Although remaining a leading county in crop income in the 1970's, income from livestock increased considerably with large cattle-feeding operations, and two-thirds of the county's average annual farm income of $92,500,000 in the early 1970's was from cattle, sheep, and hogs. The county's 1960 population was 9,583; the 1970 population was 10,509, according to the United States census.

***Parmerton, Texas.**

***Parnell, Texas.** (Hall County.)

Parnell, Texas. (Roberts County.) Parnell, the first county seat of Roberts County, had a post office from 1889 to 1898. Parnell and Miami wrangled over the courthouse site. The Creswell Land and Cattle Company, Limited, favored the Parnell site in the middle of the county twenty-two miles northwest of Miami, while people of Miami pushed its interest as the railroad town. Miami won the final election in 1898, and few traces remained of Parnell in 1972.

Grover C. Ramsey

***Parr, Archer (Archie).** Archer (more often called Archie) Parr, son of George Berham and Sarah Pamela (Givens) Parr, was born at Saluria, on Matagorda Island in Calhoun County (not at Indianola, as stated in Volume II), on December 25, 1860 (or possibly 1861). He was married to Elizabeth Allen, and they had six children (not five; one of the six, a daughter, predeceased him). Archer Parr served in the Texas Senate for twenty (not twenty-two) consecutive years; he lost his seat in the Senate when he was defeated in the election of 1934 (not 1932). His service extended from the Thirty-fourth Legislature (January, 1915) through the Forty-third Legislature (November, 1934).

BIBLIOGRAPHY: Records, Bureau of Vital Statistics, Texas State Department of Health; *Members of the Legislature of the State of Texas from 1846 to 1939* (1939); Biographical File, Barker Texas History Center, University of Texas at Austin.

Parr, George Berham. George Berham Parr, son of Elizabeth (Allen) and Archer (Archie) Parr,qv was born in San Diego, Texas, on March 7, 1901. At the age of thirteen he served as his father's page boy in the Texas Senate, so he observed as a youngster the machinations of Texas politics. He spoke Spanish fluently, another political asset in the area of South Texas which his father dominated. He attended the University of Texas (Austin) from 1921 to 1925, the last two years in the university's law school, although he did not obtain a degree. He passed the Bar examination in 1926 and was soon thereafter elected judge of Duval County, being the only candidate on the ballot—a familiar Parr technique. With his father's powerful backing he had become, at age twenty-five, Duval County's political boss, succeeding his father as the new "Duke of Duval." Through alliances with political bosses in fifteen South Texas counties, along with three directly controlled (Duval, Jim Wells, and Nueces counties), the Parr family held immense power and exerted considerable influence on state and national politics. George Parr was married to Thelma Duckworth, and they had one daughter; they were divorced about 1949, and Parr later was married to Eva Perez; they also had one daughter.

A millionaire rancher, oilman, and banker, George Parr first ran afoul of the law in 1934, when federal court charges were brought against him for income tax evasion for the year 1928. He evaded a trial (and thus avoided public airing of the sources of his income) by pleading guilty; he was fined $5,000 and given a two-year suspended prison sentence. In 1936 his probation was revoked and he served nine and one-half months in prison. In 1946 President Harry S. Truman gave him a pardon which restored his civil rights and allowed him to hold public office again. He was appointed judge again in 1949 and was reelected to that position in 1950.

In 1948, when Coke R. Stevenson,qv former governor of Texas, had apparently defeated Congressman Lyndon Baines Johnson qv for a seat in the United States Senate in the closest senatorial race in the nation's history, an amended return was sent in from Precinct 13 in Jim Wells County, a Parr stronghold, giving 201 votes for Johnson and 2 for Stevenson. This gave Johnson the Senate seat by a plurality of 87 votes, earned him the nickname of "Landslide Lyndon," and made it possible for Johnson to achieve the prominence which later enabled him to become president of the United States. Coke Stevenson's accusations of fraud were never carried to a conclusion because the voting lists from Box 13 mysteriously disappeared and U. S. Supreme Court Justice Hugo Black quashed the federal investigation.

The incident brought national attention to Parr, and during the 1950's national magazine and news media articles accused him of ruling by threats, economic boycotts, and maintaining a private army of *pistoleros* who posed as deputy sheriffs. He was accused of using tax funds obtained illegally from the county treasury and the school districts, and the Internal Revenue Service again probed into his financial affairs. The large Mexican American population in South Texas continued to support him, however, and Parr claimed that the large conservative interests were out to ruin him because he looked after the interests of the poor and Spanish-speaking people. In 1957 he was convicted and sentenced to a ten-year term for using the mails to defraud the Benavides Independent School District of tax funds, but upon appeal the U. S. Supreme Court reversed the decision in 1960. In 1963 the last dismissals were granted on numerous indictments against Parr from the 1950's investigations involving income tax evasion and theft.

George Parr was indicted again in June, 1973, for income tax evasion; convicted on March 19, 1974, he was sentenced to ten years in prison (five of them suspended) and fined $14,000. The case was on appeal when Parr committed suicide near Julian Windmill on his ranch in Duval County on April 1, 1975. He was buried in Benavides Cemetery, and many of his mourners were Mexican Americans who believed that he had been a stalwart friend to the Spanish-speaking people of South Texas.

BIBLIOGRAPHY: Records, Bureau of Vital Statistics, Texas State Department of Health; Biographical File, Barker Texas History Center, University of Texas at Austin.

Eldon S. Branda

*Parramore, James H.

*Parrilla, Diego Ortiz.

*Parris, Texas.

*Parrish, Lucien Walton.

*Parrott, Robert B.

*Parsley Hill, Texas.

Parsons, Albert Richard. Albert Richard Parsons was born on June 24, 1848, in Montgomery, Alabama. Orphaned at five, he was sent to Texas to live with an older brother, William Henry Parsons,qv editor of the Tyler *Telegraph*, who was moving to central Texas to practice law about the time of Albert's arrival. In 1859 Albert was sent to Waco for schooling; a year later he went to Galveston to learn the printer's trade as an apprentice to Willard Richardson,qv Galveston *News* qv editor. After Texas left the Union, Parsons, only thirteen, joined a local military group and took part in the capture of federal troops at Indianola. When Richardson refused to allow him to join a regular military unit, he ran away and enlisted in an artillery company at Sabine Pass. At the conclusion of his year's enlistment, he left to join his brother William, then commander of Parsons' Brigade,qv Texas Cavalry. He served as a scout for the brigade throughout the rest of the war, taking part in several campaigns including the Red River campaign.qv

Returning to Waco at the conclusion of the war, Parsons farmed and worked as a typesetter to finance six months of study at Waco University. By 1868 he was converted to Republican principles, and he established a newspaper, the *Spectator*, to advocate Negro rights. He addressed Republican rallies throughout central Texas in an attempt to organize and get out the Negro vote. He was rewarded for these activities with an appointment as assistant United States internal revenue assessor for Texas. On June 10, 1871, Parsons married Lucy Eldine Gonzales.

In 1871 Parsons was elected reading secretary for the Texas Senate, and later he was named chief deputy collector of internal revenue in Austin. He had continued newspaper writing as traveling correspondent for the Houston *Telegraph* ᑫᵛ from 1869 to about 1871 and as correspondent for the *Texas Agriculturist*. While on tour as correspondent he visited Chicago, where he located in 1873. He became a Marxist and joined the Social Democratic party. One of the most effective leaders in the radical ranks, Parsons began to travel as a propagandist for the Socialist Labor party and in 1881 was the candidate of the Socialist faction for mayor of Chicago. By 1883 he had rejected political action and claimed to be an anarchist. He became the editor of a local radical weekly, *The Alarm*, in 1884. He remained active in the labor movement and was one of the speakers at the meeting on May 4, 1886, which culminated in the Haymarket Riot. Although Parsons was not present at the rally when the bomb (that killed seven policemen) was thrown, he was indicted with seven other anarchists as an accessory to the murder. Never apprehended by the police, Parsons voluntarily appeared for the trial. Despite an eloquent statement in his defense, Parsons was found guilty and sentenced to death. Most scholars have concluded that Parsons could have saved his life by appealing to the governor for clemency, but he refused to abandon his associates. One of the six condemned to death, Parsons, along with three others, was hanged on November 11, 1887. He was survived by his wife and two children.

BIBLIOGRAPHY: Henry David, *The History of the Haymarket Affair* (1936); Lucy E. Parsons, *Life of Albert R. Parsons* (1889); *Dictionary of American Biography*, VII (1934).

James V. Reese

*Parsons, Edmund Byrd.

*Parsons, William H. William H. Parsons served as an acting brigadier general in the Confederate Army, but he was never promoted to that rank (as stated in Volume II). He served in the Twelfth Texas Legislature as a Republican senator.

BIBLIOGRAPHY: John Q. Anderson (ed.), *Campaigning with Parsons' Texas Cavalry Brigade, CSA* (1967).

*Parsons, Texas. (Kerr County.)

*Parsons, Texas. (Parker County.)

Parsons' Brigade. Parsons' Brigade was created in Arkansas in September, 1862, when the 19th and the 21st Texas Cavalry regiments and Morgan's Texas Cavalry Battalion joined the 12th Texas Cavalry Regiment, which already had seen action in skirmishes north of Little Rock that summer. In April, 1863, the 19th and 21st regiments under Colonel George Washington Carter ᑫᵛ took part in a raid on Cape Girardeau, Missouri, while the other units moved south into Louisiana under Colonel William H. Parsons.ᑫᵛ In the summer of 1863 the brigade reunited and raided Union posts west of the Mississippi River in efforts to divert Federal troops from the Vicksburg campaign. The brigade was sent to Texas in the fall of 1863, but returned to Louisiana to assist in defeating Union forces in the Red River campaign ᑫᵛ in the spring of 1864. Thereafter, the brigade served in Arkansas and Texas until the end of the war.

BIBLIOGRAPHY: *A Brief and Condensed History of Parsons' Texas Cavalry Brigade* (1892); Stephen B. Oates, *Confederate Cavalry West of the River* (1962).

Parsons' Seminary, Texas. Parsons' Seminary was one of the principal towns in Travis County in 1859. It was situated about twelve miles east of Austin and was noted for its female school.

BIBLIOGRAPHY: *Texas Almanac* (1936).

*Partridge Creek.

*Party Pledge. *See* Election Laws.

*Parvin, Texas.

*Pasadena, Texas. Pasadena, in southeastern Harris County, was incorporated in 1943 and adopted its present home-rule charter form of government in 1964. In 1950 the Washburn Tunnel, which carries traffic beneath the Houston Ship Channel,ᑫᵛ was completed and connected Pasadena with north channel towns and the western part of Houston. Since 1955 the city has built a new city hall, a library building, a park and recreation complex, and a memorial building. There has been extensive improvement and construction of water and sewage disposal facilities. In the 1960's the economy was directly influenced by the petrochemical industry ᑫᵛ and the National Aeronautics and Space Administration's Manned Spacecraft Center.ᑫᵛ The area along the Houston Ship Channel became highly industrialized, and major products of the Pasadena area were oil field equipment, machinery and tools, chemical products, iron and steel, synthetic rubber, paper, building material, cement, bags and bagging, paint, containers, petroleum, cottonseed, livestock, rice, and flour. In 1966 the town had thirty-one schools, six hospitals, three banks, eighty-five churches, a business college, a junior college, daily and weekly newspapers, and two radio stations. Of the city's 760 businesses in 1967, there were twenty-four manufacturers. The second largest city in Harris County in 1970, Pasadena reported a total of 870 businesses that year. Historic sites of the battle of San Jacinto are nearby. In 1960 Pasadena had a population of 58,737; the 1970 population was 89,277, according to the United States census. *See also* Houston Standard Metropolitan Statistical Area.

Pasalve Indians. In the late seventeenth and early eighteenth centuries the Pasalve (Pajalve,

Pastalbe, Pastalve, Paxalve) Indians ranged the area on both sides of the Rio Grande that is now northeastern Coahuila, northwestern Nuevo León, and the adjoining part of Texas south of the Edwards Plateau. Between 1698 and 1727 some of the Pasalve were at Mission Santa María de los Dolores de la Punta at modern Lampazos, Nuevo León. Swanton listed the Pasalve as probably Coahuiltecan in speech, which appears reasonable. One name variant, Pastalve, has caused confusion because, when handwritten, it is easily mistaken for Pastaluc, which is a variant of Pastaloca.

BIBLIOGRAPHY: F. W. Hodge (ed.), *Handbook of American Indians*, II (1910); P. O. Maas, *Viajes de misioneros Franciscanos á la conquista del Nuevo México* (1915); M. Orozco y Berra, *Geografía de las lenguas y carta etnográfica de México* (1864); J. R. Swanton, *Linguistic Material from the Tribes of Southern Texas and Northeastern Mexico* (1940); R. S. Weddle, *San Juan Bautista: Gateway to Spanish Texas* (1968).

T. N. Campbell

Pascagoula Indians. When first known in 1699 the Pascagoula (Pacha-Ogoula, Pascagola, Pascaboula, Paskaguna) Indians lived in southwestern Alabama and southeastern Mississippi, but in the middle eighteenth century they crossed the Mississippi and settled near the mouth of the Red River in Louisiana. In the early nineteenth century pressure from American settlers forced them farther westward. Some of the Pascagoula entered Texas and lived with the Biloxi near the Neches River in present Angelina County, and others seem to have settled on the Red River in northeastern Texas. Most of the Pascagoula in Texas probably accompanied the Biloxi to Indian Territory, now Oklahoma, but at least a few remained and evidently joined the Alabama of present Polk County (two of their descendants were found there in 1908). Some linguists have considered the Pascagoula as Siouan, others as Muskhogean.

BIBLIOGRAPHY: F. W. Hodge (ed.), *Handbook of American Indians*, II (1910); J. R. Swanton, *Indian Tribes of the Lower Mississippi Valley and Adjacent Coast of the Gulf of Mexico* (1911), *The Indians of the Southeastern United States* (1946), *The Indian Tribes of North America* (1952).

T. N. Campbell

*Paschal, Frank.

*Paschal, Franklin Lafitte.

*Paschal, George Washington. George Washington Paschal's second wife was Mrs. Marcia (Duval) Price, daughter of William Pope Duval qv (governor of Florida, 1822–1834). Paschal and Mrs. Price were married on March 25, 1852.

BIBLIOGRAPHY: *Texas State Gazette*, April 3, 1852.

*Paschal, Isaiah Addison.

*Paschal, Thomas Moore.

*Paschal County.

*Pasche, Texas.

*Pasnacan Indians. The Pasnacan [not Pasnacanes, as shown in Volume II] (Panascan, Pasnacano, Tacasnan) Indians, possibly Coahuiltecan in speech, lived near the Texas coast between the San Antonio and Nueces rivers. When first known in the

eighteenth century they were closely associated with the Orejones, Pamaque, and Piguique. Some contemporary Spanish writers considered the Pasnacan, Piguique, and Viayan as subdivisions of the Pamaque, who were linked with the area around the mouth of the Nueces River on Nueces and Corpus Christi bays. At intervals during the first half of the eighteenth century groups of Pasnacan entered at least two of the San Antonio missions—San José y San Miguel de Aguayo and San Juan Capistrano,qqv the latter in 1743. In 1754 a few Pasnacan seem to have been induced to enter Mission San Francisco Vizarron in northeastern Coahuila, along with other groups from the lower Texas coast. It is evident that the Pasnacan lost their identity in the latter part of the eighteenth century in local mission populations of Coahuila and Texas.

BIBLIOGRAPHY: F. C. Chabot, *San Antonio and Its Beginnings* (1931); F. W. Hodge (ed.), *Handbook of American Indians*, II (1910); F. C. Chabot (ed.), *Excerpts from the Memorias for the History of Texas, by Father Morfi* (1932); J. R. Swanton, *Linguistic Material from the Tribes of Southern Texas and Northeastern Mexico* (1940).

T. N. Campbell

PASO. *See* Political Association of Spanish-Speaking Organizations.

Paso de Francia. *See* San Antonio Crossing.

*Paso Real, Texas.

Pasqual Indians. This name, which appears in the baptismal records of San Antonio de Valero Mission qv of San Antonio, may be a variant of Pazagual, the name of a Coahuiltecan group represented at San Bernardo Mission qv in 1708, near present Guerrero in northeastern Coahuila. Swanton listed the Pasqual as probably Coahuiltecan in speech.

BIBLIOGRAPHY: F. W. Hodge (ed.), *Handbook of American Indians*, II (1910); P. O. Maas, *Viajes de misioneros Franciscanos á la conquista del Nuevo México* (1915); J. R. Swanton, *Linguistic Material from the Tribes of Southern Texas and Northeastern Mexico* (1940).

T. N. Campbell

*Pass Cavallo.

Password. *See* El Paso County Historical Society.

*Pastaloca Indians. In the late seventeenth century the Pastaloca (Pastalac, Pastalath, Pastaloque, Pastaluc, Pastulac, and other variants) Indians were linked with a strip of territory that lies between the Nueces and Rio Grande, an area that embraces parts of several Texas counties—Dimmit, La Salle, Maverick, Webb, and Zavala. In April, 1690, they were encountered by Spaniards on the Nueces River, probably in modern Dimmit or Zavala County, encamped with eight other groups. The next year, June, 1691, they were reported at a *ranchería* in present southern Maverick County, some ten miles north of the Rio Grande, this time with five other groups. All of the Indian bands with which the Pastaloca were associated are considered Coahuiltecan-speakers, as Swanton has indicated.

Afterward some of the Pastaloca entered two missions near modern Guerrero in northeastern

Coahuila—San Bernardo,qv known to have been there between 1703 and 1727, and San Juan Bautista,qv from 1708 to 1738. In the 1720's a few Pastaloca also entered San Antonio de Valero Mission qv of San Antonio. It is clear that the Pastaloca lost their identity among the mission Indian populations of Coahuila and Texas.

Some confusion has developed because of the fact that, when handwritten, the variant Pastaluc can easily be misread as Pastalve, a variant of Pasalve, and vice versa. Hodge equated Pastaloca with Patacal, but this is an error.

BIBLIOGRAPHY: L. Gómez Canedo, *Primeras exploraciones y poblamiento de Texas, 1686–1694* (1968); C. W. Hackett (ed.), *Pichardo's Treatise on the Limits of Louisiana and Texas*, II (1934); F. W. Hodge (ed.), *Handbook of American Indians*, II (1910); P. O. Maas, *Viajes de misioneros Franciscanos á la conquista del Nuevo México* (1915); J. R. Swanton, *Linguistic Material from the Tribes of Southern Texas and Northeastern Mexico* (1940); R. S. Weddle, *San Juan Bautista: Gateway to Spanish Texas* (1968).

T. N. Campbell

Pastate Indians. The name Pastate occurs only in a document of 1748 which lists the tribes of central and eastern Texas who had requested that missions be founded on the San Gabriel River (vicinity of present Rockdale). The recognizable names on this list indicate tribes of diverse linguistic affinity—Atakapan, Caddoan (including both Caddo and Wichita groups), Karankawan, and Tonkawan. To which of these linguistic groups the Pastate belonged cannot be determined. It is possible that the Pastate are the same as the Postito, who were apparently Coahuiltecans from west of San Antonio, but no recognizable Coahuiltecan group name appears on this list of Indian petitioners.

BIBLIOGRAPHY: H. E. Bolton, *Texas in the Middle Eighteenth Century* (1915); C. W. Hackett (ed.), *Pichardo's Treatise on the Limits of Louisiana and Texas*, I (1931).

T. N. Campbell

*Pasteal Indians. Although this name is entrenched in the literature, it is erroneous and should be removed. Pasteal is an early copyist's misreading of "Patcil" (*see* Patacal Indians), a Coahuiltecan group that ranged over northeastern Coahuila and possibly the adjoining part of Texas in the late seventeenth and early eighteenth centuries.

BIBLIOGRAPHY: F. W. Hodge (ed.), *Handbook of American Indians*, II (1910); J. R. Swanton, *Linguistic Material from the Tribes of Southern Texas and Northeastern Mexico* (1940), *The Indian Tribes of North America* (1952).

T. N. Campbell

*Pasteur Institute of Texas. The Pasteur Institute of Texas, having merged with the Bureau of Laboratories in 1928, underwent another change in 1958, when the division became the section of laboratories of the State Department of Public Health.qv The performance of laboratory tests necessary in diagnosis of rabies, polio, encephalitis, and other diseases remained an important function of the department.

Pastia Indians. In the early eighteenth century the Pastia (Pasti, Paxti) Indians lived southwest of present San Antonio, but in response to Apache pressures they moved eastward to an area between the San Antonio and Guadalupe rivers southeast of San Antonio. The evidence is reasonably clear that they were a hunting and gathering people who spoke a Coahuiltecan dialect. They were represented at two San Antonio missions—San José y San Miguel de Aguayo (after 1720) and Nuestra Señora de la Purísima Concepción de Acuña (after 1741).qqv Although the names are similar, the Pastia were not the same as the Pasteal, for Pasteal is an early copyist's misreading of "Patcal" (*see* Patacal Indians).

BIBLIOGRAPHY: H. E. Bolton, *Texas in the Middle Eighteenth Century* (1915); P. P. Forrestal, "The Solís Diary of 1767," *Preliminary Studies of the Texas Catholic Historical Society*, I (1931); M. A. Habig, *The Alamo Chain of Missions: San Antonio's Five Old Missions* (1968); F. W. Hodge (ed.), *Handbook of American Indians*, II (1910); P. O. Maas, *Viajes de misioneros Franciscanos á la conquista del Nuevo México* (1915); J. A. Morfi (C. E. Castañeda, ed.), *History of Texas, 1673–1779* (1935); G. Tous, "The Espinosa-Olivares-Aguirre Expedition of 1709," *Preliminary Studies of the Texas Catholic Historical Society*, I (1930); C. I. Wheat, *Mapping the Transmississippi West, 1540–1861*, Map No. 115 (1957); R. S. Weddle, *San Juan Bautista: Gateway to Spanish Texas* (1968).

T. N. Campbell

*Pastoren Creek.

*Pastura, Texas.

Patacal Indians. The Patacal (Patcal, Pasteal—misreading of Patcal) Indians appear to have ranged over northeastern Coahuila and perhaps the adjoining part of Texas in the late seventeenth and early eighteenth centuries. In 1727 it was recorded that the Patacal had been at mission San Juan Bautista qv near present-day Guerrero in northeastern Coahuila but had withdrawn and moved southward. They were probably Coahuiltecan in speech.

BIBLIOGRAPHY: M. Orozco y Berra, *Geografía de las lenguas y carta etnográfica de México* (1864); J. W. Powell, *Indian Linguistic Families of America North of Mexico* (1891); R. S. Weddle, *San Juan Bautista: Gateway to Spanish Texas* (1968).

T. N. Campbell

*Pataguo Indians. The Pataguo (Patagahu, Pataguaque, Patao, Pataque, Patauo, Patou, and others) Indians were first recorded in 1670, at which time they were said to be living somewhere well to the north of Monterrey, Nuevo León. In 1674–1675 they were ranging both sides of the Rio Grande in the area now embraced by northeastern Coahuila and the adjoining part of Texas south of the Edwards Plateau. In 1690 the Pataguo were visited by Spaniards at a *ranchería* on the Nueces River, probably in modern Dimmit or Zavala counties, which they shared with eight other groups, all evidently of Coahuiltecan affiliation. The next year, 1691, they were again encountered, but farther east, evidently on or near the Frio River in present Frio County, where they shared a *ranchería* with twelve other bands.

Some Pataguo entered San Francisco Solano Mission qv of northeastern Coahuila as early as 1704, but in 1708 unmissionized Pataguo were still living north of the Rio Grande. In 1718 Solano was moved to present San Antonio and renamed San Antonio de Valero Mission.qv Many Pataguo evidently moved to San Antonio, for their name appears in the Valero records in at least nine variants between 1720 and 1763.

Swanton identified both "Patague" and "Patou" as probable Coahuiltecan-speakers. These names are both variants of Pataguo. The record suggests that the Pataguo lost their ethnic identity among the mission Indians of San Antonio during the latter part of the eighteenth century.

BIBLIOGRAPHY: H. E. Bolton (ed.), *Spanish Exploration in the Southwest, 1542–1706* (1916); L. Gómez Canedo, *Primeras exploraciones y poblamiento de Texas, 1686–1694* (1968); M. A. Hatcher, "The Expedition of Don Domingo Terán de los Ríos into Texas," *Preliminary Studies of the Texas Catholic Historical Society,* II (1932); F. W. Hodge (ed.), *Handbook of American Indians,* II (1910); P. O. Maas, *Viajes de misioneros Franciscanos á la conquista del Nuevo México* (1915); Esteban L. Portillo, *Apuntes para la historia antigua de Coahuila y Texas* (1886); J. R. Swanton, *Linguistic Material from the Tribes of Southern Texas and Northeastern Mexico* (1940).

T. N. Campbell

Patalca Indians. The Patalca (Iatalca, Pataloque, Patuleco) Indians were first reported in northeastern Coahuila during the 1670's under the names Pataloque and Patuleco. Thereafter they appear under the name Patalca at Nuestra Señora de la Purísima Concepción de Acuña Mission qv in San Antonio, which they first entered in 1733. Since most of their associates were Coahuiltecans, it seems likely that the Patalca spoke a Coahuiltecan dialect.

BIBLIOGRAPHY: H. E. Bolton, "Spanish Mission Records at San Antonio," *Quarterly of the Texas State Historical Association,* X (1906–1907); H. E. Bolton, *Texas in the Middle Eighteenth Century* (1915); J. J. Figueroa Torres, *Fr. Juan Larios: Defensor de los Indios y fundador de Coahuila, 1673–1676* (1963); F. W. Hodge (ed.), *Handbook of American Indians,* II (1910); Esteban L. Portillo, *Apuntes para la historia antigua de Coahuila y Texas* (1886); R. G. Santos, "A Preliminary Survey of the San Fernando Archives," *Texas Libraries,* XXVIII (1966–1967).

T. N. Campbell

*Pataquilla Village.

*Patarabueye Indians. This name was applied by the Spanish to certain settled peoples along the Rio Grande and lower Río Conchos, in Mexico, near present Presidio. The Otomoaco of the late sixteenth century seem to have been the same people later known as Patarabueye, who are generally considered to be Jumano Indians. J. C. Kelley has used the name Patarabueye to refer to the agricultural branch of the Jumano and the name Jumano to refer to the nomadic, bison-hunting branch of the Jumano. Occasionally the Patarabueye have been identified with certain Wichita groups on the Red River, but this cannot be substantiated.

BIBLIOGRAPHY: F. W. Hodge (ed.), *Handbook of American Indians,* II (1910); J. C. Kelley, "The Historic Indian Pueblos of La Junta de los Ríos," *New Mexico Historical Review,* XXVII (1952), XXVIII (1953); J. C. Kelley, "Juan Sabeata and Diffusion in Aboriginal Texas," *American Anthropologist,* LVII (1955); W. W. Newcomb, Jr., *The Indians of Texas* (1961).

T. N. Campbell

*Patents in the Republic of Texas.

*Patilo, Texas.

*Patiri Indians. This small tribe, which is now regarded as Atakapan in language, lived in southeastern Texas during the eighteenth century. The Patiri seem to have ranged over the territory that lay between that of the Bidai and Akokisa Indians. This would place them in the area between Houston and Huntsville. From 1749 to 1751 the Patiri, along with other Atakapan-speaking groups, particularly the Akokisa, Bidai, and Deadose, were represented at San Ildefonso Mission qv near present Rockdale. After this the Patiri dropped out of sight. They probably lost their ethnic identity among the Bidai and Akokisa, who survived into the nineteenth century. Sound correspondences in the names suggest that the Patiri may have been the same people as the Petaro who in the late seventeenth century were listed in records of the La Salle Expedition qv as living in the same general area.

BIBLIOGRAPHY: P. Margry, *Découvertes et établissements des Français dans l'ouest et dans le sud de l'Amérique Septentrionale 1614–1698,* III (1879); A. F. Sjoberg, "The Bidai Indians of Southeastern Texas," *Southwestern Journal of Anthropology,* VII (1951); J. R. Swanton, *The Indians of the Southeastern United States* (1946).

T. N. Campbell

*Patman, Texas.

*Patonia, Texas.

*Patricia, Texas.

*Patrick, George Moffit.

*Patrick, James B.

*Patrick, Texas.

*Patrick Creek.

*Patrons of Husbandry. *See* Grange.

*Patroon, Texas.

*Patroon Bayou.

*Patroon College.

Patterson, Caleb Perry. Caleb Perry Patterson was born January 23, 1880, in Saltillo, Tennessee, the son of Robert Henry and Mary Anne (Creasy) Patterson. He was married to Tommie A. Cochran in Sardis, Tennessee, on August 8, 1907. The couple had no children. He earned thirteen academic degrees, among which were a B.A. and M.A., Vanderbilt University (1911); M.A., Harvard University (1916); LL.B., University of Texas (1921); and Ph.D., Columbia University (1923), where he studied under the leading authorities in the field of constitutional history and law.

He was an instructor in literature at Vanderbilt (1910–1911); professor of history and government, West Tennessee Teachers College (1912–1917); and instructor of history, Columbia (1918–1919). He began his thirty-eight years as a teacher at the University of Texas (Austin) as an instructor in government (1919), then as associate professor (1920), and full professor (1925). He served as chairman of the department for eight years, and he became professor emeritus in 1955. Patterson was a Carnegie Foundation research professor in Europe (1926) and studied the judicial system of Great Britain on a Laura Spelman Rockefeller Foundation award (1931–1932).

Patterson quickly became well known in the 1920's and was in great demand as a public speaker. He urged entry of the United States into the League of Nations, abolition of lame duck sessions of Congress, and reform of the electoral college system. Many students who later became distinguished political scientists credited their interest in the field to Patterson's inspirational teaching. With the coming of the New Deal he testified before congressional committees against President Roosevelt's court-packing proposal. In his writings he opposed centralizing government in Washington to the extent that it would eventually lead to the destruction of states' rights.

A prolific writer, he was the author of numerous books and texts and coauthor of many more; he also wrote an extraordinary number of articles on constitutional law and edited D. C. Heath's political science series. Among his books were *The Negro in Tennessee, 1790–1865* (1922), *Administration of Justice in Great Britain* (1933), *Presidential Government in the United States* (1945), and *The Constitutional Principles of Thomas Jefferson* (1953). Among his many books on Texas was *A Civil Government of Texas*, coauthored with James B. Hubbard (c. 1925).

He was an early member and president of the Southwestern Social Science Association qv (founded as the Southwestern Political Science Association; he was its first secretary-treasurer) and editor of its *Southwestern Social Science Quarterly* qv (1925–1935); he founded Pi Sigma Alpha, national honorary scholarship society in political science. In 1953 the Texas legislature commended Patterson for bringing honor to the University of Texas and the state in his writings and in his teaching. He retired from teaching in 1957. The C. P. Patterson–Thomas Jefferson Collection, established by the University of Texas (Austin) in 1961, contained important resources assembled by Patterson for the study of Jefferson's life and writings. He died in Austin on November 29, 1971, and was buried in Austin Memorial Cemetery.

BIBLIOGRAPHY: Biographical File, Barker Texas History Center, University of Texas at Austin; Austin *American*, November 29, 1971.

Patterson Settlement, Texas. Patterson Settlement was established in 1853 by George W. Patterson, John Leakey, and A. B. Dillard several miles south of the present town of Sabinal in Sabinal Canyon, Uvalde County. The Civil War and Indian depredations caused the old settlement to be abandoned. *See also* Sabinal, Texas.

BIBLIOGRAPHY: Lois M. Carmichael, The History of Uvalde County (M.A. thesis, Southwest Texas State Teachers College, 1944); *Texas Almanac* (1936).

*Pattillo, George A.

*Pattison, Texas.** Pattison, in southern Waller County, was named for James Tarrant Pattison (not his son George Madison Pattison, as stated in Volume II), who settled in the area and received a land certificate for 640 acres in December, 1839. In March, 1845, he bought 764 acres of land in the area that included the later townsite. The heirs of James Tarrant Pattison donated 150 acres to the Western Narrow Gauge Railroad for right-of-way and also donated land for a church, school, park, and cemetery. When the railroad was abandoned in 1899 that property donated to the railroad was returned to the Pattisons. In 1971 Pattison had two businesses and an estimated population of 316.

Mrs. Daniel W. Haskew

*Patton, Moses L.

*Patton, William Hester.

*Patton, Texas. (Galveston County.)

Patton, Texas. (Hemphill County.) *See* Dreyfoos, Texas.

*Patton, Texas. (McLennan County.)

*Pattonville, Texas.

Pattullo, George R. George R. Pattullo was born on October 9, 1879, in Woodstock, Ontario, Canada, the son of George Robson and Mary (Rounds) Pattullo. He attended Woodstock Collegiate Institute and engaged in newspaper work in Montreal, London, and Boston. In the summer of 1908 he left his job as Sunday editor of the Boston *Herald* and traveled west with Texas cowboy photographer Erwin E. Smith.qv For the next several years they rode and worked together through western Texas, New Mexico, and Arizona, Smith producing photographs and Pattullo writing western stories which appeared in several popular magazines, including the *Saturday Evening Post* and *Mc-Clure's*.

On November 5, 1913, Pattullo married Lucile Wilson, daughter of one of Dallas's early business leaders, J. B. Wilson. They made their home in Dallas for a short time before Pattullo became a special correspondent for the *Saturday Evening Post* with the American Expeditionary Force in World War I. Thereafter he lived mainly in New York, where he continued writing western fiction. He frequently visited Dallas, where he had extensive business and social interests. He was a member of the Players and Union clubs in New York and of the Old Guard Club of Palm Beach, Florida. Some of his books were *The Untamed* (1911), *A Good Rooster Crows Everywhere* (1939), *All Our Yesterdays* (1948), and *Some Men in Their Time* (1959). He died in New York City on July 29, 1967, and was buried at Hillcrest Mausoleum in Dallas, Texas.

BIBLIOGRAPHY: *Who's Who In America* (1960); Eldon S. Branda, "Portrait of a Cowboy as a Young Artist," *Southwestern Historical Quarterly*, LXXI (1967–1968); Dallas *Morning News*, July 30, 1967.

Patumaca Indians. The Patumaca (Patumaco, Patacama) Indians are known only from marriage records of Nuestra Señora de la Purísima Concepción de Acuña Mission qv in San Antonio, which they seem to have entered as early as 1733. At least thirty Patumaca individuals are named in these records, and one of them, Joseph Flores, served a term as governor of the Indians represented at Mission Concepción. The aboriginal range of the Patumaca is not known. However, they entered this mission at the same time as a number of Coahuiltecan groups from northeastern Coahuila and the adjacent part of Texas, which suggests that the Patumaca had the same affiliation and came from the same general area.

BIBLIOGRAPHY: H. E. Bolton, "Spanish Mission Records at San Antonio," *Quarterly of the Texas State Historical Association,* X (1906–1907); H. E. Bolton, *Texas in the Middle Eighteenth Century* (1915); F. W. Hodge (ed.), *Handbook of American Indians,* II (1910); R. G. Santos, "A Preliminary Survey of the San Fernando Archives," *Texas Libraries,* XXVIII (1966–1967).

                                                    T. N. Campbell

*Patzau Indians. The Patzau (Pacha, Pachao, Pachaug, Pasaja, Patzar, Pazac, Pucha, and other variants) Indians were first mentioned in 1684 by Juan Domínguez de Mendoza qv when he was in the western part of the Edwards Plateau. In 1690 they were encountered by Spaniards on the Nueces River, probably in present-day Dimmit or Zavala County, where they shared the same encampment with eight other Indian bands. The next year, 1691, they were seen farther east, apparently on the Frio River southwest of San Antonio. Here they shared the same temporary settlement with twelve other groups. Some Patzau entered San Francisco Solano Mission qv of northeastern Coahuila as early as 1712. When this mission was transferred from Coahuila to San Antonio in 1718 and became known as San Antonio de Valero,qv many Patzau began to arrive. Numerous variants of the name Patzau appear in the surviving baptismal, marriage, and burial records of Valero, especially between the years 1723 and 1750. For some unspecified reason Swanton listed Pachaug and Patzau as separate Coahuiltecan groups, but the evidence indicates that both names refer to the same people.

BIBLIOGRAPHY: H. E. Bolton (ed.), *Spanish Exploration in the Southwest, 1542–1706* (1916); L. Gómez Canedo, *Primeras exploraciones y poblamiento de Texas, 1686–1694* (1968); C. W. Hackett (ed.), *Pichardo's Treatise on the Limits of Louisiana and Texas,* II (1934); F. W. Hodge (ed.), *Handbook of American Indians,* II (1910); R. G. Santos, "A Preliminary Survey of the San Fernando Archives," *Texas Libraries,* XXVIII (1966–1967); J. R. Swanton, *Linguistic Material from the Tribes of Southern Texas and Northeastern Mexico* (1940).

                                                    T. N. Campbell

*Paul, James Christopher.

*Paul, Texas.

*Paul Quinn College. Paul Quinn College was founded in Austin by a small group of African Methodist Episcopal circuit-riding preachers in 1872. The institution later moved to Waco as a one-building trade school and taught newly freed slaves blacksmithing, carpentry, tanning, saddlery, and other skills.

As the African Methodist Episcopal church developed throughout the South, funds became available for a larger school. The first two acres of the present twenty-two-acre campus in east Waco were purchased in 1881. That same year, Paul Quinn College (named for Bishop William Paul Quinn, an A.M.E. missionary of the western states for almost thirty years) was chartered by the state.

The oldest liberal arts college for Negroes in Texas began with a faculty of five and an early-day curriculum which encompassed mathematics, music, Latin, theology, English, printing, carpentry, sewing, and "household work." Facilities on the new campus included the brick main building, one frame building, and "three shed rooms for young men."

Additional buildings were made possible through contributions from interested patrons of the college. In 1950 the college entered an extensive expansion program, completing a church, student union, gymnasium, and administration building by 1954. Major renovations of other buildings on campus were also made. In 1954 the Waco Chamber of Commerce launched a successful $100,000 drive to replace a girls' dormitory destroyed by fire. The campus included fifteen permanent structures by 1964.

The college was accredited by the Texas Education Agency qv and affiliated with the Council for Small Colleges and the Association of Texas Colleges and Universities.qv Ten departments of instruction were organized into three divisions: humanities, natural sciences, and social sciences. Bachelor of Arts and Bachelor of Science degrees were granted. A member of the South Central Athletic Conference, Paul Quinn College maintained varsity teams for intercollegiate competition in basketball, baseball, and track.

The library contained 28,718 volumes in 1969. In the fall of 1974 enrollment was 496, and Stanley E. Rutland was president of the college.

*Pauline, Texas.

*Paul's Store, Texas.

*Paul's Valley, Texas.

*Pausane Indians. In 1708 the Pausane (Paisano, Pausana, Payzano) Indians lived in northeastern Coahuila and perhaps also in the adjoining part of Texas. In that year some of them entered San Bernardo Mission qv near present Guerrero, Coahuila. Later the Pausane were said to be in Texas on the San Antonio River, presumably between present-day San Antonio and the coast. Before 1738 some of them entered Nuestra Señora de la Purísima Concepción de Acuña qv Mission qv at San Antonio. In 1737 about three hundred Pausane were induced to enter Mission San Francisco Vizarrón de los Pausanes near modern La Unión, northeastern Coahuila. It is clear that the Pausane spoke a Coahuiltecan dialect, but the question of whether they are the same as the Paisano of northern Tamaulipas remains open.

BIBLIOGRAPHY: V. Alessio Robles, *Coahuila y Texas en la Epoca Colonial* (1938); F. W. Hodge (ed.), *Handbook* of American Indians, II (1910); P. O. Maas, Viajes de misioneros Franciscanos á la conquista del Nuevo México (1915); J. R. Swanton, Linguistic Material from the Tribes of Southern Texas and Northeastern Mexico (1940); R. S. Weddle, San Juan Bautista: Gateway to Spanish Texas (1968).

T. N. Campbell

Pausay Indians. The Pausay (Pausal, Pausaqui, Pojosay, Pozoay) Indians were first reported in northeastern Coahuila in 1675 under the name Pausal. Thereafter they are known only from the records of San Antonio de Valero Mission,qv San Antonio, in the eighteenth century. Swanton listed them as probably Coahuiltecan in speech.

BIBLIOGRAPHY: H. E. Bolton, Texas in the Middle Eighteenth Century (1915); F. W. Hodge (ed.), Handbook of American Indians, II (1910); Esteban L. Portillo, Apuntes para la historia antigua de Coahuila y Texas (1886); R. G. Santos, "A Preliminary Survey of the San Fernando Archives," Texas Libraries, XXVIII (1966-1967); J. R. Swanton, Linguistic Material from the Tribes of Southern Texas and Northeastern Mexico (1940).

T. N. Campbell

*Paw Paw Creek.

Pawelekville, Texas. Pawelekville, in northern Karnes County, was founded in 1930 by John A. Pawelek, who opened a store on the then new State Highway 123. The chief occupations of the forty-eight inhabitants in 1966 were farming and ranching. In 1971 the estimated population was 105.

*Pawnee, Texas.

*Pawnee Indians. The Pawnee (Aguaje, Ahuahe, Avahi, Maha, Panimaha, Skidi) Indians from the Nebraska area entered Texas at various times in the late eighteenth and early nineteenth centuries. A part of the Skidi Pawnee migrated southward between 1770 and 1780 and joined the Taovaya on Red River, and this association continued into the nineteenth century. At times the name Pawnee served as a synonym for the Taovaya. In 1795 a party of Pawnee and Taovaya visited San Antonio for the purpose of establishing friendly relations with the Spanish, who were interested but took no formal steps toward cementing the relationship.

BIBLIOGRAPHY: H. E. Bolton, Athanase de Mézières and the Louisiana-Texas Frontier, I (1914); F. W. Hodge (ed.), Handbook of American Indians, I (1907), II (1910); R. C. Troike, "A Pawnee Visit to San Antonio in 1795," Ethnohistory, 11 (1964); D. H. Winfrey and J. M. Day (eds.), The Indian Papers of Texas and the Southwest, 1825–1916, I–III (1966).

T. N. Campbell

*Paxton, Texas.

*Payaya Indians. The Payaya (Paia, Paialla, Payai, Payagua, Payata, Piyai, and other variants) Indians, a Coahuiltecan-speaking group first reported about 1690, originally ranged an area that extended from San Antonio southwestward to the Frio River and beyond. However, it is with the San Antonio area that the Payaya were most consistently associated. A local stream was referred to as El Arroyo de los Payayas, and a pass through the hills northwest of San Antonio was known as Puerto de los Payayas. Yanaguana, the Payaya name for the

San Antonio River, has been preserved and was perpetuated by the Yanaguana Society qv of San Antonio. Shortly before 1709 a group of Payaya joined other Coahuiltecans and moved to the vicinity of present Milam County in east-central Texas, where they settled among Tonkawans in a locality known as Ranchería Grande.qv

The Payaya entered missions in both Coahuila and Texas. A few Payaya were baptized at San Francisco Solano Mission qv of northeastern Coahuila in 1706. The Payaya Indians were one of the groups for whom San Antonio de Valero Mission qv was established in present San Antonio in 1718, and they are mentioned in records of this mission as late as 1776. Some Payaya were also at nearby Nuestra Señora de la Purísima Concepción de Acuña Mission.qv

BIBLIOGRAPHY: L. Gómez Canedo, Primeras exploraciones y poblamiento de Texas, 1686–1694 (1968); M. A. Habig, The Alamo Chain of Missions: A History of San Antonio's Five Old Missions (1968); M. A. Hatcher, "The Expedition of Don Domingo Terán de los Ríos into Texas," Preliminary Studies of the Texas Catholic Historical Society, II (1932); F. W. Hodge (ed.), Handbook of American Indians, I (1907), II (1910); A. de León and others, Historia de Nuevo León, con noticias sobre Coahuila, Tejas, y Nuevo México (1909, 1961); P. O. Maas, Viajes de misioneros Franciscanos á la conquista del Nuevo México (1915); R. G. Santos, "A Preliminary Survey of the San Fernando Archives," Texas Libraries, XXVIII (1966–1967); J. R. Swanton, Linguistic Material from the Tribes of Southern Texas and Northeastern Mexico (1940); R. S. Weddle, San Juan Bautista: Gateway to Spanish Texas (1968).

T. N. Campbell

*Payne, John. John Payne was born on March 4, 1784, in North Carolina and died on October 14, 1848, in Sabine County (therefore, he could not have been sheriff and notary public in Sabine County after 1848, as stated in Volume II; John M. Payne, his son, may have held these posts).

Helen Gomer Schluter

*Payne, John Bayly.

Payne, Leon Roger. Leon Roger Payne, country and western singer and composer, was born on June 15, 1917, in Alba, Texas (Rains County), the son of Jesse and Gertrude (Murdock) Payne. Blind in one eye at birth, he lost the sight of the other in a childhood accident. He attended the Texas School for the Blind qv from May 17, 1922, until his graduation from there on May 31, 1935.

Payne's singing and composing career began with a Palestine, Texas, radio station. He played the guitar and several other stringed instruments, and he sang according to some critics "in the soft, smooth style of Eddie Arnold."

On August 16, 1948, Payne married Myrtie Velma Courmier, a blind girl he had known when he attended the Texas School for the Blind. They had two children and reared two other children born to his wife from a previous marriage. In that same year his composition "Lifetime to Regret" established his reputation as a composer, and in 1949 he composed "I Love You Because" (a song inspired by his wife), which became a top hit and remains a standard in country and western music. His "You've Still Got a Place in My Heart" was first recorded in 1951, but its greatest success came in the 1960's when Dean Martin and many other leading artists recorded it. Payne made many appearances on both the "Louisiana Hayride" in Shreveport and the "Grand Ole Opry" in Nashville, Tennessee, the most prestigious of country and western radio shows. Other well-known singers who recorded Payne's songs were Elvis Presley, Glen Campbell, Don Gibson, Jim Reeves,qv and George Jones. Jones recorded an album of Payne's songs in 1971.

Leon Payne died on September 11, 1969, in San Antonio, and he was buried in Sunset Memorial Park in San Antonio.

Eldon S. Branda

*Payne, Leonidas Warren, Jr.

*Payne, Texas. (Marion County.)

*Payne, Texas. (Wharton County.)

*Payne Spring, Texas.

*Paynes Gap.

*Paynes Waterhole.

*Payuguan Indians. In the late seventeenth and early eighteenth centuries the Payuguan (Paiabun, Paiuam, Pallugan, Paraguan, Payague, Payavan, and other variants) Indians ranged over a large area in northeastern Coahuila, northwestern Nuevo León, and the adjoining part of Texas south of the Edwards Pleateau. In 1690 the Payuguan were encountered by Spaniards at a temporary settlement on the Nueces River, probably in modern Dimmit or Zavala County, a settlement which they shared with eight other Indian groups. The next year they were found farther east on the Frio River southwest of San Antonio. This time twelve groups shared the same encampment.

Shortly before and after 1700 the Payuguan entered several Spanish missions in Coahuila and Nuevo León—San Francisco Solano,qv Santa María de los Dolores de la Punta, and Dulce Nombre de Jesús de Peyotes. In 1708 they were listed with groups said to be living on both sides of the Rio Grande north, northeast, and east of present Lampazos, Nuevo León, which would seem to place them between present Eagle Pass and Laredo, Texas. In 1713 a few Payuguan families were induced to move southward and take up residence at Mission Candela in Coahuila. Although the date is uncertain, it is known that a few Payuguan also entered San Bernardo Mission qv near modern Guerrero, Coahuila. In 1715 the Payuguan participated in a Coahuila Indian rebellion. Then in 1718, when San Francisco Solano Mission qv was moved from the Rio Grande to present San Antonio and renamed San Antonio de Valero,qv some of the Payuguan moved with it. It thus seems evident that later in the eighteenth century the Payuguan lost their identity in various mission Indian populations of Coahuila, Nuevo León, and Texas.

BIBLIOGRAPHY: L. Gómez Canedo, *Primeras exploraci-ones y poblamiento de Texas, 1686–1694* (1968); F. W. Hodge (ed.), *Handbook of American Indians,* II (1910); P. O. Maas, *Viajes de misioneros Franciscanos á la conquista de Nuevo México* (1915); Esteban L. Portillo, *Apuntes para la historia antigua de Coahuila y Texas* (1886); J. R. Swanton, *Linguistic Material from the Tribes of Southern Texas and Northeastern Mexico* (1940); R. S. Weddle, *San Juan Bautista: Gateway to Spanish Texas* (1968).

T. N. Campbell

Peace, John Robert. John Robert Peace, lawyer and public official, was born in Wharton, Texas, on January 24, 1917, the son of John Robert and Lillie Ellen (Stack) Peace. After attending public school in East Bernard, he studied one year at Schreiner Institute in Kerrville before transferring to the University of Texas, where he received an LL.B. degree in 1939. In that same year he began law practice in San Antonio and practiced there the remainder of his life. On November 18, 1939, he was married to Ruby McGee; they had three children.

Peace was named by Governor John Connally as a member of the University of Texas board of regents in 1967. He was chairman of the board from 1971 until 1973, and is credited with being the driving force in establishing a branch of the University of Texas in San Antonio.

Peace was executive assistant attorney general for Texas and served on the state Democratic Executive Committee from 1956 to 1960. He was chairman of the Public Safety Commission and was a trustee of St. Mary's University. He was also a director of the San Antonio Livestock Exposition, the Texas Law Enforcement Foundation, the Sam Rayburn qv Foundation, and was vice-president and general counsel of the Burke Foundation. Periodically he was a visiting professor at St. Mary's University Law School, and he served on the board of directors of the First National Bank of San Antonio, Station KLRN-TV, and Southwest Airlines. During World War II he was in the Marine Corps, from which he was retired as a first lieutenant. Peace was an avid collector of Texana. His collection of some 900 books and 500 documents dating back to the 1700's was donated to the University of Texas at San Antonio. He died at his home in San Antonio on August 17, 1974, and he was buried at Sunset Memorial Park there.

Joe B. Frantz

*Peace Party Conspiracy.

*Peach, Texas.

*Peach Creek.

*Peach Creek, Texas.

*Peach Point Plantation.

*Peach River and Gulf Railway Company.

*Peach Tree, Texas.

Peach Tree Village, Texas. Peach Tree Village, a rural community in northwestern Tyler County, was once a Coushatta Indian village. It became an Anglo American settlement about 1835 when Peter Cauble qv built a home (still there in 1970) and established a plantation. Valentine Ignatius Burch qv settled there about 1845. By the 1850's a road and mail route connected Peach Tree Village with Woodville. During the remainder of the nineteenth century Peach Tree Village served as a rural community center.

BIBLIOGRAPHY: *Tyler County Dogwood Festival* (brochures, 1950–1962); Austin Callan (ed.), *Reunion of the "Crow School"* (1929).

*Peacock, Wesley.

*Peacock, Texas.

*Peacock Military Academy.

*Peak, Junius.

*Peanut Culture. Peanut production in 1954 was centered in the county areas of Comanche-Eastland-Erath, Wilson-Karnes-Atascosa-Frio-Bexar, and Waller-Harris-Fort Bend, and in the East Texas blackland area. In that year 108,185,000 pounds of peanuts valued at over $12,000,000 were produced on 281,000 acres. Peanuts were grown on approximately 8,400 farms during the late 1950's, and twelve peanut oil mills were in operation in 1958. A 1959 survey indicated that Texas ranked third in the nation, producing 202,-300,000 pounds of peanuts valued at more than $18,800,000 on 289,000 acres of land. Irrigated acreage and the number of peanut oil mills increased in the early 1960's. A new variety of Spanish peanut was introduced in 1961, marking the first improvement in the United States derived from a controlled breeding program.

Peanuts were second only to cotton as the most valuable oilseed crop in Texas by the mid-1960's. The state ranked fifth in peanuts harvested. Over 260,000 acres in approximately 130 counties were planted in 1964, bringing in 236,440,000 pounds valued at over $25,000,000. Cash farm income in 1967 from peanuts was about $37,000,000. Irrigated peanut cultivation exceeded 70,000 acres out of 296,000 acres planted in 1968; the crop that year was 420,320,000 pounds and was valued at $48,-757,000. Peanut hay was an increasingly valuable by-product for peanut farmers.

By 1972 peanuts were grown on more than 300,-000 acres by approximately 12,500 growers in 117 counties, and the state ranked second nationally in peanut acreage. The ten leading counties were Comanche, Frio, Eastland, Atascosa, Wilson, Erath, Mason, Fannin, Houston, and Gaines. The 1972 peanut crop in Texas was 478,800,000 pounds, valued at $65,596,000.

BIBLIOGRAPHY: *Texas Agricultural Progress* (March, April, 1963); *Texas Almanac* (1955, 1963, 1967, 1969, 1973); *Texas Business Review* (March, 1960).

*Pear Ridge, Texas. Pear Ridge, a suburb of Port Arthur in Jefferson County, had a population of 3,470 in 1960 and 3,697 in 1970, according to the U. S. census report. *See also* Beaumont-Port Arthur-Orange Standard Metropolitan Statistical Area.

*Pear Valley, Texas.

*Pearce, James Edwin.

*Pearce, John Elias.

*Pearl, Texas.

*Pearl City, Texas.

*Pearland, Texas. Pearland, in Brazoria County, had a population of 1,497 in 1960 and 6,444 in 1970, an increase of 330.5 percent during the ten-year period. The city reported 100 businesses in 1970. *See also* Houston Standard Metropolitan Statistical Area.

*Pearsall, Texas. Pearsall, seat of Frio County, is the marketing and shipping center for a farming and ranching area which produces livestock, peanuts, watermelons, and vegetables. In 1964 Pearsall had a new hospital and a public library. In 1970 the town reported a total of 120 businesses, including producers of ready-mix concrete, newspapers, natural gas, and pear burners. The 1960 population was 4,957, and the 1970 population was 5,545, according to the United States census report.

Pearson, Frederick Stark. Frederick Stark Pearson was born in Lowell, Massachusetts, on July 3, 1861, son of Ambrose and Hannah Pearson. He attended Tufts College, where he received the A.M.B. degree (1883) and A.M.M. degree (1884); he was an instructor there and at Massachusetts Institute of Technology before coming to Texas in 1886 as a field engineer for a group of eastern financiers. He was married to Mabel Ward on January 5, 1887. Pearson had gained an engineering reputation in the East, first as organizer of a series of electric light companies and transportation systems, the most important of which was the Boston transportation system, and subsequently as chief engineer of the Metropolitan Street Railway in New York City.

His Texas projects were concentrated around the distribution of lumber and land development. In 1900 he established a lumber processing plant in El Paso, the El Paso Milling Company, after receiving a concession for the distribution of finished lumber milled from the Mexican sugar pine forests. In 1912 he was instrumental in chartering the Texas Land and Development Company qv in Plainview, Texas, the purpose of which was to develop raw land into finished, irrigated farms. He served as a director of the company from October 21, 1912, until his death on the *Lusitania* on May 7, 1915. He and his wife, who died with him, were survived by two sons and a daughter.

BIBLIOGRAPHY: Billy R. Brunson, The Texas Land and Development Company (Ph.D. dissertation, Texas Technological College, 1960); *Who Was Who In America* (1943).

Billy R. Brunson

*Pearson, Texas.

*Pease, Charles Henry.

*Pease, Elisha Marshall. Elisha Marshall Pease was the son of Lorrain (not Lorain, as stated in Volume II) Thompson Pease, and his wife was Lucadia Christiana (not Christina) Niles. In 1834 he toured western New York, Ohio, Michigan, Illinois, and Missouri (not the New England states). In 1866 Pease's attendance at the Convention of Southern Loyalists in Philadelphia followed (not preceded) his defeat for governor of Texas, and in 1867 he was appointed provisional governor by General Philip Henry Sheridan qv (not General William Tecumseh Sherman qv).

BIBLIOGRAPHY: Charles W. Ramsdell, *Reconstruction in Texas* (1910); John L. Waller, *Colossal Hamilton of Texas* (1968); Pease-Graham-Niles Family Papers (MS., Austin-Travis County Collection, Austin Public Library); Pease Papers (MS., Archives, Masonic Grand Lodge of Texas, Waco).

Katherine Hart
Roger A. Griffin

Pease, Julia Maria. Julia Maria Pease, the second of three daughters of Lucadia Christiana (Niles) and Elisha Marshall Pease,qv was born on March 14, 1853, in Brazoria, Texas. When her father was elected governor that same year, the family moved to Austin; in 1856 they occupied the newly completed governor's mansion. In 1859 Governor Pease purchased from James B. Shaw qv an estate northwest of Austin with a mansion, Woodlawn, built by Austin architect Abner Hugh Cook.qv It was there that "Miss Julia" lived most of her life. She was educated at Hartford Female Seminary in Connecticut, entered Vassar in 1870, and was graduated with a B.A. degree in 1875, trained in music and the arts. She accompanied her parents to Galveston in 1879 when her father was collector of customs.

When her older sister, Carrie Pease Graham, died in 1882, Carrie's three children were brought to Woodlawn to be reared by Julia and Julia's mother. With Governor Pease's death in 1883 Julia became manager of his considerable estate. For several years she lived in New York City, where the Graham children were in school.

In Austin she was active in the early days of the Texas State Historical Association qv (one of its first life members), the University Ladies Club, and the Boy Scouts (her nephews' scout troops often met at Woodlawn), and she took part in the activities of literary, historical, cultural, and philanthropic organizations. She was interested in raising funds for a hospital and in improving the conditions in the Austin jail, which she frequently visited. Her interest in preserving the trees of Austin was well known. During the 1890's she carried on an extensive correspondence with sculptress Elisabet Ney;qv during this time she and her mother were Miss Ney's patrons. In April, 1911, four years after Miss Ney's death, Julia Pease met with Mrs. Percy V. Pennybacker,qv Mrs. Joseph B. Dibrell, Miss Johanna Runge, and Miss Emma Burleson in "Formosa," Miss Ney's former studio, to discuss the preservation of both the studio and the collection of Miss Ney's works. The Texas Fine Arts Association qv was the formal organization which resulted from that meeting, and the following June the group held a formal exhibition of the artist's works. When the Pease estate surrounding Woodlawn was subdivided into Enfield and Westenfield in the early 1900's, Julia Pease may well have suggested many of the Connecticut place names and Pease-Niles family names which were used for many of the new

streets. Julia Pease died on January 19, 1918, in Austin, and was buried in Oakwood Cemetery.

BIBLIOGRAPHY: August Watkins Harris, *Minor & Major Mansions in Early Austin* (c. 1955); Katherine Hart (comp.), *Pease Porridge Hot* (1967); Vernon Loggins, *Two Romantics* (1946); "Historical Notes," *Southwestern Historical Quarterly*, XLI (1937–1938); Austin *Daily Democratic Statesman*, June 8, 1875; Austin *Statesman*, July 10, 1971; Pease-Graham-Niles Papers (MS., Austin-Travis County Collection, Austin Public Library); Biographical File, Barker Texas History Center, University of Texas at Austin; Files, Elisabet Ney Museum, Austin.

Katherine Hart

*Pease River.

†Peaster, Texas.

*Peavy, Texas.

*Pebble, Texas.

*Pecan. *See* Tree, State. For information on pecan growing and production, *see* Pecan Industry.

*Pecan Bayou.

Pecan Bowl. The Pecan Bowl postseason football game was first played at Abilene in December, 1964, and was played there each succeeding year until 1968, when the location was changed to Arlington. One of four regional playoff bowls of the NCAA College Division football plan, it was not classified as a major bowl.

George Breazeale

*Pecan Creek.

*Pecan Gap, Texas.

*Pecan Grove, Texas.

*Pecan Industry. In the 1950's Texas led the nation in the total number of pecan trees and was usually first in annual production. The 1954 crop totaled twenty-two million pounds valued at $5,886,000. Texas led all states in the production of native pecans and was second in total pecan production in 1960, accounting for more than 21 percent of the nation's total crop. In that year just over 2,000,000 trees on nearly 16,000 Texas farms produced over eight and one-half million pounds valued at $8,600,000. The 1964 agricultural census reported a total of 1,875,906 pecan trees (one-third improved varieties) on 11,074 farms.

Pecan crops vary substantially from year to year, both in production and value. The 1963 crop, for example, reached fifty-six million pounds valued at nearly $12,000,000; it was three times the crop of the previous year and twice that of the following year. In 1965 the pecan crop was a record sixty-two million pounds valued at $11,000,000, but in 1966 the state's trees yielded only eighteen million pounds valued at $5,000,000. Better indicators of the development of the pecan industry in the 1960's were the increased cultivation of improved varieties of trees, the increased use of irrigation, and the development of a mechanical harvester.

Leading pecan producing counties were Gonzales, San Saba, Bell, Hood, and Guadalupe (in order of production), and San Antonio was the principal marketing center for Texas pecans. The

1972 crop of sixty-five million pounds of pecans brought $25,500,000.

BIBLIOGRAPHY: *Texas Agricultural Progress* (Winter, 1964, Winter, 1967); *Texas Almanac* (1955, 1963, 1965, 1969, 1973).

*Pecan Point, Texas.

*Pecan Point Plantation.

*Pecan Spring.

*Pecan Spring Branch.

Peck, William Mynatt. William Mynatt Peck, son of Moses and Susan Peck, was born at Mossy Creek, Jefferson County, Tennessee, on November 11, 1821. He migrated to Texas in 1849 and settled at Mount Pleasant, Limestone County (town was later called Fairfield after the new county of Freestone was created). In 1857 he became a member of the county commission, and in 1861 he served as the delegate from Freestone County to the Secession Convention qv in Austin. He was a signer of the Texas Secession Resolution.

Peck fought in the Civil War, serving first as a private in the 19th Brigade, Texas Militia, and then as a captain in the Braxton Bragg Cavalry. He later served in the 8th Texas Infantry Regiment of Walker's Texas Division.qv Early in 1864 he was recalled to Texas and elected to the Tenth Texas Legislature from the Nineteenth Senatorial District.

Peck was married twice. His first wife, Sarah Virginia Peck, died at Fairfield in 1852. He was married a second time, to Nancy Elizabeth Forbes in 1857, and they had two children. Peck died in Fairfield on February 19, 1892, and was buried there.

BIBLIOGRAPHY: J. P. Blessington, *The Campaigns of Walker's Texas Division* (1968); John Henry Brown, *Indian Wars and Pioneers of Texas* (1896); *A Memorial and Biographical History of Navarro, Henderson, Anderson, Limestone, Freestone, and Leon Counties, Texas* (1893); E. W. Winkler (ed.), *Journal of the Secession Convention of Texas, 1861* (1912).

Chandler A. Robinson

*Pecks Lake.

*Pecos, Texas. Pecos, seat of Reeves County, reported the construction of five additional school buildings and a museum in 1964. By 1966 the town had twenty-six churches, a hospital, a library, a newspaper, and a radio station. A nursing and convalescent home was completed, and construction of municipal parks was underway in 1966. Businesses in Pecos include companies manufacturing irrigation pipes, turbine pumps, cottonseed and peanut oils, fertilizer, and food products. In 1970 the number of rated businesses was 288. The 1960 population was 12,728; the 1970 population was 12,682, according to the United States census report.

*Pecos Army Air Field.

*Pecos Bill.

*Pecos County. Pecos County, one of the leading petroleum producing counties, produced 767,-896,204 barrels of oil between 1926 and January 1, 1973. It ranked third among Texas counties in sheep raising in the 1960's.

In the early 1970's Pecos County had an average annual farm income of nearly $14 million, 60 percent of which came from cattle, sheep, goats, and hogs. Crops included cotton, grains, vegetables, and pecans.

In addition to hunting, attractions for tourists include Horsehead Crossing,qv the Annie Riggs Museum, old Fort Stockton,qv and the Dinosaur Tracks Roadside Park. The 1960 population was 11,957; the 1970 census was 13,748.

Pecos Crossing. *See* Camp Melvin, Texas.

*Pecos and Northern Texas Railway Company.

*Pecos River.

*Pecos River Railroad Company.

*Pecos Valley and Northeastern Railway Company. *See* Pecos River Railroad Company.

*Pecos Valley Railroad Company. *See* Pecos River Railroad Company.

*Pecos Valley Southern Railway Company.

Peddy, George Edwin Bailey. George Edwin Bailey Peddy was born August 22, 1892, on a farm in East Texas near Tenaha, shortly before his father's death. He was the seventh son of William Henry and Laura Gertrude (Chambers) Peddy. While still a young man he helped support his mother, then attended the University of Texas, graduating from its law school in 1920. Peddy was student body president in 1917 and led students protesting Governor James Edward Ferguson's qv political attacks on the university (he later supported Ferguson's attacks against the Ku Klux Klan qv). While still a student, he was elected to the Thirty-fifth Texas Legislature (1917) from Shelby County; he resigned, however, to accept a commission as captain in the army during World War I.

After receiving his law degree Peddy formed a law partnership in Houston with two former classmates, David Andrew Simmons qv and Dan Jackson. He served two years as assistant district attorney of Harris County and later for two years as assistant United States attorney in charge of mail fraud prosecutions. From 1925 to 1942 he practiced law as a partner with the Houston firm of Vinson, Elkins, Weems, and Francis.

After the nomination of Earle Bradford Mayfield qv for senator in the 1922 Democratic primaries and after the state Democratic convention in San Antonio, where it appeared to many that the Ku Klux Klan had gained control of the party, a mass meeting of "Independent Democrats" on September 16, 1922, in Dallas, selected Peddy to oppose Mayfield. Peddy had campaigned for James E. Ferguson as the anti-Klan candidate in the primaries. Mayfield and regular Democratic forces succeeded in keeping Peddy's name off the ballot; however, Independent Democrats finally failed to have Mayfield removed from the ballot on the grounds that his endorsement by and presumed membership in the KKK disqualified him as a Democrat and precluded his honoring the senatorial oath. Republican endorsement of Peddy also failed to win him a place on the ballot. Depending entirely on write-in votes, Peddy ran a surprisingly strong race, polling one-third (130,744 to 264,260) of the vote. Peddy challenged Mayfield's election before the U.S. Senate; the subsequent Senate investigation delayed Mayfield's seating for two years.

Peddy volunteered for military service during World War II and became a lieutenant colonel, serving as a staff officer in the 5th Infantry Division, Third Army, from the Normandy invasion to the end of the war. Peddy was deputy military governor of the city of Frankfurt in 1945. He was awarded the Bronze Star and Croix de Guerre. In 1948 he entered the contest for United States senator from Texas; he drew nearly 20 percent of the Democratic primary vote and forced his opponents, Lyndon B. Johnson qv and Coke Stevenson,qv into a runoff. He had waged his campaign on strong anti-Communist and pro-states' rights planks.

In 1921 Peddy married Gertrude Irwin; they raised two of her nephews as their foster children. Peddy was serving as chairman of the Texas Cancer Crusade when he died in Houston on June 13, 1951; he was buried in Ramah Cemetery in Tenaha.

BIBLIOGRAPHY: Seth Shepard McKay, *Texas Politics, 1906–1944* (1952); Biographical File, Barker Texas History Center, University of Texas at Austin; University Writings Collection, Academic Center, University of Texas at Austin.

Richard T. Fleming

*Peden, Edward Andrew.

*Pedernales, Texas.

*Pedernales River.

*Pedigo, Texas.

*Pedriza Creek.

*Peebles, Richard Rodgers. [This title was incorrectly listed in Volume II as Peebles, Richard Rogers.]

BIBLIOGRAPHY: R. G. White Papers (MS., Archives, University of Texas at Austin Library).

J. D. Matlock

*Peebles, Robert.

*Peede, Texas.

*Peeler, Anderson James.

*Peeler, Texas.

*Peerless, Texas.

*Peerson, Cleng.

*Peggy, Texas.

Pegleg Crossing. Pegleg Crossing of the San Saba River, located twelve miles east of Menard at the mouth of MacDougal Creek, was used almost continuously by the Spaniards from the time of the establishment of San Saba de la Santa Cruz Mission qv in 1757 until the end of the colonial period. In 1849 William Henry Chase Whiting surveyed the ford as a part of a migration road to California. It served the army as a crossing, linking Fort McKavett qv with San Antonio both before and after the Civil War. From 1867 until 1888, the San Antonio-San Diego (Southern) Stage Line used the military road and constructed a relay station,

Pegleg Station, on a hill overlooking the ford. The Western Trail qv likewise used the ford for cattle drives from south-central Texas to northern ranges and railheads. When State Highway 29 from Mason to Menard was built, Pegleg Crossing was abandoned. *See also* San Antonio-San Diego Mail Route.

BIBLIOGRAPHY: James B. Gillett, *Six Years with the Texas Rangers, 1875–1881* (1925); J. Marvin Hunter (comp.), *The Trail Drivers of Texas* (1925); Menard *News,* July 23, 1964.

J. M. Skaggs

*Pehir Village.

*Peinhoum Village.

Peirce, Thomas Wentworth. Thomas Wentworth Peirce, the son of Andrew and Betsey (Wentworth) Peirce, was born on August 16, 1818, in Dover, New Hampshire. He first visited Texas as a youth while on his way home from Cuba, where he had spent the winter because of ill health. He worked for his father (who was in trade and navigation) until 1837, when he went into business with his brother in Dover. In 1843 he entered the house of Peirce and Bacon in Boston, where he became a prominent merchant. The company's trade extended into the South, especially to Texas, where cotton, sugar, and hides were bought. In 1852 Peirce opened a branch house of the business in Galveston, with Ebenezar B. Nichols qv as a partner. The firm ran a line of fifteen packet ships to transport Texas products to the East Coast and to Europe.

Peirce became a wealthy man and was instrumental in building the Galveston, Harrisburg, and San Antonio Railway, which was later incorporated with the Southern Pacific Railroad (known as the Sunset Route), which Peirce also helped build. (*See* Pierce Junction, Texas, which at one time was spelled Peirce Junction and was named for Thomas Wentworth Peirce.)

After the death of his first wife, Mary Curtis, at their summer home in Topsfield, Massachusetts, Peirce married Cornelia Cook of Galveston (a niece of his Galveston partner, Ebenezar B. Nichols). Thomas Wentworth Peirce died in October, 1885, at Clifton Springs, New York, and was buried at Mount Auburn, Massachusetts.

BIBLIOGRAPHY: S. G. Reed, *A History of the Texas Railroads* (1941); Atlantic States Series of Biographical Reviews, *Biographical Review—Containing Life Sketches of Leading Citizens of Essex County, Massachusetts,* XXVIII (1898); Biographical File, Essex Institute (James Duncan Phillips Library, Salem, Massachusetts).

Peirce Junction, Texas. *See* Pierce Junction, Texas.

*Peissaquo Village.

*Pelham, Texas.

*Pelican, Texas.

*Pella, Texas.

*Pellegrini, Snider de.

Pellicer, Anthony Dominic. Anthony Dominic Pellicer, first bishop of San Antonio, was born on

December 7, 1824, in St. Augustine, Florida, the son of Francisco and Margarita (Juanada) Pellicer. He entered Spring Hill College, Mobile, Alabama, and was ordained on August 15, 1850, with his cousin Dominic Manucy,qv who also became a bishop in Texas. From 1850 to 1874 he served in the Diocese of Mobile, Alabama, as pastor and in several administrative positions, the highest being vicar general of the diocese.

When the western portion of the Galveston diocese, comprising territory between the Colorado and Nueces rivers and stretching from the Gulf of Mexico to El Paso County, was designated the Diocese of San Antonio in 1874, Anthony Pellicer was named its first bishop. He was consecrated in Mobile on December 8, 1874.

At this time San Antonio had a population of about 13,000, but the new diocese contained some 40,000 people scattered over a land dangerous for traveling. Within a few years, Pellicer had visited most of the parishes and missions in his diocese, but his health failed under the burden. He died on April 14, 1880, and was buried under the floor of the San Fernando de Bexar Cathedral.qv

Sister M. Claude Lane, O.P.

*Pelly, Texas. In 1947 Pelly was not consolidated with Goose Creek and Baytown (as stated in Volume II); Pelly annexed unincorporated Baytown, and later, in 1947, Pelly and Goose Creek consolidated, taking the name of Baytown.

*Peloncillo Peak.

*Pelone Indians. The name Pelone, meaning "hairless" or "bald" (not "hairy ones," as stated in Volume II), was frequently applied by the Spanish to Indian groups in which adult males customarily removed all or part of the head hair. In northeastern Mexico removal of head hair was a common practice among the Indians, and at least eight groups known during the eighteenth century were sometimes called Pelone. Nearly all of these groups were also known by other names; some, such as the Carrizo, were at times on the Texas side of the Rio Grande. In the eighteenth century the Lipan-Apache were frequently referred to as the Pelone Indians. When the name Pelone is encountered in documents, it must always be considered in some regional or local context.

BIBLIOGRAPHY: H. E. Bolton, "The Jumano Indians in Texas, 1650–1771," *Quarterly of the Texas State Historical Association*, XV (1911–1912); W. E. Dunn, "Apache Relations in Texas, 1718–1750," *Quarterly of the Texas State Historical Association*, XIV (1910–1911); F. W. Hodge (ed.), *Handbook of American Indians*, I (1907); M. D. McLean and E. del Hoyo (eds.), *Description of Nuevo León, Mexico, 1735–1740, by Don Josseph Antonio Fernández de Jáuregui Urrutia* (1964).

T. N. Campbell

*Pelotas, Texas.

*Pemberton Draw.

*Pen Branch.

*Pen Creek.

*Peña Blanca Creek.

*Peña Blanca Hills.

*Peña Blanca Mountains.

*Peña Colorado Creek.

*Peña Creek.

Peña Station. Peña Station, a mile east of present-day Hebbronville in Jim Hogg County, was a crossroads freight station and stage stop frequented by carts and wagons. The history of the station began in 1875, when Lazarro Peña bought 1,920 acres in five surveys along the waters of Santa Rosalia and Panilla, tributaries of Los Almos Creek. Peña Station (or Peña) appears on Texas maps as early as 1881, the same year the Texas-Mexican Railway Company qv built a narrow-gauge line from Corpus Christi to Laredo. Most freight to Clay Davis (see Rio Grande City) and Ringgold Barracks (see Fort Ringgold) from San Antonio and Corpus Christi went overland through Peña Station for several years. From Corpus Christi freight was often sent via railroad to Peña Station, where ox-drawn carts and wagons were loaded to take freight on to the border. From San Antonio the freight was hauled overland all the way.

When Francisco Peña refused to sell land for a townsite, the Texas-Mexican Railway Company made arrangements with James R. Hebbron for a new location for their depot. They loaded the old station on a flatcar and moved it a mile west, where Hebbronville was built. Peña Station continued to be used by stages and freighters, and it appeared on maps as a station near the railroad until 1908. In 1892 Peña had a hotel and a population of 100; around 1900 it had a store. It disappeared from the maps around 1908.

BIBLIOGRAPHY: W. H. Chatfield (comp.), *The Twin Cities of the Border* (1893); Frank C. Pierce, *A Brief History of the Lower Rio Grande Valley* (1917); Chamber of Commerce, Hebbronville, *Fiftieth Anniversary, Jim Hogg County* (1963); *The Texas Southwestern Railway Guide and Hand Book* (1892); Cartographic Collection, Barker Texas History Center, University of Texas at Austin.

Agnes G. Grimm

*Peñalosa Briceno y Berdugo, Diego Dionisio de.

Peñascal, Texas. *See* Point Peñascal.

*Penateka Comanche Indians.

*Pendell, Texas.

*Pendencia Creek.

*Pendleton, George Cassety.

Pendleton, Tom. *See* Van Zandt, Edmund Pendleton, Jr.

*Pendleton, Texas. (Bell County.)

*Pendleton, Texas. (Sabine County.) Pendleton was surveyed as a townsite by Thomas S. McFarland,qv (not William McFarland,qv as stated in Volume II). According to an entry from a portion of his journal, Thomas S. McFarland went to San Augustine on April 2, 1837, and made an agreement with Captain D. Brown to make a plat of a town to be located at Gaines [Ferry] on the Sabine

River to be called Pendleton, a family name of James Gaines.qv

BIBLIOGRAPHY: A Journal of Coincidences and Acts of Thomas S. McFarland, January 1, 1837–May 24, 1840 (MS., Archives, University of Texas at Austin Library).

Deolece Parmelee

*Penelope, Texas.

*Penfield, Texas.

*Pénicaut, André.

Penick, Daniel Allen. Daniel Allen Penick, son of Dixon Brown and Elizabeth Allen (Cochrane) Penick, was born on a farm in Cabarrus County, North Carolina, on September 7, 1869. The Penick family moved to Austin in 1882, and in 1887 Penick entered the University of Texas, where he edited *The Texas University*, a student magazine. He was active in founding the university YMCA and served as its first secretary-treasurer. He lettered in baseball for three successive years and was a member of the track team. Penick received the B.A. degree in 1891 and the M.A. in 1892.

After teaching English and Latin at the Paris, Texas, high school (1892–1893) and at Daniel Baker College in Brownwood (1893–1894), he entered Johns Hopkins University in 1894 for graduate study in Greek, Latin, and Sanskrit; he received a Ph.D. degree from there in 1898, with a dissertation which was later printed as *Herodotos In The Greek Renascence* (1902). Following a year of teaching at the Centenary Collegiate Institute in New Jersey, he returned to the University of Texas in 1899 as an instructor; he became a full professor in 1917. Penick served on the faculty continuously for fifty-six years until his retirement in 1955, never having taken a leave of absence. His principal field of instruction was New Testament Greek. In addition, he served as head of the correspondence division of the university from 1920 to 1927 and as assistant dean of the College of Arts and Sciences from 1926 to 1940.

Although his achievements as a teacher of classical languages were substantial, Penick was best known in the state and nation as a brilliantly successful tennis coach. He organized and coached the men's tennis team, starting in 1908, and continued as head tennis coach for fifty years until he retired in 1957 at the age of eighty-seven. While he was coach, his teams won all ten of the Southwest Conference qv team titles awarded, took thirty-one of the forty individual doubles championships, and captured twenty-six of the forty individual singles championships. In addition, his men won five national doubles championships and two national singles championships. Two of them were members of Davis Cup teams. In the spirit of the classical Greek period, Penick insisted that self-control was all-important. He served as president of the Southwest Conference for twelve years, from 1923 to 1935, and was president of the Texas Tennis Association for over fifty years.

Penick was a pioneer in the campus ministry movement in 1899, when he organized and taught a special Sunday school class for college students at the Highland Presbyterian Church (later renamed the University Presbyterian Church) in Austin. He was the first layman to be selected as moderator of the Presbyterian Synod of Texas.

His publications included an edition of Sallust's *Catiline* [*Bellum Catilīnae*] (1908) and, in collaboration with L. C. Procter, *Latin, First Year* and *Latin, Second Year*, elementary textbooks (1927, 1933). He was the author of papers on classical subjects and numerous articles concerned with tennis.

Penick married Chloe Parmalee Hastings on December 26, 1901; they had three children. He died on November 8, 1964, at the age of ninety-five, and was buried in Oakwood Cemetery.

Harry J. Leon

*Penick, Texas.

*Peniel, Texas.

*Peniel University. *See* Texas Holiness University.

*Penington, Sydney O.

*Penitas, Texas.

*Penitentiary System. *See* Prison System.

Penn, William Evander. William Evander Penn, an early Baptist evangelist in Texas, was born on August 11, 1832, near Old Jefferson, Rutherford County, Tennessee, to George Douglas and Telitha (Patterson) Penn. He received a meager elementary education and, at age sixteen, attended Male Academy in Trenton, Tennessee, for one year and then Union University at Murfreesburo, Tennessee, for one term. He studied with a law firm and in 1852 established his own law practice in Lexington, Tennessee. Four years later he married Corrilla Frances Sayle; they reared several foster children. Penn offered his services to the Confederacy in 1861 and was commissioned a captain in the cavalry. He was captured on a raid into Ohio and held prisoner until his exchange in 1865; he held the rank of major at the end of the war.

Penn moved to Jefferson, Texas, in 1866 to practice law; he soon began to speak as a lay preacher in Texas churches. Continuing to practice law, he conducted revivals in Texas and many other states; he also made a revival tour of Scotland and England in 1885 and 1886. He was known for his strong, musical basso, and in the latter part of his career, in the 1880's, he was co-editor of several hymn books published under the title *Harvest Bells*. He also wrote the words and music to several hymns. Penn died on April 27, 1895, and was buried at Eureka Springs, Arkansas.

BIBLIOGRAPHY: W. E. Penn, *The Life and Labors of Major W. E. Penn, "The Texas Evangelist"* (1896).

Jerry F. Dawson

*Pennall, Robert A.

*Pennell, Texas.

*Penniger, Robert G.

*Pennington, Isaac M.

*Pennington, Texas.

*Pennington College.

*Pennybacker, Mrs. Percy V.

Penoy Indians. The Penoy are known from one of the contemporary accounts (Cavelier) of the La Salle Expedition.qv These Indians seem to have lived near the Hasinai tribes, apparently to the west or southwest. Their linguistic and cultural affiliations remain undetermined.

BIBLIOGRAPHY: I. J. Cox (ed.), *The Journeys of Réné Robert Cavelier, Sieur de La Salle*, I (1905); F. W. Hodge (ed.), *Handbook of American Indians*, II (1910); J. G. Shea (ed.), *Early Voyages up and down the Mississippi* (1861).

T. N. Campbell

*Pentecost, George S.

*Peñunde Indians.

*Penwell, Texas.

*People, The.

*People's Advocate.

*People's Party.

*People's Press.

*Peoria, Texas.

*Pep, Texas.

*Pepper Creek.

*Perch Well.

*Percilla, Texas.

*Perdido Creek.

*Perdiz Creek.

*Pérez, Ignacio.

Perez, Pablo. Pablo Perez was born in Mier, Tamaulipas, Mexico, on May 14, 1812. During the 1840's he moved to the vicinity of present San Diego, Texas. There he bought property, built several stone houses, and settled several families along the east side of San Diego Creek; the settlement became known as Perezville, and Perez is considered one of the founders of San Diego.

About 1850 Perez married Vicente Barrera, heiress to the La Tinaja de Lara land grant; they had four sons. On this grant Perez established and later sold two ranches (Los Reales and El Muertecito) located north and northeast of present Alice, Texas. In 1854 he hired Felix A. von Blücher qv to survey the La Tinaja de Lara land grant which had been taken over by newcomers. This survey was partly the basis for a court order returning the grant to the Barrera heirs (which included the Perez family). Perez died on May 29, 1892.

Agnes G. Grimm

*Perico, Texas.

Perini, Vincent Charles, Jr. Vincent Charles (Bud) Perini, Jr., son of Vincent and Emma (Berkly) Perini, was born in Denver, Colorado, on January 15, 1895, and received his primary and secondary schooling in Denver. He early became familiar with the mining industry and spent several summers working in gold and silver mines north of Durango, Colorado. His undergraduate training at the University of Colorado was interrupted by World War I, when he entered the United States cavalry and rose to the rank of captain, serving on the Mexican border. At the close of the war, he returned to the University of Colorado, majoring in geology, and obtained his B.A. degree in 1919 and his M.A. degree in 1920. He began a career as a professional geologist, serving first with various state agencies in Colorado, then joining the Marland Oil Company in 1922.

Perini moved to Texas in 1923, where he lived the rest of his life. He helped establish the Marland Oil Company of Texas at Sulphur Springs, then entered a partnership under the firm name of Merry Brothers and Perini in 1924. After operating from Albany, Coleman, Cisco, Fort Worth, Paducah, and San Angelo, he settled permanently in Abilene in 1935. The partnership was dissolved in 1944, and Perini then operated as an independent.

As a geologist and oilman Perini achieved leadership in both scientific and industrial circles. He is credited with the discovery of many oil fields in west-central Texas. He served as president of the West Central Texas Oil and Gas Association for two terms, vice-president of the Independent Petroleum Association of America, vice-president of the National Stripper Well Association, and first president of the Abilene Geological Society, and he was active in many other professional, civic, and philanthropic organizations. His business interests included the Perini Mining Company, directorship in the First State Bank of Abilene, a ranch at Buffalo Gap, and various oil and gas properties.

Perini married Maxine Walker in 1936; they had three sons. He died on February 20, 1965, in Abilene and was buried in the Buffalo Gap Cemetery.

Frank B. Conselman

Perkins, Joe J. Joe J. Perkins was born in Lamar County, Texas, on March 7, 1874, the son of [?] and Elizabeth (Hunter) Perkins. He lived for a time in Montague County and undertook his first business enterprise in Decatur in 1897, a mercantile establishment called the Red Store. When he moved to Wichita Falls in 1909 he was head of the Belknap Coal Mines and had developed mining properties in Young County. In 1911 he established, with his nephew Frank Timberlake, the first of a chain of dry goods stores, the Perkins-Timberlake Stores. He also became a leader in the Texas oil industry, particularly in the Wichita Falls-Electra and West Texas areas. In the 1920's he helped organize the Texoma Oil and Refining Company, which later was sold to Continental Oil Company. He was a director and later chairman of the board of the City National Bank of Wichita Falls. His business interests included real estate, ranching, and other investments.

Perkins was known to the public primarily as a lay churchman and philanthropist. A gift in honor of his wife, who shared in his philanthropic activities, was the Lois Perkins Chapel on the campus of Southwestern University in Georgetown. He served on numerous boards of Methodist agencies and institutions. The Methodist Home for Children in Waco and Southern Methodist University received his special attention. The school of theology of Southern Methodist University received substantial gifts from him, making possible an extensive building program, and in 1945 the school was named the Perkins School of Theology.

Perkins married Lois Craddock of Wichita Falls on March 17, 1918, and they had two daughters. He died in Wichita Falls on September 15, 1960, and was buried in the Perkins mausoleum there.

Howard Grimes

*Perkins, Stephen W.

*Permanent Council.

*Permanent School Fund. *See* School Fund, Permanent.

Permanent University Fund. *See* University Fund, Permanent.

Permian Basin. The Permian Basin is located in West Texas and the adjoining area of southeastern New Mexico. It underlies an area approximately 250 miles wide and 300 miles long. The name derives from the fact that the area was downwarped before being covered by the Permian sea and the subsidence continued through much of the Permian period; consequently, it contains one of the thickest deposits of Permian rocks found anywhere. Although it is structurally a basin in the subsurface, much of the basin lies under the south end of the High Plains (Llano Estacado) and the northwestern portion of the Edwards Plateau, which are topographically high. On the west and south it extends across the Pecos River valley to mountain ranges in both New Mexico and West Texas.

The presence of rocks of Permian age was first reported by G. G. and Benjamin Franklin Shumard ^{qv} in 1858 after a study of outcrops in the Guadalupe Mountains. Later work in West Texas by Dr. Johan August Udden ^{qv} and his associates in the Bureau of Economic Geology at the University of Texas (Austin) contributed to knowledge of the age, structure, and stratigraphy of sediments found in outcrops around its Texas margin.

When the Permian sea retreated southward, it left the Permian Basin area of West Texas and New Mexico with a restricted outlet. This resulted in an inland sea where evaporation greatly exceeded fluid intake, and a great thickness of "evaporite" sediments was deposited; one of these was potash, a critical commodity during World War I, until then a product obtained from Germany. Dr. Udden's early investigations led the United States Geological Survey to concentrate much of its early effort in the search for potash in this area. The first commercial deposit was found in New Mexico in 1925. Up to 1967 all seven of the potash companies operating in the Permian Basin, representing an investment of some $200,000,000, were located in New Mexico. Texas deposits have not been developed because of the more expensive processes involved.

Much of the Permian Basin, and particularly that portion underlying the Llano Estacado, was home to the Comanche Indians until they were finally forced out by the United States Army in 1875. Because of good grasslands, most of the area was inviting to both ranchers and farmers. Since surface water was almost nonexistent, ranchers and farmers drilled water wells to sustain themselves and their livestock, and often the water well driller found evidence of oil or gas.

The first commercial oil well in the Permian Basin was completed in 1921 in Mitchell County, Texas, on the east side of the basin; completed at a total depth of 2,498 feet, it was the discovery well of the Westbrook field. Early oil prospecting was started in southeastern New Mexico about the same time as in West Texas. By 1923 it was presumed that the Permian Basin was in the form of an elliptical bowl, the subsurface strata dipping from the rim to a maximum depth in the middle. Because of this and the lack of suitable rock outcrops in the interior during the early search for oil, geological survey crews looked for surface anticlines in the Edwards Plateau and the rock outcrop areas west and south of the Pecos River. This method resulted in the discovery of several good oil fields, notably the World field in Crockett County, the McCamey field in Upton and Crane counties in 1925, and the Yates field in Pecos County in 1926. Prior to the Hobbs field discovery in 1928, all discoveries were made as a result of random drilling or surface and subsurface mapping. The Hobbs field discovery was made after magnetometer and torsion balance surveys both showed the area to be anomalous. From that time on geophysics, particularly the seismograph, was used as an exploratory tool.

By 1929 a sufficient number of oil tests had been drilled to give sketchy control for a subsurface map of the Permian Basin. Its outline was fairly well defined, and oil discoveries within the basin suggested the probability of interior folds. In 1930 Lon D. Cartwright published a report with cross section and map, showing a large positive area located in the approximate middle of the basin, which he named the "Central Basin Platform." The map showed the platform trending north-northwest across the Texas-New Mexico line into Lea County. By this time a sufficient number of wells had been drilled to show that the Central Basin Platform was a structural feature common to both states.

Because of the great distances to the markets and the lack of pipelines through which to move the oil, deep tests were not economically justified. Consequently, all oil fields discovered before 1928 were producing from Permian dolomite or sand, from depths less than 4,500 feet. A deep test was started in the Big Lake field, in Reagan County, Texas, and in 1928 a large flow of oil and gas was encountered at 8,525 feet. Fossil evidence showed the producing section to be of Ordovician age. This discovery greatly expanded the prospects for the Permian

Basin's becoming a major oil and gas producing area; however, because of the economic depression of the early 1930's few locations for deep tests were made prior to 1936. With the oncoming of World War II the need for oil was urgent, and it became economically justified to drill more and deeper tests.

During the war many new oil and gas zones were found not only in rocks of Permian and Ordovician age but also from zones in each geologic system from Permian through Cambrian and from practically every known type of subsurface trap.

Two of the largest accumulations were the Horseshoe Atoll and the Spraberry trend area. Horseshoe Atoll is a subsurface accumulation of fossiliferous limestone, as much as 3,000 feet thick, deposited during Pennsylvanian and early Permian time in the northern part of the Midland basin in West Texas. It is a horseshoe-shaped mass about ninety miles across and seventy miles from north to south. The crest of the atoll is a series of irregular hills and depressions. Oil migrated to many of these buried hills and was trapped in the porous rock, resulting in a line of oil fields nearly 200 miles in length. The Spraberry trend area is located in the region between the south end of the Llano Estacado and the north part of the Edwards Plateau. The producing structure here is basically a fractured permeability trap on a homoclinal fold about 150 miles in length. Oil production is practically continuous along its entire length; its maximum width is thirty-five miles.

The entire Permian Basin during 1966 produced a total of 607,000,000 barrels of oil and 2,300,000,000 cubic feet of gas for a total of $2,000,000,000. A cumulative total of 11,300,000,000 barrels of oil has been produced, and even with this large withdrawal the 1967 estimated reserve was 7,500,000,000 barrels. Intrastate and interstate gas pipeline systems have expanded throughout the area, and in the 1960's Midland-Odessa was the headquarters for oil and gas development in the Permian Basin area. Hundreds of millions of dollars have been spent on petrochemical refineries and supplemental construction work in the Permian Basin, and in 1969 it was rated the largest inland petrochemical complex in the United States. Some of the more commonly known Permian Basin petrochemical products were synthetic rubber, plastics, emulsion paints, solvents, food wrappers, nylon, ammonia, nitric acid, hydrogen, and fertilizer. See also Petrochemical Industry.

BIBLIOGRAPHY: Donald A. Myers, Phillip T. Stafford, Robert J. Burnside, "Geology of the Late Paleozoic Horseshoe Atoll in West Texas," *University of Texas Publication No. 5607* (1956); J. A. Udden, "Review of the Geology of Texas," *Bulletin of the University of Texas,* No. 44 (1916); Roswell Geological Society, *Oil and Gas Fields of Southeastern New Mexico* (1950); "Oil and Gas Fields in West Texas," *University of Texas Publication No. 5716* (1957); *Bulletin of the American Association of Petroleum Geologists,* No. 8, XIV (1930), Symposium Part 2, XXVI (1942), No. 2, XXXVII (1953).

Charles D. Vertrees

Permian Historical Society. The Permian Historical Society, formerly the Texas Permian Historical Society, was organized in November, 1958, in Odessa for the purpose of preserving the heritage of the Permian Basin qv of West Texas by the collection and preservation of documents, a publications program, encouragement of original research, sponsorship of quarterly programs, and the preservation and marking of sites, buildings, and objects significant in area history and culture.

The society was chartered by the state in May, 1959, and originally included the counties of Andrews, Crane, Ector, Loving, Ward, and Winkler. In 1965 "Texas" was dropped from the society's name in order to include Lea County in southeastern New Mexico; the Texas counties of Crockett, Gaines, Glasscock, Howard, Martin, Midland, Pecos, Reagan, Reeves, and Upton were also added. The first president was John A. Moravick.

The organization publishes *The Scroll*, a newsletter for members, and *The Permian Historical Society Annual*, containing articles on regional history. Two historical collections have been published in booklet form to commemorate the anniversaries of Ector and Ward counties: *Odessa, Texas, U.S.A. 1886–1961* (1961) and *Water, Oil, Sand & Sky* (1962). Permanent projects included a collection of biographical information from pioneers in the oil industry and the sponsorship of study tours to historic sites. The society has accumulated and maintained an archival collection of over seven thousand items and has participated in the establishment of six museums. Membership in 1972 was approximately 130 members, and the president was Mrs. Grace Thorman King. Chairmen of county historical survey committees and presidents of local societies served on the board.

Grace Thorman King

Permian Junior College System. The Permian Junior College System was established in 1969 as the Permian Basin Junior College System, when the Odessa Junior College District (which included Odessa College qv) voted to include the Midland Independent School District. Controversy arose when Midland citizens requested a Midland-located campus. Midland College qv was established, using existing public school facilities. With public pressure to build new facilities for Midland College, a bond issue was presented in November, 1971, to authorize construction; the bond issue was soundly defeated, mainly by the citizens of Odessa. As a result of continued controversy between the two cities, attempts were made by Midland residents to disannex from the Permian Junior College System; however, the state's attorney general determined that there was no legal authority to do so. In a special session of the legislature in October, 1972, legal authority was granted for such disannexation, and in December of that year the citizens of Midland voted to disannex and to create their own junior college district, with authority to levy taxes and issue bonds. In effect this dissolved the Permian

Junior College System at that time, although the system remained officially registered until the end of the fiscal year, August, 1973.

*Perote Prison and Prisoners.

Perpacug Indians. The Perpacug (Pexpacux) Indians appear to have ranged the Lower Rio Grande Valley near the Gulf Coast. The maps of Jiménez Moreno and G. Saldivar place them on the north bank of the river in what is now Starr County, but the surviving records do not seem to indicate such a precise location.

BIBLIOGRAPHY: W. Jiménez Moreno, "Tribus e idiomas del Norte de México," *El Norte de México y el Sur de Estados Unidos* (1944); G. Saldivar, *Los Indios de Tamaulipas* (1943).

T. N. Campbell

Perpepug Indians. In the middle eighteenth century this band lived along the lower Rio Grande below present Rio Grande City. The maps of Jiménez Moreno and G. Saldivar show them on the north bank of the river in what is now Zapata County, but the documents give only a general location. The name is said to mean "white heads," which suggests some distinctive form of head decoration, perhaps painting or a special kind of headdress.

BIBLIOGRAPHY: W. Jiménez Moreno, "Tribus e idiomas del Norte de México," *El Norte de México y el Sur de Estados Unidos* (1944); G. Saldivar, *Los Indios de Tamaulipas* (1943).

T. N. Campbell

Perrin, Texas. (Grayson County.) Perrin, in Grayson County, six miles north-northwest of Sherman, was the location of Perrin Air Force Base,qv which had been named for Lieutenant Colonel Elmer Daniel Perrin of Boerne, who was killed testing a B-26 near Baltimore, Maryland, in June, 1941. In 1970 Perrin was an unincorporated town with a population of 1,709, according to the United States census. The air force base was deactivated on June 30, 1970.

*Perrin, Texas. (Jack County.)

*Perrin Air Force Base. Perrin Air Force Base, six miles north-northwest of Sherman, conducted F-86 Sabrejet training for Air Defense Command crew members through 1959. Beginning in 1960 pilots were trained for the Convair F-102 Delta Dagger, a new series of fighter-interceptor aircraft.

Perrin was transferred to the Air Defense Command in July, 1962, and became its only F-102 training base. The air base introduced in September, 1964, a survival training program on Lake Texoma for air crew members stationed west of the Mississippi River.

The base added a training mission with the activation of the 3251st Flying Training Squadron in April, 1967, to train already qualified jet pilots as instructors for Air Training Command's undergraduate pilot training program. In 1967 the base consisted of 1,879 acres with $31,000,000 in real property, compared to its original 1,000 acres and $60,000 in real property.

In 1969 Perrin Air Force Base still conducted interceptor pilot training and T-37 instructor pilot training. The base was being used by the Aerospace Defense Command when it was deactivated on June 30, 1970, and the property was deeded to Grayson County. *See* Perrin, Texas (Grayson County.)

*Perry, Albert G.

*Perry, Cicero R. (Rufe).

*Perry, Emily Austin Bryan.

Perry, George Sessions. George Sessions Perry was born at Rockdale, Texas, on May 5, 1910, son of Andrew Preston and Laura (Van de Venter) Perry. He was educated at Rockdale public schools and at Allen Academy in Bryan, with brief college training at Southwestern University, Purdue University, and the University of Houston. In love with words, all he ever wanted to be was a writer. He looked more like a football fullback, six feet four inches tall, weighing enough to make chairs cringe. His physical exuberance was matched, unexpectedly, with a remarkable sensitivity.

He started writing at age eighteen, finished eight novels and a basket of stories "that nobody wanted to buy" until at last he made a sale to the *Saturday Evening Post* of his story "Edgar and the Dank Morass." From then on, Perry was able to sell to the big-pay magazines pretty much as he wanted, and he soon became a master craftsman of the "commercial" story and of the salable nonfiction article par excellence, later collected in such volumes as *Hackberry Cavalier* (1944), *Cities of America* (1947), *Families of America* (1949), and *Tale of a Foolish Farmer* (1951).

Perry's debut as a serious novelist was made in 1939 with *Walls Rise Up*, perhaps derivative of Steinbeck and Caldwell, but warm, droll, and immensely evocative of Texas rural life. This was followed in 1941 by the much-praised *Hold Autumn in Your Hand*, a more serious study, which won the National Book Award (1941) of the American Booksellers Association; it also received the Texas Institute of Letters qv Award for the best Texas book in 1941. The book was later filmed as *The Southerner*. In 1942 he published *Texas: A World in Itself*, a rollicking portrait of Texas, past and present.

With the coming of World War II, Perry was stationed first at San Antonio with the army air force; he later became an accredited navy war correspondent for the *New Yorker* and the *Saturday Evening Post*, covering the North African, Sicilian, and southern French coast invasions; he also covered the war in the Pacific. He could not bring himself to write fiction again. His war book, *Where Away* (1944), written in collaboration with Isabel Leighton, remains one of the most eloquent documents composed by war correspondents.

Perry's family was one of the oldest in Rockdale, Texas, and despite global traveling and success as a writer, Perry returned there often to live in the rambling old white house where he grew up; he tried both ranching and farming in the countryside. He had married Claire Elizabeth Hodges of Beaumont on February 20, 1933, and from the beginning she had an unfailing belief in his talent. They had no children.

My Granny Van (1949) was his last major work. Arthritis overtook him, and his suffering, quietly borne, was intense. Much of the time he had to wear a back brace which paralyzed normal movement, but he continued to work. Living half the year at Guilford, Connecticut, he wandered from his home there on December 13, 1956, apparently semiconscious; his body was discovered two months later in a small stream in which he had drowned. He was buried at Rockdale, Texas.

BIBLIOGRAPHY: Maxine Cousins Hairston, *George Sessions Perry: His Life and Works* (1973).

Lon Tinkle

Perry, Hally Ballinger Bryan. Hally Ballinger Bryan Perry was born in Galveston, Texas, on January 10, 1868, the daughter of Laura H. (Jack) and Guy Morrison Bryan qv and grandniece of Stephen F. Austin. She attended Hollins College in Virginia, and on November 3, 1909, married Emmett L. Perry, a cousin. They had no children. Having a deep interest in Texas history, she and a cousin, Betty Ballinger,qv organized the Daughters of the Republic of Texas qv in 1891. Her father preserved the family historical records of Moses and Stephen F. Austin, and she along with other members of her family became executors of the Austin Papers and presented them, together with the personal belongings of the Austins, to the Archives at the University of Texas (Austin). She died in Alpine, Texas, on July 27, 1955, and was buried in the State Cemetery qv at Austin.

Mrs. John S. Caldwell

*Perry, Henry.

Perry, Howard Everett. Howard Everett Perry was born in Cleveland, Ohio, on November 2, 1858, the son of Lansford and Nancy (Wilson) Perry. He attended Oberlin College and worked in his father's business, the Woods-Perry Lumber Company in Cleveland. In 1879 Perry went to Chicago, where he continued in the lumber business. On February 7, 1897, he married Grace Henderson. They had no children. Perry later joined C. M. Henderson & Co., a Chicago shoe manufacturing firm headed by his wife's father; Perry accumulated considerable wealth.

In 1887 he purchased four and one-half sections of land in Brewster County, Texas, for $5,760. Following the discovery of quicksilver qv on this property, he incorporated the Chisos Mining Company in the state of Maine on May 8, 1903; the company reported the first production that same year. Recovery continued for four decades, during which time the mine became one of the largest quicksilver producers in the nation. While secrecy surrounded the operation, it was estimated in 1934 that the company had marketed over twelve million dollars in the liquid metal. After 1936 production declined, and on October 1, 1942, the company ad-mitted insolvency. The mine was sold in bankruptcy on March 15, 1943, to the Texas Railway Equipment Company for $81,000. Operated as the Esperado Mining Company, the firm continued production until 1945, when surface installations were sold for salvage. Details of Perry's life are obscure. He maintained residence in Chicago and seldom visited the mine, but he administered absolute control through daily correspondence and a loyal administrative staff. At the beginning of World War I Perry moved to Portland, Maine. He died on December 6, 1944, in Boston, Massachusetts.

BIBLIOGRAPHY: Kenneth Baxter Ragsdale, *Quicksilver: Terlingua and the Chisos Mining Company* (1976).

Kenneth B. Ragsdale

*Perry, James Franklin.

*Perry, James Hazard.

*Perry, Louis Clausiel.

*Perry, Texas.

*Perry and Hunter Store.

*Perryton, Texas. Perryton, seat of Ochiltree County, built three new schools, a fire station, a city hall, a police station, a county jail, and a library between 1957 and 1968. An eighty-bed hospital was also completed by that date. Perryton has its own newspaper and radio station. Elevator and shipping facilities are available for wheat. Businesses in 1972 were chiefly concerned with farming, ranching, commercial cattle feeding, oil, and natural gas. The 1960 population was 7,903, an increase of over three thousand since 1950. The 1970 population was 7,810, according to the United States census report.

*Perryville, Texas.

*Pershing, Texas. (Tarrant County.)

*Pershing, Texas. (Travis County.)

*Person, Hiram K.

*Personville, Texas. A post office was established at Personville, Limestone County, in 1855 (not 1870, as stated in Volume II), and William Person was appointed postmaster at that time.

BIBLIOGRAPHY: Ray A. Walter, *A History of Limestone County* (1959).

*Pert, Texas.

*Pescadito, Texas.

Pescado Indians. The name Pescado (Spanish for "fish") was applied to certain Indians of Trans-Pecos Texas and the adjoining part of northern Chihuahua. In 1683 the Gente de Pescado ("people of the fish") were known to the Jumano, but their location was never identified. These were probably the Pescado of the eighteenth century who originally lived on the north bank of the Rio Grande near present Redford but later crossed to the south bank to live at San Antonio de los Puliques,qv apparently because of Apache pressure. These Pescado were absorbed by the Spanish-speaking population of northern Chihuahua in the late eighteenth century. The Pescado settlement near present Redford was known as Tapalcolmes, which may link the Pescado with the Topacolme, a late seventeenth-century group, apparently Concho Indians, who lived north of the Rio Grande in the same general area. J. R. Swanton seems to have erred in identifying the Pescado as Coahuiltecans.

BIBLIOGRAPHY: C. W. Hackett (ed.), *Pichardo's Treatise on the Limits of Louisiana and Texas,* I (1931); F. W. Hodge (ed.), *Handbook of American Indians,* II (1910); J. C. Kelley, "The Historic Indian Pueblos of La Junta de los Ríos," *New Mexico Historical Review,* XXVII (1952), XXVIII (1953); C. Sauer, *The Distribution of Aboriginal Tribes and Languages in Northwestern Mexico* (1934); J. R. Swanton, *Linguistic Material from the Tribes of Southern Texas and Northeastern Mexico* (1940).

T. N. Campbell

*Petao Indians. The Petao Indians are known only from records of the La Salle Expedition,qv which indicate that in the late seventeenth century these Indians lived well to the north or northeast of Matagorda Bay, possibly between the Brazos and Trinity rivers. The Petao have been erroneously equated with the Petaro and Petzare, whose names also occur on the same list of Indian groups. The affiliations of all three groups remain unknown.

BIBLIOGRAPHY: I. J. Cox (ed.), *The Journeys of Réné Robert Cavelier, Sieur de La Salle,* II (1906); F. W. Hodge (ed.), *Handbook of American Indians,* II (1910); P. Margry, *Découvertes et établissements des Français dans l'ouest et dans le sud de l'Amérique Septentrionale 1614–1698,* III (1879); H. R. Stiles (ed.), *Joutel's Journal of La Salle's Last Voyage, 1684–7* (1906).

T. N. Campbell

Petaro Indians. The Petaro Indians are known only from records of the La Salle Expedition,qv which indicate that in the late seventeenth century these Indians lived well to the north or northeast of Matagorda Bay, possibly between the Brazos and Trinity rivers. The Petaro have been erroneously equated with the Petao and Petzare, whose names also occur on the same list of Indian groups. The affiliations of all three groups are still undetermined. However, sound correspondences in the names suggest that the Petaro may be the same as the Patiri, an Atakapan-speaking group that lived in the same general area during the first half of the eighteenth century.

BIBLIOGRAPHY: F. W. Hodge (ed.), *Handbook of American Indians,* II (1910); P. Margry, *Découvertes et établissements des Français dans l'ouest et dans le sud de l'Amérique Septentrionale 1614–1698,* III (1879).

T. N. Campbell

*Peter Creek.

*Peters, Texas.

*Peters' Colony.

*Peters' Colony Controversy. *See* Hedgcoxe War.

*Peters Prairie, Texas.

*Petersburg, Texas. (Hale County.) Petersburg, in Hale County, had a population of 1,400 in 1960 and 1,300 in 1970, according to the United States census. The town had thirty-six businesses in 1970.

Petersburg, Texas. (Lavaca County.) Petersburg, first seat of Lavaca County when the county was organized in August, 1846, was located six miles south-southeast of Hallettsville. Petersburg's first post office was granted in 1848 with William T. Townsend as first postmaster. The townsite, located on 300 acres of land given by Arthur Sherill, was near Zumwalt Settlement, which Adam Zumwalt and his family had established in the early 1830's. The town was on the San Felipe–Gonzales–San Antonio and the Victoria–Columbus roads. The population in 1848 was twenty when John Williams opened a store. Town lots did not sell rapidly, and it was not until the single building which was used as courthouse, church, school, and sheriff's office burned to the ground that a court house was constructed in mid-1850. For a time county business was held in various buildings or under the trees, and prisoners were locked in barns and boarded in private homes.

In a bitterly contested election in 1852 Hallettsville was made the county seat, even though it required most of the town's manpower and arms to secure the county archives from the irate citizens of Petersburg. The matter was not settled until a final legal decision in 1860. In the 1850's E. H. Nelson and his wife established Nelson Academy, using what was the courthouse and the old Spencer Townsend tavern to house the academy's boarders. With the Civil War the school had to close for lack of pupils. In 1876 the post office was moved to Williamsburg, where John Williams operated a large storehouse, grist mill, and gin. By 1880 the town had been reduced to only one establishment.

The one building on the Petersburg site in 1963 was a home which had in its walls the old post oak lumber of the Petersburg courthouse.

BIBLIOGRAPHY: Paul C. Boethal, *History of Lavaca County* (1959).

Grover C. Ramsey

*Petersburg, Texas. (Red River County.)

*Petersville, Texas.

*Petes Creek.

*Peticado Indians.

*Petri, Friedrich Richard.

*Petrick, Texas.

*Petrified Canyon.

Petrochemical Industry. Products derived from oil and natural gas are the backbone of the giant Texas petrochemical industry, mostly concentrated along the Texas Gulf Coast and in the Permian Basin.qv The need for synthetic rubber and synthetic chemicals for explosives during World War II prompted the development of the highly specialized petrochemical industry in Texas. After 1952 the state's share in the American petrochemical industry increased dramatically, and during the 1960's Texas played an increasingly diversified role in all phases of the petrochemical industry: furnishing and processing oil and gas, producing petrochemicals, and manufacturing commercial commodities.

By 1965 more than two hundred petrochemical plants in Texas processed such basic petrochemicals as ethylene, propylene, butadiene, benzene, isoprene, and xylenes, which are the building blocks for innumerable chemical products spanning the range of the plastic, rubber, and synthetic fiber industries. By 1967 the Texas Gulf Coast petrochemical complex dominated the American production capacity of several basic petrochemical gasses and liquids, providing 82 percent of the production capacity for butadiene, 66 percent for benzene, 70 percent for ethylene, and 67 percent for styrene. In 1965 Texas supplied more than half of the national production of carbon black, another important raw material derived from natural gas; that year eighteen plants produced 1,173,000,000 pounds of carbon black (valued at $87,500,000) used in tires and rubber products, printing ink, plastics, pigments, fertilizers, and other manufactured products. In all, Texas supplied about 40 percent of all basic petrochemicals produced in the United States by 1969.

In the 1960's Texas began taking a larger part in the manufacture of plastic, synthetic fiber, and rubber products. Ethylene gas and polyethylene plastic materials (produced by subjecting ethylene to high pressures and heats in the presence of a catalyst) represented an important example of this development. By 1963 twelve Texas plants had an ethylene production capacity of 4.9 billion pounds, more than half of the nation's capacity of 8.9 billion pounds. That same year Texas manufacturers had a 1.6 billion pound production capacity for polyethylene, 80 percent of the national capacity. Still other Texas businesses used polyethylene to manufacture finished plastic commodities.

By 1967 the Texas petrochemical industry represented a capital investment approaching five billion dollars and employed about forty-five thousand workers. The largest portion of this industry was the world's largest complex of ethylene production facilities along the Texas Gulf Coast, which in 1969 developed about 15 billion pounds of production capacity.

Some of the larger chemical concerns with plants and offices in Texas are: Allied Chemical Corporation, Aluminum Company of America, Clorox Company, Continental Oil Company, Diamond Alkali Company, Dow Chemical Company, E. I. DuPont de Nemours & Company, Goodyear Tire & Rubber Company, Jefferson Chemical Company (a subsidiary of Texaco Inc.qv), Monsanto Company, Phillips Petroleum Company, Shell Chemical Company, and Union Carbide Corporation. *See also* Chemical Industries.

*Petroleum, Texas.

*Petroleum Industry. *See* Oil, Discovery and Production of; Oil, Economic Importance of; Oil, Refining of; Oil Field Machinery and Procedures; Oil Fields, Major, to 1940; Oil Fields, Major, 1940 to 1968; Oil Industry, Regulation of.

*Petrolia, Texas.

*Petrolia Oil Field.

*Petronilla, Texas.

*Petteway, Texas.

*Pettibone, Texas.

*Petticoat Lobby. *See* Women's Joint Legislative Council.

*Pettit, Texas. (Comanche County.) Pettit was originally named Fleming for Mart V. Fleming, who settled there in 1872. The name was changed to honor J. P. Pettit, an early settler, merchant, and donor of the school campus there. An abandoned stone ice house which once accompanied a store was the only reminder of this community in 1967.

Margaret Tate Waring

*Pettit, Texas. (Hockley County.)

*Pettus, Freeman.

*Pettus, John Freeman.

*Pettus, Samuel Overton.

*Pettus, William.

*Pettus, Texas.

*Petty, John.

*Petty, Texas. (Lamar County.)

*Petty, Texas. (Lynn County.)

*Petty's Chapel, Texas.

*Pettys Creek.

Petzare Indians. The Petzare (Petaz, Petçare) Indians are known only from records of the La Salle Expedition,qv which indicate that in the late seventeenth century these Indians lived well to the north or northeast of Matagorda Bay, possibly between the Brazos and Trinity rivers. The Petzare have been erroneously equated with the Petao and Petaro, whose names also occur on the same list of Indian groups. The affiliations of all three groups are unknown.

BIBLIOGRAPHY: F. W. Hodge (ed.), *Handbook of American Indians*, II (1910); P. Margry, *Découvertes et établissements des Français dans l'ouest et dans le sud de l'Amérique Septentrionale 1614–1698*, III (1879); H. R. Stiles (ed.), *Joutel's Journal of La Salle's Last Voyage, 1684–7* (1906).

T. N. Campbell

Peupuetem Indians. The Peupuetem (Peupuepuem) Indians lived on the north bank of the lower Rio Grande in the middle eighteenth century. The maps of Jiménez Moreno and G. Saldivar place them in present Cameron and Hidalgo counties, but the documents indicate only that they lived somewhere downstream from present Rio Grande City. The name is said to mean "those who speak differently."

BIBLIOGRAPHY: W. Jiménez Moreno, "Tribus e idiomas del Norte de México," *El Norte de México y el Sur de Estados Unidos* (1944); G. Saldivar, *Los Indios de Tamaulipas* (1943).

T. N. Campbell

*Peveler Creek.

*Peveto, Texas.

*Peyote.

*Peyton, Jonathan C.

*Péz, Andrés de.

*Pfeuffer, George.

*Pfeuffer, Somers V.

*Pflugerville, Texas.

*Phair, Texas.

*Phalba, Texas.

*Phantom Lake.

Pharmacy, State Board of. The State Board of Pharmacy, created in 1907 by the Texas legislature, is composed of six members appointed by the governor for six-year terms. All must be registered pharmacists, but must have no connection with any school of pharmacy.

The board administers the Texas Pharmacy Law; gives examinations for registering pharmacists; issues, renews, and revokes licenses; issues permits for retail pharmacy stores and manufacturers of drugs and medicines; maintains a registry of state pharmicists; presents pharmacy violations to prosecuting officers; and investigates alleged violations of laws concerning narcotics and drugs.

BIBLIOGRAPHY: University of Texas at Austin, *Guide To Texas State Agencies* (1972).

Pharmacy in Texas. The early history of pharmacy in Texas was closely related to that of medicine and was recorded primarily by physicians or medicine men of the period. Probably one of the first Europeans to practice pharmacy and medicine in the New World was Alvar Núñez Cabeza de Vaca,qv who reached the east coast of Texas in 1528, where Indians who greeted his party soon made him a slave. Indian medicine, herbs, and concoctions, as well as "magic," were some of the remedies he used when ordered to treat the Indians who were suffering from epidemic disease.

Spanish missionaries as early as 1682 in El Paso treated the sick and dispensed medicines; only as civil communities or military posts developed were physicians likely to appear and relieve the padres of their medical chores. Spanish physicians in Texas were only average in ability, lacked adequate drug supplies, and usually treated patients in deplorable sanitary conditions. Although their knowledge and experience in handling drugs were usually limited, Spanish doctors were the principal dispensers of drugs in colonial Texas. Many times the pioneer physicians substituted local vegetation for the usual drug remedies; in this search for available drugs they often relied upon the knowledge of medicine men and practitioners in Indian and peasant communities. They often prepared the medication at the patient's bedside from herbs carried in their saddlebags. Many of these saddlebag remedies were family formulas and were particularly adaptable.

Eventually some colonial doctors made up medicines in large quantities and placed them on the shelf in their offices or in their homes, which they called drugstores. This was one of the origins of drug manufacture and sales in Texas.

Medical conditions and drug distribution did not alter much in republican Texas. Nicholas D. Labadie,qv a French Canadian, served as a surgeon at the battle of San Jacinto and later that year opened a combination medical office and drugstore in Galveston. Other physicians also owned drugstores in combination with their medical practices. Among the first were John Logue, who opened a pharmacy in Columbus in 1844, and Joe M. Reuss, who owned a drugstore in Indianola in 1845.

The first recorded drugstores not operated by physicians were in Austin, one owned by McKinstry and Hyde, another by Robertson and Benjamin P. Johnson. Clayton Erhard came from Germany and opened an early drugstore in San Marcos. The Behrmann Drug Store was probably the first in Galveston; in it apprentice Justus J. Schott qv received his pharmaceutical training. First Behrmann's and then Schott's pharmacies were the main source of medical supplies from Europe to other drugstores and physicians in Galveston and throughout Texas. Recognizing the strategic importance of San Antonio as the future business center of southwest Texas, Frederick J. Kalteyer opened a retail drugstore there in 1854; soon he imported drugs into Texas from France and Mexico and developed a sizable wholesale drug business. It later became the San Antonio Drug Company, in operation for more than a century.

The first pharmacy in Dallas was established in 1855 by Frank A. Sayre, who advertised as a pharmacist and chemist. William Hermes, in the same year, opened a drugstore in a log cabin in La Grange. The advent of the prescribing druggist was heralded by a notice which appeared in the San Antonio *Daily Ledger and Texan* of April 27, 1860. In 1863 advertisements appeared in Houston for a drugstore owned by J. J. Schott and F. B. Colby; E. Erlenmeyer and E. F. Schmidt were listed as chemist-pharmacists, and both were dealers in drugs, medicine, perfumery, toilet soaps, and mineral waters, as well as prescriptions. The *Texas State Gazette* qv (Austin) advertised in 1865: "for sale both wholesale and retail, French Quinine, Opium, Morphine, Calomel, Raw Ginger, Arrowroot, Jamaica Ginger, Jayne's Expectorant, Mustang Linament, Bull's Sarsaparilla, Lobelia Seed, Sweet Spirits of Nitre, English Cod Liver Oil, Brown's Mixture, Radway's Ready Relief, Adcock's Porous Plasters, Brandreth's Pills, Wright's India Vegetable Pills, Extract of Colocynth and many other items." In 1866 Dr. F. C. Wilkes published *A Manual of Practice for the Diseases of Texas*, in which he reported that at least five of the remedies therein were sold in drugstores in every neighborhood in the state of Texas.

In 1873 the Morley Drug Company was established in Austin primarily as a retail-wholesale drug house. While most of its drugs came from American manufacturers and were shipped through Galveston and New Orleans, absolutely pure drugs were ordered from Germany. In the mid-nineteenth century many Texas druggists bought basic substances in bulk and acted as manufacturers, wholesalers, prescribers, and retailers of medicines.

In 1879 the Texas State Pharmaceutical Association, the first permanent organization of Texas pharmacists, was formed in Dallas. At least eighteen pharmacists participated in this attempt to organize pharmacists on a professional basis, to seek passage of legal standards for pharmacy, and to improve educational standards for pharmacists. Most early association pharmacists had been college educated, usually in Europe, prior to coming to Texas. *The Proceedings of the Annual Meeting of the Texas State Pharmaceutical Association* (1879–1889) indicate that early meetings of the association were devoted almost entirely to the study of scientific topics and round-table discussions of current problems inside and outside of the profession. Efforts were made to secure passage of a pharmacy bill by the legislature and to assure a chair of pharmacy for the University of Texas Medical Branch, which was being developed in Galveston. In 1889, the tenth anniversary of the association, the Texas Pharmacy Law was passed.

In 1893 Governor James Stephen Hogg qv urged the creation of the chair of pharmacy at the University of Texas. In that year the Twenty-third Texas Legislature added $2,500 to the budget of the university's medical branch for the purpose of establishing a school of pharmacy. Established at Galveston in 1893 with James Kennedy, a practicing physician from San Antonio, elected as the first professor of pharmacy, the school registered eleven students the first year. The course of instruction, consisting of two sessions of seven months each, was gradually increased to meet the demands of a progressing profession until it attained the status of a five-year program with a Bachelor of Science degree in pharmacy being conferred upon graduation. The early faculty was composed of physicians; by 1966 it operated with a faculty of thirty, the majority of whom held degrees in pharmacy and Doctor of Philosophy degrees. The school was moved from Galveston and became the College of Pharmacy on the main university campus in Austin in 1927. Graduate work was offered for the first time in 1948, and instruction leading to the Doctor of Philosophy degree was made available.

Other pharmacy schools were established during the early years of pharmacy in Texas, none of which have survived. The School of Pharmacy at Baylor University in Dallas opened in 1903 and operated for twenty-eight years before closing in 1931. Fort Worth Medical College, a part of Texas Christian University, offered a program of instruction in pharmacy from 1905 to 1918.

After World War II two new schools of pharmacy opened in Texas. In 1947 the board of regents of the University of Houston, then a municipal institution (but since 1963 a part of the state system of higher education), authorized the opening of a School of Pharmacy. The School of Pharmacy at Texas State University for Negroes (now Texas Southern University) was organized as an integral department in 1949.

The first law regulating the practice of pharmacy appeared in 1889, followed in 1907 by the Thirtieth Legislature's passage of a bill authorizing the governor to appoint members to the first State Board of Pharmacy.qv The Texas Health Law, which helped control drugs, was passed in 1907. The present Texas Pharmacy Law was passed in 1929; it required that an applicant for pharmacy registration in Texas be a graduate of a recognized college of pharmacy.

Early publications of interest to Texas pharmacists were *Druggists' Circular and Chemical Gazette, Daniel's Medical Journal of Texas,* and Dr. Eugene Eberle's popular *Southern Pharmaceutical Journal,* established in 1908 and bought by Walter Henry Cousins qv in 1915. In 1896 a house journal called *The Texas Druggist,* published by Felix Parsons for the Texas Drug Company, became the official publication of the Texas State Pharmaceutical Association. There were changes in official publications until 1929, when the name *The Texas Druggist* was given to the association by the Texas Drug Company; in 1962 the name was changed to *Texas Pharmacy.*

In the 1970's, through an outstanding educational system of pharmacy at the undergraduate and graduate levels, Texas had a high standard of practice in pharmacy. Extensive programs of governmental and privately financed research were being conducted, and the pharmacist was increasingly acting as a consultant with physicians, hospitals, nursing homes, and extended care facilities.

Pharmacy in Texas has moved from the practice of uncontrolled distribution of drugs of all types at the turn of the century to legal control over narcotics, barbiturates, and other drugs which are subject to abuse. The pharmacist is continually sought as an expert in the area of drug evaluation and as a consultant in all divisions of the health sciences.

BIBLIOGRAPHY: Johanna Blumel, *History of the San Antonio Drug Company and Pharmacy in Texas, 1854–1954* (1954); Pat Ireland Nixon, *A Century of Medicine in San Antonio* (1936) and *The Medical Story of Early Texas, 1528–1853* (1946); Mrs. George P. Red, *The Medicine Man In Texas* (1930); Marie Louise Giles, The Early History of Medicine in Dallas, 1841–1900 (M.A. thesis, University of Texas at Austin, 1951); Esther Jane Wood Hall, Chapters in the History of Pharmacy in Texas (M.A. thesis, University of Texas at Austin, 1953).

Esther Jane Wood Hall

*Pharr, Texas. Pharr, in south-central Hidalgo County, adopted both a home rule charter and a commission form of municipal government in 1949. Among the businesses reported in the 1960's were those concerned with irrigation equipment, clay products, mattresses, food harvesting and processing equipment, and concrete products. In 1970 Pharr had 212 businesses. The city recorded a 62 percent increase in population during the 1950's, from 8,690 in 1950 to 14,106 in 1960; the population in 1970 was 15,829, according to the United States census report. *See also* McAllen-Edinburg-Pharr Standard Metropolitan Statistical Area.

Phelan, John Henry. John Henry Phelan was born December 11, 1877, in Charlotte, North Carolina, the son of Patrick Henry and Adele (Myers) Phelan. He was educated in parochial schools there, then worked as an office boy, a shipping clerk, and finally as a traveling salesman. In January, 1902, he moved to Beaumont, Texas, where he worked as a salesman for Heisig and Norvell, wholesale grocers. He remained with the firm until 1913, when he organized the Phelan-Josey Company, later the Phelan Grocery Company, which operated as a wholesale and manufacturing firm with branches throughout East Texas.

With the beginning of the modern petroleum industry at Spindletop Oil Field qv near Beaumont, Phelan embarked on a new career and by 1907 was involved in the oil business. He, along with Miles Frank Yount,qv founded the Yount Oil Company (which later became the Yount-Lee Oil Company), organized at Sour Lake in 1915 (see Sour Lake Oil Field). In 1925, after a decline in production at Spindletop, the Yount-Lee Oil Company drilled in a deeper stratum there, and Spindletop boomed again for several years, reaching a new high in production. Phelan was a trustee of the Yount-Lee Oil Company when in 1935 it was sold to Stanolind Oil Company, a sale reputed to be at that time the largest financial transaction of its type in the nation's history.

Phelan remained chairman of the board of his grocery company and was also a director of the First National Bank of Beaumont, Standard Brass Company, Norvell-Wilder Supply Company, and several other businesses. He and his wife were philanthropists whose gifts were worldwide and ran into millions of dollars, although Phelan refused publicity and remained an anonymous donor.

He was married to Johanna (Hannah) Cunningham of Braidwood, Illinois, in June, 1905, in Chicago; they had three children. A Roman Catholic, Phelan was honored by Notre Dame University and was appointed a Knight of St. Gregory by the Pope, one of three men in Texas who had ever received that honor. John Henry Phelan died in Beaumont on May 19, 1957, and was buried at Magnolia Cemetery there.

BIBLIOGRAPHY: Marcellus E. Foster and Alfred Jones (eds.), South and Southeast Texas (1928); Dabney White and F. C. Richardson, East Texas: Its History and Its Makers, IV (1940); The Texas Gulf Coast: Its History and Development, III (1955); Biographical File, Barker Texas History Center, University of Texas at Austin.

*Phelan, Texas.

*Phelps, James Aeneas E.

*Phelps, Timothy B.

*Phelps, Texas.

*Philips, William C. [This title was incorrectly listed in Volume II as Philips, William D. Some listings of the secretaries of state of Texas give his name as D. W. C. Phillips, but this is also in error, for the "D." was picked up from "Dr." (which he was) and the second "l" in his name has continued to appear incorrectly. All copies of his signature, in his hand, read "W. C. Philips." Ed.]

William C. Philips was born in Boone County, Missouri, on January 14, 1823. In 1846 he married Martha Ann Robertson. He was graduated from Transylvania University, Lexington, Kentucky, on March 5, 1847, and practiced medicine in Missouri until 1850, when he went to California.

In December, 1853, he moved to Austin, where he set up medical practice. A strong Unionist, he wrote under the pseudonym of Vesicula Calculus and was elected president at the Union Club's first meeting in September, 1860. He left Austin during the Civil War but returned about 1866. In 1867 (not 1857, as stated in Volume II) he was appointed secretary of state of Texas. In 1871 he was chief clerk in the office of the state comptroller. Interested in stock farming, in 1896 he brought a celebrated race horse, Silent Friend, to Austin, where he and J. H. Philips offered the horse as stud from the Elmonia Stock Farm.

He continued his Republican party qv activities in the state, attending the inauguration of President James A. Garfield in 1881 and serving as delegate to both state and national Republican conventions until 1886. In 1887 he and his daughter moved to Kansas City, Missouri, where he worked as paymaster-inspector of the Metropolitan Street Railroad Company. He was living in Rocheport, Missouri, in 1906 when he committed suicide. He left a note asking that his only epitaph be, "He was Secretary of State in Texas under Governor Pease."

BIBLIOGRAPHY: Texas Almanac (1872); Pease-Graham-Niles Papers, J. M. Coleman Papers (MSS., Austin-Travis County Collection, Austin Public Library).

Elizabeth N. Kemp

*Philips, Zeno.

*Phillips, Alexander H.

*Phillips, Isham B.

*Phillips, Nelson.

*Phillips, William Battle.

*Phillips, Texas. (Hutchinson County.) Phillips, an unincorporated community in southern Hutchinson County, decreased in population from 3,605 in 1960 to 2,515 by 1970, according to the United States census report. Phillips had seven businesses in 1970.

*Phillips, Texas. (Moore County.)

*Phillips Rock.

*Phillipsburg, Texas.

*Philosophical Society of Texas. [A listing of presidents of the society between 1935 and 1949, in Volume II, failed to list Eugene Perry Locke, who was president in 1945. Ed.]

The Philosophical Society of Texas continued to hold meetings on or near December 5 of each year. Meetings have been in Dallas, Houston, San Antonio, Austin, Lufkin, College Station, San Augustine, Nacogdoches, Fort Clark, and Salado. Sessions begin at dinner on Friday evening, followed by an address. On Saturday there is a day-long series of symposiums on topics of current interest and an after-dinner address.

Presidents since 1950 have been William Lockhart Clayton,qv A. Frank Smith,qv Ernest Lynn Kurth,qv Dudley Kezer Woodward, Jr., Burke Baker,qv Jessie Andrews,qv James Pinckney Hart, Robert Gerald Storey, Lewis Randolph Bryan, Jr.,qv W. St. John Garwood, George Crews McGhee, Harry Huntt Ransom, Eugene Benjamin Germany,qv Rupert Norval Richardson, Mrs. George Alfred Hill, Jr., Edward Randall, Jr.,qv McGruder Ellis Sadler,qv William Alexander Kirkland, Richard Tudor Fleming,qv Herbert Pickens Gambrell, Harris Leon Kempner, Carey Corneis,qv Willis McDonald Tate, Dillon Anderson, Logan Wilson, Edward Clark, and Thomas H. Law (1976). Sam Hanna Acheson qv was corresponding secretary from 1939 until his death in 1972. Herbert Gambrell was recording secretary from 1941 to 1973. In December, 1973, Mary Joe Carroll and Virginia Gambrell were named secretaries of the society. On November 1, 1975, Dorman H. Winfrey was named secretary along with Mary Joe Carroll. A membership of approximately two hundred has been maintained through the years.

BIBLIOGRAPHY: Philosophical Society of Texas, *Proceedings*, XXVII (1963), XXXIV (1970).

Herbert Gambrell

Physical Fitness, Governor's Commission on. The Governor's Commission on Physical Fitness, created by the 62nd Texas Legislature in 1971, is composed of fifteen members appointed by the governor with the concurrence of the Senate for a six-year term. The members must represent all fields of physical fitness and should be widely known as professionals. The commission's responsibilities include educating the public in the need for, and benefits of, physical fitness; coordinating efforts in public and private schools, industries, and physical fitness commissions of any political subdivisions of the state or comparable agencies of other states or the federal government; encouraging development of physical fitness programs for all ages; and disseminating information by publication, conferences, lectures, workshops, and other means. The commission evaluates existing programs of physical fitness and recommends improvements and new programs to the governor and legislature. In addition to an annual report of all its activities, the commission submits an inventory of facilities of physical fitness programs to the governor and the legislature. A director is employed by the commission to serve as an administrator.

BIBLIOGRAPHY: University of Texas at Austin, *Guide To Texas State Agencies* (1972).

Physical Therapy Examiners, Texas Board of. The Texas Board of Physical Therapy Examiners, created by the 62nd Texas Legislature in 1971, is composed of nine members appointed by the governor with the concurrence of the Senate for six-year terms. The members must be practitioners of physical therapy for at least five years immediately preceding appointment to the board, and they must hold a certificate from the physical therapy curriculum of the University of Texas or an equivalent physical therapy curriculum. The board examines and licenses physical therapists and physical therapy assistants and has the power to suspend or revoke the licenses. A list of all physical therapists registered is given each year to the secretary of state's office for permanent record, and all licenses must be renewed annually through the board.

BIBLIOGRAPHY: University of Texas at Austin, *Guide To Texas State Agencies* (1972).

*Physiography of Texas. *See* Natural Regions of Texas.

*Picachos.

*Pichardo, José Antonio.

*Pickens, Lucy Holcombe.

*Pickens, Texas.

*Pickering, Texas.

*Picket, Pamelia.

*Picket Spring Branch.

Pickett, Bill. Bill Pickett was born near Liberty Hill, Texas, on the South San Gabriel River, the son of Thomas Jefferson and Virginia (Gilbert) Pickett. His birthdate is uncertain, although varying accounts place it between 1860 and 1870. His father is said to have been part Negro, white, and Indian, and his mother a full-blooded Choctaw Indian. Pickett finished the fifth grade, then began doing odd jobs in Florence, Round Rock, Taylor, and Georgetown. For a while he was a range rider and broke horses and mules on the Garret King Ranch. It was Pickett's original confrontation with a runaway steer while loading a stock car at Taylor that brought him notice and eventual fame as a "bulldogger." While holding the animal's horns and twisting its neck, Pickett also bit the steer's lip and forced it to the ground. He later perfected this act as a rodeo stunt, and it was in Fort Worth in the early 1900's that Pickett joined Zack Miller who, with his brothers Joe and George, was building up the Miller Brothers 101 Wild West Show. Pickett's style was so startling and so effective that he frequently is credited with having invented the sport, although steer wrestling with the "nose-biting" had been performed earlier. Pickett would leap from his galloping horse, "Spradley," onto the head of the running steer, grab a horn in each hand, twist the animal's nose into position so he could bite the steer's tender upper lip with his teeth; throwing up his hands to show he wasn't holding onto the animal, he would fall to one side of the steer, drag his heels along beside, until the animal went down. Although nose-biting is no longer a part of it, steer wrestling has become a standard feature of the American rodeo scene.

Continuing his association with the Millers, for the next thirty years Pickett appeared before audiences in North America, England, and Mexico, often billed as the "Dusky Demon" or "The Wonderful Negro Pickett." On the show's first trip to Madison Square Garden in New York City he performed along with men who were to become famous in the entertainment industry, Tom Mix and Will Rogers (who acted as Pickett's "hazer" during that performance). In Mexico City Pickett's performance almost caused a riot, and while he was unable to bring the Mexican bull down, he did hold onto its horns long enough to win a bet for the Miller brothers.

Pickett has been described as five feet, nine inches tall, 165 pounds, while others saw him as larger; whatever his size, all agreed that he was rugged and strong. With the decline of the Millers' fortunes in the early 1930's, Pickett retired and bought land near Chandler, Oklahoma, but he continued to visit with his old boss, Zack Miller, at the 101 Ranch near Ponca City, Oklahoma. It was while he was acting as companion and nurse to Zack, who was ill, that Pickett was injured while roping a stallion there. The horse knocked him down and stomped him. Bill Pickett died eleven days later, on April 2, 1932. In 1936 his grave on the 101 Ranch was marked by the Cherokee Strip Cowpunchers Association. In 1972 Pickett became the first Negro cowboy to be enshrined in the Rodeo Hall of the National Cowboy Hall of Fame in Oklahoma City.

BIBLIOGRAPHY: Fred Gipson, *Fabulous Empire: Colonel Zack Miller's Story* (1946); J. Gordon Bryson, *Shin Oak Ridge* (1964); Philip Durham and Everett L. Jones, *The Negro Cowboys* (1965); Glenn Shirley, *Buckskin and Spurs* (1958); Austin *American-Statesman*, December 12, 1971; Clifford P. Westermeier, "The Cowboy in His Home State," *Southwestern Historical Quarterly*, LVIII (1954–1955).

*Pickett, Edward Bradford.

*Pickett, George Bibb.

*Pickett, Texas.

*Pickett Ranch Creek.

*Pickton, Texas.

*Pickwick, Texas.

*Picoso Creek.

Pictographs and Petroglyphs. *See* Rock Art, Indian.

*Pidcoke, Texas.

*Piechar Village.

*Piedmont, Texas.

*Piedra Creek.

*Piedra Pinta Creek.

*Piedras, José de las. [The Juan N. Cortina referred to in this article in Volume II is not the Juan Nepomuceno Cortina whose biography is in Volume I; therefore, the *quod vido* by his name is in error.]

*Piedras Blancas Indians. This group is known from one Spanish encounter in 1693, at which time the Piedras Blancas (Spanish for "white stones") were foraging between the Río Sabinas and the Rio Grande in northeastern Coahuila. Their range probably extended northward across the Rio Grande into Texas. It seems likely that the Piedras Blancas were also known to the Spaniards by a native name. Swanton suggested that they probably spoke a Coahuiltecan dialect.

BIBLIOGRAPHY: L. Gómez Canedo, *Primeras exploraciones y poblamiento de Texas, 1686–1694* (1968); F. W. Hodge (ed.), *Handbook of American Indians*, II (1910); J. R. Swanton, *Linguistic Material from the Tribes of Southern Texas and Northeastern Mexico* (1940).

T. N. Campbell

*Pierce, Abel Head (Shanghai).

Pierce, Frank Cushman. Frank Cushman Pierce, son of Sarah Katharine (Cushman) and Leonard Pierce, Jr.,qv was born at Fort Davis, Texas, on December 15, 1858. Pierce's early years were spent in New England, in Buffalo, New York, and briefly in Matamoros, Mexico, where his father was U.S. consul. In late 1865 or early 1866 the family settled in Brownsville, where Pierce received some formal education in public and private schools.

In 1871 he became a telegrapher; later he was an assistant agent for the Morgan Steamship Company at Port Isabel and a seaman on the U.S.S. *Rio Bravo* during its brief career on the Rio Grande. In 1882 he moved to Indianola, Texas, where he married Kate Eichlitz, who died eight years later; they had no children. In the 1880's Pierce moved to Dallas where he worked as a business college instructor and a court reporter. He began contributing articles about Mexico and the South Texas area to Texas newspapers and magazines; he also studied law and was admitted to the Bar in Dallas in 1895. Pierce married Isabella Jane Archer on December 1, 1891; they had eight children. In 1904 Pierce resettled with his family in Brownsville; there he practiced law, organized and operated the Rio Grande Valley Abstract Company, and became a genealogist.

Pierce was one of four residents designated by General Frederick Funston of Fort Sam Houston qv and General James Parker of Fort Brown qv to assist in reassuring citizens of Mexico during the Border Incident (1915–1916) by personal contact and circulation of a manifesto in Spanish. In 1916 he compiled a handbook, *Colloquial and Idiomatic Mexican*, and in 1917 he wrote *A Brief History of the Lower Rio Grande Valley*, containing information largely obtained from conversations with longtime residents. The same year he worked with the military authorities in permanently marking the battlefields of Palo Alto, Resaca de la Palma,qqv and old Fort Brown. Pierce died on November 10, 1918, and was buried in Brownsville, Texas.

Florine Pierce Faulk
Grace Edman

Pierce, George Washington. George Washington Pierce was born in Webberville, Texas, on January 11, 1872, the son of George W. and Mary Elizabeth (Gill) Pierce. He received a B.S. degree in 1893 and an M.A. degree in 1894 from the University of Texas, then went to Harvard to earn another M.A. degree in 1899 and a Ph.D. degree in 1900. Pierce also spent a year at the University of

Leipzig. At Harvard he was appointed assistant professor in 1907, professor in 1917, and Rumford Professor from 1921 to 1940, when he became professor emeritus of physics and communication engineering. During this long tenure he also served as chairman of the Department of Physical Sciences and director of the Cruft High Tension Electrical Laboratory.

In 1910 Pierce's first book, *Principles of Wireless Telegraphy*, was published, and in that same year he received the medal of the Institute of Radio Engineers for distinguished services in radio communication. By 1920 he had published his second work, *Electric Oscillations and Electric Waves*; in 1948 he published *The Songs of Insects*.

Pierce was a fellow of the American Academy of Arts and Sciences and a member of the National Academy of Science and the Texas Academy of Science;qv he received many honors for his work in the field of radio communication, such as the 1928 Franklin medal of the Franklin Institute. He was also a member of the Philosophical Society of Texas.qv

He was first married to Florence H. Goodwin on August 12, 1904. After her death in 1945 he married Helen Russell on November 2, 1946. Pierce died in Franklyn, New Hampshire, on August 25, 1956, and was buried at Cambridge, Massachusetts.

BIBLIOGRAPHY: Austin *American*, August 28, 1956; Biographical File, Barker Texas History Center, University of Texas at Austin.

Pierce, John Leonard. John Leonard Pierce was born on April 29, 1895, in Dallas, Texas, the son of Isabella (Archer) and Frank Cushman Pierce.qv He attended West Texas Military Academy (now Texas Military Institute) and Agricultural and Mechanical College of Texas (now Texas A&M University). On June 29, 1918, he married Kate Bodine Stone; they had three children. In June, 1917, he was commissioned 2nd lieutenant, U.S. Infantry, serving with the 8th U.S. Infantry Regiment in Germany, and advanced through various grades to brigadier general by June, 1943. He was interested in the modern concept of mobile warfare and the development of armor. During World War II he served in many important capacities, including division commander of the 16th Armored Division. His decorations included the Legion of Merit with Oak Leaf Cluster and Order of the White Lion and Military Cross of Czechoslovakia. Following World War II Pierce was president of the Secretary of War's Discharge Review Board. He retired in 1946 to Brownsville and died in San Antonio on February 12, 1959. He was buried at Fort Sam Houston National Cemetery.

BIBLIOGRAPHY: *Who's Who In America* (1950).

Kate Bodine Pierce

*Pierce, Jonathan Edwards.

Pierce, Leonard, Jr. Leonard Pierce, Jr., son of Ann Laura (Prince) and Leonard Pierce, Sr., was born on September 5, 1828, in Eastport, Maine. Pierce served in the U.S. Navy in 1853 and then

resided a year in Chihuahua, Mexico, and became proficient in Spanish. On December 25, 1855, he married Sarah Katharine Cushman, of Maine; they had six children, two of whom died as infants. They lived in Texas from 1856 to 1860; during most of this period he was assistant paymaster for the U.S. Army at Fort Davis.qv He was commissioned U.S. consul at Matamoros, Mexico, on July 20, 1861. Leaving his family in Bangor, Maine, he sailed for Matamoros; arriving in November, 1861, he found the consulate destroyed by fire and this portion of Mexico torn by civil unrest. Pierce's principal responsibilities as consul were the care of refugees from Confederate territory and the military enlistment of Unionist sympathizers; during this time Pierce relocated about seven hundred refugees and sent about three hundred men to enlist in the Union Army, these men forming the nucleus of a regiment of cavalry known as the Texas Union Cavalry, which later served in Nathaniel P. Banks'qv Army of the Gulf. On August 1, 1864, Pierce requested that he be relieved of his duties, and his resignation became effective November 30, 1864. He remained in Matamoros until February 18, 1865, then moved to Buffalo, New York, before settling his family in Brownsville in late 1865 or early 1866. Because of poor health Pierce moved to Roma, Texas, but he returned to Brownsville in 1870. He died there on May 8, 1872, and was buried in the old city cemetery in Brownsville.

BIBLIOGRAPHY: Frank C. Pierce, *A Brief History of the Lower Rio Grande Valley* (1917); Consular Dispatches, Matamoros, Mexico, U.S. Department of State, National Archives (Microfilm copies, Texas Southmost College Library, Brownsville).

Florine Pierce Faulk
A. A. Champion

*Pierce, Texas.

*Pierce Junction, Texas. Pierce Junction, originally spelled Peirce Junction, was named for Thomas W. Peirce,qv Boston capitalist and one of the most active and successful railroad builders in Texas from the late 1850's until the late 1880's. Pierce Junction was the first stop on the Houston Tap and Brazoria Railroad (the Sugar Road), which ran to Stafford, Sugarland, and thence to Richmond. The original spelling, Peirce Junction, is shown on George H. Sweet's 1874 Texas railroad map; on subsequent railroad maps (1875, 1876) the junction is referred to as Pierce Junction.

BIBLIOGRAPHY: S. G. Reed, *A History of the Texas Railroads* (1941).

Walter P. Freytag

Piernas, Joseph. Joseph Joan y Domingo Piernas was born in Barcelona, Spain, on February 23, 1755, the son of Pedro Joseph Piernas, ad interim governor of Louisiana during the American Revolution, and María Gracia Ory. Entering military service as a cadet on June 1, 1765, he served at both St. Louis and New Orleans until his discharge as a lieutenant about 1780. His military career was checkered with irregularities. He went to Natchitoches, bought a plantation and slaves, and lived there for several years, but later returned to New Orleans. There he married María Adelayda Leconte in 1793 and moved to the jurisdiction of Nacogdoches. His ranch, called Santa María Adeleida, was near the Sabine River at present-day Converse, Louisiana. He frequently served as French and Spanish interpreter for Nacogdoches commandant José de Guadiana. Sending merchandise to San Antonio in 1795 in exchange for horses, he engaged in a financial dispute with Antonio Leal.qv Piernas pastured cattle along the Calcasieu River and in 1795 sought to form a settlement there, but when Spain transferred the province to France, he went to Pensacola; he resided there at least until 1815.

BIBLIOGRAPHY: Jack D. L. Holmes, "Joseph Piernas and a Proposed Settlement on the Calcasieu River, 1795," McNeese Review, XIII (1962); Jack D. L. Holmes (ed.), Documentos inéditos para la historia de la Luisiana, 1792–1810 (1963); Jack D. L. Holmes, Honor and Fidelity, The Louisiana Infantry Regiment and the Louisiana Militia Companies, 1766–1821 (1965); Jack D. L. Holmes, "Joseph Piernas and the Nascent Cattle Industry of Southwest Louisiana," McNeese Review, XVII (1966).

Jack D. L. Holmes

*Pierpont, William.

*Pierpont Place, Texas.

*Pierson, John Goodloe Warren.

*Pierson, William.

Pig War. The Pig War is the name given to the dispute between Alphonse Dubois de Saligny,qv French chargé d'affaires, and the Lamar administration that resulted in a temporary rupture of diplomatic relations between France and the Republic of Texas. It originated in 1841 in a private quarrel between the Frenchman and an Austin hotelkeeper, Richard Bullock (see Bullock House), over a matter of marauding pigs. Dubois de Saligny complained that the pigs, owned by Bullock, invaded the stables of his horses, ate their fodder, and even penetrated to his very bedroom to devour his linen and chew his papers. Bullock, charging that the Frenchman's servant had killed a number of his pigs on orders from his master, thrashed the servant and threatened the diplomat himself with a beating. Dubois de Saligny promptly invoked the "Laws of Nations," claimed diplomatic immunity for himself and his servant, and demanded the summary punishment of Bullock by the Texas government. The Frenchman was already on bad terms with the administration, especially Acting President David Gouverneur Burnet and Secretary of State James Mayfield,qqv owing to their opposition to his project of a Franco-Texian commercial and colonization company (although Mayfield had originally introduced the Franco-Texian Bill qv in the House). Saligny may have exploited the undignified wrangle with Bullock as a means to vent his spleen on the current administration of the Republic. When Mayfield refused to have the hotelkeeper punished without due process of law, the chargé d'affaires, acting without instructions from his own government, broke diplomatic relations and left the country in May, 1841. From Louisiana, where he resided over a year, he emitted occasional dire warnings of the terrible retribution that would be exacted by France.

While the French government officially supported its agent in his quarrel with Texas, it disapproved of his highhanded departure from his post and had absolutely no intention of resorting to force in behalf of this very undiplomatic and short-tempered subordinate. Thus, the "war" ended in a compromise. The Houston administration, which succeeded that of Lamar, made "satisfactory explanations" to the French government and requested the return of Dubois de Saligny. These explanations were less than Saligny had asked for, as they contained neither censure of the previous administration nor promises to punish Bullock. But aware of the disapprobation in the French Foreign Ministry, he accepted this peace offering and returned to Texas in April, 1842, to resume his official duties.

The Pig War was an isolated episode in the history of the Texas frontier with few repercussions. It was a black mark against Dubois de Saligny in the French Foreign Ministry that hurt his career, but it did not alter the policy of France toward the young Republic.

BIBLIOGRAPHY: Nancy Nichols Barker (ed. and trans.), The French Legation in Texas, I (1971); George P. Garrison (ed.), Diplomatic Correspondence of the Republic of Texas, II, Part III (1911); Nancy N. Barker, "Devious Diplomat: Dubois de Saligny and the Republic of Texas," Southwestern Historical Quarterly, LXXII (1968–1969).

Nancy N. Barker

*Pigeon Roost Prairie.

Piguique Indians. The Piguique (Piguicane, Pihuique) Indians are known only during the eighteenth century, and there is some doubt about their linguistic status. They lived along the Texas coast between the San Antonio and Nueces rivers and seasonally visited the offshore islands, particularly St. Joseph's Island and Mustang Island. This territory was a boundary zone between Karankawan- and Coahuiltecan-speakers. Since no sample of Piguique speech has survived, it is possible to argue that these people were either Karankawan or Coahuiltecan. However, the documentary evidence seems to indicate that they were Coahuiltecan in speech. Their earlier associations were with Coahuiltecan bands, particularly the Pamaque and the Pasnacane. In fact, some Spanish writers say that Piguique, Pasnacane, and Viayan were subdivisions of Pamaque. The Piguique appear to have been associated with Karankawan groups somewhat later in time. After their numbers had been greatly reduced by epidemics of measles and smallpox, the Piguique entered several missions in both northeastern Mexico and southern Texas. Some went to San Francisco Vizarron Mission south of the Rio Grande; others went to Nuestra Señora del Espíritu Santo de Zúñiga and Nuestra Señora del Refugio missions qqv near the coast; and still others went to certain San Antonio missions—Nuestra Señora de la Purísima Concepción de Acuña and San Juan Capistrano.qqv The ethnic identity of the Piguique was lost after abandonment or secularization of these various missions.

BIBLIOGRAPHY: H. E. Bolton, *Texas in the Middle Eighteenth Century* (1915); F. W. Hodge (ed.), *Handbook of American Indians*, II (1910).

T. N. Campbell

*Pike, Albert.

*Pike, Zebulon Montgomery.

*Pike, Texas.

*Pike's Peak.

*Pilancillos Creek.

*Pilar. *See* Nuestra Señora del Pilar de los Adaes Presidio; Nuestra Señora del Pilar de Nacogdoches.

*Pilgrim, Thomas J.

*Pilgrim, Texas.

*Pilgrim Creek.

*Pillans, Palmer Job.

Pillot, Joseph Eugene. Joseph Eugene Pillot, son of Teolin and Anna C. (Drescher) Pillot, was born February 25, 1886, in Houston. He attended the University of Texas and Cornell University with the intention of studying law, but he gave up that pursuit to enroll in the New York School of Fine and Applied Arts. He worked for awhile as an interior decorator in New York, then entered the workshop course in play writing at Harvard. He continued there for several years, writing and working with the Boston Community Players. He also took a drama course at Columbia.

Pillot became a successful writer of one-act plays, many of which were widely produced on stage, radio, and television. His best known play, *Two Crooks and a Lady*, was first produced at Harvard and has been called a model of construction; it has been republished and produced many times. Other plays include *My Lady Dreams*, *Hunger*, and *The Sundial*. His works have been included in many anthologies and handbooks on the technique of play writing. He was a writer of songs also; the most popular have been "As a Snow White Swan" and "Let Not Your Song End." Most of Pillot's later writing was sacred music. He also wrote poetry.

In 1955 Pillot and artist Grace Spaulding John, in cooperation with the River Oaks Garden Club, produced a prose book, *Azalea*, which was the story of a real dog and of the two iron dogs which had guarded the Pillot residence in Houston for more than a hundred years. In 1965 the family home was given to the Harris County Heritage and Conservation Society and moved to Sam Houston Park, where it was restored, furnished, and opened to the public.

He was a member of the Poetry Society of Texas qv and the 1953 president of its Houston chapter. Pillot never married. He died on June 2, 1966, and was buried in Glenwood Cemetery, Houston.

BIBLIOGRAPHY: Grace Leake, "Eugene Pillot, Playwright," *Holland's* (May, 1939); *Who's Who in the South and Southwest* (1961); Biographical File, Barker Texas History Center, University of Texas at Austin.

Julia Hurd Strong

*Pillsbury, Timothy.

*Pilot Grove, Texas.

*Pilot Grove Creek.

*Pilot Knob.

*Pilot Knob, Texas.

*Pilot Mountain.

*Pilot Point, Texas. Pilot Point, in northeastern Denton County, had a population increase from 1,254 in 1960 to 1,663 in 1970, a gain of 32.6 percent, according to the United States census report. The town had fifty businesses in 1970.

*Pin Oak, Texas.

*Pin Oak Creek.

*Pinanaca Indians. The Pinanaca (Pimanco, Pinaca, Pinanca [as shown in Volume II], Piranaca, and other variants) Indians are primarily linked with eastern Coahuila, but their range extended northward across the Rio Grande south of the Edwards Plateau. They were first recorded in 1674–1675 in northeastern Coahuila and the adjoining part of Texas, where they were said to live on roots, fruits, fish, deer, and bison. In 1687 they seem to have been associated with the Cabezas and other groups of southern Coahuila, and in 1693 they were listed as one of the Indian groups of western Coahuila and eastern Chihuahua. They survived in Coahuila until at least 1762. Their extension northward into Texas was probably connected with seasonal movement to fish in the Rio Grande and to hunt bison north of the river. Although Swanton listed the Pinanaca as probably Coahuiltecan-speakers, their linguistic status remains uncertain. Hodge suggested that the Pinanaca may have been the same people as the Pamaque of southern Texas, but no evidence supports this linkage.

BIBLIOGRAPHY: V. Alessio Robles, *Coahuila y Texas en la Epoca Colonial* (1938); H. E. Bolton (ed.), *Spanish Exploration in the Southwest, 1542–1706* (1916); J. J. Figueroa Torres, *Fr. Juan Larios: Defensor de los Indios y fundador de Coahuila, 1673–1676* (1963); W. B. Griffen, *Culture Change and Shifting Populations in Central Northern Mexico* (1969); C. W. Hackett (ed.), *Historical Documents Relating to New Mexico, Nueva Vizcaya, and Approaches Thereto, to 1773*, II (1926); F. W. Hodge (ed.), *Handbook of American Indians*, II (1910); Esteban L. Portillo, *Apuntes para la historia antigua de Coahuila y Texas* (1886); J. R. Swanton, *Linguistic Material from the Tribes of Southern Texas and Northeastern Mexico* (1940).

T. N. Campbell

*Pinckney, John M.

*Pinckney, Texas.

*Pine, Texas.

*Pine Creek.

*Pine Forest, Texas. (Hopkins County.)

Pine Forest, Texas. (Orange County.) Pine Forest, in western Orange County, increased its population from 344 in 1960 to 512 by 1970, according to the United States census report.

*Pine Island, Texas.

*Pine Island Bayou.

*Pine Lake.

*Pine Mesa.

*Pine Mills, Texas.

*Pine Mountain.

*Pine Prairie, Texas.

*Pine Spring Peak.

*Pine Springs, Texas.

*Pine Tree, Texas.

*Pine Valley, Texas. (San Jacinto County.)

*Pine Valley, Texas. (Walker County.)

*Piñeda, Alonso Álvarez de.

*Pinchill, Texas.

*Pinehurst, Texas. (Montgomery County.)

Pinehurst, Texas. (Orange County.) Pinehurst, a suburb of Orange in eastern Orange County, had a population increase from 1,703 in 1960 to 2,198 in 1970, according to the United States census report. Although incorporated, the community had no post office in 1970.

*Pineland, Texas. Pineland, a sawmill center in southwestern Sabine County, had a population decrease from 1,236 in 1960 to 1,127 in 1970, according to the United States census report. It remained, however, the county's largest town.

*Piney Creek.

Piney Point Village, Texas. Piney Point Village, in southwestern Harris County, was incorporated in 1955 with an alderman type of municipal government. In 1966 the town reported one public school and four churches. The city was restricted against any kind of business; it was exclusively a residential district. The 1960 population was 1,790; in 1970 it was 2,548, according to the United States census report. See also Houston Standard Metropolitan Statistical Area.

*Pinhook, Texas.

Piniquu Indians. In the late seventeenth and early eighteenth centuries the Piniquu Indians seem to have ranged both sides of the Rio Grande in northeastern Coahuila and the adjoining part of Texas. They were represented at San Francisco Solano Mission qv in northeastern Coahuila in 1704. It is inferred that the Piniquu spoke a Coahuiltecan dialect, since nearly all of their associates in this mission were Coahuiltecans. Although Bolton (in Hodge) indicates that some Piniquu were at San Antonio de Valero Mission qv of San Antonio, this may be an error. In 1718 San Francisco Solano was moved from Coahuila to San Antonio, where it became known as San Antonio de Valero. The Solano records were incorporated into the Valero records, leading to some confusion about the Indian groups associated with each phase of the mission's history. Bolton also equates the Minicau with the Piniquu, but this is very debatable.

BIBLIOGRAPHY: F. W. Hodge (ed.), *Handbook of American Indians*, II (1910); J. R. Swanton, *Linguistic Material from the Tribes of Southern Texas and Northeastern Mexico* (1940).

T. N. Campbell

*Pink Bollworm. See Bollworm, Pink.

*Pinks Peak.

*Pinkston, Texas.

*Pinnacle Mountains.

*Pinoak Creek.

*Pinoak Mound.

*Pinola Hill.

Pinole Indians. The Pinole Indians are known only from a Spanish document of 1693, which refers to them as "those who eat all of their food made into pinole." They are mentioned as one of fifty "nations" that lived north of the Rio Grande and "between Texas and New Mexico." This may be interpreted to mean the southern part of western Texas, since the document also states that the Apache were at war with the groups named. Nothing further is known about the Pinole.

BIBLIOGRAPHY: C. W. Hackett (ed.), *Historical Documents Relating to New Mexico, Nueva Vizcaya, and Approaches Thereto, to 1773*, II (1926).

T. N. Campbell

*Pinto, Texas.

*Pinto Canyon.

*Pinto Creek.

*Pinto Indians. In the middle of the eighteenth century the Pinto Indians, whose name is Spanish and probably refers to tattooing, ranged over northern Tamaulipas and the adjoining part of southern Texas. In 1749 one group was encountered near San Fernando, Tamaulipas; others lived on both sides of the Rio Grande, particularly in the Reynosa-McAllen sector. In 1757 there was a Pinto settlement in what is now southern Hidalgo County. Some Pinto families entered the missions of San Fernando and Nuevo Santander in northern Tamaulipas. In later times the Pinto were one of several Coahuiltecan bands along the Rio Grande below Laredo who were called Carrizo by the Spaniards. A few descendants of the Pinto were still living near Reynosa as late as 1900. Some confusion arises from the fact that the Spaniards sometimes referred to the Pakawa as Pinto (Pakawa is a Coahuiltecan word that means "tattooed"). However, it seems clear that the Indians most frequently referred to as Pinto lived nearer to the Gulf Coast than the Pakawa.

BIBLIOGRAPHY: F. W. Hodge (ed.), *Handbook of American Indians*, II (1910); W. Jiménez Moreno, "Tribus e idiomas del Norte de México," *El Norte de México y el Sur de Estados Unidos* (1944); G. Saldivar, *Los Indios de Tamaulipas* (1943); R. C. Troike, "Notes on Coahuiltecan Ethnography," *Bulletin of the Texas Archeological Society*, 32 (1962).

T. N. Campbell

*Pinto Mountain.

*Pinyon Hills.

*Pioneer, Texas.

Piou Indians. This name, about which there is much confusion, is known only from records of the La Salle Expedition,qv which indicated that the Indians so designated lived just west or southwest of the Hasinai tribes in the late seventeenth century. The confusion arises from the combination of Orcan and Piou, the names of two separate Indian groups, to give a hybridized name, Orcampiou or Orcampion (Orcamipia in Spanish). This error was made in one of the editions of Henri Joutel's qv journal. The linguistic and cultural affiliations of both Orcan and Piou remain undetermined. Piou is not to be confused with Peinhoum, which refers to another group on the same list of tribes cited as living in the area.

BIBLIOGRAPHY: I. J. Cox (ed.), *The Journeys of Réné Robert Cavelier, Sieur de La Salle*, II (1906); F. W. Hodge (ed.), *Handbook of American Indians*, II (1910); H. R. Stiles (ed.), *Joutel's Journal of La Salle's Last Voyage, 1684–7* (1906).

T. N. Campbell

*Pipe Creek.

*Pipe Creek, Texas.

*Pipe Lines. *See* Oil Industry, Regulation of; and related articles.

*Pirates of the Gulf. *See* Aury, Louis-Michel; Laffite, Jean.

*Piro Indians.

*Pirtle, Texas.

*Pischachay Creek.

*Pisek, Texas.

*Pisgah, Texas.

*Pita Indians. This presumably Coahuiltecan group is poorly documented and is known only from mission records of northeastern Mexico and Texas. Some Pita took up residence at Mission Nuestra Señora de los Dolores de la Punta, near modern Lampazos in northern Nuevo León, where they were reported in 1727. The Pita were also represented at San Antonio de Valero Mission qv at present San Antonio, established in 1718, as well as at mission San Juan Bautista qv near present-day Guerrero in northeastern Coahuila, where a few Pita were recorded as late as 1783. It seems likely that the Pita were the same people as the Pitalac, who originally lived along the Rio Grande near modern Laredo, Texas.

BIBLIOGRAPHY: F. W. Hodge (ed.), *Handbook of American Indians*, II (1910); M. Orozco y Berra, *Geografía de las lenguas y carta etnográfica de México* (1864); J. R. Swanton, *Linguistic Material from the Tribes of Southern Texas and Northeastern Mexico* (1940); R. S. Weddle, *San Juan Bautista: Gateway to Spanish Texas* (1968).

T. N. Campbell

*Pitahay Indians. The Pitahay (Pitanay, Pitijaya, Piutaay, Putaay) Indians were first reported in 1690, when they were encountered by Spaniards on one of the upper branches of the Frio River. Here they were encamped with five other groups. The next year (1691) they were seen farther down the same drainage, apparently in present-day Frio County, where they shared the same encampment with twelve other groups. In 1708 they were again reported in the same general area, and in 1713 some of them were persuaded by missionaries to move southward across the Rio Grande and enter Mission Candela of northeastern Coahuila. Although Hodge and Swanton listed the Pitahay and Putaay as separate Coahuiltecan bands, the primary sources clearly indicate that both names refer to the same population.

BIBLIOGRAPHY: H. E. Bolton, *Guide to Materials for the History of the United States in the Principal Archives of Mexico* (1913); L. Gómez Canedo, *Primeras exploraciones y poblamiento de Texas, 1686–1694* (1968); M. A. Hatcher, "The Expedition of Don Domingo Terán de los Ríos into Texas," *Preliminary Studies of the Texas Catholic Historical Society*, II (1932); F. W. Hodge (ed.), *Handbook of American Indians*, II (1910); P. O. Maas, *Viajes de misioneros Franciscanos á la conquista del Nuevo México* (1915); J. R. Swanton, *Linguistic Material from the Tribes of Southern Texas and Northeastern Mexico* (1940).

T. N. Campbell

Pitalac Indians. The Pitalac (Pitala, Pitalaque, Pittal) Indians do not appear in documents until 1708, at which time, under the name "Pittales," they were said to be living on the Rio Grande east of Mission Nuestra Señora de los Dolores de la Punta, which was near modern Lampazos in northern Nuevo León. This would place the Pitalac on the Rio Grande in the general vicinity of Laredo, possibly upstream from this city rather than downstream. Thereafter the Pitalac are known only in connection with the eighteenth-century missions of San Antonio. The record is none too clear as to which of these missions they were attached. Some seem to have been at Nuestra Señora de la Purísima Concepción de Acuña qv and possibly also at San Francisco de la Espada.qv According to Castañeda, they were also known as the Alobja. The Pitalac may have been the same people as the Pita.

BIBLIOGRAPHY: C. E. Castañeda, *Our Catholic Heritage in Texas*, II (1936); M. A. Habig, *The Alamo Chain of Missions: A History of San Antonio's Five Old Missions* (1968); F. W. Hodge (ed.), *Handbook of American Indians*, II (1910); P. O. Maas, *Viajes de misioneros Franciscanos á la conquista del Nuevo México* (1915).

T. N. Campbell

*Pitcher Creek.

*Pitchfork.

*Pitchfork Ranch. The manager of Pitchfork Ranch from 1930 to 1940 was Virgil V. Parr (not Virgil V. Paine, as stated in Volume II).

Tad Moses

*Pitic, Plan of.

*Pitts, John D. John D. Pitts served as adjutant general of Texas from March, 1848, to November, 1851 (not 1849, as stated in Volume II).

*Pittsbridge, Texas.

*Pittsburg, Texas. Pittsburg, seat of Camp County, reported industries concerned with furniture, baskets, clothing, agricultural implements, bottling, feedstuffs, and foundry and machine shop products in 1972. The town also had a hospital and nursing home. The 1960 population of 3,796 increased to 3,844 by 1970, according to the United States census report.

*Pivitot Bayou.

*Place Junction, Texas.

*Placedo Junction, Texas.

*Placid, Texas.

*Placido.

*Plains, Texas. Plains, located in an oil and agricultural area, is the seat of Yoakum County. In 1970 the town had forty-eight businesses. Plains had a 1960 population of 1,195 and a 1970 population of 1,087, according to the United States census report.

*Plains Areas of Texas. See Central Denuded Region; Coastal Plains; East Texas; Edwards Plateau; Grand Prairies and the Lampasas Cut Plain; High Plains; South Texas Plains.

*Plainview, Texas. (Coryell County.)

*Plainview, Texas. (Denton County.)

*Plainview, Texas. (Hale County.) Plainview, seat of Hale County, is a commercial center for an extensively irrigated farming area. Industries manufacture agricultural machinery, irrigation pumps, pipe and sprinkler systems, and fertilizer, as well as process castor oil, cottonseed oil, feeds, and food and dairy products. The city had 450 businesses in 1970. Site of Wayland Baptist College, Plainview reported forty-six churches, fifteen schools, three banks, two city parks, two hospitals, and a public library in the mid-1960's. Three newspapers and a radio station served the area. The 1960 population was 18,735; the 1970 census figure was 19,096, according to the United States census report.

The last two remaining trees from two hackberry groves that once were landmarks on the High Plains nearly a century ago stand in a city park between Broadway and Date streets in Plainview, near a spring which flows into Running Water Draw. Although the two founders of Plainview considered the names "Hackberry Groves" and "Running Water Draw," they chose Plainview because the view in all directions from their future town was obstructed only by the two hackberry groves.
BIBLIOGRAPHY: John A. Haislet (ed.), *Famous Trees of Texas* (1970).

*Plainview, Texas. (Sabine County.)

*Plainview Field.

*Plank, Texas.

Planning Agency Council. The Planning Agency Council, created in 1965, was composed of representatives of the Texas State Department of Health, Texas State Highway Department, Texas Industrial Commission, Texas Parks and Wildlife Department, State Soil and Water Conservation Board, Texas Employment Commission, Railroad Commission, and Texas Water Development Board.qqv The

function of the council was to coordinate state programs involving the use of federal, state, and local funds.

The 60th Texas Legislature in 1967 abolished the Planning Agency Council and established the Division of Planning Coordination of the Governor's Office and several interagency planning councils (*see* Planning Coordination, Division of, Governor's Office; *see also* Interagency Councils).
BIBLIOGRAPHY: University of Texas at Austin, *Guide To Texas State Agencies* (1966).

Planning Coordination, Division of, Governor's Office. The Division of Planning Coordination, Governor's Office, was established by the 60th Texas Legislature in 1967. The act designated the governor as the state's chief planning officer and specified the division as the focal point for coordination of state agency and regional planning activities. Among its responsibilities the division reviews grant applications and state plans which require federal assistance, develops coordination of statewide transportation, identifies Texas manpower needs, and is responsible for the Coastal Resources Management Program, which is a part of a total natural resources program. The Interagency Councils,qv set up by the same legislation in 1967, are given staff support by the division. The division and the Interagency Councils replaced the Planning Agency Council.qv

The Division of Planning Coordination is also responsible for providing financial assistance and technical support to the twenty-four Texas regional councils of governments and also serves as liaison between the state agencies and these regional councils. The division provides the coordination required between all the state agencies and the governor's office and also the administration of the Goals for Texas program. In addition, the Division of Planning Coordination works with any special program or project which responds to state and federal legislation calling for the governor to take a more active role in Texas government. In 1972 Ed Grisham served as director of the division.

*Planning and Zoning in Texas. *See also* Urban and Regional Planning in Texas; Urban Renewal in Texas.

*Plano, Texas. Plano, in Collin County, undertook major public improvements in the 1960's to accommodate a great influx of inhabitants. Much of the increase in population was a result of the adjacent expanding metropolitan area of Dallas. New industrial parks were opened, and campuses of the University of Plano and the University of Texas at Dallas (formerly the Graduate Research Center of the Southwest) were located in Plano. In 1960 the population was 3,695; by 1970 it had increased to 17,872 inhabitants, according to the United States census. Plano reported 187 businesses in 1970. *See also* Dallas Standard Metropolitan Statistical Area.

*Plantations. *See* Bernardo Plantation; Eagle Island Plantation; Ellersly Plantation; Evergreen

Plantation; Forest Hills Plantation; Glen Eden Plantation; Glenblythe Plantation; Groce's Retreat; Liendo Plantation; Monte Verdi Plantation; Orozimbo Plantation; Peach Point Plantation; Pecan Point Plantation; Retrieve Plantation; Waldeck Plantation; Wyalucing Plantation.

*Planter.

*Planter's Gazette.

*Plantersville, Texas.

*Plaska, Texas.

*Plaster, Thomas Phiney.

*Plasterco, Texas.

*Plata, Texas.

*Plateau, Texas.

*Platt, Texas.

*Playa Ladosa.

*Pleasant Creek.

*Pleasant Grove, Texas. (Dallas County.)

*Pleasant Grove, Texas. (Eastland County.)

Pleasant Grove, Texas. (Falls County.) Pleasant Grove is a rural community located in south-central Falls County west of the Brazos River. The first community church was established prior to 1887, and the school dates from about that time. By 1936 the school was a common school district and operated until September, 1953, when it was consolidated into the Rosebud Independent School District. The 1970 estimated population of Pleasant Grove was thirty-five.
BIBLIOGRAPHY: Lillian Schiller St. Romain, *Western Falls County, Texas* (1951); *Texas Almanac* (1972).

Pleasant Grove, Texas. (Lee County.) Pleasant Grove, between Tanglewood and Lexington in Lee County, was first named Brown's Gin after a man who operated a cotton gin and grocery store at the site about 1875. In 1883 a Baptist church was founded in a grove of oak trees and the present name was adopted. Ranching and farming are the chief businesses of the inhabitants. The population was about 170 in 1930; in the late 1960's the population was approximately 50.

*Pleasant Grove, Texas. (Rusk County.)

*Pleasant Grove, Texas. (San Jacinto County.)

*Pleasant Grove, Texas. (Wood County.)

*Pleasant Hill, Texas.

*Pleasant Hill, Battle of.

*Pleasant Mound, Texas.

*Pleasant Point, Texas.

*Pleasant Valley, Texas. (Dallas County.)

*Pleasant Valley, Texas. (Garza County.)

Pleasant Valley, Texas. (Potter County.) Pleasant Valley came into existence in 1922 when Quincy Ford subdivided land immediately north of Amarillo into tracts for settlement. By 1926 the town had a grocery store and a population of 250. Already a part of the Amarillo Independent School District, Pleasant Valley's first school was constructed in 1927 by the district, and it opened with four teachers. The settlement of Pleasant Valley, with approximately 5,000 inhabitants, was annexed by the city of Amarillo in 1958.

Mrs. N. P. Taylor

Pleasant Valley, Texas. (Wichita County.) Pleasant Valley, in central Wichita County just west of Wichita Falls, was incorporated with a mayor-council form of government on January 11, 1962. The town consisted of 1,286.53 acres on which several farm residences and a few small stores were located. The Pleasant Valley population, which was 323 in 1970, according to the United States census report, was primarily engaged in farming. *See also* Wichita Falls Standard Metropolitan Statistical Area.

Dora Davis

*Pleasanton, Texas. Pleasanton, in Atascosa County, was an agricultural trade center with 140 businesses, a thirty-three-bed hospital, and churches representing nine denominations in 1970. In 1960 Pleasanton had 3,467 inhabitants, and in 1970 it had 5,407, according to the United States census.

In the city square a bronze statue of a cowboy marks the area as "the birthplace of the cowboy," where men first used the techniques of handling cattle on horseback. The eight-foot monument, donated by Mr. and Mrs. Ben L. Parker of Pleasanton, was completed by an Austrian sculptor in 1970.

*Pleasants, Henry Clay.

*Pleasantville, Texas.

*Pledger, Texas.

*Plemons, William Buford.

*Plemons, Texas.

*Plentitude, Texas.

Pliska, John Valentine. John Valentine Pliska, son of Frank Joseph and Maria Anna (Lesak) Pliska, was born in Tyn, Halferstein, Moravia (now Czechoslovakia), on December 6, 1879. The Pliska family immigrated to Texas in 1896, landing in Galveston and settling at Moulton, near La Grange.

Pliska, an apprentice in his father's blacksmith and carriage shop in Europe, worked on farms and in blacksmith shops in central Texas until 1903, when he started on a trip to Mexico. The train stopped at Midland, where Pliska took a job in Greasewood Smith's blacksmith shop. Later he was a bronc buster and horseshoe maker on the Slaughter Ranch. He built his own blacksmith shop in Midland in 1904 and became well known as a brand maker for ranches in the area. The doors of his shop, which were used to test new branding irons, were preserved as a record of brand signatures through the years; they were given to and exhibited by the University of Texas at the time of the Texas Centennial.qv

In 1905 Pliska married Louise Hundle of Flatonia, and they became the parents of seven children. About this time he began building a flying machine (from his studies in aerodynamics at a balloon school in Germany, he knew the rudiments of aircraft principles). The biplane had a tricycle landing gear with delicate tubeless tires and an open cockpit built so that the pilot could move his body to help steer the craft. The steel structure was covered with shellacked canvas. The plane's engine was made in Sandusky, Ohio, by the Robertson Marine Motors Company; Pliska went there to supervise the construction and brought it back to Midland in a boxcar. Fuel was ordered from New York in five-gallon cans. Piano wires braced the wings and metal bands tipped the propeller ends. The weight of the plane, fuel, and pilot was about 750 pounds. Date of the first successful flight is uncertain; it was probably before 1910, although it followed the Wright brothers' historic 1903 flight by several years. The plane, with Pliska piloting, achieved its longest flight of about fifteen minutes and an altitude of fifty-nine feet over the old polo field south of Midland. Pliska dismantled his plane after a July 4, 1910, exhibition in Odessa and stored it in his blacksmith shop on North Baird Street.

Pliska remained a master blacksmith until his health failed in 1952, and then he retired to his model irrigated farm near Midland. He died on July 28, 1956, in Midland and was buried there. In June, 1962, his aircraft was removed from the blacksmith shop to be restored for display at the Midland Air Terminal. Ground-breaking ceremonies for a museum were held in October, 1963, and the building which housed the aircraft was dedicated at the Midland Air Terminal on October 16, 1965.

BIBLIOGRAPHY: June Hazlip, "Smithy Among the Skyscrapers." *Houston Chronicle Rotogravure Magazine*, November 22, 1953; Midland *Reporter-Telegram*, July 28, 29, 1956, October 12, 20, 1963; Austin *American-Statesman*, October 13, 1963; "Flight 1909," *Horizon* (August, 1962).

Marie Caruth

*Pluck, Texas.

*Plum, Texas.

*Plum Creek.

*Plum Creek Fight.

*Pluto, Texas.

*Plymouth, Texas.

*Pochanaquarhip. *See* Buffalo Hump.

*Pocket.

*Poe, George Washington.

*Poe, John William.

*Poe, Texas.

*Poer, Texas.

*Poesta, Texas.

*Poesville, Texas.

*Poet Laureate of Texas. Until 1961 a new poet laureate of Texas was appointed every two years; subsequently, the term was reduced to one year, with alternate poets laureate selected in 1953, 1959, and since 1963. The honorary appointment carries with it no obligations or requirements. The select-

ing committee, for the most part, chooses those whose poetry can be understood by the average reader.

BIBLIOGRAPHY: Margaret Royalty Edwards, *Poets Laureate of Texas, 1932–1966* (1966).

*Poetry, Texas.

Poetry Society of Texas. The Poetry Society of Texas, organized in 1921, grew out of a movement initiated by Therese Kayser Lindsey,qv a Tyler poet. After obtaining information from the state poetry society of Charleston, South Carolina, she called a meeting of interested persons in Dallas, where plans were made for the organization of a statewide society. Mrs. Lindsey was chosen corresponding secretary; the other charter members were Hilton Ross Greer,qv president; Karle (Wilson) Baker,qv vice-president; Clyde Walton Hill,qv treasurer; Jewell Wurtzbaugh, recording secretary, and Whitney Maxwell Montgomery qv and Louella Styles Vincent, directors. In 1922 the society published its first yearbook, received its charter under state law, and began to function actively.

The aim of the society was to encourage and enlist public support and interest in poetry. Membership was open to anyone in sympathy with the society's general aims. Membership in 1972 was approximately 850, with twenty-nine chapters across the state; headquarters were in Dallas. Active members must be native Texans, residents of Texas, or former citizens of Texas who have been active in the society in the past; associate memberships have no geographical qualifications.

Meetings are held the second Saturday evening of each month from October through June, in the Umphrey Lee Student Center, Southern Methodist University, in Dallas. The November meetings feature an annual awards dinner, and the June meetings include an annual garden party and poetry program held at Fondren Library on the Southern Methodist University campus. Meetings include lectures by distinguished speakers and poetry readings.

The society sponsored an annual book publication contest from 1925 to 1933. It holds annual and monthly contests with awards for individual poems. It has a permanent library collection in the Dallas Public Library, numbering several hundred books and pamphlets by Texas poets. Since 1922 the society has annually published a yearbook containing general information, a summary of the year's activities, and the monthly prize-winning poems of members. It also publishes a monthly news bulletin for members. Richard Sale was president of the society in 1972.

BIBLIOGRAPHY: Poetry Society of Texas, *A Book of the Year* (1939, 1962, 1972).

Sonja Fojtik

Pohl, Hugo D. Hugo D. Pohl was born in Detroit, Michigan, on March 11, 1878. He studied art under Julius Theodore Melchers in Detroit, then continued his training under Joseph W. Gies at the Detroit Museum of Art. Further study led Pohl to

New York and then to France to work under Jean Paul Laurens. Meanwhile his paintings were being exhibited in several galleries throughout the United States. In 1908 he was commissioned by the International Harvester Company in Chicago to paint murals depicting harvests in various countries; these murals on the walls of the company's new office building took eighteen months to complete.

He decided in 1918 to tour the Southwest to find themes for his work. A pioneer in the automobile trailer movement, he constructed a traveling studio on an automobile chassis and started from Chicago in July, 1919, on a long trip through the West—Colorado, New Mexico, Arizona, and California. Paintings of the California missions during this period are among his best works and provide a valuable historic record. After an interval of visits to Detroit and Washington, D. C. (where he was director of the Art League), Pohl moved to San Antonio, Texas, in the early 1920's, where he established a studio and became president and director of the San Antonio Academy of Art. Among his pupils were many artists who later became well known in Texas. In the January, 1938, issue of the San Antonio publication *Naylor's Epic Century* (*see* Naylor, Joe Oliver), Pohl was introduced as art editor, and a number of his drawings and paintings of San Antonio scenes were included.

Pohl specialized in mural decoration, genre, and historical subjects. The design for the first curtain for the municipal auditorium in San Antonio was painted by Pohl. Among his other better known paintings are the "Founding of San Antonio" and "Portrait of Mayor [Bryan] Callaghan." He died on July 20, 1960, in San Antonio. In October, 1961, the Panhandle-Plains Historical Museum qv presented an exhibit of his work, with the Coppini Academy of Fine Arts in San Antonio loaning forty pictures for the exhibition.

BIBLIOGRAPHY: Files, Alamo Museum, San Antonio; Files, Witte Memorial Museum, San Antonio; "Art in Texas: Introducing Hugo D. Pohl," *Naylor's Epic Century* (January, 1938); Frances Battaile Fisk, *A History of Texas Artists and Sculptors* (1928); Esse Forrester-O'Brien, *Art and Artists of Texas* (1935); *Who's Who in American Art* (1962).

Caroline Remy

*Poindexter, William.

*Poinsett, Joel Roberts.

*Point, Texas.

*Point Blank, Texas.

*Point Bolivar. The first known fortification on Bolivar Peninsula qv was James Long's qv Fort Las Casas (1819–1821) at Point Bolivar (*see also* Long, Jane Herbert Wilkinson; Long Expedition; Fort Travis). About this time one of Francisco Xavier Mina's qv men is said to have named the area for the South American hero, Simón Bolívar. Stephen F. Austin's 1822 *Mapa Geográfico de la Provincia de Texas* shows the name Bolivar Peninsula. An 1825 map in the University of Texas at Austin Archives shows the point marked as "Fort

de Bolivar" with a fortification drawing. The United States Coast Survey map of 1852 shows Point Bolivar with Sanderson's House marked on the Gulf side and advice to use it and a nearby lightboat in navigating the entrance to Galveston Bay. In the 1855 edition of the Coast Survey, a lighthouse is shown on the point. This lighthouse lines up with another mark, Fort Point, at the tip of Galveston Island, for navigation. The term Bolivar Roads qv continued to be used to describe the waterway between Galveston and Bolivar Peninsula.

The well-known Bolivar ferry, which connects Galveston with Bolivar Peninsula at Point Bolivar, began as a municipally owned service in the early 1930's with two diesel-powered ferries, each carrying thirty vehicles at regular intervals, reducing the distance between Galveston and Port Arthur-Beaumont by approximately sixty miles.

In 1971 the Texas Highway Department qv ran three ferries, also diesel-powered, on a twenty-four-hour schedule. The 185-foot ferries each had a capacity of four hundred passengers and fifty-two standard-size cars, and they traveled at twelve knots an hour. The ferry traveler between Point Bolivar and Galveston passes the wreckage of a World War I concrete ship, once known as the S.S. *Selma*, and Pelican Island, which was at one time two islands, Pelican Split and Pelican Island, since joined by fill from channel dredging. *See also* Point Bolivar Lighthouse.

BIBLIOGRAPHY: J. O. Dyer, *The Early History of Galveston* (1916); Earl Wesley Fornell, *The Galveston Era* (1961); Galveston Chamber of Commerce, *The Port of Galveston* (1928); Dallas *Morning News*, December 10, 1958; Cartographic Collection, Barker Texas History Center, University of Texas at Austin.

Point Bolivar Lighthouse. In 1872 the United States government constructed a lighthouse on Point Bolivar qv near the site of a fort erected in 1819 by General James Long.qv The structure was designed to serve as a guide to mariners, and in 1900 it marked the end of the north jetty, a great wall of stone built to protect Galveston harbor. The lighthouse stood 115 feet high and was constructed of solid brick masonry encased in steel plates.

The lighthouse was one of the few large structures to survive the Galveston storm of 1900 (*see* Galveston Flood). However, its use was discontinued in 1933 in favor of a more modern and less expensive aid to navigation. In 1970 the lighthouse was privately owned.

BIBLIOGRAPHY: Clarence Ousley, *Galveston in Nineteen Hundred* (1900); Galveston *Daily News*, July 11, 1936; Marker Files, Texas Historical Commission, Austin.

M. Doty

Point Comfort, Texas. Point Comfort, in Calhoun County across Lavaca Bay from Port Lavaca, was incorporated in 1953 and is a suburb of Port Lavaca. Many of the basic public facilities and improvements were built in the 1950's, including a fire station and a swimming pool. By the early 1960's a large aluminum plant and industries producing chemicals supported the town's economy. In 1969 the town had six churches, a school, and a library; ten business establishments were reported in 1970. The 1960 population was 1,453; the 1970 population was 1,446, according to the United States census report.

Point Comfort and Northern Railway Company. The Point Comfort and Northern Railway Company was chartered April 29, 1948. By 1972, of the 16.99 total miles of track operated, 12.7 miles was mainline track. The Aluminum Company of America was the major stockholder in the Point Comfort and Northern Railway Company.

*Point Enterprise, Texas.

*Point Isabel. *See* Port Isabel.

*Point Peak.

Point Peñascal. Point Peñascal, situated in present Kenedy County, was the extreme point of land, sometimes cut off from the mainland, on Laguna Madre at the southeast approach to Salt Lagoon (now Baffin Bay). Point Peñascal made up part of the region known in the nineteenth century as Rincon del Peñascal. During the Civil War the point was utilized by J. Ingalls and Company, wholesale merchandisers and dealers in salt, as a port in the contraband cotton trade. Confederate cotton was sometimes smuggled by boats of light draft along the Texas coast as far south as the point and was then consigned to Mexican teamsters who hauled it overland for sale at Matamoros. In the twentieth century this jut of land became known as Griffin's Point.

BIBLIOGRAPHY: José San Román Papers (MS., Archives, University of Texas at Austin Library); Charles W. Pressler, *Traveller's Map of the State of Texas* (1867).

Robert H. Thonhoff

*Pointers, Texas.

Pojue Indians. In 1683–1684 Juan Domínguez de Mendoza qv led an exploratory expedition from El Paso as far eastward as the junction of the Concho and Colorado rivers east of present San Angelo. In his itinerary he listed the names of thirty-seven Indian groups, including the Pojue, from which he expected to receive delegations. Nothing further is known about the Pojue, who seem to have been one of many Indian groups of north-central Texas that were swept away by the southward thrust of the Lipan-Apache and Comanche Indians in the eighteenth century.

BIBLIOGRAPHY: H. E. Bolton (ed.), *Spanish Exploration in the Southwest, 1542–1706* (1916); C. W. Hackett (ed.), *Pichardo's Treatise on the Limits of Louisiana and Texas*, II (1934).

T. N. Campbell

Polacme Indians. The Polacme (Polame) Indians seem to have been eastern Concho Indians who in the early eighteenth century lived at the town of Nuestra Señora de Guadalupe qv on the south bank of the Rio Grande near present Presidio. In 1693 the Polacme were listed among the "nations" that lived north of the Rio Grande in this area. During the eighteenth century the Polacme

appear to have been absorbed by the Spanish-speaking population of northern Chihuahua.

BIBLIOGRAPHY: C. W. Hackett (ed.), *Historical Documents Relating to New Mexico, Nueva Vizcaya, and Approaches Thereto, to 1773*, II (1926); J. C. Kelley, "Factors Involved in the Abandonment of Certain Peripheral Southwestern Settlements," *American Anthropologist*, LIV (1953); R. D. Reindorp, "The Founding of Missions at La Junta de los Ríos," *Supplementary Studies of the Texas Catholic Historical Society*, I (1938); C. Sauer, *The Distribution of Aboriginal Tribes and Languages in Northwestern Mexico* (1934).

T. N. Campbell

*Polar, Texas.

†Polecat Creek.

Poles in Texas. The first Polish immigration to America, extending from 1608 to 1775, consisted of only a few adventurers or religious refugees; it was not until the period from 1776 to 1853 that political refugees from the Napoleonic Wars, the partitions of Poland, and the Polish Revolution of 1830 influenced immigration to Texas. Early in 1818 a group of Polish veterans who had served under Napoleon were among the approximately four hundred men of various nationalities who sailed up the Trinity River and founded the military camp Champ d'Asile qv north of Galveston (near present Liberty). This short-lived colony soon dispersed because of famine and the threat of Spanish military opposition. A few Polish veterans fought in the Texas Revolution at Goliad and San Jacinto.

The greatest wave of immigration began in 1854 and lasted until the outbreak of World War I (1914). Partition of Poland by its neighbors had led to deteriorating socio-economic conditions in the homeland, and Texas offered encouragement to immigrants. Some came as early as 1830, as individuals rather than in groups, and these for the most part were absorbed into the communities where they settled. A Polish Franciscan missionary, Father Leopold Moczygemba, had been working in the areas of San Antonio, New Braunfels, and Castroville since April, 1852, and it was through his influence that a group of approximately one hundred Polish families (accounts vary as to exact number) from Upper Silesia came to south-central Texas. They sailed on the *Weser*, out of Bremen, and landed in Galveston on December 3, 1854; traveling inland, they founded Panna Maria (Virgin Mary) in Karnes County on December 24, 1854 (having the first Mass said there on Christmas Day following), on three hundred acres of land at the junction of the San Antonio and Cibolo rivers, purchased from John Twohig.qv This was the first permanent Polish colony in the United States, and ruins of the first stone buildings remain today.

Although the first year in Texas was extremely hard, they persevered, and some seven hundred of their Polish countrymen followed, arriving in Galveston on December 15, 1855; thirty additional families arrived the next year. Not all of the Polish families reached the Cibolo-San Antonio junction. Some chose to remain in the coastal communities, and others continued along the San Antonio and Medina rivers, settling in St. Hedwig, Bandera, San Antonio, and Yorktown. It was at Panna Maria, however, that the first Polish Catholic church (1855) and the first Polish school (1868) in the United States were established.

With the influx of immigrants after 1865, the central Texas towns of Cestochowa, Kosciusko, Falls City, Polania, New Waverly, Brenham, Marlin, Bremond, Anderson, Bryan, and Chappell Hill were either founded or populated by the Poles. It is estimated that by 1900 there were 16,740 Poles in Texas, concentrated in thirty-eight settlements in the following counties: Bandera, Bexar, Wilson, Karnes, DeWitt, Hays, Falls, Guadalupe, Caldwell, Matagorda, Fayette, Austin, Harris, Grimes, Washington, Brazos, Robertson, Walker, and Grayson.

For many years the Poles did not contribute directly to the political, cultural, or social life of the state; the language barrier was difficult to overcome, and many Poles chose to remain isolated rather than adapt to new situations. They did, however, contribute to the economy, being industrious farmers, artisans, and laborers. Their social life was bound up in the feasts and festivals of the Catholic church. Native Polish clergy cared for the spiritual welfare of the people, and Polish national churches were founded; there were also small numbers of Polish Jews in some of the communities. Education, at first considered unimportant, became necessary to second and third generation Poles, yet thorough "Americanization" of the Poles did not take place until after World War II.

Unlike their compatriots in other parts of the United States, the Poles in Texas did not organize large and powerful fraternal organizations, nor did they establish Polish-language presses as did other European ethnic groups. The teaching of the Polish language never developed beyond the primary level. It was not until 1971 that Polish ethnic consciousness in Texas emerged at the statewide level, with the founding of a Texas chapter of the Polish American Congress by Father John W. Yanta.

The customs, traditions, and language of the old country are still in evidence among the older group of Poles in Texas. With the exception of the Bryan, Houston, and San Antonio groups, the Polish settlements remained predominantly rural through the first half of the twentieth century. Although there are no exact census figures available, it is estimated that there were more than 40,000 citizens of Polish extraction living in Texas by 1972.

BIBLIOGRAPHY: Edward J. Dworaczyk, *The First Polish Colonies in Texas* (1936), *The Centennial History of Panna Maria, Texas* (1954); Miecislaus Haiman, *The Poles in the Early History of Texas* (1936); Jacek Przygoda, *Texas Pioneers From Poland* (1971); B. Roman Witowski, "Poles In America: A Selected Bibliography," *Polish American Studies*, XII (1955); Jan Marie Wozniak, *St. Michael's Church: The Polish National Catholic Church in San Antonio, Texas, 1855–1950* (M.A. thesis, University of Texas at Austin, 1964); Joseph A. Wytrwal, *America's Polish Heritage: A Social History of the Poles in America* (1961); X. Waclaw Kruszka, *Historya polska w Ameryce*, I, VI, VII (1905–1908); Mieczyslaw Szawleski, *Wychodztwo polskie w Stanach Zjednoczonych Ameryki* (1924); Andrzej Brozek, *Slazacy W Teksasie* (1972).

Jan L. Perkowski
Jan Marie Wozniak

*Police. See State Police.

Polignac, Camille Armand Jules Marie, Prince de. Camille Armand Jules Marie, Prince de Polignac, was born at Millemont Seine-et-Oise, France, on February 16, 1832. He was the son of the former Marie Charlotte Parkyns and Jules de Polignac, who had been president of the Council of Charles X of France. Polignac studied mathematics and music at St. Stanislas College in the 1840's. In 1853 he joined the French army and won a second lieutenant's commission in the Crimean War. He resigned in 1859, then traveled to Central America to study political economy and geography.

In 1861 he offered his services to the Confederacy and became a staff officer under P. G. T. Beauregard and Braxton Bragg. In January, 1863, he was promoted to brigadier general and in March was transferred to the Trans-Mississippi Department to become the commander of a Texas infantry brigade. He led the Texans in skirmishes at Vidalia and Harrisonburg, Louisiana, in the spring of 1864, and at Mansfield in the first major action of the Red River campaign.qv That day, Polignac rose to division commander and was soon promoted to major general after the death of Alfred Mouton. Polignac led the division throughout the remainder of the campaign and during its service in Arkansas in the fall of 1864. In January, 1865, he was sent to Napoleon III of France to request intervention on behalf ot the Confederacy but arrived too late to accomplish anything. (*See also* Polignac's Brigade.)

After the war he again traveled to Central America, did some writing, and served as a brigadier general in the Franco-Prussian War. In 1874 he married Marie Adolphine Longenberger, who died at the birth of their daughter. He married Elizabeth Margaret Knight in 1883, and they had two daughters and one son. Polignac continued to study mathematics and music until his death on November 15, 1913.

BIBLIOGRAPHY: Roy O. Hatton, "Prince Camille de Polignac and the American Civil War, 1863–1865," *Louisiana Studies*, III (1964).

Alwyn Barr

Polignac's Brigade. The 22nd, 31st, and 34th Texas Cavalry regiments were raised in the winter of 1861 and the spring of 1862 in North Texas. In the spring and summer of 1862 they were ordered into the Indian Territory and Arkansas, where they were organized into a brigade with some Indian regiments under Colonel Douglas H. Cooper. In the fall of 1862 the brigade fought at Shirley's Ford and at Newtonia, Missouri, before being driven back into Arkansas, where they were dismounted for service as infantry. The brigade was joined by the 20th Texas Cavalry, served under several commanders, and fought at Prairie Grove, Arkansas, in the late fall and winter of 1862. In January, 1863, the 15th Texas Infantry joined the brigade, which marched through snow back to Texas under the command of Colonel Joseph Warren Speight,qv leaving the 20th Texas behind in the Indian Territory.

In the spring of 1863 the brigade was sent to Louisiana, where the 22nd and the 34th were retrained as infantry, while the 15th and the 31st were joined by the 11th Texas Battalion in skirmishing and in the battles of Stirling's Plantation and Bayou Bourbeau. In the fall of 1863 the brigade was reunited under Brigadier General Camille de Polignac,qv with the addition of the 17th Texas Consolidated Dismounted Cavalry, and the later loss of the 11th Texas Battalion. The brigade skirmished at Vidalia and Harrisonburg, Louisiana, in early 1864 before joining Major General Richard Taylor's army to defeat Federal forces in the Red River campaign qv in April and May. Polignac became division commander after the battle of Mansfield qv and was succeeded by several brigade commanders, including Robert Dillard Stone,qv who was killed at Yellow Bayou, Wilburn Hill King,qv and Richard E. Harrison. In the fall of 1864 the brigade moved into Arkansas, then back to Texas, where it disbanded in May, 1865.

BIBLIOGRAPHY: Alwyn Barr, *Polignac's Texas Brigade* (1964).

Alwyn Barr

Political Association of Spanish-Speaking Organizations. The Political Association of Spanish-Speaking Organizations (PASO) grew out of the "Viva Kennedy" clubs formed during the John F. Kennedy presidential campaign of 1960. The clubs changed their name when the campaign was over to become the Political Association of Spanish-Speaking Organizations. They did not, however, change their political purposes. The main aim of the organization was to raise the standard of living for the Mexican American and at the same time insure against discrimination in employment.

PASO, an active organization of over 10,000 members, participated in the 1960's in such causes as supporting the Valley farm workers' strikes, registering voters, and helping to abolish the poll tax. The organization maintains close ties with organized labor union groups.

*Political Chief. *See* Mexican Government of Texas.

*Political Departments of Mexican Texas. *See* Mexican Government of Texas.

*Political Parties. The Democratic party qv has always been the leading political party in Texas except during Reconstruction.qv In the nineteenth century, however, Whigs, Know-Nothings, Republicans, Greenbackers, and Populists qqv provided at different times a formidable opposition, so that Texas did not become a real one-party state until after 1900, when the Republican party sank into insignificance and minor parties largely disappeared.

Several factors contributed to the Democrats' virtual monopoly of Texas politics during the first half of the twentieth century. By 1900 the Republican party in the state ceased to be important; torn by factional struggle until 1923, it then fell under the control of a political machine dominated by R. B. Creager,qv Republican national committeeman, who remained in control until his death in 1950. Creager was interested chiefly in naming the Texas delegations to Republican national conventions and in dispensing federal patronage in the state when that party held the presidency. He showed little desire to increase Republican voting strength or to take any real part in electing Republicans to state, district, or county offices. Only in the gubernatorial election of 1924 and the presidential election of 1928 were serious Republican campaigns staged, during which times a large number of Democrats voted Republican in efforts to defeat Mrs. Miriam A. Ferguson qv for governor and Alfred E. Smith for president. The former effort was unsuccessful, but the latter was successful. The dissident Democrats of these elections in Texas had no intention of becoming Republicans, and the Texas Republicans did little to induce them. Anti-Ferguson Democrats and "Hoovercrats" (for Herbert Hoover for president), respectively, simply used the Republican party as a means of trying to defeat the majority faction of the Democratic party.

Perhaps the adoption of the direct primary system of nomination in 1905 under the Terrell Election Law (*see* Election Laws) was the chief factor in insuring for the Democratic party a monopolistic place in Texas politics. This law was designed to apply mainly to the Democratic party because the primary system was made mandatory only for parties polling as many as 100,000 (later 200,000) votes for their candidates for governor in the last general election, a figure which the Republicans did not reach for many years. Thus Texas voters came to look upon the Democratic primary as the real election, because its nominees were largely unopposed in the general election and because Democratic factionalism in the primaries in reality substituted for party politics.

During the New Deal period Texas Democratic factions began to develop in a more pronounced form and to take on a definite pattern of conservatism versus liberalism. In the 1930's and 1940's minor parties developed both to the left and to the right of the state's Democratic party—"Jeffersonian Democrats" in 1936, "Democrats for Willkie" in 1940, "Texas Regulars" in 1944, and the "States' Rights" or "Dixiecrat" party in 1948. Although the Texas Republican party remained insignificant in national politics until the election of 1952, the Republican presidential vote in Texas progressively increased after 1932. Those voting for Republican presidential candidates came to be designated as "Presidential Republicans" because they still voted in Democratic primaries and for Democratic candidates for state office. The death of Creager in 1950 and the nomination of Dwight D. Eisenhower qv in 1952 resulted in a struggle for new leadership among Texas Republicans and a strong movement to carry the state for Eisenhower.

A temporary provision in the Texas election law permitted "cross-filing" of the candidates of another party, so in 1952 the Republicans cross-filed most of the Democratic candidates for statewide offices as an inducement to Democratic voters to vote for Eisenhower. Eisenhower carried Texas in 1952 largely because of the work of a strong combination of conservative Democrats under the leadership of Democratic Governor Allan Shivers. This majority faction was known as the "Shivercrats." In 1956 the strong influence of United States Senator Lyndon B. Johnson qv and Speaker of the U.S. House of Representatives Sam Rayburn qv kept the Texas Democratic organization from bolting, but they could not prevent the voters from again following Shivers and carrying the state for Eisenhower by an even larger majority. The Eisenhower vote in Texas in 1952 was 53.12 percent; in 1956 it was over 55 percent.

In 1960 Texas returned to the Democratic presidential column, casting a very thin majority for John F. Kennedy for president (along with Texan Lyndon B. Johnson for vice-president); however, the total vote for losing Republican presidential candidate Richard Milhous Nixon was greater than that given Eisenhower when he carried the state in the two previous elections. From 1952 to 1962 the newly reorganized Republican party seemed mainly interested in carrying the state for the Republican presidential ticket. In 1954, however, a Dallas Republican, Bruce Alger, was elected to Congress; in a special election in 1961 the first Republican United States senator since Reconstruction, John G. Tower, was elected. Tower's election inspired the Republicans to branch out in the regular election of 1962 and nominate candidates for many offices. They presented candidates for most statewide offices, congressional and state legislative seats, and many local offices: victories were few, but in many races the Republican vote ran high, and many thought that Texas was on the threshold of a two-party system.

The Democratic landslide of 1964, however, seemed to wipe out the start made by Republicans in Texas. As in 1962, the Republicans made many nominations, but they worked hardest in support of Barry Goldwater, the conservative Republican presidential candidate. Huge majorities were registered for most Democratic candidates. Conservative Republican support of Goldwater in Texas apparently alienated many politically moderate Texans who had been inclined to vote Republican. Nationally, the Goldwater candidacy seemed to divide the conservative and moderate wings of the Republican party. On both the state and national levels the Republican party appeared on the verge of collapse after Goldwater's overwhelming defeat. The Texas dream of a two-party system was dissipated, and the national two-party system seemed threatened as well.

That pessimistic picture, however, was wiped out by the results of the election of 1966. The election was a great encouragement to the Texas Republicans, who concentrated on reelecting Senator Tower to his first full-length term. They succeeded by a majority of over 200,000. Two Republicans were elected to the United States House of Representatives; three were elected to the lower house of the Texas legislature; and the first Republican state senator was chosen in thirty-nine years. These victories did not make Texas a two-party state, but they did mean that the Republican party was a significant factor in Texas politics. [For updated account *see* information following bibliography below. Ed.]

BIBLIOGRAPHY: Stuart A. MacCorkle and Dick Smith, *Texas Government* (1964); O. Douglas Weeks, *Texas Presidential Politics in 1952* (1953), *Texas One-Party Politics in 1956* (1957), *Texas in the 1960 Presidential Election* (1961), *Texas in 1964—A One-Party State Again?* (1965); Paul D. Casdorph, *A History of the Republican Party in Texas, 1865–1965* (1965); James R. Soukup, Clifton McCleskey, and Harry Holloway, *Party and Factional Division in Texas* (1964).

O. Douglas Weeks

In the presidential elections of 1968 and 1972, both won by Richard M. Nixon, many Texas Democrats voted for the Republican. In 1968 Texas gave a slight edge to losing Democratic candidate Hubert H. Humphrey, but in the 1972 election Texans voted overwhelmingly for Nixon (2,298,896 votes) in preference to his Democratic opponent, George McGovern (1,154,289 votes). Republican John Tower continued as United States senator, having defeated Democratic nominee Barefoot Sanders in the 1972 election. In that same year Republican Henry C. Grover, although defeated by Dolph Briscoe in an attempt to win the Texas governorship, received more votes than any other Republican gubernatorial candidate in the history of Texas. Raza Unida,qv a third political party, attracted enough voters (214,118) to entitle the party to a position on the 1974 Texas gubernatorial ballot. In the 1972 election further gains were made in the Texas legislature by the Republicans, when seventeen of their members were elected to the Texas House of Representatives and three were elected to the Texas Senate; in 1974 they ran almost as well, electing sixteen representatives and three state senators. See *also* Sharpstown Stock Fraud Scandal.

Eldon S. Branda

*Polk County. Polk County, home of the state's only Indian reservation, ranked second among Texas counties in lumber production in 1965. It had the greatest number of forested acres, with twice as much southern pine as hardwood timber. Other income was derived from rice, cotton, and petroleum and other minerals. Tourists were attracted by the Alabama-Coushatta Indian Reservation and the Big Thicket.qqv The county supported a hospital and bookmobile service and by 1966 had purchased a site for a public library-museum building. The 1960 population was 13,861; the 1970 census was 14,457.

Polk County may claim two national champion trees: a honey locust tree growing on the Alabama-Coushatta Indian Reservation and a Chinese tallow tree growing near the Goodrich Independent School. In 1968 the honey locust tree had a trunk circumference of 81 inches, was 112 feet tall, and had a crown spread of 43 feet. In 1967 the Chinese tallow tree had a girth of 103 inches, a height of 40 feet, and a crown spread of 66 feet.

BIBLIOGRAPHY: John A. Haislet (ed.), *Famous Trees of Texas* (1970).

*Polk Creek.

*Poll Tax. *See* Election Laws.

*Pollard, Amos.

Pollard, Claude. Claude Pollard was born in Carthage, Texas, on February 14, 1874, the son of Hamilton and Sarah Jane (Davis) Pollard. He attended public schools in Carthage and taught for a time before studying law. He was admitted to the Bar in 1895 and during the next fourteen years served as Panola County attorney (1895–1898), U.S. district attorney (1900–1905), and assistant attorney general of Texas (1905–1909). He married Julia S. Newton on December 27, 1897; they had two children.

In 1909 Pollard moved to Kingsville, where he served as counsel for a railway company until 1916, when he went into private law practice. While in Kingsville, he was a leader in the movement which resulted in the organization of Kleberg County, with Kingsville as the county seat. He also served as regent of South Texas State Teachers College (now Texas A&I University) and was president of the Texas Bar Association qv in 1920.

In 1926 Pollard defeated James V. Allred qv for attorney general and was reelected in 1928. He resigned before the end of his second term (serving from January, 1927, to September, 1929) to become general counsel for the Railway General Managers' Association of Texas. Pollard died in Austin on November 25, 1942, and was buried in the State Cemetery.qv

BIBLIOGRAPHY: *Texas Bar Journal*, VI (January, 1943); *Who's Who In America* (1934).

Jack Geddie

*Polley, Joseph Benjamin.

*Polley, Joseph Henry.

*Pollitt, George.

*Pollok, Texas.

*Polly's Peak.

*Polytechnic College.

*Pomeroy, Eltweed.

*Pommel Peak.

*Pompey Creek.

*Pompey Mountains.

Pomulum Indians. In the late seventeenth and early eighteenth centuries the Pomulum (Pamulam, Pamuli, Pomuluma) Indians ranged an area on both sides of the Rio Grande between present Eagle Pass and Laredo. In 1708 they were reported on the Rio Grande with eight other groups, all said to speak the same language, unquestionably Coahuiltecan. The Pomulum entered several missions in or near this area—San Bernardo qv in northeastern Coahuila, sometime after 1703; Santa María de los Dolores de la Punta, near present Lampazos, Nuevo León; and San Miguel de Aguayo at Monclova, Coahuila, reported still there as late as 1762. They seem never to have entered the missions of southern Texas.

BIBLIOGRAPHY: F. W. Hodge (ed.), *Handbook of American Indians*, II (1910); P. O. Maas, *Viajes de misioneros Franciscanos á la conquista del Nuevo México* (1915); J. A. de Morfi, "Viage de indios y diario del Nuevo-México," *Documentos para la historia de México*, I (1856); Esteban L. Portillo, *Apuntes para la historia antigua de Coahuila y Texas* (1886); J. R. Swanton, *Linguistic Material from the Tribes of Southern Texas and Northeastern Mexico* (1940); R. S. Weddle, *San Juan Bautista: Gateway to Spanish Texas* (1968).

T. N. Campbell

*Pond Creek.

*Pond Creek, Texas.

*Ponder, Texas.

*Pone, Texas.

*Ponta, Texas.

*Ponton, Andrew.

*Ponton Creek.

Pontoon Bridge Crossing. *See* Camp Melvin, Texas.

*Pontotoc, Texas.

*Pony, Texas. (Runnels County.)

*Pony, Texas. (San Saba County.)

Pool, J. P. J. P. Pool was born on July 7, 1870, at Jones Prairie, Texas, to Fanny (McKinney) and James Smith Pool. He attended public schools in Milam County, took an academic course at Baylor University, then studied law for one year (1890–1891) at the University of Texas before being admitted to the Bar in 1891.

He practiced law in Victoria in 1893 and married Jessie Dupree on April 26, 1893; they had two children. In 1898 he formed with his brother-in-law, John L. Dupree, the law firm of Dupree and Pool, which lasted until 1928, when he became a district judge. Other local and state positions held by Pool included committee clerk of the Twenty-second Texas Legislature, secretary of the Senate for the Twenty-fourth and Twenty-sixth Texas legislatures, representative of the Seventy-fourth District in the Thirtieth Legislature, county judge of Victoria County from 1909 to 1920, presiding judge of the Fourth Administrative Judicial District from 1929 to 1937, and judge of the Twenty-fourth Judicial District from 1928 to 1940. Pool died on January 19, 1940, and was buried in Evergreen Cemetery in Victoria.

BIBLIOGRAPHY: Hobart Huson, *District Judges of Re-*

fugio County (1941); *Texas Bar Journal* (April, 1940); Theora H. Whitaker, *Victoria* (1941).

Charles Spurlin

*Pool Branch.

*Pool Creek.

*Pools Creek.

*Poolville, Texas.

*Poor Hollow.

*Pope, John.

*Pope, William Henry.

*Pope, Texas.

*Pope Ranch, Texas.

*Popher Creek.

*Population of Texas. *See* Census and Census Records.

*Populist Party in Texas.

*Porcion Creek.

*Porfirio, Texas.

*Port Acres, Texas.

Port Alto, Texas. Port Alto, on the west shore of Carancahua Bay in northeastern Calhoun County, was known as Persimmon Point before its subdivision in 1939. The name "Alto" refers to the village's boat landing or "stop." Throughout its history the unincorporated community has had about ten permanent residents and one store. Vacationers and retired persons, however, increased the summer population to 205 in 1961, but the settlement was destroyed in September of that year by Hurricane Carla (*see* Hurricanes in Texas). The community was rebuilt by 1966, and the summer population numbered approximately 185 that year. In 1970 the Port Alto telephone exchange had 170 listings, indicating a probable increase in total population, both permanent and seasonal.

*Port Aransas, Texas. Port Aransas, in Nueces County, has grown rapidly as a resort because of attractive opportunities for fishing, skin diving, surfing, and camping in the area. The town's 1960 population of 824 increased to 1,218 by 1970, according to the United States census report. The population, however, frequently swells to over 10,-000 during peak periods, straining facilities and crowding highways. Besides the regular summer tourists, Port Aransas is crowded with college students at Easter, at Christmas, and between semesters. Late fall and early spring are the best times for surfing.

New construction, especially of motel and condominium apartment facilities, has increased at a rapid rate. Since the mid-1960's building has tripled and water consumption has more than tripled.

*Port Arthur, Texas. Port Arthur, in Jefferson County, continued to be a world shipping center during the 1960's. The Gulf Intracoastal Waterway,qv which runs through Port Arthur, connects the city with commerce throughout the South. The four-hundred-foot-wide, thirty-six-foot-deep chan-

nel provides the outlet to the Gulf of Mexico for the four large refineries of Port Arthur that have made the city known as the oil refining center of the world. Daily capacity of the refineries in the late 1960's exceeded 750,000 barrels of crude oil. The Port of Port Arthur is a part of the Sabine Customs District and is among the world's newest deepwater shipping facilities, boasting perhaps the largest gantry crane in North America. The city is the port headquarters for the Port Arthur District, which includes Port Arthur, Beaumont, Orange, Sabine, and Lake Charles, Louisiana.

A new bridge, Gulfgate, was constructed in the 1960's, spanning 138 feet above the Sabine-Neches Waterway qv and connecting Port Arthur with Pleasure Island. From the island one can travel down Sabine Lake Causeway to Louisiana. Another bridge, the tallest in the South (230 feet with a vertical clearance of 176 feet for ocean-going vessels), crosses the Neches River on State Highway 87 between Port Arthur and Orange.

Port Arthur was the first city in Texas to adopt the twelve-grade public school system. It was also the site of one of the outstanding business colleges in the South, Port Arthur College,qv which offered all phases of business, radio, television, and electronics education; the college became Lamar University at Port Arthur qv in 1975.

The city, incorporated in 1898, had a manager-council form of government. In the 1960's there were over seventy-five churches, three banks, two hospitals, eleven public schools, a library, a newspaper, four radio stations, and a television station. In 1960 the population was 66,676, and in 1970 it was 57,371. *See also* Beaumont-Port Arthur-Orange Standard Metropolitan Statistical Area.

*Port Arthur College. Port Arthur College, Port Arthur, continued as a vocational school, specializing in business and electronics education. A new $800,000 classroom-administration building was occupied in November, 1967. The curriculum was expanded to include a night school and special summer classes for high school undergraduates and college-preparatory students. Business classes included clerical, stenographic, secretarial, office machine, key punch, bookkeeping, and accounting courses. Included in the electronics courses were classes in broadcasting-telecasting and radio and television repair. The college continued to operate the college-owned radio station. Port Arthur College offered a lifetime placement service. The 1974–1975 regular term enrollment was 409 students.

In July, 1973, Port Arthur College was granted candidate-for-accreditation status by the Southern Association of Colleges and Schools. Two new buildings were erected to house vocational programs in 1973 and 1974, and on April 1, 1974, W. Sam Monroe succeeded his father, Madison Monroe, as president of Port Arthur College. On July 29, 1974, the board of trustees voted to merge the school with Lamar University in Beaumont; Lamar University agreed to accept the college as a branch of its system, and Port Arthur College officially became Lamar University at Port Arthur on September 1, 1975. In the fall of that year there were 388 academic students out of a total of 562 students taking credit and noncredit courses. W. Sam Monroe continued as director of the school at Port Arthur, and the radio station continued to be operated by Port Arthur College Foundation in connection with Lamar University at Port Arthur. *See also* Lamar University.

*Port Arthur Ship Channel. *See* Sabine-Neches Waterway and the Sabine Pass Ship Channel.

*Port Bolivar, Texas. *See also* Point Bolivar; Point Bolivar Lighthouse; Bolivar Peninsula.

*Port Bolivar Iron Ore Railway.

Port Caddo, Texas. Port Caddo was established when a native of San Augustine, Obediah Hendrick, Jr., was granted 660 acres by the Republic of Texas on July 7, 1838. The land was described as being in "Shelby County on the south of Ferry Lake embracing Taylor's Bluff" (later Harrison County). Hendrick envisioned a great inland port at Taylor's Bluff and divided the town into over one thousand lots with a main street. The town was incorporated, and sales of stock, lots, buildings, and homes started immediately after the survey was finished.

By 1839 wagons were arriving at Port Caddo from the east and boats were bringing people and shipments of goods to the new inland port. From its very beginning Port Caddo was a typical, boisterous frontier town, and as the westward movement gained momentum Port Caddo prospered. In the beginning, little attention was given to taxes; however, around 1839 a customs service was established at Port Caddo.

Violent and bloody conflicts arose over the collection of tariffs on imports and exports. These conflicts culminated on January 29, 1845, when the Texas Congress passed an act establishing a collectorial district including parts of Red River, Bowie, Nacogdoches, and Rusk counties. All of Harrison County was included, and Port Caddo was named the port of entry. However, there was continued refusal to pay tariffs at Port Caddo because of the progress being made toward annexation with the United States. The problem was finally resolved, and the office was closed January 31, 1846, after Texas joined the United States.

Port Caddo continued to thrive until shortly before the Civil War, when Big Cypress Bayou was opened to Jefferson, Texas; then it started into a rapid decline. In the 1870's, the big raft on the Red River was removed (*see* Red River Raft), causing the water of Caddo Lake to fall and closing the era of the riverboat to Port Caddo and Jefferson. Port Caddo continued to be identified on maps until the early 1900's, when a group purchased the area for Port Caddo Motor Club. In the 1930's the site of Port Caddo was part of the property which was bought and which became Caddo Lake State Scenic Park (*see* Parks, State).

BIBLIOGRAPHY: V. H. Hackney, *Port Caddo—A Vanished Village and Vignettes of Harrison County* (1966).

            V. H. Hackney

*Port Harlingen.

*Port Isabel, Texas. Port Isabel, in Cameron County, was supported economically by commercial fishing, shrimping, tourism, and the petroleum industry. Among the larger businesses in the 1960's were a chemical refinery, a service pipeline company, shipyards, and a frozen foods company. In 1972 there were 110 businesses. Recreational opportunities included fishing, boating, and hunting. The population in 1960 was 3,575; in 1970 it was 3,067, according to the United States census. *See also* Brownsville-Harlingen-San Benito Standard Metropolitan Statistical Area.

Port Isabel Lighthouse. A familiar landmark near Port Isabel, Texas, is a lighthouse which was contracted by the United States government in 1852. The building cost $7,000 and was intended to be a guide to the commerce of the Rio Grande. During the Civil War, however, the land and lighthouse became objects of contention. Union and Confederate forces fought several battles over the possession of the area, for both sides wanted to use the high building as a lookout tower. World War II saw the use of the Port Isabel Lighthouse as a sentinel tower until 1943, when it was declared unsafe for use. In 1970 the structure, a state historic site (*see* Parks, State), once again appeared on the charts as an approved aid to navigation.

BIBLIOGRAPHY: Leonard King, *Port of Drifting Men* (1945); Verna Jackson McKenna, *Old Point Isabel Lighthouse, Beacon of Brazos Santiago* (1956); Frank C. Pierce, *A Brief History of the Lower Rio Grande Valley* (1917); James Heaven Thompson, A Nineteenth Century History of Cameron County, Texas (M.A. thesis, University of Texas at Austin, 1965); Marker Files, Texas Historical Commission, Austin; Texas Legislative Council, *Staff Research Report* (1958).

            M. Doty

*Port Isabel and Rio Grande Valley Railway.

*Port Lavaca, Texas. Port Lavaca, seat of Calhoun County, was a rapidly growing center for marketing, fishing, livestock handling, and tourist trade during the 1960's. The city's businesses included those dealing with shell dredging, ship repairing, oil and gas, seafood (especially shrimp) processing, and manufacturing. Businesses totaled 237 in 1970. Population grew from 8,864 in 1960 to 10,491 in 1970, according to the United States census.

*Port Neches, Texas. Port Neches, in Jefferson County, is located on the bluff above the Neches River where Joseph Grigsby qv built his home after the battle of San Jacinto on land he had received from empresario Lorenzo de Zavala qv in 1834.

In the 1960's Port Neches had an industrial economy. Local plants produced synthetic rubber, road surfacing materials, petrochemicals, and oil and cement products. The city reported twenty-one churches, one bank, a park, a library, a newspaper, a radio station, and five schools. In 1966 a memorial library was completed. In 1970 eighty businesses were reported. The 1960 population was 8,696, and in 1970 it was 10,894, according to the United States census. *See also* Beaumont-Port Arthur-Orange Standard Metropolitan Statistical Area.

*Port O'Connor, Texas. The town of Port O'-Connor was laid out in 1909 on land purchased from Thomas M. O'Connor (not Thomas O'Connor qv [1819–1887], as stated in Volume II).

BIBLIOGRAPHY: Sister Margaret Rose Warburton, History of O'Connor Ranch (M.A. thesis, Catholic University of America, 1939).

Ann Fears Crawford

*Port Preston, Texas.

*Port Sullivan, Texas.

*Porter, Sophia.

*Porter, William N.

*Porter, William Sydney [pseud. O. Henry]. *See also* O. Henry Museum.

*Porter Creek.

*Porter Springs, Texas. Porter Springs, a farming and ranching community in western Houston County, was founded about 1880 on land having numerous springs and owned by Mack Porter. The population was estimated at fifty in 1970. In the 1970 United States census the Porter Springs Division, an area much greater than the community, listed a population of 1,496.

*Porters, Texas.

Porter's Bluff, Texas. Porter's Bluff, also called Taos, was established in northeast Navarro County on the Trinity River and was a shipping point in the 1870's and 1880's.

BIBLIOGRAPHY: *Texas Almanac* (1, 6).

*Porterville, Texas.

*Portilla, Felipe Roque de la.

*Portilla, José Nicolás de la.

*Portis, David Y.

*Portland, Texas. Portland, now on the boundary of San Patricio County and Nueces County, was incorporated in 1949 under general law. During the 1960's the town reported three public schools, a bank, a library, a newspaper, and nine churches. Portland's businesses were largely concerned with metal products and tourism. By 1965 Portland had completed a city hall building, added to the fire station, and improved the water and sewer systems. In 1970 eighty businesses were reported. Its 1950 population of 1,292 had almost doubled by 1960, when a figure of 2,538 was reported. In the 1970 census the population had risen to 7,302. *See also* Corpus Christi Standard Metropolitan Statistical Area.

Portscheller, Heinrich. Heinrich Portscheller, architect and builder, was born in Germany in 1840; various towns are given as his birthplace: Hamburg, Neunkirchen, or Zweibrücken in the Palatinate. The family trade was building.

Portscheller and a friend, Frederick Ellert, arrived at the Mexican port of Vera Cruz in 1865, where they were impressed into Maximilian's army. They were assigned to a unit composed of German nationals called the "Contre-Guerillas" which operated in northern Mexico. As the tide of war turned against Maximilian's forces, the northern units were often left to forage without support from central agencies and became demoralized; both Ellert and Portscheller deserted to Texas prior to June, 1866. Encouraged by the agents of General Mariano Escobedo to join the Mexican cause, both men participated in the battle of Santa Gertrudis near Camargo on June 15, 1866.

With cessation of military activities Portscheller worked as a mason at Fort Ringgold qv and later in the vicinities of Rio Grande City, Roma, and Mier. In 1879 he married Leonarda Campos; they became the parents of three daughters and a son. On February 26, 1883, Portscheller declared his intention to become a United States citizen.

After a brief residence in Mier (1879–1881) he moved his family to Roma which, along with Rio Grande City, was a flourishing trading center. Portscheller established a brickyard at Roma, organized an efficient construction crew, and began serious construction activity. His ability as a craftsman had already proved excellent, and he was a successful architect. His work shows lively experimentation, particularly in utilizing light and shadow to aesthetic advantage.

He built many fine houses and commercial structures. The cemetery at Roma contains tombs and vaults designed by Portscheller and constructed by his craftsmen. Among his Roma clients in the 1880's were Manuel Guerra, Antonio Saenz, Nestor Saenz, Pablo Ramírez, and Rafael García Ramírez. Perhaps his greatest effort was in Rio Grande City in 1886—the construction of the Silverior de la Peña building with drugstore, post office, and family living quarters.

In 1894, following an economic slump, Portscheller moved his family to Laredo, eventually building a residence and office at 1005 San Dario. He built St. Peter's Church (probably from plans prepared by others), an iron bridge in south Laredo, many cisterns, and several houses. About 1900 he went to Monterrey, Mexico, to construct a building for the Civil College (destroyed in 1962). He died in 1915 and was buried in the Protestant cemetery in Laredo.

Eugene George

*Porvenir, Texas.

*Posadas, Alonzo de.

Posalme Indians. The Posalme (Poxsalma) Indians, apparently a Concho band, lived on the north bank of the Rio Grande near present Presidio in the late seventeenth and eighteenth centuries. Their principal settlement was known as San Cristóbal. In the late eighteenth century the Posalme were absorbed by the Spanish-speaking population of the Presidio area.

BIBLIOGRAPHY: C. W. Hackett (ed.), *Historical Documents Relating to New Mexico, Nueva Vizcaya, and Approaches Thereto, to 1773*, II (1926); J. C. Kelley, "Factors Involved in the Abandonment of Certain Peripheral Southwestern Settlements," *American Anthropologist*, LIV (1952); J. C. Kelley, "The Historic Indian Pueblos of La Junta de los Ríos," *New Mexico Historical Review*, XXVII (1952), XXVIII (1953); C. Sauer, *The Distribution of Aboriginal Tribes and Languages in Northwestern Mexico* (1934).

T. N. Campbell

*Posey, Texas. (Hopkins County.)

*Posey, Texas. (Lubbock County.)

*Posideon, Texas.

*Possum, Texas.

*Possum Kingdom Lake. Morris Sheppard Dam qv and Possum Kingdom Reservoir, popularly known as Possum Kingdom Lake, are owned and operated by the Brazos River Authority qv for water supply for municipal, industrial, mining, irrigation, recreational, and power generation uses.

Construction of the dam was started May 29, 1938, and in March, 1941, the dam was completed. One month later runoff had filled the reservoir with sufficient water to start power generation. The reservoir had a capacity of 747,700 acre-feet at the top of the gates, elevation 1,000.1 feet above mean sea level, with an area of 19,800 acres. The hydroelectric power facilities consisted of two 11,250-kilowatt generating units. The drainage area above the dam was 22,550 square miles, of which 9,240 was probably noncontributing.

BIBLIOGRAPHY: Texas Water Commission, *Bulletin 6408* (1964).

Seth D. Breeding

*Post, Charles William.

*Post, Wiley.

*Post, Texas. Post, founded by and named for cereal manufacturer Charles William Post,qv was the commercial center and seat of Garza County as well as the site of textile mills and several independent oil companies during the 1960's. Among its businesses were a bank, a newspaper, a radio station, a cotton mill, and two printing firms. A hospital, two libraries, and a city-county airport, built in the 1960's, served the town. Businesses totaled 106 in 1970. The 1960 census showed a population of 4,663; the 1970 population count was 3,854, according to the United States census.

*Post Mountain.

*Post Oak, Texas.

*Post Oak Branch.

*Post Oak Creek.

*Post Oak Point, Texas.

*Postal System of the Republic of Texas.

Postito Indians. The Postito Indians, presumably Coahuiltecans, were at San José y San Miguel de Aguayo Mission,qv in San Antonio, during the eighteenth century. Here they were closely associated with the Pampopa. The Postito may be the same as the Cachopostale (Cachapostale), who lived with the Pampopa on the Nueces and Frio rivers between present San Antonio and Eagle Pass earlier in the same century. The Postito were at Mission San José until at least 1785.

BIBLIOGRAPHY: J. A. Dabbs, "The Texas Missions in 1785," *Preliminary Studies of the Texas Catholic Historical Society*, III (1940); F. W. Hodge (ed.), *Handbook of American Indians*, I (1907); J. R. Swanton, *Linguistic Material from the Tribes of Southern Texas and Northeastern Mexico* (1940).

T. N. Campbell

*Postoak, Texas. (Freestone County.)

*Postoak, Texas. (Jack County.)

*Postoak Creek.

*Postoak Ridge.

*Potato Hill.

*Potato Top Peak.

*Potawatomi Indians.

*Poteet, Texas. The population of Poteet, in north-central Atascosa County, had grown from 2,811 in 1960 to 3,013 by 1970, according to the United States census. In 1970 the town reported twenty-five businesses.

*Poth, Texas. The 1970 census showed a population of 1,296 in Poth, an increase from the 1960 population of 1,119. This Wilson County community reported thirty businesses in 1970.

**Potomac.*

*Potomac, Texas.

*Potosi, Texas.

*Potrance Creek.

*Potter, Andrew Jackson.

*Potter, Henry N.

*Potter, Reuben Marmaduke. Reuben Marmaduke Potter was married on March 23, 1853 (not March 28, 1853, as stated in Volume II).

BIBLIOGRAPHY: Frank Brown Papers (MS., Archives, University of Texas at Austin Library); *Texas State Gazette*, March 26, 1853.

Joseph Dixon Matlock

*Potter, Robert. Robert Potter was born in June, 1799, near Williamsboro in Granville County, North Carolina. He married Isabella Taylor, and they had two children. They were divorced in 1834. In the Regulator-Moderator War qv Potter was a Moderator (not a Regulator, as stated in Volume II). On March 2, 1842, Regulators (not Moderators), headed by William P. Rose,qv shot and killed Potter in Caddo Lake. His body was recovered the following day (Volume II wrongly states that his body was never recovered), and he was buried at Potter's Point on the lake. His remains were moved to the State Cemetery qv in Austin on October 9, 1928.

BIBLIOGRAPHY: Ernest C. Shearer, *Robert Potter: Remarkable North Carolinian and Texan* (1951).

*Potter and Blocker Trail.

*Potter County. In the 1960's Potter County's manufacturing income was largely derived from helium, natural gas, oil, sand, and gravel. It produced approximately 60 percent of the world's helium. Large cattle ranches occupied most of the county and accounted for three-fourths of the agricultural income. Crops included wheat and grain sorghums grown on irrigated land, while dairy products and poultry also contributed to the farm income.

Most institutions and projects of the county were joint operations with the city of Amarillo. Among these were a child welfare unit, a library, a cerebral palsy clinic, and Amarillo Medical Center.qv Amarillo College served both Potter and Randall counties, and the Amarillo branch of the Texas State Technical Institute qv served most of northwest and west Texas.

Major tourist attractions were the Alibates Flint Quarries,qv a tri-state fair, and Lake Meredith. Potter County also benefited from the tourist trade at Palo Duro Canyon State Park (see Parks, State) in Randall County. The 1960 population was 115,580; in 1970 it was 90,511, according to the United States census. See also Amarillo Standard Metropolitan Statistical Area.

*Potter Creek.

*Potters Peak.

Pottery Industry in Texas. Evidence of early use of Texas clays is plentiful in the remains of various native Indian earthenwares. The Spanish brought to the New World the potter's wheel and classical southern European earthenwares with lead glazes. Much of this type of earthenware was manufactured in Mexico, but absolute evidence of its manufacture in Texas during the Spanish Colonial period does not presumably exist.

After 1835 the entrance of large numbers of immigrants of northern European heritage into Texas created a demand for stoneware vessels. Clay suitable for stoneware was present in many parts of Texas. The earliest stoneware factory may have been in present Rusk County during the days of the Republic of Texas. Taylor Brown was granted a second-class headright to land just north of the present city of Henderson in 1839; he operated a pottery on this land, but the date of its establishment is not known. Edwin Theodore Dumble qv states in the Second Annual Report of the Geological Survey of Texas, 1890 (1891) that the clay bed near Henderson had been used for over forty years. This would indicate that the pottery was operating before 1850.

The special census of industry and manufacture for Texas in 1850 lists three other stoneware potteries operating in the state. Two of these were also in Rusk County and the other in Montgomery County. By 1860 there were at least eleven stoneware potteries operating in Texas. These were in Bastrop, Denton, Guadalupe, Henderson, Montgomery, Lee, Limestone, Rusk, Titus, and Waller counties. All of these were small potteries providing a variety of household ware such as jugs, jars, churns, and bowls for local use. The potteries in Montgomery and Waller (then Austin) counties closed soon after 1860. They were not in regions where good stoneware clays were available. The Denton potteries used clays from the Eagle Ford geological group, and the supply was excellent and plentiful. Most of the other potteries in the state have used clays from the Wilcox geological group, which are excellent for stoneware.

The pottery industry flourished during the last quarter of the nineteenth century and into the twentieth century. There were active potteries in Bastrop, Bexar (see Elmendorf, Texas), Bowie, Cass, Denton, Falls, Franklin, Guadalupe, Harris, Harrison, Henderson, Limestone, Nacogdoches, Parker, Rusk, Smith, Titus, Upshur, Wilson, and Wood counties. After 1915 there were less and less demand for heavy handmade stoneware vessels, and many of the potteries ceased functioning.

A few potteries such as the Love Field, Ideal, and Southern potteries in Dallas; the Marshall, Grubbs, and Star potteries in Marshall; the Athens Pottery in Athens; and the San Antonio and Meyer potteries in Bexar County were active between 1920 and 1950.

In 1971 the Athens Pottery was still making unglazed flower pots. Three potteries were active in the Marshall area. The Grubbs Pottery and the Star Pottery manufactured mainly unglazed flower pots. The Marshall Pottery was the largest in the state and produced glazed churns, jars, pitchers, jugs, bowls, and a variety of unglazed flower pots and planters. These were distributed over all of Texas and the neighboring states.

BIBLIOGRAPHY: Georgeanna H. Greer and Harding Black, The Meyer Family: Master Potters of Texas (1971); Georgeanna H. Greer, "Preliminary Information on the Use of the Alkaline Glaze for Stoneware in the South 1800–1970," in Stanley South (ed.), The Conference on Historic Site Archeology Papers, 1970, V (1971).

Georgeanna H. Greer

Potts, Charles Shirley. Born near Weatherford on September 22, 1872, Charles Shirley Potts was the son of Charles Brooke and Elizabeth Matilda (Shirley) Potts. He had his basic education at Weatherford College and Parker Institute and became a teacher in and near Parker County. In 1902 he was graduated with B.A. and M.A. degrees from the University of Texas, then became an assistant professor of economics and history at the Agricultural and Mechanical College of Texas (now Texas A&M University). He was graduated from the University of Texas law school in 1909; he joined the political science faculty there in 1911 and the law faculty in 1914. In 1922 he was a founding member of the Texas Law Review qv and served as first chairman of its editorial board. He earned an S.J.D. degree at Harvard Law School in 1926 and joined the faculty of law at Washington University in St. Louis. In 1927 he was named dean of the School of Law at Southern Methodist University.

His reputation was a significant factor in the school's securing approval of the American Bar Association and membership in the Association of American Law Schools. The greatest achievement of his deanship was the phasing-out of proprietary legal education in Dallas and the institution of high-standard evening legal education by the law school in 1938. Potts guided the school through the difficult years of World War II and, though he had reached the age for retirement in 1942, stayed on until 1947 after assembling a faculty to meet the deluge of applicants for legal education at the war's end.

He taught and wrote principally in the fields of criminal law and procedure and constitutional law, and he brought to these subjects a great diversity of learning and teaching experience. He worked actively in the impeachment proceedings against Governor James E. Ferguson qv and toward reform of Texas procedural law, particularly in the field of criminal law.

In 1916 he married Ada Hardeman Garrison, daughter of George P. Garrison;qv they had two children. Potts died on May 9, 1963, in Dallas and was buried there.

BIBLIOGRAPHY: Arthur L. Harding, "Charles Shirley Potts: A Memoir," *Southwestern Law Journal*, XVI (1962); Roy R. Ray, "Charles Shirley Potts," *Texas Bar Journal*, XXVI (1963).

Joseph W. McKnight

Potts, Robert Joseph. Robert Joseph Potts was born near Weatherford, Texas, on November 17, 1877, the son of Charles Brooke and Elizabeth Matilda (Shirley) Potts. He graduated with a B.A. degree from Agricultural and Mechanical College of Texas (now Texas A&M University) in 1906. On November 11, 1914, he married Esther Barnwell Davis; they had three sons.

Potts was a math instructor at A&M (1907–1909), assistant professor of civil engineering (1909–1910), associate professor and then professor of highway engineering (1910–1914). It has been disputed (with Northwestern University) whether he was the first or second professor of highway engineering in America.

Potts wrote the law passed by the Texas legislature creating the Texas Highway Department,qv which began operation in 1917. He also wrote the first specification for a state highway which permitted no stumps more than six inches in height on the roadway. He was one of the founders and the first president of the Texas branch of Associated General Contractors of America, and he served as a member of the Texas Highway Commission from 1949 to 1955. Potts was a pioneer road builder and a producer of sand and gravel for road construction. He died in Austin on April 18, 1962, and was buried at Oakwood Cemetery in Waco.

William B. Alderman

*Pottsboro, Texas.

*Pottsville, Texas.

*Poultry Production. Between 1953 and 1963 cash income from poultry, including chickens, broilers, eggs, and turkeys, ranged from $128 million to over $157 million yearly. Commercial broiler production normally exceeded one hundred million birds per year. In 1960, 126,855 farms raised chickens, 2,409 raised broilers, 49,620 sold eggs, and 11,297 raised turkeys. Leading counties in poultry sales were Shelby, Nacogdoches, and Gonzales. Eighty-five Texas poultry-dressing plants paid out over $8 million in payrolls in 1960. The gross income from poultry production in 1963 was $163 million. In 1968 Texas ranked fifth in turkey raising and gross income, eighth in production of chickens and eggs, and sixth in broiler production. That same year 13,055,000 chickens (not broilers) were raised for a gross income of $4,530,000. Egg production in 1968 reached almost 3 billion eggs at a gross income of over $90 million. Number produced and gross income from broilers and turkeys were 161,940,000 for $81,618,000 and 7,156,-000 for $27,336,000, respectively. In all, poultry and egg production amounted to just over 7 percent of the state's farm income in 1968. In 1972 the gross income of Texas producers was $4,700,000 from farm chickens, $75,404,000 from eggs, $93,-790,000 from broilers, and $33,794,000 from turkeys. Sales from turkey hatching eggs, ducks, geese, quail, pigeons, and other poultry items grossed approximately $5,000,000 annually.

BIBLIOGRAPHY: *Texas Almanac* (1963–1973).

Poverty, Alleviation of. See Community Affairs, Department of.

*Powder Creek.

Powder Horn, Texas. Powder Horn, in Calhoun County, was a shipping point during the 1850's. It was located on Powder Horn Bayou and served as the depot for Indianola. It was also a transshipment point for supplies to the interior of the state, particularly San Antonio. In 1853 the buildings at the depot consisted of five structures for supplies, a small blacksmith shop, and a stable. These structures were built on ground leased by the United States government. A 250-foot-long wharf, on which was laid a railway, was connected with the government land. In 1856 there was a semi-weekly line of steamers to New Orleans, and in 1857 Powder Horn was a troop shipping point.

BIBLIOGRAPHY: M. L. Crimmins (ed.), "Colonel J. K. F. Mansfield's Report of the Inspection of the Department of Texas in 1856," *Southwestern Historical Quarterly*, XLII (1938–1939); M. L. Crimmins (ed.), "W. G. Freeman's Report on the Eighth Military Department," *ibid.*, LI (1947–1948); Earl W. Fornell, "Texans and Filibusters in the 1850's," *ibid.*, LIX (1955–1956).

*Powderhorn Lake.

*Powderly, Texas.

*Powdermill Creek.

Powell, Benjamin Harrison. Benjamin Harrison Powell was born in Montgomery, Texas, on November 12, 1881, the son of Benjamin Harrison and Eleanor Inez (Meacham) Powell. In 1903 he received degrees of Litt.B. and LL.B. from the University of Texas, where he was an editor of the *Texan* (predecessor of the *Daily Texan* qv). In 1949 he received an honorary LL.D. degree from Sam Houston State Teachers College (now Sam Houston State University).

Powell practiced law at Huntsville with the firm of Dean, Humphrey, and Powell from 1903 until 1919, when he became judge of the 12th Judicial District. From 1920 to 1927 he served on the Commission of Appeals to the Supreme Court of Texas. In November, 1927, he resumed the practice of law in Austin.

Powell was chairman of the board of directors and president of the Texas Bar Association,qv and he served on a special committee to assist the Supreme Court in writing the Texas Rules of Civil Procedure. He was also a member of the House of Delegates of the American Bar Association, the National Conference of Commissioners on Uniform State Laws, and the American Law Institute. He strongly supported the statute requiring all Texas lawyers to belong to the State Bar of Texas,qv successor to the old voluntary Texas Bar Association.

Powell married Marian Leigh Rather on November 12, 1913; they had two sons. He died on December 3, 1960, and was buried in Oakwood Cemetery at Huntsville.

W. St. John Garwood

*Powell, Peter.

*Powell, Texas.

*Powell Creek.

*Powell Oil Field.

*Powelldale Mountains.

Powell's Cave. Powell's Cave, located in Menard County, has been known to spelunkers since 1961. Since then members of the Texas Speleological Association qv in three major projects and several smaller trips have mapped more than eight and one-half miles of cave passage, making Powell's Cave the longest cave known in Texas. The cave consists of an extensive maze level with long crevice- and tunnel-like passages below the first level. The lowest level contains a flowing stream which probably empties into nearby San Saba River. A mine shaft intersects the cave.

A. Richard Smith

*Power, James.

*Power and Hewetson Colony.

*Powers, Stephen.

*Poyner, Texas.

*Prade Ranch, Texas.

*Praha, Texas.

*Prairie Areas of Texas. *See* Grand Prairies and the Lampasas Cut Plain; Texas Prairies.

*Prairie Branch.

*Prairie Canyon.

*Prairie Creek.

*Prairie Dell, Texas.

*Prairie Dog Town Fork of Red River.

*Prairie Dogs.

*Prairie Hill, Texas. (DeWitt County.)

*Prairie Hill, Texas. (Limestone County.)

*Prairie Hill, Texas. (Washington County.)

*Prairie Lea, Texas.

*Prairie Mountain.

Prairie Mountain, Texas. Prairie Mountain community is a grouping of some twenty families located in southwestern Llano County near the mountain by that same name. The community dates to 1906 and has been variously known as Starks, Putnam, and Hickory. At one time it had a post office, cotton gin, and grocery. A noted county landmark, the two-story stone home and stone barn of pioneer teacher and surveyor R. F. (Bob) Rountree, still stands in the community. In 1971 the families of Prairie Mountain celebrated its 65th anniversary with a social hour, supper, and table games.

*Prairie Point, Texas. (Cooke County.)

Prairie Point, Texas. (Wise County.) *See* Rhome, Texas.

*Prairie Siding, Texas.

*Prairie View, Texas. (DeWitt County.)

*Prairie View, Texas. (Waller County.) Prairie View, an unincorporated community in central Waller County, increased in population from 2,326 in 1960 to 3,589 by 1970, according to the United States census report.

Prairie View A&M University. Prairie View A&M University (formerly Prairie View Agricultural and Mechanical College, and before that Prairie View University qv) doubled enrollment between 1946 and 1964, from approximately 1,500 to over 3,000 students. In 1947 the legislature changed the school's name from Prairie View University to Prairie View Agricultural and Mechanical College as a branch of the Texas A&M University System;qv still part of that system, the name was changed again, in 1973, to Prairie View A&M University. It was dedicated primarily to agriculture, engineering, military science, and natural sciences. The college offered bachelor's degrees in agriculture, arts and sciences, engineering, home economics, industrial education and technology, and nursing education.

During the period 1946–1974 the campus physical plant underwent considerable expansion. Additions included a new administration building, new dormitories and dining facilities, the Memorial Student Center, a computer center, a health and education building, additional classroom buildings, and an extensive addition to the library, which in the early 1970's contained approximately 105,000 volumes. Originally a Negro land-grant college, Prairie View followed the pattern established by the Texas A&M System by integrating in 1963. The fall enrollment for 1974 was 4,870, and the faculty numbered approximately 220. Alvin I. Thomas was president in that year. *See also* Education, Negro.

*Prairie View University. *See also* Prairie View A&M University.

*Prairieville, Texas. Prairieville, in eastern Kaufman County, was founded in 1847 (not 1870, as stated in Volume II), one of the three Norwegian settlements established by Johan Reinert Reiersen.qv A post office was established in 1854 as were the first church and cemetery. Elise Wærenskjold qv wrote in 1857 that there were a hundred people in Prairieville. During the Civil War the post office was closed, and mail for Prairieville area residents was still being sent to the Tyler post office in Smith County in 1866. In 1925 the town had ten places of business and a cotton gin, but in the 1940's the children were being sent to Marbank to school. In 1954 the post office was discontinued. By 1971 there was a population of about fifty people, a Methodist church, a Baptist church, and a general store and filling station; new homes were being built and mobile homes were being moved in, perhaps because of the nearness of Cedar Creek Reservoir and Lake. Four Mile Prairie,qv three miles east of Prairieville, was a neighboring Norwegian community.

BIBLIOGRAPHY: C. A. Clausen (ed.), *The Lady with the Pen: Elise Waerenskjold in Texas* (1961).

Mrs. C. H. Richman

*Prater, William.

*Prather, William Lambdin. William Lambdin Prather received the LL.B. degree from Washington College at Lexington, Virginia (not Lexington, Kentucky, as stated in Volume II).

Pratt, Henry Cleves. Henry Cleves Pratt was born in New Hampshire in 1803. Working on his father's farm in 1817, the boy was found to have artistic talent and ambition by Samuel F. B. Morse. Morse took him to Charleston, South Carolina, and, in 1812, to Washington, D. C., teaching him the rudiments of painting and employing him for a number of years as an assistant in his studio. In 1845 Pratt joined Thomas Cole on a painting expedition to Maine. In 1851 he joined the Bartlett Survey in Texas and the Southwest for various boundary, railroad, and wagon-road surveys, where he made hundreds of sketches, some of which he expanded into oil paintings. He also painted portraits of John Russell Bartlett and James Wiley Magoffin qqv while in the Southwest, and the number of his landscapes was extensive. "View of Smith's West Texas Ranch," an oil, is now owned by Texas Memorial Museum qv of the University of Texas, and a collection of Pratt's work, watercolors and drawings, is owned by Brown University, Providence, Rhode Island. The Bartlett Survey reports published in 1857 included thirty of Pratt's illustrations. The artist lived until 1880.

BIBLIOGRAPHY: Pauline A. Pinckney, *Painting in Texas: The Nineteenth Century* (1967).

Pauline A. Pinckney

*Prattville, Texas.

*Prehistoric Man in Texas. *See* Archaeology (not Anthropology, as stated in Volume II); Paleo-Indians.

*Premont, Texas. Premont, in Jim Wells County, was incorporated in 1939 and had a mayor-commissioner type of government. In 1967 the town had a nursing home, a bank, a library, nine churches, and a newspaper. Thirty-eight businesses were reported in 1970. In 1960 the population was 3,049, and in 1970 it was 3,282, according to the U.S. census report.

*Prendergast, Albert Collins.

*Prendergast, Davis M'Gee.

*Presbyterian Church in Texas. Three synods in Texas continue to represent the national Presbyterian denominations: the Presbyterian Church, Synod of Texas, United States; the United Presbyterian Church, Synod of Texas, United States of America; and the Cumberland Presbyterian Church, Synod of Texas. Each synod includes some churches outside of Texas.

The Synod of Texas, United States, largest of the three, doubled its membership after 1943 and conducted three major reorganizations, three program changes, and three major financial campaigns in twenty years. The reorganization began in 1950 with an effort to simplify the synod's structure and bring it into line with a recent reorganization of the national denomination. In 1955 the Texas-Mexican Presbytery was dissolved and all Spanish-speaking churches and ministers were placed in geographic presbyteries. In 1958 the number of presbyteries was reduced to six. In 1965 the synod adopted a program to simplify its agencies, to coordinate its staff, to give wider representation, especially to the laity, and to improve the reporting procedure at annual synod meetings.

Program changes included reorganization in 1951 of the twenty-five-year-old Texas Presbyterian Foundation, assets of which increased to over seven million dollars; addition of adoption and foster home care under professionally trained personnel for the children's home in 1953; and consolidation of two schools for boys and girls of Mexican descent into the Presbyterian Pan American School,qv at Kingsville. As a result of three financial campaigns the synod increased its assets fivefold and acquired a new conference center near Hunt, Texas.

Offices of the Synod of Texas, United States, located in Austin, reported 511 ministers, 419 churches, and 123,004 members with 85,201 involved in Sunday schools at the end of 1965. Its institutions included Austin College qv at Sherman, Austin Presbyterian Theological Seminary qv at Austin, Schreiner Institute qv at Kerrville, Presbyterian Pan American School qv at Kingsville, Presbyterian Children's Home and Service Agency at Dallas and Itasca (*see* Southwestern Presbyterian Home and School for Orphans), Mo-Ranch Assembly near Hunt, and the Texas Presbyterian Foundation at

Dallas. Contributions in 1965 were $15,572,100, including $3,459,218 for benevolences outside of local congregations.

The United Presbyterian Church, Synod of Texas, United States of America, received its new name in 1958 as the result of a national union between the Presbyterian Church, United States of America (which had 3,000 members in 1906, not 300, as stated in Volume II) and the United Presbyterian Church. Since there were no United Presbyterian churches in Texas, the only other change made in the synod's organization was a reduction of the number of presbyteries from twelve to six in 1960. The United Presbyterian Synod of Texas supported a Campus Christian Life ministry—largely in cooperation with the Synod of Texas, United States—on sixteen college and university campuses in the state. The synod maintained two children's homes: one at Amarillo served seventy-five children; the other, formerly Reynolds Home at Dallas, moved to Waxahachie and changed its name to United Presbyterian Homes; its facilities for seventy-eight children were erected at a cost of $878,291. In 1965 plans for development included a home for elderly citizens at the same location. Trinity University qv was the major institution of this synod.

Offices of the United Presbyterian Synod of Texas, United States of America, were at Denton. At the end of 1965 the synod reported 283 ministers in Texas, 256 churches, and 53,797 members with 35,691 participating in Sunday schools. In 1965 contributions were $5,782,142, of which $905,120 was for benevolences beyond local congregations. In 1955 a foundation was organized to handle bequests, and in 1967 its funds totaled $1,020,434.

The Cumberland Presbyterian Church, Synod of Texas, included congregations in four states and three foreign countries in 1965. Its only institution in Texas was a children's home in Denton, which in 1965 enrolled forty children. The synod office, located in Fort Worth, reported 82 ministers, 64 churches, and 8,814 members with 7,957 involved in Sunday schools at the end of 1965. Total value of all church property was $4,585,291. The Cumberland General Assembly voted to unite with the Second Cumberland Presbyterian Church (Negro), but the latter group, composed of 5,500 members, declined the invitation to become a part of this Texas synod. See also Presbyterian Education in Texas.

Malcolm L. Purcell

Presbyterian Education in Texas. Although much of what was accomplished by Presbyterians in education in the first half of the nineteenth century was the work of individuals, the Presbyterian church often assisted these personal efforts and also established several schools. Several Presbyterian clergy and laymen engaged in primary education before and after the Texas Revolution, but the first venture into higher education was Galveston University,qv promoted by W. L. McCalla, opened in December, 1840, and attended by one hundred

students by the end of the first year. McCalla intended to found a university under Presbyterian auspices since all the trustees were Presbyterian ministers, but the school charter nullified that intention by providing for state aid. The school operated until 1844. Although the University of San Augustine qv was chartered in 1837, it was not until Marcus A. Montrose qv became its president in 1842 that the school began operations; it closed after five years without awarding a degree. Presbyterians at Nacogdoches also attempted to establish a university in 1844 with an endowment of land and pledges; Reverend John May Becton qv was named to prepare a charter and the Presbytery of Brazos was to elect nine trustees. This fruitless effort lasted two years; then in 1849 the Brazos presbytery, under the urgings of Daniel Baker,qv again discussed the establishment of a college as a source of native ministers. A state charter was signed by Governor George T. Wood qv on November 22, 1849, and the next year Austin College,qv the oldest continuing Presbyterian college in Texas, opened in Huntsville. Its first years were devoted to college preparatory training, while college classes leading to a bachelor's degree began in 1853.

Cumberland Presbyterians, who had broken with the main body of Presbyterians partly in protest over high educational requirements for ministers, particularly on the frontier, showed no concern for higher education until 1848. Then each of the three Cumberland synods in Texas launched a college. Larissa College qv was established by the Brazos Synod ten miles east of Jacksonville; Chapel Hill College,qv by the Texas Synod of Daingerfield; and Ewing College,qv by the Colorado Synod at La Grange. All three schools expired with the founding of Trinity University qv at Tehuacana in 1869 under the auspices of the three Cumberland synods. In 1902 Trinity University came under the responsibility of the Presbyterian Synod of Texas, United States of America, and was moved to Waxahachie; in 1942 it was moved to San Antonio.

In 1890 Daniel Baker College qv opened at Brownwood with Brainard Taylor McClelland qv as president and with seven faculty members. The school's first board of trustees represented the Presbyterian Church, United States of America, as well as the Cumberland Presbyterian, Methodist, Christian, and Episcopalian denominations. From 1893 to 1929 the school operated under the auspices of the Presbyterian Church, United States; then the college was released to an independent board of local Brownwood people.

Little was done in Texas by Presbyterians for the education of women before 1902, although there were some unsuccessful efforts. Plans by the two major Presbyterian sects to create a university in Dallas in 1886 failed to materialize, and Tyler Female College and Synodical College qqv did not last long. More impressive were the efforts of individual Presbyterians: Victoria Female Academy qv originally under John Shive and his wife; Galveston Female Collegiate Institute (*see* Galveston Seminary) under John McCullough;qv Lamar Female Seminary qv under O. P. Starke at Paris; Bryan Female Seminary under W. H. Vernor for some years after the Civil War; and Clarksville (originally New Boston) Female Institute qv under Mrs. Eliza Todd and John Anderson qv (*see also* Clarksville Male and Female Academy; Ringwood Female Seminary; Live Oak Female Seminary). Then in 1902 Texas Presbyterian College qv for women opened at Milford with Henry Clay Evans as president and an enrollment of fifty-five students. Within five years the enrollment rose to almost 200. Until it merged with **Austin College** in 1929, it provided education for over two thousand young women.

Austin College had been founded to provide native Presbyterian ministers, but a generation later no minister had come out of the school to serve Texas. Efforts were made, therefore, to establish a theological school. The first effort was semiprivate. R. K. Smoot and Robert Lewis Dabney qv founded Austin School of Theology.qv The school soon came under the auspices of Central Texas Presbytery, United States, and sent a number of men into the Texas ministry before it closed in 1895. Four years later the Synod of Texas, United States, accepted the Stuart Seminary qv property and opened the Austin Presbyterian Theological Seminary qv in the fall of 1902. Except for four years at the time of World War I, it has continued in operation.

A special concern of Presbyterians in Texas has been the education of Spanish-speaking Texans. Early efforts were made largely by individuals such as William Cochran Blair,qv who came to Texas in 1839 as a missionary. He began a movement for a college which would attract Spanish-speaking students from both Texas and Mexico; Aranama College qv opened in 1854 but was dissolved during the Civil War. In 1854 Melinda Rankin,qv a New England teacher, opened the Rio Grande Female Institute qv for Mexican girls. Realizing the need for broader support, Miss Rankin deeded the property to a Presbyterian board of trustees. In 1858 the school was offered to Western Texas Presbytery, United Synod of the South (later the Presbyterian Church, United States), but various disagreements forestalled action. With the coming of the Civil War, Miss Rankin fled to New Orleans because of her Unionist sympathies; Hiram Chamberlain qv carried on the school until his death in 1866, but presbytery records indicate that the school continued to operate until 1875. From then until 1897 the facilities were used by the Foreign Missionary Committee of the Presbyterian Church, United States. In 1912 the Synod of Texas, United States, opened Texas Mexican Industrial Institute qv for boys at Kingsville, on a 640-acre tract donated by Henrietta King.qv J. W. Skinner headed the school, which had a program of a half-day's high school study and a half-day's work. Ten years later Presby-

terian women in Texas began establishing a similar school for girls. On October 1, 1924, Presbyterian School for Mexican Girls qv opened at Taft, offering a program that alternated study and work. In 1957 the Synod of Texas, United States, combined both schools on the Kingsville campus as the Presbyterian Pan American School.qv

Two other educational ventures by Presbyterians were Southwestern Presbyterian Home and School for Orphans,qv which was opened in 1906 near Itasca, and Schreiner Institute.qv The latter was the result of interest and philanthropy by Charles Armand Schreiner.qv Concerned for the education of West Texas ranch boys, in about 1906 Schreiner first sought the help of the Western Texas Presbytery, United States, to establish a school. After a long delay, the Synod of Texas, United States, appointed a board of trustees and engaged James Joseph Delaney qv to head Schreiner Institute, which began holding classes in 1923. After 1930 the institute received financial aid from the synod. *See also* Presbyterian Church in Texas.

BIBLIOGRAPHY: Robert Finney Miller, *A Family of Millers and Stewarts* (1909); *Presbyterian Expansion in the Synod of Texas of the Presbyterian Church, U.S.* (1927); Mabelle Agnes Purcell, *Two Texas Female Seminaries* (1951); William Stuart Red, *A History of the Presbyterian Church in Texas* (1936); William Stuart Red, *The Texas Colonists and Religion, 1821–1836* (1924); Thomas H. Campbell, *History of the Cumberland Presbyterian Church in Texas* (1936).

Malcolm L. Purcell

Presbyterian Pan American School. Presbyterian Pan American School, Kingsville, became the successor of Texas Mexican Industrial Institute qv and the Presbyterian School for Mexican Girls qv following a decision to merge the two schools. In September, 1957, the Taft campus of the Presbyterian School for Mexican Girls closed and a coeducational program began at Kingsville.

The Presbyterian Church, Synod of Texas, United States, owned, controlled, and provided the operating budget for the mission school. High school and limited college programs were offered for students fourteen years of age and older who applied through their local Presbyterian churches. Admission to the college department was by faculty nomination only; no applications were accepted. In addition to a college preparatory high school department, an intensive English department operated primarily in the summer session to enable foreign students to take regular courses.

The school sought to prepare students to finish college and enter teaching, ministerial, missionary, medical, and legal professions. All students lived in dormitories on the Kingsville campus, which accommodated sixty boys and fifty-four girls. Other facilities on the 700-acre campus included a chapel, a classroom building, an office building, a 13,000-volume library, a swimming pool, and athletic fields.

Total enrollment during 1965–1966 was 114 students, including 6 in the college department, 27 from Mexico, and 18 from other countries. In 1972 the faculty numbered thirteen members and the regular term enrollment of students was 110. Sherwood H. Reisner served as president. *See also* Presbyterian Education in Texas.

*Presbyterian School for Mexican Girls. A 200-acre tract was given by Taft Ranch interests for the founding of the Presbyterian School for Mexican Girls. The town of Taft gave $10,000 and the women of the church raised $50,000 to launch the project. A faculty of two, with Katherine Gray as principal, met with nineteen students at the opening in 1924. In 1957 the school merged with the Presbyterian Pan American School.qv *See also* Presbyterian Education in Texas.

*Presbyterian Theological Seminary. *See* Austin Presbyterian Theological Seminary.

*Prescott Creek.

President's Library. *See* Lyndon Baines Johnson Library. *See also* Lyndon Baines Johnson Birthplace, Boyhood Home, and Ranch; Lyndon B. Johnson State Historic Park (under Parks, State).

President's Ranch Trail. The President's Ranch Trail, which was dedicated on November 10, 1967, at Wimberley, is a ninety-mile route located in the counties of Hays, Blanco, and Gillespie in the Texas hill country qv and extends from the LBJ Ranch, located on Ranch Road 1 near Stonewall, to San Marcos. From the ranch two approaches are possible to Blanco, from which the main route extends to San Marcos: one, referred to as the north branch, proceeds from Ranch Road 1 via U.S. Highway 290 through Hye to Johnson City, then to Blanco via U.S. Highway 281; the other approach, referred to as the south branch, leads from the ranch to Stonewall, reaching Blanco by means of Albert, on Ranch Road 1623. The route from Blanco to San Marcos leads through Wimberley, via Ranch Roads 165 and 2325, where Ranch Road 12 leads to San Marcos.

The idea for the trail honoring Lyndon Baines Johnson's qv presidency began with a group of interested persons made up of landowners along the proposed route, as well as civic and business leaders in the hill country area. The Texas Tourist Development Agency qv gave its official sanction to the project on September 12, 1967, which paved the way for the incorporation of the President's Ranch Trail Association, Inc., in October, 1967. It was initiated as a nonprofit public service for the promotion of historic, scenic, and recreational points of interest in President Johnson's home vicinity, under the rules of the Texas Travels Trails Committee, whose policy required that the three counties involved in the project be made responsible for establishing, publicizing, and maintaining the entire trail. The total financing of the trail was also made a responsibility of the tri-county group. A ten-member board of directors was established, and C. B. Smith, Sr., of Austin and Wimberley, was elected chairman of the association.

The trail, which closely follows the route taken by pioneers and Indian tribes of the area, reflects the background of the people from whom President Johnson descended, as well as places important to his early and later life—the birthplace of Lyndon Baines Johnson; the LBJ Ranch; the Johnson family cemetery; the LBJ State Park; the Johnson family home in Johnson City; the Pedernales Electric Cooperative in Johnson City, which was brought into being under his influence as United States senator; the First Christian Church in Johnson City, to which he belonged; the Hye post office, where he mailed his first letter; the Albert post office, general store, and school building; and his alma mater, Southwest Texas State University, in San Marcos, where his student rooming house is also located. *See also* Lyndon Baines Johnson Birthplace, Boyhood Home, and Ranch; Lyndon B. Johnson State Historic Park (under Parks, State).

*Presidiales.

*Presidio, Texas.

*Presidio de Béxar. *See* San Antonio de Béxar Presidio.

*Presidio County. Presidio County, a mountainous area of the Big Bend,qv is sparsely settled except in the Marfa area. The 1960 population was 5,460, a decrease of approximately two thousand in ten years from the 7,354 in 1950; the 1970 population was 4,842. This county, the site for the filming of the movie *Giant*, is mostly occupied by large ranches, the livestock of which accounted for three-fourths of the farm income, which averaged $5,-000,000 annually in the early 1970's, when some five thousand acres of irrigated land produced cotton, alfalfa, melons, and vegetables. Deposits of silver, lead, zinc, and mica have been located and mined in the past, but in 1963 only stone and gem stones contributed to the mineral income of $24,476. The mine at Shafter was at one time one of the more important silver producers in the United States but has been inactive in recent years. Other minerals are no longer commercially mined.

*Presidio de la Junta de los Ríos. *See* Presidio del Norte.

*Presidio del Norte.

*Presidio del Pilar. *See* Nuestra Señora del Pilar de los Adaes Presidio.

Presidio del Rio Grande. *See* San Juan Bautista.

*Presidio Road. *See* Old San Antonio Road.

*Presidios and Presidial Towns.

*Presley, Texas.

Presnall, Pope A. Pope A. Presnall, son of Harrison and Susan (Applewhite) Presnall, was born near San Antonio on July 26, 1865. He attended elementary school at nearby Oak Island on the Medina River and high school in San Antonio. In the early 1880's Presnall was a cowboy on the newly opened cattle ranges west of the Pecos River. He served as county treasurer of Pecos County while Roy Bean qv was judge.

Presnall moved to Alice in 1893 and with S. B. Mosser founded a private bank known as Presnall and Mosser, Bankers (later the Alice National Bank). He also engaged in ranching. In 1897 he married Alice Clare Clark; she died in April, 1904, leaving three children. In August, 1907, he married Donia Scruggs; they had two children. Presnall became the first mayor of Alice when it was incorporated on June 2, 1904. He also served on the school board and on the Jim Wells County draft board during World War I. Presnall moved to Corpus Christi in 1933 and died there on September 3, 1958.

Agnes G. Grimm

*Pressler, Charles William.

*Preston, Texas.

*Prestridge, Texas.

*Prewetts Creek.

*Prewitt Lake.

*Price, John T.

Price, Philip Pope. Philip Pope Price, teacher, lawyer, optometrist, and rancher, was born in Warrenton, North Carolina, on November 3, 1850. He received all of his schooling in Warrenton, graduating from the small college there before his seventeenth birthday. In 1867 he came to Texas and began teaching Latin and Greek at Goliad College;qv he also taught in nearby Gonzales, Nordheim, and Yorktown. He studied law and passed the state Bar examination, but his law practice was only incidental. Because of his poor eyesight he studied optometry.

About 1900 Price moved to Duval County, where he taught school for several years and traveled throughout the region fitting and selling spectacles. In 1903 he married Elizabeth Almond; they had one child. He was Jim Wells County commissioner from 1915 to 1916 and ran unsuccessfully for county judge. He then resumed teaching at Amargosa, Texas, and taught there until 1924. From 1925 until 1934 he was superintendent of county schools in Jim Wells County. On August 31, 1943, he died at his ranch home ten miles north of Alice.

Agnes G. Grimm

*Price, Texas. (Delta County.)

*Price, Texas. (Rusk County.)

*Price Creek.

*Prices Creek, Texas.

*Priddy, Texas.

*Pride, Texas.

*Pridgen, Bolivar Jackson.

*Prieto Creek.

*Prieto Indians. These Coahuiltecan Indians are known through a single report (1794) from Nuestra Señora del Espíritu Santo de Zuñiga Mission qv near Goliad. In this report they are identified as a subdivision of the Aranama, and it is said that at that time only twelve remained. The name, which is Spanish for "dark ones," suggests that they may have had a darker skin color than other Aranama,

but it may also refer to some distinctive style of body painting.

BIBLIOGRAPHY: Esteban L. Portillo, *Apuntes para la historia antigua de Coahuila y Texas* (1886); J. R. Swanton, *Linguistic Material from the Tribes of Southern Texas and Northeastern Mexico* (1940).

T. N. Campbell

*Primary Election Laws. *See* Election Laws.

*Primer, Sylvester.

*Primera, Texas. Primera, in western Cameron County, had a population of 1,066 in 1960 and 902 in 1970, according to the United States census report.

*Primrose, Texas. (Tarrant County.)

*Primrose, Texas. (Van Zandt County.)

*Princeton, Texas. Princeton, in Collin County, had a population of 594 in 1960 and 1,105 in 1970, an increase of 86 percent in ten years, according to the United States census report. Princeton had twenty-three businesses in 1970.

*Pringle, Texas.

*Prison Commission. *See* Texas Prison Board.

Prison Rodeo. *See* Texas Prison Rodeo.

*Prison System. *See also* Corrections, Texas Department of; Corrections, Texas Board of.

Prisoners of War in Texas. During World War II Texas had approximately twice as many prisoner-of-war camps as any other state. Twenty-one prisoner base (permanent) camps were located on military installations, and over twenty branch (temporary) camps were constructed throughout the state. Approximately forty-five thousand German, Italian, and Japanese prisoners were interned in Texas from 1942 to 1945. As the war continued, a policy of maximum utilization replaced a policy of maximum security of the prisoners, which resulted in the use of over twenty-seven thousand prisoners in numerous agricultural tasks, such as picking cotton, pulling corn, and harvesting rice. The prisoners were well treated, and very few escape attempts occurred from the Texas camps. After the war almost all of the prisoners were returned to their native countries, and many expressed their desire to return to Texas; however, over one hundred prisoners who died of wounds or of natural causes are still buried in the Fort Sam Houston qv National Cemetery in San Antonio. *See also* World War II, Texas in.

BIBLIOGRAPHY: Robert W. Tissing, Jr., Utilization of Prisoners of War in the United States During World War II, Texas: A Case Study (M.A. thesis, Baylor University, 1973).

Robert W. Tissing, Jr.

*Pritchett, Henry Carr.

*Pritchett, Texas.

Proctor, Alexander Phimister. Alexander Phimister Proctor, sculptor of Texas Memorial Museum's qv "Mustangs," was born in Bozanquit, Ontario, Canada, of Canadian-English stock, on September 27, 1860, the fourth of eleven children of Alexander and Tirzah (Smith) Proctor. The family came to Clinton, Michigan, by covered wagon in 1863, stayed a year before moving to Newton, Iowa, then went to Des Moines, where the family lived on a farm on the Raccoon River and Proctor attended a one-room school. Devoted to hunting and fishing, he began his lifelong interest in the outdoors and wild animals. In 1871 the family moved to Denver, Colorado, and he spent numerous seasons hunting, sketching, and studying animal forms in the western wilderness.

Proctor began drawing at an early age, and, encouraged by his father, he began art lessons soon after the family's arrival in Denver. He learned wood engraving in the studio of J. Harrison Mills, where he also met mountain men of the West and artists from the East. His first commission was twenty illustrations for Sheriff D. J. Cook's book, *Hands Up*, in 1880. In 1884 he homesteaded on Grand Lake in Colorado, built a log cabin there, and prospected for gold, then went to California. To continue his art training he sold his homestead and went to New York, where he enrolled in the National Academy in the winter of 1885. He spent the next winter drawing at the Art Students' League. In 1887 he met sculptor John Rogers, who encouraged him to model in clay and construct armatures; his first piece, "Fawn," was pictured in *Harper's Weekly*. Since the instructors at the league and the academy were not interested in the modeling or drawing of wild animals, Proctor worked mainly on his own, with criticism coming from fellow sculptors. In 1891 he was invited to Chicago to model life-size wild animals for the World's Columbian Exposition of 1893.

On September 27, 1893, he was married to Margaret Daisy Gerow, a young sculptress who was also working for the exposition; they went to Paris, where Proctor studied French methods of sculpture. He completed horses for two equestrian statues by Augustus Saint-Gaudens: "General John A. Logan" for Grant Park, Chicago, and "General William T. Sherman" for Central Park, New York City. He, with his family, went to Paris in 1896 on a three-year Rinehart scholarship; he returned to New York to complete a copper griffin and the equestrian statue "Louis Jolliet" for the Louisiana Purchase Exposition in St. Louis in 1904.

Proctor's first Texas work was the "General Robert E. Lee and Young Soldier" for the Southern Women's Memorial Association to present to the city of Dallas for the Texas Centennial qv Exposition in 1936, and it was Proctor's sculpture identified with the West which led to his second Texas commission. In 1938 J. Frank Dobie qv contacted Proctor for his friend, Texas oilman Ralph Ogden, who wanted to give a sculptured group of mustangs to the University of Texas at Austin. The artist made a fifteen-inch-high model of a small, compact group of six mustangs and brought it to Texas, where a colt was added; the model was accepted. During the spring, summer, and fall of 1939, when Proctor was working on the "Mus-

tangs," he lived on the Tom East ranch (part of the King Ranch qv) in South Texas, where there was a herd of wild mustangs. The group was finished, but during the years of World War II the plaster model remained in the Gorham Bronze Foundry in Providence, Rhode Island, awaiting the release of critical materials needed for the casting. Finally the "Mustangs," Proctor's last large work, was dedicated at the museum on May 1, 1948, and the sculptor was present. Ralph Ogden had died, but his widow presented the statue in his name.

Proctor and his wife were the parents of eight children. He died on September 4, 1950, in Palo Alto, California, his home. He was buried beside his wife in Mt. Pleasant Cemetery, in Seattle, Washington.

BIBLIOGRAPHY: Hester Elizabeth Proctor (ed.), *Sculptor in Buckskin: An Autobiography by Alexander Phimister Proctor* (1971); J. Frank Dobie, *The Seven Mustangs* (1948); Austin *American*, September 6, 1950, January 1, 1958.

*Proctor, Frederick Cocke.

*Proctor, Texas. Proctor, located about twelve miles east of Comanche in Comanche County, had a post office, three businesses, and two active churches in the late 1960's; Proctor Reservoir was completed during that time. A large peanut-buying station, part of which occupies the abandoned school building, serves nearby farmers. Once an important point on the Fort Worth and Rio Grande Railway, the depot had disappeared by 1967. A historical marker beside the nearby highway honors Mollie Evelyn Moore Davis,qv Texas author and sister of T. O. Moore, Confederate veteran and Proctor's first postmaster. An estimated 195 people lived in the community in 1971.

Margaret Tate Waring

Proctor Reservoir. Proctor Dam and Proctor Reservoir are in the Brazos River Basin in Comanche County, nine miles northeast of Comanche on the Leon River. The project was owned by the federal government and was operated by the United States Army Corps of Engineers, Fort Worth District, for flood control and water conservation. The Brazos River Authority qv was the local cooperative agency and contracted to purchase the conservation storage for $1,707,700 with interest over a fifty-year period. Construction began on June 28, 1960, and impoundment of water began on September 30, 1963. The reservoir, which had a capacity of 374,200 acre-feet at the top of the flood-control storage space at elevation 1,197 feet above mean sea level, provided flood control, conservation storage, and recreational facilities. The drainage area of the Leon River above Proctor Dam was 1,265 square miles.

BIBLIOGRAPHY: Texas Water Commission, *Bulletin 6408* (1964).

Seth D. Breeding

*Proffitt, Texas.

*Progreso, Texas.

*Progress, Texas.

*Prohibition Movement.

*Prospect, Texas. (Clay County.)

*Prospect, Texas. (Milam County.)

*Prosper, Texas.

*Prosser, Texas.

Protestant Episcopal Church Education in Texas. The first efforts at establishing Protestant Episcopal church schools in Texas were largely made by individuals without official appointment or appropriation. The general convention of the Episcopal church in 1835 made the first provision for the election of missionary bishops for states and territories in foreign countries where the Episcopal church was not organized, and the foreign committee of the board of missions considered sending a missionary to Texas. The result was authorization without appropriation and proved to be the plight of the Episcopal church and its schools in Texas for decades.

John Wurts Cloud,qv a priest from the Diocese of Mississippi, is known to have been in Texas in 1831 and to have conducted a school at Brazoria, and Chester Newell,qv an Episcopal deacon, operated a school at Velasco in 1837. Richard Salmon qv set out for Texas in 1836 with an interest in forming a group of Episcopalians within the Austin Colony. Arriving in Velasco in October, his group disintegrated almost immediately. He later moved to Brazoria and attempted to open a school, but he was stricken with tuberculosis and was unable to work actively. In 1837 a few citizens of Matagorda united, formed Christ Church, and requested the foreign committee to appoint a missionary. This was the first parish of the Episcopal church in Texas, and Caleb Smith Ives,qv who became their first rector, was able to come only because there was sufficient money to employ him as a teacher. This parish and school flourished and provided greater continuity in year-to-year operation than any similar effort in that generation.

In 1841 Leonidas Polk, missionary bishop of the Southwest, who was making his first official visit to Texas, was impressed by the work at Matagorda. This visit led Bishop Polk to concur with the opinions of Benjamin Eaton of Galveston and Charles Gillette qv of Houston that a school was needed to support their congregations. Almost all of the first dozen Episcopalian missionaries to Texas taught school in conjunction with their pastoral duties.

For the remainder of the century it was common for a group to purchase a building, operate a school for a year or so, and then in despair sell its assets to another sect, Masonic lodge, or municipal school. In most cases both private and church schools endured a precarious existence for short periods. The fluctuating strength and effectiveness of these schools was determined by many factors, including drouth and subsequent crop failure in such places as Brazoria and Columbia, instability of the Republic of Texas currency, yellow fever in Galveston, cholera in Austin, as well as storms and floods.

The most ambitious plan of the 1840's was the effort to found diocesan schools in Anderson (Grimes County). The original plans for a boys' and girls' school failed for lack of money. Charles Gillette moved to Anderson and operated St. Paul's College,qv a primary-through-college diocesan school, for a brief period of time. The only noted success of these efforts was the training of some of the tutors to serve as clergymen of the church.

Election of the Right Reverend Alexander Gregg qv as the first bishop of Texas in 1859 gave new but brief impetus to the church and its schools. One of his ambitions was to found a strong boys' and girls' school in the diocese. He moved to San Antonio and strengthened St. Mary's Hall,qv a school for girls, which was a fulfillment of half his dream. The effort to establish a boys' school was thwarted, however, by lack of funds, leaving St. Mary's Hall the only church school existing continuously from those days to the present.

Hopes for expanding education were deterred by the confusion during the Civil War,qv and with Reconstruction qv the establishment of Episcopal church schools did not have the urgency of the past. In addition, the demand for public education was being met with increasing effectiveness by municipal schools. Between 1838 and 1874 the Episcopal church established many schools of varying levels in connection with parishes and missions in such places as Brenham, Washington-on-the-Brazos, Lockhart, Seguin, San Augustine, Marshall, Galveston, Houston, and San Antonio.

Most of the church schools begun in the previous century did not survive to witness the revival of interest in general education by the church in the 1940's. The parish day-school movement sprang from different motivation than the parochial schools of the previous century. Many communities had adequate public grade schools but no kindergartens, and churchmen moved to fill this need; however, no single motivation or approach identifies schools related to the Episcopal church. Some churches initiated schools in an effort to provide a "Christian" balance in both the content and methodology of the public schools, which were considered too "secular" in the stringent demand that they be non-sectarian.

In 1966 there were about fifty schools operated by the Episcopal church in Texas. Three of these were interparish schools; that is, they were operated jointly by more than one congregation in a particular city. They were St. James' School, Corpus Christi; St. Andrew's School, Austin; and All Saints' School, Beaumont. Most of the schools were operated and underwritten by one congregation and varied in scope from pre-school through high school. Several schools were directly affiliated with their dioceses. St. Mark's School of Texas in Dallas had diocesan affiliation as did Texas Military Institute qv in San Antonio. In the Diocese of Texas, St.

Stephen's School (outside Austin) was unique in providing high school training for both boys and girls in a boarding school setting with additional provision for day students.

Some of the original church schools severed their church ties in times of crisis. Such was the case with St. John's School, Houston, which was patterned after a New England academy and maintained no liaison with the Episcopal church or its schools. Most Episcopal schools, being the responsibility of given congregations, have been free to evolve and develop in accordance with their native leadership and particular motivation.

The social crises of the 1960's were weathered by the schools of the Episcopal church in Texas, which, in many instances, were accused of having been formed to circumvent integration. However, the formation of the Texas Episcopal School Association and the National Association of Episcopal Schools had assisted in voluntary compliance with desegregation and the establishment of basic standards for church schools. *See also* Protestant Episcopal Church in Texas.

BIBLIOGRAPHY: Lawrence Brown, *The Episcopal Church in Texas* (1963); G. L. Crocket, *Two Centuries in East Texas* (1962).

Edward M. Hartwell

*Protestant Episcopal Church in Texas.** The Episcopal church, hampered in its pastoral work during World War II because the great proportion of its clergy served in armed forces chaplaincies, was able to begin the postwar period with new leadership. The rapid growth of the cities after the war demanded the organization of many new Episcopal congregations. In Houston, for example, there were fifteen congregations in 1944; in 1964 there were thirty-five; in Dallas there were seven in 1944 and twenty-seven in 1964; in San Antonio there were six in 1944 and thirteen in 1964; not included in these figures are new churches within the larger metropolitan areas of these cities. Outside the large cities, conditions varied greatly. Many of the old county seat towns, once able to hold self-sustaining parishes with full-time rectors, saw their Episcopal churches reduced to dependent missions or were forced to share their rectors with other churches. On the other hand, the spread of the petroleum industry and allied industries made cities of what had been small towns, while improved methods in agriculture and ranching accounted for the growth of marketing centers, so that in many towns there were several congregations where one was once scarcely able to survive. By 1970 there were 450 Episcopal churches in Texas. The increased number of churches resulted in the need for more clergymen, and the need was fulfilled. In 1944 there were 152 clergy listed in the Texas jurisdiction (including Texas west of the Pecos); in 1964 there were 427. By 1970 there were 593 Episcopal clergy in Texas.

One result of the increase in population and prosperity throughout the region was that the two remaining missionary jurisdictions were able to attain the status of self-supporting and self-governing dioceses. The Missionary District of New Mexico and Southwest Texas became a diocese at the general convention of 1952. (It unsuccessfully petitioned at that time to shed its cumbersome name in favor of "Diocese of the Rio Grande.") The Missionary District of North Texas was admitted by the 1958 general convention as the Diocese of Northwest Texas. Total membership of the five Episcopal dioceses in Texas was 147,435 adult members in 1970. This figure, along with the figures on number of clergy and number of churches in Texas, includes the state of New Mexico (which is part of one of the Texas dioceses).

Along with the growth of the church was the expansion of its work in education. Additional classroom facilities for Sunday schools and many parish day schools were provided. Each of the diocese jurisdictions has either constructed or added to existing facilities for conferences and summer youth camps, and some have more than one facility to meet the needs of congregations remote from the first center.

In the field of ministry to college and university communities, student centers and chaplaincies have been provided at many colleges throughout the state. The effort to provide church liberal arts colleges has been made, but so far without lasting effect. A committee appointed by the Diocese of Texas to study the need for a four-year liberal arts college has reported from year to year, but has not recommended action.

Theological education became another acute educational need of the church in Texas in the postwar years. The need for more clergymen throughout the church was great in those years, and the number of men seeking training for ordination was too large for existing Episcopal theological schools to accommodate. In September, 1951, bishops Clinton Simon Quin qv and John Elbridge Hines authorized a tentative experiment in Austin. Three part-time faculty members began instructing an entering class, and the Austin Presbyterian Theological Seminary qv offered to enroll these students in some of their courses, using additional course offerings at the University of Texas. The Diocesan Council of January, 1951, adopted this new school and authorized its application for a state charter as the Episcopal Theological Seminary of the Southwest.qv From the outset other dioceses sent students to the seminary. In 1952 the seminary received property in the University of Texas neighborhood from Dr. and Mrs. Ernest Villavaso, Frederick Duncalf,qv and his wife, Alma Duncalf, in memory of Ernest Villavaso, Jr. Six permanent buildings, including Christ Chapel, have been erected on this site, a large library collection assembled, and a full faculty brought together. The seminary has been accredited by the American Association of Theological Schools. In recent years the dioceses of West Texas, New Mexico and Southwest Texas, Arkansas,

Northwest Texas, and Oklahoma have assumed joint ownership of the seminary.

In 1956 the Church Historical Society of the national church accepted the invitation of the Episcopal Theological Seminary of the Southwest to locate its headquarters and archives in the seminary library; this brought to Austin the official archives of the Episcopal church in the United States, for which the society is custodian.

Activity in humanitarian concerns has increased in the Episcopal church since 1945. The dioceses of West Texas, New Mexico and Southwest Texas, and Dallas have been active in missionary work with Spanish-speaking people. Homes for the elderly have been established in several places. The Diocese of Texas has built St. Luke's Hospital in the Texas Medical Center qv in Houston and acquired and enlarged Good Shepherd Hospital in Longview. The Diocese of Dallas sponsors All Saints' Hospital in Fort Worth and Gaston Hospital in Dallas. All the dioceses have cooperated in interdenominational work with migrant workers and in many other social causes. *See also* Protestant Episcopal Church Education in Texas.

BIBLIOGRAPHY: *Living Church Annual* (1945); *Episcopal Church Annual* (1965).

Lawrence L. Brown

*Providence, Texas. (Polk County.)

*Providence, Texas. (Van Zandt County.)

*Provident City, Texas.

*Provincias Internas.

*Provisional Government.

*Pruett, Texas.

*Pruit, Pleasant M.

*Pruitt, Texas.

*Pryor, Charles R.

*Pryor, Ike T.

*Pryor, William.

*Psaupsauo Indians.

*Public Domain. *See* Lands, Texas Public.

Public Employment Program. *See* Community Affairs, Department of.

*Public Health, State Department of. [Officially called the Texas State Department of Health, this department has long been identified with the name given it in 1903, when it was designated the Department of Public Health and Vital Statistics.] Although most of the department's mental health and mental retardation services were removed with the formation of the Texas Department of Mental Health and Mental Retardation qv in 1965, the State Department of Public Health grew in size and stature in the 1960's until it was a major state agency. Besides administrative services, the agency included tuberculosis control, preventive medical services, special health services, local health services, environmental sanitation services, laboratories, and records and statistics. Specific functions of personnel working through the organizational

structure included such tasks as hospital licensing, venereal disease case-finding, food and drug inspections, birth and death recording, phenylketonuria screening and dietary control to prevent one form of mental retardation, information dissemination, and disaster preparedness. In cooperation with the state agency, some sixty local health units function throughout the state, effecting public health services at the grass roots level. A migrant labor project, zoonosis control, waste water technology, air pollution control, vector control, biologics and drugs, and pesticides were areas of concentration for the department during the late 1960's.

Grant H. Burton

*Public Instruction. *See* Education; and related articles.

*Public Lands. *See* Lands, Texas Public.

*Public Safety, Department of. [This title was incorrectly listed in Volume II as Public Safety, State Department of.] The Department of Public Safety functions through the following major divisions: Personnel and Staff Services, Driver and Vehicle Records, Identification and Criminal Records, Inspection and Planning, Defense and Disaster Relief, Data Processing, Traffic Law Enforcement, and Criminal Law Enforcement. Plans and policies are still established by the Public Safety Commission.

BIBLIOGRAPHY: University of Texas at Austin, *Guide To Texas State Agencies* (1972).

Public Service Careers Program. *See* Community Affairs, Department of.

*Public Utilities, Regulation of. *See* Railroad Commission.

*Public Weigher.

*Public Welfare, State Department of. The State Department of Public Welfare was authorized in 1965 to cooperate with the federal government in administering the anti-poverty program, which had been established in 1964. The department continued in the 1970's to administer four public assistance programs for needy Texans: old age assistance, aid to the blind, aid to the permanently and totally disabled, and aid to families with dependent children. The federal government provided approximately 75 percent of the assistance funds, and the state, by appropriation from the legislature, provided the remainder.

The department also administered the Texas Medical Assistance Program (Medicaid), which helped pay the costs of medical care for many people who were eligible for public assistance. It served as the state agency responsible for administration of two food programs for the benefit of needy persons—the commodity distribution program and the food stamp program.

The department's division of social services provided many services to children, adults, and families who received financial assistance through the department. The department also had as a fundamental responsibility the protection of all children

from abuse, neglect, or exploitation. It also provided adoptive services and was responsible for licensing child-care and child-placing facilities. In 1970 the department had 3,700 employees.
BIBLIOGRAPHY: University of Texas at Austin, *Guide To Texas State Agencies* (1972).

Pucha Indians. In 1683–1684 Juan Domínguez de Mendoza qv led an exploratory expedition from El Paso as far eastward as the junction of the Concho and Colorado rivers east of present San Angelo. In his itinerary he listed the names of thirty-seven Indian groups, including the Pucha, from whom he expected to receive delegations on the Colorado River. Nothing further is known about the Pucha, who seem to have been one of many Indian groups of north-central Texas that were swept away by the southward thrust of the Lipan-Apache and Comanche Indians in the eighteenth century. However, it is possible that the Pucha were the same people as the Patzau, a Coahuiltecan band of the same period reported as living south of the Edwards Plateau and between present San Antonio and Eagle Pass. This identity cannot be demonstrated.
BIBLIOGRAPHY: H. E. Bolton (ed.), *Spanish Exploration in the Southwest, 1542–1706* (1916); C. W. Hackett (ed.), *Pichardo's Treatise on the Limits of Louisiana and Texas*, II (1934).

T. N. Campbell

Pucham Indians. The Pucham (Pueham) Indians are known only from the diary of Juan Domínguez de Mendoza, qv who in 1684 listed them as one of thirty-seven Indian groups from which delegations were expected while he was encamped in the western part of the Edwards Plateau. Since about half of the names on this list are identifiable as Coahuiltecan, it is possible that the Pucham, whose name is similar to some of these (*i.e.*, Pucha, Puguahian), are also of Coahuiltecan affiliation.
BIBLIOGRAPHY: H. E. Bolton (ed.), *Spanish Exploration in the Southwest, 1542–1706* (1916); C. E. Castañeda, *Our Catholic Heritage in Texas, 1591–1936*, II (1936); C. W. Hackett (ed.), *Pichardo's Treatise on the Limits of Louisiana and Texas*, II (1934).

T. N. Campbell

*Pueblo.

*Pueblo, Texas.

*Pueblo Indians.

*Pueblo Ruins of the Texas Panhandle. *See also* Alibates Flint Quarries.

*Puente De Piedra.

*Puertecita Mountains.

*Puerto Rico, Texas.

*Pugsley, Texas.

Puguahiane Indians. In 1683–1684 Juan Domínguez de Mendoza qv led an exploratory expedition from El Paso as far eastward as the junction of the Concho and Colorado rivers east of present San Angelo. In his itinerary he listed the names of thirty-seven Indian groups, including the Puguahiane (Paguachiane), from whom he expected to receive delegations on the Colorado River. Nothing

further is known about the Puguahiane, who seem to have been one of many Indian groups of north-central Texas that were swept away by the southward thrust of the Lipan-Apache and Comanche Indians in the eighteenth century. However, it is possible that the Puguahiane were the same people as the Pacuachiam, a Coahuiltecan band of the same period that lived south of the Edwards Plateau. This has yet to be demonstrated.
BIBLIOGRAPHY: H. E. Bolton (ed.), *Spanish Exploration in the Southwest, 1542–1706* (1916); C. W. Hackett (ed.), *Pichardo's Treatise on the Limits of Louisiana and Texas*, II (1934).

T. N. Campbell

*Pulacuam Indians. In 1690 the Pulacuam (Pulacmam, Pulacman) Indians were encountered by Spaniards on the headwaters of the "Río Medina," which could be either the present Medina River or the San Antonio River. This suggests that their range was along the southern margin of the Edwards Plateau west of present San Antonio. On the Río Medina they were encamped with five other bands, all apparently of Coahuiltecan affiliation. Swanton stated that the Pulacuam may have been Coahuiltecan or Tonkawan in speech, but none of the evidence now available supports a Tonkawan affiliation. Bolton (in Hodge) suggested that the Pulacuam may have been the same people as the Sulujam. This is a guess based on presumed phonetic resemblances in the names and is not acceptable.
BIBLIOGRAPHY: L. Gómez Canedo, *Primeras exploraciones y poblamiento de Texas, 1686–1694* (1968); F. W. Hodge (ed.), *Handbook of American Indians*, II (1910); J. R. Swanton, *Linguistic Material from the Tribes of Southern Texas and Northeastern Mexico* (1940).

T. N. Campbell

Pulaski, Texas. Pulaski, situated on a bluff on the east bank of the Sabine River nine miles east of Carthage, served as the seat for two counties, first as the temporary seat of Harrison County in 1841, and then as the seat of Panola County in 1846.

Pulaski became the seat of Panola County by an election in August, 1846, but heated opposition, led by Samuel M. Perry, forced the commissioners court to designate the community as a temporary county seat and to approve a second election to determine a permanent site.

The choice of a permanent county seat became the county's biggest political issue for the next two years, until the county electorate in a general election of July, 1848, selected the undeveloped area of Carthage as the permanent county seat. After 1848 Pulaski declined as a community, and the 1850 census reported a population of only thirty-three.
BIBLIOGRAPHY: Lawrence R. Sharp, History of Panola County, Texas, to 1860 (M.A. thesis, University of Texas at Austin, 1940); Carthage Circulating Book Club, *History of Panola County* (1935).

Pulcha Indians. The Pulcha (Pilcha, Pylcha, Vlcha) Indians are known only from a long list of Indian groups reported in 1684 by Juan Domínguez de Mendoza qv when he was in the western part of the Edwards Plateau. It is said that delegations from these Indians were expected, but no territorial ranges are specified. As the name was never reported from adjoining areas, the Pulcha may have been a local Edwards Plateau group, possibly of Coahuiltecan affiliation.

BIBLIOGRAPHY: H. E. Bolton (ed.), *Spanish Exploration in the Southwest, 1542–1706* (1916); C. E. Castañeda, *Our Catholic Heritage in Texas, 1519–1936*, II (1936); C. W. Hackett (ed.), *Pichardo's Treatise on the Limits of Louisiana and Texas*, II (1934).

T. N. Campbell

Pulique Indians. The Pulique (Puilque, Pulica) Indians are known mainly from the first half of the eighteenth century, when they lived in the village of San Antonio de los Puliques on the south bank of the Rio Grande below modern Presidio. In the late seventeenth century they were listed among "nations" that lived north of the Rio Grande in the same area. The identity of the Pulique is not clear, but some writers have identified them as a branch of the Concho Indians. In the late eighteenth century the Pulique seem to have been absorbed by the Spanish-speaking population of northern Chihuahua.

BIBLIOGRAPHY: C. W. Hackett (ed.), *Historical Documents Relating to New Mexico, Nueva Vizcaya, and Approaches Thereto, to 1773*, II (1926); J. C. Kelley, "Factors Involved in the Abandonment of Certain Peripheral Southwestern Settlements," *American Anthropologist*, LIV (1952); J. C. Kelley, "The Historic Indian Pueblos of La Junta de los Ríos," *New Mexico Historical Review*, XXVII (1952), XXVIII (1953); C. Thomas and J. R. Swanton, *Indian Languages of Mexico and Central America and Their Geographical Distribution* (1911).

T. N. Campbell

*Pulliam, Texas. (Tom Green County.)

*Pulliam, Texas. (Zavala County.)

*Pulliam Bluff.

*Pulliam Creek.

Pullin, Texas. *See* Green, Texas.

*Pullman, Texas.

*Pulp and Paper Industry. *See* Paper, Manufacture of.

*Pummel Peak.

*Pumphrey, Texas.

*Pumpville, Texas.

*Purdon, Texas.

*Purgatory Creek.

*Purísima Concepción Mission. *See* Nuestra Señora de la Purísima Concepción de los Hainai Mission; Nuestra Señora de la Purísima Concepción de Acuña Mission.

*Purísima Concepción del Socorro. *See* Nuestra Señora de la Concepción del Socorro.

*Purley, Texas.

*Purmela, Texas.

*Pursley, Texas.

*Purtis Creek.

*Purves, Texas.

*Putaay Indians. *See also* Pitahay Indians.

*Putnam, Texas.

*Putnam Mountain.

*Pyote, Texas.

Pyote Air Force Station. Pyote Air Force Station, formerly Pyote Army Air Field,qv was redesignated Pyote Air Force Station in 1959. It served as a radar site of the Air Defense Command until the summer of 1963 and then was maintained as excess property. The Air Defense Command disposed of this station in 1966, and it was taken over by the General Services Administration for sale or other disposition.

Maurer Maurer

*Pyote Army Air Field. *See also* Pyote Air Force Station.

*Pyramid Rock.

Pyron, Charles L. Charles L. Pyron was born in Marion County, Alabama, in 1819, and was educated in the normal schools of that state. In 1848 he moved to Texas, going first to Port Lavaca, and then to San Antonio, where he bought a ranch near San José y San Miguel de Aguayo Mission qv and specialized in the raising of high-grade cattle. On November 15, 1849, he married Octavia Caroline Smith, of Port Lavaca, who bore him four children.

With the secession of Texas, Pyron raised a company of troops which was mustered into state service on April 15, 1861, and into the Confederate Army on May 23, 1861, as Company B, 2nd Texas Mounted Rifles. He was stationed on the frontier at Fort Lancaster and Fort Stockton,qqv and he later joined Colonel John R. Baylor qv in Confederate Arizona. He was a major and battalion commander during General Henry H. Sibley's qv New Mexico campaign. Near Fort Craig his advance precipitated the battle of Valverde on February 21, 1862. He and his men were also the first to enter Albuquerque and to occupy Santa Fe. At Apache Canyon his small force was defeated by a Federal detachment; two days later he played a prominent role in the far larger, decisive battle of Glorieta Pass on March 28, 1862. Shortly after the close of the New Mexico campaign, he was promoted to lieutenant colonel.

Elected colonel of the reorganized 2nd Texas Cavalry on October 8, 1862, Pyron saw action in Louisiana during the Teche campaign of 1863. He was severely wounded at Lafourche Crossing on June 21, 1863. On April 16, 1864, he assumed command of the post of San Antonio, and on June 26 of that year he was placed in charge of the northern division of the Western Sub-District of Texas with headquarters at San Antonio. He held that position until April, 1865, when, because of the Union threat to the Texas coast, he was transferred to Corpus Christi to command the eastern division of the Western Sub-District. With the surrender of the Trans-Mississippi Department, Pyron returned to his ranch near San Antonio. He died on August 24, 1869.

BIBLIOGRAPHY: Charles M. Barnes, *Combats and Conquests of Immortal Heroes (1910); Ellis A. Davis and Edwin H. Grobe (eds.), New Encyclopedia of Texas (1929); U.S. War Department, The War of the Rebellion: A Compilation of the Official Records of the Union and Confederate Armies (1880–1901); U. S. Census, 1860, Bexar County, Texas (microfilm, University of Texas at Austin Library); Calhoun County Marriage Records (County Clerk's Office, Port Lavaca); Galveston Tri-Weekly News, September 1, 1869.

Martin Hardwick Hall

*Pyron, Texas.

Q

Quæstad, Carl Engebretson. Carl Engebretson Quæstad was born in 1815 in Loiten, Hedmark, Norway, and as a young man was a hunting and fishing guide and a blacksmith. He married Sedsel Oldsdatter Ringnæs in 1841 and in the 1840's came to Kaufman County, Texas. He was with the Norwegian immigrants who explored the region along the Bosque River in 1853 and was among the first settlers to secure land there. On his farm he built a masonry house, which was still standing in the 1960's. He was a cattleman, farmer, blacksmith, and mason. An inquiring intellectual, he bought books and loaned them throughout the community; he collected scientific data and in 1874 and 1882 sent collections of fossils and Indian artifacts to the Bergen Museum in Norway. He provided a home for the Swedish naturalist, Gustav Belfrage qv from 1870 to 1879. He died in 1886 and was buried at Norse, Texas, in the Norse Cemetery beside his fellow pioneer settler, Cleng Peerson.qv See also Norwegians in Texas.

BIBLIOGRAPHY: C. A. Clausen (ed.), The Lady with the Pen: Elise Waerenskjold in Texas (1961); Institute of Texan Cultures, The Norwegian Texans (1970).

*Quail, Texas.

*Quaker Colony. See also Estacado, Texas; Friendswood, Texas.

Quakers in Texas. Few Quakers (Society of Friends) were to be found in Texas until after the Civil War. Their early opposition to slavery led the Friends to bypass the Gulf Coast states. Several yearly meetings of Friends made known their opposition to accepting slaveholding Texas into the Union, primarily because Texas reserved the right to divide into five slave states. A pro-slavery, anti-abolitionist newspaper, the Anti-Quaker, appeared in Austin in March, 1842. Several individual Quakers did make their way to Texas before the 1870's, the most famous being Mifflin Kenedy.qv Early twentieth-century Quaker groups were in Lipscomb County (1910) and in View Point, Texas. Today there are two major Quaker organizations in the state, the Kansas Yearly Meeting, the earliest group, and the South Central Yearly Meeting.

The Estacado Monthly Meeting of the Society of Friends, established in Estacado, Texas (see Quaker Colony; Cox, Paris), was sponsored from Iowa. In 1893 the Friends began leaving Estacado, settling for a brief time in Alvin, Texas. They purchased 1,538 acres of land at the headwaters of Clear Creek, adjacent to Harris County, from J. C. League (see League City, Texas) in 1895 and named their settlement Friendswood at the suggestion of Frank J. Brown, one of the colony's leaders. In 1902 Friendswood Academy was established and was maintained until 1945. For a time Friendswood Monthly Meeting retained its connection with Iowa Yearly Meeting, later transferring to Rose Hill Quarterly Meeting of which League City Monthly Meeting (in 1910) was also a part. In December of the same year Friendswood Quarterly Meeting was established under the auspices of the Kansas Yearly Meeting. Meetings belonging to this group in 1970 were in Bayshore, Northshore, Friendswood, South Houston, League City, Texas City, and San Antonio, which had the San Antonio Monthly Meeting and the Friends Chapel Monthly Meeting. These meetings have pastors and their services are programmed to resemble the traditional Protestant church services more than they do traditional Friends meetings.

The Kansas Yearly Meeting in 1964 sponsored the Friends School in San Antonio. Located in the former Southern Christian College buildings, the school offered education, housing, and guidance to emotionally disturbed children who have been rejected by other child care agencies. In 1970 approximately eighty students were being cared for. These Friends in 1963 joined with an interdenominational group and established headquarters in Friendswood for CABCO (Central African Broadcasting Company)—known in Europe and Africa as CORDAC. The station, located in Bujumbura, Burundi, on the northeast shore of Lake Tanganyika, broadcasts daily missionary programs in five languages to a possible audience of ten million.

After World War II a number of individual Quakers moved to Texas, and the American Friends Service Committee began to expand its work into the state. With these two developments there began a series of meetings connected with the South Central Yearly Meeting in some of the principal Texas cities. These traditional meetings, like those in England and Pennsylvania, have no pastors or "programmed" services. Among the meetings of this traditional type are the Friends Monthly Meetings at Austin (established in 1949) and Dallas (1952), and the Live Oak Monthly Meeting in Houston (1956). Worship groups (preliminary organizations) have been formed in San Antonio, Lubbock, and Fort Worth. The South Central Yearly Meeting group is affiliated with the Texas Conference of Churches and Friends General Conference, and is active in its support of the work of the American Friends Service Committee, Friends Committee on National Legislation, and the Friends World Committee for Consultation. The American Friends Service Committee has had service programs of various kinds in Texas since the end of World War II. In 1971 there were community and peace testimony projects centered in San Antonio, Houston, and the Rio Grande Valley.

BIBLIOGRAPHY: Henry C. and Melissa S. Fellow, *Semi-Centennial Historical Sketch of Kansas Yearly Meeting of Friends* (n.d.); Sheldon Glenn Jackson, *A Short History of Kansas Yearly Meeting of Friends* (1946); Edith B. McGinnis, *The Promised Land* (1947); Ethel Mary Franklin (ed.), "Memoirs of Mrs. Annie P. Harris," *Southwestern Historical Quarterly*, XL (1936–1937); Friends World Committee, *Friends Directory* (1971–1972); Kansas Yearly Meeting of Friends, *Minutes of Ninety-ninth Annual Session* (1970).

Kenneth Carroll
Eugene Ivash

*Quanah, Texas. Quanah, seat and principal town of Hardeman County, is in an agricultural and ranching area with cattle, cotton, wheat, oats, and barley as the chief sources of income. Oil and gas production became a big industry for Quanah with the discovery of the Conley oil field southwest of the town in 1959. Principal products of local industries are sheet metal, cottonseed oil, and gypsum products, although agribusinesses were predominant. Quanah reported nineteen churches, four schools, two banks, a library, a municipal building, and a hospital in the mid-1960's. The county museum is located in Quanah. The 1960 population was 4,564; in 1970 it was 3,948, according to the United States census. Quanah reported eighty-eight businesses in 1970.

*Quanah, Acme, and Pacific Railroad.

Quanataguo Indians. The Quanataguo Indians are known from a single entry (1728) in the burial records of San Antonio de Valero Mission,qv at San Antonio. The name is given as the band affiliation of a woman who was married to a Coahuiltecan. Apparently this is the basis for J. R. Swanton's identification of the Quanataguo as Coahuiltecan in speech. However, it is possible that Quanataguo is a variant of Anathagua, a name that appears on a list of twenty-five tribes of east-central and southeastern Texas recorded in 1748 as having asked for missions in that general area. The list contains no names recognizable as Coahuiltecan; the identifiable names indicate only Caddoans (including Wichita), Tonkawans, Atakapans, and Karankawans. Quanataguo and Anathagua bear some resemblance to Quiutcanuaha, the name of a group of Indians identified in 1691 as living an unspecified distance southwest of the Hasinai Indians of eastern Texas, but no identities can be established. The affiliations of all three groups remain undetermined.

BIBLIOGRAPHY: H. E. Bolton, *Texas in the Middle Eighteenth Century* (1915); C. W. Hackett (ed.), *Pichardo's Treatise on the Limits of Louisiana and Texas*, I

(1931); F. W. Hodge (ed.), *Handbook of American Indians*, II (1910); J. R. Swanton, *Linguistic Material from the Tribes of Southern Texas and Northeastern Mexico* (1940); J. R. Swanton, *Source Material on the History and Ethnology of the Caddo Indians* (1942).

T. N. Campbell

*Quantrell, Charles W. See Quantrill, William Clarke.

*Quantrill, William Clarke.

*Quapaw Indians.

Quara Indians. In the latter part of the seventeenth century the Quara (Coara, Kouara) Indians lived north of Matagorda Bay on or near one of the major streams in present Jackson County, apparently the Lavaca River. Their village, which was visited by La Salle qv in 1687, was one of many settlements along this river. Of these various settlements, only the Quara and Anachorema villages are identified in the records of the La Salle Expedition.qv In the Quara village La Salle and his party stayed two days, during which time some 700 or 800 warriors returned with 150 prisoners, which lends support to the statement that this area was rather heavily populated. The Quara are not referred to by this name in later times and their ethnic affiliation remains unknown. Since they lived in an area dominated by Karankawa groups, it is possible that they too were Karankawan. However, on the basis of sound correspondence, it has been suggested that the Quara were the people later known as Aranama.

BIBLIOGRAPHY: C. W. Hackett (ed.), *Pichardo's Treatise on the Limits of Louisiana and Texas*, I (1931); J. G. Shea, *Early Voyages up and down the Mississippi* (1861); J. G. Shea, *Discovery and Exploration of the Mississippi Valley* (1903).

T. N. Campbell

*Quarai Indians.

*Quaras Indian Village.

*Quarry, Texas. (Shackelford County.)

*Quarry, Texas. (Washington County.)

*Quarry Creek.

*Quarter Horse. See Horse Breeding: Western (or Quarter) Horses.

**Quarterly of the Texas State Historical Association. See Southwestern Historical Quarterly.*

*Quarton, Texas.

*Quartz Knob.

*Queen City, Texas. Queen City, Cass County, reported twenty-three businesses in 1970. The town had a population in 1960 of 1,081; in 1970 the population, according to the United States census, was 1,227.

*Queens Creek.

*Queen's Peak.

Quem Indians. The Quem (Cem, Maquem, Queni, Quimi, Quimso, Quini) Indians, apparently Coahuiltecan-speakers, were first reported in 1689, when a Quem man guided Alonso de León qv to the site of La Salle's qv settlement near Matagorda

Bay. In June, 1691, the Quem and five other groups were visited by Spaniards at a *rancheria* in present southern Maverick County, some ten miles north of the Rio Grande. After 1718 a few Quem families entered San Antonio de Valero Mission qv in San Antonio. The aboriginal range of the Quem seems to have been northeastern Coahuila and the adjacent part of Texas.

BIBLIOGRAPHY: H. E. Bolton (ed.), *Spanish Exploration in the Southwest, 1542-1706* (1916); L. Gómez Canedo, *Primeras exploraciones y poblamiento de Texas, 1686-1694* (1968); M. A. Hatcher, "The Expedition of Don Domingo Terán de los Ríos into Texas," *Preliminary Studies of the Texas Catholic Historical Society*, II (1932); F. W. Hodge (ed.), *Handbook of American Indians*, II (1910).

T. N. Campbell

*Quemado, Texas.

Quepano Indians. The Quepano (Cuepano, Quepana) Indians, who were apparently Coahuiltecans, lived near Cerralvo in northeastern Nuevo León in the latter part of the seventeenth century. Some Quepano were at San Antonio de Valero Mission,qv in San Antonio, during the first half of the following century.

BIBLIOGRAPHY: H. E. Bolton, *Texas in the Middle Eighteenth Century* (1915); W. Jiménez Moreno, "Tribus e idiomas del Norte de México," *El Norte de México y el Sur de Estados Unidos* (1944); J. R. Swanton, *Linguistic Material from the Tribes of Southern Texas and Northeastern Mexico* (1940).

T. N. Campbell

*Querecho Indians.

*Queretarian Missionaries in Texas. *See* Santa Cruz de Querétaro, College of.

Quevene Indians. The Quevene (Guevene) Indians were encountered by Cabeza de Vaca qv on the Texas coast, presumably about 1528. Their area cannot be clearly identified, but it seems to have been in the middle section of the coast. They have been identified with the Cujane, a Karankawan group known to the Spanish over 150 years later. This identification is based on occupation of the same general area and phonetic similarities in the names. It cannot be proved or disproved.

BIBLIOGRAPHY: A. F. Bandelier (ed.), *The Journey of Alvar Nuñez Cabeza de Vaca* (1922); F. W. Hodge (ed.), *Handbook of American Indians*, I (1907), II (1910).

T. N. Campbell

Quibaga Indians. The Quibaga Indians are known from a single Spanish missionary report (1691) which identifies them as enemies of the Hasinai Indians of eastern Texas. The linguistic and cultural affiliations of the Quibaga remain unknown. The name is similar to that of the Quitaca, a group, possibly Wichita, that lived in the same general area during the eighteenth century, but there is no proof that the two names refer to the same people.

BIBLIOGRAPHY: J. R. Swanton, *Source Material on the History and Ethnology of the Caddo Indians* (1942).

T. N. Campbell

*Quicksand Creek.

*Quicksilver Mining in Texas. *See* Mercury Mining in Texas; Mineral Resources and Mining in Texas; Perry, Howard Everett.

Quicuchabe Indians. The Quicuchabe Indians were one of twenty Indian groups that joined Juan Domínguez de Mendoza qv on his journey from El Paso to the vicinity of present San Angelo in 1683-1684. Since Mendoza did not indicate at what point the Quicuchabe joined his party, it is impossible to determine their range or affiliations. However, the Indians between the Pecos River and the San Angelo area were being hard pressed by Apache at this time, and it seems likely that the Quicuchabe ranged somewhere between these two localities.

BIBLIOGRAPHY: H. E. Bolton (ed.), *Spanish Exploration in the Southwest, 1542-1706* (1916).

T. N. Campbell

*Quide Indians.

*Quien Sabe Ranch.

*Quigley, Texas.

Quiguaya Indians. The Quiguaya Indians are known from a single Spanish missionary report (1691), which identifies them as enemies of the Hasinai Indians of eastern Texas. The Quiguaya seem to have lived to the west of the Hasinai. Although it cannot yet be demonstrated, the Quiguaya seem to have been the same people as the Quiouaha, reported in documents (1687) pertaining to the La Salle Expedition qv as enemies of the Kadohadacho on Red River. The Quiouaha have been erroneously identified with the Kiowa Indians, who did not enter the Texas area until the nineteenth century. The affiliations of both Quiguaya and Quiouaha remain unknown.

BIBLIOGRAPHY: F. W. Hodge (ed.), *Handbook of American Indians*, I (1907), II (1910); P. Margry, *Découvertes et établissements des Français dans l'ouest et dans le sud de l'Amérique Septentrionale*, III (1879); J. R. Swanton, *Source Material on the History and Ethnology of the Caddo Indians* (1942).

T. N. Campbell

*Quihi, Texas. Quihi, in Medina County, was located on the military road from San Antonio to Fort Inge, Fort Clark, and Fort Duncan.qqv Seth Eastman and Frederick Law Olmsted qqv were among the numerous travelers who passed through the European-like settlement before the Civil War. Olmsted in 1857 described the Alsatian-style whitewashed stone houses there, with dormer windows and high-gabled, thatched roofs. Wooden second-story additions were often made later. The cemetery had wrought iron markers decorated with painted tin wreaths.

On March 10, 1846, ten families left Castroville in loaded carts and wagons, traveling ten miles to camp that night at Quihi Creek. After an Indian attack on the settlers' camp, in which five adults were killed and a boy was taken captive, the colonists built a semicircular brush fortification for protection at night. The Lipan and Kickapoo attacked in 1847, and Indian raids continued until 1874.

Each family had a townsite lot and a farm (640 acres for a married man and 320 acres for a single man). The colonists had to cultivate fifteen acres of their land to hold it, and they sold corn to the forts in the area. Drouth came in 1848–1849, followed by a cholera epidemic. The first public school was erected in 1875, and there was for a time a German-English school. A Lutheran church was built first, and later a Methodist church was built. The church bell which the Bernard Brucks family had brought from Europe was used as a warning signal against Indians, and it is today in the Catholic church in D'Hanis. The first post office was in the Louis W. Boehle house in 1855. In 1971 there were approximately ninety-six people living in Quihi. *See also* Castro, Henri; Castro's Colony.

BIBLIOGRAPHY: Lois Burkhalter, *A Seth Eastman Sketchbook, 1848–1849* (1961); Frederick Law Olmsted, *A Journey through Texas* (1857); Josie Rothe, "Quihi, Born Amid Turbulence of Old Times, Is at Peace Today," Dallas *Morning News*, August 18, 1935; Picture Files, Barker Texas History Center, University of Texas at Austin.

Crystal S. Ragsdale

*Quihi Creek.

*Quil Miller Creek.

Quin, Clinton Simon. Clinton Simon Quin, third bishop of the Diocese of Texas, Episcopal Church, was born in Louisville, Kentucky, on September 28, 1883, the son of J. B. and Nettie (Jones) Quin. After receiving the LL.B. degree from the University of Louisville, he enrolled in the Episcopal Theological Seminary in Virginia and graduated in 1908. He married Hortense Pilcher in 1909. He was rector of churches in Pewee Valley and Paducah, Kentucky, until 1917, when he was called to Trinity Church, Houston, Texas. The following year he was elected coadjutor bishop of Texas and was consecrated to that office on October 31, 1918.

Upon the death of George Herbert Kinsolving qv in October, 1928, Quin became the third bishop of Texas. He was an energetic leader and preacher, widely known for his success in youth work and for recruiting young men for the ministry of the Episcopal church. The membership of the church increased during his tenure, largely because of his pastoral work and his interest in people. He retired in 1955 after thirty-seven years as bishop. He died on November 29, 1956.

BIBLIOGRAPHY: *Clerical Directory of the Protestant Episcopal Church in the United States of America* (1956); *Journal of the Council of the Diocese of Texas* (1956).

Lawrence L. Brown

*Quincy, Texas. (Bee County.)

*Quincy, Texas. (Harrison County.)

*Quinet Indians. In the latter part of the seventeenth century this group, which is known only from documents concerning the La Salle Expedition,qv lived north of Matagorda Bay. They were among the Indians who lived nearest to Fort St. Louis.qv La Salle qv met a band of Quinet on the lower Lavaca River (present Jackson County) and made peace with them. The Quinet and Ebahamo

seem to have been closely associated, and both appear to have been Karankawan groups. After 1690 no more is heard of the Quinet under this name. It seems likely that they were later known under some other Karankawan name, possibly Cujane.

BIBLIOGRAPHY: C. W. Hackett (ed.), *Pichardo's Treatise on the Limits of Louisiana and Texas,* I (1931); J. G. Shea, *Discovery and Exploration of the Mississippi Valley* (1903).

T. N. Campbell

*Quinlan, Texas.

*Quinn Creek.

*Quintana, Texas.

*Quintania Creek.

*Quintero, José Agustín.

*Quioborique Indians.

Quiouaha Indians. The Quiouaha (Kiohican, Kiohuan, Kiohuhahan, Kiouahaa, Quiohohouan, Quiouhan) Indians are mentioned in documents (1687) pertaining to the La Salle Expedition,qv which identify them as enemies of the Kadohadacho on the Red River. The Quiouaha have been erroneously identified with the Kiowa, who did not enter the Texas area until the nineteenth century. Although it has yet to be demonstrated, the Quiouaha were probably the same people as the Quiguaya, mentioned in a single Spanish missionary report (1691) as living west of the Hasinai Indians of eastern Texas. The affiliations of both groups remain undetermined.

BIBLIOGRAPHY: F. W. Hodge (ed.), *Handbook of American Indians,* I (1907), II (1910); P. Margry, *Découvertes et établissements des Français dans l'ouest et dans le sud de l'Amérique Septentrionale,* III (1879); J. R. Swanton, *Source Material on the History and Ethnology of the Caddo Indians* (1942).

T. N. Campbell

*Quisaba Indians. In 1683–1684 Juan Domínguez de Mendoza qv led an exploratory expedition from El Paso as far eastward as the junction of the Concho and Colorado rivers east of present San Angelo. In his itinerary he listed the names of thirty-seven Indian groups, including the Quisaba, from which he expected to receive delegations. Nothing further is known about the Quisaba, who seem to have been one of many Indian groups of north-central Texas that were swept away by the southward thrust of the Lipan-Apache and Comanche Indians in the eighteenth century.

BIBLIOGRAPHY: H. E. Bolton (ed.), *Spanish Exploration in the Southwest, 1542–1706* (1916); C. W. Hackett (ed.), *Pichardo's Treatise on the Limits of Louisiana and Texas,* II (1934).

T. N. Campbell

*Quiscat.

*Quitaca Indians. The Quitaca Indians were one of twenty Indian groups that joined Juan Domínguez de Mendoza qv on his journey from El Paso to the vicinity of present San Angelo in 1683–1684. Mendoza did not indicate at what point the Quitaca joined his party. In a Spanish document of 1771 the Quitaca were mentioned as having signed a peace treaty with the Spanish, along with the Tawakoni, Yscani, and Cantona groups, all of whom are considered to be Wichita. If these were the same Quitaca mentioned by Mendoza, then the Quitaca can be identified as a Wichita people and it can be stated that Wichita groups were ranging much farther west in the seventeenth than in the eighteenth century. This identification negates J. R. Swanton's classification of the Quitaca as Coahuiltecan.

BIBLIOGRAPHY: Bexar Archives Translations, 50 (Archives, University of Texas at Austin Library); H. E. Bolton (ed.), *Spanish Exploration in the Southwest, 1542–1706* (1916); F. W. Hodge (ed.), *Handbook of American Indians*, II (1910); W. W. Newcomb, Jr., *The Indians of Texas* (1961); J. R. Swanton, *The Indian Tribes of North America* (1952).

T. N. Campbell

*Quitaque, Texas.
*Quitaque Creek.
*Quitman, John Anthony.
*Quitman, Texas. Quitman, in central Wood County, had a 1960 population of 1,237 and a 1970 population of 1,494, according to the United States census report. The town had seventy businesses in 1970.

*Quitman Arroyo.
*Quitman Canyon.
*Quitman Mountains.
*Quito, Texas.
*Quitole Indians.
*Quiutcanuaha Indians. This name is known from a Spanish missionary report (1691) which indicates that the Quiutcanuaha lived southwest of the Hasinai of eastern Texas, but the distance is unspecified. The name remotely resembles the names of other unidentified groups of the same general area, such as Anathagua and Quanataguo, but no identities can be established. The affiliations of all three groups remain undetermined.

BIBLIOGRAPHY: F. W. Hodge (ed.), *Handbook of American Indians*, II (1910); J. R. Swanton, *Source Material on the History and Ethnology of the Caddo Indians* (1942).

T. N. Campbell

*Quivi Indians.
*Quivira Province.

R

*Rábago y Terán, Felipe.
*Rábago y Terán, Pedro de.
*Rabb, Andrew.
*Rabb, John.
Rabb, Mary Crownover. Mary (Polly) Crownover Rabb was born April 8, 1805, in Buncombe County, North Carolina, the daughter of John and Mary (Chesney) Crownover. She married John Rabb qv in 1821 in Jonesboro, Arkansas, and they had nine children. On October 1, 1823, she left Arkansas with her husband and a large party of relatives to settle in Texas. In her reminiscences, *Travels and Adventures in Texas in the 1820's*, Mary Rabb described their early life in phonetically written English. The large log house where they lived in the 1830's and 1840's, on Rabb's Prairie qv in Fayette County, had one main room with a board lean-to kitchen in the back and a gallery across the front. Huge squared pine logs about sixteen feet long were used in the one-and-a-half-story house, which still stood until about 1965. The Rabbs moved to the Barton Springs area outside Austin in 1860. Mary Rabb died in Austin on October 15, 1882, and was buried beside her husband in Oakwood Cemetery there.

BIBLIOGRAPHY: Annie Doom Pickrell, *Pioneer Women in Texas* (1929); Mary Crownover Rabb, *Travels and Adventures in Texas in the 1820's* (1962); Mary Rabb Family Papers, 1823–1922 (Photocopy MS., Archives, University of Texas at Austin Library); Louis Wiltz Kemp Papers, Biographical Notebook (MS., Archives, University of Texas at Austin Library).

*Rabb, Thomas J.
*Rabb, William.

*Rabb, Texas.
*Rabbit Creek.
*Rabbit Ears Creek.
*Rabbs Creek.
*Rabb's Prairie, Texas.
*Rabb-Switch, Texas.
*Rabke, Texas.
*Race Horses. *See* Horse Breeding.
*Race Track, Texas.
*Rachal, Texas.
Radio in Texas. Perhaps the first radio broadcasting in Texas originated in Austin from a physics laboratory on the campus of the University of Texas. As part of his experiments in high-frequency radio, a physics professor, S. Leroy Brown, built radio equipment and began broadcasting weather and crop reports before World War I. During World War I, using the call letters KUT, the university's Division of Extension operated Brown's equipment to broadcast reports from the U.S. Marketing Bureau and the U.S. Department of Agriculture. By March, 1922, the station had combined with a second campus station (call letters 5XY), and with a 500-watt power rating was one of the best-equipped and most powerful stations in the nation. The usual broadcasts were from 8 to 10 p.m. on three nights a week; programming consisted of music, lectures, and agriculture and marketing reports. In addition, football games were broadcast in season and a church service was aired on Sunday. KUT carried no news broadcasts, spon-

sored programs, or commercials. Brown acted as general manager, technical director, and program director, while Orlando Murphy was the announcer. In the mid-1920's the license and equipment of this early station were assigned to a commercial company, and the facilities eventually became what is now Station KNOW in Austin.

Another early station was WRR of Dallas, owned by the city, which began broadcasting in 1920 with Dad Garrett as announcer. During these early days of broadcasting, many small, homemade radio stations went on the air on a non-commercial basis, primarily for the amusement of the operators and their neighbors.

By the end of 1922, the year that commercial radio broadcasting began in Texas, and before there was a federal agency to regulate radio broadcasters, twenty-five commercial stations were in operation in the state. Among them were WBAP, Fort Worth; KGNC, Amarillo; WFAA, Dallas; WOAI, San Antonio; KFJZ, Fort Worth; KILE, Galveston; and WACO, Waco.

Radio Station WBAP in Fort Worth established the basic format for country music variety show broadcasting (a format since taken over by Nashville's "Grand Ole Opry" and Chicago's "National Barn Dance") with a program which began on January 4, 1923, featuring fiddler, square-dance caller, and Confederate veteran Captain M. J. Bonner.

WFAA in Dallas, operating on 150 watts, held many firsts in radio broadcasting in Texas. It was the first to carry programs designed to educate; first to produce a serious radio drama series, one titled "Dramatic Moments in Texas History" and sponsored by the Magnolia Petroleum Company; first to air a state championship football game; first to join a national network (1927); and first to air inaugural ceremonies, those of Governor Ross Sterling qv in 1931. WFAA was the property of the Alfred Horatio Belo qv Corporation, publisher of the Dallas Morning News;qv Adam Colhoun, the first announcer, at times read to his listeners from that newspaper when there was nothing else to offer. Gene Finley was the first manager until Robert Poole replaced him in 1924. The station carried no newscasts; entertainment enjoyed top priority. Early programs carried the voices of the Early Birds, Eddie Dunn, Frank Munroe, Jimmie Jeffries, Pegleg Moreland, the Cass County Kids, and Dale Evans (then the wife of piano player Frank Butts and later the wife of Hollywood western star Roy Rogers). The Folger Coffee Company was WFAA's first paying advertiser, sponsoring the Bel Canto Quartet.

South Texas' first station, WOAI in San Antonio, went on the air on September 25, 1922. Founded by G. A. C. Halff, with an initial power of 500 watts, it was increased to 5,000 watts in 1925, considered powerful for the time. On February 6, 1928, WOAI joined the world's first network, the National Broadcasting Company. It eventually became a clear channel operating on 50,000 watts. WOAI was one of the first stations to employ a local news staff. One of its greatest achievements was a regular Sunday broadcast of "Musical Interpretations," featuring Max Reiter,qv conductor of the San Antonio Symphony Orchestra. Reiter also conducted the orchestra for NBC's nationwide "Pioneers of Music," originating from San Antonio's municipal auditorium.

In Houston an amateur radio club was organized in 1919 for amateur builders and operators of crystal sets, with James L. Autrey as president. The first local commercial station was WEV, owned and operated by Hurlburt Still. On May 21, 1922, the Houston Post qv broadcast a Sunday concert from the radio plant of A. P. Daniel, 2504 Bagby Street. Later that year the Houston Conservatory of Music sent out programs over Station WGAB. In 1924 the Houston Post-Dispatch absorbed a station operated by Will Horwitz and established it as KPRC, which made its debut in May, 1925. Several new stations were licensed in the next few years. KXYZ, which had first broadcast on October 20, 1930, was taken over by Jesse H. Jones qv in 1932, increasing its power to 1,000 watts two years later. When stations KPRC and KTRH installed one broadcasting plant for sending out waves simultaneously in 1936, the plant was the second of its kind in the world. Each station increased its power to 5,000 watts. KTRH became the Houston Chronicle qv station in 1937.

With the advent of television, the number of radio stations decreased. On February 1, 1971, Texas had 280 standard radio broadcasting (AM) stations and 112 frequency modulation (FM) stations. This total of 392 compared to a total of 422 two years earlier. See also Texas Association of Broadcasters; Television in Texas.

BIBLIOGRAPHY: Writers' Program of the Work Projects Administration, Houston, A History and Guide (1942); Texas Almanac (1971); Defense Research Laboratory, University of Texas, DRL Journal (No. 29, June 1, 1966); Bernard Brister, "Radio House," Southwest Review, XXIX (Spring, 1944); Bobby Wimberly, "WOAI: Texas Pioneer in Radio," Junior Historian (September, 1952).

*Radium, Texas.

*Rafael, Texas.

*Raggedy Creek.

*Ragley, Texas.

*Raglin, Henry Walton. Henry Walton Raglin (known as Ragland when he first arrived in Texas from Mississippi), was born in 1817. He joined the army of the Republic of Texas qv on May 26, 1836, as a private and was discharged on August 26, 1836. In 1837 Raglin began a long career of public service when he took a position in the auditing department of the Republic. In March, 1841, he became a traveling tax agent for the treasury department and in October was elected a corporal of the Travis Guards and Rifles qv in Austin. From November, 1841, to July, 1842, he was enrolling clerk of the Senate for the Sixth Congress of the

Republic of Texas, and again for the Ninth Congress from December, 1844, to June, 1845. He saw military service in 1842 during the Vásquez invasion (see Vásquez, Rafael). He held a job as clerk in Washington-on-the-Brazos from October, 1843, to February, 1846. In 1853 and 1854 he was enrolling clerk for the Senate during the Fifth Legislature. Raglin was one of the state's first tax collectors and was a member of the Texas Veterans Association.qv He was married to Anna Jane Magee in the "Mississippi Settlement" in Grimes County, on April 13, 1847. He died in Austin on December 7, 1882.

BIBLIOGRAPHY: Henry Walton Raglin Papers (MS., Archives, University of Texas at Austin Library); Harriet Smither (ed.), *Journals of the Sixth Congress of the Republic of Texas, 1841–1842* (1940); *Biographical Directory of the Texan Conventions and Congresses 1832–1845* (1941); *Members of the Legislature of the State of Texas from 1846 to 1939* (1939); Austin *Daily Statesman*, December 8, 1882.

Karen Collins

Ragsdale, McArthur Cullen. McArthur Cullen Ragsdale, pioneer West Texas photographer, was born on April 22, 1849, in Spartanburg, South Carolina, son of Edmund Carter and Elizabeth (Calhoun) Ragsdale. As a young man he acquired his first camera, hoping its use would finance a college education. He entered college but had to withdraw almost immediately due to financial problems. With his family, Ragsdale left South Carolina in 1868, landed in Galveston, and went by wagon to Belton. For two years he worked as an itinerant photographer, visiting towns northwestward to Brownwood and southward to Fort McKavett, Mason, and Fredericksburg. Longhorn cattle, buffalo, and remnants of Kiowa and Comanche Indian tribes became photographic subjects for Ragsdale.

In 1875 he reached Fort Concho and the nearby village of Saint Angela, where he opened a photography shop on the main trail, which later became Chadbourne Street in San Angelo. There he brought his bride, Mary Elizabeth (May) Webber and recorded scenes of the area on photographic glass plates. In 1915 he sold his studio, and the valuable collection of photographic plates was destroyed when the buyer cleaned out the studio to make way for his own things. Many prints are extant, but almost all of the important plates were lost. Ragsdale died September 14, 1944.

BIBLIOGRAPHY: J. Evetts Haley, *Focus on the Frontier* (1957).

Silas B. Ragsdale

*Ragsdale, Smith.

*Ragtown, Texas. (Garza County.)

*Ragtown, Texas. (Lamar County.)

*Raguet, Anna W. Anna W. Raguet was the eldest of eight children (not seven, as stated in Volume II) of Henry Raguet qv and Marcia Ann Towers (not Temple) Raguet. Her mother stated in her claim for a pension that her maiden name was Marcia Ann Towers, although the name is often found as Mercy Ann Towers, and this is the way the name was written on a family record of births and marriages in the Raguet family papers, now in the archives of the Barker Texas History Center at the University of Texas at Austin. This record also shows that Anna Raguet was born on January 25 (not January 15), 1819, in Newtown (not Philadelphia), Bucks County, Pennsylvania. The middle initial "W" in Anna W. Raguet's name is assumed to stand for Wynkoop, for her paternal grandmother, Anna (Wynkoop) Raguet, although examined documents bear only the initial.

The date of marriage between Anna Raguet and Robert Anderson Irion qv differs in almost every printed source. According to one family record the date was April 9, 1840, but no legal instrument has been found to substantiate that date. The records in the Nacogdoches County Courthouse show that two marriage licenses were issued, both on Monday, March 30, 1840. License number 28 states that the marriage was solemnized the previous day, Sunday, March 29 (a mystery in itself since, by law, the marriage date should not have preceded the date of the license to marry); license number 80 states that the marriage took place the same day, Monday, March 30, 1840. Both show the officiant as Adolphus Sterne.qv Anna (Raguet) and Robert Anderson Irion were the parents of five children.

BIBLIOGRAPHY: Raguet Family Papers (MS., Archives, University of Texas at Austin Library); Marriage Records, Republic of Texas, 1840 (Nacogdoches County Courthouse, Nacogdoches, Texas); Shannon Irion and Jenkins Garrett (comps.), *Ever Thine Truly: Love letters from Sam Houston to Anna Raguet* (1975); Helen Hoskins Rugeley, "Anna Raguet Irion (1819–1883)," in (Evelyn M. Carrington, ed.), *Women in Early Texas* (1975); *The Pennsylvania Magazine of History and Biography*, XXXI (1907).

Eldon S. Branda

*Raguet, Henry. Henry Raguet, son of James Michael and Anna Wynkoop (not Ann Wyncoop, as stated in Volume II) Raguet, was born on February 11 (or possibly February 20), 1796. On April 25, 1818, Henry Raguet was married to Marcia Ann Towers (not Temple, as stated in Volume II), although her name is also found as Mercy Ann Towers (see Raguet, Anna W.).

BIBLIOGRAPHY: Raguet Family Papers (MS., Archives, University of Texas at Austin Library); Frank W. Johnson (Eugene C. Barker, ed.), *A History of Texas and Texans*, IV (1914); *The Pennsylvania Magazine of History and Biography*, XXXI (1907).

Anna Kathryn Holbrook

Raht, Carlysle Graham. Carlysle Graham Raht, son of Dolph and May Raht, was born September 13, 1880, probably in Gainesville, Cooke County, and grew up on a ranch near Henrietta, Clay County. He had only a few years of formal schooling at Henrietta and at the old Fort Worth University before entering the University of Texas, where he studied the history of the Southwest. As a young man he went to the Trans-Pecos area, working as a cowboy, newspaperman, and mining engineer. Later he was a rancher and worked for the railroad.

He spent a great deal of time with old-timers in the Big Bend, collecting the history and lore of that area, about which he later wrote. His first book, *The Romance of Davis Mountains and Big Bend Country*, was published privately in 1919 by Rahtbooks Company in El Paso. The book has since become a collector's item. In 1963 Raht reestablished Rahtbooks Company in order to reprint the work.

His other books, all dealing with early days in the Southwest and somewhat autobiographical, include *Old Buck and I* (1964), *Confessions of a Fiddlefoot* (1967), *Reveries of a Fiddlefoot* (1970), and *High Dawn* (1971).

Raht served as a scout for the 8th U.S. Cavalry under General John Pershing and saw limited action against Pancho Villa.qv At the outbreak of World War II, at age 60, Raht volunteered for service and was assigned to serve with the Atomic Energy Commission. He received a citation for work in scientific research and development of the atomic bomb. He was one of the founders of the Texas Permian Historical Society (now the Permian Historical Society qv), which made him an honorary life member. His wife, Arda, was also a writer; they had one son. Raht died July 26, 1972, in Odessa and was buried there.

BIBLIOGRAPHY: San Angelo *Standard-Times*, July 28, 1972; Biographical File, Barker Texas History Center, University of Texas at Austin.

*Railroad Commission. In 1952 the Railroad Commission was directed by the legislature to organize a new division called the Liquefied Petroleum Gas Division with power to promulgate adequate regulations and standards pertaining to the liquefied petroleum gas industry in order to protect the health, welfare, and safety of the general public. *See also* Oil Industry, Regulation of.

George F. Singletary, Jr.

*Railroad Construction, Public Aid to.

*Railroad Strike of 1886. See Southwest Strike.

Railroads in Texas. [The symbol qv is omitted following names of railroads, as it can be assumed that separate articles appear on all major railroads in Texas. Ed.] Railroad development and economic growth paralleled each other for years in Texas. Because of the state's size and its lack of roads or dependable river navigation, transportation was a major problem facing early settlers of the region. Fertile farm lands, though cheap, were worth little so long as settlement was scattered and markets inaccessible. The first railroad in the United States was only seven years old in 1836, but interest in this form of transportation began in Texas with the birth of the Republic. The First Congress, on December 16, 1836, issued the first charter for a railroad west of the Mississippi River when it authorized the Texas Railroad, Navigation, and Banking Company qv to construct railroads "from and to such points . . . as selected." Despite having many leading citizens among its incorporators, as well as the sanction of Stephen F. Austin and Sam Houston, the scheme aroused the public's suspicions, mainly because of the banking provisions which were attacked by Anson Jones,qv and the company

became a major issue in the second congressional elections. This, with the panic of 1837, caused its collapse.

But the critical problem of moving people and goods increased as Texas grew. Several railroads or schemes involving railroads were chartered in the fifteen years following 1836, but no railroad was constructed. Andrew Briscoe,qv in 1840, graded two miles of the Harrisburg and Brazos Railroad, but fears of a Mexican invasion stopped the work. The first railroad built in Texas, and the second west of the Mississippi, was the Buffalo Bayou, Brazos, and Colorado, a successor to Briscoe's effort. Begun by General Sidney Sherman qv in 1852, it opened for traffic September 7, 1853, running west from Harrisburg (now a Houston suburb) twenty miles to Stafford's Point, with trips on Wednesday and Saturday, using passenger coaches made from Boston horsecars. It was financed mainly by Massachusetts capital, although William Marsh Rice, John Sealy,qqv and other Texans held stock.

The first Texas railroads were planned for specific localities, usually towns or counties. Of the ten lines operating at the beginning of the Civil War, five ran to Houston and one connected with a Houston line. Only two, the five-mile Memphis, El Paso and Pacific, near Jefferson, and the Southern Pacific, at Marshall, did not reach a seaport. The Southern Pacific (not to be confused with the later system of that name) for years was the only Texas railroad connected with another state, having linked with Shreveport, Louisiana, in 1864.

Transcontinental roads through Texas were projected well before the first line was built. In 1853 the federal government authorized surveying expeditions along five routes to determine the best way to the West Coast. The southernmost of the five crossed Texas at about the thirty-second parallel. In 1854 Captain John Pope,qv of the Topographical Engineer Corps of the United States Army, led a party of seventy-five men from Doña Ana, New Mexico, eastward through Texas, following this approximate parallel nearly 800 miles to Preston on the Red River. At about the same time the Texas Western Railroad backers sent Andrew B. Gray qv on a westward survey over somewhat the same territory as Pope's route. This was to be the route of a grandiose national system called the Atlantic and Pacific Railroad, which was never built. Gray's notes, published in 1855, and Pope's report, both favorable to a route across what was considered desert, were substantiated twenty-five years later when the Texas and Pacific was put through that region.

When rail building fever hit Texas in the 1850's it was realized that the sums required would make it virtually impossible for private enterprise to build railroads in such a thinly populated state. Some kind of public financial incentive would be necessary to attract investors from other states and foreign countries. Local bonds from cities and counties totaling $2,360,850 were issued to railroads in Texas between 1850 and 1876. State school funds were used to make loans to a few lines. The major form of incentive, however, was the state land grant. In 1852 the legislature offered eight sections (5,120 acres) for each mile of track laid. This did not stimulate building, so the grant was raised to sixteen sections in 1854, and it remained that number, with two exceptions, until land grants were discontinued in 1882.

When the Civil War began Texas had approximately 468 miles of railroad. While Texas railroads did not suffer the devastation which hit roads in the Deep South, they were severely crippled; one, the Eastern Texas, was torn up to make coastal defenses and was never rebuilt. Three other roads each lost several miles of track and much equipment when they were destroyed to prevent possible use by Federal invaders. At the war's end only four lines were intact, and they were in disrepair, faced bankruptcy, and had irregular service, if any. During Reconstruction qv little new track was built because of political and economic instability. The Constitution of 1869 qv forbade land grants for railroads. By 1870 state rail mileage was still slightly under the 600 mile mark. Construction picked up in the early 1870's, with the Houston and Texas Central pushing to Dallas and the Red River by 1873, and the Texas and Pacific (old Texas Western and Southern Pacific) reaching Dallas from Texarkana that same year. The Constitution of 1876 qv reestablished the sixteen-section land grant, and by 1880 Texas had 3,026 miles of railroad. By 1890 another 6,045 miles had been added, and in 1901 Texas railroads passed the 10,000-mile mark. By 1920, with 16,049 miles, the major building was over. In 1922 Texas lost rail mileage for the first time since the Civil War; however, the peak of 17,078 miles was not reached until 1932, and then a steady decline in mileage began. At the end of 1967 Texas had slightly more than 14,000 miles of track—the most railroad mileage of any state in the United States. By January 1, 1970, the state's railroad mileage had been reduced further, to 13,825 miles of mainline track.

Railroads received 32,153,878 acres of public lands, most of which was in West Texas; many of the present-day centers in that part of Texas were established by the railroads to draw settlers. From the sale of 27,926,563 acres of land, it has been estimated that the railroads received $42,374,870, or about $1.50 an acre.

In 1881 the Southern Pacific, building from California, bought the Galveston, Harrisburg and San Antonio Railway, which contained the Buffalo Bayou, Brazos, and Colorado Railway. That same year the Southern Pacific acquired the Texas and New Orleans Railroad, establishing the first transcontinental route through Texas, from New Orleans to San Francisco. Jay Gould qv entered the Texas railroad picture in 1879 when he bought control of the Missouri-Pacific, and within a short time he controlled one-third of the state's rail mileage, including the Missouri, Kansas, and Texas (Katy), the International-Great Northern, and the Texas and Pacific (see Missouri-Pacific System in Texas). The Santa Fe system, through several purchases, came to Texas in 1882, and in 1886 it bought the Gulf, Colorado and Santa Fe, forming the spine of a Kansas-to-Gulf network. By 1898 all ten major railroad systems operating in Texas had been established in the state, although their expansion through merger and consolidation was far from completed. These systems were: Burlington; St. Louis-San Francisco (Frisco); Missouri, Kansas, and Texas (Katy); Rock Island; Santa Fe; Missouri-Pacific; Texas and Pacific; Southern Pacific; St. Louis Southwestern (Cotton Belt); and Kansas City Southern. The Missouri, Kansas, and Texas (Katy) system was separated from the Gould empire in 1891. In 1968 the Cotton Belt was owned and operated by the Southern Pacific, and the Texas and Pacific was operated as a division of the Missouri-Pacific. These ten major systems controlled twenty-eight of the forty-five railroad properties in Texas in 1970, and they controlled 13,379 of the 13,825 total miles of mainline track in the state; the seventeen unaffiliated properties controlled only 446 miles of mainline track.

Despite power given to the state by the Constitution of 1876 to act against railroad abuses, and subsequent laws prohibiting rebates, by the middle 1880's shippers, farmers, and many officials were protesting high rates, discrimination against certain areas and crops, traffic pools, and other restrictive practices. Railroads, the most powerful industrial force in Texas, were accused of running the state through bribery, hidden monopolies, and controls, while profits were going to outside capitalists. In 1888 Attorney General James Stephen Hogg qv filed several suits, mainly against several of the Gould railroads, alleging their control by outside capital was in violation of the Texas Constitution. He also got a court decision against rail pools which set rates and divided available traffic among the larger systems. The success of these suits forced the reshuffling of the Gould empire and caused most lines to set up Texas corporations and move headquarters to Texas. The public felt, however, that even more regulation was needed, and in 1890 the establishment of a state railroad commission was the main issue in the governor's race. Hogg, using rail reform as his key, won an overwhelming victory in the race despite bitter opposition from several Texas newspapers, notably the Dallas Morning News.qv The Texas Railroad Commission,qv created in 1891, became one of the most powerful regulatory bodies in the state. Later, in the twentieth century, its importance was based on regulation of the petroleum industry in Texas, a power originally derived from its supervision of pipelines and oil storage facilities.

Although there was public and legislative objection to consolidation of subsidiary lines, the practice continued as it became more and more unprofitable to operate small, independent railroads. By the 1920's the only large company not controlled by one of the ten big systems was the 162-mile Texas-Mexican Railway Company, a majority of whose stock was owned by the Mexican National Railways.

In 1900 there began a flurry of interurban electric railway planning. The first to be built was the Denison-Sherman Railway, completed in 1901. Within fifteen years more than 400 miles of electric interurban tracks had been constructed in Texas, much of it paralleling steam locomotive roads. Eventually the state had almost exactly 500 miles of electric railway, the largest system being the Texas Electric, whose 226 miles centered in Dallas. The last interurban railway developed in the United States was the twenty-five mile Houston and North Shore, built to Goose Creek (now Baytown) in 1927. By 1950 all electric trackage had been abandoned or reverted to regular rail usage except for a short electric switching line, still operating in San Antonio in 1968.

The Texas State Railroad, a 32-mile line built between 1896 and 1909 to serve prison system foundries at Rusk, was the only state-owned railroad. The state operated it until 1921, when it was leased by the Southern Pacific.

The 1930's saw the first wholesale abandonment of trackage, and from 1933 to World War II a little more than 880 miles had been pulled up, mainly on branch lines. Even though railroads operated at from three to five times normal capacity during the war, with passenger traffic, for example, rising from 5.1 million persons in 1941 to an all-time high of 25.9 million persons in 1944, abandonment of trackage continued to far outstrip new mileage. The Burlington-Rock Island in 1936 inaugurated the first streamlined diesel passenger service in Texas with the "Sam Houston Zephyr." By 1955 virtually all Texas railroads had converted to diesel power, but the seven-mile Moscow, Camden, and San Augustine continued scheduled passenger service behind steam locomotives as late as 1962.

By 1966 the Texas Railroad Commission showed only 343 miles of unaffiliated railway trackage in Texas; most of this was connected with specific products, such as the Rockdale, Sandow, and Southern, which hauled lignite; or the trackage was a bridge line, such as the 32-mile Roscoe, Snyder, and Pacific, which connected two larger systems. At least three short lines were established in the 1950's and 1960's after parent companies abandoned them. The Georgetown Railroad and the Belton Railroad were taken over by local ownerships. When the Katy abandoned its 218-mile Texas Central branch from Waco to Rotan late in 1967, a new Texas Central line was chartered, utilizing 24 miles of the Katy. New railroads were also built for specific users after 1950. The Texas and Northern and the Point Comfort and Northern were constructed when large industries were developed in areas without rail service. In 1967 the Sabine River and Northern was building in Orange and Jasper counties.

At the close of 1966 three systems, the Southern Pacific, the Santa Fe, and the Missouri-Pacific, each operated more than 3,000 miles of track in Texas. However, the process of cutting off unprofitable mileage continued at about the same rate as in the preceding twenty years. While most major lines were enjoying increased freight tonnage, passenger travel diminished so rapidly that in 1968 only these three major systems offered any passenger service in the state. In the decade of the 1960's, the number of passengers traveling by railway was reduced from almost three million in 1959 to less than one-half million in 1969. Several of Texas' larger cities had no passenger train service at all by 1972. [For information concerning the author of the highly significant *A History of the Texas Railroads* (1941), *see* Reed, St. Clair Griffin.]

BIBLIOGRAPHY: S. G. Reed, *A History of the Texas Railroads* (1941); C. S. Potts, *Railroad Transportation in Texas* (1909); George W. Hilton and John F. Due, *The Electric Interurban Railways in America* (1960); Richard C. Overton, *Gulf to Rockies: The Heritage of the Fort Worth and Denver-Colorado and Southern Railways, 1861–1898* (1953); *Moody's Transportation Manual* (1920 et seq.); Railroad Commission of Texas, *Annual Report* (1891 et seq.); *Texas Almanac* (1967, 1971).

A. C. Greene

*Rainbolt, Texas.

*Rainbow, Texas.

*Raines, Cadwell Walton.

*Rainey, Anson.

*Rainey, Frank.

*Rainfall in Texas. *See also* Weather in Texas; Rainmaking.

*Rainmaking. [Out of alphabetical order as Rain Making on page 432, Volume II.] Modern rainmakers are scientists and technicians who document their efforts and results under the supervision of state agencies. In Texas the Water Development Board qv regulates all attempts to modify the state's weather. In order to obtain a weather modification license, the operator must convince the Water Development Board of his technical ability and also get approval for the location and dates of a specific project. The Texas law governing attempts to change weather has served as a model for similar statutes in many other states. Meteorologists estimate that it takes ten years to determine the success of rainmaking experiments because normal year-to-year rainfall variations can exceed 50 percent of the average figure.

Most of the rainmaking projects in Texas were in West Texas and the Panhandle, areas in which the average annual rainfall was fifteen to twenty-five inches, and in some years far below that level. Silver iodide was the most common chemical used for cloud seeding. Proponents claim that when this chemical is released into a cloud's base from aircraft, or carried up from the ground by air currents (if conditions are favorable), some of the silver iodide reaches the freezing point, forms ice crystals, turns to snow, and falls to the ground as rain. Rainmaking activity usually extends from early spring to late summer.

During the drouth cycle of the 1950's several Texas cities and organizations of farmers contracted with professional rainmakers to seed clouds. Fort Worth paid $20,000 to a Denver firm, and Dallas paid $52,000 a year for several years to the same firm. Total Texas payments to cloud seeders were said to have exceeded $100,000 a year in some years of the 1950's, generally with disappointing results.

In the late 1960's and early 1970's, the Plains Weather Improvement Association, a group of West Texas ranchers, spent $130,000 a year in rainmaking efforts for a large area north of Lubbock. The Upper Colorado Water District seeded an area northeast of Big Spring for two years, and the federal Bureau of Reclamation conducted cloud seeding experiments in the San Angelo area at a cost of close to $1,000,000 over a three-year period.

Because of the exceedingly dry fall and winter of 1970–1971 in northwest Texas, forty ranchers in and around Aspermont, in Stonewall County, backed a rainmaking project which promised to produce five inches of rain within thirty days from February 8, 1971. Charcoal briquettes soaked in a special chemical solution and heated to 7,200° Fahrenheit were to turn into gas which would be blown into the clouds to produce ice crystals which in turn were to cause rainfall. The project failed and the rainmakers did not collect their $10,000.

BIBLIOGRAPHY: Dallas *Times Herald*, February 7, 1971; San Antonio *Express News*, September 10, 1972.

*Rains, Emory. Emory Rains was married to Marana Anderson sometime before February 19, 1835, the date he received, as a married man, one league of land in Lorenzo de Zavala's qv colony. Emory and Marana Rains had twelve children.

BIBLIOGRAPHY: Louis Wiltz Kemp Papers, Biographical Notebook (MS., Archives, University of Texas at Austin Library).

*Rains County. Rains County, primarily a livestock-raising area, also produced some truck crops and a small amount of natural gas. The state highway department, a gas refinery, and a telephone company were businesses directly affecting the economy of the county. The major tourist attraction is Lake Tawakoni in the western part of the county. The 1960 population was 2,993; in 1970 it was 3,752, a 25 percent increase, according to the U.S. census.

*Rainy Creek.

*Raisin, Texas.

*Raiz Creek.

*Raleigh, William.

*Raleigh, Texas. (Fannin County.)

*Raleigh, Texas. (Navarro County.)

Ralls, John Robinson. John Robinson Ralls was born in Monroe County, Georgia, on November 13, 1862, the eldest son of John Robinson and Fannie Minnie (Bird) Ralls. In 1890 he moved to Bowie, Texas, and in the following years he was a merchant in Belcherville, Terrell, and finally in Ryan, Oklahoma. In 1906 he traded the Ryan store for a ten-thousand-acre ranch in Crosby County. In 1910 a short line railroad was built through his ranch to Crosbyton, bypassing the county seat at Emma. Ralls laid out a town (named after himself) on the right-of-way to serve the residents of Emma. Subdividing his ranch into quarter-section tracts for sale to prospective farmers, Ralls built homes and business houses in the town and donated land for schools and churches there. In 1906 he married Dollie M. Martin, from whom he was divorced in 1920. A Presbyterian, he died on October 3, 1921, and was buried in Ralls.

BIBLIOGRAPHY: Seymour V. Connor (ed.), *Builders of the Southwest* (1959); Ralls *Banner*, September 25, 1936.

Seymour V. Connor

*Ralls, Texas. Ralls was established in 1911 by John Robinson Ralls qv (not John E. Ralls, as stated in Volume II).

Ralls served as a market and shipping point for the west-central part of Crosby County. Agriculture was important in Ralls' economy, with cotton the leading crop, and vegetables, wheat, and grain sorghums following in importance. In the 1960's new schools were built and building proposals included a new hospital and a chamber of commerce building. A mill for the manufacture of cotton bagging was completed at a cost of $1,200,000. Among its seventy-five businesses in 1970 were cotton gins, grain elevators, feed mills, and a compress. The 1960 population was 2,229; the 1970 population was 1,962, according to the United States census.

*Ramarito, Texas.

*Rambler, The.

*Ramey, Lawrence.

Ramey, Thomas Boyd. Thomas Boyd Ramey, son of Thomas Brown and Mary Josephine (Spencer) Ramey, was born in Tyler, Texas, on August 8, 1892. He was graduated from Tyler High School in 1909, received a B.A. degree from the University of Texas in 1913, and attended law school at Columbia University in 1913–1914. He received a Master of Laws degree from the University of Texas in 1915. On June 28, 1916, he was married to Cordelia Stacy of Austin. They had three children, two of whom died in infancy.

Ramey was the senior partner of a Tyler law firm. He was an organizer and the first president of the Tyler Industrial Foundation and director of the Texas Research League.qv He was the first president of the board of trustees of Tyler Junior College and a member and chairman of the State Board of Education.qv He was also one of the organizers and first president of the Texas Rose Festival.qv

Ramey's death occurred on October 18, 1967, on the opening day of the thirtieth Texas Rose Festival. He was buried in Tyler in Oakwood Cemetery.

Thomas B. Ramey, Jr.

*Ramirena Creek.

*Ramirez, Texas.

*Ramirez y Sesma, Joaquín.

*Ramón, Diego.

*Ramón, Domingo (José Domingo).

*Ramona, Texas.

*Ramsdell, Charles William.

*Ramsdell, Texas.

*Ramsey, Frank Taylor.

*Ramsey, William F. William F. Ramsey, appointed by Governor T. M. Campbell,qv was a member of the Court of Criminal Appeals and served from January 1, 1908, to January 5, 1911 (not the Court of Civil Appeals from 1909 to 1911, as stated in Volume II). Ramsey resigned as associate justice of the Texas Supreme Court on March 29, 1912 (not May 29, 1912).

Edward Crane

*Ranch Branch.

Ranch Headquarters. *See* Ranching Heritage Center.

*Ranchería Grande. [This title was listed in Volume II as Ranchería Grande Indians.] The term "ranchería" was used by the Spanish to denote an impermanent settlement or encampment of Indians and was not used as a name for any specific Indian group. The Ranchería Grande was an Indian encampment in the general vicinity of Milam County and should not be confused with any one Indian group.

*Rancheria Hills.

*Ranchero Creek.

*Ranches. For an account of what was probably the first ranch in Texas, *see* Hernándes, Andrés.

Ranching Heritage Center. Founded in 1969 as Ranch Headquarters, an outdoor museum that was part of the Museum of Texas Tech University qv complex, the name was changed on January 31, 1975, to the Ranching Heritage Center. The center presents the true story of America's ranching past by preserving, restoring, and interpreting its buildings, furnishings, and tools. Approximately twenty historic structures, which otherwise would not be preserved, were assembled at the center. These structures were carefully selected to portray the types of construction used by ranchers over the several decades between the 1830's and the early 20th century. The building types reflect the various geographical regions through which the ranching industry passed as it spread northward and westward across Texas. Plans in 1975 included erecting a building representing the late eighteenth-century Spanish colonial period.

Incompatible building types are separated from one another by earthen berms eight to eighteen feet in height. The 40,000 cubic yards of soil which comprise the earthen berms also isolate the vastly different species of trees, grasses, and distinctive plants that accompany each structure. These berms also screen out modern evidences of civilization which surround the site. Buffalo grass has been grown to attractively cover the berms.

The oldest building in the project is the log cabin headquarters of El Capote Ranch, constructed near Gonzales before 1840. Nearby is "Hedwigs Hill," a double log cabin built near Mason in the hill country of Texas in 1853. The third building at the center is a two-story stone house built in 1873. Two rifle ports over the front door indicate the concern of the builder, whose earlier log cabin had been burned by Indians. The next house is a half-dugout, built near Matador in 1891. This structure represents ranching's move onto the arid and semi-arid plains where neither lumber nor satisfactory building stone could be obtained in substantial quantities. A two-story dugout is located on the other side of an earthen berm. The lower portion, constructed in 1890, was the original structure in the first town of Whiteface. The upper level, constructed after 1900, used the roof of the lower portion as a floor.

As transportation into treeless areas improved, ranchers began freighting lumber into their remote areas. Due to the expense of freighting lumber, these ranchers built box-and-strip houses. This type of building was a simple wooden box with a roof over it; thus, it provided a maximum amount of enclosed space from a limited supply of lumber. A rather simple box-and-strip house as well as a more elaborate box-and-strip house have been included in the collection.

A large two-story, turn-of-the-century house completes the story of the evolution of ranch dwellings. This elaborate house represents the homes of the ranchers who had survived the drouths, blizzards, and market fluctuations, consequently making their way from poverty to wealth.

A series of secondary buildings portray the working past of ranch life; among these are a barn, bunkhouse, corrals, office, carriage house, blacksmith shop, milk-and-meat house, and two restored wooden windmills. One of these windmills offers the visitor a drink of earth-cool water, unhardened by the alkali of western river reservoirs and untainted by the chemicals of municipal water systems.

The slogan, "Preservation, education, recreation, in an outdoor museum of ranching history," indicates that the center serves a wide variety of contemporary needs. One of the most enjoyable aspects of this unique outdoor living museum is that the visitor is able to come into such close relationship with the surroundings at the center. He may finger the barbs of wire which fenced in the open range, see a blacksmith working at the forge, refresh himself at the tall wooden windmill creaking in the

Texas wind, and smell sun on soil, rain on grass, and oil on leather. A Texas State Historical Survey Committee qv marker was officially dedicated at the center on October 3, 1970.

Duncan Muckelroy

*Ranchita, Texas.

*Rancho Davis, Texas. *See* Rio Grande City, Texas.

*Rancho Viejo Floodway.

*Randado, Texas.

*Randal, Horace. Horace Randal, son of Sarah (Kyle) and Leonard Randal,qv entered the United States Military Academy as a Texas appointee in 1849, spent five years (instead of the usual four) at the academy because of a deficiency in mathematics, graduating on July 1, 1854 (and thus was not the first Texas graduate from West Point, as has been claimed, for James B. McIntyre, appointed from Texas in 1849, graduated on July 1, 1853). The U.S. Military Academy records show his birthdate as 1831 (not 1833, as stated in Volume II), in which case he would have been eighteen, not sixteen, when he entered the academy; however, there is no other verification for this earlier date. He was married to Nannie Taylor on July 8, 1862; they had one son. It is possible that he was married once before and was widowed, although no official record can be found of a previous marriage.

During the Civil War he was not commissioned a brigadier general by the Confederate government (as stated in Volume II), but because of his recognized ability in commanding a brigade he was assigned to command as a brigadier general in early April, 1864, although he was not formally commissioned at the time of his death later that month, on April 30, 1864, at the battle of Jenkins' Ferry. He was first buried at the hamlet of Tulip, Arkansas, near the battlefield; later his remains were removed and reburied in Marshall, Texas.

BIBLIOGRAPHY: John Q. Anderson, *A Texas Surgeon in the C.S.A.* (1957); J. C. Haskell, *The Haskell Memoirs* (1960); Richard Taylor (Charles P. Roland, ed.), *Destruction and Reconstruction; Personal Experiences of the Late War* (1879, 1968); John D. Winters, *The Civil War in Louisiana* (1963); C. A. Evans (ed.), *Confederate Military History* (1899); U.S. War Department, *The War of the Rebellion: A Compilation of the Official Records of the Union and Confederate Armies* (1880–1901); Marshall (Texas) *Republican*, May 13, 1862, July 8, 1862, August 12, 1862, September 6, 1883; San Augustine County Records.

*Randal, Leonard.

*Randall, Edward.

Randall, Edward, Jr. Edward Randall, Jr., was born in Galveston on October 1, 1891, the son of Laura (Ballinger) and Edward Randall.qv He attended the University of Texas, University of Chicago, and University of Berlin; he received a B.A. degree from Yale in 1913 and an M.D. from the University of Pennsylvania in 1917. During World War I he was acting chief of medical services at Walter Reed Hospital.

He succeeded his father as a professor in the University of Texas Medical Branch at Galveston, where he was active for half a century. He established the John Sealy Hospital Fever Therapy Unit and other research projects. Randall was the first Texas diplomate of the National Board of Medical Examiners. He was a trustee and director of the Rosenberg Library qv for twenty-five years and served as president of the Philosophical Society of Texas qv in 1965.

Randall was married to Katherine Risher, and they were the parents of two sons and a daughter. He died on March 11, 1971, and was buried in Trinity Episcopal Cemetery in Galveston.

BIBLIOGRAPHY: Philosophical Society of Texas, *Proceedings* (1970).

*Randall County. Randall County, with 76,464 irrigated acres in 1968, ranked high among Texas counties in wheat acreage. Grain sorghums, beef cattle, and other livestock also contributed to the agricultural income. Tourist attractions included Palo Duro Canyon State Scenic Park (*see* Parks, State), Buffalo Lake,qv and the Panhandle-Plains Historical Museum qv in Canyon. The 1960 population was 33,913; the 1970 census was 53,885, a 58.9 percent increase in ten years, largely due to the growth of the city of Amarillo in the county, and the increased growth of Canyon, the county seat. *See also* Amarillo Standard Metropolitan Statistical Area.

Randal's Brigade. *See* Randal, Horace.

*Randell, Choice Boswell.

*Randolph, Cyrus Halbert. Cyrus Halbert Randolph was never clerk of the Supreme Court of Texas (as stated in Volume II).

Randolph, Frankie Carter. Frankie Carter Randolph, longtime leader of Texas liberal Democrats, was born on January 25, 1894, daughter of William T. and Maude (Holley) Carter, in Barnum, Polk County, Texas, where her father had extensive lumber interests. The family moved to Camden when she was three years old, then to Houston when she was about ten. There she went to public and private schools, then attended a girls' preparatory school, Baldwin School at Bryn Mawr, Pennsylvania. She then spent some time in Europe, studying, with a sister as tutor. On June 14, 1918, she was married to Robert D. Randolph, a pioneer naval air corps pilot during World War I and a resident of Washington, D.C.; they were the parents of two daughters.

They moved to Houston, where Mrs. Randolph was one of the founders of the Junior League, of which she was president in the early 1920's; she was prominent in Houston horse riding circles, in activities of the League of Women Voters, and in various charities. During the depression of the 1930's, she was a volunteer in the Social Service Bureau. She supported Franklin D. Roosevelt in his presidential campaigns in the 1930's and 1940's and became deeply involved in Texas politics in the liberal wing of the Democratic party. She fought for city planning, public housing, and better drainage in the low-income areas.

In 1952 she entered the Adlai Stevenson-for-president headquarters in Harris County, laid down a check for $1,000, and asked how she could help. She began organizing the card files of the precincts, working on poll tax campaigns, and attending "thousands" of precinct meetings. She was influential in the founding of the DOT (Democrats of Texas), liberal wing of the Democratic party in Texas,qv in opposition to the SDEC (state Democrats who endorsed the Republican nominee, Dwight D. Eisenhower,qv for president in 1952).

Frankie Randolph's organizational skill in precinct work in Harris County led to her election by liberal forces in 1956 to the position of national Democratic committeewoman over powerful conservative opposition, and against the wishes of then U.S. Senator Lyndon B. Johnson.qv She led the liberal-loyalist wing of the Democratic party in Harris County to sweeping victories in the county and legislative elections of 1958. She was national committeewoman until 1960, when conservative Democrats came into power and elected Hilda Blumberg Weinert.qv An outspoken woman, Frankie Randolph was a determined and forceful advocate of unchanging loyalty to the Democratic party. She was an early supporter of integrated schools, public housing, and labor unions. She backed her beliefs with her money.

In late summer, 1954, Mrs. Randolph, Minnie Fisher Cunningham,qv and Mrs. Jud Collier met in Austin to consider the establishment or support of a liberal Texas newspaper. Paul Holcomb's State Observer in Austin had recently been purchased and the name was changed to the Texas Observer.qv Frankie Randolph became its financial backer and silent partner. The paper's early issues covered the Veterans Land Board Scandal;qv Red-baiting and Communist charges against book selection by Texas libraries; charges of "subversive" influences of modern art being shown in Texas museums; and current affairs in government and politics in Austin. During the years when she was the mainstay of the Texas Observer, Mrs. Randolph was hostess, along with others, at the "Wednesday Club" luncheons at the Observer's Houston branch office on Welch Street; there were often speakers as well as forum discussions at these liberal Democratic gatherings, sometimes attended by seventy or eighty people. In November, 1967, Mrs. Randolph transferred the title of ownership of the Texas Observer to longtime editor Ronnie Dugger. She lived to witness the weakening of the liberal Democratic forces in Houston and Texas, but she always remained an inspiration to the state's liberals. Frankie Randolph died in Houston on September 5, 1972, and was buried in Glenwood Cemetery in that city.

BIBLIOGRAPHY: Austin American, September 7, 1972; Dallas Morning News, February 2, 1958; Houston Post, June 19, 1960, September 6, 1972; Texas Observer, September 13, 1954, May 23, 1956, January 15, 1957, July 11, 1958, November 6, 1959, February 9, 1962, February 2, 1968; Biographical File, Barker Texas History Center, University of Texas at Austin.

Randolph, Texas. (Bexar County.) Randolph, an unincorporated town in Bexar County, had a 1970 population of 5,329, according to the United States census. Its population was due primarily to the presence of Randolph Air Force Base.qv

*Randolph, Texas. (Fannin County.)

*Randolph Air Force Base. In April, 1945, the training instructors school at Randolph Air Force Base, near San Antonio, was replaced by the U. S. Army Air Force's pilot school, specializing in transition training for B-29 bombers. From December, 1945, to March, 1948, primary and basic pilot training was conducted at the base, but was later deleted from the program, and the wing was designated as the 3510th Basic Pilot Training Wing. In 1950 the 3510th Combat Crew Training Group was activated and there was a phase-out of the pilot training course. In 1951 the last class of aviation cadets was graduated from the base. Randolph became the home of the 3510th Combat Crew Training Wing in 1952, and for the next six years this type of training was the base's primary mission. Men were trained for B-29 and B-57 bombers and C-119 and KC-97 transports. During this period the helicopter school moved from Randolph to Gary Air Force Base qv in San Marcos.

Headquarters for the Air Training Command was moved from Illinois to Randolph Air Force Base in 1957 so that it would be more centrally located with respect to its training activities. The School of Aviation Medicine was relocated the following year at Brooks Air Force Base.qv

In 1960 Air Training Command instructor and supervisor training courses began. That same year the U. S. Air Force's basic pilot instructor school was established, with Randolph's flying training wing as the responsible agency for training rated U. S. Air Force pilots as instructors in the classroom and in the cockpit. This was the only U.S. Air Force base where pilots received training as instructors.

In June, 1963, Randolph diversified its operations when the Military Assistance Training Program located its flying and on-the-job training for officers and men at this base. More than fifty-one countries have participated in this training since it moved to Randolph. Up to 1964 Randolph had been a flying training base, but no pilot had actually won his wings there; this changed when twenty-one allied students received their wings in January, 1964.

In 1967 the Department of Defense designated Randolph as the ninth undergraduate pilot training base within the Air Training Command, and it again began to train student pilots. That same year five groups were assigned to Randolph and to the 3510th Flying Training Wing. They were the air base group, civil engineering group, maintenance and supply group, hospital group, and the flying training group, which included six squadrons responsible for primary flying training. Under the 1967 military construction bill, Randolph was to receive over one million dollars for troop housing and utilities.

*Randolph College (Cisco, Texas).

*Randolph College (Lancaster, Texas).

*Randolph Creek.

*Randon, David.

*Randon, John.

*Randon, Texas.

*Range Creek.

*Ranger, Texas. Ranger, in northwestern Eastland County, had a 1960 population of 3,313 and a 1970 population of 3,094, according to the United States census. The city had seventy businesses in 1970.

*Ranger Canyon.

*Ranger, Desdemona, and Breckenridge Oil Fields.

Ranger Junior College. Ranger Junior College, located in Ranger, Texas, was organized on September 1, 1926, and was governed by the board of trustees of the Ranger Independent School District until August, 1950. At that time the board voted to make the college a separate unit. Theodore Nicksick, Jr., became president in June, 1959. The thirty-seven-acre campus contained a physical plant of twelve permanent buildings, including administration, classroom, science, fine arts, and business buildings, as well as a gymnasium, a library, a cafeteria, and a student union. Two dormitories were provided for men and two for women. The Paramount Hotel, owned by the college, served as an auxiliary dormitory in downtown Ranger, and apartments were provided for married students in this facility. In 1969 the library contained approximately thirteen thousand volumes, and a music library housed over one hundred volumes.

The curriculum was organized into five divisions: fine arts, natural science, social science, humanities, and practical arts. Courses of instruction prepared students for further study in senior colleges or entry into business or other vocational fields. A terminal two-year program in business was also given. Student enrollment numbered 595 for the fall, 1974, term, and Jack Elsom served as president.

*Ranger Springs.

*Rangerville, Texas.

*Rankin, Frederick Harrison. Frederick Harrison Rankin, son of Margaret "Peggy" (Berry) and Robert Rankin qv (not James Rankin, as stated in Volume II), was born on February 15, 1794 (not 1795).

BIBLIOGRAPHY: Robert Rankin Pension Papers (Record Group 15, Records of the Veterans Administration, National Archives, Washington, D.C.); Records, American Revolution Bicentennial Commission of Texas (MS., Archives, Texas State Library, Austin).

Ann Patton Malone

*Rankin, George Clark.

*Rankin, Melinda.

Rankin, Robert. Revolutionary War veteran Robert Rankin was born in the colony of Virginia in 1753. He entered the service of the Continental Army in 1776, with the Third Regiment of the Virginia line, participating in the battles of Germantown, Brandywine, and Stony Point, and in the siege of Charleston, where he was captured and remained a prisoner of war until exchanged, at which time he received a promotion to lieutenant.

On October 1, 1781, during a furlough, Rankin married Margaret "Peggy" Berry in Frederick County, Virginia. He returned to active duty on October 15 and served until the war's end. Robert and Margaret Rankin were the parents of three daughters and seven sons, one of whom was Frederick Harrison Rankin.qv

The Rankin family moved to Kentucky in 1784. In 1786 Rankin was named by the Virginia legislature as one of nine trustees for the newly established town of Washington, in Bourbon County (later Mason County), Kentucky. In 1792 Rankin served as a delegate from Mason County to the Danville Convention, which drafted the first constitution of Kentucky. He also became an elector of the Kentucky Senate of 1792. The last mention of Rankin in Mason County, Kentucky, is in the 1800 census.

In 1802 the Rankin family moved to Logan County, Kentucky, then to Mississippi territory on the Tombigbee River in 1811, an area which eventually became Washington County, Alabama. Four of the Rankin sons fought in the War of 1812. The Rankin family suffered a severe financial reversal around 1819–1820, probably in conjunction with land speculation and the Panic of 1819. In July, 1828, Rankin first made an application for a pension for his Revolutionary War service.

In 1832 the Rankins moved to Joseph Vehlein's qv colony in Texas, along with the William Butler and Peter Cartwright families. Robert Rankin was issued a certificate of character by Jesse Grimes qv on November 3, 1834, as required by the Mexican government. On November 13 of the same year he applied for a land grant in Vehlein's colony and received a league and labor in October, 1835. The present town of Coldspring, San Jacinto County, is located on Rankin's original grant (*see* Coldspring, Texas). Rankin had the reputation of being a just and diplomatic man. He was a friend of Sam Houston, and his influence with the Indians in the region was well known. Houston reputedly called upon Rankin in the spring of 1836, asking him to encourage neutrality among the Indians during the crucial Texian retreat toward San Jacinto.

Toward the end of 1836 Rankin became ill, and he and his wife moved to Saint Landry Parish, Louisiana, where he died on November 13, 1837, at the age of eighty-four. His body was brought back to their home near Coldspring, in the new Republic of Texas, and he was buried in the old Butler Cemetery. In 1936 his body was reinterred at the State Cemetery qv in Austin. His widow, Peggy, lived in Texas with her sons, William and Frederick, in Polk, Montgomery, and Liberty counties until her death sometime after December, 1852.

BIBLIOGRAPHY: L. W. Kemp, Biographical Notebook (MS., Archives, University of Texas at Austin Library); Records, American Revolution Bicentennial Commission of Texas (MS., Archives, Texas State Library, Austin); Robert Rankin Pension Papers (Record Group 15, Records of the Veterans Administration, National Archives, Washington, D.C.).

Ann Patton Malone

*Rankin, Texas. (Ellis County.)

*Rankin, Texas. (Upton County.) Rankin had a 1960 population of 1,214 and a 1970 population of 1,105, according to the United States census. The town had thirty businesses in 1970.

Ranney, William Tylee. William Tylee Ranney was born in 1813, the son of William and Clarissa (Gaylord) Ranney of Middletown, Connecticut. At an early age, Ranney served as an apprentice in his uncle's tin shop, and as an artisan he developed an interest in sketching. He entered the Institute of Mechanical Arts in Brooklyn, New York, but interrupted his art studies to go to New Orleans, where he enlisted in 1836 as a volunteer in the Texas war for independence, participating in the battle of San Jacinto. He spent enough time soldiering in Texas so that many of his genre paintings are flavored with the rough life of the Texas frontier. He avoided depicting any actual war scenes, but instead portrayed the activities peculiar to the pioneers, recording in pencil sketches the hunter, trapper, and horseman.

In 1838 he returned to his studies at the institute, receiving his diploma the same year; in 1843 he advertised as a portraitist, and in 1848 he married Margaret O'Sullivan of Cork, Ireland. When the new phase of genre painting showing the Western scene gained the attention of the American public, Ranney began improvising on sketches he had made during his adventures in Texas. On the spacious grounds of his New Jersey home he was able to raise and observe horses, and he installed many relics of the Texas region. Ranney's paintings from 1846 to 1849, signed, dated, and exhibited in New York, show an absorption with the Western scene. In 1850 he was elected a member of the National Academy of Design, where he exhibited regularly. Paintings showing the flavor of the pioneer country were "Mexican War Drummer," "Study of Oak Trees," "Hunting Wild Horses," and "The Lasso."

In 1853 he became ill and thereafter produced little, but his friends continued to collect and exhibit his works. A special sale held at the National Academy of Design on December 20 and 21, 1858, realized over $7,000 for his family. At this sale Ranney's work, consisting of 108 separate pieces,

made it possible to estimate to some degree the range and extent of his genre and portrait paintings.

BIBLIOGRAPHY: Francis S. Grubar, *William Ranney* (1962); Pauline A. Pinckney, *Painting in Texas: The Nineteenth Century* (1967); University of Texas at Austin, *Paintings from the C. R. Smith Collection* (1969).

Pauline A. Pinckney

Raphael Collection. The Raphael Collection in Brownsville was composed of family pieces as well as furniture and artifacts collected by Gabriel Matthews Raphael during his years in the import business, beginning in 1866, in Brownsville and Matamoros, Mexico. Most of the pieces were from France and Scotland. The collection was located in the Stillman House Museum, owned by the Brownsville Historical Association, and was a joint presentation of Mrs. Gabriel Raphael and the Raphael children, Angus, Alice, and Claire Raphael, in April, 1960.

Grace Edman

*Rare Book Collections. Rare book collections at the library of the University of Texas at Austin have grown as a result of an intensive program of acquisitions. The library now ranks among the thirty-two great libraries in Western Europe and North America, along with the Yale, Harvard, Pierpont Morgan, and Huntington libraries, in its collections of rare books and manuscripts.

The collection began with an emphasis on pre-twentieth-century literary manuscripts and books and included the Wrenn, Aitken, and Stark libraries. By 1956 a program was begun of acquiring works of twentieth-century American and English authors. In 1958 the T. E. Hanley collection, formed over a thirty-year period, was purchased. It is particularly rich in materials of D. H. Lawrence, T. E. Lawrence, George Bernard Shaw, Ezra Pound, James Joyce, William Butler Yeats, and Dylan Thomas. A History of Science collection was developed, which included the papers of English astronomer Sir John Frederick William Herschel and of English physicist Sir Owen Willans Richardson.

Book illustrations and examples of typography used through the centuries of book production are collected for research in the art of the book. A visual accompaniment to the manuscripts and printed materials is the collection of literary iconography, paintings, sketches, sculpture, and graphics. A series of catalogs and bibliographies have been published on the resources of the rare book collections. In 1972 many of the university's rare books and manuscripts collections were housed in one library, the newly completed Harry Ransom Humanities Research Center building on the campus of the University of Texas at Austin.

June Moll

*Ratama, Texas.

Ratchford, Fannie Elizabeth. Fannie Elizabeth Ratchford, the daughter of James Wylie and Malireda (Rose) Ratchford, was born on June 5, 1888, in Paint Rock, Concho County. When she was fifteen she wrote an account of her father's experiences as assistant adjutant general in the Confederate Army, published as *Some Reminiscences of Persons and Incidents of the Civil War* (1909). Receiving both the B.A. and M.A. degrees from the University of Texas, Miss Ratchford became librarian of the university's Rare Book Collections qv in 1917, a position she held until her retirement in 1957. She helped gather and catalog the Wrenn, Aitken, and Stark collections, which, together with other holdings, gained an international reputation for the rare books library at the University of Texas at Austin. Much of her research was devoted to nineteenth-century literary forgeries (especially those connected with Thomas J. Wise, who had placed many of them in the Wrenn collection). The Brontë family, of English literary fame, also received her careful attention, and her work in this area gained wide recognition. In numerous articles and several books, she explored or edited the literary works of Charlotte and Emily Brontë from their adolescence to adulthood, including a compilation of the early writings of Charlotte Brontë, *Legends of Angria* (1933); *The Brontës' Web of Childhood* (1941); and a novel in verse by Emily Brontë, *Gondal's Queen* (1955).

Fannie Ratchford held three Guggenheim fellowships during her career, and in 1954 she received an honorary LL.D. degree from Western College for Women (Ohio). She edited or provided notes for several other important works, including *The Correspondence of Sir Walter Scott and Charles Robert Maturin* (1937); *The Story of Champ d'Asile* (c. 1937); *Letters of Thomas J. Wise to John Henry Wrenn* (1944); and an exchange of letters between H. Buxton Forman and Thomas J. Wise, *Between the Lines* (1945). She was one of the editors of the complete works of the Brontës for Oxford Press after her retirement. She died in Austin on February 9, 1974.

BIBLIOGRAPHY: *Texian Who's Who* (1937); "Our Frontispiece: Fannie Elizabeth Ratchford," *Bulletin of Bibliography*, 20 (May–August, 1950); Clara Marie Sitter, History and Development of the Rare Book Collections of the University of Texas Based on Recollections of Miss Fannie Ratchford (M.L.S. thesis, University of Texas at Austin, 1966); Austin *American*, February 25, 1954; Austin *American-Statesman*, February 10, 1974; *Daily Texan*, October 8, 1953.

*Ratcliff, Texas. (Houston County.)

*Ratcliff, Texas. (Starr County.)

*Rath, Charles.

*Rath Trail. Rath Trail ended near Double Mountain (not the Double Mountains, as stated in Volume II) in southeastern Stonewall County. [In several places in the Volume II article, the word "yoke" should be substituted for the word "yolk."]

*Ratibor, Texas.

*Ratler, Texas.

*Ratliff, Texas.

*Rattan, Texas.

*Rattlesnake Butte.

*Rattlesnake Creek.

*Rattlesnake Gap.

*Rattlesnake Mountain.

*Rattlesnake Mountains.

Raunick, Selma Marie (Metzenthin). Selma Marie Metzenthin Raunick was born in Berlin, Germany, on May 17, 1877, the daughter of Ernst Ferdinand and Marie Theresa (Pank) Metzenthin. She came from Germany with her family in October, 1886, and lived in Austin during the time her father was pastor of St. Martin's Lutheran Church, from 1886 to 1894. The Metzenthin family moved to Steelton, Pennsylvania, in 1894, where she was graduated from high school in 1897. She was married to G. A. W. Raunick in Harrisburg, Pennsylvania, in 1909, and they were divorced in 1920; they had no children, although later, after the death of her sister, Else Metzenthin Schade, Selma reared the three Schade children. Returning to Texas in 1911, she taught in the Austin Academy (a prep school located in the former home of Governor James Stephen Hogg qv) before receiving her B.A. degree in 1919 and her M.A. degree in 1922 from the University of Texas. She did graduate work at the University of Pennsylvania and at the Universite de Strasbourg (France). She later taught at Allen Junior High School, Kenilworth Hall (a private girls' school), and Texas Wesleyan College Academy qv (all in Austin), Sul Ross State Teachers College (now Sul Ross State University), and the University of Hamburg, Germany. She was associated with choral groups in Mason, where she lived for a time, and in 1930, in Austin, she founded the Friends of German Pioneers of Texas. She also lived at various times in New Braunfels and San Marcos.

Mrs. Metzenthin Raunick's numerous writings, which brought attention for the first time to the large number of Texas-German writers in various fields, include "A Survey of German Literature in Texas" (from 1820 to the 1920's) in the *Southwestern Historical Quarterly* qv (1929–1930), and two volumes (in German) of Texas-German poetry and prose, *Deutsche Schriften in Texas* (1935, 1936), which had appeared earlier in article form in the *Freie Presse für Texas.*qv Her articles on German settlers and their culture and her stories and poems appeared in both English and German language periodicals and newspapers, such as the *Freie Presse für Texas*, the *Southwest Review,*qv the *American-German Review* (1940–1950), and the Taylor *Herald*. Several of her serialized novels, including the semi-autobiographical "Die Familie Metter in Amerika" (1944), were published in the *Neu Braunfelser Zeitung.*qv She died on February 12, 1954, in San Marcos and was buried in the San Marcos cemetery.

Margaret Schade Schulze

*Raven Creek.

*Raven Hill, Texas.

*Ravenna, Texas.

*Rawlins, Roderick.

*Rawlins, Texas.

*Rawls, Amos.

*Rawls, Benjamin.

*Rawls, Daniel.

*Ray Creek.

*Ray Knob.

Rayburn, Samuel Taliaferro. Samuel Taliaferro Rayburn, Texas legislator, congressman, and long-time Speaker of the United States House of Representatives, was born near the Clinch River in Roane County, eastern Tennessee, on January 6, 1882, son of William Marion and Martha (Waller) Rayburn. In 1887 the family moved from Tennessee to a forty-acre cotton farm near Windom, Fannin County, in north-central Texas. Bonham, in the same county, eventually became Sam Rayburn's permanent residence.

At the age of eighteen, Rayburn entered East Texas Normal College (now East Texas State University); although alternately attending college and teaching school, he completed in two years the three-year normal school course leading to the B.S. degree. He taught school two years, then left teaching to pursue a long-standing ambition of becoming a lawyer and legislator, inspired in part by an acquaintance with the political career of Senator Joseph Weldon (Joe) Bailey.qv In 1906 Rayburn won a seat in the Texas House of Representatives; he attended the University of Texas law school between legislative sessions and was admitted to the State Bar qv in 1908. He was reelected to the state legislature in 1908 and 1910; in his third term he served as Speaker of the House. In 1912 he was elected to the United States Congress as a Democrat from the Fourth Texas District.

Sam Rayburn's oath of office on April 7, 1913, as a member of the House of Representatives marked the beginning of over forty-eight years of continuous service, the longest record of service in that body ever established (at the time of his death in 1961). He became majority leader in the 75th and 76th Congresses (1937–1940) and in 1940 was named Speaker of the House to fill the unexpired term of Speaker William B. Bankhead. He continued as Speaker of the United States House of Representatives in every Democratic-controlled Congress from the 76th through the 87th (1940–1961). During the two periods of Republican majorities in the House (1947–1949 and 1953–1955), he served as minority leader. On three occasions during his legislative career (1948, 1952, and 1956), he served as permanent chairman of the Democratic national convention.

Rayburn's congressional career spanned the particularly accelerated legislative activity which occurred during the administrations of Woodrow Wilson, Franklin Delano Roosevelt, and Harry S. Truman; he was a participant in the passage of most of the significant legislation of the first half of the twentieth century. During the Wilson administration, Rayburn introduced legislation for increasing the power of the Interstate Commerce Commission and during World War I sponsored the War Risk Insurance Act. During the early New Deal years, from his position as chairman of the House Committee on Interstate and Foreign Commerce, he was author of the Truth-in-Securities Act, Railroad Holding Company Bill, Public Utilities Holding Company Act, the act creating the Federal Communications Commission, and, with Senator George W. Norris, the significant Rural Electrification Act. After 1937, as majority leader and Speaker of the House, he was responsible for guiding through the House of Representatives the remaining portions of the basic New Deal program. During World War II he helped insure the legislative base and financial support for the war effort, and in the postwar years he opposed what he regarded as reactionary or inflationary legislative proposals while supporting President Truman's foreign assistance programs and his basic domestic measures.

Although a review of Sam Rayburn's legislative record reveals a pattern of broad consistence, his career is not easily reduced to categorization. Even though he sponsored or supported most of the New Deal legislation, he was regarded at the time as more of a "middle-of-the-roader" than a liberal or "New Dealer." Although he was viewed as a loyal "party man," he retained and exercised an independence of action which occasionally cut sharply across party aims, and although his complete mastery of political process made him a formidable congressional adversary, his fairness and candor within the process brought him respect from both sides of the aisle.

In 1949 "Mr. Sam" was awarded the $10,000 Collier's award for distinguished service to the nation, and this award became the basis of an endowment for establishing and maintaining the Sam Rayburn Library at Bonham. The library, completed in 1957 and dedicated by former President Truman, houses the Rayburn public and private papers, and with its related research materials, it operates as a study center for problems in contemporary American politics and government.

Sam Rayburn was married in 1927 to Metze Jones of Valley View, Texas, but the marriage ended quickly in divorce and Rayburn remained unmarried until his death at age seventy-nine on November 16, 1961. He was buried in Bonham, Texas.

BIBLIOGRAPHY: Charles Dwight Dorough, Mr. Sam (1962); The Leadership of Speaker Sam Rayburn, House Document No. 247, 87th Congress, 1st Session, 1961; Rayburn Medal, Hearing, Senate Committee on Banking and Currency, 87th Congress, 2nd Session, 1962.

Floyd F. Ewing

*Rayburn, Texas.

*Rayford, Texas.

*Rayland, Texas.

*Raymond, Charles H.

*Raymond, James Hervey.

Raymond, Texas. Raymond, twelve miles west of Henrietta in Clay County, was a switch on the Fort Worth and Denver Railroad, connecting it with the Wichita Valley Railroad. In 1966 an engine and one car made round trips daily from Raymond through Dean, Petrolia, and Byers to the Red River and Oklahoma state line near Waurika, Oklahoma.

*Raymondville, Texas. Raymondville, seat of Willacy County, is a commercial center for the truck and irrigated fruit crops produced in the surrounding area. Raymondville industries in the 1960's included a cottonseed processing plant, manufacturers of farm implements, producers of leather goods, and truck-fruit processors. Due to its location near the coast, Raymondville is a year-round recreational center. The city reported sixteen churches, a hospital, a library, a radio station, and three newspapers in the late 1960's. The 1960 population was 9,385; the 1970 population was 7,987, according to the United States census. Raymondville had 146 businesses in 1970.

Rayner, J. B. J. B. Rayner was born a slave in Raleigh, North Carolina, in 1850, the son of a white father, Kenneth Rayner, prominent in the state's public life, and a Negro mother. Rayner received his education at Shaw University and St. Augustine Collegiate Institute (both in Raleigh), although he did not receive a degree. Before coming to Robertson County, Texas, in 1881, Rayner served as a constable, magistrate, and deputy sheriff in his native state. After arriving in Texas, he taught school, preached, and worked with various societies for the advancement of his race. He was an advocate of the Booker T. Washington philosophy and worked with Negro leader Robert Lloyd Smith qv in the Farmer's Home Improvement Society.qv Rayner later became president of Conroe Normal and Industrial College at Conroe.

By 1892 Rayner had become disenchanted with the Republican party,qv which he deserted in that year to accept the tenets of Populism. Appointed by the state chairman of the Populist party qv as a stump speaker and organizer, Rayner, with a corps of Negro assistants, avidly canvassed the eastern and southeastern sections of the state. It was claimed that he converted at least twenty-five thousand Negroes to the Populist cause. He was rewarded for his efforts by an appointment to the executive committee of the Populist party in Texas. Articulate and with a sense of humor, Rayner was an effective orator and organizer among Texas Negroes. After 1898 he dropped out of politics until 1905, when he returned to the Republican party. He died on July 14, 1918.

Lawrence Rice

Rayner, Texas. Rayner was the first seat of Stonewall County. The offices were moved to Asper-

mont in 1889 after being established in Rayner in 1888.

BIBLIOGRAPHY: *Texas Almanac* (1936).

*Raypaul, Texas.

*Raywood, Texas.

Raza Unida Party. An independent political party, Raza Unida (United Race or United People) was organized in Texas in January, 1970, by a group of Chicanos qv (a name adopted primarily by younger Mexican Americans). The party was an outgrowth of research begun in the 1960's in a MAYO qv (Mexican American Youth Organization) experimental program known as the Winter Garden Project in Crystal City, Texas.

The founder was Jose Angel Gutierrez, a native of Crystal City, who with his wife, Luz, started the Winter Garden Project to make Crystal City a model of Chicano self-determination. Gutierrez, the first national party chairman, still held that position in 1973, and the national headquarters was in Crystal City.

Raza Unida party was first organized in four South Texas counties: Hidalgo County in the Rio Grande Valley, and Dimmit, La Salle, and Zavala counties in the Winter Garden area. Colorado was the second state in which Raza Unida developed. Organizational work for the party was underway in twenty-three states in 1973. Major campaigns, in addition to those in Texas and Colorado, were carried out in California, Illinois, Wisconsin, and Arizona by 1973. While organized chiefly by and for Chicanos, Raza Unida party embraced the idea of bringing dignity, self-respect, and power to all disenfranchised minorities, including Blacks, women, the poor, and the voiceless Anglo. The avowed purpose of the party was to bring social, economic, and political change and improvement to minorities through political strategy.

The Spanish name, Raza Unida, was chosen as a symbol of the party's intention to be different. The party's goal was to make all people of the electorate feel that they have the right and responsibility to have a voice in the issues that control their lives.

Raza Unida experienced its first electoral success in April, 1970, when the party's slate swept the school board elections in Crystal City. Party chairman Gutierrez was elected chairman of the school board, and two other Chicanos defeated candidates of the Democratic party.qv In that same month Raza Unida was also victorious in city council elections in Crystal City, Carrizo Springs, and Cotulla.

Reforms instituted when Raza Unida candidates won school board and city council seats in South Texas included the following: bilingual-bicultural education in elementary schools; hiring of teachers, principals, and school counselors of Mexican descent; free breakfast programs for elementary schools; additional summer educational programs for children of migrant workers; housing projects; street improvements; summer recreation programs; elimination in some schools of a discriminatory English proficiency examination; and elimination of a rule that prohibited the speaking of Spanish on school grounds.

As the party branched out to statewide elections it was less successful, and dissension developed in the party. Basic disagreements over party direction first surfaced publicly in 1971, when an urban faction led by state party chairman Mario Compean, of San Antonio, successfully challenged party-founder Gutierrez in a debate over the party's entering statewide races instead of limiting itself to county, local, and school district elections.

Gutierrez felt the organizational effort which produced the party's first victories in Crystal City should be the basis of similar drives in other communities where there were large numbers of Mexican Americans. Despite his warning that statewide losses would hurt the young party and exhaust its limited resources, the party presented candidates for state offices in 1972 and lost every race. The votes in a few races, however, including Ramsey Muniz's strong showing in the governor's race (214,118 votes) surprised some observers.

In the early 1970's Raza Unida remained successful in Crystal City elections, and the party continued receiving substantial financial assistance from federal agencies, private foundations, and churches to back local projects dealing with education, health, and other socio-economic problems. *See also* Mexican Americans in Texas.

BIBLIOGRAPHY: Mario Compean, Jose Angel Gutierrez, and Antonio Camejo, *La Raza Unida Party in Texas* (A Merit Pamphlet from Pathfinder Press, 1970); John R. Fry, "Election Night in Crystal City," *Christianity and Crisis,* 32 (November 27, 1972); Richard A. Santillan, "El Partido La Raza Unida: Chicanos in Politics," *The Black Politician* (July, 1971); *Cristal* (September, 1971); "Action Express," San Antonio *Express,* September 4, 1973.

*Razor, Texas.

Read, John Lloyd. John Lloyd Read was born at Blum, Texas, on November 16, 1898, the son of Robert McMurray and Elizabeth (Butchee) Read. He attended the Memphis, Texas, public schools, served briefly in World War I, then received a B.A. degree in 1922 and an M.A. degree in 1926, both from Baylor University. In 1938 he received a Ph.D. degree from Columbia University. His doctoral thesis, "The Mexican Historical Novel, 1826–1910," reflected a lifelong interest in Latin American culture; it was published by the *Instituto de las Españas* at Columbia in 1939. He married Mayme Barnes on December 26, 1922; they had no children.

Read began his teaching career at Decatur Baptist College, and in 1926 he became director of the Department of Spanish at Southwest Texas State Teachers College (now Southwest Texas State University). In 1946 he became chairman of the newly created division of foreign languages, a position he held until his death. He was also college registrar from 1950 to 1956 and for a time was director of the Inter-American House on campus. One of his chief interests was the improvement of opportunities for Latin American students. He died on August 4, 1959, and was buried in San Marcos City Cemetery.

*Reagan, John Henninger.

*Reagan, William Reason.

*Reagan, Texas.

*Reagan County. Reagan County's economy was based mainly on oil and gas, cattle, and sheep, but after 1948 the county expanded the production of cotton and grain sorghum by irrigation. Between 1923 and January 1, 1973, the county produced 287,167,751 barrels of oil. In the late 1960's the county reported fifty farms and seventy ranches and supported a hospital, a library, and a park. Improvements on the courthouse building were approved in 1966. County population remained sparse, numbering 3,782 in 1960, and 3,239 in 1970, according to the United States census.

*Reagan Creek.

*Reagan Wells, Texas.

*Reagor Springs, Texas.

*Real, Julius.

*Real County. Real County, though mainly a sheep, goat, and cattle ranching area, experienced a large increase in tourism during the 1960's, particularly during deer season. Another tourist attraction was Camp Wood,qv which was located on the site of the San Lorenzo de la Santa Cruz Mission.qv It is a popular area for artists. The 1960 population was 2,079; by 1970 the count was 2,013, according to the United States census.

*Reál Presidio de San Sabá. *See* San Sabá Presidio.

*Realitos, Texas.

*Reaugh, Frank.

*Rebecca, Texas.

*Rebecca Creek.

*Rebecca Creek, Texas.

*Reclamation. *See* Conservation of Natural Resources.

*Recognition of the Republic of Texas. *See* Diplomatic Relations of the Republic of Texas.

*Reconstruction in Texas.

*Record, Texas.

Records Preservation Advisory Committee. The Records Preservation Advisory Committee, created in 1965, was composed of the state librarian as chairman, secretary of state, state auditor, comptroller of public accounts, attorney general, secretary of the Senate and chief clerk of the House of Representatives. The function of the committee was to advise the records preservation officer and to work with the records management division of the state library and the historical commission.

BIBLIOGRAPHY: University of Texas at Austin, *Guide To Texas State Agencies* (1972).

*Rector, John B.

*Rector, Texas.

*Red, George Clark.

*Red, Rebecca (Stuart). Rebecca (Stuart) Red was born on October 2, 1827 (not 1826, as stated in Volume II).

Mrs. Stuart M. Purcell

*Red, Samuel Clark.

*Red, William Stuart.

*Red Arroyo.

*Red Bank, Texas.

*Red Bank Creek.

*Red Barn, Texas.

*Red Bayou.

*Red Bluff, Texas. (Harrison County.)

*Red Bluff, Texas. (Reeves County.)

*Red Bluff, Texas. (San Saba County.)

*Red Bluff Dam and Reservoir. Red Bluff Reservoir is in the Rio Grande Basin in Reeves and Loving counties, five miles north of Orla on the Pecos River, a tributary to the Rio Grande. The reservoir extends into Eddy County, New Mexico. The project is owned and operated by the Red Bluff Water Power Control District for hydroelectric power generation and irrigation. Construction of the dam began in November, 1934, and was completed in September, 1936, with impoundment of water beginning at the time of completion. The reservoir was first filled in June, 1937, and water use began in that same year. Power generation began June 6, 1937. The reservoir has a capacity of 310,000 acre-feet and a surface area of 11,700 acres at elevation 2,841.7 feet above mean sea level. The hydroelectric power plant contains two generating units having a combined capacity of 2,300 kilowatts. The contributing drainage area above Red Bluff Dam is 20,720 square miles.

BIBLIOGRAPHY: Texas Water Commission, *Bulletin 6408* (1964).

Seth D. Breeding

*Red Branch, Texas. (Grayson County.)

*Red Branch, Texas. (Leon County.)

*Red Creek.

*Red Deer Creek.

*Red Fork of Rush Creek.

*Red Hill, Texas.

*Red-Lander.

*Red Lawn, Texas.

*Red Mountain.

*Red Mud Creek.

*Red Oak, Texas.

*Red Oak Creek.

*Red Point.

*Red Ranger, Texas.

*Red River.

*Red River, Texas. (Grayson County.)

*Red River, Texas. (Hardeman County.)

Red River Army Depot. In 1972 the Red River Army Depot, formerly called the Red River Ordnance Depot,qv occupied a fifty-square-mile area northwest of Texarkana, with approximately three thousand buildings and structures. It was served by some six thousand civil service employees as well as a limited number of military personnel. The primary mission of the depot remained the receipt, storage, and issue of general supplies and ammunition to customers in the Fourth Army area, and depot maintenance of general supplies and ammunition. *See also* Lone Star Army Ammunition Plant.

BIBLIOGRAPHY: *Texas Almanac* (1963, 1970).

*Red River Boundary. *See* Boundaries of Texas.

Red River Bridge Controversy. The Red River Bridge controversy between Texas and Oklahoma occurred in July, 1931, over the opening of a newly completed free bridge, built jointly by both states, across the Red River between Denison, Texas, and Durant, Oklahoma. On July 3, 1931, the Red River Bridge Company, a private firm operating an already established toll bridge that paralleled the free span, filed a petition in the United States district court in Houston asking for an injunction preventing the Texas Highway Commission from opening the bridge. The company claimed that the highway commission had agreed in July, 1930, to purchase the toll bridge for $60,000 and to pay the company for its unexpired contract an additional $10,000 for each month of a specified fourteen-month period in which the free bridge might be opened, and that the highway commission had not fulfilled this obligation. A temporary injunction was issued on July 10, 1931, and Texas Governor Ross S. Sterling qv ordered barricades erected across the Texas approaches to the new bridge. However, on July 16 Governor William (Alfalfa Bill) Murray qv of Oklahoma opened the bridge by executive order, claiming that Oklahoma's "half" of the bridge ran north and south across the Red River, that Oklahoma held title to both sides of the river from the Louisiana Purchase Treaty of 1803, and that the state of Oklahoma was not named in the injunction. Oklahoma highway crews crossed the bridge and demolished the barricades. Governor Sterling responded by ordering a detachment of three Texas Rangers,qv accompanied by Adjutant General William Warren Sterling,qv to rebuild the barricades and protect Texas State Highway Department qv employees charged with enforcing the injunction. The Rangers arrived on the night of July 16.

On July 17 Murray ordered Oklahoma highway crews to tear up the northern approaches to the still-operating toll bridge, and traffic over the river came to a halt. On July 20 and July 21 mass meetings demanding the opening of the free bridge were held in Sherman and Denison, and resolutions to this effect were forwarded to Austin. On July 23 the Texas legislature, which was meeting in a special session, passed a bill granting the Red River Bridge Company permission to sue the state in order to recover the sum claimed in the injunction. The bridge company then joined the state in requesting the court to dissolve the injunction, which it did on July 25. The free bridge was opened to traffic and the Rangers were withdrawn on that day.

Meanwhile, a federal district court in Muskogee, Oklahoma, acting on a petition from the toll bridge company, had on July 24 enjoined Governor Murray from blocking the northern approaches to the toll bridge. Murray, acting several hours before the injunction was actually issued, declared martial law in a narrow strip of territory along the northern approaches to both bridges and then argued that this act placed him, as commander of the Oklahoma National Guard, above the federal court's jurisdiction. An Oklahoma guard unit was ordered to the bridge, and Murray, armed with an antique revolver, made a personal appearance in the "war zone," as the newspapers labeled it. No attempt was made to enforce the Oklahoma injunction, but on July 26, with the free bridge open, Murray directed the guardsmen to permit anyone who so desired to cross the toll bridge.

On July 27 Murray announced that he had learned of an attempt to close the free bridge permanently, and he extended the martial law zone to the Oklahoma boundary marker on the south bank of the Red River. Oklahoma guardsmen were stationed at both ends of the free bridge, and Texas papers spoke of an "invasion." Finally, on August 6, 1931, the Texas injunction was permanently dissolved, the Oklahoma guardsmen were withdrawn to enforce martial law in the Oklahoma oil fields, and the bridge controversy was laid to rest.

BIBLIOGRAPHY: Keith L. Bryant, *Alfalfa Bill Murray* (1968); William H. Murray, *Memoirs of Governor Murray and True History of Oklahoma,* II (1945); William W. Sterling, *Trails and Trials of a Texas Ranger* (1959); *General and Special Laws of the State of Texas Passed by the 42nd Legislature at the First Called Session* (1931); Dallas *Morning News,* July 17–25, 1931, March 22, 1953; Sherman *Daily Democrat,* July 2–August 6, 1931.

Lonn Taylor

*Red River Campaign.

*Red River County. Red River County continued as a producer of beef cattle, poultry, cotton, corn, hay, and truck crops in the 1960's. Two-thirds of the farm income was derived from livestock in the early 1970's. The county was 51 percent forested in 1967, and it milled 460,000 board-feet of lumber in three active mills in 1968. A small amount of petroleum was produced, totaling 449,580 barrels from 1951 to January 1, 1973. The county opened a fifty-acre industrial park in 1963 to encourage industry.

In 1966 Langford Lake, with 162 surface acres, was completed to provide water for the county seat of Clarksville. Tourist attractions included historic homes and sites and the birthplace of John Nance Garner.qv The 1960 population was 15,682; in 1970 it was 14,298, according to the United States census.

*Red River Indian War.

*Red River Ordnance Depot. *See also* Red River Army Depot.

*Red River Raft. *See* Red River.

*Red River Station.

*Red River, Texas, and Southern Railway Company.

*Red Rock, Texas.

*Red Rovers.

*Red Springs, Texas. (Baylor County.)

Red Springs, Texas. (Smith County.) Red Springs, in northern Smith County, was founded in 1855 in an area where numerous springs flowed from the clay hills north into the Sabine River. The community, once a center for logging and lumbering, began to decline about 1930, when the area had less timber. By 1966 only about fifteen persons inhabited the town.

*Redbank Creek.

*Redd, William Davis.

Redditt, John Sayers. John Sayers Redditt (given his middle name for his great-uncle, Joseph Draper Sayers qv), son of John David and Lewis Permellia (Miller) Redditt, was born April 4, 1899, in Center, Shelby County, Texas. He was graduated from the University of Texas law school in 1921 and opened a law practice in Lufkin that same year.

Redditt was active in civic affairs in Lufkin and was elected in 1933 to the Texas Senate, where he served until 1941. He was in the United States Army during World War II, and following that, in 1947, he was one of the founders of Winn's Variety Stores in San Antonio. Redditt held numerous state offices, including chairman of the Texas Economy Commission, chairman of the Texas Highway Commission, and president of the Texas Good Roads Association; he was cited as having been instrumental in the upgrading of Texas highways and in the improvement of the forestry service.

A member of the Texas Commission on Higher Education,qv he also served on the board of regents of the University of Texas beginning in 1961. He resigned from that board in December, 1964, two years before the end of his term, in protest of Governor John Connally's failure to approve an architect chosen by the regents to design a building at Texas Western College (now the University of Texas at El Paso). Redditt claimed his decision had nothing to do with the governor, but was a result of his objection to a new state law that gave the governor power over the choice of architects for state buildings. Redditt received a distinguished alumnus award from the University of Texas at Austin in 1971.

He was married to Hazel Lee Spears on December 27, 1928; they had two daughters. Redditt died April 13, 1973, in Lufkin, and he was buried there.

BIBLIOGRAPHY: Biographical File, Barker Texas History Center, University of Texas at Austin.

Redfield, Henry Prentice. Henry Prentice Redfield was born in Derry, New Hampshire, on May

27, 1819, the son of William and Susan (Prentice) Redfield. After the death of his father, his mother married John C. Cunningham, a friend of Moses and Stephen F. Austin, and soon thereafter the family (including Henry's brothers John Albert and William) immigrated to the Austin Colony in Texas, leaving New York in late 1830 and arriving by ship at Matagorda in 1831. They lived at San Felipe for several years, then settled on the Colorado River in lower Bastrop County on a large grant of land which became known as Cunningham's Prairie. Besides farming, the Cunninghams later ran a stagecoach inn on the old road from Austin to San Felipe.

During the Texas Revolution qv Henry Prentice Redfield joined the Army of the Republic of Texas.qv He was in Captain John Henry Moore's qv company at the battle of Gonzales qv on October 2, 1835; with Ben Milam qv at the siege of Bexar qv in early December, 1835; and, while not an actual participant in the battle of San Jacinto, he helped round up the fleeing Mexicans after the battle. Redfield continued to serve in the Texas Army in various Indian fights and was wounded in the Plum Creek fight qv on August 11, 1840. In that same year his brother William was killed in a battle involving the Republic of the Rio Grande.qv

In 1842 Henry Redfield was with Mathew Caldwell qv on the expedition against General Adrian Woll qv at San Antonio and fought in the battle of Salado qv (see also Mexican Invasions of 1842). During the Mexican War,qv in 1846, Redfield joined the 1st Texas Cavalry, United States Army, and served under General Zachery Taylor qv at the battle of Resaca de la Palma qv and the siege of Monterrey. In 1850 he was the first census taker of Bastrop County.

On September 11, 1842, Henry Prentice Redfield was married to Sarah Card of Fayette County, and they had nine children. After her death he was married to Julia Kersting of Washington County in 1872, and they had seven children. Redfield died on February 27, 1900, at Giddings and was buried in the Giddings Cemetery. An official Texas historical marker honoring Redfield was dedicated at his grave in 1971.

BIBLIOGRAPHY: L. W. Kemp and Ed Kilman, *The Battle of San Jacinto and the San Jacinto Campaign* (1947); L. W. Kemp, Biographical Notebook (MS., Archives, University of Texas at Austin Library); Files of the Texas Historical Commission, Austin; Files of the Daughters of the Republic of Texas Museum, Austin.

Jack R. McKinney

*Redfish Bay.

*Redford, Texas.

*Redgates Creek.

*Redland, Texas. (Angelina County.)

*Redland, Texas. (Wood County.)

*Redman, William Columbus.

*Redmud Creek.

*Redoak Creek.

*Redrock Creek.

*Redwater, Texas.

*Redwine, Texas.

*Redwood, Texas.

*Reece's Creek.

*Reed, Henry.

Reed, Malcolm Hiram. Malcolm Hiram Reed, son of Thomas Seldon and Dora (Connell) Reed, was born on February 22, 1876, at Gabriel Mills, Williamson County, Texas. He graduated from high school at Bertram, then attended Hill's Business College in Waco. In 1893 his father sent him to Marble Falls to merchandise goods, and he remained there in business for fifteen years; he organized and was president of the Marble Falls State Bank before moving to Austin in 1908.

His business in Austin, M. H. Reed and Company, was one of the leading cotton factors in the state; it was also a major handler of cedar timber and pecans. Reed was active in banking, real estate, and oil. Through his Yellow House Land Company (1923–1942), he purchased and resold the lands of the Yellow House Ranch qv to farmers in Hockley and Lamb counties. Reed was married twice, in 1898 to Margaret Badger, who bore him four children, and, following a 1936 divorce, to Roberta Farish Purvis; they had two daughters. He died on December 11, 1945, and was buried in Memorial Park, Austin.

BIBLIOGRAPHY: Seymour V. Connor (ed.), *Builders of the Southwest* (1959).

Roy Sylvan Dunn

Reed, St. Clair Griffin. St. Clair Griffin Reed, author of the highly significant *A History of the Texas Railroads*, was born on March 26, 1867, in Franklin Parish, Louisiana, son of Isaac Alexander and Ellen Addison (Griffin) Reed. He entered Madison (now Colgate) University, Hamilton, New York, in 1885, leaving at the end of his sophomore year because of the death of his father. Returning to Texas, he taught in Victoria High School; he later went back to Madison University, from which he was graduated in 1888. He began his railroad career immediately after graduation, taking a position as freight clerk in the office of the New York, Texas, and Mexican Railway,qv later a part of the Southern Pacific lines (see Southern Pacific System in Texas). In 1889 he received the first of many rapid promotions, becoming chief clerk to the general freight and passenger agent.

In 1905 he was promoted to division freight and passenger agent of the Louisiana and Texas Railroad (see Morgan Lines) in Lafayette, Louisiana; in 1906 he was transferred to the Houston and Texas Central Railroad;qv both companies had become part of the Southern Pacific lines. In 1911 he was promoted to assistant general freight agent, and the following year he became assistant general freight and passenger agent of the Southern Pacific lines. He remained in Dallas until 1918, when he was assigned to Houston as a corporate land and tax agent. In 1920 he was appointed assistant general freight agent of the Southern Pacific lines in Texas, and in 1924 he was promoted to assistant freight traffic manager of the Southern Pacific lines in Texas. In 1928 Reed's jurisdiction was extended to Louisiana; he later became freight traffic manager. Reed retired in 1937 after forty-nine years of continuous service with the Southern Pacific lines in Texas and Louisiana.

Reed was a member and president of the Association of Interstate Commerce Practitioners, an honorary member of the Eugene Field Society, and a contributing member of the Texas State Historical Association.qv He also belonged to the Railway and Locomotive Historical Society, located in Boston, and was a member of the Episcopal church. It was in 1941 that Reed published the historically important *A History of the Texas Railroads*; he also wrote numerous articles concerning Texas railroads for various periodicals, and his contribution of railroad articles to Volumes I and II of the *Handbook of Texas* was enormous.

On February 20, 1895, Reed married Carrie Pye in Port Lavaca; they had three sons and one daughter. He died on March 2, 1948, in Houston and was buried in Forest Park Cemetery there.

BIBLIOGRAPHY: Clarence R. Wharton (ed.), *Texas Under Many Flags* (1930); Writers Biographical File, Barker Texas History Center, University of Texas at Austin.

*Reed Plateau.

*Reed's Branch.

*Reed's Switch, Texas.

*Reedville, Texas.

*Reels, Patrick.

*Reese, Charles Keller.

*Reese, Texas. (Cherokee County.)

Reese, Texas. (Lubbock County.) Reese, an unincorporated town west of the city of Lubbock, had a 1970 population of 2,545, according to the United States census.

*Reese Air Force Base. Reese Air Force Base, adjacent to Lubbock, Texas, was reactivated in August, 1949, and the first postwar classes of pilots trained there graduated in March, 1950. From 1951 to 1957 Reese Air Force Base conducted training programs using T-6, T-28, and TB-25 aircraft. In 1959 the base discontinued B-25 training. By mid-1963 Reese Air Force Base had trained eight thousand cadets since its reactivation, and in that year the T-38 supersonic jet trainer was added to the list of training aircraft.

The training program was modified in March, 1965, with the addition of a six-week pre-flight indoctrination program in the single-engine, propeller-driven T-41A aircraft. Upon completion of this course, cadets entered a fifty-five-week primary phase training course in the T-37. The last part of the program included extensive experience in the T-38 supersonic jet trainer.

Laverne H. Neuhaus

*Reeves, George R.

Reeves, James Travis. James Travis (Jim) Reeves, country and popular singer, was born in Galloway, Panola County, on August 20, 1923, the son of Tom and Mary (Adams) Reeves. After graduation from Carthage High School in 1942 he attended the University of Texas and played for the university baseball team. He pitched briefly for Marshall and Henderson in the Class C East Texas League, but retired from baseball in 1946 following a leg injury. In 1947 he was an announcer and disc jockey at KGRI in Henderson and began singing locally under the name Sonny Day. He recorded first in 1949 for Macy, a small Houston company, but experienced no real success until 1952, when he signed a contract with Abbott records. His second Abbott recording, "Mexican Joe," brought him national popularity and led him in 1953 to employment as an announcer for KWKH, Shreveport, Louisiana, and subsequent appearances on the "Louisiana Hayride." After his second successful recording, "Bimbo," Reeves joined the Grand Ole Opry in Nashville, Tennessee, in 1955 and began recording for RCA Victor. His most successful recordings were "He'll Have To Go" and "Four Walls."

Reeves and his pianist, Dean Manuel, were killed July 31, 1964, when his private plane crashed near Nashville. He was buried in a two-acre memorial plot near Carthage, Texas, on the road to Shreveport. At the time of his death Reeves owned KGRI in Henderson and three music publishing companies. He had made three European tours and two trips to South Africa, where he starred in a film, *Kimberley Jim*. He was survived by his wife, Mary, whom he married in 1946. They had no children.

BIBLIOGRAPHY: Linnell Gentry, *A History and Encyclopedia of Country, Western, and Gospel Music* (1961); *Official WSM Grand Ole Opry History-Picture Book*, II (1961); Bill C. Malone, *Country Music, U.S.A.* (1968).

Bill C. Malone

Reeves, Malachiah. Malachiah Reeves was born on September 26, 1843, in Bibb County, Alabama, posthumous son of Reverend Malachiah Reeves and Nancy Bethel (Blakey) Reeves. His mother married William Wood when Reeves was three, and the family came to Texas in late 1849 or early 1850 by way of old Sabinetown, first settling on a farm near Chireno, Nacogdoches County. In 1860 he was living in Houston County and attended his first school; he then attended a subscription school in the spring of 1861, and in July of that year joined a "good bunch of fire-eating boys" for three years' service in the Confederate Army. In Richmond, Virginia, he was part of Louis Trezevant Wigfall's qv battalion. He was a member of Company I, 1st Texas Regiment of Hood's Texas Brigade qv when he was captured at Mechanicsville, Virginia, in 1862. His memoirs contain vivid details of his war experiences.

After the war he farmed near Pennington, Texas, and became a member of the Missionary Baptist

Church there in 1866. He married Jane Elizabeth Powers on September 23, 1875, and they had one daughter before her death in August, 1876. On January 4, 1877, he married Nancy Joanna Beall, and they lived in the Rock Hill community; they had eleven children. In 1883 the family moved to the Hopewell Church community, east of Athens; it had a school and a Baptist church and cemetery. Later it was known as Leagueville, with two general stores, a gin, and a post office. Through the years Reeves and his wife studied with the country school teachers who boarded in their home. In 1888 he was ordained to preach as a Baptist minister and served in rural churches in Henderson and Anderson counties. He was postmaster in Leagueville from August, 1906, until the post office closed early in 1907. In 1924 Reeves wrote his memoirs. He died on December 4, 1929, in Frankston and was buried in Leagueville Cemetery.

BIBLIOGRAPHY: Leila Ione Reeves Eads (comp.), Mary Joe Reeves Young (ed.), *M. Reeves and his Family* (1966); Athens *Daily Review*, September 16, 23, 1965.

R. T. *Craig*

*Reeves, Reuben A.

*Reeves County. Reeves County, an agricultural area, had many large cattle ranches and 88,000 acres of irrigated land upon which cotton, feed crops, cantaloupes, and vegetables were grown in the 1960's. The county produced over thirty-seven million barrels of oil between 1939 and 1973. Reeves County supported a hospital and libraries in Pecos and Balmorhea. Major tourist attractions included Lake Balmorhea, Balmorhea State Recreation Park (*see* Parks, State), West of the Pecos Museum, and a July rodeo. The 1960 population was 17,644; the 1970 figure was 16,526, according to the United States census.

*Refining Industry. *See* Oil, Refining of.

*Reforestation and Timber. *See* Conservation of Natural Resources.

*Refrigeration, Early History of, in Texas. Texas engineers did much of the early experimental work in the development of commercial refrigeration in the United States, although it was from Europeans (notably Scotch, English, and French), that their theories were obtained. The most interesting refrigeration history related to Texas dates from 1861 to 1885. When the natural ice supply from the north was cut off by the Civil War, men of ingenuity in Texas and Louisiana came forth with inventiveness in mechanical ice making and food preservation (*see* early account in Volume II).

After the Civil War Texas' expanding beef industry encouraged and financed the development of the mechanical cold process. Andrew Muhl, of San Antonio, in partnership with a Mr. Paggi, built an ice-making machine there in 1867 before moving it to Waco in 1871. Development of mechanical refrigeration for the Texas meat industry began in 1865 in Dallas with Thaddeus S. C. Lowe's carbon dioxide machines, which had been used to inflate the balloons he was constructing. Using dry ice made with carbon dioxide compressors, Lowe designed a ship for refrigeration, the *William Tabor*, in 1867, in competition with Henry Peyton Howard's ship, *Agnes*, to carry chilled and frozen beef by steamship to New Orleans. The *William Tabor* drew too much water to dock in New Orleans harbor, and, because Howard's ship was the first to accomplish the feat, Lowe did not receive the proper credit for his attempt; however, the singular accomplishment of a refrigerator-designed ship did establish the compressor process of refrigeration for ships delivering meat to New York and Europe.

From 1871 to 1881 the first mechanically refrigerated abattoir in the United States was planned, established, and successfully operated in Fulton, Texas, for the purpose of chilling and curing beef for shipment to Liverpool, England, and other destinations. Daniel Livingston Holden (not D. C. Holden, as stated in Volume II), his brother, Elbridge Holden, and Elbridge Holden's father-in-law, George W. Fulton,qv took part in the development of this new process of beef packing and shipping. Thomas L. Rankin, of Dallas and Denison, was a holder of twenty-four patents in the area of refrigeration and had been involved in refrigeration work with Daniel L. Holden. From 1870 to 1877 Rankin worked on the development of refrigerator and abattoir service for rail shipping of refrigerated beef from Texas and the Great Plains. In late 1873 a rail shipment of chilled beef successfully reached New York from Texas. The development made by Rankin and his Texas associates spread rapidly to other beef-shipping centers of the nation.

Another early worker in the development of ice-making machinery was Charles A. Zilker of San Antonio and Austin. Coming to Austin from Indiana in 1880, he worked in an ice plant which had been using a French machine brought from San Antonio. In 1882 Richard King qv asked Zilker and his brother, Andrew J. Zilker, to go to Brownsville to serve as engineers at an ice plant which King had bought in 1876. Returning to Austin in 1884, Zilker continued improving and designing compressor-type ice-making machinery. In business with G. W. Brackenridge,qv a San Antonio banker, Zilker established ice plants in Austin and San Antonio. After that he built ice plants in any city where he could find enough prosperous people and sufficient cooling water for compressors. In 1928 Zilker sold his ice plants (which ranged from Texas eastward to Atlanta and northward to Pittsburgh) to the Samuel Insull interests, Chicago, for one million dollars. Generally it can be said that the development of mechanical ice refrigeration in Texas and the South gave to the industry the world's principal creative progress in ice making. (For a later account, *see* Refrigeration, Since 1900, in Texas; *see also* Air Conditioning in Texas.)

BIBLIOGRAPHY: Willis R. Woolrich, *The Men Who Created Cold* (1967); Charles A. Zilker, *Sixty Years of Ice* (1940); *Daily Picayune* (New Orleans), July 13, 1869; *Tri-Weekly State Gazette* (Austin), March 23, 1870;

Flakes Bulletin (Galveston), July 13, 1860; Willis R. Woolrich, "The History of Refrigeration; 220 Years of Mechanical and Chemical Cold: 1748–1968," *ASHRAE Journal* (July, 1969); Willis R. Woolrich Papers (MS., Archives, University of Texas at Austin Library).

Willis R. Woolrich

Refrigeration, Since 1900, in Texas. By 1900 there were 766 ice plants in the United States, and Texas, with 77, had more plants than any other state, producing cheap and abundant quantities of ice. Fruit and vegetable production in Texas greatly expanded after the turn of the century, and the refrigerator car was used effectively in transporting these perishable foods to cities outside the state. Two of the most important Texas industries, highly dependent on refrigeration, were the fish and poultry processing plants. By the late 1960's there were thirty-six plants processing frozen fish and shrimp in Texas; in 1967 there were sixty-seven poultry processing firms in the state.

Texas industry contributed greatly to the manufacture of refrigerants and refrigerating equipment. Among the products made in Texas were dry ice, industrial ice boxes, ice-making machinery, industrial ice-crushing machinery, household refrigerators, commercial and domestic air-conditioning units, and air-conditioner parts. Approximately two hundred ice-manufacturing plants were still operating in Texas in 1967. Instead of supplying ice to homes, as in the past, these plants provided ice for leisure-time activities, both public and private, and for various commercial operations. (For earlier account, *see* Refrigeration, Early History of, in Texas.)

BIBLIOGRAPHY: Oscar E. Anderson, Jr., *Refrigeration in America: A History of a New Technology and Its Impact* (1953); Charles T. Clark, "The Development of Refrigeration in Texas," *Texas Business Review* (November, 1966).

Charles T. Clark

*Refugio, Texas. Refugio, seat of Refugio County, was a commercial center for petroleum, ranching, and farming in the late 1960's. The town reported eleven churches, two newspapers, a hospital, a fifty-two-bed nursing home completed in 1966, three libraries, and a municipal swimming pool. The 1960 population was 4,944; the 1970 count was 4,340, according to the United States census report. Refugio had 112 businesses in 1970.

*Refugio, Battle of.

*Refugio County. Refugio County's economy was based on agriculture and petroleum in the 1960's. A number of large ranches were located in the northern part of the county, with the farming region located in the south. In 1971 there were four gins to handle that year's cotton crop of 6,379 bales. The county ranked tenth among Texas counties in oil production in 1961 and produced over seven hundred eighty million barrels of oil from 1928 to January 1, 1973. It rose to first among South Texas oil producing counties in 1970. The Aransas National Wildlife Refuge ᑫᵛ was located on the coast. The county also supported a library

and a hospital. The 1960 population, 10,975, had declined by 13.5 percent to 9,494 in 1970, according to the United States census.

*Refugio Mission. *See* Nuestra Señora del Refugio Mission.

*Regency, Texas. *See also* Hanna Valley, Texas.

*Regidor.

*Regulator-Moderator War.

Regulatory Loan Commissioner. The 1963 Texas Regulatory Loan Act created the office of regulatory loan commissioner. Appointed by the finance commission, he was responsible for the regulation of licensed agencies engaged in making loans of up to $1,500, and he could promulgate regulations to implement the act.

BIBLIOGRAPHY: Stuart A. McCorkle and Dick Smith, *Texas Government* (1964).

Dick Smith

Rehabilitation, Texas Commission for. The Texas Commission for Rehabilitation, composed of six members appointed by the governor, was created in 1969 to rehabilitate mentally and physically handicapped persons for employment and independence. In addition to vocational training, the commission provides counseling, financial assistance, and job placement. State aid for vocational rehabilitation was first available through the State Board of Vocational Education from 1929 to 1949, and through the Division of Vocational Education and Disability Determination of the Texas Education Agency ᑫᵛ from 1949 until the Texas Commission for Rehabilitation was established.

BIBLIOGRAPHY: University of Texas at Austin, *Guide To Texas State Agencies* (1972).

*Reid, Mayne.

*Reidville, Texas.

*Reiersen, Johan Reinert. Johan Reinert Reiersen was born in Vestre (West) Moland, Norway, April 17, 1810 (not April 19, 1810, as stated in Volume II), the son of Kirsten (Gjerulfsdatter) and Ole Reiersen, a country sexton of the Lutheran church. He studied at Arendal Middleskole in southern Norway and later was forced to leave the University of Christiania (present-day Oslo) in the early 1830's because of a "youthful indiscretion." Going to Copenhagen he edited magazines and made translations from German and French into Norwegian. On August 5, 1836, he married Henriette Christiane Waldt in Copenhagen, and they had at least five sons and two daughters.

By 1839 he was in Christiansand, Norway, where, with his brother Christian, he began publishing a liberal journal, *Christianssandsposten*, in which he urged immigration to America as a way of improving the lot of Norwegian laborers. Called the "apostle of temperance," he took a strong editorial stand against liquor. His paper supported public enlightenment, freedom of conscience, Christian toleration, and public spiritedness.

In the summer of 1843 he made a trip to the United States, arriving in New Orleans. After a visit to the Norwegian settlements in the Midwest, he visited in Texas with President Sam Houston, who encouraged his idea of a Norwegian immigration project. On his return to Norway he published, in 1844, an immigrant guide, *Veiviser for norske emigranter til de forenede nordamerikanske stater og Texas (Pathfinder for Norwegian Emigrants to the United North American States and Texas)*, which had a great influence on Norwegian immigration to the United States because of its highly favorable reports on agriculture, trade and industry, public lands, and the quality of American life. Reiersen began editing, along with his brother Christian, the monthly journal *Norge og Amerika (Norway and America)* before his second trip to America (not during his first trip, as implied in Volume II). He continued editing and writing for this journal after his return to America in the summer of 1845 with his father, sister, brother, a pastor and school teacher, a carpenter, and several other men. From Texas he sent back "Sketches from Western America" for the journal which was then edited by Elise (Tvede) Wærenskjold qv until Mrs. Wærenskjold joined the Reiersens in Texas in 1847. His writings from Texas were concerned with immigrant life, contrasting conditions in Norway with those in America, and he often printed letters from newly established settlers. A land certificate for 1,476 acres of Texas land, as well as a claim for a section of land, was acquired by Reiersen's group (there is no proof that his father, Ole Reiersen, acquired the patent, as stated in Volume II). The property was located and surveyed in Henderson County.

Johan established his first colony, Normandy, in late summer or early fall of 1845 near Brownsboro. After hiring an American to build a log house for his father, he returned to New Orleans to meet his newly arrived family, his wife and their four young sons, his mother, and another sister. Illness plagued the family; a baby daughter had died at sea, and a son later died in Shreveport. In the spring or summer of 1846 Reiersen was able to move his family to Normandy.

By the end of August, 1846, another company of emigrants arrived from Christiansand, and about fifty more arrived on Christmas Eve. Eleven of these families settled in the lowlands of the Neches River, despite Reiersen's admonition that the area was not conducive to good health. A number of the group died the following summer of "climate fever," and Reiersen had to go to Cherokee County for medicine for those who were ill. In the summer of 1847 a few more families arrived, some settling in Larissa, with his brother Christian's colony of Norwegians. On New Year's Day, 1848, Reiersen and his family moved to Four Mile Prairie, where he built a log house. He also founded the town of Prairieville near there. This was the foundation of the Norwegian settlements in Van Zandt and Kauf-

man counties, some thirty-six miles from the first colony at Normandy. More colonists came in 1850 and 1853, settling near Brownsboro (Normandy) and at Four Mile Prairie.

Reiersen's wife, Henriette Christiane, died in Prairieville in 1851 at the birth of another son; some time later he married Ouline Jacobine Ørbeck Reiersen, Christian Reiersen's widow. Johan Reinert Reiersen died on September 6, 1864, in Prairieville, and he was buried on his farm near there.

BIBLIOGRAPHY: Theodore C. Blegen, *Norwegian Migration to America* (1931); Theodore C. Blegen (ed.), *Land of Their Choice: The Immigrants Write Home* (1955); Theodore C. Blegen (ed.), "Behind the Scenes of Emigration: A Series of Letters from the 1840's," *Norwegian American Studies and Records*, XIV (1944); Olaf Morgan Norlie, *History of the Norwegian People in America* (1925); C. A. Clausen (ed.), *The Lady with the Pen: Elise Waerenskjold in Texas* (1961); *Dictionary of American Biography* (1943); *Who Was Who in America, 1607–1896* (1963).

*Reilly Springs, Texas.

*Reily, James.

*Reinhardt, Texas.

Reisdorff, Joseph. Joseph Reisdorff was born October 4, 1840, in Nievenheim, Rheinprovinz, Germany. He came to the United States, studied at St. Francis Seminary, Milwaukee, Wisconsin, and was ordained a priest on March 16, 1872. He was assigned to the Archdiocese of St. Louis, Missouri, before he came to Texas in search of a more healthful climate, arriving at the north-central town of Windthorst in Archer County on December 31, 1891. A colonizer, Fr. Reisdorff traveled west through the Texas Panhandle, establishing several towns in that area. In 1895 he was in Rhineland, Knox County; in 1902 he was in Nazareth, Castro County (for his contribution to that town, *see* Nazareth, Texas); by 1907 he was in Umbarger in Randall County.

Fr. Reisdorff was interested in his German countrymen's buying their own land at low prices and building their own homes. In each town he was influential in establishing a Catholic parish with a resident priest and in seeing that a growing community was established before he set out to work in another new settlement. Very often he would place ads in German-American newspapers, particularly in the Midwest, in order to attract settlers to the region.

After a career of moving from place to place, he settled in Slaton, Lubbock County, on December 8, 1911, where he was parish priest until 1917, when he went on sick leave. Fr. Reisdorff remained in Slaton until his death on January 28, 1922. He was buried in Jefferson City, Missouri.

BIBLIOGRAPHY: Charles P. Flanagin, Origins of Nazareth, Texas (M.A. thesis, West Texas State College, 1948); Castro County Diamond Jubilee, Inc., *History of the First Seventy-Five Years of Castro County, Texas, 1891–1966* (1966); Catholic Archives, Chancery Office, Austin.

*Reiser, Texas.

*Reiter, Max.

*Rek Hill, Texas. [This title was incorrectly listed in Volume II as Reks Hill, Texas.] Since the mid-1940's the Texas State Highway Department qv has used the name Rek Hill on both their maps and signs. There was an early German settler by the name of Reck in the vicinity of Fayetteville in Fayette County, and the community may have been named for this family, although the spelling is slightly different.

Walter P. Freytag

*Reklaw, Texas.

Relampago, Texas. Relampago, in the southeast corner of Hidalgo County, has at various times been the headquarters of the Mora Tract, location of a brick-manufacturing plant, and more recently the site for Rosenthal Farms, Inc. Relampago was founded around 1900. Its population was estimated to be over two hundred in the late 1960's. Farm labor was the chief occupation of the inhabitants.

*Reliance, Texas.

Relics. Relics, a magazine published in Austin by Western Publications, Inc.,qv began as a quarterly in 1967 and became a bi-monthly publication in 1969. Available by subscription only, it had a national circulation of 15,000 in 1971.

Though devoted primarily to frontier relics and artifacts, and to public and private collections of western Americana, it does not exclude any item of American origin. Joe Austell Small was publisher and Robert Stout was editor in 1971.

Pat Wagner

*Remlig, Texas.

*Remount, Texas.

*Rendham, Texas.

*Renner, Texas.

*Reno, Texas. (Lamar County.)

*Reno, Texas. (Parker County.)

*Renova, Texas.

Rentfro, Robert Byron. Robert Byron Rentfro was born on September 25, 1874, in Montgomery County, the son of Robert Byron and Laura (Linton) Rentfro. In 1880 his family moved to Brownsville. He attended Texas Agricultural and Mechanical College (now Texas A&M University), Southwestern University, and the University of Texas law school, receiving his LL.B. degree in 1896. He practiced law with his father in Brownsville, and in 1904 he married Eleanor Russell.

Rentfro served as county attorney for Cameron County, deputy collector for the U.S. Bureau of Customs, and postmaster of Brownsville from 1907 to 1912. In 1920 he was elected to the Brownsville city commission, then was elected mayor in 1929, serving five consecutive two-year terms; thereafter, he served as city attorney for many years. Rentfro played an important role in the establishment of the Brownsville Navigation District. The deepwater port facilities at Brownsville, the district's principal objective, were completed and dedicated on May 14–16, 1936. Rentfro participated in most water control and development projects in the Lower Rio Grande Valley during his public career. He died on April 19, 1953, in Brownsville.

Eleanor Russell Rentfro

*Republic of the Rio Grande.

*Republic of Texas.

*Republican Party in Texas. With the founding of the Republican Club of Texas in 1947 by Captain J. F. Lucey of Dallas, a drive was initiated to build a potent Republican party in the state, and the party has grown steadily since that time. Dwight D. Eisenhower qv carried Texas in the 1952 presidential election, when many Democrats joined with Republicans over the tidelands controversy.qv In the same election Allan Shivers polled over 400,000 votes for governor as a Republican as a result of a unique cross-filing system which enabled Democratic candidates for state office also to run as Republicans (*see* Election Laws).

Two years later Bruce Alger of Dallas was elected as a Republican to the Eighty-fourth Congress and to four successive Congresses. Again with the help of conservative Democrats, the Republicans carried Texas for Eisenhower in 1956, although the Democrats won all the state offices. In 1960 Republican Richard M. Nixon received 1,122,323 votes to 1,168,230 for John F. Kennedy in a close race for the electoral votes of Texas. In this same election John G. Tower of Wichita Falls got over 900,000 votes as a candidate for the United States Senate against Lyndon B. Johnson,qv who was running both for the vice-presidency and the Senate. When Johnson resigned his seat in the Senate to become vice-president of the United States, Tower was elected to replace him in the special election which followed in 1961, defeating interim Senator William A. Blakley of Dallas. Tower thus became the first Republican to hold statewide elective office since Edmund Jackson Davis qv was elected governor during Reconstruction in Texas.qv

The party made a particularly strong showing in 1962, when Ed Foreman of Odessa won election to Congress, bringing the number of Republicans representing Texas in Washington to three. The party's gubernatorial candidate, Jack Cox, made a strong, though losing, race against John Connally, and seven Republicans were elected to the lower house of the state legislature, although none were elected to the more powerful Texas Senate. A nonbinding presidential preferential primary, held by the Republican party for the first time in 1964, reflecting overwhelming support for Arizona's Senator Barry Goldwater. In the general election, however, the great popularity of President Johnson as a native son cancelled out what few gains the party had made in the recent past. Congressmen Alger and Foreman both were defeated in their bids for reelection, and only one Republican, Frank Cahoon of Midland, was returned to the state legislature.

The election of 1966 was encouraging to the Republican party, for Senator Tower was reelected to his first full-length term by a majority of approximately 200,000 votes. Two Republicans were elected to the U.S. House of Representatives, three to the lower house of the state legislature, and the first Republican in thirty-nine years was elected to the Texas Senate. In 1968 Richard M. Nixon narrowly missed carrying Texas in his Republican bid for president, receiving 1,227,844 votes to Hubert H. Humphrey's 1,266,804. Republican Paul Eggers received over one million votes for governor in both 1968 and 1970, but was defeated both times by Preston Smith.

Three Republicans were elected to the U.S. House of Representatives in 1968, and they retained these three seats in 1970. In the state legislature two Republicans were elected to the Senate both in 1968 and 1970; nine Republicans were elected to the House in 1968 and ten in 1970. In the general election of 1970, Republican Congressman George Bush was defeated by Democrat Lloyd Bentsen for the U.S. Senate by a vote of 1,071,234 to 1,226,568, although Bush, along with Republican candidate for governor Paul Eggers, carried both Harris and Dallas counties, the two most populous counties in the state. In 1972 Republican President Richard M. Nixon carried Texas with 2,298,896 votes, as opposed to 1,154,289 for his Democratic opponent, George McGovern. In that same year Republican Senator John Tower was reelected over Democratic nominee Barefoot Sanders, and Republican Henry C. Grover, although defeated by Democrat Dolph Briscoe, received more votes than any other Republican candidate for governor in the history of Texas. Further gains by Republicans were made in the Texas legislature in 1972, when seventeen were elected to the House and three were elected to the Senate; these gains were consolidated in 1974, when sixteen Republicans were elected to the House and the same three Republican senators were returned to the Texas Senate. See also Political Parties.

BIBLIOGRAPHY: Paul D. Casdorph, A History of the Republican Party in Texas, 1865–1965 (1965).

Paul D. Casdorph

*Resaca Creek.

*Resaca de los Cuates.

*Resaca de los Fresnos.

*Resaca Guerra.

*Resaca de la Palma, Battle of.

*Resley Creek.

*Retama, Texas.

*Retamia Creek.

Retreat, Texas. Retreat, in Navarro County south of Corsicana, had a 1970 population of 263, according to the United States census.

*Retrieve Plantation.

*Retta, Texas.

*Reubes Creek.

*Reverchon, Julien.

*Revolution, Texas War of. See Texas Revolution.

*Rexville, Texas.

*Reynolds, George Thomas.

*Reynolds, Joseph Jones.

*Reynolds, William D.

*Reynolds, Texas.

*Reynolds Branch.

*Reynolds Creek.

*Reynolds Presbyterian College.

Rhea, Texas. Rhea, in northwestern Parmer County near the Texas-New Mexico state line, had a 1970 estimated population of ninety-eight.

*Rhea Mills, Texas.

*Rhem, Texas.

*Rhineland, Texas.

Rhoads, Joseph J. Joseph J. Rhoads was born in Marshall, Harrison County, on October 30, 1890, the son of Dennis Collins and Mary J. Rhoads. He was graduated from Central High School of Marshall with first honors in 1906; he received a B.S. degree from Bishop College with the highest honor of the class of 1910. Rhoads then served as assistant principal of the H. B. Pemberton High School in Marshall from 1910 to 1918. In 1918 he was married to Lucile O. Bridge. The following year he became an instructor at Tuskegee Institute and remained there until 1922, when he went to Yale as a student for one year. He returned to Texas in 1923 and was principal of the Booker T. Washington High School in Dallas from 1923 to 1929.

In 1929 Rhoads became the sixth president of Bishop College, the first black and alumnus of that college to head it. Located in Marshall, Rhoads distinguished himself as an educator, administrator, and militant leader for civil rights during a tenure that lasted from 1929 to 1951. In 1935 he received an M.A. degree from the University of Michigan. As president of the Texas Council of Negro Organizations and chairman of the Texas Commission on Democracy in Education, Rhoads fought for equality of opportunity for all citizens and equal salaries for black teachers in Texas. He established the Dallas branch of Bishop College, which opened in 1947, laying the foundation for the eventual move of the institution from Marshall to Dallas in 1961. The J. J. Rhoads Education Building on the new campus was named for him. Joseph J. Rhoads died October 9, 1951, and was buried in Marshall.

BIBLIOGRAPHY: Who's Who In Colored America (1950); Who's Who In America (1950).

Roland C. Hayes

*Rhoda Lake.

*Rhome, Texas.

Rhonesboro, Texas. Rhonesboro, in western Upshur County, was founded about 1900. At one time the town, with a population of five hundred, had a railroad depot, a hotel, a bank, a gin, a post office, a school, a church, and numerous businesses, but by the middle 1960's Rhonesboro reported one store and a service station. Most of the inhabitants of the area farmed, ranched, or commuted to work in Longview. The population was forty in 1970.

*Ricardo, Texas.

*Rice, James O. James O. Rice was married on November 3, 1846, to Nancy D. Gilliland.

Lucie C. Price

*Rice, Jonas Shearn.

*Rice, William Marsh. William Marsh Rice died on September 23, 1900 (not 1896, as stated in Volume II). [Some later printings of Volume II contain this correction.]

*Rice, Texas. Appointed on October 2, 1872, the first postmaster of Rice, in Navarro County, was Joseph Callaway Bartlett (not L. B. Haynie, as stated in Volume II), according to United States Post Office records, National Archives, General Services Division, Washington, D.C.

Roger A. Bartlett

*Rice Creek.

*Rice Culture. In 1970 Texas ranked a close second to Arkansas in rice production among the five states of the southern rice belt, which also included Louisiana, Mississippi, and Missouri. These states, plus California, produced almost 99 percent of the United States rice crop. Many of the rice-producing farms are in coastal areas, within trucking distance of deepwater ports where the rice is exported. The United States has ranked among the world's leading rice exporters, although it has had less than 2 percent of the world's rice acreage. Largest exports in 1968–1970 were to South Vietnam and Indonesia, with approximately three billion pounds shipped to each of those countries.

In the three decades from 1940 to 1970 the rice yield per acre in Texas more than doubled, from over two thousand pounds to over four thousand pounds per acre. The largest rice production, a record 25,408,282-hundredweight harvest, occurred in 1968; the highest per-acre harvest of 5,004 pounds per acre was in 1967. Rice farmers in 1970 produced a total of 20,782,000 hundredweight of rice from 467,000 acres harvested, for a $108 million crop, third only to cotton and grain sorghums as a moneymaking crop in Texas.

In 1970 Wharton County was the largest rice producer in the state, with a production of over three million hundredweight; Jefferson, Matagorda, and Brazoria each produced over two million hundredweight, as the next leading rice-producing counties in that order, followed by Chambers, Liberty, Colorado, Jackson, Harris, and Fort Bend counties, each producing over one million hundredweight. In the 1970's there was a limited early harvest beginning in late July and ending in early October, with peak harvest during August. The second cutting was from early October to early December with peak harvest during November.

In addition to the grain drill method still being used for planting, airplanes have been used exten-sively since the 1950's to plant, fertilize, and apply insecticides and herbicides. The farms are highly mechanized. New varieties of rice were being planted in the 1960's and 1970's. The top two long grain varieties of the five produced were Bluebelle and Belle Patna; others were Dawn, Starbonnet, and Patna. The only two medium grain varieties produced were Nato and Saturn. Texas did not raise any short grain varieties in 1970. Research in all phases of rice culture was being carried on near Beaumont at the Agriculture Research and Extension division of Texas A&M University. In 1959, after years of declining rice consumption in the United States, members of the rice industry of Arkansas, Louisiana, Mississippi, and Texas formed the Rice Council. Since that time, through the council's promotional work, rice consumption in the United States has risen from 6.1 pounds per capita in 1959 to 8.3 pounds per capita in 1968.

The Texas counties reporting rice production were divided into three groups, all on the coastal prairie: the east group consisted of Jefferson, Chambers, Liberty, Orange, Hardin, and Newton counties; the central group included Brazoria, Harris, Fort Bend, Waller, and Galveston counties; and in the west group were Wharton, Matagorda, Colorado, Jackson, Calhoun, Lavaca, Victoria, Austin, and Bowie counties. In 1970 the west group planted the largest acreage of Bluebelle and Belle Patna rice varieties, and the east group planted the largest in Nato and Dawn varieties. Rice yields in Texas have increased during the last decade because of the use of early maturing varieties with high yield potential, chemical grass control, utilization of fertilizer, and stubble-cropping practices.

Saleable by-products obtained from rice are rice hulls, used for fine abrasives, hand soap, synthetics, and commercial fertilizers; rice bran, which is high in niacin, for livestock and poultry feed; rice oil, extracted from rice bran, for a low cholesterol cooking oil; rice polish, which has a high vitamin content, used as a highly digestible livestock feed (and coming into use for human consumption); rice flour, a non-allergenic product for baking; and rice straw, a roughage feed for cattle and bedding for livestock. After harvest, large numbers of migrating coastal ducks, geese, and other waterfowl feed on the rice crop residue, and rice farmers have additional revenue from hunting leases.

Today's rice-milling procedures produce several types of rice for the consumer market: regular milled white rice, mineral-rich brown rice, par-boiled rice, and pre-cooked rice. With the influx of convenience foods, rice can now be purchased cooked, uncooked, wet, dry, frozen, and packaged in pre-mixed dishes. Rice is also used in the brewing industry in place of barley or corn. Business operations other than farming which are a part of the rice industry are rice mills, rice dryers, and irrigation and canal companies.

BIBLIOGRAPHY: Rice Council, *American Rice . . . in the Diet* (January, 1970), *Facts about American Rice* (n.d.), *What Is the Rice Council?* (n.d.); Rice Millers' Association, *Rice Acreage in the United States, 1970* (n.d.), *Rice Production in the United States, 1970* (n.d.); Texas Department of Agriculture and United States Department of Agriculture, *Texas Field Crop Statistics, 1970* (1971); U.S. Department of Agriculture, *Rice Situation*, RS-17 (March, 1971).

*Rice University. Rice University became the new name for Rice Institute in July, 1960, and in 1962 the institution celebrated the fiftieth anniversary of its opening. The quadrangle with the statue of founder William Marsh Rice qv in the center was still the nucleus of academic life, although over a dozen new buildings were added to the campus after 1950, including a stadium, a building to house the new graduate program in space science, and a nuclear laboratory. Numerous undergraduate and graduate courses were added to the curriculum.

There were two women's and six men's residential colleges, each having its own government and college master. Enrollment expanded from 1,509 students during the 1950–1951 term, to 3,525 in the fall term of 1974. The faculty grew from 108 in 1950 to 325 in 1970, when the student-faculty ratio was ten to one. The endowment was over $114 million in mid-1970. For the first time in its history Rice charged tuition in September, 1965, and students were admitted without regard to race, religion, or creed. There were 441 baccalaureate, 144 masters, and 122 Ph.D. degrees awarded in 1970. The total number of degrees awarded from 1916 to 1970 was 16,192.

The university's Fondren Library had a total of 622,110 volumes in 1970, including 8,380 art volumes acquired in that year. An item of special interest at Rice was one of the world's largest collections of Beethoven biographical materials; the library also housed one of the country's largest collections of Austrian and Austro-Hungarian historical materials. Student publications were the *Thresher, Campanile, Rice Engineer*, and others. University publications included *Architecture at Rice, Austrian History Yearbook, Rice University Review, Rice University Studies*, and *Studies in English Literature 1500–1900*. Three journals with editorial offices on campus were *High Temperature Science, Journal of the Electrochemical Society*, and *Journal of Southern History*. The Jefferson Davis Association, with headquarters at Rice, sponsored the collection, compilation, and editing of the Jefferson Davis papers for a projected twenty-volume series.

A 1969 addition to the fine arts department was the formation of the Institute for the Arts, under the directorship of Dominique de Menil. The new center sponsored film-making, photography, art lectures, and changing exhibitions ranging from classical art to modern art and other cultural media. On extended loan to Rice from the de Menil Foundation were paintings, sculptures, drawings, prints, posters, and rare books.

With the end of William Vermillion Houston's term as president in 1960, Carey Croneis qv became acting president for one year and then the university's first chancellor in 1961. Kenneth Sanborn Pitzer assumed the office of president from 1961 to 1968. Frank Everson Vandiver followed as acting president for 1969, and Norman C. Hackerman assumed the presidency in 1970.

*Riceland, Texas.

*Rice's Crossing, Texas.

*Rich Lake.

*Richards, Texas. (Grimes County.)

*Richards, Texas. (San Saba County.)

*Richards Creek.

*Richardson, Chauncey.

Richardson, Daniel Long. Daniel Long Richardson was born about 1793 and came to Sabine County, Texas, from Hancock County, Georgia, probably in 1833. He settled with his family in the area where Sabinetown was later located. A man of considerable means, he lived with his family on a large plantation and held at various times between fifty and one hundred slaves. He was married to Mary J. Ponce, also of Georgia, and they had three daughters, one of whom married David Spangler Kaufman,qv and another of whom married Franklin Barlow Sexton.qv Richardson served in the Texas Army qv from March 17 to December 19, 1836, first in Captain Henry Teal's qv company and then with Jacob Snively.qv He received a bounty warrant for his service.

Of unique interest is Richardson's purchase from George Campbell Childress qv on January 27 and 28, 1838, at Milam, Texas, the latter's headright certificate for one league and one labor of land for "one thousand dollars in hand paid."

Richardson died in Sabine County in the early part of 1849 and was buried in the cemetery at Sabinetown. The inventory of his estate included thousands of acres of land in as many as twenty-one counties, fifty-two slaves, a dwelling house, gin house, blacksmith shop, grist mill, kitchen, stables, corn cribs, farm goods, cattle, oxen, wagons, and other implements. Cash divided among four heirs amounted to approximately $120,000.

BIBLIOGRAPHY: Sam Houston Dixon and Louis Wiltz Kemp, *The Heroes of San Jacinto* (1932); Mary S. Estill, "The Education of Anna Kaufman," *Texana* (Fall, 1966); J. K. Greer, "The Committee on the Texan Declaration of Independence," *Southwestern Historical Quarterly*, XXXI (1927–1928); Daniel Long Richardson Will, Probate Court Records, Sabine County.

Mary S. Estill
Helen Gomer Schluter

*Richardson, David.

*Richardson, George F.

Richardson, Sid Williams. Sid Richardson was born on April 25, 1891, in Athens, Texas, the son of John Isidore and Nancy [Nannie] (Bradley) Richardson. He started his business career early, earning $3,500 by cattle trading while still a senior in high school in 1908. He attended Baylor University and Simmons College (now Hardin-Simmons University) for about eighteen months, then quit to become a salesman for an oil well supply company, an oil scout, and a lease purchaser; although he remained interested in the cattle business and ranching, his main concern was the oil industry. He became an independent oil producer in Fort Worth in 1919.

His finances fluctuated widely, and he accumulated wealth and lost it several times during the 1920's. He was well established as a millionaire by 1935, when he opened up the rich Keystone Oil Field in Winkler County. From his suite of offices in Fort Worth he individually leased more oil land than did several major oil companies; operated three cattle ranches; and owned the Texas State Network (a radio and television organization), a carbon black plant at Odessa, and the Texas City Refining Company. In 1936 he purchased St. Joseph's Island off the Texas coast, and he resided there when he wasn't in Fort Worth. In 1954, with his longtime friend Clinton Williams Murchison,qv he backed fellow Texan Robert Ralph Young qv in a successful fight to control the New York Central Railroad, buying 800,000 shares worth $20,000,000.

The public seldom knew of Richardson's business activities, and few knew what he looked like, for he rarely talked to reporters and did not like publicity. In politics he was a confidant of President Franklin D. Roosevelt, advising him at times during World War II in affairs concerning oil production. In 1952 he helped persuade his friend, General Dwight D. Eisenhower,qv to run for president, being one of the original "Ike for President" boosters. In 1956, however, he returned to the Democrats after the president vetoed a natural gas bill. Richardson never publicized his large contributions to civic groups, churches, libraries, and especially to Boys, Incorporated, a California organization for helping boys. On July 7, 1947, he established the Sid W. Richardson Foundation, designed to aid churches, hospitals, and schools in Texas. Richardson was considered one of the wealthiest men in the nation; some estimates of his worth ranged up to $800 million, and he was often referred to as the "bachelor billionaire."

He died apparently of a heart attack on September 30, 1959, at his St. Joseph's Island ranch home. He was buried at Athens, Texas, and many dignitaries attended the funeral, including Lyndon B. Johnson, Sam Rayburn,qqv and evangelist Billy Graham, who conducted the services. The Sid W. Richardson Foundation presented to the University of Texas at Austin a two-million-dollar gift to increase its holdings of the History of Science Collection, one of the most distinguished collections in the world, now housed in the Harry Ransom Humanities Research Center. In appreciation, the university named the new building adjacent to the Lyndon Baines Johnson Library qv the Sid W. Richardson Hall. The building, on the campus of the university, was dedicated on January 21, 1971; it houses the Lyndon B. Johnson School of Public Affairs, the Eugene C. Barker Texas History Center,

the Latin American Collection, and the Texas State Historical Association.qqv

BIBLIOGRAPHY: Austin American, October 1, 1959; Who's Who In America (1956); Biographical File, Barker Texas History Center, University of Texas at Austin.

Ben Procter

*Richardson, Stephen.

Richardson, Thomas Clarence. Thomas Clarence Richardson was born on March 25, 1877, near Cisco in Eastland County, the son of A. J. and Sarah Ann (Latham) Richardson. He attended schools in Crowell and Quanah, a teacher's normal school in Mangum, Oklahoma, and, for a short time, Texas A&M College (now Texas A&M University). He held teaching certificates from Oklahoma and Texas and was a country school teacher from 1897 to 1904. Beginning a long period of small town newspaper publishing, he founded the Wheeler County Texan, at Storey, in 1903, the Shamrock Texan in 1904, and acquired, edited, or published several others, including the Sutherland Springs Health Resort, the Floresville Advocate, and the Seadrift Success; he worked on the San Angelo Standard in 1917 and on the Bryan Daily Eagle in 1918.

In 1918 Richardson joined the extension staff of Texas A&M and became the agricultural agent for Cameron County, but he later left to operate his own farm and to manage a seed plantation. In 1923 he returned to agricultural writing; he was the first editor of Valley Farmer and Citrus Grower and a member of the editorial staffs of Farm and Ranch and Holland's Magazine.qv In 1934 he submitted to the Texas legislature the first tentative bill on the organization of soil conservation districts. After joining the staff of the Farmer-Stockman in 1943, Richardson eventually became associate editor. He wrote innumerable articles on agricultural subjects, the four-volume East Texas, Its History and Its Makers (1940), and Autobiography of the Rambling Longhorn (1959). He was a widely known and respected authority on old cattle trails in the Southwest.

Richardson was involved in the founding of at least two organizations, the Dallas Agricultural Club and the Texas Agricultural Workers Association. He was a member of the Texas Academy of Science, Texas State Historical Association, Southwestern Social Science Association,qqv and the National Agricultural History Society. In 1901 he was married to Dora Sutton of Mangum, Oklahoma; they had two daughters. Richardson died in Palestine, Texas, on November 21, 1956, and was buried at Colorado City, Texas.

BIBLIOGRAPHY: Thomas Clarence Richardson, Autobiography of the Rambling Longhorn (1959), East Texas, Its History and Its Makers, IV (1940); Texas Press Messenger, June, 1954.

Sam Whitlow

*Richardson, Walter Raleigh.

*Richardson, Wilds Preston.

*Richardson, Willard.

*Richardson, William.

*Richardson, Texas. Richardson, in Dallas and Collin counties, was largely a residential city and electronics center in the 1960's. Site of the Graduate Research Center of the Southwest (now the University of Texas at Dallas), Richardson reported twenty-one schools, eighteen churches, three parks, two banks, a library, and active theatrical and symphony groups in the mid-1960's. Among the businesses there were those manufacturing electronics equipment, industrial machinery, clothing, feeds, fertilizers, and aluminum and food products. The 1960 census listed 16,810 persons, but by 1970 the population had risen to 48,582, an increase of 189 percent, according to the United States census. *See also* Dallas Standard Metropolitan Statistical Area.

*Richardson Creek.

*Richerson Lake.

*Richland, Texas. (Bee County.)

*Richland, Texas. (Hopkins County.)

*Richland, Texas. (Navarro County.)

Richland, Texas. (Rains County.) Richland, in northern Rains County, is a small rural community. Most of the approximately one hundred inhabitants in the 1960's were farmers.

*Richland County.

*Richland Creek.

*Richland Creek, Texas.

Richland Hills, Texas. Richland Hills, an incorporated town in Tarrant County northeast of the Fort Worth metropolitan area, had a population of 7,804 in 1960 and 8,865 in 1970, according to the U.S. census report. *See also* Fort Worth Standard Metropolitan Statistical Area.

*Richland Springs, Texas.

*Richmond, Texas. The choice of the name Richmond for the early settlement in Fort Bend County evidently was made by Henry Jones,qv who named it after his birthplace, Richmond, Virginia. Henry Jones and Randal Jones qv were not brothers (as stated in Volume II), but were distantly related by marriage only. Randal Jones was born in Columbus County, Georgia.

Richmond, seat of Fort Bend County, adjoins the larger town of Rosenberg. In the early 1970's its economy was based on marketing and mineral-based industries. Canned foods, mixed feeds, oil field equipment and supplies, salt, sulphur, and steel products were among the commodities produced. Cottonseed processing was another important local industry. Richmond shared a county library with Rosenberg and was the site of the Richmond State School,qv which opened in April, 1968. The 1960 population of Richmond was 3,668; by 1970 the population had increased to 5,777, a 57.5 percent increase, according to the United States census. *See also* Houston Standard Metropolitan Statistical Area.

*Richmond Male and Female Academy.

Richmond State School. Richmond State School was opened in April, 1968, as a state school facility of the Texas Department of Mental Health and Mental Retardation.qv Located in Richmond, the school offered an intensive daily physical therapy treatment program in 1970 that resulted in improvement in 92 percent of the eighty multihandicapped children involved. The school received $21,426 from the Vocational Education Grant through the Texas Education Agency qv for twenty-two girls in the vocational homemaking program and sixteen boys in the building and grounds maintenance program. Expanded medical and dental programs have improved the basic daily care of the residents. Census at the end of 1970 was 501, and the superintendent was H. Russell White. *See* Mentally Ill and Mentally Retarded, Care of, in Texas.

BIBLIOGRAPHY: Texas Department of Mental Health and Mental Retardation, *Annual Report, 1970* (n.d.).

*Richmond *Telescope.*

Richwood, Texas. Richwood, an incorporated town located in southeast Brazoria County between Freeport and Angleton, had a population of 649 in 1960 and 1,452 in 1970, a 123.7 percent increase in population, according to the United States census.

*Rickard, George L.

*Ricker, Texas.

*Ricord, John.

Riddleville, Texas. *See* Gillett, Texas.

*Ridge, Texas. (Mills County.)

*Ridge, Texas. (Robertson County.)

*Ridgeway, Texas.

*Riesel, Texas.

*Rigaud, Antoine.

Rights of Man.

Riker, Thad Weed. Thad Weed Riker was born on November 2, 1880, in Stamford, Connecticut, the son of Thaddeus Weed and Louise Draper (Nesbitt) Riker. He received B.A. and M.A. degrees from Princeton University in 1903 and 1904; during those years Riker was a special Fellow in Latin at Princeton. In 1908 he received a B.Litt. degree from Oxford University, England, and in 1935 was awarded a D.Litt. from Oxford. He married Fannie Rhea Preston on June 2, 1923; they had two children.

He was an instructor in English history at Cornell University for the 1908–1909 academic year before coming to the University of Texas in 1909 as an instructor in modern European history. He was promoted to adjunct professor in 1913, associate professor in 1917, and professor in 1923. He was a member of the organization committee on education training in the War Plans Division, general staff, in World War I. Riker also served as visiting professor of modern history at the University of Chicago from 1931 to 1932, and as special research professor at the University of Texas in 1941.

He was the author of several books and articles, including *Henry Fox, First Lord Holland* (1911), *The Making of Roumania* (1931), *A Short History of Modern Europe* (1935), *The Story of Modern Europe* (1942), and *A History of Modern Europe* (1948). Riker was a member of the board of editors of the *Journal of Modern History* from 1928 to 1932, serving as acting editor from 1931 to 1932. He was also a member of the board of editors of the *American Historical Review* from 1943 to 1948. Riker retired from the university in 1951. He died in Austin on February 17, 1952, and was cremated in San Antonio.

BIBLIOGRAPHY: *Who's Who In America* (1950); Austin *American*, February 18, 1952; University of Texas, Documents and Minutes of the General Faculty, 1954; Biographical File, Barker Texas History Center, University of Texas at Austin.

*Riley Mountains.

*Rim Peak.

*Rinard Creek.

Rincon del Peñascal. *See* Point Peñascal.

Ring, Elizabeth L. Elizabeth L. Ring, daughter of Henry and Elizabeth L. Fitzsimmons, was born in Houston on October 31, 1857. She attended Miss Brown's Young Ladies' Boarding and Day School during the 1870's. On February 14, 1880, she was married to Henry F. Ring; they had two sons. Mrs. Ring began her career as a pioneer club woman in 1887 when she became a member of the Ladies' Reading Club and took an active part in securing better library facilities for Houston. She was also instrumental in the formation of the City Federation of Women's Clubs, and was on the state board of the Texas Federation of Women's Clubs.qv

Before the turn of the century, the Texas Federation of Women's Clubs selected her as chairman of the library committee which eventually succeeded in securing state support for rural libraries; this committee also aided in establishing traveling libraries, urged the creation of a Department of Library Science at the University of Texas, and asked for the appointment by the governor of a state library commission. She also served on committees which worked for better working conditions for women and children, for better educational and recreational facilities, and for prison reform. From 1900 she was a trustee of the Carnegie Library, later the Houston Public Library. As a trustee for the Houston Foundation, beginning in 1918, she was influential in the creation of the city recreation bureau. In 1929 she was appointed to the board of regents for Texas State College for Women (now Texas Woman's University) and served until her death. Mrs. Ring died while on vacation in Alpine, Texas, on September 8, 1941, and was buried in Glenwood Cemetery in Houston.

BIBLIOGRAPHY: Biographical File, Barker Texas History Center, University of Texas at Austin; *Texian Who's Who* (1937).

Mrs. Roland Ring

*Ringgold, Texas.

*Ringgold Barracks. *See* Fort Ringgold.

*Ringgold Creek.

*Ringness, Jens. Jens Olsen Ringness was not the inventor of the disc plow (as stated in Volume II), but rather it was his son, Ole Ringness,qv who conceived, built, and journeyed east to make a case for his invention (*see* article following). Jens Olsen Ringness located his family in Neil (not Neill's) Creek Valley, west of Clifton, Texas.

BIBLIOGRAPHY: Axel Arneson, "Norwegian Settlements in Texas," *Southwestern Historical Quarterly*, XLV (1941–1942).

Ringness, Ole. Ole Ringness was born in Løiten, Norway, on October 14, 1843, the son of Kari (Jensdatter Halstenhav) and Jens Olsen Ringness.qv The family emigrated from Norway in the fall of 1851 and arrived at Johan Reinert Reiersen's qv settlement of Prairieville in 1852, where the youngest of the four Ringness children and Ole's widowed grandmother died of typhoid fever. Continuing fever and drouth forced the family and a number of other Norwegian settlers to locate in Bosque County, west of Clifton on Neil Creek in 1854.

Ole, the first mail carrier in the community, made a regular four-day round-trip between Norman Hills post office, about seven miles west of Clifton, and Fort Worth. He was never married but bought a lot at Kimball Bend on the Brazos where his mail route crossed the river, envisioning a growing town there. He also worked on the family farm, where he observed the wheels of his conveyance cup plow being pulled through the heavy soil. He conceived the idea of a disc plow and disc harrow and made models of them successfully in his father's blacksmith shop.

In 1872 he left his home near Norse for a trip east to present his case for the patent, taking a sizeable amount of money with him for a planned trip to Norway also. His father received word from a Masonic lodge in New York that Ole had died and had been buried there by the lodge. His death occurred under mysterious circumstances, presumed to be related to the fact that he was carrying a large sum of money. The place of his burial is not known, but the date of his death is given as July 26, 1872.

The family never pursued the obtaining of a patent for Ole Ringness' invention of the disc plow and harrow, and the idea was later patented by a plow company. A model of the Ole Ringness plow, said to be one of three originals, is in the Texas Memorial Museum qv in Austin.

BIBLIOGRAPHY: Axel Arneson, "Norwegian Settlements in Texas," *Southwestern Historical Quarterly*, XLV (1941–1942).

Mrs. S. M. Ringness

*Ringwood Female Seminary.

*Rio Bravo. *See* Rio Grande.

*Rio Cibolo.

Rio Colorado Indians. In the seventeenth century Rio Colorado was the New Mexico Spanish name for the Canadian River of present New Mexico and Texas. Certain Indians on this river became known as Rio Colorado Indians. It is clear that they were Apache, and it seems likely that they formed one of the early Lipan-Apache bands of northwestern Texas and northeastern New Mexico.
BIBLIOGRAPHY: A. H. Schroeder, *A Study of the Apache Indians: The Mescalero Apache* (1960); A. B. Thomas, *After Coronado* (1935).

T. N. Campbell

*Rio Frio, Texas.

*Rio Grande.

Rio Grande Bible Institute and Language School. The Rio Grande Bible Institute and Language School, Edinburg, first began operation in 1946 as a private coeducational institution under the direction of M. C. Ehlert, president. It was founded as an evangelical, interdenominational training school primarily preparing missionaries for work in Mexico and Latin America. In 1955 the institute added a missionary language course. The administration, faculty, and staff served as missionaries and did not receive salaries.

The school offered the missionary language course, a three-year Bible course, and a Bachelor of Theology degree. The school was approved by the Texas Education Agency qv for the training of veterans, and by the United States Department of Justice, which permitted the school to receive foreign students.

In 1967 there were twelve faculty members, sixteen staff members, and nine co-workers in Mexico. The institute's library contained 3,832 volumes, and the student enrollment for the regular 1966–1967 term was 104. In the 1972–1973 term the enrollment was 165, with a faculty of fifteen. Leonard C. Hanes served as president of the institution in 1973.

*Rio Grande Boundary. *See also* Boundaries of Texas; Chamizal Dispute.

*Rio Grande Campaign.

*Rio Grande City, Texas. Rio Grande City, seat of Starr County, relied on petroleum, ranching, cotton, vegetables, and grain and hay crops for its income. The International Falcon Reservoir,qv dedicated in 1953, furnished water for crop irrigation. Historic Fort Ringgold qv was acquired by the Rio Grande City Independent School District. During the 1960's the city had businesses concerned with petroleum, clay, and food products, and in 1970, 110 businesses were reported. The 1960 population was 5,835; the 1970 population was 5,676, according to the United States census. *See also* Camargo, Mexico.

*Rio Grande City Railway Company.

*Rio Grande Compact.

*Rio Grande and Eagle Pass Railroad Company.

*Rio Grande, El Paso, and Santa Fe Railroad Company.

*Rio Grande Female Institute. [This title was incorrectly listed in Volume II as Rio Grande Female Seminary.] Presbytery records indicate that a school continued to operate after the death of Hiram Chamberlain,qv until 1875. By 1897 all school work was discontinued, and the buildings were loaned to the Foreign Mission Committee of the Presbyterian Church, United States, for eighteen years. *See* Presbyterian Education in Texas.
BIBLIOGRAPHY: William Stuart Red, *A History of the Presbyterian Church in Texas* (1936).

Malcolm L. Purcell

*Rio Grande Flood Control. The construction of river and floodway levees, begun in December, 1933, was completed in 1951. Under the provisions of the 1944 water treaty, Falcon Dam (*see* International Falcon Reservoir) was constructed jointly by the United States and Mexico from 1950 to 1954, eighty miles southeast of Laredo. The United States' share of the cost was $35,000,000. United States flood control benefits by 1966 were estimated at $220,000,000.

Construction of the international Amistad Dam (*see* Amistad Reservoir), twelve miles northwest of Del Rio, was begun in August, 1963, and completed in 1968; it was dedicated by President Richard M. Nixon and Mexico's President Gustavo Díaz Ordaz on September 8, 1969. The United States share of the cost was about $72,000,000, including rights-of-way and railroad and highway relocations. In combination with Falcon Dam the Amistad structure provided virtually complete flood protection from Rio Grande floods originating above Falcon Dam.

J. F. Friedkin

*Rio Grande Micolithic and Northern Railway.

*Rio Grande Northern Railroad.

Rio Grande Railroad. *See* Port Isabel and Rio Grande Valley Railway.

*Rio Grande Rectification Project. The program of supplemental construction, begun in 1946, was completed in 1950. *See* Chamizal Dispute.

J. F. Friedkin

Rio Grande State Center for Mental Health and Mental Retardation. The name of the Rio Grande State Center for Mental Health and Mental Retardation, formerly the Harlingen State Mental Health Clinic,qv was changed in May, 1968. The center had grown from a staff of seven in 1962 to a staff of ninety-seven in 1970. Serving twelve South Texas counties, the center had hospital facilities for forty patients, a day-care center, and an alcoholic unit. The center now operates three comprehensive community mental health centers: Kingsville Community Mental Health Center opened in October,

1970; Laredo Community Mental Health Center opened in December, 1970; and Cameron-Willacy County Center opened in May, 1970. The Rio Grande State Center for Mental Health and Mental Retardation and its community centers admitted 627 patients in 1970 with an average stay of twenty-three days each. A separate program to aid alcoholic and drug addicted patients was established in May, 1970. Treatment in the center was based on individual diagnosis with the rate of payment adjusted to the person's ability to pay. The average daily census for 1970 was forty-eight, and the director was Jorge Cardenas. *See* Mentally Ill and Mentally Retarded, Care of, in Texas.

BIBLIOGRAPHY: Texas Department of Mental Health and Mental Retardation, *Annual Report, 1970* (n.d.).

*Rio Grande Station.

*Rio Grande Valley.

*Rio Grande Water Apportionment.

*Rio Hondo, Texas. Rio Hondo, in north-central Cameron County, had a 1960 population of 1,344 and a 1970 population of 1,167, according to the United States census. The town had thirty businesses in 1970.

*Rio Medina, Texas.

Río Nueces. *See* Cuitao Indians.

*Rio de las Palmas. *See* Rio Grande.

*Rio Vista, Texas. Rio Vista, in southern Johnson County, was incorporated in 1954 and during the 1960's reported a new bank, a post office, and four churches. Eight businesses were listed in 1970, and the town was a popular stopping place for campers and tourists on their way to Whitney Reservoir. In 1960 the population was 284; the 1970 population was 370, according to the United States census. *See also* Fort Worth Standard Metropolitan Statistical Area.

*Rionel, Texas.

*Rios, Texas.

Riots in Texas. Until the last half of the nineteenth century the sparseness of the population in Texas insured against the eruption of riots in the manner in which they came about in cities in the East. For this reason, and because for a long time many places did not keep local records and the state was not involved in most local incidents, it has been difficult to record many of the riots that have taken place in Texas. Only a few incidents occurred which could be termed riots prior to the Civil War; some of these would be considered riots now, but they were a common experience in the frontier life of Texas and were viewed more lightly. The occurrence of cowboys "taking a town," for example, which often involved some destruction of property, was usually considered an innocent diversion.

Other incidents were considered riots by the legally constituted authorities, but these are now regarded in another light. Such was the affair in 1832 in which a group of citizens armed themselves to free William B. Travis, Patrick C. Jack, and Edwin Waller,qqv who had been imprisoned at Fort Anahuac qv by Colonel John Davis Bradburn (*see* Bradburn, Juan Davis).

The nearest equivalent of a riot in the early days of Texas was the feud. The first and largest of these was the Regulator-Moderator War qv along the Sabine River between 1839 and 1844, but other smaller feuds were common, especially toward the western frontier.

Mob violence at times broke into rioting, generally with the object of lynching Negroes or abolitionists; however, most lynchings occurred not as the result of rioting, but from vigilance committees which operated secretly. The greatest number of riots in Texas occurred from the onset of the Civil War until the end of the century. Numerous factors accounted for the sudden increase, but in general the unrest stemmed from the social and economic uncertainties of the times and the sense of dispossession that dominated most segments of society. Between July and December, 1870, there were 124 arrests made by the state police alone for rioting.

A riot in Limestone County in 1871 was typical of those which occurred during this period. When a Negro policeman killed a white man in Groesbeck, the animosity between Negroes and whites erupted into mob violence. Fearing threats that Negroes were going to burn the town, whites throughout the county armed themselves and gathered at Groesbeck. Governor Edmund Jackson Davis qv declared martial law and sent in state troops; he thus averted a violent breakdown of law. In 1872 a similar riot occurred at Springfield. Almost invariably the cause of rioting was racial discord. State troops were required to restore order, and members of the mobs were left unpunished even when they were identified.

In 1877 at El Paso one of the most destructive riots in the state occurred; property damage was estimated to be between twelve and thirty-one thousand dollars. Known as the Salt War,qv its immediate cause was a dispute over rights to use salt ponds which had for years been used by people on both sides of the border free of charge and were regarded by those people as in the public domain. Charles H. Howard filed a claim for the land on which the salt deposits were located. When Louis Cardis qv encouraged Mexicans and Mexican Americans to defy the claim, Howard shot him. Howard then took refuge with state troops at San Elizario, where a mob of five hundred besieged them for four days. When Howard gave himself up he was killed, and the mob overran the town. In the wake of the violence, five men were found dead and much property was destroyed. The military post at El Paso was regarrisoned, but no measures were taken against the members of the mob, many of whom were Mexican nationals.

In the 1880's and 1890's racial incidents continued to be the major cause of riots, although economic conditions also became a factor. A riot of Negro troops occurred at Fort Concho qv in 1881 when about fifty Negroes broke open an arms rack and invaded the town of San Angelo, destroying some property and wounding one man. The violence stemmed from the killing of a Negro trooper and subsided after Texas Rangers qv were sent to the area.

In 1897 state troops were called out four times to protect prisoners from mobs, in one instance failing to protect their charge from lynching. State troops were called out in 1898 to keep peace at Houston during a streetcar strike and at Galveston during a wharf strike; on two other occasions they were called upon to protect prisoners from mobs. In 1899 an epidemic of smallpox at Laredo precipitated a riot among Mexican American residents who protested being moved from their homes under quarantine. They gathered in hundreds and fired several shots in an encounter with city officials. Rangers were sent in to subdue the mob before any serious damage was done. That same year troops of the Texas Volunteer Guard (see Texas National Guard) were sent to Orange to suppress a mob organized to drive Negroes out of Orange County.

The most common cause of riots in the first half of the twentieth century was public outrage toward prisoners. Mob threats of violence to prisoners necessitated the use of state troops on four occasions in 1900. In 1901 three lynchings by mobs took place despite the calling of state troops; in two instances the troops suppressed the mobs. At Brenham rioting broke out over the employment of a Negro brakeman by a railway; it was suppressed after two days. In 1902 mob violence brought on the use of state troops three times; in one instance the mob hanged a prisoner before their arrival. Troops were called out three times on this account in 1903, twice in 1904, three times the following year, and once in 1906. In Brownsville during the latter year, Texas experienced a serious race riot involving Negro soldiers. Troops were needed on two occasions, in both 1907 and 1908; in the latter year rioting at Slocum resulted in the killing of more than ten Negroes. Other mobs in the first decade of the century resulted from strikes at Houston in 1904 and racial tension at Ragley the same year. Riots also took place in San Antonio and Fort Worth in April and May of 1913.

Houston was the scene of a riot which began on the afternoon of August 23, 1917, by about 150 Negro troops from Camp Logan,qv a temporary training center near the city. The culmination of a general uneasiness and hostility following the establishment of the camp, the riot was touched off by the arrest of a Negro woman. The soldiers seized arms and ammunition from the camp and descended on the city. With seventeen dead, mostly whites, and numerous wounded of both races, the anger of an aroused white population necessitated the declaration of martial law for four days.

In 1919 conflict between Negroes and whites resulted in the proclamation of martial law at Longview. A strike at Galveston in 1920 resulted in lawlessness which required the help of the Texas National Guard. Mexia was declared in a state of anarchy because of a riot and was placed under martial law from January to March, 1922. The Sherman race riot of 1930 stemmed from the arrest of a Negro who had assaulted a white woman; Rangers were called to protect the prisoner, but a mob set fire to the courthouse and virtually seized control of the town. When troops of the Texas National Guard arrived, they were attacked by the mob, and before martial law restored order, a number of buildings were destroyed. Enforcement of oil conservation laws in the 1930's also necessitated the use of the National Guard to suppress mob lawlessness.

The National Guard was called in September, 1937, to suppress mob violence at Marshall; they were again called in June, 1943, at Beaumont, when a white mob, outraged at the assault of a white woman by a Negro, terrorized the Negro section of town. Two died and one hundred Negro homes were destroyed. In 1955 the National Guard was used to control a riot at Rusk State Hospital.qv In May, 1967, a riot occurred among Negro students at Texas Southern University in Houston, resulting in the death of one policeman and the wounding of two students and two police officers. Though the immediate cause of the riot was the arrest of a student, the one-night-long incident was related to general racial tension. See also Lynching in Texas; Negroes in Texas.

BIBLIOGRAPHY: C. L. Sonnichsen, The El Paso Salt War, 1877 (1961), I'll Die Before I'll Run (1951); Reports of the Adjutant General of Texas (1870–1955); Houston Chronicle, May 18–20, 1967.

Marilyn Von Kohl

*Ripley, Daniel.

*Ripley, Texas.

*Ripley Creek.

*Ripperdá, Juan María Vicencio de.

*Rippy Branch.

*Risher and Hall Stage Lines.

*Rising Star, Texas. Rising Star, in southwestern Eastland County, had a 1960 population of 997 and a 1970 population of 1,009, according to the United States census. The town had twenty-four businesses in 1970.

Rister, Carl Coke. Carl Coke Rister was born in Hayrick, Coke County, Texas, on June 30, 1889, the son of Craton and Sarah (Parker) Rister. He attended the public schools of Trent and Mc-Caulley. In 1915 he was graduated from Simmons College (later Simmons University and now Hardin-Simmons University) and taught for four years in Texas public schools. He received both his M.A. (1919) and Ph.D. (1925) from George Washington University. On June 11, 1916, Rister was married to Mattie May.

From 1920 to 1929 he served successively as assistant professor, associate professor, and professor of history at Hardin-Simmons; from 1925 to 1929, Rister was editor of the *West Texas Historical Association Year Book*.qv In 1929 he became a member of the Department of History at the University of Oklahoma, was made an honorary Phi Beta Kappa in 1941, and served as chairman of the history department there from 1944 to 1945. During the years he was at this university, he also served on the summer faculties of other universities. He was research professor of history from 1945 until 1951, when he became chairman of the Department of History and the first "Distinguished Professor of History" at Texas Technological College (now Texas Tech University).

From 1946 until his death he served on the executive committee of the Mississippi Valley Historical Association and was president of that body in 1949–1950. He was a member of the American Historical Association, the Texas Institute of Letters,qv and the Texas State Historical Association.qv

In addition to a large number of articles written for historical journals, Rister was the author or co-author of thirteen books, which included *The Southwestern Frontier 1865–1881* (1928), *Border Captives . . . 1835–1875* (1940), and *Oil: Titan of the Southwest* (1949), which won the Dallas *Morning News* qv award of the Texas Institute of Letters for the best book on the Southwest in 1949. His research interests centered on the history of the Southwest after the Civil War, and he was recognized as an authority on military and Indian history during that period. Rister died at Rotan, Texas, on April 16, 1955.

BIBLIOGRAPHY: *Who's Who In America* (1950); *Who's Who in the South and Southwest* (1950).

Alfred B. Sears

*Rita, Texas.

*Rita Blanca Creek.

Rita Blanca Lake. Rita Blanca Lake is in the Canadian River Basin in Hartley County, three miles south of Dalhart on Rita Blanca Creek, a tributary of the Canadian River. The Rita Blanca Lake project is owned by the United States Soil Conservation Service. In June, 1951, the city of Dalhart obtained a ninety-nine-year lease for the operation of the project as a recreational facility without any right of diversion. The administrative agency was transferred in 1960 to the United States Fish and Wildlife Service. The project, started in 1938, was completed the following year. Very little water was impounded until the flood flow of September, 1941. The lake has a capacity of 12,100 acre-feet and a surface area of 524 acres at elevation 3,860 feet above mean sea level. The drainage area above the dam is 1,062 square miles. The lake is used for recreational purposes only.

BIBLIOGRAPHY: Texas Water Commission, *Bulletin 6408* (1964).

Seth D. Breeding

*Rita Santa, Texas.

Ritter, Woodward Maurice (Tex). Woodward Maurice (Tex) Ritter, son of James Everett and Elizabeth (Matthews) Ritter, was born on January 12, 1905, in Murvaul, Panola County. [Ritter's signature as a student at the University of Texas shows that he spelled his first name Woodard (not Woodward), and a delayed birth certificate filed in Panola County in 1942 also shows the spelling Woodard; however, all printed sources use the spelling Woodward. Ed.] He moved to Nederland, in Jefferson County, to live with a sister, and graduated from South Park High School in nearby Beaumont. He attended the University of Texas from 1922 to 1927, spending one year in the law school there, 1925–1926; as a student he was influenced by J. Frank Dobie, Oscar J. Fox, and John A. Lomax qqv—who encouraged his study of authentic cowboy songs. Ritter, more interested in music, did not take a degree; for a time he was president of the Men's Glee Club at the university. He also attended Northwestern University for one year before he began singing western and mountain songs on Radio Station KPRC in Houston in 1929. The following year he was with a musical troupe touring the South and the Midwest; by 1931 he was in New York and had joined the Theatre Guild. His role in *Green Grow the Lilacs* (predecessor to the musical, *Oklahoma*) drew attention to the young "cowboy," and he became the featured singer with the Madison Square Garden Rodeo in 1932. Further recognition led to his starring in one of the first western radio programs to be featured in New York, "The Lone Star Rangers." His early appeal to New Yorkers as the embodiment of a Texas cowboy, in spite of his roots in the rural southern music tradition, undoubtedly led to his first movie contract in 1936.

Appearing in eighty-five movies, including seventy-eight westerns, Ritter was ranked among the top ten money-making stars in Hollywood for six years. While his movies owed much to the genre begun by other singing cowboys (such as Gene Autry), Ritter used traditional folk songs in his movies rather than the modern "western" ditties; films such as *Arizona Frontier, The Utah Trail,* and *Roll Wagons Roll* earned Ritter a reputation for ambitious plots and vigorous action not always found in low-budget westerns.

Tex Ritter's successful recordings, which began with "Rye Whiskey" in 1931, included over the years "High Noon," "Boll Weevil," "Wayward Wind," "Hillbilly Heaven," and "You Are My Sunshine." "Ranch Party," a television series featuring Ritter, ran from 1959 to 1962. He was married to Dorothy Fay Southworth on June 14, 1941; they were the parents of two sons. In 1964 Tex Ritter was elected to the Country Music Hall of Fame, only the fifth person to be so honored; he also served as president of the Country Music Association from 1963 to 1965. He died in Nashville, Tennessee, on January 2, 1974; funeral services were held in Nederland, Texas, and he was buried at Oak Bluff Memorial Park in nearby Port Neches.

BIBLIOGRAPHY: George N. Fenin and William K. Everson, *The Western* (1973); Bill C. Malone, *Country Music, U.S.A.* (1968); Jim Cooper, "Tex Ritter," *Texas Parade*, XXIX (July, 1968); John Edwards, "Old Time Singers —Tex Ritter," *Country and Western Spotlight* (September, 1962); Austin *American-Statesman*, January 4, 6, 1974; Biographical File, Barker Texas History Center, University of Texas at Austin.

*Rivas, Martín de.

River Crest Reservoir. River Crest Reservoir is in the Sulphur River Basin in Red River County, seven miles southeast of Bogata. The project is owned and operated by the Texas Power and Light Company for steam turbine, condenser-cooling purposes. Construction began on April 22, 1953, and the project was completed in November, 1953. This off-channel reservoir has a capacity of 7,200 acre-feet and a surface area of 560 acres at elevation 328 feet above mean sea level. Water is pumped from the Sulphur River to maintain the elevation at this operating level.

BIBLIOGRAPHY: Texas Water Commission, *Bulletin 6408* (1964).

Seth D. Breeding

*River Junction, Texas.

*River Navigation.

River Oaks, Texas. River Oaks, in central Tarrant County, was incorporated in 1941. Between 1952 and 1960 water and sewer systems were completed and improvements were made on streets and recreational facilities. During the 1960's the town had thirteen churches, a bank, and a library. Nearby Carswell Air Force Base qv and the General Dynamics plant greatly influenced the economy. The 1960 population was 8,444; in 1970 the count was 8,193, according to the United States census. *See also* Fort Worth Standard Metropolitan Statistical Area.

*River View, Texas. (Comal County.)

*River View, Texas. (Red River County.)

Rivera, Juan. Juan Rivera was born at Socorro, New Mexico, on July 12, 1892, the son of Hijinio and Josefa (Franco) Rivera. He and his wife Maria were the parents of six children. By 1915 Rivera was in Marfa, Texas, working as a typesetter for the Marfa *Town Talk*, and in 1925 he was editing a Spanish newspaper there, *Edición Español*. Rivera moved to Presidio where, in 1947, he established his own newspaper, the *International*, discontinuing that in 1961 to publish the Presidio *Voice*, a newspaper through which he waged a constant battle for the promotion of the Presidio community. His editorials showed a concern for working people, extolled the virtues of the American form of government, and praised the glories of Presidio's climate despite its defamation by the national news services as "the hottest spot in the United States." Originally a twelve-page publication, the *Voice* soon increased to sixteen pages of articles, poems, and editorials, the whole operation, including the writing, typesetting, editing, and bill collecting, done by Rivera himself. Mixing Spanish freely into the English text and with little regard for grammar and spelling, the *Voice* was completely unorthodox; its irregular publication became one of its trademarks. Although only five hundred copies were printed each issue, the paper's unique style was widely treasured by folklorists, and selections from it were often reproduced in national publications. Although its advertising came from several states and subscriptions were taken, the paper was in constant financial difficulty; however, his newspaper survived through his singular effort and the confidence of the local people in Rivera's genuine concern for Presidio. Rivera died on February 12, 1971, in Presidio and was buried there. The Sixty-second Texas Legislature passed a joint resolution honoring his memory in March, 1971.

BIBLIOGRAPHY: Carla Black, "Benjamin Franklin of the Rio Grande," *Texas Historian*, XXXII (1971–1972); Sixty-second Texas Legislature, "Memorial—Juan Rivera, Sr." (S.C.R. No. 44, March 11, 1971).

*Rivera y Villalón, Pedro de.

*Riverby, Texas.

*Riverdale, Texas.

Riverland, Texas. Riverland, a community in northeast Clay County, was supposedly named for its location near the Red River. Chief occupations were farming, cattle raising, and the growing of grain and fruit. Many residents worked in Wichita Falls.

*Rivers, Robert Jones.

*Rivers of Texas.

*Riverside, Texas. (Comal County.)

*Riverside, Texas. (Walker County.)

*Riverside Institute.

*Riviera, Texas.

*Riviera Beach, Texas.

*Riviera Beach and Western Railway.

*Roach, Texas.

*Roane, Texas.

*Roanoke, Texas.

*Roan's Prairie, Texas.

*Roansboro, Texas.

*Roaring Springs, Texas.

*Roark, A. Jackson.

*Roark, Elijah.

*Roark, Leo.

Rob and Bessie Welder Wildlife Foundation and Refuge. The Rob and Bessie Welder Wildlife Foundation was established in 1954 as the result of a provision in the will of Robert Hughes Welder qv which provided for the creation and continuing operation of a wildlife refuge in San Patricio County. The refuge was in operation for several years before it was formally dedicated on April 22, 1961.

Welder specified that the refuge provide conditions whereby wildlife could live, forage, and propagate. He sought also to provide means and opportunities for research and education in wildlife conservation and related fields. Trustees named to oversee the refuge included two nephews, Patrick Hughes Welder and John J. Welder, Jr.; the third member was M. Harvey Weil, attorney for Robert H. (Rob) Welder. First director of the refuge was Clarence Cottam.

Situated eight miles northeast of Sinton in San Patricio County, 7,800 acres were designated out of the Welder ranch to become the refuge. The entrance was one mile southwest of the junction of U.S. Highway 77 and the Aransas River, which formed the northern boundary of the refuge. Income from oil and gas leases, as well as royalties from certain other land, was dedicated toward support of the foundation. A portion of land originally granted by the Mexican government to Welder's ancestors (see Power, James; Portilla, Felipe Roque de la), the acreage in the refuge has been owned continuously by the family, and none of its rich alluvial soils has ever been cultivated. The foundation provided for the annual giving of from three to ten fellowships and other aids to graduate students and/or eminent scientists engaged in wildlife research and related disciplines. Teacher training programs were given in summer courses, and the refuge assisted in individual studies that by 1972 led to twenty-seven Ph.D. degrees and approximately that many masters degrees from various cooperating universities. The foundation supported publication of selected accounts, among which were several numbers of a monograph series published by the *Journal of Wildlife Management* and articles in the *Journal of Mammalogy*. Among the books and studies sponsored by the foundation were *Grasses of the Texas Coastal Bend* by Frank W. Gould and Thadis W. Box (1965); *Flowering Plants and Ferns of the Coastal Bend Counties of Texas* by Fred B. Jones, Chester M. Rowell, Jr., and Marshall C. Johnston (1961); and *Whitewings: The Life, History, Status and Management of the White Winged Dove*, compiled by Clarence Cottam and James B. Trefethen (1968).

The refuge's initial physical plant included five permanent buildings of modified Spanish architecture, with furnishings of the same motif. The administration building housed staff offices, zoology and botany laboratories, a library, a museum, a lecture hall, a wildlife specimen exhibit room, a photographic laboratory, and other operational facilities. The student dormitory contained eight furnished apartments. Other buildings were a rotunda for visitors and homes for the director and assistant director. On the grounds also were a ranch house for refuge employees, a necropsy laboratory, an electronic laboratory, and a workshop-equipment storage area.

The great diversity of plant and animal life in the refuge has resulted from various factors such as soil types, water relationships, variations in mineral content in water and soil, climatic conditions, topography, and other geographic conditions related to the Texas Gulf region. More than 400 subspecies of birds have been recorded on the refuge or in its immediate vicinity. Among the native birds are the roadrunner (chaparral), scissor-tailed flycatcher, mockingbird, cardinal, Mexican grebe, gallinule, roseate spoonbill, wood ibis, and the fulvous and black-bellied tree ducks. Other wildlife there, commonly found in South Texas, include the white-tailed deer, turkey, bobwhite quail, mourning dove, jackrabbit, cottontail rabbit, armadillo, javelina, opossum, raccoon, coyote, and bobcat. More than 1,300 species of plants have been identified either on or adjacent to the refuge, and at least fifty-five species each of mammals, reptiles, and amphibians have been recorded there. The refuge sponsored weekly guided tours for the general public and lectures by wildlife conservationists and other specialists.

BIBLIOGRAPHY: *Rob and Bessie Welder Wildlife Foundation* (n.d.).

Vernen Liles
Crystal Sasse Ragsdale

*Robards, Willis L.

*Robberson, Texas.

*Robbins, Earle.

*Robbins, John W.

*Robbins, Nathaniel.

*Robbins, William.

*Robbins, Texas.

*Robbins' Ferry.

*Robbinsville, Texas.

Robert A. Welch Foundation. *See* Welch, Robert Alonzo.

*Robert Lee, Texas. Robert Lee, seat of Coke County, was the principal commercial center of the county. In 1970 the town had a hospital and there were twenty-two businesses. The 1960 population was 990; the 1970 population was 1,119, according to the United States census.

*Roberts, A. S.

*Roberts, Andrew.

*Roberts, Dan W.

*Roberts, Elisha.

*Roberts, Ingham S.

*Roberts, John S.

Roberts, Meshack. *See* Roberts, Shack.

*Roberts, Moses Fisk.

*Roberts, Noel F.

*Roberts, Oran Milo. *See also* Border, John Pelham.

*Roberts, Samuel Alexander.

*Roberts, Shack.

*Roberts, William.

*Roberts, Texas.

*Roberts County. Roberts County, in the northeastern part of the Texas Panhandle, was primarily a ranching area, although it produced almost twenty-five million barrels of oil from 1949 to January 1, 1973. About 90 percent of the $4 million average annual agricultural income came from cattle production; principal crops in the early 1970's were wheat and sorghums. The 1960 population was 1,075; the 1970 population was 967, according to the United States census.

*Roberts Creek.

*Robertson, A. B.

*Robertson, Edward.

*Robertson, Elijah Sterling Clack.

*Robertson, Felix.

*Robertson, Felix H. Felix H. Robertson was buried in Oakwood Cemetery, Waco (not at Salado, as stated in Volume II).

James H. Colgin

*Robertson, James Harvey.

*Robertson, Jerome Bonaparte. Jerome Bonaparte Robertson died on January 7, 1890 (not January 7, 1891, as stated in Volume II). He was buried in Independence, but a marker erected by Hill Junior College indicates that he was reinterred in the Robertson family plot at Oakwood Cemetery, Waco, Texas.

BIBLIOGRAPHY: Dallas *Morning News*, January 9, 1890; *Memorial and Biographical History of McLennan, Falls, Bell and Coryell Counties, Texas* (1893).

James H. Colgin

*Robertson, John C.

*Robertson, Joseph W. Joseph W. Robertson was married on September 7, 1842, to Lydia Lee.

Lucie C. Price

Robertson, Lexie Dean. Lexie Dean Robertson was born in Lindale, Texas, on July 25, 1893, daughter of Alexander Green and Lena (Ansley) Dean. She was educated in the public schools of Canton and received a B.A. degree in 1925 from Howard Payne College; she also attended North Texas State College (now North Texas State University), the University of Chicago, and the University of Oklahoma. She was married to J. F. Robertson on August 16, 1911; they had no children. For several years she was a teacher and principal in the public schools but she later devoted her full time to writing. Her poems appeared in various newspapers, anthologies, and magazines, including *Kaleidograph, Southwest Review, Holland's Magazine,*qqv *Good Housekeeping,* and *Ladies Home Journal.* Much of her poetry was of the "homespun" type, and many of her early poems concerned the oil industry. One of her volumes, *I Keep a Rainbow,* won the 1932 book award of the Poetry Society of Texas,qv an organization which she served as vice-president and councilor. After her death the society established the Lexie Dean Robertson Award. She was the first native-born poet laureate qv of Texas, from 1939 to 1941.

A charter member of the Texas Institute of Letters,qv she served as its president in 1944. Mrs. Robertson published four volumes of verse: *Red Heels* (1928), *I Keep a Rainbow* (1932), *Acorn on the Roof* (1939), and *Answer in the Night* (1948). She died in Abilene on February 16, 1954, and was buried in Rising Star.

BIBLIOGRAPHY: *Texian Who's Who* (1937); Rising Star *Record*, February 27, 1954; Margaret Royalty Edwards, *Poets Laureate of Texas* (1966).

Margaret Royalty Edwards

Robertson, Samuel Arthur. Samuel Arthur Robertson, the son of Frank Selden and Catherine (Lewis) Robertson, was born at DeWitt, Missouri, on July 10, 1867. Young Robertson left home at fifteen and went to work on railroad construction crews.

His construction engineering career began in Texas in 1887. He came to the Rio Grande Valley in 1903 while under contract to lay rails for the Gulf Coast lines from Corpus Christi to Brownsville. He purchased ten thousand acres along the Los Fresnos Resaca and organized the San Benito Townsite Company, the San Benito Land and Irrigation Company, and other companies which directed the development of San Benito and the surrounding area. He was a pioneer in developing irrigation districts and building canals and drainage systems in the Valley.

To provide access to remote land, Robertson built a network of feeder spurs to connect with the Brownsville Street and Interurban Railroad Company, which he had also promoted and built (*see* San Benito and Rio Grande Valley Railway Company). Locally the network was called "The Spiderweb" and "Sam Robertson's Backdoor Railroad"; the system connected eleven communities and brought into being the town of Rio Hondo. In 1910, when ice was being shipped from Bay City, Robertson saw the need for providing ice for refrigerator cars carrying vegetables to city markets; he soon had ice plants operating in San Benito, Harlingen, and Brownsville. He was the first postmaster of San Benito and twice was elected sheriff of Cameron County.

In 1916 Robertson served as a scout for General Pershing's army when it went into Mexico in pursuit of Pancho Villa.qv On this assignment he was captured, dragged behind a horse, beaten, and left for dead. After recovering, Robertson joined the United States Army in 1917; he organized and commanded the 16th Engineers, one of the first regiments to go to France. A lieutenant colonel in 1918, he commanded the 22nd Engineers, then was promoted to full colonel before his discharge in 1919. He was repeatedly cited for competence in building light rail lines to the front trenches under shell fire. He was awarded the Distinguished Service Medal and the Congressional Medal of Honor.

Robertson was an early advocate of the development of Padre Island; he helped develop Brazos Island with the Valley's first seaside resort, "Del

Mar," which was destroyed by the 1933 hurricane. His first wife, Adele Wedegartner, whom he married on March 17, 1907, died on November 21, 1921. He then married Maria Seidler in Vienna, Austria, on December 3, 1922. Robertson died on August 22, 1938, in Brownsville and was buried in San Antonio.

BIBLIOGRAPHY: J. L. Allhands, *Gringo Builders* (1931); S. G. Reed, *A History of the Texas Railroads* (1941); San Antonio *Daily Express*, June 14, 1909, September 7, 1911; San Benito *Light*, August 23, 1938; *Valley Morning Star*, August 23, 1938.

Verna J. McKenna

*Robertson, Sawnie,

*Robertson, Sterling Clack.

*Robertson, Texas. (Crosby County.)

*Robertson, Texas. (Jasper County.)

*Robertson Branch,

*Robertson Colony.

*Robertson County. Robertson County, in east-central Texas, was primarily a farming and ranching area. In the 1960's and early 1970's the average annual agricultural income was $13 million, three-fourths of which came from beef cattle, hogs, and poultry. The cotton crop, 22,339 bales in 1970–1971, had been increased by mechanization and irrigation. Grain sorghum production also greatly increased. The 1960 population was 16,157; the 1970 population had decreased to 14,389 according to the United States census.

*Robertson Creek.

*Robinson, Andrew.

*Robinson, George.

*Robinson, James W.

*Robinson, Jesse J.

*Robinson, Tod.

*Robinson, William. [The article in Volume II on William Robinson may refer to two men of the same name, both settlers before 1832 in the Stephen F. Austin colony and both regidors *qv* of their communities. However, the evidence is not conclusive. Ed.]

A William "Popcorn" Robinson and his wife and daughter settled along the Brazos River. He was a delegate from the Precinct of Viesca *qv* to the Conventions of 1832 and 1833.*qqv* William ("Popcorn") Robinson was listed as a commissioner when Montgomery County was chartered in 1837 and as a farmer and stockman in that county in 1850.

A William Robinson settled along the lower Colorado River and became a planter, slave owner, and real estate dealer. In October, 1830, he was named a delegate from his Colorado precinct (*see* Alfred, District of) to a meeting to be held at San Felipe in November, 1830. On October 23, 1830, a meeting to elect militia officers was called for November 13, to be held at his house on the Colorado. He was appointed treasurer of the Alfred District by the Convention of 1832. He died prior

to January 14, 1841, since on that date his heirs brought suit in district court in Colorado County against the heirs of Martha Bostic in a land title case.

BIBLIOGRAPHY: *Proceedings of the General Convention of Delegates Representing the Citizens and Inhabitants of Texas: Held at the Town of San Felipe de Austin* (1832); *Texas Gazette*, January 30, March 20, July 22, October 16, 23, 1830; *Telegraph and Texas Register*, March 3, 1841; Worth S. Ray, *Austin Colony Pioneers* (1949); Noah Smithwick, "Notes and Fragments," *Quarterly of the Texas State Historical Association*, II (1898–1899).

Margaret Craig

*Robinson, Texas. (Denton County.)

*Robinson, Texas. (McLennan County.) Robinson, located in the central part of the county, southeast of Waco, had in 1960 a population of 2,111; in 1970 it was 3,807, according to the United States census.

*Robinson Bayou.

*Robinson Branch.

*Robinson Creek.

*Robinson Peak.

*Robison, James Thomas.

*Robison, Joel Walter.

*Robison, John G.

*Robstown, Texas. Robstown, in coastal Nueces County, adopted a mayor-council form of city government in 1948, thirty-six years after its incorporation. A ten-acre park-pool complex was completed in 1963 to expand the municipal recreation facilities. Among the businesses reported in the 1960's were companies related to the petroleum industry, a ready-mix concrete producer, and portable building manufacturers. The economy of Robstown was also supported by the surrounding agricultural and petroleum interests in the area. During the decade of the 1950's the city population expanded 41 percent, from 7,278 in 1950 to 10,266 in 1960; the 1970 population was 11,217, according to the United States census. *See also* Corpus Christi Standard Metropolitan Statistical Area.

*Roby, Texas. Roby, seat of Fisher County, was the third largest town in the county in the 1960's. The town was the headquarters for a nine-county electric cooperative and the site of a hospital. Roby served as a commercial center, with twenty-two businesses reported in 1970. The 1960 population was 913 and the 1970 population was 784, according to the United States census.

*Roby and Northern Railway.

*Rochelle, Texas.

*Rochelle Creek.

*Rochester, Texas. (Haskell County.)

*Rochester, Texas. (San Saba County.)

Rock Art, Indian. Indian rock art, consisting of pictographs (drawings or paintings) and petroglyphs (carvings) created by Indians, both prehistoric and historic, exist in more than two hundred known sites in Texas, usually on cave walls or natural rock shelters along rivers or streams, or on ledges and cliff faces. There probably are a great number of sites which have not been discovered, but those examined, many containing numerous paintings or engravings, represent a wide variety of styles in different locations, reflecting many divergent Indian cultures.

While many such regions in the western United States contain more pictographs than petroglyphs, the opposite is true in Texas. Sites have been located near known Indian camp grounds; others have been found in isolated, remote areas, seemingly far from ancient or modern settlements. The art work ranges in size from one inch to eighteen feet in height and is found anywhere from the ground level to many feet above ground. Some paintings were drawn in places that could only have been reached with the use of scaffolding of some sort. Pigments taken from minerals were earth colors. Black and red were most common, but white, yellow, orange, and brown were also used, sometimes singly but most often in combinations. Subjects ranged from the whole human figure or just hands or feet, to animals of all kinds—deer, buffalo, snakes, and birds. Symbols for the sun, weather, trees, weapons, and geometric shapes were also drawn. In later times Spanish and American figures were drawn, indicating their influence on the Indian.

The purposes or meanings in the drawings cannot be positively determined, but some are clearly religious or ceremonial in nature. Some obviously depict events in a tribe or of an individual, often in hunting or warfare. Maps, dancing scenes, and tallies of some sort are recorded, as are stories or myths. A few drawings seem to be attempts at humor.

Only one site exemplifies a tradition among one group of Indians over an extended length of time. Here, at the junction of the Pecos River with the Rio Grande, and the Devils River with the Rio Grande in Val Verde County, the collection of rock art (known as the lower Pecos River style) suggests an indigenous effort. Paintings show a beginning and development, slowly refining in style, and an eventual dying out—all in a geographically limited area that was seemingly isolated from outside artistic influences. Evidences of human habitation date back many thousands of years (perhaps 10,000), but the Indian culture believed responsible for the paintings here existed in the area from about 6000 B.C. to A.D. 600 or later. These pictographs are considered to be among the finest in the world.

Farther west, in El Paso County, the rock art in Hueco Tanks State Park (see Parks, State) reflects a completely different culture. Although not a distinctive style such as that at the Pecos River site, these paintings, found in centuries-old natural cisterns, are evidence of the influence of the forebears of the Puebloan Indians who lived in Arizona and New Mexico, their influence reaching into the far western areas of Texas. Paintings in the Texas Panhandle around the Canadian River valley at Rocky

Dell in Oldham County, Alibates Creek, and others near Palo Duro Canyon are similar to the Hueco Tanks drawings. Characteristic subjects of paintings at these sites are masks, shield figures, and blanket designs, probably painted by the Mescalero Indians from A.D. 900 to 1500, though influenced by the older Puebloan culture.

There are numerous other sites across Texas, but the work seems not to be the result of any frequent or consistent rock art heritage such as that found in the Pecos River and Puebloan pictograph sites. Many are later works and are possibly the result of the influence of the ancient art on later Indians. Paintings are found throughout the Big Bend area, for instance, that are not related to the Pecos River style. Rock Pile Ranch, Fort Davis, Lewis Canyon (the one site which is mostly petroglyphs), Study Butte, Comanche Springs, and sites near Comstock are among the Big Bend group. Some of the places where rock paintings have been found are Nolan County, Winkler County, Paint Rock (near the headwaters of the Nueces and Frio Rivers), and Lehmann Rock Shelter (northwest of Fredericksburg). Most of these sites cannot be attributed to any one Indian group, and probably the drawings were done or added to by many different individuals.

The paintings and petroglyphs vary in age; some are estimated to be thousands of years old, while others date only from the 1700's and 1800's. Few paintings dated after 1850 are considered true examples of Indian rock art. In some cases the figures represented are an indication of the relative age; the absence or inclusion of horses, guns, missions, and white men (and the sequence in which they appear) helps in dating the relatively modern drawings; however, these more recent drawings, often mixed in with the older work, along with vandalism in the nineteenth and twentieth centuries, have made age determinations more difficult.

Vandalism endangers rock art more than natural weathering; recent painting over and carving into the art has destroyed much of it, and many sites have already been covered by impoundment water of dams. Unfortunately, one particular area in Texas, which has been described as having more Indian paintings per square acre than any other area in the United States, has been partly covered by Amistad Reservoir qv on the Rio Grande. Many important sites, however, are now included in state parks,qv and still others have yet to be discovered.

Although there is still much work to do in this area, some research and categorizing of Indian paintings and engravings has been done. A. T. Jackson's *Picture-Writing of Texas Indians* and Forrest Kirkland and W. W. Newcomb, Jr.'s *The Rock Art of Texas Indians* are significant works. In the latter book Olea Forrest Kirkland's qv exact scale copies of Indian rock art in watercolor are reproduced. For related articles *see* Alibates Flint Quarries; Archaeology; Palo Duro Canyon; Pueblo Ruins of the Texas Panhandle.

BIBLIOGRAPHY: A. T. Jackson, *Picture-Writing of Texas Indians* (1938); Forrest Kirkland and W. W. Newcomb, Jr., *The Rock Art of Texas Indians* (1967); Campbell Grant, *Rock Art of the American Indian* (1967); Marjorie Valentine Adams, "Pictographs On The Pecos," *Texas Parade*, XV (March, 1955); Victor J. Smith, "Indian Pictographs of the Big Bend in Texas," *Publications of the Texas Folk-Lore Society*, II (1923).

Melinda Arceneaux Wickman

*Rock Creek.

*Rock Creek, Texas. (Johnson County.)

*Rock Creek, Texas. (McLennan County.)

*Rock Creek, Texas. (Parker County.)

*Rock-Crusher, Texas.

*Rock Draw.

*Rock Hill, Texas. (Collin County.)

*Rock Hill, Texas. (Wood County.)

*Rock Hill Institute.

*Rock House, Texas.

*Rock Island, Texas. (Colorado County.)

*Rock Island, Texas. (Polk County.)

*Rock Island, Texas. (Washington County.)

*Rock Island System. In Texas in 1964 the Rock Island System operated a total of 773.8 miles of first main track, 661.1 miles through the Chicago, Rock Island, and Pacific, and 112.7 miles through the Burlington-Rock Island, of which it owned half. It also owned one-half of the Galveston Terminal and one-eighth each of the Houston Belt and Terminal and the Union Terminal.

James M. Day

Rock Spring. Rock Spring, a natural water hole at the head of Tordilla Creek near Tordilla Hill,qv in Karnes County, was one of the few places along the San Patricio Trail,qv between Oakville and San Antonio, where water was usually available. Rock Spring was shown as a place name on Mexican War maps of 1845 and maps from 1859 to 1867. At one time there was a Mexican settlement of thirty or forty people at Rock Spring, which came to be called "The Jump-off" by area ranchers.

BIBLIOGRAPHY: Robert H. Thonhoff, A History of Karnes County, Texas (M.A. thesis, Southwest Texas State College, 1963).

*Rockdale, Texas. Rockdale, in Milam County, reported an increase in population from 2,321 in 1950 to 4,481 in 1960. The establishment of a large aluminum plant in 1952, a container factory in 1958, and an industrial moldings mill in 1959 greatly influenced the growth of the community. In the 1960's Rockdale had sixteen churches, a hospital, a bank, a library, and a newspaper. In 1970 there were seventy businesses; the 1970 population was 4,655, according to the United States census.

*Rockdale, Sandow, and Southern Railroad Company.

*Rockett, Texas.

*Rockford, Texas.

*Rockhouse, Texas.

*Rocking Chair Mountains.

*Rocking Chair Ranch.

*Rockland, Texas.

*Rockland Dam.

*Rockne, Texas. Rockne was originally referred to as Hilbigsville (or Hilbig's Store, because the post office for that farming community was located in the store during the years of World War I). As early as 1878 the Sacred Heart Parish and Sacred Heart Cemetery were established when Phillip Goertz and Michael Wolf, early German settlers, each gave five acres of land for the erection of the first church, which later burned down. The present church was built nearby, along with a school. In 1900 a parochial grade school was established and classes were taught by the Sisters of Divine Providence,qv from San Antonio. From 1925 the Benedictine Sisters,qv also from San Antonio, taught children and maintained the school until it was closed in 1963. Sometime soon after March 31, 1931, the date of the death of Notre Dame University football coach Knute K. Rockne, the school children and members of the community chose the name Rockne in his honor. The post office for Rockne in 1971 was in nearby Red Rock, and the population was estimated to be about three hundred.

Alois J. Goertz

*Rockport, Texas. Rockport, seat of Aransas County, had approximately one hundred fifty businesses in the early 1970's, with emphasis on tourism, sport and commercial fishing, shipbuilding, and the oil and gas industries. A large number of schools and public buildings had been constructed by the 1960's. Fulton Harbor was completed in 1955, and Rockport Beach, Ski Basin, and Cove Harbor were completed in 1958. A $2,500,000 causeway was completed in 1966. The population was 2,989 in 1960 and increased by 29.8 percent to 3,879 by 1970, according to the United States census.

*Rocksprings, Texas. Rocksprings, in Edwards County, was named for springs near the present townsite which surfaced at a rock formation, providing water two feet deep, enough for watering stock in 1877, when rancher Vol Ross first came to the area (not named for water which poured from the walls of Llano Canyon, as stated in Volume II). The 1927 tornado which swept through Rocksprings took seventy-two (not twenty-seven) lives. The courthouse, built in 1891, stands at the apex of the watershed which divides two rivers, the South Llano on the north and the Nueces on the south. For fifty years the Balentine Hotel in Rocksprings was operated by Mr. and Mrs. J. L. Balentine, who took over operation on February 1, 1918.

Rocksprings claims the title of "Angora goat capital of the world," and is a marketing and shipping point for mohair, wool, lambs, kids, and cattle. The town supported a newspaper, *The Texas Mohair Weekly*, and a hospital in 1972. A July 4 rodeo is held annually in connection with the Old Settlers Reunion. The town reported thirty-two businesses in 1970. In 1960 the population was 1,182, and in 1970 it was 1,221, according to the United States census.

BIBLIOGRAPHY: Subject File, Barker Texas History Center, University of Texas at Austin.

*Rockwall, Texas. Rockwall, seat of Rockwall County, was chiefly a farm commercial center. Its businesses in the late 1960's and early 1970's included industries concerned with aluminum, electronics, garments, agricultural supplies, window manufacturing, and leather goods. In the mid-1960's the town reported five churches, four public schools, two hospitals, a bank, a library, and a newspaper. The population increased steadily from 1,501 in 1950 to 2,166 in 1960, and to 3,121 in 1970, doubling in twenty years.

*Rockwall College.

*Rockwall County. Rockwall County, the smallest county in Texas, was chiefly an agricultural area, with cotton as its main crop. Cotton production was 11,342 bales in 1966, 7,847 in 1968, and 6,494 in 1970. The county was largely a residential area for Dallas workers and relied on nearby counties for its recreational facilities. The 1960 population was 5,878; the 1970 population was 7,046, according to the United States census. See also Dallas Standard Metropolitan Statistical Area.

*Rockwall Creek.

*Rockwood, Texas.

*Rocky Branch, Texas.

.*Rocky Creek.

*Rocky Hill.

*Rocky Hill, Texas.

*Rodair Bayou.

*Roddy, Ephraim.

*Roddy, Texas.

*Rodeos. See also Texas Prison Rodeo.

*Rodessa Oil Field.

Rodgers, James Charles. James Charles (Jimmie) Rodgers, often called the father of modern country music, was born on September 8, 1897, at Meridian, Mississippi, the son of Aaron W. and Eliza (Bozeman) Rodgers. His father was a railroad gang foreman, and Jimmie, whose mother had died when he was four years old, grew up on the railroad. He started work as a water carrier at the age of fourteen and eventually became a brakeman; working on railroads throughout the South, he learned songs from the Negro workers, who also taught him to play the banjo and the guitar.

He was married to Carrie Cecil Williamson on April 7, 1920, and they had two daughters, one of whom died in infancy. A severe case of tuberculosis, contracted in 1924, forced Rodgers to retire from the railroad, precipitating a chain of odd jobs and migrations in the South and Southwest. He served a brief stint as an entertainer with a medicine show and for a while was a city detective in Asheville, North Carolina, where he had moved in search of a more healthful climate. He organized the Jimmie Rodgers Entertainers in Asheville, and the group performed on the local radio station, singing both popular and country music.

In 1927 Rodgers signed a contract with Victor Talking Machine Company, and his records catapulted him to almost immediate fame. He made his first recording on August 4, 1927, in Bristol, on the Tennessee-Virginia border, recording "Sleep, Baby Sleep" and "Soldier's Sweetheart." Rodgers introduced a new form to commercial hillbilly music, the blue yodel, heard best in the "Blue Yodel" series of twelve songs, simply titled "Blue Yodel No. 1," "Blue Yodel No. 2," etc. One of this series has remained one of the most popular of his songs and has become known as "T for Texas." He recorded 111 songs altogether, selling twenty million records between 1927 and 1933. He earned as much as $100,000 annually, but medical bills took most of it. Billed during his professional career as "America's Blue Yodeler" and "The Singing Brakeman," Rodgers, although unable to read music, enthralled radio, recording, and stage audiences with his portrayal of songs that seemed to catalogue the varied memories and experiences of small town and rural Americans. His records included such songs as "The One Rose," "The TB Blues," "In the Jailhouse Now," "Any Old Time," "Carolina Sunshine Girl," and "The Yodeling Ranger" (composed shortly after Rodgers was made an honorary Texas Ranger qv in Austin in 1931). Rodgers' guitar technique and his famous blue yodel, as well as the informality of his presentation, were emulated by scores of young country-western singers—Jimmie Davis, Hank Snow, Gene Autry, Ernest Tubb, Hank Williams, and others—whose success was a tribute to the country-singing star.

To seek relief from tuberculosis, Rodgers moved to the dry region of the Texas hill country, and he restricted himself to performances in the South and Southwest. During the last few years of his life Rodgers made most of his appearances in Texas. In 1929 he built a $50,000 mansion, "Blue Yodeler's Paradise," in Kerrville, but left there to live in a modest home in San Antonio in 1932. Jimmie Rodgers died on May 26, 1933, in his hotel room in New York City while on a recording trip there. He was buried in Oak Grove Cemetery at Meridian, Mississippi. Jimmie Rodgers was the first person named, by unanimous vote, to the Country Music Hall of Fame in Nashville, Tennessee, on November 3, 1961, less than one month before the death of his wife, Carrie, in San Antonio.

BIBLIOGRAPHY: Bill C. Malone, Country Music, U.S.A. (1968); Carrie Williamson Rodgers, My Husband Jimmy Rodgers (1935); Townsend Miller, "Country Music," Austin American, July 29, August 5, 1972.

Rodgers, James Woodall. J. Woodall Rodgers, Dallas attorney, mayor, and civic leader, was born at New Market, Madison County, Alabama, on May 11, 1890, the son of William Emmett and Lucy Ann (Woodall) Rodgers. He was educated in the public schools of Alabama, Vanderbilt University (B.A.,

1911), the University of Texas (LL.B., 1916), and Columbia University. In World War I he served in the United States Army Artillery, emerging as a major. He married Edna Cristler on November 10, 1920.

Rodgers practiced law in Dallas and was president of the Dallas Bar Association in 1938. He served four terms as mayor of Dallas, 1939–1947. He helped to put the city on a cash basis and took a lead in spurring Dallas' growth through planning and building Central Expressway and expanding Love Field. At his urging, the city council engaged a noted city planner to draw up a master plan for Dallas. In 1945 Dallas voters approved bond issues of $40,000,000 to put into effect parts of this plan. Rodgers was a director of several corporations, a trustee of Vanderbilt University, a leader in many civic activities, and a Presbyterian. He died in Dallas on July 6, 1961. A downtown inner expressway was named for him.

BIBLIOGRAPHY: Dallas Morning News, July 7, 1961.

Wayne Gard

Rodgers, Jimmie. See Rodgers, James Charles.

*Rodgers Creek.

*Rodney, Texas.

*Rodríguez, Agustín.

*Rodríguez, Ambrosio.

Rodríguez, Chipita. Chipita Rodríguez was the only woman ever legally hanged in Texas. Chipita (possibly a misspelling of Chepita, a diminutive of Chepa, nickname for Josefa) lived in a hut at a way station for travelers on the Welder (see Welder, Robert Hughes) ranch lands on the Aransas River on a trail that led from adjoining Refugio County down to the Rio Grande Valley and Mexico. San Patricio County court records show that in August, 1863, she, along with Juan Silvera (Juan "Chiquito"), was accused of the murder of an unknown man whose body was found in the Aransas River near Chipita's cabin. Later accounts call the man John Savage, a horse trader on his way to Mexico carrying gold for purchasing. During the 1863 fall term when the Fourteenth District Court met at San Patricio (then the county seat), the grand jurors on October 7 handed down an indictment of murder against the two. The trial lasted two days, and on October 10 Juan Silvera was convicted of second-degree murder and sentenced to five years in prison; Chipita was found guilty of first-degree murder. It was recommended that she be given mercy because of her old age and the fact that there was only circumstantial evidence against her; however, Judge Benjamin F. Neal ordered that she be hanged sometime before sunset on Friday, November 13, 1863, and that she be held in the San Patricio County jail or some other secure place until that time.

She was hanged from a mesquite tree in the Nueces River bottom near San Patricio and buried in an unmarked grave. Legends concerning the incident have gathered during the years since 1863, such as that a long-lost son of Chipita's killed Savage and fled; that Juan Silvera was really Chipita's son; that a dying man later confessed to the murder; that the gold which John Savage supposedly carried was found, either before or after the trial. Irish inhabitants in old San Patricio, recalling details of the trial, have retold the story for generations. Chipita's ghost is said to haunt the Nueces River banks where she was hanged.

BIBLIOGRAPHY: Rachel Bluntzer Hebert, *Shadows on the Nueces* (1942); Vernon Smylie, *A Noose For Chipita* (1970); Ruel McDaniel, "The Day They Hanged Chipita," *Texas Parade* (September, 1962), and "The Curse That Killed San Patricio Town," *Old West* (Winter, 1968); Cliff Blackburn, "Hanging Tree," Houston *Post*, May 15, 1960; Corpus Christi *Caller-Times*, January 18, November 13, 1959, March 24, 1963, November 13, 1970.

*Rodríguez, José María.

*Rodríguez, José Policarpo.

*Rodríguez, Juan.

*Rodríguez, ex parte.

*Rodríguez-Chamuscado Expedition.

*Roehm, Johan Conrad.

*Roemer, Ferdinand von.

*Roeser, Texas.

Roessler, Anton R. Anton R. Roessler (Rössler), born in Raab, Hungary, and possibly educated in Vienna, is known for his late nineteenth-century maps of Texas and Texas counties. For twenty years following the Civil War he was a questionable figure in the field of American geology. He added little of permanent value to the written record of the science and has been accused of plagiarism and thievery, but only through Roessler did much of the data collected by the Shumard Survey reach permanent collections (see Shumard, Benjamin Franklin).

In October of 1860 Roessler was married to Octavia Baker, and they made their home in Austin. His first recorded service in Texas was in 1860–1861 as draughtsman for the [First] Geological and Agricultural Survey of Texas (Shumard Survey). His training must have been sound, for Roessler rapidly became one of the better cartographers in Texas. With the capitulation of the Shumard Survey to the exigencies of politics and war in March, 1861, Roessler became chief draughtsman for the arsenal at Austin in 1862. Apparently he did not leave for Union territory at the start of hostilities along with the rest of his colleagues on the survey, for he later emphasized his loyalty to the Confederacy in a bitter quarrel with Samuel Botsford Buckley.qv

Roessler's participation in recovering and saving Shumard Survey materials resulted in the preservation of some of the fossils and maps. In 1868 he sent to Vienna a collection of supposedly Texas fossils, some of which were indeed from Texas; unknown to Roessler, and to the confusion of the paleontological world for many years, some items were from Nebraska. Additional fossils, presumed to be Shumard material (although some may have been collected by Roessler himself), were given to the United States National Museum and Columbia University by Roessler. If these fossils were part of the survey collections, Roessler cannot be entirely blamed for salvaging what otherwise would have been lost or destroyed during the war years when the geological survey rooms were used as a percussion cap factory.

Roessler's motives for salvaging the survey data for map making are somewhat suspect; in whatever manner he obtained the data, the maps were mostly published under the banner of the Texas Land and Immigration Company of New York. In addition to geological data of the survey, the maps contained promotional material of a later date. The Shumard Survey operated under such adverse political conditions that the maps are no longer of importance except as historical memorabilia.

Roessler made his permanent home in Austin, although in the late 1860's he was a geologist for the United States Land Office in Washington, D.C. In the 1870's he made sixteen county maps and a map of the state of Texas that bears his name; during that same period he was associated with the Texas Land and Immigration Company of New York as its secretary, and with the Texas Land and Copper Association. He died in 1893.

BIBLIOGRAPHY: S. B. Buckley, *First Annual Report of the Geographical and Agricultural Survey of Texas* (1874); James M. Day and Ann B. Dunlap (comps.), *Map Collection of the Texas State Archives, 1527–1900* (1962); S. W. Geiser, "Men of Science in Texas, 1820–1880," *Field and Laboratory*, 17 (1959); Robert T. Hill, "The Present Condition of the Knowledge of the Geology of Texas," *United States Geological Bulletin*, No. 45 (1887); Keith Young, "The Roessler Maps," *Texas Junior Science*, 17 (1965).

Keith Young

*Rogan, Charles. Charles Rogan, the only child of John Netherland (not John H., as stated in Volume II) and Mary M. (Wood) Rogan, was born on February 3, 1858, near Ripley, Mississippi. He came with his family to Lexington, Texas, in 1862 (not 1861). He attended private schools in Waco and Giddings and was a member of the first graduating class of the Agricultural and Mechanical College of Texas (now Texas A&M University) in 1879. He was appointed deputy clerk of Lee County before attending Harvard Law School from 1881 to 1883. He began practicing law in Brownwood in 1884, then served as Brown County attorney, Brownwood city attorney, and Brown County judge during the years 1885 to 1897, with the exception of a two-year period (1891–1892) when he was an elected representative of the Texas legislature, representing Brown, Comanche, and Mills counties. Rogan was married to Frances Virginia Stewart on December 1, 1885; they had one son and four daughters.

In 1897 Rogan was appointed to the board of Texas A&M, but resigned to accept the appointment of commissioner of the General Land Office qv upon the death of George W. Finger,qv in May,

1899. He served the remainder of that term, then was elected in 1900 to another term, serving until January, 1903 (he was not elected to two full terms, as implied in Volume II).

During his three and one-half years as land commissioner, Charles Rogan contributed greatly to the economic and cultural development of Texas through his dedication to the preservation and enlargement of the Permanent School Fund qv of Texas. The fund had not received one-half of the unappropriated public domain that was granted it by the Constitution of 1876,qv and it was because of Rogan's special report on November 1, 1899, that the legislature's Adjustment Act of February 23, 1900, restored 5,902,076 acres or its equivalent in cash to the Permanent School Fund.

Rogan also reversed the policy that the law fixed the maximum as well as the minimum price of school and other lands, thenceforward increasing the revenue for the Permanent School Fund.

Rogan's third and greatest contribution had to do with the retaining of mineral rights for the state. In a Supreme Court decision, *Schendell* v. *Rogan* (June, 1901), which resulted from a test case asked for by Governor Joseph Draper Sayers,qv it was held that only on state lands classified "mineral" at the time of sale could the state retain mineral rights, otherwise the minerals went to the purchaser. Under Rogan's direction, his office immediately began the tremendous task of writing the word "mineral" or its abbreviation on the land records. Up to 1901 mineral activity was confined predominantly to metallic minerals, but when oil gushed at Spindletop,qv a new era had begun. To secure time to complete the task he raised the statutory price of land under the sales law from one dollar to one hundred dollars an acre. Successors to the land commissioner's office retained these mineral designations, and thus began a new land office policy which has brought millions of dollars to the Permanent School Fund throughout the years.

Roganville, in Jasper County, was named for Charles Rogan by industrialist John Henry Kirby qv in 1899. Rogan did not seek reelection as land commissioner; he opened a law office in Austin in 1903. He served as a member of the board of the Agricultural Experiment Station System qv from 1907 to 1920, and as a dollar-a-year man for the U.S. government during World War I. He died at his home in Austin on January 12, 1932, and was buried in Oakwood Cemetery there.

BIBLIOGRAPHY: Lewis B. Cooper (dir.), Texas State Teachers Association, *The Permanent School Fund of Texas* (1934); Thomas Lloyd Miller, *The Public Lands of Texas, 1519–1970* (1972); Octavia F. Rogan, *Land Commissioner Charles Rogan and the Mineral Classification of Texas Public School Lands* (1968); Walter B. Moore, "Rogan Saved All Texans Money," Dallas *Morning News*, March 8, 1969.

Octavia F. Rogan

*Rogan, Edgar Huntley.

*Roganville, Texas.

Rogers, Arthur Birch. Arthur Birch Rogers was born on August 10, 1871, at Waxahachie, Texas, the son of James C. and Elizabeth (Wilson) Rogers. The family moved to San Marcos in 1874, and Rogers attended public schools and Coronal Institute.qv He established furniture, undertaking, and cemetery businesses in San Marcos that spanned the first half of the twentieth century. He was married to Irene Swift on September 25, 1896, and they had four children. He was one of the organizers and a president of the Hays County Fair Association in the 1920's. Rogers is best known as developer of the headwaters of the San Marcos River as a tourist and recreational attraction. In 1928 he built a hotel and a golf course at the headwaters of the river; in the 1940's his son, Paul J. Rogers, began development of the Aquarena Springs qv tourist complex, which included several historical exhibits. Rogers died in San Marcos on April 26, 1953.

Tula Townsend Wyatt

*Rogers, Edwin C.

*Rogers, Joseph Burleson.

Rogers, Lieuen Morgan. Lieuen Morgan Rogers was born on December 13, 1820, in Munroe County, Alabama, the son of Patterson and Elizabeth Blair (Long) Rogers. He came to Texas with his parents in 1836, after the battle of San Jacinto, and soon enlisted in the Texas Army,qv serving under his uncle, Edward Burleson.qv He remained in the army until 1846, when he was a first lieutenant. His father and one brother were murdered by Mexican guerrillas, and he, along with another brother, systematically sought out and killed the murderers over a period of years. In 1849–1851 Rogers filibustered for fifteen months in Cuba, where he was captured and sentenced to death; later his sentence was commuted to life in prison, but through the intercession of the American and British governments, he was released and returned to Texas.

Rogers' first wife was Annette Brightman of Goliad, who died May 5, 1862. He later married Emma Stribling of San Antonio. Having acquired land near Refugio, Rogers became prominent and active in public affairs in Refugio County. He served as chief justice of that county from 1854 to 1855 and from 1860 to 1861. While chief justice in 1861 he sponsored the organization of the "Refugio Gardes," a local home-guard company, and in that same year he was commissioned a major and assigned to command the 3rd Texas State Troops, which protected supply lines in South Texas during the Civil War.

Returning to Refugio after the war, Rogers was elected as a Democrat to the Fourteenth Texas Legislature in 1873. He participated in the Coke-Davis Controversy,qv aligning himself with Democrat Richard Coke against Republican incumbent Edmund J. Davis.qqv In 1877 Rogers again became county judge of Refugio County and continued in office until his death at Refugio on November 30,

1889. He was buried in Mount Calvary Cemetery at Refugio.

BIBLIOGRAPHY: (Mrs.) Frank DeGarmo, *Pathfinders of Texas, 1836–1846* (1951); Hobart Huson, *Refugio*, I (1953), II (1955).

Hobart Huson

*Rogers, Samuel C. A. Samuel Crawford Adustin Rogers was born on June 18, 1810 (not June 10, 1810, as stated in Volume II).

BIBLIOGRAPHY: Louis Wiltz Kemp, General Biographical Notebook (MS., Archives, University of Texas at Austin Library); Samuel C. A. Rogers, Reminiscences (MS., Archives, University of Texas at Austin Library).

*Rogers, William P.

*Rogers, Texas. Rogers, in Bell County, had a 1960 population of 936 and a 1970 population of 1,030, according to the United States census. The town had twenty-two businesses in 1970.

*Rogers Creek.

Rogers Prairie, Texas. Rogers Prairie, Leon County, was on the Old San Antonio Road qv two miles east of Normangee; possibly it was named for an early settler, Robert Rogers. It was settled when the nearby blockhouse, Fort Boggy,qv was built in 1840. Rogers Prairie post office was established on July 10, 1874, with John W. Clarkson as postmaster. Its population was forty-eight in 1880. Rogers Prairie Lodge No. 540, A.F. and A.M., was chartered there in 1881. The Trinity and Brazos Valley Railroad, built in 1906, was two miles west of the village, and as a result the post office was taken to Normangee. Rogers Prairie had six businesses, a high school, a Baptist church, and a cemetery. Only the cemetery, the Ike Carter home, and several residences of later date remained in the 1960's.

Grover Cleveland Ramsey

*Roland, Texas.

*Rolder, Texas.

*Rolla, Texas.

*Rolling Stone.

Rollingwood, Texas. Rollingwood, in Travis County, was founded and developed by George B. Hatley in 1955 in the hilly area west of Austin. By May, 1963, the village had grown sufficiently to incorporate as a municipality with a mayor-council form of government. Population in 1960 was 390; by 1970 it was 780. A residential suburb of Austin, Rollingwood maintained its own police services and volunteer fire department. It had five small service businesses and was a part of the Eanes Independent School District in the late 1960's.

Rollins, Hyder Edward. Hyder Edward Rollins was born in Abilene on November 8, 1889, the son of Nathaniel G. and Elva (Hyder) Rollins. At the age of fourteen he entered Southwestern University and, after time off for teaching in country schools, he received his first degree in 1910. He received an M.A. degree from the University of Texas in 1912 and taught English there for two years. He was a graduate student at Johns Hopkins

University in 1914–1915, then attended Harvard, where he received the Ph.D. degree in 1917.

In World War I Rollins enlisted as a private in the U.S. Army Signal Corps and served as a second lieutenant for the next two years in France. In 1919 he went to Europe on a Sheldon Traveling Fellowship, Harvard, which he had earlier declined in order to enlist. He was appointed assistant professor at New York University in 1920 and became a full professor four years later. In 1926 he returned to Harvard and succeeded George Lyman Kittredge as Gurney Professor of English there in 1939. He retired in 1956 and continued to reside in Cambridge, Massachusetts.

Rollins was the author of numerous books and articles. He was editor or coeditor of some twenty volumes in *Harvard Studies in English, Harvard Studies and Notes in Philology and Literature,* and *A New Variorum Shakespeare.* Between 1914 and 1916 he published thirteen articles on O. Henry qv and other Texas subjects. He was a recognized scholar in Elizabethan poetry, the broadside ballad, and the Romantic poets. He had an international reputation for his scholarly work on the poet Keats. He directed over one hundred doctoral dissertations while at Harvard. In 1933 he received an honorary LL.D. from Southwestern University. Rollins never married. He died on July 25, 1958, and was buried in Abilene, Texas.

Richard T. Fleming

*Roma-Los Saenz, Texas. Roma-Los Saenz, in Starr County, had a population of 1,496 in 1960; by 1970, possibly due to the construction of Falcon Dam qv and the resulting resort facilities ten miles north, the population had increased to 2,154. The town supported twenty-eight businesses in 1970. *See also* Portscheller, Heinrich.

*Roman, Richard.

*Roman Catholic Church in Texas. With the Catholic population of Texas increasing from 1,-314,705 in 1950 to 2,029,478 in 1965, it was necessary to create new dioceses from the seven established between 1847 and 1947. In 1961 the diocese of San Angelo was created from counties taken out of the Amarillo, Dallas, Austin, and El Paso dioceses; its first bishop was Thomas F. Drury. In 1965 Drury was transferred to the Corpus Christi diocese, and his successor, the Reverend Thomas A. Tschoepe of Dallas, had in his new diocese sixty-eight priests caring for some 59,000 parishioners.

In 1965 four southern counties that had been part of the Corpus Christi diocese became the diocese of Brownsville, with the Most Reverend Adolph Marx, auxiliary bishop of Corpus Christi, named the first ordinary. Upon his death that same year, he was succeeded by the Most Reverend Humberto Medieros, installed in June, 1966. The Galveston-Houston diocese was divided in half in 1966, with the eastern part, the Beaumont diocese, having the Most Reverend Vincent M. Harris as first bishop.

In 1950 there were 1,165 priests, 234 brothers, and 4,051 sisters; by 1965 the number had increased to 1,879 priests, 402 brothers, and 4,865 sisters. Facilities increased from 513 parishes and 804 missions, chapels, and stations (services held where no churches were available) to 706 and 1,130, respectively. During this period infant and adult baptisms rose from 62,418 to 80,149.

Since the first Benevolent Society for the relief of the poor was founded in Galveston in 1846, the social action program has been carried on by each bishop. From one hospital founded in Galveston in 1866 by three sisters, its charitable institutions increased by 1965 to forty-one hospitals with a total bed capacity of 5,942 and a staff of 2,000 sisters, with an annual treatment of some 530,000 patients. There were nine orphanages caring for 565 children, with 196 in foster homes; twelve homes for 744 aged guests; and seven protective institutions with 461 students. Clinics were operated in various poverty areas.

Work of the church was also carried on through groups such as Catholic Charities, St. Vincent de Paul Societies, Knights of Columbus Councils, Catholic Daughters of America, Diocesan Councils of Men and Women, Catholic Youth Organizations, and lay volunteers. Minority and national groups have participated in diocesan credit unions, insurance groups, and spiritual societies.

The Texas Catholic Conference, with headquarters in Austin, and Callam Graham as director, coordinated the work of the diocese and various church organizations. The conference served as a clearing house for information on federal and state legislation. Conference recommendations were sent to the bishops. Encountering problems in the sponsoring of the 1965 Headstart Program in many dioceses, Jack McIntosh was named director of the conference's educational department; he acted as a state coordinator in educational matters and worked directly with diocesan school superintendents.

BIBLIOGRAPHY: Files of the Catholic Archives of Texas (Austin).

Sister M. Claude Lane, O.P.

Roman Catholic Education in Texas. The Roman Catholic church, always concerned with the education and training of youth, brought its educational system to Texas in 1682 when Franciscan missionaries qv established the first mission at Corpus Christi de la Isleta qv (Ysleta) near El Paso. In mission schools the Indians were taught not only religion by a special Indian catechism, but reading and writing in the Spanish language; they were given instruction in vocational training, agriculture, and caring for the sick, along with cultural training in crafts, painting, sculpture, and music. After over one hundred years, with the secularization of the missions beginning in 1794 and finally ending in 1830, this work was abandoned. When vice-prefect Bishop John Mary Odin qv arrived in Texas in 1840, he was distressed at what appeared to be a spiritual neglect of the people, and he recommended to his superior a need for Catholic schools in Galveston and San Antonio. He organized a school in Galveston in 1842 with twenty-two pupils, one-third of whom were non-Catholics. After purchasing the Love estate in Galveston in 1845, he invited the Ursuline Sisters qv from New Orleans to open a school for young ladies. Ursuline Academy,qv at Galveston, opened on February 8, 1847. Two other schools operating in 1847 were St. Mary's School at Brown's Settlement in Lavaca County and a school for boys at Brazoria. A fourth school was listed in Houston in 1848, taught by the pastor of St. Vincent's Church there, and in 1849 schools in Castroville and Cummings Creek were reported.

With help from the New Orleans convent the Galveston Ursuline Sisters opened a girls' school in San Antonio in 1851, and in that same year the Brothers of Mary (Marists) arrived in San Antonio from France, opening St. Mary's School for boys in 1852 (see St. Mary's University). Bishop Odin established the Sisters of the Incarnate Word and Blessed Sacrament qv from Lyons, France, in Brownsville, where they opened Villa Maria Academy for girls in 1853 (after having arrived in Galveston in June, 1852). By 1856 schools for boys were reported in Brownsville and Laredo.

For training a native clergy, Bishop Odin persuaded a young missionary society in France, the Oblate Fathers of Mary Immaculate, to come to Texas in 1852 (see also Oblate Fathers Trail; Oblate College of the Southwest). They opened Immaculate Conception College and Seminary in Galveston in November, 1854, which was chartered in 1856 as St. Mary's University of Galveston and continued as such until 1924. In 1926 the original charter was amended to read "at La Porte."

In 1866 Bishop Claude-Marie Dubuis qv brought two groups from France. Two Sisters of Divine Providence qv arrived in Austin in October, 1866, and opened the first Catholic school there in December; in 1868 they opened schools in Corpus Christi and Castroville. In 1895 they established Our Lady of the Lake Academy (see Our Lady of the Lake College) in San Antonio, which was expanded into a four year college in 1913.

The second group, three Sœurs Hôpitalières, who at Bishop Dubuis's request were trained for work in Texas by the Sisters of the Incarnate Word and Blessed Sacrament in Lyons, France, opened St. Mary's Infirmary, Galveston, in 1866, and Santa Rosa Infirmary, San Antonio in 1869. These nuns, later known as Sisters of Charity of the Incarnate Word,qv opened a parochial school in connection with St. Joseph's Orphanage in 1875 and established, in 1893, Incarnate Word Academy, to which a college program was added in 1909 (see Incarnate Word College).

After the Civil War the Incarnate Word sisters of Brownsville started academies at Victoria (1866), Corpus Christi (1871), and Houston

(1873). The Ursulines formed separate communities and academies at Laredo (1868), Dallas (1874), Puebla, Mexico (1892), and at Bryan following the 1900 Galveston flood.qv The Sisters of St. Mary of Namur qv came to Waco in 1873, establishing Sacred Heart Academy. In 1885 they established Saint Ignatius Academy in Fort Worth, which became their headquarters and Our Lady of Victory College qv (now merged with the University of Dallas qv). The Sisters of Mercy qv of New Orleans arrived in Indianola in January, 1875, and opened a school in September, but within the month that building, along with most of the town, was destroyed by a hurricane; they moved to Refugio, opening their first permanent school. A second group of Mercy sisters, from San Francisco, established a school in the German community of Mariensfeld (Mariensfield, later changed to Stanton), which operated from 1894 until 1938, when it was moved to Slaton.

In 1874 Holy Cross priests, brothers, and sisters from Indiana arrived in Austin. The priests assumed charge of St. Mary's parish, and the brothers prepared buildings for a Catholic boys' school, which was formally opened in 1881 as St. Edward's School for Boys and chartered as St. Edward's College in 1885 (see St. Edward's University). The sisters established St. Mary's Academy qv in Austin in 1874 and in 1880 opened a parish school in Marshall, also called St. Mary's Academy. Five sisters of Loretto from New Mexico opened St. Joseph's School in San Elizario in 1879 but moved it to El Paso in 1892, where they also sponsored the new Sacred Heart school. Dominican sisters qv of Somerset, Ohio, moved their new foundation to Galveston in 1882 and opened a select day and boarding school for girls, Sacred Heart Academy (now Dominican High School).

The Holy Rosary School for Negroes, begun by the Dominican sisters in Galveston in 1887, grew so rapidly that a new and larger building was constructed the following year. The order also staffed the following schools: St. Mary's Cathedral, Galveston (1893); St. Mary's, Taylor (1896); and Sacred Heart, Houston (1897). With the opening of schools in Galveston and Houston in 1887, interest in education for the Negro began to increase. In 1893 Margaret Healey Murphy founded a congregation in San Antonio, the Sister-Servants of the Holy Ghost and Mary Immaculate.qv Beginning at St. Peter Claver's parish school for Negroes, they expanded to Dallas, Fort Worth, Houston, and Beaumont. Sisters of the Holy Family, a Negro community of nuns founded in 1842 in New Orleans, took charge of Holy Rosary School in Galveston in 1897, reorganizing it into a grammar and industrial training school. Their work was extended to Houston, San Antonio, Ames, and Marshall. A third group dedicated to work among Negroes, the Sisters of the Blessed Sacrament for Indians and Colored People, founded in 1891 in Philadelphia, established a school in Beaumont in 1916 and later founded schools in Port Arthur, Houston, and Orange.

Parochial schools assumed a major role in Catholic education with immigration in the nineteenth century. Schools for German, Polish, Czech, Mexican, and Anglo-Saxon children often were established along with new churches. After 1900 parochial schools increased steadily in number and quality, although many of the earlier ones closed or were consolidated with public schools.

Higher education also was an educational concern. Although St. Mary's University in Galveston (1854–1924) and the University of Dallas (1907–1927) closed, St. Mary's University qv in San Antonio and St. Edward's University qv in Austin continued to operate with increased enrollment, as have the two Catholic women's colleges in San Antonio, Our Lady of the Lake College and Incarnate Word College.qqv Recently established colleges have been Sacred Heart Dominican College qv in Houston in 1945; the University of St. Thomas qv in Houston in 1946, established by the Basilian fathers, who came to Texas in 1899; and the University of Dallas, reestablished in 1956. A trend toward junior colleges developed in the early 1960's with the opening of Our Lady of Perpetual Help College in Houston and Christopher College of Corpus Christi qv by the Sisters of the Incarnate Word and Blessed Sacrament. In a move toward coeducational universities, Maryhill College for Women was created at St. Edwards University (Austin) in 1966, administered by the Sisters of the Immaculate Heart of Mary. By 1971 Maryhill College had become a part of St. Edwards University, the sisters remaining as part of the faculty and staff.

In 1965 statistics on Roman Catholic education in Texas showed 2,645 sisters, 239 brothers, 301 priests, 20 scholastics (post-novitiate teaching assistants), and 2,455 lay teachers, a total of 5,660 teachers in 16 seminaries, 10 colleges and universities, 15 nursing schools, 28 diocesan and 46 private high schools, 346 parochial and 36 private elementary schools, and 7 protective institutions. Students enrolled totaled 1,262 seminarians, 9,156 collegians, 876 in nursing schools, 21,838 in high schools, 115,555 in elementary schools, 461 in protective schools, and 70,309 high school students and 220,829 elementary students in Confraternity of Christian Doctrine classes; this brought the total number receiving Catholic instruction to 440,000.

BIBLIOGRAPHY: C. E. Castañeda, *Our Catholic Heritage in Texas, 1519–1936*, VII (1958); Max Berger, "Education in Texas during the Spanish and Mexican Periods," *Southwestern Historical Quarterly*, LI (1947–1948); *National Catholic Almanac* (1966); *The Official Catholic Directory* (1845–1966); Catholic Archives, Chancery Office, Austin.

Sister M. Claude Lane, O.P.

*Romayor, Texas.

*Romberg, Johannes Christlieb Nathanael. [This title was incorrectly listed in Volume II as Romberg, Jannes Christlieb Nathaniel.] Johannes

Romberg's eyesight was not impaired by an accident (as stated in Volume II) but by his having had the measles. The "Prairieblume" literary club, which he founded, included German settlers from the Black Jack Springs and La Grange areas, who read and discussed their stories, articles, and poems in the tradition of the "Latin Settlements" of Texas.qv Romberg is generally conceded to be the most outstanding German Texan poet and is among the notable German American poets. Many of his poems, such as "On the Colorado River," "Winter in Texas," and "The Oaks," are of German pioneer and Texas inspiration. Romberg died on February 5, 1891, in the Black Jack Springs community and was buried beside his wife in the little country cemetery of the Trinity Lutheran Church (known as the Black Jack Lutheran Church) located off the highway from La Grange to Flatonia.

BIBLIOGRAPHY: Louise Romberg Fuchs (Helen and Gertrude Franke, trans.), *Reminiscences* (1936); Annie Romberg, *History of the Romberg Family* (1960?); Selma Metzenthin Raunick, "A Survey of German Literature in Texas," *Southwestern Historical Quarterly*, XXXIII (1929–1930), "German Verse in Texas," *Southwest Review* (Autumn, 1932), "Johannes Christlieb Nathanael Romberg," *American-German Review* (February, 1948); Johannes C. N. Romberg Papers (MS., Archives, University of Texas at Austin Library).

Crystal Sasse Ragsdale

*Romero, Antonio.

*Romero, Texas.

*Romney, Texas.

Rooke, Allen Driscoll. Allen Driscoll Rooke was born in Victoria, Texas, on July 11, 1892, son of Frank B. and Roberta (Driscoll) Rooke. After graduation from the West Texas Military Academy at San Antonio and the University of Texas, he returned to Refugio County and engaged in ranching with his father and brothers. He attended the first officers' training camp at Leon Springs in 1917, was commissioned, and served overseas on the battlefront as a captain in World War I. In 1919 he joined the family firm of F. B. Rooke and Sons, eventually becoming managing partner.

An advocate of military preparedness, he was a co-organizer in 1940 of the Royal Irish Regiment of Refugio County, precursor of the Texas Defense Guard, later the Texas State Guard.qv Upon the mustering out of the 21st Battalion of the Texas Defense Guard in 1946 he was commissioned a colonel in the Texas National Guard.qv Convinced of the value of the Texas State Guard as a permanent active militia, Rooke was active in obtaining legislation authorizing the Texas State Guard Reserve Corps, of which he was deputy corps commander and major general at the time of his death. He was a charter member and president for two terms of the Texas State Guard Association, a founder of the National Association of State Militia, and was active in lobbying Congress for national recognition and support of the state guards of the several states. After his death, an act of the Fifty-ninth

Texas Legislature, 1965, made the State Guard a permanent part of the state's military establishment.

Prominent in banking and cattlemen's associations, he was president of the First National Bank of Woodsboro and a vice-president of the Southwest Cattle Raisers' Association.qv Among his benefactions was the Rooke Foundation, Inc. He died in San Antonio on May 3, 1964.

BIBLIOGRAPHY: Hobart Huson, *Refugio*, II (1953).

Hobart Huson

*Roosevelt, Texas.

*Rooster Springs, Texas.

*Ropesville, Texas. The A. W. (not W. A., as stated in Volume II) Blankenship family arrived in the Ropesville area, Hockley County, on January 2, 1902. The 1960 population of Ropesville was 423, and the 1970 population was 483, according to the United States census.

BIBLIOGRAPHY: Seymour V. Connor (ed.), *Builders of the Southwest* (1959).

David Gracy

*Rosalia Creek.

*Rosalie, Texas.

*Rosalis, Battle of.

*Rosanky, Texas. Rosanky, in southern Bastrop County, had its first community center at Snake Prairie (not Sanke Prairie, as stated in Volume II), one and one-half miles from the present site of Rosanky. A bleak description of Snake Prairie in particular and snakes in general was written by H. F. McDanield and N. A. Taylor in *The Coming Empire; or, Two Thousand Miles in Texas on Horseback* (1877), concerning their travels in the early 1870's. Rosanky had an estimated population of 210 in 1971.

*Rosario Mission. *See* Nuestra Señora del Rosario Mission.

*Roscoe, Texas. Roscoe, in Nolan County, had a 1960 population of 1,490 and a 1970 population of 1,580, according to the United States census. The town reported forty businesses in 1970.

*Roscoe, Snyder, and Pacific Railway Company.

*Rose, Archibald Johnson.

*Rose, Moses.

*Rose, Preston Robinson.

*Rose, Victor Marion.

*Rose, William Pinckney. William Pinckney Rose was the son of John and Mary (Washington) Rose.

BIBLIOGRAPHY: John Howell McLean, *Reminiscences* (1918).

*Rose Hill, Texas. (Dallas County.)

*Rose Hill, Texas. (Harris County.)

Rose Hill, Texas. (Travis County.) Rose Hill began its first school in 1879, and by 1880 Henry Nelle donated land for a school, a church, and a cemetery. Sometimes called Nelleville, Rose Hill was located in northeast Travis County, near Manor. In 1890 settlers built the Rose Hill Luther-

an Church. It existed until 1924, when the congregation merged with St. Peter's Evangelical Lutheran Church in Elgin. The building probably was used for school as well as church purposes; only the cemetery and the foundations of the church remained in the early 1970's.

BIBLIOGRAPHY: Mary Starr Barkley, *History of Travis County and Austin, 1839–1899* (c. 1963).

Rose Hill Acres, Texas. Rose Hill Acres, an incorporated town in southeastern Hardin County, had a 1970 population of 431, according to the United States census.

*Rose Industry. In the 1950's and 1960's rose growing in Texas continued to center in Smith County, with other growing areas represented by Gregg, Cherokee, Upshur, and Van Zandt counties. In the early 1970's over fifteen million rosebushes continued to be shipped annually from Texas to points throughout the United States.

BIBLIOGRAPHY: *Texas Almanac* (1967, 1973).

*Roseborough Springs, Texas.

*Rosebud, Texas. Rosebud, in southern Falls County, continued as a farm market in the 1960's. The town was served by two hospitals, two banks, a library, and a newspaper; improvements were made in the municipal system during the mid-1960's. Rosebud's businesses included cotton gins, an auction barn, two corn shellers, a fertilizer plant, a grain warehouse, and a meat-processing plant. In 1970 fifty-five businesses were reported. The 1960 population was 1,644; the 1970 population was 1,597, according to the United States census.

*Rosedale, Texas.

*Roselawn, Texas.

*Rosenberg, Henry.

*Rosenberg, Texas. Rosenberg, in central Fort Bend County, adjoins the town of Richmond. Rosenberg serves as a center for petrochemical and sulphur industries and for food-canning plants. Cotton, rice, and grain crops grown in the surrounding area are brought into the Rosenberg-Richmond interurban area for processing. Many of the area residents work in nearby Houston. Four banks, one hospital, three newspapers, twelve schools, twenty-eight churches, and three hotels were reported during the 1960's. The town shares a library with Richmond. In 1970 Rosenberg supported 187 businesses. Rosenberg's population was 9,698 in 1960; in 1970 it was 12,098, a 24.7 percent increase, according to the United States census. *See also* Houston Standard Metropolitan Statistical Area.

*Rosenberg Library. The Rosenberg Library in Galveston is an Italian Renaissance style building of simple terra-cotta ornament and excellent proportions. It was designed by William S. Eames and Thomas C. Young, members of the St. Louis City Plan Commission and architects for the United States Custom House at San Francisco. The construction contract was let to Harry Devlin of Galveston on March 21, 1902, for $126,500. Total cost of the library site, books, and building was approximately $270,000.

In June of 1969 bids for the new Moody Memorial Wing were opened and the official ground-breaking ceremony occurred on August 6, 1969. The building, a gift of the Moody Foundation and more than 2,000 individuals and other foundations, was designed by Galveston architect Thomas M. Price, with Library Design Associates of Tulsa, Oklahoma, consulting. The new wing was due to be completed by the summer of 1971 at a cost of $1.7 million. A total of 55,000 square feet more than doubled the size of the entire building. Included in the plan, in addition to greatly expanded areas to hold the library's book collection and to provide additional seating for readers, were the Wortham Auditorium, Harris Art Gallery, Humphreys Children's Department, Randall Room, and other exhibit areas, while renovation of the old building called for the inclusion of such features as the Lykes Maritime Gallery and Hutchings Texas History Museum Gallery.

With the opening of the new Moody Wing, plans were to move the older book collection onto the main floor of the Rosenberg building to become the "Research Collection." The collection is non-circulating and includes the bulk of nineteenth- and early twentieth-century titles, little-used non-Texas Americana, old technical and reference volumes, and older foreign language titles.

The William G. Rice Room's book collection was combined with archival material previously housed in the Winterbotham Room to form the present Texas History and Archives Department. The Colonel Milo Pitcher Fox and Agness Peel Fox Rare Book Room opened in December, 1967, with an endowment of more than $200,000, and houses the library's incunabula and other valuable holdings. The Marion Lee Kempner Memorial Room was also dedicated in December, 1967.

Book circulation in 1969 was 313,942 volumes; it was accomplished by means of a bookmobile and branch libraries in LaMarque, Dickinson, and Friendswood. Circulating and non-circulating materials in the library included approximately 154,778 books; 502,930 manuscripts; 193,113 government documents; 931 museum items; 3,291 microfilms; 39,491 pamphlets; 17,746 bound periodicals; 2,913 bound volumes of newspapers; 2,387 maps; 441 framed pictures; 18,443 mounted pictures and clippings; 935 films and filmstrips; and 1,464 phonograph records.

Publications of the library have included *Samuel May Williams, 1795–1858* (1956); *The Diary of Millie Gray, 1832–1840* (1967); and *Rosenberg Library Bulletin*, a quarterly.

BIBLIOGRAPHY: The Rosenberg Library, Henry Rosenberg, 1824–1893 (1918); Minutes of the Rosenberg Library Board of Directors (1904–1970); Rosenberg Library Bulletin (New Series, 1969–1970); John D. Hyatt, "Moody Memorial Wing to Rosenberg Library," Texas Libraries (Summer, 1970).

Rosenfield, John, Jr. John Rosenfield, Jr., the son of Jennie Lind (Kramer) and Max John Rosenfield, was born in Dallas on April 5, 1900. He was educated in the Dallas public schools, attended the University of Texas, and graduated from Columbia University in New York. He worked for the New York *Evening Mail*, first as a reporter, then as a motion picture reviewer. Following brief employment as a publicity man for Paramount Pictures, he returned to Dallas in 1923 and joined the staff of the Dallas *Morning News*.qv Two years later he was asked by George B. Dealey,qv the founder of the *News*, to create an amusements department for the paper. During his forty-one years as drama and music critic for that newspaper, Rosenfield became the recognized cultural spokesman for the Southwest, contributing widely to national periodicals, as well as writing his local column, "The Passing Show." His reviews were characterized by astute judgment, dashed with keen wit. Largely through Rosenfield's influence with wealthy Dallas families, the Margo Jones Theatre [*see* Jones, Margaret Virginia (Margo)] was able to secure the financial backing which permitted its opening in June, 1947.

The Southwest Theatre Conference twice voted Rosenfield their annual award (in 1955 and 1960), and the Screen Directors Guild cited him for distinguished motion picture criticism in 1956. A member of Temple Emanu-El, he married Claire Burger in 1923 and was the father of one son. In 1957 he gave up his administrative duties with the Dallas *Morning News* but continued to write reviews until June, 1966. He died on November 26, 1966, and was buried in Dallas.

Ronald L. Davis

*Rosenthal, Texas.

*Roseville, Texas.

*Rosevine, Texas.

*Rosewood, Texas.

*Rosharon, Texas.

*Rosillo, Battle of. *See* Rosalis, Battle of.

*Rosillo Creek.

*Rosillos Mountains.

*Rosita, Texas. (Cameron County.)

Rosita, Texas. (Duval County.) Rosita, north of Rosita Creek in northeastern Duval County, had a church in 1936 but was a near ghost community in the 1970's. The town was south of the highway from Freer to San Diego. The rock store with the date 1932 set above the door was deserted in 1971.

BIBLIOGRAPHY: Bill Salter, "This Is South Texas," San Antonio Express, July 14, 23, 1971.

Rosita, Texas. (Starr County.) Rosita, in southern Starr County about seven miles west of Rio Grande City, had an estimated population of 215 in 1971, with most engaged in farming. The town had a filling station, a grocery store, and a gravel mining operation.

*Rosita Creek.

*Ross, George M. *See* Von Ross, George M.

*Ross, James J.

*Ross, Lawrence Sullivan. [The spelling of Ross's mother's first name was Catherine (not Katherine, as shown in Volume II).]

*Ross, Peter F. [Ross's mother's name was Catherine H. (Fulkerson) Ross (not Katherine H. Ross, as shown in Volume II).]

*Ross, Reuben.

*Ross, Reuben.

Ross, Robert Shapley. Robert Shapley Ross, son of Catherine (Fulkerson) and Shapley Prince Ross,qv was born April 22, 1848, at Station Creek, a ranger station near Waco. He was possibly the first white child born in the environs of present McLennan County. He attended primary school in Waco, St. Mary's in San Antonio, and Baylor University. During the Civil War he was a captain in Company D, 6th Texas Regiment, then returned to Waco, where on March 12, 1871, he married Elizabeth Anne Glenn; they had one daughter. In 1874 he was one of the organizers of the Waco Grays, a defense organization armed by the state; Ross was elected captain. The Grays numbered about sixty men, drilled once a month, and contributed to the social life of Waco.

In 1876 Ross edited the *Advance*, a Waco afternoon newspaper. Later, with his brother William Hallam Ross,qv he owned and published the *Daily Reporter*. He served as deputy sheriff of McLennan County for eight years, and from 1890 to 1894 he was county treasurer. In 1912 he was one of those responsible for bringing a group of Huaco Indians to the Waco Cotton Palace. Robert Shapley Ross died on January 11, 1923, and was buried at Oakwood Cemetery in Waco.

BIBLIOGRAPHY: John Sleeper and J. C. Hutchins (comps.), *Waco and McLennan County, Texas* (1876); Margaret Barclay, *Gibson Denison Ross Williams* (1965); Raymond L. Dillard, The Ross Family (M.A. thesis, Baylor University, 1931); Waco *Morning News*, March 16, 1922; Waco *Times-Herald*, May 16, 1912, January 11, 1923.

Merle Mears Duncan

*Ross, Shapley Prince. [The spelling of Ross's wife's first name was Catherine (not Katherine, as shown in Volume II).]

Ross, William Hallam. William Hallam Ross, youngest child of Catherine (Fulkerson) and Shapley Prince Ross qv was born August 18, 1853, in Waco. A member of the Waco Grays, an active military and social organization, he spent most of his early life in Waco. He and his brother, Robert Shapley Ross qv owned and published a newspaper, the *Daily Reporter*. On June 24, 1881, Ross married Elizabeth Anne Denison; they had eight children. Later William Hallam Ross practiced farming on land he owned in Palo Pinto County and near Stephenville in Erath County, where he brought his family. On November 14, 1913, he was appointed federal agricultural demonstration agent for Dallas County, where he was in charge of educational and demonstration farm work, a program designed to encourage farmers to operate their farms on a scientific basis. Ross was one of the first county agents in Texas. Upon retirement, he settled in Tarrant County and engaged in farming and operating a seed business. William Hallam Ross died on July 4, 1918, while visiting relatives in Belton. He was buried in Oakwood Cemetery in Waco.

BIBLIOGRAPHY: John Sleeper and J. C. Hutchins (comps.), *Waco and McLennan County, Texas* (1876); F. W. Johnson (E. C. Barker and E. W. Winkler, eds.), *A History of Texas and Texans*, V (1916); Margaret Barclay, *Gibson Denison Ross Williams* (1965); Raymond L. Dillard, The Ross Family (M.A. thesis, Baylor University, 1931); Waco *Times-Herald*, July 5, 1918, July 3, 1929.

Merle Mears Duncan

*Ross, Texas. (Brazoria County.)

*Ross, Texas. (McLennan County.)

*Ross' Brigade.

*Ross City, Texas. Ross City, in southern Howard County, was named for William Rossman, locator and developer of the town. Intending to supply the needs of a new oil field discovered in the area, Rossman bought the land in 1926 and divided it into townsite lots. For several years Ross City was a boom town and had a population of several hundred; in 1970 it was a ghost town. One residence, comprised of two rock buildings, was the only vestige left of the town.

Loyce Haynie Rossman

*Ross Creek.

*Rosser, Charles McDaniel.

*Rosser, Texas.

Rössler, Anton R. *See* Roessler, Anton R.

*Rosston, Texas.

*Rossville, Texas.

*Roswell, Texas.

*Rotan, Texas. Rotan, in Fisher County, had a 1960 population of 2,788; the 1970 count was 2,404, according to the United States census. Sixty businesses were reported in 1970.

Rothko Chapel. Rothko Chapel, a rare combination of art, architecture, and religion, was dedicated in Houston on February 27, 1971. Located there are works of two outstanding modern abstract artists, Mark Rothko and Barnett Newman. Built as an ecumenical chapel for the Institute of Religion and Human Development, it was funded by the Menil Foundation.

The idea of commissioning Mark Rothko had its origin in a 1964 visit to the artist's New York studio by John and Dominique de Menil, Houston art patrons, and they were impressed with what they felt was a religious quality in the famous artist's work. Rothko completed for them eighteen huge paintings by the spring of 1968. An abstract expressionist, he painted the fifteen-foot-high canvasses in dark, almost monochromatic, browns, blacks, purples, and reds. The octagonal chapel was built solely to display fourteen of the huge paintings, grouped as three triptychs and five singles. The four extra paintings, giving flexibility in choice for display, were stored at the Houston Museum of Fine Arts.qv

Barnett Newman's *Broken Obelisk* is a twenty-six-foot-high Corten steel sculpture, a shaft rising from a pyramid base, standing in a reflecting pool in front of the chapel. The rusty patina which had collected earlier on the sculpture while it was on display in New York and Washington was sandblasted off so that its new brownish-orange coloring would derive entirely from the Houston atmosphere. John and Dominique de Menil, who bought the sculpture, dedicated it to Martin Luther King, Jr.

The chapel itself, originally designed by architect Philip Johnson, but completed by architects Howard Barnstone and Eugene Aubry, is built of hand-molded natural sand-faced buff brick; it is windowless, but has a skylight of glass and metal webbing. The interior walls are concrete blocks covered with gray plaster; the flooring consists of eight-inch-square asphalt pavers. Simple cedar benches are the only furniture in the chapel.

BIBLIOGRAPHY: Lawrence Alloway, "Art," *The Nation*, March 15, 1971; David Snell, "Rothko Chapel—the painter's final testament," *Smithsonian*, August, 1971; Ann Holmes, "Rothko Chapel Opening," Houston *Chronicle*, February 21, 1971; Brian O'Doherty, "The Rothko Chapel," *Art In America*, 61 (January–February, 1973).

*Rough Creek.

*Rough Creek, Texas.

*Rough Hollow.

*Rough Mountain.

*Rough Riders.

*Rough Run.

*Round Head Mountain.

*Round Hill.

*Round Hole Branch.

*Round Mountain.

*Round Mountain, Texas.

*Round Prairie, Texas.

*Round Rock, Texas. Round Rock, first known as Brushy, is one of the oldest continuously settled communities in Williamson County. Settlement began in the area as early as 1834 (*see* Old Round Rock, Texas) and the community of Brushy was well known by 1840 (not 1850, as stated in Volume II), after Kenney's Fort qv was constructed in 1839 to provide protection against the Indians. Brushy took the new name of Round Rock (after a large round rock which is still in the bed of Brushy Creek) on August 24, 1854, when Jacob M. Harrell, Thomas Oatts, and other early settlers submitted the new name to the U.S. Post Office.

One of the early educational endeavors in Round Rock was Greenwood Masonic Institute (not "College," nor did the institute ever have a large enrollment, as stated in Volume II), located in the Masonic Hall in Old Round Rock and conducted by the Cumberland Presbyterian church. When the Masonic Hall burned, a new school was opened between Old Town and New Town Round Rock. The church gave up its management, and the Southern Presbyterians (not the Cumberland Presbyterian church) chartered Round Rock Institute in 1884. With the approach of a successful public school system, Round Rock Institute was closed in 1891 (not 1910). Also flourishing in the early days of New Town was the Round Rock Academy, under the direction of I. N. Stephens, Sr.

The Round Rock *Leader*, a weekly newspaper, was founded in 1896 (not 1875) and was first known as the Round Rock *Searchlight*. The name was changed probably around 1900.

In recent years various individuals and groups in Round Rock have carried forward the restoration of old and significant structures. The idea of preserving the architectural heritage of the community, especially its Old Town, is attributed to Helen Erwin and Rebecca Nelson in the early 1930's, and since then, particularly during the 1960's, to Harriett Rutland (Mrs. Erwin's daughter). Considerable effort and money have been devoted to purchasing and restoring houses, many of which are over one hundred years old, including Round Rock's first post office. Most of the buildings have been restored for use and the original decor of many has been preserved.

Round Rock had the first successful commercial cheese factory in Texas. Built by Thomas Edward and Carl A. Nelson, and managed by a Wisconsin cheesemaker, August H. Kaufman, the factory began operation in January, 1928, with the intention of bringing diversified farming to the region. Armour and Company purchased the factory in 1930 and continued production of cheddar cheeses. A cooperative of dairy farmers, Mid-Tex Producers Association, purchased the factory in 1956, and cheese production subsequently reached its peak. The factory was sold again in 1967, and it closed in October, 1968.

In the 1960's Round Rock continued to serve as a commercial center for the surrounding agricultural region. The town reported five churches and a bank; among the more than seventy commercial establishments reported were a lime kiln (since the earliest days of the railroad), rock quarries, fertilizer producers, and manufacturers of brooms, mattresses, and boats. The Lutheran Home for the Aged, the Lutheran Orphanage, and the Baptist Children's Home also served Round Rock. The Williamson County Old Settlers and the Swedish Old Settlers hold celebrations there each summer. The 1960 population was 1,878; it increased by almost 50 percent to 2,811 by 1970, according to the United States census report.

BIBLIOGRAPHY: Austin *American-Statesman*, June 29, 1969, October 4, 1970; Round Rock *Leader*, July 23, 1953.

Mrs. Starkey Duncan
Eugene N. Goodrich

*Round Timber, Texas.

*Round Top, Texas. The name Round Top was probably derived from the original settlement on the La Bahia Road qv about two miles north of the present town of Round Top, which was the location of a round top house built in 1847 by Alwin H. Soergel, an early German settler and author of an emigrant guide, *Für Auswanderungslustige*. In 1847 Viktor Bracht qv listed the Round Top House as a United States post office, with H. A. Robertson as postmaster. The early settlers in the area, largely American landholders, were the Ledbetters, Taylors, Robisons, Townsends, and Alexanders. Florida Chapel, an adjoining settlement on the south side of Cummins Creek, was also settled by Americans. In the 1840's and early 1850's Germans began to move into the area in large numbers. Among the first families were the Zapps, Henkels, Frickes, Bauers, Weyands, von Rosenbergs, Kneips, Rummels, and Schuddemagens.

The Round Top Guerrillas and the Round Top Guards were formed there and served the Confederacy during the Civil War. Round Top remained a sleepy rural German trading center with a population of 124 in 1960 and 94 in 1970, when, during that decade, it experienced a resurrection and restoration to become widely known as an historical attraction, with a number of authentically restored original houses, stores, and a church. In addition, a number of early farm houses in the surrounding rural area have been restored. Early maps relating to the Round Top area are: Hunt and Randel (1839); Charles Pressler (1851); Jacob de Cordova (1851); A. R. Roessler,qqv with early roads and railroads (1874); A. W. Spaight (1882); H. R. Bieberstein, plat map of the town of Round Top (1877); and the General Land Office Fayette County Survey Map, showing La Bahia Road (1920). *See also* Winedale Museum.

BIBLIOGRAPHY: Rudolph L. Biesele, *The History of the German Settlements in Texas, 1831–1861* (1930); Viktor Bracht (Charles Frank Schmidt, trans.), *Texas in 1848* (1931); Leonie Rummel Weyand and Houston Wade, *Early History of Fayette County* (1936); Marsha F. Jackson, *Notes on Henkel Square, Round Top, Texas* (1970); Frank Lotto, *Fayette County, Her History, and Her People* (1902).

Paul C. Ragsdale

*Round Top Academy.

*Roundup, Texas.

Rountree's Stage Stand. Rountree's Stage Stand was situated at the headquarters of the J. F. Rountree ranch in eastern Atascosa County about three miles west of Fashing. In the late 1870's the Rountrees operated a livery stable and cafe for the Corpus Christi and Brownsville stages of the San Antonio and Rio Grande Stage Company. In 1879 the Rountree Stage Stand was shown to be the only stage stop along the San Patricio Trail qv between Fairview and Oakville.

Robert H. Thonhoff

Routh, Eugene Coke. Eugene Coke Routh, an outstanding religious journalist, was born to Joseph Edward and Mary Ellen (Stramler) Routh on November 26, 1874, at Plum Grove, Texas. In 1889 he entered high school at Flatonia, and in 1893, planning a teaching career, he entered the University of Texas. After graduation in 1897 Routh became principal of a school at Winchester, then married Mary Mildred Wroe on December 20, 1897; they had six children. His first wife died in 1925, and he married Alice Routh, a distant cousin, on July 7, 1926.

While teaching in San Saba, Routh was licensed as a Baptist preacher. In 1901 he began "home mission" work in central Texas, later serving churches in Lockhart and San Antonio. In 1906 he was chairman of the committee which inaugurated San Marcos Academy. After a brief stay in the Abilene area, Routh returned to San Antonio to become editor of the *Baptist Visitor* in August, 1906. Two years later it became the *South Texas Baptist*. In 1912 this paper was merged into the *Baptist Standard* qv and Routh moved to Dallas to become associate editor; promoted to editor in 1914, he served until 1928.

Among controversial matters in his career were problems concerning evolution and the Ku Klux Klan.qv Editorially, Routh opposed the Klan and defended Baptist colleges against the charges of J. Frank Norris.qv He preferred not to be involved in the new "militant policy" demanded by the convention in 1927, resigned in 1928, and reluctantly left Dallas for Oklahoma City. From 1928 to 1943 he edited the *Baptist Messenger* for Oklahoma Baptists. For five years he edited *The Commission* for the Foreign Mission Board, doubling the circulation to 100,000 while reporting on worldwide missionary services.

Between 1929 and 1955 Routh was the author of eleven books, including *The Story of Oklahoma Baptists* (1932), *Adventures in Christian Journalism* (1951), and *Baptists on the March* (1953). He had completed forty-one years of denominational journalism when he retired in 1948, but he continued to write and preach. He was a member of the Texas State Historical Association.qv Routh died on May 12, 1966, and was buried in Laurel Land Memorial Park in Dallas.

BIBLIOGRAPHY: *Baptist Standard*, May 18, 1966; *Baptist Messenger*, May, 1966; E. C. Routh, *Adventures in Christian Journalism* (1951).

Robert C. Cotner

Routt, Joe Eugene. Joe Eugene Routt, son of Eugene Otis and Annie Belle (Clay) Routt, was born on October 18, 1914, at Chappell Hill, Texas. He attended Texas Agricultural and Mechanical College (now Texas A&M University) from 1933 to 1938, receiving a degree in animal husbandry. A guard on the varsity football team, Routt was named to the All-American football teams of 1936 and 1937, the first All-American player for A&M. He played on the 1938 College All-Star team at

Chicago and in the East-West Shrine game at San Francisco. Routt was commissioned a second lieutenant upon graduation from A&M and went on active duty in the United States Army in March, 1942. In 1942 he played for the Army West All-Star football team, playing against professional football teams. Routt was an infantry officer in World War II; he received the Bronze Star and Purple Heart decorations. He was a captain and company commander in Holland when he was killed in action on December 2, 1944. He was buried at Margraten, Holland; on April 19, 1949, he was reburied at Brenham, Texas.

Routt was married to Marilyn Maddox on March 1, 1942; they had two daughters. He was named to the National Football Foundation's Hall of Fame and in 1952 to the Texas Sports Hall of Fame.qv

BIBLIOGRAPHY: Houston *Post*, December 21, 1944; Kern Tips, *Football—Texas Style* (1964).

H. B. McElroy

*Rowden, Texas.

*Rowe, Joseph.

*Rowena, Texas. Rowena, in Runnels County, was laid out in November, 1898, by Paul J. Baron (not P. J. Barron, as stated in Volume II) and was first known as Baronsville (not Barronsville); however, the Gulf, Colorado, and Santa Fe Railroad station at this site had been named Rowena as early as 1890. This station and the one at Miles, Texas, were named by Jonathan Miles, a prominent cattleman from San Angelo, who had been instrumental in procuring the railroad right-of-way. Rowena station was named for a young lady whom Miles' son, John, was courting (not for a member of the Baron family, as stated in Volume II). In February, 1904, Paul J. Baron changed the name of his townsite to Rowena, at the request of residents of the area. Rowena was settled principally by German Americans and Czech Americans from central Texas. It was the birthplace of Bonnie Parker.qv It is the site of St. Joseph's High School, one of the few Catholic schools in West Texas. Twenty-one businesses were reported in 1970. The town had an estimated population of 446 that same year.

A. E. Skinner
Susan Miles

*Rowland, Texas.

*Rowlett, Daniel.

*Rowlett, Texas. Rowlett, in Dallas County, had a 1960 population of 1,015 and a 1970 population of 1,696, according to the United States census.

*Rowlett Creek.

*Roxana, Texas.

*Roxton, Texas.

*Roy Inks Dam and Lake. *See* Inks Dam and Lake.

*Royall, Richard Royster. [This title was incorrectly listed in Volume II as Royal, Richardson Royster.] Richard Royster Royall, son of William and Elizabeth (Bedford) Royall, was born in Halifax County, Virginia, on June 1, 1798, moved to Tuscumbia, Alabama, as a young man, and visited Texas several times between 1820 and 1831. A friend of Stephen F. Austin, Royall permanently settled in Texas in 1832, bringing his family with him to Matagorda.

Royall was married to Ann Alexander Underwood in 1819; they were the parents of four girls and two boys. His first wife died in Matagorda County on February 18, 1831; he was married again, to Elizabeth Allen Love, in Houston on January 3, 1839; they had one daughter. Royall was prominent in the affairs of Texas, serving as chairman of a central committee at San Felipe, which Stephen F. Austin had formed to act as a general supervisory body before the meeting of the Consultation qv in 1835.

According to family records, Richard Royster Royall died on June 29, 1840 (not May 29, 1840, as stated in Volume II).

BIBLIOGRAPHY: Richard Royall Family History, and Austin Papers, Vol. II, Part I (MSS., Archives, University of Texas at Austin Library); Lamar Papers (MS., Archives, Texas State Library, Austin).

*Royalty, Texas.

*Roy's Peak.

*Royse City, Texas. Royse City, on the Collin-Rockwall county line, had a 1960 population of 1,274 and a 1970 population of 1,535, according to the United States census. Thirty-five businesses were reported in 1970.

*Royston, Mart H.

*Royston, Texas.

*Royston Hill.

Royston Nave Memorial. *See* Nave, Royston.

*Roznov, Texas.

*Rubber, Manufacture of Synthetic.

Rubenstein, Jake. *See* Ruby, Jack.

*Rubí, the Marquis de.

*Ruby, G. T.

Ruby, Jack. Jack Ruby, whose real name was Jake Rubenstein, was born on March 25, 1911, in Chicago, Illinois, the son of Polish immigrants, Joseph and Fannie (Rutkowski) Rubenstein. He was placed in a foster home at the age of twelve, and at sixteen he dropped out of school to begin working at odd jobs. In 1933 he moved to San Francisco, where he sold newspaper subscriptions. He returned to Chicago in 1941, made an unsuccessful attempt to organize a union of junkyard workers, was then drafted into the army air force and was trained as a mechanic. After his discharge in 1946 Ruby moved to Dallas, where he and his sister Eva opened two nightclubs in 1947.

On November 24, 1963, he shot to death Lee Harvey Oswald,qv alleged assassin of President

John F. Kennedy (*see* Kennedy, John Fitzgerald, Assassination of) in the basement of the Dallas city jail. The shooting was witnessed by a television audience of millions. Ruby was convicted in Dallas of first degree murder, but in November, 1966, the Texas Court of Criminal Appeals ordered a new trial, ruling that a change of venue was necessary. Before a second trial could begin, he entered a Dallas hospital on December 9, 1966, and it was discovered that he was suffering from terminal lung cancer. He died in Dallas on January 3, 1967, and was buried in Westlawn Cemetery in Chicago, Illinois.

BIBLIOGRAPHY: Houston *Post*, January 4, 1967.

*Ruby, Texas.

*Rucker, Texas.

*Rucker Creek.

Ruckman, Thomas. Thomas Ruckman, founding father of Karnes County, Texas, was born in Northumberland County, Pennsylvania, on November 8, 1826. After graduating from the College of New Jersey (now Princeton University) in 1848, he taught school for one year in South Carolina. He moved in 1850 to San Antonio, where he worked for a year as a bookkeeper.

In 1851 he opened a trading post in the Mexican settlement of Alamita, located on the old Ox-Cart Road between San Antonio and Goliad. In 1852 he entered into a business partnership with Lewis S. Owings (who left in 1858 to become the first territorial governor of Arizona). Together they foresaw a metropolis arising at this roadstop and laid out a new town, which they named Helena in honor of Owings' wife, Helen Swisher Owings. When Karnes County was organized in 1854, Helena was chosen county seat. Ruckman, postmaster at Helena from 1854 to 1857, continued for nearly forty years as its leading merchant and banker. He helped found the Helena Academy in 1872.

Ruckman married (Mrs.) Jennie McCall on February 14, 1861; they had one daughter. He died on December 3, 1914, and was buried in the Masonic Cemetery of Helena.

BIBLIOGRAPHY: Thomas Ruckman Papers (Archives, University of Texas at Austin Library); Robert H. Thonhoff, A History of Karnes County (M.A. thesis, Southwest Texas State College, 1963); San Antonio *Express*, December 5, 1914.

Robert H. Thonhoff

*Rudd, Jonathon Davenport.

Rudder, James Earl. James Earl Rudder, son of Dee Forest and Annie (Powell) Rudder, was born in Eden, Texas, on May 6, 1910. He attended John Tarleton Agricultural College (now Tarleton State University) from 1927 to 1930, and he graduated from the Agricultural and Mechanical College of Texas (now Texas A&M University) in 1932 with a degree in industrial education. He was commissioned a second lieutenant of infantry in the U.S. Army Reserve in 1932. In 1933 he was a teacher

and coach at Brady, then taught and coached at John Tarleton from 1938 until called to active duty in 1941. In 1943, as a lieutenant colonel, he organized and trained the famed 2nd Ranger Battalion and led them during the 1944 Normandy invasion. His rangers suffered more than 50 percent casualties on the first day, and Rudder was wounded twice. In the winter of 1944–1945 he commanded the 109th Infantry Regiment, which played a major role in repulsing the German counter-offensive at the Battle of the Bulge. Rudder was released from active duty in 1945 with the rank of colonel. One of the most decorated American soldiers during World War II, he was awarded the Distinguished Service Cross, Legion of Merit, Silver Star, Bronze Star, the French Legion of Honor, and other decorations.

Rudder married Margaret E. Williamson of Menard on June 12, 1937, and they had five children. From 1946 to 1952 he served as mayor of Brady. He was a member of the State Board of Public Welfare from 1953 to 1955 and of the State Democratic Executive Committee from 1952 to 1956. In 1955 he was appointed commissioner of the General Land Office qv to serve out the unfinished term of Bascom Giles (*see* Veterans Land Board Scandal), and in 1956 he was elected to that office. He resigned in 1958 to become vice-president of Texas A&M, and in 1959 he became that institution's president; in 1965 he was named president of the Texas A&M University System.qv

In 1954 Rudder was promoted to the rank of brigadier general of U.S. Army Reserves; he was made a reserve major general in 1957. In 1967 President Lyndon B. Johnson qv presented Rudder the Distinguished Service Medal, the United States' highest peacetime honor. Rudder died on March 23, 1970, and was buried in Bryan.

BIBLIOGRAPHY: Austin *American*, April 3, 1963, March 24, 1970; *Who's Who in America* (1960); *Who's Who in the South and Southwest* (1969).

*Rudolph, Texas. Rudolph, in Kenedy County, was named for Rudolph Kleberg,qv United States congressman at the turn of the century.

BIBLIOGRAPHY: James L. Allhands, *Gringo Builders* (1931); Tom Lea, *The King Ranch*, II (1957).

*Rueg, Henry.

*Ruff, Texas.

Ruffini, Frederick Ernst. Frederick Ernst Ruffini (date of birth unknown) was reared in Cleveland, Ohio. He received his architectural training there and gained considerable architectural experience in Cleveland before he came to Austin in 1877 as partner to J. N. Preston. The partnership lasted two years, after which time Ruffini practiced alone. In his advertisements Ruffini listed as examples of his work many courthouses and jails as well as public and commercial buildings. Most of his courthouses have been replaced by later structures. The mansard roofed courthouse of his design in Blanco was built in 1885; it was still standing in the early 1970's, used as a frontier museum.

His outstanding buildings in Austin included the Millett Opera House; Texas School for the Deaf;qv the Hancock Building on West Pecan Street (now West Sixth Street), where Ruffini had his offices; the Hancock Opera House; and the most important of all, the Old Main Building of the University of Texas. That structure was begun in 1882, but only the west wing was completed when Ruffini died in November, 1885. The central tower and last wing were completed according to his plans following his death. The large watercolor that his brother, Oscar Ruffini,qv painted of the Old Main Building was hanging in the Barker Texas History Center qv in Sid Richardson Hall at the University of Texas at Austin in 1972. Plans for the erection and completion of the west wing of the Old Main Building are in the university archives. Of all the buildings Ruffini designed in Austin only the Millett Opera House, now much altered, was still standing in 1972.

A number of architectural drawings and watercolors of building specifications were on file in the State Archives.qv Among the collection of drawings were plans for nine courthouses in Georgetown, Franklin, San Marcos, Sulphur Springs (Hopkins County), Quitman, Longview, Corsicana, Blanco, and Henderson. Plans for jails (prisons) included those for New Braunfels, McKinney, Franklin, Groesbeck, and Burnet (with sheriff's residence).

Ruffini was married; when his wife Elsie died in October, 1885, they had three surviving children; F. E. Ruffini died less than one month later, on November 16, 1885.

BIBLIOGRAPHY: Roxanne Kuter Williamson, *Victorian Architecture in Austin* (M.A. thesis, University of Texas at Austin, 1967); F. E. Ruffini and Oscar Ruffini Papers (MSS., Archives, Texas State Library, Austin); F. E. Ruffini Papers (MS., Archives, University of Texas at Austin Library); Austin *Daily Statesman*, November 17, 18, 1885.

Drury B. Alexander

Ruffini, Oscar. Oscar Ruffini was born in Cleveland, Ohio, on August 10, 1858. His training as an architect was received in the Detroit office of Elijah E. Myers,qv the architect of the Texas state Capitol,qv and in the Austin office of his brother, Frederick E. Ruffini.qv While in his brother's office he served as a draftsman and at times as a project supervisor. He supervised the construction of the Concho County courthouse after the death of his brother. At the age of twenty he was listed in the Austin City Directory of 1878 as a draftsman.

By April, 1884, Oscar Ruffini had gained enough experience to set himself up as an architect in San Angelo, the newly established county seat of Tom Green County. His first major commission was the San Angelo courthouse, the building which established his reputation. During his long career Oscar Ruffini designed numerous courthouses, schools, residences, and commercial buildings throughout West Texas.

A collection of his architectural drawings, specifications, details, and watercolors of West Texas buildings are in the State Archives.qv These include plans for the courthouses of Concho, Mills, Sutton, Sterling, and Crockett counties. His home (and office), located in downtown San Angelo on Chadbourne Street, was moved to become part of the complex of nearby Fort Concho qv Museum. Ruffini never married. He died on January 18, 1957, in San Angelo and was buried in Fairmont Cemetery there.

BIBLIOGRAPHY: F. E. Ruffini and Oscar Ruffini Papers (MSS., Archives, Texas State Library, Austin).

Drury B. Alexander

*Rugby, Texas.

*Rugeley, John. John Rugeley, son of Henry and Elizabeth (Cook) Rugeley, was born on January 12, 1792 (not 1804, as stated in Volume II), at the Retreat Plantation, Fairfield County, Camden District, South Carolina. He was first married to Parthenia Irvin on June 12, 1814, and they had ten children. She died on May 1, 1831, and on February 12, 1833, John Rugeley married Eliza Clopton Colgin, by whom he had eleven children. He came to Texas in 1840, then brought his family with him in 1842. He died June 17 (13?), 1878, at Bay Prairie, Matagorda County, and was buried in the Rugeley family cemetery on Caney Creek in Matagorda County.

BIBLIOGRAPHY: Arda Talbot Allen, *Twenty-one Sons for Texas* (1959).

Rowland Rugeley

*Ruidosa, Texas.

*Ruiz, José Francisco. [Although the surname Ruiz may take an accent (Ruíz, as shown in Volume II), most accounts of José Francisco Ruiz show the name without an accent. Ruiz's wife's name was Josefa Hernández. Ed.] Lieutenant Colonel don Francisco Ruiz escaped the cruelties of Ignacio Elizondo,qv following the battle of the Medina River,qv and sought refuge in the *rancherías* of the Comanche Indians until 1821 (rather than in the United States, as stated in Volume II). He lived eight years with them, according to the unpublished manuscripts of Jean Louis Berlandier,qv who used Ruiz's information on the Comanches in his writings. Today the one-story, cut stone Ruiz house is on the grounds of the Witte Memorial Museum qv in San Antonio.

BIBLIOGRAPHY: Jean Louis Berlandier, *Voyage au Mexique, 1826 au 1834*, IV, and *Indigenes*, I (Photocopy MSS., Archives, University of Texas at Austin Library; original MSS., respectively, in Library of Congress, Washington, D.C., and Thomas Gilcrease Institute of American History and Art, Tulsa, Oklahoma).

Sheila M. Ohlendorf

*Rule, Texas. Rule, in Haskell County, had a 1960 population of 1,347 and a 1970 population of 1,024, according to the United States census. The town had twenty-eight businesses in 1970.

*Ruliff, Texas.

*Rumeley, Texas.

*Rump Senate.

*Run, Texas.

*Runaway Scrape.

*Runey Canyon.

*Runge, Henry.

*Runge, Texas. Runge, in Karnes County, had a 1960 population of 1,036 and a 1970 population of 1,147, according to the United States census. Twenty-two businesses were reported in 1970.

*Runnels, Hardin Richard.

*Runnels, Hiram George.

*Runnels City, Texas.

*Runnels County. Runnels County, site of the San Clemente Mission,qv has a farm income almost evenly divided between crops (grain sorghums and cotton) and livestock (cattle, hogs, poultry, sheep, and goats). The county is among the leading counties in sheep raising. There was a period of oil exploration and drilling in the county in 1949, but the pools found were small, and the agricultural economy prevailed. However, from 1927 to January 1, 1973, 101,981,519 barrels of oil had been produced. Manufacturing and government installations in the area also provided income for the county. Runnels County reported three newspapers, two libraries, and twenty-seven churches during the mid-1960's. The 1960 population was 15,016; the 1970 population was 12,108, according to the United States census.

*Running Creek.

*Runningwater, Texas.

*Runningwater Draw.

Rural Electrification in Texas. The Emergency Relief Act of 1935 gave President Franklin Delano Roosevelt the authority he needed for a rural electrification program. When, on May 11 of that year, he created the Rural Electrification Administration (REA) as a Depression relief agency similar to the Works Progress Administration qv and the Civilian Conservation Corps, rural electrification at first seemed to offer the large-scale project that was needed, since only 10 percent of the nation's farms then had central station electricity. In Texas, with fewer people and vast spaces, the figure was only 2.3 percent. It soon became clear, however, that rural electrification was not a suitable relief project. It needed small numbers of skilled men rather than large numbers of unskilled labor. By August, 1935, the agency was modified to a lending agency. It took its permanent form in 1936 with passage by Congress of the Norris-Rayburn Bill.

By that time Texas farmers were already at work. A loan to a group at Bartlett had been approved in November, 1935, for $33,000, one of the first ten loans made by REA. The Bartlett farmers had contracted to buy power from the municipal generating plant, so they were able to move ahead swiftly. Their first fifty-eight-mile line serving 120 members was energized on March 9, 1936. Members claim that date made the Bartlett project the first in the nation under REA.

Investor-owned utilities and municipalities could borrow from REA for rural electrification financing, but few did. The utilities feared uniform rate and area coverage regulations. Municipalities were not sure about their legal power to build rural lines. Utilities undertook some rural line building, but did not use REA loans. Most of the borrowers, then, were organized groups of farmers and ranchers like those at Bartlett. Each group had to convince REA officials that their project was feasible and that the loan was sound. In some areas this was difficult; for example, in Schleicher County ranchers proposed a cooperative with less than one member per mile of line. After several revisions, their loan application finally was approved after one member signed a contract guaranteeing to pay a minimum of $75 per month and several others had agreed to pay $50 monthly.

By January 1, 1965, the REA borrowers and investor-owned utilities had more than reversed the statistics on rural electrification—instead of only 2 percent of Texas farms with electricity, there were only 2 percent without electricity. By 1966 REA loans had financed seventy-seven distribution systems in Texas (seventy-six cooperatives and the Rural Electric Division of the city of Bryan) and two generation and transmission cooperatives. Together, these systems operated more than 165,000 miles of line reaching into all but ten Texas counties.

By January 1, 1971, the seventy-seven distribution systems financed by REA loans in Texas operated more than 180,089 miles of line, serving 496,083 rural connections and reaching into 246 of the 254 counties. The REA cooperatives in Texas formed a statewide association, Texas Electric Co-Ops, Inc., with headquarters in Austin. The association issued a monthly publication, Texas Co-Op Power, with a circulation of 260,000 (the largest statewide circulation in the nation), operated a transformer and repair division with its shops in Austin, and maintained a pole-treating division with a plant in Jasper. A data-processing center in Austin did the addressing and billing for sixteen co-ops serving 113,000 consumers all over Texas.

BIBLIOGRAPHY: Marquis Childs, The Farmer Takes a Hand (1952); REA Statistical Report No. 101 (1970); Texas Almanac (1965, 1971); Files of the Texas Electric Co-Ops, Austin.

Norris G. Davis

*Rural Shade, Texas.

*Rush Creek.

*Rusheagle, Texas.

*Rushing, Texas.

*Rusk, David.

*Rusk, Thomas Jefferson.

*Rusk, Texas. Rusk, seat of Cherokee County, established a new forty-seven-bed hospital in 1948 and was the site of Rusk State Hospital.qv During the 1960's the town reported seventeen churches, and among its businesses (110 in 1970) were construction companies, a hatchery, an iron ore plant, and manufacturers of boxes and crates, garments, and dairy products. Rusk remained a commercial center for the surrounding agricultural, lumber, and iron ore area. The 1960 population was 4,900; in 1970 it was 4,914, according to the United States census.

*Rusk Baptist College.

*Rusk County. Rusk County, among Texas' all-time leading oil-producing counties, produced 1,505,419,749 barrels of oil from 1930 to January 1, 1973. The county also was a leading producer of livestock and poultry, which brought in 90 percent of the $12 million average annual farm income in the early 1970's. Dairying, truck crops, and lumber contributed the remainder. The county was 50 percent forested, and it had five active lumber mills in 1968, which produced approximately 31,000 board-feet of lumber. Lake Cherokee and Striker Creek Reservoir provide recreation for the area, while historic homes and other sites attract many tourists. The 1960 population was 36,421; the 1970 count was 34,102, according to the United States census.

*Rusk County Academy.

*Rusk Educational Association.

*Rusk Masonic Institute.

*Rusk State Hospital. The average daily census of patients at Rusk State Hospital in 1964 was 1,942; by 1967, 1,886 patients were located there, and a maximum security unit for the criminally insane was a part of the facility.

During 1970 Rusk State Hospital received accreditation by the Joint Commission on Hospital Accreditation and approval to receive Medicare and Medicaid benefits by the United States Department of Health, Education, and Welfare. More and better trained professional staff workers were added, and a student practicum program was instituted with Stephen F. Austin State University and North Texas State University. The hospital in 1970 served thirty counties in the East Texas-Gulf Coast area through eight units. Future plans included new wards, a wilderness campsite, a swimming pool, and a hobby shop. The average daily census for 1970 was 1,796, and the superintendent in 1970 was L. T. Neill. *See* Mentally Ill and Mentally Retarded, Care of, in Texas.

BIBLIOGRAPHY: Board for Texas State Hospitals and Special Schools, *Report* (1964); *Texas Almanac* (1967); Texas Department of Mental Health and Mental Retardation, *Annual Report, 1970.*

*Rusk Transportation Company.

*Rusks Brook.

*Russell, Alexander J.

*Russell, Charles Arden.

Russell, David Riley. David Riley Russell was born in Fairfield on December 4, 1902, the son of Mary Sarah "Mollie" (Riley) and John Lawson Russell. He received a B.A. degree from Southern

Methodist University in 1926 and joined the staff of that school as assistant professor in the speech and theater department. He received an M.A. degree in drama from Carnegie Institute of Technology in Pittsburgh, Pennsylvania, in 1931.

Poet laureate of Texas qv from 1945 to 1947, Russell wrote four books of poetry, one of which, *Sing With Me Now* (1945), won the 1945 Texas Institute of Letters qv prize for poetry. His poems appeared in such papers and magazines as the New York *Times* and the *Southwest Review,*qv as well as in local, regional, and national anthologies. He also wrote plays which were produced at Southern Methodist University and in Dallas theaters. He was a member of several professional organizations, including the Poetry Society of Texas,qv of which he was president from 1941 to 1951, the Texas Institute of Letters, and the Texas Folklore Society.qv In 1941 Russell edited the Poetry Society's *Yearbook.*

Russell married Mrs. Agnes (Scaling) McNeny on March 30, 1956. The Mr. and Mrs. David Russell Poetry Prize in a creative writing contest was given annually at Southern Methodist University. Russell died on March 20, 1964.

Margaret Royalty Edwards

*Russell, Gordon James.

*Russell, Levi James.

*Russell, Lyman Brightman.

*Russell, Richard Robertson.

*Russell, William Jarvis.

*Russell, Texas. (Leon County.)

*Russell, Texas. (Van Zandt County.)

*Russell Creek.

*Russell Fork.

*Russellville, Texas.

*Rustler, Texas.

*Rustler Hills.

*Rustlers Creek.

*Ruter, Martin.

*Rutersville, Texas.

*Rutersville College. Rutersville College, its buildings long gone, received a United Methodist historical site marker, granted by the General Commission on Archives and History of the United Methodist Church, on May 2, 1971, in a service commemorating the 1840 establishment of the college as the first Protestant and Methodist college in Texas.

BIBLIOGRAPHY: Austin *American,* April 29, 1971.

*Rutersville Military and Monumental Academy. *See* Texas Monumental and Military Institute.

*Ruth, Texas. (Concho County.)

*Ruth, Texas. (Coryell County.)

*Rutledge, Texas.

*Ryals, Texas.

Ryder-Taylor, Henry. *See* Taylor, Henry Ryder.

*Rye, Edgar. Edgar Rye was born on June 22, 1848 (not 1849, as stated in Volume II), in Greenup County, Kentucky. It is possible that his parents were Henry W. and Mary A. Rye, although family relationships are not clearly defined.

While justice of the peace and county attorney in Shackelford County, Rye established the Albany *Tomahawk* in 1879, the town's first newspaper, and was associated with it under the names *Western Sun* and Albany *Sun* during 1880–1882. In the spring of 1883 he helped J. C. Son with the Albany *Star*, starting his lifelong career in cartooning. He was the Albany correspondent for the Fort Worth *Gazette* from 1883 to 1886 (and sporadically thereafter), representing that paper in Austin at the Twentieth Legislature in 1887. He spent ten months (not several years, as stated in Volume II) as manager of an oil and soap factory in Lerdo, Durango, Mexico, in 1887–1888 (not 1885), and sent back a series of interesting "Mexican Letters," nineteen of which were published in the Fort Worth *Gazette* and three in the Albany *News* (from June, 1887, to April, 1888).

After returning from Los Angeles, where he had been cartoonist on the Los Angeles *Cactus* (the winter of 1888–1889), he took a homestead near Oklahoma City for a few months, then returned to Albany, Texas, where he and S. F. Cook published the Albany *News*.

He was married to Marie Turley Henderson in Seguin in December, 1891, and in April, 1892, they left Albany for Rockport, where Rye operated the *New Era* and became associated with the *Texas Land News*. In late 1894 they moved to Young County, where he published the Graham *Radiator*, then to Texas City to publish the *Texas Coast News*. By 1898 they were back in north-central Texas, where he worked on the Wichita Falls *Herald* and where his wife died on October 20, 1903.

He visited the western part of the country, including California, from June to November, 1916, returned to Wichita Falls, then moved to California in January, 1917. On April 26, 1917, in San Diego, he was married a second time, to Gertrude [?], and they lived in Los Angeles. There he produced patriotic verses and cartoons. Drawing mainly from the book which had brought him fame, *The Quirt and the Spur: Vanishing Shadows of the Texas Frontier* (1909), he wrote wild west scenarios, but none were bought by the Hollywood film studios.

Edgar Rye died in Los Angeles on June 6, 1920 (not June 7, as stated in Volume II). His book *The Quirt and the Spur* was republished in a facsimile reproduction of the first edition in 1967.

BIBLIOGRAPHY: Charles E. Linck, Jr., *Edgar Rye, North Central Texas Cartoonist and Journalist* (1972); Biographical File, Barker Texas History Center, University of Texas at Austin.

*Rye, Texas.

*Rylie, Texas.

S

*S M S Ranches.

*Sabana, Texas.

*Sabana Mountains.

*Sabana River.

*Sabeata, Juan.

*Sabin, Chauncey Brewer.

*Sabina Creek.

*Sabinal, Texas. Sabinal, in Uvalde County, was the third settlement located along the Sabinal River; it followed Waresville (now the town of Utopia) to the north and Patterson Settlement qv (later abandoned) several miles to the south. Sabinal was first settled in 1853 by the Hammer family (not by the founders of the Patterson Settlement, as stated in Volume II). In 1856 a unit of U.S. Cavalry under Captain Albert C. Brackett established Camp Sabinal qv to protect the San Antonio-El Paso road, which crossed the Sabinal River at this point. The camp was subsequently occupied by Texas Rangers.qv By 1856 the Sabinal community consisted of five families, with a store and mail drop operated by Louis M. Peters.

Sabinal remained an agribusiness center and a gateway to the surrounding recreational areas during the 1960's. Forty-three businesses were reported in 1970. The 1960 population was 1,747, and the 1970 population was 1,554, according to the United States census.

BIBLIOGRAPHY: Lois Miller Carmichael, *The History of Uvalde County* (M.A. thesis, Southwest Texas State Teachers College, 1944); Clarice Gulley, "Uvalde County—First One Hundred Years," *Junior Historian*, XVII (1956–1957).

*Sabinal Christian College.

*Sabinal River.

*Sabine, Texas.

**Sabine Advocate.*

*Sabine Baptist College.

*Sabine County. Sabine County, over 80 percent forested, relied on lumbering as its chief source of income during the 1960's. The three mills in the county produced 87,438,000 board-feet of lumber in 1969. Cattle and poultry accounted for most of the other farm income. Major tourist attractions in the county were the Sam Rayburn Reservoir, Toledo Bend Reservoir, Sabine National Forest, and Red Hills Lake. The 1960 population was 7,302; the 1970 population was 7,187, according to the United States census.

*Sabine Cross Roads. *See* Mansfield, Battle of.

*Sabine and East Texas Railroad Company. *See* East Texas Railroad Company.

*Sabine and Galveston Bay Railroad and Lumber Company.

*Sabine Lake.

*Sabine National Forest. *See* National Forests in Texas.

*Sabine and Neches Valley Railway Company. In 1944 the Sabine and Neches Valley Railway Company extended from Ruliff, Texas, to Gist, Texas, a distance of 11.8 miles. It was controlled through ownership of approximately 83 percent of its capital stock by the Newton Lumber Company, which abandoned operations in April, 1945.

James M. Day

*Sabine-Neches Waterway and the Sabine Pass Ship Channel. The Sabine-Neches waterway is a Y-shaped series of channels extending from the Gulf of Mexico to Sabine Pass, then from Sabine Lake to Port Arthur; from there it extends to Orange by way of the Sabine River (not the Neches River, as stated in Volume II); it extends from Port Arthur to Beaumont by way of the Neches River.

*Sabine Pass. Located at Sabine Pass at the mouth of the Sabine River is a historic lighthouse which tended the pass for almost one hundred years. It was authorized in 1849 to be built in connection with a military reservation. Completed in 1856, it stands eighty-five feet high and is supported by buttresses that fan outward on all sides. The lighthouse witnessed the battle of Sabine Pass qv in 1863 and was in operation until 1952 when it was retired from active duty. In 1971 the lighthouse was a gift from the federal government to Lamar University, which planned research projects at the facility.

BIBLIOGRAPHY: Dallas *Morning News*, May 21, 1952; San Angelo *Standard Times*, June 20, 1971.

*Sabine Pass, Texas.

*Sabine Pass, Battle of.

*Sabine Pass, Alexandria, and Northwestern Railway Company.

Sabine Pass Lighthouse. *See* Sabine Pass.

*Sabine River.

Sabine River Authority of Texas. The Sabine River Authority of Texas, an official agency of the state, was created by the legislature in May, 1939, with jurisdiction over all of the Sabine River watershed in Texas. It was given broad powers over the conservation, storage, control, preservation, quality, and utilization of water in the Sabine River and its Texas tributaries. As a matter of policy, however, the authority has limited its activities to major projects beyond the financial means of local interests. It has no taxing power and for financing relies primarily upon revenue bonds and income from its projects. Headquarters for the authority is located in Orange. It has a nine-member

board of directors appointed by the governor, representing all sections of the watershed.

Operations in the field are directed by three administrative units. The Orange Canal Division supplies fresh water from the Sabine River by means of a pumping station and canal network for irrigation and industrial usage in Orange County; property was purchased from private interests and financed with revenue bonds in July, 1954. The Iron Bridge Division, headquartered at the Iron Bridge damsite near Point, operates Lake Tawakoni, from which water supplies are drawn by the cities of Dallas, Greenville, Terrell, and Wills Point. This project became operational on September 1, 1961. Its entire $17.5 million cost was underwritten by the city of Dallas in return for the right to withdraw up to 80 percent of the water it makes available. The Toledo Bend Division, constructed between 1964 and 1968, represents the $60 million Toledo Bend Dam development, undertaken jointly with the Sabine River Authority of Louisiana. One of the nation's largest reservoirs, the Toledo Bend Reservoir is sixty-five miles long and has 230,800 surface acres; it impounds approximately five million acre-feet of water.

Within the framework of the Sabine River Compact, the Texas authority is jointly developing with the Louisiana authority the waters of the Sabine River in the Stateline Reach between Logansport, Louisiana, and Orange, Texas. This compact was officially executed January 28, 1953, following approval by the legislatures of Louisiana and Texas, and the Congress of the United States. The Texas authority is also engaged in a program for computerized monitoring of the Sabine River at various points for water quality analysis and control.

J. Cullen Browning

Sabine River Boundary Dispute. *See* Boundaries of Texas.

Sabine River and Northern Railroad Company. The meeting to organize the Sabine River and Northern Railroad Company was held on June 11, 1965. Organized to serve as a service road for a paper mill, it began operation in 1967.

James M. Day

*Sabine Valley University.

*Sabinetown, Texas.

*Sachse, Texas.

*Sacred Heart Dominican College. *See also* Dominican College.

*Sacul, Texas.

*Sadammo Indians. The Sadammo (Caitsodammo, Sadamon, Sadujam) Indians are known from a few documents of the late seventeenth and eighteenth centuries. These sources identify the Sadammo as enemies of both the Hasinai and the Kadohadacho. Although it is generally thought that the Sadammo were Apache, this has never been proved. One French source equated the Sadammo with the Toyal, but the evidence for this was not made explicit (recent writers identify the Toyal with the Tohaha). J. R. Swanton thought that the Sadammo were the same people as the Nadamin, but in documents of the La Salle Expedition qv the Sadammo (Caitsodammo) were listed as enemies of the Kadohadacho, whereas the Nadamin were listed as their allies. It does not seem likely that the two names refer to the same people. Swanton also stated that the Sadamon were either Apachean or Tonkawan in affiliation. The status of the Sadammo remains in doubt.

BIBLIOGRAPHY: H. Folmer, "De Bellisle on the Texas Coast," *Southwestern Historical Quarterly*, XLIV (1940–1941); F. W. Hodge (ed.), *Handbook of American Indians*, I (1907), II (1910); P. Margry, *Découvertes et établissements des Français dans l'ouest et dans le sud de l'Amérique Septentrionale*, III (1879); J. R. Swanton, *Source Material on the History and Ethnology of the Caddo Indians* (1942).

T. N. Campbell

*Saddle Creek.

*Saddlers Creek.

Sadler, McGruder Ellis. McGruder Ellis Sadler was born on November 5, 1896, at Hobucken, Pamlico County, North Carolina, the son of John Daniel and Mary (Alcock) Sadler. He was graduated from Atlantic Christian College in 1919 and received an M.A. degree from Vanderbilt in 1921. The following year he attended the University of Chicago where he did graduate work in religious education. He accepted an appointment in 1922 as secretary of religious education in the Chesapeake Bay area for the United Christian Missionary Society (UCMS). He took a leave of absence to earn a B.D. degree at Yale in 1925 and later returned to Yale, receiving the Ph.D. degree in 1929.

Sadler was appointed national secretary of religious education for the UCMS shortly thereafter; a year later a division of the Rockefeller Foundation sent him to investigate Far Eastern missions and the Oriental way of life. On his return to the United States in July, 1931, he accepted the deanship at Lynchburg College in Virginia; then in 1936 he accepted the ministry at the Central Christian Church in Austin, Texas. In 1941 Texas Christian University selected him as its sixth president. In 1943 Sadler reorganized the university into seven schools and colleges (in 1946 an eighth college was added), each with its own administrative head. After the establishment of a strong undergraduate program, Sadler instituted Ph.D. work in six areas.

While president of the university Sadler also served in many other important capacities. He was elected president of the International Convention of Christian Churches in 1944, and in Amsterdam in 1948 he helped organize the World Council of Churches. He helped organize the National Council of Churches of Christ in 1950 and the Texas Council of Churches in 1953; he was elected vice-president and president of those organizations, respectively. In the fields of education and civic endeavor he was equally prominent. He was elected president of the Association of American Colleges in 1952 and served on the board of the Fort Worth Opera

Association. In 1966 he was president of the Philosophical Society of Texas.qv In 1954 the Fort Worth branch of the National Conference of Christians and Jews selected him as recipient of their annual award for outstanding services, and on November 5, 1964, the Newcomen Society in North America held a "Texas meeting" as a special recognition, commemorating his sixty-eighth birthday.

Sadler married Frances Windley Swain on September 17, 1924; they were the parents of two daughters. He retired as president of Texas Christian University on July 1, 1965; he died on September 11, 1966, in Walker County and was buried in Greenwood Mausoleum in Fort Worth.

BIBLIOGRAPHY: Amos Melton, "Indeed a Long Shadow," *This is T. C. U.* (Fall, 1965); Fort Worth *Star-Telegram*, September 12, 1966; Biographical File, Public Relations Office, Texas Christian University.

Ben Procter

*Sadler, William Turner.

*Sadler, Texas.

Saengerbund. *See* Texas State Singing Society.

*Saenz, Texas.

*Sage Creek.

*Sager, Christoph Adam.

*Sagerton, Texas.

*Saginaw, Texas. Saginaw, in northwestern Tarrant County, was incorporated in 1949 with a mayor-council form of government. During the 1960's the town reported six churches, a school, and a library. Saginaw had approximately forty businesses in 1970. The 1960 population was 1,001; the 1970 population was 2,382, according to the United States census.

St. Anthony Seminary. St. Anthony Seminary was established in 1905 by the Missionary Oblates of Mary Immaculate as a high school department and preparatory school for the San Antonio Philosophical and Theological Seminary (*see* Oblate College of the Southwest) on the same twenty-four acre tract of land north of San Antonio. The school represented the culmination of several earlier attempts to found and maintain a school for the education of Texas candidates for the Roman Catholic priesthood. Students not necessarily intending to become priests were accepted until 1911. Though the name St. Anthony's Apostolic School was the official title, the school came to be known unofficially for several decades as St. Anthony's College. In 1920 the major seminary students, those in philosophy and theology, were moved to a temporary home in Castroville, thus leaving St. Anthony's for the exclusive use of the high school and college preparatory students. The name St. Anthony's Junior Seminary was adopted in 1950 and shortened to St. Anthony Seminary in 1968.

In earlier years the bulk of the student body came from outside Texas, but since about 1945 approximately 80 percent have come from Texas. Since its beginning, the seminary has graduated nearly 450 eventual priests. Since 1936 almost the entire original plant has been replaced with larger and more modern buildings. The physical plant on the original campus includes a convent for the nuns, main building, classroom building, college-level center, chapel, gymnasium, two swimming pools, and three athletic fields. High school students are taught on campus, but the college students take classes at St. Mary's University.qv In 1970–1971 the student enrollment was 160 and the faculty numbered eleven. Ronald Walker, O.M.I., was president in 1971.

Andrew J. Grimes, O.M.I.

*St. Charles Bay.

*St. Clair Creek.

*St. Denis, Louis Juchereau de.

*St. Edward's University. Edward Sorin, founder of St. Edward's, purchased 120 acres of land for the school early in the 1870's. Later Mrs. Mary Doyle donated to the Congregation of Holy Cross her 400-acre farm which lay east of the original 120 acres. Two brothers of the Congregation of Holy Cross first occupied the farm in 1874, and it soon became known as the Catholic Farm. In 1881 a small school was established east of the present Main Building, and in 1885 it was chartered as St. Edward's College. On March 10, 1925, a new charter renamed the school St. Edward's University.

The years 1957 to 1969, during which time Holy Cross Brother Raymond Fleck was president, represented a period of unprecedented growth and expansion for St. Edward's University. Construction of ten new buildings, including five student residences, one faculty residence, a science hall, a dining hall, a central heating and cooling plant, and an ultra-modern classroom building with facilities including a computer center, television center, and language laboratory, were completed during the 1960's.

During this twelve-year period enrollment climbed from 320 to 884 students, and by 1969 the enrollment represented approximately thirty-five states and twenty foreign countries. The faculty had expanded to approximately eighty members (composed of brothers and priests of the Congregation of Holy Cross, sisters of the Immaculate Heart of Mary, priests of the Dominican order, and lay men and women educators), 50 percent of whom held doctoral or terminal degrees. Courses were being offered in twenty-six major fields of study, including six pre-professional programs. Alumni numbered approximately 3,500. About 50 percent of the St. Edward's graduates were continuing their education at a graduate level. Library holdings were 60,000 volumes.

In 1967 St. Edward's High School for boys was closed, and future concentration was to be on further expansion of the university program. In addition to physical expansion and growth, St. Edward's was changing internally, moving toward a more public, ecumenical format.

After establishment of the coordinate system of education in 1966, St. Edward's University included two colleges: Maryhill College, a women's college administered by the Sisters of the Immaculate Heart of Mary, and Holy Cross College, the men's college. In February, 1970, the two colleges were amalgamated, and St. Edward's, whose Catholic heritage stretched back nearly a century, had evolved into a private, coeducational, coordinate Christian university.

Since its founding in 1885, the university had been operated by the Congregation of Holy Cross, first by the priests, then by the brothers of that Roman Catholic order. In 1946 Edmund Hunt became the first brother-president of the school. Beginning in 1966, serious study was given to the corporate reorganization of the institution. Brother Raymond Fleck (president from 1957 to 1968), who had introduced many other innovations on the hilltop campus, played a principal role in the careful planning for this revolutionary move, and plans were approved in 1968 by the religious board who then held legal control of the university.

In the spring of 1969 legal control of the university was passed officially from the Brothers of Holy Cross to St. Edward's University Foundation. The foundation then issued a sponsoring charter to St. Edward's University, Inc., a nonprofit corporation organized expressly to operate the university. A twenty-two-person ecumenical board of trustees was appointed to represent the corporation and to govern the school. Four trustees were religious members; the remainder were laymen—community leaders in business, the professions, and civic organizations. George Van Houten was elected chairman.

Shortly afterward, laymen were named to fill key positions in the administration. Edgar L. Roy, Jr., was president in 1969, the first lay president in the history of the institution. Upon Roy's resignation, Brother Stephen Walsh was appointed president in 1972. In the fall term, 1972, there were 1,282 students (842 men and 440 women) at St. Edward's University. In 1972 an arena-style theatre, the Mary Moody Northen Theatre for the Performing Arts, was completed, and the first production was presented there on March 13–18, 1972. The Main Building, designed in Gothic Revival style by famed architect Nicholas J. Clayton,qv was built in 1888 and, following a fire in 1903, was rebuilt, using the architect's original plans; in the early 1970's the building was designated a national historic landmark under the National Historic Preservation Act, and it also received a Texas historic landmark medallion from the Texas Historical Commission.qv In the fall term, 1974, there were 1,400 students at St. Edward's University. *See also* Roman Catholic Education in Texas.

BIBLIOGRAPHY: Brother Raymond Fleck, *Report of the President, 1957–1968* (1969); Brother Silvan Mellett, *Registrar's Report on Enrollment* (1968); Kevin Robertson, *The Ninety-two Years of St. Edward's University, 1874–1966* (1966); Austin *American-Statesman*, January 20, 1974.

Rose V. Batson

*Saint Elmo, Texas.

*St. Francis, Texas.

*St. Gall, Texas. *See* Fort Stockton, Texas.

*St. Hedwig, Texas.

*Saint Jo, Texas. Saint Jo, in Montague County, had a 1960 population of 977 and a 1970 population of 1,054, according to the United States census. The town reported twenty-five businesses in 1970.

*St. John, Texas.

*St. Joseph's Island.

St. Lawrence, Texas. St. Lawrence, in the southern part of Glasscock County, was founded in 1943. The population in the 1960's was sparse, with most of the inhabitants engaged in farming.

*St. Louis, Arkansas, and Texas Railway of Texas. *See* St. Louis Southwestern Railway of Texas.

*St. Louis, Brownsville, and Mexico Railway Company. Henrietta King qv (not Richard King and Mifflin Kenedy,qqv as stated in Volume II) gave 640 acres for the townsite of Kingsville, 40 acres for railroad shops, and 75,000 acres of land in Cameron and Kleberg counties to ensure railroad right-of-way to the Rio Grande Valley; both Richard King and Mifflin Kenedy had long been dead by the time this transaction took place after the turn of the century.

In the mid-1960's the St. Louis, Brownsville, and Mexico Railway Company owned 559.8 miles of track, all of it in Texas. It was controlled by the New Orleans, Texas, and Mexico Railway Company, which owned all its capital stock. In 1956 it was consolidated with the Missouri-Pacific.

BIBLIOGRAPHY: S. G. Reed, *A History of the Texas Railroads* (1941).

*St. Louis de Caddodacho.

St. Louis-San Francisco Railway Company. On January 1, 1964, the St. Louis-San Francisco Railway Company took over the 91.03 miles of track in Texas of the St. Louis, San Francisco, and Texas, which it had formerly owned. It owns the Quanah, Acme, and Pacific Railway Company, and has a one-eighth interest in the Union Terminal.

James M. Day

*St. Louis, San Francisco, and Texas Railway Company. *See also* St. Louis-San Francisco Railway Company.

*St. Louis Southwestern Railway of Texas.

St. Mary of Namur, Sisters of. *See* Sisters of St. Mary of Namur.

St. Mary's Academy. St. Mary's Academy in Austin had its origin in 1874, when Sisters of Holy Cross qv answered a plea from the pastor of St. Mary's Church to operate a parish school. The school was a two-room cabin located on the site of the sacristy of the present St. Mary's Cathedral; at first Mother M. Angela Gillespie (American founder of the Holy Cross order of sisters) and Sister M. Austin did all the teaching and cooking for the school.

By 1875 increased enrollment required the construction of a larger building at the same site, and in 1882 the sisters purchased an additional amount of nearby land which had originally been reserved for Mirabeau B. Lamar,qv second president of the Republic of Texas. On this land, bounded by East Seventh, Brazos, East Eighth, and San Jacinto streets, a new building, four stories high and made of Travis County limestone, was opened in 1885 as a school for girls. A large north wing was added in 1901, reflecting the gradual increase in enrollment.

For over sixty years classes were regularly held in the imposing building, which became a notable landmark in downtown Austin. In 1947, however, the sisters moved the school to a ten-acre plot at Forty-first and Red River streets, formerly the E. H. Perry estate, the central features of which were a large residence of Italian Renaissance architecture and terraced formal gardens. The old school building downtown, which had been sold, was razed.

In September, 1968, the school was reorganized as a coeducational institution and its name was changed to Holy Cross High School. In part this reflected the new needs of the community following the closing of St. Edward's High School for boys (*see* St. Edward's University). Increased financial difficulties forced the closing of this long-standing educational venture in 1972, just a few years short of what would have been its centennial anniversary. Shortly thereafter the buildings and grounds were sold to a syndicate of doctors who, in 1974, resold the property to Mr. and Mrs. Marvin Henderson. The new owners purchased the site with the intention of establishing a new private, non-denominational, coeducational, and non-boarding school, initially for grades seven through ten or eleven, but eventually through twelve. Chartered as The Christian Academy of Austin, plans for the new school were formulated by 1975. Charlotte Klein, the last principal at Holy Cross High School, was named principal of the new academy, which was scheduled to open in the fall of 1975. Its only tie with the old St. Mary's Academy was the retention of the lovely site in Austin as a place for private education. *See also* Roman Catholic Education in Texas; Sisters, Holy Cross.

Marlene Joseph Glade

*St. Mary's of Aransas, Texas.

*St. Mary's College.

*St. Mary's Hall.

*St. Mary's University. St. Mary's University, San Antonio, became the fourth largest private university in Texas in 1964 when enrollment reached 3,100 students. By the fall of 1969 the enrollment had increased to 4,278. A top enrollment of 6,000 was planned by 1977, the school's 125th anniversary. Contributing to the university's growth was a coeducational program inaugurated in 1963, at which time women were admitted to all four university schools: arts and sciences, law, graduate, and business administration, the latter begun in 1959. In 1958 St. Mary's offered a bachelor of science in industrial engineering for the first time. The engineering program was expanded to include master's degrees in industrial engineering, engineering science, and operation research by 1964.

St. Mary's continued to be conducted by the St. Louis Province of the Society of Mary, a worldwide Roman Catholic teaching order of brothers and priests. The library housed 87,048 volumes in 1967 and 128,700 volumes in 1969. In 1967 the university faculty included 188 members; in 1969 the total rose to 222. The university maintained two campuses, the 130-acre Woodlawn campus in northwest San Antonio and the downtown School of Law. Campus construction kept pace with the university's growth and was to have a major impetus in the late 1960's and 1970's to provide final development of the campus. In the planning stage were a new library, a student center, an engineering building, a science addition, and a women's dormitory, to be followed by a graduate center and a law center, additional domitories, a new administration building, and multi-purpose classroom buildings.

The university's $2,500,000 budget in the mid-1960's derived 50 percent of its income from student tuition and fees, 20 percent from auxiliary enterprises, and 15 percent each from the contributed services of the Society of Mary and from donations and endowments. The Very Rev. James A. Young served as president of the college in 1974. Total enrollment for the fall term of that year was 3,564.

St. Matthew, Texas. St. Matthew, an unincorporated farming community in northern Burleson County, had a population of approximately twelve in the mid-1960's.

St. Maxent, Honorato Celestino de. Honorato Celestino de St. Maxent was born in New Orleans in 1773, the son of Gilberto Antonio de St. Maxent and Isabel LaRoche. He was the brother-in-law of Louisiana governors-general Luis de Unzaga and Bernardo de Gálvez. Choosing a military career, he fought in the defense of Orán, Africa, before joining his friend, François Honoré Fortier qv in a journey to Mexico in 1801. They returned overland from Mexico City to New Orleans in a horse and mule drive over most of southern Texas, an arduous journey which took from June 10 to December 5, 1801. (For a more detailed account of the trip, see Fortier, Honoré.) St. Maxent returned from New Orleans to Mexico overland with dispatches for the viceroy in a trip which extended from May 23 to July 24, 1805.

BIBLIOGRAPHY: Archivo de Ministerio de Asuntos Exteriores, doc. LXIX (Madrid, Spain); Archivo General de Indias, Papeles de Cuba, legs. 161-a, 161-b, 1502-a (Seville, Spain); Stanley Faye, "Privateersmen of the Gulf and their Prizes," *Louisiana Historical Quarterly*, XXII (1939); Jack D. L. Holmes, "De México a Nueva Orléans en 1801: el Diario Inédito de Fortier y St. Maxent," *Historia Mexicana*, XVI (1966).

Jack D. L. Holmes

*St. Olive, Texas.

Saint Patrick Battalion. See Irish in Texas.

*Saint Paul, Texas. (Falls County.)

*Saint Paul, Texas. (San Patricio County.)

*St. Paul's College.

St. Philip's College. St. Philip's College, San Antonio, was founded by Bishop James Steptoe Johnston qv in 1898 as St. Philip's Normal and Industrial School, and it began in an old adobe house with instruction under the direction of a missionary, Mrs. Cowan. The work continued under direction of Mrs. Perry G. Walker from 1900 to 1902. In September, 1902, Artemisia Bowden took charge of the school. Under her supervision the institution developed from an industrial school for girls to a high school and later to a first class junior college.

In September, 1927, the school opened as St. Philip's Junior College and Vocational Institute, serving the immediate needs of the Negro community of San Antonio and vicinity. The college ceased to function as a private Episcopal institution in August, 1942, and became a municipal junior college through affiliation with San Antonio College,qv under the auspices of the San Antonio Independent School District. While the name St. Philip's Junior College continued in use for legal purposes, the school was commonly referred to in its new capacity as St. Philip's College.

San Antonio College and St. Philip's College were placed under a newly created district board of trustees by citizenry vote in October, 1946; thus the San Antonio Union Junior College District replaced the San Antonio Independent School District in operation of the colleges. St. Philip's College admitted non-Negro students in June, 1955, discontinuing its former classification as an all-Negro institution of higher learning.

The college, a member of the Southern Association of Colleges and Secondary Schools and of the Association of Texas Colleges and Universities,qv was accredited by the Texas Education Agency.qv Curricula, divided into academic and pre-professional, offered associate in arts degrees and vocational certificates.

The campus, situated on the east side of San Antonio about two miles from the center of the city, occupied approximately ten acres. Campus buildings included an administration hall, classrooms, laboratories, a library, an auditorium, a student union, a gymnasium, and two shop buildings. During the 1969 fall term the college had an enrollment of 1,793 students, a faculty of 111 members and a 16,483-volume library. In 1974 John B. Murphy served as dean of St. Philip's College and Jerome F. Weynand was president of the San Antonio Junior College District administration. The fall enrollment for 1974 had increased to 5,630.

St. Thomas University. See University of St. Thomas.

*Salado, Texas.

*Salado, Battle of (1813). See Rosalis, Battle of.

*Salado, Battle of the (1842).

*Salado College.

*Salado Creek.

*Salapaque Indians. In the middle eighteenth century the Salapaque (Alapagueme, Saulapaguet, Talapagueme, Zalapagueme) Indians, apparently a Coahuiltecan band, lived on both sides of the lower Rio Grande but mainly on the south side at various points between Matamoros and Reynosa in northern Tamaulipas. Some entered missions at Reynosa and Camargo, where they remained until well after 1800; others entered San José y San Miguel de Aguayo Mission qv in San Antonio and were there as late as 1790.

BIBLIOGRAPHY: F. W. Hodge (ed.), *Handbook of American Indians*, II (1910); A. Prieto, *Historia, geografía y estadística del estado de Tamaulipas* (1878); G. Saldivar, *Los Indios de Tamaulipas* (1943); R. C. Troike, "Notes on Coahuiltecan Ethnography," *Bulletin of the Texas Archeological Society*, 32 (1962).

T. N. Campbell

*Salas, Juan de.

*Salatrillo Creek.

Salazar, Trinidad. Trinidad Salazar was born on April 16, 1862, in Cuidad Jimenez, Tamaulipas, Mexico. Orphaned when young, he sought a new life in Texas. In the 1880's he was a wool and hide buyer for the Amargosa Ranch (*see* Amargosa, Texas), then owned a general store in the Santa Cruz community, about twenty-five miles southwest of what is now Alice. Salazar married twice: Adelaida Bazan on May 20, 1886, and, after her death in 1890, Guadalupe Garza on June 23, 1894. In 1888 when the first San Antonio and Aransas Pass Railway qv train arrived at its terminal point, a new town site (which became Alice, Texas), Salazar was aboard with merchandise purchased in San Antonio. He sold goods by cart to other settlers of Alice before he set up a store. As one of Alice's original businesses, his store prospered. About 1887 he bought the Lichtenstein Hotel on the corner of First and Aransas streets and converted it into a general merchandise store; his family lived upstairs until he built a large home on Prospect Street; Salazar possessed Alice's first telephone. In 1904 he opened a large new store on South Reynolds Street, with merchandise valued at $75,000. Salazar's was the largest general merchandise store between Corpus Christi and Laredo during the first two decades of the twentieth century. Charitable and civic-minded, he was largely responsible for the construction of the Nayer School, and he often made his home available to victims of flash floods. The T. Salazar Grammar School was named in his honor. He died on September 28, 1921, at his home in Alice.

Agnes G. Grimm

*Salcedo, Manuel María de.

*Salcedo, Texas. *See* Santísima Trinidad de Salcedo.

*Salem, Texas. (Hays County.)

*Salem, Texas. (Milam County.)

*Salem, Texas. (Newton County.)

*Salem, Texas. (Smith County.)

*Salem, Texas. (Victoria County.)

*Salem Creek.

Sales Tax, Municipal. The Sixtieth Texas Legislature in 1967 authorized cities to levy a sales tax of 1 percent on a local option basis. Most of the state's voters in cities approved such a local sales tax, the collection of which became a major source of revenue for municipal governments. On January 1, 1968, there were only 14 municipalities levying such a tax; on January 1, 1971, there were 605. The state's comptroller of public accounts qv collects the municipal sales tax along with the state sales tax, then remits collections to each municipality quarterly after deducting a collection fee. *See also* Sales Tax, State.

Sales Tax, State. The sales tax in Texas, called the Limited Sales and Use Tax, was first enacted in 1961 by members of the Fifty-seventh Texas Legislature, to be effective September 1, 1961. Although it was not the first sales tax in Texas—before that time there had been a sales tax on certain items such as motor vehicles, gasoline, cigarettes, etc.—the Limited Sales and Use Tax in 1961 was the first broad-based tax in the state, although it was limited in the sense that it provided for some exemptions, such as groceries, medicines, agricultural implements, services (as such), and others. The rate of tax initially set in 1961 was 2 percent of the retail sales price of all tangible personal property not specifically exempted. In 1968 the Sixtieth Texas Legislature increased the rate to 3 percent, effective October 1, 1968. Further amendments occurred in 1969 when the Sixty-first Texas Legislature increased the rate to 3¼ percent, effective October 1, 1969, and again in 1971 when the Sixty-second Legislature increased the rate to 4 percent, effective July 1, 1971. This rate was in effect in 1972 and there had been no changes in the base of the tax by that time.

The retailer collecting the tax could deduct 1 percent of the quarterly tax due as reimbursement for collection. An additional 2 percent discount was allowed the retailer who made prepayment of the tax based upon a reasonable estimate of the liability for the quarter in which prepayment was made. *See also* Sales Tax, Municipal.

Robert S. Calvert

*Salesville, Texas.

*Saligny, Alphonse de. Although he sometimes styled himself Count, Jean Pierre Isidore Alphonse Dubois (later de Saligny) did not use this title in his official correspondence and was not in fact a member of the French nobility. *See* Dubois de Saligny; *see also* Pig War.

*Salina Indians.

Salinas, Porfirio, Jr. Porfirio Salinas, Jr., son of Porfirio and Clara (Garcia) Salinas, was born in Bastrop, Texas, on November 6, 1910, the third in a family of seven children. A few years later the family moved to San Antonio, where Salinas attended school and lived for most of his life. On February 15, 1942, he married Maria Bonilla; they had one daughter.

From his early youth he showed exceptional artistic ability, and, although he never had any formal training, he was an apprentice to artists José Arpa qv and Robert Wood. He was in the U.S. Army during World War II, and while stationed in San Antonio he painted murals at Fort Sam Houston,qv all destroyed when the temporary buildings were later razed. During the 1940's and 1950's, Salinas became one of Texas' most popular artists, noted for his colorful landscapes of bluebonnets, cactus, and huisache, and of Central and West Texas scenes. His paintings were included in the collections of J. Frank Dobie, President Lyndon B. Johnson, Sam Rayburn,qqv Price Daniel, Sr., and John B. Connally, and they hang in the national capitols of both the United States and Mexico.

Numerous reproductions of his works were made, and in 1967 *Bluebonnets and Cactus: An Album of Southwestern Paintings by Porfirio Salinas* was published, with a preface by Dewey Bradford and a biographical introduction by Joe B. Frantz. Salinas died on April 18, 1973, in San Antonio, and was buried in San Fernando Cemetery there on April 23.

BIBLIOGRAPHY: John H. Jenkins, "Porfirio Salinas," *Southwestern Art*, I (1967); New York *Times*, March 15, 1964; San Antonio *Express*, April 19, 1973; Biographical Files, Barker Texas History Center, University of Texas at Austin; Files, Institute of Texan Cultures, University of Texas at San Antonio.

John H. Jenkins

*Salinas Creek.

*Salinas Varona, Gregorio de.

*Saline Creek.

Saline Lake, Texas. *See* Jordan's Saline, Texas; Grand Saline, Texas.

*Salineno, Texas.

Salinero Indians. The name Salinero, "salt producer," was frequently used by the Spanish to refer to Indian groups that exploited local sources of salt. This name was widely used in northern Mexico and Texas. In Tamaulipas, Nuevo León, Coahuila, and Chihuahua various unrelated Indian groups were known as Salinero. The principal Salinero group in Texas lived along the Pecos River, and their range extended northward along this river into southeastern New Mexico. These Salinero are repeatedly mentioned in documents of the late seventeenth and eighteenth centuries. Sometimes the Salinero were equated with the Natage. It is clear that the Salinero were Apache Indians and that they were among the groups that eventually became known as Mescalero Apache.

BIBLIOGRAPHY: H. E. Bolton, "The Jumano Indians in Texas, 1650–1771," *Quarterly of the Texas State Historical Association*, XV (1911–1912); H. E. Bolton (ed.), *Spanish Exploration in the Southwest, 1542–1706* (1916); W. E. Dunn, "Apache Relations in Texas, 1718–1750," *Quarterly of the Texas States Historical Association*, XIV (1910–

1911); A. H. Schroeder, *A Study of the Apache Indians: The Mescalero Apaches*, Part III (1960).

T. N. Campbell

*Salisbury, Texas.

*Salmon, Richard.

*Salmon, Texas.

*Salmon Peak.

*Salomoneno Creek.

*Salona, Texas.

*Salsamora Creek.

*Salt Basin.

*Salt Branch.

*Salt City, Texas.

*Salt Creek.

*Salt Creek, Texas.

*Salt Creek Massacre. The Salt Creek Massacre, also referred to as the Warren Wagontrain Raid, occurred on May 18 (not May 17, as stated in Volume II), 1871.

BIBLIOGRAPHY: Benjamin Capps, *The Warren Wagontrain Raid* (1974); W. S. Nye, *Carbine & Lance* (rev. ed. 1969).

*Salt Draw.

*Salt Flats, Texas.

*Salt Fork of the Brazos River.

*Salt Fork of Red River.

*Salt Gap.

*Salt Gap, Texas.

*Salt Industry. Common salt production in 1954 totaled 2,876,943 short tons valued at $7,-629,531. Some of the salt brine production was transported by pipeline to chemical plants at Freeport, Corpus Christi, and Houston. In the 1960's most of the salt production in Texas came from salt domes on the Coastal Plains. Production was reported in Brazoria, Chambers, Duval, Fort Bend, Harris, Hutchinson, Jefferson, Van Zandt, Ward, and Yoakum counties. The Grand Saline mine in Van Zandt County continued to have a large output (*see* Grand Saline, Texas). In 1961 salt production increased to 4,695,000 short tons valued at $17,-682,000; this trend continued, so that by 1970 the state produced 10,269,000 short tons valued at $47,620,000.

BIBLIOGRAPHY: *Texas Almanac* (1957, 1963, 1971).

*Salt Lake.

*Salt Lakes, The.

*Salt Mountain.

*Salt Prong.

*Salt War.

*Saltgrass Draw.

*Saltillo, Mexico.

*Saltillo, Texas.

*Salty, Texas.

*Salty Creek.

*Saluria, Texas.

*Sam Houston National Forest. *See* National Forests in Texas.

*Sam Houston State Teachers College. *See also* Sam Houston State University.

Sam Houston State University. Sam Houston State University (formerly Sam Houston State Teachers College qv), Huntsville, added a student union, a music building, a graphic arts building, and a vocational agriculture laboratory to the compus in 1951. An ROTC unit was established at the college in 1952. On April 21, 1954, the institution celebrated its seventy-fifth anniversary.

By 1964 the college had an enrollment of 5,738 students, a 259-member faculty, a completely air-conditioned plant valued at $20,000,000, and a curriculum which offered nine degrees in twenty-seven subject areas, including four graduate degrees in nineteen areas. Courses and degrees for teachers and administrators at all levels of public schools and junior colleges were offered. Preparation for entrance to schools of medicine, law, engineering, dentistry, and other professions was given. Joint programs in social work and research were presented through the college by the Texas Board of Corrections qv and the Institute of Contemporary Corrections and the Behavioral Sciences.

In 1965 organization of the college into the following six schools was approved: graduate school, school of business and applied arts, school of education, school of fine arts, school of humanities, and school of science. In recognition of the broadened scope of the college, the state legislature changed the institution's name from Sam Houston State Teachers College to Sam Houston State College in 1965, and to Sam Houston State University in 1969. In 1969 enrollment reached 8,594, the faculty totaled 350, and the library contained 306,923 volumes. In the fall term, 1974, student enrollment increased to 10,144; Elliott T. Bowers was president in that year.

Sam Rayburn Dam and Reservoir. Sam Rayburn Dam and Sam Rayburn Reservoir were known as McGee Bend Dam and McGee Bend Reservoir (*see* McGee Bend Project) until December, 1963, when the dam and reservoir were renamed by congressional action. The dam and reservoir are in the Neches River Basin in Jasper County, eleven miles northwest of Jasper on the Angelina River, a tributary of the Neches River. The reservoir extends into Angelina, Sabine, San Augustine, and Nacogdoches counties.

The project is owned by the United States government, and is operated by the United States Army Corps of Engineers, Fort Worth District. The local agency for the purchase of water storage rights is the Lower Neches Valley Authority.qv The marketing agency for electric power generated at the dam is Southwestern Power Administration. The project is designed to control and regulate floods, generate power, and conserve water for municipal, industrial, agricultural, and recreational purposes. The reservoir has a total capacity of 2,852,600 acre-feet and a surface area of 114,500 acres at the top of the power storage space at an elevation of 164 feet above mean sea level. Two hydroelectric power generating units with a total capacity of 52,000 kilowatts were installed at the dam. Power generation began July 1, 1966. The drainage area at the dam is 3,449 square miles.

BIBLIOGRAPHY: Texas Water Commission, *Bulletin 6408* (1964).

Seth D. Breeding

Sam Rayburn Library. *See* Rayburn, Samuel Taliaferro.

Sam Rayburn Veterans Administration Center. *See* Veterans Administration Hospital, Bonham.

Sama Indians. The Sama Indians are known only from records pertaining to San Antonio de Valero Mission qv at San Antonio. It seems clear that the Sama were not the same as the Sana. The Sama were among the Indians for whom the mission was founded in 1719, and one document states that their language was the same as that of the Payaya, which was Coahuiltecan. The Sana did not enter this mission until the 1740's, and it is also known that their language was not Coahuiltecan.

BIBLIOGRAPHY: J. A. Dabbs, "The Texas Missions in 1785," *Preliminary Studies of the Texas Catholic Historical Society*, III (1940); F. W. Hodge (ed.), *Handbook of American Indians*, II (1910).

T. N. Campbell

Samacoalapem Indians. The Samacoalapem (Sanacualapem, Sumacoalapem) Indians, apparently Coahuiltecans, lived on the lower Rio Grande. In the middle eighteenth century their principal settlements were on the south bank of the river between Camargo and Mier, Tamaulipas. Although the evidence is not clear, it appears likely that they also ranged along the north bank.

BIBLIOGRAPHY: W. Jiménez Moreno, "Tribus e idiomas del Norte de México," *El Norte de México y el Sur de Estados Unidos* (1944); G. Saldivar, *Los Indios de Tamaulipas* (1943).

T. N. Campbell

*Samampac Indians. This group is known from only one brief meeting with Spanish travelers near the close of the seventeenth century. At this time the Samampac (Caomopac) and several other Coahuiltecan bands were ranging over the Nueces-Frio area between present San Antonio and Eagle Pass.

BIBLIOGRAPHY: F. W. Hodge (ed.), *Handbook of American Indians*, II (1910); J. R. Swanton, *The Indian Tribes of North America* (1952).

T. N. Campbell

*Sambo, Texas.

*Samfordyce, Texas.

*Samnorwood, Texas.

*Sampanal Indians. The Sampanal (Sanpanle) Indians are known only from the latter part of the seventeenth century, when they were visited by Spanish travelers on two occasions. At the first meeting the Sampanal were near the southern margin of the Edwards Plateau some fifty miles north or northeast of present Eagle Pass; at the second

they were in the Nueces-Frio area between San Antonio and Eagle Pass. It seems clear that they were
one of the many small Coahuiltecan bands that
ranged over the territory south of the Edwards
Plateau. Their identity seems to have been lost before the Spanish mission period of the eighteenth
century. However, it is possible that the name
Sampanal is a variant of Sanipao, the name of a
Coahuiltecan band that appeared in 1755 at the
Nuestra Señora de la Purísima Concepción de
Acuña Mission qv of San Antonio and remained
there until at least 1790.

BIBLIOGRAPHY: F. W. Hodge (ed.), *Handbook of
American Indians*, II (1910); J. R. Swanton, *Linguistic
Material from the Tribes of Southern Texas and North-
eastern Mexico* (1940).

T. N. Campbell

*Sample, Texas.

*Sampson, Thornton Rogers.

*Sampson, Texas.

Samuel, William M. G. William M. G. Samuel,
born in Missouri in 1815, came as an immigrant
soldier to San Antonio probably in the late 1830's.
Samuel's marksmanship ability was put to use
during the Indian wars, and in the Mexican War
he served in General John E. Wool's Army of
Chihuahua. After a term as justice of the peace of
Medina County, Samuel served as county court
commissioner, and in 1878 and 1880 he was a peace
officer and a notary public. In 1881 and 1882 he
was elected deputy sheriff of San Antonio and
helped to put under arrest persons who were ter-
rorizing the town. In 1849 he began painting pictures for the bare walls of the old Bexar County
Courthouse. These paintings were realistic views
of the homes, people, and daily scenes that he observed from the windows of the courthouse. For
almost a century his paintings, assuming the color
of the darkened, smoky walls, hung unnoticed.
Finally they were "discovered" in the 1930's. During quiet periods of Samuel's long service in the
local government, he made portraits of some of his
associates and friends. Among those identified as
Samuel's work on the walls were primitive paintings of Sam Houston, Big Foot Wallace, Deaf
Smith, José Antonio Menchaca,qqv and a self-
portrait. William Samuel died in 1902.

BIBLIOGRAPHY: Pauline A. Pinckney, *Painting in Texas:
The Nineteenth Century* (1967).

Pauline A. Pinckney

*Samuel Huston College. *See also* Huston-
Tillotson College.

*Samuella, Texas.

*San Agustín de Ahumada Presidio. An arche-
ological excavation of the second location of the
presidio, just northeast of Wallisville, Chambers
County, was conducted by the Texas Archeological
Salvage Project and the State Building Commission qv in the fall of 1965. Although much of the
site was destroyed by recent borrow pits, several

thousand Spanish Colonial and Indian artifacts
were recovered.

Curtis Tunnell

*San Ambrosia Creek.

*San Andres Creek.

*San Angelo, Texas. *See also* San Angelo Standard Metropolitan Statistical Area.

*San Angelo Army Air Field.

San Angelo Center. The San Angelo Center is
a retardate residential facility of the Texas Department of Mental Health and Mental Retardation qv
occupying facilities that were formerly the Mc-
Knight State Sanatorium.qv Opened October 7,
1969, the center was designed to supplement ha-
bilitation practices and enhance the self concept
of retardates thirty-five years old or older. Most of
the residents have little potential of returning to
community life. Census at the end of 1970 was
251, and the superintendent was J. W. Irwin. *See
also* Mentally Ill and Mentally Retarded, Care of, in
Texas.

BIBLIOGRAPHY: Texas Department of Mental Health
and Mental Retardation, *Annual Report, 1970.*

San Angelo College. *See* Angelo State University.

*San Angelo Junction, Texas.

San Angelo Reservoir. San Angelo Reservoir is
located in the Colorado River Basin in Tom Green
County, three miles northwest of San Angelo on
the North Concho River. The project is owned by
the United States government and is operated by
the United States Army Corps of Engineers, Fort
Worth District. The Upper Colorado River Authority qv purchased conservation storage space in
the reservoir for municipal, industrial, irrigational,
mining, and recreational purposes. This water supplements San Angelo's water supply. Construction
started in May, 1947; closure was completed on
March 7, 1951; and deliberate impoundment of
water began on February 1, 1952. The reservoir is
for flood control, conservation, and recreation purposes. The capacity of the conservation storage
space is 119,200 acre-feet; it has a surface area of
5,440 acres at elevation 1,908 feet above mean sea
level. The flood control storage capacity is 277,200
acre-feet between the top of the conservation storage
space and the uncontrolled spillway crest. Drainage
area is 1,488 square miles, of which 105 square
miles is probably noncontributing.

BIBLIOGRAPHY: Texas Water Commission, *Bulletin 6408*
(1964).

Seth D. Breeding

San Angelo Standard Metropolitan Statistical
Area. The San Angelo Standard Metropolitan Statistical Area, created in 1949 by the United States
Bureau of the Budget, includes the 1,534 square
miles of Tom Green County and is the market
center for a twenty-three-county agricultural region
in west-central Texas. It is a geographic transitional
area merging the Edwards Plateau qv with the rolling plains of Texas. The major metropolitan com-

munity is San Angelo, a city of 63,884 population in 1970, showing an 8.6 percent increase over the 1960 population of 58,815, according to the United States census. The total metropolitan area, identical with Tom Green County, had a 1970 population of 71,047, an increase of approximately 10 percent over the 1960 census of 64,630.

The principal agricultural activity in the metropolitan area was in livestock, particularly Rambouillet and Merino sheep and Angora (mohair) and Spanish (meat) goats. The shallow, rocky soil, not suitable for extensive cultivation, was sufficient for sheep and goat grazing, accounting for approximately 155,000 sheep and 30,000 goats raised annually in the area. Cattle were also of considerable importance; some 40,000 cattle were raised on metropolitan area ranches in 1969. Crop raising was composed principally of grain sorghum and cotton, much of it produced on irrigated land. The area lies on the fringe of the Permian Basin qv oil fields, and crude oil production of just over two million barrels in 1968 contributed to the area economy.

Water conservation and flood control projects since 1950 have resulted in San Angelo Reservoir (North Concho Lake) with a watershed capacity of 396,000 acre-feet, and Twin Buttes Reservoir (Three Rivers Lake) with 600,000 acre-feet, both dwarfing old Lake Nasworthy with its 12,390 acre-feet capacity. Increasing activity on the three lakes has made the city a popular place for water recreation enthusiasts. The impounded water cushions the city against the effects of periodic and sometimes prolonged drouths. Natural disaster experiences in the area included the tornado of 1953, resulting in 11 deaths, 159 injuries, and destruction amounting to $3,239,000. In 1957 a general flood, signaling the end of the extensive drouth of the 1950's, damaged approximately eight homes.

A young city, San Angelo was hardly more than a collection of *jacales* (huts, not jackals, as stated in Volume II) and adobe houses before 1888 when railway lines reached the site, promoting its growth. Seat of Tom Green County and business center for the large ranching and petroleum area, the city was the nation's largest market for sheep and goats, with more than eighty wool and mohair warehouses. Nearly 50 percent of the nation's mohair was handled there. In 1965 a new livestock market reporting service, sponsored jointly by the national and state departments of agriculture, was located in San Angelo. In addition to over one hundred industries, which included an international aircraft-manufacturing plant (Mitsubishi Aircraft International, Inc.), surgical supply and ceramic tile factories, clothing and slipper manufacturers, meat packers and wool processors, and a regional telephone office, the city boasted five major banks and forty-five smaller financial institutions in the mid-1960's. The San Angelo *Standard Times*, established in 1920, was the founding paper of the Harte-Hanks Newspapers, Inc., chain. Several sub-urban shopping districts now supplement downtown business and mercantile establishments. A new 7,300-acre tire testing track of the Goodyear Tire and Rubber Co. was located near the city, employing over two hundred people. San Angelo reported 976 businesses in 1970.

In 1958 Goodfellow Air Force Base qv became an air force security service training school with a detachment of Central Air Rescue and a detachment of the 6th Weather Squadron stationed there. Old Fort Concho,qv designated as a registered historic landmark, has been preserved with its twenty-two buildings; a museum was established in the post's old administration building. Cultural activities in San Angelo include the Angelo State University entertainment series, San Angelo Symphony Orchestra, and San Angelo Civic Theatre. The Miss Wool of America pageant each June, sponsored for a number of years by national and international wool organizations, was discontinued after 1972. Other annual events include a rodeo and fat stock show, steer-roping contests with nationally known performers, and the San Angelo relays for area high school track teams. The air-conditioned 6,500-seat San Angelo Coliseum, opened in the 1950's and operated by the board of city development, provided a variety of promoted entertainment.

San Angelo also has become an area medical service center with Shannon West Texas Memorial Hospital, St. John's Hospital, the Clinic Hospital of San Angelo, and the Baptist Memorials Geriatric Center providing progressive medical facilities. Facilities for those of retirement age also include Rio Concho Manor, a ten-story federally financed complex with an addition begun in 1972, and the famed old Cactus Hotel, purchased and operated by the Baptist General Convention as a retirement apartment hotel and designated as the Moody Memorial Retirement Center.

The city's educational system includes San Angelo Central High School, a showplace for its architectural plant as well as its educational planning. The Lakeview Independent School District also served a part of northeast San Angelo. In 1965 San Angelo Junior College became Angelo State College, a fully tax supported, bachelor's-degree granting institution (now Angelo State University). There were twenty-five public and parochial schools and also a business college in San Angelo in 1969. *See also* Tom Green County.

Billy M. Jones

*San Antonio. The schooner *San Antonio* had four twelve-pound guns (not seven, as stated in Volume II) and one twelve-pound (not eighteen-pound) long pivot gun. She was first named the *Asp* (not the *Asp of Baltimore*). One officer was killed and two (not three) officers were wounded in the mutiny of February 11, 1842.

BIBLIOGRAPHY: Tom Henderson Wells, *Commodore Moore and the Texas Navy* (1960).

Tom Henderson Wells

*San Antonio, Texas. *See also* San Antonio Standard Metropolitan Statistical Area.

*San Antonio Academy.

*San Antonio and Aransas Pass Railway.

*San Antonio Arsenal. The United States Arsenal at San Antonio was closed as such in 1949, although its buildings continued to be used for federal government offices. On July 19, 1972, two acres and three buildings were transferred from the federal government to the city of San Antonio as part of President Richard M. Nixon's Legacy of Parks Program, under the United States Department of the Interior's Bureau of Outdoor Recreation. The remaining three arsenal buildings on the approximately eighteen remaining acres continued to be used for federal government offices in 1972.

BIBLIOGRAPHY: Five States of Texas, Incorporated, *"Five States" Guide to Texas* (1963); *San Antonio Conservation Society Year Book 1972–1973* (1972); Files, Texas Historical Commission, Austin.

*San Antonio Aviation Center. *See* Lackland Air Force Base.

*San Antonio Bay.

*San Antonio Belt and Terminal Railway Company. The San Antonio Belt and Terminal Railway Company owned a freight and passenger terminal with 21.5 miles of industrial and outside track in San Antonio in 1964. It was leased to the Missouri-Kansas-Texas Railroad Company, which owns all its stock.

James M. Day

*San Antonio de Bexar Presidio.

San Antonio Citizens League. The Citizens League was formed in San Antonio after the Wurzbach-McCloskey 1928 congressional election contest. Harry McLeary Wurzbach,qv the Republican incumbent who had served three terms in the U.S. House of Representatives, was apparently defeated in 1928 by Augustus McCloskey,qv the Democratic nominee who had been supported by the San Antonio city political machine. After thirteen months, Wurzbach was declared the winner in the disputed election and he replaced McCloskey in the House. The league, founded by prominent citizens, declared itself against "machine rule" and demanded honest elections, honest spending of bond proceeds, only two terms for officeholders, and an end to organized gambling.

The league won most county offices in the Democratic primary in 1930, but in 1931 it failed to capture city hall; the machine's virtual monopoly of the Latin American and Negro vote was an insuperable barrier. In 1932 the league again won a sweeping victory in the county races; Negroes did not vote in the Democratic primary.

Internal dissension in the league and the death of its chief target, Mayor C. M. Chambers, combined to defeat its ticket in the 1933 city election. The weakened league rallied in 1934 to win most of the county offices, losing its district attorney, Walter Tynan, but sending its tax assessor, Maury Maverick,qv to a new congressional seat. In 1935 its candidate for mayor withdrew after the campaign

was under way, and the league then withdrew the rest of its candidates.

In 1936 the executive committee, then nine in number, quarreled over whether it should oppose its incumbent sheriff for not closing the gambling houses. By a vote of five to four the sheriff was placed on the ticket, but the four dissenters resigned and withdrew, three of them doing so publicly. Only Maverick and a few minor candidates survived the machine landslide.

While in theory the league consisted of a convention of all of the citizens of San Antonio, in practice the executive committee determined policy in campaigns and nominated candidates, and the officeholders ran the league between elections. The six campaigns waged by the league were featured by nightly rallies designed to carry the campaign to every part of town. While the executive committee was always conservative politically, the league's best-known product, Maverick, was an unqualified liberal.

Nowlin Randolph

San Antonio College. San Antonio College, San Antonio, was formally opened on September 21, 1925, as University Junior College with an enrollment of 200 students. Classes were first conducted in the old Main High School building after dismissal of high school classes for the day. Under the administration of the University of Texas and in the absence of an appropriation to support the junior college, fees were charged on a quarterly basis. The purpose of the college was to provide services and facilities in addition to those offered by the church-related colleges in San Antonio.

The state attorney general ruled in December, 1925, that operation of a junior college by the University of Texas violated the state constitution; thus, supervision of the college, known as San Antonio Junior College, passed to the San Antonio board of education for the second year of operation. Although tuition covered the cost of instruction, the city chapter of the American Association of University Women underwrote other financial needs for the 1926–1927 academic year. In 1926 the college was assigned part of the building on Alamo Street formerly occupied by the German-English School qv and later by Thomas Nelson Page Junior High School. The college then offered a full-time and evening curriculum. In 1930 the indefinite status of the college was ended when it was made part of the San Antonio School System for a five-year probationary period. Public support for the college insured its continued existence.

James Otis Loftin qv became president in 1941 and until his death in 1955 was largely responsible for the college's growth. St. Philip's Junior College (*see* St. Philip's College), a Negro institution, was transferred from the operation of the Episcopal diocese to the San Antonio Independent School District in 1942 as a branch of San Antonio Junior College. In 1945 a proposal for a Union Junior College District for metropolitan San Antonio was approved by a substantial voting majority. In August, 1946, San Antonio Junior College and St. Philip's Junior College passed from control of the board of trustees. San Antonio College was adopted as the official name in 1948.

All buildings on the thirty-seven-acre San Pedro Avenue campus were constructed after 1950 and include library, administration, classroom, and science buildings (1950), a health building (1951), a student center, a maintenance building, and an annex containing classrooms and a computer center (1954), a fine arts center (1956), the president's home (1958), a chemistry-geology building (1961), and Dewey Annex containing departmental offices (1963). The Baptist, Church of Christ, and Methodist student centers were also constructed during these years. A technical arts and a classroom-library building were under construction in 1965, and a student union building was on the drawing board.

The college, fully accredited, operated both day and evening divisions as well as a summer school program. Courses of instruction were categorized as those leading to degrees from senior institutions, technical and vocational, terminal vocation, and community service. The college participated in the Texas Educational Microwave Project, a televised program of instruction, through a Ford Foundation grant. In 1964 the enrollment was 9,100 and the faculty numbered 175. Student enrollment reached 13,638 and faculty members totaled 530 in 1969; the library contained 91,000 volumes that same year. Dean of the college in 1974 was Paul R. Culwell, and total enrollment in that year was 20,019. Jerome F. Weynand was president of the college district.

San Antonio Conservation Society. The San Antonio Conservation Society was founded by a group of historic-minded San Antonio women on March 22, 1924, after the disastrous 1921 flood resulted in flood control measures that threatened drastic physical changes in old San Antonio. The organization began at once a program of public education in conservation and preservation, including lectures and history-oriented entertainments. The society was incorporated on July 8, 1925, with the purpose of preserving and encouraging the preservation of historic buildings, objects, and places related to the history of Texas and its natural beauty; the group has remained active to the present time in the purchase, restoration, and operation of historic sites.

In 1926, after failing to preserve the old Market House, which was their original intention, the society discovered that a new river channel was to be cut and that the large downtown riverbend would be drained and cemented over. The society was instrumental in saving this riverbend of the San Antonio River, the only remaining meander that has survived rechanneling and tunneling in the city. The federal Works Progress Administration (WPA) qv provided the labor for landscaping and for construction of riverwalks, footbridges, and a riverbank theater. That mid-town area became

known as "El Paseo del Rio," with many shops and restaurants along the river. After the city purchased the Spanish Governors' Palace qv in the late 1920's, members of the society were named to supervise restoration, landscape-gardening, and furnishing, and to fill curator positions. In the early 1930's San José Granary, with some adjoining land, was purchased by the group, and the federal government through the WPA furnished labor for restoration. Soon after, the society collaborated with Bexar County agencies, the state Highway Department,qv and the Catholic church in the restoration of the church's San José y San Miguel de Aguayo Mission qv and in the reconstruction of the mission enclosure. The San José Granary in 1941 and the adjoining land in 1950 were given to the state of Texas, and the society was successful in having the entire complex of Mission San José designed as a national historic site, the first so honored in Texas.

In 1941 the society purchased property which contained the two-hundred-year-old aqueduct which carried water to San Francisco de la Espada Mission,qv designated in 1965 a national historic landmark. In 1942 an old stone house at 511 Villita Street, overlooking the riverbend, was purchased and became the society's headquarters; in 1950 nearby Cós House was acquired. In 1957 twenty-five acres of pecan bottom land near the acequia of San Juan Capistrano Mission qv were acquired, and a park was established. Scheduled for demolition in 1960, a group of three stone buildings, which had been the home of José Antonio Navarro qv (see also Navarro House Museum), was acquired and restored. In 1961 the society was given the Yturri-Edmonds home and the old Travieso Mill on Old Mission Road. Moved onto this property was the Oge Carriage House from King William Street. In 1965 sections of the old Ursuline Convent (see Ursuline Academies), designed by early architects Jules Poinsard and François Giraud, were purchased, and in 1969 this property was entered in the National Register of Historic Places. Three outstanding houses, the Eduard Steves Homestead, the Ike West Home (both on King William Street), and the Charles Zilker House on Elm Street, were acquired. In every case the society assumes ownership of historic properties only to protect, preserve, or restore them, and then finds an appropriate use for each.

The society achieved national notice for its longstanding annual Christmas season presentations of two Mexican folk celebrations, "Los Pastores" (The Shepherds) and "Los Posados" (The Inns). Also popular since its inception in 1947 is the entertainment, "Night in Old San Antonio," held each spring at the time of Fiesta San Antonio qv in La Villita.qv

Ecology was long an interest of the group. San Pedro Park was preserved as a recreational area through the society's efforts in the late 1940's; an annual tree-selling project was sponsored beginning in 1952, and trees were planted as well as sold by the organization. Travis Park, which had been deeded to the city in the 1850's, was leased by the city in 1954 to a corporation for an underground parking garage. The Conservation Society brought suit, and in a state supreme court decision in 1957 the lease arrangement was declared null and void, thus proving the society's contention that dedicated parkland had legal rights; Travis Park was therefore preserved as a city parkland.

In 1959 a projected city plan for a nine-mile north expressway to run through seven miles of public parkway (Brackenridge Park, Olmos Basin Park, and Olmos Basin) was contested by the society in two lawsuits, thus delaying the project. In this landmark case for municipal parks throughout the nation no legal decision had been reached by 1972.

In 1947 the Conservation Society added an associate membership, from which new active members were taken, and in 1955 a junior associate membership was created to enable young members to study regional history and traditions. Beginning in 1949 the society annually presented awards to persons and organizations who best served the cause of conservation. The society's charter was amended in 1962 to include members' concern for the state's natural beauty and to emphasize the educational character of the society. An adjunct to the organization, the San Antonio Conservation Society Foundation, was chartered by the state on May 19, 1970. The society has had twenty-four presidents since its organization; Emily Edwards served as the first president, 1924–1926, and Mrs. Winfield S. Hamlin held office in 1972–1973.

BIBLIOGRAPHY: Lillie Mae Hagner, *Alluring San Antonio* (1940); Charles Ramsdell, *San Antonio: A Historical and Pictorial Guide* (1959); San Antonio Conservation Society, *Conservation in San Antonio Since 1924* (1970); *San Antonio Conservation Society Year Book 1972–1973* (1972).

*San Antonio Creek.

San Antonio Crossing. San Antonio Crossing was the point on the Rio Grande where the Camino Real, or Old San Antonio Road,qv crossed the river near the presidio of San Juan Bautista,qv and the term generally referred to any one of several fords on the river near the presidio. Specifically, it was located five miles southeast of San Juan Bautista at a crossing known as Paso de Francia. Two islands divide the river into three channels at the crossing at a point where the river begins to bend from southerly to southeasterly. The King's Highway entered the Texas side at the end of a chain of high bluffs, just above the Falls of Presidio del Rio Grande, then followed an easterly course.

It is believed that the name Paso de Francia, or France Way, was applied to this crossing in 1689 when Alonso de León qv made his fourth entrada in search of the colony of Sieur de La Salle.qv De León's entry into Texas at this site is the earliest that can accurately be ascribed to Paso de Francia, though the Bosque-Larios Expedition qv of 1675 may have been the first to use this ford. Subsequent to the nearby establishment of San Juan Bautista in

1700, the Paso de Francia crossing became the principal thoroughfare for all of the Spanish entradas of exploration and colonization into Texas. The last major use of the ford was in 1836 when Antonio López de Santa Anna,qv at the head of part of his army, crossed at Paso de Francia to quell the Texan insurrectionists. In later years Paso de Francia was variously referred to as the Lower Crossing, the Las Islas or Isletas Crossing, and during the period of Anglo exploration, Kingsbury Falls or Rapids, and the Falls of Presidio del Rio Grande. In 1918 the Daughters of the American Revolution and the state of Texas placed their terminal trail marker on the east bank of this site.

Six miles upstream from Paso de Francia lies another and possibly more ancient ford. It was called Paquache (and sometimes Tlacuache) after one of the Coahuiltecan tribes indigenous to the area. This upper crossing is near the mouth of Cuervo Creek and may have first been used by Domingo Terán de los Ríos qv in 1691. During the early years of the Presidio de San Juan Bautista, it was called the Pass of Diego Ramón.qv General Adrian Woll qv forded the river at Paquache with his army when he raided San Antonio in 1842. Four years later General John E. Wool, following Woll's route, invaded Mexico via Paquache with his Army of Chihuahua. Throughout the remainder of the 19th century, due to the proximity of the new upriver towns of Eagle Pass and Piedras Negras, the Paquache Crossing was the principal ford for traffic to and from Presidio del Rio Grande. Both the United States and the Mexican governments erected small customs houses and assigned guards to oversee and regulate trade crossing the river. During the Mexican border troubles in 1916, Texas Rangers qv and detachments of troops from Fort Duncan qv camped at Paquache and at Paso de Francia. Though the crossings were no longer being used and both custom houses at Paquache were abandoned, these ancient fords were still regarded as strategic sites.

Today, ranchers in the vicinity refer to the Paquache, or upper crossing, as the "Old San Antonio Crossing" and to Cuervo Creek as "San Antonio Creek." Until the Rio Grande flood of 1954, a large Spanish *carreta* wheel could be seen partially exposed just below this upper crossing. The change and misinterpretation in place names has lent confusion to researchers trying to locate Paso de Francia. Except for the King's Highway marker at the site six miles below Paquache, the original "Old San Antonio Crossing" has long been forgotten.

BIBLIOGRAPHY: C. E. Castañeda, *Our Catholic Heritage in Texas, 1519–1936*, II (1936); W. H. Emory, *Report of the U.S.-Mexican Boundary Survey*, I (1857); J. M. Inglis, *A History of Vegetation on the Rio Grande Plain* (1964); Mrs. Lipscomb Norvell, *King's Highway* (1945); V. Alessio Robles, *Coahuila y Texas en la Epoca Colonial* (1938) and *Coahuila y Texas Desde . . . la . . . Independencia . . .* (1945); Bryant Tilden, *Notes on the Upper Rio Grande* (1847); W. H. C. Whiting, *Report of the Secretary of War* (1850).

Ben E. Pingenot

*San Antonio *Evening News*. The San Antonio *Evening News* was printed by the Harte-Hanks newspaper group which bought both the *Evening News* and the San Antonio *Express* qv in 1960–1962. In 1972 the managing editor of the *Evening News* was John Newell and the publisher was Houston H. Harte. Harte was also president of the Express Publishing Company which owned both newspapers (*see* San Antonio *Express* for other officers of the company). The daily circulation of the San Antonio *Evening News* was 67,607 in 1972.

*San Antonio Express. At the end of World War II, Frank E. Huntress, Jr., took over management of the daily morning newspaper, the San Antonio *Express* from his father, Frank E. Huntress. New holdings included a large block of stock in paper mills purchased in 1946 when a strike by Canadian loggers nearly put the paper out of business. Owner and operator of radio station WOAI in 1922, the *Express* acquired its second radio station, KYFM in 1947. In 1949 the paper bought KTSA-AM and FM radio, but sold it in 1954. That same year the *Express* added KGBS radio-television to its holdings, renaming the station KENS-TV.

The Express Publishing Company continued to be the publisher of both the *Express* and the San Antonio *Evening News,*qv and in the early 1950's there was a trend toward merging their formerly separate staffs. By 1958 high speed Goss presses enabled the company to print more than 60,000 papers an hour.

From 1960 to 1962 the Harte-Hanks newspaper group purchased the company from the Grice heirs, the Brackenridge estate, the Huntress family, and W. A. Druce, becoming sole owners of the paper. Conway Craig, president and publisher of the Corpus Christi *Caller-Times*, became president and publisher of the *Express*, and Houston H. Harte, president of the San Angelo *Standard-Times*, became vice-president. Frank Huntress, Jr., former president and publisher, became chairman of the board. In 1965 a newsroom staff of eighty-eight celebrated the 100th anniversary of the founding of the *Express*.

In 1972 the managing editor of the *Express* was Ken Kennamer; the publisher was Charles O. Kilpatrick, who was also executive editor and a vice-president of the Express Publishing Company. Other officers of the company were associate editor Sterlin Holmesley, associate executive editor Bill Wagner, vice-president James H. Smith, and president Houston H. Harte. The daily circulation of the San Antonio *Express* in 1972 was 81,936.

BIBLIOGRAPHY: Subject Files, Barker Texas History Center, University of Texas at Austin.

*San Antonio Female College.

San Antonio Fiesta. *See* Fiesta San Antonio; *see also* Fiesta de San Jacinto.

*San Antonio Greys. *See* New Orleans Greys.

*San Antonio and Gulf Shore Railway.

*San Antonio *Herald*.

*San Antonio Historical Association. The San Antonio Historical Association continued to hold meetings on the third Friday of January, February, March, May, September, October, and November in Alamo Hall; an annual dinner at a local hotel featured the president's address.

At regular meetings papers are presented which focus primarily on local topics of historical interest, although subject matter pertaining to the entire Southwest is acceptable. Most speakers are business and professional persons engaged in historical research as an avocation, but during the 1960's there was an increased participation by professors and graduate students from local universities. In 1947 the association received the publications of the Yanaguana Society qv upon that organization's dissolution. Joseph William Schmitz qv was the association's first president and cofounder in 1940, and Mrs. Q. W. Bynum was president in 1972.

Donald E. Everett

*San Antonio de la Isleta. *See* Corpus Christi de la Isleta.

*San Antonio de los Julimes Pueblo. *See* San Antonio de los Puliques Pueblo.

*San Antonio *Light*. In post World War II years the San Antonio *Light*, a William Randolph Hearst publication since 1924, attained circulation leadership in that city under publisher B. J. Horner and managing editor N. Dwight Allison. Following their retirement in 1967, William B. Bellamy was named managing editor, and Frank A. Bennack was publisher. In 1972 the *Light*, with a daily circulation of 122,292 and a Sunday circulation of 160,905, was one of the leading Hearst newspapers in the United States.

*San Antonio and Mexican Gulf Railway.

*San Antonio Mountain.

*San Antonio National Cemetery.

*San Antonio de Padua.

*San Antonio de Padua Mission. *See* San Antonio de Valero Mission.

San Antonio Philosophical and Theological Seminary. *See* Oblate College of the Southwest.

San Antonio Prairie, Texas. San Antonio Prairie, southwest of Caldwell on State Highway 21 in Burleson County, was a farming community of fifteen people in the mid-1960's.

*San Antonio de los Puliques Pueblo.

*San Antonio River.

San Antonio River Authority. The San Antonio River Authority (SARA) was organized in 1937 by the 45th Texas Legislature as a conservation and reclamation district of the state. Its jurisdiction includes the counties of Bexar, Wilson, Karnes, and Goliad within the San Antonio River Basin. This agency was originated primarily to seek development of a barge canal from the Gulf Coast inland to the city of San Antonio, and to promote flood control and soil conservation. In 1961 the legislature expanded the authority of the agency to include the conservation and use of ground, storm, flood, and unappropriated flow waters in the district; irrigation; sewage treatment; pollution prevention; development of parks and recreational facilities; forestation; and the preservation of fish.

The authority was governed by an elected twelve-member board of directors, six from Bexar and two each from Wilson, Karnes, and Goliad counties. Members were elected on a non-partisan basis to serve six-year, staggered terms. Board policies were carried out by a management organization under the manager with the assistance of two departments: operations and administrative services. The operations department coordinates and administers SARA's field activities through five divisions: water quality and supply, soil conservation, flood control, parks and recreation, and land.

The water quality and supply division is responsible for all activities relating to water conservation, storage, procurement, distribution and supply, sewage treatment, pollution prevention, and irrigation. Administration of these responsibilities resulted in the construction of a modern, authority-owned and -operated sewage treatment plant and laboratory complex in eastern Bexar County serving 5,000 people. This division also prepared the first basin-wide stream quality standards plan in Texas, the result of a basin-wide stream quality study to pinpoint pollution problems. This division also exercises regulatory control over all waste treatment plants in the San Antonio River Basin. Stream and effluent samples taken from various points in the basin are analyzed at the SARA laboratory under the auspices of the Texas Water Pollution Board and State Department of Public Health.qv

The soil conservation division is one of the oldest at SARA. In 1953 W. B. Tuttle, SARA chairman from 1937 to 1954, helped steer pilot watershed legislation through Congress and was instrumental in obtaining authorization of sixty-four of these projects for the United States. Two projects, consisting of twenty watershed flood control structures, were assigned to the San Antonio River Basin (the Calaveras Watershed in Bexar County and the Escondido in Karnes County). The projects consist of a series of flood control dams established along stream channels within a watershed, and offer flood protection, recreation, wildlife refuge, and agricultural, municipal, and industrial water use. From the two pilot projects the authority has increased basin flood protection with the development of nine structures in two additional watersheds. SARA plans call for operation and maintenance of 100 flood control structures in ten watersheds by 1975. Construction of these flood control dams is financed by the Soil Conservation Service under Public Law 566. Easement acquisition, contract administration, and operation and maintenance expenses are carried primarily by SARA.

Urban flood control is a responsibility of the flood control division of the authority. This division is responsible for the $32 million San Antonio Channel Improvement Project involving 33.9 miles of improved channel and fifty-five new, all-weather bridges. SARA buys land required for new flood control channels, builds bridges, relocates utilities, and then turns the project over to army engineers for construction at federal expense. Construction involves widening, deepening, and straightening the channels of the San Antonio River and four tributary creeks within metropolitan San Antonio. The city of San Antonio operates and maintains the completed structures.

The parks and recreation division of SARA completed, and now operates and maintains, Espada Park in south San Antonio, on the river. It also constructed two other parks in Bexar County. These recreational facilities were established using Neighborhood Youth Corps labor, a result of President Lyndon B. Johnson's qv War on Poverty program. Espada Park exhibits the Kennedy Memorial Tree, a honey locust given to SARA by Senator Ted Kennedy and transplanted from the late President John F. Kennedy's Hyannis Port home. Visitors can also view the old Espada dam, built in 1731 by Franciscan Friars for irrigation purposes, and conserved by SARA for its historical significance.

San Juan Park, situated on the San Antonio River upstream from Espada, features a mile-long lake created by SARA with an off-channel area for boat storage. This completed park will offer boating, fishing, and picnicking facilities.

Martinez Park, in eastern Bexar County, covers 117 acres, with barbecue pits throughout, and a large centralized pavilion with a stocked fishing pond, the only park in Bexar County with overnight camping facilities.

The administrative services department coordinates three divisions: legal, finance, and general services. In this capacity it is responsible for staff functions necessary to conduct the general business and administration of the authority as a governmental agency. The department also prepares the annual budget and manages personnel.

Con Mims

*San Antonio Road. *See* Old San Antonio Road.

*San Antonio-San Diego Mail Route.

*San Antonio de Senecú.

*San Antonio Southern Railway Company.

San Antonio Standard Metropolitan Statistical Area. The San Antonio Standard Metropolitan Statistical Area was originally composed of Bexar County, with 1,247 square miles, but expanded on October 18, 1963, with the addition of Guadalupe County, with 715 square miles, to bring the total area to 1,962 square miles. The 1960 population figure for the statistical area (Bexar County) was 687,151. The 1970 population for the entire metropolitan area was 864,014, including 830,460 in Bexar County and 33,554 in Guadalupe County. Historically related to San Antonio from the Spanish Colonial period, Guadalupe County towns such as Seguin, Kingsbury, and Marion have become economically linked to the Bexar metropolis since World War II. The relationship is demonstrated in the expansion and similarities of the area's businesses and industries, as well as in agricultural activities. Diversified agriculture is common to both counties, with truck crops, poultry, dairy and beef cattle, hogs, and miscellaneous crops being raised on the 1,864 farms of Bexar County and the 1,908 farms of Guadalupe County.

For Guadalupe County, oil has been a major source of income; by January 1, 1973, over 157 million barrels had been produced since its discovery in 1922. The total Guadalupe mineral value for 1967 was $10,043,211, while in Bexar County it amounted to $26,753,560. Seguin, the county seat and major city in Guadalupe County, had a 1960 population of 14,299; the 1970 population was 15,934. In 1964 the town reported twenty-eight industrial firms manufacturing or processing such items as structural steel, fibre glass cloth, brick, and cotton uniforms. Seguin had 340 businesses in 1969. The Guadalupe Valley Hospital and Texas Lutheran College,qv a four-year institution, are located there. The people of Seguin and Guadalupe County have recreational access to the Max Starcke Park on the Guadalupe River and Lake McQueeney.

The city of San Antonio is a historical, cultural, and international center in the south-central area of Texas. The Spanish Governors' Palace, the restored Spanish village of La Villita, and the San Fernando de Bexar Cathedral qqv are major attractions for tourists. Five missions are located in the city; besides the Alamo and the San José y San Miguel de Aguayo Mission,qqv which has been recently restored, there are the Nuestra Señora de la Purísima Concepción de Acuña Mission, the San Francisco de la Espada Mission, and the San Juan Capistrano Mission.qqv Along the landscaped San Antonio River, which weaves through the downtown section, are an outdoor theater, areas for art shows, and buildings and shops of historic and tourist interest. The walk along the river, called El Paseo del Rio, has been expanded and enlarged. In the summer the river is the scene for the Fiesta Noche del Rio and the King's River Parade. The Fiesta San Antonio,qv the Shrine Circus, and the San Antonio Livestock Exposition and Rodeo are popular attractions. For recreation San Antonio provides 3,275 acres of park land, including the large Brackenridge Park, which has such facilities as the Witte Memorial Museum,qv an aquarium, a Chinese sunken garden, an outdoor theater, and the third largest zoo in the nation.

Elsewhere in the city are art galleries, theaters, auditoriums, and the Joe Freeman Coliseum. The Marion Koogler McNay Art Institute qv houses an outstanding collection of art which is open free to the public; the San Antonio Little Theatre, in operation for forty-six years, is a community theater offering a varied program of entertainment. The thirty-three-year-old San Antonio Symphony sponsors guest performers, an opera festival, and pop

concerts, in addition to its regular annual fifteen subscription concerts. Important to the cultural, architectural, and business interests of the area was the 1968 HemisFair qv in celebration of the city's 250th birthday. Located on a ninety-two-acre urban renewal area tract and featuring as its theme "The Confluence of Civilization in the Americas," it attracted the participation of foreign nations as well as state and federal governments.

San Antonio has remained one of the educational centers of the Southwest with ten colleges and universities with a total enrollment of 25,000 students in 1971. St. Mary's University and Trinity University qqv have both projected Ph.D. programs as part of their expanding graduate work. The colleges include Incarnate Word College, Our Lady of the Lake College,qqv and two junior colleges combined under the San Antonio Junior College District, San Antonio College and St. Philip's College.qqv A new addition, first opened in 1973, is the University of Texas at San Antonio.qv The university will add to the existing components of the University of Texas System qv (mostly medical facilities) already in San Antonio. Also part of the educational community is the Oblate College of the Southwest,qv a fully-accredited college and seminary for the Oblate priesthood. A complement to the schools, the San Antonio Public Library serves the area with eight branch libraries, books by mail, and ready-reference information by telephone. The library offers over one million volumes, films, records, and government documents to the area residents.

Medical facilities for the metropolitan area include at least four public and eighteen private hospitals. In 1966 construction of the South Texas Medical Center was begun, including Villa Rosa Psychiatric and Rehabilitation Hospital, a Veterans Administration Hospital, and the University of Texas Medical School at San Antonio. The Bexar County Hospital, Southwest Texas Methodist Hospital, and Cerebral Palsy Treatment Center were also located at the center. Additions were planned to expand into almost all areas of medical treatment. Of particular note is the Institute for Surgical Research, a part of Brooke Army Medical Center. It is nationally known for its work in the treatment of severe burns. San Antonio is also the site for the San Antonio State Chest Hospital,qv which treats all kinds of respiratory diseases, and the San Antonio State Hospital.qv

Medical as well as other types of research are conducted at several major research laboratories. The Southwest Research Center (including the Southwest Research Institute and the Southwest Foundation for Research and Education qqv), the Southwest Agricultural Institute, and the Aerospace Medical Division are centers for extensive specialized research projects both publicly and privately funded. These are in addition to the research facilities of the Brooke Army Medical Center.

The numerous military installations in the city provide economic, industrial, and medical advantages for the area and continue San Antonio's historic military tradition. The military employed over 85,000 military and civilian personnel in San Antonio in 1971. Kelly Air Force Base qv is the largest military installation, and Brooks Air Force Base, Lackland Air Force Base, Randolph Air Force Base, and Fort Sam Houston qqv account for the other major installations. Stationed at these bases are various schools, centers, and specialized divisions in addition to the well-known medical facilities. Located at Kelly AFB is a major industrial center for repair of aircraft engines and the USAF Security Service dealing with communications security. The air force's only basic training center for recruits is at Lackland, and the headquarters for the Air Training Command is at Randolph.

In 1960 San Antonio's population was 587,718, and by 1970 it had increased to 654,153, according to the United States census. San Antonio reported 9,262 businesses in 1970. See also Bexar County; Guadalupe County. [Comal County was added to the San Antonio Standard Metropolitan Statistical Area in April, 1973. Ed.]

San Antonio State Adult Mental Health Clinic. The San Antonio State Adult Mental Health Clinic, adjacent to the San Antonio State Hospital,qv began operation in 1958. It was an out-patient treatment center for adults in need of psychiatric services. The clinic attempted to stem the advance of serious mental illness by early diagnosis and treatment and provided after-care for furloughed and discharged hospital patients. By 1970 the clinic had been absorbed by the San Antonio State Hospital. See also Mentally Ill and Mentally Retarded, Care of, in Texas.

BIBLIOGRAPHY: Board for Texas State Hospitals and Special Schools, Report (1964); Texas Department of Mental Health and Mental Retardation, Annual Report, 1970.

San Antonio State Chest Hospital. The San Antonio State Chest Hospital was opened in 1953 as the San Antonio State Tuberculosis Hospital, operating under the Board for Texas State Hospitals and Special Schools.qv The hospital was established as a replacement for the Weaver H. Baker Memorial Sanatorium,qv which was reclaimed in 1952 for air base purposes by the federal government. The hospital was designed as a TB facility and also accommodated mentally ill and mentally retarded patients with active tuberculosis. In 1964 it was the largest tuberculosis hospital in Texas. In 1965 it began operating under the State Department of Public Health.qv The hospital had facilities for one thousand patients in 1967. The surgical unit of the hospital was also utilized for patients from San Antonio State Hospital.qv Patients of all ages were admitted from thirty-six counties. In 1971 the 62nd Texas Legislature changed the name of the hospital to the San Antonio State Chest Hospital. The change reflected the expansion and reorganization from a TB hospital to a facility treating not only TB but a wide range of respiratory diseases and disorders.

Beginning in 1970 there was a gradual falling of the in-patient census and an increase in the out-patient department. Less serious respiratory cases were placed on an out-patient basis, and more serious cases, often with complicated secondary conditions were hospitalized. A new administration building was opened, and a remodeling of older facilities resulted in more flexible and smoother operations. In-service training programs were expanded, and libraries were added for the patients and for medical staff research. In 1971 physical and inhalation therapy departments experienced increased activity, and a new program of research into chronic obstructive lung disease was started.

The San Antonio State Chest Hospital remained the largest state tuberculosis hospital in Texas in 1971 and was the only state TB hospital in Texas to treat mentally ill and mentally retarded patients in addition to other patients. In 1970 visits to the out-patient clinic numbered 9,107, and in 1971 visits totaled 8,895. Average daily census for the hospital in 1970 was 515 and in 1971 was 387. The superintendent was Robert M. Inglis.

BIBLIOGRAPHY: Board for Texas State Hospitals and Special Schools, Report (1964); San Antonio State Chest Hospital, Annual Report (1970–1971).

*San Antonio State Hospital. Some of the elderly mental patients at the San Antonio State Hospital were maintained in private nursing homes on a furlough basis. Daily census of hospital patients in 1967 averaged 2,700.

In 1970 San Antonio State Hospital was accredited by the Joint Commission on Accreditation of Hospitals. The hospital also qualified for Medicare and Medicaid benefits from the United States Department of Health, Education, and Welfare by adding to the nursing staff. The hospital operated four outreach clinics in 1970 in Eagle Pass, Sinton, Beeville, and Bay City. Construction was begun for another in Del Rio. In that same year a new unit and an expanded program were developed to adapt to the admissions to the hospital. Twelve percent of admissions were narcotic addicts, and a separate unit was established to treat these specialized cases. Thirty-two percent of admissions were alcoholic patients. An expansion of the alcoholic treatment program served to meet this increasing demand on facilities. The average daily census in 1970 was 1,836, and the superintendent was Joseph G. Cocke. See also Mentally Ill and Mentally Retarded, Care of, in Texas.

BIBLIOGRAPHY: Board for Texas State Hospitals and Special Schools, Report (1964); Texas Department of Mental Health and Mental Retardation, Annual Report, 1970.

San Antonio State Tuberculosis Hospital. See San Antonio State Chest Hospital.

*San Antonio Surprise.

*San Antonio de los Tiguas. See Corpus Christi de la Isleta.

*San Antonio University. See University of San Antonio.

*San Antonio, Uvalde, and Gulf Railroad Company.

*San Antonio de Valero Mission. An archeological excavation on the grounds of the mission was carried out by the State Building Commission and the Witte Memorial Museum qqv in the summer of 1966. Foundations of adobe walls and other architectural features were uncovered, and many thousands of artifacts from the Spanish colonial and later Anglo American occupations of the site were found. Objects recovered included gun flints, gun parts, musket balls, cannon balls, knives, buttons, buckles, military insignia, coins, beads, broken bottles, food remains, nails, and shards of Spanish, Mexican, Indian, and Anglo American pottery.

Curtis Tunnell

*San Antonio *Zeitung*.

*San Augustine, Texas. San Augustine, seat of San Augustine County, is a lumbering center for the area. The city, known as "the oldest Anglo American town in Texas," instituted a tour of historical homes and places in the town in 1959. Among the town's approximately eighty businesses in 1970 were feed mills, poultry plants, and a boat manufacturer. The 1960 population was 2,584; the 1970 population was 2,539, according to the United States census.

*San Augustine County. San Augustine County, 80 percent forested, continued in the 1960's and 1970's to derive a large income from timber sales. Almost all of its $7 million average annual farm income was from cattle and poultry; vegetables were the chief crops. There was a small amount of oil production. Tourism increased with the construction of the McGee Bend Reservoir, renamed Sam Rayburn Reservoir in 1963 in honor of Samuel Taliaferro Rayburn.qv Historic homes and sites can be found throughout San Augustine County. Angelina National Forest is located in the southern part of the county and the Sabine National Forest (*see* National Forests in Texas) in the eastern part. The 1960 population was 7,722; the 1970 population was 7,858, according to the United States census.

*San Augustine University. *See* University of San Augustine.

*San Benito, Texas. San Benito, in central Cameron County, is a commercial center for an agricultural area and serves an expanding industrial region. During the mid-1960's, clothing manufacturing, vegetable packing, and other industries resulted in 200 additional jobs for area residents. A new expressway was built through San Benito, promoting the growing tourist industry. The semitropical climate attracts not only tourism but also retired people who make the San Benito area their home. The city reported 172 businesses in 1970. The 1960 population was 16,422; the 1970 population was 15,176, according to the United States census. *See also* Brownsville-Harlingen-San Benito Standard Metropolitan Statistical Area.

*San Benito and Rio Grande Valley Railway Company.

San Bernard. The schooner *San Bernard* carried four (not seven, as stated in Volume II) twelve-pound medium guns and one twelve-pound (not eighteen-pound) long pivot gun. She was first named *Scorpion* (not *Scorpion of Baltimore*), and she was sold for $150 on November 30, 1846 (not 1847).

BIBLIOGRAPHY: Tom Henderson Wells, *Commodore Moore and the Texas Navy* (1960).

Tom Henderson Wells

*San Bernard (Bernardo), Port of.

San Bernard National Wildlife Refuge. *See* Wildlife Areas in Texas.

*San Bernard River.

*San Bernardo Bay.

San Bernardo Mission. *See* San Juan Bautista.

*San Bernardo Village.

*San Caja Hill.

*San Carlos, Texas.

*San Clemente Mission.

*San Cristóbal.

*San Cristobal Creek.

*San Diego, Texas. San Diego, seat of Duval County, extends partly into neighboring Jim Wells County; it is a commercial center for the products of farms, ranches, and oil fields of the area. Near the city are gravel deposits and a quarry. San Diego had a new high school in 1966 and reported thirty-two businesses in 1970. The 1960 population of 4,351 increased to 4,490 by 1970, according to the United States census.

*San Diego Creek.

*San Diego and Gulf Railway.

*San Elizario, Texas (San Elceario).

*San Elizario Presidio (San Elzario).

*San Esteban Lake. The San Esteban Lake project was started by St. Stephens Land and Irrigation Company, but ownership has changed several times. The Pearl M. Robinson estate was listed as the owner in 1963. Previous owners were Reese Turpin and the estates of C. A. Duncan and James H. Kirk. Construction of the dam was begun in 1910 and completed in 1911. The reservoir had an original capacity of 18,770 acre-feet and a surface area of 762 acres at elevation 4,451 feet above mean sea level. San Esteban Lake was built to store water for irrigation, but because of small runoff into the lake, little irrigation has been practiced. [San Esteban Lake is often misspelled San Estaban Lake, even on some official documents and maps; however, the Water Development Board agrees the original Spanish spelling should be used. Ed.]

BIBLIOGRAPHY: Texas Water Commission, *Bulletin 6408* (1964).

Seth D. Breeding

*San Felipe.

*San Felipe de Austin, Texas.

*San Felipe Creek.

San Fernando Academy. *See* Pontotoc, Texas.

San Fernando Archives. The San Fernando Archives consist of the records of the early parish church of the settlement of San Fernando de Bexar,qv records of the six San Antonio missions, the *Libros de Gobierno,* and the *Compañía Volante de San Carlos de Parras del Alamo.* The material dates from approximately 1703 to 1858 and is the property of San Fernando de Bexar Cathedral.qv The collection was calendared and microfilmed during the late 1960's. Copies are found at the cathedral and in the Bexar County Archives.

When the San Antonio missions were ordered secularized in 1793, the records of the individual missions were given to the church of the civil settlement of San Fernando de Bexar. The records were not inventoried although repeated requests were made to the parish priest to do so. Many of the original documents were lost or destroyed during the years after 1793. Floods of 1815 and 1921, plus the church fire of 1828, destroyed many papers and stained much of what remained. Also, there are gaps in the records of the parish church due to the politics of priests during the Mexican War for Independence and the Texas Revolution. Approximately 4,000 pages of manuscript survived to the early 1800's. The records of the San Antonio missions have considerable information on the identification and tracing of Indian tribes and contain material on mission personnel and historical events. Herbert E. Bolton qv described this part of the collection in detail in *The Quarterly of the Texas State Historical Association,*qv X (1906–1907). The parochial and military records not described by Bolton have many genealogical sources, records of marriages, births, and deaths, and biographical information on some Texas personalities. They also provide significant insight to the cultural and social aspects of the community. The *Libros de Gobierno* have been considered the most important section of the San Fernando Archives, and they are the only records of their kind remaining in Texas. Within the section are documents such as the manuscript copy written by Miguel Hidalgo y Costilla qv from his prison cell in Chihuahua on May 18, 1811, a short while before his execution, wherein he states his repentance for having led the insurrection against New Spain.

BIBLIOGRAPHY: Richard Santos, "A Preliminary Survey of the San Fernando Archives," *Texas Libraries,* 28 (Winter, 1966–1967).

*San Fernando de Bexar.

San Fernando de Bexar Cathedral. A parish church at San Fernando de Bexar qv was founded by the Canary Islanders qv on July 2, 1731. Construction of the church began May 13, 1734, and was completed November 6, 1749. When the neighboring missions were secularized in 1793, their records and books were given to the parish church. These later formed a large part of the San Fernando Archives.qv A later Gothic building designed by François Giraud was built over the old church in 1868, and the transcept of the old eighteenth century church became the sacristy of the new church. In 1874 the church was declared a cathedral.

It was a center of activity during the colonial period in Texas history. Leading Texans were baptised, married, or buried at the church of San Fernando de Bexar. In 1836 Juan N. Seguin qv attempted to recover the remains of some Alamo defenders reportedly buried in the San Fernando church.

BIBLIOGRAPHY: Richard Santos, "Preliminary Survey of the San Fernando Archives," *Texas Libraries,* 28 (Winter, 1966–1967).

*San Fernando Creek.

*San Fernando de Mexico, College of.

*San Flat, Texas.

*San Francisco, Texas.

*San Francisco Creek.

*San Francisco de la Espada Mission.

*San Francisco de los Julimes Mission.

*San Francisco de los Neches Mission.

*San Francisco Ranchería.

San Francisco Solano Mission. San Francisco Solano Misson was founded on March 1, 1700, at La Ciénega de Rio Grande by Father Antonio de San Buenaventura Olivares, Father Francisco Hidalgo, and Captain Diego Ramón.qqv Nearby was the mission of San Juan Bautista,qv which had been reestablished two months earlier. The site was soon to become the Presidio de San Bautista del Rio Grande near the Paso de Francia crossing (*see* San Antonio Crossing) of the Camino Real (*see* Old San Antonio Road).

Because of the scarcity of water, the Indians eventually deserted the first location of the Solano mission. The missionaries followed them to a place fifteen leagues west of the Rio Grande and in 1703 relocated the mission there under the name of San Ildefonso. In 1708, due to the hostility of the Gavilane Indians, Solano was moved back to the Rio Grande to a site three leagues above San Juan Bautista. This third mission location was named Señor San José, and a village by that name, San José,qv exists there to the present.

In 1709 padres Olivares, Isidro Felix de Espinosa,qv and the commandant of the Presidio de San Juan Bautista, Pedro de Aguirre, with fourteen soldiers, made an entrada to the San Antonio River and promised to send missionaries to the Indians there. Seven years later Olivares, as missionary at the college Santa Cruz de Querétaro,qv was sent by college guardian, Fray Joseph Diez, to the viceroy in Mexico with the report of the entrada of Domingo Ramón (José Domingo).qv Ramón urged that Spanish forces supporting the reestablished missions in East Texas be strengthened; he maintained further that lines of communication were too long and a base nearer than Saltillo was needed for effective support. Olivares laid before the viceroy his own plan whereby the San Francisco Solano Mission should be moved to the San Antonio River along with its few remaining Jarame Indians. These he would use to teach the Payaya, Sana, and Pampoa Indians on the San Antonio River. The viceroy, the Marqués de Valero, in concert with his legal department reacted favorably to Ramón's letter and the suggestions of Olivares. A military escort of ten soldiers was to be assigned Olivares in moving Solano from the Rio Grande to the San Antonio River. Olivares was to make the journey in company with the expedition being formed by Martín de Alarcón.qv

On May 3, 1717, Olivares arrived at the missions on the Rio Grande where he sought, unsuccessfully, the soldiers he had been promised. Both the commandant at San Juan Bautista and the governor of Coahuila told Olivares that soldiers could not be spared for his assignment. He then retired to San José to await the arrival of Alarcón and to begin making preparations for moving the Solano mission. During the months that followed, Olivares was visited by more than 150 Indians, mostly chiefs from the San Antonio River, and he told them of his plans for moving to their homeland. Alarcón arrived in Coahuila on August 3, and, following several delays, began his entrada on April 9, 1718. Nine days later Fray Olivares, with his party, left San José and arrived at the San Antonio River on May 1.

With the two parts of the expedition united on that date, the San Antonio de Valero Mission qv was founded. It was called San Antonio in honor of Saint Anthony, and de Valero to honor the viceroy by whose decree the transfer was authorized. The first baptism at the new location was of a Jarame Indian boy. The entry in the baptismal record shows that San Antonio de Valero was not a new mission, but an old one transferred to a new site. Father Miguel Nuñez, who performed this first baptism, wrote: "In this Mission of San Francisco Solano situated in San Antonio de Valero, I baptized . . ." Olivares remained in charge of the mission until September 8, 1720. At that time he surrendered it to another of its original cofounders, Fray Francisco Hidalgo.

BIBLIOGRAPHY: H. H. Bancroft, History of the North Mexican States and Texas (1884); C. E. Castañeda, Our Catholic Heritage in Texas, 1519–1936, I, II (1936); Francisco Céliz (Fritz Leo Hoffmann, trans.), Diary of the Alarcón Expedition into Texas, 1718–1719 (1935); Isidro Félix de Espinosa, Crónica Apostolica . . . de esta Nueva-España . . . (1746); Edward W. Heusinger, Early Explorations and Mission Establishments in Texas (1936); V. Alessio Robles, Coahuila y Texas en la Epoca Colonial (1938); Jorge Cervera Sanchez (ed.), Descripción del Territorio del Real Presidio de San Juan Bautista, por Fray Morfi (1950).

Ben E. Pingenot

*San Francisco de los Tejas Mission.

*San Francisco de Valero.

*San Francisco Xavier de Horcasitas Mission.

*San Francisco Xavier de Nájera (Náxera) Mission. [This title was listed in Volume II as San Francisco Xavier de Naxara (Najara) Mission, but is more often found as shown here.]

*San Francisco Xavier Presidio.

*San Francisco Xavier de los Tejas Mission. See San Francisco Xavier de Horcasitas Mission.

*San Gabriel, Texas.

*San Gabriel River.

*San Gabriels, Battle on the. The battle on the San Gabriels occurred on May 15–17, 1839 (not May 17, 1838, as stated in Volume II). See also Flores, Manuel.

*San Geronimo Creek.

*San Ildefonso Creek.

*San Ildefonso Mission.

*San Isidro, Texas.

*San Jacinto. The schooner San Jacinto carried four (not seven, as stated in Volume II) twelve-pound medium guns and one nine-pound (not eighteen-pound) long brass pivot gun. The San Jacinto was first named Viper (not Viper of Baltimore), and she was lost October 31, 1840, when she dragged anchor, was grounded, and later wrecked on the shore.

BIBLIOGRAPHY: Tom Henderson Wells, Commodore Moore and the Texas Navy (1960).

Tom Henderson Wells

*San Jacinto, Texas.

*San Jacinto, Battle of.

San Jacinto Battleground Commission. The San Jacinto Battleground Commission, originally created in 1907, was composed of three members appointed by the governor. Operating under the Board of Control,qv the commission had the responsibility for the care and preservation of the San Jacinto State Park.qv The commission was abolished in 1965, and its duties were transferred to the Parks and Wildlife Department.qv

BIBLIOGRAPHY: University of Texas at Austin, Guide To Texas State Agencies (1966).

*San Jacinto Bay.

San Jacinto College. San Jacinto College, in Pasadena, Harris County, derived its name from the historical monument within sight of the campus. The junior college district encompassed five school districts on the Houston Ship Channel qv—Pasadena, Deer Park, Galena Park, La Porte, and Channelview. Classes began in 1961 in three adjoining store buildings in downtown Pasadena. An initial enrollment of 876 students increased to 3,656 students by 1965, making San Jacinto the second largest public junior college in the state.

A permanent, 143-acre campus opened in 1962 with completion of a science building; the following year a science lecture building was added. During 1964 an administration building, a gymnasium, and a music building were completed. That same year a $3,500,000 bond issue passed for construction of a library, additional classrooms, a student center, a women's gymnasium, a technical building, and art and drama additions to the fine arts building. The library housed 41,000 volumes in 1969.

In 1969 student enrollment was 6,740 and the faculty numbered 198 members. In the 1960's the college offered the first two years of four-year college curricula in both day and evening programs, and it also provided preparation for technicians in business and industrial occupations. Such programs, usually two years in length and leading to an associate degree, included data processing, engineering drafting, electronics, and police administration. The college also offered an associate degree in nursing. Thomas M. Spencer served as president of the college in 1974, when there was a fall enrollment of 8,500 students. In 1974 San Jacinto College, in addition to its South Campus in Pasadena, had a North Campus in Houston.

*San Jacinto County. San Jacinto County, 80 percent forested in 1972, had as its leading industry the production of lumber and pulpwood. Oil production also contributed to the economy. From 1940, when oil was first discovered in San Jacinto County, to January 1, 1973, nearly 19 million barrels of oil were produced. Less than $2 million of the average annual farm income was from cattle, poultry, and crops. Sam Houston National Forest (see National Forests in Texas), a major recreational facility, encompasses over 58,000 acres of San Jacinto County. The 1960 population was 6,153; the 1970 population was 6,702, according to the United States census.

*San Jacinto Heights.

San Jacinto Historical Advisory Board. The San Jacinto Historical Advisory Board, created in 1965, was composed of the chairman of the Battleship Texas qv Commission and the president of the San Jacinto Museum of History Association, as ex officio members, and three members appointed by the governor. The function of the board was to advise the Parks and Wildlife Commission (see Parks and Wildlife Department) on the proper historical development of the site and to accept all gifts and grants made for the battleground.

BIBLIOGRAPHY: University of Texas at Austin, Guide To Texas State Agencies (1970).

*San Jacinto Monument and Museum. Since September, 1966, the monument and museum have been operated by the San Jacinto Museum of History Association under contract with the Texas State Parks and Wildlife Commission (see Parks and Wildlife Department); prior to that time, and since its organization in 1938, the association's contract was with the state Board of Control.qv

*San Jacinto Mountain.

*San Jacinto Ordnance Depot. The San Jacinto Ordnance Depot continued to ship army and navy supplies between 1945 and 1950, but plans had been made for phasing out activities as soon as the decreasing need for war materials would allow. With the involvement of the United States in the Korean conflict, the need for the depot and its services again arose, and phasing out was postponed.

In 1959 the depot was declared surplus. The United States Army Corps of Engineers assumed care and custody responsibilities until disposal of the facilities could be accomplished. In October, 1964, all facilities of the San Jacinto Ordnance Depot were sold to the Houston Channel Industrial Corporation for over ten million dollars.

Carter Barcus

*San Jacinto River.

San Jacinto River Authority. The San Jacinto River Authority was created by special acts of the legislature in 1937 as the San Jacinto River Conservation and Reclamation District. Like many such agencies, it was charged with numerous duties and given a broad scope of operational latitude, although it received no appropriation of money at that time. The district was granted the power to levy taxes but has never exercised this power. The boundaries of the district embrace all of the watershed of the San Jacinto River with the exception of that part within Harris County. It can operate both within and without the boundaries. The name of the district was changed to San Jacinto River Authority in 1951 by the legislature.

The authority was actually in the "paper stage" until 1945, when the Federal Works Administration put the water system it had constructed up for sale as a war emergency measure to supply surface water to the industries located along the Houston Ship Channel.qv The original system consisted of dual canals, one being the West Canal and the Sheldon Reservoir and the other the East Canal and the Highlands Reservoir. One pump station, located on the San Jacinto River approximately one and one-half miles upstream from the present Lake Houston dam, pumped water for both canals. This station was constructed to withstand any known rises of the past.

Following a long series of negotiations, a purchase agreement with the FWA was finally completed on April 25, 1945, and the authority purchased that part of the canal and reservoir system east of the San Jacinto River. The city of Houston purchased the west half of the system. The pumping plant remained the property of the FWA and was operated by the city of Houston with operation expense shared by the authority and the city. The authority paid a total purchase price of $862,572 for the east system, which included 16 miles of canal and the 1,424-acre reservoir. Funds for the purchase of the system were provided by a bond issue and from funds on hand through collection of state tax remission revenues.

The city of Houston continued to operate the west system after the construction of Lake Houston. Later, the Sheldon Reservoir was sold by the city to the state Fish and Game Department (now a part of the Parks and Wildlife Department qv) which operates it as a game preserve and fish hatchery and offers seasonal public fishing in certain sections of the reservoir.

The original pumping arrangement continued until the summer of 1947, when a period of extremely low rainfall caused the pumping capacity of the single station to be inadequate for both systems. In order to ensure that the authority's industrial customers were served without interruption, two auxiliary pumping units were placed in operation on the east bank of the San Jacinto River near the beginning of the open section of the east canal. The drouth continued, and in 1948 two additional auxiliary units were added. These four units were used intermittently in conjunction with the main pumping plant until the filling of Lake Houston in 1954.

The authority constructed a modern electrical pump station, located at the east end of the dam of Lake Houston, which pumps water from the upstream side of the dam. The authority pays the city of Houston a monthly amount for increasing its normal flow of water plus a power saving rate based upon the increased elevation of water in the lake. The station is equipped with three electrically powered pumps, each capable of pumping twenty-five million gallons of water daily. The station was designed and constructed to accommodate an ultimate capacity of 300 million gallons daily.

The canal system of the authority runs easterly from Lake Houston, skirts Crosby to the east, and continues in a southerly direction, paralleling the Crosby-Lynchburg road until it enters the Highlands Reservoir. Below the reservoir the canal continues south until it reaches Humble's Baytown refinery. Humble has been the authority's major water customer since the system was purchased. This canal also supplies surface water to United Carbon Company and Marbon Chemical Company. The Gulf Oil Corporation qv also became one of the authority's industrial customers.

The Highlands Reservoir, since the construction of Lake Houston, has been only partially utilized for water storage. In times of excessive rainfall, large quantities of local run-off water are impounded in the reservoir, thus adding to the conservation of available surface water. At no time does the reservoir contain less than a thirty-day supply for the industrial customers. Systematic samplings of the fish population are made periodically with the results showing a good cross-section of game fish in the reservoir. There is also an abundance of trash fish which provide excellent food for the game fish.

Since 1946 the authority has provided equipment for soil conservation practices. Rates for rental of equipment such as graders and bulldozers are set so that the operation is self-supporting but accrues no profit. The San Jacinto River Authority is governed by a board of six directors who serve without salary. The directors are selected in such a manner as to represent all areas of the watershed. In 1969 W. B. Weisinger of Conroe was chairman.

*San Jacinto State Park. *See also* San Jacinto Battleground State Historic Park, under Parks, State.

San José, Mexico. San José, a tiny primitive village on the left bank of the Rio Grande eight miles north of Guerrero, Coahuila, Mexico, was founded in 1708, when the San Francisco Solano Mission qv was moved to the site from San Ildefonso. Father Francisco Hidalgo,qv president of the Rio Grande missions, superintended the erection of a stone and earthen chapel of suitable capacity with everything essential for establishing a pueblo. The Indians to which the mission ministered were the Payayas, Payoguanes, and principally Jarames (Xarames). Within a decade most of the mission's Indians had moved northward into Texas. By 1718 not one Indian neophyte remained at San José, and Father Antonio de San Buenaventura Olivares,qv the mission's original founder, moved the Solano mission to the San Antonio River, where it became the San Antonio de Valero Mission.qv

For the next 199 years San José continued without incident as a small insignificant ranchería. In 1917, however, it became the center of an international incident when a band of thieves, spawned during the turbulence of the revolution in Mexico, raided the Indio Ranch twenty-two miles below Eagle Pass and drove off 160 head of goats. This was the culmination of a number of raids against the Indio which had been going on for over a year. The next morning, December 30, 1917, Major E. C. Wells from Fort Duncan,qv with three troops of cavalry and a few Texas Rangers,qv followed the goat trail to the river. Crossing over, the trail led another mile to the village of San José, where several freshly slaughtered goats were seen hanging in trees; there was also a hobbled cow with the Indio brand. As the 150 Americans approached the village they were fired upon by Mexicans concealed in the brush. The troopers dismounted and began firing by platoons in "V" formation. The Mexicans retreated to one of the houses farther into the village where they continued shooting. The soldiers, using a machine gun, fired at the walls of the houses, whereupon the battle ended. Major Wells reported that twelve were known to have been killed, though there were seventeen burials at Piedras Negras and three at San José immediately after the fight. The Americans suffered no casualties. Mexican authorities were enraged by the incident, but as a result the governor of Coahuila organized a Ranger company, similar to the Díaz *Rurales*, which cleaned up the border area.

Today San José is inhabited by fewer than one hundred people and is still primitive. Motor vehicles are rarely seen in the village, and most of the inhabitants commute by horse- or mule-drawn wagons over the trails that lead to Guerrero and Piedras Negras. A beautiful spring serves the water needs of the village, and along its course to the river are a number of ancient stone ruins. As yet the exact site of the mission has not been found, but it was probably situated on a low hill which overlooks the village and the river.

BIBLIOGRAPHY: Francisco Céliz (Fritz Leo Hoffmann, trans.), *Diary of the Alarcón Expedition into Texas, 1718–1719* (1935); Isidro Félix de Espinosa, *Crónica Apostolica . . . de esta Nueva-España . . .* (1746); V. Alessio Robles, *Coahuila y Texas en la Epoca Colonial* (1938); Walter Prescott Webb, *The Texas Rangers* (1935).

Ben E. Pingenot

*San José, Texas.

*San José de Ayamonte Pueblo.

*San José de los Nazonis Mission.

*San José y San Miguel de Aguayo Mission.

*San Juan, Texas. San Juan, in south-central Hidalgo County, has an agricultural and commercial economy. During the mid-1960's the town reported two hospitals, ten churches, three schools (including a new one-million-dollar high school), a library, a bank, a newspaper, and a new shopping center. In 1970 San Juan reported eighty businesses. A Shrine of Our Lady of San Juan of the Valley was completed in 1954 and has attracted many tourists. The population of San Juan was 4,371 in 1960; the 1970 population was 5,070, according to the United States census. *See also* McAllen-Edinburg-Pharr Standard Metropolitan Statistical Area.

San Juan Bautista. San Juan Bautista is the generic appellation for the Spanish presidio and mission complex on the Rio Grande where the Old San Antonio Road qv entered Texas. The mission of San Juan Bautista was first founded on the Río Sabinas ten leagues northwest of Lampazos, in northern Coahuila, on June 24, 1699. Its founders were the Querétaro Franciscans, Fray Diego Salazar de San Buenaventura, Fray Francisco Hidalgo, qv and the soldier Juan Martín Treviño. Salazar was named president of the mission but soon left Hidalgo in charge of it. Troubles with the Indians forced the abandonment of San Juan, but Hidalgo, joined by padres Antonio de San Buenaventura Olivares qv and Marcos Guereña, enabled Salazar to rebuild the mission at a site farther north near the Rio Grande. On January 1, 1700, it was reestablished in the Valle de la Circuncisión at La Ciénega de Rio Grande. The mission's new location was five miles northwest of the Paso de Francia crossing (*see* San Antonio Crossing) on the Rio Grande, which Alonso de León qv had used on earlier entradas into Texas. Nearby San Francisco Solano Mission qv was founded that same year. To protect the missions from hostile Indians, the viceroy ordered Captain Diego Ramón qv with a *compañía volante* of thirty men to establish a fort nearby. The Real Presidio de San Juan Bautista del Rio Grande was founded in late July or early August, 1701, a quarter league east of the mission and was augmented with troops from the Presidio de Coahuila (Monclova). In 1702 a third mission, San Bernardo, was established northeast of the San Juan Bautista mission. With the abandonment of the East Texas missions in 1693, this Rio Grande mission outpost became the most advanced point in the northeast of New Spain. Throughout the Spanish colonial epoch, all of the entradas into Texas, both military and religious, originated from there. In 1709 Fray Olivares, Fray Isidro Felix de Espinosa,qv and the commandant of the Presidio de San Juan Bautista, Pedro de Aguirre, left San Juan Bautista and made an entrada to the Colorado River. They stopped at the future site of San Antonio and there named the San Pedro springs. Seven years later the Ramón expedition, guided by the Frenchman Louis Juchereau de Saint Denis,qv embarked from San Juan Bautista and permanently reopened the Camino Real (*see* Old San Antonio Road) across Texas. The Aguayo Expedition qv in 1721, launched from San Juan Bautista, reestablished the East Texas missions and so strengthened Spain's claim to Texas as to preclude further disputes with France. Throughout the mission period, San Juan Bautista served as a supply base and headquarters for missionary activity. Such luminaries in the Texas mission field as padres Espinosa and Antonio Margil de Jesús,qv as well as those aforementioned, either served as missionaries or presided at this Rio Grande mission establishment.

In addition to its importance in missionary activity, San Juan Bautista was also a vital link between Texas and Mexico, as well as a base for exploration and frontier defense. In 1729 Captain José Berroterán explored the Rio Grande northward from San Juan Bautista to above the mouth of the Pecos. The Garza Falcón-Músquiz expedition left San Juan Bautista on December 28, 1735, and explored the Del Rio-Dryden area before establishing the Presidio del Sacramento on the San Diego River. In 1747 a detachment from San Juan Bautista crossed the Rio Grande and followed it southward in conjunction with José de Escandón's qv exploration of the lower Rio Grande. That same year the captain of San Juan Bautista, with fifteen men, joined Pedro de Rábago y Terán qv at Presidio del Sacramento on an expedition into the Big Bend area.

In 1703 Hidalgo reported that the presidio consisted of ten *casas de terrado*, a plaza of arms of suitable size and disposition, and three missions, San Juan Bautista, San Bernardo, and San Francisco Solano, which were flat-roofed structures of stone and adobe. By 1775 San Bernardo had become the richest mission in the province with more Indians, fertile pastures, and livestock than any other, and in 1777 the mission was described by Fray Agustín Morfi qv as "a beautiful temple." However, the missions had passed their zenith and their decline was evident. Morfi observed that San Juan Bautista was threatening to fall into ruin, and he considered it unlikely that the new San Bernardo buildings would ever be finished. Waning interest in the missions had forced the college of Santa Cruz de Querétaro qv to transfer them to the Franciscan college of Nuestra Señora de Guadalupe de Zacatecas qv and the province of Guadalajara in 1772. In that same year a new royal *reglamento* named San Juan Bautista one of fifteen presidial forts along the northern frontier of New Spain, a defense against the increasing menace of hostile Apache and Comanche Indians. Though the missions were not completely secularized until 1826–1829, their decline and ultimate abandonment had brought a change much earlier in the presidial title. By the end of the eighteenth century, the name Presidio de San Juan Bautista had given way to simply Presidio del Rio Grande; still later its name was frequently shortened to "Rio Grande."

Lieutenant Zebulon Montgomery Pike ^{qv} spent a day and a night at Presidio del Rio Grande on his return to the United States in 1807, and he made note of it in his journal. During the early efforts of Mexican revolt against Spain, the governor of Texas, Manuel María de Salcedo,^{qv} and the commandant at Béjar, Colonel Simón de Herrera,^{qv} were brought to the presidio, where they were imprisoned; it was to Presidio del Rio Grande that Padre Miguel Hidalgo y Costilla ^{qv} was marching his forces when captured at Bájan below Monclova. Throughout the period of Mexican independence and Anglo colonization of Texas, Presidio del Rio Grande continued as a thoroughfare between Texas and Mexico; however, after the founding of Laredo in 1755, the volume of traffic passing through Presidio del Rio Grande began to decline as the former took precedence. In 1836 Antonio López de Santa Anna ^{qv} assembled part of his army at Presidio del Rio Grande for his march into Texas, and six years later General Adrian Woll ^{qv} launched his raid against San Antonio from there. During the Mexican War, General John Wool invaded Mexico at this point and camped his Army of Chihuahua just west of the village, the last military *entrada* to pass through Presidio del Rio Grande.

From its founding San Juan Bautista had been the capital (*cabecera*) in the Rio Grande district. In 1828, under a decree of February 21, the *cabecera* was transferred to Gigedo and in 1831 it was moved again to Nava. On March 18, 1834, Presidio del Rio Grande again became a *cabecera* when the legislature named it one of seven departments within the state of Coahuila and Texas. Before this the old presidio had experienced still another name change; under decree No. 4 of August 7, 1827, the name "Rio Grande" was changed to Villa de Guerrero; this last name change required nearly fifty years before gaining wide acceptance. Until recent years the change in place names caused some historians to doubt the actual location of the old mission and presidio.

Down to 1761 there were 1,434 baptisms at San Juan Bautista; there were 1,606 burials. The population of San Juan Bautista was 800 in 1777, 943 in 1827, and reportedly 2,000 in 1847. Its present-day population is approximately 2,700. Located thirty miles below Eagle Pass, Guerrero has changed little in size or appearance over the years.

San Juan Bautista mission reposes as a mound of stones and earth just west of the village. One mile to the northeast stands San Bernardo, a magnificent ruin, regarded as the most important in the state of Coahuila. In between lies the village which was the old presidio. Many of the original buildings are still standing, with some in use and others in ruin. The neatly frescoed walls, heavy doors, and carved beams lend an air of antiquity to the place. A small clear stream from a nearby spring, the town's water supply, flows between the village and San Bernardo, a part of the Franciscan irrigation system that has stood the test of over 250 years. San Juan Bautista, from the start, has been historically bound to Texas and especially to San Antonio. Recognizing this fact, the San Antonio Conservation Society ^{qv} made a pilgrimage to Guerrero in March, 1936, as part of their Texas Centennial activities.

BIBLIOGRAPHY: H. H. Bancroft, *History of the North Mexican States and Texas* (1884); C. E. Castañeda, *Our Catholic Heritage in Texas, 1519–1936*, I–V (1936–1942); Francisco Céliz (Fritz Leo Hoffmann, trans.), *Diary of the Alarcón Expedition into Texas, 1718–1719* (1935); Isidro Félix de Espinosa, *Crónica Apostolica . . . de esta Nueva-España . . .* (1746); Edward W. Heusinger, *Early Exploration and Mission Establishments in Texas* (1936); Paul Horgan, *Great River: The Rio Grande in North American History*, I, II (1954); V. Alessio Robles, *Coahuila y Texas en la Epoca Colonial* (1938); *Coahuila y Texas desde la Consumación de la Independencia . . . .*, I, II (1945–1946); Jorge Cervera Sanchez (ed.), *Descripción del Territorio del Real Presidio de San Juan Bautista, por Fray Morfi* (1950); Robert S. Weddle, *San Juan Bautista* (1968); Sarah S. McKeller, "Old Presidio Site at Guerrero," Eagle Pass *News Guide* (Centennial Edition, 1949).

Ben E. Pingenot

*San Juan Capistrano Mission.

San Juan Plantation. The San Juan Plantation on the Rio Grande near San Juan, Hidalgo County, is recognized as a historic landmark by an official Texas historical marker on the plantation headquarters. The founder and developer of this, the earliest and largest plantation in an area at one time considered suitable only for grazing, was John Closner,^{qv} veteran law enforcement officer for twenty-eight years, popularly called "the father of Hidalgo County." He began buying land in 1884, and by 1904 the San Juan Plantation, so named by Mrs. Closner for the Spanish translation of "John," comprised 7,000 acres. The total eventually reached 45,000 acres. By 1895 Closner had installed a pumping plant and constructed a network of canals and laterals for the first irrigation system from the Rio Grande in the area. The equipment came by water to Port Isabel and was hauled by wagon the fifty-odd miles to the plantation. Closner was the first in that area to raise alfalfa, with 700 acres flourishing under several cuttings a year; the first to experiment with tobacco crops; the first to experiment with sugar cane by cross-planting hybrid cane seed from Mexico with seed from Louisiana; and the first to experiment with commercial crops of vegetables, fruits, melons, and nuts. His findings in such diversified farming set an area-wide example.

Sugar cane from the plantation won the gold medal at the 1904 Exposition in St. Louis for the finest sugar cane in the world. At that time the plantation included 800 acres of sugar cane which was processed into *piloncillo* (cones of coarse brown sugar) for the native trade on both sides of the Rio Grande. Production of sugar processed from a 250-ton mill began when boilers for the mill arrived after many transportation difficulties and at great expense.

By 1921 sugar cane was gone from the Valley, but cotton, citrus fruits, and vegetables became important products because of the rich soil, climate, and irrigation, assets which Closner had recognized in the mid-1880's. The first telephone line in that area, installed in 1902, connected Closner's home in Hidalgo to the headquarters of the plantation. Later he constructed a line to McAllen, and the Hidalgo Telephone Company was formed with Closner as president. As the plantation progressed, the number of families of workers increased. A substantial school building was erected and equipped at a cost of $1,500 for the children of the plantation.

BIBLIOGRAPHY: *Encyclopedia of American Biography* (1937); J. L. Allhands, *Gringo Builders* (1931); San Antonio *Express*, September 7, 1911; Harlingen *Valley Morning Star*, March 28, 1965.

Verna J. McKenna

*San Juanita Creek.

*San Leon, Texas.

*San Lorenzo, Texas.

*San Lorenzo Creek.

*San Lorenzo del Realito. *See* Corpus Christi de la Isleta.

*San Lorenzo de la Santa Cruz Mission. San Lorenzo de la Santa Cruz Mission was located on the east bank of the Nueces River at the present town of Camp Wood in Real County (not at Barksdale in Edwards County, as stated in Volume II). The Texas Memorial Museum qv conducted an archeological excavation of the site in the fall of 1963. Stone and adobe foundations of eighteen structures, arranged around an enclosed plaza, were uncovered. Thousands of Spanish colonial and Indian artifacts, such as brass religious ornaments, glass beads, parts of iron weapons and tools, food remains, buttons, broken wine bottles and dishes, gun flints, and stone tools, were recovered.

Curtis Tunnell

*San Luis Advocate.

*San Luis de las Amarillas de San Sabá Presidio. *See* San Sabá Presidio.

*San Luis Island.

*San Luis Pass.

*San Manuel, Texas.

*San Marcos, Texas. San Marcos, incorporated in 1877, is the seat of Hays County. In the 1960's, it relied mainly on tourism and educational interests for its income. Among its major attractions were Aquarena Springs and Wonder Cave.qqv The opening of Gary Job Corps Training Center (*see* Job Corps Program in Texas) in 1965 on the site of Gary Air Force Base qv and the growth of Southwest Texas State College (now Southwest Texas State University) also contributed to the local economy. A newer and larger municipal library opened in 1966, and plans for a park along the San Marcos River were underway that same year. Among the 260 businesses reported in San Marcos in 1970 were the manufacturers of plastics, feeds, wool, sheet metal products, lighting fixtures, furniture, meat products, tortillas, and other foods. During the 1950's the city recorded a 27 percent population increase, and during the 1960's a 48.4 percent increase. The 1950 population was 9,980; the 1960 population was 12,713; and the 1970 population was 18,860, according to the United States census.

*San Marcos Academy. *See also* Baptist Schools in Texas.

*San Marcos Air Force Base. *See also* Gary Air Force Base.

*San Marcos de Neve.

*San Marcos River.

*San Marcos State College. *See* Southwest Texas State University.

*San Martine Creek.

*San Miguel de los Adaes Mission. *See* San Miguel de Linares de los Adaes.

*San Miguel Creek.

*San Miguel de Linares de los Adaes.

*San Nicolas Lakes.

San Pantaleón. *See* Camp Melvin, Texas.

*San Patricio, Texas.

*San Patricio, Battle of.

*San Patricio County. By the early 1970's San Patricio County derived 75 percent of its average annual agricultural income of more than $22.5 million from cotton, grain sorghums, and other crops. The beef and dairy cattle industry provided significant income, as did the fishing and shrimp industries. Oil production was increasing; daily production in 1968 was 27,920 barrels. From 1930 to January 1, 1973, over 402 million barrels of oil had been produced. Along with reclamation drainage and brush control projects, an expansion of land was under irrigation. In 1968, 19,788 acres were irrigated. Light industries producing concrete and concrete products, aluminum ingots and products, and marine hardware supplemented the economy.

During the mid-1960's county projects included the improvement and expansion of the county's airport and highways. Tourist attractions were the Rob and Bessie Welder Wildlife Foundation and Refuge qv and Lake Corpus Christi State Recreation Park (*see* Parks, State). The county celebrates its Irish heritage at an annual barbecue at San Patricio de Hibernia Church near Odem, held in honor of the early settlers from Ireland.

According to the 1960 census, San Patricio County's population of 45,021 had the fifth youngest median age in the state at 20.3 years. The 1970 population was 47,288, according to the United States census. *See also* Corpus Christi Standard Metropolitan Statistical Area; Irish in Texas.

BIBLIOGRAPHY: *Early History of San Patricio County* (1934).

*San Patricio Creek.

*San Patricio Minute Men.

San Patricio Trail. The San Patricio Trail, first beaten out by the Irish in 1830 to connect San Patricio and San Antonio, was one of the main thoroughfares of South Texas until the 1880's. Beginning at the Santa Margarita Crossing ᑫᵛ of the Nueces River near San Patricio, the trail at various times followed either its wet weather route along the west bank, or its dry weather route along the east bank of the river as far northward as Oakville; thence, the trail followed a natural course across the prairie to the San Antonio River, which was followed to San Antonio.

Due to unsettled conditions which prevailed before, during, and after the Texas Revolution, the trail fell into disuse. Because of the war with Mexico, the route was reopened by General Zachary Taylor,ᑫᵛ whose army of advance was stationed on the Nueces. The trail was used extensively during the war for the movement of troops and supplies.

In 1846 a regular line of wagons began transporting goods from Corpus Christi through San Patricio to San Antonio. A stage line was established as early as 1850. As a means of protection for settlers, travelers, and traders along the trail, the United States government established Fort Merrill ᑫᵛ on the west bank of the Nueces, about thirty miles upstream from San Patricio.

As a result of the tight Federal blockade during the Civil War, the San Patricio Trail became one of the main contraband trade routes of the Confederacy. Large amounts of arms, ammunition, supplies, and cotton were transported over the trail to and from the neutral port of Matamoros, Mexico. After the war, the trail continued to be used as a stage and post road until 1881. At different times, stages of the J. J. Ellis Corpus Christi and Laredo Line and of the Rio Grande Stage Company operated daily between San Antonio and Corpus Christi, with connections at Oakville with the coaches of the Oakville and Brownsville Stage Company. Place names along the trail at various times were Graytown, Fairview, New Hope, Rock Spring, Tordilla Mound, Tordilla, Rountree's Ranch, Belle Branch, Oakville, Fox Nation, Gussettville, Fort Merrill, Casa Blanca, Lagarta, Penitas, Santa Margarita, and Echo.

The coming of the railroad to South Texas caused the demise of the old San Patricio Trail. The International and Great Northern Railroad, from San Antonio to Laredo, and the Texas-Mexican Railroad, from Corpus Christi to Laredo, were both completed in 1881. Abandonment of the trail was precipitated by the completion of the San Antonio and Aransas Pass Railroad from San Antonio to Corpus Christi in 1886.

BIBLIOGRAPHY: Hobart Huson, *Refugio: A Comprehensive History of Refugio County from Aboriginal Times to 1953* (1953); Walter Lord (ed.), *The Fremantle Diary* (1954); Robert H. Thonhoff, The History of Karnes County, Texas (M.A. thesis, Southwest Texas State College, 1963); Corpus Christi *Gazette*, January 8, 1846; San Antonio de Bexar *Western Texian*, November 17, 1848; San Antonio *Daily Express*, December 9, 1879, November 15, 1881; San Antonio *Herald*, May 3, 1879.

Robert H. Thonhoff

*San Pedro, Texas.

*San Pedro Creek.

*San Pedro Village.

*San Perlita, Texas.

*San Pierre, Joseph.

San Román, José. José San Román, the son of Joaquin María de San Román, was born in the valley of Arcentales near Bilbao, Spain, about 1822. He came to America in the mid-1800's, settling first in New Orleans, where he established business connections with the wholesale merchandise firm of Thorn. M. Grath Co. In 1846 he went to Matamoros, Mexico, and set up a general merchandise business, supported by Grath Co., on a corner of the main plaza. During the Mexican War, San Román sold supplies to the American Army operating in Mexico. His business quickly developed, and in November, 1848, he moved his store and home to Brownsville, Texas. San Román also invested in commercial transportation, becoming himself a wholesale supplier for small stores throughout the South Texas-Tamaulipas, Mexico, region. In 1854 he bought an interest in the steamboat *Swan*(n), operating between Galveston and the mouth of the Rio Grande River. In 1855 he and John Young challenged the river transportation monopoly of M. Kenedy & Co. (*see* Kenedy, Mifflin, and King, Richard). Thereafter, San Román maintained boats on the Rio Grande (including the *Alamo* and the *José San Román*). By 1860 he carried on a private banking and credit service, owned extensive real estate in Cameron County, and was acknowledged as one of the wealthiest men in South Texas.

During the Civil War San Román became a central figure in the contraband cotton trade carried on in Brownsville and Matamoros. He acted as seller for hundreds of small and large cotton farmers west of the Mississippi River, even representing the state of Louisiana; he sold cotton to textile manufacturers in Havana, New York, Liverpool, and Bordeaux. To protect his cotton business, he moved his operations back to Matamoros in 1862.

In 1866 San Román opened a large wholesale merchandise business in Brownsville, assisted by his cousin Simon Celaya. Later San Román made places in his business for other relatives from Spain. By 1870 Celaya frequently represented the San

Román interests. For example, Celaya was instrumental in securing in 1870 a new charter for the Rio Grande Railroad, superseding the 1866 charter held by the Mifflin Kenedy, Richard King interests (*see* Port Isabel and Rio Grande Valley Railway). The line from Brownsville to Port Isabel, Texas, was completed in 1873, spelling doom for the steamboat transport business on the Rio Grande.

San Román returned to Spain in 1879, leaving his business enterprises in the hands of Celaya and several nephews.

BIBLIOGRAPHY: José San Román Papers (MS., Archives, University of Texas at Austin Library); United States Manuscript Census Returns for 1860 (microfilm copy, University of Texas at Austin Library); Frank C. Pierce, *A Brief History of the Lower Rio Grande Valley of Texas* (1917); Ralph A. Wooster, "Foreigners in the Principal Towns of Ante-Bellum Texas," *Southwestern Historical Quarterly*, LXVI (1962–1963); Ralph A. Wooster, "Wealthy Texans, 1870," *ibid.*, LXXIV (1970–1971); Brownsville *Herald*, June 29, 1930, May 10, 1936.

Edgar P. Sneed
Grace Edman

*San Roque Creek.

*San Saba, Texas. San Saba, seat of San Saba County, is a shipping point for cattle, sheep, wool, mohair, and poultry products. Among its businesses during the 1960's was a plant that crushed rock used in making terrazzo tile. Improvements made were a new post office and a wing added to the hospital. School improvements included a new physical education building and plans for a new elementary building. A twenty-four-acre park was under development in the mid-1960's. Sometimes called the "pecan capital of the world," San Saba is the center for the pecan industry in the area, and it is also a popular spot for hunting and fishing. The town reported eighty businesses in 1970. The 1960 population was 2,728; the 1970 population was 2,555, according to the United States census.

*San Saba Colonization Company. *See* Fisher-Miller Land Grant.

*San Saba County. San Saba County, predominantly a ranching area, in the early 1970's derived about 80 percent of its average annual farm income of $10 million from livestock and poultry. Pecans and peanuts are the principal crops; the county produces several million pounds of pecans in most years. Turkey and chicken ranches have become increasingly important to the county's economy; eggs are shipped to several midwestern states. The 1960 population was 6,381; the 1970 population was 5,540, according to the United States census.

*San Saba Masonic College.

*San Saba Peak.

*San Sabá Presidio.

*San Saba River.

*San Sabá de la Santa Cruz Mission.

*San Solomon Springs.

*San Teodoro Village.

*San Vicente, Texas.

*San Xavier Missions.

*San Xavier de Nájera Mission. *See* San Francisco Xavier de Nájera (Náxera) Mission.

*San Xavier Presidio. *See* San Francisco Xavier Presidio.

*San Ygnacio, Texas.

*Sana Indians. Much confusion surrounds this name because several Indian groups in Texas had names that approximated Sana, and some writers have oversimplified the picture by equating most of these with Sana. The Cana and Sama Indians, who evidently spoke Coahuiltecan dialects, are not to be confused with the Sana, who lived farther east and did not speak Coahuiltecan. Furthermore, the Cana and Sama entered two of the San Antonio missions at their inception, whereas the Sana did not appear on the mission scene until some twenty-five years later. From 1691 until 1750 the Sana were consistently associated with an area east and northeast of San Antonio, especially between the Guadalupe and Brazos rivers. When encountered by Europeans the Sana were usually occupying settlements jointly with other groups, particularly Cantona, Cava, Emet, and Tohaha. The Sana began to enter San Antonio de Valero Mission ^qv at San Antonio in the 1740's and were mentioned as living there as late as 1793. Although the records are sometimes ambiguous, the main variants of the name Sana appear to have been Chana, Chane, Jana, Xanac, and Xana. Xanna is likewise a variant of Sana, but Xanna is also recorded in 1691 as the name of a group that seems to have lived farther east, certainly east of the Trinity River and possibly as far east as western Louisiana. The status of Xanna needs further study. The Canu also remain a problem, since they cannot be satisfactorily related to any other known group. Because it appears clear that Sana did not speak Coahuiltecan, Karankawan, or Caddoan, and because in the eighteenth century they were so frequently associated with Tonkawans, the language of the Sana has been tentatively identified as Tonkawan. This appears to be a reasonable conclusion, but it is also possible that the Sana spoke some other language, perhaps one that is still unknown.

BIBLIOGRAPHY: H. E. Bolton (ed.), *Spanish Exploration in the Southwest, 1542–1706* (1916); F. W. Hodge (ed.), *Handbook of American Indians*, II (1910); Francisco Céliz (Fritz Leo Hoffmann, trans.), *Diary of the Alarcón Expedition into Texas, 1718–1719* (1935); J. R. Swanton, *The Indian Tribes of North America* (1952).

T. N. Campbell

*Sanate Adiva.

*Sanatorium, Texas.

*Sanborn, Henry B.

*Sanborn, Texas.

*Sanches Creek.

Sánchez, George Isadore. George Isidore Sánchez, one of the earliest and most outspoken educators concerned with the status of the Latin American in Texas and the Southwest, was born in Albuquerque, New Mexico, on October 4, 1906, the son of Telesfor and Juliana (Sánchez) Sánchez. He received a B.A. degree from the University of New Mexico in 1930, an M.A. degree in education from the University of Texas (Austin) in 1931, and a Ed.D. degree at the University of California at Berkeley in 1934.

His wide interest in the education problems of Latin Americans of both hemispheres led to his research and survey work for the Julius Rosenwald Fund from 1935 to 1937 on rural education in Mexico and rural and Negro education in the South. He was appointed chief technical consultant and director of the National Teachers College for the Venezuelan Ministry of Education in 1937–1938. When he joined the teaching staff of the University of Texas in 1940, he had already published *Mexico—A Revolution by Education* (1936) and *Forgotten People—A Study of New Mexicans* (1940). In 1941 he made a study of Navajo Indian education for the United States Office of Indian Affairs, which culminated in his book, *The People—A Study of the Navajos* (1948). In 1951 he directed a survey concerning the "wetback" in the Lower Rio Grande Valley, a part of a study of the Spanish-speaking people of northern Mexico residing in Texas.

At the University of Texas, George Sánchez was chairman of the Department of History and Philosophy of Education, College of Education, from 1951 to 1959; in 1959 he returned to full-time teaching in the department (renamed the Cultural Foundation of Education in 1970). He was a member of the Civil Rights Commission created in 1957 to advise the president and Congress on segregation problems and solutions. In 1961 he was appointed by President John F. Kennedy to the national advisory council of the newly formed Peace Corps; he also served on the president's fifty-man committee for a New Frontier policy in the Americas. Always concerned with minority problems, he testified in San Antonio in 1968 at the first hearing of the Civil Rights Commission devoted exclusively to Mexican American problems. He was an indefatigable writer and speaker on the socio-economic status of the Mexican American in the Southwest.

He was married to Virginia Romero on June 15, 1925, and they had two children. After a divorce from his first wife in 1947 he was married to Luisa G. Guerrero on August 30, 1947. George I. Sánchez died in Austin on April 5, 1972. *See also* Mexican American Joint Council.

*Sánchez, Luis.

*Sánchez de la Barrera y Gallardo, Tomás.

*Sanchez, Texas.

*Sancito Creek.

*Sanco, Texas.

*Sand, Texas. (Bastrop County.)

*Sand, Texas. (Dawson County.)

*Sand Creek.

Sand Flat, Texas. (Smith County.) Sand Flat

was founded about 1855 at a crossing of two roads in a flat sandy area. In 1966 the community was located in the center of the new Sand Flat oil field in northern Smith County and had approximately two hundred inhabitants, most of whom farmed or commuted to Tyler or Swan.

*Sand Flat, Texas. (Van Zandt County.)

*Sand Grove, Texas.

*Sand Hill, Texas. (Burleson County.)

*Sand Hill, Texas. (Upshur County.)

*Sand Hills.

*Sand Lake, Texas.

*Sand Mountain.

*Sand Spring Creek.

*Sandefer, Jefferson Davis.

Sanders, Morgan Gurley. Morgan Gurley Sanders was born July 14, 1878, on a farm near Ben Wheeler, Texas, in Van Zandt County, the son of Levi Lindsey and Sarah Frances (Smith) Sanders. He attended public schools in Ben Wheeler and graduated from the Alamo Institute, a school in the same village. Sanders and Percy Clark of Canton organized the Ben Wheeler *Headlight*, a weekly newspaper which they edited and published. Sanders read law, attended the University of Texas, and was admitted to the Bar in 1901. He began practicing law in Canton, county seat of Van Zandt County, and won election to the Texas legislature in 1902; he served two terms in the House. In 1910 he was elected prosecuting attorney of Van Zandt County, and in 1915–1916 he was elected district attorney of the Seventh Judicial District of Texas. He resigned from that office and resumed the practice of law in Canton.

Sanders was a delegate to many Democratic state conventions and was elected as a Democrat to the Sixty-seventh United States Congress on March 4, 1921; he served in succeeding Congresses until January 3, 1938. He was an unsuccessful candidate for renomination and resumed the practice of law in Canton. He was married to Irene Cox, and they had one son. Sanders died in Corsicana on January 7, 1956, and was buried in Hillcrest Cemetery in Canton.

Jack Geddie

*Sanders Creek.

*Sanders Hollow Creek.

*Sanderson, Texas. Sanderson, seat of Terrell County, is the principal trade center of the county and is in an area of large sheep, goat, and cattle ranches. A flood in June, 1965, caused extensive damage to the town. Thirty-two business establishments were reported in 1970. Sanderson, with about two-thirds of the county population, had a 1960 population of 2,189; the 1970 population was 1,229, according to the United States census.

*Sanderson Canyon.

*Sandi Indians.

*Sandia, Texas.

*Sandies Creek.

*Sandoval, Manuel de.

*Sandoval, Texas.

*Sandow, Texas.

*Sandstone Mountain.

Sandusky, William H. William H. Sandusky was born in 1813 in Columbus, Ohio, the son of John and Elizabeth (Clarno) Sandusky. In 1838 he established himself in Austin as an artist-draftsman, assisting in the surveying of the town and the making of a map of Austin. He served the state as a surveyor and later as registrar of the General Land Office.qv In 1840 he was appointed secretary to President Mirabeau B. Lamar, but a year later he resigned for health reasons and asked that he be given an appointment in the survey of the coast and harbors of Texas. In 1842 Sandusky married Jane McKnight, and the couple lived in Galveston, where he advertised as a maker of maps, charts, landscapes, and plans of cities and towns. He worked in Galveston until his death in 1846.

Though reflecting limited skill, his sketches of the city of Austin add important material to the early history and founding of the capital city.

BIBLIOGRAPHY: Pauline A. Pinckney, *Painting in Texas: The Nineteenth Century* (1967).

Pauline A. Pinckney

*Sandusky, Texas.

*Sandy, Texas.

*Sandy Creek.

*Sandy Creek, Texas.

*Sandy Fork of Peach Creek.

*Sandy Hill, Texas.

*Sandy Mountain.

*Sandy Point, Texas.

*Saner, Robert Edward Lee.

*Saner Junction, Texas.

*Sanford, Texas.

*Sanford and Northern Railroad.

*Sanger, Alexander.

*Sanger, Texas. Sanger, in north-central Denton County, had a 1960 population of 1,190 and a 1970 population of 1,603, according to the United States census. The town had forty businesses in 1970.

Sängerbund. See Texas State Singing Society.

*Sanipao Indians. These are Coahuiltecan Indians whose aboriginal location remains unknown. In 1755 the Sanipao appeared at Nuestra Señora de la Purísima Concepción de Acuña Mission qv of San Antonio, where they lived until at least 1790. It is possible that the name Sanipao is a variant of Sampanal, the name of another Coahuiltecan group that lived along the southern margin of the Edwards Plateau in the late seventeenth century.

BIBLIOGRAPHY: F. W. Hodge (ed.), *Handbook of American Indians*, II (1910); J. R. Swanton, *The Indian Tribes of North America* (1952).

T. N. Campbell

Sanitarian Advisory Committee. The Sanitarian Advisory Committee, composed of five members, was created in 1965 for the purpose of assisting the State Board of Health in forming rules and regulations for the examining and licensing of professional sanitarians. This program for registering professional sanitarians was administered by the division of sanitary engineering within the State Department of Health (see Public Health, State Department of). In 1973 there were approximately 875 registered sanitarians in Texas.

BIBLIOGRAPHY: University of Texas at Austin, *Guide To Texas State Agencies* (1972).

*Sansom, John William. John William Sansom was with the German American Unionists who were in the battle of the Nueces,qv and although he joined Edward Degener qv (as stated in Volume II), it was Fritz Tegener who led the Unionist group of sixty-five men; the Confederate forces were led by C. D. McRae (not James M. Duff,qv although the group included men from Duff's company). In the ensuing battle nineteen Unionists were killed and fifteen wounded (six of the wounded men later escaped), and of the rest, nine were murdered by the Confederate forces. The remainder of the German American party scattered: six were killed on October 18, 1862, while crossing the Rio Grande; eleven reached Union territory and served in the United States Army; and of the remaining twenty, some went to Mexico or California, and some remained hidden in Texas. Although various accounts differ, it appears that of the original sixty-five Unionists, a total of thirty-four men were killed (not forty-five, as stated in Volume II). John William Sansom was one of those who escaped; he later wrote an account of the battle. He died on June 19 (not June 18), 1920.

BIBLIOGRAPHY: John W. Sansom, *The Battle on the Nueces River* (c. 1905); Marcus J. Wright (comp.) and Harold B. Simpson (ed.), *Texas in the War, 1861–1865* (1965); Claude Elliott, "Union Sentiment in Texas, 1861–1865," *Southwestern Historical Quarterly*, L (1946–1947).

*Sansom, Texas. See North Uvalde, Texas.

Sansom Park Village, Texas. Sansom Park Village, in central Tarrant County, was incorporated in 1950 with an alderman form of government. By the mid-1960's the town had nine churches, a school, and numerous businesses, including a plastics company and a refrigeration plant. The 1960 population was 4,175; the 1970 population was 4,771, according to the United States census.

Santa Ana National Wildlife Refuge. See Wildlife Areas in Texas.

*Santa Anna, Antonio López de.

*Santa Anna, Texas. (Coleman County.) Santa Anna had a 1960 population of 1,320 and a 1970 population of 1,310, according to the United States census. The town had twenty-five businesses in 1970.

Santa Anna, Texas. (Jackson County.) *See* Texana, Texas.

*Santa Anna Creek.

*Santa Anna Mountains.

Santa Catarina, Texas. Santa Catarina, in northeastern Starr County, consisted of a filling station, a grocery store, and a cotton gin in the mid-1960's. The inhabitants were principally engaged in farming and ranching. The 1970 population estimate was forty-five.

*Santa Clara, Texas.

*Santa Clara Creek.

*Santa Cruz, Texas. (Duval County.)

*Santa Cruz, Texas. (Starr County.)

Santa Cruz del Cíbolo. *See* Fuerte del Santa Cruz.

*Santa Cruz de Querétaro, College of.

*Santa Cruz de San Sabá. *See* San Sabá de la Santa Cruz Mission.

*Santa Cruz Settlement.

*Santa Cruz de Tapacolmes Pueblo.

*Santa Elena, Grand Canyon of.

*Santa Fe County.

*Santa Fe Dock and Channel Company.

*Santa Fe Expedition. *See* Texan Santa Fe Expedition.

*Santa Fe Lake.

*Santa Fe Railroad System. On August 1, 1965, the Interstate Commerce Commission approved the merger of the Gulf, Colorado, and Santa Fe Railway Company with three subsidiaries of the Santa Fe system in Texas: the Kansas City, Mexico, and Orient Railway Company of Texas; the Panhandle and Santa Fe; and the Rio Grande, El Paso, and Santa Fe. The Gulf and Interstate of Texas was not included, but is still part of the system. The Santa Fe system in Texas also included one-fourth interest in the Houston Belt and Terminal Railroad, one-eighth interest in the Union Terminal, and one-third interest in the Texas City Terminal. The Santa Fe Railroad system had 5,121 miles of track in Texas on January 1, 1968.

*Santa Fe Trail.

*Santa Gertrudis Cattle.

*Santa Gertrudis Creek.

*Santa Gertrudis Ranch. *See* King Ranch.

*Santa Isabel, Texas.

*Santa Isabel Creek.

*Santa Margarita, Texas.

Santa Margarita Crossing. Santa Margarita Crossing, a natural ford across the Nueces River near San Patricio, was a point of convergence for many roads leading northward from Matamoros, Reynosa, Camargo, Mier, Revilla, and Laredo to La Bahía and San Antonio. One of the immutable landmarks of the coastal bend area, the crossing had been used since earliest times by buffaloes, Indians, explorers, soldiers, freighters, stages, and travelers. From 1830 to about 1886, the crossing was the southern terminus of the San Patricio Trail.qv A ferry was established at the site in 1846. During the Civil War the crossing was designated as a point of consignment to Mexican teamsters for contraband cotton destined for Matamoros.

BIBLIOGRAPHY: Hobart Huson, *Refugio: A Comprehensive History of Refugio County from Aboriginal Times to 1953* (1953); Robert H. Thonhoff, A History of Karnes County, Texas (M.A. thesis, Southwest Texas State College, 1963).

Robert H. Thonhoff

*Santa Maria, Texas.

*Santa Monica, Texas.

*Santa Petronilla Creek.

Santa Rita, Texas. (Cameron County.) Santa Rita was an early town in present-day Cameron County, possibly the earliest town named by English-speaking people in the area, and was the county's first seat of government. It was located on the Rio Grande, five miles from Brownsville. In the late 1700's the land on the south bank of the river was claimed by José Narciso Cavazos of Reynosa, who called it "Santa Rita," and by José Salvador de la Garza, who received the Espíritu Santo grant. It eventually became a ranch belonging to a descendant of the two. A village was built there before the establishment of Matamoros in 1826. About 1830 the river changed course and the tract was then located north of the stream.

In 1834 the Mexican government granted to John Stryker the *banco de Santa Rita*. When General Zachary Taylor's qv troops occupied Matamoros, other United States residents crossed to the Stryker place. The Texas legislative act creating Cameron County was approved in February, 1848, and Santa Rita became the county seat. An election of officers was held August 7, but organization was not completed until September 11. In December, 1848, Brownsville was voted county seat of the area, and some of the householders of Santa Rita put their buildings on wheels and rolled them to the winning site. A remnant of Santa Rita is called Villa Nueva.

BIBLIOGRAPHY: "Texas Collection," *Southwestern Historical Quarterly*, XLVIII (1944–1945); Brownsville *Herald*, May 10, 1936.

Grace Edman

*Santa Rita, Texas. (Reagan County.) *See* Rita Santa, Texas.

*Santa Rita Oil Well.

*Santa Rosa, Texas. (Cameron County.) Santa Rosa had a 1960 population of 1,572 and a 1970 population of 1,466, according to the United States census. The town had twenty businesses in 1970.

*Santa Rosa, Texas. (Willacy County.)

*Santa Rosa Lake. Santa Rosa Lake, in Wilbarger County, is owned and operated by the William Thomas Waggoner qv estate to provide a water supply for stock raising and mining. Built in 1929, the lake has an estimated capacity of 11,570 acre-feet with a surface area of 1,500 acres at elevation 1,150 feet above mean sea level. The drainage area above the dam is 336 square miles.

BIBLIOGRAPHY: Texas Water Commission, *Bulletin 6408* (1964).

Seth D. Breeding

*Santana. *See* Buffalo Hump.

*Santander, Texas.

*Santiago Draw.

*Santiago Mountains.

*Santiago Peak.

*Santísima Trinidad de Salcedo.

*Santísima Virgin de los Dolores Mission. *See* Nuestra Señora de los Dolores de los Ais Mission.

*Santísimo Nombre de María Mission.

*Santísimo Rosario Mission. *See* Nuestra Señora del Rosario Mission.

*Santleben, August.

*Santo, Texas.

*Santo Tomas Creek.

*Sap Oak, Texas.

Saracuam Indians. The Saracuam Indians are known only from a Spanish document of 1716 which merely lists them as a group of Indians encountered somewhere between Monclova, Coahuila, and eastern Texas. It cannot be established that they ever lived in Texas. J. R. Swanton doubtfully included the Saracuam in his list of Coahuiltecan bands.

BIBLIOGRAPHY: F. W. Hodge (ed.), *Handbook of American Indians*, II (1910); J. R. Swanton, *Linguistic Material from the Tribes of Southern Texas and Northeastern Mexico* (1940).

T. N. Campbell

*Saragosa, Texas.

*Sarahville de Viesca. *See* Viesca, Sarahville de.

*Saratoga, Texas.

*Sarber, Texas.

*Sarco, Texas.

*Sarco Creek.

*Sardis, Texas. (Ellis County.)

*Sardis, Texas. (Fisher County.)

*Sargent, Texas. (Matagorda County.)

*Sargent, Texas. (Reeves County.)

*Sarita, Texas. Sarita, seat of Kenedy County, is a ranch headquarters and trading center for the county. The population was an estimated 196 in 1971, when the town reported two businesses.

*Saron, Texas.

*Saspamco, Texas.

Sassory Indians. The Sassory Indians are known from one of the contemporary accounts (Cavelier) of the La Salle Expedition.qv This account indicates that in the late seventeenth century the Sassory lived near the Hasinai tribes, somewhere to the west or southwest. The Sassory have been somewhat hesitantly identified with the Nasoni, one of the Hasinai tribes, but the location of the Nasoni at that time does not agree with the location indicated for the Sassory. The linguistic and cultural affiliations of the Sassory remain undetermined.

BIBLIOGRAPHY: I. J. Cox (ed.), *The Journeys of Réné Robert Cavelier, Sieur de La Salle*, I (1905); F. W. Hodge (ed.), *Handbook of American Indians*, II (1910); J. G. Shea (ed.), *Early Voyages up and down the Mississippi* (1861).

T. N. Campbell

*Satank (Setangya).

*Satanta. Satanta, Kiowa chief who committed suicide on October 11, 1878, at the penitentiary at Huntsville, was removed from the cemetery there and reinterred at the Fort Sill military cemetery at Fort Sill, Oklahoma.

BIBLIOGRAPHY: University of Chicago, *Indian Voices* (February, 1964).

Satapayogligla Indians. This is the name of one band of Chizo Indians, who are considered by some writers to be a branch of the Concho. In the seventeenth and early eighteenth centuries the Chizo occupied the area now covered by northeastern Chihuahua, northwestern Coahuila, and the lower part of the Big Bend region of Trans-Pecos Texas.

BIBLIOGRAPHY: C. W. Hackett (ed.), *Historical Documents Relating to New Mexico, Nueva Vizcaya, and Approaches Thereto, to 1773*, II (1926); C. Sauer, *The Distribution of Aboriginal Tribes and Languages in Northwestern Mexico* (1934).

T. N. Campbell

Satatu Indians. These Indians are known only from a Spanish document of 1693 which lists the Satatu as one of fifty "nations" that lived north of the Rio Grande and "between Texas and New Mexico." This may be interpreted to mean the southern part of western Texas, since the document also mentions that the Apache were at war with the group named. Nothing further is known about the Satatu.

BIBLIOGRAPHY: C. W. Hackett (ed.), *Historical Documents Relating to New Mexico, Nueva Vizcaya, and Approaches Thereto, to 1773*, II (1926).

T. N. Campbell

*Satin, Texas.

*Satsuma, Texas.

*Sattler, Texas.

*Satuit, Texas.

*Saturn, Texas.

*Saucedo, José Antonio.

*Saucita Creek.

*Sauer, Emil.

*Saul, Thomas Stovin.

*Saunders, Bacon.

*Saunders, George W.

Saunders, Lawrence. *See* Davis, Clare Ogden; Davis, John Burton.

Saunders, Xenophon Boone. Xenophon Boone Saunders, son of Joel Boone and Mariam Lewis (Kennedy) Saunders, was born on October 21, 1828 (1831?), in Columbia, Tennessee. He was descended from Elizabeth Boone, youngest sister of Daniel Boone, and came to Texas about 1855 after attending Jackson College in Columbia, Tennessee, and Hanover College in Indiana, from which he was graduated in 1849. He read law at Indianapolis and Nashville and was admitted to the Bar in Memphis in 1854.

Saunders came first to Washington County, Texas, and later moved to Bell County about 1855, where he joined with prominent members of the Whig party to found the Belton *Independent*, Bell County's first newspaper. The paper opposed secession and built strong support for Sam Houston in central Texas.

Saunders practiced law in Belton in 1857 and in 1860 was elected Belton's first mayor. Although he had been an ardent opponent of secession and had stumped central Texas speaking against leaving the Union, Saunders was one of the first to cast his lot with his neighbors who had voted for secession. He was elected captain of Company A, 16th Texas Infantry Regiment, was later promoted to major, and participated in the battles of Perkins' Landing, Milliken's Bend, Mansfield, Pleasant Hill, and Jenkins' Ferry, part of the time commanding the regiment.

Saunders was elected a delegate from Bell and Lampasas counties to the Constitutional Convention of 1866,[qv] and in 1875, when the terms of the district judges appointed by Reconstruction Governor Edmund Jackson Davis[qv] expired, he was elected district judge; he served in that capacity until 1877, when he entered into a law partnership with A. J. Harris, a partnership which became well known in central Texas.

Saunders married Annie E. Surghnor of Leesburg, Virginia, on December 17, 1857; they had four sons and two daughters. He died on July 20, 1909, at Belton.

BIBLIOGRAPHY: John Henry Brown, *Indian Wars and Pioneers of Texas* (189?); *Memorial and Biographical History of McLennan, Falls, Bell and Coryell Counties* (1893); George W. Tyler, *History of Bell County* (1936); Marcus J. Wright (comp.) and Harold B. Simpson (ed.), *Texas in the War, 1861–1865* (1965).

Dayton Kelley

*Saus Creek.

*Sauz Creek.

*Sava, Texas.

Savings and Loan Department. In 1961 the legislature removed the regulation of state-chartered building and loan associations from the Banking Department[qv] and created a separate Savings and Loan Department. Both departments were under the supervision and control of the Finance Commission, which appointed their administrators—the banking commissioner and the savings and loan commissioner.

BIBLIOGRAPHY: Stuart A. MacCorkle and Dick Smith, *Texas Government* (1964).

Dick Smith

*Savoy, Texas.

*Savoy Male and Female College.

*Sawmill Canyon.

*Sawmill Mountain.

*Sawmills. *See* Lumber and Lumbering.

*Sawtooth Mountain.

*Sawyer, Frederick A.

*Sawyer Branch.

*Saxet, Texas.

*Sayers, Joseph Draper. Joseph Draper Sayers was elected lieutenant governor of Texas in November, 1878, and served for one term, from January, 1879, to January, 1881 (not from 1878 to 1879, as stated in Volume II).

*Sayers, Texas.

*Sayersville, Texas.

*Sayles, John.

*Sayre, Charles D.

*Scallorn, Texas.

*Scarborough, Emily Dorothy.

*Scarborough, John B.

*Scarborough, Lee Rutland.

*Scarboroughs Creek.

*Scates, William Bennett.

*Scenic Mountain.

*Sceyne, Texas.

Scharbauer, Clarence. Clarence Scharbauer was born in Albany County, New York, on August 18, 1879, the son of Christian and Jennie (McCarthy) Scharbauer. In 1889 the family migrated to Midland, Texas, to join John Scharbauer, Christian's brother, who had come to Texas in 1880 and prospered first as a sheep rancher, then as a cattle man. Clarence Scharbauer attended public school in Midland and worked for his uncle in the summers. When he was sixteen, he acquired his own herd of cattle and his own VXL brand. He attended a business school in Waco in 1898 and Baylor University in 1899, but he turned his full energies to the cattle business in 1900.

In 1901 he joined his father and uncle in the organization of the Scharbauer Cattle Company, becoming manager of the company and its ranches at the age of twenty-two. Under his guidance the company flourished until it was dissolved in 1912 into separate ranches.

In 1914 the Scharbauer Cattle Company was re-established, again with Clarence Scharbauer as manager. He also owned and operated separately three other ranches and was a leader in the raising of registered cattle. Oil was discovered on some of his property in 1935. In addition to ranching and other business interests, he built the Scharbauer Hotel in Midland in 1927. Scharbauer was active in numerous civic organizations. He married Ruth Cowden on December 1, 1908. They had two sons. He died on October 2, 1942.

BIBLIOGRAPHY: Seymour V. Connor (ed.), *Builders of the Southwest* (1959).

Seymour V. Connor

*Schattel, Texas.

*Schep Creek.

Scherer, Gideon. Gideon Scherer was born near Rural Retreat, Wythe County, Virginia, the son of Elizabeth (Spoon) and Jacob Scherer, on December 2, 1811. He studied in a country school, but he probably had more formal training, for he was a practicing minister when, about 1852, he and his wife decided to come to Texas, where Gideon could minister to the increasing number of German Lutheran immigrants arriving there. The couple made their way by the Kanawha, Ohio, and Mississippi rivers to New Orleans, then to Galveston, and finally to Columbus, where he soon organized a Lutheran church. Although not the first Lutheran church in Texas, it certainly was among the first to use the English language. Most of its members had non-German names.

In 1857 Gideon and his brother, John Jacob Scherer,qv who had come to Texas after 1852, were asked to establish a college in Columbus under the auspices of the Lutheran church; they founded Colorado College.qv Jacob Scherer, their father, who was also a minister and had come to Columbus in 1854 at the age of sixty-nine, helped by teaching classes in the college until his death in Columbus on March 2, 1860. Gideon Scherer died little more than a year later, on June 2, 1861.

W. A. Flachmeier

Scherer, John Jacob. John Jacob Scherer was born near Rural Retreat, Wythe County, Virginia, the son of Elizabeth (Spoon) and Jacob Scherer, on February 7, 1830. After some education in a country school, he attended Virginia Collegiate Institute and Pennsylvania College, completing his work there in 1852. He accepted a teaching position in the private school of a Judge Munger in San Felipe, Texas, but soon was teaching school in Columbus. He and his brother, Gideon Scherer,qv with their father, Jacob Scherer, organized Colorado College qv in Columbus under the auspices of the Lutheran church in 1857. All three of them taught in the college; his father died on March 2, 1860, and his brother died the following year. On October 19, 1863, John Jacob Scherer enlisted in the Confederate Army for a six-month period.

He returned to Virginia in 1867 and there was married to Elizabeth Katherine Killinger. They returned to Texas, where he served as president of Colorado College until 1873, when he left Texas to go back to Virginia; there he was the founder and first president of Marion College. He served as its president until 1910 and remained as president emeritus until his death in 1919.

BIBLIOGRAPHY: Goodridge Wilson, *A Brief History of Marion College* (1948); James A. Brown, "Sketches of Deceased Lutheran Ministers in the Synod of Southwest Virginia," *Lutheran Quarterly*, XXV (July, 1895).

W. A. Flachmeier

*Schermersville, Texas.

*Schertz, Texas. Schertz, northeast of San Antonio in Guadalupe County, on the Guadalupe-Bexar county line, was incorporated in 1958. The community had twenty-seven businesses in 1970. Population was 4,061 in 1970, according to the United States census.

Schiwetz, Berthold. Berthold "Tex" Schiwetz was born in Cuero, Texas, on July 23, 1909, the son of Berthold and Anna (Reiffert) Schiwetz, and brother of Texas artist Edward M. "Buck" Schiwetz. After graduation from high school in Cuero he enrolled in the Agricultural and Mechanical College of Texas (now Texas A&M University) to study business administration, although he preferred painting and drawing. During the depression of the early 1930's he had to give up his study of art to work in an office. In 1935, in his spare time, he began to carve portraits out of plaster, and for the next two years he studied sculpture under William McVey at the Houston Museum of Fine Arts.qv In 1939, at McVey's urging, he went to the Cranbrook Academy of Art in Michigan to study with sculptor Carl Milles. At the outbreak of World War II he served in Europe with the 95th Infantry Division.

By 1945 he was again in Cranbrook and spent the next five years in the Milles studio there. During the summer of 1949 he traveled with Milles to Sweden and Italy and in 1950 became his assistant. In Rome he took charge of Milles' studio at the American Academy, and during the time of Milles' illness Schiwetz supervised completion of many of the sculptor's last important works, among them the Milles fountain in the restaurant court of the Metropolitan Museum of Art and the William Volker memorial fountain in Kansas City.

After Milles' death in 1955 Schiwetz remained a year at the American Academy in Rome, but in 1956 he returned to Cranbrook as head of the sculpture department. For the next six years he worked with a select group of students there while continuing his own work. His first major show was held at Worcester Art Museum in December, 1957, and another one-man show was held in the Sculpture Center in New York on February 16, 1958. In 1962 Schiwetz left Cranbrook for Florence, Italy, where he established his studio. He worked in the Bruno Bearzi bronze foundry nearby, and there he created a number of large sculptures. In 1966, after a serious illness, he returned to the United States and lived on Ossabaw Island, off the coast of Georgia, sketching wild animals, shore birds, and shells. In 1967 he returned to Michigan to live and work in his studio at Walbri in Bloomfield Hills, Michigan. He moved to Dexter, Michigan, in 1969, establishing his home and studio, where he died in June, 1971. He was buried in Cuero. A posthumous show of fifty-two pieces of his work was held in the Birmingham Art Museum in Michigan in the latter part of 1971.

From his years in Rome Schiwetz learned the use of water as a sculptural element of design for his fountain pieces; from his Texas boyhood he recaptured the sense of joy and play in the animal and insect forms which served as numerous subjects for his sculptures; and from the Etruscans, he derived a feeling of whimsy in characterization. His forty-two-inch-high bronze "Bird Formation" is in the Worcester Art Museum. Among his fountain pieces are "Praying Mantis," "Sting Rays," and "Jonah and the Whale." His works are in private collections in Houston and in the East and Midwest; they are also in the Millesgården, Ledvigo, Sweden, the Flint Museum in Flint, Michigan, the Cleveland Museum of Art, and City Park, Philadelphia.

BIBLIOGRAPHY: *Arts* (March, 1958); Birmingham Galleries, Inc. [Michigan], *The Sculpture of Berthold "Tex" Schiwetz, 1909–1971* (1971); Worcester Art Museum, *"Tex" Schiwetz, Sculpture in Bronze* (1957), *News Bulletin and Calendar*, XXIII (May, 1958); Biographical Files, Barker Texas History Center, University of Texas at Austin; Files, Art Library, University of Texas at Austin.

Crystal Sasse Ragsdale

*Schleicher, Gustav.

*Schleicher County. Schleicher County is primarily a sheep and goat raising area. By 1970 over 90 percent of the average annual agricultural income of $4.7 million was from sheep, goats, cattle, wool, and mohair. Vegetables were grown on irrigated land; over 2,100 acres were irrigated by the mid-1960's. Oil contributed to the economy, with nearly sixty million barrels produced from 1937 to January 1, 1973. The 1960 population was 2,791; the 1970 population was 2,277, according to the United States census.

*Schmitz, John B.

Schmitz, Joseph William. Joseph William Schmitz, son of John B. and Mary (Kayser) Schmitz, was born on February 12, 1905, in Stacyville, Iowa. He attended a parochial school taught by brothers of the Society of Mary in Dyersville, Iowa, entered the Marianist novitiate at Maryhurst (near Kirkwood, Missouri), and professed his first vows in the order on August 15, 1922.

He began his teaching career in the high school department of the Marian Chaminade College in Clayton, Missouri, in 1924. Four years later he was transferred to the high school department of St. Mary's University in San Antonio, where he also completed work on his B.A. degree in English in 1931. During several leaves of absence for graduate study, he obtained an M.A. degree in history at Loyola University, Chicago, in 1934 and a Ph.D. degree from that institution in 1939. From that time on he was a permanent member of the history staff at St. Mary's, serving for many years as chairman of that department. He became vice-president and dean of the faculty there in 1961.

His books include *Thus They Lived: Daily Life in the Republic of Texas* (1936), reprinted as *Texas Culture 1836–1846* (1960); *Texas Statecraft, 1836–1845* (1941); and *The Society of Mary in Texas* (1951). He also wrote a number of articles and reviews for scholarly publication.

A member of many professional organizations, Schmitz was the first president and cofounder of the San Antonio Historical Association.qv He was a long-time member of the executive council of the Texas State Historical Association,qv to which he was elected a fellow; he was vice-president and due to succeed to the presidency of that organization the year of his death. He died on February 16, 1966, and was buried at St. Mary's University Cemetery.

BIBLIOGRAPHY: Felix Diaz Almaraz, Jr., "Joseph William Schmitz, S.M.," *Texana*, IV (Summer, 1966); *Who's Who In America* (1964); Biographical File, Barker Texas History Center, University of Texas at Austin.

Seymour V. Connor

*Schneider, Texas.

*Schoenau, Texas.

*Schoenthal, Texas.

Schoffelmayer, Victor Humbert. Victor Humbert Schoffelmayer, newspaper writer and agricultural authority, was born in 1878 in Stuttgart, Germany, and came as an infant to Chicago with his parents, who soon took him back to Germany; his father returned alone to Chicago, where he died, and Victor was nine years old when his mother brought him back to the United States. He was educated at New Engelberg College, a Benedictine boarding school in northwest Missouri, and at Josephinium College in Ohio. Ill, possibly from tuberculosis, he came to San Antonio in 1896, where he met William H. Menger of the Menger Hotel,qv who sent him to Castroville to regain his health. Later he worked for Menger as a writer on the *Southern Messenger*. He taught school briefly in Pilot Point, Texas, in 1897, studied painting under George Upp in Missouri, and then opened a piano studio in Keokuk, Iowa.

Beginning in 1905 he was a reporter on a number of newspapers in Missouri, Kansas, Iowa, and Minnesota. He was the art and music critic on the Minneapolis *Journal* before he became editor in 1913 of the *Southwest Trail*, a monthly agricultural development journal financed by the Rock Island Railroad Lines to attract settlers to the Southwest. Working out of Chicago, he edited the *Southwest Trail* at a time when there were few other agricultural bulletins published. He and his wife, Carrie, traveled over 50,000 miles a year in a special railroad car, promoting farm machinery and distributing agricultural literature. With the coming of World War I the Rock Island Lines project ended.

In December, 1917, Schoffelmayer began working for George Bannerman Dealy qv as field editor of the *Semi-Weekly Farm News*, a subsidiary of the Dallas *Morning News*;qv soon thereafter he became agricultural editor of the Dallas *Morning News*. During the 1920's and 1930's his department urged a diversified farming program for the small farmers of Texas. His insistence on the need for crop diversification led to the establishment of the Institute of Technology and Plant Industry at Southern Methodist University (later separated from the university and renamed the Texas Research Foundation qv). Schoffelmayer was in charge of radio station WFAA's Farm Hour from its beginning in the mid-1930's until his retirement in 1947, after which he served as a consultant on the staff of the Southwest Research Institute.qv During his long career he did much to advance farming and ranching methods in Texas.

He was the author of four books: *Texas at the Crossroads* (1935); *White Gold* (1941), the story of the cotton industry of the Southwest; *Here Comes Tomorrow* (1942), a study of Texas agricultural methods and related problems in European farming; and *Southwest Trails to New Horizons* (1960), an autobiography.

In 1906 he was married to Carrie Fleming of St. Louis, Missouri; after her death in 1944 he was married in 1949 to Mrs. Aimee Worthern Friedgen, of Los Angeles. Schoffelmayer died on April 30, 1962, in Durate, California.

*Schofield, Texas. (Burleson County.)

*Schofield, Texas. (Hill County.)

*School Creek.

*School Fund, Available. Since 1950–1951 the income of the state Available School Fund has increased significantly with a resultant increase in the rate per scholastic distributed to public schools. In the 1969–1970 fiscal year the Available School Fund disbursed $288,059,478.32; this amounted to a payment rate per scholastic of $117.65. There are two major revenue sources for the fund: earnings from the Permanent School Fund qv and designated tax revenues. The fund does not receive annual appropriations by the legislature from the general revenue fund (as stated in Volume II). Fund revenues are derived from portions of state ad valorem taxes; occupations taxes; license fees of various kinds; rentals of state lands, buildings, and equipment; interest on state bank deposits and on investments; and fuel taxes. In addition, the fund receives portions of monies from escheated estates and from the omnibus tax fund, into which cigarette, liquor, gasoline, and utilities taxes are paid. *See also* Education; Foundation School Program Fund; Land Appropriations; Lands, Texas Public. [The Available School Fund should not be confused with the Available University Fund.qv Ed.]

*School Fund, Permanent. The Permanent School Fund has grown steadily, receiving additional monies from oil and gas royalties and from bonuses on mineral leases. The Permanent School Fund amounted to $675,052,611.13 in July, 1966, and grew to $842,217,721.05 in July, 1970. This sum is invested and the earnings are transferred to the Available School Fund.qv The investments were distributed approximately as follows at the end of the 1966 fiscal year:

U. S. Treasury Bonds	48%
Municipal Bonds	12%
Corporate Bonds	24%
Common Stocks	16%

In the 1965–1966 fiscal year, $24,434,239.58 was transferred to the Available School Fund; in 1969–1970 the figure was $34,762,955.32. *See also* Education; Foundation School Program Fund; Land Appropriations; Lands, Texas Public; Rogan, Charles. [The Permanent School Fund should not be confused with the Permanent University Fund.qv Ed.]

J. W. Edgar

School Land Board. The School Land Board was created in 1939 when the legislature set apart and dedicated to the Permanent School Fund qv the mineral estate in riverbeds and channels and in all areas within the tidewater limits, including islands, lakes, bays, and the bed of the sea belonging to the state. All the duties of the abolished Board of Mineral Development (created in 1931) were transferred to the School Land Board. The board supervises the management, leasing, and sale of the public school lands.

Originally composed of the commissioner of the General Land Office qv and the governor as ex officio members, and one citizen member appointed by the governor, in 1965 the governor was taken off the board and was replaced by another citizen member appointed by the attorney general. Two citizen members are appointed for two-year terms while the land commissioner serves during his term of office.

BIBLIOGRAPHY: University of Texas at Austin, *Guide To Texas State Agencies* (1970).

*School Lands. *See* Land Appropriations.

*Schoolerville, Texas.

*Schools. *See* Education.

Schott, Arthur. Arthur Schott was born in 1813; in 1849 he joined the Emory Survey of the United States-Mexico border as first assistant surveyor. On the survey Schott prepared 226 drawings, 25 of these in color, which augmented the natural science aspects of the survey. His prints were remarkably successful, considering the experimentation in the use of color printing in progress at the time. In addition to bird and Indian plates he made two excellent drawings of particular documentary value: "Military Plaza—San Antonio, Texas" and "The Military Colony Opposite Fort Duncan." After the survey Schott lived in Washington, D.C., where he contributed to the Smithsonian Reports (1856–1866) on geological subjects in the Rio Grande country. A man of considerable talent, Schott, in addition to being an artist, was also a naturalist, an engineer, a physician, and a well-known musician and linguist. Schott made a scientific approach to problems in regional geography. He died in 1875.

BIBLIOGRAPHY: Pauline A. Pinckney, *Painting in Texas: The Nineteenth Century* (1967).

Pauline A. Pinckney

Schott, Justus J. Justus J. Schott was born on July 18, 1846, in Germany (possibly in the area of Hesse-Cassel), the son of Justus and Louise (Zeiss) Schott, who immigrated to Galveston, Texas, in 1850 with their six children. Yellow fever was prevalent at the time, and within two years both parents died from it. The orphaned children were taken into various homes and soon became scattered. Young Schott and his sister, Louise, were taken into the home of a family by the name of Carstens.

At the age of eight, Schott entered private school in the home of a German schoolmaster. At the age of twelve he began an apprenticeship at the Behrmann drugstore, owned by a brother of Mrs. Carstens. From then until 1867 Schott worked in the drugstore, learning pharmacy and eventually becoming manager of the store. His work was interrupted during the Civil War, when Schott presented himself for military service; he was soon released from duty because of physical disability. In December, 1867, Schott began his own business, and in 1873 he opened a drugstore on Market Street in Galveston.

In 1869 Schott began to experiment with making chewing gum. From a sea captain he obtained chicle from Mexico. Refining and adding sugar and flavoring, Schott developed a marketable product to replace the paraffin and spruce gum then in use. A pamphlet was sent across the country announcing the possibilities of chicle. Shortly thereafter the Adams Chewing Gum Company brought a $50,000 suit against Schott for infringement of patent rights; Schott, in a court case tried in New Orleans, proved that he had sent out his pamphlets before the Adams patent. Though he won the case, he did not pursue his rights further.

The J. J. Schott Drug Company, Inc., on Market Street became a gathering place for people of Galveston and was soon widely known. Schott was appointed the first chairman of the board of pharmacy examiners when it was created for the Seventh Congressional District; when a single board of examiners for the state of Texas was created, he was a member.

Schott married Christina Rhode about 1873; after her death he married Rosa Burnet. He filled his millionth prescription on January 17, 1913, and continued to fill prescriptions for another fifteen years before his death on May 6, 1928, in Galveston. He was buried in Hallettsville, Texas.

Riley Le Fevers

*Schraeder, Texas.

*Schreiner, Charles Armand.

Schreiner, Gustave Frederick. Gustave Frederick (Fritz) Schreiner, son of Mary Magdalena "Lena" (Enderle) and Charles Armand Schreiner,qv was born on March 3, 1866, in the Turtle Creek Community near Kerrville, Texas. He attended public schools in Kerrville and Comfort and the English-German school in San Antonio. In 1884–1885 he attended Von Lycker's Business College in New York City. Known as the "dean

of hill country ranchers," he participated in cattle drives in 1889 and 1890 and managed the Schreiner Land and Livestock Company from 1887 until 1962.

Schreiner was appointed to the Texas Game and Fish Commission (see Parks and Wildlife Department, Texas) for a four-year term by Governor Daniel James Moody, Jr.,qv and reappointed to a successive four-year term by Governor Ross S. Sterling.qv He did much to foster plans for the conservation of wildlife. Schreiner was cited by the commission as being primarily responsible for the preservation of the deer population in the hill country of Texas. He was also a leading thoroughbred horse breeder.

He added to the Schreiner family philanthropic traditions established by his father. He gave approximately one-half million dollars toward the operation and building of Schreiner Institute qv and left an estate valued at approximately two-and-one-half million dollars to provide a continuing income for that school after his death. He served on the board of trustees of Schreiner Institute from 1923 until 1962.

On February 15, 1892, he was married to Hulda Rummel in San Antonio. Schreiner died on May 31, 1962, in Kerrville.

BIBLIOGRAPHY: Bob Bennett, *Kerr County, Texas, 1856–1956* (c. 1956); Kerrville *Daily Times*, June 1, 1962; Kerrville *Mountain Sun*, June 6, 1962; San Antonio *Express*, February 16, 1892; Biographical File, Barker Texas History Center, University of Texas at Austin.

Joe R. Baulch

Schreiner, Louis Albert. Louis Albert Schreiner, son of Mary Magdalena "Lena" (Enderle) and Charles Armand Schreiner qv was born on December 31, 1870, on his parents' Turtle Creek ranch in Kerr County, a short time before the family moved into Kerrville, where his father had opened a general merchandise store. Louis Schreiner attended school in Comfort and the German-English School in San Antonio. He attended business college in Poughkeepsie, New York, but returned to work as bookkeeper in the Charles Schreiner bank in Kerrville. In 1918 when Charles Schreiner divided his $6 million estate among his eight children, Louis Schreiner received the bank as part of his share.

He donated land for Kerrville's first airport and, with his father and brothers, donated land for the Veterans Administration Hospital, the Texas Lions Camp for Crippled Children, and a state agricultural building. Numerous gifts were given to Schreiner Institute, including two dormitories. He was involved in organizing the local telephone company, and during the 1930's he became the only Texan among officers and directors of the National Wool Trade Association. He was a member of the Texas Sheep and Goat Raisers Association, and he is credited with the founding of the cooperative wool marketing system in Texas. During the depression years of the 1930's, Schreiner did much to encourage local ranchers to stay on their land to await the return of better times. In 1940 Louis

Schreiner's portrait, along with others, was hung in the Saddle and Sirloin Club in the Stockyards Inn in Chicago, in honor of men who had made outstanding contributions to agriculture and livestock raising in the United States.

Louis Schreiner was married to Mae Shiner on September 15, 1898, in San Antonio. They were the parents of one daughter. After Mrs. Schreiner's death in 1932, Schreiner was married to Mrs. Evaland F. Scobey in New York City on January 15, 1936. He died on September 18, 1970, and was buried in Glenrest Cemetery in Kerrville.

BIBLIOGRAPHY: Austin *American-Statesman*, September 20, 1970; Fort Worth *Star-Telegram*, December 12, 1940; San Angelo *Standard-Times*, December 13, 1967; Biographical File, Barker Texas History Center, University of Texas at Austin; Kerr County Scrapbook (Archives, University of Texas at Austin Library).

Schreiner College. *See* Schreiner Institute. [The school's name was officially changed from Schreiner Institute to Schreiner College by the board of trustees in 1973.]

*Schreiner Institute. Schreiner Institute, Kerrville, continued both a high school and a junior college department. The high school curriculum was designed to meet the needs of those preparing for college and was composed mostly of residents; the college curriculum contained the usual courses needed to complete the first two years of college work in all traditional and professional fields. Enrollment was 400 in 1965, 350 of whom could be housed in the school's dormitories. The institute faculty numbered thirty-three in 1965. In the fall of 1974 there were 440 students enrolled in the junior college department; the high school department enrollment was considerably smaller.

In the 1950's and 1960's several new facilities were added to the campus, including a student center with dining rooms, a school store, a snack bar, a swimming pool, recreation rooms, a lounge, a chapel, and publication offices (1958). Two dormitories were completed in 1961 and 1966. A new military science building (1965) and a science building (1966) were constructed, and plans called for further additions of buildings to house the library, student health service, and chapel-auditorium. In 1969 the institute library contained 11,000 volumes.

The institute was the recipient of several large gifts, principally the continued support of the founder's sons, Louis A. and Gustave F. Schreiner,qqv in excess of three million dollars between 1950 and 1965. Gustave F. Schreiner's estate also provided for a permanent endowment. The Moody Foundation of Galveston granted $250,000 for construction of the science building in 1965. Andrew Edington was president of the institution from 1950 to 1971. In October, 1971, Sam M. Junkin became president. In 1973 the school's name was officially changed from Schreiner Institute to Schreiner College. *See also* Presbyterian Education in Texas.

*Schroeder, Texas.

*Schuetze, Julius.

*Schulenburg, Texas. Schulenburg, in Fayette County, is a commercial center for an area of diversified farming. Businesses reported during the 1960's included a milk-processing plant and companies producing corrugated metal pipe, smoked meats, gardening equipment, toys, and fertilizers. There were approximately eighty businesses in 1970. Among the buildings in Schulenburg were a post office, a city hall completed in 1958, and a telephone company building completed in 1962. The town had a large park and reported eight churches in the mid-1960's. Its population was 2,207 in 1960 and 2,294 in 1970, according to the United States census.

Schuler, Anthony J. Anthony J. Schuler was born at St. Mary's, Pennsylvania, on September 20, 1869, the son of Joseph and Albertina (Algeir) Schuler. In 1876 the family moved to Colorado. Schuler received his early education from Father Matz, a missionary; when the priest was transferred to Denver (he later became bishop of Denver), Schuler accompanied him in order to continue his education. In 1886 Schuler entered the Jesuit Order and in June, 1901, was ordained a priest. He served as professor and student prefect at Sacred Heart College in Denver and later served two terms as president of that institution. He also spent six years as pastor of Immaculate Conception Church and chaplain of Hotel Dieu in El Paso.

In 1915 Schuler was appointed bishop of the diocese of El Paso and was consecrated in October of that year. He is known as the first bishop of El Paso, although John J. Brown, S.J., served for six months in that capacity before Schuler's appointment. His diocese covered an area of more than 64,000 square miles in Texas and New Mexico; it was composed of approximately 54,000 Catholics, thirty-one priests, twenty parishes, fifty-eight missions, with hospitals, academies, and parochial schools run by various religious orders of women.

During his twenty-seven years of administration, he built many churches, schools, and other institutions, including St. Patrick's Cathedral, Catholic Community Center, St. Margaret and Sacred Heart orphanages, and St. Joseph's Sanitorium. He founded the *Catholic Weekly* and the *Western American* and persuaded the *Revista Catolica* (a newspaper) to move its offices from Las Vegas to El Paso in December, 1917. He was one of the founders of Associate Charities (later called Welfare Association) and of the Community Chest.

Upon his retirement, December 1, 1942, his diocese numbered 118 priests, fifty parishes, ninety-seven missions, five academies, twelve parochial schools, four hospitals, six orphanages, three day nurseries, a maternity clinic, and two large Catholic Action centers. Bishop Schuler died on June 3, 1944, in Denver. His body was returned to El Paso, where he was buried.

BIBLIOGRAPHY: Catholic Archives, Chancery Office, Austin.

Sister M. Claude Lane, O.P.

*Schumannsville, Texas.

*Schwab City, Texas.

*Schwertner, Texas.

*Science Hall.

*Science Hall, Texas. (Hays County.)

*Science Hall, Texas. (Jasper County.)

Scientific Balloon Flight Station. *See* National Center for Atmospheric Research, Scientific Balloon Flight Station.

*Scioto Belle.

*Scobey, Robert.

⊹Scofield, Cyrus Ingerson.

Score, John Nelson Russell. John Nelson Russell Score, son of John and Katie Marie (Ebrecht) Score, was born in White Church, Missouri, on April 21, 1896. He received the B.A. degree from Scarritt-Morrisville College in Missouri in 1914 and the B.D. degree from Emory University in Georgia in 1916; he attended New College, Edinburgh, Scotland, and the University of Edinburgh in 1919, then received the Th.D. degree from the Pacific School of Religion, Berkeley, California, in 1924. He entered Methodist ministerial and religious work in 1913 and held pastorates and various positions of service and responsibility in the church both in the United States and in Europe.

During World War I, Score served as chaplain with the rank of first lieutenant in the United States Army in 1918–1919. After the war he served as chaplain with the rank of captain in the California National Guard (1925–1926) and later in the Texas National Guard.qv

On June 1, 1942, he became president of Southwestern University, Georgetown, Texas, a position he held until his death. He was a member of the board of trustees of several Methodist institutions and was active in various scholarly societies as well as civic clubs.

He was married to Margaret Ruth Smith on January 12, 1921; they had one son. Score died on September 26, 1949, and was buried in the Lois Perkins chapel on the campus of Southwestern University in Georgetown.

Forrest E. Ward

*Scotland, Texas.

Scots in Texas. Scots, as immigrants to Texas, came singly or in small groups, some as early as 1825, but they had very limited success in establishing colonies, and they dispersed rapidly throughout the population. Several Scots, working both for the U.S. government and Scottish universities, explored and mapped Texas from around 1805 to 1835.

Those settlers who came to stay fought in the Texas Revolution, and they were quickly followed into the new republic by native-born Scots or Americans of Scottish ancestry.

Among noted individuals were the McLennans, who settled in central Texas (*see* McLennan, Neil; McLennan County); George Cupples,qv

prominent early Texas physician; Jesse Chisholm,qv Scot-Cherokee trailblazer and trader; the Camerons (*see* Cameron, Ewen; Cameron, John; Cameron, William; Cameron, William Waldo); and Edmund Duncan Montgomery,qv physician and philosopher.

A number of Scottish stone workers were brought to Texas for the construction of the state capitol qv (*see also* Capitol Boycott) in the 1880's. These granite workers were responsible for much of the work on the present capitol building and other, later, construction around the state.

Although individualistic in business and settlement, Texas Scots were not slow to organize. In 1890, the Universal Order of Scottish Clans organized several lodges in Texas. The Scottish Society of Texas qv was a later organization. Both were active in 1972 and held annual clan gatherings.

John L. Davis

*Scott, Arthur Carroll. *See also* Scott and White Memorial Hospital.

*Scott, James.

*Scott, James.

*Scott, James W.

*Scott, Thomas Morton.

*Scott, William.

*Scott, William Sherley.

*Scott, William Thomas.

Scott, Zachary Thomson. Zachary Thomson Scott, son of Lewis and Abby (Boyle) Scott, was born on December 25, 1880, at Fort Worth. He graduated from the University of Texas Medical School at Galveston in 1903. In 1900, as a medical student, he was responsible for saving the lives of many people trapped by the rising waters of the Galveston flood.qv After graduation he began his practice in Clifton, in Bosque County. In 1909 he moved to Austin, where, with Thomas J. Bennett, he established the Austin Sanitarium and developed a lifelong interest in the Texas Tuberculosis Association. He instituted the sale of Tuberculosis Seals in Texas.

During World War I he served as a lieutenant commander in the navy and was in charge of a unit at the naval hospital in Gulfport, Mississippi. After the war, Scott and Frank C. Gregg established the Scott-Gregg Clinic in Austin in 1923.

Scott married Sallie Lee Masterson on June 2, 1909; they were the parents of two daughters and a son, Zachary Thomson Scott, Jr.,qv who became a well-known actor. Scott died in Austin on January 19, 1964, and was buried in Austin Memorial Park.

Scott, Zachary Thomson, Jr. Zachary Thomson Scott, Jr., the son of Sallie Lee (Masterson) and Zachary Thomson Scott,qv was born in Austin, Texas, on February 21, 1914. His acting career began at Austin High School, where Scott was active in theatrical productions. Later, while attending the University of Texas, he took leading roles in

Curtain Club productions and served as president of that organization; he was also on the track team. He interrupted his schooling at the age of nineteen to work his way to England on a freighter. There he joined a repertory company and for the next three years gained acting experience. He returned to the University of Texas in 1935 and married Elaine Anderson; in 1937 a daughter was born. Scott graduated from the university with a B.A. degree in 1939.

During this period Scott worked as director of the Little Theatre in Austin and taught dramatics at St. Mary's Academy.qv He then gave up dramatic pursuits and worked at various jobs, including that of an oil field worker, but the lure of the stage eventually caused him to move his family to New York. He was soon acting in various Broadway productions.

In 1943 Warner Brothers Studio discovered Scott while he was appearing in *Those Endearing Young Charms*. Signed for the starring role in *The Mask of Dimitrios*, he began a film career that extended through thirty motion pictures. Scott is best remembered for his work in such popular films as *Mildred Pierce*, *The Southerner*, *Hollywood Canteen*, *Danger Signal*, and *Cass Timberlane*. He received an Academy Award nomination for his portrayal in *The Southerner*.

During the 1940's Scott's roles, with the exception of *The Southerner*, were those of a suave, debonair sophisticate, but after 1950 his career broadened. He sang the lead role in a production of *The King and I* and appeared on the London stage in such productions as *Subway in the Sky*. He played numerous television roles and continued to make movies. In 1950 Scott and his wife were divorced; several years later he married actress Ruth Ford, with whom he appeared on Broadway in *Requiem for a Nun*, a play that novelist William Faulkner had written for Mrs. Scott.

He grew ill while he and his wife were doing readings from Faulkner's works at the University of Mississippi in early 1965. On October 3, 1965, Scott died. He was buried at Memorial Park in Austin, Texas.

BIBLIOGRAPHY: Austin *American*, November 5, 1943, November 3, 1953, October 4, 1965; Biographical File, Barker Texas History Center, University of Texas at Austin.

Kenneth E. Lively

*Scott, Texas. (Hidalgo County.)

*Scott, Texas. (Van Zandt County.)

*Scott Branch.

*Scott Creek.

Scott and White Memorial Hospital. Scott and White Memorial Hospital in Temple was established by Dr. Arthur Carroll Scott,qv of Gainesville, who had come to Temple in 1892 as chief surgeon for the Santa Fe Railroad hospital, and Dr. Raleigh R. White qv of Cameron, who became his partner in 1897. In 1904 they established their hospital, first in a converted house, then shortly thereafter in a onetime Catholic convent which be-

came the nucleus of a collection of thirty-one buildings in the fifty-nine years the hospital remained in that location. The hospital was first called the Temple Sanitarium, but in 1923 the name was changed to Scott and White Hospital. Dr. White died in 1917, but Dr. Scott continued with the hospital until his death in 1940. Other early doctors recruited were Dr. O. F. Gober in 1905 and Dr. Claudia Potter in 1906. The original partnership grew into one of the five largest private group medical practices in the United States and has been known to most people simply as Scott and White. Drs. M. W. Sherwood and G. V. Brindley, Sr., who came to work for the partners in 1908 and 1911, respectively, later became partners and cofounders of the Scott, Sherwood, and Brindley Foundation, which now owns the hospital's physical assets.

The hospital was converted to a nonprofit hospital-foundation by its charter of December 23, 1949; a successful fund drive for a new facility followed, and in December, 1963, the hospital moved to its present plant, a 308-bed hospital which in 1972 was valued at more than $17 million. The seven-story hospital has an unusual radial floor plan which gives it a silo effect. The hospital has been a major influence on medicine in the Southwest, pioneering in the concept of private group practice, with medical specialists pooling their talents and working as teams. Scott and White doctors are on salary and, continuing a long held practice, do not collect fees. Professional nurses have been trained there since 1904, and staff physicians and scientists are given time to carry out special research projects and prepare scientific papers. The hospital foundation is guided by a fifteen-man board of nine laymen and six doctors. It is an internationally known hospital-clinic with a large number of patients coming from other states and foreign countries, especially Mexico, for care. Nearly 100,000 patients register annually, and the staff includes more than 120 physicians and scientists plus a 1,400-member working staff. In 1972 a ten-year master plan for expansion called for a $25 million construction program.

BIBLIOGRAPHY: Larry Ingram, "Scott and White," *Texas Star* (October 15, 1972); Subject Files, Barker Texas History Center, University of Texas at Austin.

Scottish Society of Texas. The Scottish Society of Texas, first organized in 1963, represents about fifty Scottish Highland clans in Texas. The organization is a statewide association which sponsors the annual Texas Highland Games each May. For nine successive years the games were held in Austin, but in 1972 they were held at McLennan County Community College in Waco. The games consist of competition in dancing, piping, and athletic events. Judges from outside Texas, members of appropriate official governing societies, decide winners in several different traditional Scottish dances, in bagpipe bands, and in individual piping. The traditional sports events include tossing the caber, tossing the sheaf, and the hammer throw.

There are other games and events for children. A ball and a tartan parade are also featured. A festive two-day affair, the games are open to the public.

Each year the Scottish Society of Texas gives a scholarship to a McLennan County Community College student who can verify a Scottish heritage. The society functions to perpetuate Scottish traditions and to provide fellowship for Scottish Americans so that they will have a continuing awareness of their heritage. In 1972 the society had 110 members; Joe Waring was president, and Harry Gordon, one of the original organizers, served as president emeritus. In addition to the officers, a nine-member board of governors was elected. The official news sheet of the Scottish Society of Texas and the Scots of Austin was *Heather Notes*, edited by Harry Gordon. See *also* Scots in Texas.

*Scotts Creek.

*Scottsville, Texas.

*Scranton, Texas.

Screwmen's Benevolent Association. The Galveston Screwmen's Benevolent Association was a trade union of specialized longshoremen who, with the aid of screwjacks, stowed and packed the bulky cotton bales into the holds of ships before the use of the power cotton compress. Their specialized ability insured an increase in the bale capacity of a ship by 10 to 15 percent, a skill critical to the profitable operation of the shipper.

On the night of September 11, 1866, twenty-three Galveston cotton screwmen met to establish an association similar to the group in New Orleans which had been established in 1850. The very nature of the screwmen's work, equality in the five-man gangs directed by a foreman who performed the same tasks, led to the success of the union. A list of the original thirty-four members, who had signed up before the second meeting, shows only five native-born United States citizens; the others came from Ireland, England, the Scandinavian countries, Scotland, and Germany, and the membership was to retain a foreign-born majority. Qualifications for membership emphasized skill, character, and health, and applicants were subject to the vote of the whole membership, with seven black balls sufficient for rejection. Screwmen had to be hardy men to perform the demanding work, and their exceptional physical strength was a source of group pride and a legend in port cities.

In the beginning the association's main function was concern for the welfare of the membership, with relief for ill members, death benefits, and financial aid to distressed members, rather than for militant economic activities. Dr. Hamilton W. West was retained as the association's physician from 1878 to 1887. Constant concern with a favorable image kept the group from any political or religious involvement, although it was not averse to taking part in public affairs in Galveston if the association's image or its members' welfare were involved. Social activities of the association included picnics, parades, and balls, and some of the members agitated for uniforms or "regalia" for social events.

The Galveston screwmen did not seek any ties with the other screwmen's organizations in Mobile or New Orleans, nor with local labor organizations. They took no part in the Galveston longshoremen's strike in 1885. The association, early on, brought about the standardization of wages at five dollars a day (and later six dollars a day), a working day of nine hours (seven on Sunday or at night), and the enforcement of an earlier ruling that no member could work with or for any person or persons who employed Negroes to work on shipboard. By 1875 most regular screwmen were association members in what amounted to a closed shop, and the association was the largest and strongest labor organization in Galveston. Membership grew from little more than 100 in 1876 to 250 in 1880 and about 325 in 1891.

In 1879 some black longshoremen established the Cotton Jammer's Association, but in 1882 Norris Wright Cuney,qv a leading black businessman, was unable to secure stevedoring contracts for black longshoremen, although during the peak seasons of fall and winter there was a labor shortage. On November 28, 1882, the Screwmen's Benevolent Association called a general holiday for its members in opposition to the appearance of Negro workers in the cotton-screwing trade. Early the next year, however, Cuney finally broke the white longshoremen's virtual monopoly by bringing a number of black longshoremen from New Orleans so that he would have the needed workmen, and he gained the stevedoring contract with the Morgan Lines,qv one of the port's largest cotton shippers.

In March, 1883, a new Negro screwmen's association, the Screwmen's Benevolent Association No. 2, was established, and William L. Moody,qv president of the Galveston Cotton Exchange, was informed that Cuney had both men and tools to screw the cotton for shipping. The first job, however, on the ship *Albion*, on April 2, 1883, resulted in the immediate withdrawal of all white workers from the ship. A strike was called by the white association and a change made in the executive officers from those who were conciliatory to the more militant. In September a close vote within the association brought the men back to work; however, it was not an overwhelming victory for the blacks, for in the late 1880's only Cuney is known to have hired black screwmen.

The association introduced an apprenticeship system in 1885 which resulted in an increased white labor force, thereby gaining a virtual monopoly of the work at the port of Galveston. By 1891, when the association celebrated its twenty-fifth anniversary, its evolution from a benevolent society to a union was complete. During the 1890's certain developments occurred which marked the twilight of the association's quarter-century of successful labor organization. Cotton became an expanding Texas crop and each year a greater number of men was needed for the screwmen work crews; larger and more rapid steel ships began to undermine the actual economic value of cotton screwing. The closed shop went out in 1901, as did, in 1904, the rule limiting to seventy-five the number of bales which could be screwed by a gang in a normal workday; blacks took over larger and larger portions of the work. It was the introduction in Galveston of the high-density cotton compress in 1910 that ended the need for screwmen, and by World War I the screwmen were no longer a part of the necessary work force. In 1902 the association had affiliated with the national longshoremen's union as Local 307, and by 1924 all semblance of its identity was gone.

BIBLIOGRAPHY: James V. Reese, "The Evolution of an Early Texas Union: The Screwmen's Benevolent Association of Galveston, 1866–1891," *Southwestern Historical Quarterly,* LXXV (1971–1972).

*Scroggins, Texas.

*Scull, Sally.

*Scurlock, Mial.

*Scurlock, William. William Scurlock settled in Sabine County (not San Augustine, as stated in Volume II) when he came to Texas in 1834. Although his associations with San Augustine were strong—he was a member of the Masonic Red Land Lodge No. 3 there—census and tax records show that he was a resident of Sabine County; he was buried in the Abner Cemetery in Sabine County.

BIBLIOGRAPHY: *Biographical Directory of the Texan Conventions and Congresses, 1832–1845* (1941); William Tellis Parmer, A History of Freemasonry in San Augustine and Sabine Counties, Texas, Before 1900 (M.A. thesis, University of Texas, 1950).

Helen Gomer Schluter

*Scurry, Richardson A.

*Scurry, Thomas.

*Scurry, William Read. [This title was incorrectly listed in Volume II as Scurry, William Redi. Various printed works differ in the spelling of Scurry's middle name; however, his original signature on the Ordinance of Secession in February, 1861, reads William Read Scurry.]

BIBLIOGRAPHY: Texas Secession Ordinance, February 1, 1861 (Original document, Archives, Texas State Library); "A Declaration of the Causes Which Impel the State of Texas to Secede from the Federal Union," *The Standard* (Clarksville, Red River County), February 23, 1861; Marcus J. Wright (comp.) and Harold B. Simpson (ed.), *Texas in the War 1861–1865* (1965).

*Scurry, Texas.

*Scurry County. Scurry County, in West Texas, was one of the leading mineral-producing counties in Texas, ranking sixth in 1969 when minerals produced (in order of value)—petroleum, natural gas liquids, natural gas, stone, magnesium chloride, and clay—had a total value of $173,221,000. From 1923 to January 1, 1969, over 737 million barrels of oil were produced; by 1973 that total had reached 1,011,915,520 barrels. In the early 1970's Scurry County had an average annual farm income of $12 million, two-thirds of which came from livestock and poultry; the raising of beef cattle was increasing, and cotton, sorghums, and small grains were the chief crops. Major tourist attractions were Lake J. B. Thomas and the Sandstone Canyon Indian pictographs (*see* Rock Art, Indian). The population of Scurry County has been declining since 1950, when it was 22,779. In 1960 the population was 20,369; in 1970 it was 15,760, a 22.6 percent decrease in ten years, according to the United States census.

Scurry's Brigade. *See* Scurry, William Read.

*Sea Breeze, Texas.

*Seabrook, Texas. Seabrook, in Harris County, was incorporated in 1961 and had a mayor-alderman form of municipal government. Considerable damage was done to Seabrook's waterfront area in September, 1961, as a result of Hurricane Carla (*see* Hurricanes in Texas). By 1966, however, a new city hall and a new sewer treatment plant were completed, and paving and drainage projects were under construction. The town had two public schools, a bank, and six churches. In 1970, 100 businesses were reported, and the local economy was directly influenced by area chemical plants, oil production and refining, and NASA qv and its suppliers. The seafood processing industry was also important to the town. In 1970 Seabrook's population was 3,811, according to the United States census. *See also* Houston Standard Metropolitan Statistical Area.

*Seabur, Texas.

*Seadrift, Texas. Seadrift, in Calhoun County, had a 1960 population of 1,082 and a 1970 population of 1,092, according to the United States census. Fifteen businesses were reported in 1970.

*Seagoville, Texas. Seagoville, in Dallas County, had a 1960 population of 3,745 and a 1970 population of 4,390, according to the United States census. The town had 110 businesses in 1970.

*Seagraves, Texas. Seagraves, in northern Gaines County, is a rural commercial center serving a three-county area. Industries producing carbon black and other petroleum and chemical products employed several hundred people. The town reported seventy-two businesses in 1970. In the 1960's Seagraves had a thirty-bed hospital and twelve churches. Of historical interest was the old Santa Fe Railroad station that had been in the town since the early days of the area. The population was 2,307 in 1960 and 2,440 in 1970, according to the United States census.

Seale, Richard. Richard (Uncle Dick) Seale, founder of the oldest Negro church in Texas, was born (in 1797?) in a slave pen in Alexandria, Virginia. The date of his birth is uncertain, but he treasured a silver coin given to him, according to his mother, by General George Washington when the child's crying during a parade attracted Washington's attention.

Uncle Dick acquired some education and became overseer for his master, Joshua Seale, whose plantation was west of Jasper in the Indian Creek community near Bevilport, Jasper County, Texas. A devout Christian, Uncle Dick was interested in the spiritual welfare of his people; about 1850, with Joshua Seale's help, he organized the Dixie Baptist Church for the Negroes of the community, with himself as pastor. Part of the original church still stood in January, 1967, when the structure was awarded a historic building medallion. Uncle Dick died in 1875 and was buried at Indian Creek in the Seale family cemetery.

BIBLIOGRAPHY: William Seale, A History of the Dixie Baptist Church (MS., Dixie Baptist Church, Jasper, Texas); William Seale, Texas Riverman: The Life and Times of Captain Andrew F. Smyth (1966).

William Seale

*Seale, Texas. (Parker County.)

*Seale, Texas. (Robertson County.)

*Seals Creek.

*Seals of Texas.

*Sealy, John.

*Sealy, Texas. Sealy, in south-central Austin County, has an economy based on farming and ranching, although it has several important industries. During the mid-1960's Sealy had a new $250,000 livestock auction center and a rice-drying and -milling plant. Other construction projects included three new churches, a fire station, a water well, and school improvements. In 1970, seventy-five businesses were reported. The 1960 population was 2,328; the 1970 population was 2,685, according to the United States census.

*Searcy, Isham Green. Isham Green Searcy served as a penitentiary commissioner from 1883 to 1885 (not in 1881, as stated in Volume II); he was collector of internal revenue for the Third District of Texas beginning in 1885 (not 1884).

*Seat of Government. See Capitals of Texas.

*Seaton, Texas.

*Seattle, Texas.

*Seawillow, Texas.

*Seay, Frank.

*Sebastian, Texas.

*Sebastopol, Texas.

*Sebree, Texas.

*Secession Convention.

*Secession in Texas.

*Seclusion, Texas.

*Secmoco Indians. The Secmoco Indians are known only from baptismal records of San Antonio de Valero Mission qv at San Antonio. J. R. Swanton listed Secmoco as one of the Coahuiltecan bands. Intermarriage with the Papanac at the mission suggests that the Secmoco were probably from the same areas as the Papanac, that is, northeastern Coahuila and the adjoining part of Texas. Sencase, Sepunco, and Sinicu have been suggested as possible synonyms for Secmoco, but no evidence for these identifications can be found. Swanton listed a similar name, Chemoco (Chimoco), as a Coahuiltecan band, but this resulted from an error. The Chemoco were Indians at San Francisco Solano in California, not at the mission of the same name near Eagle Pass.

BIBLIOGRAPHY: H. E. Bolton, Texas in the Middle Eighteenth Century (1915); F. W. Hodge (ed.), Handbook of American Indians, II (1910); J. R. Swanton, Linguistic Material from the Tribes of Southern Texas and Northeastern Mexico (1940).

T. N. Campbell

*Seco Creek.

*Second Creek.

*Second Creek, Texas. Second Creek, in Burleson County south of Caldwell, was an unincorporated community of ten in the 1960's. Farming was the only occupation.

*Second Yegua Creek.

*Secrest, Washington H.

*Secretary of State. See also State Executive Officers, Compensation of.

*Securities Board, State. See State Securities Board.

*Security, Texas.

*Sedalia, Texas.

*Sedalia Cattle Route.

*Sedwick, Texas.

*Seefield, Texas.

*Seele, Hermann Friedrich. Hermann Friedrich Seele had three sons and two daughters (not three children, as stated in Volume II); one of his sons died in infancy. An early Texas educator, Seele was promoter of the first special school tax in Texas; he was cited posthumously as one of the eighty-four "Heroes and Heroines of Texas Education" during a 1954 centennial celebration of the public schools program. Seele is also remembered as the attorney and secretary for the Citizens Committee of New Braunfels when the heirs of the Veramendi estate brought suit to recover title to the Comal Tract. Seele was given an indefinite leave of absence from his teaching position at the New Braunfels Academy qv in 1878 so that he might represent the people of New Braunfels in the land title case, which was finally decided in favor of the citizens of New Braunfels in 1879. See also Veramendi Estate—New Braunfels.

BIBLIOGRAPHY: Rudolph L. Biesele, The History of the German Settlements in Texas, 1831–1861 (1930); Oscar Haas, "Teacher Seele Granted Leave to Plead Settlers' Land Case," New Braunfels Zeitung-Chronicle, June 27, 1966.

Ruth Seele Aniol

*Seeley Academy. See San Antonio Academy.

*Seep Spring Mountain.

*Segno, Texas.

*Segovia, Texas.

*Seguin, Erasmo.

*Seguin, Juan Nepomuceno. [This title was incorrectly listed in Volume II as Seguin, Juan Nepomucena. The following provides several other corrections in addition to material not included in the Volume II article on Juan Nepomuceno Seguin for the period before 1834 and the period after 1848, when Seguin sought permission to return to Texas from Mexico. Ed.]

Although accounts vary as to Juan Nepomuceno Seguin's exact birthdate (October 27, 28, or 29, 1806), the records of San Fernando de Bexar Cathedral qv show that Seguin was baptized there on November 3, 1806, when he was six days old; this would indicate that he was born October 28, 1806 (not October 27, as stated in Volume II). Juan N. Seguin was married to Maria Gertrudis Flores on January 18, 1826. Three months later Seguin made his first trip to New Orleans, and he was assisted by Stephen F. Austin and his brother James Austin, who alerted Anglo American colonists to lend their aid to Seguin while he journeyed to and from that city.

On April 17, 1848, after six years in Mexico, Seguin wrote Sam Houston that he desired to return to his native Texas and that he was willing to face the consequences of having served in the Mexican Army. The exact date of his return is not known; however, by November 22, 1849, he was in San Antonio, where his infant daughter was baptized. The families of Erasmo Seguin qv and Juan N. Seguin were noted in the Bexar County census of 1850. On August 16, 1852, Juan N. Seguin was elected justice of the peace of precinct 8 of Bexar County. Seguin said in his *Personal Memoirs* (1858) that he was left alone upon his return because his enemies had already destroyed him politically.

In 1855 Seguin was appointed to a committee to draw the Democratic party platform of Bexar County; in that same year he constructed a ranch home near Floresville, in an area which later became Wilson County. In 1862 he moved to Monterrey to accept a position in the army of Benito Juárez, and he served as a colonel until 1871. In 1873 he returned to Wilson County, where he applied, successfully, for a pension. By 1883 Juan N. Seguin had moved to Mexico again, where he lived with his son, Santiago, who was the mayor of Nuevo Laredo. On March 16, 1887, Seguin applied for a pension from the Mexican Army for services rendered, but he was refused on the grounds that he had been a Texas rebel; also, there was no record of his Mexican military service because he had served as an irregular cavalry commander.

Juan Nepomuceno Seguin, considered a traitor at one time by Texas and at another time by Mexico, died in Nuevo Laredo on August 27, 1890 (not 1889, as stated in Volume II). Because of his service to Texas in gaining independence from Mexico, on September 20, 1974, the remains of Seguin were transferred from the burial place in Nuevo Laredo, Mexico, to the city of Seguin, Texas, to be reinterred there.

Richard G. Santos

*Seguin, Texas. Seguin, seat of Guadalupe County, was founded in 1838 (not 1858, as stated in Volume II). [Some later printings of Volume II contain this correction.] Seguin grew rapidly in the years between 1950 and 1960, the population increasing from 9,733 to 14,299. There were approximately thirty industrial firms there by 1972, producing structural steel, aircraft parts, fiber glass cloth, brick, and industrial insulation; textiles, furniture, and food products were also produced. In 1970 Seguin had approximately 370 businesses, three banks, twenty-five churches, a sixty-bed hospital, and a four-year college, Texas Lutheran. Recreational facilities were provided by nearby Max Starcke Park on the Guadalupe River and Lake McQueeney. The 1970 population was 15,934, an 11.4 percent increase over 1960, according to the United States census.

Segujulapem Indians. In the middle eighteenth century the Segujulapem Indians, who apparently spoke a Coahuiltecan language, had settlements on the north bank of the Rio Grande in what is now Cameron and Hidalgo counties. The name is said to mean "those who live in the huisaches" (shrubs).

BIBLIOGRAPHY: W. Jiménez Moreno, "Tribus e idiomas del Norte de México," *El Norte de México y el Sur de Estados Unidos* (1944); G. Saldívar, *Los Indios de Tamaulipas* (1943).

T. N. Campbell

Segutmapacam Indians. The Segutmapacam (Sagutmapacam) Indians, apparently Coahuiltecans, lived along the lower Rio Grande. In the middle eighteenth century their principal settlements were on the south bank of the river near present Reynosa, Tamaulipas. They seem also to have foraged and camped on the Texas side of the Rio Grande.

BIBLIOGRAPHY: W. Jiménez Moreno, "Tribus e idiomas del Norte de México," *El Norte de México y el Sur de Estados Unidos* (1944); G. Saldívar, *Los Indios de Tamaulipas* (1943).

T. N. Campbell

*Sejita, Texas.

*Selden, Texas.

*Selfs, Texas.

*Selkirk, William.

*Sellman, Texas.

*Sells Creek.

*Selma, Texas.

*Selman, John.

*Selman City, Texas.

*Semicolon Court. One of the judges serving on the Supreme Court of Texas during the Reconstruction qv period (derisively termed the Semicolon Court) was Colbert Caldwell qv (not Coldwell, as shown in Volume II).

*Seminole, Texas. Seminole, seat of Gaines County, completed a new post office and a county park in the 1950's; it also remodeled its courthouse. The park facilities included an amphitheater, a community center, and a nine-hole golf course. Among the 146 businesses reported during 1970 were manufacturers of mattresses, petrochemical products, ready-mix concrete, sheet metal products, and oil field equipment. From 1950 to 1960 Seminole had a 64.8 percent increase in population, from 3,479 in 1950 to 5,737 in 1960. The next ten years showed a 12.7 percent decline, with a 1970 population of 5,007, according to the United States census.

*Seminole Canyon.

*Seminole Draw.

*Seminole Indians.

*Semonan Indians. The Semonan Indians are known from a single Spanish document (1690), which indicates only that these Indians lived somewhere between Monclova, Coahuila, and eastern Texas. J. R. Swanton doubtfully included them in his list of Coahuiltecan bands. The Semonan have been equated with the Tsepehoen and the Serecoutcha, two groups named in records of the La Salle Expedition,qv but no evidence other than presumed sound correspondences has been presented to support these identifications. The location and affiliations of the Semonan remain undetermined.
BIBLIOGRAPHY: F. W. Hodge (ed.), *Handbook of American Indians*, II (1910); J. R. Swanton, *Linguistic Material from the Tribes of Southern Texas and Northeastern Mexico* (1940).

T. N. Campbell

*Sempronius, Texas.

*Senate, Texas.

Sencase Indians. In 1737 this otherwise unidentified group of Indians was recorded at San Antonio de Valero Mission qv in San Antonio. Sencase may be a variant of some other name, possibly Siansi, the name of a Coahuiltecan group at the same mission, but this equivalence cannot be proved. It has also been suggested that Sencase is a badly garbled version of Secmoco, another Coahuiltecan band reported at this mission during the same period. This too lacks proof.
BIBLIOGRAPHY: H. E. Bolton, *Texas in the Middle Eighteenth Century* (1915); F. W. Hodge (ed.), *Handbook of American Indians*, II (1910); J. R. Swanton, *Linguistic Material from the Tribes of Southern Texas and Northeastern Mexico* (1940).

T. N. Campbell

*Senecú del Sur. *See* San Antonio de Senecú.

*Senior, Texas.

*Senterfitt, Texas.

Separate Property Law. Though unmarried adult men and women in Texas have full control of their property, married men and women are subject to the restraints of the community property law,qv and married women in Texas were long under severe restraints in dealing with their separate property. Since the Constitution of 1845,qv

every constitution of Texas, except the Constitution of 1869,qv has defined the separate property of married women as that property acquired before marriage and acquired during marriage by gift, devise, or descent. All other property of husband and wife acquired during marriage is community property. This constitutional provision (Article XVI, Section 15 of the Constitution of 1876 qv) has its antecedents in a Texas statute of 1840 and ultimately the law of Spain (Castile).

Prior to 1913 the management of the separate property of both the husband and wife was vested in the husband, but the wife's consent to disposition of her separate property was required. As a further protection to the married woman in making a disposition of her realty, it was required that the transaction be explained to her and that she make a sworn acknowledgement of the transaction, in both instances out of the presence of her husband. This requirement was instituted in 1846, repealed in part in 1963, and wholly repealed in 1967. With the legislative reform of 1913, the married woman acquired the management of her separate property, though the husband was required to join in conveyances of realty and transfers of securities. Full power of management of separate property of married women was enacted in 1963.

Since 1848, and in almost every respect since 1840, Texas statutes have defined the separate property of husbands in the same terms as that of wives. Separate property of a spouse is not subject to any liability incurred by the other spouse. As a Texas married woman lacked general contractual capacity prior to 1963, her separate property was rarely made subject to contractual liability.
BIBLIOGRAPHY: William O. Huie, *The Community Property Law of Texas* (1951); Ocie Speer, *A Treatise of the Law of Marital Rights in Texas* (1929); Joseph W. McKnight, "Recodification and Reform of Matrimonial Property Law," *Texas Bar Journal*, XXIX (1966); Joseph W. McKnight (reviewer of book by W. O. Huie), "*Texas Cases and Materials on the Law of Marital Property Rights*," *Texas Law Review*, XLVI (1967).

Joseph W McKnight

Sepinpacam Indians. In the middle eighteenth century the Sepinpacam Indians lived on the north bank of the Rio Grande in what is now Cameron and Hidalgo counties. The name, which is said to mean "salt makers," suggests that this was one of the Coahuiltecan bands that produced salt at La Sal Vieja, a salt lake in nearby Willacy County.
BIBLIOGRAPHY: W. Jiménez Moreno, "Tribus e idiomas del Norte de México," *El Norte de México y el Sur de Estados Unidos* (1944); G. Saldivar, *Los Indios de Tamaulipas* (1943).

T. N. Campbell

Sepuncó Indians. This otherwise unidentified group was represented at San Antonio de Valero Mission qv of San Antonio in 1730. It has been suggested that this name may be a variant of Secmoco, but no proof of this has been presented.
BIBLIOGRAPHY: F. W. Hodge (ed.), *Handbook of American Indians*, II (1910).

T. N. Campbell

*Serbin, Texas.

Serecoutcha Indians. The Serecoutcha (Fercontecha, Fercouteha, Tsepechoen frercutea) Indians are known only from records of the La Salle Expedition,qv which indicate that in the late seventeenth century these Indians lived inland well to the north or northeast of Matagorda Bay, probably between the Brazos and Trinity rivers. In some Spanish sources the names of two separate groups were combined to form Tsepechoen frercutea. In the French sources Tsepehoen and Fercouteha are separated by a comma. The Serecoutcha have been equated with the Semonan, but no evidence can be found to support this identification. The linguistic and cultural affiliations of the Serecoutcha remain undetermined.

BIBLIOGRAPHY: I. J. Cox (ed.), *The Journeys of Réné Robert Cavelier, Sieur de La Salle,* II (1906); F. W. Hodge (ed.), *Handbook of American Indians,* II (1910); P. Margry, *Découvertes et établissements des Français dans l'ouest et dans le sud de l'Amérique Septentrionale,* III (1879); H. R. Stiles (ed.), *Joutel's Journal of La Salle's Last Voyage, 1684–7* (1906).

T. N. Campbell

*Serecoutcha Village. See also Serecoutcha Indians.

*Sesteadero Creek.

*Setag, Texas.

*Seth, Texas.

*Seth Ward College.

*Settlers Creek.

*Seven-D Ranch.

*Seven Hundred Springs.

*Seven Knobs.

*Seven Mile Mesa.

*Seven Oaks, Texas.

Seven Pines, Texas. Seven Pines, in southern Upshur County and on the Gregg County line, became a town in 1931 during the oil boom (though the community was founded earlier); it was named for seven large pine trees at the site. In subsequent years the town dwindled to a few small businesses, and the seven pine trees were cut down. The one hundred inhabitants of the town in the 1960's were mostly oil field workers.

*Seven Points Academy.

*Seven Sisters, Texas.

Seventh-day Adventist Churches in Texas. *See* Adventist Churches in Texas.

Sevier, Clara Driscoll. *See* Driscoll, Clara.

*Sevier, Henry Hulme.

Seward, Samuel. Samuel Seward came to Texas around 1828 and purchased land on the Brazos River in Cole's Settlement, later named Independence, in Washington County. Seward is said to have bought the estate of the merchant Colbert Baker, who died prior to 1837. The old Seward home at Independence, probably the first large two-story house in the community, was built in 1855 of hand-hewn cedar. It has been photographed, and architectural drawings have been made of it by the Historic American Buildings Survey of the United States Department of the Interior.

BIBLIOGRAPHY: Worth S. Ray, *Austin Colony Pioneers* (1949); Picture File, Barker Texas History Center, University of Texas at Austin.

Seward Junction, Texas. Seward Junction, in western Williamson County at the intersection of highways 183 and 29, had two filling stations, a garage, and a population of about thirty-five in 1967. The area was first settled in 1869 by William Robinson Seward, who had helped Noah Smithwick qv build and operate a mill near Burnet in the late 1850's; Seward later served in the Home Guard near Lampasas.

*Sexton, Franklin Barlow.

*Sexton, Texas.

*Sexton City, Texas.

*Seymore, Texas.

*Seymour, Texas. Seymour, seat and chief commercial center of Baylor County, had a 1960 population of 3,789 and a 1970 population of 3,469, according to the United States census. An agribusiness center, the town had a soil testing laboratory and reported well over one hundred businesses in the early 1970's. Seymour also had a hospital and a city park.

*Shackelford, John.

*Shackelford County. Shackelford County, with a predominately petroleum and ranching economy, produced 125,872,246 barrels of oil between 1910 and January 1, 1973. In the late 1960's and early 1970's over 90 percent of the average annual agricultural income of $4.5 million was derived from beef cattle, with small grains, cotton, and sorghums contributing the remainder. A county hospital was completed in 1950 and a county library in 1961. Major tourist attractions included Fort Griffin qv (*see also* Parks, State), the Fort Griffin Fandangle qv in June, a January stock show, and hunting and fishing. The 1960 population of Shackelford County was 3,990; the 1970 population was 3,323, according to the United States census.

*Shady Grove, Texas. (Cherokee County.)

*Shady Grove, Texas. (Dallas County.)

*Shady Grove, Texas. (Hopkins County.)

*Shady Grove, Texas. (Upshur County.)

Shady Shores, Texas. Shady Shores, a residential suburb southeast of Denton in Denton County, was incorporated in October, 1960. It is crossed by U.S. Highway 77 (Interstate 35) and reaches the shore of Garza-Little Elm Reservoir. The 1970 population was 543, according to the United States census.

*Shafter, William Rufus.

*Shafter, Texas.

*Shafter Canyon.

*Shafter Lake.

Shafter Lake, Texas. Shafter Lake, in north Andrews County, was a growing town on the shores of Shafter Lake in the early 1900's. Its post office was established on July 19, 1907. During the decade 1905–1915 the town had a population of several hundred, a bank, two hotels, several general stores, two drugstores, a blacksmith shop, a Masonic lodge, three churches, and a six-room concrete block school building. Shafter Lake reached its peak, with a population of at least 500, about 1910, when the town of Andrews, ten miles to the southeast, vied with Shafter Lake for the county seat. A feud between the two towns developed. Controversy arose over each town's attempt to acquire additional qualified voters for the county seat election. In June, 1910, the election was held, and Shafter Lake lost the county seat to Andrews.

After the loss, Shafter Lake began to decline. The Llano Estacado and Pacific Railroad was projected, but only one mile was ever graded, and the newspaper publisher left Shafter Lake to found the Lubbock *Avalanche*. On January 31, 1929, the post office was discontinued. In 1962 only the K. H. Irwin house and foundations of the village buildings remained.

BIBLIOGRAPHY: *Andrews Golden Jubilee, 1910–1960* (1960).

Grover C. Ramsey

*Shaler, William.

*Shallowater, Texas. Shallowater, in northwestern Lubbock County, was a farm marketing center with processing and storage facilities. The town was incorporated in 1955 with a mayor-alderman form of government. During the 1960's Shallowater reported five churches, a school, a bank, a library, and a newspaper. In 1970 there were approximately thirty businesses. The 1960 population was 1,001; the 1970 population was 1,339, according to the United States census. *See also* Lubbock Standard Metropolitan Statistical Area.

*Shamrock, Texas. Shamrock, in Wheeler County, had a 1960 population of 3,113 and a 1970 population of 2,644, according to the United States census. The city had 116 businesses in 1970.

*Shanghai, Texas.

*Shannon, William R.

*Shannon, Texas.

*Shannon Creek.

*Sharon, Texas.

*Sharp, John.

*Sharp, Walter Benona.

*Sharp, Texas.

*Sharp Mountain.

*Sharpe, Redford.

Sharpstown Stock Fraud Scandal. Texas went through one of its traditional and periodic governmental scandals during 1971–1972, when federal accusations and then a series of state charges were leveled against nearly two dozen state officials and former state officials. Before normalcy returned, Texas politics had taken a slight shift to the left and had undergone a thorough housecleaning: the incumbent governor was labeled an unindicted co-conspirator in a bribery case and lost his bid for reelection; the incumbent Speaker of the House of Representatives and two associates were convicted felons; a popular three-term attorney general lost his job; an aggressive lieutenant governor's career was shattered; and half of the legislature was either intimidated out or voted out of office.

The scandal centered, initially, on charges that state officials had made profitable quick-turnover bank-financed stock purchases in return for the passage of legislation desired by the financier, Houston businessman Frank W. Sharp. By the time the stock fraud scandal died down, state officials also had been charged with numerous other offenses—including nepotism and use of state-owned stamps to buy a pickup truck.

In the 1972 electoral aftermath, incumbent Democrats were the big losers, although at the top level of officialdom it was a matter of conservative Democrats being replaced by less conservative Democrats. Using the scandal as a springboard, less conservative Democrats and Republicans carried the "reform" battle cry and gained a stronger foothold in the legislature, too.

The Democrats, defensively, charged that the whole scandal atmosphere in Texas was a national Republican plot, originated in the Nixon Administration's Department of Justice. But before the smoke cleared, Will Wilson, an ex-Democratic Texas attorney general, by then one of Texas' top Republicans in the federal government, was hounded from his position as chief of the criminal division of the Department of Justice because of his own business dealings with Frank Sharp.

The political tumult that was to become known as the Sharpstown stock fraud scandal started out meekly, though symbolically, on the day Texas Democrats were gathering in Austin to celebrate their 1970 election victories and inaugurate their top officials. Attorneys for the United States Securities and Exchange Commission (SEC), late in the afternoon of January 18, 1971, filed a lawsuit in Dallas federal court alleging stock fraud against former Democratic state attorney general Waggoner Carr, former state insurance commissioner John Osorio, Frank Sharp, and a number of other defendants. The civil suit also was filed against Sharp's corporations, including the Sharpstown State Bank and National Bankers Life Insurance Corporation.

But it was deep down in the supporting material of the suit that the SEC lawyers hid the political bombshells. There it was alleged that Governor Preston Smith, state Democratic chairman and state banking board member Elmer Baum, House Speaker Gus Mutscher, Jr., Representative Tommy Shannon of Fort Worth, Rush McGinty (an aide to Mutscher), and others—none of them charged in the SEC's suit—had, in effect, been bribed. The plot, according to the SEC, was hatched by Sharp himself, who wanted passage of new state bank deposit insurance legislation that would benefit his own financial empire.

The SEC said the scheme was for Sharp to grant more than $600,000 in loans from Sharpstown State Bank to the state officials, with the money then used to buy National Bankers Life stock, which would later be resold at huge profits as Sharp artificially inflated the value of his insurance company's stock.

The quarter-of-a-million-dollar profits were, in fact, made. But they weren't arranged by Sharp, the SEC said, until after Governor Smith made it possible for Sharp's bank bills to be considered at a special legislative session in September, 1969, and Mutscher and Shannon then hurriedly pushed the bills through the legislature. (Smith later vetoed the bills on the advice of the state's top bank law experts, but not until he and Baum had made their profits on the bank loan-stock purchase deal.)

The state officials denied all the charges, asserting that they had obtained the bank loans and made the stock purchases purely as business transactions unrelated to the passage of Sharp's bank bills. But as the spring of 1971 droned into summer, political pressure mounted on Smith, Baum, Mutscher, and Shannon—even on Lieutenant Governor Ben Barnes, who had been connected in several tangential ways to Frank Sharp, his companies, and the bank bills.

By the fall of 1971, when Mutscher and his associates were indicted, the politics of 1972 had begun to take shape. Incumbents moved as far away as possible, politically, from the "old system" and the current state leaders. New candidates came forward, some of them literally with no governmental experience, under a "throw the rascals out" banner.

Mutscher, Shannon, and McGinty were tried in Abilene, on a change of venue from Austin because of adverse pretrial publicity, in February and March, 1972. The indictment charged the three men with conspiracy to accept a bribe from Sharp—and District Attorney R. O. (Bob) Smith of Austin said during the trial that Governor Smith was an unindicted co-conspirator. Prosecutors acknowledged from the start that the case would be based entirely on circumstantial evidence, which produced legal technicalities inexplicable to laymen. But the jury needed only 140 minutes on March 15, 1972, after exposure to hundreds of pounds and hours of evidence, to find the Mutscher group guilty. The next day, at the request of the defendants, Judge J. Neil Daniel assessed punishment at five years' probation.

The conviction of the Abilene Three dramatically advanced the momentum of the "reform" movement, coming less than three months before primary elections at which more legislative seats were contested than in any year since World War II. (Redistricting decisions by the federal courts added to the high percentage of electoral challenges, but the Sharpstown scandal generally was credited as the main factor.)

In statewide races "reform" candidates also dominated. The Democratic governor's race saw two newcomers—liberal legislator Frances (Sissy) Farenthold of Corpus Christi and conservative rancher-banker Dolph Briscoe of Uvalde—run far ahead of Governor Smith, who was seeking a third term as governor, and Lieutenant Governor Barnes, whose seemingly inexorable rise to political prominence was ended when his reputation was tainted by the scandal. Briscoe defeated Mrs. Farenthold in the runoff and later was elected governor; but Republican candidate Henry Grover of Houston and La Raza Unida qv candidate Ramsey Muniz of Waco drew enough votes to make Briscoe Texas' first "minority" governor.

For the state's second top executive branch job, voters chose moderate Houston newspaper executive William P. Hobby, Jr., over seven other Democratic candidates as lieutenant governor—also on a "reform" theme. Reform-minded moderate Democrat John Luke Hill of Houston, a former secretary of state, left a successful private law practice to defeat the popular three-term attorney general, Crawford Martin,qv who had been criticized for his handling of the stock fraud scandal and for his own relationship with Frank Sharp.

The Democratic primary and the general election of 1972 also produced a striking change in the legislature's membership, including a half-new House roster and a higher-than-normal turnover in the Senate. Most of the newcomers were committed to "reform" in some fashion, regardless of their ideological persuasion. The voters simultaneously indicated that their confidence in the legislature had been restored to some extent, because they approved in November, 1972, an amendment allowing the legislature to sit as a constitutional convention in 1974. (The convention failed by three votes on July 30, 1974, to approve a proposed new constitution for the voters to consider. See Constitutional Convention of 1974.)

The final impact of the stock fraud scandal on Texas politics occurred during the regular session of the legislature in 1973. The lawmakers, led by new House Speaker Price Daniel, Jr., of Liberty, a moderate and son of a former governor, with active support from Attorney General Hill and Lieutenant Governor Hobby, and with verbal encouragement from Governor Briscoe, passed a series of far-reaching reform laws. Among other subjects, the legislation required state officials to disclose their sources of income, forced candidates to make public more details about their campaign finances, opened up most governmental records to citizen scrutiny, expanded the requirement for open meetings of governmental policy-making agencies, and imposed new disclosure regulations on paid lobbyists. See also Political Parties.

BIBLIOGRAPHY: Sam Kinch, Jr., and Ben Procter, *Texas Under A Cloud* (1972); Charles Deaton, *The Year They Threw The Rascals Out* (1973).

Sam Kinch, Jr.

Shary, John H. John H. Shary, son of Austrian emigrants Robert and Rose (Wazob) Shary, was born on a Saline County, Nebraska, farm on March 2, 1872. After graduation from Crete High School, he attended Doane College. Shary became a registered pharmacist at the age of eighteen, and after four years in the drug business, he joined a California redwood lumber firm for which he traveled in most of the United States and in Canada.

Shary became interested in land investments and development, particularly in Texas. Between 1906 and 1910 he and George H. Paul developed 250,-000 acres in the cotton-producing area around Corpus Christi, operating from out-of-state offices; special trains brought prospective purchasers to South Texas weekly.

In 1912 Shary became interested in the Lower Rio Grande Valley. He was impressed with the commercial potential of citrus-growing experiments by such men as A. P. Wright, J. K. Robertson, and H. H. Banker. In the next few years he bought and subdivided more than 50,000 acres of land in the Lower Rio Grande Valley and attempted to install an irrigation system. Jesse Holmon Jones ᵠᵛ helped him finance this venture. He bought most of the early experimental citrus groves, especially grapefruit, and from them he harvested some of the early commercial citrus crops after World War I. After earlier efforts to standardize the marketing of citrus crops had failed, Shary and other leading citrus producers succeeded in establishing the Texas Citrus Fruit Growers Exchange. In 1923 Shary built the first commercial citrus-packing plant in the area.

Shary headed numerous commercial firms, including banks, land companies, and newspapers, and he was a director of the Intercoastal Canal Association (see Gulf Intracoastal Waterway) and the St. Louis, Brownsville, and Mexico Railway Company.

Shary married Mary O'Brien, and they lived at Sharyland, near Mission, Texas. They also maintained homes at Omaha, Nebraska, and Branson, Missouri. Their only child, Marialice, married Allan Shivers, governor of Texas from 1949 to 1957. Shary died on November 6, 1945, in San Antonio; he was buried in a small chapel at Sharyland.

BIBLIOGRAPHY: Brownsville *Herald*, May 10, 1936; G. C. Parrish, A History of the Rio Grande Valley Citrus Industry (M.A. thesis, Texas A&I University, 1940).

Weldon Hart

*Sharyland, Texas. Sharyland, in southern Hidalgo County, between Mission and McAllen, was named for John H. Shary ᵠᵛ (not John W. Shary, as stated in Volume II).

*Shatto, Texas.

*Shavano, Texas.

*Shaw, James.

*Shaw, James B. James B. Shaw's estate, Woodlawn, became the property of the Pease family when Elisha Marshall Pease ᵠᵛ acquired it in a bill of sale executed on June 13, 1859. The Pease family used the name Woodlawn and did not rename

the estate Enfield (as stated in Volume II); the name Enfield was later given to the property around the mansion when the Pease heirs developed it as a real estate subdivision; Governor Allan Shivers bought Woodlawn (then known as the Pease Mansion) in 1956.

James B. Shaw, the original owner of the mansion, apparently did not die until sometime after April, 1883 (not in the 1870's, as stated in Volume II).

BIBLIOGRAPHY: August Watkins Harris, *Minor and Major Mansions in Early Austin, A Sequel* (1958); Austin *Statesman*, July 10, 1971; Pease-Graham-Niles Family Papers (MS., Austin-Travis County Collection, Austin Public Library).

Katherine Hart

*Shaw, Jim.

Shaw, John William. John William Shaw was born on December 12, 1863, son of Patrick and Elizabeth (Smith) Shaw, in Mobile, Alabama. After obtaining his early education in the Mobile schools, he entered the diocesan seminary at Navan, County Meath, Ireland. He attended the North American College, Rome, from 1882 to 1888, and he was ordained there on May 26, 1888.

He served in various parishes of the Mobile diocese and was its chancellor from 1896 to 1910. He was appointed coadjutor bishop of San Antonio and was consecrated on April 14, 1910. He succeeded to the See of San Antonio in 1911.

The founding of St. John's Seminary might be considered his greatest contribution to the diocese, but of no less significance was the opening of the old Spanish missions for public worship. This was the first step towards the preservation and restoration of these missions since the beginning of the Civil War.

Upon the death of Archbishop Blenk in 1918, Shaw was appointed archbishop of New Orleans. Shaw died on November 2, 1934.

BIBLIOGRAPHY: Catholic Archives, Chancery Office, Austin.

Sister M. Claude Lane, O.P.

*Shaw, William.

*Shaw Bend, Texas. (Colorado County.)

*Shaw Bend, Texas. (San Saba County.)

*Shawnee, Texas.

*Shawnee Creek.

*Shawnee Indians.

*Shawnee Trail.

*Shaws Creek.

*Shaw's Ranch, Texas.

Shearer, Gordon Kent. Gordon Kent Shearer, one of Texas' leading newspapermen, was born on January 3, 1880, in Altoona, Pennsylvania. He grew up in Pennsylvania, where he and his wife Rebecca were married, before moving to Galveston, Texas, in the early 1900's. As a teen-ager he had worked on a Philadelphia newspaper before coming to Texas, and he continued in that career on the Galveston *News* ᵠᵛ and several other Texas newspapers. At one time he published the Harlingen *Star*. Shearer became the capitol correspondent for the Scripps-Howard newspaper chain, but he was perhaps best known for his service as bureau chief for the United Press in Austin. He opened that office in 1927 and worked there for twenty years. His column, "Under the Dome," became a popular political feature. Walter Cronkite, well-known national television newsman, worked under Shearer and credited much of his early journalistic training to him. Shearer retired from newspaper work on December 31, 1947; the following year he became executive secretary of the State Parks Board;qv he was historian-research director for that board until he retired in 1961. Shearer died on May 31, 1971, in Austin and was buried in Austin Memorial Park. He was survived by one son.

BIBLIOGRAPHY: Biographical File, Barker Texas History Center, University of Texas at Austin.

*Shearn, Charles.

*Sheep Peak.

*Sheep Ranching. Texas continued to be the leading state in sheep and wool production during the 1960's and 1970's, although the total number of sheep declined from 6,063,797 in 1960 to 3,214,000 in 1973. There were approximately 14,000 Texas sheep ranchers in 1973; two thirds of the sheep were raised in west-central Texas, with Concho, Val Verde, Crockett, Pecos, and Tom Green counties the leading producers. San Angelo was the largest sheep and wool market in the nation (*see* San Angelo Standard Metropolitan Statistical Area).

BIBLIOGRAPHY: *Texas Almanac* (1963, 1973).

*Sheep Wars.

*Sheffield, Texas.

Sheffy, Lester Fields. Lester Fields Sheffy, son of W. B. and Alice (Sherwood) Sheffy, was born March 27, 1887, at Henrietta, Texas. In 1889 the family moved to Plainview, where Sheffy attended public schools. He attended Clarendon College before receiving a B.A. degree from Southwestern University in 1911 and an M.A. degree from the University of Texas in 1914. In 1923–1924 Sheffy did additional graduate work at the University of Chicago; he was awarded the Litt.D. degree by Austin College, Sherman, in 1937. Beginning his career in 1911, Sheffy served as superintendent of public schools at Stratford, Matador, and Wellington. In 1918 he joined the faculty of West Texas State Normal College (now West Texas State University) as professor of history and head of the department, a post held until his retirement in 1957.

Sheffy was a leader in the formation of the Panhandle-Plains Historical Society qv in 1921, was elected its first president, served the society as executive secretary from 1930 to 1953, and was reelected president in 1954; he edited the *Panhandle-Plains Historical Review* for eighteen years. He was active in the drive to secure funds for construction of the Panhandle-Plains Historical Museum qv and was a fellow of the Texas State Historical Association.qv Sheffy's publications included *The*

Life and Times of Timothy Dwight Hobart, 1855–1935 (1950); *The Francklyn Land and Cattle Company* (1963); and (with Ima Christina Barlow and Alyce McWilliams) *Texas* (1954). On July 26, 1911, Sheffy married Carrie Virginia Smith of Clarendon. He died on November 23, 1967, at Canyon and was buried in Plainview Cemetery.

Frederick W. Rathjen

*Shelby, David.

*Shelby, Joseph Orville. *See* Shelby Expedition.

Shelby, Thomas Hall. Thomas Hall Shelby, son of John McNitt and Josephine (Jackson) Shelby, was born in Henderson County, Texas, on June 22, 1881. At an early age he moved with his family to Wilbarger County, where he was graduated from Vernon High School. He received his B.A. degree from the University of Texas in 1907 and his M.A. degree from the University of Chicago in 1921. From 1913 to 1916 he was a professor of education at Sam Houston Normal Institute (now Sam Houston State University). After teaching and serving in administrative capacities in Texas public schools, in 1920 he became director of the extension service at the University of Texas; in 1925 he became dean of the Division of Extension and professor of education at the university, serving in this capacity until 1951. As dean, Shelby initiated extension programs which enabled thousands of teachers to complete undergraduate and graduate degrees; he gave vigorous leadership to the development of adult education in Texas.

Shelby was a life member of the Texas State Teachers Association qv and was president of that organization in 1919. He served as president of the National University Extension Association in 1929 and was named a member of the White House Conference in 1933.

A Methodist, Shelby was married to Dora Ethel Beasley on December 22, 1907; they were the parents of two children. He died at his home in Austin on November 3, 1963, and was buried in Oakwood Cemetery.

BIBLIOGRAPHY: *Who's Who In America* (1948).

Norris A. Hiett

*Shelby, Texas.

*Shelby County. Shelby County has an economy based primarily on timber, poultry, and cattle. In 1969 the eight active lumber mills produced 38,912,000 board-feet of lumber from the county's forests, which covered approximately 68 percent of the total land area. By 1970 most of the average annual agricultural income of $30 million was derived from the poultry industry, cattle, and crops. Over thirty-eight million broilers and twelve million dozen eggs were produced annually. The Toledo Bend Reservoir,qv completed in 1967, supplied water and recreational facilities for most of the county, and Sabine National Forest qv was also a tourist attraction. The 1960 population was 20,-479; the 1970 population was 19,672, according to the United States census.

*Shelby Expedition.

*Shelbyville, Texas.

*Sheldon, Texas. Sheldon, an unincorporated town in Harris County, had a 1970 population of 1,665, according to the United States census.

*Shell, Texas.

*Shell Mountain.

*Shelley, Nathan George.

*Shelving Rock.

*Shep, Texas.

*Shepard, Seth.

*Shepherd, William M.

*Shepherd, Texas. Shepherd, in San Jacinto County, was incorporated and had a population of 928 in 1970, according to the United States census.

*Shepherds Creek.

*Shepherd's Valley, Texas.

*Sheppard, John Levi.

*Sheppard, Morris.

*Sheppard Air Force Base. Since 1952 Sheppard Air Force Base has conducted training through three basic schools: the 3750th Technical School, the U.S. Air Force School of Health Care Sciences, and the 3630th Flying Training Wing. The largest and oldest school, the 3750th Technical School, trains personnel in aircraft maintenance, comptrollerships, transportation, communication, missiles, civil engineering, and field training.

The aircraft maintenance school, transferred to the base in 1949, became the largest such facility in the U.S. Air Force when fighter aircraft were added in 1969. During the 1960's Sheppard was the major center for Titan and Atlas intercontinental ballistic missile training and for Thor and Jupiter intermediate range ballistic missile training, but by 1969 all missile training except the Titan II training was phased out. Civil engineering training began at Sheppard in 1958, and the field and mobile training school was added in 1959.

The U. S. Air Force School of Health Care Sciences was located at Sheppard in 1966; it offered training in dentistry, medicine, nursing, veterinary medicine, biomedical science, and health services administration. In 1971 this was the only medical service school in the U.S. Air Force, and in that year a physicians' assistants program was added to the curriculum.

The 3630th Flying Training Wing conducted two undergraduate pilot training programs, one for the West German Air Force and another for the South Vietnamese Air Force; these programs began in 1966 and 1971, respectively. A helicopter pilot training school was in operation at Sheppard from 1965 to 1971. The Strategic Air Command had an operational wing at Sheppard from 1960 to 1965; in 1969 it became a tenant organization at Sheppard.

Other tenant units at Sheppard in 1971 were communications and weather squadrons, an aerospace rescue and recovery service detachment, a special investigations office, and two auditor general detachments.

During the 1960's more than $40 million was spent on permanent construction, such as service clubs, chapels, a gymnasium, composite dormitories, swimming pools, and a 300-bed hospital. Most of the original World War II barracks were replaced or remodeled. Sheppard Air Force Base encompassed an area of 5,082 acres valued at $115 million in 1971. Population at Sheppard in 1960 was 13,861, and in 1971 it was 17,601. The base was located about five miles north of Wichita Falls.

*Shepton, Texas.

Sheridan, Anne. Anne Sheridan, film actress, was born on February 21, 1915, in Denton, Texas, and christened Clara Lou Sheridan. For a brief period of time she attended North Texas State Teachers College (now North Texas State University). In 1933, as one of thirty-three young women chosen to promote a Paramount film by taking part in a beauty contest, she won a screen contract. Her first five pictures were westerns, and publicity releases soon billed her as the "oomph girl" of the movies. In 1939 she was under contract to Warner Brothers and soon thereafter reached stardom. One of her best known roles was in *The Man Who Came to Dinner*, with Monty Wooley and Jimmy Durante. Other major films in which she starred with leading Hollywood actors included *King's Row*, *The Unfaithful* (opposite Zachary Thompson Scott, Jr.ᵃᵛ), *Angels with Dirty Faces*, and *George Washington Slept Here*. In 1959 she turned to the stage and toured in the play *Kind Sir*. Her career in movies and television spanned more than thirty years.

Miss Sheridan was thrice married, to S. Edward Norris in 1936, George Brent in 1942, and Scott McKay in 1966. She died in Hollywood Hills, California, on January 21, 1967.

BIBLIOGRAPHY: Austin *American*, January 22, 1967; New York *Times*, January 22, 23, 1967.

*Sheridan, Philip Henry.

*Sheridan, Texas.

*Sheriff. *See also* County and Precinct Officers, Terms of.

*Sherley, Texas.

*Sherman, Sidney.

*Sherman, William Tecumseh.

*Sherman, Texas. Sherman, at the intersection of U.S. highways 75 and 82, is the seat of Grayson County. The city continued to be an industrial, commercial, and educational center during the 1960's. Sherman supported 516 businesses in 1970. Businesses included firms manufacturing surgical bandages, business machines, aluminum products, truck bodies, construction machinery, cottonseed products, asphalt pipe, and boats; the processing of grains, food, and petroleum were other Sherman enterprises. In addition to two regular hospitals, the city had a hospital devoted to the care of crippled children. Austin College and St. Joseph's Academy were located in the town, and Perrin Air Force Base qv was nearby. Population was 24,-988 in 1960; the 1970 population was 29,061, according to the United States census. *See also* Sherman-Denison Standard Metropolitan Statistical Area.

*Sherman County. Sherman County, in the Texas Panhandle and on the Oklahoma border, is among leading Texas counties in wheat production and cattle feeding. During the 1960's wheat production often exceeded 2,000,000 bushels annually and in 1967 totaled 3,222,900 bushels. Two-thirds of the $39 million average annual farm income in the early 1970's was from livestock; 200,000 cattle were fed in 1972. Sherman County irrigates over 245,000 acres. Experiments in raising sugar beets were begun early in the decade, and pinto beans were introduced as a new crop during that period. The county supported a library and the Stratford Cemetery Association. An exhibit and livestock show barn was completed during the 1960's. Sherman County had a 1960 population of 2,605 and a 1970 population of 3,657, a 40.4 percent increase, according to the United States census.

*Sherman, Denison, and Dallas Railway Company.

Sherman-Denison Standard Metropolitan Statistical Area. The Sherman-Denison Standard Metropolitan Statistical Area, composed of Grayson County in north-central Texas, was designated in April, 1967, when the populations of the two principal cities, Sherman and Denison, each reached approximately 26,000. Grayson County, a territory of 927 square miles of level to rolling terrain, had a 1970 population of 83,225, according to the United States census. The economy of the area was dependent primarily on the agricultural income from the whole county along with the business and industrial facilities of Sherman and Denison. The average annual farm income of the area during the early 1970's was approximately $15 million, with beef cattle and poultry the major source of income. Prime agricultural commodities were corn, cotton, grain, peanuts, and dairy foods.

Over 159 million barrels of oil were produced in the county from 1930 to 1973. Firms in the area manufactured machinery, surgical bandages, aluminum products, cottonseed products, asphalt pipe, boats, furniture, cotton textiles, and transit pipe. Retail sales in 1970 were over $121 million.

A four-year liberal arts school, Austin College, is located in Sherman, and Grayson County Junior College is in Denison. St. Joseph's Academy is also located in Sherman. Tourist and recreational facilities in the area are Lake Texoma and Hagerman National Wildlife Refuge.qqv The house where President Dwight David Eisenhower qv was born is in Denison, and the Eisenhower State Recreation Park (*see* Parks, State) is near Denison Dam. Per-

rin Air Force Base qv near Sherman was the major military establishment in the area until it was deactivated on June 30, 1970.

Other incorporated towns in the area (with 1970 population figures) are Whitesboro (2,927), Van Alstyne (1,981), Whitewright (1,742), Howe (1,359), Bells (778), Collinsville (768), Pottsboro (748), Gunter (647), Tom Beam (540), Tioga (456), Sadler (309), and Southmayd (222). *See also* Standard Metropolitan Statistical Areas in Texas.

*Sherman, Shreveport, and Southern Railroad Company.

*Sherry, Texas.

*Sherwood, Texas. Sherwood, in Irion County, remained the county seat until an election was held on September 7, 1936; the seat was removed to Mertzon in that year (not in 1910, as stated in Volume II). The results were questioned in court, but the election was decreed valid, and by 1937 bids were taken for a new courthouse in Mertzon. In 1971 the estimated population of Sherwood was forty-seven.

BIBLIOGRAPHY: Leta Crawford, *A History of Irion County* (1966).

*Shettles, Elijah L.

*Shields, Texas.

Shiloh, Texas. (Burleson County.) In 1966 Shiloh, in western Burleson County, was a small unincorporated farming community with a population of ten.

*Shiloh, Texas. (Denton County.)

*Shiloh, Texas. (DeWitt County.)

*Shiloh, Texas. (Limestone County.)

*Shiloh, Texas. (Rusk County.)

*Shiloh, Texas. (Williamson County.)

*Shilow Baptist Institute.

*Shin Oak Mountain.

*Shiner, Texas. Shiner, in Lavaca County, had a 1960 population of 1,945 and a 1970 population of 2,102, according to the United States census. The city had sixty businesses in 1970.

*Shingle Hills.

*Shipbuilding. With the close of World War II, the Texas shipbuilding industry reconverted its yards to peacetime production, sharply lowering employment and output. In 1943 two major Texas shipyards employed 35,000 workers; in 1963 all twenty-three yards in the state employed a total of about 4,500. The value of output in the latter year was approximately seventy million dollars, including some twenty million dollars each in the construction of non-propelled ships (principally oil and chemical barges) and in ship repair projects, and about ten million dollars in the building of self-propelled ships. Some yards were also producing fabricated metal products and industrial heating equipment.

About ten shipyards of substantial size were operating in Texas ports during 1968, half of these in the Beaumont-Port Arthur-Orange area and most of the remainder in the Houston-Galveston area. Several of these yards, in addition to constructing ships and barges, have specialized in building off-shore drilling platforms for the petroleum industry.

Boat manufacturing, though a much smaller industry than shipbuilding, grew dramatically in the state during the 1950's and 1960's with the increased interest in recreational boating. By 1963 the state had eighty-five boatbuilding plants employing a total of 1,200 workers. Production value was approximately seven million dollars in outboard motorboats, and there was a comparable aggregate value in the production of inboard motorboats, sailboats, rowboats, and other small craft. All the state's largest boat plants have been established since 1945. These large plants, as well as most of the small ones, fabricated boats of fiberglass-reinforced plastic, and many also built sheet-aluminum boats. Wood and laminated-wood boats, while still produced in Texas, accounted for a decreasing share of the output.

The state's largest boatbuilding plants in 1968 were located in Austin, Plano, Lewisville, Channelview, and Rockport, all in or near metropolitan areas where boat ownership has been high. Boats registered in 1965 by the Texas State Highway Department qv (those powered by over ten horsepower) totaled 197,104, with 33,102 in Harris County, 26,521 in Dallas County, 15,901 in Tarrant County, 9,305 in Bexar County, 7,373 in Jefferson County, 5,436 in Nueces County, 5,259 in Travis County, and the remaining 94,207 in various counties around the state.

Robert H. Ryan

*Shipman, Daniel.

*Shipman, Moses.

*Shipping, Ocean. See Ocean Shipping.

*Shiro, Texas.

*Shive, Texas. Shive, in west-central Hamilton County, had a post office from January 18, 1884, when Robert Shive was appointed postmaster, to November 30, 1936, when the mail was ordered to Hamilton (not from 1900 to 1930, as stated in Volume II). The post office was in a store operated by Robert Shive and his brother James W. Shive. Settled in the mid-1870's, Shive had a school, Union Hill, by 1883. The first German settlers came in 1885, changing somewhat the community's culture. By 1908 Shive had four churches, four stores, and a hotel. In 1970 it had two businesses, a church, and an estimated population of sixty-one.

Kathryne Baker Witty

*Shoal Creek.

*Shockley, Texas.

*Shoe Peg Mountain.

*Sholar, Texas. See Eagle Mills, Texas.

*Shook's Chapel, Texas.

Shoreacres, Texas. Shoreacres, in southeastern Harris County, was incorporated in 1949 and had a mayor-alderman form of city government. The city was zoned as residential only. During the 1960's water and sewage system improvements and additions were made. The 1950 population was 183. The 1960 population of 518 had increased to 1,872 by 1970, a 261.4 percent increase, according to the United States census. See also Houston Standard Metropolitan Statistical Area.

*Shores Creek.

*Short, Daniel McDowell.

*Short Canyon.

*Short Creek.

*Shorthorn Cattle.

*Shovel Mountain.

*Shreveport, Houston, and Gulf Railroad Company.

*Shrimp Fishing. See Marine Resources.

*Shumard, Benjamin Franklin. Benjamin Franklin Shumard's brother was G. G. Shumard (not G. C. Shumard, as stated in Volume II).

*Shumla, Texas.

*Shumla Canyon.

Siacucha Indians. The Siacucha Indians were one of twenty Indian groups that joined Juan Domínguez de Mendoza qv on his expedition from El Paso to the vicinity of present San Angelo in 1683–1684. Since Mendoza did not indicate at what point the Siacucha joined his party, it is impossible to determine their range or affiliations. However, the Indians between the Pecos River and the San Angelo area were being hard pressed by Apache at this time, and it seems likely that the Siacucha ranged between these two localities.

BIBLIOGRAPHY: H. E. Bolton (ed.), *Spanish Exploration in the Southwest, 1542–1706* (1916).

T. N. Campbell

*Siaguan Indians. In the late seventeenth century the Siaguan (Chiguan, Sciaguan, Scipxam, Xiahuan) Indians lived along the Rio Sabinas of northern Coahuila and on the great bend of the Nueces River northeast of Eagle Pass, presumably in the area covered by present Dimmit and Zavala counties. Siaguan was one of the Coahuiltecan bands for whom missions San Juan Bautista and San Francisco Solano qqv were established in northeastern Coahuila (vicinity of present Eagle Pass). Later the Siaguan were also at the nearby mission of San Bernardo. qv Apparently some Siaguan followed San Francisco Solano Mission when it was moved to San Antonio in 1718 and became known as San Antonio de Valero Mission. qv Baptismal and marriage records show that the Siaguan were present at that mission as late as 1760.

BIBLIOGRAPHY: H. E. Bolton, *Texas in the Middle Eighteenth Century* (1915); J. A. Dabbs, "The Texas Missions in 1785," *Preliminary Studies of the Texas Catholic Historical Society*, III (1940); F. W. Hodge (ed.), *Handbook of American Indians*, II (1910); J. R.

Swanton, *Linguistic Material from the Tribes of Southern Texas and Northeastern Mexico* (1940).

T. N. Campbell

Siansi Indians. In the early eighteenth century the Siansi Indians, who appear to have spoken a Coahuiltecan language, were reported at San Francisco Solano Mission qv (south of the Rio Grande near present Eagle Pass). When this mission was moved to San Antonio and became known as San Antonio de Valero Mission,qv the Siansi moved with it. It has been suggested that Siansi and Sencase are variants of the name Secmoco, but this has not been proved.

BIBLIOGRAPHY: H. E. Bolton, *Texas in the Middle Eighteenth Century* (1915); F. W. Hodge (ed.), *Handbook of American Indians*, II (1910); J. R. Swanton, *Linguistic Material from the Tribes of Southern Texas and Northeastern Mexico* (1940).

T. N. Campbell

*Sibley, Henry Hopkins. *See also* Sibley's Brigade.

*Sibley, John.

Sibley's Brigade. Sibley's Brigade was formed in August and September, 1861, in San Antonio, Texas, by Henry Hopkins Sibley.qv In June, 1861, Sibley, a former U.S. Army officer stationed in New Mexico, traveled to Richmond, Virginia, to enlist Confederate government support for his plan to raise a volunteer force and drive Federal troops from the New Mexico Territory. By promising to maintain his forces in the field without burdening the Southern treasury, he won President Jefferson Davis' qv approval. Commissioned a brigadier general on July 5, 1861, Sibley returned to San Antonio, where he recruited and trained three regiments—the 4th, 5th, and 7th Texas Cavalry regiments. The march to Fort Bliss,qv Texas, began on October 22, 1861; the regiments departed San Antonio at two-week intervals and completed the journey by mid-January, 1862.

Sibley's Brigade, reinforced by troops at Fort Bliss and numbering about 2,500 men, first occupied the Mesilla Valley of southern New Mexico and then advanced on Fort Craig, a Federal post on the Rio Grande, about midway between El Paso, Texas, and Albuquerque, New Mexico. Finding the post too well fortified, Sibley, by now a sick man, moved his force on toward the New Mexico capital. However, the Federal garrison at Fort Craig, under Colonel Edward R. S. Canby,qv sallied forth to block the invaders. In the resulting battle of Valverde (February 21, 1862), the Texans, under the immediate command of Colonel Thomas Green,qv defeated the smaller Federal force, but failed to capture Fort Craig.

Although the brigade occupied Albuquerque and Santa Fe without opposition, it failed to capture needed Federal supplies. Neither did the Confederates win the territorial population to their cause. In late March, 1862, 700 Confederate troops, under Lieutenant Colonel William Read Scurry,qv advanced northeast toward Fort Union (about twenty miles north of Las Vegas), the other major Federal post in New Mexico Territory. They encountered about 1,300 Federal troops, mostly Colorado volunteers, in Glorieta Pass. In a series of skirmishes and battles (March 26–28, 1862), Confederate forces won the field but suffered the irreplaceable loss of their supply train. Casualties on both sides were heavy.

When Colonel Canby's troops from Fort Craig and Colonel Gabriel R. Paul's men from Fort Union joined forces in early April, Sibley's Brigade, now with few supplies and little ammunition, was forced to choose between fighting its enemy, superior in numbers and equipment, and abandoning the campaign. After burying eight bronze cannon in Albuquerque, the Texans made their way down the Rio Grande, through the San Mateo Mountains, and back into Texas. By the campaign's end, Sibley's Brigade had suffered about 40 percent casualties, including about 500 dead. Disease and the hostile environment accounted for more deaths than Federal arms. Sibley's Brigade returned to San Antonio in the summer of 1862 and was disbanded.

There are indications that General Sibley had conceived the New Mexico campaign as the first phase of a grandiose scheme to conquer California and northern Mexico for the Confederacy.

BIBLIOGRAPHY: Martin Hardwick Hall, *Sibley's New Mexico Campaign* (1960); David B. Gracy II (ed.), "New Mexico Campaign Letters to Frank Starr, 1861–1862," *Texas Military History*, IV (1964).

Sico Indians. This name is known from a single Spanish missionary report (1691), which indicates that the Sico were neighbors of the Hasinai tribes of eastern Texas. It is said that the Sico lived an unspecified distance southwest of the Hasinai. The affiliations of the Sico remain undetermined.

BIBLIOGRAPHY: J. R. Swanton, *Source Material on the History and Ethnology of the Caddo Indians* (1942).

T. N. Campbell

Sicujulampaguet Indians. The Sicujulampaguet (Sicajayanpaguet, Sicalasyampaquet) Indians lived on the lower Rio Grande. In the middle eighteenth century some of their settlements were in what is now southern Hidalgo County.

BIBLIOGRAPHY: W. Jiménez Moreno, "Tribus e idiomas del Norte de México," *El Norte de México y el Sur de Estados Unidos* (1944); G. Saldivar, *Los Indios de Tamaulipas* (1943).

T. N. Campbell

Sideck, Anthony. Anthony Sideck (sometimes found as Sydeck, Saidet, Sydoc, *etc.*), probably a brother of John Baptist Sideck and Peter Sideck,qqv was a native of Louisiana. He moved to the area of Refugio, Texas, in the 1820's and settled on a ranch near John B. Sideck on the San Antonio River near Mesquite Landing. Soon afterwards the families of Peter Teal, Nicholas Fagan, and Edward McDonough, all with the Power and Hewetson Colony,qv settled in the same area. Members of four nearby Indian tribes, the Lipans, Tonkawas, Comanches, and Karankawas, worked on the settlers' ranches. The lands of Anthony and John B. Sideck were across the river from those of Don Carlos de la Garza.

Anthony Sideck, along with John B. Sideck, joined the advance guard that went to Goliad after word was received from John Joseph Linn qv that a company of Matagorda planters led by George Morse Collinsworth qv was advancing to capture Goliad, a feat accomplished on October 10, 1835 (see Goliad Campaign of 1835). Anthony Sideck was with Amon B. King's qv foray just before General José Urrea's qv assault against the Texas colonists who had fled to Nuestra Señora del Refugio Mission qv (see Goliad Campaign of 1836). He was either with the stragglers from King's company who were picked up by Urrea or with Hugh McDonald Frazer's qv company at the battle of Coleto;qv Sideck was saved from the Goliad Massacre qv by the intervention of his neighbor, Mexican officer Captain Carlos de la Garza.

He was married to Catherine (Catharine) Fagan, daughter of Nicholas Fagan. The Refugio 1850 (September) census lists "Anthony Sydoc," thirty-five years old, his wife, Catharine, twenty-five, and five children, eight years old and younger. Anthony Sideck died probably soon after that census was taken.

BIBLIOGRAPHY: Hobart Huson, *Refugio: A Comprehensive History of Refugio County from Aboriginal Times to 1953* (1953); Records (MS., General Land Office); Deed Records, Probate Minutes, Refugio County.

Talmadge Buller

Sideck, John Baptist. John Baptist Sideck (sometimes found as Sydeck, Saidet, etc.) was born in Natchitoches, Louisiana, on October 8, 1790, the son of Ursula (Schleyter [or] Chletre) and Pierre Clavis (François) Sideck. During the War of 1812 he served as a private in the Louisiana militia. In 1819, possibly as a member of the Long Expedition,qv he moved to Texas and settled on the north bank of the San Antonio River at Mesquite Landing, perhaps the earliest settler in the area before the Power and Hewetson Colony qv was established, an area which later included the families of Nicholas Fagan, Peter Teal, and Edward McDonough; a neighboring rancher was Don Carlos de la Garza. In his application for land in 1834 Sideck stated that he had been in Texas fifteen years prior to that date. His brother, Peter Sideck, and Anthony Sideck qqv (probably his brother) moved with him or came shortly thereafter.

John B. Sideck and Anthony Sideck were with the advance guard that went to Goliad after John Joseph Linn's qv message that a company of Matagorda planters under George Morse Collinsworth qv was on the way to capture Goliad, which they succeeded in doing on October 10, 1835 (see Goliad Campaign of 1835). John B. Sideck was listed as being with the group of colonists who were in Nuestra Señora del Refugio Mission qv (see Goliad Campaign of 1836) under the command of William Ward qv when it was attacked by General José Urrea,qv March 14, 1836, and was with Hugh McDonald Frazer's qv company at the battle of Co-

leto.qv Although ordered shot, he was spared in the Goliad Massacre qv through the intercession of his neighboring rancher, Mexican officer Captain Carlos de la Garza. Sideck died in 1842, and Peter Teal was granted letters of administration upon the estate.

BIBLIOGRAPHY: Hobart Huson, *Refugio: A Comprehensive History of Refugio County from Aboriginal Times to 1953* (1953); Marion J. S. Pierson, *Louisiana Soldiers in the War of 1812* (1963); Records (MS., General Land Office); Records (Immaculate Conception Church, Natchitoches, Louisiana).

Talmadge Buller

Sideck, Peter. Peter Sideck (sometimes found as Sydeck, Saidet, Sydix, etc.), an early settler in Refugio County, was born on September 20, 1874, in Natchitoches, Louisiana, the son of Ursula (Schleyter [or] Chletre) and Pierre Clavis (François) Sideck. Around 1803 he probably moved from Natchitoches to the vicinity of Opelousas, Louisiana. In 1807 a Peter Sideck unsuccessfully sought land at Prairie Anacoco, east of the Sabine River, within the Neutral Ground.qv On August 22, 1811, a land certificate was issued by the commissioners of the Western District of Orleans Territory to a Peter Sydix for two hundred acres on Beaver Creek near Bayou Chicot in St. Landre Parish. He served as a private in the militia in Louisiana during the War of 1812. It was alleged that he participated in filibustering expeditions into Texas. He had a headright certificate issued by the board of land commissioners for Montgomery County.

It is not known exactly when he moved to Refugio County, where his brother John Baptist Sideck qv resided. It appears that Peter was killed in an Indian raid on the San Antonio River in Refugio County in 1838.

BIBLIOGRAPHY: Hobart Huson, *Refugio: A Comprehensive History of Refugio County from Aboriginal Times to 1953* (1953); Probate Minutes (Refugio County); Records (Immaculate Conception Church, Natchitoches, Louisiana); Veterans' Files, War of 1812 (National Archives, Washington, D.C.).

Talmadge Buller

✦**Sidney, Texas.**

✦**Siemering, August.**

✦**Sierra Aguja.**

✦**Sierra Blanca, Texas.** Sierra Blanca, seat of Hudspeth County, was a tourist stop and commercial center for the surrounding ranching area. In the mountain standard time zone, the town was so close to the time zone boundary that its citizens operated on both mountain standard time and central standard time. At times the post office and railroads operated on central standard time while the courthouse, tourist facilities, and businesses dealing with western firms used mountain standard time. To alleviate confusion, announcements and invitations very often stipulated both times. The population of Sierra Blanca in 1970 was approximately 600.

✦**Sierra Blanca Range.**

✦**Sierra del Carmen.**

✦**Sierra de Cristo Rey.**

✦**Sierra Diablo.**

*Sierra Madera.

*Sierra Prieta.

*Sierra Tinaja Pinta.

*Sierra Vieja.

*Sierrita de la Cruz.

*Sieur de la Salle. See La Salle, René Robert Cavelier, Sieur de.

*Sigler, William N.

*Sign Cutting.

*Signal Hill, Texas.

*Signal Mountain.

*Signal Peak.

Siguipam Indians. The Siguipam Indians, who were at the San Francisco de la Espada Mission qv of San Antonio in the first half of the eighteenth century, have usually been equated with the Siupam, but certain evidence does not support this. The Siguipam are said to have lived on the coast, whereas the Siupam are linked with the interior, especially the area around present San Antonio, where they were associated with the Xarame and Sijame, who ranged westward from San Antonio when first known and were never mentioned as living near the coast. This suggests that Siguipam represents a coastal group whose name was rendered differently in other sources, possibly as Segujulapem, Segutmapacam, or Sicujulampaguet. These names refer to three presumably Coahuiltecan bands who lived on the lower Rio Grande near the coast during the eighteenth century.

BIBLIOGRAPHY: F. W. Hodge (ed.), Handbook of American Indians, II (1910); W. Jiménez Moreno, "Tribus e idiomas del Norte de México," El Norte de México y el Sur de Estados Unidos (1944); G. Saldivar, Los Indios de Tamaulipas (1943).

T. N. Campbell

*Sijame Indians. It has been suggested that the language of the Sijame (Cijame, Hijame, Xixame, Zihame) Indians was Tonkawan instead of Coahuiltecan, but the evidence seems to favor a Coahuiltecan linguistic affiliation. As early as 1698 some Sijame, whose name is said to mean "fish," entered Mission Santo Nombre de Jesus de Peyotes near present Villa Union in northeastern Coahuila, which is a good indication that they originally lived in an area of Coahuiltecan speech. In 1709 Sijame were seen at San Pedro Springs in San Antonio, where they were encamped with Xarame and Siupam, both of which were Coahuiltecan in speech. In 1716 Sijame were encountered with Tonkawan and Coahuiltecan bands at Ranchería Grande qv on the Brazos River of central Texas (Milam County area). The Sijame from Ranchería Grande began to enter San Antonio de Valero Mission qv at San Antonio in 1719, but much later, after 1740, they entered this mission in greater numbers. It was after 1740 that Tonkawan groups began to enter the same mission, and it is upon this and the earlier association with Tonkawans at Ranchería Grande that the argument for Tonkawan linguistic affiliation is based. The much earlier record of Sijame in

Coahuila indicates that they were one of many Coahuiltecan bands that fled northeastward into Texas to escape European domination and Apache pressure. Some Sijame continued to live at San Antonio de Valero until as late as 1763, and in 1777 Sijame were reported as the dominant group at Mission Santo Nombre de Jesus de Peyotes in Coahuila. It is evident that the history of the Sijame has two phases, one in Texas and the other in northeastern Mexico. J. R. Swanton listed Sijame and Hijame as separate Coahuiltecan bands, but the available data do not support this distinction.

BIBLIOGRAPHY: H. E. Bolton, Texas in the Middle Eighteenth Century (1915); F. W. Hodge (ed.), Handbook of American Indians, I (1907), II (1910); J. R. Swanton, Linguistic Material from the Tribes of Southern Texas and Northeastern Mexico (1940); R. C. Troike, "Researches in Coahuiltecan Ethnography," Bulletin of the Texas Archeological Society, 30 (1961).

T. N. Campbell

Sikes, Chase Baromeo. See Baromeo, Chase.

*Sikes, Texas.

*Silas, Texas.

*Siloam, Texas.

*Silsbee, Texas. Silsbee, in eastern Hardin County, reported six public schools, two banks, one library, fifteen churches, two newspapers, and one radio station during the mid-1960's. The town was the county's major commercial center for oil, agriculture, and lumbering, and it reported at least eleven manufacturers; businesses totaled approximately 145 in 1970. The population almost doubled in a decade, from 3,179 in 1950 to 6,277 in 1960. By 1970 the population had further increased by 15.8 percent, to 7,271, according to the United States census.

*Silver, Texas.

*Silver City, Texas. (Fannin County.)

*Silver City, Texas. (Milam County.)

*Silver City, Texas. (Navarro County.)

*Silver City, Texas. (Red River County.)

*Silver Creek.

*Silver Lake.

*Silver Lake, Texas.

*Silver and Silver Mining. No production of silver in Texas was reported by the United States Bureau of Mines after 1952, when 4,672 troy ounces valued at $4,228 were produced. Total production of silver during the period 1885–1952 was 33,303,173 fine ounces valued at $23,446,564.

BIBLIOGRAPHY: Texas Almanac (1963, 1973).

*Silver Valley, Texas.

*Silverton, Texas. Silverton, seat of Briscoe County, is a commercial center for the farms and ranches of the area. The manufacture of clay products and irrigation supplies are major local industries; there were approximately fifty-two businesses located there by 1970, and the town supported a hospital and a county newspaper. The population of Silverton increased from 857 in 1950 to 1,098 in

1960; the population in 1970 was 1,026, according to the United States census.

*Simars de Bellisle, François. *See* De Bellisle, François Simars.

*Simkins, Eldred James.

*Simkins, William Stewart.

*Simmons, David Andrew.

Simmons, Frank Elmer. Frank Elmer Simmons was born on January 15, 1880, near Friend, Nebraska. His family moved to Texas, arriving in Walker County early in 1883; in July of the same year they settled in McLennan County. Simmons attended Walker School until 1892, then Haunted Hill School, and for a short time in 1900, Salado College. He taught school in the Horn community south of McGregor in 1901. That same year he married Laura Alice Stapp.

He began his writing career as Moody correspondent for the McGregor *News* in 1895 and made numerous journalistic and historical contributions in the Coryell-McLennan county area. In 1934 Simmons was appointed by the state parks board to compile the history of Mother Neff State Park (*see* Parks, State) in Coryell County. Other published works include *History of Coryell County* (1936), *Coryell County History Stories* (1948), and a volume of poetry, *Legend of Haunted Hill and Other Poems* (1948). He began collecting snails after he had reached the age of 70, learning to classify them and furnishing detailed locality data for the state, national, and international museums where he placed them. Simmons died in his home in Oglesby on January 9, 1966.

Laura Simmons

Simmons, George Albert. George Albert Simmons, son of James William and Mary (Barry) Simmons, was born at Decatur, Texas, on January 9, 1892. After his mother's death in 1905, the family moved to Dallas, where he attended a Catholic high school; he studied for two years at the University of Dallas. Simmons entered the cottonseed-processing business and managed a cotton oil mill first at Snyder, Oklahoma, and then in Quanah, Texas. He moved to Lubbock in 1930 to manage the Lubbock Cotton Oil Mill, one of many mills and gins operated in West Texas and New Mexico by the Simmons Cotton Oil Mills, a family-owned company. A national leader in the cotton-processing industry, he served as director (1938–1954) and president (1939–1940) of the Texas Cottonseed Crushers' Association and as director (1946–1954) of the National Cotton Council. In 1952 he became chairman of the national council's beltwide pink bollworm qv committee. He was also a longtime benefactor of Texas Tech's Department of Agriculture.

Simmons married Maizie Bailey in 1914, and they had two sons. After the death of his first wife in 1932, he married Mrs. Hazel James in 1935. He died on March 22, 1954, and was buried at Lubbock.

BIBLIOGRAPHY: Seymour V. Connor (ed.), *Builders of the Southwest* (1959).

Lawrence L. Graves

*Simmons, James Wright.

Simmons, Marshall Lee. Lee Simmons (first name, Marshall, seldom used), son of D. A. and Kate B. (Swilling) Simmons, was born in Linden, Cass County, Texas, on September 9, 1873. In 1885 the family moved to Sherman in Grayson County where Lee attended public schools; he completed two years at Austin College and three years at the University of Texas, although he did not complete the requirements for a degree. He was a farmer-stockman in the early 1900's and operated a mule barn in Sherman.

In November, 1912, he was elected sheriff of Grayson County, but before he could take office he was seriously wounded in an assassination attempt. He recovered and was later elected to a second term in 1914.

Governor Pat Morris Neff qv appointed him a member of a commission to study the prison system qv of the state in 1923; the commission's report, given by Simmons to the legislature, recommended that the prison system take full advantage of its physical and human resources in the way of production of goods and to decrease the idleness of prisoners, recommendations later employed. He was appointed to the prison board by Governor Daniel James Moody, Jr.,qv and served from 1927 to 1930. In April, 1930, Simmons became general manager of the prison system with headquarters at the prison in Huntsville. The Texas Prison Rodeo qv was organized under his leadership, and improvements in prison conditions and new prison services were initiated during his term. It was he who conceived the plan which put the Texas Rangers qv on the trail of Clyde Barrow and Bonnie Parker.qqv He left the prison system in 1935 and became district clerk for the Eastern District, United States District Court; from 1943 to 1953 he was Texas-Louisiana representative in Denison for the Southwest Power Administration. Later he wrote his memoirs, entitled *Assignment Huntsville*. Simmons was married to Nola Stark in 1895, and they had one daughter. He died while on a trip to Austin on October 12, 1957, and was buried in Sherman.

BIBLIOGRAPHY: Lee Simmons, *Assignment Huntsville* (1957); Biographical File, Barker Texas History Center, University of Texas at Austin.

*Simmons, William.

*Simmons, Texas.

*Simmons Branch.

*Simmons Creek.

*Simmons University. *See* Hardin-Simmons University.

*Simms, Texas. (Bowie County.)

Simms, Texas. (Deaf Smith County.) Simms, in north-central Deaf Smith County, is not an organized community. In 1911 a school was built on land owned by Anna R. Simms. At that location in the 1960's there was a community house for the use of the farming area.

*Simms Creek.

*Simonds, Frederic William.

*Simonds, Texas.

*Simonton, Texas.

*Simpson, Friench.

Simpson, George Allen. George Allen Simpson, one of the last of the buffalo hunters, was born on February 28, 1852, in Boone County, Missouri, the son of John and Marietta (Foster) Simpson. He lived with his parents in Nebraska and then in Colorado. From there they moved to South Texas in 1867, where they proposed to drive cattle to Colorado markets by way of the Goodnight-Loving Trail,qv but the venture failed because of the danger of Indians and thieves. Simpson's father died when he was a boy, and his mother married a Mr. Gibbs, who had two sons. Simpson joined with Gibbs and his sons in forming a buffalo-hunting outfit. They hunted in the vicinity of Fort Elliott,qv where they stacked hundreds of buffalo hides at what came to be known as Hidetown, near Fort Elliott [see Mobeetie (Old), Texas], to be sent to Dodge City, where they were to be shipped to the tanneries of the East. After leaving Gibbs' outfit, Simpson hunted buffalo on his own until none were left in the area.

Simpson married Sylvania Woods at Fort Elliott on October 5, 1877; they had seven children and settled down on a farm near Canadian, Texas, where they produced vegetables and supplies for the local market and raised a few cattle. Simpson died on November 21, 1937, and was buried at Canadian.

BIBLIOGRAPHY: Files of the Panhandle-Plains Historical Museum, Canyon.

L. F. Sheffy

*Simpson, John Nicholas.

*Simpson, John P.

*Simpson, Morgan H.

*Simpson Creek.

*Simpsonville, Texas. (Matagorda County.)

Simpsonville, Texas. (Upshur County.) Simpsonville, a settlement in northwestern Upshur County, was first established as Chelsa, and a post office was opened on January 19, 1858. The name was changed to Simpsonville on April 22, 1858, beginning a long period during which the post office was discontinued and reestablished several times; it was discontinued on November 5, 1866, reestablished on November 11, 1867, discontinued on May 19, 1879, reestablished on June 16, 1879, and discontinued on August 15, 1906. Late in 1913 citizens of Simpsonville made application for another post office, but since a community in Matagorda County had established a post office with that same name about 1910, the name Simpsonville was no longer acceptable for the settlement in Upshur County. The citizens' group renamed their community Thomas in honor of O. Thomas,

who had been postmaster in the community for many years; the Thomas post office was established on February 14, 1914, and was discontinued on February 20, 1954. *See also* Thomas, Texas.

B. D. Tucker

*Sims, Bartlett.

*Sims, Charles H.

Sims, Orland LeCompte. Orland LeCompte Sims was born September 20, 1881, in Pierce City, Missouri, the son of Dunlap E. and Ella (LeCompte) Sims, who brought him to Concho County, Texas, as a child. Reared at Paint Rock and San Angelo, he was graduated from the University of Texas in 1905 with a degree in civil engineering. He returned to Concho County as a farmer and rancher, where he later served as county commissioner, as county judge from 1927 to 1935, and as a member of the Thirty-seventh Texas Legislature (1921). As county commissioner, Sims pioneered the use of tractors and heavy road-building equipment; he also helped form the Texas Good Roads Association and was credited with having named or assisted in naming most of the roads in West Texas. Always interested in area history and archaeology, Sims wrote two books—*Gun-Toters I Have Known* (1967), which recounts exploits of some of the early-day outlaws and peace officers, and *Cowpokes, Nesters, & So Forth* (1970), which relates his observations of the way the world changed from his boyhood in Paint Rock to more modern times.

Sims was married to Josephine Norton of Weatherford on December 27, 1927; they had one son. Sims died on June 8, 1973, and was buried in Fairmount Cemetery in San Angelo.

Joe B. Frantz

*Sims, Texas. (Brazos County.)

*Sims, Texas. (Matagorda County.)

*Sims Bayou.

*Sims Creek.

*Sims Valley, Texas.

Sinclair City, Texas. Sinclair City, in southeastern Smith County, was founded in 1931 as a pump station on a pipeline owned by Sinclair Oil and Refining Company. By 1966 all the company-owned houses had been removed, leaving only the pump station and a warehouse. The twenty-five inhabitants of the community in 1966 were mostly Negro farmers.

*Sindico Procurador.

Singer, John V. John V. Singer was born probably in 1793 in Rensselaer County, New York, the birthplace of his younger brother, Isaac Merrit Singer, who developed the sewing machine. Facts concerning Singer are open to conjecture, for much of his life is clothed in legend. He supposedly severed ties with his family, although years later he invested $500 in his brother's sewing machine company and reputedly received a large sum of money in return in the 1850's. He sailed to Texas about 1847 with his New Orleans-born wife, Johanna Shaw Singer, and possibly some children, to establish a shipping business in Port Isabel. Their three-masted schooner, the *Alice Sadell*, was wrecked on the coast of Padre Island in a storm. The family survived, came ashore, and salvaged materials, food, and furniture from the wrecked boat. They lived in a tent made of canvas sails until they could build a small house. In 1851 the Singers bought the old Santa Cruz ranch from the Padre Nicolás Balli qv estate, built a home on the foundation of the old house, and renamed the ranch Las Cruces. They went into the cattle business, and Singer bought and sold land on Padre and Brazos islands. They also grew vegetables, which Mrs. Singer took to Port Isabel in a skiff and to Brownsville by ox cart. Singer was appointed wreckmaster of the island and profited from salvaged materials, which may have included bars of silver.

In the 1860 United States census for Cameron County it is recorded that Singer's wife was thirty-six and that they had seven Texas-born children, the oldest a girl of fourteen. When the Civil War broke out, the Singers were ordered to leave the island because of their Union sympathies. They buried their collected treasure (said to have been over $80,000 in Spanish coins, silver bars, jewelry, and paper money). They lived for a time at Flour Bluff, south of Corpus Christi, and then on Brazos Island. Federal troops occupied the Las Cruces ranch and subsisted on the Singer cattle. When the war was over, the Singers returned to Padre Island and tried, unsuccessfully, to find their buried treasure, for wind and water had erased any remembered landmarks. After his wife's death in 1866, Singer went to Honduras; on his return he took his family to New Orleans. With his oldest son, Alexander, he went back at least twice to his "Lost City," located about twenty-five miles north of the southern tip of the island, near the present Willacy and Cameron county line, but all attempts to find the treasure failed. John Singer supposedly died in Mississippi, although the death date is not known.

BIBLIOGRAPHY: William Mahan, *Padre Island, Treasure Kingdom of the World* (1967); Vernon Smylie, *The Secrets of Padre Island* (1964); J. Lee Stambaugh and Lillian Stambaugh, *The Lower Rio Grande Valley of Texas* (1954); Writers' Round Table, *Padre Island* (1950).

Singing Society, Texas State. *See* Texas State Singing Society.

*Single Star.

*Singleton, George Washington.

*Singleton, Phillip.

*Singleton, Texas.

*Sinicu Indians. This name is known only from baptismal records at the San Antonio de Valero Mission qv of San Antonio. The published literature dealing with the Sinicu Indians is somewhat confusing. In one article (Sinicu) in the *Handbook of American Indians*, H. E. Bolton qv listed four names in the above-named baptismal records as synonyms of Sinicu, namely, Censoc, Censoo, Seniczo, and Senixzo; but in another article (San Antonio de Valero) Bolton listed both Sinicu and Siniczo, the latter being identified as a synonym for Cenizo or Seniso. Such facts as are now available suggest that all of these names are probably variants of Cenizo, the name of a well-known band of Coahuiltecan Indians who lived in northeastern Mexico during the late seventeenth and early eighteenth centuries. Some Cenizo entered the San Francisco Solano Mission qv near present Eagle Pass about 1700. In 1718, when this mission was moved to San Antonio and became known as San Antonio de Valero, the Cenizo moved with it. Hence it seems reasonable to consider Bolton's Sinicu and his synonyms for Sinicu as probable variants of Cenizo. Further analysis of the primary documents is needed for solution of this problem. J. R. Swanton listed Cenizo and Sinicu as separate Coahuiltecan bands. There is no basis for equating the Sinicu with the Semoco (Secmoco), as some writers have suggested. It is possible but not probable that the Nigco of San Antonio de Valero were Sinicu.

BIBLIOGRAPHY: F. W. Hodge (ed.), *Handbook of American Indians*, II (1910); M. D. McLean and E. del Hoyo (trans.), *Description of Nuevo León, México 1735–1740, By Don Josseph Antonio Fernández de Jáuregui Urrutia* (1964); E. L. Portillo, *Apuntes para la historia de Coahuila y Texas* (1886); J. R. Swanton, *Linguistic Material from the Tribes of Southern Texas and Northeastern Mexico* (1940).

T. N. Campbell

Siniple Indians. Siniple Indians are known only from a Spanish document of 1693 which lists the Siniple as one of fifty "nations" that lived north of the Rio Grande and "between Texas and New Mexico." This may be interpreted to mean the southern part of western Texas, since the document also mentions that the Apache were at war with the groups named. Nothing further is known about the Siniple. However, they may be the same as the Sinible, reported in the same document as living south of the Rio Grande (somewhere between Durango and present Presidio, Texas).

BIBLIOGRAPHY: C. W. Hackett (ed.), *Historical Documents Relating to New Mexico, Nueva Vizcaya, and Approaches Thereto, to 1773*, II (1926).

T. N. Campbell

*Sinks, Julia (Lee).

Sinoreja Indians. The Sinoreja (Spanish for "earless") Indians are known only from a Spanish document of 1693 which lists them as one of fifty "nations" that lived north of the Rio Grande and "between Texas and New Mexico." This may be interpreted to mean the southern part of present western Texas, since the document also mentions that the Apache were at war with the groups named. Nothing further is known about the Sinoreja.

BIBLIOGRAPHY: C. W. Hackett (ed.), *Historical Documents Relating to New Mexico, Nueva Vizcaya, and Approaches Thereto, to 1773*, II (1926).

T. N. Campbell

*Sinton, Texas. Sinton, seat of San Patricio County, is a center for farming, petroleum, and petrochemical industries, with its major businesses concerned with grain storage and oil field supplies. Principal agricultural products are cotton, grain sorghums, and beef cattle. Sinton had 170 businesses in 1970. In 1966 the town adopted a home rule charter and a city council-manager form of municipal government. In 1967 Sinton reported a newly constructed high school, a bank, a library, three hospitals, two newspapers, a radio station, sixteen churches, and varied recreational facilities. An urban renewal program was to be effected in 1969. The 1960 population was 6,008; in 1970 it was 5,563, according to the United States census. *See also* Corpus Christi Standard Metropolitan Statistical Area.

*Sion, Texas.

*Sip Bayou.

*Sipe Springs, Texas. (Comanche County.) Sipe Springs was given its name by John C. Plott (not Flott, as stated in Volume II). In 1903 Sipe Springs (pronounced "seep") had approximately twenty businesses, including two cotton gins and a hotel. Oil activity from 1918 to 1919 created a population boom. A brick schoolhouse with six classrooms and an auditorium was constructed in 1922 and was used until the county school consolidation movement began after World War II; in 1967 the school building was no longer standing. That year the community had a business district consisting of a store, which occupied the former Sipe Springs bank building, and a frame Masonic lodge building. An estimated 115 people lived in or near Sipe Springs in 1970; there were a number of farm residences, an active church, and a cemetery.

Margaret Tate Waring

*Sipe Springs, Texas. (Milam County.)

*Sipe Springs Branch.

Siquipil Indians. Siquipil, Pajalat, and Tilpacopal were three Coahuiltecan bands for whom the Nuestra Señora de la Purísima Concepción de Acuña Mission qv was established at San Antonio in 1731. The aboriginal location of the Siquipil band remains unknown. Since they entered this mission with groups from the area south of the Edwards Plateau, it is sometimes assumed that they came from this area also.

BIBLIOGRAPHY: H. E. Bolton, *Texas in the Middle Eighteenth Century* (1915); J. A. Dabbs, "The Texas Missions in 1785," *Preliminary Studies of the Texas Catholic Historical Society*, III (1940).

T. N. Campbell

*Siringo, Charles A.

*Sisk, Texas. (Erath County.)

*Sisk, Texas. (Reeves County.)

*Sister Creek.

*Sister Grove Creek.

*Sisterdale, Texas.

Sisters, Benedictine. The Benedictine Sisters, their origin going back to the sixth century in Italy, first came to Texas in 1919. Mother Ledwina and another nun first left the motherhouse at St. Mary's,

Pennsylvania, in 1911 and established a small group at the Isle of Pines, Cuba. Mother Ledwina headed a group of eight sisters in 1919, when they left Cuba for Texas, settling in Leming, a small town in Atascosa County, south of San Antonio. There they operated a convent and school (Mother Ledwina died there), before moving to San Antonio in 1926. From 1926 to 1963 the Benedictine Sisters operated a nursing home in San Antonio. In 1961 they bought approximately twenty-seven acres of hill country land at Boerne, in Kendall County. From 1961 to 1963 they improved the land, which had three substantial rock houses already there. In August, 1963, the sisters moved to the new location in Boerne and trained additional sisters there. In 1968 they opened a day and boarding school for girls, which had an average annual enrollment of forty-five girls until 1972, when the school was converted to a coeducational institution, with a kindergarten and grades one through twelve. The boarding school was being phased out so that the last boarding students would be through after the 1977–1978 school term. By the 1975–1976 term there were 210 boys and girls in attendance. The acreage of the facility had increased to 47.5 acres by 1976, and many new buildings had been constructed, including five classroom buildings, a learning center, a gym, and a chapel. The motherhouse building, one of the old rock houses, was being enlarged in that year, and there were nineteen Benedictine Sisters in residence there. Mother Aloysia Goertz was the prioress.

Eldon S. Branda

Sisters of Charity of the Incarnate Word. In 1866 three sisters of the Hospital of Antiquaille, Lyons, France, offered their services to Bishop Claude-Marie Dubuis, qv who was seeking volunteers for the mission fields of Texas. After receiving their spiritual training with the Sisters of the Incarnate Word and Blessed Sacrament, qv in Lyons, who were already active in Texas, Sisters M. Blandine Mathelin, M. Joseph Roussin, and M. Ange Escude were invested in the habit by Bishop Dubuis, who named the group the Sisters of Charity of the Incarnate Word. Arriving in Galveston on October 25, 1866, they remained with the Ursulines (*see* Sisters, Ursuline) until their convent was ready in February, 1867. They opened Charity Hospital on April 1, 1867; the hospital was later known as St. Mary's Infirmary. During the yellow fever epidemic in the summer of 1867, Mother Blandine died; Sister Joseph as superior and Sister Ange were left to carry on the work. An orphanage, which was opened for child survivors of the yellow fever epidemic, was formally established in 1874 as St. Mary's Orphanage, with a separate location and building. Other hospitals established were: St. Joseph's Infirmary, Houston (1887); Hotel Dieu, Beaumont (1896); St. Anthony's Home for the Aged, Houston (1897); St. Mary's, Port Arthur (1929); St. Theresa's, Beaumont (1934); and St. Edward's-Rischar Memorial, Cameron (1946).

The motherhouse was moved to Houston in 1925, and educational work was begun. In 1966 the Sisters of Charity of the Incarnate Word operated thirteen hospitals, two homes for the aged, five grade schools, and three schools for nurses; they also staffed the nursing department of Sacred Heart Dominican College (see Dominican College). The members numbered 421 professed sisters, 21 novices, 15 postulants, and 31 aspirants working in Texas, Louisiana, California, Arkansas, Utah, Mexico, Ireland, and Guatemala.

In 1869 the sisters began their work in San Antonio when Bishop Dubuis chose three members, Sisters Madeline, Agnes, and Pierre of the Galveston community, to open Santa Rosa Hospital. In 1875 the three nuns opened a parochial school in connection with St. Joseph's Orphanage. Their educational system has spread from Texas to Missouri, Oklahoma, Louisiana, Illinois, Mexico, Ireland, and Peru.

Because of the distance and inconveniences of travel in the early period, the San Antonio branch became independent of the Galveston group. Including the general motherhouse in San Antonio and provincial houses in St. Louis, Missouri, and Mexico City, the number of professed sisters was 1,096 in the late 1960's, with 69 novices and 17 postulants. Of this number 466 professed sisters worked at the San Antonio province and operated Incarnate Word College,qv three high schools, twenty-six elementary schools, four hospitals, three nurses' training schools, an orphanage, and a community center in the archdioceses of San Antonio and New Orleans and in the dioceses of Amarillo, Corpus Christi, Dallas-Fort Worth, and San Angelo.

BIBLIOGRAPHY: Catholic Archives, Chancery Office, Austin.

Sister M. Claude Lane, O. P.

Sisters of Divine Providence. The first two Sisters of Divine Providence, Sister Superior St. Andrew and Sister Marie Alphonse Boegler (later called Sister St. Claude), arrived in Texas from Alsace-Lorraine in October, 1866. Bishop Claude-Marie Dubuis qv sent the two nuns to Austin, where they opened the first Catholic school there in December, 1866. In 1868 the nuns opened two more schools, one in Corpus Christi (later taken over by the Sisters of Charity of the Incarnate Word qv) and the other in Castroville. The sisters' first permanent headquarters was established in Castroville and remained there until the motherhouse was moved to San Antonio in 1896. By 1872 the group had increased to seventeen members and four postulants, teaching in Fredericksburg, D'Hannis, New Braunfels, Frelsburg, Panna Maria, St. Hedwig, and Danville.

Under the leadership of Mother Mary Florence, schools were opened in Louisiana in 1887, and within a short time ten schools were in operation there, including five for Negro children. By 1907 there were ten schools in Oklahoma, including several for Indian children. At the time of the golden jubilee of the community in 1910, the order was located in two archdioceses and six dioceses and was operating sixty-nine academies and schools with a combined enrollment of nearly 10,000 children.

In 1898 the first Normal School for sisters was in operation at Castroville; by 1900 it was transferred to Our Lady of the Lake Convent and Academy (see Our Lady of the Lake College) in San Antonio. Summer courses were taught by state-approved professors for certification of the sisters to teach in the public schools. By 1915 most of these schools had been converted into parish schools or discontinued, thus ending, for the most part, some forty years of service to public education needs of rural children. In the 1960's in predominately Catholic areas, a few parish schools combined with public schools, with the sisters teaching in these schools again.

Our Lady of the Lake Academy continued to add college courses, eventually became a four-year institution, Our Lady of the Lake College, and opened its graduate school to male students. The Worden School of Social Service is part of the college system.

When the Sisters of Divine Providence celebrated the centennial year of their arrival in Texas, 1866–1966, they numbered 730 professed sisters, 32 novices, and 37 postulants; two adjunct groups to the order were the Missionary Catechists of Divine Providence (82 Catechists and 10 novices), and the Missionary Sisters of Divine Providence in Queretaro, Mexico (nine sisters). The order was represented in the archdiocese of San Antonio and in the dioceses of Austin, Brownsville, Corpus Christi, Dallas-Fort Worth, El Paso, Galveston-Houston, and San Angelo in Texas; Alexandria and Lafayette in Louisiana; Little Rock, Arkansas; Tulsa, Oklahoma; and Queretaro, Mexico. In addition to a college and school for social service, the sisters operated three hospitals, two clinics, twenty-six high schools, and sixty-four elementary schools.

BIBLIOGRAPHY: Catholic Archives, Chancery Office, Austin.

Sister M. Claude Lane, O. P.

Sisters, Dominican. Twenty Dominican sisters under the leadership of Mother Mary Agnes Magevney arrived in Galveston from Somerset, Ohio, on September 29, 1882. Bishop Nicholas Aloysius Gallagher qv had invited them to make their headquarters in Galveston in the convent recently vacated by the Sisters of Mercy.qv On October 9, the sisters opened Sacred Heart Academy, a day and boarding school (later Dominican High School, with no boarders). Holy Rosary School for Negroes was opened in 1887, and in 1893 St. Mary's Cathedral School was opened, with eight lower grades and four upper grades (a high school which closed in 1924). By 1900 the community had increased to sixty sisters, with schools in Beaumont, Taylor, and Houston. Because of the 1900 storm their boarding school was moved from Galveston to Lampasas, where St. Dominic's Villa was established; this school remained open until 1925. St. Agnes Academy, a select day and boarders' school for girls, opened in Houston in 1906; its site was transferred to a Houston suburb in 1963.

Mother Pauline Gannon, foreseeing the need for certifying teachers, accepted in 1914 a small Mexican school in Austin, Our Lady of Guadalupe, and also purchased a house near the University of Texas so that the sisters could attend summer classes. In 1918 she directed the building of Newman Hall as a residence for girls and sisters attending the university.

The Dominican sisters established Sacred Heart Dominican College (*see* Dominican College) in 1945 on the campus of the motherhouse in Houston, and in 1966 they opened a mission school in Zacapa, Guatemala.

In 1966 there were 313 professed sisters, 33 novices, and 13 postulants working in a college, two academies, seven high schools, thirty-three grade schools, three residence halls for college girls, a Montessori school, and one mission. The sisters furnished school supervisors for two dioceses, archivists for the Catholic Archives of Texas, and several other services in the chanceries of the Austin and Galveston-Houston dioceses. Dominican sisters were located in the archdiocese of Los Angeles and the dioceses of Austin; Galveston-Houston; Lafayette, Louisiana; San Diego, California; and Zacapa, Guatemala.

BIBLIOGRAPHY: Catholic Archives, Chancery Office, Austin.

Sister M. Claude Lane, O. P.

Sisters, Holy Cross. Sister M. Euphrosine, of the Holy Cross sisters, came to Texas in 1870 at the request of Bishop Claude-Marie Dubuis qv to establish schools in Corpus Christi, Nacogdoches, and Clarksville, but this early effort was unsuccessful. In 1874 four Holy Cross nuns from the general motherhouse in Notre Dame, Indiana, arrived in Austin to take over St. Mary's School, which had been operated by the Sisters of Divine Providence qv since 1866. The school was reopened near the church in a small stone house which doubled as a residence for the sisters. The nuns taught school and did all the cooking and household chores. Most of the students were boarders. In 1875 more sisters arrived, and by the 1880's the school had been expanded and improved. In 1882 a site for a permanent school was purchased in mid-town Austin, a square which in 1838 had been reserved for the residence of the president of the Republic of Texas. A stone, four-story building was completed at this location in 1885, and St. Mary's Academy qv became a first-rate day and boarding school for girls. In 1947, after selling the mid-town property, the sisters acquired the E. H. Perry estate in Austin, added to the original mansion, and discontinued the boarding of students. The academy became coeducational under the name of Holy Cross High School in September, 1968; in 1972 the school was closed.

St. Mary's Academy in Marshall was established by the sisters in 1880 and has continued in operation through the years since. In 1919 the Holy Cross

sisters took charge of Our Lady of Guadalupe School in Austin, a school begun by the Dominican nuns (*see* Sisters, Dominican) in 1914. At the request of the pastor of St. Ignatius Martyr, the sisters accepted that parish school in 1940 and assisted at the missions of San José in Creedmoor, Elroy, and Dry Creek, all in Travis County. They also worked in the missions in Round Rock and Georgetown. When St. Louis parish was established in Austin in 1953, the sisters operated its school. They also taught at Our Lady of Sorrows School in McAllen.

The sisters are in the eastern province of the order, with headquarters at Rockville, Maryland, and they numbered 424 members in the mid-1960's. The general motherhouse in Notre Dame, Indiana, headed a total membership of 1,536 Holy Cross nuns. Those in Texas in the early 1970's continued to work in the dioceses of Austin, Brownsville, and Dallas-Fort Worth.

BIBLIOGRAPHY: Catholic Archives, Chancery Office, Austin.

Sister M. Claude Lane, O. P.

Sisters of the Incarnate Word and Blessed Sacrament. The Sisters of the Incarnate Word and Blessed Sacrament, founded in 1625 in Lyons, France, was the second group of Catholic educators to come to Texas. When Bishop John Mary Odin qv asked for volunteers to work in the Texas missions, four sisters offered their services, and with Sister Superior St. Claire Valentine they arrived in Galveston on June 29, 1852. They remained with the Ursuline nuns (*see* Sisters, Ursuline) for several months, studying English and Spanish before going to Brownsville in February, 1853. The sisters' first house was a small one-story warehouse; later they secured the loan of a four-room house, and in March they opened the third school for girls in Texas. By November their first convent was completed, and a boarding and day school was conducted. At the request of Bishop Claude-Marie Dubuis,qv Sister St. Claire, along with volunteers from Europe, opened an independent house, Nazareth Academy, in Victoria on January 7, 1867. From 1874 to 1895 the sisters took part in a "community system" when parents petitioned for a public school in their community. When a demand was made for the nuns to wear secular clothes, the arrangement with the sisters ended. During this time they also opened a school for Negroes, which was forced to close because of protests by Negro Protestant ministers. A commercial school was added to Nazareth Academy in 1911; accreditation from the state was received in 1917. After 1900 the sisters taught in parochial schools established in Cuero (1916), Falls City (1924), San Antonio (1928), and La Grange (1930).

At the request of Bishop Dubuis, Sister Superior M. Ignatius McKeon of Brownsville and three sisters from Victoria opened a school in Corpus Christi on March 19, 1871. This foundation became the motherhouse of the Brownsville and Corpus Christi sisters, who have since operated Christopher College,qv a high school in Corpus Christi, and several parochial schools in the dioceses of Corpus Christi and Brownsville. In 1873 an independent institution in Houston was formed from the Victoria community. The Houston sisters operated a motherhouse, a high school, Our Lady of Perpetual Help Junior College, and Incarnate Word Academy in the Houston area, Bishop Byrne High School in Port Arthur, and other parochial schools in the Galveston-Houston, Beaumont, and Austin dioceses. Two other communities formed from the Victoria house were Shiner (1879) and Hallettsville (1882); they joined with the Victoria group in 1939 to form the Sisters of the Incarnate Word and Blessed Sacrament of San Antonio, with their motherhouse in Victoria. Besides academies and parochial schools, these sisters operated Burns Hospital in Cuero and Huth Memorial Hospital in Yoakum.

BIBLIOGRAPHY: Catholic Archives, Chancery Office, Austin.

Sister M. Claude Lane, O. P.

Sisters of Mercy. On January 6, 1875, two Sisters of Mercy from New Orleans arrived at Indianola. The Superior, Mother Mary Camillus Lucas, and Sister Mary John Berchmans were later joined by four other sisters. Scarcely had the school been opened in September when a hurricane destroyed the school and severely damaged the town. At the request of the pastor in Refugio, the sisters moved there and established their first permanent convent. The school was made public in 1890; in 1916 the sisters established Mercy Academy, which became Our Lady of Refugio Parochial School in 1940. The sisters, under the direction of Sister M. DiPazzi Lucas, established a motherhouse and opened a day and boarding school. Mercy Hospital, later to become the motherhouse, was founded in Laredo in 1894. Teaching positions in public schools were accepted in Penitas, Roma, Mercedes, Mission, Edinburg, Point Isabel, and Rio Grande City. Some of these schools became parochial, as many of the buildings belonged to the Roman Catholic church.

Mother Camillus and five sisters left Refugio to teach in the public school at San Patricio from 1876 to 1886. In 1887 they moved to Cuero, where a school and later a hospital were operated. Mother Camillus moved to Smithville in 1897 and opened a school which was operated until her death in 1911; the two remaining sisters and a postulant moved to Lockhart to run St. Ignatius School, which had been discontinued by the Sisters of Divine Providence.qv They finally disbanded in 1913, joining the Mercy sisters at Stanton, Texas.

The West Texas group of sisters, arriving from San Francisco in 1894, established an academy at Mariensfield (Stanton) and maintained it until a tornado demolished the buildings in 1938, after which they moved to join their sisters in Slaton. The Sisters of Mercy of the Southwest and West Texas joined with a number of other communities in America to form the Sisters of Mercy of the Union of the United States; they established their motherhouse in St. Louis, Missouri. These sisters continued to teach in Groom, Slaton, Edinburg, Harlingen, McAllen, Mercedes, Mission, Rio Grande City, and Refugio. They also owned hospitals in Slaton, Brownsville, and Laredo.

BIBLIOGRAPHY: Catholic Archives, Chancery Office, Austin.

Sister M. Claude Lane, O. P.

Sisters of St. Mary of Namur. In 1863 a Belgian community of sisters devoted to the education of girls arrived in Lockport, New York, and established their foundation. Upon the invitation of Bishop Claude-Marie Dubuis,qv Mother Superior Emilie brought two sisters to Waco in 1873 and opened Sacred Heart Academy in September of that year in a four-room house which also served as a convent. (The academy flourished and was replaced by a parochial school in the 1950's.) In the next few years the sisters opened academies in Corsicana (Sacred Heart, 1875); Sherman (St. Joseph's, 1876); and Denison (St. Xavier's, 1877). St. Ignatius Academy, Fort Worth, was established in 1885, but by 1910 the enrollment had outgrown the space, so that Our Lady of Victory College qv and Academy replaced it. Fort Worth became the headquarters of the community and the provincial house of the western province. In 1930 the college was opened to seculars and continued to offer higher education to young ladies; it merged with the new University of Dallas qv in 1956. The sisters established a House of Studies and a novitiate on property adjoining the university in Irving.

Other schools were opened in Wichita Falls, Beaumont, and Houston, as well as in Colorado and California. In 1965 the sisters numbered 199, with 13 novices and 4 postulants. They were represented in the archdiocese of Denver, the dioceses of Dallas-Fort Worth, Galveston-Houston, and Beaumont in Texas, and Monterey-Fresno, California. Three high schools, eighteen grade schools, and one mission were under the care of these sisters.

BIBLIOGRAPHY: Catholic Archives, Chancery Office, Austin.

Sister M. Claude Lane, O. P.

Sister-Servants of the Holy Ghost and Mary Immaculate. A new congregation devoted to the education of Negroes in the South was founded in 1893 in San Antonio by Margaret Healey Murphy, an Irish widow who had come to Texas in 1887. For several years she had tried unsuccessfully to work and teach in the Negro community. She organized a group of women as teachers dedicated to the work, depending entirely on volunteers. In 1888 St. Peter Claver Church, the first parish church in San Antonio organized solely for Negroes, and financed by Mrs. Murphy, was dedicated. She opened a small school beside the church, but it met with difficulties because of the unfriendly white neighborhood. Mrs. Murphy decided to found her congregation, and in 1893 she and two friends took vows as Sister-Servants of the Holy Ghost and Mary Immaculate. Volunteers were scarce, so in 1898 Mother Mary Margaret went to her native Ireland to seek recruits. As the years went on the community of predominantly Irish nuns, dedicated to the education of Negro children, expanded into the archdiocese of New Orleans and the dioceses of Corpus Christi, Dallas-Fort Worth, Galveston-Houston, Alexandria and Lafayette in Louisiana, and Natchez-Jackson in Mississippi. In 1966 they worked in thirty-eight schools and one home for the aged. The community numbered 262 professed sisters, 5 novices, 4 postulants, and 19 aspirants.

BIBLIOGRAPHY: Catholic Archives, Chancery Office, Austin.

Sister M. Claude Lane, O. P.

Sisters, Ursuline. The Ursuline nuns, an order founded in Italy in 1535, was the first group of Catholic educators to come to North America; they established schools in Quebec in 1639. The sisters, who had been in New Orleans since 1727, were the first order to volunteer for service in the new state of Texas. Six nuns, along with Mother Superior St. Arsene Blin, arrived in Galveston on January 19, 1847, and on February 8 they opened the first Catholic school for girls in Texas in the family home of the Love estate, purchased by Bishop John Mary Odin qv in 1845. The group, increased by volunteers from Canada, served as nurses during the Galveston yellow fever epidemics in 1848, 1853, and 1858, turned their newly built school into a hospital during the Civil War for war victims of both sides, worked during the disastrous hurricanes of 1875 and 1900, and assisted in the care of survivors of the Galveston fires of 1854 and 1882.

In 1851 three nuns of the Galveston community joined with a group from New Orleans to open the first girls' school in San Antonio. An academy for girls was opened in Laredo in 1868 by Mother Joseph Aubert and Sister Teresa Pereda. Mother Aubert also founded an Ursuline house in Puebla, Mexico, in 1892. Six of the Galveston sisters under Mother Joseph Holly established the first Catholic school in what is now the Diocese of Dallas on February 2, 1874.

When the Ursuline nuns joined a motherhouse in 1906 in Rome, Italy, the headquarters for the southern province of America was located first in Dallas, then in San Antonio. Later Kirkwood, Missouri, became the provincial house of the central province. These sisters, once semicloistered, now teach in parochial schools, maintaining the originally established academies and continuing to teach in six parochial schools in Dallas, Galveston, Laredo, and Texarkana. *See also* Ursuline Academies.

BIBLIOGRAPHY: Catholic Archives, Chancery Office, Austin.

Sister M. Claude Lane, O. P.

*Siupam Indians. The Siupam (Suipam) Indians were Coahuiltecan-speaking Indians who are known only from the vicinity of present San Antonio in the early eighteenth century. Their settlements were along the San Antonio River, particularly at San Pedro Springs, where in 1709 they were observed in a rancheria with Xarame and Sijame. The Siupam have been equated with the Siguipam of San Francisco de la Espada Mission,qv but this is not supported by acceptable evidence. The Siguipam were said to be a coastal people, whereas the Siupam were never mentioned as living near the coast.

BIBLIOGRAPHY: F. W. Hodge (ed.), *Handbook of American Indians*, II (1910); J. R. Swanton, *Linguistic Material from the Tribes of Southern Texas and Northeastern Mexico* (1940).

T. N. Campbell

Sivells Bend, Texas.

Six Flags Over Texas. Six Flags Over Texas, an amusement park adjacent to the south side of the Dallas-Fort Worth Turnpike, fifteen miles from both cities, is a project of the Great Southwest Corporation, a Texas firm with offices in Arlington. Six Flags began operations on August 5, 1961; it was constructed at a cost of $10,000,000, with expansion costs totaling $5,000,000 by 1966. Of the 115 acres in the park, 40 acres are devoted to entertainment facilities and 75 acres to a paved parking area. It is recognized as being educationally stimulating and historically representative of early Texas. An eight-foot granite Texas historical marker outside the entrance tells the story of Texas history under the flags of Spain, France, Mexico, the Republic of Texas, the Confederacy, and the United States. The park is divided into six sections, each showing the influence and growth of the state under the separate flags.

The park is circled by a narrow-gauge railway with authentic steam locomotives. Entertainment includes a ride on a runaway mine train, a log flume water ride, a spelunking cave, an astrolift sky ride, a Mexican fiesta train, two turnpikes with self-propelled sports cars, scale model antique cars, a La Salle riverboat ride, a skyhook which takes visitors 155 feet aloft, stagecoaches, and Indian war canoe rides. The Crazy Horse Saloon features musical shows, and an amphitheater features revues. Restaurants serve Southern, Mexican, and American dishes. The park is open on weekends in the spring and fall and daily from June through Labor Day.

Claude Cox

*Six Mile, Texas. (Calhoun County.)

*Six Mile, Texas. (Milam County.)

*Six-Pounder.

*Six-Shooter. See Colt Revolver.

*Six Shooter Creek.

*6666 Ranch. See Four Sixes Ranch.

*Sixmile Bayou.

*Sixmile Creek.

*Sixshooter Draw.

*Sjolander, John Peter.

*Skeen, Texas.

*Skeen Peak.

*Skeeterville, Texas.

*Skellytown, Texas.

*Skidi Pawnee Indians. *See also* Pawnee Indians.

*Skidmore, Texas.

*Skillet Creek.

*Skillman Grove Camp Meeting. *See* Bloys Camp Meeting.

*Skinout Mountain.

*Skinoux Creek.

*Skrone, Texas.

*Skull Creek.

+Skunk Creek.

*Slater, Texas.

*Slaton, Texas. Slaton, in southeastern Lubbock County, had a newspaper, a bank, a hospital, a library, sixteen churches, and three city parks in 1966. The economy was based primarily on the railroad industry, cotton and grain growing, cattle feeding, and meat processing. In 1970 there were 155 businesses reported; the chief industries were four cotton gins, a cotton compress, a grain elevator, and manufacturers of cabinet and office fixtures, heavy farm equipment, chemicals, and livestock formula. In 1960 the population was 6,568; in 1970 it was 6,583, according to the United States census.

*Slaughter, Christopher Columbus. Christopher Columbus Slaughter was married to Carrie Averill on January 17, 1877 (not 1878, as stated in Volume II). [Some later printings of Volume II contain this correction.]

Nelle Slaughter DeLoache

*Slaughter, George Webb.

*Slaughter, John B.

*Slaughter Creek.

*Slave Insurrections.

Slayden, Ellen Maury. Ellen Maury Slayden was born at the Maury family home, Piedmont, in Charlottesville, Virginia, in 1860; she received her education from tutors at home. On June 12, 1883, she married James Luther Slayden,qv a merchant and rancher in San Antonio; they had no children. Ellen Slayden served for a time in 1889 as society editor of the San Antonio *Express*.qv Upon her husband's election to Congress in 1896, they moved to Washington, where they maintained a residence for the next twenty-one years. She continued her writing, contributing to various magazines and newspapers, and was a tireless record keeper and diarist. Her notebooks concerning observations of the social and political life in Washington from 1897 to 1919 were left to her nephew Maury F. Maverick.qv Maverick's widow, Terrell Webb, together with her second husband, Walter Prescott Webb,qv had the journal published in 1962 as *Washington Wife*. Ellen Maury Slayden died in San Antonio on April 20, 1926.

Mary Shields Pearson

*Slayden, James Luther.

*Slayden, Texas.

*Sledge, Andrew.

Slick, Thomas Baker. Thomas Baker Slick was born on May 6, 1916, in Clarion, Pennsylvania, the son of Tom and Berenice (Frates) Slick. He attended and was graduated from Phillips Exeter Academy (1934) and from Yale University (1938) with a premedical biology degree. A member of Phi Beta Kappa, he did graduate work at Harvard University and at Massachusetts Institute of Technology. His extensive business interests included the Slick Oil Corporation, Slick Airways, Inc., and numerous oil, land, mineral, and cattle enterprises. He founded (by developing plans and by contributions of two million dollars and 3,800 acres of land) the Southwest Research Center in San Antonio. The center consists of the Southwest Foundation for Research and Education qv (*see also* Argyle Hotel), established to do basic biomedical research, and the Southwest Research Institute,qv established to do basic and applied research primarily in the engineering sciences for both private industry and agencies of the federal government.

Tom Slick was a trustee and governor of the Texas Research Foundation, Worchester Foundation for Experimental Biology (Shrewsbury, Massachusetts), Trinity University (San Antonio), and the San Antonio Medical Foundation. He was a member of numerous organizations, including the United World Federalists, Inc., the National Planning Association, and the American Association for the Advancement of Science. During the first part of World War II he was a "dollar-a-year" man for the War Production Board in Washington and a cargo officer in Chile for the Board of Economic Warfare. He later served in the navy in the Pacific and in Japan.

He was co-inventor of the lift slab method of building construction and several other inventions, author of *The Last Great Hope* (1951), leader of a Himalayan Snowman expedition, member of the Explorer's Club, and a collector of the works of modern artists and sculptors. Medical research remained a primary interest all of his life. He was married and divorced twice and was the father of four children. He was killed in a private plane crash near Dell, Montana, on October 6, 1962, and was buried in Mission Burial Park, San Antonio, Texas.

*Slick Mountain.

*Slickrock Creek.

*Slickrock Mountain.

*Slide, Texas.

*Slidell, Texas.

*Sligo, Texas.

*Sloan, Texas.

*Sloan Creek.

*Slocum, Milton.

*Slocum, Texas.

*Slough Creek.

*Small, Texas.

Smathers, James Field. J. Field Smathers, inventor of the electric typewriter, was born on a farm near Valley Spring, Llano County, on February 12, 1888, the son of James Jefferson and Harriet Olenzo (Spinks) Smathers. After attending a one-room country school he entered Texas Christian University in 1904. After finishing business school, he taught shorthand and typing for a year, then became a typist, accountant, and credit manager of a Kansas City, Missouri, firm in 1908. While doing the constant typing required by his position, he realized the need for some means to increase the speed and decrease the fatigue of typing, and the use of electric power seemed to him the obvious device. For more than three years he worked on the application of electric power to typewriters, and by the fall of 1912 Smathers had completed a working model and applied for a patent, which was issued the next year.

He continued to develop his idea until, in September, 1914, he perfected an electric typewriter that performed perfectly. In the early 1920's he obtained an extension of his early patent because of the delay in his work caused by his overseas military service during World War I. In 1923 the Northeast Electric Company of Rochester, New York, entered into a royalty contract with Smathers for the production of electric typewriters. However, private industrial acceptance of the concept of an electrically powered typewriter did not come until 1930, when Electric Typewriters, Inc., a subsidiary of Northeast Electric Company, put the Electromatic model on the market. This company was purchased by the International Business Machines Corporation in 1933, a step which marked the beginning of the IBM Office Products Division.

The Franklin Institute of the state of Pennsylvania awarded Smathers the Edward Longstreth Medal "for ingenuity in the invention of the electric typewriter." In 1938 he joined the Rochester staff of IBM as a consultant and worked in development engineering at Poughkeepsie until his retirement in 1953. In 1945 the Rochester Museum of Arts and Sciences awarded him a fellowship for the invention of an escapement for spacing typewriter characters variably according to their widths. An honorary award in 1966 by the alumni association of Texas Christian University recognized Smathers as a "distinguished alumnus."

He died on August 7, 1967, in Poughkeepsie, New York, and was buried in Poughkeepsie Rural Cemetery. He was survived by his wife, Mildred Eloise Gill Smathers, a son, and a daughter.

BIBLIOGRAPHY: "The Challenge That Led To An Invention," *This Is TCU* (Spring, 1967); Austin *American-Statesman*, August 10, 1967.

Betty Donovan Knox

*Smeathers, William. William Smeathers [sometimes spelled Smither(s)] was born about 1766, possibly in Virginia; he was living in Kentucky before he came to Texas. He lived at Galveston before 1821, when he accompanied Stephen F. Austin during the first days of Austin's journey to San Antonio de Bexar. Smeathers may have been one of those who, with William Little,qv built a log cabin on the big bend of the Brazos River in the fall of 1821 (*see* Fort Bend). He died in Columbia on August 13, 1837.

BIBLIOGRAPHY: *Telegraph and Texas Register* (Houston), August 19, 1837.

Marshall Jackson

*Smeathers Creek.

*Smetna, Texas.

*Smiley, Texas.

Smith, A. Frank. A. Frank Smith, son of William Angie and Mary Elizabeth (Marrs) Smith, was born in Elgin, Texas, on November 1, 1889. He received a B.A. degree from Southwestern University in 1912 and attended the Theological Seminary of Vanderbilt University from 1912 to 1914. He received a D.D. degree from Southwestern University in 1923, and an LL.D. from that institution in 1940. A Methodist minister, he served the Detroit circuit in Red River County in 1914–1915. He organized a Methodist church (later to become Highland Park Methodist Church) on the campus of Southern Methodist University in 1915. In 1930 he was elected a bishop of the Methodist Episcopal Church, South, and was the bishop in charge of the Texas Conference from 1934 until his retirement in 1960. He was a leader in the movement to unite into a single denomination the Methodist Episcopal Church and the Methodist Episcopal Church, South. Following the unification of the denomination in 1939, Smith was elected the first president of the combined Council of Bishops of the Methodist Church.

From 1940 to 1960 he was in charge of all missionary work of the Methodist church in the United States, and from 1938 to 1960 he was chairman of the board of trustees of Southern Methodist University in Dallas. In 1951 he served as president of the Philosophical Society of Texas.qv

On June 16, 1914, he was married to Bess Patience Crutchfield, a native of Blossom, Texas, and they had four children. Smith retired as a bishop in 1960 and died on October 5, 1962, at his home in Houston. He was buried in Forest Park-Lawndale Cemetery in that city.

BIBLIOGRAPHY: *Who's Who In America* (1962).

*Smith, Allen John.

*Smith, Ashbel.

*Smith, Benjamin Fort.

Smith, Charles Walker. Charles Walker Smith, son of William Burley and Sarah Ann (Sheppard) Smith, was born in Holmes County, Mississippi, on June 6, 1855. He moved with his parents to Carroll Parish, Louisiana, in 1860, then to Johnson County, Texas, in 1870, and, following his mother's death about 1871, to a community later known as Brazos Point, in northeastern Bosque County.

As a young man, Smith was a teacher and merchant near Brazos Point. In 1882, he married Emma Annie Mickey of Kimball, Texas. He founded the town of Eulogy, near Brazos Point, on July 11, 1884, where he operated a dry goods store; he was its first postmaster in 1885. Smith was ordained a minister of the Church of Christ in 1888. He moved to Floyd County in 1890 and settled on a section of land a few miles northeast of Floydada. One of the earliest preachers in the area, he was instrumental in establishing Church of Christ churches at Plainview, Silverton, Sand Hill, Petersburg, Cone, and Canyon. He also helped in the establishment of Lockney Christian College qv in 1894. Smith died on July 10, 1937, at Santa Anna, and was buried at Lockney.

William C. Horton

*Smith, Christian.

*Smith, Cornelius.

*Smith, Edmund Kirby.** Edmund Kirby Smith, in order to distinguish himself from the many other "Smiths" in the Confederate Army, began calling himself Kirby-Smith. His family continued the practice, and since his death the family has been known as Kirby-Smith.

BIBLIOGRAPHY: Joseph Howard Parks, *General Edmund Kirby Smith, C.S.A.* (1962).

Paul S. Lofton, Jr.

*Smith, Erastus (Deaf).

Smith, Erwin Evans.** Erwin Evans Smith, son of Albert A. and Mary Alice (Erwin) Smith, was born on August 22, 1886, in Honey Grove, Texas; when he was seven he moved fifteen miles west to Bonham with his mother, who had remarried after his father's death. As a boy he visited with relatives near Quanah, and he was introduced to ranch life in Hardeman and Foard counties. The cattle range so appealed to him that he began making sketches of horses and Indians, and he obtained an inexpensive camera to record what he saw. Still a youth, he rode the range in Arizona and Mexico as a regular cowhand, but he always took his camera along so that he could record what he knew was fast disappearing from the American scene. He still wanted to be an artist, however, and in 1904, at the age of eighteen, he went to Chicago to study under Lorado Taft, one of the foremost American sculptors; his intention was to create bronze sculptures of the men and beasts of the cow country, using his photographs as guides to truthfulness in his work. After two years with Taft, he returned to Texas, worked as a cowhand, and with great veracity photographed the working life of the cowboy. Constantly urging his fellow workers to go about their business as usual, and working with painstaking exactness, Smith's pictures took on the natural look of a master painter's brush. By remaining truthful to the life he knew best, he was able to capture a real and exciting portrait of the rangeland during a period when cameras and equipment were very unsophisticated.

In 1906 Smith took his photographs with him to Boston, where he studied under the eminent sculptor, Bella Lyon Pratt. He won a prize at the Boston Art Institute for his bust of a Sioux Indian, and although he continued to be associated with the Boston Museum of Fine Arts for the next three years, he hurried back to the rangeland as often as he could. In 1908 forty enlargements of his photographs of the West were stopping crowds in a downtown Boston exhibit, and two articles about him had appeared, both written by George Pattullo,qv Sunday editor of the Boston *Herald*. This success brought him to the attention of famous actors like Dustin Farnum and William S. Hart, who wanted advice on how to make their western characterizations more authentic. Pattullo became his closest friend, and they traveled together in Texas, New Mexico, and Arizona, Smith producing photographs and Pattullo writing western stories which appeared in popular magazines. In 1914 Smith returned to Texas to begin ranching on his own, but by 1917 he was bankrupt. He never married. Once his range-riding days were over, his artistic life faded, and he spent his remaining years at his place outside Bonham, where he died on September 4, 1947. He was buried in Oakwood Cemetery in Honey Grove. The last thirty years of his life seem to have been unproductive, but the early photographs remain a testimonial to his early artistic genius. Concerning his photographs, Harry Peyton Steger qv wrote in 1909 that "whether the man who took them succeeds as a painter and sculptor," he has already done a work of great importance." Over ten thousand photographs were in Smith's collection at the time of his death. In 1949 eighteen hundred plates and films were placed in the Library of Congress, Washington, D.C., and one hundred of Erwin Smith's prints were on permanent display at the Texas Memorial Museum qv in Austin. His photographs continue to be reproduced all over America as the finest pictorial account of the western rangelands.

BIBLIOGRAPHY: Eldon S. Branda, "Portrait of a Cowboy as a Young Artist," *Southwestern Historical Quarterly*, LXXI (1967–1968); J. Evetts Haley, *Life on the Texas Range* (1952).

Eldon S. Branda

*Smith, Erwin Jesse.

*Smith, Felix Ezell.** Felix Ezell Smith was the son of William Stark and Nancy A. (Roundtree) Smith.

Ludie B. Camp

Smith, Frank Chesley.** Frank Chesley Smith, a business executive and civic leader in Houston, was born on September 9, 1882, in Hickman, Kentucky, the son of Chesley Chambers and Frances (Duncan) Smith. He was a student at Vanderbilt University from 1911 to 1915 and served in the United States Army during World War I from 1917 to 1919. After the war Smith was involved in the real estate, mortgage, and banking business until 1933, when he became president of the Houston Natural Gas Corporation; he served as president until 1955, when he was named chairman of the board of directors; he was also a director of the Coleman Company in Wichita, Kansas. Highly respected in his field, Smith was one of the organizers of a research institute for the gas industry in 1939–1940, was president of the Southern Gas As-

sociation in 1943 and president of the American
Gas Association in 1953. He was chairman of the
board of trustees of the Institute of Gas Technology in Chicago from 1941 to 1943 and again in
1956.

Smith held positions with many educational institutions, serving as a governor of the University
of Houston, advisory board member of Scott and
White Memorial Hospital,qv chairman of the board
of governors of the Southwestern Research Institute,qv and a director of the Texas College of Arts
and Industries (now Texas A&I University) from
1939 to 1955 and chairman of its board from 1941
to 1952. During his association with Texas A&I,
Smith introduced possibly the first course on gas
technology in the United States; a fine arts center
on the Texas A&I campus was named in his honor.
He served as president of the Texas division of the
American Cancer Society from 1946 to 1952, and
chairman of its board of directors from 1952 to
1955, when he became honorary chairman. A member of several civic and professional organizations,
he was also elected to the Philosophical Society of
Texas.qv

Frank C. Smith was married to Elizabeth Hail on
October 26, 1920, and they had two children. He
died on January 13, 1971, in Houston and was
buried in Forest Park-Lawndale Cemetery in Houston.

BIBLIOGRAPHY: *Who's Who In America* (1960); Philosophical Society of Texas, *Proceedings*, XXXIV (1970).

*Smith, George W.** George W. Smith, who
was born in Kentucky about 1823, was not secretary of state under James Stephen Hogg qv (as
stated in Volume II), came to Texas in 1847,
was an able lawyer, and served as a district judge
before the Civil War. He attended the Constitutional Convention of 1866 qv and was elected in
June of that year as an associate justice of the Supreme Court of Texas (*see* Judicial System). The
court had been increased to five judges under the
new constitution, and Smith, along with George
Fleming Moore, Richard Coke, Stockton P. Donley, and Asa Hoxey Willie,qqv served until September 10, 1867, when they were removed by
United States General Philip Henry Sheridan qv
as an impediment to Reconstruction;qv they were
replaced by men who were supposed to be in sympathy with Congressional Reconstruction, a court
known since, derisively, as the Semicolon Court.qv

In 1873 George W. Smith, aged 50 and a widower, was a resident of Columbus and represented the
Twenty-fifth District, Colorado and Lavaca counties, in the House of Representatives of the Thirteenth Texas Legislature, which met in regular
session from January 14 to June 4, 1873. He was
cited for his ability, honesty, and laborious effort,
and as the chief author of an election law by which
frauds were prevented. A dispatch of October 24,
1873, announced his death due to yellow fever at
his home in Columbus. [This George W. Smith
(in Volume II) has been confused with other men

bearing the same name; *see* biographies below.
Ed.]

BIBLIOGRAPHY: W. J. Barker (comp.), *Directory of the
Members of the Thirteenth Legislature of the State of
Texas* (1873); J. H. Davenport, *History of the Supreme
Court of the State of Texas* (1917); Norma Shaw, The
Early History of Colorado County (M.A. thesis, South-
west Texas State Teachers College, 1939); George E. Shelly,
"The Semicolon Court of Texas," *Southwestern Historical
Quarterly*, XLVIII (1944–1945); Leila Clark Wynn, "A
History of the Civil Courts in Texas," *ibid.*, LX (1956–
1957); Dallas *Herald*, October 25, 1873.

Smith, George W.** George W. Smith was born
in Marietta, Georgia, on July 14, 1845, the son of
Aaron S. and Lucinda W. Smith. He came to Texas
before the Civil War and located in Smith County.
During the war he served with Oran M. Roberts' qv
11th Texas Infantry Regiment, Randal's Brigade,qv
the youngest of six brothers serving in the Confederacy. After the war he taught school and was admitted to the Bar, practicing in Tyler. He was the
first county judge of Smith County under the Constitution of 1875,qv and was chairman of the state
Democratic executive committee, 1880–1882. Probably he was a resident of Mitchell County when
he made the speech nominating James Stephen
Hogg qv for attorney general at the state convention in Galveston on August 10, 1886. He was a
lawyer in Colorado City in Mitchell County when
the Sweetwater Baptist Association met in August,
1890, to found Abilene Baptist College (later
Hardin-Simmons University) and named Smith to
the locating committee. Smith was also appointed to
the school's first board of trustees in 1890. [He
should not be confused with the Rev. George W.
Smith (below) who was chosen president of that
board.]

From 1891 to 1895 George W. Smith was secretary of state under Governor James S. Hogg. Thereafter he practiced law in Houston until 1898, when
he returned to Colorado City. He was married to
Laura L. Swann in Tyler in 1876, and the couple
had two sons and two daughters. Smith died in
Colorado City on January 24, 1906, and was buried
there.

BIBLIOGRAPHY: Robert C. Cotner (ed.), *Addresses and
State Papers of James Stephen Hogg* (1951); Ike W. Jay,
History of Hardin-Simmons University, 1890–1940 (M.A.
thesis, Texas Technological College, 1941); R. C. Crane,
"The Beginning of Hardin-Simmons University," *West
Texas Historical Association Year Book*, XVI (1940);
Colorado City *Weekly Record*, January 26, 1906.

Mabel B. Smith
Sawnie B. Smith

Smith, George W.** [Because the name George
W. Smith appears so often in the same period of
Texas history, although referring to different men,
the following individuals are listed to avoid con-
fusion among them and those above. *See also* Smyth,
George W.]

George W. Smith was a Baptist pastor in Gonzales, then in Abilene from 1887 to 1890; in 1890
he was presiding officer of the Sweetwater Baptist
Association, which included an area from Baird to
El Paso, a territory larger than Kentucky or Tennessee. At the sixth annual session of the association

in Sweetwater in August, 1890, he was one of the leaders in the founding of Abilene Baptist College (now Hardin-Simmons University). The Rev. Smith was named first president of the school's board of trustees (and should not be confused with the lawyer and secretary of state from Colorado City, George W. Smith, above, who was a member of that same board).

BIBLIOGRAPHY: R. C. Crane, "The Beginning of Hardin-Simmons University," *West Texas Historical Association Year Book,* XVI (1940); Ike W. Jay, History of Hardin-Simmons University, 1890–1940 (M.A. thesis, Texas Technological College, 1941).

George W. Smith was a lieutenant in the United States 9th Cavalry, and a post adjutant, in San Antonio in April and May, 1875, when he received information from John Lapham Bullis qv telling of Bullis' rescue from a party of Comanches by three Seminole Negro-Indian scouts at Eagle's Nest crossing of the Pecos.

BIBLIOGRAPHY: Kenneth Wiggins Porter, "The Seminole Negro-Indian Scouts, 1870–1881," *Southwestern Historical Quarterly,* LV (1951–1952).

George W. Smith, a carpetbagger qv from New York state, was a member of the June through August meeting of the Constitutional Convention of 1868–1869.qv He was in Jefferson, Texas, in early October, 1868, where he was the leader of Negroes in the community, who outnumbered the whites two to one. Smith was involved in a dispute with a white man, brought in a group of Negroes, and in a confrontation between the whites and Smith's group, several whites were wounded. Smith fled to the military command for protection but was turned over to Jefferson civil authorities and jailed. A group of armed men entered the jail, and Smith and several of his Negro companions were killed. Following the incident General Joseph J. Reynolds qv sent in additional troops and put Jefferson under martial law. Thirty white citizens were arrested and held in confinement for ten months. A military commission finally convicted five of the men. Although the Jefferson *Times* called Smith an "infamous scoundrel," he was hailed as a martyr by the radical press in the North.

BIBLIOGRAPHY: Charles W. Ramsdell, *Reconstruction in Texas* (1910).

G. W. Smith, a major, was stationed in Brenham in command of a battalion of the United States 17th Infantry when the town was looted and burned on the night of September 7, 1866, by members of the battalion. Although Smith was indicted and had judgments brought against him in Texas civil courts, he was protected by the military authorities in the Reconstruction qv government and was never sentenced.

BIBLIOGRAPHY: Charles W. Ramsdell, "Presidential Reconstruction in Texas," *Quarterly of the Texas State Historical Association,* XII (1908–1909).

Smith, Harriet Frances. Harriet Frances Smith was born on November 7, 1870, in Huntsville, daughter of John Lyle and Sarah (Murray) Smith. She received a diploma from the New England Conservatory of Music, studied at the University of Chicago, Cornell University, and Clark University, and received a masters degree from George Peabody College for Teachers. She taught in Montgomery, Brownwood, Paris, and Huntsville, then was director of the Department of Music at Texas Christian University when it was located in Waco. From 1914 to 1941 she taught geography at Sam Houston State Teachers College (now Sam Houston State University). She was the author, along with Darthula Walker, of *The Geography of Texas* (1923) and contributed to the *Grolier Society, Texas Outlook,* and *Journal of Geography.* She was never married. Harriet Frances Smith died November 27, 1958, in Huntsville and was buried in Oakwood Cemetery there.

BIBLIOGRAPHY: Huntsville *Item,* December 4, 1958; Faculty Biography File (MS., Sam Houston State University Library, Huntsville).

Elizabeth Oliphant
Aline Law

*Smith, Henry.

*Smith, Henry Clay (Hank).

*Smith, James.

*Smith, James Franklin.

Smith, James Norman. James Norman Smith was born in Richmond County, North Carolina, in 1789. From 1808 until 1840 he lived in Tennessee, where he farmed and taught school; James K. Polk was one of his students. In 1840 he arrived at Indianola, Texas, and made his way to the Upper Cuero Creek Settlement qv of present DeWitt County. There he began a long career of political and social leadership. He was among the organizers of the Cumberland Presbyterian church in the area and was the first elder in the region. At Clinton he continued his church work as elder, Sunday school organizer, and recruiter.

Smith's school at Upper Cuero Creek was the first organized in the area. After surveying the nearby town of Concrete in 1846, he relocated first at Cameron, then at Clinton, where he took up the duties of county clerk, a position he held from 1846 to 1865. He also operated a store in conjunction with his duties as county surveyor, Masonic leader, and schoolmaster. He died in 1875 and probably was buried beside his wife, Elizabeth Hungerford Moorehead Smith, in the Old Clinton Cemetery.

BIBLIOGRAPHY: Nellie Murphree (Robert W. Shook, ed.), *A History of DeWitt County* (1963); James Norman Smith, Memoirs (MS., Archives, University of Texas at Austin Library).

Robert W. Shook

*Smith, John.

*Smith, John Peter.

*Smith, John William. John William Smith died on January 12, 1845 (not January 13, 1845, as stated in Volume II). [Some later printings of Volume II contain this correction.]

John Dixon Matlock

Smith, Joshua G. Joshua G. Smith died in defense of the Alamo. At that time he was twenty-eight years old, single, and a resident of Bastrop,

Texas. He was born in North Carolina and had received a Spanish land grant of a quarter league in the Robertson Colony qv near present Marlin, Texas, in March, 1835.

BIBLIOGRAPHY: Amelia W. Williams, A Critical Study of the Siege of the Alamo and of the Personnel of its Defenders (Ph.D. dissertation, University of Texas, 1931).

*Smith, Merriweather W.

*Smith, Morgan L. [This title was incorrectly listed in Volume II as Smith, Morgan R.]

BIBLIOGRAPHY: Adriance Papers (MS., Archives, University of Texas at Austin Library).

*Smith, Niles F.

Smith, Oscar Blake. Oscar Blake Smith, Yale-educated clergyman and early leader in the civil rights movement, whose fifty-year ministry took him throughout the United States and to many foreign countries, spent twenty-six years ministering to the University of Texas community as pastor of the University Baptist Church in Austin.

Born January 19, 1902, in Jasper, Arkansas, to Othar Otis and Mamie Nell (Boomer) Smith, he received degrees from Ouachita College, Arkadelphia, Arkansas, in 1925, and from Yale Divinity School in 1929. He was ordained into the ministry of the Baptist church in 1923 and held his first pastorate in Crossett, Arkansas, 1925–1926. He pastored churches in Bridgeport and Rockville, Connecticut; Mexico, Missouri; and Fayetteville and Conway, Arkansas, before taking the pastorate at University Baptist Church, Austin, where he served from 1943 until his retirement in 1969. He was president of Hardin College in Mexico, Missouri, from 1930 to 1932.

When he came to Austin, Blake Smith was offered a "free pulpit," and he used it as a crusader on social and moral issues, as a compassionate pastor to minister to the personal needs of his congregation, and as an enlightened man of God to preach with intellectual integrity.

He had a flair for the unusual which he carried out with style and decorum. In his early days in Austin he wore a morning coat in the pulpit, and later he wore black clerical robes, both unusual for the informality of a usual Baptist service. To protest the firing of Homer P. Rainey as president of the University of Texas in 1944, he marched down Guadalupe Street in front of the university as the officiating minister in a student-arranged funeral cortege for the "death" of academic freedom. In a prayer before a hotly-contested University of Texas football game in Austin, he reminded the rabid fans that football is, after all, only a game.

He was an imaginative leader, an eloquent speaker, a humorous storyteller, and a sympathetic counselor. He was widely known through his weekly radio show, "Religion in Life," which was aired for fourteen years over Radio Station KTBC, Austin. He also prepared and presented several series of television shows. In 1947 he spoke at the International Christian Youth Conference in Oslo, Norway. He presented lectures on more than one hundred college campuses and spoke before count-

less groups and organizations. During World War II, and for many years afterward, he made preaching missions for the armed forces. In 1952 he spent three months preaching at military bases in England at the request of the chief of chaplains of the United States Air Force. In 1960 he traveled to American bases in Turkey and Crete, and in 1962 he lectured for air force personnel in Central America.

Austin's University Baptist Church, under Dr. Smith's leadership, was integrated long before the United States Supreme Court outlawed racial segregation. A member of his congregation described him as an honest man who reflected the character of his God. "Only God knows how many suicides never took place, how many divorces never occurred, how many failures were turned into victories, because of the counsel this man gave. . . . He was unorthodox, liberal, progressive. But he was doggedly faithful to an idea that transcends all religions: the love of God for humanity. . . . Of all the men and women who have shaped the character of Austin in the last 30 years, none has been as lastingly influential as this quiet, strong, loving man."

In addition to numerous articles, he wrote The Gospel for the Bewildered (1946), Religion in Life (1947), These Shared His Coming (1951), and From Doors to Attics (1952). He was president of the Austin Ministers Alliance, president of the Council on Religion at the University of Texas, and chairman of Austin's Human Relations Committee. An oral history on a part of his ministry is in the library at Baylor University.

Blake Smith was married to Dora Alberta Riley of Eldorado, Arkansas, on December 15, 1925; they had five sons. He died June 23, 1973, in Ithaca, New York, while visiting his oldest son, John Lee Smith, director of the social action-religion program at Cornell University. His widow died September 25, 1974; both were buried at Memorial Park Cemetery in Austin.

BIBLIOGRAPHY: Austin American-Statesman, June 24, 1973, July 8, 1973; Who's Who In America (1968).

Ernestine Wheelock

Smith, Persifor Frazer. Persifor Frazer Smith was born in Philadelphia, Pennsylvania, on November 16, 1798, son of Jonathan and Mary (Frazer) Smith. In 1815 he was graduated from the College of New Jersey (later Princeton University) with a B.A. degree. He studied law and later moved to New Orleans, where he held several judicial offices and became adjutant general of Louisiana.

He married Frances Jeanette Bureau on January 19, 1822; they had one son. Because Smith had participated in several Indian fights, he received the rank of colonel in the United States Army at the beginning of the Mexican War. He directed attacks for General Zachary Taylor qv at the battle of Monterrey, and was brevetted brigadier general for gallant service. He was transferred to General Winfield Scott's Division and served in the 1st Brigade under David Emanuel Twiggs.qv Smith's bravery brought him further distinction and the rank of brevet major general.

After the war he was assigned to command the Western Division (1st Pacific Division), and after the death of General George Mercer Brooke,qv Smith was assigned the command of the Department of Texas, which he assumed in September, 1851. He continued in this position until he was transferred to St. Louis in 1856.

After the death of his first wife, he married Anne (Millard) Armstrong, widow of Major Francis A. Armstrong, on April 18, 1854. In April, 1858, he was assigned to command the Department of Utah, but he died on May 17 of that year at Fort Leavenworth, Kansas. Smith was buried in the Laurel Hill Cemetery in Philadelphia, Pennsylvania.

BIBLIOGRAPHY: *Dictionary of American Biography*, XVII (1921); War Department Records, 1851–1858 (National Archives, Washington, D.C.).

Margaret Bierschwale

Smith, Robert Lloyd. Born a free Negro in Charleston, South Carolina, about 1861, Robert Lloyd Smith attended Avery Institute in South Carolina and the University of South Carolina; he received his B.A. degree from Atlanta University. He left his native state and came to Texas sometime during the late 1870's or early 1880's. In Oakland, Colorado County, he was principal of the Oakland Normal School in 1885. He became an aide to Booker T. Washington and an advocate of the Tuskegee line of accommodation and self-help. In 1890 Smith founded the Farmers' Home Improvement Society qv in Colorado County, an outgrowth of the earlier Village Improvement Society (1889). The organization encouraged Negro farmers toward economic independence with home and farm ownership, cooperative buying, cash purchases instead of credit buying, and raising much of their own food. The society, which sponsored agricultural fairs and paid sick and death benefits, spread over Texas, Oklahoma, and Arkansas, and, with Smith as president, branched out in succeeding years to encompass a truck growers' union, an agricultural college at Wolfe City in 1906, and the Farmers' Improvement Bank in Waco. The Woman's Barnyard Auxiliaries, with membership in twenty counties, specialized in better egg, poultry, and butter production, and the raising of improved swine for the market.

A Republican, Smith was elected to the 24th and 25th legislatures in 1894 and 1896 from predominately white Colorado County, when the whites split into Democratic and Populist party factions (*see* Populist Party in Texas). His legislative proposals primarily concerned education, race relations, and the advancement of Prairie View Normal School (now Prairie View A&M University). He was appointed deputy United States marshal for the Eastern District of Texas by President Theodore Roosevelt and served from 1902 to 1909, when he was removed during the Taft administration. Smith was active in various Negro fraternal orders and in

1915 organized and took charge of the state's Negro Extension Division to foster improved agricultural methods among Negro farmers. Smith called himself a "practical sociologist." He was married to Ruby Cobb, and the couple adopted two children. Smith died July 10, 1942, and was buried in Greenwood Cemetery in Waco, where he had lived for a number of years and had been a member of St. James United Methodist Church.

BIBLIOGRAPHY: J. Mason Brewer, *Negro Legislators of Texas* (1935); Lawrence D. Rice, *The Negro in Texas, 1874–1900* (1971); R. L. Smith, "Village Improvement Among the Negroes," *Outlook*, LXIV (March 31, 1900); Monroe N. Work (comp.), "Some Negro Members of Reconstruction Legislatures: Texas," *Journal of Negro History*, 5 (January, 1920).

Lawrence D. Rice

*Smith, Robert W.

*Smith, Robert Waverly.

*Smith, Stuart Robertson.

Smith, Temple Doswell. Temple Doswell Smith was born on August 22, 1846, in Hanover County, Virginia, on Walnut Hill plantation, the son of John Snelson Smith, Jr., and Pauline Thilman (Doswell) Smith. With his parents he migrated to Indiana in 1860. He attended the public school and studied under his father. He taught school briefly and worked for an Indianapolis hardware firm and for a New York finance firm. In 1876 he married Mary Alice Francis in Indianapolis; they had one daughter.

In 1884, along with his brother Frank, Smith joined in a banking and mercantile venture in Anson, Texas. In 1887 he founded the Bank of Fredericksburg. He also organized the First National Bank of Carthage in 1884 and the Cotton Belt State Bank in Timpson in 1897, and he headed the committee that brought the railroad into Fredericksburg in 1913. A new town along the railroad was named "Bankersmith" in his honor. He died on April 24, 1926, in San Antonio and was buried in Bayview Cemetery, Jersey City, New Jersey.

BIBLIOGRAPHY: Robert Penniger, *Fest Ausgabe zum 50-jährigen Jubiläum der Gründung der Stadt Friedrichsburg* (1896); Gillespie County Historical Society, *Pioneers in God's Hills* (1960).

Esther L. Mueller

*Smith, Thomas F.

*Smith, Thomas I.

*Smith, Thomas Slater.

Smith, Thomas Vernor. Thomas Vernor Smith, professor, politician, and author, was born in a two-room cabin at Blanket, Texas, on April 26, 1890, one of ten children of John Robert and Mary Elizabeth (Graves) Smith. He had no high school diploma, but the University of Texas admitted him on condition, and two years later, in 1915, he graduated with a B.A. degree. In 1916 he received an M.A. degree from the university. He taught English literature and philosophy from 1916 to 1917 at Texas Christian University; after serving as a private in the U.S. Army during World War I, he taught philosophy from 1919 to 1921 at the University of Texas. In 1922 he received his Ph.D. from the University of Chicago and was associated with that university as both a professor of philosophy and dean from 1922 to 1948.

During his years with the University of Chicago, Smith became involved in politics. In 1934 he was elected to the Illinois state senate as a Democrat, and later he served as chairman of the Illinois legislative council. He was Illinois congressman-at-large in the 76th United States Congress from 1939 to 1941. He gained national recognition when he engaged Senator Robert A. Taft in a series of radio debates which were later published as *Foundations of Democracy* (1939). Smith was an unsuccessful candidate for reelection in 1940. He was instrumental in organizing and producing a famed and influential program in educational radio, the "University of Chicago Round Table," the oldest educational program continuously broadcast. Smith was the moderator and a participant in this endeavor, which gained a nationwide audience. During World War II, he served in Italy as an educational director of the Allied Control Commission and in Germany was an advisor dealing with German prisoners of war. He was involved in similar duties with the Educational Mission to Japan. He left the service with the rank of colonel.

In 1948 Smith went to Syracuse University as Maxwell professor of citizenship and philosophy. Known there as the "three P professor" (poetry, politics, and philosophy) he also taught for brief periods of time at some twenty-three American universities as a visiting professor, and presented a television series on some of the campuses he visited. He was a student debator while he was at the University of Texas and continued to debate with well-known public figures throughout his life. He was a member of numerous organizations, including the American Philosophical Association and the American Political Science Association. He edited the *International Journal of Ethics* and was the author of more than twenty books and hundreds of articles. Some of his books were *The Democratic Way of Life* (1925), *Philosophers in Hades* (1932), *The Legislative Way of Life* (1940), *Discipline for Democracy* (1942), and his autobiography, *A Non-Existent Man* (1962).

He was married to Nannie Stewart, a fellow student at the University of Texas; they had two children. He retired from Syracuse in 1959 and moved to Austin, Texas, for a while, but failing health caused him to move near his family in Maryland. Smith died on May 24, 1964, in Hyattsville, Maryland, and was buried in Arlington National Cemetery.

BIBLIOGRAPHY: *Who's Who In America* (1950).

Richard T. Fleming

*Smith, Wilford B.

*Smith, William Robert.

*Smith, Texas.

*Smith Bend, Texas.

*Smith County. Smith County, in East Texas, was largely urbanized by 1966. Principal agricultural products were peaches, berries, and some field crops and livestock; the county was distinguished for the growing of roses. Smith County was 39 percent forested and had two active sawmills in 1968. Lumber and minerals were also important; mineral income amounted to $11,427,797 by 1967. In 1972 total oil production reached 167,066,081 barrels since its discovery in the county in 1931. Lake Tyler and Mud Creek Reservoir were the county's major tourist attractions. The 1960 population was 86,350; in 1970 the population was 97,096, according to the United States census. *See also* Tyler Standard Metropolitan Statistical Area.

*Smith County (Judicial).

*Smith Creek.

*Smith Ferry, Texas.

*Smith Oaks, Texas.

*Smith Point, Texas.

Smither, Harriet Wingfield. Harriet Wingfield Smither, daughter of William Goldsmith and Harriet Wilson (Wingfield) Smither, was born in Hampton, Virginia, on July 13, 1879. After the death of her parents she was reared by relatives in Georgetown, Texas. She attended St. Mary's Academy in Austin, the University of Texas, where she received a B.S. degree in 1905 and an M.A. degree in 1922, and the University of Chicago. She taught in the public schools of Dublin, Cleburne, and Fort Worth from 1905 to 1922.

In 1925 she was appointed archivist in the Texas State Library,qv a position she held until her retirement. She was a coauthor (with Clarence Ousley and R. G. Hall) of *The Student's History of Our Country* (1913). Her major contributions to the field of Texas history were in the editing of manuscript collections. These include volumes five and six of the *Papers of Mirabeau B. Lamar* (1927), *Journals of the Fourth Congress* (1929), *Journals of the Sixth Congress* (1940–1945), and the "Diary of Adolphus Sterne," which appeared in the *Southwestern Historical Quarterly*.qv

Miss Smither was known for her assistance to other scholars. On her retirement, September 30, 1953, the Texas State Library and Historical Commission qv adopted a resolution stating that "largely through the efforts of Miss Smither, the State Library has acquired one of the most complete Texana collections in existence." She died at her home in Austin, March 20, 1955, and was buried in Georgetown. On March 23 of that year the Texas Senate passed a memorial resolution in her honor.

BIBLIOGRAPHY: Austin *American-Statesman*, September 24, 1950; Austin *American*, March 21, 1955.

Dorman H. Winfrey

*Smither, Robert Goodloe.

Smithers Lake. Smithers Lake is in the Brazos River Basin in Fort Bend County, ten miles southeast of Richmond on Dry Creek. The project is owned and operated by the Houston Lighting &

Power Company as the cooling-water supply for a steam-electric generating station. Construction was started on August 22, 1956, and was completed on July 1, 1957. Water had already been impounded in a small lake, and the date for beginning of impoundment in the new lake was October 15, 1957. The lake has a capacity of 18,000 acre-feet and a surface area of 2,140 acres, at elevation 66 feet above mean sea level. Runoff is supplemented by water purchased from the canal system of the Richmond Rice Association as needed to keep the lake elevation at normal level for the plant operation. The drainage area above the dam is 24.2 square miles.

BIBLIOGRAPHY: Texas Water Commission, *Bulletin 6408* (1964).

Seth D. Breeding

*Smithfield, Texas.

*Smithland, Texas.

*Smithson Valley, Texas.

*Smithville, Texas. Smithville, in southeastern Bastrop County, is a center for the fabrication of wood (particularly cedar) products and other light manufacturing. The city had sixty businesses in 1970. A rest home was completed in 1965, and fifty low-rent houses were then being built. In 1966 the city had a bank, a newspaper, and two hospitals. A new library and city hall were completed by 1971. The population was 2,933 in 1960 and 2,959 in 1970, according to the United States census.

*Smithwick, Noah.

*Smithwick, Texas.

*Smoky Creek.

*Smoothingiron Mountain.

*Smothers Creek.

*Smugglers Bayou.

*Smyer, Texas.

*Smyrna, Texas.

*Smyth, George Washington. George Washington Smyth served as commissioner of the General Land Office ᵠᵛ from March 20, 1848, to March 1, 1852 (not to March 1, 1857, as stated in Volume II). He was nominated for Congress at a convention in Tyler in 1853 (not 1852). He was elected to the 33rd United States Congress in August, 1853, and began serving his term in December, 1853 (not March 4, 1853). Smyth served as congressman through the end of the session, to March, 1855, and did not seek reelection.

BIBLIOGRAPHY: Texas General Land Office, *Report of the Commissioner of the General Land Office, 1918–1920* (c. 1920); *Texas State Gazette*, May 14, 1853; *Biographical Directory of the American Congress, 1774–1927* (1928); Peter H. Bell, Proclamations and Correspondence of the Secretary of State and Governor, 1846–1874 (Archives, Texas State Library, Austin).

Roger A. Griffin

*Smyth, Rawleigh Portues.

*Smythe, David Porter.

*Snailum Creek.

*Snake Creek.

*Snap, Texas.

*Sneed, Sebron Graham.

*Sneed, Sebron Graham, Jr.

*Sneed, Thomas Eskridge.

*Sneed Chapel, Texas.

*Sneedville, Texas.

*Snell, Martin Kingsley.

*Snelling, James G. Soulard.

*Snell's, Texas. Snell's (known also as Snell's Bend, Snell's Landing, and Snell's Bluff) was located in the extreme northeastern part of Newton County on the Sabine River about ten miles north of Burkeville. Named for Adam H. Snell, who emigrated from Alabama and settled there in 1848, it was a boat landing, trading center, and shipping point for the surrounding area. Snell and his brother, John J., were boat masters and merchants. The post office was established in 1881, but the name was changed to Delma in 1887. The town had a mill, two stores, a warehouse, and a school, but it declined after riverboats ceased making runs. Origin of the name Delma, or why it was substituted for Snell's, is not known. Delma did not appear in the list of post offices after 1909 but was shown on maps as late as 1925.

BIBLIOGRAPHY: *Texas Almanac* (1903, 1905, 1907, 1909); *New Reference Atlas of the World* (1925).

Madeleine Martin

*Snider, Gabriel Straw.

*Snipe, Texas.

*Snively, Jacob.

*Snively Expedition.

*Snook, Texas. Snook, Texas, in Burleson County, began as a Czech farming settlement when Josef Slovacek and his family moved into the Mound Prairie area in November, 1884, after a brief stay at Ross Prairie in Fayette County; Martin Kocurek, Joe Mikula, and their families, along with other Czechs, soon followed. At first the new settlers got their supplies from nearby Tunis and Merle; they then organized a cooperative and built a store on a site known as Sebesta's Corner or Sebesta. As the community grew, a beef club (*Masová Schůza*) was organized to supply fresh beef weekly to club members, and the clubhouse became a gathering place for the farmers. By the early 1890's the cooperative store had been sold to a private owner, and two saloons, two stores, and a cotton gin, all Czech-owned, had been built. In 1895, midway between Dabney Hill (a Negro settlement) and Sebesta, the post office of Snook was located; the businesses of Sebesta gradually moved there.

In 1888 a one-room school was built between Sebesta and what is now Snook; Czech books were used and the Czech language was taught until 1891. After that date a yearly vacation school for Czech studies was held. In 1914 the old school building was torn down, and the new Moravia school was built. In 1935 the building was moved to its present location. The Snook Independent School District, completely integrated, included the former schools of Moravia, Lone Oak, Merle, and Dabney Hill, with an enrollment of over five hundred and approximately thirty teachers in 1971.

Members of the Czech community in the 1880's joined the national fraternal organization, Czechoslovak Benevolent Society (CSPS), and built a lodge hall which served as a community gathering place. When dues of the society became too high, the members at Snook started a local chapter of the Slavonic Benevolent Order of the State of Texas (SPJST) in March, 1897, and held meetings in their old hall. A new hall was built in 1910 and was rebuilt in 1911; in 1935 another hall was dedicated. Protestant church services were held in various homes from the beginning of the settlement. In 1913 the Snook Protestant community joined the Evangelical Unity of the Czech-Moravian Brethren. Later churches were Saint Jacob's Catholic Church (1917), the Assembly of God Church (1934), and Lone Oak Baptist Church. A historical marker commemorating the founding of the Snook community was dedicated in 1971. In 1970 there were approximately 300 inhabitants in Snook. *See also* Czechs in Texas.

BIBLIOGRAPHY: Robert L. Skrabanek, Social Organization and Change in a Czech-American Rural Community (Ph.D. dissertation, Louisiana State University, 1949); Austin *American-Statesman*, May 26, 1971.

*Snow Hill, Texas. (Collin County.)

Snow Hill, Texas. (Morris County.) *See* Cason, Texas.

*Snyder, Dudley Hiram.

*Snyder, Texas. Snyder, seat of Scurry County, was named for an early trader, William Henry (Pete) Snyder, who had operated a trading post there in 1878; the town's post office was established on November 21, 1885 (after Pete Snyder had moved to Colorado City), and the first postmaster was Houston B. Patterson. The town was incorporated in 1907.

When oil was discovered in the area in 1948 the town had a huge increase in population, from 3,815 in 1940 to 12,010 in 1950. The town prospered during the 1950's, with businesses engaged mostly in the production of oil and oil products. In the 1960's and early 1970's Snyder had plants engaged in the manufacture of petroleum products, agricultural by-products, bricks, mattresses, wax products, mobile homes, and magnesium products. Snyder reported 278 businesses in 1970. A county hospital was located there. In 1960 the population was 13,850; a decline was evident by 1970, when the population was 11,171, a 19.3 percent decrease in ten years, according to the United States census.

BIBLIOGRAPHY: Scurry County Historical Survey Committee, *Historical Markers in Scurry County* (1969); *Texas Almanac* (1971).

*Soap Creek.

Soash, William Pulver. William P. Soash was born on September 5, 1877, in Butler County, Iowa,

son of George and Polly (Hiserodt) Soash. After his mother died in 1883, he moved from place to place with his railroad contractor father. In 1891 his father died, and Soash then worked as a carpenter and as a deputy United States marshal.

After 1900 Soash engaged in the hardware and real estate business in Iowa and helped colonize land in the Dakotas for the John Lund Land Company. In 1905 he founded the W. P. Soash Land Company, which grew to be one of the largest land companies in the United States, with offices in more than eight states; the company acquired a 30,000-acre tract in the Texas Panhandle from the Capitol Freehold Land and Investment Company.qv Soash founded the town of Ware on the Fort Worth and Denver Railway, built a hotel there in 1906, and later added more land to the tract. Two years later Soash bought Christopher Columbus Slaughter's qv 100,000-acre Running Water Ranch on the South Plains, and he sold it to northern homeseekers. He introduced new techniques in land sales and advertising, including a company magazine, *The Golden West*, and the use of excursion trains to take interested people to the actual land location.

In 1909 Soash began his largest project when he secured 200,000 acres of Slaughter's Big Spring Ranch. The town of Soash was built about twenty miles north of Big Spring, and the company offices were moved there from Iowa. In 1912 the Soash Land Company went out of business after three years of drouth, which had stopped the influx of homeseekers. In 1917, while selling Littlefield lands (*see* George Washington Littlefield) in Lamb County, he became interested in land promotion in Florida. He served in the Texas Cavalry during World War I as a second lieutenant. In 1924 Soash and the Slaughters organized the Lone Star Land Company; he became president of this company and moved his family from McAllen to Lubbock. In 1938 Soash was engaged in selling mineral interests. Soash was married to Minnie Haase in 1900; they had two children. He died on July 10, 1961.

BIBLIOGRAPHY: Seymour V. Connor (ed.), *Builders of the Southwest* (1959); Amarillo *Globe*, August 14, 1938; Littlefield Land Company Papers (Southwest Collection, Texas Tech University; MS., Archives, University of Texas at Austin Library).

David B. Gracy II

*Soash, Texas. Soash was founded in northwestern Howard County in 1909 by William Pulver Soash,qv for whom it was named. In the early years he constructed $60,000 worth of buildings, including a hotel named for his daughter Lorna, a garage, and an office and bank building to which he moved his land company's headquarters. The Gulf, Soash, and Pacific Railroad was formed and granted a charter to build from Big Spring north to the Santa Fe line near Lubbock, but the plan did not materialize. Three years of drouth from 1909 to 1912 stopped land-selling activities, and the land company went out of business, abandoning the town.

BIBLIOGRAPHY: Laura V. Hamner interview with W. P.

Soash, November 15, 1936 (MS., Archives, University of Texas at Austin Library); W. P. Soash Papers (Southwest Collection, Texas Tech University).

Soash Land Company. *See* Soash, William Pulver.

*Socagee Bayou.

Social Science Quarterly. The *Social Science Quarterly*, formerly *The Southwestern Social Science Quarterly*,qv published jointly by the Southwestern Social Science Association qv and the University of Texas at Austin, was founded in 1920. The journal has had ten editors, eight of whom have been faculty members at the University of Texas and two at the University of Oklahoma. The first editor was C. G. Haines (1920–1921), and he was followed by H. G. James (1922–1925). For the next ten years C. P. Patterson was editor; in 1936 J. J. Rhyne of Oklahoma was appointed editor-in-chief, and the association's nine sections each elected an associate editor to work with him. The election of associate editors has continued to the present, the number changing with the number of disciplines affiliated with the association. Succeeding editors have been Carl Rosenquist (1939–1941), Ruth Allen (1942–1947), Oliver Benson of Oklahoma (1948–1953), Frederic Meyers (1953–1957), Harry E. Moore (1957–1966), and Charles M. Bonjean (1966–).

The name of *The Southwestern Social Science Quarterly* was changed to *Social Science Quarterly* in June of 1968. Circulation was 3,300 in 1971. Articles were published from all disciplines represented by the association, although some preference was shown for those with an interdisciplinary or regional appeal. Major books were reviewed in the journal, and the annual program and proceedings of the Southwestern Social Science Association were also published.

Charles M. Bonjean

Socialist Party in Texas. Two Socialist parties have existed in Texas—the Socialist Labor party and the Socialist party of Texas. Generally they favored improvements in laboring conditions, popular government, increases in taxes on large accumulations of land and wealth, and government ownership of transportation, communication, and exchange facilities. The Socialist Labor party nominated candidates for governor from 1898 to 1914 (except for 1902) without polling more than 590 votes in any election. In 1904 a group including several former Populists (*see* Populist Party in Texas) organized a Social Democratic convention and in 1906 became the Socialist party of Texas. Its voting strength increased steadily to peaks of slightly more than 25,000 in the presidential election of 1912 and in the gubernatorial elections of 1912 and 1914, when it replaced the Republican party qv as the second largest party in the state. A decline followed, and no candidates were nominated in 1922 and 1924. The party then received a few votes in state elections through 1938 and in presidential elections through 1948.

BIBLIOGRAPHY: E. W. Winkler, *Platforms of Political Parties in Texas* (1916); *Texas Almanac* (1965).

Alwyn Barr

Society for the Protection of German Emigrants in Texas. *See* Adelsverein.

*Socorro, Texas.

*Socorro del Sur. *See* Nuestra Señora de la Concepción del Socorro.

*Soda, Texas.

*Soda Lake.

**Soda Lake Herald.*

*Sodosa Creek.

*Sodville, Texas.

*Soil Conservation Board, State. The State Soil Conservation Board's name was changed to the State Soil and Water Conservation Board in 1965.

Soil and Water Conservation. The Soil Conservation Service of the United States Department of Agriculture is charged with developing and carrying out a permanent national soil and water conservation program. The program in Texas covers 99 percent of the agricultural land in the state; the work is carried out in cooperation with Texas A&M University. It was estimated that by 1975, 159,918,245 acres of agricultural land would remain in the state and, of that area, 130,112,079 acres would need conservation treatment. In 1967 approximately 500 watersheds of 250,000 acres or less, with flood or other water management problems, required cooperative action by groups of landowners or operators.

Districts organized for the purpose of providing additional fertility and water for land in Texas, and protecting that in existence, are authorized under state law; the districts are administered by a governing body of five local landowners, elected by neighboring landowners, who serve without pay. It is their function to work in cooperation with federal, state, county, city, and civic organizations which devote time and money to the program. The state office for soil and water conservation in Texas is in Temple. *See also* State Soil and Water Conservation Board.

Soil and Water Conservation Board, State. *See* State Soil and Water Conservation Board; *see also* Soil Conservation Board, State (in Volume II).

*Soils of Texas.

*Sojourner, Albert Lloyd.

*Sol Creek.

Soldier Lake. Soldier Lake, in Dimmit County, is located almost due east of Carrizo Springs and south of Espantosa Lake. It drains in a southwesterly direction (with several semidry creeks which flow northeast) into the Nueces River between Asherton and Brundage.

*Soldiers Mound.

*Soldiers and Sailors Moratorium.

*Soledad Creek.

*Soledad Hills.

*Solino, Texas.

*Solitario, The.

*Solitario Peak.

*Solms, Texas.

*Solms-Braunfels, Prince Carl of.

*Solon, Texas.

*Somerset, Texas.

*Somervell, Alexander.

*Somervell County. Somervell County, noted for its unique geological formations, is primarily a ranching and tourist area. The Somervell County program-building committee, organized in 1953, established programs for young people and did valuable work in the areas of agriculture, livestock, poultry, and pecans. Dinosaur tracks in the Paluxy River bottom near Glen Rose are an unusual tourist attraction; plans were under way in 1966 to create a park around the tracks. A flour mill, a cedar oil mill, and the Central Texas Conference Methodist camp were located in the county. The 1960 population was 2,577; in 1970 it was 2,793, according to the United States census.

*Somervell Expedition.

*Somerville, James Alexander.

*Somerville, Texas. Somerville, in Burleson County, adjacent to Somerville Reservoir, had a railroad tie manufacturing plant operated by the Atchison, Topeka, and Santa Fe Railroad. The Somerville Stampede is held each year in May in an arena built by the townspeople. The two-day rodeo was inaugurated by a Catholic priest, Robert L. Mahoney, to raise money to aid in locating a shoe factory in the town; proceeds were used to build a modern recreation center and to purchase land for a planned low-income 156-home subdivision. The 1960 population was 1,177, and in 1970 it was 1,250, according to the United States census. Twenty-eight businesses were reported in 1970.
BIBLIOGRAPHY: Austin *American-Statesman*, August 29, 1971.

Somerville Reservoir. Somerville Dam and Reservoir, in the Brazos River Basin of Burleson and Washington counties, is on Yegua Creek, two miles south of Somerville. Construction began in June, 1962. The project is owned by the United States government and operated by the United States Army Corps of Engineers, Fort Worth District. A contract was made by the federal government whereby the Brazos River Authority qv would pay $4,871,-000 for the conservation storage together with a percentage of the operating cost. The reservoir, at a conservation storage space elevation of 238 feet above mean sea level, has a capacity of 160,100 acre-feet and a surface area of 11,460 acres; it is to be used for conservation storage, recreational, and other purposes. The flood control storage capacity is 347,400 acre-feet, between elevations 238 and 258 feet above mean sea level, and the drainage area above the dam is 1,006 square miles.

BIBLIOGRAPHY: Texas Water Commission, *Bulletin 6408* (1964).

Seth D. Breeding

*Soncy, Texas.

Sonoma, Texas. Sonoma, in southeast Ellis County, had a 1960 population of 503 and a 1970 population of 678, according to the United States census.

*Sonora, Texas. Sonora, seat of Sutton County, did not develop as a trading post on the San Antonio-El Paso road (as stated in Volume II); the route bypassed Sonora because the vicinity lacked adequate water. It was the sheepherder, looking for grass, who first settled in the area. The well-drilling machine made the country habitable, and Sonora's first well was drilled in February, 1889, after which time Sonora began to grow. Robert W. Callahan built the first store and became the first postmaster on September 19, 1889 (not Peter Hurst, as stated in Volume II; there was a Pharis Hurst who was second postmaster, appointed February 15, 1890). E. F. Vander Stucken (not F. F. Van Stucken) bought out a store in 1893 which possibly had been in operation since 1890. The 66.4 mile rail line from San Angelo to Sonora via Christoval and Eldorado made its first run July 1, 1930 (not June, 1931), and returned with twenty-three carloads of wool.

Sonora had an economy in the 1950's and 1960's based primarily on livestock, an expanding tourist trade, and the oil and gas industry. The Caverns of Sonora qv were a major tourist attraction. Public works included an airport completed in 1958 and sewer and water improvements completed during the early 1960's. In 1966 Sonora reported nine churches, a hospital, a bank, a library, a weekly newspaper, and a radio station. In 1970 the town had approximately sixty businesses. A Texas A&M University agricultural research substation was located in Sonora. The 1960 population was 2,619; it declined to 2,149 by 1970, according to the United States census.
BIBLIOGRAPHY: *The Devil's River News* (Sonora), October 25, 1940; San Angelo *Evening Standard*, July 1, 2, 1930; San Antonio *Express*, July 2, 1930.

John Eaton

Sonora, Caverns of. The Caverns of Sonora are located in the western part of Sutton County, in limestone of the Cretaceous age. Discovered by a sheepherder around 1900, they were given little attention in the years following. Explorations were prevented by a pit with a sixty-foot drop near the entrance; in 1955, however, spelunkers successfully roped around it and the caverns were explored for commercial development. On July 23, 1960, the caverns were opened to the public. Outstanding features of the caves are the varied types of speleothema.

In 1965 several hundred yards of new passages were opened and an exit was cut in 108 feet of solid rock. The grounds included offices, a lunch counter, a lobby, recreational areas for children, and camping facilities. The park is open year round.

John Eaton

Sons of Confederate Veterans, Texas Division of. The Sons of Confederate Veterans was organized as the United Sons of Confederate Veterans in Richmond, Virginia, on July 1, 1896, under the auspices of its parent organization, the United Confederate Veterans. J. E. B. Stuart, son of the famous cavalry leader, was its first commander-in-chief.

The organization is composed of three departments, the Army of Northern Virginia, the Army of Tennessee, and the Army of the Trans-Mississippi. The departments are organized into divisions which generally follow state lines, each divided into local camps. From the beginning the Texas Division has had local camps in all the major cities of the state.

The organization's chief project is the preservation and maintenance of *Beauvoir*, last home of President Jefferson Davis, located at Biloxi, Mississippi, and owned by the Mississippi Division. Membership is open to men who are lineal or collateral descendants of those who served honorably in the Confederate Army or Navy, provided such applicants are over twelve years of age; those members under sixteen years of age may not vote.

H. Chilton Cook, Jr., was commander of the Texas Division in 1974. The general headquarters has been located in the War Memorial Building, Jackson, Mississippi, since 1955.

Mildred Webb Bugg

Sons of Hermann, Order of the. The Order of the Sons of Hermann in the state of Texas (also known as Hermann Sons) was the largest fraternal benefit society headquartered in Texas; its home offices were in San Antonio in 1966 when its 167 lodges had a membership of approximately 64,000. From the time of its founding in San Antonio on July 6, 1861, until 1920, the Texas order was part of a national order of the Sons of Hermann. A few men of German descent organized the order in New York City in 1840, naming it for Hermann the Defender, an early German hero known also as Arminius. By 1848 there were six Sons of Hermann groups with 800 members in the United States, and, on December 25, 1848, a national grand lodge was formed in Milwaukee.

In 1861 two representatives of the national grand lodge came to San Antonio to organize the first Hermann Sons lodge in Texas, Harmonia Lodge No. 1. It was natural for the organization to find fertile soil in San Antonio since many Germans had come to the area after 1845. On March 27, 1890, the Texas grand lodge was formed, consisting of Harmonia Lodge of San Antonio and seven other newly formed lodges in Austin, Taylor, Temple, Waco, La Grange, Brenham, and Houston. These eight lodges had a total of 242 members. Within a year ninety-two more lodges were formed. In 1896 the first sister lodge, exclusively for women, was dedicated at Sherman. In 1920 the first mixed lodge for both men and women was established in San Antonio, and that trend has continued. In 1920 the Order of the Sons of Hermann in Texas, which by then was financially stronger and had more members than all of the lodges in the rest of the United States combined, broke away from the national order of the Sons of Hermann and became autonomous and independent of the national group. Complete transition from the German language to the English language by the Texas order was begun early in the 1930's and completed by 1937. Originally all of the members were of German extraction, but only about half were of German extraction by 1965. Since 1916 the order has maintained a home for aged members at Comfort, Texas, and since 1954 it has operated its own youth summer camp for junior members on its 202-acre tract at Comfort.

Fritz Schilo

*Sons of the Republic of Texas. The Sons of the Republic of Texas was first organized on April 11, 1893, at Richmond, Texas, by F. M. O. Fenn, as Deaf Smith Lodge No. 1; S. J. Winston was elected president. Ten days later, on April 21, a state society was organized in Houston with W. A. Craddock as president. The society met with the Texas Veterans Association qv in Waco the following year and continued to meet in conjunction with that organization for several years before becoming inactive. On March 15, 1922, the society was reactivated in Houston by Odin M. Kendall, along with several members of the original group and other descendants of early Texans. Andrew Jackson Houston qv was elected president.

The objectives of the society have been to perpetuate the memory and spirit of the men and women who founded Texas, to encourage research, to promote the observance of Texas holidays, to preserve and mark historical sites, and to foster comprehensive knowledge of the state.

With the help of Jesse H. Jones,qv the society was influential in securing funds for the San Jacinto Monument.qv It helped found the San Jacinto Museum of History and promoted the observance of San Jacinto Day. Since 1951 the Sons have annually given the $1,000 Summerfield G. Roberts Award to the author of the outstanding work published on early Texas during the year. Since 1953 the organization has published *The Texian*, a periodical containing news of the society and historical articles. The organization established the David G. Burnet Park in east Harris County and assisted in establishing the New Kentucky Park in the western part of the county. They also contributed to the erection of the entrance gates at the San Jacinto Battleground. In 1957 a committee met with Governor Price Daniel and discussed plans for a state archives and library building; the group was influential in helping persuade the legislature to build the structure and to give statutory standing to the Texas State Historical Survey Committee,qv an agency originally organized on a temporary basis in 1953.

Since 1970 the society has awarded the $2,500 Presidio La Bahía Award, created by the Kathryn Stoner O'Connor Foundation (*see* La Bahía), for research into the Spanish colonial period of Texas. In that same year the organization began financing the Spanish Texas Microfilm Center, which is located in the restored Calabozo rooms at the Presidio La Bahía. With an initial grant from the O'Connor Foundation, the Sons established the center for the collection of microfilmed primary resource materials for the study of the Hispanic influence on Texas culture.

In 1972 the society's membership was approximately 1,000, with 572 junior members and 33 honorary members. An honorary unit is the Knights of the Order of San Jacinto,qv created by Sam Houston in 1842 or early in 1843; this degree is conferred for outstanding service to the state of Texas and for contributing to the development of Texas heritage; since it was reestablished in 1941, seventy-nine Knights degrees have been conferred.

BIBLIOGRAPHY: Sons of the Republic of Texas, *Year Book* (1966, 1971); *The Texian* (August, 1970, March, August, 1971); Galveston *News*, April 13, 1893; Houston *Chronicle*, March 2, 1922; Houston *Post*, April 1, 1922.

Frank E. Tritico

*Sophienburg Museum. The Sophienburg Museum in New Braunfels is located on the "hill," or *Vereinsberg* (as it became known to the German settlers and since used as a designation for that part of town). Prince Carl of Solms-Braunfels,qv as commissioner general of the Adelsverein,qv lived there in a tent during his three months' stay in the colony. He planned to build a replica of his family's castle on the hill, and although he laid the cornerstone and made the outline for the Sophienburg, no buildings were completed until after he left. On April 28, 1845, during the cornerstone ceremonies, with a firing of cannon, Prince Solms had the Austrian flag raised on the hill while the new German immigrants raised the United States flag in the town below.

A complex of buildings was built on the hill and was described by the visiting German naturalist Ferdinand Roemer,qv who stayed at the Sophienburg in 1845–1846. The main building was located on lot number thirty-six on the corner of Coll and Academy streets, facing north and the town below. It was a one-story building made of cedar logs. In Albert Schütze's *Jahrbuch für Texas* (1882), credit for the building's construction was given to the Smith brothers of Seguin, but in the *Neu Braunfelser Zeitung*,qv March 1, 1906, the work was credited to the Stuessy brothers, who had moved to New Braunfels in the 1840's. In the center of the property was a well, which covered over in 1969 when a parking lot was made for the new library adjoining the museum on the southeast. The main building of the old Sophienburg, severely damaged in 1886 (not in 1866, as stated in Volume II) by the same storm which destroyed Indianola, was torn down about the turn of the century.

In 1933, when the main portion of the Sophienburg Museum was completed, an earlier historical collection was moved there from the basement of the New Braunfels city hall, where a temporary museum had been set up in 1932. Exhibited in the limestone building, which is open to the public, are German books and manuscripts, a copy of the Solms-Braunfels archives in German, and a regional collection of old tools, musical instruments, photographs, banners, clothing, firearms, furniture, household items, paintings, and drawings.

BIBLIOGRAPHY: Oscar Haas, "Editorials and Features," New Braunfels *Herald and Zeitung*, April 8, 1971; *Sophienburg Memorial Museum* (Sophienburg Museum publication, n.d.).

Edna Feuge Faust

*Soro Creek.

*Sorrel Creek.

*Sorrell Creek, Texas.

*Sorrels, Texas.

*Sosa, Gaspar Castaño de. *See* Castaño de Sosa, Gaspar.

Souanetto Indians. The Souanetto Indians are known only from the journal of Henri Joutel qv (1787), which lists them as enemies of the Kadohadacho on the Red River. The name is similar to Zauanito, the name of another unidentified group reported to Spanish missionaries (1691) as enemies of the Hasinai Indians of eastern Texas. The Zauanito seem to have lived to the west of the Hasinai. It seems likely that Souanetto and Zauanito are names for the same people, but this cannot be proved.

BIBLIOGRAPHY: F. W. Hodge (ed.), *Handbook of American Indians*, II (1910); P. Margry, *Découvertes et établissements des Français dans l'ouest et dans le sud de l'Amérique Septentrionale*, III (1879); J. R. Swanton, *Source Material on the History and Ethnology of the Caddo Indians* (1942).

T. N. Campbell

*Soule University.

*Soules Chapel, Texas.

*Sour Lake, Texas. Sour Lake, in Hardin County, had a 1960 population of 1,602 and a 1970 population of 1,694, according to the United States census. The town had thirty businesses in 1970.

*Sour Lake Oil Field.

*Sous Creek.

*South Bend, Texas.

*South Bosque, Texas.

*South Bosque River.

*South Brady Creek.

South Camp, Texas. South Camp, in northwest Midland County, owed its existence to the Midland and Northwestern Railway. When the railroad was abandoned in the 1920's, the town was deserted.

*South Concho Draw.

*South Concho River.

*South East Texas Male and Female College.

*South Elm, Texas.

*South Fork of the Sabine River.

*South Fork of the Wichita River.

*South Franklin Peak.

*South Galveston and Gulf Shore Railroad Company.

*South Grape Creek.

*South Hanlon, Texas.

South Houston, Texas. South Houston, adjacent to Pasadena in Harris County, was founded in 1907 as Dumont by C. S. Woods of the Western Land Company. By 1910 a post office was built, and by 1913 the town was incorporated as South Houston, although the railroad station continued to bear the name of Dumont. Growers shipped the produce of local truck farms, including strawberries, figs, and various vegetables, on the tracks of the Galveston, Houston, and Henderson Railroad. The diversified industries emerging prior to 1915 were destroyed by the hurricane of that year. The development of the Houston Ship Channel qv relocated the heavy industries of the area further inland. Earlier industries manufactured railroad equipment, masonry, candy, walking toys, and an early airplane. Among the businesses reported in the 1960's were manufacturers of asphalt, wire products, oil field chemicals, and concrete conduits. These newer industries were smaller due to the lack of available land. In 1970 the city reported 192 businesses. South Houston was completely surrounded by Houston and Pasadena, which provided employment for many of South Houston's residents. South Houston was amply supplied with municipal recreation facilities and public services, including modern fire-fighting equipment, a hospital, and a library. During the 1950's the population increased 82 percent; the 1960 population was 7,523; in 1970 it was 11,527, according to the United States census. See also Houston Standard Metropolitan Statistical Area.

*South Leon Creek.

*South Liberty, Texas.

*South Llano River.

*South Mayde Creek.

*South Mesquite Creek.

*South Paint Creek.

*South Paloduro Creek.

*South Pease River.

*South Plains, Texas.

South Plains College. South Plains College, a junior college in Levelland, was authorized by a vote of Hockley County citizens in April, 1957. Three months later, $900,000 was approved for purchase of land and equipment and for construction of buildings. The college opened in 1958 with five facilities completed—administration building, library-fine arts building, agriculture-shop building, gymnasium-student center, and auditorium. The Whiteface School District joined the college district in 1958. Enrollment during the first year of operation was 574 students, and the original faculty was composed of seventeen instructors.

Three dormitories were ready for occupancy by 1960, followed by another dormitory and a cafeteria in 1961. A 1963 bond election approved construction of an agriculture building and a science building, as well as enlargement of existing facilities. A fifth dormitory was completed in 1965, bringing the value of land and buildings to over $3,500,000. A 1965 bond issue of $1,765,000 was passed for further expansion of the college. By 1967, enrollment numbered 1,392 students, and the faculty numbered sixty-eight.

The college received accreditation in 1963 by the Southern Association of Colleges and Schools. The library contained 32,000 volumes in 1969, in addition to newspapers and magazines. Curricular offerings included a two-year university parallel program, a technical-occupational program, and an adult education program. College services included bus transportation, evening classes, summer school, and student placement. By 1974 there were over one hundred faculty members, and the student enrollment was 2,338. Marvin L. Baker was president of the college in 1974.

*South Plains and Santa Fe Railway Company. See Crosbyton–South Plains and Santa Fe Railroad Company.

*South Point, Texas.

South Purmela, Texas. South Purmela, located on U. S. Highway 84 in western Coryell County, had a grocery store and garage serving approximately fifteen people located there in the 1960's. South Purmela receives its mail at Purmela, two miles north.

*South San Antonio, Texas.

South San Pedro, Texas. South San Pedro, an unincorporated town in Nueces County, had a 1970 population of 3,065, according to the United States census.

*South Shelving Rock.

South Side Place, Texas. South Side Place, in Harris County, had a 1960 population of 1,282 and a 1970 population of 1,466, according to the United States census.

*South Sulphur, Texas.

*South Sulphur River.

*South Texas Baptist College.

*South Texas Chamber of Commerce.

South Texas College of Law. South Texas College of Law, in Houston, formerly known as South Texas School of Law and Commerce,qv moved to a separate campus in the J. Robert Neal Building on Polk Street in 1964. Prior to that time, the law school and South Texas Junior College qv shared quarters in the downtown YMCA.

Between 1949 and 1965, the number of semester hours required for the LL.B. degree increased from seventy-two to eighty-six. Effective in December, 1965, the LL.B. degree was no longer offered, and students who completed requirements for graduation were awarded the Juris Doctor (J.D.) degree. Admission requirements to the law school rose from having a high school diploma in 1932, to sixty semester hours of college credit in 1938, to ninety semester hours in 1955, to passing a law school admission test after 1963, and to having a baccalaureate degree after 1965.

Under the auspices of South Texas College of Law, the *South Texas Law Journal* was established in 1953. In 1965 the law library contained 20,203 volumes, and the faculty consisted of five full-time instructors and sixteen part-time lecturers. In 1969 the library held 41,018 volumes. Accrediting agencies which approved the law school included the Supreme Court of Texas, the American Bar Association, the Texas Education Agency,qv and the Veterans Administration.

Former deans have been J. C. Hutcheson, Jr., Edgar E. Townes,qv and John C. Jackson. G. R. Walker was dean in 1974, when student enrollment was 855 and the faculty numbered approximately thirty-five.

South Texas Junior College. South Texas Junior College, in Houston, was founded in 1923 as part of the South Texas School of Law and Commerce qv and was operated as a branch of the Young Men's Christian Association of Houston and Harris County. Coeducational classes met in the central YMCA building on Louisiana Street before moving to the M&M Building on Main Street. Enrollment increased from 144 students in 1949 to 2,737 students in 1973. The faculty numbered approximately 120 in 1973.

The junior college was fully accredited and offered the first two years of college-level academic programs under five divisions: business administration, humanities, mathematics and sciences, social sciences, and physical education. An associate degree program in police administration and a certificate program for YMCA secretaries were also available. The college conducted evening classes and two six-week summer sessions. In 1969 the library contained 51,071 bound volumes. Dormitory and athletic facilities were contained in the YMCA and YWCA buildings. The college participated in intercollegiate athletics through state and national conferences. In addition to placing higher education within the financial reach of youth and employed adults, a major aim of the college was to provide counseling and testing services. W. I. Dykes served as acting president in 1974. South Texas Junior College was purchased by the University of Houston and became that school's downtown campus in the fall of 1974; at that time 3,537 students were enrolled.

*South Texas Plains.

*South Texas School of Law and Commerce. See also South Texas College of Law; South Texas Junior College.

*South Texas State Teachers College. See Texas A&I University at Kingsville; see also Texas College of Arts and Industries in Volume II.

Southern Bible College. Southern Bible College, established by the East Texas District of the Pentecostal Church of God, opened in September, 1958, in the Fulton Theater building in Houston with forty-three students and seven faculty members. A junior college program and Bible courses for ministerial students were offered.

In 1959 the general convention of the Pentecostal Church of God voted to make the college a regional school to be owned by the central and eastern regions of the church; since that time the school has operated under the general organization of the Pentecostal church in Joplin, Missouri.

The facility was moved to a temporary location in the fall of 1959, a church building on Gonzales Street, Houston. In 1963 an administration and classroom building and a gymnasium were built on a permanent site on the Beaumont Highway, Houston. Dormitories, a cafeteria, a temporary library, and other buildings for classroom space have been built since that time.

The college was an associate member of the Accrediting Association of Bible Colleges in 1968. The enrollment in the fall of 1974 was 208; the president in that year was W. McDonald.

Southern Bible Institute. See Southwestern Christian College. (Terrell.)

*Southern Kansas Railway Company of Texas. See Panhandle and Santa Fe Railway Company.

Southern Mercury. The *Southern Mercury* was the official publication of the Farmers' Alliance,qv and was probably established in 1886. Its first editor was B. R. Butler; he was followed by Clarence Ousley qv and then Milton Parks in 1891. *Southern Mercury* apparently became a Populist party qv paper in 1892 under Harry Tracy.qv

BIBLIOGRAPHY: Charles William Macune, The Farmers' Alliance (MS., Archives, University of Texas at Austin Library).

*Southern Methodist University. Southern Methodist University, situated on a 150-acre campus in suburban University Park (an incorporated residential district surrounded by Dallas), remained independent of state support and nonsectarian in its teaching, although it was related to the Methodist church. In the fall of 1974 there was an enrollment of 10,079 students, and the faculty numbered over 700. A large percentage of the student body was from out of state. Buildings constructed since the close of World War II followed the original modern Georgian style. The Owens Fine Arts Center, a new complex consisting of ten major facilities for the teaching and presentation of the arts, included art museums, performing arts theaters, and an auditorium. Total assets of the university were over $109,900,000 in 1969, including a $24,911,273 endowment fund and a physical plant valued at well over $50,000,000.

The curriculum was organized around University College and the degree-granting schools of Humanities and Sciences, Fine Arts, Business Administration, Law, Perkins School of Theology, Continuing Education (the university's adult education program), and the Institute of Technology (formerly the School of Engineering). University College began in 1964 as an academic agency to receive all beginning freshmen, counsel them, provide interdisciplinary courses, and offer gifted students a superior studies program as well as basic educational courses. Each of the degree-granting schools offered graduate programs, and the Ph.D. program was expanding. Dallas College in the downtown area served as the adult education branch of the university.

The seven university libraries contained 1,046,-714 cataloged books and pamphlets in 1969; their holdings were increasing at the rate of approximately 70,000 volumes per year. The Southern Methodist University Press, formerly the University Press of Dallas, was established in 1937 as the university's publishing division. A member of the Association of American Presses since 1945, the press maintained more than one hundred books on its current in-print list on a broad range of topics, with emphasis on the Southwest region and Americana. The press issued two magazines: *The Southwest Review* and the *Journal of the Graduate Research Center*, the latter incorporating and continuing *Field and Laboratory*, established in 1932. Willis M. Tate succeeded Umphrey Lee as president in 1954, and he held that office for eighteen years; he was named chancellor of Southern Methodist University in November, 1971, and remained in that position when Paul Hardin III became president in July, 1972.

*Southern Overland Mail. See Butterfield Overland Mail Route.

*Southern Pacific System in Texas. Five principal corporate subsidiaries merged into the Southern Pacific Company on September 30, 1955, after the approval of the stockholders of the Southern Pacific Company at a meeting on May 11, 1955. Properties involved were the railroad lines of the Southern Pacific Railroad Company, Arizona Eastern Railroad Company, Dawson Railway Company, El Paso and Rock Island Railway Company, and El Paso & Southwestern Railroad Company. The total main and branch line track amounted to approximately 4,500 miles. Before the merger these lines were owned by the respective subsidiaries but operated by the Southern Pacific Company under lease. With the merger they were operated by the Southern Pacific Company as its own property. On October 31, 1961, the Texas and New Orleans Railroad Company, the El Paso and Southwestern Railroad Company of Texas, and the El Paso Southern Railway Company were merged into the Southern Pacific Company, which in 1971 operated 3,193 first main track miles in Texas.

Joseph L. Bart, Jr.

*Southern Pacific Terminal Company. The Southern Pacific Terminal Company was incorporated July 6, 1901 (not July 1, 1901, as stated in Volume II), in Texas. It was operated by its own organization from July 9, 1901, through August 31, 1906; leased to and operated by the Galveston, Harrisburg, and San Antonio Railway Company from September 1, 1906, through February 28, 1927; leased to and operated by the Texas and New Orleans Railroad Company from March 1, 1927, through October 31, 1961; and leased and operated by the Southern Pacific Company from November 1, 1961, through August 31, 1962, at which time it was merged into the Southern Pacific Company. The company's property consisted of wharves, elevators, piers, and approximately twenty-seven miles of trackage in Galveston in 1971.

Joseph L. Bart, Jr.

Southern Sportsman. The *Southern Sportsman*, a hunting and fishing magazine published in 1936 by Joe Austell Small of Austin, Texas, was later purchased by the Steck Company of Austin. At one time circulation totaled 33,000 paid subscriptions. World War II caused its suspension, and ownership reverted to Small. Plans were made for its revival, but in early 1973 the magazine had not again been put into publication.

*Southern Transcontinental Railroad Company.

Southlake, Texas. Southlake, in Denton and Tarrant counties, had a 1960 population of 1,023 and a 1970 population of 2,031, a 98.5 percent increase, according to the United States census.

*Southland, Texas.

*Southmayd, Texas.

*Southmost, Texas.

Southmost College. See Texas Southmost College.

*Southton, Texas.

Southwest Center for Advanced Studies (SCAS). See University of Texas at Dallas.

*Southwest Conference. The Southwest Conference (officially the Southwest Athletic Conference) was first suggested in 1914 by L. Theo Bellmont, then director of athletics at the University of Texas. It was originally designated the Southwest Intercollegiate Athletic Association, but the word "intercollegiate" was dropped from the official title at the second annual meeting on May 13, 1916.

The first conference competition involved Rice and Baylor in a basketball game at Houston, January 30, 1915, with Rice winning 45–10. (The track and field meet held at the University of Texas in May, 1915, was not the first conference event, as stated in Volume II; it was, however, the first track and field meet of the conference.) Texas won the first three titles awarded in basketball, baseball, and track. By 1975 the Southwest Conference had developed seven national champions in football, three in baseball, three in golf, three semifinalists in national basketball competition, and individual national winners in track, golf, tennis, swimming, and cross country.

Members of the conference in 1975 were the University of Texas at Austin, Texas Christian University, Southern Methodist University, Baylor University, Rice University, Texas A&M University, the University of Arkansas, Texas Tech University, and the University of Houston. Texas Tech was admitted to the conference in May, 1956, climaxing a long campaign by its supporters for membership. Tech started participation in all sports except baseball and football in 1958 and became eligible to compete in football for the first time in 1960. The University of Houston was admitted in 1971; it became eligible to compete in some conference sports in 1973, in basketball in 1975, and in football in 1976.

Presidents of the conference since 1945 were Gayle Scott, TCU, 1946–1947; R. A. Leflar, Arkansas, 1948–1949; D. W. Williams, A&M, 1950; J. D. Bragg, Baylor, 1951–1952; H. E. Bray, Rice, 1953–1954; E. D. Mouzon, SMU, 1955–1956; O. B. Williams, Texas, 1957–1958; Henry B. Hardt, TCU, 1959–1960; Delbert Swartz, Arkansas, 1961–1962; Chris Groneman, A&M, 1963–1964; Alan Chapman, Rice, 1965–1966; Monroe Carroll, Baylor, 1967–1968; J. William Davis, Texas Tech, 1969–1971; Harold Jeskey, SMU, 1971–1973; and J. Neils Thompson, Texas, 1973–1975.

Howard Grubbs was executive secretary of the conference from 1950 until his retirement on September 1, 1973; he was also treasurer of the Cotton Bowl.qv He was succeeded by Cliff Speegle as executive secretary of the conference and by Wilbur Evans as executive director of the Cotton Bowl. *See also* Intercollegiate Athletics.

Wilbur Evans

Southwest Foundation for Research and Education. The Southwest Foundation for Research and Education, San Antonio, was established in 1947 with funds and land provided by Thomas Baker Slick qv for the purpose of basic biomedical research. A policy of cooperation is maintained between the foundation, specializing in the life sciences, and the Southwest Research Institute qv (founded at the same time by Thomas Slick), specializing in the physical sciences. Areas of research and experimental studies of worldwide scope are carried on by the foundation in three divisions: Biological Growth and Development, Clinical Sciences, and Microbiology and Infectious Diseases. Scientific publications by a staff of internationally trained scientists are part of the foundation's program. The Urschel Memorial Laboratory, given by Charles F. and Berenice Urschel (mother of Thomas Slick), provided the foundation with modern research facilities in 1969. In 1955 the Southwest Foundation for Research and Education

purchased the old Argyle Hotel,qv and it was leased to the board of directors of the Argyle's private club, whose members are composed of those who contribute annual financial support to medical research under way at the foundation. The foundation also relies heavily on grants from the National Institutes of Health. Harold Vagtborg, long associated with the foundation, became president emeritus in May, 1970, and Stanley W. Olson became president the same year.

*Southwest Mesa.

Southwest Research Institute. The Southwest Research Institute, with campuses at San Antonio and Houston, was founded in San Antonio as a nonprofit research organization by philanthropist Thomas Baker Slick qv in 1947. The institute works in cooperation with industry, government, and individuals to utilize scientific and technical knowledge for the benefit of mankind.

The institute operates departments in applied electromagnetics; applied physics; automotive research; bioengineering; electronic systems research; engines, fuels, and lubricants; fluids and lubrication technology; instrumentation research; chemistry and chemical engineering; materials engineering; mechanical sciences; physical and biological sciences; social and management sciences; special engineering services; and structural research.

In Corpus Christi the institute also operates an ocean science and engineering laboratory. A United States Army fuels and lubricants laboratory on the San Antonio campus is staffed by institute personnel. Since 1955 the institute has edited *Applied Mechanics Reviews*, the monthly publication of the American Society of Mechanical Engineers. The Houston campus was established in 1962 and specializes in electronics and systems engineering and in problems of air and water pollution control and solid waste disposal; it serves as the institute's immediate contact with the NASA Manned Spacecraft Center.qv A continuing program of symposia is conducted by the institute, which is also affiliated with the Institute de Investigaciones Industriales in Monterrey, Mexico.

Government and private sources provide nearly equal portions of research income. In 1970 gross revenues were derived from 462 active projects for industrial sponsors and governmental agencies. The institute staff in 1965 was 821; in 1970 it was 1,117. Harold Vagtborg served as first president of the institute; Martin Goland was president in 1970. *See also* Southwest Foundation for Research and Education.

BIBLIOGRAPHY: Southwest Research Institute, *Annual Report* (1965, 1970), *The Constant Search* (n.d.).

Jack Harmon

*Southwest Review. The *Southwest Review*, a journal of contemporary literature, criticism, and discussion, continued to be published quarterly by the Southern Methodist University Press. Allen Maxwell, who had been the magazine's managing editor before the war, became editor in late 1945, a position he held until the autumn issue of 1963, when Decherd Turner assumed the post. Turner resigned following the winter, 1965, issue, and was succeeded by Margaret L. Hartley, who had been assistant editor from 1947 to 1961 and managing editor from 1961 to 1963.

Regionalism without provincialism has been a strong emphasis of the *Southwest Review* throughout most of its career, more explicit at some periods than at others. Many well-known writers of Texas and the Southwest have contributed. The scope of the magazine's interests outside the region is illustrated by the score of contributions to the *Review* between 1916 and 1959 by the Franco-American historian Albert Guérard. Another interest of the magazine has been its encouragement of new talent; many writers have received their initial hearing in its pages.

Margaret L. Hartley

*Southwest Society of Biblical Study and Research.

*Southwest Strike.

Southwest Texas Junior College. Southwest Texas Junior College, Uvalde, was established in 1946 as a tri-county junior college serving Uvalde, Real, and Zavala counties. The campus was originally an army air corps flying school adjacent to the municipal airport. Most of the World War II buildings were replaced by modern facilities, including Garner Science Center, La Forge Hall (containing a gymnasium, auditorium, cafeteria, and lounge), Richarz Memorial Building (which housed the library containing 16,000 volumes in 1967, administration offices, and a bookstore), and a two-story women's dormitory. Since 1959 many new permanent buildings have been added.

The college provided free transportation to students living within the district. Students from other Texas counties or other states were accepted at slightly higher tuition rates. In addition to the regular enrollment in 1964–1965, night school enrollment totaled more than 200 students on campus, in Crystal City, and in Del Rio. The two-year program was designed to prepare students for eventual degrees in teaching, music, dentistry, medicine, veterinary medicine, pharmacy, laboratory technology, general education, law, business administration, physical education, and agriculture. A one-year program for prospective engineers and one-year and two-year programs in secretarial training, data processing, and nursing were also available. Former Vice-President of the United States John Nance Garner qv contributed financial aid to the college by way of an endowment.

The total enrollment at the college in the fall of 1974 was 1,606 students; the faculty numbered over sixty members. Wayne Matthews was president in 1974.

*Southwest Texas State Teachers College. *See also* Southwest Texas State University.

Southwest Texas State University. Southwest Texas State University, formerly Southwest Texas State Teachers College,qv in San Marcos, experienced a tremendous growth in enrollment after 1950, with 2,013 students in that year, 4,461 in 1964, 6,580 in 1967, and 12,894 in the fall of 1974. The full-time teaching staff increased from 94 in 1950, to 275 in 1967, and approximately 400 in 1971. The physical plant was greatly enlarged, with total plant investment expanding from $3,511,224 in 1950 to $15,418,438 in 1965. The college budget, reflecting the school's growth during that same period, increased from $1,573,245 to $6,686,696; by 1971 both these figures were further increased. Library holdings increased from 71,650 in 1950 to 243,321 in 1969.

Many curriculum changes took place, including the addition of general education requirements, new graduate programs, participation in educational television programs, enlargement of language offerings, and installation of a language laboratory. Emphasis was placed on the development of speech and hearing therapy courses and on the training of teachers for the orthopedically handicapped. Certification requirements met the standards of the Texas Education Agency.qv

The Fifty-sixth Texas Legislature changed the school's name from Southwest Texas State Teachers College to Southwest Texas State College, effective September 1, 1959; in 1969 the legislature again authorized a name change, this time to Southwest Texas State University. James H. McCrocklin succeeded James Garland Flowers qv as president of the college in 1964. In 1968 the acting president was Leland Derrick. Billy Mac Jones was appointed president in September, 1969. Jack C. Cates was named acting president in 1973, and Lee H. Smith was president in 1974. During the 1960's the school gained national attention as the alma mater of the president of the United States, Lyndon Baines Johnson.qv

Southwestern Assemblies of God College. Southwestern Assemblies of God College, Waxahachie, was established in 1927 at Enid, Oklahoma, under the leadership of P. C. Nelson. First known as Southwestern Bible School, the school moved to Fort Worth in 1941, where it merged with the South Central Bible Institute. The combined institutions came under the ownership and direction of the Texas District Council of the Assemblies of God, and the name was changed to Southwestern Bible Institute.

In 1943 the institute was moved to its present location at Waxahachie. A junior college curriculum was added to the program during the 1944–1945 term. That division, including pre-ministerial students, accounted for 80 percent of the enrollment. The institute became a regional school in 1954, with support coming from seven districts of the Assemblies of God: Arkansas, Louisiana, New Mexico, Oklahoma, North Texas, South Texas, and West Texas.

In 1963 the name was changed to Southwestern Assemblies of God College; the upper division of the curriculum was called the Southwestern College of the Bible. The campus was increased to seventy-seven acres; new facilities included a men's dormitory, a library, and married student apartments. The library contained 43,010 volumes in 1969. In the fall of 1974, 481 students were enrolled; there were approximately 20 faculty members. The junior college division was accredited by the Association of Texas Colleges and Universities.qv The Bible college division was a charter member of the American Association of Bible Colleges. Blake L. Farmer served as president in 1974.

*Southwestern Baptist Theological Seminary. Southwestern Baptist Theological Seminary, Fort Worth, grew from a one-building facility in Waco in 1908 to six main buildings and over 300 family living units on a seventy-acre campus in Fort Worth by the mid-1960's. The seminary operated schools of theology, religious education, and church music. Degree programs included the bachelor of divinity and both master and doctor of theology and of church music. Diploma courses were offered by each of the three schools for non-college students above thirty years of age and for wives of regularly enrolled students. The school claimed to be the largest evangelical seminary in the world. There were 1,845 students enrolled in the 1970–1971 regular term; there were 75 members in the faculty. Graduates numbered more than 11,000 during the first fifty-eight years of operation, and ex-students accounted for approximately one-half of the seminary-trained missionaries appointed by the Southern Baptist Foreign Mission Board. The seminary's library contained 361,345 volumes in 1969. Endowment funds for the seminary exceeded $5,000,-000 in 1965, and the institution's assets were over $16,400,000. The operating budget for 1965–1966 was $1,884,484. President of the seminary in 1971 was Robert E. Naylor. See also Baptist Church in Texas.

*Southwestern Christian Advocate. See Texas Christian Advocate.

*Southwestern Christian College. (Denton.)

Southwestern Christian College. (Terrell.) Southwestern Christian College was established in Fort Worth under the name Southern Bible Institute in the fall of 1948, with forty-five students attending. The board of trustees planned to purchase property in Fort Worth for a permanent school plant; however, an opportunity arose in 1949 to buy the site formerly occupied by Texas Military College qv in Terrell.

The move to Terrell was made in 1950, at which time the name of the school was changed to Southwestern Christian College. Although founded primarily for the education of Negro youth from the Churches of Christ, Southwestern Christian College was open to anyone. The Bible-centered junior college offered basic academic courses leading to the associate of arts degree. In the 1974 fall term, enrollment numbered 235 students, and the faculty consisted of approximately 20 members. Jack Evans was president of the college in 1974.

Southwestern Diabetic Foundation. The Southwestern Diabetic Foundation, located at Camp Sweeney, a 403-acre tract near Gainesville, is a rehabilitation and educational health center, exclusively for diabetic boys and girls. The camp, organized in 1950, was named for Dr. J. Shirley Sweeney, who was the foundation's founder and medical director; at one time the foundation was called the Sweeney Diabetic Foundation.

The camp is operated during the summer; approximately three hundred children attend sessions from three to nine weeks for treatment or training. Each camper is placed in his or her own age and development group, and a counselor is available for every four boys and girls. Sports activities and indoor crafts are important in the daily schedule. Medical supervision, such as specific diet and insulin schedule, is provided by the medical director. In 1965 the staff included camp director James V. Campbell, a registered nurse, a dietitian, three medical students, and thirty counselors, in addition to Dr. Sweeney.

While the camp serves mainly the South and Southwest, its work is national in scope; a few children attend from foreign countries. Admission is based on medical need rather than on the child's parents' geographic or financial situation. The camp operates on public donations.

*Southwestern Exposition and Fat Stock Show.

*Southwestern Historical Quarterly. The *Southwestern Historical Quarterly*, which contains articles and documents on Texas and Southwestern history, has been published by the Texas State Historical Association qv since 1897. Horace Bailey Carroll qv served as editor from 1946 to 1966. The association named Joe B. Frantz to that post at the association's seventieth annual meeting in 1966; L. Tuffly Ellis was shortly thereafter named assistant editor. A cumulative index of volumes XLI–LX (July, 1937–April, 1957) was published in 1960. The first fifty-four volumes of the *Quarterly* were reprinted in 1968.

A new format for the *Quarterly* was inaugurated, beginning with the July, 1967, issue, featuring a color reproduction of a painting on the cover, the state seal reproduced in color on the title page, a photographic section, and special color pages for the "Southwestern Collection" section. The format proved popular and has been continued in all issues of the *Quarterly* to the present time. In 1976 Joe B. Frantz continued as editor, L. Tuffly Ellis was managing editor, and Barbara J. Stockley was associate editor. The *Southwestern Historical Quarterly* and the *Handbook of Texas* (also published by the Texas State Historical Association) remain the two most important published sources for the study of Texas history.

Southwestern Historical Wax Museum. The Southwestern Historical Wax Museum, housed in the Varied Industries Building at the State Fair ᵠᵛ Park, Dallas, was opened in September, 1963, and is open year-round. Over one hundred life-like, authentically dressed wax figures are arranged in scenes depicting historical events of Texas and the old West. Wax representations of famous Texas personages include heroes, lawmen, gunslingers, political figures, athletes, and entertainers. Many modern-day personages are also represented. There is also an exhibit of three hundred antique firearms and weapons, many of which belonged to famous and infamous Southwesterners; the collection was started in the early 1890's by Harrison H. Schwend of Clay County.

Mary Alice Brown

*Southwestern Junior College. See also Southwestern Union College.

Southwestern Junior College of the Assemblies of God. See Southwestern Assemblies of God College.

Southwestern Law Journal. The *Southwestern Law Journal* was originally called *Texas Law and Legislation,* a biannual review devoted to Texas legal developments; it was founded by the faculty of the School of Law of Southern Methodist University in 1947. With the second volume the name was changed to *Southwestern Law Journal*; it became a quarterly with the third volume. Volume 2 carried the first annual survey of Texas law, expanded to cover important developments in neighboring states. Abandoned after Volume 9, these annual surveys of Texas law were reinitiated in 1967, with a full additional fifth issue devoted to this purpose. The format of the journal was substantially expanded in 1957. During the 1971–1972 academic year the journal published its twenty-sixth volume. Though subject to faculty supervision, the journal is controlled and edited by a self-perpetuating board of student editors; it is financed by law school funds and by subscribers, who numbered over 1,200 in 1972.

Joseph W. McKnight

*Southwestern Medical College of the University of Texas. See also University of Texas Southwestern Medical School at Dallas.

Southwestern Medical Foundation. See Southwestern Medical College of the University of Texas; University of Texas Southwestern Medical School at Dallas.

*Southwestern Political Science Quarterly. See Southwestern Social Science Quarterly, Social Science Quarterly; see also Southwestern Social Science Association.

*Southwestern Political and Social Science Quarterly. See Southwestern Social Science Quarterly; Social Science Quarterly; see also Southwestern Social Science Association.

*Southwestern Presbyterian Home and School for Orphans. In 1957 the new board of trustees decided to discontinue the school and enroll all children in the Itasca schools. While the school operated, it had twelve grades with an enrollment ranging from 75 to 116, with 4 to 5 teachers. See also Presbyterian Education in Texas.

Malcolm L. Purcell

*Southwestern Railway Company.

*Southwestern Social Science Association. Established at the University of Texas in 1918 (not 1920, as stated in Volume II) as the Southwestern Political Science Association, the organization changed its name to the Southwestern Political and Social Science Association in 1923 and finally to the Southwestern Social Science Association in 1931. It is the oldest regional social science association in the nation and one of the few attempting, on a regional basis, to bring the social sciences together under the same scholarly roof. The association publishes jointly with the University of Texas at Austin the *Social Science Quarterly.*ᵠᵛ

Membership, originally made up of approximately 150 teachers and public leaders interested in political science, expanded steadily except during World War II, when membership declined. By 1950 the association had 655 members representing nine disciplines. Since that time both the scope of the organization and its membership have expanded. By 1971 more than 2,200 scholars representing a dozen disciplines were members of the association. Eleven of these disciplines are organized as separate sections—accounting, economics, geography, government, decision sciences, history, sociology, management, finance, marketing, and business communication. All sections meet both independently and jointly at the general association conference held annually in early spring. Attendance at recent meetings has exceeded 2,000.

Charles M. Bonjean

*Southwestern Social Science Quarterly. See also Social Science Quarterly.

Southwestern Union College. Southwestern Union College, in Keene, was known as Southwestern Junior College ᵠᵛ from 1916 until the constituency of the Southwestern Union Conference of Seventh-day Adventists changed its official name in 1963. The junior college continued to operate a preparatory school, although the proportion of college students rose gradually. During the 1965–1966 term, 275 students (approximately 60 percent of the student body) were enrolled in college courses. At that time there were eight administrative officers, including E. C. Wines, president, and thirty faculty members. Major construction on the 140-acre campus between 1955 and 1965 included a women's dormitory, a classroom-auditorium building, a library-administration building, and a science building. The library contained 40,000 volumes by 1969. LeRoy Leiske was president in 1974 when the student enrollment reached 671.

Associate in arts and associate in science degrees were offered in a wide variety of fields. The school held memberships in the Association of Texas Colleges and Universities,qv the American Association of Junior Colleges, the Southern Association of Junior Colleges, and the Texas Junior College Association. See also Adventist Churches in Texas; Adventist Schools in Texas.

*Southwestern University. Southwestern University, Georgetown, had among its early executive officers John Howell McLean qv (not McClean, as stated in Volume II). Southwestern remained a small, liberal arts college of the Methodist church. The university curriculum in the 1960's was administered under two main branches, the College of Arts and Sciences, which had divisions of the humanities, social sciences, and natural and applied sciences, and the School of Fine Arts, which offered programs in art, sacred music, and speech and drama. Master's degrees and summer school programs were discontinued.

Buildings on the campus completed between 1950 and 1965 included a chapel, a union building, a science hall, a fine arts center, dormitories, a clinic, a power plant, a lounge, a golf pro shop, the president's home, and a religious activities center. Grounds improvements included a swimming pool, a golf course, a memorial fountain, and a mall. Construction of dormitories, a food service center, and a library addition was under way after 1965. Library holdings were enhanced in 1965 by the addition of the 2,400-volume Ed Clark collection of Texana. Southwestern's endowment grew from $1,058 to $6,259,330 in the fifteen-year period between 1950 and 1965, the fifth highest of any Methodist college in the United States.

Enrollment of the college increased following World War II to over eight hundred students. During the early 1950's attendance declined as war veterans graduated, but enrollment increased again through the 1960's. By the fall of 1974 there were 905 students, and the faculty numbered approximately seventy. Succeeding W. R. Finch as president in 1962 was L. Durwood Fleming, who remained president in 1974.

*Sowell, Andrew Jackson. One of Andrew Jackson Sowell's books, published in 1884, was Rangers and Pioneers of Texas (not Raiders and Pioneers of Texas, as stated in Volume II).

*Sowells Creek.

*Sowers, Texas.

Space Industry in Texas. For many years before the space age dawned with the orbiting of the first artificial earth satellite in the fall of 1957, Texas played an important part in the development of American military aviation and aircraft technology. Before World War II the complex of army airfields (later air force bases) surrounding San Antonio already existed, and one of the airfields, Randolph (see Randolph Air Force Base), had come to be known as the "West Point of the Air." During the war other military installations were built in the state, and the Fort Worth-Dallas area became a leading manufacturer of aircraft and aircraft equipment. The immediate postwar years, although bringing some decline of aircraft manufacture in the state, saw the growth of the U.S. Air Force School of Aviation Medicine at San Antonio into the nation's outstanding aeromedical center; at the same time it became a center for the new field of space medical research and applications.

In the 1950's, as national security needs dictated an expensive ballistic missile program involving all three military services, millions of federal dollars found their way to Texas in development and fabrication contracts to such firms with large Texas plants as the General Dynamics Corporation, the Boeing Company, and Texas Instruments. During this decade the space industry had come to Texas in the form of manufacturing operations for military rocket projects, ballistics research and testing at the U.S. Navy's Daingerfield Ordnance Test Facility, and research into the psychophysiological conditions of space flight at San Antonio.

The decision of the National Aeronautics and Space Administration in September, 1961, to locate its multimillion-dollar Manned Spacecraft Center qv in Houston, planned as the command post for the national effort to send men to the moon, was the culmination of Texas' growing identification with the development of atmospheric and extra-atmospheric transport. (For a detailed account, see also Manned Spacecraft Center.)

Charles C. Alexander

*Spade, Texas. (Lamb County.)

*Spade, Texas. (Mitchell County.)

*Spade Draw.

*Spade Ranch.

*Spaight, Ashley W.

*Spanish Bluff.

*Spanish Camp, Texas.

*Spanish Fort, Texas.

*Spanish Governors' Palace. The Spanish Governors' Palace was purchased in the late 1860's by Ernst H. Altgelt, founder of Comfort in Kendall County. He and his family lived there at various times, and the property was held by his widow, Emma Murck Altgelt, until the early 1900's. In 1928 the city of San Antonio included in a bond-issue election the funds for purchase and restoration of the building. Members of the San Antonio Conservation Society qv aided in restoring and furnishing this historic site. The Spanish Governors' Palace is maintained by the city of San Antonio as a museum open to the public.

BIBLIOGRAPHY: Emma Murck Altgelt (Guido Ransleben, Sr., trans.), "Aus Die Jahre, 1865–1910," Comfort News, January 1, 8, 1970; San Antonio Conservation Society, Conservation in San Antonio Since 1924 (1970).

Spanish Law in Texas. As an outpost of the kingdom of New Spain, the province of Texas shared with Mexico the basic law of the parent sovereign, that of Castile. This law went essentially unchanged during the tumultuous fifteen years of independent Mexican rule (1821–1836), but following her own independence, Texas adopted the law of England in preference to that of Spain (*see* English Law in Texas). Three areas of law were excepted from the wholesale adoption of English law in Texas: certain procedural rules affecting trials, the law affecting land titles and certain water rights, and a large body of rules affecting family relationships.

In spite of severe antagonism to Hispano-Mexican government, the predominantly Anglo American colonists of Texas found in the prevailing legal system a number of elements better adapted to their conditions than Anglo American legal institutions under which they had been reared in the United States. Anglo American judicial procedure was inordinately complex and operated through two different sets of courts with different rules—those of law and equity. The Castilian legal system functioned very satisfactorily with a unitary judiciary. This system appealed to the frontiersmen and they perpetuated it. Castilian court rules of pleading as understood on the frontier were simple and straightforward, as compared to the complicated English forms of action and pleadings, and so these Spanish rules were also retained. But after the Civil War, with a great influx of common law lawyers and teachers trained in the Anglo American system, this simplicity of procedural rules became more and more theoretical. The Castilian principle of venue of law suits was also favored. Whereas the English rule was that a person was sued in the court of the locality where the facts giving rise to the dispute occurred, the Spanish rule required that a person be sued where he lived, for the convenience of the defendant. Though that rule had a number of original Castilian exceptions which were retained, it acquired a great many more in the years following that tended to impede its effectiveness. The Castilian tradition also provided a model for a system of probate administration that is much simpler than the English system. The Texas institution of an independent executor, seemingly modeled on the Castilian *albacea universal*, provides for great flexibility and reduced cost in probate practice.

It is a basic rule of international law that when sovereignty changes, general law does not change until specifically altered by the new sovereign, and titles to land already acquired will not be interfered with. Hence, land title law was not varied by the change from Mexican to Texan sovereignty except insofar as the previous holders of land who had espoused the Mexican cause had their lands declared forfeited. An anomalous result of continued application of the Spanish doctrine to land grants made before the act of January 20, 1840, and those made thereafter is that different rules may apply to adjacent tracts depending on the origin of the grant. Along the seashore, for example, where the shore is flat, a common law grant may extend farther toward the ocean than an adjacent Spanish law grant because of the different system of measuring the coastal boundary. With respect to grants along rivers, there is also a difference. Grants made under Hispanic rules extend only to the bank of a navigable stream, as the sovereign was the owner of the river bed. Subsequent common law grants extend to the center line of a navigable stream. If the owner of a Hispanic grant should own both banks, however, the effect of the Small Act of 1929 is that he will own the bed of the stream as well as the banks. The law applicable to Spanish grants is also much more restrictive as to irrigation rights, since Spanish grants are not entitled to such rights unless specifically granted.

The most significant residuum of Spanish law is in the area of family relationships. Adoption was unknown in English common law. Its comparatively early institution by statute in Texas (1850) is generally attributed to the Spanish legal tradition. The law of matrimonial property is also heavily influenced by the Spanish tradition. The Anglo American frontiersman found the idea of common ownership of the gains of marriage between husband and wife much more agreeable to his society than common law principles (*see* Community Property Law; Separate Property Law). Protection of certain land and tools of husbandry and trade from creditors' claims was also appealing to him as opposed to the creditor-oriented rule of common law (*see* Homestead Law). This adoption of Hispano-Mexican principle has spread from Texas with varying degrees of liberality to other sister states. Texas law also followed the Hispanic model of allowing the husband to protect the home by giving him the right of killing his wife's paramour without punishment. There has been much criticism of this rule and strong recommendation for its abolition.

BIBLIOGRAPHY: Gerald Ashford, "Jacksonian Liberalism and Spanish Law in Early Texas," *Southwestern Historical Quarterly*, LVII (1953–1954); Joseph W. McKnight, "The Spanish Watercourses of Texas" in (Morris Forkosch, ed.), *Essays in Legal History in Honor of Felix Frankfurter* (1966); Joseph W. McKnight (reviewer of book by William O. Huie), "*Texas Cases and Materials on the Law of Marital Property Rights*," *Texas Law Review*, XLVI (1967); Joseph W. McKnight, "The Spanish Influence on the Texas Law of Civil Procedure," *Texas Law Review*, XXXVIII (1959); Joseph W. McKnight, "Origin of the Cuckoo Law," *Texas Observer*, April 2, 1965.

Joseph W. McKnight

*Spanish Pass.

*Sparenberg, Texas.

*Sparks, Sam.

*Sparks, William F.

*Sparks, Texas.

*Sparrib Creek.

*Sparta, Texas.

Speaker, Tristram E. Tristram E. (Tris) Speaker was born on April 4, 1888, in Hubbard, Texas, one of three boys and five girls. In 1905 he attended Polytechnic College in Fort Worth and in 1906 he started his baseball career as a 50-dollar-a-month player with Cleburne of the North Texas League. In 1907 he played with Houston and the Boston Red Sox and, in 1908, with Little Rock. The Boston Red Sox recalled him in 1909, and he stayed with them through 1915. During the years 1916 through 1926 he played in Cleveland. In 1920, as a $57,000-a-year manager, he led Cleveland to its first pennant. In 1927 Speaker played with Washington, and he finished his career with Philadelphia in 1928. During his twenty-two years in the major leagues he recorded a lifetime batting average of .344. In 1936 he was the seventh player named to the Baseball Hall of Fame, and in 1951 he was the first athlete named to the Texas Sports Hall of Fame.qv

At the age of thirty-six, Speaker (sometimes called the "Gray Eagle" or "Spoke") married Mary Frances Cuddihy. He died of a heart attack on a fishing trip to Lake Whitney on December 8, 1958, and was buried in the Fairview Cemetery at Hubbard.

BIBLIOGRAPHY: Austin *American*, December 9, 1958; Thomas Turner, "Gray Eagle of the Golden Era," *Texas Parade*, XXII (1961).

Mary Beth Fleischer

*Speaks, Texas.

*Spearman, Texas. Spearman, seat of Hansford County, almost doubled its population during the 1950's, with a count of 1,852 in 1950 increasing to 3,555 by 1960. In the 1960's the town had two newspapers, a hospital, and a new high school. Spearman had facilities for grain storage, and it was the county center for shipping, gas and petroleum plants, and irrigation supplies. The city had 116 businesses in 1970. By that same year the population had decreased slightly, to 3,435, according to the United States census.

Specht, Theodore. Theodore Specht was born in Braunschweig, Germany, on April 17, 1810, and became a sailing ship captain while still a young man. He was married to Maria Berger, and they immigrated to Fredericksburg, Texas. Specht built a log and rock house on the corner of Main and South Milam streets, which served as both store and home. The Comanche chief Santana qv requested a fireplace room one night for one of his wives, who there bore him a son. On December 7, 1848, Specht became the first postmaster of Fredericksburg, his store serving as a post office. Specht helped to introduce improved wheat and rye seeds to Gillespie County farmers. When the *Neu Braunfelser Zeitung* qv was published in 1852, he became its agent. After his death on June 4, 1862, his wife and seven children continued to operate the store.

BIBLIOGRAPHY: Rudolph Leopold Biesele, *The History of the German Settlements in Texas, 1831–1861* (1930); Gillespie County Historical Society, *Pioneers in God's Hills* (1960); Robert Penniger, *Fest-Ausgabe zum 50-jährigen Jubiläum der Gründung der Stadt Friedrichsburg* (1896); Fredericksburg *Radio Post*, August 28, 1941.

Esther L. Mueller

Special Schools and Special Education, Texas Education Agency. In 1951 the Texas School for the Deaf qv was placed under the jurisdiction of the Texas Education Agency,qv and in 1953 the Texas School for the Blind qv was also placed under that agency. The formerly all-Negro school, Texas Blind, Deaf, and Orphan School,qv was added to the Texas Education Agency in 1965, and the school's name was changed to the Texas Blind and Deaf School. The three schools were combined and integrated in 1966 to provide an overall residential program for deaf and blind children. In 1973 they were operated as the Texas School for the Blind, located in north Austin, and the Texas School for the Deaf, located on two campuses, in south and east Austin. Each school had its own superintendent. The division of special schools handled all administrative affairs.

The division of special education of the Texas Education Agency worked with local school officials throughout the state in developing educational programs for physically, mentally, and emotionally handicapped children. The division also worked with statewide organizations and individuals in special education programs in the public schools.

In 1969 the legislature gave the Texas Education Agency additional responsibility in establishing two regional experimental diagnostic centers for the treatment of children with learning disabilities.

BIBLIOGRAPHY: Texas State Board of Education, *Audit Report, Special Schools for the Blind and Deaf, 1970* (n.d.); University of Texas at Austin, *Guide To Texas State Agencies* (1970, 1972).

*Speck Mountain.

*Speegleville, Texas.

Speer, Ocie. Ocie Speer, son of D. and Sallie (Ellis) Speer, was born on April 1, 1869, near Alvarado, Johnson County, and was educated in the public schools there. He was married to Annie Floride Milner on December 3, 1891, and they had five daughters.

He was admitted to the Bar in 1890 and was county attorney of Fisher County from that year until 1892. He practiced law in Bowie from 1894 until 1902, when he became associate justice of the Court of Civil Appeals at Fort Worth. He returned to private law practice from 1914 until 1925, when he was appointed to the Commission of Appeals of the Supreme Court of Texas. In 1929 he again entered private law practice, this time in Austin. He served as counsel to the state banking commission from 1933 to 1939 and from 1949 to 1953; during the intervening period he was assistant to the attorney general of Texas.

Although not a supporter of Miriam Amanda Ferguson,qv he consented to represent her when she was barred from the ballot as a candidate for governor, and he succeeded in having her name placed on the ballot. By a series of suits he established a number of vacancies in the Yates Oil Field qv in Pecos County; he also argued the case involving the Texas Tidelands (*see* Tidelands Controversy) before the Supreme Court of the United States while acting as assistant attorney general.

Speer, one of the leading authorities on Texas constitutional law, was best known for his work *A Treatise on the Law of Married Women in Texas* (1901), which was republished as *A Treatise on the Law of Marital Rights in Texas* (1916, 1929). He also wrote *A Brief* (1925), which was an annotation of Texas forms and rules, *A Treatise on the Law of Special Issues in Texas* (1931), *Texas Jurists* (1936), and *A Treatise on the Law of Banks and Banking in Texas* (1952). Speer sponsored the painting of portraits for the state of all former judges of the Supreme Court of Texas, the Texas Court of Criminal Appeals, and the commissioners of those courts, which he reproduced in his book *Texas Jurists*. Speer retired from practice in 1953 and died on April 11, 1959.

BIBLIOGRAPHY: *World Biography* (1954); *Texas Bar Journal*, VIII (1945), XX (1957), XXII (1959).

Nowlin Randolph

*Speer Creek.

*Speer Institute.

Speight, Joseph Warren. Joseph Warren Speight, son of Jesse and Mary May Speight, was born on May 31, 1825, in Green County, North Carolina. Speight was educated in North Carolina, where his father was a U.S. congressman, and in Mississippi, where his father was a U.S. senator. He was admitted to the Bar in 1847 at Aberdeen, Mississippi, practiced law there, and became a Freemason; he served as grand master of all Mississippi lodges. When his health declined he moved to Waco, Texas, in January, 1854. There he engaged in farming and surveying, affiliated with a Waco Masonic lodge, and entered vigorously into the civic leadership of the new community.

He was a leading Baptist and was influential in bringing Rufus C. Burleson qv to Waco from Independence in 1861 to establish Waco University qv (which was consolidated with Baylor University qv in 1886). Speight served on the board of trustees of Waco University, and his home grounds eventually became part of the Baylor campus.

During the early years of the Civil War, he organized the 15th Texas Infantry Regiment and was commissioned a colonel. He saw much hard service in the Trans-Mississippi theater, especially in Louisiana, and he often led the brigade, to which his regiment was attached, before he resigned because of ill health in the spring of 1864 (*see* Polignac's Brigade). At the war's end Speight withdrew from the practice of law and resumed his agricultural pursuits. Described by contemporaries as being stern and austere in demeanor, he had no personal interest in politics.

Speight was one of the six men who in 1866 obtained from the legislature a charter authorizing the erection of a toll bridge across the Brazos River at Waco. Opened on January 7, 1870, it was the only bridge across that important river and was a great financial success. Speight, twice married, had a family of five children. He died at Waco on April 26, 1888, and was buried in Oakwood Cemetery.

BIBLIOGRAPHY: Alwyn Barr, *Polignac's Texas Brigade* (1964); Roger N. Conger (ed.), *A Century of Fraternity; Waco Lodge No. 92 A.F.&A.M.* (1952); John Sleeper and J. C. Hutchins (comps.), *Waco and McLennan County, Texas* (1876); William M. Sleeper and Allan D. Sanford, *Waco Bar and Incidents of Waco History* (1941); J. L. Walker and C. P. Lumpkin, *History of the Waco Baptist Association of Texas* (1897); Marcus J. Wright (comp.) and Harold B. Simpson (ed.), *Texas in the War 1861–1865* (1965); Roger N. Conger, "The Waco Suspension Bridge," *Texana*, I (1963).

Roger N. Conger

Speight's Brigade. *See* Polignac's Brigade.

Spell, Lota May. Lota May Spell, daughter of William Harold and Mildred Addie (Dashiell) Harrigan, was born February 2, 1885, at Big Spring, Texas. Her father was a superintendent of railroads in Mexico with headquarters in Mexico City and Querétaro, and so her early education was received from tutors. She began her musical studies under August Schemmel, first in San Antonio and then at Virginia Institute of Bristol, Tennessee, from 1898 to 1901, when Schemmel became director of music there. She attended the Grand Ducal Conservatory at Karlsruhe, Germany, from 1902 to 1905, where she completed her education in piano, harmony, and composition. Between 1905 and 1910 she performed as a pianist in Europe and Mexico. In 1910 she became an instructor in the Whitis Preparatory School of Austin, Texas.

On September 8, 1910, she was married to Jefferson Rea Spell, a professor of Romance languages at the University of Texas; they had one daughter. From 1910 to 1914 Mrs. Spell was head of the music department of Melrose Hall of San Antonio, during which time she also completed course work at the University of Texas, receiving the B.A. degree in 1914. She received an M.A. degree in 1919 and a Ph.D. in English in 1923 from the University of Texas. She also studied at Columbia University and the University of Chicago in the summers of 1919 and 1920. From 1921 to 1927 she served as librarian of the Genaro García Library (now the Latin American Collection qv) of the University of Texas. In the mid-1930's she was employed by the state to identify historical sites for the Texas Centennial qv celebrations and to write inscriptions for the monuments placed on those sites. She was teacher of music history and appreciation at the Texas School of Fine Arts, qv associate editor of *The Musicale* (1929–1933), associate editor of the *Southwestern Musician* (1933–1947), editor of *Texas Music News* (1946–1948), and a contributor to numerous musical journals, including *The Etude*, during her lifetime. She was intensely interested in musical education, especially that of young children, and devoted much of her lifetime to developing training tools for teaching the young. From 1939 to 1971 she taught children at her studio in Austin. She prepared bulletins for the University Interscholastic League qv to encourage musical education in the state, including the valuable work, *Music in Texas* (1936), recently reprinted.

Lota Spell's linguistic ability in German, French, Italian, Latin, and Spanish, along with her interest in music, led her into research in musical development throughout the western hemisphere, especially in the Southwest and Mexico, and this brought her wide recognition. Her articles appeared regularly in many important quarterlies and reviews, both musical and historical, and she was generous with her time and energy to encourage and assist others who were interested in these fields. Her research in Latin American culture led to her book *Pioneer Printer: Samuel Bangs in Mexico and Texas* (1963). She contributed articles on seventeenth-century Mexican poetess Sor Juana Inés de la Cruz and on nineteenth-century Mexican diplomat, dramatist, and theater empresario Manuel Eduardo de Gorostiza. At the time of her death she had completed manuscripts on Gorostiza and on Fray Pedro de Gante, one of the first music teachers in Mexico. A complete list of her numerous publications has yet to be compiled. Her correspondence, along with that of her husband, was given to the Latin American Collection of the University of Texas at Austin. The valuable Spell library was purchased by the University of Texas in the early 1960's.

She was a member and officer of many music associations, and she was named a fellow of the Texas State Historical Association.qv Lota Spell died on April 3, 1972, in Austin, and she was buried in San Antonio City Cemetery No. One.

Nettie Lee Benson

*Spence, Joseph.

*Spencer, Nancy.

*Spencer Creek.

*Sperry, Texas.

*Spicewood, Texas.

*Spichehat Indians.

Spiess, Hermann. Hermann Spiess was born around 1818 in Offenbach, Hesse-Darmstadt, Germany, the son of Luise (Werner) and Johann Balthasar Spiess; his father was a musician, linguist, pastor, writer on public education, and founder of the public education school system in Offenbach. Hermann's brother Adolf, an ardent physical culturist, had been a tutor to the young **Prince Carl of Solms-Braunfels,**qv but in 1833 was urged to flee from Giessen because of his acquaintance with members of the Frankfurt student *Putsch*, or revolt, taking Hermann with him to Burgdorf, Switzerland. Hermann returned to the Gymnasium (school) in Darmstadt in 1835, where he and Ferdinand Herff qv both passed their maturity examinations in 1838. That spring Hermann Spiess entered the University of Giessen, but the following year, because of his activities against the reactionary school government, Spiess was expelled for two and one-half years. During that time he attended Polytechnic Institute in Karlsruhe, enter-

ing the school of natural sciences. He returned to Giessen in 1842, passed the examination, and from 1842 to 1845 he was with the woods and forests commission in Darmstadt, passing the second examination in 1844. In the spring of 1845 he took a two-year leave of absence; he came to New York and traveled west to Milwaukee, then south to New Orleans, Galveston, and New Braunfels in the spring of 1846. Spiess returned to Darmstadt, but despite the promise of a secure professional career he wrote that he "could not find any peace and suffered as the entire German youth or young manhood at that time." He convinced Herff and Gustav Schleicher qv to join him in founding a communistic colony in Wisconsin. As Spiess gathered a number of young men who were interested in the plan, his work became known in Darmstadt. Contacted by an envoy of Count Carl of Castell (*see* Adelsverein), Spiess and Herff were interviewed in Wiesbaden, and they agreed to bring their colony to Texas and settle on Adelsverein lands. Herff and Spiess landed in New York in April, 1847, and continued by way of New Orleans and Galveston. Spiess went to New Braunfels and Herff remained on the coast to meet the "Darmstadters" at Indianola. (*See also* "Latin Settlements" of Texas; Bettina, Communistic Colony of.)

Count Carl sent a letter with Spiess announcing his appointment to the position of general commissioner of the Adelsverein, as John O. Meusebach qv had already made known his plan to resign as head of the Verein's colonization project. When Meusebach replaced the controversial "Dr. Schubert" [or Shubbert] (whose real name was Friedrich [or Frederic] Armand Strubberg) with Jean von Coll as colony director in Fredericksburg, Schubert refused to give up the post and would not vacate the society's living quarters. Spiess went there to settle the matter and also to regain control of Nassau Plantation (*see* Nassau Farm), a Verein-owned 5,000-acre plantation in Fayette County, which Schubert had earlier acquired by lease. After the breakdown of negotiations between Spiess and Schubert, Schubert took physical possession of Nassau Plantation, and a pre-dawn gunfight between the two factions at Nassau resulted in the death of a man named Sommers (or Summers) with the Schubert party from La Grange, and Casper Rohrdorf (*see* Swiss in Texas) with the Spiess group. In a September 27, 1848, trial in La Grange, Spiess was acquitted on the grounds of self-defense in the death of Sommers.

Spiess supervised the surveying of land for the expected Darmstadt colony on the Llano River, and a place was selected as close as possible to Fredericksburg for protection and source of supplies. A road was laid out and a river crossing was prepared. Wagons were sent to the coast in July to bring the Darmstadters to their new location, which was not actually on the exact site Spiess had chosen. They named the new colony Bettina.

Meanwhile the financial affairs of the society had continued to disintegrate, and Spiess had inherited the responsibility of keeping the colonies going. The necessity of maintaining the still dependent colonies of New Braunfels and Fredericksburg involved hundreds of mule and ox carts, wagoners, saddlers, blacksmiths, bookkeepers, and clerks. On the last days of 1847 Spiess made it known that the affairs of the society would be severely limited. The administration at Fredericksburg, as well as that at Indianola, was abolished, and a number of oxen, mules, and wagons were auctioned to meet some of the society's debts. Hermann Wilke was retained to continue the surveying of town lots and ten-acre plots, and the original deeds transferring the lands from the Verein to the settlers bear the name of Hermann Spiess.

Spiess participated in the activities of New Braunfels from the beginning. In 1848, with Ludwig Bene (afterwards his successor as Verein administrator) and Louis C. Ervendberg,qv he signed the petition for the charter of the Western Texas Orphan Asylum, for those children whose parents had died during the illnesses that plagued the colonists during their migration from the coast to New Braunfels in 1845–1846. In 1850 Spiess and a number of men formed the Guadalupe River Bridge Company to construct a toll bridge across the river in New Braunfels. During this time he also built a sawmill and a shingle mill on his property at Waco Springs, just above New Braunfels. After the strong anti-slavery statement issued at a German political meeting held in San Antonio in May, 1854, Spiess and several other Texas Germans issued a statement in the *Texas State Gazette*,qv June 18, 1854, defending the majority of their fellow settlers against the resulting press indictment that Texas Germans were pro-union and anti-slavery. (*See* German Attitude—Civil War.)

In 1851 Spiess was married to Lena Spiess,qv the Mexican girl whose story had become legend among the early German settlers. They had ten children, three of whom died in infancy. In 1867 Spiess sold his Texas property on the advice of his doctor to move to a colder climate. The family settled in Warrensburg, Missouri, where Spiess died some time after 1873.

BIBLIOGRAPHY: Rudolph L. Biesele, *The History of the German Settlements in Texas, 1831–1861* (1930); Irene Marschall King, *John O. Meusebach* (1967); Robert Penniger (ed.) and Charles L. Wisseman, Sr. (trans.), *Fredericksburg, Texas . . . The First Fifty Years* (1971); Moritz Tiling, *The History of the German Element in Texas, 1820–1850* (1913); Rudolph L. Biesele, "The Texas State Convention of Germans in 1854," *Southwestern Historical Quarterly*, XXXIII (1929–1930); Henry B. Dielmann, "Dr. Ferdinand Herff, Pioneer Physician and Surgeon," *ibid.*, LVII (1953–1954); Louis Reinhardt, "The Communistic Colony of Bettina," *Quarterly of the Texas State Historical Association*, III (1899–1900); Armin O. Huber, "Frederic Armand Strubberg, Alias Dr. Shubbert, Town-Builder, Physician, and Adventurer, 1806–1889," *West Texas Historical Association Year Book*, XXXVIII (1962); Oscar Haas Papers of Comal County (New Braunfels).

Crystal Sasse Ragsdale

Spiess, Lena. Lena (or Lina) Spiess, the Mexican wife of Hermann Spiess,qv second general commissioner of the Adelsverein,qv was born probably around 1836 in Mexico, although the early years of her life are clouded in mystery. Later in her life she selected April 22 as her birthdate. Various accounts have shown her as having been kidnapped by Comanche Indians at an early age and either given to or bought by German settlers at New Braunfels when she was three or four years old.

One account shows that the little girl was sent to a Catholic convent for a time and then became part of the household of Count Ernst Coreth, near New Braunfels, where she was taught High German and English (with a German accent) by Augusta and Minchen Schleicher, and that she then lived for a while with Hermann Spiess and his sister Luise, who had come over from Germany for a visit to Hermann's home at Waco Springs. According to this account Lena was adopted by Spiess, but upon his sister's return to Germany the child was sent to Louis C. Ervendberg's qv *Waisenhaus* (Western Texas Orphan Asylum) to live with the German children whose parents had died.

A different account says that the child was given to Dr. Ferdinand Herff qv by a Comanche Indian brave in return for an eye operation, that she was left in the care of a Miss Julie Herf, the cook at Bettina Colony,qv and then taken to the orphanage.

It is fairly certain, however, that Lena lived for a time at the *Waisenhaus*. After that the facts are known. When Lena was about fifteen, in 1851, she was married to Hermann Spiess. They became the parents of ten children and lived at Waco Springs until the family moved to Warrensburg, Missouri, in 1867. Although she had some memories of her life in Mexico, Lena Spiess never discovered who her parents were nor where she had been born. She died in Tropico, California, a Los Angeles suburb, on January 3, 1914.

BIBLIOGRAPHY: Irene Marschall King, *John O. Meusebach* (1967); Henry B. Dielmann, "Dr. Ferdinand Herff, Pioneer Physician and Surgeon," *Southwestern Historical Quarterly*, LVII (1953–1954); Oscar Haas Papers of Comal County (New Braunfels).

Crystal Sasse Ragsdale

*Spiller, George.

*Spiller Creek.

*Spiller's Store, Texas.

*Spinach Culture.** During the 1950's Texas continued to be the leading spinach-producing state, and production was concentrated in the Winter Garden area of South Texas. In 1954 more than 16,000 acres yielded 2,062,000 bushels valued at $3,608,000. Crystal City, the site of one of the world's largest spinach canneries, erected a statue of the cartoon character Popeye. In 1959, 155 Texas farmers reported growing spinach. The value of spinach, one of Texas' most publicized truck crops, ranged from $3,000,000 to $5,000,000 annually during the 1950's. Little change had taken place by 1966, although value and carlot shipments had dropped slightly. In 1968, when crop acreage was reduced due to Hurricane Beulah, the value of the spinach crop was $2,665,000 from 4,500 acres; this compared with $2,304,000 from 6,000 acres in 1967. In 1970, 5,800 acres of spinach were harvested with a value of $2,065,000.

BIBLIOGRAPHY: *Texas Almanac* (1955, 1965, 1967, 1969, 1971).

*Spindletop Bayou.

*Spindletop Oil Field. Exploration of the Spindletop Oil Field was begun by Pattillo Higgins qv (not Padillo Higgins, as stated in Volume II) in 1892. Anthony Francis Lucas qv took over operations in June, 1899 (not 1889), and the well was drilled under contract by the Hamill (not Hamil) brothers, Alfred, James, and Curt.

BIBLIOGRAPHY: James A. Clark and Michael T. Halbouty, *Spindletop* (1952); Thelma Johnson, *et al.*, *The Spindletop Oil Field* (1927); Ruth Sheldon Knowles, *The Great Gamblers: The Epic of American Oil Exploration* (1959).

Splawn, Walter Marshall William. Walter Marshall William Splawn, economist and authority on railroad law and commerce, was born on June 16, 1883, in Arlington, Texas, the son of William Butler and Mary Marshall (Collins) Splawn. He graduated from Decatur Baptist College in 1904 and from Baylor University with a B.A. degree in 1906. He also took B.A. and M.A. degrees (1908, 1914) from Yale University, and a Ph.D. from the University of Chicago in 1921. He received the LL.D. degree from Howard Payne College in Brownwood in 1923. He had read law for several years in Fort Worth and was admitted to the Bar in 1909, after having been an instructor in English at Decatur Baptist College in 1907–1908, and at Fort Worth High School in 1909–1910. He was an instructor in social science at Baylor University from 1910 to 1912, then practiced law in Fort Worth from 1912 to 1915; he again taught at Baylor from 1916 to 1919.

Splawn joined the University of Texas faculty as an economics professor in 1919; he took a leave of absence to serve on the Texas Railroad Commission qv from March, 1923, to August, 1924. The laws he helped formulate were cited as models for federal railroad reorganization laws. Splawn left the commission to become president of the University of Texas in 1924. He was president during the time that oil development of university lands was broadening the horizons of the university's future, and he was instrumental in guiding the use of these new resources.

Splawn left the university in 1927 to become dean of the graduate school and director of political sciences at the American University in Washington, D.C. He worked as referee on the War Claims Commission in 1928, and in 1930 was special counsel to the House of Representatives Interstate Commerce Committee. He was involved in the formation of numerous laws initiated during President Franklin D. Roosevelt's administration and was largely responsible for the formulation of the Railroad Holding Company Act, the Truth in Securities Act, the Securities and Exchange Act, the Utility Holding Company Act, and the Federal Communications Act. In 1934 President Roosevelt appointed Splawn to the Interstate Commerce Commission (ICC), a position he held until his retirement in 1953, serving as chairman in 1938 and 1951. He then produced a manuscript, The University of Texas: Its Origin and Growth to 1928; the two-volume work was never published, and a copy was placed in the Archives of the University of Texas at Austin. In 1957, despite blindness, he began teaching again, this time at Decatur Baptist College. In September, 1957, he returned briefly to Washington as a consultant to the House of Representatives Committee on Interstate and Foreign Commerce. Splawn was the author of several books on economics and the regulation of railroads, including *Introduction to the Study of Economics* (1922), *Consolidation of Railroads* (1924), and *Government Ownership and Operation of Railroads* (1928). He has been called the "father" of today's regulatory laws.

Splawn was married to Zola Isabel Lay of Mason, Texas, on July 21, 1912; they had two daughters. He died on January 17, 1963, in Washington, D.C., and was buried in Friends Cemetery at Lincoln, Virginia, where he had maintained a home.

BIBLIOGRAPHY: Biographical File, Barker Texas History Center, University of Texas at Austin.

*Splendora, Texas.

*Spofford, Texas.

*Spohn, Arthur Edward.

Sports Hall of Fame. *See* Texas Sports Hall of Fame.

Sports in Texas. Favorable climatic conditions have been a major factor in making Texas one of the world's foremost centers of sports activity. Competitive opportunities for the amateur athlete have been numerous, and although activity in professional sports was slow in the beginning, rapid strides took place later as interest mushroomed, spurred by sportsdom's most intriguing arena, the Astrodome qv in Houston.

Organized baseball dates back to 1888 in Texas, but the predominant sports interest through the first two-thirds of the twentieth century centered around interscholastic and intercollegiate activity. Track and field was the first competitive sport to attain a high level of organization and participation, both on the high school and the collegiate level. Football, which was celebrated for its 100th year of existence as a sport in 1969 (a centennial year in which the University of Texas at Austin won the national championship), moved into the state in the 1890's, but football did not become a household word in Texas until it had been in existence for nearly a half century. Colleges and high schools were playing it long before, but it was not until 1920 that the state determined its first scholastic (high school) football championship. In actuality, it was a co-championship (Cleburne and Houston Heights), and that initial University Interscholastic League qv season did not end until January 8, 1921. From that beginning, high school football in

Texas increased in participation and appeal to far outdistance programs in rival states. The number of participants in the UIL's unprecedented program reached 45,000 in the 1967–1968 school year, and estimated attendance at high school football contests soared to approximately 8,000,000. An additional 85,000 youngsters participated in the junior high and B-team programs in the state. In the mid-1970's, boys and girls competed (separately) for state championships in basketball, track and field, cross-country, golf, swimming, tennis, football (boys only), volleyball (girls only), and baseball (boys only). This participation was supplemented by that of the parochial schools, which also played for state titles. There were powerful intercollegiate football teams in Texas prior to the founding of the Southwest Conference qv in late 1914, but in those days only the Ivy League powers in the East received recognition. Texas colleges participated under the banner of the Southwest Intercollegiate Athletic Association prior to 1915, and many of the members retained that affiliation after the formation of the Southwest Conference. Eventually the parent organization was dissolved and was replaced by such leagues as the Texas Conference (no longer in existence), the Lone Star Conference, the Big State Conference, the Southland Conference, and the Southwestern Athletic Conference.

Trinity, Hardin-Simmons, and Howard Payne, among others, gained early football acclaim, but most of the All-American recognition and national championship consideration has gone to Southwest Conference teams. SMU, TCU, Texas A&M, and the University of Texas at Austin, in that chronological order, achieved national championships in football, with the University of Texas winning that honor on several occasions. All of the Southwest Conference schools have developed All-American players, and they have been joined by virtually every college in the state in furnishing outstanding talent to the professional leagues.

Teams from Texas have also won national championships in basketball, baseball, and golf, and they have contributed many national individual champions in track and field, tennis, swimming, and golf. The University of Houston, Abilene Christian, Pan American, the University of Texas at Arlington, North Texas State, Southwest Texas State, Prairie View A&M, and the University of Texas at El Paso have also produced national champions. Junior colleges have basked in national championship glory, including those in Tyler, Kilgore, San Jacinto, Howard County, and Henderson County. Among them they have claimed top honors in basketball, track and field, and football at the Junior Rose Bowl.

Approximately a dozen minor leagues offered organized baseball in Texas before a major league franchise was granted to Houston for the 1962 season. The Houston entry in the National League (first as the Colt 45's, later as the Houston Astros qv) initially had little success; however, history was made once the Astrodome opened in 1965. In that year the Astros had a home attendance of 2,151,470; afterward the dome became a mecca for football, rodeo, and soccer, and it housed the largest crowd (52,000) ever to see a basketball game (UCLA vs. Houston). In 1972 another major league baseball team came to Texas when the American League franchise of the Washington Senators was transferred to Arlington as the Texas Rangers Baseball Club.qv

Major league football arrived earlier. Dallas fielded a team briefly in the National Football League in 1952, but the Texans of that era did not last out the season. In 1960 Dallas was home for the Dallas Cowboys qv of the NFL and for the Dallas Texans qv of the new American Football League. The Houston Oilers qv were formed in Houston and won the first two championships of the AFL. The Dallas Texans' franchise was transferred to Kansas City in 1963, but it was not until 1966 that the Cowboys were able to capitalize on having the Dallas scene to themselves. Afterward, for two straight seasons, they won the eastern division of the NFL and finished as runners-up to the champion Green Bay Packers. During this time they began playing to full houses of 75,000. In the 1971 season the Cowboys not only won the National Conference championship, but they defeated the American Conference champion, the Miami Dolphins, in the Super Bowl early in 1972.

The years 1967 and 1968 brought to the state professional basketball (Dallas, Houston, and later San Antonio), soccer (Dallas), and returned ice hockey (Dallas, Fort Worth, Houston, and later Amarillo), after an absence of many years.

Texas produced national champions in tennis and in golf. For more than a quarter of a century Texas has produced more golf champions than any other state, both in amateur and professional ranks. Wrestling, boxing, auto racing, and horse racing (at one time) have been prominent in Texas; the only major appeal in boxing, however, has come from the amateur Golden Gloves tournaments and professional fights in the Astrodome.

Because of the increasing number of lakes in the state, water sports have flourished. Recreational activities such as fishing, boating, and water skiing are popular. The hunting of deer, wild turkey, duck, geese, and quail continues to flourish during the seasons set aside for such purposes. See also Intercollegiate Athletics; Texas Sports Hall of Fame.

Wilbur Evans

Spraberry, Texas. Spraberry, in eastern Midland County, was founded about 1951 and named for a nearby oil field. The community had a post office until 1954. In 1971 the community, with an estimated population of forty-six, consisted of a service station and a store.

Spriegel, William Robert. William Robert Spriegel, nationally known authority on personnel management, was born in Charleston, West Virginia, on May 14, 1893, the son of John William and Mary M. (Lynn) Spriegel. He received a B.A.

degree in economics in 1914 and a B.S. degree in chemistry in 1915, both from Lebanon University. Spriegel served for two years as superintendent of schools at Waynesville, Ohio, but with World War I, he became an aviator and pilot instructor. On August 6, 1918, he married Gladys Maree Strelinger, and they had two children. He continued his education after the war, receiving an M.A. degree in psychology in 1920 and a Ph.D. degree in economics in 1935, both from the University of Michigan. From 1919 to 1931 Spriegel held important managerial positions with the U.S. Rubber Company, Dodge Brothers, Fisher Body Corporation, and Charles A. Strelinger Company in Detroit. He left the industrial business world to go to the University of Michigan's School of Business Administration as assistant in policy for two years.

He began his teaching career at Western Kentucky State Teachers College in 1934, and in 1937 he went to Northwestern University, where he was management department chairman from 1939 to 1948. He also served for a while as mediator on the National War Labor Board in 1942. He joined the University of Texas faculty in 1948 as professor of management and associate dean of the College of Business Administration. Two years later he was named dean of the college and remained in that capacity until 1958. After his resignation as dean, Spriegel continued to teach through 1966, occasionally going on national lecture tours.

He was the author and coauthor of many books, some of which were *Personnel Management* (1954), *Industrial Management* (1955), and *Elements of Supervision* (1957); his numerous monographs included works on job evaluation, personnel practices in the automobile industry and colleges and universities, and training supervisors in human relations. He served as vice-president and later as president of the American Academy of Management during the mid-1950's and was one of the U.S. delegates to the International Management Congress in 1953 and 1957. He was general chairman of the Texas Personnel and Management Association and held various other positions in national professional organizations. On May 21, 1953, the Texas House of Representatives passed a resolution honoring him for "notable and constructive work in the field of Scientific Management." He died on August 28, 1972, in Austin, and was buried in Berkley, Michigan.

BIBLIOGRAPHY: *Who's Who In America* (1960); Biographical File, Barker Texas History Center, University of Texas at Austin.

*Spring, Texas.

*Spring Branch.

*Spring Branch, Texas.

*Spring Creek.

*Spring Creek, Texas. (Parker County.)

*Spring Creek, Texas. (Throckmorton County.)

*Spring Creek County.

*Spring Creek Gap.

*Spring Gap.

*Spring Gap Mountains.

*Spring Gully.

*Spring Hill.

*Spring Hill, Texas. (Bowie County.)

*Spring Hill, Texas. (Falls County.)

*Spring Hill, Texas. (Gregg County.)

*Spring Hill, Texas. (Navarro County.)

*Spring Lake.

*Spring Lake, Texas.

*Spring Mesa.

Spring Valley, Texas. (Harris County.) Spring Valley had a 1960 population of 3,004 and a 1970 population of 3,170, according to the United States census.

*Spring Valley, Texas. (McLennan County.)

*Springdale, Texas.

*Springfield, Texas. (Anderson County.)

*Springfield, Texas. (Jim Wells County.)

*Springfield, Texas. (Limestone County.)

*Springfield Lake.

*Springtown, Texas. Springtown, in Parker County, had a population of 859 in 1960, but by 1970 the population had risen to 1,194, according to the United States census. The town had twenty-eight businesses in 1970.

*Springtown Male and Female Institute.

*Sprinkle, Texas.

*Spur, Texas. Spur, the largest city in Dickens County, is a shipping point for cotton, cattle, and wheat. Construction activities in the early 1960's provided the town with several new churches, public buildings, and recreational facilities. In 1965 the Caprock Peace Officers Association began holding its annual rattlesnake rodeo and barbecue, one of the most bizarre of western festivals. A hospital, a bank, a library, and a newspaper serve the inhabitants of Spur. One mile west of the city is an agricultural experiment station operated under the auspices of the Texas A&M University System.qv White River Reservoir, fourteen miles from Spur in adjacent Crosby County, added to the city's attractions when it was completed in 1963. The 1960 population was 2,170; in 1970 it was 1,747, according to the United States census. Spur reported fifty-three businesses in 1970.

*Spur Ranch.

*Spurger, Texas.

*Spurlin, Texas.

*Spurs.

*Spy, The.

*Spy Mountain.

*Square and Compass Ranch.

*Square Top Mountain.

*Squaw Creek.

*Squirrel Creek.

*Stacy, Texas.

*Staff, Texas.

*Stafford, Adam.

*Stafford, William.

*Stafford, Texas. Stafford, in Fort Bend County, greatly increased in size during the 1950's and 1960's, expanding partially into Harris County (*see* Houston Standard Metropolitan Statistical Area). From a population of 1,485 in 1960, it continued to grow during the following decade, reaching a population of 2,906 by 1970, an increase of 95.7 percent in ten years, according to the United States census. Stafford reported forty businesses in 1970.

*Stafford's Point. *See* Stafford, Texas.

*Stagecoach Lines.

*Stairway Mountain.

*Staked Plains. *See* Llano Estacado.

Stallings, William Crider. William Crider Stallings, one of four children of Elisha and Emily Stallings, was born on September 9, 1842, near Covington, in Newton County, Georgia. Although his schooling was limited, he was self-educated by reading widely. He enlisted in the Confederate Army in the cavalry under General John F. Morgan's command and saw combat duty in Tennessee, Virginia, Maryland, and Kentucky.

In 1864 he married Modora Austin, who died soon after. In 1866 he married Martha Driggers, and the couple had five children before her death in 1876. Stallings married Ida R. Hurst in 1877, and they had ten children. In the fall of 1879 the Stallings moved to Texas and settled on a farm in the Bascomb Methodist Church community east of Tyler, and then in Chandler (Henderson County) and in Decatur and Alvord (Wise County), where he operated a blacksmith shop for several years. Later they moved to their own farm five miles west of Tyler in the Dixie community, where he lived for the rest of his life.

Before coming to Texas Stallings had become a licensed Methodist minister; he served in churches both in Georgia and Texas. He read widely on farming and plants and became known for his successful farming methods. A firm believer in farming diversification, he grew many different types of crops, specializing in corn, which he field-selected and sold as seed corn. (Later a variety of white corn, "Stallings White Corn," was named for him.) He also specialized in raising Poland-China hogs. On November 12, 1906, the Commercial Club of Tyler, a group of businessmen, met near the courthouse square and, with the cooperation of Seaman A. Knapp of the United States Department of Agriculture, appointed Stallings the first county agricultural agent in Texas and the first in the nation to serve only one county. He served in that capacity for one year in Smith County. Tyler businessmen and the Federal Bureau of Plant Industry

of the United States Department of Agriculture each paid half of Stallings' $150 monthly salary.

At a meeting of all state agents in demonstration work, held in the fall of 1907 in Washington, D.C., Stallings was appointed a district agent with the responsibility of working in his own county and supervising work in one or two nearby counties, so that in the beginning of the crop year of 1908 Stallings also supervised Cherokee County. In the fall of 1909 the East Texas districts were consolidated into only two large districts; Stallings was again a county agent, serving in Cherokee and Angelina counties for the crop year of 1910. Through Stallings' efforts the yields in both cotton and corn were increased by over 50 percent in the area, and the Smith County boys' corn club was awarded the corn trophy at the State Fair of Texas qv in Dallas.

Stallings died on January 10, 1916, and was buried in the Beaird Cemetery, four miles west of Tyler. A historical marker was placed on the courthouse square in Tyler in November, 1971, in honor of Stallings' pioneer farm demonstration work.

BIBLIOGRAPHY: Mrs. M. R. Bentley, "The Cradle of Extension Work," *Bunker's Monthly* (March, 1928); *Texas Co-Op Power* (January, 1972); Files of the Texas Historical Commission, Austin.

*Stalnaker, John William.

*Stamford, Texas. Stamford, in Jones County and partly in Haskell County, had an economy supported primarily by cotton and ranching; it had three gins, a compress, a cotton oil mill, and a delinting plant in the 1960's, and its businesses, well over one hundred in 1970, included a ladies' sportswear factory and six other manufacturers. An industrial park with a $1,200,000 building was in operation by 1964. The town was the commercial center for the surrounding area in Jones, Haskell, and Stonewall counties. Lake Stamford in Haskell County provided recreation, and the town began work on a lakeside park to enhance the attraction for tourists. The Texas Cowboy Reunion qv is held on the Fourth of July in Stamford. The 1960 population was 5,259; it had dropped to 4,558 by 1970, according to the United States census. *See also* Abilene Standard Metropolitan Statistical Area.

*Stamford College.

*Stamford Cowboy Reunion. *See* Texas Cowboy Reunion.

*Stamford and Northwestern Railway Company.

*Stampede, Texas.

*Stampede Creek.

*Stamper, Texas.

*Stamps.

*Stamps, John.

Stamps, Thomas Dodson. Thomas Dodson Stamps, son of Asa and Elizabeth (Willeford) Stamps, was born in Kingsbury, Texas, on July 23, 1893. He was graduated from the University of Texas with a Bachelor of Arts degree in 1912.

He entered the United States Army in 1914, was commissioned a second lieutenant, and received a Bachelor of Science degree from the U.S. Military Academy in 1917. He was with the U.S. Army Corps of Engineers from 1917 to 1938, and he commanded engineer troops during World War I in France and Germany with the 107th Engineers of the 32nd Infantry Division; his decorations included the Legion of Merit with Oak-Leaf Cluster and the French Legion of Honor. He received another Bachelor of Science degree, this time from Massachusetts Institute of Technology, in 1921; he rose to the rank of brigadier general by 1956.

Stamps was head of the Department of Military Art and Engineering at the U.S. Military Academy from 1938 to 1956 and dean of the academic board there from 1956 to 1957. He developed texts and atlases for studies of recent wars, and during World War II he initiated a series of paperbacks to bring the latest engineering developments to the cadets. He was active in cadet affairs and served for many years on the athletic board at West Point. Before his service at the academy he had been a construction engineer òn Mississippi River and Illinois waterways projects and served in the construction of the American Embassy in Tokyo, Japan, in 1930–1931.

He was a member of the Society of American Military Engineers, the American Society of Engineering Education, and the American Military Institute. He was co-editor of *A Short Military History of World War I* and *A Military History of World War II*; he also contributed numerous articles to technical journals. He retired as a professor at the Military Academy in 1957; from then until August, 1963, he directed military studies at the University of Maryland. Stamps married Lois Baker on October 4, 1919; they had two children. He died on April 12, 1964, at Washington, D.C., and was buried at West Point.

Richard T. Fleming

*Stamps, Texas.

Standard Metropolitan Statistical Areas in Texas. Texas, with more Standard Metropolitan Statistical Areas (SMSA) than any other state in the union, had a total of twenty-four such areas following the 1970 United States census, when the Bryan-College Station (Brazos County) area was the latest so designated. [By 1973 there were still twenty-four areas, but the Dallas and Fort Worth areas had been combined into a single statistical unit, and Killeen-Temple SMSA had been created. *See* tables following. Ed.] The state also had a higher percentage of urban and metropolitan population than the national average. In 1970 over three-fourths (79.7 percent) of the state's population lived in urban areas (as defined by the Bureau of the Census, U. S. Department of Commerce) and 73.5 percent of the population lived in the twenty-four Standard Metropolitan Statistical Areas (forty Texas counties plus Miller County, Arkansas).

The federal government designates SMSA areas,

defining dense urban populations with common economic and social characteristics. The standard definition for metropolitan areas was first issued in 1949, when they were called "Standard Metropolitan Areas." This replaced the four different definitions—metropolitan districts, metropolitan counties, industrial areas, and labor market areas—previously used for various urban areas. The primary purpose in creating a uniform definition was to enable all federal statistical agencies to utilize the same boundaries when they published data useful for analyzing metropolitan problems. In order to achieve a more objective definition of a metropolitan area, the criteria were revised and reissued in March, 1958. "Statistical" was added as an identifying phrase to describe more accurately the objectives of the definition. This concept aided in the collection of comparable statistics so that socioeconomic factors such as labor force, industrial output, and criminal records could be used in analyses. An SMSA was officially defined as one or more counties containing a core city of at least 50,000 inhabitants, or two cities with a combined population of at least 50,000, provided the smaller had at least 15,000 persons. The area must have a "metropolitan character," or at least 75 percent of its labor force in nonagricultural employment. There must be evidence of an economic and social integration between the central city and its county and outlying counties for the area to qualify as an SMSA. Measures of integration range from the percentage of labor force living outside but working within the central city, to population density, newspaper circulation, data on charge accounts, traffic volume, and others. An urban region may have more than one SMSA when the criterion of integration is lacking, such as Fort Worth, Dallas, and Sherman-Denison, where each was defined as a separate and distinct SMSA although their areas' boundaries were contiguous. Within Texas, a region such as this is often considered as a single "urban complex." [As noted above, however, Dallas and Fort Worth were combined in 1973 into a single statistical unit. Ed.]

Even though they have a common definition, the metropolitan statistical areas in Texas vary considerably. Population in the largest SMSA, Houston (in 1970), was 1,985,031, while that of the smallest (in 1970), Bryan-College Station, was 57,978. While the McAllen-Edinburg-Pharr SMSA had less than 1 percent nonwhite population in the late 1960's, Tyler had over 27 percent; Laredo had a foreign-born population of over 18 percent, while Texarkana had only 3 percent foreign-born. The population of the Austin SMSA increased by 39.3 percent between 1960 and 1970, while during the same period the SMSA populations of Odessa and McAllen-Edinburg-Pharr remained static, and those of Abilene and Brownsville-Harlingen-San Benito decreased by 5.3 percent and 7.1 percent, respectively.

The different areas also vary in their economic bases. Farm-commodity related industries are distinctive in several areas, such as cotton in Lub-

STANDARD METROPOLITAN STATISTICAL AREAS IN TEXAS IN 1970

Central Cities	Counties
Abilene	Jones, Taylor
Amarillo	Potter, Randall
Austin	Travis
Beaumont-Port Arthur-Orange	Jefferson, Orange
Brownsville-Harlingen-San Benito	Cameron
Bryan-College Station	Brazos
Corpus Christi	Nueces, San Patricio
Dallas	Collin, Dallas, Denton, Ellis, Kaufman, Rockwall
El Paso	El Paso
Fort Worth	Johnson, Tarrant
Galveston-Texas City	Galveston
Houston	Brazoria, Fort Bend, Harris, Liberty, Montgomery
Laredo	Webb
Lubbock	Lubbock
McAllen-Edinburg-Pharr	Hidalgo
Midland	Midland
Odessa	Ector
San Angelo	Tom Green
San Antonio	Bexar, Guadalupe
Sherman-Denison	Grayson
Texarkana	Bowie (and Miller County, Arkansas)
Tyler	Smith
Waco	McLennan
Wichita Falls	Archer, Wichita

CHANGES MADE IN STANDARD METROPOLITAN STATISTICAL AREAS IN TEXAS FOLLOWING THE 1970 CENSUS

Central Cities	Counties
Abilene	Callahan County was added in April, 1973.
Austin	Hays County was added in April, 1973.
Beaumont-Port Arthur-Orange	Hardin County was added in April, 1973.
Dallas-Fort Worth	The six-county Dallas area was combined with the two-county Fort Worth area, and three additional counties were added in April, 1973: Wise, Parker, and Hood counties.
Houston	Waller County was added in April, 1973.
Killeen-Temple	This SMSA was created in 1972, composed of Bell and Coryell counties.
San Antonio	Comal County was added in April, 1973.
Texarkana	Little River County (Arkansas) was added in April, 1973.
Wichita Falls	Clay County was added and Archer County was deleted in April, 1973.

bock, wool in San Angelo, and fruit and vegetables in the Lower Rio Grande Valley; the economies of Midland and Odessa are tied to oil production; Austin is a university and government center; and air force and army bases are vital to San Antonio's economy.

The number of local governments within different Texas SMSA's also varied widely. The average in Texas was thirty-nine in the late 1960's, ranging from five in Midland to more than two hundred fifty in the Dallas area, while the average number of local governments per SMSA nationally was eighty-seven, or more than twice the number in Texas metropolitan areas. Until 1963, under the liberal annexation laws of Texas, home rule cities could annex surrounding territories without the approval of the annexed areas; thus, the boundaries of the core city expanded as the metropolitan population grew, and the problem of multiple and conflicting units of government stayed at a minimum. The population density in Texas was almost half the national average, and as a result the Texas SMSA's had fewer thickly populated city slums than in other areas of the country; however, with more cars per capita, the state had correspondingly larger traffic problems.

With the creation of metropolitan statistical areas providing valuable statistical information, Texas began to recognize the necessity of helping local governments make adjustments to rapid metropolitan growth. The Fifty-ninth Texas Legislature passed measures providing for the creation of regional planning councils, and by 1967 twelve areas had established such councils and five more were forming them. The Sixtieth Legislature considered recommendations for new laws and constitutional amendments resulting from the 1966 comprehensive study of Texas metropolitan areas by the Texas Research League.[qv]

From 1950 to 1970 metropolitan development in Texas was in a period of dynamic growth, and this trend was continuing in the early 1970's. Eight new SMSA's were designated after the United States census of 1960—six in August, 1960, one in April, 1966, and one in April, 1967; one was added after the 1970 census. During the same period many additional counties were added to existing SMSA's. In 1970 the forty counties (plus Miller County, Arkansas, as part of the Texarkana SMSA) within the twenty-four Texas SMSA's had a population of 8,267,843 persons out of the state's total population of 11,196,730. In the late 1960's the Texas Research League estimated that by the year 2020 there would be additional SMSA's created in Texas, that many counties would be added to existing SMSA's, and that over 87 percent of the state's population would be metropolitan. [Additional changes since 1972 are reflected in the accompanying second table. Ed.]

Shirley Chapman

***Standard Mine, Texas.**

***Standart, Texas.**

***Standefer, Isaac.**

***Standefer, Israel.**

***Standifer, Jesse Marshall.**

***Stanfield, Texas.**

***Stanley, David Sloane.**

***Stanley, J. H. S.**

***Stanley, Texas.**

***Stanley Creek.**

***Stansel, Texas.**

***Stant Rhea Stage Stand.**

***Stanton, Texas.** Stanton, seat of Martin County, is a shipping center for livestock and a center for oil and ranching businesses. Minor industries include a cotton compress, cotton gins, and bottling, packing, and woodworking companies. Stanton holds annual livestock exhibits and capon shows. The 1960 population was 2,228; the 1970 count was 2,117, according to the United States census. Stanton had fifty-eight businesses in 1970.

***Staples, Sidney Lee.**

***Staples, Texas.**

***Stapp, Elijah.**

***Star, Texas.**

***Star Hollow Creek.**

***Star Mountain.**

Star of the West. The *Star of the West* was a two-deck, side-wheel, schooner-rigged merchant ship fired upon by Confederate batteries as she attempted to relieve Fort Sumter on January 9, 1861. Hired out of New York as a troop transport for $1,000 a day, under its master, Elisha Howes, the *Star* sailed for Texas to pick up seven companies of United States troops assembled at Indianola. On April 18, while anchored off Pass Caballo bar leading into Matagorda Bay, the ship was captured by Colonel Earl Van Dorn qv and members of two Galveston militia units, the Wigfall Guards and the Island City Rifles. Two days later the ship was taken to New Orleans, where Louisiana's Governor Moore changed its name to the C.S.S. *St. Philip*. The old name persisted, however, and the *Star* served as a naval station and hospital ship until Farragut captured New Orleans. Then the *Star* carried millions in gold, silver, and paper currency to Vicksburg and continued to Yazoo City. When Federal Lieutenant Commander Watson Smith tried to lead two ironclads and five smaller vessels through Yazoo Pass into the Tallahatchie River to attack Vicksburg from the rear, Confederate defenders hurriedly constructed Fort Pemberton, and Brigadier General William W. Loring had the *Star* sunk athwart the Tallahatchie to block the passage of the Union flotilla. In a skirmish on April 12, 1863, the Union forces suffered heavy casualties and were forced to withdraw. The owners of the *Star* collected $175,000 in damages from the United States government for their loss.

BIBLIOGRAPHY: New Orleans *Daily Crescent*, April 23, 1861; Charles B. Boynton, *History of the Navy during the Rebellion*, II (1868); U.S. War Department, *The War of the Rebellion: A Compilation of the Official Records of the Union and Confederate Armies* (1880–1901); George and Dewey Lehr (comps.), *Star of the West* Documentary (photostats from the Library of Congress and National Archives, Washington, D.C., in the Greenwood-Leflore Public Library, Greenwood, Mississippi); Jack D. L. Holmes, "The End of 'The Star of the West'," *Civil War Times*, III (1961).

Jack D. L. Holmes

Stark, Henry Jacob Lutcher. Henry Jacob Lutcher Stark was born on December 8, 1887, in Orange, Texas, the son of William H. and Miriam M. (Lutcher) Stark,qv early settlers in Orange County. Stark received his formal education in Orange, graduating from high school in 1905. He earned the B.A. degree from the University of Texas in 1910. Honorary LL.D. degrees were awarded him by Baylor University (1933) and Southwestern University at Memphis, Tennessee (1938).

Heir to one of the country's greatest lumber fortunes, he was a civil engineer and became successful in such diverse fields as rice farming, banking, real estate, and oil field drilling and exploration. By the mid-1930's he held executive positions in the Orange First National Bank, Lutcher and Moore Lumber Company, a land development corporation, a packing company, and a steel company which later became part of United States Steel Company. Business and land developments encompassed both sides of the Sabine River: lumber and land in Orange County, and oil and land in southwestern Louisiana, where during the 1920's the Stark family had operated a modern fur trapping business.

Stark was active in educational, philanthropic, and cultural affairs. Beginning in 1919 he served on the board of regents of the University of Texas for six four-year terms, three of which he was chairman of the board. In 1958 Stark's name was added to the Longhorn Hall of Fame in Austin. Because of his family's active interest in the development of Texas Woman's University, that school awarded him a distinguished service award in 1963. He was keenly interested in the National Association of Audubon Societies, the American Irish Society, the Louisiana Society for Horticultural Research, and the Texas Ornithological Society. The Shangri-La gardens and bird sanctuary in Orange were his monuments to floral beauty and the preservation of bird wildlife. The Nelda C. Stark and H. J. Lutcher Stark Foundation was organized for philanthropic purposes. The family received much attention in 1937 when it donated to the University of

Texas a giant collection of books and art objects, valued in excess of $4,000,000. When the university failed to provide adequate housing for the art collection, the Starks withdrew that part of the gift. Stark continued to acquire art treasures, giving special attention to Audubon sketches, Remington western scenes, and other subjects of regional significance. He also served as a board member of the SLI Foundation, a nonprofit corporation designed to promote the development and welfare of Southwestern Louisiana Institute at Lafayette.

Stark married Nita Hill on April 5, 1914; they had two sons. After Mrs. Stark's death he married Nelda Childers on December 16, 1943. He died on September 2, 1965, and was buried at Orange.

BIBLIOGRAPHY: Orange *Leader*, May 29, 1936, September 2, 1965; Austin *American*, September 3, 1965.

Thomas L. Charlton

*Stark, Miriam Lutcher.

Starr, Amory Reily. Amory Reily Starr, son of Harriet (Johnson) and James Harper Starr,qv was born on August 25, 1847, at Nacogdoches. He attended Nacogdoches University, which offered courses from the elementary grades to college level. During the first years of the Civil War, he ran away from home four times to join the Confederate Army and finally on July 4, 1864, was allowed to serve as a private in Company H, 4th Regiment, Texas Cavalry of Hardeman's Brigade; he served as a scout. After the Civil War he again attended Nacogdoches University and then the University of Virginia, where he received a law degree. On returning to Nacogdoches he and his friend, Peyton Forbes Edwards,qv were in law partnership for a brief period before 1873 when Starr assumed control of the James H. Starr and Son land agency, which had belonged to his father and brother, James Franklin Starr;qv the Starr family had moved to Marshall in 1870. Amory Starr was married to Georgia Mehaffey on June 4, 1872; they were the parents of four sons and two daughters.

During Reconstruction,qv Starr joined the Knights of the White Camelia.qv Because of the group's anti-Negro activities in Harrison County, officers of the federal government placed Starr and other members in the stockade at Jefferson. Since none of the group would testify against the others, the charges against them were dropped. In 1875 or 1876 Starr was one of the organizers of the Citizens party, which restored white Democrats to power and control in Harrison County in the 1878 election. He served as a member of the state Democratic executive committee, as mayor of Marshall, Texas, and was appointed a regent of the University of Texas in 1893 by Governor James Stephen Hogg.qv Starr died in Marshall on December 15, 1906, and was buried in Greenwood Cemetery there.

BIBLIOGRAPHY: John N. Cravens, *James Harper Starr: Financier of the Republic of Texas* (1950); R. P. Littlejohn, "Pioneer Marshall Man Wanted Children to Know Story of Political Heritage," Marshall *News Messenger*, January 24, 1951; James Harper Starr Papers (MS., Archives, University of Texas at Austin Library).

John N. Cravens

*Starr, Belle.

*Starr, Franklin Jefferson.

Starr, James Franklin. James Franklin Starr was born March 30, 1844, at Nacogdoches, son of Harriet (Johnson) and James Harper Starr.qv He attended local schools, including Nacogdoches University. In 1861 Starr enlisted in the Confederate Army, and he was in the New Mexico campaign under General Henry H. Sibley qv (*see* Sibley's Brigade). He participated in the battle of Galveston qv and also saw active service in Louisiana, Arkansas, and Mississippi before the war's end, when he held the rank of major. After the war he attended the University of Virginia and then returned to Marshall, Texas, to form with his father the partnership of James H. Starr and Son, a real estate and banking agency.

On June 6, 1868, Starr was married to Clara Fry Clapp. He died on January 11, 1902, and was buried in Greenwood Cemetery in Marshall.

BIBLIOGRAPHY: David B. Gracy II (ed.), "New Mexico Campaign Letters of Frank Starr, 1861–1862," *Texas Military History*, IV (1964); James Harper Starr Papers (MS., Archives, University of Texas at Austin Library); Marshall *Morning News*, January 12, 1902.

John N. Cravens

*Starr, James Harper.

*Starr County. Starr County, with a petroleum and agribusiness economy, produced over 216 million barrels of oil between 1929 and 1973, and its average annual farm income was approximately $11 million in the early 1970's. Farming, consisting of vegetables, feed crops, and cotton, was concentrated on 35,000 irrigated acres along the Rio Grande. The major tourist attraction is the International Falcon Reservoir.qv The county has a number of fine examples of nineteenth-century Rio Grande border architecture (*see* Portscheller, Heinrich). The 1960 population was 17,137; the 1970 population was 17,707, according to the U.S. census.

*Starrville, Texas.

*Starvation Creek.

*State Archives. *See* Archives of Texas.

*State Auditor.

*State Bar of Texas. The State Bar of Texas is composed of all persons licensed to practice law in the state. It is a completely self-governing body and is the administrative arm of the Supreme Court of Texas (*see* Judicial System). Members annually elect a president-elect (who automatically becomes president the following term) and a vice-president. The board of directors is the general executive agency of the Bar and it consists of twenty-eight members elected by the membership from twenty-two State Bar districts (a single member from each district, except four members from Harris County, three from Dallas County, and two from Bexar County). The directors serve three-year, staggered terms; at their discretion they appoint a full-time executive director (who is also editor-in-chief of the monthly *Texas Bar Journal*), a general counsel, a director of continuing legal education, a public relations director, a director of member services, and a managing editor of the *Texas Bar Journal*. Offices of the State Bar are located in Austin.

BIBLIOGRAPHY: University of Texas at Austin, *Guide To Texas State Agencies* (1972).

*State Bird. See Mockingbird.

State Building Commission. The State Building Commission, created by the adoption of a constitutional amendment in 1954, was composed of the governor, the attorney general, and the chairman of the Board of Control.qv An executive director is appointed by the commission, and work is carried out under his supervision in five divisions of the organization. The commission had the responsibility of planning and constructing new state buildings and remodeling existing ones. In addition, it was authorized to arrange for the acquisition of new building sites. The erection of certain monuments and historical memorials was also made the responsibility of the commission in cooperation with the Texas State Historical Survey Committee.qv In 1965 the 59th Legislature enacted into law the State Building Construction Administration Act to provide for the orderly planning of buildings constructed by the state, to provide for the adequate inspection of building construction work in progress, and to provide for reasonably accurate projection of building program requirements and estimates of the costs of proposed projects prior to legislative appropriation. The commission supervises planning and inspection of building projects for all state agencies except the Texas State Highway Department,qv institutions of higher learning (*see* Coordinating Board, Texas College and University System), the Texas Board of Corrections, the Texas Youth Council, and the Texas Department of Mental Health and Mental Retardation.qqv

BIBLIOGRAPHY: University of Texas at Austin, *Guide To Texas State Agencies* (1972).

Phil Bible

State Building Materials and Systems Testing Laboratory. *See* Community Affairs, Department of.

*State Cemetery. Qualifications for burial in the State Cemetery in Austin are stated in Article 678, *Vernon's Annotated Texas Statutes* (1964), and in the administrative regulations of the Board of Control.qv Included are members and ex-members of the Texas legislature, Confederate war veterans, elective state and ex-state officials, and officials who have been appointed by the governor and confirmed by the Texas Senate.

An exception to the regulations was the burial of author J. Frank Dobie qv in 1964 by special permission of the governor and vote of the Texas legislature. (Dobie's widow, Bertha McKee Dobie,qv was also buried there in 1974.) Miriam Amanda Ferguson,qv buried in 1961, and Daniel

James Moody,qv buried in 1966, brought to nine the number of governors interred in the State Cemetery.

BIBLIOGRAPHY: Austin *American-Statesman*, September 20, 1970.

*State Colonization Law. See Mexican Colonization Laws, 1821–1830.

*State Colored Orphans' Home.

State Commission for the Deaf. The State Commission for the Deaf was created in 1971 by the 62nd Texas Legislature. Appointed by the governor with the concurrence of the Senate, the six commission members serve six-year terms. Two of the members must be deaf persons. The commission appoints an executive director, preferably deaf or hard-of-hearing. The commission is responsible for rendering all services to the deaf except those which are by law the responsibility of the welfare, educational, or other agencies of the state. Among its duties the commission collects and dispenses information concerning the deaf, conducts a census of deaf persons in the state, and accepts any and all gifts to the state for services dealing with the deaf.

BIBLIOGRAPHY: University of Texas at Austin, *Guide To Texas State Agencies* (1972).

*State Dairy and Hog Farm. See also State Hog Farm; Texas Leander Rehabilitation Center.

State Department of Public Welfare. *See* Public Welfare, State Department of.

State Executive Officers, Compensation of. The Constitution of 1876 qv originally set the salaries for the officers in the executive branch of the state government. The governor received $4,000 annually; the attorney general, $2,000, plus fees not to exceed $2,000; the secretary of state, $2,000; and the comptroller of public accounts, the treasurer,qqv and the commissioner of the General Land Office,qv $2,500 each. In 1936 the constitution was amended to provide the following annual salaries: governor, $12,000; attorney general, $10,000; and other executive officials, $6,000 each. Constitutional stipulation of salaries received by executive officers was removed by a series of constitutional amendments in 1954, and the legislature was empowered to determine them. In 1967 state executive salaries were as follows: governor, $25,000; attorney general, $22,500; commissioner of the General Land Office, $21,000; secretary of state, $19,000; and the comptroller of public accounts and the state treasurer, $20,000 each. Senate Bill No. 7 of the 62nd Legislature in 1971 set the following salaries: governor, $58,500; attorney general, $31,000; commissioner of the General Land Office, $31,000; secretary of state, $28,000; and the comptroller of public accounts and the state treasurer, $31,000 each. Generally, compensation has been increased every two years; in 1975 the legislature determined that the following annual salaries would be paid during the fiscal year 1977: governor, $66,800; attorney general, commissioner of the General Land Office, comptroller of public accounts, and state treasurer, all $42,300; and secretary of state, $39,-

900. The lieutenant governor,qv although a part of the executive branch, does not have any executive functions; his annual salary is the same as that paid to members of the legislature, which was $7,200 in 1975. [By a 1972 constitutional amendment, effective in 1975, all of the officers mentioned here (plus the commissioner of agriculture) served for four-year terms. Ed.]

Dick Smith

*State Fair of Texas. After World War II the State Fair of Texas continued to grow in size and scope, with the building of a new livestock coliseum facilitating the holding of horse shows and rodeos. The fair is held in October of each year; new attendance records were set in 1963, 1966, 1967, 1968, and again in 1971, when an all-time record of 3,134,646 persons passed through the gates during the sixteen days of the fair. This growth allowed the exposition to keep a solid hold on the title of the biggest annual fair in the United States.

In 1966 Robert B. Cullum, president of the association, announced plans to enlarge and renovate the grounds and to remodel and redecorate State Fair Music Hall. In 1971 the fair incorporated seven museums, six exhibition halls, a large modern theater, the Cotton Bowl,qv and a complete agricultural complex on its 200-acre park. Visitors could view art exhibits, musical extravaganzas, sports spectaculars, and international displays.

Wayne Gard

*State Flower. *See* Bluebonnets.

**State Gazette.*

*State Girls Training School. *See* Gainesville State School for Girls.

State Hog Farm. The State Dairy and Hog Farm qv changed its name to the State Hog Farm in 1951. In 1964 the farm produced hogs for the Texas Blind, Deaf, and Orphan School, the Confederate Home for Men, the Mexia State School, the Travis State School, the Austin State School, and the Abilene State School;qqv the farm netted a profit. The grazing and selling of beef steers was expanded by the farm, and Buttercup Recreation Park was maintained and operated on a regular basis for patients and students at Austin eleemosynary institutions. In 1964 the central hog farm supervisor was Leonard L. Wynn. In the late 1960's the farm was converted to a recreational and educational facility for the mentally ill and mentally retarded. *See also* Texas Leander Rehabilitation Center.

BIBLIOGRAPHY: *Annual Report for the State Hog Farm* (1964).

State Judicial Qualifications Commission. The State Judicial Qualifications Commission, created in 1965, was composed of nine members: two justices of courts of civil appeals and two district judges selected by the Supreme Court (*see* Judicial System), two members of the State Bar of Texas qv chosen by the board of directors of the State Bar, and three members appointed by the governor. The concurrence of the Texas Senate was required for all appointments. The duty of the commission was to consider complaints and information regarding the disability or misconduct of judges and to make recommendations to the Supreme Court concerning the removal of judges. In 1970 the commission's jurisdiction was extended to cover all judicial officers of the state, from Supreme Court justices to justices of the peace and municipal judges. In that year both the commission and the Supreme Court were granted the power to censure judicial officers following a formal hearing.

BIBLIOGRAPHY: University of Texas at Austin, *Guide To Texas State Agencies* (1972).

*State Juvenile Training School for Boys. *See* Gatesville State School for Boys.

State Law Library. Created in 1971 to replace the libraries of the Supreme Court, the Court of Criminal Appeals, and the attorney general's office, the State Law Library maintains legal reference materials for use by members and staff of these three offices, by other commissions and agencies, and by citizens of the state. The library may transfer any of its books, papers, and publications to the library of the University of Texas at Austin law school. The library is controlled and administered by the State Law Library Board, which is composed of the chief justice of the Supreme Court, the presiding judge of the Court of Criminal Appeals, and the attorney general, or their personal representatives.

BIBLIOGRAPHY: University of Texas at Austin, *Guide To Texas State Agencies* (1972).

*State Library. *See* Texas State Library.

*State Library and Historical Commission. *See* Texas State Library and Historical Commission.

*State Line Creek.

State-Local Relations, Division of. *See* Community Affairs, Department of.

*State Motto. *See* Motto, State.

*State Orphans' Home. *See* also Corsicana State Home.

*State Police.

State Sales Tax. *See* Sales Tax, State.

State Securities Board. The State Securities Board, composed of three gubernatorial appointees serving overlapping six-year terms, was created by the Securities Act of 1957. The board appoints a securities commissioner as its administrative officer. The main function of the agency is regulating the sale of stocks, bonds, and other securities sold in Texas, as well as the persons and corporations which sell such securities. Prior to the creation of the State Securities Board, the secretary of state administered Texas laws concerning the sale of securities. In 1970 the board was authorized fifty positions of employment.

BIBLIOGRAPHY: Stuart A. MacCorkle and Dick Smith, *Texas Government* (1964); Clifton McCleskey, *Government and Politics of Texas* (1963); Wilbourn Eugene Benton, *Texas, Its Government and Politics* (1961); University of Texas at Austin, *Guide To Texas State Agencies* (1972);

William H. Tinsley, "Texas Securities Act," *Texas Municipalities* (July, August, 1954).

Dick Smith

State Soil and Water Conservation Board. Formerly called the Soil Conservation Board,qv the name was changed to the State Soil and Water Conservation Board in 1965.

*State Song. *See* "Texas, Our Texas."

*State Teachers Colleges. Names of those colleges listed in Volume II as State Teachers Colleges have been changed as follows: East Texas State Teachers College, now East Texas State University; North Texas State College, now North Texas State University; Sam Houston State Teachers College, now Sam Houston State University; Southwest Texas State Teachers College, now Southwest Texas State University; Stephen F. Austin State College, now Stephen F. Austin State University; Sul Ross State Teachers College, now Sul Ross State University; and West Texas State Teachers College, now West Texas State University.qqv

**State Topics and Texas Monthly Review.*

*State Tree. *See* Tree, State.

*State Tuberculosis Sanatorium. *See* McKnight State Sanatorium.

*Station Creek.

*Stayton, John William.

*Stayton, Texas.

*Steal Easy Mountain.

*Steamboat Mountain.

*Steamship Routes. *See* Ocean Shipping and River Navigation.

*Stedman, Nathan Alexander.

*Stedman, William.

*Steedman, Texas.

*Steel, Texas.

*Steel Production. *See* Iron and Steel Industry.

*Steele, Alphonso.

*Steele, William. William Steele served as adjutant general of Texas from January 20, 1874, to January, 1879 (not to 1885, as stated in Volume II); John B. Jones qv followed Steele as adjutant general when Jones was confirmed by the Senate on January 25, 1879.
BIBLIOGRAPHY: Clarence P. Denman, "The Office of Adjutant General in Texas, 1835–1881," *Southwestern Historical Quarterly*, XXVIII (1924–1925); Files of the Adjutant General's Department, Camp Mabry, Texas.

Sylvan Dunn

*Steele Creek.

*Steele's Store, Texas.

*Steepcreek, Texas.

*Steger, Harry Peyton.

*Steiner, Josephus Murray.

*Steiner, Ralph.

*Steiner, Texas.

Steinfeldt, John Mathias. John Mathias Steinfeldt was born in the village of Ankum, near Hanover, Germany, on August 18, 1864, the son of Sophia (Zimmerman) and Henry Steinfeldt. When he was ten, his family came to America and settled in Cincinnati, where he attended public schools. He received an art scholarship to the Cincinnati School of Design, studied piano and harmony in the College of Music in Cincinnati, and attended Dayton College in Dayton, Ohio. He studied music in New York and Paris.

He came to San Antonio in 1887, became assistant organist at San Fernando Cathedral,qv and was organist at the Jewish Temple Beth-El and the First Baptist Church. A few years after his arrival, he became organist at St. Mary's Catholic Church, a position he held for over fifty years. In 1920 he founded the San Antonio College of Music, where he taught piano and pipe organ, in addition to holding classes in Eagle Pass and Laredo. He appeared several times as soloist with the San Antonio Symphony and the Chicago Symphony. Among his compositions were a number of concert pieces, "The Song of the River" (a chorus for women's voices), and "Missa Maria Immaculata," or "Mass in G," the dedication mass for the new St. Mary's Church. He was awarded a prize by the State Federation of Music Clubs for his San Antonio-inspired composition, "La Concepción."

He was married to Vivia May Ripley on July 10, 1893, in San Antonio. They were the parents of four children. Steinfeldt died on February 28, 1946; a requiem mass was held at St. Mary's Church, where he had so long been organist, and he was buried in St. Mary's Cemetery in San Antonio.
BIBLIOGRAPHY: Ellis A. Davis and Edwin H. Grobe, *New Encyclopedia of Texas*, I (1929?); San Antonio *Evening News*, March 1, 1946; St. Mary's Church in San Antonio, *The Bulletin* (September, 1924).

Steinmark, Freddie Joe. Freddie Joe Steinmark, University of Texas football player who became a national symbol of courage and determination, was born on January 27, 1949, in Denver, Colorado, the son of Fred Gene and Gloria (Marchetti) Steinmark. His father had been a professional baseball player and encouraged him in all sports, so that Freddie had an early introduction to football, playing during his elementary and junior high school years on the Rough Riders team of the citywide Young America League in Denver. At Wheat Ridge High School there he lettered in football, baseball, and basketball; throughout his entire sports career, Steinmark's teams rarely lost a game. He ranked twenty-fifth scholastically in his high school graduating class of 530, and in his senior year he received the Golden Helmet Award from the Denver *Post* as the outstanding scholar-athlete in Colorado; he also received the Colorado Hall of Fame award as the state's outstanding high school athlete.

In 1967 Freddie Steinmark received a football scholarship to the University of Texas at Austin.

Despite his relatively small size, 5 feet, 10 inches, about 160 pounds, Steinmark was a valuable addition to the Texas Longhorn team, playing defensive back on the freshman team, also starting in that position on the varsity during his sophomore and junior years. As a sophomore he was the team's leading punt returner and was named an All-Southwest Conference qv athlete-scholar while majoring in chemical engineering. On December 6, 1969, when Texas and Arkansas were rated first and second teams in the nation, respectively, he played in the game at Fayetteville, called the "Big Shoot-out," which gave the national championship to the Texas Longhorns. The football game was important in sports annals because it determined the national football champion on the one-hundredth anniversary of college football and was witnessed by one of the largest television audiences in history. Richard M. Nixon, president of the United States, was in attendance and congratulated the team personally. Six days later Steinmark was hospitalized at the University of Texas M. D. Anderson Hospital and Tumor Institute at Houston;qv what was thought to have been a deep bruise on his left leg turned out to be a tumor, a bone sarcoma, originating from the bone itself, and not the result of a football injury. His left leg was amputated. When just twenty days later he attended on crutches the Texas-Notre Dame football game in the Cotton Bowl,qv he gained national recognition for his determination and stamina and became an inspiration to thousands of cancer victims. The game, won by Texas, was dedicated to Steinmark by his teammates. The university's board of regents took on responsibility for Steinmark's medical and educational expenses, and friends and fans were invited to contribute. The response to Steinmark's illness was nationwide. He continued his education almost immediately in the spring semester of 1970, and he helped coach the freshman defensive backs in that year. He changed his major to liberal arts and planned to enter law school.

On April 13, 1970, he and his coach, Darrell Royal, met with President Nixon at the White House to mark the annual education and fund-raising drive of the American Cancer Society. Steinmark received a special citation from the president for "steadfast faith in God, his country and himself." He traveled and spoke at various meetings and fund-raising dinners, but returned to Houston every few months for additional checkups. Despite extensive therapy the disease continued to progress. With the help of Blackie Sherrod, sports editor of the Dallas Times Herald,qv he wrote his autobiography, I Play to Win (1971), a lively account of his years as a starting defensive football safety, and a personal story of his faith in God, which became his greatest ally against despair. He was a Roman Catholic. He entered the M.D. Anderson Hospital for the last time on April 20, 1971, supposedly for influenza. He died on June 6, 1971, in Houston, and was buried in Mount Olivet Cemetery in Denver, Colorado, with his coach and many of his teammates in attendance. A personal message by special envoy was sent to the family by President Nixon. A new forty-seven-foot-high scoreboard at the remodeled Memorial Stadium on the University of Texas at Austin campus was dedicated to Freddie Steinmark on September 23, 1972.

BIBLIOGRAPHY: Freddie Steinmark, I Play to Win (1971); Austin American, June 7, 1971; Daily Texan, June 8, 11, 1971, September 23, 1972; Biographical File, Barker Texas History Center, University of Texas at Austin.

Eldon S. Branda

Stell, John D. John D. Stell, born in Georgia in 1804, served in that state's militia, attaining the rank of colonel. He sat as a lower court judge, then was elected to the Georgia Senate, becoming its president in 1853–1854. Stell also represented Georgia in the June and November, 1850, sessions of the Nashville Convention.

In 1856 the Stell family settled in Leon County, Texas. On January 8, 1861, the voters of the thirty-ninth representative district, composed of Leon and Madison counties, elected Stell to represent them at the Secession Convention qv (see also Secession in Texas). When the delegates to the convention convened on January 28, 1861, they elected Stell as president pro tempore; later he was unanimously elected vice-president of the convention. Stell was appointed by convention president Oran Milo Roberts qv to a committee (which included Pryor Lea and John Henry Brown qqv) to draw up the convention's Address to the People of Texas, presenting its case for secession. Thereafter, Stell served at the Confederate ordnance works in Tyler, Texas.

From 1856 to 1860, Stell engaged in successful business enterprises, including planting and Trinity River transportation. He was married twice and had a total of ten children. He died in 1862.

BIBLIOGRAPHY: Memorial and Biographical History of Navarro, Henderson, Anderson, Limestone, Freestone and Leon Counties, Texas (1893); Willard E. Wight (ed.), "A Letter from the Texas Secession Convention," Southwestern Historical Quarterly, LX (1956–1957); Ernest William Winkler (ed.), Journal of the Secession Convention of Texas, 1861 (1912).

*Stella, Texas. (Fayette County.)

*Stella, Texas. (Harris County.)

Stem, Jesse. Jesse Stem, Texas Indian agent from 1851 to 1853, was born about 1820, the son of Jacob and Sarah Stem, in Green Springs, Sandusky County, Ohio. He was admitted to the Bar in Columbus in 1842 and was later married to Matilda Elizabeth Pittinger; they had four daughters. Because of poor health and the consequent need for a change in climate, he sought an appointment as a commissioner or Indian agent in California during the gold rush; unsuccessful, he accepted a post as Indian agent in Texas. When he left his home in Tiffin, Ohio, he was senior partner in the law firm of Jesse and Leander Stem.

He arrived in San Antonio in February, 1851, and met Judge John H. Rollins, the only other Indian agent in Texas following the expiration of

Robert S. Neighbor's qv federal appointment. Rollins, like Stem, was an asthmatic, and he was so ill that many of his duties were taken over by the younger man, Stem, who welcomed to councils all Indians, including the hostile Comanches. These gatherings served to allay some of the sharp criticism Texans had directed at the United States government for sending ill, untrained, and uncooperative agents to Texas. Rollins and Stem were soon joined by John A. Rogers, who took the El Paso sector, and the Indian areas of Texas were divided among the three men.

Stem settled at the Grayson Ranch, four miles from San Antonio. He began writing letters to his family and to his friend Rutherford B. Hayes, later president of the United States, describing his activities. His health improved and he became interested in acquiring cheap Texas land for investment. In August, 1851, he returned to Ohio for his family, during which time Rollins died. Upon his return to Texas, Stem first settled his family in Seguin. During February and March, 1852, he met with all the Texas Indian tribes except those on the Rio Grande and the northern Comanches; he was successful in gaining the confidence of the eastern tribes as well as that of the southern Comanches. He lived in a series of frontier stations—Fort Croghan (near present Burnet), Fort Graham (while Major Henry Hopkins Sibley qv was stationed there), and Fort Belknap.qqv It was on the Clear Fork of the Brazos that he bought land, built a house, and started a farm.

When Major George T. Howard qv became superintendent of Indian agents, Stem resigned and returned to Ohio in 1853 with his family. By November he was back in Texas, accompanied by a friend, William Leppelman. In February, 1854, after a wagon loaded with supplies for his farm broke down near Fort Belknap, he and Leppelman were slain by two renegade Kickapoo Indians, who were later caught and executed by their own tribe. Stem's body was later removed to Sandusky, Ohio; his ranch was sold to Judge John A. Matthews qv and his wife, Sallie Reynolds Matthews,qv and it became part of the large Matthews ranch in Shackelford County.

BIBLIOGRAPHY: Mildred P. Mayhall, *Indian Wars of Texas* (1965); W. B. Parker, *Notes Taken during the Expedition Commanded by Capt. R. B. Marcy, U.S.A., through Unexplored Texas . . .* (1856); Rupert N. Richardson, *The Frontier of Northwest Texas, 1846–1876* (1963); Watt P. Marchman and Robert C. Cotner, "Indian Agent Jesse Stem: A Manuscript Revelation," *West Texas Historical Association Year Book*, XXXIX (1963); Jesse Stem Papers (MS., Rutherford B. Hayes Memorial Library, Fremont, Ohio); United States Office of Indian Affairs, Letter Books, 1851, 1852, 1853 (MS., Archives, University of Texas at Austin).

Mildred P. Mayhall

*Stephen. *See* Estevanico.

*Stephen Creek.

*Stephen Creek, Texas.

*Stephen F. Austin State College. *See also* Stephen F. Austin State University.

Stephen F. Austin State University. Stephen F. Austin State University (formerly Stephen F. Austin State College qv), Nacogdoches, was one of the fastest growing state-supported colleges in Texas during the 1960's. Funds for new classroom buildings were obtained through statewide referendums on constitutional amendments, and the Housing and Home Finance Agency of the federal government made dormitory financing available. The value of the physical plant was in excess of $18,000,000 in 1965. Between 1961 and 1966, eight dormitories and twelve apartment buildings were constructed. During 1966, $4,250,000 twin-tower dormitories, a $4,000,000 science building, and several classroom buildings reached the planning stage. By 1972 the university's physical plant was greatly enlarged. The library contained 331,480 volumes in 1969. During the 1974–1975 term, the faculty consisted of approximately 400 members, and the student enrollment was 10,881; Ralph W. Steen served as president.

*Stephens, Isaac W.

*Stephens, J. W.

*Stephens, John Hall.

*Stephens, John Leonard.

*Stephens County. Stephens County, with a petroleum and ranching economy, draws 90 percent of its agricultural income from livestock and poultry. Over 197 million barrels of oil were produced in the county between 1916 and 1973. Business concerns with a direct influence on the economy include those connected with oil, cattle, clothing, metal, machine shops, refining, and recreation. Significant changes in Stephens County include the completion of Hubbard Creek Reservoir and Lake Daniel qqv and the establishment of several new industries. The county supports a hospital. The 1960 population was 8,885; in 1970 it was 8,414, according to the United States census.

*Stephens Creek.

*Stephensboro, Texas.

*Stephenson, Henry.

*Stephenson's Ferry.

*Stephenville, Texas. Stephenville, seat of Erath County, is a processing center for the agricultural produce of the county. In 1953 Stephenville formed an industrial foundation, and by 1964 the city had twenty-four industries, including a creamery, hatcheries, feed mills, meat packers, a poultry dresser, a garment factory, and nurseries. By the early 1970's the city had well over two hundred businesses. Tarleton State College, in Stephenville, was elevated in 1958 to the status of a four-year senior college (now Tarleton State University, and a part of the Texas A&M University System qv). The town supported a hospital. In 1960 the population was 7,359; in 1970 it was 9,277, an increase of 26.1 percent during the ten-year period, according to the United States census.

*Stephenville North and South Texas Railway Company.

*Steppe Creek.

*Sterett, William Greene.

*Sterley, Texas.

*Sterling, Ross S.

*Sterling, W. S.

Sterling, William Warren. William Warren Sterling, son of Edward A. and Mary (Chamberlain) Sterling, was born near Belton on April 27, 1891, and spent his early years on his family's ranch before they moved to Beaumont in 1901. He entered Texas A&M at seventeen, but two years later he was working on ranches near Falfurrias and in Hidalgo County. During the "Bandit War," 1915-1916, when political unrest in Mexico spilled over the Rio Grande border, he was a posseman and scout for the 3rd United States Cavalry in Hidalgo and Cameron counties. During World War I he was commissioned a second lieutenant in the 9th Texas Infantry. Afterward he was in Mirando City as deputy sheriff and justice of the peace during the oil boom in Webb County oil fields. In 1927 Governor Dan Moody qv appointed him captain, Company D of the Texas Rangers,qv and he was sent immediately to the oil-boom town of Borger. In 1928 his Ranger headquarters were moved to Falfurrias. About this time Gutzon Borglum,qv the sculptor, used Sterling as the model (as a young man Sterling was six feet, three inches tall, and husky) for his planned Texas Ranger statue. In 1929 Sterling was in Pettus when an oil boom started there, and he helped stop the lawlessness. During the administration of Governor Ross S. Sterling qv he served as adjutant general (commander of the Texas Rangers and the Texas National Guard); in this capacity he closed the Red River bridge at Denison during the much publicized Red River bridge controversy qv between Oklahoma and Texas in 1931 Sterling resigned from the Rangers at the close of his service as adjutant general in 1933. As a colonel during World War II, he helped set up selective service for the 8th Service Command. Sterling managed the Driscoll ranches in South Texas and later appraised ranches in Texas. His book, *Trails and Trials of a Texas Ranger*, was published in 1959. He was married to Zora Lou Eckhardt, and they had two daughters. Sterling died on April 26, 1960, and was buried in Seaside Memorial Park in Corpus Christi.

BIBLIOGRAPHY: Austin *American*, August 28, 1969; Brooks County *Texan*, March 22, 1929; Corpus Christi *Caller and Daily Herald*, February 15, 16, 27, 28, 1915; Falfurrias *Facts*, April 28, 1960; *Life*, November 21, 1958.

Sterling, Texas. Sterling, Robertson County, was located two miles west of the present town of Calvert in the 1830's. Sterling C. Robertson,qv colonizer for the Nashville Company (*see* Robertson Colony) lived three miles south of the community which bore his name. Apparently the post office was local without official status. A saloon, a blacksmith shop, a livery stable, and two churches, Baptist and Presbyterian, were located there. The Presbyterian church was moved to Calvert, where it still stands. Only the cemetery of Sterling remains.

Grover C. Ramsey

*Sterling City, Texas. Sterling City, seat of Sterling County, was incorporated in 1955 with a mayor-councilman form of government. It serves as the market for the county, dealing largely with wool, lamb, mohair, and cattle produce. In the 1960's the town had six churches, a county-supported hospital, a bank, a library, and a newspaper. The 1960 population was 854; in 1970 it was 780, according to the United States census.

*Sterling County. Sterling County, an oil-producing and ranching area, derived 90 percent of its agricultural income in the early 1970's from sheep, cattle, and goats. Crops of feedstuffs were grown principally in the Concho River Valley, while an increasing amount of land was being put into pasture. The 1960 population was 1,177; in 1970 it was 1,056, according to the United States census.

*Sterling Creek.

*Sterne, Adolphus. Adolphus Sterne and his wife Eva Catherine Rosine (Ruff) Sterne were the parents of seven children. It was in the Sterne home that Sam Houston lived when he took up residence in Nacogdoches in 1833. Possibly because of the Mexican laws denying ownership of land to non-Catholics, Sam Houston was baptized into the Roman Catholic church in Nacogdoches in late 1833 or early 1834; Eva Sterne, a devout Catholic, stood as godmother to Houston (although she was considerably younger than he). Adolphus Sterne's father was a Jew and his mother was a Christian; in Texas Sterne was identified with the Roman Catholic church.

BIBLIOGRAPHY: Marquis James, *The Raven* (1929); W. P. Zuber, "Captain Adolphus Sterne," *Quarterly of the Texas State Historical Association*, II (1898-1899).

*Sterrett, Texas.

*Stetson Hats.

Stevens, James G. James G. Stevens was born in Alabama about 1823. During the period of the Republic of Texas, he moved to Hunt County, Texas, where he was a trader. In 1841 he served under Edward H. Tarrant qv at the Indian fight on Village Creek in Tarrant County. In 1862 he helped recruit the 22nd Texas Cavalry Regiment and was elected major. He became a colonel when the regiment was reorganized later that year. In the fall and winter of 1862 he led the unit at Newtonia, Missouri, and Prairie Grove, Arkansas, as part of what was to become known as Polignac's Brigade.qv In 1863, after the regiment had been dismounted to serve as infantry, Stevens resigned. He settled in Dallas, serving as a surveyor and later as a school superintendent in Dallas County. He died on May 24, 1889.

BIBLIOGRAPHY: Alwyn Barr, *Polignac's Texas Brigade*

(1964); Philip Lindsley, *A History of Greater Dallas and Vicinity* (1909).

Alwyn Barr

*Stevens, Thomas.

*Stevens, Texas.

Stevenson, Coke Robert. Coke Robert Stevenson, named for Governor Richard Coke qv by his parents, Robert Milton and Virginia (Hurley) Stevenson, was born March 20, 1888, in a log cabin in Mason County. His father was a school teacher and surveyor in various hill country areas, including Sutton County, where Coke Stevenson finished his formal schooling (a total of seven years of three-month school terms). His father opened a general mercantile store in Junction, Kimble County, and as a teen-ager Coke Stevenson went into the freight business, driving a wagon between Junction and Brady. He studied history and bookkeeping by the light of campfires, sold the freight line, and went to work as a janitor for the Junction State Bank; he was soon doing the bank's bookkeeping, and by the time he was twenty he was made cashier. He studied law at night, passed the State Bar qv in 1913, left the bank to practice law, and organized and became president of the First National Bank in Junction. As a young man he was involved in many small businesses in Kimble County, including the Junction Warehouse Company, a motion picture house, a hardware store, an automobile agency, a weekly newspaper, a drug business, and the establishment of the Las Lomas Hotel in Junction.

In Kimble County he served as county attorney (1914–1918) and as county judge (1919–1921). He was elected to the Texas House of Representatives in 1928, and he was a member of that body from 1929 to 1939, serving as Speaker of the House from 1933 to 1937, the first person ever to hold that office for two successive terms. Elected lieutenant governor of Texas, he served from 1939 to August 4, 1941, when he became governor of Texas, succeeding W. Lee O'Daniel,qv who had resigned to become United States senator. A tall, quiet, pipe-smoking, Western-type man, Stevenson was elected governor on his own in 1942; a popular wartime governor, he was reelected in 1944 by an overwhelming vote, and his tenure from August, 1941, to January, 1947, was the longest consecutive service of any Texas governor up to that time. Stevenson's record in the legislature was one which showed a concern for soil conservation laws, expansion of and a permanent financing policy for the state highway system, an enlarged building program for the University of Texas, and teacher salary increases. He was a strong believer in fiscal responsibility, and as governor he emphasized conservative financial policies; his administration began with a state treasury deficit and ended with a surplus. Not an extremist on states' rights, he was nevertheless against the centralization of governmental power, and he opposed some of the domestic policies of the Roosevelt administration.

Coke Stevenson was married to Fay Wright on December 24, 1912; they had one son. During Stevenson's first year as governor, in January, 1942, his wife died. He remained a widower until January 16, 1954, when he was married to a widow, Marguerite (King) Heap; they had one daughter.

When he left the governor's mansion qv in 1947, Stevenson returned to his 15,000-acre ranch at Telegraph, near Junction. His last political race, for United States senator in 1948, was the only one he ever lost, and it perhaps gave him more national attention than he had ever received before. That election, which he lost to Lyndon Baines Johnson qv by eighty-seven votes, may have changed the course of history, for Johnson went on to become president of the United States. The contest between Stevenson and Johnson was the closest senatorial race in the nation's history; after Stevenson appeared to be the winner, an amended return came in from Precinct 13 in Jim Wells County, a George Berham Parr qv stronghold, giving Johnson 201 votes and Stevenson only 2 votes; this decided the election in Johnson's favor, with a total state vote of 494,191 for Johnson and 494,104 for Stevenson. Stevenson contested the election, claiming there had been fraudulent votes cast in Duval County and in Precinct 13 in Jim Wells County. The dispute was carried all the way to the U.S. Supreme Court, but after the voting lists from Box 13 were lost or stolen, and the Duval County returns were burned prior to the date set by law, the federal court ruled that it did not have jurisdiction in the case. Stevenson's plea to the United States Senate was refused, and he took the defeat with bitterness. He remained disenchanted with the Democratic party qv during his long retirement from active politics. For president he supported Republicans Dwight D. Eisenhower qv in 1952 and Richard M. Nixon in 1960.

Coke Robert Stevenson died at the age of eighty-seven on June 28, 1975, in Shannon Memorial Hospital in San Angelo. He was buried on his ranch in Kimble County. *See also* Governor, Office of; Lieutenant Governor, Office of.

BIBLIOGRAPHY: Booth Mooney, *Mister Texas: The Story of Coke Stevenson* (1947); Charles E. Simons, "Log Cabin Statesman," *Texas Parade*, VI (March, 1942); Biographical File, Barker Texas History Center, University of Texas at Austin.

Eldon S. Branda

*Stevenson, James P.

*Stevenson, Robert.

*Stevenson, William. William Stevenson was the first Protestant preacher to preach in Texas when, according to his autobiography, he preached at the settlement at Pecan Point qv on the southwest side of the Red River (in present northeastern Red River County) in the fall and winter of 1815.

BIBLIOGRAPHY: Walter E. Vernon, *William Stevenson: Riding Preacher* (1964).

Walter N. Vernon

*Stevenson, Texas.

*Stewards Mill, Texas.

*Stewart, Charles.

*Stewart, Charles Bellinger.

*Stewart, Joseph H.

*Stewart, Maco.

*Stewart, Texas. (Cottle County.)

*Stewart, Texas. (Matagorda County.)

*Stewart, Texas. (Rusk County.)

*Stewart Creek.

*Stewart Heights, Texas.

*Stewarton, Texas.

*Stewartsville, Texas.

*Stieren, Texas.

*Sriff, Edward.

*Stiff Creek.

*Stiles, Texas.

Stillhouse Hollow Reservoir. Stillhouse Hollow
Dam (formerly Lampasas Dam) and Stillhouse
Hollow Reservoir are in the Brazos River Basin in
Bell County, five miles southwest of Belton on the
Lampasas River. The project is owned by the United
States government and is operated by the United
States Army Corps of Engineers, Fort Worth District. The Brazos River Authority qv purchased the
conservation storage space. The reservoir has a capacity of 235,700 acre-feet and a surface area of
6,430 acres at the conservation storage space elevation. The capacity at the top of the flood control
storage space at the spillway crest elevation of 666
feet above mean sea level is 630,400 acre-feet and
the surface area is 11,830 acres. The drainage area
above the dam is 1,318 square miles.

BIBLIOGRAPHY: Texas Water Commission, *Bulletin 6408*
(1964).

Seth D. Breeding

*Stillman, Charles.

*Stills Creek.

*Stillwell Creek.

*Stillwell Mountain.

*Stilson, Texas.

*Stilwell, Arthur Edward.

*Stink Creek.

*Stinnett, Claiborne.

*Stinnett, Texas. Stinnett, seat of Hutchinson
County, was incorporated in 1927. It is the commercial center for the surrounding grain-growing, oil,
and ranching area. In the 1960's the town reported
eight churches, one school, a bank, a library, and a
newspaper. In 1960 the population was 2,695, more
than double the 1950 population of 1,170; however, in 1970 the figure was 2,014, a 25.3 percent
decline in population during the previous decade,
according to the United States census. The town
had forty-five businesses in 1970.

Stirpes. *Stirpes*, the Texas State Genealogical
Society Quarterly, takes its name from a legal term
meaning kindred or family. The name was chosen
for the family history magazine by its first editor,
Mildred Dulaney, a professional librarian of Waco
and Fort Worth, who edited Volume I in 1961.
After that time the quarterly was edited by the
founder and president of the society, Edna Perry

Deckler, of Fort Worth. In the mid-1970's Mary
Barnett Curtis was editor. *Stirpes*, published each
March, June, September, and December, presents
data on genealogical subjects. Although emphasis
is placed on records of the Republic of Texas era
(1836–1846), published material is not limited
to the records of Texas.

BIBLIOGRAPHY: *Stirpes*, I (1961).

Edna Perry Deckler

*Stith, Texas.

Stock Fraud Scandal. *See* Sharpstown Stock
Fraud Scandal.

*Stock Yards, Texas.

*Stockard, Texas.

*Stockdale, Fletcher S. [The following entirely
replaces the Volume II article on Fletcher S. Stockdale because of the many serious biographical errors
in the earlier work. Ed.] Fletcher Summerfield
Stockdale was born in Russellville, Kentucky, in
either 1823 or 1825, one of eight children of
Thomas Ward and Laurinda (Hise) Stockdale.
After studying law and being admitted to the Kentucky Bar, Stockdale came to Texas in 1846, where
he practiced law in Anderson, Grimes County, before moving to Calhoun County.

On September 1, 1856, along with his interests
in business, farming, and law, Stockdale became
one of four men who secured a charter for the
Powderhorn, Victoria and Gonzales Railroad Company. The company plans were for construction
of a line from Powderhorn, on Matagorda Bay
(*see* Indianola, Texas), to Austin. Although the
company existed for two years, nothing substantial
came of the project.

In 1857 he was married to Mrs. Elizabeth Pryor
Bankhead Lytle; that same year he began serving
as representative of the Twenty-sixth District in
the Texas Senate. He served until 1861. As a
delegate to the state Democratic conventions in
1859 and 1860, he served on the committee on
resolutions and platforms. He was a delegate to
the national Democratic convention in Charleston
in 1860, where he was a member of the committee
on resolutions at the seceders' meeting. (*See* Secession in Texas.)

Stockdale was a leading member of the Secession Convention qv which met in Austin in 1861.
He served on the committee which drew up the
ordinance of secession and was one of the signers
of the document. From 1862 to 1863 he acted as
special aide to Governor Francis R. Lubbock.qv
Stockdale was elected lieutenant governor of Texas
on November 5, 1863, and served until June, 1865,
when he was governor for the brief period after
Governor Pendleton Murrah's qv flight to Mexico
in June, 1865, with the fall of the Confederacy.
President Andrew Johnson appointed Andrew J.
Hamilton qv provisional governor in July, and
Stockdale was one of the committee which met
Hamilton on the outskirts of Austin, escorted him
into town, and handed him the keys to the Texas
archives and capitol in August, 1865. After his

removal from office Stockdale returned to Calhoun County.

In the late 1860's in Indianola, Stockdale promoted the development of a refrigerator car for shipping beef. As president of the Indianola Railroad, he reported twelve and one-half miles of new track completed, two locomotives and other rolling stock, and depot buildings, shops, and grounds at Indianola. He moved to Cuero sometime after the town was established in 1873 as the terminus for the Gulf, Western Texas, and Pacific Railroad. He practiced law and promoted the Cuero Land and Immigration Company.

In 1868 Stockdale was a member of the Texas Senate. In the Constitutional Convention of 1875 qv he served on the committees of judiciary and land grants and participated in debates on the establishment of a free public school system in Texas. He was a delegate to the national Democratic conventions in 1872, 1876, and 1880; he was also a delegate to the state Democratic convention in 1873 and was chosen as one of the convention's eight vice-presidents. In the state Democratic convention of 1876 Stockdale was chairman of the committee on resolutions and platforms and a member of that committee again in the 1882 and 1888 conventions.

Stockdale's first wife had died on April 17, 1865. In Washington, D.C., on July 11, 1877, Stockdale married Elizabeth Schleicher, the seventeen-year-old daughter of his friend and Texas political colleague, Gustav Schleicher qv and Elizabeth Tinsley Howard Schleicher. The couple had three children. Stockdale died in Cuero on February 4, 1890, and was buried in Russellville, Kentucky. His second wife survived him. In 1946 the Texas legislature ordered a portrait of Stockdale painted and hung in the gallery of Texas governors in the capitol.qv In 1965 a historical marker was erected in his memory in Stockdale, Texas, the town which was named for him.

BIBLIOGRAPHY: J. William Davis, There Shall Also Be A Lieutenant Governor (1967); James T. Deshields, They Sat in High Places: The Presidents and Governors of Texas (1940); S. S. McKay, Debates in the Texas Constitutional Convention of 1875 (1930); S. G. Reed, A History of the Texas Railroads (1941); E. W. Winkler (ed.), Journal of the Secession Convention of Texas (1912), Platforms of Political Parties in Texas (1916); D. W. Ogletree, "Establishing the Texas Court of Appeals, 1875–1877," Southwestern Historical Quarterly, XLVII (1943–1944); Anna Irene Sanbo, "The First Session of the Secession Convention in Texas," ibid., XVIII (1914–1915); Deolece Parmelee, "Forgotten Prologue: Fletcher Summerfield Stockdale," Texana (Fall, 1964); Dallas Morning News, January 24, 1965.

*Stockdale, Texas. Stockdale, in eastern Wilson County, had a 1960 population of 1,111 and a 1970 population of 1,132, according to the United States census. The town had thirty businesses in 1970.

*Stockholm, Texas.

*Stockman, Texas.

*Stockton, Robert Field.

*Stockton, Texas.

*Stolley, George.

Stone, B. Warren. B. Warren Stone, Civil War officer, was born in Georgetown, Scott County, Kentucky, on November 5, 1817, the son of Barton W. and Celia (Bowen) Stone. He was educated at Georgetown College, Kentucky, and in 1836 moved with his father to Jacksonville, Illinois, where he remained until 1845. In 1844 he married Margaret W. Howard, daughter of Tilghman Ashurst Howard,qv the chargé d'affaires to the Republic of Texas in 1844 and friend of Sam Houston. Stone and his wife had two daughters; they lived in Memphis, Tennessee, from 1845 until November, 1851, when they moved to Dallas because of his wife's illness. Stone traveled with Sam Houston in the spring of 1851 from Baton Rouge, Louisiana, to Grand Echore, on the Red River. Following his wife's death in Dallas in 1855, he was married in February, 1857, to Sue E. Smith of Mount Sterling, Kentucky; they had at least five children. He returned to Dallas, lived outside the city in Dallas County, and continued the practice of law.

In 1861, Stone raised the 6th Texas Cavalry and commanded the regiment at Pea Ridge, Arkansas, in March, 1862. When the unit was sent east of the Mississippi River, Stone returned to Texas and raised the 2nd Texas Partisan Rangers, which served in Louisiana and Arkansas. Following the war Stone moved to Missouri, settled in Howard County, near Fayette, and devoted more time to his farm than to his law practice. He returned to Dallas in November, 1879, where he died on February 26, 1881.

BIBLIOGRAPHY: William S. Speer and John Henry Brown (eds.), Encyclopedia of the New West (1881); Marcus J. Wright (comp.) and Harold B. Simpson (ed.), Texas in the War 1861–1865 (1965); Berry B. Cobb, A History of Dallas Lawyers 1840–1890 (1934); U.S. Census, 1860, Dallas County (microfilm, Barker Texas History Center, University of Texas at Austin).

Stone, Robert Dillard. Robert Dillard Stone, a lawyer, came to Texas before the Civil War from Missouri. He enlisted in the 22nd Texas Cavalry in 1862 and was elected lieutenant of Company H. He later rose to lieutenant colonel in 1863 and commanded Polignac's Brigade qv in the Red River campaign qv from mid-April to mid-May, 1864. He was killed in action at Yellow Bayou, Louisiana, on May 18, 1864.

BIBLIOGRAPHY: Confederate Veteran, XVII (July, 1909); Alwyn Barr, Polignac's Texas Brigade (1964).

Alwyn Barr

*Stone, Samuel C.

*Stone Bayou.

*Stone City, Texas.

*Stone Creek.

*Stone Fort. See Old Stone Fort.

*Stone Point, Texas.

*Stoneburg, Texas.

*Stoneham, Texas.

*Stonewall, Texas.

*Stonewall County. Stonewall County received most of its farm income, which averaged $5 million annually in the early 1970's, from cattle, with cotton, small grains, peanuts, and other crops contributing the remainder. From 1938 to 1973 approximately 145 million barrels of oil were produced in the county. The 1960 population was 3,017; in 1970 it was 2,397, according to the United States census.

*Stonewall Institute.

*Stonewall Seminary.

*Stony, Texas.

*Stony Creek.

*Stop, Texas. *See* Blandlake, Texas.

*Storey, Leonidas Jefferson.

*Storrs, Augustus.

*Stout, Owen H.

*Stout, Texas.

*Stovall Creek.

*Stowell, Texas.

Stowers, George Arthur. George Arthur Stowers was born February 3, 1867, in Richmond County, Georgia, the son of Thomas J. Stowers. He attended public school in Atlanta, where the family had moved, worked as a messenger for Western Union Telegraph Company, was a newspaper boy for the Atlanta *Constitution*, and at thirteen was working in a mercantile store. Out of his savings from a two-dollar-a-week job in a candy company he was able at seventeen to start his own furniture store in Birmingham, Alabama, with $500 capital. By the time he was twenty-three he was operating ten stores in Alabama, Tennessee, and Texas, with San Antonio, Dallas, Waco, and Fort Worth the Texas outlets.

He moved his business from Birmingham to Dallas in 1889, but soon thereafter he located in San Antonio, where his business succeeded to the extent that it would eventually change the city's downtown skyline. His first furniture stores were on West Commerce Street; by 1910 he had built a ten-story building (a "skyscraper" at that time) at the corner of Main and Houston streets, one of the largest retail businesses in San Antonio. He also opened furniture stores in Houston and Laredo. Stowers' ranch holdings outside San Antonio were extensive.

George A. Stowers was married to Mary Agnes Perry of Philadelphia on June 5, 1896, and they had three children. He died in San Antonio on February 16, 1917, and was buried in Mission Burial Park.

BIBLIOGRAPHY: San Antonio *Express*, August 15, 1909, February 17, 1917.

S. W. *Pease*

*Straddlebug Mountain.

*Straight Creek.

*Strain, Texas.

Strake, George William. George William Strake, pioneer oilman and philanthropist, was born November 9, 1894, in St. Louis, Missouri, the son of William George and Anna (Casper) Strake.

He was educated in the public schools of St. Louis and received a B.S. degree from St. Louis University in 1917. Following World War I, in which he served in the U.S. Army Air Corps, Strake became involved in the oil industry in Mexico from 1919 to 1925; he then went to Havana, Cuba, combining an interest in mineral development and an automobile agency, losing almost all of the $250,000 he had made in Mexico. In 1927 Strake moved to the Houston area; as an independent oil man he leased land near Conroe in Montgomery County. His lease of 8,500 acres of South Texas Development Company land was the largest block of land leased up to that time for oil exploration. Although geologists claimed no oil was to be found there, and he could not get outside financial backing, Strake, after drilling many dry wells, struck oil in December, 1931. Other successful wells followed, opening up the 19,000-acre Conroe field, which proved to be the third largest oil field in the United States. Strake was probably the first oil millionaire in Houston after selling a part of his holdings to the Humble Oil and Refining Company qv for $5 million in the early 1930's. His discovery proved that the Cockfield sand was an oil producing formation and opened wildcatting in an area fifty miles wide and five hundred miles long, from Texas into Louisiana and Mississippi. Strake's oil operations eventually spread into Coastal and West Texas, New Mexico, Oklahoma, the southern states, and as far north as Michigan and Nebraska. His oil fortune was estimated to be between one hundred and two hundred million dollars. In addition to his oil interests, Strake was a director of the Mercantile-Commerce Bank and Trust Company in St. Louis, chairman of the board and president of the Aluminum Products Company in Houston, an original stockholder and founder of the Houston *Tribune*, and an officer in many other companies. In 1937 Strake represented the governor and the state of Texas at the United States presidential inauguration, and during World War II he served on the citizens' committee for the Houston-Harris County civilian defense and as Texas representative for Belgian war relief.

A devout Roman Catholic, Strake gave much of his oil fortune to numerous educational institutions, civic organizations, and charities. He was an active supporter of the Boy Scouts of America and was on its national executive board. Strake donated several thousand acres of land near Conroe to the Boy Scouts of America; named Camp Strake, it was the third largest boy scout camp in the United States. He was a founding benefactor of St. Joseph's Hospital Foundation in Houston when he donated $500,000 to that institution. He was also a generous contributor to St. Thomas University, of which he was a member of the board of trustees, and the Strake Jesuit College Preparatory School in Houston, which was named in his honor. He was on the board of the University of Notre Dame, served Our Lady of the Lake College in an advisory capacity, and was a trustee of the Institute of Chinese Culture in Washington. He was also on the board of governors of the American National Red Cross and the Southwest Research Institute,qv and he was a trustee of the National Foundation for Infantile Paralysis. Strake was cited as the most generous contributor to the Houston-Harris County United Fund charities. He was a member of numerous professional and civic organizations.

In recognition of his gifts and support, Strake received several honorary degrees and four papal honors between 1937 and 1950, including two of the Vatican's highest honors for a layman—the Order of St. Sylvester and the Order of Malta. The National Conference of Christians and Jews, of which he was a member of the national board, honored him in 1950 for outstanding contributions to business, civic, and religious affairs. On June 5, 1957, the citizens of Conroe honored Strake on the twenty-fifth anniversary of the discovery of oil in Montgomery County by dedicating a monument to him on the city hall lawn; Governor Price Daniel read a proclamation designating it George W. Strake Day in Montgomery County.

Strake was married to Susan E. Kehoe on September 10, 1924, and they had three children. He died on August 6, 1969, in Columbus, while on a trip to San Antonio, and he was buried in the Garden of Gethsemane Cemetery in Houston.

BIBLIOGRAPHY: *Who's Who in the South and Southwest* (1950); *Time*, August 15, 1969; Houston *Chronicle*, June 4, 5, 1957, August 7, 1969; Houston *Post*, May 1, 1966, August 7, 1969; Biographical File, Barker Texas History Center, University of Texas at Austin.

*Strange, James.

*Stranger, Texas.

*Stratford, Texas. Stratford, seat of Sherman County, serves both Sherman and Dallam counties as the only major commercial center in the area. An agribusiness center, Stratford had approximately eighty business establishments in 1970, and many of these were concerned with farm supply and produce. Since 1950 the town has added new church buildings, an exhibit and livestock show barn, additions to public schools, street lights, and a paved runway for the airport. Stratford had seven churches, a bank, a library, and a newspaper in 1966. The 1960 population was 1,380; in 1970 it was 2,139, a population increase of 55 percent in ten years, according to the United States census.

*Stratton, Texas.

*Stratton Ridge, Texas.

*Strawn, Texas. Strawn, in southwestern Palo Pinto County, was laid out in 1880 and 1881 on land belonging to Stephen Bethel Strawn and James N. Stuart, two early ranchers in the area prior to 1860. Stuart built the first house, in 1875, in what later became Strawn. The town was founded when the Texas and Pacific Railway reached the site. Joseph Peter Davidson was also an early settler in the area, arriving in 1856 and founding Davidsonville, the town which later merged with Strawn; another early settler in the area was W. C. Cochran (not W. W. Cockran, as stated in Volume II).

Strawn had seventeen businesses in 1970. The population in 1960 was 817; in 1970 it was 786, according to the United States census.

BIBLIOGRAPHY: Mary Whatley Clarke, *The Palo Pinto Story* (1956); Joseph Carroll McConnell, *The West Texas Frontier* (1933); B. B. Paddock (ed.), *A Twentieth Century History and Biographical Record of North and West Texas*, I (1906).

J. R. Stuart

*Straw's Mill, Texas.

*Street, Robert Gould.

Streeter, Thomas Winthrop. Thomas Winthrop Streeter, son of Frank Sherwin and Lilian (Carpenter) Streeter, was born on July 20, 1883, in Concord, New Hampshire. After graduation from St. Paul's School, Concord, in 1900, he received a B.L. degree from Dartmouth College in 1904 and an LL.B. degree from Harvard Law School in 1907. He practiced law in Boston, eventually as a member of the firm Streeter and Holmes. On June 23, 1917, he married Ruth Cheney, and they had four children. In 1917 Streeter moved to New York and began a career of business and finance. He was treasurer and then vice-president of the American International Corporation, served as a dollar-a-year man in Washington for the U.S. government during World War I, and then continued in various business enterprises in New York until 1939, when he retired from active business and devoted himself to his Americana collection for the next twenty-five years at his home in Morristown, New Jersey.

Always interested in early American history, Streeter began collecting as a young man, and in 1952 he published a bibliography of selected items from his Americana collection, *Americana—Beginnings*. While serving as chairman of the board (1923–1930) of Simms Petroleum Corporation, a Texas firm, his business trips to the state gave him the opportunity to locate and acquire books, pamphlets, broadsides, and maps relating to Texas history during the period 1795–1845. Rare items from this collection were exhibited in 1936 at the Texas Centennial qv in Dallas and at the formal opening in 1939 of the San Jacinto Monument and Museum.qv In 1944 he gave to the archives of the University of Texas the Beauregard Bryan qv Papers, the last large collection, of almost 2,000 documents, relating to the early history of the Moses Austin qv family. In 1949 he wrote the foreword to Ernest W. Winkler's qv *Check List of Texas Imprints, 1846–1860*.

Streeter assembled the largest private Texana collection ever compiled. From these and other materials which had been printed not only in Texas, but in Mexico, the United States, and Europe, he compiled and published the authoritative three-part (five-volume) work *Bibliography of Texas, 1795–1845*, the first part being *Texas Imprints* (2 vols., 1955), the second part, *Mexican Imprints Relating to Texas* (1 vol., 1956), and the third part, *United States and European Imprints Relating to Texas* (2 vols., 1960). For this definitive work and other scholarly accomplishments he received the honorary Litt.D. degree from Dartmouth College. Upon completion of the *Bibliography* he sold his Texas collection of nearly 2,000 imprints to Yale University for its Western Americana Collection, and it was placed with that university's Wagner and Coe collections.

Streeter was active in many learned societies; he was chairman of the Associates of the John Carter Brown Library, chairman of the Fellows of the Pierpont Morgan Library, president of the American Antiquarian Society, president of the American Bibliographical Society, treasurer of the New York Historical Society, fellow of the California Historical Society (and recipient of their 1962 Wagner Memorial Award), and a fellow of the Texas State Historical Association qv (and member of its advisory council for volumes I and II of the *Handbook of Texas*, published in 1952). Thomas W. Streeter died in Morristown, New Jersey, on June 12, 1965, and was buried in Peterborough, New Hampshire. In accordance with his wishes, Streeter's remaining Americana collection, composed of some 5,000 volumes ranging from discovery and exploration to first books in each of the American states, was sold in a series of seven auctions at Parke-Bernet Galleries in New York City from 1966 through 1969. Many of his books were famous ones and the last copies then available for purchase. He had wanted to give other collectors a chance to enjoy owning them as much as he had. The sales caused great interest and brought in gross receipts of $3,100,000. *See also* Texas Historical Records Survey.

BIBLIOGRAPHY: *National Cyclopedia of American Biography* (1969); *Who Was Who In America*, IV (1968); "Streeter Books To Be Sold At Parke-Bernet Auctions," *Publishers Weekly*, 190 (October 17, 1966); "Texas Collection," *Southwestern Historical Quarterly*, XLIX (1945–1946); *London Times Literary Supplement*, January 19, 1967; New York *Times*, June 13, 1965; Yale University Library, *One Hundred Forty Texas Pamphlets and Broadsides* (February, 1957); Biographical File, Barker Texas History Center, University of Texas at Austin.

Ruth Cheney Streeter

*Streeter, Texas.

*Streetman, Texas.

Street's Weekly. See Holland's Magazine.

*Stremme, Conrad C.

*Stricklin Creek.

*Striker Creek. [This title was incorrectly listed in Volume II as Strikers Creek.]

Striker Creek Reservoir. Striker Creek Reservoir is in the Neches River Basin in Rusk and Cherokee counties, eighteen miles southwest of Henderson on Striker Creek. The project is owned and operated by the Angelina and Nacogdoches Counties Water Control and Improvement District No. 1. Water is used for municipal purposes, by the Texas Power & Light Company for condenser-cooling water for a steam-electric generating station, and by the Southland Paper Company, which contracted to purchase 10,000 acre-feet of water annually. Construction began on July 23, 1956, and was completed in July, 1957. The reservoir has a capacity of 26,700 acre-feet and a surface area of 2,400 acres at normal operating elevation of 292 feet above mean sea level. The drainage area is 182 square miles.

BIBLIOGRAPHY: Texas Water Commission, *Bulletin 6408* (1964).

Seth D. Breeding

*Strikes in Texas. Prior to the maintenance by the United States government of records of work stoppages, no accurate means existed to determine the number of strikes in Texas or the extent of worker participation in the strikes known to have occurred. From scattered sources, however, it is clear that strikes did happen, with the first known strike coming as early as the era of the Republic. In September or October, 1838, the Texas Typographical Association, the first labor organization in Texas, struck the Houston publishers and secured a 25 percent wage increase. From then on, occasional work stoppages occurred, usually involving only a small number of workers and almost never a labor organization. Not until after the Civil War were there incidents that might qualify as bonafide strikes. The strikes of 1870 were typical. In January of that year, Houston telegraphers joined a short, unsuccessful nationwide strike against Western Union; in April, the Austin Typographical Union suffered a disastrous defeat; in May, Galveston brickmasons struck for a raise but returned to work without it; and, in November, the engineers and brakemen on the Houston and Texas Central Railway lost their jobs as a result of a walkout involving wages.

The first work stoppage involving more than a handful of workers occurred in June, 1872, when the management of the Houston and Texas Central Railway instituted a policy requiring all employees to sign an agreement releasing the company from all liability for accidents on the job. No union existed, yet almost all employees attended meetings demanding the withdrawal of the liability release, calling it a "death warrant." When the railroad refused, 80 percent of the operating employees walked out and all trains on the line stopped for several days. After supervisory personnel and new employees put most of the trains back into operation, all those remaining on strike were fired. Although the engineers were later rehired and the liability release was withdrawn, the strike was a disastrous failure for most of the workers.

The number of strikes clearly increased through the seventies, as the number of unions and labor militancy grew. The peak year until the middle eighties was 1877, when there were numerous small local strikes and major work stoppages among dockworkers in Galveston and railway workers on the Texas and Pacific. Both the large strikes were marked by considerable violence. The dockworkers' strike saw the first use of Negroes as strikebreakers in Texas. (*See* Screwmen's Benevolent Association.)

[*See* Strikes in Texas, in Volume II, for the period 1880 to 1945. Ed.]

The vast changes which occurred in Texas during and following World War II found perhaps no clearer substantiation than labor-management relations. The 2,500,000 man-days lost in the approximately 150 strikes during the eighteen months immediately after the war exceeded the total man-days lost in all previous strikes combined. This greatest outburst of industrial conflict in the state's history included major work stoppages in the oil, railroad, aircraft manufacturing, chemical, construction, steel, and nonferrous metals industries. The primary factors provoking the strikes included the expiration of wartime no-strike pledges, the problems created by demobilization, the drastic inflation which followed the war, and vigorous organizational drives in several industries.

When this surge of labor troubles subsided, prewar conditions did not return. In no year of the two decades following the war did the number of strikes or man-days lost fall as low as the previous high of sixty-four strikes with 198,000 man-days lost established in 1937. In each year except 1963 (when only 7,000 workers struck their jobs), the number of Texans involved in labor disputes was more than twice the prewar high of 11,800 established in 1941. The average number of workers involved per strike also reached record levels after the war, with 1,025 men per strike in 1945, 977 per strike in 1946, and over 400 per strike in nine of the twenty years following the war. During these twenty years, 790,000 strikers lost 14,257,000 man-days in 1,680 work stoppages.

While the small strike, involving relatively few men and scant man-days lost, continued to account for the majority of these work stoppages, approximately 75 percent of the man-days lost resulted from strikes in major industries. More than 100,-000 man-days were lost due to strikes in the oil industry in each of the years 1945, 1947, 1950, 1952, 1959, 1961, 1962, and 1963; in transportation and communication in 1946, 1947, 1950, 1953, 1963, and 1965; in the chemical industry in 1946, 1949, 1956, 1961, 1962, and 1963; in the steel industry in 1946, 1952, 1956, and 1959; and in construction in 1946, 1947, 1952, 1953, 1954, 1956, 1958, 1959, 1960, 1961, and 1965.

Both the industries and unions which developed most rapidly in Texas after World War II were of national or regional character; consequently major work stoppages were less frequently purely local conflicts. The nationwide steel strikes of 1952, 1956, and 1959 affected large numbers of Texas steelworkers, and longshoremen in the state's ports took part in regional strikes in 1956, 1959, 1961, 1962, and 1965. Often nationwide strikes against particular companies, such as those against Sinclair Oil Corporation in 1945 and 1952, Southwestern Bell in 1953, and Ford Motor Company in 1964 and 1967, involved Texans.

Yet the locally provoked strike of major impact did not disappear. Almost all work stoppages in construction were local conflicts. In 1962 a disagreement over job reclassifications created by automation kept 2,000 employees of American Oil Company's Texas City refinery off the job for over a year; this strike was of great importance in the adjustment to automation throughout the oil and chemical industries. In 1966 Latin American farm workers in the Rio Grande Valley began an extended strike against corporate farms, a strike which had broad social, political, and economic implications (*see* Political Association of Spanish-Speaking Organizations).

A more mature attitude toward labor relations by the unions, management, and the public characterized the postwar decades. As a result labor disputes were more peaceful, if equally acrimonious (especially in the urban areas of high union membership and activity). Occasional fisticuffs still occurred, from those marking the oil and chemical strikes of 1945 to several fights accompanying the Rio Grande Valley farm workers' strike. But rare was the kind of violence that marred the Lone Star Steel strike at Daingerfield in 1957, where bombings and shootings occurred, and a large force of Rangers and highway patrolmen were needed to restore peace.

BIBLIOGRAPHY: James V. Reese, The Worker in Texas, 1821–1876 (Ph.D. dissertation, University of Texas at Austin, 1964); U.S. Department of Labor, Bureau of Labor Statistics, *Analysis of Work Stoppages* (1945–1966).

James V. Reese

*String Prairie.

*String Prairie, Texas.

*Stringtown, Texas. [This title was incorrectly listed in Volume II as String Town, Texas.] Stringtown was located in Hays County (not Comal County, as stated in Volume II). The community got its name from the approximately six-mile-long string of houses which were built facing the old San Antonio to Austin post road (not the Camino Real or Old San Antonio Road qv), beginning near Purgatory Creek, southwest of San Marcos, to York Creek on the Hays County-Comal County line (now Farm Road 2439). Between 1850 and 1856 eighteen families settled in the community, building log homes, a store, and a one-room schoolhouse. John D. Pitts,qv called the "father of Stringtown," donated land for the schoolhouse, which was also used for church services. In the 1970's some residents of the area continued to call it Stringtown.

BIBLIOGRAPHY: Zora M. Talbot, *Stringtown* (1961).

Al Lowman

*Strip, Texas.

*Strong, Henry W.

*Strong, Sterling Price.

*Strongfield, Texas.

*Stroud, Beden.

*Stroud, Ethan A.

*Strouds Creek.

*Structure, Texas.

*Stuart, Ben C.

*Stuart, David Finney.

*Stuart, Hamilton.

Stuart, Mary Frances (Blake). Mary Frances "Fannie" (Blake) Stuart was born in December, 1837, in Lexington, Mississippi, the daughter of E. H. and Frances (Harris) Blake. In 1846 her family moved to Houston; when she was twelve she was sent to the Hartford Female Seminary in Connecticut, a journey made by oxcart, riverboat, stagecoach, and railroad. Upon completion of her education she returned to Texas and became an assistant teacher at Live Oak Female Seminary qv at Gay Hill in Washington County. At the end of the school term, December, 1860, she married a fellow teacher, Robert Cummins Stuart II, brother of Rebecca (Stuart) Red.qv The couple had four children. After living in Brenham they moved to Austin, where Stuart was a cotton factor. Mrs. Red came to Austin to open her own private school for young ladies, Stuart Seminary,qv in a new three-story stone building on Robertson Hill at East Ninth and Navasota streets, built just across the street from the Stuart home. Mrs. Stuart taught the first class in 1875. She taught again in 1886 during Mrs. Red's last illness. Fannie Stuart died on September 24, 1892, in Austin, and she was buried there.

BIBLIOGRAPHY: S. H. Dixon and L. W. Kemp, *The Heroes of San Jacinto* (1932); *Harris County Heritage Society Cook Book* (1964); Mabelle Purcell, *Two Texas Female Seminaries* (1951); Marguerite Johnston, *A Happy Worldly Abode, Christ Church Cathedral, 1839–1964* (1964); Betty Plummer, *Historic Homes of Washington County, 1821–1860* (1971); Mary Starr Barkley, *History of Travis County and Austin, 1839–1899* (1963).

Francita Stuart Koelsch

*Stuart Seminary. Mary Frances (Blake) [not Balke, as stated in Volume II] Stuart qv was the first teacher in the Stuart Seminary. The school was established by Mrs. Stuart's sister-in-law, Rebecca (Stuart) Red,qv in 1875 as the Stuart Female Seminary; it carried that name until about 1893 when the school catalog appeared with the new title, Stuart Seminary. *See also* Presbyterian Education in Texas.

BIBLIOGRAPHY: Mabelle Purcell, *Two Texas Female Seminaries* (1951).

*Stuarts Creek.

*Stubblefield, Texas.

*Stubblefield Creek.

*Stubbs, Texas.

*Stubenrauch, Joseph W.

Studer, Floyd V. Floyd V. Studer was born on July 3, 1892, at Canadian, Texas, the son of J. C. and Ella (Gallaher) Studer. He remained a resident of Canadian until he moved to Amarillo in 1925. Largely self-educated, Studer became a friend of nationally known archaeologists because of his intimate knowledge of the archaeology of the Canadian River Valley. During his youth, he became aware of the Alibates Flint Quarries qv and the Pueblo Ruins of the Texas Panhandle.qv In subsequent years he explored the Canadian River and all its tributaries between the 100th and 103rd meridians, eventually locating and mapping over two hundred Texas Panhandle pueblo sites and bringing them to the attention of leading archaeologists.

Studer was an owner of the cattle-ranching firm of J. C. Studer and Sons from 1913 until 1950; he was an officer and director of banks in Canadian and Amarillo, and he was also associated with a life insurance company. For a time he was curator of archaeology of the Panhandle-Plains Historical Museum.qv During the latter years of his life, he was a leader in securing the establishment of the Alibates Flint Quarries and Texas Panhandle Pueblo Culture National Monument (*see* Alibates Flint Quarries).

On June 15, 1915, Studer married Annie Ball Cooper of Canadian; they had two daughters. Mrs. Studer died in 1957, and Studer married Susan Cooper Bushfield on June 10, 1959. Studer died on March 31, 1966, at Amarillo, where he was buried in Llano Cemetery.

Frederick W. Rathjen

Studies in English. See also Texas Studies in Literature and Language.

*Study Butte.

*Study Butte, Texas.

*Sturgeon, Texas.

*Sturgis, Texas.

*Styx, Texas.

Suahuache Indians. These apparently Coahuiltecan Indians are known from one brief encounter with Spaniards in 1693, at which time it was said that they lived in northeastern Coahuila. It seems likely that the Suahuache were one of the numerous Coahuiltecan bands that ranged from northeastern Coahuila across the Rio Grande into the adjoining part of Texas. They may be the same as the Suajo, one of twenty Indian groups that joined Juan Domínguez de Mendoza qv on his journey from El Paso to the vicinity of present San Angelo in 1683–1684. This identification is suggested by Mendoza's statement that "some nations departed toward their land with the Indian who governed them, who is a Christian and is proficient in the Mexican language and in Castilian."

BIBLIOGRAPHY: H. E. Bolton (ed.), *Spanish Exploration in the Southwest, 1542–1706* (1916); F. W. Hodge (ed.), *Handbook of American Indians*, II (1910); J. R. Swanton, *Linguistic Material from the Tribes of Southern Texas and Northeastern Mexico* (1940).

T. N. Campbell

Suajo Indians. The Suajo Indians were one of twenty Indian groups that joined Juan Domínguez de Mendoza qv on his journey from El Paso to the vicinity of present San Angelo in 1683–1684. Since Mendoza did not indicate at what point the Suajo joined his party, it is difficult to make statements about their range and affiliation. However, the Indians between the Pecos River and the San Angelo area were being hard pressed by Apache at this time, and it may be that the Suajo ranged somewhere between these two localities. It is also possible that the Suajo were the same people as the Suahuache, who in 1693 were reported in northeastern Coahuila. This identification is suggested by Mendoza's statement that "some nations departed toward their land with the Indian who governed them, who is a Christian and is proficient in the Mexican language and in Castilian." If the two are the same, a Coahuiltecan language is indicated.

BIBLIOGRAPHY: H. E. Bolton (ed.), *Spanish Exploration in the Southwest, 1542–1706* (1916); F. W. Hodge (ed.), *Handbook of American Indians*, II (1910); J. R. Swanton, *Linguistic Material from the Tribes of Southern Texas and Northeastern Mexico* (1940).

T. N. Campbell

*Suana Indians.

*Sublett, Henry Williams. Henry Williams Sublett married Jane Bell (or Belle) Anderson on July 31, 1847.

Lucie C. Price

*Sublett, Philip A.

*Sublett, Texas.

*Sublime, Texas.

*Sudan, Texas. Sudan, in Lamb County, grew into a community of more than 1,000 people after the Santa Fe Railroad constructed a line from Lubbock, Texas, to Texico, New Mexico, in 1913. Sudan was not a terminus for the Santa Fe Railroad (as stated in Volume II). In 1960 the population of Sudan was 1,235; in 1970 it was 976, according to the United States census.

BIBLIOGRAPHY: S. G. Reed, *A History of Texas Railroads* (1941).

*Sue Peak.

*Suffolk, Texas.

*Suffrage Laws. *See* Election Laws.

*Sugar Creek.

*Sugar Land, Texas. Sugar Land, in eastern Fort Bend County near the Harris County line, was incorporated under a mayor-alderman form of government in 1959. It was a growing farm market town in the 1960's and early 1970's, and the most significant business was the large sugar refinery which gave the town its name; other businesses included those dealing with foods, feeds, and oil field equipment. Twenty-five businesses were reported in 1970. The prison farm was still located there in 1975. Sugar Land's population, according to the United States census, increased from 2,802 inhabitants in 1960 to 3,318 in 1970, an 18.4 percent increase.

*Sugar Land Railroad Company. The Sugar Land Railroad Company was sold by its owner, W. T. Eldridge, in 1925 to the New Orleans, Texas, & Mexico Railway Co. The sale became effective January 2, 1926. In 1942 the Interstate Commerce Commission ordered the road to abandon the line extending southeast from Cabell. In 1956 the road was consolidated with the Missouri-Pacific.

James M. Day

*Sugar Loaf Hill.

*Sugar Production. In the 1950's almost all Texas sugar was used for the production of syrup. Sugarcane syrup was produced in some Gulf Coast and East Texas counties, but no production figures were listed. Sorghum syrup was also produced in East Texas counties in small mills utilizing homegrown sorghum crops. In 1954 sorghum syrup production was 180,000 gallons valued at $306,000. Sugar beets were also grown, mainly in Deaf Smith and other Panhandle counties. The 1954 production of sugar beets was estimated at 135,000 bushels valued at $495,000.

Limited amounts of cane and sorghum syrup were produced in the late 1950's. In 1959 approximately one hundred farms produced 61,905 gallons of sugarcane syrup valued at $102,612. Sorghum syrup production had declined to 30,701 gallons, of which only 19,624 gallons valued at $39,248 were sold commercially.

The closing of the United States market to Cuban production stimulated the cultivation of sugar beets in the 1960's. In 1964 the state's first sugar mill for processing beets was completed at Hereford in Deaf Smith County, making a total of two sugar-producing plants in Texas. In that year approximately 539,000 tons from 26,000 acres were processed. By 1967 sugar beet production, from 29,800 acres, yielded 663,000 tons valued at $8,089,000. In 1970 the state produced 588,000 tons from 29,100 acres.

BIBLIOGRAPHY: *Texas Almanac* (1955, 1965, 1969, 1971); *Directory of Texas Manufacturers* (1966).

*Sugarloaf Mountain.

*Suggs, Texas.

*Sul Ross State Teachers College. *See also* Sul Ross State University.

Sul Ross State University. Sul Ross State University, Alpine, has had a succession of name changes, from Sul Ross State Normal College in 1920, to Sul Ross State Teachers College qv in 1923, to Sul Ross State College in 1949, and finally to the present name in 1969 by act of the Sixty-first Texas Legislature. Through the spring semester, 1966, the college had conferred 5,013 bachelor's degrees and 1,580 master's degrees. In 1969 the library contained approximately 120,000 cataloged volumes, including two special collections, the Texas-Southwest (Texana) and Aldrich collections. In the fall term of 1974 the school had an enrollment of 2,698 and a faculty of approximately 165. Bryan Wildenthal served as president from 1952 to 1965, when he was succeeded by Norman L. McNeil, who served until 1973. Hugh Meredith was president of Sul Ross State University in 1974. In that year the Uvalde Extension Center, an upper-level division offering work beyond the sophomore year, was opened in Uvalde, Texas; Louis G. Wood was director of the center, and 233 students were enrolled.

*Sullivan, Texas.

*Sullivan City, Texas.

*Sulphur, Texas. (Bowie County.)

*Sulphur, Texas. (Franklin County.)

*Sulphur Bluff, Texas.

*Sulphur Branch.

*Sulphur Creek.

*Sulphur Draw.

*Sulphur Industry. Texas at times has produced more than 90 percent of the nation's sulphur and in the 1950's continued to be a leading world producer. In 1954 production by the Frasch process (the method of drilling wells into deposits, melting the sulphur with superheated water, and forcing the molten sulphur to the surface), amounted to 3,450,000 long tons valued at $75,100,000. In addition to native sulphur produced by the Frasch process, sulphur was also being recovered from sour gas. In the 1960's Texas retained its position as one of the world's leading sulphur-producing areas, and, exclusive of the oil-gas group, it was the state's most valuable mineral. Expanded storage, shipment, and use of molten sulphur made possible significant changes, such as the employment of large tankers which carried molten sulphur to Holland, and the increased use of barge transportation which carried Texas sulphur to inland markets. In 1965 Texas production (Frasch process) amounted to 3,674,000 long tons valued at $83,282,000. The production of native frasch sulphur remained largely concentrated in Fort Bend, Jefferson, Liberty, Matagorda, and Wharton counties, and from underground Permian strata in Pecos County. In 1967, 3,448,000 long tons of (Frasch process) sulphur were produced at a value of $111,931,000. A preliminary estimate for 1970 was for a production of 2,956,000 long tons.

Two new sulphuric acid plants were built in 1966 at Houston and Port Arthur. Major oil firms were exploring tidelands leases offshore for sulphur production through sour gas purification. Other exploration and leasing included that in Pecos, Culberson, and Duval counties. Plants to extract sulphur from sour gas in 1970 were located in Andrews, Atascosa, Cass, Cochran, Crane, Ector, Franklin, Gaines, Harris, Hockley, Hopkins, Jefferson, Karnes, McMullen, Moore, Rains, Reagan, Van Zandt, and Wood counties.

BIBLIOGRAPHY: *Texas Almanac* (1955, 1965, 1967, 1969, 1971).

*Sulphur Mountain.

*Sulphur River.

Sulphur Spring, Texas. Sulphur Spring, situated at the Ojo de Agua Creek crossing of the La Bahía Road qv in southeastern Karnes County, was a place-name that appeared on maps in 1853, a year before Karnes County was created. Maps of 1859 and 1867 showed the name of Mineral Spring appearing where Sulphur Spring had been. In 1887 the town of Runge was established at the same location.

BIBLIOGRAPHY: Robert H. Thonhoff, *A History of Karnes County, Texas* (M.A. thesis, Southwest Texas State College, 1963).

*Sulphur Springs, Texas. (Hopkins County.) Sulphur Springs was incorporated possibly as early as 1852, and it was rechartered in 1871 when it became the seat of Hopkins County. The town adopted a home rule charter in 1917, and it accepted a commission-manager form of municipal government in 1947. Light industries in Sulphur Springs were engaged in the manufacture of a variety of products, including men's work clothing, women's dresses, mattresses, dairy equipment, dairy products, transmission parts, ready-mix concrete, sheet metal products, moveable shutters, high pressure valves, and petrochemical products. The city reported 298 businesses in 1970. Municipal facilities and services were considerably expanded during the 1960's. The 1960 population was 9,160; in 1970 it was 10,642, according to the United States census.

*Sulphur Springs, Texas. (San Saba County.)

*Sulphur Springs Draw.

*Sulujame Indians. The aboriginal location of the Sulujame (Chuluaam, Zolohan, Zulajan) Indians is unknown. Between 1726 and 1741 this name is included in the records of San Antonio de Valero Mission qv at San Antonio. Since in these records the Sulujame are often linked with the Pataguo and Xarame, it seems likely that they were a Coahuiltecan band from the same area, namely, the Nueces-Frio region south of the Edwards Plateau.

BIBLIOGRAPHY: F. W. Hodge (ed.), *Handbook of American Indians*, II (1910); J. R. Swanton, *Linguistic Material from the Tribes of Southern Texas and Northeastern Mexico* (1940).

T. N. Campbell

*Suma Indians. In the seventeenth and eighteenth centuries the Suma (Sume, Suna, Zuma) Indians ranged over a territory that extended from the vicinity of present El Paso westward across northwestern Chihuahua into northeastern Sonora. They entered various Spanish missions near El Paso and Casas Grandes. The Suma slowly declined in numbers and several remnants seem to have been absorbed by various local Apache groups in the late eighteenth century. A few Suma individuals were still living south of El Paso in the late nineteenth century. The affiliations of the Suma remain in doubt. Most writers profess to see little difference between the Suma and the Jumano. J. D. Forbes has recently argued that the Suma were Athapaskans, but he seems to have placed too much emphasis on their late association with Apaches.

BIBLIOGRAPHY: J. D. Forbes, "Unknown Athapaskans: The Identification of the Jano, Jocome, Jumano, Manso, Suma, and Other Indian Tribes of the Southwest," *Ethnohistory*, 6 (1959); F. W. Hodge (ed.), *Handbook of American Indians*, II (1910); A. E. Hughes, *Beginnings of Spanish Settlement in the El Paso District* (1914); C. Sauer, *The Distribution of Aboriginal Tribes and Languages in Northwestern Mexico* (1934).

T. N. Campbell

Sumi Indians. This name is known only from baptismal records (1719) at the San Antonio de

Valero Mission qv in San Antonio. The similarity of Sumi to Sumacoalapem, a variant of Samacoalapem, suggests that the two may have been the same people. The Samacoalapem lived on the south bank of the Rio Grande between Camargo and Mier, Tamaulipas, in the middle eighteenth century.

BIBLIOGRAPHY: F. W. Hodge (ed.), *Handbook of American Indians*, II (1910); W. Jiménez Moreno, "Tribus e idiomas del Norte de México," *El Norte de México y el Sur de Estados Unidos* (1944); G. Saldivar, *Los Indios de Tamaulipas* (1943).

T. N. Campbell

*Summerfield, John.

*Summerfield, Texas.

*Summit, Texas. (Bexar County.)

*Summit, Texas. (Burnet County.)

*Summit, Texas. (Milam County.)

*Summit, Texas. (Motley County.)

*Sumner, Texas.

Sumners, Hatton William. Hatton William Sumners, a Texas spokesman in Congress for thirty-four years, was born on a farm near Fayetteville in Lincoln County, Tennessee, on May 30, 1875, the son of W. A. and Anna (Walker) Sumners. In 1893 he came to Texas and lived with his grandparents at Garland. Soon afterward he began studying law in the Dallas office of McLauren and Wozencraft.

He passed the state Bar examination in 1897 and three years later was elected prosecuting attorney of Dallas County. His vigorous fight against gambling led to his defeat two years later, but in 1904 he was elected to a second term, after which he returned to the private practice of law. In 1912, as a Democrat, he was elected congressman-at-large from Texas; two years later he was elected representative of the Fifth Congressional District, made up of Bosque, Hill, Ellis, Rockwall, and Dallas counties. He was placed on the House Judiciary Committee in 1919, became its chairman in 1932, and served in that capacity for fifteen years. He represented the legislative branch of the government before the Supreme Court on four occasions, helped write the Philippine Constitution, and became a strong opponent of centralized government. He led the successful House fight against President Franklin D. Roosevelt's plan to enlarge the Supreme Court, and he was recognized as an authority on constitutional law. Opposed to executive dictation to Congress, he held that "the aggregate wisdom of the people is the only safe guide of a republic." After his retirement from Congress in 1946, he became research director of the Southwestern Legal Foundation at Southern Methodist University. He never married. Sumners died in Dallas on April 19, 1962; he was buried in Garland, Texas.

BIBLIOGRAPHY: Raymond Moley, *27 Masters of Politics* (1949); Dallas *Morning News*, April 20, 1962.

Wayne Gard

*Sumpter, Jesse.

*Sumpter, Texas.

*Sun, Texas. (Grayson County.)

*Sun, Texas. (Jefferson County.)

Sun Bowl. Established in 1935, the Sun Bowl football game, annually matching college teams in the postseason, is the oldest continuous bowl game contest in Texas and the third oldest in the nation. The Sun Bowl stadium is the home field for the University of Texas at El Paso and is located on UTEP's campus, where picturesque mountains serve as a backdrop. The bowl game is the highlight of a week-long Sun Bowl Carnival that was conceived for the purpose of providing El Pasoans with the opportunity to host friends, neighbors, and visitors during the holiday season at the end of each year. Steadily growing in stature, the Sun Bowl has attracted participants from several major athletic conferences.

Wilbur Evans

*Sunday Creek.

*Sunday Houses.

*Sundown, Texas. Sundown, in southwest Hockley County, was incorporated in 1947. A tornado in 1949 killed or injured over twenty people and caused much property damage. In 1965 a comprehensive plan for city development was adopted. Businesses in the late 1960's were connected with oil, farming, and ranching, and during that same time the town reported six churches, a school, a bank, and a library. Population was 1,186 in 1960; in 1970 it was 1,129, according to the United States census. Thirty businesses were reported in 1970.

Sunigogligla Indians. Sunigogligla (Seuliyolida, Sunigugliga) is the name of one band of Chizo Indians, who are considered by some writers to be a branch of the Concho. In the seventeenth and early eighteenth centuries the Chizo occupied the area now covered by northeastern Chihuahua, northwestern Coahuila, and the lower part of the Big Bend region of Trans-Pecos Texas.

BIBLIOGRAPHY: C. W. Hackett (ed.), *Historical Documents Relating to New Mexico, Nueva Vizcaya, and Approaches Thereto, to 1773*, II (1926); C. Sauer, *The Distribution of Aboriginal Tribes and Languages in Northwestern Mexico* (1934).

T. N. Campbell

*Suniland, Texas.

*Sunny Glen Home.

*Sunny Side, Texas.

*Sunnyside, Texas.

Sunnyvale, Texas. Sunnyvale, in eastern Dallas County, had a 1960 population of 969 and a 1970 population of 995, according to the United States census.

*Sunray, Texas. Sunray, in northern Moore County, had a 1960 population of 1,967 and a 1970 population of 1,854, according to the United States census. The town had thirty-five businesses in 1970.

Sunrise, Texas. Sunrise, an unincorporated town in central Falls County south of Marlin, had a 1960 population of 1,708 and a 1970 population of 1,213, according to the United States census.

Sunrise Beach, Texas. Sunrise Beach, one of the first lake-front subdivisions on Lake Lyndon B. Johnson, is located approximately halfway between Marble Falls and Llano in Llano County. It was founded in 1958 by developer David Miller of San Antonio as a resort and retirement area. In 1966 there were recreational facilities, motels, restaurants, and businesses concerned with building trades. The permanent population in 1970 was approximately eight hundred.

*Sunset, Texas.

*Sunset College.

*Sunset Heights, Texas.

Sunset Valley, Texas. Sunset Valley, in Travis County, was incorporated in 1954; it is a residential area adjoining Austin on the southwest. In 1966 part of the community had paved streets, natural gas, and a water system. In 1960 the population was 179; in 1970 it was 292, according to the United States census. *See also* Austin Standard Metropolitan Statistical Area.

*Sunshine Hill.

*Sunshine Hill, Texas.

*Superintendent of Public Instruction, State.

*Supplejack Creek.

**Supply.*

*Supreme Court. *See* Judicial System.

*Surface Water.

*Surfside, Texas.

*Surveying.

Surveyors Fight. *See* Battle Creek Fight.

*Susola Indians.

*Sutherland, George.

*Sutherland, John. John Sutherland settled on Cibolo Creek in Wilson County in 1849 (not in 1840 on the Cibolo River, as stated in Volume II), when he took part in the commercial development of some sulphur springs. *See also* Sutherland Springs, Texas.

Justin Van Gorden Anderson

*Sutherland, Walter.

*Sutherland Springs, Texas. Sutherland Springs, first county seat of Wilson County (1860), was founded about 1849 (not 1831, as stated in Volume II) when John Sutherland qv moved to the area and began developing the sulphur springs owned by Gideon Lee of New York City; however, settlement near the future townsite, which was to become known as "old town," was begun as early as 1831. The first permanent settlers included William Myers and Joseph H. Polley,qv whose home, "Whitehall," located on the east bank of Cibolo Creek, near "new town," was still being occupied in 1971. In 1970 the population was approximately one hundred fifty in "old town," which had a general store, a service station, and a modern post office.

BIBLIOGRAPHY: San Antonio *Express*, August 22, 1971.

*Sutherlands Creek.

*Sutton, John S.

*Sutton, William Seneca. William Seneca Sutton was the son of James Tillton and Francena Lavinia (Martin) Sutton (not Frances [Martin] Sutton, as stated in Volume II). Sutton was married to Annie Blackman (not Blackburn) Erwin on June 12, 1884.

BIBLIOGRAPHY: *Dictionary of American Biography* (1936); *Who Was Who In America* (1968).

D. Richard Bowles

*Sutton, Texas.

*Sutton County. Sutton County was organized with Sonora as the county seat on November 4, 1890. The rail line from San Angelo to Sonora, although built in 1929 (as stated in Volume II), was completed in 1930; the first train reached Sonora on July 1 of that year.

In the 1960's and early 1970's, Sutton County derived almost all of its annual agricultural income from livestock, primarily sheep, goats, cattle, and horses. The county was one of the leading Texas counties in the number of sheep and goats raised. Located in Sonora, the only town in Sutton County, was an experimental substation of the Texas A&M University System.qv A small oil industry was developing during the 1960's, but it remained small. From 1948 to January 1, 1973, a total of 2,752,335 barrels of crude oil had been produced. Tourist attractions included deer and turkey hunting, a wool and mohair show, and the Caverns of Sonora.qv The 1960 population was 3,738; in 1970 it was 3,175, according to the United States census.

*Sutton-Taylor Feud.

**Svoboda.*

*Swager Creek.

*Swain, William Jesse. William Jesse Swain served in the House of the Fourteenth Legislature (1874–1875) and in the Senate of the Sixteenth and Seventeenth legislatures (1879, 1881). In 1882 he was elected state comptroller and served from January 16, 1883, to January 18, 1887 (not 1884, as stated in Volume II). He died in Houston (not Austin) on December 20 (not December 21), 1904, and was buried in the State Cemetery.qv

BIBLIOGRAPHY: F. B. Baillio (not Baillis, as stated in Volume II), *History of the Texas Press Association* (1916); Tommy Yett (comp.), *Members of the Legislature of the State of Texas from 1846 to 1939* (1939); Houston *Daily Post*, December 21, 1904.

*Swamp City, Texas. *See also* Crews, Texas.

*Swan, Texas.

*Swan Lake.

*Swanson, Adolph Clarence.

Swartwout, Samuel. Samuel Swartwout, youngest son of Abraham and Maria (North) Swartwout, was born on November 17, 1783, in Poughkeepsie, New York. He and two older brothers became prosperous merchants in the city of New York and prominent in politics. As a young man he became closely connected with Aaron Burr,qv was one of the active supporters of the Southwest Empire scheme, and was tried and acquitted in the famous Burr conspiracy case. In the War of 1812 he was captain of a city militia company, the Iron Grays. In 1814 he married Alice Ann Cooper, by whom he had two children.

Swartwout worked hard and successfully to promote Andrew Jackson as a presidential candidate and was rewarded after the election by a very lucrative appointment as collector for the port of New York. It was during this time that the colonization of Texas by Anglo Americans was at its height, and Swartwout became interested in Texas lands. An active figure in the New Washington Association,qv his name appears frequently with other early developers of Texas. The town Swartwout, laid out in present Polk County, was one of his projects. Swartwout saved two Texas Navy qv ships, *Invincible* and *Brutus*,qqv from being sold (1836–1837) by paying their repair bills in New York.

In November, 1838, he left suddenly for Europe; subsequent investigation revealed a shortage of between one and two million dollars in customs accounts. For some time thereafter the term "Swartwouting" was synonomous with embezzlement. In 1840 he returned without funds or means of livelihood and was liable to the government for the huge sum misappropriated during his collectorship. The government finally agreed to accept as payment in full whatever he could realize from sale of his lands in Texas and New Jersey.

As early as 1845 Swartwout sought redress from Texas, citing the help he had given her in former years. These appeals continued until his death and later were renewed by his widow. Descendants petitioned the legislature from time to time until 1902. He received eight thousand dollars from the legislature, but all other appeals were of no avail. He died in New York on November 21, 1856.

BIBLIOGRAPHY: Walter Flavius McCaleb, *New Light on Aaron Burr* (1963); John F. Mines, *A Tour Around New York* (1893); *Dictionary of American Biography* (1936); *Encyclopedia of American Biography*, VI (1889); Leo Hershkowitz, " 'The Land of Promise': Samuel Swartwout and Land Speculation in Texas, 1830–1838," *New York Historical Society Quarterly*, XLVIII (1944–1945); Andrew F. Muir, "The Municipality of Harrisburg, 1835–1836," *Southwestern Historical Quarterly*, LVI (1952–1953); Louis Lenz, "Texas Money," *ibid.*, LVII (1953–1954); George F. Haugh (ed.), "History of the Texas Navy," *ibid.*, LXIII (1959–1960).

Madeleine Martin

*Swartwout, Texas.

*Swauano Creek.

*Swayne, James W.

*Swearingen, Patrick Henry.

*Swearingen, Richard Montgomery.

*Swearingen, William C.

*Swearingen, Texas.

Sweatt v. *Painter*. Racial separation by force of law had been a historic tradition in the United States prior to the decision of *Sweatt* v. *Painter* by the Supreme Court of the United States in 1950.

The manner in which segregation of the races by state action in a variety of contexts became established at law, in the face of the fourteenth amendment prohibiting a state from denying to any person within its jurisdiction the equal protection of the laws, is perhaps best revealed by the case of *Plessey* v. *Ferguson*, decided by the Supreme Court around the turn of this century. While that case involved the segregation of the races on a common carrier, the separate but equal doctrine utilized in the case to sanction segregation in that situation was subsequently recognized as applicable in a wide variety of situations, including that of segregation of the white and Negro races for public education. Among other reasons given for the approval of the separate but equal doctrine were: (1) that it was simply a recognition of a fundamental and ineradicable difference; and (2) that it was reasonable in the context of established usages, customs, and traditions of the people. Absolute equality in treatment was not necessary.

Those who sought to challenge race segregation in public education prior to *Sweatt* v. *Painter* did so primarily by contending that there was in the particular situation in question gross inequality of facilities or a complete failure to provide Negroes with higher education of the type in issue. While decisions had been rendered prior to *Sweatt* v. *Painter* indicating that the Supreme Court was shifting to a new and more exacting standing of equality that would ultimately require the state to be "color-blind" in all its activities, these decisions had not proceeded to the point of shaking the foundations of the long-established tradition of an attempt to get equality through segregation. *Sweatt* v. *Painter* did so.

Heman Marion Sweatt, a Negro, applied for admission to the University of Texas School of Law in February, 1946. His was the first application of any Negro to the University of Texas. He met all eligibility requirements for admission except for his race. On that ground he was denied admission pursuant to Article VII, Section 7, of the Texas Constitution, which read: "Separate schools shall be provided for the white and colored children, and impartial provision shall be made for both."

Mandamus proceedings were then instituted by Sweatt to require state and university officials to enroll him. The trial judge continued the case to give the state an opportunity to establish "a separate but equal" law school, and a temporary law school was forthwith opened in February, 1947, known as the School of Law of the Texas State University for Negroes. The school of law was located in a house on Thirteenth Street north of the Capitol.qv The students had access to the Supreme Court library, and several members of the law faculty of the University of Texas School of Law taught the classes. Mandamus was then denied by the state courts of Texas pursuant to the separate but equal doctrine. The Supreme Court of the United States granted certiorari and thereafter held that the Equal Protection Clause required Sweatt's admission to the University of Texas School of Law. Sweatt enrolled at the beginning of the 1950–1951 school year, as did several other Negroes.

Sweatt v. *Painter* did not establish the invalidation of race separation per se by force of law, but the criteria used by the court in the application of the separate but equal doctrine gave legal experts cause to believe that the doctrine was virtually dead. It was clear from the opinion that a good faith effort to supply equality of treatment without integration was insufficient; rather, it must be equality in fact. It was only necessary for the court to say later in *Brown* v. *Board of Education of Topeka* that equality in fact was not a possibility through a policy of separation because to separate children in public schools "from others of similar age and qualifications solely because of their race generates a feeling of inferiority as to their status in the community that may affect their hearts and minds in a way unlikely ever to be undone."

W. Page Keeton

*Sweden, Texas.

*Swedes in Texas. The 1960 census showed 1,557 foreign-born Swedes in Texas. A study of the Swedes in Texas was made during preparation for the Texas exhibit, Institute of Texan Cultures, at HemisFair qqv in San Antonio in 1968.

Carl M. Rosenquist

Sweeny, Thomas Jefferson. Thomas Jefferson Sweeny (sometimes spelled Sweeney) was born about 1818 in Tennessee, the son of John and Ann (Fuller) Sweeny. He came to Texas with his parents in the 1830's, entered the army at the age of seventeen, and served in Captain William Hester Patton's qv company. He and his brother, William Burrell Sweeny, were in the battle of San Jacinto. Thomas J. Sweeny married Diana Frances Haynie, and they were the parents of five or more children. He died in La Grange, probably in 1869, and was buried near Sweeny, a town named for his father.

BIBLIOGRAPHY: Loyce Haynie Rossman, *Rev. John Haynie—Ancestry, Life & Descendants* (1963).

Loyce Haynie Rossman

*Sweeny, Texas. [This title was incorrectly listed in Volume II as Sweeney, Texas.] Sweeny, in Brazoria County, was named for John Sweeny, an early settler in the area. Sweeny had a 1960 population of 3,087 and a 1970 population of 3,191, according to the United States census. The town listed thirty-eight businesses in 1970.

BIBLIOGRAPHY: J. L. Allhands, *Gringo Builders* (1931).

*Sweet, Alexander Edwin.

Sweet, George H. George H. Sweet was born in Ulster County, New York, about 1830. He was a Mexican War veteran and was apparently well educated. In the early 1860's, he was one of the publishers of the San Antonio *Herald*.qv He was elected captain of Company A, 15th Texas Cavalry, on January 1, 1862, and was elected colonel on March 10. Sweet's regiment marched to Arkansas

in the summer of 1862, and was dismounted to serve as infantry on July 24. Sweet and most of his men were captured at Arkansas Post on January 11, 1863. He was exchanged in the spring of 1863 and was sent to the Trans-Mississippi Department in the fall to collect the men of his regiment who had escaped from Arkansas Post. In the fall of 1864 he was the commander of Camp Ford,qv the Confederate prison at Tyler. In the summer of 1866 Sweet made a trip through Mexico and kept a travel diary.

In 1871 Sweet published an immigrant's handbook, *Texas: Her Early History, Climate, Soil, and Material Resources*. In that same year he became publisher of the *Texas New Yorker*,qv a monthly magazine published in New York and designed to promote investment in and immigration to Texas. Sweet continued this journal until 1878, when he moved to Galveston and became the publisher of the Galveston *Journal*. He sold the Galveston paper in December, 1881.

BIBLIOGRAPHY: Service Records of G. H. Sweet (Confederate Service Records, Archives, University of Texas at Austin Library); George H. Sweet, "Notes of Travel Made by Geo. H. Sweet, of San Antonio . . ." (MS., Archives, Texas State Library, Austin); R. M. Collins, *Chapters from the Unwritten History of the War Between the States* (1893); F. Lee Lawrence and Robert Glover, *Camp Ford, C.S.A.* (1964); San Antonio *Herald*, May 24, 1862; Dallas *Weekly Herald*, December 1, 1881.

Sweet, James R. James R. Sweet was born in Bridgetown, Nova Scotia, in 1818. He was married to Charlotte James, and they had two children. He established a business in Saint John, New Brunswick, but after business reverses he moved with his family to San Antonio in 1849. He was engaged in the mercantile business, speculated in mining, and bought land at the head of the San Antonio River in present-day Alamo Heights, where he built a large home. The property was later purchased by George W. Brackenridge,qv and the site is now the campus of Incarnate Word College.qv

Sweet served as mayor of San Antonio from January 1, 1859, to May 26, 1862, when he resigned to join the Confederate Army. As a lieutenant with the 33rd Texas Cavalry Regiment, he served in the Rio Grande Valley. At the end of the war, along with General John Bankhead Magruder,qv General Joseph Orville Shelby (*see* Shelby Expedition), and others, he remained in Mexico during the Reconstruction qv period. After his return to San Antonio he bought an interest in the San Antonio *Herald* qv in 1873; later, failing health forced his retirement. His son, Alexander Edwin Sweet,qv was a journalist on that same paper before gaining nationwide fame as a journalist in Galveston. James R. Sweet died in San Antonio on December 12, 1880, and was buried in City Cemetery.

BIBLIOGRAPHY: Vinton Lee James, *Frontier and Pioneer Recollections of Early Days in San Antonio and West Texas* (1938); Marcus J. Wright (comp.) and Harold B. Simpson (ed.), *Texas In The War 1861–1865* (1965); San Antonio *Express*, December 13, 1880.

S. W. Pease

*Sweet Home, Texas.

Sweet Home Colored School. Sweet Home Colored School in Guadalupe County, with three teachers, was an industrial training school for Negroes in 1917, located in an area where a number of Negroes had settled. There were also several students who transferred to the school from other districts. The school offered manual training and domestic science plus the regular curriculum, and it maintained a small farm with experimental garden plots. The complex of frame buildings included a teachers' cottage, a church, a school building, a blacksmith shop, and a bell tower from which a bell was rung each morning at 7:30 to begin the school day. George Washington Brackenridge qv was said to have been a contributor to the school's support.

BIBLIOGRAPHY: Picture File, Barker Texas History Center, University of Texas at Austin.

*Sweet Potato Culture. In the 1950's Texas sweet potatoes found a wide market in the North, Middle West, and Pacific Coast areas. In 1954 thirty thousand acres produced 1,350,000 bushels valued at $4,320,000. In 1958 Texas ranked third nationally, behind Louisiana and North Carolina, in acreage, representing 8.4 percent of the total United States sweet potato acreage, at a value of over $5,000,000. In 1960, 9,000 farmers reported sweet potato production, with more than 80 percent of the commercial acreage concentrated in twenty-five East Texas counties; sweet potatoes were also grown in the Winter Garden area of South Texas and in Bexar, Haskell, and Knox counties.

In order to increase yields, protection of sweet potato beds with plastic covers was introduced in Texas in 1962. Irrigation of limited acreage was also tried successfully on the High Plains. In 1963 Van Zandt County ranked first in the state and third in the nation in total production of sweet potatoes. During the 1960's the value of Texas production of sweet potatoes averaged over $5,000,000 annually. Planted acreage had increased in the western part of the state in the 1960's because of the availability of irrigation, but northeast Texas was still the center of sweet potato production in 1970; in that year 13,000 acres produced a crop valued at $6,-552,000.

BIBLIOGRAPHY: Texas Agricultural Experiment Station, *Miscellaneous Publications*, No. 540 (October, 1961); *Texas Almanac* (1955, 1963, 1965, 1967, 1971); *Texas Agricultural Progress* (May–June, 1963, Winter, 1965); *Texas Business Review* (May, 1960).

*Sweetwater, Texas. (Nolan County.) Sweetwater, seat of Nolan County and incorporated in 1902, was the commercial center and shipping point for several counties. During the 1960's Sweetwater businesses were chiefly concerned with the cotton, cattle, and oil industries; two gypsum products plants were also located there. Sweetwater reported 247 businesses in 1970. New buildings completed were the county-city coliseum in 1959, a health unit in 1961, a library in 1965, and a new high school in 1967. The town reported forty-two churches, a hospital, a newspaper, a radio station, and a television station in the late 1960's. The 1960 population was 13,914; in 1970 it was 12,020, according to the United States census.

Sweetwater, Texas. (Wheeler County.) *See* Mobeetie (Old), Texas.

*Sweetwater Army Air Field.

*Sweetwater Creek.

Swenson, Andrew John. Andrew John Swenson, long associated with the development and administration of the Texas division of the Swenson Land and Cattle Company, was born on November 16, 1863, in Nässjö, Jönköping Province, Sweden. He came to a Swedish settlement between Round Rock and Georgetown in Williamson County, Texas, when he was eighteen; a year later he moved to West Texas, near present Stamford, Jones County, to work for his uncle, Swen Magnus Swenson.qv After a year of fence riding, Swenson spent five years in Abilene looking after the ranching interests of the widow of his cousin John Swenson.

He visited Sweden and then returned to West Texas in 1887. In 1889 his fiancee, Selma Augusta Anderson, came from Sweden, and they were married that year in New Sweden, Travis County; they had five sons. They lived on their own place north of Anson, Jones County, for five years before moving in 1894 to the Ellerslie ranch, one of the S. M. Swenson holdings southwest of Stamford. There, on five sections of land, the SMS Ranches' qv purebred Hereford and Shorthorn cattle were developed from a start of 125 pureblood heifers. In 1897 Swenson became superintendent of the SMS Ranches, and in 1905 the family moved into Stamford. When Frank Harris, manager of the Swenson Land and Cattle Company, died in 1922, Swenson became manager, a position he held until his retirement in 1948; he was also a vice-president of the cattle company. He was a director of the Texas Cowboy Reunion qv Association from its founding in 1930, and he had numerous business affiliations with both cattle and banking. He died in his home in Stamford on February 14, 1953, and was buried in Bethel Lutheran Church Cemetery in Ericksdahl, near Stamford.

BIBLIOGRAPHY: Violeta T. Mahood, "America Changed Everything for Him," *West Texas Today* (March, 1935); Fort Worth *Star-Telegram*, March 23, 1941, February 15, 1953; Stamford *American*, February 7, 1941; Andrew J. Swenson Papers (MS., Archives, University of Texas at Austin Library).

Swenson, Axel Magnus Godfrey. Axel Magnus Godfrey (Swede) Swenson was born at Ellerslie, a Swenson ranch in Jones County, on January 21, 1900, the son of Selma (Anderson) and Andrew John Swenson.qv He lived at the Ellerslie ranch until 1907, then lived in Stamford, where he was graduated from high school in 1918. He entered the University of Texas, was a four-year letterman on the Longhorn football team, and was elected a member of the Friar's Club; he was graduated with a B.A. degree in 1923. Throughout his life he worked for the family-owned Swenson Land and Cattle Company; although the company had corporate headquarters in New York City, Swenson resided in Stamford.

In 1947 he was appointed to the University of Texas board of regents by Governor Beauford Jester.qv In 1955 Governor Allan Shivers appointed him Texas chairman of the Cowboy Hall of Fame in Oklahoma City. He was one of the founders and promoters of the Texas Cowboy Reunion qv of Stamford, Texas, and was a director of the Texas and Southwestern Cattle Raisers' Association.qv In 1964 he was elected to the University of Texas Longhorn Hall of Honor.

Swenson's father, A. J. Swenson, was a nephew of Swen (Svante) Magnus Swenson qv (see also SMS Ranches). A. M. G. Swenson was married to Harriet C. Womack on December 2, 1933, in Duncan, Oklahoma, and they had three children. Swenson died in Stamford on December 23, 1972, and was buried at Bethel Lutheran Church Cemetery in Ericksdahl, near Stamford.

BIBLIOGRAPHY: Abilene *Reporter-News*, December 24, 1972; Dallas *Morning News*, December 27, 1972; *Texas Posten*, December 28, 1972.

*Swenson, Swen Magnus. Swen Magnus Swenson's name is sometimes found as Sven M. Svenson; by the 1860's he referred to himself in official documents as Svante M. Swenson; he is also referred to as Swante M. Swenson. His first marriage was to Jeanette Long on December 12, 1843 (not ten years after his arrival in Texas—which would have been 1848—as stated in Volume II).

BIBLIOGRAPHY: Gail Swenson, S. M. Swenson and the Development of the SMS Ranches (M.A. thesis, University of Texas at Austin, 1960); S. M. Swenson Papers (MS., Archives, University of Texas at Austin Library); Biographical File, Barker Texas History Center, University of Texas at Austin.

*Swenson, Texas.

*Swietzer, Alonzo B.

*Swift, Eben.

*Swift, Timothy.

*Swift, Texas.

*Swindlers Creek.

*Swine Raising. In the 1950's Texas swine production was below the state's consumption, and large out-of-state imports from the midwestern states were necessary. Whereas in 1940, 60 percent of all Texas farms reported the raising of hogs, in 1964 only 16 percent did. The main obstacle to increased hog production was the lack of consistent corn yield in Texas. The 1954 census reported 906,000 hogs valued at $23,375,000. The introduction of hybrid corn met with some success, but only the size of Texas enabled it to rank among the top twenty swine-producing states by 1963. In 1960 Texas had 1,263,000 swine valued at $19,198,000. Ten years later, on December 1, 1970, the state had 1,419,000 hogs valued at $31,928,000. The gross income from 325,896,000 pounds of pork was $73,027,000 in 1969; this was from an average weight of 239 pounds per animal and prices averaging $21.60 per hundredweight. While production was

scattered over the state, principal concentrations were in west-central Texas, the South Plains, the southern Blacklands, the Panhandle, and northeast and East Texas; however, by 1970 Texas continued to produce less than 30 percent of the pork consumed in the state, and it ranked only fifteenth among the states in swine production.

BIBLIOGRAPHY: *Texas Almanac* (1955, 1965, 1967, 1971).

*Swisher, Bella French.

*Swisher, James Gibson. James Gibson Swisher died November 14, 1862 (not November 14, 1864, as stated in Volume II).

BIBLIOGRAPHY: Alexander Eanes Cemetery Record Book (MS., Austin-Travis County Collection, Austin Public Library).

Lucie C. Price

*Swisher, John Milton.

*Swisher County. Swisher County, in northwest Texas, in the early 1970's had an economy based on agriculture, with approximately $50 million average annual income evenly divided between crops and livestock. One of the leading counties in total farm income, with extensive irrigation, it produced wheat, grain sorghums, corn, soybeans, and cotton. While cattle raising was also important to the county, mineral production was insignificant. Most businesses were concerned with seed, meat and poultry products, feed and grain, and farm machinery. Palo Duro Canyon State Park (see Parks, State) and North Tule Lake were scenic and recreational attractions. The county supported a museum and a hospital and was responsible for the construction of North Tule Lake. Swisher County's 1960 population was 10,607; in 1970 it was 10,373, according to the United States census.

*Swiss Alp, Texas. Swiss Alp, in Fayette County, was the location of Philadelphia Lutheran Church, which was organized in 1867. In 1967 this historic church of the Lutheran Church of America (Texas-Louisiana Synod) united with two neighboring churches: Trinity Lutheran (Black Jack Springs, organized in 1875) and Salem Lutheran (Freyburg, organized in 1869 as a member of the Missouri Synod, disbanded in 1961, and reorganized in 1963). The combined membership of approximately three hundred from these three early Texas-German churches were meeting in 1971 in the Swiss Alp community in the old Philadelphia Lutheran Church, now known as the United Evangelical Lutheran Church. *See also* Romberg, Johannes C.

Swiss in Texas. There were plans for settlement of Swiss in Texas as early as 1819, when a group of Swiss merchants in Philadelphia proposed to settle 10,000 of their countrymen in Texas. Although their plans did not materialize, other Swiss people became interested in the opening of Texas to colonization. In 1821 Louis and Henry Rueg qv moved to Texas and ultimately opened a mercantile business in Nacogdoches. Tadeo Ortiz, a Creole of Guadalajara, Mexico, secured authorization from the new Mexican republic in 1822 to bring European colonists into Coahuila and Texas, with particular attention to the Swiss as well as German, Irish, and Canary Islanders;qv his plan was never realized. Stephen F. Austin, in a June 14, 1830, letter to Thomas F. Leaming, wrote that he was considering the advantages of Swiss and German immigrants because they were opposed to slavery and did not have the Anglo American mania for speculation.

The contributions of Swiss immigrants to the history of the state have been far out of proportion to their relatively small numbers. A group of German-speaking Swiss settled the community of Schoenau, between Shelby and Industry, in Austin County. They built a hall nearby for their "Harmony Verein," where they enjoyed dancing and athletics, and organized a singing society, *Helvetia Schoenau Maennerchor*, in the 1880's. The community disappeared, but the hall was still standing and in use in 1968. The population peak of the Swiss in most Texas areas was reached in the years 1890 to 1910; during this period there were Swiss settlements in Bexar, Dallas, Austin, Fayette, Travis, and Williamson counties. Vernon, in Wilbarger County, was settled by the Swiss in 1893. The 1930 census listed 1,410 persons of Swiss extraction. Craftsmen and tradesmen were predominate in number, and they tended to settle in the urban centers of Galveston, Houston, and Dallas.

Swiss immigrants who have played significant roles in Texas history include Jean Louis Berlandier,qv botanist and zoologist for the Mexican Boundary Commission in 1828; Peter Hunter Fullinwider,qv first Presbyterian missionary to Texas; and John "Dutch John" Wahrenberger,qv an Austin baker who in 1842 was said to have alerted the town's citizenry of the impending removal of the archives of the Republic in the Archive War.qv

Two Swiss military men of whom little has been written were Johann Jacob Rahm and C. Rohrdorf. Johann Jacob Rahm, a Swiss member of John Coffee Hays' qv Texas Rangers,qv was instrumental in persuading Hays to aid Germans of Henri Castro's qv colony who were stranded in San Antonio in the spring of 1844. He also aided Prince Carl of Solms-Braunfels'qv party when the springs and site of New Braunfels were located in 1845 and received an engraved gun from the prince in appreciation. The following year Rahm was killed in New Braunfels in a duel. C. Rohrdorf, a Swiss army colonel with the German Adelsverein, qv was a painter and lithographer who made numerous drawings and paintings of the early German settlements of New Braunfels and Fredericksburg; he was killed in a brief and violent encounter between two German groups contending for the possession of Nassau Farm qv in 1847, and John O. Meusebach qv is said to have bought the art collection left by the artist.

Getulius Kellersberger, brother-in-law of Johannes Romberg,qv came to Texas in the late 1840's,

became an internationally known surveyor and engineer, then returned to Texas to join the Confederacy during the Civil War. After the failure of the French colony of La Reúnion,qv a few Swiss made their homes in Dallas; among them were the naturalist Jacob Boll,qv who returned there from Europe in the 1870's, and Benjamin Lang (or Long, as he came to be known), who was the post-Civil War mayor of Dallas and the United States commissioner for the district. Two Swiss financier-philanthropists, George Henry Hermann qv of Houston and Henry Rosenberg qv of Galveston, made outstanding bequests to their cities. Cesar Maurice Lombardi qv set the editorial pattern for the Dallas *Morning News* qv during the period of his directorship; he was also on the board of directors of the Galveston *News*.qv Jacob Metzger was founder of the Metzger dairies in Dallas, and Edward Walter Eberle,qv a distinguished naval officer from the early 1900's until the beginning of World War I, was responsible for numerous innovations in modern United States naval practices.

BIBLIOGRAPHY: John Paul von Grueningen (ed.), *The Swiss in the United States* (1940); Swiss-American Historical Society, *Prominent Americans of Swiss Origin* (1932); Eloise Santerre, La Reúnion (M.A. thesis, Southern Methodist University, 1936); José María Sánchez (Carlos E. Castañeda, trans.), "A Trip to Texas in 1828," *Southwestern Historical Quarterly*, XXIX (1925–1926); Ralph A. Wooster, "Foreigners in the Principal Towns of Ante-Bellum Texas," *ibid.*, LXVI (1962–1963); Edith Louise Kelly and Mattie Austin Hatcher (eds.), "Tadeo Ortiz de Ayola and the Colonization of Texas, 1822–1833," *ibid.*, XXXII (1928–1929); Oscar Haas, "Early New Braunfels," New Braunfels *Zeitung-Chronicle*, August 2, 1964; Getulius Kellersberger, Experiences During Confederacy, 1861–1865 (MS., Archives, Texas State Library, Austin); Files of the University of Texas Institute of Texan Cultures at San Antonio.

William Field

*Switzer, David S.

*Sycamore, Texas. (Kinney County.)

*Sycamore, Texas. (Wise County.)

*Sycamore Creek.

*Sydnor, John S.

*Sylvan, Texas.

*Sylvester, James Austin.

*Sylvester, Texas.

Symonds, Henry Gardiner. Henry Gardiner Symonds, corporation executive, was born on October 15, 1903, in Pittsburgh, Pennsylvania, the son of Nathaniel G. and Amy Irene (Millberry) Symonds. Reared in Chicago, Symonds received a B.A. degree in geology from Stanford University in 1924 and an M.A. degree in business administration from Harvard in 1927. His business career began with a Chicago bank, but by 1930 Symonds had joined the Chicago Corporation as assistant treasurer, later becoming vice-president, and then moving to Corpus Christi in 1938 to manage the corporation's oil and gas interests there. In 1943 he became president of the newly established Tennessee Gas Transmission Company (renamed Tenneco in 1966) in Houston. Formed to move gas by pipeline from Texas to the northeastern United States during World War II, the company grew in the following years under Symonds' leadership to become an industrial complex of diversified interests reporting assets of over $4 billion in 1970. Major operations of the company in addition to oil and gas included chemicals, packaging, agriculture, and land development. In 1968 Symonds retired as chief executive officer of the company, but remained chairman of the board. Symonds was involved in numerous subsidiaries of Tenneco and other companies, serving either on the board or as an officer of at least a dozen companies and corporations, including General Telephone and Electronics Corporation, Packaging Corporation of America, Carrier Corporation, Philadelphia Life Insurance Company, Southern Pacific Company of San Francisco, and several South American oil companies. He served on the boards of Texas A&M University, the University of Houston, and Rice University. Symonds was counselor to the Stanford Research Institute, vice-chairman of the National Industrial Conference, a member of the Business Advisory Council of the U.S. Department of Commerce, and a member of numerous professional and civic organizations.

Symonds was married to Margaret Clover on August 11, 1928, and they had five children. He died June 1, 1971, in Houston and was buried in Oakbrook, Illinois. Tenneco Foundation in 1971 endowed a $600,000 professorship at Rice University in honor of H. Gardiner Symonds.

BIBLIOGRAPHY: *Who's Who In America* (1960); Biographical File, Barker Texas History Center, University of Texas at Austin.

*Synodical College.

Syrians in Texas. *See* Lebanese-Syrians in Texas.

T

*T Anchor Ranch.

*T Bar Ranch.

*Tabernacle Mountain.

*Tabira Indians.

*Table Gap.

*Table Mountain.

*Table Rock Creek.

*Table Top Mountain.

*Tabor, Texas.

*Tacame Indians. The Tacame (Cacame, Tacamane, Tacone, Tecamene) Indians were Coahuiltecans who in the early eighteenth century ranged over an area near the Gulf Coast between the San Antonio and Nueces rivers. This area apparently included parts of what are now known as Bee, Goliad, Refugio, and San Patricio counties. The Arcahomo of this area seem to have formed one subdivision of the Tacame. The Tacame entered three missions at San Antonio, first San Francisco de la Espada and then San Antonio de Valero and Nuestra Señora de la Purísima Concepción de Acuña.qqv In 1737 about two hundred Tacame at San Francisco de la Espada deserted the mission. Some of these were persuaded to return, but shortly thereafter they left San Francisco de la Espada and took up residence at the other missions. Most of these went to Mission Concepción, where they were reported to be living as late as 1793. The Tacame have been confused with the Thecamon, who, according to records of the La Salle Expedition,qv lived somewhere north or northeast of Matagorda Bay. There is no proof that these names refer to the same people.

BIBLIOGRAPHY: H. E. Bolton, *Texas in the Middle Eighteenth Century* (1915); C. W. Hackett (ed.), *Pichardo's Treatise on the Limits of Louisiana and Texas*, I (1931); F. W. Hodge (ed.), *Handbook of American Indians*, II (1910).

T. N. Campbell

Tackitt, J. Pleasant. J. Pleasant Tackitt (sometimes found as Tackett) was born on April 22, 1803, near Louisville, Kentucky, son of Lewis and Elizabeth (Bashum) Tackitt. He later went to Arkansas where, in 1826, he served as a licensed minister of the Methodist church. In 1835 he married Keziah F. Bruton; they had ten children. While in Arkansas he served as missionary to the Cherokee Indians and postmaster of Pope County; he was elected representative to the Arkansas general assembly in October, 1842.

In the 1850's Tackitt and his family came to Texas, settling first in Collin County and then in Parker County; they moved in 1856 to Young County about eight miles south of Fort Belknap qv near Fish Creek. Tackitt served as minister and county official and did missionary work for the Brazos Indian Reservation.qv Under his leadership the first Methodist church in Young County was established at Fort Belknap in 1858; he founded other churches in Collin and Parker counties. Because of difficulties with the Indians and his defense against them, Tackitt became known as the "fighting parson." Tackitt (or Tackett) Mountain in Young County was named for him in memory of the skirmish there in 1860 between the Tackitt family and a band of Indians led by a Comanche known to the settlers as Piny Chummy (or Pine-O-Channa). During the Civil War he served as chief justice and postmaster in Young County and as enrolling officer in the Confederate Army. In 1882 Tackitt returned to Parker County, where he died on July 2, 1886; he was buried near the Goshen church which he founded, five miles west of Springtown.

BIBLIOGRAPHY: Carrie J. Crouch, *A History of Young*

County, Texas (1956); G. A. Holland, *History of Parker County and The Double Log Cabin* (1937); Barbara Neal Ledbetter, *Civil War Days in Young County, Texas, 1861–1865* (1965); Barbara Neal Ledbetter (comp.), *The Fort Belknap of Yesterday and Today, 1851–1963* (1963); Joseph Carroll McConnell, *The West Texas Frontier* (1933); Rupert Norval Richardson, *The Frontier of Northwest Texas, 1846 to 1876* (1963).

Barbara Neal Ledbetter

*Tacoma, Texas.

Tadiva Indians. The name Tadiva (Tadiua) appears in a single Spanish document written late in the seventeenth century. As it occurs in a list of twenty-one tribes, nineteen of which are clearly Caddoan, it seems likely that Tadiva refers to a small and perhaps peripheral tribe of the southwestern or Hasinai division of Caddo Indians in eastern Texas.

BIBLIOGRAPHY: J. R. Swanton, *Source Material on the History and Ethnology of the Caddo Indians* (1942).

T. N. Campbell

*Tadmore, Texas.

Taensa Indians. The Taensa (Taenso, Tahensa, Takensa, Tenisaw, Tenza, Tinza) Indians were Muskhogean-speaking Indians who originally lived near the Mississippi River in northeastern Louisiana. In the early nineteenth century, after they had moved to southwestern Louisiana, the Taensa petitioned the Spanish government for lands in southeastern Texas. They were granted permission to settle between the Trinity and Sabine rivers, but the move was never made.

BIBLIOGRAPHY: C. E. Castañeda, *Our Catholic Heritage in Texas, 1519–1936*, V (1942); F. W. Hodge (ed.), *Handbook of American Indians*, II (1910); J. R. Swanton, *Indian Tribes of the Lower Mississippi Valley and Adjacent Coast of the Gulf of Mexico* (1911); J. R. Swanton, *The Indian Tribes of North America* (1952).

T. N. Campbell

*Taff, Joseph Alexander.

*Taft, Texas. Taft, in coastal San Patricio County, developed during the 1920's and 1930's from a company town of the Coleman-Fulton Pasture Company qv into a commercial center for growing oil industries and diversified agricultural interests of the surrounding county. The addition of an aluminum industry in the area also stimulated economic growth in the city. Seventy businesses were reported in 1970. Under its aldermanic government, water works improvements were made. A public library and a high school band hall and gymnasium were reconstructed following Hurricane Carla in 1961 (*see* Hurricanes in Texas). During the 1950's Taft's population increased 16 percent, from 2,978 in 1950 to 3,463 in 1960. In 1970 the population was 3,274. *See also* Corpus Christi Standard Metropolitan Statistical Area; Taft Southwest, Texas.

*Taft-Catarina Ranch. *See* Coleman-Fulton Pasture Company.

Taft Southwest, Texas. Taft Southwest, an unincorporated town in eastern San Patricio County, had a 1960 population of 1,927 and a 1970 population of 2,026, according to the United States census. *See also* Taft, Texas.

TAGER. *See* University of Texas at Dallas.

Tahiannihouq Indians. The Tahiannihouq (Tahinnihouq) Indians are known only from the records of the La Salle Expedition qv (1687), in which they are identified as enemies of the Kadohadacho on the Red River. There is no indication of where the Tahiannihouq lived, but it seems likely that their area was north of the Red River and hence outside of present Texas. The Tahiannihouq have been erroneously identified with the Kannehouan who, according to records of the same expedition, lived north or northeast of Matagorda Bay, possibly near the Brazos River.

BIBLIOGRAPHY: F. W. Hodge (ed.), *Handbook of American Indians*, I (1907), II (1910); P. Margry, *Découvertes et établissements des Français dans l'ouest et dans le sud de l'Amérique Septentrionale*, III (1879).

T. N. Campbell

Tahocullake Indians. Tahocullake (Hogologe, Tahogale, Tahogalewi, Tokogalgi) is the name used in Texas for a small group of Yuchi Indians who apparently accompanied the Cherokee to northeastern Texas in the early part of the nineteenth century. The Yuchi originally lived in eastern Tennessee but later also had settlements in Georgia and northern Florida. The few Tahocullake who came to Texas were probably expelled along with the Cherokee in 1839. Yuchi Indians still live in Creek, Okmulgee, and Tulsa counties, Oklahoma, but it is not known if any of these are descendants of the Tahocullake who lived so briefly in Texas.

BIBLIOGRAPHY: F. G. Speck, *Ethnology of the Yuchi Indians* (1909); D. H. Winfrey and J. M. Day (eds.), *The Indian Papers of Texas and the Southwest, 1825–1916*, I (1966).

T. N. Campbell

*Tahoka, Texas. Tahoka, seat of Lynn County, had sixty-eight businesses in 1970, many of them related to the processing, marketing, and shipping of cotton. The town had an airport, a hospital, a newspaper, a city park, a library, and twelve churches. The March livestock show and the September fair draw tourists. The population in 1960 was 3,012; the 1970 population was 2,956, according to the United States census.

*Tahoka Lake.

*Tahuunde Indians.

*Tails Creek.

*Taimamar Indians. This name (shown in Volume II as Taimamare Indians) and eight similar names—Tasmamar, Teimamar, Teneinamar, Tenimama, Ticmamar, Ticmanar, Timamar, and Tumamar—have been recorded for Coahuiltecan bands in Texas and Mexico, much to the confusion of anthropologists, historians, and linguists. The basic facts appear to be as follows. The Bosque-Larios Expedition qv of 1675 entered Texas near Eagle Pass and penetrated the southwestern part of the Edwards Plateau (Maverick, Kinney, and Edwards counties). At one point this expedition encountered

Tenimama (Teneinamar in another version), and at another point they met Teimamar (Taimamar and Tumamar in other versions). Unless the scribe of this expedition was careless, this indicates two separate bands in the area with similar names. In 1683 Teimamar were reported as living much farther west, between Durango, Mexico, and present Presidio, Texas. In 1716 Ticmanar were encountered on the Brazos River of south-central Texas. The mission records compound this confusion. Between 1700 and 1718 Ticmamar were recorded in baptismal documents at San Francisco Solano Mission qv near present Eagle Pass, and both Timamar and Ticmamar were listed in the records of San Antonio de Valero Mission qv at San Antonio (San Francisco Solano was moved to San Antonio in 1718 and renamed San Antonio de Valero). Today it is not possible to determine whether these various names refer to one band, or two, or three, or even nine. J. R. Swanton listed three of these as names for Coahuiltecan bands— Taimamar, Teneinamar, and Tumamar.

BIBLIOGRAPHY: H. E. Bolton, *Texas in the Middle Eighteenth Century* (1915), (ed.), *Spanish Exploration in the Southwest, 1542–1706* (1916); C. W. Hackett (ed.), *Historical Documents Relating to New Mexico, Nueva Vizcaya, and Approaches Thereto, to 1773*, II (1926); F. W. Hodge (ed.), *Handbook of American Indians*, I (1907), II (1910); J. R. Swanton, *Linguistic Material from the Tribes of Southern Texas and Northeastern Mexico* (1940).

T. N. Campbell

*Tait, Charles William.

*Taiton, Texas.

*Tajique Indians.

*Talamantes, Melchor de.

*Talapagueme Indians.

*Talbott Ridge, Texas.

*Talco, Texas. Talco, in Titus County, had a population of 1,024 in 1960 and 837 in 1970, according to the United States census.

*Taliaferro, Robert Hay.

*Talley Mountain.

*Tallichet, Jules Henri.

*Tallow Face Mountain.

*Tally, David.

*Tallys, Texas.

*Talpa, Texas.

*Talpacate Creek.

*Talty, Texas.

*Tama.

*Tama, Texas.

*Tamcan Indians. In the early eighteenth century the Tamcan Indians were reported as living somewhere north of the Rio Grande in the vicinity of present Eagle Pass. Nothing else is known about them. Since the Tamcan were linked with an area dominated by Coahuiltecan groups at that time, J. R. Swanton listed them as Coahuiltecans. H. E. Bolton once suggested that the name Tamcan might be a variant of either Tacame or Tonkawa. The

areas occupied do not coincide, and no specific documentary evidence has been found that will support either identification. Another possibility, also unprovable, is that the Tamcan were the same people as the Tancacoama, who lived in northern Nuevo León in the seventeenth century.

BIBLIOGRAPHY: F. W. Hodge (ed.), *Handbook of American Indians*, II (1910); W. Jiménez Moreno, "Tribus e idiomas del Norte de México," *El Norte de México y el Sur de Estados Unidos* (1944); J. R. Swanton, *Linguistic Material from the Tribes of Southern Texas and Northeastern Mexico* (1940).

T. N. Campbell

*Tamega, Texas.

*Tamina, Texas.

*Tamique Indians. These Coahuiltecan Indians were always closely associated with the Aranama, who in the early eighteenth century lived along the Guadalupe River in the vicinity of present Victoria. In 1726 Nuestra Señora del Espíritu Santo de Zuñiga Mission qv was moved from Matagorda Bay to the lower Guadalupe River for the purpose of Christianizing the Aranama and Tamique. In 1749, when the mission was again moved, this time to the San Antonio River in the vicinity of present Goliad, the Aranama and Tamique moved with it. Unlike the Aranama, the Tamique do not seem to have run away from the mission very often. In 1794, when the Tamique are last mentioned, about twenty-four individuals were still living at Mission Espíritu Santo. In this late missionary report the Tamique are listed as a subdivision of the Aranama, but this is probably the result of Spanish administrative practice. Some writers have suggested that the Tamique and the Tacame were the same people; little evidence can be found to support this identification. Some Tamique entered the San Antonio de Valero Mission qv when it was founded at San Antonio in 1718.

BIBLIOGRAPHY: H. E. Bolton, *Texas in the Middle Eighteenth Century* (1915); J. A. Dabbs, "The Texas Missions in 1785," *Preliminary Studies of the Texas Catholic Historical Society*, III (1940); P. P. Forrestal, "The Solís Diary of 1767," *Preliminary Studies of the Texas Catholic Historical Society*, I (1931); F. W. Hodge (ed.), *Handbook of American Indians*, II (1910).

T. N. Campbell

*Tampico, Texas.

*Tampico Expedition.

*Tancha Bayou.

*Tanglewood, Texas.

Tanima Indians. The Tanima (Danemme, Teneme, Tiniema) Indians, whose name means "liver eaters," were a Comanche band known by this name only after 1800. Although they ranged widely over northern Texas, the Tanima are most frequently linked with the area that lies between the upper Brazos and Red rivers. This area they shared with the Nokoni and Tenawa. Sometimes the Tanima camped with the Penateka, who lived to the south between the Brazos and Colorado rivers. The Tanima and Tenawa were frequently confused by observers who wrote about them, so that today it is not always possible to tell which band is meant.

In fact, some anthropologists think that the two names refer to the same band of Comanche.

BIBLIOGRAPHY: R. N. Richardson, *The Comanche Barrier to South Plains Settlement* (1933); J. R. Swanton, *The Indian Tribes of North America* (1952); E. Wallace and E. A. Hoebel, *The Comanches, Lords of the South Plains* (1952).

T. N. Campbell

*Tank Creek.

*Tankersly, Texas.

*Tankersly Creek.

Tannehill, Jessie C. Jessie C. Tannehill was born on December 30, 1797, in Kentucky; he was married to Jane Richardson in 1823 near Nashville, Tennessee. They came to Texas with their two children in 1827 and settled near Caney in Matagorda County. In the latter part of 1828 or early in 1829 they moved to Bastrop County, locating near the Old San Antonio Road qv at the river crossing; with the pioneer families of Stephen F. Austin's "little colony" they lived for a time in tent structures of pine poles and buffalo skins. After the town of Bastrop was laid out, Jessie Tannehill purchased five acres of land and built one of the first houses there.

Little is known of the family from 1829 to 1836. Tannehill acquired the title of "judge," and records show that on November 7, 1831, he was defeated by one vote for the office of sindico procurador qv by Moses (Mosea) Rousseau. In the early spring of 1836, when invading Mexican forces threatened the settlements along the Colorado, the Tannehills, along with other families, fled in their wagons along the Old San Antonio Road. Afterwards the Tannehills lived in Huntsville, then moved to La Grange, where they purchased property and lived until 1839. The last of their seven children was born there.

Tannehill had secured a headright of 4,428 acres (possibly in the late 1820's) on the Colorado River above Bastrop in what is now Travis County, and in 1836 Captain Robert M. Coleman qv built his stockade outpost on the northern part of the survey. The fort was abandoned in 1838; the next year the Tannehills moved onto their headright and built a two-story home of Bastrop sawmill lumber on a rise overlooking the river valley, using logs from the fort (*see* Fort Colorado) for barns and outbuildings. Although the house was moved two hundred feet north and east of the original site, it was still occupied in 1971.

Jessie Tannehill was active in the land development of Travis County, and with several others he laid out the townsite of Montopolis at about the same time Waterloo was selected as capital of the Republic of Texas. In July, 1839, lots were being sold for the new town, and sites were designated for churches, "seminars of learning," and other public buildings. The town did not develop as expected, and the area reverted to farm land. Tannehill sold the east half of his league in the 1840's, and at his wife's death in 1855 divided his holdings among his children. He probably continued to live in the Fort Prairie settlement outside Austin until his death on March 17, 1863; he was buried in the family burial ground near his home.

BIBLIOGRAPHY: Mary Starr Barkley, *History of Travis County and Austin, 1839–1899* (1963); John Holland Jenkins (John Holmes Jenkins, ed.), *Recollections of Early Texas* (1958); Gerald S. Pierce, *Texas Under Arms* (1969); Noah Smithwick, *The Evolution of a State* (1900); Bastrop *Advertiser* (pubs.), *In the Shadow of the Lost Pines* (1955).

Jack O. Miller

*Tanning Industry. *See* Leather Industry.

*Tanoan Indians.

Tanpachoa Indians. In 1583–1584 the Tanpachoa Indians were reported as living along the Rio Grande near present El Paso. Most writers consider Tanpachoa as an early name for the Manso, who in 1598 occupied the same area. This interpretation is plausible, but the Tanpachoa could have been a local group displaced by Manso invaders. The linguistic affiliation of the Manso is still being debated. Some consider that it was Athapascan (Apache), others Uto-Aztecan.

BIBLIOGRAPHY: J. D. Forbes, "Unknown Athapaskans: The Identification of the Jano, Jocome, Jumano, Manso, Suma, and Other Indian Tribes of the Southwest," *Ethnohistory*, 6 (1959); G. P. Hammond and A. Rey (eds.), *Expedition into New Mexico by Antonio de Espejo, 1582–1583, as Revealed in the Journal of Diego Pérez de Luxán, a Member of the Party* (1929); W. W. Newcomb, Jr., *The Indians of Texas* (1961); C. Sauer, *The Distribution of Aboriginal Tribes and Languages in Northwestern Mexico* (1934).

T. N. Campbell

*Tanpacuaze Indians. The Tanpacuaze (Tampaquash, Tompacua) Indians may have been a group of Pakawa who moved down the Rio Grande from the Eagle Pass area in the middle eighteenth century. Tompacua is recorded as the Comecrudo name for the Pakawa along the lower Rio Grande. As the Spaniards sometimes also referred to the Pakawa as Pinto, further confusion has arisen. Whatever its origin, the name Tanpacuaze is firmly entrenched in historical records as one of many small Coahuiltecan bands in northeastern Mexico and southern Texas. Tompacuas, a former small settlement in Hidalgo County, is evidently linked with the Tanpacuaze. Under the name Tampaquash, they figured in Indian raids on the Brownsville area as late as 1855. The argument of A. S. Gatschet that the Tanpacuaze were Karankawa who fled to Mexico in the middle of the nineteenth century does not appear to be valid, for the Tanpacuaze were mentioned as living near the Rio Grande as early as 1780. So far as is now known, there is no connection between the Tanpacuaze and the Tompacua of Florida.

BIBLIOGRAPHY: A. S. Gatschet, *The Karankawa Indians, the Coast People of Texas* (1891); F. W. Hodge (ed.), *Handbook of American Indians*, II (1910); D. H. Winfrey and J. M. Day (eds.), *The Indian Papers of Texas and the Southwest, 1825–1916*, III (1966).

T. N. Campbell

*Tantabogue Creek.

*Tanyard Branch.

Taos, Texas. *See* Porter's Bluff, Texas.

*Taovaya Indians.

*Tapado Canyon.

Taquitatome Indians. Taquitatome (Cacui-
taome) is said to be an alternate name for the Chizo
Indians who lived in the area covered by northeastern Chihuahua, northwestern Coahuila, and the
lower Big Bend region of Trans-Pecos Texas during
the seventeenth and early eighteenth centuries. See
Chizo Indians.

T. N. Campbell

*Taracone Indians.

*Taraha Indians. The Taraha (Tara, Thara)
Indians are known only from records of the La
Salle Expedition,qv which indicate that these Indians lived southwest of the Hasinai tribes, probably between the Brazos and Trinity rivers. The
Taraha did not live in Arkansas, as some have suggested, because the records clearly show that the
La Salle party visited a large Taraha village shortly
before La Salle was murdered. The linguistic and
cultural affiliations of the Taraha have not been determined. Some writers have called them Caddoan,
others Atakapan, and still others Athapascan.

BIBLIOGRAPHY: I. J. Cox (ed.), *The Journeys of Réné
Robert Cavelier, Sieur de La Salle,* I (1905); C. W.
Hackett (ed.), *Pichardo's Treatise on the Limits of Louisiana and Texas,* I (1931); F. W. Hodge (ed.), *Handbook of American Indians,* II (1910).

T. N. Campbell

*Tarantula.

Tareguano Indians. The Tareguano (Tare-
quano) Indians, a Coahuiltecan band, originally
lived in northeastern Mexico along the present
Tamaulipas-Nuevo León boundary, about halfway
between Cerralvo and Camargo. Although the evidence is not clear, the Tareguano seem to have migrated up the Rio Grande Valley and for a time
lived on the north bank of the river above Laredo.
In the latter part of the eighteenth century most of
the surviving Tareguano entered the mission at
Camargo.

BIBLIOGRAPHY: F. W. Hodge (ed.), *Handbook of
American Indians,* II (1910); W. Jiménez Moreno,
"Tribus e idiomas del Norte de México," *El Norte de
México y el Sur de Estados Unidos* (1944); G. Saldivar,
Los Indios de Tamaulipas (1943); J. R. Swanton, *Lin-
guistic Material from the Tribes of Southern Texas and
Northeastern Mexico* (1940).

T. N. Campbell

*Tariff Policies of the Republic of Texas.

*Tarkington Creek.

Tarkington Prairie, Texas. Tarkington Prairie
was founded by Burton B. Tarkington in 1822 near
the old Nacogdoches-Lynchburg trail in northern
Liberty County. The surrounding land was well
suited for crop and cattle raising, and the group of
settlers soon grew to become a thriving rural community. By the 1860's there was a store-trading
center, a blacksmith shop, a steam mill and gin, a
combination Baptist church-Masonic lodge, and a
post office. Immediately after the Civil War, many
veterans settled in the community, and trail drivers
and shippers of wagon trail goods made Tarkington

Prairie a stop along this major route to the coast.
The post office was abandoned because of the proximity of the larger post office at Cleveland. Today
the old trading center still stands, but the original
cattle trail is covered by pavement.

BIBLIOGRAPHY: Cleveland *Advocate,* November 26,
1936.

Mrs. Ben E. Pickett

*Tarleton, John.

*Tarleton State University. Tarleton State Uni-
versity (formerly Tarleton State College), Stephenville, a part of the Texas A&M University System,qv
grew from an enrollment of 900 in 1950 to 3,027
in the fall of 1972. The curriculum expanded to
include a four-year college program in 1961, with
the first degrees conferred in May, 1963. Degrees
were offered in liberal arts, sciences, general business, education, and general agriculture. Seven
buildings were added to the campus and existing
facilities received extensive remodeling. In 1969 the
library contained 97,000 volumes. W. O. Trogdon
was president in 1974, when the enrollment was
3,026.

*Tarlton, Benjamin Dudley.

*Tarpley, Texas.

*Tarrant, Edward H. Edward H. (possibly for
Hampton) Tarrant, according to information given
on census returns, was born in South Carolina in
1799 (not in North Carolina in 1796, as stated in
Volume II). Tarrant's early life is still not clearly
documented, although it appears that during the
War of 1812 he was living in Muhlenberg County,
Kentucky (not in Tennessee); his service record in
the national archives indicates that he did not leave
Kentucky during his military service, and that he
probably did not serve with General Andrew Jackson at the battle of New Orleans (as stated in
Volume II).

It is not clear when Tarrant left Kentucky, but in
the early 1820's he was in Henry County, Tennessee, where he was elected a colonel of militia in
the new frontier environment. In 1825 he helped
organize the first Masonic lodge in Paris, Tennessee,
and by 1827 he had become sheriff of Henry County.
From 1829 to the early 1830's he was a resident of
Henderson County, Tennessee, before he moved to
Texas, possibly by way of Mississippi. Tarrant apparently established his household of relatives,
hired men, and slaves in Red River County, Texas,
by November 23, 1835; on February 2, 1838,
he received a league and labor of land from the
Republic of Texas as part of a uniform grant made
to all heads of families resident in Texas on March
2, 1836. It is possible that, to complete his move,
Tarrant had returned to the United States during
the period of the Texas Revolution, for there is no
record of his participation in any of the military
events in Texas of that period (as implied in Volume II).

Elected in September, 1837, Tarrant represented
Red River County in the House of Representatives
of the Second Congress until his resignation, dated

December 12, 1837 (not April 9, 1838). Tarrant's last appearance in the House was apparently on November 11, 1837; he had decided that he could better serve the Republic by directing ranger activities against the Indians. Tarrant served as chief justice of Red River County in 1838 after Robert Hamilton qv had been nominated to that post in December, 1836; there is some question as to which of the two men actually served as first chief justice of the county.

Tarrant practiced law, engaged in farming, and took a leading role in the militia's activity against the Indians while he was chief justice; when he resigned from the post on May 30, 1839, he was one of the most prosperous men in Red River County. He was elected by popular vote on November 18, 1839, as commander, carrying the rank of brigadier general, of an organization of northeast Texas defenders known as the Fourth Brigade. His Indian-fighting career was culminated in the May, 1841, battle of Village Creek.qv

In 1847 Tarrant ran for lieutenant governor, but he was defeated by John Alexander Greer.qv He served in the House of Representatives in the Third and Fourth Texas legislatures from 1849 to 1853.

He was married to Mary Danforth on April 6, 1851. They lived on Chambers Creek near Italy, Texas, in Ellis County, but they participated in the social life of Waxahachie. In 1857 Tarrant moved part of his household to Fort Belknap, and when Indian depredations became frequent in that area, he again turned his attention to raising forces against them. While traveling from his home on Chambers Creek to Belknap, Tarrant became ill and died on August 2, 1858, at the home of William Fondren, about ten miles from Weatherford, where he was buried. He was reburied on his farm on Chambers Creek in Ellis County on January 28, 1859, and was buried a third time on March 3, 1928, in Pioneer Rest Cemetery in Fort Worth.

BIBLIOGRAPHY: Robert L. and Pauline H. Jones, "Edward H. Tarrant," *Southwestern Historical Quarterly*, LXIX (1965–1966); Rex Wallace Strickland, "History of Fannin County, Texas, 1836–1843" (Part I), *Southwestern Historical Quarterly*, XXXIII (1929–1930); *ibid*. (Part II), XXXIV (1930–1931); Biographical File, Barker Texas History Center, University of Texas at Austin.

*Tarrant, Texas. (Hopkins County.)

*Tarrant, Texas. (Tarrant County.)

*Tarrant County. Tarrant County, in north-central Texas, was the fourth most populous county in the state in 1970. Over 80 percent of the agricultural income was derived from livestock (both dairy and beef cattle, hogs, and poultry), but oats, cotton, and corn were also important. The county produced over 83 million pounds of milk in 1972 and received much of its farm income from that product. The county seat and largest city was Fort Worth, but several other towns in Tarrant County were growing in size and importance, particularly Arlington. Airplane and helicopter plants accounted for large employment in the county's predominantly urbanized economy. The county is one of the lead-

ing educational centers in Texas, with several colleges and universities. Among the recreational facilities in the area are outstanding art museums, parks, theaters, and a new convention center in Fort Worth. The population of the county was 538,-495 in 1960; in 1970 the population was 716,317, according to the United States census. *See also* Fort Worth Standard Metropolitan Statistical Area.

Tarrant County Junior College District. The Tarrant County Junior College District, Fort Worth, was established by a county vote on July 31, 1965. The school was planned as a multiple-campus institution; three sites were acquired in 1965. The South Campus, a 158-acre tract on which twenty-three buildings valued at $11,000,000 were constructed, opened in September, 1967. The Northeast Campus, a 188-acre tract, began operations in September, 1968. The Northwest Campus, a 150-acre lakeside tract, was to be developed in the mid-1970's. Although each campus was to be limited to 5,000 students, the enrollment for the two operating schools soon exceeded that figure. The South Campus, which had projected a 3,000 student enrollment and a full-time staff of 125 members in September, 1967, had by the fall of 1974 an enrollment of 9,326 students. The Northeast Campus enrolled 9,037 students for the 1974 fall semester. In addition to these regular semester students, each campus also registered non-semester students.

The colleges offer two years' work leading to associate of arts and associate of science degrees; they offer courses in thirteen occupational areas, including electronics, drafting and design, data processing, firefighting, aerospace technology, police science, nursing, and secretarial science. Community service or special courses are given when there is sufficient demand and an available qualified instructor; college credit is not given for these courses. Library holdings for the South Campus and Northeast Campus in 1969 were 20,000 volumes and 12,765 volumes, respectively. Chancellor of the junior college district in 1974–1975 was Joe B. Rushing. During that same term Charles L. McKinney was president of the South Campus and Herman L. Crow succeeded Donald M. Anthony as president of the Northeast Campus.

*Tarrant Field. *See* Carswell Air Force Base.

*Tarver, Benjamin E.

*Tarzan, Texas.

*Tascosa, Texas. The Maverick Boys' Ranch, which was established on the site of Old Tascosa in 1939, was founded by Cal Farley.qv *See also* Cal Farley's Boys Ranch.

*Tascotal Mesa.

*Tate Springs, Texas.

Tatsch, John Peter. John Peter Tatsch, master craftsman of Texas-German furniture, was born on July 26, 1822, in Irmenach, in the forested Hunsrück region of Germany. The son of Peter and Hanna Elisabeth Tatsch, he was married to Maria Elisabeth Tatsch, a distant relative who lived in the adjoining village of Beuern, Germany, on January 26, 1847. In 1852, with their two young daughters, they came to Fredericksburg, Texas; there they had three more children.

In 1857 his limestone house on North Bowie Street, just east of Town Creek, was built by stonemasons, under Tatsch's direction, in the style of the third phase of house building in Fredericksburg (after those of log, then half-timbered *Fachwerk*). Tatsch finished the house with woodwork of his own; he built an inside stairway to the attic, a departure from the usual Fredericksburg house with its characteristic outside stairway. The huge, one-of-a-kind "Dutch" or "milk bottle" chimney at one corner of the kitchen, along with the house itself, has been recorded by the Historic American Buildings Survey of the United States Department of the Interior.

Tatsch crafted smooth doors and intricate wooden latches for the barn. He set up a workshop with a lathe, making bedposts, table legs, chair rungs, and spinning wheel spokes for customers. He made such things as bedsteads and chairs to fit the specifications of the purchaser, and for his own household he devised wire mousetraps, wooden eggs for hens' nests, and a great variety of wooden bowls. His fine, large wardrobes, often with a carved star motif, have become prized among collectors of Texas primitive furniture. He used cherry, oak, and walnut woods, matching the grains, and for his slat-back chairs and rockers he used the hard wood of hackberry. From his cooper's bench he turned out churns, barrels, tubs, and buckets for local use.

Tatsch was a member of the Fredericksburg Workmen's Association, a benevolent organization founded in 1874. During the Civil War he was a member of the local group which organized to protect the area from Indian harassment. In 1892 he was a charter member of Terry Post, No. 64, of the Grand Army of the Republic. John Peter Tatsch died in Fredericksburg on May 1, 1907, and was buried in City Cemetery there. His collection of tools was given by his family to the Kammlah House, the Pioneer Museum in Fredericksburg.

BIBLIOGRAPHY: Gillespie County Historical Society, *Pioneers in God's Hills* (1960); Robert Penniger (ed.), Charles L. Wisseman, Sr. (trans.), *Fredericksburg, Texas: The First Fifty Years* (1971); Fort Worth *Star-Telegram*, October 16, 1960; Files of the University of Texas Institute of Texan Cultures at San Antonio.

*Tatum, Texas.

*Taubenhaus, Jacob Joseph.

†Tavener, Texas.

Tawakoni Crossing. *See* Carvajal Crossing.

*Tawakoni Indians.

Tax, Municipal Sales. *See* Sales Tax, Municipal.

Tax, State Sales. *See* Sales Tax, State.

*Tax Board, State or Intangible.

*Tax Board: To Calculate Ad Valorem Tax Rate.

*Tax Districts, Special.

*Taxation.

*Taxes, Assessment and Collection of. *See also* County and Precinct Officers, Terms of; Sales Tax, Municipal; Sales Tax, State.

*Taxpayers' Convention of 1871.

*Taylor, Bride Neill.

*Taylor, Charles Stanfield.

*Taylor, Creed.

Taylor, Henry Ryder. Henry Ryder Taylor (also found as Ryder-Taylor) was born in Leicester, England, on May 5, 1850, and began his journalistic career with the London *Telegraph* and *All The Year Round*. In 1881 he came to the United States and settled in San Antonio, where he was editor of the Sunday *Mirror*. He lived for about two years in Mexico City where he wrote for *The Two Republics*; he then worked in St. Louis and New York before returning to San Antonio to publish *The Texas Figaro*, a weekly paper devoted to drama, sports, society, and politics. He was one of the first reporters on the San Antonio *Daily Light* (*see* San Antonio *Light*) and was on the news staff of that paper for over twenty years. He wrote poems and was engaged in the publication of the *International Magazine* until a short time before his death.

As a youth in London he knew Charles Dickens and possibly served as the famous author's amanuensis. While living in San Antonio, he was occasionally host to (and perhaps a collaborating writer with) O. Henry (William Sydney Porter qv). In 1924 the Texas Historical and Landmarks Association qv placed a tablet on his house on South Presa Street where O. Henry supposedly worked with Taylor.

Taylor was the author of two books about San Antonio: *History of the Alamo and of the Local Franciscan Missions* (190?) and *Visitors Guide, a Reliable History of the City of San Antonio from Its Foundation in 1689 to Its Present Time* (1902). He died on July 13, 1908, in San Antonio and was buried in the Knights of Pythias Cemetery. Taylor was survived by his wife; accounts vary as to whether he had two or three daughters.

BIBLIOGRAPHY: San Antonio *Express*, July 14, 1908; San Antonio *Light*, July 14, 1908; H. Bailey Carroll, "Texas Collection," *Southwestern Historical Quarterly*, LV (1951–1952).

S. W. Pease

Taylor, James. James Taylor, son of Charles Walter and Effie (McGuyer) Taylor, was born on January 5, 1901, in Rogers, Bell County. After graduating from Rogers High School, he attended North Texas State Normal College (now North Texas State University) in Denton before entering the University of Texas, where he received both B.A. and M.A. degrees in 1927. Taylor remained at the university as an instructor of history until 1928, when he became a faculty member at Stephen

F. Austin State Teachers College (now Stephen F. Austin State University) in Nacogdoches. In 1929 he went to the University of Chicago as a teaching Fellow to do graduate work, but his studies were interrupted by the depression and he returned to Texas after a year. In 1931 he was appointed director of the Department of Social Sciences at Lamar State College of Technology (now Lamar University) in Beaumont. While there he resumed graduate work at the University of Texas and received the Ph.D. degree in 1936. Two years later he joined the faculty at Texas State College for Women (now Texas Woman's University) in Denton, where he remained until the outbreak of World War II.

In July, 1942, he joined the United States Army Air Forces and served as historian for the air units in the Pacific Ocean area during the last two years of the war, after which he was assigned to record the historic atom bomb tests at Bikini Atoll; he accompanied the mission to the Marshall Islands during the summer of 1946. Later in that year he became professor of history at Southwest Texas State Teachers College (later Southwest Texas State College and now Southwest Texas State University) in San Marcos. He was recalled to active duty during the Korean War and served in the publications section of the Department of Defense in Washington from early 1951 until September, 1952. He was co-author of a part of volume five, *The Pacific: Matterhorn to Nagasaki*, in the multi-volume work *The Army Air Forces in World War II* (1953). He returned to Southwest Texas State at San Marcos, and while there he helped organize the Texas Association of College Teachers,qv the most effective voice of faculty opinion in the state, and he became its president in 1953. He was interested in improving the academic competence of students planning to teach history in high schools, and in collaboration with others he helped establish an annual conference sponsored jointly by the Texas Council of the Social Studies and Southwest Texas State Teachers College. Taylor was appointed in 1958 to a visiting professorship at the University of Texas; upon completion of these duties he returned to Southwest Texas State College. In May, 1962, he was honored by the establishment of the James Taylor Lecture, an annual event presented each spring at the college.

Taylor was a member of numerous educational organizations and was a Fellow and member of the executive council of the Texas State Historical Association.qv He was married to Virginia Rogers Hubert on September 5, 1926; they had one child. When this marriage ended in divorce, he married Elizabeth Hindman on July 6, 1943. Taylor died on November 26, 1962, and was buried in the San Marcos City Cemetery.

Emmie Craddock

Taylor, James R. James R. Taylor, born about 1838, was educated at Larissa College in Cherokee County, Texas. He enlisted in the Confederate Army at Larissa on February 15, 1862, and was elected a captain in the 17th Texas Cavalry. When the regiment was reorganized at Little Rock, Arkansas, on May 22, he was elected colonel. He was captured with most of his regiment at Arkansas Post on January 11, 1863, and was exchanged at City Point, Virginia, in April of that same year. He then returned to the Trans-Mississippi Department where he collected men from the regiments captured at Arkansas Post to be organized as the 17th Texas Consolidated Dismounted Cavalry. The new regiment, in the fall of 1863, was attached to Polignac's Brigade qv of Texas infantry, and served throughout the remainder of the war in Louisiana, Arkansas, and Texas. Taylor was killed while acting as brigade commander at the battle of Mansfield, Louisiana, on April 8, 1864, during the Red River campaign.qv

BIBLIOGRAPHY: Alwyn Barr, *Polignac's Texas Brigade* (1964); Marcus J. Wright (comp.) and Harold B. Simpson (ed.), *Texas In The War 1861–1865* (1965); Service Records of J. R. Taylor (Civil War Biographical File, Archives, University of Texas at Austin Library, originals in National Archives, Washington, D.C.).

*Taylor, John D.

*Taylor, Joseph J.

*Taylor, M. D. K.

*Taylor, Robert H. Robert H. Taylor was an unsuccessful candidate for lieutenant governor as a Republican in 1873. He died on May 10, 1889 (not 1888, as stated in Volume II), in Bonham.

BIBLIOGRAPHY: Paul D. Casdorph, *A History of the Republican Party in Texas, 1865–1965* (1965); Dallas Morning News, May 11, 1889.

Taylor, Thomas Hendricks. Thomas Hendricks Taylor was born on July 5, 1885, at May, Brown County, the only son of Henry Percy and Frances Miranda (Lester) Taylor. He attended a local country school and the preparatory department of Howard Payne College in Brownwood. He later entered Baylor University, where he earned a B.A. degree in 1907; in 1920 he received an M.A. degree from the same university.

He began teaching at Howard Payne College in September, 1907, and remained there for forty-eight years. When Howard Payne assumed senior college status in 1913, Taylor became registrar, a position he held for three years. He became dean of the institution in 1916 and served in that capacity until October, 1929, when the board of trustees elected him president of the college.

During the twenty-six years of his tenure as president, capital funds for the school's endowment increased from thirty thousand dollars in 1929 to two and one-half million dollars in 1955, and property holdings grew from seven acres to nearly four hundred acres. During the same period the school was approved by state, regional, and national accrediting agencies. After his retirement in 1955, he compiled eighteen bound volumes of manuscript materials on Central Texas Baptist history and on Howard Payne College.

Taylor served as county chairman of the Democratic party in Brown County from 1920 to 1961 and was a member of the Baptist church. He was a member of the Texas Board of Public Welfare from 1940 to 1947. Taylor was married to Myrtle E. Evans on June 16, 1907; they had five children. He died on December 5, 1961, and was buried in Eastlawn Memorial Park at Brownwood.

T. R. Havins

Taylor, Thomas Jefferson, II. Thomas Jefferson Taylor II was born on August 29, 1874, in Autauga County, Alabama. He migrated to Texas in the mid-1890's, settling in Karnack, Harrison County. Taylor prospered as a merchant and owner of extensive farm lands. He married Minnie Lee Patillo of Alabama in 1900. They had two sons and a daughter, Claudia Alta, who married Lyndon Baines Johnson,qv thirty-sixth president of the United States. In 1934 Taylor donated to the state about two-thirds of the land composing Caddo Lake State Park (*see* Parks, State). He died on October 25, 1960, and was buried at Marshall, Texas.

*Taylor, Thomas Ulvan.

*Taylor, William S.

*Taylor, Zachary.

*Taylor, Texas.** Taylor, in southeastern Williamson County, is a center for agriculture and small industry. In the 1970's there were over two hundred businesses in Taylor, among which were a bedding factory, an iron foundry and machine shop, several mills, meat and poultry plants, and two large furniture manufacturing companies. A new library was built in 1960. The population in 1960 was 9,434; the 1970 population was 9,616, according to the United States census.

*Taylor, Bastrop, and Houston Railway Company.

*Taylor Bayou.

*Taylor Bayou, Texas.

*Taylor County.** Taylor County, rural except for the urban area around Abilene, has an economy based on agriculture, industrial manufacturing, petroleum, and banking and finance; an important addition to the economy was Dyess Air Force Base,qv which was completed in 1956. Abilene State Park (*see* Parks, State), situated in the southern part of the county, and Abilene, Kirby, and Fort Phantom Hill lakes are major tourist attractions. Located in Abilene are Abilene Christian College, McMurry College, Hardin-Simmons University, Abilene State School qqv (mental health center), West Texas Rehabilitation Center, a community theater, an orchestra, a fine arts museum, and a children's home. The population of Taylor County in 1960 was 101,078, a 59 percent increase over the 1950 figure of 63,370; however, the population in 1970 had declined to 97,853, a 3.2 percent decrease, according to the United States census. *See also* Abilene Standard Metropolitan Statistical Area.

*Taylor Creek.

*Taylor Hills.

Taylor Lake Village, Texas. Taylor Lake Village, in southeastern Harris County, was incorporated in December, 1961, and had a mayor-aldermanic form of city government. A residential community, Taylor Lake Village had no business concerns within the incorporated limits of the town. Businesses in the area influencing the local economy were NASA qv and its supporting industries. Although the town was not included as an incorporated municipality in the United States census report for 1970, Taylor Lake Village was listed as incorporated, with a population of 650, in the Texas Municipal League's qv report for 1973. *See also* Houston Standard Metropolitan Statistical Area.

*Taylor-Sutton Feud.** *See* Sutton-Taylor Feud.

*Taylors Bayou.

Taylor's Trail. Taylor's Trail, the route taken by General Zachary Taylor's qv army of occupation from the Nueces River to the Rio Grande during the Mexican War,qv was one of the most important paths of conquest used by an American army on American soil. Composed of nearly four thousand troops, Taylor's army marched 174 miles in twenty days during March, 1846, along a route from Corpus Christi to the bank of the Rio Grande opposite Matamoros.

Two possible routes had been reconnoitered and determined practicable for the advance of Taylor's army: one route coursed the entire length of Padre Island; the other route followed the coastline on the mainland to the Rio Grande. After receiving orders to advance on February 4, 1846, Taylor chose to take the mainland route. On March 4, 1846, a vanguard of sixty men under Major William Graham was dispatched to the crossing on Santa Gertrudis Creek to establish a supply depot for the main army which would follow.

On March 8, 1846, Taylor issued orders for the army of occupation to advance to the Rio Grande. The army was organized into an advance guard and three brigades for purposes of marching, convenience of camp, supply, and mutual support in case of hostilities. The advance unit, composed of the 2nd regiment of dragoons and a battery of artillery under the command of Colonel David E. Twiggs,qv left Corpus Christi on March 8, 1846. The three brigades, each followed by its own baggage and supply train, left successively at one-day intervals: the first brigade, under command of Brevet Brigadier General William Jenkins Worth,qv started on March 9; the second brigade, under Colonel James S. McIntosh, departed on March 10; the third brigade, under Colonel William Whistler, left on March 11. The main supply train of more than three hundred wagons drawn by oxen and mules followed the last column. Taylor and his staff, who planned to overtake the advance guard by the time it reached the Arroyo Colorado, were the last to leave.

The first leg of Taylor's Trail from Corpus Christi was up the Nueces River for sixteen miles; thence almost due west to Agua Dulce Creek; then south past Los Pintos, San Fernando Creek, Santa Gertrudis Creek, Escondido Creek, Los Belladeros, Santa Clara Motte, Bobido Creek, Santa Rosa Ponds, El Sauz, Paso Real, and on to the bank of the Rio Grande opposite Matamoros. The trail passed through present Nueces, Kleberg, Kenedy, Willacy, and Cameron counties.

Taylor's Trail continued to be used for many years as the main route for the stage lines which ran from San Antonio and Corpus Christi to Brownsville. A monument to mark the starting point of the trail was erected in Corpus Christi in 1934; another monument to mark a camp site on the trail was erected in 1936 about seven miles south of Sarita, Kenedy County. After Taylor crossed the Arroyo Colorado (in Cameron County near present-day Harlingen) on March 20, 1846, the Paso Real Crossing there became known also as General Taylor's Crossing.

BIBLIOGRAPHY: W. S. Henry, *Campaign Sketches of the War with Mexico* (1847); Edward J. Nichols, *Zach Taylor's Little Army* (1963); *Monuments Erected . . . to Commemorate the Centenary of Texas Independence* (1939); Robert H. Thonhoff, "Taylor's Trail in Texas," *Southwestern Historical Quarterly*, LXX (1966–1967).

Robert H. Thonhoff

*Taylorsville, Texas.

*Taylorville, Texas.

*Taza, Texas.

*Tazewell, Texas.

*Taztasagonie Indians.

Tchanhié Indians. The Tchanhié Indians are known only from records (1687) of the La Salle Expedition,qv which merely identify these Indians as enemies of the Kadohadacho on the Red River in extreme northeastern Texas. It is not known whether they lived in Texas or in adjoining parts of Oklahoma, Arkansas, or Louisiana. Their affiliations have yet to be determined.

BIBLIOGRAPHY: P. Margry, *Découvertes et établissements des Français dans l'ouest et dans le sud de l'Amérique Septentrionale*, III (1879).

T. N. Campbell

*Teacher Retirement System of Texas. In 1970 the state board of trustees to administer the teacher retirement system of Texas numbered seven members. One member was appointed by the State Board of Education,qv three members were appointed by the governor, and three teacher members were appointed by the governor after being nominated by popular ballot of the members of the retirement system.

In addition to providing a retirement fund for teachers, the retirement system provides disability benefits and death or survivor benefits. In 1970 about 27,000 monthly payments were made to annuitants and about 247,000 accounts were credited with deposits each month. There is an investment advisory committee to assist with management of the system funds, and an independent investment counsel is available for investment consulting. By law half of the funds must be invested in government and municipal bonds, and the rest may be invested in corporate stocks and bonds. Assets exceeded $1.3 billion, while actuarial liabilities were more than $2 billion. The actuarial deficit reflects the assumption of liabilities for benefits based on service prior to inception of the system and the first eighteen years of operation when member contributions were limited by law to $180 each year, but the deficit was gradually being reduced.

BIBLIOGRAPHY: University of Texas at Austin, *Guide To Texas State Agencies* (1970).

*Teachers Colleges. *See* State Teachers Colleges.

*Teacup, Texas.

Teagarden, Weldon Leo (Jack). Weldon Leo Teagarden, known as Jack Teagarden, was born in Vernon, Texas, on August 20, 1905, to Charles and Helen (Geingar) Teagarden. Part of a musical family, he started playing the trombone at age seven and was almost entirely self-taught, developing a technique of using his lips to form low notes because he could not extend the slide its full distance. This technique became a habit and a part of his style in later years. When he was fifteen he performed with an uncle's band in San Angelo. During 1921–1922 he played in the band of pianist Peck Kelley, and for a time thereafter he had his own band in Kansas City; he went to New York in 1927, making his debut as a vocalist the next year with Eddie Condon's "Makin' Friends." During the 1928–1933 period he worked with the Ben Pollack and Mal Hallett bands, and from 1934 to late 1938 he was a member of the Paul Whiteman orchestra.

From January, 1939, until early 1947 he toured with his own band; later in 1947 he joined Louis Armstrong's group, remaining until near the end of 1951. Subsequently, he formed a small band which toured widely in the United States, in Europe in 1957, and on a state department visit to the Far East from September, 1958, to January, 1959.

Teagarden appeared in the movies *Birth of the Blues*, *The Glass Wall*, and *Jazz on a Summer's Day*. He was an admired recording artist, being featured on RCA Victor, Columbia, Decca, Capitol, and MGM discs. As a jazz artist he won the 1944 *Esquire* magazine Gold Award, was highly rated in the Metronome polls of 1937–1942 and 1945, and was selected for the *Playboy* magazine All Star Band, 1957–1960. Teagarden was the featured performer at the Newport Jazz Festival of 1957. *Saturday Review* wrote that he "walked with artistic dignity all his life," and *Newsweek* praised his "mature approach to trombone jazz." It was claimed that he was the first white man to play and convey the blues.

Teagarden was married first to Ora Binyon in San Angelo, Texas, in 1923; they had two sons before they were divorced. In the 1930's he was married to and divorced from, successively, Clare Manzi of New York City and Edna "Billie" Coats. His fourth marriage was to Mrs. Adeline Barriere Gault in September, 1942; they had one son. Teagarden died in New Orleans on January 15, 1964, and was buried in Forrest Memorial Park, Hollywood, California.

BIBLIOGRAPHY: Jay D. Smith and Len Guttridge, *Jack Teagarden: The Story of a Jazz Maverick* (1960); *The New Edition of the Encyclopedia of Jazz* (1960); *Who's Who In America* (1962); *Music* (January 24, 1964); *Saturday Review* (March 14, 1964); *Newsweek* (January 27, 1964); Dallas *Times Herald*, January 16, 1964.

Clay Bailey

*Teague, Texas. Teague, in southwest Freestone County, is a railroad division point and commercial center for parts of Freestone and Limestone counties. A modern brick company was built and a fourteen-acre incorporated industrial foundation was established in the town in the 1960's. In 1970 sixty-five businesses were reported. There were also a park, a twenty-three-bed hospital, and a nursing home located at Teague. The population in 1960 was 2,728; the 1970 population was 2,867, according to the United States census.

*Teal, Henry.

Teaname Indians. The Teaname (Teana, Peana) Indians were one of numerous Coahuiltecan bands of the late seventeenth and early eighteenth centuries that lived in northeastern Coahuila but also ranged north of the Rio Grande, particularly in the southwestern part of the Edwards Plateau (Kinney County and vicinity). In 1708 they were mentioned in the records of Mission San Juan Bautista qv near Eagle Pass. Later some of the Teaname seem to have been at San Antonio de Valero Mission qv in San Antonio, where they were known as Peana. The Anna, reported in the early eighteenth century as living somewhere in southern Texas, may be the Teaname under another name.

BIBLIOGRAPHY: V. Alessio Robles, *Coahuila y Texas en la Epoca Colonial* (1938); F. W. Hodge (ed.), *Handbook of American Indians*, II (1910).

T. N. Campbell

Teanda Indians. In 1683–1684 Juan Domínguez de Mendoza qv led an exploratory expedition from El Paso as far eastward as the junction of the Concho and Colorado rivers east of present San Angelo. In his itinerary he listed the names of thirty-seven Indian groups, including the Teanda, from which he expected to receive delegations on the Colorado River. Nothing further is known about the Teanda, who seem to have been one of many Indian groups of north-central Texas that were swept away by the southward thrust of the Lipan-Apache and Comanche Indians in the eighteenth century.

BIBLIOGRAPHY: H. E. Bolton (ed.), *Spanish Exploration in the Southwest, 1542–1706* (1916); C. W. Hackett (ed.), *Pichardo's Treatise on the Limits of Louisiana and Texas*, II (1934).

T. N. Campbell

Teaselville, Texas. Teaselville was founded about 1850 just east of the Neches Saline, a natural salt flat in southwest Smith County. The Cherokee Indians worked the salt marsh in the early 1800's, and in 1839, during the Cherokee War, qv Texas troops camped about one-half mile north of the community. The campsite bears a historical marker. In the 1960's about fifty farmers and ranchers lived in the area. *See also* Tyler Standard Metropolitan Statistical Area.

*Tebo Bayou.

*Tecahuiste Indians.

*Teci, Texas.

*Teck, Texas.

*Tecolote Creek.

Tecolote Indians. The Tecolote (Spanish for "owl") Indians are known from the middle eighteenth century, when they were reported as living in settlements with other Indians along the lower Conchos River south of present Presidio. One Spanish source seems to link the Tecolote with the Otomoaco of the late sixteenth century. If this interpretation is correct, then the Tecolote can be considered as a remnant of the agricultural branch of the Jumano, sometimes referred to as Patarabueye.

BIBLIOGRAPHY: J. C. Kelley, "Factors Involved in the Abandonment of Certain Peripheral Southwestern Settlements," *American Anthropologist*, LIV (1952); J. C. Kelley, "The Historic Indian Pueblos of La Junta de los Rios," *New Mexico Historical Review*, XXVII (1952), XXVIII (1953).

T. N. Campbell

*Tecoyos Creek.

*Tecula, Texas.

*Tecumseh, Texas.

*Tecumseh Peak.

*Tee Pee City, Texas.

*Teel, George.

Teel, Trevanion Theodore. Trevanion Theodore Teel, son of Benjamin Van der Mark and Ann Gilmore (Weir) Teel, was born in Pittsburgh, Pennsylvania, on August 18, 1824. His father, a physician, moved his family to Rushville, Illinois, in 1828, to Lexington, Tennessee, in 1830, back to Rushville in 1833, and to Weston, Missouri, in 1839. Trevanion Teel received a license to practice law in Platte City, Missouri, in 1841. In 1843 he moved to Saint Joseph, Missouri, where he joined an American Fur Company expedition into the Rocky Mountains. In 1844 he was employed by a mercantile company in Evansville, Indiana.

At the outbreak of the Mexican War Teel joined the 2nd Indiana Volunteer Regiment. He was subsequently elected first lieutenant of his company and served with distinction in the battle of Buena Vista. After his discharge from the army in 1847 he settled in Saltillo, Coahuila, where his father was practicing medicine, but in 1848 the family moved to San Antonio for one month, then to Lockhart, Texas, where Teel opened a law office. In 1851 he married Emily Winans, of Bastrop. In 1856 he moved to San Antonio, where, in January, 1861, he organized Teel's Battery of light artillery. He was ordered to occupy Fort Bliss qv with John Salmon Ford, qv and from El Paso he joined Henry Hopkins Sibley's qv New Mexico campaign. His battery played an important part in the battle of Valverde, and Teel was promoted to the rank of major for distinguishing himself in that fight. When Sibley retreated from New Mexico, Teel buried eight of the Confederate cannon near the plaza in Albuquerque. In 1889 he supervised the excavation of these guns.

After the Civil War Teel became a prominent criminal lawyer in South and West Texas. In 1892 he claimed to have defended more than seven hundred clients charged with capital offenses, with not one executed, and not more than twenty convicted. He died in El Paso on July 6, 1899, and was buried in the Odd Fellows Cemetery in San Antonio.

BIBLIOGRAPHY: L. E. Daniell, *Personnel of the Texas State Government* (1892); Martin H. Hall, *Sibley's New Mexico Campaign* (1960).

*Teepee Creek.

*Tehauremet Indians.

*Tehuacana, Texas.

*Tehuacana Academy.

*Tehuacana Creek.

*Tehuacana Creek Councils.

*Tehuacana Hills.

Teich, Frank. Frank Teich, born in Lobenstein, Germany, on September 22, 1856, was the son of the poet Frederick Teich and Catherine (Horn) Teich. At the age of eight he began painting, and after his graduation from the University of Nuremberg he was apprenticed to the German sculptor Johannes Schilling; he probably worked on the German national monument, *The Watch on the Rhine*. He then studied a year under the Franciscan Brothers at Deddelbach am Main.

Teich immigrated to the United States in 1878 and traveled in Illinois, Michigan, Wisconsin, Missouri, and California. In Chicago in 1879 he contributed to the stone carving on the Cook County courthouse. By 1883 he was in Texas, locating first in San Antonio but working on different projects across the state. Teich worked under Gustav Wilke, superintending the granite cutters and inspecting the granite used in the state capitol qv building at Austin, and he also worked on the Tarrant County courthouse. In San Antonio in 1885 Teich opened a marble yard on the present site of the Medical Arts building, across from the Alamo, and worked on the construction of several buildings in the city, including the city hall and the Kampman building. Shortly afterwards, for health reasons, Teich left San Antonio for the hills around Fredericksburg. In Llano County Teich discovered a granite deposit and opened a quarry, but he soon left to spend time in Europe gathering ideas. He returned around 1901 and opened Teich Monumental Works two miles from Llano.

Teich was responsible for, or worked on, many monuments throughout Texas and other states, many of them Confederate monuments in the southern states. He completed the Confederate monument and the Fireman's monument on the capitol grounds at Austin, the Sam Houston monument in Houston, the Luther Memorial Church in Orange, the statue "Grief" over the grave of Will Scott Youree in the Scottsville cemetery near Marshall, a carved Italian marble altar in a Durango, Mexico, church, the Governor Pease monument in Austin, and two Confederate statues in Dallas. He did much work in the San Antonio area, including the Mahncke Memorial in Brackenridge Park and the altar in St. Mary's Church. He was the sculptor of the bronze statue of La Salle qv in Navasota and the monument to Shanghai Pierce qv near Blessing, Texas. Teich was in an indirect way responsible for bringing the sculptor Pompeo Coppini qv to Texas.

Frank Teich married Elvina Lang of San Antonio on October 12, 1887; they had three daughters. He died January 27, 1939, in Llano and was buried there. He has been called the father of the granite industry of Texas.

BIBLIOGRAPHY: Esse Forrester-O'Brien, *Art and Artists of Texas* (1935); Clarence R. Wharton, *Texas Under Many Flags*, IV (1930); *San Antonio Express*, March 31, 1937, January 28, 1939; Witte Memorial Museum Files, San Antonio, Texas.

*Teichmueller, Hans.

*Tejas, Presidio of. *See* Nuestra Señora de los Dolores de los Tejas Presidio.

*Tejas Indians. No single tribe of Indians called themselves Tejas, but the Caddoan tribes of East Texas used the word generally to refer to the allied tribes of their confederacy. *See also* Texas, Origin of Name.

*Tejon, Texas.

Tejón Indians. The Tejón (Texón) Indians, a Coahuiltecan band (whose name is Spanish for "badger"), lived along the south bank of the Rio Grande in the vicinity of Reynosa, Tamaulipas, when it was founded in the middle of the eighteenth century. It seems reasonable to conclude that the Tejón ranged along both sides of the river (a former railroad stop near Brownsville was known as Tejón). After Reynosa was settled, some Tejón moved to the Río San Juan about twenty-five miles from Camargo, where they remained until after 1800. Along with other Coahuiltecan bands on the lower Rio Grande, the Tejón were sometimes referred to as Carrizo. In 1886 a group of Carrizo, apparently including a few Tejón, was living near Charco Escondido about twenty miles south of Reynosa, and as late as 1907 some Tejón still lived near Reynosa at a community known as Las Prietas.

BIBLIOGRAPHY: E. A. Cervantes, *Documentos relativos a la Villa de Cinco Señores, capital de Nuevo Santander, hoy Jimenez, Tamaulipas* (1942); F. W. Hodge (ed.), *Handbook of American Indians*, II (1910); A. Prieto, *Historia, geografía y estadística del estado de Tamaulipas* (1878); G. Saldivar, *Los Indios de Tamaulipas* (1943); R. C. Troike, "Notes on Coahuiltecan Ethnography," *Bulletin of the Texas Archeological Society*, 32 (1962).

T. N. Campbell

*Tejones Creek.

*Tektites in Texas.

*Telamene Indians.

*Telegraph, Texas.

*Telegraph Service in Texas. Since 1943 Western Union has remained the only telegraph company in Texas. Since then, advances have made it one of the most modern telecommunications companies in the world. In the early 1960's ten major Texas cities and their surrounding communities were served by Western Union Telex, a direct-dial teleprinter exchange service which establishes automatic connections between subscribers in eight seconds or less, regardless of distance. A large number of additional Texas cities were added to the Telex network in 1966 and 1967. Telex subscribers throughout the state can have record and data communications with other subscribers throughout the United States and in a hundred other countries around the world through the international carriers.

Western Union's broadband exchange service allows subscribers to select broadband channels by pushbutton telephone for the automatic exchange of data, facsimile, and voice communications. Inaugurated in the fall of 1964, broadband exchange service initially was available in the Dallas and Houston areas for broadband connections to subscribers in twenty-three other large cities from coast to coast.

Also in the fall of 1964, Western Union inaugurated its new $80 million transcontinental microwave network with a main trunk running into Texas. The new system, of advanced design, was capable of handling all forms of electronic communication, including high-speed facsimile, data, telegraph, voice, and Telex services. Designed total capacity of the microwave beam system was approximately 7,000 voice channels. It was initially equipped to provide 600 voice bands which would add a basic capacity of more than 80 million telegraph channel miles, or more than fifteen times the company's existing channel mileage.

On February 9, 1972, the Western Union telegraph office at Marshall, the first telegraph office in Texas (since February 14, 1854), was closed. This was representative of the fact that Western Union was closing many small local offices around the country.

L. R. *Wilcox*

*Telegraph and Texas Register.

*Telephone, Texas.

*Telephone Service in Texas. [There have been some claims that Colonel A. H. Belo,qv of Galveston, did not have the first telephone installed in Texas (on March 18, 1878, as stated in Volume II); those who claim that it was George Washington Brackenridge,qv of San Antonio, who installed the first telephone, cite a newspaper article (San Antonio *Daily Express*, June 11, 1893) in which Brackenridge is quoted as saying, "I cannot give the exact date of the establishment of the line, but it was *about* twenty years ago." (If it had been exactly twenty years previously, or 1873, that date would have been three years prior to the 1876 date officially designated for the invention of the telephone by Alexander Graham Bell.) In the newspaper article Brackenridge says, "the wire was strung on poles from the bank to my residence, the route being by way of the government buildings. The first method of communication used was *Gray's printing telegraph*, which I think is still in use in some parts of the country. This system had at that time just been invented and it worked very successfully. The message was received in *printed* form and the line was easily operated." (All italics added.) Brackenridge goes on to say that it was sometime later that he installed a pair of receivers, "both to talk into and hear through," but he does not pinpoint the date. He concludes by saying that "the original line to my residence was replaced by a new and more direct one in 1877." It is not the intention here to support any particular claim for the installation of the first telephone in Texas, but from Brackenridge's own statement, it is obvious that he was using a printed message system on his first line, not a talking system; but it is also possible that he was using a talking system by 1877, although the evidence, being a reminiscence many years later, is not conclusive. Possibly other documents in the files of the First National Bank in San Antonio would better substantiate this claim. Ed.]

Telephone service in Texas increased rapidly after World War II. By 1955, 311 telephone companies operated in Texas, and the total number of telephones in the state had increased to 2,398,521 (all figures here include main line telephones and do not include extension telephones). On May 7, 1955, the two-millionth telephone was installed in Texas in the governor's office at Austin. In that year Texas ranked seventh in the nation in number of telephones. Southwestern Bell Telephone Company inaugurated direct distance dialing in Harlingen in 1955, and by 1963 Texas had more than 550,000 telephones on the direct distance dialing network.

On January 1, 1971, Texas had 6,266,000 telephones, operated through 108 companies. By December 31, 1972, that figure had increased to 7,058,993 telephones, served by ninety-eight companies. In that year Texans served by Southwestern Bell Telephone Company—the largest company in the state—made a daily average of 35,221,822 local and long distance calls. Houston, with 1,369,069, had the largest number of telephones of any metropolitan area in Texas. By January 1, 1975, there were 7,747,100 telephones in the state, and more than 90 percent of the telephones were on direct distance dialing. Of the ninety-six companies operating, ninety were members of the Texas Telephone Association, including Southwestern Bell Telephone Company and Mountain Bell Telephone Company in El Paso County.

BIBLIOGRAPHY: *Texas Almanac* (1955, 1963, 1971, 1973).

Television in Texas. The first television station in Texas, WBAP-TV, Fort Worth, began operating on September 27, 1947. By 1950 six stations were in operation in Texas, with three in the Dallas-Fort Worth area, two in San Antonio, and one in Houston. The rapid growth of television in its early stages prompted the Federal Communications Commission to bring all television construction to a halt in the summer of 1950 in order to allow a long-range analysis of the industry, upon which channel allocations and technical specifications could be based. At the time of the freeze only the six mentioned above were in existence. The ban was lifted in 1952, and other stations around the state soon began operations.

In the early 1950's the San Antonio and Fort Worth stations changed from kineoscope programming to broadcasting live programs by use of the coaxial cable. In 1953 four major television networks served Texas—American Broadcasting Company (ABC), Columbia Broadcasting System (CBS), National Broadcasting Company (NBC), and Dumont. In that year, network broadcasting was made possible across the state through use of facilities of the Bell Telephone System, which had invested $10 million in Texas television cables and microwave relay stations. By 1973 ABC, CBS, and NBC were the major television networks, while Dumont was no longer a principal network; the Hughes Sports Network was operating in Texas, while the Westinghouse Network (not truly a network, but a program supplier) ran special dramatic programs and documentaries. Beginning in 1954 the Spanish International Network began Spanish language television programs for the Spanish-speaking population in the El Paso-Juarez, Mexico, area. The following year San Antonio joined the network; Laredo-Nuevo Laredo, Mexico, joined in 1962, and Lubbock was added in 1970.

As an example of the early economic value of commercial television stations in Texas, in 1953 the hourly rate for television time on KRLD-TV in Dallas was $750; by 1968 the rate was $2,300 per hour. Rates varied around the state, with some of the smaller stations charging $300 per hour, but rates were increased by the 1970's. Over a period of twenty-five years the number of stations steadily increased, particularly in the larger metropolitan areas such as Houston and Dallas-Fort Worth, but some of the stations in less populated areas went out of business for lack of supporting revenue. As of September 6, 1973, there were forty-seven major television stations and five satellite television stations in Texas, for a total of fifty-two stations. A satellite station is one that is a sister-subordinate to a major station, carrying programs from the major station, but also carrying some local programs and advertising.

The first educational television in the nation was KUHT, Houston, established in 1953. Others followed in Texas during the 1960's, so that by 1973 there were the following additional educational stations in the state: KLRN, Austin-San Antonio; KERA, Dallas; KTXT, Lubbock; KNCT, Killeen; KEDT, Corpus Christi (the latter two connected with KLRN, Austin-San Antonio); and KAMU, College Station. These stations, in addition to providing locally produced programs, were connected with Educational Television (ETV), later known as National Educational Television (NET), and in 1970 as Public Broadcasting System (PBS).

In 1966 the Texas legislature provided financial aid to school districts for student ETV services, as did the National Defense Education Act (NDEA). The Educational Television Facilities Act and the Elementary and Secondary Education Act provided financial aid for purchase of broadcasting equipment.

The nation's first closed circuit television for university level classroom instruction was Texas Educational Media Program (TEMP), originally called Texas Educational Microwave Project, and was operated by the University of Texas at Austin Communication Center. Plans for the project began in 1957, and the unique transmitting equipment was designed and built by Collins Radio of Dallas and bears serial number one. TEMP covers over a seventy-mile path from Austin to San Antonio. When the system began operation it served Southwestern University in Georgetown; Texas Lutheran College in Seguin; Incarnate Word College, San Antonio College, Trinity University, St. Mary's University, and Our Lady of the Lake College in San Antonio; Southwest Texas State University in San Marcos; and the University of Texas, Huston-Tillotson College, and St. Edward's University in Austin. By 1972 the first three schools were no longer a part of the inter-college network. The program subjects, designed to supplement college studies, varied widely. Approximately fifteen courses were presented in 1971, with foreign language instruction the most popular among member schools. A two-year (1971–1973) Moody Foundation grant of $62,195 underwrote the TEMP service to the five private colleges and three public universities and colleges.

Since the end of World War II the mushrooming expansion of the television industry has affected the Texas economy in the manufacturing of parts, servicing of television sets, and construction of television stations; operation of the medium has steadily increased the demand for technical and studio personnel.

Telfener, Joseph. Joseph Telfener, an Italian count for whom Telferner, Texas, was named (although incorrectly spelled), became interested in railroad construction in Texas and was instrumental in forming a corporation called the New York, Texas, and Mexican Railway Company.qv Telfener was a well known and influential European financier who was married to an American, Ada Hungerford, on March 15, 1879, in Rome, Italy; they had four children. It was probably through his father-in-law, Colonel Daniel E. Hungerford (see Hungerford, Texas), that Telfener became interested in railroad construction in Texas, although he had prior experience in railroad building in South America. Together, Telfener and Hungerford planned a railroad which would link New York City with Mexico City. Because of the liberal land policies that Texas offered to encourage railroad construction, the line was to begin in Texas. The New York, Texas, and Mexican Railway Company charter was signed on October 18, 1880, in Paris, France, and was filed in Austin, Texas, on November 17, 1880. The company contracted with Telfener to build 350 miles of track from Richmond to Brownsville; work was begun west from Rosenberg Junction and east from Victoria in September, 1881. Count Telfener brought over 1,200 Italian workers, hoping they would remain in Texas and settle on land adjacent to the railroad line, known locally as the "Macaroni Line." Telfener was a frequent visitor to Texas; having offices in New York City, he received distinguished members of the Italian colony in New York, and his extravagant style became well known.

Construction on the railroad was slow, and there was difficulty in keeping the Italian laborers from leaving to take other jobs. On April 22, 1882, the state of Texas repealed the law granting land to companies for railroad construction, and Telfener abandoned his plans after completing only 91 miles of the original 350 planned. Expenditures for the line, completed July 4, 1882, totaled over $2 million. Telfener operated the short line until July 23, 1884, when the construction contract was annulled. The line was acquired by his brother-in-law, John W. Mackay, in January, 1885, and was then sold to the Southern Pacific Lines in September of that year. Towns along the route between Victoria and Rosenberg were named for the financiers (Telfener, Hungerford, and Mackay), for Mackay's wife (Louise), and for Telfener's daughters (Inez and Edna). Count Telfener continued other financial interests and remained prosperous until his death in Rome, Italy, on January 1, 1898.

BIBLIOGRAPHY: Ellin Berlin, *Silver Platter* (1957); S. G. Reed, *A History of the Texas Railroads* (1941); *The South American Journal and Brazil and River Plate Mail* (1880–1883); John C. Rayburn, "Count Joseph Telfener and the New York, Texas, and Mexican Railway Company," *Southwestern Historical Quarterly*, LXVIII (1964–1965).

John C. Rayburn

*Telferner, Texas. Telferner, Texas, though misspelled, was named for Italian Count Joseph Telfener qv (not Joseph Telferner, as stated in Volume II).

*Telico, Texas.

*Tell, Texas. (Childress County.)

*Tell, Texas. (Hall County.)

*Tempe Creek.

*Tempe Junction, Texas.

*Temperance and Temperance Societies. *See* Prohibition Movement.

*Temple, Edward Arthur.

Temple, Thomas Lewis Latané. Thomas Lewis Latané Temple, lumberman and industrialist, was born on March 18, 1859, in Essex County, Virginia, the son of Henry W. I. and Suzan (Jones) Temple. Left an orphan at age eleven, he briefly attended a local academy; at the age of seventeen he migrated to Arkansas. After a short period of farming and serving as deputy county clerk, he moved to Texarkana in 1877 and entered the lumber business. By 1887 he was part owner and manager of the Atlanta Lumber Company.

Temple married Georgia D. Fowlkes on December 2, 1880; they had five children. In 1893 Temple came to Angelina County, Texas, and purchased 7,000 acres of pine timberland from J. C. Diboll. He built his first sawmill, a medium circular rig, which began production in 1894. He also built the town of Diboll and developed the Southern Pine Lumber Company, as well as a complex of related Temple industries, which grew to include major sawmill operations at Diboll, Pineland, Lufkin, and Hemphill; the Temple-White Company, a major producer of mop and broom handles; Temple Associates Box Factory; Love Wood Products; Temple Builders Supply and Great Texas Lumber Company; Temple Cotton Oil Company; and the Texas-Southeastern Railroad.

Temple's philanthropies included the establishment of the Temple Memorial Library in Diboll, the Memorial Hospital in Lufkin, and the Temple Memorial Home for Crippled Children in Texarkana. Temple died on October 2, 1935, and was buried in Texarkana.

Robert S. Maxwell

*Temple, Texas. Temple, in eastern Bell County, serves as a commercial center for a large area of central Texas. Manufacturing plants produce furniture, shoes, insulation, cottonseed products, electronic products, plastics, work clothes, optical supplies, livestock and poultry feeds, and woodwork. During the 1960's Temple Junior College qv was expanded and improved. The city remained a railroad center and medical center. Several hospitals are located there, including the unique Scott and White Memorial Hospital.qv Temple is the site of a substation of the Agricultural Experiment Station System qv and is the location for state offices of the United States Soil Conservation Service. An annual pioneer day in June attracts tourists to the city. The 1960 population of Temple was 30,419; the 1970 population was 33,431, according to the United States census. For statistical purposes, in 1972 Temple was included in the Killeen-Temple Standard Metropolitan Statistical Area.qv

Temple Junior College. Temple Junior College, Temple, began as part of the Temple Public School System in 1928 and operated under that system until 1956 in the basement of Temple High School. The college created a separate school district in 1955, and in 1956 the voters passed a bond issue for construction of a new campus and retirement of bonds. The move was made to the new campus on South First Street in 1957. A complete break from the public school system came in 1959 through establishment of a college board of regents.

Student enrollment figures showed a steady increase: 117 in 1935, 392 in 1956, 1,250 in 1965, and 1,770 in the fall semester of 1974. The building program in the 1960's included an arts building, a $310,000 library, and a $325,000 science building. The college maintained a faculty of approximately sixty persons in 1969, and that same year library holdings totaled 18,178 volumes. Accredited by the Southern Association of Colleges and Schools, the college curriculum contained pre-professional, liberal arts, occupational, and adult education courses. Marvin R. Felder was president in 1974.

*Temple-Northwestern Railway Company.

*Templeton, Howard.

*Templeton, John Dickson.

*Ten Mile Creek.

*Ten Mile Draw.

*Tenaha, Texas. Tenaha, in northern Shelby County, had a 1960 population of 1,097 and a 1970 population of 1,094, according to the United States census. Thirty-three businesses were reported in 1970.

*Tenaha Creek.

*Tenark, Texas.

Tenawa Indians. The Tenawa (Denavi, Tanewa, Tannewish, Tenawit, Tenhua) Indians, whose name means "down stream," were a Comanche band known by this name only during the first half of the nineteenth century. Although they ranged widely over northern Texas, the Tenawa are most frequently linked with the area that lies between the upper Brazos and Red rivers. This area they shared with the Nokoni and Tanima bands. Sometimes the Tenawa camped with the Penataka, who lived south of the Tenawa between the Brazos and Colorado rivers. The Tenawa seem to have disappeared as a band before 1850. The Tenawa and Tanima were sometimes confused by observers who wrote about them, and today it is not always possible to tell which band is meant. In fact, some anthropologists think that the two names refer to the same band of Comanche.

BIBLIOGRAPHY: R. N. Richardson, *The Comanche Barrier to South Plains Settlement* (1933); J. R. Swanton, *The Indian Tribes of North America* (1952); E. Wallace and E. A. Hoebel, *The Comanches, Lords of the South Plains* (1952).

T. N. Campbell

*Tenehaw Municipality.

Teneryville, Texas. Teneryville, in northern Gregg County, was founded in 1931, when the Lathrop oil well came in. The town was named for G. B. Tenery, on whose land oil was discovered. In 1931 there were some two hundred people living there; in 1966 there were only four or five families. Teneryville and Tennerville (in the same county) are separate communities.

*Tenicapeme Indians. The Tenicapeme (Panaquiapeme, Tanaquiapeme, Tenaquipeme) Indians were a group of Coahuiltecans who lived on both sides of the lower Rio Grande in the second half of the eighteenth century. The name is recorded in baptismal records at Matamoros as late as 1800. Some Tenicapeme also entered San José y San Miguel de Aguayo Mission qv at San Antonio. If Tenu, Tena, and Tina are shortened forms of the same name, as seems likely, then some of the Tenicapeme were also at San Antonio de Valero Mission qv in San Antonio.

BIBLIOGRAPHY: F. W. Hodge (ed.), *Handbook of American Indians*, II (1910); G. Saldivar, *Los Indios de Tamaulipas* (1943); J. R. Swanton, *Linguistic Material from the Tribes of Southern Texas and Northeastern Mexico* (1940); R. C. Troike, "Notes on Coahuiltecan Ethnography," *Bulletin of the Texas Archeological Society*, 30 (1962).

T. N. Campbell

*Tennerville, Texas.

*Tennessee Colony, Texas.

*Tennessee Valley, Texas.

*Tenney Creek.

*Tennyson, Texas.

*Tenorio, Antonio.

*Tenoxtitlán, Texas.

*Tenth Cavalry Creek.

*Tenu Indians. The Tenu (Tena, Tina) Indians are known only from records of San Antonio de Valero Mission qv at San Antonio, and their status remains in doubt. Since they entered this mission about 1740, a time when many Tonkawan groups were also entering the mission, it has been suggested that the Tenu may have been a Tonkawan group. It is also possible to argue that they were a Coahuiltecan group and that the name is a shortened form of either Tenicapeme or Tinapihuaya. The Tenicapeme lived in northern Tamaulipas, and some members of this band were at San José y San Miguel de Aguayo Mission qv in San Antonio. Indirect evidence suggests that the Tinapihuaya originally lived on the coast between the Nueces and San Antonio rivers. Tenu identification must await better documentary evidence.

BIBLIOGRAPHY: H. E. Bolton, *Texas in the Middle Eighteenth Century* (1915); F. W. Hodge (ed.), *Handbook of American Indians*, II (1910).

T. N. Campbell

*Tepachuache Indians.

*Tepee Butte.

*Tepee Draw.

Tepelguan Indians. In 1590 Gaspar Castaño de Sosa qv encountered a group of Indians with this name in western Texas. Castaño's route had been in dispute, but recent studies have convincingly demonstrated that he followed the Pecos River and not the Rio Grande from Coahuila to the Pueblo Indian towns of northern New Mexico. This permits placement of the Tepelguan on the eastern side of the Pecos River, possibly in present Crockett County. Here the Tepelguan lived by hunting and gathering wild plant products. The identification of the Tepelguan remains in doubt. The name is very similar to that of the Tepehuane, a Uto-Aztecan group that originally occupied a large area in Durango and adjoining states in northwestern Mexico, but no one has yet considered seriously that the Tepelguan of the lower Pecos were refugees from Durango. It seems more reasonable to regard the Tepelguan of Texas as an indigenous group that lived along the lower Pecos River and perhaps also in northern Coahuila. This interpretation is supported by the fact that Tepelguan were reported north of Monterrey in Nuevo León during the late seventeenth century. These were probably the same Tepelguan that entered San Francisco Solano Mission qv near present Eagle Pass in 1706. However, further research should be directed toward determining the relationship between the Tepelguan of Texas and the Tepehuane of Durango. The resemblance in names may prove not to be fortuitous.

BIBLIOGRAPHY: F. W. Hodge (ed.), Handbook of American Indians, II (1910); W. Jiménez Moreno, "Tribus e idiomas del Norte de México," El Norte de México y el Sur de Estados Unidos (1944); A. H. Schroeder and D. S. Matson, A Colony on the Move: Gaspar Castaño de Sosa's Journal, 1590-1591 (1965).

T. N. Campbell

*Tepemaca Indians. In the last half of the eighteenth century the Tepemaca, a Coahuiltecan-speaking group, ranged along both sides of the Rio Grande between Laredo and Rio Grande City and also along the Río Alamo upstream from Mier. The Tepemaca appear to be closely related to the Cuero Quemado, who lived farther down the Rio Grande, and it has been suggested that both names refer to the same people.

BIBLIOGRAPHY: F. W. Hodge (ed.), Handbook of American Indians, II (1910); G. Saldivar, Los Indios de Tamaulipas (1943).

T. N. Campbell

*Tequesquite Creek.

*Terán, Manuel de. See Mier y Terán, Manuel de.

Terán, Pedro de. See Rabago y Terán, Pedro de.

*Terán de los Ríos, Domingo.

*Terlingua, Texas.

*Terlingua Creek.

*Terminal, Texas.

*Terocodame Indians. In the latter part of the seventeenth century the Terocodame (Codam, Hieroquodame, Oodame, Perocodame, Teroodam) Indians, who were Coahuiltecans, lived on both sides of the Rio Grande near present Eagle Pass. In 1700 San Francisco Solano Mission qv was built within their favorite settlement area, and the whole band seems to have entered as a unit. The records of this mission suggest that the Terocodame constituted the dominant band in an incipient confederation of local bands. Some of the Terocodame followed San Francisco Solano Mission when it was moved to San Antonio in 1718 and became known as San Antonio de Valero Mission.qv J. D.

Forbes has recently questioned the identification of the Terocodame as Coahuiltecan, but he presents no alternative linguistic identification.

BIBLIOGRAPHY: H. E. Bolton (ed.), Spanish Exploration in the Southwest, 1542-1706 (1916); J. D. Forbes, "Unknown Athapaskans: The Identification of the Jano, Jocome, Jumano, Manso, Suma, and Other Indian Tribes of the Southwest," Ethnohistory, 6 (1959); F. W. Hodge (ed.), Handbook of American Indians, II (1910); J. R. Swanton, Linguistic Material from the Tribes of Southern Texas and Northeastern Mexico (1940).

T. N. Campbell

*Terrell, Alexander Watkins. Alexander Watkins Terrell was born on November 3 (not November 23, as stated in Volume II), 1827. In 1863 Terrell entered the Confederate Army as a major in the 1st Texas Cavalry Regiment, Arizona Brigade (not as lieutenant colonel) and later served as a lieutenant colonel and commander of Terrell's Texas Cavalry Battalion. Terrell was promoted to colonel when the battalion expanded into Terrell's Texas Cavalry Regiment (sometimes referred to incorrectly as the 34th Texas Cavalry Regiment). He remained commander of the regiment until near the end of the war.

Terrell served four terms in the Texas Senate, beginning in the Fifteenth Legislature of 1876 and ending in the Eighteenth Legislature of 1883 (not 1875 to 1882). He also served in the Texas House of Representatives in the Twenty-second Legislature in 1891, the Twenty-eighth Legislature in 1903, and the Twenty-ninth Legislature in 1905. Governor Thomas Mitchell Campbell qv appointed Terrell to the board of regents of the University of Texas on January 29, 1909; he served until January, 1911. While on the board he was influential in securing funds to build the library building.

Terrell was married three times. His first wife was Ann Elizabeth Boulding of Howard County, Missouri; they had five children before she died in 1860. Terrell married Sarah D. Mitchell of Robinson County, Texas, and she died in 1871. Terrell's last marriage was to Mrs. Anne Holiday Anderson Jones. Terrell died on September 9 (not September 8), 1912, and was buried in the State Cemetery.qv

BIBLIOGRAPHY: L. E. Daniell, Personnel of the Texas State Government (1892); Frank W. Johnson, A History of Texas and Texans, III (1914); Marcus J. Wright (comp.) and Harold B. Simpson (ed.), Texas in the War, 1861-1865 (1965); Biographical Encyclopedia of Texas (1880); Who Was Who In America (1943); Frank Brown, "Annals of Travis County and of the City of Austin from Earliest Times to 1875," (MS., Archives, University of Texas at Austin Library); Thomas Stallings Henderson Papers (MS., Archives, University of Texas at Austin Library); Biographical Files (MS., Austin-Travis County Collection, Austin Public Library).

Terrell, Ben Stockton. Ben Stockton Terrell was born in Colorado County, Texas, on July 10, 1842, the son of Henry Terrell. He moved to Guadalupe County in 1857. In 1861 he enlisted in the 4th Texas Infantry of Hood's Brigade qv and was wounded at Seven Pines and at Sharpsburg before being transferred to Terry's Texas Rangers qv (8th Texas Cavalry). He returned to farming in Texas in 1865; the following year he went to Mexico as a trader, but in 1870 he returned to Texas to farm. He joined the Farmers' Alliance qv in 1886 and became treasurer of the Texas Alliance Exchange. In 1887, after election as national lecturer of the Alliance, he traveled widely through the South organizing new chapters and debating those who questioned Alliance goals, including Governor "Pitchfork" Bill Tilman of South Carolina. In 1891 he was elected president of the Confederation of Industrial Organizations, which included Alliance representatives, and in January, 1892, he traveled to St. Louis as a Texas delegate to the founding convention of the People's party.qv Later that year he was temporary chairman of the People's party national convention at Omaha and ran second in a bid for the vice-presidential nomination. He was defeated for Congress as the Populist candidate in the 11th District in 1892, withdrew in 1894 in favor of an independent Democratic candidate, and continued as an active party leader through 1896.

Terrell also served at various times as county and city attorney in Seguin and Guadalupe County; he was a lifelong Methodist. On February 23, 1876, he married Katie Heaner, and they had one daughter. He died on March 18, 1928.

BIBLIOGRAPHY: Seguin *Enterprise*, March 23, 1928; Galveston *Weekly News*, June 23, July 7, 28, September 1, 1892; Galveston *Daily News*, September 20, 1894, September 13, 1896; *Report of the Secretary of State of Texas* (1892).

Alwyn Barr

Terrell, Charles Vernon. Charles Vernon Terrell, son of Samuel Lafayette and Emily Catherine (Kellam) Terrell, was born in a log cabin in Wise County on May 2, 1861. He was educated in the schools of Decatur and at A&M College, which he entered in 1881. He taught at a country school for four months, then read law in a private office. After being admitted to the Bar, he was city attorney of Decatur for four years. In 1886 he was the Decatur correspondent for the Dallas *Morning News*.qv In 1892 he was elected county attorney of Wise County, a post he held for four years, during which he vigorously prosecuted cattle rustlers.

In 1896 Terrell was elected to the first of two terms as a state senator. In the legislature, he introduced the bill to establish North Texas State Teachers College (now North Texas State University) and supported bills for compulsory school attendance, uniform textbooks, and the use of public land to finance education. Terrell was elected state treasurer in 1922. After two years in that post, he became a member of the Texas Railroad Commission.qv In his fifteen years on the commission, he supported the fight for equalization of freight rates, aided in bus and truck regulation, and worked for the conservation of oil and gas through the proration of production. A portrait of Terrell was unveiled in the Texas Senate on his ninety-second birthday, May 2, 1953.

On August 9, 1893, he married Etta May, a Decatur teacher; they had two sons and a foster daughter. He died in Austin on November 17, 1959.

BIBLIOGRAPHY: C. V. Terrell, *The Terrells* (1948); Dallas *Morning News*, November 18, 1959.

Wayne Gard

Terrell, Edwin Holland. Edwin Holland Terrell was born in Brookville, Indiana, on November 21, 1848, the youngest son of Martha (Jarrell) and Williamson Terrell. After his mother's death in 1849, he was reared in the family of George Holland, an attorney in Richmond, Indiana. In 1871 Terrell graduated as valedictorian from Asbury (now DePauw) University.

He first came to Texas in 1871 as an aide to his brother, Colonel C. M. Terrell, who was stationed in San Antonio. In 1872 he accompanied his brother to Omaha, Nebraska, and the western frontier, before entering Harvard Law School. He graduated in 1873 and then studied international law and modern languages at the Sorbonne in Paris. In 1874 he was admitted to the Bar and became a partner in Barbour, Jacobs, and Terrell at Indianapolis, Indiana.

Terrell moved to San Antonio in 1877 and became vice-president of the San Antonio Gas Company and the San Antonio Board of Trade; he was also a promoter of the San Antonio and Aransas Pass Railway. In 1887 he was defeated for mayor of San Antonio; two years later he was appointed minister to Belgium by President Benjamin Harrison. He also served as United States representative to the International Congress on the Slave Trade in 1889–1890, to the International Conference on Customs Tariffs in 1890, and on the *Commission Technique*, which revised the tariff provisions of the Berlin Treaty of 1885. In 1891 he concluded a treaty of commerce, amity, and navigation between the United States and the Congo Free State with Belgian King Leopold II, who later decorated Terrell for his services. He was also one of the United States delegates to the International Monetary Conference of 1892. As a leader in the Republican party in Texas,qv Terrell was a delegate to the Republican national conventions of 1880, 1888, and 1904, and was a member of the state executive committee, 1894–1900.

On August 17, 1874, Terrell married Mary Maverick, daughter of Samuel A. Maverick qv of San Antonio. They had six children before her death in Brussels in January, 1891. On February 7, 1895, he married Lois Lasater, and they had three children. Terrell died in San Antonio on July 1, 1910.

BIBLIOGRAPHY: *Dictionary of American Biography*, XVIII (1943); *Memorial and Genealogical Record of Southwest Texas* (1894); *A Twentieth Century History of Southwest Texas* (1907).

*Terrell, Frederick.

Terrell, George Butler. George Butler Terrell was born in Alto, Cherokee County, on December 5, 1862, the son of Sam Houston and Julia (Butler) Terrell, and the grandson of George Whitfield Terrell.qv He attended the public schools of Alto,

Sam Houston State Teachers College (now Sam Houston State University), and Baylor University. From 1886 to 1903 he taught school in Cherokee County, during which time he was a member of the State Teachers Examining Committee and on the State Textbook Commission. He also engaged in farming and stock raising at Alto. He was elected to the Texas House of Representatives in 1898 and served for seven (non-consecutive) terms until 1920, when he was elected commissioner of agriculture for Texas; he was reelected to that post for four additional terms. In 1930 he was again elected to the Texas House of Representatives. In the legislature he was concerned with laws on agriculture and secured the establishment of four experiment stations; he sponsored a law requiring the grading of fruits and vegetables and a law requiring the teaching of agriculture and domestic science.

In 1932, as a Democrat, Terrell was elected U.S. congressman-at-large from Texas. He went into Congress with the New Deal but soon found himself in opposition to most New Deal measures. He was outspoken in his opposition to NRA. When he cast the only Democratic vote against a relief bill, the Civil Works Administration Act, the city council of his home town, Alto, sent a resolution to President Franklin D. Roosevelt declaring that Terrell did not represent their feelings. Terrell was stricken with paralysis in May, 1934, and later that same month declared that he would not be a candidate for reelection. He returned to Alto and resumed his interest in farming. He died in Alto on April 18, 1947, and was buried in the old Palestine Cemetery near Alto. He was survived by his wife, Allie (Turney) Terrell, and five children.

BIBLIOGRAPHY: *Biographical Directory of the American Congress, 1774–1961* (1961); *Who's Who In America* (1934); Dallas *Morning News*, February 7, May 30, 1934, April 19, 1947.

Thomas L. Miller

*Terrell, George Whitfield.

*Terrell, Henry Berryman.

*Terrell, J. O.

*Terrell, John J.

*Terrell, Texas. Terrell, in Kaufman County, had fifteen major industries in the 1960's, most of which were concerned with the manufacture of aluminum products, ice cream, clothing, paper supplies, and feeds. The town also had a cotton compress and metal and woodworks industries. Terrell is a banking and distribution center for a diversified farming area, and in the late 1960's it supported forty-three churches, four hospitals, two banks, a college, a library, a newspaper, and a radio station. Terrell had 212 businesses in 1970. Terrell State Hospital qv was located there. The 1960 population was 13,803; the 1970 population was 14,182, according to the United States census.

*Terrell County. Terrell County, with 95 percent of its income from sheep and goats, is largely a ranching area; some cattle are raised, but the value of crops is insignificant. Natural gas is produced and the mineral value runs to several million dollars annually. Tourist attractions include hunting, a July rodeo, and the ruins of Fort Meyer.qv Since 1946 several new towns have grown up along the Southern Pacific railroad. A flood in June, 1965, caused extensive damage to Sanderson, the major center of the county. The 1960 population was 2,600; the 1970 population was 1,940, according to the United States census.

*Terrell Election Law. *See* Election Laws.

*Terrell Hills, Texas. Terrell Hills, in northeastern Bexar County, was incorporated as a municipality on May 11, 1939 (not 1936 in San Antonio, as stated in Volume II). In 1945 the city of San Antonio annexed the town of Terrell Hills without an election in either community. In a lawsuit initiated by the town to prevent annexation, the court voided the annexation. Late in 1957 Terrell Hills adopted a home rule charter. The town doubled in population during a ten-year period, going from 2,708 in 1950 to 5,572 in 1960; the 1970 population was 5,225, according to the United States census.

BIBLIOGRAPHY: Edward W. Heusinger, *A Chronology of Events in San Antonio* (1951).

Terrell Reservoir. Terrell Reservoir is in the Trinity River Basin in Kaufman County, six miles east of Terrell on Muddy Cedar Creek. The project is owned and operated by the city of Terrell as a municipal water supply and for recreation purposes. Construction of the project began in February, 1955, and was completed in November, 1955. The reservoir has a capacity of 8,300 acre-feet and a surface area of 885 acres at the service spillway crest elevation of 503 feet above mean sea level. At the emergency spillway crest elevation, the capacity is 12,400 acre-feet with a surface area of 1,150 acres. The drainage area above the dam is fourteen square miles.

BIBLIOGRAPHY: Texas Water Commission, *Bulletin 6408* (1964).

Seth D. Breeding

*Terrell State Hospital. With the opening of a 400-bed air-conditioned ward in 1963, Terrell State Hospital's average daily census was 2,597 patients; in 1967 there were 2,700 patients, ranging in age from eighteen months to 100 years and including residents and students from the Denton and Lufkin state schools.qqv An outpatient clinic provided after-care treatment for eligible patients and for those referred to the clinic for evaluation and treatment.

In 1970 the hospital was organized into four geographic units and three specialty units. Although admissions to the hospital continued to increase, there was a 23 percent increase in discharges during 1970, attributed partly to the use of the unit system. Occupational therapy programs were directed for patients through sheltered workshops supported by industrial contracts, and the patients received funds for their work. With the cooperation of the community and hospital staff, two outreach programs treated 871 patients in Paris and Greenville. Recreational facilities for patients were increased at Lake Tawakoni with the addition of a swimming pool donated by the volunteer council. The average daily census for 1970 was 2,568; the hospital superintendent was Luis M. Cowley. *See also* Mentally Ill and Mentally Retarded, Care of, in Texas.

BIBLIOGRAPHY: Board for Texas State Hospitals and Special Schools, *Report* (1964); Texas Department of Mental Health and Mental Retardation, *Annual Report, 1970.*

*Terrell Wells, Texas.

*Terreros, Alonso Giraldo de.

*Terreros, Pedro Romero de.

*Terrett Draw.

*Terry, Benjamin Franklin.

Terry, David Smith. David Smith Terry was born in Christian County, Kentucky, on March 8, 1823, the second of four sons of Joseph R. and Sarah (Smith) Terry, and brother of Benjamin F. Terry.^{qv} The family moved to Hinds County, Mississippi, in 1826; the parents separated in 1834. At the urging of her brother, Benjamin Fort Smith,^{qv} Mrs. Terry and her sons joined her mother in Texas and settled on Oyster Creek in Fort Bend County.

Terry studied law in the office of T. J. B. Hadley and was admitted to the Bar in 1845 at Galveston. He served in Captain Samuel L. S. Ballowe's Company of the 1st Texas Mounted Regiment in the Mexican War and participated in the battle of Monterrey in 1846. In 1847 he was an unsuccessful candidate for district attorney of Galveston County. Terry migrated to California in 1849, briefly engaged in gold mining, and then began the practice of law in Stockton, California. In 1855 he was elected a justice of the California Supreme Court.

Terry achieved notoriety in 1856 for stabbing a member of the Vigilance Committee. After imprisonment and a secret trial by the Vigilantes, he was set free. Again he received notoriety when, partly as an aftermath of a bitter political struggle between two factions of the California Democratic party in 1859 and also to defend himself against statements made about him, he killed U.S. Senator David C. Broderick in a duel. Terry resigned from the Supreme Court, and while Broderick became a martyr and hero of the Northern sympathizers, Terry was excoriated and indicted for murder. He stood trial in 1861, but the judge directed a verdict of not guilty.

Terry came back to Texas by way of Mexico in 1863 to join the Confederate Army. He raised a cavalry regiment and was elected its colonel, but he saw no service outside of Texas. At the end of the war, he refused to accept a parole and went to Jalisco, Mexico, where he engaged in farming and ranching until he returned to Stockton, California, in 1868 to resume the practice of law. He was a member of the California Constitutional Convention of 1878–1879.

Terry married Cornelia Runnels at Galveston in 1852; they had six children. After his wife's death in 1884, he married Sarah Althea Hill in January, 1886. On August 14, 1889, during an altercation in a railroad restaurant in Lathrop, California, Terry was killed by David Neagle, the bodyguard of U.S. Supreme Court Justice Stephen J. Field, with whom Terry had had differences. He was buried in the Rural Cemetery, Stockton, California.

BIBLIOGRAPHY: A. E. Wagstaff, *Life of David S. Terry* (1892); Carroll Douglas Hall, *The Terry-Broderick Duel* (1938); A. Russell Buchanan, *David S. Terry of California* (1956); Robert H. Kroninger, *Sarah and the Senator* (1964); C. S. Potts, "David S. Terry," *Southwest Review*, XIX (1934); Notes of John Wharton Terry on David S. Terry, 1934 (MS., Bancroft Library, University of California at Berkeley).

Cooper K. Ragan

*Terry, John Wharton.

*Terry, Texas.

*Terry County. Terry County ranked among the leading Texas counties in total crop income and cotton production. In the late 1960's and early 1970's over 90 percent of the farm income, which averaged $29 million annually, came from cotton, sorghums, and small grains grown on approximately 175,000 irrigated acres. As of February 1, 1971, there were twenty-one gins in the county, producing 103,514 running bales of cotton during the 1970–1971 season. The raising of cattle and sheep was becoming increasingly important to the county's economy. Between 1940 and January 1, 1973, 151,053,360 barrels of oil had been produced in Terry County. The 1960 population was 16,286; the 1970 population was 14,118, according to the United States census.

*Terry's Chapel, Texas.

*Terry's Texas Rangers.

*Terryville, Texas.

*Tesnus, Texas.

*Tet Indians. This is the name of an Indian group that is known only by hearsay. In 1706 the Tet were reported to be living somewhere north of San Juan Bautista,^{qv} a mission on the south side of the Rio Grande near present Eagle Pass. Thereafter the Tet are not mentioned again. It seems likely that Tet is a shortened form of Tetecore, which is the name of a Coahuiltecan-speaking band that lived in northern Coahuila. Many Indian groups of northern and northeastern Coahuila crossed the Rio Grande to hunt in the southwestern part of the Edwards Plateau.

BIBLIOGRAPHY: H. E. Bolton (ed.), *Spanish Exploration in the Southwest, 1542–1706* (1916); F. W. Hodge (ed.), *Handbook of American Indians*, II (1910).

T. N. Campbell

Tetecore Indians. The Tetecore lived in Coahuila during the latter part of the seventeenth century. They may have been the same as the Tet, who in the early eighteenth century were reported as living in Texas somewhere north of Eagle Pass.

Both are assumed to have been Coahuiltecan in language.

BIBLIOGRAPHY: H. E. Bolton (ed.), *Spanish Exploration in the Southwest, 1542–1706* (1916); F. W. Hodge (ed.), *Handbook of American Indians*, II (1910).

T. N. Campbell

Tetzino Indians. This name is connected with a group of Indians who entered the San Antonio de Valero Mission qv in San Antonio about 1740. It has been argued that the Tetzino were Tonkawan because they entered this mission along with other Indians considered to be Tonkawan in affiliation. This appears to be supported by linguistic evidence. The name Tetzino may be a Spanish distortion of Titskan (the Tonkawan name for themselves was Titskan watitch, "indigenous people").

BIBLIOGRAPHY: H. E. Bolton, *Texas in the Middle Eighteenth Century* (1915); F. W. Hodge (ed.), *Handbook of American Indians*, II (1910).

T. N. Campbell

Texaco Inc. Texaco Inc. became the corporate name of the former Texas Company qv of Delaware in 1959. In the years that followed World War II, Texaco embarked on a long-range program of modernization and expansion. At the end of 1964 the company had more than 40,000 retail outlets in the United States, employed more than 56,000 people, and was the only oil company marketing under its own name in all fifty states. With total assets of $4.9 billion, it ranked as the second largest oil company and the fifth largest manufacturing company in the United States. With a net income of $577.3 million in 1964, Texaco Inc. ranked second in terms of earnings among oil companies and third among all manufacturing corporations in the United States.

During the 1960's Texaco Inc. had interests in many parts of the world. In the Middle East, the company owned a 30 percent interest in the Arabian American Oil Company, a 30 percent interest in the Trans-Arabian Pipe Line Company, and, through a wholly-owned subsidiary, a 7 percent interest in oil operations in Iran. The company owned a half interest in the Caltex group of companies, which operated in more than 70 countries in the Eastern Hemisphere. Texaco Inc. also marketed in West Africa through wholly-owned subsidiaries. It had important crude oil production on the Persian Gulf island of Bahrain and on the Indonesian island of Sumatra. It began production of crude oil in Libya at the end of 1963 and was exploring in other countries in the North Sea area. Texaco was the largest oil producer in Colombia and Trinidad, and had substantial production in Venezuela. It owned a 68 percent interest in Texaco Canada Limited, and marketed in the United Kingdom through its 75 percent-owned Regent subsidiary.

In its worldwide petroleum activities, Texaco Inc. produced 1,815,123 barrels a day, refined 1,673,532 barrels a day, and marketed 1,760,085 barrels a day during 1964. This balance between producing, refining, and marketing activities was a special characteristic of the company. At the end

of 1964 the company had eleven refineries in the United States, and a twelfth under construction. The company operated or held an interest in thirty-eight foreign refineries, and six more were under construction or planned.

James A. Clark

*Texan.

Texan, Daily. See Daily Texan.

*Texan, The.

*Texan Emigration and Land Company. See Peters' Colony.

*Texan Santa Fe Expedition.

Texana. *Texana*, a quarterly publication devoted to Texas history, was first published in January, 1963. It was edited by Robert E. Davis and published by the Texian Press of Waco. An editorial board, comprised of historians throughout the state, approved articles accepted for publication. *Texana* had a wide circulation in college and high school libraries and appealed to individuals interested in Texas history. The format is that of a historical journal; a requirement for published articles is that they be fully documented. The last issue in each volume contains an index to the volume. In 1972 Dayton Kelley was editor and Robert E. Davis was publisher.

Robert E. Davis

*Texana.

*Texana, Texas.

*Texana Academy.

Texarkana, Texas. See also Texarkana Standard Metropolitan Statistical Area.

Texarkana College. Texarkana College, Texarkana, was founded in 1927 as a public junior college and a branch of the public school system. H. W. Stilwell served both as superintendent of schools and first president of the college. The original campus consisted of a single building at 16th and Pine streets. Laboratories and a gymnasium were used jointly by the college and a high school. An election in 1941 established the Texarkana College District. Until the end of World War II, enrollment grew slowly from the first 109 students, but thereafter a rapid increase in enrollment demanded enlargement of college facilities. The college purchased a new twenty-acre campus in 1948 and began construction of an administration building and gymnasium in 1950.

The college moved to the new campus in October, 1951, when the enrollment totaled 589 students. Additional funds were voted for construction of an auditorium and classroom building in 1954, and the college and school boards agreed to separate in 1957. During 1958, $475,000 in bonds provided for construction of a student union and enlargement of the campus to eighty-eight acres. The funds also covered additions of men's and women's dormitories, music and technical buildings, a nursing center, and shops in 1959. The biology building, first segment of a science complex, was completed in 1965; it was followed by construction of the chemistry and nursing centers in 1966 and a new library in 1967. A continuing program of campus landscaping and beautification was carried on by the garden clubs of Texarkana.

Curriculum offerings included the first two years of all basic college courses and many terminal courses in business and data processing. Licensed vocational nursing, medical technology, and a two-year associate in science were programs offered in conjunction with two local hospitals. The school was approved and accredited by the Association of Texas Colleges qv and the Southern Association of Colleges and Schools. Enrollment reached 1,724 students during the 1963–1964 term, and there were fifty-six members of the faculty; library holdings during that term totaled 13,000 volumes. By 1969 library holdings had increased to 25,049 volumes, and there were eighty faculty members. J. W. Cady was president of the college during the 1973–1974 term; there were 2,822 students enrolled at that time. By 1974 the college was called Texarkana Community College, and there were 2,944 students enrolled; Levi H. Hall was acting president.

*Texarkana and Fort Smith Railway Company.

Texarkana Reservoir. Texarkana Reservoir is in the Sulphur River Basin in Bowie and Cass counties, eleven miles southwest of Texarkana on the Sulphur River. The reservoir borders Bowie and Cass counties and extends into Morris, Titus, and Red River counties. The project is owned by the United States government and operated by the United States Army Corps of Engineers, New Orleans District, for flood control and conservation purposes. The cities of Texarkana, Texas, and Texarkana, Arkansas, are authorized to divert 14,-572 acre-feet of water annually from Texarkana Reservoir for municipal use. Construction began in September, 1948, and was completed in December, 1957, at a cost of $34,200,000. The reservoir operated for temporary floodwater detention from July 2, 1953, to June 27, 1956, when deliberate impoundment began. It has a capacity of 145,300 acre-feet and a surface area of 20,000 acres at the conservation storage level elevation of 220 feet above mean sea level; it has a 2,654,300 acre-feet capacity at the spillway crest elevation of 259.5 feet. This provides a flood control storage capacity of 2,509,000 acre-feet between the two elevations. The drainage area above the dam is 3,443 square miles.

BIBLIOGRAPHY: Texas Water Commission, *Bulletin 6408* (1964).

Seth D. Breeding

Texarkana Standard Metropolitan Statistical Area. The Texarkana Standard Metropolitan Statistical Area, composed of Bowie County, Texas, and Miller County, Arkansas, and covering 1,530 square miles, was designated a metropolitan statistical area by the federal government in August, 1960, when the total population of the city of Texarkana, divided by the state line, reached 50,-006 (30,218 in Texas and 19,788 in Arkansas). The total population for the entire area in that year was 91,657 (59,971 in Bowie County, Texas, and 31,686 in Miller County, Arkansas). In 1970 the total area population was 101,198, with 67,813 in Bowie County, Texas, and 33,385 in Miller County, Arkansas. The total population of Texarkana in that year was 52,179, with 30,497 persons living on the Texas side and 21,682 residents on the Arkansas side.

The economy of this northeast Texas area has continued to grow at a steady pace, with more emphasis towards industry. The average annual agricultural income (for the Texas area only) was between $12 million and $13 million by 1970. Crops raised included cotton, corn, rice, soybeans, pecans, and truck crops; livestock and poultry accounted for 75 percent of the farm income. Industries in the area included the manufacture and marketing of lumber products, sewer tile, rockwool, sand and gravel, mobile homes and accessories, municipal hardware supplies, tires, railroad tank cars, and paper products. Also of great importance to the economy of the entire area are the Red River Army Depot, the Lone Star Army Depot, the Lone Star Army Ammunition Plant,qqv and a federal correctional unit, all in the Texarkana area. Retail trade, like the industrial growth, continued to increase steadily.

The city of Texarkana is the railroad, commercial, and industrial center for this Texas-Arkansas area, as well as the hub for portions of Oklahoma and Louisiana; it is also the educational, cultural, and medical center of the metropolitan area. Texarkana College,qv a fully accredited junior college, includes the William Buchanan Department of Nursing. The Civic Music Association, with patrons from the entire metropolitan area, brings in artists of national and international fame. Texarkana serves the area with three major hospitals and several modern clinics. Supplying water for industrial development are Lake Texarkana (*see* Texarkana Reservoir) and the Millwood Reservoir in Arkansas. Both are also important recreational sites. The Texarkana area holds annually a Four States Fair and Rodeo, plus other rodeos, band festivals, and a Miss Texarkana Pageant.

New Boston, with a 1970 population of 3,699, was the second largest town in Bowie County, Texas. Other towns in the county which had over 1,000 population in 1970 were DeKalb (2,157), Hooks (2,545), Maud (1,107), Nash (1,961), and Wake Village (2,408). Boston, the county seat of Bowie County, remained unincorporated and was not included in the 1970 census; its population was probably less than two hundred. *See* Boston, Texas; New Boston, Texas; *see also* Standard Metropolitan Statistical Areas in Texas. [Little River County, Arkansas, was added to the Texarkana Standard Metropolitan Statistical Area in April, 1973. Ed.]

Lewis Cannon
Robert G. Williams

*_Texas_.

*Texas.

Texas, Origin of Name. The word _texas_ (_tejas, tayshas, texias, thecas?, techan, teysas, techas?_) had wide usage among the Indian tribes of East Texas even before the coming of the Spanish, whose various transcriptions and interpretations gave rise to many theories about the meaning. The usual meaning was "friends," although the Hasinai applied the word to a large group of tribes—including Caddoan—to mean "allies." The Hasinai probably did not apply the name to themselves as a local group name; they did use the term, however, as a form of greeting, "hello, friend."

How and when the name _Texas_ first reached the Spanish is uncertain, but the notion of a "great kingdom of Texas," associated with a "Gran Quivira," had spread in New Spain prior to the expedition of Alonso de León qv and Don Damian Manzanet (Massanet) qv in 1689. Manzanet reported meeting Indians who proclaimed themselves _thecas_, or "friends," as he understood it, and on meeting the chief of the Nabedache (one of the Hasinai tribes), mistakenly referred to him as the "governor" of a "great kingdom of the Texas." Francisco de Jesus María, a missionary left by Manzanet among the Nabedache, attempted to correct erroneous reports about the name by asserting that the Indians in that region did not constitute a kingdom, that the chief called "governor" was not the head chief, and that the correct name of the group of tribes was not "Texas." _Texias_, according to María, meant "friends," and was simply a name applied by the tribes to the various groups allied against the Apache. Later expeditions by the Spanish for the most part abandoned the name "Texas" or else used it as an alternative to "Asinay" (Hasinai), while official Spanish documents continued to use it, later narrowing it to mean only the Neches-Angelina group of Indians and not a geographic area.

Other meanings have less evidence from contemporary accounts to support them: "land of flowers," "paradise," and "tiled roofs"—from the thatched roofs of the East Texas tribes—were never suggested by first-hand observers so far as known, though later theories connect them with _tejas_ or its variant spellings. Whatever the Spanish denotations of _Texas_, the state motto, "Friendship," carries the original meaning of the word as used by the Hasinai and their allied tribes, and the name of the state apparently was derived from the same source.

BIBLIOGRAPHY: F. W. Hodge (ed.), _Handbook of American Indians_, II (1910); Don Damian Manzanet (Lilia M. Casis, trans.), "Letter . . . Relative to the Discovery of the Bay of Espiritu Santo," _Quarterly of the Texas State Historical Association_, II (1898–1899); W. W. Newcomb, Jr., _The Indians of Texas_ (1961).

Phillip L. Fry

Texas A&I University at Corpus Christi. _See_ Texas A&I University System; _see also_ University of Corpus Christi.

Texas A&I University at Kingsville. Texas A&I University at Kingsville, formerly known as Texas College of Arts and Industries,qv had an increase in enrollment from 2,284 students in 1954 to 4,907 students in 1967, the year that the name change occurred. By that year the faculty numbered 291. University property consisted of 1,104 acres: a 149-acre main campus and an adjoining 640-acre experimental farm, a 266-acre tract awaiting development, an eighty-acre citrus and vegetable center at Weslaco, and experimental acreage plots in Bayview and northwest of Edinburg. Of the forty major buildings on the main campus, all in Spanish-style architecture, twenty-two were completed between 1950 and 1965. The master plan called for a physical plant to accommodate 8,000 students.

In 1947 the college was reorganized into six divisions: agriculture, arts and sciences, business administration, engineering, teacher education, and graduate studies. By 1965, 381 courses were offered on both undergraduate and graduate levels, including major work on the master's level in sixteen fields. Texas A&I was accredited by the Southern Association of Colleges and Schools, the Association of Texas Colleges and Universities,qv the National Association of Schools of Music, and the National Council for the Accreditation of Teacher Education. More than 179,465 volumes and approximately 4,500 reels of microfilm were held in 1967 by the university library, which also received over 1,200 current periodicals.

Athletic teams participated as members of the Lone Star Conference and were known as the Javelinas. A fortieth anniversary celebration of the institution's founding was held in 1965. Upon Ernest H. Poteet's retirement in 1962, James C. Jernigan became president. Enrollment in the fall of 1974 was 6,796, and Gerald Burns Robins was president. _See also_ Texas A&I University System.

Texas A&I University at Laredo. _See_ Texas A&I University System.

Texas A&I University System. The Texas A&I University System was created when, in addition to Texas A&I University at Kingsville,qv two upper-level institutions offering work beyond the sophomore year were founded in Laredo and Corpus Christi. Texas A&I University at Laredo was founded in 1969; in the fall of 1974 there were 758 students enrolled, and Billy F. Cowart was president. Texas A&I University at Corpus Christi was founded in 1971, and the first students were admitted in the fall of 1973; in that year the enrollment was 969, and D. Whitney Halladay was president. Enrollment increased to 1,603 in 1974. (For a history of this facility when it was a private school, _see_ University of Corpus Christi.) Chancellor of the Texas A&I University System in 1974 was James C. Jernigan.

Texas A&M University. Texas A&M University, College Station, had a student body of 8,200 in 1963, when its physical plant was valued in excess of $60,000,000; in that year on August 23, in recognition of the diversified and expanded character of the institution, the Fifty-eighth Texas Legislature changed its name from Agricultural and Mechanical College of Texas qv to Texas A&M University.

Effective June 1, 1963, a limited coeducational policy was initiated which allowed the enrollment of wives and daughters of A&M faculty, staff, employees, and students; girls pursuing a course of study not offered at any other state supported college; and females who sought an academic goal which could best be achieved at Texas A&M. In 1965 the policy was expanded to permit women to earn a degree from A&M for summer work, and by the early 1970's A&M was fully coeducational, admitting all qualified men and women to all academic studies.

By 1965 the following university divisions existed: college of agriculture, college of arts and sciences (including school of business administration), college of engineering (including school of architecture), school of military sciences, college of veterinary medicine, Texas Maritime Academy,qv and graduate college. Graduate college programs included master's degrees in the arts, business administration, computing sciences, education, engineering (aerospace, agricultural, architectural, chemical, civil, electrical, geological, industrial, mechanical, and petroleum), and science. Doctorates in education and philosophy were also offered by the graduate college, and the college of veterinary medicine offered a three-year D.V.M. program.

Texas A&M operated one of the largest cyclotrons in the nation and one of the best data processing facilities. It also had one of the most powerful nuclear reactors on any campus and opened a space research center built in cooperation with the National Aeronautics and Space Administration (see Manned Spacecraft Center).

The university library housed a collection of 610,142 volumes in 1969 and was a federal depository for United States government documents. Approximately 6,000 current serials and fifty newspapers were received by the main library. The student enrollment at Texas A&M University in the fall of 1973 was 18,410; approximately 3,000 of that total were women. By the fall of 1974 total enrollment had increased to 21,245. Jack K. Williams was president of both the university and the Texas A&M University System qv in 1974, succeeding James Earl Rudder qv in 1970. See also University Fund, Available; University Fund, Permanent.

Texas A&M University System. The Texas A&M University System (formerly Texas Agricultural and Mechanical College System qv) included Texas A&M University, Tarleton State University, Prairie View A&M University, and Moody College of Marine Sciences and Maritime Resources qqv (formerly Texas Maritime Academy qv) among its institutions of higher learning in 1973. Other components in the system were the following: Agricultural Experiment Station, Agricultural Extension Service, Texas Engineering Experiment Station, Texas Engineering Extension Service, Texas Transportation Institute, and Texas Forest Service.qqv From 1965 until 1969 the James Connally Technical Institute was part of the system, but it was separated when it became part of the Texas State Technical Institute.qv Arlington State College qv was transferred from the Texas A&M University System to the University of Texas in April, 1965, and became the University of Texas at Arlington,qv an official part of the University of Texas System,qv in March, 1967. See also University Fund, Available; University Fund, Permanent.

*Texas Academy of Science. James R. Dixon, of Texas A&M University, was president of the Texas Academy of Science in 1973.

*Texas Aeronautics Commission. See Aeronautics Commission, Texas.

*Texas Agricultural, Commercial, and Manufacturing Company. See Peters' Colony.

*Texas Agricultural Experiment Stations. See Agricultural Experiment Station System.

*Texas Agricultural Extension Service. See also Agricultural Extension Service, Texas.

*Texas Agricultural and Mechanical College System. See also Texas A&M University System.

Texas Air Control Board. See Air Control Board, Texas.

Texas Air National Guard. See Texas National Guard.

*Texas Almanac. After 1950, editions of the Texas Almanac were published with the following dates: 1952–1953, 1954–1955, 1956–1957, 1958–1959, 1961–1962, 1964–1965, 1966–1967, 1968–1969, 1970–1971, 1972–1973, and 1974–1975. Among these were three special editions: the one hundredth anniversary edition, 1956–1957; the George Bannerman Dealey qv memorial edition, 1958–1959; and the 1966–1967 edition, which observed the 110th anniversary of the first issuance of the Texas Almanac, as well as the 125th anniversary of the founding of "Texas' Oldest Business Institution," publishers of the Texas Almanac and Dallas Morning News.qv

Stuart Malcolm McGregor,qv who had edited the Texas Almanac since 1925, retired in 1961 after the publication of the 1961–1962 edition, which was dedicated to him by the publishers in recognition of his editorship. The editorial policies and format which he established were continued in later editions. In 1961 Walter B. Moore became editor of the publication. Fred R. Pass succeeded him in June, 1973.

Walter B. Moore

Texas Antiquities Committee. See Padre Island Treasure.

Texas Archeological and Paleontological Society. *See* Texas Archeological Society.

Texas Archeological Society. The Texas Archeological Society, founded to maintain professional interest and support of archeological work, was organized in October, 1928, in Abilene, primarily through the efforts of Cyrus N. Ray and E. B. Sayles. Known initially as the West Texas Archeological Society, it had a charter membership of fifty-seven. Within a few months the name was changed to the Texas Archeological and Paleontological Society; in 1929 there were approximately 105 members, 73 of them from Abilene. At the twenty-fifth annual meeting at Southern Methodist University in November, 1952, the name was changed to the Texas Archeological Society. Membership was open to any person interested in the preservation of the archeological resources of Texas. The society encouraged scholarly pursuit of archeology through cooperation with educational institutions and museums; its publications included, in addition to special works, a quarterly newsletter, *Texas Archeology*, and the annual, since 1929, *Bulletin of the Texas Archeological Society* qv (the first two volumes used the spelling, *Archaeological*, as did the society, which changed the spelling to "Archeological" in 1931). The society annually sponsors a field school, and in 1971 there was an international membership of 886, including 129 institutions.

BIBLIOGRAPHY: Floyd V. Studer, "Texas Archeological Society," *Panhandle-Plains Historical Review*, XXVIII (1955); Dee Ann Suhm, Alex D. Krieger, and Edward B. Jelks, *An Introductory Handbook of Texas Archeology* (1955); *Bulletin of the Texas Archaeological and Paleontological Society*, 1 (1929).

Michael B. Collins

*Texas, Arkansas, and Louisiana Railway.

*Texas Army. *See* Army of the Republic of Texas.

Texas Association of Broadcasters. The Texas Association of Broadcasters, founded September 18, 1951, by J. M. McDonald, manager of KCRS, Midland, provided a unified voice for Texas broadcasters; McDonald was elected first president. Activities were to range from participation in politics to public service. TAB worked for the passage of the anti-libel law in Texas (1954). In 1958 the group supported a constitutional amendment allowing the state of Texas to finance tourist advertising, assisted in setting up Texas' first "deathless weekend" safety drive, worked to coordinate a statewide disaster relief program, and instituted the Pitluk Award for outstanding community service. In 1959 permanent headquarters were created in Austin. In 1960 the Elkins Education Awards were established in addition to a program of annual awards to draw to public attention outstanding work at the local station level. The highway safety program, "Drive Lighted and Live," was started.

In 1961 separate organizations of AM, FM, and TV stations threatened TAB solidarity, but by 1964 the groups had returned to the organization.

In 1964 a college workshop at the University of Texas (Austin) began sponsoring an annual meeting of graduating high school seniors interested in broadcasting careers. In 1967 TAB had a membership of 272 and in 1968 had as one of its goals the improvement of the disaster relief program, which began as a result of the broadcasting work done during Hurricane Beulah in the Rio Grande Valley. *See also* Radio in Texas; Television in Texas.

Bonner McLane

Texas Association of College Teachers. The Texas Association of College Teachers (TACT) was organized in November, 1948, as the College Classroom Teachers Association, a section of the Texas State Teachers Association.qv Sam B. Barton, North Texas State College (now North Texas State University), was the first president, serving from 1948 to 1950. To coordinate more effectively the association's growing program, a state office with an executive secretary was established in Austin in 1953. In 1956 TACT adopted a new constitution, voting complete organizational autonomy from TSTA and becoming the Texas Association of College Teachers.

TACT is composed of local units or chapters located in the state supported colleges and universities. In 1974 the membership numbered about 3,300, in thirty chapters. The purpose of the association as stated in its constitution is to develop programs to assist in attaining a first-class system of higher education in Texas, and to strive for the highest personal standards of teaching, scholarship, and research.

TACT was largely instrumental in obtaining social security and other fringe benefits for college and university teachers, and in establishing a coordinating agency for state higher education. It continues to work for improved salaries and carries on research projects of concern to faculty personnel, providing relevant and useful information in clarifying the needs of higher education in Texas. In addition to faculty members, it works with college administrators, boards of regents, the state's Coordinating Board,qv legislators, key public officials, all organizations interested in the progress of Texas education, and the general public.

TACT's state executive board is composed of a president and eleven other officers. David Pratt of Texas A&I University was president in 1974–1975. The house of delegates consists of chapter representatives to fall and spring state meetings. *The TACT Bulletin* is published by the state office in Austin.

Mrs. Alice Calkins

Texas Association of Counties. The Texas Association of Counties, not a state agency, was created in the fall of 1969 when the Texas legislature authorized Texas counties to collect dues for an organization which would serve all county officials in the state. The association's first full-time executive director, Kenneth A. Douglas, began duties on January 1, 1973.

A non-political service organization, the association provides information concerning county government and helps to keep county officials informed about state laws which affect them.

Texas Association for Graduate Education and Research. *See* University of Texas at Dallas.

*Texas Bankers Association.

*Texas Baptist College.

*Texas Baptist Herald.

Texas Baptist Institute and Seminary. Texas Baptist Institute and Seminary, in Henderson, opened in September, 1948, in buildings of the Calvary Baptist Church. A permanent campus was located on Longview Drive after completion of an administration building in 1954. The Calvary Baptist Church appointed trustees and elected administrative officers and faculty.

The institute and seminary conducted classes on a nine-month basis in four departments: Bible and Bible languages; evangelism and Bible interpretation; church history, administration, and doctrine; and speech and English. Students wanting to do religious work could earn a certificate in English Bible. The institute also offered the B.A. and M.A. degrees in English Bible, while the seminary offered the same degrees in theology. A thesis was required for completion of both degrees.

The library contained 2,947 volumes in 1969. Building plans were for duplex apartments, classrooms, and a chapel. Enrollment fluctuated from thirty-five to seventy-four full-time students (1948–1973). In 1973 the faculty numbered ten and Ray O. Brooks served as president.

*Texas Baptist University.

*Texas Bar Association. *See* State Bar of Texas.

Texas Bible Chair. *See* Christian Church Schools in Texas.

*Texas Blind, Deaf, and Orphan School. *See also* Special Schools and Special Education; Texas School for the Blind; Texas School for the Deaf.

Texas Blind and Deaf School. *See* Special Schools and Special Education; Texas Blind, Deaf, and Orphan School; Texas School for the Blind; Texas School for the Deaf.

Texas Board of Corrections. *See* Corrections, Texas Board of.

*Texas Business Review. The *Texas Business Review* had a circulation of over 6,500 in 1964; in 1971 the circulation was 6,700. A monthly supplement was published, entitled *Construction in Texas*, containing detailed data on building permits issued in all standard metropolitan statistical areas qv and in municipalities that required building permits.

Stanley A. Arbingast

Texas Cattle Raisers' Association. *See* Cattle

Raisers' Associations (in Volume I); Texas and Southwestern Cattle Raisers' Association (in this volume).

Texas Caver. See Caves and Cave Studies in Texas.

*Texas Centennial.

*Texas Centennial of Statehood.

*Texas Central Railroad Company.

Texas Children's Home and Aid Society. *See* Gladney Home.

*Texas Christian.

*Texas Christian Advocate. The Methodists of Texas had a newspaper as early as 1847, when Robert B. Wells qv started the weekly, *Texas Christian Advocate and Brenham Advertiser* in Brenham. It was both a church and community paper. It was moved in less than a year to Houston, where Orceneth Fisher qv (Wells' father-in-law) became editor, and the name was changed to the *Texas Christian Advocate*. A year later (1849) Chauncey Richardson qv became editor, and the name of the paper was changed to the *Texas Wesleyan Banner*.qv The Methodist General Conference between 1850 and 1854 gave it official recognition. It carried much general news and was not exclusively a religious paper. The editor claimed for it the largest circulation in Texas—1,500 subscribers. Richardson resigned after a brief period when his salary was reduced during the paper's financial difficulties, and Charles Shearn,qv who contributed to the paper's financing, became editor. David Ayres qv became editor and publisher a few years later, when the paper was moved to Galveston in the early 1850's, and the name again was changed to the *Texas Christian Advocate*. When Galveston was blockaded during the Civil War, the paper was moved back to Houston until 1866, when it was returned to Galveston.

In 1866 I. G. John was elected editor and served for eighteen years. By 1884, with Louis Blaylock and William Shaw as publishers, the *Advocate* had 10,500 subscribers. Publication was moved to Dallas in 1887; in 1898 George C. Rankin qv became editor. During his seventeen-year tenure he used the editorial page to fight gambling, prostitution, liquor, dancing, disrespect for the Sabbath, and to rally Methodists to the support of the prohibition movement.qv After Rankin's death in 1915 the paper's editors included W. D. Bradfield, Andrew J. Weeks qv (1919–1922), and E. A. Hunter. From the early 1880's until 1924 Blaylock continued to provide a stable base for the paper's financing.

Through several mergers the *Advocate* was named *Southwestern Advocate* (for a short period when it served New Mexico, Oklahoma, and Texas) and then the *Christian Advocate*. It was changed back to the *Texas Christian Advocate* in 1952. In 1960, with Carl E. Keightley as editor, the paper's name was again changed, this time to the *Texas Methodist*.qv *See also* Methodist Church in Texas.

BIBLIOGRAPHY: John D. Barron, Jr., A Critical History

of the *Texas Christian Advocate*, 1849–1949 (M.A. thesis, University of Missouri, 1952); William Jesse Stone, Jr., A Historical Survey of Leading Texas Denominational Newspapers, 1846–1861 (Ph.D. dissertation, University of Texas at Austin, 1974).

Walter N. Vernon

*Texas Christian University. In 1941 McGruder Ellis Sadler qv (not E. M. Sadler, as stated in Volume II) became president of Texas Christian University, and in 1943 the school was reorganized into seven (not six) colleges or schools, each with its own administrative head. The eighth division, Harris College of Nursing, was added in 1946.

Between 1950 and 1965 the university experienced unprecedented growth. Construction, renovation, enlargement, or acquisition of twenty-five buildings was accomplished during the fifteen-year period. Included were a science building, a chapel, a student center, dormitories, a stadium, a school of business, a library, a school of education, a coliseum, a health center, apartments, offices and classrooms, a cafeteria, and a medical arts building. In 1963 the university acquired the Worth Hills Golf Course, 106 acres adjacent to the campus, bringing the total campus area to 242 acres. Since 1969 new facilities have included a tennis center, a physical sciences building, a nursing and home economics building, a health and physical education building, and a women's residence hall.

Entrance requirements were upgraded, and advanced programs leading to Ph.D. degrees were inaugurated in 1959. Research programs accelerated, with grants totaling more than $1,700,000 by 1971. Texas Christian University Research Foundation was chartered by the state in 1962. Nuclear physics research equipment, a computer center, a foreign language laboratory, radio-TV studios with an FM station (KTCU-FM), the Ames Observatory, the Institute of Behavioral Research, and the Institute for Study of Cognitive Systems were other new facilities. In 1963 Brite College of the Bible became known as Brite Divinity School. A special course division to serve as an all-university liaison with business, professional, community, and faculty groups was established in 1964.

The TCU Press was formally established in 1966 (although it had operated occasionally in previous years), and it began regular publication of books and monographs. During 1967 the university began participation in the Texas Association for Graduate Education and Research (TAGER qv) in North Texas, and it cooperated with other area colleges and industrial firms in a closed circuit TV network to provide various courses, usually at the graduate level. A faculty assembly and senate were formed in 1967–1968, and students were given a voice on most university committees. Chapters of Phi Beta Kappa and Sigma Xi have been added to the university's accrediting organizations.

The university's endowment program grew to $29.5 million by 1971, an increase of more than $7 million since 1960. The annual operating budget reached $15.9 million. By 1971 library holdings consisted of 765,000 books, documents, and periodicals, including the William Luther Lewis collection of rare books, the A. M. Pate collection on the American presidency, a substantial selection of volumes on the Southwest, and other important collections.

Student enrollment reached 6,405 during the fall semester of 1973; faculty numbered 474 that same year. James M. Moudy, who became the seventh head of the university in July, 1965, remained as chancellor in 1974, when the enrollment was 6,132. *See also* Christian Church Schools in Texas.

Jim Lehman

Texas Chronicle.

*Texas City, Texas. Texas City, an industrial city in Galveston County, had a deepwater port which ranked fifth in the state in total tonnage handled in 1969; principal exports (domestic and foreign) were chemicals and petroleum products. Tonnage in short tons handled by the port rose from over fourteen million tons in 1958 to over sixteen million in 1969. Property damage of over $67 million to the port area resulted from the disastrous explosions in April, 1947 (*see* Texas City Disaster). After Hurricane Carla in 1961 caused damages amounting to over $29 million in the Texas City-La Marque area, a project of hurricane and flood control, with a seawall and dike, was begun in 1962; it was scheduled for completion in the early 1970's. A dike, which reached five miles into Galveston Bay toward Point Bolivar, brought additional fishing and camping facilities to the area. A new library and an indoor arena for rodeos and horse shows were constructed in the 1960's. The population in 1960 was 32,065; in 1970 it was 38,908, according to the United States census. *See also* Galveston-Texas City Standard Metropolitan Statistical Area.

Texas City Disaster. One of the worst disasters in Texas history occurred on April 16, 1947, when the ship S.S. *Grandcamp* exploded at 9.12 a.m. at the docks in Texas City. The French-owned vessel, carrying explosive ammonium nitrate, caught fire early in the morning, and while attempts were being made to extinguish the fire, the ship exploded. The entire dock area was destroyed, along with the nearby Monsanto Chemical Company, other smaller companies, grain warehouses, and numerous oil and chemical storage tanks. Smaller explosions and fires were ignited by flying debris, not only along the industrial area, but throughout the city. Fragments of iron, parts of the ship's cargo, and dock equipment were hurled into businesses, houses, and public buildings. A fifteen-foot tidal wave, created by the force, swept the dock area. The concussion of the explosion, felt as far away as Port Arthur, damaged or destroyed at least 1,000 residences and buildings throughout Texas City. The ship S.S. *High Flyer*, in dock for repairs and also carrying ammonium nitrate, had been ignited by the first explosion; it was towed 100 feet from the docks

before it exploded about sixteen hours later, at
1:10 a.m. on April 17. The first explosion had
killed twenty-six Texas City firemen and destroyed
all of the city's fire fighting equipment, including
four fire trucks, leaving the city helpless in the wake
of the second explosion. No central disaster organization had been created by the city, but most of
the chemical and oil plants had disaster plans
which were quickly activated. Although power and
water were cut off, hundreds of local volunteers
began fighting the fires and doing rescue work.
Red Cross personnel and other volunteers from
surrounding cities responded with assistance until
almost 4,000 workers were operating; temporary
hospitals, morgues, and shelters were set up.

Probably the exact number of people killed will
never be known, although the ship's anchor monument records 576 persons known dead, 398 of
whom were identified and 178 listed as missing.
All records of personnel and payrolls of the Monsanto Company were destroyed, and many of the
dock workers were itinerants, making identification
difficult. Almost all persons in the dock area—
firemen, ships' crews, and spectators—were killed,
and most of the bodies were never recovered; sixty-
three bodies were buried unidentified. The number
of injured ranged in the thousands, and loss of
property totaled about $67 million. Litigation over
the Texas City disaster was finally settled in 1962
when the United States Supreme Court refused to
review an appeals court ruling that the Republic
of France, owner of the *Grandcamp*, could not be
held liable for any claims resulting from the explosion.

BIBLIOGRAPHY: American Red Cross, *Texas City Explosion* (1948); Ivy Stewart Deckard, *In the Twinkling of an
Eye* (1962); Elizabeth Lee Wheaton (comp.), *Texas City
Remembers* (1948); Fire Prevention and Engineering Bureau of Texas (and) The National Board of Fire Under-
writers, *Texas City, Texas, Disaster* (n.d.).

*Texas City Junction, Texas.

*Texas City Terminal Railway Company. The
Texas City Terminal Railway Company in 1964
was a terminal switching line with about twelve
miles of terminal track connecting the port of
Texas City with main line railroads. On December 20, 1956, an agreement was reached between
the company and ten insurance firms by which the
railroad received $3,250,000 for damages incurred
in the Texas City disaster qv of April, 1947.

James M. Day

*Texas Civil Judicial Council. The Texas Civil
Judicial Council, created by legislative statute in
1929, continued its function of making a continuous
study of and reporting on the operation, organization, and improvement of the civil courts of Texas.

Since a 1953 amendment, the council membership (all members served without compensation)
has consisted of eighteen members, nine of whom
were ex officio members: the chief justice of the
Supreme Court of Texas or his delegate from the
same court, two justices of the Courts of Civil

Appeals, two presiding judges of the Administrative Judicial Districts, the chairman and the immediate past chairman of the Senate Jurisprudence
Committee, and the chairman and the immediate
past chairman of the House Judiciary Committee;
the remaining nine members were appointed by the
governor for six-year terms and included seven
lawyers and two non-lawyer citizens, one of whom
had to be a professional journalist. Of the five ex
officio judge-members, all except the chief justice
(or his delegate) were chosen by the governor for
the terms of office qualifying them for membership.

The wide range of council activities includes
gathering and publishing current official statistics
and pertinent information on the operation of the
Texas civil judicial system. The council recommends improvements in the system and in court
procedure and publishes an annual report during
the first half of each year. It has been responsible
for numerous recommendations that have since been
embodied in law, such as the creation in 1939 of the
statutory State Bar of Texas,qv with compulsory
membership of the entire practicing Bar. It recommended the legislative adoption (1955) of the present probate code, the draft-codification (1957) of
the public school laws (with the financial aid of the
M. D. Anderson Foundation qv), and the constitutional provision for the compulsory retirement of
judges of superior courts (recommended by the
council in 1964 and made law by the voters of
Texas in November, 1965). In 1969 the council
was given the expanded authority to collect statistics
in the criminal as well as the civil judicial system.

The council has maintained its office in the Supreme Court building in Austin since 1959. An
executive secretary and a stenographer were the
only regular employees.

BIBLIOGRAPHY: Texas Civil Judicial Council, *Annual Report* (1954, 1957, 1963, 1968, 1970); University of Texas
at Austin, *Guide To Texas State Agencies* (1972).

W. St. John Garwood

*Texas Civil Service. *See* Civil Service in Texas.

*Texas Collection. The Texas Collection in the
Eugene C. Barker Texas History Center qv at the
University of Texas at Austin contains the library,
archives, and Texas newspaper collections. On
April 1, 1950, Llerena Friend became librarian;
upon her retirement in 1969 the library and the
archives were consolidated under one director,
Chester V. Kielman. In 1971 the center was located
in Sid W. Richardson qv Hall on the east campus.
The Texas newspaper collection (newspapers from
1829 forward), earlier a part of the main library's
general newspaper collection, was also housed in
the center beginning in 1971.

Library holdings included 104,000 titles in 1973,
and archival holdings were approximately seventeen
million documents in 1973. The collections serve
faculty, graduate students, and researchers at the
university at Austin, in addition to other universities and senior colleges around the country. In

1973, 1,724 researchers used the archives, and the staff handled over thirty-two thousand requests.

The University of Texas Archives Publication Program was established in the 1960's. Completed publications include *The University of Texas Archives: A Guide to the Historical Manuscript Collections in the University of Texas Library*, Volume I (1967), compiled and edited by Chester V. Kielman, with the assistance of the Dora Dieterich Bonham Fund, and a 172-reel microfilm edition of the Bexar Archives,qv which was sponsored by the National Historical Publications Commission and completed in 1971. Descriptive guides to the three segments of the microfilm edition were published in 1967, 1969, and 1971.

*Texas College. Texas College, Tyler, trained more than 4,000 graduates between its founding in 1894 and 1965. The college, a four-year liberal arts institution, offered majors in elementary education, physical education, health and recreation, home economics, English, music, biology, chemistry, mathematics, business education, and social science.

Especially concerned with the development of East Texas youths from limited financial backgrounds, Texas College provided financial aid through student loan and work-study programs. During the 1954–1955 term, the college had an enrollment of 676 students, a faculty of forty-three members, and D. R. Glass was president. Twelve years later during the 1966–1967 term, enrollment was 455 students, the faculty numbered thirty-one members, and Horace C. Savage served as president. The library housed 53,973 volumes in 1969.

Texas College continued its relationship with the Christian Methodist Episcopal church and was a member of several college associations and councils. In 1965 the value of the physical plant exceeded $1,500,000. In 1974 Allen C. Hancock was president, the enrollment was 536, and the faculty numbered approximately forty.

*Texas College of Arts and Industries. *See also* Texas A&I University.

Texas College of Mines. *See* University of Texas at El Paso.

Texas Commission on the Arts and Humanities. The Texas Commission on the Arts and Humanities, called the Texas Fine Arts Commission before a change in name by the 62nd Texas Legislature, has the duty to foster the fine arts for the enrichment and benefit of the citizens of Texas, to make vacations and visits to Texas more appealing to the world, and to attract outstanding creators in the field of fine arts through appropriate programs of education and publicity. The commission is also authorized to direct the sponsorship of art lectures and exhibitions and to compile and disseminate information on the progress of fine arts in the state.

All the duties and authorities previously vested in the Board of Mansions Supervisors qv have been assumed by the commission, and it acts in an advisory capacity to other state agencies which are concerned with acquiring or renovating works of art. The commission may also accept donations of money, property, art objects, or historical relics on behalf of the state. It is composed of eighteen members appointed by the governor, with concurrence of the Senate; members are selected from all fields representing the fine arts and from individuals widely known for their professional competence and experience with the fine arts. They serve for overlapping six-year terms.

In 1974 a plan was undertaken for the commission to work with the Humanities Research Center of the University of Texas at Austin to collect and store artifacts and memorabilia in the Hoblitzell Theater Arts Library. The collection was to serve as an official archives for Texas arts, encompassing music, dance, the visual arts, literature, architecture, and folk arts. (For an earlier account of the commission, *see* Fine Arts Commission, Texas.)

BIBLIOGRAPHY: University of Texas at Austin, *Guide To Texas State Agencies* (1972).

Texas Commission on Higher Education. *See* Coordinating Board, Texas College and University System.

*Texas Commission on Interstate Co-operation. *See* Interstate Co-operation, Texas Commission on.

Texas Commission for Rehabilitation. *See* Rehabilitation, Texas Commission for.

Texas Communities Tomorrow Program. *See* Community Affairs, Department of.

*Texas Company, The. The corporate name of the Texas Company was changed to Texaco Inc. in 1959. *See also* Texaco Inc.

*Texas Congress of Parents and Teachers. The Texas Congress of Parents and Teachers had a 1971 membership of 693,202 and was the second largest state PTA branch in the nation. It was comprised of districts organized along county lines; city, county, and school district PTA councils; and more than 2,500 local units. The governing body worked through a state executive committee and a state board of managers, and annual state conventions were held in November at selected Texas host cities. A state headquarters building in Austin was erected in 1937; a west wing was added in 1950, and a second story was added in 1957.

Through the Texas Congress Legislation Program and a legislative bulletin, the group actively supported desired state legislation that fell within the scope of parent-teacher work as it came before the Texas legislature. Leadership training seminars were held each summer in Austin for PTA delegates from all areas of the state. The Texas State Fair Association honored the Texas PTA each October by providing for a special PTA Day at the State Fair of Texas qv in Dallas. The governor normally proclaimed October as Parent-Teacher Membership Enrollment Period in Texas.

The Texas Parent-Teacher magazine, official publication of the Texas PTA, was converted in 1971 to *The Texas PTA*, a bulletin issued nine months of the year. Membership in the national PTA was over nine million.

BIBLIOGRAPHY: Texas Congress of Parents and Teachers, *State Handbook, 1966–67.*

Lea Ledger

Texas Council on Migrant Labor. *See* Labor, Texas Council on Migrant.

*Texas Courier.

*Texas Cowboy Reunion. The Texas Cowboy Reunion has sponsored annual rodeos in Stamford, Texas, since the 1930's. Guests who appeared at the reunions ranged from Will Rogers, who attended the rodeo shortly before his death, to various governors and state officials. The reunion's rodeo was the first to include cutting horse events, cowgirl sponsors, barrel racing, and approved quarter horse shows. Since their appearance in the Stamford rodeo, these events have been added to many other rodeos held throughout the nation. By 1967, in addition to the Old Timers Bunkhouse, the reunion's physical plant included a guest house to provide accommodations for visiting dignitaries. Various riding clubs and the Hardin-Simmons Cowboy Band usually participated in the reunions. *See also* Anson, Texas (in Volume I), for an account of the Cowboys' Christmas Ball in Anson.

BIBLIOGRAPHY: *The Cattleman,* XLVI (September, 1959).

*Texas Creek.

*Texas Democrat.

*Texas Dental College.

Texas Department of Corrections. *See* Corrections, Texas Department of.

*Texas Dialects. *See* Dialects, Texan.

*Texas Division. *See* Thirty-sixth Division.

*Texas Education Agency. In 1949 the legislature abolished the former State Board of Education (*see* Education, State Board of, in Volume I) and the office of State Superintendent of Public Instruction, and the Gilmer-Aikin (not Gilmer-Aiken, as stated in Volume I) Law created the Texas Education Agency as the state's administrative agent to supervise the public school system. In 1972 the agency was composed of the State Board of Education (which included the State Board for Vocational Education), the Commissioner of Education ^{qv} (selected by the board), and professional, technical, and clerical staffs.

The State Board of Education was composed of twenty-one members elected for six-year terms, with one member being elected from each congressional district of the state as they were constituted in 1949. The State Board of Education was the policy-forming body for the public schools; it adopted operating budgets on the basis of legislative appropriations, established regulations for the accreditation of schools, executed contracts for the purchase of textbooks to be used in the public schools, and invested the Permanent School Fund.^{qv} The Commissioner of Education, appointed by the board for a four-year term, was the secretary of the

board and the chief executive officer of the Texas Education Agency. One of his many duties was the issuance of teachers certificates. The professional, technical, and clerical staffs of the Texas Education Agency were under the direct supervision of the Commissioner of Education.

In general, the agency set standards and supervised the public schools of the state. Funds from the federal government for programs related to public education were handled through the Texas Education Agency. It also administered the Texas School for the Deaf, the Texas School for the Blind,^{qqv} and the state's vocational rehabilitation program. *See also* Special Schools and Special Education.

BIBLIOGRAPHY: Texas Education Agency, *Minimum Foundation School Program* (1954); Rae Files Still, *The Gilmer-Aikin Bills* (1950); Stuart A. MacCorkle and Dick Smith, *Texas Government* (1964); Clifton McCleskey, *The Government and Politics of Texas* (1963); Wilbourn Eugene Benton, *Texas, Its Government and Politics* (1961); University of Texas at Austin, *Guide To Texas State Agencies* (1972).

Dick Smith

Texas Educational Foundation. *See* Job Corps Program in Texas.

*Texas Electric Railway.

*Texas Emigrant.

*Texas Emigration and Land Company. *See* Peters' Colony.

*Texas Employment Commission.

*Texas Engineering Experiment Station. Since 1950, research discoveries at the Texas Engineering Experiment Station, part of the Texas A&M University System,^{qv} included: nuclear activation analysis techniques; effects of low-dose chronic gamma radiation on mice and rats and high-level neutron and gamma radiation on goats; a prototype for the manufacture of crop-dusting planes; computer methods for multicomponent distillation; enzyme visceration means in trash fish utilization; high-protein flours from edible oil seeds; and design of crash-landing gear and other engineering innovations for space shots.

L. J. Horn

*Texas Engineering Extension Service. In 1967 the Texas Engineering Extension Service, a part of the Texas A&M University System,^{qv} conducted courses for industrial supervisory personnel both on the campus and in local industrial areas. Many of these courses were conducted within the plant, and instruction was designed to serve the special needs of the individual company requesting training service. Extension training programs were also provided for municipal electric and rural electric linemen and telephone maintenance personnel. More recently, courses were established to train electronic technicians and heavy construction equipment operators. Drafting was offered in a twelve-week course during the summer months for persons who wished to prepare for immediate employment in industry. In the 1960's approximately fifteen thousand people per year enrolled in the courses conducted by the Engineering Extension Service staff in an effort to upgrade their knowledge and skills to meet changing employment requirements.

H. D. Beardon

*Texas Farm Bureau. The first Texas Farm Bureau was organized in the summer of 1920; within the first year it established a cotton marketing cooperative and soon after a number of other marketing cooperatives. In 1924 the organization's by-laws were amended to permit the marketing cooperatives to pay members' dues; therefore, all members automatically became members of the Farm Bureau. As the cooperatives failed or became separated from the parent organization, the Farm Bureau's membership dwindled, and by 1932 the first Farm Bureau organized in Texas had ceased operation. Increased interest in agricultural legislation and renewed efforts to organize Texas farmers and ranchers in the early 1930's resulted in the chartering of the Texas Agricultural Association in 1934. Two years later it became affiliated with the American Farm Bureau Federation, and eventually the name was changed to the Texas Farm Bureau Federation. "Federation" was dropped from the name in 1954.

In the 1930's there were never more than a few thousand members, but by 1945 membership had grown to some 7,000. By 1950 there were more than 50,000 members as new county groups were organized; the organization continued to expand yearly.

The Texas Farm Bureau initiated its first service-to-member program in 1944 with a membership contract for medical insurance. In 1946 the TFB joined with other states to found the Southern Farm Bureau Life Insurance Company. The Southern Farm Bureau Casualty Insurance Company was established in 1947 in conjunction with other southern state farm bureaus. In 1950 the TFB set up its own Texas Farm Bureau Insurance Company, offering fire and extended coverage. This company was converted into the Texas Farm Mutual Insurance Company in 1958; later, crop-hail insurance was introduced.

In the early 1960's TFB expanded its services to include promotion and development of Texas commodities for European markets. In 1966 a domestic cattle marketing program (limited to pilot counties) was begun. In 1971 a task force committee in East Texas was writing a program for feeder and stocker calf sales, and a similar committee in the Panhandle was preparing a feeder and stocker calf purchasing program. A broiler-grower service to assist producers in contract bargaining was no longer in operation in 1971, although that same year a used-hen marketing program (initiated in 1967) was successful.

A service program was instituted in 1965 for the sale of the Farm Bureau's own Safemark tires and batteries to members through independent dealers in more than 175 counties. Texas was one of about thirty states in the program.

The TFB has supported state legislation for improved animal health laws, farm-to-market road systems, an egg grading law, a tractor gas refund, an exemption from sales tax on farm machinery, appropriation of funds for agricultural research and education, and improved feed, seed, and insecticide laws.

Fifty states, plus Puerto Rico, have organized farm bureaus affiliated with the American Farm Bureau Federation. In 1968 TFB had 105,653 members in 203 organized counties; in 1971 there were 127,402 farm and ranch family members in 206 counties, and of these, about 165 had their own offices. The board of directors was composed of thirteen members, one from each of the thirteen districts in the state; officers of the organization were elected by board members from among their own number. In 1971 there were more than 300 employees of the Texas Farm Bureau and its affiliated insurance services; of these, some 200 were at the Waco headquarters. In 1973 J. T. Woodson was president and Warren Newberry was executive director.

Bill Hoover
Bill Wedemeyer

*Texas Federation of Women's Clubs. The Texas Federation of Women's Clubs is composed of fourteen districts named for their respective regions. Membership of the federation is of two types: active and associate. The federation includes seven departments of work: conservation, education, fine arts, home life, international affairs and international clubs, public affairs, and Texas heritage. Three programs are required—Federation Day, Americanism Day, and Texas Day. In cooperation with the University of Texas, the Texas Federation of Women's Clubs established Epsilon Sigma Omicron, an honorary educational sorority for clubwomen. *The Texas Clubwoman* is the federation's official publication.

Loraine J. Dudley

*Texas Female Institute.

*Texas Female Seminary.

*Texas Feuds. *See* Feuds in Texas.

*Texas Fever. *See* Cattle Tick.

Texas Film Commission. The Texas Film Commission was created by executive order of Governor Preston Smith on May 24, 1971, during the session of the 62nd Texas Legislature. Governor Smith, a former theater owner himself, thought the state should develop a film industry of its own "second to none," and said the industry would bring "a new style and added energy to our financial, educational, and cultural environment." The position of executive director was first occupied (1971–1974) by Warren Skaaren, a former member of the governor's office staff. "The goal of the commission," said Skaaren, "is to develop a film industry in Texas—encouraging and supporting the already strong film industry of our state as well as welcoming and giving full assistance to the producers from outside Texas." The commission's first 41-member advisory board included academy award-winning actress Dorothy Malone of Dallas, and Paul Baker, director of the Dallas Theater Center, in addition to bankers, legislators, and film makers.

The work program of the Texas Film Commission for 1971–1972 included advertising in trade journals, conferences, production of a catalog of film-related services, development of location scouting services, a video tape location library, a weather information service, community cooperation, development and advertisement of a Texas script and story library (a repository of scenarios or stories with Texas themes), a semi-monthly newsletter, information regarding Texas right-to-work statutes, screenwriting competition, and investment-security guidelines and motion picture law seminars. *See also* Texas Film Industry.

James R. Buchanan

Texas Film Industry. The production of motion pictures in Texas dates from at least 1909, when Gaston Melies and William F. Haddock, a noted stage actor, were in San Antonio making "horse operas." Melies was the twin brother of George Melies, one of the more important French technical innovators in film; the two had worked together before Gaston came to America. Two other brothers, Paul and Wesley Hope Tilley,qv produced silent films in Houston in 1910. The next year in San Antonio they formed the Satex Film Company, moving it to Austin in 1913. Satex studios were at 13th and Lavaca streets in Austin; their only known production was a three-reeler called *Their Lives by a Slender Thread*, which used local actors.

A project to film a series based on the siege and fall of the Alamo was chartered in San Antonio in 1913, but flopped three years later. In 1918 the noted character actor Maclyn Arbuckle qv chose the same city for its sunshine and background scenes to open a studio financed by William Clifford Hogg.qv

Not until Hollywood came to Texas did the state's film industry gain much popular or artistic success. In 1923 the Fox Film Company shot exterior scenes for *The Warrens of Virginia* in and around San Antonio. This was a seven-reeler starring Wilfred Lytell and Martha Mansfield, whose costume caught fire near the end of filming and resulted in the star's death. The film was completed, however, and later premiered in San Antonio. A Houston locale was used in *North of the 36th* (1924), directed by Irvin Willat and starring Jack Holt and Lois Wilson, but San Antonio seemed to attract the bigger productions, especially war movies. King Vidor's *The Big Parade* (1925), with John Gilbert and Renée Adorée; *Wings* (1927), with Buddy Rogers, Richard Arlen, and Clara Bow; and Victor Fleming's *The Rough Riders* (1927), filmed on the site where Theodore Roosevelt drilled his troops, all used air and army posts

around San Antonio for locations. The 1934 MGM production of *West Point of the Air* used the newly created Randolph Air Force Base qv as a locale; it starred Robert Young, Rosalind Russell, Wallace Beery, and Robert Taylor. The last of the war movies until *Air Cadet* (1951) was *I Wanted Wings* (1940), with Ray Milland, William Holden, and Veronica Lake. *High School* (1936) was filmed largely in San Antonio's Jefferson High.

The 1940's saw little film production in Texas, but by 1952, when Paramount used the Bracketville area as location for *Arrowhead*, James T. Shahan, the mayor of Bracketville, began to think of a permanent movie set for the area. Republic filmed *The Last Command* in the area in 1955, prompting Shahan to develop the Alamo Village,qv which in 1959 became the site of the largest production in Texas, when John Wayne's Batjac company moved in to film *The Alamo*. The Alamo Village set has since been used for *Two Rode Together*, for *Bandolero*, and for various television segments and commercials.

Other locations were used in Texas in the 1950's, including the Davis Mountains as a backdrop in *The Sundowners* (1950), Rio Grande City in 1952 for *Viva Zapata*, and the area around Marfa for *Giant* (1956), a film about Texas which starred Elizabeth Taylor, Rock Hudson, and James Dean. Paris and northeastern Texas were the setting for *Home from the Hill* in 1960, and scenes around Dallas were used in the 1962 production of *State Fair*.

A new wave of moviemaking in Texas began in 1962 with the filming of *Hud* in the small town of Claude; the movie was an adaptation of *Horseman Pass By*, a novel by Texas writer Larry McMurtry, and starred Paul Newman, Melvyn Douglas, and Patricia Neal. *Baby, the Rain Must Fall* (1965) was shot in Wharton, Peter Ustinov's *Viva Max* (1968) in San Antonio, and John Wayne's *Hellfighters* (1969) in Houston. *Bonnie and Clyde* (1967), an important and much discussed film, used scenes in the Dallas-Denton area for authentic background. The Astrodome qv was the setting for *Brewster McCloud* in 1970, the same year in which exterior shots for *The Andromeda Strain* were made around Shafter, and *Red, White and Black* was filmed in Old Fort Davis.qv

Presidio Productions, Inc., based in Dallas, made and released *The Mark of the Witch* (1971), while the POP Film Company of Houston in the same year released *The Windsplitter*, filmed around Columbus. Archer City was the scene of another adaptation of a Larry McMurtry novel when *The Last Picture Show* was made there in 1971; the film by Peter Bogdanovich garnered several Academy Awards. *Leaving Cheyenne*, another McMurtry novel, was the basis for a film shot in the Bastrop area in 1972.

Dallas and Houston were the moviemaking leaders in the state in the 1970's, with several film companies covering the full spectrum of production—commercial, educational, and artistic—and there were indications that the industry would continue to grow throughout the state. Dallas had forty-seven film production companies in 1974, Houston forty, and San Antonio fifteen. The Jamieson Film Company of Dallas, founded in 1916, was the first major film production company in the Southwest, and in 1972 the company was scheduled to move into a new complex of buildings and form the Masters Film Company. MFC Film Production, Inc., of Houston, headed straight into feature films starring well known actors, after its founding in 1967. The movie industry in Texas was well prepared to compete with other southwestern states in the 1970's and was aided by the creation in 1971 of the Texas Film Commission,qv designed to encourage and support the industry by various means. Media courses and radio, television, and film departments, some with fully equipped studios and sound stages, are to be found in nearly all of the major colleges and universities in Texas.

BIBLIOGRAPHY: James R. Buchanan, "A Look at the Texas Film Industry," *Texas Business Review*, XLVI (January, 1972).

James R. Buchanan

*Texas Fine Arts Association. In 1932 the Texas Fine Arts Association (TFAA) acquired the Elisabet Ney Museum qv property (formerly called Formosa, the Austin studio-home of sculptor Elisabet Ney qv) from the heirs of Ella (Dancy) Dibrell (*see* Dibrell, Joseph Burton). The TFAA operated this museum until 1941, when it was deeded to the city of Austin's parks and recreation department.

During the years following 1943 the association steadily increased both its membership and its scope of activities. Until 1959 membership was granted directly to individuals; in that year the association expanded its activities by establishing local chapters which were affiliated with the state organization by charter. A new constitution was written, and local chapters were widely distributed around the state.

In 1943 Clara Driscoll qv conveyed her homesite in Austin, Laguna Gloria, to the Texas Fine Arts Association Holding Corporation. In 1961 the management of Laguna Gloria Art Museum qv was assumed by the Austin chapter of the TFAA under the name Laguna Gloria Art Museum, Inc. The city of Austin contributed substantially each year toward the maintenance of Laguna Gloria as a museum, and the Austin Junior League helped with arrangements for local and traveling exhibitions. In 1965, by agreement and merger of the holding corporations of the Austin chapter and the state organization, control of the property rights of Laguna Gloria was granted to the Austin chapter of the TFAA. The state organization was assured of certain exhibition privileges and space for the state office.

Regionally sponsored local shows, high school scholarship competitions, a spring jury show, a fall invitational exhibition, circuit exhibitions (shown each year in over fifty communities throughout the state), and a monthly newsletter are some of the widespread activities of the Texas Fine Arts Association in their quest to stimulate interest in the fine arts in Texas.

Lucile E. Weller

Texas Fine Arts Commission. *See* Fine Arts Commission, Texas; *see also* Texas Commission on the Arts and Humanities.

*Texas Folklore Society. The Texas Folklore Society was formally organized by Leonidas W. Payne and John A. Lomax qqv on December 29, 1909 (not 1910, as stated in Volume II). Sixty-six members (not sixty-five) were enrolled that day, and charter membership, held open until April 1, 1910, totaled ninety-two.

During the following year, interest in the society was maintained by the issuance of circulars to members, but it was not until April 8, 1911, that the organization held its first formal meeting in Austin at the Main Building of the University of Texas. Annual meetings have been held regularly since 1911, except for interruptions in 1918–1921 and 1944–1945, caused by two world wars. The first item to be published by the society was a pamphlet by Will Thomas in 1912 on Negro folksongs, and the first numbered volume was a miscellany in 1916, edited by Stith Thompson,qv secretary-treasurer, and later republished under the title *Round the Levee* (1935).

By 1966 the society had published thirty-three volumes, the titles and numbers of which indicated publications in a series. The society also annually produced a book or distributed some other folklore book to its members. In addition to the annual volume, the Range Life Series was instituted by J. Frank Dobie qv in order to make unpublished true narratives available, but publication of the series was allowed to lapse after the fifth book. Paisano Books, a new series begun in 1966, bore the name of the society's emblem, the paisano or roadrunner, a symbol chosen by Dobie.

In the 1960's an extensive collection of tapes was transcribed, and the society sponsored an annual contest for college students. Membership in the organization was open to anyone interested in folklore. The society is the second oldest continuously functioning folklore organization in the United States (the oldest being the American Folklore Society). In 1964 Wilson M. Hudson at the University of Texas succeeded Mody Boatright qv as editor. Until 1971 the society maintained an office and archives on the campus of the University of Texas at Austin, although it was not a part of that institution. Francis Abernethy of Stephen F. Austin University became the secretary-editor of the Texas Folklore Society in 1971, and the office was moved to that university campus in Nacogdoches at that time. In 1973 the membership of the society was approximately four hundred and fifty.

BIBLIOGRAPHY: *Publications of the Folk-Lore Society of Texas*, I (1916); *Publications of the Texas Folk-Lore So-*

ciety, II (1922); Subject File, Barker Texas History Center, University of Texas at Austin.

Wilson M. Hudson

*Texas Forest Service. The Texas Forest Service, a part of the Texas A&M University System,qv was created as the state forestry agency of Texas. Its objectives were to persuade and aid private owners of forest land in practicing forestry and converting submarginal agricultural lands to productive forests; to protect private forest lands against forest wildfires, insects, and disease; to inform the public of the contribution that forests, a renewable natural resource, make to the economy of the state; to educate Texans in uses and abuses of forest products; and to assist forest products industries in developing new products and improving production techniques.

Service activities included control of wildfires; supplying cooperative leadership in the control of insect and disease outbreaks; operation of a tree seedling nursery, seed orchards, and seed production areas to produce higher quality tree seedlings for reforestation of private lands; research in tree improvement and wood utilization; and providing technical information to timberland owners and forest products manufacturers. The service also demonstrated forest management on a multiple-use basis on four small state forests; conducted educational programs for the prevention of fires and use of natural resources; enforced the laws which related to wildfires and insect and disease epidemics; and maintained an inventory of timber growth and removal.

From its inception, research was conducted by the service on a modest scale. In 1951 the organization launched a research program in forest tree improvement, the first southern state forestry agency to undertake such research. Attention was also given to various aspects of wood utilization. In 1957 a nursery was developed in Jasper County near Magnolia Springs. It was later converted into the Magnolia Springs Seed Orchards where pedigreed pine seeds were produced for reforestation.

In the 1970's Texas had four small state forests, ranging in size from 626 to 2,980 acres and totaling 7,089 acres. During that time the service functioned in three broad areas—education, research, and general counseling. A seventh geographical administrative district was added to the service in 1961. In September, 1962, the service created a forest pest control section with the primary responsibility of conducting surveys and coordinating control of the southern pine beetle and other forest insects and diseases which attack pine and hardwood trees. A 1,800-acre hardwood demonstration forest was leased for twenty-five years in 1964 for the purpose of continuing timber production and water conservation, as well as to serve as a habitat for wildlife.

D. A. Anderson

*Texas 40 and 8.

*Texas Frontier Centennial.

*Texas Frontier Regiment. *See* Frontier Regiment.

*Texas Gazette.

*Texas Gazette and Brazoria Commercial Advertiser.

*Texas Geographic Magazine. The last issue of the *Texas Geographic Magazine*, Volume XII, was published in the fall of 1948. Both the magazine and the Texas Geographic Society,qv which published it, failed due to lack of financial support.

Edwin J. Foscue

*Texas Geographic Society. The Texas Geographic Society ceased to exist in 1950 due to lack of financial support. The last issue of the official publication of the society, the *Texas Geographic Magazine*,qv was published in 1948.

Edwin J. Foscue

Texas Gulf Coast Historical Association. The Texas Gulf Coast Historical Association was organized in 1955 by professional and lay historians interested in collecting and preserving manuscript records reflecting the significant changes which have occurred in the upper Texas coast within the last century. The association collects archival material relating to political and social history, but it specializes in the collection of business and economic history records. Its membership in 1966 was 150 persons and corporations.

The organization was sponsored by the University of Houston, and its archives were housed in the M. D. Anderson qv Library on the university campus. In 1966 its most important collections included the Charles A. Warner collection, the John Henry Kirby qv papers, the Robert Alonzo Welch qv papers, the Imperial Sugar Company records, the Minnie Fisher Cunningham qv papers, and the Joseph Stephen Cullinan qv collection.

The association encourages research and publication in the field of its interest through the Lewis Randolph Bryan, Jr.,qv award. This prize, in the amount of $200, has been awarded annually since 1960 for a manuscript of monograph length that, in the opinion of the committee, makes an original and significant contribution to the historical literature of the Gulf Southwest in the period since 1865. It also publishes one or two numbers a year in its *Publication Series*, and by 1966 the association had published ten titles.

James A. Tinsley

*Texas and Gulf Railroad Company.

*Texas Hall of State Museum. See Hall of State.

Texas Hill Country. *See* Hill Country.

Texas Historian. See Junior Historian Movement.

*Texas Historical Board.

Texas Historical Commission. After a change in name in August, 1973, the Texas State Historical Survey Committee became the Texas Historical Commission. The Committee was created by the Texas legislature in 1953 to lead, coordinate, sponsor projects, and act as a clearing house and information center to survey, record, preserve, restore, and mark all phases of Texas history by working with and through state, regional, and local groups and individuals. The original Committee, composed of eighteen members, was appointed for six-year terms by the governor and was comprised of persons who had demonstrated interest in the preservation of Texas heritage. It had the power to prescribe uniform markers, to check the historical accuracy of inscriptions prepared for markers by any individual or group, and to certify the historical worthiness of any historical property the state may determine to purchase.

State law authorized county judges to appoint County Historical Survey Committees. Texas had 254 County Historical Survey Committees in 1966. These committees allowed the Texas State Historical Survey Committee to coordinate and cooperate in activities throughout the state. State law also allowed commissioners courts to appropriate money from the general fund to finance the activities of County Historical Survey Committees, and to erect historical markers and acquire objects of historical significance. In addition, cities and counties were authorized to spend funds to operate historical museums.

The objectives of the Texas State Historical Survey Committee were embodied in a twenty-one-point policy statement called RAMPS, which was adopted in 1964. It called for the recording, appreciation, marking, preservation, and survey of Texas history. One of the basic objectives was the erection of 5,000 official Texas historical markers in five years. The Committee deemed this action necessary because the state had not had an official marking program since the Texas Centennial qv celebration in 1936. As of January 1, 1967, a total of 3,197 markers had been erected in conjunction with the RAMPS program.

Five types of official Texas historical markers were erected to mark structures, archeological finds, mountain passes, old trails, Indian camp and burial grounds, sites of battles and skirmishes, sites related to important events in cattle, agricultural, and petroleum industries, unique weather sites, early railroads, famous gunfights, early business and educational institutions, birthplaces or homes of outstanding Texans, and the date of founding, origin of name, and history of many towns and counties, as well as towns that no longer existed.

In 1966 the Committee established two special awards to recognize individuals, groups, and organizations for completing significant restoration or preservation projects. They are known as the Texas Restoration Award and the Texas Award for Historical Preservation. After 1968 the Committee broadened its scope by conducting the state archeological program, a museum services program, and

the National Register of Historic Places programs for the state.

Truett Latimer

*Texas Historical and Landmarks Association.

*Texas Historical Records Survey. The program of the Texas Historical Records Survey became defunct in 1942, and the records were stored in the University of Texas Archives. *See also* Work Projects Administration in Texas.

BIBLIOGRAPHY: David L. Smiley, "A Slice of Life in Depression America: The Records of the Historical Records Survey," *Prologue* (Winter, 1971).

*Texas Holiness University.

Texas Industrial Commission. *See* Industrial Commission, Texas.

*Texas Industrial Congress.

Texas Institute of Letters. The Texas Institute of Letters was organized on November 9, 1936, in Dallas, inspired by the Texas Centennial qv celebration. Its purpose was the "stimulation of interest in Texas Letters, the recognition of distinctive achievement in the field, and the promotion of fellowship among those especially interested in the literary and cultural development of the state." The first book award was given in 1939 to J. Frank Dobie qv for *Apache Gold and Yaqui Silver.*

The institute was indebted to two special sources of aid in the formative period: in 1938 the Cokesbury Bookstore began sponsoring the annual meetings in Dallas; in 1946 Carr P. Collins offered an annual award of one thousand dollars for the best Texas book of the year, defined as one on a Texas subject or by a Texas author. This later became the non-fiction award when the Jesse H. Jones qv award, of the same amount, was offered by Houston Endowment Inc.qv for the best book of fiction. Both awards have continued to the present. These and six other awards, totaling over three thousand dollars, have provided special incentive to Texas writers and brought distinction to the institute.

The active membership in the early 1970's was approximately one hundred fifty members, including several members from outside the state. The annual meetings are held in alternate years in Dallas, and in such other cities as Austin, Houston, and San Antonio. The afternoon session encourages informal discussion, followed by a business meeting. The annual awards dinner, with a guest speaker and open to non-members, has become one of the outstanding literary and social occasions of the year. For the institute's contribution to the Dobie-Paisano Project, *see* Paisano Ranch.

BIBLIOGRAPHY: William H. Vann, *The Texas Institute of Letters* (1967).

William Vann

Texas Jack. *See* Omohundro, John Burwell, Jr.

*Texas Journal of Education.

*Texas Land Company.

Texas Land and Development Company. The Texas Land and Development Company was an operating company for a series of parent companies chartered in Canada and organized in Plainview, Texas, in 1912. It carried out the idea of Milton Day Henderson, a local realtor, who, in foreseeing the great agricultural potential of the South Plains, conceived a plan to bring prospective settlers to land already developed and ready to operate. The development involved buying a large tract of land, dividing it into individual farms, and preparing each farm for occupancy. Preparation included the erection of appropriate dwellings, cultivation of at least one-quarter of each farm for the planting of alfalfa or sorghum, and the installation of an irrigation system.

Since his plans were too extensive to be financed locally, Henderson interested Frederick Stark Pearson,[qv] an eastern financier and engineer, in the project. Pearson's acquisition of funds for the enterprise, through a series of complex financial maneuvers between May 3, 1912, and December 3, 1912, brought $1,557,000 to Plainview for Henderson's use in buying the land. Halbert Cyrus Randolph and his son, Peyton Beaumont Randolph, local attorneys, examined and cleared land titles and wrote checks for the land that Henderson wished to purchase. From May 12, 1912, until the end of his buying, Henderson purchased 61,360 acres of land in Hale, Floyd, and Swisher counties, of which 18,175 acres were already under cultivation.

. By the end of November, 1914, the Texas Land and Development Company had expended $618,561 on the development of its lands. In order to promote sales the company advertised in the Hale County *Herald* and in such national magazines as *Sunset* and *Country Gentleman*. Land salesmen were sent to cities throughout the Midwest to conduct prospective buyers on excursion tours to the Texas lands. Ninety-two contracts totaling 12,038 acres were sold from the beginning of 1913 to July, 1916, when sales of developed farms were suspended due to a shortage of operating capital brought about by World War I. The amount of money that the company would have received if all of the contracts had been paid in full was approximately $1,090,127. The company sold 2,621 acres of undeveloped dry farm land valued at $82,498 between October, 1916, and the end of 1919, when a plan for reorganization of the company was put into effect. Even though the attempt to develop and sell irrigated farms was not entirely successful, the Texas Land and Development Company, on two experimental farms, demonstrated that a large variety of grains, fruits, fibers, and forage, as well as hogs, could be grown successfully on the South Plains.

Under a reorganization plan in 1919, the company leased its lands to tenant farmers on a year-to-year basis and urged its tenants to purchase company land when possible. The plan was a long time in reaching fruition, however, since the company did not sell all of its lands until 1946. Ten years later, on January 31, 1956, the company officially closed.

BIBLIOGRAPHY: Billy R. Brunson, The Texas Land and Development Company (Ph.D. dissertation, Texas Tech University, 1960).

Billy R. Brunson

*Texas Law Review (first).

*Texas Law Review (second). The *Texas Law Review* (second) continued as a forum for legal scholarship at the School of Law of the University of Texas at Austin, publishing works by law professors, practitioners, and students. Circulation was more than 2,500 by 1974, and the publication remained among the most widely quoted legal journals in the nation. Former editors have become judges, legal scholars, and practicing lawyers, both in Texas and elsewhere. Between fifty-five and sixty-five law students at the university are invited to become candidates for the *Review* at the end of their first year in law school. Fourteen law students are selected at the end of their second year to serve on the board of editors. Ten to fifteen additional students may qualify as associate editors.

In 1965 the Texas Law Review Association was organized; by 1974 it was comprised of 1,200 ex-editors of the *Review*. The association met in Austin each spring at the time of the annual *Texas Law Review* banquet. The purpose of the association, other than social, was to provide financial assistance to the *Review*.

*Texas League. As of 1963 all of the Texas League teams were owned by major league clubs. In the seventy-one playing seasons through 1966, twenty-nine cities had been members of the Texas League and South Texas League. In 1966 the clubs were Albuquerque, owned by Los Angeles, Amarillo by Houston, Arkansas by the St. Louis Cardinals, Austin by Milwaukee, Dallas-Fort Worth by the Chicago Cubs, and El Paso by the San Francisco Giants. The Dixie Series, begun in 1921, was continued through 1958. In 1959 it was replaced by an international series between the Texas and Mexican leagues' pennant winners for the Pan-American championship; this series lasted for three years. In 1971 the Texas League played an interlocking schedule with the Southern Association in the Dixie Association.

By 1966 more than 10,000 individual players had participated in Texas League games since 1888. Many of the greatest figures in pro baseball wore league uniforms. More than 10 percent of the total roster played one or more years in the major leagues after leaving Texas League clubs. The figure continued to increase since the farm system often promoted players to the parent clubs. By 1974 the National Baseball Hall of Fame included several former Texas Leaguers. From its inception, the league shared with other professional circuits the status of a business operated on more of a sporting than a business basis. Local pride was always a strong incentive, engendering inter-city rivalry. Attendance grew, especially after the advent of night baseball. Teams in the league in 1974 included San Antonio, Victoria, Midland, El Paso, and

Amarillo. *See also* McCloskey, John J; Texas Sports Hall of Fame.

William B. Ruggles

Texas Leander Rehabilitation Center. The Texas Leander Rehabilitation Center, so named in the late 1960's, was formerly the State Hog Farm.qv It became a pilot program for the development of recreational and educational facilities for the mentally retarded and mentally ill of Texas. Located on seven hundred acres, seventeen miles northwest of Austin, the center had camping facilities, nature trails, and a wildlife management area. The center was under the direction of the Texas Department of Mental Health and Mental Retardation.qv

Texas Legislative Council. *See* Legislative Council, Texas.

Texas Legislature. *See* Legislature of Texas.

*****Texas Library Association.** By 1950 the Texas Library Association had inaugurated a plan for strengthening the association through district organizations and joint meetings with the Friends of Texas Libraries and other groups at association conferences. In March, 1950, the quarterly *Texas Library Journal* superseded *News Notes* as the official publication of the association. Frequent amendments to the constitution provided for the interests of public, county, college, school, and special libraries and called attention to the weaknesses of the second constitution, which resulted in the adoption of a third in 1961.

After 1950 the association concentrated on a long-range plan for library development in Texas. Conference programs, committee assignments, surveys by independent agencies, independent studies, district programs, and the 1966 First Governor's Conference on Libraries contributed to planning. In developing a state plan, the association was cognizant of such factors as the growth, mobility, urbanization, and industrialization of society; the rising level of education, resulting in broader interests and more exacting demands on library collections; the increasing rate and rising costs of published material in many forms; the scientific and technical advances which influence all means of communication; and the impact of federal programs created by the passage of the Library Services Act and subsequent legislation. A system of libraries geared to the growth, transition, expansion, and improvement of library service was envisioned. The need for a program keyed to the objectives of each library in terms of the functions and services it has to perform was recognized. Appropriate legislation and financial assistance at the state level were considered essential to the success of the program. A cooperative program which utilized available personnel and book resources was required, since no one library could hope to obtain every publication needed or the professional library staff necessary to process and service such collections of resources, were they obtainable.

Between 1902 and 1966 the Texas Library Association held fifty-three conferences. After 1944 these meetings convened annually in the larger cities of the state. The membership for 1966 was 2,323; in 1971 it was 3,720.

Fred Folmer

*****Texas Library and Historical Commission.** *See* Texas State Library and Historical Commission.

*****Texas Literary Institute.**

*****Texas, Louisiana, and Eastern Railroad Company.**

Texas-Louisiana Lutheran. The *Texas Lutheran* qv was renamed the *Texas-Louisiana Lutheran* in 1958. It became the official publication of the Texas-Louisiana Synod of the Lutheran Church in America, which was formed in 1963 from the old Evangelical Lutheran Synod of Texas and Louisiana. This periodical was not the same as the *Southern Lutheran* of the Southern District of the American Lutheran Church. David Cooper, who had been *Texas Lutheran* editor, became editor of the new publication, a position which he held in 1972. The *Texas-Louisiana Lutheran* carried church news and ecumenical items. On 15″ x 12″ newsprint, the paper usually had six pages. Circulation was 11,993 in 1971 and went to each member family in the northern, southern, and eastern districts of the synod. *See also* Lutheran Church in Texas.

W. A. Flachmeier

*****Texas and Louisiana Railroad Company.**

*****Texas Lutheran.** *See also* Texas-Louisiana Lutheran.

*****Texas Lutheran College.** In 1948 the Texas-Louisiana Synod of the United Lutheran Church joined the Texas District of the American Lutheran Church in support and management of Texas Lutheran College, a four-year liberal arts college in Seguin. In 1953 it was decided that Clifton Junior College qv would be merged with Texas Lutheran College, and so the Texas Circuit of the Evangelical Lutheran Church came to be a partner in the college.

Texas Lutheran College expanded its services and increased its enrollment. By the early 1970's there were eighteen major buildings on the 101-acre campus. Total assets were in excess of $7 million, and the library contained 68,000 books. In 1974 Joe K. Menn was president, and the enrollment totaled 1,078 for the fall term. *See also* Lutheran Church in Texas.

W. A. Flachmeier

Texas Magazine, The. The first issue of *The Texas Magazine* appeared in Austin in May, 1896, with Robert E. McCleary as editor and publisher. The content of the magazine was mainly historical, with some fiction and poetry. During its year of publication the magazine contained announcements of the beginning of the Texas State Historical Association and the activities of the Daughters of the Republic of Texas qqv and other women's organizations. As the magazine became more literary, a section called "Among Writers and Books" was added. Texas writers whose works appeared in the magazine were historians Cadwell Walton Raines and James Thomas DeShields qqv and poets William Lawrence (Larry) Crittenden and John Peter Sjolander.qv The last issue was published in June, 1897.

In August, 1897, *The Texas Magazine* was issued in Dallas, with William G. Scarff as editor and publisher and Dudley Goodall Wooten qv as editorial supervisor. During its publication of less than a year, the magazine covered a wide range of interests, including literature, current events, women's clubs, and poetry. Historical articles continued to be featured; Oran Milo Roberts, Adele Lubbock Briscoe Looscan, and John Avery Lomax qqv were contributors. The issue of April, 1898, was the last publication of *The Texas Magazine* in Dallas, although in the February-March issue of the literary magazine *Gulf Messenger*, a merger was announced for the two magazines.

The Texas Magazine, published in Houston in October, 1909, with Harry Van Denmark, editor, and Charles A. Newning, publisher, was a business and land development publication. Although fiction, serials, poems, and articles of general interest were used, editorial interest was in the opening of undeveloped regions of Texas to farming. Articles on good roads, biographies of prominent Texas businessmen, and feature stories of growing towns made up the main content, with advertisements by Texas banks and real estate developers. Numerous photographs of cities, towns, public buildings, and homes, printed on hard, slick paper, depict in detail the Texas of the early 1900's. Poetry by Sjolander and Judd Mortimer Lewis,qv as well as the writings of Katie Daffan qv continued to appear. Less and less advertising appeared in the magazine; the last issue was in August, 1913.

BIBLIOGRAPHY: Imogene Bentley Dickey, *Early Literary Magazines of Texas* (1970); "Notes and Fragments," *Quarterly of the Texas State Historical Association*, I (1897–1898); "Book Reviews and Notices," *ibid.,* XV (1911–1912); "Book Reviews and Notices," *Southwestern Historical Quarterly,* XVI (1912–1913).

*Texas Manufacturers Association. In 1974 the Texas Manufacturers Association had a membership composed of more than 4,000 business executives representing 3,300 firms, corporations, and individuals. The major objective of the association was to build and maintain an effective environment in which its members could conduct their affairs. Efforts were made to build a better labor environment, to create a better image for business and industry, to maintain fair regulation of industry, to encourage civic responsibility, to secure fair application and reasonable interpretation of tax laws, and to reduce the cost of workmen's unemployment compensation. The association continued to publish a monthly, *Texas Industry*; it also published a weekly magazine, *Executive Digest*. L. W. Gray was president of the association in 1974.

T. R. Monk, Jr.

Texas Maritime Academy. Texas Maritime Academy, Galveston, a component in the Texas A&M University System qv was the fifth state maritime academy founded in the United States and the only maritime academy on the Gulf Coast. Interest in an academy on the Gulf was expressed in 1957 by a national convention of the Propeller Club in Houston. A group of Galveston citizens, led by Rear Admiral Sherman B. Wetmore, United States Naval Reserve, initiated efforts to secure a state charter for a nautical school. Upon investigating, they learned that a law passed in 1931 provided for the establishment of such a school. The bill had lain dormant because a rider prohibited use of state funds, but in 1959 the rider was lifted and a small appropriation was authorized for the school.

The first class enrolled in September, 1962, and graduated in May, 1966, with an accredited bachelor of science degree in marine engineering or in marine transportation. Graduates were also eligible for commissions as ensigns in the naval reserve and merchant marine licenses from the coast guard as third mate or third assistant engineer.

In addition to the campus in Galveston, the academy had loan of a 15,000-ton training ship, the *Texas Clipper*, from the Maritime Administration of the United States Department of Commerce. The academy was also presented with a gift of forty acres of waterfront property and $1,000,000 to develop a waterfront campus adjacent to a proposed oceanographic center on Pelican Island at Galveston.

Freshmen attended the main campus of Texas A&M University at College Station and thereafter completed three years of training at Galveston. Each class participated in three ten-week cruises, and prospective students could sail on a cruise while pursuing a summer program of college studies. The school's founder was Captain Bennett M. Dodson of the United States Navy. In 1972–1973 the academy's enrollment was eighty-six men and one woman; the superintendent was James D. Craik. In the fall of 1973 the academy's name was changed to the Moody College of Marine Sciences and Maritime Resources.qv

Texas Mass Transportation Commission. *See* Mass Transportation Commission, Texas.

Texas Medical Association. The Texas Medical Association was organized in Austin on January 17, 1853, under that name (not Medical Association of Texas,qv as stated in Volume II under that title). Joseph Taylor of Harrison County (not George Cupples qv of San Antonio, as stated in Volume II) was elected president of an initial membership of thirty-five (not forty-eight members). Instrumental to the formal organization was a notice, signed by a group of Austin doctors, which appeared on December 11, 1852, in the *Texas State Gazette*,qv and on December 15, 1852, in the *Texas Monument*,qv calling on all authorized physicians in the state to attend a meeting in Austin on January 17, 1853, for the purpose of organizing a state medical society. The result of that meeting, lasting from January 17 to January 19, was the formal organization of the Texas Medical Association. The first officers were elected, and a constitution and bylaws were drafted.

The second meeting was held in Austin November 14 to November 16, 1853, at which time George Cupples was elected president. Dr. Cupples' presidential address has been cited as a landmark in the affairs of the association. At this meeting the name was changed to the Medical Association of Texas, and the organization was incorporated under that name by a legislative act of November 28, 1853. The association was inactive for sixteen years, then was reactivated in 1869, when the name was changed to the Texas State Medical Association. In 1901 the name was changed to the State Medical Association of Texas, and in 1951 the original name of Texas Medical Association was resumed. In 1948 the association moved its headquarters and the Memorial Library, which was established in the 1920's as a service to the physicians of Texas, from Fort Worth to Austin, where both were permanently housed. In 1966 the library collection numbered over 40,000 volumes, 800,000 reprints, and a large collection of medical motion pictures. In 1970 the association was composed of 113 component county medical societies and over 10,000 members.

BIBLIOGRAPHY: Pat Ireland Nixon, *A History of the Texas Medical Association, 1853–1953* (1953).

*Texas Medical Center. The idea for the Texas Medical Center, Houston, was conceived by the trustees of the M. D. Anderson Foundation qv in the early 1940's. The foundation planned the first units of the center to be the University of Texas Hospital for Cancer Research and the Baylor University College of Medicine.qv A 134-acre site of city-owned property, adjacent to the Hermann Hospital grounds and adjoining Hermann Park, passed to the foundation from the city in 1944, after a popular vote authorized the sale in 1943.

The Texas Medical Center, Inc., was organized and received title to the land in 1945, at which time a board of directors assumed responsibility for development and coordination of the center under the leadership of president E. W. Bertner. Designed to attract institutions related to health education, research, and patient care, the center assembled staffs, provided facilities, and developed programs necessary to assure the highest standards of attainment in medicine. The various programs were directed by independent institutions which worked jointly to strengthen each other and the center as a whole.

In 1949 a new Hermann Hospital was completed; then came three periods of extensive expansion. Between 1951 and 1953 facilities were completed for Methodist Hospital, Arabia Temple Crippled Children's Clinic, Texas Medical Center Library (Jesse H. Jones qv Library Building), Texas Children's Hospital, St. Luke's Episcopal Hospital,

University of Texas M. D. Anderson Hospital and Tumor Institute,qv and the University of Texas Dental Branch.qv

During the second period of expansion in 1959 and 1960, the Texas Institute for Rehabilitation and Research, Houston Speech and Hearing Center, Houston State Psychiatric Institute for Research and Training qv (now Texas Research Institute of Mental Sciences qv), Texas Woman's University qv College of Nursing, and the Institute of Religion and Human Development (*see* Rothko Chapel) were completed and became integral parts of the complex. During that period the Texas Medical Center joined with Baylor University College of Medicine to activate a joint administration committee, consisting of seven members, responsible for policy matters of the medical college as related to the center. Other joint committees have since been started.

Between 1963 and 1965 Ben Taub General Hospital, a city-county charity hospital staffed by Baylor University, was completed, as was an addition to Methodist Hospital, which doubled patient care facilities to 700 beds. March Culmore Hall, a residence for women, was occupied in 1963. The City of Houston Department of Public Health opened in 1965. The University of Texas began operation of a Division of Continuing Education in Medicine and the University of Texas Graduate School of Biomedical Sciences qv in the center during that period. (*See also* University of Texas Health Science Center at Houston; University of Texas System.)

In twenty years the Texas Medical Center achieved national and international recognition in education, research, and patient care, especially in the fields of heart disease, cancer, and rehabilitation. The nineteen separate institutions of the center represented a total capital investment of approximately $100 million in 1965; in 1970 it was approximately $210,234,000. The annual budget in 1965 was about $67 million, of which $15 million was designated for research. In 1970 the budget was $159,474,000 with $29,693,000 for research. In 1964 there were 1,963 students and 8,835 full-time and 951 part-time persons employed at various institutions in the center. In 1970 there were 3,196 students and 13,047 full-time and 2,145 part-time persons employed at various institutions. In 1964, 2,639 beds and 221 bassinets accommodated 88,764 in-patients, and there were 735,238 out-patient visits. In 1970, 3,256 beds and 191 bassinets accommodated 105,313 in-patients, and there were 949,662 out-patient visits. W. Leland Anderson succeeded E. W. Bertner as president of the center in 1950.

BIBLIOGRAPHY: *The Texas Medical Center* (1964); Texas Medical Center, Inc., *Annual Report* (1970).

*Texas Medical College.

*Texas Memorial Museum. The 44th Texas Legislature in 1935 appropriated funds amounting to $250,000 for planning, equipping, and managing

the Texas Memorial Museum. Centennial souvenir coins, sponsored by the Texas American Legion qv and minted by the United States government, raised an additional $94,000 with which to purchase collections for exhibits. Cost of the building itself was $392,435 (not $525,000, as stated in Volume II). Construction was begun in 1936 with President Franklin D. Roosevelt and Governor James V. Allred qv participating in ground-breaking ceremonies. The cornerstone was laid on December 13, 1937, and the museum was formally opened on January 15, 1939 (not September 15, 1938). Since the building was constructed on the campus of the University of Texas, the board of regents of the university was also designated as the board of directors of the museum. These were the only official ties between the university and the museum until 1959, when the legislature made the museum an integral part of the university.

The Texas Memorial Museum is a natural history and Texas history museum. It promotes scholarly research, acquires and preserves research and teaching collections, and disseminates information about the fields with which it deals through exhibits and other means. The museum has four exhibition floors, each one devoted to a single discipline. The ground floor has geology and paleontology displays which relate the story of the earth's history and the animals that have lived upon it, with a focus on Texas. The second (entrance) floor contains exhibits which trace Texas history from the era of Spanish missions to post-Civil War days. The third (natural history) floor features the animals and plants of Texas, among which are bison, mountain lion, and other habitat groups. Exhibits on the fourth floor, the Hall of Man, relate the story of man with particular emphasis on Texas prehistory and historic American Indians. The statue of the group of mustangs in front of the museum was the work of Alexander Phimister Proctor.qv In July, 1957, E. N. Sellards retired as director and was succeeded by W. W. Newcomb, Jr., who was still director in 1976.

W. W. Newcomb, Jr.

Texas Methodist. The *Texas Methodist*, formerly the *Texas Christian Advocate*,qv was published as a supplement in a Chicago magazine, the *Christian Advocate*, under the title "News of Texas" from 1950 to 1952. It again became a separate publication in 1952 as the *Texas Christian Advocate*, under the editorship of J. F. Simpson. Carl E. Keightley became editor on June 1, 1959, and the paper changed its name to the *Texas Methodist* in the issue of March 18, 1960. It remained the publication of the Methodist church in Texas. By the mid-1960's circulation had reached over 60,000. In 1965 the Rio Grande Conference edition in Spanish was begun. In 1967 Jon Kinslow, a newspaperman, was editor; in 1969, Spurgeon M. Dunnam III succeeded him. By 1972 the paper was serving conferences in the Northwest and in Florida, and circulation had reached an all-time high of 160,000. *See also* Methodist Church in Texas.

Carl E. Keightley

*Texas Mexican Industrial Institute. *See also* Presbyterian Pan American School; Presbyterian Education in Texas.

*Texas-Mexican Railway Company. The Texas-Mexican Railway operated, jointly with the International-Great Northern Railroad, the international bridge at Laredo and operated a line built by the United States government from Corpus Christi to the Naval Air Station at Flour Bluff. In 1964 it operated 161.4 miles of first main track in Texas.

James M. Day

*Texas-Midland Railroad Company.

*Texas Military College. Texas Military College was closed after the school term ending in the spring of 1949, and the property was offered for sale by the Louis C. Perry family. It was purchased by members of the Church of Christ, through donations, for the purpose of establishing Southwestern Christian College qv in Terrell.

Rosemary Sims

Texas Military History. In 1967 *Texas Military History* was a quarterly historical journal published in Austin by the National Guard qv Association of Texas. It was established in the spring of 1961 in response to the association's constitutional mandate to preserve and record the military history of Texas and Texans and as a project of the association's history committee. Under the editorship of Jay A. Matthews, Jr., the journal published articles on all phases of military organizations and experiences which occurred in Texas or which involved Texas units or Texans as individuals. It ceased publication in 1969 when the ownership changed to Jay A. Matthews, Jr., and the name became *Military History of Texas and the Southwest.*qv

Jay A. Matthews, Jr.

*Texas Military Institute.

Texas Monthly. An innovative new magazine reached Texas readers in the early 1970's when *Texas Monthly* appeared for the first time with the February, 1973, issue. Published by Michael R. Levy and edited by William D. Broyles, the magazine reflected a sophisticated, yet straightforward approach to contemporary life in Texas. *Texas Monthly* enjoyed an early popularity around the state, and it received notice nationally when it was given the National Magazine Award in 1974 by the Columbia University Graduate School of Journalism. In 1976 *Texas Monthly* had a circulation of approximately 200,000 paid subscribers, and it was estimated that there were 1,000,000 readers of the magazine. Editorial offices were located in Austin.

*Texas Monument.

*Texas Monumental and Military Institute.

*Texas Motto. *See* Motto, State.

Texas Municipal League. The Texas Municipal League, known as the League of Texas Municipalities qv until 1958, continued to function as a service organization for Texas cities. The central office in Austin answered inquiries dealing with problems encountered by Texas cities, developed and furnished reference material, supplied ordinances on a variety of subjects, apprised cities of legislation affecting them, and at one time sponsored training institutes for city officials and employees. Its monthly magazine, *Texas Town and City* (*Texas Municipalities* until 1958), served as a clearinghouse for official news, advertised employment opportunities, and carried relevant book reviews. An annual conference was held to discuss current problems in municipal government administration and operations, and to elect and install league officers.

A member of the National League of Cities, the Texas Municipal League had 740 member cities in August, 1974. Affiliated with it were numerous specialized groups: Association of Airport Executives, Building Officials of Texas, Texas Association of Assessing Officers, Texas City Attorneys' Association, Association of City Clerks and Secretaries of Texas, Municipal Finance Officers Association (Texas chapter), Texas Fire Chiefs' Association, Texas City Management Association, Association of Mayors, Councilmen and Commissioners, Texas Municipal Parks and Recreation Association, Association of City Personnel and Civil Service Officials of Texas, City Planners' Association of Texas, Texas Police Chiefs' Association, Texas Public Works Association, Municipal Utilities League, and Texas Municipal Librarians Association.

BIBLIOGRAPHY: Lynn F. Anderson, "A Half Century of Service to Texas Cities," *Texas Town and City*, XLIV (September, 1962).

Stephen J. Matthews

*Texas National Guard. When the Texas National Guard was reorganized after World War II, the Texas Air National Guard was created. It was officially organized in 1947; however, its antecedents lie with the 111th Observation Squadron (the aviation section of the 36th Infantry Division), which was first organized in 1923 and has served continuously since that time in either a state or federal status. During the Korean conflict, the 136th Fighter Bomber Wing of the Texas Air National Guard was the first Air National Guard wing ever to be called into federal service intact and to engage in combat. In 1972 the Texas Air National Guard consisted of thirty-three units in seven locations, with 3,180 personnel assigned.

In 1959 the Texas National Guard was reorganized for service under nuclear battlefield conditions, resulting in a reduction of some units and the elimination of the following: 112th Armored Cavalry Regiment, 124th Armored Cavalry Regiment, XLI Corps Artillery, 8th Field Artillery Group, 474th Field Artillery Battalion, 111th Ordnance Company, and 220th AAA Detachment. The personnel from these units were placed in the 36th Division and the 49th Division.

In 1961, 3,000 Texas Guardsmen assisted disaster units on the Gulf Coast during and after Hurricane Carla. Immediately thereafter, the 49th Armored Division and three transportation companies were added to active Army units because of the existing crisis in Berlin. In 1963 the total authorized strength of Texas National Guard troops was 20,961, and the total assigned strength on April 31, 1963, was 16,252. In March, 1963, the Texas Army National Guard was reorganized to complement the active Army and to provide a strong balanced force upon mobilization. The 112th, 122nd, 136th, and 1104th Transportation companies and the 100th Public Information Detachment were eliminated. Personnel from these units were placed in the 36th Infantry Division, with headquarters at Austin, the 49th Armored Division, with headquarters in Dallas, and the State Headquarters, Austin.

In 1965 the federal government allotted approximately $35,000,000 for the Army and Air National Guard of Texas; the state of Texas appropriation was $1,025,619. In 1968 the Texas National Guard was reorganized into three brigades and state-based support units with an authorized strength of approximately 17,000 Army and 3,000 Air Guard personnel. This reorganization eliminated the 36th Infantry and 49th Armored divisions. These divisions were replaced with the 36th Separate Infantry Brigade, 71st Separate Infantry Brigade (Airborne), and the 72nd Separate Infantry Brigade (Mechanized). In 1971 the 49th Armored Group was reorganized into the 49th Armored Brigade.

In 1971 Texas had an authorized strength of 17,383 Army National Guard troops with an assigned strength of 17,088 members in 123 units. The main storage, maintenance, and administrative headquarters for supply of the Texas National Guard was at Camp Mabry qv in Austin. Additional facilities for maintenance of equipment were located in Fort Worth and North Fort Hood. The federal government deeded land for use as rifle ranges and training areas by the Texas National Guard from the following sites: Camp Barkeley, Abilene; Camp Bowie, Brownwood; Camp Maxey,qqv Paris; and Eagle Mountain Lake, near Fort Worth. *See also* Texas State Guard; Thirty-sixth Division; Thirty-sixth Division Association.

Albert E. Binotti

*Texas National Register.

*Texas Navy.

*Texas-New Mexico Railway Company. On October 31, 1928, the Interstate Commerce Commission approved the Texas and Pacific Railway Company's application to acquire control by purchase of the entire capital stock of the Texas-New Mexico Railway Company.

James M. Day

*Texas and New Orleans Railroad.

*Texas New Yorker.

Texas and Northern Railway Company. The Texas and Northern Railway Company was chartered on August 4, 1948, and operates 15.3 miles of track from Daingerfield to Lone Star, Texas. It is controlled through ownership of the entire capital stock by the Lone Star Steel Company.

James M. Day

Texas Observer, The. The *Texas Observer* is a journal published biweekly in Austin. A combination newspaper and magazine, subtitled "A Journal of Free Voices," it is politically liberal and independent. During the second half of the 1950's the paper gave much space to corruption in state government—the veterans land board scandal,qv the collapsing insurance companies, and the practice of giving gifts to state officials. Its special issues on Austin lobbyists first informed the political community how the hired advocates of special interests work on and in the legislature.

Since its inception on December 13, 1954, the paper has also published special studies and reports on such subjects as slums in Texas, state taxes, conditions in the mental hospitals and reform schools, loan sharks, the Texas Railroad Commission,qv the Texas Research League,qv nursing homes, the spreading use of lie detectors in the state, integration, higher education, industrial accidents, the Texas Poll, automobile insurance rates, and state water resources. Its reporters cover the legislature each session, often focusing on controversies affecting the poor and the minorities and, conversely, the state's economic and political power structure. The paper also reports from around the state on specific events, such as violations of academic freedom, and publishes interviews with and studies of leading politicians and major candidates in Texas elections. "Political Intelligence," a regular feature, presents the staff's understandings and summations of events in state and major-city politics.

In its "issues on issues" the *Observer* has proposed a wide variety of reforms in Texas, ranging in subjects from public power development and public utility regulation to civil rights and liberties and state minimum wage laws. Editorially, the *Observer* crusaded for integration in the 1950's and was plain-spoken against politicians it regarded as indifferent to the needs of the poor. In the 1960's it gave more weight to such subjects as the Vietnam war and police behavior and more frequently raised questions about the structures of American society. While it usually endorsed liberal Democrats, it also supported Republicans. The *Observer* was particularly attentive to reporting facts concerning the 1971–1972 Sharpstown stock fraud scandal.qv

Aside from political interests, the *Observer* publishes articles, essays, and poems by many of the region's better writers. Special issues were devoted to Roy Bedichek, Walter Prescott Webb, and J. Frank Dobie qqv and were converted into a book entitled *Three Men in Texas* (University of Texas Press, 1967). The paper's list of contributing editors included Bill Brammer, Larry L. King, Elroy

Bode, Willie Morris, and other good writers. Except for 1961 and 1962 when Morris was editor, Ronnie Dugger was editor until February, 1967, at which time Greg Olds became editor and Dugger became editor-at-large. In 1970 Kaye Northcott succeeded to the editorship, joined by Molly Ivins as coeditor.

From the outset, the editor has had exclusive control of the *Observer's* editorial content. The paper was first owned by a corporation; then it was held by a partnership including Mrs. R. D. Randolph (*see* Randolph, Frankie Carter) of Houston, Democratic national committeewoman from Texas between 1956 and 1960. In 1967 Dugger became the owner and publisher. Originally it was a weekly, and for eight years, because it attracted little advertising, it lost substantial sums of money. In 1963 it became a biweekly and since then has succeeded in operating without further investment. Circulation during the period 1971–1975 averaged about thirteen thousand.

The *Observer* is generally regarded by many journals outside the state as the leading voice of liberalism in Texas.

BIBLIOGRAPHY: Richard Ray Cole, A Journal of Free Voices: The History of *The Texas Observer* (M.A. thesis, University of Texas at Austin, 1966).

Ronnie Dugger

Texas Old Missions and Forts Restoration Association. The Texas Old Missions and Forts Restoration Association (TOMFRA) was organized in 1962 as a charitable and educational society to promote the preservation and restoration of old mission and fort sites of Texas and to promote the location, excavation, and preservation of those which were unknown. The missions in which the association is most concerned are those of the Spanish and Mexican regimes, whereas the forts of major interest include those of the mid- and late nineteenth century. The association has also promoted the restoration of San Juan Bautista,qv Coahuila, the gateway for the Hispanic colonization of Texas.

The association convenes at the location of one or more historic sites for its annual meeting. There, learned papers are read, and authoritative tours of the sites are conducted. Irregular tours of various locales related to Texas history—in Texas, Mexico, and Spain—are also sponsored by the society for its members. The association publishes a quarterly newsletter, *El Campanario*, containing matters of historical and current interest; it also periodically publishes, or makes available for purchase, pictures and plans of mission and fort sites for its members.

Joseph W. McKnight

*"Texas, Our Texas."

Texas Outlook. The *Texas Outlook*, the official publication of the Texas State Teachers Association,qv had a paid circulation, limited principally to the teaching profession in Texas, of 104,387 in 1965; in 1971 the figure had risen to 146,877. The subscription price to nonmembers of the Texas State Teachers Association was $4.00 annually.

The *Outlook* served as a forum for the analysis and reporting of significant aspects of education in Texas, provided information to aid teachers in becoming informed and articulate spokesmen for the importance of education, disseminated news about professional activities, and informed educators about legal, legislative, and other governmental matters affecting them and their professional work.

Charles H. Tennyson

*Texas and Pacific Railway Company. The Texas and Pacific system is an affiliate of and controlled through stock ownership by the Missouri-Pacific system. It is primarily a "bridge line" receiving and passing on more traffic than it originates. It is the most important subsidiary of the Missouri-Pacific, operating in Texas 1,155 miles of first main track.

As of December 31, 1963, the Texas and Pacific Railway Company owned controlling stock interest in the Abilene and Southern, the Denison and Pacific Suburban, the Fort Worth Belt Railway, the Kansas, Oklahoma and Gulf, the Texas-New Mexico Railway Company, and the Weatherford, Mineral Wells, and Northwestern Railway Company. The Texas Short Line Railway operations were abandoned on March 7, 1962. In September, 1964, the Texas and Pacific purchased the Kansas, Oklahoma, and Gulf Railway and its affiliates, the Midland Valley Railroad and the Oklahoma City-Ceda-Atoha Railway, which it sold later to the Atchison, Topeka, and Santa Fe. Although in the same year a proposal was made to merge the Missouri-Pacific and the Texas and Pacific into a new organization called the Texas and Missouri-Pacific Railroad, the action was not taken.

James M. Day

*Texas Parade. *Texas Parade* in the 1970's continued to publish articles on highways, industry, tourism, business, history, and sports in Texas. Although not an official publication of the state, it was cited numerous times by the state legislature for outstanding contributions to the promotion and better understanding of Texas and Texans.

William B. Alderman

Texas Parks and Wildlife Commission. *See* Parks and Wildlife Department, Texas.

Texas Parks and Wildlife Department. *See* Parks and Wildlife Department, Texas.

Texas Permian Historical Society. *See* Permian Historical Society.

*Texas Planning Board. *See also* Planning Agency Council.

*Texas Prairies.

*Texas Presbyterian.

*Texas Presbyterian College. *See also* Presbyterian Education in Texas.

*Texas Presbyterian Home and School for Orphans. *See* Southwestern Presbyterian Home and School for Orphans.

*Texas Presbyterian University.

*Texas Press Association. In the 1960's the Texas Press Association continued to publish the monthly *Texas Press Messenger*; the association's semimonthly bulletin became a weekly publication for a time but changed back to a semimonthly in the early 1970's. The TPA promoted better advertising, received all newspapers from around the state, and maintained a clippings bureau which served 360 clients around the state. Beginning in 1961 the association presented a "Texan of the Year" award to a native-born Texan living out of the state who had contributed some noteworthy service; nine such awards were given between 1961 and 1974.

In 1970 the central headquarters of the association moved into its own office building in Austin, the first permanent building owned by the TPA. The building displayed a state historical marker commemorating Texas newspapers during the Civil War. Vernon T. Sanford, general manager since 1947, served in that capacity until 1971, when W. G. Boykin succeeded him; Lyndell Williams succeeded Boykin as general manager in the spring of 1974. The Texas Press Association had a membership of 532 in August, 1974.

*Texas Prison Board. *See also* Corrections, Texas Board of; Corrections, Texas Department of.

Texas Prison Rodeo. The first Texas Prison Rodeo was held in October, 1931, organized by Lee Simmons,qv whose headquarters were at the prison in Huntsville. Simmons saw the need for a recreational program for the prisoners and scheduled the contests for Sunday afternoons just for that purpose. Later, when the public took interest, it was billed as "Texas' Fastest and Wildest Rodeo" and has been held annually each Sunday afternoon in October for many years since.

Inmates of the Texas Prison System qv (now the Texas Department of Corrections qv) may participate in all events, although try-outs are held to prove competency. In the beginning all performers were prisoners, but in recent times professionals have been brought in because the prison population is comprised largely of former urban dwellers who know nothing about handling horses or livestock. The stock used in the rodeos comes from the prison farm system. Every prisoner in the Texas Prison System who has a clear record is permitted to attend the rodeo if he chooses; special buses are provided to take them to and from Huntsville. Proceeds from the rodeo are placed in the Department of Corrections' educational and recreational fund, which provides educational, vocational, religious, recreational, and welfare programs for the inmates. Attendance in the late 1960's reached over 100,000, and the rodeo continued to attract large crowds in the 1970's.

BIBLIOGRAPHY: Lee Simmons, *Assignment Huntsville* (1957); Biographical File, Barker Texas History Center, University of Texas at Austin.

Texas Prison System. *See* Prison System (in Volume II); *see also* Corrections, Texas Board of; Corrections, Texas Department of.

*Texas Public Lands. *See* Lands, Texas Public.

Texas Quarterly. The first number of the *Texas Quarterly* was published on February 22, 1958. As defined by the founder and original editor, Harry H. Ransom, the periodical, designed for the general literate reader, was to seek a balance among the sciences, social sciences, humanities, and fine arts. Despite its name, it was not designed to pursue regional or provincial interests alone. In its volumes leading scientists, novelists, poets, critics, scholars, statesmen, businessmen, architects, photographers, and artists have had their say, delivering what the reviewer for the London *Times Literary Supplement* described as "crisp, topical essays rather than the refurbished bottom-drawer stuff." Writers have included Sir Bernard Lovell, Robert Graves, Samuel Beckett, Allen W. Dulles, Harlow Shapley, Frank Lloyd Wright, Aaron Copland, Edward Steichen, Robert Penn Warren, Allen Tate, John Wain, J. B. Priestley, Angus Wilson, W. H. Auden, Stephen Spender, Marianne Moore, Octavio Paz, Eudora Welty, Katherine Anne Porter, Ignazio Silone, Jorge Luis Borges, Dean Rusk, and Lyndon B. Johnson.qv

The publication also produced special numbers on Mexico, Spain, Italy, Britain, and Australia, and on the art of South America. Available in both soft and hard covers, most became collector's items. In 1966 *The Muse in Mexico*, a section of the first special number, was in its third printing as a book. Other numbers of the magazine offered blocs of articles devoted to single topics, and supplements were later issued as books, among them *The Centennial Celebration of Baudelaire's "Les Fleurs du Mal,"* Richard Elman's *A Coat for the Tsar*, and George Garrett's *The Sleeping Gypsy*.

Illustrations in the *Quarterly* reflected the scope and variety of its contents. Paintings, drawings, engravings, and photographs by many artists, some especially commissioned by the periodical, have been included.

Thomas M. Cranfill

*Texas Railroad, Navigation, and Banking Company.

Texas Ranger Hall of Fame. In August, 1973, ground was broken in Waco for the site of the Texas Ranger Hall of Fame. Located adjacent to the Colonel Homer Garrison qv Museum (*see* Fort Fisher), the completed Texas Ranger Hall of Fame, which honored members of the Texas Rangers,qv was dedicated on February 7, 1976. Many state and national dignitaries attended the ceremony.

*Texas Rangers. As the frontier disappeared, Texas Ranger activities were redirected toward law enforcement among settlers, reducing the popularity of the force among some of its members and some Texans. The organization was allowed to dwindle as the need for it grew less; however, in 1935 the Rangers were reorganized and placed under the Department of Public Safety.qv Provision was made for the adoption of modern methods of detecting crime.

In 1967 the Texas Rangers were a six-company unit consisting of six captains, six sergeants, and fifty Ranger privates, a total of sixty-two men stationed in towns considered to be strategic points across the state, with headquarters in the following geographical regions: Houston, Dallas, Lubbock, Corpus Christi, Midland, and Waco. By 1971 San Antonio had replaced Corpus Christi as a company headquarters, and by September 1, 1974, the force had eight captains, seven sergeants, and seventy-nine privates, for a total of ninety-four men.

Rangers were selected from the ranks of the Texas Department of Public Safety and from other law enforcement agencies; after appointment they received special training at schools conducted by the department. They were charged with four major duties: protection of life and property through enforcement of the criminal statutes of Texas, suppression of riots and insurrections, investigation of major crimes, and the apprehension of fugitives. To enforce the law they were furnished with automobiles, armored cars, boats, and airplanes, as well as modern weapons. No longer furnished horses and saddles, each Ranger was still required to have access to such equipment.

Homer Garrison, Jr.,qv was director of the Department of Public Safety and chief of the Texas Rangers from 1938 to 1968. In 1974 the line of command was Wilson E. Speir, director of the DPS, James M. Ray, chief of criminal law enforcement, and William D. Wilson, senior captain of the Rangers.

At Dallas Love Field a bronze statue of a Ranger carried the inscription, "One Riot, One Ranger." The basic creed of the organization was put into words by an early Ranger: "No man in the wrong can stand up against a man in the right who keeps on a-comin'." *See also* Texas Ranger Hall of Fame; Fort Fisher.

Texas Rangers (Baseball Club). The Texas Rangers baseball club came to Texas in 1972 from Washington, D.C., where a franchise for professional baseball had been held for over seventy years. The move to Arlington, Texas, was authorized on September 21, 1971, by approval of American League officials and club owners. Robert E. Short was the owner of the club, and Ted Williams was manager through the first season in Texas; upon Williams' resignation, Whitey Herzog was named manager. At midpoint in the 1973 season Billy Martin became manager, replacing Herzog. In July, 1975, Martin was replaced by Frank Lucchesi as manager.

Although their first season in Texas was lackluster, the Rangers, by acquiring several new players and coaches, showed more promise in the 1973 season. Texas Stadium in Arlington was renovated to accommodate the club, and in April, 1974, a group of Fort Worth and Dallas businessmen, headed by Brad Corbett, purchased 90 percent of the Rangers organization for an estimated nine million dollars.

BIBLIOGRAPHY: Shelby Whitfield, *Kiss It Goodbye* (1973); Austin *American-Statesman*, May 30, 1974; Fort Worth *Star-Telegram*, April 3, 1974.

Texas Rangers Museum. *See* Fort Fisher.

Texas Rehabilitation Center of Gonzales Warm Springs Foundation. By 1964 the Texas Rehabilitation Center of Gonzales Warm Springs Foundation, Incorporated, previously known as the Warm Springs Foundation for Crippled Children,qv had expanded its activities to include the treatment and rehabilitation of children, teen-agers, and adults suffering from physical disabilities caused by disease or by industrial or automobile accidents, with emphasis placed on disabilities as a result of paralysis.

Edward R. Webber III

***Texas Republican** (Brazoria).*

***Texas Republican** (Marshall).*

***Texas Republican** (Nacogdoches).*

Texas Research Foundation. By 1966 the Texas Research Foundation had in use 860 acres of fields, pastures, test plots, and laboratories. After more than two decades of research, it had developed the Renner Farming System, a process of growing major cash crops for soil improvement, using rotation to improve the land, and the Renner Pasture System, which provided year-round grazing, leaving grass for hay and silage while improving the soil. The latter system helped to triple the number of beef and dairy cattle in the Dallas-Fort Worth area from 1,000,000 head in 1944 to more than 3,000,000 in 1964.

In addition, the foundation put in practice in 1962 a farm demonstration program which applied sound crop and pasture programs to fifty farms in thirty Texas counties. Research at Renner evolved new crop strains which increased yields while upgrading soil. These included grain sorghum, white corn hybrids, two varieties of soybeans, several superior grasses, and a less-seed-shattering sesame plant.

On September 1, 1972, the Texas Research Foundation was liquidated and the property and land were distributed among Texas A&M University and the University of Texas at Dallas and at Austin. A&M received 380 acres of the western portion and established the North Texas Research and Extension Center of the College of Agriculture, with plans to establish other branches of A&M. U.T. Dallas received the eastern portion of 275 acres, together with the Lundell Herbarium, Rare Book Collection, Science Library, and Reading Room, all of which were named after C. L. Lundell, the foundation's director and founder. The Lundell Herbarium and the Rare Book Collection were transferred from Renner to the University of Texas

at Austin in 1972, and a professorship in systematic botany, endowed by a gift of property valued at more than $100,000 by Dr. and Mrs. Lundell, was established there beginning in the fiscal year 1974–1975.

BIBLIOGRAPHY: *Texas Agricultural Progress*, 19 (Winter, 1973); Texas A&M University, News Information Release, August 15, September 1, 1972; University of Texas at Austin, *UT News*, January 18, 1973; Austin *American*, August 16, 1972; Dallas *Morning News*, August 4, 1972.

Wayne Gard

Texas Research Institute of Mental Sciences. The Texas Research Institute of Mental Sciences is a research and professional training facility of the Texas Department of Mental Health and Mental Retardation.qv It began operation in 1957 as the Houston State Psychiatric Institute for Research and Training.qv In 1961 it was relocated in the Texas Medical Center qv in Houston, and in 1967 it assumed its present name.

Research is directed into the basic areas of detection, correction, and prevention of mental illness and mental retardation, and concentrated studies are done in specific programs. In 1970 programs included biomedical and behavioral research into emotional and physical causes for drug and alcohol addiction, biochemical factors in mental illness, and genetic defects that cause mental retardation.

The world's first working period-analytic system was developed at the institute as a result of intensive research. This new system records and analyzes by computer the electrical impulses of the human body. The system interprets clinical electroencephalograms and traces the action of drugs in the nervous system with much greater precision than before. A new series of chemical compounds has been developed and tested for treatment of all forms of mental disease, and advancement has been made in the area of diagnostic testing of all newly-admitted children to state schools. Through this work some rare metabolic syndromes were discovered, facilitating efficiency in treatment to the extent that some children no longer needed hospitalization.

Professional instruction plays a large part in the programs at the Texas Research Institute of Mental Sciences. The training of biologists, chemists, and anatomists for research programs attracted nurses, caseworkers, counselors, pastoral trainees, psychiatry residents, and psychology interns. The institute is well recognized in the professional world, and its books and papers are valuable contributions to scientific literature. An international symposium is held annually, with varying topics drawing prominent researchers and scientists.

In addition to a research and training center, the institute functions as an outpatient clinic and was the largest outpatient center in Texas in 1970, serving at least 4,000 patients. Intensive care treatment has prevented extensive hospitalization for some patients, and research is continuing in this treatment at the institute's Center Pavilion Hospital.

The Texas Research Institute of Mental Sciences

director in 1970 was William M. McIsaac. *See* Mentally Ill and Mentally Retarded, Care of, in Texas.

BIBLIOGRAPHY: Texas Department of Mental Health and Mental Retardation, *Annual Report, 1970.*

Texas Research League. The Texas Research League was founded in 1952 as an educational, non-profit Texas corporation with headquarters in Austin. Privately supported by businesses and individuals whose contributions maintain a permanent professional research staff, the league engaged in nonpartisan research into the operations, programs, and problems of Texas state and local government. It undertook studies only upon request from governmental sources, including the governor and the legislature. In the course of its duties the league studied a wide range of state and local governmental problems and policies, including state hospitals, welfare, insurance regulation, the Department of Public Safety, the Texas Railroad Commission,qqv problems concerning state taxation and water resource development, and problems of metropolitan government. The results of research efforts were returned to the agency requesting the research, and public reports were made with the consent of the agency involved. The league did not lobby. Its studies, financed from league funds exclusively, were performed without cost to public agencies requesting them.

Alvin A. Burger

*Texas Revolution.

*Texas Revolution, Finances of.

*Texas Rose Festival.

*Texas, Sabine Valley, and Northwestern Railway Company.

*Texas and Sabine Valley Railway Company.

*Texas and St. Louis Railway Company. *See* St. Louis Southwestern Railway of Texas.

*Texas School for the Blind.** The Texas School for the Blind, in Austin, was transferred to the Texas Education Agency qv in 1953 by the Fifty-third Legislature. No longer considered an elee-mosynary institution, the school is an independent school district and participates in state and county scholastic appropriations. In the late 1960's the school was integrated and consolidated with the all-Negro Texas Blind and Deaf School (formerly called the Texas Blind, Deaf, and Orphan School qv). The school has one campus, in north Austin. It had a 1969 enrollment of 251, and the superintendent was Robert A. Hansen. *See also* Special Schools and Special Education, Texas Education Agency.

BIBLIOGRAPHY: Texas State Board of Education, *Audit Report, Special Schools for the Blind and Deaf, 1970* (n.d.); University of Texas at Austin, *Guide To Texas State Agencies* (1972).

*Texas School for the Deaf.** The Texas School for the Deaf, in Austin, was placed under the jurisdiction of the Texas Education Agency qv in 1951 by the Fifty-second Legislature, and the school was no longer considered an eleemosynary institution. Beginning in 1955 a completely new physical plant was built, and the old buildings were razed. The all-Negro Texas Blind, Deaf, and Orphan School qv was transferred to the Texas Education Agency in 1965, renamed the Texas Blind and Deaf School, and was then abolished to be merged with the Texas School for the Deaf. The new school was completely integrated, and consolidated services were provided for all deaf children. There were two campuses in operation in 1973, one in east Austin, the other in south Austin. Academically, a pupil could receive the equivalent of a ninth-grade public school education. The Texas School for the Deaf was an independent school district and participated in state and county scholastic appropriations. Enrollment in 1969 was 666, and the superintendent was Albert W. Douglas. *See also* Special Schools and Special Education, Texas Education Agency.

BIBLIOGRAPHY: Texas State Board of Education, *Audit Report, Special Schools for the Blind and Deaf, 1970* (n.d.); University of Texas at Austin, *Guide To Texas State Agencies* (1972).

Texas School of Fine Arts. Texas School of Fine Arts, Austin, was established as a private fine arts school in 1930 with accreditation by the State Department of Education. Anita Storrs Gaedcke and Miriam Gordon Landrum qv shared responsibilities for the school's direction until 1942, when Miss Landrum became sole owner and director. The institution offered both preparatory and college courses in music, speech and drama, and art. Certificates of achievement were completed through private lessons; there was no age limit.

Enrollment during the 1965–1966 term was 170 students; there were eight teachers. A charter member of the Texas Association of Music Schools, the Texas School of Fine Arts offered two six-week summer terms in addition to the long term session.

The school moved to its present location on West 11th Street in 1969. By 1973 the speech, music, and drama courses had been dropped, but art instruction continued on an individual basis and an art gallery had been added. The director was Charles Berkeley Normann, who also served as president and treasurer. Mrs. Eva Huesser joined Normann in partnership in May, 1972, serving as vice-president and corporation secretary. Both Normann and Huesser taught full-time, and a part-time instructor was also engaged. By 1973 the school had adopted a minimum age limit of twelve years; at that time the enrollment was approximately one hundred twenty students.

BIBLIOGRAPHY: Mint O. James-Reed, *Music in Austin: 1900–1956* (1957); Austin *American-Statesman,* January 29, 1972.

Texas School Journal.

Texas Sentinel.

*Texas Short Line Railway Company.

Texas Siftings.

*Texas South-Eastern Railroad Company.

Texas Southern University. Texas Southern University, Houston, was known as Texas State University for Negroes ᵠᵛ until 1951. Between 1947, when the university moved to a permanent sixty-five-acre campus, and 1967, enrollment increased from 2,303 to 4,569 students; the faculty grew from over 100 to 225 members; and the physical plant more than quadrupled in size, from one masonry building and a number of frame structures to twenty-six masonry buildings.

Undergraduate, graduate, and professional courses of study were offered by 1965. The university organization encompassed the following accredited divisions: College of Arts and Sciences, School of Business, School of Law, School of Pharmacy, School of Industries, Graduate School, and Summer School. University athletic teams, known as the TSU Tigers, participated in intercollegiate competition through the Southwestern Athletic Conference and the National Association of Intercollegiate Athletics.

The combined library facilities of Texas Southern University numbered over 179,000 volumes and 750 periodical subscriptions by 1969. Several special collections of books and materials were held, including the Heartman Collection of Negro Life and Culture, the Shaw Fine Arts Collection, and the curriculum, pharmacy branch, and law libraries.

Raphael O'Hara Lanier resigned as first president of the university in 1955 and was succeeded by Samuel M. Nabrit. In 1974 Granville M. Sawyer was president. Enrollment in that year was 7,125. *See also* Education, Negro.

Texas Southmost College. Texas Southmost College, Brownsville, was formally opened as a junior college on September 28, 1926, to serve the need for higher education in the lower Rio Grande area. The college was originally known as Brownsville Junior College.

On February 12, 1947, plans were initiated with the War Assets Administration for a college site and properties at Fort Brown,ᵠᵛ which had been deactivated after World War II. The first classes were held on the new campus in June, 1948. In November, 1949, the Southmost Union Junior College District was created, and the school was henceforth known as Texas Southmost College. Complete separation of the college from the public schools was effected in December, 1950.

In addition to several buildings obtained from the War Assets Administration, the college district built the Pink Bollworm ᵠᵛ Research Center, Cleve Tandy Liberal Arts Building, and a gymnasium. The Civic Center, owned by the city, was situated on the campus and was used jointly by the city and the college. The administration and natural sciences were housed in the former hospital buildings complex, later referred to as Gorgas Science Center, a historical landmark. Zachary Taylor Library, supported by the college, the city, and Cameron County, was housed in Fort Brown Memorial Center and administered by the college. Building plans on the

forty-five-acre campus called for additions of a library and college center, and an administration wing attached to the Tandy Building.

The college's fivefold objectives were to provide two years of college work for transfer to four-year institutions, two years of specialized work in business, professional, or technical education, part-time adult education, enrichment courses of general interest, and a center for cultural development. The college offered associate in arts and associate in business degrees, as well as certificates of completion. The institution held membership in the Southern Association of Colleges and Secondary Schools, the American Association of Junior Colleges, and the Texas Association of Junior Colleges.

Enrollment in 1950 was distributed between academic and vocational branches, with 810 and 635 students in each branch, respectively. The major portion of the 1950 academic enrollment consisted of veterans taking evening courses. By the 1964–1965 term, the vocational branch had been dropped, and 765 students were enrolled in the academic branch. The 1967 enrollment was 1,185, and the faculty numbered forty-six. During a fifteen-year period, library holdings increased from 6,800 to 41,696, and by 1969 to 55,000. Arnulfo Oliveira was president in 1974, when enrollment totaled 3,226.

*Texas and Southwestern Cattle Raisers' Association. The Texas and Southwestern Cattle Raisers' Association increased membership and expanded activities during the 1950's and 1960's, one of the most significant periods in its long history. Rains in the spring of 1957 brought an end to one of the Southwest's most severe and widespread drouths and resulted in a resurgence in membership to an all-time high of more than 13,000 members.

In the late 1950's the association's officers went to Florida to observe the results of screwworm eradication in the Southeast and to set in motion a series of events which resulted in screwworm eradication in the Southwest. The program, financed in the beginning largely from voluntary contributions by the stock industry, has perhaps been of more benefit to livestock producers than any other program in the twentieth century. Working through and with the Southwest Animal Health Research Foundation and with government agencies, the association played a major role in the program which brought about an end to the pest through release of millions of radioactive-sterilized screwworm flies.

In 1961 the association recognized the growing importance of cattle feeding in the Southwest by establishing the Cattle Feeders Division, and that same year the association established award programs for 4-H members and Future Farmers of America who had made distinguished records in livestock production and management. In little more than a decade, the Southwest had become one of the nation's leading cattle feeding areas. In 1955 there were 227,000 head of cattle fed in Texas, and in

1969 there were over two and one-half million head fed, mostly in large modern commercial feedlots utilizing tons of Texas-grown grain sorghums.

Control of cattle theft continued as one of the primary objectives of the association, and in 1966 mechanization of the mammoth TSCRA brand records was initiated. Machines were installed which quickly transcribe and record brand inspection information received daily from inspectors at markets located throughout Texas. Inspection records relating to missing or stolen cattle may also be retrieved by these machines from the brand files at a tremendous rate of speed. This mechanization is a great aid to association inspectors and other law enforcement officers in the detection and apprehension of cattle thieves and is regarded as one of the most significant strides in this field in many years. For earlier history of the association, *see* Cattle Raisers' Associations in Volume I; *see also* Cattle Brands; Cattle Drives; Cattle Industry; Cattle Rustling; Cattle Tick; Cattle Trails; *Cattleman, The.*

Dick Wilson

Texas Speleological Association. *See* Caves and Cave Studies in Texas.

Texas Sports Hall of Fame. Membership in the Texas Sports Hall of Fame was limited to those persons, male or female, living or dead, whose achievements in athletics brought lasting fame and honor to the state of Texas. Instituted in 1949 by the Texas Sports Writers Association, the Hall of Fame came into being in 1951 with the enshrinement of Tris Speaker,qv all-time outfield star with the Cleveland Indians. Installation ceremonies are held annually at a luncheon in Dallas, which has become a traditional highlight of Cotton Bowl qv Classic Week. The luncheon is co-sponsored by the Salesmanship Club of Dallas. Those honored and the sport which they represent are listed in the order of selection from 1951 to December, 1975. Tris Speaker qv (baseball); Ben Hogan (golf); Joe Routt qv (football); Babe Didrikson Zaharias qv (golf, track and field); Sam Baugh (football); Billy Disch qv (baseball); Bo McMillin qv (football); Rogers Hornsby qv (baseball); Byron Nelson (golf); Paul Tyson qv (football); Davey O'Brien (football); Cecil Smith (polo); Jimmy Kitts (football, basketball); Jimmy Demaret (golf); Dutch Meyer (football); Wilmer Allison (tennis); John Kimbrough (football); Joel Hunt (football); Clyde Littlefield (track and field, football); Fred Wolcott (track and field); Doak Walker (football); Dana X. Bible (football); Paul Richards (baseball); Bobby Morrow (track and field); Matty Bell (football); Ki Aldrich (football); Bobby Layne (football); Pete Cawthon (football); Bibb Falk (baseball); Monty Stratton (baseball); Clyde (Bulldog) Turner (football); D. A. Penick qv (tennis); John J. McCloskey qv (baseball); Cecil Grigg (football); Gerald Mann (football); Kyle Rote (football); David Greig (Skippy) Browning qv (swimming); Ray Morrison (football); Earl Meadows (track and field); Wilson Elkins (football, track, basketball); Jake Atz qv (baseball); Buddy Davis (track and field); Jack Gray (basketball); Slater Martin (basketball); George L. (Tex) Rickard qv (boxing); Willie Shoemaker (jockey); Raymond (Rags) Matthews (football); Michael Francis (Pinky) Higgins qv (baseball); Ben Lee Boynton qv (football); Johnson Blair Cherry qv (football); Lloyd Mangrum (golf); Jackie Robinson (basketball); Ad Toepperwein qv (marksmanship); Eddie Dyer qv (baseball); Wesley Bradshaw (football); J. Walter Morris qv (baseball); Howard Grubbs (football); Fred Hansen (track and field); A. J. Foyt (auto racing); Botchey Koch (football); Betty Jameson (golf); Ralph Guldahl (golf); Dick Todd (football); Homer Norton qv (football); Eddie Southern (track); Weldon Humble (football); Clarence Kraft (baseball); Bobby Wilson (football); Max Hirsch qv (horse racing); Jess Neely (football); Buster Brannon (football); Ernie Banks (baseball); Jack Johnson qv (boxing); Carl Reynolds (baseball); Pete Shotwell (football); W. J. Wisdom (basketball); H. N. Russell (football); Joe Pate (baseball); Abe Martin (football); Bill Lillard (bowling); E. O. (Doc) Hayes (basketball); Frank Bridges (football); Albert Samuel (Abb) Curtis (basketball); Lynwood (Dusty) Boggess (baseball); Lew Jenkins (boxing); John (Snipe) Conley (baseball); John (Boody) Johnson (football); Lee Trevino (golf); Randy Matson (track and field); Raymond Berry (football); Bill (Jitterbug) Henderson (football, basketball, baseball, track); Johnny Vaught (football); Bob Lilly (football); Frank Anderson (track); and Alfred (Red) Barr (swimming).

An eight-acre site in Grand Prairie was designated as the location for a planned Texas Sports Hall of Fame museum-library, but construction had not started by 1975; a fund-raising campaign was active at that time.

Wilbur Evans

Texas Staats Sängerbund. *See* Texas State Singing Society.

Texas State College for Women. *See also* Texas Woman's University.

Texas State Council of Defense.

Texas State Department of Health. *See* Public Health, State Department of.

Texas State Employment Service. *See* Texas Employment Commission.

Texas State Gazette. *See State Gazette.*

Texas State Guard. With the return of the Texas National Guard qv to state control in 1947 the Texas State Guard was deactivated as an active state militia and the Texas State Guard Reserve Corps was authorized as an inactive state militia. Membership in the Reserve Corps was limited to former members of the Texas Defense Guard, Texas

State Guard, Texas National Guard, and former members of the armed forces.

During the call to federal service in 1961 of the 49th Armored Division, units of the Texas State Guard Reserve Corps located at 49th Armored Division armories were activated as Texas State Guard units. They became an active state militia and served the state and communities in an outstanding manner until the return of the 49th.

In 1965, in order to provide a reservoir of militia strength for use by the state of Texas as a supplement to the Texas National Guard, the Fifty-ninth Texas Legislature created the Texas State Guard. The Texas State Guard is a part of the state militia of Texas within the meaning of the Second Amendment of the Constitution of the United States. A section of the revised civil statutes of Texas states that "the active Militia of Texas, herein referred to as the State Military Forces, shall consist of the organized and uniformed forces of this State which shall be known as the Texas Army National Guard, the Texas Air National Guard, and the Texas State Guard."

The Texas State Guard is organized as a cadre organization with six defense groups, whose boundaries parallel the regional boundaries of the Department of Public Safety;qv twenty battalions; and 139 security units. A Texas State Guard security unit is located at each National Guard armory with a mission of reinforcing the Texas National Guard in time of emergency and replacing the Texas National Guard units called into federal service. The 1968 cadre strength of the Texas State Guard was 1,160 officers and 1,479 enlisted men. From the time of its first organization in 1940 to January, 1968, approximately 8,270 officers and over 104,000 enlisted men served in the Texas State Guard. The Texas State Guard has as its heritage the State Militia of Texas from the period 1835 to 1903 and the Texas National Guard on state duty from 1903 to the present.

Dorsey T. Kownslar

Texas State Highway Department. *See* Highway Department, Texas State.

*Texas State Historical Association. The Texas State Historical Association continued from 1951 to 1976 to collect books and documents for the University of Texas at Austin Library, to sponsor the Junior Historian Movement qv in high schools of the state, and to publish the *Texas Historian* (formerly the *Junior Historian*), the *Southwestern Historical Quarterly*,qv and books on Texas history, including a third volume of the *Handbook of Texas*, edited by Eldon S. Branda. H. Bailey Carroll qv continued as director of the association until shortly before his death in May, 1966. He was succeeded by Joe B. Frantz. Mrs. Coral Horton Tullis qv was secretary-treasurer until her death in 1967. Presidents since 1951 have been Claude Elliott,qv Paul Adams, Ralph Steen, Merle Duncan, Fred R. Cotten,qv George P. Isbell, J. P. Bryan, Sr., Seymour V. Connor, Wayne Gard, Rupert N. Richardson, Cooper K. Ragan, Dorman H. Winfrey, Roger N.

Conger, Anne Brindley, Ralph A. Wooster, Billy Mac Jones, and Dan E. Kilgore (1976). Headquarters of the association was moved in January, 1971, to the third floor, center section, of the newly completed Sid W. Richardson qv Hall, the same building which housed the Eugene C. Barker Texas History Center.qv In 1976 Joe B. Frantz continued as director and L. Tuffly Ellis was associate director of the association.

Texas State Historical Survey Committee. *See* Texas Historical Commission.

Texas State Hospitals and Special Schools, Board for. *See* Board for Texas State Hospitals and Special Schools.

*Texas State Library. Although Texas could boast of having able state librarians and employees, the chief problem the Texas State Library faced for more than half a century was that of inadequate housing. By the 1950's the situation had become alarming, and the archives division was forced to move to a quonset hut in northwest Austin. In January, 1957, Governor Price Daniel went before the Fifty-fifth Legislature and recommended that a state archives and library building be erected to house the divisions of the state library. Before the legislature adjourned in May, the funds had been provided, and the new building was dedicated on April 10, 1962.

Built of granite from the same quarry which supplied materials for the capitol,qv the outer walls are made of "sunset red granite." The building is 257 feet long and 77 feet wide; it is approximately 60 feet tall. The building has four main floors and seven stack floors. The stacks are not open to the public. Of the approximately 100,000 square feet of floor space, the library occupied some 66,000 square feet, with the remainder occupied, until they moved out in January, 1974, by the General Land Office;qv in 1974 there were several state offices located on the fourth floor of the building.

The structure is highlighted by the flags of Spain, France, Mexico, the Republic of Texas, the Confederacy, and the United States. Embedded in the stone on the west portico are brightly colored mosaic shields of each nation. Smaller bronze emblems decorate the metal doors at the front. On each side of the building are quotations from the Constitution of the Republic and Texas' Declaration of Independence,qqv cut into the stone, along with the Texas seal. The rear of the building is embellished with six terra-cotta seals of the nations.

The first floor foyer is a Texas showcase. It has been set aside for an educational project which reflects the history of the state. Historic maps, manuscripts, and artifacts are displayed in the room. In the terrazzo floor is the wreath-and-star emblem of Texas. The main walls are polished granite, and the upper wall is sandstone. Above the center of the area is a large oval light fixture, depicting the lone star of the state with a fifty-star border.

A forty-five-foot Texas history mural decorates the upper walls of the lobby. It was created by the English artist Peter Rogers, in association with Peter Hurd, the noted western artist, and was designed in three main parts, depicting the story of Texas chronologically from left to right.

The Texas State Library services include preservation of historical documents, including past and current documents of the state government, aiding research workers, publication and display of valuable Texana, and a wide range of activities to help improve library facilities throughout the state and to stimulate use of available libraries. It is organized into five general divisions: administrative services division, archives division, division for the blind and physically handicapped, records management division, and division for library services and development (including information services department, technical services, and department of library development).

The Texas State Library also administered federal and state programs to encourage library development. The federal Library Services Act (1956) and its successor, the Library Services and Construction Act (1965) provided categorical grants to public libraries. The Texas Library Systems Act (1969) was the first legislation to provide state funds for public libraries. It gave the Texas State Library and Historical Commission qv authority to organize systems and enabled the legislature to appropriate funds for these systems.

The Regional Historical Resources Depository Act (1971) gave the Texas State Library responsibility for administering the establishment of regional depositories in academic and other libraries in order to maintain and make available the inactive records of cities, counties, and special governmental districts.

Dorman H. Winfrey

*Texas State Library and Historical Commission. Composed of five members prior to 1953, the Texas State Library and Historical Commission was increased in that year to six members, all appointed by the governor for six-year terms of office. *See also* Texas State Library.

*Texas State Military Board.

*Texas State Paper.

Texas State Pharmaceutical Association. *See* Pharmacy in Texas.

*Texas State Railroad. The Texas State Railroad lease with the Texas and New Orleans Railroad qv expired in 1962, and on November 1 of that year the Texas South-Eastern Railroad Company qv took up the lease. The railroad was originally controlled by the governor of the state and a prison commission, but it later came under the direction of a board of managers.

James M. Day

Texas State Singing Society. The first organized song festival in Texas was held on October 15 and 16, 1853, in New Braunfels, with the Germania Singing Society as host to three other male singing societies from San Antonio, Austin, and Sisterdale. At the second meeting of the group in San Antonio in May, 1854, the Texas State Singing Society was organized. A lithograph by Carl G. von Iwonski qv shows the New Braunfels *Germania Gesangverein* seated together for their portrait in 1857. Before the Civil War there were singing societies in Shelby, La Grange, Indianola, Columbus, Pedernales, Grape Creek, Boerne, and Comfort, and until 1860 these groups met annually. From 1870 to 1916 they met together every other year. On February 8, 1879, the Austin Singing Society (*Saengerrunde*) was organized.

Changes in the singing society's programs began with the introduction of piano accompaniment in 1856 and mixed choruses in 1860. In 1877 soloists and orchestras were brought from out of state; after 1880 women regularly participated in the singing groups, and in 1891 children took part. In 1881 western groups formed the West Texas Singers League (*Westtexanischen Gebirgs-Sängerbund*), which included Boerne, Comfort, Fredericksburg, Kerrville, Walhalla (Sattler), Anhalt, Smithson Valley, and later Ufnau, Honey Creek, and Twin Sisters. Large gatherings of the singing groups alternated between Galveston, Austin, Dallas, Houston, and San Antonio. In 1898 the Gillespie County Singers League was formed, which included singers' societies from Fredericksburg, Stonewall, Luckenbach, Meusebach Creek, Grapetown, and Live Oak.

Begun by the Germans, the society began to include other ethnic groups in 1894, when Anglo Americans first joined the singers. In 1913, at the Texas State Singing Society's diamond jubilee celebration, twenty-one societies assembled in Houston, and the massed choruses sang music almost exclusively by American composers. The greatest singing festival before World War I, in number of voices and excellence of performers, was held in San Antonio in 1916, directed by Arthur Claasen. During World War I the organization was inactive, and is seemed unlikely that it would reorganize, but in 1920 the Gillespie County Singers held the first revival. In 1922 a few members of several local groups met together, and by 1929 ten societies were represented in a San Antonio song festival. Gradually biennial meetings became regular, usually held in Fredericksburg and New Braunfels. During World War II, again, the society was inactive, and it had some difficulty getting started again because the organization had broken into small groups. However, these groups still met in various centers.

Among the men who devoted years of service to their singing societies were Edward Schmidt of Comfort, Carl Diengers of Boerne, Carl William Besserer of Austin, Hermann E. Dietel of Smithson Valley, Adolf W. Hopf of Fredericksburg, Ferdinand H. Ohlendorf of Galveston, and G. J. Petmecky and C. G. Guenther of New Braunfels. Through the years, in addition to singing societies in the towns previously mentioned, there was the

Guadalupe Valley Singers League (1896), which included singers' groups from Cordova, Marion, Seguin, Yorks Creek, Dietz, Schumannsville, Barbarossa, and Geronimo; in the area from Brenham to Schulenburg were High Hill, Sealey, Taylor, Bleiberville, O'Quinn, Rockdale, Schoenau (Swiss), and Piney. Parades, often under a triumphal arch, opened the festivals, with each society carrying a banner decorated with its name, home town, and insignia. The groups enjoyed dances, picnics, and visiting during the periodic singing gatherings, occasions which often lasted several days. Programs printed in German contained the names of visiting societies, the occasion, the history of the host group, and the words to songs (often translated into English). Such programs for the twenty-eighth Texas State Saengerfest in Austin (1911), the Piney Concordia in Bellville (1935), and the Salatrillo Liederkranz in Converse (1951) gave the continuing story of German singing societies in Texas.

The German name for the society is *Texas Staats Sängerbund*; most of the present members are of German descent. Through its active promotion of high musical standards among member groups, its concerts with leading conductors, soloists, and large orchestras, and its increasing encouragement of and emphasis upon American music and musicians, the Texas State Singing Society has contributed substantially to musical culture in Texas.

BIBLIOGRAPHY: Rudolph L. Biesele, *The History of the German Settlements in Texas, 1831–1861* (1930); Oscar Haas, *A Chronological History of the Singers of German Songs in Texas* (1948); *History of New Braunfels and Comal County, Texas, 1844–1946* (1968); Saengerfest Papers and Programs (Archives, University of Texas at Austin Library); Moritz P. G. Tiling, *History of the German Element in Texas from 1820 to 1850* (1913); Lota M. Spell, *Music in Texas* (1935); Carl Venth, *My Memories* (1939).

Lota M. Spell

*Texas State Teachers Association. In 1949 the Texas State Teachers Association sponsored the passage of the Minimum Foundation School Program, which provided for a $2,403 minimum salary and reorganized the Texas educational system. In 1953 the association secured the passage of four bills improving the teacher retirement system;qv in 1954 it co-sponsored legislation creating an across-the-board increase of $402 in the minimum foundation salary schedule.

The association sponsored a major legislative program in 1955 which, after its enactment into law, provided additional benefits for teachers and strengthened the teacher retirement system. In 1957 the association sponsored legislation which secured a $399 per year increase for teachers and increased allowances for administrators. In 1961 the association secured the enactment of a bill which provided an $810 base salary raise and increments for public school teachers based on teaching experience. Legislation improving the teacher retirement program was sponsored and passed in 1963, followed by another salary increase in 1964. By 1965 the association had gained a teacher pay raise bill which provided a monthly increase in salary for

teachers, a new increment schedule, and an additional amount to be used by local school boards to supplement salaries of some teachers. By 1969 the association had obtained a three-year teacher pay raise bill and a retirement bill.

The association continued many of its services, including the publication of the *Texas Outlook*.qv Membership was no longer limited to white teachers or white friends of education; by 1974, membership had increased to 152,340, about 90 percent of all Texas teachers.

Charles H. Tennyson

Texas State Technical Institute. The Texas State Technical Institute, offering courses in vocational and technical education, had four locations in 1974: Amarillo, Harlingen, Sweetwater, and Waco. The institute, first located on the site of James Connally Air Force Base qv in Waco, was established as the James Connally Technical Institute by Texas A&M University through an act of the state legislature in April, 1965. The first classes were held in January, 1966, with a student enrollment of approximately 700 and a faculty of forty-five. Twenty-one hundred acres and buildings of the James Connally Air Force Base, purchased by the state in 1967, were available to the school.

The goal of the institute was to train skilled workers for industry and business, particularly those in Texas. The teaching program was conducted in two instructional centers. The technical education center accepted high school graduates for a two-year training program in highly skilled technical occupations. The vocational skill development center prepared students for jobs requiring skilled craftsmanship; the length of study varied with the level of competence of the student.

In 1969 the Texas legislature passed a bill separating the school from the Texas A&M University System qv and created the Texas State Technical Institute. The Harlingen branch, known as the Rio Grande Campus, began operations in November, 1967. Beginning with two instructors and forty students, the school had grown to a student body of 1,262 by 1974.

Student enrollment for the 1968–1969 regular term at the James Connally Campus, Waco, was 1,374; in 1974 it was 2,702. Enrollment on the Mid-Continent Campus, Amarillo, was 1,083 in 1974. Rolling Plains Campus, Sweetwater, had an enrollment of 419 in 1974. Maurice W. Roney was president of the four Texas State Technical Institute campuses in 1974.

*Texas State University for Negroes. *See also* Texas Southern University.

Texas Studies in Literature and Language. The first issue of the quarterly, *Texas Studies in Literature and Language, A Journal of the Humanities*, appeared in the spring of 1959, under the editorship of Philip Graham, professor of English at the University of Texas at Austin. *TSLL* differed considerably from the annual *Studies in English*,qv its predecessor, which was published through 1958.

From the first, the large majority of contributors to *TSLL* were not connected with the University of Texas; for example, in the academic year 1970–1971, with Professor Ernest J. Lovell, Jr., as executive editor, the journal published in its four issues a total of forty-seven articles written by scholars and critics from thirty-eight universities in the United States and elsewhere. Of the total forty-seven articles (724 pages), thirty-two were concerned with English literature, thirteen with American literature, and two with other subjects. The range of these four issues covered every one of the usually designated fields of English and American literature, from Anglo-Saxon or Old English to the present, and these articles were read by students and professors in every state in this country, as well as in a large number of foreign countries. *TSLL*, published by the University of Texas Press,qv is financially supported by the University of Texas at Austin and is a teaching arm of the university. Contributions of significance in all areas of literature, linguistics, philosophy, social studies, and nontechnical science are considered for publication, although brief notes and book reviews are not normally accepted.

Ernest J. Lovell, Jr.

*Texas Synodical Female College.

Texas Tax Journal.

Texas Tech University. By an act of the Texas legislature, Texas Technological College,qv Lubbock, was renamed Texas Tech University, effective September 1, 1969. The college had operated six schools in 1964: agriculture, arts and sciences, business administration, engineering, home economics, and graduate. A law school was added in 1967, and a medical school was opened in 1972 (*see* Texas Tech University School of Medicine). U.S. Army and U.S. Air Force ROTC units and an extension division were also maintained. Texas Tech participated in intercollegiate athletics as a member of the Southwest Conference.qv

The first Ph.D. degree was conferred in 1952; since that date the graduate program has been enlarged to include many doctoral and master's degrees in many areas. Library facilities contained 1,200,000 catalogued items in 1969 and were expanding at the rate of 50,000 volumes annually. The library also served as a regional depository for federal documents and for the Atomic Energy Commission. Enrollment increased from 7,156 resident students in 1955 to over 17,000 in 1967. The student body was divided between undergraduate and graduate students at nearly a 12 to 1 ratio in 1964. Faculty members numbered 1,057 during the 1966–1967 term. The campus consisted of 1,839 acres, with 371 acres used for the main plant; other acreage was used for agricultural and other research and services. A research farm at Pantex consisted of 5,821 acres plus 8,000 acres on lease. The farm was the headquarters of a beef cattle center. Out of a total of 169 buildings, 103 were permanent struc-

tures and represented an original construction cost of $58,700,000. The college operating budget increased from $1,829,055 in 1945, to $5,646,838 in 1955, and to $17,646,058 in 1965. Edward Newlon Jones succeeded D. M. Wiggins as president in 1952, and Robert Cabaniss Goodwin served as president beginning in 1959. Grover E. Murray was president of the university in 1974, when enrollment totaled 21,927. *See also* Museum of Texas Tech University; Ranching Heritage Center.

Texas Tech University School of Medicine. Texas Tech University School of Medicine at Lubbock was authorized by the Sixty-first Texas Legislature in 1969. The first students, sixty-one in number, enrolled in the fall of 1972. Enrollment increased to 103 students in 1973 and 122 students in 1974.

*Texas Technological College. *See also* Texas Tech University.

Texas Times (Galveston).

Texas Tourist Development Agency. *See* Tourist Development Agency, Texas.

Texas Traffic Safety Council. *See* Traffic Safety Council, Texas.

*Texas Trail. *See* Western Trail.

*Texas Transportation Company.

Texas Transportation Institute. The Texas Transportation Institute was established in 1950 to engage in research, provide instruction at the graduate level, and serve as the research agency for the Texas State Highway Department.qv Fred J. Benson, its first executive officer, was succeeded by Charles J. Keese in 1962. The institute is a part of the Texas A&M University System.qv

Research activities were concerned with highway design and traffic engineering, highway bridges and structures, highway materials and soils, highway pavement design, vegetation control, and economic aspects of transportation. Among the educational activities sponsored by the institute were annual transportation conferences, refresher seminars for right-of-way agents, short courses in highway and traffic engineering and asphalt technology, graduate courses in various phases of transportation, and research subjects for theses and dissertations for advanced degrees. It extended information to the transportation industry through special adult education courses and publications. The institute also assisted in bringing specialists in transportation to the Texas A&M University campus.

The institute's research has provided successful solutions for many problems in transportation, resulting in more durable pavements, readily available aggregates for construction, use of lightweight concrete, prestressing and prefabricating concrete bridge structures, determination of influences of freeways on land values and uses, and sign supports that yield when struck by vehicles. Other areas of innovation include improved soil selection and use, materials testing, highway design, traffic control, and intersection illumination.

L. J. Horn

***Texas Trunk Line.** *See* Dallas, Palestine, and Southeast Railroad.

***Texas Veterans Association.**

***Texas Volunteer Guard.** *See* Texas National Guard.

Texas Water Development Board. *See* Water Development Board, Texas.

Texas Water Pollution Control Board. *See* Water Quality Board, Texas.

Texas Water Quality Board. *See* Water Quality Board, Texas.

Texas Water Rights Commission. *See* Water Rights Commission, Texas.

Texas Water Well Drillers Board. *See* Water Well Drillers Board, Texas.

***Texas Weekly.**

***Texas Wesleyan Banner.**

***Texas Wesleyan College.** Texas Wesleyan College, Fort Worth, remained a small, liberal arts college of the Methodist church. The forty-one-acre campus contained twenty-two buildings in 1965, which were valued at $3,000,000. An endowment fund exceeded $2,000,000 that year, and the annual operating budget ran over $1,000,000.

During Law Sone's presidency, the following buildings were constructed: home economics, student center, 100,000-volume-capacity library, two residence halls, dining hall, and Polytechnic Methodist Church. In addition, a home for the president was acquired and buildings were remodeled for the band, art, and speech-drama departments. A ten-year building plan called for completion of a science building, a health center, a field house, and additional residence facilities. The library housed 77,183 volumes in 1969.

Enrollment in 1969 was 2,020 students, and the faculty numbered ninety members. Forty-four percent of the teaching staff held earned doctorates. In 1963 the institution decided to concentrate on quality undergraduate programs, and the master's program in education was dropped. Bachelor's degrees in arts, science, business administration, and music continued to be offered by the college.

Texas Wesleyan College held membership in, or the approval of, seventeen education organizations, including the Southern Association of Colleges and Schools. The school was a member of the Big State Intercollegiate Athletic Conference, and students competed in basketball, track, golf, and tennis. William M. Pearce served as president in 1974, when enrollment was 1,786.

***Texas Wesleyan College Academy.**

***Texas Western College.** *See also* University of Texas at El Paso.

Texas Western Narrow Gauge Railroad. *See* Texas Western Railroad; Western Narrow Gauge Railroad.

***Texas Western Railroad.** The Missouri, Kansas, and Texas Railway Company did not acquire the Texas Western Railroad's grade and right-of-way (as stated in Volume II), but acquired a right-of-way three miles south of Pattison. The land given for the Texas Western's right-of-way was returned to the Pattison family after the Texas Western abandoned it in 1899. *See* Pattison, Texas.

***Texas v. White.**

***Texas Woman's College.**

Texas Woman's University. Texas Woman's University, known as Texas State College for Women qv until 1957, was the first institution in North Texas (Denton) to confer the Ph.D. degree, the first such degree having been conferred in 1953. The faculty numbered 379 in 1969. That same year the library housed 375,000 volumes.

The building programs completed by 1966 raised the value of the university's physical plant to approximately $28,000,000. The university owned and operated two clinical centers, one in the Texas Medical Center,qv Houston, and the other in the Southwestern Medical College of the University of Texas,qv Dallas. The major fields of study were arts and sciences, teaching, fine arts, health, physical education and recreation, household arts and sciences, nursing, library science, occupational therapy, and physical therapy. John A. Guinn served as president in 1974, when there was a total student enrollment of 7,190.

Texas Women's Political Caucus. The women's rights movement was active in Texas as early as 1926 when Rena Maverick Green qv of San Antonio was named Texas State Executive Committee chairman of the National Woman's party. That same year the organization issued a booklet, *How Texas Tax Laws Discriminate Against Women.* (*See* Community Property Law of Texas.) While the succeeding years brought some attention to the movement, it was not until July, 1971, that a statewide meeting of interested women was held in Austin to form a group which became known as the Texas Women's Political Caucus. The organization was an outgrowth of the national resurgence of interest in women's rights which came out of the civil rights movement of the 1960's. A need was felt for a women's political organization to sponsor women's issues such as welfare rights, abortion, and contraception. Equality in employment and economic opportunities, legal rights, and child care centers were among the concerns of the women members. In 1971 Texas had one woman state representative, Frances "Sissy" Farenthold of Corpus Christi, and one woman state senator, Barbara Jordan (later elected to the U.S. Congress) of Houston.

The first state convention of the TWPC was held in Austin in March, 1972, to formulate a multipartisan women's coalition for the promotion of political action and the encouragement of women's effectiveness on all political levels—as voters, as candidates, and as lobbyists for their goals. Special targets were sexism, racism, and poverty. Helen Cassidy, of Fort Worth, was elected TWPC chairperson and Jeanne Necaise, of Houston, treasurer. TWPC compiled three publications for its members in 1973, *Woman's Candidate Guide*, *How to Organize in a Local Area*, and *Legislative Report* (a rating review of legislative voting in the 1973 Texas legislature). In 1973 TWPC ran its first complete legislative program of women's issues, and there were five women representatives and one woman senator in the Texas legislature.

State headquarters for TWPC was located in Austin, and by mid-1973 there were twenty caucus groups in Texas known either by a city name (Austin Women's Political Caucus) or a county name (Harris County Women's Political Caucus). Of the 2,000 caucus members, the twenty-eight- to thirty-five-year-old age group had the highest number. Non-working as well as working women belonged to TWPC, with the major metropolitan areas furnishing the main membership. Caucus groups in the western part of the state were organized in Lubbock, Amarillo, and El Paso. TWPC members worked in decision making roles in the state Democratic executive committee and in Raza Unida.qv The first TWPC newsletter was issued in January, 1973.

The TWPC was responsible for bringing to Texas the first National Women's Political Caucus convention, held in Houston in the Rice Hotel in February, 1973. Jane Hickie was the state delegate, and Cathy Bonner, TWPC state director, was a regional delegate. Frances Farenthold was elected chairperson of the national caucus for a two-year term. *See also* Women, Status of, in Texas.

BIBLIOGRAPHY: Houston *Chronicle*, November 12, 1971, February 12, 1973; Houston *Post*, February 12, 1973; *Texas Observer*, March 5, 1973; *Texas Women's Political Caucus Newsletter*, I (January, 1973).

*Texas in World War I. *See* World War I, Texas in.

*Texas in World War II. *See* World War II, Texas in.

Texas Youth Council. *See* Youth Council, Texas.

*Texhoma, Texas.

*Texhoma City, Texas.

*Texian.

*Texian and Brazos Farmer.

*Texian Democrat.

*Texian and Emigrant's Guide.

*Texla, Texas.

*Texline, Texas.

*Texon, Texas.

*Texroy, Texas.

*Textile Industry. The textile industry in Texas has easy access to marketing areas of the nation and to the raw materials necessary to the industry. In the early 1970's there were over twenty-eight plants in Texas manufacuring items which fall into the category of textile mill products. During 1970 the industry employed 6,928 Texans, who received a payroll of nearly $23.1 million. These textile mills used Texas cotton, wool, and mohair in their fabrics. The state produced 25 percent of the nation's cotton, 97 percent of the nation's mohair, and 20 percent of its wool during 1971.

Textile mills in Texas furnished material to over 700 manufacturers in the state; in 1970 these companies employed 60,719 persons, with a payroll of $252.3 million. The mills in Texas sold their products in both national and international markets. In the late 1960's mills in Corsicana, Hillsboro, Ralls, and Houston experienced financial difficulties and were forced to close because of outdated equipment and competition from foreign imports.

Burlington Industries, Inc., an internationally known textile manufacturer, had mills located in Post, Memphis, and Sherman, Texas. These plants produced bed sheets and pillow cases from raw materials found in the state and turned out packaged products ready for distribution. Twelve plants in Texas, including these three, used cotton and synthetics to produce bed sheets, pillow cases, duck twill, canvas, Osnaburg, flannel, shirting, gingham, upholstery and drapery fabrics, and industrial fabrics.

Two carpet mills were operating in the 1970's in Hillsboro and Marlin. Nine knitting mills produced such items as ladies' ready-to-wear, men's wear, knit and doubleknit sportswear fabrics, athletic clothing, hosiery, sweaters, and shirts. Two mills produced glass yarn, woven fiberglass cloth, and fibrous glass reinforcement, and three mills produced such items as cordage, twine, yarn, and reinforced polyethylene fabric. Three mills used wool and mohair in the production of drapery fabrics, neckties, scarves, blankets, upholstery fabrics, uniform goods, coating materials, and flannels. Various other mills produced bias tape, bags, waistbanding, surgical dressing, and medical and baby products. With the advent of solvent scouring, dyeing, and finishing, the way was opened for further expansion in individual mills and in the number of mills operated without the use of water and the consequent pollution of water resources.

The natural fibers of cotton, wool, and mohair were often used in combination with synthetic fibers, depending on the design, color, and purpose of the fabric. Knitted fabrics came to the fashion forefront in the late 1960's because knitted weaves had great elasticity, needed no ironing, and had considerable body. Knitting machines could be changed quickly to alter the pattern and weave to follow the new styles. Woven fabrics producers met the competition with the development of stretch woven fabrics and by changing their patterns and designs more often than before.

BIBLIOGRAPHY: University of Texas at Austin, Publications of the Natural Fibers & Food Protein Committee of Texas (formerly the Cotton Research Committee of Texas).

William F. Harris

Teya Indians. The Teya Indians, known only from records of the Coronado Expedition qv in the middle sixteenth century, seem to have lived in the eastern part of the Texas Panhandle and the adjoining part of Oklahoma, particularly along the Canadian River Valley. Their linguistic and cultural affiliations remain uncertain. Some writers identify them as Apache and others as Wichita. The Teya were fairly numerous, practiced agriculture, and lived in thatched houses, all of which appear to link them with later Wichita groups of Oklahoma and northern Texas. The Teya are not to be confused with the Tejas or Texas, another name for the southwestern group of Caddo tribes better known as Hasinai, who lived in eastern Texas.

BIBLIOGRAPHY: D. A. Gunnerson, "The Southern Athabascans: Their Arrival in the Southwest," *El Palacio*, LXIII (1956); G. P. Hammond and A. Rey, *Narratives of the Coronado Expedition* (1940); W. W. Newcomb, Jr., *The Indians of Texas* (1961); A. H. Schroeder, "A Re-analysis of the Routes of Coronado and Oñate into the Plains in 1541 and 1601," *Plains Anthropologist*, VII (1962); W. R. Wedel, *Prehistoric Man on the Great Plains* (1961); G. P. Winship, *The Coronado Expedition, 1540–1542* (1896).

T. N. Campbell

***Thackwell, Texas.**

***Thalia, Texas.**

Tharp, Benjamin Carroll. Benjamin Carroll Tharp was born in Pankey, Grimes County, Texas, on November 16, 1885, the son of Edwin H. and Angelina Victoria (McJunkin) Tharp. He enrolled in Sam Houston Normal Institute (now Sam Houston State University) in 1908 and was graduated in 1910. He came to the University of Texas in 1911 and received a B.A. degree in 1914 and an M.A. degree in 1915. He was plant pathologist at the State Department of Agriculture qv from 1915 to 1917 and associate professor of biology at Sam Houston Normal from 1917 to 1919, when he joined the University of Texas faculty as an instructor in botany. His work on the ecological survey in 1921, concerning the age of trees along the Red River, contributed to the settlement of the Texas-Oklahoma boundary dispute (*see* Boundaries of Texas). Tharp received the Ph.D. degree in 1925 from the University of Texas and in that year was named an associate professor; he was a full professor from 1933 until his retirement in 1956. He was also assistant dean of the College of Arts and Sciences from 1928 to 1934.

A highly respected academician, Tharp's approach to Texas vegetation was essentially that of a naturalist, and he probably knew the vegetation of the state better than anyone in his own time. He was director of the University of Texas Herbarium from 1943 until 1956, and his studies and collection of Texas flora resulted in publications which strongly influenced such writers as Roy Bedichek, J. Frank Dobie, and Walter P. Webb.qqv His first comprehensive treatment of the vegetation of Texas was "The Structure of Texas Vegetation East of the 98 Meridian," published in the *University of Texas Bulletin* (1926). *The Vegetation of Texas* (1939) was a later, more comprehensive study. "A Pollen Profile from a Texas Bog," published jointly with J. E. Potzger of Butler University in 1947, was one of the first studies in the southern United States to determine vegetational shifts and climate changes through the use of pollen profile sequences. His last major work was *Texas Range Grasses* (1952). He was co-editor of Mary S. Young's qv 1914 journal of botanical explorations in Trans-Pecos Texas, published in the *Southwestern Historical Quarterly* qv in 1962.

Tharp, who has been called the "Father of Texas Ecology," was a life member of the Texas Academy of Science qv and a member of other state and national societies. He was married to Norris Ophelia Wallis on September 16, 1914, and they had two sons. He died in Austin on November 29, 1964, and was buried in Austin Memorial Park.

BIBLIOGRAPHY: *Who's Who In America* (1960); Austin American, November 30, 1964; Biographical File, Barker Texas History Center, University of Texas at Austin.

***Tharp, Texas.**

***Thatcher, Thomas.**

Thaxter, Texas. Thaxter, in northwest Midland County, owed its existence to the Midland and Northwestern Railway Company. When the railroad was abandoned in the 1920's, the town went out of existence.

***Thayer, Texas.**

***The Grove, Texas.**

***The Knobbs, Texas.** The Knobbs (*see* Yegua Knobs), at the headwaters of Yegua Creek, was the place of settlement in the 1840's and 1850's of people from the mountains or hills of the Carolinas, Virginia, Tennessee, Georgia, Alabama, and Mississippi. Their log houses and shake-covered roofs were made from the native pin oaks, and the board-covered wattle and daub chimneys were a constant fire threat to the wooden houses. From the end of the Civil War to the 1890's, feuding and slayings among the various groups in The Knobbs area brought about the formation of vigilante committees in neighboring McDade, Bastrop, Oak Hill, and Giddings. Feud killings on Christmas Eve and Christmas Day, 1883, left seven men dead. When the courthouse at Giddings burned, the records which might have revealed much of the background and facts of the feuds were destroyed.

BIBLIOGRAPHY: George King Martin, "Land of the Noose—Yegua Knobbs," *Old West*, 5 (Spring, 1969).

***Theater in Texas.** With the decline of touring professional theater, mainly because of traveling costs, some major Texas cities organized their own resident professional companies and productions. Dallas was a pioneer, with the outdoor Starlight Operetta in the amphitheater in State Fair Park; its productions became known as State Fair Musicals when they moved into the auditorium in 1951; the name was changed again, to Dallas Summer Musicals, and a large local company was headed by imported "name" Broadway actors. There were counterparts in large arena operations in Fort Worth's Casa Mañana and in the Houston Music Theater.

Margo Jones qv continued her resident professional Theatre-in-the-Round in Dallas until her death in 1955. In Houston Nina Vance not only continued the Alley Theatre qv but, aided by foundation grants and local donors, moved theater production to the Jesse H. Jones Hall for the Performing Arts,qv when it was opened in mid-town Houston in November, 1968. Another resident professional theater, allied with Trinity University as its graduate school of drama, was operated by Paul Baker in the Dallas Theater Center, which was designed by Frank Lloyd Wright and opened in 1959.

In the late 1930's and early 1940's a few universities, notably Baylor and the University of Texas (Austin), organized full-scale drama departments offering bachelor's and master's degrees; the University of Texas later added a doctoral program. In the 1960's virtually every college in the state offered degree courses in theater (some in connection with speech), and many had buildings with elaborate and flexible playing facilities, along with sophisticated technical equipment.

With the increase in vacation travel in Texas, a number of outdoor amateur dramatic productions were introduced. At Palo Duro Canyon, *Texas*, a history-based drama, is presented annually over a period of weeks. Robert E. Nail qv began the Fort Griffin Fandangle qv in Albany in 1938, and it continues to be produced each year on the Watt Matthews Ranch. Most of these outdoor productions were cast with local talent. *See also* Little Theater Movement; Music in Texas.

Gynter Quill

Theatre-in-the-Round, Margo Jones. *See* Jones, Margaret Virginia (Margo); Theater in Texas.

Thecamon Indians. The Thecamon (Tecamenez, Tecamon, Teheaman) Indians are known only from records of the La Salle Expedition,qv which indicate that in the late seventeenth century these Indians lived inland north of Matagorda Bay, apparently not far from the Colorado River. The Thecamon have been confused with the Tacame, a Coahuiltecan group that also lived near the coast but much farther to the southwest, between the San Antonio and Nueces rivers. There is no proof that these two names refer to the same people. The linguistic and cultural affiliations of the Thecamon remain undetermined.
BIBLIOGRAPHY: I. J. Cox (ed.), *The Journeys of René Robert Cavelier, Sieur de La Salle*, II (1906); F. W. Hodge (ed.), *Handbook of American Indians*, II (1910); H. R. Stiles (ed.), *Joutel's Journal of La Salle's Last Voyage, 1684-7* (1906).

T. N. Campbell

*Thedford, Texas.

*Thelma, Texas. (Bexar County.)

*Thelma, Texas. (Limestone County.)

*Theodore, Adah Bertha. *See* Menken, Adah Isaacs.

*Theon, Texas.

*Thermo, Texas.

*Theuvenins Creek.

*Thicket, Texas. D. J. Williams, G. W. Brown, and H. P. Geisendorf owned the original sawmill at Thicket, in Hardin County; they operated the mill from 1904 until 1917 (not from 1909 to 1920, as stated in Volume II), when it was dismantled and sold, along with all of the housing.

Two other mills operated in this community in the early 1920's, one owned by H. P. Geisendorf and the other by D. L. Williams, son of the original owner. After abandonment of the millsite, the post office was moved to the White Oak community about two miles away. The population of Thicket in the late 1960's was approximately one hundred.

Lois Williams Parker

*Thickety Creek.

*Third Creek.

*Third Yegua Creek.

*Thirty-sixth Division. After World War II the 36th Division was reorganized, and the division headquarters received federal recognition in late 1946, with the remainder of the division being federally recognized in that year and in 1947. The division continued to grow until the Texas National Guard qv was reorganized in 1959. At that time some units were exchanged with the 49th Armored Division in order to better align the two divisions geographically. In 1965 the 36th Infantry Brigade (Separate) was formed, primarily of 36th Infantry Division units. This brigade was a high priority unit of the Selected Reserve Force with the capability of moving from home station to mobilization station in seven days. In December, 1967, and January, 1968, the 36th Infantry Division was eliminated due to reorganization of the reserve forces. A portion of the division became a part of the 71st Infantry Brigade (Airborne) which is the only reserve forces airborne brigade in the United States Army. Both the 36th Infantry Brigade (Separate) and the 71st Infantry Brigade (Airborne) are successor units to the 36th Infantry Division. *See also* Thirty-sixth Division Association; Walker, Fred Livingood; Lost Battalion.
BIBLIOGRAPHY: United States Army, 36th Division (Richard A. Huff, ed.), *A Pictorial History of the 36th "Texas" Infantry Division* (194–?); United States Army, 36th Division, *The Story of the 36th Infantry Division* (n.d.); Fred L. Walker, *From Texas To Rome* (1969); Robert L. Wagner, *The Texas Army* (1972).

Albert E. Binotti

Thirty-sixth Division Association. The 36th Division Association was founded in January, 1946, at a meeting in Brownwood of veterans who served with the Thirty-sixth Division qv during World War II. Among the association's founders were H. Miller Ainsworth (first president), William H. Martin, Carl L. Phinney, Richard B. Dunbar, and the division's wartime commander, General Fred L. Walker.qv The association holds annual reunions in order to perpetuate the comradeship engendered by their common service. The association sponsored the publication of *A Pictorial History of the 36th "Texas" Infantry Division* in the late 1940's. After September, 1947, membership in the association was open to anyone assigned to the division in World War I or II. On Veterans Day, 1959, on the state Capitol qv grounds in Austin, an eleven-foot granite monument was dedicated by the association to the members of the 36th Division who were killed in both world wars. Another monument exists near the Salerno site where the 36th Division led the allied invasion into Italy in 1943. In May, 1972, the 36th Division Association sponsored a return trip to Salerno for its members. *The T-Patcher*, the official newsletter, is published quarterly. The 1972 annual reunion was held in Dallas, and the president was Roger Cannon.

James I. Eddins

Thomas, Albert. Albert Thomas, son of James and Lonnie (Langston) Thomas, was born on April 12, 1898, in Nacogdoches. He was graduated from Rice Institute (now Rice University) with a B.A. in 1920 and took a law degree from the University of Texas in 1926. Thomas served as a second lieutenant in the army during World War I, and in 1922 he married Lera Millard of Nacogdoches. He was admitted to the Texas Bar in 1927 and served as attorney for Nacogdoches County until 1930, when he moved to Houston as assistant United States attorney. In 1936 Thomas was elected to the United States House of Representatives, an office which he held until his death, at which time his wife was elected to complete his term.

Ranking eleventh in seniority in the House at the time of his death, Thomas had served since 1949 as chairman of the House subcommittee on independent office appropriations; he was also a member of the subcommittee on defense appropriations and a member of the joint committee on atomic energy. In 1950 Thomas was elected chairman of the Texas House delegation, and in 1964 he was named chairman of the House Democratic caucus.

Thomas played a leading role in securing the location of the Manned Spacecraft Center qv in Houston in 1961. A high point in his career came in November, 1963, when President John F. Kennedy, who had requested that Thomas not retire from public office, and Vice-President Lyndon B. Johnson qv came to Houston to honor Thomas at a testimonial dinner (*see* Kennedy, John Fitzgerald, Assassination of). On February 15, 1966, Thomas died in his Washington home; he was buried in Houston.

BIBLIOGRAPHY: Houston *Post*, February 16, 1966; *Who's Who In America* (1966).

*Thomas, Benjamin.

*Thomas, Cullen Fleming.

*Thomas, David.

*Thomas, Ezekiel.

*Thomas, George Henry.

*Thomas, Jacob.

*Thomas, Nathan.

Thomas, Stephen Seymour. Stephen Seymour Thomas, one of America's distinguished portrait painters, was born in San Augustine, Texas, on August 20, 1868, the son of James Edwards and Mary Landon (Blount) Thomas. He began painting and drawing at an early age and attended the Art Students' League in New York from 1885 to 1888, studying under William Merritt Chase and James Carroll Beckwith. At the age of twenty he was in Paris, studying at the Académie Julian and at the École des Beaux Arts. He painted both genre and landscape subjects and exhibited for twenty consecutive years at the Paris Salon, where he received his first honors in 1891. The salon hung the first two paintings he submitted, and in 1892 his painting, "Victime Innocente," was exhibited there and afterwards was widely reproduced. The painting's success insured him an entry in *Who's Who In America* at the age of twenty-four and brought him a number of commissions. His last exhibit at the Paris Salon was "Portrait of M. Antonin Dubost," president of the French Senate. During the 1890's he won a number of honors, including a bronze medal at the 1900 Paris Exposition, two gold medals (1901, 1904) at the Paris Salon, the Hors Concours Salon award in 1904, and a gold medal at the Munich Internationale. In 1905 he was decorated in France with the Cross of the Legion of Honor.

Thomas was commissioned to paint a portrait of Sam Houston for the Texas building at the 1893 World's Fair in Chicago. Following its exhibition at the fair, the huge equestrian portrait was shown in the Paris Salon, then presented in 1920 by Colonel and Mrs. Francis Drake to the city of Houston; it was finally hung in the San Jacinto Monument and Museum.qv Thomas painted portraits of many famous personages, among them several of President Woodrow Wilson, one of which hangs in the White House in Washington, D. C. Thomas balanced his career as a portrait painter with numerous landscape works.

A large collection of Thomas' paintings was given by the artist's daughter, Mrs. Jean Haskell, to be hung in the S. Seymour Thomas Memorial Room in the Ezekiel W. Cullen qv Home in San Augustine, Texas. His "Lady and Dog" was part of the collection of the Metropolitan Museum of Art; other works were in private collections and museums, both in America and abroad.

Thomas was married to Helen M. Haskell in London on October 11, 1892; they had one daughter. He died at his home in La Crescenta, California, in March, 1956, and was buried there.

BIBLIOGRAPHY: Pauline A. Pinckney, *Painting in Texas: The Nineteenth Century* (1967); *Who's Who In America* (1952).

Jean Haskell

*Thomas, Texas. Thomas, in northwestern Upshur County, was first called Chelsa, then Simpsonville in 1858, before it was named for O. Thomas (not for Thomas Creek, as stated in Volume II) in 1914; O. Thomas had for many years been postmaster of the settlement when it was known as Simpsonville. The Thomas post office was opened on February 14, 1914, and was closed on February 20, 1954. In 1970 the Thomas community had an estimated population of two hundred. *Se also* Simpsonville, Texas.

B. D. Tucker

*Thomas Creek.

Thomas Toby.

*Thomason, John William, Jr. John William Thomason, Jr., was the son of Sue (Goree) Thomason (not Sue Gores Thomason, as stated in Volume II). Thomason's studies also included one year at Sam Houston Normal Institute (now Sam Houston State University). One of his books was titled *Salt Winds and Gobi* (not *Gold*) *Dust.* Thomason was buried in Oakwood Cemetery in Huntsville.

BIBLIOGRAPHY: Roger Willock, *Lone Star Marine* (1961).

John Payne
Aline Law

*Thomaston, Texas.

*Thompson, Alexander.

*Thompson, Algernon P.

*Thompson, Ben.

*Thompson, Charlton W.

Thompson, Ernest Othmer. Ernest Othmer Thompson was born in Alvord, Texas, on March 24, 1892, the son of Lewis Oliver and Lee Agnes (Murray) Thompson. He married May Peterson on June 9, 1924. His wife died on October 8, 1952, and on October 29, 1953, he married Myda Bivins. Thompson attended Virginia Military Institute in 1914 and received an LL.B. degree from the University of Texas in 1917. Texas Technological College (now Texas Tech University) and Texas Christian University awarded him honorary LL.D. degrees in 1934 and 1951.

Thompson was admitted to the Texas Bar in 1917 and began law practice in Amarillo. In 1932 he was appointed to the Railroad Commission qv of Texas. During his years on the commission Thompson earned a national reputation as an authority on oil and gas conservation. In 1937 he attended the World Petroleum Congress in Paris as President Franklin D. Roosevelt's personal representative. In 1945 he conducted a world survey of oil for Secretary of War Robert Patterson. Thompson was a member of the Interstate Oil Compact Commission from 1935 to 1965, serving three terms as chairman. The American Petroleum Institute in 1951 cited Thompson as the world's greatest authority on conservation. He was also an important figure in the growth of the Texas National Guard,qv holding the rank of lieutenant general upon his retirement in 1957 after thirty-four years in the guard. Thompson retired from the Railroad Commission in January, 1965, after completing thirty-two years of service. He died on June 29, 1966, in Amarillo and was buried in the State Cemetery.qv

BIBLIOGRAPHY: Dallas *Morning News*, June 29, 1966; *Who's Who In America* (1952).

*Thompson, Frances Judith Somes (Trask).

*Thompson, George.

*Thompson, James E.

*Thompson, Jesse.

Thompson, Milton John. Milton John Thompson, aerodynamics professor and engineer, was born July 28, 1904, in Grand Rapids, Michigan, the son of Schuyler D. and Jennie L. (Albertson) Thompson. He was educated in the local schools and a junior college there. He received a B.S. degree in aeronautical engineering from the University of Michigan in 1925 and an M.S. degree from the same school the following year. After two years at that university as an instructor of engineering mathematics, he won a Guggenheim fellowship in 1928 to study at the Warsaw Polytechnical Institute in Poland. He received his Sc.D. degree in aerodynamics in 1930 in Poland. Returning to the University of Michigan, Thompson was assistant professor in the Department of Aeronautical Engineering until 1937, when he became associate professor. During that time he was active in wind tunnel projects and also became well known as a consultant in aeronautical engineering.

In 1941 Thompson accepted a professorship at the University of Texas in the Department of Mechanical Engineering. Through his efforts (and due to the importance of aviation in the war), the university's Department of Aeronautical Engineering was established in 1942, with Thompson as chairman. Thompson often toured the United States, Europe, and the Middle East as a lecturer. Stressing the future of aerodynamics, he predicted that 90 percent of ocean travel after World War II would be by air and that man would double the speed of sound in supersonic jets. For most of 1945 he was on leave from the university to serve as supervisor of aerodynamics at the Applied Physics Laboratory of Johns Hopkins University. Returning to Austin he and C. P. Boner established the Defense Research Laboratory at the University of Texas, and Thompson served as associate director of that laboratory until shortly before his death. In 1958 the university's Department of Aeronautical Engineering became the Department of Aerospace Engineering because of the new emphasis on aerospace courses and the research in travel outside the earth's atmosphere. Thompson remained as chairman of the new department. He coauthored several books and wrote many articles and scientific papers. He has been called the founder of the Department of Aerospace Engineering at the University of Texas; his special field was flight performance of aerospace vehicles. Thompson was married to Helen B. Frank on August 22, 1931; they had two children. He died on July 23, 1971, in Austin, and he was buried in Austin Memorial Park.

BIBLIOGRAPHY: *Who's Who In America* (1960); Biographical Files, Barker Texas History Center, University of Texas at Austin.

Thompson, Paul Jennings. Paul Jennings Thompson was born in Quincy, Illinois, on September 26, 1890. After graduation from high school in Kahoka, Missouri, he worked for two years on the Clark County *Courier*, then enrolled at the University of Missouri to study journalism. After graduation in 1914 he was successively assistant editor of the Clark County *Courier*, editor of the Macon (Missouri) *Republican*, and a member of the advertising staff of the Cedar Valley *Times* (Vinton, Iowa). He volunteered for the army in World War I and was sent to Camp McArthur,qv near Waco, Texas, where he met and later married Bess Gentry Park. After the war he worked for a year on the Billings, Montana, *Gazette*; he then accepted an invitation to join the journalism faculty at the University of Texas as an adjunct professor.

His career as a journalism educator was marked by many distinctions. In 1927 he became chairman of the Department of Journalism at the University of Texas. He was instrumental in designing the Texas Student Publications, Inc., a model organization for the production of student publications which has been widely adopted by other universities. He opposed overloading the curriculum with professional courses and helped to steer journalism education throughout the country into the pattern of the liberal arts degree. He helped to found the Southwest Journalism Congress and served as its president. He was elected president of the American Association of Schools and Departments of Journalism in 1946–1947, and he was one of the designers of the national accreditation program in journalism education. On May 1, 1953, he received the University of Missouri Honor Award for Distinguished Service in Journalism.

With Ward Mayborn,qv Texas publisher, Thompson established a system of summer internships on Texas newspapers for journalism students. Due to his efforts, a scholarship program for journalism students was developed. In March, 1949, four hundred former students gathered at a dinner in his honor, and a sum of $2,000 from more than one thousand ex-students was presented to him to use for journalism education. When he retired in 1959 from the directorship of the school of journalism, five hundred students gathered at another dinner in his honor. After his retirement he began writing a book on the ethics of journalism. The manuscript was completed before he died on May 22, 1964.

DeWitt C. Reddick

*Thompson, Robert Andrew.

Thompson, Stith. Stith Thompson, one of the world's leading authorities on folklore, was born in Bloomfield, Kentucky, on March 7, 1885, the son of John Warden and Eliza (McClaskey) Thompson. He was a student at Butler College in Indianapolis, Indiana, took a B.A. degree at the University of Wisconsin in 1909, an M.A. degree at the University of California in 1912, and a Ph.D. degree at Harvard University in 1914. Thompson was married to Louise Faust on June 14, 1918; they had two daughters.

He came to the University of Texas (Austin) as an instructor in English in 1914 and remained there until 1918. As secretary-treasurer of the Texas Folklore Society,qv Stith Thompson edited the first numbered volume of that society's *Publications* (1916). In 1935 it was reprinted under the title *Round the Levee*, in the preface of which J. Frank Dobie qv said that Thompson "worked up a membership to support him, and by issuing this volume glued the Society together, setting a precedent for a long line of succeeding volumes that have made the Texas organization the best known among all state organizations of its kind in the nation."

After leaving the University of Texas, Thompson was a professor of English at Colorado College (1918–1920), the University of Maine (1920–1921), and Indiana University (1921–1955). At Indiana University he taught courses in folklore, and he was dean of that university's Graduate School from 1947 to 1950. He was the U.S. delegate to the International Folklore Congress in Paris in 1937 and was an official in various international folklore meetings. The author, coauthor, or translator of numerous books and articles on folklore, he was perhaps best known for his work on the classification of motifs in folk tales. His six-volume *Motif-Index of Folk-Literature* (1932–1937) is considered the international key to traditional material, and it has been said that Thompson was responsible for putting the study of folklore in the United States on a solid, scholarly basis.

After he retired as Distinguished Service Professor of English and Folklore at Indiana University in June, 1955, he returned to the University of Texas (where he had begun his career) as a visiting professor of English during the spring semester of 1956. Thompson and his wife traveled widely after his retirement, but he continued to work in the field of folklore. He wrote an autobiography in two parts and presented a bound, typewritten copy of each to the University of Texas at Austin (*see* bibliography below).

Stith Thompson died on January 13, 1976, in Columbus, Indiana; he was buried in the family cemetery outside Springfield, Kentucky.

BIBLIOGRAPHY: Stith Thompson, *Folklorist's Progress* (Autobiographical typescript, 1956, Barker Texas History Center, University of Texas at Austin); Stith Thompson, *Second Wind: A Sequel after Ten Years to Folklorist's Progress* (1966, *ibid.*); *Who's Who In America* (1952); University of Texas at El Paso, *The American Folklore Newsletter*, IV (Winter, 1976); Biographical File, Barker Texas History Center, University of Texas at Austin.

Eldon S. Branda

*Thompson, Thomas M.

*Thompson, Waddy.

*Thompson, Wells.

*Thompson Creek.

*Thompsons, Texas.

*Thompson's Ferry.

*Thompsonville, Texas. (Gonzales County.)

*Thompsonville, Texas. (Jim Hogg County.)

*Thomson, Alexander, Jr.

*Thomson, Thaddeus Austin. Thaddeus Austin Thomson was married to Annie Eloise Anderson (not Henderson, as stated in Volume II).

Katherine Hart

*Thorn, Frost.

*Thornberry, Texas.

*Thorndale, Texas. Thorndale, in Milam County, had a population of 995 in 1960 and 1,031 in 1970, according to the United States census.

*Thornson Creek.

*Thornton, Francis W.

Thornton, Robert Lee. Robert Lee Thornton was born near Hico, in Hamilton County, on August 10, 1880, the son of William Travis and Polly Ann (Weatherby) Thornton. When he was seven years old, the family moved to Ellis County, where he obtained fragmentary schooling and learned to pick five hundred pounds of cotton a day. After working for two years as a clerk in a general store in Bristol, he borrowed money to take an eight-week course in bookkeeping in Dallas. In 1905, while a salesman for a candy company, he married Mary Metta Stiles of Waxahachie. In 1916 he and his wife's two brothers raised $20,000, $6,-000 of it in cash, and started a bank with Thornton as president. The bank, which lent money on mules and automobiles, along with other collateral, grew rapidly and became the Mercantile National Bank, the third largest in Dallas.

Thornton became president of the Dallas Chamber of Commerce, 1933–1936; president of the State Fair of Texas,qv 1945–1963; and mayor of Dallas, 1953–1961. He also helped form the Dallas Citizens Council, was a leader in many civic organizations, and was a director in at least a dozen corporations. As mayor, with the motto, "Keep the dirt flying," he had a large part in expanding airport facilities, enlarging the city hall, building a new library and downtown auditorium, and increasing the city's water supply. Thornton Freeway was named for him. He died in Dallas on February 15, 1964.

BIBLIOGRAPHY: George Sessions Perry, "The Duke of Dallas," *Saturday Evening Post* (June 11, 1955); Dallas *Morning News*, February 16, 1964.

Wayne Gard

*Thornton, Texas.

*Thornton Creek.

*Thorp Spring, Texas.

*Thorp Spring Christian College.

*Thouching Creek.

*Thrall, Homer S.

*Thrall, Texas. Thrall, in Williamson County, was the site of the greatest rainfall recorded in United States history, during an eighteen-hour period on September 9, 1921; on that day 36.40 inches of rain fell there. (*See also* Weather in Texas.) Thrall had a population of 631 in 1960 and 619 in 1970, according to the United States census.

*Threadgill Creek.

*Three D Ranch. See Waggoner Ranch.

*Three Hundred. *See* Old Three Hundred.

*Three Leagues, Texas.

*Three Mile Creek.

*Three Mile Peak.

*Three Mounds.

*Three Rivers, Texas. Three Rivers, in Live Oak County, had a population of 1,932 in 1960 and 1,761 in 1970, according to the United States census.

*Threemile Creek.

*Thrift, Texas.

*Thrifty, Texas.

*Throckmorton, James Webb.

*Throckmorton, William Edward.

*Throckmorton, Texas. Throckmorton, county seat of Throckmorton County, had thirty businesses in 1970, serving an area devoted to the production of cattle and oil. In 1966 the town reported six churches, a city park, a twenty-six-bed hospital, a library, and a newspaper. The population in 1960 was 1,299; in 1970 the count was 1,105, according to the United States census.

*Throckmorton County. The stone ranch house near the old California Trail was built in 1856 by Lieutenant Newton Curd Givens qv (not Gibson, as stated in Volume II). In 1970 Throckmorton County had an economy based on cattle and oil, though some wheat, cotton, and small grains were raised. Between 1924 and 1973, 78,916,968 barrels of oil had been produced in the county. The county held its centennial celebration in 1958 at Throckmorton, the county seat. Tourist attractions included Camp Cooper and the site of the Comanche Indian Reservation,qqv in addition to Camp Wilson and Throckmorton Reservoir. The population was 2,767 in 1960; the count was 2,205 in 1970, according to the United States census.

*Thurber, Texas. *See also* Children of God.

*Thurmond, Alfred Sturgis.

*Thurmond, Columbus Lafayette.

*Thurston, Algernon Sidney.

*Tick Fever. *See* Cattle Tick.

*Ticky Creek.

Tidelands. Controls of the oil resources of the tidelands were given to the various states in May, 1953. By 1954, 131 undersea producing oil and gas wells were brought in. Most of these were in Louisiana. The offshore drilling activities in Texas remained lean until 1967, when activity picked up as companies began testing the federal acreage available to them from the United States' first sale off the state. A total of 102 wells were drilled in 1967, compared with 58 in 1966. Of those wells drilled in 1967, fifty-three were on state leases and forty-nine on federal leases. The General Land Office qv reported receipts of over $200 million from Texas tidelands during the period May 23, 1953, to August 31, 1972; this figure included bonuses, rentals, and royalties. *See also* Tidelands Controversy.

James A. Clark

Tidelands Controversy. The tidelands controversy between the United States and Texas involved the title to 2,608,774 acres of submerged land in the Gulf of Mexico between low tide and the state's Gulfward boundary three leagues (10.35 miles) from shore.

Texas, first acquiring this land by establishing and maintaining itself as an independent nation, reserved this as well as all other unsold land when it entered the Union in 1845. Ownership of the property by the state of Texas was recognized by officials of the United States for more than 100 years. After oil was discovered under state leases, applicants for cheaper federal leases and federal officials began to assert national ownership in the same manner as they had done against California and other coastal states.

The contest was not confined to Texas. All states became concerned over their long-recognized titles to lands beneath their navigable waters. It became a national issue, resulting in three Supreme Court decisions against the states, three acts of Congress in favor of the states, two presidential vetoes against the states, and a major issue in a presidential campaign, before the states finally won the victory. It was the most serious conflict of the century between the states and the federal government.

The federal claims were branded as an attempted "expropriation" and "steal" by outraged officials of Texas and many of the other states. In 1949 a statewide public opinion poll reported that the people of Texas considered it to be the most important public issue facing the state. Public indignation ran higher in Texas than elsewhere because this land had been dedicated to and was a source of revenue for the public school fund (*see* School Fund, Available; School Fund, Permanent). Furthermore, Texas held title not only under the general rule of law theretofore applicable to all states, but under the specific provisions of the Annexation Agreement between the Republic of Texas and the United States. State officials, the Texas legislature, the Democratic and Republican state conventions, the Texas congressional delegation, and many citizens groups resolved to resist the federal claims and seek congressional action recognizing continued state ownership.

The history of the Texas side of this controversy began in 1836 at San Jacinto, where Texas won its independence from Mexico. While still on the battlefield, General Sam Houston sketched out the boundaries of the new nation. They were enacted into law by the First Congress of the Republic of Texas on December 19, 1836. The boundary in the Gulf was described as follows:

". . . beginning at the mouth of the Sabine river, and running West along the Gulf of Mexico *three leagues* from land . . ."

In 1837 this boundary act was sent to President Andrew Jackson, and it was read to the United States Senate. With full knowledge, the United States officially recognized the independence of the Republic of Texas, and President Jackson said,

"The title of Texas to the territory she claims is identified with her independence. . . ." With its own navy the Republic of Texas maintained and defended its three-league boundary in the Gulf of Mexico during the nine years that it existed as an independent nation.

This was the boundary in the Gulf when negotiations were held between the Republic of Texas and the United States for annexation. The Congress of Texas insisted that the United States recognize and defend the established boundaries. General Sam Houston would not agree to annexation until he obtained an assurance from President Polk on this subject. On June 15, 1845, Polk vowed to "maintain the Texian title to the extent which she claims it to be. . . ."

Before Texas entered the Union, the Supreme Court of the United States had already written two decisions holding that lands beneath all navigable waters within the boundaries of the original states "were not granted by the Constitution to the United States, but were reserved to the States respectively . . ." and that "the new States have the same rights, sovereignty and jurisdiction over this subject as the original States." One of these decisions (*Pollard* v. *Hagan*, 3 How. 212, 1845) was later cited with approval and followed by 52 Supreme Court decisions and 244 federal and state court decisions.

In addition to this already established general rule of law under which Texas would retain ownership of its submerged lands after admission as a new state, the Republic of Texas received the following specific assurances relating to all of its lands in the Annexation Agreement tendered by the United States on March 1, 1845.

"That Congress doth consent that the territory properly included within and rightfully belonging to the Republic of Texas, may be erected into a new State, to be called the State of Texas. . . .

". . . and said State shall also retain all the vacant and unappropriated lands lying within its limits. . . ."

After the war between the United States and Mexico, the Texas legislature passed a resolution urging its congressional delegation to insist on the original Texas boundary being followed in the treaty with Mexico, and this boundary commencing "in the Gulf of Mexico, *three leagues* from land, opposite the mouth of the Rio Grande" was written into the Treaty of Guadalupe Hidalgo ᵠᵛ in 1848. Texas' three-league Gulfward boundary was again recognized and followed in the Gadsden Treaty between the United States and Mexico in 1853.

On many other occasions between 1845 and 1948 the United States recognized this boundary and Texas' ownership of the submerged lands within such boundary. When federal officials needed sites for lighthouses, fortifications, and jetties in the Gulfward areas, they obtained grants from the Texas legislature. Thus, with no adverse claims against the title to this property, the Texas legislature authorized the School Land Board ᵠᵛ to execute mineral leases on this land for the benefit of the public school fund. These leases, sold to the highest bidders, had yielded many millions of dollars before any federal claims were asserted.

Other coastal states, relying upon their general title under the Constitution and the long line of Supreme Court opinions, were receiving revenues from oil, kelp, shell, sand, marl, fish, ports, docks, piers, and expensive building sites on filled land along the coasts of Florida and New York.

The earliest adverse claims against any of the states were asserted by applicants for federal oil leases under the federal law which granted leases at twenty-five cents per acre on any undeveloped lands owned by the United States. This was not one one-hundredth of the price per acre averaged by the states for the leases they had sold under state laws. By 1950 there were 1,031 federal lease applicants who had blanketed the coasts of Texas, California, and Louisiana with applications for leases on lands already covered by state leases.

The first lawsuit asserting federal ownership of tidelands was filed by the United States against California in 1946. The federal claim was based on allegations that original ownership of the land was held by the United States before California was created as a state; that former Supreme Court cases adjudicating state ownership were erroneous and should be overruled; that long recognition of state ownership by federal officials did not bar federal action; that paramount federal governmental rights in the tidelands area were inconsistent and incompatible with state ownership; and that no state could hold ownership of lands underlying the marginal sea belt below low tide.

Because this lawsuit was based on claims broad enough to be applied against other states, the attorneys general of all other states filed an *amicus curiae* brief in opposition to the federal claim, and Price Daniel (attorney general for the state of Texas, 1947–1953) presented oral argument on their behalf before the Supreme Court of the United States. In 1946, while the suit was pending, Congress passed a bill recognizing and confirming state ownership of the property, but this bill was vetoed by President Harry Truman.

In 1947, by a split decision, the Supreme Court decided against California in an opinion by Justice Hugo L. Black. The language and theory of this opinion were so shocking to state officials and leading lawyers of the nation that the American Bar Association, the Council of State Governments, the Governors Conference, most of the state legislatures, the National Association of Attorneys General, and the American Title Association immediately urged that Congress again act to overthrow the result and theories announced in the decision. It became one of the most widely criticized opinions in the history of the court.

Justice Black conceded that the states had claimed and possessed their submerged lands in good faith under the language of numerous Supreme Court decisions indicating "that the Court then believed that States not only owned tidelands and soil under navigable inland waters, but also owned soils under navigable waters within their territorial jurisdiction, whether inland or not." But since oil and other property involved might be necessary to the national defense and the conduct of international affairs, Justice Black reasoned that the case should not be controlled by "bare legal title" or "mere property ownership." He said:

"The crucial question on the merits is not merely who owns the bare legal title to the lands under the marginal sea. The United States here asserts rights in two capacities transcending those of a mere property owner."

It was the new theory that federal "paramount rights" may be exercised to take oil and other property without ownership and without compensation that excited fears that the rule might be applied equally to lands beneath inland waters of all the states and eventually to private property.

However, until after the presidential election of 1948, there was still hope that Texas' special title retained under the Annexation Agreement would be recognized by federal officials and that this state would not be sued. On the day he argued the California case, March 13, 1947, United States Attorney General Tom Clark handed to the press a statement saying that a decision in that case would not apply to Texas; that "as a Republic it owned all of the lands within its boundaries, including the marginal sea commonly called tidelands. This area was under the sovereignty of Texas during the Republic and was retained by it under the provisions of the Act of Admission." During the presidential campaign, President Truman said in Austin on September 20, 1948: "Texas is in a class by itself; it entered the Union by Treaty." Even former Secretary of the Interior Harold L. Ickes, a champion of the fight against state ownership, said in a national television address, October 14, 1948: "Parenthetically, Texas may have the legal right to its tidelands, because it came into the Union voluntarily and as an independent country."

Texas went Democratic in the 1948 election, and shortly after the election President Truman directed the attorney general to file suit against Texas. Motion for summary judgment (without hearing evidence) was made on behalf of the United States. Texas made a strong plea, supported by eleven of the world's authorities on international law, in support of its title to the property as an independent nation; its retention of the land under the terms of the international agreement by which it became a state; and its right to introduce evidence on both points.

By a vote of four to three, the Supreme Court decided against Texas, thereby, for the first time in its history, denying a state the right to introduce evidence in a contested lawsuit. The majority opinion by Justice William O. Douglas recognized Texas' ownership as a Republic, but held that transfer of national sovereignty to the United States and admission as a state on an equal footing with the other states accomplished a transfer of this land to the United States.

On motion for rehearing, again supported by leading authorities on the interpretation of international agreements, Texas urged that transfer of national sovereignty does not carry with it the ownership of lands specifically retained by solemn agreement; that the "equal footing" provision was not submitted to or accepted by the Republic of Texas; and that there was no "equal footing" as far as lands and debts were concerned, because Texas was the only state required to assume its own public debt and permitted to retain all of its unsold lands. The court corrected its erroneous citation on "equal footing" but did not change the result of its decision.

In 1952 Congress again passed a bill restoring to the states the title to all submerged lands within their respective boundaries, but for the second time, President Truman vetoed the bill.

In the presidential campaign of 1952, General Dwight D. Eisenhower ^{qv} made special recognition of the rights of Texas under the Annexation Agreement as well as the long-recognized rights of the other states under earlier Supreme Court decisions. He declared in favor of state ownership legislation and said he would sign the bill if it were enacted again by Congress. The Republican platform agreed. On the other hand, the Democratic nominee, Adlai Stevenson, said he would veto such a bill if enacted again by Congress. In Texas this became the foremost issue in the 1952 campaign. The state Democratic Convention placed Stevenson's name on the ticket but then passed a resolution urging all members of the Texas Democratic party to vote for Eisenhower, and Eisenhower carried the state in the November election.

In 1953 Congress made the restoration of submerged lands one of the first orders of business. Price Daniel, then United States senator from Texas, was coauthor of the legislation in the Senate, where it survived what was then the longest filibuster in Senate history (twenty-seven days) and finally won a substantial majority in both Houses. President Eisenhower signed the measure on May 22, 1953. One of the pens used by the president in affixing his signature was presented to the Texas Memorial Museum ^{qv} in a ceremony conducted by the University of Texas.

As an aftermath, one last battle was pitched against Texas in 1957, when the Republican attorney general, Herbert Brownell, filed suit against the state, alleging that its legal boundary and therefore its tideland ownership extended only three miles instead of three leagues (10.35 miles) into the Gulf. This was resented in Texas, primarily because President Eisenhower, the Congress, and Attorney General Brownell himself had specifically recognized three leagues as the extent of the Texas boundary and ownership during the hearings and pendency of the 1953 legislation. The Brownell action sought to take away two-thirds of the Texas property.

President Eisenhower publicly disagreed with the position taken by the Department of Justice with respect to the Texas boundary. Nevertheless, Texas

was forced to defend its boundary in the Supreme Court of the United States. Texas prevailed in this lawsuit, which was decided on June 1, 1960, and now holds thoroughly litigated and firmly established title to its three-league Gulfward boundary and the 2,608,774 acres within such boundary. As of August 31, 1966, the General Land Office reported that the Texas public school fund had received $156,312,000 from leases, rentals, and royalties on this property, and that sixteen fields had been discovered with eighty producing wells.

BIBLIOGRAPHY: An Act to define the boundaries of the Republic of Texas (in) H. P. N. Gammel (comp.), *The Laws of Texas 1822–1897*, I (1193–1194); Joint Resolution of the Congress of Texas, June 23, 1845, *ibid.*, II (1225); Ordinance of the Convention of Texas, July 4, 1845, *ibid.*, II (1228–1230); Texas Annexation Agreement, Joint Resolution of the Congress of the United States, March 1, 1845, 28th Cong., 2nd Sess., 5 Stat. 797; *U.S. v. California*, 332 U.S. 19; *U.S. v. Texas*, 339 U.S. 707; Brief for the State of Texas in Opposition to Motion for Judgment, *United States v. Texas*, No. 13, Original in the Supreme Court of the United States, October Term, 1949; National Association of Attorneys General, *Every State Has Submerged Lands* (1948); Price Daniel, *Sovereignty and Ownership in the Marginal Sea* (1950); "Symposium on the Texas Tidelands Case," *Baylor Law Review*, III (1951); Ernest Bartley, *The Tidelands Oil Controversy* (1953).

Price Daniel

*Tidwell, Texas. (Hunt County.) Tidwell had one store in 1900, which was operated by J. I. Money (not J. J. Mooney, as stated in Volume II). Money also operated the telephone switchboard in Tidwell at one time; he was listed in the 1880 census of Hunt County as a farmer, age twenty-nine.

Bush Prather
Fletcher Warren

*Tidwell, Texas. (Williamson County.)

*Tidwell Prairie, Texas.

*Tierra Alta, Texas.

*Tierra Blanca Creek.

*Tierra Vieja Mountains.

*Tiffin, Texas.

*Tiger Creek.

Tigertown, Texas. Tigertown (also known as Tiger Point), one of thirteen towns laid out in Washington County before or during the period of the Republic, was located about six miles southwest of Brenham. In 1856 a post office was listed for Tigertown, but by 1902 the site was only a cotton field.

BIBLIOGRAPHY: Wilfred O. Dietrich, *The Blazing Story of Washington County* (1950); Harry Haynes, "Death of Early Towns in Washington County—What Death Hath Wrought," Galveston *News*, August 17, 1902.

Tigua Indians. The Tigua (Tiguex, Tiwa, Tihua, possibly Cheguas) Indians in Texas are a remnant of the original Tiwa-speaking Pueblo that came to El Paso in 1680 and settled in Ysleta del Sur, establishing their mission church, Corpus Christi de los Tihuas de Ysleta, in 1682. In 1751 Spain issued a grant to the Tiguas of thirty-six square miles, centered at the mission. The Texas legislature in 1871 incorporated the settlement of

Ysleta (without the consent of the Tiguas), and their lands, amounting to some 20,000 acres, were sold, with only some 300 acres remaining in Indian hands. In 1874 the incorporation act was repealed by the legislature, but by the early 1970's only about three acres remained in private Tigua ownership.

Four Tiguas took part in the defeat of the Apaches under Victorio qv at Sierra Vieja Pass, in Presidio County, near Valentine. Present Tiguan descendants live in or near the town of Ysleta, about twelve miles southeast of El Paso; the community was annexed by El Paso in 1955, and the Tiguas were unable to pay the accompanying rise in property taxes. An attempt to clarify the status of the group resulted in a ruling of the U.S. Indian Bureau in 1961 that the Tiguas had been the responsibility solely of the state of Texas since 1845.

In 1966 the state began an investigation into the legal ownership of Tigua land. Since few of the original documents were extant, the only formal evidence to connect the town of Ysleta with the Ysleta Grant (made in 1751, and affirmed in the Relinquishment Act passed by the Texas legislature in 1854) was the extensive references in deed records, church records, and other legislative acts. By May, 1967, Texas had recognized the Tiguas as a Texas Indian tribe and had put them under the trusteeship of the Commission for Indian Affairs,qv in effect acknowledging them as the oldest identifiable ethnic group in the state. In 1968 a federal law was signed recognizing the Tigua Indians as a tribe and transferring all responsibilities to the state of Texas.

In a 1971 study of the ninety-one Tigua families living in the *Barrio Indio*, a section of Ysleta, thirty-two families had an annual income of $1,000 or less; fifteen of the thirty-two had no income other than welfare payments. A number of men worked in building trades or were employed in Project Bravo of the U.S. Department of Labor. A few of the women worked in nearby clothing manufacturing plants. Half of the Tiguas were under twenty-one. Of the 439 persons of the Tigua community, 20 percent had had no formal education, but of the 142 children under the age of ten, all were in school in 1971.

By the early 1970's conditions for the Tiguas had begun to improve. The Indians filed suit in the federal courts for restitution of their original Spanish land grant. They claimed the U.S. had violated the Treaty of Guadalupe Hidalgo,qv which guaranteed the integrity of Spanish and Mexican grants. In 1972, $1.7 million in state and federal grants was pledged to them; Texas budgeted $237,151 for the Tiguas, most of it for buying and developing land. In 1972 the tribal property included seven acres, with buildings to be used as offices. A hacienda dating from 1744 had been restored to serve as a community building. A housing project was in the planning stage.

The Tiguas have been Catholic for some three hundred years; on July 12, they celebrate the annual field mass in honor of St. Anthony, their patron saint. Unlike other tribes in the El Paso area,

however, the Tiguas have largely resisted absorption into the Mexican culture. The traditional rituals and ceremonies which they have retained differ little from those at Isleta, New Mexico, their ancestral pueblo. The Tiguas enjoy their own tribal government, which oversees secular and ceremonial affairs. Another source of pride is Hueco Tanks,qv now Hueco Tanks State Park (*see* Parks, State), where some 2,000 pictographs are preserved (*see* Rock Art, Indian). According to legend, *El Wiede*, the spirit, dwells at Hueco Tanks and created the Tiguas there. A twenty-acre archeological site near Hueco Tanks was donated to the tribe by Horizon Properties Corporation. The land, which contained the ruins of a thirteenth-century pueblo, was to be developed as a tourist attraction, providing employment and tribal revenue. Miguel Pedraza was the tribal governor in 1971.

BIBLIOGRAPHY: Tom Diamond (comp.), *Pueblo de la Ysleta del Sur* (1970); C. L. Sonnichsen, *Pass of the North* (1968); Brad Cooper, "Return of the Tiguas," *Texas Parade*, 32 (March, 1972); Bob Miles, "New Hope for an Ancient People," *Texas Star*, February 20, 1972; Alan Minter, "The Tigua Indians of the Pueblo de Ysleta del Sur, El Paso County, Texas," *West Texas Historical Association Year Book*, XLV (1969); Don Walden, "The Wiede at Hueco Tanks," *Texas Observer*, July 16, 1971; University of Texas at Austin, *Guide To Texas State Agencies* (1972).

*****Tiguex Indians.** *See also* Tigua Indians.

*****Tilden, Texas.** Tilden, county seat of McMullen County, is the commercial center for a ranching area. The city boasts a natural gas processing plant. In 1967 it reported two churches, a public school, and a library. In 1970 ten businesses were reported. Between 1962 and 1964 Boot Hill Cemetery was restored and landscaped. Although population figures for Tilden were not included in the United States census report, the estimates were 485 for 1960 and 416 for 1970.

*****Tilijae Indians.** In the latter part of the seventeenth century the Tilijae (Filifae, Tilijaya, Tilixae, Tilyaya, Tiloja) Indians, who spoke a Coahuiltecan language, ranged over a territory that extended from present Monclova, Coahuila, northward across the Rio Grande to the southern margin of the Edwards Plateau in Texas. They were most closely linked with the Nueces River in the area now covered by Dimmit, Zavala, and Uvalde counties. The Tilijae were reported at the mission of La Caldera in Coahuila before 1700, and later they were also reported at the mission of San Juan Bautista qv near present Eagle Pass. They were among the Coahuiltecan groups for which San Juan Capistrano Mission qv was established at San Antonio in 1731, and their name appears as early as 1733 in the records of nearby Nuestra Señora de la Purísima Concepción de Acuña Mission.qv

BIBLIOGRAPHY: H. E. Bolton, *Texas in the Middle Eighteenth Century* (1915); F. W. Hodge (ed.), *Handbook of American Indians*, II (1910); J. R. Swanton, *Linguistic Material from the Tribes of Southern Texas and Northeastern Mexico* (1940).

T. N. Campbell

*****Tillar, Benjamin Johnston.** Benjamin Johnston Tillar was associated with the Bush and Tillar

Cattle Company (not the Tush and Tillar Cattle Company, as stated in Volume II).

Tilley, Wesley Hope. Wesley Hope Tilley was born in Springfield, Illinois, on December 23, 1885, the son of Joseph Edgar and Millee (Davis) Tilley. After graduation from high school in Springfield, Tilley studied music privately in St. Louis, Missouri. He and his brother, Paul, were among the pioneers of film making in Texas. In 1910 they were producing silent films in Houston, and in 1911 they moved to San Antonio where they formed the Satex Film Company. They made one-reel silent films and showed them on a screen at night in front of the Alamo. Their attempt at film making there was successful enough, but they moved to Austin in 1913. With assets of $25,000 they reestablished the Satex Film Company and added a finishing plant for processing motion picture film.

The Satex Company was the only company manufacturing silent films south of St. Louis at that time and the first film company in the United States to make three-reel movies. That same year the company folded because of financial difficulties, even though six movies had been made and released nationally. Tilley later joined the Hagenbeck Circus band and toured with them for two years in Germany. He returned to Austin and taught music. During World War I Tilley taught code, construction, and electronics of radio for the U. S. Army Air Corps in Austin. On January 31, 1920, Tilley married Helen Grist of Austin. They had one son. Tilley was director of the Ben Hur Shrine band in Austin for thirty-eight years and served as secretary-treasurer for the Federation of Musicians (Local 433) in Austin from 1943 to 1964. He died June 24, 1972, in Austin. *See also* Texas Film Industry.

James R. Buchanan

*Tillotson College. *See also* Huston-Tillotson College.

*Tilmon, Texas.

Tilpacopal Indians. The Tilpacopal, Pajalat, and Siquipil were three Coahuiltecan bands for whom Nuestra Señora de la Purísima Concepción de Acuña Mission qv was established at San Antonio in 1731. The aboriginal location of the Tilpacopal remains unknown, but it seems likely that they ranged the area south of the Edwards Plateau.
BIBLIOGRAPHY: H. E. Bolton, *Texas in the Middle Eighteenth Century* (1915); F. W. Hodge (ed.), *Handbook of American Indians*, II (1910).

T. N. Campbell

*Timber. *See* Lumber and Lumbering in Texas.

*Timber, Texas.

*Timber Creek.

*Timber Mountain.

*Time, Texas.

*Timm City, Texas.

*Timmons Creek.

*Timpson, Texas. Timpson, in Shelby County, had a population of 1,120 in 1960 and 1,254 in 1970, according to the United States census.

*Timpson and Henderson Railway.

*Tin Horn War.

*Tin Smelting in Texas. In 1951 the production of America's largest tin smelter, in Texas City, was interrupted by a revolution in Bolivia, the source of the smelter's ore. For two years no long-term contract for tin ore was negotiated. The smelter, the only source of refined tin in the United States, produced approximately 50 percent of the tin used by United States consumers in 1952.

By 1953 the Texas City smelter was able to handle all grades of tin from pure alluvial to low-grade primary ore. The annual capacity of the two-step, natural gas-fired reverberatory furnace was 96,000 tons, with 99.75 percent purity or better.

In 1955 the $13,000,000 facility was put up for sale by the Office of Defense Mobilization, thereby blocking a move to close the government-owned plant. Wah Chang Company, a well-known tungsten firm, purchased the smelter in 1958. By 1956 production of tin had fallen to 17,600 tons, much less than the 43,000 tons produced in 1946. Obtaining ore remained a problem during the late 1950's, and although there were tin minerals in the Trans-Pecos and Burnet-Llano areas, no Texas ore was mined.

Wah Chang produced 11,597 tons of tin ingots in 1960, as well as some ferro metals such as tungsten metal powder and tantalum columbium oxides. In 1964 the Texas City plant produced 3,958 tons of tin and began to recover molybdenum; a year later the plant doubled its tin-producing capacity. *See also* Minerals in Texas.
BIBLIOGRAPHY: *Texas Business Review* (September, 1952, July, 1953, October, 1955, May, 1958, February, 1964, August, 1964, September, 1964); U. S. Bureau of Mines, *Minerals Yearbook*, III (1954); U. S. Bureau of Mines, *Minerals Yearbook*, I, III (1964).

*Tinapihuaya Indians. The Tinapihuaya (Tinipijuay), presumably a Coahuiltecan-speaking group, are known only from records of San Francisco Vizarron de los Pausanes Mission, near present-day La Unión in northeastern Coahuila, a mission which they entered in 1737 along with the Pausane and Piguique. Since the Pausane and Piguique were brought there from the Texas coastal plain (between the Nueces and San Antonio rivers), it seems likely that the Tinapihuaya also came from the same area.
BIBLIOGRAPHY: F. W. Hodge (ed.), *Handbook of American Indians*, II (1910); J. A. de Morfi, "Viaje de indios y diario del Nuevo-México," *Documentos para la historia de México*, I (1856); M. Orozco y Berra, *Geografía de las lenguas y carta etnográfica de México* (1864); E. L. Portillo, *Catecismo geográfico, político e historico del estado Coahuila de Zaragoza* (1897); J. R. Swanton, *Linguistic Material from the Tribes of Southern Texas and Northeastern Mexico* (1940).

T. N. Campbell

*Tinata de la Piedra.

Tiniba Indians. The Tiniba Indians are known from a single Spanish missionary report (1691), which indicates that they lived an unspecified distance southwest of the Hasinai tribes of eastern Texas. Their affiliations remain undetermined.

BIBLIOGRAPHY: J. R. Swanton, *Source Material on the History and Ethnology of the Caddo Indians* (1942).

T. N. Campbell

*Tinnins, Texas.

*Tinsley, James W.

*Tinsley Creek.

*Tioga, Texas.

*Tiopane Indians. The Tiopane (Sayupane) Indians appear to have lived between San Antonio and the coast during the first half of the eighteenth century, but their range cannot be more precisely determined. Perhaps the most significant clue is provided by a contemporary statement that the Tiopane were among the Indian groups that served as a buffer between Espíritu Santo de Zuñiga Mission qv (near present Goliad) and the Apache to the west and northwest. This suggests that the Tiopane lived along the San Antonio River in the general vicinity of present Karnes County. Although the published records are not entirely clear, the Tiopane seem to have been represented at two of the San Antonio missions—Nuestra Señora de la Purísima Concepción de Acuña and San José y San Miguel de Aguayo.qqv Their linguistic affiliation remains in doubt. J. R. Swanton thought that the Tiopane were either Coahuiltecan or Karankawan in language. If their range as suggested above is accurate, it seems more likely that they were Coahuiltecan. The name of the Tiopane is so similar to that of the Tiopine that these two groups have sometimes been confused. In fact, some writers have suggested that the two names represent the same people.

BIBLIOGRAPHY: H. E. Bolton, *Texas in the Middle Eighteenth Century* (1915); F. W. Hodge (ed.), *Handbook of American Indians*, II (1910); J. R. Swanton, *Linguistic Material from the Tribes of Southern Texas and Northeastern Mexico* (1940).

T. N. Campbell

Tiopine Indians. The status of this group remains in doubt because of certain complications in the records. The first is that the name Tiopine is so similar to that of the Tiopane that the two have been confused. In fact, some writers have thought that both names may refer to the same people. The second is that San Antonio mission records indicate that after 1750 the Tiopine became known as the Chayopine. It is not certain whether this involved combining the survivors of two or more groups and referring to them by a new name (as was sometimes done for administrative convenience) or simply using another form of the same name for the same people (as was also done at times). The solution to this problem must await detailed analysis of the primary documents. For details on the ethnohistory of Tiopine-Chayopine, *see* Chayopine Indians.

T. N. Campbell

*Tip Top, Texas.

*Tipoy Village.

Tippit, J. D. J. D. Tippit was the Dallas policeman who was killed on November 22, 1963, while attempting to apprehend a person identified as Lee Harvey Oswald,qv alleged assassin of President John F. Kennedy (*see* Kennedy, John Fitzgerald, Assassination of). His parents were Edgar Lee and Lizzie Mae (Rush) Tippit. He was born on September 18, 1924, in Red River County, Texas. He completed ten grades of public school, served in the United States Army from July, 1944, to June, 1946, and attended a Veterans Administration vocational training school at Bogata, Texas, from 1950 to 1952. In July, 1952, Tippit joined the Dallas police force. In eleven years as a patrolman, he compiled a good record. On December 26, 1946, Tippit married Marie Frances Gasaway. They had three children. He was buried in Laurel Land Cemetery in South Dallas.

BIBLIOGRAPHY: *Hearings Before the President's Commission on the Assassination of President John F. Kennedy*, XXIV (1964).

Tips, Kern. Kern Tips, son of Robert and Mary (Kern) Tips, was born on August 23, 1904, in Houston. He was married to Nancy Tucker, and they had two children. Tips received his college education at the Agricultural and Mechanical College of Texas (now Texas A&M University) and at Rice Institute. While studying at Rice, he was a sports reporter for the Houston *Chronicle* qv from 1924 through 1926, when he became sports editor of that newspaper, and he served in that capacity through 1934. His association with radio began as a sportscaster in 1926 and later as a newscaster in 1930. He served as general manager of Houston radio station KPRC from 1935 through 1946. On January 1, 1947, Tips joined the advertising agency of Wilkinson-Schiwetz & Tips. In September, 1954, when the firm merged with McCann-Erickson, Inc., one of the world's largest advertising agencies, Tips became a vice-president of that firm. In September, 1966, he retired from service with McCann-Erickson, Inc., and embarked on a "fourth career" as producer and narrator of a syndicated series of five-minute sports radio shows broadcast throughout the Southwest. He continued in the activity through June, 1967, a short time before his death.

Tips was perhaps best known as the "Voice of the Southwest Conference," having spent thirty-two years broadcasting Southwest Conference qv football games. During that period he was associate producer and narrator of Humble Oil and Refining Company's qv "Southwest Conference Highlights." His voice was beamed around the world through the facilities of the Armed Forces Radio Service network. Tips served as a member of the board of directors of the National Association of Broadcasters from 1939 to 1940, as a member of the NBC Affiliates Council in 1941, as an advisor to the Office of War Information during World War II, and as director of Civilian Defense of Houston and Harris County, 1943–1945. In 1959 he was selected as the man who had contributed most to radio and television in Texas in the first annual award of the Association of Broadcasting Executives in Texas. He was recipient of the only award ever made by the Southwest Football Officials Association for distinguished service to the sport. He was voted Texas Sportscaster of the Year in a national poll, an honor he was accorded five consecutive years, and he received many other testimonials and awards from clubs, associations, and educational institutions. Tips was the author of *Football—Texas Style*. On August 3, 1967, Kern Tips died in Houston.

Sylvia Gunn

*Tira, Texas.

Tirkle Community, Texas. *See* Harmony (Kent County), Texas.

Tishim Indians. This name is known only from baptismal records of San Antonio de Valero Mission qv in San Antonio. The mother of a baptized child was recorded as Tishim, the father Yojuane. The Tishim may be the same as the Tixemu, who in 1683 were reported as one of the Texas groups known to the Jumano, some of whom traveled widely in the interior of Texas. If so, a Tonkawan affiliation is suggested by the fact that the Tishim woman was married to a Yojuane (the Yojuane were Tonkawans). The similarity of Titskan, the Tonkawa name for themselves, to both Tishim and Tixemu also suggests the same relationship. J. R. Swanton considered the Tishim to be either Coahuiltecan or Tonkawan in language.

BIBLIOGRAPHY: C. W. Hackett (ed.), *Pichardo's Treatise on the Limits of Louisiana and Texas*, I (1931); F. W. Hodge (ed.), *Handbook of American Indians*, II (1910); J. R. Swanton, *Linguistic Material from the Tribes of Southern Texas and Northeastern Mexico* (1940).

T. N. Campbell

*Titus, Andrew Jackson.

*Titus, James.

*Titus County. Titus County, 30 percent forested, had two mills capable of producing 20,000 board-feet of hardwood lumber daily in 1964, but by 1970 there was only one mill and no recorded production. Between 1936 and January 1, 1973, there were 164,422,158 barrels of oil produced. The agricultural income is derived largely from livestock, with farming limited to truck crops, fruits, and feed crops. Titus County was among the leading counties in the production of broilers. The 1960 population was 16,785; in 1970 it was 16,702, according to the United States census.

*Tivoli, Texas.

*Tivydale, Texas.

Tixemu Indians. This name appears on a list of tribes (recorded in 1683 at El Paso) known to the Jumano Indians, some of whom traveled extensively in the interior of Texas. Unfortunately the location of the Tixemu is not given. The Tishim, represented by at least one individual at San Antonio de Valero Mission qv of San Antonio in the middle eighteenth century, were probably the Tixemu known to the Jumano. If so, a Tonkawan linguistic affiliation is suggested by the fact that a Tishim woman at San Antonio was married to a Yojuane. The Yojuane were Tonkawans, and several other names on the Jumano list are identifiable as Tonkawan. The similarity of Titskan, the Tonkawa name for themselves, to both Tixemu and Tishim also suggests

the same relationship. J. R. Swanton considered the Tishim to be either Coahuiltecan or Tonkawan in language.

BIBLIOGRAPHY: C. W. Hackett (ed.), *Pichardo's Treatise on the Limits of Louisiana and Texas*, I (1931); F. W. Hodge (ed.), *Handbook of American Indians*, II (1910); J. R. Swanton, *Linguistic Material from the Tribes of Southern Texas and Northeastern Mexico* (1940).

T. N. Campbell

Tlacopsel Indians. The Tlacopsel (Acopsel, Lacopsel, Tlascopsel) Indians were an Atakapan group of southeastern Texas. The location of their settlements remains unknown, but it is believed that they lived in the same general area as the Bidai and Deadose. They are known only during the eighteenth century, mainly in connection with Indian requests for missions in east-central Texas.

BIBLIOGRAPHY: H. E. Bolton, *Texas in the Middle Eighteenth Century* (1915); F. W. Hodge (ed.), *Handbook of American Indians*, II (1910); A. S. Gatschet and J. R. Swanton, *A Dictionary of the Atakapa Language* (1932).

T. N. Campbell

*Tlascalan Indians. *See also* Tlaxcalan Indians.

*Tlascopsel Indians. *See also* Tlacopsel Indians.

Tlaxcalan Indians. The Tlaxcalan (Tlascalan, Tlaxcaltecan, Tlaxcalteco) Indians of central Mexico, who spoke a Uto-Aztecan language, aided Cortez in his conquest of the Aztec empire and received certain privileges in return. This relationship of mutual aid and trust continued into later times, and Tlaxcalans often assisted the Spaniards on the frontier in exploration, warfare, and colonization. A Tlaxcalan was with Antonio de Espejo qv in Trans-Pecos Texas and New Mexico in 1582–1583. In 1688 a Tlaxcalan scout was sent by the governor of Coahuila to check on La Salle's qv colony on the Texas coast, and this same Tlaxcalan reported the presence of Jean Henri qv (presumably a survivor of the La Salle Expedition qv) among Coahuiltecan Indians near the Rio Grande. Shortly thereafter Tlaxcalan auxiliary soldiers were with several expeditions that sought La Salle's Fort St. Louis qv and were also with Domingo Terán de los Ríos qv in the Hasinai country of eastern Texas. In 1759 Tlaxcalan auxiliaries were with Diego Ortiz Parilla in his disastrous punitive campaign against the Comanche and their allies on the Red River. Although there were plans to settle Tlaxcalans at several strategic places in Texas, relatively few actually settled there (nine families arrived at San Sabá Mission qv in 1757). However, Tlaxcalan colonists were fairly numerous at various places on or just south of the Rio Grande, as at El Paso (refugees from northern New Mexico after the Pueblo Indian rebellion of 1680), at San Juan Bautista qv near present Eagle Pass (settled there about 1700 to help instruct and control the Coahuiltecan Indians at near by missions), and in the lower Rio Grande Valley (invited by José de Escandón qv to settle in his new colony of Nuevo Santander in the 1750's). Descendants of these early Tlaxcalan settlers still live along the Rio Grande, and some are undoubtedly living in Texas today.

BIBLIOGRAPHY: C. Gibson, *Tlaxcala in the Sixteenth*

Century (1952); M. Simmons, "Tlascalans in the Spanish Borderlands," *New Mexico Historical Review*, XXXIX (1964).

T. N. Campbell

*Toaa Indians. See also Tohaha Indians.

Toapa and Toapari Indians. These names are known from a single Spanish document of 1683 which identifies them as friends of the Jumano, a tribe noted for wide travel across Texas. It seems likely that both lived somewhere in west-central Texas. Their affiliations remain unknown.

BIBLIOGRAPHY: C. W. Hackett (ed.), *Pichardo's Treatise on the Limits of Louisiana and Texas*, I (1931).

T. N. Campbell

*Tobacco Culture. In the 1950's there was no commercial production of tobacco in Texas. By 1965 one tobacco processor was operating in Texas, but no estimated tobacco acreage had been reported. When the H. W. Finck Cigar Company of San Antonio was founded in 1893, it was one of nineteen tobacco-processing companies in the city, and tobacco was still being grown in Texas. In the early 1970's it was the sole remaining tobacco company and it continued to market "Travis Club," its own brand of cigars.

BIBLIOGRAPHY: Institute of Texan Cultures, *The German Texans* (1970); *Texas Almanac* (1955, 1963, 1965); *Directory of Texas Manufacturers* (1966).

Tobin, Edgar. Edgar Tobin, son of William G. and Ethel (Murphy) Tobin, was born in San Antonio on September 7, 1897. He was a graduate of San Antonio Military Academy. Tobin was a member of Captain Eddie Rickenbacker's "Hat in the Ring" air squadron during World War I; he earned the title "ace" after he had downed five enemy planes and an observation balloon. He returned to San Antonio after the war and started the Tobin Aerial Surveys firm. He established a reputation in mapping operations for oil firms, first entering the commercial mapping field for Humble Oil and Refining Company.ᑫᵛ During World War II his company mapped the entire United States for the federal government, and he served as special civilian adviser to General H. H. Arnold, U.S. Army Air Forces. In San Antonio he was a generous contributor to many charitable organizations.

Tobin was married to Margaret Batts (a regent of the University of Texas from 1947 to 1955 and daughter of Robert Lynn Batts ᑫᵛ) on November 10, 1926, in Austin; they had a son and a daughter. Tobin died January 10, 1954, near Shreveport, Louisiana, in a plane crash which took the lives of eleven other prominent businessmen, one of whom was Thomas Elmer Braniff.ᑫᵛ Tobin was buried in Sunset Memorial Park in San Antonio. At the time of his death his company was the largest aerial mapping firm in the world. The Edgar Tobin Foundation was established in San Antonio.

BIBLIOGRAPHY: Dallas *Morning News*, January 11, 12, 1954; San Antonio *Express*, January 11, 12, 1954.

Tobin, John Wallace. John Wallace Tobin was born in San Antonio on June 27, 1867, the son of Josephine (Smith) and William Gerard Tobin.ᑫᵛ He received his education at St. Mary's Academy

and St. Mary's College. At the age of twenty, he was commissioned 2nd lieutenant in the Texas militia as a member of the Belknap Rifles,ᑫᵛ a San Antonio volunteer organization.

In 1893 Tobin was elected city councilman. He resigned before completing the term to become chief of the San Antonio fire department. In 1897 he was Bexar County treasurer. In 1900 he began his tenure as sheriff of Bexar County; he was reelected every two years until 1908 and again from 1910 to 1923, a total of twenty-one years. He was known as the "gunless sheriff."

Tobin's ambition was to become mayor of San Antonio, following in the footsteps of his grandfather, John William Smith,ᑫᵛ San Antonio's first mayor after Texas became a republic. He succeeded in 1923 and was mayor until his death in 1927. The period of his office was marked by many public improvements, including the construction of Olmos Dam, the widening and straightening of the San Antonio River, a street improvement project, the renovation of the city hall, and the construction of a municipal auditorium.

An Episcopalian, Tobin was married to Minnie Thornton on August 15, 1906. They had a daughter, who died in childhood. Tobin died on November 10, 1927, and was buried in City Cemetery No. 1 in San Antonio.

Zelime Vance Gillespie

*Tobin, Patrick Henry.

Tobin, William Gerard. William Gerard Tobin was born in South Carolina on May 21, 1833. In October, 1853, he came to San Antonio with his brother, Dan Tobin. Two months after his arrival he was married to Josephine Smith, daughter of John William Smith,ᑫᵛ former mayor of San Antonio. They were the parents of ten children.

Tobin was a member of the Texas Rangers ᑫᵛ for a short time in 1855, and in 1856 he served as San Antonio's city marshal. In 1859 he was captain of a company of San Antonio volunteers and served under Samuel Peter Heintzelman ᑫᵛ of the U.S. Army during Juan Nepomuceno Cortina's ᑫᵛ raids along the border near Brownsville. When Texas seceded from the Union, Tobin was commissioned captain in the Confederate Army and served throughout the war.

After the war Tobin returned to San Antonio; during the 1870's he leased the Vance building, once a Confederate headquarters, and converted it into a hotel, the Vance House. He was an early advocate of Texas-type Mexican foods and in 1881 negotiated with the United States government to sell canned chili con carne to the army and navy. In the mid-1880's he organized an extensive factory for the canning of chili con carne and other Mexican food specialties. Tobin's death, a few days after the canning operation had been started, ended further development of the project. He died at his home on July 28, 1884, and was buried in City Cemetery No. 1 in San Antonio.

BIBLIOGRAPHY: William Corner, *San Antonio de Bexar* (1890); Edward W. Heusinger, *A Chronology of Events in San Antonio* (1951); M. L. Crimmins, "Colonel Robert E.

Lee's Report on Indian Combats in Texas," *Southwestern Historical Quarterly*, XXXIX (1935–1936); *Frontier Times* (July, 1929); San Antonio *Express*, July 31, September 5, 1869, June 8, 14, September 7, 1871, January 19, 1882, July 15, 29, September 7, 1884, October 23, 1908.

Zelime Vance Gillespie

Tobo Indians. The Tobo Indians are known from a single Spanish missionary report (1691) which lists them among the groups that lived southeast of the Hasinai. Since the distance is not given, it is impossible to tell whether the Tobo area was in eastern Texas or western Louisiana. Their affiliations are unknown.

BIBLIOGRAPHY: J. R. Swanton, *Source Material on the History and Ethnology of the Caddo Indians* (1942).

T. N. Campbell

***Toboso Indians.** In the seventeenth century the Toboso Indians occupied the Bolsón de Mapimí of Coahuila and Chihuahua, and in the following century they frequently raided Spanish settlements to the east in Nuevo León. It is likely that they sometimes crossed the Rio Grande, but records of Toboso in Texas are rare. However, a few Toboso found their way to Nuestra Señora del Refugio Mission qv near the Texas coast. Baptismal records indicate their presence at this mission between 1807 and 1828. The Toboso are frequently identified as Athapaskans (Apache), but more recent research has produced enough evidence to indicate that the Toboso language was probably Uto-Aztecan.

BIBLIOGRAPHY: J. D. Forbes, "Unknown Athapaskans: The Identification of the Jano, Jocome, Jumano, Manso, Suma, and Other Indian Tribes of the Southwest," *Ethnohistory*, 6 (1959); F. W. Hodge (ed.), *Handbook of American Indians*, II (1910); M. D. McLean and E. del Hoyo (eds.), *Description of Nuevo León, Mexico (1735–1740), by Don Josseph Antonio Fernández de Jáuregui Urrutia* (1964); C. Thomas and J. R. Swanton, *Indian Languages of Mexico and Central America and Their Geographical Distribution* (1911).

T. N. Campbell

***Toby and Brother Company.**

***Tod, John Grant.** John Grant Tod was a commander in the Texas Navy qv (not commander of the navy, as stated in Volume II).

Rosa Tod Hamner

Tod, John Grant, Jr. John Grant Tod, Jr., son of Abigail Fisher (West) and John Grant Tod,qv was born in Richmond, Fort Bend County, on January 14, 1864. In 1866 his family moved to nearby Harrisburg, where he resided the rest of his life. He received an LL.B. degree from Yale in 1885 and practiced law in Houston. He served as county judge of Harris County, 1892–1896, and district judge, 1896–1900. He was secretary of state during the second term of the administration of Governor Joseph Draper Sayers.qv He took an active part in the development of the Houston Ship Channel,qv including the extension of the channel through Irish Bend (later the Deer Park area) in 1905. In 1890 he was married to Osceola Morriss, and the couple had two daughters. Tod died in Galveston on February 20, 1918, and was buried in Glendale Cemetery in Harrisburg. *See also* Todville, Texas.

BIBLIOGRAPHY: Marilyn McAdams Sibley, *The Port of Houston* (1968); Harris County Historical Society, Inc., *Houston, A History and Guide* (1942); John Leslie Dickson, The Houston Ship Channel (M.A. thesis, George Peabody College for Teachers, 1929); Texas Bar Association, *Proceedings* (1919).

Rosa Tod Hamner

Tod, Texas. *See* Todville, Texas.

***Tod Mountain.**

***Todd, George T.**

***Todd, William Smith.**

***Todd, Texas.** (Grimes County.)

***Todd, Texas.** (Harris County.) [This title was incorrect in Volume II and should be deleted. *See* Todville, Texas. Ed.]

***Todd City, Texas.**

***Toddville, Texas.** [This title was incorrect in Volume II and should be deleted. *See* Todville, Texas. Ed.]

***Todos Santos Creek.**

Todville, Texas. Todville (also known as Tod), in Harris County, was founded by John Grant Tod, Jr.qv in 1900 as a subdivision on the western shore of Galveston Bay, near the town of Seabrook. Originally named Morrisstown in honor of Ritson Morriss, the original grantee of the land, the site soon became popularly known as Todville, and it is now officially so designated.

Rosa Tod Hamner

Toepperwein, Adolph. Adolph (Ad) Toepperwein was born in Boerne, Kendall County, on October 16, 1869, the son of German immigrants, Johanna (Bergman) and Ferdinand Toepperwein. Soon after, the family moved to Leon Springs, where Ferdinand Toepperwein was a well-known gunsmith. When Adolph was thirteen his father died, and the boy went to San Antonio, first working in a crockery shop and then as a cartoonist for the San Antonio *Express*.qv After seeing the famed "Doc" W. F. Carter in an exhibition of marksmanship, he began perfecting his own shooting talents. In 1889 he quit his newspaper job and went to New York with San Antonio theater manager George Walker, looking for a vaudeville job.

In 1901, after touring with a circus for eight years, Toepperwein began his fifty-year association with the Winchester Repeating Arms Company as an exhibition publicity agent and sales representative. In 1903 he was married to Elizabeth Servaty, of New Haven, Connecticut, who had never fired a gun in her life. Within two years the Toepperweins were traveling as a team, billed as "The Famous Topperweins" (their name Americanized). She became an outstanding woman marksman, representing American Powder Mills. They traveled throughout the world until her death in 1945.

Ad Toepperwein's first official record was made at the St. Louis World's Fair in 1904. In 1906 during a three-day exhibition, he made 19,999 hits out of 20,000 hand-thrown wood blocks. It was at the San Antonio fairgrounds in December, 1907, that he made his famous world record, using a 1903 model Winchester .22 automatic. At about twenty-five feet he didn't miss a single hand-thrown wood chip out of 8,000 and missed only four out of the remaining 5,000 during sixty-eight and one-half hours of target shooting. He attracted both rural and townspeople to exhibits wherever Winchester guns were sold. After his retirement in 1951 Toepperwein conducted a shooting camp in Leon Springs. He was elected to the Texas Sports Hall of Fame.qv

Ad Toepperwein died in San Antonio on March 4, 1962, and was buried beside his wife in Mission Burial Park. A Toepperwein museum was opened in May, 1973, on the Lone Star Brewery grounds in San Antonio to house some of the memorabilia of the team's long years of marksmanship.

BIBLIOGRAPHY: Charles M. Barnes, *Combats and Conquests of Immortal Heroes* (1910); Norman B. Wiltsey, "Rifleman in Retrospect," *Frontier Times*, 38 (August–September, 1964); Austin *American-Statesman*, December 27, 1969; San Antonio *Express*, August 5, 1894, May 26, 1901, January 28, 1945.

*Tohaha Indians.** The Tohaha (Teao, Thoaga, Toaa, Toaha, Toao, Tooja, Tohahe, Tohaka, Tuxaha) Indians are not to be confused with the Toho, although they both lived in the same area and were closely associated. Both are generally considered to be Tonkawan groups, but this has never been satisfactorily demonstrated. In the late eighteenth century the Tohaha were most frequently encountered by Europeans on the lower Guadalupe and Colorado rivers (but not near the coast), where they often shared the same settlements with other groups, particularly Cantona, Cava, Emet, and Sana. They were never reported in missions, at least under this name or its variants. Some modern writers have equated the Toyal with the Tohaha. (In Volume II the Tohaha and Toaa were treated as separate groups, but there is no basis for this separate treatment. The literature makes it clear that these are variant names for the same people.)

BIBLIOGRAPHY: H. E. Bolton (ed.), *Spanish Exploration in the Southwest, 1542–1706* (1916); C. W. Hackett (ed.), *Historical Documents Relating to New Mexico, Nueva Vizcaya, and Approaches Thereto, to 1773*, II (1926); F. W. Hodge (ed.), *Handbook of American Indians*, I (1907), II (1910); P. Margry, *Découvertes et établissements des Français dans l'ouest et dans le sud de l'Amérique Septentrionale*, III (1879); J. R. Swanton, *Source Material on the History and Ethnology of the Caddo Indians* (1942).

T. N. Campbell

Toho Indians. The Toho (Thoo, Tohan, Tohau, Tojo, Tokau, Too, Tou, Toxo, Tuu) Indians are not to be confused with the Tohaha, although both lived in the same area and were often closely associated. It is generally thought that both were Tonkawan groups, but this cannot be proved conclusively. In the late seventeenth century the Toho and Tohaha were most frequently encountered by the Spanish along the lower Guadalupe and Colorado rivers (but not on the coast), where they shared villages with other groups, particularly the Cantona, Cava, Emet, and Sana. In 1740 some of the Toho entered San Antonio de Valero Mission qv at San Antonio and were reported there as late as 1765. Attempts to link the Toho with the Atayo of Cabeza de Vaca qv are not very convincing because over 150 years separate the initial records of the two groups. Identification of Toho with the Tohau (Tohan, Tokau) of

the La Salle Expedition qv records is generally accepted and is supported by the fact that both Tohau and Tohaha appear on the same list of localized groups. H. E. Bolton qv once called attention to the similarity of certain variants of Toho, particularly Tuu and Tou, to Tup and Top, two group names that have never been satisfactorily explained. Bolton's suggestion deserves serious attention and should be tested. (In Volume II the Tojo [Toho] and Too were listed as separate groups, but the literature shows that these are variants of the same name.)

BIBLIOGRAPHY: H. E. Bolton, *Texas in the Middle Eighteenth Century* (1915) and (ed.), *Spanish Exploration in the Southwest, 1542–1706* (1916); F. W. Hodge (ed.), *Handbook of American Indians*, I (1907), II (1910); P. Margry, *Découvertes et établissements des Français dans l'ouest et dans le sud de l'Amérique Septentrionale*, III (1879).

T. N. Campbell

*Tohookatokie Indians.**

*Tojo Indians.** *See also* Toho Indians.

Tojuma Indians. In 1683–1684 Juan Domínguez de Mendoza qv led an exploratory expedition from El Paso as far eastward as the junction of the Concho and Colorado rivers east of present San Angelo. In his itinerary he listed the names of thirty-seven Indian groups, including the Tojuma (Toijuma), from whom he expected to receive delegations. Nothing further is known of the Tojuma, who seem to have been one of many Indian groups of north-central Texas that were swept away by the southward thrust of the Lipan-Apache and Comanche Indians in the eighteenth century.

BIBLIOGRAPHY: H. E. Bolton (ed.), *Spanish Exploration in the Southwest, 1542–1706* (1916); C. W. Hackett (ed.), *Pichardo's Treatise on the Limits of Louisiana and Texas*, II (1934).

T. N. Campbell

Tokamak. The Texas Tokamak, a device to test the basic concepts necessary to harness the energy-producing mechanism of the hydrogen bomb for peaceful purposes, was dedicated in November, 1971, at the University of Texas at Austin, in the lobby of the physics-math-astronomy building, which was nearing completion. The project, which had been developing since 1965 in the university's Center for Plasma Physics and Thermonuclear Research, will attempt to harness the powerful energy of the hydrogen bomb for controlled light, heat, and power.

The Tokamak was named for a similar machine invented in the Soviet Union in the 1960's which was designed to prove the feasibility of a new method of heating plasmas (rapid moving streams of gas atoms) to the enormous temperatures required to produce thermonuclear fusion. The advantages of fusion, as opposed to fission, are an almost limitless supply of fuel, no radioactive waste products, no possibility of runaway nuclear accidents, and a potential plant efficiency of 80 percent in converting nuclear energy into electric power. The Texas Tokamak is a one-million-dollar doughnut-shaped aluminum bottle housed in a laboratory about the size of a gymnasium. The University of Texas laboratory was one of five in the country, the others being government laboratories at Princeton, Oak Ridge, Los Alamos, and Livermore. The fusion laboratory was originally begun as a partnership between the university and ten investor-owned utilities in Texas— the Texas Atomic Energy Research Foundation. The Edison Electric Institute, representing the utility industry on a nationwide basis, joined in support of the laboratory, as did the federal government through the Atomic Energy Commission and the National Science Foundation.

A major breakthrough in the project came in the fall of 1974 when the Fusion Research Center at the University of Texas at Austin achieved temperatures of over 200 million degrees, Fahrenheit, in the Tokamak. The previous record for heating in a confinement device was 20 to 30 million degrees, F., achieved at Princeton. For a fusion reaction to occur, a temperature of at least 100 million degrees, F. (10,000 times hotter than the surface of the sun), must be achieved and confined for at least a full second. Although the temperature was achieved in the Tokamak, it could only be confined for ten thousandths of a second. Research continued in extending the confinement time.

BIBLIOGRAPHY: James Overton, "The Texas Tokamak is Dedicated," *Texas Times* (December, 1971); *Daily Texan*, February 25, October 2, 1974.

*Tokio, Texas. (McLennan County.)

*Tokio, Texas. (Terry County.)

*Tolar, Texas.

*Tolbert, Texas.

*Toledo, Texas.

Toledo Bend Reservoir. Toledo Bend Dam and Toledo Bend Reservoir are on the Sabine River, fourteen miles northeast of Burkeville, Texas. The reservoir extends into Newton, Sabine, Shelby, and Panola counties in Texas, and Sabine and DeSoto parishes in Louisiana. The project is owned and operated by the Sabine River Authority of Texas qv for the use of the Texas share of the waters of the Sabine River. A compact has been made for the division of the waters between Texas and Louisiana. Construction started in May, 1964. The reservoir has a capacity of 4,661,000 acre-feet and a surface area of 186,500 acres at the maximum operating level 173 feet above mean sea level. Of this, 1,668,-200 acre-feet is for power generation and conservation use, and the remainder is for power-head storage and emergency water supply. The drainage area above the dam is 7,178 square miles. The hydroelectric power installation consists of two generating units, with all auxiliary equipment, having a total installed capacity of 80,750 kilowatts.

BIBLIOGRAPHY: Texas Water Commission, *Bulletin 6408* (1964).

Seth D. Breeding

*Toledo y Dubois, José Álvarez de.

*Toler, Daniel J.

*Tollett Creek.

*Tollette, Texas.

*Tolosa, Texas.

*Tolsa, Eugenio.

*Tom, John Files.

*Tom, William.

*Tom Ball Creek.

*Tom Bean, Texas.

*Tom Creek.

*Tom Green County. Tom Green County, a recreational center for a large part of West Texas, had three lakes in its vicinity: Lake Nasworthy, San Angelo Reservoir, and Twin Buttes Reservoir. Other tourist attractions included restored Fort Concho, qv a stock show, and the Miss Wool of America Pageant each June (discontinued after 1972). The county supported wholly or in part a library, a welfare unit, a health department, a child welfare unit, and Angelo State College (now Angelo State University).

Tom Green County was the market center for a twenty-three-county agricultural region in west-central Texas. The economy was largely urbanized and centered in San Angelo, although sheep and cattle raising were of major importance throughout the area. Tom Green County ranked third among Texas counties in the number of sheep raised in the 1960's and early 1970's. Its principal city, San Angelo, was the nation's largest market for sheep and goats. Cotton, sorghums, and feed crops were grown on the county's irrigated acres. By January 1, 1973, over 43 million barrels of oil had been produced; the county also produced some natural gas. The 1960 population was 64,630; the 1970 population was 71,047. *See also* San Angelo Standard Metropolitan Statistical Area.

*Tom Nunn Hill.

*Tomas, Chief.

*Tomato, Texas.

*Tomball, Texas. Tomball, in Harris County, had a population of 1,713 in 1960. In 1970 the United States census reported 2,734, almost a 60 percent increase in population over the 1960 figure.

*Tomkins, Augustus M.

*Tona, Texas.

*Tone, Thomas J.

*Tong, James F.

*Tongue River.

*Tonk Creek.

*Tonkawa Indians.

*Tonqua, Texas.

*Tonti, Henri de.

*Tonzaumacagua Indians.

*Too Indians. *See also* Toho Indians.

*Tool, Texas.

*Toomey, De Lally Prescott.

*Toomey, Texas.

*Toon College.

Top Indians. At present the Top (Thop) Indians cannot be clearly distinguished from the Tup. Two groups may be involved, or the two names may refer to the same people. *See* Tup Indians.

T. N. Campbell

Topacolme Indians. The Topacolme (Tapacolme, Tapalcolme) Indians, apparently a Concho group, lived in Trans-Pecos Texas in the late seventeenth and early eighteenth centuries. They seem to have lived on both sides of the Rio Grande in the vicinity of present Redford. Since a settlement of the Pescado Indians was known as Tapalcolme, it seems likely that Pescado was an alternate name for the Topacolme.

BIBLIOGRAPHY: C. W. Hackett (ed.), *Historical Documents Relating to New Mexico, Nueva Vizcaya, and Approaches Thereto, to 1773*, II (1926); J. C. Kelley, "Factors Involved in the Abandonment of Certain Peripheral Southwestern Settlements," *American Anthropologist*, LIV (1952); J. C. Kelley, "The Historic Indian Pueblos of La Junta de los Ríos," *New Mexico Historical Review*, XXVII (1952), XXVIII (1953); C. Sauer, *The Distribution of Aboriginal Tribes and Languages in Northwestern Mexico* (1934).

T. N. Campbell

*Topsey, Texas.

*Torbert, Texas.

*Torcer, Texas.

Tordilla, Texas. Tordilla, situated in eastern Atascosa County about three miles northwest of Fashing, was a stage stop and post office along the old San Patricio Trail qv from 1878 to 1888. In the early 1900's the old stage stand was converted into what was called Stage Stand School. A hand-dug, boulder-lined well was all that remained of Tordilla in 1963.

Robert H. Thonhoff

Tordilla Hill. [This title was incorrectly listed in Volume II as Tornillo Hill.] Tordilla Hill derived its name from the color of the soil in the region. The word "tordilla" is a Spanish adjective which means gray, grizzled, or the color of a thrush. The hill was one of the most prominent landmarks for travelers along the old San Patricio Trail qv and became widely known for being the site of one of the first uranium discoveries in Texas in 1954. It is located in the northwestern part of Karnes County near the Atascosa County line (not in the southwestern part of the county, as stated under the wrong title in Volume II). *See also* Uranium Mining.

BIBLIOGRAPHY: *South Texas Geological Society 1958 Fall Field Trip* (December 5, 1958); Robert H. Thonhoff, *A History of Karnes County, Texas* (M.A. thesis, Southwest Texas State College, 1963).

Tordilla Mound, Texas. Tordilla Mound was a post office in Atascosa County from August 4, 1858, to April 15, 1859. It was probably a stage stop along the San Patricio Trail qv near Tordilla Hill qv and the natural water hole at Rock Spring, qv where ruins of two old stone buildings were found in 1963.

Robert H. Thonhoff

Toreme Indians. The Toreme Indians were one of twenty Indian groups that joined Juan Domínguez de Mendoza qv on his expedition from El Paso to the vicinity of present San Angelo in 1683–1684. Since Mendoza did not indicate at what point the Toreme joined his party, it is impossible to determine their range or affiliations. However, the Indians between the Pecos River and the San Angelo area were being hard pressed by Apache at this time, and it seems likely that the Toreme ranged between these two localities.

BIBLIOGRAPHY: H. E. Bolton (ed.), *Spanish Exploration in the Southwest, 1542–1706* (1916).

T. N. Campbell

Tornadoes in Texas. The greatest number of tornadoes (also called cyclones or twisters) occur in the United States through a belt running along the eastern edge of the Great Plains from Iowa to Texas. They are most frequent in Texas during the months of April, May, and June. From 1916 through 1963, 865 deaths and considerable economic loss were attributed to 1,505 tornadoes. During 1957, 145 were observed touching the ground; in 1967, 232 were recorded; and in 1972 there were 144 tornadoes observed in Texas.

Tornadoes often appear suddenly, inflicting great damage in one brief blow; towns have been flattened and entire families wiped out in minutes. One tornado hit White Deer, Higgins, and Glazier in April, 1947, cut a trail one-and-one-half miles wide, and traveled a total of 221 miles across parts of Texas, Oklahoma, and Kansas. The tornado cloud has a twisting tail, or funnel, which operates like a suction tube. The funnel moves erratically across the ground, smashing some buildings, skipping others, and changing directions.

Thus, in the tornado aftermath there are inexplicable mysteries which are recounted until they become folklore. Among the oddities and freakish sights related in Texas tornado tales are such things as live, plucked chickens, willowy straws driven into posts, corn cobs imbedded in tree trunks, houses intact but shifted from foundations, whole large roofs displaced a few inches, and heavy equipment carried great distances. According to one account, a tornado in the Cedar Creek community, in May, 1868, "blew cattle into the air, lodging them in trees, sucked all water from the Brazos River for a short distance and dumped a fifty-pound fish on dry land."

The destructive potential of tornadoes has increased as Texans have become more urbanized. Two tornadoes simultaneously swept through different portions of Austin on May 4, 1922, inflicting damage of $350,000 and killing thirteen persons. The most completely photographed tornado in history moved slowly through Oak Cliff and West Dallas on April 2, 1957. There were 574 buildings, mainly homes, damaged; two hundred persons were injured; ten were killed; and economic loss amounted to about $4,000,000.

May 6, 1930, was a day besieged by tornadoes. For about twelve hours massive turbulence occurred from West Texas to deep East Texas and as far south as Kenedy in Karnes County. That morning windstorms struck Austin, Spur, and Abilene; from noon until 9:30 p.m. at least sixteen other places suffered severely. There were at least three separate tornadoes. At mid-afternoon tornadic winds ravaged Bynum, Irene, Mertens, Frost, and Ennis, killing forty-one persons, injuring many more, and damaging crops and buildings in excess of $2,000,000. Frost was left in ruins, the jail being practically the only building which withstood the assault. Later in the evening another tornado struck Kenedy, Runge, and Nordheim, resulting in thirty-six lives lost, thirty-four injuries, and $127,000 in damages. Finally, a nighttime tornado at Bronson in Sabine County caused additional damage and two deaths. Spur, San Antonio, and Gonzales also reported deaths because of the storm. A total of eighty-two persons lost their lives in the turbulence of May 6, 1930, and damage totaled almost $2,500,000.

A large part of Goliad was destroyed in four minutes on Sunday, May 18, 1902, by a tornado which struck without warning. In a strip about two blocks wide and one mile long in the western part of town, one hundred houses were ripped into rubble, as were a Methodist church, a newly constructed Baptist church and parsonage, and a Negro Methodist church filled with worshipers. Damage was estimated at $125,000. Several hundred persons were injured, and 114 people died, almost all of whom were buried in one long trench, for there was no time to dig separate graves or conduct individual funerals. For decades to come, this was noted as Texas' greatest tornado tragedy. Among the long-remembered oddities wrought by the strong wind was the fact that no pieces of steel from stoves or other household implements were ever recovered. Neither was any trace found of a long steel bridge.

Not until May 11, 1953, would a single tornado kill so many Texans again. This time there was a warning. The weather bureau announced that tornadoes were a possibility somewhere along a line extending from San Angelo to Waco. Early that afternoon a tornado swept through three miles of small houses in the Lake View portion of San Angelo, and later another funnel twisted through five miles of Waco. At San Angelo eleven persons were killed and one hundred fifty-nine were injured; the damage amounted to over $3,250,000. At Waco—immune to tornadoes, according to an Indian legend—losses were much greater. In a two-mile square of downtown Waco, buildings were lifted by the funnel and dropped in masses of broken bricks, splintered wood, and crushed plaster. Tons of glass flew through the air. Within seconds the business district was wrecked, left in a pile of debris. Some 196 business buildings were demolished, 376 others were damaged to the extent that they were unsafe, 2,000 automobiles were damaged, 150 homes were destroyed, 250 other homes were seriously damaged, and an additional 450 homes were less seriously damaged. Total damages were approximately $51,000,000. A total of 1,097 persons were injured and 114 perished, the same number as in Goliad half a century earlier.

In the spring of 1970 a series of tornadoes wreaked havoc across the South Plains. On April 17 and 18, a group of twisters leapfrogged across the country from Whitharral to Clarendon, injuring one hundred fifty people and killing twenty-three along two 175-mile-long corridors. The town of Plainview (which has more tornadoes than any other place in the U.S.) suffered heavy damage, and sixteen people were killed when a funnel touched down at the resort village of Sherwood Shores, on Greenbelt Lake. On the night of May 11, exactly seventeen years after the Waco disaster, a tornado swept through the business and residential districts of Lubbock. The winds turned vehicles into missiles and toppled brick buildings. When it was over, a swath eight miles long and a mile wide had been cut through the city. In a fifteen-square-mile area, designated as the storm area, 8,800 structures were damaged, while 250 businesses and 1,040 houses were destroyed. Fifteen- and twenty-story buildings had their facades blown off. In addition, at Texas Tech University—not included in the storm area assessment—widespread "minor" damage occurred, which amounted to one-half million dollars. Altogether, twenty-six people were killed, two thousand were injured, and property damage of over $200,000,000 was sustained.

To meet the increasing threat of tornadoes in Texas, improved systems of forecasting, spotting, tracing, and warning have been instituted. *See also* Hurricanes in Texas; Weather in Texas.

BIBLIOGRAPHY: Snowden D. Flora, *Tornadoes of the United States* (1954); Harry Estill Moore, *Tornadoes over Texas* (1958); Catherine Young Clack, "The Bellevue Tornado of April 26, 1906," *Southwestern Historical Quarterly,* LXIII (1959–1960); Frederic Simonds, "The Austin, Texas, Tornadoes of May 4, 1922," University of Texas *Bulletin No. 2307* (February 15, 1923); *Climatological Data,* XXXV (May, 1930); National Academy of Sciences Report, *The Lubbock Storm of May 11, 1970* (1970); *Texas Almanac* (1961, 1963, 1965); Austin *American,* April 19, 20, May 24, 1970; Austin *Statesman,* May 12, 13, 1970; Corsicana *Daily Sun,* May 7, 1930; Goliad *Advance-Guard,* June 2, 1960; *Karnes County News,* May 8, 1930; J. H. Baker Diary, 1858–1918 (MS., Archives, University of Texas at Austin Library).

Roy Sylvan Dunn

✝Torneros Creek.

*Tornillo, Texas.

*Tornillo Creek.

*Tornillo Hill. [This title was incorrect in Volume II and should be deleted, since there is no Tornillo Hill in southwestern Karnes County. There is a Tordilla Hill, however, located in northwestern Karnes County. *See* Tordilla, Texas; Tordilla Hill; Tordilla Mound, Texas. Ed.]

*Toro, Texas.

*Toro Creek.

*Toronto, Texas.

*Toronto Mountain.

*Torrey, David K.

*Torrey, John F.

*Torrey, Thomas S.

*Torrey Trading Houses.

*Tortuga Indians. The Tortuga Indians, who were probably Coahuiltecan in speech, lived in northeastern Mexico during the eighteenth century. They are most firmly linked with a locality on the Tamaulipas-Nuevo León boundary about halfway between Mier and Cerralvo. One source (Uhde) also links the Tortuga with the Texas coast, particularly the section between the Nueces and the Rio Grande. This is based upon hearsay and needs better documentation. Some writers have suggested that the Tortuga may have been Tonkawans, but this has yet to be demonstrated and appears to be very unlikely.

BIBLIOGRAPHY: F. W. Hodge (ed.), *Handbook of American Indians*, II (1910); W. Jiménez Moreno, "Tribus e idiomas del Norte de México," *El Norte de México y el Sur de Estados Unidos* (1944); G. Saldivar, *Los Indios de Tamaulipas* (1943); A. Uhde, *Die Länder am untern Rio Bravo del Norte* (1861).

T. N. Campbell

*Tortugas Creek. [Out of alphabetical order on page 791, Volume II.]

*Tosca, Texas.

*Toto, Texas.

*Toudouze, Gustave.

Tourism in Texas. While tourism as a major source of revenue for Texas is a relatively recent phenomenon, the state's role as a visitor destination may be traced far back into history. The origin of tourism in Texas might be rooted in the coastal map produced in 1519 by Texas' discoverer, Alonso Álvarez de Piñeda,qv for map making and map distribution remain a keystone of modern tourist promotion. Similarly, active visitor promotion in Texas could be traced to Alvar Nuñez Cabeza de Vaca,qv whose reports in 1536 of seven golden cities of Cibola induced Francisco Vásquez de Coronado qv and 1,000 troops to make a tour of West Texas in a fruitless search for riches.

Promotional literature in pre-Republic Texas was beamed at potentially permanent residents, although at least one guidebook for casual visitors, Mary Austin Holley's qv *Tourist Guide to Texas*, was published in 1835. A number of guides to Texas were published during its decade as a republic and during its early days of statehood. In Melinda Rankin's qv *Texas in 1850*, the author wrote as shamelessly as any contemporary publicist that "a traveller, passing through Texas during the months of April and May, would not fail of pronouncing it to be the most charming spot on earth."

Before and after the Civil War, railroad development in Texas gave impetus to travel for pleasure and adventure. Stagecoach, steamship, and riverboat lines made deliberate bids for recreational traffic, posting special excursion rates, and promoting the charms and comforts of Texas with various items of literature. Between 1873 and 1878 commercial buffalo hunts promoted cooperatively by railroads and private entrepreneurs drew many hunters, who helped spread the state's fame as an outdoorsman's paradise, a status it has retained.

The salubrious climate of Texas has long drawn visitors, and various health spas have flourished since the 1850's. The Hot Wells health resort of San Antonio, a pioneer tourist attraction throughout the last half of the nineteenth century, attracted visitors by the thousands through such imaginative devices as a race track featuring ostriches. In the early 1900's the Rio Grande Valley and the Texas coast, principally around Galveston, became popular as winter resorts. By 1922 the fame of Texas as a winter retreat was so well established that President Warren G. Harding vacationed at length in the Rio Grande Valley.

Early writers of Western novels, such as Rex Beach and Zane Gray, helped to publicize Texas as "cowboy country," an image Texans would later seek to soften. The guides to Texas written in the cowland idiom by Charles A. Siringo qv and sold in paperback on west-bound trains are said to have outsold the Bible between 1885 and 1900.

Except for the increased construction of highways after 1917 (*see* Highway Development in Texas), which was a decided advantage for travelers, Texas did not formally enter into the field of tourism until the centennial year of statehood in 1936. Then, at the request of the legislature, the Texas State Highway Department qv established information bureaus at principal entry points to counsel visitors drawn to Texas by the centennial qv celebration at Dallas. The information bureaus were so popular among visitors that the legislature asked that they be operated permanently as a service to tourists. By the early 1970's such bureaus were in operation on the Texas border (or near it) at Amarillo, Anthony, Denison, Gainesville, Langtry, Laredo, Orange, Texarkana, Waskom, and Wichita Falls, and in the rotunda of the state capitol qv at Austin.

Since 1936 the highway department has published annually a new edition of a Texas travel map for tourists. Printed in four colors and lavishly illustrated with photographs depicting outstanding tourist destinations, the map's distribution exceeded a million copies in 1967. The highway department has also published a wide range of informational, statistical, and safety materials since 1936 to assist travelers on Texas highways.

Until 1958 publication of literature designed primarily to attract visitors to Texas was proscribed by the "carpetbagger clause" in the Constitution of 1876.qv Inserted by Texans with recent memories of Reconstruction qv and concomitant "carpetbaggers" and "scalawags," the constitutional provision made it unlawful to expend any state funds for the attraction of immigrants; by various court interpretations, tourists were ruled to be immigrants. In 1958, enlightened by findings that tourism in Texas was declining despite a growing thirty billion dollar annual vacation expenditure among Americans, Texans voted a constitutional amendment to allocate tax monies to attract visitors. In 1960, under the revised constitution, the Texas highway department published the first brochure specifically designed to lure tourists to the state, and since that time it has developed a large spectrum of promotional pieces.

In 1963 the legislature authorized the state's first tourist-advertising budget and established the Texas

Tourist Development Agency qv as a part of the governor's executive department. The agency was charged to create a responsible and accurate national and international image of Texas through creative advertising and public relations.

Within the purview of the Texas Tourist Development Agency, Texas became the first state to base its national advertising schedules upon motivational research findings. Depth-interviews were conducted nationwide by the Belden Associates opinion polling firm of Dallas and supplemented quantitatively by the national Gallup Poll to guide the agency in developing its advertising programs. Texas tourist advertising in national publications emphasized scenic and cultural diversity, pleasant climate, abundant water, good accommodations, and sophisticated activities to offset the research firms' findings that large numbers of Americans felt Texas to be a desert land peopled largely by cowboys and oilmen and devoid of such nationally favored vacation charms as inland water, beaches, forests, mountains, historic sites, and cosmopolitan cities. In its first three years the tourist development agency, in cooperation with various tourist-oriented businesses over the state, also hosted four tours of Texas for nationally known travel writers and editors, resulting in worldwide publicity on the emerging "Vacationland Texas." A $12,000 exhibit dramatizing the message of "Texas for a World of Difference," the theme of early Texas tourist advertising, was sponsored by both the tourist development agency and private businesses. It began touring the nation's principal travel and vacation shows in 1967. In the late 1960's the Texas highway department estimated that the number of out-of-state pleasure travelers in Texas increased sizably over the non-advertising years.

While developing and promoting tourism in Texas was the primary responsibility of the state's tourist development agency, other state agencies were involved on an ancillary basis. The Texas highway department remained most active in tourism through its travel and information division, operation of tourist bureaus, production of travel-promotion literature, maintenance of extensive photograph files, and tourist counseling. Many programs of the Texas State Historical Survey Committee and the Texas Parks and Wildlife Department qqv were keyed to a growing awareness of the economic importance of tourism. The role of the newly-formed Texas Fine Arts Commission (now the Texas Commission on the Arts and Humanities) and the Texas Film Commission qqv was anticipated to bear similarly upon the state's efforts to recruit additional visitors.

By the late 1960's the total tourism effort had helped excite increased interest of investment capital in building additional facilities to accommodate and entertain those vacationing in Texas. The most outstanding developments aimed at entertaining visitors were Six Flags Over Texas, qv of Dallas-Fort Worth, and HemisFair qv (1968) in San Antonio. Other outstanding attractions include the As-trodome qv in Houston; Aquarena Springs qv in San Marcos; the outdoor drama, Texas, at Palo Duro Canyon; and the Sea-Arama ocean show at Galveston. A large number of cities, towns, and geographic regions, such as San Antonio, El Paso, Dallas-Fort Worth, Corpus Christi, Padre Island National Seashore, the Rio Grande Valley, the Guadalupe Mountains National Park, and Big Bend National Park qqv were also considered tourist attractions. Lyndon B. Johnson's qv election as president caused a notable increase of tourists to the Texas Hill Country qv and to the Lyndon B. Johnson State Historic Park (see Parks, State), the Lyndon Baines Johnson Birthplace, Boyhood Home, and Ranch, qv and the Lyndon Baines Johnson Library qv in Austin.

Keith Elliott

Tourist Development Agency, Texas. The Texas Tourist Development Agency was created in 1963 with a six-member advisory board and an executive director. The agency was created for the promotion of tourism in Texas; it coordinates efforts of several state agencies in matters relating to tourism. The tourist agency cooperates with the Texas State Highway Department, qv the state parks, qv and other agencies in advertising by radio, television, newspapers, and other media. The agency also provides consultant assistance to communities initiating tourist programs, and it publishes a monthly newsletter. In 1965 the agency was expanded and additional projects were added. The legislature authorized the agency's participation in HemisFair qv to represent the state, and these efforts later resulted in the Institute of Texan Cultures. qv Among other projects, the agency sponsors tours for the nation's travel writers and agents, a touring exhibit on Texas, and the Texas Arts and Crafts Fair in Kerrville. A news and features bureau was added, and the agency began using national opinion polls to help formulate advertising programs. Texas was the first state to use such motivational research in promotion of tourism. In 1969 the agency board was expanded to nine members. Frank Hildebrand was executive director in 1972. See also Tourism in Texas.

BIBLIOGRAPHY: University of Texas at Austin, *Guide To Texas State Agencies* (1972).

*Tours, Texas.

Tov Indians. The Tov Indians are known only from San Antonio de Valero Mission qv at San Antonio shortly before this mission was secularized in the late eighteenth century. It seems likely that Tov is a variant of either Top or Tup. It is reported that Tup Indians entered the mission sometime after 1755. It is still uncertain whether Top and Tup refer to two separate groups or to a single group.

BIBLIOGRAPHY: J. A. Dabbs, "Texas Missions in 1785," *Preliminary Studies of the Texas Catholic Historical Society*, III (1940); F. W. Hodge (ed.), *Handbook of American Indians*, II (1910).

T. N. Campbell

*Tow, Texas.

*Towash.

James Stephen Hogg qv in 1890, but in 1891 he was involved in the split between alliance leaders on membership of the newly established Railroad Commission.qv In 1892 he was a leader of the Jeffersonian Democrats, a group which merged into the Populist party qv (*see also* People's party).

Tracy spoke to and organized clubs throughout the South and served as a delegate to the party's state and national conventions. From Dallas he also published the party's papers, the *Southern Mercury* qv and the *Texas Advance*. He continued as a Populist leader through 1900, when he led a bolt from the state convention by those who favored returning to the Democratic party.qv

In his later years Tracy moved to the Panhandle and became an active member of the Farmers' Union qv of Texas, serving on its legislative committee. In 1914 he campaigned to have the union endorse James Edward Ferguson qv for governor. He died at Tulia on March 29, 1915.

BIBLIOGRAPHY: Roscoe Martin, *The People's Party in Texas* (1933); Ernest W. Winkler, *Platforms of Political Parties in Texas* (1916); Dallas *Morning News*, March 31, 1915.

Alwyn Barr

*Tracy, Texas.

*Tradinghouse Creek.

Traffic Safety, Office of. *See* Community Affairs, Department of.

Traffic Safety Council, Texas. The Texas Traffic Safety Council, created in 1957, was composed of an executive committee including the governor, the director of the State Department of Public Safety,qv the state highway engineer, the commissioner of education, the director of the Department of Public Welfare,qv and one citizen member. The governor could appoint other members. The functions of the council were to plan a cooperative program of traffic safety among several state agencies and to conduct research in the field of traffic safety.

BIBLIOGRAPHY: University of Texas at Austin, *Guide To Texas State Agencies* (1964).

*Trail Drivers Association.

*Trail Drivers and Driving.

*Trails.

Train Wreck Stunt. One of the most spectacular publicity stunts ever staged took place in Texas on September 15, 1896, when two steam locomotives from the Missouri, Kansas, and Texas railroad were run at each other at an estimated speed of 90 miles an hour. The stunt was the idea of William George Crush, a passenger agent for the M. K. & T.; he evidently thought the event would attract enough passengers on special trains to pay for the affair. Some 50,000 persons, arriving on thirty trains, assembled in a field between Waco and West to view the event. The result was catastrophic, if not spectacular. Two people were killed and many were injured when the two boilers exploded. The railroad settled all claims by the injured as fast as they were presented. As far as is known, no similar stunt has ever been tried again.

BIBLIOGRAPHY: J. Marvin Hunter, Sr., "A Pre-arranged Head-on Collision," *Frontier Times*, 27 (May, 1950).

*Trammels, Texas.

*Trammel's Trace.

*Tranquitas Creek.

*Trans-Pecos.

Transportation Commission, Texas Mass. *See* Mass Transportation Commission, Texas.

Transportation Institute, Texas. *See* Texas Transportation Institute.

*Trap Mountain.

*Trask, Frances. *See* Thompson, Frances Judith Somes (Trask).

*Travis, Charles Edward.

*Travis, William Barret.

*Travis, Texas.

*Travis County. *See also* Austin Standard Metropolitan Statistical Area.

*Travis Guards and Rifles.

*Travis Peak.

*Travis Peak, Texas.

Travis State School. Established as a branch of the Austin State School qv in 1933 as the Austin State School Farm Colony,qv the institution became a separate facility in 1949. It acquired its present name in 1961. It once served as a halfway house for retarded males who were trainable and who were from rural backgrounds. In July, 1968, there were 1,800 enrolled as mentally retarded. All students were transfers. Ten ward buildings and necessary service buildings were completed in 1963. A special education program was conducted for those able to benefit from classroom instruction. In 1970 the school received a grant from the Hospital Improvement Project, which made possible the use of a unit system of treatment. A new Vocational Evaluation and Training Center, with a capacity of over three hundred residents, was opened and staffed through a grant from the Texas Rehabilitation Commission. A swimming pool, administration building, and five full-time physicians were added that same year. The census at the end of 1970 was 1,754, and the superintendent was Robert L. Breckenridge. *See* Mentally Ill and Mentally Retarded, Care of, in Texas.

BIBLIOGRAPHY: Board for Texas State Hospitals and Special Schools, *Report* (1964); Texas Department of Mental Health and Mental Retardation, *Annual Report, 1970*.

*Trawick, Texas.

*Traylor, John H.

*Traylor, Melvin Alvah. Melvin Alvah Traylor was president of the First National Bank of Ballinger, Texas (not Dillinger, Texas, as stated in Volume II). He married Dorothy Arnold Yerby (not Kirby).

BIBLIOGRAPHY: *Dictionary of American Biography* (1936).

Treasure. *See* Padre Island Treasure.

*Treasurer, State. *See also* State Executive Officers, Compensation of.

*Treasury Robbery.

*Treat, James.

*Treaties, Commercial. *See* Diplomatic Relations of the Republic of Texas.

Treaty Oak. The Treaty Oak of Austin is a 500-year-old live oak tree (*Quercus virginiana*) with a branch spread of 110 feet. It stands in a lot on Baylor Street, between West Fifth and West Sixth streets, on property acquired by the city of Austin in 1937. The tree was a landmark and a popular picnic spot for Austin citizens before the town engulfed it in the 1880's. It takes its name from a local story that Stephen F. Austin signed a treaty with the Indians under its branches, but there is little foundation for this belief. In 1927 the giant oak was admitted to the American Forestry Association's Hall of Fame.

BIBLIOGRAPHY: Austin *American*, April 25, 1915, January 26, 1922, June 11, 1937, May 22, 1953; Treaty Oak File, Austin-Travis County Collection, Austin Public Library.

*Treaty of Annexation. *See* Annexation of Texas.

*Treaty of 1819. *See* Adams-Oñis Treaty.

*Treaty of 1884.

*Treaty of Guadalupe Hidalgo. *See* Guadalupe Hidalgo, Treaty of.

*Treaty, Slave Trade, with Britain. *See* Diplomatic Relations of the Republic of Texas.

*Treaty of Velasco. *See* Velasco, Treaties of.

*Tredway, Texas.

*Tree, State.

Tree Farming. A certified tree farm is any privately owned forest land voluntarily used for growing trees. The owner protects his timber from fire, insects, diseases, and destructive grazing, and he harvests his trees in a way to insure reestablishment of the forest. There are no membership dues in the tree farm program, no subsidies, and no assessments; the tree farmer grows trees as a crop because it is good business. A certificate of membership in the American Tree Farm System is given by the industrial forestry industry, which often provides private landowners with trees for replanting and in many cases provides mechanical tree planters, free of charge or at nominal cost, to assist landowners in tree planting.

Begun in 1941, the American Tree Farm System was active in forty-seven of the fifty states by 1960. Each year about 3,000,000 acres were added to its rolls; the total area in certified tree farms in the United States was over 55,000,000 acres in 1961. More than 1,900 technical foresters served as inspectors to help maintain good standards of forest management on private certified tree farms.

The repeated growing of tree crops was the primary objective of tree farming, but this objective usually resulted in additional benefits, such as watershed protection, preservation of the soil, and recreation and maintenance of forage for game. The United States Department of Agriculture assists in the program, with a forestry headquarters located at the Agricultural Extension Service qv at Texas A&M University.

Most of the timber-growing and wood-processing activity in Texas occurs in the piney woods of East Texas. This area provides the raw material for a great variety of industries, adding nearly a billion dollars annually to the economy of Texas. In the 1960's approximately 12,000,000 acres of pine-hardwood forest lands were owned by some 160,000 individual timber growers. Most of these were small timber holdings under 500 acres in size. The wood-using industries owned about 30 percent, or a little over 3,000,000 acres. Privately owned lands made up about 93 percent of the East Texas forest lands, while public holdings, mostly in the national forests of Texas, accounted for 7 percent.

In addition to the piney woods, some timber-growing and wood-processing activity occurs in the post oak region, an area skirting the East Texas tree-growing region and extending to the south as far as Wilson County. Some forty sawmills operated in this area. A considerable amount of fence post material was harvested in the cedar brakes, an area adjoining the post oak region to the west, extending into Sutton County and as far north as Menard and as far south as Uvalde. Some lumber and cross-ties were produced from timber harvested in the coastal forest, a small area located in the Brazoria County–Fort Bend County areas and in a considerable part of Jackson County.

On March 1, 1973, there were 1,914 officially recognized tree farms in Texas, according to the Texas Forestry Association; the total area was 4,083,517 acres. Texas ranked sixth in the nation in number of tree farms and sixth in tree farm acreage *See also* Texas Forest Service.

BIBLIOGRAPHY: American Forest Products Industries, *Industrial Forestry in the United States* (1961); *Texas Almanac* (1973).

*Trees of Texas.

Trementina Indians. The Trementina (Nementina) Indians ranged the Canadian River area of Texas and New Mexico in the late seventeenth century. They seem to have been an early Lipan-Apache band. The Trementina were either closely associated with the Limita or were the same people. In contemporary documents both names were sometimes equated with Cipayne, the name from which Lipan probably evolved.

BIBLIOGRAPHY: J. M. Espinosa, *Crusaders of the Rio Grande* (1942); A. H. Schroeder, *A Study of the Apache Indians: The Mescalero Apaches*, Part III (1960); A. B. Thomas, *After Coronado* (1935).

T. N. Campbell

Trenckmann, William Andreas. William Andreas Trenckmann, son of Andreas Friedrich and Johanna (Jokusch) Trenckmann, was born on August 23, 1859, at Millheim, Austin County, one of the Latin Settlements.qv His father (1809–1883), formerly owner and director of a private school in Magdeburg, Germany, had left Germany in the wake of the revolution of 1848 and soon settled as a farmer near Cat Spring, Texas; he was the first president of Cat Spring *Landwirtschaftlicher Verein*, the oldest agricultural society in Texas (*see* Cat Spring, Texas).

As a child, W. A. Trenckmann attended the Millheim frontier school of Ernst F. Maetze,qv whose example influenced him for life. In 1876, at the age of seventeen, he joined the first class to enter the Agricultural and Mechanical College of Texas (now Texas A&M University). He was valedictorian of the first class, graduating in 1879.

Trenckmann started his career as a teacher in Frelsburg, and he later taught in Shelby; he was principal of the Bellville school when he married Mathilde Miller on April 20, 1886.

In 1891 he commenced publication of *Das Wochenblatt*, a German language weekly newspaper. He edited and published it continuously for over forty-two years, until its sale in 1933; he continued to write for it until his death in 1935. From the time of its first publication, the paper soon became a respected voice in the Texas German communities and beyond, primarily as a means of informing and educating German-speaking immigrants and their descendants about politics, current issues at all levels, and about American institutions. A staunch supporter of civil liberties and free elections, Trenckmann opposed Sunday laws, Prohibition,qv the Ku Klux Klan,qv and even before his rise to power, Adolph Hitler and the National Socialist movement. When the United States entered World War I, it was particularly gratifying to Trenckmann that Albert Sidney Burleson,qv postmaster general, issued permit no. 1 to *Das Wochenblatt*, exempting it from censorship imposed on war news and discussion appearing in German publications.

Also a literary writer, Trenckmann contributed numerous stories, essays, reviews, and larger works in serialized form or in special issues to *Das Wochenblatt*; he produced a series of calendars as annual supplements and a booklet, *Austin County* (1899), the first geographical and historical account of the county. During his years in the Texas legislature, he wrote *Die Lateiner am Possum Creek* (1907), one of the very few works of fiction to treat the plight of the Texas Germans who supported the Union in the Civil War. In 1903 he published a play, *Der Schulmeister von Neu-Rostock*. In later years he serialized his memoirs, *Erlebtes und Beobachtetes* (1931–1933).

Trenckmann was a member of the legislature from 1905 to 1909, when he moved with his wife and four children from Bellville to Austin. He served as a member and chairman of the board of directors of the Agricultural and Mechanical College of Texas; he was asked to become its president, but he did not accept. He also served as chairman of the board of directors of the Blind Institute.qv

A complete file of *Das Wochenblatt* is available at the library of the University of Texas at Austin. Several of Trenckmann's larger works have been translated. He died in Austin on March 22, 1935.

BIBLIOGRAPHY: Charles Nagel, *A Boy's Civil War Story* (1934); Selma Metzenthin-Raunick, *Deutsche Schriften in Texas*, II (1936); Austin *American*, March 23, 1935; H.S.R. No. 124, Forty-fourth Texas Legislature.

Clara Trenckmann Studer

*Trent, Texas.

*Trenton, Texas.

*Tres Cuevas Mountain.

*Tres Hermanas Mountains.

*Tres Palacios Bay.

*Tres Palacios Creek.

*Trespalacios, José Felix.

*Trevat, Texas.

*Trevino, Texas.

*Trickham, Texas.

Trigg, Edna Westbrook. Edna Westbrook Trigg, Texas' first home demonstration agent, was born in Milam County on December 30, 1868, the daughter of Ervin and Rachel (Walker) Westbrook. She attended a community school in Liberty, Milam County, and earned her teaching certificate by attending summer normal schools conducted in Cameron. In 1911, when she was principal of a school in the Liberty community, she was chosen by the United States Department of Agriculture to supervise the girls tomato clubs in Milam County. During the summer of 1912 Edna Trigg organized eleven clubs, holding each club member responsible for cultivating one-tenth of an acre in tomatoes and selling the fresh tomatoes or saving them for canning. In August, 1912, she organized the first exhibit of the girls' products in Milano; she also organized exhibits at the Rockdale Fair Association and at the State Fair of Texas qv in 1913.

That first year, four girls who had been tomato club members started bank accounts, and others earned scholarships, including a $1,200 scholarship given by Mary Eleanor Brackenridge.qv The following year Mrs. Trigg organized canning and poultry clubs which both boys and girls could join, but because no money was available the work was stopped in 1915. Interrupting her work as school principal at Liberty, the chamber of commerce at Childress asked her to teach a two-month canning school at a salary of $100. Here Mrs. Trigg learned a new process of canning with a steam pressure cooker mounted on a gasoline burner.

In 1915 she was appointed home demonstration agent in Denton County, and again she met with the difficulty of being a "government woman" whose job it was to tell rural women how to improve their rural living situations. She borrowed $350 to buy steam pressure cookers, placed them in twenty communities to encourage canning, and after a number of canning sessions, she sold the cookers to community members. In 1916 Edna Trigg became the first official county home demonstration agent in Texas.

During World War I she attended patriotic meetings to encourage people to buy Liberty Bonds and to grow and can their own food; she continued to hold weekly canning meetings, and during this time she also served on the staff of the College of Industrial Arts (now Texas Woman's University), overseeing courses in methods and assuring professionalism in home demonstration work.

Edna Westbrook was married to Charles Letman Trigg in 1892; they had two children. She died on November 15, 1946, and was buried in the I.O.O.F. Cemetery in Denton. A Texas State Historical Survey Committee qv marker honoring her was placed on the courthouse square in Cameron in October, 1970.

BIBLIOGRAPHY: Lynda Bowers, "Texas' First Home Demonstration Agent," *Texas Agricultural Progress*, 17 (Winter, 1971); Cora Melton Cross, "The Story of Home Demonstration Work," *Texas Monthly*, V (May, 1930); Kathryn Kahler, "Texas' First Home Demonstration Agent," *Texas Historian*, XXXII (1971–1972); Files of the Texas Agricultural Extension Service, Texas A&M University, College Station.

*Trigger Mountain.

*Trimmer Creek.

*Trinidad, Texas. Trinidad, in western Henderson County, reported seventeen businesses in 1970, including a regional power plant, a chemical fertilizer plant, a gas company, and a ready-mix concrete plant. The city had a modern air-conditioned high school, four churches, and one bank. One of the newest and largest lakes in Texas, the Cedar Creek Reservoir, was located immediately north and east of Trinidad. The 1960 population was 786; the 1970 population was 1,079, according to the United States census.

*Trinidad Creek.

Trinidad Lake. The Trinidad Lake project was started and completed in 1925. The lake has a capacity of 7,800 acre-feet and a surface area of 753 acres at elevation 285 feet above mean sea level. Water is pumped from the river to maintain this level. There is no significant drainage area to contribute material runoff to this off-channel storage.

BIBLIOGRAPHY: Texas Water Commission, *Bulletin 6408* (1964).

Seth D. Breeding

*Trinity, Texas. (Kaufman County.)

*Trinity, Texas. (Trinity County.) Trinity, the leading commercial center for the lumbering-farming Trinity County area, in 1967 had seven churches, a hospital, a bank, a library, and a newspaper. In 1970 fifty businesses were reported. The 1960 population was 1,787; the 1970 population was 2,512, according to the United States census.

*Trinity and Brazos Valley Railway Company. *See* Burlington-Rock Island Railroad Company.

*Trinity, Cameron, and Western Railroad Company.

*Trinity City, Texas.

*Trinity County. Trinity County, with 87 percent of its land area forested, had two mills with an output capacity of 15,000 board-feet of lumber daily in 1964. Cattle production composes the major agricultural enterprise, although some corn and other crops are grown. Tourist attractions include the Davy Crockett National Forest qv and historical points of interest on the Trinity River. The 1960 population was 7,539; the 1970 population was 7,628, according to the United States census.

*Trinity County (Judicial).

*Trinity Lutheran College.

*Trinity Lutheran Homes.

*Trinity Mills, Texas.

*Trinity River. *See also* Trinity River Authority of Texas; Trinity River Navigation Projects.

Trinity River Authority of Texas. The Trinity River Authority of Texas, a political subdivision of the state, was created in 1955 by the Fifty-fourth Legislature, and comprised Tarrant, Dallas, Ellis, Navarro, and Chambers counties and generally that portion of the following counties that lie within the watershed of the Trinity River: Kaufman, Henderson, Anderson, Freestone, Leon, Houston, Trinity, Madison, Walker, San Jacinto, Polk, and Liberty. The authority is governed by a board of directors appointed by the governor with the advice and consent of the Senate. There are seventeen counties in the authority, represented by twenty-four directors, of which Dallas County has four, Tarrant County, three, and each of the remaining counties, one. There are two directors-at-large.

The authority was given the responsibility of effectuating flood control, conservation, and beneficial use of storm and flood waters in the Trinity River watershed. The authority prepared a master plan for the Trinity River Basin in 1957, which was being implemented by the authority in the following ways: (1) construction of Livingston Reservoir to provide water supply to the immediate authority area and to the city of Houston; (2) purchase of storage space for water supply within multi-purpose federal reservoirs, including the Navarro Mills, Bardwell, and Wallisville projects; (3) construction of water treatment facilities for the city of Ennis; (4) construction and operation of a regional sewage collection and treatment system for the cities of Farmers Branch, Grand Prairie, Irving, and Dallas.

Robert N. Tharp

*Trinity River High School.

*Trinity River Navigation Projects. In 1955 at the request of the privately-supported Trinity Improvement Association, the Texas legislature set up the Trinity River Authority,qv with twenty-four directors appointed for six-year terms. The TRA began working with other public and private organizations to plan the development of the Trinity River Basin.

In 1960 construction began on the Navarro Mills Dam and Reservoir on Richland Creek, sixteen miles southwest of Corsicana. This $10,400,000 flood-control and water-conservation project, completed in 1963, was planned by the Fort Worth District, United States Army Corps of Engineers. The lake covers 11,700 acres and has a capacity of 212,209 acre-feet. It provides water for Corsicana and other communities in addition to reducing flood damages to farmlands and towns. The dam, like others on Trinity tributaries, also helps to give a more stable river flow needed for navigation.

In 1963 the plan for making the Trinity River navigable by barges was approved by the U.S. Army Corps of Engineers. In 1965 Congress included, in that year's omnibus Rivers and Harbors Act, authorization for the long-sought Trinity River barge canal, estimated to cost $911,000,000. This project included a 365-mile canalization of the river from its mouth on the Gulf of Mexico to Dallas and Fort Worth. The authorization carried no appropriation but recommended that $83,000,000 be granted to start the work.

In 1966 the U.S. Army Corps of Engineers awarded an $889,978 contract for construction of part of the proposed Wallisville Reservoir, intended to bring Trinity River barge traffic forty miles upstream, as far as Liberty. By the 1970's aerial mapping had cleared the way for advance engineering, and federal funds had been appropriated to help the Texas State Highway Department qv raise bridges to navigation level, but further progress was dependent on congressional funding.

Wayne Gard

*Trinity and Sabine Railway Company.

*Trinity University. Trinity University, San Antonio, continued under the auspices of the Synod of Texas, United Presbyterian Church. It was founded as a result of the consolidation of three earlier Cumberland Presbyterian colleges: Ewing College, Larissa College, and Chapel Hill College qqv (not Chappell Hill Male and Female Institute,qv as stated in Volume II). The university moved from the eighty-acre Woodlawn campus to the new Skyline campus of one hundred acres atop Trinity Hill in 1952. Enrollment increased from 1,638 students in 1950 to 3,412 students in 1974, and the faculty increased from 153 to 219 members during that time. During a fifteen-year period, undergraduate offerings expanded from nineteen to twenty-six major subjects, and a graduate school was added with sixteen departments. Doctoral programs in five or six fields were scheduled by 1969.

In 1950 library facilities consisted of 44,653 volumes and 277 periodicals housed in a quonset hut, contrasted with 325,000 volumes and more than 1,200 periodicals housed in the Chapman Graduate Center and George Storch Memorial Library by 1969. The Research Institute for Human Relations worked on problems in psychology in 1950. Later, research in natural sciences and the humanities was conducted under the faculty research and development committee with the aid of governmental and private grants.

More than thirty buildings were constructed between 1950 and 1965. In 1962 James W. Laurie, president of the university since 1951, announced a fifty-million-dollar centennial program, two-thirds of which was planned for endowment of scholarships, professorial chairs, increased faculty salaries, and library holdings. The other third was projected to complete the basic campus master plan before 1969, the university's centennial year. In 1974 the president of the university was Duncan Wimpress. *See also* Presbyterian Education in Texas.

*Trinity Valley and Northern Railway Company.

*Trinity Valley Southern Railroad Company.
*Triple Butte.
*Tripp, Texas.
*Tri-State College.
*Trobough, John.

Trost, Henry Charles. Henry Charles Trost was born on March 5, 1860, in Toledo, Ohio. His parents, who had come from Germany in 1850, were Ernest and Wilhelmina (Frank) Trost. An art school graduate at seventeen, he worked for three years as a draftsman in a Toledo architectural firm. He moved to Pueblo, Colorado, in 1880 and lived there for several years; he worked on designs for the World's Industrial and Cotton Exposition building at the Cotton Centennial, which opened in New Orleans in 1884, and possibly worked with architect Nicholas J. Clayton qv in Galveston from 1883 to 1884. In 1885 he was in Topeka, Kansas, where he worked on designs of the senate chamber of the Kansas state capitol in association with the firm of Haskell and Wood. He moved to Chicago about 1886, where he lived for twelve years and was a charter member of the Chicago Architects Sketch Club and an official in two ornamental iron work companies in the 1890's. In 1898 he was living in Tucson, where he designed buildings for the University of Arizona, the Carnegie Library, and the first Owl Club building (mission style, with details of design similar to those of Chicago architect Louis Sullivan).

He moved to El Paso in 1904 and formed an architectural firm with his three brothers and a nephew. In 1906 he completed the W. W. Turney house, the classic mansion which later became, with alterations, the El Paso Museum of Art. The interior of the house showed the influence of the Prairie School design. His own house, similar to Frank Lloyd Wright's Susan Lawrence Dana house in Springfield, Illinois, was still standing in El Paso in 1970. It had mission-style furniture, leaded glass windows, partial room partitions, and textiles of his own design.

Among the numerous homes and commercial buildings which he designed was the Francisco Hotel in Albuquerque, with its pueblo-like exterior and Spanish colonial lobby decoration. In 1914 he designed the first four buildings of the State School of Mines and Metallurgy (later Texas Western College, now the University of Texas at El Paso). His design of the El Paso courthouse is somewhat reminiscent of the municipal building he designed in Dallas. The "twin" tower buildings, the Lohrs Tower (1928) in Phoenix and the Bassett Tower (1930) in El Paso, are both setback skyscrapers with strong vertical emphasis and sparingly applied ornament. Trost died in El Paso on September 19, 1933; his library was given to Rice University in 1954 and was dispersed into the Fondren Library's working collection.

BIBLIOGRAPHY: Lloyd C. Engelbrecht, "Henry Trost: The Prairie School in the Southwest," *The Prairie School Review*, VI (1969); Frank W. Johnson, *A History of Texas and Texans*, IV (1914).

*Trotti, Texas.

*Troublesome Creek.

*Troup, Texas. Troup, in Cherokee and Smith counties, had a population of 1,667 in 1960; in 1970 the population was 1,668. *See also* Tyler Standard Metropolitan Statistical Area.

*Trout Creek.

*Troutman, Johanna.

*Troy, Texas. (Bell County.)

Troy, Texas. (Comanche County.) *See* Cora, Texas.

Troy, Texas. (Freestone County.) Troy, also called Pine Bluff and Sand Town, was settled in the middle 1840's in eastern Freestone County on the Trinity River near the Comanche Trail crossing, and it was for a time the most important settlement in the county. It was a port for steamboats plying the river; roads from Troy led to Houston, via Springfield and Franklin, and to Nacogdoches and Shreveport in Louisiana, via Rusk. On November 4, 1850, Troy became the first post office established in Freestone County. The only traces of Troy by 1970 were stumps of trees that once lined the main street.

Llewellyn Notley

*Truby, Texas.

*Truce, Texas.

True West. *True West*, a magazine publishing true accounts of every facet of the pioneer West, was established by Joe Austell Small in 1953 as a quarterly. In 1954 it became a bi-monthly and in 1961 was incorporated into Western Publications, Inc.[qv] The magazine is distributed worldwide and in 1974 had a circulation of over 185,000. It is edited and published in Austin, Texas, and until his death in 1963, Walter Prescott Webb [qv] was historical consultant. In 1974 Pat Wagner was editor.

Joe Small

*Truehart, James L.

*Trueheart, Henry Martyn.

*Trueloves, Texas.

*Truett, George W.

*Truitt, James.

*Truitt, James W.

*Trujillo Creek.

*Trumbull, Texas.

*Truscott, Texas.

*Trusts. *See* Anti-Trust Regulation.

*Tryon, William Milton.

*Tryon, Texas.

Tsepehoen Indians. The Tsepehoen (Tsepcoen, Tsepechoen, Tsepehouen) Indians are known only from records of the La Salle Expedition.[qv] These documents indicate that in the late seventeenth century the Tsepehoen lived inland well to the north or northeast of Matagorda Bay, probably near the Brazos River. They have been equated with the Semonan, who are known only in Spanish documents, but there is no evidence other than partial sound correspondences which supports this identification. It seems likely that the two are unrelated. In some Spanish sources Tsepehoen appears as Tsepechoen frercutea, but this is an erroneous combination of two separate names, Tsepehoen and Fercutea, which are separated by a comma in French sources. The affiliations of the Tsepehoen remain undetermined.

BIBLIOGRAPHY: I. J. Cox (ed.), *The Journeys of Réné Robert Cavelier, Sieur de La Salle*, II (1906); F. W. Hodge (ed.), *Handbook of American Indians*, II (1910); H. R. Stiles (ed.), *Joutel's Journal of La Salle's Last Voyage, 1684-7* (1906).

T. N. Campbell

Tsera Indians. These Indians are known only from records of the La Salle Expedition.[qv] According to these documents, the Tsera lived inland well to the north or northeast of Matagorda Bay, probably near the Brazos River. On Henri Joutel's [qv] list of tribes Tsera was followed by Bocherete (Bocrette), and in some French and Spanish books a hybrid name was unfortunately produced—Tserabocherete or Tserabocrette. The linguistic and cultural affiliations of both Tsera and Bocherete remain undetermined.

BIBLIOGRAPHY: I. J. Cox (ed.), *The Journeys of Réné Robert Cavelier, Sieur de La Salle*, II (1906); F. W. Hodge (ed.), *Handbook of American Indians*, II (1910); H. R. Stiles (ed.), *Joutel's Journal of La Salle's Last Voyage, 1684-7* (1906).

T. N. Campbell

*Tuanca Indians.

*Tubbes, Texas.

*Tuberculosis, State Hospitals for.

Tuberculosis Advisory Committee. The Tuberculosis Advisory Committee, created in 1965, consisted of twelve members appointed by the governor from medical and other specified fields. Its function was to advise the State Board of Health,[qv] the state commissioner of health, and the director of the division of tuberculosis services, and to work with other agencies in making recommendations toward the eradication of the disease.

BIBLIOGRAPHY: University of Texas at Austin, *Guide To Texas State Agencies* (1972).

*Tucara Indians.

*Tuck Branch.

*Tucker, James B.

Tucker, Philip Crosby, Jr. Philip Crosby Tucker, Jr., son of Philip Crosby and Mary C. M. (McCloskey) Tucker, was born at Vergennes, Addison County, Vermont, on February 14, 1826. He completed the course of study offered in the public schools in Vergennes, Vermont, but there is no known reference to further formal education. He began to read law, however, in his father's office and started his Vermont law practice under the guidance of his father. This arrangement continued without great financial success, but it did provide him with training and experience for his later professional life in Texas.

Tucker left Vermont on October 31, 1852, for Texas, arrived at Galveston the following November, and opened his Texas law practice. He purchased the Samuel May Williams qv home in 1858, which he occupied for the remainder of his life. (In his will Tucker provided that Tucker Masonic Lodge No. 297 should inherit the property subject to a life tenancy for his family. The lodge sold the property, and later it was converted into a museum by the Galveston Historical Society.qv Tucker had served as president of that society from 1885 to 1894.)

During the Civil War, Tucker joined the Confederate Army in the defense of Galveston; with the rank of major he was assigned to the staff of General John Bankhead Magruder.qv On February 8, 1867, he introduced the Scottish Rite of Freemasonry into Texas by beginning the communication of the degrees of that rite to a class of eight Galveston Masons. By 1966 the rite had grown to 61,-750 members.

Tucker's first wife, a widow by the name of Harrison whom he married before the outbreak of the war, died shortly after the marriage. Tucker then married Mary C. (?); they had five children. After her death Tucker married Isabella T. Baldwin on March 13, 1881; they had one son. Tucker died in the House of the Temple at Washington, D.C., on July 9, 1894. His body was returned to Galveston and interred in the Episcopal Cemetery.

James D. Carter

Tucker, Thomas F. Thomas F. Tucker, son of Elizabeth (Matthews) and William H. Tucker, was born in Barnwell District, South Carolina, on February 22, 1818. Following the death of his parents, Tucker, with his four younger brothers, came from Mississippi to Shelby County, Texas, in 1841. There he was married to Frances Adeline Duncan in May, 1845; they were the parents of sixteen children. During the Mexican War, he enlisted (in May, 1847) and served in a company commanded by John Coffee (Jack) Hays.qv He was mustered out at Veracruz, Mexico, in May, 1848, and soon after moved his family to Harrison County.

At the beginning of the Civil War Tucker enlisted at the town of Elysian Fields in Captain Sterling Brown Hendrick's qv Company. He was subsequently promoted through all the grades to that of colonel in 1864. He was in charge of Camp Ford,qv northeast of Tyler, in early November, 1863, when the first large group of Northern prisoners (those captured in Louisiana) were brought there. He was in the 17th Consolidated Regiment, Texas Dismounted Cavalry, which saw combat service in Louisiana in 1864.

In 1869 the Tuckers moved to southeast San Augustine County. In 1879 Tucker established a ranch on California Creek in present Haskell County, above MacKenzie Crossing. In the spring of 1880 the family moved into the rock house which John Alexander Matthews and his wife Sallie Ann Reynolds Matthews qqv had built in 1877. When Haskell County was organized in 1885, Tucker was elected the first county judge; his son, Alex D. Tucker, was the first sheriff and tax collector. Thomas F. Tucker died in Haskell on May 21, 1886,

and was buried in the Haskell Cemetery. *See also* Haskell County; Haskell, Texas.

BIBLIOGRAPHY: F. Lee Lawrence and Robert W. Glover, *Camp Ford, C.S.A.* (1964); R. E. Sherrill, *Haskell County History* (1965); Leon Mitchell, Jr., "Camp Ford," *Southwestern Historical Quarterly*, LXVI (1962–1963); R. E. Sherrill, "Early Days in Haskell County," *West Texas Historical Association Year Book*, III (1927); James Tucker Papers, 1863–1893 (MS., Archives, University of Texas at Austin Library); U.S. War Department, *The War of the Rebellion: A Compilation of the Official Records of the Union and Confederate Armies* (1880–1901).

Cooper K. Ragan

*Tucker, Texas. (Anderson County.)

*Tucker, Texas. (McCulloch County.)

*Tuckertown, Texas.

Tucubante Indians. The Tucubante Indians are known from a document of 1754, which identifies them as part of a large group of Apache and remnants of other tribes encamped near present Eagle Pass. It is said that these Apache were the same as those living near San Antonio, who were mainly Lipan-Apache. The group near Eagle Pass also included Natage (Mescalero Apache). It thus appears that Tucubante was the name of one band of Lipan-Apache.

BIBLIOGRAPHY: W. E. Dunn, "Apache Relations in Texas, 1718–1750," *Quarterly of the Texas State Historical Association*, XIV (1910–1911); J. D. Forbes, "Unknown Athapaskans: The Identification of the Jano, Jocome, Jumano, Manso, Suma, and Other Indian Tribes of the Southwest," *Ethnohistory*, 6 (1959).

T. N. Campbell

*Tuetini Indians.

Tugumlepem Indians. These presumably Coahuiltecan-speaking Indians lived on the extreme southern part of the Texas coast. In the middle eighteenth century their settlements were between present Port Isabel and Brownsville in eastern Cameron County.

BIBLIOGRAPHY: W. Jiménez Moreno, "Tribus e idiomas del Norte de México," *El Norte de México y el Sur de Estados Unidos* (1944); G. Saldivar, *Los Indios de Tamaulipas* (1943).

T. N. Campbell

*Tule Creek.

*Tule Lake.

*Tule Mountain.

*Tuleta, Texas.

*Tulia, Texas. Tulia, county seat of Swisher County, is a commercial center for a large farming area. In 1967 the town had nineteen churches, six public schools, a hospital, a library, a newspaper, a radio station, and plans for a modern airport. One hundred fifty-six business establishments were reported in 1970. The 1960 population was 4,410; the 1970 population was 5,294, according to the United States census.

*Tulip, Texas.

Tullis, Coral Horton. Coral Horton Tullis, the daughter of John Thomas and Collistia (Polk) Horton, was born on October 18, 1882, in Elmo, Kaufman County, Texas. Her mother was a third cousin of President James K. Polk. Mrs. Tullis graduated from Quanah High School in 1898 and Terrill

School in Denton in 1901. She taught in the Travis County schools from 1901 to 1903 and in the Austin public schools from 1904 to 1906. In 1906 she was married to John Ledbetter Tullis, and they were the parents of four children.

From 1912 to 1922, they lived in Lane County, Oregon, but returned to Austin in 1922. Mrs. Tullis entered the University of Texas, earning a B.A. degree in 1924, along with a Phi Beta Kappa key, and in 1927 she took an M.A. degree. Mrs. Tullis became a member of the university's history department in 1924, and in 1959, at the time of her retirement from the faculty, she was an assistant professor of history. During most of her years on the University of Texas campus, Mrs. Tullis was identified with the work of the Texas State Historical Association.qv She was corresponding secretary from 1927 to 1942; in 1942 (with the death of Charles William Ramsdell,qv who had held the position of treasurer from 1907) the association combined the offices of corresponding secretary and treasurer; Mrs. Tullis was elected annually to that position from 1942 until her retirement in 1967. Historians had great respect for her knowledge of the association and its *Southwestern Historical Quarterly*.qv In 1937, when the association was forty years old, the editors of the *Quarterly* requested Mrs. Tullis to compile a list of all articles printed in the magazine up to that year. The July, 1937, issue (Vol. XLI, No. 1) carried her compilation of "Publications of the Texas State Historical Association, July, 1897, through April, 1937."

At its 71st annual meeting in 1967, the association honored Mrs. Tullis at the time of her retirement, after forty years of service, with an inscribed silver tray. Mrs. Tullis died in Austin on June 22, 1967, and she was buried in the family plot at Quanah. Beginning at the 1968 annual meeting of the Texas State Historical Association, the Coral Horton Tullis Memorial Award was presented annually to the person who in the previous year had made the greatest contribution to Texas history.

Dorman H. Winfrey

*Tulsa, Texas.

*Tulsita, Texas.

*Tumlinson, Elizabeth.

*Tumlinson, James.

*Tumlinson, John James.

*Tumpataguo Indians.

*Tumpzi Indians.

*Tundra, Texas.

Tunica Indians. The Tunica (Canicon, Janequo, Tanico, Toniqua) Indians originally lived in present western Mississippi, but early in the eighteenth century pressure from the Chickasaw forced them to cross the Mississippi and settle near the mouth of the Red River in Louisiana. Sometime between 1784 and 1803 they moved up the Red River to the vicinity of present Marksville, Louisiana. A part of these later joined the Atakapa in southwestern Louisiana, which probably explains the report that in 1886 a few Tunica were living in the vicinity of Beaumont, Texas. The Tunica seem to have ranged widely at all times. In the late seventeenth and eighteenth centuries they were in frequent contact with the Caddoan groups of both Louisiana and Texas. It seems likely that one group of Tunica was actually living in eastern Texas in the middle eighteenth century, since the name Tanico occurs on a list of Texas tribes that petitioned the Spanish for missions in east-central and southeastern Texas. Some of the Marksville Tunica moved to Indian Territory, now Oklahoma, in the middle nineteenth century and eventually lost their identity among the Chickasaw. Others survived in the Marksville area until as late as 1930.

BIBLIOGRAPHY: F. W. Hodge (ed.), *Handbook of American Indians*, II (1910); J. R. Swanton, *Indian Tribes of the Lower Mississippi Valley and Adjacent Coast of the Gulf of Mexico* (1911), *Source Material on the History and Ethnology of the Caddo Indians* (1942), and *The Indians of the Southeastern United States* (1946).

T. N. Campbell

*Tunis, Texas.

*Tup Indians.** The status of the Tup Indians is not clear because at present it is impossible to determine whether or not the Tup were the same people as the Top. Both names were connected with two of the missions established on the San Gabriel River near present Rockdale in the middle eighteenth century. H. E. Bolton qv made much of the point that the Tup were represented at Nuestra Señora de la Candelaria Mission,qv which was founded for Karankawan groups only. As both Tup and Top appear in records pertaining to this mission, it would seem that both names refer to a single Karankawan band. However, in another article Bolton also stated that the Top were represented at San Francisco Xavier de Horcasitas Mission,qv which was founded for Tonkawan groups only. If considered alone, this evidence would indicate that the Top were Tonkawan and hence distinct from the Tup. Since both Tup and Top were represented at the first named mission, we have an inconsistency that cannot be resolved until the original manuscript sources are reexamined. Some of the Tup are said to have entered San Antonio de Valero Mission qv at San Antonio after the San Gabriel missions were abandoned in 1755. These may be the Tov who were reported there in 1785. Bolton once called attention to the similarity of the names Tup and Top to certain variants of the name Toho, particularly Tuu and Tou. This possible linkage deserves serious consideration.

BIBLIOGRAPHY: H. E. Bolton, "The Founding of the Missions on the San Gabriel River," *Southwestern Historical Quarterly*, XVII (1913–1914) and *Texas in the Middle Eighteenth Century* (1915); C. W. Hackett (ed.), *Pichardo's Treatise on the Limits of Louisiana and Texas*, I (1931), II (1934); F. W. Hodge (ed.), *Handbook of American Indians*, II (1910).

T. N. Campbell

*Tupelo, Texas.

*Turcotte, Texas.

*Turkey, Texas.

*Turkey Bend, Texas.

*Turkey Creek.

*Turkey Creek, Texas.

*Turkey Mountain.

*Turkey Peak.

Turkey Production. *See* Poultry Production.

*Turkey Slough.

Turkey Trot. The town of Cuero's first Turkey Trot, staged to herald the opening of the fall marketing season, was held in 1912. The celebration in the "Turkey Capital of the World" was inspired by the annual practice of turkey buyers who drove flocks of birds into Cuero after buying them from outlying farms.

J. C. Howerton, publisher of the Cuero *Daily Record*, is credited with having suggested the name for the celebration; the Cuero Fair and Turkey Trot Association organized the first celebration, inaugurating many of the activities that have since become traditional. In the thirteenth Turkey Trot, in 1967, some 3,000 turkeys walked in the parade down several blocks of Esplanade and Main streets in Cuero, but after large numbers of the broad-breasted, feedlot turkeys collapsed, the event was thought to be impractical, and a seven-county South Texas Livestock Show was inaugurated. As part of Cuero's centennial in 1972, the Turkey Trot was revived, and the fourteenth celebration was held October 20–23 with hardy range-raised turkeys used in the parade.

BIBLIOGRAPHY: D. L. Prentice, "Turkeys Trot for Cuero Centennial," *Texas Star*, October 15, 1972; Austin *American*, November 12, 1940; New York *Times*, October 20, 1940; San Antonio *Express*, March 4, 1934, August 9, 1954; *Texas Review*, November, 1951.

*Turlington, Texas.

*Turnbow Mountain.

*Turner, Amasa. Amasa Turner, born on November 9, 1800, in Scituate, Massachusetts, was the son of Harris and Jael (Whiton) Turner. He was married to Julia Morse on December 17, 1826 (not 1827, as stated in Volume II), according to a letter the bride wrote on January 4, 1827, and verified by the 1826 marriage index in Mobile, Alabama. Amasa Turner came to Texas in 1835 (not 1833). In 1839 and 1840 he improved a plantation on Cedar Bayou, Harris County, and divided his time between there and Galveston until 1848, when he moved to Lavaca County. He was elected to represent Lavaca and Gonzales counties in the House of Representatives of the Fourth Legislature, 1851–1853 (not the Fifth Legislature, 1850–1851, as stated in Volume II), and he was again elected, this time to represent Lavaca and DeWitt counties, in the House of Representatives (not the Senate) of the Fifth Legislature, 1853–1854 (not the Sixth Legislature, 1852–1853). In 1865 Amasa Turner moved to Gonzales, where he died on July 21, 1877.

BIBLIOGRAPHY: Letter of Julia Morse Turner, January 4, 1827 (in possession of Helen H. Rugeley, Austin, Texas); Amasa Turner Papers (MS., Archives, University of Texas at Austin); *Members of the Legislature of the State of Texas from 1846 to 1939* (1939).

Helen H. Rugeley

*Turner, Avery.

*Turner, Ezekiel B.

*Turner, John.

*Turner, Thomas Fontaine.

*Turner Hall Convention.

*Turnersville, Texas. (Coryell County.)

*Turnersville, Texas. (Travis County.)

*Turnertown, Texas.

*Turney, William Ward.

*Turney, Texas.

*Turney Peak.

*Turnham Bluff.

*Turnover Creek.

*Turpentine, Texas.

*Turtle Bayou.

*Turtle Bayou, Texas.

*Turtle Bayou Resolutions.

*Turtle Creek.

*Tusane Indians. The Tusane (Tuzane) Indians are known only from San Juan Bautista qv mission near present Eagle Pass. Since they were also referred to as Carrizo, a name frequently applied to Coahuiltecan bands along the Rio Grande below Laredo, it is believed that they originally ranged that area. The name Tusonid also occurs in the records of San Juan Bautista and may be a variant of Tusane.

BIBLIOGRAPHY: F. W. Hodge (ed.), *Handbook of American Indians*, II (1910); E. L. Portillo, *Apuntes para la historia de Coahuila y Texas* (1886); J. R. Swanton, *Linguistic Material from the Tribes of Southern Texas and Northeastern Mexico* (1940).

T. N. Campbell

*Tuscaloosa, Texas.

*Tuscola, Texas.

*Tuscosso Creek.

*Tusolivi Indians. The Tusolivi (Fusolibi) Indians are known only from Spanish records of the early eighteenth century. In 1709 the Tusolivi were encountered on the Colorado River southeast of present Austin in association with Simomo (Simaomo) and Yojuane. Their presence in this area and their association with one tribe of undisputed Tonkawan affiliation have led to their identification as probably Tonkawan.

BIBLIOGRAPHY: C. W. Hackett (ed.), *Pichardo's Treatise on the Limits of Louisiana and Texas*, II (1934); F. W. Hodge (ed.), *Handbook of American Indians*, II (1910).

T. N. Campbell

Tusonid Indians. The Tusonid Indians are known only as a group of Indians, presumably of Coahuiltecan affiliation, associated with San Juan Bautista qv mission (near present Eagle Pass) in the eighteenth century. It is possible that Tusonid is a variant of Tusane, the name of a Coahuiltecan band also referred to as Carrizo, which was associated with the same mission.

BIBLIOGRAPHY: F. W. Hodge (ed.), *Handbook of American Indians*, II (1910); E. L. Portillo, *Apuntes para la historia de Coahuila y Texas* (1886); J. R. Swanton, *Linguistic Material from the Tribes of Southern Texas and Northeastern Mexico* (1940).

T. N. Campbell

*Tuttles Creek.

*Tuxedo, Texas.

Tweedy, Joseph. Joseph Tweedy, pioneer sheep ranchman of Knickerbocker, Tom Green County, was born in New York City on March 17, 1849, to a family of clothing merchants who had settled in Danburg, Connecticut. With three friends he sailed from New York to Galveston in April, 1876. The men bought Mexican ewes and merino rams and herded sheep on the Frio River between Fort Clark and Fort Duncan. Indian depredations drove them to explore the Concho River country around San Angelo, later an international center of the wool industry. Along with John Arden of California, Tweedy and his partners drove the first sheep into this area in the spring of 1877. Headquarters of their Knickerbocker Ranch on Dove Creek, still operated by the Tweedy family, became the town of Knickerbocker. Tweedy was an organizer and first president of the Wool Growers' Association formed at San Angelo in 1881, supporting scab inspection laws, herd and fencing laws, and rambouillet sheep. When wool prices fell in 1884, some ranch holdings were sold and other partners withdrew. Tweedy served as a long-term county commissioner for Tom Green County, as bank director, and as a civic leader in San Angelo. His San José Irrigation Company, chartered on Dove Creek in 1885, was one of the earliest ventures in irrigation in Texas. Tweedy also pioneered in pecan budding and grafting. He died in San Angelo on January 24, 1928.

Mrs. A. M. Tweedy

*Twelve-Mile Coleto Creek.

*Twelve Mile Creek.

*Twelve Mile Mountain.

Twichell, Willis Day. Willis Day Twichell was born on March 24, 1864, in Hastings, Minnesota, to Daniel Wilson and Sarah Catharine (Coons) Twichell. He was graduated from the National Normal University, Lebanon, Ohio, in 1883, with a degree in civil engineering. Immediately thereafter, he began the practice of civil engineering in Springfield, Ohio. Two years later, in November, 1885, he was employed by an immigration company in Texas to stake out the proposed county seat at Garden City in Glasscock County.

In January, 1886, in Big Spring, Twichell met William S. Mabry,qv a surveyor employed by the Capitol Syndicate.qv The syndicate was then building the capitol at Austin, for which it was being paid in land for its services. On this land the syndicate had set up the XIT Ranch.qv Mabry began looking for a surveyor to assist him when the syndicate decided to fence the southern portion of the ranch and create the Yellow Houses Division (see Yellow Houses, Texas), to which a large herd of cattle would be delivered on July 1, 1886. The surveyors would map out the fence lines, locate watering places, divisional headquarters, and line camps for several hundred thousand acres of land. Twichell took the job, and the surveying party left Colorado City on January 29, 1886. After completing work on the Yellow Houses Division, Twichell began surveying the Spring Lake Division, which adjoined on the north.

Twichell's basic education in cadastral surveying, astronomy, physics, and mathematics provided a technical knowledge which he used in perfecting the methods of surveying lands in Texas, unique as compared to the long-used, inexact system of following directions indicated by a magnetic compass. With cadastral surveying, Twichell's east-west survey lines corrected for the curvature of the earth's surface.

During 1887–1888, Twichell and Mabry maintained an office together in Tascosa, but in 1890 Twichell moved his office to Amarillo. There on September 4, 1895, he was married to Eula Trigg, and they had five children. Twichell worked as a state surveyor (his first and last appointment bonds dated November 10, 1900, and March 1, 1916), though he kept his office in Amarillo until he moved to Austin in 1918. Retiring from active business on January 1, 1934, to become a consultant, he moved to San Angelo, where he lived until his death on September 23, 1959.

Later cadastral surveyors retracing his lines found them to be of high accuracy. His survey records, composed of many field books, working sketches, some 200 finished maps, field notes, and about 50,000 pages of correspondence, were purchased by six major oil companies a short time before Twichell's death, and they are in a private depository in Midland, Texas.

BIBLIOGRAPHY: Alice D. Gracy, "Willis Day Twichell," *Panhandle-Plains Historical Review*, XVIII (1945); Sue Watkins (ed.), *One League to Each Wind* (1965).

Alice Duggan Gracy

*Twichell, Texas.

*Twiggs, David Emanuel.

*Twin Branch.

*Twin Buttes.

Twin Buttes Reservoir. Twin Buttes Dam and Twin Buttes Reservoir are in the Colorado River Basin in Tom Green County, eight miles southwest of San Angelo on the South Concho River, Spring Creek, and Middle Concho River. The project is owned by the United States government, and is operated by the United States Bureau of Reclamation, Amarillo office, for flood control, conservation, irrigation, and recreation purposes. Local agencies cooperating in the project are the San Angelo Water Supply Corporation for municipal water supply, and Tom Green County Water Control and Improvement District No. 1 for irrigation water. Construction started on May 3, 1960, and was completed on February 13, 1963. Deliberate impoundment of water began on December 1, 1962. This project is above Lake Nasworthy and can release water from storage to keep Lake Nasworthy at a constant level; downstream requirements will be further regulated by this reservoir. The reservoir has a controlled capacity of 640,600 acre-feet, at elevation 1,969 feet, of which 454,400 acre-feet is allocated to flood control. The drainage area above the dam is 3,724 square miles, of which 1,178 square miles is probably noncontributing.

BIBLIOGRAPHY: Texas Water Commission, *Bulletin 6408* (1964).

Seth D. Breeding

*Twin Creek.

*Twin Lakes.

*Twin Mountains.

*Twin Peaks.

*Twin Sister Peaks.

*"Twin Sisters."

*Twin Sisters, Texas.

*Twitty, Texas.

*Two-Buckle Ranch.

*Two Draw Lake.

*Two Mile, Texas.

*Two Mile Creek.

*Twohig, John.

*Tyacappan Village.

*Tye, Texas.

*Tyler, George W.

*Tyler, Orville Thomas.

*Tyler, Texas. Tyler, county seat of Smith County, had an economy based on agriculture (especially rose bushes), oil, and manufacturing. Tyler had 125 manufacturing and processing plants in 1964, employing 7,825 workers. The city was served by a modern air terminal building, a civic theater, and a symphony orchestra. In addition to its municipal rose gardens, Tyler had seventy-five azalea gardens and azalea trails. In 1967 Tyler had seventy-five churches, five hospitals, three colleges, two libraries, two newspapers, three radio stations, and a television station. Sewer and water systems improvements and street-paving projects were completed in 1967. In 1970 Tyler reported a total of 1,416 businesses. The 1960 population was 51,230; the 1970 population was 57,770, according to the United States census. *See also* Tyler Standard Metropolitan Statistical Area.

*Tyler Bluff.

Tyler Commercial College. *See* Metropolitan Technical Insitute.

*Tyler County. Tyler County, 94 percent forested, had seven mills capable of producing 144,000 board-feet of lumber daily in 1967. Livestock raising was second to lumbering in economic importance to the county. The petroleum industry produced 25,321,371 barrels of oil between 1937 and January 1, 1973. In 1963 Governor Allan Shivers gave a library and museum to the county. Significant county improvement projects include an airport completed in 1961 and the Martin Dies, Jr.,qv State Recreation Park, which was completed in 1965. Other tourist attractions included the Big Thicket,qv John Henry Kirby State Forest and Museum, Town Bluff (Dam B) Lake, and Fort Terán.qv The 1960 population was 10,666; the 1970 figure was 12,417, according to the United States census.

*Tyler Female College.

Tyler Junior College. Tyler Junior College, Tyler, was originally established in 1926 as part of the Tyler public school system and operated under that plan until September, 1946. Voters established a new independent Tyler Junior College District in November, 1945, and authorized a tax levy for support of the college, including a bond issue for erection of a new college plant on its own campus, separating it from the public school system. Harry E. Jenkins was made president of the college, and under his direction enrollment increased from less than 200 students to 5,340 in 1974.

Since 1946 the junior college district was enlarged by extension to eight neighboring school districts; each district voted to become part of the college district for junior college purposes. The college operated under statutory authority by its board of trustees, composed of ten members elected for six-year terms. Between 1946 and 1965, twelve major buildings were added to the sixty-six-acre campus. Private gifts accounted for the strong financial status of the college. Notable additions included a collection of rare paintings, donated by Watson W. Wise, and the J. S. Hudnall Planetarium. Curricula consisted of a two-year liberal arts program and an adult education program, which were accredited by the Southern Association of Colleges. The library housed 34,000 volumes in 1969.

*Tyler Southeastern Railway.

Tyler Standard Metropolitan Statistical Area. The Tyler Standard Metropolitan Statistical Area, East Texas' first metropolitan area, was recognized in August, 1960, when the 1960 census reported the population of Tyler as 51,230. The metropolitan area consists of Smith County, covering 934 square miles, with a total 1960 census population of 86,350; by 1970 the population of the county had increased to 97,096, and the city of Tyler had a population of 57,770. Besides Tyler, the area includes Flint, Bullard, Troup, Arp, Whitehouse, Winona, Lindale, Silver Lake, and a portion of Overton. The area is located on the western edge of the piney woods section of central East Texas and is surrounded by forests, low hills, and streams. The climate and soil are suitable for diversified agriculture, which accounts for the financial significance of fruit, vegetables, and livestock production. The area supplies more than half of the nation's rose bushes. The raising of livestock has contributed to the agricultural income, with the consolidation of small individual holdings into extensive cattle-raising units. In 1950 Smith County had over five thousand farms; by 1960 there were fewer than three thousand. Agricultural importance decreased, but there was a great expansion of industrial interests.

The petroleum industry has been important to the area since the discovery of oil in East Texas and has produced more than 167,000,000 barrels of oil (1931–1973), contributing to an annual income of more than seventeen million dollars by 1973. Other industries, centered mainly in the city of

Tyler, were competing with the oil industry in terms of the number of people employed. By 1966, even though the petroleum industry still represented the largest actual monetary expenditure, the metal and fabricating industries involved more persons.

By the middle 1960's, Tyler had 125 manufacturing plants employing more than 8,000 workers. The more important industries included aluminum foundries, petroleum and chemical plants, concrete block plants, a tire factory, machinery manufacturers, and air-conditioning and refrigeration plants. Other significant industries were connected with timber production and the manufacturing of clothing. Other towns in the metropolitan area contributed to the industrial picture. Troup, with a 1970 population of 1,668, was a commercial outlet for vegetable shipping. It also had a clay refractory and a wood products company. In Lindale, population 1,631, there was a fruit-canning company and a clay products plant. Arp, with its population of 816, specialized in the construction of oil field machinery and equipment. Bullard, Winona, and Gresham all had lumber companies, while Owentown was an important industrial complex.

The area expanded its water system with a 45,000 acre-foot reservoir called the Mud Creek Project. This reservoir also added a tourist recreation center to the existing Lake Tyler, Bellwood Lake, and Tyler State Park. Other tourist attractions include Tyler's October Rose Festival, its azalea gardens and trails, and a September fair.

As a medical center for the area, Tyler expanded its hospital facilities in building programs during the 1960's. The East Texas Chest Hospital qv is at nearby Owentown. Higher education is provided by Tyler Junior College, which had an enrollment of 5,340 in 1974, and by Texas College, which had 536 students in that same year. An upper-level institution, Tyler State College, opened in 1973. See also Standard Metropolitan Statistical Areas in Texas.

Robert K. Peters
Wiley W. Jenkins

Tyler State College. Tyler State College was established in 1971 with its own nine-member board of regents by the 62nd Texas Legislature. The college opened for classes in January, 1973, and accepted only junior, senior, and graduate level students. Located in temporary quarters in Tyler, the college has acquired a 200-acre tract of land for future development as its campus. The president was James Stewart. Enrollment in the fall of 1974 was 874 students.

BIBLIOGRAPHY: University of Texas at Austin, *Guide To Texas State Agencies* (1972).

*Tyler Tap Railroad.

*Tyler University.

*Tyler's Bluff, Texas.

*Tynan, Texas.

*Tyng, George.

*Type, Texas.

Tyson, Paul. Paul Tyson was born in Hope, Arkansas, on October 25, 1886; he moved with his parents, Marvin and Sue (McDonald) Tyson, to Santa Anna, Texas, in 1890, entered Texas Christian University (when it was still located in Waco) in 1904 with the intention of pursuing a medical career, and played football and baseball at TCU for four years. A good athlete, he was offered a professional major league baseball contract, but he refused it.

Tyson began work on a master's degree in biology at TCU before going to Tyler High School in 1911 for a brief period as a science teacher and football supervisor; he then taught for two terms at Denison High School. It was at Waco High School that Tyson began his extraordinary coaching career, beginning in 1913; during the following twenty-eight years he became the best known high school coach in the United States because of his legendary football teams. He had only two leaves of absence during that time—one in 1918, to serve in the army, and the other in 1931, to spend a season with Pop Warner, noted football coach at Stanford University.

Under his direction the Waco Tigers won four state high school championships (1922, 1925, 1926, and 1927) and were in the finals on three occasions (1923, 1924, and 1939). In twenty-one years, from 1921 to 1941, his teams won 167 games, lost 30, and tied in 9 games. His most outstanding season was in 1927, the year he invented the spin play; in that year his Waco team was recognized as the unofficial national schoolboy champion after soundly defeating Cathedral Latin High School of Cleveland, Ohio, in a post-season game, by a score of 40 to 14. Tyson was widely respected and was often sought after for advice by college coaches. Knute Rockne, great Notre Dame football coach, once remarked that Tyson knew more about football than any man in America.

In 1942 Tyson left Waco High School to coach at South Park High School in Beaumont; he later coached at Jesuit High School in Dallas, worked as a counselor at Woodrow Wilson High School in Dallas, and taught at Westminster College at Tehuacana. In 1949 he returned to coaching, going to Daniel Baker College; he was preparing for his second season there when he died on September 9, 1950, in Brownwood. He was buried in Waco, the city in which he had been most successful. Tyson never married. He was elected to the Texas Sports Hall of Fame qv and also to the Texas High School Coaches Association Hall of Honor in 1963.

*Tyson, Texas.

U

*U Lazy S Ranch.

*Udden, Johan August.

*Ufnau, Texas.

*Ugalde, Juan de.

*Ugarte, José Joaquín.

*Ugartechea, Domingo de.

*Uhland, Texas.

*Ujuiap Indians. The Ujuiap (Ajuyap, Auju-iap) Indians are known only from the records of San Antonio de Valero Mission qv in San Antonio, which indicate that they entered that mission after 1740 and remained there until at least 1755. Their original location and linguistic affiliation remain unknown. H. E. Bolton qv thought that they might be Tonkawan because they entered the mission during the same period as a number of groups considered to be Tonkawans. However, this argument is weakened by the fact that Karankawan and Coahuiltecan groups also entered the mission during the same period. Although it cannot be demonstrated by documentary evidence, it is possible that the Ujuiap were descendants of the Ijiaba (Iciaba), who were Coahuiltecans and lived along the Río San Juan in northeastern Mexico during the latter part of the seventeenth century.

BIBLIOGRAPHY: Genaro García (ed.), Documentos inéditos ó muy raros para la historia de México, XXV (1909); F. W. Hodge (ed.), Handbook of American Indians, II (1910).

T. N. Campbell

Umalayapem Indians. The Umalayapem (Humalayapem) Indians, who probably spoke Coahuiltecan, lived on the lower Rio Grande. In the middle of the eighteenth century their principal settlements were on the south bank of the Rio Grande between Camargo and Reynosa, Tamaulipas. They sometimes foraged and camped on the Texas side of the river, principally in the area of present Starr and Hidalgo counties.

BIBLIOGRAPHY: W. Jiménez Moreno, "Tribus e idiomas del Norte de México," El Norte de México y el Sur de Estados Unidos (1944); G. Saldivar, Los Indios de Tamaulipas (1943).

T. N. Campbell

*Umbarger, Texas.

Uncertain, Texas. Uncertain, on the shores of Caddo Lake in Harrison County, was incorporated in 1961. That year most of the community's 213 citizens were fishing camp operators. The population in 1970 was 202, according to the United States census. Situated on the site of Uncertain Landing, the town was so named because steamboat captains in earlier days often had trouble mooring their vessels. It was also the site of an old hunting, fishing, and boating society called the Uncertain Club, which existed in the early twentieth century. The town limits are irregular in shape, being designed to include most of the restaurants and fishing camps along part of the Caddo Lake shoreline.

*Underground Water. Underground water includes all water that occurs below the earth's surface, occupying interstices or voids of pervious rocks and soil; like surface water, it is derived principally from precipitation which falls upon the earth's surface and percolates downward under gravity. Underground water in the zone of saturation may occur in either water table (unconfined) aquifers or artesian (confined) aquifers. Confined water is generally under pressure greater than atmospheric pressure, and wells penetrating a confined aquifer will permit water to rise above the confining strata. If sufficient pressure exists flowing wells may result. In the case of water table aquifers, water is derived from local precipitation; but in the case of artesian aquifers, water may enter the permeable strata ten or even hundreds of miles from the point where it is intercepted by wells.

Most geologic formations in Texas contain water, but only a relatively few yield abundant supplies. Those formations yielding abundant supplies which have been classified as major aquifers include: the Gulf Coast aquifer, which corresponds to the Gulf Coast: Carrizo-Wilcox aquifer, just north of the Gulf Coast aquifer; Trinity Group aquifer, mainly North-Central Texas; Edwards-Trinity aquifer, identified with the Edwards Plateau area; Edwards aquifer, corresponding to the Balcones Fault zone; Ogallala aquifer, roughly the High Plains area; and Alluvium aquifer, in widespread areas in Texas but occurring principally in West Texas.

Underground water is a principal water resource in Texas, and its importance as a source of supply for municipal, industrial, and irrigation uses, as well as domestic and livestock purposes, is immeasurable. It is estimated that over 10,338,272 acre-feet of underground water was pumped in 1969 for municipal, industrial, and cropland irrigation purposes.

Many of the large cities and nearly all of the smaller cities and communities in Texas supply their water needs from municipally-owned wells or from a combination of surface and underground water sources. In 1969, 1,871 Texas municipal water systems were dependent solely upon underground water for their municipal needs. An additional 160 municipal water systems used both surface water and underground water, and 341 municipal water systems depended solely upon surface water. Municipal pumpage of underground water by these systems in 1969 was on the order of 1,040,740 acre-feet.

The largest single use of underground water in Texas is for irrigation, about 76 percent of all irrigation water coming from underground sources. More underground water is used for irrigation in Texas than for all other uses combined. In 1969 about 8,768,000 acre-feet of underground water was pumped to irrigate approximately 6,712,000 acres of land throughout Texas. Heavily irrigated areas using underground water are the High Plains region, Winter Garden area, Pecos-Coyanosa, and the Salt Basin areas in the Trans-Pecos. Of all water pumped for irrigation purposes in Texas, 73 percent is produced in the High Plains; Hale, Lamb, Castro, Parmer, and Swisher counties, five adjoining counties in the southern High Plains, produced 28 percent of all the underground water pumped for irrigation in Texas.

In addition to municipal and irrigation uses, many industries have developed underground water supplies for cooling and industrial processes. About 529,532 acre-feet of underground water was pumped for industrial purposes in 1969. Characteristics of underground water which make it particularly desirable for industry are its uniform temperature and uniform quality at a given source. Although all underground water contains mineral matter derived principally from soil and rocks through which it moves, its quality and temperature will generally remain constant at a given locality unless it is contaminated by human activities.

Several factors have contributed to the development and widespread use of underground water as a supply source in Texas. Nearly all of the geologic formations in the state yield some water, generally in sufficient quantities for domestic and livestock purposes. Where it is available in sufficient quantities, underground water is generally cheapest to develop, since it does not need the extensive pipelines and treatment facilities required for surface supplies. Unlike surface water, which flows in definite and limited channels, underground water can often be developed at the point of use, requiring little or no transportation. Large areas of Texas deficient in rainfall and having few perennial streams available for water supply contain vast quantities of underground water in storage.

Underground water is particularly desirable for municipal and industrial purposes because of its uniform quality and temperature, because it is not highly susceptible to contamination, and because it usually requires little treatment. Underground water, unlike surface water which is the property of the state of Texas, is the exclusive property of the owner of the land surface, and it is subject to barter, sale, or lease and not subject to the complicated and often conflicting riparian and appropriative doctrines governing surface water rights. Except for a few statutes pertaining to conservation, protection, and waste, the state of Texas does not regulate the production or use of underground water. Some local control is exercised by underground water conservation districts, which are empowered to promulgate rules and regulations for conserving, preserving, protecting, and recharging underground

water reservoirs within their boundaries, including well spacing and well permitting.

Bernard B. Baker

*Underwood, Ammon.

Underwood, Arch Stobo. Arch Stobo Underwood was born in Hillsboro, Texas, on January 29, 1893, the son of Harris F. and Mary (Turner) Underwood. He attended the public schools of Athens, Texas. On February 19, 1915, he married Minnie Quickenstedt, and they had four children.

In 1925 he established the Texas Compress and Warehouse Co. in Athens, which became the parent company of a network of facilities in twenty South Plains area towns. He served as that company's president and general manager until his retirement in 1968. He also was a director of the First National Bank in Dallas, the Southwestern Life Insurance Co., and the Fort Worth and Denver Railway. He resigned from all three in 1961.

As an active Presbyterian, Underwood served on the board of directors of Trinity University for thirty-five years and was instrumental in moving the university from Waxahachie to San Antonio in 1942.

Known as a political "king-maker" and possibly the state's greatest modern cotton-marketer, Underwood frequently held gigantic parties and barbecues at his Lake Undy home near Athens. He was a friend and frequent guest of former Presidents Franklin D. Roosevelt, Harry S. Truman, Lyndon B. Johnson,qv House Speaker Sam Rayburn,qv and others in high government positions. Underwood died in Lubbock on April 7, 1972, and was buried in Westhaven Mausoleum there.

BIBLIOGRAPHY: *Texian Who's Who* (1937); Dallas *Morning News*, April 18, 1972.

*Union, Texas. (Hopkins County.)

*Union, Texas. (Lubbock County.)

Union, Texas. (Terry County.) Union was founded in 1919. It was serving a farming area with a school, a gin, and a general store in 1966. In 1970 the estimated population of Union was eighty-five people.

*Union, Texas. (Wilson County.)

*Union Academy.

*Union Bower, Texas.

*Union Grove, Texas.

*Union Hill, Texas.

*Union League of Texas. *See* Loyal Union League.

*Union Party.

*Union Regulation in Texas. Since the passage of the union regulatory laws of 1947, little significant legislation in the area has been enacted. In 1951 the legislature sought to strengthen the "right to work" provisions of previous legislation by making violations by either the employer or union "conspiracies in the restraint of trade" and thereby invoking the penalties under the state's anti-trust laws. The "open shop" policy was enhanced in 1955 by legislation making it illegal for a union member, or members, to strike or picket to force an employer to recognize the union or to force other employees to accept the union as a bargaining agent if the union does not actually represent a majority of the employees working when the strike began. The act likewise established the procedures for holding an election to determine the sentiments of the employees, procedures clearly designed to make the union's organization efforts more difficult. Failure to gain a majority of all employees, not just those voting, opened the union to the possibility of a damage suit by the employer.

A series of court cases challenging the state union regulatory laws led to some modifications, but for the most part the laws were upheld. The narrow limitations on secondary boycotts were struck down by the courts, and the provisions for registration of union organizers with the secretary of state were modified by the Supreme Court to apply only to professional union organizers. The requirement that all working agreements, including a check-off for union dues, be filed with the secretary of state was declared unconstitutional, as were the limitations on collection of fees, dues, fines, and assessments by local unions and abridgements of the unions' right to expel members. The requirements on financial reports were modified slightly by judicial decision. All other provisions, when challenged, were upheld in principle if not in specific application or definition. Several of the regulatory provisions have never been invoked, and thus their constitutionality is still not clear. No union, for example, has been charged with anti-trust violation, nor has any been sued for damages for breach of contract.

The major reason for so little state activity in the area of union regulation was the passage, in 1947 and 1959, of the relatively strict Taft-Hartley and Landrum-Griffin acts, which imposed federal controls similar to those established by Texas, making further state legislation unnecessary. *See* Labor Organizations; *see also* Strikes in Texas.

James V. Reese

*Union Terminal Company. All of the major systems operating in Texas except the Missouri-Pacific system owned one-eighth interest in the Union Terminal Company in 1964. It operated 2.1 miles of terminal track in Dallas.

James M. Day

*Union Valley, Texas.

*Unitarian Church. *See also* Unitarian Universalist Association.

Unitarian Universalist Association. The Unitarian Universalist Association was formed as a result of a 1961 merger of the American Unitarian Association and the Universalist Church of America. Historically, the Unitarian concept of one God stood in contradistinction to the generally accepted Trinitarian view of God in three persons. The rejection of the divinity of Jesus followed naturally, and it was supplanted by the recognition of the importance of the basic strengths and values of the man Jesus and of all men. The Universalists historically spoke against the predestination theory and

affirmed their faith in the power of love. For over a century, both groups have run parallel courses and have shared common concerns. In this country much of the early growth of the two denominations was closely connected to the transcendentalist movement of the early nineteenth century in the New England area.

In Texas there were two Unitarian Universalist churches in 1906, with a membership of 118. After World War II much growth was evidenced by the establishment of what is called the "fellowship movement." Lay-led groups were formed in a number of cities and towns. In 1973 there were sixteen churches and eighteen fellowships in Texas, with a combined membership of 3,571. *See also* Unitarian Church.

Russell W. Lockwood

United Church of Christ. Formerly called the Congregational Church in Texas,qv the United Church of Christ was formed on May 1 and 2, 1963, when the South Central Conference of the United Church of Christ was created as a successor to the Texas Association of the Central South Conference of Congregational Christian Churches.

*United Daughters of the Confederacy, Texas Division of. Since 1939 the Texas Division has awarded scholarships yearly to worthy boys and girls and the Albert Sidney Johnston qv saber to the outstanding cadet at Texas A&M University.

Under the administration of Mrs. R. W. Widener, president from 1962 to 1964, approval of the membership was obtained to close the Confederate Woman's Home qv in Austin. The home had been deeded to the state of Texas in 1911, and all expenses of its operation since that date had been paid by the state. The home was officially closed in September, 1966; only one Confederate widow remained living at that time.

During the 1960's the Texas Division erected a monument in Little Mound Cemetery, near Gilmer, honoring Emma Sansom, a Confederate heroine from Alabama. It also erected a monument in Hereford honoring the memory of three donors of a tract of land which was deeded to the Texas Division over forty years ago. The organization was influential in persuading the state to erect a marker at Baytown, near the site of Bayland Orphans' Home for Boys,qv and was responsible for improvements made to the Texas Confederate Museum in Austin.

In 1968 the Texas Division had seventy-four chapters with a membership of 2,696. The junior organization, the Children of the Confederacy, had twenty chapters.

Helen Reaves Ramsey

United States Arsenal, San Antonio. *See* San Antonio Arsenal.

*United States Naval Air Stations. *See* Naval Air Station, Corpus Christi, Texas; Naval Air Station, Dallas, Texas; Naval Auxiliary Air Station, Beeville, Texas; Naval Auxiliary Air Station, Kingsville, Texas.

United States Naval Inactive Ship Maintenance Facility, Orange, Texas. The presence of the United States Navy in Orange dates from August, 1940, when the navy established the office of supervisor of shipbuilding to oversee the construction of twenty-four landing craft. With the naval construction boom brought by World War II, the Orange facility grew, and the office of supervisor of shipbuilding represented the navy at shipyards along the entire Texas coastline.

In November, 1945, with the cessation of hostilities, emphasis at the Orange installation shifted from shipbuilding to logistical support and to demobilization of naval craft, and the United States Naval Station, Orange, Texas, was established. The primary mission of the station was to provide logistic and industrial support for the inactivation ("mothballing") and berthing of the Texas Group, U. S. Sixteenth Fleet.

In December, 1959, the Department of the Navy reorganized its activity in Orange. It had fulfilled its primary mission of inactivating ships and was by then performing maintenance and preservation operations on those ships already mothballed. Therefore, the U. S. Naval Station, Orange, Texas, was deactivated, and the facility became the Texas Group, Atlantic Reserve Fleet, with the mission of preparing for the activation of mothballed vessels moored there. Many of the functions associated with a naval station were discontinued, mainly those related to the dockside support of active ships.

In October, 1966, following a reorganization of the Department of the Navy, the Orange installation was again reorganized: from the Texas Group, Atlantic Reserve Fleet, it became the United States Naval Inactive Ship Maintenance Facility under the Naval Ship Systems Command (formerly the Bureau of Ships). Its mission, however, remained essentially the same—inactivation, security, maintenance, and activation of naval ships—and its security and routine maintenance force consisted of approximately 122 civilian employees. Inactivation and activation of ships, as well as all major overhaul work, were accomplished on a contract basis by local civilian industry. In 1971 thirteen officers and twenty-nine enlisted men were attached to the facility.

Some 170 vessels, mostly of a combat type and representing almost a two-billion-dollar defense investment, were moored at the facility in 1971. Many of the ships had distinguished World War II records, such as the U.S.S. *Revenge*, a minesweeper which was the first United States ship to enter Tokyo Bay after the Japanese surrender. *See also* Naval Station, Orange, Texas, in Volume II.

T. V. Aldert

United States Naval Station. See United States Naval Inactive Ship Maintenance Facility, Orange, Texas.

United States v. Texas. See Greer County.

Unity, Texas.

*Universal City, Texas. In 1970 Universal City, in Bexar County, had 7,613 inhabitants, according to the United States census. In that year the city reported eighty businesses.

University of Corpus Christi. The University of Corpus Christi, Corpus Christi, was chartered on April 1, 1947, as Arts and Technological College. A four-year liberal arts college affiliated with the Baptist General Convention of Texas, the institution's first campus was Chase Field,qv a deactivated naval air training field at Beeville. In August, 1947, the college moved to temporary quarters at Cuddihy Field in Corpus Christi. The board of trustees changed the school's name to the University of Corpus Christi in October, and in December of the same year the school was moved again, permanently, to Ward Island on Ocean Drive, occupying the former naval radar training school. The total number of students in attendance for the 1949–1950 term was 556.

By 1965 six buildings were completed, including dormitories, an administration building, a science building, and a library. The university continued to use the frame buildings formerly occupied by the navy.

The school offered bachelor's degrees in twenty areas by 1964. The library moved to fully equipped (fireproof) quarters in 1963. Holdings increased from 13,220 to 57,000 volumes between 1955 and 1969. Student activities included varsity competition in football, basketball, and tennis, as well as intramural competition in several other sports. By the regular 1964–1965 term, 711 students were registered and there was a faculty of thirty-nine members. By 1972 enrollment had decreased to 501 students. Kenneth A. Maroney was president in 1972. The University of Corpus Christi was subsequently sold and became a part of the Texas A&I University System;qv the first students were admitted to the new school in the fall of 1973. In the fall of 1974 Texas A&I University at Corpus Christi had an enrollment of 1,603 students, and its president was D. Whitney Halladay.

University of Dallas. First opened in 1907, the University of Dallas operated until 1927. In the 1950's the need for a Catholic four-year institution of higher learning in the Diocese of Dallas-Fort Worth again became evident. In 1955 a thousand-acre tract of land in the northwest Dallas metropolitan area was purchased, and plans were made for a four-year, coeducational diocesan college, with graduate work to be added as soon as practicable. The Most Reverend Thomas K. Gorman, bishop of Dallas-Fort Worth, was chancellor of the school.

The university opened in September, 1956, in Irving, with a freshman class of 269 students and a teaching and administrative staff composed of laymen, diocesan and Cistercian priests, and Sisters of St. Mary of Namur.qv The Sisters' junior college for women in Fort Worth, Our Lady of Victory College,qv was absorbed into the university. Affiliated with the Catholic University of America, the university was also a member of the National Catholic

Education Association, the Association of Texas Colleges,qv and the Southern Association of Colleges and Schools.

Departments of instruction were grouped into six major divisions: fine arts, language and literature, philosophy and theology, physical and natural sciences, social sciences, and education. The student-faculty ratio was kept at approximately eleven to one, and 60 percent of the professors held earned Ph.D. degrees. A graduate program was initiated in 1966, permitting students to earn advanced degrees through the Ph.D. By 1969 the school's physical plant numbered over twenty-four buildings, including a library housing 70,000 volumes. Enrollment increased to 948 students in the 1966–1967 regular term; members of the faculty in that year totaled 85. Professional or pre-professional training was offered in law, business management, engineering-science (in cooperation with the Science Research Center), medicine, nursing (in cooperation with the St. Paul School of Nursing of Dallas), and teacher education. Enrollment in the fall of 1974 was 1,717 students. Donald A. Cowan served as president of the university. See also Roman Catholic Education in Texas.

*University of Eastern Texas.

University Fund, Available. The Available University Fund is income which is derived from the Permanent University Fund.qv For more detailed information, see University Fund, Permanent. See also University of Texas (in Volume II); University of Texas at Austin; Agricultural and Mechanical College of Texas (in Volume I); Land Appropriations; Lands, Texas Public. [The Available University Fund should not be confused with the Available School Fund qv (which benefits the Texas public school system, kindergarten through the twelfth grade). Ed.]

University Fund, Permanent. The Permanent University Fund consists of approximately 2,100,-000 acres of land, predominantly in West Texas, together with cash and securities. The principal of the fund cannot be spent for any purpose, since it must be kept as a permanent endowment. About two-thirds of the income (Available University Fund qv) from the Permanent University Fund is available to the University of Texas System,qv which is charged with the responsibility for management of the fund. The Texas A&M University System,qv since September 1, 1934, has received one-third of the income from the fund arising from the 1,000,000 acres of land appropriated by the Constitution of 1876 qv and the land appropriated by the Act of 1883, except income from grazing leases.

The income from the Permanent University Fund may be pledged to secure the payment of bonds or notes to be issued for the purpose of constructing, equipping, or acquiring buildings at components of the Texas A&M University System (including Texas A&M University, Prairie View A&M University, Tarleton State University, Agricultural Experiment Station System, Texas Agricultural Exten-

sion Service, Texas Engineering Experiment Station, and Texas Forest Service,qv but not including, as of March, 1976, Moody College of Marine Sciences and Maritime Resources qv) and six components of the University of Texas System (University of Texas at Austin, University of Texas Medical Branch at Galveston, University of Texas Southwestern Medical School at Dallas, University of Texas at El Paso, University of Texas Health Science Center at Houston, and University of Texas System Cancer Center qqv). The remainder of the University of Texas System's two-thirds portion of the Available University Fund, after debt service on the University of Texas System Permanent University Fund bonds outstanding, goes to the University of Texas at Austin. The remainder of Texas A&M University System's one-third portion of the Available University Fund, after debt service on the Texas A&M University System's Permanent University Fund bonds, goes to Texas A&M University.

Additions to the Permanent University Fund come primarily from royalties on mineral production on university lands and from bonuses on mineral lease sales. Income to the Available University Fund is derived from the income on investments of the Permanent University Fund, principally in bonds and stocks. See also University of Texas (in Volume II); University of Texas at Austin; Agricultural and Mechanical College of Texas (in Volume I); Land Appropriations; Lands, Texas Public. [The Permanent University Fund should not be confused with the Permanent School Fund qv (which benefits the Texas public school system, kindergarten through the twelfth grade). Ed.]

*University of Houston. The University of Houston, located in Houston, became the home of the nation's first educational television station, KUHT, in 1953. Accreditation from the Southern Association of Colleges and Secondary Schools was received in 1954. Two years later the M. D. Anderson Foundation qv gave $1,500,000 to endow six professorships, and the Ford Foundation awarded the university $1,300,000 to supplement faculty salaries.

A sixty-member board of governors, comprised of prominent Houstonians, including the fifteen regents provided for by a 1945 legislative act, held its first meeting in 1957. In 1959 the board of governors sought state financial assistance and admission as an independent unit in the state system of higher education. Admission to the state system was voted in 1961, to become effective in September, 1963. The university was thereafter guided by a nine-member board of regents appointed by the governor.

In 1960 the university chartered a foundation for research on a 1,603-acre tract of land at Camp Wallace,qv and several research projects were begun for the National Aeronautics and Space Administration qv in 1962. By 1964 research contracts in progress reached the million-dollar level annually.

In 1964 the university was composed of nine separate colleges: architecture, arts and sciences, business administration, engineering, education, law, optometry, pharmacy, and technology; there was also a downtown school and graduate school. The university possessed a forty-million-dollar, debt-free physical plant on a 300-acre main campus. Approximately twenty million dollars in buildings and additions, half financed by bonds, were under construction by the late 1960's, including a chemistry and pharmacy building, a religion center, a library addition, general classroom and engineering buildings, a university center, and a student services building. Library collections totaled 520,689 volumes in 1969, and the university faculty totaled about 1,350 members. Enrollment by the 1968 fall term was 23,713 students, and by 1974, 29,389 students were registered. In 1974 Philip G. Hoffman served as president. In 1974 the university operated two branch campuses, at Clear Lake City and at Victoria, which offered upper-division courses only. In that same year a branch, Downtown College, was operating at One Main Plaza, Houston.

*University Interscholastic League. In the mid-1960's one and one-quarter million pupils in elementary, intermediate, and high school grades annually entered into the more than fifty different activities sponsored by the University Interscholastic League. Added to the full-time staff of the organization was a director of journalism. The Drama Loan Library had increased its holdings to 25,000 plays, 500 play collections, 425 play production books, and 400 volumes devoted to one form or another of public speaking. (Activities of the organization included most of those described in Volume II.) The work of the league continued to be financed by three sources in approximately equal parts: state appropriation, membership fees, and a percentage of football gate receipts. The annual budget in the 1960's averaged $75,000.

BIBLIOGRAPHY: University of Texas Bureau of Public School Service, *Constitution and Contest Rules of the University Interscholastic League for 1966–1967* (1966).

Rhea H. Williams

*University Lands. *See* Land Appropriations; University Fund, Available; University Fund, Permanent.

*University Park, Texas. University Park, in Dallas County, had a 1960 population of 23,202 and a 1970 population of 23,498, according to the United States census. *See also* Dallas Standard Metropolitan Statistical Area.

University of Plano. The University of Plano was chartered by the state in May, 1964, as a private, coeducational, nondenominational institution of senior rank. Classes first met during the fall of 1965 in two leased buildings in downtown Dallas. Facilities on a 760-acre campus in Plano were ready for occupancy by April, 1966, and included dormitories, a student center, and a former World's Fair pavilion (donated by the Malaysian government), which was reconstructed as an administration-library-classroom building.

The university also operated an academy for students with learning problems and a school of ex-

perimental education, both of which remained in Dallas. Efforts were underway to begin a preparatory school at Plano in September, 1966. The college of liberal arts curriculum offered majors in English, foreign languages, history, politics, and economics, leading to bachelor of arts degrees.

During the 1968–1969 term, the university reported 267 students and a faculty of thirty-one members. Library holdings in 1969 totaled 20,000 volumes. In 1972 the university had 206 students registered and a faculty of thirty-three; Donald G. Scott served as president.

University of St. Thomas. The bishop of Galveston, the Most Reverend Christopher E. Byrne, D.D., announced establishment of the University of St. Thomas in May, 1945. The Basilian Fathers of Toronto chose the T. P. Lee mansion in Houston as the site for the Catholic coeducational university. Pope Pius XII bestowed his blessing in March, 1946, and the university program began with a series of adult education courses in November of that year.

Following renovation of the original buildings and erection of a science building during the summer of 1947, the first undergraduate classes opened with sixty students and a faculty of four Basilian fathers and seven lay professors. Several private homes in the neighborhood were purchased for residence facilities, and a library and a social science building (1954), a student center (1955), an auditorium-fine arts building (1958), and a cafeteria and students' commons (1960) were added.

The Southern Association of Colleges and Secondary Schools granted accreditation in 1954, and the university established an endowed chair in history in 1957. A new phase of university development began in 1961, when the Basilian fathers started a center for seminarians taking undergraduate courses. In 1962 a modern languages laboratory and a computer center were installed. By that year the faculty had grown to forty-nine members, twenty-two Basilians and twenty-seven lay professors. The student body numbered 598.

Restricted to undergraduate work, the curriculum provided courses leading to B.A. degrees in the following subjects: art history, biology, chemistry, classical languages, economics, education, English, history, mathematics, modern languages, philosophy, physics, and sociology. A biology building was completed in 1966. A library, a chemistry building, and dormitory facilities were completed in the late 1960's.

In the 1966–1967 regular term there were 961 students taught by a seventy-member faculty. In 1969 the library held 45,000 volumes. By 1974 enrollment had increased to 1,718 students, and the faculty numbered approximately 120. Patrick O. Braden was president.

*University of San Antonio.

*University of San Augustine. By 1840 the University of San Augustine had a grant of 17,712 acres of land. Three leagues of the land were sold, and the money was invested in a building, but the first board of trustees rented the building to a Presbyterian, J. M. Rankin, for an academy. In 1842 Marcus A. Montrose,qv became the president. A Presbytery of Eastern Texas was organized at San Augustine in 1843 to assist the school, but the university closed after five years without awarding a degree. *See also* Presbyterian Education in Texas.

BIBLIOGRAPHY: William Stuart Red, *A History of the Presbyterian Church in Texas* (1936); Dan Ferguson, "The Antecedents of Austin College," *Southwestern Historical Quarterly*, LIII (1949–1950).

Malcolm L. Purcell

*University of Texas. *See also* University of Texas at Austin; University of Texas System.

*University of Texas, Medical Branch of. *See also* University of Texas Medical Branch at Galveston; University of Texas Medical School at Houston; University of Texas Medical School at San Antonio; University of Texas Southwestern Medical School at Dallas; University of Texas System (which refers to numerous other medical components within the system, each of which may also be found under its own title).

University of Texas at Arlington. The University of Texas at Arlington, founded in 1895 as Arlington College, a private institution, had a succession of names. By 1917 the college became state supported. The Texas legislature changed the name to North Texas Agricultural and Mechanical College in 1923, and then to Arlington State College qv in 1949. Arlington State College acquired senior college status in 1959. The college was transferred from the Texas A&M University System qv to the University of Texas in April, 1965. In March, 1967, the Texas legislature changed the name to the University of Texas at Arlington and made it an official part of the University of Texas System.qv

Since the early 1950's the most notable step in the college's growth was promotion from junior college to senior institution status in the fall of 1959. In 1965, B.A. and B.S. degrees were offered in fifteen fields of arts and sciences and five fields of engineering. Two-year terminal programs in commercial and technical fields continued, as well as academic transfer programs of two-year duration. Master's degree programs in the fields of economics, electrical engineering, engineering mechanics, mathematics, psychology, and physics were offered for the first time in the fall of 1966. A major building program completed eighteen projects totaling approximately $14,-225,000 in the fifteen-year period from 1950 to 1965. Library volumes, budget, and staff were augmented proportionately, with 400,000 books on the shelves in 1969.

In 1967 the regular term enrollment of students was 11,501, and the faculty numbered 486. By the 1974 fall term, enrollment reached 15,434. In 1974 Wendell Nedderman was president. *See* Arlington State College (in Volume I); *see also* University of Texas System.

University of Texas at Austin. On March 6, 1967, the Sixtieth Texas Legislature changed the official name of the main university of the University of Texas qv to The University of Texas at Aus-

tin. The main university at Austin was the largest component institution in the University of Texas System.qv It also included the University of Texas McDonald Observatory at Mount Locke and the University of Texas Marine Science Institute at Port Aransas.qqv Research was also undertaken on extensive off-campus acreage at the Balcones Research Center and the Brackenridge Tract in Austin.

Valued in excess of $100,000,000 by 1965, the physical plant of the main university comprised seventy-six permanent buildings used for classroom, laboratory, administration, library, dormitory, and service facilities set on a campus of more than 232 acres. Nineteen buildings were constructed or acquired between 1950 and 1965. The university was granted the right of eminent domain in 1965 to purchase various properties adjacent to the campus on the north, east, and south. In 1972 the main campus consisted of more than 110 buildings on a plot of nearly 300 acres. The Lyndon Baines Johnson Library,qv housing presidential papers, was completed in 1971 on the university campus with university funds. It was staffed and operated by the federal government.

Major physical assets in the science-engineering fields included a nuclear reactor, a radio telescope, a computation center, an electron microscope, and a particle accelerator. (*See also* Tokamak.) University research was broadened and deepened in many areas, ranging through such fields as nuclear physics, water resources, linguistics, medicine, astronomy, marine sciences, computation, chemistry, and the humanities.

In the 1966–1967 regular term the main university enrolled 27,345 students, including 4,307 students in the graduate school. The faculty, numbering more than 1,800, included nine of the state's fourteen members of the National Academy of Sciences. By the mid-1960's, nearly two dozen endowed and named academic positions were established to attract and retain leading faculty scholars. The university also approved the establishment of endowed lectureships which extended temporary appointments to prominent authorities in various fields. In the fall of 1974 student enrollment was 41,841.

In 1975 the main university had eight colleges and five schools, which included fifty departments plus a division of general and comparative studies. There were more than fifty organized research units.

In 1975 the university was still the only southwestern member of the Association of American Universities, an organization of forty-six universities of the highest academic standing in the United States and Canada. The national Office of Education reported that Texas led all other institutions in the South in number of doctoral degrees granted. Through August, 1974, the university had granted 169,678 academic degrees (bachelor's, master's, and doctoral). Of that number, 30,548 were graduate degrees.

The key factor in the university's program was its library, largest within a one-thousand-mile radius of Austin, with 3,518,690 volumes in 1975. Particularly notable were the collections in English and American literature, Texas and Southern history, Latin American culture, theater history, and the history of science. The Undergraduate Library and Academic Center offered a variety of opportunities for independent learning, such as open shelf collections associated with special research collections, exhibits, and lecture programs. The new Harry Ransom Humanities Research Center housed rare books and special collections. A new general library building was under construction in 1975.

The Permanent University Fund,qv an endowment provided by university-owned oil lands in West Texas, had assets which exceeded $445,000,000 in 1965, an increase of $329,500,000 over the 1950 value. By August 31, 1974, the permanent fund had increased to $724,286,159. The Available University Fund,qv primarily interest from investment of the permanent endowment, was shared with Texas A&M University,qv which received one-third. Although the available fund was largely responsible for the main university's physical plant, built without tax money, an increasing portion was combined with private gifts to develop new teaching and research programs. The university derived its support from state appropriations, the available fund, student fees, and miscellaneous sources. The 1974–1975 educational and general budget was $85,434,374, of which $48,047,352 was used for instructional purposes.

Presidents of the university since 1950 were: Theophilus S. Painter qv (1946–1952), James Clay Dolley (acting, 1952), Logan Wilson (1953–1960), Harry Ransom (1960–1961), and Joseph R. Smiley (1961–1963). Between 1963 and 1967 the office of the president of the main university was abolished, and the chancellor of the system, Harry Ransom, assumed the additional duties. In 1967 the presidency was reestablished and Norman Hackerman became president (1967–1970). Bryce Jordan served as acting president from 1970 until 1971, when Stephen H. Spurr became president. In 1974 Spurr was relieved of his duties as president, with some controversy, and Lorene Lane Rogers served as acting president from September, 1974, until September 12, 1975, when she was named the fifteenth president of the University of Texas at Austin, the first woman to be named president of a major state university. See University of Texas (in Volume II); see also University of Texas System; Alcalde; Daily Texan; Eugene C. Barker Texas History Center; Latin American Collection; Rare Book Collections; Texas Collection; Texas Memorial Museum; University Fund, Available; University Fund, Permanent; University of Texas Press; University of Texas Tower, Murders at the.

University of Texas at Dallas. The University of Texas at Dallas was chartered as the Graduate Research Center of the Southwest on February 14, 1961. Located in Dallas, Richardson, and Plano, the center was established as a private, nonprofit institution to conduct scientific research in the public interest and to advance graduate education in the Southwest. On January 1, 1967, the center became the Southwest Center for Advanced Studies (SCAS). In September, 1969, the center became a part of the University of Texas System qv as an upper-level institution, and it was renamed the University of Texas at Dallas.

In 1962 a laboratory for earth and planetary sciences was formed in the center as the first of five planned interdisciplinary research and academic groupings. The earth and planetary sciences laboratory included divisions in geosciences, atmospheric and space sciences, and mathematics and mathematical physics. A 1,266-acre campus site, approximately eighteen miles north of downtown Dallas on the Dallas-Collin county line, was established in July, 1962.

By 1963 the faculty and staff had increased from nineteen to one hundred members, and $615,835 in sponsored research projects plus $101,804 in unsponsored research had been allocated. A magnetic observatory, placed in operation in July, 1963, was a cooperative effort of the center, industry, and government. The United States Coast and Geodetic Survey provided personnel for day-to-day observations and transmittal of data. A laboratory of computer sciences was formed in October of the same year.

By 1964 the center faculty and staff increased to 184 members, and sponsored research for the 1963–1964 fiscal period increased to $1,893,286. A laboratory of molecular sciences and a division of genetics were organized in February, 1964, and the Founders Building, the first major structure on the campus, was formally opened in October of that year. In 1965, of the total investment in development, $3,200,853 was for buildings and site improvement, $1,003,196 was for scientific equipment and furnishings, and $3,856,298 was for land purchases, making a total capital investment of $8,060,347.

A magnetic facility was moved from the Massachusetts Institute of Technology to the campus in 1965 and operated as a regional center for research in solid state physics with high magnetic fields. In the summer of 1965, seven private educational and research institutions combined to expand graduate education programs in North Texas and chartered the Texas Association for Graduate Education and Research (TAGER). Under the initial plan, TAGER sponsored doctoral programs in biology, chemistry, engineering, geoscience, mathematics, and physics. Post-doctoral programs were conducted at the center with appointees teaching at institutions belonging to the TAGER group.

The American Cancer Society supported continuing research into the use of a negative pion beam for cancer therapy, a special center project. Other major groups supporting center research included the National Aeronautics and Space Administration,qv the United States Air Force, the National Science Foundation, the Atomic Energy Commission, the National Institutes of Health, the United States Public Health Service, and the American Chemical Society.

Lloyd V. Berkner served as first president of the center and later as director of the laboratories and chairman of the executive committee. Gifford Johnson became the center's second president in 1965. Bryce Jordan was named first president of the University of Texas at Dallas in July, 1970. The first official enrollment at the University of Texas at Dallas was fifty-six students in 1970–1971; in 1974 enrollment was 700. Junior and senior level undergraduate students were to be admitted beginning in September, 1975. *See also* University of Texas System.

BIBLIOGRAPHY: Graduate Research Center of the Southwest, *Annual Report, 1964–1965* (1965); *Advance*, II (1965).

Alfred T. Mitchell

*University of Texas Dental Branch. The University of Texas Dental Branch, now named the University of Texas Dental Branch at Houston, was established as a private school in 1905. By action of the Forty-eighth Texas Legislature it became a branch of the University of Texas and was opened as a state institution in 1943 under the name University of Texas Dental Branch. The school was renamed by the Sixtieth Texas Legislature in 1967 and became a part of the University of Texas System.qv

The branch completed a new building in May, 1955, made possible by funds raised by the citizens of Houston, a grant from the M. D. Anderson Foundation,qv and appropriation by the Fifty-second and Fifty-third legislatures. A graduate program leading to the degree of Master of Science in Dentistry was instituted in April, 1961. The University of Texas Dental Science Institute at Houston was established in February, 1964, as the research arm of the University of Texas Dental Branch at Houston. Clinical and hospital facilities, as well as a library housing 21,612 volumes in 1969, served students. The student body increased from 239 in 1950 to 507 in 1967; during the same period the faculty increased from fifty-seven to ninety-eight. Located in the Texas Medical Center,qv the dental branch was composed of the University of Texas Dental School and the University of Texas Dental Science Institute. In October, 1972, the University of Texas Dental Branch at Houston, with its school and institute, became a part of the University of Texas Health Science Center at Houston.qv Enrollment in the fall of 1974 was 667 students, and John V. Olson served as dean. *See also* University of Texas System.

University of Texas Dental School at San Antonio. The University of Texas Dental School at San Antonio was created by the Sixty-first Texas Legislature in 1969. In October, 1972, the dental school became a part of the University of Texas Health Science Center at San Antonio.qv Located in the South Texas Medical Center in San Antonio, the school enrolled ninety-four students in the fall of 1973, and J. Duncan Robertson was acting dean. Philip J. Boyne became dean in 1974, when the student enrollment was 112. *See also* University of Texas System.

University of Texas at El Paso. The University of Texas at El Paso, formerly Texas Western College,qv was renamed and remained a branch of the University of Texas System qv in 1967. The school grew in all areas from 1950 through the 1960's. The value of endowments increased from $439,238 in 1950 to $1,163,032 in 1965. Building values likewise increased, from $3,594,511 to $11,387,403 over the fifteen-year period, and construction of a two-million-dollar physical science-mathematics building was planned. In 1950 the college enrolled 2,165 students and employed 133 faculty members. By the fall of 1974 enrollment was 11,418. The library holdings grew from 51,500 volumes in 1950 to 300,000 in 1969. The college offered thirteen degrees in its schools of engineering and in the arts and sciences. Arleigh B. Templeton served as president in 1974. *See* Texas Western College; *see also* University of Texas System.

University of Texas Environmental Science Park. The University of Texas Environmental Science Park, located in Bastrop County in the Smithville-Bastrop area, was established to study man's interaction with his environment. The park is composed of two parts off State Highway 21—the Camp Swift Division, an animal study area, and the Buescher Division, an ecology study area adjacent to Buescher State Park (*see* Parks, State). The idea for this type of natural study area originated in the mid-1960's with Dr. R. Lee Clark of the University of Texas M. D. Anderson Hospital and Tumor Institute qv and interested persons in Smithville. A legislative bill to activate the park was signed in April, 1971, and $100,000 for the planning stage of the park was allocated. The bill gave administration of the park to M. D. Anderson Hospital and permitted the hospital to receive gifts and grants from outside sources.

The Buescher Division of over 700 acres of almost pristine forest land was to be used in studies of natural flora and fauna and man's effect on them, and problems of health and disease. A human impact study on the ecologic effect of human use of land was made, comparing the effects of the 500,-000 visitors in 1971 in Bastrop State Park to the effects of visitors on adjacent Buescher State Park, which received about one-fourth that number of visitors. The Camp Swift Division was planned for veterinary resources and animal studies, including the raising of specific animals for experimentation.

The potential uses for both divisions were myriad, and laboratories for health research, a library, and facilities for conferences and seminars were planned, as well as public environmental education for tourists visiting the parks.

In October, 1972, the environmental science park became a part of the University of Texas System Cancer Center.qv *See also* University of Texas System.

BIBLIOGRAPHY: *Texas Times*, December, 1971.

University of Texas Graduate School of Biomedical Sciences at Dallas. The University of Texas Graduate School of Biomedical Sciences at

Dallas was founded in 1972 as a graduate division of the University of Texas Health Science Center at Dallas.[qv] In the fall of 1974 the school enrolled 172 students and the dean was Ronald W. Estabrook.

University of Texas Graduate School of Biomedical Sciences at Galveston. The University of Texas Graduate School of Biomedical Sciences at Galveston is a division of the University of Texas Medical Branch at Galveston.[qv] In 1974 the school enrolled 103 students and J. Palmer Saunders was dean.

University of Texas Graduate School of Biomedical Sciences at Houston. The University of Texas Graduate School of Biomedical Sciences at Houston was established by the Fifty-eighth Texas Legislature in 1963 to conduct graduate courses in areas related to medical education and research. The new school, located in the Texas Medical Center,[qv] absorbed the University of Texas Postgraduate School of Medicine, which had been a separate component institution of the University of Texas System [qv] since its activation in 1948. The postgraduate school of medicine was renamed the Division of Continuing Education in the Graduate School of Biomedical Sciences but was transferred to the University of Texas Medical School at Houston [qv] in 1969. In October, 1972, the University of Texas Graduate School of Biomedical Sciences at Houston became a part of the University of Texas Health Science Center at Houston.[qv] In 1968 enrollment was 76 students, and by 1974 it had grown to 160 students. Dean of the school in 1974 was Alfred G. Knudson.

University of Texas Graduate School of Biomedical Sciences at San Antonio. The University of Texas Graduate School of Biomedical Sciences at San Antonio was founded in November, 1972, as a graduate division of the University of Texas Health Science Center at San Antonio.[qv] In the fall of 1974 the school enrolled sixty-three students. Armand J. Guarino was dean at that time.

University of Texas Health Science Center at Dallas. The University of Texas Health Science Center at Dallas was established in October, 1972, as one of four centers across the state to coordinate the medical and health units of the university system. Included in the health center at Dallas in 1973 were the University of Texas Southwestern Medical School at Dallas, the University of Texas Graduate School of Biomedical Sciences at Dallas, and the University of Texas School of Allied Health Sciences at Dallas.[qqv] President of the University of Texas Health Science Center at Dallas in 1974 was Charles C. Sprague. *See also* University of Texas System.

University of Texas Health Science Center at Galveston. *See* University of Texas Medical Branch at Galveston.

University of Texas Health Science Center at Houston. The University of Texas Health Science Center at Houston was established in October, 1972, as one of four centers across the state to coordinate the medical and health units of the university system. Included in the health science center at Houston in 1973 were the University of Texas Dental Branch at Houston (formerly named the University of Texas Dental Branch [qv]), the University of Texas Medical School at Houston, the University of Texas Graduate School of Biomedical Sciences at Houston, the University of Texas School of Public Health at Houston, and the University of Texas Speech and Hearing Institute at Houston.[qqv] Acting president of the University of Texas Health Science Center at Houston in 1972 was John V. Olson. Charles A. Berry was president in 1974. *See also* University of Texas System.

University of Texas Health Science Center at San Antonio. The University of Texas Health Science Center at San Antonio was established in October, 1972, as one of four centers across the state to coordinate the medical and health units of the university system. Included in the health center at San Antonio in 1973 were the University of Texas Medical School at San Antonio, the University of Texas Dental School at San Antonio, and the University of Texas Graduate School of Biomedical Sciences at San Antonio.[qqv] President of the University of Texas Health Science Center at San Antonio in 1974 was Frank Harrison. *See also* University of Texas System.

University of Texas at Houston. Although authorized by the Sixtieth Texas Legislature in March, 1967, as the University of Texas at Houston, the title covering those university biomedical institutions located there was changed by October, 1972. *See* University of Texas Health Science Center at Houston; *see also* University of Texas System.

University of Texas Institute of Texan Cultures at San Antonio. The University of Texas Institute of Texan Cultures at San Antonio had component institutional status in the University of Texas System [qv] from July, 1970, until February, 1973, when it became a part of the University of Texas at San Antonio. *See* Institute of Texan Cultures; *see also* University of Texas at San Antonio; University of Texas System.

University of Texas M. D. Anderson Hospital and Tumor Institute at Houston. The University of Texas M. D. Anderson Hospital and Tumor Institute at Houston was authorized in 1941 by the Forty-seventh Texas Legislature as the Texas State Cancer Hospital with a Division of Cancer Research to be controlled and managed by the University of Texas. The hospital began operations in 1944. The institution was named M. D. Anderson Hospital and Tumor Institute in 1954; its present name was authorized by the Texas legislature in March, 1967. The institution is located in the Texas Medical Center.[qv]

In October, 1972, the University of Texas M. D. Anderson Hospital and Tumor Institute became a part of the University of Texas System Cancer Center.[qv] *See* M. D. Anderson Foundation; *see also* University of Texas System; University of Texas Environmental Science Park.

University of Texas McDonald Observatory at Mount Locke. The University of Texas McDonald Observatory at Mount Locke received a new thirty-six-inch reflector in 1956, designed to take the load of observation of brighter stars off the eighty-two-inch reflector. Many other auxiliary instruments were provided to make the most effective use of the faint light collected by the telescopes. In addition to photographic emulsions, photoelectric cells were increasingly employed.

The University of Texas at Austin qv assumed administration and operation of the observatory in 1963. A major building program was undertaken, and a 107-inch telescope, the third largest in the world, was put into operation in 1968. It was constructed jointly by the university and the National Aeronautics and Space Administration.qv In 1967, when the University of Texas System qv became statewide, the observatory remained a part of the astronomy department of the University of Texas at Austin. *See also* McDonald Observatory (in Volume II); Harvard Radio Astronomy Station; University of Texas System.

University of Texas Marine Science Institute at Port Aransas. The University of Texas Marine Science Institute at Port Aransas was established in 1941 as a project of the zoology department of the University of Texas, through the initiative of E. J. Lund and with the aid of the general education board. Early studies were made in biophysics and physiology from a building and pier of the U.S. Army Corps of Engineers along the jetty of Aransas Pass inlet. Eleven acres of land on the barrier island (Mustang-Padre Island) were obtained from the federal government, and construction of a new high pier and two frame buildings was completed in 1945. At that time continuous all-year work began with a resident staff, the institute journal was started, and the first Ph.D. program was completed.

In 1948 a building was added to the pier and to the lower area. Work on the physiology of oysters in the late 1940's under Lund was followed by studies in ichthyology, taxonomy, ecology, general distribution of invertebrate fauna, estuarine ecology related to salinity gradients, and paleoecology. A boat suitable for operations on the Gulf shelf was added. Gradual diversification, including a resident marine geology program, a 4,000-volume library, regular summer teaching, and taxonomic reference collections, was followed by formal association with campus teaching departments in 1956. Resident faculty programs in marine microbiology, marine botany, and marine chemistry were added in 1958 and 1959. A new headquarters, research building, and boat basin were constructed in 1960. Research facilities included two diesel motor vessels, several smaller craft, walk-in constant temperature rooms, concrete ponds, autoclave and dark rooms, radioactive storage and handling room, and recirculating seawater system. With turtle grass flats, mud-bottomed bays, oyster reefs, continental shelf environments,

rock jetties, open beaches, oil drilling platforms, and bird rookeries close by, a variety of environments was available for study in the subtropical climate.

The institute engaged primarily in basic research and graduate instruction. An integrated teaching program in marine science was offered through the institute and related departments of science and engineering on the main campus of the university. The institute served the Southwest region through its program for visiting classes, investigators, and summer students. Studies for development of state marine resources were also conducted. In 1967 the institute became a part of the University of Texas System,qv under the administrative control of the University of Texas at Austin.qv

By law the institute director was an ex officio member of the General Land Office.qv Donald E. Wohlschlag was appointed director of the institute in September, 1965, succeeding Howard T. Odum. Patrick L. Parker was director in 1974. *See also* University of Texas System.

University of Texas Medical Branch at Galveston. In March, 1967, the University of Texas Medical Branch at Galveston, formerly the Medical Branch of the University of Texas,qv was so renamed. It consisted of a school of medicine and a school of nursing, with technical curricula, a postgraduate program, and a multi-hospital complex.

Buildings on the campus constructed since 1950 include the Gail Borden qv Building (1953), which houses the departments of biochemistry, physiology, microbiology, pharmacology, and the library; the 641-patient John Sealy Hospital and R. Waverly Smith Memorial Pavilion (1954); the Rosa and Henry Ziegler Hospital (1954), for patients with diseases of the chest; and the Randall Pavilion (1960), formerly the Negro hospital, which closed in 1958 and reopened after extensive remodeling for the needs of psychiatric patients.

The outpatient building, on the site of the old John Sealy Hospital and connected to the new hospital, opened its first three floors in 1964. Those floors provided space for an emergency room, X-ray facilities, clinic, and department of obstetrics and gynecology. When completed, the fourth through sixth floors provided clinic and research facilities for the departments of surgery, medicine, and neurology and psychiatry. The Sealy-Smith Professional Building, opened in 1964, furnished offices for many physicians who served as part-time members of the staff; the building also contained offices of the Sealy-Smith Foundation.

The Shrine Burn Institute, completed in 1965, contained facilities for research, medical training, and professional care of severely burned children. The institute, the first such endeavor in the United States, had thirty beds and was a philanthropic project of the Shriners of North America. Several dormitories were added to the campus, and extensive remodeling of the Keiller and Graves buildings (Galveston State Psychopathic Hospital) was completed.

Research facilities added since 1950 included a twelve-bed clinical study center for patient care and research in the prevention and management of diseases; a behavioral science laboratory in the department of neurology and psychiatry, which related the nervous system to behavior in parallel experiments involving humans and lower animals; a research computation center which made computers available for research data analysis; a birth defects center, designed for treatment of congenital malformations and for research into the causes of birth defects; and a center in the pediatrics department for genetic studies in mental retardation. During the 1964 fiscal year research grants exceeding three million dollars were awarded the faculty from various private and government sources. Endowments provided additional funds for research, construction, and professional chairs.

In 1960 the medical school curriculum was revised to include electives; thus, certain students were permitted to select an alternate program to complete medical school in three calendar years. By the regular 1974–1975 term, 735 students were enrolled; the faculty numbered about 300. The medical branch library was rated nationally among the first six medical school libraries in total number of journals received. Bound volumes in the stacks totaled approximately 99,000 by 1969.

During the 1970's plans included a twenty-two-million-dollar building program encompassing a new clinical science building, a basic science building, an animal care center, a library, an additional laboratory, a conference center with a six-hundred-seat auditorium, a building for the school of nursing, a children's center, and other renovations and expansions. In addition to the medical school, the medical branch at Galveston included the University of Texas Graduate School of Biomedical Sciences at Galveston and the University of Texas School of Allied Health Sciences at Galveston.qqv

Chief administrative officers of the medical branch since 1950 have been: Chauncey D. Leake, executive vice-president and dean, 1942–1955; John B. Truslow, executive director and dean, 1956–1964; and Truman G. Blocker, Jr., executive director and dean, 1964–1974. William C. Levin became president on September 1, 1974. See University of Texas, Medical Branch of (in Volume II); see also University of Texas System; University of Texas System School of Nursing.

University of Texas Medical School at Houston. The University of Texas Medical School at Houston was established in 1969 by the Sixty-first Texas Legislature to provide for the teaching and training of medical students, medical technicians, and other technicians in the practice of medicine. Classes opened in 1970 but were held in three other schools while classrooms were constructed in the Texas Medical Center.qv In October, 1972, the University of Texas Medical School at Houston became a part of the University of Texas Health Science Center at Houston.qv Enrollment in the fall of 1974 was 148

students, and Cheves Smythe served as dean. See also University of Texas System.

University of Texas Medical School at San Antonio. The University of Texas Medical School at San Antonio, originally named the South Texas Medical School, was authorized by the Fifty-sixth Texas Legislature in 1959. Construction of the school, located on a 100-acre site donated by the San Antonio Medical Foundation in the South Texas Medical Center complex in San Antonio, was not begun until 1966. In September, 1966, fifteen students enrolled and carried on their studies in the University of Texas medical schools in Dallas and Galveston until facilities could be completed in San Antonio. In March, 1967, the legislature renamed the school the University of Texas Medical School at San Antonio and made it a part of the university system. In September, 1968, a twelve-million-dollar facility opened its doors to 105 students, 56 of whom were freshmen, the remainder, transfers. A full-time faculty of eighty-four members taught under the new system, which abandoned the nine-month school session in favor of periods allowing from four to six weeks off during the year. The Bexar County Hospital, also within the medical center, was built integrally with the medical school as a teaching hospital. A further innovation was student-patient contact from the first year of study. F. Carter Pannill, Jr., was the school's first dean.

In October, 1972, the University of Texas Medical School at San Antonio became a part of the University of Texas Health Science Center at San Antonio.qv Enrollment in the fall of 1974 was 473 students, and Stanley Crawford was dean. See also University of Texas System.

University of Texas of the Permian Basin. The University of Texas of the Permian Basin was created as an upper-level coeducational institution by the Sixty-first Texas Legislature in 1969. The school opened in the fall of 1973 with an enrollment of 1,112. It is located on the 600-acre McKnight Site near Odessa. President of the school in 1973 was B. H. Amstead. In 1974 enrollment was 1,352 and V. R. Cardozier served as acting president; Cardozier was named permanent president on September 12, 1975. See also University of Texas System.

University of Texas Press. Although certain publications printed by the University of Texas printing division have borne the imprint "University of Texas Press" since the early 1900's, there was no organization by that name until 1950. In that year the University of Texas Press was established as a division of the University of Texas under the supervision of a faculty advisory committee and with a director appointed by the president of the university. By 1970 the press had published over 400 books, a large number of which were works dealing with Latin America and translations of Latin American fiction, poetry, and history. Perhaps the best known of these is Eloise Roach's translation of Juan Ramón Jiménez's *Platero y Yo* (1957). Other publications in the same field include translations of Jorge Luis Borges' *Otros In-*

quisiciones (1964), Agustín Yáñez's *Al Filo del Agua* (1963), Daniel Cosío Villegas' *Extremos de América* (1964), the poems of Rubén Darío (1965), and Garcilaso de la Vega's *The Florida of the Inca* (1951) and *Royal Commentaries of the Incas* (1965). The most monumental undertakings of the press have been the publication of the thirteen-volume *Handbook of Middle American Indians,* of which nine volumes were in print in 1970, and the two-volume *The Bird Life of Texas* (1974), by Harry Church Oberholser.qv The Latin American publications program of the press has received financial assistance from a number of sources, including grants from the Rockefeller Foundation and a revolving fund contributed to by the Pan American Sulphur Company.

Another large segment of the press' output has been comprised of books dealing with the history and natural history of Texas and the Southwest. Of these, the most popular has been Mary Motz Will's and Howard S. Irwin's *Roadside Flowers of Texas* (1961). The press has also published scholarly works and translations in a number of specialized fields, including literature, art, geology, mathematics, education, history, botany, biology, anthropology, and law. In addition to books, the press also publishes and distributes a number of monograph series and learned journals.

When the press opened in 1950, it employed three persons. It published three books during its first year of activity. In 1970 it employed thirty-two persons and was publishing an average of forty books per year. In 1965 it opened a London office in cooperation with six other university presses. Frank Wardlaw, the first director, was appointed to that position in 1950 and held that office until mid-1974. Philip D. Jones was named director, effective August 1, 1974.

BIBLIOGRAPHY: University of Texas Press, *Books in Print, 1969* (1969); Austin *American-Statesman,* April 10, 1966; *Texas Times,* February, 1968, January, 1969.

University of Texas at San Antonio. The University of Texas at San Antonio was established by the Sixty-first Texas Legislature in 1969 as a co-educational institution. Located on a 600-acre site in northwest San Antonio, the school began enrolling students in the fall of 1973, when 1,113 registered. The University of Texas Institute of Texan Cultures at San Antonio qv became a part of the University of Texas at San Antonio in February, 1973. Peter T. Flawn was president in 1974, when 1,620 students were enrolled. *See also* University of Texas System.

University of Texas School of Allied Health Sciences at Dallas. The University of Texas School of Allied Health Sciences at Dallas was approved by the board of regents in 1968; it first enrolled students in 1970. The school is a professional health educational institution for the undergraduate and certificate level. In October, 1972, it became a part of the University of Texas Health Science Center at Dallas.qv In the fall of 1974 enrollment was 174

students. John W. Schermerhorn served as dean that year. *See also* University of Texas System.

University of Texas School of Allied Health Sciences at Galveston. The University of Texas School of Allied Health Sciences at Galveston is a division of the University of Texas Medical Branch at Galveston.qv The school enrolled 164 students in the fall of 1974, when the dean was Robert K. Bing. *See also* University of Texas System.

University of Texas School of Allied Health Sciences at Houston. The University of Texas School of Allied Health Sciences at Houston is a division of the University of Texas Health Science Center at Houston.qv The school enrolled thirty students in the fall of 1974, when Alton Hodges was acting dean. *See also* University of Texas System.

*University of Texas School of Mines. *See* Texas Western College; University of Texas at El Paso.

University of Texas School of Public Health at Houston. The University of Texas School of Public Health was authorized by the Texas legislature in 1947. In March, 1967, the legislature renamed the school the University of Texas School of Public Health at Houston, and, located in the Texas Medical Center,qv it was first funded and activated in 1967 at Houston. In October, 1972, it became a part of the University of Texas Health Science Center at Houston.qv Enrollment for the fall of 1974 was 346 students, and Reuel A. Stallones served as dean. *See also* University of Texas System.

University of Texas Southwestern Medical School at Dallas. The University of Texas Southwestern Medical School at Dallas, formerly Southwestern Medical College of the University of Texas,qv Dallas, was renamed in 1967. In October, 1972, the medical school became a part of the University of Texas Health Science Center at Dallas,qv one of four centers coordinating biomedical units of the University of Texas System qv across the state.

In 1955 the campus site on Harry Hines Boulevard was occupied, and during the following ten years, administrative, faculty, and business offices, classrooms, laboratories, and research facilities were completed. The medical library, organized in 1943, contained approximately 68,000 volumes and 1,250 serial publications by 1964; by 1969 the library contained 87,288 volumes.

The Southwestern Medical Foundation worked in cooperation with regents of the university to continue to promote medical education, research, and the development of the Southwestern Medical Center. Fifteen hospitals in Dallas and its vicinity were utilized in teaching programs of the school.

The medical school granted doctor of medicine and master of medical arts degrees. A combined course leading to a bachelor of arts degree was offered on the basis of three years undergraduate work at the main university and one year at the medical school. Both M.A. and Ph.D. degrees were awarded by the graduate school of the main university on the basis of work completed in certain departments of the medical school, including anatomy, biochemistry, biophysics, microbiology, pharmacology, and radiobiology. A Ph.D. in clinical psychology might also be obtained from the medical school, which further provided numerous postgraduate programs for medical practitioners.

During the regular 1964–1965 term, the medical school had an enrollment of 400 students and a faculty of 152 members. In the fall of 1974 the enrollment was 627. Frederick J. Bonte was dean of the school in 1974. *See* Southwestern Medical College of the University of Texas (in Volume II); *see also* University of Texas System.

University of Texas Speech and Hearing Institute at Houston. The University of Texas Speech and Hearing Institute at Houston, formerly the Houston Speech and Hearing Clinic, became a part of the University of Texas System ᵠᵛ in 1971. From 1971 to October, 1972, it was designated the Division of Communicative Disorders of the University of Texas Graduate School of Biomedical Sciences at Houston.ᵠᵛ In October, 1972, the institute was renamed the University of Texas Speech and Hearing Institute at Houston and became a part of the University of Texas Health Science Center at Houston.ᵠᵛ *See also* University of Texas System.

University of Texas System. The University of Texas higher education system was reorganized statewide in 1967. Ranking among the ten largest systems of higher education in the nation, the system coordinated existing components and newly established institutions. The system is composed of general academic institutions, health science centers, a cancer center, and a nursing school. The University of Texas at Austin ᵠᵛ was the largest component institution in the system, and it included the University of Texas McDonald Observatory at Mount Locke and the University of Texas Marine Science Institute at Port Aransas.ᵠᵠᵛ Other general academic institutions within the system were the University of Texas at Arlington, the University of Texas at Dallas, the University of Texas at El Paso, the University of Texas of the Permian Basin, and the University of Texas at San Antonio.ᵠᵠᵛ

The health science centers, the cancer center, and the nursing school were organized in October, 1972, to coordinate university-wide programs in specific health areas. Under the administrative control of each of these three medical units there were several individual institutions. In 1974 the health science centers were (1) the University of Texas Health Science Center at Dallas,ᵠᵛ including the University of Texas Southwestern Medical School at Dallas, the University of Texas Graduate School of Biomedical Sciences at Dallas, and the University of Texas School of Allied Health Sciences at Dallas;ᵠᵠᵛ (2) the University of Texas Medical Branch at Galveston,ᵠᵛ including the University of Texas Medical School at Galveston, the University of Texas Graduate School of Biomedical Sciences at Galveston,ᵠᵛ the University of Texas School of Allied Health Sciences at Galveston,ᵠᵛ the Uni-

versity of Texas Marine Biomedical Institute at Galveston, and the University of Texas Medical Branch Hospitals at Galveston; (3) the University of Texas Health Science Center at Houston,ᵠᵛ including the University of Texas Medical School at Houston, the University of Texas Dental Branch, the University of Texas Graduate School of Biomedical Sciences at Houston, the University of Texas School of Allied Health Sciences at Houston, the University of Texas School of Public Health at Houston, and the University of Texas Speech and Hearing Institute at Houston;ᵠᵠᵛ and (4) the University of Texas Health Science Center at San Antonio,ᵠᵛ including the University of Texas Medical School at San Antonio, the University of Texas Dental School at San Antonio, and the University of Texas Graduate School of Biomedical Sciences at San Antonio.ᵠᵠᵛ The University of Texas System Cancer Center ᵠᵛ was composed of the University of Texas M. D. Anderson Hospital and Tumor Insitute at Houston and the University of Texas Environmental Science Park.ᵠᵠᵛ The University of Texas System School of Nursing ᵠᵛ included the University of Texas School of Nursing at Austin, the University of Texas School of Nursing at El Paso, the University of Texas School of Nursing at Fort Worth, the University of Texas School of Nursing at Galveston, the University of Texas School of Nursing at Houston, and the University of Texas School of Nursing at San Antonio.

The University of Texas System is governed by a nine-member board of regents selected from different parts of the state, nominated by the governor, and appointed by the senate for six-year terms. In 1973 the regents of the University of Texas System were Dan C. Williams, Jenkins Garrett, Frank C. Erwin, Jr., Mrs. Lyndon B. Johnson, A. G. McNeese, Jr., Joe T. Nelson, Frank N. Ikard, Joe M. Kilgore, and John Robert Peace.ᵠᵛ By 1975 Garrett, Erwin, Ikard, Kilgore, and Peace were replaced on the board by Thomas H. Law, James E. Bauerle, Walter Sterling, Edward Clark, and Allan Shivers. Chancellors of the system have included: James Pinckney Hart (1950–1954) and Logan Wilson, acting chancellor from January through September, 1954. The chancellor's office was discontinued at that time, and the office of president of the University of Texas System was instituted. Logan Wilson became president in October, 1954, and held the office until 1960, when the chancellorship form of administration was reinstated, and Wilson held the office of chancellor from 1960 to 1961. Harry Huntt Ransom held the office of chancellor from 1961 to 1971, when Charles LeMaistre was appointed chancellor, an office which he still occupied in 1975. *See also* University Fund, Available; University Fund, Permanent.

University of Texas System Cancer Center. The University of Texas System Cancer Center was established in October, 1972, to coordinate university-wide programs in cancer studies. In 1973 the center included the University of Texas M. D. Anderson Hospital and Tumor Institute at Houston and the

University of Texas Environmental Science Park qqv at Smithville. President of the University of Texas System Cancer Center in 1973 was R. Lee Clark. *See also* University of Texas System.

University of Texas System School of Nursing. The University of Texas System School of Nursing was established in 1890 as the John Sealy Hospital School for Nurses. It was originally organized as an independent school under a board of women managers. In 1897 it was transferred to the University of Texas and became the School of Nursing, one of the divisions of the medical branch. The board of regents of the University of Texas in May, 1967, renamed the school the University of Texas Nursing School (System-wide). In 1968 the school was composed of the University of Texas Graduate Nursing School at Austin, the University of Texas (Undergraduate) Nursing School at Austin, and the University of Texas (Clinical) Nursing School at Galveston.

In 1969 the Sixty-first Texas Legislature established a clinical nursing school in San Antonio and a four-year nursing school in El Paso. In 1971 the Sixty-second Texas Legislature established an undergraduate nursing school in Tarrant County. The legislature also authorized the nursing school to place clinical nursing students in Houston, enrolling them in the existing clinical nursing school in Galveston.

In October, 1972, the University of Texas Nursing School (System-wide) was renamed the University of Texas System School of Nursing, and the components of the system were the University of Texas School of Nursing at Austin, the University of Texas School of Nursing at El Paso, the University of Texas School of Nursing at Fort Worth, the University of Texas School of Nursing at Galveston, the University of Texas School of Nursing at Houston, and the University of Texas School of Nursing at San Antonio. Enrollment at the various schools in fall, 1974, was 1,058 students in Austin (all included in the total headcount of the main campus), 562 students in El Paso (371 of which were included in the total headcount of the main campus), 451 students in Fort Worth (all included in the total headcount of the main campus), 190 students in Galveston, 340 students in Houston, and 377 students in San Antonio. Marilyn D. Willman was president of the University of Texas System School of Nursing in 1974. *See also* University of Texas System.

University of Texas Tower, Murders at the. *See* Whitman, Charles Joseph.

*Unojita Indians. In 1683–1684 Juan Domínguez de Mendoza qv led an exploratory expedition from El Paso as far eastward as the junction of the Concho and Colorado rivers east of present San Angelo. In his itinerary he listed the names of thirty-seven Indian groups, including the Unojita, from which he expected to receive delegations. Nothing further is known about the Unojita, who seem to have been one of many Indian groups of north-central Texas that were swept away by the

southward thrust of the Lipan-Apache and Comanche Indians in the eighteenth century.

BIBLIOGRAPHY: H. E. Bolton (ed.), *Spanish Exploration in the Southwest, 1542–1706* (1916); C. W. Hackett (ed.), *Pichardo's Treatise on the Limits of Louisiana and Texas,* II (1934).

T. N. Campbell

Unpuncliegut Indians. The Unpuncliegut (Hunzpunzliegut) Indians, who probably spoke Coahuiltecan, lived on the southern part of the Texas coast. In the middle eighteenth century their settlements were along the mainland shore of the Laguna Madre in present Cameron and Willacy counties.

BIBLIOGRAPHY: W. Jiménez Moreno, "Tribus e idiomas del Norte de México," *El Norte de México y el Sur de Estados Unidos* (1944); G. Saldivar, *Los Indios de Tamaulipas* (1943).

T. N. Campbell

*Upland, Texas.

*Upper Colorado River Authority. *See* Colorado River Authorities.

*Upper Cuero Creek Settlement.

Upper Guadalupe River Authority. The Upper Guadalupe River Authority was created in 1939 by the Forty-sixth Texas Legislature "to control, develop, store, preserve and distribute" the waters of the upper Guadalupe and its tributaries. Because of problems unique to the hilly terrain and a narrow drainage basin in the Guadalupe headwater area, the creating act limited this conservation and reclamation district specifically to Kerr County. However, the authority functions cooperatively with the ten-county downriver region served by the Guadalupe-Blanco River Authority.qv

To be prepared for projected population growth, the authority in 1964 employed the Ambursen Engineering Corporation of Texas to undertake a preliminary investigation of the Upper Guadalupe River Basin. This report was completed and accepted in 1966, and a presentation study of a damsite in Kerr County was accepted for filing by the Texas Water Rights Commission qv in October of that same year. In a further effort to determine the total water resources available to residents of Kerr County, the authority in 1965 entered into a contract with the Texas Water Development Board,qv the United States Geological Survey, and the city of Kerrville, Texas, to conduct a study of ground water in the area of the authority. A report on the latter was submitted in 1968.

The authority is governed by a nine-man board of directors appointed by the governor for six-year overlapping terms. Operating revenue accrues from an ad valorem tax of five cents per one hundred dollars assessed valuation of property in the area served. Headquarters are in Kerrville.

W. E. Syers

*Upper Keechi Creek.

*Upper Meyersville, Texas.

Upper Nueces Reservoir. Upper Nueces Reservoir is in the Nueces River Basin in Zavala County, six miles north of Crystal City. The present dam and reservoir, located upstream from an earlier dam, was built by the Zavala and Dimmit counties' Water Improvement District No. 1 for irrigation and water supply. The original dam, built in 1926, was damaged by high water in October, 1927, and was repaired. The construction contract for the present dam and spillway was awarded on October 16, 1947, and the project was completed in March, 1948. The reservoir has a capacity of 7,590 acre-feet and a surface area of 316 acres at spillway crest elevation of 598 feet above mean sea level. The drainage area above the dam is estimated to be 2,160 square miles.

BIBLIOGRAPHY: Texas Water Commission, *Bulletin 6408* (1964).

Seth D. Breeding

*Upper Yorktown, Texas.

*Upshur County. Upshur County shifted from an agricultural to a nonagricultural economy after 1950. By 1963 only sixty-eight acres were planted in cotton. Major farm products were poultry, beef, dairy products, peaches, and truck crops. By 1965 the petroleum industry had gained major economic importance in the county; from 1931 to January 1, 1973, 252,549,352 barrels of oil had been produced, with oil exploration increasing yearly. With 59 percent of its land area forested, Upshur County had two mills capable of producing 30,000 board-feet of lumber daily in 1966. In the early 1950's several steel and iron plants were located in the county. Tourist attractions include Lake O' the Pines and the October Yamboree at Gilmer. The population in 1960 was 19,793; in 1970 it was 20,976, according to the United States census.

*Upson, Christopher C.

*Upton, John Cunningham.

*Upton, William Felton.

*Upton, Texas.

*Upton County. Upton County produced over 470,000,000 barrels of oil from 1925 to January 1, 1973. In 1970 the oil and gas industry was valued at over $76,000,000. Ranching contributes about one million dollars annually to the county. The farm income is mainly derived from sheep, cattle, and poultry. The population in 1960 was 6,239; in 1970 the population had decreased to 4,697, according to the United States census.

*Uracha Indians. This name is known only from a single entry (1764) in the baptismal records at San Antonio de Valero Mission qv in San Antonio. It may refer to the Orancho, who were mentioned by Juan Domínguez de Mendoza qv in 1684 as one of the Indian groups he was expecting to arrive at San Clemente,qv a temporary mission established on the Colorado River east of present San Angelo. No clues have yet been found to the linguistic and cultural affiliations of either group. J. R. Swanton listed Uracha as speaking a Coahuiltecan language, but he presented no evidence in support of this identification. The available evidence suggests occupation somewhere between San Antonio and the Pecos River.

BIBLIOGRAPHY: H. E. Bolton (ed.), *Spanish Exploration in the Southwest, 1542–1706* (1916); F. W. Hodge (ed.), *Handbook of American Indians*, II (1910); J. R. Swanton, *Linguistic Material from the Tribes of Southern Texas and Northeastern Mexico* (1940).

T. N. Campbell

Uranium Mining in Texas. Rare-earth minerals, including several uranium minerals, were mined for many years from a pegmatite dike on Baringer Hill in Llano County. This locality, now beneath the waters of Lake Buchanan, was made famous by William E. Hidden of Tiffany fame, who wrote of the rare minerals there and conducted the mining operations for a time.

In the intensive exploration for uranium following World War II a broad search was made in the Trans-Pecos region and in the red-bed region east of the High Plains, as well as in the Central Mineral region (the Llano Uplift). Several prospects in these regions were reported by geologists of the United States Geological Survey, the Atomic Energy Commission, and the Bureau of Economic Geology at the University of Texas (Austin). In the fall of 1954, G. H. Strodtman, a pilot for Jaffe-Martin and Associates, oil operators of San Antonio, discovered high radioactivity near old Deweesville in western Karnes County while making airborne radiometric surveys in exploring for oil. Some leases in the radioactive areas were acquired by the operators. About the same time or shortly thereafter, Clarence Ewers, while searching for opalized wood and testing for radioactivity with a hand counter near Tordilla Hill qv—a prominent *cuesta* (hill) in the western tip of Karnes County—discovered high radioactivity at the northern foot of the hill and found yellow uranium minerals both in sandstone rock exposures and in the soil in shallow pits that he dug nearby. "Sulfur," probably a misidentification of yellow uranium minerals, had been reported in the 1920's as occurring in this area.

Since the Texas Coastal Plain had previously been considered unlikely country for uranium, the discovery of ore of commercially interesting grade and quantity was a great surprise to many, and the discovery was followed by a mad scramble for leases and feverish prospecting by all known methods. By the summer of 1956 about fifteen prospects had been located along a narrow strip 300 miles long, extending from the vicinity of the Colorado River in Fayette County into Starr County to a few miles north of the Rio Grande. One eight-ton load of high-grade, hand-picked ore was taken from shallow pits at the foot of Tordilla Hill to a mill at Grants, New Mexico, in December, 1958. The first large-scale mining was begun in July, 1959, just west of old Deweesville, on Lyssy, Gembler, and Korzekwa properties. By December, 1960, the San Antonio Mining Company, a locally operating subsidiary of Climax Molybdenum Company, had mined and stockpiled one hundred thousand tons of moderately low-grade ore—pending the building of a processing mill. In 1961 a processing mill, built and operated by Susquehanna-Western, Inc., using an acid-leach, solvent-extraction process, started production of "yellow cake" that assays about 78 percent uranium oxide. In the spring of 1966, after original contracts with the Atomic Energy Commission had been fulfilled, the mill was shut down for a few months, but in June, 1966, it resumed operation under a new contract with the Atomic Energy Commission to furnish uranium concentrate to the West German government. All mining from 1961 to June, 1967, had been done by Susquehanna-Western, Inc., but by the fall of 1966 other companies were actively securing leases in the region.

The open-pit mines are as large as 120 feet deep and 500 feet wide; they are located mainly along a line extending from one mile east to four miles northeast of Tordilla Hill. However, ore has been produced from a mine fourteen miles northeast of Tordilla Hill (three miles east of Falls City) and from another, twenty-four miles southwest of Tordilla Hill (ten miles northwest of Three Rivers, in Live Oak County).

Recent exploration for uranium has been concentrated along a strip ten to twenty miles wide and about two hundred miles long, extending from Gonzales to Duval County.

BIBLIOGRAPHY: Dolan Hoye Eargle and John Luther Snider, *A Preliminary Report on the Stratigraphy of the Uranium-bearing Rocks of the Karnes County Area, South-Central Texas* (University of Texas Bureau of Economic Geology, RI 30, 1957).

D. Hoye Eargle

Urban and Regional Planning in Texas. From 1937 to 1957 only limited action occurred in the areas of planning and zoning in Texas. (For earlier history, *see* Planning and Zoning in Texas, Volume II.) In 1957 the legislature authorized the State Department of Public Health qv to provide planning assistance for political subdivisions and to accept grants from the federal government under the provisions of the Federal Housing Act of 1954 and from other sources. This was the beginning of the Urban Planning Assistance Program in Texas, designed primarily to assist communities with a population of fifty thousand or less. Over one hundred Texas cities have taken part in this program, developing comprehensive plans to guide their growth. Legislation was passed to give cities which were unzoned the authority to enforce building restrictions laid down by a plan or other instrument affecting subdivisions inside their boundaries, thereby giving a tool to guide the development of the cities.

The urban renewal legislation passed in 1957 led to comprehensive planning in several cities which took part; enabling legislation required a referendum before a program could be undertaken in a community, and some declined to participate. Feasibility studies were undertaken by some cities to determine what their respective needs were before undertaking any such program.

The Federal Aid Highway Act of 1962 required twenty-two urban places (of over fifty thousand population) in Texas to engage in comprehensive, cooperative, and continuing planning processes in order to participate in the development of transportation systems under the act; failure to cooper-ate would have meant exclusion from the program. The coordination of such urban planning has been done by the urban section of the Texas State Highway Department. qv

Although Fort Worth in 1909 and Dallas in 1910 demonstrated the first individual city planning efforts, the success was curtailed by inaction or incompletion. In the late 1920's, when the legislature began to take an interest in planning, citizen interest increased as well. In 1956 Fort Worth generated interest through the Gruen Plan for the redevelopment of its central business district. The plan was based on a regional socioeconomic analysis with application to the city's projected growth potential and land-use requirements, including the rehabilitation of downtown areas. The Dallas-Fort Worth metropolitan area felt the need for regional planning in that their projected population for 1980 was two and one-half million people within the many incorporated communities in Dallas and Tarrant counties. The same need was felt in other areas as well. Lack of state enabling legislation and the lack of a sufficient planning budget for the regional plan resulted in the failure of the Dallas-Tarrant County Regional Planning Group in 1955. The North Texas Council of Governments was making an effort to solve those problems which had been recognized ten years previously. By the middle of July, 1966, there were eight such metropolitan organizations in Texas, with more being formed.

The Lower Rio Grande Valley regional planning was given a boost in 1957 with a regional land-use sketch plan, projected to the year 2010, done as a demonstration project by the graduate city planning program of the University of Texas at Austin. In 1960 the necessity of the harmonious development of contiguous cities and regions on both sides of the Texas-Mexico border was recognized by the architects of Mexico and the United States in the "Charter of El Paso," which called for planning in the area as one region, not as two. The Texas Senate, in 1962, set up the Border Conference Committee to make studies of cooperation and development in common along the border, and with other border states of the United States, as well as with Mexico. In July, 1966, this committee and similar ones from California, New Mexico, Arizona, Nuevo León, Tamaulipas, Coahuila, Sonora, and Baja California met to discuss health, welfare, tourism, commercial interchange, culture, agriculture, livestock, wildlife, and international relations. Mexico had recently launched a border development program aimed at making the border a center of industry and tourism. State enabling legislation was needed to make this international regional cooperation feasible all along the border. The Planning Agency Council qv was set up as a part of the governor's office in 1965 in an effort to coordinate the activities of the various planning groups and to make available to towns information about government-sponsored programs in which they were eligible to participate. (*See* Planning Coordination, Division of, Governor's Office.)

The Texas Social Welfare Association, founded in 1909, has aimed at furthering the coordination of planning efforts. Surveys have been conducted at the request of small towns, helping them to develop and to take advantage of programs for development. In 1966 a diagnostic survey was undertaken at Mission, Texas, to determine what the citizens wanted and needed before urban renewal began economic and physical planning. The program was based on the opinion that problems developing in areas that had been rehabilitated stemmed from a lack of social information and consideration when physical and economic plans were drawn up for the areas. Trained interviewers were sent in to determine what the people of Mission wanted, and efforts to involve the citizens deeply in the planning process were made. This consideration of the social problems was considered an important step forward in planning in Texas.

A trend appeared to be developing in Texas toward greater coordination of planning efforts on the regional instead of the city level, possibly leading to a much more productive use of Texas' natural resources. See also Urban Renewal in Texas.

BIBLIOGRAPHY: League of Women Voters (Waco), *Blueprint for Planning* (1965); Hugo and Martha Leipziger-Pearce, *History of Urban Planning in Texas* (1965).

Hugo Leipziger-Pearce

Urban Renewal in Texas. Urban Renewal was the name given in 1954 to an expanded program of federal financial assistance, designed to revitalize urban areas through conservation, rehabilitation, and clearance action. On August 22, 1957, the Texas urban renewal law, granting Texas cities the authority to undertake urban renewal projects, became effective. The legislation came as a result of widespread interest in urban renewal among Texas cities, several of which had already initiated applications for federal renewal assistance under their home rule charter powers.

The program provided for an advance of federal funds to plan an urban renewal project, grants of a certain percentage of the net project costs, and temporary loans for the project. Cities of more than fifty thousand people could receive grants amounting to two-thirds of their net project costs; communities of fewer than fifty thousand people could receive grants which covered three-fourths of their net project costs. An urban renewal project consisted of the rehabilitation and conservation of sound but deteriorating structures, the acquisition of land and structures beyond rehabilitation or needed for public improvements, the clearance of land, the relocation of displaced project residents, and the installation of site improvements. Cleared land was offered for sale to public or private redevelopers; however, under certain circumstances, cleared land could be retained for planned public reuse.

In order to participate in the federal program, it was necessary for the city to possess legal power to use eminent domain for urban renewal purposes, i.e., the acquisition of private and public property for resale to private and public redevelopers. In Texas, where the home rule charter movement had

received widespread and enthusiastic acceptance, a considerable segment of legal opinion asserted that Texas home rule cities possessed the necessary urban renewal power. Several home rule cities amended their charters to provide specifically for the exercise of eminent domain. This action came just prior to the enactment of the state enabling legislation and was never tested in the courts.

As originally drafted, the state urban renewal law followed the provisions of so-called "Model Legislation." As enacted, however, the Texas urban renewal law contained a significant departure from the "Model Act," in that it provided that no city could embark on an urban renewal program without first gaining approval in an election.

Between 1957 and 1966 some fifty-four urban renewal elections were held by Texas cities. Thirty-six favorable verdicts and eighteen defeats were recorded for the program. The margins in both victory and defeat were overwhelming, with only seven elections being relatively close votes (five approving, two disapproving).

The program grew steadily during its early history in Texas. In August, 1966, there were a total of forty-nine projects in twenty Texas cities; twenty-seven projects were in execution, and the remaining twenty-two were developing plans for execution. The federal grant reserved for these projects totaled $85,122,627, and a total of 1,333.7 acres of land was to have been cleared and sold to public and private redevelopers. As of June 30, 1966, approximately one-third of that land had already been sold.

Seventeen of the twenty Texas communities were engaged in renewal projects involving rehabilitation of existing structures. Midway in 1966, 1,778 residential structures in these projects had been successfully brought to an acceptable standard by their owners, some with the assistance of special low-interest loans and some using special rehabilitation loans and grants.

By 1966 a total of 2,800 project families had been successfully relocated into decent, standard housing. Fifty-three percent, or 1,494 of these families, were able to purchase their own homes, 1,096, or 39 percent, were relocated in private rental housing; and the remaining 8 percent, or 210 families, were relocated into low-rent public housing units.

The Waco project, completed in June, 1964, was the first completed urban renewal project in Texas. The project involved the acquisition and clearance of sixty-three acres of badly deteriorated residential housing. The land was sold to Baylor University, which was redeveloping the land for university uses. In 1966 the city of Waco had six other urban renewal projects under way, with a combined capital grant reservation of $5,083,843. The combined projects, which included a general neighborhood renewal plan covering the central business district, included over one thousand acres of the city's area.

HemisFair qv in San Antonio occupied a ninety-two-acre site acquired and cleared by the city's urban renewal agency with the help of a $12,206,000 federal grant. Permanent reuse for most of the site was planned as a civic center, as well as a location for federal and state agency buildings. The Grand Prairie program, with two urban renewal projects and one code enforcement program under way, was proving highly successful in both the physical and social aspects of rehabilitation in residential areas. Austin, after experiencing considerable delays, was involved in urban renewal projects in the 1960's, seeking to upgrade residential areas and to enhance properties around the Capitol qv complex and the University of Texas campus.

During the 1960's three major concepts or policy trends were clearly emerging from the program on the national level. The most readily discernible trend was the shift in program emphasis from one dealing almost exclusively with the physical environment to one which included the socioeconomic aspect of urban life. Educational and training aids were made available through the Office of Economic Opportunity so that individuals could improve their earning ability; there was an attempt to alleviate social problems at the same time that housing and physical environment were being improved.

Another trend was the intensification of efforts to effect metropolitan or regional coordination in the approach to common urban problems. States were encouraged, through the availability of various federal planning grants, to establish some form of organization that could prepare plans for solving the traditional problems of overlapping and conflicting governmental jurisdictions in urban areas. In Texas the Planning Agency Council,qv created by the Fifty-ninth Legislature, represented an initial step in that direction. A further step was the constitutional amendment adopted by the voters on November 8, 1966, authorizing the consolidation of governmental functions between political subdivisions within counties of 1.2 million or more inhabitants (only Harris County at that time).

The third significant trend was the concept of positive guidance to achieve urban development goals in both the physical and socioeconomic environment. The execution of this concept was rather tentative, and it was expected that the new technology of computer and space science would greatly affect the manner of solving urban problems. *See also* Urban and Regional Planning in Texas.

BIBLIOGRAPHY: C. E. Schermbeck, "A New Era in Urban Development," *Public Affairs Comment*, XII (March, 1966).

C. E. Schermbeck

*Urbana, Texas.

*Urbantke, Carl.

*Urrea, José de. [This title was incorrectly listed in Volume II as Urrea, José.] José de Urrea was born in 1797 in the presidio of Tucson, Sonora (now Arizona). He was a military cadet in the presidial company of San Rafael Buenavista in 1809 and a lieutenant in 1816, participating in battles in Jalisco and Michoacán. In 1821 he supported the Plan of Iguala of Agustín de Iturbide.qv He participated in the anti-Iturbide Plan of Casa Mata and the siege of San Juan de Uluá. Affiliated with

the Plan of Montaño, Urrea was separated from army service, but in 1829 he reentered and fought in Tampico with Santa Anna qv against Isidro Barradas. He intervened in the Plan of Jalapa against the government of Vicente Román Guerrero qv and when Anastasio Bustamante qv came to power (1829–1830), Urrea was named to the secretariat of the command in Durango. He was made a lieutenant colonel in 1831. In July, 1832, along with Santa Anna, he declared for Gómez Pedraza, and in 1834 he assumed the command of the permanent regiment of Cuautla, near Cuernavaca, after having received the rank of colonel from Francisco Ellorriaga, whom he had supported. As acting general in July, 1835, he was sent to fight the Comanches in Durango, where he was commandant general and then governor in September and October.

He participated in the expedition to Texas in 1836 and was engaged in the conflicts at San Patricio, Agua Dulce, and Coleto.qqv Urrea was opposed to the withdrawal of Mexican troops ordered by the captive Santa Anna after the battle of San Jacinto. In 1837 he was named commandant general of the departments of Sinaloa and Sonora. In December, upon being passed over for the appointment of governor, he proclaimed the two departments under the federal system, whereupon he was designated constitutional governor and protector. He then turned over his executive office to the vicegovernor and marched on opposing forces at Mazatlán, where he was defeated. He fled to Guaymas and finally to Durango, where he became involved in yet another uprising. In 1839 he was captured and sent to Perote Prison.qv Later during an imprisonment in Durango he was rescued by his partisans to take part in a revolt. In 1842 he assumed the executive power of Sonora, which he held until May, 1844. In 1846 he fought against the United States in the Mexican War.qv He died in 1849.

BIBLIOGRAPHY: *Diccionario Porrúa de Historia, Biografía y Geografía de México* (1965).

Shelia M. Ohlendorf

*Urrutia, Joseph de (José).

*Ursuline Academies.

Ursuline Nuns. *See* Sisters, Ursuline; *see also* Ursuline Academies.

Uscapem Indians. The Uscapem (Iscapan) Indians, who were probably Coahuiltecans, lived on the lower Rio Grande. In the middle eighteenth century their main settlements were east of Reynosa, Tamaulipas. They also foraged and camped on the Texas side of the river, particularly in Cameron and Hidalgo counties.

BIBLIOGRAPHY: W. Jiménez Moreno, "Tribus e idiomas del Norte de México," *El Norte de México y el Sur de Estados Unidos* (1944); G. Saldivar, *Los Indios de Tamaulipas* (1943); C. Thomas and J. R. Swanton, *Indian Languages of Mexico and Central America and Their Geographical Distribution* (1911).

T. N. Campbell

*Usher, Patrick.

*Utaca Indians. In the late seventeenth century Utaca Indians were reported as living on both sides of the Rio Grande in western Texas and adjoining

Mexico. Their locations were never specified. In one document the Utaca were listed among tribes that lived between Durango, Mexico, and present Presidio, Texas; in another document they were listed among Texas tribes who were known to the Jumano Indians, a group that traveled widely in Texas. Although proof is lacking, the Utaca of these documents may be the same as the Quitaca encountered during the same period by Juan Domínguez de Mendoza [qv] on his journey from El Paso to the vicinity of San Angelo. These Quitaca seem to have been related to the Wichita of later times.

BIBLIOGRAPHY: C. W. Hackett (ed.), *Historical Documents Relating to New Mexico, Nueva Vizcaya, and Approaches Thereto, to 1773*, II (1926); C. W. Hackett (ed.), *Pichardo's Treatise on the Limits of Louisiana and Texas*, I (1931); F. W. Hodge (ed.), *Handbook of American Indians*, II (1910).

T. N. Campbell

*Utley, Texas.

*Utopia, Texas.

Utopian Socialists in Texas. *See* Bettina, Communistic Colony of; Cabet, Étienne; Considérant, Victor Prosper; Herff, Ferdinand; La Réunion; Utopia, Texas; Wolski, Kalikst.

*Uvalde, Texas. Uvalde, seat of Uvalde County, was laid out by German Texan architect William C. A. Thielepape (not Thielepope, as shown in Volume II). At one time known as the "honey capital of the world" Uvalde had a drastically reduced honey production in the early 1970's because of land clearance and extensive use of herbicides and pesticides. Uvalde had a United States fish hatchery and a tire test track, in addition to industries concerned with vegetable packing and processing, feeds, mining, and garment making. By 1970 the city had twenty-five churches, two banks, a hospital, a library, a newspaper, and a radio station. Southwest Texas Junior College and a new Texas A&M Research and Extension Center were located in Uvalde. Uvalde Extension Center, an upper-level center offering work beyond the sophomore year, was a division of Sul Ross State University (Alpine) in 1974.

Former Vice-President John Nance Garner,[qv] before his death, donated his brick home to the city for a museum and library in memory of his wife, Mariette Rheiner Garner. Uvalde was the birthplace and home of the present Texas governor, Dolph Briscoe, Jr. The population of Uvalde in 1960 was 10,293; in 1970 the count was 10,764, according to the United States census.

*Uvalde County. Uvalde County has an economy based on livestock. In 1966, 90 percent of the agricultural income was from cattle, sheep, goats, wool, and mohair. At that time there were 21,000 acres of irrigated land on which vegetables and cotton were grown. The average annual income from agriculture in the early 1970's was approximately $15 million, two-thirds of which came from livestock. Crops produced included wheat, corn, oats, and vegetables.

There was also a $1 million annual income from cedar post sales.

Garner State Park in the Frio River Canyon and the towns of Utopia and Concan were popular recreation attractions; Fort Inge and Camp Sabinal [qqv] were historic sites of interest. Uvalde County was also a major deer and turkey hunting area. From October to February beehives from all over the United States are brought into the county to take advantage of the many flowering plants of the season. Local honey production, however, was drastically reduced after 1969. Population in 1960 was 16,814; in 1970 it was 17,348, according to the United States census.

Uvalde County Limestone Rock Asphalt. The only limestone rock asphalt found to date in Texas in sufficient quantity and of marketable quality is located on approximately 75,000 to 100,000 acres in the southwest portion of Uvalde County and the southeast portion of Kinney County. It is an area of sedimentary limestone, quite porous, and every interstice is filled with bitumen. The strata are ten or twelve feet to forty or fifty feet in thickness. Natural erosion has brought to view most of the locations yet found, and it could not be said just what size the deposit may be, or if it is a continuous mass under the surface. The bitumen content varies from 1 percent, or less, to 20 percent in one known location. Its depth has not been proven below an approximate two hundred feet.

The first production in this locality was during the years of 1885 to 1895, by the Lathe Carbon Company, for the purpose of extracting the bitumen from the stone and to recover the ichthyol from the bitumen. Their operation was of short duration but was the beginning of activity where the community of Blewett is now. About 1898 the contracting firm of Parker-Washington from San Antonio surfaced several blocks of Market Street near its intersection with St. Mary's Street with material very crudely handled, which made a smooth and impervious surface for approximately twelve years. The street was torn out when the road was widened and otherwise improved. The first production of limestone rock asphalt for street and road surfacing was at the Blewett location in 1912. From 1920 to 1935 there was a total of six firms engaged in this work, but not all at the same time. No combined record is known to have been kept, but many millions of tons have been produced and used by cities of Texas and the Texas State Highway Department.[qv] In 1970 there were two firms in operation—Uvalde Rock Asphalt Company (continuous since 1912) and White's Uvalde Mines (since 1923). Their combined production during the late 1960's was one and three-quarter million tons or more yearly. *See also* Asphalt Belt Railway; Blewett, Texas; Dabney, Texas; Whitesmine, Texas.

John H. White

*Uvalde and Northern Railroad.

V

*Valda, Texas.

*Valdasta, Texas.

Valdéz, José Antonio. José Antonio Valdéz, the *bachiller padre*, was ordained a Roman Catholic priest at an early age and remained a controversial figure throughout his career in Texas. He was a participant in the 1813 battle of the Medina River qv and was cited for bravery; thereafter he remained in Texas as chaplain to Spanish and Mexican garrisons. He was chaplain to the Alamo garrison in 1815 and 1817; from 1817 until 1836 he was chaplain to the garrison at La Bahía-Goliad, although he was stationed at Nacogdoches several times during this period. In 1819 he accompanied the royal troops to Nacogdoches to repel James Long's qv first invasion. In 1821 he was at La Bahía qv where he conversed with Stephen F. Austin, who subsequently wrote that Valdéz was a well-educated, cultured, and affable gentleman. He was known for his courage, and he fought along with the troops in military encounters.

While at Goliad in 1820–1821, he applied to the Spanish governor of Texas, Antonio María Martínez qv for a grant of land, but no action was taken. Valdéz was commissioned as a chaplain in Agustín de Iturbide's qv army and probably was active on the patriot side. In 1824 he renewed his petition to the *Diputación Provincial de Tejas* and its president, José Antonio Saucedo,qv and was granted four leagues in the fork of the Guadalupe–San Antonio rivers. It appears that he already had established a ranch on the land at the time of his application. This ranch, which he operated until the early 1840's, was situated below the settlement on the Carlos de la Garza ranch. (*See* Carlos Rancho, Texas.) The padre officiated at the chapel on the Carlos ranch as well as at La Bahía.

In 1827 Padre Valdéz intervened on behalf of the Indians and negotiated the peace between them and the Austin colonists. The treaty, dated May 13, 1827, was signed at La Bahía, the padre being one of the signers. After the capture of Goliad in October, 1835, by George Morse Collinsworth's qv expedition, most of the Mexican population along with the padre evacuated to the Carlos ranch which, until the battle of San Jacinto, became the center of Texas Mexican resistance to the Anglo Texans. Valdéz was the leader of the loyalist resistance, probably organized the guerrillas who harassed Philip Dimitt's and James Walker Fannin's qqv garrisons, and cooperated with José Urrea's qv army in its invasion of Texas.

It was to break up this activity that Fannin dispatched the Red Rovers qv and some of Burr H. Duval's qv company to capture Valdéz and destroy the counter-revolutionists. Valdéz and other leaders were captured on one of these expeditions and ac-companied Fannin on the latter's retreat. They "dug in" during the battle of Coleto,qv and were liberated by Fannin's surrender. Valdéz and the Mexicans at Goliad apparently returned to their homes, but not for long. Many of them accompanied Vicente Filisola's qv retreat and probably took the archives of Goliad with them (the latter probability indicated by the presence of the papers in the Mexican national archives). The resurgent Texian troops appear to have visited the padre's ranch and reduced it to ruins, although there is some indication that Valdéz remained in possession of the property until 1843.

Valdéz apparently regarded his grant of 1824 as valid and did not apply as colonist of the Power and Hewetson Colony,qv which appears to have recognized and respected the grant to the extent of the four sitios called for, but to have questioned the excess. The colonial surveyors set apart four leagues at the *Paso de los Apaches*, and the empresarios admitted María de Jesusa Travieso and her son as colonists and granted them the remainder of the concession of 1824. Señora Travieso, who was the widow of a Spanish army officer, was the reputed wife of the padre and was said to have borne him several children.

During the early years of the Republic, Valdéz was priest of Bexar. Bishop John Mary Odin,qv after his arrival in Texas, unfrocked Valdéz and another priest at Bexar for their alleged "loose morals."

BIBLIOGRAPHY: C. E. Castañeda, *Our Catholic Heritage in Texas*, VI (1950); Hobart Huson (ed.), *Dr. J. H. Barnard's Journal* (1949); Hobart Huson, *Refugio*, I (1953); Virginia H. Taylor (trans., ed.), *The Letters Of Antonio Martínez, Last Spanish Governor Of Texas, 1817–1822* (1957); "Journal of Stephen F. Austin on his First Trip to Texas, 1821," *Southwestern Historical Quarterly*, VII (1903–1904).

Hobart Huson

*Valdez, Juan.

*Vale Creek.

*Valentine, Texas. Valentine, the smaller of the only two towns in Jeff Davis County, is a shipping point for cattle, lambs, and wool. The town reported five businesses in 1970. In 1960 the population was 420; by 1970 it had declined to 213, according to the United States census.

*Valentine Branch.

*Valenzuelo Creek.

*Valera, Texas.

*Valley Branch.

*Valley Creek.

*Valley Ford, Texas.

*Valley Mills, Texas. Valley Mills, a retail market and shipping point for Bosque County, and extending into McLennan County, claimed to have "the best water in Texas." In 1960 the population was 1,061; the count was 1,022 in 1970, according to the United States census.

*Valley Spring, Texas. [This title was incorrectly listed in Volume II as Valley Springs, Texas.]

*Valley View, Texas. (Comal County.)

*Valley View, Texas. (Cooke County.)

*Valley View, Texas. (DeWitt County.)

*Valley View, Texas. (Mitchell County.)

Valley View, Texas. (Runnels County.) In 1966 Valley View, in central Runnels County, consisted of a Baptist church building built in 1946 and a filling station. The Pearce school, built in 1887, was the first building on the site of Valley View, but it was not until 1908, when the Valley View Baptist Church began meeting in the old school building, that the present name was acquired. In 1923 the Runnels City Baptist Church building, originally constructed in 1886, was secured and moved to Valley View, and the old Pearce school building became a barn on the J. A. Patterson farm.

Valley View, Texas. (Upshur County.) Valley View, in central Upshur County, was founded about 1880. In the 1960's a large rural high school for Negroes and several small businesses and residences were located there.

Valley View, Texas. (Wichita County.) Valley View, in southwestern Wichita County, was founded in 1889. The community in the 1960's served a farming area.

*Valley Wells, Texas.

*Val Verde, Texas.

*Val Verde County. Val Verde County, named for the Civil War battle usually known as Valverde (and sometimes as Val Verde, as shown in Volume II), is one of Texas' leading sheep, lamb, and wool producing counties. First among Texas counties in the number of sheep raised in the 1950's and 1960's, it was also the leading sheep county in the United States in the early 1970's, with approximately 250,-000 head; goats numbered 200,000. Crop farming and dairy production were decreasing, but agriculture still accounted for 10 percent of the employment in the county in the mid-1960's. Most employment is in trade and services, with the accent on government jobs. Tourist attractions include Judge Roy Bean's qv saloon at Langtry, San Felipe Springs, and Fort Hudson.qv Amistad Dam, which was designed to eliminate the destructive floods which have occurred in the area, and Amistad Reservoir qv were also tourist and recreation attractions. The 1960 population was 24,461; in 1970 it was 27,471, according to the United States census, an increase of 12.3 percent. Approximately three-fourths of the county's population lived in the city of Del Rio.

*Van, Texas. (Leon County.)

*Van, Texas. (Van Zandt County.) Van had a 44.4 percent change in population in a decade, increasing from 1,103 in 1960 to 1,593 by 1970, according to the United States census.

*Van Oil Field.

*Vanall, Texas.

*Van Alstyne, Texas. Van Alstyne, in southeastern Grayson County, had approximately forty businesses in 1970, including manufacturers of clothing, building tile, and tire patches. There was a cotton gin and a plant which distributed stone for commercial use. Population in 1960 was 1,608; in 1970 it was 1,981, according to the United States census.

*Vanca Indians. This group is known from one chance meeting with Spanish travelers near the end of the seventeenth century. At this time the Vanca and several other Coahuiltecan bands ranged over the Nueces-Frio area between San Antonio and Eagle Pass.

BIBLIOGRAPHY: F. W. Hodge (ed.), Handbook of American Indians, II (1910).

T. N. Campbell

Vance, James Milton. James Milton Vance was born in San Antonio on March 11, 1857, the son of Frances E. (Tabor) and William Vance.qv He was educated at the old German-English School,qv San Antonio; Earlham Academy, Richmond, Indiana; and the University of the South, Sewanee, Tennessee.

His father was a merchant in San Antonio, and Vance's first business venture was in a partnership grocery store, Vance and Edwards, at the corner of Houston and Navarro streets from 1877 to 1881; this was the first store opened on Houston Street, now San Antonio's main business street. For reasons of health he gave up the store and established Hillside Dairy Ranch five miles north of the city, where he resided until his death.

He built up an outstanding dairy herd and became known throughout the state for his interest in dairying and agriculture. His was perhaps the first registered dairy herd in the Southwest. Hillside Ranch became a show place and was extensively written about in Texas farm papers before the turn of the century. Vance first introduced the DeLaval cream separator in Texas and became agent for the entire state and a large part of northern Mexico.

He was one of the organizers of the San Antonio International Fair and served as its secretary-manager from 1899 until its close in 1909. He was active on the board of directors of the San Antonio Chamber of Commerce, with special interest in the highway and agriculture departments, and was chairman of the latter for many years. He helped organize the Texas Jersey Cattle Club, the State Dairymen's Association, the Lone Star Poultry Association, and the Texas Farmers Congress. He was president of the Bexar County chapter of the Texas Pioneer Association at the time of his death. Vance belonged to the Episcopal church. He was appointed food administrator for Bexar County by Herbert Hoover and served in that capacity throughout World War I.

He was married to Mary Ellen Tobin on September 10, 1878; they had three daughters. Vance died on January 26, 1930, and was buried in the Tobin family plot in City Cemetery No. 1 in San Antonio.

BIBLIOGRAPHY: Frederick C. Chabot, With the Makers of

San Antonio (1937); *DeLaval Monthly* (September, 1908); *Texas Farm and Ranch* (October 19, 1895).

Zelime Vance Gillespie

Vance, William. William Vance was born in Ireland on December 13, 1813. He came to the United States with his father and brothers in 1826 and settled in New York. His father became engaged in the mercantile business, and William and his brothers followed in that line of work.

With his brothers, James and John, William operated establishments in both Arkansas and New Orleans, Louisiana, under the firm name of Vance and Brothers. With the outbreak of the Mexican War, he was appointed commissary agent for the American forces and came to San Antonio in 1845 with General Winfield Scott's army. Following the Mexican War, he and his brothers located permanently in San Antonio in 1848. Their mercantile store in San Antonio was on Alamo Plaza, opposite the present location of Joske's department store.

Vance and Brothers built the first army barracks in San Antonio, located at the present corner of Travis and St. Mary's streets. They also built a two-story building adjoining the barracks (facing Houston Street), which served as an army headquarters. The building was later converted into a hotel known as the Vance House. It has since remained a hotel location and is now the site of the Gunter Hotel.

The Vance firm was active in many endeavors; they operated an overland transportation system by stage, and once they contracted to return a nine-year-old boy, who had been kidnapped by Indians and rescued by Kit Carson, to his home in Brady, Texas. After the failure of an army project to train fifty-seven camels as prairie mounts for the cavalry, they bought most of them and sold them to a circus.

Vance was an early business leader of San Antonio and had extensive real estate holdings. He served as city alderman from 1860 to 1862, and he was an agent for the Confederacy in export trade.

Vance married Frances E. Tabor on June 4, 1856, in New York; they had a son James Milton Vance,qv and three daughters. He died on October 2, 1878, and was buried in the Masonic Cemetery in San Antonio.

Zelime Vance Gillespie

*Vance, Texas. (Colorado County.)

*Vance, Texas. (Real County.) [Out of alphabetical order on page 829, Volume II.]

*Vancourt, Texas.

Vandale, Earl. Earl Vandale was born on June 28, 1882, in Roane County, West Virginia, the son of John Andrew Adam and Olive A. (Crislip) Vandale. He received his formal education in the public schools and the University of West Virginia, where he studied law in 1902–1903. After teaching in rural schools between 1900 and 1908, he went into the oil and gas business, first in West Virginia, then in Ohio, in Oklahoma, and finally in Texas, where he was employed by the Magnolia Petroleum Company in 1922. By 1923 he was in the High Plains area of West Texas; from 1925 until his death in 1952 he made his home in Amarillo.

Vandale's business specialty was as a buyer, and he sharpened what must have been a native talent into a fine art. Just as he was tremendously successful in his vocation of acquiring oil and gas lands and leases, he was also successful in his avocation of purchasing rare books and documents relating to Texas. His initial interest, primarily in West Texas, grew not only to be statewide but also to encompass events, persons, and places related to or associated with the state as a whole. Within little more than two decades, Vandale had one of the largest and most valuable collections of Texas books then in private hands. He was aided in this achievement by the purchase of the H. P. N. Gammel qv collection, in addition to many other smaller collections from other estates. He submitted bids at auctions all over the nation and as far away as London, England; with his special buying ability, very often he was able to purchase from collectors who initially had no desire to sell. His pride and interest in books was not confined to acquisition, for he read his books as well and gave appraisals of their accuracy.

Vandale retired from his position with the Magnolia Petroleum Company on January 1, 1947. In 1948 he sold his Texana collection to the University of Texas to become a part of the Eugene C. Barker Texas History Center.qv He immediately started a second collection, broadening his field to include Western Americana. He referred to this collection as his "Mountain Men and Bad Boy Books."

Vandale was married first to Grace A. Burke on December 23, 1911; they had one son. His wife died on May 19, 1920, and he was married again, on March 21, 1925, to Vada Lee Davis. Vada Vandale had originally protested the expansion of the library from living room to guest room, to dining room, to halls. Soon, however, she too had book collector's fever and shared both the work and the enthusiasm in acquiring the second collection. After her death in 1960 Vandale's son, John, gave the Western Americana collection to the University of Texas to be a unit in the undergraduate Academic Center, the collection dedicated to the memory of Earl and Vada Vandale.

Although the University of Texas was the major beneficiary of Vandale's abilities and generosities, he also made significant contributions to libraries throughout West Texas and particularly to the Panhandle–Plains Historical Museum qv at West Texas State College (now West Texas State University) in Canyon. Under the auspices of the Panhandle-Plains Historical Society,qv he established the Vandale historical writing contest. He was particularly enthusiastic about and a generous contributor to the Junior Historian Movement qv of the Texas State Historical Association.qv Vandale was a member of the executive council and an officer of the Texas State Historical Association and served as its president from 1949 to 1951. He died in Amarillo on November 9, 1952, and was buried there.

BIBLIOGRAPHY: J. Evetts Haley, *Earl Vandale on the Trail of Texas Books* (1965); *Texian Who's Who* (1937).

Mary Joe Carroll

*Vandalia, Texas.

*Van Demark, Harry Van Deusen.

*Vanderbilt, Texas.

*Vanderpool, Texas.

*Van Der Stucken, Frank Valentine.

Vandeveer, Logan. Logan Vandeveer was born in Casey County, Kentucky, in 1815 or 1816. [The surname Vandeveer is spelled about eight different ways in official records, but the spelling used here is the way Logan Vandeveer actually spelled it, according to documents bearing his own signature.] He first came to Texas in 1833, returned to Kentucky for a short time, and then came back to Texas in 1835 with his close friend William H. Magill; the two men settled in the municipality of Mina qv (later Bastrop County). Vandeveer enlisted in the Texas Army qv on February 28, 1836, serving in the first regiment of Texas Militia and in the company of Mina Volunteers. He was wounded in the battle of San Jacinto and was discharged June 1, 1836. Vandeveer and Magill entered the Ranger service and fought Indians throughout the Bastrop area.

Vandeveer was married to Lucinda Mays (also spelled Mayes) in 1838 or 1839 in Bastrop County, and (by some accounts) they had seven children (although by the time of the 1850 census in what is now Burnet County, only four children were recorded). In 1838 Vandeveer received a land grant in the area that is now the city of Austin, but when the Republic decided on that site as the capital, his land was relinquished. He then received tracts of land in what is now Burnet County (for his war service) and purchased additional tracts there, land which is now part of the town of Burnet. By 1849 he and his family were living in Hamilton, also called Hamilton Valley (present Burnet), which was developing around Fort Croghan.qv Vandeveer and Magill secured a contract to provide beef and foodstuff for the fort, and by 1851 Vandeveer had another contract to furnish beef to Fort Mason, fifty miles distant. Vandeveer was influential in the petition to the state legislature in 1852 for the creation of Burnet County; he was also instrumental in having Burnet (formerly Hamilton) named county seat. Vandeveer, in that same year, was named Burnet's first postmaster. About 1854 Vandeveer and an associate by the name of Taylor erected the first permanent building in Burnet; it served as a post office and store and later (as it still did in the 1970's) as headquarters for the local Masonic lodge. In 1853 Vandeveer established the first school in Burnet, a one-room log cabin, and he brought in William H. Dixon, an Oxford University graduate, to teach French, Latin, and Greek, in addition to the more elementary lessons for the younger children.

In the late summer of 1855 Vandeveer, with a brother and three other men, took a large herd of cattle to Louisiana. He developed yellow fever near New Orleans and died on September 2, 1855, in the Parish of Plaquemines, where he was buried.

BIBLIOGRAPHY: Logan Vandeveer Papers (MS., Archives, Texas State Library, Austin); The Highlander (Marble Falls), April 13, 20, 27, 1972.

Frank C. Rigler
Tad Moses

Vandiver, Harry Shultz. Harry Shultz Vandiver, internationally known mathematician and professor at the University of Texas at Austin, was born on October 21, 1882, in Philadelphia, Pennsylvania, the son of Ida Frances (Everett) and John Lyon Vandiver. He attended the University of Pennsylvania in 1904–1905, was associated with John L. Vandiver, a customshouse broker, in Philadelphia from 1900 to 1919, and was a member of the United States Naval Reserve from 1917 to 1919. From 1919 to 1924 he was an instructor of mathematics at Cornell University. He began teaching at the University of Texas in 1924 as an associate professor of pure mathematics. In 1935 he was made a full professor. The university named him Distinguished Professor of Applied Mathematics and Astronomy in 1947, and he retired in 1966. At various times he was a visiting professor at the University of Chicago, Princeton University, the University of Indiana, and Notre Dame University.

Throughout his scholarly career he received numerous research appointments, including four Heckscher Research Foundation grants at Cornell University (1920–1923), two Guggenheim Memorial Fund grants (1927, 1930), and two Penrose Research grants from the American Philosophical Society (1934, 1940). He won the prestigious Frank Cole Prize of the American Mathematical Society (1931) for his paper "Fermat's Last Theorem," a study of the number theory of Pierre de Fermat, a seventeenth-century French lawyer and amateur astronomer. Vandiver's international reputation was established with this paper. He was the author of more than 175 scholarly articles contributing to such fields as number theory, finite algebras, fields, rings, and groups. He was recognized as a leading contributor on the history of mathematics, as well as on the laws of reciprocity, cyclotomic and relative Abelian algebraic fields, and constructive algebraic theories. He was a member of numerous scholarly organizations and was at various times editor of *Annals of Math* and *Journal of Mathematical Analysis and Applications*.

Vandiver was married to Maude Folmsbee Everson on July 25, 1923, and the couple had one son, Frank E. Vandiver, historian and educator. Harry Vandiver died on January 4, 1973, in Austin and was buried in Austin Memorial Park.

BIBLIOGRAPHY: Austin *American*, November 7, 1945, January 5, 1973; *Daily Texan*, February 24, 1955; Biographical File, Barker Texas History Center, University of Texas at Austin.

*Van Dorn, Earl.

*Van Dorn, Isaac.

*Vandyke, Texas.

*Vanetta, Texas.

*Vanham Branch.

*Van Horn, James Judson.

*Van Horn, Texas. Van Horn, seat of Culberson County, built a community center, three schools, and a new courthouse in the 1960's. Mining, ranching, and some farming support the economy of the town, which had three cotton gins and a carrot- and onion-packing shed. The 1960 population was 1,953; in 1970 the population was 2,240, according to the United States census, and the town had eighty businesses.

*Van Horn Creek.

*Van Horn Mountains.

*Van Horne, Jefferson.

*Vann, Texas.

*Van Ness, Cornelius.

*Van Ness, George.

*Van Raub, Texas.

*Van Vleck, Texas. Van Vleck, in Matagorda County, had a population of 1,051 in 1970, according to the United States census.

Van Zandt, Edmund Pendleton, Jr. [pseud. Tom Pendleton]. Edmund Pendleton Van Zandt, Jr., was born in Fort Worth on June 30, 1916, the son of Ethel (Young) and Edmund Pendleton Van Zandt. He attended schools in Fort Worth, the old Preston High School, and Texas Christian University, and he was graduated from the University of Texas. He was an honor graduate of Southern Methodist University Law School in 1949, where he was editor-in-chief of the SMU law review. He entered military service during World War II in 1942 and was a captain in the United States Marine Corps, serving as an overseas intelligence officer, Pacific Marine Air Wing, and later as secretary of the Naval Air Mission in Lima, Peru.

Van Zandt worked for oil companies in various jobs, as roustabout, oil scout, and foreign oil concession negotiator, in Venezuela and London. He returned to the United States in 1962 to become assistant to the president of the General American Oil Company of Texas at Dallas. In 1963 he joined the Fort Worth National Bank.

In 1952 Collier's magazine bought his two-part fiction serial, "Deep Test." Under the nom de plume Tom Pendleton he wrote The Iron Orchard, the story of a typical oil career blended with social satire. It won the Texas Institute of Letters qv fiction award in 1966 jointly with Larry McMurtry's The Last Picture Show. Hodak, a novel set in South America, was published in 1969, and Seventh Girl was published in 1970.

Edmund Pendleton Van Zandt died in Fort Worth on July 22, 1972, and memorial services were held there. He was married to Durelle Alexander, and they were the parents of three children.

BIBLIOGRAPHY: Dallas Morning News, November 20, 1966, March 27, 1969; Fort Worth Star-Telegram, September 7, 1952, July 22, 1972; Houston Chronicle, December 4, 1966; Biographical Files, Barker Texas History Center, University of Texas at Austin.

*Van Zandt, Isaac.

*Van Zandt, Khleber Miller.

*Van Zandt, Richard Lipscomb.

*Van Zandt, Free State of. See Free State of Van Zandt.

*Van Zandt County. Van Zandt County, one of the leading counties in the production of salt, has a diversified agriculture, including cattle raising, dairying, and the cultivation of truck crops and cotton. It was the leading Texas county in beef-breeding cows, with a $7.9 million cattle income in 1970. In 1963 the county ranked first in the state and third in the nation in production of sweet potatoes, and it continued in the 1970's as a leading producer. Total oil production in the county was over 385 million barrels between 1929 and January 1, 1973. Lake Tawakoni is the major tourist attraction. The 1960 population was 19,091; in 1970 it was 22,155, according to the United States census.

*Vaquero.

Vaquero Indians. The name Vaquero ("cow people") was applied by the Spanish to the nomadic bison-hunting Indians of present northwestern Texas and eastern New Mexico during the late sixteenth and early seventeenth centuries. They were evidently the same as the Querecho reported earlier in the same area by members of the Coronado Expedition.qv It is generally believed that the Vaquero were ancestral to the Apaches who later became known as Mescalero and Lipan, particularly the latter.

BIBLIOGRAPHY: G. P. Hammond and A. Rey (eds.), Don Juan de Oñate, Colonizer of New Mexico, 1595–1628 (1953); M. E. and C. H. Opler, "Mescalero Apache History in the Southwest," New Mexico Historical Review, XXV (1950); Albert H. Schroeder, A Study of the Apache Indians: The Mescalero Apaches, Part III (1974); Albert H. Schroeder, "A Re-analysis of the Routes of Coronado and Oñate into the Plains in 1541 and 1601," Plains Anthropologist, 7 (1962).

T. N. Campbell

*Vara.

*Varisco, Texas.

*Varner, Martin.

*Varners Creek.

*Varona, Gregorio de Salinas. See Salinas Varona, Gregorio de.

*Vasco, Texas.

*Vashti, Texas.

*Vásquez, Rafael. Rafael Vásquez was born in 1804 in Mexico City. He was appointed brevet brigade general in 1839 and was commandant general of Jalisco (state) in 1851–1852. Vásquez died March 9, 1854, in Mexico City.

BIBLIOGRAPHY: Service Records, Historical Archives of the Defense Ministry, Mexico City.

S. W. Pease

*Vattman, Texas. See also Vattmannville, Texas.

Vattmannville, Texas. Vattmannville, in southern Kleberg County, was named for a Catholic priest named Vattmann upon whose advice, apparently, a Catholic church was built on the site. The community was being called Vattmannville by 1909. In 1966 the place consisted of a small Catholic church, a parochial grade school, a community recreation hall, and several other buildings to house the priest and assistants. Vattmannville, or Vattman as local people often call and spell it, is more a community center for nearby farming families than a town. Approximately a dozen people lived there in the 1960's.

*Vaughn, Horace Worth.

*Vaughn, Texas.

*Veach, Texas.

*Veal, William G.

*Veale Creek.

*Vealmoor, Texas.

*Veals, Texas.

*Veal's Station, Texas.

*Veatch, John Allen.

*Vega, Texas. Vega, the seat, market, and shipping point for Oldham County, was incorporated in 1927 with a commission form of government. In 1967 Vega reported four churches, two schools, a bank, and a newspaper. The town also has grain elevators, farm implement houses, county and United States government offices, and several motels. Vega is the location of a county pavilion constructed in 1966. Businesses totaled forty in 1970. The 1960 population was 658; in 1970 the population was 839, according to the United States census, and this figure represented more than one-third of the population of Oldham County.

*Vehlein, Joseph.

*Velasco, Texas. See also Brazosport, Texas.

*Velasco, Battle of.

*Velasco, Treaties of.

*Velasco, Brazos, and Northern Railroad. See Houston and Brazos Valley Railway.

*Velasco Herald.

*Velasco Terminal Railway Company. See Houston and Brazos Valley Railway.

Velazquez, Eulalio. Eulalio Velazquez, a native of Mexico whose date of birth is not known, published the first regional Spanish newspaper, El Cosmopolita, in Alice, Texas, from 1903 to 1914. He also ran a private school on the second floor of the building in which he published his weekly newspaper. Here he taught Spanish and commercial and agricultural courses. He was a graduate of Baylor University School of Business in Waco, and he was also an accountant. Velazquez was an early contributor, through his progressiveness, to the cultural and material improvement of the Spanish-speaking citizens of the South Texas area.

In 1914 he moved to Kingsville and within a few months moved to Eagle Pass. In 1920 he returned to Mexico, where he lived successively in Chihuahua, Queretaro, Orizaba, and Veracruz. He died in Veracruz on September 18, 1941.

                                  Agnes G. Grimm

*Velma, Texas.

*Venado Bayou.

*Venado Indians. In the eighteenth century the Venado (Benado) Indians, whose name is Spanish for "deer," ranged from the vicinity of Duval County in southern Texas southward across the Rio Grande to the area around Cerralvo in northeastern Nuevo León. The Venado were among several Coahuiltecan groups for which San Juan Capistrano Mission qv was established in 1731 at San Antonio. Later, in 1757, many Venado entered the mission at Camargo, just south of the Rio Grande, and some were reported at this mission as late as 1807. The Venado were also represented at Mission San Francisco Vizarron in northeastern Coahuila.

BIBLIOGRAPHY: F. W. Hodge (ed.), Handbook of American Indians, II (1910); W. Jiménez Moreno, "Tribus e idiomas del Norte de México," El Norte de México y el Sur de Estados Unidos (1944); J. R. Swanton, Linguistic Material from the Tribes of Southern Texas and Northeastern Mexico (1940).

                                  T. N. Campbell

Vende Flechas Indians. These Coahuiltecan Indians are known through a single missionary report (1794) from Nuestra Señora del Espíritu Santo de Zuñiga Mission qv near Goliad. In this report they are listed as a subdivision of the Aranama, and at that time only six Vende Flechas remained. The name, which is Spanish for "arrow sellers," suggests specialization in a particular craft. Presumably the original territory of the Vende Flechas was the same as that of the Aranama.

BIBLIOGRAPHY: E. L. Portillo, Apuntes para la historia de Coahuila y Texas (1886).

                                  T. N. Campbell

Vending Commission, Texas. The Texas Vending Commission was created by the legislature in 1971 to regulate the vending machine industry. The commission is composed of nine members: three ex officio members (or their representatives)—the director of the state's Department of Public Safety, qv the commissioner of consumer credit, and the attorney general—and six members appointed by the governor, with the concurrence of the Senate, for overlapping terms of six years. No more than three of the appointed members may be at the time of appointment, or have been at any other time, owners or operators of any coin-operated machine. An executive director is employed by the commission as its chief administrative officer.

The commission collects an annual occupational tax levied on owners of coin-operated machines and licenses the operation of these machines. The commission makes rules and regulations for the enforcement and collection of the revenues, and it may suspend licenses for a period of at least one year for violation of its rules. Regulations also require that owners of music, skill, or any pleasure coin-operated machines not have concurrent financial interests in, or unauthorized dealings with, businesses selling alcoholic beverages. The commission can initiate investigations and hearings and can take other necessary measures to enforce this prohibition, including the initiation of civil proceedings through the attorney general's office.

BIBLIOGRAPHY: University of Texas at Austin, Guide To Texas State Agencies (1972).

*Venth, Carl.

*Venus, Texas.

*Vera, Texas.

*Veramendi, Juan Martín.

Veramendi Estate—New Braunfels. A suit to clear title to the Comal Tract, where New Braunfels is located, had originally been instituted by the heirs of Juan Martín Veramendi qv in 1852 for the purpose of recovering land settled by the Germans in 1845; in 1854 the Supreme Court of Texas decided in favor of the Veramendi heirs. The New Braunfels citizens offered to pay the debt (principal together with accrued interest) owed by the bankrupt German Emigration Company, the Adelsverein,qv but the heirs refused to accept the money. The case was brought up again in December, 1876, when the heirs of the Veramendi estate filed suit in the United States Circuit Court, demanding possession of the land. Hermann Friedrich Seele qv was the attorney and secretary for the Citizens Committee of New Braunfels which opposed the Veramendi claims; the case was finally settled on April 24, 1879, when the court rendered a decision in favor of the New Braunfels citizens. A bronze plaque with the text of the decision was placed on the pedestal of the statue in Landa Park,qv honoring the German pioneers of New Braunfels. *See also* Solms-Braunfels, Prince Carl of.

BIBLIOGRAPHY: Rudolph L. Biesele, *The History of the German Settlements in Texas, 1831–1861* (1930); Oscar Haas, "Teacher Seele Granted Leave to Plead Settlers' Land Case," New Braunfels *Zeitung-Chronicle*, June 27, 1966.

*Verand, Texas.

*Verdaguer, Peter.

*Verde Creek.

*Verdi, Texas.

Verhalen, Texas. Verhalen, a railroad switch on the Pecos Valley Southern Railway in Reeves County, was built in 1910 and named for a local farmer. There was never a town at the site.

*Verhelle, Texas.

*Veribest, Texas.

*Vernon, Texas. Vernon, seat of Wilbarger County, reported twenty-one churches, three banks, a library, two newspapers, and a radio station in the late 1960's. Businesses included those concerned with agricultural supplies and processing, seed breeding, milling of cotton and alfalfa, and manufacture of mobile homes and garments. The city was also an oil center in North Texas. Vernon had a second hospital completed in 1967, and it had plans for a geriatrics hospital. The 1960 population was 12,141; the 1970 population was 11,454, according to the United States census. In 1972 there were approximately 265 businesses in Vernon.

Vernon Center. The Vernon Center was opened early in 1970 and dedicated on May 28, 1970, as a state hospital facility of the Texas Department of Mental Health and Mental Retardation.qv Formerly a part of the Wichita Falls State Hospital,qv the center at Vernon received its first patients from the Wichita Falls hospital and also from direct admissions. Units were established geographically for alcoholics, ambulatory geriatrics, and mental retardates. Three outreach clinics were operational, with six more planned. Average daily census in 1970 was 491, and the superintendent was Frankie E. Wil-

liams. *See* Mentally Ill and Mentally Retarded, Care of, in Texas.

BIBLIOGRAPHY: Texas Department of Mental Health and Mental Retardation, *Annual Report, 1970.*

Vernon Regional Junior College. The voters of Wilbarger County approved the creation of a county junior college district in an election on January 20, 1970. A board of seven trustees was elected on January 22, and on April 9, 1970, David L. Norton was named president of Vernon Regional Junior College. A campus site, which in 1973 totaled 100 acres, was acquired at the intersection of U.S. Highways 70 and 287. The first phase of the building program included an Academic Science Center, Administration-Fine Arts Building, Applied Arts Center, Resource Material Center, and Student Activity Center. The college opened in the fall of 1972. Designed as a comprehensive community junior college, the curriculum included academic and technical-vocational subjects. There were 608 students in the first class, and 799 students were enrolled in the fall of 1974. Jim M. Williams was president in 1974.

*Verona, Texas.

*Vesey, Texas.

Vesicula Calculus. *See* Philips, William C.

*Veterans Administration Hospital, Amarillo. The Veterans Administration Hospital at Amarillo, for general medical and surgical patients, had a plant consisting of a four-story main building, a dietetics building, nurses' quarters, staff quarters, a chapel, recreation buildings, and five service and utility buildings. In April, 1973, the authorized bed capacity of the hospital was 146, and the staff included eleven full-time, thirty-eight consulting, and two attending doctors; there were thirty-five full-time nurses and one part-time nurse. One hundred twelve patients were treated at that time.

Veterans Administration Hospital, Big Spring. The Veterans Administration Hospital at Big Spring was established in 1950 for the general medical and surgical treatment of veterans. As of April, 1973, there were 250 authorized beds at the facility, with 226 patients there at that time. The staff included fifteen full-time and forty-five consulting doctors; there were fifty-three full-time nurses and one part-time nurse.

Veterans Administration Hospital, Bonham. The Veterans Administration Hospital at Bonham was completed in October, 1951. It had a capacity of 401 beds in April, 1973, including 230 domiciliary, 71 hospital (for general medical and surgical patients), and 100 nursing home care units. Three hundred sixty-eight patients resided in the hospital at that time. The hospital staff included eleven full-time, thirteen consulting, and four attending doctors; thirty full-time nurses were on the staff.

In 1970 the hospital was renamed the Sam Rayburn Veterans Administration Center. It is one of two centers in Texas (the other at Temple), where domiciliary beds are provided for veterans who do not necessarily need medical care, but who, having no home or relatives to care for them, live at the center.

*Veterans Administration Hospital, Dallas. In April, 1973, the Veterans Administration Hospital at Dallas had an authorized bed capacity of 775. The hospital, which handled general medical and surgical, tuberculosis, and neuro-psychiatric patients, had a resident population of 625 patients at that time. The hospital staff included 77 full-time, 9 part-time, 128 consulting, and 117 attending doctors; there were 180 full-time and 6 part-time nurses. In April, 1973, no patients remained on the hospital's waiting list. Increasingly, in the 1960's and 1970's, the hospital at Dallas (along with the one in Houston) was also used as a treatment center for alcoholism and drug addiction.

*Veterans Administration Hospital, Houston. The Veterans Administration Hospital at Houston was the largest unit in Texas in bed capacity in 1973, having a total authorization of 1,330. Several new buildings were constructed in the 1950's and 1960's, including a six-story building housing psychiatric patients and a seven-story building housing out-patient service and a research department. In a teaching capacity, the hospital was affiliated with five schools of nursing and the Baylor University College of Medicine for the training of medical students, interns, and residents. The hospital, which handled 1,194 general medical and surgical, tuberculosis, neuro-psychiatric, and nursing home care patients in April, 1973, employed seventy-one full-time, thirty-five part-time, one hundred eight consulting, and one hundred sixty-eight attending doctors on its staff. Two hundred sixty-eight full-time and twelve part-time nurses completed the Houston staff. In April, 1973, fifty-seven patients remained on the hospital's waiting list. Increasingly, in the 1960's and 1970's, the hospital at Houston (along with the one in Dallas) was also used as a treatment center for alcoholism and drug addiction.

*Veterans Administration Hospital, Kerrville. The Veterans Administration Hospital at Kerrville (referred to as Legion Branch, as shown in Volume II) treated general medical and surgical and tuberculosis patients. In April, 1973, the authorized bed capacity was 346, and 303 patients were being treated. The hospital staff included seventeen full-time, one part-time, and thirty-four consulting doctors; there were sixty-six full-time and two part-time nurses. At that time, twenty-two patients remained on the hospital's waiting list. The hospital was essentially for intermediate care of long-term patients.

*Veterans Administration Hospital, McKinney. In the 1950's and in the early 1960's, the McKinney Veterans Administration Hospital had an operating bed capacity of 812. On September 30, 1965, this hospital was closed down and its patients were transferred to other operating institutions. In June, 1966, the Texas Educational Foundation, Inc., through contract with the Office of Economic Op-

portunity, located the McKinney Center for Women in the hospital's facilities. *See also* Job Corps Program in Texas.

Veterans Administration Hospital, Marlin. The Veterans Administration Hospital at Marlin was established in 1950 for the general medical and surgical treatment of veterans. The facility has 222 authorized beds, and as of April, 1973, three patients were on the hospital's waiting list, while 196 patients were in the hospital. The staff included eleven full-time, one attending, and four consulting doctors; there were also one part-time and twenty-seven full-time nurses. The hospital was essentially for intermediate care of long-term patients.

Veterans Administration Hospital, San Antonio. The Veterans Administration Hospital at San Antonio admitted its first patient on October 29, 1973, and was officially dedicated on November 17, 1973, as the Audie L. Murphy [qv] Memorial Veterans Hospital. At capacity the facility was able to treat 700 in-patients, 180 of whom were neuro-psychiatric, the remainder general medical and surgical patients.

Veterans Administration Hospital, Temple. The Veterans Administration Hospital at Temple was established in 1946. Prior to that date, the facility was known as the McCloskey General Hospital (*see* McCloskey Veterans Administration Center, in Volume II). Treatment is available for general medical and surgical, tuberculosis, and neuro-psychiatric patients. In April, 1973, the authorized bed capacity was 740; 650 patients were being treated, and 95 patients remained on the hospital's waiting list. The staff included fifty-seven full-time, seven part-time, eighty-six consulting, and three attending doctors; there were also one hundred fifty-five full-time nurses on the staff.

Officially a Veterans Administration center, one of two in Texas (the other at Bonham), the center also provides 552 domiciliary beds for veterans who do not necessarily need medical care, but who, having no home or relatives to care for them, live at the center.

*Veterans Administration Hospital, Waco. The Veterans Administration Hospital at Waco, the largest such installation in Texas in the late 1960's with a capacity of 1,515 beds in November, 1968, was second to the facility at Houston in terms of bed capacity by 1973. The hospital, which exclusively cared for neuro-psychiatric patients, had a total of 1,066 patients in April, 1973, with no patients on the waiting list. The bed capacity was reduced to 1,100, and the hospital's staff included three part-time and thirty-three full-time doctors, assisted by one hundred eight full-time and two part-time nurses in April, 1973.

*Veterans Administration Hospitals in Texas. By 1951 construction had been completed on veterans hospitals in Big Spring, Bonham, and Marlin. The Veterans Administration Hospital, McKinney,[qv] was closed on September 30, 1965. Hospitals in operation in April, 1973, included Veterans Administration Hospital, Amarillo,qv with a capacity for 146 general medical and surgical patients; Veterans Administration Hospital, Big Spring,qv with a capacity for 250 general medical and surgical patients; Veterans Administration Hospital, Bonham,qv with a capacity for 401 general medical and surgical, domiciliary, and nursing home care patients; Veterans Administration Hospital, Dallas, qv with a capacity for 775 general medical and surgical, tuberculosis, and neuro-psychiatric patients; Veterans Administration Hospital, Houston,qv with a capacity for 1,330 general medical and surgical, tuberculosis, neuro-psychiatric, and nursing home care patients; Veterans Administration Hospital, Kerrville,qv with a capacity for 346 general medical and surgical and tuberculosis patients; Veterans Administration Hospital, Marlin,qv with a capacity for 222 general medical and surgical patients; Veterans Administration Hospital, Temple,qv with a capacity for 740 general medical and surgical, tuberculosis, neuro-psychiatric, and domiciliary patients; and Veterans Administration Hospital, Waco,qv with a capacity for 1,100 neuro-psychiatric patients.

The hospitals at Houston and Dallas are also used as treatment centers for alcoholism and drug addiction. Those at Bonham and Temple are centers with domiciliary beds, units for veterans who do not necessarily need medical care, but who, having no home or relatives to care for them, live at the centers. The Veterans Administration Hospital, San Antonio,qv admitted its first patient on October 29, 1973, with a bed capacity of 700, equipped for 180 neuro-psychiatric and 520 general medical and surgical patients.

Veterans' Affairs Commission. The Veterans' Affairs Commission was created by the legislature in 1947 as the successor to the office of the Veterans' State Service Officer,qv whose duties the new agency absorbed. The commission was composed of five gubernatorial appointees who served six-year overlapping terms and appointed the executive director. The agency's duties included assisting veterans or their survivors in filing, processing, and settling claims, and in explaining policies of the Veterans Administration, as well as federal and state laws which affected veterans.

Veterans of Foreign Wars in Texas. The first Veterans of Foreign Wars post in Texas was instituted on June 26, 1917, in San Antonio. It was known as Fort Sam Houston Post No. 76 and was organized by Arthur W. Pigott, "father of the VFW in Texas." Pigott joined the VFW in 1913 while on duty in San Francisco, California; after he transferred to Fort Sam Houston qv in 1916, he requested permission to organize a post there.

The post, with some twenty charter members, was short-lived, for with the beginning of World War I every member of the post went to war, a distinction that few other VFW posts could claim. Post 76 was reactivated about 1920 and was still active in 1974, with a membership of 550 members.

The Department of Texas, Veterans of Foreign Wars, was officially founded on April 21, 1921, when a charter was issued by the national headquarters of the organization. At the time of chartering, Texas had five VFW posts. They were Fort Sam Houston Post No. 76, San Antonio; Dallas Post No. 156, Dallas; Herbert D. Dunlavy Post No. 581, Houston; Camp Bowie Post No. 708, Fort Worth; and Buddy Moore Post No. 688, Palestine. During the early years of the Department of Texas organization, membership ranged from a low of 221 to a high of 969 at the end of the first administration. Department of Texas General Order No. 1 was issued on May 1, 1921, establishing temporary department headquarters in Houston. In the same directive R. H. McLeod of Houston was recorded as having been duly elected and installed as department commander.

The first new post organized within the Department of Texas was Davis-Seamon Post No. 812 in El Paso, mustered on July 25, 1921. Organization of other units followed. On July 15, 1921, the territory of the Department of Texas was enlarged by the admission of the state of Louisiana. The designation then was changed to the Department of Texas-Louisiana, and this additional territory increased the membership of the department by thirty-three, all members of Crescent City Post No. 351 in New Orleans. Later the New Orleans post withdrew from the department, and this action permitted the department to revert back to its original name.

The permanent headquarters of the department have been in Austin since August, 1946, with the first offices located at 801 Rio Grande Street. In 1966 the department headquarters were moved to the fifth floor of a modern five-story building, owned by the organization, at the corner of East 11th and San Jacinto streets.

In 1974 the Department of Texas consisted of twenty-eight districts, with 421 active posts. Each district elected a commander, who, with other elected and appointed statewide officers, comprised a council of administration which governed the finances and assets of the Department of Texas.

In 1974 the membership of the VFW in Texas was approximately 80,000; the year before, when it had reached a membership of 75,000, it became the largest veterans organization in the state. A state convention was held each year at a designated city, and department officers were elected at that time; a mid-year meeting was convened for the purpose of mid-year reports.

The Department of Texas produced one national commander-in-chief, Ted C. Connell of Killeen, who served during 1960–1961. Another Texan and past department commander, Julian Dickenson, held the key administrative office in the national organization in 1974. He was first appointed to that office in 1950; known as the adjutant general, Dickenson directed the national headquarters staff in Kansas City, Missouri.

Membership in the VFW was limited to veterans who served overseas in time of war or national emergency and had been awarded a decoration, ribbon, or occupation medal. The department's annual programs provided recognition for outstanding achievements by posts in all activities. An important part of the Veterans of Foreign Wars in Texas was the Ladies' Auxiliary, which also had districts corresponding to the VFW districts.

The objectives of the Veterans of Foreign Wars were fraternal, patriotic, historical, and educational. The motto was "Honor the Dead by Helping the Living." The official publication of the department was the *Texas VFW News*, a tabloid newspaper published monthly except August. It was begun in February, 1947, with Bruce M. Francis as its first editor. In 1973 F. M. Robinson was named editor.

F. M. Robinson

Veterans' Land Board. A constitutional amendment in 1946 authorized the establishment of the Veterans' Land Board. The board was constituted in 1949 and was composed of the governor, attorney general, and commissioner of the General Land Office,qv who were to administrate the Veterans' Land Program. The amendment authorized the legislature to empower the board to issue $25 million in bonds, the proceeds of which were to be used by the board for buying land to resell to Texas veterans of World War II. Another amendment in 1951 increased the amount of bonds that could be issued to $100 million and authorized the legislature to extend the benefits of the act to Texas veterans with service subsequent to 1945. Benefits of the program were made available to veterans of the Korean conflict, and in 1967 an amendment extended these benefits to veterans of Vietnam. Another constitutional amendment in 1956 changed the composition of the board to the commissioner of the General Land Office and two gubernatorial appointees and increased the amount of bonds to be issued to $200 million. Originally the veteran could purchase a minimum of twenty (later fifteen) acres of land, but no sale to any one veteran could exceed $7,500 in cost. In 1967 the maximum amount allowed was $10,000 to any one veteran, and in June, 1973, the minimum amount of land that could be purchased was reduced to ten acres. At that time the veteran was required to make a 5 percent down payment on the selling price, the balance payable at an interest rate of 5.5 percent over a forty-year period. On April 24, 1975, the maximum loan was increased to $15,000; all other existing requirements remained the same. *See also* Veterans' Land Board Scandal.

BIBLIOGRAPHY: Wilbourn Eugene Benton, *Texas, Its Government and Politics* (1961); Clifton McCleskey, *The Government and Politics of Texas* (1963); Stuart A. MacCorkle and Dick Smith, *Texas Government* (1964); University of Texas at Austin, *Guide To Texas State Agencies* (1972).

Dick Smith

Veterans' Land Board Scandal. Violation of the intent and purpose of the Veterans' Land Program through fraud and bribery was first brought to light in November, 1954, by Roland Kenneth Towery, managing editor for the Cuero *Record*. On looking into a report that two Cuero businessmen were entertaining Negro men after hours at the country club, Towery found that the two had paid the Negro caretaker at the club ten dollars for every

veteran he could persuade to sign an application for purchase of land under the Veterans' Land Act.

This act had been voted into law by the people of Texas in November, 1946, after proposal by the legislature. The plan was to issue $25 million in bonds, the proceeds of which were to be used by the state to buy land and to resell it to veterans at 3 percent interest on forty-year loans. In February, 1951, another $75 million was voted to be made available for such purchases. The only stipulations on the purchase were that the loan could not be for more than $7,500 and the tracts could not be less than twenty acres. A 5 percent down payment in cash was required, and the land had to be held for three years before resale. The law covering the program specifically provided for the permissibility of "block sales," which allowed two or more veterans to join together to buy land or let the state buy the land for them and resell it to them at twenty or more acres each. The reason for allowing such grouping was the realization that it would be difficult for veterans to buy twenty acres or more for as little as $7,500. It was this block sale of land which led directly to the intervention of promoters and the scandal which followed.

The administration of the Veterans' Land Program was delegated by law to a Veterans' Land Board qv made up of the governor, attorney general, and commissioner of the General Land Office.qv The commissioner of the land office was designated as the chairman of the board.

On investigating the report concerning the activities of the two Cuero men, Towery found that the veterans who were signing applications to buy land were not aware that they were doing so, having been told by unscrupulous land promoters that they were getting the land free or that they were applying for soldiers' cash bonuses. Amounts varying from ten to three hundred dollars were paid to veterans for their signatures. Many of those who signed were barely literate.

Towery took what he had learned to DeWitt County Attorney Wiley Cheatham, who revealed that he had been investigating reported irregularities in the land program since September, rumors having reached him that local veterans were receiving bills from the state for payments on land they did not know they had bought. Cheatham pledged Towery to secrecy until he could go to Austin and check with state officials on the matter. On his return to Cuero on November 5, 1954, he authorized Towery to print whatever he chose, saying that he had received no help or encouragement from officials in Austin.

Towery decided to check on the matter himself. He obtained an appointment with Bascom Giles, commissioner of the General Land Office and chairman of the board of the Veterans' Land Board. Giles at once denied any irregularities in the program in DeWitt County, attributing such reports to "politics" and the machinations of a former appraiser for the land office who had been fired.

Towery, struck by the fact that Giles was defending himself against charges of which he had not been accused, wrote the story for the Cuero *Record* on November 14, 1954. The story and those which followed won a Pulitzer Prize for Towery in 1955 for distinguished reporting of local affairs. It also set off an intensive investigation by the office of the attorney general under John Ben Shepperd (who was a member of the Veterans' Land Board at the time of the investigation), the Department of Public Safety qv under Homer P. Garrison,qv the state auditor's office, and the Senate General Investigating Committee. Governor Allan Shivers, as a member of the Veterans' Land Board, was also actively involved in the investigation.

Irregularities in the program were found to exist in DeWitt, Lavaca, Victoria, Dimmit, Uvalde, Zavala, and Bexar counties. Once investigations were begun, numerous charges were filed against various persons accused of taking part in the improper use of state monies and violating veterans' personal rights; twenty persons were indicted in nine counties; prison terms were ultimately assessed against Bascom Giles (often referred to as "the father of the Veterans' Land Bill"), who was indicted first in Austin on March 5, 1955, and charged with conspiracy to commit theft of $83,500 in state money in Veterans' Land Board deals. He was finally sentenced to serve six years in the state penitentiary at Huntsville, having received thirteen sentences totaling seventy-five years which were to be served concurrently. He entered prison in January, 1956, and was released in December, 1958. He was also heavily fined, and he paid back over $80,000 in judgments in civil suits which were filed against him. He was the first elected state official to enter prison for a crime committed while in office (though not in office at the time he was sentenced, since he declined to accept a ninth term as land commissioner, to which he had recently been reelected). Only two other persons, B. R. Sheffield of Brady and T. J. McLarty of Cuero, served prison sentences as a result of the crimes committed.

Civil suits forced the promoters to buy back the land and keep up the payments, and the state subsequently recovered most of the money. In order to prevent similar illegal proceedings in the future, steps were taken by the legislature to tighten loopholes in the land program. The Veterans' Land Program was still in existence in 1975. *See* Veterans' Land Board.

BIBLIOGRAPHY: Newspaper Files, Legislative Reference Division, Texas State Library, Austin.

Elizabeth Kaderli

***Veterans' State Service Officer.** *See also* Veterans' Affairs Commission.

***Vial, Pedro.**

***Viana, Francisco.** Francisco Viana was born in Málaga, Spain, in 1750. He served as a cadet in the Malta Cavalry and the Queen's Dragoons from 1763 to 1767, when he was promoted to ensign in the Mexican Dragoons. He served in Mexico for more than thirty-three years. He was commissioned a lieutenant on January 9, 1778, and advanced to captain on June 22, 1792. He led Mexican troops against marauding Apaches in Chihuahua and served as adjutant to his general on numerous occasions. He crushed the revolt of Zacualco and pursued smugglers and bandits in the Cañadas of Ceutla and Fistla. As interim *corregidor* of Real de Minas de Bolaños, he investigated complaints from the settlers against the Real Audiencia de Guadalajara in matters involving the militia and payment of tribute by the miners.

Acting in conjunction with Simón de Herrera,qv Viana organized Spanish defenses along the Sabine River and challenged American forces in the Neutral Ground qv between the Sabine and Arroyo Hondo in 1805–1806. As commandant of Nacogdoches in 1806, he ordered the reoccupation of Bayou Pierre and San Francisco de los Tejas Mission.qv Viana was the go-between in the negotiations of Herrera and General James Wilkinson, which resulted in the Neutral Ground agreement of November 5, 1806.

BIBLIOGRAPHY: C. E. Castañeda, *Our Catholic Heritage in Texas*, V (1942); C. W. Hackett (ed.), *Pichardo's Treatise on the Limits of Louisiana and Texas*, III (1941); Jack D. L. Holmes, "Showdown on the Sabine: General James Wilkinson *vs.* Lieutenant-Colonel Simón de Herrera," *Louisiana Studies*, III (1964).

Jack D. L. Holmes

***Viayan Indians.** This Coahuiltecan band is occasionally mentioned in eighteenth-century sources. A significant clue to Viayan identity is provided by one of these sources, which lists the Viayan and Piguique as subdivisions of the Pamaque. This suggests that the Viayan once lived in the same general area as the Pamaque and Piguique, that is, near the Gulf Coast between the San Antonio and Nueces rivers.

BIBLIOGRAPHY: F. W. Hodge (ed.), *Handbook of American Indians*, II (1910).

T. N. Campbell

***Viboras, Texas.**

***Vickery, Texas.**

***Vicksburg and El Paso Railroad.** *See* Texas Western Railroad.

***Victor, Texas.** (Erath County.)

***Victor, Texas.** (Harris County.)

Victor Braunig Lake. Victor Braunig Lake, formerly known as East Lake, is in the San Antonio River Basin in Bexar County, fifteen miles southeast of San Antonio on the Arroyo Seco. The project is owned and operated by San Antonio as a source for condenser-cooling water for a steam-electric generating plant. Construction began on June 6, 1961, and was completed in December, 1962. The lake has a capacity of 26,500 acre-feet and a surface area of 1,350 acres at operating water level elevation of 507 feet above mean sea level. The drainage area of the lake is nine square miles.

BIBLIOGRAPHY: Texas Water Commission, *Bulletin 6408* (1964).

Seth D. Breeding

***Victoria, Texas.** (Limestone County.)

***Victoria, Texas.** (Victoria County.) Victoria, seat of Victoria County, was a marketing and processing center for a cattle and oil area. The growth of industries in Victoria caused the population to double from 1950 to 1960. Among the recently built or expanded industries were producers of synthetic fiber raw material, oil field equipment, sand and gravel, concrete, and boats. In 1967 the city reported forty-eight churches, three hospitals, four banks, two libraries, two newspapers, three radio stations, and Victoria College.qv In 1970, 950 business establishments were reported. The population was 33,047 in 1960; the count in 1970 was 41,349, according to the United States census.

*Victoria *Advocate*.

Victoria College. Victoria College, Victoria, was established as a junior college of the Victoria school system on February 4, 1925. Classes first met in Patti Welder Junior High School while another adjoining building was constructed to house the college. Community growth during World War II and the postwar years provided the impetus to expand the college into a countywide institution in 1947.

In 1948 a $750,000 bond issue passed for the purpose of building a new campus. A separate forty-acre tract with four new buildings in northeast Victoria was occupied at the start of the 1949–1950 session. The board of trustees changed the name from Victoria Junior College to Victoria College in 1949. Another bond issue, for $700,000, provided funds in 1957 for a library (which contained 22,000 volumes in 1969), a science building, and other improvements. Eight permanent buildings were in use by 1965.

The evening school, an extension of the day school, offered academic courses and a limited number of technical and vocational courses. In addition to two-year associate of arts transfer programs, Victoria College offered a twelve-month vocational nursing course.

Between 1949 and 1965, enrollment increased from 240 to 1,184 students. By the 1974–1975 regular term, enrollment was 1,919, and the faculty numbered about sixty-five. Roland E. Bing served as president of the college in 1974.

*Victoria County. Victoria County, with an agricultural and oil economy, was rapidly becoming industrialized in the 1960's. Cattle raising was extensive, with grain sorghums, cotton, and other crops also contributing to the farm income, which averaged $11 million annually in the early 1970's. The petroleum industry produced 195,180,025 barrels of oil from 1931 to January 1, 1973. The barge canal connecting Victoria and the Gulf Intracoastal Waterway qv was newly constructed. The 1960 population was 46,475; in 1970 it was 53,766, according to the United States census.

*Victoria Creek.

*Victoria Female Academy. *See also* Presbyterian Education in Texas.

*Victoria Male Academy.

*Victoria Peak. The name "Victoria Peak" was changed (corrected) in 1959 by official action of the U.S. Board on Geographic Names to "Victorio Peak," since it was originally named for the Apache Indian chief, Victorio.qv *See* Victorio Peak; *see also* Victorio Canyon.

Michael H. McKann

*Victorio. Victorio, an Apache Indian chief, and his band of renegades were defeated for the first time on August 6, 1880, at the battle of Rattlesnake Springs (exact site unknown, since the springs no longer flow, but possibly located near the mouth of Victorio Canyon). They were forced to flee southward to Mexico, where in his last stand in the Tres Castillos Mountains, on October 16 (possibly October 14), 1880, Victorio and most of his band were killed in a battle with Mexican troops under the command of Colonel Joaquin Terrazas. A small number of the Indians escaped and returned to Texas to continue their depredations. The last Indian battle in Texas, which annihilated the remnants of Chief Victorio's band, was fought on the western rim of Victorio Canyon on January 29, 1881. *See also* Victorio Canyon; Victorio Peak.

BIBLIOGRAPHY: William Roger Lemmons, *The Recreation Potential of Victorio Canyon, Texas* (1971); Dan L. Thrapp, *Victorio and the Mimbres Apaches* (1974).

Michael H. McKann

Victorio Canyon. Named for Victorio,qv the Apache Indian chief, Victorio Canyon is located on the boundary between Hudspeth and Culberson counties, approximately twenty miles north of Van Horn. The canyon is a deep gorge with some sheer cliffs plunging 1,800 feet to the desert floor. The most spectacular scenery, found in a side canyon known as Little Victorio Canyon, has soaring, cathedral-like pinnacles. Within Victorio Canyon the Texas Parks and Wildlife Department qv established the Sierra Diablo Wildlife Management Area (*see* Wildlife Areas in Texas), where they have reintroduced the once-native bighorn sheep. Victorio Canyon was the area in which the battle of Rattlesnake Springs (near the mouth of the canyon and since dried up) took place, where Victorio and his band of renegades were defeated on August 6, 1880. The last Indian battle in Texas was fought on the western rim of Victorio Canyon on January 29, 1881. *See* Victorio; *see also* Victorio Peak.

BIBLIOGRAPHY: William Roger Lemmons, *The Recreation Potential of Victorio Canyon, Texas* (1971); Dan L. Thrapp, *Victorio and the Mimbres Apaches* (1974); Lyndon B. Johnson School of Public Affairs, University of Texas at Austin, *Victorio Canyon: A Natural Area Survey, Part IV* (1973).

Michael H. McKann

Victorio Peak. Victorio Peak, located in western Culberson County at the eastern edge of the Sierra Diablo Mountains, approximately twenty miles north of Van Horn, rises to an elevation of 6,350 feet (not 6,432 feet, as stated in Volume II under the title Victoria Peak). Victorio Peak was named for the Apache Indian chief, Victorio.qv The peak is located on the eastern rim of a spectacular canyon, Victorio Canyon, also named after the Indian chieftain. For many years maps of the area showed the name as Victoria Peak, but in 1959 the U.S.

Board on Geographic Names, by recognizing the name's true origin, approved the spelling "Victorio Peak" for all federal mapping. However, in 1975, when the U.S. Geological Survey was mapping the area again, a proposal was made to change the name back to Victoria Peak. Subsequent research found no support for the change, and it only strengthened the claim that the peak was named for Victorio. Sources did reveal that there has always been confusion by the non-Spanish-speaking Americans on how to spell the Apache chief's name. Military dispatches issued by the military officers engaged in battle with Victorio often spelled his name "Victoria," an incorrect feminine form of the name, and perhaps this was the origin of the misspelling. *See also* Victorio Canyon.

BIBLIOGRAPHY: William Roger Lemmons, *The Recreation Potential of Victorio Canyon, Texas* (1971); Dan L. Thrapp, *Victorio and the Mimbres Apaches* (1974); Lyndon B. Johnson School of Public Affairs, University of Texas at Austin, *Victorio Canyon: A Natural Area Survey*, Part IV (1973); Records, Culberson County Historical Commission, Van Horn, Texas.

Michael H. McKann

*Victory Field.

*Vidaurri, Texas.

Vidix Indians. This name is known from a single Spanish missionary report (1691), which indicates that the Vidix were neighbors of the Hasinai tribes of eastern Texas and lived an unspecified distance to the southwest. The name Vidix suggests identity with the Bidai, who lived in the same area, but the "Bidey" are also listed in the same report. The linguistic and cultural affiliations of the Vidix remain undetermined.

BIBLIOGRAPHY: J. R. Swanton, *Source Material on the History and Ethnology of the Caddo Indians* (1942).

T. N. Campbell

*Vidor, Texas. Vidor, in western Orange County, had grown by 1970 to include 111 businesses and served an industrialized area. One shopping center was completed and a second was under construction in the late 1960's. The school system included three elementary schools, one junior high school, and one high school. The 1960 population was 4,938; the 1970 population was 9,738, almost doubling in ten years, according to the United States census. *See also* Beaumont-Port Arthur-Orange Standard Metropolitan Statistical Area.

*Vieja Pass.

*Vieja Peak.

*Vienna, Texas.

*Viesca, Agustín.

*Viesca, José María.

*Viesca, Precinct of.

*Viesca, Sarahville de.

*View, Texas. (Comal County.)

*View, Texas. (Taylor County.)

*Vigilantes and Vigilance Committees.

*Vigo Park, Texas.

*Villa, Francisco (Pancho).

*Villa, Texas. (Hudspeth County.)

*Villa, Texas. (Mills County.)

*Villafaña, Angel de.

*Village Creek.

*Village Creek, Texas.

*Village Creek, Battle of.

*Village Mills, Texas.

*Villareal Creek.

Villareales, Texas. Villareales, in southern Starr County, west of Rio Grande City on U.S. Highway 83, had about eighty-five inhabitants in 1966, mostly engaged in farming.

*Villas, Texas.

*Villegas, Texas.

*Vince, Allen.

*Vince, Richard.

*Vince, Robert.

*Vince, William.

*Vincent, Texas.

*Vince's Bayou.

*Vince's Bridge. Controversy has surrounded Vince's Bridge since the battle of San Jacinto, when observers and participants gave conflicting accounts of the location and destruction of the bridge. Recent investigation supports the statements of earlier writers who believed the bridge was located on Sims Bayou,[qv] on the survey of Allen Vince,[qv] and not on Vince's Bayou,[qv] on the property of William Vince [qv] (as stated in Volume II). Allen Vince built and owned the structure, and no record shows that he ever owned land in the William Vince sitio; contemporary references to "the Vince Bridge" or to the bridge "on the bayou of that name" reflect the confusion caused by the adjoining lands of the two brothers and the close proximity of the two streams.

Frédéric Gaillardet,[qv] an early observer of Texas events, wrote in 1839 that the "bridge over Sims Bayou was the only means of retreat which lay open to the Mexicans" and that General Sam Houston's first command was to destroy it. Other early historians accepted Vince's Bayou as the site, but some later historians, after observing the location of the present historical marker at Vince's Bayou, have called the entire episode a myth. Vince's Bayou was hardly deep enough—despite heavy rains—or long enough to delay reinforcements reaching the Mexican Army, but Sims Bayou is a larger body of water and would take longer to head if the bridge were down. Santa Anna, in his attempted escape, came to a burned bridge on what he thought was the headwaters of Buffalo Bayou, and his secretary thought it was on the Brazos. Both could hardly have mistaken a small stream such as Vince's Bayou for much larger streams. Santa Anna was captured after being delayed by the burned structure, and Amasa Turner's [qv] account states specifically that Santa Anna was captured near "Sims Bayou," although most accounts place his capture at Vince's Bayou.

The idea for destroying the bridge has been credited to several participants, but mainly to Erastus (Deaf) Smith [qv] and to General Houston, who credited himself with the idea in a speech before the United States Congress. Houston's version was contradicted, however, by Moseley Baker,[qv] and by most accounts the idea was originally that of Deaf Smith. It is probable then that Smith proposed the idea, that after some debate Houston authorized it, and that Smith and others attempted to cut the span with axes. Since nearly every witness after the battle relates that the bridge was burned, it is also probable that Smith, with little time and few men, finally had to set fire to it.

The strategic importance of Vince's Bridge is more easily explained by its location on Sims Bayou. Its destruction prevented reinforcements from reaching Santa Anna by keeping news of his defeat from reaching General Vicente Filisola,[qv] his second-in-command, and also from General José Urrea,[qv] who had a division on the west bank of the Brazos River. In addition, the escape of nearly all of the Mexican survivors was prevented, including that of their commander. Further, if the destruction of the bridge was announced to the Texans just before the battle, as related in many accounts, they knew that there was little hope for retreat by either army.

BIBLIOGRAPHY: George L. Charlton, "Vince's Bridge: Question Mark of the San Jacinto Campaign," *Southwestern Historical Quarterly*, LXVIII (1964–1965); R. B. Humphrey, "The Vinces of Vince's Bayou," *Southern Historical Research Magazine*, I (1936); John H. Jenkins (ed.), "Amasa Turner's Account of the Texas Revolution," *Texana*, I (1963); Frédéric Gaillardet (James L. Shepherd, III, trans.), *Sketches of Early Texas and Louisiana* (1966); Chester Newell, *History of the Revolution in Texas* [1838] (1935); Edward Stiff, *The Texan Emigrant* [1840] (1968).

Phillip L. Fry

*Vine Grove, Texas.

*Vineyard, Texas.

*Vinson, Robert Ernest.

Vinson, William Ashton. William Ashton Vinson, son of John and Mary Elizabeth (Brice) Vinson, was born on a farm near White Oak, South Carolina, on December 22, 1874. After his parents moved to a farm near Sherman, Texas, in October, 1887, he attended public school in Sherman for two years and then entered Austin College Preparatory School. In 1896 he graduated from Austin College with second honors in his class. After graduation he began the study of law in the offices of Judge W. W. Wilkins in Sherman, took the Bar examination in open court, and received his license to practice.

In 1899 the partnership of Wilkins, Vinson and Batsell was formed, and he remained in this partnership until 1909. He married Ethel Clayton Turner of Sherman, on December 19, 1900; they had three daughters. On September 19, 1909, he and his family moved to Houston where he joined the firm of Lane, Walters and Storey. He remained with this firm until 1915, when he formed a law partnership with E. W. Townes under the name of Townes & Vinson. In 1917, after the death of Townes, James A. Elkins, who was then living in Huntsville, came to Houston and helped Vinson form the law firm which became Vinson, Elkins & Weems. This law firm became the largest in Houston and one of the largest in the nation.

Vinson was a director and general counsel of the Great Southern Life Insurance Company. In 1940 he was appointed by the Texas Supreme Court to serve on a committee to prepare a code of civil procedure for all Texas civil courts. He was also a member of the Texas committee on interpretation of rules of civil procedure. He served as a member of the library board of the Houston Public Library and was president of the library board from 1926 until he retired in April, 1951. He was also active in the establishment of the USO centers in Houston. Vinson died at his home on October 26, 1951, and was buried in the Forest Park Cemetery in Houston.

Ann Hornak

Vinta Indians. This name is known from a single Spanish missionary report (1691), which indicates that the Vinta were neighbors of the Hasinai tribes of eastern Texas. It is said that they lived an unspecified distance to the southeast of the Hasinai. The name suggests Caddoan affiliation (a Kadohadacho chief of the nineteenth century was known as Bintah, "the wounded man").

BIBLIOGRAPHY: J. R. Swanton, *Source Material on the History and Ethnology of the Caddo Indians* (1942).

T. N. Campbell

*Vinton, Texas.

*Viola, Texas.

*Violet, Texas.

*Violet Creek.

Virginia City, Texas. Virginia City, in Bailey County, about twenty-five miles southwest of Muleshoe, was platted on March 13, 1909, by Mathew C. Vaughn and Samuel D. McCloud. It was said by some that Virginia City was a bogus scheme to sell land and that the railroad which was graded through the town was a hoax. The town quickly vanished.

BIBLIOGRAPHY: Roysten E. Willis, *Ghost Towns of the South Plains* (M.A. thesis, Texas Technological College, 1941).

*Virginia Point, Texas.

*Vista, Texas.

*Vistador Creek.

*Vistula, Texas.

*Viterbo, Texas.

*Vivian, Texas.

*Voca, Texas.

*Vogel, Texas.

*Vogel's Valley, Texas.

*Vogelsang, Texas.

Voice of the Mexican Border. *Voice of the Mexican Border* was a magazine devoted to the history of the Big Bend Country; it was edited by Alice Jack Shipman, daughter of Pat Dolan, first sheriff of Jeff Davis County. The first issue was published in September, 1933, in Marfa, Texas, and was copyrighted in the same year. Publication was sporadic, and it is believed that only nine issues were printed, the last in 1938. At least one edition was published in El Paso. The magazine's staff in 1933 consisted of "Jack Shipman, sole owner, and editor"; O. L. Shipman (her husband), secretary-treasurer; and James H. Leaverton, assistant editor. Copies of the magazine are difficult to find, and they now bring premium prices.

Pat Wagner

Volente, Texas. Volente, about twenty miles northwest of Austin, on Lake Travis in Travis County, served as a post office from 1886 to 1909. The first postmaster was Andrew J. Stanford; the last was Allie Cluck Anderson. The inhabitants moved to the hillsides when the valley site of Volente was submerged by Lake Travis in 1934. In 1956 the community, then named Dodd City, reverted to the original name Volente. In the 1960's the village was unincorporated and had no post office.

*Volga, Texas.

*Volunteer Guard. *See* Texas National Guard.

*Von Bauer, J. H.

Von Behr, Ottomar. Baron Ottomar von Behr was born in 1810, the son of a high official of the duchy of Anhalt-Cöthen, Germany. He was a friend of geographer-naturalist Alexander von Humboldt and of Bettina von Arnim (*see* Bettina, Communistic Colony of).

It is not clear when von Behr first came to Texas, but he was in Houston in 1846 when he met an acquaintance, Hermann Spiess,qv and they returned to Europe together. Gustav Dresel,qv agent of the Adelsverein,qv wrote from Galveston in 1847 that von Behr and his family had arrived from Germany and were staying with him. It was the same year that von Behr's book for German immigrants— *Guter Rath für Auswanderer nach den Vereinigten Staaten von Nordamerika, mit besonderer Berücksichtigung von Texas*—was published in Leipzig.

Nicolaus Zink qv founded a settlement on the Sister creeks in 1847, and von Behr, following soon after, was the second settler. It is said that von Behr was the one who named the settlement Sisterdale (*see* Sisterdale, Texas). This colony of German intellectuals was an important stop forty-six miles from San Antonio on the historic Pinta (Pintas) Trace, which led to Fredericksburg and on west. In the Galveston *Zeitung,* June 7, 1848, von Behr's name appeared on a list of prominent Texas Germans who would vouch for the favorable Texas climate, the land and land prices, the farming potential, and the friendliness of the Indians.

The Comal County census of 1850 lists Ottomar von Behr (age 35), his wife, Louisa Katzfass (age 27), and three children. In October, 1853, von Behr was one of the four singers from Sisterdale who attended the first *Saengerfest* in New Braunfels (*see* Texas State Singing Society). He raised a breed of sheep that he had developed by crossing those he had brought from Germany with a Mexican breed. In his complex of log and *fachwerk* cabins on the banks of the Guadalupe he had a lending

library (possibly the first in Texas), held court as justice of the peace of his precinct, and is said to have operated the post office. He was a meteorologist and a naturalist. Prominent travelers, among them Prince Paul of Würtemberg, John Russell Bartlett,qv and Frederick Law Olmsted,qv visited the von Behr household and commented on its contents of books, pictures, and a harpsichord in the wilderness culture of the Latin colony (*see* "Latin Settlements" in Texas).

Von Behr owned property in Germany and made regular trips back there to collect his rents; on one trip he took his daughters by his first marriage to enroll in school. He died on a later trip to Germany in 1856. His wife remained in Texas to rear their four children, whose descendants were living in the Sisterdale area in the 1970's.

BIBLIOGRAPHY: John Russell Bartlett, *Personal Narrative of Explorations and Incidents in Texas, New Mexico, California, Sonora, and Chihuahua,* I (1854); Rudolph Leopold Biesele, *The History of the German Settlements in Texas, 1831–1861* (1930); Viktor Bracht (Charles Frank Schmidt, trans.), *Texas in 1848* (1931); Samuel Wood Geiser, *Naturalists of the Frontier* (1948); Frederick Law Olmsted, *A Journey Through Texas* (1857); Dresel Papers, Hermann Spiess Papers (MSS., Oscar Haas Archives, New Braunfels).

Paul C. Ragsdale

*Von Blücher, Felix A.

*Von Claren, Oscar.

*Von Ormy, Texas. Count Adolph von Ormy and his wife possibly had as many as twenty servants (not two hundred, as stated in Volume II) working in the house and on the grounds of the castle-like residence they purchased from Enoch Jones,qv original owner and builder. The town of Von Ormy had a population of approximately 264 in 1971.

Frank X. Tolbert

*Von Ross, George M.

*Vontress, Texas.

Von Wrede, Friedrich Wilhelm, Jr. Friedrich Wilhelm von Wrede, Jr., was born in Germany on December 31, 1820, the son of Demoiselle Margarete Henriette Charlotte (Greven) and Friedrich Wilhelm von Wrede, Sr.qv He came to the United States with his parents on the sailing vessel *Manko,* arriving at New Orleans on January 5, 1836.

After extensive travels with his father to East Texas, St. Louis, and New York, he returned to Germany in 1843. In 1844 he returned to Texas as secretary to Prince Carl of Solms-Braunfels,qv who was sent to Texas by the Adelsverein qv to make arrangements for the settling of German immigrants. Von Wrede was one of the group who accompanied John O. Meusebach,qv Solms' successor, to the San Saba River in West Texas to make a peace treaty with the Indians (*see* Meusebach-Comanche Treaty).

He later entered private business in Fredericksburg, and from 1850 to 1851 he was county clerk of Gillespie County. He represented that area in the Eighth Texas Legislature, from 1859 to 1861. With the beginning of the Civil War in 1861 he enlisted in the Gillespie Rifles, 31st Brigade, under Captain Charles H. Nimitz.qv

Friedrich Wilhelm von Wrede, Jr., was married to Sophie Bonzano (sister of Mary Bonzano, who was married first to Henry Kessler qv and then to Henry Francis Fisher qv); the von Wredes had four children who were born in Fredericksburg. Sometime after February 2, 1865, the family returned to Germany, where another child was born about 1866. They lived in Wiesbaden, Germany, from 1866 to 1871. No records beyond 1871 have been found.

BIBLIOGRAPHY: Friedrich W. von Wrede (Chester W. Geue, trans.), *Sketches of Life in the United States of North America and Texas* (1970); Kirchen-buch of the Protestant Congregation, Fredericksburg, Texas (Book No. I, 1865); Gillespie County Courthouse Records; Solms-Braunfels Archives (MS., Archives, University of Texas at Austin Library); Texas Confederate Index (Microfilm, Archives, Texas State Library, Austin).

Chester W. Geue

Von Wrede, Friedrich Wilhelm, Sr. Friedrich Wilhelm von Wrede, Sr., was born in Oberhausen, Detmold, Germany, on February 18, 1786, the son of Friedrich von Wrede and his second wife Johannette Lucie Christiane von Bardeleben. Details of his early life are not well known, although judging from the book he wrote, he must have been well educated. He served in the Hessian army for ten years, during which time he fought against Napoleon at Waterloo; he was discharged in 1817, after attaining the rank of captain. Von Wrede was married in Detmold on May 12, 1813, to Demoiselle Margarete Henriette Charlotte Greven, of Bielefeld, Germany; they had one son, Friedrich Wilhelm von Wrede, Jr.qv In the years following his military service von Wrede planned to immigrate to Texas, and on January 5, 1836, he, his wife, and their son arrived in New Orleans on the ship *Manko*. Threats of war with Mexico prevented him from settling in Texas, although he visited the state long enough to qualify for a grant of land in Van Zandt County. After his wife's death in New Orleans in 1837, von Wrede, sometimes accompanied by his son, traveled and made notes of his observations in America. He returned to Germany in June, 1843, joining his son

there (who had arrived eight days earlier); with the editorial help of Emil Drescher, in Cassel, he compiled and published *Lebensbilder aus den vereinigten Staaten von Nordamerika und Texas* (1844). [This was translated and edited over one hundred years later, by Chester W. Geue, with the title *Sketches of Life in the United States of North America and Texas* (1970).]

Von Wrede's *Sketches*, an epistolary travel book, is a generally realistic account of the opportunities and difficulties of colonists on the American frontier, especially in Texas. The book helped to influence prospective German settlers to come to Texas (*see* Germans in Texas), despite the negative effect of von Wrede's own violent death in Texas the following year. Von Wrede returned to Texas in 1844 as an official of the Adelsverein qv with, in Emil Drescher's words, "the joyful anticipation of sketching for the German motherland, new pictures of the flourishing health and well-being of its daughter colony in Texas." For a time von Wrede was manager of the Adelsverein's Nassau Farm qv in Fayette County. On October 24, 1845, while camping on a return trip from Austin to New Braunfels, von Wrede and Oscar von Claren qv were killed and scalped by Indians at a place referred to as Live Oak Spring, ten to twelve miles from Austin, probably near Manchaca Springs. They were buried at the site of the massacre by United States soldiers, who gave them military honors.

BIBLIOGRAPHY: Rudolph Leopold Biesele, *The History of the German Settlements in Texas, 1831–1861* (1930); Samuel Wood Geiser, *Naturalists of the Frontier* (1948); Friedrich W. von Wrede (Chester W. Geue, trans.), *Sketches of Life in the United States of North America and Texas* (1970); Solms-Braunfels Archives (MS., Archives, University of Texas at Austin Library); Solms-Braunfels Archives (MS., Sophienburg Museum, New Braunfels).

Chester W. Geue

*Voss, Texas.

*Votaw, Texas.

*Voth, Texas.

*Vreeland, Texas.

W

*Waco, Texas. Waco, county seat of McLennan County, was a trade, manufacturing, and agricultural processing center in the mid-1970's. The city was the home of several United States government agencies, including the Veterans Administration regional office and a new federal Youth Corps project. Waco was also the site of the Texas State Technical Institute qv (formerly the James Connally Technical Institute), established by the Texas A&M University System,qv and Baylor University.

On May 11, 1953, a tornado struck the downtown area of Waco, killing 114 persons and injuring hundreds more. Some 196 business buildings and 150 homes were destroyed (*see* Tornadoes in Texas).

The city quickly began rebuilding, however, and in 1964, Waco was the first city in Texas to complete an urban renewal project (*see* Urban Renewal in Texas). Between 1957 and 1962 eight new parks, a new fire station, and a $450,000 library were constructed.

In the mid-1960's the city reported one hundred thirty-seven churches, thirty-six public schools, four libraries, six banks, three newspapers, six radio stations, two television stations, four hospitals, and an airport. Waco's population in 1960 was 97,808. In 1970 the population was 95,326, making Waco the state's thirteenth largest city, according to the

United States census. *See also* Waco Standard Metropolitan Statistical Area.

*Waco Army Air Field. *See* Connally Air Force Base; James Connally Air Force Base.

*Waco, Beaumont, Trinity, and Sabine Railway Company.

*Waco Classical School.

*Waco County.

*Waco *Examiner.*

*Waco Female College. F. C. Wilkes qv (not F. C. Wilks, as stated in Volume II) was one of the founders of Waco Female College.

*Waco Female Seminary.

*Waco Indians.

*Waco and Northwestern Railroad Company.

Waco Reservoir. Waco Dam and Waco Reservoir are in the Brazos River Basin in McLennan County, two miles west of Waco on the Bosque River. The Waco Reservoir Project is owned and operated jointly by the United States Army Corps of Engineers, Fort Worth District; the city of Waco; and the Brazos River Authority.qv This reservoir inundated old Lake Waco. A new dam was started on June 13, 1958, and was completed in 1965. The reservoir serves for flood control, conservation storage, and recreational purposes. At conservation storage elevation of 455 feet above mean sea level, the capacity is 152,500 acre-feet with a surface area of 7,260 acres. The reservoir has 573,900 acre-feet of flood control storage capacity, and the drainage area above the dam is 1,652 square miles.

BIBLIOGRAPHY: Texas Water Commission, *Bulletin 6408* (1964).

Seth D. Breeding

*Waco Springs.

*Waco Springs, Texas.

Waco Standard Metropolitan Statistical Area. The Waco Standard Metropolitan Statistical Area, created in 1949 by the United States Bureau of the Budget, covers the 1,034 square miles of McLennan County near the center of Texas. The county is bisected by the Brazos River, which is joined within the corporate limits of Waco by the Bosque River. The 1960 population for the county was 150,091. In 1970 the population was 147,553, according to the United States census. In addition to the city of Waco, other towns within the Waco SMSA, with their 1970 populations, are: Bellmead, 7,698; Beverly Hills, 2,289; Lacy-Lakeview, 2,558; Northcrest, 1,669; Robinson, 3,807; Woodway, 4,819; McGregor, 4,365; Moody, 1,286; West, 2,406; and Mart, 2,183. Smaller communities are: Speegleville, Crawford, China Spring, Axtell, Lorena, Bruceville, Eddy, Rosenthal, Downsville, Elm Mott, Leroy, Ross, and South Bosque.

During the years following World War II there was a significant change in the basic economy of the Waco area. Historically a planting region and a major inland cotton-producing and marketing center, the area shifted to industrial and commercial development in the postwar years. The number of owner-operated farms dwindled with an attendant increase in urban residence and employment. By the mid-1970's manufacturing industries represented the leading source of family income. Principal manufactured products included automobile tires, glass containers, structural steel, cement, church furniture, textiles, toys, millwork, laundry machinery, and corrugated fiberboard and cartons. The important Rocketdyne facility at McGregor was a primary supplier of solid fuel propellants for the military, and during 1966 a large plant was established in Waco for production of bomb casings.

Agricultural produce, however, remained an important supplement to the Waco area economy. In 1960 McLennan County ranked sixth among Texas counties in the number of farms. In the early 1970's the agricultural income averaged over $23 million annually, with cotton, grain sorghums, livestock, and poultry products the leading contributors. The city of Waco was a major producer of processed poultry, and McLennan County was the headquarters for several farm organizations, including the Texas Farm Bureau,qv the Texas Cotton Association, and the Texas Certified Seed Association.

Waco, the county seat, was the industrial, commercial, and marketing center for the county. With a 1960 population of 97,808, Waco was also the population center of the county. In 1970 the city's population was 95,326. Waco was headquarters for an air force unit and contained a branch of the Federal Aviation Administration. The city maintained army, navy, marine, and national guard reserve units.

Long renowned as an educational center, Waco is the home of Baylor University, established initially by the Baptist denomination at Independence in 1845. Also at Waco are Paul Quinn College, established there in 1872 by the African Methodist Episcopal church; Texas State Technical Institute; and McLennan Community College,qqv a new two-year junior institution. It is also the headquarters for the Masonic Grand Lodge of Texas. The Armstrong Browning Library qv at Baylor houses the most extensive collection in existence of the works and personal effects of the poet Robert Browning and his wife, poet Elizabeth Barrett Browning.

Waco Reservoir qv provides recreation for the area. Within the city of Waco are the 680-acre Cameron Park and several smaller parks; nearby is Mother Neff State Park (*see* Parks, State). Other tourist attractions include the old suspension bridge across the Brazos in Waco which is, along with several old historic homes, being preserved by the Heritage Society of Waco. The area celebrates annually with the Heart O' Texas Fair and Rodeo. *See also* Waco, Texas; Standard Metropolitan Statistical Areas in Texas.

BIBLIOGRAPHY: *Texas Almanac* (1967, 1969, 1971, 1973).

Roger N. Conger

*Waco State Home. Waco State Home was placed under the administration of the Texas Youth Council qv by the Fifty-fifth Texas Legislature. On

August 31, 1965, the multiservice program of the home was caring for 288 children. Of this number, 239 were in residence at the home, 10 were in paid foster homes, and 38 were either with relatives on temporary home trial placements, in pre-adoptive placements, in free foster homes, in job placements, or in college. In 1970 there were 300 children in the home, and those of scholastic age attended Waco public schools on an annual contract basis, rather than attending school on the grounds. The superintendent at that time was J. Ludwick.

BIBLIOGRAPHY: Texas Youth Council, *Annual Report* (1965); *Texas Almanac* (1971).

William T. Field

*Waco Tap Railroad Company. *See* Waco and Northwestern Railroad Company.

*Waco *Times-Herald*.

*Waco University.

Wade, Houston. Houston Wade was born in Fayetteville, Fayette County, on August 14, 1882, the son of Ida (Meitzen) and Tyler Wade. He worked for the La Grange *Journal* until the early 1900's, when he moved to Houston; there he was employed with the postal service until 1940, when he retired to his farm near Hackberry in Lavaca County.

Wade was one of the organizers of the Sons of the Republic of Texas,qv and he served on its state executive committee for many years. He discovered the original document, drawn by Sam Houston, that founded the Order of San Jacinto,qv an honorary order of knights which was revived by the Sons of the Republic of Texas in 1941. He worked on the project to compile the first complete list of the men of Captain Nicholas Mosby Dawson's qv command, who were slain in the Dawson Massacre.qv (The manuscript of this work is in the Archives of the University of Texas at Austin.)

Wade wrote articles on Texas heroes that were published, mainly in the 1930's, in the Masonic *Texas Grand Lodge Magazine*. His books and brochures include *An Early History of Fayette County* (1936), written in collaboration with Leonie Rummel Weyand; *Thumbnail History of Fayette County* (1941); and *David Wade, A Texas Pioneer* (1943). Books that he compiled were *The Dawson Men of Fayette County* (1932); *Masonic Dictionary, Republic of Texas* (1935); *Notes and Fragments of the Mier Expedition* (1937); and *David G. Burnet Letters* (1944). Houston Wade's papers, including his scrapbooks and biographical sketches of the men of the Mier Expedition,qv are in the Archives of the Texas State Library.qv Wade was also an advocate of historical markers; he took part in the erection of a monument to Father Michael Muldoon qv near Hostyn and the memorial tower on Monument Hill qv near La Grange. He died on October 30, 1947, in Hallettsville and was buried in Fayetteville. He was survived by his wife, Ida Carson Wade.

BIBLIOGRAPHY: "Texas Collection," *Southwestern Historical Quarterly*, LI (1947–1948); Houston *Post*, November 1, 1947.

Hobart Huson

*Wade, John M.

*Wade, Nathan.

*Wadsworth, Texas. (Hale County.)

*Wadsworth, Texas. (Matagorda County.)

*Waelder, Jacob.

*Waelder, Texas. Waelder, in Gonzales County, had a population of 1,270 in 1960 and 1,138 in 1970, according to the United States census.

Wærenskjold, Elise Amalie. Elise Amalie Wærenskjold was born on February 19, 1815, in Dypvåg parsonage, Kristiansand diocese, Norway, the daughter of Lutheran minister Nicolai (Niels) Seiersløv and Johanne Elisabeth (Meldahl) Tvede, both of whose families were Danish-born patriots of the newly formed independent country of Norway. She was educated at home by private tutors, and at nineteen she became a teacher, a rare step for a woman at that time. In Norway she is still remembered as a woman leader (*foregangskvinne*). After teaching in Tønsberg she went to Lillesand and opened a handicraft school for girls which, although denied public funds, remained open until after 1845. In 1839 she married a young sea captain, Svend Foyn, who was to become the founder of Norway's whaling industry, a powerful and wealthy figure in modern Norwegian history. The marriage, which began without the customary reading of bans, ended in an amicable separation in 1842, and the couple maintained a friendship throughout their long lives. Elise assumed her maiden name, signing "E. Tvede" to the articles on temperance she had begun to write. No doubt influenced by her father's stand for temperance, she became involved in the movement and in 1843 published a pamphlet on the evil effects of the use of brandy.

When Christian and Johan Reinert Reiersen qv immigrated to Texas, she assumed the editorship of their magazine *Norge og Amerika*, a position which she held from 1846 until she immigrated to Texas in 1847. She joined Reiersen's colony of Normandy in October, 1847, and on September 10, 1848, married the leader of the immigrating party, Danish Norwegian Wilhelm Wærenskjold, not knowing that her divorce had not become final. She was notified when the divorce was granted in Norway on January 10, 1849. The Wærenskjolds acquired rights to a square mile of land at Four Mile Prairie, Van Zandt County, where a number of Norwegian settlers had moved, and expected to raise cattle; but the Civil War ended their plans, and Wilhelm went into milling, farming, and contracting. During the 1850's their three sons were born. The couple took an active part in the life of the Norwegian community, in the affairs of the Lutheran church, and in the temperance movement among the settlers. In January, 1866, their youngest son died, and in November of the same year Wilhelm was murdered by an Anglo American.

Through the hard years of drouth, locust plagues, and poverty on her farm, Elise Wærenskjold sold magazine subscriptions, books, and garden seeds, and she taught school. Then, at long last, she asked for and received financial aid from her former husband, Svend Foyn. Her numerous letters from the late 1840's until the mid-1890's remain an invaluable source of information on Norwegian immigrant life in Texas. She maintained a lively interest in current European literature, subscribed to Norwegian, German, and English newspapers, and constantly requested books in her letters home. She wrote for Norwegian publications, defending the Norwegian settlements against detractors, and later wrote of the settlers themselves and their descendants. She steadfastly held to her early belief in freedom for women; except for her opposition to slavery before the Civil War, she had little interest in American politics. She died on January 22, 1895, at the home of her eldest son, Otto Wærenskjold, in Hamilton, Texas, after having lived at Four Mile Prairie for forty-six years.

BIBLIOGRAPHY: Theodore C. Blegen, *Land of Their Choice* (1955); C. A. Clausen (ed.), *The Lady with the Pen: Elise Wærenskjold in Texas* (1961); Carlton C. Qualey, *Norwegian Settlement in the United States* (1938); Institute of Texan Cultures, *The Norwegian Texans* (1970); Estelle G. Nelson, *A First Lady of Texas* (1943); Philip D. Jordan, "J. Tolmer—Spurious Traveler," *Southwestern Historical Quarterly*, LXV (1961–1962).

Crystal Sasse Ragsdale

*Waggener, Leslie.

*Waggener, Leslie, Jr.

*Waggoner, Daniel.

*Waggoner, William Thomas.

*Waggoner Ranch.

*Wagner, Texas. (Hartley County.)

*Wagner, Texas. (Hunt County.)

*Wagner Creek.

*Wagon Wheel.

*Wagram, Texas.

*Wahrenberger, John.

Wainwright, Jonathan Mayhew. Jonathan Mayhew ("Skinny") Wainwright was born in Walla Walla, Washington, on August 23, 1883, the son of Robert Powell Page and Josephine (Serrell) Wainwright. Following in the footsteps of his father, he entered West Point, graduated in 1906, and took his first troop command with a cavalry unit on the Texas border. During his forty-five years of army service he was stationed at Texas forts in the cavalry at various times. He was promoted through the grades to brigadier general by 1938.

In October, 1940, he was assigned to duty in the Philippines under the command of General Douglas MacArthur. When MacArthur left Bataan, the command was turned over to Lieutenant General Wainwright, who was taken prisoner by the Japanese at the surrender of Corregidor.

Wainwright spent three and one-half years in Japanese prison camps. He returned to the United States at the end of the war, at which time he was awarded the Congressional Medal of Honor and made a full general in September, 1945. He was assigned command of the Fourth Army at Fort Sam Houston in San Antonio, Texas, in January, 1946,

and retired from that command on August 31, 1947. Having formed an affection for Texas during his tours of duty there, he decided to make it his home.

He was married to Adele Howard Holley on February 18, 1911, and they had one son. On September 2, 1953, Wainwright died in Brooke Army Hospital, San Antonio. He was buried with full military honors at Arlington National Cemetery on September 9, 1953.

*Waite, Carlos Adolphus.

*Waka, Texas.

*Wake, Texas.

*Wake Village, Texas. Wake Village, in Bowie County, had a population of 1,140 in 1960 and 2,408 in 1970, according to the United States census.

Wakefield, Paul Louis. Paul Louis Wakefield, son of John Henry and Della (Hogg) Wakefield, was born at Lovelady, Houston County, on May 6, 1895. He attended the public schools at Lovelady and studied at the University of Texas, where he majored in journalism.

He served as an enlisted man in the United States Army in France in World War I. As a newspaperman immediately after the war, Wakefield was with the United Press in Paris and New York. He was on the staff of the Houston *Chronicle* qv for ten years and was Texas correspondent for the New York *Herald-Tribune* during the time of Stanley Walker's qv editorship. He also wrote special correspondence for the old New York *World*. In 1927 he was appointed first lieutenant in the Texas National Guard.qv Over the years he rose to the grade of major general, and in 1949 he was appointed state director of selective service; he retired in 1955.

Wakefield was active in Texas politics, serving as an aide to governors Ross S. Sterling and Coke R. Stevenson.qqv He was appointed to the planning board of the Public Works Administration (PWA) in 1934, was at one time a member of the staff of Vice-President John Nance Garner,qv and served as an assistant to Jesse Holman Jones.qv

Paul Wakefield was married on January 24, 1928, to Eleanor L. Wilson; they had one son. The marriage ended in divorce, and on December 22, 1946, he was married to (Miss) William Lois LaLonde in San Antonio. Wakefield died in Austin on March 23, 1961, and was buried in Austin Memorial Park.

William Boyd Sinclair

*Wakefield, Texas.

*Waketon, Texas.

*Walburg, Texas.

*Waldeck, Texas.

*Waldeck Plantation. Waldeck Plantation was operated and owned by Morgan L. Smith qv (not Morgan R. Smith, as stated in Volume II).

BIBLIOGRAPHY: Adriance Papers (MS., Archives, University of Texas at Austin Library).

*Waldrip, Texas.

*Wales, Texas.

*Walhalla, Texas.

*Walker, Alexander Stuart.

*Walker, Alexander Stuart, Jr.

*Walker, Andrew J. (Andy).

Walker, Fred Livingood. Fred Livingood Walker, commander of the 36th Texas Infantry Division (see Thirty-sixth Division) during the Italian campaigns of World War II, was born on June 11, 1887, in Fairfield County, Ohio, the son of Belle (Mason) and William Henry Walker. During his college days (1907–1911) at Ohio State University, he was a member of the Ohio Cavalry and was graduated as an engineer in 1911. He entered the army that year, following a competitive examination, and as a second lieutenant he was stationed in San Antonio.

From 1911 to 1914 he served with the 13th Infantry Regiment in the Philippines. From 1914 to 1916 he was stationed in Eagle Pass and served under General John J. Pershing during the punitive expedition into Mexico. In 1917, at the beginning of World War I, he was sent overseas, and in 1918 he was in the second battle of the Marne; for exceptional gallantry in combat he was awarded the Distinguished Service Cross. After the war he was assigned as an instructor at the Infantry School, Fort Benning, Georgia; he was commandant of Shattuck School in Faribault, Minnesota, from 1927 to 1932, and was graduated in 1933 from the Army War College in Washington, D.C., where he served as instructor from 1934 to 1937. He was then assigned to the 15th Infantry at Tientsin, China. In 1941 he was in San Antonio as a brigadier general, assistant commander of the 2nd Division.

From September, 1941, to July, 1944, Walker commanded the 36th Texas Infantry Division. In World War II, after a brief period in North Africa, the 36th Division made a successful landing on September 18, 1943, at Salerno, in southern Italy, the first American troops to invade the continent of Europe. Walker was awarded the Distinguished Service Medal for his leadership. He commanded the division through the battles of the Rapido River, Cassino, and Mt. Artemisio on the drive north through Rome and beyond; all were successful except the battle at the Rapido River, an attempt which General Walker advised against because of insuperable odds, and this failure resulted in heavy casualties for the division.

Walker was awarded the Distinguished Service Cross with Oak Leaf Cluster for his part in the Italian campaign before he left Italy to assume command of the Infantry School at Fort Benning, Georgia, in July, 1944. After the war, in January, 1946, the Thirty-sixth Division Association,qv composed of division veterans, met in Brownwood, Texas, and passed a resolution calling for a congressional investigation of the battle of the Rapido River, a defeat which they charged was due to the inefficiency and inexperience of General Mark W. Clark, who had ordered the attack contrary to the repeated recommendations of the subordinate commanders. The United States congressional committees of military affairs in both the House of Representatives and the Senate invited witnesses to appear, but the Congress did not order a full-scale investigation.

Concerning the Italian campaign Walker wrote "My Story on the Rapido River Crossing" (Army, September, 1952) and "The 36th Was A Great Fighting Division" (Southwestern Historical Quarterly,qv July, 1968). His book From Texas to Rome (1969) is his journal of the division's World War II experience. In recognition of Walker's service with the 36th Division, his portrait was hung in the state capitol qv in Austin. After Walker's retirement from the regular army as a major general on April 30, 1946, he was appointed lieutenant general and commander of the Texas National Guard qv by Governor Coke Stevenson,qv to reorganize the guard, a post he held for fourteen months.

Walker was married to Frances "Julia" Martin Messmore on August 19, 1911; they had a daughter and two sons. After Mrs. Walker's death in June, 1961, Walker was married to Margaret Millikan on August 30, 1962. Fred L. Walker died at Walter Reed Army Hospital in Washington, D.C., on October 6, 1969, and was buried in Kirkersville, Ohio, where he had made his home. The Walker diaries and papers were left in the possession of his son, Lieutenant Colonel Charles W. Walker.

BIBLIOGRAPHY: Martin Blumenson, Bloody River (1970); Robert L. Wagner, The Texas Army (1972); Fred L. Walker, From Texas To Rome (1969); New York Times, October 8, 1969; Biographical File, Barker Texas History Center, University of Texas at Austin.

Walker, Jacob. Jacob Walker was born in May, 1799, in Tennessee. He later moved to Nacogdoches, and in November, 1827, he married Sara Anne Vauchere (or Vochery). As witnessed by Mrs. Almaron Dickenson,qv survivor of the siege and fall of the Alamo, he was the last man killed in that battle.

Jessie McIlroy Smith

*Walker, James.

Walker, John George. John George Walker, son of John G. and Sarah (Caffery) Walker, was born in Cole County, Missouri, on July 22, 1822. Educated at Jesuit College (later St. Louis University), Walker was commissioned into the United States Army at the beginning of the Mexican War as a first lieutenant of Company K, Colonel Persifor Frazer Smith's qv regiment of mounted riflemen; he received a severe wound and was brevetted captain for gallantry. Following the Mexican War he was stationed at frontier posts in California, Oregon, Arizona, and New Mexico and was commissioned a captain on June 30, 1851. He served on the Texas frontier against the Indians from 1854 to 1856. In 1861 he was a captain in the garrison at Fort Union, New Mexico.

Walker resigned his commission and was appointed a major of cavalry in the Confederate Army in August, 1861. Serving initially in Virginia, he received rapid promotions, and on November 8, 1862, he became a major general after having commanded a division in the Maryland campaign. On

January 1, 1863, Walker assumed command of the newly organized Texas Division, then at Little Rock, Arkansas. Under his leadership this division became known as "Walker's Texas Division" qv and "Walker's Greyhounds." Following the Red River Campaign,qv in which Walker sustained a serious wound at the battle of Pleasant Hill,qv he relinquished command of the division and assumed command of the District of West Louisiana; subsequently, Walker was made commander of the District of Texas, New Mexico, and Arizona, and served in that capacity until April, 1865, when he took command of John Austin Wharton's qv cavalry corps.

After the war, uncertain of the future, Walker joined other senior Confederates in fleeing to Mexico. He was in Havana by August, 1865, and then proceeded to England, where he resided and acted as agent for a company engaged in promoting a Confederate colony in Venezuela. Walker returned to the United States in 1868. In later years he served as United States consul in Bogotá, Colombia, and as special commissioner to the South American republics on behalf of the Pan-American Convention.

Walker was married to Sophie M. Baylor in New Orleans on April 10, 1858. He died in Washington, D.C., on July 20, 1893, and was buried at Winchester, Virginia.

Walker's first year of Confederate service has frequently been confused with that of another officer of the same name—Captain, later Lieutenant Colonel, John G. Walker, 8th Texas Cavalry (Terry's Texas Rangers qv), who was his cousin.

BIBLIOGRAPHY: Joseph P. Blessington, *The Campaigns of Walker's Texas Division* (1875); Ezra J. Warner, *Generals in Gray* (1959); Alfred J. and Kathryn A. Hanna, *Confederate Exiles in Venezuela* (1960); Sarah A. Dorsey, *Recollections of Henry Watkins Allen* (1866).

Lester N. Fitzhugh

*Walker, Moses B.

*Walker, Richard Sheckle.

*Walker, Samuel Hamilton. Samuel Hamilton Walker was born in Prince Georges County, Maryland, on February 24, 1817 (not 1810, as stated in Volume II). He enlisted at age nineteen with the Washington City Volunteers for the Indian Wars and served from June, 1836, to May, 1837, in the war against the Creek Indians, although he did not engage in combat during this time. Walker came to Texas in January, 1842 (not 1836); he first served in Captain (not Colonel) Jesse Billingsley's qv company at the time of the Adrian Woll qv invasion of 1842 and later became captain of a company under John Coffee Hays.qv He was not sent to New York to order Colt revolvers qv in 1839 (as stated in Volume II). During the Mexican War Walker fought in the battle of Monterrey in September, 1846 (not 1847, as stated in Volume II), with General William Jenkins Worth qv (erroneously called General T. J. Worth in Volume II).

The first correspondence between Samuel Colt and Walker was in November, 1846, while Walker was in Washington to accept and execute the oath of office as captain of Company C, First United States Mounted Rifles, Regular United States Army. He had accepted the appointment earlier that year while serving as lieutenant colonel of the First Texas Mounted Rifles. Colt asked Walker for his opinion of the revolvers which had been used by the Texas Navy and the Texas Rangers,qqv hoping to enlist Walker's aid in getting a contract from the War Department. Subsequent correspondence and a meeting in New York in December led to a contract signed on January 4, 1847, incorporating many basic changes over the old Paterson Number Five model. The arms were to be manufactured by the Eli Whitney Company, and Walker suggested even more changes after the first model was made, to refine the sights, enlarge the handle, and simplify the accessories. The first order was for 1,000 pistols to arm the First United States Mounted Rifles, though some were diverted to the regiment of John Hays. The first shipment of the Walker-Colt revolvers was sent to Veracruz and apparently reached the Mounted Riflemen after the death of Walker.

BIBLIOGRAPHY: Henry W. Barton, "The United States Cavalry and the Texas Rangers," *Southwestern Historical Quarterly*, LXIII (1959–1960); Samuel Colt (J. E. Parsons, ed.), *Samuel Colt's Own Record* (1949); William B. Edwards, *The Story of Colt's Revolver: The Biography of Colonel Samuel Colt* (1953).

Hugh D. Adair

Walker, Stanley. Stanley Walker, son of Cora (Stanley) and Walter Walker was born on October 21, 1898, on a ranch fifteen miles northeast of Lampasas. He attended the Unity Community country school near School Creek and was graduated from the Lampasas high school. He attended the University of Texas, studying journalism, from 1915 to 1918, and while in Austin he worked as a reporter on the Austin *American*.qv In 1918–1919 he worked for the Dallas *Morning News*;qv he sold several articles about Texas to the New York *Herald*, and this led to a job in New York City in 1920 as a reporter and rewrite man for that newspaper, which later became the New York *Herald-Tribune*. He became night city editor in 1926, and two years later he was appointed city editor (1928–1935). Walker quickly became one of the best known city editors of that time, a period of speakeasies when celebrities and gangsters alike sought his attention. Known as a dapper little man, from his post on the *Herald-Tribune* he made and unmade people, phrases, and places.

From those years came his first two books, *The Night Club Era* (1933) and *City Editor* (1934). In 1935 he resigned from the staff of the *Herald-Tribune* and took the managing editor's job with William Randolph Hearst's New York *Mirror*. Six months later he resigned that post and wrote his most widely known book, *Mrs. Astor's Horse* (1935), a who's who of American celebrities which took a nonchalant, cynical view of life that was characteristic of the newspapers of the 1920's and 1930's. Walker was on the staff of the *New Yorker* for a time, worked for the Columbia Broadcasting Company's "Home Front" (a daytime newspaper of the air for women listeners), and wrote numerous articles for over a dozen leading magazines. In the 1940's he wrote a promotional book for each of the Republican presidential candidates, Thomas E. Dewey (*Dewey: An American of This Century*) and Wendell Willkie (*This is Wendell Willkie*).

Walker was married to Mary Louise Sandefer on January 2, 1923; they had a daughter and a son. His wife died on January 29, 1944, and Walker was married to Ruth Alden Howell of Washington, D.C., on January 19, 1946.

Disenchanted by postwar New York, Stanley Walker left the city at the age of forty-seven in January, 1946, and returned with his second wife to Lampasas, where he stayed for the remainder of his life. In a prophetic article, "Farewell to New York" (*Saturday Evening Post*, August 17, 1946), he gave his reasons for leaving—the disadvantages of urban life, which later were recognized as major sociological and environmental problems. In the years which followed he wrote numerous articles on Texas and two books about the state, *Home to Texas* (1956) and *Texas* (1962). After learning that he had a fatal illness, Walker gave a farewell celebration for old-time friends at the Driskill Hotel in Austin. He committed suicide at his Lampasas ranch on the following day, November 25, 1962.

Since that time, the Stanley Walker Memorial Award for literary excellence in Texas daily and weekly newspapers has been awarded each year by the Texas Institute of Letters.qv The Stanley Walker Memorial Award for excellence in reporting is awarded periodically to students in the School of Journalism of the University of Texas at Austin.

BIBLIOGRAPHY: *Literary Digest*, October 3, 1936; George Fuermann, "Deep in His Lone Star Heart," *New York Times Book Review*, October 28, 1962; Lucius Beebe, "I Saw the Elephant," *Holiday* (September, 1950); *Texas Observer*, November 30, 1962; Biographical File, Barker Texas History Center, University of Texas at Austin.

*Walker, Thomas.

*Walker, Walton Harris.

*Walker, William.

*Walker, William E.

*Walker County. Walker County, with an economy based partly on the forestry industry, also relied on farming and livestock raising. Over 70 percent forested, the county had five active lumber mills in 1969. During the 1960's some farm land was converted to cattle grazing. By 1970 some 90 percent of the total farm income of $6.5 million came from livestock, dairying, poultry, and poultry products. Major tourist attractions are the Sam Houston National Forest (*see* National Forests in Texas) which covers 53,461 acres in the southeastern portion of the county, the 2,122-acre Huntsville State Recreation Park (*see* Parks, State), and the prison rodeo.qv A diagnostic unit of the Prison System qv was completed in 1964, and the Huntsville-Walker County Library was also completed in the late 1960's. The 1960 population of 21,475 increased to 27,680 by 1970, according to the United States census.

*Walker Creek.

*Walker Peak.

*Walkers Branch.

*Walkers Creek.

*Walkers Creek, Texas.

Walker's Texas Division. Walker's Texas Division was organized at Camp Nelson, near Austin, Arkansas, in October, 1862. The only division in Confederate service composed of troops from a single state, it took its name from Major General John George Walker,qv who took command from its organizer, Brigadier General Henry Eustace McCulloch,qv on January 1, 1863. During its existence it was commonly called the "Greyhound Division," or "Walker's Greyhounds," in tribute to its special capability to make long, forced marches from one threatened point to another in the Trans-Mississippi Department. It attempted to relieve the siege of Vicksburg by attacking the Federal troops at Milliken's Bend in June, 1863.

The high point of its service was during the early months of 1864, when it opposed Federal Major General Nathaniel P. Banks' qv invasion of Louisiana by way of the Red River valley. On April 8–9, 1864, it was committed with other Confederate forces in the battles of Mansfield and Pleasant Hill,qqv halting Banks' advance on Shreveport and Marshall. On April 10, 1864, with Thomas J. Churchill's and William H. Parsons' qv divisions, it began a forced march north to intercept Federal Major General Frederick Steele, who was moving from Little Rock to Camden, Arkansas, in cooperation with Banks' invasion from the south.

Steele reached Camden on April 15, then evacuated it on the 27th. On the 30th he was overtaken by Walker's Division at Jenkins' Ferry on the Saline River, fifty-five miles north of Camden. The ensuing fighting was desperate, costing the lives of two of the three brigade commanders of the division, Brigadier General William Read Scurry and Brigadier General Horace Randal.qqv Steele completed his withdrawal to Little Rock, ending the last real threat to western Louisiana and Texas during the war.

In June, 1864, Walker was directed to assume command of the District of West Louisiana, and Major General John Horace Forney took command of the division. During March and April, 1865, the division marched to Hempstead, Texas, where it disbanded on May 19, 1865.

Initially, the division was made up of four brigades: First Brigade, composed of the 12th (usually called "8th"), 18th, and 22nd Texas infantry regiments, the 13th Texas Cavalry (dismounted), and Haldeman's Texas Battery; Second Brigade, composed of the 11th and 14th Texas infantry regiments, the 28th Texas Cavalry (dismounted), the 6th (Gould's) Texas Cavalry Battalion (dismounted), and Daniel's Texas Battery; Third Brigade, composed of the 16th, 17th, and 19th Texas infantry regiments, the 16th Texas Cavalry (dismounted), and Edgar's Texas Battery; Fourth Brigade, composed of the 10th Texas Infantry and the 15th,

18th, and 25th Texas cavalry regiments (dismounted).

The original regiments of the Fourth Brigade were detached from the division shortly after its organization, and these were captured intact at Arkansas Post on January 11, 1863. Late in the war another Fourth Brigade was reconstituted when the 16th and 18th Texas infantry regiments and the 28th and 34th Texas cavalry regiments (dismounted) were assigned to the division. At the same time the 29th Texas Cavalry (dismounted) was added to the First Brigade and the 2nd Regiment of Texas Partisan Rangers (dismounted) to the Third Brigade. For a brief period, during the Jenkins' Ferry phase of the Red River Campaign,qv the 3rd Texas Infantry was assigned to the Third Brigade, but this regiment was ordered to return to Texas shortly thereafter.

Brigade commanders in Walker's Texas Division were: First Brigade, Colonel Overton C. Young,qv Brigadier General James M. Hawes, Brigadier General Thomas Neville Waul,qv and Brigadier General Wilburn Hill King,qv Second Brigade, Brigadier General Horace Randal and Brigadier General Robert P. Maclay; Third Brigade, Colonel George M. Flournoy,qv Brigadier General Henry Eustace McCulloch, Brigadier General William Read Scurry, and Brigadier General Richard Waterhouse;qv Fourth Brigade, Colonel (later Brigadier General) James Deshler.qv

The fighting service of Walker's Texas Division was less arduous than that of many similar commands in the Army of Northern Virginia and the Army of Tennessee. It operated efficiently, however, under peculiar difficulties unknown east of the Mississippi River, and it deserved major credit for preserving Texas from Federal invasion.

BIBLIOGRAPHY: Joseph P. Blessington, *The Campaigns of Walker's Texas Division* (1875); Mark Mayo Boatner, *Civil War Dictionary* (1959); Ezra J. Warner, *Generals in Gray* (1959).

Lester N. Fitzhugh

*Walkerton, Texas.

*Wall, Texas.

*Wallace, Benjamin C.

*Wallace, Benjamin Rush.

*Wallace, Caleb.

Wallace, Daniel Webster. Daniel Webster (80 John) Wallace, a Negro cowhand who became a prominent Mitchell County ranchman, was born near Inez, in Victoria County, on September 15, 1860, the son of Will and Mary (Barber) Wallace, both slaves. About three months before his birth, his mother had been sold to the O'Daniel family; he grew up with the O'Daniel sons, M. H. and Dial, and remained in close contact with the family all of his life. Tiring of his job chopping cotton near Flatonia, Fayette County, he joined a cattle drive in 1877. He had never ridden a cow pony before but followed the herd to Runnels and Taylor counties to where the present town of Buffalo Gap is located. For a short time he worked for Sam Gholson, a veteran Indian fighter, then for John

Nunn's N.U.N. cattle outfit on the headwaters of the Brazos River as a horse wrangler and horse breaker. Sixteen months later he joined Clay Mann's outfit on the rangeland near Colorado City, Mitchell County.

During the more than twenty years he worked for Mann he saw every phase of open range cow work. He saw the Texas and Pacific Railroad built beyond Colorado City and worked for such cattle men as Christopher Columbus Slaughter, Isaac L. Ellwood,qqv A. B. "Sug" Robertson, C. A. "Gus" O'Keefe, and for the Bush and Tillar Cattle Company (*see* Benjamin Johnson Tillar). He acquired the nickname "80 John" from his long association with Clay Mann, whose brand was "80."

Wallace had little formal education, acquiring that which he had during two winters at a school in Navarro County in the 1880's. On April 8, 1888, Wallace was married to Laura Dee Owen of Navarro County; they had four children. Not long after his marriage, as the free grass and open range was disappearing, Wallace began buying sections of land southeast of Loraine in Mitchell County, where some of his family still live. His Durham cattle brand was a D triangle; on his Herefords he used a D on the right hip and a running W on one side. He was a member of the Texas and Southwestern Cattle Raisers' Association qv for thirty years. He died on March 28, 1939, and was buried on his home place, which is marked by a state historical marker. The D. W. Wallace school in Colorado City was named in his honor in the mid-1950's.

BIBLIOGRAPHY: Hettye Wallace Branch, *The Story of "80 John"* (1960); *Cattleman* (February, 1936, April, 1939, June, 1946, March, 1951); R. C. Crane, "D. W. Wallace ('80 John'), A Negro Cattleman on the Texas Frontier," *West Texas Historical Association Year Book,* XXVIII (1952).

Martha Earnest

Wallace, David Richard. David Richard Wallace was born on November 10, 1825, on a small farm near Greenville, North Carolina, the son of Warren and Phoebe (Powell) Wallace. He attended schools in Greenville, graduated from Wake Forest College in 1850, taught at Warrenton Institute and Greenville Academy, and then pursued the study of medicine at New York City Medical College, where he received a medical degree in 1853. Wallace returned to Greenville and formed a partnership to practice medicine with another physician.

In December, 1855, he took his mother with him to Bastrop, Texas; several months later he moved to Independence, where Baylor University was then located, formed a partnership with another doctor, and taught Latin and Greek at Baylor. In 1861 when the faculty of that school moved to Waco to open Waco University, Wallace moved also, continuing to practice medicine and to teach at the university. In 1862 he reported to the 15th Texas Infantry Regiment as a surgeon and served throughout the war. At the close of the war he was surgeon for the Department of Southern Texas.

Wallace returned to Waco, formed a partnership with J. H. Sears for the general practice of medicine, and also went into the drug business. He was appointed superintendent of the State Lunatic Asylum (later renamed Austin State Hospital qv) and served in that position from 1874 until 1879. In 1883 he was appointed to help establish the North Texas Lunatic Asylum (later renamed Terrell State Hospital qv); he was appointed superintendent there but resigned in 1891 to return to Waco. He did not enter the general practice of medicine again; instead, he specialized in nervous diseases and was often called upon for advice in the treatment of insanity. He believed that the insane should not be hidden away but should be treated for illness. In this respect Wallace was a pioneer in the psychiatric field in Texas.

Wallace was prominent in civic and business enterprises, as well as professional medical groups. He was awarded an honorary degree by Baylor University and an honorary membership in the American Psychological Association.

In 1857 Wallace was married to Arabella Daniel; they had five children. His wife died in 1868, and three years later he was married to her sister, Susan Lavinia Robert, a widow with one son; they had one son. Wallace died on November 21, 1911, in Waco, and he was buried in Oakwood Cemetery.

BIBLIOGRAPHY: Doris Dowell Moore, The Biography of Doctor D. R. Wallace (1966); George Plunkett Red, The Medicine Man in Texas (1930); Merle M. Duncan, "David Richard Wallace," Texana, I (1963); "The Death of Senator Coke," Southwestern Historical Quarterly, LXIII (1959–1960); Waco Daily Times-Herald, November 21, 1911; Waco News-Tribune, November 22, 1911.

Merle Mears Duncan

Wallace, Edward Seccomb. Edward Seccomb Wallace was born in Ansonia, Connecticut, on June 15, 1897, the son of Frederic William and Grace Mary (Seccomb) Wallace. He was graduated from Phillips-Andover Academy at Andover, Massachusetts, and Evans School in Mesa, Arizona. He received a B.A. degree from Yale, an M.A. from Harvard, and a Ph.D. from Boston University. His studies at Yale were interrupted by World War I when he entered the army and was sent to Love Field, qv Texas, for flight training. He received his commission there on March 22, 1918, and continued with advanced training at Ellington Field, qv Texas.

During World War II Wallace served with the U.S. Army Air Forces in the North Africa and Sicily campaigns. Following the war he lived in San Antonio, where he served for a time as military historian (civilian status) for the air force. Wallace taught at South Kent School, South Kent, Connecticut; Northeastern University, Boston, Massachusetts; Suffolk University, Boston; and Pan American College, Edinburg, Texas. A student of southwestern military history, Wallace traveled widely in Texas and northern Mexico and was indefatigable in tracing old trails and locating Indian camps and battlefield sites.

He wrote four books of narrative history with a southwestern background: *General William Jenkins Worth, Monterey's Forgotten Hero* (1953); *The Story of the U. S. Cavalry, 1775–1942* (1954), which he coauthored with Major General John K. Herr; *The Great Reconnaissance* (1955); and *Destiny and Glory* (1957). His *The Great Reconnaissance* is considered outstanding among books relating to topographical engineers and was selected by Lawrence Clark Powell as one of the 100 best books written about the American West.

Wallace was a member of the Texas State Historical Association qv and a frequent contributor of articles to the *Southwestern Historical Quarterly*, qv *American Heritage*, and various Western publications. Beginning in 1956 Wallace spent several winters in Eagle Pass, Texas. He died at his home in Millington Green, East Haddam, Connecticut, on November 13, 1964.

Ben E. Pingenot

*Wallace, Joseph Washington Elliot.

*Wallace, W. A. A. (Bigfoot).

*Wallace, Texas.

*Wallace Creek.

*Wallace Creek, Texas.

*Wallach, William Douglas. At the time of his death Wallach was married to the former Margaret Newton of Washington, D.C., and the couple had four daughters.

BIBLIOGRAPHY: Evening Star (Washington, D.C.), December 1, 1871.

*Waller, Edwin.

*Waller, Texas. Waller, in eastern Waller and northwestern Harris counties, had a population of 900 in 1960 and 1,123 in 1970, according to the United States census.

*Waller County. Waller County, 18 percent forested, had petroleum resources evaluated at $34,-500,000 in 1963. Total crude oil production between 1934 and January 1, 1973, was 16,321,556 barrels. In the early 1970's about 60 percent of the $11.5 million average annual farm income came from livestock, and timber and crops constituted the other main income sources. The population was 12,071 in 1960 and 14,285 in 1970, according to the United States census. See also Houston Standard Metropolitan Statistical Area.

*Waller Creek.

*Walleye Creek.

*Walling, Elisha.

*Walling, Jesse. According to the county court records of Rusk County, Jesse Walling died at Millville (now a ghost town) in Rusk County (not in Whitney in Hill County, as implied in Volume II). His body was moved from Millville to Walling Bend Cemetery on the Brazos River in Bosque County, about six miles from Whitney in Hill County. When the building of Lake Whitney Dam flooded the Walling Bend Cemetery, all burials, including that of Jesse Walling, were moved to the Whitney city cemetery.

Maida Jaggers

*Walling, John.

*Walling, Thomas J.

*Walling, Texas.

*Wallis, Texas. Wallis, in Austin County, had a population of 1,028 in 1970, according to the United States census.

*Wallis Ranch, Texas.

*Wallisville, Texas.

*Walnut Creek.

*Walnut Springs, Texas.

*Waloope Creek.

*Walsh, Charles Clinton.

*Walsh, William C. William C. Walsh was elected chief clerk of the Texas House of Representatives in January, 1873. Later he was appointed commissioner of the General Land Office qv by Governor Richard Bennett Hubbard qv upon the death of Land Commissioner Johann Jacob Groos qv in June, 1878 (not 1873, as stated in Volume II); he served in that position until 1887.

*Walsh, Texas. (San Jacinto County.)

*Walsh, Texas. (Travis County.)

Walter, Hulda Saenger. Hulda Saenger Walter, an early writer of German verse in Texas, was born in Fredericksburg, Gillespie County, on January 7, 1867. She was the daughter of William and Henriette (Klingelhoefer) Saenger. Hulda Saenger's first poem, written when she was eleven years old, was "Jesu meine Zuversicht." She married Fred Walter on October 2, 1890; they were the parents of a daughter. Throughout her life Hulda Walter published poems in such Texas newspapers as Das Wochenblatt qv and the Waco Post, as well as in Die Amerika, Die Abendschule, and Die Deutsche Hausfrau. Two of her poems were presented by Mrs. Lyndon B. Johnson, wife of the president of the United States, to Frau Luise Erhard, wife of German Chancellor Ludwig Erhard, to commemorate a conference held by their husbands at the Lyndon Baines Johnson qv ranch in 1963. Hulda Saenger Walter died in Fredericksburg on January 6, 1929, and was buried there.

BIBLIOGRAPHY: Gillespie County Historical Society, Pioneers in God's Hills (1960); Selma Metzenthin Raunick, "A Survey of German Literature in Texas," Southwestern Historical Quarterly, XXXIII (1929–1930); "Texas Collection," ibid., L (1946–1947).

*Walter, Texas.

Walter Prescott Webb Great Frontier Foundation. See Friday Mountain Ranch.

*Walthall, James Du Bose.

Walthall, Texas. Walthall, four miles south of Ballinger in Runnels County, came into existence as a stop on the stage line that connected Fort Concho and Camp Colorado.qqv The settlement, located at the crossing of the Colorado River, consisted of a house, a dugout, and a store. In 1877 a post office was established. The town, never having more than a half dozen families, began to decline when A. B. Hutchison closed the store and moved to Runnels City in 1886.

*Walton, William M. William M. Walton practiced law in Austin after the Civil War with W. P. de Normandie. (Walton was not using the name

"W. P. de Normadie," as stated in Volume II.) In addition to his law practice, Walton also wrote The Life and Adventures of Ben Thompson (1884).

BIBLIOGRAPHY: William M. Walton, An Epitome of My Life (1965).

*Walton, Texas. (Clay County.)

*Walton, Texas. (Van Zandt County.)

*Wamba, Texas.

*Wanderers Creek.

*Wanderer's Retreat, Texas.

*Wander's Creek.

*Waneta, Texas.

*Waples, Joseph.

*Waples, Texas.

*Ward, Lafayette.

*Ward, Matthias.

*Ward, Seth.

*Ward, Thomas William.

*Ward, William.

*Ward County. Ward County, engaged in raising some cotton, grains, alfalfa, and livestock, is also a leading oil-producing county. Mineral resources in the county were evaluated at $93,525,000 in 1973. Between 1928 and January 1, 1973, 497,-303,534 barrels of oil had been produced. The major tourist attraction is the Monahans Sandhills State Scenic Park (see Parks, State). Industries in the county include the manufacture and processing of oil field equipment and tools, the bottling of soft drinks, the production and refining of natural gas, butane, propane, and sodium sulphate, the making of ready-mix concrete, and a regional steam-electric power plant. The county supports a library. The population was 14,917 in 1960 and 13,019 in 1970, according to the United States census.

*Ward County (Judicial).

*Ward Creek.

*Warda, Texas.

*Warden Creek.

*Wardville, Texas.

*Ware, William.

*Ware, Texas. Ware, in Dallam County, was founded by William Pulver Soash qv on a tract of land he purchased from the Capitol Freehold Land and Investment Company, Limited,qv in 1905 for the purpose of colonization. Early in 1907 he built a hotel to accommodate land prospectors he brought into the area.

BIBLIOGRAPHY: Laura V. Hamner, interview with W. P. Soash, November 15, 1936 (MS., Archives, University of Texas at Austin Library); Seymour V. Connor (ed.), Builders of the Southwest (1959).

Waresville, Texas. See Utopia, Texas.

*Warfield, Charles A.

*Warfield, Texas.

*Warfield Expedition.

*Waring, Texas. Waring, in Kendall County, was named for R. P. M. Waring, who gave the right-of-way for the San Antonio and Aransas Pass Rail-

way when the line was extended from San Antonio to Kerrville in 1887. The settlement was originally known as Waringford. In 1888 the post office at the adjacent settlement of Windsor, across the Guadalupe River, was moved to Waringford. On February 10, 1901, Waringford became officially known as Waring (a post office designation). The post office is said to have been in eight different locations since its founding and to have had possibly seven postmasters by the early 1970's, when it served almost one hundred families. The last train went through Waring on May 30, 1970.

BIBLIOGRAPHY: San Antonio *Express*, August 2, 1972; Kendall County Scrapbook (MS., Archives, University of Texas at Austin Library).

*Warm Springs Foundation for Crippled Children. *See also* Texas Rehabilitation Center of Gonzales Warm Springs Foundation.

*Warner, Phoebe Kerrick.

*Warren, Abel.

Warren, David Mathias. David Mathias Warren, Panhandle publisher and banker, was born at South Greenfield, Missouri, on July 19, 1894, the son of Wilburn Henry and Kate (Speer) Warren. After attending public schools at Lockwood and South Greenfield, Missouri, he entered the University of Missouri in 1914; he was graduated with a bachelor of journalism degree in 1917. He worked briefly on newspapers in Missouri, Kentucky, and Wyoming.

In 1918 Warren came to Texas and took a job as telegraph editor of the Amarillo *Daily News*. This started a long association with the publishers, J. E. Nunn and J. L. Nunn. He became city editor and then managing editor. After sale of the Amarillo paper to Gene Howe and associates, Warren was made secretary-treasurer and general manager of the newly formed Nunn-Warren Publishing Company in 1926, a newspaper chain serving much of the Texas Panhandle and eastern New Mexico. The corporation was split in 1932, Warren retaining papers in Panhandle, Hereford, Friona, Borger, and Spearman. Warren himself edited the Panhandle *Herald*.qv Midway in his career, he disposed of his newspapers and entered the banking field, heading banks in Panhandle and Borger.

Warren's major public interests were newspapers and history, and he collected a large library on these subjects. He was a life member of numerous historical societies, including the Texas State Historical Association,qv the Southern Historical Association, and the Panhandle-Plains Historical Society.qv He was also active in academic affairs and in 1944 was appointed to the University of Texas board of regents, on which he served two six-year terms. He was credited with hastening the establishment of the journalism library and the construction of the journalism building. Warren was married to Alvah D. Meyer of Amarillo on October 2, 1923; they had two sons. He died on January 23, 1958, in Amarillo and was buried there in Llano Cemetery. He had anonymously established the fund which, at his death, was named the David M. Warren and Alvah

Warren Journalism Scholarship Fund in his memory.

BIBLIOGRAPHY: H. Bailey Carroll, "Texas Collection," *Southwestern Historical Quarterly*, LXII (1958–1959).

Olin Hinkle

*Warren, John.

*Warren, Texas.

*Warren Central Railroad Company.

Warren City, Texas. Warren City, in northwestern Gregg and southeastern Upshur counties, was founded and incorporated in 1952. The population was 167 in 1960 and 150 in 1970, according to the United States census. The town was named for the Warren Petroleum Corporation, which manufactures gas and is the town's main industry. Utilities are from Gladewater, with the exception of a city-owned water system.

*Warren and Corsicana Pacific Railroad.

Warren Wagontrain Raid. *See* Salt Creek Massacre.

*Warrenton, Texas.

Warriner, Phanuel Warner. Phanuel Warner Warriner was born in Wilbraham, Massachusetts, on March 17, 1798 (or 1799). He received a B.S. degree from Hamilton College in Clinton, New York, in 1826 and a theological degree from Andover Theological Seminary in Newton Center, Massachusetts, in 1829; he was ordained to the ministry in the Park Presbyterian Church in Boston on September 24, 1829. He was married to Apphia Garrison of New Hampshire on September 28, and the same year he became the first settled pastor of the First Presbyterian Church in Monroe, Michigan Territory, where he remained until 1834. From then until 1839 he was pastor of the Presbyterian congregation in White Pigeon, St. Joseph County.

Warriner came to the Republic of Texas about 1840 to serve as a representative of the American Home Missionary Society in Sabine, San Augustine, and Jasper counties. He preached at various places in the area until he became the regular pastor of the Presbyterian church of San Augustine in 1844. Soon after his arrival he became a teacher in the chartered, non-sectarian University of San Augustine,qv and he also served as head of the Ladies' Academy of the university. He, along with Marcus A. Montrose, John May Becton,qqv and J. H. McKnight, formed the Presbytery of Eastern Texas on February 4, 1843, and agreed to "cooperate with the trustees of the university with their advice, sanction, and protection." This move by the Presbyterian leaders created a conflict with the Methodists, who then organized a school of their own, the Wesleyan Male and Female College.qv The rivalry between the two schools led to the ultimate closing of both in 1847 and the subsequent formation of the non-denominational University of Eastern Texas.qv That same year Warriner took a leading part in the establishment of the Masonic lodge in San Augustine.

For many years he was the agent for the American Bible Society in Texas and traveled and preached over much of the upper eastern part of the state.

After 1863 his health began to fail, and he was no longer active in the missionary field. At the time of the Sabine County census of 1850 Warriner was fifty-two, his wife was forty-four, and they had four children. Warriner died in Tyler, Smith County, on November 3, 1879.

BIBLIOGRAPHY: George Louis Crockett, *Two Centuries in East Texas* (1932); William Tellis Parmer, *A Centennial History of Sexton Lodge, Sabine County, Texas, 1860–1960 and Jackson Lodge, Sabine County, 1847–1957* (1960); Jessie Guy Smith, *Heroes of the Saddle Bags* (1951); Dan Ferguson, "Antecedents of Austin College," *Southwestern Historical Quarterly,* LIII (1949–1950).

Helen Gomer Schluter

*Warring Creek.

*Warsaw, Texas. (Kaufman County.)

*Warsaw, Texas. (San Augustine County.)

*Washboard Canyon.

*Washboard Creek.

*Washburn, Texas.

*Washington, Alexander Hamilton. [This title was listed in Volume II as Washington, Hamilton.] Alexander Hamilton Washington was born on March 5, 1805, the son of Sarah (Rootes) and Warner Washington, Jr., near Berryville in Clarke County, Virginia. His great-grandfather was John Washington, an uncle of George Washington. Hamilton Washington grew up in Clarke County, worked on his father's farms, and about 1838 he moved to Vicksburg, Mississippi, to practice law.

In 1840 Abner G. A. Beazley (not A. C. A. Beazley, as stated in Volume II), who was married to Hamilton Washington's sister, placed money and property in his brother-in-law's charge to be invested in Texas. Washington acquired the property on the William G. Logan qv league, which was located on the Trinity River about forty miles north of Liberty, Texas. The league later became part of San Jacinto County.

The plantation became the site of the Confederacy's farthest-inland Texas naval station. On December 18, 1862, Commander William W. Hunter, Confederate Navy, the superintendent of Texas coastal defenses, established his headquarters on the Logan league. This naval station was abandoned in April, 1863.

Hamilton Washington was a Confederate Army volunteer in December, 1862, and was commissioned an aide with the rank of major on the staff of General John Bankhead Magruder.qv His principal duties were to put the lower valley of the Trinity River in the best possible state of defense, to construct flatboats and transport supplies down the Trinity to Confederate forces along the Texas coast, and to use the Alabama and Coushatta Indians qqv in his activities along the Trinity. An Indian cavalry company was assigned to assist him. Hamilton Washington resigned his commission on August 28, 1864.

At the end of the war he was nearly bankrupt and in declining health. His final public service was a tour of duty as agent for the Coushatta Indians during the administration of Governor James Webb Throckmorton,qv August 9, 1866, to August 8, 1867.

BIBLIOGRAPHY: Rose M. E. MacDonald, *Clarke County, A Daughter of Frederick* (1943); John W. Wayland, *The Washingtons and Their Homes* (1944); Curtis Chappelear, "Early Landowners in the Benjamin Harrison and Robert Carter Nicholas Tracts," *Proceedings of Clarke County Historical Association,* VII (1948); Howard N. Martin, "Texas Redskins in Confederate Gray," *Southwestern Historical Quarterly,* LXX (1966–1967); U. S. War Department, *The War of the Rebellion: A Compilation of the Official Records of the Union and Confederate Armies* (1880–1901); *Official Records of the Union and Confederate Navies in the War of the Rebellion* (1894–1927).

Howard N. Martin

*Washington, James H.

*Washington, Lewis M. Henry.

*Washington, Thomas Pratt.

Washington, Walter Owen. Walter Owen Washington, son of Ella (Maxwell) and Thomas Pratt Washington (and grandson of Thomas Pratt Washington qv), was born in Travis County on September 24, 1883. He received his early education in a country school near Austin. He was graduated from the University of Texas in 1904 with a degree in civil engineering and returned in 1908 for graduate work in mining engineering. In the interim he worked on railroad location surveys in Texas and western Mexico, and in 1909 he opened an engineering office in McAllen. He was an officer in the engineering corps during World War I. After the war he became a partner in the firm of Whiteaker and Washington and maintained an office in San Antonio until 1923.

Washington provided engineering service for many Texas counties and was county engineer of Cameron County from 1920 to 1939. He pioneered advanced practices in the construction of concrete highways, particularly in rigid control over water-cement ratios for strength in concrete pavement mixes. Washington supervised construction of the Rio Grande Valley's flood control system of levees and floodways in Cameron County. In 1939–1940 he was construction engineer for a WPA federal water control and irrigation canal program in Willacy County. As Brownsville's city engineer, 1941–1942, he supervised the building of runways and facilities at the municipal airport. During 1943–1945 he was supervising engineer for the construction of synthetic rubber plants at Corpus Christi and Ingleside, Texas. His last thirty-five years were spent in Brownsville.

He was active in numerous professional and historical associations and received various awards for his work. He married Bernice Beth Haskell on October 17, 1910, in Greenville, Texas; they had six children. Washington died on July 4, 1954, and was buried in Oakwood Cemetery in Austin.

BIBLIOGRAPHY: *Texas and Texans,* IV (1914); *County Progress,* 9 (February, 1932); *Who's Who in Texas* (1947); *Who's Who in Engineering: A Biographical Dictionary* (1948); *Texas Professional Engineer,* 7 (July-August, 1948); Brownsville *Herald,* June 3, 1951, July 5, 1954.

Bernice H. Washington
Grace Edman

*Washington, Texas. *See* Washington-on-the-Brazos.

*Washington-on-the-Brazos. Recent archeological excavations in the Washington State Park,qv conducted by the University of Texas at Austin and the State Building Commission,qqv have uncovered remains of the old Independence Hall where the Texas Declaration of Independence qv was signed. Thousands of historic artifacts—buttons, buckles, printer's type, gun parts and musket balls, nails, tools, knives, marbles, food remains, and fragments of bottles and dishes—from the early village of Washington were recovered at these excavations.

Curtis Tunnell

*Washington County. Washington County, with a small production of oil, is a leading beef cattle, hog, and poultry-raising area. Also contributing to the farm income are cotton and grain crops. During the 1960's the county attracted a number of businessmen who developed several large plantations. Also during the 1960's the county was among the leading dairy counties. Major businesses of the county are concerned with agricultural produce, manufacturing, and tourism. The county supports a junior college and a library. County improvement projects include the Somerville Reservoir, additions to Blinn Memorial College,qv a new airport, and a United States government building. The 1960 population was 19,145; the 1970 population was 18,842, according to the United States census.

*Washington County Railroad.

*Washington Masonic School.

*Washington State Park. *See also* Parks, State.

*Washita River.

*Washout Mountain.

*Waskom, Texas. Waskom, in Harrison County, had a population of 1,336 in 1960 and 1,460 in 1970, according to the United States census.

*Wasp Creek.

Wasson, Alonzo. Alonzo Wasson was born at Fort Smith, Arkansas, on April 13, 1870, son of Alonzo and Sarah Jane (Tealy) Wasson. Soon after his birth the family moved to Texas. After attending the public school at Gainesville and St. Vincent's College in Cape Girardeau, Missouri, he began newspaper work in Texas in 1891. He wrote for several papers, including the Dallas *Morning News*, the San Antonio *Express*,qqv the Kansas City *Times*, and the St. Louis *Globe-Democrat*. In 1905 he rejoined the staff of the Dallas *Morning News* and rose to editor-in-chief before retiring in 1929. From his farm near Austin he continued to send editorial correspondence to the *Morning News* until his death on August 11, 1952. His wife was Loretto Smith, whom he married on November 21, 1906.

BIBLIOGRAPHY: Philosophical Society of Texas, *Proceedings, 1952*, XVII (1953); *Texian Who's Who* (1937).

*Wasson, Texas.

*Wastella, Texas. Wastella, in Nolan County, was named for Wastella Neely, the eldest daughter of W. H. Neely. (The name is not a combination of two names, as stated in Volume II.)

Mrs. Wastella Neely Cornett

*Watauga, Texas.

*Watch Mountain.

Water Agencies and Programs, Local. Several units of local government in Texas were authorized to engage in water programs. Counties, cities, and many other kinds of water districts were authorized by statute to undertake certain projects. The extent to which the several units actually exercised their authority, however, varied considerably.

Early in the state's development, counties were relied upon to undertake certain water functions. They were authorized to clear and improve streams for navigation and to make drainage and flood control improvements on petition of specified members of property owners. These programs were limited, however, because constitutional provisions permited only a special assessment tax to finance such improvements. The county remained the only unit of local government authorized to perform these services until 1904, when the constitution was amended to permit the establishment of special districts. After that time these new units assumed most of the duties of making the improvements.

Counties, however, continued to participate in water programs as administrative areas of the state government. They were responsible for enforcing state laws, including fish and game laws and water laws pertaining to water districts. Under the general water law statutes, the commissioners court of a county was empowered to create numerous kinds of water districts. The county board appointed the governing boards of levee, drainage, and navigation districts, and the boards of water control and preservation districts situated in only one county. Counties also had a certain amount of supervisory authority over general law water districts. The county auditor, in a county having an auditor, had general supervision over all the books and records of all the county officers, including those of the water districts.

After the constitutional amendment of 1904, water districts became the most important unit of local government to undertake water programs. Water districts in Texas direct all the major water programs, including flood control, drainage, navigation, irrigation, domestic, commercial, and industrial water supply, sewage disposal, power supply, ground water control, mosquito control, soil conservation, and recreation. These tasks of supplying and/or controlling water often involve the construction of levees, dams, lakes, and power facilities, or the channelling, clearing, and maintenance of streams and rivers.

By 1966 there were over 793 water districts in the state, counting all districts created under both general and special laws. The thirteen types of general law water districts were water control and improvement, water improvement, water control and preservation, water power control, water supply, fresh water supply, underground water conservation, municipal water, irrigation, levee improvement, drainage, navigation, and conservation and reclamation.

There was little control over water districts by either state agencies or the public, and this caused a great deal of criticism. The rapid multiplication of disparate, often overlapping water districts made it impossible for even the most conscientious citizen to understand their problems and activities. As a result, in 1961 the state legislature enacted a provision which provided that no types of water district except water control and improvement districts and underground water conservation districts could thereafter be created. The legislature also empowered the Texas Water Commission qv to supervise and coordinate activities of water districts. The prohibition on creating other types of districts, however, was declared unconstitutional in the case of *Harris County Fresh Water Supply District, No. 55* v. *Carr* in 1963. As a result, it was still possible in the 1960's to create any of the types of general law water districts.

Cities had a vital concern in maintaining adequate municipal water supply. Texas cities could construct municipal water systems and issue the bonds required to construct them if such construction and bonding were approved in popular elections. Cities were also authorized to construct sewer systems and sewage disposal plants, most of which had to be financed by means of voter-approved bond issues. Flood protection measures were also undertaken by cities, since many cities were located on or near streams subject to overflow. Home rule cities had the power to improve any river or stream within the city and to levy a special assessment on the property owners especially benefited. They could also establish improvement districts to undertake such projects.

Texas cities located on navigable streams could acquire land for the purpose of establishing and maintaining wharves, docks, railway terminals, and other aids to navigation. They could also deed this property to the federal government for the improvement of navigation. Any city situated within the territorial limits of a navigation district and having a deepwater port could purchase, construct, own, and maintain dikes, spillways, seawalls, and breakwaters to protect the city. Furthermore, the city could elevate and reclaim submerged or low lands along the waterfront, dredge channels, build and operate drydocks, piers, wharves, and boat basins. To finance these improvements for their harbors, coastal cities could issue bonds. Texas cities could also generate, purchase, and distribute hydroelectric power, own and operate municipal electric plants, and contract with other generating agencies for electrical energy.

See (in Volumes I and II) Drainage Districts; Irrigation Districts; Navigation Districts; Water Control and Improvement Districts; Water Engineers, Board of; Water Improvement Districts; Water Law; Water Power; Water Resources; Water Supply Districts; *see also* (in this volume) the articles which follow.

John T. Thompson

Water Commission, Texas. The Board of Water Engineers qv became the Texas Water Commission by legislative act in 1961. The governor appointed the three members for six-year terms and designated one as chairman. The chairman also served as the administrative officer of the commission. The most important new function assigned to the commission was that of making statewide plans for maximum development of the water resources of the state. In 1965 most of the functions of the Texas Water Commission not related to the question of water rights were transferred to the Texas Water Development Board.qv At the same time, the name of the Texas Water Commission was changed to the Texas Water Rights Commission.qv

BIBLIOGRAPHY: Stuart A. MacCorkle and Dick Smith, *Texas Government* (1964); University of Texas at Austin, *Guide To Texas State Agencies* (1972).

Dick Smith

Water Conservation. *See* Soil and Water Conservation.

*Water Control and Improvement Districts. *See also* Water Agencies and Programs, Local.

Water Development Board, Texas. The Texas Water Development Board was created in 1957 to provide loan assistance to political subdivisions for development of surface water supply projects that could not be financed through commercial channels. The responsibility of the board was increased in 1963, when it was given the authority to acquire and develop water conservation storage facilities. In 1965 most of the functions and responsibilities of the Texas Water Commission qv not related to the question of water rights were transferred to the Texas Water Development Board. The responsibility for the preparation of a comprehensive state water plan, in progress in 1967, was also given to the board. The Texas Water Development Board is composed of six members appointed for six-year terms (overlapping) by the governor with the advice and consent of the Senate. Each member must be from a different section of the state and must have at least ten years of successful business or professional experience. One member is selected from each of the following fields: engineering, law, public or private finance, and agriculture; and two members are selected from the public at large.

BIBLIOGRAPHY: University of Texas at Austin, *Guide To Texas State Agencies* (1972).

Howard B. Boswell

*Water Engineers, Board of. *See also* Texas Water Rights Commission.

*Water Improvement Districts. *See also* Water Agencies and Programs, Local.

*Water Law. *See also* Water Agencies and Programs, Local (and all *see* references following that article).

Water Pollution Control Board, Texas. *See* Water Quality Board, Texas.

*Water Power. By July, 1966, hydroelectric power plants with a total generating capacity of 463,280 kilowatts had been installed at twenty major sites in Texas and on boundary streams. At that time installations with a total capacity of

212,750 kilowatts were under construction at Toledo Bend Dam on the Sabine River and Amistad
Dam on the Rio Grande (the latter inundating two
existing units—Devils Lake,qv 1,800 kilowatts, and
Lake Walk,qv 1,350 kilowatts). By the early 1970's
these projects were completed, and hydroelectric
power plants with a total generating capacity of
672,880 kilowatts were at the following locations:

Denison Dam (Lake Texoma qv), on the Red
River five miles north of Denison, had two generating units, with a combined capacity of 70,000
kilowatts, installed in March, 1945.

Toledo Bend Dam (see Toledo Bend Reservoir),
completed in the late 1960's on the Sabine River
fourteen miles northeast of Burkeville, had two
generating units with a combined capacity of
80,750 kilowatts.

Sam Rayburn Dam,qv on the Angelina River
eleven miles northwest of Jasper, had two generating units with a combined capacity of 52,000 kilowatts. Generation of power began on July 1, 1966.

Morris Sheppard Dam qv (Possum Kingdom
Lake qv), on the Brazos River eleven miles southwest of Graford, had two generating units, installed
in 1941, with a combined capacity of 22,500
kilowatts.

Whitney Dam,qv on the Brazos River seven miles
southwest of Whitney, had two generating units,
installed in 1953, with a combined capacity of
30,000 kilowatts.

Buchanan Dam,qv on the Colorado River eleven
miles west of Burnet, had three generating units,
installed in 1938, with a combined capacity of
33,750 kilowatts.

Inks Dam,qv on the Colorado River ten miles
west of Burnet, had one 12,500-kilowatt generating
unit installed in June, 1938.

Alvin Wirtz Dam (Lake Lyndon B. Johnson qv),
on the Colorado River four miles west of Marble
Falls, had two generating units, installed in June,
1951, with a combined capacity of 45,000 kilowatts.

Max Starcke Dam (Marble Falls Lake qv), on
the Colorado River at Marble Falls, had two generating units, installed in September, 1951, with a
combined capacity of 32,000 kilowatts.

Mansfield Dam qv (Lake Travis qv), on the Colorado River twelve miles northwest of Austin, had
three generating units, installed in 1941, with a
combined capacity of 67,500 kilowatts.

Tom Miller Dam (Lake Austin qv), on the Colorado River at Austin, had two generating units, installed in March, 1940, with a combined capacity
of 13,500 kilowatts.

TP-1 Dam (Lake Dunlap qv), on the Guadalupe
River nine miles northwest of Seguin, had two generating units, installed in 1928, with a combined
capacity of 3,600 kilowatts.

Abbott Dam (TP-3, Lake McQueeney qv), on the
Guadalupe River five miles west of Seguin, had two
generating units, installed in 1928, with a combined
capacity of 2,800 kilowatts.

TP-4 Dam (Lake Placid; see Guadalupe-Blanco
River Authority), on the Guadalupe River three

miles southwest of Seguin, had one 2,400-kilowatt
generating unit installed in March, 1932.

TP-5 Dam (Lake Nolte qv), on the Guadalupe
River three miles southeast of Seguin, had two generating units, installed in November, 1927, with a
combined capacity of 2,480 kilowatts.

H-4 Dam (Lake Gonzales; see H-4 Reservoir),
on the Guadalupe River four miles southeast of Belmont, had one generating unit, installed in 1931,
with a capacity of 2,400 kilowatts.

H-5 Dam (Wood Lake; see Guadalupe-Blanco
River Authority), on the Guadalupe River three
miles southwest of Gonzales, had one 2,400-kilo-
watt generating unit installed in October, 1931.

Red Bluff Dam,qv on the Pecos River five miles
north of Orla, had two generating units, installed
in June, 1937, with a combined capacity of 2,300
kilowatts.

Amistad Dam (see Amistad Reservoir), on the
Rio Grande twelve miles northwest of Del Rio, had
two hydroelectric power plants of 66,000 kilowatts
capacity each, one on the United States side and the
other on the Mexican side of the river. This installation, completed in the late 1960's, inundated Devils
Lake qv Dam (which had one generating unit, installed in 1928, with a capacity of 1,800 kilowatts)
and Lake Walk qv Dam (which had one generating
unit, installed in 1929, with a capacity of 1,350
kilowatts), both on Devils River northwest of
Del Rio.

International Falcon Reservoir,qv on the Rio
Grande three miles west of Falcon Heights, had a
hydroelectric power plant on each side of the river
at the dam, each plant having three 10,500-kilowatt
generating units. Generation of electricity began in
October, 1954.

BIBLIOGRAPHY: Texas Water Commission, Bulletin 6408
(1964).

Seth D. Breeding

Water Quality Board, Texas. The first separate
state agency that was interested solely in state water
pollution control was the Texas Water Pollution
Advisory Council, created in 1953. It consisted of
five ex officio members and was purely advisory.
The Texas Pollution Control Act of 1961 created
the Texas Water Pollution Control Board, which
was empowered to issue permits and to generally
control pollution. The Texas Water Quality Act of
1967 created the Texas Water Quality Board,
which assumed the functions, powers, duties, and
responsibilities of the Water Pollution Control
Board.

The Texas Water Quality Board consists of
seven members, the executive director of the Texas
Water Development Board,qv the state commissioner of health, the executive director of the Parks
and Wildlife Department,qv the chairman of the
Railroad Commision,qv and three members appointed from the public. Except for the deletion of
the requirement that the governor appoint the
members from private life to represent agriculture,
industries, and the general public, respectively, the
membership of the Texas Water Quality Board is
the same as that of the Water Pollution Control

Board which preceded it. The membership of the board is designed to assure effective coordination among state agencies interested in water quality control and to give the general public maximum representation.

*Water Resources. *See* Surface Water; Underground Water; Artesian Wells; Rainfall in Texas; Rainmaking; Rivers of Texas; Irrigation; Water Agencies and Programs, Local (and all *see* references following that article).

Water Rights Commission, Texas. The name of the Texas Board of Water Engineers qv was changed in 1962 to Texas Water Commission,qv and again in 1965 to Texas Water Rights Commission. The members of the governing body of the agencies have been the same in number and selected in the same manner as for the original board, except that an act passed by the legislature in 1965 specified that the three commissioners be selected from separate areas of the state rather than from water divisions.

Numerous functions have been assigned to the commission over the years. The responsibility for cancelling existing water rights when they are not being utilized was assigned to the board in 1955. The Texas Water Planning Act of 1957 added the responsibility of preparing and implementing a statewide plan for the development, conservation, and beneficial use of the water resources of Texas. Two results of the 1957 planning act were the resumption of topographic mapping by the state in 1958 and the preparation of plans for meeting the state's long-range water requirements. The planning function of the board, however, was transferred in 1965 to the Texas Water Development Board.qv The legislature in 1961 added several more functions, including responsibilities relative to the detection, prevention, and elimination of pollution of the waters of the state; the licensing of water well drillers; the inspection during construction of projects of water control and improvement districts; and the functions of the state reclamation engineer.

BIBLIOGRAPHY: University of Texas at Austin, *Guide To Texas State Agencies* (1972).

Seth D. Breeding

*Water Supply Districts. *See also* Water Agencies and Programs, Local.

*Water Valley, Texas.

Water Well Drillers Board, Texas. The Texas Water Well Drillers Board, created in 1965, was composed in 1972 of the executive director of the Texas Water Development Board,qv the executive director of the Texas Water Quality Board,qv the chairman of the state Board of Health (*see* Public Health, State Department of), as ex officio members, and six water well drillers chosen from geographical regions of the state. The primary duties of the board were the licensing and regulation of water well drillers and the prevention of underground water pollution.

BIBLIOGRAPHY: University of Texas at Austin, *Guide To Texas State Agencies* (1972).

*Waterhole Creek.

Waterhouse, Richard. Richard Waterhouse, also known as Richard Waterhouse, Jr., the eldest son of Richard E. Waterhouse qv and Mary Thomas (Lane) Waterhouse, was born on January 12, 1832, in Rhea County, Tennessee. As a boy, during the Mexican War, he served as a private in Company H of the 4th Regiment of Tennessee Volunteers, which was commanded by his father. In 1849 he moved with his parents to San Augustine, Texas, where he was associated with his father in business. Waterhouse was married to Rosalie Wallace on December 30, 1858; they had two children. In 1859 or 1860 he moved to Jefferson, where, in association with his father and others, he engaged in the mercantile business under the titles Waterhouse & Lockhart; Waterhouse, Wallace & Company; and Richard Waterhouse & Company.

Soon after the outbreak of the Civil War, Waterhouse recruited the 19th Texas Volunteer Infantry in and around Jefferson and, on May 13, 1862, was commissioned its colonel. All of his war service was in the Trans-Mississippi Department of the Confederacy. Under the command of Henry E. McCulloch,qv he participated in the battle of Milliken's Bend.

In April, 1864, he fought in William Read Scurry's qv Brigade at the battles of Mansfield and Pleasant Hill qqv during the Red River Campaign,qv and at the following battle of Jenkins' Ferry in Arkansas.

In recognition of his ability, Waterhouse was assigned to a command as a brigadier general by General Edmund Kirby Smith;qv he was to assume command of the Trans-Mississippi Department on April 30, 1864. The appointment was later made official by President Jefferson Davis,qv took effect on March 17, 1865, and was confirmed the following day by the Confederate Senate on the last date on which it convened.

After the war, Waterhouse returned to Jefferson, where he engaged in mercantile, shipping, and real estate operations until his death on March 20, 1876, while on a business trip to Waco. He was buried in Oakwood Cemetery at Jefferson.

BIBLIOGRAPHY: G. L. Crocket, *Two Centuries in East Texas* (1932); J. P. Blessington, *Campaigns of Walker's Texas Division* (1876); U. S. War Department, *The War of the Rebellion: A Compilation of the Official Records of the Union and Confederate Armies* (1880–1901); Ezra J. Warner, *Generals in Gray* (1959); Waco *Daily Examiner*, March 21, 22, 1876; Houston *Telegraph*, March 21, 22, 24, 1876.

Palmer Bradley

Waterhouse, Richard E. Richard E. Waterhouse, son of Richard Green Waterhouse, of Rhea County, Tennessee, was born on August 11, 1805, at Knoxville. He was married to Mary Thomas Lane at Athens, Tennessee, on March 20, 1831; they had eleven children. He was captain of a company which took part in the Seminole War in 1837, and during the Mexican War he served as a major of the Tennessee Mounted Volunteers from June, 1846, to May, 1847. He later served as colonel of the 4th Regiment of Tennessee Volunteers from November, 1847, to August, 1848. He was a member of the Tennessee legislature from 1841 to 1842.

In 1849 Waterhouse moved with his family to San Augustine, Texas, where he engaged in the mercantile business and acquired large landholdings. In 1857 and again in 1859 he was elected representative to the Texas legislature from San Augustine County. His store was robbed and he was murdered in San Augustine on December 31, 1863. The murder attracted wide attention but was never satisfactorily solved.

BIBLIOGRAPHY: William DeRyee and R. E. Moore, *Texas Album of the Eighth Legislature* (1860); G. L. Crocket, *Two Centuries in East Texas* (1932); William Hugh Robarts, *Mexican War Veterans* (1887).

Palmer Bradley

*Waterloo, Texas. (Grayson County.)

*Waterloo, Texas. (Travis County.)

*Waterloo, Texas. (Williamson County.)

*Waterman, Texas.

*Waters Mountain.

*Waters-Pierce Case.

*Watkins, Jesse.

Watkins, Theophilus. Theophilus Watkins was born in Kentucky in 1819. He was married to Susan Williams, and they had one daughter. After his wife's death he came to Texas in 1845 with his brother, Charles, and lived for a time near the present site of Sabinal, on land later known as Watkins' Flat. In 1848 he went to California, but returned to Kentucky in 1850; he came back to Texas in 1854, this time bringing his daughter. He was a captain at Fort Inge qv near Uvalde, and his company protected the area from Indian attacks. On December 1, 1867, he was married in Kentucky to Frances Anna Elizabeth Mosely; they had six children.

They settled in the valley of the Frio River, Frio Canyon, in what later became Real County, where Watkins saw the possibilities for an irrigation system with water from the Frio River. In 1868, together with F. Smith and Newman Patterson, he constructed a ditch ten miles long and five feet wide, with a depth ranging from three to four feet. It was a gravity canal supplied with water by means of a dam built of brush and gravel on the main Frio River. The ditch was not put into full operation until a charter was granted to the Lombardy Irrigation Company on August 20, 1875. The ditch was still in operation in the 1960's, and the dam had been rebuilt a number of times. Watkins died in 1883 and was buried in the cemetery at Rio Frio.

BIBLIOGRAPHY: Grace Lorene Lewis, A History of Real County, Texas (M.A. thesis, University of Texas at Austin, 1956).

Sallie Lewis

*Watrous, John Charles.

*Watson, William.

*Watson, Texas. (Comanche County.)

*Watson, Texas. (Red River County.)

*Watson Branch, Texas.

*Watson's Store, Texas.

*Watsonville, Texas.

*Watters Park, Texas.

*Watts, Arthur Thomas.

*Watts, Texas. (Limestone County.)

*Watts, Texas. (Robertson County.)

*Watts Creek.

*Watts Creek, Texas.

*Wattsville, Texas.

*Waugh, Beverly.

Waugh, Julia Nott. Julia Nott Waugh, Texas writer, was born on August 9, 1888, near Goliad at the ranch home of her parents, Mary (Ray) and Thomas H. Nott, a pioneer physician of the old town of St. Mary's of Aransas. She attended Mrs. Shive's private school in Goliad and St. Mary's Hall in San Antonio; she received a B.A. degree from the University of Texas in 1913. She also attended Columbia University and a school in Paris, France.

Although she traveled widely, Julia Nott Waugh made her home in San Antonio, where she became prominent in literary, historical, and conservationist circles, and served for several years as a director of the Yanaguana Society.qv She wrote *Castro-Ville and Henry Castro—Impresario* (1934), which included a translation from the French of Auguste Frétellière's manuscript, "Adventures of a Castrovillian, 1834–1844." J. Frank Dobie qv described her Castro history as being "the best written monograph dealing with any aspect of Texas that I have read." From her interest in Mexican folk traditions of San Antonio she wrote *The Silver Cradle* (1955). She contributed articles, dealing principally with Texas pioneer days and with Mexican customs and manners, to national and Texas publications.

She was married to George F. Waugh, an officer in the United States Army, in 1914, and after the war she joined him at his station in Europe. The marriage ended in divorce about 1927. She died in the Algonquin Hotel in New York (where she often stayed) on January 18, 1958, and she was buried in the family plot in Oak Hill Cemetery in Goliad. Her will, which was probated in San Antonio, bequeathed her personal library to the Goliad County Library.

Hobart Huson

*Waukegan, Texas.

*Waul, Thomas N. Thomas Neville Waul died near Greenville on July 28 (not July 27, as stated in Volume II), 1903, and was buried at Fort Worth.

BIBLIOGRAPHY: Marcus J. Wright and Harold B. Simpson, *Texas in the War, 1861–1865* (1965); Death Certificate (County Clerk's Office, Hunt County).

*Waul's Legion.

*Wavell, Arthur Goodall.

*Waverly, Texas.

*Waxahachie, Texas. During the 1960's Waxahachie, seat of Ellis County, was rapidly becoming industrialized. The population increased from 12,749 in 1960 to 13,452 in 1970, according to the United States census. Local industries included a cotton oil mill, feed and poultry processing plants, and businesses manufacturing clothing, furniture, and fiberglass. Many residents commuted to work in Dallas. In 1970 the city had 222 businesses and a hospital. The Texas Baptist Home for Children and the Southwestern Junior College of the Assemblies of God qv were located in Waxahachie. The Confederate Powder Mill was nearby. See also Dallas Standard Metropolitan Statistical Area.

*Waxahachie Creek.

*Waxahachie Tap Railroad Company. See Central Texas and Northwestern Railroad Company.

*Way, Texas.

*Wayland, J. H.

*Wayland, Texas.

*Wayland Baptist College. Wayland Baptist College, Plainview, remained a junior college until 1947, when it first offered senior college courses. It was accredited by the Southern Association of Colleges and Schools in 1956, and it was the oldest surviving institution of higher learning in the Panhandle and South Plains of Texas. The school opened its doors to all races in 1951, thus becoming the first Texas college to integrate voluntarily. Wayland showed a gradual increase in enrollment over the years, with 345 men and 365 women enrolled as regular students by the fall of 1964. In the 1974–1975 regular term the enrollment was 932. Additional students took noncredit workshops and participated in conferences. The building program during the 1960's included completion of a dugout track and stadium and an auditorium, the center of a fine arts complex.

The faculty numbered over fifty members in 1972. The library contained 43,000 volumes in 1965; by 1969 holdings had increased to 50,805 volumes. One of the distinctive features of the college was its concern for international relations. It annually held an international relations conference, to which ambassadors and statesmen from foreign countries were invited. Roy C. McClung was president in 1974.

*Wayne, Texas.

*Wayside, Texas.

*Weadington Creek.

*Wealthy, Texas.

Weather in Texas. Weather in Texas is widely varied because of the state's enormous size, its great elevation differences, and its peculiar geographic position between the high plateau of the Rocky Mountains and the Gulf of Mexico. The state's daily weather rather than its average weather (climate) is of more concern to Texans because of meteorological instability which results in storms, floods, drouths, and unseasonable weather fronts.

Climate. The climate varies from east to west and north to south; but in general the state exhibits three types of climate—maritime, continental, and mountain. Maritime climate, a modified marine type with fairly uniform temperatures, mild winters, and humid summers, is found along the Gulf of Mexico. Continental climate, marked by very rapid changes and extremes in temperature, prevails over the remainder of the state except for the Trans-Pecos area, which has a mountain climate, characterized by temperatures somewhat cooler than continental. Differences in latitude, elevation, and distance from moisture sources (principally the Gulf of Mexico) justify ten separate climate subdivisions. Although there is throughout Texas a relatively low average humidity, a gentle southerly wind, and much sunshine, the variety of climates makes possible a diversity of agricultural production, from forests in the east to grassy plains in the west, from hard wheat in the north to grapefruit in the south and rice and sugar cane in the southeast.

Weather Records. The voluminous records kept by the Spanish bureaucratic officials who administered Texas for so many decades rarely mentioned the weather directly; however, through the years various other sources—diaries, travel accounts, correspondence, newspapers, and medical records of military posts—reveal that the weather in Texas was of concern to early explorers, missionaries, dignitaries, Anglo American colonists, other immigrants, and temporary residents. By 1855 Texas had twenty-one weather stations reporting data which were published; these were decreased in number during the Civil War, and by 1870, when federal weather service officially began (February 9, 1870), Texas had fourteen weather stations at scattered settlements and military posts. The United States Congress passed an act on October 1, 1890, transferring all meteorological services formerly carried on by the army signal corps to a newly created weather bureau under the secretary of agriculture, effective July 1, 1891. Texas had seventy-eight stations in 1890 and one hundred twelve in 1900; the number of stations continued to increase until by the early 1970's there were approximately one thousand weather observers around the state, mostly private citizen volunteers reporting to the federal government, in addition to forty-one major stations and offices operated by the federal weather bureau (which in 1971 became a part of the National Oceanic and Atmospheric Administration). In addition, the United States Air Force air weather service maintained stations at military installations in Texas.

Temperature. In Texas there is a wide range of temperatures. The northwest experiences rather low winter readings, while other areas have very high summer temperatures. The hottest month is August. The highest readings come from three areas: Rio Grande City to Cotulla to Eagle Pass; the Upper Rio Grande from Presidio to Candelaria; and along the Red River from Childress to Chillicothe into Oklahoma at Hollis and Altus. Extended subfreezing weather is rare, and outdoor work is seldom stopped for more than forty-eight to seventy-two hours at a time. In parts of South Texas subfreezing temperatures usually occur only for a few hours prior to sunrise, and some winters are without freezes. The shortest average growing season—180 days—occurs at Muleshoe and Dalhart, the longest —341 days—at Galveston. The highest temperature ever recorded at a weather station in Texas was 120 degrees at Seymour on August 12, 1936; the lowest was 23 degrees below zero at Tulia on February 12, 1899, and again that same temperature at Seminole on February 8, 1933.

Significant snowfall is usually confined to the mountainous and High Plains areas. Vega, at an elevation of 4,000 feet, averages twenty-four inches annually. Measurable snow fell at Brownsville only once in about seventy-five years, and the temperature there drops to freezing during only four out of ten years. A well known winter phenomenon is the "norther," a blustery, cold wind from the north, with or without moisture, which rapidly reduces temperature. Extreme conditions, such as strong winds and subfreezing temperatures accompanied by snow, occur at times, but these blizzards are usually confined to the western and northwestern portions of the state. Blizzards were particularly damaging to the cattle industry during the nineteenth century.

One of the greatest heavy-snow anomalies in history occurred on February 14–15, 1895, when Houston, Orange, Stafford, and Columbia each received 20 inches of snow and Galveston received 15.4 inches. Cold waves with snow and ice were severe in the winter of 1947–1948 and again in 1948–1949. From January 25 to February 2, 1949, a winter storm paralyzed traffic as far south as San Antonio, damaged telephone and telegraph lines, and inflicted millions of dollars of damage on citrus and truck crops in the Lower Rio Grande Valley. In January, 1951, a freeze extended into the Gulf, killing an estimated 30,000 tons of fish. In February, 1956, a blizzard which dumped thirty-three inches of snow at Hale Center resulted in twenty deaths, while the blizzard of March 22–25, 1957, marooned four thousand persons and caused ten deaths and heavy livestock losses. Two severe ice and snow storms during December and January, 1972–1973, paralyzed traffic as far south as Corpus Christi, damaging electric and telephone lines and causing extensive agricultural losses in North Texas and the Panhandle. A drastic fuel shortage which coincided with the storm resulted in a curtailment of electric and other services and caused additional hardship and financial loss.

Storms. The most destructive storms that strike Texas are hurricanes and tornadoes. A typical hurricane has a diameter of 700 miles, but as a rule affects only the coastal region of the state. Tornadoes, on the other hand, with swirling winds up to 500 miles per hour, range across the whole state.

Sandstorms and dust storms are frequent in late winter and early spring and are most intense and bothersome in west and northwest Texas. Resulting from extreme differences in barometric pressure in adjacent areas, the storms occur when high pressure areas move in from the west and northwest. Because plowed land releases soil high in humus content, sandstorms are now quite rare, having been replaced by dust storms. The Dust Bowl qv in northwest Texas, western Oklahoma, Kansas, and Nebraska in the 1930's was the result of exceptional drouth after destruction of the grassy covering of the ranges. Two of the worst soil-blowing storms were those of February 24–25, 1956, and January 25, 1965.

Turbulent weather, especially thunderstorms, is often accompanied by hail. Although hail risk is comparatively small (the greatest risk being in the Panhandle and South Plains), Texas ranks high nationally in losses due to hail. In the thirty-year period ending with 1953, there were thirty-three hailstorms which resulted in damages of $100,000 or more each; a dozen of these inflicted damages of at least $1,000,000. Such storms may injure or kill animals and, in some cases, people. Hailstorms are damaging to crops, but many storms in rural areas are never reported for official tabulation; those inflicting severe damage to cities, however, usually receive publicity.

On May 8, 1926, a particularly severe hailstorm hit the area of Dallas. For ten minutes, in a path from one to fifteen miles wide and running from twenty-five miles north of the city to twenty-five miles southeast, hailstones as large as twelve inches in circumference damaged roofs, windows, automobiles, and crops. Some sections of Dallas looked as though they had been riddled by machine-gun fire. Scores of citizens were injured and many animals were killed.

Rainfall. Although average rainfall varies from fifty-six inches in east Texas to eight inches in extreme west Texas, not all moisture deficiencies occur in the west. Each of several rainfall belts is subject to great variation. There are also seasonal differences. As a result of spring thunderstorms, April and May are peak periods of precipitation except in the Trans-Pecos area, where afternoon showers occur during the summer. Heavy rainstorms and flooding, however, can strike any section at any time of the year. Flooding, usually of short duration, takes place somewhere in Texas almost every year.

During the rainstorm of June 27–July 1, 1899, an average of 8.9 inches fell over 66,000 square miles, and 17 inches fell over 7,000 square miles. At Turnersville, in Coryell County, 33 inches fell during three days of this deluge. Thirty-five lives were lost, and property damages amounted to $9,000,000. Another heavy rainstorm occurred on September 6–10, 1921. At Taylor, in Williamson County, 17 inches were recorded during the first day, and a total of 30 inches fell during a two-day period, while the same storm poured an 18-hour total of 36.4 inches on nearby Thrall—a record for the nation. Damages were estimated at $17,000,000, and 224 lives were lost in the resulting flood.

See also Drouths in Texas; Hurricanes in Texas; Rainfall in Texas (in Volume II); Rainmaking; Tornadoes in Texas.

BIBLIOGRAPHY: Isaac Monroe Cline, *Storms, Floods and Sunshine* (1945); William G. Hoyt and Walter B. Langbein, *Floods* (1955); Snowden D. Flora, *Hailstorms of the United States* (1956); A. M. Vance and Robert L. Lowry, Jr., *Excessive Rainfall in Texas* (1934); Robert B. Orton, *Climates of the States: Texas* (1969); Edward Hake Phillips, "The Texas Norther," *Southwestern Historical Quarterly,* LIX (1955–1956); *Texas Game and Fish* (May, 1951); *Texas Almanac* (1965, 1971).

Roy Sylvan Dunn

*Weatherford, Jefferson.

*Weatherford, Texas. Weatherford, county seat of Parker County and market and shipping point for agricultural products of the area, derived much of its income from beef and dairy cattle, fruits, and vegetables. Other major businesses were connected with oil field equipment, brick, stone products, trailers, ceramics, fertilizer, and electronics. In the 1960's the town reported a college, three banks, two libraries, thirty-three churches, a newspaper, and a radio station. The city purchased ninety acres for future expansion of Weatherford College and built two new schools and a bank building. A new hospital supplemented the city's four nursing homes. Nearby Weatherford Lake provided recreational facilities and a water supply for the town. The proximity of the greatly expanding Fort Wolters qv affected Weatherford in population and construction activities. The 1960 population was 9,759; in 1970 the number had increased to 11,750, according to the United States census. The city had 237 businesses in 1970.

*Weatherford College. Weatherford College, Weatherford, ceased to be operated by Southwestern University qv on May 31, 1949, four years after they merged. The merger agreement stated that if Southwestern should decide to terminate administration, Weatherford College would first be offered to the city of Weatherford and then to Parker County.

Under the state junior college law, the total property valuations in the city were too low to qualify the city for administration of the school, and the continuation of Weatherford College came before the people of Parker County in a special election on August 6, 1949. Three propositions passed: to establish a Parker County Junior College District, coextensive with county boundaries; to set up a board of trustees for operation of the college; and to place a $.30 tax rate on each $100 valuation of taxable property for the college.

Enrollment increased from 260 students during the 1950–1951 school year to 792 students in 1964–1965 and 1,270 in fall, 1974. In 1965 a $520,000 bond issue was approved to supplement federal financing of an auditorium-fine arts building, a library-classroom building, and a physical education building. In 1969 library volumes totaled 21,000. Further expansion of the school was projected on a new ninety-acre campus in southeast Weatherford, as the cost of acquiring land around the original campus was prohibitive. The faculty included approximately fifty members in 1974, and E. W. Mince served as president of the college.

Weatherford Lake. Weatherford Lake is in the Trinity River Basin in Parker County, seven miles east of Weatherford on the Clear Fork of the Trinity River. The lake is owned and operated by the city of Weatherford for municipal and industrial water supply. Construction of the project began in June, 1956, and was completed on March 15, 1957. The lake has a capacity of 19,600 acre-feet and a surface area of 1,280 acres at the spillway crest

elevation of 896 feet above mean sea level. The drainage area above the dam is 109 square miles.

BIBLIOGRAPHY: Texas Water Commission, *Bulletin 6408* (1964).

Seth D. Breeding

*Weatherford, Mineral Wells, and Northwestern Railway Company.

*Weatherly, Texas.

*Weatherred, Francis Marcus, I.

*Weatherred, William Wallace.

*Weaver, Texas.

*Weaver H. Baker Memorial Sanatorium. The Weaver H. Baker Memorial Sanatorium was reclaimed in 1952 for air base purposes by the federal government; the institution was replaced in 1953 by the San Antonio State Tuberculosis Hospital, which in 1971 was renamed the San Antonio State Chest Hospital.qv

*Weaver Springs, Texas.

*Webb, James.

*Webb, Joseph.

Webb, Walter Prescott. Walter Prescott Webb was born on April 3, 1888, to Casner P. and Mary Elizabeth (Kyle) Webb on a farm in Panola County, Texas. The family moved several times in Texas before settling in Stephens County; there and in Eastland County young Webb went to school intermittently before finishing Ranger High School and receiving a teaching certificate. After teaching at a succession of one-teacher schools Webb entered the University of Texas, where he alternated college attendance with teaching positions at country and small-town schools. He received all three of his regular degrees from the University of Texas— the B.A. in 1915, M.A. in 1920, and Ph.D. in 1932. He also received honorary degrees from the University of Chicago, Southern Methodist University, and Oxford University in England.

Webb was teaching in Main High School in San Antonio when he was invited to join the history department of the University of Texas in 1918. He remained on the university's faculty for the next forty-five years, except for visiting professorships elsewhere. In 1933 he became professor of history, and in 1952 he was named Distinguished Professor of History. He also was a visiting professor at Stephen F. Austin State College (now Stephen F. Austin State University); University of North Carolina; University of West Virginia; University of Alaska; Rice University; University of Houston; Harvard University; Queens College, Oxford (Harmsworth Professor, 1942–1943); and University of London (Harkness Professor, 1938).

From 1939 to 1946 Webb was director of the Texas State Historical Association,qv where he originated such features of the association's program as *The Handbook of Texas*, the Junior Historian Movement,qv book publication, the annual book auction, and the "Texas Collection" section of the *Southwestern Historical Quarterly*.qv He was president of the Mississippi Valley Historical Association, 1954–1955, and of the American Historical Association, 1957–1958.

Webb was one of the charter members and later a fellow of the Texas Institute of Letters.qv He was also a fellow of the Texas State Historical Association, as well as a member of the Philosophical Society of Texas.qv He held two Guggenheim fellowships, acted as special advisor to Senator (and later Vice-President) Lyndon Baines Johnson qv on water needs of the South and West, and received a $10,000 award from the American Council of Learned Societies for distinguished service to scholarship. The United States Bureau of Reclamation also gave him an award for distinguished service to conservation. He was an invited speaker to an international historical congress in Paris, and the Second International Congress of Historians of the United States and Mexico examined his Great Frontier thesis as its sole topic during its 1958 meeting. Webb had earlier won the Carr P. Collins Award of $1,000 of the Texas Institute of Letters for his book The Great Frontier (1952).

In all, Webb wrote or edited more than twenty books. The best known are The Great Plains (1931), which won the Loubat Prize for the best book over a five-year period and was chosen a quarter century later by a national panel of historians as the most significant work of history by a living author; The Texas Rangers (1935); Divided We Stand (1937); The Great Frontier (1952); The Handbook of Texas (1952); More Water for Texas (1954); and An Honest Preface (1959). At the time of his death he was working on a television series on American civilization under a grant from the Ford Foundation.

Webb was married on September 16, 1916, to Jane Elizabeth Oliphant, who died on June 28, 1960. They had one daughter. On December 14, 1961, he was married to Mrs. Terrell (Dobbs) Maverick (widow of Maury Maverick qv) of San Antonio. Walter Prescott Webb was killed in an automobile accident near Austin on March 8, 1963, and was buried in the State Cemetery qv by proclamation of Governor John Connally. See also Friday Mountain Ranch.

Joe B. Frantz

Webb, William Graham. William Graham Webb was born in Covington, Newton County, Georgia, on November 11, 1824. He received his education in Athens and Cassville, Georgia, and shortly after 1842 moved to La Grange, in Fayette County, Texas, where, on December 30, 1846, he was commissioned lieutenant colonel of the 3rd Regiment, 2nd Brigade, 4th Division of the Texas Militia for service in the Mexican War.qv

During the years between the Mexican War and the Civil War,qv Webb practiced law in La Grange. On May 14, 1848, he was married to Sarah Ann Amelia Hill, sister of James Monroe Hill and John Christopher Columbus Hill;qqv they had one daughter and three sons. On April 14, 1860, Webb was commissioned a brigadier general and authorized to organize the 22nd Brigade of the Texas Militia. On

April 29, 1862, he was appointed a receiver under the Act for the Sequestration of the Estates of Alien Enemies for the counties of Colorado, Comal, Fayette, Gonzales, Guadalupe, and Hays. Webb was commissioned on June 17, 1862, for a four-year term (to date from May 17, 1862) as brigadier general of the 22nd Brigade, Texas State Troops, by Governor Francis Richard Lubbock.qv It appears that his report early in 1863 to General John Bankhead Magruder qv caused the latter to place Austin, Colorado, and Fayette counties under martial law. At an unknown date he relinquished his general's commission.

In December, 1863, with the rank of captain in the Confederate Army, he recruited his own unattached company of cavalry; records indicate that this unit was operating in Grimes County in the fall of 1864; by the end of the year he had returned to civilian life and resumed the duties of Confederate States receiver. Before the end of the war his territory apparently had been greatly enlarged from the original six counties.

After the war Webb resumed the practice of law in La Grange. He was appointed administrator of the then nonexistent University of Texas by Governor James Webb Throckmorton qv on January 5, 1867. Also in 1867 he purchased the Daily Telegraph (originally the Telegraph and Texas Register qv) and moved to Houston to take over its management. Upon suspension of publication of the Telegraph in 1873, he practiced law in Houston until February, 1885, when he moved to Albany, Texas, to join his son in the formation of a law, loan, land, and livestock firm.

After three years in Albany, Webb returned to central Texas and lived in Austin, where he died on March 9, 1902. He was buried in La Grange.

Joseph E. Blanton

*Webb, Texas. (Tarrant County.)

*Webb, Texas. (Webb County.)

Webb Air Force Base. Webb Air Force Base, located just outside of Big Spring, Howard County, was originally the site of Big Spring Army Air Force Bombardier School,qv built during World War II to serve as a bombardier training center. In 1945, at the end of the war, the army installation was closed and the property was used as a county airport. The base was reactivated in October, 1951, and opened in 1952 as a pilot training center. In the planning and building stages the base was called Big Spring Air Force Base, but on May 18, 1952, the base was formally named for First Lieutenant James L. Webb, a native of Big Spring, who was lost on a military flight on June 16, 1949, off Hokkaido, Japan. On May 26, 1971, Webb Air Force Base received over twelve hundred acres of land as a gift from the city of Big Spring. In 1973 the base was the headquarters of the 78th Flying Training Wing.

*Webb County. Webb County had an agricultural economy, with two-thirds of the farm income being derived from livestock and poultry. It was one of the leading beef-producing counties, with the

principal breeds being Santa Gertrudis, Hereford, Charolais, and Brahman. Both irrigated and dry-land farming were practiced, with additional acreage given to dairy cattle and truck crops. From 1921 to January 1, 1973, total production of crude oil amounted to 89,807,740 barrels. The county-owned Casa Blanca Lake near Laredo provided a place for water sports. The 1960 population was 64,791; the 1970 count rose to 72,859, according to the United States census. See also Laredo Standard Metropolitan Statistical Area.

*Webber, Charles Wilkins.

Webber, John Ferdinand. John Ferdinand Webber was born in Vermont in 1793. In the War of 1812 he served as a private in Captain S. Dickinson's company, 31st United States Infantry, from May 23, 1813, to May 31, 1814, during which time he fought in the battle of Shadage Woods. He was in Austin's colony as early as 1826 and received a headright on June 22, 1832. Some time earlier he was married (before the Reverend Michael Muldoon,qv according to an affidavit of his widow) to a slave, Silvia Hector. On June 11, 1834, John Cryer emancipated Silvia and her three children. The Webbers had at least eight additional children.

Webber did not participate in the Texas Revolution. He was the first settler on Webber's Prairie in Travis County. Beginning in the 1840's newcomers from the Deep South resented Webber's racially mixed marriage, and ultimately he moved his household. In 1853 he bought several leagues of land fronting on the Rio Grande downstream from the town of Hidalgo. There he established Webber's Ranch, where his family farmed in poverty. A Unionist, he fled to Mexico during the Confederate occupation of the Rio Grande Valley. He returned in May, 1865, and received a pension from the United States in 1872.

Webber died at his home on July 19, 1882, and he was buried in the family cemetery on the levee road, a short distance above the Donna, Texas, pump. His widow, "Aunt Puss," died about 1891. The hamlet of Webberville in Travis County bears his name.

BIBLIOGRAPHY: Edna (Turley) Carpenter, Tales from the Manchaca Hills (1960); Noah Smithwick, The Evolution of a State (1900); J. Lee Stambaugh and Lillian J. Stambaugh, The Lower Rio Grande Valley of Texas (1954); Deed Records of Travis and Hidalgo Counties; Pension Records (National Archives, Washington, D.C.).

Andrew Forest Muir

*Webberville, Texas.

Webbville, Texas. Webbville is the name given to the terminus of Farm Road 2806 in northeastern Coleman County. In 1966 a country store, Webb's Store, existed at the site. In 1973 the estimated population of the community was fifty.

*Webster, Texas. Webster, in southern Harris County, is in the Houston Standard Metropolitan Statistical Area.qv Its population grew from 329 in 1960 to 2,231 by 1970, an increase of 578.1 percent, according to the United States census. In the early 1970's the town reported forty businesses, a post office, and a bank. Webster's dramatic growth may be attributed in part to its close proximity to the Manned Spacecraft Center.qv

*Webster County.

*Webster Creek.

Webster Massacre. The massacre of the Webster party by Comanche Indians occurred in August, 1839, near the headwaters of Brushy Creek in present Williamson County. John Webster, leading a party of thirteen to establish a settlement in West Texas, discovered a large force of Indians between the north and south forks of the San Gabriel River. The Webster party tried to gain the security of the settlements on the Colorado. Overtaken near Brushy Creek, the party formed defenses by arranging their wagons in a square. In the ensuing battle all the men of the party were killed, and Mrs. Webster and her two children were captured. Mrs. Webster and her daughter escaped from the Comanches several months later, when the Indians were encamped near San Antonio to attend a council for prisoner exchange (see Council House Fight). Mrs. Webster's son, who was held by another group of Indians, was ransomed after two years of captivity.

In 1936 the Texas Centennial qv Commission erected a monument one and six-tenths miles east of Leander at the place of burial of the massacre victims.

BIBLIOGRAPHY: Frank Brown, Annals of Travis County and the City of Austin (MS., Archives, University of Texas at Austin Library); J. W. Wilbarger, Indian Depredations in Texas (1889); William S. Red (ed.), "Allen's Reminiscences of Texas, 1838–1842," Southwestern Historical Quarterly, XVII (1913–1914); Monuments Erected . . . to Commemorate the Centenary of Texas Independence (1939).

Peyton O. Abbott

*Weches, Texas.

Wecter, Dixon. Dixon Wecter was born in Houston on January 12, 1906, the son of John Joseph and Eugenia (Dixon) Wecter. Valedictorian of the high school graduating class of Colorado City in 1921, at the age of fifteen he entered Baylor University, where he received an A.B. degree in 1925. He took a master's degree at Yale in 1926 and was one of thirty-two Rhodes Scholars in 1928, identifying himself with Merton College of Oxford. Illness forced him to return to the United States in 1930. He returned to Yale and received his doctorate in 1936.

Wecter began his teaching career in 1933 as an instructor at the University of Denver. The following year he joined the faculty of the University of Colorado, and in 1939 he became professor of American literature at the University of California at Los Angeles. In 1942–1943 he held a Guggenheim Fellowship, and in 1945 he became visiting professor of American history at the University of Sydney, Australia. In 1946 and 1947 he was lecturer at the University of Chicago, and in 1949 the state department employed him on a cultural mission to South America. At Los Angeles, Wecter was associated with the Henry E. Huntington Library and served as chairman of its permanent research staff from

1946 to 1949. At this time he became the Margaret Byrne Professor of American History at the University of California at Berkeley.

As a social historian, Wecter published widely during his lifetime in the *Atlantic Monthly*, *The Saturday Review of Literature*, *The Virginia Quarterly Review*, and the New York *Times*. His books include *The Saga of American Society* (1937), *Edmund Burke and His Kinsmen* (1939), *The Hero in America* (1941), and *When Johnny Comes Marching Home* (1944), for which he won the Houghton Mifflin Life-in-America Prize. He also received the Commonwealth Club's "Gold Medal for Literary Achievement" for *The Age of the Great Depression* (1948). He served as associate editor of *The Literary History of the United States* and as literary editor of the Mark Twain estate from 1946 until the time of his death. He edited Mark Twain's letters to Mrs. Fairbanks in 1949 and *The Love Letters of Mark Twain* in 1950; he left an unfinished volume, *Sam Clemens of Hannibal*, to be published posthumously.

Baylor University awarded him the Litt.D. in 1945, and Rockford College granted him the LL.D. in 1950. Wecter died on June 24, 1950, after having delivered the centennial address for the California Library Association. He was buried in Denver and was survived by his wife, Elizabeth (Farrar) Wecter, whom he had married on December 28, 1937.

BIBLIOGRAPHY: *Current Biography* (1944); *Directory of American Scholars* (1942); *Twentieth Century Authors* (1955); *Who Was Who In America*, III (1960).

Lois Smith Murray

*Weekly Citizen. See Citizen, The.

*Weekly Dispatch (Matagorda).

*Weekly Dispatch (San Antonio).

*Weekly Galvestonian. See Galvestonian.

*Weekly Houstonian. See Houstonian.

*Weekly Texian.

*Weeks, Andrew Jackson.

Weeks, Oliver Douglas. Oliver Douglas Weeks, son of Dana Oliver and Gertrude (Douglas) Weeks, was born in Marion, Ohio, on September 4, 1896. He was a noted author and an authority on American, Southern, and Texas politics and political theory.

Weeks earned a B.A. degree from Ohio Wesleyan University in 1918 and an M.A. from the University of Wisconsin in 1919. He taught political science briefly at Morningside College in Sioux City, Iowa, from 1920 to 1922, and then returned to the University of Wisconsin to earn a Ph.D. in 1924. He was a teaching assistant in political science at that university from 1922 to 1924 before going to the University of Texas as an instructor of government, 1924–1925. After a brief interval at Western Reserve University, 1925–1926, Weeks returned to Texas in 1926, where he taught until his retirement in 1966. He was married to Julien Elizabeth Devereux on June 21, 1927; they had two children.

He became a full professor of government in 1933 and was chairman of the government department from 1935 to 1947 and from 1950 to 1957. He took one brief leave of absence, 1945–1946, to teach at Shrivenham-American University in Shrivenham, England, and at Biarritz-American University (United States Army) at Biarritz, France.

Weeks was a member of the American Political Science Association, the Southwestern Social Science Association,qv and the Southern Political Science Association. He was the first president of the Southwestern Political Science Association (1963), book review editor of the *Southwestern Social Science Quarterly* qv from 1926 to 1945, and was a frequent contributor of articles to publications of the University of Texas Institute of Public Affairs and other professional journals. Widely known for his books on national and regional politics, he wrote *The Democratic Victory of 1932* (1933), *Two Legislative Houses or One* (1938), *Research in the American State Legislative Process* (1947), *Texas Presidential Politics in 1952* (1953), and *Texas One-Party Politics in 1956* (1957).

Weeks died in Austin on October 30, 1970, and was buried in Memorial Park there.

BIBLIOGRAPHY: Austin *American-Statesman*, October 31, 1970; *Who's Who In America* (1960); *Who's Who in the South and Southwest* (1961); Biographical File, Barker Texas History Center, University of Texas at Austin.

*Weems, Mason Locke.

*Weesatche, Texas.

*Wegefarth County.

*Wehdem, Texas.

*Weimar, Texas. In the late 1960's Weimar, in western Colorado County, reported a hospital, a newspaper, a library, two banks, and sixty-eight businesses. The city is a dairy and pecan-marketing center, but special emphasis is put on poultry and egg production and shipping. Four feed mills serve the local poultry industry, which produces turkeys as well as chickens. Important improvements in public facilities and the construction of a nursing home were completed in 1967. The 1960 population was 2,006; by 1970 it had increased to 2,104, according to the United States census.

*Weinert, Ferdinand C.

Weinert, Hilda Blumberg. Hilda Blumberg Weinert was born on April 19, 1889, in the farming community of Schumansville, Guadalupe County, the daughter of Emma Henrietta (Meyer) and Henry J. Blumberg, descendants of early German settlers of the area. She was graduated in 1906 from Seguin High School and in 1907 attended Southwest Texas Normal School in San Marcos (now Southwest Texas State University). She taught school in La Vernia in 1908 and in Seguin for several years. She was married to Hilmar H. Weinert on June 23, 1915, and the couple had one daughter.

Hilda Weinert, who came to be known as Texas' "Mrs. Democrat," served as a delegate to every national Democratic convention from 1936 to 1968, and missed only one county and one state committee meeting during those years. In 1938 the State Democratic Committee admitted women to its membership for the first time, and Hilda Weinert was chosen to represent her district. She became the first woman vice-chairman of the State Democratic Executive Committee and served as national committeewoman from 1944 to 1957 after Clara Driscoll's qv sixteen years as national committeewoman. In 1957 the liberal Democrat group put in their candidate, Frankie Randolph,qv who held the position until 1960, after which Mrs. Weinert was reinstated. Mrs. Weinert, a loyal Democrat, supported Adlai Stevenson in the national presidential election in 1952, when the Democratic State Executive Committee supported the Dwight D. Eisenhower qv Republican ticket.

During World War II, President Franklin Delano Roosevelt appointed her a consultant in civil defense; President Harry S. Truman appointed her to the Board of National Prisons for Women. October 13, 1964, was declared "Hilda B. Weinert Day" by Governor Price Daniel, and her portrait, painted by Herman De Jori, was hung in the state capitol.qv She served as regent of Texas Lutheran College for twenty-one years. In 1956 she received the Texas Heritage Foundation medal. She was, at the time of her death, chairman of the board of the Seguin State Bank and Trust Company and of several companies formerly headed by her husband, who died in 1956. Hilda Blumberg Weinert died on May 23, 1971, at her home in Seguin, and was buried in San Geronimo Cemetery in Guadalupe County.

BIBLIOGRAPHY: Austin *American*, July 23, 1944, June 16, 21, 1953, May 24, 1971; Dallas *Morning News*, July 22, 23, 1944; Seguin *Gazette*, May 27, 1971; Biographical File, Barker Texas History Center, University of Texas at Austin.

*Weinert, Texas.

Weingarten, Joseph. Joseph Weingarten, the son of Harris and Beili (Weidinger) Weingarten, was born in Galicia, Poland, on October 8, 1884, and came to the United States with his parents as a child. The family lived first in Richmond, Texas, and then in Houston. Weingarten was educated in the public schools and at Massey Business College. In 1901 he and his father opened their first grocery store, in downtown Houston. J. Weingarten, Incorporated, was formed in 1914, but it was not until 1920 that Weingarten opened a second store. Advertising "Better Food for Less," he pioneered in self-service and cash-and-carry shopping. By 1926 he was operating six stores. The number had grown to twelve in 1938, twenty-five in 1951, and seventy in 1967.

Weingarten was a director of both the Burlington-Rock Island Railroad and the Ampal-American Israel Corporation; he was a member of the board of the National Association of Food Chains and was the first president of the Super Market Institute of America. He also served as a board member of the Texas Medical Center,qv Medical Research Foundation of Texas, and Baylor Medical Foundation; he worked for the Jewish Theological Seminary of America (New York) and B'nai B'rith, the worldwide Jewish fraternal and social organization. In recognition of his service, Weingarten was awarded the Brotherhood Award of the National Conference of Christians and Jews in 1952.

Impressed during a visit to Israel in 1950 by the common greeting *Shalom Aleichen* (peace be unto you), Weingarten began a personal effort to promote world peace. In 1959 he traveled widely and conversed with international figures, and in 1960 he founded the World Institute for World Peace Foundation, which, in turn, established a chair for peace studies at Rice University and a center for the study of peace at Wayne State University in Detroit.

On May 6, 1923, Weingarten was married to Malvina Kessler; they had two sons and a daughter. He died on February 26, 1967. At the time of his death the World Institute for World Peace Foundation planned an eighty-three-acre peace center on Trinity Bay.

BIBLIOGRAPHY: *Who's Who In America* (1966); *Who's Who In World Jewry* (1965); "Golden Anniversary," *Houston* (April, 1951); Houston *Post*, August 7, 1966, February 27, 1967; Houston *Chronicle*, February 27, 1967.

David G. McComb

*Weir, Texas.

*Weirs Creek.

*Weirville, Texas.

Weisberg, Louis. Louis Weisberg was born on January 13, 1891, in Waco, McLennan County, the son of Edith (Adelman) and Louis Weisberg. An honor graduate of Waco High School, he was awarded a scholarship to the University of Texas, received a B.S. degree in chemistry there, and then took a Ph.D. in chemical engineering from Massachusetts Institute of Technology. He was a Phi Beta Kappa and a teaching assistant in both schools. Following his graduation from MIT he served with the United States Army in World War I. He went to France with the first contingent of chemists and was active in the French underground. He developed an antidote for mustard gas, which had killed or incapacitated thousands during the war. Afterwards he settled first in Washington, D.C., and then opened his own laboratory in New York City; he continued to practice his profession independently for nearly forty years. He was an internationally-known chemical consultant. During World War II he worked with the Manhattan Project, which developed the atom bomb. He also developed and patented a process for chromium plating. After the war he gave up his laboratory and retired.

He lived in Stamford, Connecticut, where he helped organize Temple Sinai. He also lived in New York City and later in Dallas. He was married to Lillian Krohn in Austin in 1919. The couple had no children. He was a sponsor of the New York Shakespeare Festival and a member of many professional chemists' organizations. Louis Weisberg died in Dallas on March 23, 1972, and was buried in Beth Israel Cemetery in Austin.

BIBLIOGRAPHY: Austin *American*, March 27, 1972.

*Weiser, Harry Boyer.

Welch, Robert Alonzo. Robert Alonzo Welch, son of Alexander Chambers and Mary (Gary)

Welch, was born on February 15, 1872, near New-berry, South Carolina. At the age of fourteen he borrowed fifty dollars and on August 5, 1886, boarded a train for Texas, where he was met in Houston by his cousin, Chris Welch, founder of the Welch Academy, a Houston school for boys. During his first few years in Houston Robert Welch worked for several different firms. In 1891 he went to work as bookkeeper, later doubling as salesman, for the Bute Company, a paint firm that also sold insecti-cides. There he remained until July 1, 1927, at which time he resigned as secretary-treasurer but stayed on as a member of the firm's board of di-rectors.

He became interested in oil when the Spindletop Oil Field [qv] came in near Beaumont, Texas, in 1901, and he was soon nicknamed "Pete" by his friends because of his intense interest in petroleum. He bought an acre in the middle of the Spindletop field and sold it for a $15,000 profit, a sale he was soon to regret since the land brought $1 million a few weeks later. It provided him, however, with money to invest in the Goose Creek Oil Feld,[qv] which later brought him a handsome profit.

In 1905 he made another important oil deal, for drilling rights on the Gaillard lease twenty-five miles southeast of Houston, near Goose Creek. Drilling began in 1907. The hole was dry, but he decided to buy additional acreage in that area anyway; he founded the Ashbel Smith Land Com-pany that same year, naming himself president. The profits from this venture were the beginning of the fortune he was to make in oil, sulphur, banking, and real estate in Houston and surrounding areas.

Welch never married. He died in a Houston hos-pital on December 27, 1952, and was buried in the Glenwood Cemetery. He left an estate valued at ap-proximately $42 million, the bulk of which went to a trust fund for the support of chemical research in Texas "for the benefit of mankind." He had asked that the fund be called the "Houston Foundation," but this name was changed after his death to the "Robert A. Welch Foundation." Because he realized that chemistry might not always play the leading role in the world that it had during his lifetime, Welch stipulated that his trustees must make the support and encouragement of chemical research their sole concern only for ten years; after that peri-od the research area was to be left to the judgment of the trustees.

The institutions to benefit most from the Welch Foundation funds have been those in the University of Texas System.[qv] Large sums have also been given to M. D. Anderson Hospital in Houston, Texas A&M University, Rice University, Prairie View A&M University, the University of Houston, Bay-lor University, and Texas Southern University.[qqv]

Because he died without heirs other than his sis-ter, who was already privately wealthy, Welch also specified in his will that 15 percent of the net value of his estate be divided among his employees. The amount thus divided was approximately $7,500,000.

Another $500,000 was set aside for extending financial aid to employees.

BIBLIOGRAPHY: Biographical File, Barker Texas History Center, University of Texas at Austin; James A. Clark, *A Biography of Robert Alonzo Welch* (1963).

James A. Clark

*Welch, Texas.

Welch Foundation. *See* Welch, Robert Alonzo.

*Welcome, Texas.

Welder, Rob and Bessie, Wildlife Foundation and Refuge. *See* Rob and Bessie Welder Wildlife Foundation and Refuge.

Welder, Robert Hughes. Robert "Rob" Hughes Welder was born March 26, 1891, at the Welder ranch north of Sinton, San Patricio County, the son of John J. and Eliza (Hughes) Welder and a de-scendant of two early Texas empresarios, Felipe Roque de la Portilla and James Power.[qqv] A rancher and outdoorsman all of his life, he created the Rob and Bessie Welder Wildlife Foundation and Ref-uge,[qv] which came into existence in 1954 as a result of a provision in his will which set aside 7,800 acres of uncultivated ranchland for the refuge. Other bequests made by Welder included a 300-acre tract, the Rob and Bessie Welder Park, bequeathed to the city of Sinton for a city park. His father had earlier given a park to the city.

Robert Hughes Welder was married to Helen Field Power in Victoria, Texas, on April 17, 1912; they had three daughters. The marriage ended in divorce, and on November 3, 1951, he and Mrs. Bessie Knowlan Utley, of Sinton, were married. There were no children by this marriage. Welder died on December 31, 1953, and was buried in the family burial ground on the Welder ranch.

*Weldon, Texas. (DeWitt County.)

*Weldon, Texas. (Houston County.)

*Welfare, Texas. The name of Welfare, in Ken-dall County, between Boerne and Comfort, is pos-sibly a derivation of the German word *Wohlfahrt*, "pleasant trip." In 1846 the settlement was called Boyton, but the name was changed to Welfare when a branch of the Texas and New Orleans Railroad went through there from San Antonio to Kerrville.

BIBLIOGRAPHY: Kendall County Scrapbook (MS., Ar-chives, University of Texas at Austin Library).

*Wellborn, Olin.

*Wellborn, Texas.

*Wellington, Texas. Wellington, seat of Col-lingsworth County, is a ranching and farming cen-ter, with grain elevators, cotton gins, and a cotton compress. Located there are manufacturers of mat-tresses, concrete, pool tables, and ranching equip-ment. In 1970 the town had eighty businesses. By 1970 the town had a high school, a hospital, a clinic, public parks, a public golf course, and a county li-brary. The population was 3,137 in 1960 and 2,884 in 1970, according to the United States census.

*Wellman, Texas.

*Wells, Francis F.

*Wells, James B.

*Wells, James B., Jr. James B. Wells, Jr., married Pauline J. Kleiber (not Kleibar, as stated in Volume II). Wells was chairman of the state Democratic Executive Committee for two terms—1900–1904 (not 1902–1906).

BIBLIOGRAPHY: Ernest William Winkler (ed.), *Platforms of Political Parties in Texas* (1916); W. H. Chatfield, *The Twin Cities* (1959); James B. Wells Papers (MS., Archives, University of Texas at Austin Library).

*Wells, Lysander.

*Wells, Robert Barnard.

Wells, Thomas Henderson. Tom Henderson Wells, son of Eleanor (Henderson) and Peter Boyd Wells (and descendant of Thomas Stalworth Henderson qv and Wayman F. Wells qv), was born in Austin, Travis County, on June 3, 1917. He attended the University of Texas, Creighton University, and Old Dominion College. He was graduated from the United States Naval Academy at Annapolis in 1940. During World War II he served with the United States Navy in the Pacific and was aboard the carrier *Hornet* when it was sunk in October, 1942. He was awarded twelve battle stars for his World War II service and four stars for his services in the Korean conflict; he was also awarded the Bronze Star as a destroyer captain.

Wells was executive officer of the Naval ROTC program at the University of Texas from 1952 to 1954 and associate professor of naval science there. Wells retired from the regular navy as a commander in 1960. He received both his M.A. degree (1961) and Ph.D. degree (1963) from Emory University. He was associate professor of history at Northwestern State College, Natchitoches, Louisiana, at the time of his death.

His first book, *Commodore Moore and the Texas Navy* (1960) established his place as an authority on the navies of the South and of Texas. His later writings include the section entitled "The Navies," in *Civil War Books: A Critical Bibliography* (1967); a U.S. Navy pamphlet, *The Texas Navy* (1968); and a publication of his M.A. thesis, *The Slave Ship Wanderer* (1968). *The Confederate Navy: A Study in Organization* (1971), originally his Ph.D. dissertation, was published posthumously; the work had earlier been awarded the triennial prize by the United Daughters of the Confederacy qv for the best book of high merit in the field of Southern history relevant to the Confederacy. He contributed to the *Dictionary of American Fighting Ships* and wrote numerous articles for scholarly history publications; he also wrote a weekly column in the Natchitoches *Times*.

Tom Wells was married to Carolyn McConnell of Philadelphia, Pennsylvania, on December 28, 1943, and they were the parents of seven children. He died at his home in Natchitoches, Louisiana, on April 16, 1971, from injuries which he had received in an automobile accident three weeks earlier. He was buried in Pineville Military Cemetery in Alexandria, Louisiana.

BIBLIOGRAPHY: Austin *American-Statesman*, August 28, 1960, April 17, 1971; *Daily Texan*, December 18, 1951, October 21, 1960; Houston *Chronicle*, December 11, 1960;

Houston *Post*, November 6, 1960; Biographical File, Austin-Travis County Collection, Austin Public Library.

*Wells, Wayman F. Wayman F. Wells married Mary Emily Bacon on March 11, 1849 (not 1848, as stated in Volume II).

Lucie C. Price

*Wells, Texas. (Cherokee County.)

*Wells, Texas. (Jack County.)

*Wells, Texas. (Lynn County.)

*Wells Creek.

*Wells Creek, Texas.

*Welview, Texas.

*Wenasco, Texas.

*Wends in Texas. The Texas Wends were one of the ethnic groups featured by the Institute of Texan Cultures,qv which opened at HemisFair qv in the spring of 1968. An extensive file of photographs and bibliographical material was collected by the institute in 1967 during the preparatory work for the show. Among the features in the exhibit were photographs of Wendish brides in their black wedding gowns and a *Lebenswecker* (life awakener), an instrument like that used in acupuncture, brought by the Wends from Lusatia, their European homeland. Two years later the institute featured an exhibit on Wendish printing (eight Wendish characters are added to the German alphabet to give the Wendish phonetics). Featured in the show was the German newspaper *Deutsches Volksblatt*, published in Giddings, Lee County, from 1899 to 1938 by John Andrew Proske. Church bulletins, handbills, and funeral notices in Wendish, in addition to occasional columns in Wendish and English, appeared in this German language newspaper. On August 29, 1929, the seventy-fifth anniversary of the founding of Serbin, an article on the Wends in Texas appeared in the paper.

BIBLIOGRAPHY: Anne J. Blasig, *The Wends of Texas* (1954); Jack DeVere Rittenhouse, *Wendish Language Printing in Texas* (1962); P. E. Kretzman, "The Early History of the Wendic Lutheran Colony in the State of Texas," *Concordia Historical Institute Quarterly*, III (July, 1930); Arthur C. Repp, St. Paul's and St. Peter's Lutheran Churches, Serbin, Texas, 1855–1905 (M.A. thesis, St. Mary's University, 1940); Frederick Simpich, "The Wends of Speewald," *National Geographic* (March, 1923); Herbert Tuttle, "The Prussian Wends, and Their Home," *Harper's New Monthly Magazine*, LIV (1876–1877).

Wentworth, Texas. (Sutton County.) Wentworth, located three miles south of Sonora, came into existence in the late 1880's after A. J. Winkler drilled a well on the site. It consisted of twelve to twenty families of sheepmen, with a store-post office; a school-church was built by the Masons. Wentworth lost the election for the county seat to Sonora in 1890 and no longer existed by 1893.

John Eaton

*Wentworth, Texas. (Van Zandt County.)

*Wesco, Texas.

*Weser, Texas.

*Weslaco, Texas. Weslaco, in Hidalgo County, continued to be a centrally located citrus and vegetable marketing and processing center in the 1960's and 1970's. Its industries centered on agricultural businesses, with some cattle feeding and clothing manufacturing. Experiment and laboratory operations of Texas A&M, Texas A&I, and the United States Department of Agriculture were located in Weslaco. In the late 1960's Weslaco reported nine schools, thirty churches, two banks, a hospital, a library, a newspaper, a radio station, and a television station. The population in 1960 was 15,649, more than double that of 1950. In 1970 the population was 15,313, according to the United States census. The city reported approximately 275 businesses in 1973.

Wesley, Carter Walker. Carter Walker Wesley, a prominent black lawyer and publisher, was born in Houston on April 29, 1892, the son of Harry and Mabel (Green) Wesley. Educated at Fisk University in Nashville, Tennessee, where he received a B.A. degree in 1917, and Northwestern University in Illinois, where he received a J.D. degree in 1922, Wesley practiced law in Muskogee, Oklahoma, from 1922 to 1927. In 1927 he moved to Houston to engage in the construction and brokerage business, and there he became associated with the Houston *Informer*, a newspaper for blacks. He was auditor of the paper in 1929, vice-president in 1930, and treasurer and general manager by the end of 1932; he later became publisher of the newspaper. Wesley also owned the Dallas *Express*, one of a group of papers published by Freedmen's Publishing Company. The Houston *Informer* at one time had a statewide circulation of 45,000, and it was a crusading voice for equal rights for blacks before the integration of hotels, restaurants, and theaters in Texas in the early 1960's. Heman Marion Sweatt was a former circulation manager for the Houston *Informer*, and Wesley helped plan Sweatt's case in the suit against the University of Texas, a suit which eventually overturned the "separate but equal" policy of Texas schools (*see Sweatt* v. *Painter*).

Wesley was a founder of the 120-member National Newspaper Publishers Association. He was a veteran of World War I, and in 1948 he was sent to Germany along with ten other black publishers to investigate claims of discrimination against black servicemen. Wesley was married to Doris Wooten in 1933; they were the parents of three children. Wesley died November 10, 1969, in Houston, and he was buried in Paradise Cemetery North in that city.

BIBLIOGRAPHY: *Who's Who in Colored America* (1950); *International Library of Negro Life and History, 1970 Year Book* (1970); *The Informer and Texas Freeman* (Houston), November 13, 1969.

*Wesley, Texas.

*Wesley College.

*Wesleyan Male and Female College.

*Wesson, Texas.

*West, Charles Shannon. [This title was incorrectly listed in Volume II as West, Charles Sherman. Some later printings of Volume II contain this correction.] The exact date that Charles Shannon West was married to Florence Randolph Duval was September 1, 1859, according to Travis County marriage records. West was associate justice of the Texas Supreme Court from December 23, 1882 (not 1881, as stated in Volume II), to September 29, 1885. He died at his home in Austin on October 23, 1885 (not October 28, 1885).

BIBLIOGRAPHY: Lucie Clift Price (comp.), *Travis County, Texas, Marriage Records, 1840–1882* (1973); Leila Clark Wynn, "A History of the Civil Courts in Texas," *Southwestern Historical Quarterly*, LX (1956–1957); Austin *Daily Statesman*, October 24, 1885.

+West, Claiborne.

*West, Duval. Duval West was the son of Florence Randolph (Duval) and Charles Shannon West qv (not Charles Sherman West, as stated in Volume II).

West, Elizabeth Howard. Elizabeth Howard West, one of seven children of Mary Robertson (Waddell) and James Durham West, was born on March 27, 1893, in Pontotoc, Mississippi. She received both B.A. and M.A. degrees from the University of Texas, where she majored in history. She taught in rural Mississippi and in Bryan and Austin, Texas. In 1906 she moved to Washington, D.C., to take a position in the Library of Congress, first in the catalog division and later in the manuscript division, where she was responsible for compiling the Calendar of the Papers of Martin Van Buren and the Calendar of the New Mexico Papers (incomplete).

In 1911 Miss West became archivist at the Texas State Library,qv a position she held until 1915. From 1915 to 1918 she was librarian of the Carnegie Library in San Antonio, her first administrative position. Through her library bulletins, improved reading lists, services to special groups, and newspaper articles about the library, and through series of lectures sponsored by the library, she improved the quality of library service. In 1918 she returned to Austin as state librarian and became the first woman in Texas to head a department in state government. She gave the library new direction and worked for reduced political control of the library as well as for tenure and higher salaries for library personnel. She also stimulated the creation of county libraries and inaugurated in Texas the state library service to the blind. In 1925 Miss West became librarian at Texas Technological College (now Texas Tech University), where she continued to place emphasis on service. She was responsible for compiling such library holdings as the *British Museum Catalogue of the Printed Books* and *Encyclopedia Universal Europea-Americana* (both publications of the Carnegie Endowment for World Peace), for gathering records of West Texas ranches, and for assembling important papers connected with the James Bowie qv estate. Granted a leave of absence, Miss West spent 1930 to 1932 in Spain as research assistant for the Library of Congress. In 1942 she became librarian emeritus of Texas Tech. She died in Pensacola, Florida, on January 4, 1948.

She was an active member of many organizations, and her published works included catalogs of manuscript collections; translations (mainly from the Spanish); and contributions to the *Dictionary of American Biography*, the *Dictionary of American History*, the *Handbook of Texas Libraries*, and many periodicals and newspapers.

BIBLIOGRAPHY: Goldia Ann Hester, Elizabeth Howard West, Texas Librarian (M.A. thesis, University of Texas at Austin, 1965).

Dorman H. Winfrey

*West, James Marion.

*West, Milton H.

*West, Texas. West, in McLennan County, had a population of 2,352 in 1960 and 2,406 in 1970, according to the United States census. *See also* Waco Standard Metropolitan Statistical Area.

*West Amarillo Creek.

*West Aransas Creek.

*West Bank, Texas.

*West Bay.

*West Bernard Creek.

*West Caddo Peak.

*West Caney Creek.

*West Columbia, Texas. West Columbia, in Brazoria County, had an economy based on agriculture, oil, and sulphur. In the 1960's many major oil companies had producing wells in or near West Columbia, and the area boasted the largest cattle population in Texas. Recreational opportunities included hunting, fishing, and swimming. The Varner-Hogg Plantation (*see* Parks, State) was completely restored, and attracted many visitors every year. The population was 2,947 in 1960 and 3,335 in 1970, an increase of 13.2 percent over the ten-year period, according to the United States census.

*West Columbia Oil Field.

*West Creek.

*West End, Texas.

*West Fork of the Trinity River.

*West Hamilton, Texas.

*West Knott, Texas.

West Lake Hills, Texas. West Lake Hills, in Travis County, was incorporated in 1953. Located on the west side of Lake Austin at the edge of the Edwards Plateau, the community served as a residential area for Austin jobholders and received mail through the city of Austin. In the early 1960's West Lake Hills obtained a fire engine and firefighting equipment through voluntary contributions of its residents. The community was in the Eanes Independent School District. The population was 714 in 1960 and 1,488 in 1970, an increase of 108.4 percent over the ten-year period, according to the United States census. *See also* Austin Standard Metropolitan Statistical Area.

West Mountain, Texas. West Mountain, named for an elevation in southern Upshur County, was founded by Isaac Moody, the second white man to settle in the county. At one time the community had a large school. Though the chief business of the surrounding area was farming, most of the inhabitants of West Mountain were retired or worked in nearby towns. The town had a population of 194 in 1970, according to the United States census.

*West Mud Creek.

*West Nona, Texas.

*West Nueces River.

West Orange, Texas. West Orange, in southeastern Orange County, was incorporated in 1954 and two years later adopted both a home rule charter and a council form of municipal government. Many employees of the Gulf Coast industrial complex live in this residential area. The population was 4,848 in 1960 and 4,787 in 1970, according to the United States census. *See also* Beaumont-Port Arthur-Orange Standard Metropolitan Statistical Area.

*West Point, Texas.

*West Salt Creek.

*West San Jacinto River.

*West Sandy Creek.

*West Scrap, Texas.

*West Shawnee Trail.

*West Sweden, Texas.

*West Texas Chamber of Commerce.

West Texas Children's Home. The West Texas Children's Home, in Monahans, Ward County, was established by the Fifty-ninth Texas Legislature in 1965, with administrative activities to be conducted by the Texas Youth Council.qv A sum of $200,000 was appropriated for the repair, renovation, furnishing, and equipping of the facilities of Pyote Air Force Station,qv which had closed. The home, created for the care of dependent and neglected children, opened in 1966 with over one hundred students; in 1973 there were approximately 230 students at the home and Fred Conradt was superintendent.

BIBLIOGRAPHY: Texas Youth Council, *Annual Report* (1965); *Texas Almanac* (1973).

William T. Field

*West Texas Historical Association. The West Texas Historical Association, with headquarters since its organization in 1924 at Hardin-Simmons University in Abilene, continued to publish the *West Texas Historical Association Year Book*. A cumulative index of the *Year Book*, volumes 1–45, was compiled and edited by Escal F. Duke in 1972. Rupert N. Richardson, an editor of the publication since its inception, was still editor in 1975, and this longtime intimacy with the organization was typical of members of the West Texas Historical Association. Emmett M. Landers was secretary of the association from 1929 and secretary-treasurer from 1931 to 1942. Mrs. Joseph (Madge M.) Grba was secretary-treasurer in 1975, having served in that capacity since 1943 (and as acting secretary in 1942, when she was Madge Moore Landers, widow of the previous holder of this office).

The association's first president, Royston Campbell Crane,qv remained in that office from 1924 until 1949, when he became president-emeritus. Presidents since that time have been Martin Lalor Crimmins qv (1949–1951), Ernest Wallace (1951–1952), J. W. Williams (1952–1954), Seth Shepard McKay (1954–1955), James T. Padgitt (1955–1957), Floyd F. Ewing, Jr. (1957–1959), Ben O. Grant (1959–1961), W. E. Brown (1961–1963), R. Ernest Lee, Sr. (1963–1965), Fred R. Cotten qv (1965–1967), John Berry (1967–1969), Escal F. Duke (1969–1971), Kenneth F. Neighbours (1971–1973), and Ralph A. Smith (1973–1975).

West Texas Historical Association Year Book. See West Texas Historical Association.

West Texas Historical and Scientific Society. The first president of the West Texas Historical and Scientific Society was H. T. Fletcher, who was elected by the board of directors at a meeting held on February 26, 1926. The society's first publication, *Sul Ross State Teachers College Bulletin,* was published on December 1, 1926, at Alpine, Texas. Most of the society's publications have included a variety of materials dealing with historical, scientific, and related topics. Beginning with number eight this policy was altered to include only one theme. In 1936 the Centennial qv Commission of Control provided money for a permanent museum at Alpine. The museum (now called Museum of the Big Bend) was located on the campus of Sul Ross State Teachers College (now Sul Ross State University).

The last publication of the society was the *Sul Ross State College Bulletin,* dated September 1, 1964. Clifford B. Casey was president in 1966. About 1967 the college took over the museum from the society, and for several years the organization held few meetings. On March 26, 1972, Joe S. Graham was elected president of the society, and in February, 1973, a symposium on the Big Bend was held in Alpine; plans for publication of the papers read at that meeting were in progress in early 1975. Although the West Texas Historical and Scientific Society was no longer associated with Sul Ross State University, the planned publication was to be published by the Sul Ross Press, with funds provided by the society. There were plans to publish under a new name (not as the Sul Ross *Bulletin*) and a new format. Graham continued as president of the society until the summer of 1973, when Hallie Stilwell was elected president; she was still president in 1975.

Louise B. McCrabb
Joe S. Graham

*West Texas Military Academy.

West Texas Museum. *See* Museum of Texas Tech University.

West Texas Museum Association. *See* Museum of Texas Tech University.

*West Texas Normal and Business College.

*West Texas State College. *See also* West Texas State University.

West Texas State University. West Texas State University, Canyon, received authorization from the Texas legislature in 1963 to reorganize and to change its name from West Texas State College qv (first known as West Texas State Normal College from 1910 to 1923, and as West Texas State Teachers College from 1923 to 1949). The latest change in name, giving university status, recognized the school's expanded scope and purpose and gave greater impetus to the drive for academic excellence. Administrative reorganization included the college of arts and sciences with three divisions (humanities, social sciences, and science); the school of business; the school of teacher education; and the graduate school.

There was a marked expansion of the physical plant, curriculum and program development, enrollment, and faculty, along with an increased emphasis on research. Construction of the Kilgore Research Center's first unit signaled the emergence of the university as a research focal point. The center housed an electronic computer system, laboratories, rooms for low-temperature physics research, and a library, in addition to offices for twenty researchers. Cooperative research agreements were made with several agencies, including the National Science Foundation. Of the major buildings on campus, twenty were constructed or greatly modified during the 1950–1965 period. Other additions included an applied science building to house the agricultural and industrial education departments, a $350,000 enlargement of the library (which contained 146,108 volumes in 1969), a $700,000 expansion of the Panhandle-Plains Historical Museum,qv an administration building, and a building for the school of business.

Enrollment climbed from 1,913 students in 1950 to more than 4,500 in 1964. The fall, 1974, regular-term enrollment was 6,645; at that time Lloyd I. Watkins served as president.

West University Place, Texas. West University Place, in southwestern Harris County, was chosen for a community of country homes by Governor Ben W. Cooper of Tennessee in 1910. The first lots were sold in 1917 by A. D. Foreman, who had named the development West University Place because of its proximity to Rice Institute (now Rice University). The town was incorporated in 1925 and adopted a home-rule charter in 1940 with a council-manager form of city government. In 1923 there were approximately forty families living in the city. By the late 1930's and early 1940's the city had experienced a period of fast growth and was said to be the second fastest growing city in the nation. The city was completely surrounded by Houston and used the schools of the Houston Independent School District, one of which was within the city limits. The city maintained its own water and waste disposal plants and police and fire departments. As West University Place was predominately a residential area, there were few businesses within the city limits; the economy was influenced greatly by Houston businesses. In the mid-1960's.

there were six churches and a library in the city. The 1950 population of 17,074 had decreased to 14,628 by 1960 and to 13,317 by 1970, according to the United States census. *See also* Houston Standard Metropolitan Statistical Area.

***West Vernon, Texas.**

***West Yegua Creek.**

***Westall, Thomas.**

***Westbrook, Texas.** (Mitchell County.)

***Westbrook, Texas.** (Robertson County.)

***Westcott, Texas.**

***Western, Thomas G.**

******Western Advocate.***

***Western (or Upper) Cross Timbers.**

***Western Land and Livestock Company.**

***Western Narrow Gauge Railroad.** In 1877 the western terminus of the Texas Western Narrow Gauge Railroad was the townsite of Pattison (not Patterson, as stated in Volume II). *See also* Pattison, Texas; Texas Western Railroad.

BIBLIOGRAPHY: Corrie Pattison Haskew (comp.), *Historical Records of Austin and Waller Counties* (1969).

Western Publications, Inc. Western Publications, Inc., in Austin, was comprised of several widely read magazines: *True West*, *Frontier Times*, *Old West*, and *Relics*.[qqv] In 1971 the firm also published *Badman*, *Gold!*, and *Wanderlust*. The publishing firm was owned by Joe Austell Small.

Western Sportsman. *Western Sportsman* was a magazine founded by Charles Waterman in Denver, Colorado, in 1937. The publication covered hunting and fishing activities in eleven western states, and it gained a circulation of slightly over 30,000. Publication was suspended during World War II, and Joe Austell Small, of Austin, Texas, bought the magazine at that time. In 1947 Small revived *Western Sportsman* and built it into the first regional outdoor magazine to become a financial success. He sold it in 1957, but publication was thereafter suspended, and the magazine's ownership reverted to Small. Plans were made for its revival, but in early 1975 the magazine had not again been put into publication.

Joe Small

Western Texas College. Western Texas College, in Snyder, is a public coeducational community college. It enrolled its first students in fall, 1971, and by fall, 1972, had fifty faculty members. The enrollment in fall, 1974, was 1,034; Robert L. Clinton served as president.

***Western Trail.** The Western Trail (also called Dodge City Trail and Fort Griffin Trail) was opened in 1876 and became the principal thoroughfare for Texas cattle en route to northern railheads and ranges after 1879. When the successful Indian campaigns of 1874–1875 by Ranald Slidell Mackenzie[qv] and Nelson A. Miles ended the threat of Indian raids in northwest Texas, Texans began abandoning the farmer-laden Chisholm Trail[qv] through East Texas for the more direct and less congested Western Trail.

The Western Trail was not one path but an intricate complex. From Brownsville cattlemen used a feeder route of the Chisholm known as the Matamoros Trail northward through Santa Rosa, George West, Three Rivers, San Antonio, Beckman, Leon Springs, Boerne, and Comfort to Kerrville. Another feeder, the Old Trail, began at Castroville and headed northward through Bandera and Camp Verde to Kerrville, where the two principal feeders merged into the trunk route. From that point the main trail proceeded northwestward, forded the East Fork of the James River near present Noxville (Kimble County) and the Llano at Beef Trail Crossing at the mouth of Red Creek, passed through London, crossed the San Saba at Pegleg Crossing[qv] and Brady Creek west of the town of Brady, and exited the hill country through Cow Gap, where it was joined by feeders from Mason, San Saba, and Lampasas counties. From Cow Gap, it proceeded across the Colorado at Waldrip and passed through Coleman, where it was intersected by the Jinglebob Trail from Trickham and by one of the two feeders from Tom Green County. Past Coleman, it fanned out through Belle Plain, Baird, and Clyde and reunited at Albany, where the Potter and Bacon Trail (*see* Potter and Blocker Trail) departed northwestward through the Llano Estacado to Colorado. Continuing northward from Albany, the Western Trail forded the Clear Fork near Fort Griffin at the old Butterfield-Military Road Crossing, where the second feeder from Tom Green County and Buffalo Gap joined the trunk. Thence it continued northward through Throckmorton, forded the Brazos at Seymour and the Pease at present Vernon, and then veered northeastward to Doan's Store and the crossing of the Prairie Dog Town Fork of the Red River, first used as a cattle crossing in 1870 by George Lyons (preceding Maxwell and Morris, who used the crossing in 1874, as stated in Volume II); Hige Nail, trail boss for the Adams brothers of Uvalde, used the same crossing in 1876. Seeing the advantages of trail-supplied business at the ford, Jonathan and Corwin F. Doan (not C. F. Doan alone, as stated in Volume II) moved their trading post (*see* Doan's Crossing and Store) from Fort Sill to the ford of the Red River in 1878.

Three alternate paths through the Indian Territory converged upon Dodge City. The principal route crossed the North Fork of the Red River north of present Warren, the Washita near present Butler, and the Canadian south of Camargo, veered fifteen miles southwest of Camp Supply, traversed the Cimarron at the mouth of Redoubt Creek and entered Dodge from the south. The second alternate, used to avoid the Kiowa-Comanche Reservation, reached Dodge by passing through Greer County (then under Texas jurisdiction) and near the Antelope Hills. The last alternate to Dodge followed the divide between the Salt and Elm forks from Mangum to the Texas line, forded the North Fork of the Red River near present Shamrock, Sweetwater Creek near Mobeetie, and the Canadian at the present town of the same name, and proceeded on to Dodge.

Two routes were used to reach ranges beyond Dodge City. One, the International (or proposed National) Trail, left the trunk before reaching Dodge City, starting from near Camp Supply, headed west through the Oklahoma Panhandle, turned north directly south of the Colorado-Kansas border, and roughly paralleled that line to the U.S.-Canadian border. The other path extended north from Dodge through Ogallala, Nebraska, to ranges on the Missouri River.

Although several factors were involved in forcing the closing of the Western Trail, the most important reason was the "Texas fever" qv controversy. As the disease, carried north by Texas cattle, threatened to destroy all northern cattle, most northern states and territories in 1885 enacted quarantines restricting the importation of Texas cattle during the warm months. Texas Congressman James Francis Miller,qv in an effort to guarantee trailing, on January 7, 1886, introduced a resolution in the United States House of Representatives that would have placed non-Texas segments of the Western-International Trail under federal control, but the "National Trail" issue died in committee. Thereafter, Texans began using the state's railroad facilities to transport livestock to market. The last reported drive on the Western Trail was in 1893 by John Rufus Blocker qv to Deadwood, South Dakota.

BIBLIOGRAPHY: J. Marvin Hunter (comp.), *The Trail Drivers of Texas* (1925); J. M. Skaggs, The Great Western Cattle Trail in Texas (M.A. thesis, Texas Tech University, 1965); H. S. Tennant, "The Two Cattle Trails," *Chronicles of Oklahoma*, XIV (1934).

J. M. Skaggs

Westfall, Edward Dixon. Edward Dixon Westfall was born on December 22, 1820, in Knox County, Indiana. His father, Abraham, moved the family to Jasper County, Illinois, in 1841. Edward Westfall left Illinois in 1843 to go to Missouri, intending to join a wagon train to Oregon. Instead he traveled and held various jobs until he came to Texas in 1845.

Westfall moved from Hopkins County, Texas, to San Antonio in 1846. The Mexican War qv had broken out, and he joined the company of Captain John Conner in Colonel Peter Hansborough Bell's qv regiment. Later he served in Captain William G. Crump's company.

After the war, in 1848, Westfall built a cabin on the Leona River about one hundred miles from San Antonio and about thirty miles from Fort Inge,qv near the present site of Uvalde. He spent the next twenty-nine years in that vicinity, farming under the constant threat of Indian raids and serving as a guide for settlers, Rangers, and soldiers. He was a stage guard for William A. A. (Big Foot) Wallace qv when Wallace had the contract to carry mail to El Paso. When Wallace was commissioned by Governor Peter H. Bell to raise a company of Rangers for frontier defense, Westfall was one of his lieutenants. Wallace and Westfall were lifelong friends.

During the Civil War, Westfall moved near Camp Wood; in 1874 he moved to Bexar County, where he farmed on Calaveras Creek about sixteen miles from San Antonio. He married Josephine Susan Dillon in 1881.

Westfall's journals, which he kept from 1886 to his death in 1897, reveal that he was a man who loved to read, although he had little formal education. When he died on June 12, 1897, he left his estate to his wife and stipulated that after her death it was to be applied to the establishment of a free public library in San Antonio, or if one were already established, to be used for improving existing service. By the time Mrs. Westfall died, on January 4, 1940, San Antonio had a public library system, and in June, 1963, the Westfall Branch Library, built partially with the proceeds from Westfall's estate and partially from city funds, was opened. Both Westfall and his wife were buried at Elmendorf.

BIBLIOGRAPHY: Andrew Jackson Sowell, *Early Settlers and Indian Fighters of Southwest Texas* (1900); Irwin and Kathryn Sexton, "Edward Dixon Westfall: Early Texas Climatologist, Philosopher, and Philanthropist," *Southwestern Historical Quarterly*, LXVIII (1964–1965); Journals of Edward Westfall, 1886–1897 (MS., San Antonio Public Library).

Irwin and Kathryn Sexton

*Westfield, Texas.

*Westhoff, Texas.

*Westminster, Texas. [This title was incorrectly listed in Volume II as Westminister, Texas.]

*Westminster College. [This title was incorrectly listed in Volume II as Westminister College.] Westminster College continued as a junior college at Tehuacana, affiliated with Southwestern University, until 1950, when it closed. The property was sold to the Congregational Methodist church, which opened another junior college there. *See* Westminster Junior College and Bible Institute.

*Westminster Encampment. [This title was incorrectly listed in Volume II as Westminister Encampment.] Following the transfer of the equipment and program of the Westminster Encampment to the Presbyterian Mo-Ranch Assembly at Hunt, Texas, in 1949, the original encampment property was acquired by and incorporated into the campus of Schreiner Institute.qv

F. H. Junkin

Westminster Junior College and Bible Institute. Westminster Junior College and Bible Institute, Tehuacana, Limestone County, was the successor of the Congregational Methodist Bible School, which opened in Dallas in 1944 under the leadership of Marvin Sheffield, Otho Jennings, and J. T. Upchurch. W. E. Bruce replaced Jennings as the superintendent of the school in the fall of 1944 and directed the school for nine years. During that time a three-year course in Bible and supporting subjects was offered primarily for ministers and missionaries. On March 21, 1953, property was purchased at Tehuacana by the Congregational Methodist church, and the Congregational Methodist Bible School was moved to that location. The property at Tehuacana had a long church history;

it had first been used by Trinity University,qv a Presbyterian school, from 1869 to 1902. Then the property was sold to the Methodist Protestant church, which moved its school, Westminster College,qv to the location; that school operated at Tehuacana until 1950. The campus was unoccupied until 1953, when it was opened by the Congregational Methodist church as Westminster Junior College and Bible Institute. The school's program was expanded to include the basic junior college curriculum.

The campus consisted of twelve buildings, including housing for faculty and students. Nine thousand volumes, in addition to pamphlets, magazines, newspapers, and documents, were held in the library in 1969. The school operated under the auspices of the Congregational Methodist church but was not a sectarian school. It offered an associate of arts degree. The Bible Institute, a department of the college, offered a four-year curriculum leading to the degree of bachelor of religion. In 1968–1969 the college had a faculty numbering fifteen and a student body of ninety-five, but by 1970 the student body had decreased to sixty; Elmo McGuire was president. In 1971 thirty-five students and seven teachers of the Westminster Junior College and Bible Institute moved from Tehuacana, Texas, to a forty-acre campus at Florence, Mississippi, a location called the "geographical center" of the Congregational Methodist church.

*Westmoorland College.

*Weston, Texas.

*Westover, Ira.

*Westover, Texas.

Westover Hills, Texas. Westover Hills, in Tarrant County, was a residential community west of Fort Worth. Incorporated in 1939, the town had a population of 307 in 1960 and 374 in 1970, according to the United States census. See also Fort Worth Standard Metropolitan Statistical Area.

*Westphalia, Texas.

*Westville, Texas. (DeWitt County.)

*Westville, Texas. (Trinity County.)

Westway, Texas. Westway, Deaf Smith County, was given that name by a Judge Slaton of Hereford in 1923 because of its location west of Hereford. The first settlement had been the Tierra Blanca camp of the XIT Ranch qv in 1898. Lewis Arnold filed on a section of land bordering the campsite, traded a horse for a house, and moved the house to his claim, thus becoming the first settler at what was to become Westway. The eastern line of the XIT Ranch practically halved the settlement. In 1919 a school was built at the town on land given by Slaton. In 1927 Phineas Short started a store, and in 1930 a Baptist church was also established. In the 1960's Westway had a church, a store, a parsonage, and several residences. The chief occupation of the inhabitants was ranching.

Westworth Village, Texas. Westworth Village, in western Tarrant County, was incorporated in 1941 with an aldermanic form of government. With one grocery store, three churches, and two public schools in the 1960's, the village was primarily a residential area. The population was 3,321 in 1960 and 4,578 in 1970, an increase of almost 38 percent during the ten-year period, according to the United States census. See also Fort Worth Standard Metropolitan Statistical Area.

*Wetmore, Texas.

*Wetsel, Texas.

*Weymiller Butte.

*Wharey, James Blanton.

**Wharton.* The brig *Wharton* was first named *Colorado* (not *Colorado of Baltimore,* as stated in Volume II). Under command of Captain Edwin Ward Moore, the *Wharton* was at New York City from December 10, 1839, until January 21, 1840, when she left after a sharp dispute over United States neutrality laws which forbade recruiting by foreign nations. The *Wharton* was transferred to the United States Navy on May 11, 1846 (not June, 1846), and was sold for fifty dollars on November 30, 1846 (not 1847).

BIBLIOGRAPHY: Tom Henderson Wells, *Commodore Moore and the Texas Navy* (1960).

Tom Henderson Wells

*Wharton, Clarence Ray.

*Wharton, John Austin.

*Wharton, John Austin.

*Wharton, Lawrence Hay.

*Wharton, Sarah Ann (Groce).

*Wharton, Turner A.

*Wharton, William Harris.

*Wharton, Texas. Wharton, county seat of Wharton County, is the center for a farming and oil area. By 1970 a new one-hundred-bed hospital and a high school had been completed, the Wharton Industrial Foundation was developed, an industrial park was purchased, and five buildings had been added to Wharton County Junior College. In 1966 the city reported thirteen churches, two hospitals, a library, two newspapers, and a radio station. There were 156 businesses in Wharton in 1970, largely concerned with sulphur and rice. Excluding a rather large unincorporated area next to the city limits, the 1960 population of Wharton was 5,734; the 1970 population was 7,881, according to the United States census, thus showing a 37.4 percent increase over the ten-year period.

*Wharton College.

*Wharton County. Wharton County had an economy based on sulphur, oil, cattle, and the cultivation of rice, cotton, grain sorghums, and vegetables. By 1972 the yearly mineral income of the county was $53,881,000. Between 1925 and January 1, 1973, the county produced 230,537,121 barrels of crude oil. In the early 1970's Wharton was among the leading counties in total farm and livestock products sales, with an average annual farm income of $40.4 million. It was the leading rice-producing county and was third among counties in beef cattle. The 1960 population was 38,152; the 1970 population was 36,729, according to the United States census.

Wharton County Junior College. Wharton County Junior College, Wharton, a state-supported institution, opened in 1946 following a county bond election which approved its establishment. First-year enrollment numbered approximately 130 students, and ten instructors were employed.

The school's enrollment grew steadily, from 523 students in 1954, to 946 in 1959, to 1,513 in 1964, and to 1,820 in 1974. The faculty grew in number to over ninety members by the fall of 1974. Wharton County Junior College served students drawn principally from Wharton, Matagorda, Brazoria, Fort Bend, Colorado, and Jackson counties. The expanded enrollment permitted broad curriculum offerings, including two years of any pre-professional major, as well as vocational and technical courses to meet the needs of industry along the Gulf Coast.

The campus master plan in the 1960's anticipated facilities for 2,500 students. Two-thirds of the financing came from state tax sources, while the remaining funds were gathered from district taxes and tuition fees. Several donations to the Wharton County Junior College Foundation were used to provide scholarships, assist building projects, and purchase library books and specialized equipment. Library holdings in 1969 consisted of 31,000 volumes. Theodore Nicksick, Jr., was president of the college in 1974.

*Wheat Production. The largest Texas wheat harvest was produced in 1947 when 7,310,000 acres yielded 124,270,000 bushels. In the 1950's wheat was almost totally a cash crop. Although it declined in importance as a food grain during this period, it still ranked third in crop value. In 1954, 30,894,000 bushels valued at over $67,000,000 were produced on over 3,000,000 acres. Almost all Texas wheat was of the red winter class and was grown primarily on the High Plains. The crop suffered one of the worst drouths in Texas history, which began in the winter of 1950 and continued throughout the decade. In 1955 a combination of extreme drouths and insect infestation reduced the annual yield of wheat to only 14,326,000 bushels. Yields increased during the late 1950's, however, to the extent that the average annual production for the period from 1954 to 1958 totaled 36,000,000 bushels. Texas wheat found a good market in the Northeast and was exported to that area via coastal shipping.

In 1961 Texas wheat acreage yielded 86,956,000 bushels, the third largest crop on record. The value of the 1963 wheat harvest from the 4,655,000 acres under cultivation had declined to $64,095,000, but in 1968 the crop of 84,150,000 bushels raised on 3,825,000 acres was valued at $106,029,000. The size and value of the crop decreased in 1969, and again in 1970, when 54,408,000 bushels valued at $70,730,000 were harvested from 2,267,000 acres. Leading wheat-producing counties in the late 1960's and early 1970's were Carson, Castro, Deaf Smith,

Floyd, Hansford, Hartley, Moore, Ochiltree, Parmer, Swisher, Sherman, and Wilbarger. Amarillo, Plainview, Lubbock, and Wichita Falls, as well as the Dallas-Fort Worth area, were the centers for more than seven large flour mills in the state. *See also* Agriculture in Texas.

BIBLIOGRAPHY: *Texas Almanac* (1955, 1963, 1965, 1967, 1971, 1973); Texas Agricultural Experiment Station *Bulletin*, No. 948 (March, 1960); *Texas Agricultural Progress* (July–August, 1960); *Texas Business Review* (April, 1959, July, 1960).

*Wheatland, Texas. (Dallas County.)

*Wheatland, Texas. (Hardeman County.)

*Wheatlands, Texas.

*Wheeler, Royal T.

*Wheeler, Thomas Benton.

*Wheeler, Texas. Wheeler, seat of Wheeler County, is the commercial center for a farming, ranching, and oil area. In 1970 the town had sixty businesses, as well as five churches, a hospital, a library, a bank, one newspaper, and a new high school. The population was 1,174 in 1960 and 1,116 in 1970, according to the United States census.

*Wheeler County. In the 1960's and 1970's Wheeler County had three major income sources—livestock, crops, and petroleum and natural gas. Grain sorghums, wheat, and cotton were grown on 7,500 irrigated acres in 1968. In the 1972–1973 season 10,489 bales of cotton were processed by the four active gins in the county. Between 1921 and January 1, 1973, the county produced 68,850,668 barrels of crude oil. An annual St. Patrick's Day celebration is held at Shamrock. The county's historic sites include Old Mobeetie [*see* Mobeetie (Old), Texas] and Fort Elliott.qv The population was 7,947 in 1960 and 6,434 in 1970, according to the United States census.

*Wheeler Creek.

*Wheelock, Edwin M. Edwin Miller Wheelock was born in New York City on August 30, 1829, the son of Charles and [?] (Brown) Wheelock. He was a graduate of the Harvard University schools of law and divinity. In 1857 he was ordained minister of the Unitarian society at Dover, New Hampshire. His sermon about John Brown on November 27, 1859, was widely published in the North, and, as a result, Virginia offered a $1,500 reward for Wheelock's capture. In 1862 he resigned his pastorate to become chaplain of the 15th New Hampshire Infantry; he accompanied his regiment to New Orleans, where he was assigned the duty of investigating freedmen's complaints of cruelty. Later he served on a military board which established freedmen's schools in Louisiana.

After the war he was placed in charge of educational activities of the Freedmen's Bureau qv in Texas and, in 1867 (not 1866, as stated in Volume II), was appointed superintendent of public education by Governor Elisha Marshall Pease.qv In the early 1870's he was one of the editors of the Austin *State Journal*, the official newspaper of the Republican state administration. He was reporter for the state supreme court, 1870–1872, and superintendent of the Texas School for the Blind,qv 1872–1874. In 1887 he organized the Unitarian society in Spokane, Washington, and served as minister for two years. He then returned to Austin where he again served as a Unitarian minister in the early 1890's.

Wheelock was married to Ellen M. Brackett at Somerville, Massachusetts, on September 22, 1855; they had a son and a daughter. He died in Austin on October 29, 1901, and was buried in Oakwood Cemetery there.

BIBLIOGRAPHY: Biographical File, Barker Texas History Center, University of Texas at Austin; Ralph Lewis Lynn, The Educational Points of View and Services of the Texas State Superintendents of Public Instruction (M.A. thesis, Baylor University, 1946).

*Wheelock, Eleazer Louis Ripley.

Wheelock, Frank Emerson. Frank Emerson Wheelock was born in Holland, New York, on April 11, 1863, the son of William Efner and Louisa Diane (Farrington) Wheelock. After his mother's death, his family moved to Wisconsin; in 1876 they moved to Illinois and the following year to Minneapolis, Minnesota, where Wheelock finished school.

He began working for the I O A Ranch qv in northwest Texas in 1887 and became general manager two years later; he continued to manage the ranch until it was dissolved in 1901. In 1890, with the financial support of John T. Lofton and James Harrison of Fort Worth, Wheelock became manager of a venture to lay out a town a short distance north of the Monterey townsite. The town was named Lubbock. On December 19, 1890, Wheelock, Lofton, and Harrison agreed with W. E. and H. Rayner, promoters of Monterey, to set up a new Lubbock, and all worked for its success, with Wheelock managing affairs. He served as the town's first mayor and was on the first Lubbock County Commission. In addition, he introduced the first cotton gin in the county and helped to bring the railroad to Lubbock.

Wheelock was a Methodist and a member of various organizations. He was a rancher and partner with Irvin L. Hunt in a mercantile firm. On December 9, 1891, he was married to Sylva Belle Hunt; they had seven children. Wheelock died in Lubbock on June 28, 1932, and was buried there.

BIBLIOGRAPHY: Seymour V. Connor (ed.), Builders of the Southwest (1959).

*Wheelock, Texas.

*Wheelock Creek.

*Wheelwright, George Washington.

*Whetstone, Peter.

*Whig Party in Texas. Whig party members in Texas took an active part in both the 1848 and 1852 presidential elections. Although the delegates chosen at the state convention in Galveston in May, 1848, failed to attend the Whig national convention in June, the Texas convention authorized the Louisiana delegation to cast the Texas votes for the nomination of Zachary Taylor.qv Whig electors William Beck Ochiltree, Benjamin Holland Epperson, Ed-

ward H. Tarrant,qqv and James W. Allen campaigned vigorously for Taylor. "Rough and Ready Clubs" were formed in Galveston and Houston; the club in Galveston was burned in November during a violent confrontation between Whigs and Democrats. Whig candidates Taylor and Millard Fillmore received 31 percent of the total votes cast in Texas, carrying Victoria, Nueces, and Cameron counties and running strongly in ten other counties.

The 1849–1850 national controversy over the Compromise of 1850 qv weakened the Texas Whigs somewhat, but the party ran two candidates in the 1851 state elections: Benjamin Holland Epperson for governor and William Beck Ochiltree for United States representative from the Eastern District. Both were easily defeated.

During 1852, a presidential election year, the Whigs held two conventions, one at Tyler for the Eastern District and one at Houston for the Western District; a delegation was sent to the national convention to support the candidacy of Millard Fillmore. Even though the nomination went to Winfield Scott, the Texas Whigs campaigned actively. Scott received 26 percent of the total votes cast in Texas, but because the votes were spread more evenly across the state than in 1848, Scott did not carry a single county. In the 1853 state elections Ochiltree, running as a Whig candidate, came in second in the governor's race.

BIBLIOGRAPHY: Randolph Campbell, "The Whig Party of Texas in the Elections of 1848 and 1852," Southwestern Historical Quarterly, LXXIII (1969–1970).

*Whip-handle Dispatch.

*Whirlwind Mesa.

*Whitaker, William.

*White, Ambrose B.

*White, Amy.

*White, Francis Menefee.

*White, James Phelps. James Phelps White was born on December 21, 1856 (not December 2, as stated in Volume II). He helped organize Oldham County in 1880–1881; in 1882 he and his brother, Thomas David, went into partnership with George Washington Littlefield,qv when the Littlefield Cattle Company was organized in Texas. In 1901 Littlefield bought the Yellow House Ranch qv on the South Plains, and Phelps was made manager. When Littlefield decided to colonize a portion of the ranch. White served as general manager of the Littlefield Lands Company qv from 1912 to 1915. In Roswell, New Mexico, White founded the J. P. White Company, which administered his extensive farming and ranching interests in that state, and built a four-story building to house it. White was married to Lou Tomlinson of Fort Worth on July 22, 1903; they had four children.

BIBLIOGRAPHY: David B. Gracy II, "George Washington Littlefield, Portrait of a Cattleman," Southwestern Historical Quarterly, LXVIII (1964–1965); George W. Littlefield Collection (Archives, University of Texas at Austin Library); Mrs. Julian C. Lane, Key & Allied Families (1931); James D. Shinkle, Fifty Years of Roswell History (1965).

David Gracy

*White, James Taylor.

*White, John Preston.

*White, John Will.

*White, Joseph. Joseph White was born in Georgia. He died in San Felipe de Austin on June 14, 1830. In October, 1830, alcalde Thomas Barnett qv published notice that Zeno Philips,qv administrator of Joseph White's estate, would have a public sale at White's last residence, of half a league of land on Clear Creek, west of Galveston Bay; two lots; a Negro woman slave; household and kitchen furniture; and personal property. White, in a similar capacity, had announced a public sale in October, 1829, in San Felipe.

BIBLIOGRAPHY: *Texas Gazette*, October 13, 1829, June 19, October 30, 1830.

White, Matthew G. Matthew G White was born in Charlotte County, Virginia, in 1775, the son of John and Mary White. He was married to Lucy Price; they immigrated to Mississippi before 1800, became plantation owners near Liberty (the county seat of Amite County), and reared a family of ten children. In 1825 White and his son-in-law, Hugh Blair Johnston,qv were leaders of some forty-two families who immigrated to the Atascosito District of Texas (*see* Atascosito Road) which then encompassed the lands of southeast Texas lying between the San Jacinto and Sabine rivers and south of the Nacogdoches District.

White signed the official census of the Atascosito District in 1826, which listed 331 names. In April, 1831, the Mexican government granted White the league of land on which he had settled, that being on the east bank of the Trinity River adjacent to the present city of Liberty (now encompassed within the city limits and an area on which much of the south Liberty oil field was later located). While serving as alcalde of the district in 1831, White helped establish the town of Liberty, but he was drowned in Self's Bayou, shortly before the town was officially named that same year by Francisco Madero,qv land commissioner for Texas. The name of the district was also changed from Atascosito to Liberty, and White's son-in-law, Hugh B. Johnston, was elected alcalde.

BIBLIOGRAPHY: Mary Eloise de Garmo, *Pathfinders of Texas, 1836–1846* (1951); Mary McMillan Osburn (ed.), "The Atascosito Census of 1826," *Texana*, I (1963); MS. papers in the possession of Miriam Partlow, Price Daniel, and Bill Daniel (Liberty, Texas).

Houston Daniel

*White, Owen Payne.

*White, Raleigh R. *See also* Scott and White Hospital.

*White, Reuben.

*White, Sam Addison. Sam Addison White, who had been mayor of Victoria, Victoria County, in 1863, continued in that office when no elections were held in 1864. He was appointed district judge in 1865 by the provisional governor of Texas, Andrew Jackson Hamilton.qv

BIBLIOGRAPHY: Roy Grimes (ed.), *300 Years in Victoria County* (1968).

Hobart Huson

White, Taylor. *See* White, James Taylor.

*White, Walter C.

*White, William C.

*White, Texas. (El Paso County.)

*White, Texas. (Titus County.)

*White Bluff Creek.

*White Canyon.

White Citizens Councils in Texas. White Citizens Councils were first established in Mississippi following the United States Supreme Court decision of May 17, 1954, when the court reversed the 1895 ruling in *Plessy* v. *Ferguson*, which provided for "separate but equal" accommodations for Negroes; more specifically, the court declared that racial segregation in public schools was unconstitutional. The formation of White Citizens Councils to oppose integration was the immediate reaction of some Southerners, and the movement spread to areas of Texas. B. E. Masters, president emeritus of Kilgore Junior College, was an early supporter of the philosophy which encouraged the formation of councils in Texas, and he organized the first local council in Kilgore. Some state legislators openly favored laws which would maintain the status quo in the state's segregation practices, and Representative Joe N. Chapman of Sulphur Springs called for all lawful means to promote states' rights and prevent integration in Southern schools. In addition to the council at Kilgore, councils were formed in Palestine, Texarkana, and other communities, mainly in the eastern part of the state. In 1957 a membership of 25,000 Texans was claimed by some members, but there was no accurate count available. While the groups advocated nonviolence, they encouraged a social and economic boycott against both Negroes and whites who were active in local desegregation activities.

The White Citizens Councils never had widespread popularity or influence in the state, and Texans, for the most part, supported antidiscrimination legislation in the late 1950's. The Texas Board of Education allowed state funds for desegregated school districts, and the Texas Commission on Race Relations, sponsored by the Ford Foundation's Southern Regional Council, helped organize committees in localities where the White Citizens Councils were especially active. Early in the 1960's the councils faded into obscurity, and it is probable that many of their members joined the newly organized John Birch Society, which held strong segregationist views.

*White City, Texas. (Gaines County.)

*White City, Texas. (San Augustine County.)

*White City, Texas. (Wilbarger County.)

*White Creek.

*White Deer, Texas. White Deer, in Carson County, had a population of 1,057 in 1960 and 1,092 in 1970, according to the United States census.

*White Deer Creek.

*White Hall, Texas.

*White Lake.

*White Man's Union Associations.

*White Mound, Texas.

*White Oak, Texas. (Gregg County.) White Oak, in Gregg County, had a population of 1,250 in 1960 and 2,300 in 1970, an increase of 84 percent during the ten-year period, according to the United States census.

White Oak, Texas. (Hopkins County.)

*White Oak Bayou. *See also* Whiteoak Bayou.

*White Oak Creek. *See also* Whiteoak Creek.

*White River.

White River Reservoir. White River Dam and White River Reservoir are in the Brazos River Basin in Crosby County, sixteen miles southeast of Crosbyton on the White River. The project is owned and operated by the White River Municipal Water District to supply water to Post, Spur, Ralls, and Crosbyton. Construction began on September 12, 1962, and the dam was completed on November 21, 1963. The reservoir has a total capacity of 38,200 acre-feet (200 acre-feet is dead storage) and a surface area of 1,808 acres at service spillway crest elevation of 2,369 feet above mean sea level. The drainage area of the White River above the dam is 172 square miles.

BIBLIOGRAPHY: Texas Water Commission, *Bulletin 6408* (1964).

Seth D. Breeding

*White Rock, Texas. (Hunt County.)

*White Rock, Texas. (Red River County.)

*White Rock Creek.

White Rock Lake. White Rock Lake is on White Rock Creek in the Trinity River Basin in Dallas County in northeast Dallas. White Rock Lake is owned and operated by the city of Dallas to supply a small part of the city's municipal water needs, and to supply water for condenser cooling at a steam-electric generating plant. White Rock Dam was started in 1910 by the city of Dallas and completed in 1911. The reservoir had an original capacity of 18,160 acre-feet and a surface area of 1,254 acres at spillway crest elevation of 458.1 feet above mean sea level. A survey in 1956 determined the capacity as 12,300 acre-feet with a surface area of 1,095 acres. The drainage area is 100 square miles.

BIBLIOGRAPHY: Texas Water Commission, *Bulletin 6408* (1964).

Seth D. Breeding

White Settlement, Texas. White Settlement, in western Tarrant County, was incorporated in 1948 with a mayor-council form of government. In 1966 the community reported twenty-four churches, a hospital, a bank, a library, and two newspapers. The General Dynamics and Bell Helicopter plants greatly influenced the economy of the city. The 1960 population was 11,513; the 1970 count was 13,449, according to the United States census. *See also* Fort Worth Standard Metropolitan Statistical Area.

*White Star, Texas.

White Stone, Texas. White Stone, in southwestern Williamson County, south of Leander, was originally a rural school. The building later became one of several residences in the farming and ranching area. The community had a filling station and a small grocery store in the late 1960's.

*Whited, Texas.

*Whiteface, Texas.

*Whitefish Creek.

*Whiteflat, Texas. (Motley County.)

*Whiteflat, Texas. (Nolan County.)

*Whitehall, Texas.

*Whitehouse, Texas. Whitehouse, in Smith County, had a population of 842 in 1960 and 1,245 in 1970, an increase of almost 48 percent over the ten-year period, according to the United States census. *See also* Tyler Standard Metropolitan Statistical Area.

*Whiteland, Texas.

*Whitely, Texas.

*Whiteman.

*Whitenton, William Maynard.

*Whiteoak Bayou.

*Whiteoak Creek.

*Whites Bayou.

*Whites Creek.

*Whitesboro, Texas. (Grayson County.) Whitesboro, a farming and recreational center in western Grayson County, had a population of 2,485 in 1960 and 2,927 in 1970, according to the United States census. Many of the town's businesses were connected with the petroleum industry, while others dealt with garment manufacturing and meat processing. Whitesboro also had a bank and a newspaper.

*Whitesboro, Texas. (Hamilton County.) *See also* Whiteway, Texas.

*Whitesboro Normal School.

*Whitesides, Boland.

*Whitesides, Henry.

*Whitesides, James.

*Whitesides, William B.

*Whitesmine, Texas.

Whiteway, Texas. Whiteway (formerly Whitesboro), in southeast Hamilton County, was established to serve the needs of motorists between Jonesboro and Hamilton. At one time its population was fourteen; in 1966 four inhabitants were reported. Whiteway was named for Steve White, a local resident, whose sons established and operated the filling station, garage, body shop, and grocery store.

W. W. Standifer

*Whitewright, Texas. Whitewright, in southeastern Grayson County, had a population of 1,315 in 1960 and 1,742 in 1970, according to the United States census.

*Whitfield, John Wilkins.

*Whitfield, Texas.

*Whitfield's Legion.

*Whitharral, Texas.

*Whiting, Nathaniel.

*Whiting, Samuel.

*Whitlock, William.

Whitman, Charles Joseph. Charles Joseph Whitman was born in Lake Worth, Florida, on June 24, 1941, the oldest of three sons of Margaret and Charles A. Whitman, Jr. He attended Sacred Heart grade and junior high schools, was an Eagle Scout at twelve, and graduated from St. Ann's High School in West Palm Beach in 1959. He enlisted in the Marine Corps on July 6, 1959, and was stationed for a year and a half at Guantánamo Bay, Cuba. He passed a test to enter officer training, was sent to a preparatory school in Bainbridge, Maryland, and then to the University of Texas at Austin in September, 1961, to major in engineering. There he met Kathleen F. Leissner, and they were married on August 17, 1962, at Needville, Texas, her home town. Because of low grades he was ordered back to duty as an enlisted man in the Marine Corps on February 12, 1963. While still in the service he attended East Carolina State College in the summer of 1964. He was discharged on December 4, 1964, and returned to Austin, reentering the University of Texas in the spring of 1965 to study architectural engineering. In the summer of 1965 he attended Alvin Junior College and then continued at the University of Texas in the 1965–1966 school year. He also worked part time and was a scoutmaster. In the spring of 1966 his mother left his father and moved to Austin to be near her eldest son. On March 29 Whitman sought medical and psychiatric advice at the university health center, but he failed to return as directed for further assistance. On July 22 he visited the University of Texas tower observation deck with his brother John.

During the pre-dawn hours of August 1, 1966, Whitman killed his mother in her apartment and his wife at their residence. Later in the morning he bought a variety of ammunition and a shotgun; about 11:30 A.M. he went to the university tower, taking with him in a footlocker six guns, knives, food, and water. After clubbing the receptionist (who later died) on the twenty-eighth floor about 11:45 A.M., he killed two persons and wounded two others who were coming up the stairs from the twenty-seventh floor. On the observation deck of the tower, at an elevation of 231 feet, Whitman then opened fire on persons crossing the campus and on nearby streets, killing ten more people and wounding thirty-one more (one of whom died a week later). Police arrived and returned his fire, while other policemen worked their way into the tower. Several of the dead and wounded were moved to cover by students and other citizens while the firing continued. At 1:24 P.M. police and a deputized private citizen reached the observation deck, where police officers Ramiro Martinez and Houston McCoy shot and killed Whitman. Altogether, seventeen persons were killed, including Whitman, and thirty were wounded in one of the worst mass murders in modern United States history. An autopsy on Whitman's body revealed a brain tumor, but medical authorities disagreed over its effect on Whitman's actions. His body was returned to Lake Worth, Florida, for burial.

BIBLIOGRAPHY: Austin *American* (and) Austin *Statesman*, August 1–8, 1966; Subject File, Barker Texas History Center, University of Texas at Austin.

Alwyn Barr

*Whitmore, George W.

*Whitney, Texas. Whitney, in Hill County, had a population of 1,050 in 1960 and 1,371 in 1970, according to the United States census. The town had approximately sixty businesses in 1970.

*Whitney Dam and Reservoir. The Whitney Reservoir project, in the Brazos River Basin in Hill and Bosque counties, is owned by the United States government and operated by the United States Army Corps of Engineers, Fort Worth District, for flood control and the generation of electric power. Construction began on May 12, 1947, and the main dam and spillway were completed in April, 1951. The reservoir has a capacity of 379,100 acre-feet and a surface area of 15,800 acres. The reservoir's storage capacity of 1,620,400 acre-feet, between elevations 520 feet and 571 feet above mean sea level, is for flood control. The drainage area above the dam is 26,170 square miles, of which 9,240 square miles is probably noncontributing. The power plant has two 15,000-kilowatt generating units with all auxiliaries for delivery of energy to the transmission system. The energy is sold to the Brazos Electric Power Cooperative, Inc., for distribution in the area. The first unit was activated on June 25, 1953.

BIBLIOGRAPHY: Texas Water Commission, *Bulletin 6408* (1964); *Texas Almanac* (1971).

Seth D. Breeding

*Whitsett, Texas.

*Whitson, Texas.

*Whitt, Texas.

*Whittaker, Texas.

*Whitten, Texas. *See also* Whitton, Texas.

*Whittenburg, Texas.

Whitton, Texas. [This title was incorrectly listed in Volume II as Whitten, Texas.] Whitton, in southwestern Van Zandt County, was founded probably about 1860 by members of the Whitton family, the descendants of whom still live in the vicinity. On a mail route from Canton, the Whitton community in the late 1960's and early 1970's was in an agricultural region that also served as a residential area for commuting industrial workers.

*Whitworth Draw.

*Whon, Texas.

Whooping Crane. The whooping crane did not become specifically identified with Texas until the 1930's, when several of that endangered species were noticed wintering on Blackjack Peninsula, between St. Charles Bay and San Antonio Bay. In December, 1937, on the advice of wildlife specialists, the United States Bureau of Biological Survey, forerunner of the United States Fish and Wildlife Service, purchased the peninsula and transformed it into the Aransas Migratory Waterfowl Refuge (later Aransas National Wildlife Refuge qv). There the migrating families of the only whooping cranes on earth came under the surveillance of the federal government. In October and November each year the birds make the 2,500-mile flight to Texas from the breeding grounds in Wood Buffalo National Park, Alberta, Canada, about five hundred miles south of the Arctic Circle.

The whooping crane, somewhat over four feet tall (and with a wing span of approximately seven feet), is the tallest of North American birds. The bird was named and identified *Grus americana alba* by English naturalist Mark Catesby in South Carolina in the 1720's. The number of whooping cranes, which had been declining since 1870, reached a dangerously low count in the winter of 1938–1939, when only fourteen birds were officially listed. In the winter of 1948–1949 there were thirty birds recorded; ten years later there were thirty-two. In 1965–1966 there were forty-four, and in 1971–1972 the number was fifty-nine; however, during the winter of 1972–1973 the count was down to fifty-one.

A number of whooping cranes have survived in captivity, most of them at the Audubon Park Zoo in New Orleans. One bird, Rosie, was the property of the United States government; she survived in Texas after being captured (injured) near Lometa in Lampasas County in May, 1955. Rosie stayed in the San Antonio Zoo until 1964, when she was transferred to Audubon Park Zoo in New Orleans in an attempt to mate her with one of the several whooping cranes there. In 1966 Rosie was returned to San Antonio accompanied by a male, Crip, and the pair produced one surviving chick, Tex, which was taken to the Patuxent Wildlife Research Center at Laurel, Maryland. Rosie died in June, 1971, but Crip was still in the San Antonio Zoo in May, 1973.

Hazards to whooping crane survival at the Aransas Refuge, as listed by the Whooping Crane Conservation Association, were extensive waterfowl hunting in the immediate vicinity of the refuge; encroachment of vacation cabins near the birds' feeding territories; and boats plying the Gulf Intracoastal Waterway,qv which passes through the area within viewing distance of the birds. A United States Army Air Force bombing range on nearby Matagorda Island, oil explorations, and ranching operations in the vicinity have also been threats to whooping crane survival since the late 1930's.

BIBLIOGRAPHY: Robert Porter Allen, *The Whooping Crane* (1952); Robert Porter Allen, *On the Trail of Vanishing Birds* (1957); Faith McNulty, *The Whooping Crane* (1966); Austin *American-Statesman*, March 18, 1973; *Panola Watchman* (Carthage), December 20, 1971.

*Whythe, Robert L.

*Wichita County. Wichita County was a crossroads for Indians long after they had been moved from Texas into the Indian Territory of Oklahoma. In May, 1872 (not 1874, as stated in Volume II) Henry W. Strong qv and ten other men under the leadership of Lieutenant John A. McKinney (not General Ranald Slidell Mackenzie,qv who was in general command of the frontier forces at that time) followed a party of Indians from Jack County to the Red River. They met on the crest of a hill not far from the present site of the Wichita Falls courthouse. It was James H. Banta (not Mark Banta, who was only three years old at the time) who located on Beaver Creek in 1877. S. L. Fowler (not S. W. Fowler) drilled an oil well on his farm in Wichita County in 1918. Oil as well as gas showings in water well drilling were reported in the county as early as 1901 to 1909; although oil leases were made before 1911, it was not until April 1, 1911, when the Clayco No. 1 was brought in, that the Electra Oil Field qv was fully realized.

Wichita County ranked eighth among Texas counties in oil production in 1961. By January 1, 1973, the county had produced 689,090,389 barrels of oil since 1910. The second largest income producer was beef cattle. There was some production of wheat, sorghum, cotton, guar, and other crops. Native grapes and small orchards were located in the county. Major economic concerns of the county were Sheppard Air Force Base,qv Midwestern University, and manufacturing businesses located in the Wichita Falls area. Lake Wichita, in the southeastern part of the county, was a recreation area. Population was 123,528 in 1960 and 121,862 in 1970, according to the United States census. *See also* Wichita Falls Standard Metropolitan Statistical Area.

BIBLIOGRAPHY: Henry W. Strong, *My Frontier Days and Indian Fights on the Plains of Texas* (1926).

*Wichita Daily Times. The *Wichita Daily Times* published its first evening edition on May 14, 1907 (not May 17, 1907, as stated in Volume II).

                    Louise Kelly

*Wichita Falls, Texas. Lake Wichita, begun in 1900, was completed in 1901 (not 1907, as stated in Volume II). The Times Publishing Company was organized in 1907 (not 1904). Wichita Falls, county seat of Wichita County and commercial center for an extensive area in both Texas and Oklahoma, reported 145 churches, three hospitals, a college, two libraries, a newspaper, five radio stations, and two television stations in 1966. Completed in the mid-1960's were a fire station and a police station, renovation of city hall and one of the libraries, and improvements on parks. Lake Arrowhead (in nearby Clay County), a water supply for the city, was completed in 1966. The population of Wichita Falls was 101,724 in 1960 and 97,564 in 1970, according to the United States census. *See also* Wichita Falls Standard Metropolitan Statistical Area.

BIBLIOGRAPHY: *Directory of Newspapers and Periodicals* (1958); Texas Water Development Board, Report 48, *Dams and Reservoirs in Texas, Historical and Descriptive Information* (December 31, 1966).

Wichita Falls Junior College. *See* Midwestern University.

*Wichita Falls and Northwestern Railway Company of Texas.

*Wichita Falls and Oklahoma Railway Company.

*Wichita Falls Railway Company.

*Wichita Falls, Ranger, and Fort Worth Railroad.

*Wichita Falls and Southern Railway Company.

Wichita Falls Standard Metropolitan Statistical Area. The Wichita Falls Standard Metropolitan Statistical Area between 1960 and 1973 was composed of Wichita and Archer counties, which cover 1,524 square miles in the north-central plains of Texas. Archer County, with a population of 6,110, and Wichita County, with a population of 123,528, had a combined 1960 census count of 129,638. In 1970 the two-county statistical area had a population of 127,621, according to the United States census (Wichita County, 121,862; Archer County, 5,759). The major city in the area, Wichita Falls, with a population of 101,724 in 1960 and 97,564 in 1970, is located in the southeastern part of Wichita County; Burkburnett, near the Oklahoma border in northeastern Wichita County, is the area's second largest city, with a population of 7,621 in 1960 and 9,230 in 1970.

The economy of the area was based primarily on petroleum production, agriculture, and manufacturing. Between 1910 and January 1, 1973, the two-county area produced over one billion barrels of oil, and in the year 1972 alone it produced over twelve million barrels. Nearly all of Archer County's farm income, averaging $11.5 million annually in the early 1970's, was from the raising of livestock; Wichita County had during the same period an average annual farm income of $7.6 million, two-thirds of it from beef and dairy cattle, hogs, and poultry. Grains and cotton were the chief crops.

Wichita Falls, the industrial and commercial center of the metropolitan area, was also the distribution center for a large area of Texas and Oklahoma. Numerous oil companies were located there, and manufacturers produced hospital supplies, clothing, and industrial equipment. Sheppard Air Force Base,qv a missile training center, also augmented the economy and population of the city. Midwestern University, a four-year accredited college, was located in Wichita Falls, and many of its students came from the metropolitan area. In the 1960's the city also supported a symphony orchestra, the Midwestern Chamber Music String Ensemble, the Civic Music Association, the Civic Playhouse, the Broadway Theater League, the Art Association, and the Great Books Discussion Committee, in addition to other cultural organizations associated with the university.

Lake Kickapoo in Archer County, Lake Wichita in Wichita County, Lake Arrowhead in Clay County, and numerous smaller lakes provided water supply and recreation for the whole metropolitan area. Of historical significance was Camp Cureton qv in Archer County, the site of a Texas Ranger qv station for the Frontier Regiment.qv

Several smaller cities in Wichita County contributed to the area's industrial income. Burkburnett,

which had a 21 percent increase in population between 1960 and 1970, had plants which produced machinery, plastics, chemical products, and rodeo equipment. Iowa Park had a 76 percent increase in population during the ten-year period, with census counts of 3,295 in 1960 and 5,796 in 1970. Plants there produced fertilizers, bullets, and oil field equipment. Electra, also in Wichita County, was an agribusiness and oil center, although its population decreased from 4,759 in 1960 to 3,895 in 1970.

The largest town in Archer County was Archer City, the county seat. It had a population of 1,974 in 1960 and 1,722 in 1970, a decrease of almost 13 percent during the ten-year period. Next largest town in the county was Holliday, with a population of 1,139 in 1960 and 1,048 in 1970. Other trading centers were Windthorst, Megargel, Lakeside City, and Scotland. Windthorst and Scotland were established around the turn of the century as German-Catholic settlements.

In 1973 Archer County was no longer included in the Wichita Falls Standard Metropolitan Statistical Area. Clay County was added, and the new two-county statistical area covered 1,713 square miles and, based on the 1970 census, had a total population of 129,941. Henrietta, the seat of Clay County, had a 1970 population of 2,897; the town had plants which produced mobile homes and boots and saddles. *See also* Standard Metropolitan Statistical Areas in Texas.

*Wichita Falls State Hospital. In 1951 the Vernon State Home, in Vernon, was activated as a branch of the Wichita Falls State Hospital, and in 1964 cared for an average of 431 aged psychotic patients. Daily census of the two institutions in 1967 was 2,359. An outpatient clinic was operated to provide follow-up care for the patients furloughed or discharged from the hospital. Early in 1970 the branch at Vernon was separated from the Wichita Falls facility. *See* Vernon Center.

In that same year the treatment program at Wichita Falls State Hospital was expanded by the addition of special programs for geriatric and mentally retarded patients, a new physical therapy department, an outpatient clinic for children under ten years old, and a new outpatient clinic at Mineral Wells. The training program for professional staff was also expanded. The average daily census for 1970 was 1,348, a reduction from previous years. The superintendent in 1970 was Bernard Rappaport. *See* Mentally Ill and Mentally Retarded, Care of, in Texas.

BIBLIOGRAPHY: Board for Texas State Hospitals and Special Schools, *Report* (1964); Texas Department of Mental Health and Mental Retardation, *Annual Report, 1970.*

*Wichita Falls and Wellington Railway Company.

*Wichita Indians.

*Wichita River.

*Wichita Valley Railroad Company.

*Wichita Valley Railway Company.

*Wickeland, H.

*Wickett, Texas.

*Wickliffe, Charles Anderson.

*Wickson Creek.

*Wied, Texas.

*Wieland, Texas.

*Wiergate, Texas.

*Wiess, Simon.

*Wiess, Texas.

*Wiess's Bluff, Texas.

*Wigfall, Louis Trezevant.

*Wiggins, Texas. (Cass County.)

*Wiggins, Texas. (McLennan County.)

Wight, Lyman. Lyman Wight, Mormon leader, became the second chief justice and judge of probate court of Gillespie County in 1850, when he contested the election in which he had been defeated by Johann Jost Klingelhoefer qv (who had not at that time become a naturalized citizen). After attending only five sessions of commissioners court, Wight refused further participation, and a new election was held in August, 1851; Klingelhoefer, by then a United States citizen, was elected and became the county's third chief justice.

BIBLIOGRAPHY: Davis Britton (ed.), *The Reminiscences and Civil War Letters of Levi Lamoni Wight* (1970); Robert Penniger (Charles L. Wisseman, Sr., trans.), *Fredericksburg, Texas: The First Fifty Years* (1971); Gillespie County Historical Society, *Pioneers in God's Hills* (1960); Probate Court Minutes, Volume A, Gillespie County.

*Wightman, Elias R.

*Wightman, Texas.

*Wihan, Texas.

*Wilbarger, John Wesley.

*Wilbarger, Josiah Pugh.

*Wilbarger, Mathias.

Wilbarger County. Wilbarger County gained its income from oil production, ranching, and farming. Between 1915 and January 1, 1973, 212,984,-235 barrels of crude oil had been produced in the county. Cattle, hogs, and poultry accounted for one-half of the farm income, while crops, including cotton, grains, vegetables, and guar, made up the other half; the average annual farm income amounted to $16 million in the early 1970's. Most of the guar grown in Texas was produced around a processing plant in Wilbarger County. The county partially supports a library and owns an airport. Vernon, the county seat, is the location of a mental health center (*see* Vernon Center), a drug treatment center, Vernon Regional Junior College, and the Red River Valley Museum. Lockett, southwest of Vernon, is the site of Texas A&M Research and Extension Center. There are many historic sites in the county, including Doan's Crossing (*see* Doan's Crossing and Store). The population of Wilbarger County was 17,748 in 1960 and 15,355 in 1970, according to the United States census.

*Wilbarger Creek.

*Wilbarger Peak.

*Wilburn Branch.

*Wilco, Texas.

*Wilcox, John A.

Wilcox, Sebron Sneed. Sebron (Seb) Sneed Wilcox, son of Nathan Miles and Minnie Genevieve (Sneed) Wilcox, was born on December 9, 1884, at Burnet, Texas. His family moved to Georgetown while he was a boy, and he attended schools there. At the age of fifteen he entered Southwestern University; he left there without having graduated and moved to Austin to study shorthand and typing.

On October 27, 1907, Wilcox married Stella Marie Jones; they had one daughter. In succession Wilcox worked for the Houston and Texas Central Railway Company in Houston, the attorney general's office in Austin, and the law firm of Pierce and Hawkins in Brownsville. In September, 1911, Wilcox was appointed court reporter for the Forty-ninth District in Laredo, and he remained in this position until he retired in December, 1958.

Wilcox was an ardent student of Texas history, and it was through his efforts that the Laredo Archives qv (dating from a 1749 document, but predominantly 1768 to 1846, and miscellaneous papers up to 1875) were saved from destruction. He assisted the Texas Historical Records Survey qv in seeing that the documents were copied correctly, and copies of those completed portions of the typescripts were placed in the Archives Division of the Texas State Library, qv the University of Texas at Austin Library, the National Archives in Washington, D.C., and in Laredo, Texas.

Wilcox wrote several articles based on the Laredo Archives, which were published in the *Southwestern Historical Quarterly*. qv He was one of the founders of the Laredo Historical Society and a member of the Texas Historical Commission qv for Webb County; he helped secure three monuments for Laredo during the Texas Centennial qv celebration. Wilcox died in Laredo on May 12, 1959, and was buried in the Laredo Catholic Cemetery. After his death his family, carrying out his wish, donated his research materials to the library at St. Mary's University in San Antonio. This material included a fine collection of rare books about Texas, copies of his own writings on local history, an almost complete file of the Laredo *Times*, and, most important, the original manuscript materials of the Laredo Archives.

BIBLIOGRAPHY: Walter Prescott Webb, "Texas Collection," *Southwestern Historical Quarterly*, XLIV (1940-1941); Seb S. Wilcox, "The Spanish Archives of Laredo," *ibid.*, XLIX (1945-1946); H. Bailey Carroll, "Texas Collection," *ibid.*, LXV (1961-1962).

Rogelia O. Garcia

*Wilcox, Texas. (Burleson County.)

*Wilcox, Texas. (Gray County.)

*Wilcox, Texas. (Somervell County.)

*Wild Cat Creek.

*Wild Horse Creek.

*Wild Horse Draw.

*Wilda, Texas.

*Wildcat Mountain.

Wildcats and Wildcatters. A wildcat well is a well drilled in the hope of finding oil where none is known to exist, and a wildcatter is one who makes it his business to drill such wells. Since there is no method of determining the presence of oil in any structure except by drilling, the discovery well in every field is a wildcat, and since of all the wildcat wells drilled about one in sixteen produces oil, the wildcatter is by temperament a gambler who takes calculated risks, hoping that his successes will more than offset his failures. As the cost of drilling went up over the years, agreements by which the risks were shared by several companies or individuals became common.

In an economy in which a continuing supply of petroleum was essential, the wildcatter was regarded as a public benefactor; thus, in the oil industry the term "wildcat" and its derivatives developed an honorific meaning formerly lacking, although in other industries the connotation is less rewarding. In labor history, for example, a wildcat strike is one not authorized by the union, and thus the term has a negative effect. In business during the first half of the nineteenth century, the term "wildcat" was applied to any unsound or unreliable enterprise, but especially to unsound banking. Before the national banking acts of 1843–1864, banks sometimes issued notes beyond their power to redeem. The notes of one such bank in Michigan bore on one side the engraving of a panther, and when the notes became worthless they were known throughout the country as wildcat money; thus, wildcat banks were unsafe banks. The term spread to mining, and in 1864 Mark Twain applied it to worthless and often fraudulent mining stock. One who helped remove the stigma from the word was Ida Tarbell, who in her attack on Standard Oil in 1903, noted that the Rockefeller group refused to assume the risks of exploratory drilling, thus forcing upon them the wildcatter, whose resources were comparatively meager. When the term was first used in Texas cannot be determined, but it was in general use before World War I.

Mody C. Boatright

Wildenthal, Bryan. Bryan Wildenthal, son of Bernard and Aissa (Wadgyman) Wildenthal, was born on April 10, 1904, in Cotulla, Texas. He attended Cotulla public schools before entering Southwest Texas State Teachers College (now Southwest Texas State University) in San Marcos; he was graduated from there in 1925, at which time he was appointed auditor of the school. He held that position while he continued his education at the University of Texas in Austin, where in 1927 he earned an M.A. degree in economics.

In 1928 he was married to Doris Kellam; they had two children. He became business manager for Southwest Texas State, a position he held until 1940, when he was appointed a professor of economics. During World War II, on a leave of absence, Wildenthal served as general assistant to the secretary of the Red Cross in the Pacific area. He returned to Southwest Texas State following the war. In 1950 he was appointed president of a junior college, Angelo College (now Angelo State University). In 1952 he was appointed president of Sul Ross State College (now Sul Ross State University) in Alpine, and he served in that capacity until his death on June 1, 1965; he was buried in the San Marcos cemetery.

Ida Stevenson Vernon

*Wilderville, Texas.

*Wildhorse Creek.

*Wildhorse Mountain.

*Wildhurst, Texas.

Wildlife Areas in Texas. In 1975 ten state wildlife management areas existed in Texas, encompassing approximately 190,000 acres. In many of the state-owned areas, supervised public hunting and fishing were permitted if surplus game existed. The areas were as follows:

Black Gap Wildlife Management Area, 102,258 acres, was established in Brewster County fifty-five miles south of Marathon. Principal game species were mule deer, javelina, antelope, and scaled (blue) quail.

Chaparral Wildlife Management Area, 15,200 acres, was established in Dimmit and La Salle counties eight miles east of Artesia Wells to the north of FM Road 133. Principal game species were white-tailed deer, javelina, bobwhite and scaled (blue) quail, and wild turkey.

Gene Howe Wildlife Management Area, 5,821 acres, was established in Hemphill County seven miles east of Canadian. Principal game species were white-tailed deer, bobwhite quail, and wild turkey.

Gus Engeling Wildlife Management Area, 10,941 acres, was established in Anderson County twenty miles northwest of Palestine. Principal game species were white-tailed deer and bobwhite quail.

J. D. Murphree Wildlife Management Area, 8,407 acres, was established in Jefferson County five miles southwest of Port Arthur. Principal game species were migratory waterfowl.

Kerr Wildlife Management Area, 6,493 acres, was established in Kerr County fifteen miles west of Hunt on the North Fork of the Guadalupe River. Principal game species were white-tailed deer and wild turkey.

Las Palomas Wildlife Management Area, 666 acres, was divided into six main units: Cameron County—the Longoria unit, which was five miles north of Santa Rosa, and the Voshell unit, which was one mile southwest of Brownsville; Hidalgo County—the Adams unit, which was two miles southeast of Weslaco; Willacy County—the Fredericks unit, which was two miles northwest of Sebastian; Starr County—the Grulla unit, which was one mile south of the village of La Grulla, and the Prieta unit, which was nine miles west of Rio Grande City. Principal game species were white-winged dove and chachalaca. Since these tracts were nesting sanctuaries, no hunting was permitted.

Matador Wildlife Management Area, 28,184 acres, was established in Cottle County eleven miles northwest of Paducah. Principal game species were quail and wild turkey.

Sheldon Wildlife Management Area, 2,503 acres, was established in Harris County nineteen miles northeast of Houston. Although principal game species were migratory waterfowl, this area was a waterfowl sanctuary and no hunting was permitted. Fishing was permitted in the reservoir.

Sierra Diablo Wildlife Management Area, 7,791 acres, was established in Culberson County approximately twenty miles north of Van Horn. Principal game species were mule deer and desert bighorn sheep.

Although not classified as wildlife management areas, the Texas legislature authorized several bird sanctuaries in the state, including the following: Vingt et Un Islands, located in Galveston Bay, sponsored by the Audubon Society, the Garden Clubs of Houston, and the Houston Outdoor Nature Club; Connie Hagar Sanctuary, which bordered on Rockport (see Hagar, Conger Neblett); Lake Corpus Christi Sanctuary, which included all of the lake's waters except portions in Jim Wells and Nueces counties; Ingleside Cove Sanctuary, which included waters in San Patricio and Nueces counties; and Wichita County Wildlife Refuge, located near Wichita Falls.

In 1975 there were also ten federal wildlife refuges in Texas; they were the following:

Anahuac National Wildlife Refuge, 9,837 acres in Chambers County on the upper Gulf Coast, was established in 1963 as a wintering ground for four species of geese and many waterfowl, and as a year-round home for mottled ducks.

Aransas National Wildlife Refuge,qv 54,829 acres in Aransas, Refugio, and Calhoun counties, was established in 1937, and is well known as the wintering ground of the whooping crane,qv which is in danger of extinction. The refuge also supports the endangered Attwater's prairie chicken and is a wintering ground for migratory waterfowl. White-tailed deer and peccaries are also present.

Attwater's National Wildlife Refuge, approximately 4,400 acres on the San Bernard River, five miles northeast of the town of Eagle Lake in Colorado County, was purchased by the United States government in the early 1970's as a refuge for the endangered Attwater's prairie chicken; the government was purchasing more land in 1975.

Brazoria National Wildlife Refuge, 6,525 acres along the Texas Gulf Coast in Brazoria County, fifteen miles southeast of Angleton, was set aside in 1966 as a waterfowl wintering area. It supports limited numbers of mourning doves and bobwhites.

Buffalo Lake National Wildlife Refuge (see Buffalo Lake), 7,664 acres in Randall County in the Texas Panhandle, was a reservoir and land area transferred from the Forest Service in 1958. An important resting area for waterfowl during migrations, winter populations occasionally reach 1,000,-000 ducks. Canada geese were abundant, numbering up to 40,000.

Hagerman National Wildlife Refuge,qv 11,320 acres on the Big Mineral Arm of Lake Texoma in Grayson County, was established in 1946 as a waterfowl migration and wintering area; bobwhite and deer are also present.

Laguna Atascosa National Wildlife Refuge,qv 45,147 acres in the lower Rio Grande Valley in Cameron County, was established in 1946 as a waterfowl area. The refuge winters as many as 1,000,000 ducks, often including the continent's largest concentration of redheads; it also supports deer, turkeys, and small mammals.

Muleshoe National Wildlife Refuge,qv 5,809 acres in Bailey County in the Texas Panhandle, was established in 1935; it is important to waterfowl in fall and winter and often winters 750,000 ducks and large concentrations of sandhill cranes.

San Bernard National Wildlife Refuge, 14,915 acres located twenty-five miles southwest of Angleton in Brazoria County, was acquired in 1968. The refuge provides coastal marsh and some freshwater habitat for migrating waterfowl and is a nesting habitat for mottled ducks.

Santa Ana National Wildlife Refuge, 1,981 acres on the bank of the Rio Grande near Alamo in Hidalgo County, was established in 1943; the refuge is well known for its many birds that are found elsewhere, mainly in Mexico. Famous for its display of native trees and shrubs as well as birdlife, it is a popular winter attraction for bird watchers.

Private refuges were also located in Texas. The Audubon Society sponsored many sanctuaries, some of which were South Bird Island, located at Laguna Madre southeast of Flour Bluff, one of the two wintering grounds in the United States for the white pelican; Second-Chain Islands, between San Antonio and Mesquite bays on the coast; Green Island, located at Laguna Madre at the mouth of the Arroyo Colorado; Lydia Ann Island, north of Port Aransas; and Swan Island, located at Copano Bay near Rockport. The Rob and Bessie Welder Wildlife Foundation and Refuge qv was another private refuge; located eight miles northeast of Sinton in San Patricio County, it contained a great variety of birds and nonmigratory wildlife.

*Wildorado, Texas.

*Wildorado Creek.

*Wiley College. Wiley College, Marshall, had a regular term enrollment of 573 students in 1974. The forty-six-acre campus was improved and modernized during the 1960's with an extensive building program. A Christian coeducational institution, Wiley College was accredited by the Southern Association of Colleges and Secondary Schools, the Texas Education Agency,qv the university senate of the Methodist church, and the American Medical Association. College affiliations included the Association of American Colleges and Universities, the United Negro Fund, and the Association of Texas Colleges and Universities.qv

Major divisions of the curriculum were education and teacher training, humanities, natural sciences and mathematics, and social sciences and business.

B.S. and B.A. degrees were offered. Pre-professional training in medicine, nursing, dentistry, and law were also available, as well as a cooperative program in engineering with New York University. In addition to the residence program, the college operated Saturday extension classes. The library contained 30,000 volumes in 1969. Robert E. Hayes served as president in 1974.

*Wilke, Texas.

*Wilkerson Creek.

Wilkes, Franklin Collett. Franklin Collett Wilkes, born about 1822, came to Texas as a Methodist minister in the 1850's. In 1857, while serving as the local pastor, he became the first president of Waco Female College.qv He then served as presiding elder of the Galveston district of the Methodist church in Texas during 1858. Once the Civil War had begun, he joined the Confederate Army. On April 24, 1862, at Hempstead, he was elected colonel of the 24th Texas Cavalry, which marched to Arkansas that summer. Wilkes and most of his regiment were captured at Arkansas Post on January 11, 1863, exchanged at City Point, Virginia, in April, and returned to active duty with the Army of Tennessee around Chattanooga. In July, 1864, Wilkes was transferred to the Retired Invalid Corps and assigned to the District of Texas. In September, however, he was captured in Tensas Parish, Louisiana, and again imprisoned, first in Fort Lafayette and later in Fort Warren. He was exchanged in March, 1865, and in April he made a personal effort to arrange a cease-fire in the Trans-Mississippi area.

After the war he returned to the ministry and served in Brenham in 1866 and in Austin from 1869 to 1873. He was also general agent for Bayland Orphan's Home for Boys qv and traveled over the state seeking funds for its maintenance. The home (and farm) for Civil War orphans was established by interested Houston and Galveston men soon after the Civil War and was located on Galveston Bay in Harris County. Wilkes was chaplain of the Texas Senate in 1881. He resigned because of poor health and moved to Lampasas, where he died on December 8, 1881. He was buried in that city.

BIBLIOGRAPHY: Macum Phelan, *A History of Early Methodism in Texas, 1817–1866* (1924), *A History of the Expansion of Methodism in Texas, 1867–1902* (1937); Dallas *Weekly Herald*, July 20, 27, 1872, January 13, December 14, 1881; Service Records (Civil War Biographical File, Archives, University of Texas at Austin Library).

Alwyn Barr

*Wilkins, Jane.

*Wilkins Creek.

*Wilkinson, Alfred Ernest.

*Wilkinson, James.

*Wilkinson, Texas.

*Willacy, John G.

*Willacy County. Willacy County has an economy based on agribusiness and the production of oil. Between 1936 and January 1, 1973, the county produced 75,252,149 barrels of crude oil. In the early 1970's Willacy County had an average annual farm income of $24.8 million, 80 percent of which came from crops, mainly cotton, sorghums, vegetables, and fruit. In the 1972–1973 season 66,625 bales of cotton were produced, and there were ten active gins in the county. Willacy County was a leader in the production of cabbage, green corn, onions, and Irish potatoes. An onion fiesta was held annually in April to celebrate the largest truck crop. Production of citrus fruits was also high. Tourist attractions include the Laguna Atascosa National Wildlife Refuge qv and access to the Gulf of Mexico. Willacy County had a population of 20,084 in 1960 and 15,570 in 1970, according to the United States census.

*Willamar, Texas.

*Willard, Texas.

*Willawalla Creek.

*William Beaumont General Hospital. William Beaumont General Hospital, at El Paso, was housed in a new, $17.5 million, twelve-story building, which was dedicated on July 1, 1972. The hospital, with a capacity of 611 beds, handled more than 917,000 outpatient visits and admitted about 15,500 inpatients annually. It had approximately 1,400 military and 900 civilian personnel.

William Beaumont was a fully accredited hospital with residency and intern-training programs, and it offered special training courses for army nurses, hospital administrators, clinical clerks, and orthopedic workers.

*William Carey Crane College.

William Harris Reservoir. William Harris Reservoir is in the San Jacinto-Brazos coastal basin in Brazoria County, eight miles northwest of Angleton, and is an off-channel project between the Brazos River and Oyster Creek. The project is owned and operated by the Dow Chemical Company as an industrial water supply for several affiliated plants near Freeport. Construction of the project was completed in July, 1947. The reservoir has a normal capacity of 12,000 acre-feet and a surface area of 1,663 acres at normal maximum water surface elevation of 43 feet above mean sea level. Water is obtained for the reservoir by pumping from the Brazos River and is released from the reservoir by gravity flow to Oyster Creek. From there it flows through the channel to a pumping plant which lifts the water to a canal system and small retention reservoir. The water is then distributed by a gravity canal system to the various places of use at the industrial plants.

BIBLIOGRAPHY: Texas Water Commission, *Bulletin 6408* (1964).

Seth D. Breeding

William Marsh Rice University. See Rice University.

*William Penn, Texas.

William Robbins. See Liberty.

*Williams, Augustus.

Williams, Daniel Mortimer. Daniel Mortimer Williams, lawyer, writer, and editor, was born on October 17, 1890, in Childress, Childress County, the son of Thomas Arnold Barlow and Rebecca

(Raworth) Williams; he was the twin brother of David Reichard Williams.qv Dan Williams received a B.A. degree and a law degree (1917) from the University of Texas. As editor of the *Daily Texan* qv he allowed women to work on the *Texan* staff for the first time, praised the university for allowing women to participate in drama for the first time, and lashed out at high prices that students were having to pay as consumers.

He served in the United States Army from 1917 to 1919 and during the latter year attended the Sorbonne in Paris, France. Returning to Texas, he was county attorney of Childress County for a year and then became an English instructor at the University of Texas. In 1920 and 1921 he was editor of the Tampico *Tribune* in Tampico, Mexico; he then went to New York City and was a writer and editor on the New York *World* and the New York *Telegram*; he was appointed chief editorial writer on the New York *World Telegram*. During the years from 1922 to 1937 he crusaded for civil liberties, for laws to promote safety at sea, for safe food and milk regulations in New York City, and for numerous programs such as bank investment and deposit protection, health and welfare reforms, and work programs for the unemployed.

In the early 1940's, during World War II, he went to Washington, D.C., and as a correspondent for the Trans-Radio Press he covered the White House and the State Department. From 1946 to 1948 he wrote columns for the Washington *Post*, and he contributed to the *New Republic*, the *New Yorker*, and many other magazines. He was active in the founding of the American Newspaper Guild and was a member of the American Civil Liberties Union. He was married to Jean Lockwood in June, 1921; the couple had two children. He died on November 1, 1969, and was buried in Rockdale, Texas.

Jean Dugger

Williams, David Reichard. David Reichard Williams, who developed the indigenous Texas ranch-style house, was born in Childress, Childress County, on October 17, 1890. He was the son of Thomas Arnold Barlow and Rebecca (Raworth) Williams and the twin brother of Daniel Mortimer Williams.qv Most of his early education was obtained at home and through correspondence courses, and at the age of fifteen he began work with the Fort Worth and Denver City Railway System, first in construction work and then in the company's repair shops in Childress. From 1912 to 1916 he studied architecture at the University of Texas, where he also did art work for the *Cactus* and the *Daily Texan*.qv In 1916, without having received a degree, he took a job as a civil engineer for Gulf Oil Corporation qv in Tampico, Mexico, where he planned buildings, pipelines, pumping stations, narrow-gauge railways, camps, and small hospitals. For two and one-half years, between 1920 and 1923, he traveled, studied, and sketched in Europe. In 1924 he began work as an architect in Texas, with headquarters in Dallas.

The distinctive type of house which he developed was based on his study of early Texas homes, many of which were built by German and Czech settlers. The Williams house, designed for roomy comfort, caught the summer breeze but protected against glare. This sturdy, functional type of home, designed to meet regional needs, was adopted by many other architects. From 1933 to 1950 Williams worked for various government agencies as planner and consultant. The Woodlake Cooperative Agricultural Community for Depression-displaced farm families was under his supervision and planning (*see* Woodlake, Texas, in Trinity County). He helped plan the Matanuska Valley farm community near Anchorage, Alaska, served as deputy administrator of the National Youth Administration (NYA), and wrote the architectural style manual, *NYA Architecture: Design and Standards*. He worked on the restoration and reconstruction of La Villita qv in San Antonio in 1939 and during World War II worked for the government designing numerous defense housing projects. After the war he assisted in United Nations work, restoring agricultural areas and fisheries in China and constructing resettlement housing for European refugees in Venezuela. His last years were spent in Lafayette, Louisiana, where he promoted the idea of a bayou-type, raised-cottage style of colonial French architecture. In 1960 the American Institute of Architects elected him a fellow. He was married to Louise Lyle Givens on December 31, 1934; they had one daughter. David Williams died in Lafayette on March 10, 1962, and was buried there. Most of his papers were placed in the archives of the University of Southwestern Louisiana in Lafayette. His photographs of early Texas houses, which inspired his use of indigenous architecture, are in the archives of the School of Architecture of the University of Texas at Austin; copies were placed in the Library of Congress.

BIBLIOGRAPHY: Wayne Gard, "The Ranch-house Goes to Town," *Better Homes and Gardens* (June, 1937); *Life* (June 9, 1941); Dallas *Morning News*, February 26, 1949, November 11, 1957, February 29, March 11, 1960, March 11, 1962.

Wayne Gard

*Williams, Frank Alvin.

*Williams, George I.

*Williams, Guinn. Guinn Williams was the son of Minnie (Thompson) and W. W. Williams. He was married to Minnie Lee Leatherwood.

BIBLIOGRAPHY: Wise County Scrapbook (MS., Archives, University of Texas at Austin Library).

Williams, Guinn, Jr. Guinn "Big Boy" Williams, Jr., the son of Minnie Lee (Leatherwood) and Guinn Williams,qv was born on April 26, 1899, in Decatur, Wise County, and was raised on the family ranch. By 1919 he was in Hollywood working as an extra in films, and during slack times in movie making he often rode wild horses in rodeos. He worked with Tom Mix and Harry Carey during the early part of his career and in 1928 began to have bit parts which grew into character and supporting roles. Will Rogers gave Williams, who was six feet, two inches tall, his nickname when they were working in films together. Comic roles, mainly in westerns, became his trademark in the variety of over one hundred films he played in from 1928 until 1962. He played in such non-western films as *My Man*, with Fanny Brice (1928), *The Littlest Rebel*, with Shirley Temple (1935), and *A Star Is Born*, with Janet Gaynor (1937). He was in the John Wayne movie *The Alamo* (1960); his last film was *The Comancheros* (1962). An expert polo player, he owned a ranch near Spofford, Kinney County, until shortly before his death in Van Nuys, California, on January 6, 1962. Williams was survived by his wife, Dorothy, and one son.

BIBLIOGRAPHY: Leslie Halliwell, *The Filmgoer's Companion* (1970); John T. Weaver (comp.), *Forty Years of Screen Credits, 1929–1969* (1970); New York *Times*, January 7, 1962.

*Williams, Henry.

*Williams, Henry Howell.

*Williams, John.

*Williams, John A.

*Williams, John R.

*Williams, Lemuel Hardin.

*Williams, Leonard H.

*Williams, Nathaniel Felton.

*Williams, Oscar Waldo.

*Williams, Robert H.

*Williams, Robert R.

*Williams, Samuel May.

*Williams, Solomon.

*Williams, Stephen.

*Williams, Thomas.

*Williams, Walter Erskine.

*Williams, William D.

*Williams, William M.

*Williams Bayou.

*Williams Creek.

*Williams Ranch, Texas.

*Williamson, Robert McAlpin.

*Williamson County. Williamson County is essentially an agricultural area, with 60 percent of its farm income coming from crops, mainly cotton, corn, sorghums, and oats. Cattle, hogs, sheep, goats, and poultry supply the rest. The average annual farm income in the early 1970's was approximately $26 million. The county's twenty gins turned out 62,458 bales of cotton during the 1972–1973 season. There was also a small amount of oil produced; between 1915 and January 1, 1973, total crude oil production had reached 9,067,384 barrels. Tourist attractions include Cobb Caverns, Inner Space Cavern, the gravestone of Sam Bass, the site of the battle of Brushy Creek, Kenney's Fort,qqv and San Gabriel Park. Between 1960 and 1966 about forty small dams had been constructed on the Brushy Creek watershed, and dams on the San Gabriel River were

proposed. The population was 35,044 in 1960 and 37,305 in 1970, according to the United States census.

*Williamson Creek.

*Willie, Asa Hoxey.

*Willie, James.

*Willis, Texas. Willis, in northern Montgomery County, had a population of 975 in 1960. By 1970 this number had grown to 1,577, an increase of 61.7 percent. At that time the town listed thirty businesses. *See also* Houston Standard Metropolitan Statistical Area.

*Willis Creek.

*Willis Male and Female College.

*Willoughby Branch.

*Willow, Texas.

*Willow Bayou.

*Willow Branch.

*Willow City, Texas.

*Willow Creek.

*Willow Grove, Texas.

*Willow Marsh Bayou.

*Willow Mountain.

*Willow Springs, Texas. (Fayette County.)

*Willow Springs, Texas. (San Jacinto County.)

*Willow Water Hole Bayou.

*Willowhole, Texas.

Wills, James Robert (Bob). James Robert (Bob) Wills was born on March 6, 1905, near Kosse in Limestone County, Texas, the first of ten children born to John and Emmaline (Foley) Wills. In 1913 his family moved to Hall County, where they settled on the Ogden Ranch between Memphis and Estelline. In the early 1920's the family moved to a combination farm and ranch between Little Red River and Big Red River. It was while Bob Wills lived in Hall County that he learned to play the violin, and in 1915 he played the instrument at his first dance. He played for ranch dances in West Texas for the next fourteen years, and his life and career were greatly influenced by that environment. During that time Wills brought together two streams of American folk music to create his own distinctive art form, called western swing. He had first learned frontier fiddle music from his father and grandfather, but he also learned blues and jazz from Negroes, who were his earliest playmates and co-workers in the cotton fields of East and West Texas. He played fiddle music with the heat of blues and the swing of jazz, creating a new music that could as properly be called western jazz as western swing.

In 1929 Wills moved to Fort Worth, where he performed on several radio stations, organized a band which became the Light Crust Doughboys,qv and worked for a future governor of Texas and United States senator, W. Lee O'Daniel.qv In 1934 Wills moved to Oklahoma, where he made radio and musical history with his broadcasts over Station

KVOO. During his years in Tulsa (1934–1943), he and his new group, the Texas Playboys, continued to develop the swinging western jazz he had pioneered in West Texas, adding drums and horn sections of brass and reeds. Wills' recording of his famous composition of "New San Antonio Rose" (1940) took him out of the provincialism of the Southwest and made him a national figure in popular music. In the same year he went to Hollywood and made the first of his nineteen movies.

Wills was married and divorced several times between 1935 and 1941. On August 10, 1942, he was married to Betty Anderson, and they remained married for nearly thirty-three years, until his death in 1975; they had four children. Wills had two children by former marriages.

Wills joined the army in December, 1942. After World War II he had his greatest success, grossing nearly one-half million dollars during some years. In 1957 he was elected to the American Society of Composers, Authors and Publishers. In 1968 he was elected to the Country Music Hall of Fame, although Wills never thought of his music as "country." His influence in popular American music was extensive: he was a creator of western swing in the Southwest and on the West Coast, a founding father of country-and-western music in Nashville, a transitional figure in rock and roll, and an influence on country rock in Austin.

In 1969 the governor and legislature of Texas honored Wills for his contribution to American music, one of the few original musical forms Texas and the Southwest have produced. The day after the ceremonies in Austin, Wills had a crippling stroke. He died on May 13, 1975, and was buried in Memorial Park in Tulsa, Oklahoma.

BIBLIOGRAPHY: Ruth Sheldon, *Hubbin' It: The Life of Bob Wills* (1938); Charles R. Townsend, *San Antonio Rose: The Life and Music of Bob Wills* (1976).

Charles R. Townsend

*Wills Point, Texas. Wills Point, in northern Van Zandt County near Lake Tawakoni, was an important cotton raising and shipping center, although by the early 1970's it had acquired a more diverse economy. The raising of livestock, truck farming, and some industry brought in a major portion of the income of the town. The manufacture of ladies' garments there gave employment to several hundred people. In 1970 Wills Point reported seventy-five businesses, a hospital, a library, a nursing home, a bank, seven churches, and a weekly newspaper. The population was 2,281 in 1960 and 2,636 in 1970, according to the United States census.

*Willson, Charles.

*Willson, Samuel A.

Wilmans, Edith Eunice Therrel. Edith Eunice Therrel Wilmans, first woman elected to the Texas legislature, was born on December 21, 1882, at Lake Providence, East Carroll Parish, Louisiana, the daughter of Benjamin Franklin and Mary Elizabeth (Grier) Therrel. She attended public schools in Dallas, where her parents had moved in 1885. She was married to Jacob Hall Wilmans, on December

25, 1900; they had three daughters. In 1914 Edith Wilmans helped organize the Dallas Equal Suffrage Association; later she helped organize the Dallas Housewives League and the Democratic Women of Dallas County, and she was president of the Democratic Women's Association of Texas.

To learn more about the legal problems involved in improving the status of women and children, she studied law and was admitted to the Bar in 1918. In 1922 she was elected to the Thirty-eighth Texas Legislature, representing Dallas County, District 50, in 1923, the year her husband died. While in the legislature she endorsed legislation for child support and child care and for the creation of the Dallas County District Court of Domestic Relations. She served only one term in the legislature, and in 1924 and 1926 she ran unsuccessfully for governor. In 1929 she was married to Henry A. Born of Chicago; the marriage ended in divorce, and she returned to Dallas to practice law. She ran for the legislature again in 1935, but was defeated; that same year she bought a farm home near Vineyard, Jack County. She was a candidate for the Thirteenth District Congressional seat in 1948 and again in a 1951 special election, losing both races. In 1958 Edith Wilmans returned to Dallas to live, and she died there on March 21, 1966; she was buried in Hillcrest Memorial Park in Dallas.

BIBLIOGRAPHY: Dallas *Morning News*, July 8, 1951.

Edith Eunice Wilmans Malone

*Wilmer, Texas. Wilmer, in Dallas County, increased dramatically in size in the 1950's as the Dallas urban area expanded to include it. It had a population of 1,785 in 1960 and 1,922 in 1970. *See also* Dallas Standard Metropolitan Statistical Area.

*Wilmeth, Texas.

*Wilson, Augusta Jane (Evans). *See* Evans, Augusta Jane.

Wilson, Charlotte. *See* Baker, Karle (Wilson).

*Wilson, Francis.

*Wilson, Hugh.

*Wilson, James Charles.

*Wilson, James Theodore Dudley.

*Wilson, John.

*Wilson, Robert. Robert Wilson, son of James and Elizabeth (Hardcastle) Wilson, was the father of two sons (not one, as stated in Volume II). The sons were James Theodore Dudley Wilson qv and John R. Wilson (who died in Houston in 1855, the year before his father's death).

BIBLIOGRAPHY: Amelia W. Williams and Eugene C. Barker (eds.), *The Writings of Sam Houston, 1813–1863*, II (1939); *History Of Texas Together With A Biographical History Of The Cities Of Houston And Galveston* (1895); *Biographical Directory of the Texan Conventions and Congresses, 1832–1845* (1941).

Wilson, Roscoe. Roscoe Wilson was born on March 5, 1881, in Brazoria, Texas, the son of Eugene Joseph and Della (Sweeney) Wilson. After finishing public school in Houston, he studied law in his father's office and was admitted to the Bar in 1903. He opened his own law office in Lubbock in 1909 and established the firm of Wilson, Randal, and Kilpatrick there in 1925. He was a director of the First National Bank of Lubbock and one of the founders of the Lubbock Building and Loan Association. On June 22, 1912, he was married to Alice Effie Brownfield.

Wilson was active in civic affairs in Lubbock; he belonged to a number of city, business, and fraternal organizations and served on a number of special boards and committees, including the charter commission for the city of Lubbock. He aided in the establishment of St. Pauls-on-the-Plains Episcopal Church and was a member of the Lubbock school board. Wilson was a member of the local committee which secured the site for Texas Technological College (now Texas Tech University). He helped induce the state to locate the institution in Lubbock and was appointed in 1929 to the college's board of directors, on which he served until his death on February 13, 1936. A Lubbock elementary school was named in his honor, and in 1936 *La Ventana*, the Texas Tech yearbook, was dedicated to him.

BIBLIOGRAPHY: Seymour V. Connor (ed.), *Builders of the Southwest* (1959).

Seymour V. Connor

Wilson, Samuel Calhoun. Samuel Calhoun Wilson, the son of James Reed and Ella Louise (Calhoun) Wilson, was born on January 5, 1877, in Walker County. He attended public schools in Huntsville and was graduated from Sam Houston Normal Institute (later named Sam Houston State Teachers College and now Sam Houston State University). He also studied at the University of Texas, the University of Chicago, George Peabody College, and Cornell University. He was married in November, 1905, to Sammie Logan; they had three children.

Wilson became a member of the faculty of Sam Houston Normal Institute as a young man, and his career was intimately associated with the growth of that institution. For twenty-nine years he was director of the school's agriculture department, and for a number of those years Sam Houston Normal Institute was the only normal school in the United States which was authorized to give teacher training in vocational agriculture under the provisions of the Smith-Hughes Act; under Wilson's direction, the department which he founded came to be recognized as one of the most outstanding in the South. Toward the close of his career he was given a life membership in the Texas Vocational Association, which honored him as "the father of vocational agriculture in Texas."

Wilson belonged to a number of professional and honorary societies; he was president of the Texas Vocational Association and of the Texas State Teachers Association.qv During World War I he was employed by the Department of the Interior as supervisor of farm production in southern states. He was the author of numerous articles on educational topics, and he was responsible for several conferences on rural life and education which met in Huntsville under the sponsorship of the federal government. Wilson died on October 21, 1939, in Huntsville; he was buried in Oakwood Cemetery there.

BIBLIOGRAPHY: Faculty Biographies, 1879–1940 (MS., Sam Houston State University Library); *Texian Who's Who* (1937).

Aline Law

*Wilson, Stephen Julian.

*Wilson, Texas. (Collin County.)

*Wilson, Texas. (Comanche County.)

*Wilson, Texas. (Lynn County.)

*Wilson Branch.

*Wilson County. Wilson County, a highly diversified farming area, had an average annual farm income of $16.5 million in the early 1970's. Major agricultural produce included grain sorghums, coastal bermuda, vegetables, peanuts, and watermelons; cattle (both beef and dairy), hogs, and poultry contributed approximately two-thirds of the farm income. A watermelon jubilee is held each June in Stockdale, and a peanut festival is held each October in Floresville. Between 1941 and January 1, 1973, the county produced 14,162,333 barrels of crude oil. The population of Wilson County was 13,267 in 1960 and 13,041 in 1970, according to the United States census.

*Wilson Creek.

*Wilson Draw.

*Wilson Lake.

*Wilson Springs, Texas.

*Wimberley, Texas.

*Winan Creek.

*Winch, Joel C. C.

*Winchell, Texas.

*Winchester, Texas.

*Winchester Quarantine.

*Wind River.

Windcrest, Texas. Windcrest is an incorporated town in eastern Bexar County; its growth during the 1960's reflected the urban expansion of San Antonio. The town's population was 441 in 1960 and 3,371 in 1970, an increase of 664.4 percent, according to the United States census. *See also* San Antonio Standard Metropolitan Statistical Area.

Windmills in Texas. Before the introduction of windmills to Texas, inhabitable land was confined to areas where a constant water supply was available. There was no way for vast areas to be settled without a life-giving supply of water. The coming of the windmill made it possible to pump water from beneath the ground, and soon whole new areas of the state were opened up to settlers.

The first windmills in Texas were of the European style, built by Dutch and German immigrants for grinding meal and powering light industry. What Texans needed most, however, was a windmill that pumped water. Because of its bulk and need for constant attention, the European windmill was impractical for this purpose.

The solution to this problem came in 1854, when Daniel Halladay (sometimes found as "Hallady" or "Halliday") built the first American windmill in Ellington, Connecticut. He added to his mill a vane, or "tail," as it was called by Texas cowhands, that functioned to direct the wheel into the wind. The wheel was a circle of wood slats radiating from a horizontal shaft and set at angles to the wind, designed so that centrifugal force would slow it in high winds; thus, the machine was self-regulating and operated unattended. Its simple direct-stroke energy converter consisted of only a shaft and a small flywheel to which the sucker rod was pinned. This compact mechanism was mounted on a four-legged wood tower which could be constructed over a well in one day.

Railroad companies immediately recognized windmills as an inexpensive means of providing water for steam engines and for attracting settlers to semiarid regions through which they planned to lay track. In 1860 the Houston Tap and Brazoria Railroad purchased the right to manufacture and use James Mitchell's "Wind Wheel" on its right-of-way from Houston to Wharton, Texas. By 1873 the windmill had become an important supplier of water for railways, small towns where there were no public water systems, and small farms.

Many of the very early mills were crude, inefficient, homemade contraptions. One of the popular makeshift mills was a wagon wheel with slats nailed around it to catch the wind, mounted on half an axle. The axle was fastened securely to a post erected beside the well. A sucker rod was pinned to the edge of the hub. It was stationary and worked only when the wind blew in the right direction. The windmills used later on the big ranches were the more dependable factory-made windmills.

Windmills moved to the ranches when the use of barbed wire began in Texas in the late 1870's. At first the water holes, springs, creeks, and rivers were fenced, so that the back lands had no access to water. In the midst of the ensuing fence cutting and fighting, some ranchers began drilling wells and experimenting with windmills. Most of these experiments were unsuccessful, however, due to lack of knowledge concerning the proper size of the windmill in relation to the depth and diameter of the well.

One of the earliest successful experiments was made eight miles north of Eldorado, in Schleicher County, by C. C. Doty. A nomadic sheepman, Doty moved his flock into that area in 1880 and found abundant water in shallow wells. By 1882, however, a drouth had dried his wells; he ordered a drilling rig from Fort Scott, Arkansas, bored a fifty-two-foot well, and erected a Star windmill, which successfully supplied water for his 4,000 head of stock.

Watering stock with windmills spread rapidly over the Edwards and Stockton plateaus, into the Trans-Pecos country, and down into the Rio Grande plains. The practice then moved northward into the Panhandle, where Eastern land speculators began buying, fencing, and running stock on the land until it became ripe for colonization. Among the first of these speculators to indirectly bring windmills to North Texas was the Magnolia Cattle and Land Company, organized by Major W. V. Johnson. In 1884 the company bought two-thirds of the state-owned land in Borden County, land which had natural water resources and had long been unofficially claimed for grazing by Christopher Columbus Slaughter.qv When Johnson fenced the land, Slaughter was forced into the use of windmills to supply water for his cattle.

By 1886 the Matador Land and Cattle Company, Limited,qv and the Francklyn Land and Cattle Company began using windmills to water stock. The largest of the Eastern land speculators, the Capitol Syndicate,qv began using windmills on its XIT Ranch qv in 1887, and by 1900 it had 335 in operation.

On the coastal prairies of Texas the Coleman-Fulton Pasture Company qv erected twenty-two windmills in San Patricio County during 1885 and 1886, but it was not until the King Ranch qv began extensive use of the windmill in 1890 that the practice began to spread rapidly over that area. By 1900 windmills were a common sight in Texas. Inhabitable land was no longer limited to regions with a natural water supply. The windmill made the most remote areas habitable.

The use of windmills created two of the most colorful characters of the West, the driller and the windmiller, and altered the lifestyle of another, the range rider. The driller was usually a loner and seldom seen by anyone except the range rider and windmiller. He followed the fence crews and guessed at where he might find water, then bored wells with his horse-powered drilling rig. When the driller was successful the windmiller followed and set up a mill. Owners of the larger ranches usually employed several windmillers to make continuous rounds, checking and repairing windmills. The windmillers lived in covered wagons and only saw headquarters once or twice a month.

The early mills had to be greased twice a week, and this was the range rider's job. He kept a can (or beer bottle) containing grease tied to his saddle. When he rode up to a mill that was squeaking, he would climb it, hold the wheel with a pole until he could mount the platform, and then let the wheel turn while he poured grease over it. The range rider was always in danger of attacks from swarms of wasps which hung their clustered cells beneath the windmill's platform; there was the added danger of falling from the tower when such attacks occurred.

The windmill industry's shift in 1888 to the back-geared, all-steel mill created heated debates in Texas livestock and farming circles. Most ranchers and farmers welcomed the new steel windmill because its galvanized wheel and tower held up better in harsh weather; also, its gear system was better able to take advantage of the wind, thus enabling the windmill to run more hours per day. The back-geared mill could also pump deeper and larger-diameter wells. Those who favored the old wood mill argued that the steel mill was more likely to break because of its high speed, that it was not as easily repaired as the wood mill, and that when parts had to be ordered the steel mill might be inoperative for days. Though sales of wood mills continued, they declined steadily, so that by 1912 few were being sold.

The last major development in the windmill came in 1915. A housing which needed to be filled with oil only once a year was built around the mill's gears. This relieved the range rider of his biweekly greasing chores and somewhat diminished the windmiller's job. Because of the dependability of this improved windmill, worries over water shortages were eased for the rancher, farmer, and rural dweller. This mill was the prime supplier of water in rural Texas until 1930, when electric and gasoline pumps began to be widely used.

Though Texas became the largest user of windmills in the United States, there were never more than three active manufacturers of windmills in Texas at one time. Only two Texas manufacturers, the Axtell Company in Fort Worth and the San Antonio Machine and Supply Company, produced windmills on a large scale. The last water-pumping windmill patented in the United States, however, was invented by a native Texan, W. W. Welborn, in 1951, in the small southwestern town of Carrizo Springs, Dimmit County. It was a specialized mill designed for pumping water from depths of 700 to 2,000 feet. By the time this giant mill had been developed, the windmill market had declined so far that it could support no new mills.

At their peak in 1928, windmill manufacturers in the United States produced 99,050 units a year, 26,000 of which were exported; 50 percent of the remainder were sold in Texas. The last census of windmill manufacturers was taken in 1963; that year only 7,562 units were sold, and approximately 3,000 of those were sold in Texas.

Windmills remain an important supplier of water for Texas cattlemen. The King Ranch in the late 1960's kept 262 mills running continuously and 100 complete spares in stock. Stocking spare mills is a common practice among ranchers who depend on the windmill to supply water for cattle in remote pastures. Because the windmill has been confined for the most part to remote areas, it has become a symbol of a lonely and primitive life, fitting for the pioneer Texans it first served.

BIBLIOGRAPHY: J. Evetts Haley, *The XIT Ranch of Texas* (1953); R. D. Holt (ed.), *Schleicher County or Eighty Years of Development in Southwest Texas* (1930); Walter Prescott Webb, *The Great Plains* (1931); Joe M. Carmichael, "Water from the Wind," *Cattleman*, XXXVI (October, 1949).

Daniel B. Welborn

*Windom, Texas.

Windsor, Texas. (Kendall County.) Windsor, in western Kendall County, was established as a post office on April 26, 1880, on the north bank of the Guadalupe River, with Mrs. Lucy A. Wentworth as the first postmistress. In 1887 a township of Waringford was established across the river on the south bank, and the post office was moved there from Windsor the following year. *See* Waring, Texas.

BIBLIOGRAPHY: San Antonio *Express*, August 2, 1972.

*Windsor, Texas. (McLennan County.)

*Windthorst, Texas.

*Winedale, Texas. *See also* Winedale Museum.

Winedale Museum. The Winedale Museum, located in the Winedale community in northeast Fayette County near Round Top, includes several outstanding examples of early Texas architecture. The Sam Lewis house, a two-story frame house of eight rooms with a galleried porch across the front and an open hall or "dog-trot" through the center of the structure, combines both Anglo American and German architectural features. The original portion of the house was probably a one-room house built by William S. Townsend in 1834. Townsend sold the farm in 1840 to John York,qv who in turn sold it to Samuel K. Lewis qv in 1848. Lewis enlarged the house to its present form. Utilizing a braced frame construction, the house was built of local cedar which was sawed in heavy square timbers. The plan of the house, with a central open hall, two rooms on each side of the hall, and chimneys in the gable ends, is typical of the Anglo American house, while the window details and woodwork suggest the work of German craftsmen.

In 1859 the public road from Brenham to La Grange was relocated to run by the Lewis farm, and for a brief period it may have served as a depot on the Sawyer and Risher stage line from Brenham to La Grange to Austin. It is also believed that the Lewises were responsible for the remarkable interior decoration, a feature which adds much distinction to the building. The decoration consists of a painted ceiling, borders, and overmantel panels found in the major rooms. The most elaborate work is on the ceiling of the second-floor parlor; a green parrot appears in the center of the ceiling. The paintings, consisting of a classic medallion and garland design with a floral border, are the work of a skilled professional painter and are believed to have been done by Rudolf Melchior, a member of a family of German artists who came to the United States in 1853 and settled at Round Top in the 1860's.

In 1882 Lewis' heirs sold the farm to Josef G. Wagner, whose son lived there until his death in 1960. In 1963 Ima Hogg,qv daughter of James Stephen Hogg,qv purchased the property, which consisted of more than 130 acres of land and several related buildings, in order to preserve the Lewis home (sixty additional acres were purchased in 1972). Under Ima Hogg's direction, an extensive restoration program was carried out. The search for materials began at Winedale, where timber was cut on the Lewis farm itself (as was the original cedar in the house), and extended to Massachusetts, where square nails were found which were similar to those in the old building. The timber, all cedar, was put together in the medieval carpentry style of notched and pegged joints. The siding was made of cedar, and the roof was of cedar shake. Much of the original iron hardware—doorknobs, locks, and hinges—remained. In 1965 Miss Hogg gave the property and buildings to the University of Texas at Austin to be used as an outdoor museum and study center.

In addition to the Lewis house, the Winedale property included two handsome barns. The older one, a transverse-crib barn, was composed of two double log cabins covered by one large roof; the cabins were oak with cedar roofs. The other barn, made of handsome timber trusses, featured an open, central space. Both barns were restored, and the larger one was equipped with two dressing rooms and a small stage for the presentation of programs. Also on the grounds were a log kitchen, where open fireplace cooking was done, and a smokehouse, for curing meat and storing preserves.

After 1965 three additional buildings were moved to the site: Hazel's Lone Oak, a typical Texas dog-run house of the 1850's, now used as an office and visitor center; Lauderdale House, a Greek-revival farmhouse built in 1858 by a Somerville, Texas, planter, restored for use now as a dormitory for visiting scholars; and McGregor-Grimm House, an elaborately decorated two-story Greek-revival farmhouse built in 1861 by a Washington County planter, restored and opened to the public in April, 1975.

This collection of nineteenth century buildings on the 190-acre site which comprises the Winedale Museum is a part of the University of Texas at Austin; a faculty advisory committee is appointed by the president of the university. Lonn Taylor, appointed curator in 1970, was director of the museum in 1975. Examples of meetings held annually at the museum are an agricultural history conference, a preservation seminar, and a museum administrators seminar. A continuing program sponsored by the museum is a regional survey of vernacular architecture. An annual Winedale Festival, extending over two weekends in April, offers concerts and theatrical performances to the general public.

Drury B. Alexander

*Winfield, Edward H.

*Winfield, Texas.

*Winfree, Texas.

*Wing, Martin Carroll.

*Wingate, Texas.

*Wink, Texas. Wink, in Winkler County, had a population of 1,863 in 1960 and 1,023 in 1970, a decrease of approximately 45 percent during the ten-year period, according to the United States census. In 1970 the town listed sixteen businesses.

*Winkler, Clinton M.

Winkler, Ernest William. Ernest William Winkler, son of Charles August and Katarina Louisa (Huber) Winkler, was born on January 21, 1875, near The Grove, on the border of Coryell and Bell counties. He completed the normal course at Blinn Memorial College at Brenham in 1894; he entered the University of Texas in September, 1895, and graduated with his class in 1899, although he taught for one year, 1896–1897, at the Eden community near Seguin.

Winkler was a tutor in history at the university while working on his M.A. degree in 1899–1900 and in the summer of 1900 was employed to separate and sort materials in the Bexar Archives.qv

From 1900 to 1903 he taught history at Blinn College; he worked on the college paper there and assisted in indexing the *Quarterly of the Texas State Historical Association* (now *Southwestern Historical Quarterly* qv). From 1910 to 1937 he was associate editor of the *Quarterly*, a member of the editorial committee until 1959, and a fellow of the Texas State Historical Association.qv

In the fall of 1903 Winkler became translator and classifier of manuscripts for the Texas State Library.qv In 1905 he went to Mexico to acquire Mexican materials and to select documents to be copied for the archives collection. Upon the death of Cadwell Walton Raines qv in August, 1906, Winkler succeeded him as state librarian. In 1907 he transferred to the state's agriculture department as chief clerk, but he returned as state librarian in 1909, under the newly created Texas State Library and Historical Commission;qv he served as secretary of the commission and editor of *Texas Libraries*. To carry out the obligation of the commission to print the state's archives, he edited the *Secret Journals of the Senate of the Congress of the Republic of Texas* (1911) and the *Journal of the Secession Convention of Texas, 1861* (1912). He assisted Eugene Campbell Barker qv in editing the historical portion of Francis White Johnson's qv *History of Texas and Texans* (1914). He served as president of the Texas Library Association qv in 1912.

In April, 1915, under political pressure, Winkler was forced out of the state librarianship. He became assistant librarian and bibliographer at the University of Texas Library in the fall of that year. In 1916 he became reference librarian and curator of Texas books. Winkler was one of the administrators of the Littlefield Fund for Southern History and was active in the examination and purchase of Southern materials. In 1921 he appraised and negotiated the details of the purchase of the Genaro García Collection, which became the foundation for the Latin American Collection qv at the University of Texas. He became librarian of the University of Texas in 1923, and during the eleven years of his administration there was a vast expansion of library holdings, particularly in the collection of historical materials. Although on modified service after 1945, Winkler continued his work as a bibliographer; he gave help and encouragement to Thomas Winthrop Streeter qv in the preparation of Streeter's *Bibliography of Texas, 1795–1845* (1956, 1960) and was himself assigned the task of collecting and editing the *Check List of Texas Imprints, 1846–1860* (1949), which appeared serially in the *Southwestern Historical Quarterly* before its publication in book form. For that book he received the Schreiner Award. He became ill in 1950, and the last task of his active career was participation in the opening of the Eugene C. Barker Texas History Center qv in April, 1950.

Winkler held emeritus status from the time of his full retirement in October, 1951, until his death in Austin on February 8, 1960. He was survived by his widow, Johanne Tabea (Kuehne) Winkler, whom he married on December 22, 1904, and by one son and four daughters. He was buried in the country cemetery near the Moody-Leon Methodist Church on the Coryell and McLennan county line.

Llerena Friend

*Winkler, Texas.

*Winkler County. Winkler County, with mainly an oil economy, produced 852,178,659 barrels of crude oil between 1926 and January 1, 1973. In the 1960's experiments were begun with irrigated alfalfa fields, and most of the $620,000 average annual farm income in the 1970's was from beef cattle. The county supported three community centers, a library and branch library, a hospital, and an airport. The major tourist attraction was Monahans Sandhills State Scenic Park (*see* Parks, State). The population of Winkler County was 13,652 in 1960 and 9,640 in 1970, a decrease of 29.4 percent during the ten-year period, according to the United States census.

*Winnie, Texas. Winnie, an unincorporated community in Chambers County, had a population of 1,114 in 1960 and 1,543 in 1970, an increase of 38.5 percent during the ten-year period, according to the United States census. The community listed seventy-two businesses in 1970.

*Winnsboro, Texas. Winnsboro, on the border between Wood and Franklin counties, is a marketing center for a truck-farming area. Since 1950 a new hospital, a modern high school, and a 917-acre lake were completed. Winnsboro's "Autumn Trails," a fall nature show, featured little theater productions, arts and crafts, music conventions, and other events. In 1970 the city reported 116 businesses, eight churches, a hospital, a library, and a newspaper. The city's population was 2,675 in 1960 and 3,064 in 1970, a 14.5 percent increase over the ten-year period, according to the United States census.

*Winona, Texas.

*Winston, George Tayloe.

*Winter Garden Region.

*Winter Haven, Texas.

Wintergreen, Texas. Wintergreen, a ghost town of Karnes County, was situated at the crossing of the Victoria-San Antonio and the lower Helena-Gonzales roads. It appeared on maps of the 1858–1868 period, and Civil War maps gave it the designation of "Wintergreen P. O.," indicating that it was a Confederate post office.

Robert H. Thonhoff

Winters, James Washington. James Washington Winters was born in Giles County, Tennessee, on January 21, 1817, the son of James and Rhoda (Creel or Beal) Winters. The family moved from Memphis, Tennessee, to Texas in 1834 and settled between the eastern and western forks of the San Jacinto River in what is now Montgomery County. He and his father and brothers joined volunteer forces to repel Martín Perfecto de Cós qv on his entry into Texas, but by the time they reached San

Felipe in December, 1835, Cós had already been defeated in the siege of Bexar.qv On March 12, 1836, Winters joined a group of some eighteen persons who formed a company on the San Bernard under Captain William Ware qv with the intention of stopping the Mexicans at DeWees Crossing on the Colorado River, but they were ordered by Sam Houston to fall back. They later joined Houston and were part of the group ordered to intercept Santa Anna qv at Lynch's Ferry.qv Winters served in Sidney Sherman's qv division at the battle of San Jacinto. He witnessed Santa Anna's surrender.

He was married to Percy Tullis in Montgomery County on September 14, 1837. Following the Civil War they lived in Tuxpan, Mexico, for a time. After his wife's death Winters returned to Texas and was married to Elizabeth Weir. Winters was the father of eight children.

In 1901 Winters was appointed by the Texas Veterans Association qv to serve on a commission to identify and locate historic spots on the San Jacinto battlefield for the purpose of marking them with granite shafts. A narrative of the battle of San Jacinto (along with an early account of his life) was recounted by Winters in 1901 and published in the *Quarterly of the Texas State Historical Association* (now the *Southwestern Historical Quarterly* qv) in October, 1902. Winters died at his home near Big Foot, Frio County, on the night of November 13 (or the morning of November 14), 1903, and was buried in the Brummett Cemetery nearby.

BIBLIOGRAPHY: James Washington Winters, "An Account of the Battle of San Jacinto," *Quarterly of the Texas State Historical Association*, VI (1902–1903); Sam Houston Dixon and Louis Wiltz Kemp, *The Heroes of San Jacinto* (1932); Louis Wiltz Kemp, San Jacinto Notebook (MS., Archives, University of Texas at Austin Library); Galveston *Daily News*, November 17, 1903; San Antonio *Daily Express*, November 17, 1903.

Winters, John Howard. John Howard Winters, son of John William and Frances Ruth (Hatchett) Winters, was born in Stephenville on December 10, 1901. He attended John Tarleton Agricultural College (now Tarleton State University) and Simmons College (now Hardin-Simmons University). He was married to Guydelle Vineyard on August 8, 1921, and they had one son. Winters taught school in Amarillo in 1922 and remained in that city's school system for four years; he then entered the wholesale grain business and was manager of a milling and grain company in Guthrie, Oklahoma, in 1928–1929. He returned to the Panhandle area and continued in the grain business until 1943. He served on the Amarillo school board and the Amarillo College board from 1931 to 1933. He was county commissioner of Potter County from 1937 to 1943, and he served as president of the Texas County Judges and Commissioners Association in 1941–1942.

In August, 1943, Winters was appointed executive director of the State Department of Public Welfare,qv a position he held for twenty-three years, serving under five governors. Known as an able administrator, Winters was named president of the American Public Welfare Association in 1953. His title as a state department head was changed to commissioner of welfare in 1957, and he remained in that position until his death in Austin on December 1, 1966. He was buried in Austin Memorial Park.

*Winters, Texas. Winters, in north-central Runnels County, serves a predominantly farming area. A factory for the manufacture of air coolers was established in 1958, and a plant for the manufacture of outdoor lighted signs began operation in 1959. Winters' grain mill expanded considerably during the 1960's, and the town's retail business was second only to Ballinger in Runnels County. The town had ninety-six businesses in 1970. The population of 3,266 in 1960 had decreased to 2,907 by 1970, according to the United States census.

*Wintuisen, Tomás Felipe.

*Wipprecht, Rudolph.

*Wire Hollow Creek.

Wirtz, Alvin Jacob. Alvin Jacob Wirtz was born in Columbus, Colorado County, on May 24, 1888, son of Dora (Dent) and Lewis Milton Wirtz. He attended Columbus public schools and the University of Texas, where he earned an LL.B. degree in 1910. He joined the law firm of Caruthers and Brown in Eagle Lake, near his hometown, and on November 18, 1913, he married Kittie Mae Stamps; they had one daughter. They moved to Seguin, where he practiced law from 1917 to 1934. In 1922 the district which included Guadalupe County elected him to the Texas Senate, where he served until 1930.

Wirtz's initial interest in hydroelectric power came with his involvement in developing the Guadalupe River by constructing a chain of privately-owned dams and hydroelectric projects. Emery, Peck and Rockwood, a subsidiary of Samuel Insull's industrial holdings, built the dams and later began construction of Hamilton Dam (see Hamilton Dam, Texas) on the Colorado River. When the stock market crash of 1929 toppled the Insull empire, Wirtz was appointed receiver, on behalf of Texas creditors, of the state's Insull properties, including the unfinished dam project. He then promoted the formation of the Lower Colorado River Authority.qv In the Texas Senate he wrote the legislation (which was ultimately passed in 1934) creating the authority as a state agency. In 1934 Wirtz moved to Austin, where he organized the law firm of Powell, Wirtz, Rauhut and Gideon. He specialized in oil and water law and was appointed general counsel to the newly-created Lower Colorado River Authority. Working closely with United States Representative Lyndon Baines Johnson,qv he helped the authority secure grants and loans from the Public Works Administration, the Reconstruction Finance Corporation, and the Rural Electrification Administration. He also aided in the formation of rural electric cooperatives in counties throughout central Texas. Although irrigation, flood control, and inexpensive hydroelectric power in the rural counties resulted from the river developments, the projects were completed only after a long and spirited struggle against the private utility companies. Wirtz's leadership and legal expertise throughout the public power fight were instrumental in the project's fulfillment. (See also Rural Electrification in Texas.)

As an early supporter of the political career of Lyndon B. Johnson, Wirtz helped the young congressman obtain numerous federal projects for the Tenth Congressional District, enlisted powerful supporters for Johnson's early campaigns, and aided the future president's U.S. Senate races in 1941 and 1948. In 1948 he represented the candidate before the canvassing subcommittee of the Democratic State Executive Committee and led the successful fight in which Johnson was declared winner (by eighty-seven votes) over Coke R. Stevenson qv in the contested election.

An influential figure in Democratic politics, Wirtz was a delegate to the 1928, 1932, and 1940 Democratic national conventions. He actively promoted Franklin D. Roosevelt's renomination bids in 1940 and 1944. He served as chairman of the National Youth Administration's advisory board for Texas and as director of the Austin housing authority. In January, 1940, President Roosevelt appointed Wirtz undersecretary of the Department of the Interior, a position he resigned in May, 1941, to return to his Austin law firm and to aid Johnson's U.S. Senate campaign against W. Lee O'Daniel.qv During World War II he acted as negotiator for the president's cabinet committee for Saudi Arabian oil.

In addition to his extensive knowledge of public power, Wirtz was also an expert in oil and gas law, and he represented such prominent clients as Brown and Root Company of Houston and independent petroleum producer Sid Williams Richardson.qv Early in his career he gained a reputation as a staunch advocate of civil liberties, and in 1939 he successfully led the defense of Maury Maverick qv during an indictment regarding campaign practices in San Antonio. Wirtz died on October 27, 1951, in Austin, and he was buried in the State Cemetery.qv

BIBLIOGRAPHY: *National Cyclopaedia of American Biography*, XLI (1956); *Who's Who In America* (1950).

Michael L. Gillette

*Wise, Henry A.

*Wise County. In 1960 Wise County ranked fourth among Texas counties in number of dairy cows, with 13,318, and in 1968, with 13,800, it tied for third with Erath County. In the 1970's it was still one of the leading dairy counties and also produced beef cattle, hogs, goats, and poultry. Crops included sorghums, small grains, pecans, peanuts, vegetables, and fruit. Minerals, valued at $46,818,-000 in 1971, included petroleum, natural gas, natural gas liquids, clays, stone, sand, and gravel. The county produced 52,095,883 barrels of crude oil between 1942 and January 1, 1973. The largest youth fair in the state was held each spring in Wise County. Wise County Park on Lake Bridgeport was completed in 1965, and in 1966 the first phase of a master plan to develop Lake Bridgeport into a 3,800-acre recreation site was completed. Tourist attractions included a rodeo, an old settlers reunion, a county-sponsored museum in Decatur, Lake

Bridgeport, and Eagle Mountain Reservoir. The population was 17,012 in 1960 and 19,687 in 1970, an increase of 15.7 percent over the ten-year period, according to the United States census. *See also* Dallas-Fort Worth Standard Metropolitan Statistical Area.

*Witcher, Texas.

Withers, Harry Clay. Harry Clay Withers was born on November 20, 1880, at Denton, the son of John Allen and Mary (Coleman) Withers. He was educated in the public schools of Denton and at the Haskell Institute, Durant, Oklahoma. At the age of nineteen he enlisted in the 33rd United States Volunteer Infantry during the Spanish-American War and took part in sixteen engagements in the Philippine Insurrection campaign (1899–1901). He began his newspaper career with the Denton *Record Chronicle* in 1901. After a brief period with the Houston *Post* qv in 1903 he joined the editorial staff of the Dallas *Morning News* qv in 1904. He was married to Annie Sinclair on January 23, 1907.

Withers advanced from reporter to sports editor of the Dallas *Morning News* in 1905; later he became its city editor, managing editor, and executive editor, except for the period when he worked for that newspaper's affiliate, the Dallas *Journal*, as city editor (1914–1918) and managing editor (1918–1938). During and after World War II, while he was managing editor of the Dallas *Morning News*, he wrote numerous analytical news articles, most of which were also broadcast over Radio Station WFAA.

Withers was one of the originators of the Dallas Crime Commission, a chairman of the board of development of Southern Methodist University, and a director of the A. H. Belo Corporation (*see* Belo, Alfred Horatio). He was awarded an honorary LL.D. degree by Southwestern University in 1947. He died on April 24, 1959, at Dallas and was buried in Hillcrest Memorial Cemetery. In a resolution by Senator Lyndon Baines Johnson qv in the United States Senate, Withers was described as the dean of Texas newspaper editors, and the senate voted to adjourn on May 7, 1959, in his memory.

BIBLIOGRAPHY: *Who's Who In America* (1950); *Texian Who's Who* (1937); Dallas *Morning News*, April 25, 1959; *Congressional Record*, May 7, 1959.

Sam Acheson

Witt, Edgar E. Edgar E. Witt was born on January 28, 1876, in Bell County, the son of James Monroe and Elizabeth (Simpson) Witt. He received his early education in the schools at Salado and received an LL.B. degree from the law department of the University of Texas in 1903; he then entered law practice in Waco.

In 1914 Witt was elected to the House of Representatives of the Thirty-fourth Texas Legislature. In 1918 Witt entered the military service as a captain and was sent to Paris, France; while there a vacancy occurred in the Texas Senate, and his name was entered as a candidate in a special election, which he won. He served in the Senate until 1930, and it was largely through his efforts that the bill

creating the Tenth Court of Civil Appeals was passed over the veto of the acting governor. He was twice elected lieutenant governor of Texas, in 1930 and 1932. He ran for governor in 1934 but was defeated by James V. Allred.qv

Witt remained active in his law practice in Waco until President Franklin D. Roosevelt appointed him chairman of the special Mexican Claims Commission (1935–1938) and again in 1943, chairman of the United States Mexican Claims Commission, an office he held until 1947. President Harry S. Truman appointed him chief commissioner of the Indian Claims Commission, and he served in that capacity until his retirement in June, 1960. Witt remained an active member of the Democratic party qv throughout his life. He was married to Gwynne Johnstone on June 6, 1904; they had no children. He died on July 11, 1965, in Austin and was buried in the family plot in Oakwood Cemetery in Waco.

Jake Tirey

*Witte Memorial Museum. The Witte Memorial Museum, celebrating its fiftieth anniversary in San Antonio in 1976, focused on four main areas of interest. The natural history museum is devoted to Texas wildlife and ecology, paleontology, anthropology, herpetology, ornithology, entomology, geology, and pre-Columbian anthropology and archaeology. Of particular interest are the E. M. Barron Mineral and Gem Collection and the Lone Star Hall of Wildlife and Ecology, which opened in March, 1971.

The history museum houses items relating to the Spanish colonial era, Texas pioneers, the Confederacy, and postbellum Texas to the 1930's; other items include arms and armor, stamps and coins, and costumes of Fiesta de San Jacinto.qv Antique cars, as well as a collection of horse-drawn vehicles, are housed in the San Antonio Museum of Transportation (formerly called the Witte Confluence Museum) in HemisFair qv Plaza.

The historic houses section focuses particularly on the 1800 to 1840 period and contains the Twohig House, the Ruiz House, and the Navarro House (all three moved to the present site from downtown San Antonio), and the reconstruction of both a hill country log cabin and an East Texas log cabin. In the early 1970's a project was underway to restore those houses (and furnish them) as examples of early Texas architecture and home life; by 1975 restoration of the Twohig and Navarro houses was completed.

The art museum houses selections of early American art, early Texas painters, contemporary American art, sculpture, drawings, prints, glass, china, porcelain, and other decorative and folk arts. A definitive collection of German-Texas furniture had been assembled by the museum by the early 1970's, and a summer long exhibit of Texas decorative arts, including early Texas furniture, was held in 1973. Some of the activities of the Witte Memorial Museum included guided tours, lectures, films, gallery talks, concerts, dance recitals, arts festivals, drama, hobby workshops, formally organized education programs for children and adults, and inter-museum loan and circulating exhibitions. The museum shop was renovated in 1971 with fixtures from a turn-of-the-century country store.

The San Antonio Museum Association, operating the Witte Memorial Museum and the San Antonio Museum of Transporation, in the fall of 1973 purchased the old Lone Star Brewery on Jones Avenue to be developed into the San Antonio Museum of Art. The old brewery was named as a national historic site.

Mrs. Ellen D. Schulz Quillin was the Witte Memorial Museum's first curator, and Eleanor R. Onderdonk qv was the first art curator. William A. Burns was director of the museum in the 1960's; he was succeeded by Jack R. McGregor in 1970, who remained as director in 1975.

*Witting, Texas.

*Wizard Wells, Texas.

Wochenblatt, Das. See Trenckmann, William Andreas.

*Woden, Texas.

*Wofford, Texas.

*Wokaty, Texas.

*Woldert, John George.

*Wolf Creek.

*Wolf Creek Lake.

*Wolf Flat, Texas.

*Wolf Mountain.

*Wolf Ridge.

*Wolfe City, Texas. Wolfe City, in Hunt County, had a population of 1,317 in 1960 and 1,433 in 1970, according to the United States census. The town listed thirty-one businesses in 1970.

Wolfenberger, Samuel. Samuel Wolfenberger was born in Wytheville, Virginia, on April 8, 1804, the son of Benjamin and Elizabeth (Mueller) Wolfenberger. From 1821 to 1824 he worked in various communities in Virginia, including Amsterdam, where he learned the trade of wagonmaker and wheelwright. In 1825 he was in Tennessee, where in Hawkins County in 1827 he was married to Caroline Fleshheart (or Fliesart); they became the parents of eight children.

In 1830 the Wolfenbergers moved to Marion County, Missouri, and then to Texas in 1831, settling in the area which was to become the Municipality of Mina qv and in later years Bastrop; there he worked as a wheelwright. He fought under Lieutenant William Jarvis Russell's qv command in the battle of Velasco qv in June, 1832. In 1834 he was named alcalde of the Municipality of Mina and helped form the first of the Committees of Safety and Correspondence qv on May 8, 1835. On November 28, 1835, at San Felipe de Austin he was named one of the commissioners responsible for the organization of the Texas Militia within the jurisdiction of Mina. Earlier that month, on November 17, he had enlisted in the Mina Volunteers for the campaign in San Antonio de Bexar and took part in the siege of Bexar qv in early December, 1835. He was discharged from the Texas Army qv in San Antonio on December 17, 1835. There is no record of Wolfenberger having served in the Texas Army during spring, 1836, although within a year after that he served as second sergeant in Robert M. Coleman's qv company of rangers (forerunner of the Texas Rangers qv) with headquarters at Coleman's Fort on the Colorado. During this time he also served as coroner and as assessor and administrator for the probate court of Bastrop County. In 1839 he was named county tax collector. In 1884 he received a league and labor of land in Bastrop County on Walnut Creek. Wolfenberger had registered his SW cattle brand as early as 1833, when he began ranching. From 1848 until the time of his death he raised cotton and with his sons was engaged in freighting goods on the Old San Antonio Road.qv In August, 1854, Wolfenberger, C. Meriday, and W. E. Stone were designated trustees for school district 19, later called Wolf Ridge; they located the school on land purchased on Cedar Hollow Creek.

Samuel Wolfenberger died on April 10, 1860, and was buried about ten miles southwest of Bastrop in the Wolfenberger cemetery, which was still maintained by members of the family in the 1970's. The state of Texas placed a marker at his grave in 1957.

Deed L. Vest

*Wolfforth, Texas. Wolfforth, in southwestern Lubbock County, was incorporated in 1950 and since that date completed installation of a city water and sewer system and paved its streets. The town reported four churches, three schools, one bank, and one library in the late 1960's. In 1970 the town reported thirty businesses. The population was 597 in 1960 and 1,090 in 1970, an increase of almost 83 percent, according to the United States census. See also Lubbock Standard Metropolitan Statistical Area.

*Wolfpen Creek.

*Woll, Adrian.

Wolski, Kalikst. Kalikst Wolski was born in 1816 of landed gentry stock in Potoczek, province of Lublin, Poland. He studied in the Piarist school in Warsaw but left to join Polish forces in the uprising against Russia in November, 1830. When the revolt failed, Wolski went to France and studied engineering. He had a part in the building of French railroads and in the construction of the dikes at Dieppe. As an ardent socialist he feared reprisals from the government of Louis Napoleon (III) and came to the United States in 1852, arriving first in New York. He visited Buffalo for several months and traveled as far west as Chicago, but he returned to New York City, where he remained for over a year. He visited the socialist Cooperative Agricultural Association of the North American Phalanx at Red Bank, New Jersey, and was interested in the women's liberation movement of the period.

Victor Prosper Considérant,qv the heir and disciple of Utopian thinker Charles Fourier, wrote Wolski in New York and asked him to go to New Orleans to meet the first group of colonists who were bound for Texas to found the colony, La Réunion,qv near Dallas. Wolski, who was selected as guide because of his knowledge of the English language, met the first group of Belgian and French settlers in New Orleans when they arrived in February, 1855. In early March they went by ship to Galveston, then to Houston, and then by foot and oxcart to the site of the proposed colony. The party of thirty-seven (including four teamsters) arrived in May, and Wolski remained at La Réunion until mid-November, long enough to convince himself that the project would fail. He returned to New Orleans, and little is known about the next four years of his life there. Apparently he had a daughter, Anna (mother unknown), who was educated in the Ursuline Convent in New Orleans and who was to figure prominently in the life of the Polish and American actress, Helena Modjeska. Wolski returned to Poland in 1860 or 1861 and settled in the Austrian portion of the divided Polish state, principally in Kraków and Zakopane. Wolski's account of his experiences in America, a great deal of it about Texas, was published in serial form in the Warsaw illustrated weekly *Kłosy* (Ears of Grain) in the mid-1860's. A revised version of these articles was published as a book, *Do Ameryki i w Ameryce* (To America and in America), in 1876; a second edition was issued by Wolski himself in 1877, and this volume was translated into English as *American Impressions* in 1968. Although Wolski wrote other historical works, he never again wrote about America. He died on January 22, 1885. *See also* Utopian Socialists in Texas.

BIBLIOGRAPHY: Kalikst Wolski (Marion Moore Coleman, trans.), *American Impressions* (1968).

Marion Moore Coleman

*Wolters, Jacob F.

Wolters Air Force Base. See Fort Wolters.

*Womack, Texas. (Bosque County.)

*Womack, Texas. (Colorado County.)

*Woman Suffrage. *See also* Women, Status of, in Texas.

Women, Status of, in Texas. Women who came to Texas in the early nineteenth century were ill-prepared for the trials and hardships that awaited them. Courage and determination were as much required of women as of men, and women helped build the houses, tended the livestock, and slept on crude beds of logs with rope or rawhide lacings for springs. A gun was always close at hand in anticipation of the ever-dreaded attack from Indians.

The legal status of women was also quite different from that of the mid-twentieth century. Women were not allowed to vote, hold office, or sit on a jury. The colonists were governed by the civil law of Spain and Mexico, but the settlers also brought with them the traditions and prejudices of the English common law. As said by Sir William Blackstone, the famous eighteenth-century English judge (who had a profound influence on American jurisprudence), "Husband and wife are one and that one is the husband."

Under the community property law of Mexico the husband managed not only the property acquired by the joint efforts of husband and wife, but also the property owned by the wife before marriage and that which she received after marriage by inheritance or gift. He alone had the right to convey property. A married woman could not make a contract or prosecute a lawsuit. (*See* Community Property Law of Texas.)

The statute relating to witnesses to a will provided: "The following persons cannot be witnesses to a will—a minor under fourteen, a woman, a dumb person, a homicide, or similar offender, an apostate, a Moor or a Jew." In lawsuits the statute permitted a woman of good reputation to be a witness except in a suit relating to a will, but "if she has been convicted of adultery," the statute provided, "or of bad reputation, her testimony will not be competent."

An early law book describing the prohibition under Mexican law of a woman being a lawyer declared, "No woman, however learned she may be, can act as an advocate for others in court. There are two reasons for this; first because it is neither proper nor honorable for a woman to assume masculine duties, mingling publicly with men in order to argue cases for others; second, because in ancient times the wise men forbade it, on account of a woman called Calphernia [Carfania], who was so shameless that she annoyed the judges with her speeches, so that they could do nothing with her." With such laws in effect it is not surprising that there were few famous women of the colonial days of Texas. One whose name is still recalled was Jane Long,qv known as "The Mother of Texas" because she was the first woman of English descent to enter Texas and to bear the first child of such parentage in the colony. Sophia Suttonfield Porter qv was perhaps the most interesting woman of the early days of statehood; she was described as "a woman Paul Revere" after she warned Confederates of the approach of Federal scouts.

Texas also had its women outlaws in the nineteenth century, the best known of whom was Belle Starr,qv often referred to as the outlaw queen of the Indian Territory. Usually a woman could become widely known only through some unique experience, such as that of Cynthia Ann Parker,qv who was kidnaped by Indians in 1836 in a raid on Fort Parker,qv lived among the Indians for twenty-five years, married a chief of the Comanches, and became essentially one of them before being forced to join the white community against her will (an action which probably contributed to her death soon afterward).

Perhaps the most talented Texas woman of the nineteenth century was Elisabet Ney,qv who was born in Germany in 1833. She became a famous European sculptor before coming to Texas in 1872 with her husband. She is best known in this country for her statues of Stephen F. Austin, Sam Houston, and other Texas public figures. Elisabet Ney was one of the first in Texas to rebel against the inferior status of women.

Whether women of early Texas (except for Elisabet Ney) were satisfied with their lowly status is not known. At any rate they made no public outcry, and it was not until 1893 that the first Texas Equal Rights Association was organized. Its objectives were "to advance education and equal rights of women and to secure suffrage to them by appropriate national and state legislation."

At this time there was no constitutional prohibition against women holding most state and county offices; however, women could not be members of the legislature or serve as officials of cities, towns, or villages, since the constitution provided that only qualified electors were eligible for these offices, and women, of course, were not electors.

No women ran for office, however, and their efforts were confined to trying to secure the vote for women. Foremost among the women active in the suffrage movement was Minnie Fisher Cunningham,qv who was president of the Galveston Equal Suffrage Association and of the Texas association. As a child she was amazed at the injustice that disfranchised her sex, and when she became a woman she spent her time speaking, compaigning, and organizing. In 1917 she lobbied in Austin for woman suffrage, and after women's enfranchisement she ran, unsuccessfully, for United States senator and later for governor. At a gathering of representative women in Austin, she declared, "Opportunity arising in the whirlwind of current events must be snatched off the griddle by women who see the issues of the day."

Other women who worked for the suffrage amendment were Jessie Daniel Ames, Jane LeGette Yelvington McCallum,qv Marguerite Reagan Davis, and Annie Webb Blanton.qv Mrs. Ames was the first president of the Texas League of Women Voters, which was formed from the old suffrage organization. Emma (Grigsby) Meharg qv became the first woman secretary of state (1925–1926) under Governor Miriam Amanda Ferguson.qv She was followed by Jane Y. McCallum, who served under two governors, Dan Moody (1927–1931) and Ross S. Sterling qqv (1931–1933). Mrs. Davis was secretary of the Texas Suffrage Association and the first woman presidential elector from Texas. Her husband, John Davis, was later a state senator and clerk of the Democratic national convention in 1924. The first woman officeholder was Mrs. L. P. Carlisle, who was appointed county clerk of Hunt County in 1902 to succeed her husband. In 1918, at the behest of Governor William P. Hobby qv and women leaders, the legislature granted women the right to vote in primaries.

Annie Webb Blanton was the first woman to run for office after the enfranchisement of women in the primaries. In 1918 she was elected state superintendent of public instruction and served for two terms. Prior to her election she had served as president of the Texas State Teachers Association qv and as vice-president of the National Education Association. It has been said that she advanced the cause of rural education and awakened men and women to educa-

tional needs more than any other person in the history of Texas.

Gradually women began to run for and be elected to county and state offices. The first woman state legislator was Edith Eunice Therrel Wilmans qv of Dallas, a Ku Klux Klan qv candidate elected in 1922; in 1924 Miriam Amanda Ferguson ran for governor and was elected on an anti-Klan ticket. By 1931 there were four women in the Texas House of Representatives and one in the Senate; since then, except for one session, there have always been women in the legislature. An increasing number held county offices, particularly that of county treasurer, which was the lowest paid county office. There are now women on school boards, city councils, and various commissions and boards of city, county, and state government.

Oveta Culp Hobby was appointed by President Dwight David Eisenhower qv as secretary of health, education and welfare in 1953, and before that she was head of the Women's Army Corps (WAC) during World War II. The first woman state district judge was appointed in 1935; in 1971 two state district judges, one federal judge, two domestic relations judges, and one county judge were women.

The legal status of women also showed a marked improvement. Women obtained the right to serve on juries in 1954. By the 1970's they could contract, bring suits in their own name, and manage their separate property and that part of the community property derived from their earnings or income from their separate property. This progress was achieved at a very slow pace, and the role of women in the early 1970's was still one of tokenism. Around the state there was usually one woman among nine members on a city council or school board. In 1970, of one hundred twenty-six members on college and university boards, only eight were women, and four of those were on the board of Texas Woman's University (as required by the legislature). In 1971 Claudia Taylor (Lady Bird) Johnson was appointed a regent of the University of Texas, an appointment which brought the number to nine women on college and university boards.

At times women's progress seemed to go backward. In 1919 Annie Webb Blanton was elected superintendent of public instruction, yet there has never been a woman in that position since. Mrs. Ferguson remained the only woman governor Texas has ever had. No woman has served as secretary of state since Jane Y. McCallum during Governor Sterling's term. In 1931 there were four women in the Texas House of Representatives; there were never that many again over a period of forty years; in 1971 there was one woman, Barbara Jordan, in the Texas Senate, and one woman, Frances "Sissy" Farenthold, in the Texas House of Representatives. Perhaps it was their strong representation that encouraged other women to run, for by 1973 five women were in the House and one woman was in the Senate; two years later that number had again increased, with the same women reelected and two additional women elected to the Texas House of Representatives. No Texas district had ever sent a woman to the United States Congress until March, 1966, when Lera Thomas was elected from Houston to fill the unexpired term of her deceased husband, Albert Thomas.qv The first Texas woman to be elected on her own to serve in the United States Congress was Barbara Jordan, from Houston in 1972; she was also the first black woman in the South to be elected to Congress.

The most important reason for lack of progress has been tradition and custom. In 1905 President Grover Cleveland, commenting on the demand by some women to vote, declared, "Sensible and responsible women do not want to vote. The relative positions to be assumed by men and women in the working out of our civilization were assigned long ago by a higher intelligence than ours." To many women it seemed hardly fair to charge the good Lord with this decision. But tradition and custom continued to keep women from realizing their full potential. Girls were reared by most mothers to get married and have children, boys to have careers. In school women were discouraged from taking courses in engineering, law, and architecture, usually considered men's fields. Industry and business continued to recruit boys on college campuses for executive positions, but not girls. Regardless of a college degree a young woman found that in many instances only a secretary's job was open to her in business.

The attitude that the election of women to public office was a usurping of the male right to govern still prevailed among some people at the beginning of the 1970's. In a 1970 Gallup poll the question was asked, "Would you vote for a woman if she were the nominee of your party?" Of those responding, 14 percent answered that they would not. Some people considered the idea of women participating in government or working in executive positions as funny. When the Civil Rights Act barring discrimination on the basis of race, religion, or ethnic origin was debated in Congress, a group of Southerners thought they would defeat the legislation and at the same time cause a little merriment by adding the word "sex"; thus, with high humor, an amendment was adopted prohibiting discrimination on the basis of sex. But contrary to the wishes of the Southern group the law was passed outlawing sex discrimination, as well as that of race, ethnic origin, and religion.

Custom and tradition were not the only reasons for the slow progress of women; the attitude of women themselves held them back. Many were satisfied with their role, while others, who wanted to make a greater contribution, were too humble about their abilities and did not ask for the jobs they were capable of doing. Still others did not want to take the trouble to do anything about their position; inertia held them back.

The question remained in the 1970's: what did women need to do to become policy makers and to participate fully in the community? Women's groups generally endorsed the philosophy that they needed first to believe in themselves and in what they were capable of doing; that the attitude of people gener-

ally (both men and women) needed to be changed so that women would be accepted as individuals and not just as women; that women needed to be aggressive, to have courage, to speak out against prejudice and discrimination, and to have the zeal of the early suffragettes. Susan B. Anthony, when she was over eighty years old, declared, "Failure is impossible." *See also* Woman Suffrage; Women's Joint Legislative Council; Texas Women's Political Caucus.

Sarah T. Hughes

*Women's Joint Legislative Council.

Women's Political Caucus, Texas. *See* Texas Women's Political Caucus.

*Women's Property Rights. *See* Community Property Law of Texas.

*Wonder Cave.

*Wood, David L.

*Wood, George T. George T. Wood was defeated in his attempts to regain the governorship of Texas in 1851 and 1853 (not 1852, as stated in Volume II).

BIBLIOGRAPHY: Clarksville *Standard*, July 30, August 13, 1853.

Roger A. Griffin

Wood, James Ralph. James Ralph Wood, son of Judson Hiram and Frances (Jones) Wood, was born on April 9, 1896, in Sherman; his grandfather, John Wright Wood, an Alabama lawyer, came to Texas before the Civil War to farm in Rusk County.

Wood was valedictorian of the Sherman High School graduating class in 1914 and attended the University of Texas at Austin. After returning from France, where he served as an infantry captain in World War I, he entered the University of Texas law school, graduating with an LL.B. degree in 1921.

He practiced law with his father in Sherman until 1927, when he joined a Dallas law firm. In 1945 he became general counsel and vice-president of Southwestern Life Insurance Company; he served as president of the company from 1948 to 1962, when he was named chairman of the board.

He was a trustee of the Dallas Museum of Fine Arts, the Southwestern Medical Foundation, the Texas Research Foundation,qqv and the Southwestern Legal Foundation; he was a director of the Dallas Citizens Council, the State Fair of Texas,qv and the Dallas Grand Opera Association. He was also a member of the Dallas Historical Society and the Philosophical Society of Texas.qqv

Wood was married to Kathleen Cook on June 5, 1923; they had two sons. He died in Dallas on December 9, 1973.

BIBLIOGRAPHY: *Who's Who In America* (1968); Biographical File, Barker Texas History Center, University of Texas at Austin.

*Wood, John Howland.

*Wood County. In 1973 Wood County remained 49 percent forested with pine and hardwoods. In 1968 there were four lumber mills in the county that produced 775 million board-feet of softwood lumber and 257 million board-feet of hardwood lumber. Over 90 percent of Wood County's $11 million average annual farm income came from beef and dairy cattle, hogs, and poultry. The county was also a leading producer of strawberries, watermelons, and sweet potatoes. Between 1941 and January 1, 1973, nearly 630 million barrels of oil had been produced. The minerals of Wood County, which included petroleum, natural gas, sand and gravel, and clays, were valued at $137,859,000 in 1971. Four new lakes were completed in 1962, one in each of the county's four precincts. The county population in 1960 was 17,653; in 1970 the population was 18,589, according to the United States census.

*Wood Hollow Creek.

*Wood Hollow Mountains.

*Wood Slough.

*Woodal, Texas.

*Woodbine, Texas.

*Woodbury, Jesse.

*Woodbury, John Lucius.

*Woodbury, Texas.

Woodhouse, Humphrey Eugene. Humphrey Eugene Woodhouse, son of Humphrey Woodhouse, was born in Wethersfield, Connecticut, on December 4, 1822. Having acquired a rudimentary education, he went to New York at the age of fourteen and obtained a position with a wholesale and retail house that dealt in shipping to foreign countries. In 1847 the firm sent him on a merchant vessel to Brazos Santiago, Texas, in charge of merchandise which was unloaded at Point Isabel (now Port Isabel). From there Woodhouse proceeded to Matamoros where, after selling his merchandise, he entered the commercial house of Samuel A. Belden.

Woodhouse moved to Brownsville on August 24, 1848, and there he went into business selling goods in his own building. In 1854 he entered a partnership with Charles Stillman,qv and they extended their merchandising trade far into the interior of Mexico. Woodhouse withdrew from the firm in 1859 and continued importing and exporting alone; he then established a line of packet ships between Brazos Santiago and New York; he competed with the Morgan Lines qv in the shipping trade between New Orleans and Padre Island. During the following years Woodhouse owned or had an interest in about fifty ships of various classes and tonnage. He built a wharf and a warehouse at Point Isabel, where he also operated a general store. He had a business in Matamoros, as well as the original one in Brownsville. At one time Woodhouse lived in New Orleans, although for the most part he made his home in Brownsville, where he built a house in 1856. During the Civil War his operations were chiefly confined to Matamoros, where he maintained a home; after the war he reopened his business at Brownsville.

Woodhouse was one of the leading border merchants who opposed the high freight rates charged by the steamboat partnership of Richard King and Mifflin Kenedy.qqv Woodhouse, with Joseph Kleiber, John S. (Rip) Ford,qqv Simon Celaya, and others incorporated the Rio Grande Railroad Company (see Port Isabel and Rio Grande Valley Railway) and built the narrow-gauge railroad from Point Isabel to Brownsville by 1871. In 1892 Woodhouse reported for taxation over 16,000 acres of ranch land in central Cameron County, listing himself as "resident owner."

He was married to Augusta Olcutt of New York City in 1856; they had one daughter. Augusta Woodhouse died after three years of their marriage, and in 1865 Woodhouse was married to Mary Belknap; they had six children. Woodhouse died on September 18, 1899, and was buried in the Old Cemetery in Brownsville.

BIBLIOGRAPHY: John Henry Brown, *Indian Wars and Pioneers of Texas* (n.d.); W. H. Chatfield (comp.), *The Twin Cities of the Border* (1893); LeRoy P. Graf, The Economic History of the Lower Rio Grande Valley, 1820–1875 (Ph.D. dissertation, Harvard University, 1942; copy in Barker Texas History Center, University of Texas at Austin); Woodhouse, Kleiber, and Garden Papers (MS., Archives, Texas Southmost College).

Grace Edman

*Woodlake, Texas. (Grayson County.)

*Woodlake, Texas. (Trinity County.) The planning and construction of the Woodlake Cooperative Agricultural Community for Depression-displaced farm families in 1933–1934 was under the supervision of David Reichard Williams.qv

*Woodland, Texas. (Hopkins County.)

*Woodland, Texas. (Red River County.)

Woodland Hills, Texas. Woodland Hills, an incorporated community in Dallas County, had a population of 339 in 1960 and 366 in 1970, according to the United States census.

*Woodlawn, Texas.

Woodlawn Mansion. *See* Shaw, James B.; Pease, Julia Maria.

*Woodman, W. H.

*Woodmyer, Texas.

*Woodrow, Texas. (Hardin County.)

*Woodrow, Texas. (Lubbock County.)

*Woods, James B.

*Woods, Norman B.

Woods, Peter Cavanaugh. Peter Cavanaugh Woods was born at Shelbyville, Tennessee, on December 30, 1819, the son of Sarah (Davidson) and Peter Woods. Sometime after his graduation from Louisville Medical Institute (Kentucky) in 1842, he met and married Georgia V. Lawshe; they had seven children. In 1850 Woods and his family moved from Water Valley Mississippi, to Bastrop, Texas; in 1853 they moved to San Marcos, where he practiced medicine.

In 1861 Woods recruited and became captain of Company A, 32nd Texas Cavalry (officially designated the 36th Texas Cavalry by the Confederate Congress). When the regiment was organized, he was elected colonel and commanded the unit throughout the war in the Rio Grande Valley, along the Texas coast, and in the Red River campaign.qv Woods was severely wounded in the battle at Yellow Bayou on May 18, 1864.

After the war Woods returned to farming and the practice of medicine at San Marcos. He served in the Constitutional Convention of 1866.qv After his wife's death in 1872, he married Ella Reeves Ogletree in 1874, and they had five children. Woods died on January 27, 1898, and was buried in San Marcos.

BIBLIOGRAPHY: *Memorial and Genealogical Record of Southwest Texas* (1894); *Confederate Veteran*, VI (1898); Merritt B. Pound, *Benjamin Hawkins, Indian Agent* (1951); Alwyn Barr, *Polignac's Texas Brigade* (1964); T. F. Harwell, *Stars & Bars* (1947).

Wilton Woods

*Woods, Zadock.

*Woods, Texas.

*Woods Creek.

*Woods' Fort.

*Woods Spring.

*Woodsboro, Texas. Woodsboro, in Refugio County, had a population of 2,081 in 1960 and 1,839 in 1970, according to the United States census. In 1970 the town listed fifty-five businesses.

*Woodson, Texas.

*Woodville, Texas. Woodville, county seat of Tyler County, was incorporated in 1929. It is a commercial center for a lumbering and livestock-raising area. In 1970 the town had eighty business establishments, thirteen churches, a hospital, a bank (which was enlarged in 1966), a library, and a newspaper. Landscaping of the courthouse, post office, and hospital was completed in 1967. The population was 1,920 in 1960 and 2,662 in 1970, an increase of 38.6 percent during the ten-year period, according to the United States census.

*Woodward, John.

*Woodward, Texas.

*Woodward Creek.

Woodway, Texas. Woodway, in central McLennan County, was founded in 1951 and incorporated in 1955 with a population of approximately 250. The population was 1,244 in 1960 and 4,819 in 1970, an increase of over 287 percent during the decade, according to the United States census. The community had a school system, several churches, and a business area of shops and stores. The name of the city was derived from the names of two residential areas, Midway and Westwood. *See also* Waco Standard Metropolitan Statistical Area.

*Wool Production. *See* Sheep Ranching; Textile Industry.

*Wooldridge, A. P. Alexander Penn Wooldridge, son of Absalom Davis and Julia Webber (Stone) Wooldridge, was chairman of the committee on location of the University of Texas for the city of Austin in 1881 (not for the board of regents, as stated in Volume II). Although he was never a member of the University of Texas board of regents, Wooldridge served as secretary to the board from its fourth meeting on August 17, 1882, until Sep-

tember, 1894, and thus had some influence on early university policies. He was the eighth president (not the first, as stated in Volume II) of the Texas Bankers Association,qv having been elected to that office on May 12, 1892.

BIBLIOGRAPHY: Minutes of the Board of Regents, University of Texas at Austin, November 15, 1881–September 10, 1894; *Proceedings of the Eighth Annual Convention of the Texas Bankers Association Held at Waco, Texas, May 10, 11, 12, 1892* (n.d.); Ruth Ann Overbeck, *Alexander Penn Wooldridge* (1963).

*Wooley Branch.

Woolfolk, Joseph Alfred. Joseph Alfred Woolfolk was born on April 19, 1836, in Mead County, Kentucky, the son of John A. and Mahala A. (Harris) Woolfolk. He was graduated from the University of Missouri and then from the law school of the University of Louisville in 1858; that same year he came to Texas and settled in the frontier town of Belknap, Young County, where he practiced law. He was a member of a ranger company organized in Keechi Valley, with headquarters at Belknap, and during the Civil War he served the Confederacy in Tennessee.

After the war he returned to Louisville, where he worked in the law office of his uncle. There he was married to Elizabeth J. Lewis on February 9, 1865; they were the parents of nine children. Woolfolk returned to Texas in 1867, went into the cattle business in Weatherford, Parker County, and also maintained his law practice. His family joined him the following year. Woolfolk was one of the two lawyers appointed to defend the Kiowa chiefs, Big Tree and Satanta,qqv who were charged with murder in connection with the Salt Creek Massacre,qv in one of the most sensational cases tried in Texas; the Indians were convicted. Woolfolk returned to Young County and practiced law; he held several positions in the county before he retired to his farm near Newcastle. He died on May 23, 1919, and was buried in the Woolfolk cemetery one mile northwest of Fort Belknap.qv

BIBLIOGRAPHY: James Cox, *Historical and Biographical Record of the Cattle Industry and the Cattlemen of Texas* (1959); C. C. Rister, "The Significance of the Jacksboro Indian Affair of 1871," *Southwestern Historical Quarterly*, XXIX (1925–1926).

Barbara N. Ledbetter

*Wooster, Texas.

*Wooten, Dudley Goodall.

*Wooten, Goodall Harrison.

*Wooten, Joe Sil.

*Wooten, Thomas Dudley.

*Wooten Wells, Texas.

Work, Philip Alexander. Philip Alexander Work, son of John and Frances (Alexander) Work, was born in Cloverport, Breckinridge County, Kentucky, on February 17, 1832. He came with his family to Velasco, Texas, in 1838 and several years later settled in Town Bluff, Tyler County; his father established a plantation a few miles below Town Bluff. After receiving a good education, Work was admitted to the Bar in Woodville in 1853. Work enlisted and served with the rank of first sergeant for four months in Captain John George Walker's qv Company B, Mounted Battalion of Texas Volunteers, when Governor Elisha Marshall Pease qv in the fall of 1854 issued a call for volunteers to protect the Texas frontier from Indian depredations; the volunteers were then mustered into the United States regular army, and Work later received a federal pension for this service.

Work was one of the two delegates from Tyler County to attend the Secession Convention qv in 1861, but before the convention reconvened on March 2, he resigned to raise a company of Texas militia, which was known locally as the Woodville Rifles. When it was mustered into the Confederate Army at New Orleans in May, 1861, it became Company F of the 1st Texas Infantry Regiment, Hood's Texas Brigade.qv Upon reorganization of the regiment in May, 1862, in Virginia, Work, who had already been promoted to major, was elected lieutenant colonel. He became the regimental commander on June 27, during the battle of Gaines' Mill after Colonel Alexis T. Rainey was wounded. Thereafter, Work commanded the 1st Texas Infantry in the battles of Malvern Hill, Freeman's Ford, Thoroughfare Gap, Second Manassas, Boonesboro Gap, Sharpsburg or Antietam, Fredericksburg, and Gettysburg. At Sharpsburg his regiment suffered 82.3 percent casualties, the greatest percentage of losses sustained by any regiment, Union or Confederate, in a single day of fighting during the war. His father, Dr. John Work, was the assistant surgeon of the 1st Texas Infantry from October, 1862, to July, 1864.

Philip Work succeeded to the command of Hood's Brigade on the third day of the battle of Gettysburg. On September 18, 1863, before the battle of Chickamauga, he became ill and had no further field service with his regiment; his resignation as lieutenant colonel of the 1st Texas Infantry Regiment on November 12, 1863, was accepted by the War Department in January, 1864. He returned to Texas and, after recovering his health, raised and commanded a company in Colonel David Smith Terry's qv Texas Cavalry Regiment from the fall of 1864 to the end of the war.

Work resumed his law practice in Woodville, but in October, 1865, he moved to New Orleans, where he practiced law and was in the steamboat business. After 1874 he resided in Hardin County, Texas, where he attained eminence as a land lawyer. He also was the owner of the steamboat *Tom Parker*, which navigated the Neches River. In his later years Work wrote several accounts of his wartime experiences, but only fragments of these manuscripts have been preserved. At Woodville on May 8, 1855, he was married to Adeline F. Lea, and they were the parents of four children. He died on March 17, 1911, and was buried in the old Hardin cemetery near Kountze.

BIBLIOGRAPHY: Philip A. Work Papers (MS., in possession of Cooper K. Ragan, Houston); U.S. War Department, *The War of the Rebellion: A Compilation of the Official Records of the Union and Confederate Armies* (1880–1901); J. B. Polley, *Hood's Texas Brigade* (1910); Cooper K. Ragan, "Tyler County Goes to War," *Texas Military History*, I (1961); Pension Records, Indian Wars (MS., National Archives, Washington, D.C.).

Cooper K. Ragan

Work Projects Administration in Texas. The Work Projects Administration (WPA) was originally named the Works Progress Administration when it was established as a national agency on May 6, 1935, by an executive order of President Franklin D. Roosevelt. Harry Hopkins, who had been chief of the Federal Emergency Relief Administration (FERA) and the Civil Works Administration (CWA) during 1933 and 1934, was appointed head of the new WPA, which succeeded these organizations. The name of the agency was changed to Work Projects Administration on July 1, 1939, when it was made a part of the Federal Works Agency, but its continuity was unbroken and the purposes of the WPA remained the same. It was established as an anti-Depression relief measure and lasted until it was phased out in 1943, after it was rendered unnecessary by increased employment and reduced relief rolls.

Prior to the WPA the problems of unemployment in Texas had been faced by Governor Miriam Amanda Ferguson,qv who issued an executive order creating the Texas Relief Commission in March, 1933. The commission used FERA funds, enabling Texans to participate in various early New Deal programs such as construction and white-collar projects of the Civil Works Administration and the camp programs of the Civilian Conservation Corps (CCC).

One CWA program, the Public Works of Art Project (PWAP) of 1933–1934, employed dozens of Texas artists in the decoration of public buildings, but the program was not administered by the Texas Relief Commission. Due to the PWAP administrative procedures under the United States Treasury Department, payrolls were routed through federal customs officers in the sixteen CWA regions, and expenditures were authorized by the federal government.

The FERA, under which these projects had been organized, was discontinued in December, 1935. Prior to that, in July, 1935, Texas had established an administration in San Antonio, directed by H. P. Drought, to coordinate WPA activities. The WPA functioned in Texas until after unemployment had begun to fall off sharply in 1942. The phase-out was completed in 1943, and the final report of state administrator Drought was written in March of that year.

Under the WPA 600,000 persons in Texas were helped to provide subsistence for themselves and their families. According to its regulations anyone employed by the WPA had to be the economic head of his family and had to be certified as destitute on the rolls of the Texas Relief Commission. People of both sexes and of all races were employed. WPA wages in Texas ranged from forty-five to about seventy-five dollars per month. Peak employment under the Texas WPA program was 120,000 persons in February, 1936. This figure perhaps reflects the level of administrative efficiency at that time rather than the need for employment, since the peak caseload of the relief commission came later, in February, 1939, when 218,291 of the unemployed were on relief rolls. Soon after that time the name of the state relief organization was changed by legislative act in September, 1939, to the State Department of Public Welfare.qv State WPA administrator Drought blamed the increase in caseload in 1939 on widespread crop failure in Texas in that year. The caseload remained high from 1939 through 1942, always staying between 120,000 and 150,000, while the number of workers employed by the WPA was never more than half of the caseload figure. The biggest drop in caseload in Texas did not come until the period February–October, 1942, when a reduction of 75 percent occurred, with a proportional drop in WPA employment. The major reason for a worker's leaving WPA relief employment was that of finding other work, although some were forced off by lack of adequate project funds. The 1942 drop in Texas WPA employment was undoubtedly due to the increase of business activity following United States entry into World War II.

Activities of the Work Projects Administration in any given area of the country were dependent on the needs and skills of the persons on relief in that area, since the main prerequisite for WPA employment was one's certified relief status. In Texas this had the effect of limiting projects in the arts. There was only one attempt at a theater project, which lasted only a month. There were no programs in painting or sculpture. This fact is deceptive, however, since Texans were being employed by the Treasury Department's relief art project and section of fine arts during approximately the same period that the WPA was in effect. At least seventy separate mural projects were carried out by Texans under these two projects.

The WPA activities in Texas were varied. As its art project the state conducted an excellent survey of folk art objects for the Index of American Design. There were so few artists on relief rolls that better-than-average craftsmen had to be employed and trained on the job. The objects were listed and pictorial records were made of them. The original plates for this index are on deposit at the National Gallery of Art in Washington, D.C.

The WPA Archeological Survey studied the Indians of Texas. This study entailed the location, mapping, and excavation of Indian villages, camp sites, and burial mounds (a total of fifty sites in all); the collection of specimens from these locations; and the analysis of all resultant information and material. In the paleontologic-mineralogic survey, WPA workers, again under the supervision of professional scientists, worked many sites in Texas for fossils, mineral resources, and combinations of both. As war requirements increased, work became involved with mineral investigation, especially for the location of road materials and mineral resources designated as strategic.

The music program in Texas consisted of the organization of groups of musicians into ensembles of various sizes, including dance bands, a Mexican folk group, and two Latin-style orchestras. The program also included teaching in CCC camps, in underprivileged parts of three metropolitan areas, and in public schools having no musical curriculum.

A broad adult education program was instituted to provide instruction in such basic areas as literacy and citizenship, in vocational training and home economics, and in foreign languages and other academic subjects.

Programs designed primarily to answer the needs of unemployed women were a child protection program, for training in the care of pre-school children; a clothing program, for the operation of shops which trained workers to make and repair garments and shoes for free distribution to the needy; a feeding program, which included storage and distribution of relief food, as well as the provision of school lunches, matron service, gardening, and food preservation; a housekeeping aid program, which trained women to fill positions as domestic workers and provided emergency aid in home services; and a health service program, which provided training and personnel for work in health agencies and institutions.

The American Imprints Inventory employed library workers and supervisors, first as a part of the Texas Historical Records Survey qv program and later in cooperation with the library service program. This inventory included books, pamphlets, broadsides, broadsheets, maps, newspapers, and periodicals in public, semipublic, and private collections in the state for the period from the beginning of printing into the nineteenth century; it calendared or transcribed three major manuscript collections. Copies of these materials were deposited at the University of Texas and other institutions. This program also included compilation of a list of all libraries in Texas.

Other archival and literary programs were the research and records programs, which provided clerical labor to public agencies for the installation or improvement of records systems; the library training program, which covered every phase of library science; and the library service program, which gave support in labor, funds, or technical knowledge to all types of libraries in Texas. Perhaps the best known was the WPA writers' project, which conducted large-scale research into the state's cultural history and its geographical points of interest. This work resulted in many publications, including several state and local guides to Texas. All manuscript materials from the writers' project were deposited in the University of Texas at Austin Archives.

The greatest single area of WPA public spending in Texas was construction. As in most of the other WPA projects in Texas, one-fourth of the construction costs had to be provided by sponsors. This was a regulation imposed by the Texas WPA administrators, there being no federal requirement for matching monies. Construction projects included parks, swimming pools, highways, bridges, stadiums, and other public buildings.

Recreational facilities were increased, but recreational leadership and organizational help were also boosted under the WPA. An attempt was made to provide leisure-time activities for persons of all ages, races, and economic groups during all seasons of the year. The WPA in Texas built and organized pre-school play centers, playgrounds, community recreation centers, toy loan centers, athletic leagues, boys clubs, girls clubs, and, during the period of World War II, centers for all branches of armed forces personnel. All recreational programs were begun with the idea of establishing permanent facilities.

BIBLIOGRAPHY: Texas WPA Papers, Record Group 69 (MS., National Archives, Washington, D.C.); Arthur M. Schlesinger, Jr., *The Age of Roosevelt* (1960); Lionel V. Patenaude, The New Deal in Texas (Ph.D. dissertation, University of Texas at Austin, 1953); Mallory B. Randle, "Texas Muralists of the PWAP," *Southwestern Art*, I (1966).

Mallory B. Randle

Works Progress Administration in Texas. *See* Work Projects Administration in Texas.

World Institute for World Peace Foundation. *See* Weingarten, Joseph.

*World War I, Texas in.

*World War II, Texas in. *See also* Prisoners of War in Texas; Chennault, Claire Lee; Eisenhower, Dwight David; Krueger, Walter; Murphy, Audie Leon; Nimitz, Chester William; Wainwright, Jonathan Mayhew; Walker, Fred Livingood.

*Worley, Texas.

*Worser Creek.

Worsham, Israel. Israel Worsham was born in 1820, the son of Jeremiah and Catherine (Landrum) Worsham, who came from Alabama to Texas, crossing the Sabine River on December 31, 1829, to settle in Austin's colony, where they received headright grant number five (a league and labor of land).

Israel Worsham received land certificate number thirty-five, 320 acres in Montgomery County on March 27, 1839, from the Republic of Texas. In fall, 1842, he volunteered for service in the Somervell Expedition qv and served as a captain in that punitive campaign. He represented Montgomery County in the House of Representatives of the Sixth Texas Legislature (1855–1856); he was again elected to that body, representing Montgomery, Grimes, and Brazos counties in the Eleventh Texas Legislature (1866).

During the Civil War he was a member of the home guard and was appointed a major, commanding the Montgomery County companies. He supplied the Confederate Army with slaves to drive wagons of provisions from his plantation, for which he was never reimbursed "for want of funds."

In 1867 Worsham wrote the description of Montgomery County for the *Texas Almanac*. He was a member of a Masonic lodge (number twenty-five), the Council of Labourers (a secret organization similar to that of the Grange qv), and the Texas Veterans Association.qv He donated land for railroad right-of-way, was active in affairs of the Methodist church, and served as an election judge. He was married to Emily Womack; they had four daughters and one son. Israel Worsham died in 1882 and was buried in the family cemetery on his plantation in Montgomery County on the old Post Road to Houston.

Ella K. Daggett Stumpf

*Worsham, William Benjamin.

*Worth, William Jenkins.

*Worth County.

*Wortham, Louis J.

*Wortham, William Amos.

*Wortham, William B.

*Wortham, Texas. Wortham, in Freestone County, had a population of 1,087 in 1960 and 1,036 in 1970, according to the United States census.

*Worthing, Texas.

*Wozencraft, Alfred Prior.

Wozencraft, Frank Wilson. Frank Wilson Wozencraft was born in Dallas on January 7, 1892, the son of Virginia Lee (Wilson) and Alfred Prior Wozencraft.qv He received a B.A. degree from the University of Texas in 1913 and an LL.B. degree in 1914. He began his law practice in his father's office in Dallas. From 1916 to 1919 he worked for Southwestern Bell Telegraph and Telephone Company as assistant general attorney for Texas. During this time, 1917 to 1919, he also served as a captain in the United States Army.

In 1919 Wozencraft was elected mayor of Dallas, the youngest person (up to that time) ever selected for that position. In 1921 he turned down renomination to return to law practice in Dallas; ten years later he joined the legal department of the Radio Corporation of America in New York, serving successively as assistant general attorney, general solicitor, vice-president, and general counsel. He resigned in 1942 to serve in the army during World War II, first as a lieutenant colonel and then as a full colonel with the American-British Combined Chiefs of Staff. After the war he went into private law practice in Washington, D.C., from 1945 to 1963, when he retired and returned to Dallas.

During the 1920's Wozencraft was active in the work of the League of Texas Municipalities,qv and he was given the title of honorary president for life. He was a member of the Philosophical Society of Texas qv and was its vice-president in 1966. He was an active member of the national executive board of the Boy Scouts of America.

Wozencraft was married to Mary Victoria McReynolds in 1921; they had two sons. He died in Dallas on September 3, 1966, and was buried in Greenwood Cemetery.

BIBLIOGRAPHY: *Who's Who In America* (1960); Dallas *Times Herald*, September 4, 1966; Dallas *Morning News*, September 5, December 26, 1966; Houston *Post*, September 5, 1966.

*Wrays, Texas.

*Wright, Charles.

*Wright, Claiborne.

*Wright, David.

*Wright, Edward Bingham.

*Wright, George W.

*Wright, James.

*Wright, James G.

*Wright, Jefferson. Jefferson Wright, born in 1798 in Mount Sterling, Kentucky, was a practicing artist before he came to Texas. Little is known of his art training, although at the age of twenty-four he met the great American portraitist Thomas Sully through his friend Matthew H. Jouett. It is possible that he studied with these two older artists in their studios.

In the spring of 1837 Wright came to Texas and announced in a Houston newspaper his intention of painting portraits for the citizens of that city. Advertising and the influential friendship of Sam Houston, whose portrait he painted, brought him commissions from many prominent political figures, among them Juan N. Seguin.qv

Along with Sam Houston, Thomas Weston, and Anson Jones,qv he became one of the founders of the local Masonic order in Houston. He served briefly as an Indian agent. When the artist was at the height of his popularity in the early 1840's, he temporarily lost some patronage when he sketched some politicians in uncomplimentary positions, implying that they straddled issues. In late 1842 his portrait work was interrupted by a period of active military duty. Wright was a member of the Somervell Expedition,qv but when this episode was over he came back to East Texas and resumed painting portraits. In his twelve years in Texas he contributed greatly to the Republic by painting portraits of its heroes in a simple, vigorous manner. In May, 1846, he returned to his home in Kentucky for a visit; he became ill and died there.

BIBLIOGRAPHY: Pauline A. Pinckney, *Painting in Texas: The Nineteenth Century* (1967).

Pauline A. Pinckney

*Wright, Travis G.

*Wright, William B. William Bacon Wright was born in Columbus, Georgia, on July 4, 1830, the son of John Wright. He was graduated from Princeton University, then he returned to Georgia, studied law, and was admitted to the Bar when he was nineteen. Soon afterward he moved to Eufaula, Barbour County, Alabama. In 1854 (not 1855, as stated in Volume II) he moved to Paris, Texas.

After serving in the Civil War he lived for a time in Clarksville, Red River County, and continued the practice of law. In 1873 he returned to Paris, Texas, and it was from that district that he was elected a member of the Constitutional Convention of 1875.qv During the 1880's Wright and his family lived in Dallas, where he practiced criminal law. They moved to San Antonio in 1888, and Wright entered into the banking business.

William Bacon Wright was married to a Miss Greer of Georgia in 1849, and they had four children. After her death he was married to Pink Gates of Mississippi in 1868; they had six children. He

died in San Antonio on August 10, 1895, and was buried in City Cemetery No. 1 in that city.

BIBLIOGRAPHY: San Antonio *Express*, August 11, 1895.

Lucie C. Price
Eugene W. Bowers

*Wright City, Texas.

*Wright Creek.

*Wright's Creek.

*Wrights Knobs.

*Wrightsboro, Texas.

Wueste, Louisa Heuser. Louisa Heuser Wueste was born in Gummersbach, Germany, on June 6 (or 9), 1806 (or 1803), the daughter of Daniel and Louisa (Yügel) Heuser. Her early interest in painting was stimulated by her father's successful business in the manufacture and importation of paints and the discussions of painting techniques among her two sisters and their artist husbands. Louisa studied portraiture at the Düsseldorf School of Art, and her works show the influence of her teacher, August Wilhelm Sohn, an eminent artist.

In 1821 Louisa was married to Peter William Leopold Wueste, a physician. The rearing of their three children interrupted her art career, but after her husband's death she returned to painting. Her son and two daughters left Germany in 1852, and in 1857 Louisa Wueste joined them in San Antonio. There, with the anxieties of the pre-Civil War period and the dangers of actual war, she found little public interest in painting; nevertheless, she established a studio in 1861 and gave art instruction while continuing her painting. A number of her family portraits (which she did not sign) remained in the possession of her descendants. Her landscapes and still lifes were signed with her initials, "L. W."

Louisa Wueste left San Antonio in the early 1870's to live with her son, Daniel, in Eagle Pass, where she found little encouragement for her art; however, her interest was stimulated there by the life of the Mexican people along the Rio Grande. Her paintings completed during this period reflect the color and vigor of this new influence. She died on September 28, 1874, in Eagle Pass, and she was buried in the Wueste family plot in the Eagle Pass cemetery.

BIBLIOGRAPHY: Pauline A. Pinckney, *Painting in Texas: The Nineteenth Century* (1967).

*Wurzbach, Charles Louis.

*Wurzbach, Emil Frederich.

*Wurzbach, Harry McLeary.

*Wuthrich Hill, Texas.

*Wyalucing Plantation. The Wyalucing Plantation building was demolished in 1962.

*Wyatt, Peyton S.

*Wyatt, Texas.

*Wylie, Texas. (Collin County.) Wylie, near Lavon Reservoir, is in a rich agricultural area which yields cotton, corn, and small grains. Manufacturers produce children's wear, transformers, and auto parts. Wylie reported forty-two businesses in 1970.

The population was 1,804 in 1960 and 2,675 in 1970, an increase of over 48 percent during the ten-year period, according to the United States census. *See also* Dallas Standard Metropolitan Statistical Area.

*Wylie, Texas. (Taylor County.)

*Wylie Mountains.

*Wyly, Alfred Henderson.

Wynne, Angus Gilchrist. Angus Gilchrist Wynne, an attorney, oil man, and University of Texas benefactor, was born on January 12, 1886, in Wills Point, Texas, the son of William Benjamin and Margaret Welch (Henderson) Wynne. He attended the University of Texas from 1903 to 1907, taking law courses in his final year. Wynne was admitted to the Texas Bar in 1909, began his practice at Wills Point, and became a prominent Dallas attorney and business leader. He was president of the Texas Bar Association qv in 1939 and served as

chairman of the University of Texas Development Board from 1948 to 1951. He was one of the incorporators of the University of Texas Law School Foundation in 1952, and in 1957 he became chairman of the building development committee for the Warm Springs Foundation for Crippled Children qv (*see also* Texas Rehabilitation Center of Gonzales Warm Springs Foundation). In 1969 Wynne established and endowed a law professorship at the University of Texas law school in honor of his father, William Benjamin Wynne.

Angus Gilchrist Wynne was married to Nemo Shelmire on April 17, 1912; they had two sons. Wynne died December 17, 1974, in Dallas.

*Wynne, Richard M.

*Wynnewood, Texas.

*Wynns, Archibald.

*Wyser's Bluff, Texas.

X

*XIT Ranch. The XIT Ranch covered parts of ten counties (not nine, as stated in Volume II), since it included a small portion of Cochran County.

*Xabe.

Xanna Indians. In a Spanish missionary report of 1691 the Xanna were listed among the tribes that lived to the southeast of the Hasinai Caddo of eastern Texas, which suggests that their area was either in eastern Texas or western Louisiana and that the Xanna were not the same as the Sana who at the same time lived southwest of the Hasinai between the Guadalupe and Brazos rivers. However, one document clearly indicates that the name Sana was occasionally rendered as Xanna. The status of Xanna remains uncertain.

BIBLIOGRAPHY: C. W. Hackett (ed.), *Pichardo's Treatise on the Limits of Louisiana and Texas*, IV (1946); J. R. Swanton, *Source Material on the History and Ethnology of the Caddo Indians* (1942).

T. N. Campbell

*Xarame Indians. The Xarame (Charame, Chaulama, Jarame, Shiarame, Zarame) Indians are not to be confused with Xaraname (Aranama) of the coastal region, although both groups are considered to have spoken Coahuiltecan languages. The aboriginal range of the Xarame seems not to have been the area around San Antonio, as some historians have asserted. Such evidence as exists suggests that the Xarame originally ranged south of the Edwards Plateau in a strip of territory that extended from the Nueces and Frio rivers southwestward across the Rio Grande into northeastern Coahuila. They were one of the four Coahuiltecan bands for which the original mission of San Juan

Bautista qv was established in 1699 on the Río Sabinas of Coahuila. Shortly afterward, when this mission was moved to the Rio Grande near present Eagle Pass, these Xarame moved with it. Other Xarame entered the nearby San Francisco Solano Mission qv when it was founded in 1700. In 1716 still other Xarame were represented at Ranchería Grande,qv where groups of Coahuiltecan and Tonkawa refugees had assembled near the Brazos River to escape both Apache and Spanish domination. In 1718, when San Francisco Solano Mission was moved from the Rio Grande to San Antonio and became known as the San Antonio de Valero Mission,qv some of the Xarame went with it, forming a nucleus of mission-trained Indians who helped give instruction to other Coahuiltecan bands gathered there. Xarame are mentioned in the records of San Antonio de Valero as late as 1776. Marriage records of Nuestra Señora de la Purísima Concepción de Acuña Mission qv in San Antonio contain the names of Xarame Indians who entered this mission in 1733 and later. J. R. Swanton listed Harame and Xarame as separate Coahuiltecan bands, but he did not explain why he made this judgment.

BIBLIOGRAPHY: F. W. Hodge (ed.), *Handbook of American Indians*, II (1910); J. R. Swanton, *The Indian Tribes of North America* (1952).

T. N. Campbell

Xeripam Indians. The Xeripam Indians are known from a single Spanish document (1708) which lists the Indian groups that lived north of the present Eagle Pass area. It has been noted that Xeripam resembles Ervipiame, the name of a Tonkawan group, but the name Ervipiame also appears in the same document. Although the Xeripam were not included in J. R. Swanton's list of identified Coahuiltecan bands, it seems likely that they were one of the many small Coahuiltecan bands of the Eagle Pass area.

BIBLIOGRAPHY: F. W. Hodge (ed.), *Handbook of Amer-* *ican Indians*, II (1910); J. R. Swanton, *Linguistic Material from the Tribes of Southern Texas and Northeastern Mexico* (1940).

T. N. Campbell

*Xinesi.

*X-Ray, Texas.

Y

*Y E Mesa.

*Yakwal Indians. The Yakwal (Tonkawa for "drifted ones") Indians are known only from Tonkawa folklore. According to a legend collected by A. S. Gatschet, part of the Tonkawa were once isolated by land submergence on the Texas coast. Many years later the main body of Tonkawa found these people living near present Galveston and called them Yakwal. It is not known how much historical truth remains in this traditional record. A. F. Sjoberg has suggested that the Yakwal may refer to the Mayeye, a Tonkawan group that joined the Karankawa near the coast in the late eighteenth century.

BIBLIOGRAPHY: F. W. Hodge (ed.), *Handbook of American Indians*, II (1910); A. F. Sjoberg, "The Culture of the Tonkawa, A Texas Indian Tribe," *Texas Journal of Science*, V (1953).

T. N. Campbell

*Yamparika Indians.

*Yanaguana Society. The Yanaguana Society in San Antonio was dissolved in March, 1947, and the articles of dissolution were filed with the secretary of state on May 23 of that year. Minutes, membership records, books, and thirteen paintings by Theodore Gentilz qv were given to the Daughters of the Republic of Texas qv and are now in the DRT library on the Alamo grounds. "Yanaguana" was the Payaya Indian name for the tribe's village, at the site of present San Antonio, when the Spanish expedition under the first governor, Domingo Terán de los Ríos,qv arrived there in June, 1691, accompanied by Fray Damian Massanet.qv Mary Frances Norton (not Miss Frances Norton, as stated in Volume II) was one of the charter members of the society, along with Frederick Charles Chabot, William Aubrey,qqv Frost Woodhull, and Harry Hertzburg.

Martha Doty Freeman

*Yancey, Texas.

*Yankee Creek.

*Yantis, J. E.

*Yantis, Texas.

*Yarboro, Texas.

*Yarboro Creek.

*Yard, Texas.

*Yarrellton, Texas.

*Yatasi Indians.

*Yates, Andrew Janeway.

*Yates, Texas.

*Yates Oil Field.

*Yates Peak.

*Ybarbo, Antonio Gil. *See* Ibarvo, Antonio Gil.

*Ybdacax Indians. This name is known only from a single hearsay report. In the early eighteenth century it was given as the name of a group that lived somewhere north of San Juan Bautista,qv a mission on the south side of the Rio Grande near present Eagle Pass. This would place the Ybdacax south of the Edwards Plateau in Texas, an area dominated by Coahuiltecan-speakers.

BIBLIOGRAPHY: F. W. Hodge (ed.), *Handbook of American Indians*, II (1910); J. R. Swanton, *Linguistic Material from the Tribes of Southern Texas and Northeastern Mexico* (1940).

T. N. Campbell

*Yearling Head Mountain.

*Yeary, John.

*Yegua, Texas.

*Yegua Creek.

*Yegua Knobs.

*Yell, Archibald.

*Yell Settlement, Texas.

*Yellow Bayou.

*Yellow Branch.

*Yellow House, Texas. [This is an incorrect title on page 943 of Volume II. For correction of errors in that article, *see* Yellow Houses, Texas. Ed.]

*Yellow House Creek.

*Yellow House Peak.

Yellow House Ranch. The Yellow House Ranch, covering 312,175 acres in Lamb, Hockley, Bailey, and Cochran counties, was created in July, 1901, when Major George Washington Littlefield qv purchased the southern, or Yellow Houses, division of the XIT Ranch qv for two dollars an acre. (*See* Yellow Houses, Texas, for origin of the name.)

The ranch headquarters was located at the base of the Yellow Houses bluff (in present Hockley County) because of the availability of spring water there. For the same reason, the Yellow Houses site had been a landmark and favorite campsite on the old trail across the plains from the headwaters of the Brazos River to Fort Sumner on the Pecos River. To tap this source of water further, eighty-one windmills were constructed on the ranch, one of which measured 128 feet from the base to the top of the fan and was reputed to have been the tallest windmill in the world.

The manager of the ranch was James Phelps White,qv who, as Littlefield's nephew and partner, owned one-quarter interest in the spread. Both White and Littlefield were known as astute cattlemen, and they rarely suffered losses of cattle from severe weather or from prairie fires, such as the fire in 1906, which burned off some 220,000 acres on the Yellow House Ranch. At the most, they ran 27,000 head of cattle, branded LFD. Although Herefords were the principal stock, the ranch also carried some Black Angus for a time, and in the 1920's White stocked the ranch with a few buffalo.

Though little oil was found beneath the ranch itself, one of the first wells in this oil region was drilled in 1912 at South Camp, about six miles north-northwest of Levelland.

In June, 1912, Littlefield contracted with the Santa Fe Railroad to build a segment of its main line from Lubbock to Texico, New Mexico, across his land. In August he created the Littlefield Lands Company qv to sell the northeastern corner of 79,040 acres for farms and to open the town of Littlefield in Lamb County. In April, 1923, after Littlefield's death, the remainder of the ranch was sold by White and the Littlefield estate to the Yellow House Land Company and was subdivided for sale as farms. The towns of Pep and Whitharral in Hockley County were opened by the company on this acreage. Later some 20,000 acres surrounding the old ranch headquarters were returned to cattle grazing. The Yellow House Ranch was owned and operated in the late 1960's by White's son, George Littlefield White.

BIBLIOGRAPHY: David B. Gracy II, *Littlefield Lands: Colonization on the Texas Plains, 1912–1920* (1968); *Lamb County Leader* (Littlefield), August 18, 1938; J. Evetts Haley, *George W. Littlefield, Texan* (1943).

David B. Gracy II

Yellow Houses, Texas. [This title was incorrectly listed in Volume II as Yellow House, Texas.] Yellow Houses, in the northwestern part of present Hockley County (earlier in Lamb County) was the site of headquarters of the Yellow Houses division (or southern division) of the XIT Ranch qv from the opening of the ranch in 1884–1885 (not 1880, as stated in Volume II); the official divisions of the ranch were not made until 1887. Yellow Houses, as shown on maps of 1884 and 1891 was in southern Lamb County when it was part of the XIT Ranch, but all maps since a re-survey was made in 1912 by a state surveyor, W. D. Twichell,qv show Yellow Houses in Hockley County. In earlier times the Spanish called the site Casas Amarillas, and the name Yellow Houses continued in modern times, fitting because of the high limestone bluff of yellowish hue, which from a distance and from certain points of view has the appearance of walls of a great city; with the caves in the face of the cliff the image often appears as a group of yellow houses. In 1901 George W. Littlefield qv bought the Yellow Houses division of the XIT Ranch and it became known as Yellow House Ranch.qv

BIBLIOGRAPHY: XIT Maps, Hockley and Lamb Counties (Map Collection, Barker Texas History Center, University of Texas at Austin); Maps of Lamb County, 1884, 1891, and Map of George W. Littlefield's Ranch, Lamb and Hockley Counties, 1913 (General Land Office, Austin); J. Evetts Haley, *George W. Littlefield, Texan* (1943) and *The XIT Ranch of Texas* (1953); Cordia Sloan Duke and Joe B. Frantz, *6,000 Miles of Fence* (1961); Lewis Nordyke, *Cattle Empire* (1949).

Eldon S. Branda

*Yellow Lake.

*Yellow Pine, Texas.

**Yellow Stone.*

Yelvington, Leonard Ramsey. Leonard Ramsey Yelvington, son of Jesse Leonard and Sarah Gillespie (Ramsey) Yelvington, was born on February 5, 1913, in West Point, Fayette County, Texas. He attended public schools in Smithville until the mid-1920's, when the family moved to San Antonio.

After graduating from Brackenridge High School in San Antonio, Ramsey Yelvington entered Howard Payne College. He transferred to Baylor University the following fall and studied dramatics with Paul Baker. Yelvington left Baylor before graduating (lacking only three credits) and worked in various radio stations around the state. During World War II he served for three years in the U.S. Army Corps of Engineers at Fort Lewis, Washington, and wrote for the base newspaper.

After the war Yelvington worked briefly with a radio station in San Antonio, then moved to Wimberley to write and raise livestock. He began writing stories and published a book of short stories with a hill country setting, *The Roaring Kleinschmids* (1950). Encouraged by Paul Baker, he turned to writing plays. Yelvington's *Home to Galveston* (his first play), *Cocklebur*, and *The Long Gallery* were produced by Baker at Baylor University in the early 1950's. *The Long Gallery* was also produced Off Broadway in 1958. *Women and Oxen*, *A Cloud of Witnesses* (published in 1959), and *Shadow of an Eagle* (produced at Dallas Theater Center) compose Yelvington's *A Texian Trilogy* He received Danforth and Rockefeller grants for his writing.

In 1961 he received an M.A. degree from Baylor and joined Southwest Texas State University as playwright-in-residence and professor of speech and drama. Yelvington wrote numerous plays which James Barton directed in the SWTSU, Glade (outdoor theater at San Marcos Academy), and Mission San José theaters.

He was married to Louise Durham on October 16, 1942; they had two daughters. Yelvington's eighteenth full-length play, *The Folklorist*, directed by his daughter, Harriet Yelvington Smith, opened in the SWTSU Theatre July 23, 1973. Yelvington died two days later, July 25, in San Marcos.

Ramsey Yelvington, a devout Baptist, was a member of the Texas Folklore Society, the Texas State Historical Association, the Texas Institute of Letters, and the Philosophical Society of Texas.qqv He helped found and served as president of the Texas Playwright's Company.

BIBLIOGRAPHY: Paul Baker, "Introduction," (in) Ramsey Yelvington, *A Cloud of Witnesses* (1959); Biographical File, Barker Texas History Center, University of Texas at Austin.

Elton Abernathy

Yemé Indians. The Yemé Indians, a Coahuiltecan band of northeastern Mexico, were one of several groups commonly referred to as Carrizo, who ranged both sides of the Rio Grande. In the early nineteenth century the Yemé lived in the vicinity of Laredo. They may be the same as the Ymic who in 1708 were on the Rio Grande near the mission at San Juan Bautista qv (near present Eagle Pass). It is remotely possible that the Yemé and Ymic were descendants of either the Imimule or the Imipecte, who lived in northeastern Nuevo León during the seventeenth century.

BIBLIOGRAPHY: F. W. Hodge (ed.), *Handbook of American Indians*, II (1910); W. Jiménez Moreno, "Tribus e idiomas del Norte de México," *El Norte de México y el Sur de Estados Unidos* (1944); J. R. Swanton, *Linguistic Material from the Tribes of Southern Texas and Northeastern Mexico* (1940).

T. N. Campbell

*Yero, Texas.

*Yescas, Texas.

*Yesner, Texas.

*Ygnacio Creek.

*Yguace Indians.

Ylame Indians. The Ylame Indians were one of twenty Indian groups that joined Juan Domínguez de Mendoza qv on his journey from El Paso to the vicinity of present San Angelo in 1683–1684. Since Mendoza did not indicate at what point the Ylame joined his party, it is not possible to determine their range or affiliations. However, the Indians between the Pecos River and the San Angelo area were being hard pressed by Apache at this time, and it seems likely that the Ylame ranged somewhere between these two localities.

BIBLIOGRAPHY: H. E. Bolton (ed.), *Spanish Exploration in the Southwest, 1542–1706* (1916).

T. N. Campbell

*Yman Indians.

*Ymic Indians.** The Ymic Indians, apparently a Coahuiltecan band, lived on the Rio Grande near the mission at San Juan Bautista qv (near present Eagle Pass). It seems likely that these Indians were the same as the Yemé who in the early nineteenth century lived in the vicinity of Laredo. If so, the Ymic are among the various Coahuiltecan bands of southern Texas and northeastern Mexico who came to be known as Carrizo. It is remotely possible that the Ymic and Yemé were descendants of either the Imimule or the Imipecte, who lived in northeastern Nuevo León during the seventeenth century.

BIBLIOGRAPHY: F. W. Hodge (ed.), *Handbook of American Indians*, II (1910); W. Jiménez Moreno, "Tribus e idiomas del Norte de México," *El Norte de México y el Sur de Estados Unidos* (1944); J. R. Swanton, *Linguistic Material from the Tribes of Southern Texas and Northeastern Mexico* (1940).

T. N. Campbell

Ynsfrán, Pablo Max. Pablo Max Ynsfrán was born in Asunción, Paraguay, on July 30, 1894, the son of Facundo D. and Francisca (Jiménez) Ynsfrán. After graduation in 1911 from the Colegio Nacional de Asunción, he entered the Escuela de Notariado of the law school of the Universidad Nacional of Paraguay; he received the legal degree of Escribano Notario in 1918. Between 1918 and 1921 he served in the Paraguayan Ministry of Education.

During the years from 1920 to 1928, Ynsfrán was professor of philosophy and Roman history in the Colegio Nacional de Asunción, professor of literature in the Escuela Normal, secretary to the Paraguayan delegation at the Fifth Pan American Conference in Santiago, Chile, in 1923, and a member of the Chamber of Deputies (national congress) of Paraguay (1924–1928). From 1929 to 1933 he was chargé d'affaires of the Paraguayan legation in Washington, D.C., and while there he attended the School of Foreign Service of Georgetown University. In 1933 he returned to Paraguay to become president of the State Bank (Oficina de Cambios), where he continued until 1936. He was a member of the boundary commission of Paraguay from 1933 to 1936, and of the governing board of the Agricultural Bank of Paraguay in 1934–1935; during this same period he was a member of the board of primary education of the Paraguayan government. From 1938 to 1940 he was counselor of the Paraguayan legation in Washington, D.C., and chargé d'affaires. He returned to Paraguay in 1940 and was minister of economy, public works, and colonization, and at that same time he was one of the editors of the United Press Association.

In 1942 Ynsfrán came to the University of Texas as a visiting lecturer in the Department of Romance Languages. He remained with the University of Texas in Austin until his retirement in 1963; he also taught government and economics courses. He was a long-time member of the executive committee of the Institute of Latin American Studies from the time of its organization at the university in 1942.

Ynsfrán translated several works into Spanish and wrote many articles which appeared in both North and South American scholarly journals. He was the author of *Sobre latinismo* (1927) and *La expedición norteamericana contra el Paraguay, 1858–1859*, I (1954), II (1958); he edited and annotated *The Epic of the Chaco: Marshal Estigarribia's Memoirs of the Chaco War, 1932–1935* (1950); and he compiled indexes to two important manuscript collections: *Catálogo del archivo de don Lucas Alamán que se conserva en la Universidad de Texas, Austin* (1954) and *Catálogo de los manuscritos del archivo de don Valentín Gómez Farías obrantes en la Universidad de Texas, Colección Latinoamericana* (1968).

Pablo Ynsfrán was married to Carmen Gatti in Asunción, Paraguay, on December 22, 1924; they were the parents of one son. Ynsfrán died in Temple, Texas, on May 7, 1972, and was buried in the Italian cemetery in Asunción, Paraguay.

*Yoakum, Benjamin Franklin.

*Yoakum, Charles H.

*Yoakum, Franklin L.

*Yoakum, Henderson King.

*Yoakum, Texas. Yoakum, on the Lavaca-DeWitt county line, is a trading center for products from both counties. The city's approximately 170 businesses in the early 1970's included several dealing in leather goods and meat packing, food processing, metal works, a cannery, a newspaper, a radio station, and two banks. A hospital, a nursing home, a library, a municipal park, and a municipal airport served the community. Yoakum is a railway division point and the site of a highway department office. Since 1960 the city has sponsored an annual Wildflower Trail in springtime, featuring guided tours and wildflower art exhibits. The population of Yoakum was 5,761 in 1960 and 5,755 in 1970, according to the United States census.

*Yoakum County. Yoakum County, on the New Mexico border, continued as one of the leading oil-producing counties in Texas. Between 1936 and January 1, 1973, 688,524,896 barrels of oil had been produced. Minerals, including petroleum, natural gas liquids, natural gas, and salt accounted for an average annual income of $171 million. The county's agricultural income, from sorghums, cotton, alfalfa, watermelons, castor beans, beef cattle, and hogs, averaged $10.5 million annually in the early 1970's. Over 86,000 acres of land were irrigated.

Yoakum County supported two libraries, a hospital, a rodeo park, and two airports. Between 1950 and 1960 the county's population almost doubled, but by 1970 the population had declined somewhat. According to the United States census the population was 4,339 in 1950, 8,032 in 1960, and 7,344 in 1970.

*Yojuane Indians. The Yojuane (Diujuan, Iacovane, Iojuan, Joyvan, Yacavan, Yocuana, Yujuane) Indians, a Tonkawan people, are known mainly from the eighteenth century, when they ranged over a large area in east-central Texas that extended from the Colorado River east of Austin northward to the Red River. However, in the second half of the eighteenth century the Yojuane were largely confined to the southern portion of this range. They were at San Francisco Xavier de Horcasitas Mission qv near present Rockdale between 1748 and 1756. In the nineteenth century the Yojuane were rarely mentioned, and it is clear that they were included among the bands called Tonkawa during that period. These Tonkawa were assembled on the Brazos Indian Reservation qv of present Young County in the 1850's and in 1859 were moved to Indian Territory, now Oklahoma. After the Civil War some of the Tonkawa returned to northern Texas, where they lived until 1884. In that year they were moved back to Indian Territory. Today the Tonkawa are extinct as an ethnic group.

BIBLIOGRAPHY: H. E. Bolton, *Athanase de Mézières and the Louisiana-Texas Frontier, 1768–1780* (1914), and *Texas in the Middle Eighteenth Century* (1915); F. W. Hodge (ed.), *Handbook of American Indians*, I (1907), II (1910); A. F. Sjoberg, "The Culture of the Tonkawa, A Texas Indian Tribe," *Texas Journal of Science*, V (1953); D. H. Winfrey and J. M. Day (eds.), *The Indian Papers of Texas and the Southwest, 1825–1916*, I–V (1966).

T. N. Campbell

*Yokum Gang.

*Yo-Lo-Digo Creek.

*Yorica Indians. The Yorica (Corica, Goxica) were Coahuiltecan-speaking Indians who in the last half of the seventeenth century lived in northeastern Coahuila, but sometimes crossed the Rio Grande to hunt in the southwestern part of the Edwards Plateau. The Bosque-Larios Expedition qv of 1675 encountered fifty-four Yorica and Hape adults a few miles north of the Rio Grande near present Eagle Pass. They were loaded with dried bison meat that was being taken back to their settlements south of the river. Baptismal records indicate that some of the Yorica entered the San Antonio de Valero Mission qv of San Antonio in the eighteenth century.

BIBLIOGRAPHY: V. Alessio Robles, *Coahuila y Texas en la Epoca Colonial* (1938); H. E. Bolton (ed.), *Spanish Exploration in the Southwest, 1542–1706* (1916); F. W. Hodge (ed.), *Handbook of American Indians*, II (1910).

T. N. Campbell

*York, John.

*York Creek.

*York Creek Ridge, Texas.

*Yorks Creek.

*Yorktown, Texas. Yorktown, the commercial center of southwestern DeWitt County, undertook several community improvement projects in the 1960's, including the building of low rent housing and a program for town beautification. There were approximately seventy-five businesses in the early 1970's, including feed companies, a grain elevator, and a cotton gin. The town, with a mayor-council government, supported a hospital, a library, a nursing home, public and parochial schools, two newspapers, and two banks. The population of Yorktown was 2,527 in 1960 and 2,411 in 1970, according to the United States census.

*Yougeen, Texas.

*Young, Charles G.

*Young, Hugh Franklin.

*Young, James.

Young, Mary Sophie. Mary Sophie Young was born in Glendale, Ohio, on September 20, 1872, the daughter of Charles Huntington and Emma

Adams (Sainer) Young. She attended Ohio public schools, Harcourt Place Seminary, and Wellesley College, from which she received a B.A. degree in 1895. From that time until 1906 she taught in schools in Missouri, Illinois, Kansas, and Wisconsin, at the same time taking correspondence courses from the University of Chicago. She attended the University of Chicago from 1906 to 1910, when she received a Ph.D. degree from that institution.

In the fall of 1910 Mary Young came to the University of Texas as a tutor in botany; she was promoted to the rank of instructor the following year. In 1912 she was assigned to teach a course in taxonomy and put in charge of the university's herbarium. She found Austin a most strategic area for collecting specimens, being situated on a line where the eastern and western flora meet. Despite numerous difficulties encountered in her frequent field trips, she greatly enriched the holdings of the herbarium through the collection of new Texas specimens and the exchange of duplicates with other states. In 1917 Mary Young's *A Key to the Families and Genera of the Wild Plants of Austin, Texas* was published as *University of Texas Bulletin No. 1754*; this work and another, *The Seed Plants, Ferns and Fern Allies of the Austin Region*, published in 1920 as *University of Texas Bulletin No. 2065*, reflected her pioneer work in the field of plant classification in the Austin area.

Mary S. Young also collected specimens in other areas in central Texas, but the subject which she became most interested in was the flora of West Texas. With the exception of the summer of 1917 (which she spent in the Panhandle area), she spent the summers of 1914 through 1918 in the Trans-Pecos area of Texas. Encountering difficulties as a woman traveling over large areas of the wildest and most mountainous Texas country, she brought back hundreds of plants not previously represented in the university's herbarium. She became ill early in 1919 and died of cancer on March 5, 1919. Mary Sophie Young was buried in Oakwood Cemetery in Austin. Her journal for the summer, 1914, expedition to the Trans-Pecos area was published posthumously in two issues of the *Southwestern Historical Quarterly* qv (January, April, 1962).

BIBLIOGRAPHY: B. C. Tharp, "Recollections of Dr. M. S. Young," *The Alcalde*, VIII (January, 1921); B. C. Tharp and Chester V. Kielman (eds.), "Mary S. Young's Journal of Botanical Explorations in Trans-Pecos Texas, August–September, 1914," *Southwestern Historical Quarterly*, LXV (1961–1962).

*Young, Maud Jeannie (Fuller).

Young, Overton C. Overton C. Young was born in Georgia about 1825. He moved to Texas in the 1840's and by 1860 was a wealthy planter in Brazoria County. He was married and had five children. On December 1, 1861, he was commissioned colonel of the 12th Texas Infantry, which, because of considerable confusion, was generally known as the 8th Texas Infantry. Young's regiment in the summer of 1862 marched to Arkansas, where it joined McCulloch's—later Walker's—Texas in-

fantry division (*see* Walker's Texas Division). From September through December, Young commanded one brigade, and thereafter he led his regiment in several campaigns in Arkansas and Louisiana throughout the remainder of the war. He was wounded during the battle of Jenkins Ferry in the Red River Campaign qv in the spring of 1864.

BIBLIOGRAPHY: Service Records of Overton Young (Civil War Biographical File, Archives, University of Texas at Austin Library, originals in National Archives, Washington, D.C.); U. S. Census, 1860, Brazoria County, Texas (microfilm, University of Texas at Austin Library); Joseph P. Blessington, *The Campaigns of Walker's Texas Division* (1875).

Young, Robert Ralph. Robert Ralph Young, son of David John and Mary Arabella (Moody) Young, was born at Canadian, Texas, on February 14, 1897. His mother was the daughter of Robert Moody,qv a prominent rancher and banker. Young attended Culver Military Academy (1912–1914) and the University of Virginia (1914–1916), but he left Virginia without graduating, married, and went to work in 1916 as a powder-cutter in the E. I. Dupont de Nemours powder plant at Carney's Point, New Jersey. By 1920 he had left Dupont and, using an inheritance from his grandfather, he bought a food-dehydrating company. This business failed, and in 1922 Young joined General Motors, where he became assistant treasurer in 1928. He left General Motors and became an investment consultant in 1929; in 1931 he formed a brokerage partnership with Frank Kolbe and bought a seat on the New York Stock Exchange in order to speculate in stocks. By 1942 he owned a controlling interest in the Alleghany Corporation, a railroad holding company. As chairman of the board of the Chesapeake and Ohio Railroad, he launched a well-publicized campaign for the modernization of railroad passenger service and became one of the first railroaders in the country to introduce lightweight, high-speed diesel passenger trains on his lines. He regarded himself as a crusader against the management of railroads by banking interests. In 1954, after a long proxy struggle, and with the aid of Clinton Williams Murchison and Sid Williams Richardson,qqv he gained control of the New York Central Railroad and became chairman of the board of that corporation.

Young was an amateur poet and bibliophile. In 1953 he donated a number of documents dealing with Texas history, including a valuable collection of microfilms of documents in the Archivo General de las Indias in Seville, to the University of Texas at Austin. He was posthumously awarded the Distinguished Service Medal of the Texas Heritage Foundation for his efforts to compile a library of Texas historical documents.

Young was married to Anita Ten Eyck O'Keefe on April 27, 1916. They had one daughter, who died in 1941. He committed suicide at his Palm Beach, Florida, home on January 25, 1958, and was buried in Saint Mary's Cemetery in Newport, Rhode Island. The New York Central's electronic freight-yard in Elkhart, Indiana, was named in his honor.

BIBLIOGRAPHY: Joseph Borkin, *Robert R. Young, the Populist of Wall Street* (1969); *Who's Who In America* (1952); New York *Times*, January 26, 1958; Biographical File, Barker Texas History Center, University of Texas at Austin.

Young, Stark. Stark Young was born in Como, Mississippi, on October 11, 1881, the son of Alfred Alexander and Mary (Stark) Young. He received a B.A. degree from the University of Mississippi in 1901 and an M.A. degree from Columbia University in 1902. He was an instructor in English at the University of Mississippi from 1904 to 1907 before becoming associated with the University of Texas as an instructor in English literature (1907–1910) and professor of general literature (1910–1915). In 1909 he organized and was the first director of the Curtain Club, the student dramatic organization at the University of Texas. Before leaving Austin, Young founded and edited (in 1915) the *Texas Review* (which in 1924 was renamed the *Southwest Review* qv and was transferred to Southern Methodist University).

From 1915 to 1921 Young was professor of English at Amherst College; he then moved to New York City, and for three years, 1921 to 1924, he was on the editorial staff of the *New Republic*. He was also associate editor of *Theatre Arts Monthly* from 1921 to 1940 and served as dramatic critic of the New York *Times* in 1924–1925. From 1925 to 1947 he was again on the editorial staff of the *New Republic*. For extended periods during his writing career, Young resided in Florence, Italy; he was a lecturer in that country for the Westinghouse Foundation in 1931, and he was given the honorary title of Commander of the Order of the Crown of Italy.

Young's writings comprise a great body of work, including novels, plays, books on the theater, translations of Chekhov's works, critical and aesthetic essays, short stories, and poetry. Some of his works include a volume of verse, *The Blind Man at the Window* (1906); *Three Plays* (1919); a collection of essays on the theater, *The Flower in Drama* (1923); a collection of short stories, *The Street of the Islands* (1930); and many articles in periodicals. One of his novels, *So Red The Rose* (1934), was made into a film. He never married. Young died on January 6, 1963, at Fairfield, Connecticut, and was buried at Como, Mississippi.

BIBLIOGRAPHY: *Who's Who In America* (1950).

Richard T. Fleming

*Young, William Cocke.

*Young, William Hugh. William Hugh Young died on November 28, 1901, and was buried in the Confederate Cemetery in San Antonio.

Palmer Bradley

*Young, Texas.

*Young County. Young County in the early 1970's had an economy based on oil, agribusinesses, and tourism. Minerals, including petroleum, natural gas, natural gas liquids, sand, and gravel brought in an average annual income of $13 million. The average annual farm income was $6.5 million, 80 percent of which came from the production of beef cattle, hogs, sheep, and goats; the chief crops were wheat, sorghums, and cotton.

Possum Kingdom Lake and Lake Graham qqv attract visitors for fishing, boating, and water sports, and restored Fort Belknap qv is a tourist attraction. In the early 1970's approximately 300,000 acres in the county were leased for hunting. The population of Young County was 17,254 in 1960 and 15,400 in 1970, according to the United States census.

*Youngsboro, Texas.

*Youngsport, Texas. Youngsport, in Bell County, was a community during the Reconstruction qv period, having a single store there in the late 1860's. A post office was established there by 1872 (not 1884, as stated in Volume II). In 1970 the estimated population of Youngsport was thirty.

BIBLIOGRAPHY: George W. Tyler, *History of Bell County* (1966); *Texas Almanac* (1872, 1972).

*Yount, Miles Frank.

Youth Council, Texas. The Texas Youth Council was created in 1949 as the Texas State Youth Development Council. It was reorganized in 1957 as the Texas Youth Council, and its board was reduced from nine to three members, all appointed by the governor for six-year terms. It had responsibility for the state's juvenile correctional institutions, including Gatesville State School for Boys, Mountain View School for Boys, Gainesville State School for Girls, Crockett State School for Girls, qqv Brownwood Statewide Reception Center for Delinquent Girls, and Brownwood State Home and School for Girls. The council also had supervision over the care of dependent and neglected children at Waco State Home, Corsicana State Home, and West Texas Children's Home. qqv

BIBLIOGRAPHY: University of Texas at Austin, *Guide To Texas State Agencies* (1964, 1967, 1972).

Dick Smith

Youth Opportunity Program, Governor's. *See* Community Affairs, Department of.

*Yowani Indians.

*Yowell, Texas.

Yoyehi Indians. In 1683–1684 Juan Domínguez de Mendoza qv led an exploratory expedition from El Paso as far eastward as the junction of the Concho and Colorado rivers east of present San Angelo. In his itinerary he listed the names of thirty-seven Indian groups, including the Yoyehi (Yoyci), from which he expected to receive delegations on the Colorado River. Nothing further is known about the Yoyehi, who seem to have been one of many Indian groups of north-central Texas that were swept away by the southward thrust of the Lipan-Apache and Comanche Indians in the eighteenth century.

BIBLIOGRAPHY: H. E. Bolton (ed.), *Spanish Exploration in the Southwest, 1542–1706* (1916); C. W. Hackett (ed.), *Pichardo's Treatise on the Limits of Louisiana and Texas*, II (1934).

T. N. Campbell

*Yprande Indians.

*Ysbupue Indians. The Ysbupue Indians are known from a single Spanish document (1708) which lists the Indian groups that lived north of present Eagle Pass. J. R. Swanton has identified them as Coahuiltecan-speakers.

BIBLIOGRAPHY: F. W. Hodge (ed.), *Handbook of American Indians*, II (1910); J. R. Swanton, *Linguistic Material from the Tribes of Southern Texas and Northeastern Mexico* (1940).

T. N. Campbell

*Yscani Indians.

*Ysleta, Texas. *See also* Tigua Indians.

*Ysopete.

Yturria, Francisco. Francisco Yturria, son of Manuel and Paula Navarro (Ortuzu) Yturria, was born in Santander, Tamaulipas, Mexico, in 1832. He was married to Felicitas Treviño, daughter of Ignacio Treviño, an original Spanish grantee of five leagues and two labors in Cameron County; they had two children, a son and a daughter.

Yturria began his career in business by working as a clerk for Charles Stillman,qv one of the founders of Brownsville, and by purchasing lands adjoining those of his wife's inheritance. At the time of his death in 1912, Yturria owned 130,000 acres in Cameron, Hidalgo, Willacy, Kenedy, and Starr counties. He established and operated the Francisco Yturria Bank of Brownsville under a private charter; he also established a bank in Matamoros. Prior to the coming of the railroad in 1904, trading was done in Mexican money; however, for the payment of taxes this money was exchanged at the Yturria bank for United States coin. Silver and gold were kept in sacks, and these were stored in a vault which in the 1960's was on display in the lobby of the National Bank of Commerce of Brownsville. The original bank building was still used as an office for the Yturria interests.

The vast Punta del Monte Rancho was the headquarters of a 72,000-acre tract of land in Willacy and Kenedy counties which produced 2,000 steers per year. In later years the headquarters was a stop on the Alice-Brownsville stagecoach line. Yturria often combined his cattle drives with Richard King,

Mifflin Kenedy, and Charles Stillman,qqv and the herds required approximately three hundred cowboys for the trip to Dodge City. On these occasions Yturria would travel by boat to New Orleans and by train to Kansas, where he sold the cattle; he returned to Texas by way of New York, where he made his deposits in the Hanover National Bank.

During the Civil War he had a monopoly on the sale of cotton through Mexico; he was one of the wealthiest and one of the most influential men of his time in southwest Texas. Yturria died on June 12, 1912, in Brownsville.

BIBLIOGRAPHY: J. L. Allhands, *Gringo Builders* (1931); W. H. Chatfield, *The Twin Cities of the Border and the Country of the Lower Rio Grande* (1893).

Verna J. McKenna

*Yucatan Expedition. *See* Texas Navy.

*Yucca, Texas.

Yué Indians. The Yué Indians were one of several groups commonly referred to as Carrizo, who ranged over parts of northeastern Mexico and extreme southern Texas in the eighteenth century. It is generally believed that all Carrizo bands spoke Coahuiltecan dialects. In the early nineteenth century a group of Yué still lived near Camargo in Tamaulipas.

BIBLIOGRAPHY: F. W. Hodge (ed.), *Handbook of American Indians*, II (1910); J. R. Swanton, *Linguistic Material from the Tribes of Southern Texas and Northeastern Mexico* (1940).

T. N. Campbell

*Yuta Indians.

Yxandi Indians. The Yxandi (Sandi, Ysandi) Indians are known only from the 1730's, when they were closely associated with the Lipan and other Apache groups in west-central Texas, particularly along the San Saba River. They were probably one of several bands that later came to be spoken of collectively as Lipan-Apache.

BIBLIOGRAPHY: H. E. Bolton, "The Jumano Indians in Texas, 1650–1771," *Quarterly of the Texas State Historical Association*, XV (1911–1912); F. C. Chabot (ed.), *Excerpts from the Memorias for the History of Texas, by Father Morfi* (1932); W. E. Dunn, "Apache Relations in Texas, 1718–1750," *Quarterly of the Texas State Historical Association*, XIV (1910–1911).

T. N. Campbell

Z

*Zabcikville, Texas.

*Zacatecan Missionaries in Texas. *See* Nuestra Señora de Guadalupe de Zacatecas, College of.

*Zacatosa Creek.

*Zack, Texas.

Zacpo Indians. Zacpo is the name of an otherwise unidentified group of Indians listed in baptismal records of the San Antonio de Valero Mission qv in San Antonio.

BIBLIOGRAPHY: H. E. Bolton, *Texas in the Middle Eighteenth Century* (1915).

T. N. Campbell

Zaharias, Mildred Ella (Babe) Didrikson. Mildred Ella Didrikson Zaharias, named the greatest woman athlete of the first half of the twentieth century by vote of the Associated Press, was born on June 26, 1914, in Port Arthur, Texas, the sixth of seven children of Ole and Hannah Marie (Olson) Didrikson. At the age of three and a half she moved with her family to Beaumont, where she attended public schools. In 1930 she moved to Dallas to play basketball for the Employers Casualty Company's national championship basketball team; employed in that company's office, she also began her track and field career while there.

As a young girl Mildred Didrikson was given the nickname "Babe" because of her unusual athletic ability at a time when the baseball player Babe Ruth was the best known athlete in America.

In 1932 Babe singlehandedly won the team championship at the national Amateur Athletic Union (AAU) women's track and field meet, defeating the whole team of Illinois girls, thirty points to twenty-two points. In that same year she won two gold medals at the Olympic games, placing first in the women's eighty-meter hurdles and the javelin throw. In December, 1932, she became a professional and went into show business for a short time, singing and playing a harmonica. She moved to California in 1933 and then returned to Texas. In 1934 she toured with professional women's basketball and baseball teams, and in 1935 she began her golf career.

On December 23, 1938, she was married to Theodore Vetoyanis, a wrestler from Pueblo, Colorado, who had changed his name to George Zaharias. From 1940 to 1950 Babe Zaharias won every major golf title, including the World Open and the National Open. In April, 1953, she was operated on for cancer, and few people believed she would ever play golf again; however, she came back to win more professional golf tournaments, including the National Open. During her career she had played for many cancer fund benefits, and she continued that work throughout her three-year illness, setting up a national fund for cancer research. In 1953 she was elected to the Texas Sports Hall of Fame,qv and in 1955 she was elected to the Helms Athletic Foundation Hall of Fame. She maintained a home in Tampa, Florida, before she died of cancer at John Sealy Hospital in Galveston on September 27, 1956; she was buried in Beaumont. In 1968 an official Texas historical marker was placed at her graveside.

BIBLIOGRAPHY: Babe Didrikson Zaharias and Harry Paxton, *This Life I've Led* (1955); *Current Biography* (1956); Austin *Statesman*, September 27, 1956.

Mary Beth Fleischer

*Zambrano, Juan Manuel.

Zanzenburg, Texas. Zanzenburg (sometimes found as Zanzenberg) was the original name for Center Point in Kerr County. Archival records of the United States Post Office in Washington, D.C., show that the post office at Zanzenburg (with that spelling) was established on November 25, 1859, and that the post office retained that spelling until the name of the town was changed to Centrepoint on September 25, 1872. It is not known when the change in spelling to Center Point occurred, but post office records show that the town was listed as Center Point by 1896.

Zanzenburg had been in existence for several years before the first post office was established. In the 1856 election to determine the seat of Kerr County, the residents of Zanzenburg cast the deciding votes for the Anglo American colony of Brownsborough (later Kerrsville, now Kerrville) over the German settlement of Comfort. The first sessions of the commissioners court were held on the George M. Ridley farm across the Guadalupe River from Zanzenburg.

When the post office was moved to the south side of the Guadalupe River in 1872, the name was changed to Centrepoint (later Center Point) because the location was halfway between Kerrville and Comfort and was also about halfway between Fredericksburg and Bandera.

BIBLIOGRAPHY: Bob Bennett, *Kerr County, Texas, 1856–1956* (1956); Guido E. Ransleben, *A Hundred Years of Comfort in Texas* (1954); Matilda Marie Real, A History of Kerr County, Texas (M.A. thesis, University of Texas at Austin, 1942); United States Post Office Records (Civil Archives Division of the National Archives, General Services Administration, Washington, D.C.).

*Zapalac, Texas.

*Zapata, Antonio.

*Zapata, Texas. Zapata, seat of Zapata County, was built in 1952–1953 to replace the historic town of Zapata, which was inundated by International Falcon Reservoir qv in 1953. The city, with approximately fifty businesses in the early 1970's, served as a market and tourist center for the county. The population was 2,031 in 1960 and 2,102 in 1970, according to the United States census.

*Zapata County. Zapata County is an area of ranching, oil production, and irrigated farming. From 1919 to January 1, 1973, 35,971,921 barrels of oil had been produced. Natural gas, petroleum, and stone accounted for the county's $4 million average annual mineral income in the early 1970's. Eighty percent of the $4.2 million average annual farm income was from the raising of beef cattle; cotton, melons, onions, and carrots were the major agricultural crops. Tourism became an important industry to the county after International Falcon Reservoir qv was completed in the early 1950's. Three towns in the county, Zapata, Falcon, and Lopeno, had to be relocated on higher ground when the Falcon Reservoir inundated that area. Zapata County had a population of 4,393 in 1960 and 4,352 in 1970, according to the United States census.

*Zapp, Texas.

*Zaragosa, Texas.

Zaragoza, Ignacio Seguín. Ignacio Seguín Zaragoza, Mexican military hero, was born on March 24, 1829, at Presidio La Bahía (*see* La Bahía) in the state of Coahuila and Texas (near present Goliad, Texas). He was the second son of Miguel G. Zaragoza of Veracruz, Mexico, and María de Jesús Seguín of Bexar (San Antonio), who was a kinsman of Erasmo Seguín.qv With Mexico's defeat in the Texas Revolution, Miguel Zaragoza, an infantryman, moved his family from Goliad to Matamoros, where Ignacio Zaragoza entered the school of San Juan. When his father was transferred to Monterrey in 1844, Ignacio entered a seminary there. In 1846 he left the seminary and entered the mercantile business for a short time. He joined the state militia and in 1852 became a captain. He declared for the liberal forces and the Plan de Ayutla,

Mexico's first serious effort to create a democratic and constitutional government.

Zaragoza took part in the battles against the armies of Santa Anna qv in the 1850's. On January 21, 1857, while on an important army assignment in San Luis Potosí, Zaragoza was unable to attend his own marriage to Rafaela Padilla in Monterrey, so his brother, Miguel, served as his proxy. Ignacio Zaragoza and his wife had four children; three sons died in infancy, and a daughter, Rafaela, died in the 1920's.

During the years of the War of the Reform, 1857 to 1860 (the struggle between conservative powers and liberal forces led by Benito Juárez), Zaragoza took part in a number of military engagements. In December, 1860, Juárez sent Zaragoza to inspect the defenses of Veracruz, Mexico's main port of entry on the Gulf of Mexico. In early 1861 he was made minister of war and navy in Juárez's parliamentary ministry. In mid-July, 1861, Juárez declared a two-year moratorium on Mexico's European debts, and in December a fleet of Spanish ships forced the surrender of Veracruz; soon thereafter the forces of France and England joined the Spanish. Juárez put Zaragoza in command of the Army of the East, and in February, 1862, a month after his wife's death in Mexico City, Zaragoza began work on the defenses of Puebla. Early in 1862 the English and Spanish withdrew; French forces attacked Puebla in a battle which lasted the entire day of May 5, 1862, the now famed "Cinco de Mayo." Zaragoza's well-armed, well-trained men forced the withdrawal of the French troops from Puebla to Orizaba. The number of French reported killed ranged from 476 to 1,000, although many of the French troops were already ill from their stay in the coastal lowlands. Mexican losses were reported to be approximately eighty-six. In mid-August Zaragoza went to Mexico City, where he was feted as a hero. When he returned to his troops in Puebla he became ill with typhoid fever, and he died there on September 8, 1862.

A state funeral was held in Mexico City with interment at the Panteón de San Fernando. On September 11, 1862, President Juárez issued a decree changing the name of the city of Puebla de los Angeles to Puebla de Zaragoza and making Cinco de Mayo a national holiday. Zaragoza became one of the great national heroes of Mexico. Songs have been written in his honor, and schools, plazas, and streets have been named either "Zaragoza" or "Cinco de Mayo." Each year on May 5, Zaragoza societies meet throughout Mexico and in a number of Texas towns, including Goliad, where a restoration has been undertaken at Ignacio Zaragoza's birthplace. In May, 1971, the Texas legislature designated land adjacent to Presidio La Bahía at Goliad as General Zaragoza State Historic Site, where in 1973 archeological work was begun. (See Parks, State.)

BIBLIOGRAPHY: Rodolfo Llano Arroyo, Ygnacio Zaragoza (1962); Wilfrid Hardy Callcott, Liberalism in Mexico, 1857–1929 (1965); Ricardo Covarrubias, Anales de la

Vida del C. General de División Don Ignacio Zaragoza (1962); Guillermo Colín Sánchez, Ignacio Zaragoza (1963); San Antonio Express, May 7, 1971.

Zauanito Indians. The Zauanito Indians are known only from a single Spanish missionary report (1691), which identifies them as enemies of the Hasinai Indians of eastern Texas. They appear to have lived west of the Hasinai. The name is similar to Souanetto, the name of another unidentified group listed by Henri Joutel qv (1687) as enemies of the Kadohadacho on the Red River. It seems likely that these names refer to the same people, but this cannot be proved.

BIBLIOGRAPHY: F. W. Hodge (ed.), Handbook of American Indians, II (1910); P. Margry, Découvertes et établissements des Français dans l'ouest et dans le sud de l'Amérique Septentrionale, III (1879); J. R. Swanton, Source Material on the History and Ethnology of the Caddo Indians (1942).

T. N. Campbell

*Zavala. Captain John T. K. Lothrop qv took command of the steamship-of-war *Zavala* on March 4, 1840. The *Zavala*, with the *Austin* and the *San Bernard*,qqv took part in the capture of San Juan Bautista (now Villahermosa), in the state of Tabasco, Mexico, on November 20, 1840.

BIBLIOGRAPHY: Tom Henderson Wells, Commodore Moore and the Texas Navy (1960).

Tom Henderson Wells

*Zavala, Lorenzo de. See De Zavala, Lorenzo.

*Zavala, Texas. (Angelina County.) [This is an incorrect title on page 951 of Volume II. See Zavalla, Texas. Ed.]

*Zavala, Texas. (Jasper County.)

*Zavala County. Zavala County, in the southwestern part of the state called Texas' Winter Garden, produces spinach, sorghums, cotton, onions, corn, and many other vegetables, all on irrigated land. Beef and dairy cattle, goats, sheep, and poultry are raised on large ranches and small farms. The county's $15.7 million average annual farm income in the early 1970's was evenly divided between crops and livestock. With many agribusinesses, including packing plants for vegetables, Zavala was the leading county in the Winter Garden truck-farming area.

Between 1937, when petroleum production began in the county, and January 1, 1969, 2,522,986 barrels of oil had been produced; however, in 1972 alone the county produced 1,820,833 barrels, so that by January 1, 1973, total production of oil since the industry began in the county was 6,088,918 barrels. The total mineral value, which also included some natural gas, was approximately $3.5 million annually in the early 1970's.

Tourist attractions include hunting, fishing, and the Popeye statue (a symbol for spinach) in Crystal City. The population of Zavala County was 12,696 in 1960 and 11,370 in 1970, according to the United States census.

*Zavalla, Texas. [This title was incorrectly listed in Volume II as Zavala, Texas.] Zavalla, located in Angelina County, reported two schools there in 1967. The population estimate for the town was five hundred and fifty in 1960 and nine hundred in 1970, although those figures are possibly higher than an actual count would have shown.

*Zeirath, Texas.

*Zephyr, Texas.

*Zerván, Federico.

*Zigzag, Texas.

*Ziler, Texas.

Zink, Nicolaus. Nicolaus Zink, whose name was given to the Zinkenburg qv (or Zink's fort), the first German structure in New Braunfels, was born in Bamberg, Bavaria, Germany, on February 4, 1812. A civil engineer (and former Bavarian army officer), he came with his wife Louise (von Kheusser) Zink to Texas in 1844 along with other German settlers under the auspices of the Adelsverein qv and the leadership of Prince Carl of Solms-Braunfels.qv

During the three months from December, 1844, to March, 1845, Zink supervised the move of approximately half of the German immigrants bound for New Braunfels from Indianola, by way of Victoria, McCoy's Creek, and Seguin. On March 21, 1845, the immigrants' wagons and pushcarts under Zink's command arrived at the site that was to become New Braunfels on the east bank of Comal Creek. Here on the rise of land where Saints Peter and Paul Catholic Church was later built, Zink supervised the erection of a palisade to enclose the first tent settlement. The site was called Zinkenburg, and the Germans lived there until houses could be built. Zink made the original survey for the townsite of New Braunfels, as well as adjoining farmland, and Zink Street was named for him. He was given twenty-five acres in New Braunfels and approximately one hundred acres of farmland outside the town, which he divided into tracts for sale. In 1846 he was hauling passengers and merchandise from Houston to New Braunfels. In the fall of 1847 he was divorced from his wife for "unhappy differences."

In 1847 Zink left New Braunfels with the intention of going to Fredericksburg, but instead settled on land on Sister Creek, where he built a large log house with an upper story, the first building in what was to be Sisterdale, the most famed of the "Latin settlements" of Texas.qv Zink gained the reputation of being a successful farmer, of holding his own against the Comanches, and of getting a good price for the wheat he sold to the quartermasters of the neighboring army encampments.

In 1850 he and his second wife, Elisabeth, sold their house and several acres of land to Edward Degener qv and began operation of a grist mill on Baron Creek south of Fredericksburg. In 1853 Zink was living in the newly established town of Comfort. In the 1870 Kendall County census Zink was listed as a fifty-nine-year-old shinglemaker with an English wife, Agnes, who was thirty-four years of age. Zink then settled in Spanish Pass, between

Comfort and Boerne. He died on November 3, 1887, and was buried on a knoll near his home at Welfare.

BIBLIOGRAPHY: Guido E. Ransleben, *A Hundred Years of Comfort in Texas* (1954); Moritz Tiling, *History of the German Element in Texas from 1820–1850* . . . (1913); Adolf Paul Weber, *Deutsche Pioniere*, II (1894); Rudolph L. Biesele, "Early Times in New Braunfels and Comal County," *Southwestern Historical Quarterly*, L (1946–1947); San Antonio *Express*, March 4, 1934; Oscar Haas Archives, New Braunfels.

Crystal Sasse Ragsdale

Zinkenburg. Zinkenburg was the name given the first fortress on the site which became New Braunfels in Comal County. The fort was named in honor of Nicolaus Zink,qv a German civil engineer who came to Texas in 1844 with other German immigrants under the sponsorship of the Adelsverein qv and under the leadership of Prince Carl of Solms-Braunfels.qv The settlers arrived at the site on March 21, 1845. Zinkenburg was located on a steep rise on the east bank of Comal Creek; Nicolaus Zink supervised construction of the fort, which consisted of a palisade enclosing a tent city. The fort had two bastions with cannon to protect the settlers until the Sophienburg (*see* Sophienburg Museum) could be completed. It was at the Zinkenburg that Prince Carl reputedly received Lipan-Apache chief Castro qv and offered him wine and German cake. Daily target practice was held at the fort to avert the danger of an Indian attack. Fritz Goldbeck, a German poet who lived at the Zinkenburg as a fourteen-year-old boy, described in poetry the wagons and white tents of the settlers within the stockade. In 1850 a Catholic church was built on the site, at the corner of present Zink Street and Castell Avenue. The original log church has been enclosed within the walls of the present Saints Peter and Paul Catholic Church.

BIBLIOGRAPHY: Rudolph Leopold Biesele, *The History of the German Settlements in Texas, 1831–1861* (1930); Fritz Goldbeck, *Seit fünfzig Jahren* (1896); Oscar Haas, *History of New Braunfels and Comal County, Texas, 1844–1946* (1968); "Early New Braunfels," New Braunfels *Herald*, December 19, 1963; Gerald S. Pierce, *Texas Under Arms* (1969); Selma Metzenthin-Raunick, "German Verse in Texas," *Southwest Review* (Autumn, 1932).

Crystal Sasse Ragsdale

*Zionville, Texas.

*Zipperlandville, Texas.

*Zita, Texas.

*Zoar, Texas.

*Zodiac Settlement. *See* Mormons in Texas.

Zonomi Indians. This name is known from a single Spanish missionary report (1691), which indicates that the Zonomi were neighbors of the Hasinai tribes of eastern Texas. It is said that they lived an unspecified distance southeast of the Hasinai. The affiliations of the Zonomi remain undetermined.

BIBLIOGRAPHY: J. R. Swanton, *Source Material on the History and Ethnology of the Caddo Indians* (1942).

T. N. Campbell

*Zorn, Texas.

*Zoro Creek.

*Zorquan Indians. The Zorquan (Zerquan) Indians entered San Antonio de Valero Mission qv in San Antonio about 1740, but this is all that is now known about them. Since many Tonkawan Indian groups from south-central Texas entered this mission at approximately the same time, H. E. Bolton thought that Zorquan was probably a Tonkawan group from the same area. It is also possible that Zorquan is a Spanish distortion of Yojuane, the name of a prominent Tonkawan band. J. R. Swanton listed the Zorquan as a Coahuiltecan band, but he presented no evidence in support of this linguistic identification. Today it seems best to regard the linguistic status of the Zorquan as undetermined.

BIBLIOGRAPHY: H. E. Bolton, *Texas in the Middle Eighteenth Century* (1915); F. W. Hodge (ed.), *Handbook of American Indians*, II (1910); J. R. Swanton, *The Indian Tribes of North America* (1952).

T. N. Campbell

*Zuber, Abraham.

*Zuber, William Physick. [This title was incorrectly listed in Volume II as Zuber, William Physich.]

BIBLIOGRAPHY: William Physick Zuber (Janis Boyle Mayfield, ed.), *My Eighty Years in Texas* (1971).

*Zuehl, Texas.

*Zulch, Texas.

*Zunkerville, Texas.

*Zybach, Texas.